VOLUME II

Lewis's
Medical-Surgical Nursing

Assessment and Management of Clinical Problems

Eleventh Edition

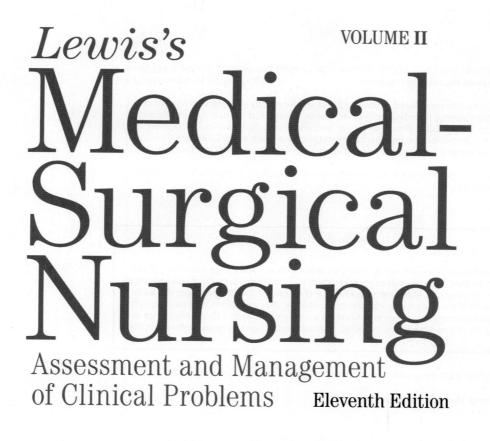

Mariann M. Harding, RN, PhD, FAADN, CNE
Professor of Nursing
Kent State University at Tuscarawas
New Philadelphia, Ohio

Section Editors

Jeffrey Kwong, RN, DNP, MPH, ANP-BC, FAAN, FAANP
Professor
Division of Advanced Nursing Practice
School of Nursing
Rutgers University
Newark, New Jersey

Dottie Roberts, RN, EdD, MSN, MACI, OCNS-C, CMSRN, CNE
Executive Director
Orthopaedic Nurses Certification Board
Chicago, Illinois

Debra Hagler, RN, PhD, ACNS-BC, CNE, CHSE, ANEF, FAAN
Clinical Professor
Edson College of Nursing and Health Innovation
Arizona State University
Phoenix, Arizona

Courtney Reinisch, RN, DNP, FNP-BC
Undergraduate Program Director
Associate Professor
School of Nursing
Montclair State University
Montclair, New Jersey

ELSEVIER

Elsevier
3251 Riverport Lane
St. Louis, Missouri 63043

Notice

Practitioners and researchers must always rely on their own experience and knowledge in evaluating and using any information, methods, compounds or experiments described herein. Because of rapid advances in the medical sciences, in particular, independent verification of diagnoses and drug dosages should be made. To the fullest extent of the law, no responsibility is assumed by Elsevier, authors, editors or contributors for any injury and/or damage to persons or property as a matter of products liability, negligence or otherwise, or from any use or operation of any methods, products, instructions, or ideas contained in the material herein.

Previous editions copyrighted 2017, 2014, 2011, 2007, 2004, 2000, 1996, 1992, 1987, and 1983.

International Standard Book Number: 978-0-323-55149-6

Senior Content Strategist: Jamie Blum
Senior Content Development Specialist: Rebecca Leenhouts
Publishing Services Manager: Julie Eddy
Book Production Specialist: Clay S. Broeker
Design Direction: Amy Buxton

Printed in Canada

Last digit is the print number: 9 8 7 6 5 4 3 2

MARIANN M. HARDING, RN, PHD, FAADN, CNE

Mariann Harding is a Professor of Nursing at Kent State University Tuscarawas, New Philadelphia, Ohio, where she has been on the faculty since 2005. She received her diploma in nursing from Mt. Carmel School of Nursing in Columbus, Ohio; her Bachelor of Science in nursing from Ohio University in Athens, Ohio; her Master of Science in Nursing as an adult nurse practitioner from the Catholic University of America in Washington, DC; and her doctorate in nursing from West Virginia University in Morgantown, West Virginia. Her 29 years of nursing experience have primarily been in critical care nursing and teaching in licensed practical, associate, and baccalaureate nursing programs. She currently teaches medical-surgical nursing, health care policy, and evidence-based practice. Her research has focused on promoting student success and health promotion among individuals with gout and facing cancer.

JEFFREY KWONG, RN, DNP, MPH, ANP-BC, FAAN, FAANP

Jeffrey Kwong is a Professor at the School of Nursing at Rutgers, the State University of New Jersey. He has worked for over 20 years in the area of adult primary care with a special focus on HIV. He received his undergraduate degree from the University of California—Berkeley, his nurse practitioner degree from the University of California—San Francisco, and completed his doctoral training at the University of Colorado—Denver. He also has a Master of Science Degree in public health with a focus on health education and behavioral sciences from the University of California—Los Angeles, and he was appointed a Hartford Geriatric Interprofessional Scholar while completing his gerontology education at New York University. In addition to teaching, Dr. Kwong maintains a clinical practice at Gotham Medical Group in New York City. He is a Fellow in the American Association of Nurse Practitioners.

DOTTIE ROBERTS, RN, EdD, MSN, MACI, CMSRN, OCNS-C, CNE

Dottie Roberts received her Bachelor of Science in nursing from Beth-El College of Nursing, Colorado Springs, Colorado; her Master of Science in adult health nursing from Beth-El College of Nursing and Health Sciences; her Master of Arts in curriculum and instruction from Colorado Christian University, Colorado Springs, Colorado; and her EdD in healthcare education from Nova Southeastern University, Ft. Lauderdale, Florida. She has over 25 years of experience in medical-surgical and orthopaedic nursing and holds certifications in both specialties. She has also taught in two baccalaureate programs in the Southeast and is certified as a nurse educator. She currently serves as contributing faculty for the RN-BSN program at Walden University. For her dissertation, Dottie completed a phenomenological study on facilitation of critical-thinking skills by clinical faculty in a baccalaureate nursing program. She has been Executive Director of the Orthopaedic Nurses Certification Board since 2005 and editor of *MEDSURG Nursing,* official journal of the Academy of Medical-Surgical Nurses, since 2003. Her free time is spent traveling, reading, and cross-stitching.

DEBRA HAGLER, RN, PhD, ACNS-BC, CNE, CHSE, ANEF, FAAN

Debbie Hagler is a Clinical Professor in the Edson College of Nursing and Health Innovation at Arizona State University in Phoenix. She is Deputy Editor of *The Journal of Continuing Education in Nursing*. She received her Practical Certificate in Nursing, Associate Degree in Nursing, and Bachelor of Science in Nursing from New Mexico State University. She earned a Master of Science from the University of Arizona and a doctorate in Learning and Instructional Technology from Arizona State University. Her clinical background is in adult health and critical care nursing. Her current role focuses on supporting students through the Barrett Honors program and helping faculty members develop their scholarly writing for publication.

COURTNEY REINISCH, RN, DNP, FNP-BC

Courtney Reinisch is the Undergraduate Program Director and Associate Professor for the School of Nursing at Montclair State University. She earned her Bachelor of Arts in biology and psychology from Immaculata University. She received her Bachelor of Science in nursing and Masters of Science in family practice nurse practitioner degree from the University of Delaware. She completed her Doctor of Nursing Practice degree at Columbia University School of Nursing. Courtney's nursing career has focused on providing care for underserved populations in primary care and emergency settings. She has taught in undergraduate and graduate nursing programs in New York and New Jersey. Courtney enjoys playing tennis, snowboarding, reading, and spending time with her family and dogs. She is the biggest fan for her nieces and nephews at their soccer games, cross-country events, and track meets. She is an active volunteer in the Parents Association of her son's school and advocates for the needs of students with learning differences and the LGBTQ community.

Vera Barton-Maxwell, PhD, APRN, FNP-BC, CHFN
Assistant Professor
Advanced Nursing Practice, Family Nurse
  Practitioner Program
Georgetown University
Washington, District of Columbia
  Nurse Practitioner
Center for Advanced Heart Failure
West Virginia University Heart and Vascular
  Institute
Morgantown, West Virginia

Cecilia Bidigare, MSN, RN
Professor
Nursing Department
Sinclair Community College
Dayton, Ohio

Megan Ann Brissie, DNP, RN, ACNP-BC, CEN
Acute Care Nurse Practitioner
Neurosurgery
Duke Health
Durham, North Carolina
Adjunct Instructor
College of Nursing
University of Cincinnati
Cincinnati, Ohio

Diana Taibi Buchanan, PhD, RN
Associate Professor
Biobehavioral Nursing and Health Systems
University of Washington
Seattle, Washington

Michelle Bussard, PhD, RN
RN to BSN Online eCampus Program Director
College of Health and Human Services
Bowling Green State University
Bowling Green, Ohio

Kim K. Choma, DNP, APRN, WHNP-BC
Women's Health Nurse Practitioner
Independent Consultant and Clinical
  Trainer
Kim Choma, DNP, LLC
Scotch Plains, New Jersey

Marisa Cortese, PhD, RN, FNP-BC
Research Nurse Practitioner
Hematology/Oncology
White Plains Hospital
White Plains, New York

Ann Crawford, RN, PhD, CNS, CEN
Professor
Department of Nursing
University of Mary Hardin-Baylor
Belton, Texas

Kimberly Day, DNP, RN
Clinical Assistant Professor
Edson College of Nursing and Health Innovation
Arizona State University
Phoenix, Arizona

Deena Damsky Dell, MSN, RN, APRN, AOCN(R), LNC
Oncology Advanced Practice Registered
  Nurse
Sarasota Memorial Hospital
Sarasota, Florida

Hazel Dennison, DNP, RN, APNc, CPHQ, CNE
Director of Continuing Nursing Education
College of Health Sciences, School of Nursing
Walden University
Minneapolis, Minnesota
Nurse Practitioner
Urgent Care
Virtua Health System
Medford, New Jersey

Jane K. Dickinson, PhD, RN, CDE
Program Director/Lecturer
Diabetes Education and Management
Teachers College Columbia University
New York, New York

Cathy Edson, MSN, RN
Nurse Practitioner
Emergency Department
Team Health—Virtua Memorial
Mt. Holly, New Jersey

Jonel L. Gomez, DNP, ARNP, CPCO, COE
Nurse Practitioner
Ophthalmic Facial Plastic Surgery
  Specialists
Stephen Laquis, MD
Fort Myers, Florida

Sherry A. Greenberg, PhD, RN, GNP-BC, FGSA
Courtesy-Appointed Associate Professor
Nursing
Rory Meyers College of Nursing
New York University
New York, New York

Diana Rabbani Hagler, MSN-Ed, RN, CCRN
Staff Nurse
Intensive Care Unit
Banner Health
Gilbert, Arizona

Julia A. Hitch, MS, APRN, FNPCDE
Nurse Practitioner
Internal Medicine—Endocrinology
Ohio State University Physicians
Columbus, Ohio

Haley Hoy, PhD, APRN
Associate Professor
College of Nursing
University of Alabama in Huntsville
Huntsville, Alabama
Nurse Practitioner
Vanderbilt Lung Transplantation
Vanderbilt Medical Center
Nashville, Tennessee

Melissa Hutchinson, MN, BA, RN
Clinical Nurse Specialist
MICU/CCU
VA Puget Sound Health Care System
Seattle, Washington

Mark Karasin, DNP, APRN, AGACNP-BC, CNOR
Advanced Practice Nurse
Cardiothoracic Surgery
Robert Wood Johnson University Hospital
New Brunswick, New Jersey
Adjunct Faculty
Center for Professional Development
School of Nursing
Rutgers University
Newark, New Jersey

Patricia Keegan, DNP, NP-C, AACC
Director Strategic and Programmatic
  Initiatives
Heart and Vascular Center
Emory University
Atlanta, Georgia

Kristen Keller, DNP, ACNP-BC, PMHNP-BC
Nurse Practitioner
Trauma and Acute Care Surgery
Banner Thunderbird Medical Center
Glendale, Arizona

Anthony Lutz, MSN, NP-C, CUNP
Nurse Practitioner
Department of Urology
Columbia University Irving Medical Center
New York, New York

Denise M. McEnroe-Petitte, PhD, RN
Associate Professor
Nursing Department
Kent State University Tuscarawas
New Philadelphia, Ohio

Amy Meredith, MSN, RN, EM Cert/Residency
APN-C Lead and APN Emergency
    Department
Emergency Department
Southern Ocean Medical Center
Manahawkin, New Jersey

Helen Miley, RN, PhD, AG-ACNP
Specialty Director of Adult Gerontology
Acute Care Nurse Practitioner Program
School of Nursing
Rutgers University
Newark, New Jersey

Debra Miller-Saultz, DNP, FNP-BC
Assistant Professor of Nursing
School of Nursing
Columbia University
New York, New York

Eugene Mondor, MN, RN, CNCC(C)
Clinical Nurse Educator
Adult Critical Care
Royal Alexandra Hospital
Edmonton, Alberta
Canada

Brenda C. Morris, EdD, RN, CNE
Clinical Professor
Edson College of Nursing and
    Health Innovation
Arizona State University
Phoenix, Arizona

Janice A. Neil, PhD, RN, CNE
Associate Professor
College of Nursing, Department of
    Baccalaureate Education
East Carolina University
Greenville, North Carolina

Yeow Chye Ng, PhD, CRNP, CPC, AAHIVE
Associate Professor
College of Nursing
University of Alabama in Huntsville
Huntsville, Alabama

Mary C. Olson, DNP, APRN
Nurse Practitioner
Medicine, Division of Gastroenterology and
    Hepatology
New York University Langone Health
New York, New York

Madona D. Plueger, MSN, RN, ACNS-BC CNRN
Adult Health Clinical Nurse Specialist
Barrow Neurological Institute
Dignity Health
St. Joseph's Hospital and Medical Center
Phoenix, Arizona

Matthew C. Price, MS, CNP, ONP-C, RNFA
Orthopedic Nurse Practitioner
Orthopedic One
Columbus, Ohio
Director
Orthopedic Nurses Certification Board
Chicago, Illinois

Margaret R. Rateau, PhD, RN, CNE
Assistant Professor
School of Nursing, Education, and Human
    Studies
Robert Morris University
Moon Township, Pennsylvania

Catherine R. Ratliff, RN, PhD
Clinical Associate Professor and Nurse
    Practitioner
School of Nursing/Vascular Surgery
University of Virginia Health System
Charlottesville, Virginia

Sandra Irene Rome, MN, RN, AOCN
Clinical Nurse Specialist
Blood and Marrow Transplant Program
Cedars–Sinai Medical Center
Los Angeles, California
Assistant Clinical Professor
University of California Los Angeles School
    of Nursing
Los Angeles, California

Diane M. Rudolphi, MSN, RN
Senior Instructor of Nursing
College of Health Sciences
University of Delaware, Newark
Newark, Delaware

Diane Ryzner, MSN, APRN, CNS-BC, OCNS-C
Clinical Nursing Transformation Leader
Orthopedics
Northwest Community Healthcare
Arlington Heights, Illinois

Andrew Scanlon, DNP, RN
Associate Professor
School of Nursing
Montclair State University
Montclair, New Jersey

Rose Shaffer, MSN, RN, ACNP-BC, CCRN
Cardiology Nurse Practitioner
Thomas Jefferson University Hospital
Philadelphia, Pennsylvania

Tara Shaw, MSN, RN
Assistant Professor
Goldfarb School of Nursing
Barnes-Jewish College
St. Louis, Missouri

Cynthia Ann Smith, DNP, APRN, CNN-NP, FNP-BC
Nurse Practitioner
Renal Consultants, PLLC
South Charleston, West Virginia

Janice Smolowitz, PhD, DNP, EdD
Dean and Professor
School of Nursing
Montclair State University
Montclair, New Jersey

Cindy Sullivan, MN, ANP-C, CNRN
Nurse Practitioner
Department of Neurosurgery
Barrow Neurological Institute
Phoenix, Arizona

Teresa Turnbull, DNP, RN
Assistant Professor
School of Nursing
Oregon Health and Science University
Portland, Oregon

Kara Ann Ventura, DNP, PNP, FNP
Director
Liver Transplant Program
Yale New Haven
New Haven, Connecticut

Colleen Walsh, DNP, RN, ONC, ONP-C, CNS, ACNP-BC
Contract Assistant Professor of Nursing
College of Nursing and Health Professions
University of Southern Indiana
Evansville, Indiana

Pamela Wilkerson, MN, RN
Nurse Manager
Primary Care and Urgent Care
Department of Veterans Affairs
Veterans Administration, Puget Sound
Tacoma, Washington

Daniel P. Worrall, MSN, ANP-BC
Nurse Practitioner
Sexual Health Clinic
Nurse Practitioner
General and Gastrointestinal Surgery
Massachusetts General Hospital
Boston, Massachusetts
Clinical Operations Manager
The Ragon Institute of MGH, MIT, and
    Harvard
Cambridge, Massachusetts

TEST BANK

Debra Hagler, RN, PhD, ACNS-BC, CNE, CHSE, ANEF, FAAN
Clinical Professor
Edson College of Nursing and Health Innovation
Arizona State University
Phoenix, Arizona

CASE STUDIES
Interactive and Managing Care of Multiple Patients Case Studies

Mariann M. Harding, RN, PhD, FAADN, CNE
Professor of Nursing
Kent State University at Tuscarawas
New Philadelphia, Ohio

Brenda C. Morris, EdD, RN, CNE
Clinical Professor
Edson College of Nursing and Health Innovation
Arizona State University
Phoenix, Arizona

POWERPOINT PRESENTATIONS

Bonnie Heintzelman, RN, MS, CMSRN
Assistant Professor of Nursing
Pennsylvania College of Technology
Williamsport, Pennsylvania

Michelle A. Walczak, RN, MSN
Associate Professor of Nursing
Pennsylvania College of Technology
Williamsport, Pennsylvania

TEACH FOR NURSES

Margaret R. Rateau, RN, PhD, CNE
Assistant Professor
School of Nursing, Education, and Human Studies
Robert Morris University
Moon Township, Pennsylvania

Janice Sarasnick, RN, PhD, CHSE
Associate Professor of Nursing
Robert Morris University
Moon Township, Pennsylvania

NCLEX EXAMINATION REVIEW QUESTIONS

Mistey D. Bailey, RN, MSN
Lecturer, Nursing
Kent State University Tuscarawas
New Philadelphia, Ohio

Shelly Stefka, RN, MSN
Lecturer, Nursing
Kent State University Tuscarawas
New Philadelphia, Ohio

STUDY GUIDE

Collin Bowman-Woodall, RN, MS
Assistant Professor
Samuel Merritt University
San Francisco Peninsula Campus
San Mateo, California

CLINICAL COMPANION

Debra Hagler, RN, PhD, ACNS-BC, CNE, CHSE, ANEF, FAAN
Clinical Professor
Edson College of Nursing and Health Innovation
Arizona State University
Phoenix, Arizona

EVIDENCE-BASED PRACTICE BOXES

Linda Bucher, RN, PhD, CEN, CNE
Emerita Professor
University of Delaware
Newark, Delaware

NURSING CARE PLANS

Collin Bowman-Woodall, RN, MS
Assistant Professor
Samuel Merritt University
San Francisco Peninsula Campus
San Mateo, California

Kristen Ryan Barry-Rodgers, RN, BSN, CEN
Emergency Department Charge and Staff Nurse
Virtua Memorial Hospital
Mt. Holly, New Jersey

Michelle Bussard, PhD, RN
RN to BSN Online eCampus
  Program Director
College of Health and Human Services
Bowling Green State University
Bowling Green, Ohio

Margaret A. Chesnutt, MSN, FNP, BC, CORLN
Nurse Practitioner
Primary Care
Veterans Administration Medical Center
Decatur, Georgia

Ann Crawford, RN, PhD, CNS, CEN
Professor
Department of Nursing
University of Mary Hardin-Baylor
Belton, Texas

Jonel L. Gomez, DNP, ARNP, CPCO, COE
Nurse Practitioner
Ophthalmic Facial Plastic Surgery Specialists
Stephen Laquis, MD
Fort Myers, Florida

Jennifer Hebert, MSN, RN-BC, NE-BC
Manager, Patient Care Services
Nursing Administration
Sentara Princess Anne Hospital
Virginia Beach, Virginia

Haley Hoy, PhD, APRN
Associate Professor
College of Nursing
University of Alabama in Huntsville
Huntsville, Alabama
Nurse Practitioner
Vanderbilt Lung Transplantation
Vanderbilt Medical Center
Nashville, Tennessee

Coretta M. Jenerette, PhD, RN, CNE, AOCN
Associate Professor
School of Nursing
University of North Carolina at
  Chapel Hill
Chapel Hill, North Carolina

Beth Karasin, MSN, APN, AGACNP-BC, RNFA, CNOR
Advanced Practice Nurse
Neurosurgery
Atlantic Neurosurgical Specialists
Morristown, New Jersey

Mark Karasin, DNP, APRN, AGACNP-BC, CNOR
Advanced Practice Nurse
Cardiothoracic Surgery
Robert Wood Johnson University Hospital
New Brunswick, New Jersey
Adjunct Faculty
Center for Professional Development
School of Nursing
Rutgers University
Newark, New Jersey

Kristen Keller, DNP, ACNP-BC, PMHNP-BC
Nurse Practitioner
Trauma and Acute Care Surgery
Banner Thunderbird Medical Center
Glendale, Arizona

Suzanne M. Mahon, DNSc, RN, AOCN(R), AGN-BC
Professor
Division of Hematology/Oncology
Department of Internal Medicine
Adult Nursing, School of Nursing
Saint Louis University
St. Louis, Missouri

Helen Miley, RN, PhD, AG-ACNP
Specialty Director of Adult Gerontology
Acute Care Nurse Practitioner Program
School of Nursing
Rutgers University
Newark, New Jersey

Linda L. Morris, PhD, APN, CCNS, FCCM
Clinical Nurse Educator
Associate Professor of Physical Medicine and Rehabilitation
  and Anesthesiology
Academy Department
Shirley Ryan Ability Lab
Northwestern University Feinberg School of Medicine
Chicago, Illinois

Louise O'Keefe, PhD, CRNP
Assistant Professor and Director
Faculty and Staff Clinic
College of Nursing
University of Alabama in Huntsville
Huntsville, Alabama

Catherine R. Ratliff, RN, PhD
Clinical Associate Professor and Nurse Practitioner
School of Nursing/Vascular Surgery
University of Virginia Health System
Charlottesville, Virginia

Lori M. Rhudy, RN, PhD, CNRN, ACNS-BC
Clinical Associate Professor
School of Nursing
University of Minnesota
Minneapolis, Minnesota
Nurse Scientist
Division of Nursing Research
Mayo Clinic
Rochester, Minnesota

Cynthia Ann Smith, DNP, APRN, CNN-NP, FNP-BC
Nurse Practitioner
Renal Consultants, PLLC
South Charleston, West Virginia

Janice Smolowitz, PhD, DNP, EdD
Dean and Professor
School of Nursing
Montclair State University
Montclair, New Jersey

Charity L. Tan, MSN, ACNP-BC
Acute Care Nurse Practitioner
Neurological Surgery
University of California Davis Health
Sacramento, California

Kara Ann Ventura, DNP, PNP, FNP
Director
Liver Transplant Program
Yale New Haven
New Haven, Connecticut

Robert M. Welch, MSN, FNP, CRNO
Nurse Practitioner
Ophthalmology—Retina
Neveda Retina Associates
Reno, Nevada

Mary Zellinger, APRN-CCNS, MN, ANP-BC, CCRN-CSC, FCCM
Clinical Nurse Specialist
Cardiovascular Critical Care
Nursing Department
Emory University Hospital
Atlanta, Georgia

To the Profession of Nursing and to the Important People in Our Lives

Mariann

*My husband Jeff, our daughters
Kate and Sarah,
and my parents, Mick and Mary.*

Jeff

*My parents, Raymond and Virginia,
thank you for believing in me and
providing me the opportunity to become a nurse.*

Dottie

*My husband Steve and my children Megan, E.J., Jessica, and Matthew, who have
supported me through four college degrees and countless writing projects; and to
my son-in-law Al, our grandsons Oscar and Stephen, and my new daughter-in-law
Melissa.*

Debbie

*My husband James, our children Matthew,
Andrew, Amanda, and Diana, and our granddaughter Emma.*

Courtney

To future nurses and the advancement of health care globally.

The eleventh edition of *Lewis's Medical-Surgical Nursing: Assessment and Management of Clinical Problems* incorporates the most current medical-surgical nursing information in an easy-to-use format. This textbook is a comprehensive resource containing the essential information that students need to prepare for class, examinations, clinical assignments, and safe and comprehensive patient care. The text and accompanying resources include many features to help students learn key medical-surgical nursing content, including patient and caregiver teaching, gerontology, interprofessional care, cultural and ethnic considerations, patient safety, genetics, nutrition and drug therapy, evidence-based practice, and much more.

To address the rapidly changing practice environment, all efforts were directed toward building on the strengths of the previous editions while delivering this more effective new edition. To help students and faculty members focus on the most important concepts in patient care, most chapters open with a conceptual focus that introduces students to the common concepts shared by patients experiencing the main exemplars discussed in the chapter. This edition features more body maps and has many new illustrations. Lengthy diagnostic tables in the assessment chapters have been separated into specific categories, including radiologic studies and serology studies. The previously combined visual and auditory content is now in separate chapters focusing on the assessment and management of vision and hearing disorders. New Promoting Population Health boxes address strategies to improve health outcomes.

For a text to be effective, it must be understandable. In this edition, great effort has been put into improving the readability and lowering the reading level. Students will find more clear and easier-to-read language, with an engaging conversational style. The narrative addresses the reader, helping make the text more personal and an active learning tool. The language is more positive. For example, particular side effects and complications are referred to as *common,* as opposed to *not uncommon.*

International Classification for Nursing Practice (ICNP) nursing diagnoses, one of the terminologies recognized by the American Nurses Association, are used throughout the text and ancillary materials. The language is similar to that of NANDA-I. ICNP nursing diagnoses are used in many facilities worldwide to document nursing care in electronic health records. By introducing students to the ICNP nursing diagnoses, students will learn a more shared vocabulary. This should translate into the more accurate use of diagnostic language in clinical practice across healthcare settings.

Contributors were selected for their expertise in specific content areas; one or more specialists in a given subject area have thoroughly reviewed each chapter to increase accuracy. The editors have undertaken final rewriting and editing to achieve internal consistency. The comprehensive and timely content, special features, attractive layout, full-color illustrations, and student-friendly writing style combine to make this the textbook used in more nursing schools than any other medical-surgical nursing textbook.

ORGANIZATION

Content is organized into 2 major divisions. The first division, Sections 1 through 3 (Chapters 1 through 16), discusses general concepts related to the care of adult patients. The second division, Sections 4 through 13 (Chapters 17 through 68), presents nursing assessment and nursing management of medical-surgical problems. At the beginning of each chapter, the Conceptual Focus helps students focus on the key concepts and integrate concepts with exemplars affecting different body systems. Learning Outcomes and Key Terms assist students in identifying the key content for that chapter.

The various body systems are grouped to reflect their interrelated functions. Each section is organized around 2 central themes: assessment and management. Chapters dealing with assessment of a body system include a discussion of the following:

1. A brief review of anatomy and physiology, focusing on information that will promote understanding of nursing care
2. Health history and noninvasive physical assessment skills to expand the knowledge base on which treatment decisions are made
3. Common diagnostic studies, expected results, and related nursing responsibilities to provide easily accessible information

Management chapters focus on the pathophysiology, clinical manifestations, diagnostic studies, interprofessional care, and nursing management of various diseases and disorders. The nursing management sections are presented in a consistent format, organized into assessment, nursing diagnoses, planning, implementation, and evaluation. To emphasize the importance of patient care in and across various clinical settings, nursing implementation of all major health problems is organized by the following levels of care:

1. Health Promotion
2. Acute Care
3. Ambulatory Care

SPECIAL FEATURES

The 6 competencies for registered nursing practice identified by QSEN serve as the foundation of the text and are highlighted in the core content, case studies, and nursing care plans.

- *New!* **Nursing Management** tables and boxes focus on the actions nurses need to take to deliver safe, quality, effective patient care.
- *New!* **Diagnostic Studies** tables focus on the specific type of study, such as interventional, serologic, or radiologic, with more detailed information on interpreting results and associated nursing care.
- **Cultural and ethnic health disparities** content and boxes in the text highlight risk factors and important issues related to the nursing care of various ethnic groups. A special Culturally Competent Care heading denotes cultural and ethnic content related to diseases and disorders. Chapter 2 (Health Equity and Culturally Competent Care) discusses health status differences among groups of people related to access to care, economic aspects of health care, gender and cultural issues, and the nurse's role in promoting health equity.
- **Interprofessional care** is highlighted in special Interprofessional Care sections in all management chapters and Interprofessional Care tables throughout the text.

- **Focused Assessment boxes** in all assessment chapters provide brief checklists that help students do a more practical "assessment on the run" or bedside approach to assessment. They can be used to evaluate the status of previously identified health problems and monitor for signs of new problems.
- **Safety Alert boxes** highlight important patient safety issues and focus on the National Patient Safety Goals.
- **Pathophysiology Maps** outline complex concepts related to diseases in a flowchart format, making them easier to understand.
- **Patient and caregiver teaching** is an ongoing theme throughout the text. Chapter 4 (Patient and Caregiver Teaching) emphasizes the increasing importance and prevalence of patient management of chronic illnesses and conditions and the role of the caregiver in patient care.
- *New!* **Conceptual Focus** at the beginning of each chapter helps students focus on the key concepts and integrate concepts with exemplars affecting different body systems.
- **Gerontology and chronic illness** are discussed in Chapter 5 (Chronic Illness and Older Adults) and included throughout the text under Gerontologic Considerations headings and in Gerontologic Differences in Assessment tables.
- **Nutrition** is highlighted throughout the textbook. Nutritional Therapy tables summarize nutritional interventions and promote healthy lifestyles in patients with various health problems.
- *New!* **Promoting Population Health boxes** present health care goals and interventions as they relate to specific disorders, such as diabetes and cancer, and to health promotion, such as preserving hearing and maintaining a healthy weight.
- **Extensive drug therapy** content includes Drug Therapy tables and concise Drug Alerts highlighting important safety considerations for key drugs.
- **Genetics content** includes:
  - Genetics in Clinical Practice boxes that summarize the genetic basis, genetic testing, and clinical implications for genetic disorders that affect adults
  - A genetics chapter that focuses on practical application of nursing care as it relates to this important topic
  - Genetic Risk Alerts in the assessment chapters, which call attention to important genetic risks
  - Genetic Link headings in the management chapters, which highlight the specific genetic bases of many disorders
- **Gender Differences** boxes discuss how women and men are affected differently by conditions such as pain and hypertension.
- **Check Your Practice boxes** challenge students to think critically, analyze patient assessment data, and implement the appropriate intervention. Scenarios and discussion questions are provided to promote active learning.
- **Complementary & Alternative Therapies boxes** expand on this information and summarize what nurses need to know about therapies such as herbal remedies, acupuncture, and yoga.
- **Ethical/Legal Dilemmas boxes** promote critical thinking for timely and sensitive issues that nursing students may deal with in clinical practice—topics such as informed consent, advance directives, and confidentiality.
- **Emergency Management tables** outline the emergency treatment of health problems most likely to require emergency intervention.

- **Nursing care plans** on the Evolve website focus on common disorders or exemplars. These care plans incorporate ICNP nursing diagnoses, Nursing Interventions Classification (NIC), and Nursing Outcomes Classification (NOC) in a way that clearly shows the linkages among NIC, NOC, and nursing diagnoses and applies them to nursing practice.
- Coverage on delegation and prioritization includes:
  - Specific topics and skills related to delegation and the nurse's role in working with members of the interprofessional team, which are detailed in Nursing Management tables.
  - Delegation and prioritization questions in case studies and Bridge to NCLEX Examination Questions.
  - Nursing interventions throughout the text, listed in order of priority.
  - Nursing diagnoses in the nursing care plans, listed in order of priority.
- **Assessment Abnormalities tables** in assessment chapters alert the nurse to commonly encountered abnormalities and their possible etiologies.
- **Nursing Assessment tables** summarize the key subjective and objective data related to common diseases. Subjective data are organized by functional health patterns.
- **Health History tables** in assessment chapters present key questions to ask patients related to a specific disease or disorder.
- **Evidence-based practice** is covered in Applying the Evidence boxes and evidence-based practice-focused questions in the case studies. Applying the Evidence boxes use a case study approach to help students learn to use evidence in making patient care decisions.
- **Informatics boxes and content** in Chapter 4 (Patient and Caregiver Teaching) reflect the current use and importance of technology as it relates to patient self-management.
- **Bridge to NCLEX® Examination Questions** at the end of each chapter are matched to the Learning Outcomes and help students learn the important points in the chapter. Answers are provided just below the questions for immediate feedback, and rationales are provided on the Evolve website.
- **Case Studies** with photos bring patients to life. Management chapters have case studies at the end of the chapters. These cases help students learn how to prioritize care and manage patients in the clinical setting. Unfolding case studies are included in each assessment chapter, and case studies that focus on managing care of multiple patients are included at the end of each section. Discussion questions with a focus on prioritization, delegation, and evidence-based practice are included in all case studies. Answer guidelines are provided on the Evolve website.

LEARNING SUPPLEMENTS FOR STUDENTS

- The handy **Clinical Companion** presents approximately 200 common medical-surgical conditions and procedures in a concise, alphabetical format for quick clinical reference. Designed for portability, this popular reference includes the essential, need-to-know information for treatments and procedures in which nurses play a major role. An attractive and functional four-color design highlights key information for quick, easy reference.
- An exceptionally thorough **Study Guide** contains over 500 pages of review material that reflect the content found in

the textbook. It features a wide variety of clinically relevant exercises and activities, including NCLEX-format multiple choice and alternate format questions, case studies, anatomy review, critical thinking activities, and much more. It features an attractive four-color design and many alternate-item format questions to better prepare students for the NCLEX examination. An answer key is included to provide students with immediate feedback as they study.

- The **Evolve Student Resources** are available online at *http://evolve.elsevier.com/Lewis/medsurg* and include the following valuable learning aids organized by chapter:
  - Printable **Key Points** summaries for each chapter.
  - 1000 NCLEX examination **Review Questions.**
  - **Answer Guidelines** to the case studies in the textbook.
  - **Rationales for the Bridge to NCLEX® Examination Questions** in the textbook.
  - 55 **Interactive Case Studies** with state-of-the-art animations and a variety of learning activities, which provide students with immediate feedback. Ten of the case studies are enhanced with photos and narration of the clinical scenarios.
  - Customizable **Nursing Care Plans** for over 60 common disorder or exemplars.
  - **Conceptual Care Map Creator.**
  - **Audio glossary** of key terms, available as comprehensive alphabetical glossary and organized by chapter.
  - **Fluids and Electrolytes Tutorial.**
  - **Content Updates.**
- More than just words on a screen, **Elsevier eBooks** come with a wealth of built-in study tools and interactive functionality to help students better connect with the course material and their instructors. In addition, with the ability to fit an entire library on one portable device, students have the ability to study when, where, and how they want.

TEACHING SUPPLEMENTS FOR INSTRUCTORS

- The **Evolve Instructor Resources** (available online at *http://evolve.elsevier.com/Lewis/medsurg*) remain the most comprehensive set of instructor's materials available, containing the following:
  - **TEACH for Nurses Lesson Plans** with electronic resources organized by chapter to help instructors develop and manage the course curriculum. This exciting resource includes:
    - Objectives
    - Pre-class activities
    - Nursing curriculum standards
    - Student and instructor chapter resource listings
    - Teaching strategies, with learning activities and assessment methods tied to learning outcomes
    - **Case studies** with answer guidelines
  - The **Test Bank** features over 2000 NCLEX examination test questions with text page references and answers coded for NCLEX Client Needs category, nursing process, and cognitive level. The test bank includes hundreds

of prioritization, delegation, and multiple patient questions. All alternate-item format questions are included. The ExamView software allows instructors to create new tests; edit, add, and delete test questions; sort questions by NCLEX category, cognitive level, nursing process step, and question type; and administer and grade online tests.
- The **Image Collection** contains more than 800 full-color images from the text for use in lectures.
- An extensive collection of **PowerPoint Presentations** includes over 125 different presentations focused on the most common diseases and disorders. The presentations have been thoroughly revised to include helpful instructor notes/teaching tips, unfolding case studies, illustrations and photos not found in the book, new animations, and updated audience response questions for use with iClicker and other audience response systems.
- Course management system.
- Access to all student resources listed above.
- The **Simulation Learning System (SLS)** is an online toolkit that helps instructors and facilitators effectively incorporate medium- to high-fidelity simulation into their nursing curriculum. Detailed patient scenarios promote and enhance the clinical decision-making skills of students at all levels. The SLS provides detailed instructions for preparation and implementation of the simulation experience, debriefing questions that encourage critical thinking, and learning resources to reinforce student comprehension. Each scenario in the SLS complements the textbook content and helps bridge the gap between lecture and clinical. The SLS provides the perfect environment for students to practice what they are learning in the text for a true-to-life, hands-on learning experience.

ACKNOWLEDGMENTS

The editors are especially grateful to many people at Elsevier who assisted with this revision effort. In particular, we wish to thank the team of Jamie Blum, Rebecca Leenhouts, Denise Roslonski, Clay Broeker, and Julie Eddy. In addition, we want to thank Kristin Oyirifi in marketing. We also wish to thank our contributors and reviewers for their assistance with the revision process.

We are particularly indebted to the faculty, nurses, and student nurses who have put their faith in our textbook to assist them on their path to excellence. The increasing use of this book throughout the United States, Canada, Australia, and other parts of the world has been gratifying. We appreciate the many users who have shared their comments and suggestions on the previous editions.

We sincerely hope that this book will assist both students and clinicians in practicing truly professional nursing.

Mariann M. Harding
Jeffrey Kwong
Dottie Roberts
Debra Hagler
Courtney Reinisch

CONTENTS

CONCEPTS EXEMPLARS

Acid–Base Balance
Chronic Kidney Disease
Diarrhea
Metabolic Acidosis
Metabolic Alkalosis
Respiratory Acidosis
Respiratory Alkalosis

Cellular Regulation
Anemia
Breast Cancer
Cervical Cancer
Colon Cancer
Endometrial Cancer
Head and Neck Cancer
Leukemia
Lung Cancer
Lymphoma
Melanoma
Prostate Cancer

Clotting
Disseminated Intravascular
    Coagulopathy
Pulmonary Embolism
Thrombocytopenia
Venous Thromboembolism

Cognition
Alzheimer's Disease
Delirium

Elimination
Benign Prostatic Hypertrophy
Chronic Kidney Disease
Constipation
Diarrhea
Intestinal Obstruction
Pyelonephritis
Prostatitis
Renal Calculi

Fluids and Electrolytes
Burns
Hyperkalemia
Hypernatremia
Hypokalemia
Hyponatremia

Gas Exchange
Acute Respiratory Failure
Acute Respiratory Distress Syndrome
Asthma

Chronic Obstructive Pulmonary Disease
Cystic Fibrosis
Lung Cancer
Pulmonary Embolism

Glucose Regulation
Cushing's Syndrome
Diabetes Mellitus

Hormonal Regulation
Addison's Disease
Hyperthyroidism
Hypothyroidism

Immunity
Allergic Rhinitis
Anaphylaxis
HIV Infection
Organ Transplantation
Peptic Ulcer Disease

Infection
Antimicrobial Resistant Infections
Health Care–Associated Infections
Hepatitis
Pneumonia
Tuberculosis
Urinary Tract Infection

Inflammation
Appendicitis
Cholecystitis
Glomerulonephritis
Pancreatitis
Pelvic Inflammatory Disease
Peritonitis
Rheumatoid Arthritis

Intracranial Regulation
Brain Tumor
Head Injury
Meningitis
Seizure Disorder
Stroke

Mobility
Fractures
Low Back Pain
Multiple Sclerosis
Osteoarthritis
Parkinson's Disease
Spinal Cord Injury

Nutrition
Gastroesophageal Reflux Disease
Inflammatory Bowel Disease
Metabolic Syndrome
Malnutrition
Obesity

Perfusion
Acute Coronary Syndrome
Atrial Fibrillation
Cardiogenic Shock
Endocarditis
Heart Failure
Hyperlipidemia
Hypertension
Hypovolemic Shock
Mitral Valve Prolapse
Peripheral Artery Disease
Septic Shock
Sickle Cell Disease

Reproduction
Early Pregnancy Loss
Ectopic Pregnancy
Infertility

Sleep
Insomnia
Sleep Apnea

Sensory Perception
Cataracts
Glaucoma
Hearing Loss
Macular Degeneration
Otitis Media

Sexuality
Erectile Dysfunction
Leiomyomas
Menopause
Sexually Transmitted Infection

Thermoregulation
Frostbite
Heat Stroke
Hyperthyroidism

Tissue Integrity
Burns
Pressure Injuries
Wound Healing

DIAGNOSTIC STUDIES TABLES

DRUG THERAPY TABLES

GENETICS IN CLINICAL PRACTICE BOXES

GERONTOLOGIC ASSESSMENT DIFFERENCES TABLES

HEALTH HISTORY TABLES

INFORMATICS IN PRACTICE BOXES

INTERPROFESSIONAL CARE TABLES

NURSING ASSESSMENT TABLES

NURSING MANAGEMENT BOXES

NUTRITIONAL THERAPY TABLES

PATIENT & CAREGIVER TEACHING TABLES

PROMOTING HEALTH EQUITY

PROMOTING POPULATION HEALTH BOXES

38

Assessment: Gastrointestinal System

Kara Ann Ventura

We can't help everyone, but everyone can help someone.

Ronald Reagan

(e) http://evolve.elsevier.com/Lewis/medsurg

CONCEPTUAL FOCUS

Elimination
Fluids and Electrolytes

Nutrition

LEARNING OUTCOMES

1. Describe the structures and functions of the organs of the gastrointestinal tract.
2. Describe the structures and functions of the liver, gallbladder, biliary tract, and pancreas.
3. Distinguish the processes of ingestion, digestion, absorption, and elimination.
4. Explain the processes of biliary metabolism, bile production, and bile excretion.
5. Link the age-related changes of the gastrointestinal system to the differences in assessment findings.
6. Obtain significant subjective and objective assessment data related to the gastrointestinal system from a patient.
7. Perform a physical assessment of the gastrointestinal system using appropriate techniques.
8. Distinguish normal from abnormal findings of a physical assessment of the gastrointestinal system.
9. Describe the purpose, significance of results, and nursing responsibilities related to diagnostic studies of the gastrointestinal system.

KEY TERMS

absorption, p. 830
bilirubin, p. 832
borborygmi, Table 38.10, p. 842
cheilosis, Table 38.10, p. 841
deglutition, p. 829

digestion, p. 830
endoscopy, p. 846
hematemesis, Table 38.10, p. 841
Kupffer cells, p. 832
melena, Table 38.10, p. 842

pyorrhea, Table 38.10, p. 841
pyrosis, Table 38.10, p. 842
steatorrhea, Table 38.10, p. 842
tenesmus, Table 38.10, p. 842
Valsalva maneuver, p. 832

The gastrointestinal (GI) system, also called the *digestive system,* consists of the GI tract and its associated organs and glands. Included in the GI tract are the mouth, esophagus, stomach, small intestine, large intestine, rectum, and anus. The associated organs are the liver, pancreas, and gallbladder (Fig. 38.1). Problems that change physiologic processes or associated organs affect a person's ability to maintain nutritional status and eliminate waste.

STRUCTURES AND FUNCTIONS OF GASTROINTESTINAL SYSTEM

The GI tract extends around 30 ft (9 m) from the mouth to the anus. The GI tract is essentially a tube composed of 4 layers. From the inside to the outside, these layers are (1) mucosa lining; (2) submucosa connective tissue, which contains glands, blood vessels, and lymph nodes; (3) muscle; and (4) serosa. The muscular coat has 3 smooth muscle layers: the oblique (inner) layer, circular (middle) layer, and longitudinal (outer) layer.

Parasympathetic and sympathetic branches of the autonomic nervous system (ANS) innervate the GI tract. The parasympathetic (cholinergic) system is mainly excitatory. The sympathetic (adrenergic) system is mainly inhibitory. For example, parasympathetic stimulation increases peristalsis and sympathetic stimulation decreases it. Both sympathetic and parasympathetic afferent fibers relay sensory information.

The GI tract has its own nervous system: the enteric nervous system (ENS) or intrinsic nervous system. The ENS system regulates motility and secretion along the entire GI tract. The ENS is composed of 2 networks: (1) Meissner plexus in the

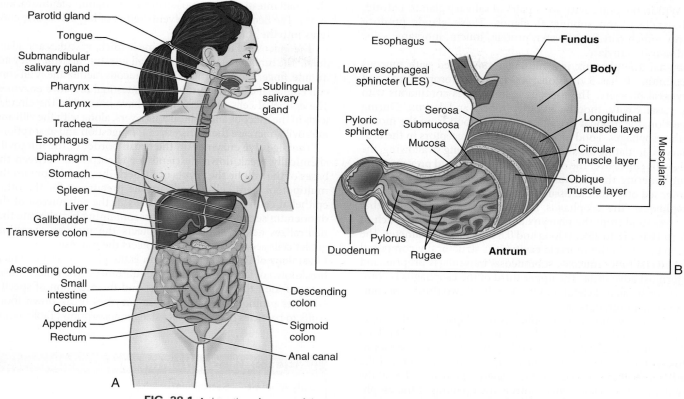

FIG. 38.1 A, Location of organs of the gastrointestinal system. B, Parts of the stomach.

submucosa and (2) Auerbach (myenteric) plexus between the muscle layers. The submucosal plexus controls secretion and is involved in many sensory functions. The myenteric plexus is the major nerve supply to the GI tract and controls GI movements. Although the ENS receives innervation from the ANS, it functions independently of the brain and spinal cord.

Circulation in the GI system is unique in that venous blood draining the GI tract organs empties into the portal vein, which then perfuses the liver. This allows the liver to clean the blood of bacteria and toxins from the GI tract. The celiac artery, superior mesenteric artery (SMA), and the inferior mesenteric artery (IMA) supply arterial blood to the GI tract. The stomach and duodenum receive their blood supply from the celiac axis. The distal small intestine to mid large intestine receives its blood supply from branches of the hepatic and SMA. The distal large intestine through the anus receives its blood supply from the IMA. The GI tract and accessory organs receive 25% to 30% of the cardiac output at rest and 35% or more after eating. Because such a large percent of the cardiac output perfuses these organs, the GI tract is a major source from which to divert blood flow during exercise, stress, or injury.

The peritoneum almost completely covers the abdominal organs. The 2 layers of the peritoneum are the *parietal layer,* which lines the abdominal cavity wall, and the *visceral layer,* which covers the abdominal organs. The peritoneal cavity is the potential space between the parietal and visceral layers. The 2 folds of the peritoneum are the mesentery and omentum. The mesentery attaches the small intestine and part of the large intestine to the posterior abdominal wall. It contains blood and lymph vessels. The omentum hangs like an apron from the stomach to the intestines. It contains fat and lymph nodes.

The main function of the GI system is to supply nutrients to body cells. This is accomplished through the processes of (1) *ingestion* (taking in food), (2) *digestion* (breaking down food), and (3) *absorption* (transferring food products into circulation). *Elimination* is the process of excreting the waste products of digestion.

Ingestion

Ingestion is the intake of food. *Appetite,* the desire to ingest food, influences how much food a person eats. An appetite center is found in the hypothalamus. Several factors, including hypoglycemia, an empty stomach, and a decrease in body temperature, stimulate appetite. The hormone *ghrelin* released from the stomach mucosa plays a role in appetite stimulation. Another hormone, *leptin,* is involved in appetite suppression. (See Chapter 40 for a discussion of ghrelin and leptin.) The sight, smell, and taste of food can stimulate appetite. Stomach distention, illness (especially accompanied by fever), hyperglycemia, nausea and vomiting, and certain drugs (e.g., amphetamines) inhibit appetite.

Deglutition, or swallowing, is the mechanical portion of ingestion. The organs involved in deglutition are the mouth, pharynx, and esophagus.

Mouth. The mouth consists of the lips and oral (buccal) cavity. The lips surround the opening of the mouth and function in speech. The hard and soft palates form the roof of the oral cavity. The oral cavity contains the teeth, used in *mastication* (chewing), and the tongue. The tongue is a solid muscle mass. It aids in chewing and moving food to the back of the throat for swallowing. The taste receptors (taste buds) are on the sides and tip of the tongue. The tongue is also important in speech.

Within the oral cavity are 3 pairs of salivary glands: parotid, submaxillary, and sublingual glands. These glands produce saliva, which consists of water, protein, mucin, inorganic salts, and salivary amylase.

Pharynx. The pharynx is a muscular tube lined with mucous membrane. It has 3 divisions: nasopharynx, oropharynx, and laryngeal pharynx. The mucous membrane is continuous with the nasal cavity, mouth, auditory tubes, and larynx. During ingestion, the oropharynx is the route for food from the mouth to the esophagus. Food or liquid stimulates receptors in the oropharynx, initiating the swallowing reflex. During swallowing, the epiglottis closes over the opening to the larynx and prevents food from entering the respiratory tract. The tonsils and adenoids, composed of lymphoid tissue, help the body prevent infection.

Esophagus. The esophagus is a hollow, muscular tube that receives food from the pharynx and moves it to the stomach. It is 7 to 10 in (18 to 25 cm) long and 0.8 in (2 cm) in diameter. The esophagus is in the thoracic cavity. It is structurally composed of 4 layers: inner mucosa, submucosa, muscularis propria, and outermost adventitia. The upper third of the esophagus is composed of striated skeletal muscle. The distal two thirds are composed of smooth muscle.

Between swallows, the esophagus is collapsed and the *upper esophageal sphincter* (UES) closed. With swallowing, the UES relaxes and a peristaltic wave moves the bolus into the esophagus. The muscular layers contract *(peristalsis)* and propel the food to the stomach. The *lower esophageal sphincter* (LES) at the distal end of the esophagus controls the opening of the esophagus into the stomach. It stays contracted except during swallowing, belching, or vomiting. The LES is an important barrier that normally prevents reflux of acidic gastric contents into the esophagus.

Digestion and Absorption

Stomach. The stomach's functions are to store food, mix food with gastric secretions, and empty contents in small boluses into the small intestine. The stomach absorbs only small amounts of water, alcohol, electrolytes, and certain drugs.

The stomach is usually J shaped and lies obliquely in the epigastric, umbilical, and left hypochondriac regions of the abdomen (Fig. 38.5 later in the chapter). It always contains gastric fluid and mucus. The 3 main parts of the stomach are the fundus (cardia), body, and antrum (Fig. 38.1). The pylorus is a small portion of the antrum proximal to the pyloric sphincter. The LES and pyloric sphincter guard the entrance to and exit from the stomach.

The stomach wall has 4 layers. The serous (outer) layer of the stomach is continuous with the peritoneum. The muscular layer consists of the longitudinal (outer) layer, circular (middle) layer, and oblique (inner) layer. The mucosal layer forms folds called rugae that have many small glands. In the fundus the glands contain (1) chief cells, which secrete pepsinogen and (2) parietal cells, which secrete hydrochloric (HCl) acid, water, and intrinsic factor. The secretion of HCl acid makes gastric juice acidic. This acidic pH helps protect us against ingested organisms. Intrinsic factor promotes cobalamin (vitamin B_{12}) absorption in the small intestine.

Small Intestine. The primary functions of the small intestine are digestion and **absorption**, the uptake of nutrients from the gut lumen to the bloodstream. The small intestine is a coiled tube about 23 ft (7 m) in length and 1 to 1.1 in (2.5 to 2.8 cm) in diameter. It extends from the pylorus to the ileocecal valve.

The small intestine is composed of the duodenum, jejunum, and ileum. The ileocecal valve prevents reflux of large intestine contents into the small intestine.

The mucosa of the small intestine is thick, vascular, and glandular. The functional units of the small intestine are *villi*. They are minute, fingerlike projections in the mucous membrane. Villi contain epithelial cells that produce the intestinal digestive enzymes. The epithelial cells on the villi also have *microvilli*. The circular folds in the mucous and submucous layers, along with the villi and microvilli, increase the surface area for digestion and absorption.

The digestive enzymes on the brush border of the microvilli chemically break down nutrients for absorption. Between the bases of the villi lie the crypts of Lieberkühn, which contain the multipotent stem cells. These are the precursors for the other epithelial cell types. Brunner's glands in the submucosa of the duodenum secrete an alkaline fluid containing bicarbonate that neutralizes acidic fluids and protects the mucosa. Intestinal goblet cells secrete mucus that protects the mucosa.

Physiology of Digestion. Digestion is the physical and chemical breakdown of food into absorbable substances. The timely movement of food through the GI tract and the secretion of specific enzymes promote digestion. These enzymes break down foodstuffs to particles of appropriate size for absorption (Table 38.1).

TABLE 38.1 Gastrointestinal Secretions

Daily Amount (mL)	Secretions/ Enzymes	Action
Salivary Glands		
1000–1500	Salivary amylase	Initiation of starch digestion
Stomach		
2500	HCl acid	Activation of pepsinogen to pepsin
	Intrinsic factor	Essential for cobalamin absorption in ileum
	Lipase	Fat digestion
	Pepsinogen	Protein digestion
Small Intestine		
3000	Aminopeptidases	Protein digestion
	Amylase	Carbohydrate digestion
	Enterokinase	Activation of trypsinogen to trypsin
	Lactase	Lactose to glucose and galactose
	Lipase	Fat digestion
	Maltase	Maltose to 2 glucose molecules
	Peptidases	Protein digestion
	Sucrase	Sucrose to glucose and fructose
Pancreas		
700	Amylase	Starch to disaccharides
	Chymotrypsin	Protein digestion
	Lipase	Fat digestion
	Trypsinogen	Protein digestion
Liver and Gallbladder		
1000	Bile	Emulsification of fats and aid in absorption of fatty acids and fat-soluble vitamins (A, D, E, K)

The process of digestion begins in the mouth, where food is chewed, mechanically broken down, and mixed with saliva. Saliva helps us swallow by lubricating food. Saliva contains amylase, which breaks down starches to maltose. Chewing and the sight, smell, thought, and taste of food stimulate the release of saliva. A person makes about 1 L of saliva each day. After swallowing, food moves through the esophagus to the stomach. No digestion or absorption occurs in the esophagus.

Both GI secretion and motility are under neural and hormonal control. Food entering the stomach and small intestine triggers the release of hormones into the bloodstream (Tables 38.2 and 38.3). These hormones play important roles in the control of HCl acid secretion, production and release of digestive enzymes, and motility.

In the stomach, muscle action mixes the food with gastric secretions to form *chyme,* which is now ready for absorption. Protein digestion begins with the release of pepsinogen from chief cells. The stomach's acidic environment results in the conversion of pepsinogen to its active form, pepsin. Pepsin begins the breakdown of proteins. There is minimal digestion of starches and fats. The stomach also serves as a reservoir for food, releasing it slowly into the small intestine. The length of time that food stays in the stomach depends on the composition of the food. The average meal stays in the stomach for 3 to 4 hours.

In the small intestine, the physical presence and chemical nature of chyme stimulates motility and secretion. Secretions involved in digestion include enzymes from the pancreas, bile from the liver, and enzymes from the small intestine (Table 38.1). Carbohydrates are broken down to monosaccharides, fats to glycerol and fatty acids, and proteins to amino acids. Enzymes on the brush border of the microvilli complete the digestion process. These enzymes break down disaccharides to monosaccharides and peptides to amino acids for absorption.

The absorption of most of the end products of digestion occurs in the small intestine. The movement of the villi enables these end products to come in contact with the absorbing membrane. Monosaccharides, fatty acids, amino acids, water, electrolytes, vitamins, and minerals are absorbed.

Elimination

Large Intestine. The large intestine is a hollow, muscular tube around 5 to 6 ft (1.5 to 1.8 m) long and 2 in (5 cm) in diameter. The 4 parts of the large intestine are shown in Fig. 38.2.

The most important functions of the large intestine are water and electrolyte absorption. The large intestine also forms feces and serves as a reservoir for the fecal mass until defecation occurs. Feces are composed of water (75%), bacteria, unabsorbed minerals, undigested foodstuffs, bile pigments, and desquamated (shed) epithelial cells. The large intestine secretes mucus, which acts as a lubricant and protects the mucosa.

Microorganisms in the colon contribute to digestion by (1) producing vitamin K and some B vitamins and (2) breaking down proteins that are not digested or absorbed in the small intestine into amino acids. Bacteria deaminate the amino acids, resulting in ammonia. Ammonia is carried to the liver, where it is converted to urea. Urea is excreted by the kidneys. Bacteria produce gas that escapes the colon through the anus, a phenomenon called *flatulence* or *flatus.* If an infection or antibiotics alter the normal microbiome, an overgrowth of pathogenic bacteria can occur and cause disease.

The movements of the large intestine are usually slow. However, propulsive (mass movements) peristalsis does occur. Food entering the stomach and duodenum triggers gastrocolic and duodenocolic reflexes, resulting in peristalsis in the colon. These reflexes are more active after the first daily meal and often result in bowel evacuation.

Defecation is a reflex action involving voluntary and involuntary control. Feces in the rectum stimulate sensory nerve endings that produce the desire to defecate. The reflex center for defecation is in the parasympathetic nerve fibers in the sacral part of the spinal cord. These fibers produce contraction of the rectum and relaxation of the internal anal sphincter. When a

TABLE 38.2 Phases of Gastric Secretion

Stimulus to Secretion	Secretion
Cephalic (nervous)	
Sight, smell, taste of food (before food enters stomach). Initiated in the CNS and mediated by the vagus nerve.	HCl acid, pepsinogen, mucus
Gastric (hormonal and nervous)	
Food in antrum of stomach, vagal stimulation.	Release of gastrin from antrum into circulation to stimulate gastric secretions and motility
Intestinal (hormonal)	
Presence of chyme in small intestine.	*Acidic chyme* (pH <2): Release of secretin, gastric inhibitory polypeptide, cholecystokinin into circulation to decrease HCl acid secretion
	Chyme (pH >3): Release of gastrin from duodenum to increase acid secretion

TABLE 38.3 Hormones Controlling GI Secretion and Motility

Hormone	Source	Activating Stimuli	Function
Gastrin	Gastric and duodenal mucosa	Stomach distention, partially digested proteins in pylorus	Stimulates gastric acid secretion and motility. Maintains lower esophageal sphincter tone.
Cholecystokinin	Duodenal mucosa	Fatty acids and amino acids in small intestine	Contracts gallbladder and relaxes sphincter of Oddi. Allows increased flow of bile into duodenum. Release of pancreatic digestive enzymes.
Gastric inhibitory peptide	Duodenal mucosa	Fatty acids and lipids in small intestine	Inhibits gastric acid secretion and motility.
Secretin	Duodenal mucosa	Acid entering small intestine	Inhibits gastric motility and acid secretion. Stimulates pancreatic bicarbonate secretion.

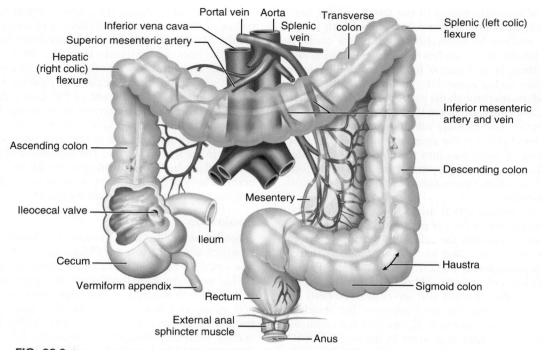

FIG. 38.2 Anatomic locations of the large intestine. (From Patton KT, Thibodeau GA: *Anatomy and physiology*, ed 8, St Louis, 2013, Mosby.)

person feels the desire to defecate, they can voluntarily relax the external anal sphincter. An acceptable environment for defecation is usually needed or the urge to defecate will be ignored. If defecation is suppressed for long periods, problems can occur, such as constipation or fecal impaction.

The Valsalva maneuver, often referred to as "bearing down," can promote defecation. During this maneuver, the person inspires deeply and holds the breath, closing the airway, while contracting abdominal muscles and bearing down. This increases both intraabdominal and intrathoracic pressures and reduces venous return to the heart. The heart rate temporarily decreases along with a decrease in cardiac output. This results in a transient drop in BP. When the patient relaxes, thoracic pressure falls, resulting in a sudden flow of blood into the heart, increased heart rate, and an immediate rise in BP. The Valsalva maneuver may be contraindicated in the patient with a head injury, eye surgery, heart problems, hemorrhoids, abdominal surgery, or liver cirrhosis with portal hypertension.

Liver, Biliary Tract, and Pancreas

Liver. The liver is the largest internal organ in the body, weighing around 3 lb (1.36 kg). It lies in the right epigastric region (Fig. 38.5 later in the chapter). Most of the liver is enclosed in peritoneum. It has a fibrous capsule that divides it into right and left lobes (Fig. 38.3).

The functional units of the liver are lobules. A lobule consists of rows of hepatic cells *(hepatocytes)* arranged in cords that radiate out from a central vein. Capillaries called *sinusoids* lie between the rows of hepatocytes. Sinusoids are lined with Kupffer cells, which carry out phagocytic activity, removing bacteria and toxins from the blood. The hepatic cells secrete bile into tiny canals called *canaliculi*. These merge with other canals to form larger, interlobular bile ducts, which unite into the 2 main left and right hepatic ducts.

The liver has a rich blood supply. The portal circulatory system brings blood to the liver from the stomach, intestines, spleen, and pancreas. About 25% of the blood supply comes from the hepatic artery, a branch of the celiac artery. The other 75% comes from the portal vein. The portal vein carries absorbed products of digestion directly to the liver. Once in the liver, the portal vein branches and comes in contact with each lobule.

The liver performs many functions and is essential for life. It has metabolic, secretory, vascular, and storage functions (Table 38.4). The hepatic cells constantly make bile. Bile consists of water, cholesterol, bile salts, electrolytes, fatty acids, and bilirubin. It provides the alkaline medium needed for the action of pancreatic lipase. Bile salts are needed for fat emulsification and digestion.

Bilirubin Metabolism. The liver constantly makes bilirubin, a pigment derived from the breakdown of hemoglobin (Fig. 38.4). When released into the bloodstream, it binds to albumin. This form of bilirubin is called *unconjugated*. It is insoluble in water and transported to the liver. In the liver, unconjugated bilirubin is conjugated with glucuronic acid and excreted in bile into the intestine. *Conjugated* bilirubin is soluble in water. In the intestines, bacterial action reduces bilirubin to stercobilinogen and urobilinogen. Stercobilinogen accounts for the brown color of stool. A small amount of urobilinogen is reabsorbed into the blood, where it is returned to the liver through the portal circulation. There, it is excreted again in the bile or entered into circulation and excreted by the kidneys.

Biliary Tract. The biliary tract consists of the gallbladder and ducts that connect the liver, gallbladder, and duodenum. The gallbladder is a pear-shaped sac found below the liver. The gallbladder's function is to concentrate and store bile. It holds around 45 mL of bile. The presence of fat in the upper duodenum triggers the release of cholecystokinin, which causes the gallbladder to contract and release bile.

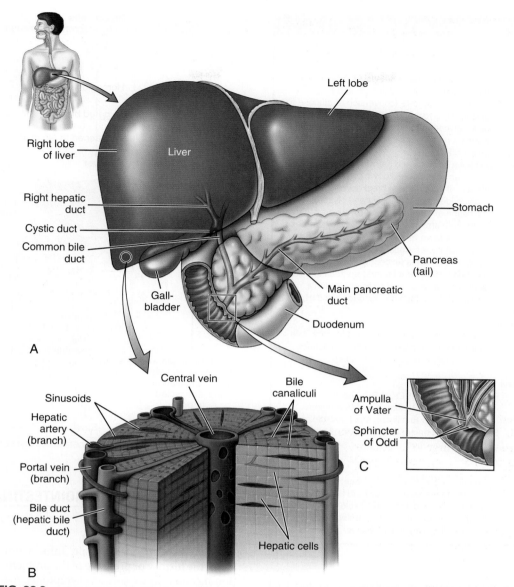

FIG. 38.3 A, Gross structure of the liver, gallbladder, pancreas, and duct system. B, Liver lobule. C, Entrance of the common bile duct into the duodenum.

The hepatic ducts receive bile from the canaliculi in the liver lobules. The left and right hepatic ducts merge with the cystic duct from the gallbladder to form the common bile duct. Bile moves down the common bile duct to enter the duodenum at the ampulla of Vater (Fig. 38.3). The pancreatic duct also enters the duodenum at this point.

Pancreas. The pancreas is a long, slender gland lying behind the stomach and in front of the first and second lumbar vertebrae. It consists of a head, body, and tail. The peritoneum covers the anterior surface of the pancreas. The pancreas has lobes and lobules. The pancreatic duct extends along the gland and enters the duodenum through the common bile duct at the ampulla of Vater (Fig. 38.3).

The pancreas has both exocrine and endocrine functions. The exocrine function contributes to digestion through the production and release of enzymes (Table 38.1). The endocrine function occurs in the islets of Langerhans, whose β cells secrete insulin and amylin; α cells secrete glucagon; δ cells secrete somatostatin; and F cells secrete pancreatic polypeptide.

Gerontologic Considerations: Effects of Aging on Gastrointestinal System

The process of aging changes the functional ability of the GI system. Diet, alcohol intake, and obesity affect organs of the GI system, making it a challenge to separate the sole effects of aging from lifestyle. Many factors can lead to a decrease in appetite and make eating less pleasurable. Caries and periodontal disease can lead to loss of teeth. Taste buds decline in number and the sense of smell lessens, leading to decreased ability to taste. With less saliva, a very dry mouth *(xerostomia)* is common.[1]

Age-related changes in the esophagus include delayed emptying, resulting from smooth muscle weakness; reduced UES opening; and an incompetent LES. Although GI motility decreases with age, secretion and absorption are less affected.

TABLE 38.4 Functions of Liver

Function	Description
Metabolic Functions	
Blood clotting	Synthesis of prothrombin (factor I), fibrinogen (factor II) and factors V, VII, IX, and X.
Carbohydrate metabolism	Performs glycogenesis (conversion of glucose to glycogen), glycogenolysis (process of breaking down glycogen to glucose), gluconeogenesis (formation of glucose from amino acids and fatty acids).
Detoxification	Inactivation of drugs and harmful substances and excretion of their breakdown products.
Fat metabolism	Synthesis of lipoproteins, breakdown of triglycerides into fatty acids and glycerol, formation of ketone bodies, synthesis of fatty acids from amino acids and glucose, synthesis and breakdown of cholesterol.
Protein metabolism	Synthesis of nonessential amino acids, synthesis of plasma proteins (except gamma globulin), synthesis of clotting factors. Bacteria in colon deaminate amino acids to form ammonia (NH_3). which is then changed to urea (NH_4).
Secretory Functions	
Bile production	Formation of bile, which contains bile salts, bile pigments (mainly bilirubin), and cholesterol.
Bilirubin	Conjugation and secretion of bilirubin.
Vascular Functions	
Blood filtration	Breakdown of old RBCs, WBCs, bacteria, and other particles. Breakdown of hemoglobin from old RBCs to bilirubin and biliverdin.
Blood reservoir	Serves as temporary storage for blood within general circulation.
Storage Functions	
Storage	Stores glucose in form of glycogen; vitamins, including fat-soluble (A, D, E, K) and water-soluble (B_1, B_2, cobalamin, folic acid); fatty acids; minerals (iron, copper); and amino acids in form of albumin and β-globulins.

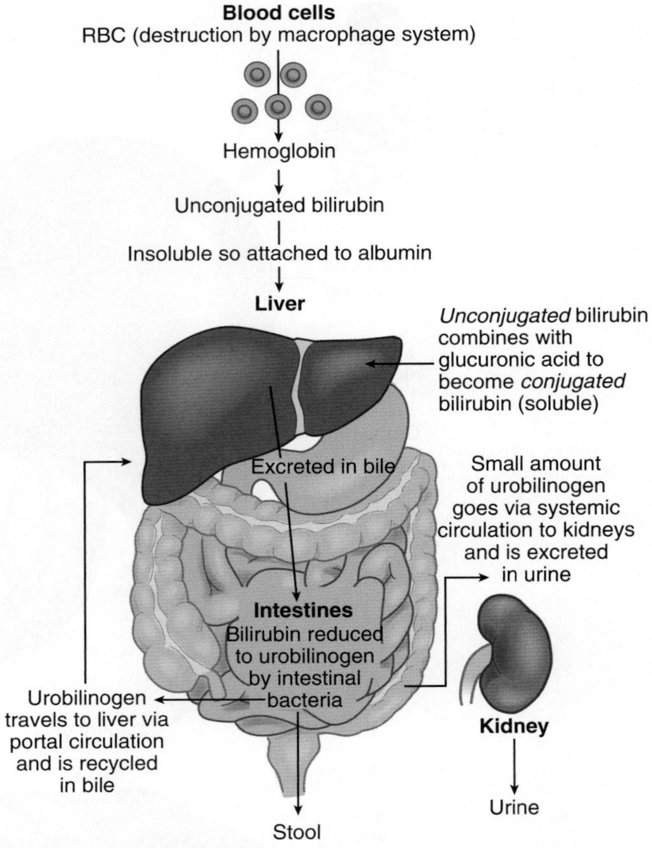

The older adult often has a decrease in intrinsic acid and HCl acid secretion (*hypochlorhydria*).[1]

Constipation affects 30% to 40% of adults over age 60.[2] Factors that may increase the risk for constipation include slower peristalsis, anorectal dysfunction, inactivity, decreased dietary fiber, inadequate fluid intake, and constipating medications. Neurologic, cognitive, and metabolic problems may play a role. See Chapter 42 for a detailed discussion of constipation.

The liver size decreases after 50 years of age but results of liver function tests stay within normal ranges. Age-related enzyme changes in the liver decrease the liver's ability to metabolize drugs and hormones.[1]

The size of the pancreas is unaffected by aging. It does undergo structural changes, such as fibrosis, fatty acid deposits, and atrophy. Gallbladder diseases increase with age.[3]

Older adults, especially those over 85, are at risk for decreased food intake. The inability to obtain food affects nutritional intake. Economic constraints may reduce the number of fresh fruits and vegetables consumed and thus the amount of fiber. Immobility limits the ability to prepare meals. Age-related changes in the GI system and differences in assessment findings are outlined in Table 38.5.

FIG. 38.4 Bilirubin metabolism and conjugation.

ASSESSMENT OF GASTROINTESTINAL SYSTEM

Subjective Data

Important Health Information

Past Health History. Obtain information from the patient about the history or presence of the problems related to GI functioning and fully explore any symptoms. Ask about any abdominal pain, nausea, vomiting, abdominal distention, jaundice, heartburn, dyspepsia, changes in appetite, hematemesis, indigestion, bloating, and trouble swallowing. Review the patient's bowel habits. Ask about diarrhea, constipation, melena, rectal bleeding and excessive gas, Document related conditions, such as food intolerance or allergies, lactose intolerance, and anemia. Ask the patient about a history or presence of diseases such as reflux, gastritis, hepatitis, colitis, gallstones, hemorrhoids, peptic ulcer, cancer, diverticuli, or hernias.

Ask the patient about weight history. Explore in detail any unexplained or unplanned weight loss or gain within the past 6 to 12 months. Discuss any history of chronic dieting and repeated weight loss and gain.

Medications. Assess the patient's past and current use of medications. Ask about the reason for taking the medication, its name, the dose and frequency, length of time taken, its effect, and any side effects. It is critical to include information about over-the-counter (OTC) medications, prescription drugs, herbal products, vitamins, probiotics, and nutritional supplements. Many medications cause side effects in the GI system. GI problems can affect drug absorption and effectiveness.

TABLE 38.5 Gerontologic Assessment Differences

Gastrointestinal System

Expected Aging Changes	Differences in Assessment Findings
Mouth	
Atrophy of gingival tissue	Poor-fitting dentures
Decreased taste buds, decreased sense of smell	Decreased sense of taste (especially salty and sweet)
Decreased volume of saliva	Dry oral mucosa
Gingival retraction	Loss of teeth, dental implants, dentures, difficulty chewing
Esophagus	
Lower esophageal sphincter pressure decreased, motility decreased	Epigastric distress, dysphagia, potential for hiatal hernia and aspiration
Abdominal Wall	
Decreased number and sensitivity of sensory receptors	Less sensitivity to surface pain
Thinner and less taut	More visible peristalsis, easier palpation of organs
Stomach	
Atrophy of gastric mucosa, decreased blood flow	Food intolerances, signs of anemia as result of cobalamin malabsorption, slower gastric emptying
Small Intestines	
Slightly decreased motility and secretion of most digestive enzymes	Indigestion, slowed intestinal transit, delayed absorption of fat-soluble vitamins
Liver	
Decreased protein synthesis, ability to regenerate decreased	Decreased drug and hormone metabolism
Decreased size and lowered position	Easier palpation because of lower border extending past costal margin
Large Intestine, Anus, Rectum	
Decreased anal sphincter tone and nerve supply to rectal area	Fecal incontinence
Decreased muscular tone, decreased motility	Flatulence, abdominal distention, relaxed perineal musculature
Increased transit time, decreased sensation to defecation	Constipation, fecal impaction
Pancreas	
Pancreatic ducts distended, lipase production decreased, pancreatic reserve impaired	Impaired fat absorption, decreased glucose tolerance

TABLE 38.6 Gastrointestinal Surgeries

Procedure	Description
Appendectomy	Removal of appendix
Cholecystectomy	Removal of gallbladder
Choledochojejunostomy	Opening between common bile duct and jejunum
Choledocholithotomy	Opening into common bile duct for removal of stones
Colectomy	Removal of colon
Colostomy	Opening into colon
Esophagoenterostomy	Removal of part of esophagus with segment of colon attached to remaining part
Esophagogastrostomy	Removal of esophagus and anastomosis of remaining part to stomach
Gastrectomy	Removal of stomach
Gastrostomy	Opening into stomach
Glossectomy	Removal of tongue
Hemiglossectomy	Removal of half of tongue
Herniorrhaphy	Repair of a hernia
Ileostomy	Opening into ileum
Mandibulectomy	Removal of mandible
Pyloroplasty	Enlargement and repair of pyloric sphincter area
Vagotomy	Resection of branch of vagus nerve

Many chemicals and drugs are potentially hepatotoxic (see *livertox.nih.gov*) and result in significant harm unless monitored closely. For example, chronic high doses of acetaminophen and nonsteroidal antiinflammatory drugs (NSAIDs) may be hepatotoxic. NSAIDs may predispose a patient to upper GI bleeding, with an increasing risk as the person ages. Other medications, such as antibiotics, may change the normal bacterial composition in the GI tract, resulting in diarrhea. Antacids and laxatives may affect medication absorption. Ask the patient about laxative or antacid use, including the kind and frequency.

Surgery or Other Treatments. Obtain information about hospitalizations for any problems related to the GI system. Record any abdominal or rectal surgery, including the year, reason for surgery, postoperative course, and blood transfusions. Terms related to common GI surgeries are listed in Table 38.6.

TABLE 38.7 Health History

Gastrointestinal System

Health Perception–Health Management
- Describe any measures used to treat GI symptoms such as diarrhea or constipation.
- Do you smoke?* Do you drink alcohol?*
- Are you exposed to any chemicals on a regular basis?* Have you been exposed in the past?*
- Have you recently traveled outside the United States?*

Nutritional-Metabolic
- Describe your usual daily food and fluid intake.
- Do you take any supplemental vitamins or minerals?*
- Have you had any changes in appetite or food tolerance?*
- Has there been any weight change in the past 6 to 12 months?*
- Are you allergic to any foods?*

Elimination
- Describe the frequency and time of day you have bowel movements. What is the consistency of the bowel movement?
- Do you use laxatives or enemas?* If so, how often?
- Have there been any recent changes in your bowel pattern?*
- Do you have any pain with bowel movements or pain relieved by bowel movements?
- Describe any skin problems caused by GI problems.
- Do you need any assistive equipment, such as ostomy equipment, raised toilet seat, commode?

Activity-Exercise
- Do you have limitations in mobility that make it hard for you to obtain and prepare food?*

Sleep-Rest
- Do you have any problem sleeping because of a GI problem?*
- Are you awakened by symptoms such as gas, abdominal pain, diarrhea, or heartburn?*

Cognitive-Perceptual
- Have you had any change in taste or smell that has affected your appetite?*
- Do you have any heat or cold sensitivity that affects eating?*
- Does pain interfere with food preparation, appetite, or chewing?*
- Do pain medications cause constipation, diarrhea, or appetite suppression?*

Self-Perception–Self-Concept
- Describe any changes in your weight that have affected how you feel about yourself.
- Have you had any changes in normal elimination that have affected how you feel about yourself?*
- Have any symptoms of GI disease caused physical changes that are a problem for you?*

Role-Relationship
- Describe the impact of any GI problem on your usual roles and relationships.
- Have any changes in elimination affected your relationships?*
- Do you live alone? Describe how your family or others assist you with your GI problems.

Sexuality-Reproductive
- Describe the effect of your GI problem on your sexual activity.

Coping–Stress Tolerance
- Do you have GI symptoms in response to stressful or emotional situations?*
- Describe how you deal with any GI symptoms that result.

Value-Belief
- Describe any culturally specific health beliefs about food and food preparation that may influence the treatment of your GI problem.

*If yes, describe.

Functional Health Patterns. Key questions to ask a patient with a GI problem are outlined in Table 38.7.

Health Perception–Health Management Pattern. Ask about the patient's health practices related to the GI system, such as maintaining normal body weight, proper dental care, adequate nutrition, and effective elimination habits.

Ask about recent foreign travel with possible exposure to hepatitis or parasitic infestation. Explore any sexual and drug use behaviors that may increase risk for hepatitis exposure. Determine whether the patient has received hepatitis A and B vaccination.

Assess the patient for habits that directly affect GI functioning. The intake of alcohol in large quantities or for long periods has detrimental effects on the stomach mucosa. Chronic alcohol exposure causes fatty infiltration of the liver and can cause damage, leading to cirrhosis and hepatocellular cancer. Obtain a history of cigarette smoking. Nicotine is irritating to the GI tract mucosa. Cigarette smoking is related to GI cancers (especially mouth and esophageal cancers), esophagitis, and ulcers. Smoking delays the healing of ulcers.

Family history is an important part of this health pattern. About one third of cases of colorectal cancer occur in patients with a family history. Because of the relationship between colorectal and breast cancer, ask about a history of either type of cancer in the family.

GENETIC RISK ALERT

Colorectal Cancer
- Colorectal cancer may run in families if first-degree relatives (parents, siblings) or many other family members (grandparents, aunts, uncles) had colorectal cancer. This is especially true when family members are diagnosed with colorectal cancer before age 50
- Genetic conditions associated with an increased risk for colorectal cancer include:
- Hereditary nonpolyposis colorectal cancer (HNPCC). It is caused by mutations in several different genes.
- Familial adenomatous polyposis (FAP). FAP is characterized by multiple polyps that are noncancerous at first but eventually develop into cancer if not treated. Most cases of FAP are due to mutations of the adenomatous polyposis coli (APC) gene.

Inflammatory Bowel Disease (IBD)
- People with IBD have a genetic predisposition or susceptibility to the disease.
- First-degree relatives have a 5- to 20-fold increased risk for developing IBD.

Nutritional-Metabolic Pattern. A thorough nutritional assessment is essential. Take a diet history and ask about both content and amount or portion size. Food preferences and preparation may vary by culture. Open-ended questions allow the patient to express beliefs and feelings about the diet. For example, you can say, "Please tell me about your food and beverage intake over the past 24 hours." A 24-hour dietary recall can be used to analyze the adequacy of the diet. Help the patient recall the preceding day's food intake, including early morning and nighttime intake, snacks, liquids, and vitamin supplements. You can then evaluate the diet in relation to recommended servings for dietary intake using a guide such as MyPlate (www.choosemyplate.gov). A 1-week recall may provide more information on usual dietary patterns. Compare weekday and weekend dietary intake patterns in relation to both the quality and quantity of food.

Ask the patient about the use of sugar and salt substitutes, caffeine intake, and amount of fluid and fiber intake. Note any changes in appetite, food tolerance, and weight. Anorexia and weight loss may indicate cancer or inflammation. Decreased food intake also can be the consequence of economic problems or depression.

Ask about food allergies and dietary intolerances, including lactose and gluten. Have the patient describe the allergic response and any GI symptoms.

Elimination Pattern. Elicit a detailed account of the patient's bowel elimination pattern. Note the frequency, time of day, and usual stool consistency. Ask about the presence of pain with bowel movements, if bowel movements relieve pain, and any recent changes in bowel patterns. Explore the use of laxatives and enemas, including type, frequency, and results.

Document the amount and type of fluid and fiber intake. These influence the frequency and consistency of stools. Inadequate fiber intake can be associated with constipation. Look for any association between a skin and GI problem. Food allergies can cause skin lesions, pruritus, and edema. Diarrhea can result in redness, irritation, and pain in the perianal area. External drainage systems, such as an ileostomy or ileal conduit, may cause local skin irritation.

Activity-Exercise Pattern. Activity and exercise affect GI motility. Immobility is a risk factor for constipation. Assess ambulatory status to determine if the patient can secure and prepare food. If the patient is unable to do these tasks, see if a family member or an outside agency is meeting this need. Note any limitation in the ability to feed oneself. Assess for access to a toilet. Identify the use of and access to supplies such as a commode or ostomy supplies.

Sleep-Rest Pattern. GI symptoms can interfere with the quality of sleep. Nausea, vomiting, diarrhea, indigestion, and bloating can produce sleep problems. Ask the patient if GI symptoms affect sleep or rest. For example, a patient with gastroesophageal reflux disease (GERD) may wake with burning epigastric pain.

A patient may have a bedtime ritual that involves a specific food or beverage. Herbal teas may be sleep inducing. Document individual routines and comply with these whenever possible to avoid sleeplessness. Hunger can prevent sleep, and a light, easily digested snack may be helpful.

Cognitive-Perceptual Pattern. Sensory changes can result in problems related to acquiring, preparing, and ingesting food. Changes in taste or smell can affect appetite and eating pleasure. Vertigo can make shopping or standing at a stove difficult and dangerous. Heat or cold sensitivity can make certain foods painful to eat. Problems in expressive communication limit the patient's ability to state personal dietary preferences.

Both acute and chronic pain influence dietary intake. Behaviors associated with pain include avoiding activity, fatigue, and disrupted eating patterns. For patients receiving opioid medications, assess for decreased appetite, constipation, nausea, and sedation.

Self-Perception–Self-Concept Pattern. Many GI and nutritional problems affect the patient's self-perception. Overweight and underweight persons may have problems related to self-esteem and body image. Repeated attempts to achieve a personally acceptable weight can be discouraging and depressing for some people. The way a person recounts a weight history can alert you to potential problems in this area.

The need for external devices to manage elimination, such as a colostomy or an ileostomy, may be challenging for some patients. The patient's willingness to engage in self-care and to discuss this situation provides you with valuable information related to body image and self-esteem.

The altered physical changes often associated with advanced liver disease can be disturbing for the patient. Jaundice and ascites cause significant changes in external appearance. Assess the patient's attitude about these changes.

Role-Relationship Pattern. Problems related to the GI system, such as cirrhosis, hepatitis, ostomies, obesity, and cancer, may affect the patient's ability to maintain usual roles and relationships. A person may need to leave a job or reduce work hours. Changes in body image and self-esteem can affect relationships.

Sexuality-Reproductive Pattern. Changes related to sexuality and reproductive status can result from problems of the GI system. For example, obesity, jaundice, and ascites could decrease the acceptance of a potential sexual partner. An ostomy can affect the patient's confidence related to sexual activity. Your sensitive questioning can identify potential problems.

Anorexia can affect the reproductive status of a female patient. Obesity leads to reduced fertility and increased miscarriage rates in women.

Coping-Stress Tolerance Pattern. Determine what is stressful for the patient and what coping mechanisms the patient uses. Factors outside the GI tract can influence its functioning. Both psychologic and emotional factors, such as stress and anxiety, influence GI functioning in many people. Stress can manifest as anorexia, nausea, epigastric and abdominal pain, or diarrhea. It can worsen some diseases of the GI system, such as peptic ulcer disease, irritable bowel syndrome, and IBD. However, never attribute GI symptoms solely to psychologic factors.

Value-Belief Pattern. Assess the patient's spiritual and cultural beliefs about food and food preparation. Whenever possible, respect these preferences. Determine if any value or belief could interfere with planned interventions. For example, if the patient with anemia is a vegetarian, you will need to consider how to increase dietary intake of iron-rich foods other than meat. Thoughtful assessment and consideration of the patient's beliefs and values usually increase adherence and satisfaction.

Objective Data
Physical Examination
Mouth

Inspection. Inspect the mouth for symmetry, color, and size. Observe for abnormalities such as pallor or cyanosis, cracking, ulcers, or fissures. The dorsum (top) of the tongue should have a thin white coating. The undersurface should be smooth. Observe for any lesions. Using a tongue blade, inspect the buccal mucosa and note the color, any areas of pigmentation, and any lesions. Dark-skinned persons normally have patchy areas of pigmentation. In assessing the teeth and gums, look for caries; loose teeth; abnormal shape and position of teeth;

CASE STUDY

Subjective Data

(© iStockphoto/ Thinkstock.)

A focused subjective assessment of L.C. revealed the following information:

- **Past Medical History:** Negative history for medical or surgical problems.
- **Medications:** None.
- **Health Perception–Health Management:** L.C. states he has not been feeling well for the past several weeks. He feels weak and is easily fatigued. Denies exposure to chemicals. No recent travel outside of the United States. Smokes 1 pack of cigarettes per day for 20 yrs. Drinks 3 to 4 bottles of beer per day.
- **Nutritional-Metabolic:** L.C. is 5 ft, 9 in tall and weighs 140 lb (BMI: 20.7 kg/m^2). States has been losing weight over the past several months and does not have an appetite. No food allergies.
- **Elimination:** States has had alternating episodes of constipation and diarrhea. He noticed some bright red blood in stools. Has not had a bowel movement for 4 days.
- **Cognitive-Perceptual:** Rates pain as a 9 on a scale of 0 to 10. States pain comes and goes in waves. Prefers to lie still with knees flexed and drawn into his abdomen.

Discussion Questions

1. Which subjective assessment findings are of most concern to you?
2. Based on these subjective assessment findings, what should be included in the physical assessment? What would you be looking for?
3. What would be your priority assessment?

You will learn more about physical examination of the gastrointestinal system in the next section.
(See p. 840 for more information on L.C.)

Answers available at *http://evolve.elsevier.com/Lewis/medsurg.*

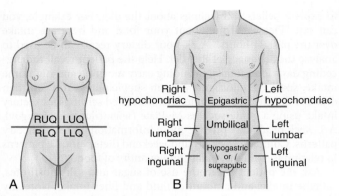

FIG. 38.5 A, Abdominal quadrants. **B,** Abdominal regions. *LLQ,* Left lower quadrant; *LUQ,* left upper quadrant; *RLQ,* right lower quadrant; *RUQ,* right upper quadrant.

and swelling, bleeding, discoloration, or gingival inflammation. Note any distinctive breath odor.

Inspect the pharynx by tilting the patient's head back and depressing the tongue with a tongue blade. Observe the tonsils, uvula, soft palate, and anterior and posterior pillars. Tell the patient to say "ah." The uvula and soft palate should rise and remain in the midline.

Palpation. Palpate any suspicious areas in the mouth. Note ulcers, nodules, indurations, and areas of tenderness. The mouth of the older adult needs careful assessment. Pay attention to dentures (e.g., fit, condition), the ability to swallow, and the tongue, and note any lesions. Ask the patient with dentures to remove them during an oral examination to allow for good visualization and palpation of the area.

Abdomen. We use 2 systems to anatomically describe the surface of the abdomen. One system divides the abdomen into 4 quadrants by a perpendicular line from the sternum to the pubic bone and a horizontal line across the abdomen at the umbilicus (Fig. 38.5, A, and Table 38.8). The other system divides the abdomen into 9 regions (Fig. 38.5, B). Only the epigastric, umbilical, and suprapubic or hypogastric regions are commonly assessed.

For the abdominal examination, good lighting should shine across the abdomen. The patient should be in the supine position and as relaxed as possible. To help relax the abdominal muscles, have the patient slightly flex the knees and raise the head of the bed slightly. The patient should have an empty bladder. Use warm hands when doing the abdominal examination to avoid eliciting muscle guarding. Ask the patient to breathe slowly through the mouth.

The standard approach for examining the abdomen is appropriate for an older adult. The abdomen may be thinner and laxer unless the patient is obese.

Inspection. Assess the abdomen for skin changes (color, texture, scars, striae, dilated veins, rashes, lesions), umbilicus (location and contour), symmetry, contour (flat, rounded [convex], concave, protuberant, distended), observable hernias or masses, and movement (pulsations, peristalsis). A normal aortic pulsation may be seen in the epigastric area. Look across the abdomen tangentially (across the abdomen in a line) for peristalsis. Peristalsis is not normally visible in an adult but may be visible in a thin person.

Auscultation. When you examine the abdomen, auscultate before percussion and palpation because these latter procedures may alter the bowel sounds. Use the diaphragm of the stethoscope to auscultate bowel sounds because they are relatively high pitched. Use the bell of the stethoscope to detect lower pitched sounds. Warm the stethoscope in your hands before auscultating to help prevent abdominal muscle contraction. Listen in the epigastrium and in all 4 quadrants. Start in the right lower quadrant because bowel sounds are normally present there. Listen for bowel sounds for at least 2 minutes. Do not count bowel sounds. Determine if they are normal, hypoactive, or hyperactive.

The frequency and intensity of bowel sounds vary depending on the phase of digestion. Normal sounds are relatively high pitched and gurgling. Stomach growling or loud gurgles (*borborygmi*) indicate hyperperistalsis. The bowel sounds are high pitched (rushes and tinkling) when the intestines are under tension, as in intestinal obstruction. Listen for decreased or absent bowel sounds. A perfectly "silent abdomen" is uncommon.[4] If you are patient and listen for several minutes, you will often find the bowel sounds are not absent but are hypoactive. If you do not hear bowel sounds, note the amount of time you listened in each quadrant without hearing bowel sounds.

Listen for vascular sounds. A *bruit*, best heard with the bell of the stethoscope, is a swishing or buzzing sound and indicates turbulent blood flow. Normally you should not hear aortic bruits.

Percussion. The purpose of percussing the abdomen is to estimate the size of the liver and determine the presence of fluid, distention, and masses. Sound waves vary according to the density of underlying tissues. Air produces a higher pitched, hollow sound termed *tympany.* Fluid or masses produce a

TABLE 38.8 Structures Located in Abdominal Regions

Right Upper Quadrant	Left Upper Quadrant	Right Lower Quadrant	Left Lower Quadrant
• Liver and gallbladder • Pylorus • Duodenum • Head of pancreas • Right adrenal gland • Portion of right kidney • Hepatic flexure of colon • Portion of ascending and transverse colon	• Left lobe of liver • Spleen • Stomach • Body of pancreas • Left adrenal gland • Portion of left kidney • Splenic flexure of colon • Portion of transverse and descending colon	• Lower pole of right kidney • Cecum and appendix • Portion of ascending colon • Bladder (if distended) • Right ovary and fallopian tube • Uterus (if enlarged) • Right spermatic cord • Right ureter	• Lower pole of left kidney • Sigmoid flexure • Part of descending colon • Bladder (if distended) • Left ovary and fallopian tube • Uterus (if enlarged) • Left spermatic cord • Left ureter

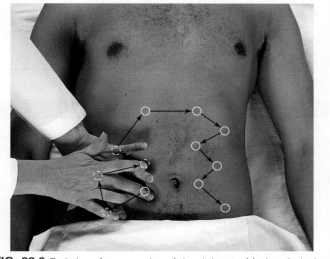

FIG. 38.6 Technique for percussion of the abdomen. Moving clockwise, percuss lightly in all 4 quadrants. (From Jarvis C: *Physical examination and health assessment,* ed 6, St Louis, 2012, Saunders.)

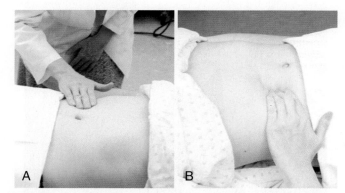

FIG. 38.7 A, Technique for light palpation of the abdomen. B, Technique for deep palpation.

short, high-pitched sound with little resonance termed *dullness.* Lightly percuss all 4 quadrants of the abdomen and assess the distribution of tympany and dullness (Fig. 38.6). Tympany is the predominant percussion sound of the abdomen.

To percuss the liver, start below the umbilicus in the right midclavicular line and percuss lightly upward until you hear dullness. This is the lower border of the liver. Next, start at the nipple line in the right midclavicular line and percuss downward between ribs to the area of dullness indicating the upper border of the liver. Measure the height or vertical space between the 2 borders to determine the size of the liver. The normal range of liver height in the right midclavicular line is 2.4 to 5 in (6 to 12.7 cm).

Palpation. Use palpation to assess the abdominal organs and detect any tenderness, distention, masses, or fluid. Palpation is important because it may reveal a tumor. Begin with light palpation. Palpate any areas in which the patient reports tenderness last.

Use *light palpation* to detect tenderness or cutaneous hypersensitivity, muscular resistance, masses, and swelling. Help the patient relax for deeper palpation. Keep your fingers together and press gently with the pads of the fingertips, depressing the abdominal wall about 0.4 in (1 cm). Use smooth movements and palpate all quadrants (Fig. 38.7, *A*).

Use *deep palpation* to delineate abdominal organs and masses (Fig. 38.7, *B*). Use the palmar surfaces of your fingers to press more deeply. Again, palpate all quadrants and note

the location, size, and shape of masses, as well as the presence of tenderness. During these maneuvers, observe the patient's facial expression because it will provide nonverbal cues of discomfort or pain.

An alternative method for deep abdominal palpation is the two-hand method. Place 1 hand on top of the other and apply pressure to the bottom hand with the fingers of the top hand. With the fingers of the bottom hand, feel for organs and masses. Practice both methods of palpation to determine which is most effective.

Check a problem area on the abdomen for rebound tenderness by pressing in slowly and firmly over the painful site. Withdraw the palpating fingers quickly. Pain on withdrawal of the fingers indicates peritoneal inflammation. Because assessing for rebound tenderness may produce pain and severe muscle spasm, it should be done at the end of the examination and only by an experienced practitioner.

To palpate the liver, place your left hand behind the patient to support the right eleventh and twelfth ribs (Fig. 38.8). The patient may relax on your hand. Press the left hand forward and place the right hand on the patient's right abdomen lateral to the rectus muscle. The fingertips should be below the lower border of liver dullness and pointed toward the right costal margin. Gently press in and up. The patient should take a deep breath with the abdomen so that the liver drops and is in a better position for palpation. Try to feel the liver edge as it comes down to the fingertips. During inspiration, the liver edge should feel firm, sharp, and smooth. Describe the surface and contour and any tenderness. If the patient has chronic obstructive pulmonary disease, large lungs, or a low diaphragm, the liver may be palpated 0.4 to 0.8 in (1 to 2 cm) below the right costal margin.

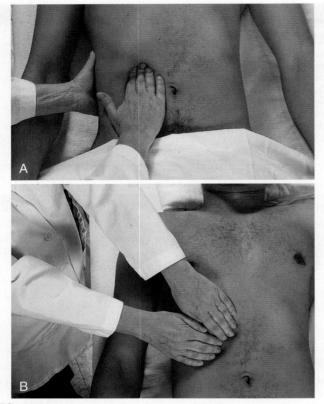

FIG. 38.8 A, Technique for liver palpation. B, Alternative technique to palpate liver with fingers hooked over the costal region. (From Jarvis C: *Physical examination and health assessment*, ed 6, St Louis, 2012, Saunders.)

To palpate the spleen, move to the patient's left side. Place your right hand under the patient, and support and press the patient's left lower rib cage forward. Place your left hand below the left costal margin and press it in toward the spleen. Ask the patient to breathe deeply. The fingertips can feel the tip or edge of an enlarged spleen. The spleen is normally not palpable. If it is palpable, do not continue because manual compression of an enlarged spleen may cause it to rupture.

Rectum and Anus. Inspect perianal and anal areas for color, texture, masses, rashes, scars, erythema, fissures, and external hemorrhoids. Palpate any masses or unusual areas with a gloved hand.

For the digital examination of the rectum, place a gloved, lubricated index finger against the anus while having the patient gently bear down (Valsalva maneuver). Then, as the sphincter relaxes, insert the finger. Point the finger toward the umbilicus. Try to get the patient to relax. Insert the finger into the rectum as far as possible and palpate all surfaces. Assess any nodules, tenderness, or irregularities. Use the gloved finger to remove a stool sample and check it for occult blood. However, a single guaiac-based fecal occult blood test has limited sensitivity in detecting colorectal cancer.

Findings of a normal physical assessment of the GI system are given in Table 38.9. Table 38.10 outlines assessment abnormalities. Gerontologic differences in the GI system and differences in assessment findings are described in Table 38.5. A *focused assessment* is used to evaluate the status of previously identified GI problems and to monitor for signs of new problems. A focused assessment of the GI system is shown on this page.

CASE STUDY
Objective Data: Physical Examination

(© iStockphoto/Thinkstock.)

A focused assessment of L.C. reveals the following: BP 120/74, heart rate 110, respiratory rate 24, temperature 100.4° F (38° C). Abdomen firm and slightly distended. High-pitched bowel sounds in upper quadrants. No bowel sounds auscultated in left lower quadrant. Mild abdominal palpation elicits pain.

Discussion Questions
1. Which physical assessment findings are of most concern to you?
2. Based upon the subjective and objective assessment data presented so far, what would be 3 priority nursing diagnoses?
3. What diagnostic studies do you think may be ordered for L.C.?

You will learn more about diagnostic studies related to the gastrointestinal system in the next section.
(See p. 847 for more information on L.C.)

Answers available at *http://evolve.elsevier.com/Lewis/medsurg*.

FOCUSED ASSESSMENT
Gastrointestinal System

Use this checklist to make sure the key assessment steps have been done.

Subjective
Ask the patient about any of the following and note responses.

Loss of appetite	Y	N
Abdominal pain	Y	N
Changes in stools (e.g., color, blood, consistency, frequency, pain)	Y	N
Nausea, vomiting	Y	N
Painful swallowing	Y	N

Objective: Diagnostic
Check the following results for critical values.

Endoscopy: colonoscopy, sigmoidoscopy, esophagogastroduodenoscopy	✓
CT scan	✓
Radiologic series: upper GI, lower GI	✓
Stool for occult blood or ova and parasites	✓
Liver function tests	✓

Objective: Physical Examination
Inspect

Skin for color, scars, petechiae, and other lesions.	✓
Abdominal contour for symmetry and distention	✓
Perianal area for intact skin, hemorrhoids	✓

Auscultate*

Bowel sounds	✓

Palpate

Abdominal quadrants using light touch	✓
Abdominal quadrants using a deep technique	✓

*NOTE: Perform auscultation before palpation.

DIAGNOSTIC STUDIES OF GASTROINTESTINAL SYSTEM

Tables 38.11 and 38.12 present common diagnostic studies of the GI system. Selected diagnostic studies are described in more detail in the following discussion.

For most diagnostic studies, make sure a signed consent form for the procedure has been completed and is in the medical record. The HCP doing the procedure is responsible for explaining the procedure and obtaining written consent. You have a key role in teaching patients about the procedures. When preparing the patient, it is important to ask about any known allergies to drugs, iodine, shellfish, or contrast media.

Many GI system diagnostic procedures require (1) measures to cleanse the GI tract and (2) ingestion or injection of a contrast medium or a radiopaque tracer. Often the patient has a series of GI diagnostic tests done. Monitor the patient closely to ensure adequate hydration and nutrition during the testing period.

Some diagnostic studies are especially difficult and uncomfortable for the older adult. Adjustments may be needed during the preparation, especially for those with certain health conditions (e.g., diabetes).[5] Make sure to consider any physical limitations when positioning the older patient during testing. Close monitoring is needed to avoid problems, such as dehydration from prolonged fluid restriction and diarrhea from bowel-cleansing procedures.

Radiologic Studies

Upper Gastrointestinal Series. An upper GI series with small bowel follow-through provides visualization of the oropharyngeal area, esophagus, stomach, and small intestine. The procedure consists of the patient swallowing contrast medium (a thick barium solution or gastrograffin) and then assuming different positions on the x-ray table. The movement of the contrast medium is observed with fluoroscopy, and a series of x-rays are taken. An upper GI series is useful in identifying esophageal strictures, polyps, tumors, hiatal hernias, foreign bodies, and ulcers.

Lower Gastrointestinal Series. The purpose of a lower GI series, or a barium enema, is to observe (using fluoroscopy) the colon filling with contrast medium and to observe (by x-ray) the filled colon. The patient receives an enema of contrast medium. This procedure identifies polyps, tumors, and other lesions in the colon. Adding air contrast after the barium provides better visualization (Fig. 38.9). Because the patient must retain the barium, an older or immobile patient may not tolerate it very well.

TABLE 38.9 Normal Physical Assessment of Gastrointestinal System

Mouth
- Moist and pink lips
- Pink and moist buccal mucosa and gingivae without plaques or lesions
- Teeth in good repair
- Protrusion of tongue in midline without deviation or twitches
- Pink uvula (in midline), soft palate, tonsils, and posterior pharynx
- Swallows smoothly without coughing or gagging

Abdomen
- Flat without masses or scars. No bruises
- Bowel sounds in all quadrants
- No abdominal tenderness; nonpalpable liver and spleen
- Liver 10 cm in right midclavicular line
- Generalized tympany

Anus
- Absence of lesions, fissures, and hemorrhoids
- Good sphincter tone
- Rectal walls smooth and soft
- No masses
- Stool soft, brown, and heme negative

TABLE 38.10 Assessment Abnormalities

Gastrointestinal System

Finding	Description	Possible Etiology and Significance
Mouth		
Acute marginal gingivitis	Friable, edematous, painful, bleeding gingivae	Irritation from ill-fitting dentures or orthodontic appliances, calcium deposits on teeth, food impaction
Candidiasis	White, curdlike lesions surrounded by erythematous mucosa	*Candida albicans*
Cheilitis	Inflammation of lips (usually lower) with fissuring, scaling, crusting	Often unknown
Cheilosis	Softening, fissuring, and cracking of lips at angles of mouth	Riboflavin deficiency
Geographic tongue	Scattered red, smooth (loss of papillae) areas on dorsum of tongue	Unknown
Glossitis	Reddened, ulcerated, swollen tongue	Exposure to streptococci, irritation, injury, vitamin B deficiencies, anemia
Herpes simplex	Benign vesicular lesion	Herpesvirus
Leukoplakia	Thickened white patches	Premalignant lesion
Pyorrhea	Recessed gingivae, purulent pockets	Periodontitis
Smooth tongue	Red, slick appearance	Cobalamin deficiency
Ulcer, plaque on lips or in mouth	Sore or lesion	Cancer, viral infections
Esophagus and Stomach		
Dyspepsia	Burning or indigestion	Peptic ulcer disease, gallbladder disease
Dysphagia	Difficulty swallowing, sensation of food sticking in esophagus	Esophageal problems, cancer of esophagus
Eructation	Belching	Gallbladder disease
Hematemesis	Vomiting of blood	Esophageal varices, bleeding peptic ulcer
Nausea and vomiting	Feeling of impending vomiting, expulsion of gastric contents through mouth	GI infections, common manifestation of many GI diseases; stress, fear, and pathologic conditions

TABLE 38.10 Assessment Abnormalities

Gastrointestinal System—cont'd

Finding	Description	Possible Etiology and Significance
Odynophagia	Painful swallowing	Cancer of esophagus, esophagitis
Pyrosis	Heartburn, burning in epigastric or substernal area	Hiatal hernia, esophagitis, incompetent lower esophageal sphincter
Abdomen		
Absence of liver dullness	Tympany on percussion	Air from viscus (e.g., perforated ulcer)
Absent bowel sounds	No bowel sounds on auscultation	Peritonitis, paralytic ileus, obstruction
Ascites	Accumulated fluid within abdominal cavity, eversion of umbilicus (usually)	Peritoneal inflammation, heart failure, metastatic cancer, cirrhosis
Borborygmi	Waves of loud, gurgling sounds	Hyperactive bowel as result of eating
Bruit	Humming or swishing sound heard through stethoscope over vessel	Partial arterial obstruction (narrowing of vessel), turbulent flow (aneurysm)
Distention	Excessive gas accumulation, enlarged abdomen, generalized tympany	Obstruction, paralytic ileus
Hepatomegaly	Enlargement of liver, liver edge >1–2 cm below costal margin	Metastatic cancer, hepatitis, venous congestion
Hernia	Bulge or nodule in abdomen, usually appearing on straining	Inguinal (in inguinal canal), femoral (in femoral canal), umbilical (herniation of umbilicus), or incisional (defect in muscles after surgery)
Hyperresonance	Loud, tinkling rushes	Intestinal obstruction
Masses	Lump on palpation	Tumors, cysts
Nodular liver	Enlarged, hard liver with irregular edge or surface	Cirrhosis, cancer
Rebound tenderness	Sudden pain when fingers withdrawn quickly	Peritoneal inflammation, appendicitis
Splenomegaly	Enlarged spleen	Chronic leukemia, hemolytic states, portal hypertension, some infections
Rectum and Anus		
Fissure	Ulceration in anal canal	Straining, irritation
Hemorrhoids	Thrombosed veins in rectum and anus (internal or external)	Portal hypertension, chronic constipation, prolonged sitting or standing, pregnancy
Mass	Firm, nodular edge	Tumor, cancer
Melena	Abnormal, black, tarry stool containing digested blood	Cancer, bleeding in upper GI tract from ulcers, varices
Pilonidal cyst	Opening of sinus tract, cyst in midline just above coccyx	Probably congenital
Steatorrhea	Fatty, frothy, foul-smelling stool	Chronic pancreatitis, biliary obstruction, malabsorption problems
Tenesmus	Painful and ineffective straining at stool. Sense of incomplete evacuation	Inflammatory bowel disease, irritable bowel syndrome, diarrhea secondary to GI infection (e.g., food poisoning)

TABLE 38.11 Diagnostic Studies

Gastrointestinal System

Study	Description and Purpose	Nursing Responsibility
Endoscopy Colonoscopy	Directly visualizes entire colon up to ileocecal valve with flexible fiberoptic scope. Patient's position is changed frequently during procedure to assist with advancement of scope to cecum. Used to diagnose or detect inflammatory bowel disease, polyps, tumors, and diverticulosis and dilate strictures. Procedure allows for biopsy and removal of polyps without laparotomy.	*Before:* Bowel preparation prior varies depending on HCP. Patient should avoid fiber for up to 72 hr prior, then either a clear or full liquid diet 24 hr before. Bowel cleansing should follow a split-dose regimen. The evening before the procedure, the patient should drink a cleansing solution. The second dose should begin 4–6 hr before the procedure. A split-dose regimen started early morning the day of a procedure provides better cleansing for patients scheduled in the afternoon. Encourage the patient to drink all the solution. Stools will be clear or clear yellow liquid when the colon is clean. Bisacodyl tablets or suppositories may be given before the cleansing solution to remove the bulk of the stool. Explain to patient that a flexible scope will be inserted while patient in side-lying position and sedation will be given. *After:* Patient may have abdominal cramps caused by stimulation of peristalsis because the bowel is constantly inflated with air during procedure. Teach patients about pain post-colonoscopy and the characteristics of this pain. Tell patients if pain lasts longer than 24 hr to notify HCP. Check vital signs. Observe for rectal bleeding and manifestations of perforation (e.g., malaise, abdominal distention, tenesmus).

TABLE 38.11 Diagnostic Studies
Gastrointestinal System—cont'd

Study	Description and Purpose	Nursing Responsibility
Endoscopic retrograde cholangiopancreatography (ERCP)	Fiberoptic endoscope (using fluoroscopy) is orally inserted into descending duodenum. Then common bile and pancreatic ducts are cannulated. Contrast medium is injected into ducts to allow for direct visualization of structures. Can be used to retrieve a gallstone from distal common bile duct, dilate strictures, biopsy, and diagnose pseudocysts.	*Before:* Explain procedure. Keep patient NPO 8 hr before. Ensure consent form is signed. Give sedation immediately before and during procedure. Give antibiotics if ordered. *After:* Check vital signs. Assess for perforation or infection. Pancreatitis is most common complication. Check for return of gag reflex.
Esophagogastroduodenoscopy (EGD)	Directly visualizes mucosal lining of esophagus, stomach, and duodenum with flexible endoscope. Test may use video imaging to visualize stomach motility. Detects inflammation, ulcerations, tumors, varices, or Mallory-Weiss tears. Biopsies may be taken. Varices can be treated with band ligation or sclerotherapy.	*Before:* Keep patient NPO for 8 hr. Ensure consent form is signed. Give preoperative medication if ordered. Explain to patient that local anesthesia may be sprayed on throat before insertion of scope and that patient will be sedated during procedure. *After:* Keep patient NPO until gag reflex returns. Gently tickle back of throat to determine reflex. Use warm saline gargles for relief of sore throat. Check temperature q15–30min for 1–2 hr (sudden temperature spike is sign of perforation).
Laparoscopy (peritoneoscopy)	Visualize peritoneal cavity and contents with laparoscope. Double-puncture peritoneoscopy permits better visualization of abdominal cavity, especially liver. Done in operating room. Can obtain biopsy specimen.	*Before:* Ensure consent form is signed. Keep patient NPO 8 hr. Give preoperative sedative medication. Ensure bladder and bowels are emptied. *After:* Observe for complications of bleeding and bowel perforation after the procedure.
Sigmoidoscopy	Directly visualizes rectum and sigmoid colon with lighted flexible endoscope. Sometimes a special table is used to tilt patient into knee-chest position. Used to detect tumors, polyps, inflammatory and infectious diseases, fissures, hemorrhoids.	*Before:* Bowel preparation similar to colonoscopy. Explain to patient knee-chest position, need to take deep breaths during insertion of scope, and possible urge to defecate as scope is passed. Encourage patient to relax and let abdomen go limp. *After:* Observe for rectal bleeding after polypectomy or biopsy.
Video capsule endoscopy	Patient swallows a vitamin-sized capsule with camera, which provides endoscopic visualization of GI tract (Fig. 38.11). Camera takes >50,000 images during test, relaying them to monitoring device that patient wears on a belt. Images then downloaded to computer. Used to look at areas of GI tract not accessible by upper and lower endoscopy.	*Before:* Keep patient NPO for 8 hr. May have bowel preparation similar to colonoscopy. After swallowing capsule, clear liquids resumed in 2 hr and food in 4 hr. *After:* 8 hr after swallowing device, patient returns to have monitoring device removed. Tell patient that capsule is disposable and will be present in a bowel movement.
Radiology		
Cholangiography		
• Magnetic resonance cholangiopancreatography (MRCP)	Use of MRI technology to obtain images of biliary and pancreatic ducts.	Same as MRI.
• Percutaneous transhepatic (PTC)	Under local anesthesia and monitored anesthesia care, a long needle is passed into liver (under fluoroscopy) and into bile duct. Bile is removed, and radiopaque contrast medium directly injected into biliary system. Used to determine filling of hepatic and biliary ducts.	*Before:* Assess patient's medications for contraindications, precautions, or complications with use of contrast medium. Keep patient NPO for 8–12 hr before test. Start prophylactic IV antibiotics 1 hr prior. *After:* Observe patient for signs of hemorrhage, bile leakage, and infection. Observe safety precautions until sedation wears off. Maintain bed rest for 6 hr.
• Surgical cholangiogram	Contrast medium is injected into common bile duct during surgery on biliary structures.	*Before:* Explain that anesthetic will be used. Assess patient's medications for contraindications, precautions, or complications with use of contrast medium.
Computed tomography (CT) scan	Noninvasive radiologic examination allows for exposures at different depths. Using oral and IV contrast medium accentuates density differences. Detects biliary tract, liver, and pancreatic disorders.	*Before:* Before contrast medium used, evaluate renal function. Assess if patient is allergic to shellfish since the contrast is iodine based. Patient may need to be NPO prior. *During:* Warn patient that contrast injection may cause a feeling of being warm and flushed. Patient must lie completely still during scan. *After:* Encourage patient to drink fluids to avoid renal problems with any contrast.

Continued

TABLE 38.11 Diagnostic Studies

Gastrointestinal System—cont'd

Study	Description and Purpose	Nursing Responsibility
Defecography	Uses fluoroscopy or MRI to assess the shape and position of the rectum during defecation. Using a lubricated small plastic tip, fill rectum and anus with barium. Oral barium allows small bowel to be visualized. The person then sits on a toilet-like seat attached to the x-ray table and is asked to push and empty the rectum. Images are taken while person is sitting at rest, straining, squeezing, and during defecation. Detects pelvic floor abnormalities.	*Before:* Keep patient NPO for 2 hr. 2 enemas are given 2 hr before, 15 min apart. Oral barium is given 1 hr before.
Gastric emptying breath test (GEBT)	Noninvasive test that measures CO_2 in a patient's breath. Used to diagnose delayed gastric emptying. Baseline breath test done. Then patient eats a special test meal that includes a scrambled egg mix and *Spirulina platensis*, a protein enriched with carbon-13. It is measured in breath samples collected at multiple time points after the meal.	*Before:* Teach patient to be NPO after midnight and that the test takes 4 hr. *During:* Can be done in any clinical setting. It does not require special training or special precautions related to radiation.
Lower GI or barium enema	Fluoroscopic x-ray examination of colon using contrast medium, which is given rectally (enema) (Fig. 38.9). Double-contrast or air-contrast barium enema is test of choice. Air is infused after the barium flows through transverse colon. Used to detect the presence of tumors, diverticula, and polyps.	*Before:* Give laxatives and enemas until colon is clear of stool evening before procedure. Follow clear liquid diet evening before procedure. Keep patient NPO for 8 hr before test. Teach patient about the barium enema. Explain that cramping and urge to defecate may occur during procedure and patient may be placed in various positions on tilt table. *After:* Give fluids, laxatives, or suppositories to help in expelling barium. Observe stool for passage of contrast medium. Tell patient that stool may be white for up to 72 hr.
Magnetic resonance imaging (MRI)	Noninvasive procedure using radiofrequency waves and a magnetic field. IV contrast medium (gadolinium) may be used. Used to detect hepatobiliary disease, hepatic lesions, and sources of GI bleeding and stage colorectal and other cancers.	*Before:* Check for pregnancy, allergies, and renal function. Have patient remove all metal objects. Ask about any history of surgical insertion of staples, plates, dental bridges, or other metal appliances. Remove metallic foil patches. Patient may need to be fasting. Assess for claustrophobia and the need for antianxiety medication. *During:* Patient must lie completely still during scan.
Nuclear imaging scans (scintigraphy)	Tracer doses of a radioactive isotope are injected IV, and a scanning device picks up radioactive emission, which is recorded on paper. Shows size, shape, and position of organ. Identifies functional disorders and structural defects.	*Before:* Tell patient that the substance used contains only traces of radioactivity and poses little to no danger. Schedule no more than 1 radionuclide test a day. Explain to patient need to lie flat during scanning.
• Gastric emptying studies	Assesses ability of stomach to empty solids. Patient eats cooked egg containing ^{99m}Tc and toast with water. Images are obtained at 0, 1, 2, and 4 hr later. Used to study gastric emptying disorders caused by ulcers, ulcer surgery, diabetes, cancer, or functional disorders.	Same as above.
• Hepatobiliary scintigraphy (HIDA)	Patient is given IV injection of ^{99m}Tc and positioned under camera to record distribution of tracer dose in liver, biliary tree, gallbladder, and proximal small intestine. Used to identify obstructions of bile ducts (gallstones, tumors), diseases of gallbladder, and bile leaks.	Same as above.
• Scintigraphy of GI bleeding	^{99m}Tc–labeled sulfur colloid or ^{99m}Tc labeling of the patient's own RBCs to determine the site of active GI blood loss. Sulfur colloid or patient's RBCs are injected, then images of abdomen taken at intermittent intervals.	Same as above.
Small bowel series	Contrast medium is ingested, and films taken every 30 min until medium reaches terminal ileum.	*Before:* Explain procedure, including the need to drink contrast medium and assume various positions on x-ray table. Keep patient NPO for at least 8 hr. Tell patient to avoid smoking after midnight. *After:* Take measures to prevent contrast medium impaction (fluids, laxatives). Tell patient that stool may be white for up to 72 hr.

TABLE 38.11 Diagnostic Studies
Gastrointestinal System—cont'd

Study	Description and Purpose	Nursing Responsibility
Upper gastrointestinal (GI) or barium swallow	Fluoroscopic x-ray study using contrast medium. Used to diagnose structural abnormalities of esophagus, stomach, and duodenum.	Same as for small bowel series.
Ultrasound	Noninvasive procedure using high-frequency ultrasound waves, which are passed into body structures and recorded as they are reflected. Used to show size and configuration of an organ.	
• Abdominal ultrasound	A conductive gel is applied to skin, and a transducer is placed on the area. Detects abdominal masses (tumors, cysts), gallstones, biliary and liver disease.	*Before:* Teach patient to be NPO for 8–12 hr. Air or gas can reduce quality of images. Food intake can cause gallbladder contraction, resulting in suboptimal study.
• Endoscopic ultrasound (EUS)	Small ultrasound transducer is installed on tip of endoscope. Because EUS transducer gets close to the organ(s) being examined, images obtained are more accurate and detailed than those provided by traditional ultrasound. Detects and stages esophageal, gastric, rectal, biliary, and pancreatic tumors and abnormalities.	Same as esophagogastroduodenoscopy (EGD).
• Ultrasound elastography (Fibroscan)	Transient elastography uses an ultrasound transducer to assess level of liver fibrosis. Used to monitor patients with chronic liver disease.	*Before:* Explain the need to lie in dorsal decubitus position with right arm in extreme abduction.
Virtual colonoscopy	Combines CT scanning or MRI with computer virtual reality software. Air is introduced via a tube placed in rectum to enlarge colon to enhance visualization. Images obtained while patient is on back and abdomen. Computer combines images to form 2-D and 3-D pictures that are viewed on monitor. Detects intestine and colon diseases, including polyps, cancer, diverticulosis, and lower GI bleeding.	*Before:* Bowel preparation similar to colonoscopy.

TABLE 38.12 Laboratory Studies
Gastrointestinal System

Test	Reference Interval	Description and Purpose
Blood Studies		
Amylase	60–120 U/L (30–220 U/L)	Enzyme secreted by pancreas. Important in diagnosing acute pancreatitis. Level of amylase peaks in 24 hr and then returns to normal in 48–72 hr
Gastrin	25–100 pg/mL when fasting	Hormone secreted by cells of the antrum of the stomach, the duodenum, and the pancreatic islets of Langerhans
Lipase	0–160 U/L	Enzyme secreted by pancreas. Important in diagnosing pancreatitis. Level stays higher longer than serum amylase in acute pancreatitis
Fecal Tests		
Fecal analysis	Note form, consistency, and color. Specimen examined for mucus, blood, pus, parasites, and fat content	Teach patient to keep diet free of red meat for 24–48 hr before occult blood test
Stool culture	Normal intestinal flora	Tests for the presence of bacteria, including *Clostridium difficile*

Virtual Colonoscopy. *Virtual colonoscopy* combines CT scanning or MRI to produce images of the colon and rectum less invasively. It requires radiation and prior cleansing of the colon but no sedation.

Compared to conventional colonoscopy, virtual colonoscopy provides a better view inside the colon that is narrow from inflammation or a growth.[6] If a polyp is found, it will have to be removed by conventional colonoscopy. Virtual colonoscopy may be less sensitive in obtaining information on the details and color of the mucosa and in detecting small (less than 10 mm) or flat polyps.

Ascending colon   Transverse colon   Descending colon

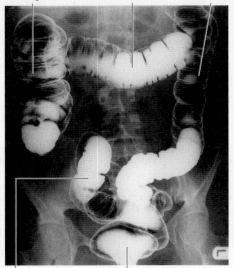

Sigmoid colon   Rectum

FIG. 38.9 Barium enema x-ray showing the large intestine. (From Drake RL, Vogl W, Mitchell AWM: *Gray's anatomy for students,* ed 3, Edinburgh, 2014, Churchill Livingstone.)

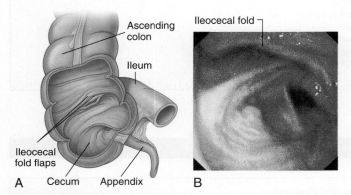

Ascending colon

Ileum

Ileocecal fold flaps

A   Cecum   Appendix

Ileocecal fold

B

FIG. 38.10 **A,** Illustration showing the ileocecal junction and the ileocecal fold. **B,** Endoscopic image of the ileocecal fold. (From Drake RL, Vogl W, Mitchell AWM: *Gray's anatomy for students,* ed 3, Edinburgh, 2015, Churchill Livingstone.)

Endoscopy

Endoscopy refers to the direct visualization of a body structure through an endoscope. An endoscope is a fiberoptic instrument with a light and camera attached, allowing the ability to take video and still pictures (Fig. 38.10). Some endoscopes have a channel through which to pass instruments, such as biopsy forceps and cytology brushes.

Endoscopy can examine the esophagus, stomach, duodenum, and colon. *Endoscopic retrograde cholangiopancreatography* (ERCP) visualizes the pancreatic, hepatic, and common bile ducts. Endoscopy is often combined with diagnostic procedures, including biopsy, cytologic studies, invasive, and therapeutic

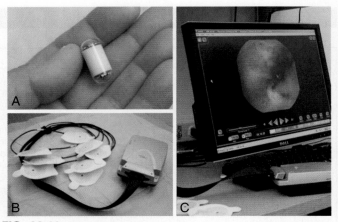

FIG. 38.11 Capsule endoscopy. **A,** The pill-sized video capsule has its own camera and light source. **B,** As it travels through the GI tract, it sends messages through sensing electrodes placed on the chest and abdomen to a data recorder worn on a waist belt. **C,** After the test, the images are viewed on a computer. (From Dye CE, Gaffney RR, Dykes TM, et al: Endoscopic and radiographic evaluation of the small bowel in 2012, *Am J Med* 125:1228e1, 2012.)

procedures. Examples include polypectomy, sclerosis or banding of varices, cauterization of bleeding sites, common bile duct stone removal, and balloon dilation.

The major complication of GI endoscopy is perforation through the structure being studied. Many endoscopic procedures require short-acting IV sedation. All endoscopic procedures require informed, written consent. Specific endoscopy procedures are discussed in Table 38.11.

Capsule endoscopy is a noninvasive approach to visualize the GI tract (Fig. 38.11). Colon capsule endoscopy is useful in diagnosing small bowel disease and monitoring inflammation in patients with IBD. Its sensitivity in detecting small lesions, colonic polyps, and colorectal cancer is under investigation.[7]

Liver Function Studies

Liver function tests (LFTs) are laboratory (blood) studies that reflect hepatic disease. Table 38.13 describes the most common LFTs.

Liver Biopsy

The purpose of a liver biopsy is to obtain hepatic tissue to use to establish a diagnosis of cancer or assess and stage fibrosis. It may be done to follow the progress of liver disease, such as chronic hepatitis.

The 2 types of liver biopsy are open and closed. The *open method* involves making an incision and removing a wedge of tissue. It is done in the operating room with the patient under general anesthesia, often with another surgical procedure. The *closed,* or *needle, biopsy* is a percutaneous procedure. It is often done with ultrasound or CT guidance. The HCP administers a local anesthetic, then inserts a needle between 6th and 7th or 8th and 9th intercostal spaces on the right side to obtain specimen of hepatic tissue. Table 38.14 outlines the nursing management of a patient undergoing a liver biopsy.

TABLE 38.13 Liver Function Tests

Test	Reference Interval	Description and Purpose
Bile Formation and Excretion		
Serum bilirubin		Measures liver's ability to conjugate and excrete bilirubin, distinguishing between unconjugated (indirect) and conjugated (direct) bilirubin in plasma
• Total	0.3–1.0 mg/dL (5.1–17 μmol/L)	Measures direct and indirect total bilirubin
• Direct	0.1–0.3 mg/dL (1.7–5.1 μmol/L)	Measures conjugated bilirubin. High in obstructive jaundice
• Indirect	0.2–0.8 mg/dL (3.4–12 μmol/L)	Measures unconjugated bilirubin. High in hepatocellular and hemolytic conditions
Urinary bilirubin	0 or negative	Measures urinary excretion of conjugated bilirubin
Hemostatic Function		
Prothrombin time (PT)	11–12.5 sec	Determination of prothrombin activity
Vitamin K	0.1–2.2 ng/mL (0.22–4.88 nmol/L)	Essential cofactor for many clotting factors
Lipid Metabolism		
Cholesterol (serum)	200 mg/dL (<5.2 mmol/L), varying with age	Synthesized and excreted by liver. High in biliary obstruction. Low in cirrhosis and malnutrition
Protein Metabolism		
α-Fetoprotein	<10 ng/mL (<10 mcg/L)	Sign of hepatocellular cancer
Ammonia	10–80 mcg/dL (6–47 μmol N/L)	Conversion of ammonia to urea normally occurs in liver. Increase can result in hepatic encephalopathy secondary to liver cirrhosis
Protein (serum)	• Albumin: 3.5–5.0 g/dL (35–50 g/L) • Globulin: 2.3–3.4 g/dL (23–34 g/L) • Total protein: 6.4–8.3 g/dL (64–83 g/L)	Measures serum proteins made by liver
Serum Enzymes		
Alanine aminotransferase (ALT)	4–36 U/L	High in liver damage and inflammation
Alkaline phosphatase (ALP)	30–120 U/L (0.5–2.0 μkat/L)	Originates from bone and liver. Serum levels rise when excretion is impaired because of obstruction in biliary tract
γ-Glutamyl transpeptidase (GGT)	Male and Female > 45: 8–38 U/L Female < 45: 5–27 U/L	Present in biliary tract, not in skeletal or heart muscle. High in hepatitis and alcoholic liver disease. More sensitive for liver dysfunction than ALP
Aspartate aminotransferase (AST)	0–35 U/L (0.0–0.58 μkat/L)	High in liver damage and inflammation

TABLE 38.14 Nursing Management
Care of the Patient Undergoing Liver Biopsy

Preprocedure
• Perform baseline assessment, including vital signs, pulse oximetry.
• Withhold food and fluids for 8–12 hr before.
• Check patient's coagulation status (prothrombin time, clotting or bleeding time).
• Give sedative and other drugs, as ordered.
• Obtain type and crossmatch.
• Teach patient and caregiver about procedure and postprocedure care. Explain need to hold breath after expiration when needle is inserted.
• Ensure informed consent has been signed.

Postprocedure
• Check vital signs to detect internal bleeding q15min × 2, q30min × 4, q1hr × 4.
• Notify HCP of dyspnea, cyanosis, and restlessness, which may occur with pneumothorax.
• Keep patient lying on right side for minimum of 2 hr to splint puncture site. Then maintain bed rest for 12–14 hr, as ordered.
• Apply a small dressing over the needle insertion site.
• Teach patient and caregiver about discharge care including signs and symptoms to report to HCP (e.g., site complications) and any activity restrictions. Tell patient to avoid straining or coughing, which cause increased intraabdominal pressure.

CASE STUDY
Objective Data: Diagnostic Studies

(© iStockphoto/ Thinkstock.)

The ED physician performs a rectal examination and finds a palpable mass. The following diagnostic tests are ordered:
• CBC
• Electrolytes
• Liver function tests
• Urinalysis
• CT scan of the abdomen
• Colonoscopy

The CBC reveals an Hgb of 6.8 g/dL and Hct of 20%. The WBC count is normal. The electrolytes, liver function tests, and urinalysis are within normal limits. The CT scan reveals pockets of gas and fluid in the ascending colon and 2 medium-sized tumors in the transverse colon.

Discussion Questions
1. Which diagnostic study results are of most concern to you?
2. With this information, what other diagnostic studies would you expect to be ordered for L.C.?
3. What are the interprofessional team's priorities for L.C. at this time?

Case study continued in Chapter 42 on p. 966.

Answers available at *http://evolve.elsevier.com/Lewis/medsurg.*

BRIDGE TO NCLEX EXAMINATION

The number of the question corresponds to the same-numbered outcome at the beginning of the chapter.

1. A patient is admitted to the hospital with a diagnosis of diarrhea with dehydration. The nurse recognizes that increased peristalsis resulting in diarrhea can be related to
   a. sympathetic inhibition.
   b. mixing and propulsion.
   c. sympathetic stimulation.
   d. parasympathetic stimulation.

2. A patient has a high blood level of indirect (unconjugated) bilirubin. One cause of this finding is that
   a. the gallbladder is unable to contract to release stored bile.
   b. bilirubin is not being conjugated and excreted into the bile by the liver.
   c. the Kupffer cells in the liver are unable to remove bilirubin from the blood.
   d. there is an obstruction in the biliary tract preventing flow of bile into the small intestine.

3. As gastric contents move into the small intestine, the bowel is normally protected from the acidity of gastric contents by the
   a. inhibition of secretin release.
   b. secretion of mucus by goblet cells.
   c. release of pancreatic digestive enzymes.
   d. release of gastrin by the duodenal mucosa.

4. A patient is jaundiced, and her stools are clay colored. This is *most* likely related to
   a. decreased bile flow into the intestine.
   b. increased production of urobilinogen.
   c. increased bile and bilirubin in the blood.
   d. increased production of cholecystokinin.

5. An 80-yr-old man states that, although he adds a lot of salt to his food, it still does not have much taste. The nurse's response is based on the knowledge that the older adult
   a. should not have any changes in taste.
   d. has a loss of taste buds, especially for sweet and salt.
   c. has some loss of taste but no problems chewing food.
   d. loses the sense of taste because the ability to smell is decreased.

6. When the nurse is assessing the health perception–health maintenance pattern as related to gastrointestinal function, an appropriate question to ask is
   a. "What is your usual bowel elimination pattern?"
   b. "What percentage of your income is spent on food?"
   c. "Have you traveled to a foreign country in the last year?"
   d. "Do you have diarrhea when you are under a lot of stress?"

7. During an examination of the abdomen the nurse should
   a. position the patient in the supine position with the bed flat and knees straight.
   b. listen for bowel sounds in the epigastrium and all four quadrants for 2 minutes.
   c. describe bowel sounds as absent if no sound is heard in a quadrant after 2 minutes.
   d. use the following order of techniques: inspection, palpation, percussion, auscultation.

8. Normal physical assessment findings of the gastrointestinal system are *(select all that apply)*
   a. nonpalpable spleen.
   b. borborygmi in upper right quadrant.
   c. tympany on percussion of the abdomen.
   d. liver edge 2 to 4 cm below the costal margin.
   e. finding of a firm, nodular edge on the rectal examination.

9. In preparing a patient for a colonoscopy, the nurse explains that
   a. a signed permit is not needed.
   b. sedation will be used during the procedure.
   c. one cleansing enema part of the required preparation.
   d. light meals should be eaten for 3 days before the procedure.

1. d, 2. b, 3. b, 4. a, 5. b, 6. c, 7. b, 8. a, c, 9. b

For rationales to these answers and even more NCLEX review questions, visit *http://evolve.elsevier.com/Lewis/medsurg*.

ⓔ EVOLVE WEBSITE/RESOURCES LIST

http://evolve.elsevier.com/Lewis/medsurg
Review Questions (Online Only)
Key Points
Answer Keys for Questions
- Rationales for Bridge to NCLEX Examination Questions
- Answer Guidelines for Case Studies on pp. 835, 838, 840, and 847
Conceptual Care Map Creator
Audio Glossary
Supporting Media
- Animation
- Rectal Examination
Content Updates

REFERENCES

1. Lichtenstein AH: Optimal nutrition for the older adults. In: Rippe JM: *Nutrition in lifestyle medicine*, New York, 2017, Humana Press.
*2. Emmanuel A, Mattace-Raso F, Neri MC, et al: Constipation in older people: A consensus statement, *Int J Clin Pract* 1:71, 2017.
3. Matsumoto T, Seno H: Updated trends in gallbladder and other biliary tract cancers worldwide, *Clin Gastroenterol Hepatol* 16:339, 2018.
4. Jarvis C: *Physical examination and health assessment*, ed 7, St Louis, 2016, Saunders.
*5. Ho SB, Hovsepians R, Gupta S: Optimal bowel cleansing for colonoscopy in the elderly patient, *Drugs Aging* 34:163, 2017.
6. National Digestive Diseases Information Clearinghouse: Virtual colonoscopy. Retrieved from *www.niddk.nih.gov/health-information/health-topics/diagnostic-tests/virtual-colonoscopy/Pages/diagnostic-test.aspx*.
7. Yu S, Sridhar S, Chamberlain SM: Capsule endoscopy: Diagnostic and therapeutic procedures in gastroenterology, New York, 2018, Springer.

*Evidence-based information for clinical practice.

Nutritional Problems

Mariann M. Harding

*They may forget your name, but they will never forget
how you made them feel.*

Maya Angelou

ⓔ http://evolve.elsevier.com/Lewis/medsurg

LEARNING OUTCOMES

1. Relate the essential components of a well-balanced diet to their impact on health outcomes.
2. Describe the etiology, clinical manifestations, and interprofessional and nursing management of malnutrition.
3. Describe the components of a nutritional assessment.
4. Explain the indications, complications, and nursing management related to the use of enteral nutrition.
5. Explain the indications, complications, and nursing management related to the use of parenteral nutrition.
6. Compare the etiology, clinical manifestations, and nursing management of eating disorders.

KEY TERMS

This chapter focuses on problems related to nutrition. A review of normal nutrition provides a basis for evaluating nutritional status. We need sufficient energy, protein, and other nutrients to maintain health. Many problems affect nutrition by changing the way we ingest, absorb, digest, and metabolize nutrients. These changes can lead to malnutrition, and health problems which affect functional status and quality of life. This makes it important for nurses to incorporate assessment and interventions aimed at promoting optimal nutrition.

NUTRITIONAL PROBLEMS

Nutrition is the sum of processes by which one takes in and uses nutrients. We view nutritional status on a continuum from undernutrition to normal nutrition to overnutrition. Any change in nutrient intake or use can cause nutritional problems. Nutritional problems occur in all ages, cultures, ethnic groups, and socioeconomic classes and across all educational levels.

Many factors influence nutritional status. A person establishes attitudes toward food and eating habits early. Dietary intake often reflects cultural or religious preferences. A person or family's financial status influences the type and amount of nutritious food they can buy.[1]

NORMAL NUTRITION

Nutrition is important for energy, growth, and maintaining and repairing body tissues. Optimal nutrition (in the absence of any underlying disease process) results from eating a balanced diet. The major components of the basic food groups are macronutrients (carbohydrates, fats, proteins), micronutrients (vitamins, minerals, electrolytes), and water. Optimal nutrition and daily physical activity are essential for a healthy lifestyle.

Body type, age, gender, medications, physical activity, and the presence or absence of disease influence a person's daily caloric requirements. Adjustments in caloric intake are necessary depending on changes in health status and daily activity level. There are several ways to estimate caloric need. The Mifflin–St. Jeor equation calculates daily adult energy (calorie) requirements based on resting metabolic rate (Table 39.1).[2] A simpler way to estimate daily calories needed is by kilocalories

TABLE 39.1 Estimating Daily Energy (Calorie) Requirements

Mifflin–St. Jeor Equation

For each gender, use the formula below to calculate energy expenditure:

Men: 10 × weight (kg) + 6.25 × height (cm) − 5 × age (yr) + 5
Women: 10 × weight (kg) + 6.25 × height (cm) − 5 × age (yr) − 161

To determine total daily calorie needs, the energy expenditure is multiplied by the appropriate activity factor, as follows:

1.200 = sedentary (little or no exercise)
1.375 = lightly active (light exercise/sports 1–3 days/wk)
1.550 = moderately active (moderate exercise/sports 3–5 days/wk)
1.725 = very active (hard exercise/sports 6–7 days a wk)
1.900 = extra active (very hard exercise/sports and physical job)

Example

Man: Weight 180 lb (82 kg); height 5 ft, 10 in (178 cm); age 50, very active

Energy expenditure = 10 (82) + 6.25 (178) − 5 (50) + 5 × 1.725 = 2911

Woman: Weight 150 lb (68 kg); height 5 ft, 6 in (168 cm); age 60; lightly active

Energy expenditure = 10 (68) + 6.25 (168) − 5 (60) −161 × 1.375 = 1745

TABLE 39.2 Nutritional Therapy

Foods High in Protein

Complete Proteins	Incomplete Proteins
• Eggs	• Grains (e.g., corn)
• Fish	• Legumes (e.g., navy beans, soybeans, peas)
• Meats	• Nuts (e.g., peanuts)
• Milk and milk products (e.g., cheese)	• Seeds (e.g., sesame seeds, sunflower seeds)
• Poultry	

per kilogram (kcal/kg). An average adult should consume 20 to 25 cal/kg body weight to lose weight, 25 to 30 cal/kg to maintain body weight, and 30 to 35 cal/kg to gain weight.[3] Energy needs may be greater during illness.

Carbohydrates, the body's main source of energy, yield about 4 cal/g. We classify them as either simple or complex, depending on the number of sugars they have. Simple carbohydrates come in 2 forms: monosaccharides (e.g., glucose, fructose), which are found in fruits and honey, and disaccharides (e.g., sucrose, maltose, lactose). They are found in foods such as table sugar, malted cereal, and milk.. Complex carbohydrates (polysaccharides) include starches, such as cereal grains, potatoes, and legumes.

Carbohydrates are the chief protein-sparing ingredient in a nutritionally sound diet. The Dietary Reference Intake (DRI) recommendations are that 45% to 65% of total calories should come from carbohydrates.[3] A person should take around 14 g of dietary fiber per 1000 calories eaten per day from fruits, vegetables, and whole grains. This equals roughly 28 to 30 g for a typical 2000-calorie diet. We should choose food and beverages with little added sugar or caloric sweeteners.

Fats are a major source of energy for the body. One gram of fat yields 9 calories. Fats are stored in adipose tissue and the abdominal cavity. They act as carriers of essential fatty acids and fat-soluble vitamins. Fats give us a feeling of satiety after eating. Fat intake should be no more than 20% to 35% of total calories.[3]

Fats can be divided into (1) potentially harmful (saturated fat and *trans* fat) and (2) healthier dietary fat (monounsaturated and polyunsaturated fat). One type of polyunsaturated fat, omega-3 fatty acids, may be especially beneficial to your heart. Omega-3 fatty acids (found in some types of fatty fish) appear to decrease the risk for coronary artery disease.[4]

Diets high in excess calories, usually in the form of fats, contribute to the development of obesity. We should consume less than 10% of calories from saturated fatty acids (about 20 g of saturated fat per day in a 2000-calorie diet) and choose foods with no *trans*-fatty acids.

Proteins are an essential part of a well-balanced diet. They are needed for tissue growth, repair, and maintenance; body

regulatory functions; and energy production. Ideally, 10% to 35% of daily caloric needs should come from protein.[3] The recommended daily protein intake is 0.8 to 1 g/kg of body weight. For the normal healthy person of average body size, this equals about 45 to 65 g of protein daily. One gram of protein yields 4 calories. Amino acids are the fundamental units of protein structure. We classify the 22 amino acids as essential or nonessential. The body can make nonessential amino acids if an adequate supply of protein is available. The body cannot make the 9 essential amino acids. Their availability depends totally on dietary sources. We obtain them from both animal and plant sources. *Complete proteins* contain all the essential amino acids. Proteins that lack one or more of the essential amino acids are *incomplete proteins*. Table 39.2 lists foods high in protein.

Vitamins are organic compounds needed in small amounts for normal metabolism. Vitamins function primarily in enzyme reactions that facilitate amino acid, fat, and carbohydrate metabolism. A diet consisting of foods from the 5 basic food groups is essential for obtaining the recommended dietary allowances of essential vitamins. Vitamins are divided into 2 categories: *water-soluble* vitamins (vitamin C and the B-complex vitamins) and *fat-soluble* vitamins (vitamins A, D, E, and K). Since the body stores excess fat-soluble vitamins, consuming too much can result in toxicity. There are upper limits for vitamins A, D, and E.

PROMOTING POPULATION HEALTH

Health Impact of a Well-Balanced Diet

- Reduces risk for anemia
- Maintains normal body weight and prevents obesity
- Maintains good bone health and reduces risk for osteoporosis
- Lowers the risk for developing high cholesterol and type 2 diabetes
- Decreases the risk for heart disease, hypertension, and certain types of cancers

Mineral salts (e.g., magnesium, iron, calcium) make up about 4% of the total body weight. The body needs minerals to build and repair tissues, regulate body fluids, and assist in various functions. Minerals needed in amounts greater than 100 mg/day are *major minerals*. Minerals present in minute amounts are *trace elements*. Table 39.3 lists the major minerals and trace elements. Some minerals are stored and can be toxic if taken in excess amounts. The amount of minerals needed daily varies from a few micrograms of trace minerals to 1 g or more of the major minerals, such as calcium, phosphorus, and sodium. A well-balanced diet usually meets the daily requirements of minerals. However, deficiency and excess states can occur.

TABLE 39.3 Major Minerals and Trace Elements

Major Minerals	Trace Elements
• Calcium	• Chromium
• Chloride	• Copper
• Magnesium	• Fluoride
• Phosphorus	• Iodine
• Potassium	• Iron
• Sodium	• Manganese
• Sulfur	• Molybdenum
	• Selenium
	• Zinc

TABLE 39.4 Nutritional Therapy

Foods High in Iron

These foods provide 25%–39% of the Dietary Reference Intake (DRI) of iron.

Food	Selected Serving Size
Breads, Cereals, and Grain Products	
Farina, regular or quick cooked (enriched)	⅔ cup
Oatmeal, instant, fortified, prepared (enriched)	⅔ cup
Ready-to-eat cereals, fortified (enriched)	1 oz
Meat, Poultry, Fish, and Alternatives	
Beef liver, braised	3 oz
Chicken or turkey liver, braised	½ cup diced
Clams: steamed, boiled, or canned (drained)	3 oz
Oysters: baked, broiled, steamed, or canned (undrained)	3 oz
Pork liver, braised	3 oz
Soybeans, cooked	½ cup

VEGETARIAN DIET

There are many types of vegetarians and no strict definition of the word "vegetarian." The common element among all vegetarians is the exclusion of red meat from the diet. Many vegetarians are *vegans,* who are pure or total vegetarians and eat only plants, or *lacto-ovo-vegetarians.* They eat plants, dairy products, and eggs.

Without a well-planned diet, vegetarians can have vitamin or protein deficiencies. Plant protein, although a lesser quality than animal protein, fulfills most protein requirements. Combinations of vegetable protein foods (e.g., cornmeal, kidney beans) can increase the nutritional value. Milk made from soybeans or almonds is an excellent protein source and should be calcium fortified. Vegans and lacto-ovo-vegetarians are also at risk for iron deficiency. Table 39.4 lists examples of foods high in iron.

The primary deficiency for a strict vegan is lack of cobalamin (vitamin B_{12}).[5] We obtain cobalamin from animal protein, special supplements, or foods fortified with the vitamin. Vegans not using cobalamin supplements are susceptible to the development of megaloblastic anemia and the neurologic signs of cobalamin deficiency. Other deficiencies that may be present in a vegan diet include calcium, zinc, and vitamins A and D.

Culturally Competent Care: Nutrition

People have unique cultural heritages that may affect eating customs and nutritional status. Each culture has its own beliefs and behaviors related to food and the role that food plays in the cause and treatment of disease. Culture and religion can influence which foods are considered edible, how they are prepared, when they are eaten, and how and who prepares them. For example, some religions, such as Judaism and Islam, have specific laws about food. Assess the extent to which Jewish or Muslim patients adhere to Kosher or Halal dietary practices to ensure that we serve proper meals. The websites Kosher Quest (*www. kosherquest.org*) and the Islamic Food and Nutrition Council of America (*www.ifanca.org*) provide detailed information.

Assess the patient's diet history and implement needed dietary changes. Avoid cultural stereotyping by not making assumptions or generalizations about diet based on a person's cultural background. Dietary habits differ considerably within and among ethnic groups. Acculturation, the process by which immigrants adopt the lifestyle of a new culture, can affect dietary practices.

It is important to know whether the patient eats "traditional foods" associated with the culture. Assess the impact of eating traditional foods on health. For example, traditional foods eaten by some Asian Americans may be high in fiber and low in fat and cholesterol. The diet may be low in calcium because of limited dairy product intake. "Soul food," identified with some blacks, includes foods such as collard greens and vegetables prepared with pork; beans; fried meats; grits; and cornbread. This diet may increase the risk for diabetes and heart disease.

Considering cultural beliefs is important when planning and monitoring acceptance of dietary changes. Culture can influence the perception of body weight and size. Ask the patient or family about how culture affects dietary choices and weight maintenance. For example, in some cultures obesity does not carry the stigma that it does in Western cultures. This may make teaching about weight reduction harder. A Jewish patient who eats only Kosher food may find comfort in knowing that an enteral feeding formula is Kosher. Another example of culturally sensitive planning is adjusting meal plans for the Muslim patient observing Ramadan (the Islamic month of *fasting,* in which Muslims refrain from eating and drinking during daylight hours).

MALNUTRITION

Malnutrition is a deficit, excess, or imbalance of essential nutrients. It may occur with or without inflammation. Malnutrition affects body composition and functional status. Other terms used to describe malnutrition include *undernutrition* and *overnutrition.*

Undernutrition occurs when nutritional reserves are depleted, and nutrient and energy intake are not sufficient to meet daily needs or added metabolic stress.[6] *Overnutrition* refers to the ingestion of more food than is required for body needs, as in obesity.

Malnutrition is a problem in both developing and developed countries across the care continuum (community, hospital, long-term care). Prevalence rates for malnutrition in the hospital setting range from 30% to 50%.[7] The prevalence of malnutrition in older adults based on the Mini Nutritional Assessment (MNA) ranges from about 3% (community-dwelling older adults) to 30% (rehabilitation settings).[8]

Etiology

Several terms describe the types and causes of adult malnutrition. Older terms still used in some settings include *primary* or *secondary protein-calorie malnutrition* (PCM), *marasmus,* and *kwashiorkor.* Marasmus and kwashiorkor describe forms of malnutrition seen in children in developing countries. You should not use these terms to describe malnutrition in adults.

The following cause-based terms are the preferred ones to use in clinical practice settings, since they indicate the interaction and importance of inflammation on nutritional status (Fig. 39.1).[9]

- *Starvation-related malnutrition,* or primary PCM, occurs when nutritional needs are not met. In primary PCM, there is chronic starvation without inflammation (e.g., anorexia nervosa).
- *Chronic disease–related malnutrition,* or secondary PCM, is related to conditions that have sustained mild to moderate inflammation. This occurs when dietary intake does not meet tissue needs, although it would under normal conditions. Examples of conditions associated with this type of malnutrition include organ failure, cancer, rheumatoid arthritis, and obesity.
- *Acute disease–related or injury-related malnutrition* is related to acute disease or injury states with marked inflammatory response (e.g., major infection, burns, trauma, surgery).

Contributing Factors

Many factors contribute to the development of malnutrition, including socioeconomic factors, physical illnesses, incomplete diets, and drug-nutrient interactions. Table 39.5 lists conditions that increase the risk for malnutrition.

Socioeconomic Factors. Persons or families with limited financial resources may have *food insecurity* (inadequate access). Food insecurity is a major public health problem. It affects the overall quality of food that is available in both quantity and nutritional value. Those with food insecurity usually choose less expensive "filling" foods, which are more energy dense (high fat) and lack nutritional value. This type of diet increases the risk for nutrient deficiencies.

To help obtain food, people may use "safety net programs." These include food assistance programs; housing and energy subsidies; and in-kind contributions from relatives, friends, food pantries, or charitable organizations. Consult with social workers to help patients gain access to government and local programs, such as Meals on Wheels, that deliver nutritious meals to homebound people.

The "heat or eat" phenomenon is problematic, as those with limited economic resources struggle to pay household utility bills or put food on the table. Older adults on a fixed income have an added burden of deciding on whether to pay for medications or food. You and the dietitian can help patients in making food choices that meet nutritional requirements while staying within their limited resources.

Physical Illnesses. Malnutrition is a common consequence of illness, surgery, injury, or hospitalization. The hospitalized patient, especially the older adult, is at risk for becoming malnourished. Prolonged illness, major surgery, sepsis, draining wounds, burns, hemorrhage, fractures, and immobilization can all contribute to malnutrition. Undernutrition can worsen a pathologic condition. An existing deficiency state is likely to become more severe during illness.

Anorexia, nausea, vomiting, diarrhea, abdominal distention, and abdominal cramping may accompany gastrointestinal (GI) disease. Any combination of these symptoms interferes with normal food consumption and metabolism. In addition, a patient may restrict intake to a few foods or fluids that may not be nutritious out of fear of worsening an existing GI problem.

Malabsorption syndrome is the impaired absorption of nutrients from the GI tract. Decreases in digestive enzymes or in bowel surface area can quickly lead to a deficiency state. Many drugs have undesirable GI side effects and alter normal digestive and absorptive processes. For example, antibiotics can change the normal flora of the intestines. This decreases the body's ability to make biotin, a B-complex vitamin whose production depends on that gut flora.

Fever accompanies many illnesses, injuries, and infections, with a concomitant increase in the body's basal metabolic rate (BMR) and nitrogen loss. Each degree of temperature increase on the Fahrenheit scale raises the BMR by about 7%. Without an

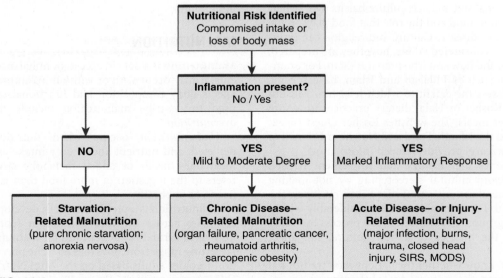

FIG. 39.1 Definitions of malnutrition. *MOD,* Multiple organ dysfunction; *SIRS,* systemic inflammatory response syndrome. (From Nix, S: *Williams' basic nutrition and diet therapy,* ed 15, St Louis, 2018, Elsevier.)

increase in caloric intake, the body uses protein stores to supply calories and protein depletion develops. After the body temperature returns to normal, the rate of protein breakdown and resynthesis may stay increased for several weeks.

Consider the nutritional requirements of a patient who is not overtly ill but having diagnostic studies. This patient may be nutritionally fit on entering the hospital but can become malnourished because of the dietary restrictions imposed by multiple diagnostic studies.

Incomplete Diets. Vitamin deficiencies are rare in most developed countries. When vitamin imbalances do occur, they usually involve several vitamins, rather than a single one. This may happen with a person with a pattern of alcohol and drug use, those who are chronically ill, and those who follow poor dietary practices. Persons who had surgery on the GI tract may be at risk for vitamin deficiencies. For example, resection of the terminal ileum poses a risk for deficiencies of fat-soluble vitamins. After a gastrectomy, patients need cobalamin supplements. Because intrinsic factor (normally made in the stomach) is not available to bind with cobalamin, cobalamin cannot be absorbed in the ileum. Followers of fad diets or poorly planned vegetarian diets are also at risk.

Manifestations of vitamin imbalances range from skin conditions to neurologic signs. The recommended dietary allowances for essential vitamins and manifestations of imbalances are outlined in Table 39.6.

Drug-Nutrient Interactions. A *drug-nutrient interaction* occurs when a drug affects the use of nutrients in the body. Many drug and food or beverage interactions may occur. Potential adverse interactions include incompatibilities, altered drug effectiveness, and impaired nutritional status. Many drugs have side effects, such as changes in taste, appetite, and nausea. Grapefruit juice can increase the absorption of some drugs, enhancing their effect. Drug-nutrient interactions can also occur with the use of herbs and dietary supplements. Monitor and prevent these potential interactions for patients in the hospital and at home.

Pathophysiology of Starvation

Knowing the pathophysiology of the starvation process will help you understand the physiologic changes that occur in malnutrition. Initially, the body selectively uses carbohydrates (glycogen) rather than fat and protein to meet metabolic needs. These carbohydrate stores, found in the liver and muscles, are minimal. They may be totally depleted within 18 hours. During the early phase of starvation, protein is used only in its normal participation in cellular metabolism.

However, once carbohydrate stores are depleted, the body converts skeletal protein to glucose for energy. Alanine and glutamine are the first amino acids used in *gluconeogenesis,* the process by which the liver forms glucose. The resulting plasma glucose allows metabolic processes to continue. When these amino acids are used as energy sources, the person may be in negative nitrogen balance (nitrogen excretion exceeds nitrogen intake).

Within 5 to 9 days, the body uses fat to supply much of the needed energy. In prolonged starvation, fat provides up to 97% of calories, conserving protein. Depletion of fat stores depends on the amount available. Fat stores are generally used up in 4 to 6 weeks. Once fat stores are gone, the body uses visceral and body proteins, including those in internal organs and plasma.

TABLE 39.5 Conditions That Increase the Risk for Malnutrition

- Chronic alcohol use
- Decreased mobility that limits access to food or its preparation
- Dementia
- Depression
- Drugs with antinutrient or catabolic properties (e.g., corticosteroids, antibiotics)
- Excessive dieting to lose weight
- Need for increased nutrients because of hypermetabolism or stress (e.g., infection, trauma, fever)
- No oral intake and/or receiving standard IV solutions for 10 days (adults) or for 5 days (older adults)
- Nutrient losses from malabsorption, dialysis, diarrhea, or wounds
- Swallowing disorders (e.g., head and neck cancer)

TABLE 39.6 Recommended Daily Vitamin Intake and Manifestations of Deficiencies

Vitamin	Dietary Reference Intake	Manifestations of Deficiencies
A (retinol)	*Men:* 900 mcg/retinol equivalents* *Women:* 700 mcg/retinol equivalents	Dry, scaly skin. Increased susceptibility to infection, night blindness, anorexia, eye irritation, keratinization of respiratory and GI mucosa, bladder stones, anemia, retarded growth
D	*Adults ages 19–70:* 600 IU *Adults age >70:* 800 IU	Muscular weakness, excessive sweating, diarrhea and other GI problems, bone pain, active or healed rickets, osteomalacia
E	*Adults:* 15 mg	Neurologic deficits
K	*Men:* 120 mcg *Women:* 90 mcg	Blood coagulation problems
B₁ (thiamine)	*Men:* 1.2 mg *Women:* 1.1 mg	Anorexia, fatigue, nervous irritability, constipation, paresthesias, insomnia
B₆ (pyridoxine)	*Men ages 19–50:* 1.3–1.7 mg *Men age >51:* 1.7 mg *Women ages 19–50:* 1.3–1.5 mg *Women age >51:* 1.5 mg	Seizures, dermatitis, anemia, neuropathy with motor weakness, anorexia
B₁₂ (cobalamin)	*Adults:* 2.4 mcg	Megaloblastic anemia, anorexia, glossitis, sore mouth and tongue, pallor, neurologic problems (e.g., depression, dizziness), weight loss, nausea, constipation
C	*Men:* 90 mg *Women:* 75 mg	Bleeding gums, loose teeth, easy bruising, poor wound healing, scurvy, dry, itchy skin
Folate (folic acid)	*Adults:* 400 mcg	Impaired cell division and protein synthesis, megaloblastic anemia, anorexia, fatigue, sore tongue, diarrhea, forgetfulness

*1 retinol equivalent = 10 international units vitamin A activity from β-carotene or 3.33 international units vitamin A activity from retinol.

They rapidly decrease because they are the only remaining body source of energy available.

If a malnourished patient has surgery, physical trauma, or an infection, the stress response is superimposed on the starvation response. The body uses protein stores for energy to meet the increased metabolic energy expenditure.

As protein depletion continues, liver function becomes impaired and protein synthesis decreases. The decrease in protein synthesis lowers plasma oncotic pressure. A major function of plasma proteins, primarily albumin, is to maintain the osmotic pressure of blood. When the oncotic pressure decreases, body fluids shift from the vascular space into the interstitial compartment. Eventually albumin leaks into the interstitial space along with the fluid. Edema becomes observable. Often edema in the patient's face and legs masks the underlying muscle wasting.

As the total blood volume decreases, the skin appears dry and wrinkled. As fluids shift to the interstitial space, ions also move. Sodium (the main extracellular ion) increases in amount within the cell. Potassium (the main intracellular ion) and magnesium shift to the extracellular space. The sodium-potassium exchange pump has high-energy needs, using 20% to 50% of all calories ingested. When the diet is extremely deficient in calories and essential proteins, the pump will fail. This leaves sodium inside the cell (along with water), and the cell expands.

The liver is the body organ that loses the most mass during protein deprivation. Fat gradually infiltrates the liver due to decreased synthesis of lipoproteins. Death will rapidly ensue if the person does not receive dietary protein and necessary nutrients.

Impact of Inflammation. Inflammation affects nutrient metabolism and is an important part of nutritional status. During the starvation process, there is a decreased BMR, sparing of skeletal muscle, and decreased protein breakdown. However, in inflammatory states, there are changes in the expression of proinflammatory (e.g., interleukin-6 [IL-6]) and antiinflammatory cytokines (e.g., IL-10). These cytokine changes result in increased protein and skeletal muscle breakdown, increased BMR, increased glucose turnover, decreased negative acute phase protein (albumin, prealbumin) production, and increased positive acute phase protein (e.g., C-reactive protein [CRP]) production.[10]

Clinical Manifestations and Diagnostic Studies

The manifestations of malnutrition range from mild to emaciation and death (Fig. 39.2). The most obvious signs are seen in the skin (dry and scaly skin, brittle nails, rashes, hair loss), mouth (crusting and ulceration, changes in tongue), muscles (decreased mass and weakness), and CNS (mental changes, such as confusion, irritability). The speed at which malnutrition develops depends on the quantity and quality of the protein intake, caloric value, illness, and person's age.

The manifestations result from numerous interactions at the cellular level. As protein intake declines, the muscles (the largest store of protein in the body) become wasted and flabby. This leads to weakness and fatigability. Decreased protein is available for tissue repair, causing delayed wound healing. The person is more susceptible to infections. Both humoral and cell-mediated immunity are deficient. Leukocytes decrease in the peripheral blood. Impaired phagocytosis occurs because of the lack of energy needed to drive the process. Many malnourished persons are anemic because they lack iron and folic acid (necessary building blocks for red blood cells [RBCs]).

The diagnosis of malnutrition is best determined by body composition, including a thorough history of weight loss,

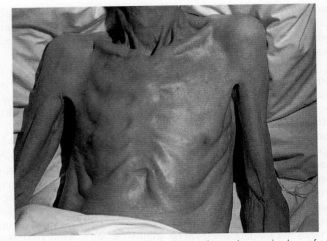

FIG. 39.2 Severe malnutrition results in wasting and extensive loss of adipose tissue. (From Kamal A, Brockelhurst JC: *Color atlas of geriatric medicine*, ed 2, St Louis, 1991, Mosby.)

nutrient intake, and measures of functional status. Obtain vital signs, height, and weight. Assess and document the patient's physical state and each body system. Table 39.7 outlines the assessment and findings of the patient with malnutrition.

Laboratory Studies. Serum albumin has a half-life of 20 to 22 days. In the absence of marked fluid loss (e.g., from hemorrhage or burns), the serum albumin value lags behind actual protein changes by more than 2 weeks. This makes albumin a poor indicator of acute changes in nutritional status. Prealbumin, a protein made by the liver, has a half-life of 2 days. It is a better indicator of recent or current nutritional status. However, the extent to which visceral proteins, including albumin and prealbumin, are true markers of malnutrition is questionable.

Albumin and prealbumin are *negative acute phase proteins*. This means that during an inflammatory response, the liver decreases synthesis of these proteins. So low or below normal levels of albumin and prealbumin may indicate an inflammatory state rather than accurately depicting nutritional status. One way to determine if low albumin and prealbumin levels are due to malnutrition is to measure CRP, a *positive acute phase protein*. CRP typically increases during inflammation. A high CRP and low albumin or prealbumin suggest that inflammation is driving the change in albumin and prealbumin levels.[11]

Serum electrolyte levels reflect changes taking place between the intracellular and extracellular spaces. The serum potassium level often increases. The RBC count and hemoglobin level indicate the presence and degree of anemia. The total lymphocyte count decreases with malnutrition. Calculate it by multiplying the percent of lymphocytes times the total white blood cell (WBC) count. Liver enzyme levels may increase with malnutrition. Serum levels of both fat-soluble and water-soluble vitamins usually decrease. Low serum levels of fat-soluble vitamins correlate with the presence of *steatorrhea* (fatty stools).

❖ NURSING AND INTERPROFESSIONAL MANAGEMENT: MALNUTRITION

◆ Nursing Assessment

As a nurse, you are responsible for nutritional screening across care settings. Nutritional screening identifies those who are malnourished or at risk for malnutrition. The Joint Commission

TABLE 39.7 Nursing Assessment
Malnutrition

Subjective Data

Important Health Information

- *Past health history:* Severe burns, major trauma, hemorrhage, draining wounds, bone fractures with prolonged immobility, chronic renal or liver disease, cancer, malabsorption syndromes, GI obstruction, infectious diseases, acute (e.g., trauma, sepsis) or chronic inflammatory condition (e.g., rheumatoid arthritis)
- *Medications:* Corticosteroids, chemotherapy, diet pills, dietary supplements, herbs
- *Surgery or other treatments:* Recent surgery, radiation

Functional Health Patterns

- *Health perception–health management:* Alcohol or drug use. Malaise, apathy
- *Nutritional-metabolic:* Increase or decrease in weight, weight problems. Increase or decrease in appetite, typical dietary intake, food preferences and aversions, food allergies or intolerance. Ill-fitting or absent dentures. Dry mouth, problems chewing or swallowing, bloating, or gas. ↑ Sensitivity to cold, delayed wound healing
- *Elimination:* Constipation, diarrhea, nocturia, decreased urine output
- *Activity-exercise:* Increase or decrease in activity patterns. Weakness, fatigue, decreased endurance
- *Cognitive-perceptual:* Pain in mouth. Paresthesias, loss of position and vibratory sense
- *Role-relationship:* Change in family (e.g., loss of a spouse), financial resources
- *Sexual-reproductive:* Amenorrhea, impotence, decreased libido

Objective Data

General

- Listless, cachectic, underweight for height

Eyes

- Pale or red conjunctivae, gray keratinized epithelium on conjunctiva (Bitot's spots). Dryness and dull appearance of conjunctivae and cornea, soft cornea. Blood vessel growth in cornea. Redness and fissuring of eyelid corners

Integumentary

- Dry, brittle, sparse hair with color changes and lack of luster, alopecia. Dry, scaly lips. Fever blisters, angular crusts and lesions at corners of mouth (cheilosis). Brittle, ridged nails. Decreased tone and elasticity of skin. Cool, rough, dry, scaly skin with brown-gray pigment changes. Reddened, scaly dermatitis, scrotal dermatitis. Slight cyanosis, peripheral edema

Respiratory

- Decreased respiratory rate, ↓ vital capacity, crackles, weak cough

Cardiovascular

- Increased or decreased heart rate, ↓ BP, dysrhythmias

Gastrointestinal

- Swollen, smooth, raw, beefy red tongue (glossitis), hypertrophic or atrophic papillae. Dental cavities, absent or loose teeth, discolored tooth enamel. Spongy, pale, receded gums with a tendency to bleed easily, periodontal disease. Ulcerations, white patches or plaques. Redness, swelling of oral mucosa. Distended, tympanic abdomen. Ascites, hepatomegaly, decreased bowel sounds, steatorrhea

Neurologic

- Decreased or loss of reflexes, tremor; irritability, confusion, syncope, peripheral neuropathy

Musculoskeletal

- Decreased muscle mass with poor tone, "wasted" appearance, bow-legs, knock-knees, beaded ribs, chest deformity, prominent bony structures

Possible Diagnostic Findings

- ↓ Hemoglobin and hematocrit, ↓ mean corpuscular volume (MCV), mean corpuscular hemoglobin (MCH), or mean corpuscular hemoglobin concentration (MCHC). Altered serum electrolyte levels, especially hyperkalemia. ↓ BUN and creatinine, ↓ serum albumin, transferrin, and prealbumin. ↑ CRP, ↓ lymphocytes, ↑ liver enzymes, ↓ serum vitamin levels

---

requires nutritional screening for all patients within 24 hours of admission, with a detailed nutrition assessment if a patient is at risk. Following a standard approach to nutritional screening, using valid and reliable tools, will accurately identify those at risk. Many nutritional screening and assessment tools are available. Hospital-specific screening tools review common admission assessment data, including history of weight loss, intake before admission, use of nutritional support, chewing or swallowing issues, and skin breakdown.

The Malnutrition Universal Screening Tool (Fig. 39.3) and Nutrition Risk Screening are common tools used with adults in acute care. The MNA assesses nutrition status in older adults. In long-term care, the Minimum Data Set (MDS) form is used to obtain nutrition information.[12] In home care settings, the Outcome and Assessment Information Set (OASIS) is used to collect information on diet, oral intake, dental health, swallowing problems, and any need for meal assistance.

If screening identifies a person at nutritional risk, perform a full nutritional assessment. A nutritional assessment is a comprehensive approach that includes medical, nutritional, and medication histories; physical examination; anthropometric measurements; and laboratory data (Table 39.8). Nutritional assessment provides the basis for nutritional intervention.

Obtain a complete diet history from the patient or caregiver. Assessing the foods eaten over the past week reveals a great deal about the patient's diet habits and knowledge of good nutrition. Often the patient's nutritional state is not the reason for seeking medical care. However, it may be a contributing factor to the disease and have an impact on management and recovery.

Anthropometric Measurements. Obtain height, weight, and girth measurements. Calculate the body mass index (BMI). We often use waist circumference and hip-to-waist ratio to assess nutritional status (see Chapter 40). Obtaining accurate measures of weight and height are critical. When possible, measure the patient's actual height rather than using the patient's self-report. Alternatives to standing height (stature) measurements include arm demi-span and knee-height measurements. The *arm demi-span* is the distance from a point on the midline at the suprasternal notch to the web between the middle and ring fingers with the arm horizontally outstretched. For persons confined to bed, using a Luft ruler is an alternative to standing height.

When assessing weight, obtain a detailed weight history, noting weight loss. Ask whether the weight loss was intentional or unintentional and the period over which it took place. A loss of more than 5% of usual body weight over 6 months (whether intentional or unintentional) is a critical indicator for further

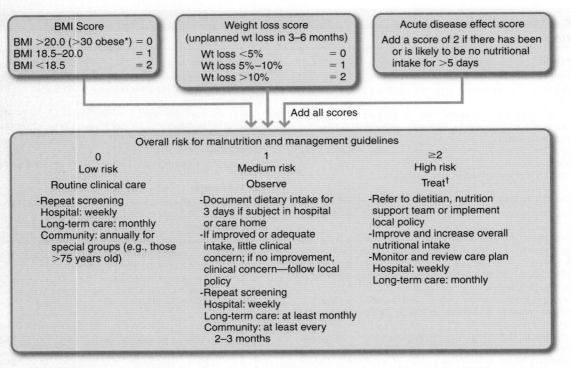

FIG. 39.3 The Malnutrition Universal Screening Tool (MUST) for adults. (Adapted from Mahan LK, Raymond JL: *Krause's food & the nutrition care process*, ed 14, St Louis, 2016, Saunders.)

TABLE 39.8 Components of Nutritional Assessment

Anthropometric Measurements
- Height and weight
- Body mass index (BMI)
- Rate of weight change
- Amount of weight loss

Physical Examination
- Physical appearance
- Muscle mass and strength
- Dental and oral health

Health History
- Personal and family history
- Acute or chronic illnesses
- Current medications, herbs, supplements
- Cognitive status, depression

Diet History
- Chewing and swallowing ability
- Changes in appetite or taste
- Food and nutrient intake
- Availability of food

Laboratory Data
- Glucose
- Electrolytes
- Lipid profile
- Blood urea nitrogen (BUN)
- Albumin, prealbumin, C-reactive protein

Functional Status
- Ability to perform basic and instrumental activities of daily living
- Handgrip strength
- Performance tests (e.g., timed walk tests)

assessment, especially in the older adult.[13] If an involuntary weight loss exceeds 10% of the usual weight, determine the reason. Unintentional weight loss is important to consider in the obese person. Latent malnutrition may be present despite excess body weight. Determine the patient's current weight in relation to ideal body weight.

Body mass index (BMI) is a measure of weight for height (see Fig. 40.6). A BMI of less than 18.5 kg/m² is considered underweight, normal weight is a BMI between 18.5 and 24.9 kg/m², and overweight is a BMI between 25 and 29.9 kg/m². A BMI of 30 kg/m² or greater is obese. BMIs outside the normal weight range are associated with increased morbidity and mortality.

Measure skinfold thickness at various sites (indicators of subcutaneous fat stores) and midarm muscle circumference (indicator of protein stores). The sites most reflective of body fat are those over the biceps and triceps, below the scapula, above the iliac crest, and over the upper thigh. The measures obtained are compared with standards for healthy persons of the same age and gender. Both skinfold thickness and midarm circumference may decrease in malnutrition. Shifts in hydration status influence these measurements. These measurements are most beneficial when done serially and by persons trained in anthropometry.

Functional Measurements. Functional assessment focuses on performance of activities of daily living (ADLs) tools. The tools used most often are the Katz Index and Lawton Scale.[14] Measuring muscle strength can assess physical functional status, an important outcome of nutrition status. Handgrip strength is measured with a hand dynamometer. Timed gait and chair stands are markers of lower extremity strength.

◆ Nursing Diagnoses

Nursing diagnoses for the patient with malnutrition include:
- Impaired nutritional status
- Impaired nutritional intake
- Fluid imbalance
- Risk for impaired tissue integrity

◆ Planning

The overall goals are that the patient with malnutrition will (1) achieve an appropriate weight, (2) consume a specified number of calories per day on an individualized diet, and (3) have no adverse consequences related to malnutrition or nutritional therapies.

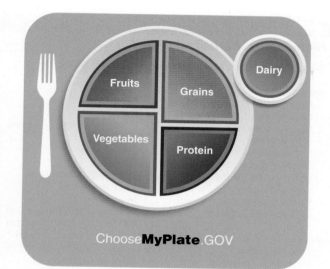

FIG. 39.4 MyPlate is the primary food group symbol that serves as a reminder to make healthy food choices and to build a healthy plate at mealtimes. It is a visual cue that shows the 5 food groups from which to select healthy foods. The plate is divided into 4 slightly different-sized quadrants, with fruits and vegetables taking up half the space and grains and protein making up the other half. The vegetables and grains portions are the largest portion. Next to the plate is a blue circle for dairy, which could be a glass of milk or a food, such as cheese or yogurt. For more information, see *www.choosemyplate.gov*. (From US Department of Agriculture, Center for Nutrition Policy and Promotion: *Guidance on use of USDA's MyPlate and statements about amounts of food groups contributed by foods on food product labels*, Washington, DC.)

◆ Nursing Implementation

◆ **Health Promotion.** It is part of your role to teach and reinforce healthy eating habits. Use MyPlate, the Dietary Guidelines for Americans, and Nutrition Facts food labels to promote healthy nutrition. The MyPlate approach is a visual guide for sensible meal planning. It helps Americans eat healthfully and make good food choices. MyPlate focuses on the proportions of 5 food groups (grains, protein, fruits, vegetables, and dairy) that you should eat at each meal (Fig. 39.4 and Table 39.9). At the health professionals' link at *www.choosemyplate.gov*, you can download daily food plans, sample menus, and tips for how to be physically active. These materials are valuable to use in patient teaching. MyPlate materials for older adults are available at *https://hnrca.tufts.edu/myplate/*.

There are many resources to help people eat a nutritious diet and maintain a healthy weight. Electronic and print sources are available for determining nutritional information in commonly consumed foods. Many food products have Nutrition Facts labels (Fig. 39.5). Consumer and health professional education materials on Nutrition Facts labels are available on the U.S. Food and Drug Administration (FDA) website *(www.fda.gov/Food/LabelingNutrition/ucm20026097.htm)*.

Help the patient find reliable Internet sources that provide evidence-based food and nutrition recommendations. Interactive web-based programs and mobile device applications are available to track physical activity, calories, nutrients, and foods eaten. Mobile device applications help with making healthy eating choices easier. Some use built-in barcode scanners to scan foods quickly and give individual food items' nutrition facts. Users can compare items for their nutrition benefit and cost. Other applications give information on portion sizes

TABLE 39.9 Nutritional Therapy
MyPlate Tips for a Healthy Lifestyle

Making food choices for a healthy lifestyle can be as simple as using these 10 tips. Use the ideas in this list to (1) balance your calories, (2) choose foods to eat more often, and (3) cut back on foods to eat less often.

1. Balance calories	• Find out how many calories you need for a day as a first step in managing your weight. Go to *www.choosemyplate.gov* to find your calorie level. • Being physically active also helps you balance calories.
2. Enjoy your food, but eat less	• Take the time to enjoy your food as you eat it. • Eating too fast or when your attention is elsewhere may lead to eating too many calories. • Pay attention to hunger and fullness cues before, during, and after meals. Use them to recognize when to eat and when you have had enough.
3. Avoid over-sized portions	• Use a smaller plate, bowl, and glass. • Portion out foods before you eat. • When eating out, choose a smaller size portion, share a dish, or take home part of your meal.
4. Foods to eat more often	• Eat more vegetables, fruits, whole grains, and fat-free or 1% milk and dairy products. • These foods have the nutrients you need for health, including potassium, calcium, vitamin D, and fiber. • Make them the basis for meals and snacks.
5. Make half your plate fruits and vegetables	• Choose red, orange, and dark-green vegetables such as tomatoes, sweet potatoes, and broccoli, along with other vegetables, for your meals. • Add fruit to meals as part of main or side dishes or as dessert.
6. Switch to fat-free or low-fat (1%) milk	• They have the same amount of calcium and other essential nutrients as whole milk. • They have fewer calories and less saturated fat.
7. Make half your grains whole grains	• To eat more whole grains, substitute a whole-grain product for a refined product. • For example, eat whole-wheat bread instead of white bread, or brown rice instead of white rice.
8. Foods to eat less often	• Cut back on foods high in solid fats, added sugars, and salt. • Limit cakes, cookies, ice cream, candies, sweetened drinks, pizza, and fatty meats such as ribs, sausages, bacon, and hot dogs. • Use these foods as occasional treats, not everyday foods.
9. Compare sodium in foods	• Use the Nutrition Facts label (Fig. 39.4) to choose lower sodium versions of foods, such as soup, bread, and frozen meals. • Select foods labeled "low sodium," "reduced sodium," or "no salt added."
10. Drink water instead of sugary drinks	• Cut calories by drinking water or unsweetened beverages. • Soda, energy drinks, and sports drinks are a major source of added sugar and calories in American diets.

Source: US Department of Agriculture Center for Nutrition Policy and Promotion: Nutrition education series, DG Tips Sheet No 1, June 2011. Retrieved from *www.choosemyplate.gov* and *www.health.gov/dietaryguidelines*.

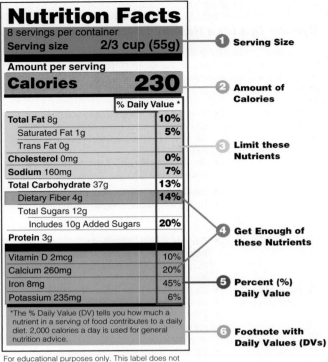

Nutrition Facts

8 servings per container

Serving size	2/3 cup (55g)

Amount per serving

Calories **230**

	% Daily Value *
Total Fat 8g	**10%**
Saturated Fat 1g	**5%**
Trans Fat 0g	
Cholesterol 0mg	**0%**
Sodium 160mg	**7%**
Total Carbohydrate 37g	**13%**
Dietary Fiber 4g	**14%**
Total Sugars 12g	
Includes 10g Added Sugars	**20%**
Protein 3g	
Vitamin D 2mcg	10%
Calcium 260mg	20%
Iron 8mg	45%
Potassium 235mg	6%

*The % Daily Value (DV) tells you how much a nutrient in a serving of food contributes to a daily diet. 2,000 calories a day is used for general nutrition advice.

1 Serving Size

2 Amount of Calories

3 Limit these Nutrients

4 Get Enough of these Nutrients

5 Percent (%) Daily Value

6 Footnote with Daily Values (DVs)

For educational purposes only. This label does not meet the labeling requirements described in 21 CFR 101.9.

FIG. 39.5 Sample of a Nutrition Facts label. (From US Department of Health and Human Services, *Nutrition facts label*, Silver Spring, MD.)

TABLE 39.10 Nutritional Therapy

High-Calorie, High-Protein Diet

Suggestions for foods for a high-calorie, high-protein diet include:

Breads and Cereals
- Buttermilk biscuits, muffins, banana bread, zucchini bread
- Granola and other cereals with dried fruit
- Hot cereals (oatmeal, cream of wheat) prepared with milk, added fat (butter or margarine), and sugar
- Potatoes prepared with added fat (butter and whole milk)

Vegetables
- Fried vegetables
- Vegetables prepared with added fat (margarine, butter)

Fruits
- Canned fruit in heavy syrup
- Dried fruit

Meat
- Casseroles
- Fried meats
- Meats covered in cream sauces or gravy
- Peanut butter

Milk and Milk Products
- Ice cream
- Milkshakes
- Whipping cream, heavy cream
- Whole milk and milk products (yogurt, ice cream, cheese)
- Whole milk with added nutritional supplements

---

and adjustments needed to reduce calories, sodium, or fat in the diet based on the user's height, weight, and activity level.

Acute Care. Collaborate with the HCP and dietitian to identify patients with malnutrition and implement appropriate interventions to meet the patient's nutritional needs. Assess nutritional state during your assessment of the patient's other physical problems. Identify risk factors for malnutrition and why they exist. With increased stress, such as surgery, severe trauma, and sepsis, the patient needs more calories and protein. Wound healing requires increased protein synthesis. The patient having major surgery who is malnourished or is at risk for malnutrition needs several weeks of increased protein and calorie intake preoperatively to promote healing postoperatively.

Teach the patient and caregiver the importance of good nutrition and the reason for recording the daily weight, intake, and output. Measure weight and height on admission, then routinely assess the person's weight. Daily weights give an ongoing record of body weight gain or loss. Rapid gains and losses are usually the result of shifts in fluid balance. In conjunction with accurate recording of food and fluid intake, body weight gives a clearer picture of the patient's fluid and nutritional state.

If the patient can take food by mouth, obtain a daily calorie count and diet diary to give an accurate record of food intake. You and the dietitian can help the patient and family in selecting high-calorie and high-protein foods (unless medically contraindicated). Table 39.10 gives examples of high-calorie, high-protein foods. Offering foods preferred by the patient enhances intake. Encourage the family to bring the patient's favorite foods from home.

Make sure the environment is conducive to eating. Provide a quiet environment. Offer oral hygiene and hand hygiene. Help the patient to a comfortable position and place the bedside table at the right height. Clear the bedside table of clutter. Place urinals, bedpans, and emesis basins out of sight. If needed, open cartons and packages. Protect mealtime from unnecessary interruptions by performing nonurgent care before or after mealtime.

The undernourished patient usually needs to have between-meal supplements. These may consist of items prepared in the dietary department or commercially prepared products. Eating these items provides extra calories, proteins, fluids, and nutrients. If the patient is unable to consume enough nutrition with a high-calorie, high-protein diet, consider adding oral liquid nutritional supplements.

Some patients may benefit from appetite stimulants, such as megestrol acetate or dronabinol (Marinol), to improve intake. Enteral nutrition (EN) may be an option in the patient who is still unable to take in enough calories (Fig. 39.6). Contraindications for EN include GI obstruction, prolonged ileus, severe diarrhea or vomiting, and enterocutaneous fistula. If EN is not possible, consider starting parenteral nutrition (PN).

Ambulatory Care. Many patients are discharged on a therapeutic diet. Discharge preparation for both the patient and caregiver is essential. Teach them about the cause of the undernourished state and ways to avoid the problem in the future. They need to be aware that undernourishment, whatever the cause, can recur and that adhering to their diet for a few weeks cannot fully restore a normal nutritional state. It may take many months to reach this goal.

Assess their ability to follow the dietary instructions considering past eating habits, religious and ethnic preferences, age, income, resources, and state of health. Emphasize the need for continual follow-up care to achieve and maintain rehabilitation. In your discharge planning, ensure proper follow-up, such as visits by the home health nurse and outpatient dietitian referrals.

Determine the need for nutritious meals and snacks after discharge from the hospital. If access to a dietitian is limited, you may be the main source of nutritional information. In your assessment, consider the availability and acceptability of community resources that provide meals, such as Meals on Wheels, senior congregate feeding sites, and the Supplemental Nutrition Assistance Program (SNAP). SNAP allows low-income households, regardless of age, to buy more food of a greater variety.

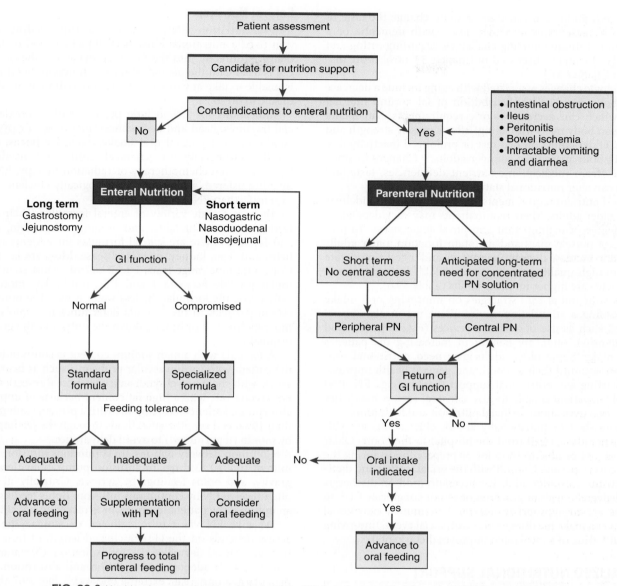

FIG. 39.6 Nutritional support algorithm. (Adapted from Ukleja A, Freeman KL, Gilbert K, ASPEN Board of Directors: Standards for nutrition support: Adult hospitalized patients, *Nutr Clin Pract* 25:403, 2010.)

Keeping a diet diary for 3 days at a time is one way to analyze and reinforce healthful eating patterns. These records are also helpful in the follow-up care. Encourage self-assessment of progress by having the patient weigh himself or herself once or twice a week and keep a weight record.

◆ **Evaluation**

The expected outcomes are that the patient who is malnourished will

• Achieve and maintain optimal body weight
• Consume a well-balanced diet
• Has no adverse outcomes related to malnutrition
• Maintain optimal physical functioning

Gerontologic Considerations: Malnutrition

Nutrition affects quality of life, functional status, and health in older adults. They are particularly vulnerable to malnutrition across care settings. You play a key role in assessing the physiologic, functional, environmental, dietary, psychologic, and social factors related to nutritional risk in older adults. Older hospitalized adults with malnutrition are more likely to have poor wound healing, pressure injuries, infections, decreased muscle strength, postoperative complications, and increased morbidity and mortality risks. They are less able to regain body weight after periods of undernutrition due to illness or surgery.

Older adults may report little or no appetite, problems with eating or swallowing, inadequate servings of nutrients, and fewer than 2 meals per day. Limited incomes may cause them to restrict the number of meals or the dietary quality of meals eaten. Social isolation is a problem in older adults. Those who live alone may lose their desire to cook and report decreased appetite. Functional limitations may affect the ability to feed oneself, buy food, or cook and prepare meals. Some may lack transportation to buy food.

Chronic illnesses associated with aging can affect nutritional status. For example, depression and dysphagia (from a stroke) can affect intake. Poor oral health from gum disease, missing teeth, or dry mouth can impair the ability to chew and swallow food.[15] Medications can cause dry mouth, change the taste of food, or decrease appetite. Older adults with dementia or a stroke present unique nursing challenges regarding eating and feeding. (Dementia is discussed in Chapter 59. Strokes are discussed in Chapter 57.)

Physiologic changes associated with aging include a decrease in lean body mass and redistribution of fat around internal organs, which can decrease caloric requirements. Sarcopenia (loss of lean body mass with aging) affects muscle strength and function. Older adults on bed rest or prolonged inactivity lose more lean body mass than younger adults.[16] Changes in smell and taste (from medications, nutrient deficiencies, taste-bud atrophy) can alter nutritional status.

General nutrient requirements and healthy eating guidelines apply to older adults. Their requirements may vary depending on the degree of malnutrition and physiologic stress. To prevent loss of muscle mass and maintain function, older adults may need to increase their protein intake and ingest a moderate amount of high-quality protein at each meal.[17] Daily vitamin D requirements are higher for older adults (Table 39.6).

Focus your initial care strategies on improving oral intake and providing a stimulating environment for meals. Special strategies, such as use of adaptive devices (e.g., large-handled eating utensils), often are helpful in increasing the patient's dietary intake. Some older adults may need nutritional support therapies until their strength and general health improve. Before starting any nutritional support therapy (e.g., EN, PN) for an older patient unable to give consent, review his or her advance directives about artificial nutrition and hydration.

Malnourished or nutritionally at-risk older adults are vulnerable when discharged from the hospital to the home. Older adults may not be able to shop for or prepare foods during the initial recovery period. Consult with the social worker and dietitian to ensure the older adult has access to food on discharge. Home-delivered meals or groceries or senior congregate feeding programs are an appropriate referral. Community nutritional programs can make mealtime a pleasant, social event. Improving the social setting of a meal often improves dietary intake.

SPECIALIZED NUTRITIONAL SUPPORT

If patients are unable to maintain or achieve adequate nutritional status, nutritional support may be needed. For a decision-making plan related to nutritional support, see Fig. 39.6.

Some agencies have nutritional support teams composed of a physician, nurse, dietitian, and pharmacist. The team's function is to oversee the nutritional support of select inpatients and outpatients. The nutritional support nurse on that team is a key resource for issues about patients' nutrition and nutritional access.

Oral Feeding

Oral supplements are widely used as an adjunct to meals and fluid intake in the patient whose nutritional intake is deficient. They provide advanced nutrition and calories and are relatively inexpensive. These include milkshakes, puddings, or commercially available products (e.g., Carnation Instant Breakfast, Ensure, Boost). Oral liquid supplements have a role in improving the nutritional status of older adults. Do not use supplements as meal substitutes, use them as snacks between meals. In long-term care, using these beverages instead of water for oral medication administration increases caloric intake.

Enteral Nutrition

Enteral nutrition (EN), also known as tube feeding, is nutrition (e.g., a nutritionally balanced liquefied food or formula) delivered directly into the GI tract, bypassing the oral cavity. EN is used with the patient who has a functioning GI tract but is unable to take any or enough oral nourishment or when it is unsafe to do so.

Indications for EN include persons with anorexia, orofacial fractures, head and neck cancer, neurologic or psychiatric conditions that prevent oral intake, extensive burns, or critical illness (especially if mechanical ventilation is needed), and those receiving chemotherapy or radiation therapy. EN is easily administered, safer, more physiologically efficient, and less expensive than PN.

There is a wide variety of enteral formulas. Their concentration, flavor, osmolality, and amounts of protein, sodium, and fat vary. There are special formulas for patients with diabetes and liver, kidney, or lung disease. Most are lactose free. Concentrations range from 1 to 2 cal/mL. Most standard formulas provide between 1 and 1.5 cal/mL. The more calorically dense the formula, the less water it has. The number and size of particles in the formula determines its osmolality. The more hydrolyzed or broken down the nutrients, the greater the osmolality.

A formula with a high sodium content is contraindicated in the patient with cardiovascular problems, such as heart failure. Those with short bowel syndrome or ileocecal resection should not receive one with a high fat content because of impaired fat absorption. Patients receiving EN with a protein content greater than 16% need supplemental fluids through the feeding tube or by mouth (if permitted) to avoid dehydration.

Common delivery options are continuous infusion or intermittent (bolus) feedings by infusion pump, bolus feedings by gravity, and bolus feedings by syringe. Critically ill patients often receive EN by continuous infusion. Bolus feeding may be an option if the patient improves or is receiving EN at home.[17]

We give EN via a tube, catheter, or stoma. The type of access depends on the (1) anticipated length of time EN will be required, (2) degree of risk for aspiration, (3) patient's clinical status, (4) adequacy of digestion and absorption, and (5) patient's anatomy (e.g., extreme obesity).[12] Fig. 39.7 shows the locations of commonly used enteral feeding tubes.

Orogastric, Nasogastric, and Nasointestinal Tubes. Nasally and orally placed tubes (orogastric, nasogastric [NG], nasoduodenal, nasojejunal) are appropriate for short-term feeding (less than 4 weeks). Nasoduodenal and nasojejunal tubes are transpyloric tubes. They are used when pathophysiologic conditions call for feeding the patient below the pyloric sphincter. Placement into the small intestine decreases the chance of regurgitating gastric contents into the esophagus and aspiration.[17] However, the patient can still aspirate gastric secretions if the stomach is not emptying properly.

Polyurethane or silicone feeding tubes are long, small in diameter, soft, and flexible. This design decreases the risk for mucosal damage from prolonged placement. These tubes are radiopaque, making their position readily identified by x-ray. A stylet is used for tube placement in a comatose patient because the ability to swallow is not essential during insertion. A complication that can result from using a stylet is increased risk for perforation.

While smaller feeding tubes have many advantages over tubes with wider lumens, such as the standard decompression

NG tube, there are some disadvantages. Because of the small diameter and length, these tubes clog easily. They are harder to use for checking residual volumes. They are particularly prone to occlusion if you do not thoroughly crush and dissolve oral drugs before administration. Failure to flush the tubing before and after giving drugs or checking residual volume can cause tube occlusion. Vomiting or coughing can dislodge the tubes. They can become knotted or kinked. Problems with a tube may require removal and insertion of a new tube, which adds to cost and patient discomfort.

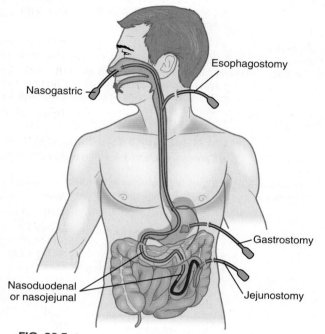

FIG. 39.7 Common enteral feeding tube placement locations.

Gastrostomy and Jejunostomy Tubes. If feedings are needed for an extended time, tubes can be placed in the stomach (gastrostomy) or small bowel (jejunostomy). A gastrostomy tube can be placed surgically, radiologically, or endoscopically (Fig. 39.7). The patient must have an intact, unobstructed GI tract. The esophageal lumen must be wide enough to pass the endoscope for percutaneous endoscopic gastrostomy (PEG) tube placement (Fig. 39.8). PEG tube and radiologically placed gastrostomy tube procedures have fewer risks than surgical placement. The procedure requires IV sedation and local anesthesia. IV antibiotics are given before the procedure.

For the patient with chronic reflux, feeding through a jejunostomy (J-tube) may be necessary to reduce the risk for aspiration. Jejunostomy tubes are placed either endoscopically or with open or laparoscopic surgery. Combination gastrojejunostomy (G-J) tubes allow for simultaneous gastric decompression and small bowel feeding. When a patient has a G-J tube, it is important to know which port is the gastric and which is the jejunal.

The tube is either premarked or marked at the skin insertion site. Enteral feedings can start within 24 hours after a surgically placed gastrostomy or jejunostomy tube without waiting for flatus or a bowel movement. Most other PEG tube feedings can start within 4 hours of insertion, although agency policies may vary.[17]

EN and Safety. You have a critical role in ensuring that EN is administered safely. Aspiration and dislodged tubes are important safety concerns. Nursing management of enteral feeding is addressed in Table 39.11.

Accidental tube removal can result in delayed feedings and potential discomfort with tube replacement. The management of common problems in patients receiving EN is outlined in Table 39.12. A nursing care plan for the patient receiving EN (eNursing Care Plan 39.1) is available on the website for this chapter.

Specific care and teaching related to feeding tubes and EN are discussed in the following section. Remember that is important

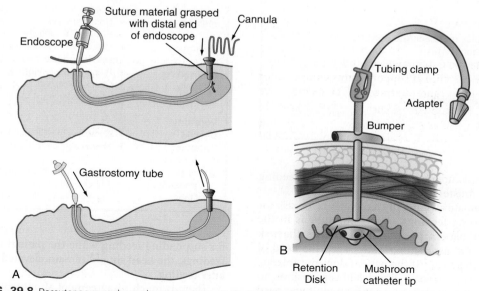

FIG. 39.8 Percutaneous endoscopic gastrostomy. **A,** Gastrostomy tube placement via percutaneous endoscopy. With use of endoscopy, a gastrostomy tube is inserted through the esophagus into the stomach and then pulled through a stab wound made in the abdominal wall. **B,** A retention disk and bumper secure the tube.

TABLE 39.11 Nursing Management

EN

Maintaining EN Infusions
- Check tube placement before feeding and before each medication administration.
- Assess for bowel sounds before feeding.
- Flush NG or gastrostomy tube as needed.
- Evaluate nutritional status of patient receiving enteral feedings.

Ensuring Patient Safety
- Give medications in the safest form possible.
  - Dilute viscous liquid medications.
  - Use liquid medications only if they are designated safe for enteral use.
  - Do not add medications to enteral feeding formula.
  - If using tablets, only use immediate-release forms.
  - Crush drugs to a fine powder and dissolve in 30–60 mL of purified water.
- Employ measures to decrease aspiration risk.
- Keep head of bed elevated to 30- to 45-degree angle.
- Check for GVR per agency policy.
- Assess regularly for complications related to tubes and enteral feedings (e.g., aspiration, diarrhea, abdominal distention, hyperglycemia, fecal impaction).
- Teach patient and caregiver about home EN and tube care.

Delegate to Licensed Practical/Vocational Nurse (LPN/VN)
- Insert NG tube for stable patient.
- Flush NG and gastrostomy tubes.
- Give bolus or continuous enteral feeding for stable patient.
- Remove NG tube.
- Give medications through NG or gastrostomy tube to stable patient.
- Provide skin care around gastrostomy or jejunostomy tubes.

Oversee Unlicensed Assistive Personnel (UAP)
- Provide oral care to patient with NG, gastrostomy, or jejunostomy tube.
- Weigh patient who is receiving EN.
- Keep the head of bed elevated 30–45 degrees.
- Report patient symptoms (e.g., nausea, diarrhea) that may indicate problems with EN to RN or LPN.
- Alert RN or LPN about infusion pump alarms.
- Empty drainage devices and measure output.

Collaborate With Dietitian
- Evaluate nutritional status of patient receiving EN.
- Select appropriate EN formula.
- Monitor for and manage complications related to EN.
- Teach patient and caregiver about home EN.

Collaborate With Pharmacist
- Select appropriate form of each medication being given enterally.
- Determine if medication must be given separately.

TABLE 39.12 Nursing Management

EN Problems

Problems and Causes	Management
Constipation	
Decreased fluid intake	• Increase fluid intake if not contraindicated.
	• Give total fluid intake of 30 mL/kg body weight.
Formula	• Change formula to one with more fiber content.
	• Give as-needed laxative.
Inactivity	• Encourage ambulation unless contraindicated.
	• Collaborate with physical therapy to promote activity.
Dehydration	
Diarrhea, vomiting	• Decrease rate or change formula.
	• Check drugs that patient is receiving, especially antibiotics.
	• Avoid bacterial contamination of formula and equipment.
Fluid intake	• Increase intake and check amount and number of feedings.
	• Increase amount of fluid intake if appropriate.
High-protein formula	• Change formula to one with less protein.
Hyperosmotic diuresis	• Check blood glucose levels often.
	• Change formula to one with less glucose.
Diarrhea	
Contaminated formula	• Refrigerate unused formula and record date opened.
	• Discard outdated formula.
	• Discard formula left standing for longer than manufacturer's guidelines.
	• 8 hrs for ready-to-feed formulas (cans)
	• 4 hrs for reconstituted formula
	• 24 hrs for closed-system enteral formulas
	• Use closed system.
Feeding too fast	• Dilute or decrease rate of feeding.
	• Change to continuous feedings.
	• Stop excess water boluses.
Formula	• Change to formula that has more fiber or is less hypertonic.
	• Change to continuous feedings.
Infection	• Obtain stool culture for fecal leukocyte determination, *C. difficile*, and/or toxin assay.
Medications	• Check for drugs that may cause diarrhea (e.g., sorbitol in liquid medications, antibiotics).
Tube moving distally	• Properly secure tube before beginning feeding.
	• Check placement before each bolus feeding or at least every 4 hrs if continuous feedings.
Vomiting	
Delayed gastric emptying	• Consult with HCP about use of prokinetic drug.
	• Follow agency policy to manage GRV.
Improper placement of tube	• Replace tube in proper position.
	• Check tube position before each bolus feeding and every 4 hrs if continuous feedings.

to teach the patient and caregiver how to care for the feeding tube and properly administer EN.

Aspiration Risk. Evaluate all enterally fed patients for risk for aspiration. Before starting feedings, ensure the tube is in the right position. Proper patient positioning decreases the risk for aspiration. To prevent aspiration, always keep the head of bed elevated 30 to 45 degrees.[17] If the patient does not tolerate a backrest elevation, use a reverse Trendelenburg position to elevate the head of the bed, unless contraindicated. If you need to lower the head of the bed for a procedure, quickly returning the patient to at least 30 degrees is critical. Follow agency policy

for suspending feeding while the patient is supine. With bolus feedings, the head should remain elevated for 30 to 60 minutes after feeding.

There is much disagreement about whether to check gastric residual volume (GRV) when giving feedings into the stomach. Some think an increased GRV increases the risk for aspiration.

Other research does not support the practice. Follow your agency policy for checking GRV. Common protocols call for checking GRV every 6 to 8 hours in non–critically ill patients and before each bolus feeding.

Other measures to decrease aspiration risk include giving feedings continuously, minimizing the use of sedation, and performing frequent oral suctioning, if needed. Promotility drugs, such as erythromycin or metoclopramide, improve gastric emptying and may reduce aspiration risk.

Tube Position. Obtain x-ray confirmation of newly inserted nasal or orogastric tubes to confirm proper position before starting feedings or medications. Smaller feeding tubes can pass directly into the bronchus on insertion without any obvious respiratory manifestations. Do not rely on the auscultation method to determine between gastric and respiratory or gastric and small bowel placement. Placing a tube under electromagnetic guidance reduces the risk for misplacement associated with blind insertion.[17] Capnography, a direct monitor of breath-to-breath CO_2 level, can determine tube placement in the respiratory tract. However, it still requires x-ray confirmation to verify location before feeding.[17]

Maintain proper placement of the tube after starting feedings. To determine if a tube is still in the proper position, mark the exit site of the tube at the time of the initial x-ray and check the tube external length at regular intervals.[17] Consider applying a nasal bridle in patients who try to pull out a tube or for whom taping the nose is difficult.

A small bowel tube may dislocate upward into the stomach, or the tube's tip can dislocate upward into the esophagus. If you see a significant increase in the external length, use other bedside tests to help determine whether the tube has become dislocated. These measures include assessing aspirate color and pH. Because each of these measures has limitations, confirm placement with more than one test. If you are checking GVR, watch for unexpected changes in volume. An increase in GVR may indicate displacement of a small intestine tube into the stomach.[18]

Site Care. Skin care around gastrostomy and jejunostomy tube sites is important because the action of digestive juices irritates the skin. Assess the skin around the feeding tube daily for signs of redness and maceration. Monitor bumper tension and routinely check for pressure injury.

To keep the skin clean and dry, initially rinse it with sterile water and dry it. Apply a dressing until the site is healed. After that, wash with mild soap and water. A protective ointment (zinc oxide, petroleum gauze) or a skin barrier (Karaya, Stomahesive) may be used on the skin around the tube. If the skin is irritated, consider using other types of drain or tube pouches. Consult a wound, ostomy, and continence nurse (WOCN) if problems occur.

Tube Patency. All enteral feedings require routine flushing. Flush feeding tubes in adults with 30 mL of warm tap water every 4 hours during continuous feedings or before and after each bolus feeding. Use sterile water in immunocompromised and critically ill patients. Always flush tubes between each medication and after all medications are given. Flush clogged tubes with warm water, using a back-and-forth motion. If that does not work, a pancreatic enzyme solution, an enzymatic declogging kit, or mechanical devices for clearing feeding tubes are options.[17]

Misconnection. An *enteral feeding misconnection* is an inadvertent connection between an enteral feeding system and

TABLE 39.13 Nursing Management
Decreasing Enteral Feeding Misconnections

The following are tips to help you decrease your risk for making an enteral feeding misconnection:

1. Teach visitors, LPN/VNs, and UAP to notify the nurse if an enteral feeding line becomes disconnected and not to reconnect any line.
2. Do not change or adapt IV or feeding devices because it may compromise the safety features incorporated into their design.
3. Do not use an IV pump or IV tubing to deliver an enteral feeding.
4. When making a reconnection or connecting any new device or infusion, trace lines back to their origins and ensure connections are secure.
5. When patient arrives on a new unit or setting or during shift hand-off, recheck connections and trace all tubes.
6. Route tubes and catheters that have different purposes in unique and standardized directions (e.g., route IV lines toward the patient's head and enteral lines toward the feet).
7. Label or color-code feeding tubes and connectors.
8. When there are multiple access points and/or several bags hanging, place proximal and distal labels on all tubings.
9. Check the patient's vital signs after making any connection.
10. Identify and confirm a solution's label, since a 3-in-1 PN solution can look like an enteral nutrition formulation bag. Label the bags with large, bold statements such as "WARNING! For Enteral Use Only—NOT for IV Use."
11. Make all connections under proper lighting conditions.

a nonenteral system, such as an IV line, a peritoneal dialysis catheter, or a tracheostomy tube cuff. With an enteral feeding misconnection, nutritional formula intended for the GI tract is given IV or into the respiratory tract. Severe patient injury and death can result from tubing misconnection. Table 39.13 gives tips to decrease the risk for enteral feeding misconnections.

Gerontologic Considerations: Enteral Nutrition

EN is used in the older patient to improve nutritional status. Because of physiologic changes associated with aging, the older adult is more vulnerable to complications associated with EN, especially fluid and electrolyte imbalances. Complications such as diarrhea can leave the patient dehydrated. Decreased thirst perception or impaired cognitive function decreases the patient's ability to seek needed fluids.

With aging, there is an increased risk for glucose intolerance. As a result, the older patient may be more susceptible to hyperglycemia from the high carbohydrate load of some EN formulas. The older adult with compromised cardiovascular function (e.g., heart failure) will have a decreased ability to handle large volumes of formula. If this happens, the patient may need a more concentrated formula (2.0 cal/mL). The older adult has an increased risk for aspiration caused by gastroesophageal reflux disease (GERD), delayed gastric emptying, hiatal hernia, or decreased gag reflex. Physical mobility, fine motor movement, and visual system changes associated with aging may contribute to problems managing EN in the home setting.

Parenteral Nutrition

Parenteral nutrition (PN) is the administration of nutrients directly into the bloodstream. PN is used when the GI tract cannot be used for the ingestion, digestion, and absorption of essential nutrients. Table 39.14 lists common reasons for the use of PN. PN is a relatively safe method of providing complete nutritional support.

TABLE 39.14 **Common Indications for PN**	
• Chronic severe diarrhea and vomiting • Complicated surgery or trauma • GI obstruction • GI tract anomalies and fistulae	• Intractable diarrhea • Severe anorexia nervosa • Severe malabsorption • Short bowel syndrome

Composition. PN is customized to meet the needs of each patient. The composition is reformulated as the patient's condition changes. This requires you to collaborate with the interprofessional team in delivering PN to the patient.

Commercially prepared PN base solutions are available. These base solutions contain dextrose and protein in the form of amino acids. The pharmacy adds prescribed electrolytes (e.g., sodium, potassium, chloride, calcium, magnesium, phosphate), vitamins, and trace elements (e.g., zinc, copper, chromium, selenium, manganese) to meet the patient's needs. A 3-in-1 or total nutrient admixture containing an IV fat emulsion, dextrose, and amino acids is widely used. Premixed PN solutions require mixing the dextrose and amino acid chambers prior to use. Standard electrolytes are available in some premixed solutions. Multivitamins can be added before use.[19]

Calories. Calories in PN mainly come from carbohydrates in the form of dextrose and by fat in the form of fat emulsion. Dextrose 100 to 150 g/day (1 g provides about 3.4 calories, as opposed to oral carbohydrates, which provide 4 calories) has a protein-sparing effect. Providing adequate nonprotein calories in the form of glucose and fat allows the use of amino acids for wound healing and not for energy. However, overfeeding can lead to metabolic complications. To minimize these problems, the recommended energy intake is 25 to 30 cal/kg/day in a non-obese patient.[19]

Fat-emulsion solutions of 10%, 20%, and 30% are available. Fat emulsions supply about 1 cal/mL (10% solution) or 2 cal/mL (20% solution). Fat emulsions primarily contain soybean or safflower triglycerides with egg phospholipids added as an emulsifier. They supply a large number of calories in a small amount of fluid. This is beneficial when the patient is at risk for fluid overload.

IV fat emulsions should provide up to 20% to 30% of total calories of PN. Most stable patients receive 1 g/kg/day. The maximum daily lipid dose is 2.5 g/kg/day. Critically ill patients may not tolerate this dose and may receive less than 1 g/kg/day. Serum triglyceride levels are done at the beginning of PN and then closely monitored. Give IV fat emulsions administered separately over 12 hours.[19] The infusion rate should not exceed 0.5 mL/kg/hr.

Fat emulsions are contraindicated in the patient with a problem with fat metabolism, such as hyperlipidemia. They are used cautiously in the patient at risk for fat embolism (e.g., fractured femur) and the patient with an allergy to eggs or soybeans.

Protein. Protein is provided at the rate of 1 to 1.5 g/kg/day depending on the patient's needs. In a nutritionally depleted patient who is under the stress of illness or surgery, protein requirements can exceed 150 g/day (2 g/kg/day) to ensure a positive nitrogen balance. Burn and multiple trauma patients may need more than 2 g/kg protein.[20] Protein needs may be lower than 1 g/kg and restricted in those with end-stage renal disease who are not on dialysis.

Electrolytes. The exact amount of electrolytes needed depends on the patient's health problem and on serum electrolyte levels. Assess individual requirements daily at the beginning of therapy and then several times a week as the treatment progresses. The following are ranges for average daily electrolyte requirements for adult patients without renal or liver impairment:

• Sodium: 1 to 2 mEq/kg
• Potassium: 1 to 2 mEq/kg
• Magnesium: 8 to 20 mEq
• Calcium: 10 to 15 mEq
• Phosphate: 20 to 40 mmol

Trace Elements and Vitamins. Zinc, copper, manganese, selenium, and chromium are added according to the patient's condition and needs. Monitor levels of these elements. The daily addition of a multivitamin preparation to the PN generally meets the vitamin requirements. The HCP may order additional amounts.

Methods of Administration. PN is given as central PN or peripheral parenteral nutrition (PPN). Central PN and PPN differ in nutrient content and tonicity, which is measured in milliosmoles (mOsm; the concentration of particles in a fluid).

Central Parenteral Nutrition. Central PN is indicated when long-term support is needed or when the patient has high protein and caloric requirements. We give central PN through a central venous catheter or a peripherally inserted central catheter (PICC) whose tip lies in the superior vena cava (see Chapter 16). Central PN solutions are hypertonic, measuring at least 1600 mOsm/L. The high glucose content ranges from 20% to 50%. Central PN must be infused in a large central vein so that rapid dilution can occur. The use of a peripheral vein for hypertonic, central PN solutions would cause irritation and thrombophlebitis.

Peripheral Parenteral Nutrition. PPN is given through a peripherally inserted catheter or vascular access device into a large vein. PPN is used when (1) nutritional support is needed for only a short time, (2) protein and caloric requirements are not high, (3) the risk for a central catheter is too great, or (4) to supplement inadequate oral intake.

Compared with central PN, PPN has fewer nutrients. While this makes PPN less hypertonic, it still has an osmolality of up to 800 mOsm/L. This increases the risk for phlebitis. Another potential complication is fluid overload. PPN requires large volumes of fluid, which many patients cannot tolerate.

❖ NURSING MANAGEMENT: PARENTERAL NUTRITION

Nursing management of patients receiving PN is outlined in Table 39.15 and eNursing Care Plan 39.2, available on the website for this chapter.

◆ Complications

Complications associated with PN are related to either the catheter or the PN infusion itself (Table 39.16).

Refeeding syndrome can occur any time a malnourished patient starts aggressive nutritional support. It is characterized by fluid retention and electrolyte imbalances (hypophosphatemia, hypokalemia, hypomagnesemia). Hypophosphatemia is the hallmark of refeeding syndrome. It is associated with serious outcomes, including dysrhythmias, respiratory arrest, and neurologic problems (e.g., paresthesias). Conditions that predispose patients to refeeding syndrome include long-standing malnutrition states, such as chronic alcohol use, vomiting and diarrhea, chemotherapy, and major surgery.

TABLE 39.15 **Nursing Management**
PN Infusions

Preparation of PN Solutions
- All PN solutions must be prepared by a pharmacist or trained technician using strict aseptic techniques under a laminar flow hood.
- Add nothing to PN solutions after they are prepared in the pharmacy.
- Limit number of people involved in preparing and administering PN to reduce risk for infection.
- PN solutions are ordered daily to adjust to the patient's current needs.
- PN solution label shows the nutrient content, all additives, time mixed, and expiration date and time.
- Solutions are good for 24 hrs and must be refrigerated until 30 min before use.

Maintaining PN Infusions
- Follow proper aseptic techniques to reduce infection risk.
- Use a 0.22-micron filter with parenteral solutions not containing fat emulsion and a 1.2-micron filter with solutions containing fat emulsion.
- Change filters and IV tubing with each new PN container or every 24 hr.
- Label tubing and filter with date and time they are put into use.
- If a multilumen catheter is present, use a dedicated line for PN.
- Do not draw blood from a line dedicated for PN unless absolutely necessary.
- Control the infusion rate. Give PN using an infusion pump.
- Set an alarm to alert for tubing obstruction.
- Periodically check the volume infused because pump malfunctions can change the rate.

Ensuring Patient Safety
- Before starting PN, check label and ingredients in solution to make sure they match what the HCP ordered.
- A second RN should verify infusion pump settings before beginning PN.
- Trace the administration tubing to the point of origin in the body at the start of the infusion and at all handoffs.
- Check the solution for leaks, color changes, particulate matter, clarity, and fat emulsions cracking (separating into layers). If present, promptly return it to the pharmacy for replacement.
- Discontinue a PN solution and replace it with a new solution if bag is not empty at the end of 24 hr. At room temperature, the solution (especially when containing fat emulsion) is a good medium for microorganism growth.
- If fat emulsions are infused separately from the PN solution, the preferred delivery method is a continuous low volume delivered over 12 hr.

Hyperglycemia
- Check glucose blood levels at bedside q4–6hr with glucose-testing meter.
- Maintain a glucose range of 140–180 mg/dL. Give sliding scale doses of insulin to keep the glucose level in normal range.

Hypoglycemia
- If a PN formula bag should empty before the next solution is available, a 10% or 20% dextrose solution (based on the amount of dextrose in the central PN solution) or 5% dextrose solution (based on the amount of dextrose in the peripheral PN solution) can be given to prevent hypoglycemia.

Catheter-Related Infections
- Carefully assess the catheter site for signs of inflammation and infection. Phlebitis can readily occur because of the hypertonic infusion. Catheter-related infection and septicemia can occur:
  - Local manifestations: erythema, tenderness, and exudate at the catheter insertion site
  - Systemic manifestations: fever, chills, nausea, vomiting, and malaise
- Immunosuppressed patients are at high-risk for infection. Note subtle signs in patients receiving chemotherapy, corticosteroids, or antibiotics, which can mask signs of infection.
- To reduce the risk for infection, catheters with antibiotic or antiseptic surfaces may be used.
- Follow agency policy for changing catheter dressings and other central line infection prevention measures (see Chapter 16).
- If you suspect an infection during a dressing change, send a culture specimen of the site and drainage and notify the HCP at once.
- If a catheter-related infection is suspected, blood cultures are drawn. A chest x-ray is taken to detect changes in pulmonary status.

Transitioning to Oral Nutrition
- Encourage oral nourishment and keep a careful record of intake. A general rule is that 60% of caloric needs should be met orally or through EN before discontinuing PN.
- Begin with clear liquids and advance as tolerated to a soft diet.

Assessing Effectiveness
- Monitor initial vital signs q4–8hr.
- Weigh patient daily as a measure of the patient's hydration status.
- Maintain accurate intake and output record.
- Determine the cause of any weight changes (e.g., fluid gained from edema, actual increase or decrease in tissue weight).
- Assess blood levels of glucose, electrolytes, and urea nitrogen.
- CBC and hepatic enzyme studies are obtained a minimum of 3 times per week until stable and then weekly as the patient's condition warrants.

TABLE 39.16 **Complications of PN**

Metabolic Problems	Catheter-Related Problems
- Altered renal function	- Air embolus
- Essential fatty acid deficiency	- Catheter-related sepsis
- Hyperglycemia, hypoglycemia	- Dislodgment
- Hyperlipidemia	- Hemorrhage
- Liver dysfunction	- Occlusion
- Refeeding syndrome	- Phlebitis
	- Pneumothorax, hemothorax, and hydrothorax
	- Thrombosis of vein

◆ Home Nutritional Support

Home PN or EN is an accepted mode of nutritional therapy for the person who does not need hospitalization but needs continued nutritional support. Some patients successfully receive home therapy for many months, even years. It is important for you to teach the patient and caregiver about catheter or tube care, proper technique in mixing and handling of the solutions and tubing, and side effects and complications.

Home nutritional therapies are expensive. Specific criteria must be met for expenses to be reimbursed. The discharge planning team must be involved early to help plan for such issues. Home nutritional support may be a burden for the patient and caregivers and affect quality of life. Tell the family about support groups, such as the Oley Foundation (*www.oley.org*), that provide peer support and advocacy.

EATING DISORDERS

Eating disorders are psychiatric conditions associated with physiologic alterations and risk for death. The manifestations of eating disorders vary across gender, age, socioeconomic status, and race and ethnicity. Patients with eating disorders may be hospitalized for fluid and electrolyte problems; dysrhythmias; and nutritional, endocrine, and metabolic disorders. Menstrual problems may occur in women of childbearing age. Many of the nutritional problems associated with these disorders require you to implement a nutritional plan of care.

The 3 most common types of eating disorders are anorexia nervosa, bulimia nervosa, and binge-eating disorder. *Binge-eating disorder* is less severe than bulimia nervosa and anorexia nervosa. Those with binge-eating disorder do not have a distorted body image and are often overweight or obese.

Eating disorders also occur in some who are health conscious. For example, men with *bigorexia* or muscle dysmorphia (an extreme concern with becoming more muscular) may use steroids or other drugs to increase muscle mass. They may also use supplements and protein shakes to increase their body weight and mass.

The *female athlete triad* is a syndrome in which eating disorders, amenorrhea, and osteoporosis are present. The triad occurs in females taking part in sports that emphasize leanness and low body weight.

ANOREXIA NERVOSA

Anorexia nervosa (AN) is characterized by restricting energy intake, difficulties in maintaining an appropriate weight, an intense fear of gaining weight or being fat, and distorted body image.[21] People with AN generally restrict the number of calories and the types of food they eat. Some people exercise compulsively, purge via vomiting and laxatives, and/or binge eat. AN manifests as unwillingness to maintain a healthy weight, refusal to eat, continuous dieting, detailed food rituals, and avoiding social situations.[21] Common assessment findings include signs of malnutrition, extreme thinness, hypothermia, and muscle weakness (Fig. 39.9).

Diagnostic studies often show osteopenia or osteoporosis, iron-deficiency anemia, a high blood urea nitrogen level from marked intravascular volume depletion, and abnormal renal function. A lack of dietary potassium and potassium loss in the urine lead to potassium deficiency. Manifestations of potassium deficiency include muscle weakness, dysrhythmias, and renal failure. Leukopenia; hypoglycemia; and decreased sodium, magnesium, and phosphorus may be present.

Treatment involves a combination of nutritional support and psychiatric care. Nutritional care focuses on reaching and maintaining a healthy weight, normal eating patterns, and perception of hunger and satiety. The patient may be hospitalized if there are medical complications that cannot be managed in an outpatient therapy program. Nutritional repletion is closely supervised to ensure consistent and ongoing weight gains. Refeeding syndrome is a rare but serious complication of refeeding programs. The patient may need EN or PN.

Improved nutrition, however, is not a cure for AN. The underlying psychiatric issues must be addressed by identifying problematic personal and family interactions, followed by personal and family counseling.

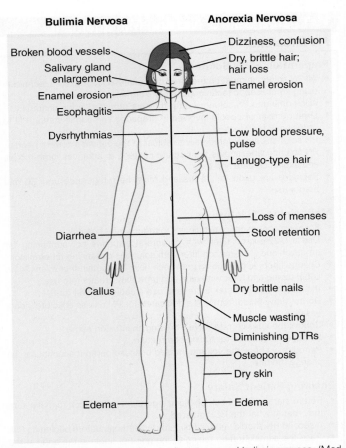

FIG. 39.9 Manifestations of anorexia nervosa and bulimia nervosa. (Modified from Mahan LK, Raymond JL: *Krause's food & the nutrition care process*, ed, 14, St Louis, 2016, Saunders.)

BULIMIA NERVOSA

Bulimia nervosa (BN) is a disorder characterized by episodes of binge eating with inappropriate compensatory behaviors to avoid weight gain (vomiting, laxative misuse, overexercise).[21] Like those with AN, the person with BN is concerned with body image and often goes to great lengths to conceal abnormal eating habits.[21] They may have normal weight for height, or their weight may fluctuate with bingeing and purging. There may have signs of frequent vomiting, such as macerated knuckles, swollen salivary glands, broken blood vessels in the eyes, and dental problems (Fig. 39.9). Abnormal laboratory values, including hypokalemia, metabolic alkalosis, and increased serum amylase, may occur from frequent vomiting.

The cause of BN is unclear. It is thought to be similar to that of AN. Some persons with BN report substance use, anxiety, affective disorders, and personality changes. Over time, problems associated with BN become increasingly hard to deal with effectively. A treatment combination of psychologic counseling (i.e., cognitive behavioral therapy) and nutritional counseling is essential.

Fluoxetine (Prozac) is the only FDA-approved antidepressant for treating BN. It may not be appropriate for all patients with BN. Education and emotional support for the patient and family are vital. Support groups, such as the National Association of Anorexia Nervosa and Associated Disorders (ANAD) *(www.anad.org)*, are helpful to those affected by these disorders.

CASE STUDY
Undernutrition

Patient Profile

M.S. is a 70-yr-old white woman who was recently admitted to the inpatient medical unit with a diagnosis of malnutrition.

Subjective Data

(© iStockphoto/ Thinkstock.)

- Reports 30-lb weight loss in past 2 mo
- Recently had a thrombotic stroke with hemiparesis and dysphagia
- Has a history of rheumatoid arthritis
- Has had nothing by mouth for the past 24 hr and just started EN via PEG tube
- Lives with her daughter, who is at her bedside

Objective Data
Physical Examination

- Has left-sided weakness
- BP is 150/90 mm Hg
- 5 ft, 4 in tall, weight 100 lb
- PEG tube recently placed

Laboratory Results

- Serum albumin 2.9 g/dL
- Prealbumin 11.0 mg/dL
- C-reactive protein 0.9 mg/L

Discussion Questions

1. What are M.S.'s risk factors for malnutrition?
2. What is her BMI?
3. What are contributing factors to her developing dysphagia and malnutrition?
4. What should you include in a successful weight gain program for M.S.?
5. For which complications of EN could M.S. be at risk?
6. *Priority Decision:* What is the priority of the nursing care for M.S.?
7. *Priority Decision:* Based on the assessment data presented, what are the priority nursing diagnoses? Identify any collaborative problems.
8. *Collaboration:* Which interventions could be delegated to unlicensed assistive personnel (UAP)?
9. *Evidence-Based Practice:* M.S.'s daughter tells you that her mother's abdomen appears bloated and she wonders if she should massage it.
10. *Collaboration:* What is the interprofessional team's top priority at this time for M.S.?
11. *Safety:* To ensure M.S.'s safety, what nursing interventions are needed considering M.S.'s recent weight loss?

Answers available at *http://evolve.elsevier.com/Lewis/medsurg*

BRIDGE TO NCLEX EXAMINATION

The number of the question corresponds to the same-numbered outcome at the beginning of the chapter.

1. The percentage of daily calories for a healthy person consists of
   a. 50% carbohydrates, 25% protein, 25% fat, and <10% of fat from saturated fatty acids.
   b. 65% carbohydrates, 25% protein, 25% fat, and >10% of fat from saturated fatty acids.
   c. 50% carbohydrates, 40% protein, 10% fat, and <10% of fat from saturated fatty acids.
   d. 40% carbohydrates, 30% protein, 30% fat, and >10% of fat from saturated fatty acids.

2. Place in order the substrates the body uses for energy during starvation, beginning with 1 for the first component and ending with 4 for the last component.
   a. skeletal protein.
   b. glycogen.
   c. visceral protein.
   d. fat stores.

3. A complete nutritional assessment including anthropometric measurements is *most* important for the patient who
   a. has a BMI of 25.5 kg/m².
   b. reports episodes of nightly nocturia.
   c. reports a 5-year history of constipation.
   d. reports an unintentional weight loss of 10 lb in 2 months.

4. Which method is *best* to use when confirming initial placement of a blindly inserted small-bore NG feeding tube?
   a. X-ray
   b. Air insertion
   c. Observing patient for coughing
   d. pH measurement of gastric aspirate

5. A patient is receiving peripheral parenteral nutrition. The solution is completed before the new solution arrives on the unit. The nurse gives
   a. 20% intralipids.
   b. 5% dextrose solution.
   c. 0.45% normal saline solution.
   d. 5% lactated Ringer's solution.

6. A patient with anorexia nervosa shows signs of malnutrition. During initial refeeding, the nurse carefully assesses the patient for *(select all that apply)*
   a. hypokalemia.
   b. hypoglycemia.
   c. hypercalcemia.
   d. hypomagnesemia.
   e. hypophosphatemia.

1. a, 2. b, a, d, c, 3. d, 4. a, 5. b, 6. a, d, e

For rationales to these answers and even more NCLEX review questions, visit *http://evolve.elsevier.com/Lewis/medsurg.*

ⓔ EVOLVE WEBSITE/RESOURCES LIST

http://evolve.elsevier.com/Lewis/medsurg
Review Questions (Online Only)
Key Points
Answer Keys for Questions
- Rationales for Bridge to NCLEX Examination Questions
- Answer Guidelines for Case Study on p. 867
Nursing Care Plans
- eNursing Care Plan 39.1: Patient Receiving Enteral Nutrition
- eNursing Care Plan 39.2: Patient Receiving Parenteral Nutrition
Conceptual Care Map Creator
Audio Glossary
Content Updates

REFERENCES

*1. Dave JM, Thompson DI, Svendsen-Sanchez A, et al : Perspectives on barriers to eating healthy among food pantry clients, *Health Equity* 1:28, 2017.

2. Mifflin MD, St. Jeor ST, Hill LA, et al: A new predictive equation for resting energy expenditure in healthy individuals, *Am J Clin Nutr* 51:242, 1990. (Classic)

3. US Department of Health and Human Services, US Department of Agriculture: 2015-2020 Dietary guidelines for Americans, ed 8. Retrieved from *www.health.gov/dietaryguidelines/2015-scientific-report.*

*4. Elagizi A, Lavie CJ, Marshall K, et al: Omega-3 polyunsaturated fatty acids and cardiovascular health: A comprehensive review, *Prog Cardiovasc Dis* 61:76, 2018.

5. Moll R, Davis B: Iron, vitamin B_{12} and folate, *Medicine* 45:198, 2017.

6. Nix, S: *Williams' basic nutrition and diet therapy,* ed 15, St Louis, 2018, Elsevier.

*7. Sriram K, Sulo S, VanDerBosch G, et al: A comprehensive nutrition-focused quality improvement program reduces 30-day readmissions and length of stay in hospitalized patients, *JPEN* 41:384, 2017.

*8. Cereda E, Pedrolli C, Klersy C, et al: Nutritional status in older persons according to healthcare setting: A systematic review and meta-analysis of prevalence data using MNA®, *Clin Nutr* 35:1282, 2016.

9. White JV, Guenter P, Jensen G, et al: Consensus statement of the Academy of Nutrition and Dietetics/ASPEN: Characteristics recommended for the identification and documentation of adult malnutrition, *J Acad Nutr Diet* 112:730, 2012. (Classic)

10. Naisbitt C, Davies S: Starvation, exercise and the stress response, *Anaesth Intensive Care Med* 18:508, 2017.

*11. Bharadwaj S, Ginoya S, Tandon P, et al: Malnutrition: Laboratory markers vs nutritional assessment, *Gastroenterol Rep* 4:272, 2016.

12. Mahan LK, Raymond JL: *Krause's food & the nutrition care process,* ed 14, St Louis, 2016, Saunders.

*13. Park SY, Wilkens LR, Maskarinec G, et al: Weight change in older adults and mortality: The Multiethnic Cohort Study, *Int J Obes* 42:205, 2018.

14. Russell MK: Clinical assessment of undernutrition, *Adv Nutr Dietetics Nutr Suppl* 6:74, 2018.

*15. Hengeveld LM, Wijnhoven HA, Olthof MR, et al: Prospective associations of poor diet quality with long-term incidence of protein-energy malnutrition in community-dwelling older adults: The Health, Aging, and Body Composition Study, *Am J Clin Nutr* 107:155, 2018.

*16. Biolo G, Pišot R, Mazzucco S, et al: Anabolic resistance assessed by oral stable isotope ingestion following bed rest in young and older adult volunteers: Relationships with changes in muscle mass, *Clin Nutr* 36:1420, 2017.

*17. Cardon-Thomas DK, Riviere T, Tieges Z, et al: Dietary protein in older adults: Adequate daily intake but potential for improved distribution, *Nutrients* 9:184, 2017.

*18. Boullata JI, Carrera AL, Harvey L, et al: ASPEN safe practices for enteral nutrition therapy, *JPEN* 41:15, 2017.

*19. Mehta NM, Skillman HE, Irving SY, et al: Guidelines for the provision and assessment of nutrition support therapy in the pediatric critically ill patient: Society of Critical Care Medicine and ASPEN, *JPEN* 41:706, 2017.

*20. Guenter P, Worthington P, Ayers P, et al: Standardized competencies for parenteral nutrition administration: The ASPEN model, *Nutr Clin Pract* 33:295, 2018.

21. National Eating Disorders Association: Learn. Retrieved from: *www.nationaleatingdisorders.org/.*

*Evidence-based information for clinical practice.

40

Obesity

Mariann M. Harding

Helping one person might not change the whole world,
but it could change the world for the one person.

Paul Shane Spear

ⓔ http://evolve.elsevier.com/Lewis/medsurg

CONCEPTUAL FOCUS

Coping
Functional Ability

Nutrition
Self-Management

LEARNING OUTCOMES

1. Discuss the epidemiology and etiology of obesity.
2. Explain the health risks associated with obesity.
3. Compare the classification systems for determining a person's body size.
4. Discuss nutritional therapy and exercise plans for the obese patient.
5. Distinguish among the bariatric surgical procedures used to treat obesity.
6. Describe the nursing and interprofessional management related to conservative and surgical therapies for obesity.
7. Describe the etiology, clinical manifestations, and nursing and interprofessional management of metabolic syndrome.

KEY TERMS

bariatric surgery, p. 879
body mass index (BMI), p. 875
extreme obesity, p. 875

lipectomy, p. 885
metabolic syndrome, p. 885
obese, p. 875

obesity, p. 869
overweight, p. 875
waist-to-hip ratio (WHR), p. 876

OBESITY

Obesity is an excessively high amount of body fat or adipose tissue (Fig. 40.1). Obesity is a global problem because it is a major risk factor for leading causes of death, including type 2 diabetes, heart disease, and certain cancers. Overweight persons often have a number of other problems, such as problems with mobility and sleeping, that affect health.

The consequences of obesity extend beyond the physical changes. Social stigma can take an emotional toll on a person's psychologic well-being. Many have problems related to altered body image, depression, and low self-esteem and withdraw from social interaction. Attitudes about obesity can create biases and discrimination against people who are obese. Obesity must be viewed and treated as a chronic disease similar to other chronic diseases, such as diabetes and hypertension.

Epidemiology of Obesity

The obesity problem is a public health crisis. After decades of rising obesity rates among adults, the rate of increase is beginning to slow, but rates are still far too high. Currently, about 40% of adults in the United States are obese. Significant geographic, racial and ethnic, and income disparities exist. Obesity rates are highest in the South (Fig. 40.2) and among blacks, Hispanics, and lower income, less-educated Americans[1] (Fig. 40.3).

🌐 PROMOTING HEALTH EQUITY
Obesity

- Hispanics (47%) and blacks (46.8%) have the highest rates of obesity.
- Among women, blacks have the highest prevalence of being obese, with 17% having extreme obesity.
- Among men, Hispanics (43.1%) have the highest prevalence of being obese.
- Asian Americans have the lowest prevalence of being obese or extremely obese.

Obesity in adulthood is often a problem that begins in childhood or adolescence. One in 10 children becomes obese as early as age 2 to 5.[1] Reversing the childhood obesity crisis is key to addressing the overall obesity epidemic.

Etiology and Pathophysiology

Obesity is an increase in body weight beyond the body's physical requirements. This results in an abnormal increase and accumulation of fat cells. However, the processes leading to and sustaining the obese state are complex and still undergoing investigation.

In obesity, there is an increase in the number of adipocytes *(hyperplasia)* and an increase in their size *(hypertrophy)*. Adipocyte *hypertrophy* is a process by which adipocytes can increase their volume several thousand times to accommodate large increases in lipid storage. When storage of existing fat cells is exceeded, preadipocytes are triggered to become adipocytes. This process occurs primarily in the visceral (intraabdominal) and subcutaneous tissues. The process of *hyperplasia* of adipocytes is greatest from infancy through adolescence.

Most obese persons have *primary obesity,* which is excess calorie intake over energy expenditure for the body's metabolic demands. Others have *secondary obesity,* which can result from various congenital anomalies, chromosomal anomalies,

metabolic problems, central nervous system (CNS) lesions and disorders, or drugs (e.g., corticosteroids, antipsychotics).

The cause of obesity involves genetic and biologic factors that are influenced by environmental and psychosocial factors. While each of these factors can and should be considered individually, in reality they are interrelated.

Genetic Link

A genetic predisposition to obesity may be present in as many as 70% of those who are obese.[2] Several genes that are linked to obesity have been found. Genes appear to influence how calories are stored and energy released. "Energy-thrifty" genes, once protective against long periods when food was not available, are now maladaptive in societies in which food availability is no longer an issue. Genes may be responsible for why 2 people living in the same environment can vary considerably in body size.

A strong link exists between a gene known as *FTO* (fat mass and obesity-associated gene) and body mass index (BMI). Variants of this gene may explain why some people become overweight while others do not. People with a certain allele of the *FTO* gene appear to have an increased appetite, reduced satiety, and higher calorie intake.[2] More research is needed to better understand the role of genes in obesity.

Physiologic Regulatory Mechanisms in Obesity. Research has focused on the physiologic regulatory processes that control eating behavior, energy metabolism, and body fat metabolism. Knowing how appetite is triggered and energy is spent gives important information for understanding obesity and specific targets for the development of drugs.

The hypothalamus, gut, and adipose tissue synthesize hormones and peptides that stimulate or inhibit appetite (Fig. 40.4). The hypothalamus is a major site for regulating appetite. Neuropeptide Y, made in the hypothalamus, is a powerful appetite stimulant. When it is imbalanced, it leads to overeating and

FIG. 40.1 The obesity epidemic has taken its toll on both adults and children in the United States. (© iStock.com/IPGGutenbergUKLtd.)

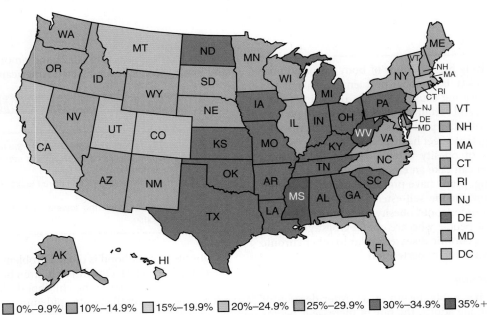

0%–9.9%   10%–14.9%   15%–19.9%   20%–24.9%   25%–29.9%   30%–34.9%   35%+

FIG. 40.2 Percent of obese adults (BMI >30 kg/m²) in the United States. Alabama, Arkansas, Louisiana, Mississippi, and West Virginia have the highest rates of obesity. Colorado has the lowest rate at 22.3%. 20 states have rates at or above 30%, 47 states have rates of at least 25%, and every state is above 20%. (Source: Trust for America's Health, Robert Wood Johnson Foundation. The state of obesity. 2017. Retrieved from *http://stateofobesity.org*.)

obesity. Hormones and peptides made in the gut and adipocyte cells affect the hypothalamus and have a critical role in appetite and energy balance (Table 40.1). When overeating develops at an early age and continues into adulthood, one's ability to sense fullness *(satiety)* is altered.

Leptin, secreted from adipocytes when they fill with fat, acts in the hypothalamus to suppress appetite and increase fat metabolism. A genetic deficiency of leptin causes extreme obesity. However, most obese persons have high leptin levels, suggesting they are leptin resistant. This may be due to a

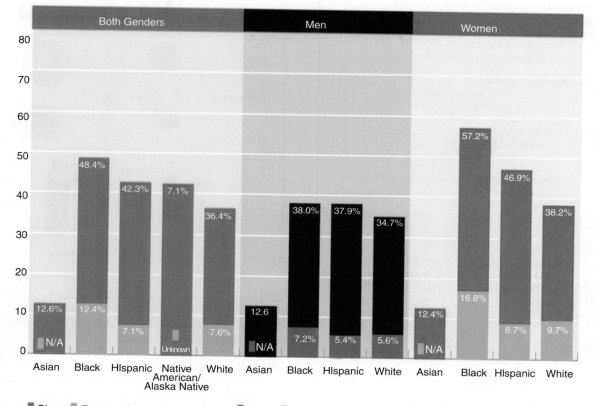

FIG. 40.3 Obesity affects some groups disproportionately. Among U.S. adults, black and Hispanic populations have higher rates of obesity than do white populations. (Source: Trust for America's Health, Robert Wood Johnson Foundation. The state of obesity. 2017. Retrieved from *http://stateofobesity.org.*)

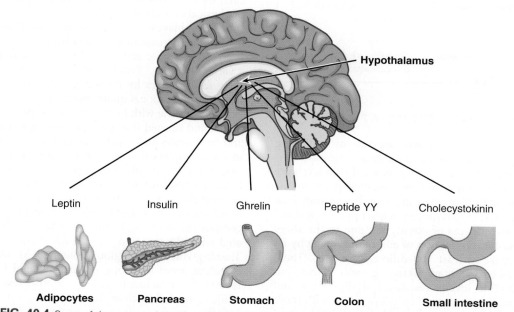

FIG. 40.4 Some of the common hormones and peptides that interact with the hypothalamus to control and influence eating patterns, metabolic activities, and digestion. Obesity disrupts this balance (Table 40.3).

TABLE 40.1 Hormones and Peptides in Obesity

Where Produced	Normal Function	Alteration in Obesity
Anorexins (Suppress Appetite)		
Cholecystokinin		
Small intestine	Inhibits gastric emptying Sends satiety signals to hypothalamus	Unknown role
Glucagon-Like Peptide-1 (GLP-1)		
Small intestine	Stimulates insulin secretion from pancreas Increases satiety (mediated by GLP-1 receptors in brain)	Unknown role
Insulin		
Pancreas	Decreases appetite	Increased insulin secretion, which stimulates ↑ liver synthesis of triglycerides and ↓ HDL production
Leptin		
Adipocytes	Suppresses appetite and hunger Regulates eating behavior	Obesity is associated with high levels Leptin resistance develops so obese people may lose the effect of appetite suppression
Peptide YY		
Colon	Inhibits appetite by slowing GI motility and gastric emptying	Circulating levels are decreased. ↓ Release after eating
Orexins (Stimulate Appetite)		
Ghrelin		
Stomach (primarily)	Stimulates appetite ↑ After food deprivation ↓ In response to food in the stomach	Normal postprandial decline does not occur, which can lead to increased appetite and overeating
Neuropeptide Y		
Hypothalamus	Stimulates appetite	Imbalance causes increased appetite

TABLE 40.2 Portion Sizes: 40 Years Ago vs. Today

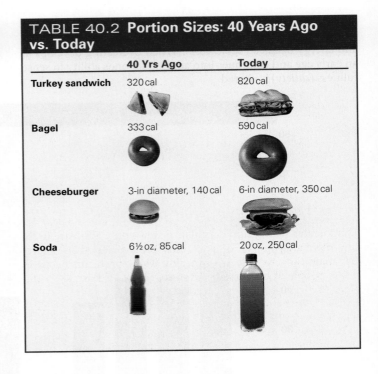

	40 Yrs Ago	Today
Turkey sandwich	320 cal	820 cal
Bagel	333 cal	590 cal
Cheeseburger	3-in diameter, 140 cal	6-in diameter, 350 cal
Soda	6½ oz, 85 cal	20 oz, 250 cal

failure to make enough leptin receptors or producing faulty receptors.

Ghrelin, a gut hormone, regulates appetite by inhibiting leptin. It acts in the hypothalamus and the brain's pleasure centers to stimulate hunger. In a nonobese person, ghrelin levels are higher when a person is hungry and decrease in response to eating. Ghrelin is thought to play a part in compulsive eating. Low ghrelin levels after gastric bypass surgery helps suppress appetite.[3]

The 2 major consequences of obesity are due to the sheer increase in fat mass and production of adipokines made by fat cells. Adipocytes make at least 100 different proteins. These proteins, secreted as enzymes, adipokines, growth factors, and hormones, contribute to insulin resistance, dyslipidemia, and high blood pressure. Excess visceral fat is associated with more alterations of adipokines. This causes people with abdominal (android) obesity more complications of obesity.[4] An increased release of cytokines from fat cells may disrupt immune factors and predispose the person to certain cancers.

Environmental Factors. Environmental factors play a key role in obesity. In today's culture, people have greater access to food (particularly prepackaged and fast foods) and soft drinks, which have poor nutritional quality. In addition, eating outside of the home interferes with the ability to control the quality and quantity of food. Portion size of meals has increased dramatically (Table 40.2). Underestimating portion sizes and therefore caloric intake is common. Lack of physical exercise is another factor that contributes to weight gain and obesity. With increases in the use of technology, labor-saving devices, and cars, we expend less energy in our everyday lives. Elimination of physical education programs in schools, along with increased time spent playing video games and watching TV, has contributed to the increase in sedentary habits.

Socioeconomic status is a known risk factor for obesity in a variety of ways.[5] People with low incomes may try to stretch their food dollars by buying less expensive foods that often have poor nutritional quality with a greater caloric content. For example, people with low incomes are more likely to buy pasta, bread, and canned fruit packed with sugar rather than chicken and fresh fruits and vegetables. Low-income residents may live in environments that do not accommodate outdoor activities (e.g., safe playgrounds, walking tracks, tennis, swimming pools).

Psychosocial Factors. People use food for many reasons besides its nutritional value. Associations with food begin in childhood, such as the use of food for comfort or rewards. The social component of eating begins early in life when food is associated with pleasure and fun at such events as birthday parties, Thanksgiving, and religious holidays. "Mindless eating" refers to eating more than one normally would because of outside factors. These factors include the food's presentation and eating while distracted, such as when studying or watching television. Mindless eating leads to consuming unnecessary calories and an increase in body weight.

♥ PROMOTING POPULATION HEALTH
Health Impact of Maintaining a Healthy Weight

- Lowers the risk for hypertension and high cholesterol
- Increases chance for longevity and better quality of life
- Reduces the risk for developing type 2 diabetes
- Reduces the risk for heart disease, stroke, and gallbladder disease
- Reduces the risk for breathing problems, including sleep apnea and asthma
- Decreases the risk for developing osteoarthritis, low back pain, and certain types of cancers

HEALTH RISKS ASSOCIATED WITH OBESITY

Hippocrates wrote that "corpulence is not only a disease itself, but the harbinger of others," thus recognizing that obesity has major adverse effects on health. Many problems occur in obese people at higher rates than in people of normal weight (Fig. 40.5).

Mortality rates rise as obesity increases, especially when obesity is associated with visceral fat.[1] In addition to these problems, obese patients have a reduced quality of life. Fortunately, most of these conditions can improve if a person loses weight.

Cardiovascular Problems

Obesity is a significant risk factor for cardiovascular disease (CVD) and stroke in both men and women. Android obesity is the best predictor of these risks and is linked with increased low-density lipoproteins (LDLs), high triglycerides, and decreased high-density lipoproteins (HDLs).[6] Hypertension can occur because of increased circulating blood volume, abnormal vasoconstriction, increased inflammation (damaging blood vessels), and increased risk for sleep apnea (raises BP). Excess body fat can lead to chronic inflammation throughout the body, especially in blood vessels, thus increasing the risk for heart disease.

Diabetes

Obesity is a major risk factor for the development of type 2 diabetes. Hyperinsulinemia and insulin resistance, common features of type 2 diabetes, are also found in obesity. The term *diabesity* reflects the combined effects of diabetes and obesity.

Excess weight decreases the effectiveness of insulin. When insulin does not work effectively, too much glucose stays in the bloodstream. Thus more insulin is made to compensate. Pancreatic β cells (cells that make insulin) may get overworked and become worn out. Over time, the pancreas is no longer able to keep blood glucose in normal range. Adiponectin, a peptide that increases insulin sensitivity, is decreased in obese people.

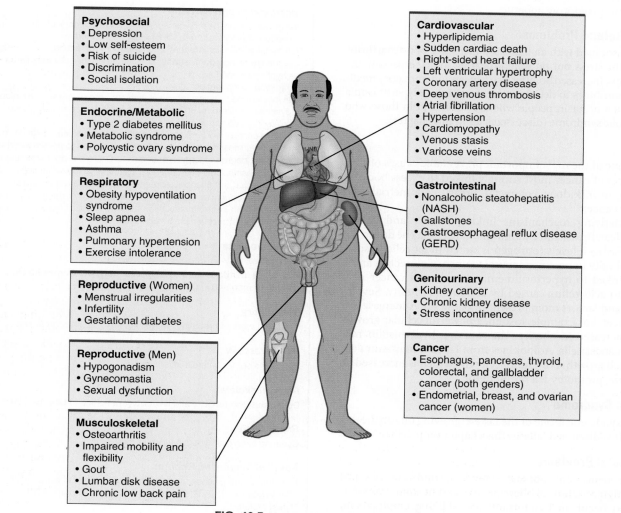

Psychosocial
- Depression
- Low self-esteem
- Risk of suicide
- Discrimination
- Social isolation

Endocrine/Metabolic
- Type 2 diabetes mellitus
- Metabolic syndrome
- Polycystic ovary syndrome

Respiratory
- Obesity hypoventilation syndrome
- Sleep apnea
- Asthma
- Pulmonary hypertension
- Exercise intolerance

Reproductive (Women)
- Menstrual irregularities
- Infertility
- Gestational diabetes

Reproductive (Men)
- Hypogonadism
- Gynecomastia
- Sexual dysfunction

Musculoskeletal
- Osteoarthritis
- Impaired mobility and flexibility
- Gout
- Lumbar disk disease
- Chronic low back pain

Cardiovascular
- Hyperlipidemia
- Sudden cardiac death
- Right-sided heart failure
- Left ventricular hypertrophy
- Coronary artery disease
- Deep venous thrombosis
- Atrial fibrillation
- Hypertension
- Cardiomyopathy
- Venous stasis
- Varicose veins

Gastrointestinal
- Nonalcoholic steatohepatitis (NASH)
- Gallstones
- Gastroesophageal reflux disease (GERD)

Genitourinary
- Kidney cancer
- Chronic kidney disease
- Stress incontinence

Cancer
- Esophagus, pancreas, thyroid, colorectal, and gallbladder cancer (both genders)
- Endometrial, breast, and ovarian cancer (women)

FIG. 40.5 Health risks associated with obesity.

Obesity complicates the management of type 2 diabetes by increasing insulin resistance and glucose intolerance. These factors make drug treatment for diabetes less effective.

Gastrointestinal and Liver Problems

Gastroesophageal reflux disease (GERD) and gallstones are more prevalent in obese people. Gallstones occur due to supersaturation of the bile with cholesterol. Nonalcoholic steatohepatitis (NASH) is a condition in which lipids are deposited in the liver, resulting in a fatty liver. NASH is associated with increased hepatic glucose production. NASH can eventually progress to cirrhosis and can be fatal. Weight loss can improve NASH.

Respiratory and Sleep Problems

The increased fat mass associated with obesity may lead to sleep apnea and obesity hypoventilation syndrome. The increased distribution of fat around the diaphragm causes reduced chest wall compliance, increased work of breathing, and decreased total lung capacity. Sleep apnea results from increased fat around the neck, leading to snoring and hypoventilation while sleeping. Weight loss can improve lung function.

Poor sleep and sleep deprivation may increase appetite. Sleep deprivation has been associated with obesity. Building up a sleep debt over a matter of days can impair metabolism and disrupt hormone levels. The level of leptin falls in people who are sleep deprived, thus promoting appetite.

Musculoskeletal Problems

Obesity is associated with an increased incidence of osteoarthritis because of the stress put on weight-bearing joints, especially the knees and hips. Increased body fat also triggers inflammatory mediators and contributes to deterioration of cartilage. Hyperuricemia and gout often occur in people who are obese and in those who have metabolic syndrome (discussed later in this chapter).

Cancer

Obesity is one of the most important preventable causes of cancer. The types of cancer most strongly linked to excess body fat are thyroid, liver, kidney, colorectal, breast, endometrial, and gallbladder cancer.[1,7]

The underlying mechanisms linking obesity and cancer remain unclear. Breast and endometrial cancer may be due to the increased estrogen levels (estrogen is stored in fat cells) associated with obesity in postmenopausal women. Colorectal cancer has been linked to hyperinsulinemia. Esophageal cancer may be related to acid reflux caused by abdominal obesity. Several hormones and factors often present in obese states increase the risk for cancer. For example, insulin, a powerful cellular growth factor, is increased in obesity. The resulting hyperinsulinemia may affect cancer cells. Adipokines from fat cells may stimulate or inhibit cell growth. For example, leptin, which is increased in obese people, promotes cell proliferation.

Metabolic Syndrome

Metabolic syndrome is one of the fastest-growing obesity health concerns. It is discussed later in this chapter on p. 885.

Psychosocial Problems

The consequences of obesity extend beyond the physical changes. Stigmatization of obese people, and in some cases discrimination, occurs in 3 important areas of living: employment, education, and health care. The social stigma associated with obesity has an emotional toll on a person's psychologic well-being. Many obese persons have low self-esteem, withdraw from social interaction, and have major depression.[8]

❖ NURSING AND INTERPROFESSIONAL MANAGEMENT: OBESITY

◆ Nursing Assessment

The first step in the treatment of obesity is to determine whether any physical conditions are present that may be causing or contributing to obesity. This requires a thorough history and physical examination (Table 40.3). Before you begin, examine your

---

TABLE 40.3 Nursing Assessment
Patients With Obesity

Subjective Data

Important Health Information

Past health history: Time of obesity onset; diseases related to metabolism and obesity, including hypertension, CVD, stroke, cancer, chronic joint pain, respiratory problems, diabetes, cholelithiasis, metabolic syndrome

Medications: Thyroid preparations, diet pills, herbal products

Surgery or other treatments: Prior weight-reduction procedures (bariatric surgery)

Functional Health Patterns

Health perception–health management: Family history of obesity; perception of problem; methods of weight loss tried

Nutritional-metabolic: Amount and frequency of eating; overeating in response to boredom, stress, specific times, or activities; history of weight gain and loss

Elimination: Constipation

Activity-exercise: Typical physical activity; drowsiness, somnolence; dyspnea on exertion, orthopnea, paroxysmal nocturnal dyspnea

Sleep-rest: Sleep apnea, use of CPAP

Cognitive-perceptual: Feelings of rejection, depression, isolation, guilt, or shame; meaning or value of food; adherence to prescribed reducing diets, degree of long-term commitment to a weight loss program

Role-relationship: Change in financial status or family relationships; personal, social, and financial resources to support a reducing diet

Sexuality-reproductive: Menstrual irregularity, heavy menstrual flow in women, birth control practices, infertility; effect of obesity on sexual activity and attractiveness to significant other

Objective Data

General

Body mass index ≥30 kg/m^2; waist circumference: woman >35 in (89 cm), man >40 in (102 cm)

Respiratory

Increased work of breathing; wheezing; rapid, shallow breathing

Cardiovascular

Hypertension, tachycardia, dysrhythmias

Musculoskeletal

Decreased joint mobility and flexibility; knee, hip, and low back pain

Reproductive

Gynecomastia and hypogonadism in men

Possible Diagnostic Findings

Elevated serum glucose, cholesterol, triglycerides; chest x-ray showing enlarged heart; ECG showing dysrhythmia; abnormal liver function test results

own personal beliefs and any potential biases related to obesity. If you associate obesity with a lack of willpower and overindulgence, you may convey your attitude to patients. They may experience shame in a setting that claims to be a caring one.

When assessing a person who is overweight or obese, be sensitive and nonjudgmental in asking specific and leading questions about weight, diet, and exercise (Table 40.4). In doing so, you can often obtain information that the patient may have withheld out of embarrassment or shyness. Patients need to understand the reason for questions asked about weight or dietary habits. You must be ready to respond to their concerns.

CHECK YOUR PRACTICE

You are working in the hypertension clinic, and the provider has asked you to do an assessment on a 54-yr-old man for referral to a weight loss program. He is 5 ft, 9 in and weighs 242 lb. His BP has been hard to control with drugs and diet. While you are trying to do an assessment (using the questions in Table 40.4), he interrupts you and asks you if he can leave. He angrily tells you, "I do not want to give up my favorite foods, quit drinking, or exercise. Do you understand that?"
• How would you respond to him?

Assess a patient's willingness to change and potential for change. If people are not ready for change, offer them the opportunity to return for further discussion when they are ready to discuss their weight again and make lifestyle changes.

When obtaining the history, explore genetic and endocrine factors, such as hypothyroidism, hypothalamic tumors, Cushing syndrome, hypogonadism in men, and polycystic ovary syndrome in women. Laboratory tests of liver function and thyroid function, a fasting glucose level, and a lipid panel (triglyceride level, LDL and HDL cholesterol levels) aid in evaluating the cause and effects of obesity. When no organic cause (e.g., hypothyroidism) is associated with obesity, the disorder should be considered a chronic, complex disease.

Assess for any co-morbid diseases associated with obesity (e.g., hypertension, sleep apnea). These obesity-related complications require special treatment.

TABLE 40.4 Assessing Patients With Obesity

When assessing patients with obesity and before selecting a weight loss strategy, ask the following questions:
• What is your history with weight gain and weight loss?
• Are other family members overweight?
• How has your body weight affected your health?
• What do you think contributes to your weight?
• What does food mean to you? How do you use food (e.g., to relieve stress, provide comfort)?
• Describe your motivation for losing weight.
• What have you already tried to lose weight? Was it successful? If not, why not?
• Would you like to manage your weight differently? If so, how?
• What sort of barriers do you think impede your weight loss efforts?
• Are there any major stresses that will make it hard to focus on weight control?
• How much time can you devote to exercise on a daily or weekly basis?
• Describe the support you have from family and/or friends for losing weight.

As part of the initial nursing physical examination, assess each body system with particular attention to the organ system in which the patient has expressed a problem or concern. Measurements used with the obese person may include height (without shoes), weight (obtain in a private location and in a gown, if possible), waist circumference, and BMI. Have the right equipment to take these measurements. Provide special chairs, examination tables, and scales that can accommodate an obese person.

◆ Classifications of Body Weight and Obesity

An important part of your patient assessment is to determine and classify a patient's body weight. Common assessment methods include BMI, waist circumference, waist-to-hip ratio (WHR), and body shape. The most widely used and endorsed measures are BMI and waist circumference. These measures are cost-effective, reliable, and easily used in all practice settings.

◆ **Body Mass Index.** The most common measure of obesity is the body mass index (BMI). BMI is calculated by dividing a person's weight (in kilograms) by the square of the height in meters (Fig. 40.6). Table 40.5 shows the classification of overweight and obesity by BMI. Persons with a BMI less than 18.5 kg/m² are considered underweight. A BMI between 18.5 and 24.9 kg/m² reflects a normal body weight. A BMI of 25 to 29.9 kg/m² is classified as being overweight. Those with values at 30 kg/m² or above are considered obese. The term extreme obesity (*morbid* or *severe obesity*) is used for those with a BMI greater than 40 kg/m².

$$BMI\ (kg/m^2) = \frac{Weight\ (pounds) \times 703}{Height\ (inches)^2}$$

Weight in Pounds

Height	120	130	140	150	160	170	180	190	200	210	220	230	240	250
4'6	29	31	34	36	39	41	43	46	48	51	53	56	58	60
4'8	27	29	31	34	36	38	40	43	45	47	49	52	54	56
4'10	25	27	29	31	34	36	38	40	42	44	46	48	50	52
5'0	23	25	27	29	31	33	35	37	39	41	43	45	47	49
5'2	22	24	26	27	29	31	33	35	37	38	40	42	44	46
5'4	21	22	24	26	28	29	31	33	34	36	38	40	41	43
5'6	19	21	23	24	26	27	29	31	32	34	36	37	39	40
5'8	18	20	21	23	24	26	27	29	30	32	34	35	37	38
5'10	17	19	20	22	23	24	26	27	29	30	32	33	35	36
6'0	16	18	19	20	22	23	24	26	27	28	30	31	33	34
6'2	15	17	18	19	21	22	23	24	26	27	28	30	31	32
6'4	15	16	17	18	20	21	22	23	24	26	27	28	29	30
6'6	14	15	16	17	19	20	21	22	23	24	25	27	28	29
6'8	13	14	15	17	18	19	20	21	22	23	24	25	26	28

Height in Feet and Inches

☐ Underweight ☐ Normal weight ☐ Overweight ☐ Obese ☐ Extreme obesity

FIG. 40.6 Body mass index (BMI) chart. Healthy weight: BMI 18 to 24.9 kg/m²; overweight: BMI 25 to 29.9 kg/m²; obesity: BMI 30 kg/m². BMI = weight (kg)/height (m²).

TABLE 40.5 Classification of Overweight and Obesity

| | BMI (kg/m^2) | Obesity Class | DISEASE RISK RELATIVE TO NORMAL WEIGHT AND WAIST CIRCUMFERENCE | |
			Men ≤40 in (102 cm) Women ≤35 in (89 cm)	Men >40 in (102 cm) Women >35 in (89 cm)
Underweight	<18.5	—	—	—
Normal	18.5–24.9	—	—	—
Overweight	25.0–29.9	—	Increased	High
Obesity	30.0–34.9	Class I	High	Very high
	35.0–39.9	Class II	Very high	Very high
Extreme obesity	≥40.0	Class III	Extremely high	Extremely high

Source: National Heart, Lung, and Blood Institute: Classification of overweight and obesity by BMI, waist circumference, and associated disease risks. Retrieved from *www.nhlbi.nih.gov/health/public/heart/obesity/lose_wt/bmi_dis.htm*.

Though BMI provides an overall assessment of fat mass, we must consider BMI in relation to the patient's age, gender, and body build. For example, a body builder may have a BMI associated with obesity, but because of a high muscle mass, the BMI would not be an accurate assessment. In contrast, in those who have lost body mass (e.g., older adults), the BMI would underestimate the degree of obesity. For this reason, other measures must be combined with the BMI for an accurate evaluation of a person's weight.

◆ **Waist Circumference.** *Waist circumference* is another way to assess and classify a person's weight. The average waist size has increased by more than 1 inch (from 37.6 inches to 38.8 inches) in the past decade. Health risks increase if the waist circumference is greater than 40 inches in men and greater than 35 inches in women.[9] People who have visceral fat with android obesity have an increased risk for CVD and metabolic syndrome (discussed later in this chapter).

◆ **Waist-to-Hip Ratio.** The **waist-to-hip ratio (WHR)** is another method used to assess obesity. This ratio describes the distribution of both subcutaneous and visceral adipose tissue. Calculate the WHR by dividing the waist measurement by the hip measurement. A WHR less than 0.8 is best. A WHR greater than 0.8 indicates more truncal fat, which puts a person at a greater risk for health complications.

◆ **Body Shape.** *Body shape* is another way of identifying those who are at a higher risk for health problems (Table 40.6). People with fat primarily in the abdominal area, an *apple-shaped body,* have *android obesity.* Those with fat distribution in the upper legs, a *pear-shaped body,* have *gynoid obesity.* Genetics has an important role in determining a person's body shape and weight.

◆ Nursing Diagnoses

Nursing diagnoses for the patient with obesity may include:
- Obesity
- Activity intolerance
- Impaired physical mobility
- Disturbed body image

◆ Planning

The overall goals are that the obese patient will (1) modify eating patterns, (2) take part in a regular physical activity program, (3) achieve and maintain weight loss to a specified level, and (4) minimize or prevent health problems related to obesity.

◆ Nursing Implementation

Obesity is one of the most challenging health problems. For most patients, successful weight management will be a hard,

TABLE 40.6 Relationship Between Body Shape and Health Risks

Body Shape	Characteristics	Health Risks
Android (apple)	• Fat primarily in abdominal area • Fat also distributed over upper body (neck, arms, shoulders) • Greater risk for obesity-related complications	• Heart disease • Diabetes • Breast cancer • Endometrial cancer • Visceral fat more active, causing ↓ insulin sensitivity • ↑ Triglycerides • ↓ HDL cholesterol • ↑ BP • ↑ Free fatty acid release into blood
Gynoid (pear)	• Fat mainly in the upper legs • Has a better prognosis but hard to treat	• Osteoporosis • Varicose veins • Cellulite • Subcutaneous fat traps and stores dietary fat • Trapped fatty acids stored as triglycerides

lifelong project. Obesity treatment begins with patients understanding their weight history and deciding on a plan that is best for them. It is rare to find an obese person who has not tried to lose weight. Some people have met with limited and temporary success, and others have met only with failure.

You are in a key position to help obese patients by (1) helping them explore and deal with their negative experiences and (2) teaching other health professionals about stigma and biases experienced by obese patients. Although health care for obese people has greater demands, HCPs often do not address these needs. HCPs are often reluctant to counsel patients about obesity for a variety of reasons, including (1) time constraints during appointments make it hard, (2) weight management may be viewed as professionally unrewarding, (3) reimbursement for weight management services is hard to obtain, and (4) many HCPs do not feel knowledgeable about giving weight loss advice.

Despite knowing benefits of weight loss, most people find the process tough. Achieving an "ideal" BMI is not necessary and may not be a realistic goal. Modest weight loss of even 3% to 5% of starting weight can have clinical benefits, and greater weight losses produce greater benefits.[10] In general, the average weight loss program (except for bariatric surgery) results in a 10% reduction of body weight. This average should not be considered a failure since it is associated with significant health benefits.[10]

Exploring a person's motivation for weight loss is essential for overall success. Using principles from motivational interviewing (see Chapter 4), you can help patients understand their desire to lose weight and gain confidence in achieving weight loss.

Focusing on the reasons for wanting to lose weight may help patients develop strategies for a weight loss program. Any supervised plan of care must be directed at 2 different processes: (1) successful weight loss, which requires a short-term energy deficit, and (2) successful weight control, which requires long-term behavior changes.

Together with other members of the interprofessional care team, you have a key role in planning for and managing the care of an obese patient. A holistic approach for weight loss must be used that includes nutritional therapy, exercise, behavior modification, and, for some, drugs or surgical intervention (Table 40.7). Combining more than one aspect supports more effective weight loss and weight control efforts. While teaching patients, stress healthy eating habits and adequate physical activity as lifestyle patterns to develop and maintain.

♥ PROMOTING POPULATION HEALTH

Maintaining a Healthy Weight

- Weigh yourself regularly.
- Consume 5 or more servings of fruits and vegetables daily.
- Choose whole grain foods, such as brown rice and whole wheat bread.
- Avoid highly processed foods made with refined white sugar, flour, and saturated fat.
- Avoid foods that are high in "energy density" or have a lot of calories in a small amount of food.
- Take part in physical activity:
  - 150 minutes of moderate-intensity aerobic activity (i.e., brisk walking) every week
  - Muscle-strengthening activities on 2 or more days a week

◆ **Nutritional Therapy.** There are no "magic" diets for weight loss. No one diet is superior for weight loss. All diets can work if they reduce caloric intake compared to expenditure and are one to which the patient will adhere.[11] The ability to adhere to a diet and degree of weight loss strongly depends on the patient's

TABLE 40.7 **Interprofessional Care**

Obesity

Diagnostic Assessment	Management
• History and physical examination	• Management of co-morbidities
• Family history	• Lifestyle interventions
• BMI, waist circumference, waist-to-hip ratio	• Taking part in weight loss program
• Assessment of health risks and co-morbidities	• Support groups
	• Behavior modification
	• Nutritional therapy
	• Exercise
	• Behavior modification
	• Support groups
	• Drug therapy (Table 40.9)
	• Surgical therapy (Table 40.10)

motivation. Restricting dietary intake so that it is below energy requirements is a cornerstone for any weight loss or maintenance program. Table 40.8 presents an example of a 1200-calorie diet. It is best to recommend a dietary approach in which calorie restriction includes all food groups. In general, recommend a diet that includes adequate amounts of fruits and vegetables, gives enough bulk to prevent constipation, and meets daily vitamin A and vitamin C requirements. Lean meat, fish, and eggs provide sufficient protein and the B-complex vitamins. Patients will find it easier to incorporate such a change into their lifestyle and not become as bored with their food options.

A very-low-calorie diet plan that limits calories to a total of 800 or less per day may be prescribed if rapid weight loss is needed.[11] These diets are not sustainable on a long-term basis. They should be provided only by trained professionals in a medical care setting. Persons on very-low-calorie diets need frequent professional monitoring because the severe energy restriction places them at risk for multiple health complications.

Many people try to lose weight by following one of the many fad diets that offer the enticement of quick weight loss with little effort. Often, these quick weight-reduction diets (found in the popular media) advocate eliminating one category of foods (e.g., carbohydrates). Therefore these should be discouraged. Low-carbohydrate diets do produce a rapid weight loss but reduce the ability to get adequate amounts of fiber, vitamins, and minerals. Restrictive diets are hard to maintain on a long-term basis. The more restrictive the diet, the greater the demand for intense discipline in the face of an intense desire to eat foods not allowed on the diet.

The degree of success of any diet depends in part on the amount of weight to be lost. A moderately obese person will

TABLE 40.8 **Nutritional Therapy**

1200-Calorie–Restricted Weight-Reduction Diet

General Principles
1. Eat regularly. Do not skip meals.
2. Measure foods to determine the correct portion size.
3. Avoid concentrated sweets, such as sugar, candy, honey, pies, cakes, cookies, and regular sodas.
4. Reduce fat intake by baking, broiling, or steaming foods.
5. Maintain a regular exercise program for successful weight loss.

Sample Meal Plan

Meal	Exchanges	Menu Plan
Breakfast	1 meat	1 hard-boiled egg
	2 breads	1 slice toast
		¾ cup dry cereal (unsweetened)
	1 fruit	½ small banana
	1 fat	1 tsp margarine
	1 dairy	1 cup low-fat milk
	Beverage	Coffee
Lunch	2 meats	Cheese enchiladas (made with 2 oz
	2 breads	cheese, 2 corn tortillas, lettuce, chili
	Vegetable	sauce)
	1 fruit	Fresh grapes (12)
	Beverage	Diet soda
Dinner	2 meats	2 oz baked chicken
	1 bread	Corn on the cob with 1 tsp margarine
	1 fat	
	Vegetable	Tossed salad and 1 Tbsp salad dressing
	1 fruit	¾ cup strawberries
	1 milk	1 cup low-fat milk

obviously reach a weight goal more easily than a person with extreme obesity. Because men have a higher percent of lean body mass, they are often able to lose weight more quickly than women. Women have a higher percent of body fat, which is metabolically less active than muscle tissue. Postmenopausal women are particularly prone to weight gain, especially increased abdominal fat.

Setting a realistic and healthy goal, such as losing 1 to 2 lb per week, should be mutually agreed on at the beginning of a weight loss program. Trying to lose too much too fast usually results in a sense of frustration and failure for the patient. You can help patients understand that losing large amounts of weight in a short period causes skin and underlying tissue to lose elasticity and tone. Slower weight loss offers better cosmetic results.

Inevitably, the patient reaches plateau periods during which no weight is lost. These plateaus may last from several days to several weeks. Remind the patient that plateaus are normal occurrences during weight reduction. A weekly check of body weight is a good method of monitoring progress. Daily weighing is not recommended because of fluctuations that result from retained water (including urine) and feces. Teach the patient to record the weight at the same time of the day, wearing the same type of clothing.

EVIDENCE-BASED PRACTICE

Obesity Interventions and Faith-Based Organizations

J.W. is a 39-yr-old black woman who is 5 ft, 6 in tall and weighs 196 lb. You work in the clinic that she visits for health care. Your clinic is referring patients who would benefit from losing weight to community and hospital-based weight loss programs. She tells you she has been trying to lose weight by "watching what she eats" and that she is "not sure what else she can do." In further talks with her, you learn she is an active member of her neighborhood church.

Making Clinical Decisions

Best Available Evidence. Obesity is highest among racial and ethnic minority groups in the United States. Many faith-based organizations (FBOs) provide programs that have helped obese persons improve weight-related behaviors (e.g., increase in physical activity and fruit and vegetable intake) and lose weight. Successes in these programs have been more notable for females. Overall, programs that offer comprehensive and intensive behavioral interventions for weight loss are an option for weight management.

Clinician Expertise. You know it is important for J.W. to engage in a weight loss program that will help her to adopt and maintain healthy behaviors. You also know that FBOs can play a major role in providing health promotion programs in the black community.

Patient Preferences and Values. J.W. says she is interested in learning about a weight loss program at her church.

Implications for Nursing Practice

1. Why is it important to discuss with J.W. her motivation for starting a weight loss program at her church?
2. How will you help J.W. to set realistic short- and long-term goals related to weight loss? How may these goals differ?
3. At each clinic visit, how will you support J.W.'s efforts to lose weight?

References for Evidence

Lv N, Azar KM, Rosas LG, et al.: Behavioral lifestyle interventions for moderate and severe obesity: a systematic review, *Prev Med* 100:180, 2017.

Tucker CM, Wippold GM, Williams JL, et al.: A CBPR study to test the impact of a church-based health empowerment program on health behaviors and health outcomes of black adult churchgoers, *J Racial Ethn Health Disparities* 4:70, 2017.

There is no clear consensus on the number of meals a person on a diet should eat. Some advocate several small meals per day because the body's metabolic rate is temporarily increased right after eating. However, patients eating several small meals a day might consume more calories unless they carefully adhere to portion sizes and total daily calorie allotment.

When a person first starts a weight loss program, food portion sizes must be carefully determined to stay within the dietary guidelines. Portion sizes over the past 40 years have increased considerably (Table 40.2). Food portions can be weighed using a scale, or everyday objects can be used as a visual cue to determine portion sizes. The size of a woman's fist or a baseball is equivalent to a serving of vegetables or fruit. The recommended portion size of meat is 3 oz. This is about the size of a person's palm or a deck of cards. A serving of cheese is about the size of a thumb or 6 dice. The standard size for chopped vegetables is ½ cup, according to MyPlate guidelines (see Table 39.9). A portion size quiz is available at *www.nhlbi.nih.gov/health/educational/wecan/eat-right/portion-distortion.htm*.

Another aspect of the American diet to consider is which foods contribute the most calories—animal sources, fruits, grains, or vegetables. Two thirds or more of a person's diet should be plant-source foods, and the other one third or less should be from animal protein. Being aware of personal consumption habits and striving for the two-thirds to one-third ratio is a simple goal that one can achieve without weighing and measuring foods at every meal. Once this ratio is part of meal planning, the patient can gradually reduce portions as they gradually increase activity levels to achieve healthy weight loss. A list of healthy or low-calorie foods serves as a good reference and allows the patient to dine out on occasion. Furthermore, the patient who carefully follows the prescribed diet may not need to take vitamin supplements.

Encourage the appropriate fluid intake in the form of water. Alcoholic and sugary beverages should be limited or avoided, since they increase caloric intake and are low in nutritional value.

◆ **Exercise.** Exercise is an essential part of a weight loss program. Patients should exercise daily, preferably 30 minutes to an hour, with a goal of more than 10,000 steps per day.[11] There is no evidence that increased activity promotes an increase in appetite or leads to dietary excess. In fact, exercise has the opposite effect. The addition of exercise results in more weight loss than dieting alone and has a favorable effect on body fat distribution.

The type of exercise (e.g., high intensity versus low intensity) does not seem to affect overall weight loss. More intensive activity may result in weight loss with a reduced time commitment, making it preferable to some people. Exercise is especially important in supporting weight loss. Higher levels of physical activity, 200 to 300 minutes per week, are recommended to maintain weight loss or minimize weight regain in the long term.[11]

Explore ways to incorporate exercise in daily routines. It may be as simple as parking farther from their place of employment or taking the stairs versus an elevator. Encourage a person to use a pedometer to track progress toward meeting the 10,000 steps a day goal. However, success may be walking one third of the recommended steps with incremental increases over time. Patients can swim and cycle, which both have long-term benefits. Joining a health club can be another way of getting exercise. Stress to patients that engaging in weekend exercise only or in spurts of strenuous activity is not helpful and can be dangerous.

◆ **Behavior Modification.** The assumptions behind behavior modification are: (1) obesity is a learned disorder caused by overeating and (2) often the critical difference between an obese person and a person of normal weight is the cues that regulate eating behavior. Therefore most behavior-modification programs deemphasize the diet and focus on how and when to eat. Ideally, behavior intervention should begin with counseling sessions with a trained interventionist. Persons who are in a behavioral therapy program are more successful in maintaining their losses over an extended time than those who do not take part in such training.[12]

Various behavioral techniques for patients engaged in a weight loss program include (1) self-monitoring, (2) stimulus control, and (3) rewards. *Self-monitoring* may involve keeping a record of the type and time food was consumed, what the person was doing, and how the person was feeling when eating. By looking at the cues and events before eating, the person can identify areas in which to make behavior changes to break the chain of events and prevent overeating. These eating behaviors must be changed, or any weight loss will only be temporary.

Stimulus control is aimed at eliminating cues in the environment that trigger eating. For example, if the patient overeats while watching television, limiting eating to a certain area (e.g., kitchen table) can be an effective way to weaken the link between eating and television watching. The more often the person does not eat in front of the television, the less likely television watching will trigger overeating.

Rewards may be incentives for weight loss. Short- and long-term goals are useful benchmarks for earning rewards. It is important that the reward for a specified weight loss not be associated with food, such as dinner out or a favorite treat. Reward items do not need to have a monetary component. For example, time for a hot bath or an hour of pleasure reading would be an enjoyable reward for many people. Praise your patient's successes, even small ones, at every opportunity. Changing existing behaviors is hard.

◆ **Support Groups.** People who are on a weight management plan are often encouraged to join a group in which others are also trying to change their eating habits. Many self-help groups offer support and information on dieting tips. For example, Take Off Pounds Sensibly (TOPS) (*www.tops.org*) is the oldest nonprofit organization of this type. Behavior modification is an integral part of the program, along with nutrition education. Weight Watchers International (*www.weightwatchers.com*), Jenny Craig (*www.jennycraig.com*), and Nutrisystem (*www.nutrisystem.com*) are probably the most successful commercial weight-loss programs.[13] Weight Watchers offers a food plan that is nutritionally balanced and practical to follow. Group leaders, all of whom have successfully lost weight with Weight Watchers, teach members various behavior-modification techniques.

There are many commercial weight-reduction centers. Most programs are staffed by nurses and dietitians. These weight-reduction centers are cost prohibitive for those with limited financial resources. Most programs offer special prepackaged foods and supplements that a person must buy as part of the weight-reduction plan. The person only consumes these prescribed foods and drinks until an agreed-on amount of weight is lost. The person is encouraged to buy the same type of foods for the maintenance phase of the program, lasting from 6 months to 1 year. Behavior-modification training is part of these programs. People must learn how to adjust their diet once they are no longer using the commercial products. This can be challenging for many. The person may regain weight lost once the restricted food program is completed.[13]

In recent years, many employers have begun weight loss programs at the workplace. The reason for such programs is that better health repays the cost of the programs through improved work performance, decreased absenteeism, less hospitalization, and lower insurance costs. Both employees and employers report benefiting from such programs.

◆ **Drug Therapy**

Drugs should never be used alone. Rather, drugs should be part of a comprehensive weight loss program that includes reduced-calorie diet, exercise, and behavior modification. They should be reserved for adults with a BMI of 30 kg/m^2 or greater (obese) or adults with a BMI of 27 kg/m^2 or greater (overweight) who have at least 1 weight-related condition, such as hypertension, type 2 diabetes, or dyslipidemia.[10,14] There are currently 5 obesity drugs for long-term management approved by the FDA (Table 40.9).

◆ **Appetite-Suppressing Drugs.** Sympathomimetic amines suppress appetite by increasing the availability of norepinephrine in the brain, thus stimulating the CNS. Sympathomimetics fall into 2 groups: amphetamines and nonamphetamines. Amphetamines have a much higher abuse potential than nonamphetamines. The FDA does not recommend or approve amphetamines for either short- or long-term weight loss.

We usually do not use nonamphetamines for weight loss because of the potential for abuse. If used, they should be used only short term (for 3 months or less). These drugs include phentermine (Adipex, Lomaira, Suprenza), diethylpropion (Tenuate), and phendimetrazine (Bontril). Adverse effects include palpitations, tachycardia, overstimulation, restlessness, dizziness, insomnia, weakness, and fatigue.

◆ **Nursing Interventions Related to Drug Therapy.** Drugs will not cure obesity. People must understand that without substantial changes in food intake and increased physical activity, they will gain weight when drug therapy is stopped.

As with any drug treatment, there are side effects (Table 40.9). Careful evaluation for other medical conditions can help determine which drugs, if any, would be advisable for a given patient. Many insurance companies do not cover the cost of weight loss drugs.

Your role related to drug therapy is to teach the patient about proper administration, side effects, and how the drugs fit into the overall weight loss plan. Changing drug dosages without consultation with the HCP can have detrimental effects. Stress that diet and exercise plans are the cornerstones of permanent weight loss. Finally, discourage patients from buying over-the-counter diet aids unless recommended by an HCP.

BARIATRIC SURGICAL THERAPY

Bariatric surgery, surgery on the stomach and/or intestines to help a person with extreme obesity lose weight, has become a viable option for treating obesity. Surgery is currently the only treatment that has a successful and lasting impact for sustained weight loss for those with extreme obesity.[15]

Criteria guidelines for bariatric surgery include having a BMI of 40 kg/m^2 or more or a BMI of 35 kg/m^2 or more with other significant co-morbidities (e.g., hypertension, type 2 diabetes, heart failure, sleep apnea).

TABLE 40.9 Drug Therapy

Obesity

Drug	Mechanism of Action	Nursing Considerations
bupropion/naltrexone (Contrave)	• *bupropion:* antidepressant • *naltrexone:* opioid antagonist	• Common side effects: nausea, constipation, headache, dizziness, insomnia, dry mouth • Suicidal thoughts and behaviors and neuropsychiatric reactions can occur • Can increase BP and heart rate. Should not be used in patients with uncontrolled hypertension • Can cause seizures. Must not be used in patients who have seizure disorder
liraglutide (Saxenda)	• Glucagon-like peptide 1 (GLP-1) agonist • Induces satiety	• Used to treat type 2 diabetes • Injected • Side effects: thyroid tumors, pancreatitis
lorcaserin (Belviq)	• Selective serotonin (5-HT) agonist • Suppresses appetite and creates a sense of satiety	• Side effects: headache, dizziness, fatigue, nausea, dry mouth, constipation
orlistat (Xenical, Allī [low-dose form available over the counter])	• Blocks fat breakdown and absorption in intestine • Inhibits the action of intestinal lipases, resulting in undigested fat excreted in feces	• Associated with stool leakage, flatulence, diarrhea, abdominal bloating, especially if a high-fat diet is consumed • Severe liver injury may occur • May need fat-soluble vitamin supplements
phentermine/topiramate ER (Qsmyia)	• *phentermine:* Sympathomimetic • *topiramate:* Decreases appetite	• Common side effects: dizziness, insomnia, dry mouth • Do not use in patients with glaucoma or hyperthyroidism • Must avoid pregnancy • Can increase heart rate. Should not be used in patients with uncontrolled hypertension or heart disease

Most people who undergo bariatric surgery successfully improve their overall quality of life. In addition to losing weight, outcomes include improved glucose control with improvement or reversal of diabetes, normalization of BP, decreased total cholesterol and triglycerides, decreased GERD, and decreased sleep apnea.[16]

Insurance coverage for bariatric surgery varies. Those who cover surgery often require extensive documentation. This often includes taking part in a supervised weight loss program for around 6 months and a psychologic evaluation.

Although overall mortality is very low, several complications can arise from surgery. Therefore, having surgery is carefully considered. Candidates for surgery must be screened for psychologic, physical, and behavioral conditions that have been associated with poor surgical outcomes. These include untreated depression, binge eating disorders, and drug and alcohol abuse that may interfere with a commitment to lifelong behavioral changes. Other contraindications to surgery include illnesses that are known to reduce life expectancy and are not likely to improve with weight reduction. These include advanced cancer; end-stage kidney, liver, and cardiopulmonary disease; severe coagulopathy; or inability to follow nutritional recommendations.

Bariatric surgeries fall into 1 of 3 broad categories: restrictive, malabsorptive, or a combination of malabsorptive and restrictive (Table 40.10 and Fig. 40.7). In *restrictive procedures,* the stomach is reduced in size (less food eaten). In *malabsorptive procedures,* the small intestine is shortened or bypassed (less food absorbed). Most procedures are done laparoscopically. These patients have fewer wound infections, shorter hospital stays, and a faster recovery period.

Restrictive Surgeries

Restrictive bariatric surgery reduces either the size of the stomach, which causes the patient to feel full more quickly, or the amount allowed to enter the stomach. In these surgeries,

digestion is not altered, so the risk for anemia or cobalamin deficiency is low. The most common restrictive surgeries include adjustable gastric banding and sleeve gastrectomy.

Adjustable Gastric Banding. Laparoscopic *adjustable gastric banding* (AGB) involves limiting the stomach size with an inflatable band placed around the fundus of the stomach (Fig. 40.7, *A*). This restrictive procedure can be done using a Lap-Band or Realize Band system. The band is connected to a subcutaneous port that can be inflated or deflated (by fluid injection in the HCP's office) to change the stoma size to meet the patient's needs as weight is lost. The restrictive effect of the band creates a sense of fullness as the upper part of the stomach now accommodates less than the average stomach. The band then causes a delay in stomach emptying, providing patients with further satiety.

The procedure can be either modified or reversed at a later date, if needed. AGB is the preferred option for patients who are surgical risks because it is a less invasive approach. Because it is restrictive only, patients must follow a strict diet to lose weight and not regain weight.

Sleeve Gastrectomy (Gastric Sleeve). In the sleeve gastrectomy (gastric sleeve), about 75% of the stomach is removed, leaving a sleeve-shaped stomach (Fig. 40.7, *B*). Although the stomach is drastically reduced in size, its function is preserved. Removing most of the stomach results in the elimination of hormones made in the stomach that stimulate hunger, such as ghrelin.

Research is ongoing on a new procedure called *endoscopic sleeve gastroplasty.* It involves using an endoscope rather than making a surgical incision. When the endoscope reaches the stomach, the surgeon places sutures in the stomach, making it smaller and changing its shape.

Gastric Plication. Gastric plication is a minimally invasive weight-loss surgery that reduces the size of the stomach. It is done by folding the stomach wall inward, and then sutures are placed to secure the folded stomach wall. This reduces the stomach volume by as much as 70%. An advantage is reversibility, since there is no gastric resection.

TABLE 40.10 Surgical Therapy for Obesity

Description	Advantages	Disadvantages
Restrictive Surgery		
Adjustable Gastric Banding (AGB) (Lap-Band, Realize Band) (Fig. 40.7, A)		
• Inflatable band encircles stomach • Creation of gastric pouch with about 30 mL (1 oz) capacity • Later stretches to 60–90 mL (2–3 oz) • Upper gastric pouch connected by very narrow channel to lower section of stomach	• Food digestion occurs through normal process • Band can be adjusted to ↑ or ↓ restriction • Can be reversed • Absence of dumping syndrome • Lack of malabsorption • Low complication rate	• Some nausea and vomiting initially (eating too much too quickly) • Food intolerance, gastric dysmotility, regurgitation • Problems with adjustment device • Band may slip or erode into stomach wall • Gastric perforation or obstruction may occur, requiring surgery • Weight loss may be more limited than with other types of surgery
Sleeve Gastrectomy (Gastric Sleeve) (Fig. 40.7, B)		
• About 75% of stomach removed • Creation of sleeve-shaped stomach with 60–150 mL (2–5 oz) capacity	• Function of stomach preserved • No bypass of intestine • Avoids complications of obstruction, anemia, vitamin deficiencies	• Weight loss may be more limited than with other types of surgery • Leakage related to stapling • Irreversible
Gastric Plication		
• Adapted version of sleeve gastrectomy (gastric sleeve) • Sleeve created by suturing rather than removing stomach	• Minimal surgery compared to sleeve gastrectomy • No rerouting of intestines • Maintains natural nutrient absorption capabilities	• Requires hospital stay of 24–48 hr • Nausea common after procedure • Risks include stomach leakage from sutured areas, blockage of stomach from swelling or fold too tight
Intragastric Balloon		
• Involves placing a deflated balloon into stomach • Balloon then filled with saline and occupies space in stomach	• Most are placed endoscopically as an outpatient procedure • Does not require invasive surgery	• Can only be left in place for 6 mos • Once device is in stomach, patients may have nausea, vomiting, abdominal pain, indigestion, gastric ulcers
Malabsorptive Surgery		
Biliopancreatic Diversion (BPD) With or Without Duodenal Switch (Fig. 40.7, C)		
• 70% of the stomach removed horizontally • Anastomosis between stomach and intestine • Decreases the amount of small intestine available for nutrient absorption • Duodenal switch cuts the stomach vertically and is shaped like a tube	• Able to eat larger meals than with gastric bypass or banding procedures • Less food intolerance • Rapid weight loss • Greater long-term weight loss	• Abdominal bloating, diarrhea, foul-smelling gas (steatorrhea) • 3 or 4 loose bowel movements a day • Malabsorption of fat-soluble vitamins • Iron deficiency • Protein-calorie malnutrition • Dumping syndrome • Most complicated of weight loss surgeries
Combination of Restrictive and Malabsorptive Surgery		
Roux-en-Y Gastric Bypass (RYGB) (Fig. 40.7, D)		
• Surgery on stomach to create a pouch (restrictive) • Small gastric pouch connected to jejunum • Remaining stomach and first segment of small intestine are bypassed (malabsorptive)	• Better weight loss results than with restrictive procedures • Lower incidence of malnutrition and diarrhea • Rapid improvement of weight-related co-morbidities • Good long-term results	• Leak at site of anastomosis • Anemia: iron deficiency, cobalamin deficiency, folic acid deficiency • Calcium deficiency • Dumping syndrome • Irreversible
Implanted Gastric Stimulation Device		
Maestro Rechargeable System (Fig. 40.8)		
• Device implanted into abdomen • Works like a pacemaker to deliver electrical impulses to vagus nerve, which tells brain when stomach is full	• Least invasive of weight loss surgeries • Procedure done on outpatient basis	• Device must be charged 1–2 times/wk • If battery completely drained, device needs to be reprogrammed • Side effects include nausea, vomiting, heartburn, belching, swallowing problems

Intragastric Balloons. Intragastric balloon weight-loss systems use a gastric balloon to occupy space in the stomach. The balloon does not change or alter the stomach's natural anatomy. It is designed to help patients feel more full, curb the appetite, and reduce food intake. Patients should follow a diet and exercise plan to help with weight loss efforts.

The balloons are less invasive than having gastric bypass surgery. Most are placed endoscopically, while the patient is under mild sedation. The HCP places the balloon into the stomach through the mouth. Once in place, the balloon is filled with saline so that it expands. The balloon can be filled with different amounts of saline (from 400 to 700 mL).

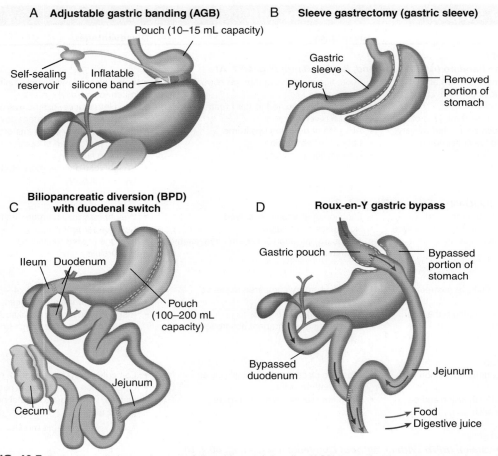

FIG. 40.7 Bariatric surgical procedures. **A,** Adjustable gastric banding (AGB) uses a band to create a gastric pouch. **B,** Sleeve gastrectomy involves creating a sleeve-shaped stomach by removing about 75% of the stomach. **C,** Biliopancreatic diversion (BPD) with duodenal switch procedure creates an anastomosis between the stomach and intestine. **D,** Roux-en-Y gastric bypass procedure involves constructing a gastric pouch whose outlet is a Y-shaped limb of small intestine.

With newer balloons, the patient swallows the balloon in a capsule that is attached to a microcatheter. The balloon is inflated with nitrogen gas through the microcatheter. After inflation, the catheter is detached and removed, leaving the balloon in the stomach.[17] When it is time to remove a balloon, it is first deflated and then removed using another endoscopic procedure.

Balloons should not be used in patients who have had gastrointestinal or bariatric surgery or who have inflammatory bowel disease, large hiatal hernia, delayed gastric emptying, or active *Helicobacter pylori* infection. Patients may have vomiting, nausea, abdominal pain, and feelings of indigestion. Other potential risks are gastric ulcers and balloon deflation.

Combination of Restrictive and Malabsorptive Surgery
Roux-en-Y Gastric Bypass. The Roux-en-Y gastric bypass (RYGB) procedure is a combination of restrictive and malabsorptive surgery. This surgical procedure is the most common bariatric procedure done in the United States. It is considered the gold standard among bariatric procedures. Overall, it has low complication rates, has excellent patient tolerance, and sustains long-term weight loss.

The RYGB involves creating a small gastric pouch and attaching it directly to the small intestine using a Y-shaped limb of the small bowel (Fig. 40.7, *D*). After the procedure, food bypasses 90% of the stomach, the duodenum, and a small segment of jejunum.

A complication of the RYGB is *dumping syndrome,* in which gastric contents empty too rapidly into the small intestine, overwhelming its ability to digest nutrients. Symptoms can include vomiting, nausea, weakness, sweating, faintness, and, on occasion, diarrhea. Patients are discouraged from eating sugary foods after surgery to avoid dumping syndrome. Because sections of the small intestine are bypassed, poor absorption of iron can cause iron-deficiency anemia. Patients need to take a multivitamin with iron and calcium supplements. Chronic anemia caused by cobalamin deficiency may occur. This problem can usually be managed with parenteral or intranasal cobalamin.

Implantable Gastric Stimulation
An implantable gastric stimulation device (e.g., Maestro Rechargeable System) consists of a pacemaker-like electrical pulse generator, wire leads, and electrodes that are implanted in the abdomen (Fig. 40.8). The Maestro System works by sending intermittent electrical pulses to the vagus nerve, which is involved in regulating stomach emptying and signaling to the brain that the stomach feels empty or full. External controllers allow the patient to charge the device and allow HCPs to adjust

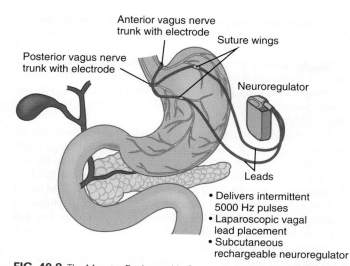

• Delivers intermittent 5000 Hz pulses
• Laparoscopic vagal lead placement
• Subcutaneous rechargeable neuroregulator

FIG. 40.8 The Maestro Rechargeable System is an electrical stimulator that is surgically implanted into the abdomen. It works by sending intermittent electrical pulses to the vagus nerve, which is involved in regulating stomach emptying and signaling to the brain that the stomach feels empty or full.

the device's settings to provide optimal therapy. Adverse events include nausea, heartburn, problems swallowing, belching, and chest pain.

❖ NURSING MANAGEMENT: PERIOPERATIVE CARE OF THE OBESE PATIENT

◆ Nursing Implementation

This section discusses general nursing considerations for the care of the obese patient who is having surgery. Special nursing considerations are described for the patient who is having bariatric surgery (Table 40.11). See Chapters 17 through 19 for more on care of the surgical patient.

◆ Preoperative Care.
Special considerations are needed for the obese patient, especially the patient with extreme obesity, who is having surgery. Before surgery, interview the patient to identify past and current health information and any assistive devices currently in use (e.g., continuous positive airway pressure [CPAP] for sleep apnea). Co-morbidities related to obesity increase the risk for complications in the perioperative period. You may need to coordinate care with the patient's specialists.

Have a plan in place before the patients arrive so that they receive optimal care and do not feel like they are a burden to the nursing staff. You must have available appropriate-size hospital gowns, beds that accommodate an increased body size, and necessary patient transfer equipment. A larger BP cuff size is needed to avoid measurement errors. Ensure that an oversized BP cuff is available and placed in the patient's room.

Consider how the patient will be weighed and transported throughout the hospital. A wheelchair with removable arms that is large enough to safely accommodate the patient and pass easily through doorways should be available.

You may need to use alternative assessment techniques to perform assessment of heart, lung, and bowel sounds. For example, because of the large chest wall, breath and heart sounds are often distant. You can use an electronic stethoscope to amplify lung, heart, and bowel sounds.

Teach the patient proper coughing and deep breathing techniques and methods of turning and positioning to prevent

TABLE 40.11 Nursing Management
Care of the Patient Undergoing Bariatric Surgery

Preoperative
- Assess for use of assistive devices. Note any physical limitations or mobility issues.
- Perform baseline assessment, including vital signs, pulse oximetry, height, weight, BMI, skin condition, nutrition status, and heart, lung, and bowel sounds.
- Assess baseline laboratory values and diagnostic test results (e.g., pulmonary function tests).
- Teach patient and caregiver about procedure and postoperative care. Review proper coughing and deep breathing techniques, incentive spirometer use, and methods of turning and positioning to prevent pulmonary complications.
- Explain the need for frequent assessment and interventions to prevent VTE.
- Have available proper-sized hospital gowns, beds, BP cuffs, and transfer equipment.

Immediate Postoperative
- Perform assessment and compare to baseline: vital signs, pulse oximetry, and heart and lung sounds.
- Assess abdominal wound for the amount and type of drainage, condition of the incision, and signs of infection.
- Observe for anastomosis leak (tachycardia, fever, tachypnea, chest and abdominal pain).
- Help patient turn, cough and deep breath, and use incentive spirometer at least every 2 hrs.
- Protect the incision against any straining that accompanies turning and coughing.
- Give pain medications as needed.
- Position the patient upright at a minimum of a 45-degree angle.
- Maintain IV and/or oral fluid intake and monitor urine output.
- Institute measures to prevent VTE.
- Nutrition
  - Start with room temperature water and low-sugar clear liquids.
  - Teach the patient to avoid drinking with a straw.
  - Begin with 15 mL every 10–15 minutes, gradually increase to 90 mL every 30 min.
  - Move to a low-fat, full-liquid diet after 48 hrs if tolerating clear liquids.
  - Observe for dehydration (thirst, decreased urine output, headache, dizziness).

pulmonary complications after surgery. If possible, show how to use a spirometer before surgery. Spirometer use helps prevent and treat postoperative lung congestion. Practicing these strategies preoperatively can help the patient perform them correctly postoperatively. If the patient uses CPAP at home for sleep apnea, make arrangements for the use of a machine while the patient is hospitalized.

Excess adipose tissue may make obtaining venous access difficult. A longer IV catheter is helpful (longer than 1 in) to go through the overlying tissue to the vein. It is important that the cannula is far enough into the vein so it is not dislodged or infiltrated.

Special Considerations for Bariatric Surgery.
Ensure that the patient scheduled for bariatric surgery understands the surgical procedure. Your teaching depends on the type of procedure and surgical approach (Table 40.10). Stress that we will frequently assess vital signs and general assessment to monitor for complications. Tell the patient that they will be assisted with ambulation soon after surgery and encouraged to cough and deep breathe to prevent pulmonary complications.

◆ **Postoperative Care.** The initial postoperative care focuses on careful assessment and immediate intervention for cardiopulmonary complications, thrombus formation, anastomosis leaks, and electrolyte imbalances. The transfer from surgery may require many staff members. During the transfer, keep the patient's airway stabilized and give attention to managing the patient' pain. Maintain the patient's head at a 45-degree angle to reduce abdominal pressure and increase lung expansion.[18]

The body stores anesthetics in adipose tissue, thus placing patients with excess adipose tissue at risk for resedation. As adipose cells release anesthetics back into the bloodstream, the patient may become sedated after surgery. If this happens, be prepared to perform a head-tilt or jaw-thrust maneuver and keep the patient's oral and nasal airways open.

Diligence in turning and ambulation postoperatively will prevent complications from surgery. The patient will typically begin walking the evening after surgery and then at least 3 or 4 times each day. Assist the patient as needed. The patient may be reluctant to move or may not have the stamina to walk even a short distance. In either situation, you will need help moving an obese patient.

Obesity can cause a patient's breathing to become shallow and rapid. The extra adipose tissue in the chest and abdomen compresses the diaphragmatic, thoracic, and abdominal structures. This compression restricts the chest's ability to expand, preventing the lungs from working as efficiently as they would otherwise. The patient retains more CO_2 with less O_2 delivered to the lungs. This results in hypoxemia, pulmonary hypertension, and polycythemia.

After surgery, the risk for venous thromboembolism (VTE) is increased. Intermittent pneumatic compression devices or compression stockings with low-dose heparin decrease the risk for VTE. Active and passive range-of-motion exercises are a frequent part of daily care.[18]

Wound infection, dehiscence, and delayed healing are potential problems for all obese patients. Assess the patient's skin for any complications related to wound healing. Keep skinfolds clean and dry to prevent dermatitis and bacterial or fungal infections.

Special Considerations for Bariatric Surgery. Patients have considerable abdominal pain after bariatric surgery (Table 40.11). Give pain medications as needed during the immediate postoperative period (first 24 hours). Be aware that pain could be from an anastomosis leak rather than typical surgical pain. Abdominal wounds require frequent observation for the amount and type of drainage, condition of the incision, and signs of infection. Monitor vital signs to help identify problems, such as infection or anastomosis leak.

Give room temperature water and low-sugar clear liquids as soon as the patient is fully awake and there is no evidence of any anastomosis leaks. Begin with 15-mL increments every 10 to 15 minutes. Gradually increase intake to a goal of 90 mL every 30 minutes by postoperative day 1. Teach the patient to avoid gulping fluids or drinking with a straw to reduce the incidence of air swallowing. The patient who tolerates clear liquids may begin a low-fat, full-liquid diet on postoperative day 3.

◆ **Ambulatory and Home Care**

Special Considerations for Bariatric Surgery. The patient who has undergone major surgical treatment for obesity has not been successful in the past in following or maintaining a prescribed diet. Now the patient must reduce oral intake because of the anatomic changes from the surgical procedure. The patient must

clearly understand the proper diet. A dietitian is usually part of the bariatric team and helps the patient with the transition to the new diet.

Patients usually are discharged on a full-liquid diet. Within 10 to 14 days after surgery, depending on tolerance, the patient may begin a pureed or soft foods diet with vitamin supplementation. Most patients transition to the usual diet 4 to 6 weeks after surgery.[19]

The usual diet is high in protein and low in carbohydrates, fat, and roughage. It should consist of 6 small feedings daily. Many need a protein supplement once or twice a day for the first few months after surgery to meet their protein needs.[19] Patient should not consume fluids with meals. Fluids and foods high in carbohydrate tend to promote diarrhea and symptoms of dumping syndrome. Calorie-dense foods should be avoided to permit more nutritionally sound food to be consumed. Teach the patient to eat slowly and stop eating when feeling full.

Weight loss is considerable during the first 6 to 12 months. Although behavior modification is not necessarily an intended outcome with these surgical procedures, it becomes an unexpected secondary gain. For example, a person who has had bariatric surgery cannot overeat or binge eat without consequences (e.g., vomiting, abdominal pain). The patient may fail to lose weight if the stomach pouch is too large. An outlet that is much too small may result in the patient losing too much weight. Some patients have been known to overeat when they return home and gain rather than lose weight.

Stress the importance of long-term follow-up care, in part because of potential complications. Teach patients to inform the HCP of any changes in their physical or emotional condition. Nutritional deficiencies are expected after malabsorptive bariatric surgery, including anemia, vitamin deficiencies, and diarrhea. Patients should take multivitamins with folate, calcium, vitamin D, iron, and vitamin B_{12} for life.[20] Peptic ulcer formation, dumping syndrome, and small bowel obstruction may be seen late in the recovery and rehabilitation stage.

INFORMATICS IN PRACTICE

Use of Smart Phone for Weight Loss

- Phone apps (e.g., My Fitness Pal) are available to help track calories, weight, exercise, and eating patterns.
- Tracking systems give immediate access to nutritional information for better dietary decision making.
- Some apps can scan the barcode of foods in the grocery store and give nutritional information.
- Calorie tracker apps can be used to monitor daily calorie intake and keep a record of weight loss progress.
- With text messaging, a phone "buddy" can provide support when a person's will power is lacking.
- Share progress with friends and family. Some weight loss apps sync with social media accounts so that a person can share milestones on Twitter and Facebook.

Several potential psychologic problems may arise after surgery. Assess social functioning, self-esteem, sexual life, and activities of daily living in follow-up care. Some patients feel guilty that they had to achieve weight loss by surgical intervention rather than by the "sheer willpower" of reduced dietary intake and exercise. Be ready to provide support and assist the patient in moving away from such negative feelings.

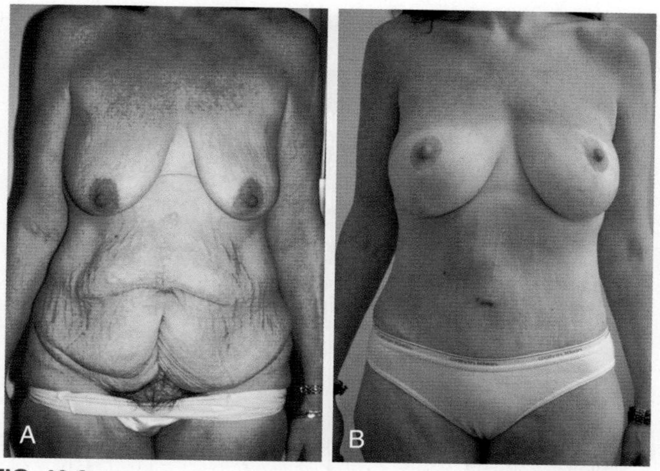

FIG. 40.9 A, Preoperative view of a 37-yr-old woman with massive weight loss who had gastric bypass surgery. B, Postoperative view 2½ years after abdominoplasty. She underwent breast surgery, thigh lift, back lift with excision of excess skin of the lower back and upper buttocks, and upper arm surgery. (From Shermak MA: Contouring the epigastrium, *Aesthet Surg J* 25:506, 2005.)

By 6 to 8 months after surgery, most patients have lost considerable weight and are able to see how much their appearance has changed. Help the patient adjust to a new body image. Massive weight loss may leave the patient with large quantities of flabby skin that can result in problems related to altered body image (Fig. 40.9). Discuss this possible outcome with the patient before surgery and again during the rehabilitation phase. Cosmetic surgery may alleviate this situation. Do not hesitate to encourage counseling for unresolved psychologic issues.

Often one result of bariatric surgery is the return of fertility in women. Pregnancy complications can result from anemia and nutritional deficiencies. Furthermore, depending on the type of surgery, intestinal obstructions and hernias may occur with pregnancy. Women must carefully consider the risk for pregnancy after bariatric surgery. In general, encourage women to postpone pregnancy for 12 to 18 months after bariatric surgery.

❓ CHECK YOUR PRACTICE

You are working in the bariatric surgery outpatient clinic. When you walk into the clinic room where a 36-yr-old woman is waiting for her follow-up visit, you find her distraught and crying. You ask her what is wrong. She responds, "I am a total failure. I have been fat all my life, and I had to have this horrible surgery to help me. Why couldn't I do it on my own?"
• What is an effective way for you to handle this situation?

◆ **Evaluation**

The expected outcomes are that the obese patient will
• Have long-term weight loss
• Have improvement in obesity-related co-morbidities
• Integrate healthy practices into daily routines
• Monitor for adverse side effects of surgical therapy
• Have an improved self-image

Gerontologic Considerations: Obesity in Older Adults

The prevalence of obesity is increasing in older people. The number of obese older persons has markedly risen because of increases in both the total number of older persons and the

percent of the older adults who are obese. Obesity is more common in older women than in older men. A decrease in energy expenditure is an important contributor to a gradual increase in body fat with age.

Obesity in older adults can worsen age-related declines in physical function and lead to frailty and disability. Obesity is associated with decreased survival. Those who are obese live 6 to 7 years less than people of normal weight.

Obesity worsens many changes associated with aging. Excess body weight places more demands on arthritic joints. The mechanical strain on weight-bearing joints can lead to premature immobility. Excess intraabdominal weight can cause problems with urinary incontinence. Excess weight may contribute to hypoventilation and sleep apnea.

Obesity affects the quality of life for older adults. Weight loss can improve physical functioning and obesity-related health complications. The same therapeutic approaches for obesity discussed earlier also apply to the older adult.

COSMETIC SURGICAL THERAPY

Lipectomy

Lipectomy (adipectomy) is done to remove unsightly flabby folds of adipose tissue (Fig. 40.9). There is no evidence that regeneration of adipose tissue occurs at the surgical sites. However, Stress to the patient that surgical removal does not prevent obesity from recurring, especially if lifetime eating habits stay the same. Although body image and self-esteem may improve with such procedures, these operations are not without complications. Do not underestimate the dangerous effects of anesthesia and the potential for poor wound healing in the obese patient.

Liposuction

Another cosmetic surgical procedure is liposuction, or suction-assisted lipectomy. It is used for cosmetic purposes and not for weight reduction. This surgical intervention helps improve facial appearance or body contours. A good candidate is a person who has achieved weight reduction and has excess fat under the chin, along the jaw line, in the nasolabial folds, over the abdomen, or around the waist and upper thighs. A long, hollow, stainless steel cannula is inserted through a small incision over the fatty tissue to be suctioned. This surgical procedure is not usually recommended for an older person because the skin is less elastic and will not accommodate the new underlying shape.

METABOLIC SYNDROME

Metabolic syndrome is a group of metabolic risk factors that increase a person's chance of developing CVD, stroke, and diabetes. About 1 in 3 adults have metabolic syndrome. The syndrome is more prevalent in those 60 years of age and older.[21]

Metabolic syndrome is a cluster of health problems, including obesity, hypertension, abnormal lipid levels, and high blood glucose. Metabolic syndrome is diagnosed if a person has 3 or more of the conditions listed in Table 40.12.

Etiology and Pathophysiology

The main underlying risk factor for metabolic syndrome is insulin resistance related to excess visceral fat (Fig. 40.10). Insulin resistance is the decreased ability of the body's cells to respond to the action of insulin. The pancreas compensates by secreting more insulin, resulting in hyperinsulinemia.

TABLE 40.12 Criteria for Metabolic Syndrome

Any 3 of the 5 measures are needed to diagnose metabolic syndrome:

Measure	Criteria
Waist circumference	≥40 in (102 cm) in men
	≥35 in (89 cm) in women
Triglycerides	>150 mg/dL (1.7 mmol/L)
	OR
	Drug treatment for high triglycerides
HDL cholesterol	<40 mg/dL (0.9 mmol/L) in men
	<50 mg/dL (1.1 mmol/L) in women
	OR
	Drug treatment for high cholesterol
BP	≥130 mm Hg systolic BP
	OR
	≥85 mm Hg diastolic BP
	OR
	Drug treatment for hypertension
Fasting blood glucose	≥100 mg/dL
	OR
	Drug treatment for elevated glucose

Source: National Heart, Lung, and Blood Institute: How is metabolic syndrome diagnosed? Retrieved from *www.nhlbi.nih.gov/health/health-topics/topics/ms/diagnosis*.

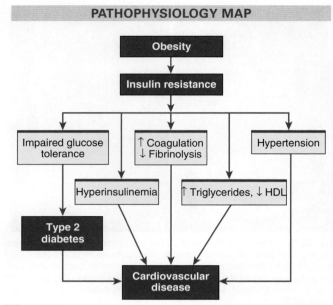

FIG. 40.10 Relationship among insulin resistance, obesity, diabetes, and CVD.

Other characteristics include hypertension, increased risk for clotting, and abnormalities in cholesterol levels. The net effect of these conditions is an increased prevalence of coronary artery disease.

Clinical Manifestations and Diagnostic Studies

The signs of metabolic syndrome are impaired fasting blood glucose, hypertension, abnormal cholesterol levels, and obesity. Medical problems develop over time if the condition is not addressed. Patients with this syndrome are at a higher risk for heart disease, stroke, diabetes, renal disease, and polycystic ovary syndrome. Patients who have metabolic syndrome and smoke are at an even higher risk.

❖ NURSING AND INTERPROFESSIONAL MANAGEMENT: METABOLIC SYNDROME

There is no specific management of metabolic syndrome. Interventions focus on reducing the major risk factors of CVD and type 2 diabetes: reducing LDL cholesterol, stopping smoking, lowering BP, losing weight, and reducing glucose levels. There are no specific medications for metabolic syndrome. Patients receive cholesterol-lowering and antihypertensive drugs as needed. Metformin (Glucophage) can lower glucose levels and enhance the cells' sensitivity to insulin. Obese patients may be candidates for bariatric surgery.

For long-term risk reduction, the person needs to maintain a healthy weight, increase physical activity, and follow healthy diet habits. You can help patients by giving information on healthy diets, exercise, and positive lifestyle changes. The diet, which should be low in saturated fats, should promote weight loss. Weight reduction and maintaining a lower weight are a priority in those with abdominal obesity and metabolic syndrome.

Because sedentary lifestyles contribute to metabolic syndrome, increasing regular physical activity will lower a patient's risk factors. In addition to helping with weight reduction, regular exercise decreases triglyceride levels and increases HDL cholesterol levels in those with metabolic syndrome.

CASE STUDY
Obesity

(© Thinkstock.)

Patient Profile

S.R. is a 48-yr-old white woman who comes to the clinic reporting hip pain.

Subjective Data

- States that it is "getting hard to get around"
- Reports gradual weight gain of 40 lbs over past 20 yrs
- Lives in a rural community with no sidewalks
- Spends her free time watching television
- Reports a history of type 2 diabetes, shortness of breath, hypertension, and osteoarthritis
- Had knee replacement surgery at age 46 for osteoarthritis
- Tried orlistat (Xenical) but hated the side effects

Objective Data

Physical Examination

- 5 ft, 6 in tall; weighs 230 lb; BMI 37 kg/m², waist circumference of 40 in
- Has obese, nontender, soft round, abdomen
- BP 160/100 mm Hg
- Moderate pain with range of motion of both hips

Laboratory Results

- Fasting blood glucose 250 mg/dL (13.9 mmol/L)
- Total cholesterol 205 mg/dL (5.3 mmol/L)
- Triglyceride 298 mg/dL (3.36 mmol/L)
- HDL cholesterol 31 mg/dL (0.8 mmol/L)
- LDL cholesterol 114 mg/dL

CASE STUDY
Obesity—cont'd

Interprofessional Care
- Referral to a community weight loss program
- Consultation with bariatric surgeon
- Diagnosed with bilateral osteoarthritis of the hips

Discussion Questions

1. What are S.R.'s risk factors for obesity?
2. Of the possible complications of obesity, which ones does S.R. have? Why did she develop them?

3. **Patient-Centered Care:** How would you help S.R. in designing a successful weight loss and weight management program?
4. **Collaboration:** How could a comprehensive community weight loss program be beneficial to S.R.?
5. What are S.R.'s risk factors for metabolic syndrome?
6. Is S.R. a candidate for bariatric surgery? Why or why not?
7. **Evidence-Based Practice:** S.R. tells you that she is not sure surgery will work for her. She asks you, "What is the best surgery for me?"

Answers available at *http://evolve.elsevier.com/Lewis/medsurg.*

BRIDGE TO NCLEX EXAMINATION

The number of the question corresponds to the same-numbered outcome at the beginning of the chapter.

1. Which statement *best* describes the etiology of obesity?
   a. Obesity primarily results from a genetic predisposition.
   b. Psychosocial factors can override the effects of genetics in causing obesity.
   c. Obesity is the result of complex interactions between genetic and environmental factors.
   d. Genetic factors are more important than environmental factors in the etiology of obesity.

2. Health risks associated with obesity include *(select all that apply)*
   a. colorectal cancer.
   b. rheumatoid arthritis.
   c. polycystic ovary syndrome.
   d. nonalcoholic steatohepatitis.
   e. systemic lupus erythematosus.

3. The obesity classification that is *most* often associated with cardiovascular health problems is
   a. primary obesity.
   b. secondary obesity.
   c. gynoid fat distribution.
   d. android fat distribution.

4. The *best* nutritional therapy plan for a person who is obese
   a. is high in animal protein.
   b. is fat-free and low in carbohydrates.
   c. restricts intake to under 800 calories per day.
   d. lowers calories with foods from all the basic groups.

5. This bariatric surgical procedure involves creating a gastric pouch that is reversible, and no malabsorption occurs. Which surgical procedure is this?
   a. Vertical gastric banding
   b. Biliopancreatic diversion
   c. Roux-en-Y gastric bypass
   d. Adjustable gastric banding

6. A patient with extreme obesity has undergone Roux-en-Y gastric bypass surgery. In planning postoperative care, the nurse anticipates that the patient
   a. may have severe diarrhea early in the postoperative period.
   b. will not be allowed to ambulate for 1 to 2 days postoperatively.
   c. will require nasogastric suction until the drainage is pale yellow.
   d. may have limited amounts of oral liquids during the early postoperative period.

7. Which criteria must be met for a diagnosis of metabolic syndrome? *(select all that apply)*
   a. Hypertension
   b. High triglycerides
   c. Elevated plasma glucose
   d. Increased waist circumference
   e. Decreased low-density lipoproteins

1. c, 2. a, c, d, 3. d, 4. d, 5. d, 6. d, 7. a, b, c, d

For rationales to these answers and even more NCLEX review questions, visit *http://evolve.elsever.com/Lewis/medsurg.*

EVOLVE WEBSITE/RESOURCES LIST

http://evolve.elsevier.com/Lewis/medsurg
Review Questions (Online Only)
Key Points
Answer Keys for Questions
- Rationales for Bridge to NCLEX Examination Questions
- Answer Guidelines for Case Study on p. 886
Student Case Study
- Patient With Obesity and Osteoarthritis
Conceptual Care Map Creator
Audio Glossary
Content Updates

REFERENCES

1. Centers for Disease Control and Prevention: Overweight and obesity. Retrieved from *www.cdc.gov/obesity/data/adult.html.*
*2. Albuquerque D, Nóbrega C, Manco L, et al: The contribution of genetics and environment to obesity, *BMJ* 123:73, 2017.
*3. Dimitriadis GK, Randeva MS, Miras AD: Potential hormone mechanisms of bariatric surgery, *Curr Obes Rep* 6:253, 2017.
*4. Shibata R, Ouchi N, Ohashi K, et al: The role of adipokines in cardiovascular disease, *J Cardiol* 70:329, 2017.
5. Robert Wood Johnson Foundation. The state of obesity. Retrieved from *https://stateofobesity.org/resources/.*
*6. Björnson E, Adiels M, Taskinen MR, et al : Kinetics of plasma triglycerides in abdominal obesity, *Curr Opin Lipidol* 28:11, 2017.

7. The link between obesity and cancer (editorial), *Lancet* 390:1716, 2017.

*8. Rotenberg KJ, Bharathi C, Davies H, et al: Obesity and the social withdrawal syndrome, *Eating Behaviors* 26:167, 2017.

9. Centers for Disease Control and Prevention: Assessing your weight. Retrieved from *www.cdc.gov/healthyweight/assessing/index.html.*

*10. Acosta A, Streett S, Kroh MD, et al: White paper AGA: POWER—Practice guide on obesity and weight management, education and resources, *Clin Gastroenterol Hepat* 515:631, 2017.

11. Bray GA, Frühbeck G, Ryan DH, et al: Management of obesity, *Lancet* 387:1947, 2016.

*12. Lv N, Azar KM, Rosas LG, et al: Behavioral lifestyle interventions for moderate and severe obesity: A systematic review, *Prev Med* 100:180, 2017.

13. Alfaris N, Minnick A, Hong P, et al: A review of commercial and proprietary weight loss programs. In: Mechanik J, Kushner R, eds: *Lifestyle medicine: A manual for clinical practice,* New York, 2016, Springer.

14. Igel LI, Kumar RB, Saunders KH, et al: Practical use of pharmacotherapy for obesity, *Gastroenterol* 152:1765, 2017.

*15. Gadde KM, Martin CK, Berthoud HR, et al: Obesity: Pathophysiology and management, *J Am Coll Cardiol* 71:69, 2018.

*16. Adams TD, Davidson LE, Litwin SE, et al: Weight and metabolic outcomes 12 years after gastric bypass, *NEJM* 377:1143, 2017.

17. Genco A, Maselli R, Casella G, et al: *Intragastric balloon treatment for obesity,* New York, 2016, Springer.

*18. Thorell A, MacCormick AD, Awad S, et al: Guidelines for perioperative care in bariatric surgery: Enhanced Recovery After Surgery (ERAS) Society recommendations, *World J Surg* 40:2065, 2016.

*19. Dagan SS, Goldenshluger A, Globus I, et al: Nutritional recommendations for adult bariatric surgery patients, *Adv Nutr* 8:382, 2017.

*20. Cooley M: Preventing long-term poor outcomes in the bariatric patient postoperatively, *DCCN* 36:30, 2017.

*21. Moore JX, Chaudhary N, Akinyemiju T: Metabolic syndrome prevalence by race/ethnicity and sex in the United States, *PCD* 14:24, 2017.

*Evidence-based information for clinical practice.

41

Upper Gastrointestinal Problems

Kara Ann Ventura

Anywhere I see suffering that is where I want to be,
doing what I can.

Princess Diana

http://evolve.elsevier.com/Lewis/medsurg

CONCEPTUAL FOCUS

Fluids and Electrolytes	Pain	Stress
Nutrition	Sleep	Tissue Integrity

LEARNING OUTCOMES

1. Describe the etiology, complications, and interprofessional and nursing management of nausea and vomiting.
2. Relate the etiology, clinical manifestations, and interprofessional and nursing management of common oral inflammations and infections.
3. Describe the etiology, clinical manifestations, complications, and interprofessional and nursing management of oral cancer.
4. Explain the types, pathophysiology, clinical manifestations, complications, and interprofessional and nursing management of gastroesophageal reflux disease and hiatal hernia.
5. Relate the pathophysiology, clinical manifestations, complications, and interprofessional management of esophageal cancer, diverticula, achalasia, and esophageal strictures.

6. Distinguish between acute and chronic gastritis, including the etiology, pathophysiology, and interprofessional and nursing management.
7. Compare and contrast gastric and duodenal ulcers, including the etiology, pathophysiology, clinical manifestations, complications, and interprofessional and nursing management.
8. Describe the clinical manifestations and interprofessional and nursing management of stomach cancer.
9. Explain the common etiologies, clinical manifestations, and interprofessional and nursing management of upper gastrointestinal bleeding.
10. Identify common types of foodborne illnesses and nursing responsibilities related to food poisoning.

KEY TERMS

achalasia, p. 904
Barrett's esophagus, p. 897
dysphagia, p. 894
esophageal cancer, p. 901
esophagitis, p. 897

gastritis, p. 915
gastroesophageal reflux disease (GERD), p. 896
hiatal hernia, p. 900
Mallory-Weiss tear, p. 891
nausea, p. 889

peptic ulcer disease (PUD), p. 904
stomach (gastric) cancer, p. 911
stress-related mucosal disease (SRMD), p. 917
vomiting, p. 889

Several upper gastrointestinal (GI) problems and the care of the patient undergoing upper GI surgery are discussed in this chapter. These include nausea and vomiting, oral and gastric cancers, gastroesophageal reflux, ulcerative disease, inflammatory and infectious bowel disorders, GI bleeding, and structural problems. Conceptually, patients with impaired GI function may have malnutrition from impaired nutritional intake. Many are at risk for altered fluid, electrolyte, and acid-base balance. Problems with eating, drinking, or talking may cause pain and impair the ability to communicate. Pain can disrupt sleep and cause fatigue. Difficulty swallowing increases the risk for aspiration.

NAUSEA AND VOMITING

Nausea and vomiting are the most common manifestations of GI disease. Although nausea and vomiting can occur independently, they are closely related and usually treated as one problem. Nausea is a feeling of discomfort in the epigastrium with a conscious desire to vomit. Vomiting is the forceful ejection of partially digested food and secretions (*emesis*) from the upper GI tract.

Etiology and Pathophysiology

Nausea and vomiting occur in a wide variety of GI disorders and in many conditions unrelated to GI disease. These include pregnancy; infection; central nervous system (CNS) problems (e.g., meningitis, tumor); cardiovascular disease (CVD) (e.g., myocardial infarction, heart failure); metabolic disorders (e.g. psychologic factors (e.g., stress, fear); and when the GI tract becomes overly irritated, excited, or distended. Patients may have nausea and vomiting after surgery with general anesthesia or as a drug side effect (e.g., chemotherapy, opioids). Women are more likely to have nausea and vomiting associated with anesthesia and motion sickness.[1]

A vomiting center in the medulla coordinates the multiple components involved in vomiting. This center receives input from various stimuli. Neural impulses reach the vomiting center via afferent pathways through branches of the autonomic nervous system. Receptors for these afferent fibers are found in the GI tract, kidneys, heart, and uterus. When stimulated, these receptors relay information to the vomiting (emetic) center, which then initiates the vomiting reflex (Fig. 41.1).

Vomiting is a complex act. It requires the coordinated activity of several structures: closure of the glottis, deep inspiration with contraction of the diaphragm in the inspiratory position, closure of the pylorus, relaxation of the stomach and lower esophageal sphincter (LES), and contraction of the abdominal muscles with increasing intraabdominal pressure. These simultaneous activities force the stomach contents up through the esophagus, into the pharynx, and out the mouth.

The chemoreceptor trigger zone (CTZ), found in the brainstem, responds to chemical stimuli from drugs, toxins, and labyrinthine stimulation (e.g., motion sickness). Once stimulated, the CTZ transmits impulses directly to the vomiting center. This action activates the autonomic nervous system, resulting in both parasympathetic and sympathetic stimulation. Sympathetic activation causes tachycardia, tachypnea, and diaphoresis. Parasympathetic stimulation causes relaxation of the LES, an increase in gastric motility, and a pronounced increase in salivation.

Clinical Manifestations

Nausea is subjective. *Anorexia* (lack of appetite) usually accompanies nausea. When nausea and vomiting occur over a long period, dehydration can develop rapidly. Water and essential electrolytes (e.g., potassium, sodium, chloride, hydrogen) are lost. As vomiting persists, the patient may have severe electrolyte imbalances, extracellular fluid volume loss, decreased plasma volume, and eventually circulatory failure.

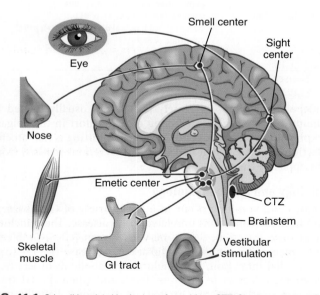

FIG. 41.1 Stimuli involved in the act of vomiting. *CTZ,* Chemoreceptor trigger zone. (Modified from McKenry L, Tessier E, Hogan M: *Mosby's pharmacology in nursing,* ed 22, St Louis, 2006, Mosby.)

Metabolic alkalosis can result from loss of gastric hydrochloric (HCl) acid. Metabolic acidosis can occur with vomiting of small intestine contents. However, metabolic acidosis is less common than metabolic alkalosis. Weight loss resulting from fluid loss can occur in a short time with severe vomiting.

Interprofessional Care

In managing nausea and vomiting, the goals of care are to determine and treat the underlying cause, recognize and correct any complications, and provide symptomatic relief.

Drug Therapy. The use of drugs to treat nausea and vomiting depends on the cause of the problem (Table 41.1). Many antiemetic drugs act in the CNS via the CTZ to block the neurochemicals that trigger nausea and vomiting. When the cause has not been determined, use drugs with caution. Using antiemetics before knowing the cause can mask the underlying disease process and delay diagnosis and treatment.

💊 DRUG ALERT Promethazine Injection

- Do not give into an artery or under the skin because of the risk for severe tissue injury.
- When given IV, it can leak out of the vein and cause severe damage to surrounding tissue.
- Deep muscle injection is the preferred route of injection administration.

5-HT$_3$ (Serotonin) receptor antagonists are effective in reducing chemotherapy-induced vomiting (CINV), postoperative nausea and vomiting (PONV), and nausea and vomiting related to migraine headache and anxiety. Dexamethasone is given with other antiemetics to manage acute and delayed CINV. Neurokinin-1 receptor antagonists (NK$_1$RAs) (e.g., aprepitant [Emend], rolapitant [Varubi]), can treat CINV and PONV.[2]

💊 DRUG ALERT Metoclopramide (Reglan)

- Chronic use or high doses carry the risk for tardive dyskinesia.
- Tardive dyskinesia is a neurologic condition characterized by involuntary and repetitive movements of the body (e.g., extremity movements, lip smacking).
- Tardive dyskinesia may persist after stopping the drug.

An oral cannabinoid (e.g., dronabinol) may be part of the regimen to manage CINV. Because of the potential for abuse as well as drowsiness and sedation, this is an option only when other therapies are not effective.

❖ NURSING MANAGEMENT: NAUSEA AND VOMITING

◆ Nursing Assessment

Each patient with a history of prolonged and persistent nausea or vomiting needs a thorough nursing assessment. You should have a basic understanding of the common conditions associated with nausea and vomiting and be able to identify the patient who is at high risk. Assess the patient for precipitating factors and describe the contents of the emesis. Table 41.2 presents subjective and objective data to obtain from a patient with nausea and vomiting.

When food is the precipitating cause of nausea and vomiting, help the patient identify the specific food. Determine when it was eaten, prior history with the food, and whether anyone else who ate the food is sick. Emesis containing

TABLE 41.1 Drug Therapy

Nausea and Vomiting

Drug	Mechanism of Action	Side Effects
Anticholinergics		
scopolamine transdermal	Block cholinergic pathways to vomiting center	Xerostomia, somnolence
Antihistamines		
dimenhydrinate (Dramamine) diphenhydramine hydroxyzine meclizine (Antivert)	Block histamine receptors that trigger nausea and vomiting	Dry mouth, hypotension, sedative effects, rashes, constipation
Cannabinoids		
dronabinol (Marinol) nabilone (Cesamet)	Inhibit vomiting control mechanism in the medulla oblongata	Xerostomia, amnesia, ataxia, confusion, coordination problems, dizziness, somnolence
Corticosteroids		
dexamethasone	Not well understood how it prevents nausea and vomiting	Hyperglycemia, insomnia, euphoria
5-HT$_3$ (Serotonin) Antagonists		
granisetron ondansetron (Zofran) palonosetron (Aloxi)	Block action of serotonin	Constipation, diarrhea, headache, fatigue, malaise, increased liver function tests
Phenothiazines		
chlorpromazine prochlorperazine promethazine Prokinetic	Act in the CNS level of the chemoreceptor trigger zone (CTZ). Block dopamine receptors that trigger nausea and vomiting	Dry mouth, hypotension, sedative effects, rashes, constipation
Metoclopramide (Reglan)	Inhibit action of dopamine. ↑ Gastric motility and emptying	CNS side effects ranging from anxiety to hallucinations, extrapyramidal side effects, including tremor and dyskinesias
Substance P/Neurokinin-1 Receptor Antagonists		
aprepitant (Emend) netupitant and palonosetron (Akynzeo) rolapitant (Varubi)	Block interaction of Substance P at NK-1 receptor	Headache, hiccups, fatigue, constipation, diarrhea, anorexia

partially digested food several hours after a meal indicates gastric outlet obstruction or delayed gastric emptying. The presence of fecal odor and bile after prolonged vomiting suggests intestinal obstruction below the level of the pylorus. Bile in the emesis suggests obstruction below the ampulla of Vater.

The color of the emesis helps determine the presence and source of any bleeding. Bright red blood occurs with active bleeding. This could be due to a **Mallory-Weiss tear** (disruption of the mucosal lining near the esophagogastric junction), esophageal varices, gastric or duodenal ulcer, or cancer. Vomitus with a "coffee-grounds" appearance is related to gastric bleeding. The blood changes to dark brown because of its interaction with HCl acid.

It is important to discern among vomiting, regurgitation, and projectile vomiting. *Regurgitation* is an effortless process in which partially digested food slowly comes up from the stomach. Retching or vomiting rarely occurs before it. *Projectile vomiting* is a forceful expulsion of stomach contents without nausea. It often occurs with brain and spinal cord tumors.

The timing of nausea and vomiting can help determine its cause. Early morning vomiting is common in pregnancy. Emotional stressors may elicit vomiting during or right after eating. Those with *cyclic vomiting syndrome* have recurring episodes of nausea, vomiting, and fatigue that last from a few hours up to 10 days.

◆ **Nursing Diagnoses**

Nursing diagnoses for the patient with nausea and vomiting may include:
- Nausea
- Fluid imbalance
- Electrolyte imbalance
- Impaired nutritional intake

More information on nursing diagnoses and interventions are in eNursing Care Plan 41.1 (available on the website for this chapter).

◆ **Planning**

The overall goals are that the patient with nausea and vomiting will (1) have minimal or no nausea and vomiting, (2) have normal electrolyte levels and hydration status, and (3) return to a normal pattern of fluid balance and nutrient intake.

◆ **Nursing Implementation**

◆ **Acute Care.** Most people with nausea and vomiting are at home. When nausea and vomiting persist, the patient may need hospitalized to diagnose the underlying problem. Until we confirm

TABLE 41.2 Nursing Assessment

Nausea and Vomiting

Subjective Data

Important Health Information

Past health history: GI disorders, chronic indigestion, food allergies, pregnancy, infection, CNS problems, recent travel, eating disorders, metabolic disorders, cancer, CVD, renal disease

Medications: Antiemetics, digitalis, opioids, ferrous sulfate, aspirin, aminophylline, alcohol, antibiotics, chemotherapy. General anesthesia

Surgery or other treatments: Recent surgery

Functional Health Patterns

Nutritional-metabolic: Amount, frequency, character, and color of vomitus. Dry heaves. Anorexia, weight loss

Activity-exercise: Weakness, fatigue

Cognitive-perceptual: Abdominal tenderness or pain

Coping–stress tolerance: Stress, fear

Objective Data

General

Lethargy, sunken eyeballs

Integumentary

Pallor, dry mucous membranes, poor skin turgor

Gastrointestinal

Amount, frequency, character (e.g., projectile), content (undigested food, blood, bile, feces), and color of vomitus (red, coffee-grounds, green-yellow)

Urinary

Decreased output, concentrated urine

Possible Diagnostic Findings

Altered serum electrolytes (especially hypokalemia), metabolic alkalosis, abnormal upper GI findings on endoscopy or abdominal x-rays

---

a diagnosis, the patient is NPO and given IV fluids. The patient with persistent vomiting, a possible bowel obstruction, or paralytic ileus may need a nasogastric (NG) tube connected to suction to decompress the stomach. Secure the NG tube to prevent its movement in the nose and back of the throat, because this can stimulate nausea and vomiting.

With prolonged vomiting, there is a chance of dehydration and acid-base and electrolyte imbalances. Record intake and output, monitor vital signs, and assess for signs of dehydration. Provide physical and emotional support. Maintain a quiet, odor-free environment. Observe for changes in the patient's physical comfort and mentation. The risk for pulmonary aspiration is a concern when vomiting occurs in older or unconscious patients or in patients with conditions that impair the gag reflex. To prevent aspiration, put the patient who cannot manage self-care in a semi-Fowler's or side-lying position.

◆ **Nutritional Therapy.** The patient with severe vomiting needs IV fluid therapy with electrolyte and glucose replacement until able to tolerate oral intake. Start oral nutrition beginning with clear liquids once symptoms have subsided. A patient may be reluctant to resume fluid intake because of fear of symptoms recurring. Water is the initial fluid of choice for oral rehydration. Have the patient sip small amounts of fluid (5 to 15 mL) every 15 to 20 minutes. Other options include carbonated beverages with the carbonation removed at room temperature and

warm tea. Extremely hot or cold liquids are often hard to tolerate. Broth and sports drinks (e.g., Gatorade) are high in sodium, so give them with caution. Dry toast, crackers, and plain gelatin may be helpful.

As the patient's condition improves, provide a diet high in carbohydrates and low in fat. Bland foods, such as a baked potato, rice, cooked chicken, and cereal, are ideal. Many patients do not tolerate coffee, spicy foods, highly acidic foods, and those with strong odors. Tell the patient to eat food slowly and in small amounts to prevent overdistending the stomach. Liquids taken between meals rather than with meals reduce overdistention. Consult a dietitian about nutritious foods that the patient can tolerate.

❓ CHECK YOUR PRACTICE

You are caring for a newly admitted 76-yr-old man who reports vomiting for the past 3 days. He says, "I cannot keep anything down, not even water."

- What assessment do you need to perform?
- What findings would show he is dehydrated?
- What are your priority nursing interventions?

◆ **Ambulatory Care.** Teach the patient and caregiver (1) how to manage the unpleasant sensation of nausea, (2) methods to prevent nausea and vomiting, and (3) ways to maintain fluid and nutritional intake. Tell them to keep the immediate environment quiet, free of noxious odors, and well ventilated. Avoiding sudden changes of position and unnecessary activity are helpful. Encourage the use of relaxation techniques, frequent rest periods, effective pain management strategies, and diversional tactics. Cleansing the face and hands with a cool washcloth and providing mouth care between episodes increase the person's comfort level. When symptoms occur, stop all foods and drugs until the acute phase is over.

If you suspect a medication is the cause, notify the (HCP at once. The HCP can change the dose or prescribe a new drug. Tell the patient that stopping the drug without consulting the HCP may have adverse effects on the person's health. The patient should take an antiemetic drug only if prescribed by the HCP. Taking over-the-counter (OTC) drugs to relieve symptoms may make the problem worse.

Some patients find that acupressure or acupuncture at specific points is effective in reducing PONV.[3] Others use herbs, such as ginger and peppermint oil. Relaxation breathing exercises, changes in body position, or exercise may help some patients.

🌿 COMPLEMENTARY & ALTERNATIVE THERAPIES

Ginger

Scientific Evidence

- May be effective for nausea and vomiting in pregnancy when used at recommended doses for short periods
- May help CINV if used with antiemetic drugs

Nursing Implications

- Few adverse effects reported with short-term use
- May interact with anticoagulants and increase risk for bleeding
- Use with caution in people with gallbladder disease

Source: *www.nccih.nih.gov/health/ginger.*

TABLE 41.3 Infections and Inflammation of the Mouth

Infection or Inflammation	Etiology	Manifestations	Treatment
Aphthous stomatitis (canker sore)	• Recurrent and chronic form of infection • Related to systemic disease, trauma, stress, or unknown causes	• Ulcers of mouth and lips, causing extreme pain • Ulcers surrounded by erythematous base	• Corticosteroids (topical or systemic) • Tetracycline oral suspension
Gingivitis	• Neglected oral hygiene, malocclusion, missing or irregular teeth, faulty dentistry • Eating soft rather than fibrous foods	• Inflamed gingivae and interdental papillae • Bleeding during tooth brushing • Development of pus, abscess formation with loosening of teeth (periodontitis)	• Prevention through health teaching, dental care, gingival massage, professional cleaning of teeth • Eat fibrous foods • Conscientious brushing habits with flossing
Herpes simplex (cold sore, fever blister) (see Table 23.6)	• Herpes simplex virus (type 1 or 2) • Predisposing factors of upper respiratory tract infections, excessive exposure to sunlight, food allergies, emotional tension, onset of menstruation	• Lip lesions, mouth lesions, vesicle formation (single or clustered) • Shallow, painful ulcers	• Spirits of camphor, corticosteroid cream, mild antiseptic mouthwash, viscous lidocaine • Remove or control predisposing factors • Antiviral agents (e.g., acyclovir [Zovirax], valacyclovir [Valtrex])
Oral candidiasis (moniliasis or thrush)	• *Candida albicans* (yeastlike fungus) • Debilitation • Prolonged high-dose antibiotic or corticosteroid therapy	• Pearly, bluish white "milk-curd" membranous lesions on mucosa of mouth and larynx • Sore mouth, yeasty halitosis	• Miconazole buccal tablets (Oravig) • Nystatin or amphotericin B as oral suspension or buccal tablets • Good oral hygiene
Parotitis (inflammation of parotid gland, surgical mumps)	• *Staphylococcus* species usually • *Streptococcus* species occasionally • Debilitation and dehydration with poor oral hygiene • Extended NPO status	• Pain in area of gland and ear • Absence of salivation • Purulent exudate from gland, erythema, ulcers	• Antibiotics, mouthwashes, warm compresses • Preventive measures, such as chewing gum, sucking on hard candy (lemon drops) • Adequate fluid intake
Stomatitis (inflammation of mouth)	• Trauma, pathogens, irritants (tobacco, alcohol) • Renal, liver, and hematologic diseases • Side effect of chemotherapy and radiation	• Excess salivation • Halitosis • Sore mouth	• Remove or treat cause • Oral hygiene with soothing solutions, topical medications • Soft, bland diet
Vincent's infection (acute necrotizing ulcerative gingivitis, trench mouth)	• Fusiform bacteria, Vincent spirochetes • Predisposing factors of stress, excessive fatigue, poor oral hygiene • Nutritional deficiencies (B and C vitamins)	• Painful, bleeding gingivae • Eroding necrotic lesions of interdental papillae • Ulcerations that bleed • Increased saliva with metallic taste, fetid mouth odor • Anorexia, fever, general malaise	• Physical and mental rest • Avoid smoking and alcohol • Soft, nutritious diet • Correct oral hygiene habits • Topical applications of antibiotics • Mouth irrigations with chlorhexidine and saline solutions

◆ **Evaluation**

The expected outcomes are that the patient with nausea and vomiting will

- Be comfortable, with minimal or no nausea and vomiting
- Have electrolyte levels within normal range
- Be able to maintain adequate intake of fluids and nutrients

Gerontologic Considerations: Nausea and Vomiting

The older adult with nausea and vomiting needs careful assessment and monitoring, especially during periods of fluid loss and rehydration therapy. They are more likely to have cardiac or renal problems that places them at greater risk for life-threatening fluid and electrolyte imbalances. Excess fluid and electrolytes replacement may have adverse consequences for a person with heart failure or renal disease. The older adult with a decreased level of consciousness has a high risk for aspirating. Close monitoring of the patient's physical status and level of consciousness during episodes of vomiting is important.

Older adults are particularly susceptible to the CNS side effects of antiemetic drugs. These drugs may cause confusion and increase fall risk. Doses should be reduced and efficacy closely evaluated. Use safety precautions for these patients (e.g., removing rugs that may cause slipping).

ORAL INFLAMMATION AND INFECTIONS

Inflammations and infections of the oral cavity are shown in Table 41.3. They may be due to specific mouth diseases or related to systemic disorders, such as leukemia or vitamin deficiency. The patient who is immunosuppressed (e.g., receiving chemotherapy for cancer) or using corticosteroid inhalant treatment for asthma is at risk for oral infections (e.g., candidiasis). Oral infections may predispose the patient to infections in other body organs. For example, the oral cavity is a potential reservoir for respiratory pathogens. Oral pathogens are associated with diabetes and heart disease.[4]

Managing these problems focuses on identifying the cause, eliminating infection, providing comfort measures, and maintaining nutritional intake. They can severely impair oral ingestion. Regular and good oral and dental hygiene reduces oral infections and inflammation.

ORAL CANCER

There are 2 types of oral cancer: *oral cavity cancer,* which starts in the mouth, and *oropharyngeal cancer,* which develops in the part of the throat just behind the mouth (the oropharynx). *Head and neck squamous cell carcinoma* (HNSCC) is a broad term used for cancers of the oral cavity, pharynx, and larynx. Most oral cancer lesions occur on the lower lip. Other common sites are the lateral border and undersurface of the tongue, labial commissure, and buccal mucosa. Annually 51,540 Americans are diagnosed with oral cancer. An estimated 10,030 people die from the disease.[5]

Oral cancer is more common after age 35. The average age at diagnosis is 65 years. It is 2 times more common in men than in women. The 5-year survival rate is 84% for localized cancer and 65% for all stages of oral cavity and pharynx cancer combined.[5] Lip cancer has the most favorable prognosis of any of the oral tumors. The visibility of lip lesions usually leads to an earlier diagnosis.

⊕ PROMOTING HEALTH EQUITY

Oral, Pharyngeal, and Esophageal Problems

Nausea and Vomiting
- Asian Americans, Middle Easterners, and blacks are more likely to have nausea and vomiting than whites

Cancers of Oral Cavity and Pharynx
- Incidence and mortality rates are higher in black men than in whites
- Death rates from oral cancer are decreasing in whites and increasing in nonwhites

Esophageal Cancer
- Highest incidence is in non-Hispanic white men
- Lowest incidence occurs in Asian Americans, Pacific Islanders, and Hispanics.

Stomach Cancer
- Asian Americans and Pacific Islanders, Hispanics, and blacks have higher rates of stomach cancer than non-Hispanic whites
- Asian Americans have higher survival rates than other ethnic groups

Etiology and Pathophysiology

Although the exact cause of oral cancer is unknown, there are predisposing factors (Table 41.4). Of those with oral cancer, 75% to 90% report either using tobacco or a history of frequent alcohol use. More than 30% of patients with cancer of the lip have outdoor occupations, showing that prolonged exposure to sunlight is a risk factor. Irritation from the pipe stem resting on the lip is a factor in pipe smokers. Human papillomavirus (HPV) contributes to 25% of oral cancer cases. HPV-associated oropharyngeal cancer is associated with multiple sexual partners, especially multiple oral sex partners.[6]

Clinical Manifestations

The common manifestations are shown in Table 41.4. Patients may report nonspecific symptoms such as chronic sore throat, sore mouth, and voice changes. *Leukoplakia,* called "smoker's patch," is a white patch on the mouth mucosa or tongue. It is a precancerous lesion, although less than 15% actually transform into cancer cells. The patch becomes *keratinized* (hard and leathery). This is described as hyperkeratosis. Leukoplakia is the result of chronic irritation, especially from smoking. *Erythroplasia* (erythroplakia), a red velvety patch on the mouth or tongue, is another precancerous lesion. More than 50% of cases of erythroplasia progress to squamous cell cancer. About 30% of patients with oral cancer have an asymptomatic neck mass.

Cancer of the lip usually appears as an indurated, painless ulcer on the lip. The first sign of cancer of the tongue is an ulcer or area of thickening. Soreness or pain of the tongue may occur, especially when eating hot or highly seasoned foods. Lesions are most likely to develop in the proximal half of the tongue. Some patients have limited tongue movement. Later symptoms include increased salivation, slurred speech, dysphagia (difficulty swallowing), toothache, and earache.

Diagnostic Studies

Diagnostic tests are done to identify oral dysplasia, which is a precursor to oral cancer (Table 41.5). Oral exfoliative cytologic study involves scraping the suspicious lesion and spreading the scraping on a slide for microscopic examination. The toluidine blue test is a screening test for oral cancer. When toluidine blue is applied topically to stain an area, cancer cells preferentially take up the dye. A negative cytologic smear or negative toluidine blue test does not necessarily rule out cancer. Once cancer is diagnosed, CT scan, MRI, and positron emission tomography (PET) are used for staging cancer.

TABLE 41.4 Types and Characteristics of Oral Cancer

Location	Predisposing Factors	Clinical Manifestations	Treatment
Lip	Constant overexposure to sun, ruddy and fair complexion, recurrent herpetic lesions, irritation from pipe stem, syphilis, immunosuppression	Indurated, painless ulcer	Surgical excision, radiation
Oral cavity	Poor oral hygiene, tobacco usage (pipe and cigar smoking, snuff, chewing tobacco), chronic alcohol intake, chronic irritation (jagged tooth, ill-fitting prosthesis, chemical or mechanical irritants), HPV	Leukoplakia, erythroplakia, ulcerations, sore spot, rough area, pain, dysphagia, a lump or thickening in the cheek A sore throat or a feeling that something is stuck Difficulty chewing and speaking (later signs)	Surgery (mandibulectomy, radical neck dissection, resection of buccal mucosa), internal and external radiation
Tongue	Tobacco, alcohol, chronic irritation, syphilis	Ulcer or area of thickening, soreness, or pain Limited tongue movement Increased salivation, slurred speech, dysphagia, toothache, earache (later signs)	Surgery (hemiglossectomy or glossectomy), radiation

Interprofessional Management: Oral Cancer

Management usually consists of surgery, radiation, chemotherapy, or a combination of these. The curative treatments are usually surgery and radiation.

Surgical Therapy. Surgery is the most effective treatment, especially for early-stage disease.[7] The procedure done depends on the location and extent of the tumor. Some patients with small tumors in the mouth and throat are candidates for minimally invasive robotic-assisted surgery. However, many of the operations are radical procedures involving extensive resections. Some examples are partial *mandibulectomy* (removal of the mandible), *hemiglossectomy* (removal of half of the tongue), *glossectomy* (removal of the tongue), resections of the buccal mucosa and floor of the mouth, and radical neck dissection.

Radical neck dissection includes wide excision of the primary lesion with removal of the regional lymph nodes, the deep cervical lymph nodes, and their lymphatic channels. The following structures are removed or transected depending on the extent of the primary lesion: sternocleidomastoid muscle and other closely associated muscles, internal jugular vein, mandible, submaxillary gland, part of the thyroid and parathyroid glands, and spinal accessory nerve. The patient usually has a tracheostomy. Drainage tubes inserted into the surgical area are connected to suction to remove fluid and blood. Head and neck surgery is described in more detail in Chapter 26.

Nonsurgical Therapy. Radiation therapy may be used alone to treat small cancers or when lesions cannot be removed. Patients usually do not have radiation before surgery because it is hard to remove radiated tissue. The tissue becomes fibrotic and heals slower. Most patients begin radiation about 6 weeks after surgery.

Chemotherapy can shrink lesions before surgery, decrease metastasis, sensitize cancer cells to radiation, or treat distant metastases. Common chemotherapy drugs include fluorouracil, cisplatin, carboplatin, paclitaxel, docetaxel, and hydroxyurea. A common combination is cisplatin and fluorouracil.[8] This combination is more effective than either drug alone. (Chemotherapy is discussed in Chapter 15.)

Palliative treatment is the best management when the prognosis is poor, the cancer is inoperable, or the patient decides against surgery. Palliation aims to treat the symptoms and make the patient more comfortable. If it becomes hard for the patient to swallow, placing a gastrostomy tube will allow for adequate nutritional intake. Give analgesic drugs freely. Frequent suctioning of the oral cavity is needed when swallowing becomes difficult. Other palliative and end-of-life nursing measures are discussed in Chapter 9.

Nutritional Therapy. Many patients are malnourished before surgery. They may need placement of a percutaneous endoscopic gastrostomy (PEG) and enteral nutrition (EN) before

radiation treatment or surgery. After radical neck surgery, the patient may be unable to ingest nutrients orally because of mucositis, swelling, location of sutures, or difficulty swallowing. PN is given for the first 24 to 48 hours. After that time, EN is given via NG, gastrostomy, or jejunostomy tube. (See Chapter 39 for information on EN.) Cervical esophagostomy and pharyngostomy are options for some patients.

Assess for feeding tolerance and adjust the amount, time, and formula if nausea, vomiting, diarrhea, or distention occurs. Give small amounts of water when the patient can swallow. Observe for choking. Suctioning may be needed to prevent aspiration.

❖ NURSING MANAGEMENT: ORAL CANCER

◆ Nursing Assessment

Subjective and objective data to obtain from a patient with oral cancer are outlined in Table 41.6.

◆ Nursing Diagnoses

Nursing diagnoses for the patient with oral cancer may include the following:
- Impaired nutritional intake
- Acute pain
- Anxiety

◆ Planning

The overall goals are that the patient with cancer of the oral cavity will (1) have a patent airway, (2) be able to communicate, (3) have adequate nutritional intake to promote wound healing, and (4) have relief of pain and discomfort.

TABLE 41.5 Interprofessional Care
Oral Cancer

Diagnostic Assessment	Management
• History and physical examination	• Surgical therapy
• Biopsy	• Surgical excision of the tumor
• Oral exfoliative cytology	• Radical neck dissection
• Toluidine blue test	• Radiation therapy
• CT, MRI, PET scans	• Chemotherapy
	• Nutrition therapy

TABLE 41.6 Nursing Assessment
Oral Cancer

Subjective Data
Important Health Information
Past health history: Recurrent oral herpetic lesions, HPV infection or vaccination, syphilis, exposure to sunlight
Medications: Immunosuppressants
Surgery or other treatments: Removal of prior tumors or lesions

Functional Health Patterns
Health perception–health management: Alcohol and tobacco use, pipe smoking. Poor oral hygiene
Nutritional-metabolic: Reduced oral intake, weight loss, difficulty chewing food, increased salivation, intolerance to certain foods or temperatures of food
Cognitive-perceptual: Mouth or tongue soreness or pain, toothache, earache, neck stiffness, dysphagia, difficulty speaking

Objective Data
Integumentary
Indurated, painless ulcer on lip. Painless neck mass

Gastrointestinal
Areas of thickening or roughness, ulcers, leukoplakia, or erythroplakia on the tongue or oral mucosa. Limited tongue movement. Increased salivation, drooling. Slurred speech. Foul breath odor

Possible Diagnostic Findings
Positive exfoliative smear cytology (microscopic examination of cells removed by scraping), positive biopsy

◆ Nursing Implementation

You play a key role in the early detection and treatment of oral cancer. Identify patients at risk (Table 41.4) and provide information about predisposing factors. Review information about smoking cessation with the patient who smokes. Warn adolescents and teenagers about the danger of using snuff or chewing tobacco and electronic cigarettes. Smoking cessation is discussed in Chapter 10 and Tables 10.3 to 10.6.

Because early detection of oral cancer is important, teach the patient to report unexplained pain or soreness of the mouth, unusual bleeding, dysphagia, sore throat, voice changes, or swelling or lump in the neck. Refer any person with an ulcerative lesion that does not heal within 2 to 3 weeks to the HCP.

♥ PROMOTING POPULATION HEALTH

Health Impact of Good Oral Hygiene

- Improves quality of life
- Lowers risk for teeth loss
- Reduces pain and disability
- Aids in early detection of oral and craniofacial cancers
- Decreases cost of care needed from dental professionals
- Decreases risk for periodontal disease, gingivitis, and dental caries

Preoperative care for the patient who will have a radical neck dissection must consider the patient's physical and psychosocial needs. Physical preparation is the same as that for any major surgery, with special emphasis on oral hygiene. Explanations and emotional support should include information on postoperative communication and feeding. Explain the surgical procedure and ensure that the patient understands the information. See Chapter 26 and eNursing Care Plan 26.2 for more information about the nursing management of a patient undergoing a radical neck dissection.

◆ Evaluation

The expected outcomes are that the patient with oral cancer will

- Have no respiratory complications
- Be able to communicate
- Maintain an adequate nutritional intake to promote wound healing
- Have minimal pain and discomfort with eating, drinking, and talking

ESOPHAGEAL DISORDERS

GASTROESOPHAGEAL REFLUX DISEASE

Gastroesophageal reflux disease (GERD) is a chronic symptom of mucosal damage caused by reflux of stomach acid into the lower esophagus. GERD is not a disease but a syndrome. GERD is the most common upper GI problem. About 15 million Americans have GERD symptoms (heartburn or regurgitation) each day.[9]

Etiology and Pathophysiology

GERD has no one single cause (Fig. 41.2). GERD results when the reflux of acidic gastric contents into the esophagus overwhelms the esophageal defenses. Gastric HCl acid and pepsin secretions in refluxate cause esophageal irritation and

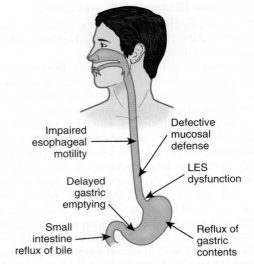

FIG. 41.2 Factors involved in the pathogenesis of GERD.

TABLE 41.7 **Factors Affecting Lower Esophageal Sphincter Pressure**	
Decrease Pressure	• Progesterone
• Alcohol	• Theophylline
• Chocolate (theobromine)	• Fatty foods
• Drugs	• Nicotine
• Anticholinergics	• Peppermint, spearmint
• β-Adrenergic blockers	• Tea, coffee (caffeine)
• Calcium channel blockers	
• Diazepam (Valium)	**Increase Pressure**
• Morphine sulfate	• Bethanechol (Urecholine)
• Nitrates	• Metoclopramide (Reglan)

inflammation *(esophagitis).* If it contains intestinal proteolytic enzymes (e.g., trypsin) and bile, this further irritates the esophageal mucosa. The degree of inflammation depends on the amount and composition of the gastric reflux and on the esophagus's mucosal defense mechanisms.

One of the primary factors causing GERD is an incompetent LES. Normally, the LES acts as an antireflux barrier. An incompetent LES lets gastric contents move from the stomach to the esophagus when the patient is supine or has an increase in intraabdominal pressure.

Decreased LES pressure can be due to certain foods and drugs (Table 41.7). Obesity is a risk factor. In an obese person the intraabdominal pressure is increased, which can worsen GERD. Cigarette and cigar smoking can contribute to GERD. Hiatal hernia, discussed in the next section, often causes GERD.

Clinical Manifestations

The symptoms of GERD vary from person to person. Persistent mild symptoms (i.e., more than twice a week) or moderate to severe symptoms once a week is considered GERD.

Heartburn *(pyrosis)* is the most common symptom. Heartburn is a burning, tight sensation felt intermittently beneath the lower sternum and spreading upward to the throat or jaw. It may occur after ingesting food or drugs that decrease the LES pressure or directly irritate the esophageal mucosa. An HCP should evaluate heartburn that occurs more than twice a

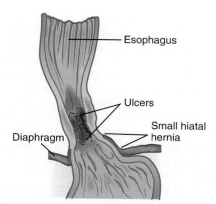

FIG. 41.3 Esophagitis with esophageal ulcerations.

TABLE 41.8 Interprofessional Care

GERD and Hiatal Hernia

Diagnostic Assessment
- History and physical examination
- Upper GI endoscopy with biopsy and cytologic analysis
- Esophagram (barium swallow)
- Motility (manometry) studies
- pH monitoring (laboratory or 24 hr ambulatory)
- Radionuclide studies

Management
Conservative
- Elevate head of bed on 4- to 6-in blocks
- Avoid reflux-inducing foods (fatty foods, chocolate, peppermint)
- Avoid alcohol
- Reduce or avoid acidic pH beverages (colas, red wine, orange juice)

Drug Therapy (Table 41.10)
- PPIs
- H_2 receptor blockers
- Antacids
- Prokinetic drug therapy

Surgical Therapy
- Nissen fundoplication
- Toupet fundoplication

Endoscopic Therapy
- Intraluminal valvuloplasty
- Radiofrequency ablation

---

week, is severe, is associated with dysphagia, or occurs at night and wakes a person from sleep. Older adults who report the recent onset of heartburn should receive medical evaluation.

GERD-related chest pain can mimic angina. It is described as burning; squeezing; or radiating to the back, neck, jaw, or arms. Chest pain is more common in older adults with GERD. Unlike angina, GERD-related chest pain is relieved with antacids.

Patients may have dyspepsia or regurgitation. *Dyspepsia* is pain or discomfort centered in the upper abdomen (mainly in or around the midline as opposed to the right or left hypochondrium). Regurgitation is often described as hot, bitter, or sour liquid coming into the throat or mouth.

A person with GERD may report respiratory symptoms, including wheezing, coughing, and dyspnea. Nighttime discomfort and coughing can awaken the person, resulting in disturbed sleep patterns. Otolaryngologic symptoms include hoarseness, sore throat, a *globus sensation* (sense of a lump in the throat), hypersalivation, and choking.

Complications

Complications of GERD are due to the direct local effects of gastric acid on the esophageal mucosa. Esophagitis (inflammation of the esophagus) is a common complication of GERD. Esophagitis with esophageal ulcerations is shown in Fig. 41.3. Repeated esophagitis may lead to scar tissue formation, stricture, and dysphagia.

Another complication of chronic GERD is Barrett's esophagus (BE) (esophageal metaplasia). *Metaplasia* is the reversible change from one type of cell to another type because of an abnormal stimulus. In BE, the flat epithelial cells in the distal esophagus change into columnar epithelial cells. These cell changes are primarily due to GERD. However, some people with no history of GERD develop BE.

About 5% to 20% of people with chronic GERD have BE.[10] Other risk factors include being over age 60, being male, being white, and having central obesity. BE is a precancerous lesion that increases the patient's risk for esophageal cancer. Because of this risk, those with BE undergo surveillance endoscopy or radiofrequency ablation as recommended.

Respiratory complications of GERD include cough, bronchospasm, laryngospasm, and cricopharyngeal spasm. These complications are due to gastric secretions irritating the upper air*way. Asthma, chronic bronchitis, and pneumonia may develop from aspiration into the respiratory system. Dental erosion, especially in the posterior teeth, may result from acid reflux into the mouth.

Diagnostic Studies

GERD is often diagnosed based on symptoms and the patient's response to behavioral and drug therapies. Diagnostic tests are done when usual therapy is ineffective or when complications are suspected. Diagnostic studies done to determine the cause of the GERD are shown in Table 41.8.

Endoscopy is useful in assessing the LES competence and the degree of inflammation (if present), potential scarring, and strictures. Biopsy and cytologic specimens can distinguish stomach or esophageal cancer from BE. In addition, the degree of dysplasia (low grade versus high grade) is determined. Manometric studies measure pressure in the esophagus and LES and esophageal motility function. Ambulatory esophageal pH monitoring is an option for those with refractory symptoms and no evidence of mucosal inflammation. Radionuclide tests can detect reflux of gastric contents and the rate of esophageal clearance.

❖ NURSING AND INTERPROFESSIONAL MANAGEMENT: GERD

Most patients with GERD can successfully manage the condition through lifestyle modifications, drug therapy, and nutrition therapy. These approaches require patient teaching and adherence to therapies. When these therapies are ineffective, surgery is an option (Table 41.8).

◆ Lifestyle Modifications

Teach the patient with GERD to avoid factors that trigger symptoms. The head of the bed is elevated 30 degrees. This can be done using pillows or with 4- to 6-in blocks under the bed. The patient should not be supine for 2 to 3 hours after a meal. A patient and caregiver teaching guide is shown in Table 41.9.

Encourage patients who smoke to stop. If needed, refer the patient to community resources for help in stopping smoking. See Chapter 10 for more information related to smoking

TABLE 41.9 Patient & Caregiver Teaching

GERD

Include the following instructions when teaching the patient and caregiver about managing GERD:

1. Explain the reason for a low-fat diet.
2. Have the patient to eat small, frequent meals to prevent gastric distention.
3. Explain the reason for avoiding alcohol, smoking (causes an almost immediate, marked decrease in lower esophageal sphincter pressure), and beverages that contain caffeine.
4. Tell the patient to not lie down for 2–3 hr after eating, wear tight clothing around the waist, or bend over (especially after eating).
5. Have the patient avoid eating within 3 hr of bedtime.
6. Have the patient to sleep with head of bed elevated on 4- to 6-in blocks (gravity fosters esophageal emptying).
7. Provide information about drugs, including reason for their use and common side effects.
8. Discuss strategies for weight reduction if appropriate.
9. Encourage patient and caregiver to share concerns about lifestyle changes and living with a chronic problem.

cessation. If stress causes symptoms, discuss measures to cope with stress. (See Chapter 6 for stress management techniques.)

◆ Drug Therapy

Drug therapy for GERD focuses on decreasing the volume and acidity of reflux, improving LES function, increasing esophageal clearance, and protecting the esophageal mucosa (Table 41.10). Proton pump inhibitors (PPIs) and histamine (H_2) receptor blockers are the most common and effective treatments for symptomatic GERD.[11] The goal of HCl acid suppression treatment is to reduce the acidity of the gastric refluxate. Patients who are symptomatic with GERD but do not have esophagitis (*nonerosive GERD*) achieve symptom relief with PPIs and H_2 receptor blockers.

Both PPIs and H_2 receptor blockers are available in prescription or OTC preparations. Teach the patient about side effects. Tell the patient to take medications as prescribed and not to stop without checking with the HCP. Have patients contact the HCP if symptoms persist.

PPIs are more effective in healing esophagitis than H_2 receptor blockers. PPIs also decrease the incidence of esophageal strictures, a complication of chronic GERD. Therapy should start with once-daily dosing, taken before the first meal of the day. Long-term use of PPIs may be associated with decreased bone density, kidney disease, vitamin B_{12} and magnesium deficiency, and increased risk for dementia.[12]

DRUG ALERT Proton Pump Inhibitors (PPIs)

- Long-term use or high doses may increase the risk for fractures of hip, wrist, and spine.
- Patients should take the lowest dose for the shortest duration needed to treat their condition.
- Use may increase the risk for *C. difficile* infection in hospitalized patients.[12]

H_2 receptor blockers reduce symptoms and promote esophageal healing in 50% of patients. The onset of action of H_2 receptor blockers is 1 hour. Depending on the specific drug, therapeutic effects last up to 12 hours. We can give famotidine, ranitidine, and cimetidine orally or IV. Nizatidine is only available orally. Some preparations combine an H_2 receptor blocker with an antacid. For example, Pepcid Complete includes famotidine, calcium carbonate, and magnesium hydroxide.

Adjunctive treatments include antacids and prokinetic drugs. Antacids produce quick, short-lived relief of heartburn. Common antacids consist of magnesium hydroxide or aluminum hydroxide as single preparations or in various combinations (Table 41.10). The neutralizing effects of antacids taken on an empty stomach last only 20 to 30 minutes. They are most effective taken 1 to 3 hours after meals and at bedtime. When taken after meals, their effects may last 3 to 4 hours.

Antacids with or without alginic acid (e.g., Gaviscon) may be useful in patients with mild, intermittent heartburn. In patients with moderate to severe or frequent symptoms or patients with esophagitis, antacids are not effective in relieving symptoms or healing lesions. After an acute phase of bleeding, antacids may be given hourly, either orally or through the NG tube. If an NG tube is in place, periodically aspirate the stomach contents and test the pH level. If pH is less than 5, intermittent suction may be used, or the frequency or dosage of the antacid or antisecretory agent increased.

The type and dosage of antacid given depend on side effects and potential drug interactions. Antacids high in sodium are used cautiously in older adults and patients with CVD, liver, and renal disease. Patients with renal failure should not take magnesium preparations because of the risk for magnesium toxicity. An antacid combination of aluminum and magnesium decreases the side effects of both.

Antacids can interact unfavorably with many drugs. They enhance the effects of some drugs, like benzodiazepines and pseudoephedrine. In many instances, antacids decrease the absorption rates of other drugs, such as thyroid hormones, phenytoin, and tetracycline. Before antacid therapy begins, inform the HCP of any drugs that a patient is taking.

Prokinetics increase LES pressure and improve gastric emptying, which may result in a small improvement in regurgitation and vomiting. Common agents include cisapride, metoclopramide (Reglan), bethanechol, and baclofen. However, many have significant side effects, so their use is limited only to those with known delayed gastric emptying.[13]

◆ Nutritional Therapy

No specific diet is used to treat GERD. Some patients may need to avoid foods that decrease LES pressure, such as chocolate, peppermint, fatty foods, coffee, and tea (Table 41.7), which predispose them to reflux. Certain foods (e.g., tomato-based products, orange juice, cola, red wine) may irritate the esophagus.

Tell the patient to avoid late evening meals, nighttime snacking, and milk, especially at bedtime, since it increases gastric acid secretion. Small, frequent meals and drinking fluids between meals help prevent overdistention of the stomach. Increased saliva production by chewing gum and oral lozenges may help with mild symptoms. Recommend weight reduction if the patient is overweight.

◆ Surgical Therapy

Surgical therapy (*antireflux* surgery) is reserved for patients with complications, such as esophagitis, medication intolerance, stricture, BE, and persistent severe symptoms. The goal of surgical therapy is to reduce reflux by enhancing the integrity of the LES. Most surgical procedures are done laparoscopically. The fundus of the stomach is wrapped around the lower part of the esophagus to reinforce and repair the defective barrier. Nissen and Toupet fundoplications are common laparoscopic antireflux surgeries.

TABLE 41.10 Drug Therapy

GERD and Peptic Ulcer Disease (PUD)

Drug	Mechanism of Action	Side Effects
Proton Pump Inhibitors (PPIs) dexlansoprazole (Dexilant) esomeprazole (Nexium) lansoprazole (Prevacid) omeprazole (Prilosec) omeprazole and sodium bicarbonate (Zegerid) pantoprazole (Protonix) rabeprazole (Aciphex)	↓ HCl acid secretion by inhibiting the proton pump (H^+-K^+-ATPase) responsible for the secretion of H^+ ↓ Irritation of the esophageal and gastric mucosa	Headache, abdominal pain, nausea, diarrhea, vomiting, flatulence
Histamine (H_2) Receptor Blockers cimetidine famotidine (Pepcid) nizatidine (Axid) ranitidine (Zantac)	Block the action of histamine on the H_2 receptors to ↓ HCl acid secretion ↓ Conversion of pepsinogen to pepsin ↓ Irritation of the esophageal and gastric mucosa	Headache, abdominal pain, constipation, diarrhea
Antacids, Acid Neutralizers *Single Substance* aluminum hydroxide (Amphojel) calcium carbonate (Tums) sodium bicarbonate (Alka-Seltzer) sodium citrate (Bicitra) *Aluminum and Magnesium* Gelusil, Maalox, Mylanta aluminum/magnesium trisilicate (Gaviscon)	Neutralize HCl acid Taken 1–3 hr after meals and at bedtime	*Aluminum hydroxide:* Constipation, phosphorus depletion with chronic use *Calcium carbonate:* Constipation or diarrhea, hypercalcemia, milk-alkali syndrome, renal calculi *Magnesium preparations:* Diarrhea, hypermagnesemia *Sodium preparations:* Milk-alkali syndrome if used with large amounts of calcium. Use with caution in patients on sodium restrictions
Cholinergic bethanechol (Urecholine)	↑ Lower esophageal sphincter pressure, improve esophageal emptying, increase gastric emptying	Lightheadedness, syncope, flushing, diarrhea, stomach cramps, dizziness
Cytoprotective sucralfate (Carafate)	Act to form a protective layer and serve as a barrier against acid, bile salts, and enzymes in the stomach	Constipation
Prokinetic metoclopramide (Reglan)	Block effect of dopamine ↑ Gastric motility and emptying Reduce reflux	CNS side effects ranging from anxiety to hallucinations Extrapyramidal side effects (tremor and dyskinesias similar to Parkinson's disease)
Prostaglandin (Synthetic) misoprostol (Cytotec)	Protect lining of stomach *Cytoprotective:* Increase production of gastric mucus and mucosal secretion of bicarbonate *Antisecretory:* ↓ HCl acid secretion	Abdominal pain, diarrhea, GI bleeding, uterine rupture if pregnant

Laparoscopic fundoplication is often an outpatient procedure. However, patients at risk for complications, including those with prior upper abdominal surgeries or co-morbidities (e.g., cardiac disease, obesity), may be hospitalized after the procedure. A small number of patients have complications, including gastric or esophageal injury, splenic injury, pneumothorax, perforation, bleeding, infection, and pneumonia.

After surgery, reflux symptoms should decrease. However, recurrence is possible. In the first month after surgery, the patient may report mild dysphagia caused by edema, but it should resolve. Teach the patient to report persistent symptoms, such as heartburn and regurgitation.

A LINX Reflux Management System is an option for patients who have symptoms despite maximum medical management. A LINX system is a ring of small, flexible magnets enclosed in titanium beads and connected by titanium wires. Once implanted laparoscopically into the LES, the ring strengthens the weak LES. Under resting (nonswallowing) conditions, the magnetic attraction between the beads helps keep a weak LES closed to prevent reflux. When the person swallows, the force of pressure associated with the movement of fluids or foods overwhelms the magnetic forces and the fluid or food passes to the stomach. Adverse events with the system include difficulty swallowing, nausea, and pain when swallowing food. Tell patients who have a LINX system not to have an MRI as it could cause serious harm.

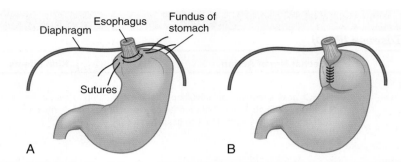

FIG. 41.4 Nissen fundoplication. **A,** Fundus of stomach is wrapped around distal esophagus. **B,** The fundus is then sutured to itself. (Modified from Doughty DB, Jackson DB: *Mosby's clinical nursing series: Gastrointestinal disorders,* St Louis, 1993, Mosby.)

◆ Endoscopic Therapy

Alternatives to surgical therapy include endoscopic mucosal resection (EMR) and radiofrequency ablation. The heat energy delivered through radiofrequencies creates lesions, which we think thicken the LES. For patients with high-grade dysplasia, EMR can be used as a diagnostic test to obtain biopsy samples. Biopsy results determine whether cancer is present.

HIATAL HERNIA

Hiatal hernia is herniation of part of the stomach into the esophagus through an opening, or hiatus, in the diaphragm. We also call it a *diaphragmatic hernia* or *esophageal hernia*. Hiatal hernias are the most common abnormality found on x-ray examination of the upper GI tract. They are common in older adults and occur more often in women.

There are 2 types of hiatal hernias (Fig. 41.4):
1. *Sliding:* The junction of the stomach and esophagus is above the diaphragm, and a part of the stomach slides through the hiatal opening in the diaphragm. This occurs when the patient is supine. The hernia usually goes back into the abdominal cavity when the patient is standing upright. This is the most common type.
2. *Paraesophageal* or *rolling:* The fundus and greater curvature of the stomach roll up through the diaphragm, forming a pocket alongside the esophagus. The esophagogastric junction stays in the normal position. Acute paraesophageal hernia is a medical emergency.

Etiology and Pathophysiology

Many factors contribute to the development of a hiatal hernia. Structural changes (weakening of the muscles in the diaphragm around the esophagogastric opening) occur with aging. Factors that increase intraabdominal pressure may predispose patients to developing a hiatal hernia. These include obesity, pregnancy, ascites, tumors, intense physical exertion, and heavy lifting on a continual basis.

Clinical Manifestations and Complications

Some people with hiatal hernia are asymptomatic. When present, manifestations of hiatal hernia are similar to those described for GERD on pp. 896-897.

Complications that may occur with hiatal hernia include GERD, esophagitis, hemorrhage from erosion, stenosis (narrowing of the esophagus), ulcerations of the herniated part of the stomach, strangulation of the hernia, and regurgitation with tracheal aspiration.

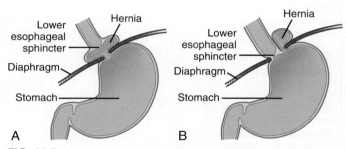

FIG. 41.5 **A,** Sliding hiatal hernia. **B,** Rolling or paraesophageal hernia.

Diagnostic Studies

An esophagram (barium swallow) may show the protrusion of gastric mucosa through the esophageal hiatus. Endoscopic visualization of the lower esophagus gives information on the degree of mucosal inflammation or other abnormalities. Other tests done are the same as those for GERD (Table 41.8).

NURSING AND INTERPROFESSIONAL MANAGEMENT: HIATAL HERNIA

Conservative therapy of hiatal hernia is similar to that described for GERD (pp. 897-898). Teach the patient to reduce intraabdominal pressure by eliminating constricting garments and avoiding lifting and straining.

Surgical approaches to hiatal hernias can include reduction of the herniated stomach into the abdomen, *herniotomy* (excision of the hernia sac), *herniorrhaphy* (closure of the hiatal defect), fundoplication, and *gastropexy* (attachment of the stomach below the diaphragm to prevent reherniation). The goals are to reduce the hernia, provide an acceptable LES pressure, and prevent movement of the gastroesophageal junction.

Surgery to repair hiatal hernia is often done laparoscopically by either Nissen or Toupet techniques (Fig. 41.5). The approach used (thoracic or abdominal) depends on the patient.

👤 Gerontologic Considerations: GERD and Hiatal Hernia

The incidence of hiatal hernia and GERD increases with age. Hiatal hernia is associated with weakening of the diaphragm, obesity, kyphosis, or other factors (e.g., wearing girdles) that increase intraabdominal pressure. Older patients may take drugs known to decrease LES pressure (e.g., nitrates, calcium channel blockers, antidepressants). Other agents, such as nonsteroidal antiinflammatory drugs (NSAIDs) and potassium, can irritate the esophageal mucosa, causing *medication-induced esophagitis.*

Some older adults with hiatal hernia and GERD are asymptomatic or have less severe symptoms. The first sign may be a serious problem, such as esophageal bleeding from esophagitis or respiratory complications (e.g., aspiration pneumonia) due to aspiration of gastric contents.

The clinical course and management of GERD and hiatal hernia in the older adult are similar to those for the younger adult. Changes in lifestyle, including smoking cessation and elevating the head of the bed on blocks may be challenging for the older adult.

Laparoscopic procedures reduce the risk associated with surgical repair. An older patient with heart and lung problems may not be a good candidate for surgical intervention.

ESOPHAGEAL CANCER

Esophageal cancer is not common. However, the rates are increasing. In the United States, around 17,280 new cases are diagnosed and 15,850 deaths occur from esophageal cancer each year.[5] The overall 5-year survival rate is 19%.

Most esophageal cancers are adenocarcinomas. The others are squamous cell tumors. Adenocarcinomas arise from the glands lining the esophagus and resemble cancers of the stomach and small intestine. The incidence of esophageal cancer increases with age. Those between 65 and 75 are at greatest risk. The incidence is higher in men than in women.

Etiology and Pathophysiology

The cause of esophageal cancer is unknown. Key risk factors include BE, smoking, excess alcohol use, and obesity. For example, current smoking or a history of smoking is associated with a twofold higher risk for esophageal cancer. Those with injury to the esophageal mucosa (e.g., from occupational exposure to asbestos and cement dust) are at greater risk. *Achalasia*, a condition marked by delayed emptying of the lower esophagus, is associated with squamous cell cancer.

Most esophageal tumors occur in the middle and lower portions of the esophagus. The tumor usually appears as an ulcerated lesion. It may penetrate the muscular layer and extend outside the wall of the esophagus. Many patients have advanced disease at the time of diagnosis. The cancer spreads via the lymph system, with the liver and lung being common sites of metastasis.

Clinical Manifestations and Complications

By the time the patient has symptoms, the tumor is often advanced. Progressive dysphagia is the most common symptom. It may be described as a substernal feeling that food is not passing. Initially the dysphagia occurs only with meat, then with soft foods, and eventually with liquids.

Pain develops late. It occurs in the substernal, epigastric, or back areas and usually increases with swallowing. The pain may radiate to the neck, jaw, ears, and shoulders. If the tumor is in the upper third of the esophagus, symptoms, such as sore throat, choking, and hoarseness, may occur. Most patients lose weight. When esophageal stenosis (narrowing) is severe, regurgitation of blood-flecked esophageal contents is common.

Hemorrhage occurs if the cancer erodes through the esophagus and into the aorta. Esophageal perforation with fistula formation into the lung or trachea sometimes develops. The tumor may enlarge enough to cause esophageal obstruction, particularly in the later stages.

TABLE 41.11 Interprofessional Care
Esophageal Cancer

Diagnostic Assessment	Management

• History and physical examination
• Endoscopy of esophagus with biopsy
• Endoscopic ultrasonography
• Esophagram (barium swallow)
• Bronchoscopy
• CT, MRI, PET scans
	• Surgical therapy
	  • Esophagectomy
	  • Esophagoenterostomy
	  • Esophagogastrostomy
	• Endoscopic therapy
	  • Dilation
	  • Endoscopic mucosal resection
	  • Laser therapy
	  • Photodynamic therapy
	  • Radiofrequency ablation
	  • Stent or prosthesis placement
	• Radiation therapy
	• Chemotherapy

Diagnostic Studies

Endoscopic biopsy is required to diagnose esophageal cancer. Endoscopic ultrasonography (EUS) is important in staging esophageal cancer. Esophagram (barium swallow) may show narrowing of the esophagus at the tumor site (Table 41.11).

Interprofessional Management

The treatment of esophageal cancer depends on the tumor's location and whether invasion or metastasis is present. Esophageal cancer usually has a poor prognosis because it is often diagnosed at an advanced stage. The best results occur with a multimodal approach, including surgery, endoscopic ablation, chemotherapy, and radiation therapy. Depending on the location and cancer spread, only chemotherapy and radiation may be used. Palliative therapy consists of restoring swallowing function and maintaining nutrition and hydration.

Surgical Therapy. The types of surgical procedures done are (1) removal of part or all of the esophagus *(esophagectomy)* with use of a Dacron graft to replace the resected part, (2) resection of a portion of the esophagus and anastomosis of the remaining portion to the stomach *(esophagogastrostomy),* and (3) resection of a portion of the esophagus and anastomosis of a segment of colon to the remaining portion *(esophagoenterostomy).* The surgical approaches may be open (thoracic, abdominal incision) or laparoscopic.

Minimally invasive esophagectomy (e.g., laparoscopic vagal nerve–sparing surgery) is being done more often. It has the advantage of using smaller incisions, decreasing intensive care unit (ICU) and hospital stays, and producing fewer pulmonary complications.

Endoscopic Therapy. Endoscopic therapy includes photodynamic therapy, EMR, and radiofrequency ablation. In photodynamic therapy, the patient receives an IV injection of porfimer sodium (Photofrin), a photosensitizer. Although most tissues absorb porfimer, cancer tissue absorbs it to a greater degree. The HCP directs light towards the cancerous area using a fiber passed through an endoscope. The light reacts with porfimer, starting a reaction that destroys the cancer cells. Patients must avoid direct sunlight for up to 6 weeks after the procedure.

EMR is an option for some small, very early stage cancers. It involves the removal of cancer tissue using an endoscope. Radiofrequency ablation uses electric currents to kill cancer cells by heating them.

Dilation, stent placement, or both can relieve obstruction. Dilation increases the lumen of the esophagus. It often relieves dysphagia and allows for improved nutrition. There are various types of dilators. Placement of stents or expandable stents may help when dilation is no longer effective. Stents allow food and liquid to pass through the stenotic area of the esophagus. Self-expandable metal stents are available with features to prevent stent migration and tumor ingrowth. Stents placed before surgery may help improve the patient's nutritional status.

Endoscopic laser therapy may be used in combination with dilation. Laser therapy can be repeated if obstruction recurs as the tumor grows. Sometimes these procedures are combined with radiation therapy.

Radiation Therapy. Depending on the type and stage of esophageal cancer, the patient may receive chemotherapy with or without radiation therapy. Concurrent therapy is given for palliation of symptoms, especially dysphagia, and to increase survival. Some patients receive radiation therapy before surgery.

Chemotherapy. Many different chemotherapy drugs can be used to treat esophageal cancer. The preferred regimens are carboplatin and paclitaxel, cisplatin with capecitabine (Xeloda), cisplatin and fluorouracil, and oxaliplatin with either fluorouracil or capecitabine. DCF (docetaxel, cisplatin, fluorouracil) is an option for metastatic disease. Other treatments include ECF (epirubicin [Ellence], cisplatin, fluorouracil) and irinotecan (Camptosar).[14] Chemotherapy is discussed in Chapter 15.

Targeted Therapy. Some esophageal cancers have too much HER-2 protein on their cell surfaces, which helps cancer cells to grow. Trastuzumab (Herceptin) is a drug that targets the HER-2 protein and kills the cancer cells. This drug can cause heart damage, so it is not given with other chemotherapy drugs that also cause heart damage, such as epirubicin.[14]

Ramucirumab (Cyramza), an angiogenesis inhibitor, binds to the receptor for *vascular endothelial growth factor* (VEGF), a compound that stimulates blood vessel growth. Thus it prevents VEGF from binding to the receptor and signaling the body to make more blood vessels. This can help slow or stop the growth and spread of cancer. Ramucirumab treats advanced cancers that start at the gastroesophageal junction. Targeted therapies are discussed in Chapter 15.

Nutritional Therapy. After esophageal surgery IV fluids are given. A jejunostomy, gastrostomy, or esophagostomy feeding tube may be placed to feed the patient depending on the type of surgery (e.g., esophagogastrectomy). A swallowing study is often done before allowing the patient to have oral fluids. When starting fluids, give water (30 to 60 mL) hourly and gradually progress to small, frequent, bland meals. Place the patient in an upright position for 2 hours after to prevent regurgitation. With EN, observe the patient for signs of intolerance to the feeding or leakage of the feeding into the mediastinum. Symptoms that indicate leakage are pain, increased temperature, and dyspnea. (EN is discussed in Chapter 39.)

❖ NURSING MANAGEMENT: ESOPHAGEAL CANCER

◆ Nursing Assessment

Ask the patient about a history of GERD, hiatal hernia, achalasia, BE, and tobacco and alcohol use. Assess the patient for progressive dysphagia and *odynophagia* (burning, squeezing pain while swallowing). Ask about the type of substances (e.g., meats, soft foods, liquids) that cause dysphagia. Assess the patient for pain (substernal, epigastric, or back areas), choking, heartburn, hoarseness, cough, anorexia, weight loss, and regurgitation.

◆ Nursing Diagnoses

Nursing diagnoses for the patient with esophageal cancer include:
- Chronic pain
- Impaired nutritional intake
- Impaired nutritional status
- Risk for aspiration
- Anxiety

◆ Planning

The overall goals are that the patient with esophageal cancer will (1) have relief of symptoms, including pain and dysphagia; (2) achieve optimal nutritional intake; and (3) have a quality of life appropriate to stage of disease and prognosis.

◆ Nursing Implementation

◆ Health Promotion. Counsel the patient with GERD, BE, or hiatal hernia about the importance of regular follow-up evaluation. Health counseling should focus on smoking cessation and reducing risk factors for GERD (Table 41.7). Maintaining good oral hygiene and dietary habits (e.g., intake of fresh fruits and vegetables) is important. Encourage patients to seek medical attention for any esophageal problems, especially dysphagia.

◆ Acute Care

Preoperative Care. The patient and caregiver usually react with shock, disbelief, and depression when given the diagnosis of esophageal cancer. Provide emotional and physical support, provide information, clarify test results, and maintain a positive attitude with respect to the patient's immediate recovery and long-term survival.

In addition to general preoperative teaching and preparation, pay attention to the patient's nutritional needs. Many are poorly nourished because of the inability to ingest adequate amounts of food and fluids. A high-calorie, high-protein diet is recommended. Some patients need a liquid form of this diet. Others may need IV fluid replacement or parenteral nutrition (PN). Teach the patient and caregiver how to keep an intake and output record and assess for signs of fluid and electrolyte imbalance. Some treatment protocols include preoperative radiation and chemotherapy.

Meticulous oral care is essential. Cleanse the mouth thoroughly, including the tongue, gingivae, and teeth or dentures. It may be necessary to use swabs or a gauze pad and to scrub the mouth, including the tongue. Milk of Magnesia with mineral oil helps remove crust formation.

Teaching should include information about chest tubes (with a planned open thoracic approach), IV lines, NG tubes, pain management, gastrostomy or jejunostomy feeding, turning, coughing, and deep breathing. (General preoperative care is discussed in Chapter 17.)

Postoperative Care. During the immediate postoperative period, the patient usually receives care in the ICU for 1 to 2 days. In addition to usual postoperative complications, dysrhythmias may result from the proximity of the pericardium to the surgical site. Other complications include anastomotic leaks, fistula formation, interstitial pulmonary edema, and acute respiratory distress related to the disruption of the mediastinal lymph nodes.

The patient usually has an NG tube in place for 5 to 7 days. The drainage may be bloody for 8 to 12 hours. The drainage gradually changes to greenish yellow. Assessing the drainage, maintaining the tube, and providing oral and nasal care are key nursing responsibilities. Do not irrigate the NG tube, reposition it, or reinsert it without consulting the HCP.

If the chest cavity is entered, postoperative drainage is achieved with chest tube insertion. Assess the amount and type of drainage. Notify the HCP of excess drainage (e.g., over 400 to 600 mL in 8 hours). Chest surgery and drainage tubes are discussed in Chapter 27.

Because of the location of the surgery and the patient' general condition, implement measures to prevent respiratory complications. Have the patient turn, cough and deep breathe, and use an incentive spirometer every 2 hours. Follow VTE prophylaxis measures and provide effective pain management. Position the patient in a semi-Fowler's or Fowler's position to prevent reflux and aspiration of gastric secretions. When the patient can drink fluids or eat, maintain the upright position for at least 2 hours after eating to assist with gastric emptying.

◆ **Ambulatory Care.** Many patients need long-term follow-up care after surgery for esophageal cancer. The patient may need chemotherapy and radiation treatment after surgery. Encourage and assist the patient in maintaining adequate nutrition. A permanent feeding gastrostomy may be needed. The patient usually is afraid and anxious about the cancer diagnosis. Know what the HCP has told the patient about the prognosis and provide appropriate counseling.

Referral to a palliative care or home health nurse may be needed. (See Chapter 15 for the care of the cancer patient and Chapter 9 for a discussion of palliative and end-of-life care.)

◆ Evaluation

The expected outcomes are that the patient with esophageal cancer will

- Maintain a patent airway
- Have relief of pain
- Be able to swallow comfortably and consume adequate nutritional intake
- Have a quality of life appropriate to stage of disease and prognosis

OTHER ESOPHAGEAL DISORDERS

Eosinophilic Esophagitis

Eosinophilic esophagitis (EoE) is characterized by swelling of the esophagus from an infiltration of *eosinophils*. People with EoE often have a personal or family history of other allergic diseases. The most common food triggers are milk, egg, wheat, rye, and beef. Environmental allergens, such as pollens, molds, cat, dog, and dust mite allergens, may be involved in the development of EoE.

Patients may have severe heartburn, difficulty swallowing, food impaction in the esophagus, nausea, vomiting, and weight loss. The diagnosis is based on symptoms and biopsy findings of eosinophils infiltrating esophageal tissue obtained from endoscopy.

Allergy skin testing helps to determine the person's allergens. A trial of avoiding the foods to which the person has positive allergy tests is the first treatment. Other common treatments include the use of PPIs (Table 41.10) and corticosteroids. Corticosteroids are used to treat EoE when avoiding allergic triggers does not relieve symptoms.

Corticosteroids may be used orally (prednisone) or as a topical therapy with inhaled corticosteroids (e.g., fluticasone

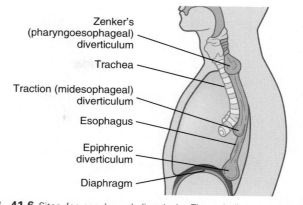

FIG. 41.6 Sites for esophageal diverticula. These hollow outpouchings may occur just above the upper esophageal sphincter (Zenker's), near the midpoint of the esophagus (traction), and just above the lower esophageal sphincter (epiphrenic). (Modified from Price SA, Wilson LM: *Pathophysiology: Clinical concepts of disease processes*, ed 6, St Louis, 2003, Mosby.)

[Flovent]). The patient takes a puff of fluticasone, and rather than inhaling it, swallows the medication. This directly delivers the drug to the esophagus. The most common side effect is a yeast infection of the throat (esophageal candidiasis).

Esophageal Diverticula

Esophageal diverticula are saclike outpouchings of 1 or more layers of the esophagus. They occur in 3 main areas: (1) above the upper esophageal sphincter *(Zenker's diverticulum)*, which is the most common location; (2) near the esophageal midpoint (traction diverticulum); and (3) above the LES (epiphrenic diverticulum) (Fig. 41.6). Zenker's diverticula occur commonly in people older than 60 years.

Typical symptoms include dysphagia, regurgitation, chronic cough, aspiration, and weight loss. Food becomes trapped in the outpouches. This causes tasting sour food and smelling a foul odor. Complications include malnutrition, aspiration, and perforation. Endoscopy or barium studies can easily establish a diagnosis.

There is no specific treatment. Some patients find that they can empty the pocket of food that collects by applying pressure at a certain point on the neck. The diet may have to be limited to foods that pass more readily (e.g., blenderized foods). Surgical treatment may be needed if nutrition is disrupted. Endoscopic stapling diverticulotomy or diverticulostomy is associated with decreased complications compared with the open approaches. The most serious surgical complication is esophageal perforation.

Esophageal Structures

The most common cause of *esophageal strictures* (or narrowing) is chronic GERD. The ingestion of strong acids or alkalis, external beam radiation, and surgical anastomosis can also create strictures. Trauma, such as throat lacerations and gunshot wounds, can lead to strictures because of scar formation. Strictures can cause dysphagia and regurgitation, leading to weight loss.

Strictures can be dilated using mechanical *bougies* (dilating instruments) or balloons. Dilation may be done with or without endoscopy, or with fluoroscopy. Surgical excision with anastomosis is sometimes needed. The patient may have a temporary or permanent gastrostomy.

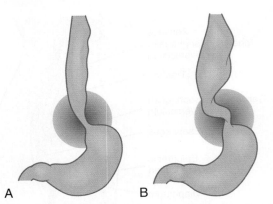

FIG. 41.7 Esophageal achalasia. **A,** Early stage, showing tapering of lower esophagus. **B,** Advanced stage, showing dilated, tortuous esophagus.

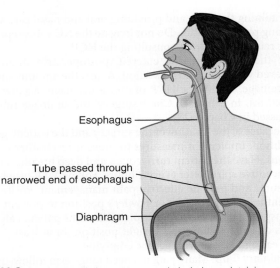

FIG. 41.8 Pneumatic dilation can treat achalasia by maintaining an adequate lumen and decreasing lower esophageal sphincter (LES) tone. (Modified from Price SA, Wilson LM: *Pathophysiology: Clinical concepts of disease processes,* ed 6, St Louis, 2003, Mosby.)

Achalasia

In achalasia, peristalsis of the lower two thirds (smooth muscle) of the esophagus is absent. Achalasia is a rare, chronic disorder. The exact cause is unknown. With achalasia, the pressure in the LES increases along with incomplete relaxation. Esophageal obstruction at or near the diaphragm occurs. Food and fluid accumulate in the lower esophagus. The result is dilation of the esophagus above the tapered affected segment of the lower esophagus (Fig. 41.7). There is a selective loss of inhibitory neurons, resulting in unopposed contraction of the LES.

The onset of achalasia is usually slow. Dysphagia is the most common symptom and occurs with both liquids and solids. Patients may report a globus sensation and/or substernal chest pain (similar to angina pain) during or right after a meal. About a third have nighttime regurgitation. *Halitosis* (foul-smelling breath) and the inability to eructate (belch) can occur. Patients may report symptoms of GERD and regurgitation of sour-tasting food and liquids, especially when they are lying down. Weight loss is common.

Diagnosis is made with esophagram (barium swallow), manometric evaluation (high-resolution manometry), and/or endoscopic evaluation. Treatment focuses on symptom management. The goals of treatment are to relieve dysphagia and regurgitation, improve esophageal emptying by disrupting the LES, and prevent the development of megaesophagus (enlargement of the lower esophagus).

Endoscopic pneumatic dilation involves dilating the LES muscle using balloons of progressively larger diameter (3.0, 3.5, and 4.0 cm) (Fig. 41.8). It is an outpatient procedure. If this is ineffective, the next option is a Heller myotomy, done laparoscopically. In this procedure, the HCP cuts through the muscles of the LES, allowing food to pass. Because GERD with esophagitis and stricture is a common complication, the patient often has anti-reflux surgery at the same time. The patient typically returns to usual activities 1 to 2 weeks afterward.

Medical therapy is less effective than invasive procedures. The injection of botulinum toxin endoscopically into the LES gives short-term relief of symptoms and improves esophageal emptying. It works by promoting relaxation of the smooth muscle. This treatment is used for older patients for whom surgery and pneumatic dilation may not be appropriate due to other chronic illnesses.

Nitrates (e.g., isosorbide dinitrate) and calcium channel blockers (e.g., nifedipine [Procardia]) relax the LES and may improve dysphagia. They are taken sublingually 10 to 30 minutes before meals. Side effects (e.g., headache), drug tolerance, and short duration of action limit their use. Symptomatic treatment consists of eating a semisoft diet, eating slowly, drinking fluid with meals, and sleeping with the head elevated.

Esophageal Varices

Esophageal varices are dilated, tortuous veins occurring in the lower part of the esophagus because of portal hypertension. Esophageal varices are a common complication of liver cirrhosis. They are discussed in Chapter 43.

DISORDERS OF THE STOMACH AND UPPER SMALL INTESTINE

PEPTIC ULCER DISEASE

Peptic ulcer disease (PUD) is a condition characterized by erosion of the GI mucosa from the digestive action of HCl acid and pepsin. Any part of the GI tract that is in contact with gastric secretions is susceptible to ulcer development. This includes the lower esophagus, stomach, duodenum, and margin of a gastrojejunal anastomosis after surgical procedures. PUD affects about 4.5 million people in the United States each year.[15]

Types

Peptic ulcers are classified as acute or chronic, depending on the degree and duration of mucosal involvement, and gastric or duodenal, according to the location. The *acute ulcer* (Fig. 41.9) is associated with superficial erosion and minimal inflammation. It is of short duration and resolves quickly when the cause is identified and removed. A chronic ulcer (Fig. 41.10) is one of long duration, eroding through the muscular wall with the formation of fibrous tissue. It is present continuously for many months or intermittently throughout the person's lifetime. Chronic ulcers are more common than acute erosions.

Although gastric and duodenal ulcers are both considered PUD, they are different in their incidence and presentation (Table 41.12).

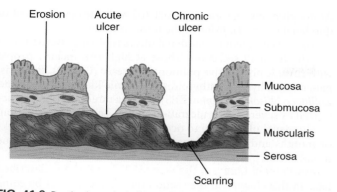

FIG. 41.9 Peptic ulcers, including an erosion, an acute ulcer, and a chronic ulcer. Both the acute ulcer and the chronic ulcer may penetrate the entire wall of the stomach. (Modified from Price SA, Wilson LM: *Pathophysiology: Clinical concepts of disease processes*, ed 6, St Louis, 2003, Mosby.)

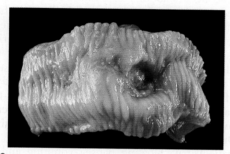

FIG. 41.10 Peptic ulcer of the duodenum. (From Kumar V, Abbas AK, Aster JC, Fausto N: *Robbins and Cotran pathologic basis of disease*, ed 8, Philadelphia, 2010, Saunders.)

Etiology and Pathophysiology

Peptic ulcers develop only in an acid environment. However, an excess of HCl acid is not necessary for ulcer development. Pepsinogen, the precursor of pepsin, changes to pepsin in the presence of HCl acid and a pH of 2 to 3. When food or antacids neutralize the stomach acid level or drugs block acid secretion, the pH increases to 3.5 or more. At a pH of 3.5 or more, pepsin has little or no proteolytic activity.

The pathophysiology of ulcer development is outlined in Fig. 41.11. The back diffusion of HCl acid into the gastric mucosa results in cellular destruction and inflammation. Histamine is released from the damaged mucosa. This results in vasodilation, increased capillary permeability, and further secretion of acid and pepsin. Fig. 41.12 shows the interrelationship between the mucosal blood flow and disruption of the gastric mucosal barrier. Several factors damage the mucosal barrier.

Helicobacter Pylori. The major risk factor for PUD is infection with *Helicobacter pylori*. 80% of gastric and 90% of duodenal ulcers are related to *H. pylori*. In the United States, *H. pylori* affects 20% of persons younger than 30 years and 50% of those older than 60 years. Infection likely occurs during childhood with transmission from family members to the child, possibly through a fecal-oral or oral-oral route. The rate is highest in black and Hispanic people.[15] Although most people with *H. pylori* never develop ulcers, it appears that those infected with *CagA*-positive strains are more likely to have PUD.[16]

In the stomach, the bacteria can survive a long time by colonizing the gastric epithelial cells within the mucosal layer. The bacteria make urease, which metabolizes urea-producing

TABLE 41.12 Comparison of Gastric and Duodenal Ulcers

Gastric Ulcers	Duodenal Ulcers
Lesion	
Superficial, smooth margins. Round, oval, or cone shaped	Penetrating (associated with deformity of duodenal bulb from healing of recurrent ulcers)
Location of Lesion	
Predominantly antrum, also in body and fundus of stomach	First 1–2 cm of duodenum
Gastric Secretion	
Normal to decreased	Increased
Incidence	
Greater in women	Greater in men, but increasing in women (especially postmenopausal)
Peak age 50–60 yr	Peak age 35–45 yr
Increased cancer risk	No increase in cancer risk
H. pylori infection in 80%	*H. pylori* infection in 90%
↑ With incompetent pyloric sphincter and bile reflux	Associated with other diseases (e.g., COPD, pancreatic disease, hyperparathyroidism, ZES, chronic renal failure)
Clinical Manifestations	
Burning or gaseous pressure in epigastrium	Burning, cramping, pressure-like pain across midepigastrium and upper abdomen. Back pain with posterior ulcers
Pain 1–2 hr after meals. If penetrating ulcer, aggravation of discomfort with food	Pain 2–5 hr after meals and midmorning, midafternoon, middle of night. Periodic and episodic. Pain relief with antacids and food
Recurrence Rate	
High	High

ammonium chloride and other damaging chemicals. Urease activates the immune response with both antibody production and the release of inflammatory cytokines. This leads to increased gastric secretion and causes tissue damage, leading to PUD.

Medication-Induced Injury. NSAID use is responsible for most non–*H. pylori* peptic ulcers. NSAIDs inhibit prostaglandin synthesis, increase gastric acid secretion, and reduce the integrity of the mucosal barrier. NSAID use in the presence of *H. pylori* further increases the risk for PUD. Patients taking corticosteroids or anticoagulants with NSAIDs have a higher risk for PUD.[15] Corticosteroids affect mucosal cell renewal and decrease its protective effects.

Lifestyle Factors. High alcohol intake is associated with acute mucosal lesions. Alcohol and smoking stimulate acid secretion. Coffee (caffeinated and decaffeinated) is a strong stimulant of gastric acid secretion. Smoking and psychologic distress, including stress and depression, can delay the healing of ulcers once they have developed.

Gastric Ulcers. Gastric ulcers can occur in any part of the stomach. They most often occur in the antrum. Gastric ulcers are less common than duodenal ulcers. Gastric ulcers are more prevalent in women and those over 50 years of age. Because of the peak incidence of gastric ulcers in older adults, the mortality rate from

PATHOPHYSIOLOGY MAP

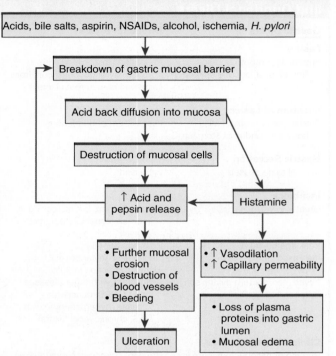

FIG. 41.11 Disruption of gastric mucosa and pathophysiologic consequences of back diffusion of acids.

PATHOPHYSIOLOGY MAP

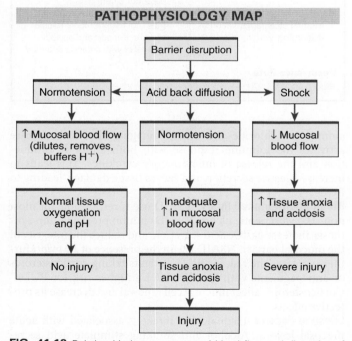

FIG. 41.12 Relationship between mucosal blood flow and disruption of the gastric mucosal barrier.

gastric ulcers is greater than that from duodenal ulcers. Gastric ulcers are more likely than duodenal ulcers to cause an obstruction. *H. pylori*, NSAIDs, and bile reflux are the main risk factors.

Duodenal Ulcers. Duodenal ulcers account for about 80% of all peptic ulcers. Duodenal ulcers occur at any age, but the incidence is especially high between 35 and 45 years of age.

Although many factors are associated with the development of duodenal ulcers, *H. pylori* is the most common.

The development of duodenal ulcers is often associated with a high HCl acid secretion. Those at high risk include people with chronic obstructive pulmonary disease (COPD), cirrhosis, pancreatitis, hyperparathyroidism, chronic kidney disease, and *Zollinger-Ellison syndrome* (ZES). ZES is a rare condition characterized by severe peptic ulceration and HCl acid hypersecretion.

Duodenal ulcers tend to occur continuously for a few weeks or months and then disappear for a time, only to recur some months later.

Stress-Related Mucosal Disease (SRMD). SRMD is described later in this chapter in the section on acute upper GI bleeding on p. 917.

Clinical Manifestations

In gastric ulcers, the discomfort is generally high in the epigastrium and occurs about 1 to 2 hours after meals. The pain is described as "burning" or "gaseous." If the ulcer has eroded through the gastric mucosa, food tends to worsen the pain. For some patients, the earliest symptoms are due to a serious complication, such as perforation.

In duodenal ulcers, symptoms occur when gastric acid comes in contact with the ulcers. With meal ingestion, food is present to help buffer the acid. Symptoms occur generally 2 to 5 hours after a meal. The pain is described as "burning" or "cramplike." It is most often in the midepigastric region beneath the xiphoid process. Duodenal ulcers can also cause back pain.

Some patients have bloating, nausea, vomiting, and early feelings of fullness. Not all patients with ulcers will have pain or discomfort. *Silent* peptic ulcers are more likely to occur in older adults and those taking NSAIDs. The presence or absence of symptoms is not related to the size of the ulcer or the degree of healing.

Diagnostic Studies

Endoscopy is the most accurate procedure to determine the presence and location of an ulcer.[15] It allows for direct viewing of the gastric and duodenal mucosa (Fig. 41.13). During endoscopy, tissue specimens are taken to determine if *H. pylori* is present and rule out stomach cancer. Endoscopy can also assess the degree of ulcer healing after treatment.

Several noninvasive and invasive tests are available to confirm *H. pylori* infection. The gold standard for diagnosing *H. pylori* infection is a biopsy of the antral mucosa with testing for urease (rapid urease testing). Urea is a by-product of the metabolism of *H. pylori* bacteria. Noninvasive tests include serology, stool, and breath testing. The urea breath and stool antigen tests can identify active infection. Stool tests are not as accurate as the urea breath test. Antibody tests for *H. pylori* can remain positive for years. They are not good for evaluating treatment results.

A barium contrast study may be used to diagnose gastric outlet obstruction or for ulcer detection in those who cannot undergo endoscopy. High fasting serum gastrin levels may show the presence of a possible gastrinoma (ZES). A secretin stimulation test can discern a gastrinoma from other causes of hypergastrinemia.

Laboratory tests, including a CBC, liver enzyme studies, serum amylase, and stool examination, may be done. A CBC may show anemia from ulcer bleeding. Liver enzyme studies help detect any liver problems (e.g., cirrhosis) that may complicate ulcer treatment. Stools are tested for blood. A serum amylase evaluates pancreatic function if we suspect posterior duodenal ulcer penetration of the pancreas.

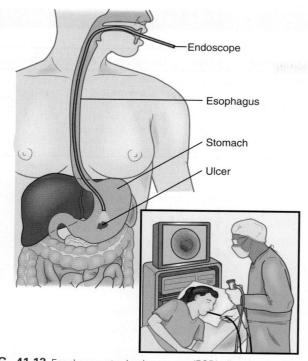

FIG. 41.13 Esophagogastroduodenoscopy (EGD) directly visualizes the mucosal lining of the stomach with a flexible endoscope. Ulcers or tumors can be directly seen and biopsies obtained.

Labels: Endoscope, Esophagus, Stomach, Ulcer

Interprofessional Management

Conservative Care. Treatment begins after diagnostic studies confirm the presence of PUD (Table 41.13). The regimen consists of adequate rest, drug therapy, smoking cessation, dietary modifications (if needed), and long-term follow-up care. The aim of treatment is to decrease gastric acidity and enhance mucosal defense mechanisms.

Patients are generally treated in ambulatory care clinics. Pain disappears after 3 to 6 days, but ulcer healing is much slower. Complete healing may take 3 to 9 weeks, depending on ulcer size, treatment plan, and patient adherence. Endoscopic examination is the most accurate method to monitor ulcer healing. The usual follow-up endoscopic evaluation is done 3 to 6 months after diagnosis and treatment.

Aspirin and nonselective NSAIDs are stopped for 4 to 6 weeks. When aspirin must be continued, co-administration with a PPI, H_2 receptor blocker, or misoprostol may be prescribed. Patients receiving low-dose aspirin (LDA) for CVD and stroke risk who have a history of ulcer disease or complications may need to receive long-term treatment with a PPI. Enteric-coated aspirin decreases localized irritation but does not reduce the overall risk for GI bleeding.

Smoking has an irritating effect on the mucosa and delays mucosal healing. The patient should either stop or severely reduce smoking. (See Chapter 10 for ways to promote smoking cessation.) Adequate rest, both physical and emotional, is important for ulcer healing and may require some changes in the patient's daily routine. Avoiding or restricting alcohol use will enhance healing.

Drug Therapy. Medications are a key part of therapy (Table 41.10). Drug therapy focuses on reducing gastric acid secretion and, if needed, eliminating *H. pylori* infection. Patients with *H. pylori* infection need treatment with antibiotics and a PPI. After

TABLE 41.13 Interprofessional Care

Peptic Ulcer Disease

Diagnostic Assessment
- History and physical examination
- Upper GI endoscopy with biopsy
- Endoscopic ultrasound
- *H. pylori* testing of breath, urine, blood, tissue
- Complete blood cell count
- Liver enzymes
- Serum amylase
- Stool testing for blood

Management

Conservative Therapy
- Adequate rest
- Smoking and alcohol cessation
- Stress management (see Chapter 6)

Drug Therapy (Tables 41.10 and 41.14)
- Antibiotics for *H. pylori*
- PPIs
- Adjunctive therapy
  - H2-receptor blockers
  - Cytoprotective drugs
  - Antacids

Acute Exacerbation Without Complications
- NPO
- NG suction
- Adequate rest
- IV fluid replacement

Drug Therapy (Tables 41.10 and 41.14)
- Antibiotics for *H. pylori*
- PPIs
- Adjunctive therapy
  - H_2 receptor blockers
  - Cytoprotective drugs
  - Antacids
  - Sedatives

Acute Exacerbation With Complications (Hemorrhage, Perforation, Obstruction)
- NPO
- NG suction
- IV PPI
- Bed rest
- IV fluid replacement (lactated Ringer's solution)
- Blood transfusions
- Stomach lavage (possible)

Surgical Therapy
- Gastric outlet obstruction: Pyloroplasty and vagotomy
- Perforation: Simple closure with omentum graft
- Ulcer removal or reduction
  - Billroth I and II
  - Vagotomy and pyloroplasty

the ulcer has healed, many patients can stop PPI therapy. Some may need to continue low-dose maintenance therapy.

Because ulcers often recur, interrupting or stopping therapy can have harmful results. Strict adherence to the prescribed drug regimen is important. Encourage the patient to adhere to therapy and continue with follow-up care as prescribed. Teach the patient and caregiver about each drug prescribed, why it is

TABLE 41.14 Drug Therapy

H. pylori *Infection*

Drug Class	Drug	Triple Therapy	Bismuth Quadruple Therapy	Non-Bismuth Quadruple Therapy
Acid suppression	PPI	20–40 mg, 2 times daily	20–40 mg, 2 times daily	20–40 mg, 2 times daily
Standard antibiotics	Amoxicillin	1gram, 2 times daily		1 g, 2 times daily
	Bismuth compound		2 tablets, 2 times daily	
	Clarithromycin	500 mg, 2 times daily		500 mg, 2 times daily
	Metronidazole		500 mg, 3 times daily	500 mg, 2 times daily
	Tetracycline		500 mg, 4 times daily	

ordered, and the expected benefits. Review what to do if pain and discomfort recur or there is blood in vomitus or stools.

Antibiotic Therapy. Eradicating *H. pylori* is the most important part of treating PUD in patients positive for *H. pylori*. Antibiotic therapy is prescribed concurrently with a PPI for 14 days (Table 41.14). If the patient has a penicillin allergy, metronidazole is used instead of amoxicillin in the triple-drug regimen. Bismuth can be given alone or as part of a combination capsule (Pylera) containing bismuth, tetracycline, and metronidazole. Because of the existence of antibiotic-resistant organisms, a growing number of patients do not have *H. pylori* eradicated with a single round of therapy.

Proton Pump Inhibitors. PPIs are more effective than H_2 receptor blockers in reducing gastric acid secretion and promoting ulcer healing. PPIs are used in combination with antibiotics to treat ulcers caused by *H. pylori*.

Cytoprotective Drug Therapy. Sucralfate is used for short-term ulcer treatment. It provides mucosal protection for the esophagus, stomach, and duodenum. Sucralfate does not have acid-neutralizing capabilities. Since it is most effective at a low pH, give it at least 60 minutes before or after an antacid. Adverse side effects are minimal. It binds with cimetidine, digoxin, warfarin, phenytoin, and tetracycline, reducing their bioavailability.

Adjunct Drugs. H_2 receptor blockers and antacids may be used as adjunct therapy to promote ulcer healing. Antacids increase gastric pH by neutralizing HCl acid. As a result, they reduce the acid content of chyme reaching the duodenum. Some antacids (e.g., aluminum hydroxide) can bind to bile salts, thus decreasing the damaging effects of bile on the gastric mucosa.

Misoprostol is a synthetic prostaglandin analog prescribed to prevent gastric ulcers caused by NSAIDs and LDA. It has protective and some antisecretory effects on gastric mucosa. People who need chronic NSAID therapy, such as those with osteoarthritis, may benefit from its use. However, it can cause diarrhea and abdominal pain. It is teratogenic and must be used with caution in women of childbearing potential.

Tricyclic antidepressants (e.g., imipramine, doxepin) may be prescribed for some patients. They may contribute to overall pain relief through their effects on afferent pain fiber transmission. In addition, they have varying degrees of anticholinergic properties, which result in reduced acid secretion.

Anticholinergic drugs are sometimes used for PUD treatment. Anticholinergics are associated with several side effects, such as dry mouth, warm skin, flushing, thirst, tachycardia, dilated pupils, blurred vision, and urine retention.

Nutritional Therapy. There is no specific diet used to treat PUD. Patients should eat and drink foods and fluids that do not cause any distressing symptoms. Foods that may cause gastric

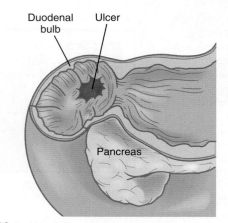

FIG. 41.14 Duodenal ulcer of the posterior wall penetrating the head of the pancreas, resulting in walled-off perforation.

irritation include pepper, carbonated beverages, broth (meat extract), and hot, spicy foods. Caffeine-containing beverages and foods can increase symptoms in some patients. Teach the patient to avoid alcohol use because it can delay healing.

Surgical Therapy. With the use of drug therapy and endoscopic therapy to treat PUD, surgery is used less often. Surgery is done on patients with complications that are unresponsive to medical management or concerns about stomach cancer. Gastric surgeries are described later in this chapter on p. 914.

Complications

The 3 major complications of chronic PUD are hemorrhage, perforation, and gastric outlet obstruction.[16] All these complications are considered emergency situations and may need surgical intervention.

Hemorrhage. Hemorrhage is the most common complication of PUD. Duodenal ulcers cause more upper GI bleeding episodes than gastric ulcers.

Perforation. Perforation is considered the most lethal complication of PUD. Perforation risk is highest with large penetrating duodenal ulcers (Fig. 41.14). However, the mortality rate associated with perforation of gastric ulcers is higher. The patient with gastric ulcers is older and often has concurrent medical problems, which accounts for the higher mortality rate.

With perforation, the ulcer penetrates the serosal surface with spillage of either gastric or duodenal contents into the peritoneal cavity. The contents entering the peritoneal cavity may contain air, saliva, food particles, HCl acid, pepsin, bacteria, bile, and pancreatic fluid and enzymes.

The manifestations of perforation are sudden and dramatic in onset. During the initial phase (0 to 2 hours after perforation), the patient has sudden, severe upper abdominal pain that quickly spreads throughout the abdomen. The pain radiates to the back and shoulders. Food or antacids do not relieve the pain. The abdomen appears rigid and boardlike as the abdominal muscles try to protect from further injury. The patient's respirations become shallow and rapid. The heart rate is elevated, and the pulse is weak. Bowel sounds are usually absent. Nausea and vomiting may occur.

If the condition is untreated, bacterial peritonitis may occur within 6 to 12 hours. The intensity of peritonitis is proportional to the amount and duration of the spillage through the perforation. It is hard to determine from symptoms alone whether a gastric or duodenal ulcer has perforated, because the manifestations of peritonitis are the same (see Chapter 42).

The immediate focus of managing a patient with a perforation is to stop the spillage of gastric or duodenal contents into the peritoneal cavity and restore blood volume. An NG tube can provide continuous aspiration and gastric decompression to stop spillage through the perforation. For duodenal aspiration, the tube is placed as near to the perforation site as possible to facilitate decompression.

Circulating blood volume is replaced with lactated Ringer's and albumin solutions. These solutions substitute for the fluids lost from the vascular and interstitial space as peritonitis develops. Blood replacement in the form of packed RBCs may be needed. A central venous pressure line and an indwelling urinary catheter may be inserted and monitored hourly. The patient with a history of heart disease needs ECG monitoring or placement of a pulmonary artery catheter for accurate assessment of left ventricular function. Broad-spectrum antibiotic therapy is started immediately to treat bacterial peritonitis.

Small perforations may spontaneously seal themselves and symptoms cease. Spontaneous sealing occurs because of fibrin production in response to the perforation. This can lead to fibrinous fusion of the duodenum or gastric curvature to adjacent tissue (mainly the liver) and strictures that can obstruct the flow of intestinal contents and the passage of stool.

Larger perforations need immediate surgical closure. Whether the patient has an open or laparoscopic repair depends on the location of the ulcer and HCP preference. The procedure involving the least risk to the patient is simple oversewing of the perforation and reinforcement of the area with a graft of omentum. Excess gastric contents are suctioned from the peritoneal cavity during the surgical procedure.

Gastric Outlet Obstruction. Both acute and chronic PUD can cause gastric outlet obstruction. Obstruction in the distal stomach and duodenum is the result of edema, inflammation, pylorospasm, or fibrous scar tissue formation. With obstruction the patient reports discomfort or pain that is worse toward the end of the day as the stomach fills and dilates. Belching or self-induced vomiting may provide some relief. Vomiting is common and often projectile. The vomitus may contain food particles that were ingested hours or days before. Constipation occurs because of dehydration and decreased diet intake from anorexia. Over time dilation of the stomach and visible swelling in the upper abdomen may occur.

The aim of therapy for obstruction is to decompress the stomach, correct any existing fluid and electrolyte imbalances, and improve the patient's general state of health. An NG tube is used as described previously. With continuous decompression for several days, the ulcer can begin healing and the

---

TABLE 41.15 Nursing Assessment
Peptic Ulcer Disease

Subjective Data
Important Health Information

Past health history: Chronic kidney disease, pancreatic disease, COPD, serious illness or trauma, hyperparathyroidism, cirrhosis of the liver, ZES

Medications: Aspirin, corticosteroids, NSAIDs
Surgery or other treatments: Complicated or prolonged surgery

Functional Health Patterns

Health perception–health management: Chronic alcohol use, smoking, caffeine use. Family history of PUD
Nutritional-metabolic: Weight loss, anorexia, nausea and vomiting, hematemesis, dyspepsia, heartburn, belching
Elimination: Black, tarry stools
Cognitive-perceptual:
- *Duodenal ulcers:* Burning, midepigastric or back pain occurring 2–5 hr after meals and relieved by food; nighttime pain common
- *Gastric ulcers:* High epigastric pain occurring 1–2 hr after meals. Food may precipitate or worsen pain.

Coping–stress tolerance: Acute or chronic stress

Objective Data
General

Anxiety, irritability

Gastrointestinal

Epigastric tenderness

Possible Diagnostic Findings

Anemia. Guaiac-positive stools. Positive blood, urine, breath, or stool tests for *H. pylori.* Abnormal upper GI endoscopic and barium studies

---

inflammation and edema will subside. Pain relief results from the decompression.

IV fluids and electrolytes are replaced according to the degree of dehydration, vomiting, and electrolyte imbalance shown by laboratory studies. A PPI or H_2 receptor blocker is used if the obstruction is due to an active ulcer. Balloon dilation can open a pyloric obstruction. Surgery may be needed to remove scar tissue.

❖ NURSING MANAGEMENT: PEPTIC ULCER DISEASE

◆ Nursing Assessment

Subjective and objective data to obtain from a patient with PUD are outlined in Table 41.15.

◆ Nursing Diagnoses

Nursing diagnoses related to PUD may include:
- Acute pain
- Lack of knowledge
- Nausea

Additional information on nursing diagnoses and interventions for the patient with PUD are in eNursing Care Plan 41.2 available on the website for this chapter.

◆ Planning

The overall goals are that the patient with PUD will (1) adhere to the prescribed therapeutic regimen, (2) see a reduction in or absence of discomfort, (3) have no signs of GI complications, (4) have complete healing of the peptic ulcer, and (5) make appropriate lifestyle changes to prevent recurrence.

◆Nursing Implementation

◆**Health Promotion.** You play an important role in identifying patients at risk for PUD. Early detection and effective treatment of ulcers are important aspects of reducing morbidity risks associated with PUD. Patients who are taking ulcerogenic drugs (e.g., NSAIDs, LDA) are at risk for PUD. Encourage patients to take these drugs with food. Teach patients to report symptoms related to gastric irritation, including epigastric pain, to their HCP.

◆ **Acute Care.** During an acute exacerbation, the patient often reports increased pain, nausea, and vomiting. Some may have bleeding. Initially, many patients try to cope with the symptoms at home before seeking medical care.

During the acute phase, the patient may be NPO for a few days, have an NG tube connected to intermittent suction, and receive IV fluid replacement. Explain to the patient and caregiver the reasons for these therapies so they understand that the advantages far outweigh any temporary discomfort. Regular mouth care relieves the dry mouth. Cleaning and lubricating the nares facilitate breathing and decrease soreness. Analysis of gastric contents may include pH testing and analysis for blood, bile, or other substances. When the stomach is empty of gastric secretions, pain decreases and ulcer healing begins.

The volume of fluid lost, the patient's signs and symptoms, and laboratory test results (hemoglobin, hematocrit, electrolytes) determine the type and amount of IV fluids given. Take vital signs initially and then at least hourly to detect and treat shock. Give IV fluids as ordered and record intake and output.

Physical and emotional rest is helpful to ulcer healing. The patient's environment should be quiet and restful. Give pain medications as ordered. A mild sedative or tranquilizer has beneficial effects when the patient is anxious and apprehensive. Use good judgment before sedating a person who is becoming increasingly restless because the drug could mask the signs of shock from upper GI bleeding.

Hemorrhage. Changes in vital signs and an increase in the amount and redness of aspirate often signal massive upper GI bleeding. With bleeding, the patient's pain often decreases because the blood helps neutralize the acidic gastric contents. It is important to maintain the patency of the NG tube so that blood clots do not obstruct the tube. If the tube becomes blocked, the patient can develop abdominal distention. Use interventions similar to those described for upper GI bleeding on pp. 918–920.

Perforation. If the patient with an ulcer develops manifestations of a perforation, notify the HCP immediately. Take vital signs promptly and record them every 15 to 30 minutes. Temporarily stop all oral or NG drugs and feedings. If perforation exists, anything taken orally can add to the spillage into the peritoneal cavity and increase discomfort. Give IV fluid as ordered to replace the depleted plasma volume. Giving pain medications provides comfort.

Those with confirmed perforation will start on antibiotic therapy. If the perforation does not seal spontaneously, surgical closure is needed. Since surgery is done as soon as possible, there may not be time to prepare the patient and family.

Gastric Outlet Obstruction. Gastric outlet obstruction can happen at any time. It is most likely to occur in the patient whose ulcer is close to the pylorus. The onset of symptoms is usually gradual. Constant NG aspiration of stomach contents can help relieve symptoms. This allows edema and inflammation to subside and permits normal flow of gastric contents through the pylorus.

Regularly irrigate the NG tube with a normal saline solution per agency policy to assist proper functioning. It may be helpful to reposition the patient from side to side so that the tube tip is not constantly lying against the mucosal surface. Maintain accurate intake and output records, especially of the gastric aspirate.

To check for ongoing obstruction, clamp the NG tube intermittently and measure the gastric residual volume. The frequency and amount of time the tube is clamped are related to the amount of aspirate obtained and the patient's comfort level. A common method is to clamp the tube overnight (usually 8 to 12 hours) and measure the gastric residual volume in the morning. When the aspirate falls below 200 mL, it is within a normal range and the patient can begin oral intake of clear liquids. Oral fluids begin at 30 mL/hr and then gradually increase in amount. As the amount of gastric residual decreases, solid foods are added, and the tube removed.

If the patient has resumed oral feedings and you note symptoms of obstruction, promptly inform the HCP. Generally, all that is needed to treat the problem is to resume gastric aspiration so that the edema and inflammation resulting from the acute episode resolve. IV fluids with electrolyte replacement keep the patient hydrated during this period. If conservative treatment is not successful, surgery is done after the acute phase has passed.

◆ **Ambulatory Care.** Patients with PUD have specific needs to prevent recurrence and complications. Teaching should cover aspects of the disease process, drugs, lifestyle changes (alcohol use, smoking), and regular follow-up care. Table 41.16 provides a patient and caregiver teaching guide for PUD.

Knowing the causes of PUD may motivate the patient to become involved in care and improve adherence to therapy. Work with the dietitian to elicit a dietary history and plan ways to incorporate any needed dietary modifications into the patient's home and work setting.

Teach the patient about prescribed drugs, including their actions, side effects, and dangers if omitted for any reason. Make

---

TABLE 41.16 Patient & Caregiver Teaching

Peptic Ulcer Disease (PUD)

Include the following instructions when teaching the patient and caregiver about management of PUD:

1. Avoiding foods that cause epigastric distress, such as acidic foods.
2. Avoid cigarettes. Smoking promoting ulcer development and delays ulcer healing.
3. Reduce or eliminate alcohol use.
4. Avoid OTC drugs unless approved by the HCP. Many preparations contain ingredients, such as aspirin, that should not be taken unless approved by the HCP. Check with the HCP about the use of NSAIDs.
5. Do not interchange brands of PPIs, antacids, or H₂ receptor blockers that you can buy OTC without checking with the HCP. This can lead to harmful side effects.
6. Take all medications as prescribed. This includes both antisecretory and antibiotic drugs. Not taking medications as prescribed can cause a relapse.
7. It is important to report any of the following:
   - Increased nausea or vomiting
   - Increased epigastric pain
   - Bloody emesis or tarry stools
8. Stress can be related to signs and symptoms of PUD. Learn and use stress management strategies (see Chapter 6).
9. Share concerns about lifestyle changes and living with a chronic illness.

sure the patient knows not to take OTC drugs (e.g., NSAIDs, LDA) unless approved by the HCP. Some H$_2$ receptor blockers and PPIs are available without a prescription. Tell the patient to check with the HCP before switching from a prescription to an OTC preparation to avoid side effects and incorrect dosing. Obtain information about the patient's psychosocial status. Knowledge of lifestyle, occupation, and coping behaviors can be helpful in planning care. The patient may be reluctant to talk about personal subjects, the stress at home or on the job, the usual methods of coping, or dependence on drugs or alcohol.

The patient may not be honest about habitual use of alcohol or cigarettes. Provide information about the negative effects of alcohol and cigarettes on PUD and ulcer healing. Changes such as smoking cessation and alcohol abstinence are hard for many people. The patient may do better in reducing, rather than totally eliminating, use of these substances. However, the goal is total cessation.

PUD is a chronic, recurring disorder. Teach patients with chronic PUD about potential complications, and what to do until they see the HCP. Emphasize the need for long-term follow-up care. Encourage the patient to seek immediate intervention if symptoms return. Some patients do not adhere to the plan of care and have repeated exacerbations. Patients quickly learn that they often have no discomfort when they omit prescribed drugs, smoke, or drink alcohol. Consequently, they make no or few changes in their lifestyle. After an acute exacerbation, the patient is likely to be more amenable to following the plan of care and open to suggestions for changes in lifestyle.

◆ Evaluation

Expected outcomes are that the patient with PUD will
- Have pain controlled without the use of analgesics
- States an understanding of the treatment plan
- Commit to self-care and management of the disease
- Have no complications (hemorrhage, perforation)

Gerontologic Considerations: Peptic Ulcer Disease

The morbidity and mortality rates associated with PUD in older adults are higher than for younger adults because of concurrent health problems and a decreased ability to withstand hypovolemia. Monitor older adults who use NSAIDs for osteoarthritis for PUD. In older patients, pain may not be the first symptom associated with an ulcer. For some patients the first sign is frank gastric bleeding or a decrease in hematocrit.

The treatment and management of PUD in older adults are similar to those in younger adults. The emphasis is on preventing gastritis and PUD. This includes teaching the patient to take NSAIDs and other gastric-irritating drugs with food, milk, or antacids. Teach the patient to avoid irritating substances, adhere to the PPI therapy as prescribed, and report abdominal pain or discomfort to the HCP.

STOMACH CANCER

Stomach (gastric) cancer is an adenocarcinoma of the stomach wall (Fig. 41.15). It accounts for more than 26,240 new cancer cases and 10,800 deaths annually.[5] The rate of stomach (particularly distal) cancer has been steadily declining in the United States. However, cancer in the proximal gastric and gastroesophageal junction is increasing.

Asian Americans, Pacific Islanders, Hispanics, and blacks have higher rates of stomach cancer than non-Hispanic whites. In the United States the incidence is higher in men than in women by a 2:1 ratio. Stomach cancer mostly affects older people. The average age of people at the time of diagnosis is 68.[5]

At the time of diagnosis, only 10% to 20% of patients have disease confined to the stomach. The 5-year survival rate in this group is 71%. However, more than 50% have advanced metastatic disease. The overall 5-year survival rate of all people with stomach cancer is about 31%.[5]

Etiology and Pathophysiology

While many factors are implicated in the development of stomach cancer, no single causative agent has been identified. Stomach cancer probably begins with a nonspecific mucosal injury because of infection (*H. pylori*), autoimmune-related inflammation, repeated exposure to irritants such as bile or NSAIDs, and tobacco use.

Stomach cancer has been associated with diets high in smoked foods, salted fish and meat, and pickled vegetables. Whole grains and fresh fruits and vegetables are associated with reduced rates of stomach cancer. Infection with *H. pylori*, especially at an early age, is a risk factor for stomach cancer. It is possible that *H. pylori* and resulting cell changes can induce a sequence of transitions from dysplasia to cancer. People with lymphoma of the stomach (mucosa-associated lymphoid tissue [MALT]) are at higher risk of stomach cancer.

Other predisposing factors include atrophic gastritis, pernicious anemia, adenomatous polyps, hyperplastic polyps, and *achlorhydria* (absent or low production of gastric HCl). Smoking and obesity both increase the risk for stomach cancer. Although first-degree relatives of patients with stomach cancer are at increased risk, only about 10% of stomach cancers have an inherited component.[17]

Stomach cancer spreads by direct extension and typically infiltrates rapidly to the surrounding tissue and liver. Seeding of tumor cells into the peritoneal cavity occurs late in the course of the disease.

Clinical Manifestations

Stomach cancers often spread to adjacent organs before any distressing symptoms occur. Manifestations include unexplained weight loss, indigestion, abdominal discomfort or pain, and signs and symptoms of anemia. The patient may report *early satiety,* or a sense of being full sooner than usual. Anemia is common. It is caused by chronic blood loss as the lesion erodes through the mucosa or from pernicious anemia (caused by loss of intrinsic factor). The person appears pale and weak. They

FIG. 41.15 Stomach cancer. Gross photograph showing an ill-defined, excavated central ulcer *(arrow)* surrounded by irregular, heaped-up borders. (From Kumar V, Abbas AK, Aster JC, Fausto N: *Robbins and Cotran pathologic basis of disease,* ed 8, Philadelphia, 2010, Saunders.)

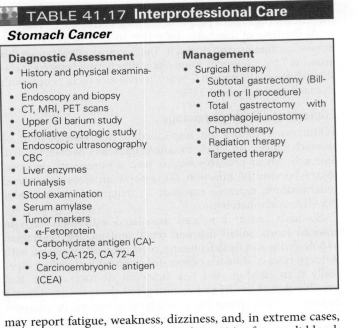

TABLE 41.17 Interprofessional Care

Stomach Cancer

Diagnostic Assessment	Management
• History and physical examination	• Surgical therapy
• Endoscopy and biopsy	• Subtotal gastrectomy (Billroth I or II procedure)
• CT, MRI, PET scans	• Total gastrectomy with esophagojejunostomy
• Upper GI barium study	• Chemotherapy
• Exfoliative cytologic study	• Radiation therapy
• Endoscopic ultrasonography	• Targeted therapy
• CBC	
• Liver enzymes	
• Urinalysis	
• Stool examination	
• Serum amylase	
• Tumor markers	
• α-Fetoprotein	
• Carbohydrate antigen (CA)-19-9, CA-125, CA 72-4	
• Carcinoembryonic antigen (CEA)	

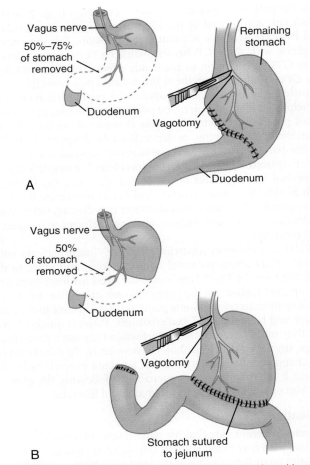

FIG. 41.16 A, Billroth I procedure (subtotal gastric resection with gastroduodenostomy anastomosis). **B,** Billroth II procedure (subtotal gastric resection with gastrojejunostomy anastomosis).

may report fatigue, weakness, dizziness, and, in extreme cases, shortness of breath. The stool may be positive for occult blood. Supraclavicular lymph nodes that are hard and enlarged suggest metastasis via the thoracic duct. The presence of ascites is a poor prognostic sign.

Diagnostic Studies

The diagnostic studies for stomach cancer are outlined in Table 41.17. Upper GI endoscopy is the best diagnostic tool. The stomach can be distended with air during the procedure, stretching the mucosal folds. Tissue biopsy and histologic examination are important in diagnosing stomach cancer.

Endoscopic ultrasound, CT, MRI, and PET scanning can be used to stage the disease. Laparoscopy is done to determine peritoneal spread.

Blood studies detect anemia and determine its severity. Increased liver enzymes and serum amylase levels may mean liver and pancreatic involvement. Stool examination provides evidence of occult or gross bleeding. The presence of tumor markers can help diagnose cancer.

Interprofessional Management

The treatment of choice for stomach cancer is surgical removal of the tumor. Preoperative management focuses on correcting nutritional deficits and treating anemia. Transfusions of packed RBCs correct the anemia. If gastric outlet obstruction occurs, gastric decompression may be needed before surgery.

Surgical Therapy. The surgical aim is to remove as much of the stomach as required to remove the tumor and a margin of normal tissue. The location and extent of the lesion, the patient's physical condition, and the HCP's preference determine the specific surgery used (e.g., open versus laparoscopic).

Lesions in the antrum or pyloric region are generally treated by either a Billroth I or II procedure (Fig. 41.16). When the lesion is in the fundus, a total gastrectomy with esophagojejunostomy is done (Fig. 41.17). When metastasis has occurred to adjacent organs, such as the spleen, ovaries, or bowel, the surgical procedure is extended as needed. If the tumor extends into the transverse colon, partial colon resection is done.

Chemotherapy and Radiation Therapy. A number of chemotherapy drugs can be used to treat stomach cancer. These include fluorouracil, capecitabine (Xeloda), carboplatin, cisplatin, docetaxel (Taxotere), epirubicin (Ellence), irinotecan (Camptosar), oxaliplatin (Eloxatin), and paclitaxel. Combination therapies are preferred as the drugs affect different phases of the cell cycle. Examples of combination therapy include ECF (epirubicin, cisplatin, fluorouracil) and docetaxel, irinotecan, oxaliplatin, or cisplatin with fluorouracil or capecitabine.[18] Intraperitoneal administration of chemotherapy agents may also be used to treat metastatic disease. Chemotherapy is discussed in Chapter 15.

Radiation therapy may be used together with chemotherapy to reduce the recurrence or as a palliative measure to decrease tumor mass and provide temporary relief of obstruction.

Targeted Therapy. Trastuzumab (Herceptin) and ramucirumab (Cyramza) are targeted therapies used to treat stomach cancer. About 20% of patients with stomach cancer have too much HER-2 on the surface of the cancer cells. Trastuzumab targets the HER-2 protein and kills the cancer cells. Ramucirumab binds to the receptor for VEGF and prevents VEGF from binding to the receptor, thus preventing the growth and spread of cancer. These drugs are used to treat esophageal cancer and were discussed on p. 902.

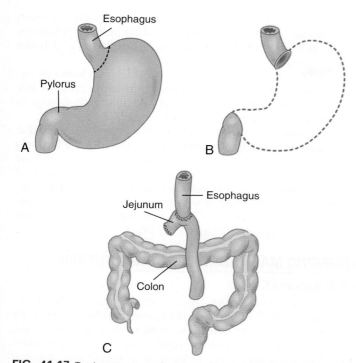

FIG. 41.17 Total gastrectomy for stomach cancer. **A,** Normal anatomic structure of the stomach. **B,** Removal of the stomach (total gastrectomy). **C,** Anastomosis of the esophagus with the jejunum (esophagojejunostomy).

❖ NURSING MANAGEMENT: STOMACH CANCER

◆ Nursing Assessment

The assessment of a person with stomach cancer is similar to that for PUD (Table 41.15). Important data to obtain from the patient and caregiver include a nutritional assessment, a psychosocial history, the patient's perceptions of the health problem and need for care, and a physical examination.

The nutritional assessment obtains information about appetite and changes in eating patterns over the previous 6 months. Determine the patient's normal weight and any recent weight changes. Unexplained weight loss and anorexia are common. Evaluate the patient's nutritional status. Cachexia may be present if oral intake has been reduced for an extended period. A malnourished patient does not respond well to chemotherapy or radiation therapy and is a poor surgical risk. The patient may report a history of vague abdominal symptoms, including dyspepsia and intestinal gas discomfort or pain. If the patient reports pain, explore where and when it occurs and how it is relieved.

Determine the patient's personal perception of the health problem and method of coping with hospitalization, diagnostic tests, and procedures. A possible diagnosis of cancer and a treatment plan that may include surgery, chemotherapy, or radiation treatment is stressful. If surgery is planned, assess the patient's expectations about surgery (cure or palliation) and how the patient has responded to previous surgical procedures.

◆ Nursing Diagnoses

Nursing diagnoses for the patient with stomach cancer include:
- Impaired nutritional intake
- Impaired nutritional status
- Acute pain
- Anxiety

◆ Planning

The overall goals are that the patient with stomach cancer will (1) have minimal discomfort, (2) achieve optimal nutritional status, and (3) maintain a degree of spiritual and psychologic well-being appropriate to the disease stage.

◆ Nursing Implementation

◆ Health Promotion. Your role in the early detection of stomach cancer focuses on identifying the patient at risk because of specific disorders such as *H. pylori* infection, pernicious anemia, and achlorhydria. Be aware of symptoms associated with stomach cancer and the significant findings on physical examination. Symptoms often occur late and mimic other conditions, such as PUD. Poor appetite, weight loss, fatigue, and persistent stomach distress are symptoms of stomach cancer. Encourage patients with a positive family history of stomach cancer to undergo diagnostic evaluation if anemia, PUD, or vague epigastric distress are present. It is important that you recognize the possibility of stomach cancer in a patient who is treated for PUD and does not get relief with prescribed therapy.

Acute Care. When diagnostic tests confirm cancer, the patient and family generally react with shock, disbelief, and depression. Provide emotional and physical support, provide information, clarify test results, and maintain a positive attitude with respect to the patient's immediate recovery and long-term survival.

Because of changes in appetite and early satiety, the patient may be malnourished. Surgery may be delayed until the patient is more physically able to withstand it. A positive nutritional state enhances wound healing and the ability to deal with infection and other possible postoperative complications. The patient may better tolerate several small meals a day than 3 regular meals. It may be challenging to persuade the patient to eat when he or she has no appetite and is depressed. Getting the patient's caregiver to help with meals and encourage intake may be beneficial. Diet may be supplemented by commercial liquid supplements and vitamins. If the patient is unable to ingest oral feedings, the HCP may prescribe EN or PN (see Chapter 39).

If needed, packed RBCs and fluid volume restoration may be given during the preoperative period. The preoperative teaching plan and the postoperative care of the patient having stomach cancer surgery is described in the next section on gastric surgery.

Radiation therapy or chemotherapy is used as an adjuvant to surgery or for palliation. Your role is to provide detailed instructions, reassure the patient, and ensure completion of the designated number of treatments. Start by assessing the patient's knowledge of these therapies. Teach the patient about skin care, need for nutrition and fluid intake, and the use of antiemetic drugs. Specific care of the patient receiving chemotherapy and radiation therapy is discussed in Chapter 15.

Ambulatory Care. When chemotherapy or radiation treatment is continuing after discharge, a referral to home health care may be beneficial. The home health nurse can help with recovery, determine the degree of patient adherence, and provide support to the patient and caregiver. Provide the patient with a list of community agencies (e.g., American Cancer Society) that are available before the patient goes home. Encourage the patient to adhere to the prescribed therapies, keep appointments for chemotherapy administration or radiation treatments, and keep the HCP informed of changes in physical condition. Recurrence of cancer is common, and patients need regular follow-up examinations and imaging assessments. Long-term management of the cancer patient is discussed in Chapter 15.

◆ Evaluation

Expected outcomes are that the patient with stomach cancer will
- Have no or minimal discomfort, pain, or nausea
- Achieve optimal nutritional status
- Maintain a degree of psychologic well-being appropriate to the disease stage

GASTRIC SURGERY

Gastric surgeries are done to treat stomach cancer, as well as polyps, perforation, chronic gastritis, and PUD. Surgeries include partial gastrectomy, gastrectomy, vagotomy, and pyloroplasty. Partial gastrectomy with removal of the distal two thirds of the stomach and anastomosis of the gastric stump to the duodenum is a *gastroduodenostomy* or *Billroth I* operation (Fig. 41.16, *A*). If the gastric stump is anastomosed to the jejunum, the surgery is a *gastrojejunostomy* or *Billroth II* operation (Fig. 41.16, *B*). A total gastrectomy involves resection of the lower esophagus, removal of the entire stomach, and anastomosis of the esophagus to the jejunum.

Vagotomy is the severing of the vagus nerve, either totally *(truncal)* or selectively *(highly selective vagotomy)*. These procedures decrease gastric acid secretion. *Pyloroplasty* consists of surgical enlargement of the pyloric sphincter to facilitate the easy passage of contents from the stomach. It is often done after vagotomy or to enlarge an opening that is constricted from scar tissue.

Postoperative Complications

As with all surgeries, acute postoperative bleeding at the surgical site can occur. Monitoring of patients is similar to that described later under acute upper GI bleeding. The most common long-term postoperative complications from gastric surgery are (1) dumping syndrome, (2) postprandial hypoglycemia, and (3) bile reflux gastritis.

Dumping Syndrome. *Dumping syndrome* is the direct result of surgical removal of a large part of the stomach and pyloric sphincter. Normally, gastric chyme enters the small intestine in small amounts. After surgery, the stomach no longer has control over the amount of gastric chyme entering the small intestine. Therefore a large bolus of hypertonic fluid enters the intestine and causes fluid to be drawn into the bowel lumen. This creates a decrease in plasma volume, distention of the bowel lumen, and rapid intestinal transit.

Symptoms begin within 15 to 30 minutes after eating. The patient usually describes feelings of generalized weakness, sweating, palpitations, and dizziness. These symptoms are due to the sudden decrease in plasma volume. The patient may have abdominal cramps, *borborygmi* (audible abdominal sounds made by hyperactive intestinal peristalsis), and the urge to defecate. These manifestations usually last less than 1 hour after eating. A short rest period after each meal reduces the chance of dumping syndrome.

Postprandial Hypoglycemia. *Postprandial hypoglycemia* is a variant of dumping syndrome. It is the result of uncontrolled gastric emptying of a bolus of fluid high in carbohydrate into the small intestine. The bolus of concentrated carbohydrate results in hyperglycemia and the release of excess amounts of insulin into the circulation. This results in reflex hypoglycemia.

Symptoms are similar to those of any hypoglycemic reaction and include sweating, weakness, mental confusion, palpitations, tachycardia, and anxiety. Symptoms generally occur 2 hours after eating.

Bile Reflux Gastritis. Gastric surgery that involves either reconstruction or removal of the pylorus can result in reflux of bile into the stomach. Prolonged contact with bile causes damage to the gastric mucosa, chronic gastritis, and PUD.

The main symptom is continuous epigastric distress that increases after meals. Vomiting relieves the distress, but only temporarily. Although only a small number of patients have bile reflux gastritis, caution the patient to notify the HCP of any continuous epigastric distress after meals. Cholestyramine (Questran), given before or with meals, has been used successfully to treat this problem. Cholestyramine binds with the bile salts that are the source of gastric irritation.

❖ NURSING MANAGEMENT: GASTRIC SURGERY

◆ Preoperative Care

Surgery can involve either laparoscopic or open surgical techniques. The HCP will provide the necessary information about the procedure and expected outcomes, so the patient can make an informed decision. Help the patient and caregiver by answering their questions. Teach them what to expect after surgery, including comfort measures, pain relief, coughing and breathing exercises, use of an NG tube, and IV fluid administration (see Chapter 17 for more on preoperative care).

◆ Postoperative Care

Postoperative care focuses on maintaining fluid and electrolyte balance, preventing respiratory complications, maintaining comfort, and preventing infection. Complications include atelectasis, pneumonia, anastomotic leak, deep vein thrombosis, pulmonary embolus, and bleeding. Morbidly obese patients have a higher risk for many postoperative complications.

After surgery, an NG tube is used for decompression. This decreases pressure on suture lines and allows edema and inflammation resulting from surgical trauma to resolve. Observe the gastric aspirate for color, amount, and odor. Small volumes of bloody drainage from the NG can be expected for the first 2 to 3 hours because bleeding at the anastomotic site is common. Report bright red bleeding that does not decrease after this period or bleeding that becomes excessive (more than 75 mL/hr) immediately to the HCP. The NG aspirate should gradually darken within the first 24 hours after surgery. Normally the color changes to yellow-green within 36 to 48 hours. After total gastrectomy, the NG tube does not drain a large quantity of secretions because removing the stomach has eliminated the reservoir capacity.

Observe the NG tube closely because blood easily clots and clogs the tube. Notify the HCP immediately if the tube stops draining or appears obstructed with blood. If the tube becomes clogged, the HCP may order periodic gentle irrigations with normal saline solution. It is essential that the NG suction is working and that the tube stays patent so that accumulated gastric secretions do not put a strain on the anastomosis. This can lead to distention of any remaining part of the stomach and result in (1) rupture of the sutures, (2) leakage of gastric contents into the peritoneal cavity, (3) hemorrhage, and (4) abscess formation. If the tube must be replaced or repositioned, call the HCP to perform this task because of the danger of perforating the gastric mucosa or disrupting the suture line.

While the NG tube is connected to suction, maintain IV therapy. Before the NG tube is removed, the patient begins clear liquids to determine the tolerance level. In a partial gastrectomy, the stomach may be aspirated within 1 or 2 hours to assess the amount remaining and its color and consistency. When fluids are well tolerated, the NG tube is removed. Solids are added gradually with the goal of resuming a normal diet.

Closely observe the patient for an anastomotic leak and notify the HCP at once if one is suspected. A leak occurs when there is a breakdown of the suture line in an anastomosis that allows gastric or intestinal contents to enter the abdomen or mediastinum. It requires immediate treatment to prevent sepsis and death. Signs and symptoms include tachycardia, dyspnea, fever, abdominal pain, anxiety, and restlessness.

Since most procedures are done laparoscopically, the risk for respiratory complications is reduced. In an open surgical approach, the incision is relatively high in the epigastrium and respiratory complications may occur. Respiratory assessment includes respiratory rate and rhythm, pulse rate and rhythm, and signs of pneumothorax (e.g., dyspnea, chest pain, cyanosis). Have the patient cough and deep breathe to expand the lungs. Pain may interfere with deep breathing and coughing. Encourage the patient to splint the area with a pillow. Splinting also protects the abdominal suture line from rupturing during deep breathing and coughing. Encourage early ambulation and frequent position changes.

Give pain medications as needed. Be aware that pain could be from an anastomosis leak rather than typical surgical pain. Abdominal wounds need frequent observation for the amount and type of drainage, condition of the incision, and signs of infection. Monitor vital signs to help identify problems such as infection, hemorrhage, or anastomosis leak. Implement measures to control nausea and vomiting. Measure and record the intake and output and obtain daily weights.

◆ **Nutritional Therapy.** Understanding the patient's surgery and the resulting anatomy is important. Long-term, many patients have malnutrition, metabolic bone disease, anemia, and weight loss. Nutrition interventions help minimize the occurrence of expected complications and maximize nutrient intake (Table 41.18). Start nutrition teaching as soon as the immediate postoperative period has passed. The dietitian usually provides dietary instructions. You must reinforce them. Following dietary measures will decrease symptoms and is essential to long-term adherence.

Postoperative wound healing may be impaired because of poor nutritional intake. Give potassium and vitamin supplements as ordered. For those who were malnourished preoperatively, a small bowel feeding tube may be placed intraoperatively. EN may be started on postoperative day 1 and adjusted depending on how oral intake is tolerated. Some may be discharged with nighttime tube feedings. PN is an option if the patient is not able to tolerate oral nutrition.

Pernicious anemia is a long-term complication of total gastrectomy and may occur after partial gastrectomy. It is due to the loss of intrinsic factor, which is made by the parietal cells. *Intrinsic factor* is essential for the absorption of cobalamin in the terminal ileum. Because it is essential for the growth and maturation of RBCs, the lack of cobalamin results in pernicious anemia and neurologic complications. The patient will require cobalamin replacement therapy (see Chapter 30). Patients should take multivitamins with folate, calcium, vitamin D, and iron for life.

TABLE 41.18 Nutritional Therapy

Postgastrectomy Dumping Syndrome

The amount of time these restrictions should be followed varies. The HCP decides the proper amount of time to remain on this prescribed diet according to the patient's clinical condition and progress.

Purposes
- Slow the rapid passage of food into the intestine
- Control symptoms of dumping syndrome (dizziness, sense of fullness, diarrhea, tachycardia), which sometimes occurs after a partial or total gastrectomy

Diet Principles
- Divide meals into 6 small feedings to avoid overloading the stomach and intestine at mealtimes.
- Do not take fluids with meals but at least 30–45 min before or after meals. This helps prevent distention or a feeling of fullness.
- Avoid concentrated sweets (e.g., honey, sugar, jelly, jam, candies, sweet pastries, and sweetened fruit) because they sometimes cause dizziness, diarrhea, and a sense of fullness.
- Protein consumption is unlimited to promote rebuilding of body tissues. Meat and eggs are specific foods to increase in the diet.
- Milk contains lactose, which may be hard to digest. Introduce milk and milk products slowly several weeks after surgery.
- Avoid carbonated beverages and foods that are gas forming to help prevent gastric distention.
- Low-roughage and raw foods are allowed as tolerated a few weeks after surgery.
- Increase complex carbohydrates (e.g., bread, vegetables, rice, potatoes) and fats to meet energy needs.

Because partial gastrectomy decreases the stomach's reservoir, patients must reduce their meal size accordingly. For the first few weeks after surgery, the patient should consume soft, bland foods with low fiber and high complex carbohydrates and protein content. Teach the patient to eat in small portions and not to drink fluids with meals. Simple sugars, lactose, and fried foods should be avoided. Teach the patient to avoid extreme temperatures in food and to chew food thoroughly.

To avoid hypoglycemic episodes, teach the patient to limit the amount of sugar consumed with each meal and eat small, frequent meals with moderate amounts of protein and fat. The immediate ingestion of sugared fluids or candy relieves hypoglycemic symptoms.

◆ **Ambulatory Care.** Patients who have had a total gastrectomy and are debilitated may need skilled care after discharge. For those going home, assist the patient and caregiver with symptom management. Make plans for pain relief, including comfort measures and the judicious use of analgesics. Teach wound care (if needed) to the primary caregiver. Dressings, special equipment, or special services may be needed. Collaborate with the dietitian to provide teaching about the diet that will optimize nutrition.

GASTRITIS

Gastritis, an inflammation of the gastric mucosa, is one of the most common problems affecting the stomach. Gastritis may be acute or chronic and diffuse or localized.

Etiology and Pathophysiology

Gastritis occurs as the result of a breakdown in the normal gastric mucosal barrier. This mucosal barrier normally protects the

TABLE 41.19 Causes of Gastritis

Drugs	**Environmental Factors**
• Aspirin	• Radiation
• Bisphosphonates	• Smoking
• Corticosteroids	
• Digitalis	**Diseases/Disorders**
• Iron supplements	• Burns
• Nonsteroidal antiinflamma-	• Crohn's disease
tory drugs (NSAIDs)	• Large hiatal hernia
	• Physiologic stress
Diet	• Reflux of bile and pancreatic
• Alcohol	secretions
• Large amounts of spicy, irri-	• Renal failure
tating foods	• Sepsis
	• Shock
Microorganisms	
• *H. pylori*	**Other Factors**
• *Cytomegalovirus*	• Endoscopy procedures
• *Mycobacterium* species	• Nasogastric tube
• *Salmonella* organisms	• Psychologic stress
• *Staphylococcus* organisms	
• *Treponema pallidum* (syphilis)	

stomach tissue from the corrosive action of HCl acid and pepsin. When the barrier is broken, HCl acid and pepsin can diffuse back into the mucosa. This back diffusion results in tissue edema, disruption of capillary walls with loss of plasma into the gastric lumen, and possible hemorrhage.

Risk Factors. Risk factors and causes of gastritis are listed in Table 41.19. Some risk factors are discussed in this section.

Drug-Related Gastritis. Drugs contribute to the development of acute and chronic gastritis. NSAIDs and corticosteroids inhibit the synthesis of prostaglandins that are protective to the gastric mucosa. This makes the mucosa more susceptible to injury. Factors that increase the risk for NSAID-induced gastritis include being female; being over age 60; having a history of ulcer disease; taking anticoagulants, LDA, or corticosteroids; and having a chronic disorder, such as CVD. Some drugs such as digoxin and alendronate (Fosamax) have direct irritating effects on the gastric mucosa.

Diet. Dietary indiscretions can cause acute gastritis. After an alcoholic drinking binge, acute damage to the gastric mucosa can range from localized injury of superficial epithelial cells to destruction of the mucosa with mucosal congestion, edema, and hemorrhage. Prolonged damage induced by repeated alcohol use results in chronic gastritis. Eating large quantities of spicy, irritating foods can cause acute gastritis.

Helicobacter Pylori. A key cause of chronic gastritis is *H. pylori* infection. *H. pylori* infection causes acute gastritis in most infected persons. Chronic gastritis may develop in some. Prolonged inflammation leads to functional changes in the stomach and may cause stomach cancer. *H. pylori* was discussed earlier in this chapter on p. 905.

Other Risk Factors. Although not as common as *H. pylori*, other bacterial, viral, and fungal infections are associated with chronic gastritis. Gastritis can occur from reflux of bile salts from the duodenum into the stomach because of anatomic changes after surgical procedures (e.g., gastroduodenostomy, gastrojejunostomy). Prolonged vomiting may cause reflux of bile salts. Intense emotional responses and CNS lesions may cause inflammation of the mucosal lining from hypersecretion of HCl acid.

Autoimmune Gastritis. Autoimmune metaplastic atrophic gastritis (also called *autoimmune atrophic gastritis*) is an inherited condition in which there is an immune response directed against parietal cells. It most often affects women of northern European descent. Patients often have other autoimmune disorders. The loss of parietal cells leads to low chloride levels, inadequate production of intrinsic factor, cobalamin (vitamin B_{12}) malabsorption, and pernicious anemia. It is associated with an increased risk of stomach cancer.

Clinical Manifestations

The symptoms of *acute gastritis* include anorexia, nausea and vomiting, epigastric tenderness, and a feeling of fullness. Hemorrhage is often associated with alcohol use and at times, is the only symptom. Acute gastritis is self-limiting, lasting from a few hours to a few days. Complete healing of the mucosa is expected.

The manifestations of *chronic gastritis* are like those of acute gastritis. Some patients are asymptomatic. However, when parietal cells are lost because of atrophy, the source of intrinsic factor is also lost. *Intrinsic factor* is essential for cobalamin absorption. The lack of cobalamin results in pernicious anemia. Cobalamin deficiency anemia is discussed in Chapter 30.

Diagnostic Studies

Acute gastritis is usually diagnosed based on the patient's symptoms and a history of drug or alcohol use. Occasionally, an endoscopic examination with biopsy is required to make the diagnosis. Breath, urine, serum, stool, and gastric tissue biopsy tests are done to assess for *H. pylori* infection. A CBC may show anemia from blood loss or lack of intrinsic factor. Stools are tested for occult blood. Serum tests for antibodies to parietal cells and intrinsic factor may be done. A tissue biopsy can rule out gastric cancer.

❖ NURSING AND INTERPROFESSIONAL MANAGEMENT: GASTRITIS

◆ Acute Gastritis

Eliminating the cause and preventing or avoiding it in the future are generally all that is needed to treat acute gastritis. The plan of care is supportive and similar to that described for nausea and vomiting. If vomiting is present, rest, NPO status, and IV fluids may be prescribed. Antiemetics are given (Table 41.1). Monitor for dehydration. It can occur rapidly in acute gastritis with vomiting.

In severe cases of acute gastritis, an NG tube may be used to (1) monitor for bleeding, (2) lavage the precipitating agent from the stomach, or (3) keep the stomach empty and free of noxious stimuli. Clear liquids are resumed when symptoms have subsided. Reintroduce solids gradually.

If the patient is at risk for hemorrhage, frequently check vital signs and test the vomitus for blood. All the management strategies discussed in the section on upper GI bleeding apply to the patient with severe gastritis (see pp. 917–920).

Drug therapy focuses on reducing irritation of the gastric mucosa and providing symptomatic relief. H_2 receptor blockers (e.g., ranitidine, cimetidine) or PPIs (e.g., omeprazole) reduce gastric HCl acid secretion (Table 41.10). Teach the patient about the therapeutic effects of PPIs and H_2 receptor blockers.

❖ Chronic Gastritis

The treatment of chronic gastritis focuses on evaluating and eliminating the specific cause (e.g., cessation of alcohol use,

TABLE 41.20 **Types of Upper GI Bleeding**	
Type	**Manifestations**
Obvious bleeding	
• Hematemesis	Bloody vomitus appearing as fresh, bright red blood or "coffee-grounds" appearance (dark, grainy digested blood).
• Melena	Black, tarry stools (often foul smelling) caused by digestion of blood in the GI tract. Black appearance is from the presence of iron.
Occult bleeding	Small amounts of blood in gastric secretions, vomitus, or stools not apparent by appearance. Detectable by guaiac test

TABLE 41.21 **Causes of Upper GI Bleeding**	
Stomach and Duodenum	**Esophagus**
• Drug-induced	• Esophageal varices
• Corticosteroids	• Esophagitis
• NSAIDs	• Mallory-Weiss tear
• Salicylates	
• Erosive gastritis	**Systemic Diseases**
• Polyps	• Blood dyscrasias (e.g., leukemia, aplastic anemia)
• PUD	• Renal failure
• Stress-related mucosal disease	
• Stomach cancer	

abstinence from drugs, *H. pylori* eradication). Antibiotic combinations are used to eradicate *H. pylori* (Table 41.14). The patient with pernicious anemia needs lifelong cobalamin therapy (see Chapter 30).

The patient undergoing treatment for chronic gastritis may have to adapt to lifestyle changes and strictly adhere to a drug regimen. Some patients find a nonirritating diet consisting of 6 small feedings a day helpful. Smoking is contraindicated in all forms of gastritis. An interprofessional team approach in which the HCP, nurse, dietitian, and pharmacist provide consistent information and support will increase the patient's success in making these changes.

UPPER GASTROINTESTINAL BLEEDING

In the United States, 250,000 hospital admissions occur each year for upper GI bleeding.[19] About 60% of these are adults over age 65. Though the mortality rate is still around 2.5%, this rate has decreased over the past few decades due to advances in the prevention and treatment of upper GI bleeding.

Etiology and Pathophysiology

Although the most serious loss of blood from the upper GI tract is characterized by a sudden onset, insidious occult bleeding can be a major problem. The severity of bleeding depends on whether the origin is venous, capillary, or arterial. Types of upper GI bleeding are described in Table 41.20. Bleeding from an arterial source is profuse, and the blood is bright red because it has not been in contact with gastric HCl acid secretion. In contrast, coffee-grounds vomitus means that the blood has been in the stomach for some time. *Melena* (black, tarry stools) occurs with slow bleeding from an upper GI source. The longer the passage of blood through the intestines, the darker the stool color because of the breakdown of hemoglobin and release of iron.

Discovering the cause of the bleeding is not always easy. A variety of areas in the GI tract may be involved. Table 41.21 lists the common causes of upper GI bleeding.

Stomach and Duodenal Origin. Peptic ulcers, due to *H. pylori* infection and the use of NSAIDS, are the most common causes of upper GI bleeding. About 25% of people on chronic NSAIDs (e.g., ibuprofen) develop ulcer disease; of these, 2% to 4% will bleed. Even LDA is associated with a risk for GI bleeding. Many OTC preparations contain aspirin. Obtain a careful medication history whenever upper GI bleeding is suspected.

Stress-related mucosal disease (SRMD), also called *physiologic stress ulcers,* describes mucosal damage in the GI tract ranging from small single lesions to multiple gastric ulcers

and major bleeding. SRMD most often occurs in critically ill patients who have had severe burns, trauma, or major surgery. Patients with coagulopathy, liver disease, or organ failure and those receiving renal replacement therapy are at highest risk for SRMD.[20]

Esophageal Origin. Bleeding from the esophagus is likely due to chronic esophagitis, Mallory-Weiss tear, or esophageal varices. Chronic esophagitis can be caused by GERD, smoking, alcohol use, and the ingestion of drugs irritating to the mucosa. Esophageal varices most often occur from cirrhosis of the liver. Esophageal varices are discussed in Chapter 43.

Diagnostic Studies

Endoscopy is the primary tool for diagnosing the source (e.g., esophageal varices, PUD, gastritis) of upper GI bleeding. Angiography is used when endoscopy cannot be done or when bleeding persists after endoscopic therapy. Angiography requires preparation and setup time and may not be appropriate for a high-risk, unstable patient. In this procedure, a catheter is inserted into the femoral artery and advanced to the left gastric or superior mesenteric artery until the site of bleeding is found.

Laboratory studies include CBC, blood urea nitrogen (BUN), serum electrolytes, prothrombin time, partial thromboplastin time, liver enzymes, arterial blood gases (ABGs), and a type and crossmatch for possible blood transfusions. All vomitus and stools are tested for gross and occult blood.

Monitor the patient's laboratory studies to estimate the effectiveness of therapy. The hemoglobin and hematocrit values are not of immediate help in estimating the degree of blood loss, but they provide a baseline for guiding further treatment. The initial hematocrit may be normal and may not reflect the loss until 4 to 6 hours after fluid replacement, since initially the loss of plasma and RBCs is equal.

Assess the patient's BUN level. During a significant hemorrhage, GI tract bacteria break down proteins, resulting in increased BUN levels. An increased BUN level may also show renal hypoperfusion or renal disease.

Interprofessional Management

A massive upper GI hemorrhage is a loss of more than 1500 mL of blood or 25% of intravascular blood volume. Although 80% to 85% of patients with massive hemorrhage spontaneously stop bleeding, the cause must be identified and treatment started at once.

Emergency Assessment and Management. A complete history of events leading to the bleeding episode is deferred until emergency care has been started. To facilitate early intervention, focus your physical examination on identifying signs and symptoms of shock, such as tachycardia, weak pulse, hypotension, cool extremities, prolonged capillary refill, and apprehension. (Shock is discussed in Chapter 66.)

Urine output is one of the best measures of vital organ perfusion. An indwelling urinary catheter is inserted so that hourly output can be accurately assessed. Hemodynamic monitoring provides an accurate and quick assessment of blood flow and pressure in the cardiovascular system (see Chapter 65). A central venous pressure line may be used for fluid volume status assessment. If the patient has a history of valvular heart disease, coronary artery disease, or heart failure, a pulmonary artery catheter may be needed. Give supplemental O_2 to increase blood O_2 saturation.

The patient is at risk for perforation and peritonitis. Do a thorough abdominal examination. Note the presence of a tense, rigid, boardlike abdomen and the presence or absence of bowel sounds.

The type and amount of fluids infused are based on physical and laboratory findings. Generally, an isotonic crystalloid solution (e.g., lactated Ringer's solution) is started. Whole blood, packed RBCs, and fresh frozen plasma may be used for volume replacement in massive hemorrhage. When upper GI bleeding is less profuse, infusion of isotonic saline solution followed by packed RBCs restores the hematocrit more quickly and does not create complications related to fluid volume overload. (The use of blood transfusions and volume expanders is discussed in Chapter 30.)

Endoscopic Therapy. The first-line management of upper GI bleeding is endoscopy. Endoscopy within the first 24 hours of bleeding is important for diagnosis, determining the need for surgical intervention, and providing treatment.

The goal of endoscopic hemostasis is to coagulate or thrombose the bleeding vessel. Several techniques are used, including (1) mechanical therapy with clips or bands, (2) thermal ablation, and (3) injection (e.g., epinephrine, alcohol). Clips and bands directly compress the bleeding vessel. Thermal ablation cauterizes tissue through applying heat to the bleeding site. Common devices include neodymium:yttrium-aluminum-garnet (YAG) laser, monopolar or bipolar electrocoagulation, heater probes, and argon plasma coagulation (APC).[21]

For variceal bleeding, other strategies include variceal ligation, injection sclerotherapy, and balloon tamponade (see Chapter 43).

Surgical Therapy. Surgical intervention is needed when bleeding continues regardless of the therapy provided and when the site of the bleeding has been identified. Surgery may be done if the patient continues to bleed after rapid transfusion of up to 2000 mL of whole blood or is still in shock after 24 hours. The site of the hemorrhage determines the choice of surgery. Mortality rates increase considerably in older patients.

Drug Therapy. During the acute phase of upper GI bleeding, drugs are used to decrease bleeding, decrease HCl acid secretion, and neutralize the HCl acid that is present. Empiric PPI therapy with high-dose IV bolus and subsequent infusion to decrease acid secretion is often started before endoscopy (Table 41.10). Efforts are made to reduce acid secretion because the acidic environment can alter platelet function and interfere with clot stabilization. This may decrease the amount of bleeding and need for endoscopic therapy.

After an acute phase of bleeding, antacids may be given hourly, either orally or through the NG tube. If an NG tube is in place, the stomach contents should be aspirated and tested periodically for pH level. If pH is less than 5, intermittent suction may be used or the frequency or dosage of the antacid or antisecretory agent increased.

❖ NURSING MANAGEMENT: UPPER GASTROINTESTINAL BLEEDING

◆ Nursing Assessment

A thorough nursing assessment is an essential first step as you begin care of the patient admitted with upper GI bleeding. The patient may not be able to give specific information about the cause of the bleeding until immediate physical needs are met. Perform an immediate nursing assessment while you are getting the patient ready for initial treatment. The assessment includes the patient's level of consciousness, vital signs, skin color, and capillary refill. Check the abdomen for distention, guarding, and peristalsis. Immediate determination of vital signs indicates whether the patient is in shock from blood loss and provides a baseline BP and pulse for monitoring the progress of treatment. Signs and symptoms of shock include low BP; rapid, weak pulse; increased thirst; cold, clammy skin; and restlessness. Monitor vital signs every 15 to 30 minutes. Inform the HCP of any significant changes.

Once the immediate interventions have begun, the patient or caregiver should answer the following questions: Is there a history of bleeding episodes? Has the patient received blood transfusions? Were there any transfusion reactions? Are there any other illnesses (e.g., liver disease, cirrhosis) or medications that may contribute to bleeding or interfere with treatment? Does the patient have a religious preference that prohibits the use of blood or blood products?

Subjective and objective data to obtain from the patient or caregiver are outlined in Table 41.22.

◆ Nursing Diagnoses

Nursing diagnoses for the patient with upper GI bleeding include:

- Impaired cardiac output
- Fluid imbalance
- Ineffective tissue perfusion
- Anxiety

◆ Planning

The overall goals are that the patient with upper GI bleeding will (1) have no further GI bleeding, (2) have the cause of the bleeding identified and treated, (3) return to a normal hemodynamic state, and (4) have minimal or no symptoms of pain or anxiety.

◆ Nursing Implementation

◆ Health Promotion. Although not all cases of upper GI bleeding can be prevented, you have an important role in identifying patients at high risk. Always consider the patient with a history of chronic gastritis, cirrhosis, or PUD at high risk. The patient who has had an upper GI bleeding episode is more likely to have another bleed. Patients on daily LDA to reduce CVD risk are at risk for upper GI bleeding, especially those over 60 years old with a history of PUD.

Teach the patient who takes regular doses of drugs that cause GI toxicity (peptic ulcer formation, bleeding), such as corticosteroids and NSAIDs, about the risk for GI bleeding. They may need to receive long-term treatment with a PPI, H_2 receptor blocker, or misoprostol. Taking these drugs with meals or snacks lessens their direct irritation.

TABLE 41.22 Nursing Assessment
Upper GI Bleeding

Subjective Data

Important Health Information

Past health history: Precipitating events before bleeding episode, prior bleeding episodes and treatment, PUD, esophageal varices, esophagitis, acute and chronic gastritis, stress-related mucosal disease
Medications: Aspirin, NSAIDs, corticosteroids, anticoagulants

Functional Health Patterns

Health perception–health management: Family history of bleeding, smoking, alcohol use
Nutritional-metabolic: Nausea, vomiting, weight loss, thirst
Elimination: Diarrhea. Black, tarry stools. Decreased urine output. Sweating
Activity-exercise: Weakness, dizziness, fainting
Cognitive-perceptual: Epigastric pain, abdominal cramps
Coping–stress tolerance: Acute or chronic stress

Objective Data

General

Fever

Integumentary

Clammy, cool, pale skin. Pale mucous membranes, nail beds, and conjunctivae. Spider angiomas, jaundice, peripheral edema

Respiratory

Rapid, shallow respirations

Cardiovascular

Tachycardia, weak pulse, orthostatic hypotension, slow capillary refill

Gastrointestinal

Red or coffee-grounds vomitus. Tense, rigid abdomen, ascites. Hypoactive or hyperactive bowel sounds. Black, tarry stools

Urinary

Decreased urine output, concentrated urine

Neurologic

Agitation, restlessness. Decreasing level of consciousness

Possible Diagnostic Findings

↓ Hematocrit and hemoglobin, hematuria. Guaiac-positive stools, emesis, or gastric aspirate. ↓ Levels of clotting factors, ↑ liver enzymes, abnormal endoscopy results

---

✚ TABLE 41.23 Emergency Management
Acute GI Bleeding

Assessment Findings	Interventions
Abdominal and GI Findings • Abdominal pain • Abdominal rigidity • Hematemesis • Melena • Nausea **Hypovolemic Shock** • ↓ BP • ↓ Pulse pressure • Tachycardia • Cool, clammy skin • ↓ Level of consciousness • ↓ Urine output (<0.5 mL/kg/hr) • Slow capillary refill	• Initial • If unresponsive, assess circulation, airway, and breathing. • If responsive, monitor airway, breathing, and circulation. • Establish IV access with large-bore catheter and start fluid replacement therapy. Insert a second large-bore catheter if shock present. • Give O₂ via nasal cannula or nonrebreather mask. • Initiate ECG monitoring. • Obtain blood for CBC, clotting studies, and type and crossmatch as appropriate. • Insert NG tube as needed. • Insert indwelling urinary catheter. • Give IV PPI therapy to decrease acid secretion. • Ongoing Monitoring • Monitor vital signs, level of consciousness, O₂ saturation, ECG, bowel sounds, and intake/output. • Assess amount and character of emesis. • Keep patient NPO. • Provide reassurance and emotional support to patient and caregiver.

Acute Care. Emergency management of acute GI bleeding is outlined in Table 41.23. Place IV lines, preferably 2, with a 16- or 18-gauge needle for fluid and blood replacement. Give fluid or blood replacement as ordered. An accurate intake and output record is essential so that the patient's hydration status can be assessed. Measure the urine output hourly. If a central venous pressure line or pulmonary artery catheter in place, record these readings every 1 to 2 hours. Use ECG monitoring to evaluate cardiac function. Close monitoring of vital signs, especially in the patient with CVD, is important because dysrhythmias may occur.

❓ CHECK YOUR PRACTICE

You are admitting a 71-yr-old man to the unit from the emergency department. He has a diagnosis of upper GI bleeding. He reports heartburn and pain (6 on a scale of 10) in the upper epigastric region and has just had a 250 mL coffee-grounds emesis.
• What assessment data do you need to obtain?
• What are the priority nursing interventions for this man?

Teach the at-risk patient to avoid known gastric irritants, such as alcohol and smoking, and to take only prescribed medications. OTC drugs can be harmful because they may contain ingredients (e.g., aspirin) that increase the risk for bleeding. Review how to test vomitus or stools for occult blood. Teach them to report positive results promptly to the HCP. Stress the importance of treating an upper respiratory tract infection promptly. Severe coughing or sneezing can increase pressure on the already fragile varices and may result in massive hemorrhage (see Chapter 43).

Patients with blood dyscrasias (e.g., aplastic anemia) or liver dysfunction or those who are taking chemotherapy drugs are at risk due to a decrease in clotting factors and platelets. Teach patients about their disease process, drugs, and increased risk for GI bleeding.

Observe the older adult or the patient with CVD closely for signs of fluid overload. However, volume overload and pulmonary edema are concerns in all patients who are receiving large amounts of IV fluids within a short time. Auscultate breath sounds and closely observe the respiratory effort. Keep the head of the bed elevated to provide comfort and prevent aspiration.

When an NG tube is present, pay special attention to keeping it in proper position and checking the aspirate for blood. Although gastric lavage (room temperature, cool, or iced) is used in some agencies, its effectiveness as a treatment for upper GI bleeding is questionable. When lavage is used, around 50 to

TABLE 41.24 Bacterial Food Poisoning

Type and Cause	Sources	Manifestations	Treatment and Prevention
Botulism Toxin from *Clostridium botulinum*; ingested toxin absorbed from gut and blocks acetylcholine at neuromuscular junction	Improperly canned or preserved food, home-preserved vegetables (most common), preserved fruits and fish, canned commercial products	*Onset:* 12–36 hr *GI:* Nausea, vomiting, abdominal pain, constipation, distention *Central nervous system:* Headache, dizziness, muscular incoordination, weakness, inability to talk or swallow, diplopia, breathing problems, paralysis, delirium, coma	*Treat:* Maintain ventilation, polyvalent antitoxin, guanidine hydrochloric acid (enhances acetylcholine release) *Prevent:* Correct processing of canned foods, boiling of suspected canned foods for 15 min before serving
Clostridial *Clostridium perfringens*	Meat or poultry dishes cooked at lower temperature (stew, pot pie), rewarmed meat dishes, gravies, improperly canned vegetables	*Onset:* 8–24 hr Diarrhea, nausea, abdominal cramps, vomiting (rare), midepigastric pain	*Treat:* Symptomatic, fluid replacement *Prevent:* Correct preparation of meat dishes. Serving food immediately after cooking or rapid cooling of food
Escherichia coli *E. coli* O157:H7	Contaminated beef, pork, milk, cheese, fish, cookie dough	*Onset:* 8 hr to 1 wk (varies by strain) Bloody stools, hemolytic uremic syndrome, abdominal cramping, profuse diarrhea	*Treat:* Symptomatic, fluid and electrolyte replacement *Prevent:* Correct preparation of food
Salmonella *Salmonella typhimurium* (grows in gut)	Improperly cooked poultry, pork, beef, lamb, and eggs	*Onset:* 8 hr to several days Nausea and vomiting, diarrhea, abdominal cramps, fever, and chills	*Treat:* Symptomatic, fluid and electrolyte replacement *Prevent:* Correct preparation of food
Staphylococcal Toxin from *Staphylococcus aureus*	Meat, bakery products, cream fillings, salad dressings, milk Skin and respiratory tract of food handlers	*Onset:* 30 min to 7 hr Vomiting, nausea, abdominal cramping, diarrhea	*Treat:* Symptomatic, fluid and electrolyte replacement, antiemetics *Prevent:* Immediate refrigeration of foods, monitoring food handlers

100 mL of fluid is instilled at a time into the stomach. The lavage fluid may be aspirated from the stomach or drained by gravity. When aspiration is the method used, it is important not to aspirate if you feel resistance. The tip of the NG tube may be up against the gastric mucosal lining. When resistance is a factor, use the gravity method.

Approach the patient in a calm manner to help decrease the level of anxiety. Use caution when giving sedatives for restlessness because it is one of the warning signs of shock and may be masked by the drugs.

Assess the stools for blood (black-tarry, bright red). Black, tarry stools are not usually associated with a brisk hemorrhage but are indicative of prolonged bleeding. Determine if menses or bleeding are possible sources of blood in the stools. When vomitus contains blood, but the stool contains no gross or occult blood, the hemorrhage is thought to be of short duration.

When beginning oral nourishment, observe the patient for symptoms of nausea and vomiting and a recurrence of bleeding. Feedings initially consist of clear fluids. They are given hourly until tolerance is determined. Gradually introduce foods if the patient has no signs of discomfort.

When hemorrhage is the result of chronic alcohol use, closely observe the patient for delirium tremens as alcohol withdrawal takes place. Symptoms indicating the onset of delirium tremens are agitation, uncontrolled shaking, sweating, and hallucinations. (Alcohol withdrawal is discussed in Chapter 10.)

Ambulatory Care. Teach the patient and caregiver how to avoid future bleeding episodes. Ulcer disease, drug or alcohol use, liver and respiratory diseases can all cause upper GI bleeding. Help the patient and caregiver to be aware of the consequences of not adhering to drug therapy.

Emphasize not to take any drugs (especially aspirin, NSAIDs) other than those prescribed by the HCP. Support the patient in smoking and alcohol cessation because they are sources of irritation and interfere with tissue repair. Long-term follow-up care may be needed because of possible recurrence. Teach the patient and caregiver what to do if an acute hemorrhage occurs in the future.

◆ **Evaluation**

The expected outcomes are that the patient with upper GI bleeding will
- Have no upper GI bleeding
- Maintain normal fluid volume
- Return to a normal hemodynamic state
- Understand potential risk factors and make lifestyle modifications

FOODBORNE ILLNESS

Foodborne illness (food poisoning) is a nonspecific term that describes acute GI symptoms such as nausea, vomiting, diarrhea, and cramping abdominal pain caused by the intake of contaminated food or liquids.[22] There are more than 250 foodborne illnesses. Each year 1 in 6 Americans, or 48 million, gets a foodborne illness. Of these, 128,000 are hospitalized and around 3000 die.[22]

Bacteria account for most foodborne illnesses. The most common source is raw foods that become contaminated during growing, harvesting, processing, storing, shipping, or final preparation. Bacteria multiply quickly when the temperature of food is between 40 and 140 degrees. So, bacteria can multiply if hot food is not kept hot enough or cold food not cold enough. The most common bacterial food poisonings are described in Table 41.24.

Focus interventions on preventing infection. Teaching includes correct food preparation and cleanliness, adequate cooking, and refrigeration (Table 41.25). For the hospitalized

TABLE 41.25 Patient & Caregiver Teaching
Preventing Food Poisoning

Include these instructions when teaching the patient and caregiver how to prevent food poisoning.

1. Cook all ground beef and hamburger thoroughly.
   - Use a digital instant-read meat thermometer to ensure thorough cooking (ground beef can turn brown before disease-causing bacteria are killed).
   - Cook ground beef until a thermometer inserted into several parts of the patty, including the thickest part, reads at least 160° F.
   - People who cook ground beef without using a thermometer can decrease their risk for illness by not eating ground beef patties that are still pink in the middle.
2. If you are served an undercooked hamburger or other ground beef product in a restaurant, send it back for further cooking. Ask for a new bun and a clean plate.
3. Avoid spreading harmful bacteria. Keep raw meat separate from ready-to-eat foods. Wash hands, counters, and utensils with hot soapy water after they touch raw meat. Never place cooked hamburgers or ground beef on the unwashed plate that held raw patties. Wash meat thermometers in between tests of patties that need more cooking.
4. Drink only pasteurized milk, juice, or cider. Commercial juice with an extended shelf-life that is sold at room temperature (e.g., juice in cardboard boxes, vacuum-sealed juice in glass containers) has been pasteurized. Juice concentrates are heated enough to kill pathogens.
5. Wash fruits and vegetables thoroughly, especially those you will not be cooking.
6. Do not eat raw food products that are supposed to be cooked. Follow package directions for cooking at proper temperatures.
7. People who are immunocompromised should avoid eating alfalfa sprouts until the safety of the sprouts can be ensured.

patient, emphasize correcting fluid and electrolyte imbalances from diarrhea and vomiting. With botulism, additional assessment and care related to neurologic symptoms are indicated (see Chapter 60).

***Escherichia coli* O157:H7 Poisoning.** Most strains of *Escherichia coli* are harmless and live in the intestines of healthy humans and animals. *E. coli* O157:H7 makes a powerful toxin and can cause severe illness with hemorrhagic colitis and kidney failure. In the very young and older adults, *E. coli* O157:H7 can be life threatening.

E. coli O157:H7 is found primarily in undercooked meats, particularly poultry and hamburger. *E. coli* outbreaks have occurred with contaminated leafy vegetables, fruits, and nuts. Infection can occur after drinking raw milk, unpasteurized or contaminated fruit juices and after swimming in or drinking sewage-contaminated water. Person-to-person contact in families, nursing homes, and child care centers is an important mode of transmission.

Illness starts 1 to 10 days after swallowing the organism and lasts 5 to 10 days. Manifestations include diarrhea (often bloody), vomiting, and abdominal cramping pain. The diarrhea is variable, ranging from mild to bloody. It may start out as watery but may progress to bloody. Systemic complications, including hemolytic uremia and thrombocytopenic purpura, and even death can occur.

Infection with *E. coli* O157:H7 is diagnosed by detecting the bacteria in the stool. All people who suddenly have diarrhea with blood should have a stool culture for *E. coli* O157:H7.

Treatment involves hydration to maintain blood volume. There is no evidence that antibiotic therapy improves the course of disease. We think that treatment with some antibiotics may precipitate kidney complications. Patients should avoid antidiarrheal agents, such as loperamide (Imodium). Other therapies may include dialysis and plasmapheresis.

A small number of patients, especially young children and older adults, develop hemolytic uremic syndrome (HUS). With HUS, the RBCs are destroyed and the kidneys fail. It is a life-threatening condition usually treated in an ICU. Blood transfusions and kidney dialysis are often needed. The mortality rate is around 5%. About one third of people with HUS have abnormal kidney function for years afterward. A few need long-term dialysis. Other long-term complications of HUS include hypertension, seizures, blindness, and paralysis.

CASE STUDY
Peptic Ulcer Disease

(© iStockphoto/ Thinkstock.)

Patient Profile

F.H., a 40-yr-old male immigrant from Vietnam, has a 1-yr history of epigastric distress. Increasingly, it is not relieved by over-the-counter omeprazole (Prilosec). He is scheduled for an upper endoscopy this morning.

Subjective Data

- Reports increasing substernal pain, especially 2 to 3 hr after eating
- Currently avoids alcohol and is taking an over-the-counter PPI
- Smoking history of 1 pack of cigarettes per day for 20 yr
- Has had increasing fatigue with exercise
- Reports occasional black bowel movement
- Takes Chinese medicine for frequent back pain

Objective Data

Physical Examination
- Height 5 ft, 5 in tall and weight 140 lb

Diagnostic Studies
- Endoscopy reveals a duodenal ulcer
- Hgb 10.2 g/dL; Hct 30%
- Histology of biopsied tissue reveals *H. pylori* infection

Interprofessional Care
- omeprazole 20 mg twice daily × 10 days
- clarithromycin 500 mg twice daily × 10 days
- amoxicillin 1 gram twice daily × 10 days

Discussion Questions

1. Explain the pathophysiology of peptic ulcer disease.
2. What are the risk factors for duodenal ulcers? Which of these did F.H. have?
3. What is the pathophysiology of *H. pylori*?
4. **Priority Decision:** Based on the assessment data provided, what are the priority nursing diagnoses? Are there any collaborative problems?
5. **Patient-Centered Care:** How will you consider F.H.'s cultural preferences in planning care?
6. **Priority Decision:** What are the priority nursing interventions for F.H.?
7. What lifestyle interventions would you recommend for F.H.?
8. **Evidence-Based Decision:** F.H. asks you if the treatment will work and this will be the end of his problems. How will you respond?
9. **Collaboration:** What referrals may be indicated?

■ BRIDGE TO NCLEX EXAMINATION

The number of the question corresponds to the same-numbered outcome at the beginning of the chapter.

1. M.J. calls the clinic and tells the nurse that her 85-yr-old mother has been nauseated all day and has vomited twice. Before the nurse hangs up and calls the HCP, she should tell M.J. to
   a. administer antiemetic drugs and assess her mother's skin turgor.
   b. give her mother sips of water and elevate the head of her bed to prevent aspiration.
   c. offer her mother large quantities of Gatorade to decrease the risk for sodium depletion.
   d. give her mother a high-protein liquid supplement to drink to maintain her nutritional needs.

2. The nurse explains to the patient with Vincent's infection that treatment will include
   a. tetanus vaccinations.
   b. viscous lidocaine rinses.
   c. amphotericin B suspension.
   d. topical application of antibiotics.

3. The nurse teaching young adults about behaviors that put them at risk for oral cancer includes
   a. discouraging use of chewing gum.
   b. avoiding use of perfumed lip gloss.
   c. avoiding use of smokeless tobacco.
   d. discouraging drinking of carbonated beverages.

4. Which instructions would the nurse include in a teaching plan for a patient with mild gastroesophageal reflux disease (GERD)?
   a. "The best time to take an as-needed antacid is 1 to 3 hours after meals."
   b. "A glass of warm milk at bedtime will decrease your discomfort at night."
   c. "Do not chew gum; the excess saliva will cause you to secrete more acid."
   d. "Limit your intake of foods high in protein because they take longer to digest."

5. A patient who has undergone an esophagectomy for esophageal cancer develops increasing pain, fever, and dyspnea when a full-liquid diet is started postoperatively. The nurse recognizes that these symptoms are *most* indicative of
   a. an intolerance to the feedings.
   b. extension of the tumor into the aorta.
   c. leakage of fluids into the mediastinum.
   d. esophageal perforation with fistula formation into the lung.

6. The pernicious anemia that may accompany gastritis is due to
   a. chronic autoimmune destruction of cobalamin stores in the body.
   b. progressive gastric atrophy from chronic breakage in the mucosal barrier and blood loss.
   c. a lack of intrinsic factor normally produced by acid-secreting cells of the gastric mucosa.
   d. hyperchlorhydria from an increase in acid-secreting parietal cells and degradation of RBCs.

7. The nurse is teaching the patient and family that peptic ulcers are
   a. caused by a stressful lifestyle and other acid-producing factors, such as *H. pylori.*
   b. inherited within families and reinforced by bacterial spread of *Staphylococcus aureus* in childhood.
   c. promoted by factors that cause oversecretion of acid, such as excess dietary fats, smoking, and alcohol use.
   d. promoted by a combination of factors that cause erosion of the gastric mucosa, including certain drugs and *H. pylori.*

8. An optimal teaching plan for an outpatient with stomach cancer receiving radiation therapy should include information about
   a. cancer support groups, alopecia, and stomatitis.
   b. nutrition supplements, ostomy care, and support groups.
   c. prosthetic devices, wound and skin care, and grief counseling.
   d. wound and skin care, nutrition, drugs, and community resources.

9. The teaching plan for the patient being discharged after an acute episode of upper GI bleeding includes information about the importance of *(select all that apply)*
   a. limiting alcohol intake to 1 serving per day.
   b. only taking aspirin with milk or bread products.
   c. avoiding taking aspirin and drugs containing aspirin.
   d. only taking drugs prescribed by the health care provider.
   e. taking all drugs 1 hour before mealtime to prevent further bleeding.

10. Several patients come to the urgent care center with nausea, vomiting, and diarrhea that began 2 hours ago while attending a large family reunion potluck dinner. You ask the patients specifically about foods they ingested containing
    a. beef.
    b. meat and milk.
    c. poultry and eggs.
    d. home-preserved vegetables.

1. b, 2. d, 3. c, 4. a, 5. c, 6. c, 7. d, 8. d, 9. c, d, 10. b

For rationales to these answers and even more NCLEX review questions, visit *http://evolve.elsevier.com/Lewis/medsurg.*

ⓔ EVOLVE WEBSITE/RESOURCES LIST

http://evolve.elsevier.com/Lewis/medsurg

Review Questions (Online Only)

Key Points

Answer Keys for Questions
- Rationales for Bridge to NCLEX Examination Questions
- Answer Guidelines for Case Study on p. 921

Student Case Studies
- Patient With Oral Cancer
- Patient With Peptic Ulcer Disease

Nursing Care Plans
- eNursing Care Plan 41.1: Patient With Nausea and Vomiting
- eNursing Care Plan 41.2: Patient With Peptic Ulcer Disease

Conceptual Care Map Creator

Audio Glossary

Content Updates

REFERENCES

*1. Matthews C: A review of nausea and vomiting in the anaesthetic and post anaesthetic environment, *J Perioper Pract* 27:224, 2017.

*2. Bošnjak SM, Gralla RJ, Schwartzberg L: Prevention of chemotherapy-induced nausea, *Support Care Cancer* 25:1661, 2017.

*3. Nguyen LA, Lee L: Complementary and alternative medicine for nausea and vomiting. In: Koch KL, Hasler WL, eds: *Nausea and vomiting*, New York, 2017, Springer.

*4. Dietrich T, Webb I, Stenhouse L, et al: Evidence summary: The relationship between oral and cardiovascular disease, *British Dental Jour* 222:381, 2017.

5. National Cancer Institute: SEER stat fact sheets. Retrieved from *http://seer.cancer.gov/statfacts/html*.

*6. de Martel C, Plummer M, Vignat J, et al: Worldwide burden of cancer attributable to HPV by site, country and HPV type, *Int J Cancer* 141:664, 2017.

7. The Oral Cancer Foundation. Surgery for oral cancer. Retrieved from *https://oralcancerfoundation.org/treatment/surgery/*.

8. American Cancer Society. Treating oral cancer. Retrieved from *www.cancer.org/cancer/oral-cavity-and-oropharyngeal-cancer/treating.html*.

9. American Gastroenterological Association. GERD. Retrieved from *www.gastro.org/patient-care/conditions-diseases/gerd*.

*10. Mansour NM, El-Serag HB, Anandasabapathy S: Barrett's esophagus: Best practices for treatment and post-treatment surveillance, *Ann Cardiothoracic Surg* 6:75, 2017.

*11. Sandhu DS, Fass R: Current trends in the management of gastroesophageal reflux disease, *Gut Liver* 12:7, 2018.

*12. Nehra AK, Alexander JA, Loftus CG, et al: Proton pump inhibitors: Review of emerging concerns, *Mayo Clinic Proc* 93:240, 2018.

*13. Gyawali CP, Fass R. Management of gastroesophageal reflux disease, *Gastroenterology* 154:302, 2018.

14. American Cancer Society. Treating esophageal cancer. Retrieved from *www.cancer.org/cancer/esophagus-cancer/treating.html*.

15. Prasad MA, Friedman LS, Anania FA: Peptic ulcer disease. In: Srinivasan S, Friedman L, eds:*Sitaraman and Friedman's essentials of gastroenterology*, ed 2, Oxford, United Kingdom, 2018, John Wiley & Sons Ltd.

16. Lanas A, Chan FK: Peptic ulcer disease, *Lancet* 390:613, 2017.

17. Gigek CO, Chen ES, Smith MA: Epigenetic alterations in stomach cancer. In: Patel V, Preedy VR, eds: *Handbook of nutrition, diet, and epigenetics*, New York, 2017, Springer.

18. American Cancer Society. Treating stomach cancer. Retrieved from *www.cancer.org/cancer/stomach-cancer/treating.html*.

*19. Abougergi MS: Epidemiology of upper gastrointestinal hemorrhage in the USA: Is the bleeding slowing down? *Digestive Diseases and Science* 63:1091, 2018.

*20. Barletta JF, Mangram AJ, Sucher JF, et al: Stress ulcer prophylaxis in neurocritical care, *Neurocrit Care* 19:1, 2017.

21. Rey JW, Hoffman A, Teubner D, et al: *Therapeutic endoscopy in the gastrointestinal tract*, New York, 2018, Springer.

22. National Digestive Diseases Information Clearinghouse. Bacteria and foodborne illness. Retrieved from *www.niddk.nih.gov/health-information/health-topics/digestive-diseases/foodborne-illnesses/Pages/facts.aspx*.

*Evidence-based information for clinical practice.

42

Lower Gastrointestinal Problems

Mariann M. Harding

In this life we cannot do great things. We can only do small things with great love.

Mother Teresa

http://evolve.elsevier.com/Lewis/medsurg

CONCEPTUAL FOCUS

Acid-Base Balance
Elimination
Fluids and Electrolytes

Inflammation
Nutrition
Pain

Stress

LEARNING OUTCOMES

1. Explain the common etiologies and interprofessional and nursing management of diarrhea, fecal incontinence, and constipation.
2. Describe common causes of acute abdominal pain and nursing management of the patient after a laparotomy.
3. Describe the interprofessional and nursing management of acute appendicitis, peritonitis, and gastroenteritis.
4. Compare and contrast the inflammatory bowel diseases of ulcerative colitis and Crohn's disease, including pathophysiology, clinical manifestations, complications, and interprofessional and nursing management.
5. Distinguish among small and large bowel obstructions, including causes, clinical manifestations, and interprofessional and nursing management.

6. Describe the clinical manifestations and interprofessional and nursing management of colorectal cancer.
7. Select nursing interventions to manage the care of the patient after bowel resection and ostomy surgery.
8. Distinguish between diverticulosis and diverticulitis, including clinical manifestations and interprofessional and nursing management.
9. Compare and contrast the types of hernias, including etiology and surgical and nursing management.
10. Describe the types of malabsorption syndromes and interprofessional care of celiac disease, lactase deficiency, and short bowel syndrome.
11. Describe the types, clinical manifestations, and interprofessional and nursing management of anorectal conditions.

KEY TERMS

anal fistula, p. 965
appendicitis, p. 937
celiac disease, p. 960
constipation, p. 929
Crohn's disease, p. 939
diarrhea, p. 924
diverticulitis, p. 957
fecal incontinence, p. 928

fistula, p. 958
gastroenteritis, p. 939
hemorrhoids, p. 963
hernia, p. 959
inflammatory bowel disease (IBD), p. 939
intestinal obstruction, p. 945
irritable bowel syndrome (IBS), p. 936
lactase deficiency, p. 962

ostomy, p. 952
paralytic ileus, p. 945
peritonitis, p. 938
short bowel syndrome (SBS), p. 962
steatorrhea, p. 960
ulcerative colitis (UC), p. 939

The wide variety of gastrointestinal (GI) problems discussed in this chapter include diarrhea, constipation, and fecal incontinence; inflammatory and infectious bowel problems; bowel trauma; bowel obstructions; colorectal cancer; abdominal and bowel surgery (including ostomy formation); and malabsorption problems. Conceptually, patients often have problems with impaired elimination and nutrition. Many have inflammation and pain and are at risk for altered fluid and electrolyte balance. Promoting optimal bowel habits and nutrition are common goals.

DIARRHEA

Diarrhea is the passage of at least 3 loose or liquid stools per day.[1] It may be acute, lasting 14 days or less, or persistent, lasting longer than 14 days. Chronic diarrhea lasts 30 days or longer.

Etiology and Pathophysiology

The primary cause of acute diarrhea is ingesting infectious organisms (Table 42.1). Viruses cause most cases of infectious diarrhea in the United States. While some viral infections can

TABLE 42.1 Causes and Manifestations of Acute Infectious Diarrhea

Type of Organism	Manifestations	Source of Infection/Susceptibility
Bacterial		
Campylobacter jejuni	• Diarrhea, abdominal cramps, and fever. Sometimes nausea and vomiting • Lasts about 7 days	• Undercooked poultry and unpasteurized milk • Most frequent in summer months
Clostridium difficile	• Watery diarrhea, fever, anorexia, nausea, abdominal pain	• Prolonged use of antibiotics followed by exposure to feces-contaminated surfaces • Spores on hands and environmental surfaces are extremely hard to kill
Clostridium perfringens	• Diarrhea, abdominal cramps, nausea, and vomiting • Occurs 6–24 hr after eating contaminated food and lasts about 24 hr	• Associated with meats, gravies, stews, dried or precooked foods • Can cause serious illness in anyone, especially older adults
Enterohemorrhagic Escherichia coli (e.g., E. coli O157:H7)	• Severe abdominal cramping, bloody diarrhea, and vomiting • Low-grade fever • Usually lasts 5–7 days	• Can cause serious illness, especially in older adults • May progress to life-threatening renal failure • Transmitted in water or food contaminated with infected feces
Enterotoxigenic E. coli	• Watery or bloody diarrhea, abdominal cramps • Nausea, vomiting, and fever may be present • Mean duration >60 hr	• Most common cause of traveler's diarrhea • Transmitted in water or food contaminated with infected feces
Salmonella	• Diarrhea, fever, and abdominal cramps • Lasts 4–7 days	• Reservoir is poultry, reptiles, and other animals (especially turtles, lizards, snakes, chicks, and young birds) • Can be transmitted by handling animals • Found in undercooked poultry, meat, and foods prepared with raw eggs
Shigella	• Diarrhea (sometimes bloody), fever, and stomach cramps • Usually lasts 5–7 days • Postinfection arthritis may occur	• Transmitted via fecal-oral route or in food or water contaminated with infected feces • Can contaminate recreational water
Staphylococcus	• Nausea, vomiting, abdominal cramps, and diarrhea • Usually mild • May cause illness in as little as 30 min • Lasts 1–3 days	• 25%–50% of people are carriers in mucous membranes, skin, or hair • Transmitted in food contaminated by food workers who are carriers or through contaminated milk and cheese
Parasitic		
Cryptosporidium	• Watery diarrhea • Lasts about 2 wks • May have abdominal cramps, nausea, vomiting, fever, dehydration, weight loss • May be fatal in those who are immunocompromised (e.g., AIDS)	• Lives in human intestines • Transmitted in stool of infected human or animal • Outer shell allows it to live for long periods outside of body and makes it resistant to chlorine • Common cause of waterborne disease (swimming pools, lakes, drinking water, food contaminated with feces)
Entamoeba histolytica	• Diarrhea, abdominal cramping • Only 10%–20% are ill, and symptoms are usually mild	• Fecally contaminated food, water, or hands • Most common in developing countries • In the United States, high-risk groups include travelers, recent immigrants, and homosexual men
Giardia lamblia	• Abdominal cramps, nausea, diarrhea • May interfere with nutrient absorption	• Highly contagious • Transmitted via fecal-oral route • Found in fresh lakes and rivers. Can be transmitted in swimming pools, water parks, and hot tubs
Viral		
Norovirus (Norwalk-like virus)	• Nausea, vomiting, diarrhea, stomach cramping • Rapid onset. Lasts 1–2 days	• Very contagious • Virus is present in stool and emesis
Rotavirus	• Fever, vomiting, and profuse watery diarrhea • Lasts 3–8 days	• Highly contagious • Transmitted mainly by fecal-oral route

be deadly, most are mild and last less than 24 hours. So, most patients rarely seek treatment.

Bacterial infection with *Escherichia coli* O157:H7, a type of enterohemorrhagic *E. coli*, is a common cause of bloody diarrhea in the United States. It is transmitted by undercooked beef or chicken contaminated with the bacteria or in fruits and vegetables exposed to contaminated manure. Other pathologic *E. coli* strains are endemic in developing countries and often cause traveler's diarrhea. *Giardia lamblia* is the most common intestinal parasite that causes diarrhea in the United States.

Infectious organisms attack the intestines in different ways. Some organisms (e.g., Rotavirus A, Norovirus, *G. lamblia*) change the secretion and/or absorption of enterocytes in the small intestine and do not cause inflammation. Other organisms (e.g., *Clostridium difficile*) impair absorption by destroying cells, causing inflammation in the colon, and producing toxins that cause damage.

Secretory diarrhea is a common result of bacterial or viral infections. It occurs when ingested pathogens survive in the GI tract long enough to absorb into the enterocytes. The resulting chain reaction changes cell permeability and causes the oversecretion of water and sodium and chloride ions into the bowel.

Organisms enter the body in contaminated food (e.g., *Salmonella* in undercooked eggs and chicken) or contaminated drinking water (*G. lamblia* in contaminated lakes or pools). Travelers often get diarrhea, especially if they travel to countries with poorer sanitation than their own. Infection can spread from person to person via the fecal-oral route. For example, adult day care workers can transmit infection from one resident to another if they do not wash their hands after changing soiled diapers or linens.

A person's age, gastric acidity, intestinal microflora, and immune status influence susceptibility to pathogenic organisms. Older adults are most likely to have life-threatening diarrhea. Since stomach acid kills ingested pathogens, taking drugs to decrease stomach acid (e.g., proton pump inhibitors [PPIs]) increases the chance that pathogens will survive.[2]

The healthy human colon contains short-chain fatty acids and bacteria, such as *E. coli*. These organisms aid in fermentation and provide a microbial barrier against pathogenic bacteria. Antibiotics kill the normal flora, making the person more susceptible to pathogenic organisms. For example, patients receiving broad-spectrum antibiotics (e.g., carbapenems, cephalosporins, piperacillin/tazobactam) are susceptible to pathogenic strains of *C. difficile*.[2] *C. difficile* infection (CDI) causes the most serious antibiotic-associated diarrhea and is a common cause of hospital-acquired GI illness in the United States.

People who are immunocompromised because of disease (e.g., human immunodeficiency virus [HIV]) or immunosuppressive drugs are susceptible to GI tract infection. Immunocompromised patients receiving jejunal enteral nutrition (EN) are especially prone to CDI and other foodborne infections. Jejunostomy and nasointestinal feedings, which bypass the stomach's acid environment, do not contain the poorly digestible fiber that normal colonic bacteria need for survival.

Diarrhea is not always due to infection. Drugs and specific food intolerances can cause diarrhea. Large amounts of undigested carbohydrate in the bowel, lactose intolerance, and certain laxatives (e.g., lactulose, sodium phosphate, magnesium citrate) produce osmotic diarrhea. *Osmotic diarrhea* results from rapid GI transit that prevents fluid and electrolyte absorption. Bile salts and undigested fats lead to excess fluid secretion into the GI tract. Diarrhea from celiac disease and short bowel syndrome result from malabsorption in the small intestine.

Clinical Manifestations

Infections that attack the upper GI tract (e.g., Norovirus, *G. lamblia*) usually produce large-volume, watery stools, cramping, and periumbilical pain (Table 42.1). Patients have either a low-grade or no fever and often have nausea and vomiting before the diarrhea begins. Infections of the colon and distal small bowel (e.g., *Shigella, Salmonella, C. difficile*) cause fever and frequent bloody diarrhea with a small volume.

Leukocytes, blood, and mucus may be present in the stool, depending on the causative agent. Severe diarrhea may cause life-threatening dehydration, electrolyte problems (e.g., hypokalemia), and acid-base imbalances (metabolic acidosis). CDI can progress to severe colitis and intestinal perforation.

Diagnostic Studies

Stool cultures are usually done only in patients who are very ill; have a fever, bloody diarrhea, or diarrhea lasting longer than 3 days; or were exposed during an outbreak.[1] Those with travelers' diarrhea lasting 14 days or longer should be evaluated

TABLE 42.2 Drug Therapy
Antidiarrheal Drugs

Drug	Mechanism of Action
bismuth subsalicylate (Pepto-Bismol)	Decreases secretions and has weak antibacterial activity. Used to prevent traveler's diarrhea
calcium polycarbophil (FiberCon)	Bulk-forming agent that absorbs excess fluid from diarrhea to form a gel. Used when intestinal mucosa cannot absorb fluid
diphenoxylate with atropine (Lomotil)	Opioid and anticholinergic. Decreases peristalsis and intestinal motility
loperamide (Imodium, Pepto Diarrhea Control)	Inhibits peristalsis, delays transit, increases absorption of fluid from stools
octreotide acetate (Sandostatin)	Suppresses serotonin secretion, stimulates fluid absorption from GI tract, decreases intestinal motility
paregoric (camphorated tincture of opium)	Opioid. Decreases peristalsis and intestinal motility

for parasitic infections. Stools are examined for blood, mucus, white blood cells (WBCs), and parasites. Cultures reliably identify infectious organisms. Multiple-pathogen stool tests can detect common viral, parasitic, and bacterial organisms from a single stool sample.

Blood cultures should be done in those with signs of sepsis or systemic infection (e.g., high fever) or who are immunocompromised.[1] The WBC count may be high. People with long-standing diarrhea can develop anemia from iron and folate deficiencies. Increased hematocrit, blood urea nitrogen (BUN), and creatinine levels are signs of fluid deficit.

In patients with chronic diarrhea, measuring stool electrolytes, pH, and osmolality helps determine whether the diarrhea is from decreased fluid absorption or increased fluid secretion. Measuring stool fat and undigested muscle fibers may show fat and protein malabsorption conditions. Some patients with secretory diarrhea have high serum levels of GI hormones, such as vasoactive intestinal polypeptide and gastrin.

Interprofessional Care

Treatment of diarrhea depends on the cause. Acute infectious diarrhea is usually self-limiting. The major concerns are preventing transmission, replacing fluid and electrolytes, and protecting the skin. Most patients tolerate oral fluids. Solutions containing glucose and electrolytes (e.g., Pedialyte) may be enough to replace losses from mild diarrhea. If losses are severe, it will be necessary to give parenteral fluids, electrolytes, vitamins, and nutrition. Teach the patient to avoid foods and drugs that cause diarrhea.

Antidiarrheal agents have limited short-term use. They coat and protect mucous membranes, absorb irritating substances, inhibit intestinal transit, decrease intestinal secretions, or decrease central nervous system stimulation of the GI tract (Table 42.2). Antidiarrheal agents are contraindicated in treating some infectious diarrheas because they potentially prolong exposure to the organism.[1] They are used cautiously in inflammatory bowel disease (IBD) because of the danger of causing *toxic megacolon* (colonic dilation greater than 5 cm).

Antibiotics rarely have a role in treating acute diarrhea. They are given only for certain infections or when the infected person is severely ill or immunosuppressed. The 2 antibiotics recommended for empiric therapy in adults are a fluoroquinolone, such as ciprofloxacin, and azithromycin.[1]

***Clostridium difficile* infection.** CDI is a particularly hazardous health care–associated infection (HAI). The risk for contracting CDI is highest in patients receiving antimicrobial, chemotherapy, gastric acid–suppressing, or immunosuppressive agents. *C. difficile* spores can survive for up to 70 days on objects, including commodes, telephones, bedside tables, and floors. Health care workers who do not adhere to strict infection control precautions can transmit *C. difficile* from patient to patient. Meticulous hand washing with soap and water is extremely important in limiting the spread of *C. difficile*. *Lactobacillus* probiotics may be used to prevent CDI or as an adjunct therapy to help prevent the risk for recurrent CDI.[3]

CDI is treated with either oral vancomycin (125 mg 4 times a day) or fidaxomicin (200 mg twice daily) for 10 days. All nonessential antibiotics, stool softeners, laxatives, and antidiarrheal agents should be stopped. Metronidazole is an option when patients are unable to be treated with vancomycin or fidaxomicin. Patients with severe, complicated CDI with shock, hypotension, ileus, or megacolon should receive vancomycin 500 mg 4 times daily orally with IV metronidazole. Patients with ileus can receive vancomycin via enema.

Recurrent CDI occurs in about 20% of patients. The risk increases with the use of additional antibiotics and CDI recurrences. *Fecal microbiota transplantation* (FMT) is emerging as the most effective treatment for recurrent CDI.[3] FMT reestablishes healthy intestinal flora by infusing fecal bacteria obtained from healthy donor stool into the patient's colon. To perform an FMT, feces obtained from the donor is pureed into a liquid, slurry consistency using saline, water, or pasteurized cow's milk. The donor stool is then placed in the GI tract via an enema, nasoenteral tube, or during colonoscopy. The major concern with FMT is the potential for transmitting infectious agents in the donor stool. Using feces from donors who have intimate physical contact with the recipient and careful screening minimize this risk. Most patients have diarrhea immediately after the procedure.

❖ NURSING MANAGEMENT: ACUTE INFECTIOUS DIARRHEA

◆ Nursing Assessment

Begin the nursing assessment with a thorough history and physical examination (Table 42.3). Ask the patient to describe their stool pattern and associated symptoms. Focus on the duration, frequency, character, and consistency of stool and the relationship to other symptoms, such as pain and vomiting. Ask about medical conditions that may cause diarrhea and whether the person is taking drugs, such as antibiotics and laxatives, which are known to cause diarrhea, decrease stomach acidity, or cause immunosuppression. Determine whether the patient has traveled to a foreign country or been at a day care facility recently and if other family members are ill. Ask about food preparation practices, food intolerances (e.g., milk), and changes in diet and appetite.

Assess for fever and signs of dehydration (dry skin, low-grade fever, orthostatic changes in pulse and BP, decreased and concentrated urine). Assess the abdomen for distention, pain, and guarding. Inspect the perineal skin for signs of redness and breakdown from the diarrhea.

TABLE 42.3 Nursing Assessment

Diarrhea

Subjective Data

Important Health Information

Past health history: Recent travel, hospitalization, infections, stress. Diverticulitis or malabsorption, metabolic disorders, IBD, IBS

Medications: Laxatives or enemas, magnesium-containing antacids, sorbitol-containing suspensions or elixirs, antibiotics, methyldopa, digitalis, colchicine; OTC antidiarrheal drugs

Surgery or other treatments: Stomach or bowel surgery, radiation

Functional Health Patterns

Health perception–health management: Chronic laxative use, malaise

Nutritional-metabolic: Ingestion of fatty and spicy foods, food intolerances. Anorexia, nausea, vomiting, weight loss. Thirst

Elimination: Increased stool frequency, volume, and looseness. Change in color and character of stools. Steatorrhea, abdominal bloating. Decreased urine output

Cognitive-perceptual: Abdominal tenderness, abdominal pain and cramping, tenesmus

Objective Data

General

Lethargy, sunken eyeballs, fever, malnutrition

Integumentary

Pallor, dry mucous membranes, poor skin turgor, perianal irritation

Gastrointestinal

Frequent soft to liquid stools that may alternate with constipation, altered stool color. Abdominal distention, hyperactive bowel sounds. Pus, blood, mucus, or fat in stools. Fecal impaction

Urinary

Decreased output, concentrated urine

Possible Diagnostic Findings

Abnormal serum electrolyte levels. Anemia, leukocytosis, eosinophilia, hypoalbuminemia. Positive stool cultures. Ova, parasites, leukocytes, blood, or fat in stool. Abnormal sigmoidoscopy or colonoscopy findings. Abnormal lower GI series

---

◆ Nursing Diagnoses

Nursing diagnoses for the patient with acute infectious diarrhea include:

* Diarrhea
* Fluid imbalance
* Electrolyte imbalance

For more information on nursing diagnoses and interventions for diarrhea, see eNursing Care Plan 42.1 on the website for this chapter.

◆ Planning

The overall goals are that the patient with diarrhea will have (1) cessation of diarrhea and resumption of normal bowel patterns; (2) normal fluid, electrolyte, and acid-base balance; (3) normal nutritional status; and (4) no perianal/perineal skin breakdown.

◆ Nursing Implementation

Consider all cases of acute diarrhea as infectious until the cause is known. Strict infection control precautions are needed to prevent the illness from spreading to others. Wash your hands with soap and water before and after contact with each patient and when handling body fluids of any kind. Flush vomitus and stool in the toilet. Teach the patient principles of hygiene, infection control, and the potential dangers of an illness that is infectious to themselves and others. Discuss proper food handling, cooking, and storage with the patient and caregiver (see Tables 41.24 and 41.25).

Viruses and *C. difficile* spores are extremely hard to kill. Alcohol-based hand cleaners and ammonia-based disinfectants are ineffective. Vigorous cleaning with soap and water does not kill everything. Immediately put patients with CDI in isolation. Ensure that visitors and all providers wear gloves and gowns. Give infected patients their own disposable stethoscopes and thermometers. Consider all objects in the room contaminated. Ensure surfaces and equipment are disinfected with a 10% bleach solution or a disinfectant labeled as *C. difficile* sporicidal.

FECAL INCONTINENCE

Etiology and Pathophysiology

Fecal incontinence is the involuntary passage of stool. It occurs when the normal structures that maintain continence are damaged or disrupted. Defecation is a voluntary action when the neuromuscular system is intact (see Chapter 38). Problems with motor function (contraction of sphincters and rectal floor muscles) and/or sensory function (ability to perceive the presence of stool or have the urge to defecate) can result in fecal incontinence. Contributing factors include altered bowel habits, weakness or disruption of the internal or external anal sphincter, damage to the pudendal nerve or other nerves that innervate the anorectum, and damage to the anal tissue (Table 42.4).

For women, obstetric trauma is the most common cause of sphincter disruption. Childbirth, aging, and menopause contribute to the development of fecal incontinence. Anorectal surgery can damage the sphincters and pudendal nerves. Radiation for prostate cancer decreases rectal compliance. Neurologic conditions, including stroke and multiple sclerosis, interfere with defecation.

People with normal functioning defecation can have incontinence if immobility prevents prompt access to a toilet or stool is accidentally discharged with diarrhea. Chronic constipation can lead to *fecal impaction,* a collection of hardened feces in the rectum or sigmoid colon that a person cannot expel. Incontinence occurs as liquid stool seeps around the hardened feces. Fecal impaction is a common problem in older adults with limited mobility. Constipated persons tend to strain during defecation. Straining contributes to incontinence because it weakens the pelvic floor muscles.

Diagnostic Studies and Interprofessional Care

The diagnosis and effective management of fecal incontinence require a thorough health history and physical examination. Ask the patient about the number of incontinent episodes per week, stool consistency and volume, and the degree that incontinence interferes with work and social activities. A rectal examination can reveal reduced anal canal muscle tone and contraction strength of the external sphincter, as well as detect internal prolapse, rectocele, hemorrhoids, masses, and fecal impaction. Other tests, such as anorectal manometry, anorectal ultrasonography, and anal electromyography, are done when symptoms persist after treating underlying problems or certain problems need further evaluation.[4]

TABLE 42.4 **Common Causes of Fecal Incontinence**	
Anal Sphincter Weakness	**Neurologic Disease**
• Anorectal infection	• Brain tumor
• Injury	• Congenital abnormalities (e.g., spina bifida, myelomeningocele)
• Anorectal surgery for hemorrhoids, fistula, and fissures	• Dementia
• Childbirth injury	• Diabetes
• Perineal trauma or pelvic fracture	• Multiple sclerosis
• Internal sphincter thinning	• Neuropathy
	• Spinal cord lesions
Functional	• Stroke
• Physical or mobility impairments affecting toileting ability (e.g., frail older person who cannot get to the bathroom in time)	**Pelvic Floor Dysfunction**
	• Fistula
	• Rectal prolapse
Inflammatory	**Other**
• Inflammatory bowel disease	• Chronic constipation
• Radiation	• Denervation of pelvic muscles from chronic straining
	• Diarrhea
	• Fecal impaction

Treatment of incontinence depends on the cause. Maintaining normal stool consistency and a bowel management program are important. This includes regular defecation, a high-fiber diet, and increased intake of caffeine-free fluids. Dietary fiber supplements or bulk-forming laxatives, like psyllium (e.g., Metamucil), increase stool bulk, firm consistency, and promote the sensation of rectal filling. Patients may need to reduce the intake of foods that cause diarrhea and rectal irritation. Common triggers include caffeine, products containing artificial sweeteners, dairy products, high gas–producing vegetables (e.g., broccoli, cabbage, cauliflower), and vegetables containing insoluble fiber (e.g., lettuce, tomatoes, corn).

Fecal incontinence from fecal impaction usually resolves after manual removal of the hard feces and cleansing enemas. Antidiarrheal agents (e.g., loperamide) are useful in slowing intestinal transit.

Physical therapy and biofeedback training can improve awareness of rectal sensation, coordinate internal and external anal sphincters, and increase the strength of external sphincter contraction. Biofeedback training requires intact sensory and motor nerves and motivation to learn. It is a safe, painless, and effective treatment.[4]

Mild electrical stimulation of the sacral nerves targets communication problems between the brain and nerves that control the pelvic floor muscles and sphincters. Electrical stimulation can improve quality of life. Some patients may achieve complete continence.[4]

For patients who do not respond to conservative measures, treatment with dextranomer/hyaluronic acid gel (Solesta) may be used. In this treatment, the gel is injected into the deep submucosa of the patient's anal canal. It works by building up tissue in the anal area, narrowing the anal canal and allowing muscles to more adequately close. No anesthesia is given. Postinjection pain and bleeding may occur.

Surgery (e.g., sphincter repair procedures) is an option when other conservative treatments fail, the patient has a full-thickness prolapse, or the anal sphincter needs repair. A colostomy is sometimes needed.

❖ NURSING MANAGEMENT: FECAL INCONTINENCE

◆ Nursing Assessment

Fecal incontinence is embarrassing, uncomfortable, and irritating to the skin. Its unpredictable nature makes it hard to maintain school and work activities and hampers social or intimate contact. Be sensitive to the patient's feelings when discussing incontinence.

Ask about bowel patterns before the incontinence developed; current bowel habits; stool consistency, volume, and frequency; and symptoms, including pain during defecation and a feeling of incomplete evacuation *(tenesmus).* The Bristol Stool Scale is helpful to assess stool consistency. Assess whether the patient has a sensation of urgency to evacuate the bowel or sensation of passing flatus and leaking stool. Ask about daily activities (mealtimes and work), diet, and family and social activities and the degree that incontinence interferes with these activities.

Check the perineal area for irritation or breakdown. Patients who have fecal incontinence are at risk for *incontinence-associated dermatitis* (IAD).[4] IAD results from chemical irritants in the feces causing skin damage. Symptoms include redness, skin loss, and rash. The location of IAD is usually the perianal or perineal area, buttocks, or upper thighs. Fungal infection is common and seen as a dark red center surrounded by satellite lesions. Your assessment is important in distinguishing IAD from pressure injury development.

◆ Nursing Implementation

Regardless of the cause of fecal incontinence, bowel training is effective for many patients. Bowel elimination occurs at regular intervals in most people. Knowing the patient's usual bowel pattern can help you plan a bowel program that will achieve optimal stool consistency and establish predictable bowel elimination patterns. For the hospitalized patient, placement on a bedpan, help to a bedside commode, or walks to the bathroom at a regular time daily help to establish regular defecation. The best time to schedule elimination is within 30 minutes after breakfast.

If these techniques are not effective in reestablishing bowel regularity, administer bisacodyl, a glycerin suppository, or a small phosphate enema 15 to 30 minutes before the usual evacuation time. These preparations stimulate the anorectal reflex. Since stimulation will not occur unless the suppository or enema touches the rectal wall, first check for stool in the rectum and digitally remove it before inserting the laxative. Once a regular pattern is established, stop these drugs. Digital stimulation is another method for stimulating the anorectal reflex. It is often included in bowel programs for people with neurogenic bowels (e.g., from spinal cord injury). Irrigating the rectum and colon (usually with tap water) at regular intervals is another way to achieve continence in patients with neurogenic bowel.

Maintaining perineal skin integrity is a priority, especially in the bedridden patient. Feces can contaminate wounds, damage skin, cause bladder infections, and spread infections such as *C. difficile.* Fecal containment is essential. One way to contain stool is a stool management system (e.g., Flexi-Seal, DigniCare, Actiflo). These systems funnel liquid stool from the rectum into a containment system. Common features include a retention cuff that sits above the anal sphincter and soft tubing that extends from this cuff to a secure hub that allows a person to change the containment canister when it is full. A system can remain in place for weeks. Their use may decrease the risk for CDI, skin damage from exposure to stool, IAD, and pressure injuries. Do not use a rectal tube or urinary catheter as a stool catheter. They

can reduce the responsiveness of the rectal sphincter and irritate or ulcerate the rectal mucosa.

Perform frequent skin assessments when using absorbent products. Incontinence pads are an option when the patient is in bed. Briefs should be used only during ambulation or when sitting in a chair. Make sure they are changed promptly after each episode of incontinence.

Use absorbent products in combination with a defined skin care program. This includes prompt cleansing, moisturizing, and skin protection. Cleanse the skin gently, using a skin cleanser rather than soap and water. Options include a cotton cloth moistened with a hydrating skin cleansing foam, incontinence clean-up cloths, or baby wipes. Avoid products that contain alcohol as they can cause drying of the skin and discomfort if skin is irritated. Pat the skin dry or use a blow dryer on a cool setting. Do not rub the skin dry. Apply a moisture barrier and, if needed, a skin barrier cream for more protection. For patients unable to care for themselves at home, you should teach caregivers how to maintain skin integrity.

Fecal incontinence is an overwhelming burden for most patients. Be sensitive to their fears. Teach them ways to reduce incontinence episodes and better cope with them when they do occur. Help patients identify food triggers that may worsen symptoms. Encourage them to avoid those foods and exercise after meals. Tell them to try to use bathrooms when they are available. Patients may be more confident when they use discreet, disposable briefs or pads. Have them wear dark-colored clothing that they can quickly remove for toileting. Ready access to a spare set of clothing and cleansing cloths is important.

CONSTIPATION

Constipation is characterized by difficult or infrequent bowel movements, often accompanied by excessive exertion during defecation or a feeling of incomplete evacuation.[5] Constipation is a symptom, not a disease. It can be acute, usually lasting less than 1 week, or chronic, lasting over 3 months.

Etiology and Pathophysiology

Risk factors associated with chronic constipation include a low-fiber diet, decreased physical activity, or ignoring the defecation urge. Ignoring the urge to defecate for a prolonged period can cause the muscles and mucosa of the rectum to become insensitive to the presence of feces. In addition, the prolonged retention of feces results in drying of stool due to water absorption. The harder and drier the feces, the harder it is to expel. Emotions, including anxiety, depression, and stress, affect the GI tract and can contribute to constipation.

Constipation occurs with diseases that slow GI transit and hamper neurologic function, such as diabetes, Parkinson's disease, and multiple sclerosis (Table 42.5). Many drugs, especially opioids, cause constipation (Table 42.6).[5]

Some people think they are constipated if they do not have a daily bowel movement. This can result in chronic laxative use and *cathartic colon syndrome,* a condition in which the colon becomes dilated and atonic (lacking muscle tone). Ultimately, the person cannot defecate without a laxative.

Clinical Manifestations

The clinical presentation varies from a mild discomfort to a more severe event mimicking an "acute abdomen." Stools are absent or hard, dry, and difficult to pass. Abdominal distention, bloating, increased flatulence, and increased rectal pressure may be present.

TABLE 42.5 Diseases Associated With Constipation

Colonic Disorders
- Cancer
- Diverticular disease
- Inflammatory bowel disease
- Intestinal stenosis
- Intussusception
- Luminal or extraluminal obstructing lesions
- Rectocele
- Prolapse

Systemic Disorders
Collagen Vascular Disease
- Amyloidosis
- Systemic lupus erythematosus
- Systemic sclerosis (scleroderma)

Metabolic/Endocrine
- Chronic renal failure
- Diabetes
- Hypercalcemia/hyperparathyroidism
- Hypokalemia
- Hypothyroidism
- Pheochromocytoma
- Pregnancy

Neurologic Disorders
- Autonomic neuropathy (from diabetes)
- Hirschsprung's megacolon
- Multiple sclerosis
- Neurofibromatosis
- Parkinson's disease
- Spinal cord lesions or injury
- Stroke

TABLE 42.6 Drugs Associated With Constipation

Cardiovascular	• Antihypertensives • Furosemide • Hypolipidemics (cholestyramine, colestipol, statins)
GI	• Antacids containing aluminum, calcium • Antidiarrheals • Proton-pump inhibitors • Supplements (e.g., bismuth, calcium, iron)
Central nervous system	• Antidepressants (tricyclics, selective serotonin reuptake inhibitors) • Antiepileptics (carbamazepine, phenytoin, clonazepam) • Antipsychotics (butyrophenones, phenothiazines, barbiturates) • Benzodiazepines
Other	• Analgesics (opiates and derivatives) • Antitussives (codeine, dextromethorphan)

Hemorrhoids are a common complication of chronic constipation. They result from venous engorgement caused by repeated *Valsalva maneuvers* (straining) and venous compression from hard, impacted stool. The Valsalva maneuver may have serious outcomes for patients with heart failure, cerebral edema, hypertension, and coronary artery disease. During straining, the patient inspires deeply and holds the breath while contracting abdominal muscles and bearing down. This increases both intraabdominal and intrathoracic pressures and reduces venous return to the heart. The heart rate temporarily decreases along with a decrease in cardiac output. This results in a transient drop in arterial pressure. When the patient relaxes, thoracic pressure falls, resulting in a sudden flow of blood into the heart, increased heart rate, and an immediate rise in arterial pressure. These changes may be fatal for the patient who cannot compensate for the sudden increased blood flow returning to the heart.

Rectal mucosal ulcers and fissures may occur from stool stasis or straining. Diverticulosis is another potential complication of chronic constipation. It is more common in older patients.

In the presence of *obstipation* (absolute constipation with no passage of gas or stool) or fecal impaction secondary to constipation, colonic perforation may occur. Perforation, which is life threatening, causes abdominal pain, nausea, vomiting, fever, and a high WBC count.

Diagnostic Studies and Interprofessional Care

In most patients, the diagnosis of constipation is based on findings from a thorough history and physical examination. The physical should include an abdominal examination, inspection of the perianal and rectal region, and a digital rectal examination. Concerning signs include a sudden, persistent change in bowel habits (>6 weeks) in those over 50 years, rectal bleeding or bloody stools, iron deficiency anemia, weight loss, significant abdominal pain, family or personal history of colorectal cancer (CRC) or inflammatory bowel disease and palpable mass.[5] If any of these are present, tests are needed to rule out serious disease, such as CRC. These may include abdominal x-rays, barium enema, and colonoscopy or sigmoidoscopy.

Increasing dietary fiber, fluid intake, and exercise can prevent many cases of constipation.[6] Laxatives (Table 42.7) and enemas are an option in treating constipation. All promote bowel movements, but each class works differently. Which one a patient receives depends on the severity and duration of the constipation and the patient's health. Daily bulk-forming laxatives (psyllium) can prevent constipation because they work like dietary fiber and do not cause dependence. In patients with chronic constipation who do not respond to diet and lifestyle modifications, osmotic laxatives are the next recommended treatment. Stimulant laxatives are given to patients who do not respond to osmotic laxatives. Enemas are fast acting and can give immediate treatment of constipation but must be used cautiously. Agents containing sodium phosphate and magnesium can cause electrolyte imbalances in older adults and patients with heart and kidney problems.

Other therapies target specific patient needs. Peripherally acting opioid receptor antagonists (e.g., methylnaltrexone, naldemedine, naloxegol) decrease constipation caused by opioid use. They do not block the analgesic effects of opioids. Biofeedback therapy may help patients who have constipation because of *anismus* (uncoordinated contraction of the anal sphincter during straining).

A patient with severe constipation related to bowel motility or mechanical disorders may need more intense treatment. Diagnostic studies include anorectal manometry, GI tract transit studies, balloon expulsion test, and defecography. A patient with unrelenting constipation may need a colostomy, ileostomy, or continent fecal diversion. These procedures are discussed later in this chapter.[6]

Nutritional Therapy. Diet is a key factor in preventing and treating constipation. Many patients have improved symptoms when they increase their dietary fiber intake. Dietary fiber is found in fruits, vegetables, and grains (Table 42.8). Wheat bran and prunes are especially effective for preventing and treating constipation. Whole wheat and bran are high in insoluble fiber.

Dietary fiber adds to the stool bulk directly by attracting water. Adequate fluid intake (2 L/day) is essential. Large, bulky stools move through the colon much more quickly than small stools. However, the recommended fluid intake may be contraindicated in a patient with heart disease or renal failure. Tell the patient that increasing fiber intake may initially increase gas production because of fermentation in the colon, but this effect decreases over several days.

TABLE 42.7 Drug Therapy

Constipation

Mechanism of Action	Indications	Example	Comments
Bulk Forming Absorbs water. Increases bulk, thereby stimulating peristalsis *Action:* Usually within 24 hr	Acute and chronic constipation, irritable bowel syndrome, diverticulosis	methylcellulose (Citrucel) psyllium (Metamucil, Konsyl, Hydrocil, Fiberall)	Contraindicated in patients with abdominal pain, nausea, and vomiting and those suspected of having appendicitis, biliary tract obstruction, or acute hepatitis. Must be taken with fluids (≥8 oz). Best choice for initial treatment of constipation
Emollients Lubricate intestinal tract and soften feces, making hard stools easier to pass. Do not affect peristalsis *Action:* Softeners in 72 hr, lubricants in 8 hr	Acute and chronic constipation, fecal impaction, anorectal conditions	*Softeners:* docusate (Colace, Surfak) *Lubricants:* mineral oil (Fleet Mineral Oil Enema)	Can block absorption of fat-soluble vitamins, such as vitamin K, which may increase risk for bleeding in patients on anticoagulants
Prosecretory Agents Increases intestinal fluid secretion through direct action on epithelial cells, speeding colonic transit *Action:* Usually within 24 hr	Chronic idiopathic constipation, irritable bowel syndrome with constipation (women only)	linaclotide (Linzess) lubiprostone (Amitiza) plecanatide (Trulance)	Contraindicated in patients with history of mechanical GI obstruction. Can cause nausea and watery diarrhea
Saline and Osmotic Solutions Cause retention of fluid in intestinal lumen, reducing stool consistency and increasing volume *Action:* Within 15 min–3 hr	Chronic constipation, bowel preparation for diagnostic tests and surgery	lactulose magnesium salts (magnesium citrate, Milk of Magnesia) sodium phosphates (Fleet Enema, Phospho-soda) polyethylene glycol (MiraLAX, GoLYTELY)	May cause abdominal distention and diarrhea. Overuse of magnesium or sodium phosphates in older adults or those with renal failure can lead to fluid and electrolyte imbalances; least effective agents in this class
Stimulants Increases peristalsis and speeds colonic transit by irritating colon wall and stimulating enteric nerves *Action:* Usually within 12 hr	Acute constipation, bowel preparation for diagnostic tests and surgery	anthraquinones (cascara sagrada, senna) phenolphthalein: sennosides (Ex-Lax), bisacodyl (Correctol, Dulcolax)	Cause melanosis coli (brown or black pigmentation of colon). Most widely abused laxatives. Should not be used in patients with impaction or obstipation

EVIDENCE-BASED PRACTICE

Probiotics and Constipation

L.R. is an 82-yr-old woman with decreased mobility due to a recent hip fracture. During a check-up visit at the orthopedic clinic, L.R. states she is having discomfort due to constipation. She tells you she is following her discharge instructions, "drinking lots of water," and trying to increase fiber in her diet.

Making Clinical Decisions

Best Available Evidence. Quality of life decreases with increased severity in constipation symptoms. Many patients with constipation have modifiable risk factors related to their lifestyle. These include low-fiber diet, poor hydration, and/or sedentary lifestyle. In adults with constipation, there is an association between the use of probiotics, especially products containing *Bifidobacterium longum* and *Bifidobacterium lactis,* and significant improvements in gut transit time, stool frequency, and stool consistency.

Clinician Expertise. You know that diet, fluid intake, and activity can play a key role in treating and preventing constipation. You recently read about the potential benefit of probiotics in relieving constipation.

Patient Preferences and Values. L.R. asks if you know of anything else she can do as she does not want to take any more drugs.

Implications for Nursing Practice

1. What information would you share with L.R. about probiotics and constipation?
2. What data would you want from L.R. about her diet, activity, medications, and fluid intake?
3. Why is it important for you to know about alternative therapies? What is your role in supporting patients who want alternatives to drug therapy?

References for Evidence

Martinez-Martinez MI, Calabuig-Tulsa R, Cauli O: The effects of probiotics as a treatment for constipation in elderly people: A systematic review, *Arch Gerontol Geriatr* 71:142, 2017.

Serra J, Mascort-Roca J, Marzo-Castillejo M, et al.: Clinical practice guidelines for the management of constipation in adults: Part 2: Diagnosis and treatment, *Gastroenterol Hepatol* 40:303, 2017.

TABLE 42.8 Nutritional Therapy
High-Fiber Foods

	Fiber/Serving (g)	Serving Size	Calories/ Serving
Vegetables			
Asparagus	3.5	½ cup	18
Beans			
• Navy	8.4	½ cup	80
• Kidney	9.7	½ cup	94
• Lima	8.3	½ cup	63
• Pinto	8.9	½ cup	78
• String	2.1	½ cup	18
Broccoli	3.5	½ cup	18
Carrots, raw	1.8	½ cup	15
Corn	2.6	½ medium ear	72
Peas, canned	6.7	½ cup	63
Potatoes			
• Baked	1.9	½ medium	72
• Sweet	2.1	½ medium	79
Squash, acorn	7.0	1 cup	82
Tomato, raw	1.5	1 small	18
Fruits			
Apple	2.0	½ large	42
Blackberries	6.7	¾ cup	40
Orange	1.6	1 small	35
Peach	2.3	1 medium	38
Pear	2.0	½ medium	44
Raspberries	9.2	1 cup	42
Strawberries	3.1	1 cup	45
Grain Products			
Bread, whole wheat	1.3	1 slice	59
Cereal			
• All Bran (100%)	8.4	⅓ cup	70
• Corn Flakes	2.6	¾ cup	70
• Shredded Wheat	2.8	1 biscuit	70
Popcorn	3.0	3 cups	62

❖ NURSING MANAGEMENT: CONSTIPATION

◆ Nursing Assessment

Determine the patient's usual defecation patterns and habits. Ask the patient about the onset and duration of symptoms; the shape and consistency of the stool; and any difficulty with evacuation. Is the patient straining during defecation? Is there a feeling of incomplete evacuation or the need to use fingering to expel the feces? Ask about diet, exercise, laxative use, and history that could contribute to problems with defecation. Table 42.9 outlines the subjective and objective data you should obtain from a patient with constipation.

◆ Nursing Implementation

Tailor the nursing management of constipation to your assessment of the patient's symptoms. Teach the patient about the role of diet, adequate fluid intake, and regular exercise in preventing and treating constipation (Table 42.10). Emphasize the importance of a high-fiber diet. Teach the patient to establish a regular time to defecate and not to suppress the urge to defecate. Discourage the use of laxatives and enemas.

Defecation is easiest when the person is sitting on a commode with the knees higher than the hips. The sitting position

TABLE 42.9 Nursing Assessment
Constipation

Subjective Data
Important Health Information
Past health history: Colorectal disease, neurologic dysfunction, bowel obstruction, environmental changes, cancer, IBD, diabetes
Medications: Aluminum and calcium antacids, antidepressants, hypolipidemics, antipsychotics, diuretics, opioids, iron, PPIs, antidiarrheals

Functional Health Patterns
Health perception–health management: Chronic laxative or enema use. Rigid beliefs about bowel function. Malaise
Nutritional-metabolic: Changes in diet or mealtime. Fiber and fluid intake. Anorexia, nausea
Elimination: Change in usual bowel patterns. Hard, difficult-to-pass stool, decrease in stool frequency and amount. Flatus, abdominal distention. Straining, tenesmus, rectal pressure. Fecal incontinence (if impacted)
Activity-exercise: Daily activity routine. Immobility, sedentary lifestyle
Cognitive-perceptual: Dizziness, headache, anorectal pain. Abdominal pain on defecation
Coping–stress tolerance: Acute or chronic stress

Objective Data
General
Lethargy

Integumentary
Anorectal fissures, hemorrhoids, abscesses

Gastrointestinal
Abdominal distention. Hypoactive or absent bowel sounds. Palpable abdominal mass. Fecal impaction. Small, hard, dry stool. Stool with blood

Possible Diagnostic Findings
Guaiac-positive stools. Abdominal x-ray showing stool in lower colon

allows gravity to aid defecation, and flexing the hips straightens the angle between the anal canal and rectum so that stool flows out more easily. Place a footstool in front of the toilet to promote flexion of the hips. It is challenging to defecate while sitting on a bedpan. For a patient in bed, raise the head of the bed as high as the patient can tolerate.

The sights, odors, and sounds of defecation embarrass most people. Provide as much privacy as possible and use an odor eliminator. Encourage patients to maintain abdominal muscle tone. Prompt patients to contract abdominal muscles several times a day. Sit-ups and straight-leg raises can help improve abdominal muscle tone.

For the patient whose perceived constipation is related to rigid beliefs about bowel function, start a discussion about these concerns. Give appropriate information on normal bowel function and discuss the adverse consequences of overuse of laxatives and enemas.

ACUTE ABDOMINAL PAIN AND LAPAROTOMY
Etiology and Pathophysiology

Acute abdominal pain is pain of recent onset. It may signal a life-threatening problem, so it requires immediate attention. Causes include damage to organs in the abdomen and pelvis, which leads to inflammation, infection, obstruction, bleeding, and perforation (Fig. 42.1). Perforation of the GI tract results in irritation of the *peritoneum* (serous membrane lining the abdominal cavity) and peritonitis. Hypovolemic shock occurs from

TABLE 42.10 Patient & Caregiver Teaching

Constipation

Include the following instructions when teaching the patient and caregiver about management of constipation.

1. **Eat Dietary Fiber**

   Eat 20 to 30 g of fiber per day. Gradually increase the amount of fiber eaten over 1 to 2 wk. Fiber softens hard stool and adds bulk to stool, promoting evacuation. Eat prunes or drink prune juice daily. Prunes stimulate defecation.

   • Foods high in fiber: raw vegetables and fruits, beans, breakfast cereals (All Bran, oatmeal)
   • Fiber supplements: Metamucil, Citrucel, FiberCon

2. **Drink Fluids**

   Fluid softens hard stools. Drink 2 L per day. Drink water or fruit juices. Avoid caffeinated coffee, tea, and cola. Caffeine stimulates fluid loss through urination.

3. **Exercise Regularly**

   Walk, swim, or bike at least 3 times per wk. Contract and relax abdominal muscles when standing or by doing sit-ups to strengthen muscles and prevent straining. Exercise stimulates bowel motility and moves stool through the colon.

4. **Establish a Regular Time to Defecate**

   First thing in the morning or after the first meal of the day is the best time because people often have the urge to defecate at this time.

5. **Do Not Delay Defecation**

   Respond to the urge to have a bowel movement as soon as possible. Delaying defecation results in hard stools and a decreased "urge" to defecate. Water is absorbed from stool by the intestine over time. The colon becomes less sensitive to the presence of stool in the rectum.

6. **Record Your Bowel Elimination Pattern**

   Develop a habit of recording on your calendar when you have a bowel movement. Regular monitoring of bowel movement will help you identify a problem early.

7. **Avoid Laxatives and Enemas**

   Do not overuse laxatives and enemas, because they cause dependence. People who overuse them become unable to have a bowel movement without them.

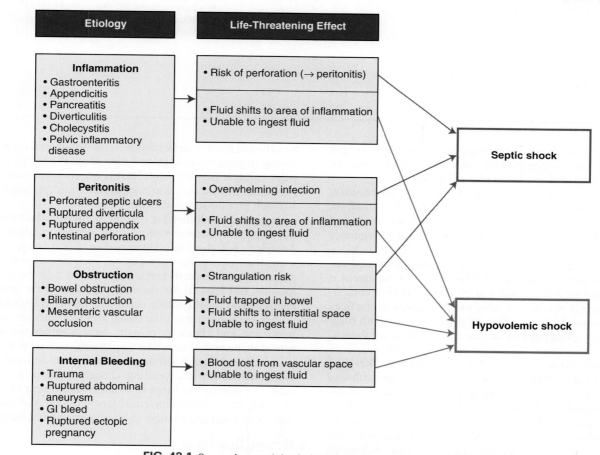

FIG. 42.1 Cause of acute abdominal pain and pathophysiologic sequelae.

bleeding or obstruction and peritonitis causing large amounts of fluid to move from the vascular space into the abdomen.

Clinical Manifestations

Pain is the most common symptom of an acute abdominal problem. The patient may have nausea, vomiting, diarrhea, constipation, flatulence, fatigue, fever, rebound tenderness, and bloating.

Diagnostic Studies and Interprofessional Care

Diagnosis begins with a complete history and physical examination. Description of the pain (frequency, timing, duration, location), accompanying symptoms, and sequence of symptoms (e.g., pain before or after vomiting) provide vital clues about the origin of the problem. Note the patient's position. The fetal posture is common with peritoneal irritation (e.g., appendicitis),

TABLE 42.11 Emergency Management

Acute Abdominal Pain

Etiology	Assessment Findings	Interventions
Inflammation • Appendicitis • Cholecystitis • Diverticulitis • Gastritis • Inflammatory bowel disease • Pancreatitis • Pyelonephritis **Vascular Problems** • Mesenteric vascular occlusion • Ruptured aortic aneurysm **Gynecologic Problems** • Pelvic inflammatory disease • Ruptured ectopic pregnancy • Ruptured ovarian cyst **Infectious Disease** • *Escherichia coli* O157:H7 • *Giardia* • *Salmonella* **Other** • Obstruction or perforation of abdominal organ • GI bleeding or ischemia • Myocardial infarction • Trauma	**Abdominal and GI Findings** • Diffuse, localized, dull, burning, or sharp abdominal pain or tenderness • Rebound tenderness • Abdominal distention • Abdominal rigidity • Nausea and vomiting • Diarrhea • Hematemesis • Melena **Hypovolemic Shock** • ↓ BP • ↓ Pulse pressure • Tachycardia • Cool, clammy skin • ↓ Level of consciousness • ↓ Urine output (<0.5 mL/kg/hr)	**Initial** • Ensure patent airway. • Apply O_2 via nasal cannula or nonrebreather mask. • Establish IV access with large-bore catheter and infuse warm normal saline or lactated Ringer's solution. Insert another large-bore catheter if shock present. • Obtain blood for CBC and electrolyte levels. • Obtain blood for amylase level, pregnancy tests, clotting studies, and type and crossmatch as appropriate. • Insert indwelling urinary catheter. • Obtain urinalysis. • Insert NG tube as needed. **Ongoing Monitoring** • Monitor vital signs, level of consciousness, O_2 saturation, and intake/output. • Assess quality and amount of pain. • Assess amount and character of emesis. • Anticipate surgical intervention. • Keep patient NPO.

a supine posture with outstretched legs with visceral pain, and restlessness with a seated posture with bowel obstructions or obstructions from kidney stones and gallstones.

Physical examination includes examination of the abdomen, rectum, and pelvis. A complete blood count (CBC), urinalysis, abdominal x-ray, and ECG are done, along with an ultrasound or CT scan. Women of childbearing age may need a pregnancy test to rule out an ectopic pregnancy.

Emergency management of the patient with acute abdominal pain is shown in Table 42.11. The goal of management is to identify and treat the cause and monitor and treat complications, especially shock. Carefully use pain medications (e.g., morphine) to provide pain relief without interfering with diagnostic accuracy when patients have nontraumatic acute abdominal pain.

An immediate surgical consult may be needed. The HCP may perform a diagnostic laparoscopy to inspect the surface of abdominal organs, obtain biopsy specimens, perform laparoscopic ultrasounds, and remove organs. A laparotomy is done when laparoscopic techniques are inadequate. If the cause of the acute abdomen can be surgically removed (e.g., inflamed appendix) or surgically repaired (e.g., ruptured abdominal aneurysm), surgery is considered definitive therapy.

❖ NURSING MANAGEMENT: ACUTE ABDOMINAL PAIN

◆ Nursing Assessment

For the patient with acute abdominal pain, take vital signs immediately and again at frequent intervals. Increased pulse and decreasing BP indicate impending shock. A fever suggests an inflammatory or infectious process. Intake and output measurement gives essential information about the adequacy of vascular volume. Altered mental status occurs with poor cerebral perfusion. Skin color, skin temperature, and peripheral pulse strength give information about perfusion.

Inspect the abdomen for distention, masses, abnormal pulsation, symmetry, hernias, rashes, scars, and pigmentation changes. Auscultate bowel sounds. Decreased or absent bowel sounds in a quadrant may occur with a bowel obstruction, peritonitis, or paralytic ileus. Perform gentle palpation to help determine the location and level of the patient's pain. Assess for involuntary guarding and rigidity, which occur with peritoneal irritation.

Ask the patient about the onset, location, intensity, duration, frequency, and character of pain. Note whether the pain has spread or moved to new sites (quadrants) and what makes the pain worse or better. Ask if the pain is associated with other symptoms, such as nausea, vomiting, changes in bowel and bladder habits, or vaginal discharge in women. Assessment of vomiting includes the amount, color, consistency, and odor of the emesis. Ask about usual and changes in bowel patterns and habits.

◆ Nursing Diagnoses

Nursing diagnoses for the patient with acute abdominal pain include:

- Acute pain
- Fluid imbalance
- Risk for infection

◆ Planning

The overall goals are that the patient with acute abdominal pain will have (1) relief of abdominal pain, (2) resolution of inflammation, (3) freedom from complications (especially hypovolemic shock), and (4) normal nutritional status.

◆ Nursing Implementation

General care for the patient with acute abdominal pain involves managing fluid and electrolyte imbalances, pain, and anxiety. Assess the quality and intensity of pain at regular intervals. Provide medication and other comfort measures. Maintain a calm environment and give information to help decrease anxiety. A nasogastric (NG) tube with low suction may decrease vomiting and relieve discomfort from gastric distention. Conduct ongoing assessments of vital signs, intake and output, and level of consciousness, which are key indicators of hypovolemic shock.

◆ Acute Care

Preoperative Care. Preoperative care includes the emergency care of the patient described in Table 42.11 and general care of the preoperative patient (see Chapter 17).

Postoperative Care. Postoperative care depends on the type of surgical procedure. See eNursing Care Plan 19.1, a general plan for the postoperative patient, on the website for Chapter 19.

After surgery, some patients will have an NG tube with low suction to empty the stomach and prevent gastric dilation. If the upper GI tract was entered, drainage from the NG tube may be dark brown to dark red for the first 12 hours. Later it should be light yellowish brown, or it may have a greenish tinge because of bile. If a dark red color continues or you see bright red blood, notify the HCP because of the risk for hemorrhage. "Coffee-grounds" granules in the drainage mean the blood has been changed by acidic gastric secretions.

Nausea and vomiting are common after a laparotomy and result from the surgery, decreased peristalsis, or pain medications. Antiemetics, such as ondansetron (Zofran), promethazine (Phenergan), and aprepitant (Emend), may be ordered. Monitor fluid and electrolyte status along with BP, heart rate, and respirations. See Chapter 41 for further discussion of managing nausea and vomiting.

Swallowed air and reduced peristalsis from decreased mobility, manipulation of the abdominal organs during surgery, and anesthesia can result in abdominal distention and gas pains. Early ambulation helps restore peristalsis, expel flatus, and reduce gas pain. Gradually, as intestinal activity increases, distention and gas pain disappear.

◆ Ambulatory Care.
Preparation for discharge begins soon after surgery. Teach the patient and caregiver about any modifications in activity, care of the incision, diet, and drug therapy. Initially the patient starts on clear liquids after surgery and then, if tolerated, progresses to a regular diet.

Early ambulation speeds recovery, but normal activities are resumed gradually, with planned rest periods. Patients generally have restrictions not to lift anything heavier than a few pounds. The patient and caregiver should be aware of any possible complications. Teach them to notify the HCP at once if fever is greater than 101°F (38.6°C), vomiting, pain, weight loss, incisional drainage, or changes in bowel function occur.

◆ Evaluation

The expected outcomes are that the patient with acute abdominal pain will:

- Have resolution of the cause of the acute abdominal pain
- Experience relief of abdominal pain and discomfort
- Be free from complications, especially hypovolemic shock and sepsis
- Have normal fluid, electrolyte, and nutritional status

ABDOMINAL TRAUMA

Etiology and Pathophysiology

Injuries to the abdominal area usually are a result of blunt trauma or penetrating injuries. Common injuries of the abdomen include lacerated liver, ruptured spleen, mesenteric artery tears, diaphragm rupture, urinary bladder rupture, great vessel tears, renal or pancreas injury, and stomach or intestine rupture.

Blunt trauma often occurs with motor vehicle accidents, direct blows, and falls. It may not be obvious because it does not leave an open wound. Both compression injuries (e.g., direct blow to the abdomen) and shearing injuries (e.g., rapid deceleration in a motor vehicle crash allowing some tissue to move forward while other tissues stay stationary) occur with blunt trauma. *Penetrating injuries* occur when a gunshot or stabbing produces an obvious, open wound into the abdomen.

When solid organs (liver, spleen) are injured, bleeding can be profuse, resulting in hypovolemic shock. When contents from hollow organs (e.g., bladder, stomach, intestines) spill into the peritoneal cavity, the patient is at risk for peritonitis. In addition, abdominal compartment syndrome can develop.

Abdominal compartment syndrome, or abdominal hypertension, is excessively high pressure in the abdomen. Anything that increases the volume in the abdominal cavity (e.g., edematous organs, bleeding) increases abdominal pressure. This high pressure restricts ventilation, potentially leading to respiratory failure. The high pressure decreases cardiac output, venous return, and arterial perfusion of organs. Decreased perfusion to the kidneys can lead to renal failure.

Clinical Manifestations

Careful assessment provides important clues to the type and severity of injury. Intraabdominal injuries are often associated with rib fractures, fractured pelvis, spinal injury, and thoracic injury. If the patient was in an automobile accident, a contusion or abrasion across the lower abdomen may indicate internal organ trauma due to seat belt use. Seat belts can produce blunt trauma to abdominal organs by pressing the intestine and pancreas into the spinal column.

Classic manifestations of abdominal trauma are (1) guarding and splinting of the abdominal wall (indicating peritonitis); (2) a hard, distended abdomen (occurs with intraabdominal bleeding); (3) decreased or absent bowel sounds; (4) abrasions or bruising over the abdomen; (5) abdominal pain; (6) hematemesis or hematuria; and (7) signs of hypovolemic shock (Table 42.12). Ecchymosis around the umbilicus (*Cullen's sign*) or flanks (*Grey Turner's sign*) may mean retroperitoneal hemorrhage. Loss of bowel sounds occurs with peritonitis. If the diaphragm ruptures, you can hear bowel sounds (if present) in the chest. Auscultation of bruits is indicative of arterial damage.

Diagnostic Studies

Laboratory tests include a baseline CBC and urinalysis. Even when bleeding, the patient will have normal hemoglobin and hematocrit because fluids are lost at the same rate as the red blood cells. Deficiencies are evident after fluid resuscitation begins. Blood in the urine may be a sign of kidney or bladder damage. Other laboratory work includes arterial blood gases, prothrombin time, electrolytes, BUN and creatinine, and type and crossmatch (in anticipation of possible blood transfusions). An abdominal CT scan and focused abdominal ultrasound are

✚ TABLE 42.12 Emergency Management

Abdominal Trauma

Etiology	Assessment Findings	Interventions
Blunt • Falls • Motor vehicle collisions • Pedestrian event • Assault with blunt object • Crush injuries • Explosions **Penetrating** • Knife • Gunshot wounds • Impalement • Other missiles	**Hypovolemic Shock** • ↓ Level of consciousness • Tachypnea • Tachycardia • ↓ BP • ↓ Pulse pressure **Surface Findings** • Abrasions or ecchymoses on abdominal wall, flank, or peritoneum • Open wounds: lacerations, eviscerations, puncture wounds, gunshot wounds • Impaled object **Abdominal and GI Findings** • Nausea and vomiting • Hematemesis • Absent or decreased bowel sounds • Hematuria • Abdominal distention • Abdominal rigidity • Abdominal pain with palpation • Rebound tenderness	**Initial** • If unresponsive, assess circulation, airway, and breathing. • If responsive, monitor airway, breathing, and circulation. • Apply appropriate O_2 therapy. • Control external bleeding with direct pressure or sterile pressure dressing. • Establish IV access with 2 large-bore catheters and infuse normal saline or lactated Ringer's solution. • Obtain blood for type and crossmatch and CBC. • Remove clothing. • Stabilize impaled objects with bulky dressing—*do not remove.* • Cover protruding organs or tissue with sterile saline dressing. • Insert indwelling urinary catheter if there is no blood at the meatus, pelvic fracture, or boggy prostate. • Obtain urine for urinalysis. • Insert NG tube if no evidence of facial trauma. • Anticipate diagnostic peritoneal lavage. **Ongoing Monitoring** • Monitor vital signs, level of consciousness, O_2 saturation, and urine output. • Maintain patient warmth using blankets, warm IV fluids, or warm humidified O_2.

the most common diagnostic methods, but the patient must be stable before going for CT.

Diagnostic peritoneal lavage can detect blood, bile, intestinal contents, and urine in the peritoneal cavity. It is generally used only for unstable patients to identify blood in the peritoneum.

❖ Interprofessional and Nursing Care

Emergency management of abdominal trauma is outlined in Table 42.12. Volume expanders or blood given if the patient is hypotensive. An NG tube with low suction will decompress the stomach and prevent aspiration. Frequent ongoing assessment is needed to monitor fluid status, detect deterioration in condition, and determine the need for surgery. The decision about whether to do surgery depends on clinical findings, diagnostic test results, and the patient's response to conservative management. Do not remove an impaled object until skilled care is available. Removal may cause further injury and bleeding.

CHRONIC ABDOMINAL PAIN

Chronic abdominal pain may originate from abdominal structures or be referred from a site with the same or a similar nerve supply. The pain is often described as dull, aching, or diffuse. Common causes of chronic abdominal pain include irritable bowel syndrome (IBS), peptic ulcer disease, chronic pancreatitis, hepatitis, pelvic inflammatory disease, adhesions, and vascular insufficiency.

Diagnosing the cause of chronic abdominal pain begins with a thorough history and description of specific pain characteristics, including severity, location, frequency, duration, and onset. The assessment includes factors that increase or decrease the pain, such as eating, defecation, and activities. Endoscopy, CT scan, MRI, laparoscopy, and barium studies may be done.

Treatment for chronic abdominal pain depends on the underlying cause.

IRRITABLE BOWEL SYNDROME

Irritable bowel syndrome (IBS) is a disorder characterized by chronic abdominal pain or discomfort and alteration of bowel patterns. Patients may have diarrhea or constipation, alternating periods of both.

IBS has no known organic cause. Psychologic stressors (e.g., depression, anxiety, panic disorders, posttraumatic stress disorder) are associated with the development and exacerbation of IBS. Patients often have a history of GI infections and adverse reactions to food. Dietary intolerances that may contribute to symptoms include gluten and fermentable oligo-, di-, and monosaccharides and polyols (FODMAPs).[7] Examples of oligosaccharides are wheat and rye products, some fruits and vegetables, onions, garlic, legumes, and nuts. The disaccharide lactose is found in milk and milk products. Fructose is a monosaccharide found in honey, apples, pears, and high-fructose corn syrup. Polyols are found in apples, pears, stone fruits, cauliflower, mushrooms, and artificial sweeteners, like sorbitol.[8]

IBS is diagnosed solely on symptoms. The Rome IV criteria for diagnosing IBS require the presence of abdominal pain and/or discomfort at least 1 day per week for 3 months that is associated with 2 or more of the following: related to defecation, change in stool frequency, or change in the stool form.[7] Depending on the stool patterns, IBS is categorized as IBS with constipation (IBS-C), IBS with diarrhea (IBS-D), IBS mixed, and IBS unsubtyped. Other common symptoms include abdominal distention, nausea, flatulence, bloating, urgency, mucus in the stool, and sensation of incomplete evacuation. Non-GI symptoms may include fatigue, headache, and sleep problems.

The key to accurate diagnosis is a thorough history and physical examination. Ask patients to describe symptoms, health history (including psychosocial factors, such as stress and anxiety), family history, and drug and diet history. Determine if and how IBS symptoms interfere with school, work, or recreational activities. Diagnostic tests are used to rule out other disorders, such as colorectal cancer, IBD, endometriosis, and malabsorption disorders (lactose intolerance, celiac disease).

No single therapy is effective for all patients with IBS. Treatment may include dealing with psychologic factors, dietary changes, and drugs to regulate stool output and reduce discomfort. Patients may benefit from keeping a diary of symptoms, diet, and episodes of stress to help identify any factors that trigger the IBS symptoms. Cognitive behavior therapy and stress management techniques may help a patient cope. Participating in regular exercise reduces bloating and constipation and reduces stress-related symptoms.

Review with the patient foods that are high in FODMAPs and teach them to follow a low-FODMAP diet.[8] If dairy products tend to cause symptoms, yogurt may be the best option because of the lactobacillus bacteria it contains. Probiotics can improve symptoms. Tell the patient with flatulence to avoid common gas-producing foods, such as broccoli and cabbage. For those with constipation, encourage an intake of enough dietary fiber to produce soft, painless bowel movements.

Drug therapy focuses on the dominant bowel symptom and pain. The opioid agonist eluxadoline (Viberzi) decreases colonic contractions to reduce diarrhea and pain. It is contraindicated in those without a gallbladder. An option for women with IBS-D is alosetron (Lotronex). Because of serious side effects (e.g., severe constipation, ischemic colitis), it is available only in a restricted access program. Other treatments for IBS-D include loperamide, antidepressants, and antispasmodic medications (hyoscyamine, dicyclomine). Antispasmodics decrease GI motility and smooth muscle spasms, reducing pain and diarrhea.[8]

💊 DRUG ALERT Alosetron (Lotronex)

- Taking this drug can cause severe constipation and ischemic colitis (reduced blood flow to intestines).
- Teach the patient to stop the drug and contact the HCP if constipation, rectal bleeding, bloody diarrhea, or abdominal pain occurs.

Women with IBS-C may benefit from lubiprostone (Amitiza). Men or women with IBS-C can take linaclotide (Linzess). It is contraindicated in patients with a history of mechanical obstruction or prior bowel surgery.

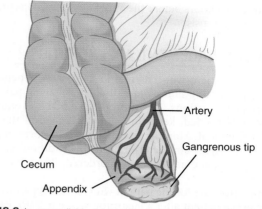

FIG. 42.2 In appendicitis the blood supply of the appendix is impaired by inflammation and bacterial infection, which may result in gangrene.

▌INFLAMMATORY DISORDERS

APPENDICITIS

Appendicitis is inflammation of the appendix, a narrow blind tube that extends from the inferior part of the cecum (Fig. 42.2). It is the most common reason for emergency abdominal surgery.

Etiology and Pathophysiology

About 7% of people will develop appendicitis sometime during their lifetime.[9] It is most common in those 10 to 30 years of age. A common cause of appendicitis is obstruction of the lumen by a fecalith (accumulated feces). Obstruction results in distention; venous engorgement; and the accumulation of mucus and bacteria, which can lead to gangrene, perforation, and peritonitis.

Clinical Manifestations

Diagnosis can be difficult because many patients do not have classic symptoms. Appendicitis typically begins with dull periumbilical pain, followed by anorexia, nausea, and vomiting. The pain is persistent and continuous, eventually shifting to the right lower quadrant and localizing at *McBurney's point* (halfway between the umbilicus and right iliac crest). A low-grade fever may develop. Further assessment reveals localized tenderness, rigidity, rebound tenderness, and muscle guarding. Coughing, sneezing, and deep inhalation worsen pain. The patient usually prefers to lie still, often with the right leg flexed. The older adult may report less severe pain, slight fever, and discomfort in the right iliac fossa.

Diagnostic Studies and Interprofessional Care

Patient examination includes a complete history, physical examination, and a differential WBC count. Most patients have a mildly to moderately high WBC count. A urinalysis is done to rule out genitourinary conditions that mimic appendicitis. CT scan is the preferred diagnostic procedure. However, ultrasound and MRI are options.

If there is a delay in diagnosis and treatment, the appendix can rupture and the resulting peritonitis can be fatal. The standard treatment of appendicitis is an immediate *appendectomy* (surgical removal of appendix).[9] If the inflammation is localized, surgery should be done as soon as the diagnosis is made. Antibiotics and fluid resuscitation are started before surgery.

If the appendix has ruptured and there is evidence of peritonitis or an abscess, giving parenteral fluids and antibiotic therapy for 6 to 8 hours before the appendectomy helps prevent dehydration and sepsis.

❖ NURSING MANAGEMENT: APPENDICITIS

Managing the patient who has manifestations of appendicitis focuses on preventing fluid volume deficit, relieving pain, and preventing complications. To ensure the stomach is empty in case surgery is needed, keep the patient NPO until the HCP evaluates the patient. Monitor vital signs and perform ongoing assessment to detect any deterioration in condition. Give IV fluids, analgesics, and antiemetics as ordered. Provide comfort measures.

Postoperative care for the patient who had an appendectomy is similar to the patient after a laparotomy (see p. 935). Patients are usually discharged within 24 hours after an uncomplicated laparoscopic appendectomy. Ambulation begins a few hours after surgery, and the diet is advanced as tolerated. Those who had a perforation usually have a longer length of stay and need IV antibiotic therapy. Most patients resume normal activities 2 to 3 weeks after surgery.

> ### ❓ CHECK YOUR PRACTICE
>
> A 28-yr-old female patient comes to the emergency department with acute abdominal pain.
> - What manifestations would make you suspect appendicitis is the cause of the patient's abdominal pain?

PERITONITIS

Etiology and Pathophysiology

Peritonitis results from a localized or generalized inflammatory process of the peritoneum. Causes of peritonitis are listed in Table 42.13. Primary peritonitis occurs when blood-borne organisms enter the peritoneal cavity. For example, the ascites that occurs with cirrhosis of the liver provides an excellent liquid environment for bacteria to flourish. Organisms can enter the peritoneum during peritoneal dialysis.

Secondary peritonitis is much more common. It occurs when abdominal organs perforate or rupture and release their contents (bile, enzymes, and bacteria) into the peritoneal cavity. Common causes include a ruptured appendix, perforated gastric or duodenal ulcer, severely inflamed gallbladder, and trauma from gunshot or knife wounds.

Intestinal contents and bacteria irritate the normally sterile peritoneum and produce an initial chemical peritonitis. Bacterial peritonitis develops a few hours later. The resulting inflammatory response leads to massive fluid shifts (peritoneal edema) and adhesions as the body tries to wall off the infection.

Clinical Manifestations

Abdominal pain is the most common symptom of peritonitis. A universal sign is tenderness over the involved area. Rebound tenderness, muscular rigidity, and spasm are other signs of peritoneal irritation. Patients may lie still and take only shallow breaths because movement worsens the pain. Abdominal distention, fever, tachycardia, tachypnea, nausea, vomiting, and altered bowel habits may be present. These manifestations vary, depending on the severity and acuteness of the underlying condition. Complications include hypovolemic shock, sepsis,

TABLE 42.13 Causes of Peritonitis

Primary
- Blood-borne organisms
- Cirrhosis with ascites
- Genital tract organisms

Secondary
- Appendicitis with rupture
- Blunt or penetrating trauma to abdominal organs
- Diverticulitis with rupture

- Ischemic bowel disorders
- Pancreatitis
- Perforated intestine
- Perforated peptic ulcer
- Peritoneal dialysis
- Postoperative (breakage of anastomosis)

TABLE 42.14 Interprofessional Care

Peritonitis

Diagnostic Assessment
- History and physical examination
- CBC, including WBC differential
- Serum electrolytes
- Abdominal x-ray
- Abdominal paracentesis and culture of fluid
- CT scan or ultrasound
- Peritoneoscopy

Management
Preoperative or Nonoperative
- NPO status
- IV fluid replacement
- NG to low-intermittent suction
- O_2 PRN
- Parenteral nutrition as needed

Drug Therapy
- Antibiotic therapy
- Analgesics (e.g., morphine)
- Antiemetics as needed

Postoperative
- NPO status
- NG to low-intermittent suction
- Semi-Fowler's position
- IV fluids with electrolyte replacement
- PN as needed
- Blood transfusions as needed

Drug Therapy
- Antibiotic therapy
- Sedatives and opioids
- Antiemetics as needed

intraabdominal abscess formation, paralytic ileus, and acute respiratory distress syndrome. Peritonitis can be fatal if treatment is delayed.

Diagnostic Studies and Interprofessional Care

A CBC is done to determine elevations in WBC count and hemoconcentration from fluid shifts (Table 42.14). Peritoneal aspiration may be done with the fluid analyzed for blood, bile, pus, bacteria, fungus, and amylase content. An abdominal x-ray may show dilated loops of bowel consistent with paralytic ileus, free air if perforation has occurred, or air and fluid levels if an obstruction is present. Ultrasound and CT scans may be useful in identifying ascites and abscesses. Peritoneoscopy may be helpful in the patient without ascites. It allows for direct examination of the peritoneum and the ability to obtain biopsy specimens for diagnosis.

Patients with milder cases of peritonitis or those who are poor surgical risks receive conservative care. Treatment consists of antibiotics, NG suction, analgesics, and IV fluid administration. Surgery is indicated to locate the cause of the inflammation, drain purulent fluid, and repair any damage (e.g., perforated organs).

❖ NURSING MANAGEMENT: PERITONITIS

◆ Nursing Assessment

Assessment of the patient's pain, including the location, is important and may help to determine the cause of peritonitis. Assess for the presence and quality of bowel sounds, increasing abdominal distention, abdominal guarding, nausea, fever, and manifestations of hypovolemic shock.

◆ Nursing Diagnoses

Nursing diagnoses for the patient with peritonitis include:
- Acute pain
- Fluid imbalance
- Impaired gas exchange
- Risk for infection

◆ Planning

The overall goals are that the patient with peritonitis will have (1) resolution of inflammation, (2) relief of abdominal pain, (3) freedom from complications (especially sepsis and hypovolemic shock), and (4) normal nutritional status.

◆ Nursing Implementation

The patient with peritonitis is extremely ill and needs skilled supportive care. Establish IV access so that you can give replacement fluids lost to the peritoneal cavity and have access for antibiotic therapy. Monitor the patient for pain and response to analgesics. You may position the patient with knees flexed to increase comfort. Sedatives may relieve anxiety and promote rest.

Accurate monitoring of intake and output and electrolyte status is essential to determine replacement therapy. Frequently monitor vital signs. Give antiemetics to decrease nausea and vomiting and prevent further fluid and electrolyte losses. Place the patient on NPO status. The patient may need an NG tube to decrease gastric distention and further leakage of bowel contents into the peritoneum. Give low-flow oxygen therapy as needed.

If the patient had an open surgical procedure, drains are inserted to remove purulent drainage and excess fluid. Postoperative care is similar to that for the patient who had a laparotomy (see p. 935).

GASTROENTERITIS

Gastroenteritis is an inflammation of the mucosa of the stomach and small intestine. Features of *acute gastroenteritis* are sudden diarrhea accompanied by nausea, vomiting, fever, and abdominal cramping. Viruses are the most common cause of gastroenteritis (Table 42.1).

Norovirus is a leading cause of foodborne outbreaks of acute gastroenteritis. Laboratory testing to identify norovirus is useful when a number of people simultaneously have gastroenteritis and there is a clear avenue for virus transmission, such as a shared location or food.

Most cases of gastroenteritis are self-limiting. Encourage oral fluids containing glucose and electrolytes (e.g., Pedialyte) to prevent and treat dehydration. Older adults and chronically ill patients may be unable to consume enough fluids to make up for fluid loss. If dehydration occurs, IV fluid replacement may be needed. Nursing management of the patient with gastroenteritis is the same as for the patient with acute diarrhea (see p. 927).

INFLAMMATORY BOWEL DISEASE

Inflammatory bowel disease (IBD) is a chronic inflammation of the GI tract characterized by periods of remission interspersed with periods of exacerbation. We classify IBD as either Crohn's disease or ulcerative colitis (UC) based on clinical manifestations (Table 42.15). As the name suggests, ulcerative colitis is usually limited to the colon. Crohn's disease can involve any segment of the GI tract from the mouth to the anus.

About 1.3 million Americans have IBD. It often begins during the teenage years and early adulthood. IBD has a second peak in the 6th decade. The incidence and frequency of IBD varies depending on geographic location and racial or ethnic background. The highest rates are in the Northern Hemisphere and industrialized nations.[10] The risk for having IBD is greater in urban compared with rural areas and those of white and Ashkenazic Jewish origin than in other racial and ethnic groups.[10] The strongest risk factor is family history. Many people with IBD have a family member with the disorder.

Etiology and Pathophysiology

We do not know the exact cause of IBD. IBD is an autoimmune disease involving an immune reaction to a person's own intestinal tract. We think that it results from an overactive, inappropriate, or sustained immune response to environmental and bacterial triggers, probably in a genetically susceptible person. The resulting inflammation causes widespread tissue destruction.

Environmental factors, such as diet, smoking, and stress, increase susceptibility by changing the environment of the GI microbial flora. We think that dietary factors unique to industrialized countries contribute to the development of IBD. High intake of refined sugar, total fats, polyunsaturated fatty acid (PUFA), and omega-6 fatty acids is associated with an increased risk for IBD. Eating fewer raw fruits, vegetables, omega-3–rich foods, and dietary fiber decrease risk.[11] Use of nonsteroidal antiinflammatory drugs (NSAIDs), antibiotics, and oral contraceptives are associated with increased risk.[12]

Genetic Link

IBD occurs more often in family members of people with IBD, especially monozygotic twins. To date, we have found over 200 genes associated with IBD. Certain genetic mutations are associated with Crohn's disease, others with UC, and many with both.

The number of gene variations suggests that IBD is a group of diseases that produce similar types of mucosal destruction. The path from genetic mutation to abnormal immune responses varies depending on which gene or genes are affected. Several of the genes are involved in protective functions of the intestines. Others have a role in the immune system, especially in the maturation and function of T cells.

TABLE 42.15 Comparison of Ulcerative Colitis and Crohn's Disease

Characteristic	Ulcerative Colitis	Crohn's Disease
Clinical		
Usual age at onset	Teens to mid-30s. After 60	Teens to mid-30s. After 60
Abdominal pain	Common, severe constant	Common, cramping
Diarrhea	Common	Common
Fever (intermittent)	During acute attacks	Common
Malabsorption and nutritional deficiencies	Minimal incidence	Common
Rectal bleeding	Common	Sometimes
Tenesmus	Common	Rare
Weight loss	Rare	Common, may be severe
Pathologic		
Location	Usually starts in rectum and spreads in a continuous pattern up the colon	Occurs anywhere along GI tract. Most common site is distal ileum
Cobblestoning of mucosa	Rare	Common
Depth of involvement	Mucosa	Entire thickness of bowel wall (transmural)
Distribution	Continuous areas of inflammation	Healthy tissue interspersed with areas of inflammation (skip lesions)
Pseudopolyps	Common	Rare
Small bowel involvement	Minimal	Common
Complications		
Cancer	Increased incidence of colorectal cancer after 10 yrs of disease	Increased incidence of small intestinal cancer. Increased incidence of colorectal cancer but less than with ulcerative colitis
C. difficile infection	Increased incidence and severity	Increased incidence and severity
Perforation	Common (because of toxic megacolon)	Common (because inflammation involves entire bowel wall)
Perianal abscess and fistulas	Rare	Common
Strictures	Occasional	Common
Toxic megacolon	More common	Rare

Genetic variation may explain differences in patient responses to drug therapies for IBD.

Many of the major genes related to Crohn's disease, including *NOD2*, *ATG16L1*, *IL23R*, and *IRGM*, are involved in immune system function. The proteins made from these genes help the immune system sense and respond appropriately to bacteria in the lining of the GI tract. *NOD2* gene changes are associated with a form of Crohn's disease that affects the ileum in persons of northern European descent. Changes in the *NOD2* gene trigger an abnormal immune response that allows bacteria to grow unchecked and invade intestinal cells. This causes chronic inflammation and digestive problems.[13]

IBD is more likely to occur in those with other genetic syndromes, including cystic fibrosis. An increased prevalence occurs in the presence of other inflammatory disorders with genetic susceptibility, such as psoriasis and multiple sclerosis.

Pattern of Inflammation in Ulcerative Colitis vs. Crohn's Disease. The pattern of inflammation differs between Crohn's disease and UC (Fig. 42.3). Crohn's disease can occur anywhere in the GI tract from the mouth to the anus. It most often involves the distal ileum and proximal colon. Segments of normal bowel can occur between diseased portions, so-called "skip" lesions. The inflammation in Crohn's disease involves all layers of the bowel wall. Typically, ulcerations are deep, longitudinal, and penetrate between islands of inflamed edematous mucosa, causing the classic cobblestone appearance. Strictures at the areas of inflammation can cause bowel obstruction. Since the inflammation goes through the entire wall, microscopic leaks can allow bowel contents to enter the peritoneal cavity and form abscesses or produce peritonitis. In active Crohn's disease, fistulas are common.

Inflammatory bowel disease (IBD)

Crohn's disease   Ulcerative colitis

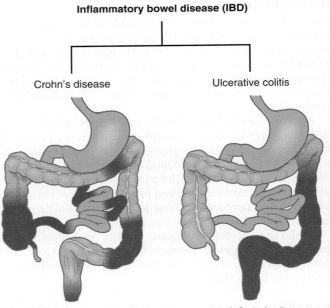

FIG. 42.3 Comparison of distribution patterns of Crohn's disease and ulcerative colitis.

UC usually starts in the rectum and moves in a continual fashion toward the cecum. Although mild inflammation may occur in the terminal ileum, UC is a disease of the colon and rectum. The inflammation and ulcerations occur in the mucosal layer, the innermost layer of the bowel wall. Fistulas and abscesses are rare since inflammation does not extend through

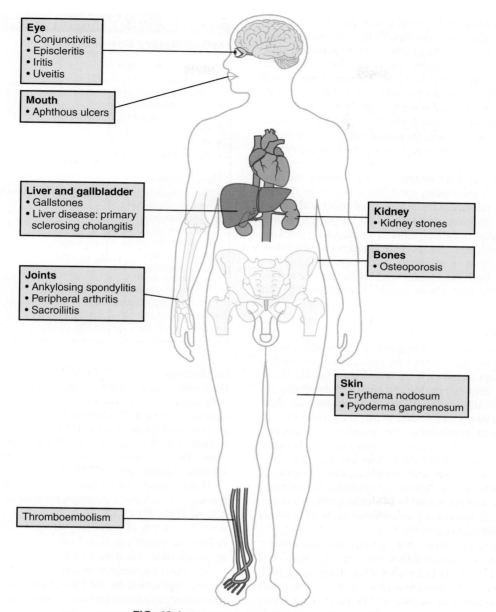

Eye
- Conjunctivitis
- Episcleritis
- Iritis
- Uveitis

Mouth
- Aphthous ulcers

Liver and gallbladder
- Gallstones
- Liver disease: primary sclerosing cholangitis

Joints
- Ankylosing spondylitis
- Peripheral arthritis
- Sacroiliitis

Kidney
- Kidney stones

Bones
- Osteoporosis

Skin
- Erythema nodosum
- Pyoderma gangrenosum

Thromboembolism

FIG. 42.4 Extraintestinal manifestations of IBD.

all bowel wall layers. Because water and electrolytes are not absorbed through inflamed mucosa, diarrhea with large fluid and electrolyte losses is common. Breakdown of cells results in protein loss through the stool. Areas of inflamed mucosa form *pseudopolyps,* tongue-like projections into the bowel lumen.

Clinical Manifestations

Both forms of IBD are chronic disorders with mild to severe acute exacerbations that occur at unpredictable intervals over many years. Although the manifestations of Crohn's disease and UC are similar (diarrhea, weight loss, abdominal pain, fever, fatigue), there are differences (Table 42.15).

In Crohn's disease, diarrhea and cramping abdominal pain are common symptoms. If the small intestine is involved, weight loss occurs from inflammation of the small intestine causing malabsorption. Rectal bleeding sometimes occurs with Crohn's disease, although not as often as with UC.

In UC, the primary problems are bloody diarrhea and abdominal pain. Pain may vary from the mild lower abdominal cramping associated with diarrhea to severe, constant pain associated with acute perforations. With *mild disease,* diarrhea may consist of no more than 4 semiformed stools daily that contain small amounts of blood. The patient may have no other manifestations. In *moderate disease,* the patient has increased stool output (up to 10 stools/day), increased bleeding, and systemic symptoms (fever, malaise, mild anemia, anorexia). In *severe disease,* diarrhea is bloody, contains mucus, and occurs 10 to 20 times a day. In addition, fever, rapid weight loss greater than 10% of total body weight, anemia, tachycardia, and dehydration are present.

Complications

Patients with IBD have both local (confined to the GI tract) and systemic (extraintestinal) complications (Fig. 42.4). GI tract complications include hemorrhage, strictures, perforation (with possible peritonitis), abscesses, fistulas, CDI, and colonic dilation (toxic megacolon). Toxic megacolon is more common with UC. Patients with toxic megacolon are at risk for perforation and may need an emergency colectomy. Perineal abscess and fistulas occur in up to a third of patients with Crohn's disease. CDI increases in frequency and severity in patients with IBD.

IBD is related to an increased risk for colorectal cancer. Those with Crohn's disease are at increased risk for small intestinal cancer. Cancer screening at regular intervals is important in persons with IBD.

People with IBD may have systemic complications, such as multiple sclerosis and ankylosing spondylitis. Some are related to the inflammatory activity in the bowel. They occur with active inflammation and improve when the IBD improves. Other complications include malabsorption, liver disease (primary sclerosing cholangitis), and osteoporosis. Routine liver function tests are important because primary sclerosing cholangitis can lead to liver failure. Both men and women with IBD are at risk for osteoporosis. They need a bone density scan at baseline and every 2 years.

Diagnostic Studies

The diagnosis of IBD includes ruling out diseases with similar symptoms and figuring out whether the patient has Crohn's disease or UC. The symptoms of early Crohn's disease are like those of IBS. Diagnostic studies provide information about disease severity and complications. A CBC typically shows iron-deficiency anemia from blood loss. A high WBC count may be a sign of toxic megacolon or perforation. Decreased serum sodium, potassium, chloride, bicarbonate, and magnesium levels occur due to fluid and electrolyte losses from diarrhea and vomiting. Hypoalbuminemia is present with severe disease because of poor nutrition or protein loss. Increased erythrocyte sedimentation rate, C-reactive protein, and WBCs reflect inflammation. The stool is examined for blood, pus, and mucus. Stool cultures can determine if infection is present.

Imaging studies, such as double-contrast barium enema, small bowel series (small bowel follow through), transabdominal ultrasound, CT, and MRI, are useful for diagnosing IBD. Colonoscopy allows for examination of the entire large intestine lumen and sometimes the most distal ileum. The HCP can determine the extent of inflammation, ulcerations, pseudopolyps, and strictures and obtain biopsy specimens for a definitive diagnosis. Since a colonoscope can enter only the distal ileum, capsule endoscopy (see Chapter 38) may be needed to diagnose Crohn's disease in the small intestine.

Interprofessional Care

The goals of treatment of IBD are to (1) rest the bowel, (2) control the inflammation, (3) combat infection, (4) correct malnutrition, (5) provide symptomatic relief, and (6) improve quality of life. There is no cure for IBD. Treatment relies on drugs to treat the inflammation and maintain remission (Table 42.16). Several drugs are available to treat IBD. Since the recurrence rate is high after surgical treatment of Crohn's disease, drugs are the preferred treatment. Hospitalization is needed if the patient does not respond to drug therapy, the disease is severe, or complications are suspected.

Drug Therapy. The goal of drug treatment in IBD is to induce and maintain remission. Five major classes of drugs are used: aminosalicylates, antimicrobials, corticosteroids, immunomodulators,

TABLE 42.16 Interprofessional Care

Inflammatory Bowel Disease

Diagnostic Assessment
- History and physical examination
- CBC, erythrocyte sedimentation rate
- Serum chemistries
- Testing of stool for occult blood and infection
- Capsule endoscopy
- Radiologic studies with barium contrast
- Sigmoidoscopy and/or colonoscopy with biopsy

Management
- High-calorie, high-vitamin, high-protein, low-residue, lactose-free (if lactase deficiency) diet
- Elemental diet or PN
- Drug therapy (Table 42.17)
  - Aminosalicylates
  - Antimicrobials
  - Biologic therapies
  - Corticosteroids
  - Immunosuppressants
- Physical and emotional rest
- Referral for counseling or support group
- Surgical therapy (Table 42.18)

and biologic therapies (Table 42.17). Drug choice depends on the location and severity of inflammation. Patients are treated with either a "step-up" or a "step-down" approach. With the step-up approach, the patient with mild symptoms begins with an aminosalicylate or antimicrobial and adds a more toxic medication (e.g., biologic therapies) when initial therapies do not work. The step-down approach uses immunosuppressant and biologic therapy first.[14]

Drugs containing 5-aminosalicylic acid (5-ASA) remain the mainstay to achieve and maintain remission and prevent flare-ups of IBD. They include sulfasalazine (Azulfidine) and the new generation of sulfa-free drugs (olsalazine, mesalamine). Aminosalicylates can treat both UC and Crohn's disease. They are much more effective for UC.[14]

The exact mechanism of action of 5-ASA is unclear. We think topical application to the intestinal mucosa suppresses proinflammatory cytokines and other inflammatory mediators. People can take aminosalicylates orally or rectally. Oral forms are available with different coatings that affect where the medication is released along the GI tract. This allows more effective treatment of specific symptoms. Rectal forms include suppositories and enemas. Rectal use offers the advantage of delivering the 5-ASA directly to the affected tissue. This is useful in treating inflammation in the rectum and/or large intestine. The combination of oral and rectal therapy is better than oral or rectal therapy alone.

Corticosteroids can help achieve remission in IBD. They are given for the shortest possible time because of the side effects associated with long-term use. Patients with disease in the left colon, sigmoid, and rectum benefit from suppositories, enemas, and foams because they deliver the corticosteroid directly to the inflamed tissue with minimal systemic effects. Oral prednisone is given to patients with mild to moderate disease who did not respond to either 5-ASA or topical corticosteroids. Those with severe inflammation may need a short course of IV corticosteroids. Corticosteroids must be tapered to very low levels when surgery is planned to prevent postoperative complications (e.g., infection, delayed wound healing, fistula formation).

TABLE 42.17 Drug Therapy
Inflammatory Bowel Disease

Class	Action	Examples
5-Aminosalicylates (5-ASA)	Decrease inflammation by suppressing proinflammatory cytokines and other inflammatory mediators	*Systemic:* balsalazide (Colazal), mesalamine (Pentasa), olsalazine (Dipentum), sulfasalazine (Azulfidine) *Topical:* 5-ASA enema (Rowasa), mesalamine suppositories
Antimicrobials	Prevent or treat secondary infection	ciprofloxacin (Cipro), clarithromycin (Biaxin), metronidazole (Flagyl)
Biologic therapies	Inhibit the cytokine tumor necrosis factor (TNF)	adalimumab (Humira), certolizumab pegol (Cimzia), golimumab (Simponi), infliximab (Remicade)
	Prevent migration of leukocytes from bloodstream to inflamed tissue	natalizumab (Tysabri), vedolizumab (Entyvio)
Corticosteroids	Decrease inflammation	*Systemic:* corticosteroids (prednisone, budesonide [Uceris]); hydrocortisone or methylprednisolone (IV for severe IBD) *Topical:* hydrocortisone suppository or foam (budesonide, Cortifoam) or enema (Cortenema)
Immunosuppressants	Suppress immune response	azathioprine, cyclosporine, methotrexate, 6-mercaptopurine

Immunosuppressants (6-mercaptopurine, azathioprine) are given for several reasons. They can maintain remission after corticosteroid therapy. Patients who do not respond to aminosalicylates, corticosteroids, or antibiotics; have side effects from corticosteroids; or have fistulas may benefit. These drugs require regular CBC monitoring because they can suppress the bone marrow and lead to inflammation of the pancreas or liver. They have a delayed onset of action and are not useful for acute flare-ups.

Methotrexate is most useful in patients with Crohn's disease who cannot stop corticosteroid use without a flare-up or in whom other drugs have been ineffective. Many patients have flu-like symptoms with use. Some develop bone marrow depression and liver dysfunction. Correct dosing is critical to minimize the risk for toxicity. Careful monitoring of the CBC and liver enzymes is essential. Advise women of childbearing age to avoid pregnancy because use causes birth defects and fetal death.

Biologics reduce IBD-related inflammation by blocking specific proteins that play a role in inflammation. There are 2 main classes: anti–tumor necrosis factor (TNF) agents and integrin receptor antagonists.

The anti-TNF agent infliximab (Remicade) is given IV to induce and maintain remission in patients with Crohn's disease and in patients with draining fistulas who do not respond to conventional drug therapy. The other anti-TNF agents are given subcutaneously.[15] The anti-TNF agents have similar side effects. The most common ones are upper respiratory and urinary tract infections, headaches, nausea, joint pain, and abdominal pain. More serious effects include reactivation of hepatitis and tuberculosis (TB); opportunistic infections; and cancers, especially lymphoma. Patients need to know the risks before starting therapy. They are tested for TB and hepatitis before treatment begins and cannot receive live virus immunizations. Teaching includes how to prevent infection and recognize early signs and symptoms (e.g., fever, cough, malaise, dyspnea).

Integrin receptor antagonists include natalizumab (Tysabri) and vedolizumab (Entyvio). They inhibit leukocyte adhesion by blocking α4-integrin, an adhesion molecule. Use is limited to those who have not had an adequate response with other therapies (corticosteroids, immunosuppressants, anti-TNF agents). Both are given by IV infusion. Their use is associated with increased risk for infection, hepatotoxicity, and hypersensitivity reactions. Because of the risk for progressive multifocal

TABLE 42.18 Indications for Surgical Therapy for IBD

- Drainage of abdominal abscess
- Failure to respond to conservative therapy
- Fistulas
- Inability to decrease corticosteroids
- Intestinal obstruction
- Massive hemorrhage
- Perforation
- Severe anorectal disease
- Suspicion of cancer

leukoencephalopathy, natalizumab is available only through a restricted program.

The biologic agents do not work for everyone. They are costly and may produce allergic reactions. They are immunogenic, meaning that patients receiving them often make antibodies against them. Immunogenicity leads to acute infusion reactions and delayed hypersensitivity-type reactions. The drugs are most effective when given at regular intervals. Infusion reactions are more likely if a drug is stopped and then restarted.

Surgical Therapy
Ulcerative Colitis. Indications for surgery for UC are outlined in Table 42.18. Surgical procedures used include (1) total proctocolectomy with ileal pouch/anal anastomosis (IPAA) and (2) total proctocolectomy with permanent ileostomy. Since UC affects only the colon, a total proctocolectomy is curative. The most common surgical procedure for UC is a total proctocolectomy with IPAA. For more detail, see the discussion on bowel resection and ostomy surgery later in this chapter on p. 952.

Crohn's Disease. Surgery for Crohn's disease is usually done for complications such as strictures, obstructions, bleeding, and fistula (Table 42.18). Most patients with Crohn's disease eventually need surgery. The most common surgery involves resecting the diseased segments with reanastomosis of the remaining intestine. Unfortunately, the disease often recurs at the anastomosis site. Repeated removal of sections of the small intestine can lead to short bowel syndrome. *Short bowel syndrome (SBS)* occurs when either surgery or disease leaves too little small intestine surface area to maintain normal nutrition and hydration. Lifetime fluid boluses and parenteral nutrition (PN) may be needed. For more detail, see the discussion on short bowel syndrome later in this chapter on p. 962.

The other common surgery for Crohn's disease is a stricture-plasty. This opens narrowed areas obstructing the bowel. Since the intestine stays intact, it reduces the risk for developing short-bowel syndrome and its associated complications. Recurrences at the site are uncommon.

Nutritional Therapy. An individualized diet is an important part of treating IBD. Patients with IBD need a balanced, healthy diet with enough calories, protein, and nutrients. Consult a dietitian about dietary recommendations. The goals of diet management are to (1) provide adequate nutrition without worsening symptoms, (2) correct and prevent malnutrition, (3) replace fluid and electrolyte losses, and (4) prevent weight loss.

Nutritional deficiencies are due to decreased oral intake, blood loss, and, depending on the location of the inflammation, impaired absorption. Patients may reduce food intake to reduce diarrhea. Inflammatory mediators reduce appetite. Blood loss and malabsorption lead to iron-deficiency anemia (see Chapter 30). The patient may need oral iron supplements. Parenteral or IV iron is an option for those who cannot tolerate oral iron or if anemia is severe. Zinc deficiency can result from ostomies or diarrhea. Zinc supplements may be needed.[16]

Disease of the terminal ileum reduces absorption of cobalamin and bile acids. Reduced cobalamin contributes to anemia. Those who develop anemia should receive cobalamin injections. Bile salts are important for fat absorption and contribute to osmotic diarrhea. Cholestyramine, an ion-exchange resin that binds unabsorbed bile salts, helps control diarrhea.

Drug therapy can contribute to nutritional problems. Patients taking sulfasalazine should take 1 mg folate (folic acid) daily.[16] Those receiving corticosteroids are prone to osteoporosis and need calcium supplements. Potassium supplements may be needed with corticosteroids.

During an acute exacerbation, patients with IBD may not be able to tolerate a regular diet. Liquid enteral feedings are preferred over PN because atrophy of the gut and bacterial overgrowth occur when the GI tract is not used. EN is high in calories and nutrients, lactose free, and easily absorbed. They help achieve remission and improve nutritional status. EN is discussed in Chapter 39.

There are no universal food triggers for IBD, but some may find that certain foods cause diarrhea. A food diary helps to identify problem foods to avoid. Patients are typically taught to then avoid or limit foods that cause GI distress or worsen symptoms.

❖ NURSING MANAGEMENT: INFLAMMATORY BOWEL DISEASE

◆ Nursing Assessment

Table 42.19 outlines the subjective and objective data you should obtain from a patient with IBD.

◆ Nursing Diagnoses

Nursing diagnoses for the patient with IBD include:

- Diarrhea
- Impaired nutritional status
- Difficulty coping
- Chronic pain

For more information on nursing diagnoses and interventions for IBD, see eNursing Care Plan 42.2 on the website for this chapter.

TABLE 42.19 Nursing Assessment

Inflammatory Bowel Disease

Subjective Data

Important Health Information

Past health history: Infection, autoimmune disorders
Medications: Antidiarrheal drugs

Functional Health Patterns

Health perception–health management: Family history of ulcerative colitis or Crohn's disease. Fatigue, malaise
Nutritional-metabolic: Nausea, vomiting; anorexia. Weight loss
Elimination: Diarrhea. Blood, mucus, or pus in stools
Cognitive-perceptual: Lower abdominal pain (worse before defecation), cramping, tenesmus

Objective Data

General

Intermittent fever, emaciated appearance, fatigue

Integumentary

Pale skin with poor turgor, dry mucous membranes. Skin lesions, anorectal irritation, skin tags, cutaneous fistulas

Gastrointestinal

Abdominal distention, hyperactive bowel sounds, abdominal cramps

Cardiovascular

Tachycardia, hypotension

Possible Diagnostic Findings

Anemia, leukocytosis. Electrolyte imbalance, hypoalbuminemia, vitamin, and trace metal deficiencies. Guaiac-positive stool. Abnormal sigmoidoscopy, colonoscopy, and/or barium enema findings

---

◆ Planning

The overall goals are that the patient with IBD will (1) have fewer and less severe acute exacerbations, (2) maintain normal fluid and electrolyte balance, (3) be free from pain or discomfort, (4) adhere to medical regimens, (5) maintain nutritional balance, and (6) have an improved quality of life.

◆ Nursing Implementation

◆ **Acute Care.** During the acute phase, focus your attention on hemodynamic stability, pain control, fluid and electrolyte balance, and nutritional support. Maintain accurate intake and output records. Monitor the number and appearance of stools. Assess for the presence of blood in stools and emesis. Give IV fluids, electrolytes, analgesics, and antiinflammatory drugs as prescribed. Monitor serum electrolytes, CBC, and vital signs, being alert for changes related to diarrhea and dehydration. If the patient has orthostatic hypotension, teach the patient to change position slowly and use safety precautions.

Help the patient stay clean, dry, and free of odor until the diarrhea is under control. Place a deodorizer in the room. Meticulous perianal skin care using plain water (no harsh soap) with a moisturizing skin barrier cream prevents skin breakdown. Dibucaine, witch hazel, sitz baths, and other soothing compresses or ointments may reduce perianal irritation and pain.

Calculate the adequacy of the daily calorie intake. Obtain a daily weight. Assess the abdomen, including bowel sounds, as needed. Consult with a dietitian about diet modifications and the need for nutritional supplements.

Postoperative care after surgical procedures for IBD is similar to that described later in this chapter in the intestinal and ostomy surgery section (see p. 952) and in the general nursing care plan for the postoperative patient (see eNursing Care Plan 19.1 on the website for Chapter 19).

◆ **Ambulatory Care.** IBD is a chronic illness. Assist the patient in accepting the chronicity of IBD and learning ways to cope with its recurrent, unpredictable nature. Teaching includes (1) the importance of rest and diet management, (2) perianal care, (3) drug action and side effects, (4) symptoms of recurrence of disease, (5) when to seek medical care, and (6) ways to reduce stress. Excellent teaching resources, written in easily comprehensible language are available from the Crohn's and Colitis Foundation of America (*www.crohnscolitisfoundation.org*).

It is important to establish rapport and encourage the patient to talk about self-care. Ask patients what you can do to promote their self-care. An explanation of all procedures and treatments helps to build trust, decrease apprehension, and increase self-control. Once you have established a therapeutic relationship, talk with smokers who have Crohn's disease about quitting since smoking is associated with more severe disease.

The patient and caregiver may need your help setting realistic short- and long-term goals. Patients may have severe fatigue, which limits their energy for physical activity. Rest is important. Patients may lose sleep because of frequent episodes of diarrhea and abdominal pain. Nutritional deficiencies and anemia worsen fatigue and leave the patient feeling weak. Teach them to schedule activities around rest periods.

Many patients have intermittent exacerbations and remissions of symptoms. Given the chronicity and uncertainty related to the frequency and severity of flares, the patient may have frustration, depression, and anxiety. Psychotherapy and behavioral therapies may help patients deal with their feelings about the disease and help to manage their symptoms. Because of the relationship between emotions and the GI tract, teach the patient ways to manage stress (see Chapter 6). Suggest the patient seek support through a local or online support group from the Crohn's and Colitis Foundation of America.

◆ **Evaluation**

The expected outcomes are that the patient with IBD will
• Have a decrease in the number of diarrhea stools
• Maintain body weight within a normal range
• Be free from pain and discomfort
• Use effective coping strategies

Gerontologic Considerations: Inflammatory Bowel Disease

A second peak in occurrence of IBD is in the 6th decade. The cause, natural history, and clinical course of IBD are similar to those seen in younger patients. However, in the older patient, proctitis and left-sided UC are more common. Diagnosis is sometimes difficult in older adults since IBD can be confused with CDI, diverticulitis, or colitis.

The interprofessional care of IBD is also similar; however, challenges exist. Drug therapy and surgery have an increased risk for adverse events, hospitalization, and mortality. Older adults are more prone to adverse events from corticosteroids. Immunosuppressant and biologic therapies have a higher risk for infection and cancer. Anemia and malnutrition are more common.[17] They are more vulnerable to volume depletion from diarrhea. Those with physical limitations may have trouble handling fecal urgency and multiple trips to the bathroom without help.

INTESTINAL OBSTRUCTION

Intestinal obstruction occurs when intestinal contents cannot pass through the GI tract. The obstruction may occur in the small (SBO) or large (LBO) intestine. It can be partial or complete, simple or strangulated. Partial obstructions do not completely occlude the intestinal lumen, allowing for some fluid and gas to pass through. They usually resolve with conservative treatment. A complete obstruction totally occludes the lumen and usually requires surgery. A simple obstruction has an intact blood supply; a strangulated one does not.

Types of Intestinal Obstruction

The causes of intestinal obstruction are either mechanical or nonmechanical.

Mechanical. In *mechanical obstruction,* there is a physical obstruction of the intestinal lumen. Most intestinal obstructions occur in the small intestine. Surgical adhesions are the most common cause of SBO.[18] They can occur within days of surgery or years later (Fig. 42.5). Other causes of SBO are hernia, cancer, strictures from Crohn's disease, and intussusception after bariatric surgery. The most common cause of LBO is colorectal cancer (malignant obstruction) followed by diverticular disease. Other causes include adhesions, ischemia, volvulus, and Crohn's disease.[19]

Nonmechanical. A *nonmechanical obstruction* occurs with reduced or absent peristalsis due to altered neuromuscular transmission of the parasympathetic innervation to the bowel. It may result from a neuromuscular or vascular disorder. Paralytic ileus (lack of intestinal peristalsis and bowel sounds) is the most common form of nonmechanical obstruction. It occurs to some degree after any abdominal surgery. It can be hard to know if a postoperative obstruction is due to paralytic ileus or adhesions. One clue is that bowel sounds usually return before postoperative adhesions develop. Other causes of paralytic ileus include peritonitis, inflammatory responses (e.g., acute pancreatitis, acute appendicitis), electrolyte abnormalities (especially hypokalemia), and thoracic or lumbar spinal fractures.

Pseudo-obstruction is a mechanical obstruction without any cause found on radiologic imaging. It is a GI motility disorder. There are several conditions associated with pseudo-obstruction. These include major surgery, electrolyte imbalance, neurologic conditions, medications, sepsis, cancer, trauma, and burns.[20]

Vascular obstructions are rare. They are the result of an interference with the blood supply to a part of the intestines. The most common causes are emboli and atherosclerosis of the mesenteric arteries. Emboli may originate from thrombi in patients who have chronic atrial fibrillation, diseased heart valves, and prosthetic valves. Venous thrombosis may occur in conditions of low blood flow, such as heart failure and shock.

Etiology and Pathophysiology

About 6 to 8 L of fluid enter the small intestine daily. Most of the fluid is absorbed before it reaches the colon. Around 75% of intestinal gas is swallowed air. When an obstruction occurs, fluid, gas, and intestinal contents accumulate proximal to the obstruction. Distention reduces fluid absorption and initially

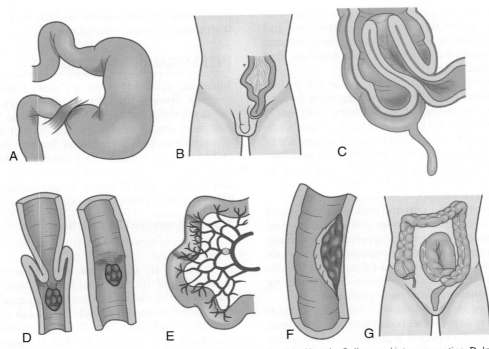

FIG. 42.5 Bowel obstructions. **A**, Adhesions. **B**, Strangulated inguinal hernia. **C**, Ileocecal intussusception. **D**, Intussusception from polyps. **E**, Mesenteric occlusion. **F**, Neoplasm. **G**, Volvulus of the sigmoid colon.

stimulates intestinal secretions. Distal to the obstruction, the bowel empties, and then collapses. As distention increases in the proximal bowel, intraluminal bowel pressure rises. The increased pressure leads to an increase in capillary permeability and extravasation of fluids and electrolytes into the peritoneal cavity. Eventually the intestinal muscle becomes fatigued, and peristalsis stops. Retention of fluids in the intestine and peritoneal cavity leads to a severe reduction in circulating blood volume. This leads to hypotension and hypovolemic shock.

If blood flow is inadequate, bowel tissue becomes ischemic, then necrotic, and the bowel may perforate. In the most dangerous situation the bowel becomes so distended that the blood flow stops, causing edema, cyanosis, and gangrene of a bowel segment. This is called *intestinal strangulation* or *intestinal infarction*. If not quickly corrected, the bowel will become necrotic and rupture, leading to infection, septic shock, and death.

The location of the obstruction determines the extent of fluid, electrolyte, and acid-base imbalances. If the obstruction is high (e.g., upper duodenum), metabolic alkalosis may result from the loss of gastric hydrochloric (HCl) acid through vomiting or NG intubation and suction. When the obstruction is in the small intestine, dehydration occurs rapidly. Dehydration and electrolyte imbalances do not occur early in large bowel obstruction. If the obstruction is below the proximal colon, solid fecal material accumulates until symptoms of discomfort appear.

Clinical Manifestations

The 4 hallmark clinical manifestations of an obstruction are abdominal pain, nausea and vomiting, distention, and constipation. The order and degree these appear vary by the cause, location, and type of obstruction (Table 42.20). Colicky abdominal pain is usually the first symptom. In SBO, the pain is often of sudden onset. It occurs at 4- to 5-minute intervals for proximal obstructions and less often for distal obstructions. The

TABLE 42.20 **Manifestations of Small and Large Intestinal Obstructions**			
	SMALL INTESTINE		**Large Intestine**
Manifestation	**Proximal**	**Distal**	
Onset	Rapid	Rapid	Gradual
Vomiting	Frequent and copious	Less frequent	Late or absent
Pain	Colicky, cramping, occurs at frequent intervals	Colicky, occurs more intermittently	Persistent, cramping
Bowel movement	Feces for a short time	Gradual constipation	Obstipation
Abdominal distention	Minimal	Increased	Increased

nature of the vomiting gives a clue to the level of obstruction. In a proximal obstruction, patients rapidly develop nausea and vomiting. It may be projectile and contain bile. Vomiting usually gives temporary relief from abdominal pain in higher obstructions. Vomiting from a more distal small bowel obstruction is more gradual in onset and more fecal and foul smelling. Bowel sounds may be high-pitched above the area of obstruction. Bowel sounds are usually absent with paralytic ileus.

Signs of LBO include abdominal distention, either obstipation or a marked change in bowel function, and lack of flatus. The patient has persistent, cramping abdominal pain. Bowel sounds are usually present and become progressively hypoactive. Vomiting is rare. Strangulation causes severe, constant pain that is rapid in onset.[19]

With both types, abdominal tenderness and rigidity occur. The patient appears acutely ill, with signs of dehydration and sepsis. These include tachycardia, dry mucous membranes, and hypotension. The patient's temperature may rise above 100°F (37.8°C).

Diagnostic Studies

Perform a thorough history and physical examination. Imaging can identify an obstruction and guide decisions about surgery. Abdominal x-rays, CT scan, or contrast enema may be done. Sigmoidoscopy or colonoscopy provides direct visualization of an LBO.

Blood tests include a CBC and blood chemistries. A high WBC count may mean strangulation or perforation. Increased hematocrit values may reflect hemoconcentration. Decreased hemoglobin and hematocrit values may mean bleeding from cancer or strangulation with necrosis. Serum electrolytes, BUN, and creatinine are monitored to assess the degree of dehydration. Metabolic alkalosis can develop from vomiting.

Interprofessional Care

Treatment of a bowel obstruction depends on the cause. If a strangulated obstruction or perforation is present, the patient will need emergency surgery to relieve the obstruction and survive. In some, especially those due to surgical adhesions, an obstruction may resolve without surgery.

Surgery may involve simply resecting the obstructed segment of bowel and anastomosing the remaining healthy bowel back together. Partial or total colectomy, colostomy, or ileostomy may be done when extensive obstruction or necrosis is present. Sometimes, an obstruction can be removed nonsurgically. Colonoscopy offers a means to remove polyps, dilate strictures, and remove and destroy tumors with a laser.

The initial treatment includes placing the patient on NPO status, providing IV fluid therapy with either normal saline or lactated Ringer's solution, and giving IV antiemetics. If needed, insert an NG tube for decompression and give ordered electrolyte replacement. Obtain blood cultures and start IV antibiotic therapy. Some patients need PN to allow bowel rest and improve nutritional status before surgery.

The treatment goal for a patient with a malignant obstruction is to regain patency and resolve the obstruction. Stents can be placed via endoscopic or fluoroscopic procedures. They are used for palliative purposes or as "a bridge to surgery," allowing a patient to avoid emergency surgery.[19] This gives the interprofessional team time to correct fluid volume problems and treat other problems, thus improving surgical outcomes. Corticosteroids with antiemetic properties that decrease edema and inflammation may be used with stent placement.

❖ NURSING MANAGEMENT: INTESTINAL OBSTRUCTION

◆ Nursing Assessment

Intestinal obstruction is a potentially life-threatening condition. Major concerns are preventing fluid and electrolyte deficiencies and early recognition of deterioration in the patient's condition (e.g., hypovolemic shock, sepsis, bowel strangulation). Nursing assessment begins with a detailed patient history and physical examination. Determine the location, duration, intensity, and frequency of abdominal pain.

Record the onset, frequency, color, odor, and amount of vomitus. Assess bowel function, including the passage of flatus. Auscultate for bowel sounds and document their character and location. Inspect the abdomen for scars, visible masses, and distention. Assess whether abdominal tenderness or rigidity is present. Measure the abdominal girth. Check for signs of peritoneal irritation (e.g., muscle guarding, rebound pain). If the HCP decides to wait to see if the obstruction resolves on its own, assess the patient regularly. Notify the HCP of changes in vital signs, changes in bowel sounds, decreased urine output, increased abdominal distention, and pain.

Maintain a strict intake and output record, including emesis and tube drainage. A urinary catheter allows for hourly monitoring of urine output. Report if the urine output is less than 0.5 mL/kg of body weight per hour. This indicates inadequate vascular volume and the potential for acute kidney injury. Rising serum creatinine and BUN levels are other indicators of acute kidney injury.

◆ Nursing Diagnoses

Nursing diagnoses for the patient with intestinal obstructions include:

- Acute pain
- Fluid imbalance

◆ Planning

The overall goals are that the patient with an intestinal obstruction will have (1) relief of the obstruction and return to normal bowel function, (2) minimal to no discomfort, and (3) normal fluid and electrolyte and acid-base status.

◆ Nursing Implementation

Monitor the patient closely for signs of dehydration and electrolyte imbalances. Give IV fluids as ordered. Assess for signs and symptoms of fluid imbalance. Some patients, especially older adults, may not tolerate rapid fluid replacement. Monitor serum electrolyte levels closely. A patient with a high intestinal obstruction is more likely to have metabolic alkalosis. A patient with a low obstruction is at greater risk for metabolic acidosis. The patient is often restless and constantly changes position to relieve the pain. Provide comfort measures and promote a restful environment. Nursing care of the patient after surgery for an intestinal obstruction is similar to care of the patient after a laparotomy (see p. 935).

With an NG tube in place, oral care is extremely important. Vomiting leaves an unpleasant taste in the patient's mouth, and fecal odor may be present. The patient breathes through the mouth, drying the mouth and lips. Provide frequent oral care and water-soluble lubricant for the lips. Check the nose for signs of irritation from the NG tube. Clean and dry this area daily, apply water-soluble lubricant, and retape the tube. Check the NG tube every 4 hours for patency.

POLYPS OF LARGE INTESTINE

Colonic polyps arise from the mucosal surface of the colon and project into the lumen. They may be *sessile* (flat, broad based, and attached directly to the intestinal wall) or *pedunculated* (attached to the intestinal wall by a thin stalk). Polyps tend to be sessile when small and become pedunculated as they enlarge (Fig. 42.6). They may be found anywhere in the large intestine. As patients age, polyps are increasingly present in the proximal colon. Rectal bleeding and occult blood in the stool are the most common signs, but most patients with polyps are asymptomatic.

Types of Polyps

The most common types of polyps are hyperplastic and adenomatous. *Hyperplastic polyps* are noncancerous. They rarely grow larger than 5 mm and never cause clinical symptoms. Other benign polyps include inflammatory polyps, lipomas, and juvenile polyps.

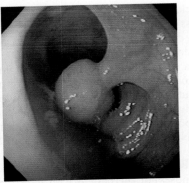

FIG. 42.6 Endoscopic image of pedunculated polyp in descending colon. (Courtesy David Bjorkman, MD, University of Utah School of Medicine, Department of Gastroenterology. In McCance KL, Huether SE: *Pathophysiology: The biologic basis for disease in adults and children*, ed 6, St Louis, 2010, Mosby.)

Adenomatous polyps are neoplastic and closely linked to colorectal adenocarcinoma. There are 3 types: tubular, tubulovillous, and villous. Villous or large adenomatous polyps are more likely to have cancers develop in them. Removing adenomatous polyps decreases the occurrence of colorectal cancer.

Genetic Link

Familial adenomatous polyposis (FAP) is the most common polyposis syndrome (see the Genetics in Clinical Practice box), causing 1% of all CRCs. FAP is a genetic disorder characterized by hundreds or sometimes thousands of polyps in the colon that appear during adolescence and early adulthood. They eventually become cancerous, usually by age 40. Since CRC is inevitable,

GENETICS IN CLINICAL PRACTICE

Familial Adenomatous Polyposis (FAP)

Genetic Basis
- Autosomal dominant FAP
  - Classic form of disease
  - Mutations in adenomatous polyposis coli (*APC*) gene
  - Normally this is a tumor suppressor gene involved in DNA repair
  - Normally this gene makes a protein that keeps polyps from developing in the colon
  - 50% of the offspring of a patient with FAP carry the *FAP* gene
- Autosomal recessive FAP
  - Autosomal recessive disorder
  - Mutations in the *mutY* homolog (*MUTYH*) gene
  - Normally this gene is involved in DNA repair
  - Characterized by fewer polyps, typically <100

Incidence
- Affects 1 in 7000 to 22,000 people
- Equally affects men and women

Genetic Testing
- DNA testing is available

Clinical Implications
- Anyone with a family history of FAP should undergo genetic testing during childhood
- If the FAP gene is present, colorectal screening begins at puberty, and annual colonoscopy begins at age 16
- Persons with a family history of FAP can benefit from genetic counseling

TABLE 42.21 Risk Factors for Colorectal Cancer

- Alcohol (≥4 drinks/wk)
- Cigarette smoking
- Family history of colorectal cancer (first-degree relative)
- Family or personal history of familial adenomatous polyposis (FAP)
- Family or personal history of hereditary nonpolyposis colorectal cancer (HNPCC) syndrome
- Obesity (body mass index ≥30 kg/m²)
- Personal history of colorectal cancer, inflammatory bowel disease, or diabetes
- Red meat (≥7 servings/wk)

the colon and rectum are removed, usually by age 25, by proctocolectomy with an IPAA or an ileostomy. Patients with classic FAP are at risk for cancers of the thyroid, stomach, small intestine, liver, and brain, so lifetime cancer surveillance is essential.

Diagnostic Studies and Interprofessional Care

Colonoscopy, sigmoidoscopy, barium enema, and virtual colonoscopy (CT or MRI colonography) are used to discover polyps. Colonoscopy is preferred because it allows evaluation of the total colon. All polyps are considered abnormal and should be removed (*polypectomy*). Polyps can be removed during colonoscopy or sigmoidoscopy. They cannot be removed during barium enema and virtual colonoscopy. After polypectomy, watch the patient for rectal bleeding, fever, severe abdominal pain, and abdominal distention, which may indicate hemorrhage or perforation.

COLORECTAL CANCER

Of cancers that affect both men and women, colorectal cancer (CRC) is the third leading cause of cancer-related deaths and the third most common cancer in men and women. Annually about 140,250 people in the United States are diagnosed with CRC and 50,600 people die from CRC.[21]

CRC is more common in men than in women. The risk for CRC increases with age, with about 90% of new CRC cases detected in people older than 50. However, while the incidence of CRC in people over 50 years is decreasing, the number of cases in people aged 20 to 49 years is rising and expected to continue to do so.[22] This is thought to be related to diet, physical inactivity, and increasing rates of obesity.

PROMOTING HEALTH EQUITY

Colorectal Cancer

- Blacks are most likely to develop colorectal cancer (CRC).
- Blacks are more likely to die of CRC than any other ethnic group.
- Cancer may occur at an earlier age in blacks and Hispanics.
- Hispanics are the least likely to undergo CRC screening.

Etiology and Pathophysiology

Unlike some other cancers, no single risk factor accounts for most cases of CRC (Table 42.21). The risk is highest in those with first-degree relatives with CRC and people with IBD. About 20% of cases of CRC occur in patients with a family history of CRC. Hereditary forms of CRC, including FAP and hereditary nonpolyposis colorectal cancer (HNPCC) syndrome (Lynch syndrome), account for another 10% of cases.

About 30% to 50% of people with CRC have an abnormal *KRAS* gene. The *KRAS* gene, which is primarily involved in regulating cell division, belongs to a class of genes known as *oncogenes*. When mutated, oncogenes have the potential to cause normal cells to become cancerous.

GENETICS IN CLINICAL PRACTICE

Hereditary Nonpolyposis Colorectal Cancer (HNPCC) or Lynch Syndrome

Genetic Basis
- Autosomal dominant disorder
- Mutations in *MSH2, MLH1, MSH6,* or *PMS2* genes
- These genes are involved with the repair of mistakes in DNA replication

Incidence
- Affects 1 in 500 to 2000 people

Genetic Testing
- DNA testing is available

Clinical Implications
- Accounts for 3% to 5% of all CRC
- Depending on the genetic mutation, the risk for developing CRC is from 50% to 80%
- If colon polyps are present, they occur at an earlier age than do polyps in the general population and are more prone to become cancerous
- Have increased risk for stomach, brain, ovary, uterus, skin, urinary tract, small bowel, and bile ducts cancers
- People with HNPCC need to have a colonoscopy every year
- Women with HNPCC should undergo ovarian and endometrial cancer screening

Maintaining a healthy weight, being physically active, limiting alcohol use, not smoking, and eating a diet with large amounts of fruits, vegetables, and grains may decrease the risk for CRC.

CRC usually starts as a polyp on the inner lining of the colon or rectum that grows over a period of 10 to 20 years. Most polyps are adenomas, which arise from the cells that make mucus. As the tumor grows, the cancer invades and penetrates the wall of colon or rectum (Fig. 42.7). Eventually cancer cells gain access to the lymph nodes and vascular system and spread to distant sites. Since venous blood leaving the colon and rectum flows through the portal vein and the inferior rectal vein, the liver is a common site of metastasis. The cancer spreads from the liver to other sites, including the lungs, bones, and brain. CRC can also spread directly into adjacent structures.

Clinical Manifestations

CRC develops slowly, and symptoms do not appear until the disease is advanced. Common manifestations include iron-deficiency anemia, rectal bleeding, abdominal pain, and change in bowel habits.

Physical findings may include:
- *Early disease:* None or nonspecific findings (fatigue, weight loss)
- *More advanced disease:* Abdominal tenderness, palpable abdominal mass, hepatomegaly, ascites

Bleeding can occur with both right- and left-sided CRC. Bleeding on the right side is more common than on the left side. It is often unrecognized, and an early manifestation is often anemia. Hematochezia (fresh blood in the stool) is more often caused by left-sided CRC than right-sided CRC.

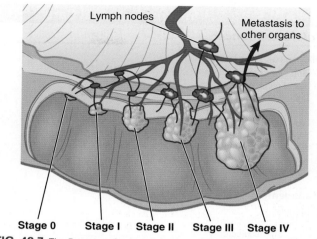

FIG. 42.7 The 5 stages of colorectal cancer. Stage 0 cancer has not grown beyond the mucosal layer. Stage I cancer has grown beyond the mucosa into the submucosa, but no lymph nodes are involved. Stage II cancer has grown beyond the submucosa into the muscle, but there is no lymph node involvement or metastasis. Stage III cancer is any tumor with lymph node involvement but no metastasis. Stage IV cancer is any tumor with lymph node involvement and metastasis.

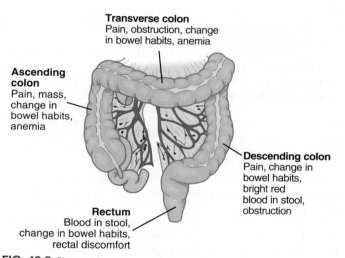

FIG. 42.8 Signs and symptoms of colorectal cancer by location of primary cancer. (Modified from McCance KL, Huether SE: *Pathophysiology: The biologic basis for disease in adults and children,* ed 6, St Louis, 2010, Mosby.)

Right-sided cancers are more likely to cause diarrhea. Left-sided cancers are usually detected later and could present with bowel obstruction (Fig. 42.8). Complications of CRC include obstruction, bleeding, perforation, peritonitis, and fistula formation.

Diagnostic Studies

Obtain a thorough history with close attention to family history (Table 42.22). Since symptoms of CRC do not become evident until the disease is advanced, there is an increased emphasis on screening. Beginning at age 45 and continuing until age 75, men and women at average risk for developing CRC should have screening tests to detect both polyps and cancer based on 1 of these testing schedules:
- Flexible sigmoidoscopy (every 5 years)
- Colonoscopy (every 10 years)

TABLE 42.22 Interprofessional Care

Colorectal Cancer

Diagnostic Assessment
- History and physical examination
- Digital rectal examination
- Testing of stool for occult blood
- CBC
- Liver function tests
- Barium enema
- Sigmoidoscopy and/or colonoscopy with biopsy
- Abdominal CT scan, ultrasound, or MRI
- Carcinoembryonic antigen (CEA) test

Management
- Surgery
  - Right hemicolectomy
  - Left hemicolectomy
  - Abdominal-perineal resection
  - Laparoscopic colectomy
- Chemotherapy
- Targeted therapy
- Radiation therapy

TABLE 42.23 TNM Classification of Colorectal Cancer

T	**Primary Tumor**
T_x	Cannot assess primary tumor because of incomplete information.
T_{is}	Carcinoma in situ. Cancer is in earliest stage and has not grown beyond mucosa layer.
T_1	Tumor has grown beyond mucosa into the submucosa.
T_2	Tumor has grown through submucosa into muscularis propria.
T_3	Tumor has grown through the muscularis propria into the pericolorectal tissues.
T_4	Tumor invades the visceral peritoneum or invades or adheres to adjacent organ or structure.
N	**Lymph Node Involvement**
N_x	Cannot assess lymph nodes.
N_0	No regional lymph node involvement is found.
N_1	Cancer is found in 1 to 3 nearby lymph nodes.
N_2	Cancer is found in 4 or more nearby lymph nodes.
M	**Metastasis**
M_x	Cannot assess presence of metastasis.
M_0	No distant metastasis seen.
M_1	Distant metastasis is present.

TABLE 42.24 Classification System Used to Stage Colorectal Cancer

Stage*	TNM†	5-Yr Survival Rate (%)
0	$T_{is}\ N_0\ M_0$	>96
I	$T_1\ N_0\ M_0$	92
	$T_2\ N_0\ M_0$	87
II	$T_3\ N_0\ M_0$	70–80
III	Any T, $N_{1-2}\ M_0$	53–84
IV	Any T, any N, M_1	12

*Staging system is shown in Fig. 42.7.
†See Table 42.23.

- Double-contrast barium enema (every 5 years)
- CT colonography (virtual colonoscopy) (every 5 years)
- Tests that primarily find cancer include:
  - High-sensitivity fecal occult blood test (FOBT) (every year), *or*
  - Fecal immunochemical test (FIT) (every year)
  - Stool DNA test (every 3 years)

Colonoscopy is the gold standard for CRC screening. It allows the entire colon to be examined, biopsies obtained, and polyps removed and sent to the laboratory for examination. People at average risk for CRC should undergo colonoscopy every 10 years beginning at age 45.

Persons at risk (Table 42.21) should begin screening earlier and have screening done more often. Those who have a first-degree relative who developed CRC before age 60 or have 2 first-degree relatives with CRC should have a colonoscopy every 5 years beginning at age 40 or 10 years earlier than when the youngest relative developed cancer. Those who have 1 first-degree relative who had CRC after age 60 should have a colonoscopy every 10 years beginning at age 40.[23]

Less favorable, but acceptable, screening methods include stool testing for fecal blood. The FOBT and FIT look for blood in the stool. Stool tests must be done yearly since tumor bleeding occurs at intervals and may easily be missed if a single test is done. Stool DNA tests (PreGen-Plus, Cologuard) can detect DNA mutations that may occur with CRC.

Once tissue biopsies confirm the diagnosis of CRC, the patient needs a CBC to check for anemia and liver function tests. A CT scan or MRI of the abdomen will be done to detect liver metastases, retroperitoneal and pelvic disease, and depth of penetration of tumor into the bowel wall. However, liver function tests may be normal even when metastasis has occurred.

Carcinoembryonic antigen (CEA) is a complex glycoprotein sometimes made by CRC cells. It may be used to monitor for disease recurrence after surgery or chemotherapy but is not a good screening tool because of the large number of false-positive findings. CEA levels also may be increased in noncolon cancers (e.g., gastric, pancreatic, breast, thyroid cancers) as well as some noncancerous conditions, like IBD, pancreatitis, cirrhosis, and chronic obstructive pulmonary disease.

Interprofessional Care

The prognosis and treatment of CRC correlates with pathologic staging of the disease. The most commonly used staging system is the tumor, node, metastasis (TNM) staging (Table 42.23). As with other cancers, prognosis worsens with greater size and depth of tumor, lymph node involvement, and metastasis (Table 42.24).

Surgical Therapy. Goals of surgical therapy include (1) complete resection of the tumor, (2) a thorough exploration of the abdomen to determine if the cancer has spread, (3) removing all lymph nodes that drain the area where the cancer is located, (4) restoring bowel continuity so that normal bowel function will return, and (5) preventing surgical complications.

Some polyps can be removed during colonoscopy, while others require surgery. Polypectomy during colonoscopy can be used to resect CRC in situ. It is considered successful when the resected margin of the polyp is free of cancer, the cancer is well differentiated, and there is no apparent lymphatic or blood vessel involvement.

The decision for surgical treatment depends on the staging and location of the cancer and the ability to restore normal bowel function and continence. Surgical removal of stage I cancer includes removing the tumor and at least 5 cm of intestine on either side of it, plus nearby lymph nodes. The remaining cancer-free ends are sewn back together (anastomosis). Laparoscopic surgery is sometimes used for stage I tumors, especially those in the left colon. Low-risk stage II tumors are treated with wide resection and reanastomosis. Chemotherapy is used after surgery for high-risk stage II tumors. Stage III tumors are treated with surgery and chemotherapy. Radiation and chemotherapy may be done before surgery to reduce tumor size.

When the tumor is not resectable or metastasis is present, palliative surgery can control hemorrhage or relieve a malignant bowel obstruction. Chemotherapy and radiation can control the spread and provide pain relief. A few patients with limited lung or liver metastases can achieve a cure after primary and metastatic tumor resection and chemotherapy. In rectal cancer, the location and size of the tumor determines the course of treatment. Local excision may be an option. If the tumor is in the distal rectum (1 to 2 cm from the anorectal junction) and the sphincters cannot be preserved, the patient will undergo an *abdominal-perineal resection (APR)*. An APR involves removing the entire rectum with the tumor, and the patient will have a permanent colostomy.

If the tumor is in the mid or proximal rectum, it may be possible to preserve the sphincters with a low anterior resection (LAR). A LAR involves removing the rectum and anastomosing the colon to the anal canal. A temporary ileostomy or colostomy may be done to divert stool and allow time for the anastomosis to heal. Another option if the anal sphincters remain is for the HCP to create an alternative reservoir with either a colonic J-pouch or coloplasty. A LAR is increasingly common because of advancements in laparoscopy and stapling techniques.

Chemotherapy and Targeted Therapy. Chemotherapy can be used to shrink the tumor before surgery, as an adjuvant therapy after colon resection, and as palliative treatment for non-resectable cancer. Adjuvant chemotherapy is recommended for patients with stage III tumors. Current protocols include varying doses of fluorouracil and leucovorin alone or in combination with oxaliplatin (Eloxatin) or irinotecan (Camptosar). The preferred protocol includes oxaliplatin. Oral fluoropyrimidines (e.g., capecitabine [Xeloda]) in combination with oxaliplatin are an alternative to fluorouracil/leucovorin.[24]

Several targeted therapies have a role in treating metastatic CRC. Angiogenesis inhibitors, which inhibit the blood supply to tumors, include aflibercept (Zaltrap), bevacizumab (Avastin), and ramucirumab (Cyramza). Cetuximab (Erbitux) and panitumumab (Vectibix) block the epidermal growth factor receptor. These drugs are often given with a combination chemotherapy regimen (e.g., fluorouracil/leucovorin/oxaliplatin).

Regorafenib (Stivarga) is a multikinase inhibitor that blocks several enzymes that promote cancer growth. It, or Lonsurf, a combination of trifluridine and tipiracil, are given to patients with metastatic CRC who are no longer responding to other therapies. Trifluridine impairs DNA function and angiogenesis. Tipiracil prevents the rapid metabolism of trifluridine, thus increasing its bioavailability.

Radiation Therapy. Some patients may receive radiation therapy as an adjuvant to surgery and chemotherapy or as a palliative measure for those with metastatic cancer. As a palliative measure, the primary goal is to reduce tumor size and provide symptomatic relief. Radiation therapy is described in Chapter 15.

TABLE 42.25 **Nursing Assessment**
Colorectal Cancer
Subjective Data
Important Health Information
Past health history: Previous breast or ovarian cancer, familial polyposis, villous adenoma, adenomatous polyps, IBD
Medications: Medications affecting bowel function (e.g., laxatives, antidiarrheal drugs)
Functional Health Patterns
Health perception–health management: Family history of colorectal, breast, or ovarian cancer; weakness, fatigue
Nutritional-metabolic: High-calorie, high-fat, low-fiber diet. Anorexia, nausea and vomiting, weight loss
Elimination: Change in bowel habits, alternating diarrhea and constipation, defecation urgency. Rectal bleeding, mucoid stools. Black, tarry stools. Increased flatus, decrease in stool caliber. Feelings of incomplete evacuation
Cognitive-perceptual: Abdominal and low back pain, tenesmus
Objective Data
General
Pallor, cachexia, lymphadenopathy (later signs)
Gastrointestinal
Palpable abdominal mass, distention, ascites, and hepatomegaly (liver metastasis)
Possible Diagnostic Findings
Anemia. Guaiac-positive stools, palpable mass on digital rectal examination. Positive sigmoidoscopy, colonoscopy, barium enema, or CT scan. Positive biopsy

---

❖ NURSING MANAGEMENT: COLORECTAL CANCER

◆ Nursing Assessment

Table 42.25 outlines the subjective and objective data you should obtain from a patient with CRC.

◆ Nursing Diagnoses

Nursing diagnoses for the patient with CRC include:
- Diarrhea or constipation
- Anxiety
- Difficulty coping

◆ Planning

The overall goals are that the patient with CRC will have (1) normal bowel elimination patterns, (2) quality of life appropriate to the disease progression, (3) relief of pain, and (4) feelings of comfort and well-being.

◆ Nursing Implementation

◆ Health Promotion.
Encourage all persons over 45 to have regular CRC screening. Help identify those at high risk who need screening at an earlier age. Discuss with patients how taking part in cancer screening helps decrease mortality rates. Realize that barriers exist, including lack of accurate information and fear of diagnosis.

Endoscopic and radiographic procedures can only reveal polyps when the bowel has been adequately prepared. Provide teaching about bowel cleansing for outpatient diagnostic procedures and give cleansing preparations to inpatients (see more on diagnostic procedures in Chapter 38).

◆ **Acute Care.** Nursing care for the patient after a colon resection is discussed in depth in the next section. If enough healthy bowel remained that the HCP could reconnect the bowel ends, normal bowel function is maintained. Routine postoperative care is appropriate. Patients with more extensive surgery (e.g., APR) may have an open wound and drains (e.g., Jackson-Pratt, Hemovac) and a permanent ostomy. Postoperative care includes sterile dressing changes, care of drains, and patient and caregiver teaching about the ostomy. Ostomy care is discussed in the next section on pp. 954–957.

◆ **Ambulatory Care.** Psychologic support for the patient and caregiver dealing with the diagnosis of cancer is important. Discuss the patient's feelings about the prognosis and future screening. Patients need much emotional support. The special needs of the cancer patient are discussed in Chapter 15. You may need to address issues surrounding palliative care, end-of-life issues, and hospice (see Chapter 9).

Patients with CRC need to know how to manage changes that result from cancer and cancer treatment. Those who had sphincter-sparing surgery may have diarrhea and incontinence of feces and gas. They may need antidiarrheal drugs or bulking agents to control the diarrhea, but overuse can result in constipation. A consult with a dietitian or wound, ostomy, and continence nurse (WOCN) may help patients and caregivers understand how to manage food and fluid options. Ostomy rehabilitation, including teaching and ongoing support, should be available for all ostomy patients. Patients with skin changes from incontinence and/or radiation therapy will need help with managing these conditions.

◆ **Evaluation**

The expected outcomes for the patient with CRC are that the patient will

- Have minimal changes in bowel elimination patterns
- Achieve optimal nutritional intake
- Experience quality of life appropriate to disease progression
- Have feelings of comfort and well-being

BOWEL RESECTION AND OSTOMY SURGERY

Surgical resection of the bowel may be done to (1) remove cancer; (2) repair a perforation, fistula, or traumatic injury; (3) relieve an obstruction or stricture; and (4) treat an abscess, inflammatory disease, or hemorrhage. For example, if a person has stage III CRC, the HCP will remove the diseased part of the colon along with a certain margin of healthy tissue. It may be a prophylactic procedure for those with complications from IBD. Patients at high risk for CRC, such as those with FAP, and patients with UC may have a total colectomy and an ileostomy.

Depending on the problem being treated, the following surgical procedures may be done:

- *Total proctocolectomy with IPAA:* 2 surgeries, 8 to 12 weeks apart. The first includes colectomy, rectal mucosectomy, ileal pouch (reservoir) construction, ileoanal anastomosis, and temporary ileostomy. A diverting ileostomy is done, and an ileal pouch is created and anastomosed directly to the anus (Fig. 42.9). The second involves closure of the ileostomy to direct stool toward the new pouch.

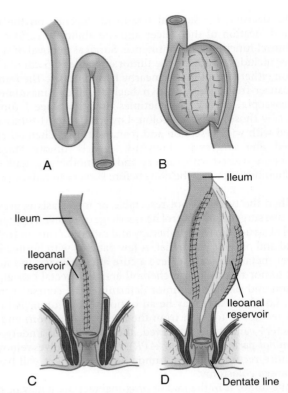

FIG. 42.9 Ileoanal pouch (reservoir). **A,** Formation of a pouch. **B,** Posterior suture lines completed. **C,** J-shaped configuration for ileoanal pouch (J-pouch). **D,** S-shaped configuration for ileoanal pouch (S-pouch).

- *Proctocolectomy with a permanent ileostomy:* Removal of the colon, rectum, and anus with closure of the anal opening. The end of the terminal ileum is brought out through the abdominal wall to form a permanent ileostomy.
- *Right hemicolectomy:* Removal of ascending colon and hepatic flexure with the ileum anastomosed to transverse colon.
- *Left hemicolectomy:* Removal of splenic flexure, descending colon, and sigmoid colon with the transverse colon anastomosed to rectum.
- *Anterior rectosigmoid resection:* Removal of part of descending colon, the sigmoid colon, and upper rectum with the descending colon anastomosed to remaining rectum.
- *Abdominal-perineal resection (APR):* Removal of the entire rectum with creation of a permanent colostomy.
- *Low anterior resection (LAR):* Removal of the rectum and with anastomosis of the colon to the anal canal. A temporary ileostomy or colostomy may be done to divert stool and allow time for the anastomosis to heal. After 8 to 12 weeks, the ostomy can be "taken down," and the ends of the colon surgically reconnected.

Ostomy. An **ostomy** is a surgically created opening on the abdomen that allows the discharge of body waste when the normal elimination route is no longer possible. The outermost part that is visible is a *stoma.* The stoma is the result of the large or small bowel being brought to the outside of the abdomen and sutured in place. When a stoma is created as a fecal diversion, feces will drain through the stoma instead of the anus.

Ostomies are named according to their location and type (Fig. 42.10). An ostomy in the ileum is an ileostomy. An ostomy in the colon is a colostomy. The ostomy is further characterized

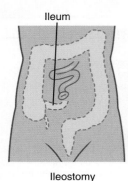
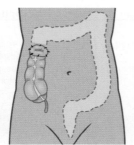
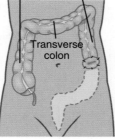
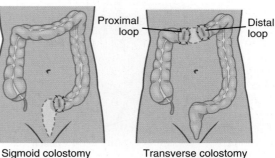

| Ileostomy | Ascending colostomy | Descending colostomy | Sigmoid colostomy single-barreled | Transverse colostomy double-barreled |

FIG. 42.10 Types of ostomies.

TABLE 42.26 **Comparison of Ileostomy and Colostomy**				
		COLOSTOMY		
Characteristic	**Ileostomy**	**Ascending**	**Transverse**	**Sigmoid**
Stool consistency	Liquid to semiliquid	Semiliquid	Semiliquid to semiformed	Formed
Fluid requirement	Increased	Increased	Possibly increased	No change
Bowel regulation	No	No	No	Yes, if there is a history of a regular bowel pattern
Pouch and skin barriers	Yes	Yes	Yes	Dependent on regulation
Indications for surgery	Ulcerative colitis, Crohn's disease, diseased or injured colon, familial polyposis, trauma, cancer	Perforating diverticulum in lower colon, trauma, rectovaginal fistula, inoperable tumors of colon, rectum, or pelvis	Same as for ascending	Cancer of the rectum or rectosigmoid area, perforating diverticulum, trauma

by its anatomic site (e.g., ascending, transverse, sigmoid). The more distal the ostomy, the more functioning bowel remains and the more likely that the intestinal contents will resemble the feces that would have been eliminated from an intact colon and rectum. Ileostomy output will be a liquid to thin paste since it did not enter the colon. Patients have no control over ileostomy drainage; it is involuntary. An ileostomy drains frequently, and the patient must wear an ostomy appliance (pouch) to collect the drainage. In contrast, sigmoid colostomy output resembles normal formed stool. Some patients can regulate emptying time with colostomy irrigation and may not need to wear a pouch. See Table 42.26 for a comparison of colostomies and ileostomies.

Ostomies may be temporary or permanent. For example, the person with a draining fistula may need a temporary ostomy to prevent stool from reaching the diseased area. Cancer involving the rectum requires a permanent ostomy if all bowel distal to the ostomy is removed.

Permanent ostomies may be continent or traditional. *Continent ileostomies* (e.g., Koch pouch, Barnett Continent Ileal Reservoir) use 40 to 45 cm of the terminal ileum to fashion an internal pouch, nipple valve, and abdominal stoma. The pouch replaces the rectum as a reservoir for stool. It can hold around 500 mL of material. Continent ostomies are an option for patients who have had a prior APR with ileostomy for UC or FAP. Patients must be motivated and compliant. They must drain the pouch manually by inserting a catheter through the nipple valve. At first, this is done every 1 to 2 hours. As the pouch enlarges, the frequency decreases to 4 times daily and as needed.

They must keep the stool consistency relatively fluid by following a low-residue diet.

The major types of traditional ostomies include end, double-barreled, and loop ostomy.

End Stoma. An end stoma is made by dividing the bowel and bringing out the proximal end as a single stoma, making a colostomy or ileostomy. The distal part of the GI tract is surgically removed or the distal segment is oversewn and left in the abdominal cavity with its mesentery intact. If the distal bowel is removed, the stoma is permanent. When the distal bowel is oversewn and not removed, the procedure is called a *Hartmann's pouch* (Fig. 42.11). With a Hartmann's pouch, the potential exists for the bowel to be reanastomosed and the stoma closed (referred to as a *takedown*).

Loop Stoma. A loop stoma is made by bringing a loop of bowel to the abdominal surface and then opening the anterior wall of the bowel to provide fecal diversion. This results in 1 stoma with a proximal opening for feces and a distal opening for mucus drainage from the distal colon. An intact posterior wall separates the 2 openings. A plastic rod holds the loop of bowel in place for 7 to 10 days after surgery to prevent it from slipping back into the abdominal cavity (Fig. 42.12). A loop stoma is usually temporary.

Double-Barreled Stoma. To create a double-barreled stoma, the HCP divides the bowel and both the proximal and distal ends are brought through the abdominal wall as 2 separate stomas (Fig. 42.10). The proximal stoma is the functioning stoma. The distal, nonfunctioning stoma is a *mucus fistula*. A double-barreled stoma is usually temporary.

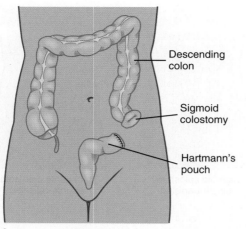

FIG. 42.11 Sigmoid colostomy. Distal bowel is oversewn and left in place to create Hartmann's pouch.

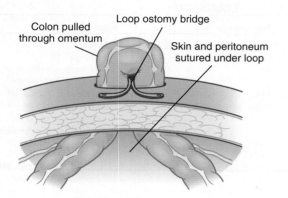

FIG. 42.12 Loop colostomy.

TABLE 42.27 **Characteristics of Stoma**

Characteristic	Description or Cause
Color	
Rose to brick-red	Viable stoma mucosa.
Pale	May indicate anemia.
Blanching, dark red to purple	Indicates inadequate blood supply to the stoma or bowel.
Edema	
Mild to moderate edema	Normal in initial postoperative period. Trauma to the stoma.
Moderate to severe edema	Obstruction of the stoma, allergic reaction to food, gastroenteritis.
Bleeding	
Small amount	Oozing from stoma mucosa when touched is normal because of its high vascularity.
Moderate to large amount	Could indicate lower GI bleeding, coagulation factor deficiency, stomal varices secondary to portal hypertension.

the bag. Being able to see the stoma makes caring for it easier. Whenever possible, it should be discreetly hidden under clothing and appropriate for normal activities.

◆ Postoperative Care

If the patient's wound is closed or partially closed, assess the incision for suture integrity and signs and symptoms of wound inflammation and infection. A patient who has an open wound with packing needs meticulous care. Reinforce dressings and change them often during the first several hours postoperatively when drainage is likely to be profuse. Carefully assess all drainage for amount, color, and consistency. The drainage is usually serosanguineous.

Assess the wound regularly and record bleeding, excess drainage, and unusual odor. Monitor for edema, erythema, and drainage around the suture line, as well as fever and a high WBC count. Observe the skin around any drains for signs of inflammation. Keep the area around the drain clean and dry. Complications that can occur include delayed wound healing, hemorrhage, fistulas, and infections.

If an ostomy is present, assess the stoma and place a clear pouching system that protects the skin and contains drainage and odor. The stoma should be rosy pink to red and mildly swollen (Table 42.27). A dusky blue stoma indicates ischemia; a brown-black stoma indicates necrosis. Assess and document stoma color every 4 hours and ensure that there is no excess bleeding. Report any sustained color changes or bleeding to the HCP. Edema will resolve over the first 6 weeks.

The colostomy starts functioning when peristalsis returns. Record the volume, color, and consistency of the drainage. When a colostomy is done on a colon that was not cleaned out before surgery, stool will drain when peristalsis returns. If the bowel was cleansed preoperatively, it will not begin producing stool until a few days after the patient is eating again. Excessive amounts of gas are common during the first 2 weeks. Because this can be distressing to patients, assure them this is temporary.

In the first 24 to 48 hours after surgery, the amount of drainage from an ileostomy may be negligible. When peristalsis returns, ileostomy output may be as high as 1500 to 1800 mL/24 hr.

❖ NURSING MANAGEMENT: BOWEL RESECTION AND OSTOMY SURGERY

◆ Preoperative Care

Psychologic preparation and emotional support are particularly important as the person begins to cope with potential changes in body image and elimination. The patient and caregiver should understand the extent of surgery planned. It is normal for the patient and caregiver to have questions concerning the procedures. Provide the patient opportunities to share concerns and questions. This will enhance the patient's feelings of control and ability to cope.

Care that is unique to ostomy surgery includes (1) psychologic preparation for the ostomy, (2) educational preparation, and (3) selecting the best site for the stoma. Ideally, the management of patients facing ostomy surgery begins preoperatively. If available, a WOCN should visit with the patient and caregiver to determine the patient's ability to perform self-care, identify support systems, and determine any modifications that could promote learning during recovery.

A WOCN should choose the site where the ostomy will be and mark the abdomen before surgery. The site should be within the rectus muscle, on a flat surface, and in a place that the patient is able to see. Stomas placed outside the rectus muscle increase the chance of developing a hernia. A flat site makes it much easier to create a good seal and avoid leakage from

If the small bowel is shortened by surgery, drainage may be greater. This is because the patient has lost the absorptive functions provided by the colon and the delay provided by the ileocecal valve. Observe the patient for signs and symptoms of fluid and electrolyte imbalance, particularly potassium, sodium, and fluid deficits. Over a period of days to weeks, the proximal small bowel adapts and increases fluid absorption. Then, feces will thicken to a paste-like consistency and the volume decrease to around 500 mL/day. Patients, especially those with Crohn's disease, are at risk for developing a bowel obstruction during the first 30 days postoperatively.

After an IPAA, initially, patients may have 4 to 6 stools or more daily. Adaptation over the next 3 to 6 months will result in fewer bowel movements. The patient can control defecation at the anal sphincter.

After intraoperative manipulation of the anal canal, transient incontinence of mucus may occur. Have the patient start Kegel exercises about 4 weeks after surgery to strengthen the pelvic floor and sphincter muscles (see Table 45.18). Perianal skin care is important to protect the epidermis from mucous drainage and maceration. Teach the patient to gently clean the skin with a mild cleanser, rinse well, and dry thoroughly. A moisture barrier ointment and a perineal pad may be used. Some patients have phantom rectal pain or still feel as if they need to have a bowel movement. This is normal and often subsides over time. Be astute in distinguishing phantom sensations from perineal abscess pain.

◆ Colostomy Care

Two major aspects of nursing care for the patient with an ostomy are (1) patient and caregiver teaching about ostomy care and (2) emotional support as the patient copes with a radical change in body image. With shorter hospital stays, patient teaching should focus on the critical aspects that patients need to master. Teaching must include (1) basic skills about managing the ostomy (e.g., changing the pouch), (2) diet, and (3) how to get help for problems. Home care and outpatient follow-up may be helpful, especially if there is access to a WOCN. Patient and caregiver teaching is outlined in Table 42.28. Nursing care for the patient with an ostomy is discussed in eNursing Care Plan 42.3 on the website.

An appropriate pouching system is vital to protect the skin and provide dependable stool collection. Most pouching systems have an adhesive skin barrier and a pouch to collect the feces. Most skin barriers are made of pectin-based or karaya mediums with hydrocolloid properties. Adhesion occurs in 2 phases. First, the wafer's backing has adhesive material that forms an immediate bond with the skin. Second, the hydrocolloids interface with the moisture on the skin to form a tighter seal. Caulking strips or "paste" around the stoma may help ensure a secure seal.

If the abdominal stoma site has bends or creases, it is hard to get a good seal and the skin barrier will pull away faster. Since excess weight of collected stool pulls the wafer away from the skin, empty ostomy bags when one-third full.

Use a transparent pouch in the initial postoperative period so that you can easily assess stoma viability and pouch application by the patient. Each time the pouch is changed, assess the skin for irritation. If the peristomal skin is irritated and raw, more products may have to be applied. Do not allow feces to remain on the skin or irritation will quickly develop. If a pouch has failed, it must be changed at once.

TABLE 42.28 Patient & Caregiver Teaching
Ostomy Self-Care

Include the following points when teaching the patient and/or caregiver about self-care of an ostomy:

1. Explain what an ostomy is and how it functions.
2. Describe the underlying condition that resulted in the need for an ostomy.
3. Demonstrate and allow the patient and caregiver to practice the following activities:
   - Remove the old skin barrier, cleanse the skin, and correctly apply new skin barriers.
   - Apply, empty, clean, and remove the pouch.
   - Empty the pouch before it is one-third full to prevent leakage.
4. Irrigate the colostomy to regulate bowel elimination (optional).
5. Explain how to contact the wound, ostomy, and continence nurse (WOCN) with questions.
6. Describe how to obtain ostomy supplies.
7. Explain dietary and fluid management.
   - Identify a well-balanced diet and dietary supplements to prevent nutritional deficiencies.
   - Identify foods to avoid to reduce diarrhea or gas (see Table 42.29).
   - Promote fluid intake of least 3000 mL/day to prevent dehydration (unless contraindicated).
   - Increase fluid intake during hot weather, excess perspiration, and diarrhea to replace losses and prevent dehydration.
   - Describe symptoms of fluid and electrolyte imbalance.
   - Explain how to contact the dietitian with questions.
   - Explain how to recognize problems (fluid and electrolyte deficits, fever, diarrhea, skin irritation, stomal problems) and how to contact the HCP and/or WOCN.
8. Describe community resources to assist with emotional and psychologic adjustment to the ostomy.
9. Explain the importance of follow-up care.
10. Describe the ostomy's potential effects on sexual activity, social life, work, and recreation and ways to manage these changes.

NURSING MANAGEMENT
Ostomy Care

Although licensed practical/vocational nurses (LPN/VNs) and unlicensed assistive personnel (UAP) provide much of the ostomy care for patients with established ostomies, patients with new ostomies have complex needs and require frequent assessment, planning, intervention, and evaluation by a registered nurse (RN).

Role of Nursing Personnel
Registered Nurse (RN)
- Assess and document stoma and peristomal skin appearance.
- For patient with a new ostomy, assess patient's psychologic preparation for ostomy care.
- Choose appropriate ostomy pouching system for patient.
- Place ostomy pouching system for a new ostomy.
- Monitor the volume, color, and odor of the ostomy drainage.
- Develop plan of care for skin care around the ostomy.
- Teach ostomy care and skin care to patient and caregiver.
- Irrigate new colostomy, if indicated.
- Teach colostomy irrigation to patient and caregiver.
- Teach patient and caregivers about appropriate dietary choices (Table 42.29).
- Delegate to UAP:
  - Empty ostomy bag and measure liquid contents.
  - Place the ostomy pouching system for an established ostomy.
  - Assist stable patient with colostomy irrigation.

TABLE 42.29 Nutritional Therapy
Effects of Food on Stoma Output

Odor Producing	Gas Forming	Diarrhea Causing
Alcohol	Beans	Alcohol
Asparagus	Beer	Beer
Broccoli	Cabbage family	Cabbage family
Cabbage	Carbonated beverages	Coffee
Eggs	Cheeses (strong)	Fruits (raw)
Fish	Onions	Green beans
Garlic	Sprouts	Spicy foods
Onions		Spinach

A colostomy in the ascending and transverse colon has semiliquid stools. Have the patient use a drainable pouch. A drainable pouch may last up to 4 to 7 days. A colostomy in the sigmoid or descending colon has semiformed or formed stools. The patient can use a drainable pouch or choose a disposable, closed end pouch changed every day. Optional charcoal filters can deodorize and automatically release flatus. They are available for both drainable and nondrainable pouches.

Another option is colostomy irrigation. It may be used to stimulate emptying of the colon. Patients who irrigate may not need a regular pouch as they may be able to regulate when the colon empties. Regularity is possible only when the stoma is in the distal colon. The patient may need to wear only a pad or small pouch over the stoma as little or no spillage should occur between irrigations. Irrigation requires manual dexterity and adequate vision. People who irrigate regularly should have ostomy bags available in case they develop diarrhea.

Teach the patient about the importance of fluids and a healthy diet. The effect of food on stoma output is individual. Most patients with colostomies can eat anything they want. However, some choose to avoid certain foods because of possible increased gas, odor, or stoma output (Table 42.29). Teach patients to chew their food very well to reduce the chance of blockage.

The patient can resume activities of daily living within 6 to 8 weeks but should avoid heavy lifting. The patient's physical condition determines when they can resume sports. Swimming with an ostomy pouch intact is not a problem. The patient can bathe and shower with or without the pouching system in place because water does not harm the stoma.

◆ Ileostomy Care
Nursing care for a patient with an ileostomy is similar to that for a patient with a colostomy. Because the stool from an ileostomy is caustic to the skin, a secure pouching system is important. This is easier with stoma protrusion of at least 1 to 1.5 cm. When the stoma is flat, recessed, or in a crease, seepage occurs and results in altered skin integrity. The patient must wear a pouch at all times since regularity is not possible with an ileostomy. An open-ended, drainable pouch is best so drainage can be easily emptied. A drainable pouch usually lasts for 4 to 7 days.

Patients need to increase fluid intake to at least 2 to 3 L/day or more when there are excess fluid losses from heat and sweating. They may need to ingest added sodium. Patients must learn signs and symptoms of fluid and electrolyte imbalance so that they can take appropriate action.

The ileostomy patient is susceptible to obstruction because the lumen is less than 1 inch in diameter. It may narrow further at the point where the bowel passes through the fascia/muscle layer of the abdomen. Foods such as nuts, raisins, popcorn, coconut, mushrooms, olives, stringy vegetables, foods with skins, dried fruits, and meats with casings must be chewed extremely well before swallowing.

◆ Psychologic Adaptation to an Ostomy
The patient's response to a new ostomy is highly individualized. Some have minimal difficulty and view their ostomy positively. It may be curative if their presenting condition was UC or a step toward remission if the diagnosis was CRC. Other patients may have a grief reaction from the loss of a body part and a change in body image. They may be angry, depressed, or resentful. Anxiety and fear are normal. Concerns about stool leaking, odor, sounds of flatus, pouch reliability, and changes in normal lifestyle are all valid worries. Accurate information, emotional support, and mastering basic skills will help patients learn to live a full life with an ostomy and accept the changes in body appearance.

The patient's emotional state may limit the ability to take part in teaching and ostomy care. Discuss with the patient the psychologic impact of the stoma and its effect on body image and self-esteem. Help the patient identify ways of coping with depression and anxiety resulting from the illness, surgery, or postoperative problems. Support from the caregiver, family, and friends is vital. It reassures the patient of their value despite having the ostomy. Encourage patients to share their concerns and ask questions. Provide information in an easily understood manner and help patients develop confidence and competence in managing the stoma.

New ostomy patients will have questions on a variety of topics ranging from managing gas to intimacy to travel. Give the names and contact information for support groups. The Wound Ostomy Continence Nurses Society (www.wocn.org), local support groups, and United Ostomy Associations of America (www.ostomy.org) provide practical information about living with an ostomy. Online support groups are also available. Most hospitals have a visitor's program. These programs give the patient and caregiver an opportunity to talk with a person who has adjusted well to an ostomy and had some of the same feelings and concerns they have.

◆ Sexual Function
Help the patient understand if specific aspects of surgery and treatment have the potential for sexual dysfunction. Pelvic surgery can disrupt nerve and vascular supplies to the genitalia. Pelvic radiation can reduce blood flow to the pelvis by causing scarring in the small blood vessels. Chemotherapy can alter sexual function. The patient's overall physical health influences sexual desire. Generalized fatigue caused by illness can decrease desire. Understanding this information can help patients plan the timing of sexual activity.

Problems with sexual dysfunction depend on the surgical technique used. Unfortunately, any pelvic surgery that removes the rectum has the potential of damaging the parasympathetic nerve plexus. The HCP should discuss the possibility with the patient.

For men, the main concern may be erection and ejaculation. Erection depends on intact parasympathetic and nonadrenergic noncholinergic nerves as well as adequate blood supply. Sympathetic nerve damage in the presacral area can disrupt the ability to ejaculate. This can occur with the APR procedure. Sexual dysfunction may be temporary and resolve in 3 to 12

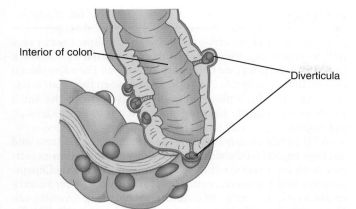

FIG. 42.13 Diverticula are outpouchings of the colon. When they become inflamed, the condition is diverticulitis. The inflammatory process can spread to the surrounding area in the intestine.

months. Nerve-sparing surgical techniques are used when possible to preserve sexual function.

For women, nerve damage can result in vaginal dryness and decreased sensation in the vagina and clitoris, making arousal and achieving orgasm more challenging. Experimenting with positions and using lubrication may help. A woman with an ostomy can still become pregnant.

Sexual function and sexuality concerns affect most patients with an ostomy. The patient with a stoma may fear rejection by a partner or that others will not find them desirable. Discuss sexuality and sexual function. Help the patient realize that it takes time to adjust to the pouch and to body changes before feeling secure with sexual functioning.

Teach the patient to empty the pouch before sexual activities. Some may apply a smaller pouch during sexual activity. Women may consider wearing open panties, a short slip, or similar lingerie. Men may consider wearing a wrap or cummerbund around the midsection to secure the pouch. There are many types of pouch covers that patients can make or purchase.

DIVERTICULOSIS AND DIVERTICULITIS

Diverticula are saccular dilations or outpouchings of the mucosa that develop in the colon (Fig. 42.13). Diverticulosis is the presence of multiple noninflamed diverticula. **Diverticulitis** is inflammation of 1 or more diverticula, resulting in perforation into the peritoneum. Clinically, diverticular disease covers a spectrum from asymptomatic, uncomplicated diverticulosis to diverticulitis with complications, such as perforation, abscess, fistula, and bleeding. Diverticula are common, especially in older adults, but most people never develop diverticulitis.

Etiology and Pathophysiology

Diverticula may occur anywhere in the GI tract but are most common in the left (descending, sigmoid) colon. They seem to occur at weak points in the intestinal wall, such as where the blood vessels pass through the muscle layer. The cause is thought to include both genetic and environmental factors. We think the main contributing factors are constipation and a lack of dietary fiber. The disease is more prevalent in Western, industrialized populations, where people tend to consume diets low in fiber and high in refined carbohydrates. Diverticula are uncommon in vegetarians. Other risk factors are obesity, inactivity, smoking, excess alcohol use, and NSAID use.

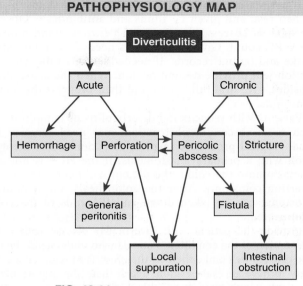

FIG. 42.14 Complications of diverticulitis.

Clinical Manifestations and Complications

Most patients with diverticulosis have no symptoms. Those with symptoms typically have abdominal pain, bloating, flatulence, and changes in bowel habits. In more serious situations, the diverticula bleed or diverticulitis develops. The most common signs and symptoms of diverticulitis are acute pain in the left lower quadrant, distention, decreased or absent bowel sounds, nausea, vomiting, and systemic symptoms of infection (fever, leukocytosis with a shift to the left). Older adults with diverticulitis may be afebrile, with a normal WBC count and little, if any, abdominal tenderness. Diverticulitis can cause erosion of the bowel wall and perforation into the peritoneum (Fig. 42.14). A localized abscess develops when the body walls off the perforated area. Peritonitis develops if it cannot be contained. Bleeding can be extensive but usually stops spontaneously.

Diagnostic Studies

Diverticular disease can be asymptomatic. It is typically found during routine sigmoidoscopy or colonoscopy. Diagnosis of diverticulitis is based on the history and physical examination (Table 42.30). The preferred diagnostic test is a CT scan with oral contrast. Abdominal and chest x-ray rule out other causes of acute abdominal pain.

❖ Interprofessional and Nursing Care

A high-fiber diet, mainly from fruits and vegetables with a decreased intake of fat and red meat, is the best way to prevent diverticular disease. High levels of physical activity seem to decrease the risk. Currently there is no evidence to support the theory that diverticulitis can be prevented by avoiding nuts and seeds.

In acute diverticulitis, the goal of treatment is to let the colon rest and the inflammation subside. Some patients can be managed at home with a clear liquid diet, bed rest, and analgesics. Hospitalization is needed if symptoms are severe, the patient is unable to tolerate oral fluids, there are systemic manifestations of infection (fever, significant leukocytosis), or the patient has co-morbid conditions (e.g., immunosuppression).

If hospitalized, the patient is kept on NPO status, placed on bed rest, and given IV fluids and antibiotics.[25] Observe for signs of abscess, bleeding, and peritonitis and monitor the WBC count. Give analgesics as needed. Maintain strict intake and output records. If needed, an NG tube with low suction will provide decompression. When the acute attack subsides, give oral fluids first and then progress the diet to semisolids.

Patients with reoccurring diverticulitis or complications, such as an abscess or obstruction, may need surgery. The usual surgical procedure involves resection of the involved colon with a primary anastomosis. If the HCP is not able to anastomose the colon, the patient will have a temporary diverting colostomy. After the colon heals, the temporary colostomy can be taken down and the ends of the colon reconnected.

Provide the patient with diverticular disease with a full explanation of the condition. Patients who understand the disease process well and adhere to the prescribed regimen are less likely to have an exacerbation. Teach them the importance of following a high-fiber diet (Table 42.8) and encourage a fluid intake of at least 2 L/day. The patient does not have to avoid nuts, seeds, and corn.

A patient with diverticular disease should avoid increased intraabdominal pressure because it may precipitate an attack. Factors that increase intraabdominal pressure are straining at stool, vomiting, bending, heavy lifting, and wearing tight, restrictive clothing. Weight reduction is important for the obese person with diverticular disease.

TABLE 42.30 Interprofessional Care

Diverticulosis and Diverticulitis

Diagnostic Assessment

- History and physical examination
- Testing of stool for occult blood
- CBC
- Urinalysis
- Barium enema
- Colonoscopy with biopsy
- Blood culture
- CT scan with oral contrast
- Abdominal and/or chest x-ray

Management

Conservative Therapy

- High-fiber diet
- Dietary fiber supplements
- Stool softeners
- Anticholinergics
- Clear liquid diet
- Weight reduction (if overweight)

Acute Care: Diverticulitis

- Antibiotic therapy
- NPO status
- IV fluids
- Analgesics
- NG suction
- Surgery
- Possible resection of involved colon
- Possible temporary colostomy

FISTULAS

A fistula is an abnormal tract between 2 hollow organs or a hollow organ and the skin. Fistulas are named by the track that they take from one body part to another. For example, an enterocutaneous fistula is an opening between the small intestine and skin. An enterovaginal fistula is between the small intestine and vagina, allowing stool and gas to drain through the vagina.

A GI fistula occurs between the lumen of the GI tract and another organ. GI fistulas are a serious complication associated with increased morbidity and mortality, extended hospital stays, and increased costs. Most fistulas occur after surgery or are associated with IBD, cancer, or radiation. Fistulas can form with diverticulitis, pancreatitis, and trauma.[26] Fistulas are classified as simple or complex and by the amount of output. A simple fistula has only one short, direct tract. A complex fistula is associated with an abscess, involves multiple organs, and may open into the base of a wound. High-output fistulas drain more than 500 mL/day, moderate-output fistulas drain 200 to 500 mL/day, and low-output fistulas drain less than 200 mL/day.

Fever and abdominal pain are early signs of a fistula. Other manifestations depend on the type of fistula. With an enterocutaneous fistula, there may be pus or intestinal contents draining through the skin opening. Patients with a colocutaneous (colon to skin) fistula may have stool or pus draining through the opening. If a colovesical (colon to urinary tract) fistula is present, manifestations include fecaluria (passing stool with urination), recurrent urinary tract infections, dysuria, and hematuria.

❖ Interprofessional and Nursing Care

A draining fistula can be disheartening for the patient and caregiver and a time-consuming challenge for HCPs. Managing a fistula requires (1) identifying the fistula tract, (2) maintaining fluid and electrolyte balance, (3) controlling infection, (4) protecting the surrounding skin, (5) managing output, and (6) providing nutritional support. Most fistulas heal spontaneously. Surgery may be needed to treat the complications.

Appropriate fluid and electrolyte replacement can be challenging, especially when the patient has a high-output fistula. Monitor the volume of fistula output as this guides replacement therapies and nutritional support. Assess the character of the drainage, noting the color, consistency, and odor. Monitor laboratory values. Low serum levels of potassium, magnesium, and phosphorus from the loss of GI fluids are common. Give IV fluids and electrolyte replacement as ordered. Keep an accurate intake and output record. Many patients are NPO as this reduces intestinal output. They may receive acid suppression with a proton-pump inhibitor and antimotility agents (e.g., loperamide). Cholestyramine and octreotide decrease GI secretions.[26] Measure vital signs frequently and be alert for signs of dehydration.

Malnutrition is a significant problem, particularly if the patient is NPO or has a small intestinal fistula. Consult a dietitian. High-calorie, high-protein PN or EN is needed to provide enough calories and protein to replace losses and support healing.[26] Many patients need trace element (e.g., copper, zinc, magnesium) and vitamin supplements.

Maintaining skin integrity and optimizing healing is essential. Consult a WOCN if available. Low-output fistulas may

CHECK YOUR PRACTICE

A 51-yr-old woman is 4 days postop after a proctocolectomy for ulcerative colitis. You note 2.5 cm of erythema in the center of her incision with heavy, foul-smelling tan drainage pooling on her skin. Suspecting she is developing an enterocutaneous fistula, you notify the HCP and WOCN.

- What will you do to protect her skin?

be managed with a simple absorbent dressing. A high-output enterocutaneous fistula often needs advanced techniques, including specialty pouches; barrier creams, powders, and sealants to protect the skin; and negative pressure wound therapy.

HERNIAS

A **hernia** is a protrusion of the viscus (e.g., the intestine) through an abnormal opening or a weakened area in the wall of the cavity in which it is normally contained. A hernia may occur in any part of the body, but it usually occurs within the abdominal cavity. *Reducible* hernias easily return into the abdominal cavity. Reducing can be done manually or may occur spontaneously when the person lies supine. *Irreducible,* or *incarcerated,* hernias cannot be placed back into the abdominal cavity. They have abdominal contents trapped in the opening. Strangulation occurs if the blood supply to the contents trapped in an irreducible hernia becomes compromised. The result is an acute intestinal obstruction. Gangrene and necrosis of the hernia contents are possible.

GENDER DIFFERENCES
Hernia

Men
- Inguinal hernias are more common in men.
- Men have a 25% lifetime risk for developing a groin hernia.
- Men undergo 90% of the 850,000 groin hernia repairs done annually in the United States.

Women
- Femoral hernias are more common in women, particularly older women.
- Women have less than a 5% lifetime risk for developing a groin hernia.

Types

An *umbilical hernia* occurs when the rectus muscle is weak (as with obesity) or the umbilical opening does not close after birth (Fig. 42.15, *A*). A *femoral hernia* occurs when there is a protrusion through the femoral ring into the femoral canal. It appears as a bulge below the inguinal ligament. Femoral hernias easily strangulate (Fig. 42.15, *B*).

The *inguinal hernia* is the most common type of hernia and occurs at the point of weakness in the abdominal wall where the spermatic cord (in men) or the round ligament (in women) emerges (Fig. 42.15, *C*).

Ventral or *incisional hernias* are due to weakness of the abdominal wall at the site of a previous incision. They occur most often in those who are obese, have had multiple surgical procedures in the same area, or have had inadequate wound healing because of poor nutrition or infection. Peristomal hernias are ventral hernias.

Clinical Manifestations

Pain is the classic symptom of a hernia. It may worsen with activities that increase intraabdominal pressure, such as lifting, coughing, and straining. A hernia may be readily visible, especially when the person tenses the abdominal muscles. If the hernia becomes strangulated, the patient will have severe pain and symptoms of a bowel obstruction, such as vomiting, cramping abdominal pain, and distention.

❖ Interprofessional and Nursing Care

Diagnosis of a hernia is usually based on history and physical examination findings. Ultrasound, CT, and MRI can help identify a hernia and determine the contents. Laparoscopic surgery is the treatment of choice. The surgical repair of a hernia, known as a *herniorrhaphy,* is usually an outpatient procedure. Reinforcing the weakened area with wire, fascia, or mesh is known as a *hernioplasty.* Emergency surgery is needed for strangulated hernias or inflamed, irreducible hernias. Surgery for strangulated hernias involves resecting the involved area with possible placement of a temporary colostomy.

After a hernia repair, the patient may have problems voiding. Measure intake and output. Observe for a distended bladder. Scrotal edema is a painful complication after an inguinal hernia repair. A scrotal support with application of an ice bag and elevating the scrotum may help relieve pain and edema. Encourage

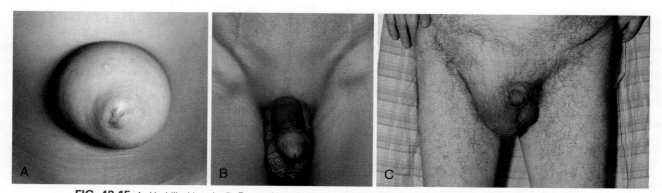

FIG. 42.15 A, Umbilical hernia. B, Femoral hernias (note swelling below the inguinal ligaments). C, Right inguinal hernia. (*A* and *B,* From Zitelli BJ, McIntire SC, Nowalk AJ: *Zitelli and Davis' atlas of pediatric physical diagnosis,* ed 6, Philadelphia, 2012, Saunders. *C,* From Swartz MH: *Textbook of physical diagnosis: History and examination,* ed 6, Philadelphia, 2010, Saunders.)

deep breathing, but not coughing. Teach patients to splint the incision and keep their mouths open when coughing or sneezing is unavoidable. The patient may be restricted from heavy lifting (>10 lb) for 6 to 8 weeks.

MALABSORPTION SYNDROME

Malabsorption results from impaired absorption of fats, carbohydrates, proteins, minerals, and vitamins. The stomach, small intestine, liver, and pancreas regulate normal digestion and absorption. Digestive enzymes ordinarily break down nutrients so that absorption can take place. Malabsorption may occur if this process is interrupted at any point. Several problems can cause malabsorption (Table 42.31). Lactose intolerance is the most common malabsorption disorder, followed by IBD, celiac disease, tropical sprue, and cystic fibrosis.

The most common signs of malabsorption are weight loss, diarrhea, and **steatorrhea** (bulky, foul-smelling, yellow-gray, greasy stools with putty-like consistency) (Table 42.32). Steatorrhea does not occur with lactose intolerance.

Tests to determine the cause of malabsorption include qualitative examination of stool for fat (e.g., Sudan III stain), a 72-hour stool collection for quantitative measurement of fecal fat, serologic testing for celiac disease, and fecal elastase testing to determine if there is pancreatic insufficiency. Near-infrared reflectance analysis (NIRA) for fecal fat is available at some centers in the United States.

Other diagnostic studies include a CT scan and endoscopy to obtain a small bowel biopsy specimen. A small bowel barium enema can identify abnormal mucosal patterns. Capsule endoscopy is useful in assessing the small intestine for changes in mucosal integrity and inflammation. Tests for carbohydrate malabsorption include the D-xylose test and the lactose tolerance test. Laboratory studies include a CBC, measurement of prothrombin time (to see if vitamin K absorption is adequate), serum vitamin A and carotene levels, serum electrolytes, cholesterol, and calcium. Treatment depends on the cause.

CELIAC DISEASE

Celiac disease is an autoimmune disease that causes damage to the small intestinal mucosa. It is triggered by ingesting gluten, a protein in wheat, barley, and rye.[27] It can occur at any age and has a wide variety of symptoms. *Celiac sprue* and *gluten-sensitive enteropathy* are other names for celiac disease.

Celiac disease is not the same disease as *tropical sprue*, a chronic disorder occurring primarily in tropical areas. Tropical sprue causes progressive disruption of jejunal and ileal tissue,

---

TABLE 42.31 Causes of Malabsorption

Bacterial Proliferation
- Parasitic infection
- Tropical sprue

Biochemical or Enzyme Deficiencies
- Biliary tract obstruction
- Chronic pancreatitis
- Cystic fibrosis
- Lactase deficiency
- Pancreatic insufficiency
- Zollinger-Ellison syndrome

Disturbed Lymphatic and Vascular Circulation
- Heart failure
- Ischemia
- Lymphangiectasia
- Lymphoma

Small Intestinal Mucosal Disruption
- Celiac disease
- Crohn's disease
- Whipple's disease

Surface Area Loss
- Billroth II gastrectomy
- Distal ileal resection, disease, or bypass
- Short bowel syndrome

TABLE 42.32 Manifestations of Malabsorption

Manifestations	Pathophysiology
Cardiovascular	
Hypotension	Dehydration
Peripheral edema	Protein malabsorption, protein loss in diarrhea
Tachycardia	Hypovolemia, anemia
Gastrointestinal	
Diarrhea	Impaired absorption of water, sodium, fatty acids, bile salts, and carbohydrates
Flatulence	Bacterial fermentation of unabsorbed carbohydrates
Glossitis, cheilosis, stomatitis	Deficiency of iron, riboflavin, cobalamin, folic acid, and other vitamins
Steatorrhea	Undigested and unabsorbed fat
Weight loss	Malabsorption of fat, carbohydrates, and protein leading to loss of calories. Marked reduction in caloric intake or increased use of calories
Hematologic	
Anemia	Impaired absorption of iron, cobalamin, and folic acid
Hemorrhagic tendency	Vitamin C deficiency. Vitamin K deficiency inhibiting production of clotting factors II, VII, IX, and X
Integumentary	
Brittle nails	Iron deficiency
Bruising	Vitamin K deficiency
Dermatitis	Fatty acid deficiency, zinc deficiency, niacin, and other vitamin deficiencies
Hair thinning and loss	Protein deficiency
Musculoskeletal	
Bone pain	Osteoporosis from impaired calcium absorption. Osteomalacia secondary to hypocalcemia, hypophosphatemia, inadequate vitamin D
Muscle wasting	Protein malabsorption
Tetany	Hypocalcemia, hypomagnesemia
Weakness, muscle cramps	Anemia, electrolyte depletion (especially potassium)
Neurologic	
Altered mental status	Dehydration
Night blindness	Thiamine deficiency, vitamin A deficiency
Paresthesias	Cobalamin deficiency
Peripheral neuropathy	Cobalamin deficiency

resulting in nutrition problems. It is treated with folic acid and tetracycline.

Celiac disease affects about 1 in 100 people worldwide.[28] First-degree relatives of someone with celiac disease have a 4% to 15% chance of developing the disorder. It is associated with other autoimmune diseases, particularly rheumatoid arthritis, type 1 diabetes, and thyroid disease. It is slightly more common in women. Symptoms often begin in childhood.

Etiology and Pathophysiology

Three factors necessary for developing celiac disease are genetic predisposition, gluten ingestion, and an immune-mediated response.

Genetic Link

About 90% to 95% of patients with celiac disease have human leukocyte antigen (HLA) allele HLA-DQ2. The other 5% to 10% have HLA-DQ8. However, not everyone with these genetic markers develops celiac disease, and some people with celiac disease do not have these HLA alleles.

As with other autoimmune diseases, the tissue destruction that occurs with celiac disease is the result of chronic inflammation. Gluten contains specific peptides called *prolamines*. Partial digestion of gluten releases the prolamine peptides, which are absorbed into the intestinal submucosa. In genetically susceptible persons, the peptides bind to HLA-DQ2 and/or HLA-DQ8 and activate an inflammatory response. Inflammation damages the microvilli and brush border of the small intestine, decreasing the amount of surface area available for nutrient absorption. Damage is most severe in the duodenum, probably because it has more exposure to gluten. The inflammation lasts as long as gluten ingestion continues.

Clinical Manifestations

Classic manifestations of celiac disease include foul-smelling diarrhea, abdominal pain, flatulence, abdominal distention, and malnutrition.[27] Some people have no obvious GI symptoms and may instead have atypical signs and symptoms. These include joint pain, osteoporosis, dental enamel hypoplasia, fatigue, peripheral neuropathy, and reproductive problems. An intensely pruritic, vesicular skin lesion, called *dermatitis herpetiformis*, is sometimes present and occurs as a rash on the buttocks, scalp, face, elbows, and knees.

Protein, fat, and carbohydrate absorption is affected. Weight loss, muscle wasting, and other signs of malnutrition may be present. Abnormal serum folate, iron, and cobalamin levels can occur. Iron-deficiency anemia is common. Patients may have lactose intolerance and need to refrain from lactose-containing products until the disease is under control. Inadequate calcium intake and vitamin D absorption can lead to decreased bone density and osteoporosis.

Diagnostic Studies

Early diagnosis and treatment can prevent complications. Screening is recommended for close relatives of patients known to have the disease, young patients with decreased bone density, those with anemia if other causes are ruled out, and certain autoimmune diseases.

Celiac disease is confirmed by a combination of findings from the history and physical examination, serology testing, and histologic analysis of small intestine biopsies.[27] Have the patient complete diagnostic testing before starting a gluten-free

diet, since the diet will change the results. Serologic testing for immunoglobulin A (IgA) antitissue transglutaminase and IgA endomysial antibody offer good sensitivity and specificity. Histologic evidence is the gold standard for confirming the diagnosis. Biopsies show flattened mucosa and noticeable losses of villi. Genotyping involves testing for HLA-DQ2 and/or HLA-DQ8 antigens.

Interprofessional and Nursing Care

A gluten-free diet (Table 42.33) is the only effective treatment for celiac disease. Most patients need to stay on a gluten-free diet for the rest of their lives. Periodic nutrition evaluations and laboratory monitoring are done to monitor for anemia and malnutrition. The patient should undergo bone density screening every 2 to 3 years.[28]

Refer all patients for a dietary consultation. You can work with a dietitian to teach the patient how to eat a nutritionally adequate diet while staying within a budget. Teach the patient to avoid wheat, barley, oats, and rye products. Although pure oats do not contain gluten, wheat, rye, and barley can contaminate oat products during the milling process. Teach the patient to read medication and food labels. Some medications and many food additives, preservatives, and stabilizers contain gluten. The patient needs to know where to buy gluten-free products. Good sources are health food stores, many grocery stores, and through Internet sites.

Maintaining a gluten-free diet can be hard, particularly when traveling or eating in restaurants. Many with celiac disease describe feeling embarrassed or like a burden when having to discuss gluten-free menu options with restaurant staff or when dining in other's homes. Mobile phone users will find apps listing gluten-free menu options at popular restaurants helpful. Many restaurants now indicate which food choices are gluten

---

TABLE 42.33 Nutritional Therapy

Celiac Disease

Foods to Eat
- Butter
- Cheese, cottage cheese
- Coffee, tea, and cocoa
- Corn tortillas
- Eggs
- Flax, corn, and rice
- Fresh fruits
- Gluten-free flour breads, crackers, pasta, and cereals
- Meat, fish, poultry (not marinated or breaded)
- Peanut butter
- Potatoes
- Soy products
- Tapioca
- Unflavored milk
- Yogurt

Foods to Avoid
- Baked goods, including muffins, cookies, cakes, pies
- Barley
- Bread, including wheat bread, white bread, "potato" bread
- Flour
- Gluten stabilizers
- Oats
- Pasta, pizza, bagels
- Rye
- Wheat

free. The Celiac Sprue Association website (*www.csaceliacs.info*) and the Celiac Disease Foundation (*www.celiac.org*) provide suggestions for maintaining a gluten-free diet and living with celiac disease.

LACTASE DEFICIENCY

Lactase deficiency is a condition in which the lactase enzyme is deficient or absent. Lactase is the enzyme that breaks down lactose into 2 simple sugars: glucose and galactose. Primary lactase insufficiency is often a result of genetic factors. Certain ethnic or racial groups, especially those with Asian or African ancestry, develop low lactase levels in childhood. Less common causes include low lactase levels resulting from premature birth and congenital lactase deficiency, a rare genetic disorder. Lactose malabsorption can occur when conditions leading to bacterial overgrowth promote lactose fermentation in the small bowel or when intestinal mucosal damage interferes with absorption. The latter occurs with IBD and celiac disease.

Symptoms of lactose intolerance include bloating, flatulence, cramping abdominal pain, and diarrhea. Diarrhea results from the excess, undigested lactose in the small intestine attracting water molecules, which prevents them from being properly absorbed. Symptoms generally occur within 30 minutes to several hours after drinking a glass of milk or ingesting a milk product. Lactose intolerance is diagnosed with a lactose tolerance test, a lactose hydrogen breath test, or genetic testing.

Treatment consists of eliminating lactose from the diet by avoiding milk and milk products, and/or replacing lactase with commercially available preparations. A lactose-free diet generally results in prompt resolution of symptoms. Many lactose-intolerant persons are aware of their condition. They likely have been avoiding lactose-containing products and using lactose-free milk products. Lactase enzyme (Lactaid) is available as an over-the-counter (OTC) product. It breaks down the lactose present in ingested milk. A number of milk products treated with lactase enzyme are readily available.

The diet may gradually advance to a low-lactose diet as tolerated. Many lactose-intolerant persons may not have symptoms if they have lactose in small amounts. Cheese has less lactose than milk and ice cream. Live culture yogurt has less lactose because the bacteria help digest the lactose. Teach the patient to read labels to detect any hidden sources of milk products. Some people tolerate lactose better if taken with meals. Teach the patient that adhering to the diet is important. Since avoiding milk and milk products can lead to calcium deficiency, supplements may be needed to prevent osteoporosis.

SHORT BOWEL SYNDROME

Short bowel syndrome (SBS) is a condition in which the small intestine does not have enough surface area to absorb enough nutrients. This leaves the person unable to meet energy, fluid, electrolyte, and nutritional needs to stay healthy on a normal diet. Causes of SBS include diseases that damage the intestinal mucosa, surgical removal of too much small intestine (e.g., with Crohn's disease, cancer), and congenital defects.

SBS is likely to develop in patients with a loss of around 75% of the small intestine. The length and area of the remaining small intestine and the presence of the colon affect the patient's outcome. If the terminal ileum and ileocecal valve are intact, the remaining intestine undergoes adaptive changes that are most pronounced in the ileum. The villi and crypts increase in size, and the absorptive capacity of the remaining intestine increases. When the colon is present, fluid and electrolyte absorption increase. Those with an end jejunostomy often have little to no adaptation.

Clinical Manifestations

SBS results in reduced nutrient, fluid, and electrolyte absorption. This leads to dehydration, weight loss, diarrhea, malnutrition, vitamin deficiencies, and electrolyte imbalances. Other manifestations include abdominal pain, flatulence, and steatorrhea. The patient may develop lactase deficiency and bacterial overgrowth. Those who do not receive appropriate nutrition may have manifestations associated with specific deficiencies. For example, patients may have peripheral neuropathy from vitamin B_{12}, vitamin E, copper, or thiamine deficiencies or fatigue due to anemia from decreased folate or iron.[29]

Interprofessional Care

The treatment goals are that the patient will have fluid and electrolyte balance, normal nutritional status, and control of diarrhea. The main treatment is nutritional support involving PN, EN, medications, and a tailored diet. In the immediate period after massive bowel resection, patients receive PN to replace fluid, electrolyte, and nutrient losses and to rest the bowel. Those with severe resections will need PN indefinitely. EN and a normal diet are gradually resumed to stimulate the remaining intestine to function better. Some can eventually stop PN.

Refer the patient to a dietitian. The ideal diet is high in protein and complex carbohydrates and low in fat and concentrated sweets. Oral supplements of calcium, zinc, and multivitamins may be needed. Soluble fiber is encouraged if the colon is present. The patient should eat at least 6 small meals per day to increase the time of contact between food and the intestine. Oral intake may be supplemented with elemental nutrient formulas and tube feeding during the night. Patients with severe malabsorption may need PN (see Chapter 39).

Patients often take multiple medications to help control fecal output. PPIs, H_2 blockers, α-adrenergic receptor agonists (e.g., clonidine), or octreotide reduce excess fluid secretion. Opioid antidiarrheal drugs decrease intestinal motility (Table 42.2). For patients who have limited ileal resections, cholestyramine reduces diarrhea resulting from unabsorbed bile acids by increasing their excretion in feces. Bile acids stimulate intestinal fluid secretion and reduce colonic fluid absorption. Antibiotic therapy is used if bacterial overgrowth is contributing to diarrhea.

Three drugs have FDA approval for the treatment of SBS: somatropin, glutamine, and teduglutide (Gattex). Somatropin enhances intestinal adaption and increases the flow of water, electrolytes, and nutrients into the bowel. Glutamine improves intestinal absorption. Teduglutide increases the surface area of the intestine and improves intestinal absorption of fluids and nutrients.

Intestinal transplantation is done at a few specialized transplant centers in the United States. It is considered the only long-term treatment option for patients with intestinal failure who have significant complications from PN or nutrition failure. The leading cause of intestinal failure is SBS. Transplantation may include the intestine alone, liver and intestine, or multivisceral combinations (stomach, duodenum, jejunum, ileum, colon, and/or pancreas).

GASTROINTESTINAL STROMAL TUMORS

Gastrointestinal stromal tumors (GISTs) are a rare form of cancer that originates in cells found in the wall of the GI tract. These cells, known as *interstitial cells of Cajal,* help control the movement of food and liquid through the stomach and intestines. About 60% of GISTs are in the stomach; 25% are in the small intestine; and the rest are in the esophagus, colon, or peritoneum.[30] Most GISTs occur in people between the ages of 50 and 70. While the exact cause of GISTs is unknown, genetic mutations likely play a role. A few GISTs occur in people with familial mutations in either the KIT or platelet-derived growth factor receptor a (PDGFRa) or in those with neurofibromatosis type 1.[30]

The manifestations of GISTs depend on the part of the GI tract affected. Early manifestations are often subtle, including early satiety, fatigue, bloating, nausea or vomiting, and a change in bowel habits. Because these manifestations are like those of many other GI problems, early detection of the cancer is difficult. Later manifestations may include GI bleeding and obstruction caused by growth of the tumor. GISTs are often found during imaging for other problems. Diagnosis is based on histologic examination of biopsied tissue. Endoscopic ultrasound, CT, or MRI are used to determine the extent of disease.

Surgery offers the only permanent cure. Often, though, GISTs have metastasized by the time of diagnosis or commonly recur. GISTs are unresponsive to conventional chemotherapy. The discovery of genetic mutations led to the development of tyrosine kinase inhibitor drugs (e.g., imatinib mesylate [Gleevec], sunitinib, regorafenib [Stivarga]) that are effective against certain GISTs.[31]

ANORECTAL PROBLEMS

HEMORRHOIDS

Hemorrhoids are dilated hemorrhoidal veins. They may be internal (occurring above the internal sphincter) or external (occurring outside the external sphincter) (Figs. 42.16 and 42.17). In affected persons, hemorrhoids appear periodically, depending on the amount of anorectal pressure.

Etiology and Pathophysiology

Hemorrhoids develop because of increased anal pressure and weakening of the connective tissue that supports the hemorrhoidal veins. Weakened supporting tissue allows for downward displacement of the hemorrhoidal veins, causing them to dilate. Blood flow through the veins of the hemorrhoidal plexus is impaired. An intravascular clot in the venule results in a thrombosed external hemorrhoid. Many factors increase the risk for hemorrhoids, including pregnancy, constipation, straining to defecate, diarrhea, heavy lifting, prolonged standing and sitting, obesity, and ascites.[31]

Clinical Manifestations

Hemorrhoids are the most common reason for bleeding with defecation. Internal hemorrhoids most often cause painless bright red bleeding with stools, on the toilet paper, or dripping into the toilet water. If internal hemorrhoids become constricted, the patient will report pain. Internal hemorrhoids can prolapse into the anal canal or externally. Symptoms of prolapse include pressure with defecation and a protruding mass.

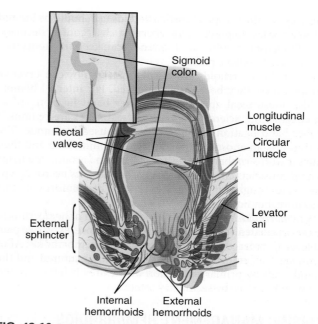

FIG. 42.16 Anatomic structures of the rectum and anus with external and internal hemorrhoids.

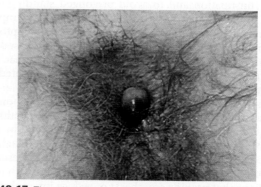

FIG. 42.17 Thrombosed external hemorrhoids. (From Townsend CM, Beauchamp RD, Evers BM, et al: *Sabiston textbook of surgery: The biological basis of modern surgical practice,* ed 19, Philadelphia, 2012, Saunders.)

External hemorrhoids are reddish blue and seldom bleed. There may be itching, burning, and edema. They usually do not cause pain unless thrombosis (blood clots) is present. Thrombosed hemorrhoids are a bluish-purple tinge and palpable at the anal orifice. They usually cause pain and inflammation. The clot can erode through the overlying stretched skin, causing bleeding with defecation. Constipation or diarrhea can worsen these symptoms.

Diagnostic Studies and Interprofessional Care

It is easy to diagnose external hemorrhoids visual inspection and digital examination. Digital examination, anoscopy, and sigmoidoscopy are used to diagnose internal hemorrhoids.

Therapy is based on the cause and the patient's symptoms. A high-fiber diet and increased fluid intake prevent constipation and reduce straining, which allows engorgement of the veins to subside. The resulting stool bulk may decrease stool leakage and itching. Ointments, such as dibucaine; creams, suppositories, and impregnated pads that contain antiinflammatory agents (e.g., hydrocortisone); or astringents and anesthetics (e.g., witch hazel, benzocaine), may shrink the mucous membranes and relieve discomfort. Topical corticosteroids use should be limited to 1 week or less to prevent side effects, such as contact dermatitis and mucosal atrophy. Stool softeners can keep the stools soft. Sitz baths help relieve pain.

External hemorrhoids are usually managed by conservative therapy unless they become thrombosed. For internal hemorrhoids, nonsurgical approaches (rubber band ligation, infrared coagulation, sclerotherapy, laser treatment) are options.[31] Rubber band ligation is the most widely used technique. The HCP inserts an anoscope to identify the hemorrhoid and then ligates it with a rubber band. The rubber band around the hemorrhoid constricts circulation. The tissue becomes necrotic, separates, and sloughs off. There is some local discomfort with this procedure, but no anesthetic is needed.

A *hemorrhoidectomy* is the surgical excision of hemorrhoids. Surgery is needed when there is marked prolapse, excessive pain or bleeding, or large or multiple thrombosed hemorrhoids. After removing the hemorrhoids, the tissue is either sutured and the wound heals by primary intention or the area is left open and healing takes place by secondary intention.

NURSING MANAGEMENT: HEMORRHOIDS

Conservative nursing management includes teaching ways to prevent constipation and to avoid prolonged standing or sitting and proper use of OTC drugs for hemorrhoidal symptoms. Teach the patient to seek medical care for severe symptoms of hemorrhoids (e.g., excessive pain and bleeding, prolapsed hemorrhoids). Sitz baths (15 to 20 minutes, 2 or 3 times each day) may help to reduce discomfort and swelling associated with hemorrhoids.

Nursing care after a hemorrhoidectomy focuses on pain control and promoting wound healing. Be aware that although the procedure is minor, the pain is severe and feared by many. There are several analgesic regimens, using a combination of medications. Most patients receive multimodal analgesia. This may involve an opioid and NSAID in conjunction with topical preparations that provide anesthesia or reduce internal sphincter spasms, such as topical lidocaine, 2% diltiazem, and glyceryl trinitrate.

The patient usually dreads the first bowel movement and often resists the urge to defecate. Give pain medication before the bowel movement to reduce discomfort. Stool softeners (e.g., docusate) and bulking agents are given to help form a soft, bulky stool that is easier to pass. If the patient does not have a bowel movement within 2 or 3 days, an oil-retention enema is given.

Sitz baths are started 1 or 2 days after surgery and continued for 1 to 2 weeks. A warm sitz bath provides comfort and keeps the anal area clean. A sponge ring in the sitz bath helps relieve pressure on the area. Initially, do not leave the patient alone because of the possibility of weakness or fainting. Teach the patient that pressure relief cushions are acceptable to ease discomfort when sitting. Tell the patient not to use a pressure relief ring or "doughnut" because they can reduce blood flow to the area.

The patient may have packing in the rectum to absorb drainage, with a T-binder to hold the dressing in place. Packing is usually removed on the first or second postoperative day. Assess for rectal bleeding, especially in patients taking clopidogrel or oral anticoagulants. The patient may be embarrassed when the dressing is changed. Provide as much privacy as possible.

Teach the patient care of the anal area, symptoms of complications (especially bleeding), and ways to avoid constipation and straining. Hemorrhoids may recur. Sometimes, anal strictures develop, requiring dilation. Regular checkups are important to prevent any further problems.

ANAL FISSURE

An *anal fissure* is a skin ulcer or a crack in the lining of the anal wall. Many times, the inciting event is trauma from passing hard stools. Other fissures are related to trauma (anal intercourse, foreign body insertion, such as endoscope), local infection (syphilis, gonorrhea, *Chlamydia*, herpes simplex virus, HIV), or inflammation. An anal fissure is acute when it is of recent onset (less than 6 weeks), and chronic if it has been present for a longer period. Chronic fissures have a characteristic appearance that includes perianal skin tag and fibrotic edges.[32]

Anal tissue ulcerates because of ischemia caused by a combination of high pressure in the internal anal sphincter and poor blood supply to the area. The ischemic tissue may ulcerate spontaneously or when traumatized by factors such as hard stools, which would not normally cause tissue breakdown. Ischemia must be corrected for a fissure to heal.

The hallmark of an anal fissure is severe anal pain. It tends to be worse with defecation and with direct pressure on the site (e.g., sitting). Acute fissures tend to bleed slightly. Patients may report red blood on the toilet paper. Constipation results because of fear of pain associated with bowel movements.

Anal fissures are easy to diagnose with a physical examination. Conservative care with fiber supplements, increased fluid intake, sitz baths, and topical analgesics is successful in most cases, especially if the fissure is acute. Topical preparations, including nitrates and calcium channel blockers, decrease rectal anal pressure and allow the fissure to heal without sphincter damage. Local injections of botulinum toxin can decrease rectal anal pressure. They are most effective when combined with nitrates. Pain is managed by softening stools with a bulk-producing agent (psyllium) or stool softener and warm sitz baths (15 to 20 minutes, 3 times per day).[32]

If conservative treatment fails, a lateral internal sphincterotomy is the recommended surgical procedure. It carries the risk for postoperative incontinence. Postoperative nursing care is the same as the care for the patient who had a hemorrhoidectomy.

ANORECTAL ABSCESS

An *anorectal abscess* is a collection of perianal pus (Fig. 42.18). The abscess results from obstruction of the anal glands, leading to infection and abscess formation. Abscess formation occurs with anal fissures, trauma, or IBD. The most common causative organisms are *E. coli*, staphylococci, and streptococci. Manifestations include local severe pain and swelling, foul-smelling drainage, tenderness, and fever. Sepsis can occur as a complication. Anorectal abscesses are diagnosed by rectal examination.

Anorectal abscesses require surgical drainage. Larger abscesses need packing afterward with impregnated gauze or placement of drains (e.g., Penrose) to promote drainage. The area then heals by granulation. Patients who have diabetes or cellulitis or are immunocompromised (e.g., chemotherapy) may need antibiotic therapy. Nursing care includes warm, moist heat applications and changing packing daily. The patient is usually more comfortable lying on the abdomen or side. A low-fiber

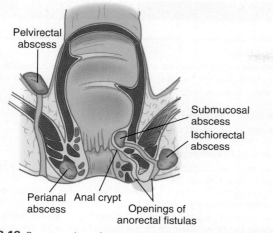

FIG. 42.18 Common sites of anorectal abscesses and fistula formation.

diet is given. The patient may leave the hospital with the wound still open. Teach the patient about wound care and the importance of sitz baths, thorough cleaning after urinating or bowel movements, and follow-up visits with the HCP.

ANAL FISTULA

An anal fistula is an abnormal tunnel leading from the anus or rectum. It may extend to the outside of the skin, vagina, or buttocks and often precedes an abscess. Anal fistulas are a complication of Crohn's disease and may resolve when drug treatment achieves remission of the disease. About 50% of anal fistulas are due to anorectal abscess.

Feces may enter the fistula and cause an infection. There may be persistent, bloody or purulent discharge, or stool leakage from the fistula. The patient may need to wear a pad to avoid staining clothes.

Surgical treatment of an anal fistula depends on the location and nature of the fistula. In a fistulotomy, the HCP opens the fistula and healthy tissue is allowed to granulate in the wound. Care is the same as after a hemorrhoidectomy. Options for complex fistulas include ligation of the intersphincteric fistula tract (LIFT) or the use of rectal flaps, setons, plugs, or fibrin glue injections to seal the fistula.

ANAL CANCER

Anal cancer is uncommon in the general population, but the incidence is increasing. In the United States around 8200 people are diagnosed with anal cancer each year.[33] It mainly occurs in older adults, with the average age being in the early 60s. Human papillomavirus (HPV) is associated with about 80% of the cases of anal cancer. Those at high risk for anal cancer include smokers, HIV-positive homosexual men, people who are immunocompromised (e.g., posttransplant immunosuppression), and women with cervical, vaginal, or vulvar cancer.[33]

Rectal bleeding is the most common presenting sign. Other symptoms include rectal pain, fullness, and changes in bowel habits. Some patients have no symptoms, which leads to delayed diagnosis and treatment.

It is especially important to screen high-risk persons using digital rectal examination (DRE) and anal Pap tests. In an anal Pap test, the anal lining is swabbed and the cells examined to identify any cell changes (e.g., dysplasia, neoplasia). High-resolution anoscopy allows for visualization of the mucosa and biopsy. An endoanal (endorectal) ultrasound may be done.

Treatment of anal cancer depends on the size and depth of the lesions. Cancer therapy involves surgery or a combination of low-dose radiation and chemotherapy. Chemotherapy regimens include combinations of mitomycin, cisplatin, and fluorouracil.[33] Options for precancerous lesions are surgical removal or treatment with topical imiquimod (Aldara) and fluorouracil. If the tumor involves the rectum and is large enough to require removing the anal sphincters, the anus will be sutured shut and a permanent ostomy created.

PILONIDAL SINUS

A *pilonidal sinus* is a small tract under the skin between the buttocks in the sacrococcygeal area. It is thought to be of congenital origin. It may have several openings and is lined with epithelium and hair, hence the name *pilonidal* ("a nest of hair"). The skin is moist, and movement of the buttocks causes the short, wiry hair to penetrate the skin. If the irritated skin becomes infected, it forms a pilonidal cyst or abscess. There are no symptoms with a pilonidal sinus unless there is an infection. Then the patient may have pain and swelling at the base of the spine.

An abscess requires incision and drainage. The wound may be closed or left open to heal by secondary intention. The wound is packed, and sitz baths ordered. Nursing care includes warm, moist heat applications when an abscess is present. The patient is usually more comfortable lying on the abdomen or side. Teach the patient to avoid contaminating the dressing when urinating or defecating and to avoid straining whenever possible.

CASE STUDY
Colorectal Cancer

(©iStockphoto/
Thinkstock)

Patient Profile

L.C., a 58-yr-old Native American man, is from a Pueblo tribe in northern New Mexico. L.C.'s wife and family drove 50 miles to take him to the Indian Health Service hospital because of his deteriorating health (see the case study in Chapter 38 on p. 835).

Subjective Data

See the case study in Chapter 38 on p. 838.

Objective Data

Physical Examination

See the case study in Chapter 38 on p. 840.

Laboratory Tests

- CT scan and colonoscopy show 2 medium-sized tumors in the transverse colon

Interprofessional Care

Surgical Procedure

- Had a transverse hemicolectomy with lymph node biopsies
- Pathology results: Adenocarcinoma, has invaded the muscle wall of colon, 2 of 5 lymph nodes are positive for cancer

Postoperative

- Feels like his life has ended and does not want to leave hospital
- States that there is "no one" to take care of him at his home and he is far away from the hospital

Follow-Up Treatment

Scheduled for outpatient chemotherapy

Discussion Questions

1. What signs and symptoms of colorectal cancer did L.C. have (see the case study in Chapter 38)?
2. What stage of CRC does L.C. probably have? What treatment is recommended for this stage of CRC?
3. How could you provide emotional support to L.C. and his family?
4. *Patient-Centered Care:* What is a culturally sensitive way for you to support L.C. and his family in making decisions about his continued health care?
5. *Priority Decision:* Based on the assessment data, what are the priority nursing diagnoses? Are there any collaborative problems?
6. *Priority Decision:* What are the priority nursing interventions for L.C. at this stage of his illness?
7. *Collaboration:* What referrals may be indicated at this time?
8. *Evidence-Based Practice:* L.C. is worried that other members of his family may have colon cancer. What can you tell him about the recommendations for colorectal cancer screening?
9. *Quality Improvement:* What outcomes would indicate nursing interventions were successful?

Answers available at *http://evolve.elsevier.com/Lewis/medsurg.*

▌ BRIDGE TO NCLEX EXAMINATION

The number of the question corresponds to the same-numbered outcome at the beginning of the chapter.

1. The *most* appropriate therapy for a patient with acute diarrhea caused by a viral infection is to
   a. increase fluid intake.
   b. administer an antibiotic.
   c. administer an antimotility drug.
   d. quarantine the patient to prevent spread of the virus.

2. A 35-yr-old female patient is admitted to the emergency department with acute abdominal pain. Which medical diagnoses should you consider as possible causes of her pain? *(select all that apply)*
   a. Gastroenteritis
   b. Ectopic pregnancy
   c. Gastrointestinal bleeding
   d. Irritable bowel syndrome
   e. Inflammatory bowel disease

3. Assessment findings suggestive of peritonitis include *(select all that apply)*
   a. rebound tenderness.
   b. a soft, distended abdomen.
   c. dull, intermittent abdominal pain.
   d. shallow respirations with bradypnea.
   e. observing that the patient is lying still.

3. In planning care for the patient with Crohn's disease, the nurse recognizes that a major difference between ulcerative colitis and Crohn's disease is that Crohn's disease
   a. often results in toxic megacolon.
   b. causes fewer nutritional deficiencies than ulcerative colitis.
   c. often recurs after surgery, while ulcerative colitis is curable with a colectomy.
   d. is manifested by rectal bleeding and anemia more often than is ulcerative colitis.

4. The nurse performs a detailed assessment of the abdomen of a patient with a possible bowel obstruction, knowing that manifestations of an obstruction in the large intestine are *(select all that apply)*
   a. persistent abdominal pain.
   b. marked abdominal distention.
   c. diarrhea that is loose or liquid.
   d. colicky, severe, intermittent pain.
   e. profuse vomiting that relieves abdominal pain.

5. A patient with stage I colorectal cancer is scheduled for surgery. Patient teaching for this patient would include an explanation that
   a. chemotherapy will begin after the patient recovers from the surgery.
   b. both chemotherapy and radiation can be used as palliative treatments.
   c. follow-up colonoscopies will be needed to ensure that the cancer does not recur.
   d. a wound, ostomy, and continence nurse will visit the patient to identify the site for the ostomy.

6. The nurse determines a patient undergoing ileostomy surgery understands the procedure when the patient states
   a. "I should only have to change the pouch every 4 to 7 days."
   b. "The drainage in the pouch will look like my normal stools."
   c. "I may not need to wear a drainage pouch if I irrigate it daily."
   d. "Limiting my fluid intake should decrease the amount of output."

7. In contrast to diverticulitis, the patient with diverticulosis
   a. has rectal bleeding.
   b. often has no symptoms.
   c. usually develops peritonitis.
   d. has localized cramping pain.

8. A nursing intervention that is *most* appropriate to decrease postoperative edema and pain after an inguinal herniorrhaphy is to
   a. apply a truss to the hernia site.
   b. allow the patient to stand to void.
   c. support the incision during coughing.
   d. apply a scrotal support with an ice bag.

9. The nurse determines that the goals of dietary teaching have been met when the patient with celiac disease selects from the menu
   a. scrambled eggs and sausage.
   b. buckwheat pancakes with syrup.
   c. oatmeal, skim milk, and orange juice.
   d. yogurt, strawberries, and rye toast with butter.

10. What should a patient be taught after a hemorrhoidectomy?
    a. Take mineral oil before bedtime.
    b. Eat a low-fiber diet to rest the colon.
    c. Use oil-retention enemas to empty the colon.
    d. Take prescribed pain medications before a bowel movement.

1. a, 2. a, b, c, d, e, 3. a, 4. c, 5. a, b, 6. c, 7. a, 8. d, 9. b, 10. d, 11. d

For rationales to these answers and even more NCLEX review questions, visit *http://evolve.elsevier.com/Lewis/medsurg*.

ⓔ EVOLVE WEBSITE/RESOURCES LIST

http://evolve.elsevier.com/Lewis/medsurg
Review Questions (Online Only)
Key Points
Answer Keys for Questions
- Rationales for Bridge to NCLEX Examination Questions
- Answer Guidelines for Case Study on p. 966
Student Case Study
- Patient With Ulcerative Colitis
Nursing Care Plans
- eNursing Care Plan 42.1: Patient With Acute Infectious Diarrhea
- eNursing Care Plan 42.2: Patient With Inflammatory Bowel Disease
- eNursing Care Plan 42.3: Patient With a Colostomy/Ileostomy
Conceptual Care Map Creator
Audio Glossary
Content Updates

REFERENCES

*1. Shane AL, Mody RK, Crump JA, et al: 2017 IDSA clinical practice guidelines for the diagnosis and management of infectious diarrhea, *Clin Infect Dis* 65:e45, 2017.

*2. Watson T, Hickok J, Fraker S, et al: Evaluating the risk factors for hospital-onset *Clostridium difficile* infections in a large healthcare system, *Clin Infect Dis* 66:1957-1959, 2018.

*3. McDonald LC, Gerding DN, Johnson S, et al: Clinical practice guidelines for *Clostridium difficile* infection in adults and children: 2017 Update by the IDSA and SHEA, *Clin Infect Dis* 66:e1, 2018.

4. Chabkraborty S, Bharucha AE: Fecal incontinence. In: Barden E, Shaker R, eds: *Gastrointestinal motility disorders*, New York, 2018, Springer.

*5. Serra J, Mascort-Roca J, Marzo-Castillejo M, et al: Clinical practice guidelines for the management of constipation in adults: Definition, etiology and clinical manifestations, *Gastroenterol Hepatol* 40:132, 2017.

6. Camilleri M, Ford AC, Mawe GM, et al: Chronic constipation, *Nat Rev Dis Primers* 3:1, 2017.

7. Weaver KR, Melkus GD, Henderson WA: Irritable bowel syndrome, *AJN* 117:48, 2017.

*8. Ireton-Jones C: The low FODMAP diet: Fundamental therapy in the management of IBS, *Curr Opin Clin Nutr Metab Care* 20:414, 2017.

9. Braslow B: Management of appendicitis. In: Khwaja KA, Diaz JJ (eds.), *Minimally invasive acute care surgery*, New York, 2018, Springer.

10. Centers for Disease Control and Prevention: Epidemiology of the IBD. Retrieved from *www.cdc.gov/ibd/ibd-epidemiology.htm*.

*11. Shivashankar R, Lewis JD: The role of diet in inflammatory bowel disease, *Curr Gastroenter Reports* 19:22, 2017.

*12. Shouval D, Rufo P: The role of environmental factors in the pathogenesis of IBD, *JAMA Pediatric* 171:999, 2017.

*13. Venema U, Werna TC, Voskuil MD, et al: The genetic background of inflammatory bowel disease: from correlation to causality, *J Pathol* 241:146, 2017.

14. Crohn's and Colitis Foundation: IBD medications. Retrieved from *www.ibdetermined.org/ibd-information/ibd-treatment/ibd-medication.aspx*.

*15. Bots S, Gecse K, Barclay M, et al: Combination immunosuppression in IBD, *Inflamm Bowel Dis* 24:539, 2018.

16. Flier LC, Welstead LA: Nutrition matters. In: Cohen R, ed: *Inflammatory bowel disease*, New York, 2017, Humana Press.

*17. John ES, Katz K, Saxena M, et al: Management of inflammatory bowel disease in the elderly, *Curr Treat Options Gastroenterol* 14:285, 2016.

*18. Reddy SR, Cappell MS: A systematic review of the clinical presentation, diagnosis, and treatment of small bowel obstruction, *Curr Gastroenterol Rep* 9:28, 2017.

19. Alavi K, Friel CM: Large bowel obstruction. In: Steele SR, Hull TL, Read TE, Saclarides TJ, Senagore AJ, Whitlow CB, eds: *The ASCRS textbook of colon and rectal surgery*, New York, 2016, Springer.

20. Toevs CC, Mazellan K, Kohr R: Ogilvie's syndrome, *Am Surg* 83:217, 2017.

21. American Cancer Society: Key statistics for colorectal cancer. Retrieved from *www.cancer.org/cancer/colon-rectal-cancer/about/key-statistics.html*.

*22. Ansa BE, Coughlin SS, Alema-Mensah E, et al: Evaluation of colorectal cancer incidence trends in the United States (2000–2014), *J Clin Med* 7:22, 2018.

23. American Cancer Society: Colorectal cancer screening guidelines. Retrieved from *www.cancer.org/cancer/colon-rectal-cancer/detection-diagnosis-staging/acs-recommendations.html*.

24. National Cancer Institute: Colon cancer treatment. Retrieved from *www.cancer.gov/types/colorectal/hp/colon-treatment-pdq#link/_125*.

*25. Ellison DL: Acute diverticulitis management, *Crit Care Nurs Clin North Am* 30:67, 2018.

*26. Ortiz LA, Zhang B, McCarthy MW, et al: Treatment of enterocutaneous fistulas, then and now, *Nutr Clin Pract* 32:508, 2017.

*27. Leonard MM, Sapone A, Catassi C, et al: Celiac disease and nonceliac gluten sensitivity, *JAMA* 318:647, 2017.

28. Celiac Disease Foundation: Celiac disease. Retrieved from *https://celiac.org/celiac-disease/understanding-celiac-disease-2/what-is-celiac-disease/*.

29. Boutte HJ, Rubin DC: Short bowel syndrome. In: Barden E, Shaker R, eds: *Gastrointestinal motility disorders*, New York, 2018, Springer.

*30. Nishida T, Blay JY, Hirota S, et al: The standard diagnosis, treatment, and follow-up of gastrointestinal stromal tumors based on guidelines, *Gastric Cancer* 19:3, 2016.

*31. American Society of Colon and Rectal Surgeons: Clinical practice guidelines for the management of hemorrhoids. Retrieved from *www.fascrs.org/physicians/clinical-practice-guidelines*.

32. American Society of Colon and Rectal Surgeons: Anal fissure, *Dis Colon Rectum* 61:293, 2018.

33. Eng C, Shridhar R, Chan E, et al: Anal cancer. *The American Cancer Society's Oncology in Practice: Clinical Management* 9:149, 2018.

*Evidence-based information for clinical practice.

43

Liver, Biliary Tract, and Pancreas Problems

Mary C. Olson

*Never define yourself by your relationship status, income,
or looks. It is your kindness, generosity, and compassion
that counts.*

Brigette Nicole

http://evolve.elsevier.com/Lewis/medsurg

CONCEPTUAL FOCUS

Infection	Nutrition
Inflammation	Pain

LEARNING OUTCOMES

1. Distinguish among the types of viral hepatitis, including etiology, pathophysiology, clinical manifestations, and complications.
2. Describe the interprofessional and nursing management of the patient with viral hepatitis.
3. Describe the pathophysiology, clinical manifestations, complications, and interprofessional care of the patient with nonalcoholic fatty liver disease.
4. Explain the etiology, pathophysiology, clinical manifestations, complications, and interprofessional and nursing management of the patient with cirrhosis.
5. Describe the clinical manifestations and management of liver cancer.

6. Distinguish between acute and chronic pancreatitis related to pathophysiology, clinical manifestations, complications, interprofessional care, and nursing management.
7. Explain the clinical manifestations and interprofessional and nursing management of the patient with pancreatic cancer.
8. Describe the pathophysiology, clinical manifestations, and interprofessional care of gallbladder disorders.
9. Describe the nursing management of the patient undergoing surgical treatment of cholecystitis and cholelithiasis.

KEY TERMS

acute liver failure, p. 989
acute pancreatitis, p. 992
ascites, p. 982
asterixis, p. 984
cholecystitis, p. 998
cholelithiasis, p. 998
chronic pancreatitis, p. 996

cirrhosis, p. 980
esophageal varices, p. 982
gastric varices, p. 982
hepatic encephalopathy, p. 983
hepatitis, p. 968
hepatorenal syndrome, p. 984
jaundice, p. 971

nonalcoholic fatty liver disease (NAFLD), p. 979
nonalcoholic steatohepatitis (NASH), p. 979
paracentesis, p. 985
portal hypertension, p. 982
spider angiomas, p. 980

Nursing management of patients with a wide range of liver, pancreatic, and gallbladder problems is the focus of this chapter. These organs are closely positioned together anatomically and highly associated in their digestive functions. Liver and pancreatic problems can lead to altered nutrient absorption and use, causing malnutrition and impaired elimination. Inflammation may be present, with the patient having pain, nausea, and vomiting. Nursing care focuses on helping the patient and caregiver manage symptoms and develop ways to cope with the diagnosis and, sometimes, prognosis. Health promotion focuses on reducing risk through immunizations and avoiding substance use.

DISORDERS OF THE LIVER

HEPATITIS

Hepatitis is inflammation of the liver. Hepatitis is most often caused by viruses. It also can be caused by substances (e.g., alcohol, medications, chemicals), autoimmune diseases, and metabolic problems.

Viral Hepatitis

There are several types of viral hepatitis. We designate each type by a letter (A, B, C, D, E). The different types have similar

TABLE 43.1 Characteristics of Hepatitis Viruses

Incubation Period and Mode of Transmission	Sources of Infection	Infectivity
Hepatitis A Virus (HAV) *Incubation:* 15–50 days (average 28) • Fecal-oral (primarily fecal contamination and oral ingestion)	• Contaminated food, milk, water, shellfish • Crowded conditions (e.g., day care, nursing home) • Persons with subclinical infections, infected food handlers, sexual contact, IV drug users • Poor personal hygiene • Poor sanitation	• Most infectious during 2 wk before onset of symptoms • Infectious until 1–2 wk after the start of symptoms
Hepatitis B Virus (HBV) *Incubation:* 115–180 days (average 56–96) • Percutaneous (parenteral) or mucosal exposure to blood or blood products • Sexual contact • Perinatal transmission	• Contaminated needles, syringes, and blood products • HBV-infected mother (perinatal transmission) • Sexual activity with infected partners. Asymptomatic carriers • Tattoos or body piercing with contaminated needles	• Before and after symptoms appear • Infectious for months • Carriers continue to be infectious for life
Hepatitis C Virus (HCV) *Incubation:* 14–180 days (average 56) • Percutaneous (parenteral) or mucosal exposure to blood or blood products • High-risk sexual contact • Perinatal contact	• Blood and blood products • Needles and syringes • Sexual activity with infected partners, low risk	• 1–2 wk before symptoms appear • Continues during clinical course • 75%–85% go on to develop chronic hepatitis C and remain infectious
Hepatitis D Virus (HDV) Incubation: 2–26 wk • HBV must precede HDV • Chronic carriers of HBV always at risk	• Same as HBV • Can cause infection only when HBV is present	• Blood infectious at all stages of HDV infection
Hepatitis E Virus (HEV) *Incubation:* 15–64 days (average 26–42 days) • Fecal-oral route • Outbreaks associated with contaminated water supply in developing countries	• Contaminated water, poor sanitation • Found in Asia, Africa, and Mexico • Not common in United States but is increasing in some areas	• Not known • May be similar to HAV

manifestations, but their modes of transmission and disease course vary (Table 43.1). Some can lead to chronic liver disease. Other less common viruses can also cause liver disease. These include cytomegalovirus (CMV), Epstein-Barr virus (EBV), herpesvirus, coxsackievirus, and rubella virus.

Hepatitis A Virus. Hepatitis A is a self-limiting infection that can cause a mild flu-like illness and jaundice. In more severe cases, it can cause acute liver failure. Hepatitis A virus (HAV) is a ribonucleic acid (RNA) virus. It is transmitted primarily through the fecal-oral route. It often occurs in small outbreaks caused by fecal contamination of food or drinking water. Poor hygiene, improper handling of food, crowded situations, and poor sanitary conditions are contributing factors.

Transmission occurs between family members, institutionalized persons, and children in day care centers. Foodborne outbreaks are usually due to food contaminated by an infected food handler. People at increased risk for infection include drug users (both injection and noninjection drugs), men who have sex with men (MSM), and persons traveling to developing countries.

The greatest risk for transmission occurs before clinical symptoms appear. The virus is found in feces 1 to 2 weeks before the onset of symptoms and at least 1 week after the onset of illness (Fig. 43.1). This means it can be carried and transmitted by persons who have undetectable, subclinical infections. It is present only briefly in blood, usually less than 3 weeks. Fecal excretion can occur in infants for months.

Anti-HAV (antibody to HAV) immunoglobulin M (IgM) appears during the acute phase. Detection of hepatitis A IgM

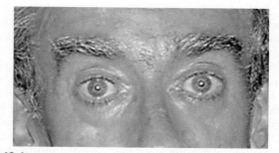

FIG. 43.1 Jaundiced patient. (From Butcher GP: *Gastroenterology: An illustrated colour text*, London, 2004, Churchill Livingstone.)

indicates acute hepatitis. Hepatitis A IgG without anti-HAV IgM indicates past infection. IgG antibody provides lifelong immunity (Fig. 43.2). HAV vaccination and thorough hand washing are the best measures to prevent outbreaks. In the United States, the incidence of infection has declined since we started vaccinating at-risk persons and children (beginning 12 to 24 months).[1]

Hepatitis B Virus. Hepatitis B virus (HBV) is a blood-borne pathogen that can cause either acute or chronic hepatitis. The incidence of HBV infection has decreased in areas where the use of the HBV vaccine is widespread.[2]

Asians and Pacific Islanders have an incidence of HBV of up to 8%. Perinatal transmission is the most common mode of transmission in this population and often results in chronic HBV infection.[2]

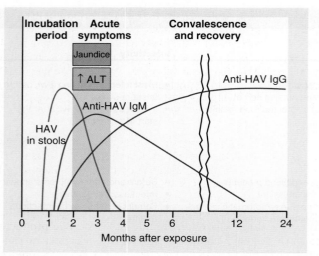

FIG. 43.2 Course of infection with hepatitis A virus *(HAV)*. *ALT*, Alanine aminotransferase. (From McCance KL, Huether SE: *Pathophysiology: The biologic basis for disease in adults and children*, ed 6, St Louis, 2010, Mosby.)

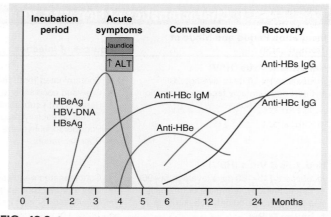

FIG. 43.3 Course of infection with hepatitis B virus *(HBV)*. *ALT*, Alanine aminotransferase; *anti-HBc*, antibody to hepatitis B core antigen; *anti-HBe*, antibody to HBeAg; *anti-HBs*, antibody to HBsAg; *HBeAg*, hepatitis B e antigen; *HBsAg*, hepatitis B surface antigen. (From McCance KL, Huether SE: *Pathophysiology: The biologic basis for disease in adults and children*, ed 6, St Louis, 2010, Mosby.)

HBV is a deoxyribonucleic acid (DNA) virus. It can be transmitted in several ways: (1) perinatally from mothers infected with HBV to their infants; (2) percutaneously (e.g., IV drug use, accidental needle-stick punctures); or (3) via small cuts on mucosal surfaces and exposure to infectious blood, blood products, or other body fluids (e.g., semen, vaginal secretions, saliva).

Sexual transmission is a common mode of HBV transmission. MSM (especially those practicing unprotected anal intercourse) are at an increased risk for HBV infection. Most believe that casual encounters, like hugging, kissing, and sharing utensils, do not transmit the disease.

Other at-risk persons include those who live with chronically HBV-infected persons, patients on hemodialysis, health care personnel, public safety workers, IV drug users, recipients of blood products, and Native Alaskans, Pacific Islanders, and Native Americans.

HBV has been detected in almost every body fluid. Infected semen, cervicovaginal secretions, and saliva contain much lower concentrations of HBV than blood, but the virus can be transmitted via these secretions. If gastrointestinal (GI) bleeding occurs, feces can be contaminated with the virus from the blood. There is no evidence of fecal-oral transmission. Organ and tissue transplantation is another potential source of infection. However, in some patients with acute hepatitis B, there is no readily identifiable risk factor.

HBV is a complex structure with 3 distinct antigens: surface antigen (HBsAg), core antigen (HBcAg), and e antigen (HBeAg). Each antigen, along with its corresponding antibody, may appear or disappear in serum depending on the phase of infection and immune response.

In most people who acquire HBV infection as an adult, the infection completely resolves without any long-term complications. In those who develop chronic HBV infections, the liver may range from a normal-appearing liver to severe liver inflammation and scarring (fibrosis). Around 25% of those who become chronically HBV-infected in childhood die from complications of chronic liver disease, including liver cancer.[3]

Screening for HBV usually includes identifying those at high risk for infection and testing the blood for the presence of hepatitis B surface antigen (HBsAg), hepatitis B antibody (anti-HBs), and hepatitis B core antibody (anti-HBc). The presence of anti-HBs in the blood indicates immunity from the HBV vaccine or from past HBV infection (Fig. 43.3). HBsAg in the serum for 6 months or longer after infection indicates chronic HBV infection.

Hepatitis C Virus. Hepatitis C virus (HCV) causes a type of hepatitis that can result in both acute illness and chronic infection. Acute hepatitis C, which can be mild in presentation, can be hard to detect unless a diagnosis is made with laboratory testing. The most common causes of acute hepatitis C outbreaks are among injection drug users and MSM with HIV infection.

HCV is an RNA virus that is blood-borne and primarily transmitted percutaneously. The most common mode of HCV transmission is the sharing of contaminated needles and equipment among injection drug users. High-risk sexual behavior (e.g., unprotected sex, multiple partners), especially among MSM, is associated with increased risk for transmission.

After a needle-stick exposure or sharps exposure to HCV-positive blood, the transmission rate is 0.1%. The risk for perinatal HCV transmission is 4% to 7% per pregnancy. Persons who were given blood or blood products before 1992 (when blood product testing for HCV began) are at higher risk for chronic HCV infection and should be routinely tested.[4] Some patients with HCV infection cannot identify a source of infection.

Most patients usually develop chronic infection. However, because signs and symptoms of HCV infection are generally mild, most people are unaware of their infection. HCV is the most common cause of chronic liver disease and liver failure. About 20% to 30% develop cirrhosis and eventually liver failure and/or liver cancer.[4] Along with chronic HBV, HCV accounts for most cases of liver cancer. HCV hepatitis is the most common reason for liver transplantation in the United States.

Because of the 15- to 20-year delay between infection and the manifestations of liver damage, long-term effects of HCV infection pose important health care challenges.

Persons at risk for HCV infection are also at risk for HBV and HIV infections. About 30% to 40% of HIV-infected patients also have HCV. This high rate of co-infection is primarily related to IV drug use. Co-infection with HIV and HCV places the patient at greater risk for progression to cirrhosis.

People in the United States born between 1945 and 1965 and those at increased risk should be screened for HCV infection. This includes people who engage in high-risk sexual practices, injection drug users, those who may have had blood or blood products prior to 1992, and/or those who have abnormal liver function tests. A positive antibody test for HCV (anti-HCV) is usually enough for a diagnosis.[2] However, a positive viral load is needed to confirm active infection because anti-HCV can also indicate a past infection.

EVIDENCE-BASED PRACTICE
Screening and Testing of Hepatitis C

You are caring for S.B., a 32-yr-old man who often visits the community clinic with health concerns. He arrives today saying he feels "tired." He tells you a friend was recently diagnosed with HCV and he wants "a shot" to keep from "getting it." You see on S.B.'s medical record that he injects drugs and has not been tested for HCV.

Making Clinical Decisions

Best Available Evidence. Currently, most HCV-infected persons are undiagnosed and therefore untreated. It is recommended that patients with known risk factors for HCV be tested. Rapid diagnostic tests (RDTs), including oral HCV antibody (Ab) RDTs, have excellent sensitivity and specificity compared to laboratory-based methods for HCV Ab detection.

Clinician Expertise. You know a major risk factor for HCV is injection drug use. You understand early diagnosis of HCV is important for best patient outcomes and prevention of transmission to others.

Patient Preferences and Values. S.B. tells you he is "busy today," but he can come back tomorrow for HCV testing.

Implications for Nursing Practice

1. What information would you provide to S.B. on HCV testing, symptoms, and transmission?
2. Since S.B. is now willing to be tested for HCV, how would you determine barriers to the informed consent process?
3. Should S.B. test positive for HCV, what other information will you provide him?

References for Evidence

Center for Disease Control and Prevention: Viral Hepatitis: Hepatitis C FAQs for Health Professionals. Retrieved from *www.cdc.gov/hepatitis/hcv/hcvfaq.htm.*

Tang W, Chen W, Amini A, et al.: Diagnostic accuracy of tests to detect hepatitis C antibody: A meta-analysis and review of the literature, *BMC Infect Dis* 17:695, 2017.

Hepatitis D Virus. Hepatitis D virus (HDV), also called *delta virus,* is uncommon in the United States. HDV is a defective single-stranded RNA virus that cannot survive on its own. It requires HBV surface Ag to serve as its outer shell. So, only those who are infected with HBV can be infected with HDV. It can be acquired at the same time as HBV or a person with HBV can be infected with HDV later. HDV is transmitted like HBV. It can cause a range of illness, from an asymptomatic chronic carrier state to acute liver failure. There is no vaccine for HDV. However, vaccination against HBV reduces the risk for HDV co-infection.[3]

Hepatitis E Virus. Like hepatitis A, the hepatitis E virus (HEV) is an RNA virus transmitted by the fecal-oral route. The usual mode of transmission is drinking contaminated water. HEV infection occurs primarily in developing countries, with epidemics reported in India, Asia, Mexico, and Africa. Only a few

cases of HEV have been reported in the United States. These have been primarily in persons who recently traveled to an HEV-endemic area. It is generally acute and self-resolving, but chronicity in immunosuppressed persons, such as liver transplant recipients, has been reported. Pregnant women may be affected severely, with reported mortality rates of up to 10%. An IgM antibody assay is available to test for acute hepatitis E.[3]

Pathophysiology

Liver. In viral hepatitis, hepatocytes become targets of the virus in one of 2 ways: through direct action of the virus (as in HCV infection) or through a cell-mediated immune response to the virus (as in HBV and HCV infection).[3]

During acute viral hepatitis, large numbers of infected hepatocytes are destroyed. The destruction of hepatocytes leads to a wide range of liver-related dysfunction. Bile production, coagulation, blood glucose, and protein metabolism can be affected. Detoxification and processing of drugs, hormones, and metabolites (e.g., ammonia from protein catabolism) may be disrupted.

After resolution of an acute infection, liver cells can regenerate. If no complications occur, the liver can resume its normal appearance and function. In certain cases, the acute hepatitis can become so severe and irreversible that people develop liver failure or die.

Chronic viral hepatitis can be insidious and silent, causing persistent and continual destruction of infected hepatocytes. Over time scar tissue can develop, which leads to fibrosis and compromised liver function. Fibrosis can lead to cirrhosis and liver failure. Cirrhosis is a generally irreversible condition that can increase one's risk for liver dysfunction, portal hypertension, and primary liver cancer. Cirrhosis is discussed later in this chapter.

Systemic Effects. In the early phases of hepatitis infection, antigen-antibody complexes between the virus and its corresponding antibody may form circulating immune complexes. The circulating immune complexes activate the complement system (see Chapter 11). The manifestations of this activation are rash, angioedema, arthritis, fever, and malaise. *Cryoglobulinemia* (abnormal proteins found in the blood), glomerulonephritis, vasculitis, and involvement of other organs can occur from immune complex activation.

Clinical Manifestations and Complications

The manifestations of the different viral hepatitis infections can be classified into acute hepatitis and chronic hepatitis (Table 43.2).

Acute Hepatitis. Many patients with acute hepatitis have no symptoms and may not even know they have been infected. However, others may have intermittent or ongoing anorexia, lethargy, nausea, vomiting, skin rashes, diarrhea or constipation, malaise, fatigue, myalgias, arthralgias, other flu-like symptoms, and right upper quadrant tenderness (caused by liver inflammation).

Although the acute phase of viral hepatitis varies depending on the type of hepatitis, it usually lasts from 1 to 6 months. During this time, the patient may have a decreased sense of smell and find food repugnant. Smokers may have distaste for cigarettes. Physical examination often reveals hepatomegaly, lymphadenopathy, abdominal tenderness, and sometimes splenomegaly. The acute phase is the period of maximal infectivity.

A patient in the acute phase of hepatitis may be *icteric* (jaundiced) or anicteric. Jaundice, a yellowish discoloration of body tissues, results from a change in normal bilirubin metabolism or disruption of the flow of bile into the hepatic or biliary duct systems. The types of jaundice are described in Table 43.3. The urine may appear darker due to excess bilirubin being excreted by the kidneys. If conjugated bilirubin cannot pass into the intestines from the liver because of obstruction or inflammation of the bile ducts, the stools will be clay colored.

Pruritus (intense generalized itching) sometimes accompanies jaundice. It occurs from the accumulation of bile salts beneath the skin. Itching can be intolerable to the patient.

As jaundice fades, the convalescent phase begins. The convalescent phase can last for weeks to months, with an average of 2 to 4 months. During this period, patients typically have malaise and easy fatigability. Hepatomegaly remains for several weeks. Splenomegaly (if present) subsides during this period.

Most patients with acute viral hepatitis recover completely. Almost all cases of acute hepatitis A resolve. However, some patients may have a relapse in the first 2 to 3 months after the infection. The disappearance of jaundice does not mean the patient has totally recovered. Some HBV infections and most HCV infections result in chronic hepatitis.

The overall mortality rate for acute hepatitis is less than 1%. The mortality rate is higher in older adults and those with underlying debilitating illnesses (including chronic liver disease).

Complications that can result from acute hepatitis are acute liver failure, chronic hepatitis, cirrhosis of the liver, portal hypertension, and liver cancer.

Acute Liver Failure. Sometimes, acute liver failure (fulminant hepatic failure) may occur, which is a serious condition with a poor prognosis. Manifestations include encephalopathy, GI bleeding, disseminated intravascular coagulation (DIC), fever with leukocytosis, renal manifestations (oliguria, azotemia), ascites, edema, hypotension, respiratory failure, hypoglycemia, bacterial infections, thrombocytopenia, and coagulopathies. Liver transplantation is usually the cure for these patients. Acute liver failure is discussed in this chapter on p. 989.

Chronic Hepatitis. Manifestations of chronic hepatitis are shown in Table 43.2. Chronic HBV is more likely to develop in infants born to infected mothers and in those who acquire the infection before age 5 than in those who acquire the virus after age 5.[3]

Problems with the patient's cellular immune response may be important in the development of the chronic HBsAg carrier state and the progression of acute HBV to chronic HBV. More than 50% of immunocompromised adults who are acutely infected with HBV progress to chronic infection.[3]

HCV infection is more likely than HBV to become chronic. As previously mentioned, many patients with chronic HCV infection develop chronic liver disease, cirrhosis, portal hypertension, and liver cancer. Risk factors for progression to cirrhosis include male gender, alcohol use, concomitant fatty liver disease, and excess iron deposition in the liver. In some patients, co-infection with HIV may cause complications or require treatment modification. Manifestations of chronic hepatitis include

---

TABLE 43.2 Manifestations of Hepatitis

Acute Hepatitis	Chronic Hepatitis
• Anorexia	• ALT, AST elevations (may be normal in some people)
• Clay-colored stools	• Ascites and lower extremity edema
• Dark urine	• Asterixis ("liver flap")
• Decreased sense of taste and smell	• Bleeding abnormalities (thrombocytopenia, easy bruising, prolonged clotting time)
• Diarrhea or constipation	• Fatigue, malaise
• Fatigue, lethargy, malaise	• Hepatic encephalopathy: confusion, difficulty concentrating, easy agitation
• Flu-like symptoms (e.g., headache)	• Hepatomegaly
• Hepatomegaly	• Increased bilirubin
• Jaundice	• Jaundice
• Low-grade fever	• Myalgias and/or arthralgias
• Lymphadenopathy	• Palmar erythema
• Myalgias and/or arthralgias	• Spider angiomas
• Nausea, vomiting	
• Pruritus	
• Right upper quadrant tenderness	
• Splenomegaly	
• Weight loss	

TABLE 43.3 Classification of Jaundice

	Hemolytic Jaundice	Hepatocellular Jaundice	Obstructive Jaundice
Causes	• Blood transfusion reactions, hemolytic anemia, sickle cell crisis	• Cirrhosis, hepatitis, liver cancer	• Cirrhosis, hepatitis, liver cancer • Common bile duct obstruction from stone(s), biliary strictures, pancreatic cancer, sclerosing cholangitis
Description	• Caused by increased breakdown of RBCs, which produces an increased amount of unconjugated bilirubin in blood • Liver is unable to handle increased load	• Results from liver's altered ability to take up bilirubin from blood or to conjugate or excrete it • In hepatocellular disease, damaged hepatocytes leak bilirubin	• Results from decreased or obstructed flow of bile through liver or biliary duct system • Obstruction may occur in intrahepatic or extrahepatic bile ducts • Intrahepatic obstructions are due to swelling or fibrosis of the liver's canaliculi and bile ducts
Diagnostic Findings			
Serum Bilirubin			
Unconjugated (indirect)	↑	↑	↑
Conjugated (direct)	Normal	↑ or ↓ (severe disease)	↑
Urine Bilirubin	Negative	↑	↑
Urobilinogen			
Stool	↑	Normal, ↓	↓
Urine	↑	Normal, ↑	↓

anemia and coagulation problems (easy bruising, bleeding). Since the liver produces clotting factors, clotting and bleeding times can be impaired or prolonged.

Skin manifestations may include spider angiomas, palmar erythema, and gynecomastia. Some patients have spleen, liver, or cervical lymph node enlargement.

In patients with severe liver damage, *hepatic encephalopathy* is a potentially life-threatening spectrum of neurologic, psychiatric, and motor disturbances. Hepatic encephalopathy results from the liver's inability to remove toxins (especially ammonia) from the blood. Hepatic encephalopathy is discussed later in this chapter on p. 983.)

Ascites, a common manifestation of hepatitis (especially chronic hepatitis), is the accumulation of excess fluid in the peritoneal cavity. Fluid accumulates due to reduced protein levels in the blood, which reduces the plasma oncotic pressure. Ascites is discussed later in this chapter on p. 982.

Diagnostic Studies

The only definitive way to distinguish among the types of viral hepatitis is by testing the patient's blood for the specific antigen or antibody. In some types of viral hepatitis, the blood can be tested for the viral load (viral level). Tests for the different types of viral hepatitis are outlined in Table 43.4. Many liver function tests show significant abnormalities, as shown in Table 43.5.

Several tests are available to determine the presence of HCV. The screening test for HCV infection is HCV antibody testing. Antibodies can be detected within 4 weeks of infection. If the antibody test is positive, HCV RNA testing is done to assess for chronic infection. A positive result confirms chronic infection. A few patients may have a false-positive HCV antibody result with a negative HCV RNA test. If recent HCV infection is suspected, HCV RNA testing is usually done because it may take several weeks or longer for HCV antibodies to develop.

HCV RNA testing may be used for immunocompromised patients (e.g., patient with HIV). Because of altered or delayed antibody response to HCV, these patients may not have detectable antibody levels even if they are infected with HCV.

Viral genotype testing is done in patients undergoing drug therapy for HBV or HCV infection. HBV has at least 8 different genotypes (A to H). In some centers, HBV genotyping is done before starting treatment. HBV genotype may be useful in predicting disease course and treatment outcomes. HBV core Ab (HBVcAb) IgG indicates that the patient has a history of HBV infection. HBV may reactivate in these patients if they become immunosuppressed.

HCV has 6 genotypes and more than 50 subtypes. In the United States, 75% of HCV infections are caused by HCV genotype 1. For patients who test positive for HCV, genotyping is done before drug therapy is started. The genotype determines the choice and duration of therapy. It is one of the strongest predictors of a patient's response to drug therapy.

A liver biopsy is done in acute hepatitis only if diagnosis is in doubt. In chronic hepatitis, a liver biopsy allows for histologic examination of liver cells and determination of the degree of inflammation, fibrosis, or cirrhosis that may be present. A patient who has a bleeding disorder may not be a candidate for a percutaneous liver biopsy because of the risk for bleeding. In these patients, a transjugular biopsy may be an alternative. This type of biopsy consists of obtaining liver tissue through a rigid cannula introduced into a hepatic vein, typically using jugular venous access.

Techniques for noninvasive assessment of liver fibrosis are increasingly replacing the need for liver biopsy. One option is the use of ultrasound elastography (e.g., FibroScan), which uses

TABLE 43.4 Diagnostic Studies

Viral Hepatitis

Virus	Tests	Significance
A	Anti-HAV immunoglobulin M (IgM)	Acute infection
	Anti-HAV immunoglobulin G (IgG)	Previous infection or immunization
		Not routinely done in clinical practice
B	HBsAg (hepatitis B surface antigen)	Marker of infectivity
		Present in acute or chronic infection
		Positive in chronic carriers
	Anti-HBs (hepatitis B surface antibody)	Indicates previous infection with HBV or immunization
	HBeAg (hepatitis B e antigen)	Indicates high infectivity
		Used to determine the clinical management of patients with chronic hepatitis B
	Anti-HBe (hepatitis B e antibody)	Indicates previous infection
		In chronic hepatitis B, indicates a low viral load and low degree of infectivity
	Anti-HBc (antibody to hepatitis B core antigen) IgM	Indicates acute infection
		Does not appear after vaccination
	Anti-HBc IgG	Indicates previous infection or ongoing infection with hepatitis B
		Does not appear after vaccination
	HBV DNA quantitation	Indicates active ongoing viral replication
		Best indicator of viral replication and effectiveness of therapy in patient with chronic hepatitis B
	HBV genotyping	Indicates the genotype of HBV
C	Anti-HCV (antibody to HCV)	Marker for acute or chronic infection with HCV
	HCV RNA quantitation	Indicates active ongoing viral replication
	HCV genotyping	Indicates the genotype of HCV
D	Anti-HDV	Present in past or current infection with HDV
	HDV Ag (hepatitis D antigen)	Present within a few days after infection
E	Anti-HEV IgM and IgG	Present 1 wk–2 mo after illness onset
	HEV RNA quantitation	Indicates active ongoing viral replication

A, Hepatitis A virus (HAV); *B,* hepatitis B virus (HBV); *C,* hepatitis C virus (HCV); *D,* hepatitis D virus (HDV); *E,* hepatitis E virus (HEV).

TABLE 43.5 Diagnostic Findings in Acute Hepatitis

Test	Abnormal Finding	Etiology
Alkaline phosphatase	Moderately ↑	Impaired excretory function of liver
γ-Glutamyl transpeptidase (GGT)	↑	Liver cell injury
Aminotransferases		
• Aspartate aminotransferase (AST)	↑ in acute phase Decreases as jaundice disappears	Liver cell injury
• Alanine aminotransferase (ALT)	↑ in acute phase Decreases as jaundice disappears	Liver cell injury
Prothrombin time	Prolonged	↓ prothrombin production by liver
Serum proteins		
• Albumin	Normal or ↓	Liver cell injury
• γ-Globulin	Normal or ↓	Impaired clearance from liver
Total bilirubin (serum)	Increased to about 8–15 mg/dL (137–257 μmol/L)	Liver cell injury
Urinary bilirubin	↑	Conjugated hyperbilirubinemia
Urinary urobilinogen	↑ 2–5 days before jaundice	Decreased urobilinogen reabsorption

TABLE 43.6 Interprofessional Care
Viral Hepatitis

Diagnostic Assessment
- History and physical examination
- Liver function tests (ALT, AST, alkaline phosphatase, bilirubin, γ-glutamyl transpeptidase [GGT])
- PT time and INR
- Hepatitis testing
  - *Hepatitis A:* Anti-HAV IgM, anti-HAV IgG, or HAV total antibody
  - *Hepatitis B:* HBsAg, anti-HBs, HBeAg, anti-HBe, anti-HBc IgM and IgG, HBV DNA quantitation, HBV genotyping
  - *Hepatitis C:* Anti-HCV, HCV RNA quantitation, HCV genotyping
  - *Hepatitis D:* Anti-HDV, HDV Ag
- FibroScan
- FibroSure (FibroTest)

Management
Acute and Chronic
- Well-balanced diet
- Vitamin supplements
- Rest (degree of strictness varies)
- Avoiding alcohol and drugs detoxified by liver

Chronic HBV and HCV
- Drug therapy (Table 43.7)

HAV, Hepatitis A virus; *HB,* hepatitis B; *HBeAg,* hepatitis B e antigen; *HBsAg,* hepatitis B surface antigen; *HBV,* hepatitis B virus; *HCV,* hepatitis C virus; *HDV Ag,* hepatitis D antigen; *HDV,* hepatitis D virus.

an ultrasound transducer to determine the degree of liver fibrosis.[5] FibroSure (FibroTest) is an example of one of several biomarkers that uses the results of serum tests to assess the extent of hepatic fibrosis.

Interprofessional Care

There is no specific treatment for acute viral hepatitis. Most patients are managed at home. Emphasis is on providing adequate nutrition and measures to rest the body and help the liver to regenerate and repair (Table 43.6). Rest reduces the metabolic demands on the liver and promotes liver cell regeneration. The degree of rest depends on the severity of symptoms, but usually alternating periods of activity and rest are adequate. Counseling should include the importance of avoiding alcohol and notifying contacts for testing and prophylaxis, if indicated.

In patients with chronic viral hepatitis, care may involve hepatologists, infectious disease specialists, pharmacists, dietitians, and mental health or substance use specialists. The role and extent of involvement of team members is based on the patient's specific needs.

Drug Therapy

Acute Hepatitis. There are no drug therapies for treating acute HAV infection. Treatment of acute HBV may be indicated only in patients with severe hepatitis and liver failure.

In acute hepatitis C, some patients may choose to be monitored for spontaneous clearance of the infection. For patients who choose treatment, one of the direct-acting antivirals (DAAs) may be used.[6] DAAs are discussed later in the section on chronic hepatitis.

Supportive drug therapy may include antihistamines for generalized itching and antiemetics for nausea. These drugs include promethazine (Phenergan) and ondansetron (Zofran).

COMPLEMENTARY & ALTERNATIVE THERAPIES
Milk Thistle (Silymarin)

Scientific Evidence
People have used milk thistle for liver disorders, including hepatitis, cirrhosis, and gallbladder problems.
- Clinical trials of milk thistle for liver diseases have mixed results.
- Silymarin was no better than placebo for chronic hepatitis C in people who had not responded to standard antiviral treatment.
- The 2008 Hepatitis C Antiviral Long-Term Treatment Against Cirrhosis (HALT-C) study found that patients with hepatitis C who used silymarin had fewer and milder symptoms of liver disease and better quality of life but no change in virus activity or liver inflammation.

Nursing Implications
- Well tolerated in recommended doses. Some people report GI side effects
- May lower blood glucose
- May interfere with the liver's cytochrome P450 enzyme system

Source: National Center for Complementary and Alternative Therapy: Milk thistle. Retrieved from *www.nccih.nih.gov/health/milkthistle/ataglance.htm.*

Chronic Hepatitis B. Drug therapy for chronic HBV focuses on decreasing the hepatitis B viral load and liver enzymes, and in turn, slowing the rate of disease progression. Long-term goals are preventing the development of cirrhosis, portal hypertension, liver failure, and liver cancer. Current drug therapies for chronic HBV do not eradicate the virus but suppress viral replication and prevent complications of infection. First-line therapies now include primarily nucleoside and nucleotide analogs (Table 43.7) and sometimes interferon therapy.[7]

TABLE 43.7 Drug Therapy
Viral Hepatitis B and C

Drug Class	Examples	Mechanism of Action	Indication
Immune modulator	pegylated interferon (Pegasys, PegIntron)	Has antiviral, antiproliferative, immune-regulating actions	Chronic hepatitis B and C*
Nucleoside and nucleotide analogs	entecavir (Baraclude) lamivudine (Epivir HBV) telbivudine (Tyzeka) tenofovir (Vemlidy, Viread)	Inhibits HBV DNA polymerase enzyme by competing with natural substrates. Prevents viral replication	Chronic hepatitis B
Direct-acting antivirals for hepatitis C			
• NS3/4A protease inhibitors	simeprevir (Olysio) glecaprevir† grazoprevir† paritaprevir† voxilaprevir†	Blocks viral protease enzyme. Prevents viral replication in genotype 1 HCV	Chronic hepatitis C
• NS5A inhibitors	daclatasvir (Daklinza) elbasvir† ledipasvir† ombitasvir† pibrentasvir† velpatasvir†	Blocks nonstructural protein 5A (NS5A) at early stage in RNA HCV replication	Chronic hepatitis C
• NS5B polymerase inhibitors	dasabuvir† sofosbuvir (Sovaldi)	Nucleotide inhibitor and non-nucleoside inhibitor of HCV polymerase. Prevent replication of RNA HCV	Chronic hepatitis C
Combination therapies	elbasvir + grazoprevir (Zepatier) ledipasvir + sofosbuvir (Harvoni) ombitasvir + paritaprevir + ritonvir‡ + dasabuvir (Viekira Pak) Pibrentasvir + glecaprevir (Mavyret) velpatasvir + sofosbuvir (Epclusa) velpatasvir + sofosbuvir + voxilaprevir (Vosevi)	Drugs are combined in single tablet. Drugs may be from the same or different classes.	Chronic hepatitis C

*Use of all oral or noninterferon therapies for chronic hepatitis C is preferred.
†Used only in combination therapy.
‡CYP3A inhibitor used to enhance the pharmacokinetics of the other agents.

Nucleoside and nucleotide analogs. Nucleoside and nucleotide analogs inhibit viral DNA replication. HBV reproduces by making copies of its viral DNA nucleosides and nucleotides. The nucleoside and nucleotide analog drugs mimic normal building blocks for DNA but are actually faulty viral DNA building blocks. Once they become incorporated into the viral DNA, they halt DNA synthesis.

Nucleoside and nucleotide analogs do not prevent all viral reproduction, but they can substantially lower the amount of virus in the body. These medications include lamivudine (Epivir), adefovir (Hepsera), entecavir (Baraclude), telbivudine (Tyzeka), and tenofovir (Viread). These oral medications are used to treat chronic HBV when there is evidence of significant active viral replication and liver inflammation.[7]

These drugs also reduce viral load, decrease liver damage, and decrease serum liver enzyme levels. Most patients with HBV need long-term treatment. When these drugs are stopped, many patients' (except those who have seroconverted) HBV DNA and liver enzyme levels return to pretreatment levels.

Severe exacerbations of hepatitis B can develop after ending treatment. If these drugs are stopped for any reason, closely monitor liver function for several months.

Interferon. Interferon is a naturally occurring immune protein made by the body during an infection to recognize and respond to pathogens. It has antiviral, antiproliferative, and immune-modulating effects. (Interferon is discussed in Chapter 13). Pegylated interferon (PEG-Intron, Pegasys) is given by subcutaneous injection.

The many side effects with interferon therapy, including flu-like symptoms (e.g., fever, malaise, fatigue), make adhering to therapy hard for some patients. Currently, the availability of better tolerated and more effective oral treatments limits interferon use. However, it is still among the first-line options recommended by hepatology societies.

Patients receiving interferon should have blood counts and liver function tests every 4 to 6 weeks. Depression is a side effect of interferon. Patients must be screened for depression and other mood disorders before starting interferon treatment and monitored frequently while on therapy.

Chronic Hepatitis C. Treatment of chronic hepatitis C is patient specific and based on the genotype of the HCV, severity of liver disease, and presence of other health problems (e.g., HIV). The goal of drug therapy is eradicating the virus and preventing HCV-related complications. Treatment for HCV primarily includes the use of DAAs (Table 43.7), which block proteins needed for HCV replication.

With DAAs, patients typically complete a 12-week regimen with oral drugs. Almost all (>95%) of those who complete treatment with the DAAs are now able to cure their chronic HCV infection.[6]

DRUG ALERT Ribavirin (Rebetol, Ribasphere)

- May cause severe birth defects. During treatment, women taking the drug and women whose male partners are taking the drug must avoid pregnancy.
- Monitor hemoglobin and hematocrit as it may cause anemia.
- Used only for specific populations.

Many patients with HIV also have HCV. Patients who have stable HIV and intact immune systems (CD4+ counts greater than 200/μL) receive HCV treatment with the goal of eradicating HCV and reducing the risk for progression to cirrhosis. HCV treatment may reduce CD4+ counts and increase the patient's risk for anemia and leukopenia.

Patients with advanced fibrosis or cirrhosis can undergo drug therapy if liver decompensation (e.g., ascites, variceal rupture, jaundice, wasting, encephalopathy) is not present.

Nutritional Therapy. No special diet is needed in the treatment of viral hepatitis. Emphasis is placed on a well-balanced diet that the patient can tolerate. During acute viral hepatitis, adequate calories are important because the patient usually loses weight. If fat content is poorly tolerated because of decreased bile production, it should be reduced. Vitamin supplements, particularly B-complex and vitamin K, are often given. If anorexia, nausea, and vomiting are severe, IV solutions of glucose or supplemental enteral nutrition (EN) therapy may be used. Fluid and electrolyte balance must be maintained.

❖ NURSING MANAGEMENT: VIRAL HEPATITIS

◆ Nursing Assessment

Subjective and objective data that should be obtained from a person with hepatitis are outlined in Table 43.8.

◆ Nursing Diagnoses

Nursing diagnoses for the patient with viral hepatitis may include:
- Impaired nutritional intake
- Activity intolerance
- Risk for bleeding

Additional information on nursing diagnoses and interventions for the patient with hepatitis is presented in eNursing Care Plan 43.1 available on the website for this chapter.

◆ Planning

The overall goals are that the patient with viral hepatitis will (1) have relief of discomfort, (2) be able to resume normal activities, and (3) return to normal liver function without complications.

◆ Nursing Implementation

Health Promotion. Viral hepatitis is a public health problem. Your role is important in the prevention and control of this disease. It is helpful to understand the epidemiology of the different types of viral hepatitis when considering appropriate control measures. Preventive and control measures for hepatitis A, B, and C are outlined in Table 43.9.

A suggested guideline for general practice to prevent you from contracting viral hepatitis from diagnosed and undiagnosed patients and carriers is for you to wear disposable gloves, goggles, and gowns (sometimes) when fecal or blood contamination is likely in handling (1) soiled bedpans, urinals, and catheters and (2) when the patient's bed linens are soiled by body excreta or secretions.

Hepatitis A. Viral hepatitis outbreaks are usually due to HAV. Preventive measures include personal and environmental hygiene and health education to promote good sanitation. Hand washing is the most important precaution. Teach about careful hand washing after bowel movements and before eating.

Vaccination is the best protection against HAV. All children at 1 year of age should receive the vaccine. Adults at risk should

---

TABLE 43.8 Nursing Assessment
*Hepatitis**

Subjective Data

Important Health Information

Past health history: Hemophilia, cancer, exposure to infected persons, ingestion of contaminated food or water. Exposure to benzene, carbon tetrachloride, or other hepatotoxic agents. Crowded, unsanitary living conditions. Exposure to contaminated needles. Recent travel, organ transplant recipient, exposure to new drug regimens, hemodialysis, transfusion of blood or blood products before 1992. HIV status (if known)

Medications: Use and misuse of acetaminophen, new prescription, over-the-counter, or herbal medications or supplements

Functional Health Patterns

Health perception–health management: IV drug and chronic alcohol use. Malaise, distaste for cigarettes (in smokers), high-risk sexual behaviors

Nutritional-metabolic: Weight loss, anorexia, nausea, vomiting. Feeling of fullness in right upper quadrant

Elimination: Dark urine, light-colored stools, constipation or diarrhea, skin rashes, hives

Activity-exercise: Fatigue, arthralgias, myalgias

Cognitive-perceptual: Right upper quadrant pain and liver tenderness, headache, itching

Role-relationship: Exposure as health care worker, resident in long-term care institution, incarceration, homelessness

Objective Data

General

Low-grade fever, lethargy, lymphadenopathy

Integumentary

Rash or other skin changes, jaundice, icteric sclera, injection sites

Gastrointestinal

Hepatomegaly, splenomegaly

Possible Diagnostic Findings

Elevated liver enzyme levels. ↑ Serum total bilirubin, hypoalbuminemia, anemia, bilirubin in urine and increased urobilinogen, prolonged PT time, positive tests for hepatitis, including anti-HAV IgM, HBsAg, anti-HBs, HBeAg, anti-HBe, anti-HBc IgM and IgG, HBV DNA quantitation, anti-HCV, HCV RNA quantitation, anti-HDV, HDV Ag. Abnormal liver scan, abnormal results on liver biopsy

*Tailor history questions to the type of hepatitis.
HAV, Hepatitis A virus; *HBcAg,* hepatitis B core antigen; *HBeAg,* hepatitis B e antigen; *HBsAg,* hepatitis B surface antigen; *HBV,* hepatitis B virus; *HCV,* hepatitis C virus; *HDV Ag,* hepatitis D antigen; *HDV,* hepatitis D virus.

---

also receive the vaccine. These include people who travel to areas with increased rates of hepatitis A, MSM, injecting and noninjecting drug users, persons with clotting factor disorders (e.g., hemophilia), and persons with chronic liver disease.

HAV vaccine is inactivated HAV protein. There are 2 forms of HAV vaccine in the United States: Havrix and Vaqta. Primary immunization consists of 1 dose given IM in the deltoid muscle. A booster is recommended 6 to 12 months after the first dose to ensure adequate antibody titers and long-term protection. Primary immunization provides immunity within 30 days after 1 dose in more than 95% of those vaccinated.

Twinrix, a combined HAV and HBV vaccine, is available for people over 18 years of age. Immunization consists of 3 doses, given on a 0-, 1-, and 6-month schedule, the same

TABLE 43.9 Preventive Measures for Viral Hepatitis

Hepatitis A
General Measures
- Hand washing
- Proper personal hygiene
- Environmental sanitation
- Control and screening (signs, symptoms) of food handlers
- Serologic screening for those carrying virus
- Active immunization: HAV vaccine

Use of Immune Globulin
- Early administration (1–2 wk after exposure) to those exposed
- Prophylaxis for travelers to areas where hepatitis A is common if not vaccinated with HAV vaccine

Special Considerations for Health Care Personnel
- Wash hands after contact with a patient or removal of gloves
- Use infection control precautions

Hepatitis B and C
Percutaneous Transmission
- Screening of donated blood
- *HBV:* HBsAg
- *HCV:* Anti-HCV
- Use of disposable needles and syringes

Sexual Transmission
- Acute exposure: HBIG administration to sexual partner of HBsAg-positive person
- HBV vaccine series given to uninfected sexual partners
- Condoms used for sexual intercourse

General Measures
- Hand washing
- Avoid sharing toothbrushes and razors
- HBIG administration for one-time exposure (needle stick, contact of mucous membranes with infectious material)
- Active immunization: HBV vaccine

Special Considerations for Health Care Personnel
- Use infection control precautions
- Reduce contact with blood or blood-containing secretions
- Handle the blood of patients as potentially infective
- Dispose of needles properly
- Use needleless IV access devices when available

HAV, Hepatitis A virus; *HBIG,* hepatitis B immune globulin; *HBsAg,* hepatitis B surface antigen; *HBV,* hepatitis B virus; *HCV,* hepatitis C virus.

schedule as that used for the single HBV vaccine. Twinrix may be given to high-risk persons, including patients with chronic liver disease, users of illicit IV drugs, patients on hemodialysis, MSM, and people with clotting factor disorders who receive therapeutic blood products. The side effects of the vaccine are mild and usually limited to soreness and redness at the injection site.

Isolation is not needed for HAV infection. For a patient with HAV infection, use infection control precautions. Place the patient who is incontinent of stool or has poor personal hygiene in a private room.

Both hepatitis A vaccine and immune globulin (IG) are used to prevent HAV infection after exposure to an infected person *(postexposure prophylaxis).* The vaccine is used for preexposure prophylaxis. IG can be given either before or after exposure. IG gives temporary (1 to 2 months) passive immunity and is

effective for preventing hepatitis A if given within 2 weeks after exposure. IG is recommended for persons who do not have anti-HAV antibodies and were exposed by close (household, day care center) contact with persons who have HAV or foodborne exposure. Because patients with HAV are most infectious just before the onset of symptoms (the preicteric phase), those exposed through household contact or foodborne outbreaks should receive IG. Although IG may not prevent infection in all persons, it may lessen the illness to a subclinical infection. When hepatitis A occurs in a food handler, IG should be given to all other food handlers at the establishment. Patrons may need to receive IG.

Persons exposed to HAV who have received a dose of HAV vaccine more than 1 month previously or who have a history of laboratory-confirmed HAV infection do not need IG.

Hepatitis B. The best way to reduce HBV infection is to identify those at risk, screen them for HBV, and vaccinate those who are not infected. Teach those at high risk for contracting HBV to reduce risks by following good hygienic practices, including hand washing and using gloves when expecting contact with blood. Patients should not share razors, toothbrushes, and other personal items. Teach patients to use a condom for sexual intercourse. In addition, the partner should be vaccinated.

The HBV vaccine is the best means of prevention. The HBV vaccines (Recombivax HB, Engerix-B) contain HBsAg, which promotes the synthesis of specific antibodies directed against HBV. The vaccine is given in a series of 3 IM injections in the deltoid muscle. The second dose is given within 1 month of the first dose and the third dose within 6 months of the first. The vaccine is more than 95% effective. Minor reactions include transient fever and soreness at the injection site. The vaccine can be given in pregnancy.

The first dose of hepatitis B vaccine should be given at birth, with the vaccine series completed by age 6 to 18 months. Older children and adolescents who did not receive the hepatitis B vaccine should be vaccinated.[3] It is important to vaccinate adults who are in the at-risk groups and are not immune. Household members of the patient with HBV should be tested and vaccinated if they are HBsAg and antibody negative. Hepatitis vaccination is recommended for patients with chronic kidney disease before they start dialysis. Dialysis patients should routinely have their antibody titer levels checked to determine the need for revaccination.

For postexposure prophylaxis, the HBV vaccine series and hepatitis B immune globulin (HBIG) are given. HBIG has antibodies to HBV and confers temporary passive immunity. HBIG is prepared from plasma of donors with a high titer of anti-HBs. HBIG is recommended for postexposure prophylaxis in cases of needle stick, mucous membrane contact, or sexual exposure and for infants born to mothers who are positive for HBsAg. Ideally HBIG should be given within 24 hours of exposure. Giving antiviral therapy (e.g., tenofovir) to pregnant women in the third trimester with viral levels over 200,000 IU/mL can prevent the small risk for neonatal infection that may occur even with postnatal immunization and vaccination.

The Centers for Disease Control and Prevention (CDC) recommends following standard precautions for the patient with HBV (see Table 14.9). This includes using disposable needles and syringes and disposing of them in puncture-resistant units without recapping, bending, or breaking.

Hepatitis C. No vaccine is currently available for hepatitis C. Therefore it is important to identify those at high risk for contracting HCV and teach them how to reduce their risks. Primary measures to prevent HCV transmission include (1) screening of blood, organ, and tissue donors; (2) using infection control precautions; and (3) modifying high-risk behavior.

In the United States, there are many people who have undiagnosed hepatitis C. Therefore the CDC recommends universal screening for all persons born between 1945 and 1965.[4] The CDC does not recommend IG or antiviral agents (e.g., interferon) for postexposure prophylaxis for HCV infection (e.g., needle-stick exposure from an infected patient). After an acute exposure (e.g., needle stick), the person should have anti-HCV testing done. For the person exposed to HCV, baseline anti-HCV and ALT levels should be measured, with follow-up testing at 4 to 6 months. Testing for HCV RNA may be done after 4 to 10 weeks.[4]

◆ **Acute Care.** In patients with hepatitis, assess for the presence and degree of jaundice. In light-skinned persons, jaundice is usually seen first in the sclera of the eyes and later in the skin. In dark-skinned persons, jaundice is seen in the hard palate of the mouth and inner canthus of the eyes. The urine may have a dark brown or brownish red color from bilirubin excretion from the kidneys. Comfort measures to relieve itching, headache, and arthralgias are helpful.

? CHECK YOUR PRACTICE

You are caring for a 32-yr-old man who has acute hepatitis A. He has severe nausea and vomiting. He is admitted to the hospital for IV hydration and monitoring. The patient says, "I'm so weak and I feel like I'm going to vomit all the time. Isn't there something you can do to help me?"

• How would you handle this situation?
• What information and teaching will you give him?

Ensuring that the patient receives adequate nutrition is not always easy. The anorexia and distaste for food may cause nutritional problems. Assess the patient's tolerance of specific foods and eating pattern. Small, frequent meals may be preferable to 3 large ones and may help prevent nausea. Often a patient with hepatitis finds that anorexia is not as severe in the morning, so it is easier to eat a good breakfast than a large dinner. Include measures to stimulate the appetite, such as mouth care, antiemetics, and attractively served meals in pleasant surroundings, in the care plan. Drinking carbonated beverages and avoiding very hot or cold foods may help ease anorexia. Adequate fluid intake (2500 to 3000 mL/day) is important.

Rest is a critical factor in promoting hepatocyte regeneration. Assess the patient's response to the rest and activity plan. Modify it as needed based on liver function tests and symptoms.

Psychologic and emotional rest is as essential as physical rest. Limited activity may produce anxiety and restlessness in some patients. Diversion activities, such as reading and hobbies, may help a patient cope with the plan of care and ensure adequate rest.

◆ **Ambulatory Care.** Most patients with viral hepatitis are cared for at home. Assess the patient's knowledge of nutrition and provide any needed dietary teaching. Caution the patient about overexertion and the need to follow the HCP's advice about when to return to work. For patients who have fatigue, tell them to plan activities after periods of rest when energy levels are highest. Teach the patient and caregiver how to prevent

transmission to other family members and symptoms to report to the HCP.

Assess the patient for any signs of complications. These include bleeding tendencies with increasing prothrombin (PT) time values, manifestations of encephalopathy, sudden increase in weight and abdominal girth (may indicate fluid retention and/or ascites), bloody or tarry stools, vomiting of blood, or elevated liver enzymes.

Teach the patient to have regular follow-ups for at least 1 year after the diagnosis of hepatitis. Because relapses occur with hepatitis B and C, teach the patient the symptoms of recurrence and the need for follow-up evaluations. All patients with chronic HBV or HCV should avoid alcohol as it can accelerate disease progression.

Note that patients who are positive for HBsAg (chronic carrier status) or HCV antibody cannot be blood donors.

◆ **Evaluation**

Expected outcomes are that the patient with hepatitis will
• Maintain food and fluid intake adequate to meet nutritional needs
• Avoid alcohol and other hepatotoxic agents
• Show gradual increase in activity tolerance
• Perform daily activities with scheduled rest periods

DRUG- AND CHEMICAL-INDUCED LIVER DISEASES

Alcohol use is the most frequent cause of both acute and chronic liver disease. It can cause injury and necrosis of liver tissue. Alcohol use can cause a spectrum of manifestations, ranging from mild elevation in liver enzymes to acute alcoholic hepatitis. It may also cause advanced fibrosis and cirrhosis, which usually occurs after decades of excess alcohol use. Patients may have serious liver disease caused by another chronic disease (e.g., chronic HCV infection) in combination with alcoholic liver disease, which can compound the problem.

Acute alcoholic hepatitis is a syndrome of hepatomegaly, jaundice, elevated liver enzymes (AST, ALT, alkaline phosphate), and low-grade fever with possible ascites and prolonged PT time. These manifestations may improve if alcohol intake ceases.

Even at the end-stage of cirrhosis, abstinence can result in significant reversal in some patients. If liver function does not recover after abstaining from alcohol for 6 months or longer, liver transplantation may be considered.

Chemical hepatotoxicity is liver injury caused by exposure to certain compounds (e.g., carbon tetrachloride, gold compounds). Some agents can cause hepatotoxicity, while others may induce cholestasis, necrosis, or liver cancer. Fortunately, because of the decreased use of these agents, the incidence of chemically induced liver toxicity has decreased since the 1980s.

Drug-induced liver injury (DILI) can present similarly to other forms of liver disease. The main cause of DILI is antimicrobial agents, especially amoxicillin-clavulanate. Many drugs (prescription, OTC, diet and herbal supplements) can cause an increase in liver enzymes and, in severe cases, jaundice and acute liver failure. The pattern of injury depends on the drug causing the reaction. The most common cause of acute liver failure is acetaminophen. In patients with chemical hepatotoxicity or DILI, all drugs identified as the cause of liver injury should be stopped.[3]

💊 **DRUG ALERT Acetaminophen (Tylenol)**

- Safe when taken at recommended levels.
- Its prevalence in a variety of pain relievers, fever reducers, and cough medicines may mean that patients do not realize they are taking several drugs that all contain acetaminophen and overdose may occur.
- Acute liver failure can occur because of overdosing, either intentionally or unintentionally.
- The FDA has asked drug manufacturers to limit the strength of acetaminophen in prescription drug products to 325 mg per tablet, capsule, or other dosage unit, making these products safer.
- Combining the drug with alcoholic beverages increases the risk for liver damage.

AUTOIMMUNE, GENETIC, AND METABOLIC LIVER DISEASES

Autoimmune Hepatitis

Autoimmune hepatitis is a chronic inflammatory disorder of the liver in which the patient's own immune system attacks the liver. The cause of this condition is unknown. Autoimmune hepatitis is characterized by the presence of autoantibodies and high levels of serum immunoglobulins. It often occurs with other autoimmune diseases.

Most patients with autoimmune hepatitis are women. Laboratory tests useful in the diagnosis include antinuclear antibody (ANA), anti–smooth muscle antibody (ASMA), and antimitochondrial antibody (AMA) testing. A liver biopsy is often done to confirm the diagnosis and guide the treatment decision.[8]

Although autoimmune hepatitis can cause acute liver failure, the spectrum of disease is variable. Most patients develop chronic hepatitis. Untreated autoimmune hepatitis can progress to cirrhosis. Prednisone with or without azathioprine (Imuran) is the recommended treatment for active autoimmune hepatitis. Cyclosporine (Gengraf), tacrolimus (Prograf, FK506), budesonide (Entocort), methotrexate, mercaptopurine, and mycophenolate mofetil (CellCept) are options in those who do not respond to prednisone and azathioprine.[8] Mycophenolate is most often used for patients intolerant to azathioprine.

Wilson's Disease

Wilson's disease is an autosomal recessive disorder involving cellular copper transport. A defect in biliary excretion leads to accumulation of copper in the liver, causing progressive liver injury and cirrhosis. About 30 people per million have Wilson's disease. It usually appears between ages 5 and 35.[9]

Once cirrhosis occurs, copper leaks into the plasma, leading to multiple complications, including neurologic, hematologic, and renal disease. The hallmark of Wilson's disease is corneal Kayser-Fleischer rings. These are brownish red rings seen in the cornea near the limbus on eye examination. Low serum ceruloplasmin levels and markedly elevated copper concentrations from liver biopsy samples are present. Diagnosis is based on clinical findings, including the corneal rings and neurologic symptoms. First-degree relatives of patients with Wilson's disease should be screened for the disease.

The recommended first treatment of symptomatic patients or those with active disease is chelating agents, such as D-penicillamine (Cuprimine) or trientine (Syprine). They promote the excretion of urinary copper. Zinc acetate (Galzin), another therapy, interferes with copper absorption. Once we have reduced the amount of copper in the body, treatment focuses on preventing copper from building up again. Liver transplantation may be an option with severe liver damage.

Hemochromatosis

Hemochromatosis is a condition in which excess iron accumulates in the body. It is primarily caused by a genetic defect *(hereditary hemochromatosis)*. It also can be caused by liver disease and chronic blood transfusions used to treat thalassemia and sickle cell disease. Hemochromatosis is discussed in Chapter 30.

Primary Biliary Cholangitis

Primary biliary cholangitis (PBC), formerly known as primary biliary cirrhosis, is a chronic disease of the small bile ducts of the liver.[3] In PBC, there is a T cell–mediated attack of the small bile duct cells, resulting in loss of bile ducts and cholestasis (blockage of bile flow). Over time, this leads to liver fibrosis and cirrhosis.

Most patients diagnosed with PBC are middle-aged women. The disease is associated with other autoimmune disorders, such as rheumatoid arthritis, Sjögren's syndrome, and scleroderma. High serum alkaline phosphatase levels, AMAs, ANAs, and serum lipid levels occur in patients with PBC.

The goals of treatment are suppressing ongoing liver damage, preventing complications, and symptom management. Drugs for PBC include ursodeoxycholic acid (ursodiol [Actigall]), a bile acid, and obeticholic acid (Ocaliva). It decreases bile in the liver. Management focuses on preventing or minimizing malabsorption, skin disorders, such as itching and xanthomas (cholesterol deposits in the skin), hyperlipidemia, vitamin deficiencies, anemia, and fatigue. Cholestyramine is used to treat itching. Patients are monitored for progression to cirrhosis. Liver transplantation is an option for end-stage liver disease in patients with PBC.

Primary Sclerosing Cholangitis

Primary sclerosing cholangitis (PSC) is a disease of unknown cause characterized by chronic inflammation, fibrosis, and strictures (narrowing) of the medium and large bile ducts both inside and outside the liver.[3] Most patients with PSC also have ulcerative colitis or, less often, Crohn's disease. Complications of PSC can include cholangitis, cholestasis with jaundice, bile duct cancer, and cirrhosis.

Drug therapy has no proven benefit, although many HCPs use ursodiol. Treatment is directed at reducing the incidence of biliary complications and screening for bile duct and colorectal cancer, which is related to the high incidence of ulcerative colitis. Patients with advanced liver disease may need liver transplantation.

Nonalcoholic Fatty Liver Disease and Nonalcoholic Steatohepatitis

Nonalcoholic fatty liver disease (NAFLD) refers to a wide spectrum of liver diseases ranging from a fatty liver (steatosis) to nonalcoholic steatohepatitis (NASH) to cirrhosis. The term *nonalcoholic* is used because NAFLD and NASH occur in people who do not consume excess amounts of alcohol.

The fundamental characteristic of NAFLD is the accumulation of fatty infiltration in the hepatocytes. In NASH, the fat accumulation is associated with varying degrees of inflammation and fibrosis of the liver. If NASH is untreated, it can become a serious liver disease leading to cirrhosis, liver cancer, and liver failure.

Currently, NAFLD is increasing because of the growing number of people who are obese. NAFLD occurs in 90% to 95% of severely obese children and adults. NASH occurs in 8% to 20% of obese persons with NAFLD.[3] NAFLD should be considered in patients with risk factors, including obesity, diabetes, hyperlipidemia, and hypertension (also known as *metabolic syndrome*).

Elevated liver function tests (ALT, AST) are often the first sign of NAFLD. Ultrasound and CT scans can be used to diagnose NAFLD. Definitive diagnosis is by a liver biopsy.

There is no currently approved medication for NAFLD.[10] The goal of therapy is weight loss of at least 10% of body weight, if overweight or obese and exercise. Reducing risk factors, including hyperlipidemia, hypertension, and diabetes, is important.

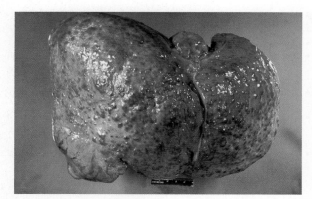

FIG. 43.4 Cirrhosis that developed from alcohol use. The characteristic diffuse nodularity of the surface is due to the combination of regeneration and scarring of the liver. (From Kumar V, Abbas AK, Aster JC, et al: *Robbins and Cotran pathologic basis of disease*, ed 8, Philadelphia, 2010, Saunders.)

🌐 PROMOTING HEALTH EQUITY
Liver, Pancreas, and Gallbladder Disorders

Hepatitis
- Hepatitis C has a higher incidence among blacks than whites.
- Hepatitis B has a higher incidence among Asian Americans and Pacific Islanders.
- Deaths caused by hepatitis C are more common in blacks.

Liver and Pancreatic Cancer
- Primary liver cancer has a highest incidence in Hispanics, followed by blacks and whites.
- Pancreatic cancer occurs more often among blacks than whites.

Gallbladder Disease
- Whites and Native Americans have a higher incidence of gallbladder disease than blacks or Asian Americans

---

CIRRHOSIS

Cirrhosis is the end stage of liver disease. Cirrhosis is characterized by extensive degeneration and destruction of the liver cells. This results in the replacement of liver tissue by fibrosis (scar tissue) and regenerative nodules that occur from the liver's attempt to repair itself (Fig. 43.4). The development of cirrhosis usually happens after decades of chronic liver disease.

Etiology and Pathophysiology

Any chronic liver disease, including disease from excess alcohol use and NAFLD, can cause cirrhosis. The most common causes of cirrhosis in the United States are chronic hepatitis C infection and alcohol-induced liver disease. In patients with alcohol-induced liver disease, controversy exists as to the degree to which malnutrition adds to the damage caused by the alcohol itself. Some cases of nutrition-related cirrhosis have resulted from extreme dieting, malabsorption, and obesity. Environmental factors and genetic predisposition may lead to the development of cirrhosis, regardless of dietary or alcohol intake.

Around 20% of patients with chronic hepatitis C and 25% of those with chronic hepatitis B develop cirrhosis.[3] Chronic inflammation and cell necrosis from viral hepatitis can result in progressive fibrosis and cirrhosis. Chronic hepatitis combined with alcohol use has a synergistic effect in accelerating liver damage.

Biliary causes of cirrhosis include primary biliary cholangitis (PBC) and primary sclerosing cholangitis (PSC). Both are described earlier in this chapter.

Cardiac cirrhosis includes a spectrum of hepatic problems that result from long-standing, severe, right-sided heart failure. It causes hepatic venous congestion, parenchymal damage, necrosis of liver cells, and fibrosis over time. Treatment is aimed at managing the patient's underlying heart failure.

In cirrhosis, the liver cells try to regenerate, but the regenerative process is disorganized. This results in abnormal blood vessel and bile duct architecture. The overgrowth of new and fibrous connective tissue distorts the liver's normal lobular structure, resulting in lobules of irregular size and shape with impeded blood flow. Eventually, irregular and disorganized liver regeneration, poor cellular nutrition, and hypoxia (from inadequate blood flow and scar tissue) result in decreased liver function.

Clinical Manifestations

Early Manifestations. Patients may be unaware of their liver condition because there are few symptoms in early-stage disease. If a person does have symptoms, these may include fatigue or an enlarged liver. Blood tests may show normal liver function (compensated cirrhosis). The diagnosis of cirrhosis is often made later when a patient presents with symptoms of more advanced liver disease.

Late Manifestations. Late manifestations result from liver failure and portal hypertension (Fig. 43.5). Jaundice, peripheral edema, and ascites develop gradually. Other late manifestations include skin lesions, hematologic problems, endocrine problems, and peripheral neuropathies (Fig. 43.6). In the advanced stages, the liver becomes small and nodular. Liver function is dramatically impaired.

Jaundice. Jaundice results from decreased ability to conjugate and excrete bilirubin into the small intestines (Table 43.3). There is an overgrowth of connective tissue in the liver, which compresses the bile ducts and leads to an obstruction. This results in an increase in the bilirubin in the vascular system, and jaundice occurs. The jaundice may be minimal or severe, depending on the degree of liver damage.

Skin Lesions. Various skin manifestations often occur with cirrhosis. **Spider angiomas** (*telangiectasia* or *spider nevi*) are small, dilated blood vessels with a bright red center point and spiderlike branches. They occur on the nose, cheeks, upper trunk, neck, and shoulders. *Palmar erythema* (a red area that blanches with pressure) occurs on the palms of the hands. Both lesions are due to an increase in circulating estrogen due to the damaged liver's inability to metabolize steroid hormones.

PATHOPHYSIOLOGY MAP

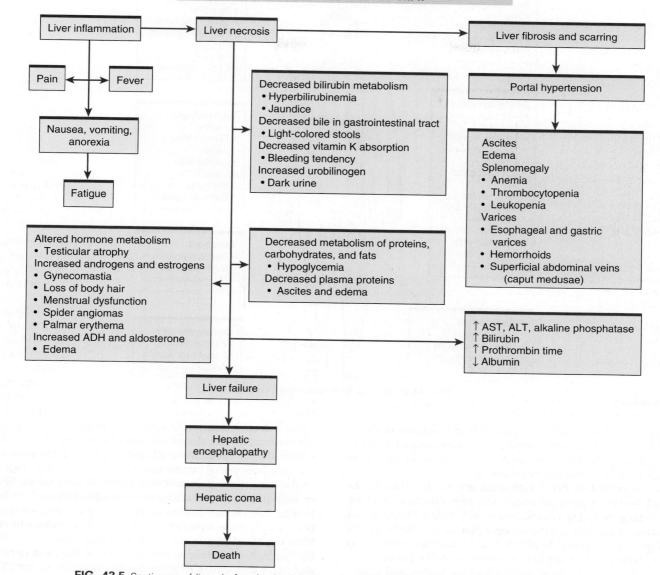

FIG. 43.5 Continuum of liver dysfunction in cirrhosis and resulting manifestations. (Adapted from Huether SE, McCance KL: *Understanding pathophysiology*, ed 5, St Louis, 2012, Mosby.)

Hematologic Problems. Hematologic problems include thrombocytopenia, leukopenia, anemia, and coagulation disorders. We think thrombocytopenia, leukopenia, and anemia are caused by the splenomegaly that results from backup of blood from the portal vein into the spleen (portal hypertension). Overactivity of the enlarged spleen results in increased removal of blood cells from circulation. Anemia can result from inadequate red blood cell (RBC) production and survival, poor diet, poor absorption of folic acid, and bleeding from varices.

The coagulation problems result from the liver's inability to make prothrombin and other factors essential for blood clotting. Manifestations of coagulation problems (bleeding tendencies) include epistaxis, purpura, petechiae, easy bruising, gingival bleeding, and heavy menstrual bleeding.

Endocrine Problems. The liver plays a vital role in the metabolism of hormones, such as estrogen and testosterone. In men with cirrhosis, gynecomastia (benign growth of the glandular tissue of the male breast), loss of axillary and pubic hair, testicular atrophy, and impotence with loss of libido may occur because of increased estrogen levels. Younger women with cirrhosis may develop amenorrhea, and older women may have vaginal bleeding. If the liver does not metabolize aldosterone properly, it can lead to hyperaldosteronism with sodium and water retention and potassium loss.

Peripheral Neuropathy. Peripheral neuropathy is a common finding in alcoholic cirrhosis. It is probably due to a dietary deficiency of thiamine, folic acid, and cobalamin. The neuropathy usually results in sensory and motor symptoms, but sensory symptoms may predominate.

Complications

Major complications of cirrhosis are portal hypertension, esophageal and gastric varices, peripheral edema, abdominal ascites, hepatic encephalopathy (mental status changes, including

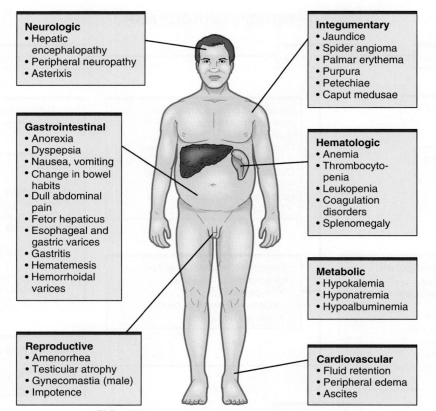

Neurologic
• Hepatic encephalopathy
• Peripheral neuropathy
• Asterixis

Integumentary
• Jaundice
• Spider angioma
• Palmar erythema
• Purpura
• Petechiae
• Caput medusae

Gastrointestinal
• Anorexia
• Dyspepsia
• Nausea, vomiting
• Change in bowel habits
• Dull abdominal pain
• Fetor hepaticus
• Esophageal and gastric varices
• Gastritis
• Hematemesis
• Hemorrhoidal varices

Hematologic
• Anemia
• Thrombocytopenia
• Leukopenia
• Coagulation disorders
• Splenomegaly

Metabolic
• Hypokalemia
• Hyponatremia
• Hypoalbuminemia

Reproductive
• Amenorrhea
• Testicular atrophy
• Gynecomastia (male)
• Impotence

Cardiovascular
• Fluid retention
• Peripheral edema
• Ascites

FIG. 43.6 Systemic manifestations of liver cirrhosis.

coma), and hepatorenal syndrome. Patients who are cirrhotic but who have no obvious complications have *compensated cirrhosis*. Those who have 1 or more complications of their liver disease have *decompensated cirrhosis*.

Portal Hypertension and Esophageal and Gastric Varices. In patients with cirrhosis, the liver undergoes structural changes. These changes lead to obstruction of blood flow in and out of the liver. This results in increased pressure within the liver's circulatory system (portal hypertension). Portal hypertension is characterized by increased venous pressure in the portal circulation, splenomegaly, large collateral veins, ascites, and gastric and esophageal varices.

As a way of reducing pressure, the body develops alternate circulatory pathways, referred to as *collateral circulation*. The collateral channels often form in the lower esophagus, anterior abdominal wall, parietal peritoneum, and rectum. Varicosities (distended veins) develop in areas where the collateral and systemic circulations communicate, resulting in esophageal and gastric varices, *caput medusae* (ring of varices around the umbilicus), and hemorrhoids.

Esophageal varices are a complex of tortuous, enlarged veins at the lower end of the esophagus. Gastric varices are found in the upper part of the stomach. These varices are fragile and do not tolerate high pressure, so they can bleed easily. Large varices are more likely to bleed. Esophageal varices can cause variceal hemorrhages with a 5-year mortality of 20%.[11] The patient may present with melena or hematemesis. Ruptured esophageal varices are the most life-threatening complication of cirrhosis and considered a medical emergency.

Peripheral Edema and Ascites. Peripheral edema occurs in the lower extremities and presacral area. Peripheral edema can occur before, concurrently with, or after ascites development. Edema results from decreased colloidal oncotic pressure from impaired liver synthesis of albumin and increased portacaval pressure from portal hypertension.

Ascites is the accumulation of serous fluid in the peritoneal or abdominal cavity. It is a common manifestation of cirrhosis. Several mechanisms lead to ascites. One mechanism of ascites occurs with portal hypertension, which causes proteins to shift from the blood vessels into the lymph space (Fig. 43.7). When the lymphatic system is unable to carry off the excess proteins and water, they leak into the peritoneal cavity. The osmotic pressure of the proteins pulls more fluid into the peritoneal cavity (Table 43.10).

A second mechanism of ascites formation is hypoalbuminemia resulting from the liver's decreased ability to synthesize albumin. The hypoalbuminemia results in decreased colloidal oncotic pressure.

A third mechanism of ascites is hyperaldosteronism, which occurs when the damaged hepatocytes metabolize aldosterone. The increased aldosterone level causes increased sodium reabsorption by the renal tubules. Sodium retention, combined with an increase in antidiuretic hormone in blood, leads to further water retention and edema. Edema decreases intravascular volume with decreased renal blood flow and glomerular filtration.

Ascites is manifested by abdominal distention with weight gain (Fig. 43.8). If the ascites is severe, the increase in abdominal pressure from the fluid accumulation may cause eversion of the umbilicus. Abdominal striae with distended abdominal wall veins may be present. Patients may have signs of dehydration (e.g., dry tongue and skin, sunken eyeballs, muscle weakness) and a decrease in urine output. Hypokalemia is common. It is

PATHOPHYSIOLOGY MAP

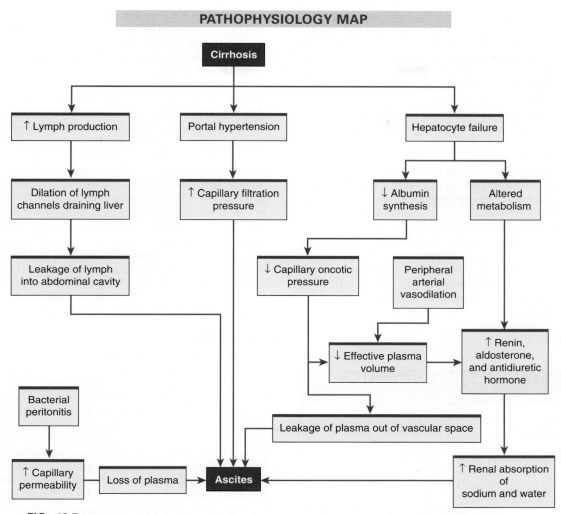

FIG. 43.7 Mechanisms for development of ascites. (Adapted from Huether SE, McCance KL: *Understanding pathophysiology*, ed 5, St Louis, 2012, Mosby.)

TABLE 43.10 Factors Involved in Ascites

Factor	Mechanism
Decreased serum colloidal oncotic pressure	Impaired liver synthesis of albumin Loss of albumin into peritoneal cavity
Hyperaldosteronism	↑ Aldosterone secretion stimulated by ↓ renal blood flow ↓ Liver catabolism of circulating aldosterone
Impaired water excretion	↑ Antidiuretic hormone stimulated by ↓ renal blood flow
Increased flow of hepatic lymph	Leaking of protein-rich lymph from surface of cirrhotic liver
Portal hypertension	↑ Resistance of blood flow through liver

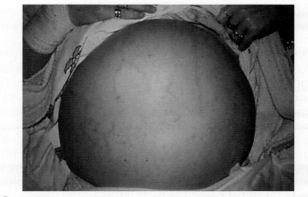

FIG. 43.8 Gross ascites. (From Butcher GP: *Gastroenterology: An illustrated colour text,* London, 2004, Churchill Livingstone.)

due to an excessive loss of potassium caused by hyperaldosteronism. Low potassium levels can also result from diuretic therapy used to treat the ascites.

Because of decreased immune function associated with cirrhosis, patients with ascites are at risk for *spontaneous bacterial peritonitis* (SBP). SBP is a bacterial infection of the ascitic fluid. In SBP, bacteria normally found in the intestines move into the peritoneal space. The bacteria most often responsible

for the infection are a gram-negative enteric pathogen, such as *Escherichia coli*. SBP is a common complication of hospitalized patients with cirrhosis and ascites. Worsening vasodilation contributes to the development of SBP.[11]

Hepatic Encephalopathy. Hepatic encephalopathy is a neuro-psychiatric manifestation of liver disease. The pathogenesis is multifactorial. It includes the neurotoxic effects of ammonia, abnormal neurotransmission, astrocyte swelling, and inflammatory cytokines. A major source of ammonia is the bacterial and enzymatic deamination of amino acids in the intestines. The ammonia that results from deamination normally goes to the liver via the portal circulation and is converted to urea. The kidneys then excrete urea. When blood is shunted past the liver via the collateral vessels or the liver is so damaged that it is unable to convert ammonia to urea, the levels of ammonia in the systemic circulation increase. The ammonia crosses the blood-brain barrier and produces neurologic toxic manifestations.

Factors that increase ammonia in the circulation may precipitate hepatic encephalopathy (Table 43.11). Hepatic encephalopathy can occur after placement of a transjugular intrahepatic portosystemic shunt (TIPS). TIPS reduces portal hypertension by diverting blood flow around the liver. (TIPS is discussed on p. 986.)

Manifestations include changes in neurologic and mental responsiveness; impaired consciousness; and inappropriate behavior, ranging from sleep problems to trouble concentrating to deep coma. Changes may occur (1) suddenly from an increase in ammonia in response to bleeding varices or infection or (2) gradually as blood ammonia levels slowly increase. We often use a grading system to classify the stages of hepatic encephalopathy (Table 43.12).

A characteristic manifestation is asterixis (flapping tremors). This may take several forms, with the most common involving the arms and hands. When asked to hold the arms and hands stretched out, the patient is unable to hold this position and performs a series of rapid flexion and extension movements of the hands.

Impairments in writing involve difficulty in moving the pen or pencil from left to right and *apraxia* (inability to construct simple figures). Other signs include hyperventilation, hypothermia, tongue fasciculations, and grimacing and grasping reflexes. *Fetor hepaticus* (musty, sweet odor of the patient's breath) occurs in some patients. This odor is from the accumulation of digestive by-products that the liver is unable to degrade.

Hepatorenal Syndrome. Hepatorenal syndrome is a type of renal failure with azotemia, oliguria, and intractable ascites. In this syndrome, the kidneys have no structural abnormality. The cause is complex. The final common pathway is likely to be portal hypertension along with liver decompensation, resulting in splanchnic and systemic vasodilation and decreased arterial blood volume. As a result, renal vasoconstriction occurs, and renal failure follows. Liver transplantation can reverse renal failure. In the patient with cirrhosis, hepatorenal syndrome can follow diuretic therapy, GI hemorrhage, or paracentesis.

Diagnostic Studies

Patients with cirrhosis have abnormalities in most of their liver function tests. Enzyme levels, including alkaline phosphatase, AST, ALT, and γ-glutamyl transpeptidase (GGT), are initially high due to their release from inflamed liver cells. However, in end-stage liver disease, AST and ALT levels may be normal due to the death and loss of hepatocytes. Patients will also have low serum total protein and albumin, increased serum bilirubin (Table 43.3) and globulin levels, and prolonged PT time. Low cholesterol levels reflect the changes in fat metabolism.

Although a liver ultrasound may be able to detect cirrhosis, it is not a reliable diagnostic test for cirrhosis. Ultrasound elastography (Fibroscan) is a noninvasive test used to quantify the degree of liver fibrosis. A liver biopsy, which may be done to identify liver cell changes, is the gold standard for a definitive diagnosis of cirrhosis.

Interprofessional Care

The goal of treatment is to slow the progression of cirrhosis and to prevent and treat any complications. Interprofessional care measures are listed in Table 43.13. Management of specific problems associated with cirrhosis is described next.

Ascites. Management of ascites focuses on sodium restriction, diuretics, and fluid removal.[12] Patients may need to limit sodium intake to 2 g/day. Very low sodium intake can result in reduced

TABLE 43.11 Factors Precipitating Hepatic Encephalopathy

Factor	Mechanism
Cerebral depressants (e.g., opioids)	↓ Metabolism by liver, causing ↑ drug levels and cerebral depression
Constipation	↑ Production of ammonia from bacterial action on feces
Dehydration	Potentiates ammonia toxicity
GI hemorrhage	↑ Ammonia in GI tract
Hypokalemia	Potassium needed by brain to metabolize ammonia
Hypovolemia	↑ Blood ammonia because of hepatic hypoxia Impaired cerebral, hepatic, and renal function because of ↓ blood flow
↑ Metabolism	↑ Workload of liver
Infection	↑ Metabolic rate and cerebral sensitivity to toxins
Metabolic alkalosis	Facilitation of transport of ammonia across blood-brain barrier Increased renal production of ammonia
Paracentesis	Loss of sodium and potassium ions ↓ Blood volume
Uremia (renal failure)	Retention of nitrogenous metabolites

TABLE 43.12 Grading Scale for Hepatic Encephalopathy

Grade	Level of Consciousness	Intellectual Function	Neurologic Findings
0	Normal to minimal change	Subtle to no change in personality, behavior, memory, concentration	Asterixis absent May have abnormal psychometric test
1	Lack of awareness, sleep disturbance	Short attention span, impaired computational skills, personality change, decrease in short-term memory, mild confusion, depression	Incoordination, asterixis may be absent
2	Lethargy, drowsiness	Disoriented to time, inappropriate behavior, deficits in executive function	Asterixis, abnormal reflexes
3	Somnolent, arousable	Disoriented to time, loss of meaningful conversation, marked confusion, incomprehensible speech	Asterixis, abnormal reflexes
4	Not arousable, comatose	Absent	Decerebrate May be responsive to painful stimuli

TABLE 43.13 Interprofessional Care

Cirrhosis of the Liver

Diagnostic Assessment

- History and physical examination
- Liver function tests (ALT, AST, alkaline phosphatase, bilirubin, γ-glutamyl transpeptidase [GGT])
- Serum albumin
- Serum electrolytes
- PT time
- Complete blood count
- Liver biopsy (percutaneous needle)
- Liver ultrasound (e.g., FibroScan)
- Upper endoscopy (esophagogastroduodenoscopy)
- CT scan, MRI

Management

Conservative Therapy

- Rest
- B-complex vitamins
- Avoiding alcohol
- Minimizing or avoiding aspirin, acetaminophen, and NSAIDs

Ascites

- Low-sodium diet
- Diuretics
- Paracentesis (if needed)

Esophageal and Gastric Varices

- Endoscopic band ligation or sclerotherapy
- Balloon tamponade
- Transjugular intrahepatic portosystemic shunt (TIPS)

Drug Therapy

- Nonselective β-blocker (e.g., propranolol [Inderal])
- octreotide (Sandostatin)
- vasopressin

Hepatic Encephalopathy

Drug Therapy

- Antibiotics (rifaximin [Xifaxan])
- lactulose

---

nutritional intake and malnutrition. The patient is usually not on restricted fluids unless severe ascites develops. When caring for patients with ascites, accurately monitor fluid and electrolyte balance. An albumin infusion may help maintain intravascular volume and adequate urine output by increasing plasma colloid oncotic pressure.

Diuretic therapy is an important part of management. Often a combination of drugs that work at multiple sites of the nephron is more effective than a single agent. Spironolactone (Aldactone) is an effective diuretic, even in patients with severe ascites. Spironolactone is also an antagonist of aldosterone and is potassium sparing. Other potassium-sparing diuretics include amiloride (Midamor) and triamterene (Dyrenium). A high-potency loop diuretic (e.g., furosemide [Lasix]), is often used in combination with a potassium-sparing drug.

Tolvaptan (Samsca), a vasopressin-receptor antagonist, can correct hyponatremia, a common problem in patients with cirrhosis. It causes an increase in water excretion, resulting in an increase in serum sodium concentration.

A **paracentesis** is a sterile procedure in which a catheter is used to withdraw fluid from the abdominal cavity.

This procedure can diagnose a medical condition or relieve pain, pressure, or difficulty breathing. In the patient with cirrhosis, this procedure is done for the person with impaired respiration or abdominal discomfort caused by severe ascites who does not respond to diuretic therapy. It is only a temporary measure of palliation because the fluid tends to reaccumulate rapidly.[12]

TIPS (discussed later in this section) is used to treat ascites that does not respond to diuretics. A peritoneovenous shunt is a surgical procedure that provides continuous reinfusion of ascitic fluid into the venous system. It is rarely used due to the high rate of complications.

Esophageal and Gastric Varices. The main therapeutic goal for esophageal and gastric varices is to prevent bleeding and variceal rupture by reducing portal pressure. The patient who has esophageal and/or gastric varices should avoid alcohol, aspirin, and nonsteroidal antiinflammatory drugs (NSAIDs).

All patients with cirrhosis should have an upper endoscopy (esophagogastroduodenoscopy [EGD]) to screen for varices. Patients with varices at risk for bleeding are often started on a nonselective β-blocker (nadolol [Corgard] or propranolol [Inderal]) to reduce the risk of hemorrhage. β-Blockers decrease high portal pressure, which decreases the risk for rupture.

When variceal bleeding occurs, the first step is to stabilize the patient and manage the airway. IV therapy is started and may include giving blood products. Care then moves toward stopping the bleeding, identifying the source, and applying interventions to prevent further bleeding. Management that involves a combination of drug therapy and endoscopic therapy is more successful than either approach alone.

Drug therapy for bleeding varices may include the somatostatin analog octreotide (Sandostatin) or vasopressin. Both produce vasoconstriction of the splanchnic arterial bed, decrease portal blood flow, and decrease portal hypertension. Currently, octreotide is used more often because it has fewer side effects than vasopressin.

At the time of endoscopy, band ligation or sclerotherapy of varices may be used to prevent rebleeding. Endoscopic variceal ligation (EVL, or "banding") is done by placing a small rubber band (elastic O-ring) around the base of the *varix* (enlarged vein). Sclerotherapy involves injecting a sclerosing solution into the swollen veins through a needle placed through the endoscope.

Balloon tamponade is an option when endoscopy does not control acute esophageal or gastric variceal hemorrhage. Balloon tamponade controls the hemorrhage by mechanical compression of the varices. Several types of tubes are available. The Sengstaken-Blakemore tube has 2 balloons, gastric and esophageal, with 3 lumens: 1 for the gastric balloon, 1 for the esophageal balloon, and 1 for gastric aspiration. Two other types of balloons are the Minnesota tube (a modified Sengstaken-Blakemore tube with an esophageal suction port above the esophageal balloon) and the Linton-Nachlas tube.

! SAFETY ALERT Balloon Tamponade

- Label each lumen to avoid confusion.
- Secure the tube to prevent movement of the tube that could result in occlusion of the airway.
- Deflate balloons for 5 minutes every 8 to 12 hr per agency policy to prevent tissue necrosis.

Supportive measures during an acute variceal bleed include giving fresh frozen plasma and packed RBCs, vitamin K, and proton pump inhibitors (PPIs; e.g., pantoprazole). Lactulose and rifaximin (Xifaxan) may be given to prevent hepatic encephalopathy from breakdown of blood and the release of ammonia in the intestine. Antibiotics are given to prevent bacterial infection.

Because of the high incidence of recurrent bleeding with each bleeding episode, continued therapy is necessary. Long-term management of patients who have had an episode of bleeding includes nonselective β-blockers, repeated band ligation of the varices, and portosystemic shunts in patients who develop recurrent bleeding.

Shunting Procedures. Nonsurgical and surgical methods of shunting blood away from the varices are available. Shunting procedures tend to be done more after a second major bleeding episode than during an initial bleeding episode. *Transjugular intrahepatic portosystemic shunt (TIPS)* is a nonsurgical procedure in which a tract (shunt) between the systemic and portal venous systems is created to redirect portal blood flow. A catheter is placed in the jugular vein and then threaded through the superior and inferior vena cava to the hepatic vein. The wall of the hepatic vein is punctured, and the catheter is directed to the portal vein. Stents are positioned along the passageway, overlapping in the liver tissue and extending into both veins.

This procedure reduces portal venous pressure and decompresses the varices, thus controlling bleeding. TIPS does not interfere with a future liver transplantation. Limitations of TIPS include the increased risk for hepatic encephalopathy (toxin-containing blood bypasses the liver) and stenosis of the stent.

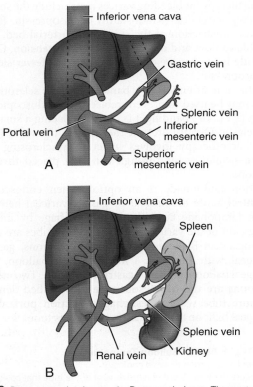

FIG. 43.9 Portosystemic shunts. **A,** Portacaval shunt. The portal vein is anastomosed to the inferior vena cava, diverting blood from the portal vein to the systemic circulation. **B,** Distal splenorenal shunt. The splenic vein is anastomosed to the renal vein. The portal venous flow stays intact while esophageal varices are selectively decompressed. (The short gastric veins are decompressed.) The spleen conducts blood from the high pressure of the esophageal and gastric varices to the low-pressure renal vein.

TIPS is contraindicated in patients with severe hepatic encephalopathy, liver cancer, severe hepatorenal syndrome, and portal vein thrombosis.

Various surgical shunting procedures can decrease portal hypertension by diverting some of the portal blood flow while allowing adequate liver perfusion. Currently, the surgical shunts most often used are the portacaval shunt and the distal splenorenal shunt (Fig. 43.9).

Hepatic Encephalopathy. The goal of management of hepatic encephalopathy is to reduce ammonia formation. Lactulose, a drug that traps ammonia in the gut, reduces ammonia formation in the intestines. We can give it orally, as an enema, or through a nasogastric (NG) tube. The drug's laxative effect expels the ammonia from the colon. Antibiotics, such as rifaximin, also may be given, especially in patients who do not respond to lactulose. Regular and frequent bowel movements are necessary to minimize the ammonia buildup, so use measures to prevent constipation.

Control of hepatic encephalopathy also involves treatment of precipitating causes (Table 43.10). This includes lowering dietary protein intake, preventing and controlling GI bleeds, and, in the case of a bleed, removing the blood promptly from the GI tract to decrease the protein accumulation in the gut.

Drug Therapy. There is no specific drug therapy for cirrhosis. However, several drugs are used to treat symptoms and complications of advanced liver disease (Table 43.14).

Nutritional Therapy. The diet for the patient who has cirrhosis without complications is high in calories (3000 cal/day). It is high in carbohydrate content with moderate to low levels of fat. Protein restriction may be needed for some patients right after a severe flare of symptoms (i.e., episodic hepatic encephalopathy). However, protein restriction is rarely needed in patients with cirrhosis and persistent hepatic encephalopathy. For many, malnutrition is a more serious clinical problem than hepatic encephalopathy.[3]

TABLE 43.14 **Drug Therapy**	
Cirrhosis	
Drug	**Mechanism of Action**
Diuretics	
furosemide (Lasix)	Acts on distal tubule and loop of Henle to ↓ reabsorption of sodium and water
spironolactone (Aldactone)	Blocks actions of aldosterone, potassium sparing
Other Therapy	
lactulose	Acidifies feces in bowel and traps ammonia, causing its elimination in feces
magnesium sulfate	Corrects hypomagnesemia that may occur with liver dysfunction
nadolol (Corgard) propranolol (Inderal)	Reduces portal venous pressure and esophageal variceal bleeding
neomycin sulfate rifaximin (Xifaxan)	↓ Bacterial flora, thus reducing ammonia formation
octreotide (Sandostatin) vasopressin	Hemostasis and control of bleeding in esophageal and gastric varices, constricts splanchnic arterial bed
PPIs (e.g., pantoprazole [Protonix])	↓ Gastric acidity
Vitamin K	Corrects clotting abnormalities from decreased vitamin K levels

A patient with alcoholic cirrhosis often has protein-calorie malnutrition. Oral nutritional supplements containing protein from branched-chain amino acids that are metabolized by the muscles may be needed. These supplements provide protein that the liver can more easily metabolize. Parenteral nutrition or EN are used with severe cases of malnutrition (see Chapter 39).

The patient with ascites and edema is placed on a low-sodium diet. The degree of sodium restriction depends on the patient's condition. Teach the patient and caregiver about the degree of restriction. Table salt is a well-known source of sodium. Other foods high in sodium include canned soups and vegetables, many frozen foods, salted snacks (e.g., potato chips), nuts, smoked meats and fish, crackers, breads, baking soda, olives, pickles, ketchup, and beer. Teach the patient to read labels for sodium content (see Fig. 34.5). Offer suggestions about how to make the diet more palatable. Seasonings, like garlic, parsley, onion, lemon juice, and spices may make food more appetizing. Collaborate with a dietitian about dietary strategies.

❖ NURSING MANAGEMENT: CIRRHOSIS

◆ Nursing Assessment

Subjective and objective data that should be obtained from a person with cirrhosis are outlined in Table 43.15.

◆ Nursing Diagnoses

Nursing diagnoses for the patient with cirrhosis may include:
- Impaired nutritional status
- Ineffective tissue perfusion
- Activity intolerance
- Fluid imbalance

Additional information on nursing diagnoses and interventions for the patient with cirrhosis is presented in eNursing Care Plan 43.2 available on the website for this chapter.

◆ Planning

The overall goals are that the patient with cirrhosis will (1) have relief of discomfort, (2) have minimal to no complications (ascites, esophageal varices, hepatic encephalopathy), and (3) return to as normal a lifestyle as possible.

◆ Nursing Implementation

◆ **Health Promotion.** Common risk factors for cirrhosis include alcohol use, malnutrition, viral hepatitis, biliary obstruction, obesity, and right-sided heart failure. Prevention and early treatment of cirrhosis focus on reducing or eliminating these risk factors. Urge patients to abstain from alcohol. Encourage those with chronic alcohol use to enroll in support programs that help patients maintain sobriety. (The treatment of alcohol use is discussed in Chapter 10.)

Adequate nutrition, especially for the person who uses alcohol and other people at risk for cirrhosis, is essential to promote normal liver regeneration. Identify and treat acute hepatitis early so that it does not progress to chronic hepatitis and cirrhosis. Bariatric surgery for morbidly obese persons reduces the incidence of NAFLD.

◆ **Acute Care.** Nursing care for the patient with cirrhosis focuses on conserving the patient's strength while maintaining muscle strength and tone. When the patient needs complete bed rest, implement measures to prevent pneumonia, thromboembolic problems, and pressure injuries. Modify the activity and rest

---

TABLE 43.15 Nursing Assessment
Cirrhosis

Subjective Data
Important Health Information

Past health history: Viral, toxic, or idiopathic hepatitis. Alcohol use, metabolic syndrome, chronic biliary obstruction and infection, severe right-sided heart failure

Medications: Adverse reaction to any medication. Use of anticoagulants, aspirin, NSAIDs, acetaminophen

Functional Health Patterns

Health perception–health management: Chronic alcohol use. Weakness, fatigue
Nutritional-metabolic: Anorexia, weight loss, dyspepsia, nausea and vomiting, gingival bleeding. Dry, yellow skin, bruising
Elimination: Dark urine, decreased urine output, light-colored or black stools, flatulence, change in bowel habits.
Cognitive-perceptual: Dull, right upper quadrant or epigastric pain. Numbness, tingling of extremities. Itching
Sexuality-reproductive: Impotence, amenorrhea

Objective Data
General

Fever, cachexia, wasting of extremities

Integumentary

Icteric sclera, jaundice, petechiae, ecchymoses, spider angiomas, palmar erythema, alopecia, loss of axillary and pubic hair, peripheral edema

Respiratory

Shallow, rapid respirations. Epistaxis

Gastrointestinal

Abdominal distention, ascites, distended abdominal wall veins, palpable liver and spleen, foul breath. Hematemesis. Black, tarry stools. Hemorrhoids

Neurologic

Altered mentation, asterixis

Reproductive

Gynecomastia, testicular atrophy, and impotence (men); loss of libido (men and women); amenorrhea or heavy menstrual bleeding (women)

Possible Diagnostic Findings

Anemia, thrombocytopenia; leukopenia. ↓ Serum albumin, potassium. Abnormal liver function studies. ↑ INR, ↓ platelets, ↑ ammonia, ↑ bilirubin levels. Abnormal abdominal ultrasound, CT, or MRI

---

schedule according to signs of improvement (e.g., decreasing jaundice, improvement in liver function studies).

Anorexia, nausea and vomiting, pressure from ascites, and poor eating habits all interfere with adequate intake of nutrients. Oral hygiene before meals may improve the patient's taste sensation. Make between-meal snacks available so that the patient can eat them at times when food is best tolerated. Offer preferred foods whenever possible. Explain the reason for any dietary restrictions to the patient and caregiver.

Nursing assessment and care should include the patient's physical status. Is jaundice present? Where is it seen—sclera, skin, hard palate? What is the progression of jaundice? If the pruritis accompanies jaundice, use measures to relieve itching. Cholestyramine or hydroxyzine (Atarax) may help. Other

TABLE 43.16 Nursing Management
Care of the Patient Undergoing Paracentesis

Preprocedure

- Have the patient void or insert an indwelling catheter.
- Obtain baseline vital signs and pulse oximetry. Weigh patient, inspect and palpate abdomen, and assess abdominal girth. Assess bladder for distention and determine last voiding.
- Assess baseline laboratory values (e.g., CBC, electrolytes, coagulation studies).
- Give any sedation or analgesia, if ordered.
- Teach patient to remain immobile during the procedure.
- Help the patient to a high-Fowler (sitting) position with feet on the floor.

Postprocedure

- Perform assessment and compare to baseline: vital signs, pulse oximetry, abdominal girth, abdominal pain. Note any signs of hypovolemia.
- Have the patient sit on the side of the bed or place in high-Fowler's position.
- Label and send the fluid for laboratory analysis.
- Check the dressing for bleeding and/or leakage of ascitic fluid.
- Give IV fluid and/or albumin as ordered.
- Measure any drainage and describe the collected fluid.
- Reweigh the patient and monitor intake and output.
- Maintain bedrest per agency protocol.

measures to relieve itching include baking soda or moisturizing bath oils (Alpha Keri), lotions containing calamine, antihistamines, soft or old linens, and control of the temperature (not too hot and not too cold). Keep the patient's nails short and clean. Teach patients to rub with their knuckles rather than scratch with their nails when they cannot resist scratching.

Note the color of urine and stools and assess for improvement or normalization of color. When jaundice is present, the urine is often dark brown, and the stool is gray or tan.

Edema and ascites require your assessment and intervention. Accurate calculation and recording of intake and output, daily weights, and measurements of extremities and abdominal girth help in the ongoing assessment of the location and extent of the edema. Mark the abdomen with a permanent marker so that you measure the girth at the same location each time.

Immediately before a paracentesis, have the patient void to prevent puncturing of the bladder during the procedure. Other nursing care associated with a paracentesis is outlined in Table 43.16.

Dyspnea is a frequent problem for the patient with severe ascites and can lead to pleural effusions. A semi-Fowler's or Fowler's position allows for maximal respiratory efficiency. Use pillows to support the arms and chest to increase the patient's comfort and ability to breathe.

Meticulous skin care is essential because the edematous tissues are prone to breakdown. Use an alternating-air pressure mattress or other special mattress. A turning schedule (minimum of every 2 hours) must be adhered to rigidly. Support the abdomen with pillows. If the abdomen is taut, cleanse it gently. The patient will tend to avoid moving because of abdominal discomfort and dyspnea. Range-of-motion exercises are helpful. Implement measures such as coughing and deep breathing to prevent respiratory problems. The lower extremities may be elevated. If scrotal edema is present, a scrotal support gives some comfort.

When the patient is taking diuretics, monitor serum sodium, potassium, chloride, and bicarbonate levels. Monitor renal function (blood urea nitrogen [BUN], serum creatinine) routinely and with any change in the diuretic dosage. Observe for signs of fluid and electrolyte imbalance, especially hypokalemia. Dysrhythmias, hypotension, tachycardia, and generalized muscle weakness may occur with hypokalemia. Muscle cramping, weakness, lethargy, and confusion may be present with hyponatremia from water excess.

Observe for and provide nursing care for any hematologic problems. These include bleeding tendencies, anemia, and increased susceptibility to infection.

Assess the patient's response to altered body image resulting from jaundice, spider angiomas, palmar erythema, ascites, and gynecomastia. The patient may have anxiety and embarrassment about these changes. Explain these phenomena and be a supportive listener. Provide nursing care with concern and encouragement to help the patient maintain his or her self-esteem.

? CHECK YOUR PRACTICE

You are caring for a 69-yr-old male patient with advanced cirrhosis who just underwent banding for esophageal varices. The UAP tells you that the patient's BP is 80/60 mm Hg and he is hard to arouse.
- What is your concern?
- What would you do?

Bleeding Varices. If the patient has esophageal or gastric varices, observe for any signs of bleeding from the varices, such as hematemesis and melena. If hematemesis occurs, assess the patient for hemorrhage, call the HCP, and be ready to transfer the patient to the endoscopy suite and/or assist with equipment to control the bleeding. Maintain the patient's airway. Patients with bleeding varices are usually admitted to the intensive care unit (ICU).

Balloon tamponade is an option for patients who have bleeding that is unresponsive to band ligation or sclerotherapy. When balloon tamponade is used, explain to the patient and caregiver the use of the tube and how the balloon is inserted. Check the balloons for patency. It is usually the HCP's responsibility to insert the tube by either the nose or mouth. Then the gastric balloon is inflated with 250 mL of air, and the tube is retracted until resistance (lower esophageal sphincter) is felt. The tube is secured by placing a piece of sponge or foam rubber at the nostrils (nasal cuff). For continued bleeding, the esophageal balloon is then inflated. A sphygmomanometer is used to measure and maintain the desired pressure at 20 to 40 mm Hg. An x-ray verifies the balloon's position.

Nursing care includes monitoring for complications of rupture or erosion of the esophagus, regurgitation and aspiration of gastric contents, and occlusion of the airway by the balloon. If the gastric balloon breaks or is deflated, the esophageal balloon will slip upward, obstructing the airway and causing asphyxiation. If this happens, cut the tube or deflate the esophageal balloon. Keep scissors at the bedside. Minimize regurgitation by oral and pharyngeal suctioning and by keeping the patient in a semi-Fowler's position.

The patient is unable to swallow saliva because the inflated esophageal balloon occludes the esophagus. Encourage the patient to expectorate and provide an emesis basin and tissues. Frequent oral and nasal care offers relief from the taste of blood and irritation from mouth breathing.

ETHICAL/LEGAL DILEMMAS
Rationing

Situation

T.H., a 43-yr-old female patient with cirrhosis of the liver, is frequently admitted to the hospital. She has been told that her continued alcohol use will inevitably lead to her death. She now has GI bleeding and needs blood transfusions. She has a rare blood type that is hard to match. Should you ask for an ethics consultation?

Ethical/Legal Points for Consideration

- *Rationing*, or the controlled distribution of scarce resources, is a difficult ethical problem. The needs of an individual patient or group of patients are weighed against the needs of many patients, who may have a greater chance of recovery, and the availability of the necessary resources.
- Health interests can supersede the interests or rights of a person. For example, in anticipation of an anthrax attack, the government could confiscate all relevant antibiotics and restrict their use to treat the disease.
- Two individual rights that must be considered regarding rationing are the (1) constitutional right to privacy and (2) right to consent to or refuse medical procedures and therapy.
- The competent adult is the only person who may consent to or refuse treatment for his or her health care problems.
- If T.H. consents to a blood transfusion, an intervening party may be allowed to refuse that treatment only given substantial intervening circumstances and not as a threat to compel adherent future behavior.
- If involved parties cannot reach an agreement, legal intervention by way of a court order may become necessary.

Discussion Questions

1. Do you think patients with diseases that have a behavioral component, like substance use, deserve aggressive treatment?
2. Would you request an ethics committee consultation in T.H.'s case?

Hepatic Encephalopathy. Nursing care of the patient with hepatic encephalopathy focuses on maintaining a safe environment, sustaining life, and assisting with measures to reduce the formation of ammonia. Patients with hepatic encephalopathy may be confused and at risk for falls or other injuries. Assess the patient's (1) level of responsiveness (e.g., reflexes, pupillary reactions, orientation), (2) sensory and motor abnormalities (e.g., hyperreflexia, asterixis, motor coordination), (3) fluid and electrolyte imbalances, (4) acid-base imbalances, and (5) response to treatment measures.

Assess the neurologic status, including an exact description of the patient's behavior, at least every 2 hours. Plan your care of the patient based on the severity of the encephalopathy. In patients with altered levels of consciousness or whose airway may become compromised, have emergency equipment readily available. Any GI bleeding may worsen encephalopathy. Institute measures to prevent falls or injuries.

. Control factors known to precipitate encephalopathy as much as possible, including anything that may cause constipation (e.g., dehydration, opioid drugs). Measures to minimize constipation are important to reduce ammonia production. Give drugs, laxatives, and enemas as ordered. Encourage fluids, if not contraindicated. Assess the patient taking lactulose for diarrhea and excessive fluid and electrolyte losses.

◆ **Ambulatory Care.** The patient with cirrhosis may be faced with a prolonged course and the chance of life-threatening problems and complications. The patient and caregiver need to understand the importance of continual health care and medical supervision.

TABLE 43.17 Patient & Caregiver Teaching
Cirrhosis

When teaching the patient and caregiver about management of cirrhosis, do the following:

1. Explain that cirrhosis is a chronic illness and requires continual health care.
2. Teach the symptoms of complications and when to seek medical attention to enable prompt treatment.
3. Teach the patient to avoid potentially hepatotoxic over-the-counter drugs, because the diseased liver is unable to metabolize them.
4. Encourage abstinence from alcohol because continued use increases the rate of liver disease progression and risk for liver complications.
5. Teach the patient with esophageal or gastric varices to avoid aspirin and NSAIDs to prevent hemorrhage.
6. Teach the patient with portal hypertension and varices that straining at stool, coughing, sneezing, and retching and vomiting may increase the risk for variceal hemorrhage.

Supportive measures include proper diet, rest, avoiding potentially hepatotoxic OTC drugs, such as acetaminophen in high doses, and abstaining from alcohol. Abstinence from alcohol is important and results in improvement in most patients. However, some patients find abstinence extremely hard and need emotional support. Explore your own attitude toward the patient whose cirrhosis is from chronic alcohol use. Always provide care without being condescending or judgmental. Treat patients with respect and concern for their well-being (see Chapter 10).

Cirrhosis is a chronic disease, and people can live many years with symptoms and complications from cirrhosis. The patient is affected not only physically but also psychologically, socially, and economically. Major lifestyle changes may be needed, especially if chronic alcohol use is the primary cause. Provide information about community support programs, such as Alcoholics Anonymous, for help with chronic alcohol use.

Teach the patient and caregiver about complications and when to seek medical attention (Table 43.17). Include instructions about adequate rest periods, how to detect early signs of complications, skin care, drug therapy side effects, observation for bleeding, and protection from infection.

Referral to a community or home health nurse may help ensure patient adherence to prescribed therapy. Home care for the patient with cirrhosis focuses on helping the patient with activities of daily living while maintaining the highest level of wellness possible.

◆ **Evaluation**

Expected outcomes are that the patient with cirrhosis will
- Maintain food and fluid intake adequate to meet nutritional needs
- Maintain skin integrity with relief of edema and itching
- Have normal fluid and electrolyte balance
- Acknowledge and get treatment for a substance use problem

ACUTE LIVER FAILURE

Acute liver failure, or *fulminant hepatic failure*, is a potentially life-threatening clinical syndrome.[3] It is characterized by a rapid onset of severe liver dysfunction in someone with no history of liver disease. It is often accompanied by hepatic encephalopathy.

The most common cause of acute liver failure is drugs, usually acetaminophen. Other drugs that can cause acute liver failure include isoniazid, sulfa-containing drugs, and anticonvulsants. Drugs can cause hepatocyte damage by disrupting essential intracellular processes or causing an accumulation of toxic metabolic products. Other causes can include viral hepatitis, especially HBV. Hepatitis A is a less common cause.

Outcomes depend on the cause. Cerebral edema, cerebellar herniation, and brainstem compression are the most common causes of death. Treatment of cerebral edema is described in Chapter 56. Liver transplantation is associated with a significant survival benefit in patients with a low probability of spontaneous recovery.

Clinical Manifestations and Diagnostic Studies

Manifestations of acute liver failure include jaundice, coagulation abnormalities, and encephalopathy. Changes in cognitive function are often the first clinical sign. Patients are susceptible to a wide variety of complications, including cerebral edema, renal failure, hypoglycemia, metabolic acidosis, sepsis, and multiorgan failure.

Serum bilirubin is high, and the PT time is prolonged. Liver enzyme levels (AST, ALT) are often markedly increased. Other laboratory tests include blood chemistries (especially glucose, since hypoglycemia may be present and need correction), complete blood count (CBC), acetaminophen level, screening for other drugs and toxins, viral hepatitis serology (especially HAV and HBV), serum ceruloplasmin (enzyme synthesized in liver) and α_1-antitrypsin levels, iron levels, ammonia levels, and autoantibodies (ANAs and ASMAs).

CT or MRI can provide information about the liver size and contour, presence of ascites or tumors, and patency of the blood vessels.

◆ Interprofessional and Nursing Care

Since acute liver failure may progress rapidly, with hour-by-hour changes in consciousness, the patient is usually transferred to the ICU once the diagnosis is made. Planning for transfer to a transplant center should begin in patients with grade 1 or 2 encephalopathy because they may worsen rapidly. Early transfer is important because the risks involved with patient transport may increase or even prevent transfer if stage 3 or 4 encephalopathy develops (Table 43.12).

Renal failure is a frequent complication of liver failure. It may be due to dehydration, hepatorenal syndrome, or acute tubular necrosis. The frequency of renal failure may be even greater with acetaminophen overdose or other toxins with which direct renal toxicity occurs. Although few patients die of renal failure alone, it often increases the mortality risk and may worsen the prognosis. Protect renal function by maintaining adequate fluid balance, avoiding nephrotoxic agents (e.g., aminoglycosides, NSAIDs), and promptly identifying and treating infection.

Monitoring and management of hemodynamic and renal function, as well as glucose, electrolytes, and acid-base status, are critical. Conduct frequent neurologic evaluations for signs of increased intracranial pressure. Position the patient with the head elevated at 30 degrees. Avoid excessive patient stimulation. Maneuvers that cause straining or Valsalva-like movements may increase intracranial pressure (ICP). ICP monitoring is discussed in Chapter 56.

Assess the patient regularly for baseline level of consciousness and orientation and report any changes to the HCP. Avoid the use of any sedatives due to their effects on mental status. The effects can be confused with worsening encephalopathy. Only minimal doses of benzodiazepines should be used due to their delayed metabolism by the failing liver. Closely observe the patient to prevent injuries and pad bedrails to avoid injury from possible seizures. Monitor intake and output for renal function and provide good skin and oral care to avoid breakdown and infection.

Changes in level of consciousness may compromise nutritional intake. Many patients receive vitamin supplementation. Other factors, such as coagulation problems, may influence whether EN is started. An NG tube may be irritating to the nasal and esophageal mucosa and cause bleeding.

LIVER CANCER

Primary liver cancer starts in the liver. The most common types of liver cancer are hepatocellular carcinoma (HCC) (75% of cases) and intrahepatic cholangiocarcinoma (bile duct cancer). In 2018 there were about 40,710 cases of HCC and 28,920 HCC deaths in the United States. Worldwide liver cancer is the fifth most common cancer and second common cause of cancer death.[13]

Liver cancer is the most common cause of death in patients with cirrhosis. Cirrhosis caused by hepatitis C is the most common cause of HCC in the United States, followed by NAFLD. About 2% of patient with cirrhosis develop liver cancer each year.

In primary liver cancer, lesions may be singular or numerous and nodular or diffusely spread over the entire liver. Some tumors infiltrate other organs, such as the gallbladder, or move into the peritoneum or the diaphragm. Primary liver cancer often metastasizes to the lung.

Metastatic cancer in the liver is more common than primary liver cancer (Fig. 43.10). The liver is a common site of metastatic

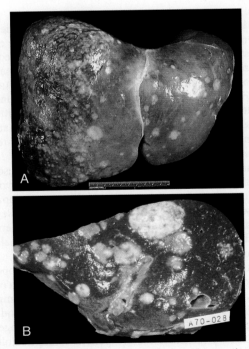

FIG. 43.10 Multiple hepatic metastases from a primary colon cancer. **A,** Gross specimen showing outside of liver. **B,** Liver section showing metastatic lesions. (*A,* From Kumar V, Abbas AK, Fausto N: *Robbins and Cotran pathologic basis of disease,* ed 7, Philadelphia, 2005, Saunders. *B,* From Kumar V, Abbas AK, Aster JC, et al: *Robbins and Cotran pathologic basis of disease,* ed 8, Philadelphia, 2010, Saunders.)

growth because of its high rate of blood flow and extensive capillary network. Cancer cells in other parts of the body are often carried to the liver via the portal circulation.

Clinical Manifestations and Diagnostic Studies

The manifestations of early liver cancer can be absent or subtle. They are often a result of the underlying cirrhosis rather than from the actual liver tumor(s). The patient may present with hepatomegaly, splenomegaly, fatigue, peripheral edema, ascites, and other complications from portal hypertension. In late stages, patients will often have fever/chills, jaundice, anorexia, weight loss, palpable mass, and right upper quadrant pain.

Diagnostic and screening for liver cancer are ultrasound, CT, and MRI. Recent advancements in MRI scanning have allowed for accurate diagnosis of liver cancers without the need for a percutaneous biopsy.[13] Sometimes, a biopsy may be done when the results of diagnostic imaging studies are inconclusive or tissue is needed to guide treatment. Risks of a biopsy include bleeding and potential tumor cell seeding along the needle tract. Therefore a biopsy is generally not done unless a diagnosis cannot be made by CT or MRI and clinical presentation. Serum α-fetoprotein (AFP) levels combined with ultrasound have a high rate of detection of early-stage HCC. (AFP is discussed in Chapter 15.)

❖ Interprofessional and Nursing Care

Prevention of liver cancer focuses on identifying and treating chronic hepatitis B and C viral infections. Treatment of chronic alcohol use may lower the risk for liver cancer. Screening for at-risk patients (e.g., those with cirrhosis) usually involves a combination of serum AFP and CT, MRI, or ultrasound imaging of the liver.

Treatment of liver cancer depends primarily on the stage of cancer: number, size, and location of tumors; involvement of any blood vessels; patient age and overall health; and extent of underlying liver disease. Surgical liver resection (partial hepatectomy) offers the best chance for a cure. However, only about 15% of people have enough healthy liver tissue for this to be an option. The underlying cirrhosis and portal hypertension often compromise liver function and may cause liver failure after surgery. Furthermore, many patients are diagnosed at an advanced stage of cancer when surgery is not an option. For those patients who have early-stage liver cancer and impaired liver function, liver transplantation offers a good prognosis.

Nonsurgical therapies include percutaneous ablation, chemoembolization, radioembolization, and sorafenib (Nexavar) oral therapy.[13] In ablation, a thin needle is inserted into the core of the tumor. Then various substances can be injected (ethanol, acetic acid) and the temperature of the probe (radiofrequency, microwave, cryotherapy) can be altered to destroy the tumor. This procedure can be done percutaneously, laparoscopically, or through an open incision. It is typically limited by the number, size, and location of liver tumors. It is usually offered to patients with early-stage liver cancer. Although complications are not common, they can include infection, bleeding, dysrhythmias, and skin burn.

In patients with multinodular HCC or intermediate-stage liver cancer, embolization of the tumors is another intervention. There are 2 options typically used: transarterial chemoembolization (TACE) or transarterial radioembolization (TARE). TACE and TARE are minimally invasive procedures done by interventional radiologists. A catheter is placed via the femoral artery or radial artery and advanced to the arterial blood supply of the tumors in the liver. Either a chemotherapy drug (TACE) or radioactive beads (TARE) along with embolizing agents are then injected into the arteries of the tumor(s) region. TACE works by shutting off the blood supply to the tumors and exposing liver tumor cells to the chemotherapy agent. TARE destroys the tumor(s) by slowly releasing radioactive material directly to the site of the tumor. It can take up to 3 months for complete results.

In patients with advanced HCC, sorafenib (Nexavar) is typically the first-line treatment. It is a kinase inhibitor, a type of targeted therapy, that blocks certain proteins (kinases) that play a role in tumor growth and cancer progression (see Table 15.13). This drug has the potential to slow tumor progression and prolong life.

Nursing interventions focus on keeping the patient as comfortable as possible. Since these patients have the same problems as any patient with advanced liver disease, the nursing interventions discussed for cirrhosis of the liver apply to these patients (see p. 987).

Although the prognosis for patients with liver cancer is poor, it is improving with early screening and surveillance programs for those with chronic hepatitis and/or cirrhosis. The cancer often progresses rapidly, with patients having complications from the advancing cancer and declining liver function. Without treatment, death may occur within 6 to 12 months, most often from hepatic encephalopathy or massive blood loss from GI bleeding.

LIVER TRANSPLANTATION

Liver transplantation has become an option for many people with end-stage liver disease or localized HCC. Liver disease related to chronic viral hepatitis is the leading reason for liver transplantation. Other reasons include congenital biliary abnormalities (biliary atresia), inborn errors of metabolism, sclerosing cholangitis, acute liver failure, and chronic end-stage liver disease. In 2018, 11,514 patients were listed for a liver transplant in the United States with 8250 patients undergoing a transplant.[3]

Liver transplant candidates must go through a rigorous transplant evaluation prior to being placed on the transplant list. This is done to confirm the diagnosis of end-stage liver disease and to assess for other co-morbid conditions (e.g., cardiovascular disease, chronic kidney disease) that may affect the patient's surgical outcome. The evaluation includes physical examination, laboratory tests (CBC, liver function tests), cardiac and pulmonary evaluations, endoscopy, CT scan, and psychologic testing. Potential recipients receive counseling about cigarette smoking and alcohol abstinence. Contraindications for liver transplant include severe extrahepatic disease, advanced HCC or other cancer, ongoing drug or chronic alcohol use, and inability to understand or adhere with the rigorous posttransplant care.

Liver transplantation is done using both deceased (cadaver) and live donor livers. The live donor liver transplant was first developed for children whose parents wanted to serve as donors. Today, some liver transplant centers are performing live liver transplant procedures for adults. In this procedure, the living person donates a part of his or her liver to another. However, live liver donation poses potential risks to the donor, including biliary problems, hepatic artery thrombosis, wound infection, postoperative ileus, and pneumothorax.

Because of the limited number of donor livers, when a liver becomes available for transplant it may be divided into 2 parts (split liver transplant) and implanted into 2 recipients. The decision to use a split donor liver is based on the donor's size and health. The recipients of the split liver generally are smaller than the donor. The success rate associated with split liver transplantation is somewhat lower than that associated with whole organ transplantation.

Postoperative complications of liver transplant include bleeding, infection, and rejection. However, the liver is subject to a less aggressive immunologic attack than other organs, like the kidneys. Transplants and immunosuppressive therapy are discussed in Chapter 13.

Immunosuppressive therapy generally involves a combination of corticosteroids, a calcineurin inhibitor (cyclosporine or tacrolimus), and an antiproliferative agent (e.g., azathioprine). Tacrolimus is superior to cyclosporine in liver transplantation. Standard immunosuppressive regimens often change over the course of the recipient's life. Corticosteroid withdrawal may be done and is relatively safe to do in liver transplant recipients.

About 80% of patients live more than 5 years after liver transplant. Long-term survival depends on the cause of liver failure (e.g., localized HCC, chronic hepatitis B or C, biliary disease). Patients who have liver disease from hepatitis B or C often have reinfection of the transplanted liver. For patients with hepatitis B, treatment after surgery with IV HBIG and a nucleoside or nucleotide analog (used to treat HBV infection) has reduced the rates of reinfection of the transplanted liver. For patients with HCV, treatment with the new direct-acting antivirals (DAAs) that can cure HCV infection has provided the opportunity to use HCV-positive liver grafts. The need for liver transplant may decrease in the HCV population. Research is ongoing to decide if DAAs should be started before or after transplant.

The patient who had a liver transplant needs highly skilled nursing care, either in an ICU or other specialized unit. Postoperative nursing care includes assessing neurologic status; monitoring for signs of hemorrhage; preventing pulmonary complications; electrolyte levels, and urine output; and monitoring for manifestations of infection and rejection. Common respiratory problems are pneumonia, atelectasis, and pleural effusions. To prevent these complications, encourage the patient to cough, deep breathe, use incentive spirometry, and frequently reposition. Measure the drainage from the Jackson-Pratt drain, NG tube, and T tube and note the color and consistency of the drainage at regular intervals.

The first 2 months after surgery are critical for monitoring for infection. Causes of infection can be viral, fungal, or bacterial. Fever may be the only sign of infection. Adhering to the medication regimen can be hard, especially in the beginning. Emotional support and teaching for the patient and caregiver are essential to the success of the patient with a liver transplant.

👤 Gerontologic Considerations: Liver Disease in the Older Adult

The incidence of liver disease increases with age. The liver's size and metabolic breakdown of drugs decrease, and hepatobiliary function is changed. The liver has a decreased capacity to respond to injury. This especially applies to regeneration after injury. Transplanted livers take longer to regenerate in the older adult compared with the younger adult.

Older adults are particularly vulnerable to drug-induced liver injury. This is due to several factors, including the increased use of multiple prescription and OTC drugs, which can lead to drug interactions and potential drug toxicity. Age-related decreases in liver function result in decreased drug metabolism and a decreased ability to recover from drug-induced injury.

A growing number of older adults have chronic hepatitis C and the resulting cirrhosis. Antibodies to HCV and elevated liver enzymes may be found during a routine health assessment in asymptomatic patients.

Lifetime health behaviors may influence the development of chronic liver disease in the older adult. Chronic alcohol use and obesity can contribute to cirrhosis, fatty liver inflammation (NASH), and liver failure. Because of many older adults' concomitant cardiovascular and lung diseases and possible anticoagulant therapy, variceal bleeding can cause significant morbidity and mortality and needs immediate medical intervention. In the older adult with liver disease, hepatic encephalopathy is sometimes misdiagnosed as dementia and often overlooked.

Because older adults tend to have more co-morbid conditions, transplantation may have more risks for complications. Therefore older adults may not be good candidates for liver transplants.

▌DISORDERS OF THE PANCREAS

ACUTE PANCREATITIS

Acute pancreatitis is an acute inflammation of the pancreas. Spillage of pancreatic enzymes into surrounding pancreatic tissue causes autodigestion and severe pain. The degree of inflammation varies from mild edema to severe hemorrhagic necrosis.

Etiology and Pathophysiology

Many factors can cause injury to the pancreas. In the United States, the most common cause is gallbladder disease (gallstones), which is more common in women. The second most common cause is chronic alcohol use. This is more common in men.

Other less common causes include drug reactions, pancreatic cancer, and hypertriglyceridemia (serum levels over 1000 mg/dL).[14] Biliary sludge and microlithiasis, which is a mix of cholesterol crystals and calcium salts, can be present in patients with acute pancreatitis.

The most common pathogenic mechanism in acute pancreatitis is autodigestion of the pancreas (Fig. 43.11). The causative factors injure pancreatic cells or activate the pancreatic enzymes in the pancreas rather than in the intestine. This may be due to reflux of bile acids into the pancreatic ducts through an open or distended sphincter of Oddi. This reflux may be caused by blockage created by gallstones. Obstruction of pancreatic ducts results in pancreatic ischemia.

The exact mechanism by which chronic alcohol use predisposes a person to pancreatitis is not known. We think that alcohol increases the production of digestive enzymes in the pancreas.

The pathophysiologic involvement of acute pancreatitis is classified as either *mild pancreatitis* (also known as *edematous* or *interstitial pancreatitis*) or *severe pancreatitis* (also called *necrotizing pancreatitis*) (Fig. 43.12). In severe pancreatitis, about half the patients have permanent decreases in pancreatic endocrine and exocrine function. Patients with severe pancreatitis are at high risk for developing pancreatic necrosis, organ failure, and septic complications, resulting in an overall fatality rate of 5%.[14]

PATHOPHYSIOLOGY MAP

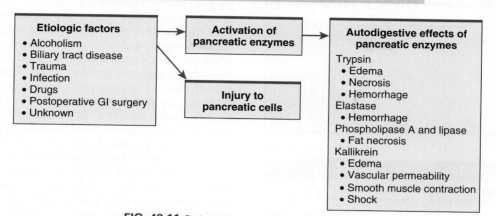

Etiologic factors
- Alcoholism
- Biliary tract disease
- Trauma
- Infection
- Drugs
- Postoperative GI surgery
- Unknown

Activation of pancreatic enzymes

Injury to pancreatic cells

Autodigestive effects of pancreatic enzymes
Trypsin
- Edema
- Necrosis
- Hemorrhage
Elastase
- Hemorrhage
Phospholipase A and lipase
- Fat necrosis
Kallikrein
- Edema
- Vascular permeability
- Smooth muscle contraction
- Shock

FIG. 43.11 Pathogenic process of acute pancreatitis.

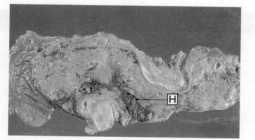

FIG. 43.12 In acute pancreatitis, the pancreas appears edematous and is often hemorrhagic *(H)*. (From Stevens A, Lowe J: *Pathology: Illustrated review in colour,* ed 2, London, 2000, Mosby.)

Clinical Manifestations

Abdominal pain is the main manifestation of acute pancreatitis. The pain is due to distention of the pancreas, peritoneal irritation, and obstruction of the biliary tract. The pain is usually in the left upper quadrant, but it may be mid-epigastric. It often radiates to the back due to the retroperitoneal location of the pancreas. The pain has a sudden onset. It is described as severe, deep, piercing, and continuous or steady. Eating worsens the pain. It often starts when the patient is recumbent. Pain is not relieved by vomiting and may be accompanied by flushing, cyanosis, and dyspnea. The patient may assume various positions involving flexion of the spine to try to relieve the severe pain.

Other manifestations include nausea and vomiting, low-grade fever, leukocytosis, hypotension, tachycardia, and jaundice. Abdominal tenderness with muscle guarding is common.

Bowel sounds may be decreased or absent. Paralytic ileus may occur and causes marked abdominal distention. The lungs are often involved with crackles present. Intravascular damage from circulating trypsin (a proteolytic enzyme) may cause areas of cyanosis or greenish to yellow-brown discoloration of the abdominal wall. Other areas of ecchymoses are the flanks (*Grey Turner' spots* or *sign,* a bluish flank discoloration) and the periumbilical area (*Cullen's sign,* a bluish periumbilical discoloration). These result from seepage of bloodstained exudate from the pancreas and may occur in severe cases.

Shock may occur from hemorrhage into the pancreas, toxemia from the activated pancreatic enzymes, or hypovolemia due to fluid shift into the retroperitoneal space (massive fluid shifts).

Complications

The severity of acute pancreatitis depends on the extent of pancreatic destruction. Acute pancreatitis can be life threatening. Some patients recover completely, others have recurring attacks, and others develop chronic pancreatitis.

Two significant local complications of acute pancreatitis are pseudocyst and abscess. A *pancreatic pseudocyst* is an accumulation of fluid, pancreatic enzymes, tissue debris, and inflammatory exudates surrounded by a wall next to the pancreas. Manifestations are abdominal pain, palpable epigastric mass, nausea, vomiting, and anorexia. The serum amylase level is often high. CT, MRI, and endoscopic ultrasound (EUS) may detect a pseudocyst. The cysts usually resolve spontaneously within a few weeks but may perforate, causing peritonitis or rupture into the stomach or the duodenum. Treatment options include surgical drainage, percutaneous catheter placement and drainage, and endoscopic drainage.

When a pseudocyst gets infected, a *pancreatic abscess* results from extensive necrosis in the pancreas. It may rupture or perforate into adjacent organs. Manifestations of an abscess include upper abdominal pain, abdominal mass, high fever, and leukocytosis. Pancreatic abscesses need prompt surgical drainage to prevent sepsis.

The main systemic complications of acute pancreatitis are cardiovascular and pulmonary (pleural effusion, atelectasis, pneumonia, and acute respiratory distress syndrome [ARDS]). The pulmonary complications are due to the passage of exudate containing pancreatic enzymes from the peritoneal cavity through transdiaphragmatic lymph channels. Enzyme-induced inflammation of the diaphragm occurs, with the result being atelectasis caused by reduced diaphragm movement. Trypsin can activate prothrombin and plasminogen, increasing the patient's risk for intravascular thrombi, pulmonary emboli, and DIC. Hypotension can occur from fluid shifts and sepsis.

Tetany, which can be caused by hypocalcemia, is a sign of severe disease. It is due in part to the combining of calcium and fatty acids during fat necrosis. We do not understand the exact mechanisms of how or why hypocalcemia occurs. Patients with severe acute pancreatitis are at risk for abdominal compartment syndrome from intraabdominal hypertension and edema.

Diagnostic Studies

The primary diagnostic tests for acute pancreatitis are serum amylase and lipase (Table 43.18). The serum amylase level is

TABLE 43.18 Diagnostic Findings
Acute Pancreatitis

Laboratory Test	Abnormal Finding
Serum amylase	↑
Serum lipase	↑
Urinary amylase	↑
Blood glucose	↑
Serum calcium	↓
Serum triglycerides	↑

TABLE 43.19 Interprofessional Care
Acute Pancreatitis

Diagnostic Assessment
- History and physical examination
- Serum amylase and lipase
- Blood glucose
- Serum calcium
- Serum triglycerides
- Flat plate of the abdomen
- Abdominal ultrasound
- Endoscopic ultrasound (EUS)
- MRCP
- ERCP
- Contrast-enhanced CT of pancreas
- Chest x-ray

Management
- NPO with NG tube to suction
- Albumin (if shock present)
- IV calcium gluconate (10%) (if tetany present)
- Lactated Ringer's solution

Drug Therapy
- Pain medication (e.g., morphine)
- PPI (e.g., omeprazole [Prilosec])
- Antibiotics (if necrotizing pancreatitis)

usually high early and stays high for 24 to 72 hours. Serum lipase level, which is high in acute pancreatitis, is an important test because other disorders (e.g., mumps, cerebral trauma, renal transplantation) may increase serum amylase levels. Other serum findings include an increase in liver enzymes, triglycerides, glucose, and bilirubin and a decrease in calcium.

Diagnostic evaluation of acute pancreatitis is directed at determining the cause. An abdominal ultrasound, x-ray, or contrast-enhanced CT scan may identify pancreatic problems. CT scan is the best imaging test for pancreatitis and related complications, such as pseudocysts and abscesses. ERCP is an option (although ERCP can cause acute pancreatitis), along with EUS, magnetic resonance cholangiopancreatography (MRCP), and angiography. Chest x-rays may show atelectasis and pleural effusions.

Interprofessional Care

Goals of interprofessional care for acute pancreatitis include (1) relief of pain, (2) prevention or alleviation of shock, (3) reduction of pancreatic secretions, (4) correction of fluid and electrolyte imbalances, (5) prevention or treatment of infections, and (6) removal of the precipitating cause, if possible (Table 43.19).
Conservative Therapy. Treatment of acute pancreatitis is focused on supportive care, including aggressive hydration, pain

management, management of metabolic complications, and minimization of pancreatic stimulation. Treatment and control of pain are very important. IV opioid analgesics may be given. Pain medications may be combined with an antispasmodic agent. Atropine and other anticholinergic drugs are avoided when paralytic ileus is present because they can decrease GI mobility, making the problem worse. Other drugs that relax smooth muscles (spasmolytics), such as nitroglycerin or papaverine, may be used. Supplemental O_2 is used to maintain O_2 saturation greater than 95%. In patients with severe pancreatitis, serum glucose levels are closely monitored for hyperglycemia.

If shock is present, blood volume replacements are used. Plasma or plasma volume expanders, such as dextran or albumin, may be given. Lactated Ringer's solution or other electrolyte solutions can correct fluid and electrolyte problems. Central venous pressure readings can help determine fluid replacement requirements. Vasoactive drugs, such as dopamine, may be needed to increase systemic vascular resistance in those with hypotension.

❓ CHECK YOUR PRACTICE

You are a nurse working in the emergency department. Your patient is a 45-yr-old woman who reports acute abdominal pain in her left upper quadrant. She is diagnosed with acute pancreatitis. She tells you, "I've been waiting in this emergency room for 8 hours and I'm starving. Why can't I get something to eat? My pain is so bad; I think it's becoming worse because you won't give me food."
- How would you respond?
- What information and teaching would you give her?

It is important to reduce or suppress pancreatic enzymes to decrease stimulation of the pancreas and allow it to rest. This is achieved in several ways. First, the patient is NPO. Second, NG suction may be used to reduce vomiting and gastric distention and to prevent gastric acidic contents from entering the duodenum. Certain drugs are given to suppress gastric acid secretion (Table 43.20). With resolution of the pancreatitis, the patient resumes oral intake. For the patient with severe acute pancreatitis who does not resume oral intake, EN support may be started.

The inflamed and necrotic pancreatic tissue is a good medium for bacterial growth. In patients with acute necrotizing pancreatitis, infection is the leading cause of morbidity and mortality. Therefore it is important to prevent infections. Because many of the organisms come from the intestine, enteral feeding reduces the risk for necrotizing pancreatitis. Monitor the patient closely so that antibiotic therapy can be started early if necrosis and infection occur. Endoscopic- or CT-guided percutaneous aspiration with Gram stain and culture may be done.
Surgical Therapy. When the acute pancreatitis is related to gallstones, an urgent ERCP plus endoscopic *sphincterotomy* (severing of the muscle layers of the sphincter of Oddi) may be done. Laparoscopic cholecystectomy may follow ERCP to reduce the potential for recurrence. Surgical intervention may be needed when the diagnosis is uncertain and for patients who do not respond to conservative therapy.

Those with severe acute pancreatitis may need drainage of necrotic fluid collections. This is done surgically, under CT guidance, or endoscopically. Percutaneous drainage of a pseudocyst can be done, and a drainage tube left in place.
Drug Therapy. Several different drugs are used to prevent and treat problems associated with pancreatitis (Table 43.20). Currently, there are no drugs that cure pancreatitis.

TABLE 43.20 Drug Therapy
Acute and Chronic Pancreatitis

Drug	Mechanism of Action
Acute Pancreatitis	
Antacids	Neutralize gastric hydrochloric (HCl) acid secretion
	↓ Production and secretion of pancreatic enzymes and bicarbonate
Antispasmodics (e.g., dicy-clomine [Bentyl])	↓ Vagal stimulation, motility, pancreatic outflow (↓ volume and concentration of bicarbonate and enzyme secretion) Contraindicated in paralytic ileus
Carbonic anhydrase inhibi-tor (acetazolamide)	↓ Volume and bicarbonate concentration of pancreatic secretion
Morphine	Pain relief
PPIs (e.g., omeprazole [Prilosec])	↓ HCl acid secretion (HCl acid stimulates pancreatic activity)
Chronic Pancreatitis	
Insulin	Treat diabetes or hyperglycemia, if needed
Pancreatic enzyme products (pancrelipase [Pancrease, Zenpep, Creon, Viokace])	Replacement therapy for pancreatic enzymes

TABLE 43.21 Nursing Assessment
Acute Pancreatitis

Subjective Data
Important Health Information
Past health history: Biliary tract disease, alcohol use, abdominal trauma, duodenal ulcers, infection, metabolic disorders
Medications: Thiazides, NSAIDs
Surgery or other treatments: Surgical procedures on the pancreas, stomach, duodenum, or biliary tract. Endoscopic retrograde cholangiopancreatography (ERCP)

Functional Health Patterns
Health perception–health management: Chronic alcohol use, fatigue
Nutritional-metabolic: Nausea and vomiting, anorexia
Activity-exercise: Dyspnea
Cognitive-perceptual: Severe midepigastric or left upper quadrant pain that may radiate to the back, worsened by food and alcohol intake, unrelieved by vomiting

Objective Data
General
Restlessness, anxiety, low-grade fever

Integumentary
Flushing, diaphoresis, discoloration of abdomen and flanks, cyanosis, jaundice. Decreased skin turgor, dry mucous membranes

Respiratory
Tachypnea, basilar crackles

Cardiovascular
Tachycardia, hypotension

Gastrointestinal
Abdominal distention, tenderness, and muscle guarding. Decreased bowel sounds

Possible Diagnostic Findings
↑ Serum amylase and lipase, leukocytosis, hyperglycemia, hypocalcemia, abnormal ultrasound and CT scans of pancreas, abnormal ERCP or MRCP

Nutritional Therapy. Initially, the patient with acute pancreatitis is on NPO status to reduce pancreatic secretion. Depending on the severity of the pancreatitis, EN is started. Because of infection risk, parenteral nutrition is reserved for patients who cannot tolerate EN (see Chapter 39). If IV lipids are given, monitor blood triglyceride levels. In cases of moderate to severe pancreatitis, the patient may need enteral feeding via a jejunal feeding tube.

When food is allowed, small, frequent feedings are given. The diet is high in carbohydrate content because that is the least stimulating to the exocrine part of the pancreas. Suspect intolerance to oral foods when the patient reports pain, has increasing abdominal girth, or has increased serum amylase and lipase levels. Supplemental fat-soluble vitamins may be given.

❖ NURSING MANAGEMENT: ACUTE PANCREATITIS

◆ Nursing Assessment

Subjective and objective data that should be obtained from a person with acute pancreatitis are outlined in Table 43.21.

◆ Nursing Diagnoses

Nursing diagnoses for the patient with acute pancreatitis may include:

- Acute pain
- Fluid imbalance
- Electrolyte imbalance
- Impaired nutritional intake

Additional information on nursing diagnoses and interventions for the patient with acute pancreatitis is presented in eNursing Care Plan 43.3 available on the website for this chapter.

◆ Planning

The overall goals are that the patient with acute pancreatitis will have (1) relief of pain, (2) normal fluid and electrolyte balance, (3) minimal to no complications, and (4) no recurrent attacks.

◆ Nursing Implementation

◆ Health Promotion. The major factors involved in health promotion are (1) assessing the patient for predisposing and etiologic factors and (2) encouraging early treatment of these factors to prevent acute pancreatitis. Encourage the patient to cease alcohol intake, especially if they have had pancreatitis before. Recurrent attacks of pancreatitis may become milder or disappear if alcohol use is stopped. Encourage early diagnosis and treatment of biliary tract disease, such as gallstones.

◆ Acute Care. During the acute phase, it is important to monitor vital signs. Hypotension, fever, and tachypnea may compromise hemodynamic stability. Monitor the response to IV fluids. Closely monitor fluid and electrolyte balance. Frequent vomiting, along with gastric suction, may result in decreased chloride, sodium, and potassium levels.

Respiratory failure may develop in the patient with severe acute pancreatitis. Assess respiratory function (e.g., lung sounds, O_2 saturation levels). If ARDS develops, the patient may need intubation and mechanical ventilation support.

> ⚠ **SAFETY ALERT Respiratory Distress in Acute Pancreatitis**
> - Assess for respiratory distress in the patient with severe acute pancreatitis.
> - Listen to lung sounds and monitor O_2 saturation on a regular basis.

Because hypocalcemia can occur, observe for symptoms of tetany, including jerking, irritability, and muscular twitching. Numbness or tingling around the lips and in the fingers is an early sign of hypocalcemia. Assess the patient for a positive Chvostek's sign or Trousseau's sign (see Fig. 16.15). Give calcium gluconate (as ordered) to treat symptomatic hypocalcemia. Monitor serum magnesium levels since hypomagnesemia may develop.

Because abdominal pain is a primary symptom of pancreatitis, a major focus of your care is pain relief. Pain and restlessness can increase the metabolic rate and contribute to hemodynamic instability. Opioids may be used for pain relief. Assess and document the duration of pain relief. Comfortable positioning, frequent changes in position, and relief of nausea and vomiting help reduce the restlessness that usually accompanies the pain. Assuming positions that flex the trunk and draw the knees up to the abdomen may decrease pain. A side-lying position with the head elevated 45 degrees decreases tension on the abdomen and may help ease the pain.

For the patient who is on NPO status or has an NG tube, provide frequent oral and nasal care to relieve the dryness of the mouth and nose. Oral care is essential to prevent parotitis. If the patient is taking anticholinergics to decrease GI secretions, the mouth will be especially dry. If the patient is taking antacids to neutralize gastric acid secretion, they should be sipped slowly or inserted in the NG tube.

Observe for fever and other manifestations of infection in the patient with acute pancreatitis. Respiratory tract infections are common, which causes the patient to take shallow, guarded abdominal breaths. Measures to prevent respiratory tract infections include turning, coughing, deep breathing, and assuming a semi-Fowler's position.

Other important assessments are observation for signs of paralytic ileus, renal failure, and mental changes. Determine the blood glucose level to assess damage to the β cells of the islets of Langerhans in the pancreas.

If patients have surgery to drain necrotic fluid or treat a cyst, they may need special wound care for an anastomotic leak or a fistula. To prevent skin irritation, use skin barriers (e.g., Stomahesive, Karaya Paste), pouching, and drains. In addition to protecting the skin, pouching allows a more accurate determination of fluid and electrolyte losses and increases patient comfort. Sterile pouching systems are available. Consult with a clinical specialist or wound, ostomy, and continence nurse (WOCN).

Ambulatory Care. After acute pancreatitis, the patient may need home care follow-up. Because of loss of physical and muscle strength, physical therapy may be needed. Continued care to prevent infection and detect any complications is important. Counseling about abstinence from alcohol is important to prevent the patient from experiencing future attacks of acute pancreatitis and development of chronic pancreatitis. Because nicotine can stimulate the pancreas, smoking should be avoided.

Teach the patient and caregiver about the treatment plan, including the importance of taking the required medications and following the recommended diet. Dietary teaching should include fat restriction because fats stimulate the secretion of cholecystokinin, which then stimulates the pancreas. Encourage carbohydrates as they are less stimulating to the pancreas. Teach the patient to avoid crash and binge dieting because they can precipitate attacks.

Teach the patient and caregiver to recognize and report symptoms of infection, diabetes, or steatorrhea (foul-smelling, fatty stools). These changes indicate ongoing destruction of pancreatic tissue and pancreatic insufficiency. The patient may need exogenous enzyme supplementation.

◆ Evaluation

The expected outcomes are that the patient with acute pancreatitis will
- Have adequate pain control
- Maintain adequate fluid and electrolyte balance
- Be knowledgeable about the treatment plan to restore health
- Get help for alcohol use and smoking cessation (if needed)

CHRONIC PANCREATITIS

Chronic pancreatitis is a continuous, prolonged, inflammatory, and fibrosing process of the pancreas. The pancreas is progressively destroyed as it is replaced by fibrotic tissue. Strictures and calcifications may occur in the pancreas.

Etiology and Pathophysiology

Chronic pancreatitis can be due to chronic alcohol use; obstruction caused by gallstones, tumor, pseudocysts, or trauma; and systemic diseases (e.g., systemic lupus erythematosus), autoimmune pancreatitis, and cystic fibrosis. Some patients may not have an identifiable risk factor (idiopathic pancreatitis). Chronic pancreatitis may follow acute pancreatitis, but it may also occur in the absence of any history of an acute condition.

The most common cause of obstructive pancreatitis is inflammation of the sphincter of Oddi associated with gallstones. Cancer of the ampulla of Vater, duodenum, or pancreas can also cause this type of chronic pancreatitis.

The most common cause of nonobstructive pancreatitis (the most common type of chronic pancreatitis) is chronic alcohol use. There is inflammation and sclerosis, mainly in the head of the pancreas and around the pancreatic duct. In some people who drink alcohol, a genetic factor may predispose them to the direct toxic effect of the alcohol on the pancreas.

Clinical Manifestations

As with acute pancreatitis, a major manifestation of chronic pancreatitis is abdominal pain. The patient may have episodes of acute pain, but it usually is chronic (recurrent attacks at intervals of months or years). The attacks may become more frequent until they are almost constant, or they may decrease as pancreatic fibrosis develops. The pain is found in the same areas as in acute pancreatitis, but is usually described as a heavy, gnawing feeling or sometimes as burning and cramp-like. Food or antacids do not relieve the pain.

Other manifestations include symptoms of pancreatic insufficiency, including malabsorption with weight loss, constipation, mild jaundice with dark urine, steatorrhea, and diabetes. The steatorrhea may become severe, with voluminous, foul-smelling, fatty stools. Some abdominal tenderness may be present.

Chronic pancreatitis is associated with a variety of complications. These include pseudocyst formation, bile duct or duodenal obstruction, pancreatic ascites or pleural effusion, splenic vein thrombosis, pseudoaneurysms, and pancreatic cancer.

Diagnostic Studies

Confirming the diagnosis of chronic pancreatitis can be hard. The diagnosis is based on the patient's signs and symptoms, laboratory studies, and imaging. In chronic pancreatitis, serum amylase and lipase levels may be increased slightly or not at all, depending on the degree of pancreatic fibrosis. Serum bilirubin and alkaline phosphatase levels may be increased. There is usually mild leukocytosis and a high sedimentation rate.

ERCP can visualize the pancreatic and common bile ducts. Imaging studies, such as CT, MRI, MRCP, abdominal ultrasound, and EUS, can show a variety of changes, including calcifications, ductal dilation, pseudocysts, and enlargement of the pancreas.

Stool samples are examined for fecal fat content. Deficiencies of fat-soluble vitamins and cobalamin, glucose intolerance, and diabetes may occur in those with chronic pancreatitis. A secretin stimulation test can assess the degree of pancreatic dysfunction.

❖ Interprofessional and Nursing Care

When the patient with chronic pancreatitis has an acute attack, the therapy is identical to that for acute pancreatitis. At other times, the focus is on prevention of further attacks, relief of pain, and control of pancreatic exocrine and endocrine insufficiency. It sometimes takes frequent doses of analgesics (morphine, fentanyl patch [Duragesic]) to relieve the pain if dietary measures and enzyme replacement are not effective.

Diet, pancreatic enzyme replacement, and control of diabetes are ways to control the pancreatic insufficiency. Small, bland, frequent meals that are low in fat content are recommended to decrease pancreatic stimulation. Smoking is associated with accelerated progression of chronic pancreatitis. Teach the patient not to consume alcohol and caffeinated beverages. If the patient is dependent on alcohol, refer the patient to other resources as needed (see Chapter 10).

Pancreatic enzyme products, such as pancrelipase (Pancrease, Zenpep, Creon, Viokace), contain amylase, lipase, and trypsin. They are used to replace the deficient pancreatic enzymes. The enzymes are usually enteric coated to prevent their breakdown or inactivation by gastric acid. They are usually taken with meals and snacks. Teach the patient and caregiver to monitor stools for steatorrhea to help determine the effectiveness of the enzymes. Bile salts may be given to help with fat-soluble vitamin (A, D, E, and K) absorption and prevent further fat loss.

If diabetes develops, it is controlled with insulin (most often) or oral hypoglycemic agents. Teach the patient about testing blood glucose levels and drug therapy (see Chapter 48). While acid-neutralizing drugs (e.g., antacids) and acid-inhibiting drugs (e.g., H_2 receptor blockers, PPIs) may be given to control gastric acidity, they have little overall effect on patient outcomes. Antidepressants can reduce any neuropathic pain associated with chronic pancreatitis.

Treatment of chronic pancreatitis sometimes requires endoscopic therapy or surgery. When biliary disease is present or obstruction or pseudocyst develops, surgery may be needed. Surgical procedures can divert bile flow or relieve ductal obstruction. A choledochojejunostomy diverts bile around the ampulla of Vater, where there may be spasm or hypertrophy of the sphincter. In this procedure, the common bile duct is anastomosed into the jejunum. Another type of surgical diverting procedure is the Roux-en-Y pancreato-jejunostomy, in which the pancreatic duct is opened and an anastomosis made with the jejunum. Pancreatic drainage procedures can relieve ductal obstruction and are often done with ERCP. Some patients may have an ERCP with sphincterotomy and/or stent placement at the site of obstruction. These patients need follow-up procedures, such as ERCP, to either exchange or remove the stent.

PANCREATIC CANCER

There is a high mortality rate of pancreatic cancer with the incidence almost equal to the mortality rates. The median age at diagnosis is around 71 years of age.[15] Most pancreatic tumors are adenocarcinomas that begin in the epithelium of the ductal system. More than half of the tumors occur in the head of the pancreas. As the tumor grows, the common bile duct becomes obstructed and obstructive jaundice develops. Tumors starting in the body or the tail often remain silent until their growth is advanced. Most cancers have metastasized at the time of diagnosis. The signs and symptoms of pancreatic cancer are similar to those of chronic pancreatitis. The prognosis of a patient with cancer of the pancreas is poor. Most patients die within 5 to 12 months of diagnosis. The 5-year survival rate is only 8%.[15]

Etiology and Pathophysiology

The cause of pancreatic cancer is unknown. Risk factors for pancreatic cancer include chronic pancreatitis, diabetes, age, cigarette smoking, family history of pancreatic cancer, high-fat diet, and exposure to chemicals, such as benzidine. Blacks have a higher incidence of pancreatic cancer than whites. The most established risk factor is cigarette smoking. Smokers are 2 to 3 times more likely to develop pancreatic cancer than nonsmokers. The risk is related to both the duration and number of cigarettes smoked.

Clinical Manifestations

Common manifestations include abdominal pain (dull, aching), anorexia, rapid and progressive weight loss, nausea, and jaundice. The most common manifestations with cancer of the head of the pancreas are pain, jaundice, and weight loss. In general, pain is common and is related to the cancer's location. The pain is often in the upper abdomen or left hypochondrium and often radiates to the back. It is often related to eating and occurs at night. Extreme, unrelenting pain is related to extension of the cancer into the retroperitoneal tissues and nerve plexuses. Pruritus may accompany obstructive jaundice. Weight loss is due to poor digestion and absorption caused by lack of digestive enzymes from the pancreas.

Diagnostic Studies

Abdominal ultrasound or EUS, spiral CT scan, ERCP, MRI, and MRCP are the most often used diagnostic imaging techniques for pancreatic diseases, including cancer. EUS involves imaging the pancreas with the use of an endoscope positioned in the stomach and duodenum. EUS also allows for fine-needle aspiration of the tumor for pathologic examination. CT scan is often the first study and gives information on metastasis and vascular involvement of the tumor. ERCP allows visualization of the pancreatic duct and biliary system. With ERCP, pancreatic secretions and tissue can be obtained for biopsy and analysis of tumor markers. MRI, PET, PET/CT scans and MRCP may be done to confirm a cancer diagnosis and determine staging. They can also monitor progress and response to therapy.

Tumor markers are used both for diagnosing pancreatic cancer and monitoring the response to treatment. Cancer-associated antigen 19-9 (CA 19-9) is increased in pancreatic cancer. It is the most commonly used tumor marker. However, CA 19-9 also can be increased in gallbladder cancer or in benign conditions, such as acute and chronic pancreatitis, hepatitis, and biliary obstruction.

Interprofessional Care

Surgery is the most effective treatment for pancreatic cancer. Only 15% to 20% of patients have resectable tumors at the time of diagnosis. With the use of neoadjuvant chemotherapy (treatment before surgery), more patients can eventually become surgical candidates. The type of surgery depends on the size and location of the tumor. Pancreatic head tumors require the classic Whipple procedure or pancreaticoduodenectomy (Fig. 43.13). In the Whipple surgery, the proximal pancreas (proximal pancreatectomy), along with duodenum (duodenectomy), distal segment of the common bile duct and distal part of the stomach (partial gastrectomy) are removed together followed by a surgical anastomosis of the pancreatic duct, common bile duct, and stomach to the jejunum. Pancreatic body and/or tail tumors require a distal pancreatectomy procedure. Sometimes, a total pancreatectomy is done. It causes diabetes and the patient is dependent on exogenous insulin and pancreatic enzyme supplementation for life. If the pancreatic tumor cannot be removed surgically, palliative measures, such as a cholecystojejunostomy, to relieve biliary obstruction and/or endoscopically placed biliary stents, can be done.

Radiation therapy alone has little effect on survival but may be effective for pain relief. External radiation is most common, but implantation of internal radiation seeds into the tumor has been used. The current role of chemotherapy is limited and can have a significant side effect profile. Chemotherapy usually consists of fluorouracil and gemcitabine (Gemzar) either alone or in combination with agents such as capecitabine (Xeloda), paclitaxel (Abraxane), erlotinib (Tarceva), or irinotecan (Onivyde). Erlotinib is a targeted therapy drug (see Chapter 15).

❖ NURSING MANAGEMENT: PANCREATIC CANCER

Because the patient with pancreatic cancer has many of the same problems as the patient with pancreatitis, nursing care includes many of the same measures (see sections on acute and chronic pancreatitis on pp. 995 and 996). Provide symptomatic and supportive nursing care. This includes giving medications and providing comfort measures to relieve pain. Psychologic support is essential, especially during times of anxiety or depression.

Adequate nutrition is an important part of the nursing care plan. Frequent and supplemental feedings may be needed. Include measures to stimulate the appetite as much as possible and to manage anorexia, nausea, and vomiting. If the patient is undergoing radiation therapy, observe for adverse reactions, such as anorexia, nausea, vomiting, and skin irritation.

The prognosis for a patient with pancreatic cancer is poor. A significant part of the nursing care is helping the patient and caregiver cope with the diagnosis and prognosis. Chapter 9 provides information on palliative and end-of-life care.

▮ DISORDERS OF THE BILIARY TRACT

CHOLELITHIASIS AND CHOLECYSTITIS

The most common disorder of the biliary system is **cholelithiasis** (stones in the gallbladder) (Fig. 43.14). The gallstones may lodge in the neck of the gallbladder or in the cystic duct. **Cholecystitis** (inflammation of the gallbladder wall) is usually associated with gallstones. They usually occur together, although a person can have gallstones without cholecystitis. Cholecystitis may present acutely or chronically.

Gallbladder disease is a common health problem in the United States. Up to 10% of American adults have cholecystitis caused by gallstones. The actual number is not known because many persons with stones are asymptomatic. *Cholecystectomy* (removal of the gallbladder) is among the most common surgical procedures done in the United States.

Gallstones are more common in women, especially multiparous women and women over 40 years of age. Postmenopausal

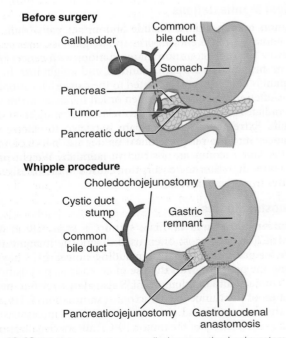

FIG. 43.13 Whipple procedure or radical pancreaticoduodenectomy. This surgical procedure involves resecting the proximal pancreas, adjoining duodenum, distal part of the stomach, and distal part of the common bile duct. An anastomosis of the pancreatic duct, common bile duct, and stomach to the jejunum is done. (From Butcher GP: *Gastroenterology: An illustrated colour text*, London, 2004, Churchill Livingstone.)

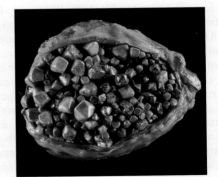

FIG. 43.14 Cholesterol gallstones in a gallbladder that was removed. (From Kumar V, Abbas AK, Aster JC, et al: *Robbins and Cotran pathologic basis of disease*, ed 8, Philadelphia, 2010, Saunders.)

women on estrogen replacement therapy and younger women on oral contraceptives are at an increased risk for gallbladder disease. Oral contraceptives affect cholesterol production and increase gallbladder cholesterol saturation. Other factors that increase the occurrence of gallbladder disease are a sedentary lifestyle, a familial tendency, and obesity. Obesity causes increased secretion of cholesterol in bile. The incidence of gallbladder disease is especially high in the Native American population.

GENDER DIFFERENCES
Cholelithiasis

Men
- Incidence is lower in men than in women.
- Gender differences in incidence decrease after age 50.

Women
- Pregnancy is the greatest risk factor for increased prevalence in women.
- Obesity increases the risk, especially for women.

Etiology and Pathophysiology

Cholelithiasis. The cause of gallstones is unknown. They develop when the balance that keeps cholesterol, bile salts, and calcium in solution is changed so that these substances precipitate. Conditions that upset this balance include infection and changes in cholesterol metabolism. In patients with gallstones, the bile secreted by the liver is supersaturated with cholesterol (lithogenic bile). The bile in the gallbladder then becomes supersaturated with cholesterol and precipitation of cholesterol occurs in the gallbladder.

Other components of bile that precipitate into stones are bile salts, bilirubin, calcium, and protein. Mixed cholesterol stones, which are mainly cholesterol, are the most common gallstones.

Changes in the composition of bile are significant in gallstone formation. Bile stasis leads to progression of the supersaturation and changes in the chemical composition of the bile (biliary sludge). Immobility, pregnancy, and inflammatory or obstructive lesions in the biliary system decrease bile flow. Hormonal factors during pregnancy may cause delayed emptying of the gallbladder, resulting in bile stasis.

The stones may stay in the gallbladder or migrate to the cystic duct or the common bile duct. They cause pain as they pass through the ducts, and they may lodge in the ducts and cause an obstruction. Small stones are more likely to move into a duct and cause obstruction. Table 43.22 describes the changes and manifestations that occur when the stones obstruct the common bile duct. If the blockage occurs in the cystic duct, the bile can continue to flow into the duodenum directly from the liver. However, when the bile in the gallbladder cannot escape, this stasis of bile may lead to cholecystitis.

Cholecystitis. Cholecystitis is most often associated with obstruction caused by gallstones or biliary sludge. Cholecystitis in the absence of obstruction (acalculous cholecystitis) occurs most often in older adults and in patients who are critically ill. Acalculous cholecystitis is also associated with prolonged immobility and fasting, prolonged parenteral nutrition, and diabetes. We think the main cause of this illness is bile stasis. Critically ill patients are more predisposed because of increased bile viscosity due to fever and dehydration and because of prolonged

TABLE 43.22 Manifestations of Obstructed Bile Flow

Manifestation	Etiology
Bleeding tendencies	Lack of or ↓ absorption of vitamin K, resulting in ↓ production of prothrombin
Clay-colored stools	No bilirubin reaching small intestine to be converted to urobilinogen
Dark amber to brown urine, which foams when shaken	↑ Water-soluble (conjugated) bilirubin elimination in urine
Fever and chills	Bacterial reflux from biliary tract to systemic circulation
Intolerance for fatty foods	No bile in small intestine for fat digestion
Jaundice	No bile flow into duodenum, bilirubin accumulates in blood
Pruritus	Deposition of bile salts in skin tissues
Steatorrhea	Undigested fatty components of food are eliminated in stool. Occurs because no bile in small intestine, thus preventing emulsion, digestion, and absorption of fat
Urobilinogen absent in urine	No bilirubin reaching small intestine to be converted to urobilinogen

absence of oral feeding resulting in a decrease or absence of cholecystokinin-induced gallbladder contraction. Other risk factors include adhesions, cancer, anesthesia, and opioids.

Once acalculous cholecystitis is present, secondary infection with enteric pathogens, including *E. coli, Enterococcus faecalis, Klebsiella, Pseudomonas,* and *Proteus,* is common. Perforation occurs in severe cases.

Inflammation is the major pathophysiologic condition. It may be confined to the mucous lining or involve the entire wall of the gallbladder. During an acute attack of cholecystitis, the gallbladder is edematous and hyperemic, and it may be distended with bile or pus. The cystic duct is also involved and may become occluded. The wall of the gallbladder becomes scarred after an acute attack. Decreased functioning will occur if large amounts of tissue become fibrotic.

Clinical Manifestations

Gallstones may produce a range of symptoms. The severity depends on whether the stones are stationary or mobile and whether obstruction is present. When a stone is lodged in the ducts or when stones are moving through the ducts, spasms may result in response to the stone. This sometimes causes severe pain, which is termed *biliary colic,* even though the pain is rarely colicky. The pain is more often steady. The pain can be excruciating and accompanied by tachycardia, diaphoresis, and prostration. The severe pain may last up to an hour, and when it subsides, there is residual tenderness in the right upper quadrant. The attacks of pain often occur 3 to 6 hours after a high-fat meal or when the patient lies down.

When total obstruction occurs, symptoms related to bile blockage occur (Table 43.22). If the common bile duct is obstructed, no bilirubin will reach the small intestine to be converted to urobilinogen. Thus the kidneys will excrete bilirubin, causing dark amber to brown urine.

Manifestations of cholecystitis vary from indigestion to moderate to severe pain, fever, chills, and jaundice. Initial symptoms of acute cholecystitis include indigestion and acute pain and tenderness in the right upper quadrant. Pain may be referred to the right shoulder and scapula. The pain may be accompanied by nausea and vomiting, restlessness, and diaphoresis. Inflammation results in leukocytosis and fever. Physical findings include right upper quadrant or epigastrium tenderness and abdominal rigidity. Chronic cholecystitis may present with a history of fat intolerance, dyspepsia, heartburn, and flatulence.

Complications

Complications of gallstones and cholecystitis include gangrenous cholecystitis, subphrenic abscess, pancreatitis, *cholangitis* (inflammation of biliary ducts), biliary cirrhosis, fistulas, and rupture of the gallbladder, which can cause bile peritonitis. In older adults and those with diabetes, gangrenous cholecystitis and bile peritonitis are the most common complications of cholecystitis. *Choledocholithiasis* (stone in the common bile duct) may occur, producing symptoms of obstruction.

Diagnostic Studies

Ultrasound is often used to diagnose gallstones (see Table 38.11). It is especially useful for patients with jaundice (because it does not depend on renal function) and for patients who are allergic to contrast medium. ERCP allows for visualization of the gallbladder, cystic duct, common hepatic duct, and common bile duct. Bile taken during ERCP is sent for culture to identify possible infecting organisms.

Percutaneous transhepatic cholangiography is the insertion of a needle directly into the gallbladder duct followed by injection of contrast materials. It is generally done after ultrasound shows a bile duct blockage.

Laboratory tests may reveal an increased WBC count because of inflammation. Serum enzymes (e.g., alkaline phosphatase, ALT, and AST), direct and indirect bilirubin levels, and urinary bilirubin levels may be increased if an obstructive process is present (Table 43.3). Serum amylase is increased if there is pancreatic involvement.

Interprofessional Care

Once gallstones become symptomatic, definitive surgical intervention with cholecystectomy is usually needed. However, in some cases, conservative therapy may be considered.

Conservative Therapy

Cholelithiasis. The treatment of gallstones depends on the stage of disease. Bile acids (cholesterol solvents), such as ursodeoxycholic acid (Ursodiol) and chenodeoxycholic acid (Chenodiol), are used to dissolve stones. However, the gallstones may recur. We usually do not treat gallstones with drugs because of the high use and success of laparoscopic cholecystectomy.

ERCP with endoscopic sphincterotomy (papillotomy) may be used to remove stones (Fig. 43.15). ERCP allows for visualization of the biliary system, dilation (balloon sphincteroplasty), and placement of stents and sphincterotomy. Special catheters with wire baskets or inflatable balloon tip may be used for stone removal.[16] When a stent is placed, it is generally removed or changed after a few months.

Extracorporeal shock-wave lithotripsy (ESWL) is an alternative treatment used when endoscopic approaches cannot remove stones. In ESWL, a lithotripter uses high-energy shock waves to disintegrate gallstones. It usually takes 1 to 2 hours to disintegrate the stones. After they are broken up, the fragments pass through the common bile duct and into the small intestine. Usually ESWL and oral dissolution therapy are used together.

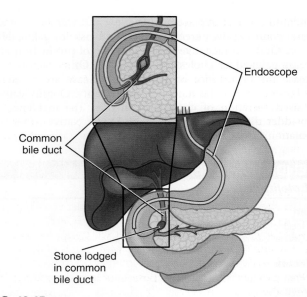

Endoscope
Common bile duct
Stone lodged in common bile duct

FIG. 43.15 During endoscopic sphincterotomy, an endoscope is advanced through the mouth and stomach until its tip sits in the duodenum opposite the common bile duct. *Inset,* After widening the duct mouth by incising the sphincter muscle, the HCP advances a basket attachment into the duct and snags the stone.

TABLE 43.23 Interprofessional Care
Cholelithiasis and Acute Cholecystitis

Diagnostic Assessment
- History and physical examination
- Ultrasound
- ERCP
- Percutaneous transhepatic cholangiography
- Liver function tests
- White blood cell count
- Serum bilirubin

Management
Conservative Therapy
- IV fluid
- NPO with NG tube, later progressing to low-fat diet
- Antiemetics
- Analgesics
- Fat-soluble vitamins (A, D, E, and K)
- Anticholinergics (antispasmodics)
- Antibiotics (for secondary infection)
- Transhepatic biliary catheter
- ERCP with sphincterotomy (papillotomy)
- Extracorporeal shock-wave lithotripsy

Dissolution Therapy
- ursodeoxycholic acid (ursodiol [Actigall])

Surgical Therapy
- Laparoscopic cholecystectomy
- Incisional (open) cholecystectomy

Cholecystitis. During an acute episode of cholecystitis, treatment focuses on pain control, control of infection with antibiotics, and maintaining fluid and electrolyte balance (Table 43.23). Treatment is supportive and focused on symptom management. If nausea and vomiting are severe, NG tube insertion and gastric decompression may be used to prevent further gallbladder stimulation. A cholecystostomy may be used to drain purulent material from the obstructed gallbladder. Opioids are given for pain management. Anticholinergics may be used to decrease GI secretions and counteract smooth muscle spasms.

Surgical Therapy. Laparoscopic cholecystectomy is the treatment of choice for symptomatic gallstones. About 90% of cholecystectomies are done laparoscopically. In this procedure, the gallbladder is removed through 1 to 4 small punctures in the abdomen. The HCP makes a small cut below the umbilicus and inserts a needle into the area. CO_2 gas is passed into the abdomen to expand the area, which allows the HCP to see the organs more clearly and gives more room to work. A laparoscope, which has a camera attached, and grasping forceps are inserted into the abdomen through the punctures. Using closed-circuit monitors to view the abdominal cavity, the HCP retracts and dissects the gallbladder and removes it with grasping forceps. This is a safe and routine procedure with minimal morbidity and quick recovery time.

Most patients have minimal postoperative pain and are discharged the day of surgery or the day after. They can usually resume normal activities and return to work within 1 week. The main complication is injury to the common bile duct. The few contraindications to laparoscopic cholecystectomy include peritonitis, cholangitis, gangrene or perforation of the gallbladder, portal hypertension, and serious bleeding disorders.

Some patients may need an incisional (open) cholecystectomy. This involves removing the gallbladder through a right subcostal incision. A T tube may be inserted into the common bile duct during surgery when a common bile duct exploration is part of the surgical procedure (Fig. 43.16). This ensures patency of the duct until the edema from the trauma of exploring and probing the duct has subsided. It also allows excess bile to drain while the small intestine is adjusting to receiving a continuous flow of bile.

Transhepatic Biliary Catheter. The transhepatic biliary catheter can be used preoperatively in biliary obstruction and in hepatic dysfunction from obstructive jaundice. It also can be inserted for palliative care when inoperable liver, pancreatic, or bile duct cancer obstructs bile flow. The catheter is used when endoscopic drainage has been unsuccessful. The catheter is inserted percutaneously and allows for decompression of obstructed

extrahepatic bile ducts so that bile can flow freely. After placement of the catheter into the obstructed duct internally, the external catheter is connected to a drainage bag. Encourage patients to replace fluids lost in the drainage bag with electrolyte-rich drinks. Cleanse the skin around the catheter insertion site daily with an antiseptic. Observe for bile leakage at the insertion site and any signs or symptoms of sudden abdominal pain, nausea, fever, or chills that may signal an occluded or malfunctioning drain.

Drug Therapy. The most common drugs used in the treatment of gallbladder disease are analgesics, anticholinergics (antispasmodics), fat-soluble vitamins, and bile salts. Morphine may be used initially for pain management. Anticholinergics, such as atropine and other antispasmodics, may be used to relax the smooth muscle and decrease ductal tone.

The patient with chronic gallbladder disease or any biliary tract obstruction may need fat-soluble vitamin (A, D, E, and K) replacement. Bile salts may be given to help digestion and vitamin absorption.

Cholestyramine may provide relief from pruritus. Cholestyramine is a resin that binds bile salts in the intestine, increasing their excretion in the feces. It comes in powder form that is mixed with milk or juice. Side effects include nausea, vomiting, diarrhea or constipation, and skin reactions. Cholestyramine may bind with other medications, so check drug-to-drug interactions.

Nutritional Therapy. People have fewer gallbladder problems if they eat smaller, more frequent meals with some fat at each meal to promote gallbladder emptying. If obesity is a problem, a reduced-calorie diet is indicated. The diet should be low in saturated fats (e.g., butter, shortening, lard) and high in fiber and calcium. Rapid weight loss should be avoided because it can promote gallstone formation.

After a laparoscopic cholecystectomy, teach the patient to have liquids for the rest of the day and eat light meals for a few days. After an incisional cholecystectomy, the patient will progress from liquids to a regular diet once bowel sounds have returned. The amount of fat in the postoperative diet depends on the patient's tolerance of fat. A low-fat diet may be helpful if the flow of bile is reduced (usually only in the early postoperative period) or if the patient is overweight. Sometimes the patient must restrict fats for 4 to 6 weeks. Otherwise, no special diet is needed other than to eat nutritious meals and avoid excess fat intake.

❖ NURSING MANAGEMENT: GALLBLADDER DISEASE

◆ Nursing Assessment

Subjective and objective data that should be obtained from a person with gallbladder disease are outlined in Table 43.24.

◆ Nursing Diagnoses

Nursing diagnoses for the patient with gallbladder disease treated surgically may include:
- Acute pain
- Lack of knowledge

◆ Planning

The overall goals are that the patient with gallbladder disease will have (1) relief of pain and discomfort, (2) no complications postoperatively, and (3) no recurrent attacks of cholecystitis or gallstones.

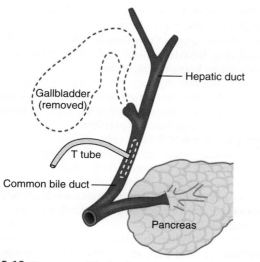

FIG. 43.16 Placement of T tube. *Dotted lines* show parts removed.

TABLE 43.24 Nursing Assessment

Cholecystitis or Cholelithiasis

Subjective Data
Important Health Information
Past health history: Obesity, multiparity, infection, cancer, extensive fasting, pregnancy
Medications: Estrogen or oral contraceptives
Surgery or other treatments: Abdominal surgery

Functional Health Patterns
Health perception–health management: Positive family history, sedentary lifestyle
Nutritional-metabolic: Weight loss, anorexia, indigestion, fat intolerance, nausea and vomiting, dyspepsia, chills
Elimination: Clay-colored stools, steatorrhea, flatulence. Dark urine
Cognitive-perceptual: Moderate to severe pain in right upper quadrant that may radiate to the back or scapula. Itching

Objective Data
General
Fever, restlessness

Integumentary
Jaundice, icteric sclera, diaphoresis

Respiratory
Tachypnea, splinting during respirations

Cardiovascular
Tachycardia

Gastrointestinal
Palpable gallbladder, abdominal guarding, and distention

Possible Diagnostic Findings
↑ Serum liver enzymes, alkaline phosphatase, and bilirubin. Absence of urobilinogen in urine, ↑ urinary bilirubin, leukocytosis. Abnormal gallbladder ultrasound

◆ **Nursing Implementation**

◆ **Health Promotion.** Be aware of predisposing factors for gallbladder disease in general health screening. Teach patients from ethnic groups in which the disease is more common, such as Native Americans, the early manifestations and to see their HCP if these manifestations occur. Patients with chronic cholecystitis may not have acute symptoms and may not seek help until jaundice and biliary obstruction occur. Earlier detection in these patients is important so that they can be managed with a low-fat diet and monitored more closely.

Acute Care. Nursing goals for the patient undergoing conservative therapy include (1) treat pain, (2) relieve nausea and vomiting, (3) provide comfort and emotional support, (4) maintain fluid and electrolyte balance and nutrition, and (5) observe for complications.

The patient with acute cholecystitis or gallstones often has severe pain. Give the drugs ordered to relieve the pain as needed before pain becomes severe. Observe for side effects of the drugs as part of the continued assessment. Nursing comfort measures, such as a clean bed, comfortable positioning, and oral care, are appropriate.

Some patients have more severe nausea and vomiting than others. For these patients, an NG tube and gastric

decompression may be ordered. Eliminating intake of food and fluids prevents further stimulation of the gallbladder. Oral hygiene, care of nares, accurate intake and output measurements, and maintaining suction should be a part of the nursing care plan. For patients with less severe nausea and vomiting, antiemetics are usually adequate. When the patient is vomiting, provide comfort measures, such as frequent mouth rinses. Remove any vomitus at once from the patient's view. If itching occurs with jaundice, use measures to relieve itching. These can include antihistamines or other treatments as previously discussed.

Assess for progression of the symptoms and development of complications. Observe for signs of obstruction of the ducts by stones. These include jaundice; clay-colored stools; dark, foamy urine; steatorrhea; fever; and increased WBC count.

When manifestations of obstruction are present (Table 43.22), bleeding may result from decreased prothrombin production by the liver. Common sites to observe for bleeding are the mucous membranes of the mouth, nose, gingivae, and injection sites. When giving injections, use a small-gauge needle and apply gentle pressure after the injection. Know the patient's PT time and use it as a guide in the assessment process.

Assessment for infections includes monitoring vital signs. A temperature elevation with chills and jaundice may indicate choledocholithiasis.

Your care of the patient after ERCP with papillotomy includes assessment to detect complications, such as pancreatitis, perforation, infection, and bleeding. Monitor the patient's vital signs. Abdominal pain, fever, and increasing amylase and lipase may indicate acute pancreatitis. The patient should be on bed rest for several hours and should be NPO until the gag reflex returns. Teach the patient the need for follow-up if the stent is to be removed or changed.

Postoperative Care. Postoperative nursing care after a laparoscopic cholecystectomy includes monitoring for complications, such as bleeding, making the patient comfortable, and preparing the patient for discharge. Patients may report referred pain to the shoulder because of the CO_2 that the HCP uses to inflate the abdominal cavity during surgery. It may not be released or absorbed by the body. The CO_2 can irritate the phrenic nerve and diaphragm, causing some difficulty in breathing. Placing the patient in the Sims' position (on left side with right knee flexed) helps move the gas pocket away from the diaphragm. Encourage deep breathing along with movement and ambulation. NSAIDs or codeine can usually relieve pain. The patient is allowed clear liquids and can walk to the bathroom to void. Most patients go home the same day.

Postoperative nursing care for incisional cholecystectomy focuses on adequate ventilation and prevention of respiratory complications. Other nursing care is the same as general postoperative nursing care (see Chapter 19).

If the patient has a T tube (Fig. 43.16), maintain the system and monitor T-tube function and drainage. The T tube is usually connected to a closed gravity drainage system. If the Penrose or Jackson-Pratt drain or the T tube is draining large amounts of bile, it is helpful to use a sterile pouching system to protect the skin. Encourage the patient to replace any lost fluids and electrolytes.

Ambulatory Care. When the patient has conservative therapy, nursing management depends on the patient's symptoms and on whether surgical intervention is planned. Dietary teaching

TABLE 43.25 Patient & Caregiver Teaching
Postoperative Laparoscopic Cholecystectomy

Postoperative teaching should include:

1. Remove the bandages on the puncture sites the day after surgery and you can shower.
2. Notify your HCP if any of the following signs and symptoms occurs:
   - Redness, swelling, bile-colored drainage or pus from any incision
   - Severe abdominal pain, nausea, vomiting, fever, chills
3. You can gradually resume normal activities.
4. Return to work within 1 wk of surgery.
5. You can resume your usual diet, but a low-fat diet is usually better tolerated for several weeks after surgery.

is usually needed. The diet is usually low in fat. The patient may need to take fat-soluble vitamin supplements. If needed, review a weight-reduction diet. Teach the patient signs and symptoms of obstruction (e.g., stool and urine changes, jaundice, itching). Explain the importance of continued health care follow-up.

The patient who undergoes a laparoscopic cholecystectomy is discharged soon after the surgery, so home care and teaching are important (Table 43.25).

After an incisional cholecystectomy, tell the patient to avoid heavy lifting for 4 to 6 weeks. Usual sexual activities, including intercourse, can be resumed as soon as the patient feels ready, unless otherwise instructed by the HCP.

Sometimes the patient needs to remain on a low-fat diet for 4 to 6 weeks. If so, an individualized dietary teaching plan is needed. A weight-reduction program may be helpful if the patient is overweight. Most patients tolerate a regular diet with no problems but should avoid excess fats.

◆ Evaluation

The overall expected outcomes are that the patient with gall-bladder disease will

- Appear comfortable and have pain relief
- State knowledge of activity level and dietary restrictions

GALLBLADDER CANCER

Gallbladder cancer is the sixth most common GI cancer in the United States.[17] Most gallbladder cancers are adenocarcinomas. They are often found incidentally as the patient is asymptomatic. The majority have advanced disease at the time of diagnosis.

The early symptoms are insidious and similar to those of chronic cholecystitis and gallstones, which makes the diagnosis difficult. Later symptoms are usually those of biliary obstruction.

Diagnosis and staging of gallbladder cancer are done using EUS, abdominal ultrasound, CT, MRI, and/or MRCP. Unfortunately, gallbladder cancer often is not detected until the disease is advanced. When it is found early, surgery can be curative. Several factors influence successful surgical outcomes, including the depth of cancer invasion, extent of liver involvement, venous or lymphatic invasion, and lymph node metastasis. Extended cholecystectomy with lymph node dissection has improved outcomes for those with gallbladder cancer.

When surgery is not an option, endoscopic stenting of the biliary tract can reduce obstructive jaundice. Adjuvant therapies, including radiation therapy and chemotherapy, may be used depending on the disease state. Overall, gallbladder cancer has a poor prognosis.

Nursing management involves palliative care with special attention to nutrition, hydration, skin care, and pain relief. Nursing care measures used for patients with cholecystitis and gallstones and for the patient with cancer (see Chapter 15) are appropriate.

CASE STUDY
Cirrhosis of the Liver

Patient Profile

M.B., a 58-yr-old male rancher who lives in rural Wyoming, is admitted with a diagnosis of cirrhosis of the liver. He has been vomiting for 2 days and noticed blood in the toilet when he vomited. He lives 40 miles from the nearest hospital. He had one of his ranch hands drive him to the hospital. His medical history includes chronic hepatitis C, depression, and stage II chronic kidney disease.

(© sbeagle/iStock/Thinkstock.)

Subjective Data

- Has been estranged from his 2 children since his divorce 3 years ago
- Has had cirrhosis for 12 yrs
- Acknowledges that he had been drinking heavily for 20 yrs but has been sober for the past 2 yrs
- Reports experiencing anorexia, nausea, and abdominal discomfort

Objective Data
Physical Examination

- Has moderate ascites
- Has jaundice of sclera and skin
- Has 4+ pitting edema of the lower extremities
- Liver and spleen are palpable

Laboratory Values

- Total bilirubin: 15 mg/dL (257 mmol/L)
- AST: 190 U/L (3.2 µkat/L)
- ALT: 210 U/L (3.5 µkat/L)
- Platelets: 45,000/µL
- eGFR: 62 mL/min
- ECG is below:

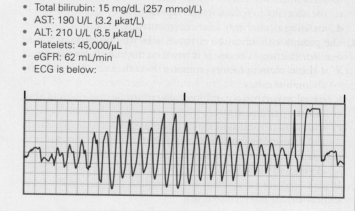

Discussion Questions

1. What are possible causes of cirrhosis? What type of cirrhosis does M.B. likely have?
2. Describe the pathophysiologic changes that occur in the liver as cirrhosis develops.

Continued

CASE STUDY

Cirrhosis of the Liver—cont'd

3. List M.B.'s clinical manifestations of liver failure. For each manifestation, explain the pathophysiologic basis.
4. Explain the significance of the results of his laboratory values and ECG findings.
5. If M.B. begins to show signs and symptoms of hepatic encephalopathy, what would you monitor? What measures would be used to control or decrease the encephalopathy?
6. What are possible causes of his GI bleeding?
7. *Priority Decision:* Based on the assessment data, what are the priority nursing diagnoses? Are there any collaborative problems?

8. *Priority Decision:* What are the priority nursing interventions for a patient at this stage of his illness?
9. *Evidence-Based Practice:* M.B. discusses his prognosis with you. He says, "There is no hope. I might as well keep drinking." How would you respond to his statement?
10. *Safety:* Given M.B.'s bleeding history and current laboratory values, identify areas of injury risk and specify actions you will take to ensure patient safety.
11. Develop a conceptual care map for M.B.

Answers and corresponding conceptual care map available at *evolve.elsevier.com/Lewis/medsurg.*

BRIDGE TO NCLEX EXAMINATION

The number of the question corresponds to the same-numbered outcome at the beginning of the chapter.

1. A patient with hepatitis A is in the acute phase. The nurse plans care for the patient based on the knowledge that
   a. itching is a common problem with jaundice in this phase.
   b. the patient is most likely to transmit the disease during this phase.
   c. gastrointestinal symptoms are not as severe in hepatitis A as they are in hepatitis B.
   d. extrahepatic manifestations of glomerulonephritis and polyarteritis are common in this phase.

2. A patient with acute hepatitis B is being discharged. The discharge teaching plan should include instructions to
   a. avoid alcohol for the first 3 weeks.
   b. use a condom during sexual intercourse.
   c. have family members get an injection of immunoglobulin.
   d. follow a low-protein, moderate-carbohydrate, moderate-fat diet.

3. A patient has been told that she has elevated liver enzymes caused by nonalcoholic fatty liver disease (NAFLD). The nursing teaching plan should include
   a. having genetic testing done.
   b. recommending a heart-healthy diet.
   c. the necessity to reduce weight rapidly.
   d. avoiding alcohol until liver enzymes return to normal.

4. The patient with advanced cirrhosis asks why his abdomen is so swollen. The nurse's response is based on the knowledge that
   a. a lack of clotting factors promotes the collection of blood in the abdominal cavity.
   b. portal hypertension and hypoalbuminemia cause a fluid shift into the peritoneal space.
   c. decreased peristalsis in the GI tract contributes to gas formation and distention of the bowel.
   d. bile salts in the blood irritate the peritoneal membranes, causing edema and pocketing of fluid.

5. In planning care for a patient with metastatic liver cancer, the nurse should include interventions that
   a. focus primarily on symptomatic and comfort measures.
   b. reassure the patient that chemotherapy offers a good prognosis.
   c. promote the patient's confidence that surgical excision of the tumor will be successful.
   d. provide information needed for the patient to make decisions about liver transplantation.

6. Nursing management of the patient with acute pancreatitis includes *(select all that apply)*
   a. administering pain medication.
   b. checking for signs of hypocalcemia.
   c. providing a diet low in carbohydrates.
   d. giving insulin based on a sliding scale.
   e. monitoring for infection, particularly respiratory tract infection.

7. A patient with pancreatic cancer is admitted to the hospital for evaluation of treatment options. The patient asks the nurse to explain the Whipple procedure that the surgeon has described. The explanation includes the information that a Whipple procedure involves
   a. creating a bypass around the obstruction caused by the tumor by joining the gallbladder to the jejunum.
   b. resection of the entire pancreas and the distal part of the stomach, with anastomosis of the common bile duct and the stomach into the duodenum.
   c. removal of part of the pancreas, part of the stomach, the duodenum, and the gallbladder, with joining of the pancreatic duct, the common bile duct, and the stomach into the jejunum.
   d. removal of the pancreas, the duodenum, and the spleen, and attachment of the stomach to the jejunum, which requires oral supplementation of pancreatic digestive enzymes and insulin replacement therapy.

8. The nurse caring for a patient with suspected acute cholecystitis would anticipate *(select all that apply)*
   a. ordering a low-sodium diet.
   b. administration of IV fluids.
   c. monitoring of liver function tests.
   d. administration of antiemetics for patients with nausea.
   e. insertion of an indwelling catheter to monitor urinary output.

9. Teaching in relation to home management after a laparoscopic cholecystectomy should include
   a. keeping the bandages on the puncture sites for 48 hours.
   b. reporting any bile-colored drainage or pus from any incision.
   c. using over-the-counter antiemetics if nausea and vomiting occur.
   d. emptying and measuring the contents of the bile bag from the T tube every day.

1. a, 2. b, 3. b, 4. b, 5. a, 6. a, b, e, 7. c, 8. b, c, d, 9. b.

For rationales to these answers and even more NCLEX review questions, visit *evolve.elsevier.com/Lewis/medsurg.*

ⓔ EVOLVE WEBSITE/RESOURCES LIST

evolve.elsevier.com/Lewis/medsurg
Review Questions (Online Only)
Key Points
Answer Keys for Questions
- Rationales for Bridge to NCLEX Examination Questions
- Answer Guidelines for Case Study on p. 1003
- Answer Guidelines for Managing Care of Multiple Patients Case Study (Section 9) on p. 1006

Student Case Studies
- Patient With Acute Pancreatitis and Septic Shock
- Patient With Cholelithiasis/Cholecystitis
- Patient With Cirrhosis
- Patient With Hepatitis

Nursing Care Plans
- eNursing Care Plan 43.1: Patient With Acute Viral Hepatitis
- eNursing Care Plan 43.2: Patient With Cirrhosis
- eNursing Care Plan 43.3: Patient With Acute Pancreatitis

Conceptual Care Map Creator
- Conceptual Care Map for Case Study on p. 1003

Audio Glossary
Content Updates

REFERENCES

1. Centers for Disease Control and Prevention: Viral hepatitis—Hepatitis A information—United States. Retrieved from *www.cdc.gov/hepatitis/hav/index.htm*.
2. Centers for Disease Control and Prevention: Viral hepatitis—Hepatitis B information—United States. Retrieved from *www.cdc.gov/hepatitis/hbv/index.htm*.
3. Friedman LS, Martin P: *Handbook of liver disease,* ed 4, Philadelphia, 2018, Elsevier.
4. Centers for Disease Control and Prevention: Viral hepatitis—Hepatitis C information—United States. Retrieved from *www.cdc.gov/hepatitis/hcv/index.htm*.
5. Barr R: Shear wave liver elastography, *Abdom Radiol* 43:800, 2018.
*6. American Association for the Study of Liver Diseases: Recommendations for testing, managing, and treating hepatitis C—United States. Retrieved from *www.hcvguidelines.org/full-report/initial-treatment-hcv-infection*.
*7. Terrault N, Lok A, McMahon B, et al: Update on prevention, diagnosis, and treatment of chronic hepatitis B: AASLD 2018 hepatitis B guidance, *Hepatology* 67:4, 2018.
8. Liberal R, de Boer YS, Andrade RJ, et al: Expert clinical management of autoimmune hepatitis in the real world, *Aliment Pharmacol Ther* 45:723, 2017.
9. Kathawala M, Hirschfield GM: Insights into the management of Wilson's disease, *Therap Adv Gastroenterol* 10:889, 2017.
10. Lazaridis N, Tsochatzis E: Current and future treatment options in non-alcoholic steatohepatitis, *Expert Rev Gastroenterol Hepatol* 11:4 357, 2017.
*11. Garcia-Tsao G: Current management of the complications of cirrhosis and portal hypertension: Variceal hemorrhage, ascites, and spontaneous bacterial peritonitis, *Dig Dis* 34:382, 2016.
12. Tsochatzis E, Gerbes A: Hepatology snapshot: Diagnosis and treatment of ascites, *J Hepatol* 67:184, 2017.
*13. Heimbach J, Kulik L, Finn R, et al: AASLD guidelines for the treatment of hepatocellular carcinoma, *Hepatology* 67:358, 2018.
*14. Crockett S, Wani S, Gardner T, et al: American Gastroenterological Association Institute guideline on initial management of acute pancreatitis, *Gastroenterol* 154: 1096, 2018.
15. Munoz A, Chakravarthy D, Gong J, et al: Pancreatic cancer: Current status and challenges, *Curr Pharm Rep* 3:396, 2017.
*16. Doshi B, Yasuda I, Ryozawa S, et al: Current endoscopic strategies for managing large bile duct stones, *Dig Endosc* 30:59, 2018.
17. Rahman R, Simoes E, Schmaltz C, et al: Trend analysis and survival of primary gallbladder cancer in the United States: A 1973–2009 population-based study, *Cancer Med* 6:874, 2017.

CASE STUDY

Managing Care of Multiple Patients

You are working on the medical-surgical unit and have been assigned to care for the following 5 patients. You have 1 LPN and 1 UAP who are assigned to help you.

Patients

(© iStockphoto/ Thinkstock.)

L.C. is a 58-yr-old Native American man admitted from the ED with acute abdominal pain. A CT scan and colonoscopy showed 2 medium-sized tumors in the transverse colon. A hemicolectomy was done 4 days ago. The adenocarcinoma had spread to the muscle of the colon wall, and there were 2 positive lymph nodes. He is scheduled to be discharged today.

(© iStockphoto/ Thinkstock.)

M.S. is a 70-yr-old white woman who was recently admitted to the unit with generalized weakness and malnutrition. She is 5 ft, 4 in tall and weighs 100 lb, with a 30-lb weight loss in past 2 months. Her medical history includes a recent thrombotic stroke with hemiparesis and dysphagia. She has had nothing by mouth for the past 24 hours and just started EN via PEG tube.

(© Christa Brunt/ iStock/ Thinkstock.)

S.R. is a 48-yr-old white woman admitted with hip pain. She has a history of type 2 diabetes, hypertension, and osteoarthritis. She is 5 ft, 6 in tall and weighs 230 lb. Her most recent BP was 160/110 mm Hg. Her morning laboratory results reveal high fasting blood glucose, total cholesterol, LDL cholesterol, and triglycerides. Her HDL cholesterol is low. Her cardiac enzymes and ECG are all within normal limits. She is scheduled to have a cardiac stress test at 10 AM.

(© iStockphoto/ Thinkstock.)

F.H., a 40-yr-old male immigrant from Vietnam, has a 1-yr history of epigastric distress. He had an upper endoscopy a few weeks ago, which revealed a duodenal ulcer and *H. pylori*. He was started on omeprazole, clarithromycin, and amoxicillin for 10 days. He came to the ED yesterday with severe epigastric pain and melena. His Hgb is 8.2 g/dL and Hct is 26%. He was admitted and put on a pantoprazole (Protonix) continuous infusion and is scheduled for a repeat EGD today.

(© sbeagle/ iStock/ Thinkstock.)

M.B. is a 58-yr-old man admitted with a diagnosis of upper GI bleeding. He has been vomiting for 2 days and noticed blood in the toilet when he vomits. He has had cirrhosis for 12 yr and admits to drinking heavily for 20 yr but has been sober for the past 2 yr. He currently reports anorexia, nausea, and abdominal discomfort. He has moderate ascites, jaundice of sclera and skin, 4+ pitting edema of the lower extremities, and palpable liver and spleen. His bilirubin and liver enzymes are all high. His platelet and RBC counts are low.

Discussion Questions

1. **Priority Decision:** After receiving report, which patient should you see first? Provide a rationale for your decision.

2. **Collaboration:** Which tasks could you delegate to the LPN? *(select all that apply)*
   a. Administer a bolus enteral tube feeding to M.S.
   b. Assess L.C.'s dressing, pain level, and bowel sounds.
   c. Administer a scheduled dose of oral lactulose solution to M.B.
   d. Because she speaks Vietnamese, teach F.H.'s wife about his disease.
   e. Perform bedside glucometer reading and administer oral medications to S.R.

3. **Priority Decision:** Which diagnostic finding should you report to the health care provider immediately?
   a. Hemoglobin 7.9 g/dL and hematocrit 25% for F.H.
   b. Serum albumin 2.7 g/dL and prealbumin 11.2 g/dL for M.S.
   c. Cholesterol 250 mg/dL and triglycerides 202 mg/dL for S.R.
   d. Total bilirubin 3.2 mg/dL with positive urine bilirubin for M.B.

4. **Priority Decision:** As you are assessing M.B., the LPN informs you that F.H. just vomited a large amount of bright red blood. What initial action would be *most* appropriate?
   a. Have the LPN administer an antiemetic to F.H.
   b. Ask the LPN to notify F.H.'s health care provider.
   c. Leave M.B.'s room to perform a focused assessment on F.H.
   d. Ask the UAP to obtain a unit of packed RBCs from the blood bank.

Case Study Progression

When you enter F.H.'s room, he tells you that his pain actually feels somewhat relieved since he vomited. However, you note that his skin is cool and clammy, his BP is 90/54 mm Hg, and his heart rate is 116 bpm. You notify his HCP.

4. Which interventions would you expect the HCP to order for F.H.? *(select all that apply)*
   a. Stat hemoglobin and hematocrit
   b. Emergent endoscopy with band ligation
   c. Discontinue the pantoprazole (Protonix) infusion
   d. Start a second IV site and administer a 500 mL normal saline bolus
   e. Contact HCP and notify operating room that patient is unstable and needs surgery

5. **Priority Decision:** After giving a bolus feeding of enteral nutrition to M.S., it would be *most* important to
   a. assess for gastric residual.
   b. obtain an abdominal x-ray.
   c. keep head of bed elevated 30 to 45 degrees.
   d. record the total amount of fluid administered.

6. Which intervention to treat ascites would you expect the HCP to order for M.B.? *(select all that apply)*
   a. Paracentesis
   b. 2 g sodium diet
   c. Diuretic therapy
   d. 1800 mL/day fluid restriction
   e. Shunt insertion from peritoneum to heart

7. **Management Decision:** As you enter the nurse's station, you overhear derogatory comments made by the UAP to the LPN about S.R.'s weight. Which response would be *most* appropriate?
   a. Report the incident to charge nurse for follow-up.
   b. Talk to the UAP to discuss a possible HIPAA violation.
   c. Talk to S.R. about the impact of UAP's bias on the patient's self-image.
   d. Set up an in-service to teach staff members to recognize obesity as a disease process.

Answers and rationales available at *http://evolve.elsevier.com/Lewis/medsurg.*

44

Assessment: Urinary System

Teresa Turnbull

Wherever there is a human being, there is an opportunity for a kindness.

Seneca

ⓔ http://evolve.elsevier.com/Lewis/medsurg

CONCEPTUAL FOCUS

Elimination   Fluids and Electrolytes

LEARNING OUTCOMES

1. Identify the anatomic location and functions of the kidneys, ureters, bladder, and urethra.
2. Explain the physiologic events involved in the formation and passage of urine from glomerular filtration to voiding.
3. Obtain significant subjective and objective data related to the urinary system from a patient.
4. Link the age-related changes of the urinary system to the differences in assessment findings.
5. Perform a physical assessment of the urinary system using appropriate techniques.
6. Distinguish normal from abnormal findings of a physical assessment of the urinary system.
7. Describe the purpose, significance of results, and nursing responsibilities related to diagnostic studies of the urinary system.
8. Evaluate findings of a urinalysis.

KEY TERMS

costovertebral angle (CVA), p. 1015
creatinine, p. 1018
cystoscopy, Table 44.11, p. 1019

glomerular filtration rate (GFR), p. 1009
glomerulus, p. 1008
nephron, p. 1008

renal biopsy, Table 44.11, p. 1020
urinalysis, p. 1018

Adequate kidney function is essential to health. If a person has complete kidney failure and treatment is not provided, death is inevitable. This chapter discusses the structures and functions, assessment, and diagnostic studies of the urinary system.

STRUCTURES AND FUNCTIONS OF URINARY SYSTEM

The *upper urinary system* consists of 2 kidneys and 2 ureters. The *lower urinary system* consists of a urinary bladder and urethra (Fig. 44.1). Urine is formed in the kidneys, drains through the ureters to be stored in the bladder, and then passes out of the body through the urethra.

Kidneys

The kidneys are the principal organs of the urinary system. The primary functions of the kidneys are to (1) regulate the volume and composition of extracellular fluid (ECF) and (2) excrete waste products from the body. The kidneys also function to control BP, make erythropoietin, activate vitamin D, and regulate acid-base balance.

Macrostructure. The paired kidneys are bean-shaped organs located retroperitoneally (behind the peritoneum) on either side of the vertebral column at about the level of the twelfth thoracic (T12) vertebra to the third lumbar (L3) vertebra. Each kidney weighs 4 to 6 oz (113 to 170 g) and is about 5 in (12.5 cm) long. The right kidney, positioned at the level of the twelfth rib, is lower than the left. An adrenal gland lies on top of each kidney.

Each kidney is surrounded by a considerable amount of fat and connective tissue that cushions, supports, and helps the kidney maintain its position. A thin, smooth layer of fibrous membrane called the *capsule* covers the surface of each kidney. The capsule protects the kidney and serves as a shock absorber if this area is traumatized from a sudden force or strike. The

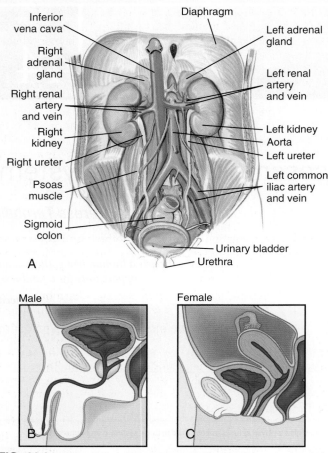

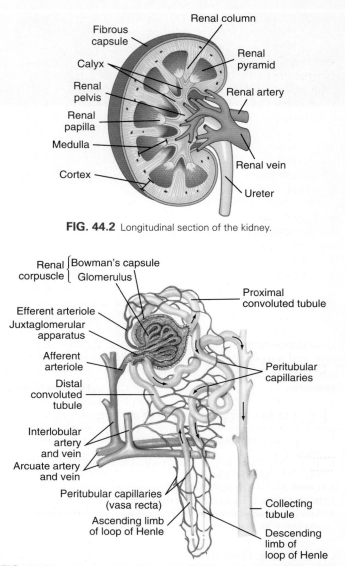

FIG. 44.1 Organs of the urinary system. **A,** Upper urinary tract in relation to other anatomic structures. **B,** Male urethra in relation to other pelvic structures. **C,** Female urethra.

FIG. 44.2 Longitudinal section of the kidney.

FIG. 44.3 The nephron is the basic functional unit of the kidney. This illustration of a single nephron unit shows the surrounding blood vessels. (Modified from Thibodeau GA, Patton KT: *The human body in health and disease,* ed 4, St Louis, 2005, Mosby.)

hilus on the medial side of the kidney serves as the entry site for the renal artery and nerves and as the exit site for the renal vein and ureter.

The *parenchyma* is the actual tissue of the kidney (Fig. 44.2). The outer layer of the parenchyma is the *cortex,* and the inner layer is the *medulla.* The medulla consists of a number of pyramids. The apices (tops) of these pyramids are the *papillae,* through which urine passes to enter the calyces. The minor calyces widen and merge to form major calyces, which form a funnel-shaped sac called the *renal pelvis.* The minor and major calyces transport urine to the renal pelvis, from there it drains through the ureter to the bladder. The renal pelvis can store a small volume of urine (3 to 5 mL).

Microstructure. The nephron is the functional unit of the kidney. Each kidney has around 1 million nephrons. Each nephron is composed of the glomerulus, Bowman's capsule, and a tubular system. The tubular system consists of the proximal convoluted tubule, loop of Henle, distal convoluted tubule, and collecting tubules (Fig. 44.3). The glomerulus, Bowman's capsule, proximal tubule, and distal tubule are in the cortex of the kidney. The loop of Henle and collecting tubules are in the medulla. Several collecting tubules join to form a single collecting duct. The collecting ducts eventually merge into a pyramid that empties via the papilla into a minor calyx.

Blood Supply. Blood flow to the kidneys, around 1200 mL/min, accounts for 20% to 25% of the cardiac output. Blood reaches

the kidneys via the renal artery, which arises from the aorta and enters the kidney through the hilus. The renal artery divides into secondary branches and then into still smaller branches, each of which forms an afferent arteriole. The afferent arteriole divides into a capillary network, the **glomerulus,** which is a collection of up to 50 capillaries (Fig. 44.3). The capillaries of the glomerulus unite in the efferent arteriole. This efferent arteriole splits to form a capillary network, the peritubular capillaries, which surround the tubular system. All peritubular capillaries drain into the venous system. The renal vein empties into the inferior vena cava.

Physiology of Urine Formation. Urine formation is the outcome of a complex, multistep process of filtration, reabsorption, secretion, and excretion of water, electrolytes, and metabolic waste products. Although urine formation is the result of this process, the primary functions of the kidneys are to filter the blood and maintain the body's internal homeostasis.

Glomerular Function. Urine formation begins at the glomerulus, where blood is filtered. The glomerulus is a semipermeable membrane that allows filtration (Fig. 44.3). The hydrostatic pressure of the blood within the glomerular capillaries causes a portion of blood to be filtered across the semipermeable membrane into Bowman's capsule. There, the filtered portion of the blood (glomerular filtrate) begins to pass down to the tubule. Filtration is more rapid in the glomerulus than in ordinary tissue capillaries because the glomerular membrane is porous. The glomerular filtrate is similar in composition to blood except that it lacks blood cells, platelets, and large plasma proteins. Under normal conditions, capillary pores are too small to allow the loss of these large blood components. However, in many kidney diseases, capillary permeability increases, which allows plasma proteins and blood cells to pass into the urine.

The amount of blood filtered each minute by the glomeruli is expressed as the glomerular filtration rate (GFR). The normal GFR is about 125 mL/min. The peritubular capillary network reabsorbs most of the glomerular filtrate before it reaches the end of the collecting duct. Therefore only 1 mL/min (on average) is excreted as urine.

Tubular Function. The tubules and collecting ducts are responsible for the reabsorption of essential materials and excretion of nonessential ones (Table 44.1). They carry out these functions by reabsorption and secretion. *Reabsorption* is the passage of a substance from the lumen of the tubules through the tubule cells and into the capillaries. This process involves both active and passive transport mechanisms. Tubular *secretion* is the passage of a substance from the capillaries through the tubular cells into the lumen of the tubule. Reabsorption and secretion cause many changes in the composition of the glomerular filtrate as it moves through the entire length of the tubule.

In the proximal convoluted tubule, about 80% of the electrolytes are reabsorbed. Normally, this includes all glucose, amino acids, and small proteins. As reabsorption continues in the loop of Henle, water is conserved, which is important for concentrating the filtrate. The descending loop is permeable to water and moderately permeable to sodium, urea, and other solutes. In the ascending limb, chloride ions (Cl^-) are actively reabsorbed, followed by passive reabsorption of sodium ions (Na^+). About 25% of the filtered sodium is reabsorbed in the ascending limb.

Two important functions of the distal convoluted tubules are final regulation of water balance and acid-base balance. Antidiuretic hormone (ADH) is needed for water reabsorption in the kidney and is important in water balance. ADH makes the distal convoluted tubules and collecting ducts permeable to water. This allows water to be reabsorbed into the peritubular capillaries and eventually returned to the circulation.

Osmoreceptors in the anterior hypothalamus detect decreases in plasma osmolality. These osmoreceptors send neural input to *superoptic nuclei cells* in the hypothalamus. These superoptic nuclei cells have neuronal axons that end in the posterior pituitary gland and act to inhibit secretion of ADH. In the absence of ADH, the tubules are essentially impermeable to water. Thus any water in the tubules leaves the body as urine.

Aldosterone (released from the adrenal cortex) acts on the distal tubule to cause reabsorption of Na^+ and water. In exchange for Na^+, potassium ions (K^+) are excreted. The secretion of aldosterone is influenced by both circulating blood volume and plasma concentrations of Na^+ and K^+.

Acid-base regulation involves reabsorbing and conserving most of the bicarbonate (HCO_3^-) and secreting excess hydrogen ions (H^+). The distal tubule has different ways to keep the pH of ECF within a range of 7.35 to 7.45 (see Chapter 16).

Myocyte cells in the right atrium secrete a hormone, atrial natriuretic peptide (ANP), in response to atrial distention from an increase in plasma volume. ANP acts on the kidneys to increase sodium excretion. At the same time, ANP inhibits renin, ADH, and the action of angiotensin II on the adrenal glands, thereby suppressing aldosterone secretion. These combined effects of ANP result in the production of a large volume of dilute urine. ANP also causes relaxation of the afferent arteriole, thus increasing the GFR.

The renal tubules are also involved in calcium balance. The parathyroid gland releases parathyroid hormone (PTH) in response to low serum calcium levels. PTH maintains serum calcium levels by causing increased tubular reabsorption of calcium ions (Ca^{2+}) and decreased tubular reabsorption of phosphate ions (PO_4^{2-}). In kidney disease the effects of PTH may have a major effect on bone metabolism.

Vitamin D is a hormone that we obtain in the diet or synthesize by the action of ultraviolet radiation on cholesterol in the skin. These forms of vitamin D are inactive and go through 2 more steps to become metabolically active. The first step occurs in the liver; the second step occurs in the kidneys. Active vitamin D is essential for the absorption of calcium from the gastrointestinal (GI) tract. The patient with kidney failure (also called *renal failure*) will have a deficiency of the active metabolite of vitamin D and problems with calcium and phosphate balance (see Chapter 47).

In summary, the basic function of nephrons is to cleanse blood plasma of unnecessary substances. After the glomerulus has filtered the blood, the tubules select the unwanted from the wanted portions of tubular fluid. Essential constituents are returned to the blood, and dispensable substances pass into urine.

Other Functions of Kidneys. The kidneys participate in red blood cell (RBC) production and BP regulation. Erythropoietin is a hormone made in the kidneys and secreted in response to hypoxia and decreased renal blood flow. Erythropoietin stimulates RBC production in the bone marrow. A deficiency of erythropoietin occurs in kidney failure, leading to anemia.

Renin is important in the regulation of BP. Renin is made and secreted by the kidney's juxtaglomerular cells (Fig. 44.4). Renin is released into the bloodstream in response to decreased renal perfusion, decreased arterial BP, decreased ECF, decreased serum Na^+ concentration, and increased urinary

TABLE 44.1 Functions of Nephron Segments

Segment	Function
Glomerulus	Selective filtration
Proximal tubule	Reabsorption of 80% of electrolytes and water, glucose, amino acids, HCO_3^- Secretion of H^+ and creatinine
Loop of Henle	Concentration of filtrate Reabsorption of Na^+ and Cl^- in ascending limb and water in descending loop
Distal tubule	Reabsorption of water (regulated by ADH) and HCO_3^- Regulation of Ca^{2+} and PO_4^{2-} by parathyroid hormone Regulation of Na^+ and K^+ by aldosterone Secretion of K^+, H^+, ammonia
Collecting duct	Reabsorption of water (requires ADH)

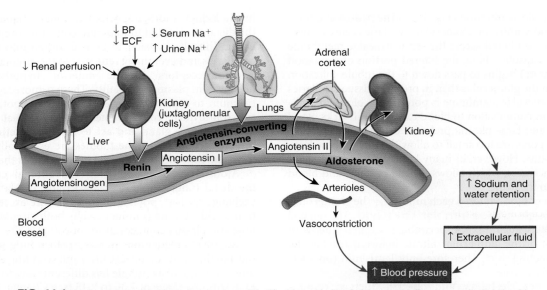

FIG. 44.4 Renin-angiotensin-aldosterone system. (Modified from Herlihy B, Maebius N: *The human body in health and disease,* ed 4, Philadelphia, 2011, Saunders.)

Na+ concentration. The plasma protein angiotensinogen (from the liver) is activated to angiotensin I by renin. Angiotensin I is then converted to angiotensin II by angiotensin-converting enzyme (ACE). ACE is found on the inner surface of all blood vessels, with especially high levels in the vessels of the lungs. Angiotensin II stimulates the release of aldosterone from the adrenal cortex. This causes Na+ and water retention, leading to increased ECF volume. Angiotensin II also causes increased peripheral vasoconstriction. An elevated BP inhibits renin release. Excessive renin production caused by impaired renal perfusion may be a contributing factor in causing hypertension (see Chapter 32).

Most body tissues synthesize prostaglandins (PGs) from the precursor arachidonic acid in response to appropriate stimuli. (See Chapter 11 and Fig. 11.2 for a more detailed discussion of PGs.) In the kidney, PG synthesis (mainly PGE_2 and PGI_2) occurs primarily in the medulla. These PGs have a vasodilating action, thus increasing renal blood flow and promoting Na+ excretion. They counteract the vasoconstrictive effect of substances such as angiotensin and norepinephrine. Renal PGs may have a systemic effect in lowering BP by decreasing systemic vascular resistance. The significance of renal PGs is related to the kidneys' role in causing hypertension. In renal failure with a loss of functioning tissue, these renal vasodilator factors are also lost, which may contribute to hypertension (see Chapter 46).

Ureters

The ureters are tubes that carry urine from the renal pelvis to the bladder (Fig. 44.1). Each ureter is about 10 to 12 inches (25 to 30.5 cm) long and 0.08 to 0.3 inches (0.2 to 0.8 cm) in diameter. Arranged in a meshlike outer layer, circular and longitudinal smooth muscle fibers contract to promote the peristaltic, 1-way flow of urine through the ureters. Distention, neurologic and endocrine influences, and drugs can affect these muscle contractions.

The narrow area where each ureter joins the renal pelvis is the *ureteropelvic junction* (UPJ). Subsequently, the ureters insert into either side of the bladder base at the *ureterovesical junctions* (UVJs). Because the ureteral lumens are narrowest at these junctions, the UPJ and UVJ are often sites of obstruction. The narrow ureteral lumens can be easily obstructed internally (e.g., urinary stones) or externally (e.g., tumors, adhesions, inflammation). Sympathetic and parasympathetic nerves, along with the vascular supply, surround the mucosal lining of the ureters. Stimulation of these nerves during passage of a stone may cause acute, severe pain, termed *renal colic.*

Because the renal pelvis holds only 3 to 5 mL of urine, kidney damage can result from a backflow of more than that amount of urine. The UVJ relies on the ureter's angle of bladder insertion and muscle fiber attachments with the bladder to prevent the backflow *(reflux)* of urine, which predisposes a person to an ascending infection. The distal ureter enters the bladder laterally at its base, courses along obliquely through the bladder wall for about 1.5 cm and intermingles with muscle fibers of the bladder base. Circular and longitudinal bladder muscle fibers adjacent to the imbedded ureter help secure it. When bladder pressure rises (e.g., during voiding or coughing), muscle fibers that the ureter shares with the bladder base contract first, promoting ureteral lumen closure. Next, the bladder contracts against its base, ensuring UVJ closure and prevention of urine reflux through the junction.

Bladder

The urinary bladder is located behind the symphysis pubis and anterior to the vagina and rectum (Fig. 44.5). Its primary functions are to serve as a reservoir for urine and to eliminate waste products from the body. Like the stomach, the bladder is a stretchable, saclike organ that contracts when it is empty.

The *trigone* is the triangular area formed by the 2 ureteral openings and bladder neck at the base of the bladder. The trigone is attached to the pelvis by many ligaments and does not change its shape during bladder filling or emptying. The bladder muscle *(detrusor)* is composed of layers of intertwined smooth muscle fibers. These fibers are capable of considerable distention during bladder filling and contraction during emptying. It is attached to the abdominal wall by an umbilical ligament, the *urachus.* Because of this attachment, as the bladder fills it rises

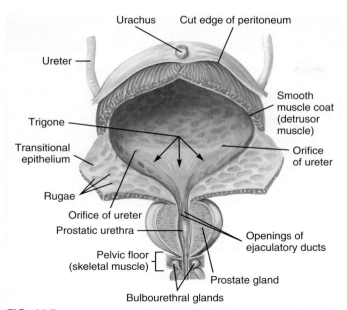

FIG. 44.5 Male urinary bladder. (Modified from Thibodeau GA, Patton KT: *Anatomy and physiology*, ed 6, St Louis, 2007, Mosby.)

toward the umbilicus. The dome and the anterior and lateral aspects of the bladder expand and contract.

Normal adult urine output is around 1500 mL/day, which varies with food and fluid intake. The volume of urine at night is less than half of that formed during the day because of hormonal influences (e.g., ADH). This diurnal pattern of urination is normal. Typically, a person will urinate 5 or 6 times during the day and occasionally at night.

On average, 200 to 250 mL of urine in the bladder cause moderate distention and the urge to urinate. When the quantity of urine reaches 400 to 600 mL, the person feels uncomfortable. Bladder capacity varies with the person, but generally ranges from 600 to 1000 mL. Evacuation of urine is termed *urination, micturition,* or *voiding.*

The bladder has the same mucosal lining as that of the renal pelvises, ureters, and bladder neck. The bladder is lined by transitional cell epithelium referred to as the *urothelium.* Unique to the urinary tract, the urothelium is resistant to absorption of urine. This means that after waste products (made by the kidneys) have left the kidneys, they cannot be reabsorbed in the urinary system. Microscopically, urothelium is only several cells deep. However, as urine enters the bladder, these cells can stretch to accommodate filling. As the bladder empties, the urothelium resumes its multicellular layer formation.

Transitional cell cancers in one section of the urinary tract can easily metastasize to other urinary tract areas given that the mucosal lining throughout the urinary tract is the same. Cancer cells may move down from upper urinary tract cancers and embed in the bladder, or large bladder tumors can invade the ureter. Cancer recurrence within the bladder is common.

Urethra

The urethra is a small tube that incorporates the smooth muscle of the bladder neck and extends to the striated muscle of the external meatus. The urethra's primary functions are to (1) control voiding and (2) serve as a conduit for urine from the bladder to the outside of the body during voiding.

The female urethra is 1 to 2 in (2.5 to 5 cm) long and lies behind the symphysis pubis but anterior to the vagina (Fig. 44.1, *C*). The male urethra, which is about 8 to 10 in (20 to 25 cm) long, starts at the bladder neck and extends the length of the penis (Fig. 44.1, *B*).

Urethrovesical Unit

Together, the bladder, urethra, and pelvic floor muscles form the *urethrovesical unit.* Voluntary control of this unit is defined as *continence.* Stimulating and inhibiting impulses are sent from the brain through the thoracolumbar (T11 to L2) and sacral (S2 to S4) areas of the spinal cord to control voiding. Bladder distention stimulates stretch receptors within the bladder wall. Impulses are transmitted to the sacral spinal cord and then to the brain, causing a desire to urinate.

If you cannot void at a given time, inhibitor impulses in the brain are stimulated and transmitted back through the thoracolumbar and sacral nerves innervating the bladder. In a coordinated fashion, the detrusor muscle accommodates to the pressure (does not contract) while the sphincter and pelvic floor muscles tighten (contract) to resist bladder pressure.

If you can void, cerebral inhibition is voluntarily suppressed. Impulses are transmitted via the spinal cord for the bladder neck, sphincter, and pelvic floor muscles to relax and for the bladder to contract. The sphincter closes, and the detrusor muscle relaxes when the bladder is empty.

Any disease or trauma that affects the function of the brain, spinal cord, or nerves that directly innervate the bladder, bladder neck, external sphincter, or pelvic floor can affect bladder function. These conditions include diabetes, multiple sclerosis, paraplegia, and tetraplegia (quadriplegia). Drugs affecting nerve transmission can affect bladder function.

Gerontologic Considerations: Effects of Aging on Urinary System

Anatomic changes in the aging kidney include a 20% to 30% decrease in size and weight between ages 30 and 90 years. By the seventh decade of life, 50% of glomeruli have lost their function.[1] Atherosclerosis accelerates the decrease of renal size with age.

Physiologic changes in the aging kidney include decreased renal blood flow, due in part to atherosclerosis, resulting in a decreased GFR. Changes in hormone levels (including ADH, aldosterone, ANP) result in decreased urinary concentrating ability and changes in the excretion of water, sodium, potassium, and acid. Despite these changes, older adults maintain homeostasis unless they encounter diseases or other physiologic stressors. After abrupt changes in blood volume, acid load, or other insults, the kidney may not be able to function effectively because much of its renal reserve has been lost.[1]

Physiologic changes occur in the aging urethra and bladder. The female urethra, bladder, vagina, and pelvic floor undergo a loss of elasticity and muscle support. Consequently, older women are more prone to bladder infections and incontinence. The prostate surrounds the proximal urethra. As men age, the prostate enlarges and may affect urinary patterns, causing hesitancy, retention, slow stream, and bladder infections.

Constipation, often experienced by older adults, can affect urination. Partial urethral obstruction may occur because of the rectum's close proximity to the urethra. Age-related changes in the urinary system and differences in assessment findings are outlined in Table 44.2.

TABLE 44.2 Gerontologic Assessment Differences

Urinary System

Gerontologic Changes	Differences in Assessment Findings
Kidney	
• ↓ Amount of renal tissue	• Less palpable
• ↓ Number of nephrons and renal blood vessels. Thickened basement membrane of Bowman's capsule and glomeruli	• ↓ Creatinine clearance, ↑ BUN level, ↑ serum creatinine
• ↓ Function of loop of Henle and tubules	• Changes in drug excretion, nocturia, loss of normal diurnal excretory pattern because of ↓ ability to concentrate urine; less concentrated urine
Ureter, Bladder, and Urethra	
• ↓ Elasticity and muscle tone	• Palpable bladder after urination because of retention
• Weakening of urinary sphincter	• Stress incontinence (especially during Valsalva maneuver), dribbling of urine after urination
• ↓ Bladder capacity and sensory receptors	• Frequency, urgency, nocturia, overflow incontinence
• Estrogen deficiency leading to thin, dry vaginal tissue	• Stress or overactive bladder, dysuria
• ↑ Prevalence of unstable bladder contractions	• Overactive bladder
• Prostatic enlargement	• Hesitancy, frequency, urgency, nocturia, straining to urinate, retention, dribbling

TABLE 44.3 Potentially Nephrotoxic Agents

Antibiotics	Other Drugs	Other Agents
• amikacin	• captopril	• Gold
• amphotericin B	• cimetidine	• Heavy metals
• bacitracin	• cisplatin	
• cephalosporins	• cocaine	
• gentamicin	• cyclosporine	
• neomycin	• ethylene glycol	
• polymyxin B	• heroin	
• streptomycin	• lithium	
• sulfonamides	• methotrexate	
• tobramycin	• nitrosoureas (e.g., carmustine)	
• vancomycin	• nonsteroidal antiinflammatory drugs (e.g., ibuprofen, indomethacin)	
	• phenacetin	
	• quinine	
	• rifampin	
	• salicylates (large quantities)	

CASE STUDY

Patient Introduction

(© iStockphoto/Thinkstock.)

A.K. is a 28-yr-old black man who comes to the emergency department (ED) in acute distress with severe abdominal pain. The pain began about 6 hours ago after he finished a 10-mile run as part of his training for a marathon. He says that the pain has steadily increased and he is nauseous. His urine is a dark, smoky color.

Discussion Questions

1. What are the possible causes of A.K.'s abdominal pain, nausea, and urine color?
2. What type of assessment would be most appropriate for A.K.: comprehensive, focused, or emergency? On what basis did you make that decision?
3. What assessment questions will you ask him?

You will learn more about A.K. and his condition as you read through this assessment chapter.

(See p. 1015 for more information on A.K.)

ASSESSMENT OF URINARY SYSTEM

Subjective Data

Important Health Information

Past Health History. Ask the patient about the presence or history of kidney disease or other urologic problems. Note specific urinary problems, such as cancer, infections, benign prostatic hyperplasia (BPH), and stones. Ask about other health problems that may affect kidney function, including hypertension, diabetes, gout, connective tissue disorders (e.g., systemic lupus erythematosus), hepatitis, human immunodeficiency virus (HIV) infection, neurologic conditions (e.g., stroke, back injury), and trauma.[2]

Medications. An assessment of the patient's current and past use of medications is important. Include over-the-counter drugs, prescription drugs, and herbal therapies. Drugs affect the urinary tract in several ways. Many drugs can be nephrotoxic (Table 44.3). Certain drugs may alter the quantity and character of urine output (e.g., diuretics). Several drugs change the color of urine. Phenazopyridine (Pyridium) turns urine orange. Nitrofurantoin (Macrodantin) turns urine dark yellow to brown. Anticoagulants may cause hematuria. Many antidepressants, calcium channel blockers, antihistamines, and drugs used for neurologic and musculoskeletal disorders affect the ability of the bladder or sphincter to contract or relax normally.

Surgery or Other Treatments. Ask the patient about hospitalizations related to renal or urologic diseases and all urinary problems during past pregnancies. Inquire about the duration, severity, and patient's perception of any problem and its treatment. Document past surgeries, especially pelvic surgeries, and urinary tract instrumentation (e.g., catheterization). Ask the patient about any radiation or chemotherapy treatment for cancer.

Functional Health Patterns. Key questions to ask a patient with problems related to the renal system are listed in Table 44.4.

Health Perception–Health Management Pattern. Ask about the patient's general health. Abnormal kidney function may be suspected if the patient reports changes in weight or appetite, excess thirst, fluid retention, headache, pruritus, blurred vision, or "feeling tired all the time." An older adult may report malaise and nonlocalized abdominal discomfort as the only symptoms of a urinary tract infection (UTI). In older adults with a UTI, family members may report the patient is disoriented, has fallen, or has increased confusion.

Obtain a smoking history. Cigarette smoking is a major risk factor for bladder and kidney cancer. Smokers who also work with cancer-causing chemicals have an especially high risk for bladder cancer.

TABLE 44.4 Health History

Urinary System

Health Perception–Health Management
- How is your energy level compared with 1 yr ago?
- Do you notice any visual changes?*
- Have you ever smoked? If yes, how many packs per day?
- Tell me about the types of jobs you have had.

Nutritional-Metabolic
- How is your appetite?
- Has your weight changed over the past year?*
- Do you take vitamins, herbs, or any other supplements?*
- How much and what kinds of fluids do you drink daily?
- How many dairy products and how much meat do you eat?
- Do you drink coffee? Colas? Tea?
- Do you spice your food heavily?*

Elimination
- Are you able to sit through a 2-hr meeting or ride in a car for 2 hr without urinating?
- Do you awaken at night with the desire to urinate? If so, how many times does this occur during an average night?
- Do you ever notice blood in your urine?* If so, at what point in the urination does it occur?
- Have you noticed any change in the color or smell of your urine?*
- Do you ever pass urine when you do not intend to? When?
- Do you use special devices or supplies for urine elimination or control?*
- How often do you move your bowels?
- Do you ever have constipation or diarrhea?*
- Do you ever have problems controlling your bowels?*

Activity-Exercise
- Have you noticed any changes in your ability to perform your usual daily activities?*
- Do certain activities worsen your urinary problem?*
- Has your urinary problem caused you to alter or stop any activity or exercise?*
- Do you need help moving or getting to the bathroom?*

Sleep-Rest
- Do you awaken at night from an urge to urinate?* How does this disturb your sleep?
- Do you awaken at night from pain or other problems and urinate as a matter of routine before returning to sleep?*
- Do you have daytime sleepiness and fatigue because of nighttime urination?*

Cognitive-Perceptual
- Do you ever have pain when you urinate?* If so, where is the pain?

Self-Perception–Self-Concept
- How does your urinary problem make you feel about yourself?
- Do you perceive your body differently since you have developed a urinary problem?

Role-Relationship
- Does your urinary problem interfere with your relationships with family or friends?*
- Has your urinary problem caused a change in your job status or affected your ability to carry out job-related responsibilities?*

Sexuality-Reproductive
- Has your urinary problem caused any change in your sexual pleasure or performance?*
- Do hygiene concerns interfere with sexual activities?

Coping–Stress Tolerance
- Do you feel able to manage the problems associated with your urinary problem? If not, explain.
- What strategies are you using to cope with your urinary problem?

Values-Beliefs
- Has your present illness affected your belief system?*
- Are your treatment decisions related to your urinary problem in conflict with your value system?*

*If yes, describe.

Exposure to certain chemicals can affect the urinary system. Aromatic amines and some organic chemicals increase the risk for bladder cancer. Phenol and ethylene glycol are examples of nephrotoxic chemicals. Obtain an occupational history. Machinists, painters, hairdressers, printers, and truck drivers have an increased incidence of bladder cancer.[3]

Information about places where a patient has lived is important. Persons living in the Southeast part of the United States have the highest incidence of urinary stones. This may be caused by the higher mineral content of the soil and water.[4] A person living in Middle Eastern countries or Africa can acquire certain parasites that can cause cystitis or bladder cancer.

GENETIC RISK ALERT

- Polycystic kidney disease and congenital urinary tract abnormalities (e.g., Alport syndrome [congenital nephritis]) are genetic disorders.
- A family history of certain renal or urologic problems increases the chance of similar problems occurring in the patient.
- For any disease reported in the health history, ask if other family members also have/had the same or similar diseases.

Nutritional-Metabolic Pattern. The usual quantity and types of fluid a patient drinks are important in relation to urinary tract disease. Dehydration may contribute to UTIs, stone formation, and kidney failure. Large intake of specific foods, such as dairy products or foods high in proteins, may lead to stone formation. Asparagus may cause the urine to smell musty. Red urine caused by beet ingestion may be mistaken for bloody urine. Caffeine, alcohol, carbonated beverages, some artificial sweeteners, or spicy foods often worsen urinary inflammatory diseases. Green tea and some herbal teas cause diuresis. An unexplained weight gain may be the result of fluid retention from a kidney problem. Anorexia, nausea, and vomiting can dramatically affect fluid status and require careful monitoring.

Elimination Pattern. Questions about urine elimination patterns are the cornerstone of the health history in the patient with a lower urinary tract disorder. Begin with asking how the patient manages urine elimination. Ask about daytime (diurnal) voiding frequency and the frequency of nocturia. Pelvic organ prolapses, particularly advanced anterior vaginal prolapse, may cause suprapubic pressure, frequency, urgency, and incontinence from urinary retention. Ask about other bothersome lower urinary tract symptoms, including urgency, incontinence, or urinary retention. Table 44.5 lists some common manifestations of urinary tract disorders.

TABLE 44.5 Manifestations of Urinary System Disorders

General Manifestations	SPECIFIC MANIFESTATIONS RELATED TO URINARY SYSTEM				
	Edema	Pain	Patterns of Urination	Urine Output	Urine Composition
• Anorexia	• Ankle	• Dysuria	• Change in stream	• Anuria	• Color (red, brown, yellowish green)
• Blurred vision	• Ascites	• Flank or costovertebral angle	• Dribbling	• Oliguria	• Concentrated
• Change in weight	• Facial (periorbital)	• Groin	• Dysuria	• Polyuria	• Dilute
• Chills	• Generalized edema	• Suprapubic	• Frequency		• Hematuria
• Cognitive changes	• Sacral		• Hesitancy of stream		• Pyuria
• Excessive thirst			• Incontinence		
• Fatigue			• Nocturia		
• Headaches			• Retention		
• High BP			• Stress incontinence		
• Nausea and vomiting			• Urgency		

Changes in the color and appearance of urine are often significant and need evaluated. If blood is visible in the urine, determine if it occurs at the beginning of, throughout, or at the end of urination. This is harder for the female patient.

Assess bowel function. Problems with fecal incontinence may signal neurologic causes for bladder problems because of shared nerve pathways. Constipation and fecal impaction can partially obstruct the urethra, causing inadequate bladder emptying, overflow incontinence, and infection.

Determine the patient's method of managing a urinary problem. A patient may already be using a catheter or collection device. Sometimes a patient must assume a specific position to urinate or perform maneuvers, such as pressing on the lower abdomen (Credé's method) or straining (Valsalva maneuver), to empty the bladder.

Activity-Exercise Pattern. Assess the patient's level of activity. A sedentary person is more likely to have stasis of urine than an active person and thus be predisposed to infection and stones. Demineralization of bones in a person with limited physical activity can cause increased urine calcium precipitation.

An active person may find that increasing activity worsens the urinary problem. The patient who has had prostate surgery or who has weakened pelvic floor muscles may leak urine when trying certain activities, such as running. Some men develop chronic inflammatory prostatitis or epididymitis after heavy lifting or long-distance driving.

Sleep-Rest Pattern. Nocturia is a common and a particularly bothersome symptom that often leads to sleep deprivation, daytime sleepiness, and fatigue. It occurs in multiple problems affecting the lower urinary tract, including urinary incontinence, urinary retention, and interstitial cystitis. Nocturia may be related to polyuria from kidney disease, poorly controlled diabetes, alcohol use, excess fluid intake, liver disease, heart failure, or obstructive sleep apnea.

When assessing nocturia, determine whether the need to urinate causes the person to arise from sleep or whether pain or other symptoms interrupt sleep. Ask if the person urinates as a matter of habit before returning to bed. Up to 1 episode of nocturia is considered normal in younger adults, and up to 2 episodes are acceptable in adults ages 65 years or older. If an older adult has more than 2 episodes during the night, assess the amount and timing of fluid intake. This information will help determine whether further investigation is needed.

Cognitive-Perceptual Pattern. Assess the level of mobility, visual acuity, and dexterity. These are important factors to evaluate in a patient with urologic problems, especially when urine retention or incontinence is a problem. Determine if the patient is alert, understands instructions, and can recall instructions when needed.

If urinary incontinence is present, ask how the patient is managing the problem. Recognize that incontinence is often distressing and embarrassing. Discuss the problem with the patient with sensitivity in a nonjudgmental manner.

A frequent symptom of renal and urologic problems is pain, including dysuria, groin pain, costovertebral pain, and suprapubic pain. Assess pain and document the location, character, and duration. The absence of pain when other urinary symptoms exist is significant. Many urinary tract cancers are painless in the early stages.

Self-Perception–Self-Concept Pattern. Problems associated with the urinary system, such as incontinence, urinary diversion procedures, and chronic fatigue (may occur with anemia), can result in loss of self-esteem and a negative body image.

Role-Relationship Pattern. Urinary problems can affect many aspects of a person's life, including the ability to work and relationships with others. These factors have important implications for future treatment and management of the patient's condition.

Urinary system problems may be serious enough to cause problems in job-related and social situations. Chronic dialysis therapy often makes regular employment or management of home and family responsibilities difficult. Concurrent poor health and negative body image can seriously affect existing roles.

Sexuality-Reproductive Pattern. Assess the effect of renal problems on the patient's sexual satisfaction. Problems related to personal hygiene and fatigue can negatively affect sexual relationships. Although urinary incontinence is not directly associated with sexual dysfunction, it often has a devastating effect on self-esteem and social and intimate relationships. Counseling both the patient and partner may be needed.

Objective Data
Physical Examination
Inspection. Assess for changes in the following:
- *Skin:* Pallor, yellow-gray cast, excoriations, changes in turgor, bruises, texture (e.g., rough, dry skin) (see Table 22.9 for assessment of dark-skinned persons)
- *Mouth:* Stomatitis, ammonia breath odor
- *Face and extremities:* Generalized edema, peripheral edema
- *Abdomen:* Abdominal contour for midline mass in lower abdomen (may indicate bladder distention and urinary retention) or unilateral mass (sometimes seen in adults, indicating kidney enlargement from large tumor or polycystic kidney)

CASE STUDY—cont'd

Subjective Data

(© iStockphoto/ Thinkstock.)

A focused subjective assessment of A.K. revealed the following information:

Past Medical History: History of 1 isolated incidence of gout 6 years ago. He stopped drinking alcohol with no further occurrence. Appendectomy 12 years ago.

Medications: None.

Health Perception–Health Management: A.K. states that he is usually healthy. He does not smoke or drink alcohol. He has never had this type of pain before. Describes the pain as being sharp and colicky (coming in waves). Rates the pain as 9 on a scale of 0 to 10.

Nutritional-Metabolic: A.K. is currently on a high-protein diet as he trains for the marathon. He eats a lot of chicken, beef, and seafood. He drinks milk-based protein shakes and water after exercising but admits that he does not think he drinks enough to replace fluid loss from perspiration. He drinks coffee for energy but denies eating chocolate or other sweets. He avoids sodas.

Elimination: Denies any history of problems with urination, constipation, or diarrhea. This is the first time he has ever noticed a change of color in his urine.

Activity-Exercise: Prides himself on his ability to exercise and run without difficulty.

Sleep-Rest: Does not awaken at night to urinate.

Cognitive-Perceptual: Denies pain on urination.

Self-Perception–Self-Concept: Believes he can monitor himself and maintain a healthy lifestyle.

Coping–Stress Tolerance: Worried that this pain may interfere with his marathon training.

Discussion Questions

1. Which subjective assessment findings are of most concern to you?
2. What would be your priority assessment of A.K.?
3. What should be included in the physical assessment? What would you be looking for?

You will learn more about the physical examination of the urinary system in the next section.

(See p. 1016 for more information on A.K.)

Answers available at *http://evolve.elsevier.com/Lewis/medsurg.*

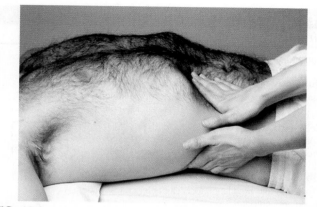

FIG. 44.6 Palpating the right kidney. (From Brundage DJ: *Renal disorders,* St Louis, 1992, Mosby.)

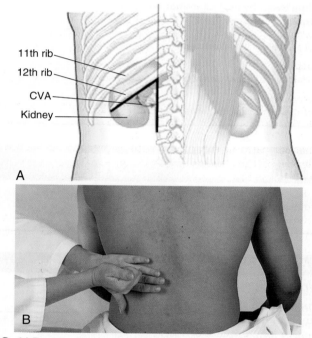

11th rib
12th rib
CVA
Kidney

A

B

FIG. 44.7 A, Costovertebral angle. B, Indirect fist percussion of the costovertebral angle *(CVA).* To assess the kidney, place one hand over the twelfth rib at the CVA on the back. Thump that hand with the ulnar edge of the other fist. (From Jarvis C: *Physical examination and health assessment,* ed 7, St Louis, 2016, Saunders.)

- *Weight:* Weight gain from edema. Weight loss and muscle wasting in kidney failure
- *General state of health:* Fatigue, lethargy, and decreased alertness

Palpation. The kidneys are posterior organs protected by the abdominal organs, ribs, and heavy back muscles. A landmark useful in locating the kidneys is the costovertebral angle (CVA) formed by the rib cage and the vertebral column. The normal-sized left kidney is rarely palpable because the spleen lies directly on top of it. Occasionally the lower pole of the right kidney is palpable.

To palpate the right kidney, place your left (anterior) hand behind and support the patient's right side between the rib cage and the iliac crest (Fig. 44.6). Elevate the right flank with the left hand. Use your right hand to palpate deeply for the right kidney. The lower pole of the right kidney may be felt as a smooth, rounded mass that descends on inspiration. If the kidney is palpable, note its size, contour, and tenderness. Kidney enlargement is suggestive of cancer or other serious renal pathologic conditions.

The urinary bladder is normally not palpable unless it is distended with urine. If the bladder is full, it may be felt as a smooth, round, firm organ and is sensitive to palpation.

Percussion. Tenderness in the flank area may be detected by fist percussion *(kidney punch).* This technique is performed by striking the fist of one hand against the dorsal surface of the other hand, which is placed flat along the posterior CVA margin (Fig. 44.7). Normally this type of percussion should not elicit pain. If CVA tenderness and pain are present, it may indicate a kidney infection or polycystic kidney disease.[5]

A bladder does not percuss until it contains at least 150 mL of urine. If the bladder is full, dullness is heard above the symphysis pubis. A distended bladder may be percussed as high as the umbilicus.

Auscultation. Use the diaphragm of the stethoscope to auscultate bowel sounds, since the bowels can affect the urinary system.

FOCUSED ASSESSMENT
Urinary System

Use this checklist to ensure that the key assessment steps have been done.

Subjective

Ask the patient about any of the following and note responses.

Painful urination	Y	N
Changes in color of urine (blood, cloudy)	Y	N
Change in characteristics of urination (decreased, excessive)	Y	N
Problems with frequent nighttime urination (nocturia)	Y	N

Objective: Diagnostic

Check the following laboratory results for critical values.

Blood urea nitrogen	✓
Serum creatinine	✓
Urinalysis	✓
Urine culture and sensitivity	✓

Objective: Physical Examination

Inspect

Abdomen	✓
Urinary meatus for inflammation or discharge	✓

Palpate

Abdomen for bladder distention, masses, or tenderness	✓

Percuss

Costovertebral angle for tenderness	✓

TABLE 44.6 Normal Physical Assessment of Urinary System

- No costovertebral angle tenderness
- Nonpalpable kidney and bladder
- No palpable masses

Table 44.6 shows how to record the normal physical assessment findings of the urinary system. Table 44.7 describes assessment abnormalities of the urinary system. Assessment findings may vary in the older adult. Table 44.2 presents the age-related changes in the urinary system and differences in assessment findings. Use a *focused assessment* to evaluate the status of previously identified urinary system problems and to monitor for signs of new problems. A focused assessment of the urinary system is outlined in the box on this page.

CASE STUDY—cont'd
Objective Data: Physical Examination

(© iStockphoto/ Thinkstock.)

A focused assessment of A.K. reveals the following: A.K. is lying with his knees bent and drawn to his abdominal area. He appears restless and keeps moving from back to side to reduce his discomfort. Vital signs are as follows: BP 156/70, apical pulse 108, respiratory rate 24, temperature 37.4° C, O_2 saturation 96% on room air. Awake, alert, and oriented × 3. Lungs are clear to auscultation. Apical pulse is regular. Abdomen nondistended with + bowel sounds in all 4 quadrants. No rebound tenderness. Positive left costovertebral tenderness. Voiding small amounts of dark, smoky urine.

Discussion Questions

1. Which physical assessment findings are of most concern to you?
2. Based on the results of the subjective and physical assessment findings, what diagnostic studies do you think may be ordered for A.K.?

You will learn more about diagnostic studies related to the urinary system in the next section.

(See p. 1022 for more information on A.K.)

Answers available at *http://evolve.elsevier.com/Lewis/medsurg*.

TABLE 44.7 Assessment Abnormalities
Urinary System

Finding	Description	Possible Etiology and Significance
Anuria	Technically no urination (24-hr urine output <100 mL)	Acute kidney injury, end-stage renal disease, bilateral ureteral obstruction
Burning on urination	Stinging pain in urethral area	Urethral irritation, UTI, urethral calculus
Dysuria	Painful or difficult urination	UTI, interstitial cystitis, urethral calculus, and wide variety of pathologic conditions
Enuresis	Involuntary nocturnal urination	Lower urinary tract disorder
Frequency	↑ Incidence of urination	Acutely inflamed bladder, retention with overflow, excess fluid intake, intake of bladder irritants, urethral calculus
Hematuria	Blood in the urine	Cancer of genitourinary tract, blood dyscrasias, kidney disease, UTI, stones in kidney or ureter, anticoagulants
Hesitancy	Delay or difficulty in initiating urination	Partial urethral obstruction, benign prostatic hyperplasia
Incontinence	Inability to voluntarily control discharge of urine	Neurogenic bladder, bladder infection, injury to external sphincter
Nocturia	Frequent urination at night	Kidney disease with impaired concentrating ability, bladder obstruction, heart failure, diabetes, post renal transplant, excess evening and nighttime fluid intake
Oliguria	↓ Amount of urine in a time period (24-hr urine output of 100–400 mL)	Severe dehydration, shock, transfusion reaction, kidney disease, end-stage renal disease
Pain	Suprapubic pain (related to bladder), urethral pain (irritation of bladder neck), flank pain, CVA tenderness	Infection, urinary retention, foreign body in urinary tract, urethritis, pyelonephritis, renal colic, stones
Pneumaturia	Passage of urine containing gas	Fistula connections between bowel and bladder, gas-forming UTI
Polyuria	Large volume of urine in a time period	Diabetes, diabetes insipidus, chronic kidney disease, diuretics, excess fluid intake, obstructive sleep apnea
Retention	Inability to urinate even though bladder contains excess amount of urine	Finding after pelvic surgery, childbirth, catheter removal, anesthesia; urethral stricture or obstruction; neurogenic bladder
Stress incontinence	Involuntary urination with ↑ pressure (sneezing or coughing)	Weakness of sphincter control, lack of estrogen, urinary retention

DIAGNOSTIC STUDIES OF URINARY SYSTEM

Many diagnostic studies are used to assess problems of the urinary system. Tables 44.8, 44.9, 44.10, and 44.11 describe the most common studies. Select studies are described in more detail here.

Many radiologic studies require the use of a bowel preparation the evening before the study to clear the lower GI tract of feces and flatus. Because the kidneys lie in a retroperitoneal location, colon contents can obstruct visualization of the urinary tract. If the bowel preparation does not adequately clear the lower GI tract, the study may be unsuccessful and need rescheduled. Common bowel preparations include enemas, magnesium citrate, and bisacodyl (Dulcolax) tablets or suppositories. Patients with kidney failure should not receive some bowel preparations, such as magnesium citrate and Fleet enema, because the kidneys cannot excrete the magnesium (see Chapter 46).

Iodine-based contrast media used in some diagnostic studies may cause contrast-induced kidney injury (CIN) and allergic reactions. Keeping the patient hydrated is important. Some patients may need IV fluids started hours before the procedure.[6] N-acetylcysteine, a renal vasodilator and antioxidant, is sometimes given to reduce the incidence of CIN. It can be given by oral or IV route.

When a patient has multiple diagnostic studies, it is important to maintain hydration.[6] The patient is at risk for dehydration when they have had nothing by mouth for consecutive days, extended time in the radiology department, and bowel preparations. Severe dehydration, especially in debilitated or older patients and patients with diabetes, may lead to acute kidney injury. Ensure that the patient is properly hydrated and given adequate nourishment between studies. Check with the HCP about insulin dosage for patients with diabetes who are NPO.

TABLE 44.8 Urinalysis

General examination of urine to establish baseline information or provide data to establish a tentative diagnosis and determine whether further studies are needed.
Before: Wash perineal area before collecting specimen.
During: Try to obtain first urinated morning specimen.
After: Ensure specimen is examined within 1 hr of urinating.

Test	Normal	Abnormal Finding	Possible Etiology and Significance
Bilirubin	None	Present	Liver disorders. May appear before jaundice is visible (see Chapter 43)
Casts	None Occasional hyaline	Present	Molds of the renal tubules that may contain protein, WBCs, RBCs, or bacteria. Noncellular casts (hyaline in appearance) occasionally found in normal urine
Color	Amber yellow	Dark, smoky color	Hematuria
		Yellow-brown to olive green	Excess bilirubin
		Orange-red or orange-brown	phenazopyridine (Pyridium)
		Cloudiness of freshly voided urine	UTI
		Colorless urine	Excess fluid intake, kidney disease, or diabetes insipidus
Culture for organisms	No organisms in bladder<10^4 organisms/mL result of normal urethral flora	Bacteria counts >10^5/mL	UTI; most common organisms are *E. coli*, enterococci, *Klebsiella*, *Proteus*, and streptococci
Glucose	None	Glycosuria	Diabetes, low renal threshold for glucose reabsorption (if blood glucose level is normal). Pituitary disorders
Ketones	None	Present	Altered carbohydrate and fat metabolism in diabetes and starvation; dehydration, vomiting, severe diarrhea
Odor	Aromatic	Ammonia-like odor	Urine allowed to stand
		Unpleasant odor	UTI
Osmolality	50–1200 mOsm/kg (50–1200 mmol/kg)	<50 mOsm/kg >1200 mOsm/kg	Tubular dysfunction. Kidney lost ability to concentrate or dilute urine
pH	4.6–8.0 (average, 6.0)	>8.0	UTI. Urine allowed to stand at room temperature (bacteria decompose urea to ammonia)
Protein	Random protein (dipstick): 0–trace	Persistent proteinuria	Characteristic of acute and chronic kidney disease, especially involving glomeruli. Heart failure.
	24-hr protein (quantitative): 50–80 mg/day		In absence of disease: high-protein diet, strenuous exercise, dehydration, fever, emotional stress, contamination by vaginal secretions
RBCs	0–4/hpf	<4.0	Respiratory or metabolic acidosis
		>4/hpf	Stones, cystitis, cancer, glomerulonephritis, tuberculosis, kidney biopsy, UTI, trauma
Specific gravity	1.005–1.030	Low	Dilute urine, excess diuresis, diabetes insipidus
	Maximum concentrating ability of kidney in morning urine (1.025–1.030)	High	Dehydration, albuminuria, glycosuria
		Fixed at about 1.010	Renal inability to concentrate urine; end-stage renal disease
WBCs	0–5/hpf	>5/hpf	UTI or inflammation

hpf, High-powered field.

TABLE 44.9 Diagnostic Studies

Urine

Study	Description and Purpose	Nursing Responsibility
Composite urine collection	Measures specific components, such as electrolytes, glucose, protein, 17-ketosteroids, catecholamines, creatinine, and minerals. Composite urine specimens are collected over a period ranging from 2–24 hr.	*During:* Have patient urinate and discard this first urine specimen. Note this time as the start of the test. Save all urine from subsequent urinations in a container for designated period. At end of period, ask patient to urinate, and this urine is added to container. Remind patient to save all urine during study period. Specimens may need refrigerated or preservatives added to container used for collecting urine.
Concentration test	Evaluates renal concentration ability. Measured by specific gravity readings. *Reference interval:* 1.005–1.030.	*Before:* Have patient fast after given time in evening (in usual procedure). *During:* Collect 3 urine specimens at hourly intervals in morning.
Creatinine clearance	Creatinine is a waste product of protein breakdown (primarily body muscle mass). Clearance of creatinine by kidney approximates the GFR. Calculated as follows: $$\text{Creatinine clearance} = \frac{\text{Urine creatinine (mg/dL)} \times \text{Urine volume (mL/min)}}{\text{Serum creatinine (mg/dL)}}$$ Reference interval: *Male:* 107–139 mL/min/1.73 m^2 *Female:* 87–107 mL/min/1.73 m^2 (corrected for body surface area).	*During:* Collect 24-hr urine specimen. Discard first urination when test is started. Save urine from all subsequent urinations for 24 hr. Have patient urinate at end of 24 hr and add specimen to collection. Ensure that serum creatinine is measured during 24-hr period.
Protein determination		
• Dipstick (Albustix, Combistix)	Detects protein (primarily albumin) in urine. *Reference interval:* 0 to trace.	*During:* Dip end of stick in urine and read result by comparison with color chart on label as directed. Grading is from 0 to 4+. Interpret with caution. Positive result may not indicate significant proteinuria. Some drugs may give false-positive readings.
• Quantitative protein test	A 24-hr collection gives a more accurate indication of amount of protein in urine. Persistent proteinuria usually indicates glomerular kidney disease. *Reference interval:* 50–80 mg/day (mainly albumin).	*During:* Perform 24-hr urine collection as above.
Residual urine	Determines amount of urine left in bladder after urinating. Finding may be abnormal in problems with bladder innervation, sphincter impairment, benign prostatic hyperplasia, or urethral strictures. *Reference interval:* ≤50 mL urine (increases with age).	*During:* Immediately after patient urinates, catheterize patient or use bladder ultrasound equipment. If a large amount of residual urine is obtained, HCP may want catheter left in bladder.
Urine culture ("clean catch," "midstream")	Confirms suspected UTI and identifies causative organisms. *Normally,* bladder is sterile, but urethra contains bacteria and a few WBCs. *Reference interval:* If properly collected, stored, and handled: <10^3 organisms/mL usually indicates no infection. 10^3–10^5/mL is usually not diagnostic. Test may need repeated. >10^5/mL indicates infection.	*During:* Use sterile container for collection of urine. Touch only outside of container. *For women:* Wipe the periurethral area from front to back, dry the area thoroughly with sterile swab, separate labia with one hand. *For men:* Retract foreskin (if present), cleanse glans around urethra, replace foreskin after cleaning. After cleaning, have patient start voiding, and collect the specimen 1 to 2 seconds after voiding starts. The initial voided urine flushes out most contaminants in the urethra and perineal area. Catheterization may be needed if patient is unable to cooperate with procedure.
Urine cytologic study	Identifies abnormal cellular structures that occur with bladder cancer. Used to follow the progress of bladder cancer after treatment.	*During:* Obtain specimens by voiding, catheterization, or bladder irrigation. Do not use morning's first voided specimen because epithelial cells may change in appearance in urine held in bladder overnight. *After:* Specimen should be fresh or brought to laboratory within the hour. An alcohol-based fixative is then added to preserve the cellular structure.

Urine Studies

Urinalysis. Urinalysis is one of the first studies done to evaluate disorders of the urinary tract (Table 44.8). Results from the urinalysis may show abnormalities, suggest the need for further studies, or show progression in a previously diagnosed disorder.

Although a specimen may be collected at any time of the day for a routine urinalysis, it is best to obtain the first specimen urinated in the morning. This concentrated specimen is more likely to contain abnormal constituents if they are present in the urine. The specimen should be examined within 1 hour of urinating. Otherwise, bacteria multiply rapidly, RBCs hemolyze, *casts* (molds of renal tubules) disintegrate, and the urine becomes alkaline because of urea-splitting bacteria. If it is not possible to send the specimen to the laboratory immediately, refrigerate it. However, for the best results, coordinate specimen collection with routine laboratory hours.

Creatinine Clearance. A common test used to analyze urinary system disorders is creatinine clearance. Creatinine is a waste product made by muscle breakdown. Urinary excretion of creatinine is a measure of the amount of active muscle tissue in the

TABLE 44.10 Blood Studies
Urinary System

Test	Reference Interval	Significance
Bicarbonate	22–26 mEq/L (22–26 mmol/L).	Most patients in renal failure have metabolic acidosis and low serum HCO_3^- levels.
Blood urea nitrogen (BUN)	10–20 mg/dL (3.6–7.1 mmol/L)	Used to detect renal problems. Concentration of urea in blood is regulated by rate at which kidney excretes urea. Nonrenal factors may increase BUN (e.g., rapid cell destruction from infections, fever, GI bleeding, trauma, athletic activity, excessive muscle breakdown).
BUN/creatinine ratio	12:1–20:1	Increased ratio may be due to conditions that decrease blood flow to kidneys (e.g., heart failure, dehydration, GI bleeding) or increased dietary protein. A decreased ratio may occur with liver disease (from decreased urea formation) and malnutrition.
Calcium (total)	9.0–10.5 mg/dL (2.25–2.62 mmol/L)	Main mineral in bone and aids in muscle contraction, neurotransmission, and clotting. In kidney disease, decreased reabsorption of Ca^{2+} leads to renal osteodystrophy.
Creatinine	*Male:* 0.6–1.2 mg/dL (53–106 µmol/L) *Female:* 0.5–1.1 mg/dL (44.97 µmol/L)	More reliable than BUN as a determinant of renal function. Creatinine is a product of muscle and protein metabolism. It is released at a constant rate.
Phosphorus	3.0–4.5 mg/dL (0.97–1.45 mmol/L).	Phosphorus balance is inversely related to Ca^{2+} balance. In kidney disease, phosphorus levels are high because the kidney is the primary excretory organ.
Potassium	3.5–5.0 mEq/L (3.5–5.0 mmol/L)	Kidneys excrete majority of body's potassium. In kidney disease, K^+ determinations are critical because K^+ is one of the first electrolytes to become abnormal. High K^+ levels >6 mEq/L can lead to muscle weakness and cardiac dysrhythmias.
Sodium	136–145 mEq/L (136–145 mmol/L)	Main extracellular electrolyte determining blood volume. Values usually stay within normal range until late stages of renal failure.
Uric acid	*Male:* 4.0–8.5 mg/dL (0.24–0.51 mmol/L) *Female:* 2.7–7.3 mg/dL (0.16–0.43 mmol/L)	Used as screening test for disorders of purine metabolism. Can indicate kidney disease. Values depend on renal function, rate of purine metabolism, and dietary intake of food rich in purines.

TABLE 44.11 Diagnostic Studies
Urinary System

Study	Description and Purpose	Nursing Responsibility
Endoscopy Cystoscopy	Inspects interior of bladder with a tubular lighted scope (cystoscope) (Fig. 44.10). Can be used to insert ureteral catheters, remove stones, obtain biopsy specimens of bladder lesions, and treat bleeding lesions. Lithotomy position is used. Procedure may be done using local or general anesthesia, depending on patient's needs and condition. Complications include urinary retention, urinary tract hemorrhage, bladder infection, and perforation of bladder.	*Before:* Give IV fluids if general anesthesia is to be used. Ensure consent form is signed. Explain procedure to patient. Give preoperative medication. *After:* Explain that burning on urination, pink-tinged urine, and urinary frequency are expected effects. Observe for bright red bleeding, which is not normal. Help with ambulation because orthostatic hypotension may occur. Offer warm sitz baths, heat, mild analgesics to relieve discomfort.
Radiologic Procedures Computed tomography (CT) scan (CT urogram)	Visualizes kidneys, ureters, and bladder. Can detect tumors, abscesses, suprarenal masses (e.g., adrenal tumors), and obstructions. Done with or without contrast media. Contrast is iodine based.	*Before:* Before contrast medium used, evaluate renal function. Assess if patient is allergic to shellfish, since the contrast is iodine based. Patient may need to be NPO 4 hr prior to study. *During:* Warn patient that contrast injection may cause a feeling of being warm and flushed. Patient must lie completely still during scan. *After:* Encourage patient to drink fluids to avoid renal problems with any contrast.
Cystogram	Visualizes bladder and evaluates vesicoureteral reflux. Evaluates patients with neurogenic bladder and recurrent UTIs. Can delineate abnormalities of bladder (e.g., diverticula, stones, tumors). Contrast media is instilled into bladder via cystoscope or catheter.	*Before:* Explain procedure to patient. *During:* If done via cystoscope, follow nursing care related to cystoscopy.
Intravenous pyelogram (IVP)	Visualizes urinary tract after IV injection of contrast media. Evaluates size and shape of kidneys, ureters, and bladder. Cysts, tumors, and ureteral obstructions distort normal appearance of these structures. Patient with decreased renal function should not have IVP because contrast media can be nephrotoxic.	*Before:* Cathartic or enema given night before. Assess patient for iodine sensitivity to avoid anaphylactic reaction. *During:* Warn patient that contrast injection may cause a feeling of being warm and flushed. *After:* Force fluids to avoid renal problems with contrast.
Kidneys, ureters, bladder (KUB)	X-ray examination of abdomen and pelvis. Delineates size, shape, and position of kidneys, ureter, and bladder. Can see radiopaque stones and foreign bodies.	*Before:* No special preparation needed.

TABLE 44.11 Diagnostic Studies

Urinary System—cont'd

Study	Description and Purpose	Nursing Responsibility
Loopogram	Detects obstructions, anastomotic leaks, stones, and reflux when patient has a urinary pouch or ileal conduit. Because urinary diversions are created with bowel, there is risk for absorption of contrast media.	*Before:* Explain procedure to patient. *During:* Monitor patient for reactions to the contrast media.
Magnetic resonance angiography	Visualizes renal vasculature. Gadolinium-enhanced studies allow visualization of renal artery.	Same as renal arteriogram. Does not require femoral artery puncture
Magnetic resonance imaging (MRI)	Visualizes kidneys. Not proven useful for detecting urinary stones or calcified tumors.	*Before:* Oral and/or IV contrast injection may be used. Check for pregnancy, allergies, and renal function before test. Have patient remove all metal objects. Remove metallic foil patches. Contraindicated for persons with implanted metallic devices or other metal fragments unless noted to be MRI safe. Ask about any history of surgical insertion of staples, plates, dental bridges, or other metal appliances. Patient may need to be fasting. Assess for claustrophobia and the need for antianxiety medication. *During:* Patient must lie completely still during scan.
Nephrostogram (Antegrade pyelogram)	Evaluates upper urinary tract when patient has allergy to contrast media, decreased renal function, or abnormalities that prevent passage of a ureteral catheter. Contrast media may be injected percutaneously into renal pelvis or via a nephrostomy tube that is already in place when determining tube function or ureteral integrity after trauma or surgery.	*Before:* Explain procedure and prepare patient as for IVP. *During and after:* Watch for signs of complications (e.g., hematuria, infection, hematoma).
Renal arteriogram (angiogram)	Visualizes renal blood vessels. Can aid in diagnosing renal artery stenosis (Fig. 44.8), extra or missing renal blood vessels, and renovascular hypertension. Can aid in distinguishing between a renal cyst and renal tumor. Included in workup of a potential renal transplant donor. A catheter is inserted into the femoral artery and passed up the aorta to the level of renal arteries (Fig. 44.9). Contrast media is injected to outline renal blood supply.	*Before:* Cathartic or enema may be used the night before. Before injection of contrast material, assess for iodine sensitivity. Tell patient a transient warm feeling may be felt along the course of blood vessel when contrast media is injected. *After:* Place a pressure dressing over femoral artery injection site. Observe site for bleeding and inflammation. Have patient maintain bed rest with affected leg straight. Take peripheral pulses in the involved leg every 30–60 min to detect occlusion of blood flow (from thrombus or emboli).
Renal biopsy	Obtains renal tissue for examination to determine type of kidney disease or to follow progress of kidney disease. Usually done as a skin (percutaneous) biopsy through needle insertion into lower lobe of kidney under CT or ultrasound guidance. Absolute contraindications are bleeding disorders, single kidney, and uncontrolled hypertension. Relative contraindications include suspected renal infection, hydronephrosis, and possible vascular lesions.	*Before:* Type and crossmatch patient for blood. Ensure consent form is signed. Assess coagulation status through patient history, medication history, CBC, hematocrit, prothrombin time, and bleeding and clotting time. Patient should not be taking aspirin or warfarin. *After:* Apply pressure dressing and keep patient on affected side for 30–60 min. Bed rest for 24 hr. Vital signs every 5–10 min, first hour. Assess for flank pain, hypotension, decreasing hematocrit, fever, chills, urinary frequency, dysuria, and gross or microscopic hematuria. Inspect biopsy site for bleeding. Teach patient to avoid lifting heavy objects for 5–7 days and to not take anticoagulant drugs until allowed by HCP.

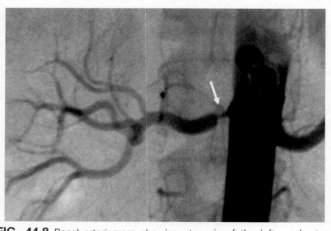

FIG. 44.8 Renal arteriogram showing stenosis of the left renal artery *(arrow)*. (From Staub D, Zeller T, Trenk D: Predicting blood pressure improvement after revascularization for renal artery stenosis, *Eur J Vasc Endovasc* 40:599, 2010.)

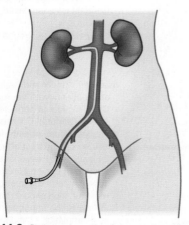

FIG. 44.9 Catheter insertion for a renal arteriogram.

TABLE 44.11 Diagnostic Studies
Urinary System—cont'd

Study	Description and Purpose	Nursing Responsibility
Renal scan	Evaluates anatomic structures, perfusion, and function of kidneys. IV radioactive isotopes are injected. Radiation detector probes are placed over kidney and scintillation counter monitors radioactive material in kidney. Radioisotope distribution in kidney is scanned and mapped. Shows location, size, and shape of kidney and assesses blood flow, glomerular filtration, tubular function, and urinary excretion. Abscesses, cysts, and tumors may appear as cold spots because of nonfunctioning tissue. Monitors function of a transplanted kidney.	*Before:* No diet or activity restriction. Tell patient that there should not be any pain or discomfort during test.
Renal ultrasound	Detects renal or perirenal masses (tumors, cysts) and obstructions. Small external ultrasound probe is placed on patient's skin. Conductive gel is applied to skin. Noninvasive procedure involves passing sound waves into body structures and recording images as they are reflected. Computer interprets tissue density based on sound waves and displays it in picture form. Can be used safely in patients with renal failure.	*Before:* Explain procedure to patient. No bowel preparation needed. *During:* Because radiation exposure is avoided, repeated images can be obtained over a brief period.
Retrograde pyelogram	X-ray of urinary tract taken after injection of contrast material into kidneys. May be done if an IVP does not visualize the urinary tract or has decreased renal function. A cystoscope is inserted, and ureteral catheters are inserted through it into renal pelvis. Contrast media is injected through catheters.	*Before:* Prepare patient as for IVP. Tell patient that there may be pain from distention of pelvis and discomfort from cystoscope. Anesthesia may be given for procedure. *After:* Complications similar to those for cystoscopy.
Urethrogram	Similar to a cystogram. Contrast media is injected retrograde into urethra to identify strictures, diverticula, or other urethral pathologic conditions. When urethral trauma is suspected, a urethrogram is done before catheterization.	*Before:* Explain procedure to patient.
Voiding cystourethrogram (VCUG)	Voiding study of bladder opening (bladder neck) and urethra. Bladder is filled with contrast media. Fluoroscopic films are taken to visualize bladder and urethra. After urination, another film is taken to assess for residual urine. Can detect abnormalities of lower urinary tract, urethral stenosis, bladder neck obstruction, vesicoureteral reflux, and prostatic enlargement.	*Before:* Explain procedure to patient.
Urodynamic Studies		
Cystometrogram	Evaluates bladder's capacity to contract and expel urine. Involves insertion of catheter and instillation of water or saline solution into bladder. Measurements of pressure exerted against bladder wall are recorded. If abdominal pressure is measured, a second tube is inserted into rectum or vagina. This tube is attached to a small fluid-filled balloon to allow pressure recording.	*Before:* Explain procedure to patient. *During:* Ask patient about sensations of bladder filling, usually including the first desire (urge) to urinate, a strong desire to urinate, and perception of bladder fullness. *After:* Observe patient for manifestations of UTI after procedure.
Radionuclide cystography (RNC)	Detects and grades vesicoureteral reflux. Like VCUG with a small dose of radioisotope tracer instilled into the bladder via urethral catheter. More sensitive than VCUG, and radiation dose is 1/1000 that of the VCUG.	*Before:* Explain procedure to patient as in VCUG.

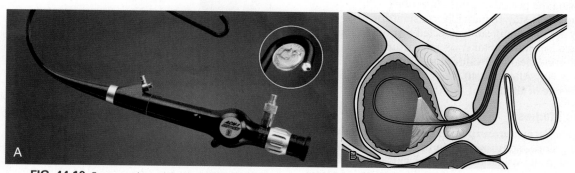

FIG. 44.10 Cystoscopic examination of the bladder in a man. **A,** Flexible cystonephroscope. **B,** Scope inserted into bladder. (*A,* Courtesy Circon Corporation, Santa Barbara, CA.)

TABLE 44.11 Diagnostic Studies

Urinary System—cont'd

Study	Description and Purpose	Nursing Responsibility
Sphincter electromyography (EMG)	Recording of electrical activity created when nervous system stimulates muscle tissue. By placing needles, percutaneous wires, or patches near the urethra, pelvic floor muscle activity can be assessed. During the cystometrogram, sphincter EMG is used to identify voluntary pelvic floor muscle contractions and response of these muscles to bladder filling, coughing, and other provocative maneuvers.	*Before:* Explain procedure to patient.
Urine flow study (uroflow)	Measures urine volume in a single voiding expelled in a period. Used to (1) assess the degree of outflow obstruction caused by such conditions as benign prostatic hyperplasia, (2) assess bladder or sphincter dysfunction effects on voiding, and (3) evaluate effects of treatment for lower urinary tract problems. Graphic displays can illustrate straining and intermittent flow patterns or other abnormal voiding disorders. *Normal maximum flow rate:* Men: 20–25 mL/sec; women: 25–30 mL/sec. Volume voided and patient's age can affect the flow rate.	*Before:* Explain procedure to patient. *During:* Ask the patient to start the test with a comfortably full bladder, urinate into a designated container, and try to empty completely. *After:* Measure residual urine volume immediately after a urinary flow study because this will help identify degree of chronic urinary retention that is often associated with abnormal flow patterns.
Videourodynamics	Combination of cystometrogram, sphincter EMG, and/or urinary flow study with anatomic imaging of the lower urinary tract, typically via fluoroscopy. Used in selected cases to identify an obstructive lesion and characterize anatomic changes in bladder and lower urinary tract	*Before:* Explain procedure to patient.
Voiding pressure flow study	Combines a urinary flow rate, cystometric pressures (intravesical, abdominal, and detrusor pressures), and sphincter EMG for detailed evaluation of micturition. It is completed by assisting the patient to a specialized toilet to urinate while the various pressure tubes and EMG apparatus remain in place.	*Before:* Explain procedure to patient.
Whitaker study	Measures the pressure differential between renal pelvis and bladder. Ureteral obstruction can be assessed. Percutaneous access to renal pelvis obtained by placing a catheter in renal pelvis. A catheter is placed in bladder. Fluid is perfused through the percutaneous tube or needle at a rate of 10 mL/min. Pressure data are then collected. Pressure measurements are combined with fluoroscopic imaging to find the level of obstruction.	*Before:* Explain procedure to patient.

body, not of body weight. Therefore people with larger muscle mass have higher values. Because almost all creatinine in the blood is normally excreted by the kidneys, creatinine clearance is the most accurate indicator of renal function. The result of a creatinine clearance test closely approximates that of the GFR. A blood specimen to measure serum creatinine should be obtained during the period of urine collection.

Creatinine levels stay remarkably constant for each person because they are not significantly affected by protein ingestion, muscular exercise, water intake, or rate of urine production. Normal creatinine clearance values range from 87 to 139 mL/min (Table 44.10). After age 40, the creatinine clearance rate decreases at a rate of about 1 mL/min/yr.

Urodynamic Studies

Urodynamic studies measure urinary tract function. Urodynamic tests study the storage of urine within the bladder and the flow of urine through the urinary tract to the outside of the body. A combination of techniques may be used for a detailed assessment of urinary function (Table 44.11).

CASE STUDY—cont'd

Objective Data: Diagnostic Studies

(© iStockphoto/Thinkstock.)

The HCP orders the following initial diagnostic studies for A.K.:
- CBC, basic metabolic panel (electrolytes, BUN, creatinine)
- Urinalysis, culture if indicated
- Renal ultrasound

A.K.'s CBC and metabolic panel results are within normal limits. His urinalysis shows moderate hematuria and the renal ultrasound shows several stones in the left ureter. There is no hydronephrosis at present. The HCP prescribes IV opioids for pain management and admits A.K. to a medical unit for further observation.

Discussion Questions

1. Which diagnostic study results are abnormal?
2. Which diagnostic study results are of most concern to you?

Answers available at *http://evolve.elsevier.com/Lewis/medsurg.*

BRIDGE TO NCLEX EXAMINATION

The number of the question corresponds to the same-numbered outcome at the beginning of the chapter.

1. A renal stone in the pelvis of the kidney will change kidney function by interfering with the
   a. structural support of the kidney.
   b. regulation of the concentration of urine.
   c. entry and exit of blood vessels at the kidney.
   d. collection and drainage of urine from the kidney.

2. A patient with kidney disease has oliguria and a creatinine clearance of 40 mL/min. These findings most directly reflect abnormal function of
   a. tubular secretion.
   b. glomerular filtration.
   c. capillary permeability.
   d. concentration of filtrate.

3. The nurse identifies a risk for urinary stones in a patient who relates a health history that includes
   a. hyperaldosteronism.
   b. serotonin deficiency.
   c. adrenal insufficiency.
   d. hyperparathyroidism.

4. Diminished ability to concentrate urine, associated with aging of the urinary system, is attributed to
   a. a decrease in bladder sensory receptors.
   b. a decrease in the number of functioning nephrons.
   c. decreased function of the loop of Henle and tubules.
   d. thickening of the basement membrane of Bowman's capsule.

5. During physical assessment of the urinary system, the nurse
   a. performs fist percussion to detect tenderness in the flank area.
   b. expects a dull percussion sound when 100 mL of urine is present in the bladder.
   c. percusses above the symphysis pubis to determine the level of urine in the bladder.
   d. palpates the lower pole of the right kidney as a smooth mass that descends on expiration.

6. Normal findings expected by the nurse on physical assessment of the urinary system include (select all that apply)
   a. nonpalpable bladder.
   b. nonpalpable left kidney.
   c. auscultation of renal artery bruit.
   d. no CVA tenderness elicited by a kidney punch.
   e. full bladder percusses as dullness above the symphysis pubis.

7. A diagnostic study that evaluates renal blood flow, glomerular filtration, tubular function, and excretion is a(n)
   a. IVP.
   b. VCUG.
   c. renal scan.
   d. loopogram.

8. On reading the urinalysis results of a dehydrated patient, the nurse would expect to find
   a. a pH of 8.4.
   b. RBCs of 4/hpf.
   c. color: yellow, cloudy.
   d. specific gravity of 1.035.

1. d, 2. b, 3. d, 4. c, 5. a, 6. a, b, d, e, 7. c, 8. d

For rationales to these answers and even more NCLEX review questions, visit *http://evolve.elsevier.com/Lewis/medsurg*.

ⓔ EVOLVE WEBSITE/RESOURCES LIST

http://evolve.elsevier.com/Lewis/medsurg
Review Questions (Online Only)
Key Points
Answer Keys for Questions
  • Rationales for Bridge to NCLEX Examination Questions
  • Answer Guidelines for Case Study on pp. 1012, 1015, 1016, and 1022
Conceptual Care Map Creator
Audio Glossary
Content Updates

REFERENCES

*1. Denic A, Lieske JC, Chakkera HA, et al: The substantial loss of nephrons in healthy human kidneys with aging *JASN* 28:313, 2017.

*2. Webster AC, Nagler EV, Morton RL, et al: Chronic kidney disease, *Lancet* 389:1238, 2017.

3. American Cancer Society: Bladder cancer risk factors. Retrieved from *www.cancer.org/cancer/bladder-cancer/causes-risks-prevention/risk-factors.html*.

*4. Ziemba JB, Matlaga BR: Epidemiology and economics of nephrolithiasis, *Investig Clin Urol* 58:299, 2017.

5. Jarvis C: *Physical examination and health assessment*, 7th ed, St Louis, 2016, Saunders.

*6. Fähling M, Seeliger E, Patzak A, et al: Understanding and preventing contrast-induced acute kidney injury, *Nat Rev Nephrol* 13:169, 2017.

45

Renal and Urologic Problems

Cynthia Ann Smith

Caring about others, running the risk of feeling, and leaving an impact on people, brings happiness.

Harold Kushner

ⓔ http://evolve.elsevier.com/Lewis/medsurg

CONCEPTUAL FOCUS

Elimination
Fluids and Electrolytes

Infection
Pain

LEARNING OUTCOMES

1. Discuss the pathophysiology, clinical manifestations, and interprofessional and nursing management of urinary tract infections, cystitis, urethritis, and pyelonephritis.
2. Distinguish the etiology, clinical manifestations, and nursing and interprofessional management of acute poststreptococcal glomerulonephritis, Goodpasture syndrome, and chronic glomerulonephritis.
3. Describe the common causes, clinical manifestations, and interprofessional and nursing management of nephrotic syndrome.
4. Compare and contrast the etiology, clinical manifestations, and interprofessional and nursing management of various types of urinary calculi.
5. Distinguish the common causes and management of renal trauma, renal vascular problems, and hereditary kidney diseases.
6. Describe the clinical manifestations and nursing and interprofessional management of kidney and bladder cancers.
7. Describe the common causes and management of urinary incontinence and urinary retention.
8. Distinguish among urethral, ureteral, suprapubic, and nephrostomy catheters regarding indications for use and nursing responsibilities.
9. Explain the nursing management of the patient undergoing nephrectomy or urinary diversion surgery.

KEY TERMS

calculus, p. 1035
cystitis, p. 1025
glomerulonephritis, p. 1032
Goodpasture syndrome, p. 1033
hydronephrosis, p. 1035
ileal conduit, p. 1055
interstitial cystitis (IC), p. 1031

lithotripsy, p. 1038
nephrolithiasis, p. 1035
nephrosclerosis, p. 1041
nephrotic syndrome, p. 1034
polycystic kidney disease (PKD), p. 1041
pyelonephritis, p. 1025
renal artery stenosis, p. 1041

stricture, p. 1040
urethritis, p. 1025
urinary incontinence (UI), p. 1045
urinary retention, p. 1050
urinary tract infection (UTI), p. 1024
urosepsis, p. 1025

A wide range of renal and urologic disorders contribute to impaired elimination. The diverse causes of these disorders are grouped by common problems, such as infectious, immunologic, obstructive, traumatic, cancerous, and neurologic mechanisms. This chapter discusses disorders of the upper urinary tract (kidneys and ureter) and lower urinary tract (bladder and urethra). Many patients are at risk fluid, electrolyte, and acid-base imbalances because of the kidneys' vital role in homeostasis. The person may have discomfort and incontinence and problems with disrupted sleep or skin integrity.

INFECTIOUS AND INFLAMMATORY DISORDERS OF URINARY SYSTEM

URINARY TRACT INFECTION

Urinary tract infections (UTIs) are infections that affect the urinary tract. They are the second most common bacterial disease and the most common bacterial infection in women.[1] *Escherichia coli* is the most common pathogen causing a UTI. It causes 70% to 95% of cases without urinary tract structural abnormalities or stones (Table 45.1). It is seen primarily in

TABLE 45.1 Common Causes of Urinary Tract Infections

- *Candida albicans*
- *Enterobacter*
- *Enterococcus*
- *Escherichia coli*
- *Klebsiella*
- *Proteus*
- *Pseudomonas*
- *Serratia*
- *Staphylococcus*
- Streptococci

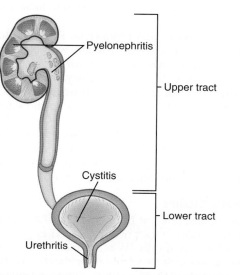

FIG 45.1 Sites of infectious processes in the upper and lower urinary tracts.

women.[2] *Candida albicans* is the second most common pathogen, causing UTIs associated with indwelling catheter use or asymptomatic colonization.

Bacterial counts of 10^5 colony-forming units per milliliter (CFU/mL) or higher typically indicate a clinically significant UTI. However, counts as low as 10^2 to 10^3 CFU/mL in a person with signs and symptoms are indicative of UTI.

Although fungal and parasitic infections may cause UTIs, this is uncommon. UTIs from these causes sometimes occur in patients who are immunosuppressed, have diabetes, have kidney problems, or received multiple courses of antibiotic therapy. These types of UTIs may occur in persons who live in or have traveled to certain developing countries.

Classification of Urinary Tract Infection

A UTI can be broadly classified as an upper or lower UTI according to its location within the urinary system (Fig. 45.1). We use specific terms to delineate the location of a UTI. For example, **pyelonephritis** implies inflammation (usually caused by infection) of the renal parenchyma and collecting system. **Cystitis** is an inflammation of the bladder, while **urethritis** is an inflammation of the urethra. **Urosepsis** is a UTI that has spread systemically. It is a life-threatening condition requiring emergency treatment.

Classifying a UTI as complicated or uncomplicated is also useful. *Uncomplicated UTIs* occur in an otherwise normal urinary tract and usually only involve the bladder. *Complicated UTIs* occur in a person with a structural or functional problem in the urinary tract. Examples include obstruction, stones, catheters, abnormal genitourinary (GU) tract, acute kidney injury (AKI), chronic kidney disease (CKD), renal transplant, diabetes,

TABLE 45.2 Risk Factors for Urinary Tract Infections

Anatomic Factors
- Congenital defects leading to obstruction or urinary stasis
- Fistula exposing urinary stream to skin, vagina, or fecal stream
- Obesity
- Shorter female urethra and colonization from normal vaginal flora

Factors Compromising Immune Response
- Aging
- Diabetes
- HIV infection

Factors Increasing Urinary Stasis
- Extrinsic obstruction (tumor, fibrosis compressing urinary tract)
- Intrinsic obstruction (stone, tumor of urinary tract, urethral stricture, BPH)
- Renal impairment
- Urinary retention (e.g., neurogenic bladder)

Foreign Bodies
- Catheters (indwelling, external condom catheter, ureteral stent, nephrostomy tube, intermittent catheterization)
- Urinary tract instrumentation (cystoscopy)
- Urinary tract stones

Functional Disorders
- Constipation
- Voiding dysfunction with detrusor sphincter muscle incoordination

Other Factors
- Habitual delay of urination ("nurse's bladder," "teacher's bladder")
- Pregnancy
- Menopause
- Multiple sex partners (women)
- Poor personal hygiene
- Use of spermicidal agents, contraceptive diaphragm (women), bubble baths, feminine sprays

or neurologic diseases. They can also occur when a person has developed antibiotic resistance, is immunocompromised, has pregnancy-induced changes, or has recurrent infection. The person with a complicated infection is at risk for pyelonephritis, urosepsis, and renal damage.

Etiology and Pathophysiology

The urinary tract above the urethra is normally sterile. Several mechanical and physiologic defense mechanisms aid in maintaining sterility and preventing UTIs. These defenses include normal voiding with complete emptying of the bladder, ureterovesical junction competence, and ureteral peristaltic activity that propels urine toward the bladder. Antibacterial characteristics of urine are maintained by an acidic pH (less than 6.0), high urea concentration, and abundant glycoproteins that interfere with the growth of bacteria. A change in any of these defense mechanisms increases the risk for a UTI (Table 45.2).

The organisms that usually cause UTIs originate in the perineum and are introduced via the ascending route from the urethra. Most infections are caused by gram-negative bacilli normally found in the gastrointestinal (GI) tract. However, gram-positive organisms, such as streptococci, enterococci, and *Staphylococcus saprophyticus,* can also cause UTIs.

A common factor contributing to ascending infection is urologic instrumentation (e.g., catheterization, cystoscopic

TABLE 45.3 Lower Urinary Tract Symptoms (LUTS)

Symptoms	Description
Emptying Symptoms	
Dysuria	• Painful or difficult urination
Hesitancy	• Difficulty starting urine stream
	• Delay between initiation of urination (because of urethral sphincter relaxation) and beginning of flow of urine
	• Diminished urinary stream
Intermittency	• Interruption of urinary stream while voiding
Postvoid dribbling	• Urine loss after completion of voiding
Urinary retention or incomplete emptying	• Inability to empty urine from bladder
	• Caused by atonic bladder or obstruction of urethra
	• Can be acute or chronic
Storage Symptoms	
Incontinence	• Involuntary or accidental urine loss or leakage
Nocturia	• Awakened by urge to void 2 or more times during sleep
	• May be diurnal or nocturnal depending on sleep schedule
Nocturnal enuresis	• Adults: loss of urine during sleep
Urgency	• Sudden, strong, or intense desire to void immediately
	• Often accompanied by frequency
Urinary frequency	• More than 8 times in 24-hr period
	• Often <200 mL each voiding

examinations). Instrumentation allows bacteria that are normally present at the opening of the urethra to enter the urethra or bladder. Sexual intercourse promotes "milking" of bacteria from the vagina and perineum and may cause minor urethral trauma that predisposes women to UTIs.

UTIs can result from hematogenous transmission, in which blood-borne bacteria invade the kidneys, ureters, or bladder from elsewhere in the body. For a kidney infection to occur in this manner, there must be prior injury to the urinary tract, such as obstruction of the ureter, damage caused by stones, or renal scars.

UTIs are the most common health care–associated infection (HAI). They are primarily associated with use of an indwelling catheter. *Catheter-associated urinary tract infections (CAUTIs)* are often caused by *E. coli* and, less often, *Pseudomonas* organisms. CAUTIs are often underrecognized and undertreated, leading to extended hospital stays, increased health care costs, and patient morbidity and mortality.[3]

Clinical Manifestations

Manifestations of UTIs range from painful urination in uncomplicated urethritis or cystitis to severe systemic illness associated with abdominal or back pain, fever, sepsis.

Lower urinary tract symptoms (LUTS) occur in patients who have UTIs of the upper urinary tract, as well as those confined to the lower tract. Symptoms are related to either bladder storage or bladder emptying (Table 45.3). These include dysuria, frequency (voiding more than every 2 hours), urgency, and suprapubic discomfort or pressure. The urine may contain grossly visible blood (hematuria) or sediment, giving it a cloudy appearance. Infection of the upper urinary tract (involving the renal parenchyma, pelvis, and ureters) typically causes fever, chills, and flank pain. A UTI confined to the lower urinary tract does not usually have systemic manifestations. People with significant bacteriuria may have no symptoms or may have nonspecific symptoms, such as fatigue or anorexia.

Remember that the characteristic manifestations of a UTI are often absent in older adults. Older adults tend to have nonlocalized abdominal discomfort rather than dysuria and suprapubic pain. They may have cognitive impairment or generalized clinical deterioration. Because older adults are less likely to have a fever with a UTI, temperature is an unreliable indicator of a UTI.[4]

Multiple problems may produce LUTS similar to the symptoms of a UTI. For example, patients with bladder tumors or those receiving intravesical chemotherapy or pelvic radiation usually have urinary frequency, urgency, and dysuria. Interstitial cystitis/painful bladder syndrome (discussed on p. 1031) produces urinary symptoms that are similar to and sometimes confused with a UTI.

A small number of healthy persons have some bacteria colonizing the bladder. This condition is called *asymptomatic bacteriuria*. It does not justify screening or treatment except in pregnant women and those undergoing urologic procedures.

Diagnostic Studies

In a patient suspected of having a UTI, first obtain a dipstick urinalysis to identify the presence of nitrites (indicating bacteriuria), white blood cells (WBCs), and leukocyte esterase (an enzyme present in WBCs, indicating pyuria). Microscopic urinalysis can confirm these findings. After confirmation of bacteriuria and pyuria, a urine culture may be done. A urine culture is needed in persistent bacteriuria, recurring UTIs (more than 2 or 3 episodes per year), or complicated, CAUTI, or HAI UTIs. Urine also may be cultured when the infection is unresponsive to empiric therapy or the diagnosis is questionable.

A voided midstream technique (*clean-catch urine sample*) is preferred for obtaining a urine culture in most circumstances (see Table 44.9). When an adequate clean-catch specimen cannot be obtained, catheterization may be needed. A specimen obtained by catheterization provides more accurate results than a clean-catch specimen.

A urine culture with *sensitivity testing* can determine the bacteria's susceptibility to a variety of antibiotic drugs. The results allow the HCP to choose an antibiotic known to be capable of destroying the bacteria causing a UTI in a specific patient.

Some patients need imaging studies of the urinary tract. An ultrasound or CT scan may be done when obstruction of the urinary system is suspected or UTIs recur.

Interprofessional Care

The interprofessional care and drug therapy of UTIs are outlined in Table 45.4. Once a UTI has been diagnosed, appropriate antimicrobial therapy is started. An antibiotic may be chosen based on the HCP's best judgment (*empiric therapy*) or the results of sensitivity testing.

Uncomplicated UTIs are treated with a short-term course of antibiotics, typically for 3 days. In contrast, complicated UTIs need a longer period of treatment, lasting 7 to 14 days or more.[4,5] Many residents of long-term care facilities, especially women, have chronic asymptomatic bacteriuria. However, we usually only treat symptomatic UTIs.

First-choice drugs to treat uncomplicated or initial UTIs are trimethoprim/sulfamethoxazole (TMP/SMX), nitrofurantoin,

TABLE 45.4 Interprofessional Care

Urinary Tract Infection

Diagnostic Assessment

- History and physical examination
- Urinalysis (midstream, "clean-catch" voided specimen)
- Urine for culture and sensitivity (if indicated)
- Imaging studies of urinary tract (if indicated): CT scan , ultrasound, cystoscopy

Management

Uncomplicated UTI

- Patient teaching
- Adequate fluid intake (6 8-oz glasses/day)

Drug Therapy

- Antibiotics
  - fluconazole (in patients with fungal UTI)
  - fosfomycin (Monurol)
  - nitrofurantoin (Macrodantin, Macrobid)
  - TMP/SMX (Bactrim, Bactrim DS)
  - trimethoprim alone (in patients with sulfa allergy)
  - phenazopyridine (Pyridium)

Recurrent UTI

- Repeat urinalysis
- Urine culture and sensitivity testing
- Adequate fluid intake (6 8-oz glasses/day)
- Repeat patient teaching
- Imaging studies of urinary tract (if indicated): see above

Drug Therapy

- Antibiotic: nitrofurantoin, TMP/SMX
- Sensitivity-guided antibiotic therapy: ampicillin, amoxicillin, first-generation cephalosporin, fluoroquinolones
- 3- to 6-month trial of suppressive or prophylactic antibiotic regimen
- Postcoital antibiotic prophylaxis: cephalexin, nitrofurantoin, TMP/SMX

TABLE 45.5 Nursing Assessment

Urinary Tract Infection

Subjective Data

Important Health Information

Past health history: Previous UTI. Urinary stones, reflux, strictures, or retention. Neurogenic bladder, pregnancy, benign prostatic hyperplasia, bladder cancer, sexually transmitted infection.
Medications: Antibiotics, anticholinergics, antispasmodics
Surgery or other treatments: Recent urologic instrumentation (catheterization, cystoscopy)

Functional Health Patterns

Cognitive-perceptual: Suprapubic or low back pain, bladder spasms, dysuria, burning on urination
Elimination: Urinary frequency, urgency, hesitancy, dysuria, nocturia
Health perception–health management: Urinary hygiene practices. Lassitude, malaise
Nutritional-metabolic: Nausea, vomiting, anorexia. Chills and fever
Sexuality-reproductive: Multiple sex partners, use of spermicidal agents or contraceptive diaphragm (women)

Objective Data

General

Fever, chills, dysuria
Atypical presentation in older adults: afebrile, absence of dysuria, loss of appetite, altered mental status

Urinary

Hematuria. Cloudy, foul-smelling urine

Possible Diagnostic Findings

Leukocytosis. Urinalysis positive for bacteria, pyuria, RBCs, WBCs, and nitrites. Positive urine culture. Ultrasound, CT scan, MRI, Voiding cystourethrogram (VCUG), and cystoscopy showing urinary tract abnormalities

---

cephalexin, and fosfomycin.[5] TMP/SMX has the advantages of being inexpensive and taken twice daily. A disadvantage is *E. coli* resistance to TMP/SMX, β-lactams, and ciprofloxacin, which is an increasing problem in the United States. Nitrofurantoin can be given 3 or 4 times daily, but a twice-daily formulation is available.

Other antibiotics used in the treatment of uncomplicated UTI include ampicillin, amoxicillin, and cephalosporins. Fluoroquinolones (e.g., levofloxacin, ciprofloxacin) should be used to treat only complicated UTIs. In patients with UTIs from fungi, fluconazole (Diflucan) is the preferred therapy.

DRUG ALERT Nitrofurantoin (Macrodantin)

- Avoid use if the patient's creatinine clearance < 30 mL/min.
- Notify HCP at once if fever, chills, cough, chest pain, dyspnea, rash, or numbness or tingling of fingers or toes develops.

A urinary analgesic, such as oral phenazopyridine, may relieve discomfort caused by severe dysuria. Phenazopyridine is an azo dye excreted in urine, where it exerts a topical analgesic effect on the urinary tract mucosa. It is taken up to 2 concurrent days. Teach patients that this drug causes the urine to turn orange or red.

Patients who have repeated UTIs may receive prophylactic or suppressive antibiotics. A low dose of TMP/SMX, nitrofurantoin, or another antibiotic taken daily may prevent recurring UTIs. A single dose may be taken after an event likely to provoke a UTI, such as sexual intercourse. Although suppressive therapy is often effective on a short-term basis, this strategy is limited because of the risk for antibiotic resistance, which leads to breakthrough infections with increasingly virulent pathogens.

❖ NURSING MANAGEMENT: URINARY TRACT INFECTION

◆ Nursing Assessment

Subjective and objective data that should be obtained from a patient with a UTI are shown in Table 45.5.

◆ Nursing Diagnoses

Nursing diagnoses for the patient with a UTI may include:
- Impaired urinary system function
- Acute pain
- Lack of knowledge

More information on nursing diagnoses and interventions for the patient with a UTI is presented in eNursing Care Plan 45.1 (available on the website for this chapter).

◆ Planning

The overall goals are that the patient with a UTI will have (1) relief from bothersome symptoms, (2) no upper urinary tract involvement, and (3) no recurrence.

◆ Nursing Implementation

◆ Health Promotion. It is important to recognize people who are at risk for a UTI. These include debilitated persons, older adults,

patients who are immunocompromised (e.g., cancer, diabetes), and patients treated with immunosuppressive drugs or corticosteroids. Health promotion activities can help decrease the frequency of UTIs and provide for early detection of infection. These activities include teaching preventive measures, including (1) emptying the bladder regularly and completely, (2) evacuating the bowel regularly, (3) wiping the perineal area from front to back after voiding and defecation, and (4) drinking an adequate amount of liquid each day.

To estimate the amount of fluid intake a person should have in 24 hours, take the person's weight in pounds, and divide that number in half. The result is the number of ounces of fluid a person should have per day. Thus a 150-lb person would need 75 oz/day. The person will obtain about 20% of this fluid from food, which leaves 60 oz (1775 mL) by drinking, or just over 7 8-oz glasses of fluid.

Routine and thorough perineal hygiene is important for all hospitalized patients, especially after using a bedpan, after a bowel movement, or if fecal incontinence is present. Answer call lights quickly and offer the bedpan or urinal to bedridden patients at frequent intervals. These measures can prevent incontinence and decrease the number of incontinence episodes.

Prevention of CAUTI. All patients undergoing catheterization of the urinary tract are at risk for developing CAUTI. You play a key role in preventing CAUTI. Avoiding unnecessary catheterization and early removal of indwelling catheters are the most effective means for reducing CAUTI. Always follow aseptic technique during these procedures. Wash your hands before and after contact with each patient. Wear gloves for care of urinary catheters. The American Nurses Association offers an evidence-based clinical tool for decreasing CAUTI.[6] Special measures for the care of urethral catheters are discussed later in this chapter on p. 1052.

◆ **Acute Care.** Acute care for a patient with a UTI includes ensuring adequate fluid intake unless contraindicated. Maintaining adequate fluid intake may be hard because of the patient feeling that fluid intake will make the pain and urinary frequency associated with a UTI worse. Tell patients that fluids will increase frequency of urination but will also dilute the urine, making the bladder less irritable. Fluids will help flush out bacteria before they have a chance to colonize in the bladder. Caffeine, alcohol, citrus juices, chocolate, and highly spiced foods or beverages should be avoided because they are potential bladder irritants.

Application of local heat to the suprapubic area or lower back may relieve the discomfort associated with a UTI. Have the patient apply a heating pad (turned to its lowest setting) against the back or suprapubic area. A warm shower or sitting in a tub of warm water filled above the waist can also give temporary relief.

Teach the patient about the prescribed drug therapy, including side effects. Emphasize the importance of taking the full course of antibiotics. Often patients stop antibiotic therapy once symptoms disappear. This can lead to inadequate treatment, recurrence of infection, and/or bacterial resistance to antibiotics.

Sometimes a second drug or a reduced dosage of drug is given after the first course to suppress bacterial growth in patients susceptible to recurrent UTI. Teach the patient to monitor for signs of improvement (e.g., cloudy urine becomes clear) as well as a decrease in or cessation of symptoms. Tell patients to promptly report any of the following to their HCP: (1) persistence of bothersome LUTS beyond the antibiotic treatment course, (2) onset of flank pain, or (3) fever.

TABLE 45.6 Patient & Caregiver Teaching

Urinary Tract Infection

When teaching a patient and caregiver measures to prevent a recurrence of a urinary tract infection (UTI), include:

1. Take all antibiotics as prescribed. Symptoms may improve after 1–2 days of therapy, but organisms may still be present.
2. Practice appropriate hygiene, including:
   - Carefully clean the perineal region by separating the labia in females, or in males pulling back the foreskin if present when cleansing.
   - Wipe from front to back after urinating.
   - Cleanse with warm soapy water after each bowel movement.
3. Empty the bladder before and after sexual intercourse.
4. Void regularly, about every 3–4 hours during the day.
5. Maintain adequate fluid intake.
6. Avoid vaginal douches and harsh soaps, bubble baths, powders, and sprays in the perineal area.
7. Report to the HCP symptoms or signs of recurrent UTI (e.g., fever, cloudy urine, pain on urination, urgency, frequency).

◆ **Ambulatory Care.** Home care for the patient with a UTI should emphasize the importance of adhering to the drug regimen. Your responsibility is to teach the patient and caregiver about the need for ongoing care (Table 45.6). This includes: (1) taking antimicrobial drugs as ordered, (2) maintaining adequate daily fluid intake, (3) voiding regularly (every 3 to 4 hours), (4) voiding before and after intercourse, and (5) temporarily stopping the use of a diaphragm.

If treatment is complete and the symptoms are still present, teach the patient to get follow-up care. Recurrent symptoms because of bacterial persistence or inadequate treatment typically occur within 1 to 2 weeks after completion of therapy. If the patient has followed the treatment plan, a relapse indicates the need for further evaluation.

◆ **Evaluation**

The expected outcomes are that the patient with a UTI will
- Have normal urinary elimination patterns
- Report relief of bothersome urinary tract symptoms
- State knowledge of the treatment plan

ACUTE PYELONEPHRITIS

Etiology and Pathophysiology

Pyelonephritis is an inflammation of the renal parenchyma (Fig. 45.2) and collecting system, including the renal pelvis. The most common cause is bacterial infection. Fungi, protozoa, or viruses can also infect the kidney.[7]

Urosepsis is a systemic infection arising from a urologic source. Its prompt diagnosis and effective treatment are critical because it can lead to septic shock and death unless promptly treated. Septic shock is discussed in Chapter 65.

Pyelonephritis usually begins with colonization and infection of the lower urinary tract via the ascending urethral route. Bacteria normally found in the intestinal tract, including *E. coli* or *Proteus, Klebsiella,* or *Enterobacter* species, often cause pyelonephritis. A preexisting factor can be present, like *vesicoureteral reflux* (retrograde [backward] movement of urine from lower to upper urinary tract) or dysfunction of the lower urinary tract (e.g., obstruction from benign prostatic hyperplasia [BPH], stricture, urinary stone). For residents of

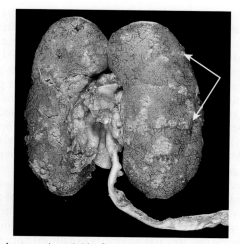

FIG 45.2 Acute pyelonephritis. Cortical surface shows grayish-white areas of inflammation and abscess formation *(arrows)*. (From Kumar V, Abbas AK, Aster JC, et al: *Robbins and Cotran pathologic basis of disease*, ed 8, Philadelphia, 2010, Saunders.)

long-term care facilities, CAUTI is a common cause of pyelonephritis and urosepsis.

Acute pyelonephritis often starts in the renal medulla and spreads to the adjacent cortex. Pregnancy-induced physiologic changes in the urinary system are one of the most important risk factors for acute pyelonephritis. Recurring episodes of pyelonephritis, especially in the presence of obstructive abnormalities, can lead to *chronic pyelonephritis* (discussed later).

Clinical Manifestations and Diagnostic Studies

The classic manifestations of acute pyelonephritis include (1) fever/chills, (2) nausea/vomiting (3) malaise, and (4) flank pain. They may include the LUTS, such as dysuria, urgency, and frequency. *Costovertebral angle tenderness* to percussion (costovertebral angle [CVA] pain) is typically present on the affected side. In some cases of pyelonephritis, renal scarring and decreased kidney function can occur, which can be potentially life-threatening.

Urinalysis results may show pyuria, bacteriuria, and varying degrees of hematuria. White blood cell (WBC) casts found in the urine may indicate involvement of the renal parenchyma. Urine cultures with sensitivities are done when pyelonephritis is suspected. Blood cultures may be done on hospitalized patients with more severe illness.

Ultrasounds may be done to identify anatomic abnormalities, hydronephrosis, renal abscesses, or an obstructing stone. CT scans are the preferred imaging studies. They can assess for signs of infection in the kidney and complications of pyelonephritis, such as impaired renal function, scarring, chronic pyelonephritis, or abscesses.

Interprofessional Care

The diagnostic tests and interprofessional care of acute pyelonephritis are outlined in Table 45.7. Patients with severe infections or complicating factors, such as nausea and vomiting with dehydration, need hospitalized.

The patient with mild symptoms may be treated as an outpatient with antibiotics for 7 to 14 days (Table 45.7). Parenteral antibiotics are often given initially in the hospital to rapidly establish high serum and urinary drug levels.[7] When initial treatment resolves acute symptoms and the person can

TABLE 45.7 Interprofessional Care

Acute Pyelonephritis

Diagnostic Assessment

- History and physical examination
- Urinalysis
- Urine for culture and sensitivity
- Imaging studies: ultrasound (initially), CT scan, cystoscopy, voiding cystourethrogram (VCUG)
- CBC count with WBC differential
- Blood culture (if bacteremia is suspected)
- Percussion for flank (CVA) pain

Management
Mild Symptoms

- Outpatient management or short hospitalization
- Adequate fluid intake
- NSAIDs or antipyretic drugs
- Follow-up urine culture and imaging studies

Drug Therapy

- Empirically selected broad-spectrum antibiotics: ampicillin, fluoroquinolones (ciprofloxacin, levofloxacin), or TMP/SMX if infection expected to be susceptible
- Short course of IV antibiotics, such as aztreonam, ceftriaxone, ciprofloxacin, or levofloxacin, may be indicated
- Switch to sensitivity-guided therapy when results of urine and blood culture are available

Severe Symptoms

- Hospitalization
- Adequate fluid intake (parenteral initially; switch to oral fluids as nausea, vomiting, and dehydration subside)
- NSAIDs or antipyretic drugs to reverse fever and relieve discomfort
- Follow-up urine culture and imaging studies

Drug Therapy

- Parenteral antibiotics
  - Empirically selected broad-spectrum antibiotics: aminoglycosides without or with ampicillin, extended spectrum cephalosporins, extended-spectrum penicillin-carbapenem
  - Switch to sensitivity-guided antibiotic therapy when results of urine and blood culture are available
- Oral antibiotics when patient tolerates oral intake

tolerate oral fluids and drugs, the person may be discharged on a regimen of oral antibiotics for an additional 14 to 21 days. Symptoms and signs typically improve or resolve within 48 to 72 hours after starting therapy.

Relapses may be treated with a 6-week course of antibiotics. Antibiotic prophylaxis also may be used for recurrent infections. The effectiveness of therapy is based on the presence or absence of bacterial growth on urine culture.

Urosepsis is characterized by bacteriuria and bacteremia (bacteria in blood). Close observation and vital sign monitoring are essential. Prompt recognition and treatment of septic shock may prevent irreversible damage or death.

❖ NURSING MANAGEMENT: ACUTE PYELONEPHRITIS

◆ Nursing Assessment

Subjective and objective data that should be obtained from a patient with pyelonephritis are similar to those for the patient with a UTI (Table 45.5).

◆ Nursing Diagnoses

Nursing diagnoses for the patient with pyelonephritis include those for the patient with a UTI (see p. 1027).

◆ Planning

The overall goals are that the patient with pyelonephritis will have (1) normal renal function, (2) normal body temperature, (3) no complications, (4) relief of pain, and (5) no recurrence of symptoms.

◆ Nursing Implementation

Health promotion and maintenance measures are similar to those for cystitis (see p. 1031). Early treatment for cystitis can prevent ascending infections. Because patients with structural abnormalities of the urinary tract are at high risk for infection, stress the need for regular medical care.

Nursing interventions vary depending on the severity of symptoms. These include teaching the patient about the disease process with emphasis on (1) continuing medications as prescribed, (2) having a follow-up urine culture, and (3) recognizing signs of recurrence or relapse (Table 45.6). In addition to antibiotic therapy, encourage the patient to drink at least 8 glasses of fluid every day, even after the infection has been treated. Rest will increase patient comfort.

The patient who has frequent relapses or reinfections may receive long-term, low-dose antibiotics. Making certain the patient understands the reason for therapy is important to increase adherence.

◆ Evaluation

The expected outcomes for the patient with pyelonephritis are the same as for UTI (see p. 1028).

CHRONIC PYELONEPHRITIS

In *chronic pyelonephritis* the kidneys become inflamed, develop fibrosis (scarring) leading to loss of renal function, and can atrophy (shrink). Chronic pyelonephritis is usually the result of significant anatomic abnormalities, such as vesicoureteral reflux or recurring infections involving the upper urinary tract. However, it may occur in the absence of an existing infection, recent infection, or history of UTIs.

Radiologic imaging studies can confirm the diagnosis of chronic pyelonephritis and possible contributing factors. A renal biopsy can show the loss of functioning nephrons, infiltration of the parenchyma with inflammatory cells, and fibrosis.

The level of renal function in chronic pyelonephritis depends on whether 1 or both kidneys are affected, the extent of scarring, and the presence of coexisting infection. Chronic pyelonephritis can progress to end-stage renal disease (ESRD). Monitoring and treating infection and correcting any underlying contributing factors are important. Nursing and interprofessional management of the patient with CKD is discussed in Chapter 46.

URETHRITIS

Urethritis is inflammation of the urethra. Causes of urethritis include a bacterial or viral infection, *Trichomonas* or monilial infection (especially in women), chlamydial infection, and gonorrhea (especially in men).

In men, the causes of urethritis are usually sexually transmitted. Purulent discharge can indicate a gonococcal urethritis.

A clear discharge typically signifies a nongonococcal urethritis. (Sexually transmitted infections are discussed in Chapter 52.) Urethritis produces bothersome LUTS, including dysuria, urgency, and frequency, similar to those seen with cystitis.

In women, urethritis is hard to diagnose. It often produces bothersome LUTS, but urethral discharge may not be present.

Treatment of urethritis is based on identifying and treating the cause and providing symptomatic relief. Drugs used for bacterial infections include TMP/SMX, doxycycline (Vibramycin), ceftriaxone, and nitrofurantoin. Metronidazole (Flagyl) and tinidazole (Monistat) are options for treating *Trichomonas* infection. Drugs, such as nystatin, clotrimazole, or fluconazole, may be used for monilial infections. In chlamydial infections, doxycycline or azithromycin may be used. For treatment of gonococcal urethritis, the preferred first-line treatment is azithromycin 1 g orally with 250 mg intramuscular ceftriaxone. Women with negative urine cultures and no pyuria usually do not respond to antibiotics.

Warm sitz baths may temporarily relieve bothersome symptoms. Teach the patient to (1) avoid using vaginal deodorant sprays, (2) properly cleanse the perineal area after bowel movements and voiding, and (3) avoid sexual intercourse for at least 7 days. Teach patients with sexually transmitted urethritis to refer their sex partners for evaluation and testing if they had sexual contact in the 60 days before the onset of the patient's symptoms or diagnosis.

URETHRAL DIVERTICULA

Urethral diverticula are localized outpouchings of the urethra. Typically, they result from enlargement of obstructed periurethral glands. In women, who have a higher incidence than men, the diverticula protrude into the anterior vaginal wall. The rare cases reported in males usually are associated with congenital lower urinary tract anomalies or surgical trauma.

The periurethral glands are found along the entire length of the urethra, with the majority draining into the distal third of the urethra. Skene's glands are the largest of these glands. Causes of urethral diverticula include urethral trauma, vaginal delivery, urethral instrumentation, urethral dilation, and frequent infections of the periurethral glands.

Symptoms include dysuria, postvoid dribbling, frequency (voiding more often than every 2 hours), urgency, suprapubic discomfort or pressure, dyspareunia, and a feeling of incomplete bladder emptying. Urinary incontinence is often present. However, many women have no symptoms.

The urine may contain gross blood (hematuria) or sediment, which gives it a cloudy appearance. An anterior vaginal wall mass may be felt on physical examination. When palpated, the mass is often quite tender and expresses purulent discharge through the urethra.

Radiographic studies, such as ultrasound and MRI, are helpful in determining the size of the diverticulum in relation to the urethral lumen. A voiding cystourethrography (VCUG) may be done but has a lower sensitivity than that of ultrasound and MRI. A urethroscopy may be of benefit.

Surgical options include transvaginal diverticulectomy, marsupialization (creation of a permanent opening) of the diverticular sac into the vagina (*Spence procedure*), and urethroscopic surgical excision. Stress urinary incontinence, infection, bleeding, and urethral-vaginal fistula are potential complications of the surgery.

INTERSTITIAL CYSTITIS/PAINFUL BLADDER SYNDROME

Interstitial cystitis (IC) is a chronic, painful inflammatory disease of the bladder characterized by symptoms of urgency, frequency, and pain in the bladder and/or pelvis. IC is often called bladder pain syndrome or painful bladder syndrome (PBS). The term *IC/PBS* refers to cases of urinary pain that cannot be attributed to other causes, such as UTI or urinary stones. IC/PBS is more common in women, affecting about 3 to 8 million women and 1 to 4 million men each year.[8]

The cause of IC/PBS is unknown. It is likely multifactorial. Possible causes include neurogenic hypersensitivity of the lower urinary tract, changes in mast cells in the muscle and/or mucosal layers of the bladder, infection with an unusual organism (e.g., slow-growing virus), or production of a toxic substance in the urine.

Clinical Manifestations and Diagnostic Studies

The 2 primary manifestations of IC/PBS are pain and bothersome LUTS (e.g., frequency, urgency). People with severe cases may void as often as 60 times in a day, including nighttime urination. The pain is usually in the suprapubic area, but may involve the vagina, labia, or entire perineal region, including the rectum and anus. The pain varies from mild to severe. The pain can be worsened by bladder filling, postponed urination, physical exertion, pressure against the suprapubic area, certain foods, or emotional distress. Voiding temporarily relieves pain. Bothersome LUTS are similar to a UTI. The condition is often misdiagnosed as a recurring or chronic UTI or, in men, chronic prostatitis.

The patient may have periods of remission and exacerbation. Women often report pain that occurs before menstruation. Sexual intercourse or emotional stress worsen pain. Some patients have symptoms that disappear altogether after a period of weeks to months. Others have persistent symptoms over months to years.

IC/PBS is a diagnosis of exclusion. A careful history and physical examination are necessary to rule out other disorders that produce similar symptoms, such as cancer, UTI, or endometriosis. Urine cultures do not find any bacteria or other organisms in the urine. Cystoscopic examination may reveal a small bladder capacity, Hunner lesions (distinct inflammatory areas on the bladder wall), and glomerulations (superficial ulcerations with pinpoint bleeding), but these findings are not always present.

Interprofessional Care

Because the cause of IC/PBS is unknown, no single treatment consistently reverses or relieves symptoms. Various therapies have been effective, including nutritional and drug therapy. People with IC/PBS do not respond to antibiotic therapy. They rarely need surgical therapy.

Eliminating foods and beverages that are likely to irritate the bladder may provide some relief from symptoms. Typical bladder irritants include caffeine; alcohol; citrus products; carbonated drinks; chocolate; foods containing vinegar, curries, or hot peppers; and foods or beverages likely to lower urinary pH, including fruits such as cranberries. An over-the-counter (OTC) dietary supplement called *calcium glycerophosphate* (Prelief) alkalinizes the urine and may provide relief from the irritating effects of certain foods. Recipes and menus for a well-balanced diet that is specifically designed to avoid bladder-irritating foods and beverages are available at the website for the Interstitial Cystitis Association (*www.ichelp.org*).

Because stress can worsen or cause flare-ups of IC/PBS symptoms, stress management techniques such as relaxation breathing and imagery (see Chapter 6) may be helpful. Using lubrication or changing positions may decrease pain associated with sexual intercourse.

The tricyclic antidepressants, amitriptyline (preferred) and nortriptyline, may reduce burning and urinary frequency. Pentosan (Elmiron) is the only oral agent approved for the treatment of patients with symptoms of IC. It enhances the protective effects of the glycosaminoglycan layer of the bladder and relieves pain by reducing the irritative effects of urine on the bladder wall. These drugs provide relief over time (weeks to months) but do not give the immediate relief that may be needed for an acute exacerbation of symptoms. A short course of opioid analgesics may be used for immediate relief. Antihistamine therapy, such as hydroxyzine, may be of use.

Pelvic physical therapy and bladder hypodistention therapy may be useful. Dimethyl sulfoxide (DMSO) can be directly instilled into the bladder through a small catheter. This drug desensitizes pain receptors in the bladder wall. Heparin, lidocaine, or sodium bicarbonate can be instilled into the bladder to relieve acute IC/PBS symptoms. Like pentosan, we think they enhance the protective properties of the glycosaminoglycan layer of the bladder. Intradetrusor botulism toxin and use of cyclosporine A have been found to be of some help.

While uncommon, surgery can be considered to improve severe, debilitating pain. Sacral neuromodulation or fulguration (using high-frequency energy to destroy a lesion) and resection of Hunner lesions are options. Urinary diversion, such as an ileal conduit, without or with removal of the bladder, is an option when other measures fail. Unfortunately, some patients have reported pain within the urinary diversion, which means that some factor in the urine may contribute to IC/PBS in certain cases.

❖ NURSING MANAGEMENT: INTERSTITIAL CYSTITIS/PAINFUL BLADDER SYNDROME

Assess the characteristics of the pain associated with IC/PBS. Ask the patient about specific dietary or lifestyle factors that relieve pain or make it worse. Teach the patient to keep a bladder log or voiding diary over a period of at least 3 days to determine voiding frequency and patterns of nocturia. Keeping a pain record at the same time may be useful.

A UTI may occur during IC/PBS management because of diagnostic instrumentation and frequent bladder instillations. A UTI is likely to cause an acute exacerbation of bothersome LUTS and urinary frequency, as well as dysuria (not typically associated with IC/PBS), odorous urine, and hematuria.

Review with the patient good nutrition, particularly in light of the broad dietary restrictions often necessary to control IC-related pain. Advise the patient to take a multivitamin containing no more than the recommended dietary allowance for essential vitamins and to avoid high-potency vitamins, because they may irritate the bladder. The patient should avoid clothing that creates suprapubic pressure, including pants with tight belts or restrictive waistlines. Educational materials about diet, coping with the need for frequent urination, and coping with the emotional burden of IC/PBS are available from the Interstitial

Cystitis Association (*www.ichelp.org*). Reassurance that IC/PBS is a real condition experienced by others and that it can be treated may relieve the anxiety, anger, guilt, and frustration related to having chronic pain and voiding dysfunction in the absence of a clear-cut diagnosis and treatment strategy.

GENITOURINARY TUBERCULOSIS

Genitourinary tuberculosis (GUTB) is the second most common type of extrapulmonary tuberculosis. Between 2% and 20% of patients with pulmonary TB will develop GUTB. Onset can occur 1 to 46 years after the primary lung infection.[9,10] When the kidney is first infected with bacilli, the patient is often asymptomatic. Sometimes the patient will have fatigue and develops a low-grade fever. As the lesions ulcerate, infection descends to the bladder and other GU organs. The patient has cystitis, frequent urination, burning on voiding, and epididymitis (in men). Hematuria, pyuria, and symptoms of a UTI are the first manifestations in most patients with GUTB.

A diagnosis of GUTB is based on finding *Mycobacterium tuberculosis* bacilli in the urine. Radiographic tests include plain radiographs, CT scan, IV pyelography, and VCUG. These studies help determine the extent and severity of the disease. Tuberculin skin test results are positive in most patients, but this finding only means that the person has had previous inhalation of mycobacteria rather than active disease.

Long-term complications of GUTB depend on the duration of the disease. Scarring of the renal parenchyma, calcifications, hydronephrosis, and the development of ureteral strictures occur. The earlier treatment is started, the less likely renal failure will develop. The patient may need long-term urologic follow-up. Nursing and interprofessional management of the patient with TB is discussed in Chapter 27.

IMMUNOLOGIC DISORDERS OF KIDNEY

GLOMERULONEPHRITIS

Glomerulonephritis (inflammation of the glomeruli) affects both kidneys equally and is the third leading cause of ESRD in the United States. Although the glomerulus is the primary site of inflammation, tubular and interstitial changes as well as vascular scarring and hardening (*glomerulosclerosis*) within the kidney can occur.[11]

A variety of conditions are associated with glomerulonephritis. These range from kidney infections, drugs toxic to the kidneys, problems with the immune system, and systemic diseases (Table 45.8). Glomerulonephritis can be acute or chronic.

TABLE 45.8 Causes and Risk Factors for Glomerulonephritis (GN)

Cause or Risk Factor	Description	Cause or Risk Factor	Description
Conditions Causing Scarring of Glomeruli		**Infections**	
Diabetic nephropathy	• Primary cause of end-stage renal disease in the United States (see Chapter 46) • Microvascular changes of diffuse glomerulosclerosis involving thickening of the glomerular basement membrane	Infective endocarditis	• Bacteria can cause an infection of 1 or more of the heart valves (see Chapter 36) • People at risk include those with a heart defect, such as a damaged or artificial heart valve • Bacterial endocarditis is associated with GN, but the exact cause is not known
Focal segmental glomerulosclerosis	• Characterized by scattered scarring of glomeruli • May result from another disease or occur for unknown reasons	Poststreptococcal glomerulonephritis	• GN may develop 1–2 wk after a streptococcal throat infection or, rarely, a skin infection (impetigo) • Antibodies (Ab) to strep antigen (Ag) develop and the Ag-Ab deposit in the glomeruli, causing inflammation
Hypertension	• Nephrosclerosis is a complication of hypertension • GN can cause hypertension	Viral infections	• Viral infections can trigger GN • Common viruses include HIV, hepatitis B, and hepatitis C viruses
Immune Diseases		**Vasculitis**	
Goodpasture syndrome	• Autoimmune disorder that causes lung and kidney disease • Causes bleeding into lungs and GN	Polyarteritis	• Autoimmune disease that affects small and medium blood vessels • Can affect any organ but common in heart, kidneys, and intestines
Immunoglobulin A (IgA) nephropathy	• Results from deposits of IgA in the glomeruli • Characterized by recurrent episodes of hematuria	Wegener's granulomatosis	• Form of vasculitis affecting small and medium blood vessels • Most often affects kidneys, lungs, and upper respiratory tract
Scleroderma	• Disease of unknown cause characterized by widespread changes in connective tissue and vascular lesions in many organs (see Chapter 64) • In the kidney, vascular lesions are associated with fibrosis • Severity of renal involvement varies	**Other Causes**	
		Amyloidosis	• Caused by infiltration of tissues with amyloid (hyaline substance) • Hyaline bodies consist largely of protein • Kidney involvement is common • Proteinuria is often the first clinical manifestation
Systemic lupus erythematosus (SLE)	• Autoimmune disorder characterized by the involvement of several tissues and organs, particularly joints, skin, and kidneys (see Chapter 64) • GN often occurs in SLE and has a poor prognosis	Illegal drug use	• People who use these drugs are at increased risk for GN

GN, Glomerulonephritis.

With *acute glomerulonephritis,* symptoms come on suddenly and may be temporary or reversible. An example of this is acute poststreptococcal glomerulonephritis (discussed in the next section). *Chronic glomerulonephritis* is slowly progressive glomerulonephritis that can lead to irreversible renal failure (discussed later in this chapter).

Diagnostic studies and a comprehensive history, including any recent infection, such as a sore throat or upper respiratory tract infection, or a diagnosis of diabetes, aid in identifying the type of glomerulonephritis present.

Acute Poststreptococcal Glomerulonephritis

Acute poststreptococcal glomerulonephritis (APSGN) is a common type of acute glomerulonephritis. It is most common in children, young adults, and adults older than 60 years. APSGN develops about 1 to 2 weeks after an infection of the tonsils, pharynx, or skin (e.g., streptococcal sore throat, impetigo) by nephrotoxic strains of group A β-hemolytic streptococci.[12] The person makes antibodies to the streptococcal antigen. Although the exact mechanism is not known, tissue injury occurs as the antigen-antibody complexes are deposited in the glomeruli, complement is activated (see Chapter 11), and inflammation results.

Manifestations include generalized body edema, hypertension, oliguria, hematuria, and varying degrees of proteinuria. Fluid retention occurs because of decreased glomerular filtration. At first, edema appears in low-pressure tissues, such as those around the eyes (*periorbital edema*). Later it progresses to involve the total body, with ascites or peripheral edema in the legs. Smoky urine indicates bleeding in the upper urinary tract. The degree of proteinuria varies with the severity of the glomerulonephropathy. Hypertension primarily results from increased extracellular fluid volume. The patient may have abdominal or flank pain. Sometimes the patient may be asymptomatic, and the problem is found on routine urinalysis.

The diagnosis of APSGN is based on a complete history and physical examination. An immune response to the streptococci is often shown by assessment of antistreptolysin-O (ASO) titers. The finding of decreased complement components (especially C3 and CH50) indicates an immune-mediated response. A renal biopsy may be done to confirm the disease.

Dipstick urinalysis and urine sediment microscopy can reveal significant numbers of erythrocytes. Erythrocyte casts are highly suggestive of APSGN. Proteinuria may range from mild to severe. Blood tests include blood urea nitrogen (BUN) and serum creatinine to assess the extent of renal impairment.

❖ NURSING AND INTERPROFESSIONAL MANAGEMENT: ACUTE POSTSTREPTOCOCCAL GLOMERULONEPHRITIS

More than 95% of patients with APSGN recover completely or improve rapidly with conservative management. Accurate recognition and assessment are critical since chronic glomerulonephritis can develop if the patient is not treated appropriately.

Management focuses on symptomatic relief. Rest is recommended until the signs of glomerular inflammation (proteinuria, hematuria) and hypertension subside. Restricting sodium and fluid intake and diuretics can reduce edema. Severe hypertension is treated with antihypertensive drugs. Dietary protein intake may be restricted if there is evidence of an increase in nitrogenous wastes (e.g., increased BUN). The dietary protein restriction varies with the degree of proteinuria. Low-protein, low-sodium, fluid-restricted diets are discussed in Chapter 46.

Antibiotics should be given only if the streptococcal infection is still present. Corticosteroids and cytotoxic drugs are not of value in treating APSGN.

One of the most important ways to prevent APSGN is to encourage early diagnosis and treatment of sore throats and skin lesions. If a culture is positive for streptococci, treatment with the appropriate antibiotic therapy is essential. Encourage the patient to take the full course of antibiotics to ensure that the bacteria have been eradicated. Good personal hygiene is a key factor in preventing the spread of cutaneous streptococcal infections.

In most cases, recovery from the acute glomerulonephritis is complete. However, if progressive involvement occurs and chronic glomerulonephritis develops, ESRD can result.

Chronic Glomerulonephritis

Chronic glomerulonephritis is a syndrome of permanent and progressive renal fibrosis. It can progress to ESRD. Most types of glomerulonephritis and nephrotic syndrome can eventually lead to chronic glomerulonephritis. Some people who develop chronic glomerulonephritis have no history of kidney disease. The cause of a patient's chronic glomerulonephritis may not be found. Although not common, an inherited disorder (e.g., Alport syndrome [see p. 1043]) may be the cause.

With chronic glomerulonephritis, symptoms develop slowly over time. Patients are often unaware that progressive kidney impairment is occurring. They do not realize that they have severe kidney impairment until a diagnostic evaluation is done. Chronic glomerulonephritis is often discovered coincidentally with the finding of an abnormality on a urinalysis, high BP, or increased serum creatinine.

The syndrome is characterized by proteinuria, hematuria, and the slow development of uremia (see Chapter 46) because of decreasing renal function. Chronic glomerulonephritis progresses insidiously toward ESRD over a course of several years.

Manifestations include varying degrees of hematuria (ranging from microscopic to gross), proteinuria, and urinary excretion of various formed elements, including red blood cells (RBCs), WBCs, and casts. Increased BUN and serum creatinine levels are common. Ultrasound and CT scan are the preferred diagnostic measures. However, a renal biopsy may be done to determine the exact cause of the glomerulonephritis.

The patient's history provides vital information related to glomerulonephritis. Assess exposure to drugs (e.g., nonsteroidal anti-inflammatory drugs [NSAIDs]), microbial infections, and viral infections (e.g., hepatitis). Evaluate the patient for more generalized conditions involving immune disorders, such as systemic lupus erythematosus (SLE). The patient may not recall any history of renal problems.

Treatment depends on the cause of the chronic glomerulonephritis and includes supportive and symptomatic care. Management of CKD is discussed in Chapter 46.

Goodpasture Syndrome

Goodpasture syndrome is an autoimmune disease characterized by antibodies that attack the glomerular and alveolar basement membranes. Damage to the kidneys and lungs results when binding of the antibody causes an inflammatory reaction mediated by complement activation (see Chapter 11).

Goodpasture syndrome is a rare disease that occurs primarily in older children and adults, especially those in their 30s to 60s. The manifestations can include flu-like and pulmonary symptoms, such as cough, mild shortness of breath, hemoptysis, crackles, and pulmonary insufficiency. Renal involvement includes hematuria, weakness, pallor, and anemia. It can proceed quickly to renal failure. Pulmonary hemorrhage usually occurs and may precede glomerular abnormalities by weeks or months.

Current management includes corticosteroids, immunosuppressive drugs (e.g., cyclophosphamide, azathioprine [Imuran]), plasmapheresis (see Chapter 13), rituximab, and dialysis. Plasmapheresis removes the circulating anti–glomerular basement membrane (GBM) antibodies, and immunosuppressive therapy inhibits further antibody production. Renal transplantation can be tried after the circulating anti-GBM antibody titer decreases. Although the disease may recur in the transplanted kidney, this is not a contraindication to transplantation.

Encourage smoking cessation. The patient receives nursing care appropriate for a critically ill patient who has AKI (see Chapter 46) and respiratory distress (see Chapter 67). Death is often from hemorrhage in the lungs and respiratory failure.

Rapidly Progressive Glomerulonephritis

Rapidly progressive glomerulonephritis (RPGN) is a type of glomerular disease with glomerular crescent formations. In contrast to chronic glomerulonephritis, which develops slowly and progresses over many years, RPGN is characterized by rapid, progressive loss of renal function over days to weeks.

RPGN can occur in a variety of situations: (1) as a complication of inflammatory or infectious disease (e.g., APSGN, Goodpasture syndrome), (2) as a complication of a systemic disease (e.g., SLE), (3) or as an idiopathic disease.

Manifestations include hypertension, edema, proteinuria, hematuria, and RBC casts. Treatment is directed toward correction of fluid overload, hypertension, uremia, and inflammatory injury to the kidney. Treatment includes corticosteroids, cyclophosphamide, and plasmapheresis. Dialysis therapy and transplantation are used as maintenance therapy for the patient with RPGN who has progressed to ESRD. After kidney transplantation, RPGN may recur.

NEPHROTIC SYNDROME

Nephrotic syndrome results when the glomerulus is excessively permeable to plasma protein, causing proteinuria that leads to low plasma albumin and tissue edema.

Etiology and Clinical Manifestations

Common causes of nephrotic syndrome are listed in Table 45.9. About one third of patients with nephrotic syndrome have a systemic disease, such as diabetes or SLE.[13]

The characteristic manifestations of nephrotic syndrome include peripheral edema, massive proteinuria, hypertension, hyperlipidemia, hypoalbuminemia, and foamy urine. The increased glomerular membrane permeability found in nephrotic syndrome is responsible for the massive excretion of protein in the urine. This results in decreased total serum protein and subsequent edema formation. Ascites and *anasarca* (massive generalized edema) develop if there is severe hypoalbuminemia.

TABLE 45.9 **Causes of Nephrotic Syndrome**	
Primary Glomerular Disease • Acute glomerulonephritis • Membranous glomerulopathy • Primary nephrotic syndrome • Rapidly progressive glomerulonephritis **Extrarenal Causes** **Allergens (Minimal Change Disease)** • Bee sting • Pollen **Cancers** • Hodgkin's lymphoma • Leukemias • Solid tumors of lungs, colon, stomach, breast	**Drugs** • captopril • heroin • NSAIDs • penicillamine **Infections** • Bacterial (streptococcal, syphilis) • Protozoal (malaria) • Viral (hepatitis, HIV, mononucleosis) **Multisystem Disease** • Amyloidosis • Diabetes • SLE

The diminished plasma oncotic pressure from the decreased serum proteins stimulates hepatic lipoprotein synthesis, which results in hyperlipidemia. At first, cholesterol and low-density lipoproteins are high. Later, triglyceride levels increase. Fat bodies (fatty casts), often appear in the urine, causing foamy urine.

Immune responses are altered in nephrotic syndrome. As a result, infection is a primary cause of morbidity and mortality. Calcium and skeletal abnormalities may occur, including hypocalcemia, blunted calcium response to parathyroid hormone, hyperparathyroidism, and osteomalacia.

Hypercoagulability is a serious issue for those with nephrotic syndrome. Hypercoagulability increases the risk for arterial and venous thromboembolism, including pulmonary embolism and deep vein or renal thrombus.

❖ Interprofessional and Nursing Care

Specific treatment of nephrotic syndrome depends on the cause. The goals are to cure or control the primary disease and relieve the symptoms. Corticosteroids and cyclophosphamide may be used in the treatment of nephrotic syndrome. Prednisone has been effective to varying degrees for some causes of nephrotic syndrome (e.g., membranous glomerulonephritis, lupus nephritis). Managing diabetes is an important consideration for nephrotic syndrome related to diabetes.

Angiotensin-converting enzyme inhibitor or angiotensin receptor blocker drugs are used to try to reduce urine protein losses. Diuretics (typically loop diuretics) can improve edema.

The treatment of hyperlipidemia includes lipid-lowering agents (see Table 33.6). Anticoagulant therapy may be needed if thrombosis is present.

The patient is placed on a low-sodium (less than 2.3 g/day), moderate-protein (1 to 2 g/kg/day) diet. If urine protein losses are high (more than 10 g/day), more protein may be recommended. Patients with nephrotic syndrome are usually anorexic and have the potential to become malnourished from the excess loss of protein in the urine. Serve small, frequent meals in a pleasant setting to encourage better dietary intake.

A major nursing intervention for a patient with nephrotic syndrome focuses on the management of edema. Assess the edema by (1) weighing the patient daily, (2) accurately recording intake and output, and (3) measuring abdominal girth or extremity size. Compare this information daily to assess the effectiveness of treatment. Clean the edematous skin carefully. Avoid trauma to the skin. Monitor the effectiveness of diuretic therapy.

Because the patient with nephrotic syndrome is susceptible to infection, teach the patient to avoid exposure to persons with known infections. Support for the patient, especially in helping cope with an altered body image, is essential because of the embarrassment and shame often associated with the edematous appearance.

OBSTRUCTIVE UROPATHIES

Urinary obstruction refers to any anatomic or functional condition that blocks or impedes the flow of urine (Fig. 45.3). It may be congenital or acquired. Damaging effects from urinary tract obstruction affect the system above the level of the obstruction. The severity of these effects depends on the location, duration of obstruction, amount of pressure or dilation, and presence of urinary stasis or infection. Infection increases the risk for irreversible damage.[14]

When obstruction occurs at the level of the bladder neck or prostate, significant bladder changes can occur. Detrusor muscle fibers *hypertrophy* (increase in size) to contract harder to push urine out a narrower pathway. Over a long period, the detrusor loses its ability to compensate for this resistance, eventually leading to a large residual urine volume in the bladder.

When *bladder outlet obstruction* is present, pressure increases during bladder filling or storage and can be transmitted to the ureter. This pressure leads to *reflux* (backflow, or backward movement, of urine), *hydroureter* (ureteral dilation and distention), vesicoureteral reflux (backflow of urine from the lower to upper urinary tract), and *hydronephrosis* (dilation or enlargement of the renal pelvises and calyces) (Fig. 45.4). Chronic pyelonephritis and renal atrophy may develop. If only 1 kidney is obstructed, the other kidney may try to compensate by enlarging.

Partial obstruction may occur in the ureter or at the ureteropelvic junction (UPJ) (where the renal pelvis narrows into the ureter). If the pressure stays low or moderate, the kidney may continue to dilate with no noticeable loss of function. Urinary stasis and reflux increase the risk for pyelonephritis. If only 1 kidney is involved, and the other kidney is functioning, the patient may be asymptomatic.

If both kidneys or only 1 functioning kidney is involved (e.g., if the patient has only 1 kidney), changes in renal function (e.g., increased BUN and serum creatinine levels) occur. Progressive obstruction can lead to renal failure. Treatment requires finding and relieving the blockage. This can include insertion of a tube (e.g., urethral or ureteral), surgical correction of the primary problem, or diversion of the urinary stream above the level of blockage.

URINARY TRACT CALCULI

In their lifetime, 13% of men and 7% of women in the United States will have **nephrolithiasis,** or kidney stone disease. The term **calculus** refers to the stone, and *lithiasis* refers to stone formation.

Most patients are middle-aged adults. The risk for developing kidney stones increases with age.[15] Stone formation is more frequent in whites than in blacks, Hispanics, and Asians.

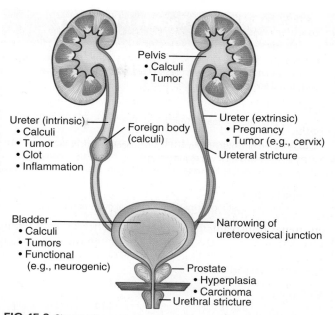

FIG 45.3 Sites and causes of upper and lower urinary tract obstruction.

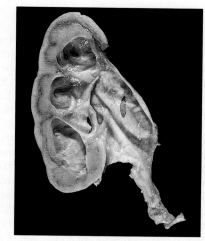

FIG 45.4 Hydronephrosis of the kidney. Note the marked dilation of the pelvis and calyces and thinning of the renal parenchyma. (From Kumar V, Abbas AK, Aster JC, et al: *Robbins and Cotran pathologic basis of disease,* ed 8, Philadelphia, 2010, Saunders.)

The incidence is higher in persons with a family history of stone formation. Stones recur in up to 50% of patients. In the United States, the incidence of stone disease is highest in the Southeast, followed by the Southwest and Midwest. Stone formation occurs more often in the summer months, supporting the possible contributing factors of a hot climate and dehydration.

GENDER DIFFERENCES
Urinary Tract Stones

Men
- Most likely to have urinary stones, except for struvite stones

Women
- More likely to have struvite stones associated with UTI

TABLE 45.10 Risk Factors for Urinary Tract Stones

Climate
- Warm climates that cause increased fluid loss, low urine volume, and increased solute concentration in urine

Diet
- Excess amounts of tea or fruit juices that increase urinary oxalate level
- Large intake of dietary proteins that increases uric acid excretion
- Large intake of salt, low calcium intake
- Low fluid intake that increases urinary concentration

Genetic Factors
- Family history of stone formation, cystinuria, gout, or renal acidosis

Lifestyle
- Immobility
- Obesity
- Sedentary occupation

Metabolic
- Abnormalities that result in increased urine levels of calcium, oxalate, uric acid, or citric acid

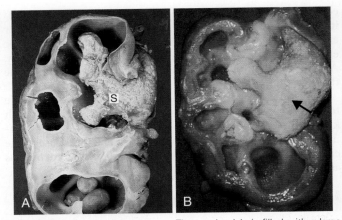

FIG 45.5 **A,** Renal staghorn stone. The renal pelvis is filled with a large stone that is shaped to its contours, resembling the horns of a stag *(S).* **B,** Imbedded staghorn stone *(arrow)* in hydronephrotic, infected, nonfunctioning kidney. (*A,* From Stevens A, Lowe JS, Scott I: *Core pathology: Illustrated review in color,* ed 3, London, 2009, Mosby Ltd. *B,* From Bullock N, Doble A, Turner W, et al: *Urology: An illustrated colour text,* London, 2008, Churchill Livingstone.)

Etiology and Pathophysiology

Many factors are involved in the incidence and type of stone formation, including climatic, dietary, genetic, metabolic, and lifestyle influences (Table 45.10). No single theory accounts for stone formation in all cases. Crystals, when in a supersaturated concentration, can precipitate and unite to form a stone. Keeping urine dilute and free flowing reduces the risk for recurrent stone formation in many people.

We think kidney stones form when certain crystal-forming substances are not diluted by the kidney and/or there is reduced ability of the kidneys to keep the crystals from sticking together. Urinary pH, solute load, and inhibitors in the urine affect the formation of stones. The higher the pH (alkaline), the less soluble are calcium and phosphate. The lower the pH (acidic), the less soluble are uric acid and cystine. When a substance is not very soluble in fluid, it is more likely to precipitate out of solution.

Other key factors in stone formation include obstruction with associated urinary stasis and UTI with urea-splitting bacteria (e.g., *Proteus, Klebsiella, Pseudomonas,* and some species of staphylococci). These bacteria cause the urine to become alkaline and contribute to the formation of struvite stones. Infected stones, trapped in the kidney (Fig. 45.5), may assume a staghorn configuration as the stone branches to occupy a larger part of the collecting system. These stones can lead to a renal infection, hydronephrosis, and loss of kidney function.

Genetic factors may contribute to urine stone formation. Cystinuria, an autosomal recessive disorder, causes a markedly increased excretion of cystine.

⊕ PROMOTING HEALTH EQUITY

Urologic Disorders

- Urinary tract stones are more common among whites than blacks.
- Uric acid stones are more common in Jewish men.
- Bladder cancer has a higher incidence among white men than black men.
- Urinary incontinence is underreported because culturally it is seen as a social hygiene problem causing patient embarrassment.

Types of Urinary Stones

The 5 major categories of stones are (1) calcium oxalate, (2) calcium phosphate, (3) cystine, (4) struvite (magnesium ammonium phosphate), and (5) uric acid (Table 45.11). Calcium stones can exist as calcium oxalate, calcium phosphate, or a mixture of both. Although calcium stones are the most common, stone composition may be mixed. Stones can be found in various locations in the urinary tract (Figs. 45.3 and 45.5).

Clinical Manifestations

The first symptom of a kidney stone is usually severe pain that begins suddenly. Typically, a person feels a sharp, severe pain in the flank area, back, or lower abdomen. People describe the pain as the most excruciating that a person can endure. We call this pain *renal colic.* It results from the stretching, dilation, and spasm of the ureter in response to the obstructing stone. Nausea and vomiting may occur due to the severe pain.

Urinary stones cause manifestations when they obstruct urinary flow. Common sites of obstruction are at the UPJ and ureterovesical junction (UVJ). The type of pain is determined by the location of the stone. If the obstruction is in a calyx or at the UPJ, the patient may have dull costovertebral flank pain or renal colic. Pain resulting from the passage of a stone down the ureter is intense and colicky. If the stone is nonobstructing, pain may be absent.

Patients with renal colic have a hard time being still. They go from walking to sitting to lying down, and then they repeat the process. Some people refer to this as the "kidney stone dance."

The patient may be in mild shock with cool, moist skin. As a stone nears the UVJ, pain moves around toward the abdomen and down toward the lower quadrant. Men may have testicular pain, while women may have labial pain. Both men and women can have groin pain. The patient may have manifestations of a UTI with dysuria, fever, and chills.

Diagnostic Studies

Stones are easily diagnosed with either a noncontrast helical (spiral) CT scan or ultrasound. A complete urinalysis helps confirm the diagnosis of a urinary stone by assessing for hematuria

TABLE 45.11 Types of Urinary Tract Stones

Characteristics	Predisposing Factors	Treatment
Calcium Oxalate Small, can easily get trapped in ureter. More frequent in men than in women. *Incidence:* 35%–40%	Idiopathic hypercalciuria, hyperoxaluria, independent of urinary pH, family history	Increase hydration. Reduce dietary oxalate, animal protein, and sodium (see Table 45.12). Encourage increased intake of calcium, fruits, and vegetables. Give thiazide diuretics. Give potassium citrate to maintain alkaline urine. Avoid vitamin C and calcium supplements.
Calcium Phosphate Mixed stones (typically), with struvite or oxalate stones. *Incidence:* 8%–10%	Alkaline urine, primary hyperparathyroidism	Increase hydration. Treat underlying causes and other stones. Reduce dietary sodium and animal protein intake. Increase dietary calcium intake. Avoid vitamin C supplements.
Cystine Genetic autosomal recessive defect. Defective absorption of cystine in GI tract and kidney, excess concentrations causing stone formation. *Incidence:* 1%–2%	Acidic urine	Increase hydration. Give α-penicillamine, captopril or tiopronin to prevent cystine crystallization. Give potassium citrate to keep urine alkaline.
Struvite (Magnesium Ammonium Phosphate) 3–4 times more common in women. Always associated with urinary tract infections. Large staghorn type (usually) (Fig. 45.5). *Incidence:* 10%–15%	Urinary tract infections (usually *Proteus*)	Give antimicrobial agents, acetohydroxamic acid. May need surgery to remove stone. Take measures to acidify urine.
Uric Acid Predominant in men, high incidence in Jewish men. *Incidence:* 5%–8%	Gout, acidic urine, inherited condition	Reduce urinary concentration of uric acid. Alkalinize urine with potassium citrate. Give allopurinol. Reduce dietary purines (see Table 45.12).

and crystalluria. Measuring urine pH is useful in the diagnosis of struvite stones (tendency to alkaline or high pH) and uric acid or cystine stones (tendency to acidic or low pH).

Retrieval and analysis of the stone(s) is important in the diagnosis of the underlying problem contributing to stone formation. The patient's serum calcium, phosphorus, sodium, potassium, bicarbonate, uric acid, BUN, and creatinine levels are measured. Patients who have recurrent stone formation should have a 24-hour urinary measurement of calcium, phosphorus, magnesium, sodium, oxalate, citrate, cysteine, sulfate, potassium, uric acid, and total urine volume.

Interprofessional Care

Evaluation and management of a patient with renal stones consist of 2 concurrent approaches. The first approach is directed toward managing the acute attack by treating the pain, infection, and/or obstruction. Give opioids to relieve renal colic pain. NSAIDs can be considered if there is no contraindication based upon the renal function. Most stones are 4 mm or less in size and pass spontaneously. However, it may take weeks for a stone to pass.

α-Adrenergic blockers, such as tamsulosin (Flomax) or terazosin, which relax the smooth muscle in the ureter, can help stone passage. These drugs also relax the muscle tissue in the prostate in men with BPH.

The second approach is directed toward evaluating the cause of the stone formation and preventing further stone development. Obtain information from the patient, including a family history of stone formation; geographic residence; nutritional assessment, including fluid intake and the intake of vitamins A, C, and D; activity pattern (active or sedentary); history of prolonged illness with immobilization or dehydration; and any history of disease or surgery involving the GI or genitourinary tract. Include any prior episodes of stone formation, prescribed and OTC medications, and use of dietary supplements.

Therapy for active stone formers requires a comprehensive management approach, with the primary emphasis on teaching. Adequate hydration, dietary sodium restrictions, dietary changes, and drugs are used to minimize urinary stone formation (Table 45.11). Depending on the specific problem underlying the stone formation, various drugs are prescribed. These drugs prevent stone formation in several ways. These include altering urine pH, preventing excessive urinary excretion of a substance, or correcting a primary disease (e.g., hyperparathyroidism).

Treatment of struvite stones requires control of infection. This may be difficult if the stone is still in place. In addition to antibiotics, acetohydroxamic acid may be used to treat kidney infections that result in the continual formation of struvite stones. Acetohydroxamic acid inhibits the chemical action caused by the persistent bacteria and can slow struvite stone formation. Stones may have to be removed surgically if the infection cannot be controlled.[16]

Endourology, lithotripsy, or open surgical stone removal may be used in the following situations: (1) stones too large for spontaneous passage (usually greater than 7 mm); (2) stones associated with bacteriuria or symptomatic infection; (3) stones causing impaired renal function; (4) stones causing persistent pain, nausea, or paralytic ileus; (5) inability of patient to be treated medically; and (6) patient with only 1 kidney.[16]

Endourologic Procedures. If the stone is in the bladder, a cystoscopy is done to remove small stones. For large stones (Fig. 45.6), a *cystolitholapaxy* is done. In this procedure, large stones are

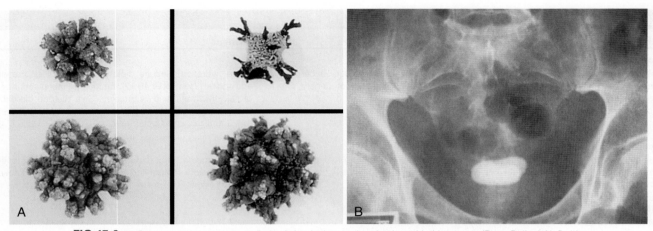

FIG 45.6 A, Calcium oxalate stones. B, Plain abdominal x-ray showing large bladder stone. (From Bullock N, Doble A, Turner W, et al: *Urology: An illustrated colour text*, London, 2008, Churchill Livingstone.)

broken up with an instrument called a *lithotrite* (stone crusher), using mechanical crushing or laser energy. The bladder is then irrigated, and the crushed stones washed out. A *cystoscopic lithotripsy* uses ultrasonic waves to break up stones. Complications associated with these procedures include hemorrhage, retained stone fragments, and infection.

Flexible *ureteroscopes* can be used to remove stones from the renal pelvis and upper urinary tract. Ultrasonic, laser, or electrohydraulic lithotripsy may be used in conjunction with ureteroscopy to break up the stone.

In *percutaneous nephrolithotomy,* a nephroscope is inserted into the kidney pelvis through a track (using a sheath) in the skin. The track is created in the patient's back. The kidney stones can be fragmented using ultrasound, electrohydraulic, or laser lithotripsy. The stone fragments are removed, and the pelvis is irrigated. A percutaneous nephrostomy tube can be left in place to make sure that the ureter is not obstructed. Complications include bleeding, injury to adjacent structures, and infection.

Lithotripsy. Lithotripsy is a procedure used to eliminate stones from the urinary tract. Lithotripsy techniques include (1) laser lithotripsy, (2) extracorporeal shock-wave lithotripsy (ESWL), (3) percutaneous ultrasonic lithotripsy, and (4) electrohydraulic lithotripsy. *Laser lithotripsy* is used to shatter ureteral and large bladder stones (bladder stones are described earlier). To access ureteral stones, a ureteroscope is used to get close to the stone. A small fiber is inserted up the scope so that the tip (which emits the laser energy) can come in contact with the stone. A holmium laser in direct contact with the stone is commonly used. The intense energy breaks the stone into small pieces, which can be extracted or flushed out. Because of the type of laser energy, no other tissue is affected. This minimally invasive treatment usually requires general anesthesia.

In *extracorporeal shock-wave lithotripsy (ESWL),* a noninvasive procedure, the patient is anesthetized (spinal or general) to ensure they maintain the same position during the procedure. The HCP uses fluoroscopy or ultrasound to focus the lithotripter over the affected kidney. Then, a high-voltage spark generator produces high-energy acoustic shock waves that shatter the stone without damaging the surrounding tissues. The small pieces of stone are then excreted in the urine. A complication of ESWL is steinstrasse, in which the ureter is blocked by those smaller pieces.

In *percutaneous ultrasonic lithotripsy* an ultrasonic probe is placed in the renal pelvis via a percutaneous nephroscope inserted through a small flank incision. The HCP positions the probe against the stone. The probe produces ultrasonic waves, which break the stone into sand-like particles. The patient receives general or spinal anesthesia.

In *electrohydraulic lithotripsy* the probe is positioned directly on a stone, but it breaks the stone into small fragments that are removed by forceps or suction. A continuous saline irrigation flushes out the stone particles, and all the outflow drainage is strained so that the particles can be analyzed. Stones can also be removed by basket extraction.

Complications of lithotripsy are rare but include hemorrhage, infection, and obstruction. Hematuria is common after lithotripsy procedures. The first few times that the patient voids, the urine is bright red. As the bleeding subsides, the urine becomes dark red or a smoky color. Antibiotics are usually given after the procedure to reduce the risk for infection.

Afterward, the patient usually has moderate to severe colicky pain. A self-retaining ureteral stent is often placed after the procedure to help the passage of sand (shattered stone) and prevent sand buildup within the ureter, which may lead to obstruction. The stent is typically removed within 2 weeks after lithotripsy. If a stone is large or positioned in the mid or distal ureter, other treatment, such as surgery, may be needed. Encourage fluids to help dilute the urine and reduce the pain from passing stone fragments.

Surgical Therapy. A small group of patients need open surgical procedures. The primary indications for surgery include pain, infection, and obstruction. The type of open surgery done depends on the location of the stone. A *nephrolithotomy* is an incision into the kidney to remove a stone. A *pyelolithotomy* is an incision into the renal pelvis for stone removal. If the stone is in the ureter, a *ureterolithotomy* is done. A *cystotomy* may be indicated for bladder stones. For open surgery on the kidney or ureter, a flank incision directly below the diaphragm and across the side is usually preferred. The most common complications after surgical procedures for stone removal are related to hemorrhage.

Nutritional Therapy. To manage an obstructing stone, the patient should drink adequate fluids to avoid dehydration. Forcing excess fluids is not advised because it does not promote spontaneous passage of stones in the urine. Forcing fluids may increase the pain or precipitate the development of renal colic.

EVIDENCE-BASED PRACTICE
Preventing Recurrent Kidney Stones

You are caring for K.D. a 41-yr-old man who is being discharged home after successful kidney stone retrieval. This was his first kidney stone and he says it was "very painful." He asks you, "Can anything be done to prevent another stone?" You see on the chart that the stone was composed of calcium oxalate and that he has gout.

Making Clinical Decisions

Best Available Evidence. Increased fluid intake (about 3 L/day) to produce 2.5 L/day of urine decreases the risk for recurrent calcium stones in patients with a prior stone. Dietary calcium intake should be 1000 to 1200 mg/day. Addition of drugs (e.g., thiazide diuretics, potassium citrate, allopurinol) for persons with recurrent calcium stones can further reduce risk. Nutritional counseling (e.g., registered dietician) for these patients is recommended.

Clinician Expertise. You know risk factors for kidney stone formation include low fluid intake and having conditions such as gout, obesity, diabetes, and/or primary hyperparathyroidism. You understand preventive measures may decrease the chance of recurrent kidney stones after the first incidence.

Patient Preferences and Values. K.D. states it may be hard to increase his fluid intake and he wants to know if a drug is available instead.

Implications for Nursing Practice

1. Why is it important for K.D. to understand the link between increased fluid intake and stone recurrence?
2. How would you help him identify ways to increase his fluid intake?
3. How would you respond to K.D.'s request for a drug to prevent recurrence?

Reference for Evidence

Dion M, Ankawi G, Chew B, et al.: CUA guideline on the evaluation and management of the kidney stone patient—2016 Update, *Can Urol Assoc J* 10:E347, 2016.

After an episode of urolithiasis, encourage a high fluid intake (around 3 L/day) to produce a urine output of at least 2.5 L/day. High urine output prevents supersaturation of minerals (i.e., dilutes the concentration of urine) and promotes excretion of minerals within the urine, thus preventing stone formation. Increasing fluid intake is particularly important for patients at risk for dehydration, including those who (1) are active in sports, (2) live in a dry climate, (3) perform physical exercise, (4) have a family history of stone formation, or (5) work outside or in an occupation that requires a great deal of physical activity. Water is the preferred fluid. Limit consumption of colas, coffee, and tea because high intake of these beverages tends to increase the risk for recurring urinary stones.

A low-sodium diet is recommended, since high-sodium intake increases calcium excretion in the urine. Foods high in calcium, oxalate, and purines are shown in Table 45.12.

❖ NURSING MANAGEMENT: URINARY TRACT CALCULI

◆ Nursing Assessment

Subjective and objective data that should be obtained from a patient with urinary tract stones are outlined in Table 45.13.

◆ Nursing Diagnoses

Nursing diagnoses for the patient with urinary tract stones include:

- Impaired urinary system function
- Acute pain
- Lack of knowledge

TABLE 45.12 Nutritional Therapy
Urinary Tract Stones

Depending on the type of stone, modifying the diet can be helpful in preventing reoccurrence.

Calcium

High: Milk, cheese, ice cream, yogurt, sauces containing milk; all beans (except green beans), lentils; fish with fine bones (e.g., sardines, kippers, herring, salmon); dried fruits, nuts; Ovaltine, chocolate, cocoa

Oxalate

High: Dark roughage, spinach, rhubarb, asparagus, cabbage, tomatoes, beets, nuts, celery, parsley, runner beans; chocolate, cocoa, instant coffee, Ovaltine, tea; Worcestershire sauce

Purine

High: Sardines, herring, mussels, liver, kidney, goose, venison, meat soups, sweetbreads
Moderate: Chicken, salmon, crab, veal, mutton, bacon, pork, beef, ham

TABLE 45.13 Nursing Assessment
Urinary Tract Stones

Subjective Data
Important Health Information

Past health history: Recent or chronic UTI. Immobilization. Previous urinary tract stones, obstruction, or kidney disease with urinary stasis. Gout, BPH, hyperparathyroidism, chronic diarrhea
Medications: Prior use of medication for prevention of stones or treatment of UTI, allopurinol, analgesics, loop diuretics, thiazide diuretics
Surgery or other treatments: External urinary diversion, long-term indwelling urinary catheter

Functional Health Patterns

Health perception–health management: Family history of urinary tract stones, sedentary lifestyle
Nutritional-metabolic: Nausea, vomiting. Dietary intake of purines, calcium ingestion, salt excess, oxalates, phosphates and use of OTC supplements. Low fluid intake. Chills
Elimination: Decreased urine output, urinary urgency, frequency, feeling of bladder fullness
Cognitive-perceptual: Acute, severe, colicky pain in flank, back, abdomen, groin, or genitalia. Burning on urination, dysuria. Anxiety

Objective Data
General

Guarding, back pain, fever, dehydration

Integumentary

Warm, flushed skin or pallor with cool, moist skin (mild shock)

Gastrointestinal

Abdominal distention, absence of bowel sounds

Urinary

Oliguria, hematuria, tenderness on palpation of renal areas, passage of stone or stones

Possible Diagnostic Findings

↑ BUN and serum creatinine levels. Urinalysis showing RBCs, WBCs, pyuria, crystals, casts, minerals, bacteria. ↑ Uric acid, calcium, phosphorus, oxalate, or cystine values on 24-hr urine sample. Stones or anatomic changes on KUB x-ray, CT scan or renal/bladder US. Direct visualization of obstruction on cystoureteroscopy

More information on nursing diagnoses and interventions for the patient with urinary tract stones is presented in eNursing Care Plan 45.2 (on the website for this chapter).

◆ Planning

The overall goals are that the patient with urinary tract stones will have (1) relief of pain, (2) no urinary tract obstruction, and (3) knowledge of ways to prevent recurrence of stones.

◆ Nursing Implementation

Most people who have had urinary stones can lower their risk for recurrence by changing their lifestyle and dietary habits. Adequate fluid intake is important to produce a urine output of around 2.5 L/day. Consult with the HCP about specific recommendations for fluid intake in a given person. The moderately active, ambulatory person should drink about 3 L/day. Fluid intake must be higher in the active person who works outdoors or who regularly engages in athletic activities.

Preventive measures for a person who is on bed rest or is immobile for a prolonged time include maintaining an adequate fluid intake, turning the patient every few hours, and helping the patient sit or stand, if possible, to maximize urinary flow.

Other preventive measures focus on reducing metabolic or secondary risk factors. For example, dietary restriction of purines may be helpful for the patient at risk for developing uric acid stones. Teach the patient the dosage, scheduling, and potential side effects of drugs used to reduce the risk for stone formation (Table 45.11). Some patients may be taught to self-monitor urinary pH or urine output.

Pain management and patient comfort are primary nursing responsibilities when managing a patient who has an obstructing stone and renal colic. To ensure that any spontaneously passed stones are retrieved, strain all urine voided by the patient using a gauze or a urine strainer. Encourage ambulation to promote movement of the stone from the upper to the lower urinary tract. To ensure safety, tell the patient who has acute renal colic to ask for help when ambulating, particularly if opioid analgesics are being given.

◆ Evaluation

The expected outcomes are that the patient with urinary tract stones will
- Maintain free flow of urine with minimal hematuria
- Report satisfactory pain relief
- State understanding of disease process and ways to prevent recurrence

STRICTURES

A ureteral or urethral stricture is a narrowing of the lumen of the ureter or urethra.

Ureteral Strictures

Ureteral strictures can affect the entire length of the ureter, from the UPJ to UVJ. While these can be congenital, they are usually from adhesions or scar formation after surgery or radiation. They may be due to extrinsic factors, such as large tumors in the peritoneal cavity. Depending on its severity, ureteral obstruction can threaten the function of the kidney.

Manifestations include mild to moderate colic, flank pain and CVA tenderness. This pain may be moderate to severe in intensity, especially if the patient drinks a large volume of fluids, such as alcohol, over a brief period. Infection is unusual unless a stone or foreign object, such as a stent or nephrostomy tube, is present.

The discomfort and obstruction of a ureteral stricture may be temporarily bypassed by placing a stent using endoscopy or by diverting urinary flow via a nephrostomy tube inserted into the renal pelvis of the affected kidney. Definitive correction requires dilation with a balloon or catheter. If the stricture is severe or recurs after initial balloon or catheter dilation, it is surgically incised using an endoscopic procedure (*endoureterotomy*). In select patients, an open surgical approach may be needed to excise the stenotic area and reanastomose the ureter to the contralateral ureter (*ureteroureterostomy*) or to the renal pelvis. Alternatively, distal ureteral strictures may be treated by a *ureteroneocystostomy* (reimplantation of the ureter into the bladder wall).

Urethral Strictures

A *urethral stricture* is the result of fibrosis or inflammation of the urethral lumen. Causes of urethral strictures include trauma, urethritis (particularly after gonococcal infection), surgical intervention or repeated catheterizations (iatrogenic), or a congenital defect of the urethra. Once the process of inflammation and fibrosis begins, the lumen of the urethra narrows and its compliance (ability to close or open in response to bladder filling or voiding) is compromised. Meatal stenosis, a narrowing of the urethral opening, is common.

Manifestations associated with a urethral stricture include a diminished force of the urinary stream, straining to void, sprayed stream, postvoid dribbling, or a split urine stream. The patient may report feelings of incomplete bladder emptying with urinary frequency and nocturia. Moderate to severe obstruction of the bladder outlet may lead to acute urinary retention. The patient may have a history of urethritis, difficulty with insertion of a urinary catheter, or trauma involving the penis or the perineum. However, many patients are unable to recall any such events, thus leading to a diagnosis of an idiopathic stricture. A history of UTI is common, particularly if the stricture involves the distal urethra. Retrograde urethrography (RUG), ultrasound urethrography, cystourethrogram, and VCUG are used to identify stricture length, location, and caliber.

Initial management focuses on dilation. A metal instrument (urethral sound) may be placed, or a series of progressively larger stents (filiforms and followers) can be placed into the urethra to expand its lumen in a stepwise fashion. Although this process is initially successful, stenosis often recurs. Recurrences may be managed by teaching the patient to repeatedly dilate the urethra by self-catheterization using a soft (coudé-tip, red rubber) catheter every few days. Alternatively, an endoscopic or open surgical procedure (*urethroplasty*) may be a more definitive therapy for an obstructive urethral stricture. Shorter strictures may be treated by resecting the fibrotic area followed by reanastomosis of the urethra. Longer strictures may require the use of a skin flap as a substitute urethral segment.

RENAL TRAUMA

Renal trauma can be blunt or penetrating. *Blunt trauma* is the most common cause. Injury to the kidney should be considered in sports injuries, motor vehicle accidents, and falls.

Renal trauma is especially likely when the patient injures the abdomen, flank, or back. Around 10% of patients with abdominal trauma also have renal trauma. *Penetrating injuries* may result from violent encounters (e.g., gunshot, stabbing incidents).

The severity of renal trauma depends on the extent of the injury. Obtain a history of trauma to the area of the kidneys. Gross or microscopic hematuria may be present. Diagnostic studies include urinalysis, ultrasound, CT, or MRI evaluation. Renal arteriography also may be done. Both the injured kidney and the uninvolved kidney should be evaluated. Treatments range from bed rest, fluids, and analgesia to exploratory surgery and repair or nephrectomy.[17]

Nursing interventions depend on the type of trauma and the extent of any associated injuries. Interventions related to renal trauma include (1) assess the cardiovascular status and monitor for shock, especially in a penetrating injury; (2) ensure adequate fluid intake and monitor intake and output; (3) provide for pain relief and comfort measures; and (4) assess for hematuria and myoglobinuria.

RENAL VASCULAR PROBLEMS

Vascular problems involving the kidney include (1) nephrosclerosis, (2) renal artery stenosis, and (3) renal vein thrombosis.

NEPHROSCLEROSIS

Nephrosclerosis is sclerosis of the small arteries and arterioles of the kidney. The decreased blood flow results in ischemia, interstitial fibrosis, and necrosis of parts of the kidney. *Benign nephrosclerosis,* which usually occurs in adults older than 60 years of age, is caused by vascular changes from hypertension and atherosclerosis. Atherosclerotic vascular changes account for most of the loss of renal function associated with aging. The degree of nephrosclerosis is related to the severity of hypertension. In the early stages, the patient with benign nephrosclerosis may have normal renal function, with the only detectable abnormality being hypertension.

Accelerated nephrosclerosis (malignant nephrosclerosis) is associated with a significantly high BP, which can be as high as 300/150 mm/Hg, with small focal hemorrhages developing in the kidneys. It begins suddenly and is a medical emergency. It is characterized by systolic BP ≥180 and/or diastolic BP ≥120 mm/Hg with evidence of new or ongoing organ damage. Renal insufficiency progresses rapidly.

The availability and use of antihypertensive drugs have improved the prognosis for patients with benign and malignant nephrosclerosis. Treatment for benign nephrosclerosis is the same as that for essential hypertension (see Chapter 32). Malignant nephrosclerosis is treated with aggressive antihypertensive therapy. The prognosis for a patient with untreated or refractive malignant hypertension is poor. These conditions can lead to death.

RENAL ARTERY STENOSIS

Renal artery stenosis is a partial occlusion of 1 or both renal arteries and their major branches. It can be due to atherosclerotic narrowing or fibromuscular hyperplasia. Renal artery stenosis can be a cause of secondary hypertension.

When hypertension develops suddenly, renal artery stenosis should be considered, especially in patients under 30 or over 50 years of age and in those with no family history of hypertension. This contrasts with the age distribution for developing primary hypertension, which is 30 to 50 years of age.

Diagnostic tests used to assess for renal artery stenosis include a renal duplex Doppler ultrasonography, CT or MRI angiography, and renal arteriogram (the gold standard).

The goals of therapy are to control BP and restore perfusion to the kidney. Percutaneous transluminal renal angioplasty, with or without stenting, is the procedure of choice, especially in older patients who are poor surgical risks.

Surgical revascularization of the kidney is needed when decreased blood flow causes renal ischemia or when renovascular hypertension is present. Revascularization of the kidney may result in the patient's BP becoming normotensive. The surgical procedure usually involves anastomosis between the kidney and another major artery, usually the splenic artery or aorta. In certain cases of unilateral renal involvement, unilateral nephrectomy may be indicated.

RENAL VEIN THROMBOSIS

Renal vein thrombosis may occur unilaterally or bilaterally. Causes include trauma, extrinsic compression (e.g., tumor, aortic aneurysm), renal cell cancer, pregnancy, contraceptive use, and nephrotic syndrome.

The patient has flank pain, hematuria, fever, or nephrotic syndrome. Anticoagulation (e.g., heparin, warfarin [Coumadin]) is important to treat the high incidence of pulmonary emboli. Corticosteroids may be used for the patient with nephrotic syndrome. Surgical thrombectomy may be done instead of or along with anticoagulation.

HEREDITARY KIDNEY DISEASES

Hereditary kidney diseases involve developmental abnormalities of the renal parenchyma. Most inherited structural abnormalities are cystic. However, cysts may develop because of obstructive uropathies, metabolic problems, or neurologic diseases. Cysts may be evaluated to rule out tumors.

POLYCYSTIC KIDNEY DISEASE

Polycystic kidney disease (PKD) is one of the most common life-threatening genetic diseases in the world. It affects 600,000 people in the United States. PKD is the fourth leading cause of ESRD, affecting 5% of those with ESRD. A nongenetic PKD (acquired cystic kidney disease [ACKD]) is seen in those with severe kidney scarring and damage who typically require dialysis. After 5 years on dialysis, 90% of patients will have ACKD.[18]

Genetic Link

PKD has 2 hereditary forms: one manifests in childhood and one in adulthood. The childhood form of PKD is a rare autosomal recessive disorder that is often rapidly progressive (see the Genetics in Clinical Practice box). The adult form of PKD is an autosomal dominant disorder and accounts for 90% of all PKD cases (see Figs. 12.4 and 12.5). If 1 parent has the disease, there is a 50% chance that the disease will pass to the child.

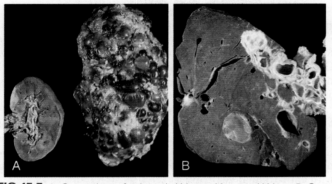

FIG 45.7 A, Comparison of polycystic kidney with normal kidney. B, Cysts in the liver. (*A,* From Brundage DJ: *Renal disorders,* St Louis, 1992, Mosby. *B,* From Kumar V, Abbas AK, Fausto N: *Robbins and Cotran pathologic basis of disease,* ed 7, Philadelphia, 2005, Saunders.)

Adult PKD involves both kidneys and occurs in both men and women. The cortex and medulla are filled with large, thin-walled cysts that are several millimeters to several centimeters in diameter (Fig. 45.7). The cysts enlarge and destroy surrounding tissue by compression. The cysts are filled with fluid and may contain blood or pus. PKD kidneys appear enlarged and look like they are filled with golf balls.

Adult PKD can be symptomless for many years. Signs and symptoms usually develop between 30 and 40 years of age.[18] Symptoms appear when the renal cysts begin to enlarge. Often the first manifestations are hypertension, hematuria (from rupture of cysts), or a feeling of pain or heaviness in the back, side, or abdomen. However, the first manifestation can be a UTI or urinary stones.

Chronic pain is the most common problem in persons with PKD. The pain can be constant and severe. Bilateral, enlarged kidneys are often palpable on physical examination. Many people have no symptoms, which can delay diagnosis.

PKD can affect the liver (liver cysts [Fig. 45.7]), heart (abnormal heart valves), blood vessels (aneurysms), and intestines (diverticulosis). The most serious complication is a cerebral aneurysm, which can rupture.

Diagnosis is based on manifestations, family history, ultrasound (best screening measure), or CT scan (provides more precise images). The disease usually progresses from loss of kidney function to ESRD by age 60 in 50% of patients.[18]

❖ Interprofessional and Nursing Care

There is no cure for PKD at present. A major aim of treatment is to prevent or treat infections of the urinary tract. Nephrectomy may be done if pain, bleeding, or infection becomes a chronic, serious problem. Dialysis and kidney transplant may be needed to treat ESRD (see Chapter 46).

When the patient begins to have progressive renal failure, the interventions depend on the remaining renal function. Nursing measures are those used for management of ESRD. They include diet modification, fluid restriction, drugs (e.g., antihypertensives), and help for the patient and family in coping with the chronic disease process and financial concerns.

The patient who has adult PKD often has children by the time the disease is diagnosed. The patient needs appropriate counseling about plans for having more children. Genetic counseling should be provided for the children. More resources can be found at the PKD Foundation website *(www.pkdcure.org)*.

❓ CHECK YOUR PRACTICE

You are doing a rotation in the dialysis unit. You have been doing vital sign checks on a 45-yr-old man who receives dialysis 3 times/wk. When you ask him why he is on dialysis, he tells you that he has polycystic kidney disease. After further discussion, he tells you that he has 1 son who is now 23 years old, but they are estranged. He does not want to tell him about his medical problems or why he is on dialysis.
• How would you respond to this patient?

MEDULLARY CYSTIC DISEASE

Medullary cystic disease is a hereditary disorder that occurs in older adults. Most cysts occur in the medulla. The kidneys are asymmetric in shape and are significantly scarred. Defects in the kidneys' concentrating ability result in polyuria. Other manifestations include hypertension, progressive renal failure, severe anemia, and metabolic acidosis. Genetic counseling may be helpful in family planning. Treatment measures are those related to ESRD (see Chapter 46). A similar disease, familial juvenile nephronophilisis, is found in young children. It can also affect the nervous system and eyes.

ALPORT SYNDROME

Alport syndrome, also known as *chronic hereditary nephritis,* is an inherited disease that primarily affects the glomeruli. The basic defect is a mutation in a gene for collagen that results in altered synthesis of the glomerular basement membrane.[19]

There are 3 genetic types of Alport syndrome: sex-linked, autosomal recessive type, and autosomal dominant type. In sex-linked, the most common type, the earliest manifestation is hematuria. These patients have progressive hearing loss and deformities of the lens of the eye. The other types of Alport syndrome cause hematuria but not deafness or lens deformities.

Males are affected earlier and more severely than females. The disease is often diagnosed in the first decade of life. Alport syndrome causes progressive kidney damage, leading to ESRD. Children with the autosomal recessive type usually develop ESRD by their teens or young adult years. People with autosomal dominant Alport syndrome usually live well into middle age before ESRD develops.

As there is no specific treatment currently available, treatment measures are supportive. Corticosteroids and cytotoxic drugs are not effective. Kidney transplantation is usually successful in people with Alport syndrome and is considered the best treatment. The disease does not recur after kidney transplantation.

URINARY TRACT TUMORS

KIDNEY CANCER

Tumors that arise from the cortex, pelvis, or calyces may be benign or cancerous. *Kidney cancer* is more common. In the United States, about 65,340 new cases of kidney cancer are diagnosed each year, and about 14,970 people die from kidney cancer.[20]

Most cases of kidney cancer are renal cell carcinomas (adenocarcinoma) (Fig. 45.8). It occurs twice as often in men as in women. The average age at diagnosis is 64 years. It is uncommon in those under 45 years old. Smoking and obesity are significant risk factors. An increased incidence is found in first-degree relatives of people who have or had renal cell cancer. Other risk

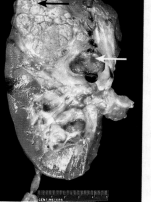

FIG 45.8 Cross section of kidney with renal cell cancer. The cancer *(black arrow)* is on the pole of the kidney. Note that the renal vein is involved and thrombosed *(white arrow).* (From Kumar V, Abbas AK, Fausto N: *Robbins and Cotran pathologic basis of disease,* ed 7, Philadelphia, 2005, Saunders.)

factors include ACKD, hypertension, and exposure to asbestos, cadmium, and gasoline.

Clinical Manifestations and Diagnostic Studies

Early-stage kidney cancer usually has no symptoms, so many patients go undiagnosed until the disease has significantly progressed. Many kidney cancers are diagnosed as incidental findings on imaging studies used to evaluate symptoms for unrelated conditions.

Kidney tumors can cause symptoms by compressing, stretching, or invading structures near or within the kidney. The most common presenting symptoms are hematuria and flank pain. Other manifestations include weight loss, fever, hypertension, hypercalcemia, and a palpable mass in the flank or abdomen. A varicocele may be present.

About 33% of patients have metastasis at the time of diagnosis. Local extension of kidney cancer into the renal vein and vena cava is common (Fig. 45.8). The most common sites of metastases include lungs, liver, and long bones.

CT scan is often used in the diagnosis and can detect small kidney tumors. Ultrasound examinations have improved the ability to determine between a solid mass tumor and a cyst. This is significant because most masses detected on imaging are cysts. Angiography, biopsy, and MRI are used in the diagnosis of renal tumors. Radionuclide isotope scanning can detect metastases.

❖ Interprofessional and Nursing Care

Preventive measures, including quitting smoking, maintaining a healthy weight, controlling BP, and reducing exposure to toxins, can help reduce the incidence of kidney cancer. Patients in high-risk groups should be aware of their increased risk for kidney cancer. Teach them about early manifestations (e.g., hematuria, hypertension). A cure for kidney cancer may be possible when it is detected early and treated.

Interprofessional care of the patient with kidney cancer is outlined in Table 45.14. Staging of kidney cancer provides a basis for determining treatment options. The following is a simple description of staging of kidney cancer:

Stage I: The tumor can be up to 7 cm in diameter and is confined to the kidney.

Stage II: The tumor is larger than a stage I tumor and is still confined to the kidney.

Stage III: The tumor extends beyond the kidney to the surrounding tissue and may have spread to a nearby lymph node.

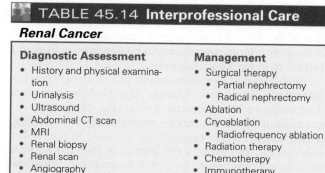

TABLE 45.14 Interprofessional Care

Renal Cancer

Diagnostic Assessment	Management
• History and physical examination	• Surgical therapy
• Urinalysis	• Partial nephrectomy
• Ultrasound	• Radical nephrectomy
• Abdominal CT scan	• Ablation
• MRI	• Cryoablation
• Renal biopsy	• Radiofrequency ablation
• Renal scan	• Radiation therapy
• Angiography	• Chemotherapy
	• Immunotherapy
	• Targeted therapy

Stage IV: Cancer spreads outside the kidney to multiple lymph nodes or to distant parts of the body, such as bones, brain, liver, or lung.

The treatment of choice for some kidney cancers is a partial nephrectomy (for smaller tumors), simple total nephrectomy, or a radical nephrectomy (for larger tumors). Radical nephrectomy involves removal of the kidney, adrenal gland, surrounding fascia, part of the ureter, and draining lymph nodes. Nephrectomy can be performed by a conventional (open) approach or laparoscopically (see discussion of nephrectomy on p. 1053). Other treatment options include cryoablation (freezing technique) and radiofrequency ablation (destroying tumor by using radiofrequency heat). These procedures can be used when surgery is not an option (e.g., patient has co-morbid conditions) and for small renal tumors.

Kidney cancer is relatively resistant to most chemotherapy drugs. While kidney cancer can be resistant to radiation therapy, it may be useful in certain situations, such as metastasis to bone or lungs.

Immunotherapy, including α-interferon and interleukin-2 (IL-2), is another treatment option in metastatic disease. (The use of α-interferon and IL-2 is discussed in Chapter 15.) Another type of drug used as immunotherapy is nivolumab (Opdivo). This drug targets PD-1, a protein on T cells that normally helps keep these cells from attacking other cells in the body. By blocking PD-1, this drug boosts the immune response against cancer cells. This can shrink some tumors or slow their growth.

Targeted therapy is another treatment option for metastatic kidney cancer. Kinase inhibitors, a class of targeted therapies, block certain proteins (kinases) that play a role in tumor growth and cancer progression. Kinase inhibitors include sunitinib (Sutent), sorafenib (Nexavar), cabozantinib (Cabometyx), and axitinib (Inlyta). Bevacizumab (Avastin), sunitinib (Sutent), and pazopanib (Votrient) inhibit the formation of new blood vessel growth to the tumor. Temsirolimus (Torisel) and everolimus (Afinitor) inhibit a specific protein known as the mechanistic target of rapamycin (mTOR).[21] These drugs are discussed in Table 15.13. The mechanisms of action are shown in Fig. 15.16.

The diagnosis of kidney cancer is devastating. Often the disease may already be metastasized by the time a person is diagnosed. The nursing care of the patient with cancer is discussed in Chapter 15.

BLADDER CANCER

Bladder cancer is the most common cancer of the urinary system.[22] About 81,190 new cases of bladder cancer are diagnosed annually, and about 17,240 deaths related to bladder cancer are reported every year. Cancer of the bladder is most common in older adults; 90% of cases occur in those over the age of 55. Bladder cancer is far more common in men than in women and in whites than in blacks or Hispanics.[23]

The most frequent cancerous tumor of the urinary tract is transitional cell cancer of the bladder. Most bladder tumors are papillomatous growths within the bladder (Fig. 45.9).

About half of bladder cancers are related to cigarette smoking. Other risk factors include exposure to dyes used in the rubber and other industries. Others at risk include women treated with radiation for cervical cancer; patients who received cyclophosphamide, docetaxel, or gemcitabine; and those who have indwelling catheters for long periods.[22] People with chronic, recurrent

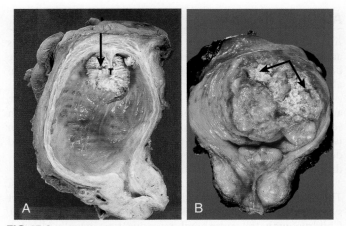

FIG 45.9 A, Papillary transitional cell cancer *(T)* seen arising from the dome of the bladder as a cauliflower-like lesion *(arrow).* B, Opened bladder showing advanced stage bladder cancer. Yellow areas are ulcerations and necrosis *(arrows).* (*A,* From Stevens A, Lowe J: *Pathology: Illustrated review in colour,* ed 2, London, 2000, Mosby. *B,* From Kumar V, Abbas AK, Fausto N: *Robbins and Cotran pathologic basis of disease,* ed 7, Philadelphia, 2005, Saunders.)

urinary tract stones, often in the bladder, and chronic lower UTIs have an increased risk for squamous cell cancer of the bladder.

Clinical Manifestations and Diagnostic Studies

Microscopic or gross, painless hematuria (chronic or intermittent) is the most common manifestation of bladder cancer. Bladder irritability with dysuria, frequency, and urgency may occur.

When cancer is suspected, obtain urine specimens to identify any cancer or atypical cells. Exfoliated cells from the bladder's epithelial surface can be detected in voided specimens. Other urine tests assess for specific factors associated with bladder cancer, such as bladder tumor antigens. Bladder cancers can be detected using CT, ultrasound, or MRI. The presence of cancer is confirmed by cystoscopy and biopsy.[24]

❖ NURSING AND INTERPROFESSIONAL MANAGEMENT: BLADDER CANCER

Most bladder cancers are diagnosed at an early stage when the cancer is treatable. Before treatment is started, bladder cancers are graded based on the cell type and staged based on the extent and invasiveness of the cancer. We use a grading system to classify the cancerous potential of tumor cells, using a scale from well differentiated (closely resembling the normal tissue) to undifferentiated (poorly differentiated) (see p. 239 in Chapter 15).

The clinical staging of bladder cancer is determined by the depth of invasion of the bladder wall and surrounding tissue. The following is a simple description of staging of bladder cancer:

Stage I: Cancer is in the inner lining of the bladder but has not invaded the bladder muscle wall.

Stage II: Cancer has invaded the bladder wall but is still confined to the bladder.

Stage III: Cancer has spread through the bladder wall to surrounding tissue. It may have spread to the prostate in men or the uterus or vagina in women.

Stage IV: Cancer has spread to the lymph nodes and other organs, such as lungs, bones, or liver.

TABLE 45.15 Interprofessional Care

Bladder Cancer

Diagnostic Assessment
- History and physical examination
- Urinalysis
- Urine cytology studies
- Cystoscopy with biopsy
- Ultrasound
- CT scan

Management
- Surgical therapy
  - Transurethral resection with fulguration
  - Laser photocoagulation
  - Open loop resection with fulguration
  - Cystectomy (segmental, partial, or radical)
- Radiation therapy
- Intravesical immunotherapy
  - Bacille Calmette-Guérin (BCG)
  - α-interferon (Intron A)
- Intravesical chemotherapy
  - doxorubicin
  - epirubicin
  - gemcitabine
  - mitomycin
  - thiotepa
  - valrubicin (Valstar)
- Systemic chemotherapy and immunotherapy

Interprofessional care of bladder cancer includes surgery, radiation, chemotherapy, and intravesical therapy (Table 45.15).

◆ Surgical Therapy

Surgical therapies include a variety of procedures. *Transurethral resection of the bladder tumor* (TURBT) is used for superficial lesions of the bladder's inner lining. The HCP uses a wire loop inserted through the cystoscope to remove the tumor and tissue, which are sent for pathologic evaluation. The base can be treated by fulguration, which burns the base of the tumor, or by use of a high-energy laser to kill the cancer cells. This procedure is also used to control bleeding in the patient who is a poor operative risk or who has advanced tumors. The primary disadvantages of this approach are reoccurrence of the bladder cancer at another site and potential for scarring and/or limited ability to hold urine with repeated TURBT procedures.[25]

A *segmental cystectomy (partial cystectomy)* is used to treat larger tumors or those that involve only 1 area of the bladder. The part of the bladder wall containing the tumor is removed along with a margin of normal tissue.

When the tumor is invasive or involves the trigone (the area where the ureters insert into the bladder) and the patient is free from metastasis beyond the pelvic area, a radical cystectomy is the treatment of choice. A *radical cystectomy* involves removal of the bladder, prostate, and seminal vesicles in men and the bladder, uterus, cervix, urethra, anterior vagina, and ovaries in women. After a radical cystectomy, a new way must be created for urine to leave the body. This surgical technique is called a *urinary diversion* (discussed later in this chapter).[25]

Postoperative instructions for any of these procedures include drinking a large volume of fluid for the first week after

the procedure. Teach the patient to monitor the color and consistency of the urine. The urine is pink for the first several days after the procedure, but it should not be bright red or contain blood clots. For 7 to 10 days after tumor resection, the patient may see dark red or rust-colored flecks in the urine. These may be from the healing tumor resection site.

Give opioid analgesics and stool softeners for a brief period after the procedure. Help the patient and family cope with fears about cancer, surgery, and sexuality. Emphasize the importance of regular follow-up care. Follow-up cystoscopies are needed on a regular basis after surgery for bladder cancer.

◆ Radiation Therapy, Chemotherapy, and Immunotherapy

Radiation therapy can be used in combination with cystectomy or as the primary therapy when the cancer is inoperable or the patient refuses surgery. Chemotherapy drugs and immunotherapy can be used to treat bladder cancer.

◆ Intravesical Therapy

Chemotherapy with local instillation of immunotherapy or chemotherapy can be delivered directly into the bladder by a urethral catheter.[24] *Intravesical therapy* is usually started at weekly intervals for 6 to 12 weeks. The drug is instilled directly into the patient's bladder and retained for about 2 hours. The patient's bladder must be empty before instillation. Change the patient's position every 15 minutes during the instillation for maximum contact in all areas of the bladder. Maintenance therapy after the initial induction regimen may be beneficial.

Bacille Calmette-Guérin (BCG), a weakened strain of *Mycobacterium bovis,* is the treatment of choice for carcinoma in situ. BCG stimulates the immune system rather than acting directly on cancer cells in the bladder. When BCG fails, α-interferon, in addition to BCG, may be used. Other treatments that can be used when BCG fails include mitomycin, epirubicin, gemcitabine, valrubicin, and thiopeta (an alkylating agent).[24]

Most patients have irritative voiding symptoms and hemorrhagic cystitis after intravesical therapy. Thiotepa can significantly reduce WBC and platelet counts in some people when absorbed into the circulation from the bladder wall. BCG may cause flu-like symptoms, increased urinary frequency, hematuria, or systemic infection. Other side effects of chemotherapy (e.g., nausea, vomiting, hair loss) do not occur with intravesical chemotherapy.

Encourage patients to increase their daily fluid intake and to quit smoking. Assess the patient for secondary UTI and stress the need for routine urologic follow-up. The patient may have fears or concerns about sexual activity or bladder function that must be addressed. Because of the high rate of disease recurrence and progression in bladder cancer, follow-up studies are important.

BLADDER DYSFUNCTION

URINARY INCONTINENCE

Urinary incontinence (UI) is an involuntary leakage of urine. Although incontinence is more prevalent among older adults, it is not a natural consequence of aging. UI has traditionally been viewed as a social or hygienic problem. It has a major effect on quality of life and contributes to serious health problems, especially in older adults.

GENDER DIFFERENCES
Urinary Incontinence

Men
- A common manifestation of BPH and prostate cancer in men
- More likely to have overflow incontinence caused by urinary retention

Women
- Prevalence of UI is higher in women than men
- More likely to have stress and urge incontinence than men

Etiology and Pathophysiology

UI occurs when bladder pressure exceeds urethral closure pressure. Anything that interferes with bladder or urethral sphincter control can result in UI. Using the acronym *DRIP*, the causes can include *D*: delirium, dehydration, depression; *R*: restricted mobility, rectal impaction; *I*: infection, inflammation, impaction; and *P*: polyuria, polypharmacy. Patients may have more than 1 type of incontinence (Table 45.16). The combination of stress and urge incontinence is referred to as mixed incontinence.

Diagnostic Studies

The basic evaluation for UI includes a focused history, physical assessment, and bladder log or voiding record whenever possible. Obtain information related to the onset of UI, factors that provoke urinary leakage, and associated conditions. Pay special attention to factors known to produce transient UI, particularly when the onset of urine loss is sudden. Whenever possible, ask the patient to keep a bladder log or voiding diary documenting the timing of urinations, episodes of urinary leakage, and frequency of nocturia for a period of 1 to 7 days (minimum of 3 days if possible). This record can be kept by nursing staff if the person is in an inpatient or long-term care facility.

Begin the physical examination with an assessment of general health and functional issues associated with urination, including mobility, dexterity, and cognitive function. A pelvic examination includes careful inspection of the perineal skin for signs of erosion or rashes related to UI and existence of pelvic organ prolapse. Assess local innervation and pelvic floor muscle strength, including a digital examination of the pelvic floor muscle to determine weakness or tension.

A urinalysis can identify factors contributing to transient UI (e.g., UTI, diabetes). Measure postvoid residual (PVR) urine in the patient undergoing evaluation for UI. The PVR volume is obtained by asking the patient to void, followed by catheterization or use of a bladder ultrasound (preferably within 10 to 20 minutes).

Urodynamic testing is needed in select cases of UI. Imaging studies of the upper urinary tract (e.g., ultrasound) are done when UI is associated with UTIs or evidence of upper urinary tract involvement.

Interprofessional Care

Many cases of UI can be cured or significantly improved. Transient, reversible factors are first corrected, followed by management of the type of UI (Table 45.16). In general, less invasive treatments are tried before more invasive methods (e.g., surgery). Nevertheless, the choice of the initial treatment is patient specific, based on patient preference, the type and severity of UI, and associated anatomic defects.

Several behavioral therapies may be used to improve UI (Table 45.17). Pelvic floor muscle training (Kegel exercises) is used to manage stress, urge, or mixed UI (Table 45.18).[26] Biofeedback can help the patient identify, isolate, contract, and relax the pelvic muscles (see the Complementary & Alternative Therapies box).

COMPLEMENTARY & ALTERNATIVE THERAPIES
Biofeedback

Scientific Evidence
Biofeedback is helpful in treating a variety of medical conditions: urinary incontinence, asthma, Raynaud's disease, irritable bowel syndrome, hot flashes, headaches, hypertension, seizure disorders, and nausea and vomiting associated with chemotherapy.

Nursing Implications
- Feedback from monitoring equipment can teach patients to control certain involuntary body responses, such as urinary incontinence.
- Although biofeedback is considered safe, patients should consult a qualified professional before using biofeedback.

Drug Therapy. Drug therapy varies according to the UI type (Table 45.19). In stress UI, drugs have a limited role in the management. Bladder sphincter tone and urethral resistance can be increased with α-adrenergic agonists, but they have limited benefit. In urge and reflex UI, drugs play a key role.

Anticholinergic drugs (muscarinic receptor blockers) block the action of acetylcholine at muscarinic receptors. They relax the bladder muscle and inhibit overactive detrusor contractions (Table 45.19). Side effects include dry mouth and eyes, constipation, blurred vision, and sleepiness.

Botox (onabotulinumtoxin A) can be used to treat UI from detrusor overactivity. Botox is injected into the bladder, resulting in relaxation of the bladder, an increase in its storage capacity, and a decrease in UI.

DRUG ALERT Antimuscarinic Agents

- Overdosage can result in severe anticholinergic effects.
- These effects include GI cramping, diaphoresis, eye pain, blurred vision, and urinary urgency.

Surgical Therapy. Surgical techniques vary depending on the type of UI. Surgical correction of stress UI is aimed at making the urinary structures more receptive to intraabdominal pressure and augmenting the urethral resistance of the internal sphincter. It may involve repositioning the urethra and/or creating a backboard of support to stabilize the urethra and bladder neck and make them more receptive to changes in intraabdominal pressure. Another technique for stress UI augments the urethral resistance of the intrinsic sphincter with a sling or periurethral injectable.

Retropubic colposuspension and pubovaginal sling placement appear to be most effective. Typically, both procedures are done through low transverse incisions. Complications specific to the retropubic suspensions include postoperative voiding dysfunction, urgency, and vaginal prolapse.

Placement of a suburethral sling, using the person's own fascia, cadaveric fascia, or a synthetic material, can correct stress UI in women. Complications include vascular and bowel injury, urinary retention, mesh or sling erosion, infection, urgency, and bladder perforation. Suburethral slings have success rates

TABLE 45.16 Types of Urinary Incontinence

Description	Causes	Treatment
Functional Incontinence • Loss of urine resulting from cognitive, functional, or environmental factors	• Older adults often have problems that affect balance and mobility (e.g., severe arthritis) • Cognitive problems (e.g., dementia)	• Modifying the environment or care plan to facilitate regular, easy access to toilet and promote patient safety • Includes better lighting, ambulatory assistance equipment, clothing alterations, timed voiding, different toileting equipment
Incontinence After Trauma or Surgery • In women, vesicovaginal or urethrovaginal fistula may occur • In men, change in continence involves proximal urethral sphincter (bladder neck and prostatic urethra) and distal urethral sphincter (external striated muscle)	• Fistulas may occur during pregnancy, after delivery of baby, after hysterectomy or invasive cancer of cervix, or after radiation therapy • Incontinence is a postoperative complication of transurethral, perineal, or retropubic prostatectomy	• External condom catheter • Penile clamp • Placement of artificial implantable sphincter • Surgery to correct fistula • Urinary diversion surgery to bypass urethra and bladder
Overflow Incontinence • Occurs when pressure of urine in overfull bladder overcomes sphincter control • Leakage of small amounts of urine is frequent throughout day and night • Urination may occur frequently in small amounts • Bladder stays distended and is usually palpable	• Caused by bladder or urethral outlet obstruction (bladder neck obstruction, urethral stricture, pelvic organ prolapse) or by underactive detrusor muscle caused by myogenic or neurogenic factors (e.g., herniated disc, diabetic neuropathy) • May occur after anesthesia and surgery (e.g., hemorrhoidectomy, herniorrhaphy, cystoscopy) • Neurogenic bladder (flaccid type).	• Urinary catheterization to decompress bladder • Use Credé or Valsalva maneuver • α-Adrenergic blockers (Table 45.19) • 5α-Reductase inhibitors (Table 45.19) to decrease outlet resistance • Bethanechol (Urecholine) to enhance bladder contractions • Intermittent catheterization • Intravaginal device, such as a pessary, to support prolapse • Surgery to correct underlying problem
Reflex Incontinence • Condition occurs when no warning or stress precedes periodic involuntary urination • Urination is frequent, moderate in volume, and occurs equally during day and night	• Spinal cord lesion above S2 interferes with central nervous system inhibition • Disorder results in detrusor hyperreflexia and interferes with pathways coordinating detrusor contraction and sphincter relaxation	• Treat underlying cause • Bladder decompression to prevent ureteral reflux and hydronephrosis • Intermittent self-catheterization • Baclofen or diazepam to relax external sphincter • Prophylactic antibiotics • Surgical sphincterotomy
Stress Incontinence • Sudden increase in intraabdominal pressure causes involuntary passage of urine • Can occur during coughing, laughing, sneezing, or physical activities, such as heavy lifting, exercising • Leakage usually is in small amounts and may not be daily	• Most common in women with relaxed pelvic floor musculature (from delivery, use of instrumentation during vaginal delivery, or multiple pregnancies) • Structures of female urethra atrophy when estrogen decreases • Prostate surgery for BPH or prostate cancer	• Pelvic floor muscle exercises (e.g., Kegel exercises), weight loss if obese, cessation of smoking, topical estrogen products, external condom catheters or penile incontinence clamp in men, surgery • Urethral inserts, patches, or bladder neck support devices (e.g., incontinence pessary) to correct underlying problem

Urge Incontinence
• Often referred to as overactive bladder
• Occurs randomly when involuntary urination is preceded by urinary urgency
• Leakage is periodic but frequent and usually in large amounts
• Nocturnal frequency and incontinence are common
	• Caused by uncontrolled contraction or overactive detrusor muscle
	• Bladder escapes central inhibition and contracts reflexively
	• Conditions include:
	  • Nervous system disorders (e.g., stroke, Alzheimer's disease, brain tumor, Parkinson's disease)
	  • Bladder disorders (e.g., carcinoma in situ, radiation effects, interstitial cystitis)
	  • Interference with spinal inhibitory pathways (e.g., cancer in spinal cord, spondylosis)
	  • Bladder outlet obstruction or conditions of unknown cause
		• Treat underlying cause
		• Biobehavioral interventions (bladder retraining with urge suppression, decrease in dietary irritants, bowel regularity, pelvic floor muscle exercises)
		• Anticholinergic drugs (Table 45.19)
		• Calcium channel blockers (Table 45.19)
		• mirabegron (Myrbetriq)
		• Vaginal estrogen creams
		• Containment devices (e.g., external condom catheters)
		• Absorbent products

TABLE 45.17 Interventions for Urinary Incontinence

Intervention	Description
Lifestyle Modifications	Self-management to reduce or eliminate risk factors, including: • Smoking cessation • Weight reduction • Good bowel regimen • Reduction of bladder irritants (e.g., caffeine, aspartame artificial sweetener, citrus juices) • Fluid modifications for those with urge incontinence
Scheduled Voiding Regimens	
Bladder retraining and urge-suppression strategies	Scheduled toileting with progressive voiding intervals. Includes teaching of urge-control using relaxation and distraction techniques, self-monitoring, reinforcement techniques, and other strategies, such as conscious contraction of pelvic floor muscles.
Habit retraining	Scheduled toileting with adjustments of voiding intervals (longer or shorter) based on the person's voiding pattern.
Prompted voiding	Scheduled toileting that requires prompts to void from a caregiver (typically every 3 hr). Used in conjunction with operant conditioning techniques to reward people for maintaining continence and appropriate toileting.
Timed voiding	Toileting on a fixed schedule (typically every 2–3 hr during waking hours).
Pelvic Floor Muscle Rehabilitation	
Biofeedback	See Complementary & Alternative Therapies box on p. 1046.
Electrical stimulation	Application of low-voltage electric current to sacral and pudendal afferent fibers through vaginal, anal, or surface electrodes. Used to inhibit bladder overactivity and improve awareness, contractility, and efficiency of pelvic muscle contraction.
Pelvic floor muscle (Kegel) exercises or training	Table 45.18.
Vaginal weight training	Active retention of vaginal weights (devices designed and shaped to exercise and strengthen pelvic floor muscles) at least twice a day. Typically used in combination with pelvic floor muscle exercises.
Anti-Incontinence Devices	
Incontinence clamps (penile compression devices)	Mechanical fixed compression applied to the penis to prevent any flow or leakage via the urethra. Must be released to void.
Intraurethral occlusive device (urethral plug)	Single-use device that is worn in the urethra to provide mechanical obstruction to prevent urine leakage. Removed for voiding.
Intraurethral valve pump	Replaceable urinary prosthesis for use in women who have impaired detrusor contractility (cannot contract muscles to push urine out of the bladder). Draws urine out to empty bladder and blocks urine flow when continence is desired.
Intravaginal support devices (pessaries and bladder neck support prostheses)	Devices support bladder neck, relieve minor pelvic organ prolapse, and change pressure transmission to the urethra.
Containment Devices	
Absorbent products	Variety of reusable and disposable pads and undergarment systems.
External collection devices	External catheter (condom) systems (e.g., penile sheaths) direct urine into a drainage bag. Most often used by men.

comparable to those of colposuspension or slings and are associated with shorter recovery periods. An artificial urethral sphincter can be used in men with intrinsic sphincter deficiency and severe stress UI.

A bulking agent can be injected underneath the mucosa of the urethra to correct stress UI in women or men. Bulking agents include glutaraldehyde cross-linked bovine collagen (GAX collagen), autologous fat, carbon beads, carbon hydroxyapatite, and polydimethylsiloxane injections. Although treatment with bulking agents avoids the risk associated with open surgery, reinjection is typically needed after several years.

In artificial sphincter surgery, the bladder sphincter that no longer works is replaced with an artificial one. A silicone inflatable ring is placed around the urethra (internally), and the patient inflates it to stop the flow and deflates it when the need to empty occurs. The patient must be able to work the pump that is placed internally. This procedure is usually used only as a last resort in a patient who is cognitively aware and able to use the artificial sphincter.[27]

❖ NURSING MANAGEMENT: URINARY INCONTINENCE

It is important to recognize both the physical and emotional problems associated with UI. Maintain and enhance the patient's dignity, privacy, and feelings of self-worth. This involves a 2-step approach with (1) containment devices to manage existing urinary leakage and (2) a definitive plan to reduce or resolve the factors leading to UI.

❓ CHECK YOUR PRACTICE

You are doing BP and glucose screening at the community senior center. While you are checking the BP on a 78-yr-old woman, she starts to sob quietly. You tell her that her BP is 134/84 and gently place your hand on her arm. You ask her what is wrong. She tells you, "I have to pee all the time. I soak the bed and my husband won't sleep with me anymore. I am washing sheets and my clothes all the time. Our whole house smells like urine."
• How would you respond to her?

TABLE 45.18 Patient Teaching

Pelvic Floor Muscle (Kegel) Exercises

Include the following instructions when teaching the patient to perform Kegel exercises:

What Is the Pelvic Floor Muscle?

- Your pelvic floor muscle provides support for your bladder and rectum and, in women, the vagina and uterus.
- If it weakens or is damaged, it cannot support these organs and their position can change.
- This causes problems with the normal bladder and rectal function.
- If you have a weak pelvic floor muscle, you may want to do special exercises to make the muscle stronger, prevent unwanted urine leakage, and lessen urinary urgency.

Finding the Pelvic Floor Muscle

- Without tensing the muscles of your leg, buttocks, or abdomen, imagine that you are trying to control the passing of gas or pinching off a stool.
- Or imagine you are in an elevator full of people and you feel the urge to pass gas. What do you do?
- You tighten or pull in the ring of muscle around your rectum—your pelvic floor muscle.
- You should feel a lifting sensation in the area around the vagina or a pulling in of your rectum.

How to Do the Exercises

There are 2 different kinds of exercises—short squeezes and long squeezes.

1. To do the *short squeezes*, tighten your pelvic floor muscle quickly, squeeze hard for 2 seconds, and then relax the muscle. Also, when you have strong urinary urges, try to tighten your pelvic floor muscle quickly and hard several times in a row until the urge passes.
2. To do the *long squeezes*, tighten the muscle for 5–10 seconds before you relax.

  Do both of these exercises 40–50 times each day.

When to Do These Exercises

- You can do these exercises anytime and anywhere.
- You can do these exercises in any position but sitting or lying down may be the easiest.

How Long Does It Take Before I Notice a Change?

After 4–6 weeks of doing these exercises, you should start to see less urine leakage and urinary urgency.

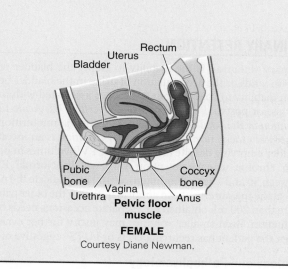

Courtesy Diane Newman.

Management options are reviewed in Tables 45.17 and 45.18. They include lifestyle interventions such as teaching the patient about consuming an adequate volume of fluids and reducing or eliminating bladder irritants, particularly caffeine and alcohol, from the diet. Have the patient maintain a regular, flexible schedule of urination, usually every 2 to 3 hours while awake. Advise patients to quit smoking because this habit increases the risk for stress UI. Teach patients about the relationships among constipation, UI, and urinary retention. Aggressive management of constipation is recommended. Begin with ensuring adequate fluid intake, increasing dietary fiber, lightly exercising, and judiciously using stool softeners. The management of constipation is discussed in Chapter 42.

Behavioral treatments include scheduled voiding regimens (timed voiding, habit training, prompted voiding), bladder retraining, and pelvic floor muscle training. Assess how the patient contains urine and offer alternative devices when indicated. Many women use feminine hygiene pads. Many men and women may use household products, such as rags, paper towels, or folded toilet tissue. Unfortunately, none of these products is designed to wick urine away from the skin, prevent soiling of clothing, and reduce or eliminate odor.

Provide information on products specifically designed to contain urine. For example, patients with mild to moderate UI often benefit from incontinent pads containing superabsorbent material, designed to absorb many times its weight in water. Patients with higher volume urine loss or those with both urinary and fecal incontinence may need disposable or reusable incontinence protective underwear, briefs, or pad/pant systems.

In inpatient or long-term care facilities, nursing management of UI includes maximizing toilet access. This may take the form of offering the urinal or bedpan or helping the patient to the bathroom every 2 to 3 hours or at scheduled times. Ensure that toilets are accessible to patients and provide privacy to allow effective urine elimination.

NURSING MANAGEMENT
Caring for the Patient With Incontinence

All members of the interprofessional care team are responsible for decreasing the risk for incontinence and preventing complications, such as skin breakdown, in patients who have UI. The RN plays a key role in delivering interventions to prevent and manage UI.
- Assess for risk factors for incontinence or urinary retention.
- Determine type of incontinence that patient is experiencing.
- Develop plan of care to decrease incontinence.
- Teach patient ways to decrease incontinence, such as pelvic floor muscle (Kegel) exercises.
- Assist patient in choosing appropriate products to contain urine.
- Delegate to the LPN/VN:
  - Use bladder scanner to estimate the postvoid residual volume (PVR).
  - Catheterize patient and measure PVR.
  - Give medications to decrease incontinence or urinary retention.
- Oversee UAP:
  - Help incontinent patient to commode or bedpan at regular intervals.
  - Clean patient and provide skin care.
  - Notify RN about new-onset incontinence in a previously continent patient.

URINARY RETENTION

Urinary retention is the inability to empty the bladder when a person voids or the accumulation of urine in the bladder because of an inability to void. In some cases, it is associated with urinary leakage or postvoid dribbling, called *overflow UI*. *Acute urinary retention* is the total inability to pass urine via micturition. It is a medical emergency. *Chronic urinary retention* is an incomplete bladder emptying despite urination. The PVR volumes in patients with chronic urinary retention vary widely. Normal PVR is between 50 and 75 mL. Findings over 100 mL indicate the need to repeat the measurement. An abnormal PVR in the older patient of more than 200 mL obtained on 2 separate occasions needs further evaluation. Even smaller volumes may justify further evaluation when the patient has recurring UTIs or LUTS suggestive of UTI.

Etiology and Pathophysiology

Urinary retention is caused by 2 different dysfunctions of the urinary system: bladder outlet obstruction and deficient detrusor (bladder muscle) contraction strength. *Bladder outlet obstruction* leads to urinary retention when the blockage is so severe that the bladder can no longer evacuate its contents despite a detrusor contraction. A common cause of obstruction in men is an enlarged prostate.

Deficient detrusor contraction strength leads to urinary retention when the muscle is no longer able to contract with enough force or for enough time to completely empty the bladder. Common causes are neurologic diseases affecting sacral segments 2, 3, and 4; long-standing diabetes; overdistention; chronic alcoholism; and drugs (e.g., anticholinergic drugs).

Diagnostic Studies

The diagnostic studies for urinary retention are the same as the ones for UI (see p. 1046).

Interprofessional Care

Behavioral therapies that were described for UI may be used in the management of urinary retention. Scheduled toileting and

TABLE 45.19 Drug Therapy
Voiding Dysfunction

Class and Mechanism of Action	Drug
α-Adrenergic Agonists	
Increase urethral resistance	pseudoephedrine
α-Adrenergic Blockers	
Reduce urethral sphincter resistance to urinary outflow	alfuzosin (Uroxatral) doxazosin (Cardura) tamsulosin (Flomax) terazosin
5α-Reductase Inhibitors	
Suppress androgen resulting in epithelial atrophy and decrease in prostate size	dutasteride (Avodart) finasteride (Proscar)
β₃-Adrenergic Agonist	
Improves bladder's storage capacity by relaxing bladder muscle during filling	mirabegron (Myrbetriq)
Anticholinergics (Muscarinic Receptor Blockers)	
Reduce overactive bladder contractions in urge urinary incontinence Relax bladder muscle during filling and improves the storage capacity of bladder	darifenacin (Enablex) fesoterodine (Toviaz) flavoxate (Urispas) oxybutynin (Ditropan XL, Oxytrol Transdermal System) solifenacin (VESIcare) tolterodine (Detrol, Detrol LA) trospium chloride
Calcium Channel Blockers	
Reduce smooth muscle contraction strength May reduce burning pain of interstitial cystitis	diltiazem (Cardizem) nifedipine verapamil (Calan)
Hormone Therapy	
Local application reduces urethral irritation and increases host defenses against UTI	estrogen cream (Premarin) estrogen vaginal ring (Estring)
Tricyclic Antidepressants	
Reduce sensory urgency and burning pain of interstitial cystitis Reduce overactive bladder contractions	amitriptyline imipramine (Tofranil)

double voiding may be effective in chronic urinary retention with moderate PVR volumes. *Double voiding* is an attempt to maximize bladder evacuation. The patient is asked to void, sit on the toilet for 3 to 4 minutes, and void again before exiting the bathroom.

For acute or chronic urinary retention, catheterization may be needed. Intermittent catheterization allows the patient to remain free of an indwelling catheter with its associated risk of CAUTI and urethral irritation. In some situations, an indwelling catheter is preferred (e.g., if the patient is unwilling or unable to perform intermittent catheterization). An indwelling catheter is also used when urethral obstruction makes intermittent catheterization uncomfortable or infeasible.

Drug Therapy. Several drugs may be given to promote bladder evacuation. For the patient with obstruction at the level of the bladder neck, an α-adrenergic blocker may be prescribed. These drugs relax the smooth muscle of the bladder neck and prostatic urethra and may decrease urethral resistance. Examples of α-adrenergic blockers are listed in Table 45.19. They are indicated in patients with BPH or bladder neck or detrusor sphincter dyssynergia (muscle incoordination).

Surgical Therapy. Surgical interventions are used to manage urinary retention caused by obstruction. Transurethral or open surgical techniques are used to treat benign or cancerous prostatic enlargement, bladder neck contracture, urethral strictures, or dyssynergia of the bladder neck. Pelvic reconstruction using an abdominal or transvaginal approach can correct bladder outlet obstruction in women with severe pelvic organ prolapse.

While surgery has had a minimal role in the management of urinary retention caused by deficient detrusor contraction strength, a few new procedures may be of benefit. Sacral neuromodulation involves a stimulator device and placement of a lead wire into the S3 foramen. Placement of an intraurethral valve pump, which empties the patient's bladder on command, may be an option.

❖ NURSING MANAGEMENT: URINARY RETENTION

Acute urinary retention is a medical emergency that requires prompt recognition and bladder drainage. Insert a catheter as ordered. Use a catheter with a retention balloon in anticipation of the need for an indwelling catheter.

Teach the patient with acute urinary retention and the patient predisposed to these episodes ways to minimize risk. Teach the patient to drink small amounts throughout the day and avoid the intake of large volumes of fluid over a brief period. Tell the patient (if chilled) to warm up before trying to void. They should avoid excess alcohol intake because it leads to polyuria and a diminished awareness of the need to void until the bladder is distended.

Have the patient who is unable to void drink a cup of coffee or brewed caffeinated tea to create or maximize urinary urgency. Tell patients that sitting in a tub of warm water or taking a warm shower may help them void. If these measures do not lead to successful urination, have the patient seek immediate care.

Patients with chronic urinary retention may be managed by behavioral methods, indwelling or intermittent catheterization, surgery, or drugs. Scheduled toileting and double voiding are the primary behavioral interventions used for chronic retention. Scheduled toileting can reduce, rather than expand, bladder capacity. In this case, have the patient void every 3 to 4 hours regardless of the desire to void. This is particularly useful in the patient with chronic overdistention, diabetes, or chronic alcoholism with a large bladder capacity and diminished or delayed sensations of bladder filling and urgency.

CATHETERIZATION

INDICATIONS FOR AND COMPLICATIONS OF CATHETERIZATION

Indications for short-term urinary catheterization are listed in Table 45.20. Unacceptable reasons for catheterization include (1) routine acquisition of a urine specimen for laboratory analysis and (2) convenience of the nursing staff or the patient's family. The risk for CAUTI is too high to allow catheterization of a patient for the convenience of hospital personnel or family members.

TABLE 45.20 Indications for Urinary Catheterization

Indwelling Catheter
- Relieve urinary retention caused by lower urinary tract obstruction, paralysis, or inability to void
- Bladder decompression preoperatively and operatively for lower abdominal or pelvic surgery
- Facilitate surgical repair of urethra and surrounding structures
- Splinting of ureters or urethra to promote healing after surgery or other trauma in area
- Accurate measurement of urine output
- Contamination of stage III or IV pressure injuries with urine that has impeded healing, despite appropriate personal care for the incontinence
- Terminal illness or severe impairment, which makes positioning or clothing changes uncomfortable, or which is associated with intractable pain

Intermittent (Straight, in and out) Catheter
- Relieve urinary retention caused by lower urinary tract obstruction, paralysis, or inability to void
- Study of anatomic structures of urinary system
- Urodynamic testing
- Collect sterile urine sample in certain situations
- Instill medications into bladder
- Measure residual urine after voiding (postvoid residual [PVR]) if portable ultrasound not available

Complications that are seen with long-term use (more than 30 days) of indwelling catheters include CAUTI, bladder spasms, periurethral abscess, chronic pyelonephritis, urosepsis, urethral trauma or erosion, fistula or stricture formation, and stones. Catheterization for sterile urine specimens may be needed if the patient has a history of complicated UTI. A catheter should be the last resort to provide the patient with a dry environment to prevent skin breakdown and protect dressings or skin lesions.

Urinary catheterization is often used in the management of the hospitalized patient. However, it is not without serious complications. As previously discussed on p. 1028, CAUTIs are the most common HAI. Scrupulous aseptic technique is mandatory when a urinary catheter is inserted. After insertion, maintenance and protection of the closed drainage system are major nursing responsibilities. Do not routinely irrigate the catheter; this should be done only if ordered.

While the patient has a catheter in place, maintain catheter, manage fluid intake, provide for the patient's comfort and safety, and prevent infection. Address the psychologic implications of urinary drainage. Patient concerns can include embarrassment related to exposure of the body, an altered body image, and fear that care of the catheter will result in increased dependency.

CATHETER CONSTRUCTION

Catheter materials include Teflon-coated latex, silicone elastomer, plastic, and hydrogel-coated silicone or latex. Catheters coated with silver or antimicrobial agents may prevent CAUTIs.

Catheters vary in construction materials, tip shape (Fig. 45.10), and size of the lumen. A coudé-tip catheter is often used in men. Catheters are sized according to the French scale. Each French unit (F) equals 0.33 mm of diameter. The diameter listed is the internal diameter of the catheter. The size used varies with the patient's size and the purpose of catheterization. In women,

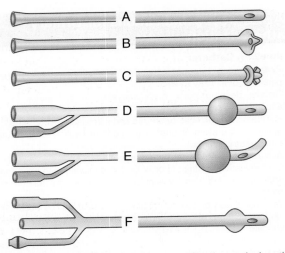

FIG 45.10 Types of urinary catheters. **A,** Simple urethral catheter. **B,** Mushroom-tip de Pezzer catheter (can be for suprapubic catheterization). **C,** Wing-tip Malecot catheter (wings hold catheter in place for temporary drainage). **D,** Indwelling urethral catheter with inflated balloon. **E,** Indwelling Tiemann catheter with coudé-tip (slightly curved tip allows for passage past obstruction). **F,** 3-way indwelling catheter (third lumen can be used for irrigation).

urethral catheter sizes 14F to 16F are the most common. In men, sizes 14F to 18F are used. Balloon sizes are either 5 or 30 mL. The primary problem resulting from too large a catheter is tissue erosion from excessive pressure on the meatus or urethra.

TYPES OF CATHETERS

Four routes are used for urinary tract catheterization: urethral, ureteral, suprapubic, and via a nephrostomy tube.

Urethral Catheterization

Urethral catheterization, the most common route of catheterization, involves the insertion of a catheter through the external meatus into the urethra, past the internal sphincter, and into the bladder.

Ureteral Catheters

The *ureteral catheter* is placed through the ureters into the renal pelvis. The catheter is inserted either (1) by being threaded up the urethra and bladder to the ureters under cystoscopic observation or (2) by surgical insertion through the abdominal wall into the ureters. The ureteral catheter is used after surgery to splint the ureters and to prevent them from being obstructed by edema. Record the urine volume from the ureteral catheter separately from that of other urinary catheters.

The patient is often kept on bed rest while a ureteral catheter is in place until the HCP orders ambulation. The self-retaining ureteral catheter is often inserted after a lithotripsy procedure or when ureteral obstruction from adjacent tumors or fibrosis threatens renal function. A double-J ureteral catheter is often used and allows the patient to ambulate. One end coils up in the kidney pelvis, while the other coils in the bladder.

Check the placement of the ureteral catheter frequently and avoid tension on the catheter. The catheter drains urine from the renal pelvis, which has a capacity of 3 to 5 mL. If the volume of urine in the renal pelvis increases, tissue damage to the pelvis will result from pressure. Do not clamp the ureteral catheter. If the HCP orders irrigation of the ureteral catheter, use strict aseptic technique. If the output is decreased, notify the HCP immediately.

Nursing Management
Care of the Patient With a Urethral Catheter

The following measures can be used to manage patients with a urethral catheter and prevent a CAUTI.
- Determine need for catheterization, but HCP must order.
- Choose appropriate type and size of catheter.
- Insert catheter in patient with urethral trauma, pain, or obstruction.
- Develop plan of care to decrease risk for infection in patient with indwelling catheter.
- Teach catheter care to the patient, particularly one who is ambulatory.
- Use a sterile, closed drainage system in short-term catheterization.
- Do not disconnect the distal urinary catheter and proximal drainage tube except for catheter irrigation (if ordered and indicated).
- Use sterile technique whenever the collecting system is open. If frequent irrigations are necessary in short-term catheterization to maintain catheter patency, a triple-lumen catheter may be preferable, permitting continuous irrigations within a closed system.
- A routine catheter change is not needed if the patient is catheterized for less than 2 weeks. For long-term use of an indwelling catheter, replace the catheter based on patient assessment and not on a routine changing schedule.
- If ordered, aspirate small volumes of urine for culture from the catheter sampling port using a sterile syringe and needle. Prepare the puncture site with an antiseptic solution.
- With long-term use of a catheter, a leg bag may be used. If the collection bag is reused, wash it in soap and water and rinse thoroughly. When it is not reused immediately, fill it with ½ cup of vinegar and drain. Vinegar is effective against *Pseudomonas* and other organisms and eliminates odors.
- Remove the catheter as early as possible. Intermittent catheterization and external catheters are alternatives that are associated with fewer cases of bacteriuria and CAUTI.
- Ensure that UAP:
  - Maintain unobstructed downhill flow of urine.
  - Empty the collecting bag regularly and accurately record the urine output.
  - Provide perineal care (once or twice a day and when needed), cleaning the meatus-catheter junction with soap and water.
  - Do not use lotion or powder near the catheter.
  - Anchor catheter using a securement device. Anchor catheter to upper thigh in women and lower abdomen in men to prevent catheter movement and urethral tension.

Check the drainage often (at least every 1 or 2 hours). It is normal for some urine to drain around the ureteral catheter into the bladder. Accurately record the urine output from the ureteral and urethral catheters. Sometimes a ureteral catheter may be used as a stent and is not expected to drain. It is important to check with the HCP as to the type of catheter and what to expect.

Suprapubic Catheters

Suprapubic catheterization is the simplest and oldest method of urinary diversion. The 2 methods of insertion of a suprapubic catheter into the bladder are (1) through a small incision in the abdominal wall and (2) using a trocar. A suprapubic catheter is placed while the patient is under general anesthesia for another surgical procedure or at the bedside with a local anesthetic. The catheter may be sutured into place. Tape the catheter to prevent dislodgment. The care of the tube and catheter is similar to that of the urethral catheter. A pectin-base skin barrier (e.g., Stomahesive) is effective in protecting the skin around the insertion site from breakdown.

The suprapubic catheter is used in temporary situations, such as bladder, prostate, and urethral surgery. It is also used on a long-term basis in some patients.

A suprapubic catheter is prone to poor drainage because of mechanical obstruction of the catheter tip by the bladder wall, sediment, and clots. To ensure patency of the tube (1) prevent tube kinking by coiling the excess tubing and maintaining gravity drainage, (2) have the patient turn from side to side, and (3) milk the tube. If these measures are not effective, obtain an order from the HCP to irrigate the catheter using sterile technique.

If the patient has bladder spasms that are hard to control, urinary leakage may result. Oxybutynin or other oral antispasmodics or belladonna and opium (B&O) suppositories may be prescribed to decrease bladder spasms.

Nephrostomy Tubes

The *nephrostomy tube* (catheter) is inserted on a temporary basis to preserve renal function when a ureter is completely obstructed. The tube is inserted through a small flank incision directly into the pelvis of the kidney and attached to connecting tubing for closed drainage. The principle is the same as with the ureteral catheter—that is, the catheter should never be kinked, compressed, or clamped. If the patient has excessive pain in the area or if there is excess drainage around the tube, check the catheter for patency. If irrigation is ordered, use strict aseptic technique. Gently instill no more than 5 mL of sterile saline solution at one time to prevent overdistention of the kidney pelvis and renal damage. Infection and secondary stone formation are complications associated with the insertion of a nephrostomy tube.

Intermittent Catheterization

An alternative approach to a long-term indwelling catheter is *intermittent catheterization,* often referred to as "straight" catheterization or "in-and-out" catheterization. The main goal of intermittent catheterization is to prevent urinary retention, stasis, and compromised blood supply to the bladder caused by prolonged pressure.[28]

It is being used more often in conditions such as neurogenic bladder (e.g., spinal cord injuries, chronic neurologic diseases) and bladder outlet obstruction in men. This type of catheterization is used in the oliguric and anuric phases of AKI to reduce the chance of infection from an indwelling catheter. Intermittent catheterization is also used postoperatively after a surgical procedure to treat UI.

The technique consists of inserting a urethral catheter into the bladder every 3 to 5 hours. Some patients perform intermittent catheterization only once or twice a day to measure residual urine and to ensure an empty bladder.

The techniques and protocols for intermittent catheterization vary. Catheters can be sterile (single use) or clean (multiple use). Catheters can be coated (prelubricated) or uncoated. Research on intermittent catheterization shows no convincing evidence that any specific technique (sterile or clean), catheter type (coated or uncoated), method (single-use or multiple-use), person (self or other), or strategy is better than any other for all clinical settings.[28]

The design of single-use, self-lubricating, silicone-coated (closed-sterile) systems is useful for patients who have recurrent UTIs or need to catheterize while at work or during travel. Teach patients to wash and rinse the catheter and their hands with soap and water before and after catheterization. Lubricant is necessary for men and may make catheterization more comfortable for women. The patient, caregiver, or HCP may insert the catheter.

Sterile technique is used for catheterization in the hospital or long-term care facility. For home care, a clean technique that includes good hand washing with soap and water is used. Teach the patient to observe for signs of UTI so that treatment can be started early. Some patients are placed on prophylactic antibiotics. Urethral damage from intermittent catheterization in men is similar to problems seen with indwelling catheterization. Complications include urethritis, urethral sphincter damage (especially if there is a forceful catheterization against a closed sphincter), urethral stricture, and creation of a false passage.

SURGERY OF THE URINARY TRACT

RENAL AND URETERAL SURGERY

The most common indications for nephrectomy are a renal tumor, polycystic kidneys that are bleeding or severely infected, massive traumatic injury to the kidney, and the elective removal of a kidney from a donor to be transplanted. Surgery involving the ureters and kidneys is most often done to remove stones that become obstructive, correct congenital anomalies, and divert urine when necessary.

Surgical Procedure

Nephrectomy can be performed by a conventional (open) approach or laparoscopically. In the open approach, an incision of about 6 to 10 inches is made through several layers of muscle. The incision can be made in the flank or abdominal area.

Laparoscopic Nephrectomy. *Laparoscopic nephrectomy* can be done to remove a diseased kidney or obtain a kidney from a living donor for transplant into a person with ESRD. With a laparoscopic nephrectomy, there are 3 to 5 puncture sites. One incision is to view the kidney, and another to dissect it. The laparoscope has a miniature camera so that the surgeons can watch what they are doing on a video monitor. Once dissected, the kidney is maneuvered into a nylon or polyurethane impermeable sack and then safely removed from the patient. Compared with conventional nephrectomy, the laparoscopic approach is less painful, involves a shorter hospital stay, and has a much faster recovery.

Preoperative Management

The basic needs of the patient undergoing renal and ureteral surgery are similar to those of any patient who has surgery (see Chapters 17 through 19). It is important preoperatively to ensure adequate fluid intake and a normal electrolyte balance. Tell the patient that if there is a flank incision, surgery will require a hyperextended, side-lying position. This position often causes the patient to have muscle aches after surgery. If a nephrectomy is planned, it is important that the patient have 1 working kidney to maintain normal renal function.

Postoperative Management

Specific postoperative needs of a patient are related to urine output, respiratory status, and abdominal distention.

Urine Output. In the immediate postoperative period, measure and record the urine output at least every 1 or 2 hours. Measure drainage from the various catheters and record it separately. Do not clamp or irrigate the catheter or tube without a specific order. The total urine output should be at least 0.5 mL/kg/hr. It is important to assess for urine drainage on the dressing and to estimate this amount. Observe and monitor the color and consistency of urine. Urine with increased amounts of mucus, blood, or sediment may occlude the drainage tubing or catheter.

Weigh the patient daily using the same scale and have the patient wear similar clothing and dressings each time. A significant change in daily weight can indicate retention of fluids, which places the patient at cardiovascular risk for developing heart failure. Fluid retention can increase the work required of the remaining kidney to perform its functions.

Respiratory Status. A nephrectomy can be performed through a flank incision just below the diaphragm. Postoperatively, it is important to ensure adequate ventilation. The patient is often reluctant to turn, cough, and breathe deeply because of the incisional pain. Give adequate pain medication to ensure the patient's comfort and ability to perform coughing and deep-breathing exercises. Have the patient use an incentive spirometer every 2 hours while awake. Early and frequent ambulation helps maintain respiratory function.

Abdominal Distention. Abdominal distention is present to some degree in most patients who have had surgery on their kidneys or ureters. It is often due to paralytic ileus caused by manipulation and compression of the bowel during surgery. Oral intake is restricted until bowel sounds are present (usually 24 to 48 hours after surgery). IV fluids are given until the patient can take oral fluids. Progression to a regular diet follows.

URINARY DIVERSION

Urinary diversion may be performed with or without cystectomy. Urinary diversion procedures are done when urinary flow is blocked. Common causes include bladder cancer, neurogenic bladder, congenital anomalies, strictures, trauma to the bladder, and chronic bladder inflammation. Numerous urinary diversion techniques and bladder substitutes are possible, including an incontinent urinary diversion, a continent urinary diversion catheterized by the patient, or an orthotopic neobladder bladder so that the patient voids urethrally.[29] Types of surgical procedures for urinary diversion are described in Table 45.21 and Fig. 45.11.

TABLE 45.21 **Urinary Diversion Surgery**			
Description	**Advantages**	**Disadvantages**	**Special Considerations**
Cutaneous Ureterostomy			
Ureters are excised from bladder and brought through abdominal wall, and stoma is created. Ureteral stomas may be created from both ureters, or ureters may be brought together, and one stoma created.	No need for major surgery.	External appliance necessary because of continuous urine drainage. Possibility of stricture or stenosis of small stoma.	Periodic catheterizations may be needed to dilate stomas to maintain patency.
Ileal Conduit			
Ureters are implanted into part of ileum or colon that has been resected from intestinal tract. Abdominal stoma is created.	Relatively good urine flow with few physiologic alterations.	External appliance necessary to continually collect urine.	Surgical procedure is complex. Postoperative complications may be increased. Reabsorption of urea by ileum occurs. Meticulous attention is necessary to care for stoma and collecting device.
Nephrostomy			
Catheter is inserted into pelvis of kidney. Procedure may be done to 1 or both kidneys and may be temporary or permanent. It is most often done in advanced disease as palliative procedure.	No need for major surgery.	High risk for renal infection. Predisposition to stone formation from catheter.	Nephrostomy tube may have to be changed every month. Never clamp the catheter.

Isolated ileal segment with ureters implanted in posterior portion of segment

A Ileal segment anastomosed to sigmoid colon

Protruding abdominal stoma

B Isolated ileal segment with ureters implanted in posterior portion of segment

Left ureter anastomosed to right ureter

Cutaneous ureterostomy on abdomen

C

Cutaneous ureterostomy on abdomen

Catheter

Stab wound on skin

Tape anchor

Drainage tubing

D Bilateral nephrostomy tubes inserted into renal pelvis; catheters exit through an incision on each flank, or there may be just one kidney

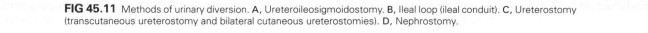

FIG 45.11 Methods of urinary diversion. **A,** Ureteroileosigmoidostomy. **B,** Ileal loop (ileal conduit). **C,** Ureterostomy (transcutaneous ureterostomy and bilateral cutaneous ureterostomies). **D,** Nephrostomy.

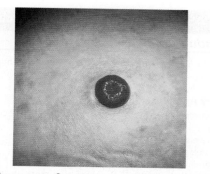

FIG 45.12 Urinary stoma. Symmetric, no skin breakdown, protrudes about 1.5 cm. Mucosa is healthy red. This configuration is flat when the patient is upright or supine. (Courtesy Lynda Brubacher, Virginia Mason Hospital, Seattle, WA.)

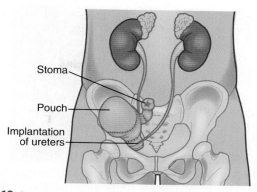

FIG 45.13 Creation of a Kock pouch with implantation of ureters into one intussuscepted part of the pouch and creation of a stoma with the other intussuscepted part.

Incontinent Urinary Diversion

Incontinent urinary diversion is diversion to the skin, requiring an appliance. The simplest form is the cutaneous ureterostomy. However, complications including scarring and strictures of the ureter, have led to the more frequent use of ileal or colonic conduits. The most common incontinent urinary diversion procedure is the **ileal conduit** (ileal loop). In this procedure a 6- to 8-in (15- to 20-cm) segment of the ileum is converted into a conduit for urinary drainage. The colon (colon conduit) can be used instead of the ileum. The ureters are anastomosed into one end of the conduit, and the other end of the bowel is brought out through the abdominal wall to form a stoma (Fig. 45.12). Although the bowel segment is still supported by the mesentery, it is completely isolated from the intestinal tract. The bowel is anastomosed and continues to function normally.

Because there is no valve and no voluntary control over the stoma, drops of urine flow from the stoma every few seconds, requiring a permanent external collecting device. The visible stoma and need for external collection devices are disadvantages of this procedure. The lifelong need to care for and deal with the stoma and collection devices may be difficult. These problems have led to the increasing use of continent diversions and neobladder bladder substitutes.

Continent Urinary Diversions

A *continent urinary diversion* is an intraabdominal urinary reservoir that can be catheterized. Continent diversions are internal pouches created similarly to the ileal conduit. Reservoirs are constructed from the ileum, ileocecal segment, or ascending colon. Large segments of bowel are altered to prevent peristaltic action. A surgically created valve and the large, low-pressure reservoir helps prevent involuntarily leakage. The patient with a continent reservoir needs to self-catheterize every 4 to 6 hours but does not need to wear external attachments. Patients may wear a small bandage on the stoma to collect any mucous drainage or excess drainage. Examples of continent diversions are the Kock (Fig. 45.13), Mainz, Indiana, and Florida pouches. The main difference among the various diversions is the segment of bowel used. For example, the Indiana pouch uses part of the ilium and right colon as a reservoir. It has become a popular form of continent urinary diversion.

Orthotopic Bladder Reconstruction

Orthotopic bladder reconstruction, or orthotopic neobladder, is the construction of a new bladder in the bladder's normal anatomic position, with discharge of urine through the urethra. The neobladder is surgically shaped from various segments of the intestines to make a low-pressure reservoir. An isolated segment of the distal ileum is often preferred. The ureters and urethra are sutured into the neobladder. Various procedures include the hemi-Kock pouch, Studer pouch, and W-shaped ileoneobladder.

Orthotopic bladder reconstruction has become a more viable option for both men and women if cancer does not involve the bladder neck or urethra. Ideal patients have normal renal and liver function, longer than 1- to 2-year life expectancy, adequate motor skills, and no history of inflammatory bowel disease or colon cancer. Obese patients and those with inflammatory bowel disease are not good candidates. The advantage of orthotopic bladder substitution is that it allows for natural micturition. Incontinence is a possible problem with this technique, and intermittent catheterization may be needed.

❖ NURSING MANAGEMENT: URINARY DIVERSION

Preoperative Management

Teaching is important for the patient awaiting cystectomy and urinary diversion surgery. Assess the patient's ability and readiness to learn before starting a teaching program. The patient's anxiety and fear may be decreased by providing more information. However, anxiety and fear may also interfere with learning. Involve the patient's caregiver and family in the teaching process.

Discuss the psychosocial aspects of living with a stoma (including clothing, changes in body image and sexuality, exercise, and odor). This may allay some fears. The patient with an orthotopic neobladder may have problems with incontinence. Discuss patients' concerns about sexual activities and let them know that counseling is available. A wound, ostomy, and continence nurse (WOCN) should be involved in the preoperative phase of the patient's care. A visit from an ostomate can be helpful. Additional interventions are discussed in eNursing Care Plan 45.3 for the patient with an ileal conduit (on the website for this chapter).

Postoperative Management

Plan nursing interventions during the postoperative period to prevent surgical complications, such as atelectasis (see Chapter 19). After pelvic surgery, there is an increased incidence of thrombophlebitis and UTI. Removal of part of the bowel increase the risk of paralytic ileus and small bowel obstruction. The patient is kept NPO, and a nasogastric tube may be needed for a few days.

Prevent injury to the stoma and maintain urine output. Tell the patient that mucus in the urine is a normal occurrence. The mucus is secreted by the mucosa of the intestine (which was

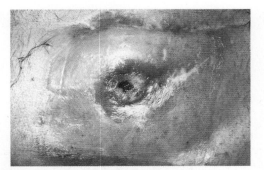

FIG 45.14 Ammonia salt encrustation from alkaline urine. (Courtesy Lynda Brubacher, Virginia Mason Hospital, Seattle, WA.)

used to create the ileal conduit) in response to the irritating effect of urine. Encourage a high fluid intake to "flush" the ileal conduit or continent diversion.

When an ileal conduit is created, provide meticulous care for the skin around the stoma. Alkaline encrustations with dermatitis may occur when alkaline urine comes in contact with exposed skin (Fig. 45.14). The urine is kept acidic to prevent alkaline encrustations. Other common peristomal skin problems include yeast infections, product allergies, and shearing-effect excoriations. Changing appliances (pouches) is described in Table 45.22. A properly fitting appliance is essential to prevent skin problems. The appliance should be about 0.1 in (0.2 cm) larger than the stoma. It is normal for the stoma to shrink within the first few weeks after surgery.

Teach the patient with a continent diversion (e.g., Indiana pouch) to catheterize at first every few hours. Over time this can be extended to every 4 to 6 hours. Irrigation of the pouch with normal saline or sterile water is often needed.

Patients with a neobladder may have postoperative urinary retention and need catheterization. It may take up to 6 months for them to regain bladder control. Patients empty their neobladders by relaxing their outlet sphincter muscles and bearing down with their abdominal muscles. Since there is no longer neurologic feedback between the reservoir and the brain, the patient should not expect a normal desire to void. To avoid bladder overdistention, patients should void at least every 2 to 4 hours, sit during voiding, and practice pelvic floor muscle relaxation to aid voiding. Follow-up x-ray studies include a "pouchogram" 3 to 4 weeks after surgery to assess for healing.

Acceptance of the surgery and changes in body image is needed to ensure the patient's best adjustment to a urinary diversion. Patient concerns include fear that the stoma will be offensive to others and will interfere with sexual, personal, professional, and recreational activities. Advise the patient that few activities will be restricted because of the urinary diversion. Meeting and sharing feelings with similar patients can help.

Discharge teaching after an ileal conduit includes teaching the patient about symptoms of obstruction or infection and care of the ostomy. The patient with an ileal conduit is fitted for a permanent appliance 7 to 10 days after surgery. It may have to be refitted later, depending on the degree of stoma healing and shrinkage.

Appliances are made of a variety of products, including natural and synthetic rubbers, plastics, and metals. Most appliances have a faceplate that adheres to the skin, a collecting pouch, and an opening to drain the pouch. The faceplate may be secured to the skin with glues, adhesives, or adherent synthetic wafers. Some appliances do not need adhesives because their design

TABLE 45.22   Patient & Caregiver Teaching

Ileal Conduit Appliances

Include the following instructions when teaching a patient or a caregiver how to change an ileal conduit appliance:

Temporary Appliance
1. Cut hole in pouch to fit over stoma (pouch 0.1 in [0.2 cm] larger than stoma).
2. Remove old pouch.
3. Clean area gently and remove old adhesive.
4. Wash area with warm water.
5. Place wick (rolled-up 4 × 4–in pad) over stoma to keep area dry during rest of procedure.
6. Dry skin around stoma.
7. Apply tincture of benzoin or other skin protectant around stoma to area where pouch will be placed.
8. Apply pouch by first smoothing its edges toward side and lower part of body.
9. Remove wick and complete application of bag.
10. If patient is usually in bed, apply bag so that it lies toward side of body.
11. If patient is ambulatory, apply bag so that it lies vertically.
12. Connect drainage tubing to pouch.
13. Keep drainage pouch on same side of bed as stoma.

Permanent Appliance*
1. Keep appliance in place for 2–14 days.
2. Change appliance when fluid intake has been restricted for several hours.
3. Sit or stand in front of mirror.
4. Moisten edge of faceplate with adhesive solvent and gently remove.
5. Clean skin with adhesive solvent.
6. Wash skin with warm water (may be done while showering).
7. Dry skin and inspect.
8. Place wick (rolled-up 4 × 4–inch pad) over stoma to keep skin free of urine.
9. Apply skin cement to faceplate and skin.
10. Place appliance over stoma.
11. Wash removed appliance with soap and lukewarm water; soak in distilled vinegar; rinse with lukewarm water and air dry.

*Many disposable appliances with self-adhesive backing are used as permanent appliances.

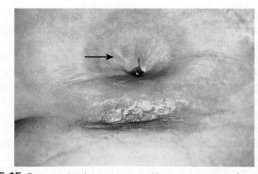

FIG 45.15 Retracted urinary stoma with pressure sore from faceplate above stoma *(arrow)*. (Courtesy Lynda Brubacher, Virginia Mason Hospital, Seattle, WA.)

relies on pressure to keep the pouch in place. If improperly fitted or applied, the faceplate may cause skin problems (Fig. 45.15). Tell the patient and caregiver about where to buy supplies, emergency telephone numbers, location of ostomy clubs, and follow-up visits with a WOCN. Follow-up with an HCP is imperative to monitor the patient's recovery, detect any complications, and assess renal function.

CASE STUDY

Painful Bladder and Frequent Urination

(© marilook/iStock/Thinkstock.)

Patient Profile

L.T., a 38-yr-old woman, comes to the HCP's office today for the eighth time in the past year for a history of pelvic pain with urinary frequency during the day, nocturia, and urgency to void. All previous urine cultures have been negative for bacteria. A recent evaluation by her gynecologist was negative for endometriosis.

Subjective Data

- Has a history of suprapubic and vaginal pain, urinary frequency and urgency
- Reports bladder pain that increases with bladder filling
- States this is her third attack of suprapubic pain and painful urination in 2 months
- Constant pain and discomfort has been physically and emotionally exhausting
- Is worried that she has cancer, and no one cares
- Has had 4 pregnancies with uneventful vaginal deliveries
- Normal menstrual cycles
- Her husband and she rarely have sexual intercourse because she has pain with intercourse
- Has a bowel movement every day. Denies constipation and/or diarrhea
- Recalls having many UTIs as a child

Objective Data

Physical Examination

- Lungs are clear. BP 132/86. Heart rate 86/min. Respiratory rate 18/min. Abdomen soft, tender in suprapubic region.

Diagnostic Studies

- Urinalysis obtained today: normal
- Previous urine cytology ordered to rule out cancer: normal
- Recent referral to urologist for cystoscopy which was done a few weeks ago

Interprofessional Care

- Cystoscopy results indicated glomerulations and Hunner lesions
- Urologist diagnosed interstitial cystitis
- Urologist prescribed pentosan (Elmiron), which she has not started yet
- Follow-up in 4 weeks with the urologist

Discussion Questions

1. After taking the patient's history, would you consider a UTI as a cause of her symptoms? Why or why not?
2. What additional testing and patient information would be helpful?
3. What is the significance of the cystoscopy findings?
4. What is the reason for the use of pentosan (Elmiron)?
5. ***Priority Decision:*** What are the priority nursing diagnoses for L.T.?
6. ***Patient-Centered Care:*** How can you help L.T. deal with her diagnosis and treatment plan?
7. Collaboration: Why is it important to get a dietitian involved in L.T.'s care?
8. ***Evidence-Based Practice:*** L.T. asks you how she can control her interstitial cystitis. How would you respond?

Answers available at *http://evolve.elsevier.com/Lewis/medsurg.*

BRIDGE TO NCLEX EXAMINATION

The number of the question corresponds to the same-numbered outcome at the beginning of the chapter.

1. The nurse teaches the female patient who has frequent UTIs that she should
   a. take tub baths with bubble bath.
   b. void before and after sexual intercourse.
   c. take prophylactic sulfonamides for the rest of her life.
   d. restrict fluid intake to prevent the need for frequent voiding.

2. One of the nurse's *most* important roles in relation to acute poststreptococcal glomerulonephritis (APSGN) is to
   a. promote early diagnosis and treatment of sore throats and skin lesions.
   b. encourage patients to obtain antibiotic therapy for upper respiratory tract infections.
   c. teach patients with APSGN that long-term prophylactic antibiotic therapy is needed to prevent recurrence.
   d. monitor patients for respiratory symptoms that indicate the disease is affecting the alveolar basement membrane.

3. The edema that occurs in nephrotic syndrome is due to
   a. increased hydrostatic pressure caused by sodium retention.
   b. decreased aldosterone secretion from adrenal insufficiency.
   c. increased fluid retention caused by decreased glomerular filtration.
   d. decreased colloidal osmotic pressure caused by loss of serum albumin.

4. A patient is admitted to the hospital with severe renal colic. The nurse's *first priority* in management of the patient is to
   a. administer opioids as prescribed.
   b. obtain supplies for straining all urine.
   c. encourage fluid intake of 3 to 4 L/day.
   d. keep the patient NPO in preparation for surgery.

5. The nurse recommends genetic counseling for the children of a patient with
   a. nephrotic syndrome.
   b. chronic pyelonephritis.
   c. malignant nephrosclerosis.
   d. adult-onset polycystic kidney disease.

6. The nurse identifies a risk factor for kidney and bladder cancer in a patient who relates a history of
   a. aspirin use.
   b. tobacco use.
   c. chronic alcohol use.
   d. use of artificial sweeteners.

7. In planning nursing interventions to increase bladder control in the patient with urinary incontinence, the nurse includes (*select all that apply*)
   a. teaching the patient to use Kegel exercises.
   b. clamping and releasing a catheter to increase bladder tone.
   c. teaching the patient biofeedback mechanisms to train pelvic floor muscles.
   d. counseling the patient concerning choice of incontinence containment device.
   e. developing a fluid modification plan, focusing on decreasing intake before bedtime.

8. A patient with a ureterolithotomy returns from surgery with a nephrostomy tube in place. Postoperative nursing care of the patient includes
   a. clamping the tube for 10 minutes every hour to decrease spasms.
   b. encouraging fluids of at least 2 to 3 L/day after nausea has subsided.
   c. notifying the provider if nephrostomy tube drainage is more than 30 mL/hr.
   d. irrigating the nephrostomy tube with 10 mL of normal saline solution as needed.

9. A patient has had a cystectomy and ileal conduit diversion. Four days after surgery, you note mucous shreds in the drainage bag. The nurse should
   a. notify the provider.
   b. notify the charge nurse.
   c. irrigate the drainage tube.
   d. document it as a normal observation.

1. b, 2. a, 3. d, 4. 5. d, 6. b, 7. a, 8. c, 9. d

For rationales to these answers and even more NCLEX review questions, visit *http://evolve.elsevier.com/Lewis/medsurg*.

ⓔ EVOLVE WEBSITE/RESOURCES LIST

http://evolve.elsevier.com/Lewis/medsurg
Review Questions (Online Only)
Key Points
Answer Keys for Questions
- Rationales for Bridge to NCLEX Examination Questions
- Answer Guidelines for Case Study on p. 1057
Student Case Studies
- Patient With Bladder Cancer and Urinary Diversion
- Patient With Glomerulonephritis and Acute Kidney Injury
Nursing Care Plans
- eNursing Care Plan 45.1: Patient With a Urinary Tract Infection
- eNursing Care Plan 45.2: Patient With Urinary Tract Calculi
- eNursing Care Plan 45.3: Patient With an Ileal Conduit
Conceptual Care Map Creator
Audio Glossary
Content Updates

REFERENCES

1. National Institute of Diabetes and Digestion and Kidney Diseases: Kidney and urologic diseases statistics for the United States. Retrieved from *www.niddk.nih.gov/health-information/health-topics/urologic-disease/urinary-tract-infections-in-adults/Pages/facts.aspx*.
2. Brusch JL, Bavaro MF, Cunha BA, et al: Cystitis in females. Retrieved from *http://emedicine.medscape.com/article/233101-overview*.
3. Brusch JL, Bronze MS: Catheter-related urinary tract infection (UTI). Retrieved from *https://emedicine.medscape.com/article/2040035-overview#a1*.
4. Chu CC, Lowder J:. Diagnosis and treatment of urinary tract infections across age groups, *Am J Obstet Gynecol* 219:40, 2018.
*5. University of Rochester: Guidelines for the diagnosis and management of urinary tract infections. Retrieved from *www.rochesterpatientsafety.com/Images_Content/Site1/Files/Pages/UTI_Treatment_Guidelines.pdf*.
6. American Nurses Association: ANA CAUTI prevention tool. Retrieved from *www.nursingworld.org/practice-policy/work-environment/health-safety/infection-prevention/ana-cauti-prevention-tool/*.
*7. European Association of Urology: Urological infections guidelines. Retrieved from *http://uroweb.org/guideline/urological-infections/#3*.
8. National Institute for Diabetes and Digestive and Kidney Diseases: Interstitial cystitis/painful bladder syndrome. Retrieved from *www.niddk.nih.gov/health-information/health-topics/urologic-disease/interstitial-cystitis-painful-bladder-syndrome*.
9. Lessnau K, Kim ED, Pais VM: Tuberculosis of the genitourinary system: Overview of GUTB. Retrieved from *http://emedicine.medscape.com/article/450651-overview*.
10. Figueiredo AA, Lucon AM, Srougi M: Urogenital tuberculosis, *Microbiol Spectr.* 5, 2017.
11. National Institute of Diabetes and Digestion and Kidney Diseases: Glomerular diseases. Retrieved from *www.niddk.nih.gov/health-information/kidney-disease/glomerular-diseases*.
12. Bhimma R: Acute poststreptococcal glomerulonephritis. Retrieved from *https://emedicine.medscape.com/article/980685-overview*.
13. Cohen EP, Batuman V: Nephrotic syndrome. Retrieved from *http://emedicine.medscape.com/article/244631-overview*.
14. US National Library of Medicine: Obstructive uropathy. Retrieved from *https://medlineplus.gov/ency/article/000507.htm*.
*15. Canadian Urological Association: CUA guidelines on the evaluation and medical management of the kidney stone patient—2016 Update, *Can Urol Assoc J* 10:E347, 2016.
*16. American Urological Association/Endourology Society: Surgical management of stones: AUA/Endourology Society guidelines. Retrieved from *www.auanet.org/guidelines/surgical-management-of-stones-(aua/endourological-society-guideline-2016)*.
*17. American Urological Association: Urotrauma. Retrieved from *www.auanet.org/guidelines/urotrauma-(2014-amended-2017)*.
18. National Kidney Foundation: Polycystic kidney disease. Retrieved from *www.kidney.org/atoz/content/polycystic*.
19. Genetics Home Reference: Alport syndrome. Retrieved from *https://ghr.nlm.nih.gov/condition/alport-syndrome#diagnosis*.
20. American Cancer Society: Key statistics about kidney cancer 2018. Retrieved from *www.cancer.org/cancer/kidney-cancer/about/key-statistics.html*.
*21. American Urological Association: Renal mass and localized renal cancer: AUA guidelines. Retrieved from *www.auanet.org/guidelines/renal-mass-and-localized-renal-cancer-new-(2017)*.
22. Farling KB: Bladder cancer: Risk factors, diagnosis, and management, *Nurse Pract* 42:26, 2017.
23. American Cancer Society: Key statistics about bladder cancer 2018. Retrieved from *www.cancer.org/cancer/bladder-cancer/about/key-statistics.html*.
*24. American Urological Association, Society of Urologic Oncology: Diagnosis and treatment of non-muscle invasive bladder cancer: AUA/SUO joint guidelines. Retrieved from *www.auanet.org/guidelines/non-muscle-invasive-bladder-cancer-(aua/suo-joint-guideline-2016)*.
*25. American Urological Association, American Society of Clinical Oncology, American Society of Radiation Oncology, Society of Urologic Oncology: Treatment of non-metastatic muscle-invasive bladder cancer: AUA/ASCO/ASTRO/SUO guidelines. Retrieved from *www.auanet.org/guidelines/muscle-invasive-bladder-cancer-new-(2017)*.
*26. Palmer MH, Willis-Gray MG: Overactive bladder in women, *AJN* 117:34, 2017.
*27. American Urological Association, Society of Urodynamics: Female pelvic medicine and urogenital reconstruction: Surgical treatment of female stress urinary incontinence: AUA/SUFU guidelines. Retrieved from *www.auanet.org/guidelines/stress-urinary-incontinence-(sui)-new-(aua/sufu-guideline-2017)*.
*28. Southern Health National Health Services Foundation Trust: Urinary catheter care guidelines. Retrieved from www.southernhealth.nhs.uk/_resources/assets/inline/full/0/70589.pdf.
29. National Institute for Diabetes and Digestive and Kidney Diseases: Urinary diversion. Retrieved from *www.niddk.nih.gov/health-information/health-topics/urologic-disease/urinary-diversion*.

*Evidence-based information for clinical practice.

46

Acute Kidney Injury and Chronic Kidney Disease

Hazel Dennison

Too often we underestimate the power of a touch, a smile, a kind word, a listening ear, or the smallest act of caring, all of which have the potential to turn a life around.

Leo Buscaglia

http://evolve.elsevier.com/Lewis/medsurg

CONCEPTUAL FOCUS

Acid-Base Balance
Adherence

Coping
Elimination

Fluids and Electrolytes
Nutrition

LEARNING OUTCOMES

1. Outline criteria used to classify acute kidney injury using the acronym RIFLE (*Risk, Injury, Failure, Loss, End-stage renal disease*).
2. Relate the clinical course of acute kidney injury.
3. Explain the interprofessional and nursing management of a patient with acute kidney injury.
4. Define chronic kidney disease and delineate its 5 stages based on the glomerular filtration rate.
5. Identify risk factors that contribute to the development of chronic kidney disease.
6. Describe the significance of cardiovascular disease in people with chronic kidney disease.
7. Explain the conservative interprofessional care and related nursing management of the patient with chronic kidney disease.
8. Distinguish among renal replacement therapy options for persons with end-stage renal disease.
9. Compare and contrast nursing interventions for patients on peritoneal dialysis and hemodialysis.
10. Discuss the role of nurses in the management of patients who receive a kidney transplant.

KEY TERMS

acute kidney injury (AKI), p. 1059
acute tubular necrosis (ATN), p. 1061
anuria, p. 1062
arteriovenous fistula (AVF), p. 1076
arteriovenous grafts (AVGs), p. 1076
automated peritoneal dialysis (APD), p. 1075
azotemia, p. 1059

chronic kidney disease (CKD), p. 1065
CKD mineral and bone disorder (CKD-MBD), p. 1068
continuous ambulatory peritoneal dialysis (CAPD), p. 1075
continuous renal replacement therapy (CRRT), p. 1079

dialysis, p. 1073
end-stage renal disease (ESRD), p. 1065
hemodialysis (HD), p. 1073
oliguria, p. 1061
peritoneal dialysis (PD), p. 1073
uremia, p. 1066

Kidney failure, also called *renal failure,* is the partial or complete impairment of kidney function. It results in an inability to excrete metabolic waste products and water. Kidney failure contributes to problems with all body systems. All patients have problems with fluid, electrolyte, and acid-base imbalance. Adhering to dietary therapies and the treatment plan can be challenging. The patient must deal with changes in lifestyle, occupation, family relationships, and self-image that can lead to withdrawal and depression. The patient grieves the loss of kidney function and independence.

Kidney failure is classified as acute or chronic (Table 46.1). Acute kidney injury (AKI) has a rapid onset. Chronic kidney disease (CKD) is gradual with a progressive decline in kidney function.

ACUTE KIDNEY INJURY

Acute kidney injury (AKI) is the term used to encompass the entire scope of the syndrome, ranging from a slight deterioration in kidney function to severe impairment. AKI is characterized by a rapid loss of kidney function. This loss is accompanied by a rise in serum creatinine and/or a reduction in urine output. AKI can develop over hours or days with progressive elevations of blood urea nitrogen (BUN), creatinine, and potassium with or without a reduction in urine output. The severity of dysfunction can range from a small increase in serum creatinine or reduction in urine output to the development of **azotemia**, an accumulation of nitrogenous waste products (urea nitrogen, creatinine) in the blood.

Although AKI is potentially reversible, it has a high mortality rate.[1] AKI usually affects people with other life-threatening conditions (Table 46.2).[2] AKI often follows severe, prolonged hypotension, hypovolemia, or exposure to a nephrotoxic agent. Hospitalized patients develop AKI at a high rate (1 in 5) and have a high mortality rate. When AKI develops in patients in intensive care units (ICUs), the mortality rate can be as high as 70% to 80%.[3,4]

Etiology and Pathophysiology

The causes of AKI are multiple and complex. We categorize them as prerenal, intrarenal (or intrinsic), and postrenal causes (Table 46.2 and Fig. 46.1).

Prerenal. *Prerenal* causes of AKI are factors that reduce systemic circulation, causing a reduction in renal blood flow. The decrease in blood flow leads to decreased glomerular perfusion and filtration of the kidneys.

It is important to distinguish prerenal oliguria from the oliguria of intrarenal AKI. In prerenal oliguria there is no damage to the kidney tissue (parenchyma). The oliguria is caused by a decrease in circulating blood volume (e.g., severe dehydration, heart failure [HF], decreased cardiac output). Prerenal

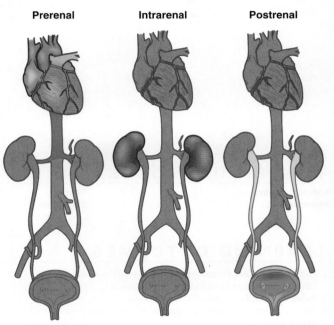

FIG. 46.1 Prerenal, intrarenal, and postrenal causes of AKI.

TABLE 46.1 Comparison of Acute Kidney Injury and Chronic Kidney Disease

	Acute Kidney Injury	Chronic Kidney Disease
Onset	Sudden	Gradual, often over many years
Most common cause	Acute tubular necrosis	Diabetic nephropathy
Diagnostic criteria	Acute reduction in urine output *AND/OR* Elevation in serum creatinine	GFR <60 mL/min/1.73 m² for >3 mo *AND/OR* Kidney damage >3 mo
Reversibility	Potentially	Progressive and irreversible
Primary cause of death	Infection	CVD

TABLE 46.2 Common Causes of Acute Kidney Injury

Prerenal	Intrarenal	Postrenal
Decreased Cardiac Output • Cardiogenic shock • Dysrhythmias • HF • MI **Decreased Peripheral Vascular Resistance** • Anaphylaxis • Neurologic injury • Septic shock **Decreased Renovascular Blood Flow** • Bilateral renal vein thrombosis • Embolism • Hepatorenal syndrome • Renal artery thrombosis **Hypovolemia** • Burns • Dehydration • Excessive diuresis • GI losses (diarrhea, vomiting) • Hemorrhage • Hypoalbuminemia	**Interstitial Nephritis** • Allergies: antibiotics (sulfonamides, rifampin), NSAIDs, ACE inhibitors • Infections: bacterial (acute pyelonephritis), viral (Epstein-Barr), fungal (candidiasis) **Nephrotoxic Injury** • Chemical exposure: ethylene glycol, lead, arsenic, carbon tetrachloride • Contrast media • Drugs: aminoglycosides (gentamicin, amikacin), amphotericin B • Hemolytic blood transfusion reaction • Severe crush injury **Other Causes** • Acute glomerulonephritis • Malignant hypertension • Prolonged prerenal ischemia • Thrombotic disorders • Toxemia of pregnancy • Systemic lupus erythematosus	• BPH • Bladder cancer • Calculi formation • Neuromuscular disorders • Prostate cancer • Spinal cord disease • Strictures • Trauma (back, pelvis, perineum)

oliguria is readily reversible with appropriate treatment.[5] With a decrease in circulating blood volume, autoregulatory mechanisms that increase angiotensin II, aldosterone, norepinephrine, and antidiuretic hormone try to preserve blood flow to essential organs. Prerenal azotemia results in a reduction in sodium excretion (less than 20 mEq/L), increased sodium and water retention, and decreased urine output.

Prerenal conditions contribute to intrarenal AKI. If decreased perfusion persists for an extended time, the kidneys lose their ability to compensate and damage to kidney parenchyma occurs (intrarenal damage).

Intrarenal. *Intrarenal* causes of AKI (Table 46.2) include conditions that cause direct damage to the kidney tissue, resulting in impaired nephron function. The damage from intrarenal causes usually results from prolonged ischemia, nephrotoxins (e.g., aminoglycoside antibiotics, contrast media), hemoglobin released from hemolyzed red blood cells (RBCs), or myoglobin released from necrotic muscle cells.

Nephrotoxins can cause obstruction of intrarenal structures by crystallizing or causing damage to the epithelial cells of the tubules. Hemoglobin and myoglobin can block the tubules and cause renal vasoconstriction. Kidney diseases, such as acute glomerulonephritis and systemic lupus erythematosus (SLE), may also cause AKI.

Acute tubular necrosis (ATN) is the most common intrarenal cause of AKI in hospitalized patients. It is primarily the result of ischemia, nephrotoxins, or sepsis. Ischemic and nephrotoxic ATN is responsible for 90% of intrarenal AKI cases.[6,7] Severe kidney ischemia causes a disruption in the basement membrane and patchy destruction of the tubular epithelium. Nephrotoxic agents cause necrosis of tubular epithelial cells, which slough off and plug the tubules. Other risks associated with developing ATN while in the hospital include major surgery, shock, blood transfusion reaction, muscle injury from trauma, and prolonged hypotension. ATN is potentially reversible if the basement membrane is not destroyed and the tubular epithelium regenerates.

Postrenal. *Postrenal* causes of AKI involve mechanical obstruction in the outflow of urine. With the flow of urine obstructed, urine refluxes into the renal pelvis, impairing kidney function. The most common postrenal causes are benign prostatic hyperplasia (BPH), prostate cancer, stones, trauma, and extrarenal tumors. Bilateral ureteral obstruction leads to *hydronephrosis* (kidney dilation), increase in hydrostatic pressure, and tubular blockage, resulting in a progressive decline in kidney function. If bilateral obstruction is relieved within 48 hours of onset, complete recovery is likely. Prolonged obstruction can lead to tubular atrophy and irreversible kidney fibrosis. Postrenal causes of AKI account for less than 10% of AKI cases.[8]

Clinical Manifestations

Prerenal and postrenal AKI that has not caused intrarenal damage usually resolves quickly with treatment. When parenchymal damage occurs due to either prerenal or postrenal causes, or when parenchymal damage occurs directly as with intrarenal causes, AKI has a prolonged course. Clinically, AKI may progress through phases: oliguric, diuretic, and recovery. When a patient does not recover from AKI, CKD may develop.

The RIFLE classification describes the stages of AKI (Table 46.3). *Risk*, the first stage of AKI, is followed by *Injury*, which is the second stage. Then AKI increases in severity to the last, or third, stage, *Failure*. The 2 outcome variables are *Loss* and *End-stage renal disease.*[9,10]

Oliguric Phase. The most common manifestations of AKI are discussed in this section.

Urinary Changes. The most common initial manifestation of AKI is oliguria, a reduction in urine output to less than 400 mL/day. Oliguria usually occurs within 1 to 7 days of the injury to the kidneys. If the cause is ischemia, oliguria often occurs within 24 hours. When nephrotoxic drugs are involved, the onset may be delayed for as long as 1 week. This phase lasts on average 10 to 14 days but can last months in some cases. The longer the oliguric phase lasts, the poorer the prognosis for complete recovery of kidney function.[1]

TABLE 46.3 RIFLE Classification for Staging Acute Kidney Injury

Stage	GFR Criteria	Urine Output Criteria	Clinical Example
Risk	Serum creatinine increased × 1.5 *OR* GFR decreased by 25%	Urine output <0.5 mL/kg/hr for 6 hr	• 68-yr-old woman with type 2 diabetes, hypertension, CAD, CKD • Scheduled to undergo emergency coronary artery bypass graft • Serum creatinine is 1.8 mg/dL (increased), weight 60 kg • Calculated GFR is 35 mL/min/1.73 m² • Has stage 3b CKD
Injury	Serum creatinine increased × 2 *OR* GFR decreased by 50%	Urine output <0.5 mL/kg/hr for 12 hr	• During surgery, she is hypotensive for a sustained period • Diagnosed with acute tubular necrosis • After surgery: serum creatinine is 3.6 mg/dL, urine output reduced to 28 mL/hr
Failure	Serum creatinine increased × 3 *OR* GFR decreased by 75% *OR* Serum creatinine >4 mg/dL with acute rise ≥0.5 mg/dL	Urine output <0.3 mL/kg/hr for 24 hr (oliguria) *OR* Anuria for 12 hr	• 72 hours after surgery, develops ventilator-associated pneumonia and sepsis while in ICU • Serum creatinine rises to 5.2 mg/dL, urine output drops to 10 mL/hr • BP remains low despite dopamine therapy
Loss	Persistent acute kidney failure. Complete loss of kidney function >4 wk	—	• Starts on continuous venovenous hemodialysis • After 3 wk of therapy she has a cardiopulmonary arrest and does not survive
End-stage renal disease	• Complete loss of kidney function >3 mo	—	•

Nonoliguric AKI has a urine output greater than 400 mL/day. About 50% of patients will be nonoliguric, making the initial diagnosis more difficult.[7]

While changes in urine output generally do not correspond to changes in glomerular filtration rate (GFR), they can be helpful in distinguishing the cause of AKI. For example, anuria (no urine output) is usually seen with urinary tract obstruction. Oliguria is often seen with prerenal causes. Nonoliguric AKI occurs with acute interstitial nephritis and ATN.[8]

A urinalysis may show casts, RBCs, and white blood cells (WBCs). Casts form from mucoprotein impressions of the necrotic renal tubular epithelial cells, which slough into the tubules. The specific gravity may be fixed at around 1.010, with urine osmolality at about 300 mOsm/kg (300 mmol/kg). This is the same specific gravity and osmolality of plasma, thus reflecting tubular damage with a loss of concentrating ability by the kidney. Proteinuria may be present if AKI is related to glomerular membrane dysfunction.

Fluid Volume. Hypovolemia (volume depletion) has the potential to worsen all forms of AKI. Fluid replacement is often enough to treat many forms of AKI, especially prerenal causes. When urine output decreases, fluid retention occurs. The severity of the manifestations depends on the extent of the fluid overload. In the case of reduced urine output (anuria and oliguria), the neck veins may become distended with a bounding pulse. Edema and hypertension may develop. Fluid overload can eventually lead to HF, pulmonary edema, and pericardial and pleural effusions.

Metabolic Acidosis. In the normal kidney, excess hydrogen ions are excreted to maintain a physiologic balance of the blood pH. Impaired kidneys cannot excrete hydrogen ions or the acid products of metabolism. Serum bicarbonate (HCO_3^-) production decreases from defective reabsorption and regeneration of HCO_3^- ions. Serum HCO_3^- is depleted through buffering of acidic hydrogen ions and metabolic end products. The patient with severe acidosis may develop Kussmaul respirations (rapid, deep respirations) to try to compensate by increasing CO_2 exhalation.

Sodium Balance. Damaged tubules cannot conserve sodium. Urinary sodium excretion may increase, resulting in normal or below-normal levels of serum sodium. Excess sodium intake is avoided because it can lead to volume expansion, hypertension, and HF. Uncontrolled hyponatremia or water excess can lead to cerebral edema.

Potassium Excess. The kidneys normally excrete 80% to 90% of the body's potassium. In AKI the serum potassium level increases because the kidney's normal ability to excrete potassium is impaired. The risk for hyperkalemia increases if AKI is caused by massive tissue trauma because the damaged cells release potassium into the extracellular fluid (ECF). Bleeding and blood transfusions may cause cellular destruction, releasing more potassium into the ECF. Metabolic acidosis worsens hyperkalemia as hydrogen ions enter the cells, and potassium is driven out of the cells into the ECF.

While patients with hyperkalemia are often asymptomatic, some may have weakness with severe hyperkalemia. Because cardiac muscle is intolerant of acute increases in potassium, emergency treatment of hyperkalemia is needed.

Acute or rapid development of hyperkalemia may result in signs that are apparent on electrocardiogram (ECG). These changes include peaked T waves, widening of the QRS complex, and ST segment depression. Progressive changes in the ECG related to increasing potassium levels are shown in Fig. 16.14.

Hematologic Disorders. Several hematologic disorders occur in patients with AKI. Hospital-acquired AKI often occurs in patients who have multiorgan failure. Leukocytosis is often present. The most common cause of death in AKI is infection. The most common sites of infection are the urinary and respiratory systems.

Waste Product Accumulation. The kidneys are the primary excretory organs for urea (an end product of protein metabolism) and creatinine (an end product of endogenous muscle metabolism). BUN and serum creatinine levels are increased in kidney disease. An increased BUN level also can be caused by dehydration; corticosteroids; or catabolism resulting from infections, fever, severe injury, or GI bleeding. The best serum indicator of AKI is creatinine because it is not affected by other factors.

Neurologic Disorders. Neurologic changes can occur as the nitrogenous waste products accumulate in the brain and other nervous tissue. The manifestations can be as mild as fatigue and difficulty concentrating and escalate to seizures, stupor, and coma.

Diuretic Phase. During the diuretic phase of AKI, daily urine output is usually around 1 to 3 L but may reach 5 L or more. The nephrons are still not fully functional even as urine output increases. The high urine volume is caused by osmotic diuresis from the high urea concentration in the glomerular filtrate and the inability of the tubules to concentrate the urine. In this phase, the kidneys have recovered their ability to excrete wastes but not to concentrate the urine. Hypovolemia and hypotension can occur from massive fluid losses.

Patients who develop an oliguric phase will have greater diuresis as kidney function returns. Large losses of fluid and electrolytes require patient monitoring for hyponatremia, hypokalemia, and dehydration. The diuretic phase may last 1 to 3 weeks. Near the end of this phase, the patient's acid-base, electrolyte, and waste product (BUN, creatinine) values stabilize.

Recovery Phase. The recovery phase begins when the GFR increases, allowing the BUN and serum creatinine levels to decrease. Major improvements occur in the first 1 to 2 weeks of this phase. Kidney function may take up to 12 months to stabilize. The patient's overall health, severity of kidney injury, and number and type of complications influence the outcome of AKI. Some patients do not recover and progress to end-stage renal disease (ESRD). The older adult is less likely to have a complete recovery of kidney function. Patients who recover may achieve clinically normal kidney function but remain in an early stage of CKD.

Diagnostic Studies

A thorough history is essential for diagnosing the cause of AKI. Consider prerenal causes when there is a history of dehydration, hypotension, or blood loss. Suspect intrarenal causes if the patient has been exposed to potentially nephrotoxic drugs or contrast media used in a radiologic study. A history of changes in the urinary stream, stones, BPH, or bladder or prostate cancer suggests postrenal causes.

Although changes in urine output and serum creatinine occur relatively late in the course of AKI, they are known diagnostic indicators. An increase in serum creatinine may not be evident until there is a loss of more than 50% of kidney function. The rate of increase in serum creatinine is important as a diagnostic indicator in determining the severity of injury.

Urinalysis is an important diagnostic test. Urine sediment containing abundant cells, casts, or proteins suggests intrarenal disorders. The urine osmolality, sodium content, and specific gravity help in distinguishing the causes of AKI. Urine sediment may be normal in both prerenal and postrenal AKI. In intrarenal problems, hematuria, pyuria, and crystals may be seen. Other testing may be needed (Table 46.4). A kidney ultrasound is often the first test done. It provides imaging without exposure to potentially nephrotoxic contrast agents. It is useful for evaluating for kidney disease and obstruction of the urinary collection system. A renal scan can assess abnormalities in kidney blood flow, tubular function, and the collecting system. A CT scan can identify lesions, masses, obstructions, and vascular anomalies. A renal biopsy is the best method for confirming intrarenal causes of AKI.

Having an MRI or magnetic resonance angiography (MRA) study with the contrast media gadolinium is not advised in patients with kidney failure. Giving gadolinium can be potentially fatal.

In patients with normal kidney function, contrast media poses minimal risk. In patients with kidney disease, *contrast-induced nephropathy* (CIN) can occur when contrast media for diagnostic studies causes nephrotoxic injury. In patients with diabetes receiving metformin, the drug should be held for 48 hours prior to and after the use of contrast media to decrease the risk for lactic acidosis. The best way to avoid CIN is to avoid exposure to contrast media by using other diagnostic tests, such as ultrasound. If contrast media must be given to a high-risk patient, the patient needs to have optimal hydration and the lowest possible dose of the contrast agent. Nursing interventions to ensure adequate fluid intake and hydration can decrease the risks associated with contrast media. Other treatment options to prevent CIN are controversial, such as giving HCO_3^- or sodium chloride solutions or prophylactic *N*-acetylcysteine.

Interprofessional Care

Because AKI is potentially reversible, the primary goals of treatment are to eliminate the cause, manage the signs and symptoms, and prevent complications while the kidneys recover (Table 46.4). The first step is to determine if there is adequate intravascular volume and cardiac output to ensure adequate perfusion of the kidneys. Diuretic therapy may be given and usually includes loop diuretics (e.g., furosemide [Lasix], bumetanide [Bumex]) or an osmotic diuretic (e.g., mannitol). If AKI is already established, forcing fluids and diuretics will not be effective and may be harmful. Closely monitor fluid intake during the oliguric phase of AKI.

The general rule for calculating the fluid restriction is to add all losses for the previous 24 hours (e.g., urine, diarrhea, emesis, blood) plus 600 mL for insensible losses (e.g., respiration, diaphoresis). For example, if a patient excreted 300 mL of urine on Tuesday with no other losses, the fluid allocation on Wednesday would be 900 mL.

Hyperkalemia is one of the most serious complications in AKI because it can cause life-threatening dysrhythmias. Therapies used to treat high potassium levels are listed in Table 46.5. Both insulin and sodium bicarbonate are temporary measures for treating hyperkalemia by promoting a transient shift of potassium into the cells. Potassium will eventually diffuse back

---

TABLE 46.4 Interprofessional Care

Acute Kidney Injury

Diagnostic Assessment
- History and physical examination
- Identify precipitating cause
- Serum creatinine and BUN levels
- Serum electrolytes
- Urinalysis
- Renal ultrasound
- Renal scan
- CT scan

Management
- Treat precipitating cause
- Fluid restriction (600 mL plus previous 24-hr fluid loss)
- Nutritional therapy
  - Adequate protein intake (0.6–2 g/kg/day) depending on degree of catabolism
  - Enteral nutrition
  - Parenteral nutrition
  - Dietary restrictions (potassium, phosphate, sodium)
- Measures to lower potassium (if high) (Table 46.5)
- Calcium supplements or phosphate-binding agents
- Dialysis (if necessary)
- Continuous RRT (if necessary)

TABLE 46.5 Therapies for High Potassium Levels

Calcium Gluconate IV
- Generally used in advanced cardiac toxicity (evidence of hyperkalemic ECG changes)
- Raises the threshold for excitation, resulting in dysrhythmias

Dietary Restriction
- Potassium intake is limited to 40 mEq/day
- Primarily used to prevent recurrent elevation, not for acute elevation

Hemodialysis
- Most effective therapy to remove potassium
- Works within a short time

Patiromer (Veltassa)
- Oral suspension that binds potassium in GI tract
- Used to treat patients with CKD
- Do not use as an emergency drug for life-threatening hyperkalemia
- Has a delayed onset of action
- Do not give to a patient with a paralytic ileus as bowel necrosis can occur

Regular Insulin IV
- Potassium moves into cells when insulin is given
- IV glucose given concurrently to prevent hypoglycemia
- When effects of insulin decrease, potassium shifts back out of cells

Sodium Bicarbonate
- Can correct acidosis and cause a shift of potassium into cells

Sodium Polystyrene Sulfonate (Kayexalate)
- Given by mouth or retention enema
- When resin is in the bowel, potassium is exchanged for sodium
- Produces osmotic diarrhea, allowing for evacuation of potassium-rich stool
- Removes 1 mEq of potassium per 1 g of drug
- Do not give to a patient with a paralytic ileus as bowel necrosis can occur

into the bloodstream. Calcium gluconate raises the threshold at which dysrhythmias occur, temporarily stabilizing the myocardium. Only sodium polystyrene sulfonate (Kayexalate), patiromer (Veltassa), and dialysis remove potassium from the body.

Conservative therapy may be all that is necessary until kidney function improves. If conservative therapy is not effective in treating AKI, then *renal replacement therapy* (RRT) is used. Controversy exists about the timing of RRT in AKI.[11] The most common indications for RRT in AKI are (1) volume overload, resulting in compromised cardiac and/or pulmonary status; (2) high serum potassium level; (3) metabolic acidosis (serum HCO_3^- level less than 15 mEq/L [15 mmol/L]); (4) BUN level greater than 120 mg/dL (43 mmol/L); (5) significant change in mental status; and (6) pericarditis, pericardial effusion, or cardiac tamponade. Although laboratory values provide rough parameters, the best guideline is the clinical status of the patient.

Of the several RRT therapy options available, there is no consensus about the best approach.[10] Even though peritoneal dialysis (PD) is a viable option for RRT, it is not often used. Intermittent hemodialysis (HD) and continuous renal replacement therapy (CRRT) have both been used effectively.

CRRT is provided continuously over 24 hours through cannulation of a vein or catheter placement. CRRT has much slower blood flow rates compared with intermittent HD. HD is the method of choice when changes are needed emergently. It is technically more complicated because it requires specialized staff and equipment and vascular access. The patient needs anticoagulation therapy to prevent blood clotting when the blood makes contact with the extracorporeal dialysis circuit. Rapid fluid shifts during HD may cause hypotension. (RRT and CRRT are discussed later in this chapter on pp. 1076–1080.)

Nutritional Therapy. The goal of nutritional management in AKI is to provide adequate calories to prevent catabolism despite restrictions that prevent electrolyte and fluid problems and azotemia. Nutritional intake must maintain adequate caloric intake (providing 30 to 35 kcal/kg and 0.8 to 1.0 g of protein per kilogram of desired body weight) to prevent the breakdown of body protein.

Adequate energy should primarily be from carbohydrate and fat sources to prevent ketosis from endogenous fat breakdown and gluconeogenesis from muscle protein breakdown. Essential amino acids may be supplemented. Potassium and sodium are regulated per plasma levels. Sodium is restricted as needed to prevent edema, hypertension, and HF. Dietary fat intake is increased so that the patient receives at least 30% to 40% of total calories from fat. Fat emulsion IV infusions given as a nutritional supplement provide a good source of nonprotein calories. If a patient cannot maintain adequate oral intake, enteral nutrition is the preferred route for nutritional support (see Chapter 39). When the gastrointestinal (GI) tract is not functional, parenteral nutrition (PN) is necessary to provide adequate nutrition. The patient treated with PN may need daily HD or CRRT to remove the excess fluid. Concentrated PN formulas are available to minimize fluid volume.

❖ NURSING MANAGEMENT: ACUTE KIDNEY INJURY

◆ Nursing Assessment

A number of assessments are essential for developing an interprofessional plan of care.[12] Daily weights, strict intake and output, and vital signs are key. Daily monitoring of a patient's urine output has prognostic implications and is crucial for determining therapy and daily fluid volume replacement. Examine the urine for color, specific gravity, glucose, protein, blood, and sediment. Assess the patient's general appearance, including skin color, edema, neck vein distention, and bruises. If a patient is receiving dialysis, observe the access site for inflammation and exudate. Evaluate the patient's mental status and level of consciousness. Assess the oral mucosa for dryness and inflammation. Auscultate the lungs for crackles and wheezes or decreased breath sounds. Monitor the heart for an S_3 gallop, murmurs, or a pericardial friction rub. Assess ECG readings for dysrhythmias. Review all laboratory values and diagnostic test results.

◆ Nursing Diagnoses

Nursing diagnoses for the patient with AKI include:
- Electrolyte imbalance
- Fluid imbalance
- Risk for infection
- Anxiety

◆ Planning

The overall goals are that the patient with AKI will (1) completely recover without any loss of kidney function, (2) maintain normal fluid and electrolyte balance, (3) have decreased anxiety, and (4) adhere to and understand the need for careful follow-up care.

◆ Nursing Implementation

◆ **Health Promotion.** Prevention and early recognition of AKI are the most important aspects of care. Prevention is directed primarily toward identifying and monitoring high-risk populations, controlling exposure to nephrotoxic drugs and industrial chemicals, and preventing prolonged episodes of hypotension and hypovolemia. In the hospital, factors that increase the risk for developing AKI are preexisting CKD, older age, massive trauma, major surgical procedures, extensive burns, HF, sepsis, and obstetric complications.

Carefully monitor the patient's weight, intake and output, and fluid and electrolyte balance. Assess and record extrarenal losses of fluid from vomiting, diarrhea, hemorrhage, and increased insensible losses. Prompt replacement of significant fluid losses helps prevent ischemic tubular damage associated with trauma, burns, and extensive surgery. Intake and output records and the patient's weight are valuable indicators of fluid volume status. Aggressive diuretic therapy for the patient with fluid overload from any cause can lead to a reduction in renal blood flow.

Monitor kidney function in persons who are taking drugs that are potentially nephrotoxic (see Table 44.3). Nephrotoxic drugs should be used sparingly in the high-risk patient. When these drugs must be used, they should be given in the smallest effective doses for the shortest possible periods. Caution the patient about abuse of over-the-counter (OTC) analgesics (especially nonsteroidal antiinflammatory drugs [NSAIDs]), as these may worsen kidney function in the patient with mild CKD.

Angiotensin-converting enzyme (ACE) inhibitors can decrease perfusion pressure and cause hyperkalemia. If other measures, such as diet modification and diuretics, cannot control the hyperkalemia, ACE inhibitors may have to be reduced or stopped. However, ACE inhibitors are often used to prevent proteinuria and progression of kidney disease, especially in patients with diabetes.[13]

◆ **Acute Care.** The patient with AKI is critically ill and may have co-morbid diseases or conditions (e.g., diabetes, cardiovascular disease [CVD]) in addition to kidney injury. Focus on the patient holistically since they will have many physical and emotional needs. Usually the changes caused by AKI arise suddenly. The patient needs help in understanding that kidney disease may affect the entire body's functions.

You have a key role in managing fluid and electrolyte balance during the oliguric and diuretic phases. Observe and record accurate intake and output. Take daily weights with the same scale at the same time each day to detect excessive gains or losses of body fluid (1 kg is equivalent to 1000 mL of fluid). Assess for signs and symptoms of hypervolemia (in the oliguric phase) or hypovolemia (in the diuretic phase), potassium and sodium problems, and other electrolyte imbalances that may occur in AKI (see Chapter 16).

Because infection is the leading cause of death in AKI, meticulous aseptic technique is critical. Protect the patient from those with infectious diseases. Be alert for local manifestations of infection (e.g., swelling, redness, pain) as well as systemic manifestations (e.g., fever, malaise, leukocytosis).

If a patient with renal failure has an infection, it is important to recognize that the temperature may not always be high. Patients with AKI have a blunted febrile response to an infection (e.g., pneumonia). If antibiotics are used to treat an infection, the type, frequency, and dosage must be carefully considered because the kidneys are the primary route of excretion for many antibiotics. Dosages may be decreased depending on the patient's level of kidney function if the drug is eliminated by the kidneys. Nephrotoxic drugs (see Table 44.3) should be used judiciously.

Perform skin care and take measures to prevent pressure injuries as mobility may be impaired. Mouth care is important to prevent stomatitis, which develops when ammonia (made by bacterial breakdown of urea) in saliva irritates the mucous membranes.

INFORMATICS IN PRACTICE
Computer Monitoring of Antibiotic Safety

- Many patients receiving antibiotic therapy are at risk for kidney failure.
- Set the computer to alert you about elevated creatinine levels and, if possible, send you a text message.
- By notifying the HCP early, medications can be stopped or doses decreased and the patient's kidney function preserved.

◆ **Ambulatory Care.** Recovery from AKI is highly variable and depends on whether other body systems fail, the patient's general condition and age, the length of the oliguric phase, and the severity of nephron damage. Protein and potassium intake are dictated by kidney function. Regular evaluation of kidney function is necessary. Teach the patient the signs and symptoms of recurrent kidney disease. Emphasize measures to prevent the recurrence of AKI.

The long-term convalescence of 3 to 12 months may cause psychosocial and financial hardships for the patient, caregiver, and family. Make appropriate referrals for counseling. If the kidneys do not recover, the patient will need to transition to life on chronic dialysis or possible transplantation.

◆ **Evaluation**

The expected outcomes are that the patient with AKI will
- Regain and maintain normal fluid and electrolyte balance
- Adhere to the treatment regimen
- Have no complications
- Have a complete recovery

Gerontologic Considerations: Acute Kidney Injury

The GFR declines with age. In older adults, impaired function of other organ systems from CVD or diabetes can increase the risk for developing AKI. The aging kidney is less able to compensate for changes in fluid volume, solute load, and cardiac output.

Although the causes of AKI in older adults are similar to younger adults, they are at an increased risk for AKI. Dehydration is a predisposing factor and tends to occur more often in older adults. Dehydration can occur from polypharmacy (diuretics, laxatives, drugs that suppress appetite or consciousness), acute febrile illnesses, and immobility.

Other common causes of AKI in the older adult include hypotension, diuretic therapy, aminoglycoside therapy, obstructive disorders (e.g., BPH), surgery, infection, and contrast media. Mortality rates are similar for older and younger patients. Patients over 65 years of age are less likely to recover from AKI. Despite this, age is not a barrier to offering RRT.[11]

CHRONIC KIDNEY DISEASE

Chronic kidney disease (CKD) involves progressive, irreversible loss of kidney function. More than 26 million American adults, or 1 out of every 9, have CKD. CKD is much more common than AKI (Table 46.1). We partially attribute the increasing prevalence of CKD to increased risk factors, including an aging population, increased rates of obesity, and increased incidence of diabetes and hypertension.

Because the kidneys are highly adaptive, kidney disease is often not recognized until there has been considerable loss of nephrons. Patients with CKD are often asymptomatic, resulting in CKD being underdiagnosed and untreated. It is thought that about 70% of people with CKD are unaware that they have the disease.[14]

CKD has many different causes. The leading ones are diabetes (about 50%) and hypertension (about 25%) (Table 46.6). Less common causes include glomerulonephritis, cystic diseases, and urologic diseases.[15] Kidney diseases are discussed in Chapter 45.

Kidney Disease Improving Global Outcomes (KDIGO) Clinical Practice Guidelines defines CKD as either the presence of kidney damage or a decreased GFR less than 60 mL/min/1.73 m² for longer than 3 months. The stages of CKD are shown in Table 46.7. The last stage of kidney disease, **end-stage renal disease (ESRD)**, occurs when the GFR is less than 15 mL/min.

TABLE 46.6 Risk Factors for Chronic Kidney Disease

Risk Factors	Prevention and Management
Age >60 yr	Prevent insult or injury to kidneys
Cardiovascular disease	Institute aggressive risk factor reduction
Diabetes	Achieve optimal glycemic control
Ethnic minority (e.g., black, Native American)	Teach about ↑ risk and assist with appropriate screening (BP measurement, urinalysis)
Exposure to nephrotoxic drugs	Limit exposure and give sodium bicarbonate as treatment
Family history of CKD	Teach about ↑ risk and assist with appropriate screening
Hypertension	Maintain BP in normal range with ACE inhibitors or ARBs

TABLE 46.7 Stages of Chronic Kidney Disease

Description	GFR (mL/min/1.73 m²)	Clinical Action Plan
Stage 1 Kidney damage with normal or ↑ GFR	≥90	Diagnosis and treatment CVD risk reduction Slow progression
Stage 2 Kidney damage with mild ↓ GFR	60–89	Estimation of progression
Stage 3a Moderate ↓ GFR	45–59	Evaluation and treatment of complications
Stage 3b Moderate ↓ GFR	30–44	More aggressive treatment of complications
Stage 4 Severe ↓ GFR	15–29	Preparation for renal replacement therapy (dialysis, kidney transplant)
Stage 5 Kidney failure	<15 (or dialysis)	Renal replacement therapy (if uremia present and patient desires treatment)

Source: Alseiari M, Meyer KB, Wong JB: Evidence underlying KDIGO (Kidney Disease: Improving Global Outcomes) guideline recommendations: A systematic review, *Am J Kidney Dis* 67:417, 2016.

At this point, RRT (dialysis or transplantation) is required to maintain life.

Over half a million Americans are receiving treatment (dialysis, transplant) for ESRD. Despite all the technologic advances in life-sustaining treatment with dialysis, patients with ESRD have a high mortality rate. As the stage of kidney disease progresses, the mortality rate increases. Mortality rates are as high as 19% to 24% for patients with ESRD on dialysis.[14,16]

The prognosis and course of CKD are highly variable depending on the cause, patient's condition and age, and adequacy of health care follow-up. Some people live normal, active lives with kidney disease, while others may rapidly progress to ESRD (stage 5).

Since 1972, the United States has covered most of the costs of providing dialysis through Medicare benefits. Under Title XVIII of the Social Security Act, ESRD was recognized as a disability. Medicare pays for 80% of eligible charges. The state, private insurance, or patient covers the rest.[16]

Clinical Manifestations

As kidney function deteriorates, all body systems become affected. The manifestations result from retained urea, creatinine, phenols, hormones, electrolytes, and water. **Uremia** is a syndrome in which kidney function declines to the point that symptoms may develop in multiple body systems (Fig. 46.2). It often occurs when the GFR is 15 mL/min or less. The manifestations of uremia vary among patients depending on the cause of the kidney disease, co-morbid conditions, age, and degree of adherence to the prescribed medical regimen. Many patients

PROMOTING HEALTH EQUITY
Chronic Kidney Disease

- Has a high incidence in minority populations, especially blacks and Native Americans
- Hypertension and diabetes are more common in blacks and Native Americans

Blacks
- The risk for CKD as a complication of hypertension is significantly higher in blacks
- Have the highest rate of CKD, nearly 4 times that of whites

Native Americans
- Have a rate of CKD twice that of whites
- Rate of CKD is 6 times higher among Native Americans with diabetes than among other ethnic groups with diabetes

Hispanics
- Rate of CKD in Hispanics is 1.5 times higher than in non-Hispanic whites

are tolerant of the changes caused by declining kidney function because they occur gradually.

Urinary System. In the early stages of CKD, patients usually do not report any change in urine output. Since diabetes is the primary cause of CKD, polyuria may be present, but not necessarily from kidney disease. As CKD progresses, patients have increasing difficulty with fluid retention and need diuretic therapy. After a period on dialysis, patients may develop anuria.

Metabolic Disturbances

Waste Product Accumulation. As the GFR decreases, the BUN and serum creatinine levels increase. The BUN increase is not only from kidney disease but also protein intake, fever, corticosteroids, and catabolism. For this reason, serum creatinine clearance determinations (calculated GFR) are considered more accurate indicators of kidney function than BUN or creatinine (Table 46.8). Significant increases in BUN contribute to nausea, vomiting, lethargy, fatigue, impaired thought processes, and headaches.

Altered Carbohydrate Metabolism. Impaired glucose metabolism, resulting from cellular insensitivity to the normal action of insulin, causes defective carbohydrate metabolism. Mild to moderate hyperglycemia and hyperinsulinemia may occur.

Insulin and glucose metabolism may improve (but not to normal values) after starting dialysis. Patients with diabetes who needed insulin before starting dialysis may need less insulin therapy when they start dialysis and their kidney disease progresses. Patients with diabetes who develop uremia may need less insulin than before the onset of CKD. Insulin, which depends on the kidneys for excretion, stays in the circulation longer. Insulin dosing must be individualized, and glucose levels monitored carefully.

CHECK YOUR PRACTICE

You are working in a community-based dialysis unit. One of your patients is a 56-yr-old woman who has been on HD for 3 weeks. You are reviewing her medications with her and she is surprised that her dose of glargine insulin has been decreased. She tells you, "I have been a diabetic for 30 years, and this is the first time ever that my dose of insulin has been decreased."

- How would you respond?

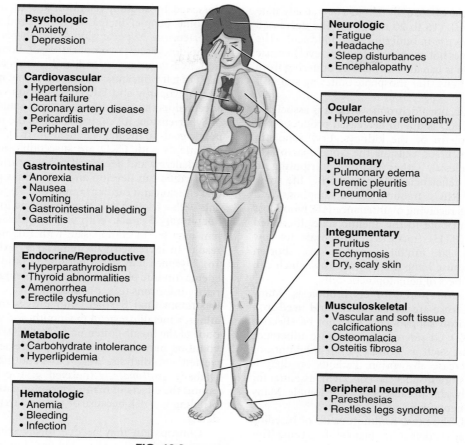

Psychologic
- Anxiety
- Depression

Cardiovascular
- Hypertension
- Heart failure
- Coronary artery disease
- Pericarditis
- Peripheral artery disease

Gastrointestinal
- Anorexia
- Nausea
- Vomiting
- Gastrointestinal bleeding
- Gastritis

Endocrine/Reproductive
- Hyperparathyroidism
- Thyroid abnormalities
- Amenorrhea
- Erectile dysfunction

Metabolic
- Carbohydrate intolerance
- Hyperlipidemia

Hematologic
- Anemia
- Bleeding
- Infection

Neurologic
- Fatigue
- Headache
- Sleep disturbances
- Encephalopathy

Ocular
- Hypertensive retinopathy

Pulmonary
- Pulmonary edema
- Uremic pleuritis
- Pneumonia

Integumentary
- Pruritus
- Ecchymosis
- Dry, scaly skin

Musculoskeletal
- Vascular and soft tissue calcifications
- Osteomalacia
- Osteitis fibrosa

Peripheral neuropathy
- Paresthesias
- Restless legs syndrome

FIG. 46.2 Possible manifestations of CKD.

TABLE 46.8 Indicators of Kidney Function

This example shows why serum creatinine alone is a poor indicator of kidney function. Calculation of GFR is considered the best index to estimate kidney function as shown by the following example.

Estimation of GFR	TYPE OF PATIENT	
	76-Yr-Old Black Woman (Weight 56 kg)	28-Yr-Old Black Man (Weight 74 kg)
Serum creatinine	1.4 mg/dL	1.4 mg/dL
GFR, estimated by the Cockcroft-Gault formula*	30.2 mL/min	82.2 mL/min
GFR, estimated by MDRD equation†	47 mL/min/1.73 m²	64 mL/min/1.73 m²

*Cockcroft-Gault GFR = (140 − Age) × (Weight in kilograms) × (0.85 if female)/(72 × Cr).
†GFR as estimated by MDRD equation calculator can be accessed at www.mdrd.com.
Cr, Creatinine; *GFR,* glomerular filtration rate; *MDRD,* modification of diet in renal disease.

Elevated Triglycerides. Hyperinsulinemia stimulates hepatic production of triglycerides. Many patients with uremia develop dyslipidemia, with increased very-low-density lipoproteins (VLDLs), increased low-density lipoproteins (LDLs), and decreased high-density lipoproteins (HDLs). The altered lipid metabolism is related to decreased levels of the enzyme lipoprotein lipase, which is important in the breakdown of lipoproteins. Most patients with CKD die from CVD.[17]

Electrolyte and Acid-Base Imbalances

Potassium. Hyperkalemia is a serious electrolyte disorder associated with CKD. Fatal dysrhythmias can occur when the serum potassium level reaches 7 to 8 mEq/L (7 to 8 mmol/L). Hyperkalemia results from the decreased excretion of potassium by the kidneys, the breakdown of cellular protein, bleeding, and metabolic acidosis. Potassium may come from foods, dietary supplements, drugs, and IV infusions.

Sodium. Sodium may be high, normal, or low in kidney disease. Because of impaired sodium excretion, sodium is retained with water. If large quantities of water are retained, dilutional hyponatremia occurs. Sodium retention can contribute to edema, hypertension, and HF. Sodium intake is patient specific but is generally restricted to 2 g/day.

Calcium and Phosphate. Calcium and phosphate changes are discussed in the section on the musculoskeletal system on pp. 1068–1069.

Magnesium. Magnesium is primarily excreted by the kidneys. Hypermagnesemia is generally not a problem unless the patient is ingesting magnesium (e.g., Milk of Magnesia, magnesium citrate, antacids containing magnesium). Manifestations can include absent reflexes, decreased mental status, dysrhythmias, hypotension, and respiratory failure.

Metabolic Acidosis. Metabolic acidosis results from the kidneys' impaired ability to excrete excess acid and from defective reabsorption and regeneration of HCO_3^-. The average adult makes 80 to 90 mEq of acid per day. This acid is normally buffered by HCO_3^-. In kidney disease, plasma HCO_3^-, which is an indirect measure of acidosis, usually falls to a new steady state at around 16 to 20 mEq/L (16 to 20 mmol/L). The decreased plasma HCO_3^- reflects its use in buffering metabolic acids. The HCO_3^- level generally does not progress below this level because hydrogen ion production is usually balanced by buffering from demineralization of the bone (the phosphate buffering system).

Hematologic System

Anemia. A normocytic, normochromic anemia is associated with CKD. Anemia in CKD is due to decreased production of the hormone erythropoietin by the kidneys. Erythropoietin normally stimulates precursor cells in the bone marrow to make RBCs (erythropoiesis). Other factors contributing to anemia are nutritional deficiencies, decreased RBC life span, increased hemolysis of RBCs, frequent blood samplings, and GI bleeding. For patients receiving maintenance HD, blood loss in the dialyzer can contribute to the anemic state. Increased parathyroid hormone (PTH) (made to compensate for low serum calcium levels) can inhibit erythropoiesis, shorten survival of RBCs, and cause bone marrow fibrosis, which can result in decreased numbers of hematopoietic cells.

We need sufficient iron stores for erythropoiesis. Many patients with kidney disease are iron deficient and need iron supplementation. Oral iron supplements may not be effective for the person with CKD. GI side effects can cause adherence difficulties. Medications, such as proton pump inhibitors or phosphate binders, decrease absorption. Patients on dialysis may need IV iron to restore iron levels. Folic acid, essential for RBC maturation, is dialyzable because it is water soluble. Many patients receive supplemental folic acid (1 mg/day).[18]

Bleeding Tendencies. The most common cause of bleeding in uremia is a qualitative defect in platelet function. This dysfunction is caused by impaired platelet aggregation and impaired release of platelet factor III. Changes in the coagulation system occur due to increased concentrations of both factor VIII and fibrinogen. The altered platelet function, hemorrhagic tendencies, and GI bleeding susceptibility can usually be corrected with regular HD or PD.

Infection. Patients with advanced CKD have an increased susceptibility to infection. This is due to changes in WBC function and altered immune response and function. Both cellular and humoral immune responses are suppressed. Other factors contributing to the increased risk for infection include hyperglycemia and external trauma (e.g., catheters, needle insertions into vascular access sites).

Cardiovascular System.

The most common cause of death in patients with CKD is CVD. Leading causes of death are myocardial infarction (MI), ischemic heart disease, peripheral arterial disease, HF, cardiomyopathy, and stroke.[17] CVD and CKD are so closely linked that if patients develop cardiac events (e.g., MI, HF), kidney function is evaluated. Traditional CVD risk factors, such as hypertension and increased lipids, are common in CKD patients.

CVD may be related to vascular calcification and arterial stiffness. Calcium deposits in the vascular medial layer are associated with stiffening of the blood vessels. The mechanisms involved are multifactorial. They include (1) vascular smooth muscle cells changing into chondrocytes or osteoblast-like cells, (2) high total body amount of calcium and phosphate resulting from abnormal bone metabolism, (3) impaired renal excretion, and (4) drug therapies to treat the bone disease (e.g., calcium-phosphate binders).[19]

Hypertension, which is prevalent in patients with CKD, is both a cause and a consequence of CKD. Hypertension is worsened by sodium retention and increased ECF volume.[20] In some people, increased renin production contributes to hypertension. Hypertension and diabetes are contributing risk factors for vascular complications.[19] Long-standing hypertension, ECF volume overload, and anemia contribute to development of left ventricular hypertrophy that may eventually lead to cardiomyopathy and HF. Hypertension can cause retinopathy, encephalopathy, and nephropathy. Because of the many effects of hypertension, BP control is one of the most important therapeutic goals in the management of CKD.[20]

Patients with CKD are susceptible to dysrhythmias from hyperkalemia and decreased coronary artery perfusion. Uremic pericarditis can develop and sometimes progresses to pericardial effusion and cardiac tamponade. Pericarditis typically presents with a friction rub, chest pain, and low-grade fever.

Respiratory System.

With severe acidosis, the respiratory system may try to compensate with Kussmaul breathing, which results in increased CO_2 removal by exhalation (see Chapter 16). Dyspnea may occur because of fluid overload, pulmonary edema, uremic pleuritis (pleurisy), pleural effusions, and respiratory infections (e.g., pneumonia).

Gastrointestinal System.

Stomatitis with exudates and ulcerations, a metallic taste in the mouth, and *uremic fetor* (a urinous odor of the breath) often occur in CKD. Anorexia, nausea, and vomiting may develop if CKD progresses to ESRD and is not treated with dialysis. Weight loss and malnutrition may occur. Diabetic *gastroparesis* (delayed gastric emptying) can compound the effects of malnutrition for patients with diabetes. GI bleeding is a risk because of mucosal irritation and the platelet defect.

Constipation may be due to ingesting iron salts or calcium-containing phosphate binders. Limitations on fluid intake and physical inactivity can increase the risk for constipation.

Neurologic System.

Neurologic changes are expected as kidney disease progresses. They are the result of increased nitrogenous waste products, electrolyte imbalances, metabolic acidosis, and atrophy and demyelination of nerve fibers.

The central nervous system (CNS) becomes depressed, resulting in lethargy, apathy, decreased ability to concentrate, fatigue, irritability, and altered mental ability. Seizures and coma may result from a rapidly increasing BUN and hypertensive encephalopathy.

Peripheral neuropathy initially manifests as a slowing of nerve conduction to the extremities. The patient may describe paresthesias in the feet and legs as a burning sensation. Eventually, motor involvement may lead to bilateral foot drop, muscular weakness and atrophy, and loss of deep tendon reflexes. Muscle twitching, jerking, *asterixis* (hand-flapping tremor), and nocturnal leg cramps may occur. In patients with diabetic neuropathy, uremic neuropathy can compound symptoms.[21] Those with advanced stage 5 CKD may develop restless legs syndrome (see Chapter 58).

Dialysis should improve general CNS manifestations and may slow or halt the progression of neuropathies. Motor neuropathy may not be reversible. The treatment for neurologic problems is dialysis or transplantation. Altered mental status, a late manifestation of CKD stage 5, rarely occurs unless the patient has chosen not to have RRT.

Musculoskeletal System.

CKD mineral and bone disorder (CKD-MBD) develops as a systemic disorder of mineral and bone metabolism caused by progressive deterioration in kidney function (Fig. 46.3). Activated vitamin D is necessary to

PATHOPHYSIOLOGY MAP

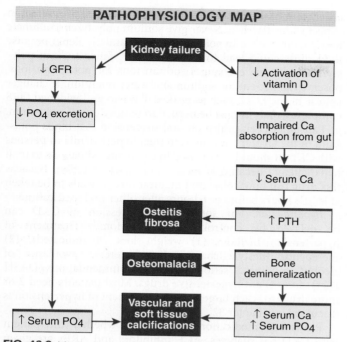

FIG. 46.3 Mechanisms of CKD-MBD. *GFR*, Glomerular filtration rate; *PTH*, parathyroid hormone.

optimize absorption of calcium from the GI tract. As kidney function deteriorates, less vitamin D is converted to its active form, resulting in decreased serum levels. Low levels of active vitamin D result in decreased serum calcium levels.[19]

Serum calcium levels are regulated primarily by PTH. When hypocalcemia occurs, the parathyroid gland secretes PTH, which stimulates bone demineralization, releasing calcium from the bones. Phosphate is also released, leading to high serum phosphate levels. Hyperphosphatemia results from decreased phosphate excretion by the kidneys. It decreases serum calcium levels and further reduces the kidneys' ability to activate vitamin D.

Low serum calcium, increased phosphate, and decreased vitamin D contribute to the stimulation of the parathyroid gland and excretion of PTH. PTH acts on the bone to increase remodeling and increase serum calcium levels. The accelerated rate of bone remodeling causes a weakened bone matrix and places the patient at a higher risk for fractures.

Normally plasma calcium is found ionized or free (physiologically active form) or bound to protein. Low ionized calcium levels can lead to tetany (see Chapter 16). However, in CKD, it is unusual for hypocalcemia to be symptomatic. In the acidotic state associated with CKD, more calcium is in the ionized form than is bound to protein.

CKD-MBD is a common complication of CKD and results in skeletal complications, vascular and soft tissue (extraskeletal) complications. Skeletal complications include (1) *osteomalacia* (results from demineralization from slow bone turnover and defective mineralization of newly formed bone) and (2) *osteitis fibrosa* (decalcification of the bone and replacement of bone tissue with fibrous tissue).

Soft tissue complications result from vascular calcifications. Vascular calcifications are a significant contributing factor to CVD. Irritation from calcium deposits in the eye can cause "uremic red eye." Intracardiac calcifications can disrupt the conduction system and cause cardiac arrest.

Integumentary System. A small number of patients develop refractory pruritus that can have a devastating impact on their well-being and quality of life. Pruritus has multiple causes, including dry skin, calcium-phosphate deposition in the skin, and sensory neuropathy. It is more common in patients receiving dialysis than in the earlier stages of CKD. The itching may be so intense that it can lead to bleeding or infection from scratching. Uremic frost is an extremely rare condition in which urea crystallizes on the skin. This is usually seen only when BUN levels are extremely high (e.g., over 200 mg/dL).

Reproductive System. Both men and women can have infertility and a decreased libido. Women usually have low levels of estrogen, progesterone, and luteinizing hormone, causing anovulation and menstrual changes (usually amenorrhea). Menses and ovulation may return after starting dialysis. Men have loss of testicular consistency, decreased testosterone levels, and low sperm counts.

Sexual dysfunction may be caused by anemia, which causes fatigue and decreased libido. Peripheral neuropathy can cause impotence in men and anorgasmia in women. Other factors that may cause changes in sexual function are psychologic problems (e.g., anxiety, depression), physical stress, and medication side effects. Sexual function may improve with maintenance dialysis and become normal with successful transplantation.

Patients who become pregnant while receiving dialysis have been able to carry a fetus to term, but there is significant risk to the mother and infant. Pregnancy in patients with a kidney transplant is more common, but there is still considerable risk to both the mother and fetus.

Psychologic Changes. Personality and behavioral changes, emotional lability, withdrawal, and depression often occur in patients with CKD. Fatigue and lethargy contribute to the feeling of illness. The changes in body image caused by edema, integumentary changes, and access devices (e.g., fistulas, catheters) may lead to anxiety and depression. Decreased ability to concentrate and slowed mental activity can give the appearance of dullness and disinterest in the environment. The patient must deal with significant changes in lifestyle, occupation, family responsibilities, and financial status. Long-term survival depends on medications, dietary restrictions, dialysis, and possibly transplantation. The patient grieves the loss of kidney function and independence.

Diagnostic Studies

Persistent proteinuria is usually the first sign of kidney damage. Screening for CKD involves a dipstick evaluation of protein in the urine or evaluation for albuminuria, which is not detected with routine urinalysis. The urine of patients with diabetes must be examined for albuminuria if no protein is present on routine urinalysis. A person with persistent proteinuria (1+ protein on standard dipstick testing 2 or more times over a 3-month period) should have further assessment of risk factors and a diagnostic workup with blood and urine tests to evaluate for CKD.

A urinalysis can detect RBCs, WBCs, protein, casts, and glucose. A renal ultrasound is usually done to detect any obstructions and determine the size of the kidneys. Other diagnostic studies (Table 46.9) help establish the diagnosis and cause of CKD. A kidney biopsy may be necessary to provide a definitive diagnosis.

Serum creatinine alone poorly reflects kidney function. GFR is the preferred measure to determine kidney function. Several

TABLE 46.9 Interprofessional Care

Chronic Kidney Disease

Diagnostic Assessment
- History and physical examination
- Identification of reversible kidney disease
- Renal ultrasound, renal scan, CT scan
- Renal biopsy
- BUN, serum creatinine, and creatinine clearance levels
- Serum electrolytes
- Lipid profile
- Urinalysis
- Protein-to-creatinine ratio in first morning voided specimen
- Hematocrit and hemoglobin levels

Management
- Correction of extracellular fluid volume overload or deficit
- RRT (dialysis, kidney transplant)
- Nutritional therapy (Tables 46.10 and 16.6)
- Measures to lower potassium (Table 46.5)

Drug Therapy
- Calcium supplementation, phosphate binders, or both
- Antihypertensive therapy
- ACE inhibitors or ARBs
- Erythropoietin therapy
- Lipid-lowering drugs
- Adjustment of drug dosages to degree of renal function

GFR calculators are available. The equations used most often to estimate GFR are the Cockcroft-Gault formula and Modification of Diet in Renal Disease (MDRD) Study equation (Table 46.8). MDRD is the preferred method.[22]

Interprofessional Care

The overall goals of CKD therapy are to preserve existing kidney function, reduce the risks for CVD, prevent complications, and provide for the patient's comfort. Early recognition, diagnosis, and treatment can prevent the progression of kidney disease. It is important that patients with CKD receive appropriate referral to a nephrologist early in the course of the disease. Every effort is made to detect and treat potentially reversible causes of kidney failure (e.g., HF, dehydration, infections, nephrotoxins, urinary tract obstruction, glomerulonephritis, renal artery stenosis).

Patients with CKD have a high incidence of CVD. More patients die from CVD than live to need dialysis. When a patient has CKD, therapy is aimed at treating CVD in addition to slowing the progression of kidney disease (Table 46.9).

A focus on stages 1 through 4 (Table 46.7) before the need for dialysis (stage 5) includes the control of hypertension, hyperparathyroidism, CKD-MBD, anemia, and dyslipidemia. The next section focuses primarily on the drug and nutritional aspects of care.

Drug Therapy

Hyperkalemia. Multiple strategies are used to manage hyperkalemia (Table 46.5). These include restricting high-potassium foods and drugs. Acute hyperkalemia may need treatment with IV glucose and insulin or IV 10% calcium gluconate.

Sodium polystyrene sulfonate, a cation-exchange resin, is often given to lower potassium levels in stage 4 CKD. Sodium polystyrene sulfonate has an osmotic laxative action and ensures evacuation of the potassium from the bowel. Tell the patient to expect some diarrhea. Never give sodium polystyrene sulfonate to a patient with a hypoactive bowel (paralytic ileus) because fluid shifts could lead to bowel necrosis. Since sodium polystyrene sulfonate exchanges sodium ions for potassium ions, observe the patient for sodium and water retention. If changes appear in the ECG, such as peaked T waves and widened QRS complexes, dialysis may be needed to remove excess potassium.

Patiromer (Veltassa) is an oral suspension that binds potassium in the GI tract. It is used to treat hyperkalemia in persons with CKD. It should not be used in emergency situations to treat hyperkalemia because of its delayed onset of action. Because this drug can bind other oral medications, it needs to be taken at least 6 hours before or 6 hours after other oral medications.

Hypertension. For some, the progression of CKD can be delayed by controlling hypertension.[20] Treatment of hypertension includes (1) weight loss (if indicated), (2) therapeutic lifestyle changes (e.g., exercise, avoidance of alcohol, smoking cessation), (3) diet recommendations (DASH Diet), and (4) antihypertensive drugs. Most patients need 2 or more drugs to reach target BP. The treatment of hypertension is discussed in Chapter 32.

Prescribed medications depend on whether the patient with CKD has diabetes. ACE inhibitors and ARBs are given to patients with diabetes and those with nondiabetic proteinuria. They decrease proteinuria and may delay the progression of CKD. They must be used with caution as they can further decrease the GFR and increase serum potassium levels.

Measure the BP with the patient in the supine, sitting, and standing positions to monitor the effect of antihypertensive drugs. Teach the patient and caregiver how to monitor the BP at home and what readings require immediate intervention.

CKD-MBD. It is hard to determine what type of bone disease a patient may have by just looking at the serum levels of calcium, phosphorus, PTH, and alkaline phosphatase. The gold standard for diagnosis is a bone biopsy.

Interventions for CKD-MBD include limiting dietary phosphorus, giving phosphate binders, supplementing vitamin D, and controlling hyperparathyroidism.[19] Phosphate intake is not usually restricted until the patient needs RRT. At that time, phosphate is usually limited to about 1 g/day, but dietary control alone is usually inadequate.

Phosphate binders include calcium-based binders, calcium acetate, and calcium carbonate. They bind phosphate in the bowel and then excrete it in the stool. Giving calcium may increase the calcium load and place the patient at increased risk for vascular calcifications. So, when calcium levels are increased or there is evidence of existing vascular or soft tissue calcifications, non–calcium-based phosphate binders may be used. These include lanthanum carbonate (Fosrenol); sevelamer carbonate (Renvela;, and iron-based, calcium-free phosphate binders, such as sucroferric oxyhydroxide (Velphoro) and ferric citrate (Auryxia).

To be most effective, give phosphate binders with each meal. Constipation is a frequent side effect of phosphate binders. Stool softeners may be needed.

Because bone disease (osteomalacia) is associated with excess aluminum, aluminum preparations should be used with caution in patients with kidney disease. Do not use magnesium-containing antacids (e.g., Maalox, Mylanta) because magnesium depends on the kidneys for excretion.

Hypocalcemia is a problem in the later stages of CKD due to the inability of the GI tract to absorb calcium in the absence of active vitamin D. If hypocalcemia persists even if the serum phosphate levels are normal, supplemental calcium and vitamin D should be given. Assess vitamin D levels to determine the need for supplementation. If the levels are low (serum values less than 30 ng/mL), vitamin D is given in the form of cholecalciferol.

Treatment of secondary hyperparathyroidism in ESRD patients requires the activated form of vitamin D because the kidneys cannot activate vitamin D. Active vitamin D is available as oral or IV calcitriol (Rocaltrol), IV paricalcitol (Zemplar), or oral or IV doxercalciferol (Hectorol). Their use can reduce the high PTH levels. Cinacalcet (Sensipar), a calcimimetic agent, is used to control secondary hyperparathyroidism. Calcimimetics mimic calcium and increase the sensitivity of the calcium receptors in the parathyroid glands. As a result, the parathyroid glands detect calcium at lower serum levels and decrease PTH secretion.

If parathyroid disease becomes severe, a subtotal or total parathyroidectomy may be done to decrease the synthesis and secretion of PTH. In most cases, a total parathyroidectomy is done and parathyroid tissue transplanted into the forearm. The transplanted cells make PTH as needed. If PTH production becomes excessive, some cells can be removed from the forearm.

Hypercalcemia may occur with calcium and vitamin D supplementation. If hypercalcemia occurs, vitamin D may be withheld, and calcium-based phosphate binders replaced with non–calcium-based phosphate binders.

Anemia. Anemia in CKD is caused by a decreased production of erythropoietin by the kidneys. Exogenous erythropoietin (EPO) is used to treat anemia. It is available as epoetin alfa (Epogen, Procrit), which can be given IV or subcutaneously, usually 2 or 3 times per week. Darbepoetin alfa (Aranesp) is longer acting and can be given weekly or biweekly.

Hemoglobin and hematocrit levels may take 2 to 3 weeks to increase. Higher hemoglobin levels (more than 12 g/dL) and higher doses of EPO are associated with a higher rate of thromboembolic events and increased risk for death from serious CV events (MI, HF, stroke). The recommendation is to use the lowest possible dose of EPO to treat anemia.

Treatment of CKD-related anemia is patient specific with the goal being to reduce the need for blood transfusions. There is no target hemoglobin or widely accepted EPO dosing strategy. Teach people who are prescribed EPO about the risks and benefits and allow them to decide about their treatment plan.

EPO can increase BP and is contraindicated in uncontrolled hypertension. The underlying mechanism is related to the hemodynamic changes (e.g., increased whole blood viscosity) that occurs as the anemia is corrected.

EPO therapy may lead to iron deficiency from the increased demand for iron to support erythropoiesis. Iron supplementation is recommended if the plasma ferritin concentrations fall below 100 ng/mL. Most CKD patients receive iron supplementation.

Although iron can be given by mouth or IV, the enteral route is limited due to GI side effects, which decrease patient adherence. Oral iron should not be taken at the same time as phosphate binders because calcium binds the iron, preventing its absorption. Tell the patient that iron may make the stool dark in color. Most patients receiving HD are prescribed IV iron sucrose (Venofer) or sodium ferric gluconate complex (Ferrlecit). Supplemental folic acid (1 mg/day) is usually given because it is needed for RBC formation and is removed by dialysis.

Blood transfusions are avoided unless the patient has an acute blood loss or has symptomatic anemia (i.e., dyspnea, excess fatigue, tachycardia, palpitations, chest pain). Transfusions increase the development of antibodies, thus making it harder to find a compatible donor for kidney transplantation. Multiple blood transfusions may lead to iron overload because each unit of blood has about 250 mg of iron.

Dyslipidemia. Dyslipidemia, a risk factor for CVD, is a common problem in CKD. Statins (HMG-CoA reductase inhibitors), such as atorvastatin (Lipitor), are used to lower LDL cholesterol levels (see Table 33.6). Statins should be used in patients with CKD, especially those with diabetes, not yet on dialysis. [23]

Fibrates (fibric acid derivatives), such as gemfibrozil (Lopid), are used to lower triglyceride levels (see Table 33.6) and can increase HDLs. Specific drugs used in these classes depend on the individual patient response and HCP recommendation.

Complications of Drug Therapy. The kidneys partially or totally excrete many drugs. CKD causes decreased elimination that leads to an accumulation of drugs and the potential for drug toxicity. Drug doses and frequency of administration are adjusted based on the severity of the kidney disease. Increased sensitivity may result as drug levels increase in the blood and tissues. Drugs of particular concern include digoxin, diabetic agents (metformin, glyburide), antibiotics (e.g., vancomycin, gentamicin), and opioid drugs.

Nutritional Therapy

Protein Restriction. The current diet for the person with CKD is designed to maintain good nutrition (Table 46.10). Calorie-protein malnutrition is a potential and serious problem that results from altered metabolism, anemia, proteinuria, anorexia, and nausea. Other factors leading to malnutrition include depression and complex diets that restrict protein, phosphorus, potassium, and sodium. Frequent monitoring of laboratory parameters, especially serum albumin, prealbumin, and ferritin, and anthropometric measurements are necessary to evaluate nutritional status. All patients with CKD should be referred to a dietitian for nutritional teaching.

For the patient undergoing dialysis, protein is not routinely restricted. For CKD stages 1 through 4, many HCPs encourage a diet with normal protein intake. Teach patients to avoid high-protein diets and supplements because they may overburden the diseased kidneys. [24]

Dietary protein guidelines for PD differ from those for HD because of protein loss through the peritoneal membrane. During PD, protein intake must be high enough to compensate for the losses so that the nitrogen balance is maintained. The recommended protein intake is at least 1.2 g/kg of ideal body weight (IBW) per day. This can be increased depending on the patient's needs.

For patients with malnutrition or inadequate caloric or protein intake, commercially prepared products that are high in protein but low in sodium and potassium are available (e.g., Nepro, Amin-Aid). As an alternative, liquid or powder breakfast drinks may be bought at the grocery store.

Fluid Restriction. Water and any other fluids are not routinely restricted in patients with CKD stages 1 to 5 who are not receiving HD. To reduce fluid retention, diuretics are often used. Patients on HD have a more restricted fluid intake than patients receiving PD. For those receiving HD, as their urine output decreases, fluids are restricted. Recommended fluid intake depends on the daily urine output. Generally, 600 mL (from insensible loss) plus an amount equal to the previous day's urine output is allowed for a patient receiving HD.

TABLE 46.10 Nutritional Therapy

Chronic Kidney Disease

	Pre-ESRD	Hemodialysis	Peritoneal Dialysis
Calcium	About 1000–1500 mg/day	Patient specific	Patient specific
Calories	30–35 kcal/kg/day	30–35 kcal/kg/day	25–35 kcal/kg/day (includes calories from dialysate glucose absorption)
Fluid allowance	As desired or depends on urine output	Urine output plus 600–1000 mL	Unrestricted if weight and BP controlled and residual renal function
Iron	Supplement recommended if receiving erythropoietin	Supplement recommended if receiving erythropoietin	Supplement recommended if receiving erythropoietin
Phosphate	Patient specific or 1.0–1.8 g/day	Patient specific or about 0.6–1.2 g/day	Patient specific or about 0.6–1.2 g/day
Potassium	Based on laboratory values	Patient specific or about 2–4 g/day	Usually not restricted
Protein	Patient specific or 0.6–1.0 g/kg/day (low protein)	1.2 g/kg/day	1.2–1.3 g/kg/day
Sodium	Patient specific or 1–3 g/day	Patient specific or 2–3 g/day	Patient specific or 2–4 g/day

Foods that are liquid at room temperature (e.g., gelatin, ice) are counted as fluid intake. Space fluid allotment throughout the day so that the patient does not become thirsty. Teach patients to limit fluid intake so that weight gains are no more than 1 to 3 kg between dialyses (*interdialytic weight gain*).

Sodium and Potassium Restriction. Teach patients with CKD to restrict sodium. Sodium-restricted diets may vary from 2 to 4 g/day. Teach the patient to avoid high-sodium foods, such as cured meats, pickled foods, canned soups and stews, frankfurters, cold cuts, soy sauce, and salad dressings (see Table 34.8). Potassium restriction depends on the kidneys' ability to excrete potassium. Salt substitutes should be avoided in potassium-restricted diets because they contain potassium chloride.

Dietary restrictions for potassium range from about 2000 to 3000 mg (39 mg = 1 mEq). Teach patients receiving HD which foods are high in potassium and to avoid them (see Table 16.6). Patients using PD do not usually need potassium restrictions. They may need oral potassium supplementation because of the loss of potassium with dialysis exchanges.

Phosphate Restriction. As kidney function deteriorates, phosphate elimination by the kidneys is decreased and the patient begins to develop hyperphosphatemia. By the time a patient reaches ESRD, phosphate is limited to around 1 g/day. Foods that are high in phosphate include meat and dairy products (e.g., milk, ice cream, cheese, yogurt, pudding). Many foods that are high in phosphate are also high in protein. Since patients on dialysis are encouraged to eat a diet containing protein, phosphate binders are essential to control the phosphate level.

❖ NURSING MANAGEMENT: CHRONIC KIDNEY DISEASE

◆ Nursing Assessment

Obtain a complete history of any existing kidney disease or family history of kidney disease. Some kidney disorders, including Alport syndrome and polycystic kidney disease, have a genetic component. Other disorders that can lead to CKD are diabetes, hypertension, and SLE.

Because many drugs are potentially nephrotoxic, ask the patient about both current and past use of prescription and OTC drugs and herbal preparations. Decongestants and antihistamines that contain pseudoephedrine and phenylephrine cause vasoconstriction and lead to an increase in BP. Magnesium and

aluminum from antacids can accumulate in the body because they cannot be excreted. Some antacids have high levels of salt, contributing to hypertension.

NSAIDs (aspirin, ibuprofen, naproxen) can contribute to the development of AKI and progression of CKD, especially when taken in higher doses than recommended. If taken as prescribed, these analgesics are usually considered safe.

Assess the patient's dietary habits and discuss any problems with intake. Measure the patient's height and weight and evaluate any recent weight changes.

The chronicity of kidney disease and the long-term treatment affect virtually every area of a person's life, including family relationships, social and work activities, self-image, and emotional state. Assess the patient's support systems. The choice of treatment modality may be related to support systems available.

◆ Nursing Diagnoses

Nursing diagnoses for patients with CKD include:
- Fluid imbalance
- Electrolyte imbalance
- Impaired nutritional status
- Difficulty coping

More information on nursing diagnoses and interventions for the patient with CKD is presented in eNursing Care Plan 46.1, available on the website for this chapter.

◆ Planning

The overall goals are that a patient with CKD will (1) show knowledge of and ability to adhere to the therapeutic plan, (2) take part in decision making for the plan of care and future treatment modality, (3) have effective coping strategies, and (4) continue with activities of daily living within physiologic limitations.

◆ Nursing Implementation

◆ Health Promotion. Identify those at risk for CKD. At-risk persons include those diagnosed with diabetes or hypertension and people with a history (or a family history) of kidney disease or repeated urinary tract infections (UTIs). They should have regular checkups that include a routine urinalysis and calculation of the estimated GFR.

People with diabetes need to have their urine checked for albuminuria if routine urinalysis is negative for protein. Teach patients with diabetes to report any changes in urine appearance

TABLE 46.11 Patient & Caregiver Teaching

Chronic Kidney Disease

Include the following information in the teaching plan for the patient and caregiver:

1. Dietary (sodium, potassium, phosphate) and fluid restrictions.
2. Common problems patient will encounter in modifying diet and fluid intake.
3. Signs and symptoms of electrolyte imbalance, especially high potassium.
4. Alternative ways of reducing thirst, such as sucking on ice cubes, lemon, or hard candy.
5. Reasons for prescribed drugs and common side effects. *Examples:*
   - Phosphate binders (including calcium supplements used as phosphate barriers) should be taken with meals.
   - Take calcium supplements prescribed to treat hypocalcemia on an empty stomach, but not at the same time as iron supplements.
   - Iron supplements should be taken between meals.
6. The importance of reporting any of the following: weight gain >4 lb (2 kg), increasing BP, shortness of breath, edema, increasing fatigue or weakness, or confusion or lethargy
7. Need for support and encouragement. Share concerns about lifestyle changes, living with a chronic illness, and decisions about type of dialysis or transplantation.

(color, odor), frequency, or volume to the HCP. If a patient needs a potentially nephrotoxic drug, it is important to monitor kidney function with serum creatinine, BUN, and GFR. Those at risk must take measures to prevent or delay the progression of CKD. Most important are measures to reduce the risk or progression of CVD. These include glycemic control for patients with diabetes (see Chapter 48), BP control (see Chapter 32), and lifestyle modifications, including smoking cessation.

♥ PROMOTING POPULATION HEALTH

Prevention and Detection of Chronic Kidney Disease

- Early detection and treatment are the primary methods for reducing CKD.
- Ensure proper diagnosis and treatment of diabetes as it is the leading cause of CKD.
- Monitor BP to detect elevations so that treatment can be started early.
- Treat hypertension appropriately and aggressively as it is the second leading cause of CKD.

◆ **Acute Care.** Most of the care of the patient with CKD occurs on an outpatient basis. In-hospital care is needed for management of complications and for kidney transplantation (if applicable).

◆ **Ambulatory Care.** Encourage patients to take part in their care. Teach the patient and caregiver about the diet, drugs, and follow-up medical care (Table 46.11). The patient needs to understand the drugs and common side effects. Because patients with CKD take many medications, a pillbox organizer or a list of the drugs and the times of administration may be helpful. Tell the patient to avoid OTC medications, such as NSAIDs and aluminum- and magnesium-based laxatives and antacids. Teach the patient to take daily BP readings and watch for signs and symptoms of fluid overload, hyperkalemia, and other electrolyte imbalances.

The dietitian should meet with the patient and caregiver on a regular basis for diet planning. A diet history and consideration of cultural variations help with diet planning and adherence. The rate of progression of CKD is dependent on the type of kidney disease and presence of other co-morbid conditions.

The patient can complete an evaluation for a kidney transplant prior to the need to start dialysis. Patients may receive a transplant before ever having to start dialysis. Even though transplantation offers the best therapeutic management for many ESRD patients, the critical shortage of donor organs limits this option for many patients.

Most patients need either PD or HD. Most patients use HD. Explain to the patient and caregiver what is involved in PD or HD and home HD modalities, transplantation, and palliative care. Offer information about all treatment options so that the patient can be involved in the decision-making process, giving a sense of control over life-altering decisions. Tell the patient that even while on dialysis, transplant is still an option. Let the patient know that if a transplanted organ fails, the patient can return to dialysis.

It is important to respect the patient's choice to not receive treatment. Patients themselves often start the conversation about palliative care. Focus the discussion on moving from the curative approach to promotion of comfort care and consideration of hospice care. Listen to the patient and caregiver, allowing them to do most of the talking and pay special attention to their hopes and fears. (Palliative and end-of-life care is discussed in Chapter 9.)

◆ Evaluation

The expected outcomes are that the patient with CKD will maintain

- Fluid and electrolyte levels within normal ranges
- An acceptable weight with no more than a 10% weight loss

▌DIALYSIS

Dialysis is the movement of fluid and molecules across a semipermeable membrane from one compartment to another. Clinically, dialysis is a technique in which substances move from the blood through a semipermeable membrane and into a dialysis solution (*dialysate*). It corrects fluid and electrolyte imbalances and removes waste products in kidney failure. It also can be used to treat drug overdoses.

The 2 methods of dialysis available are **peritoneal dialysis (PD)** and **hemodialysis (HD)** (Table 46.12). In PD the peritoneal membrane acts as the semipermeable membrane. In HD an artificial membrane (usually made of cellulose-based or synthetic materials) is used as the semipermeable membrane and is in contact with the patient's blood.

Dialysis is begun when the patient's uremia can no longer be adequately treated with conservative medical management. Generally, this is when the GFR is less than 15 mL/min/1.73 m². This criterion can vary widely in different clinical situations. The nephrologist determines when to start dialysis based on the patient's clinical status. Certain uremic complications, including encephalopathy, neuropathies, uncontrolled hyperkalemia, pericarditis, and accelerated hypertension, indicate a need for immediate dialysis.

Most patients with ESRD are treated with dialysis because (1) there is a lack of donated organs, (2) some patients are physically or mentally unsuitable for transplantation, or (3) some

TABLE 46.12 Comparison of Peritoneal Dialysis and Hemodialysis

Advantages	Disadvantages
Peritoneal Dialysis (PD)	
• Immediate initiation in almost any hospital	• Bacterial or chemical peritonitis
• Less complicated than hemodialysis	• Protein loss into dialysate
• Portable system with CAPD	• Exit site and tunnel infections
• Fewer dietary restrictions	• Self-image problems with catheter placement
• Rather short training time	• Hyperglycemia
• Usable in patient with vascular access problems	• Surgery for catheter placement
• Less cardiovascular stress	• Contraindicated in patient with multiple abdominal surgeries, trauma, unrepaired hernia
• Home dialysis possible	• Requires completion of education program
• Preferable for patient with diabetes	• Catheter can migrate
	• Best instituted with willing partner
Hemodialysis (HD)	
• Rapid fluid removal	• Vascular access problems
• Rapid removal of urea and creatinine	• Dietary and fluid restrictions
• Effective potassium removal	• Heparinization may be necessary
• Less protein loss	• Extensive equipment necessary
• Lowering of serum triglycerides	• Hypotension during dialysis
• Home dialysis possible	• Added blood loss that contributes to anemia
• Temporary access can be placed at bedside	• Specially trained personnel necessary
	• Surgery for permanent access placement
	• Self-image problems with permanent access

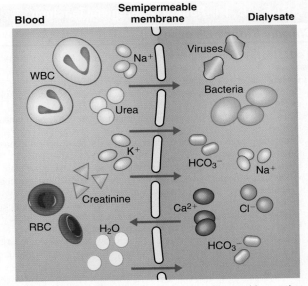

FIG. 46.4 Osmosis and diffusion across a semipermeable membrane.

the dialysate (osmotic gradient) with the addition of glucose. In HD, the gradient is created by increasing pressure in the blood compartment (positive pressure) or decreasing pressure in the dialysate compartment (negative pressure). ECF moves into the dialysate because of the pressure gradient. The excess fluid is removed by creating a pressure differential between the blood and the dialysate solution with a combination of positive pressure in the blood compartment and negative pressure in the dialysate compartment.

PERITONEAL DIALYSIS

Although PD was first used in 1923, it did not come into widespread use for chronic treatment until the 1970s with the development of soft, pliable peritoneal solution bags and the introduction of the concept of continuous PD. In the United States, about 12% of patients receiving dialysis treatments are on PD.

Catheter Placement

Peritoneal access is obtained by inserting a catheter through the anterior abdominal wall (Fig. 46.5). The catheter is about 24 in (60 cm) long and has 1 or 2 Dacron cuffs. The cuffs act as anchors and prevent the migration of microorganisms into the peritoneum. Within a few weeks, fibrous tissue grows into the Dacron cuff, holding the catheter in place and preventing bacterial penetration into the peritoneal cavity. The tip of the catheter rests in the peritoneal cavity. It has many perforations spaced along the distal end of the tubing, allowing fluid movement through the catheter.

The technique for catheter placement varies. It is usually placed surgically so that the catheter can be seen directly, minimizing potential complications. Patient preparation for catheter insertion includes emptying the bladder and bowel, weighing the patient, and obtaining a signed consent form. After placement, PD may be started at once with low-volume exchanges or delayed for 2 weeks pending healing and sealing of the exit site. Once the catheter incision site is healed, the patient may shower and then pat the catheter and exit site dry.[25] Daily catheter

patients do not want transplants. An increasing number of people, including older adults and those with complex medical problems, are receiving maintenance dialysis. A patient's age is not a factor in determining candidacy for dialysis.

General Principles of Dialysis

Solutes and water move across the semipermeable membrane from the blood to the dialysate or from the dialysate to the blood per concentration gradients. The principles of diffusion, osmosis, and ultrafiltration are involved in dialysis (Fig. 46.4). *Diffusion* is the movement of solutes from an area of greater concentration to an area of lesser concentration. In kidney failure, urea, creatinine, uric acid, and electrolytes (potassium, phosphate) move from the blood to the dialysate with the net effect of lowering their concentration in the blood. RBCs, WBCs, and plasma proteins are too large to diffuse through the pores of the membrane. Small-molecular-weight substances can pass from the dialysate into a patient's blood, so the purity of the water used for dialysis is monitored and controlled.

Osmosis is the movement of fluid from an area of lesser concentration to an area of greater concentration of solutes. Glucose is added to the dialysate and creates an osmotic gradient across the membrane, pulling excess fluid from the blood.

Ultrafiltration (water and fluid removal) results when there is an osmotic gradient or pressure gradient across the membrane. In PD, excess fluid is removed by increasing the osmolality of

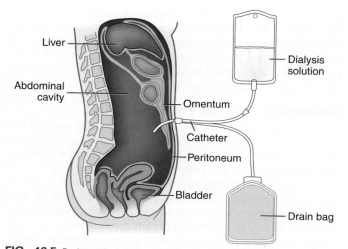

FIG. 46.5 Peritoneal dialysis showing peritoneal catheter inserted into peritoneal cavity.

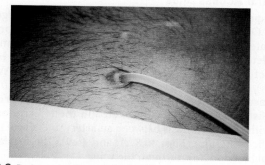

FIG. 46.6 Peritoneal catheter exit site. (Courtesy Mary Jo Holechek, Baltimore, MD.)

care varies. Some patients just wash with soap and water and go without a dressing (Fig. 46.6). Others need daily dressing changes. Showering is preferred to bathing.

In PD it is critical to maintain aseptic technique to avoid peritonitis. Several tubing connections and devices are commercially available to help maintain an aseptic system. Teach all patients to examine their catheter site for signs of infection.

Dialysis Solutions and Cycles

PD is done by putting dialysis solution into the peritoneal space. The 3 phases of the PD cycle are inflow (fill), dwell (equilibration), and drain. Together, the 3 phases are an *exchange*. For manual PD, a period of about 30 to 50 minutes is needed to complete an exchange. During *inflow*, a prescribed amount of solution, usually 2 L, is infused through an established catheter over about 10 minutes. The flow rate may be decreased if the patient has pain. After the solution has been infused, the inflow clamp is closed.

The next part of the cycle is the *dwell* phase, or equilibration, during which diffusion and osmosis occur between the patient's blood and peritoneal cavity. The duration of the dwell time is usually between 4 and 6 hours. *Drain* time takes 15 to 30 minutes. It may be facilitated by gently massaging the abdomen or changing position. The cycle starts again with the infusion of another 2 L of solution.

PD solutions vary. The choice of the exchange volume is primarily determined by the size of the peritoneal cavity. An

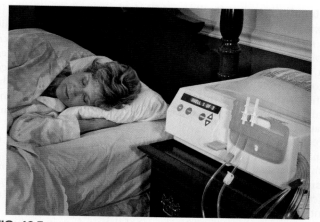

FIG. 46.7 Automated PD that can be used while the patient is sleeping.

average-size person typically uses a 2-L exchange. A larger person may need a 3-L exchange volume. Smaller exchange volumes are used for patients with a smaller body, pulmonary compromise (the added pressure of the large volume may cause respiratory problems), or inguinal hernias.

Ultrafiltration (fluid removal) during PD depends on osmotic forces. Dextrose is the most commonly used osmotic agent in PD solutions. It is relatively safe and inexpensive. It is associated with high rates of peritoneal glucose absorption, leading to problems with hypertriglyceridemia, hyperglycemia, and long-term peritoneal membrane dysfunction.

Alternatives to dextrose PD solution include icodextrin and amino acid solutions. Icodextrin is a commercially available iso-osmolar preparation. It induces ultrafiltration by its oncotic effect. Amino acid PD solutions are available and used mainly for patients who need nutritional supplementation.

Peritoneal Dialysis Systems

Automated Peritoneal Dialysis. Automated peritoneal dialysis (APD) is the most popular form of PD because it allows patients to do dialysis while they sleep. An automated device called a *cycler* delivers the dialysate for APD (Fig. 46.7). The size of a cycler is similar to a DVD player. The automated cycler times and controls the fill, dwell, and drain phases. The machine cycles 4 or more exchanges per night with 1 to 2 hours per exchange. Alarms and monitors are built into the system to make it safe for the patient to sleep while dialyzing. The patient disconnects from the machine in the morning and usually leaves fluid in the abdomen during the day.

It is hard to achieve the required solute and fluid clearance solely with nighttime APD. One or 2 daytime manual exchanges may be prescribed to ensure adequate dialysis.

Continuous Ambulatory Peritoneal Dialysis. Continuous ambulatory peritoneal dialysis (CAPD) is done every few hours during the day. The patient may perform an exchange of 2 L of peritoneal dialysate 4 times daily, with dwell times averaging 4 hours. A common schedule includes exchanges at 7 AM, 12 noon, 5 PM, and 10 PM.

In CAPD, the person instills 2 to 3 L of dialysate from a plastic bag into the peritoneal cavity through a disposable administration line. The bag and line are then disconnected. After the equilibration period, the line is reconnected to the catheter, the dialysate (effluent) is drained from the peritoneal cavity, and a new 2- to 3-L bag of dialysate solution is infused.

Complications of Peritoneal Dialysis

Exit Site Infection. Infection of the peritoneal catheter exit site is most often caused by *Staphylococcus aureus* or *Staphylococcus epidermidis* (from skin flora). Manifestations include redness at the site, tenderness, and drainage. Superficial exit site infections caused by these organisms generally resolve with antibiotic therapy. If not treated immediately, subcutaneous tunnel infections may progress and may cause peritonitis, necessitating catheter removal.

Peritonitis. Peritonitis results from contact contamination or an exit site or tunnel infection. Most often it occurs because of improper technique when connections for exchanges are contaminated. Peritonitis is usually caused by *S. aureus* or *S. epidermidis*. It rarely results from bacteria in the intestine crossing into the peritoneal cavity.

The main manifestations are abdominal pain, rebound tenderness, and cloudy peritoneal effluent with a WBC count greater than 100 cells/µL (more than 50% neutrophils) or bacteria in the peritoneal effluent shown by Gram stain or culture. GI manifestations may include diarrhea, vomiting, abdominal distention, and hyperactive bowel sounds. Fever may or may not be present. To determine if the peritoneal effluent is cloudy, drain the effluent and place the drained bag on reading material, such as a newspaper. If you cannot read the print through the effluent, it is cloudy.

Cultures, Gram stain, and a WBC differential of the peritoneal effluent are used to confirm the diagnosis of peritonitis. Antibiotics can be given orally, IV, or intraperitoneally. In most cases, the patient is treated on an outpatient basis.

The formation of adhesions in the peritoneum can result from repeated infections and interferes with the peritoneal membrane's ability to act as a dialyzing surface. Repeated infections may require the removal of the peritoneal catheter and a temporary or permanent change of modality to HD.

Hernias. Increased intraabdominal pressure from the dialysate volume can cause hernias to develop in predisposed persons, such as multiparous women and older men. After hernia repair, PD often can be resumed after several days using small dialysate volumes and keeping the patient supine.

Lower Back Problems. Increased intraabdominal pressure can cause or worsen lower back pain. The lumbosacral curvature is increased by intraperitoneal infusion of dialysate. Orthopedic binders and a regular exercise program for strengthening the back muscles are helpful for some patients.

Bleeding. After peritoneal catheter placement, it is common for the PD effluent drained after the first few exchanges to be pink or slightly bloody from trauma associated with catheter insertion. Bloody effluent over several days or the new appearance of blood in the effluent can indicate active intraperitoneal bleeding. If this occurs, check the BP and hematocrit. Blood may be present in the effluent of women who are menstruating or ovulating. This requires no intervention.

Pulmonary Complications. Atelectasis, pneumonia, and bronchitis may occur from repeated upward displacement of the diaphragm, resulting in decreased lung expansion. Longer dwell times increase the risk for pulmonary problems. Frequent repositioning and deep-breathing exercises can help. When the patient is lying in bed, elevate the head of the bed to prevent these problems.

Protein Loss. The peritoneal membrane is permeable to plasma proteins, amino acids, and polypeptides. These substances are lost in the dialysate fluid. The amount of loss is usually about 0.5 g/L of dialysate drainage, but it can be as high as 10 to 20 g/day. This loss may increase to as much as 40 g/day during episodes of peritonitis as the peritoneal membrane becomes more permeable. Unresolved peritonitis is associated with excessive protein loss that can result in malnutrition. PD may need to stop temporarily or sometimes permanently.

Effectiveness of Chronic Peritoneal Dialysis

Mortality rates are similar between in-center HD patients and PD patients for the first few years. After about 2 years, mortality rates for patients receiving PD increase, especially for the older person with diabetes and patients with a prior history of CVD.[25]

The primary advantage of PD is its simplicity and that it is a home-based program, increasing patient participation in their care. Learning the self-management skills needed to do PD usually involves a 3- to 7-day training program. There is no need for special water systems. Equipment setup is relatively simple.

HEMODIALYSIS

Vascular Access Sites

HD requires a very rapid blood flow and access to a large blood vessel. Obtaining vascular access is one of the hardest problems associated with HD. Enough time is needed for evaluation and consideration of the best arteriovenous (AV) access for HD. The types of vascular access include AV fistulas (AVFs), AV grafts (AVGs), and temporary vascular access.[26]

Arteriovenous Fistulas and Grafts. A subcutaneous arteriovenous fistula (AVF) is usually created in the forearm or upper arm with an anastomosis between an artery and a vein (usually cephalic or basilic) (Figs. 46.8, *A*, and 46.9). The fistula allows arterial blood to flow through the vein.

The vein becomes "arterialized," increasing in size and developing thicker walls. The arterial blood flow is essential to provide the rapid blood flow needed for HD. As the fistula matures, it is more amenable to repeated venipunctures. Maturation may take 6 weeks to months. AVF should be placed at least 3 months before starting HD. A fistula is the preferred access for HD.[26]

Normally, a *thrill* (buzzing sensation) can be felt by palpating the fistula, and a *bruit* (rushing sound) can be heard with a stethoscope. The thrill and bruit are created by arterial blood moving at a high velocity through the vein.

? CHECK YOUR PRACTICE

You are rotating to the inpatient dialysis unit today. It is your first time working with HD patients. You are helping a hemodialysis tech "hook-up" a 56-yr-old man to HD. He has been on HD for 5 years due to polycystic kidney disease. You take his vital signs, palpate his AV fistula, and then use your stethoscope to auscultate the AV fistula. You are concerned because you feel a super-strong pulse and hear a very loud "whoosh" sound. The patient turns to you and just smirks, "I bet you have never had a thrill like that."

- You are very flustered and not sure how to respond. What should you say to him?

AVFs are harder to create in patients with a history of severe peripheral vascular disease (e.g., people with diabetes), those with prolonged IV drug use, and obese women. These persons may need a synthetic graft.

Arteriovenous grafts (AVGs) are made of synthetic materials (polytetrafluoroethylene [PTFE, Teflon]) and form a "bridge" between the arterial and venous blood supplies. Grafts are

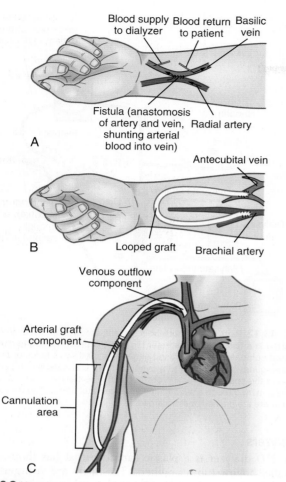

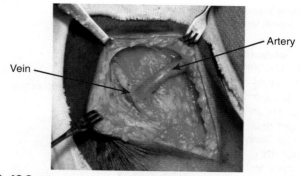

FIG. 46.9 AVF created by anastomosing an artery and a vein. (Courtesy Dr. Stephen Van Voorst, MD.)

FIG. 46.8 Vascular access for hemodialysis. **A,** AVF. **B,** AVG. **C,** HeRO Graft.

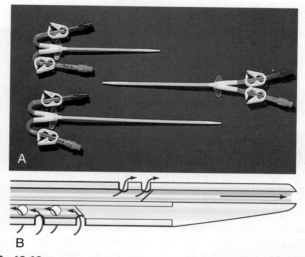

FIG. 46.10 Temporary double-lumen vascular access catheter for acute hemodialysis. **A,** Soft, flexible double-lumen tube is attached to a Y hub. **B,** The distance between the arterial intake lumen and the venous return lumen typically provides recirculation rates of 5% or less. (A, Courtesy Quinton Instrument Co., Seattle, WA.)

placed under the skin and are surgically anastomosed between an artery (usually brachial) and a vein (usually antecubital) (Fig. 46.8, *B*). An interval of 2 to 4 weeks is usually needed to allow the graft to heal, but it may be used earlier. Because grafts are made of artificial materials, they are more likely than AVFs to become infected and tend to form clots. When AVG infections occur, they may need surgical removal, since it is hard to completely resolve the infection from the synthetic material.

A common problem in patients on HD is central venous stenosis (CVS) or occlusion. CVS is serious and has a greater impact than peripheral venous stenosis because the central veins are the final pathway for blood flow to the heart. As CVS progresses, vascular access for HD is often lost.

HeRO (Hemodialysis Reliable Outflow) *Graft* is a special bridge access used in patients when other access options are exhausted. It consists of 2 pieces: a reinforced tube to bypass blockages in veins and a dialysis graft anastomosed to an artery to be accessed for HD (Fig. 46.8, *C*). The HeRO Graft is placed under the skin, like both a fistula and standard graft. The HeRO Graft bypasses the venous system and provides blood flow directly from a target artery to the heart. It may be harder to auscultate the bruit or feel the thrill in this type of access because of the absence of a venous anastomosis.

Surgical creation of AV access for HD has several risks. These include distal ischemia (*steal syndrome*) and pain because too much arterial blood is being shunted or "stolen" from the distal extremity. Manifestations of steal syndrome are pain distal to the access site, numbness or tingling of fingers that may worsen during dialysis, and poor capillary refill. Aneurysms can develop in the AV access and can rupture if left untreated.

> **! SAFETY ALERT** AV Fistulas and Grafts
> - Never perform BP measurements, IV line insertion, or venipuncture in an extremity with AV access.
> - These special precautions are taken to prevent infection and clotting of the vascular access.
> - When a patient is hospitalized, place signs in patient's room and label the arm with a band that says, "No BP, blood draws, or IV in this arm."

Temporary Vascular Access. When immediate vascular access is needed, catheterization of the internal jugular or femoral vein is done. A flexible catheter inserted at the bedside into 1 of these large veins gives access to the circulation without surgery (Fig. 46.10). The catheters usually have a double external lumen with an internal septum separating the 2 internal segments. One lumen is used for blood removal and the other for blood return (Fig. 46.11, *A* and *B*). Temporary catheters have high rates of infection, dislodgment, and malfunction. A patient should not be discharged from the hospital with a temporary catheter in place.

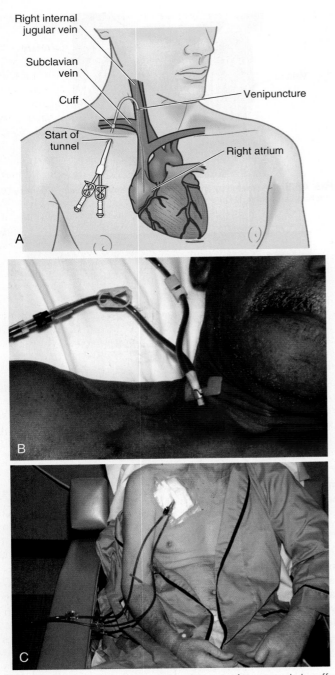

FIG. 46.11 A, Right internal jugular placement for a tunneled, cuffed semipermanent catheter. B, Temporary hemodialysis catheter in place. C, Long-term cuffed hemodialysis catheter. (B and C, Courtesy Dr. Stephen Van Voorst, MD.)

Long-term cuffed HD catheters are often used for temporary vascular access. These catheters give temporary access while the patient is waiting for fistula placement or as long-term access when other forms of access have failed. They exit on the upper chest wall and are tunneled subcutaneously to the internal or external jugular vein (Fig. 46.11, C). The catheter tip rests in the right atrium. It has 1 or 2 subcutaneous Dacron cuffs that prevent infection from tracking along the catheter and anchor the catheter, eliminating the need for sutures.

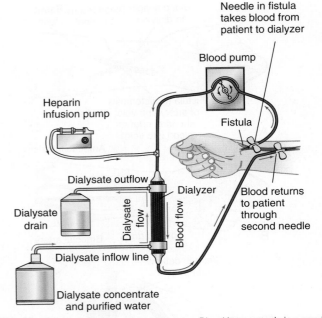

FIG. 46.12 Parts of a hemodialysis system. Blood is removed via a needle inserted in a fistula or via catheter lumen. It is propelled to the dialyzer by a blood pump. Heparin is infused either as a predialysis bolus or through a heparin pump continuously to prevent clotting. Dialysate is pumped in and flows in the opposite direction of the blood. The dialyzed blood is returned to the patient through a second needle or catheter lumen. Old dialysate and ultrafiltrate are drained and discarded.

Dialyzers

The HD dialyzer is a plastic cartridge that has thousands of parallel hollow tubes or fibers. The fibers are semipermeable membranes made of cellulose-based or other synthetic materials. The blood is pumped into the top of the cartridge and dispersed into all the fibers. Dialysis fluid (*dialysate*) is pumped into the bottom of the cartridge and bathes the outside of the fibers. Ultrafiltration, diffusion, and osmosis occur across the pores of this semipermeable membrane. When the dialyzed blood reaches the end of the thousands of semipermeable fibers, it converges into a single tube that returns it to the patient. Dialyzers differ in surface area, membrane composition and thickness, clearance of waste products, and removal of fluid.

Procedure for Hemodialysis

The needles used for HD are large bore, usually 14 to 16 gauge. They are inserted into the fistula or graft to obtain vascular access. One needle is placed to pull blood from the circulation to the HD machine, and the other needle is used to return the dialyzed blood to the patient. The needles are attached via tubing to dialysis lines. If a patient has a catheter, the 2 blood lines are attached to the 2 catheter lumens. The needle closer to the fistula (red catheter lumen) pulls blood from the patient to the dialyzer using a blood pump. Blood is returned from the dialyzer to the patient through the second needle (blue catheter lumen).[27]

When blood comes in contact with a foreign material, such as the dialyzer, it tends to clot. Heparin is added to the blood to prevent clotting.

In addition to the dialyzer, a dialysate delivery and monitoring system is used (Fig. 46.12). This system pumps the dialysate through the dialyzer, countercurrent to the blood flow. To end

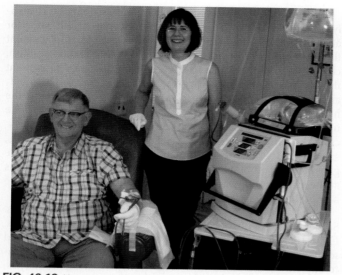

FIG. 46.13 Home hemodialysis is growing in popularity, and machines are more compact. (From NxStage Medical, Inc, Lawrence, MA.)

the treatment, a saline solution is used to return the blood in the extracorporeal circuit back to the patient through the vascular access. The needles are removed from the patient, and firm pressure is applied to the venipuncture sites until the bleeding stops.

Before beginning treatment, assess fluid status (weight, BP, peripheral edema, lung and heart sounds), condition of vascular access, and temperature. The difference between the last postdialysis weight and the present predialysis weight determines the ultrafiltration or the amount of weight (from fluid) to be removed. While the patient is on dialysis, take vital signs at least every 30 to 60 minutes because rapid BP changes may occur.

Settings and Schedules for Hemodialysis. Most HD patients are treated in a community-based center and dialyze for 3 to 4 hours 3 days per week. Most people sleep, read, talk, or watch television during HD.

Other schedule options for HD are short daily HD and long nocturnal HD. The patient receiving long nocturnal HD has the advantage of sleeping while dialyzing. Each nocturnal treatment lasts 6 to 8 hours, and the patient dialyzes up to 6 times per week.

In addition to in-center HD, home HD is available (Fig. 46.13). The use of home HD often depends on a patient's family support. One of the main advantages of home HD is that it allows greater freedom in choosing dialysis times. In short daily HD, the patient dialyzes for 2½ to 3 hours per session 5 to 6 days per week. Short daily HD is usually done at home.

Patients who choose daily dialysis or nocturnal dialysis may have fewer uremic symptoms, tend to need fewer medications, and have fewer dialysis-related side effects (e.g., hypotension, cramps). In addition, they have more autonomy. Although daily home HD offers the potential of significant health benefits, only about 2% of HD patients dialyze at home.

Complications of Hemodialysis

Hypotension. Hypotension that occurs during HD primarily results from rapid removal of vascular volume (hypovolemia), decreased cardiac output, and decreased systemic vascular resistance. The drop in BP may cause light-headedness, nausea, vomiting, seizures, vision changes, and chest pain from cardiac ischemia. The usual treatment for hypotension includes

decreasing the volume of fluid removed and infusing 0.9% saline solution.

Muscle Cramps. We do not completely understand the cause of muscle cramps in HD. Factors associated with developing muscle cramps include hypotension, hypovolemia, high ultrafiltration rate, and low-sodium dialysis solution. Treatment includes reducing the ultrafiltration rate and giving fluids (saline, glucose, mannitol). Hypertonic saline is not recommended since the sodium load can be problematic. Hypertonic glucose is preferred.

Loss of Blood. Blood loss may result from blood not being completely rinsed from the dialyzer, accidental separation of blood tubing, dialysis membrane rupture, or bleeding after removing the needles at the end of HD. If a patient has received too much heparin or has clotting problems, postdialysis bleeding can occur. It is essential to rinse back all blood, avoid excess anticoagulation, and hold firm but nonocclusive pressure on access sites until the risk for bleeding has passed.

Hepatitis. Hepatitis B used to have an unusually high prevalence in dialysis patients, but the incidence today is low. Lower transfusion requirements, screening, and recommendations for vaccinations have lowered the incidence. Outbreaks of hepatitis B still occur, likely from breaks in infection control practices. To prevent transmission, all patients and personnel in dialysis units receive hepatitis B vaccine.

Currently, hepatitis C virus (HCV) causes most cases of hepatitis in dialysis patients. (Hepatitis is discussed in more detail in Chapter 43.) About 10% of patients undergoing dialysis in the United States are positive for anti-HCV, which indicates a previous infection. Infection control precautions are mandated in caring for the patient with hepatitis C to protect the patient and staff (see Chapter 14). Currently no vaccine is available for hepatitis C.

Effectiveness of Hemodialysis

HD is still an imperfect therapy for management of ESRD. It cannot fully replace the normal biologic functions of the kidneys. It can ease many of the symptoms of CKD and, if started early, can prevent certain complications. It does not alter the accelerated rate of CVD and the related high mortality rate.

The yearly death rate of patients receiving maintenance HD is around 19% to 24%. CVD (stroke, MI) causes most deaths. Infectious complications are the second leading cause of death.[27]

Adaptation to maintenance HD varies considerably. At first, many patients feel positive about the dialysis because it makes them feel better and keeps them alive, but there is often great ambivalence about whether it is worthwhile. Dependence on a machine is a reality. In response to their illness, dialysis patients may be nonadherent or depressed and show suicidal tendencies. The primary nursing goals are to (1) help the patient to maintain a healthy self-image and (2) return the patient to the highest level of function possible, including returning to work.

CONTINUOUS RENAL REPLACEMENT THERAPY

Continuous renal replacement therapy (CRRT) is a method for treating AKI. It provides a means by which uremic toxins and fluids are removed while acid-base status and electrolytes are adjusted slowly and continuously in a hemodynamically unstable patient. The principle of CRRT is to dialyze patients in a more physiologic way (over 24 hours), just like the kidneys. CRRT is contraindicated if a patient has life-threatening manifestations of uremia (hyperkalemia, pericarditis) that need rapid treatment. CRRT can be used in conjunction with HD.

Several types of CRRT are available (Table 46.13). CRRT often uses the venovenous approaches of continuous venovenous hemofiltration (CVVH), continuous venovenous hemodialysis (CVVHD), and continuous venovenous hemodiafiltration (CVVHDF).

Vascular access for CRRT is achieved by using a double-lumen catheter (as used in HD [Fig. 46.10]) placed in the jugular or femoral vein. A blood pump propels the blood through the circuit. A highly permeable, hollow-fiber hemofilter removes plasma water and nonprotein solutes, which are collectively termed *ultrafiltrate*. The ultrafiltration rate (UFR) may range from 0 to 500 mL/hr. Under the influence of hydrostatic pressure and osmotic pressure, water and nonprotein solutes pass out of the filter into the extracapillary space and drain through the ultrafiltrate port into a collection device (drainage bag) (Fig. 46.14). The remaining fluid continues through the filter and returns to the patient via the return port of the double-lumen catheter.

TABLE 46.13 **Continuous Renal Replacement Therapies**		
Therapy	**Abbreviation**	**Purpose**
Continuous venovenous hemofiltration	CVVH	Removes fluid and solutes Requires replacement fluid
Slow continuous ultrafiltration	SCUF	Simplified version of CVVH Removes fluid No fluid replacement required
Continuous venovenous hemodialysis	CVVHD	Removes fluids and solutes Requires dialysate and replacement fluid
Continuous venovenous hemodiafiltration	CVVHDF	Removes fluids and solutes Requires dialysate and replacement fluid

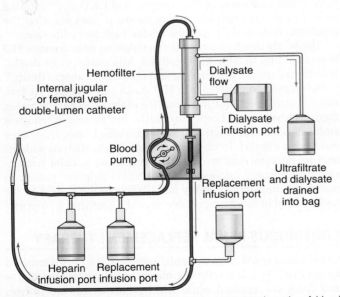

FIG. 46.14 Basic schematic of continuous venovenous therapies. A blood pump is required to pump blood through the circuit. Replacement ports are used for instilling replacement fluids and can be given prefilter or postfilter. Dialysate port is used for infusing dialysis solution. Regardless of modality, ultrafiltrate is drained via the ultrafiltration drain port.

As ultrafiltrate drains out of the hemofilter, fluid and electrolyte replacements can be infused through a port found before or after the filter as the blood returns to the patient. Replacement fluid is designed to replace volume and solutes, such as sodium, chloride, HCO_3^-, and glucose. The infusion rate of replacement fluid is determined by the degree of fluid and electrolyte imbalance. Replacement fluid infused into the infusion port before the hemofilter allows for greater clearance of urea and can decrease filter clotting. An infusion port after the filter dilutes intravascular fluid and decreases the concentration of unwanted solutes, such as BUN, creatinine, and potassium. Anticoagulants are given to prevent blood clotting. They may be infused as a bolus at the initiation of CRRT or through an infusion port before the hemofilter.

The type of CRRT can be customized to the patient's needs. Some types involve the introduction of replacement fluids. CVVHD and CVVHDF use dialysate. Dialysis fluid is attached to the distal end of the hemofilter, and the fluid is pumped countercurrent to the blood flow (Fig. 46.14). As in hemodialysis, diffusion of solutes and ultrafiltration via hydrostatic pressure and osmosis occur. This is an ideal treatment for a patient who needs both fluid and solute control but cannot tolerate the rapid fluid shifts associated with HD.

Several features of CRRT differ from HD:
- The blood pump in CRRT runs at a slower (150 mL/min average) rate. This may improve hemodynamic stability.
- Continuous rather than intermittent. Fluid volume can be removed over days (24 hours to more than 2 weeks) versus hours (3 to 4 hours).
- Solute removal can occur by *convection* (no dialysate required) in addition to osmosis and diffusion.
- Causes less hemodynamic instability (e.g., hypotension)
- Does not need constant monitoring by a specialized HD nurse but does require a trained ICU nurse
- Does not require complicated HD equipment

CRRT can be continued as long as 30 to 40 days. The hemofilter should be changed every 24 to 48 hours because of loss of filtration efficiency or potential for clotting. The ultrafiltrate should be clear yellow. Specimens may be obtained for serum chemistries. If the ultrafiltrate becomes bloody or blood tinged, suspect a rupture in the filter membrane. Stop treatment to prevent blood loss.

Specific nursing interventions include obtaining weights and monitoring and documenting laboratory values daily to ensure adequate fluid and electrolyte balance. Assess hourly intake and output, vital signs, and hemodynamic status. Although reductions in central venous pressure and pulmonary artery pressure are expected, there should be little change in mean arterial pressure or cardiac output. Assess and maintain the patency of the CRRT system. Care for the patient's vascular access site to prevent infection. Once the patient's AKI is resolved or there is a decision to withdraw treatment, CRRT is stopped and the needle(s) removed.

WEARABLE ARTIFICIAL KIDNEY

The wearable artificial kidney (WAK) has recently been developed and is approved for use to improve the quality of life of an ESRD patient. The WAK is a miniaturized dialysis machine that can be worn on the body. The carrier resembles a tool belt. The device connects to a patient via a catheter. Like conventional dialysis machines, it is designed to filter the blood of

ESRD patients. Unlike current portable or stationary dialysis machines, it can run continuously on batteries. The present version weighs about 10 lb, but future modifications could make it lighter and more streamlined.[28]

KIDNEY TRANSPLANTATION

Major advances have been made in kidney transplantation since the first live donor kidney transplant was done in 1954 between identical twins. These advances include organ procurement and preservation, surgical techniques, tissue typing and matching, immunosuppressant therapy, and prevention and treatment of graft rejection. A general discussion of organ transplantation is in Chapter 13.

Even though kidney transplantation is the best treatment option available to patients with ESRD, fewer than 4% ever receive a transplant. This is due to the large disparity between the supply and demand for kidneys. Every year thousands are waiting for kidney transplants (more than 100,000 are currently on the list), yet only about 17,000 transplants take place every year. Most die while waiting. Transplants from a deceased (cadaveric) donor usually require a prolonged waiting period, with differences in waiting time depending on age, gender, and race. Average wait times in the United States for a deceased kidney usually range from 2 to 5 years.[29-31]

Kidney transplantation is very successful, with 1-year graft survival rates over 90% for deceased donor transplants and 95% for live donor transplants.[30] An advantage of kidney transplantation when compared with dialysis is that it reverses many of the pathophysiologic changes associated with renal disease. It eliminates the dependence on dialysis and the accompanying dietary and lifestyle restrictions. Transplantation is less expensive than dialysis after the first year.

Recipient Selection

Appropriate recipient selection is important for a successful outcome. Candidacy is determined by a variety of medical and psychosocial factors that vary among transplant centers. Some transplant programs exclude patients who are morbidly obese or who continue to smoke despite smoking cessation interventions. A careful evaluation is done to identify and minimize potential complications after transplantation. Certain patients, particularly those with CVD and diabetes, are considered high risk. They must be carefully evaluated and then monitored closely after transplantation.

For a small number of patients who are approaching ESRD, a *preemptive transplant* (before dialysis is required) is possible if they have a living donor. This approach is best for patients with diabetes, who have a much higher mortality rate on dialysis than nondiabetics.

Contraindications to transplantation include advanced cancer, refractory or untreated heart disease, chronic respiratory failure, extensive vascular disease, chronic infection, and unresolved psychosocial disorders (e.g., nonadherence to medical regimens, alcohol use, drug use). Being HIV-positive or having hepatitis B or C infection is not a contraindication to transplantation.

Surgical procedures may be done before transplantation based on the results of the recipient evaluation. Coronary artery bypass or coronary angioplasty may be needed for advanced coronary artery disease. Cholecystectomy may be necessary for patients with a history of gallstones, biliary obstruction, or cholecystitis. On rare occasions, bilateral nephrectomies are done for patients with refractory hypertension, recurrent UTIs, or grossly enlarged kidneys from polycystic kidney disease. In general, the recipient's own kidneys are not removed before receiving a kidney transplant.

Histocompatibility Studies

Histocompatibility studies, including human leukocyte antigen (HLA) testing and crossmatching, are discussed in Chapter 13 on p. 205.

Donor Sources

Kidneys for transplantation are obtained from compatible blood-type deceased donors, blood relatives, emotionally related (close and distant) living donors (e.g., spouses, distant cousins,), and altruistic living donors who are known (friends) or unknown to the recipient. Living donation accounts for around 27% of all kidney transplants in the United States. Most transplant centers regard them as the preferred donation modality. [31]

ETHICAL/LEGAL DILEMMAS
Allocation of Resources

Situation

T.H., a transplant nurse coordinator, is considering her feelings about 2 patients who are being evaluated for placement on the deceased kidney transplant waiting list. One patient is a 40-yr-old black schoolteacher. She is married and has 2 children. The other patient is a 22-yr-old unemployed white man. He misses 3 or 4 dialysis treatments per month and does not take his antihypertensive drugs consistently.

Ethical/Legal Points for Consideration

- Ethical principles that are important in the allocation of human organs include utility and justice.
- Allocation policies based on utility require we use standardized outcome measures to give a rough estimate about which allocation would produce the greatest good. Factors considered include patient survival, quality of life, availability of alternative treatments, and age.
- We must give equal respect and concern to each patient. Allocation based on social characteristics (e.g., race, socioeconomic class, gender) conflict with the principle of justice and violate constitutional law.
- Constitutional laws prohibit discrimination based on race, gender, religion, and ethnic background. It is highly unlikely that these standard prohibitions will change. It is possible that definitions of unhealthy behavior, such as substance use, alcohol use, smoking, and obesity, may be used to screen out candidates.
- Nurses are concerned about social justice because of their health advocacy role. Today the situation is immensely more complex because of the cost and availability of care.

Discussion Questions

1. What does the American Nurses Association Code of Ethics say about how you as a nurse should view patients?
2. What are your thoughts about which patient should receive the next available kidney transplant?
3. Can you assign value to the lives of various patients? Who is worth more?

Live Donors. Live donors undergo an extensive evaluation to ensure that they are in good health and have no history of disease that would place them at risk for developing kidney disease or operative complications. Crossmatches are done at the time of the evaluation and about a week before the transplant to ensure that no antibodies to the donor are present or that the antibody titer is below the allowed level. Advantages of a live donor kidney include (1) better patient and graft survival rates regardless of histocompatibility match, (2) immediate organ availability, (3) immediate function due to minimal *cold time* (kidney out of body and not getting blood supply), and (4) the opportunity to have the recipient in the best possible medical condition because the surgery is elective.

The potential donor sees a nephrologist for a complete history and physical examination and laboratory and diagnostic studies. Laboratory studies include a 24-hour urine study for creatinine clearance and total protein, complete blood count, and chemistry and electrolyte profiles. Hepatitis B and C, HIV, and cytomegalovirus (CMV) testing is done to assess for transmitted diseases. An ECG and chest x-ray are done. A renal ultrasound and renal arteriogram or 3-dimensional CT scan is done to ensure that the blood vessels supplying each kidney are adequate and that no anomalies exist and to determine which kidney will be used in the transplant.

A transplant psychologist or social worker determines if the person is emotionally stable and able to deal with the issues related to organ donation. All donors must be informed about the risks and benefits of donation, the potential short- and long-term complications, and what to expect during the hospitalization and recovery phases. Kidney donation is considered safe without any long-term health consequences. Although the recipient's insurance covers the costs of the evaluation and surgery, no compensation is available for lost wages during the posthospitalization recovery period. This period can last 6 weeks or longer.

When there is ABO incompatibility between a donor and recipient, paired donor exchange is a viable alternative. *Paired organ donation,* in which one donor/recipient pair who are incompatible or poorly matched with each other find another donor/recipient pair with whom they can exchange kidneys. Thus a spouse (person A) who wants to donate a kidney to his wife (person B) but is incompatible is paired with another donor/recipient pair involving a son with ESRD (person C) and his mother (person D). In this example, person A would donate his kidney to person C, and person D would donate her kidney to person B. Paired organ donation is the practice of matching biologically incompatible donor/recipient pairs to permit transplantation of both candidates with a well-matched organ.

Another option for ABO incompatibility or a positive crossmatch between the donor and recipient is to use plasmapheresis to remove antibodies from the recipient. This allows transplant candidates to receive kidneys from live donors with blood types that we have traditionally considered incompatible. After the transplant, the patient undergoes more plasmapheresis treatments.

Deceased Donors. Deceased (cadaver) kidney donors are relatively healthy persons who have an irreversible brain injury and are declared brain dead. The most common causes of injury are cerebral trauma from motor vehicle accidents or gunshot wounds, intracerebral or subarachnoid hemorrhage, and anoxic brain damage caused by cardiac arrest. The brain-dead donor must have effective CV function and be supported on a ventilator to preserve the organs.

Even if the donor carried a signed donor card, permission from the donor's legal next of kin is still requested after brain death has been declared. That is why it is important for you to talk with your family about your wishes before losing the capacity to convey your desires.

In deceased kidney donation, the kidneys are removed and preserved. They can be preserved for up to 72 hours. Most transplant surgeons prefer to transplant kidneys before the cold time (time outside of the body when being transported from the deceased donor to the recipient) reaches 24 hours. Prolonged cold time increases the chance that the kidney will not function immediately, and ATN may develop.

The United Network for Organ Sharing (UNOS) distributes deceased donor kidneys using an objective computerized point system. A new kidney allocation system (KAS) started in early 2015 after several years of refinement. All donor kidneys receive a kidney donor profile index (KDPI). The KDPI includes 10 donor factors that evaluate the risk for a kidney transplant failure. The KDPI can help predict how long a kidney may function. Each kidney transplant candidate gets an individual Estimated Post-Transplant Survival (EPTS) score. This score ranges from 0 to 100 percent. The score is related to how long a candidate will need a functioning kidney transplant when compared with other candidates. For example, a person with an EPTS score of 20% is likely to need a kidney longer than 80% of other candidates. The EPTS score is based on age, length of time on dialysis, previous transplants, and having diabetes.[32]

When a donor becomes available, the donor's key information is compared with the data of all patients awaiting transplantation locally and nationwide. When a kidney arrives at the recipient's transplant center, a final crossmatch is done. It must be negative for the deceased donor transplantation to proceed.

The only exception is if a patient needs an emergency transplant or if a donor and recipient match on all 6 HLA antigens (zero antigen mismatch). The patient meeting either of these criteria goes to the top of the list. Emergency transplants receive priority because the patient is facing imminent death if not transplanted. If a zero antigen mismatch patient is found nationally, since statistically these grafts have better survival rates, one of the donor kidneys must be sent to that recipient's transplant center regardless of location.

Surgical Procedure

Live Donor. A transplant surgeon performs the live donor nephrectomy. The donor's surgery begins 1 to 2 hours before the recipient's surgery. The recipient is surgically prepared for the kidney transplant in a nearby operating room.

Laparoscopic donor nephrectomy is the most common technique for removing a kidney in a living donor. (Laparoscopic nephrectomy is discussed in Chapter 45.) After the kidney is removed, it is flushed with a chilled, sterile electrolyte solution and prepared for immediate transplant into the recipient. The use of a laparoscopic donor nephrectomy procedure is minimally invasive, with fewer risks and shorter recovery time than an open procedure. The laparoscopic approach significantly decreases hospital stay, pain, operative blood loss, debilitation, and length of time off work. For these reasons, the number of people willing to donate a kidney has increased significantly.

For an *open (conventional) nephrectomy,* the donor is placed in the lateral decubitus position on the operating table so that the flank is exposed laterally. An incision is made at the level of the eleventh rib. The rib may have to be removed to give adequate visualization of the kidney.

Kidney Transplant Recipient. The transplanted kidney is usually placed extraperitoneally in the iliac fossa. The right iliac fossa is preferred to facilitate anastomoses of the blood vessels and ureter and minimize the occurrence of paralytic ileus. A urinary catheter is placed into the bladder, and an antibiotic solution is instilled to distend the bladder and decrease the risk for

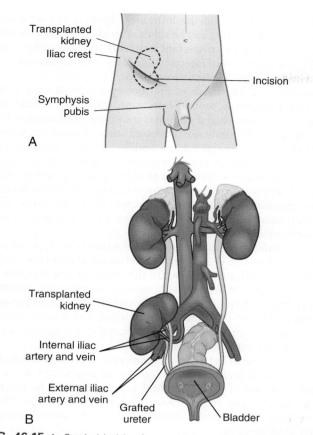

FIG. 46.15 A, Surgical incision for a renal transplant. B, Surgical placement of transplanted kidney.

infection. A crescent-shaped incision is made extending from the iliac crest to the symphysis pubis (Fig. 46.15).

Rapid revascularization is critical to prevent ischemic injury to the kidney. The donor artery is anastomosed to the recipient's internal iliac (hypogastric) or external iliac artery. The donor vein is anastomosed to the recipient's external iliac vein. When the anastomoses are complete, the clamps are released, and blood flow to the kidney is reestablished. The kidney should become firm and pink. Urine may begin to flow from the ureter at once. The donor ureter is then tunneled through the bladder submucosa before entering the bladder cavity and being sutured in place. This approach is called *ureteroneocystostomy*. This allows the bladder wall to compress the ureter as it contracts for micturition, thereby preventing reflux of urine up the ureter into the transplanted kidney. Transplant surgery takes about 3 to 4 hours.

❖ NURSING MANAGEMENT: KIDNEY TRANSPLANT RECIPIENT

◆ Preoperative Care

Nursing care of the patient in the preoperative phase includes emotional and physical preparation for surgery. Because the patient and caregiver may have been waiting years for the kidney transplant, a review of the operative procedure and what can be expected in the immediate postoperative recovery period is necessary. Stress that there is a chance the kidney may not function at once, and dialysis may be needed for days to weeks. Review the need for immunosuppressive drugs and measures to prevent infection.

To ensure the patient is in the best physical condition for surgery, an ECG, chest x-ray, and laboratory studies are done. Dialysis may be needed before surgery for fluid overload or hyperkalemia. Because dialysis may be needed after transplantation, the patency of the vascular access must be maintained. Label the vascular access extremity "dialysis access, no procedures" to prevent use of that extremity for BP measurement, blood drawing, or IV infusions. A patient on PD must empty the peritoneal cavity of all dialysate solution before going to surgery and have the PD catheter capped.

◆ Postoperative Care

◆ **Live Donor.** Postoperative care for the donor is similar to that after open (conventional) or laparoscopic nephrectomy (see Chapter 45). Closely monitor renal function to assess for impairment and the hematocrit to assess for bleeding. Donors usually have more pain than the recipient. Donors who had an open surgical approach may have more pain than those after a laparoscopic approach.

Donors who had an open approach are usually discharged from the hospital in 4 or 5 days and return to work in 6 to 8 weeks. With a laparoscopic approach, donors are discharged from the hospital in 2 to 4 days and return to work in 4 to 6 weeks. The surgeon sees the donor 1 to 2 weeks after discharge.

Nurses caring for the living donor must acknowledge the precious gift that this person has given. The donor has taken physical, emotional, and financial risks to help the recipient. It is vital that the donor is not forgotten after surgery. The donor will need support if the donated organ does not work at once or for some reason fails.

◆ **Kidney Transplant Recipient.** The priority during the postoperative period is maintaining fluid and electrolyte balance. Kidney transplant recipients require close monitoring and spend the first 12 to 24 hours in the ICU. Large volumes of urine may be made soon after the blood supply to the transplanted kidney is reestablished. This diuresis is due to the (1) new kidney's ability to filter BUN, which acts as an osmotic diuretic; (2) abundance of fluids given during the surgery; and (3) initial renal tubular dysfunction, which inhibits the kidney from concentrating urine normally. Urine output during this phase may be as high as 1 L/hr and gradually decreases as the BUN and serum creatinine levels return toward normal. Urine output is replaced with fluids milliliter for milliliter hourly for the first 12 to 24 hours.

Central venous pressure readings are essential for monitoring fluid status. Dehydration must be avoided to prevent renal hypoperfusion and renal tubular damage. Electrolyte monitoring to assess for hyponatremia and hypokalemia often associated with rapid diuresis is critical. Treatment with potassium supplements or infusion of 0.9% normal saline may be needed. IV sodium bicarbonate may be given if the patient develops metabolic acidosis from a delay in the return of kidney function.

ATN in the transplanted kidney can occur because of prolonged cold times causing ischemic damage or the use of marginal cadaveric donors (those who are medically suboptimal). While the patient is in ATN, dialysis is needed to maintain fluid and electrolyte balance. Some patients have high-output ATN with the ability to excrete fluid but not metabolic wastes or electrolytes. Other patients have oliguric or anuric ATN. These patients are at risk for fluid overload in the immediate postoperative period and must be assessed closely for the need for dialysis. ATN can last from days to weeks, with gradually improving kidney function. Most patients with ATN are discharged from the hospital on dialysis. This is extremely discouraging for the patient, who needs reassurance that renal function usually improves. Dialysis is discontinued when urine output increases and serum creatinine and BUN begin to normalize.

A sudden decrease in urine output in the early postoperative period is a cause for concern. It may be due to dehydration, rejection, a urine leak, or obstruction. A common cause of early obstruction is a blood clot in the urinary catheter. Catheter patency must be maintained since the catheter stays in the bladder for 3 to 5 days to allow the ureter-bladder anastomosis to heal. If you suspect blood clots, gentle catheter irrigation (if ordered) can reestablish patency.

With a hospital length of stay averaging 4 to 5 days, identify and address discharge planning and teaching needs early. Patient teaching ensures a smooth transition from the hospital to home. Include how to recognize signs of rejection, infection, and any complications of surgery. Frequent blood tests and clinic visits help to detect rejection early.

Immunosuppressive Therapy

The goal of immunosuppression is to adequately suppress the immune response to prevent rejection of the transplanted kidney while maintaining sufficient immunity to prevent overwhelming infection. Immunosuppressive therapy is discussed in Chapter 13.

Complications of Transplantation

Complications of PD, HD, and kidney transplantation are compared in Table 46.14.

Rejection. Rejection is one of the major problems after kidney transplantation. Rejection can be hyperacute, acute, or chronic. The types of rejection are discussed in Chapter 13 on p. 206. Patients with chronic rejection may be placed on the transplant list to be retransplanted before dialysis is required.

Infection. Infection is a significant cause of morbidity and mortality after transplantation.[32] The transplant recipient is at risk for infection because of suppression of the body's normal defense mechanisms by surgery, immunosuppressive drugs, and the effects of ESRD. Underlying systemic illness, such as diabetes or SLE, malnutrition, and older age, can further compound the negative effects on the immune response. The signs and symptoms of infection can be subtle. You must be astute in your assessment of kidney transplant recipients because prompt diagnosis and treatment of infection improves patient outcomes.

The common infections seen in the first month after transplantation are like those of any postoperative patient. These include pneumonia, wound infections, UTIs, and IV line and drain infections. Fungal and viral infections are common due to the patient's immunosuppressed state. Fungal infections include *Candida, Cryptococcus,* and *Aspergillus* organisms and *Pneumocystis jiroveci.* Fungal infections are hard to treat, require prolonged treatment periods, and often involve the administration of nephrotoxic drugs. Transplant recipients usually receive prophylactic antifungal drugs to prevent these infections, such as clotrimazole, fluconazole (Diflucan), and trimethoprim/sulfamethoxazole (Bactrim).

Viral infections, including CMV, Epstein-Barr virus, herpes simplex virus (HSV), varicella-zoster virus, and polyomavirus (e.g., BK virus), can be primary infections or reactivations of existing disease. Primary infections occur as new infections after transplantation from an exogenous source such as the donated organ or a blood transfusion. Reactivation occurs when a virus exists in a patient and becomes reactivated after transplantation because of immunosuppression.

CMV is one of the most common viral infections. If a recipient has never had CMV and receives an organ from a donor with a history of CMV, antiviral prophylaxis will be needed (e.g., ganciclovir, valganciclovir [Valcyte]). To prevent HSV infections, oral acyclovir (Zovirax) is given for several months after the transplant.

Cardiovascular Disease. CVD is the leading cause of death after renal transplantation.[32] Transplant recipients have an increased incidence of atherosclerotic vascular disease. Hypertension, dyslipidemia, diabetes, smoking, rejection, infections, and increased homocysteine levels (many of which existed prior to the transplant) can all contribute to CVD. Immunosuppressants can worsen hypertension and dyslipidemia.

Teach the patient to control risk factors, such as high cholesterol, triglycerides, and blood glucose and weight gain. Adherence to the prescribed antihypertensive regimen is essential to prevent CV events and damage to the new kidney.

Cancers. The overall incidence of cancer in kidney transplant recipients is greater than in the general population, primarily because of immunosuppressive therapy. Not only do immunosuppressants suppress the immune system to prevent rejection, they also suppress the ability to fight infection and the production of abnormal cells, including cancer cells.

The most common types of cancer after transplant are (1) skin cancers—basal and squamous cell cancers and melanoma—and (2) *posttransplant lymphoproliferative disorder (PTLD).* Most PTLDs are of B-cell origin, associated with Epstein-Barr virus (EBV), and cause aggressive lymphomas (Hodgkin's and non-Hodgkin's lymphoma). Most cases of PTLD occur within the first year of transplant.

Patients are also at risk for cancers of the colorectum, breast, cervix, liver, stomach, oropharynx, anus, vulva, and penis. Regular screening for cancer is an important part of the transplant recipient's preventive care. Teach the patient to avoid sun exposure by using protective clothing and sunscreens to minimize the incidence of skin cancers.

Recurrence of Original Kidney Disease. Recurrence of the original disease that destroyed the native kidneys occurs in

TABLE 46.14 Complications of Dialysis and Transplantation

Peritoneal Dialysis (PD)	Hemodialysis (HD)	Transplantation
• Abdominal pain	• CVD	• Cancers
• Carbohydrate abnormalities	• Disequilibrium syndrome	• Corticosteroid-related complications
• Catheter outflow	• Exsanguination	• CVD
• CVD	• Hepatitis	• Recurrence of kidney disease
• Encapsulating sclerosing peritonitis	• Hypotension	• Susceptibility to infection
• Exit site infection	• Infection, including sepsis	• Transplant rejection
• Hernias	• Muscle cramp	• Hyperacute
• Lipid abnormalities		• Acute
• Lower back pain		• Chronic
• Peritonitis		
• Protein loss		
• Pulmonary problems		
• Atelectasis		
• Pneumonia		
• Bronchitis		

some kidney transplant recipients. It is most common with certain types of glomerulonephritis, immunoglobulin A (IgA) nephropathy, diabetic nephropathy, and focal segmental sclerosis. Disease recurrence can result in the loss of a functioning kidney transplant. Patients must be advised before transplantation if they have a disease known to recur.

Corticosteroid-Related Complications. Aseptic necrosis of the hips, knees, and other joints can result from chronic corticosteroid therapy and renal osteodystrophy. Other significant problems related to corticosteroids include peptic ulcer disease, diabetes, cataracts, dyslipidemia, infections, and cancers. The use of tacrolimus and other immunosuppressants has allowed corticosteroid doses to be much lower than they were in the past.

Many transplant programs have started corticosteroid-free drug regimens because of the problems of long-term corticosteroid use. Other centers withdraw patients from corticosteroids after transplantation. For patients who stay on corticosteroids, vigilant monitoring for side effects and prompt treatment is essential. Corticosteroid therapy as immunosuppression is discussed in Chapter 13 on p. 207.

Gerontologic Considerations: Chronic Kidney Disease

The incidence of CKD in the United States is increasing most rapidly in older adults. The most common diseases leading to renal disease in older adults are hypertension and diabetes.[33]

The care of older patients is particularly challenging, not only because of the normal physiologic changes of aging but also because of the disabilities, chronic diseases, and co-morbid conditions that occur with aging. Physiologic changes include decreased cardiopulmonary function, bone loss, immunodeficiency, altered protein synthesis, impaired cognition, and altered drug metabolism. Malnutrition is common in these patients for a variety of reasons, including lack of mobility, social isolation, physical disability, and impaired cognitive function.

When conservative therapy for CKD is no longer effective, the older patient needs to consider the best treatment modality based on physical and emotional health, personal preferences, and availability of support. Quality-of-life measures show no justification for excluding the older adult from dialysis programs. Rationing dialysis based on age alone is not a reasonable decision for health care professionals to make. Older adults have successfully used dialysis, especially PD. Many choose treatment with in-center HD due to a lack of help in the home and reluctance to manage the technology of home HD or PD. Establishing vascular access for HD may be difficult because of atherosclerotic changes.

Although transplantation is an option, older adults must be carefully screened to ensure that the benefits of transplantation outweigh the risks.[34] Although a living donor is preferable, this may not be an option for many older patients.

The most common cause of death in older ESRD patients is CVD (MI, stroke), followed by withdrawal from dialysis. If a competent patient decides to withdraw from dialysis, it is essential to support the patient and family. Ethical issues (see the Ethical/Legal Dilemmas box) to consider in this situation include patient competency, benefit versus burden of treatment, and futility of treatment. Withdrawal from treatment is not a failure if the patient is well informed and comfortable with the decision.

ETHICAL/LEGAL DILEMMAS
Withdrawing Treatment

Situation

L.R., a 70-yr-old patient with diabetes and ESRD, has been on dialysis for 10 years. He tells you that he wants to stop his dialysis. His quality of life has diminished during the past 2 years since his wife died. He is not a transplant candidate.

Ethical/Legal Points for Consideration

- Informed consent includes the legal right to refuse treatment. However, the right to refuse may be more difficult if (1) it is contrary to the wishes of family and friends, (2) the treatment still appears to have effectiveness, and (3) the treatment has been in place for some time.
- Quality-of-life decisions often outweigh the benefit against the burden of treatment. When a treatment becomes too burdensome, the patient, if competent, may request to withdraw the treatment.
- It must be determined whether some other treatable problem, such as depression, may be clouding the patient's judgment.
- Although there is no ethical or legal difference between withdrawing treatment and withholding treatment, withdrawing treatment feels different because it requires an action.
- Some health care professionals become conflicted when asked to withdraw treatment, since they may think they are contributing to the patient's premature death.
- If a decision is made to withdraw treatment, the interprofessional care team, patient, and family should develop a follow-up plan that includes palliative care and hospice support.

Discussion Questions

1. How should you respond to L.R.'s request?
2. What is the American Nurses Association's position on withdrawing or withholding treatment that no longer benefits the patient or causes suffering?

CASE STUDY
Chronic Kidney Disease

(© iStockphoto/ Thinkstock.)

Patient Profile

M.B. is a 56-yr-old black college professor. He is seen by his primary care provider for a routine physical examination. He has not seen an HCP in a little over a year. He reports generalized malaise, frequent urination, and "increasing thirst." His medical history is significant for borderline hypertension and dyslipidemia. He smokes 1 pack of cigarettes per day. His efforts to quit have been unsuccessful.

Subjective Data

- Family history: father died of an MI at age 62, brother had coronary artery bypass graft (CABG) at age 50, mother died from complications of diabetes
- Becomes "winded" when walking from his car to his office at the university
- Wakes up at night to urinate and has more frequent urination
- Increasing thirst

Continued

CASE STUDY

Chronic Kidney Disease—cont'd

Objective Data

Laboratory Data
- Calculated creatinine clearance using the MDRD equation: 42 mL/min/1.73 m^2
- Serum creatinine 2.5 mg/dL
- BUN 35 mg/dL
- Serum glucose 264 mg/dL
- Hgb 13 g/dL
- Serum cholesterol 236 mg/dL

Physical Examination
- Weight 220 lb, height 5 ft, 11 in
- BP 168/104 mm Hg

Discussion Questions

1. What do you think caused M.B.'s kidney disease?
2. What stage of chronic kidney disease does he have?
3. Identify the abnormal diagnostic study results and why each would occur.
4. *Priority Decision:* Based on the assessment data provided, what are the priority nursing diagnoses? Are there any collaborative problems?
5. What are the most important treatment measures that the interprofessional team can provide for M.B.?
6. *Patient-Centered Care:* What are the nursing interventions that would help promote M.B.'s self-management of his disease process?
7. *Collaboration:* How can the interprofessional team work together with M.B. to decide on the best form of renal replacement therapy?
8. *Evidence-Based Practice:* M.B. tells you that he has not been taking his BP medications regularly. When he asks you how important they are, what will you tell him?

Answers available at *http://evolve.elsevier.com/Lewis/medsurg.*

BRIDGE TO NCLEX EXAMINATION

The number of the question corresponds to the same-numbered outcome at the beginning of the chapter.

1. RIFLE defines the first 3 stages of AKI based on changes in
   a. blood pressure and urine osmolality.
   b. fractional excretion of urinary sodium.
   c. estimation of GFR with the MDRD equation.
   d. serum creatinine or urine output from baseline.

2. During the oliguric phase of AKI, the nurse monitors the patient for *(select all that apply)*
   a. hypotension.
   b. ECG changes.
   c. hypernatremia.
   d. pulmonary edema.
   e. urine with high specific gravity.

3. If a patient is in the diuretic phase of AKI, the nurse must monitor for which serum electrolyte imbalances?
   a. Hyperkalemia and hyponatremia
   b. Hyperkalemia and hypernatremia
   c. Hypokalemia and hyponatremia
   d. Hypokalemia and hypernatremia

4. A patient is admitted to the hospital with chronic kidney disease. The nurse understands that this condition is characterized by
   a. progressive irreversible destruction of the kidneys.
   b. a rapid decrease in urine output with an elevated BUN.
   c. an increasing creatinine clearance with a decrease in urine output.
   d. prostration, somnolence, and confusion with coma and imminent death.

5. Nurses can screen patients at risk for developing chronic kidney disease. Those considered to be at increased risk include *(select all that apply)*
   a. older black patients.
   b. patients more than 60 years old.
   c. those with a history of pancreatitis.
   d. those with a history of hypertension.
   e. those with a history of type 2 diabetes.

6. Patients with chronic kidney disease have an increased incidence of cardiovascular disease related to *(select all that apply)*
   a. hypertension.
   b. vascular calcifications.
   c. a genetic predisposition.
   d. hyperinsulinemia causing dyslipidemia.
   e. increased high-density lipoprotein levels.

7. Nutritional support and management are essential across the entire continuum of chronic kidney disease. Which statements are true related to nutritional therapy? *(select all that apply)*
   a. Sodium and salt may be restricted in someone with advanced CKD.
   b. Fluid is not usually restricted for patients receiving peritoneal dialysis.
   c. Decreased fluid intake and a low-potassium diet are part of the diet for a patient receiving hemodialysis.
   d. Decreased fluid intake and a low-potassium diet are part of the diet for a patient receiving peritoneal dialysis.
   e. Decreased fluid intake and a diet in protein-rich foods are part of a diet for a patient receiving hemodialysis.

8. An ESRD patient receiving hemodialysis is considering asking a relative to donate a kidney for transplantation. In helping the patient decide about treatment, the nurse informs the patient that
   a. successful transplantation usually provides better quality of life than that offered by dialysis.
   b. if rejection of the transplanted kidney occurs, no further treatment for the renal failure is available.
   c. hemodialysis replaces the normal functions of the kidneys, and patients do not have to live with the continual fear of rejection.
   d. the immunosuppressive therapy after transplantation makes the person ineligible to receive other treatments if the kidney fails.

9. To assess the patency of a newly placed arteriovenous graft for dialysis, the nurse should *(select all that apply)*
   a. monitor the BP in the affected arm.
   b. irrigate the graft daily with low-dose heparin.
   c. palpate the area of the graft to feel a normal thrill.
   d. listen with a stethoscope over the graft to detect a bruit.
   e. assess the pulses and neurovascular status distal to the graft.

10. A kidney transplant recipient has had fever, chills, and dysuria over the past 2 days. What is the *first* action that the nurse should take?
    a. Assess temperature and initiate workup to rule out infection.
    b. Reassure the patient that this is common after transplantation.
    c. Provide warm covers to the patient and give 1 gram oral acetaminophen.
    d. Notify the nephrologist that the patient has manifestations of acute rejection.

1. d, 2. b, d, 3. c, 4. a, 5. a, b, 6. a, b, 7. a, b, d, 8. a, b, c, 9. c, d, e, 10. a

For rationales to these answers and even more NCLEX review questions, visit *http://evolve.elsevier.com/Lewis/medsurg*.

EVOLVE WEBSITE

http://evolve.elsevier.com/Lewis/medsurg
Review Questions (Online Only)
Key Points
Answer Keys for Questions
- Rationales for Bridge to NCLEX Examination Questions
- Answer Guidelines for Case Study on p. 1085
- Answer Guidelines for Managing Care of Multiple Patients Case Study (Section 10) on p. 1088

Student Case Studies
- Patient With Glomerulonephritis and Acute Kidney Injury
- Patient With Kidney Transplant

Nursing Care Plan
- eNursing Care Plan 46.1: Patient With Chronic Kidney Disease

Conceptual Care Map Creator
Audio Glossary
Content Updates

REFERENCES

*1. Moriama N, Saito S, Ishihara S, et al: Early development of acute kidney injury is an independent predictor of in-hospital mortality in patients with acute myocardial infarction, *J Cardiol* 69:1, 2017.

2. Thornburg B: Acute kidney injury, *Nursing* 46:24, 2016.

3. Bevc S, Ekart R, Hois R: The assessment of acute kidney injury in critically ill patients, *Eur J Int Med* 45:54, 2017.

*4. Omotoso BA, Abdel-Rahman EM, Xin W, et al: Dialysis requirement, long-term major adverse cardiovascular events (MACE) and all-cause mortality in hospital acquired acute kidney injury (AKI): A propensity-matched cohort study, *J Nephrol* 29:847, 2016.

*5. Nash DM, Przech S, Wald R, et al: Systematic review and meta-analysis of renal replacement therapy modalities for acute kidney injury in the intensive care unit, *J Crit Care* 41:138, 2017.

*6. Abdel-Basset E, Walid A, Maha A, et al: Early versus delayed initiation of continuous renal replacement therapy in critically ill patients with acute kidney injury, *Egy J Hosp Med* 69:2219, 2017.

*7. Perez-Fernandez X, Sabater-Riera J, Sileanu F, et al: Renal: Clinical variables associated with poor outcome from sepsis-associated acute kidney injury and the relationship with timing of initiation of renal replacement therapy, *J Crit Care* 40:154, 2017.

*8. Greer R, Yang L, Crews D, et al: Hospital discharge communications during care transitions for patients with acute kidney injury: A cross-sectional study, *BMC Health Serv Res* 16:449, 2016.

*9. Zarbock A, Gerb J, Van Aken H, et al: Early versus late initiation of renal replacement therapy in critically ill patients with acute kidney injury, *JAMA* 148:558, 2016.

*10. Izawa J, Uchino S, Takinami M: A detailed evaluation of the new acute kidney injury criteria by KDIGO in critically ill patients, *J Anesthesiol* 30:215, 2016.

11. Loiselle M: Decisional needs assessment to help patients with advanced chronic kidney disease make better dialysis choices, *Nephrol Nurs J* 43:463, 2016.

*12. Alseiari M, Meyer KB, Wong JB: Evidence underlying KDIGO guideline recommendations: A systematic review, *Am J Kidney Dis*, 67:417, 2016.

*13. Flack JM, Calhoun D, Schifrin EL: The new ACC/AHA hypertension guidelines for the prevention, detection, evaluation, and management of high blood pressure in adults, *Am J Hypertension* 31:133, 2018.

*14. Galbraith L, Jacobs C, Hemmelgarn B, et al: Chronic disease management interventions for people with chronic kidney disease in primary care: a systematic review and meta-analysis, *Neph Dialysis Transpl* 33:112, 2017.

15. National Institute of Diabetes and Digestive and Kidney Diseases: US Renal Data System: 2017 annual data report: Epidemiology of kidney disease in the US. Retrieved from *www.usrds.org/adr.aspx*.

16. US Department of Health and Human Services: ESRD: General information. Retrieved from *www.cms.gov/Medicare/End-Stage-Renal-Disease/ESRDGeneralInformation/index.html*.

*17. Ettehad D, Emdin CA, Kiran A, et al: Blood pressure lowering for prevention of cardiovascular disease and death: A systematic review and meta-analysis, *Lancet* 387:10022, 2016.

18. Coyne D, Goldsmith D, Macdougall L: New options for the anemia of chronic kidney disease, *Kidney Int* 7:157, 2017.

*19. Ketteler M, Block GA, Evenepoel P: Executive summary of the 2017 KDIGO CKD-MBD guideline update: What's changed and why it matters, *Kidney Int* 92:26, 2017.

*20. Malhotra R, Nguyen H, Benevente, et al: Association between more intensive versus less intensive blood pressure lowering and risk of mortality in chronic kidney disease stages 3-5: A systematic review and meta-analysis, *JAMA Int Med* 177:1498, 2017.

*21. Natale P, Ruospo M, Saglimbene VM, et al: Interventions for improving sleep quality with chronic kidney disease. *Cochrane Database Syst Rev*, CD012625, 2017.

22. Saran R, Robinson B, Abbott KC, et al: US Renal Data System 2016 annual data report: Epidemiology of kidney disease in the United States, *Am J Kidney Dis* 69:S688, 2017.

23. National Kidney Foundation: NKF Kidney Disease Outcomes Quality Initiative. Retrieved from *www.kidney.org/professionals/guidelines/guidelines_commentaries*.

*24. Perez-Torres A, Garcia EG, Garcia-Llana H, et al: Improvement in nutritional status in patients with chronic kidney disease by a nutritional program with no impact on renal function and determined by male sex. *J Renal Nutrition* 27:303, 2017.

25. National Kidney and Urologic Diseases Information Clearinghouse: Treatment methods for kidney disease: Peritoneal dialysis. Retrieved from *http://kidney.niddk.nih.gov/health-information/kidney-failure/peritoneal-dialysis*.

26. Debus ES, Grundmann RT: *Evidence-based therapy in vascular surgery*, New York, 2017, Springer.

27. National Kidney and Urologic Diseases Information Clearinghouse: Treatment methods for kidney disease: hemodialysis. Retrieved from *http://kidney.niddk.nih.gov/health-information/kidney-disease/kidney-failure/hemodialysis*.

28. Lee CJ, Rossi PJ: Portable and wearable dialysis devices for the treatment of patients with ESRD. In: Shalhub S, Dua A, Shin S, eds: *Hemodialysis access: Fundamentals and advanced management*, Basel, Switzerland, 2017, Springer.

29. Hart A, Smith JM, Skeans MA, et al: OPTN/SRTR 2016 annual data report: Kidney, *Amer J Transplant* 18:18, 2018.

*30. Neuberger JM, Bechstein WO, Kuypers DR, et al: Practical recommendations for long term management of modifiable risk factors in kidney and liver transplant recipients: A guidance report and clinical checklist on managing modifiable risk in transplantation, *Transplantation* 101:S1, 2017.

*31. Mathur AK, Chang YH, Steidley DE, et al: Patterns of care and outcomes in cardiovascular disease after kidney transplantation in the United States, *Transplant Direct* 3:e26, 2017.

32. Organ procurement and transplant network kidney allocation system. Retrieved from *https://optn.transplant.hrsa.gov/learn/professional-education/kidney-allocation-system/*.

*33. Wongrakpanich S, Susantitaphong P, Isaranuwatchai S, et al: Dialysis therapy and conservative management of advanced chronic kidney disease in the elderly: A systematic review, *Nephron* 137:178, 2017.

34. O'Hare AM, Song MK, Moss AH: Research priorities for palliative care for older adults with advanced kidney disease, *J Palliative Med* 20:453, 2017.

*Evidence-based information for clinical practice.

CASE STUDY

Managing Care of Multiple Patients

You are working on the medical-surgical unit and have been assigned to care for the following 4 patients. You are also assigned to receive the next new admission to the clinical unit. You have 1 UAP on your team to help you.

Patients

(© iStockphoto/Thinkstock.)

A.K., a 28-yr-old black man, was admitted for observation after a renal ultrasound found several stones in the left ureter. A.K. came to the ED with sharp, colicky left flank pain for which the HCP prescribed IV opioids. His last pain medication was given 2 hours ago. His current pain level is 4 on a scale of 1 to 10. He is voiding dark, smoky-colored urine. His vital signs are within normal limits. He has positive costovertebral tenderness.

(© iStockphoto/Thinkstock.)

S.U., a 29-yr-old Hispanic woman with type 1 diabetes, was admitted with acute pyelonephritis following a recent UTI. She has bilateral flank pain and has abdominal tenderness to palpation. Her temperature is 101.5°F (38.6°C). Her urinalysis shows pyuria and hematuria. The WBC is high at 14,800/μL. Blood culture results are pending. IV antibiotics have been started. Most recent blood glucose is 215 mg/dL.

(© iStockphoto/Thinkstock.)

M.B., a 56-yr-old black college professor, was admitted with uncontrolled hypertension. He was recently diagnosed with CKD. He smokes at least 1 pack of cigarettes per day and is having some nicotine withdrawal symptoms. His BP on admission was 224/102 mm Hg. He is receiving IV metoprolol (Lopressor) 5 mg q4hr prn for SBP >180 mm Hg. His most recent BP 3 hr ago was 174/86 mm Hg. Laboratory results show a BUN of 66 mg/dL and serum creatinine of 3.2 mg/dL.

(© iStockphoto/Thinkstock.)

D.M., an 82-yr-old woman, was admitted to the ED with severe dehydration, heart failure, and acute kidney injury. Her daughter found her unconscious and lying on the floor. She is confused. Her serum potassium is 6.3 mEq/L. Her urine output for the past 8 hours was 90 mL.

Discussion Questions

1. *Priority Decision:* After receiving report, which patient should you see first? Second? Provide a rationale for your decision.

2. *Collaboration:* Which tasks could you delegate to the UAP (select all that apply)?
   a. Obtain vital signs on M.B.
   b. Strain A.K.'s voided urine.
   c. Report D.M.'s potassium level to the HCP.
   d. Measure D.M.'s urine output and report the results to the RN.
   e. Assess S.U. for manifestations of sepsis and diabetic ketoacidosis.

3. *Priority Decision:* As you are assessing D.M., the UAP tells you that M.B.'s BP is 190/96. He is asymptomatic. Additionally, the charge nurse tells you that you will be receiving a patient with heart failure from the ED within the next 20 minutes. Which action would be *most* appropriate?
   a. Ask the charge nurse to assign the new admission to someone else.
   b. Have the UAP admit the new patient while you administer M.B.'s IV metoprolol.
   c. Call the ED and have them hold the new admission until after you have assessed all your patients.
   d. Ask the charge nurse to give M.B.'s IV metoprolol while you complete your assessment of D.M. and S.U.

Case Study Progression

As you complete your assessment of D.M., you note her apical pulse is irregular. She has 1+ pitting edema in her lower extremities. Her BP is 160/90 mm Hg, heart rate 108 beats/min, and respiratory rate 28/min. Auscultation of her lungs reveals crackles in the bases and O₂ saturation is 92% on room air. You notify her HCP.

4. Which interventions would you expect the HCP to order for D.M.? *(select all that apply)*
   a. Administer IV Kayexalate.
   b. Obtain arterial blood gas levels.
   c. Administer 40 mg of furosemide IV push.
   d. Prepare her for hemodialysis and notify her family.
   e. Obtain a 12-lead ECG and start continuous ECG monitoring.

5. *Priority Decision:* Which concern has the *highest* priority when planning care for A.K.?
   a. Acute pain
   b. Infection risk
   c. Risk for injury
   d. Difficulty coping

6. *Priority Decision:* You begin S.U.'s scheduled infusion of IV ceftriaxone. Which parameters are the *most* important to monitor while she is receiving this drug?
   a. PT and INR
   b. BUN and creatinine
   c. CBC with differential
   d. Liver function studies

7. Which statement would be *most* appropriate when teaching S.U. about her kidney infection?
   a. "The damage to your kidneys will likely require dialysis."
   b. "You will need to be in the hospital for a 2-week course of IV antibiotics."
   c. "It is very important that you maintain adequate hydration to flush your kidneys."
   d. "You will not need further antibiotics once you are discharged from the hospital."

8. *Collaboration:* As the UAP prepares the room for the patient being admitted from the ED, you overhear her telling a co-worker that she does all your work for you. What is your *best* initial action?
   a. Report the incident to the charge nurse for follow-up.
   b. Ask the UAP to discuss her concerns with you in private.
   c. Tell the UAP how much you appreciate and value her input on your team.
   d. Immediately clarify the situation by telling the UAP all the tasks you are completing.

Assessment: Endocrine System

Julia A. Hitch

> *Our compassion and acts of selflessness take us to the deeper truths.*
>
> **Amma**

http://evolve.elsevier.com/Lewis/medsurg

CONCEPTUAL FOCUS

Homeostasis
Hormonal Regulation

Reproduction
Stress

LEARNING OUTCOMES

1. Describe the common characteristics and functions of hormones.
2. Identify the locations of the endocrine glands.
3. Describe the functions of hormones secreted by the pituitary, thyroid, parathyroid, and adrenal glands and the pancreas.
4. Describe the locations and roles of hormone receptors.
5. Obtain significant subjective and objective assessment data related to the endocrine system from a patient.

6. Perform a physical assessment of the endocrine system using the appropriate techniques.
7. Link age-related changes in the endocrine system to differences in assessment findings.
8. Distinguish normal from common abnormal findings of a physical assessment of the endocrine system.
9. Describe the purpose, significance of results, and nursing responsibilities related to diagnostic studies of the endocrine system.

KEY TERMS

aldosterone, p. 1095
antidiuretic hormone (ADH), p. 1093
catecholamines, p. 1094
circadian rhythm, p. 1090
corticosteroid, p. 1095

cortisol, p. 1095
hormones, p. 1089
insulin, p. 1095
negative feedback, p. 1090
positive feedback, p. 1090

thyroxine (T_4), p. 1094
triiodothyronine (T_3), p. 1094
tropic hormones, p. 1093

STRUCTURES AND FUNCTIONS OF ENDOCRINE SYSTEM

Glands

Endocrine glands include the hypothalamus, pituitary, thyroid, parathyroids, adrenals, pancreas, ovaries, testes, and pineal gland (Fig. 47.1). These glands make and release special chemical messengers called *hormones*. The endocrine system has 5 general functions: (1) a role in reproductive and central nervous system (CNS) development in the fetus, (2) stimulating growth and development during childhood and adolescence, (3) sexual reproduction, (4) maintaining homeostasis, and (5) responding to emergency demands.[1]

Hormones

Hormones are chemical substances made by endocrine glands that control and regulate the activity of certain target cells or organs. Many are made in one part of the body and control and regulate the activity of certain cells or organs in another part of the body. The thyroid gland makes the hormone thyroxine, which affects many body tissues when released directly into the circulation. Other hormones act locally on cells where they are released and never enter the bloodstream. We call this local effect *paracrine action*. The action of sex steroids on the ovary is an example of paracrine action.

Most hormones have common characteristics, including (1) secretion in small amounts at variable but predictable rates,

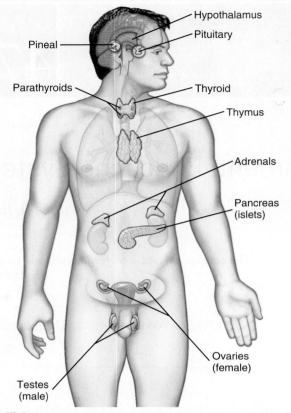

FIG. 47.1 Location of the major endocrine glands. The parathyroid glands lie on the posterior surface of the thyroid gland. (Modified from Patton KT, Thibodeau GA: *Anatomy and physiology,* ed 8, St Louis, 2013, Mosby.)

(2) regulation by feedback systems, and (3) ability to bind to specific target cell receptors. Table 47.1 reviews the major hormones, the glands or tissues that make the hormones, their target organs or tissues, and their functions.

There is a strong connection between the endocrine system and nervous system. *Catecholamines* (e.g., epinephrine), secreted by the adrenal gland, travel through the bloodstream and affect multiple organ systems. These same substances, when secreted by nerve cells in the brain and peripheral nervous system, act as neurotransmitters, sending important impulses across nerve synapses.[1]

Organs can act as endocrine glands by secreting hormones. For example, the kidneys secrete erythropoietin, a substance that stimulates red blood cell production. The heart secretes atrial natriuretic peptide (ANP). The gastrointestinal (GI) tract secretes many peptide hormones (e.g., gastrin), that aid in digestion. These hormones are discussed in their respective assessment chapters.

Hormone Receptors. Hormones exert their effects by recognizing their target tissues and attaching to receptor sites in a "lock-and-key" type of mechanism. This means a hormone will act only on cells that have a receptor specific for that hormone (Fig. 47.2).

Lipid-Soluble and Water-Soluble Hormones. We classify hormones by their chemical structure as either lipid soluble or water soluble. The differences in solubility become important in understanding how the hormone interacts with the target cell (Fig. 47.3). Lipid-soluble hormones (steroids, thyroid) are bound to plasma proteins as they travel to target cells. They cross the cell membrane by simple diffusion. Water-soluble hormones (insulin, growth hormone, prolactin) circulate freely in the blood and act directly on target tissues.

Regulation of Hormonal Secretion. Specific mechanisms control endocrine activity by either stimulating or inhibiting hormone synthesis and secretion. These include positive and negative feedback, nervous system control, and physiologic rhythms.

Simple Feedback. Negative feedback relies on the blood level of a hormone or other chemical compound regulated by the hormone (e.g., glucose). It is the most common type of endocrine feedback system. It results in the gland increasing or decreasing the release of a hormone. Negative feedback functions like a thermostat. Cold air in a room activates the thermostat to release heat. Warm air signals the thermostat to turn off the heater. An example of negative feedback is calcium and parathyroid hormone (PTH) regulation. Low blood levels of calcium stimulate the parathyroid gland to release PTH. PTH acts on the bone, intestine, and kidneys to increase blood calcium levels. The increased blood calcium level then inhibits further PTH release (Fig. 47.4).

With positive feedback, increasing hormone levels cause another gland to release a hormone that then stimulates further release of the first hormone. Something must stop the release of the first hormone (e.g., follicle death) or its release will continue. The ovarian hormone estradiol works by this type of feedback. Increased levels of estradiol made by the follicle during the menstrual cycle result in the production and release of follicle-stimulating hormone (FSH) by the anterior pituitary. FSH causes further increases in estradiol until the death of the follicle. This results in a drop of FSH serum levels.

Nervous System Control. Nervous system activity directly affects some endocrine glands. Pain, fear, sexual excitement, and other stressors can stimulate the nervous system to control hormone secretion. For example, when the CNS senses or perceives stress, the sympathetic nervous system (SNS) secretes catecholamines (e.g., epinephrine), which maximize heart and lung function and vision to deal with the stress more effectively. Chronic exposure to some stressors can cause persistent increases in heart rate and BP and changes in the endocrine system. This puts patients at risk for chronic disease, such as hypertension and heart disease. Stress-related effects are discussed in Chapter 6.

Rhythms. A common physiologic rhythm is the circadian rhythm. It is a 24-hour rhythm that is driven by sleep-wake or dark-light 24-hour (diurnal) cycles. Hormone levels and the responsiveness of target tissues fluctuate predictably during these cycles. Cortisol, made by the adrenal cortex, rises early in the day, declines toward evening, and rises again toward the end of sleep to peak by morning (Fig. 47.5). Growth hormone, thyroid-stimulating hormone, and prolactin levels peak during sleep. Reproductive cycles are often longer than 24 hours *(ultradian)*. An example is the menstrual cycle. These rhythms are important to consider when interpreting laboratory results for hormone levels.

Hypothalamus

Although many refer to the pituitary gland as the "master gland" of the endocrine system, most of its functions rely on its interrelationship with the hypothalamus, which lies next to the pituitary gland. The hypothalamus releases substances that either stimulate or inhibit the production and release of

TABLE 47.1 Endocrine Glands and Hormones

Hormones	Target Tissue	Functions
Anterior Pituitary (Adenohypophysis)		
Adrenocorticotropic hormone (ACTH)	Adrenal cortex	Fosters growth of adrenal cortex Stimulates corticosteroid secretion
Gonadotropic hormones • Follicle-stimulating hormone (FSH) • Luteinizing hormone (LH)	Reproductive organs	Stimulate sex hormone secretion, reproductive organ growth, reproductive processes
Growth hormone (GH), or somatotropin	All body cells	Promotes protein anabolism (growth, tissue repair) and lipid mobilization and catabolism
Melanocyte-stimulating hormone (MSH)	Melanocytes in skin	↑ Melanin production in melanocytes to make skin darker
Prolactin	Ovary and mammary glands in women	Stimulates milk production in lactating women. ↑ Response of follicles to LH and FSH
	Testes in men	Stimulates testicular function in men
Thyroid-stimulating hormone (TSH), or thyrotropin	Thyroid gland	Stimulates synthesis and release of thyroid hormones, growth and function of thyroid gland
Posterior Pituitary (Neurohypophysis)		
Antidiuretic hormone (ADH)	Renal tubules, vascular smooth muscle	Promotes reabsorption of water from the renal tubules, vasoconstriction
Oxytocin	Uterus, mammary glands	Stimulates milk secretion, uterine contractility
Thyroid		
Calcitonin	Bone tissue	Regulates calcium and phosphorus serum levels. ↓ Serum Ca^{2+} levels
Thyroxine (T_4)	All body tissues	Precursor to T_3
Triiodothyronine (T_3)	All body tissues	Regulates metabolic rate of all cells and processes of cell growth and tissue differentiation
Parathyroids		
Parathyroid hormone (PTH) or parathormone	Bone, intestine, kidneys	Regulates calcium and phosphorus serum levels. Promotes bone demineralization and ↑ intestinal absorption of Ca^{2+}. ↑ Serum Ca^{2+} levels
Adrenal Medulla		
Epinephrine (adrenaline)	Catecholamine	↑ In response to stress. Enhances and prolongs effects of sympathetic nervous system
Norepinephrine (noradrenaline)	Catecholamine	↑ In response to stress. Enhances and prolongs effects of sympathetic nervous system
Adrenal Cortex		
Androgens (e.g., dehydroepiandrosterone [DHEA], androsterone) and estradiol	Reproductive organs	Promote growth spurt in adolescence, secondary sex characteristics, and libido in both sexes
Corticosteroids (e.g., cortisol, hydrocortisone)	All body tissues	Promote metabolism. ↑ In response to stress. Antiinflammatory
Mineralocorticoids (e.g., aldosterone)	Kidney	Regulate sodium and potassium balance and thus water balance
Pancreas (Islets of Langerhans)		
Amylin (from β cells)	Liver, stomach	↓ Gastric motility, glucagon secretion, and endogenous glucose release from liver. ↑ Satiety
Glucagon (from α cells)	General	Stimulates glycogenolysis and gluconeogenesis
Insulin (from β cells)	General	Promotes glucose transport from the blood into the cell
Pancreatic polypeptide	General	Influences regulation of pancreatic exocrine function and metabolism of absorbed nutrients
Somatostatin	Pancreas	Inhibits insulin and glucagon secretion
Gonads		
Women: Ovaries		
Estrogen	Reproductive system, breasts	Stimulates development of secondary sex characteristics, preparation of uterus for fertilization and fetal development. Stimulates bone growth
Progesterone	Reproductive system	Maintains lining of uterus needed for successful pregnancy
Men: Testes		
Testosterone	Reproductive system	Stimulates development of secondary sex characteristics, spermatogenesis

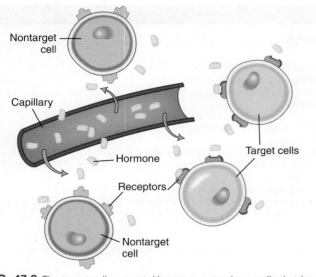

FIG. 47.2 The target cell concept. Hormones act only on cells that have receptors specific to that hormone, since the shape of the receptor determines which hormone can react with it. This is an example of the lock-and-key model of biochemical reactions.

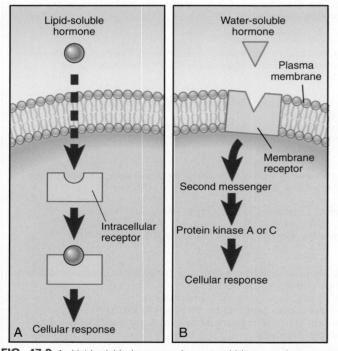

FIG. 47.3 A, Lipid-soluble hormones (e.g., steroid hormones) penetrate the cell membrane and interact with intracellular receptors. B, Water-soluble hormones (e.g., protein hormones) bind to receptors in the cell membrane. The hormone-receptor interaction stimulates various cell responses. (Modified from McCance KL, Huether SE: *Pathophysiology: The biologic basis for disease in adults and children*, ed 6, St Louis, 2010, Mosby.)

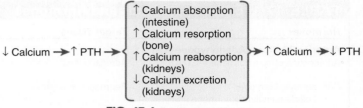

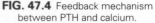

FIG. 47.4 Feedback mechanism between PTH and calcium.

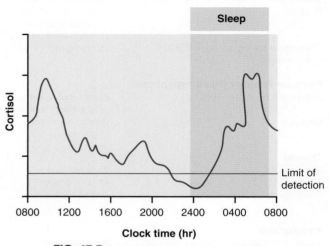

FIG. 47.5 Circadian rhythm of cortisol secretion.

TABLE 47.2 **Hormones of the Hypothalamus**

The following hormones from the hypothalamus target the anterior pituitary:

Releasing Hormones
- Corticotropin-releasing hormone (CRH)
- Thyrotropin-releasing hormone (TRH)
- Growth hormone–releasing hormone (GHRH)
- Gonadotropin-releasing hormone (GnRH)
- Prolactin-releasing factor (PRF)

Inhibiting Hormones
- Somatostatin (inhibits growth hormone release)
- Prolactin-inhibiting factor (PIF)

hormones from the pituitary gland (Table 47.2). Examples of these hormones include corticotropin-releasing hormone and thyrotropin-releasing hormone. Somatostatin inhibits growth hormone release.

Neurons in the hypothalamus receive input from the CNS, including the brainstem, limbic system, and cerebral cortex. These neurons create a circuit that helps coordinate the endocrine system and autonomic nervous system (ANS). The hypothalamus also coordinates the expression of complex behavioral responses, such as anger, fear, and pleasure.

Pituitary

The pituitary gland *(hypophysis)* is in the sella turcica under the hypothalamus at the base of the brain above the sphenoid bone (Fig. 47.1). The infundibular *(hypophyseal)* stalk connects the pituitary and hypothalamus. This stalk relays information between the hypothalamus and pituitary, creating a strong neuroendocrine connection. The pituitary consists of 2 major parts, the anterior lobe *(adenohypophysis)* and posterior lobe *(neurohypophysis)*. A smaller intermediate lobe makes melanocyte-stimulating hormone (MSH).

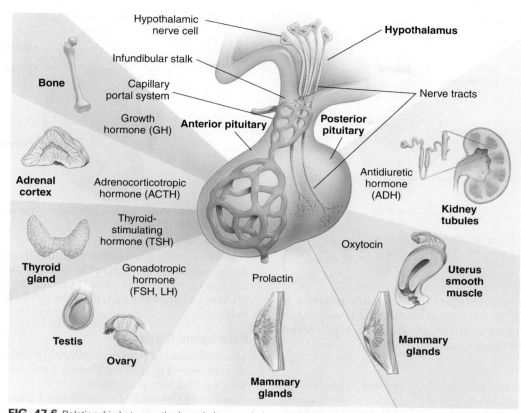

FIG. 47.6 Relationship between the hypothalamus, pituitary, and target organs. The hypothalamus communicates with the anterior pituitary via a capillary system and with the posterior pituitary via nerve tracts. The anterior and posterior pituitary hormones are shown with their target tissues. (Modified from Patton KT, Thibodeau GA: *Anatomy and physiology,* ed 8, St Louis, 2013, Mosby.)

Anterior Pituitary. The anterior lobe of the pituitary accounts for 80% of the gland by weight. The hypothalamus regulates the anterior lobe through releasing and inhibiting hormones. These hypothalamic hormones reach the anterior pituitary through a network of capillaries known as the *hypothalamus-hypophyseal portal system.* These releasing and inhibiting hormones in turn affect the secretion of 6 hormones from the anterior pituitary (Fig. 47.6).

We refer to several hormones secreted by the anterior pituitary as **tropic hormones**. Tropic hormones control the secretion of hormones by other glands. Thyroid-stimulating hormone (TSH) stimulates the thyroid gland to secrete thyroid hormones. Adrenocorticotropic hormone (ACTH) stimulates the adrenal cortex to secrete corticosteroids. FSH stimulates secretion of estrogen and the development of ova in women and sperm in men. Luteinizing hormone (LH) stimulates ovulation in women and secretion of sex hormones in both men and women.

Growth hormone (GH) affects the growth and development of all body tissues. It has many biologic actions, including a role in protein, fat, and carbohydrate metabolism. *Prolactin,* or lactogenic hormone, stimulates the breast development needed for lactation after childbirth.

Posterior Pituitary. The posterior pituitary is composed of nerve tissue and is essentially an extension of the hypothalamus. Communication between the hypothalamus and posterior pituitary occurs through nerve tracts. The hormones secreted by the posterior pituitary, **antidiuretic hormone (ADH)** and oxytocin, are made in the hypothalamus. These hormones travel down the

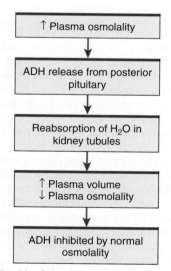

FIG. 47.7 Relationship of plasma osmolality to ADH release and action.

nerve tracts from the hypothalamus to the posterior pituitary and are stored there until stimuli trigger their release (Fig. 47.6).

The major physiologic role of ADH (also called *arginine vasopressin*) is to regulate fluid volume. It causes the renal tubules to reabsorb water, making the urine more concentrated. A rise in plasma osmolality or hypovolemia causes specialized neurons in the hypothalamus, known as *osmoreceptors,* to stimulate ADH release from the posterior pituitary (Fig. 47.7). When ADH release is inhibited, renal tubules do not reabsorb

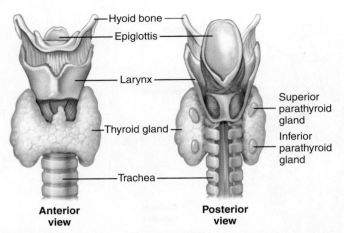

FIG. 47.8 Thyroid and parathyroid glands. Note the surrounding structures. (From Thibodeau GA, Patton KT: *The human body in health and disease*, ed 4, St Louis, 2005, Mosby.)

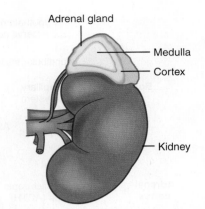

FIG. 47.9 The adrenal gland is composed of the adrenal cortex and the adrenal medulla.

water, resulting in a more dilute urine. Volume receptors in large veins, heart atria, and carotid arteries that sense pressure changes (from hypovolemia) also contribute to ADH control. ADH is also a potent vasoconstrictor.

Pineal Gland

The pineal gland is in the brain. It is composed of photoreceptive cells. Its primary function is the secretion of the hormone *melatonin*. Melatonin secretion increases in response to exposure to the dark and decreases in response to light exposure. The gland helps to regulate circadian rhythms and the reproductive system at the onset of puberty.

Thyroid Gland

The thyroid gland is in the anterior part of the neck in front of the trachea. It consists of 2 encapsulated lateral lobes connected by a narrow isthmus (Fig. 47.8). The thyroid gland is highly vascular. Its size is related to TSH secretion by the anterior pituitary. The 3 hormones made and secreted by the thyroid gland are thyroxine (T_4), triiodothyronine (T_3), and calcitonin.

Thyroxine and Triiodothyronine. Thyroxine (T_4) accounts for 90% of thyroid hormone made by the thyroid gland. However, triiodothyronine (T_3) is much more potent and has greater metabolic effects. The thyroid gland directly secretes about 20% of circulating T_3. The rest comes from the conversion of T_4 after its release into the bloodstream. Iodine is required for the synthesis of both T_3 and T_4. Both hormones affect metabolic rate, caloric requirements, O_2 consumption, carbohydrate and lipid metabolism, growth and development, brain function, and other nervous system activities. More than 99% of thyroid hormones are bound to plasma proteins, especially thyroxine-binding globulin made by the liver. Only the unbound "free" hormones are biologically active.

TSH from the anterior pituitary gland stimulates thyroid hormone production and release. When circulating levels of thyroid hormone are low, the hypothalamus releases thyrotropin-releasing hormone (TRH). TRH causes the anterior pituitary to release TSH. High circulating thyroid hormone levels inhibit the secretion of both TRH from the hypothalamus and TSH from the anterior pituitary gland.

Calcitonin. *Calcitonin* is made by C cells (parafollicular cells) of the thyroid gland in response to high circulating calcium levels. Calcitonin lowers serum calcium levels by (1) inhibiting the transfer of calcium from the bone to blood, (2) increasing calcium storage in bone, and (3) increasing renal excretion of calcium and phosphorus. Calcitonin and PTH regulate calcium balance.

Parathyroid Glands

There are usually 2 pairs of parathyroid glands lying behind each thyroid lobe (Fig. 47.8). Although there are usually 4 glands, their number may range from 2 to 6.

Parathyroid Hormone. The parathyroid glands secrete parathyroid hormone (PTH), also called *parathormone*. Its major role is to regulate serum calcium levels. PTH increases serum calcium levels by acting on bone, the kidneys, and indirectly on the GI tract. PTH stimulates the transfer of calcium from the bone into the blood. In the kidney, PTH promotes calcium reabsorption (moving calcium from the renal tubules back into the bloodstream) and phosphate excretion. PTH stimulates the renal conversion of vitamin D to its most active form (1,25-dihydroxyvitamin D_3). This form of vitamin D promotes calcium and phosphorus absorption in the GI tract. PTH secretion is regulated by a negative feedback system. When serum calcium or magnesium levels are low, PTH secretion increases. When serum calcium or active vitamin D levels are high, PTH secretion falls.

Adrenal Glands

The adrenal glands are small, paired, highly vascular glands located on the upper part of each kidney. Each gland consists of 2 parts: medulla and cortex (Fig. 47.9). Each part has distinct functions and act independently from the other.

Adrenal Medulla. The adrenal medulla is the inner part of the adrenal gland. It consists of sympathetic postganglionic neurons. The medulla secretes the catecholamines *epinephrine* (adrenaline), *norepinephrine* (noradrenaline), and *dopamine*. We consider catecholamines neurotransmitters when they are secreted by neurons and hormones when they are secreted by the adrenal medulla. They are an essential part of the SNS's "fight or flight" response.

Adrenal Cortex. The adrenal cortex is the outer part of the adrenal gland. It secretes several steroid hormones, including *glucocorticoids, mineralocorticoids,* and *androgens*. Cholesterol is the precursor for steroid hormone synthesis. Glucocorticoids (e.g., cortisol) are named for their effects on glucose metabolism. They inhibit the inflammatory response and are considered antiinflammatory. Mineralocorticoids (e.g., aldosterone) are essential for maintaining fluid and electrolyte balance. The term **corticosteroid** refers to both glucocorticoids and mineralocorticoids.

Cortisol. Cortisol, the most abundant and potent glucocorticoid, is necessary to maintain life and protect the body from stress. It is secreted in a diurnal pattern (Fig. 47.5). A negative feedback mechanism controls cortisol secretion. The release of corticotropin-releasing hormone (CRH) from the hypothalamus stimulates the secretion of ACTH by the anterior pituitary.

A major function of cortisol is regulating blood glucose concentration by stimulating hepatic glucose formation (*gluconeogenesis*). Cortisol inhibits peripheral glucose use in the fasting state, inhibits protein synthesis, and stimulates the mobilization of glycerol and free fatty acids. It helps maintain vascular integrity and fluid volume through its action on mineralocorticoid receptors. Cortisol decreases the inflammatory response by stabilizing the membranes of cellular lysosomes and preventing increased capillary permeability. Stress, burns, infection, fever, acute anxiety, and hypoglycemia increase cortisol levels.

Aldosterone. **Aldosterone** is a potent mineralocorticoid that maintains extracellular fluid volume. It acts on the renal tubule to promote renal reabsorption of sodium and excretion of potassium and hydrogen ions. Hyponatremia, hyperkalemia, and angiotensin II stimulate aldosterone synthesis and secretion. ANP and hypokalemia inhibit aldosterone synthesis and release.

Adrenal Androgens. The adrenal cortex secretes small amounts of androgens. They are converted to sex steroids in peripheral tissues: testosterone in men and estrogen in women. The most common adrenal androgens are dehydroepiandrosterone (DHEA) and androstenedione. Because they are precursors to other sex steroids, their actions are like those of testosterone and estrogen. In postmenopausal women, the major source of estrogen is the peripheral conversion of adrenal androgens to estrogen.

Pancreas

The pancreas is a long, tapered, lobular, soft gland located behind the stomach and anterior to the first and second lumbar vertebrae. The pancreas has both exocrine and endocrine functions. The hormone-secreting part of the pancreas is the *islets of Langerhans.* The islets account for less than 2% of the gland. They consist of 4 types of hormone-secreting cells: α, β, delta, and F cells. The α cells make and secrete the hormone glucagon. The β cells make and secrete insulin and amylin. Delta cells make and secrete somatostatin. F (or PP) cells secrete pancreatic polypeptide.

Glucagon. Pancreatic α cells release *glucagon* in response to low blood glucose levels, protein ingestion, and exercise. Glucagon increases blood glucose, providing fuel for energy by stimulating glycogenolysis (breakdown of glycogen into glucose), gluconeogenesis (formation of glucose from noncarbohydrate molecules), and ketogenesis. Glucagon and insulin function in a reciprocal manner to maintain normal blood glucose levels.

Insulin. Insulin is the main regulator of metabolism and storage of ingested carbohydrates, fats, and proteins. Insulin facilitates glucose transport into cells, transport of amino acids across muscle membranes, and the synthesis of amino acids into protein in the peripheral tissues. However, the brain, nerves, lens of the eye, hepatocytes, erythrocytes, and cells in the intestinal mucosa and kidney tubules are not dependent on insulin for glucose uptake. After a meal, insulin is responsible for how we use and store nutrients (*anabolism*). An increased blood glucose

TABLE 47.3 Gerontologic Assessment Differences

Endocrine System

Changes	Clinical Significance
Thyroid	
Atrophy of thyroid gland	↑ Incidence of hypothyroidism with aging
↓ secretion of T₃, T₄, TSH	Most older adults maintain adequate thyroid function
↑ Nodules	Thyroid hormone replacement dose lower in older adults
Parathyroid	
↑ Secretion of PTH	↑ Calcium resorption from bone
↑ Basal level of PTH	Hypercalcemia, hypercalciuria (may reflect defective renal mechanism)
Adrenal Cortex	
Adrenal cortex becomes more fibrotic and slightly smaller	↓ Metabolic clearance rate for glucocorticoids
↓ Metabolism of cortisol	
↓ Plasma levels of adrenal androgens and aldosterone	
Adrenal Medulla	
↑ Secretion and basal level of norepinephrine	↓ Responsiveness to β-adrenergic agonists and receptor blockers
↓ β-Adrenergic receptor response to norepinephrine	May partly explain ↑ incidence of hypertension with aging
Pancreas	
↑ Fibrosis and fatty deposits in pancreas	May partly contribute to ↑ incidence of diabetes with advanced aging
↑ Glucose intolerance with ↓ sensitivity to insulin	
Gonads	
Women: ↓ Estrogen secretion	Have menopausal symptoms
	↑ Risk for arteriosclerosis and osteoporosis
Men: ↓ Testosterone secretion	Men may or may not have symptoms

level is the major stimulus for insulin synthesis and secretion. Low blood glucose levels, glucagon, somatostatin, hypokalemia, and catecholamines usually inhibit insulin secretion.

Gerontologic Considerations: Effects of Aging on Endocrine System

Normal aging has many effects on the endocrine system (Table 47.3). These include (1) decreased hormone production and secretion, (2) altered hormone metabolism and biologic activity, (3) decreased responsiveness of target tissues to hormones, and (4) changes in circadian rhythms.

Assessing the effects of aging on the endocrine system may be difficult because the subtle changes of aging may mimic manifestations of endocrine disorders. Endocrine problems may manifest differently in an older adult than in a younger person. Older adults may have multiple co-morbidities and take medications that change the body's usual response to endocrine function. Symptoms of endocrine problems, such as fatigue, constipation, or mental impairment, may be attributed to aging, resulting in delayed treatment.

ASSESSMENT OF ENDOCRINE SYSTEM

Endocrine problems generally result from too much or too little of a specific hormone. The onset of symptoms is often gradual. Subtle or vague symptoms are often attributed to other physiologic or psychologic causes. Patients may present with fluid and electrolyte imbalances, altered tissue perfusion, inadequate coping mechanisms, changes in heart rhythm, or changes in skin integrity that can be interpreted as many other conditions. Alternatively, patients may present with acute symptoms that are life threatening and demand immediate intervention.

CASE STUDY
Patient Introduction

(© iStockphoto/Thinkstock.)

L.M. is a 35-yr-old Hispanic woman who comes to the clinic saying she is "just not feeling well." Her husband, H.M., is with her. L.M. states that she has gained a lot of weight despite trying to watch her diet and just seems to be getting more and more tired. H.M. voices concerns about the changes in his wife's energy level.

Discussion Questions

1. What are the possible causes of L.M.'s weight gain, fatigue, and irritability?
2. What would be your priority assessment of L.M.?
3. What questions would you ask L.M.?

You will learn more about L.M. and her condition as you read through this assessment chapter.
(See p. 1098 for more information on L.M.)

Answers available at *http://evolve.elsevier.com/Lewis/medsurg.*

Subjective Data

Information obtained from the patient can provide important clues as to the functioning of the endocrine system. You will need to obtain a thorough history from the patient and/or a caregiver if the patient's mental acuity is compromised.

Important Health Information

Past Health History. Patients with endocrine disorders often present with nonspecific complaints. The chief complaint may relate to not just one but a group of symptoms. The most common presenting problems include fatigue, weakness, menstrual irregularities, and weight changes. It is important to determine if the onset of symptoms has been gradual or sudden and what the patient has done about them.

Because some of the more general signs of problems are the easiest to overlook, you must evaluate any reported or observed changes in weight, appetite, skin, libido, mental acuity, emotional stability, or energy levels.

Medications. Ask about the use of all medications (both prescription and over-the-counter), herbs, and dietary supplements. Ask about the reason for taking the drug, the dosage, and the length of time the drug has been taken. In particular, ask about the use of hormone replacements. Knowing that the patient is currently taking hormone replacements, such as insulin, thyroid hormone, or corticosteroids (e.g., prednisone), should alert you to potential adverse drug events. For example, corticosteroids may increase blood glucose levels and cause bone loss with long-term use. Thyroid preparations may cause tachycardia or dysrhythmias. Drug-to-drug interactions and adverse effects of nonhormonal medications can contribute to endocrine problems.

Surgery or Other Treatments. Ask about past medical, surgical, and obstetric history, including number of pregnancies and live births. Assess growth patterns and stages of physical and emotional development. For example, knowing about radiation therapy to the head and neck is important when you suspect thyroid or pituitary problems.

Functional Health Patterns. Key questions to ask the patient with an endocrine problem are outlined in Table 47.4.

Health Perception–Health Management Pattern. Heredity plays a key role in the development of endocrine problems. Ask about first-degree relatives with diabetes, thyroid disease, or endocrine gland cancers, since these conditions have a familial tendency. A genetic assessment of family members may be needed.

GENETIC RISK ALERT

Pituitary
- Nephrogenic diabetes insipidus can be inherited as a sex-linked or autosomal disorder.

Thyroid
- Genetics has a role in many cases of hypothyroid and hyperthyroid disorders.
- Hashimoto's thyroiditis, the most common cause of hypothyroidism, and Graves' disease, a cause of hyperthyroidism, are autoimmune disorders. Both likely result from a combination of genetic and environmental factors.[2]

Multiple Endocrine Neoplasia
- Multiple endocrine neoplasia (MEN) involves tumors in 2 or more different endocrine glands.
- There are several types of MEN. Mutations of *MEN1, RET,* and *CDKN1B* genes determine the type.
- The features of MEN are relatively consistent within a family.
- A common tumor associated with MEN type 2 is medullary thyroid cancer.[2]

Diabetes
- Genetics has a strong role in the development of type 1 and type 2 diabetes.

Nutritional-Metabolic Pattern. Changes in appetite and weight can indicate an endocrine problem. Ask about a history of weight distribution and changes. Weight loss with increased appetite may occur with hyperthyroidism or diabetes. Weight gain may occur with hypothyroidism or hypocortisolism. Obese persons are more likely to develop type 2 diabetes.

Ask if there have been problems with nausea, vomiting, or diarrhea. An enlarged thyroid gland can cause difficulty swallowing or a change in neck size. Increased SNS activity, including nervousness, palpitations, sweating, and tremors, may occur with thyroid problems or a rare tumor of the adrenal medulla (*pheochromocytoma*). Heat or cold intolerance occur with hyperthyroidism or hypothyroidism, respectively.

Ask about changes in the patient's skin, especially on the face, neck, hands, or body creases. Changes in skin texture and skin that seems thicker or drier may suggest an endocrine problem. A patient with hypothyroidism or excess GH may have skin that feels coarse or leathery. Ask if the patient has noticed any change in the distribution of hair anywhere on the body.

TABLE 47.4 Health History

Endocrine System

Health Perception–Health Management

- What is your usual day like?
- Have you noticed any changes in your ability to perform your usual activities compared with last year? 5 years ago?*

Nutritional-Metabolic

- What are your weight and height?
- How much do you want to weigh?
- Have there been any changes in your appetite or weight?*
- Have you noticed any changes in the distribution of the hair anywhere on your body? *
- Have you noticed any changes in the color of your skin, especially on your face, neck, hands, or body creases? *
- Has the texture of your skin changed? For example, does it seem thicker and drier than it used to?*
- Have you noticed any difficulty swallowing, throat pain, or hoarseness? Is the top button on your shirt or blouse hard to button?*
- Do you feel more nervous than you used to? Do you notice your heart pounding or that you sweat when you do not think you should be sweating?
- Do you have difficulty holding things because of shakiness of your hands?*
- Do you feel that most rooms are too hot or too cold? Do you often have to put on a sweater, or feel as though you need to open windows when others in the room seem comfortable?*
- Do you have, or have you had any wounds that were slow to heal?*

Elimination

- Do you have to get up at night to urinate? If so, how many times? Do you keep water by your bed at night?
- Have you ever had a kidney stone?*
- Describe your usual bowel pattern. Have you noted any bowel changes?*
- Do you use anything, such as laxatives, to help you move your bowels?*

Activity-Exercise

- What is your usual activity pattern during a typical day?
- Do you have a planned exercise program? If yes, what is it and have you had to make any changes in this routine lately? If so, why, and what kinds of changes?
- Do you have fatigue with or without activity?*
- Have you had any trouble with breathing?*

Sleep-Rest

- How many hours do you sleep at night? Do you feel rested on awakening?
- Are you ever awakened by sweating during the night?*
- Do you have nightmares?*

Cognitive-Perceptual

- How is your memory? Have you noticed any changes?*
- Have you had any blurring or double vision?*
- When was your last eye examination?

Self-Perception–Self-Concept

- Have you noticed any changes in your physical appearance or size?*
- Are you concerned about your weight?*
- Do you feel you are able to do what you think you can do? If not, why not?
- Does your health problem affect how you feel about yourself?*

Role-Relationship

- Do you have a support system or partner? Are you married? Do you have any children? Do you think you are able to take care of your family and home? If not, why not?
- Where do you work? What kind of work do you do? Are you able to do what is expected of you and what you expect of yourself?
- Are you retired? What type of work did you do before you retired? How do you spend your time now that you have retired?

Sexuality-Reproductive

Women

- When did you start to menstruate? Was this earlier or later than other women in your family?
- When was your last menstrual period? Do you have scant, heavy, or irregular menstrual flows?
- How many children have you had? How much did they weigh at birth? Were you told you had diabetes during any pregnancy?*
- Are you menopausal? If so, for how long?
- Are you trying to get pregnant but cannot?*
- Are you postmenopausal? If so, do you have any bleeding from your uterus?

Men

- Have you noticed any changes in your ability to get and maintain an erection?*
- Are you trying to have children but cannot?*

Coping–Stress Tolerance

- What kind of stressors do you have?
- How do you deal with stress or problems?
- What is your support system? To whom do you turn when you have a problem?

Value-Belief

- Do you think medicine should still be taken even though you feel okay?
- Do any of your prescribed therapies cause any conflict in your value-belief system?*

*If yes, describe.

Elimination Pattern. Because maintaining fluid balance is a major role of the endocrine system, questions related to fluid intake and elimination patterns may uncover endocrine problems. For example, increased thirst and urination can indicate diabetes (pancreas disorder) or diabetes insipidus (pituitary disorder). Ask about the frequency and consistency of bowel movements. Diarrhea can occur with hyperthyroidism or thyroid cancer. Constipation occurs with hypothyroidism, hypoparathyroidism, and hypopituitarism.

Activity-Exercise Pattern. Determine if there are any acute or gradual changes in energy level or persistent fatigue. A patient with chronic fatigue secondary to hypothyroidism, hypocortisolism, or diabetes may report changes in activity level.

Sleep-Rest Pattern. Ask the patient how many hours they typically sleep, and if they feel rested on awakening. Sleep problems can result from nocturia, nightmares, anxiety, depression, or insomnia that occur with diabetes or thyroid problems.

Cognitive-Perceptual Pattern. Memory deficits may occur with hypothyroidism and changes in sodium levels. Inappropriate secretion of antidiuretic hormone (SIADH) or pituitary tumors can cause hyponatremia. These issues can occur gradually. Gathering information from patient and family about memory, cognitive abilities, and balance can increase the chances of an earlier diagnosis.

Self-Perception–Self-Concept Pattern. Many endocrine disorders may affect a patient's self-esteem because of associated changes in physical appearance. For example, weight gain associated with hypothyroidism or exophthalmos and goiter associated with hyperthyroidism can cause problems related to body image.

Role-Relationship Pattern. Questions related to roles and relationships can highlight depression, chronic fatigue, and sleep problems. With chronic fatigue, depression, and anxiety, patients and their families will have stressed relationships. Questions related to home life and the patients' ability to fulfill their role in the family will aid in identifying problems.

Sexuality-Reproductive Pattern. The endocrine system regulates GH, prolactin, LH, FSH, testosterone, and estrogen. Therefore, menstrual problems, hirsutism, infertility, decreased libido, and growth disorders can be a result of endocrine disorders. Some women develop hypothyroidism during or after menopause. Other patients begin to develop type 2 diabetes during middle age when sex hormones are changing. Document the presence of abnormal secondary sex characteristics, such as facial hair *(hirsutism)* in women. Obtain a detailed history of menstruation and pregnancy. Menstrual problems can occur with disorders of the ovaries and pituitary, thyroid, and adrenal glands. A history of large-birth-weight babies or gestational diabetes increases the risk for developing type 2 diabetes later in life. Male sexual problems may include impotence, infertility, or the lack of development of secondary sexual characteristics. Retrograde ejaculation can occur in diabetes.

Coping–Stress Tolerance Pattern. Because stress worsens some endocrine conditions, ask patients about their stress level and usual coping patterns. Patients with adrenal insufficiency have difficulty dealing with stress. These patients are at risk for developing hypotension and fluid and electrolyte imbalance.

Value-Belief Pattern. Determining a patient's ability to make lifestyle changes is an important nursing function. Identify the patient's value-belief patterns so that you can help to determine appropriate treatment plans. This is especially important in a condition such as diabetes, which may require major lifestyle changes. Other disorders, such as hypothyroidism or hypocortisolism, may be managed with medications but need lifelong monitoring.

Objective Data

Except the thyroid and testes, most endocrine glands are inaccessible to direct examination. Assessment can be accomplished using objective data from the physical examination and diagnostic tests. It is essential to understand the actions of hormones in order to assess the function of a gland by monitoring the target tissue.

Physical Examination. Use the following general examination when evaluating endocrine function.[3] Specific clinical findings for the various endocrine problems are discussed in Chapters 48 and 49. Endocrine disorders may cause changes in mental and emotional status. Throughout the examination, assess the patient's orientation, alertness, memory, cognitive abilities, affect, personality, and appropriateness of their behavior.

Take a full set of vital signs at the beginning of the examination. Variations in temperature, heart rate, and BP can occur

---

Subjective Data

A focused subjective assessment of L.M. revealed the following information:

- **Past Medical History:** Denies any medical or surgical history. Has not seen an HCP for 8 yr.
- **Medications:** None.
- **Health Perception–Health Management:** L.M. works as a receptionist for a local law firm and says it is all she can do to make it through the work day. She often wakes up with a headache and goes to bed with the same headache, describing it as a dull, throbbing ache between her eyes. She does not have the energy she had 5 yr ago or even 6 mo ago. She used to enjoy gardening and going out with friends but now can barely manage work and coming home.

(© iStockphoto/ Thinkstock.)

- **Nutritional-Metabolic:** L.M. reports a steady weight gain over the past 6 mo, mainly in her abdominal area. She feels as if she looks pregnant but knows that is not possible. Her appetite has decreased, but she is not able to lose any weight. She says she feels "bloated." She reports growth of facial hair and notices she is bruising easily. L.M. denies difficulty with swallowing, hoarseness, palpitations, or tremors.
- **Elimination:** Denies any changes or problems with urination or bowel movements.
- **Activity-Exercise:** L.M. states that she has no ambition to exercise. She is just too tired at the end of the workday and has no energy on the weekends either. She reports leg cramps with walking.
- **Sleep-Rest:** Sleeps 10+ hr at night but does not feel rested on awakening.
- **Cognitive-Perceptual:** L.M. is worried she is going crazy. She finds herself easily angered and irritable, often snapping at co-workers and her husband. She says this is not her usual self. At first, she thought it was because she was dealing with a constant, dull headache. Lately, she has noticed that her vision is blurry and that is making work and life more stressful. She says her headache hurts between her eyes. She rates the pain as a 4 on a scale of 0 to 10 and states that ibuprofen does not ease the pain. The pain is typically worse on arising in the morning. It slowly decreases during the day.
- **Self-Perception–Self-Concept:** L.M. hates the way she looks. She says when she looks in the mirror, she cannot believe what she sees. She feels as if she has aged 10 yr over the past 6 mo and has gained weight in her face, neck, and trunk. She is concerned that her scalp hair is thinning, and she is growing a beard. She tells you she feels "old and ugly"!
- **Coping–Stress Tolerance:** L.M. states that she is finding it harder to cope with the stresses of her job, her relationship with her husband, and life in general. She believes her emotions are very "raw and labile," so different from the easy-going, smiling person she had once prided herself in being.

Discussion Questions

1. Which subjective assessment findings are of most concern to you?
2. Based on the subjective assessment findings, what should you include in the physical assessment? What would you be looking for?

You will learn more about the physical examination of the endocrine system in the next section.

(See p. 1099 for more information on L.M.)

---

with a variety of endocrine-related problems. Obtain height and weight. Calculate body mass index (BMI) to assess nutritional status.

Integument. Assess the color and texture of the skin, hair, and nails. Note the overall skin color as well as pigmentation and bruising. Decreased skin pigmentation can occur in hypopituitarism, hypothyroidism, and hypoparathyroidism. Hyperpigmentation, or "bronzing" of the skin, especially on

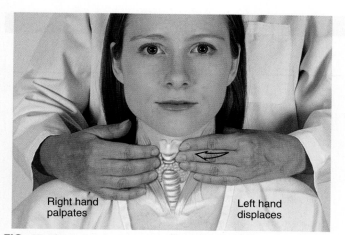

Right hand palpates

Left hand displaces

FIG. 47.10 Posterior palpation of the thyroid gland. (From Jarvis C: *Physical examination and health assessment*, ed 6, St Louis, 2012, Saunders.)

knuckles, elbows, knees, genitalia, and palmar creases, is a classic finding in a form of adrenal insufficiency known as *Addison's disease*. Palpate the skin for texture and moisture. Examine hair distribution on the head, face, trunk, and extremities. Assess the hair's appearance and texture. Hair loss, excess hair growth, or dull, brittle hair may suggest endocrine problems. Assess for delayed wound healing.

Head. Inspect the size and contour of the head. Facial features should be symmetric. Hyperreflexia and facial muscle contraction upon percussion of the facial nerve (*Chvostek's sign*) may occur in hypoparathyroidism. Inspect the eyes for position, symmetry, and shape. Large and protruding eyes (exophthalmos) are associated with hyperthyroidism. Assess visual acuity using a Snellen eye chart. Visual field loss may occur with a pituitary tumor. In the mouth, inspect the buccal mucosa, condition of teeth, and tongue size. Note hair distribution on the scalp and face. Hearing loss is common in acromegaly from excess GH.[4]

Neck. The thyroid gland is not usually visible during inspection. A feature that distinguishes the thyroid from other masses in the neck is its upward movement on swallowing. Inspect the neck while the patient swallows a sip of water. The neck should appear symmetric without lumps or bulging.

Palpate the thyroid for its size, shape, symmetry, and tenderness and for any nodules. *Goiter,* an enlarged thyroid gland, can occur with hyperthyroidism or hypothyroidism. Be careful not to press too hard or massage an enlarged thyroid gland. This can cause a sudden release of thyroid hormone into an already overloaded system. An experienced clinician should perform palpation in patients with a known diagnosis of hyperthyroidism.

Perform palpation using a posterior or anterior approach. For *anterior palpation,* stand in front of the patient, with the patient's neck flexed. Place your thumb horizontally with the upper edge along the lower border of the cricoid cartilage. Then move your thumb over the isthmus as the patient swallows water. Place your fingers laterally to the anterior border of the sternocleidomastoid muscle and palpate each lateral lobe before and while the patient swallows water.

For *posterior palpation,* stand behind the patient (Fig. 47.10). With the thumbs of both hands resting on the nape of the patient's neck, use your index and middle fingers of both hands to feel for the thyroid isthmus and for the anterior surfaces of the lateral lobes. To relax the neck muscles, ask the patient to flex the neck slightly forward and to the right. Displace the thyroid

cartilage to the right with your left hand and fingers. Palpate with your right hand after placing the thumb deep and behind the sternocleidomastoid muscle with the index and middle fingers in front of it. Ask the patient to swallow water and feel for the thyroid to move up. In a normal person, the thyroid is often not palpable. If palpable, it usually feels smooth with a firm consistency. It is not tender with gentle pressure.[5] If nodules, enlargement, asymmetry, or hardness (abnormal findings) are present, refer the patient for further evaluation. Auscultate the lateral lobes of an enlarged thyroid gland with the stethoscope bell to hear a *bruit,* a soft swishing sound that can occur with a goiter or hyperthyroidism.

Thorax. Inspect the thorax for shape and characteristics of the skin. Note the presence of breast gynecomastia in men. Auscultate lung sounds and heart sounds. Note any adventitious lung sounds (wheezing, decreased sounds) or extra heart sounds. Signs of fluid overload or heart failure may be present in patients with SIADH or hypothyroidism.

Abdomen. Inspect the contour of the abdomen and note the symmetry and color. Cushing syndrome (hypercortisolism) causes the skin to be fragile, resulting in purple-blue striae across the abdomen. Note general obesity or truncal obesity. Auscultate bowel sounds.

Extremities. Assess the size, shape, symmetry, and general proportion of hands and feet. Patients with acromegaly from pituitary tumors may have large hands and feet. Inspect the skin for changes in pigmentation, lesions, and edema. Assess muscle strength and deep tendon reflexes. In the upper extremities, assess for tremors by placing a piece of paper on the outstretched fingers, palm down. Muscular spasms of the hand elicited on application of an occlusive BP cuff for 3 minutes (*Trousseau's sign*) may occur in hypoparathyroidism.

Genitalia. Inspect the genital hair distribution pattern, since it may be changed with hormone problems.

Assessment abnormalities related to the endocrine system are outlined in Table 47.5. A focused assessment of the endocrine system is shown on p. 1101.

CASE STUDY—cont'd

Objective Data: Physical Examination

(© iStockphoto/ Thinkstock.)

A focused assessment of L.M. reveals the following: L.M. is sitting on the edge of the examination table. She appears somewhat anxious. Her BP is 190/80, heart rate 84, respiratory rate 20, temp 98.6° F (37° C). Her weight is 160 lb, and she is 5 ft, 4 in tall. L.M.'s face is reddened and puffy. She appears to have a lump on the back of her neck and shoulders. There is some acne on her face, along with some hair growth on her upper lip and chin area. Her abdomen is protruding, but her arms and legs are thin. She has +1 edema in her ankles bilaterally. There are several bruises on her upper and lower extremities, as well as purple stretch marks on her abdomen.

Discussion Questions

1. Which physical assessment findings are of most concern to you?
2. Based upon the subjective and objective assessment data presented so far, what are 3 priority nursing diagnoses?
3. What diagnostic studies would you expect to be ordered?

You will learn more about diagnostic studies related to the endocrine system in the next section.

(See p. 1106 for more information on L.M.)

Answers available at *http://evolve.elsevier.com/Lewis/medsurg.*

TABLE 47.5 Assessment Abnormalities

Endocrine System

Finding	Description	Possible Etiology and Significance
Cardiovascular		
Chest pain	Angina caused by increased metabolic demands, effusions	Hyperthyroidism, hypothyroidism
Dysrhythmias	Tachycardia, atrial fibrillation	Hypothyroidism, hyperthyroidism, hypoparathyroidism, hyperparathyroidism, pheochromocytoma
Fluid overload or signs of heart failure	Crackles in the lungs, peripheral edema, shortness of breath	SIADH, hypothyroidism, myxedema
Hypertension	High BP caused by ↑ metabolic demands and catecholamines	Hyperthyroidism, pheochromocytoma, Cushing syndrome
Gastrointestinal		
Constipation	Passage of infrequent hard stools	Hypothyroidism, hyperparathyroidism
Head and Neck		
Exophthalmos	Eyeball protrusion from orbits	Occurs in hyperthyroidism because of fluid accumulation in eye and retroorbital tissue
Goiter	Generalized enlargement of thyroid gland	Hyperthyroidism, hypothyroidism, iodine deficiency
Moon face	Periorbital edema and facial fullness	Cushing syndrome because of ↑ cortisol secretion
Myxedema	Puffiness, periorbital edema, masklike affect	Hydrophilic mucopolysaccharides infiltrating dermis in patients with hypothyroidism
Thyroid nodule(s)	Localized enlargement of thyroid gland	May be benign or malignant
Visual changes	↓ Visual acuity and/or ↓ peripheral vision	Pituitary gland enlargement or tumor leading to pressure on optic nerve
Integument		
Bruises easily	Multiple bruises over various parts of body	Cushing syndrome
Changes in hair distribution	Hair loss	Hypothyroidism, hyperthyroidism, ↓ pituitary secretion
	↓ Axillary and pubic hair	Cortisol deficiency
	Hirsutism (excess facial hair on women)	Cushing syndrome, prolactinoma (a pituitary tumor)
Changes in skin texture	Thick, cold, dry skin	Hypothyroidism
	Thick, leathery, oily skin	GH excess (acromegaly)
	Warm, smooth, moist skin	Hyperthyroidism
Depigmentation (vitiligo)	Patchy areas of light skin	May be a marker of autoimmune endocrine disorders
Edema	Generalized edema	Mucopolysaccharide accumulation in tissue in hypothyroidism
Hyperpigmentation	Darkening of the skin, especially in skinfolds and creases	Increased secretion of MSH from Addison's disease, acanthosis nigricans
Skin ulceration	Areas of ulcerated skin, most often found on legs and feet	Peripheral neuropathy and peripheral vascular disease, which are contributory factors in the development of diabetic foot ulcers
Striae	Purplish red marks below the skin surface. Usually seen on abdomen, breasts, and buttocks	Cushing syndrome
Musculoskeletal		
Changes in muscular strength or muscle mass	Generalized weakness and/or fatigue	Common with many endocrine problems, including pituitary, thyroid, parathyroid, and adrenal problems
		Diabetes, diabetes insipidus
	↓ Muscle mass	Specifically seen in GH deficiency and Cushing syndrome from protein wasting
Enlargement of bones and cartilage	Coarsening of facial features. ↑ In size of hands and feet over a period of several years	Gradual enlargement and thickening of bony tissue occurring with GH excess in adults as seen in acromegaly secondary to pituitary dysfunction
Neurologic		
↑ Deep tendon reflexes	Hyperreflexia	Hyperthyroidism, hypoparathyroidism
Lethargy	State of mental sluggishness or somnolence	Hypothyroidism
Seizure	Sudden involuntary contraction of muscles	Consequence of a pituitary tumor
		Hypervolemia and hyponatremia with SIADH
		Complications of diabetes, severe hypothyroidism
Tetany	Intermittent involuntary muscle spasms usually involving the extremities	Severe hypocalcemia that can occur with hypoparathyroidism
Nutrition		
Changes in weight	Weight loss	Hyperthyroidism caused by ↑ in metabolism, type 1 diabetes, diabetic ketoacidosis
	Weight gain	Hypothyroidism, Cushing syndrome, type 2 diabetes

TABLE 47.5 Assessment Abnormalities

Endocrine System—cont'd

Finding	Description	Possible Etiology and Significance
Glucose levels altered	↑ Serum glucose	Diabetes, Cushing syndrome, GH excess
Reproductive		
Changes in reproductive function	Menstrual irregularities, ↓ libido, ↓ fertility, impotence	Pituitary hypofunction, GH excess, thyroid problems, adrenocortical problems
Other		
↓ Urine output	↓ Water reabsorption from kidney tubules	SIADH
Polydipsia	Excessive thirst	Extreme water losses in diabetes (with severe hyperglycemia), diabetes insipidus, dehydration
Polyuria	Excess urine output	Diabetes (from hyperglycemia) or diabetes insipidus (associated with ↓ ADH)
Thermoregulation	Cold insensitivity	Hypothyroidism caused by a slowing of metabolic processes
	Heat intolerance	Hyperthyroidism caused by excessive metabolism

FOCUSED ASSESSMENT

Endocrine System

Use this checklist to ensure the key assessment steps have been done.

Subjective

Ask the patient about any of the following and note responses.

Excessive or increased thirst	Y	N
Excess or decreased urination	Y	N
Excessive hunger	Y	N
Heat or cold intolerance	Y	N
Excessive sweating	Y	N
Recent weight gain or loss	Y	N

Objective: Diagnostic

Check the following laboratory results for critical values.

Potassium	✓
Glucose	✓
Sodium	✓
Glycosylated hemoglobin (A1C)	✓
Thyroid studies: TSH, T_3, T_4	✓
Serum osmolality	✓

Objective: Physical Examination

Inspect/Measure

Body temperature	✓
Height and weight	✓
Alertness and emotional state	✓
Skin for changes in color and texture	✓
Hair for changes in color, texture, and distribution	✓

Auscultate

Heart rate, BP	✓

Palpate

Extremities for edema	✓
Skin for texture and temperature	✓
Neck for thyroid size, shape	✓

DIAGNOSTIC STUDIES OF ENDOCRINE SYSTEM

Diagnostic studies of the endocrine system are shown in Tables 47.6 and 47.7. Pertinent findings from the history and physical examination guide the selection of diagnostic studies. Imaging studies can identify pituitary tumors, thyroid nodules, or adrenal tumors. Laboratory studies may include direct measurement of the hormone level or an indirect measure of gland function by evaluating blood or urine components affected by the hormone, such as glucose or electrolytes. We can also measure the releasing or stimulating hormone. For example, we can evaluate thyroid function by measuring TSH.

We can assess hormones with constant basal levels, such as T_4, with a single measurement. Note the time of the sample collection on the laboratory slip. Information about night shift work is important for hormones with circadian or sleep-related secretion (e.g., cortisol). Evaluating other hormones may require multiple blood samplings, such as in suppression tests (e.g., dexamethasone) and stimulation tests (e.g., glucose tolerance). In these situations, it is often necessary to obtain IV access to give the testing medication and fluids and draw multiple blood samples.

Pituitary gland problems can manifest in a wide variety of ways because of the number of hormones produced. Many diagnostic studies evaluate these hormones either directly or indirectly.

Several tests are available to evaluate thyroid function. The most sensitive and accurate laboratory test is the measurement of TSH. Thus it is often the first diagnostic test done to evaluate thyroid function.[6] Follow-up tests ordered when the TSH level is abnormal include total T_4, free T_4, and total T_3. Free T_4 is the unbound thyroxine and more accurately reflects thyroid function than total T_4.

The only hormone secreted by the parathyroid glands is PTH. Because PTH regulates serum calcium and phosphate levels, these levels reflect abnormalities in PTH secretion. For this reason, diagnostic tests for the parathyroid gland typically include PTH, serum calcium, and serum phosphate levels.

Tests associated with the adrenal cortex function focus on measuring blood plasma and urine levels of the 3 types of hormones secreted: glucocorticoids, mineralocorticoids, and androgens. Urine studies often require a 24-hour urine collection to eliminate the impact of short-term fluctuations in plasma hormone levels.

The tests used to evaluate glucose metabolism are important in the diagnosis and management of diabetes. See Chapter 48 for information about diagnostic studies for diabetes.

TABLE 47.6 Serology and Urine Studies

Endocrine System

Study	Reference Interval	Purpose and Description	Nursing Responsibility
Adrenal Studies *Blood Studies*			
Adrenal steroid precursors • Androstenediones (AD) • Dehydroepiandrosterone DHEA) • Dehydroepiandrosterone sulfate (DHEA S) • 11-Deoxycortisol	AD • *Female:* 0.05–2.05 ng/mL • *Male:* 0.04–1.06 ng/mL DHEA • *Female:* 0.14–7.88 ng/mL • *Male:* 0.11–6.73 ng/mL DHEA S • *Female:* 7–488 mcg/dL • *Male:* 7–371 mcg/dL 11-Deoxycortisol • *Adults:* 10–79 ng/dL	Assesses for congenital adrenal hyperplasia, sex hormones abnormalities, adrenal or gonadal tumors.	*Before:* Tanner stage I–V of physical development needed for accurate assessment. Determine date of last menstrual period (LMP) for females. Test should be done 1 wk before or after menstrual cycle. *After:* Note date of LMP on laboratory slip.
Adrenocorticotropic hormone (ACTH, corticotropin)	• *Female:* 6–58 pg/mL • *Male:* 7–69 pg/mL	Measures amount of ACTH made by the anterior pituitary gland. Levels determine if there is an overproduction or underproduction of cortisol, and whether cause is an adrenal gland or pituitary gland abnormality.	*Before:* Patient should be NPO after midnight. Do morning blood draw between 6 and 8 AM. *During:* Use prechilled blood tube and place on ice.
ACTH stimulation test with cosyntropin (Cortisol stimulation test)	*Rapid test:* Cortisol levels increase more than 7 mcg/dL higher than baseline *24-Hour test:* Cortisol levels >40 mcg/dL *3-Day test:* Cortisol levels greater than 40 mcg/dL	Used to evaluate cause of adrenal insufficiency. If cortisol levels increase after cosyntropin injection, the cause of adrenal insufficiency is the pituitary gland. If there is no or little rise in cortisol levels, the cause of adrenal insufficiency is the adrenal gland.	*Before:* Obtain baseline cortisol level at beginning of cosyntropin infusion. *During:* Inject bolus of IV cosyntropin with a plastic syringe. Draw cortisol samples 30 and 60 min after bolus. Monitor site and rate of IV infusion. Ensure sample collection at appropriate times.
Aldosterone	*Supine:* 3–10 ng/dL (0.08–0.30 nmol/L) *Upright:* • *Female:* 5–30 ng/dL (0.14–0.08 nmol/L) • *Male:* 6–22 ng/dL (0.17–0.61 nmol/L)	Used to identify hyperaldosteronism. Helps distinguish primary aldosteronism from adrenal disease versus secondary aldosteronism from extraadrenal disease.	*Before:* Usually morning blood sample is preferred. Tell patient that the required position (supine/sitting/standing) must be maintained for 2 hr before specimen is drawn.
Cortisol (hydrocortisone, serum cortisol)	• *8 AM:* 5–23 mcg/dL (138–635 nmol/L) • *4 PM:* 3–13 mcg/dL (83–359 nmol/L)	Measures serum cortisol level to evaluate adrenal activity. Cortisol levels are normally highest in the morning, slowly drop during the day, and are lowest around midnight.	*Before:* Sample should be drawn in morning. Note if patient works night shift. Mark time of blood draw on laboratory slip. Stress and excessive physical activity produce elevated results.
Dexamethasone suppression (DST, prolonged/rapid DST, cortisol suppression test, ACTH suppression test)	Prolonged method: • *Low dose:* >50% reduction of plasma cortisol and 17-hydroxycorticosteroid (17-OCHS) • *High dose:* >50% reduction of plasma cortisol and 17-OCHS Rapid (overnight) method: • Plasma cortisol levels suppressed to <2 mcg/dL	Helps to identify and determine cause of adrenal hyperactivity (e.g., Cushing syndrome).	*Before:* Patient should fast for 8–10 hr prior. Do not test acutely ill patients or those under stress. Stress-stimulated ACTH may override suppression. Screen patient for drugs, such as estrogen and corticosteroids, that may give false-positive results. *Overnight method:* Dexamethasone 1 mg (low dose) or 4 mg (high dose) is given at 11 PM to suppress secretion of corticotropin-releasing hormone. Plasma cortisol sample is drawn at 8 AM.
Metanephrine, plasma free (fractionated metanephrines)	*Normetanephrine:* <0.5 nmol/L or 18–111 pg/mL by HPLC *Metanephrine:* <0.9 nmol/L or 12–60 pg/mL by HPLC	Used to identify pheochromocytoma of the adrenal or extraadrenal glands.	*Before:* Ask about recent history of vigorous exercise, high stress levels, or starvation (may artificially ↑ levels). Assess for drugs (e.g., caffeine, alcohol, levodopa, nitroglycerin, acetaminophen, and those containing epinephrine or norepinephrine) that can alter results.
Urine Studies			
Cortisol (hydrocortisone, urine cortisol, free cortisol)	24-Hour specimen: <100 mcg/24 hr (<276 nmol/day)	Measures urine cortisol level to evaluate adrenal activity.	*Before:* Explain 24-hr urine collection and need to avoid stressful situations and excessive physical exercise. Assess for drug use (e.g., reserpine, diuretics, phenothiazines, insulin, amphetamines) that may alter results.

TABLE 47.6 Serology and Urine Studies—cont'd

Endocrine System

Study	Reference Interval	Purpose and Description	Nursing Responsibility
17-Hydroxycorticosteroids (17-OCHS)	24-Hour specimen: *Adults:* • *Male:* 3–10 mg/24 hr (8.3–27.6 µmol/day) • *Female:* 2–8 mg/24 hr (5.2–22.1 µmol/day)	Measures 17-OCHS, a cortisol metabolite, to evaluate adrenocortical function. Older adults may have slightly lower values.	*Before:* Explain 24-hr urine collection and need to avoid stressful situations and excessive physical exercise. Assess for drug use (e.g., erythromycin, spironolactone) that may alter results.
17-Ketosteroids (17-KS)	24-Hour specimen: • *Male:* 6–20 mg/24 hr (20–70 µmol/day) • *Female:* 6–17 mg/24 hr (20–60 µmol/day)	Evaluates adrenocortical and gonadal functions by measuring urinary androgen metabolites. Older adults may have slightly lower values.	*Before:* Explain 24-hr urine collection.
Vanillylmandelic acid (VMA)	24-Hour specimen: <6.8 mg/24 hr (<35 µmol/24 hr)	Measures the excretion of catecholamine metabolite. Used to identify catecholamine-producing tumors, such as pheochromocytoma.	*Before:* Explain 24-hr urine collection. Must follow VMA-restricted diet 2–3 days before and during the urine collection. *During:* Keep 24-hr urine collection at pH <3.0 with HCl acid as preservative. Keep on ice.

Pancreatic Studies
Blood Studies

Study	Reference Interval	Purpose and Description	Nursing Responsibility
C-Peptide (connecting peptide insulin, insulin C-peptide, proinsulin C-peptide)	*Fasting:* 0.78–1.89 ng/mL (0.26–0.62 nmol/L) *1 hour after glucose load:* 5–12 ng/mL	Measures amount of C-peptide, which is released with insulin. Distinguishes between type 1 (low levels) and type 2 diabetes (normal or high levels).	*Before:* Patient should fast 8–12 hr prior. Water intake is allowed.
Glucagon	50–100 pg/mL (50–100 ng/L)	Assesses for glucagonoma (α islet cell tumor). Evaluates pancreatic function, especially in people with diabetes who have low blood glucose (hypoglycemia).	*Before:* Patient should fast 8–12 hr prior. Water intake is allowed.
Glucose (blood sugar, fasting blood glucose [FBG])	*Fasting* (defined as no caloric intake for at least 8 hr): 74–106 mg/dL (4.1–5.9 mmol/L) *Casual* (defined as any time of day): ≤200 mg/dL (<11.1 mmol/L)	Aids in the diagnosis of diabetes.	*Before:* Patient should fast 8-12 hr prior. Water intake is allowed. Assess for the many drugs that may influence results.
Glucose, postprandial (2-hour postprandial glucose [2-hr PPG])	*0–50 yr:* <140 mg/dL (<7.8 mmol/L) *50–60 yr:* <150 md/dL *60 yr and older:* <160 mg/dL	Aids in the diagnosis of diabetes.	*Before:* Patient should fast 8–12 hr, then eat a meal of at least 75 g of carbohydrate. Patient must fast after eating this meal until blood is drawn. No exercise during test.
Glucose tolerance test (GTT, oral glucose tolerance [OGTT])	*Nonpregnancy:* *Fasting:* <110 mg/dL (<6.1 mmol/L *1 hr:* <180 mg/dL (<11.1 mmol/L) *2 hr:* <140 mg/dL (<7.8 mmol/L)	Assesses glucose levels in people with symptoms of (hypoglycemia). Aids in the diagnosis of diabetes.	*Before:* Patient should fast 8–12 hr prior. Many drugs may influence results, including caffeine and smoking. Ensure that patient's diet 3 days before test includes 150–300 g of carbohydrate with intake of at least 1500 cal/day.
Glycosylated hemoglobin (GHb, GHB, glycohemoglobin, hemoglobin A1C [Hb A1C], diabetic control index, glycated protein)	*Nondiabetic adult/child:* 4%–5.6% *Prediabetes:* 5.7%–6.4% *Good diabetic control:* <7%[7]	Measures the average blood glucose for the past 90 days. Used to diagnose and screen diabetes treatment plans.	*Before:* Tell patient that fasting is not necessary and that blood sample will be drawn.
Insulin assay	6–26 µU/mL (43–186 pmol/L)	Assesses insulin levels in people with symptoms of hypoglycemia. Assesses for insulinomas and carbohydrate and lipid absorption abnormalities.	*Before:* Patient should fast 8–12 hr prior. Water intake is allowed.

Urine Studies

Study	Reference Interval	Purpose and Description	Nursing Responsibility
Glucose (urine sugar)	*Random specimen:* negative *24-hour specimen:* 50–300 mg/day (0.3–1.7 mmol/day)	Measures amount of glucose in the urine. Assesses diabetes management.	*Before:* Use freshly voided urine. Many drugs alter glucose readings. Follow directions exactly to avoid errors.
Ketones	None or negative	Measures amount of ketones in the urine. Assesses for diabetic ketoacidosis, a life-threatening condition seen most often in people with type 1 diabetes.	*Before:* Use freshly voided urine specimen. Test is often done with glucose test. Follow directions exactly. Certain drugs can produce false-positive or false-negative results.

Continued

TABLE 47.6 Serology and Urine Studies—cont'd

Endocrine System

Study	Reference Interval	Purpose and Description	Nursing Responsibility
Parathyroid Studies *Blood Studies* **Calcium (total)**	9.0–10.5 mg/dL (2.25–2.62 mmol/L)	Assesses the function of the parathyroid gland and calcium absorption.	*Before:* Patient must fast 8–12 hr prior. Assess for drug use (e.g., albuterol, heparin, diuretics) that may alter results. *After:* Keep sample on ice.
Calcium (ionized)	4.5–5.6 mg/dL (1.05–1.3 mmol/L)	Free form of total calcium. Unchanged by inconsistent serum albumin levels that occur in certain populations, such as critically ill patients.	As above.
Parathyroid hormone (PTH, parathormone)	*Intact (whole):* 10–65 pg/mL (10–65 ng/L) *N terminal:* 8–24 pg/mL *C terminal:* 50–330 pg/mL	Used to determine the cause of changes in calcium levels caused by parathyroid or nonparathyroid problems. Monitored in patients with chronic kidney disease, especially those on dialysis.	*Before:* Patient should fast 8–12 hr prior. Obtain sample in the morning. *During:* Obtain serum calcium level at same time. *After:* Mark time of blood draw on laboratory slip.
Phosphate (PO4), phosphorus (P)	3.0–4.5 mg/dL (0.97–1.45 mmol/L)	Measures amount of inorganic phosphate in the blood. Assesses for disorders related to calcium and phosphorus disorders.	*Before:* Patient must fast 8–12 hr prior. If possible, hold IV fluids containing glucose for 8 hr prior.
Pituitary Studies *Blood Studies* **Antidiuretic hormone (ADH, vasopressin, Arginine vasopressin [AVP])**	1–5 pg/mL	Assesses for diabetes insipidus (DI) or SIADH.	*Before:* Patient must fast 8–12 hr prior.
Gonadotropins • **Follicle-stimulating hormone (FSH) assay** • **Luteinizing hormone (LH assay, Lutropin)**	*FSH (Adult)* • *Male:* 1.42–15.4 IU/L • *Female:* *Follicular phase:* 1.37–9.9 IU/L *Ovulatory phase:* 6.17–17.2 IU/L *Luteal phase:* 1.09–9.2 IU/L *Postmenopause:* 19.3–100.6 IU/L *LH (Adult)* • *Male:* 1.24–7.8 IU/L • *Female:* *Follicular phase:* 1.68–15 IU/L *Ovulatory phase:* 21.9–56.6 IU/L *Luteal phase:* 0.61–16.3 IU/L *Postmenopause:* 14.2–52.3 IU/L	Assesses for pituitary, puberty or infertility conditions and menopause.	*Before:* Tell patient that fasting is not necessary and that blood sample will be drawn. *During:* Note on the laboratory slip time of LMP or whether woman is menopausal.
Growth hormone (GH, human growth hormone [HGH], somatotropin hormone [SH])	• *Men:* <5 ng/mL • *Women:* <10 ng/mL	Evaluates GH secretion and pituitary gland function.	*Before:* Patient must fast 8–12 hours prior. Emotional and physical stress may alter results. Indicate patient fasting status and recent activity level on the laboratory slip.
GH stimulation (GH provocation, insulin tolerance test [ITT], arginine test)	GH levels >10 mg/mL	Aids in identifying GH deficiency and conditions caused from decreased pituitary hormone production.	*Before:* Patient must fast 10-12 hours prior. Water is allowed on morning of test. Establish IV access for medication administration and blood sampling. *During:* Continually assess for hypoglycemia and hypotension. Keep 50% dextrose and 5% dextrose IV solution at the bedside in case severe hypoglycemia occurs.
Insulin-like growth factor (IGF-1, somatomedin C, insulin-like growth factor binding proteins [IGF BP])	42–110 ng/mL	Evaluates GH and pituitary gland function. Provides a more accurate reflection of mean plasma concentration of GH because it is not subject to circadian rhythm and fluctuations.	*Before:* Patient must fast 8–12 hr prior.

TABLE 47.6 Serology and Urine Studies—cont'd

Endocrine System

Study	Reference Interval	Purpose and Description	Nursing Responsibility
Urine Studies			
Water deprivation (ADH stimulation)	Neurogenic DI: >9% rise in urine osmolality Nephrogenic DI: <9% rise in urine osmolality Psychogenic polydipsia: <9% rise in urine osmolality	Distinguishes among neurogenic, nephrogenic, or psychogenic DI.	Before: Obtain baseline weight and urine and plasma osmolality. Should be done only if serum sodium is normal and urine osmolality is <300 mOsm/kg. During: Patient may need to fast. Severe dehydration may occur. Assess urine hourly for volume and specific gravity. Send hourly urine samples to laboratory for osmolality determination. Send blood samples for sodium and osmolality every 2 hr. Stop test and rehydrate if patient's weight drops >2 kg at any time. After: Rehydrate with oral fluids. Check orthostatic BP and pulse to ensure adequate fluid volume.
Thyroid Studies			
Blood Studies			
Antithyroglobulin antibody (thyroid autoantibody, thyroid antithyroglobulin antibody, thyroglobulin antibody, thyroid peroxidase antibody [TPO])	<116 IU/mL	Measures thyroid antibody levels. Aids in diagnosing autoimmune thyroid disease and separates it from other forms of thyroiditis. One or more antibody tests may be ordered depending on symptoms.	Before: Explain blood draw procedure to the patient.
Thyroglobulin (Tg, thyrogen-stimulated thyroglobulin)	• Male: 0.5–53 ng/mL • Female: 0.5–43.0 ng/mL	Identifies functioning thyroid tissue and thyroid cancer cells. Used primarily as a tumor marker for patients being treated for thyroid cancer.	As above.
Thyroid-stimulating hormone (TSH, thyrotropin)	2–10 µU/mL	Most sensitive diagnostic test for evaluating thyroid function. Helps in distinguishing primary (thyroid), secondary (pituitary), and tertiary (hypothalamus) hypothyroidism.	As above.
Thyroxine-binding globulin (TBG, thyroid-binding globulin)	10–19 yr: • Male: 1.4–2.6 mg/dL • Female: 1.4–3.0 mg/dL 20 yr: 1.7–3.6 mg/dL Oral contraceptives: 1.5–5.5 mg/dL	Measures TBG, the main thyroid hormone protein carrier. Used to assess thyroid function when T_4 and T_3 levels are abnormal.	As above.
Thyroxine, total and Free (T_4, thyroxine screen, FT_4)	Free T_4: 0.8–2.8 ng/dL (10–36 pmol/L) Total T_4: • Male: 4–12 mcg/dL (51–154 nmol/L) • Female: 5–12 mcg/dL (64–154 nmol/L) • >60 yr: 5–11 mcg/dL (64–142 nmol/L)	Used to evaluate thyroid function and monitor thyroid replacement or suppressive therapy. Free T_4 levels not affected by protein levels like total T_4 is, so it is thought to be more precise marker of thyroid function.	As above.
Triiodothyronine (total T_3 radioimmunoassay [T_3 by RIA], free T_3)	16–20 yr: 80–210 ng/dL 20–50 yr: 70–205 ng/dL (1.2–3.4 nmol/L) >50 yr: 40–180 ng/dL (0.6–2.8 nmol/L)	Evaluates thyroid function. Free T_3 measures the active component of total T_3. Used to diagnose hyperthyroidism if TSH is abnormal and T_4 levels are normal. May be used to monitor drug therapy.	As above.
T_3 uptake (thyroid hormone–binding ratio [THBR], T_3 resin uptake)	24%–39%	Use in conjunction with T_4 to assess thyroid function. Indirectly measures binding capacity of thyroid-binding globulin	As above.

TABLE 47.7 Radiologic Studies

Endocrine System

Study	Description and Purpose	Nursing Responsibility
Adrenal arteriography (angiography; adrenal)	Assesses for arterial obstructive conditions and/or tumors of the adrenal glands.	*Before*: Assess for allergies, especially to contrast dye. Have patient fast 6–12 hr prior. Give sedative and other drugs, as ordered. *During*: Patient will feel flushed when dye is injected. *After:* Check pressure dressing site after procedure. Monitor BP, pulse, and circulation distal to injection site. Place compression device over site. Maintain IV and/or oral fluid intake.
Computed tomography (CT)	*Abdominal:* Used to detect adrenal hyperplasia and tumors or pancreatic abnormalities, such as pancreatitis, tumors, or cysts. *Brain:* Used to detect a pituitary tumor and its size. *Neck:* Can locate thyroid nodules and assess for thyroid cancer.	*Before:* Before contrast medium used, evaluate renal function. Assess if patient is allergic to shellfish since the contrast is iodine based. Patient may need to be NPO 4 hr prior to study. If the patient is taking metformin, hold it the day of the test to prevent hypoglycemia or acidosis. *During:* Warn patient that contrast injection may cause a feeling of being warm and flushed. Patient must lie completely still during scan. *After:* Encourage patient to drink fluids to avoid renal problems with any contrast.
Magnetic resonance cholangiopancrea-tography (MRCP)	Assesses for the source of pancreatitis and can detect pancreatobiliary tumors.	*Before:* Patient may need to be fasting. Oral and/or IV contrast injection may be used. Check for pregnancy, allergies, and renal function. *During:* Patient must lie completely still during scan.
Magnetic resonance imaging (MRI)	*Abdominal:* Can distinguish benign tumors from adrenal cancers. *Brain:* Study of choice for radiologic evaluation of the pituitary gland and hypothalamus. Used to identify tumors in these glands.	*Before:* Oral and/or IV contrast injection may be used. Check for pregnancy, allergies, and renal function before test. Have patient remove all metal objects. Ask about any history of surgical insertion of staples, plates, dental bridges, or other metal appliances. Remove metallic foil patches. Patient may need to be fasting. Assess for claustrophobia and the need for antianxiety medication. *During:* Patient must lie completely still during scan.
Parathyroid scan (parathyroid scintigraphy)	Used to find the parathyroid glands. Radioactive isotopes are taken up by cells in parathyroid glands. Obtains image of the glands and any abnormally active areas.	*Before:* Check for iodine allergy. Some foods and medications are restricted a few weeks before the scan.
Radioactive iodine (RAIU) uptake	Direct measure of thyroid activity and evaluates function of thyroid nodules. For 2–4 hours: 3%–19%. *For 24 hr:* 11%–30%	*Before:* Radioactive iodine given orally or IV. Check for allergies. *During:* Uptake by the thyroid gland is measured with a scanner at several time intervals, such as 2–4 hr and at 24 hr. *After:* Encourage patient to increase fluid intake as radionuclide takes 6–24 hr to be eliminated from body.
Thyroid scan	Used to evaluate nodules of thyroid. Benign nodules appear as warm spots because they take up radionuclide. Cancer tumors appear as cold spots because they tend not to take up radionuclide.	*Before:* Radioactive isotopes are given orally or IV. Check for allergies. *After:* Encourage patient to increase fluid intake as radionuclide takes 6–24 hr to be eliminated from body.
Thyroid ultrasound	Evaluates thyroid nodules to determine size and characteristics (cystic or solid tumors). Used to observe management and surveillance of nodules and unaffected portions of the gland.	*Before:* Explain that gel and a transducer will be used over the neck. The test lasts 15 min. No fasting or sedation required.

CASE STUDY—cont'd

Objective Data: Diagnostic Studies

(© iStockphoto/Thinkstock.)

The HCP orders the following initial diagnostic studies to be drawn in the morning after an 8-hr fast:
- CBC, basic metabolic panel (electrolytes, BUN, creatinine)
- Fasting blood glucose (FBG)
- TSH, free T$_4$
- Plasma cortisol levels
- Plasma ACTH levels

CBC results reveal a WBC of 12,200/μL and a decreased lymphocyte count at 800 cells/μL. The rest of the CBC is within normal limits (WNL). The FBG is 130 mg/dL. The plasma cortisol and ACTH levels are high. Thyroid studies are WNL.

Discussion Questions

1. Which diagnostic study results are of most concern to you?
2. Do you expect the HCP to order any other diagnostic studies for L.M.?
3. What are the interprofessional team's priorities for L.M. at this time?

Answers available at *http://evolve.elsevier.com/Lewis/medsurg.*

BRIDGE TO NCLEX EXAMINATION

The number of the question corresponds to the same-numbered outcome at the beginning of the chapter.

1. A characteristic common to all hormones is that they
   a. circulate in the blood bound to plasma proteins.
   b. influence cellular activity of specific target tissues.
   c. accelerate the metabolic processes of all body cells.
   d. enter a cell and change the cell's metabolism or gene expression.

2. A patient is receiving radiation therapy for cancer of the kidney. The nurse monitors the patient for signs and symptoms of damage to the
   a. pancreas.
   b. thyroid gland.
   c. adrenal glands.
   d. posterior pituitary gland.

3. A patient has a serum sodium level of 152 mEq/L (152 mmol/L). The normal hormonal response to this situation is
   a. release of ADH.
   b. release of ACTH.
   c. secretion of aldosterone.
   d. secretion of corticotropin-releasing hormone.

4. All cells in the body are believed to have intracellular receptors for
   a. insulin.
   b. glucagon.
   c. growth hormone.
   d. thyroid hormone.

5. When obtaining subjective data from a patient during assessment of the endocrine system, the nurse asks specifically about
   a. energy level.
   b. intake of vitamin C.
   c. employment history.
   d. frequency of sexual intercourse.

6. An appropriate technique to use during physical assessment of the thyroid gland is
   a. asking the patient to hyperextend the neck during palpation.
   b. percussing the neck for dullness to define the size of the thyroid.
   c. having the patient swallow water during inspection and palpation of the gland.
   d. using deep palpation to determine the extent of a visibly enlarged thyroid gland.

7. Endocrine disorders often go unrecognized in the older adult because
   a. symptoms are often attributed to aging.
   b. older adults rarely have identifiable symptoms.
   c. endocrine disorders are relatively rare in the older adult.
   d. older adults usually have subclinical endocrine disorders that minimize symptoms.

8. Abnormal findings during an endocrine assessment include (*select all that apply*)
   a. excess facial hair on a woman.
   b. blood pressure of 100/70 mm Hg.
   c. soft, formed stool every other day.
   d. 3-lb weight gain over last 6 months.
   e. hyperpigmented coloration in lower legs.

9. A patient has a total serum calcium level of 3 mg/dL (1.5 mEq/L). If this finding reflects hypoparathyroidism, the nurse would expect further diagnostic testing to reveal
   a. decreased serum PTH.
   b. increased serum ACTH.
   c. increased serum glucose.
   d. decreased serum cortisol levels.

1. b, 2. c, 3. a, 4. d, 5. a, 6. c, 7. a, 8. a, e, 9. a

For rationales to these answers and even more NCLEX review questions, visit *http://evolve.elsevier.com/Lewis/medsurg*.

ⓔ EVOLVE WEBSITE/RESOURCES LIST

http://evolve.elsevier.com/Lewis/medsurg
Review Questions (Online Only)
Key Points
Answer Keys for Questions
- Rationales for Bridge to NCLEX Examination Questions
- Answer Guidelines for the Case Study on pp. 1096, 1098, 1099, and 1106
Conceptual Care Map Creator
Audio Glossary
Supporting Media
- Animations
  - Overview of the Endocrine System
  - Thyroid and Parathyroid Glands
  - Thyroid Secretion
Supporting Media
Content Updates

REFERENCES

1. Huether SE, McCance K: *Understanding pathophysiology*, ed 6, St Louis, 2017, Elsevier.
2. Stratakis CA: *Genetics of endocrine disorders*, St Louis, 2017, Elsevier.
3. Jarvis C: *Physical examination and health assessment*, ed 7, St Louis, 2016, Saunders.
*4. Vilar L, Vilar CF, Lyra R, et al: Acromegaly: Clinical features at diagnosis, *Pituitary* 20:22, 2017.
5. Parsa AA, Gharib H: *Thyroid nodules*, New York, 2018, Humana.
6. Pagana K, Pagana T, Pagana TN: *Mosby's manual of diagnostic and laboratory tests*, ed 13, St Louis, 2017, Mosby.
*7. American Diabetes Association: Standards of medical care in diabetes—2018, *Diabetes Care* 41:S13, 2018.

*Evidence-based information for clinical practice.

48

Diabetes Mellitus

Jane K. Dickinson

Wherever a man turns he can find someone who needs him.

Albert Schweitzer

ⓔ http://evolve.elsevier.com/Lewis/medsurg

CONCEPTUAL FOCUS

Glucose Regulation
Infection
Nutrition

Self-Management
Sensory Perception

LEARNING OUTCOMES

1. Describe the pathophysiology and clinical manifestations of diabetes mellitus.
2. Distinguish between type 1 and type 2 diabetes mellitus.
3. Describe the interprofessional care of a patient with diabetes.
4. Describe the role of nutrition and exercise in managing diabetes mellitus.
5. Discuss the nursing management of a patient with newly diagnosed diabetes mellitus.
6. Describe the nursing management of a patient with diabetes mellitus in the ambulatory and home care settings.
7. Relate the pathophysiology of acute and chronic complications of diabetes mellitus to the clinical manifestations.
8. Explain the interprofessional care and nursing management of a patient with acute and chronic complications of diabetes mellitus.

KEY TERMS

This chapter discusses the pathophysiology, manifestations, complications, and management of diabetes. The long-term complications associated with diabetes can make it a devastating disease. Diabetes is the leading cause of adult blindness, end-stage renal disease, and nontraumatic lower limb amputations. It is a major contributing factor to heart disease and stroke. Managing diabetes requires daily decisions about food intake, blood glucose monitoring, medication, and exercise. You play a vital role in promoting the patient's self-management of diabetes through providing comprehensive patient and caregiver education.

DIABETES MELLITUS

Diabetes mellitus (DM), most often referred to as diabetes, is a chronic multisystem disease characterized by hyperglycemia from abnormal insulin production, impaired insulin use, or both. Diabetes is a serious health problem throughout the world. Its prevalence is rapidly increasing. Currently in the United States, an estimated 29.1 million people, or 9.3% of the population, have diabetes. 86 million more people have prediabetes.[1]

About 8.1 million people with diabetes have not been diagnosed and are unaware that they have the disease. Diabetes is the seventh leading cause of death in the United States.[2] Adults with diabetes have heart disease death rates and risk for strokes that are 2 to 4 times higher than adults without diabetes. In addition, more than half of adults with diabetes have hypertension and high cholesterol levels.[2]

Etiology and Pathophysiology

Current theories link the causes of diabetes, singly or in combination, to genetic, autoimmune, and environmental factors (e.g., virus, obesity). Regardless of its cause, diabetes is primarily a disorder of glucose metabolism related to absent or insufficient insulin supply and/or poor use of the available insulin.

The American Diabetes Association (ADA) recognizes 4 different classes of diabetes. The 2 most common are type 1 and type 2 diabetes (Table 48.1). The 2 other classes are gestational diabetes and other specific types of diabetes with various causes.

Normal Glucose and Insulin Metabolism. Insulin is a hormone made by the β cells in the islets of Langerhans of the pancreas. Under normal conditions, insulin is continuously released into

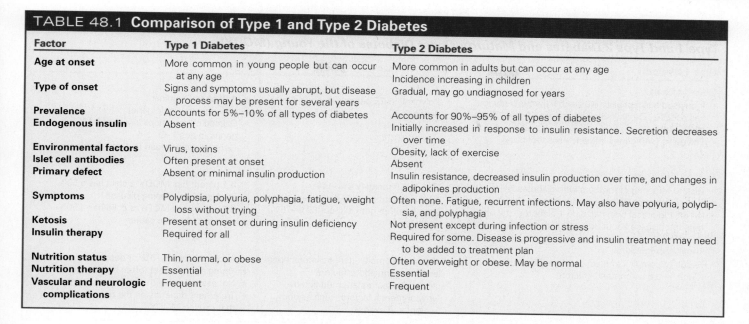

TABLE 48.1 Comparison of Type 1 and Type 2 Diabetes

Factor	Type 1 Diabetes	Type 2 Diabetes
Age at onset	More common in young people but can occur at any age	More common in adults but can occur at any age Incidence increasing in children
Type of onset	Signs and symptoms usually abrupt, but disease process may be present for several years	Gradual, may go undiagnosed for years
Prevalence	Accounts for 5%–10% of all types of diabetes	Accounts for 90%–95% of all types of diabetes
Endogenous insulin	Absent	Initially increased in response to insulin resistance. Secretion decreases over time
Environmental factors	Virus, toxins	Obesity, lack of exercise
Islet cell antibodies	Often present at onset	Absent
Primary defect	Absent or minimal insulin production	Insulin resistance, decreased insulin production over time, and changes in adipokines production
Symptoms	Polydipsia, polyuria, polyphagia, fatigue, weight loss without trying	Often none. Fatigue, recurrent infections. May also have polyuria, polydipsia, and polyphagia
Ketosis	Present at onset or during insulin deficiency	Not present except during infection or stress
Insulin therapy	Required for all	Required for some. Disease is progressive and insulin treatment may need to be added to treatment plan
Nutrition status	Thin, normal, or obese	Often overweight or obese. May be normal
Nutrition therapy	Essential	Essential
Vascular and neurologic complications	Frequent	Frequent

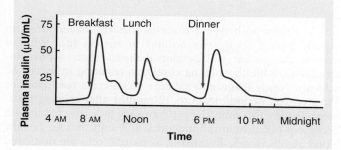

FIG. 48.1 Normal endogenous insulin secretion. After meals, insulin concentrations rise rapidly in blood and peak at about 1 hour. Then insulin concentrations promptly decline toward preprandial values as carbohydrate absorption from the GI tract declines. After carbohydrate absorption from the GI tract is complete and during the night, insulin concentrations are low and fairly constant, with a slight increase at dawn.

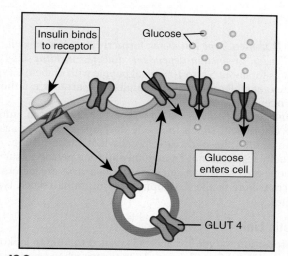

FIG. 48.2 Normal glucose metabolism. Insulin binds to receptors along the cell walls of muscle, adipose, and liver cells. Glucose transport proteins (GLUT 4s) then attach to the cell wall and allow glucose to enter the cell, where it is either stored or used to make energy.

the bloodstream in small amounts, with increased release when food is ingested (Fig. 48.1). Insulin lowers blood glucose and facilitates a stable, normal glucose range of about 74 to 106 mg/dL (4.1 to 5.9 mmol/L). The amount of insulin secreted daily by an adult is about 40 to 50 U, or 0.6 U/kg of body weight.

Insulin promotes glucose transport from the bloodstream across the cell membrane to the cytoplasm of the cell (Fig. 48.2). Cells break down glucose to make energy. Liver and muscle cells store excess glucose as glycogen. The rise in plasma insulin after a meal inhibits gluconeogenesis, enhances fat deposition of adipose tissue, and increases protein synthesis. For this reason, insulin is an *anabolic*, or storage, hormone. The fall in insulin level during normal overnight fasting promotes the release of stored glucose from the liver, protein from muscle, and fat from adipose tissue.

Skeletal muscle and adipose tissue have specific receptors for insulin and are considered insulin-dependent tissues. Insulin is required to "unlock" these receptor sites, allowing the transport of glucose into the cells to be used for energy. Other tissues (e.g., brain, liver, blood cells) do not directly depend on insulin for glucose transport but require an adequate glucose supply for normal function. Although liver cells are not considered

insulin-dependent tissue, insulin receptor sites on the liver facilitate uptake of glucose and its conversion to glycogen.

Other hormones (glucagon, epinephrine, growth hormone [GH], cortisol) work against the effects of insulin. They are *counterregulatory hormones.* These hormones increase blood glucose levels by (1) stimulating glucose production and release by the liver and (2) decreasing the movement of glucose into the cells. The counterregulatory hormones and insulin work together to maintain blood glucose levels within the normal range by regulating the release of glucose for energy during food intake and periods of fasting.

Insulin is synthesized from its precursor, proinsulin. Enzymes split proinsulin to form insulin and C-peptide, and the 2 substances are released in equal amounts. Therefore measuring C-peptide in serum and urine is a useful clinical indicator of pancreatic β-cell function and insulin levels.

⚛ GENETICS IN CLINICAL PRACTICE

Type 1 and Type 2 Diabetes and Maturity-Onset Diabetes of the Young (MODY)

Type 1 Diabetes	Type 2 Diabetes	MODY
Genetic Basis		
• Increased susceptibility (40%–50%) when a person has specific human leukocyte antigens (HLA-DR3, HLA-DR4) • Polygenic (>40 genes influence susceptibility)	• Polygenic (>25 genes influence susceptibility)	• Autosomal dominant • Monogenic (single gene) • Caused by mutations in any of 6 MODY genes (types 1–6) • Gene mutations lead to β-cell dysfunction
Risk to Offspring		
• Risk to offspring of mothers with diabetes is 1%–4% • Risk to offspring of fathers with diabetes is 5%–6% • When 1 identical twin has type 1 diabetes, the other gets the disease about 30%–40% of the time	• Risk to offspring is 8%–14% • When 1 identical twin has type 2 diabetes, the other gets it about 60%–75% of the time	• If 1 parent has MODY, a child has a 50% chance of developing disease • If 1 parent has MODY, a child has a 50% chance of being a carrier
Clinical Implications		
• Result of complex interaction of genetic, autoimmune, and environmental factors	• Result of complex genetic interactions and other metabolic factors • Metabolic factors are modified by environmental factors, such as body weight and exercise.	• Accounts for 1%–5% of people with diabetes • Young age of onset (often before age 25) • Not associated with obesity or hypertension • Treatment depends on the genetic mutation that caused MODY

Type 1 Diabetes. *Type 1 diabetes,* formerly known as *juvenile-onset diabetes* or *insulin-dependent diabetes mellitus (IDDM),* accounts for about 5% to 10% of all people with diabetes. Type 1 diabetes generally affects people under 40 years of age, although it can occur at any age.[3]

Etiology and Pathophysiology. Type 1 diabetes is an autoimmune disorder in which the body develops antibodies against insulin and/or the pancreatic β cells that make insulin. This eventually results in not enough insulin for a person to survive. A genetic predisposition and exposure to a virus are factors that may contribute to the development of immune-related type 1 diabetes.

⚛ Genetic Link

Predisposition to type 1 diabetes is related to human leukocyte antigens (HLAs) (see Chapter 13). In theory, when a person with certain HLA types is exposed to a viral infection, the β cells of the pancreas are destroyed, either directly or through an autoimmune process. The HLA types associated with an increased risk for type 1 diabetes include HLA-DR3 and HLA-DR4.

Idiopathic diabetes is a form of type 1 diabetes that is strongly inherited and not related to autoimmunity. It only occurs in a small number of people with type 1 diabetes, most often of Hispanic, African, or Asian ancestry.[3] *Latent autoimmune diabetes in adults* (LADA), a slowly progressing autoimmune form of type 1 diabetes. It occurs in adults and is often mistaken for type 2 diabetes.

Onset of Disease. In type 1 diabetes, the islet cell autoantibodies responsible for β-cell destruction are present for months to years before the onset of symptoms. Manifestations develop when the person's pancreas can no longer make enough insulin to maintain normal glucose. Once this occurs, the onset of symptoms is usually rapid. Patients often are initially seen with impending or actual ketoacidosis. The patient usually has a history of recent and sudden weight loss and the classic symptoms of *polydipsia* (excessive thirst), *polyuria* (frequent urination), and *polyphagia* (excessive hunger).

The person with type 1 diabetes requires insulin from an outside source *(exogenous insulin)* to sustain life. Without insulin, the patient will develop diabetes-related ketoacidosis (DKA), a life-threatening condition resulting in metabolic acidosis. Newly diagnosed patients may have a remission, or "honeymoon period," for 3 to 12 months after starting treatment. During this time, the patient needs little injected insulin because β-cell insulin production is still sufficient for healthy blood glucose levels. Eventually, as more β cells are destroyed and blood glucose levels increase, the honeymoon period ends and the patient will require insulin on a permanent basis.

Type 2 Diabetes. *Type 2 diabetes,* formerly known as *adult-onset diabetes* or *non–insulin-dependent diabetes mellitus (NIDDM),* accounts for about 90% to 95% of people with diabetes.[2] Many risk factors contribute to the development of type 2 diabetes. These include being overweight or obese, being older, and having a family history of type 2 diabetes. Although the disease is seen less often in children, the incidence is increasing due to the increasing prevalence of childhood obesity. Type 2 diabetes is more prevalent in some ethnic populations. Blacks, Asian Americans, Hispanics, Native Hawaiians or other Pacific Islanders, and Native Americans have a higher rate of type 2 diabetes than whites.[2]

🌐 PROMOTING HEALTH EQUITY

Diabetes

- Native Americans and Alaska Natives have highest prevalence for both men (14.9%) and women (15.3%).
- Pima Indians in Arizona have the highest rate of diabetes in the world (50% of adults).
- Native American and Alaska Native women are twice as likely to die from diabetes as white women.
- Rates are higher among blacks (12.7%) and Hispanics (12.1%) than among whites (7.4%) and Asians (8.0%).
- Blacks are twice as likely as whites to die from diabetes.

Etiology and Pathophysiology. Type 2 diabetes is characterized by a combination of inadequate insulin secretion and insulin resistance. The pancreas usually makes some *endogenous* (self-made) insulin. However, the body either does not make enough insulin or does not use it effectively, or both. The presence of endogenous insulin is a major distinction between type 1 and type 2 diabetes. In type 1 diabetes, there is an absence of endogenous insulin.

Genetic Link

Although we do not fully understand the genetics of type 2 diabetes, it is likely multiple genes are involved. We have found genetic mutations that lead to insulin resistance and a higher risk for obesity in many people with type 2 diabetes. Persons with a first-degree relative with the disease are 10 times more likely to develop type 2 diabetes.

Metabolic abnormalities have a role in the development of type 2 diabetes (Fig. 48.3). The first factor is insulin resistance, a condition in which body tissues do not respond to the action of insulin because insulin receptors are unresponsive, are insufficient in number, or both. Most insulin receptors are located on skeletal muscle, fat, and liver cells. When insulin is not properly used, the entry of glucose into the cell is impeded, resulting in hyperglycemia. In the early stages of insulin resistance, the pancreas responds to high blood glucose by producing greater amounts of insulin (if β cell function is normal). This

creates a temporary state of hyperinsulinemia that coexists with hyperglycemia.

A second factor in the development of type 2 diabetes is a marked decrease in the ability of the pancreas to make insulin, as the β cells become fatigued from the compensatory overproduction of insulin or when β-cell mass is lost. The underlying basis for the failure of β cells to adapt is unknown. It may be linked to the adverse effects of chronic hyperglycemia or high circulating free fatty acids. In addition, the α cells of the pancreas increase production of glucagon.

This leads to a third factor, which is inappropriate glucose production by the liver. Instead of properly regulating the release of glucose in response to blood levels, the liver does so in a haphazard way that does not correspond to the body's needs at the time.

A fourth factor is altered production of hormones and cytokines by adipose tissue *(adipokines).* Adipokines secreted by adipose tissue appear to play a role in glucose and fat metabolism and are likely to contribute to the development of type 2 diabetes.[4] We think adipokines cause chronic inflammation, a factor involved in insulin resistance, type 2 diabetes, and cardiovascular disease (CVD). The 2 main adipokines thought to affect insulin sensitivity are adiponectin and leptin. Finally, the brain, kidneys, and gut have roles in the development of type 2 diabetes. We are continuously learning more about metabolic factors in the development of type 2 diabetes.[4]

People with *metabolic syndrome* have an increased risk for developing type 2 diabetes. Metabolic syndrome has 5 components: increased glucose levels, abdominal obesity, high BP, high levels of triglycerides, and decreased levels of high-density lipoproteins (HDLs) (see Table 40.12). A person with 3 of the 5 components is considered to have metabolic syndrome.[5] Overweight persons with metabolic syndrome can reduce their risk for diabetes through a program of weight loss and regular physical activity. See Chapter 40 for more about metabolic syndrome.

Onset of Disease. The disease onset in type 2 diabetes is usually gradual. The person may go for many years with undetected hyperglycemia and few, if any, symptoms. Many people are diagnosed on routine laboratory testing or when they undergo treatment for other conditions, and elevated glucose or glycosylated hemoglobin (A1C) levels are found. The signs and symptoms of hyperglycemia develop when about 50% to 80% of β cells are no longer secreting insulin. At the time of diagnosis, the average person has had type 2 diabetes for 6½ years.

Prediabetes. Persons diagnosed with prediabetes are at increased risk for developing type 2 diabetes. Prediabetes is defined as impaired glucose tolerance (IGT), impaired fasting glucose (IFG), or both. It is an intermediate stage between normal glucose homeostasis and diabetes, in which the blood glucose levels are elevated but not high enough to meet the diagnostic criteria for diabetes.[6] A diagnosis of IGT is made if the 2-hour oral glucose tolerance test (OGTT) values are 140 to 199 mg/dL (7.8 to 11.0 mmol/L). IFG is diagnosed when fasting blood glucose levels are 100 to 125 mg/dL (5.56 to 6.9 mmol/L).

Persons with prediabetes usually do not have symptoms. However, long-term damage to the body, especially the heart and blood vessels, may already be occurring. It is important for patients to undergo screening and to understand risk factors for diabetes. People with prediabetes can take action to prevent or delay the development of type 2 diabetes. Encourage those with prediabetes to have their blood glucose and A1C checked

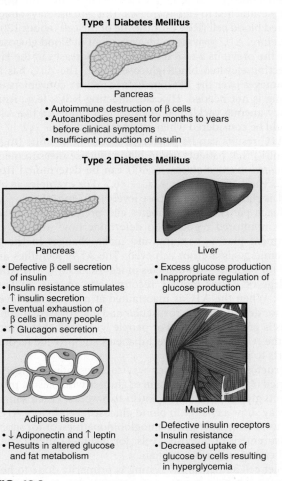

Type 1 Diabetes Mellitus

Pancreas

- Autoimmune destruction of β cells
- Autoantibodies present for months to years before clinical symptoms
- Insufficient production of insulin

Type 2 Diabetes Mellitus

Pancreas

- Defective β cell secretion of insulin
- Insulin resistance stimulates ↑ insulin secretion
- Eventual exhaustion of β cells in many people
- ↑ Glucagon secretion

Liver

- Excess glucose production
- Inappropriate regulation of glucose production

Adipose tissue

- ↓ Adiponectin and ↑ leptin
- Results in altered glucose and fat metabolism

Muscle

- Defective insulin receptors
- Insulin resistance
- Decreased uptake of glucose by cells resulting in hyperglycemia

FIG. 48.3 Altered mechanisms in type 1 and type 2 diabetes.

regularly and monitor for symptoms of diabetes, such as fatigue, frequent infections, or slow-healing wounds. Maintaining a healthy weight, exercising regularly, and making healthy food choices reduce the risk for developing overt type 2 diabetes in people with prediabetes.

Gestational Diabetes. *Gestational diabetes* develops during pregnancy and occurs in about 2% to 10% of pregnancies in the United States.[7] Women with gestational diabetes have a higher risk for cesarean delivery, and their babies have increased risk for perinatal death, birth injury, and neonatal complications. Women who are at high risk for gestational diabetes are screened at the first prenatal visit. Those at high risk include women who are obese, are of advanced maternal age, or have a family history of diabetes. Women with an average risk for gestational diabetes are screened using an OGTT at 24 to 28 weeks of gestation. Most women with gestational diabetes have normal glucose levels within 6 weeks postpartum. Women with a history of gestational diabetes have up to a 63% chance of developing type 2 diabetes within 16 years.[7] Gestational diabetes and managing the pregnant patient with diabetes are specialized areas not covered in detail in this chapter. Consult an obstetric text for more information.

Other Specific Types of Diabetes. Diabetes occurs in some people because of another medical condition or treatment of a medical condition that causes abnormal blood glucose levels. Conditions that may cause diabetes can result from injury to, interference with, or destruction of the β-cell function in the pancreas. These include Cushing syndrome, hyperthyroidism, recurrent pancreatitis, cystic fibrosis, hemochromatosis, and parenteral nutrition. Common drugs that can induce diabetes include corticosteroids (prednisone), thiazides, phenytoin (Dilantin), and atypical antipsychotics (e.g., clozapine [Clozaril]). Diabetes caused by medical conditions or drugs can resolve when the underlying condition is treated or the drug is discontinued.

Clinical Manifestations

Type 1 Diabetes. Because the onset of type 1 diabetes is rapid, the first manifestations are usually acute. The classic symptoms are *polyuria, polydipsia,* and *polyphagia.* The osmotic effect of excess glucose in the bloodstream causes polydipsia and polyuria. Polyphagia is a result of cellular malnourishment when insulin deficiency prevents cells from using glucose for energy. Weight loss may occur because the body cannot get glucose and instead breaks down fat and protein to try to make energy. Weakness and fatigue may result because body cells lack needed energy from glucose. Ketoacidosis, a complication most common in those with untreated type 1 diabetes, is associated with additional manifestations. It is discussed later in this chapter.

Type 2 Diabetes. The manifestations of type 2 diabetes are often nonspecific. It is possible a person with type 2 diabetes will have classic symptoms associated with type 1 diabetes, including polyuria, polydipsia, and polyphagia. Some of the more common manifestations associated with type 2 diabetes are fatigue, recurrent infections, recurrent vaginal yeast or candida infections, prolonged wound healing, and vision problems.

Diagnostic Studies

The diagnosis of diabetes is made using 1 of the following 4 methods:

1. A1C of 6.5% or higher
2. Fasting plasma glucose (FPG) level of 126 mg/dL (7.0 mmol/L) or greater. *Fasting* is defined as no caloric intake for at least 8 hours

3. A 2-hour plasma glucose level of 200 mg/dL (11.1 mmol/L) or greater during an OGTT, using a glucose load of 75 g
4. In a patient with classic symptoms of hyperglycemia (polyuria, polydipsia, unexplained weight loss) or hyperglycemic crisis, a random plasma glucose level of 200 mg/dL (11.1 mmol/L) or greater

If a patient is seen with a hyperglycemic crisis or clear symptoms of hyperglycemia (polyuria, polydipsia, polyphagia) with a random plasma glucose level of 200 mg/dL or greater, repeat testing is not needed. Otherwise, criteria 1 through 3 require confirmation by repeat testing to rule out laboratory error. It is preferable for the repeat test to be the same test used initially. For example, if a random elevated blood glucose is used for the initial measurement, that same measure should be used to confirm a diagnosis.

The accuracy of laboratory results depends on adequate patient preparation and attention to the many factors that may influence the results. For example, factors that can falsely elevate values include recent severe restrictions of dietary carbohydrate, acute illness, drugs (e.g., contraceptives, corticosteroids), and restricted activity, such as bed rest. A patient with impaired gastrointestinal (GI) absorption or who has recently taken acetaminophen may have false-negative results.

A1C measures the amount of glycosylated hemoglobin (Hgb) as a percentage of total Hgb. For example, A1C of 6.5% means that 6.5% of the total Hgb has glucose attached to it. The amount of glycosylated Hgb depends on the blood glucose level. When blood glucose levels are elevated over time, the amount of glucose attached to Hgb increases. This glucose stays attached to the red blood cell (RBC) for the life of the cell (about 120 days). Therefore, A1C provides a measurement of blood glucose levels over the previous 2 to 3 months, with increases in the Hb A1C reflecting elevated blood glucose levels. The A1C has several advantages over the FPG, including greater convenience, since fasting is not needed. Diseases affecting RBCs (e.g., iron deficiency anemia, sickle cell anemia) can influence the A1C and should be considered when interpreting results.

A1C results can be converted to the same units (mg/dL or mmol/L) that patients use in blood glucose measurements. An *estimated average glucose* (eAG) can be determined from the A1C. The $eAG = 28.7 \times A1C - 46.7$. For example, an A1C of 8.0% is equivalent to a glucose level of 183 mg/dL.

Teach patients with diabetes and prediabetes to have their A1C monitored regularly to determine how well the current treatment plan is working and make changes in the plan if glycemic goals are not achieved. The ADA identifies an A1C goal for patients with diabetes of less than 7.0%. The American College of Endocrinology recommends an A1C of less than 6.5%. When the A1C is maintained at near-normal levels, the risk for developing microvascular and macrovascular complications is greatly reduced. For people with prediabetes, monitoring the A1C can detect overt diabetes and provide feedback on efforts to prevent diabetes.

Fructosamine is another way to assess glucose levels. It is formed by a chemical reaction of glucose with plasma protein. It reflects glycemia in the previous 1 to 3 weeks. Fructosamine levels may show a change in blood glucose levels before A1C does. It is used for people with hemoglobinopathies, or for short-term measurement of glucose levels, for instance, after a change in medication or during pregnancy.

Islet cell autoantibody testing is primarily done to help distinguish between autoimmune type 1 diabetes and diabetes from other causes. Autoantibodies can develop to 1 or several autoantigens, including GAD65, IA-2, or insulin.

Interprofessional Care

The goals of diabetes management are to reduce symptoms, promote well-being, prevent acute complications related to hyperglycemia and hypoglycemia, and prevent or delay the onset and progression of long-term complications. These goals are most likely to be met when the patient maintains blood glucose levels as near to normal as possible. Patient teaching, which enables the patient to become the most active participant in their own care, is essential to achieve glycemic goals. Nutrition therapy, drug therapy, exercise, and self-monitoring of blood glucose are the tools used in managing diabetes (Table 48.2).

The 3 major types of glucose-lowering agents (GLAs) used in the treatment of diabetes are insulin, oral agents (OAs), and noninsulin injectable agents. All persons with type 1 diabetes require insulin. For some people with type 2 diabetes, a healthy eating plan, regular physical activity, and maintaining a healthy body weight are enough to attain optimal blood glucose levels. Eventually, most people will need medication management because type 2 diabetes is a progressive disease.

Drug Therapy: Insulin

Exogenous (injected) insulin is needed when a patient has inadequate insulin to meet specific metabolic needs. People with type 1 diabetes require exogenous insulin to survive. They often use multiple daily injections of insulin (often 4 or more) or continuous insulin infusion via an insulin pump to adequately manage blood glucose levels. People with type 2 diabetes may need exogenous insulin during periods of severe stress, such as

TABLE 48.2 Interprofessional Care

Diabetes

Diagnostic Assessment
- History and physical examination
- Blood tests, including fasting blood glucose, postprandial blood glucose, A1C, fructosamine, lipid profile, BUN and serum creatinine, electrolytes, islet cell autoantibodies
- Urine for complete urinalysis, albuminuria, and acetone (if indicated)
- BP
- ECG (if indicated)
- Funduscopic examination (dilated eye examination)
- Dental examination
- Neurologic examination, including monofilament test for sensation to lower extremities
- Ankle-brachial index (ABI) (if indicated) (see Table 37.3)
- Foot (podiatric) examination
- Monitoring of weight

Management
- Patient and caregiver teaching and follow-up programs
- Nutrition therapy (Table 48.8)
- Exercise therapy (Tables 48.9 and 48.10)
- Self-monitoring of blood glucose (SMBG) (Table 48.11)

Drug Therapy
- Insulin (Fig. 48.3 and Tables 48.3 and 48.4)
- OAs and noninsulin injectable agents (Table 48.7)
- Enteric-coated aspirin (81–162 mg/day)
- ACE inhibitors (see Table 32.6)
- Angiotensin II receptor blockers (ARBs) (see Table 32.6)
- Antihyperlipidemic drugs (see Table 33.6)

illness or surgery. Since type 2 diabetes is a progressive disease, over time, the combination of nutrition therapy, exercise, OAs, and noninsulin injectable agents may no longer adequately manage blood glucose levels. At that point, exogenous insulin is added as part of the management plan. People with type 2 diabetes may also need up to 4 injections per day to adequately maintain their blood glucose levels. Insulin pumps also can be used for patients with type 2 diabetes.

Types of Insulin. Today, people use only genetically engineered human insulin made in laboratories. The insulin is derived from common bacteria (e.g., *Escherichia coli*) or yeast cells using recombinant deoxyribonucleic acid (DNA) technology. In the past, insulin was extracted from beef and pork pancreases. These forms of insulin are no longer available.

Insulins differ by their onset, peak action, and duration (Fig. 48.4). They are categorized as rapid-acting, short-acting, intermediate-acting, and long-acting insulin (Table 48.3).

Insulin Plans. Examples of insulin plans are shown in Table 48.4. The insulin approach that most closely mimics endogenous insulin production is the basal-bolus plan (often called *intensive or physiologic insulin therapy*). It consists of multiple daily insulin injections (or an insulin pump) together with frequent self-monitoring of blood glucose (or a continuous glucose monitoring system). Injections include rapid- or short-acting (bolus) insulin before meals and intermediate- or long-acting (basal) background insulin once or twice a day. The goal is to achieve a glucose level as close to normal as possible, as much of the time as possible. This is referred to as "time in range."

Other, less intense plans can promote healthy blood glucose levels for some people. Ideally, the patient and the HCP will work together to choose a plan. Selection criteria are based on the desired and feasible blood glucose levels and the patient's lifestyle, food choices, and activity patterns. If a less intense plan is not giving the person optimal results, the HCP may encourage a more intense approach.

Mealtime Insulin (Bolus). To manage postprandial blood glucose levels, the timing of rapid- and short-acting insulin in relation to meals is crucial. Rapid-acting synthetic insulin analogs, which include aspart (NovoLog), glulisine (Apidra), and lispro (Humalog), have an onset of action of about 15 minutes. They should be injected within 15 minutes of mealtime. The rapid-acting analogs most closely mimic natural insulin secretion in response to a meal.

Short-acting regular insulin has an onset of action of 30 to 60 minutes. It is injected 30 to 45 minutes before a meal to ensure that the insulin is working at the same time as meal absorption. Because timing an injection 30 to 45 minutes before a meal is hard for some people to do with their lifestyles, the flexibility that rapid-acting insulins offer is preferred by those taking insulin with their meals.[8] Short-acting insulin is more likely to cause hypoglycemia because of a longer duration of action.

Long- or Intermediate-Acting (Basal) Background Insulin. In addition to mealtime insulin, people with type 1 diabetes use a long- or intermediate-acting basal (background) insulin to maintain blood glucose levels in between meals and overnight. Without 24-hour background insulin, people with type 1 diabetes are more prone to developing DKA. Many people with type 2 diabetes who use OAs will need basal insulin to adequately manage blood glucose levels.

The long-acting insulins include degludec (Tresiba), detemir (Levemir), and glargine (Lantus, Toujeo, Basaglar). This type of insulin is released steadily and continuously. For most people,

INSULIN PREPARATION	ONSET, PEAK, DURATION	EXAMPLE
Rapid acting lispro (Humalog) aspart (NovoLog) glulisine (Apidra)	*Onset:* 10–30 min *Peak:* 30 min–3 hr *Duration:* 3–5 hr	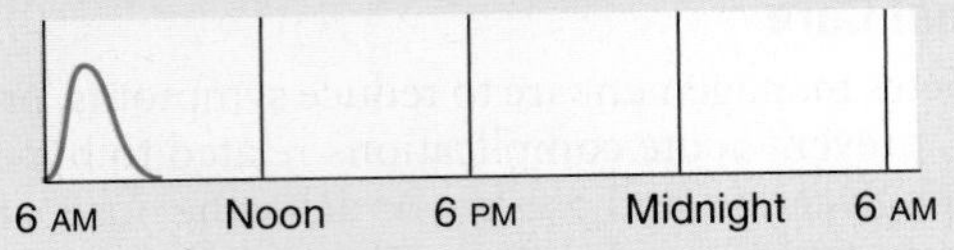 6 AM Noon 6 PM Midnight 6 AM
Short acting Regular (Humulin R, Novolin R)	*Onset:* 30 min–1 hr *Peak:* 2–5 hr *Duration:* 5–8 hr	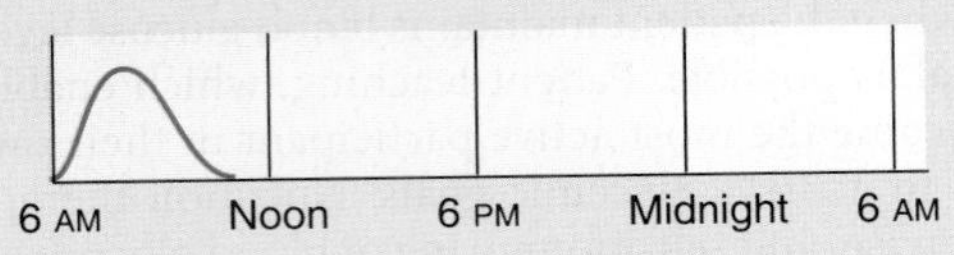 6 AM Noon 6 PM Midnight 6 AM
Intermediate acting NPH (Humulin N, Novolin N)	*Onset:* 1.5–4 hr *Peak:* 4–12 hr *Duration:* 12–18 hr	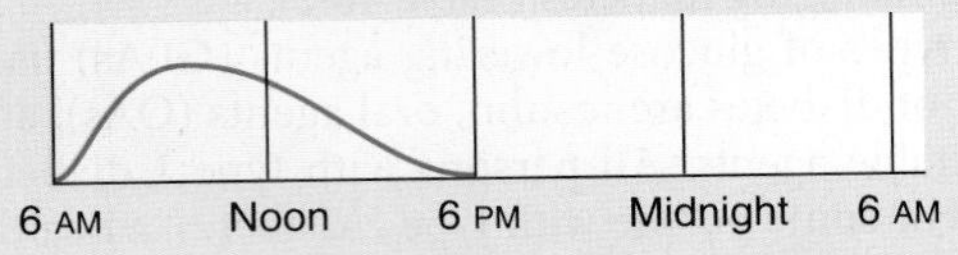 6 AM Noon 6 PM Midnight 6 AM
Long acting glargine (Lantus) detemir (Levemir) degludec (Tresiba)	*Onset:* 0.8–4 hr *Peak:* Less defined or no pronounced peak *Duration:* 16–24 hr	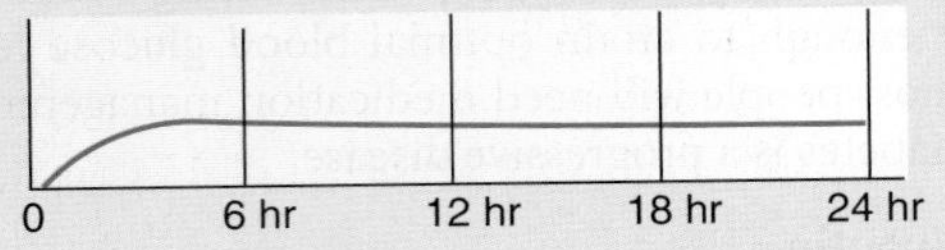 0 6 hr 12 hr 18 hr 24 hr
Inhaled insulin Afrezza	*Onset:* 12–15 min *Peak:* 60 min *Duration:* 2.5–3 hr	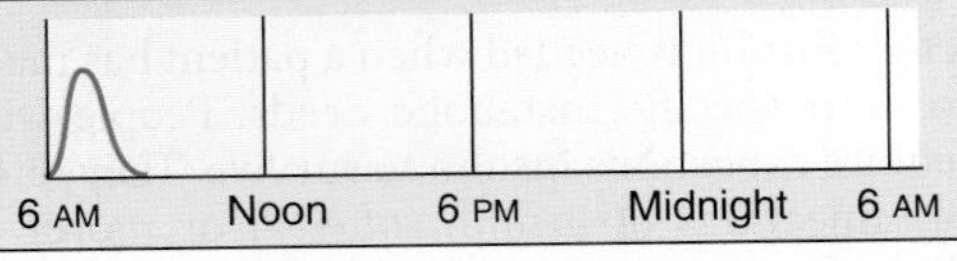 6 AM Noon 6 PM Midnight 6 AM

FIG. 48.4 Commercially available insulin preparations showing onset, peak, and duration of action. Individual patient responses to each type of insulin are different and affected by many different factors.

TABLE 48.3 Drug Therapy

Types of Insulin

Classification	Examples
Rapid-acting insulin	aspart (NovoLog) glulisine (Apidra) lispro (Humalog)
Short-acting insulin	regular (Humulin R, Novolin R)
Intermediate-acting insulin	NPH (Humulin N, Novolin N)
Long-acting insulin	degludec (Tresiba) detemir (Levemir) glargine (Basaglar, Lantus, Toujeo) insulin glargine (Basaglar)
Combination therapy (premixed)	aspart protamine/aspart 70/30* (NovoLog Mix 70/30) degludec/aspart 70/30 (Ryzodeg) lispro protamine/lispro 75/25* (Humalog Mix 75/25) lispro protamine/lispro 50/50* (Humalog Mix 50/50) NPH/regular 70/30* (Humulin 70/30, Novolin 70/30) NPH/regular 50/50* (Humulin 50/50)
More concentrated insulin	Humulin R U-500 Toujeo U-300 (insulin glargine)
Inhaled insulin	Afrezza

*These numbers refer to percentages of each type of insulin.

it does not have a peak of action. The action time for long-acting insulin varies (Fig. 48.4). Although they can be given once daily, detemir is often given twice daily. Because they lack peak action time, the risk for hypoglycemia from this type of insulin is greatly reduced. Glargine and detemir must not be diluted or mixed with any other insulin or solution in the same syringe. If OAs and long-acting insulin are not adequate to achieve glycemic goals, mealtime insulin may be added.

Intermediate-acting insulin (NPH) can be used as a basal insulin. It has a duration of 12 to 18 hours. The disadvantage of NPH is that it has a peak ranging from 4 to 12 hours, which can result in hypoglycemia. NPH can be mixed with short- and rapid-acting insulins. It should never be given IV.

? CHECK YOUR PRACTICE

You are preparing your patient's order for NPH insulin. When you look at the vial, you notice that it is cloudy. You are thinking that you should throw away the vial because has become contaminated.
• Before you take this action, what should you do?

All insulins are clear solutions except NPH, lispro protamine, and aspart protamine. They are cloudy because they contain a protein called protamine, which makes them work longer. These insulins must be gently agitated before administration.

Combination Insulin Therapy. For those who want to use only 1 or 2 injections per day, a short- or rapid-acting insulin is mixed with intermediate-acting insulin in the same syringe. This allows the patient to have both mealtime and basal coverage without having to give 2 separate injections. Although this may be more appealing to the patient, most patients achieve optimal blood glucose levels with basal-bolus therapy. Patients may mix the 2 types of insulin themselves or use a commercially premixed formula or pen (Table 48.3). Premixed formulas offer

TABLE 48.4 Drug Therapy

Insulin Regimens

Regimen	Type of Insulin and Frequency	Action Profile	Comments
Once a day Single dose	Intermediate (NPH) *At bedtime*	 7 AM Noon 6 PM Midnight 7 AM	1 injection should provide nighttime coverage.
	OR Long-acting (degludec [Tresiba], detemir [Levemir], glargine [Lantus]) *In AM or at bedtime*	 7 AM Noon 6 PM Midnight 7 AM	1 injection may last up to 24 hr with fewer defined peaks and less chance for hypoglycemia. Does not cover postprandial blood glucose levels.
Twice a day Split-mixed dose	NPH and regular or rapid (both regular and rapid are shown on the diagram) *Before breakfast and at dinner*	 7 AM Noon 6 PM Midnight 7 AM	2 injections provide coverage for 24 hr. Patient must eat at certain times to avoid hypoglycemia.
Three times a day Combination of mixed and single dose	NPH and regular or rapid (both regular and rapid are shown on the diagram) *Before breakfast* + Regular or rapid *Before dinner* + NPH *At bedtime*	 7 AM Noon 7 PM 9 PM Midnight 7 AM	3 injections provide coverage for 24 hr, especially during early AM hours. Decreased potential for 2–3 AM hypoglycemia
Basal-bolus Multiple dose	Regular or rapid (both regular and rapid are shown on the diagram) *Before breakfast, lunch, and dinner* + Long-acting (degludec, detemir, or glargine) *Once or twice a day* OR Regular or rapid (both regular and rapid are shown on the diagram) *Before breakfast, lunch, and dinner* + NPH *Twice a day*	 7 AM Noon 6 PM Midnight 7 AM 7 AM Noon 6 PM Midnight 7 AM	More flexibility is allowed at mealtimes and for amount of food intake. Good postprandial coverage. Preprandial blood glucose checks and following an individualized plan is necessary. Patients with type 1 diabetes require basal insulin to cover 24 hr. Most physiologic approach, except for pump

———— Rapid-acting (lispro, aspart, glulisine) insulin.
———— Short-acting (regular) insulin.
– – – – – – Intermediate-acting (NPH) or long-acting (glargine, detemir, degludec) insulin.

convenience to patients, who do not have to draw up and mix insulin from 2 different vials. This is especially helpful to those who lack the visual, manual, or cognitive skills to mix insulin themselves. However, the convenience of these formulas limits the potential for optimal blood glucose levels because there is less opportunity for flexible dosing based on need.

Storage of Insulin. As a protein, insulin has special storage considerations. Extreme temperatures alter the insulin molecule and can make it less effective. Insulin vials and pens in use may be left at room temperature for up to 4 weeks unless the room temperature is higher than 86° F (30° C) or below freezing (less than 32° F [0° C]). Teach patients to avoid prolonged exposure to direct sunlight. A patient who is traveling in hot climates may store insulin in a thermos or cooler to keep it cool (not frozen). Store unopened insulin vials and pens in the refrigerator.

Patients who are traveling or caregivers of patients who are sight impaired or who lack the manual dexterity to fill their own syringes may prefill insulin syringes. Prefilled syringes with 2 different insulins are stable for up to 1 week when stored in the refrigerator. Syringes with only 1 type of insulin are stable up to 30 days.

Teach patients to store syringes in a vertical position with the needle pointed up to avoid clumping of suspended insulin in the needle. Before injection, gently roll prefilled syringes between the palms 10 to 20 times to warm the insulin and resuspend the particles. Some insulin combinations cannot be prefilled and stored because the mixture can alter the onset, action, and/or peak times of either insulin. Consult a reference as needed when mixing and prefilling different types of insulin.

Administration of Insulin. Routine doses of insulin are given by subcutaneous injection. Regular insulin can be given IV when immediate onset of action is desired. Insulin is not taken orally because it is inactivated by gastric fluids. Teach patients to avoid injecting insulin IM because rapid and unpredictable absorption could result in hypoglycemia.

Insulin Injection. The steps in giving a subcutaneous insulin injection are outlined in Table 48.5. Teach this technique to new insulin users and review it periodically with long-term users.

TABLE 48.5 Patient & Caregiver Teaching
Preparing an Insulin Injection

Include the following instructions when teaching the patient and caregiver about insulin therapy:

1. Wash hands thoroughly.
2. Always inspect insulin bottle before using it. Make sure that it is the proper type and concentration, expiration date has not passed, and top of bottle is in perfect condition. Insulin solutions (except for NPH, lispro protamine, aspart protamine) should look clear and colorless. Discard if it appears discolored or if you see particles in the solution.
3. For intermediate-acting insulins (which are normally cloudy), gently roll the insulin bottle between the palms of hands to mix the insulin. Clear insulins do not need to be agitated.
4. Choose proper injection site (Fig. 48.5).
5. Ensure that the site is clean and dry.
6. Push the needle straight into the skin (90-degree angle). If you are very thin, muscular, or using an 8- or 12-mm needle, you may need to pinch the skin and/or use a 45-degree angle.
7. Push the plunger all the way down, leave needle in place for 5 sec to ensure that all insulin has been injected, and then remove needle.
8. Destroy and dispose of single-use syringe safely.

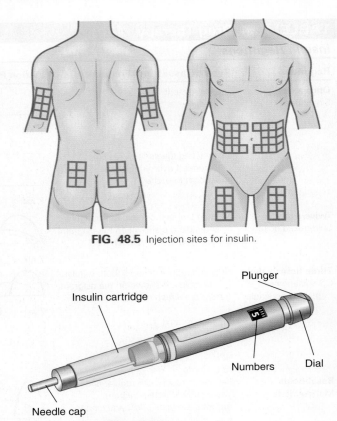

FIG. 48.5 Injection sites for insulin.

FIG. 48.6 Parts of insulin pen.

Never assume that because the patient already uses insulin, they know and practice the correct insulin injection technique. The patient may not have understood prior instructions, or changes in eyesight may result in inaccurate preparation.[9] The patient may not see air bubbles in the syringe or may improperly read the scale on the syringe. The patient receiving mixed insulins in the same syringe needs to learn the proper technique for combining them if commercially prepared premixed insulins are not used.

The speed with which peak serum concentrations are reached varies with the injection site. The fastest subcutaneous absorption is from the abdomen, followed by the arm, thigh, and buttock. Although the abdomen is often the preferred injection site, other sites work well (Fig. 48.5). Caution the patient about injecting into a site that is to be exercised. For example, injecting into the thigh and then going jogging could increase body heat and circulation. This could increase the rate of insulin absorption and speed the onset of action, resulting in hypoglycemia.

Teach patients to rotate the injection within and between sites. This allows for better insulin absorption. It may be helpful to think of the abdomen as a checkerboard, with each ½-in square representing an injection site. Injections are rotated systematically across the board, with each injection site at least ½ to 1 inch away from the previous injection site. It can be helpful to inject fast-acting insulin into faster-absorbing sites and slow-acting insulin into slower absorbing sites.

Most commercial insulin is available as U100. This means that 1 mL contains 100 U of insulin. U100 insulin must be used with a U100-marked syringe. Disposable plastic insulin syringes are available in a variety of sizes, including 1.0, 0.5, and 0.3 mL. The 0.5-mL size may be used for doses of 50 U or less. The 0.3-mL syringe can be used for doses of 30 U or less. The 0.5- and 0.3-mL syringes are in 1-unit increments. This provides more accurate delivery when the dose is an odd number. The 1.0-mL syringe is necessary for patients who inject more than 50 U of insulin. The 1.0-mL syringe is in 2-unit increments. When patients change from a 0.3- or a 0.5-mL to a 1.0-mL syringe, tell them of the dose increment difference.

Insulin syringe needles come in 3 lengths: 6 mm (½ in), 8 mm (5/16 in), and 12.7 mm (½ in).[10] Needle gauges vary among syringes. The needle gauges available are 28, 29, 30, and 31. The higher the gauge number, the smaller the diameter, thus resulting in a more comfortable injection. Only the person using the syringe should recap the needle; never recap a needle used for a patient. To prepare the site, routine hygiene, such as washing with soap and rinsing with water, is adequate. This applies primarily to patient self-injection technique. When injection occurs in a health care agency, policy usually mandates site preparation with alcohol to prevent health care–associated infection (HAI).

Insulin injections are typically given at a 90-degree angle. For extremely thin or muscular patients in the hospital, perform injections at a 45-degree angle. At home, patients inject at a 90-degree angle using the shortest needle desired. Pinching up of the skin to avoid IM injection is no longer done because of the use of short needles.

An insulin pen is a compact portable device loaded with an insulin cartridge that serves the same function as a needle and syringe (Fig. 48.6). Pen needles are available in lengths of 4 mm (5/32 in), 5 mm (3/16 in), 8 mm (5/16 in), and 12.7 mm (½ in) and in 3 gauges: 29, 31, and 32. Insulin pens offer convenience and flexibility. They are portable and compact, are more discreet than using a vial and syringe, and provide consistent and accurate dosing. For patients with poor vision, the pen is a better option, since they can hear the clicks of the pen as the dose is selected. Insulin pens come packaged with printed instructions, including pictures of the steps to take when using the pen. These instructions are helpful when teaching new users and reviewing technique with current users of a pen.

Insulin Pump. An *insulin pump* delivers a continuous subcutaneous insulin infusion through a small device worn on the belt,

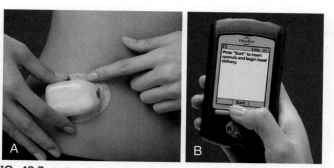

FIG. 48.7 A, OmniPod Insulin Management System. The Pod holds and delivers insulin. **B,** The Personal Diabetes Manager (PDM) wirelessly programs insulin delivery via the Pod. The PDM has a built-in glucose meter. (Courtesy of Insulet Corporation.)

in a pocket, or under clothing. Insulin pumps use rapid-acting insulin. It is loaded into a reservoir or cartridge and connected via plastic tubing to a catheter inserted into the subcutaneous tissue. Insulet Corporation has an insulin pump that is a tubing-free system (Fig. 48.7). All insulin pumps are programmed to deliver a continuous infusion of rapid-acting insulin 24 hours a day, known as the *basal rate*. Basal insulin can be temporarily increased or decreased based on carbohydrate intake, activity changes, or illness. Pump users need different basal rates at different times of the day.

At mealtime, the user programs the pump to deliver a bolus infusion of insulin appropriate to the amount of carbohydrate ingested and an additional amount, if needed, to bring down or "correct" high preprandial blood glucose. The infusion set is changed every 2 to 3 days and placed in a new site to avoid infection and promote good insulin absorption. Insulin pump users check their blood glucose level at least 4 times per day and/or use a continuous glucose monitoring system. Monitoring 8 times or more per day is common.

A major advantage of the insulin pump is the potential for keeping blood glucose levels in a tighter range with a goal of eliminating both high and low glucose. With careful programming and constant monitoring, this is possible because insulin delivery is similar to the normal physiologic pattern. Pumps offer users more flexibility with meal and activity patterns. Potential challenges of insulin pump therapy include infection at the insertion site, an increased risk for DKA if the insulin infusion is disrupted, the cost of the pump and supplies, and being attached to a device.[11]

Problems With Insulin Therapy. Problems associated with insulin therapy include hypoglycemia, allergic reactions, lipodystrophy, hypertrophy, and the Somogyi effect. Hypoglycemia is discussed in detail later in this chapter. Guidelines for assessing patients treated with insulin and other GLAs are outlined in Table 48.6.

Allergic Reactions. Local inflammatory reactions to insulin may occur, such as itching, erythema, and burning around the injection site. Local reactions may be self-limiting within 1 to 3 months or may improve with a low dose of antihistamine. A true insulin allergy, which is rare, is manifested by a systemic response with urticaria and possibly anaphylactic shock. Preservative in the insulin and the latex or rubber stoppers on the vials have been implicated in allergic reactions.

Lipodystrophy and Hypertrophy. Lipodystrophy (loss of subcutaneous fatty tissue) may occur if the same injection sites are used frequently. The use of human insulin has significantly reduced

TABLE 48.6 **Assessing the Patient Treated With Glucose-Lowering Agents**	
Category	**Assessment**
For Patient With Newly Diagnosed Diabetes or for Reevaluation of Medication Plan	
Affective	• What emotions and attitudes are patient and caregiver displaying concerning diagnosis of diabetes and insulin or OA treatment?
Cognitive	• Is patient or caregiver able to understand why insulin or OAs are being used as part of diabetes management?
	• Is patient or caregiver able to understand concepts of asepsis, combining insulins, and side effects of medications?
	• Is patient able to remember to take >1 dose/day?
	• Does patient take medications at right times in relation to meals?
Psychomotor	• Is patient or caregiver physically able to prepare and give accurate doses of the drugs?
For Patient Follow-up	
Effectiveness of therapy	• Is patient having symptoms of hyperglycemia?
	• Does blood glucose record show blood glucose levels in or out of the target range?
	• Is A1C in a healthy range and consistent with glucose records?
Self-management behaviors	• If patient is having hyperglycemia or hypoglycemia, how are those episodes managed?
	• Has patient determined reason for hyperglycemia or hypoglycemia?
	• How much insulin or OA is patient taking and at what time of day? Is patient adjusting insulin dose? Under what circumstances and by how much?
	• Has the exercise pattern changed?
	• Is patient making healthy food choices? Are meals taken at times corresponding to peak insulin action?
Side effects of therapy	• Is atrophy or hypertrophy present at injection sites?
	• Has patient had hypoglycemia? If so, how often? What time of day? What were the symptoms of hypoglycemia?
	• Are there reports of nightmares, night sweats, or early morning headaches?
	• Has patient had a skin rash or GI upset since taking OAs?
	• Has patient gained or lost weight?

the risk for lipodystrophy. *Atrophy*, which is uncommon, is the wasting of subcutaneous tissue and presents as indentations in injection sites. *Hypertrophy* happens more often and is a thickening of the subcutaneous tissue. It eventually regresses if the patient does not use the site for at least 6 months. Injecting into a hypertrophied site may result in erratic insulin absorption.

Somogyi Effect and Dawn Phenomenon. Hyperglycemia in the morning may be due to the Somogyi effect. A high dose of insulin causes a decline in blood glucose levels during the night. As a result, counterregulatory hormones (e.g., glucagon, epinephrine, GH, cortisol) are released. They stimulate lipolysis, gluconeogenesis, and glycogenolysis, which in turn cause rebound hyperglycemia. The danger of this effect is that when blood glucose levels are measured in the morning, hyperglycemia is apparent and the patient (or the HCP) may increase the insulin dose.

If a patient has morning hyperglycemia, checking blood glucose levels between 2:00 and 4:00 AM for hypoglycemia will help determine if the cause is the Somogyi effect. The patient may report headaches on awakening and recall having night sweats or nightmares.

The **dawn phenomenon** is also characterized by hyperglycemia that is present on awakening. Two counterregulatory hormones (GH and cortisol), which are excreted in increased amounts in the early morning hours, may be the cause of this phenomenon. The dawn phenomenon affects many people with diabetes and tends to be most severe when GH is at its peak in adolescence and young adulthood.

Careful assessment is needed to diagnose the Somogyi effect or dawn phenomenon because the treatment for each differs. The treatment for Somogyi effect is a bedtime snack, reducing the dose of insulin, or both. The treatment for dawn phenomenon is an increase in insulin or an adjustment in administration time. Your assessment must include insulin dose, injection sites, and variability in the time of meals or insulin administration. Ask the patient to measure and document bedtime, nighttime (between 2:00 and 4:00 AM), and morning fasting blood glucose levels on several occasions. If the predawn levels are less than 60 mg/dL (3.3 mmol/L) and signs and symptoms of hypoglycemia are present, the insulin dosage should be reduced. If the 2:00 to 4:00 AM blood glucose is high, the insulin dosage should be increased. Counsel the patient on appropriate bedtime snacks.

Inhaled Insulin. Afrezza is a rapid-acting inhaled insulin. It is given at the beginning of each meal or within 20 minutes after starting a meal. Afrezza must be used in combination with long-acting insulin in patients with type 1 diabetes. It should not be used to treat diabetic ketoacidosis. Patients with chronic lung disease, such as asthma or COPD, or who smoke, should not use Afrezza because bronchospasm can occur. Other common adverse reactions are hypoglycemia, cough, and throat pain or irritation.

Drug Therapy: Oral and Noninsulin Injectable Agents

OAs and noninsulin injectable agents work to improve the mechanisms by which the body makes and uses insulin and glucose. These drugs primarily work on 3 defects of type 2 diabetes: (1) insulin resistance, (2) decreased insulin production, and (3) increased hepatic glucose production (Fig. 48.8). These drugs may be used in combination with agents from other classes or with insulin to achieve blood glucose goals. OAs and noninsulin injectable agents are listed in Table 48.7.

Biguanides. The most widely used OA is metformin. It is the only drug in the biguanide class available in the United States. Metformin is the most effective first-line treatment for type 2 diabetes.[8] Forms of metformin include Glucophage (immediate release), Glucophage XR (extended release), Fortamet (extended release), and Riomet (liquid). The primary action of metformin is to reduce glucose production by the liver. It enhances insulin sensitivity at the tissue level and improves glucose transport into the cells. It also has beneficial effects on plasma lipids.

Because it may cause moderate weight loss, metformin may be useful for people with type 2 diabetes and prediabetes who

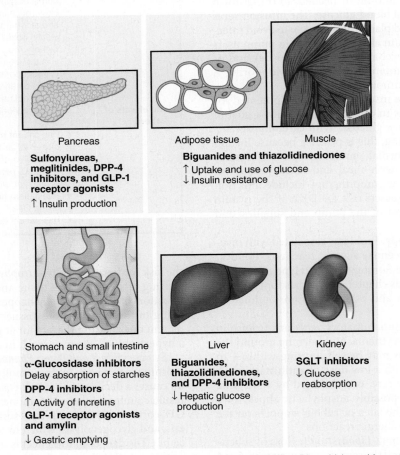

FIG. 48.8 Sites and mechanisms of action of type 2 diabetes drugs. *DDP-4,* Dipeptidyl peptidase; *GLP-1,* glucagon-like peptide-1; *SGLT,* sodium-glucose co-transporter.

TABLE 48.7 Drug Therapy

Oral Agents and Noninsulin Injectable Agents

Type	Mechanism of Action	Side Effects
Oral Agents		
α-Glucosidase Inhibitors		
acarbose (Precose) miglitol (Glyset)	Delays absorption of complex carbohydrates (starches) from GI tract	Gas, abdominal pain, diarrhea
Biguanides		
metformin (Fortamet Glucophage, Glucophage XR, Glumetza, Riomet)	↓ Rate of hepatic glucose production. ↑ Insulin sensitivity. Improves glucose uptake by tissues, especially muscles	Diarrhea, lactic acidosis. Must be held 1–2 days before IV contrast media given and for 48 hr after
Dipeptidyl Peptidase-4 (DPP-4) Inhibitors		
alogliptin (Nesina) linagliptin (Tradjenta) saxagliptin (Onglyza) sitagliptin (Januvia)	Enhances activity of incretins. Stimulates release of insulin from pancreatic β-cells. ↓ Hepatic glucose production	Pancreatitis, allergic reactions
Dopamine Receptor Agonists		
bromocriptine (Cycloset)	Activates dopamine receptors in central nervous system. Unknown how it improves glucose levels	Orthostatic hypotension
Meglitinides		
nateglinide (Starlix) repaglinide (Prandin)	Stimulates a rapid and short-lived release of insulin from the pancreas	Weight gain, hypoglycemia
Sodium-Glucose Co-Transporter 2 (SGLT2) Inhibitors		
canagliflozin (Invokana) dapagliflozin (Farxiga) empagliflozin (Jardiance) ertugliflozin (Steglatro)	↓ Renal glucose reabsorption and ↑ urinary glucose excretion	↑ Risk for genital infections and UTIs. Hypoglycemia
Sulfonylureas		
glimepiride (Amaryl) glipizide (Glucotrol, Glucotrol XL) glyburide (DiaBeta, Glynase)	Stimulates release of insulin from pancreatic islets. ↓ Glycogenolysis and gluconeogenesis. Enhances cellular sensitivity to insulin	Weight gain, hypoglycemia
Thiazolidinediones		
pioglitazone (Actos) rosiglitazone (Avandia)	↑ Glucose uptake in muscle. ↓ Endogenous glucose production	Weight gain, edema *pioglitazone:* May ↑ risk for bladder cancer and worsen HF. *rosiglitazone:* May ↑ risk for cardiovascular events (e.g., MI, stroke)
Combination Oral Therapy		
Actoplus Met, Actoplus Met XR	Same as for metformin and pioglitazone	See side effects for individual drugs
Duetact	Same as for pioglitazone and glimepiride	
Glucovance	Same as for metformin and glyburide	
Glyxambi	Same as for empagliflozin and linagliptin	
Janumet, Janumet XR	Same as for metformin and sitagliptin	
Jentadueto	Same as for linagliptin and metformin	
Kazano	Same as for alogliptin and metformin	
Kombiglyze	Same as for saxagliptin and metformin	
Oseni	Same as for alogliptin and pioglitazone	
PrandiMet	Same as for metformin and repaglinide	
Segluromet	Same as for metformin and ertugliflozin	
Steglujan	Same as for sitagliptin and ertugliflozin	
Synjardy	Same as metformin and empagliflozin	
Xigduo	Same as for dapagliflozin and metformin	
Noninsulin Injectable Agents		
Amylin Analogs		
pramlintide (Symlin)	Slows gastric emptying, decreases glucagon secretion and endogenous glucose output from liver. ↑ Satiety	Hypoglycemia, nausea, vomiting, ↓ appetite, headache
Glucagon-Like Peptide-1 (GLP-1) Receptor Agonists		
albiglutide (Tanzeum) dulaglutide (Trulicity) exenatide (Byetta) exenatide extended-release (Bydureon) liraglutide (Victoza) lixisenatide (Adlyxin) semaglutide (Ozempic)	Stimulates release of insulin, ↓ glucagon secretion, and slow gastric emptying. ↑ Satiety	Nausea, vomiting, hypoglycemia, diarrhea, headache

are overweight or obese. It is also used to prevent type 2 diabetes in those with prediabetes who are younger than age 60 and have risk factors, such as hypertension or a history of gestational diabetes.

Patients who are undergoing surgery or radiologic procedures that involve the use of a contrast medium need to temporarily discontinue metformin before surgery or the procedure. This reduces the risk of contrast-induced kidney injury (CIN) (see Chapter 44). They should not resume the metformin until 48 hours afterward, once their serum creatinine has been checked and is normal.

DRUG ALERT Metformin

- Do not use in patients with kidney disease, liver disease, or heart failure. Lactic acidosis is a rare complication of metformin accumulation.
- IV contrast media that contain iodine pose a risk for CIN, which could worsen metformin-induced lactic acidosis.
- To reduce risk for CIN, discontinue metformin 2 days before the procedure.
- May be resumed 48 hours after the procedure, assuming kidney function is normal.
- Do not use in people who drink excess amounts of alcohol.
- Take with food to minimize GI side effects.

Sulfonylureas. Sulfonylureas include glimepiride (Amaryl), glipizide (Glucotrol, Glucotrol XL), and glyburide (DiaBeta, Glynase). The primary action of sulfonylureas is to increase insulin production by the pancreas. Therefore hypoglycemia is the major side effect.

Meglitinides. Like sulfonylureas, nateglinide (Starlix) and repaglinide (Prandin) increase insulin production by the pancreas. However, because they are more rapidly absorbed and eliminated than sulfonylureas, they are less likely to cause hypoglycemia. When taken just before meals, pancreatic insulin production increases during and after the meal, mimicking the normal response to eating. Teach patients to take meglitinides any time from 30 minutes before each meal right up to the time of the meal. These drugs should not be taken if a meal is skipped.

α-Glucosidase Inhibitors. These drugs, also known as "starch blockers," work by slowing down carbohydrate absorption in the small intestine. Acarbose (Precose) and miglitol (Glyset) are the available drugs in this class. Taken with the first bite of each main meal, they are most effective in lowering postprandial blood glucose. Their effectiveness is measured by checking 2-hour postprandial glucose levels.

Thiazolidinediones. Thiazolidinediones, sometimes called "insulin sensitizers," include pioglitazone (Actos) and rosiglitazone (Avandia). They are most effective for people who have insulin resistance. These agents improve insulin sensitivity, transport, and use at target tissues. Because they do not increase insulin production, they do not cause hypoglycemia when used alone. However, these drugs are rarely used today because of their adverse effects. Rosiglitazone is associated with adverse cardiovascular events (e.g., myocardial infarction [MI]) and can be obtained only through restricted access programs. Pioglitazone can worsen heart failure (HF) and is associated with an increased risk for bladder cancer.

Dipeptidyl Peptidase-4 (DPP-4) Inhibitors. Normally, the intestines release incretin hormones throughout the day. When glucose levels are normal or elevated, incretins increase insulin synthesis and release from the pancreas and decrease hepatic glucose production. Levels increase in response to a meal. The 2 main incretin hormones are gastric inhibitory peptide [GIP]

and glucagon-like peptide-1 [GLP-1]). They are quickly inactivated by the enzyme dipeptidyl peptidase-4 (DPP-4).

DPP-4 inhibitors (also known as *gliptins*) come in pill form. They include alogliptin (Nesina), linagliptin (Tradjenta), saxagliptin (Onglyza), and sitagliptin (Januvia). DPP-4 inhibitors block the action of DPP-4, which inactivates incretin hormones. The result is an increase in insulin release, decrease in glucagon secretion, and decrease in hepatic glucose production. Since the DPP-4 inhibitors are glucose dependent, they lower the potential for hypoglycemia. The main benefit of these drugs over other medications with similar effects is the absence of weight gain as a side effect.

Sodium-Glucose Co-Transporter 2 (SGLT2) Inhibitors. Normally, sodium glucose transporters reabsorb glucose from the kidneys back into the blood stream. Sodium-glucose co-transporter 2 (SGLT2) inhibitors work by blocking the reabsorption of glucose by the kidney, increasing urinary glucose excretion. Drugs in this class include canagliflozin (Invokana), dapagliflozin (Farxiga), and empagliflozin (Jardiance).

Dopamine Receptor Agonist. Bromocriptine (Cycloset) is a dopamine receptor agonist that improves glucose levels. The mechanism of action is unknown. We think patients with type 2 diabetes have low levels of dopamine activity in the morning. These low dopamine levels may interfere with the body's ability to control blood glucose. Bromocriptine increases dopamine receptor activity. It can be used alone or as an add-on to another type 2 diabetes treatment.

Combination Oral Therapy. Many combination drugs are currently available (Table 48.7). These drugs combine 2 different classes of medications to treat diabetes. One advantage of combination therapy is that the patient takes fewer pills, thus improving medication taking.

Glucagon-Like Peptide-1 Receptor Agonists. Albiglutide (Tanzeum), dulaglutide (Trulicity), exenatide (Byetta), exenatide extended-release (Bydureon), liraglutide (Victoza), and lixisenatide (Adlyxin) simulate GLP-1 (an incretin hormone), which is decreased in people with type 2 diabetes. These drugs increase insulin synthesis and release from the pancreas, inhibit glucagon secretion, slow gastric emptying, and reduce food intake by increasing satiety.

These drugs may be used as monotherapy or adjunct therapy for patients with type 2 diabetes who have not achieved optimal glucose levels on OAs. These drugs are given using a subcutaneous injection in a prefilled pen. Byetta is given twice daily. Liraglutide is given once daily. Albiglutide, dulaglutide, and Bydureon are given once every 7 days. The delayed gastric emptying that occurs with these drugs may affect the absorption of oral medications. Advise patients to take fast-acting oral medications at least 1 hour before injecting a GLP-1 agonist drug.

DRUG ALERT Exenatide (Byetta)

- Acute pancreatitis and kidney problems have been associated with its use.

DRUG ALERT Liraglutide (Victoza) and Dulaglutide (Trulicity)

- Do not use in patients with a personal or family history of medullary thyroid cancer.
- Acute pancreatitis has been associated with its use.

Amylin Analogs. Pramlintide (Symlin) is the only available amylin analog. Amylin, a hormone secreted by the β cells of the pancreas in response to food intake, slows gastric emptying, reduces glucagon secretion, and increases satiety. Pramlintide is used in addition to mealtime insulin in patients with type 1 or type 2 diabetes who have elevated blood glucose levels on insulin therapy. It is only used concurrently with insulin and is not a replacement for insulin. Pramlintide is given before meals subcutaneously into the thigh or abdomen. It cannot be injected into the arm because absorption from this site is too variable. The drug cannot be mixed in the same syringe with insulin.

The concurrent use of pramlintide and insulin increases the risk for severe hypoglycemia during the 3 hours after injection, especially in patients with type 1 diabetes. Teach patients to eat a meal with at least 250 calories and keep a form of fast-acting glucose on hand in case hypoglycemia develops. When pramlintide is used, the bolus dose of insulin should be reduced.

DRUG ALERT Pramlintide (Symlin)
- Can cause severe hypoglycemia when used with insulin.

Other Drugs Affecting Blood Glucose Levels. Both the patient and the HCP must be aware of drug interactions that can potentiate hypoglycemia and hyperglycemia effects. For example, β-adrenergic blockers can mask symptoms of hypoglycemia and prolong the hypoglycemic effects of insulin. Thiazide and loop diuretics can worsen hyperglycemia by inducing potassium loss, although low-dose thiazide therapy is usually considered safe.

Nutrition Therapy

Individualized nutrition therapy, consisting of counseling, education, and ongoing monitoring, is a cornerstone of care for people with diabetes and prediabetes.[12] Changing eating habits can be challenging for many people. Achieving nutrition goals requires a coordinated team effort that considers the person's behavioral, cognitive, socioeconomic, cultural, and religious backgrounds and preferences. Because of these complexities, it is recommended that a dietitian with expertise in diabetes management work with the person who has diabetes. The dietitian starts with a nutrition assessment and develops an individualized food plan. Other team members may include nurses, certified diabetes educators (CDEs), clinical nurse specialists, social workers, and other HCPs.

Guidelines from the ADA state that, within the context of an overall healthy eating plan, a person with diabetes can eat the same foods as a person who does not have diabetes. This means that the same principles of healthy nutrition that apply to the general population also apply to the person with diabetes. Table 48.8 describes nutrition guidelines for patients with diabetes. According to the ADA, the overall goal of nutrition therapy is to help people with diabetes make healthy food choices that will lead to achieving and/or maintaining safe and healthy blood glucose levels. Additional specific goals include:

- Maintain blood glucose levels as close to normal as safely possible to prevent or reduce the risk for complications of diabetes.
- Achieve lipid profiles and BP levels that reduce the risk for CVD.
- Prevent or slow the rate of development of chronic complications of diabetes by modifying nutrient intake and lifestyle.
- Address individual nutrition needs while considering personal and cultural preferences and respecting the person's willingness or ability to change eating and dietary habits.
- Maintain the pleasure of eating by encouraging a variety of healthy food choices.

TABLE 48.8 Nutrition Therapy
Diabetes

Component	Recommendations
Total carbohydrate	• Include carbohydrate from fruits, vegetables, grains, legumes, and low-fat milk • Monitor by carbohydrate counting, exchange lists, or use of appropriate proportions • Fiber intake at 25–30 g/day • Nonnutritive sweeteners are safe when consumed within FDA daily intake levels
Protein	• Individualize goals • High-protein diets are not recommended for weight loss
Fat	• Individualize goals • Minimize *trans* fat • Dietary cholesterol <200 mg/day • ≥2 servings of fish per week to provide polyunsaturated fatty acids
Alcohol	• Limit to moderate amount (maximum 1 drink per day for women, 2 drinks per day for men) • Consume alcohol with food to reduce risk for nocturnal hypoglycemia in those using insulin or drugs that promote insulin secretion • Moderate alcohol consumption has no acute effect on glucose and insulin concentrations • Carbohydrates taken with the alcohol (mixed drink) may raise blood glucose

Source: American Diabetes Association: Lifestyle management: Standards of medical care in diabetes, *Diabetes Care* 41:S38, 2018.

Type 1 Diabetes. People with type 1 diabetes base their meal planning on usual food intake and preferences balanced with insulin and exercise patterns. The patient coordinates insulin dosing with eating habits and activity pattern in mind. Day-to-day consistency in timing and amount of food eaten makes it much easier to manage blood glucose levels, especially for those using conventional, fixed insulin regimens. Patients using rapid-acting insulin can adjust the dose before each meal based on the current blood glucose level and the carbohydrate content of the meal. Intensified insulin therapy, such as multiple daily injections or the use of an insulin pump, allows considerable flexibility in food selection and can be adjusted for changes from usual eating and exercise habits. This does not diminish or replace the need for healthy food choices and a well-balanced diet.

Type 2 Diabetes. Nutrition therapy in type 2 diabetes emphasizes achieving glucose, lipid, and BP goals. Modest weight loss has been associated with improved insulin sensitivity. Therefore weight loss is recommended for all persons with diabetes who are overweight or obese.[13]

There is no one proven strategy or method. A nutritionally adequate meal plan with appropriate serving sizes, a reduction of saturated and *trans* fats, and low carbohydrates can decrease calorie consumption. Spacing meals is another strategy that spreads nutrient intake throughout the day. A weight loss of 5% to 7% of body weight often improves blood glucose levels, even if desirable body weight is not achieved. Weight loss is best achieved by a moderate decrease in calories and an increase in caloric expenditure. Regularly exercising and adopting new behaviors and attitudes can promote long-term lifestyle changes. Monitoring blood glucose levels, A1C, lipids, and BP gives feedback on how well the goals of nutrition therapy are being met.

Food Composition. A healthy balance of nutrients is essential to maintain blood glucose levels and overall health. Energy from food intake can be balanced with the patient's energy output. Teach patients to plan their individual meal plan with their lifestyle and health goals in mind. The following are general recommendations for nutrient balance.

Carbohydrate. Carbohydrates include sugars, starches, and fiber. They are an important source of energy, fiber, vitamins, and minerals and needed by all people, including those with diabetes. Foods containing carbohydrate from whole grains, fruits, vegetables, and low-fat dairy are part of a healthy meal plan. The ADA recommends individualizing carbohydrate intake as there is no ideal amount for all people with diabetes.

All persons benefit from including dietary fiber as part of a healthy meal plan. The current recommendation for the general population is 25 to 30 g/day.[13]

Nutritive and nonnutritive sweeteners may be included in a healthy meal plan in moderation. Nonnutritive sweeteners include the sugar substitutes saccharine, aspartame, sucralose, stevia, neotame, and acesulfame-K.

Fat. Dietary fat provides energy, transports fat-soluble vitamins, and provides essential fatty acids. The ADA recommends individualizing saturated fat intake. Less than 200 mg/day of cholesterol and limited *trans* fats are recommended as part of a healthy meal plan. Decreasing fat and cholesterol intake helps reduce the risk for CVD. Healthy fats are those that come from plants, such as olives, nuts, and avocados.

Protein. The amount of daily protein in the diet for people with diabetes and normal renal function is the same as for the general population. The ADA recommends individualizing protein intake. Teach patients to choose lean protein whenever possible.

Alcohol. Alcohol inhibits gluconeogenesis (breakdown of glycogen to glucose) by the liver. This can cause severe hypoglycemia in patients on insulin or OAs that increase insulin secretion. Create a trusting environment in which patients feel comfortable being honest about their alcohol use because its use can make blood glucose harder to manage.

Moderate alcohol consumption can be safely incorporated into the meal plan if the person is monitoring blood glucose levels and not at risk for other alcohol-related problems. Moderate consumption is defined as 1 drink per day for women and 2 drinks per day for men. A patient can reduce the risk for alcohol-induced hypoglycemia by eating carbohydrates when drinking alcohol. On the other hand, mixed drinks often contain sweetened mixers and can increase blood glucose levels. To decrease the carbohydrate content, recommend using sugar-free mixes and drinking dry, light wines.

Patient Teaching Related to Nutrition Therapy. Most often, the dietitian initially teaches the principles of nutrition management. Whenever possible, work with dietitians as part of an interprofessional diabetes care team. Some patients who have limited insurance coverage or live in remote areas do not have access to a dietitian. In these cases, you may need to assume responsibility for teaching basic nutrition principles to patients with diabetes.

Carbohydrate counting is a meal planning technique used to keep track of the amount of carbohydrate eaten with each meal and per day. Teach patients to keep carbohydrate intake within a healthy range. The amount of total carbohydrate per day depends on blood glucose levels, age, weight, activity level, patient preference, and prescribed medications. A serving size of carbohydrate is 15 g. A typical adult usually starts with 45 to 60 g

of carbohydrate per meal. For some patients, insulin doses are tailored to the amount of carbohydrate foods that a patient will consume at the meal, with a set number of units of insulin given per gram of carbohydrate (e.g., 1 U/15 g carbohydrate, 2 U/25 g carbohydrate). Teach the patient about the foods that contain carbohydrate, how to read food labels, and appropriate serving sizes.

Diabetes exchange lists are another method for meal planning. Instead of counting carbohydrate, the person is given a meal plan with specific numbers of helpings from a list of exchanges for each meal and snack. The exchanges are starches, fruits, milk, meats, vegetables, fats, and free foods. The patient chooses foods from the various exchanges based on the prescribed meal plan. This method may be easier for some patients than carbohydrate counting. It also encourages a well-balanced meal plan. Another advantage is that this approach helps the patient limit portion sizes and overall food intake, an important part of weight management.

MyPlate was developed by the U.S. Department of Agriculture (USDA) to represent national nutrition guidelines for people with or without diabetes. This simple method helps the patient see the amount of vegetables, starch, and meat that fills a 9-in plate. The recommendation is that each meal has half of the plate filled with nonstarchy vegetables, one fourth filled with a starch, and one fourth filled with a protein (*www.diabetes.org/food-and-fitness/food/planning-meals/create-your-plate*). An 8-oz glass of nonfat milk and a small piece of fresh fruit complete the meal.[12]

Whenever possible, include family members and caregivers in nutrition education and counseling, especially the person who cooks for the household. However, the responsibility for maintaining a healthy eating plan still belongs to the person with diabetes. Reliance on another person to make health decisions interferes with the patient's ability to develop self-care skills, which are essential in managing diabetes. Foster independence, even in patients with visual or cognitive impairment. It is important to discuss traditional foods with the patient. Individualize food choices considering the patient's preferences and culturally appropriate foods.

Exercise

Regular, consistent exercise is an essential part of diabetes and prediabetes management.[14] The ADA recommends that people with diabetes engage in at least 150 min/wk (30 minutes, 5 days/week) of a moderate-intensity aerobic physical activity (Table 48.9). The ADA encourages people with type 2 diabetes to perform resistance training 3 times a week unless contraindicated.[15]

TABLE 48.9 Activities That Affect Caloric Expenditure

Light Activity (100–200 kcal/hr)	Moderate Activity (200–350 kcal/hr)	Vigorous Activity (400–900 kcal/hr)
• Fishing	• Active housework	• Aerobic exercise
• Light housework	• Bicycling (light)	• Bicycling (vigorous)
• Secretarial work	• Bowling	• Hard labor
• Teaching	• Dancing	• Ice skating
• Walking casually	• Gardening	• Outdoor sports
	• Golf	• Running
	• Roller skating	• Soccer
	• Walking briskly	• Tennis
		• Wood chopping

Exercise decreases insulin resistance and can have a direct effect on lowering blood glucose levels. It contributes to weight loss, which further decreases insulin resistance. The therapeutic benefits of regular physical activity may result in a decreased need for diabetes medications to reach target blood glucose goals in people with type 2 diabetes. Regular exercise may also help reduce triglyceride and low-density lipoprotein (LDL) cholesterol levels, increase HDL, reduce BP, and improve circulation.

Encourage patients to be active every day and to seek medical clearance before starting a new or more intensive exercise program. Patients start slowly with gradual progression toward the desired goal. Patients who use insulin, sulfonylureas, or meglitinides are at increased risk for hypoglycemia when they increase physical activity, especially if they exercise at the time of peak drug action or eat too little to maintain adequate blood glucose levels. This can also occur if a normally sedentary patient with diabetes has an unusually active day.

The glucose-lowering effects of exercise can last up to 48 hours after the activity, so it is possible for hypoglycemia to occur long after the activity. Patients who use drugs that can cause hypoglycemia should exercise about 1 hour after a meal or have a 10- to 15-g carbohydrate snack and check their blood glucose before exercising. It is preferable not to increase caloric intake for exercise. If needed, they can eat small carbohydrate snacks every 30 minutes during exercise to prevent hypoglycemia. Patients using drugs that place them at risk for hypoglycemia should always carry a fast-acting source of carbohydrate, such as glucose tablets or hard candies, when exercising. If they have frequent lows from exercise, the medication dose may need to be lowered. Table 48.10 describes exercise guidelines for patients with diabetes.

The body can perceive strenuous activity as a stress, causing a release of counterregulatory hormones and a temporary elevation of blood glucose. In a person with type 1 diabetes who has hyperglycemia and ketones, exercise can worsen these conditions. Teach these patients to delay activity if the blood glucose level is over 250 mg/dL and ketones are present in the urine. If hyperglycemia is present without ketosis, it is not necessary to postpone exercise.[12]

Monitoring Blood Glucose

Self-monitoring of blood glucose (SMBG) is a critical part of diabetes management. By providing a current blood glucose reading, SMBG lets the patient make decisions about food intake, activity patterns, and medication dosages. It produces accurate records of daily glucose fluctuations and trends and alerts the patient to acute episodes of hyperglycemia and hypoglycemia. SMBG provides patients with a tool for achieving and maintaining specific glycemic goals. It is recommended for all patients who use insulin to manage their diabetes. Other patients with diabetes use SMBG to help achieve and maintain glycemic goals and monitor for acute fluctuations in blood glucose related to drugs, food, and exercise.

The frequency of SMBG depends on several factors. These include the patient's glycemic goals, type of diabetes, medication regimen, patient's ability to check blood glucose independently, access to supplies and equipment, and patient's willingness and ability to do so. The recommendation for patients who use multiple insulin injections or insulin pumps is to monitor their blood glucose 4 to 8 times each day. Patients using less frequent insulin injections, noninsulin therapy, or nutrition management will monitor as often as needed to achieve their glycemic goals.[9]

Patients who perform SMBG use portable blood glucose monitors. A wide variety of blood glucose monitors are available (Fig. 48.9). Disposable lancets are used to get a small drop of capillary blood (usually from a finger stick) that is placed in a reagent strip. After a specified time, the monitor displays a digital reading of the capillary blood glucose value. The technology of SMBG is rapidly changing. Newer, more convenient systems are introduced on an ongoing basis.

Some systems allow the user to collect blood from alternative sites, such as the forearm or palm. Alternative site use is not recommended with rapidly changing blood glucose readings, during pregnancy, or when symptoms of low blood glucose are present. The data from some glucose monitors can be uploaded

---

TABLE 48.10 Patient & Caregiver Teaching
Exercise for Patients With Diabetes

Include the following information in the exercise teaching plan for the patient and caregiver:

1. Exercise does not have to be vigorous to be effective. The blood glucose-reducing effects of exercise can be reached with activity such as brisk walking.
2. Choose exercises that are enjoyable to foster regularity.
3. Use properly fitting footwear to avoid rubbing or injury.
4. The exercise session includes a warm-up period and a cool-down period. Start the exercise program gradually and increase slowly.
5. Exercise is best done after meals, when the blood glucose level is rising.
6. Exercise plans are patient specific and monitored by the HCP.
7. Monitor blood glucose levels before, during, and after exercise to determine the effect exercise has on blood glucose levels at specific times of the day.
8. Before exercise, if blood glucose ≤100 mg/dL, eat a 15-g carbohydrate snack. After 15 to 30 min, recheck blood glucose levels. Delay exercise if <100 mg/dL.
9. Before exercise, if blood glucose ≥250 mg/dL in a person with type 1 diabetes and ketones are present, delay vigorous activity until ketones are gone. Drink fluids.
10. Exercise-induced hypoglycemia may occur several hours after the completion of exercise.
11. Planned or spontaneous exercise can still occur when taking a glucose-lowering medication.
12. It is important to compensate for extensive planned and spontaneous activity by monitoring blood glucose levels and making adjustments in the insulin dose (if taken) and food intake.

FIG. 48.9 Blood glucose monitors are used to measure blood glucose levels. (© iStock.com/kolesnikovserg.)

to a computer and reviewed by HCPs, allowing for more frequent and efficient adjustment of the plan of care if needed.

Continuous glucose monitoring (CGM) systems are another route for monitoring glucose. More people with type 1 diabetes are using CGMs. These systems are slowly being used by people with type 2 diabetes as well. Insurance coverage and cost are the most common limiting factors. Some insulin pumps have CGM integrated as part of the system. Flash glucose monitoring is another option. It allows users to wave a reader over a subcutaneous sensor and get glucose readings at any time (Fig. 48.10).

Using a sensor inserted subcutaneously, the systems display glucose values that are updated every 1 to 5 minutes. CGM assesses interstitial glucose, which lags behind blood glucose by 5 to 10 minutes.[16] The patient inserts the sensor using an automatic insertion device. Data are sent from the sensor to a transmitter, which displays the glucose value on either an insulin pump or a pager-like receiver. The CGM can be used with or without an insulin pump. Newer CGMs can "share" data with a smart phone.

CGMs help the patient and HCP identify trends and patterns in glucose levels. The goal is to increase "time in range" (70 to 180 mg/dL) and have fewer highs and lows. They are useful for managing insulin therapy or when continuous blood glucose readings are clinically important. The patient is alerted to episodes of hypoglycemia and hyperglycemia, thus allowing corrective action to be quickly taken. Some systems need finger-stick measurements using a blood glucose monitor to calibrate the sensor and to make treatment decisions. In 2016 the FDA approved making insulin dosing decisions based on a CGM reading, without first checking a finger-stick blood glucose value.

Blood glucose meters available today are reliable when used consistently and correctly. It is not necessary to compare meter readings to laboratory readings. If the A1C result does not correspond to the blood glucose readings on the home meter, it is a good idea to troubleshoot any problems with the meter, strips, or hand washing technique.

Because errors in monitoring technique can cause errors in management strategies, comprehensive patient teaching is essential. Initial instruction should be followed with regular reassessment. Review the instructions that come with each product. If a product has a control solution, teach patients to use and interpret control solutions. Control solution should be used when first using a blood glucose meter or when there is a reason to believe that the readings are not correct. Table 48.11 lists the steps to include when teaching the patient how to perform SMBG.

People with type 1 diabetes often check their blood glucose before meals. This is because many patients use insulin pumps or multiple daily injections and base the insulin dose on the carbohydrates in a meal or make adjustments if the preprandial value is above or below target. Checking blood glucose 2 hours after the first bite of food helps a person determine if the bolus insulin dose was adequate for that meal.

Teach patients to monitor blood glucose whenever hypoglycemia is suspected and then take immediate action. During times of illness, check blood glucose levels at 4-hour intervals to determine the effects of the illness on glucose levels. Teach the patient to monitor blood glucose before and after exercise to determine the effects of exercise on blood glucose levels. This is especially important in the patient with type 1 diabetes.

A patient who is visually impaired, cognitively impaired, or limited in manual dexterity needs careful evaluation of the degree to which SMBG can be done independently. Nurses preparing patients for discharge from the hospital and nurses working in home health and outpatient settings may need to identify caregivers who can assume this responsibility. Adaptive devices are available to help patients with certain limitations. These include talking meters and other equipment for the visually impaired.

Bariatric Surgery

Bariatric surgery may be an option for patients with type 2 diabetes, especially if the diabetes or associated co-morbidities are hard to manage with lifestyle and drug therapy. Patients with

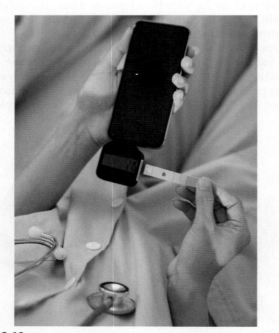

FIG. 48.10 Glucometers that connect to a smartphone allow the patient to measure blood glucose, log the measurements in an app, and share the results with health care providers. (© DragonImages/iStock.com.)

TABLE 48.11 **Patient & Caregiver Teaching**
Self-Monitoring of Blood Glucose (SMBG)
Include the following instructions when teaching the patient and caregiver about SMBG: 1. Wash and dry hands completely. It is not necessary to clean the site with alcohol, and it may interfere with test results.   2. If it is hard to get an adequate drop of blood for testing, warm the hands in warm water or let the arms hang dependently for a few minutes before making the finger puncture.   3. A lancing device is usually used. Place the lancet in the device, following the instructions that come with it. If the puncture is made on the finger, use the side of the finger pad rather than near the center. Fewer nerve endings are along the side of the finger pad. If using an alternative site (e.g., forearm), special equipment may be needed. Refer to manufacturer's instructions for alternative site use, except during hypoglycemia episodes.   4. Set lancing device to make a puncture just deep enough to get a sufficiently large drop of blood. Unnecessarily deep punctures may cause pain and bruising. Current meters need very small amounts of blood.   5. Follow instructions on monitor for checking the blood glucose level.   6. Record results. Compare with personal blood glucose goals.

type 2 diabetes who have undergone bariatric surgery need life-long lifestyle support and monitoring. Bariatric surgery is discussed in Chapter 40.

Pancreas Transplantation

Pancreas transplantation is an option for select patients with type 1 diabetes. Usually it is done for patients who have end-stage renal disease (ESRD) and have had or plan to have a kidney transplant. Kidney and pancreas transplants are often done together, or a pancreas may be transplanted after a kidney transplant. If renal failure is not present, the ADA recommends that pancreas transplantation be considered only for patients who exhibit these 3 criteria: (1) a history of frequent, acute, and severe metabolic complications (e.g., hypoglycemia, hyperglycemia, ketoacidosis) requiring medical attention; (2) clinical and emotional problems with the use of exogenous insulin therapy that are so severe as to be incapacitating; and (3) consistent failure of insulin-based management to prevent acute complications.

Successful pancreas transplantation can improve quality of life, primarily by eliminating the need for exogenous insulin and frequent blood glucose measurements. Transplantation can eliminate acute complications experienced by patients with type 1 diabetes (e.g., hypoglycemia, hyperglycemia). However, transplantation is only partially successful in reversing the long-term renal and neurologic complications of diabetes. The patient will need lifelong immunosuppression to prevent rejection of the organ. Complications can result from immunosuppressive therapy. Immunosuppressive therapy is discussed in Chapter 13.

Pancreatic islet cell transplantation is another potential treatment measure. During this procedure, the islets are harvested from the pancreas of a deceased organ donor. Most recipients need the use of 2 or more pancreases. The islets are infused via a catheter through the upper abdomen into the portal vein of the liver. With only the islets transplanted, pain and recovery time are less than with whole pancreas transplants. Currently, this procedure is experimental in the United States. Research is continuing to investigate the best ways to implant the islet cells and prevent their rejection.

Culturally Competent Care: Diabetes

Because culture can have a strong influence on dietary preferences and meal preparation practices, culturally competent care has special relevance for the patient with diabetes. For example, certain ethnic and cultural groups, such as Hispanics, Native Americans, blacks, and Asians and Pacific Islanders have a high incidence of diabetes. The increased prevalence can be attributed to genetic predisposition, environmental factors, and dietary choices.

Explore the influences of culture on food choices and meal planning with the patient as part of the health history. When teaching about nutrition, consider the patient's cultural food preferences. Nutrition resources specifically designed for members of different cultural groups are available from the ADA.

❖ NURSING MANAGEMENT: DIABETES

◆ Nursing Assessment

Table 48.12 provides initial subjective and objective data to gather from a person with diabetes. After the initial assessment, perform periodic patient assessments on a regular basis.

TABLE 48.12 Nursing Assessment
Diabetes

Subjective Data
Important Health Information
Past health history: Mumps, rubella, coxsackievirus, or other viral infections. Recent trauma, infection, or stress. Pregnancy, gave birth to infant >9 lb. Chronic pancreatitis, Cushing syndrome, acromegaly, family history of type 1 or type 2 diabetes
Medications: Use of insulin or OAs, corticosteroids, diuretics, phenytoin (Dilantin)
Surgery or other treatments: Any recent surgery

Functional Health Patterns
Health perception–health management: Positive family history, malaise
Nutrition-metabolic: Obesity, weight loss (type 1), weight gain (type 2). Thirst, hunger, nausea and vomiting. Poor healing (especially involving the feet), eating habits
Elimination: Constipation or diarrhea, frequent urination, frequent bladder infections, nocturia, urinary incontinence
Activity-exercise: Muscle weakness, fatigue
Cognitive-perceptual: Abdominal pain, headache, blurred vision, numbness or tingling of extremities, pruritus
Sexuality-reproductive: ED, frequent vaginal infections, vaginal dryness or pain, ↓ libido
Adaptation: Depression, irritability, apathy
Value-belief: Health beliefs, commitment to lifestyle changes involving food, medication, and activity patterns

Objective Data
Eyes
Soft, sunken eyeballs.* History of vitreal hemorrhages, cataracts

Integumentary
Dry, warm, inelastic skin. Pigmented lesions (on legs), ulcers (especially on feet), loss of hair on toes, acanthosis nigricans

Respiratory
Rapid, deep respirations (Kussmaul respirations)*

Cardiovascular
Hypotension.* Weak, rapid pulse*

Gastrointestinal
Dry mouth, vomiting.* Fruity breath*

Neurologic
Altered reflexes, restlessness, confusion, stupor, coma*

Musculoskeletal
Muscle wasting*

Possible Findings
Serum electrolyte abnormalities. Fasting blood glucose level ≥126 mg/dL. OGTT >200 mg/dL, random glucose ≥200 mg/dL. Leukocytosis. ↑ BUN, creatinine, triglycerides, cholesterol, LDL, VLDL. ↓ HDL. A1C >6.0% (A1C >7.0% in those with diagnosed diabetes), glycosuria, ketonuria, albuminuria. Acidosis

*Indicates manifestations of diabetes-related ketoacidosis (DKA).

◆ Nursing Diagnoses

Nursing diagnoses related to diabetes may include:
- Lack of knowledge
- Hyperglycemia
- Hypoglycemia

- Risk for injury
- Impaired peripheral neurovascular function

Additional information on nursing diagnoses and interventions for the patient with diabetes is presented in eNursing Care Plan 48.1 available on the website.

◆ Planning

The overall goals are for the patient with diabetes to (1) engage in self-care behaviors to actively manage diabetes, (2) have few or no hyperglycemia or hypoglycemia emergencies, (3) maintain blood glucose levels at normal or near-normal levels, (4) reduce the risk for chronic complications from diabetes, and (5) adjust lifestyle to accommodate the diabetes plan with minimum stress. The goal is for the patient with diabetes to safely and effectively fit diabetes into life, rather than living life around diabetes.

◆ Nursing Implementation

◆ **Health Promotion.** Your role in health promotion is to identify, monitor, and teach the patient at risk for diabetes. Obesity is the main risk factor for type 2 diabetes. The ADA recommends routine screening for type 2 diabetes for all adults who are overweight or obese (BMI 25 kg/m^2 or greater) or have 1 or more risk factors. For people who do not have risk factors for diabetes, begin screening at age 45. Table 48.13 provides criteria to screen for prediabetes and diabetes. If results are normal, repeat screening at 3-year intervals.[3]

Many other factors put a person at an increased risk for diabetes. These include age, ethnicity (being Native American, Hispanic, black, Asian, Pacific Islander), having a baby that weighed more than 9 lb at birth, history of gestational diabetes, and a family history of diabetes. A diabetes risk test is available at *www.diabetes.org/risk-test.jsp*. The diabetes risk test

determines if the person is at risk for prediabetes or diabetes based on the number of risk factors present.

Primary prevention is a cost-effective approach. Current recommendations for primary prevention include lifestyle modifications for at-risk people. A modest weight loss of 5% to 7% of body weight and 150 minutes of physical activity a week lowered the risk for developing type 2 diabetes by 34% to 58%.[17]

♥ PROMOTING POPULATION HEALTH
Preventing Diabetes

- Increase level of exercise by aiming for 150 minutes of moderate activity each week.
- Maintain a healthy weight through a nutritionally balanced diet.
- If overweight, lose weight and take part in a regular exercise program.
- Follow a diet low in fat, total calories, and processed foods and high in whole grains, fruits, and vegetables.
- If overweight and over age 45, get screened for diabetes yearly.
- Avoid cigarette smoking or tobacco products.
- Limit consumption of alcohol to moderate levels.
- Follow the prescribed treatment plan for hypertension.

◆ **Acute Care.** Acute situations involving the patient with diabetes include hypoglycemia, DKA, and hyperosmolar hyperglycemic syndrome (HHS). Nursing management for these situations is discussed in more detail later in this chapter. Other areas of acute care relate to management during acute illness and surgery.

Acute Illness and Surgery. Both emotional and physical stress can increase the blood glucose level and result in hyperglycemia. Because stress is unavoidable, certain situations may require more intense treatment, such as extra insulin and more frequent blood glucose monitoring, to maintain glycemic goals and avoid hyperglycemia.

Acute illness, injury, and surgery may evoke a counterregulatory hormone response, resulting in hyperglycemia. Even common illnesses, such as a viral upper respiratory tract infection or the flu, can cause this response. Encourage patients with diabetes to check blood glucose at least every 4 hours during times of illness. Teach acutely ill patients with type 1 diabetes and a blood glucose greater than 240 mg/dL (13.3 mmol/L) to check urine for ketones every 3 to 4 hours.

Teach patients to contact the HCP when glucose levels are over 300 mg/dL twice in a row or urine ketone levels are moderate to high. A patient with type 1 diabetes may need an increase in insulin to prevent DKA. Elevated blood glucose levels can lead to poor healing and infection. Insulin therapy may be needed for a patient with type 2 diabetes to prevent or treat hyperglycemia symptoms and avoid an acute hyperglycemia emergency. In critically ill patients, insulin therapy may be started if the blood glucose is persistently greater than 180 mg/dL. These patients have a higher targeted blood glucose goal, which is usually 140 to 180 mg/dL. Food intake is important during times of stress and illness, when the body needs extra energy. If patients can eat normally, they can continue with their regular meal plan while increasing the intake of noncaloric fluids, such as water, sugar-free gelatin, and other decaffeinated beverages, and continue taking OAs, noninsulin injectable agents, and insulin as prescribed. When illness causes patients to eat less than normal, they can continue to take OAs, noninsulin injectable agents, and/or insulin as prescribed while supplementing food intake with carbohydrate-containing fluids. Examples include

TABLE 48.13 Screening for Diabetes in Asymptomatic, Undiagnosed Persons

Who to Screen

1. Consider screening all adults who are overweight (BMI >25 kg/m^2) and have additional risk factors:
   - First-degree relative with diabetes
   - Physically inactive
   - Members of a high-risk ethnic population (e.g., black, Hispanic, Native American, Asian American,* Pacific Islander)
   - Women who delivered a baby weighing >9 lb or were diagnosed with gestational diabetes
   - Hypertensive (≥140/90 mm Hg) or on therapy for hypertension
   - HDL cholesterol level ≤35 mg/dL (0.90 mmol/L) and/or a triglyceride level ≥250 mg/dL (2.82 mmol/L)
   - Women with polycystic ovary syndrome
   - A1C ≥5.7%, IGT, or IFG on previous screening
   - Other conditions associated with insulin resistance (e.g., acanthosis nigricans)
2. In the absence of the above criteria, screening for diabetes should begin at age 45 yr.
3. If results are normal, repeat screening at least every 3 years, with more frequent screening depending on initial results and risk status.

What Measurements Are Used

To screen for diabetes or to assess risk of future diabetes, A1C, FPG, or 2-hour OGTT is appropriate.

Source: American Diabetes Association: Standards of medical care in diabetes, *Diabetes Care* 41:S15, 2018.
*Consider screening Asian Americans with a BMI of 23 kg/m^2 or higher.

low-sodium soups, juices, and regular, sugar-sweetened decaffeinated soft drinks. It is important to tell the patient to contact an HCP if they are unable to keep down food or fluid.

During the intraoperative period, adjustments in the diabetes plan can be made to ensure safe and healthy blood glucose levels. The patient is given IV fluids and insulin (if needed) just before, during, and after surgery when there is no oral intake. Explain to the patient with type 2 diabetes who has been on OAs that this is a temporary measure, not a sign of worsening diabetes.

When caring for an unconscious surgical patient receiving insulin, be alert for signs of hypoglycemia, such as sweating, tachycardia, and tremors. Frequent monitoring of blood glucose can prevent episodes of severe hypoglycemia.

◆ **Ambulatory Care.** Successful diabetes management involves ongoing interaction among the patient, caregiver, and interprofessional team. It is important that a CDE be involved in the care of the patient and family. Because diabetes is a complex chronic condition, a great deal of patient contact takes place in outpatient and home settings. The major goal of patient care in these settings is to enable the patient (with the help of a caregiver as needed) to reach an optimal level of independence in self-care activities. Unfortunately, many patients face challenges in reaching these goals. Diabetes increases the risk for other chronic conditions that can affect self-care activities. These include visual impairment, lower extremity problems that affect mobility, and other functional limitations related to a stroke.

An important nursing function is to assess the ability of patients and caregivers in performing activities such as SMBG and insulin injection. Assistive devices for self-administration of insulin include syringe magnifiers, vial stabilizers, and dosing aids for the visually impaired. In some cases, referrals are made to help the patient achieve the self-care goal. These may include an occupational therapist, a social worker, a home care nurse, a home health aide, or a dietitian.

A diagnosis of diabetes affects the patient in many profound ways. Self-management of the disease is demanding. Patients with diabetes continually face lifestyle choices that affect the foods they eat, their activities, and demands on their time and energy. The requirements of scheduled meals, SMBG, medication, and insulin management may interfere with the patient's other responsibilities. Any change in the daily routine can be hard. In addition, they face the challenge of preventing or dealing with the devastating complications of diabetes.

Careful assessment of what it means to the patient to have diabetes is a good starting point for teaching. The goals of teaching are mutually determined by the patient and you, based on individual needs and therapeutic requirements. Identify the patient's support system, and include them in planning, teaching, and counseling. When family members and other persons close to the patient are included, they can support the patient's self-care behaviors. They can also provide care if self-care is not possible. Encourage the family and caregivers to provide emotional support and encouragement as the patient deals with the reality of living with a chronic disease.

Insulin Therapy. Nursing responsibilities for the patient receiving insulin include proper administration, assessment of the patient's response to insulin therapy, and teaching the patient about administration, storage, and side effects of insulin (Table 48.5). Table 48.6 lists guidelines for assessing a patient using GLAs, including insulin and OAs.

Assessment of the patient who is a new user of insulin includes evaluating their ability to safely manage this therapy. This includes the ability to understand the interaction of insulin, food, and activity and to recognize and treat the symptoms of hypoglycemia appropriately. If the patient does not have the cognitive skills to do these things, identify and teach another responsible person. The patient or caregiver must have the cognitive and manual skills needed to prepare and inject insulin. Otherwise, additional resources will be needed to assist the patient. For patients with cognitive, physical, and other barriers, consider referral to a CDE. A CDE has the specialized knowledge and skills to promote self-care behaviors for these patients.

Many patients are fearful when they first begin using insulin. Some find it hard to self-inject because they are afraid of needles or the pain associated with an injection. Others may think that they do not need insulin or that they will be hypoglycemic after an injection. Explore the patient's underlying fears before beginning the teaching. Assessing the patient's beliefs and concerns about starting insulin will guide the teaching, counseling, and plan of care. Having open discussion with patients, providing educational materials and programs, and working with a CDE are all beneficial for patients starting insulin.

Follow-up assessment of the patient who has been using insulin therapy includes inspecting injection sites for signs of lipodystrophy and other reactions, reviewing insulin preparation and injection technique, taking a history of the occurrence of hypoglycemia, and assessing how the patient managed hypoglycemia. A review of the patient's recorded blood glucose readings is vital in assessing how the patient is doing and making any needed adjustments.

Oral and Noninsulin Injectable Agents. Your responsibilities for the patient taking OAs and noninsulin injectable agents are similar to those for the patient taking insulin. Proper administration, assessment of the patient's use of and response to these drugs, and teaching the patient and family are all essential nursing actions.

Your assessment is valuable in determining the most appropriate drug for a patient. Factors such as the patient's mental status, eating habits, home environment, learning ability, resources, attitude toward diabetes, and medication history all play a significant role in determining the most appropriate drug. For example, frail older adults who live alone are at high risk for severe hypoglycemia because low blood glucose is often undetected or untreated. This is especially true if the patient has cognitive impairment. In these cases, an OA that does not cause hypoglycemia, or a shorter-acting OA, would be most appropriate.

Patient teaching is essential. Some patients may assume that their diabetes is not a serious condition if they are only taking a pill to treat it. Teach the patient that OAs will help manage blood glucose and help prevent serious long- and short-term complications of diabetes. Discuss how OAs and noninsulin injectable agents are used in addition to food choices and activity as therapy for diabetes and the importance of following their meal and activity plans. Teach patients not to take extra pills if they have overeaten. If the patient uses sulfonylureas and metformin, teach the patient about the prevention, recognition, and management of hypoglycemia.

Personal Hygiene. The potential for infection requires diligent skin and dental hygiene practices. Because of the susceptibility to periodontal disease, encourage daily brushing and flossing and regular dental visits. When having dental work done, have the patient tell the dentist they have diabetes.

Routine care includes regular bathing, with an emphasis on foot care. Advise patients to inspect their feet daily, avoid going barefoot, and wear shoes that are supportive and comfortable. If cuts, scrapes, or burns occur, treat them promptly and monitor them carefully. Wash the area and apply a nonabrasive or nonirritating antiseptic ointment. Cover the area with a dry, sterile pad. Teach patients to notify the HCP at once if the injury does not begin to heal within 24 hours or if signs of infection develop.

Medical Identification and Travel. Teach the patient to always carry medical identification indicating that they have diabetes. Police, paramedics, and many private citizens are aware of the need to look for this identification when working with sick or unconscious persons. An identification card (Fig. 48.11) can supply valuable information, such as the name of the HCP; the type of diabetes; and the type and dosage of insulin, noninsulin injectable agents, or OAs.

Travel for a patient with diabetes requires planning. Being sedentary for long periods may raise the person's glucose level. Encourage the patient to get up and walk at least every 2 hours to lower the risk for deep vein thrombosis and prevent elevation

I have DIABETES

If unconscious or behaving abnormally, I may be having a reaction associated with diabetes or its treatment.

If I can swallow, give me a sweet drink, orange juice, LifeSavers, or low-fat milk.

If I do not recover promptly, call a physician or send me to the hospital.

If I am unconscious or cannot swallow, do not attempt to give me anything by mouth, but call 911 or send me to the hospital immediately.

FIG. 48.11 Medical alerts. A patient with diabetes should carry a card and wear a bracelet or necklace that indicates diabetes. If the patient with diabetes is unconscious, these measures will ensure prompt and appropriate attention.

NURSING MANAGEMENT
Caring for the Patient With Diabetes

You will need to collaborate with many health care team members to deliver, delegate, and coordinate care based on the patient's status.
- Assess for risk factors for prediabetes and type 1 and type 2 diabetes.
- Teach the patient and caregiver about diabetes management, including SMBG, insulin, noninsulin injectables, OAs, nutrition, physical activity, and managing hypoglycemia.
- Develop a plan to avoid hypoglycemia or hyperglycemia in a patient with DM who is acutely ill or having surgery.
- Assess for acute complications and implement appropriate actions for hypoglycemia, DKA, and HHS.
- In patients having acute complications, perform or directly supervise actions, including IV fluid and insulin administration.
- Assess for chronic complications, including CVD, retinopathy, nephropathy, neuropathy, and foot complications.
- Teach the patient and caregiver about prevention and management of chronic complications related to diabetes.
- Oversee LPN/VNs, and in some states and settings UAP, administer insulin, noninsulin injectable agents, and OAs to stable patients.

Collaborate With Other Team Members
Dietitian
- Obtain a diet history from the patient.
- Work with patient and caregiver to create an individualized meal plan.
- Provide instructions for meal plan as needed.

Physical Therapist
- Assess patient's current level of fitness.
- Develop an exercise plan with the patient.

Occupational Therapist
- Teach with patient with vision impairment how to use devices to draw up and measure insulin.
- Provide teaching on how to use a talking blood glucose monitor or use any blood glucose monitor one handed.
- Develop protective techniques for activities that involve exposure to heat, cold, and sharp objects.

Social Worker
- Aid the patient in finding resources to meet medical and financial needs.
- Help with coping with diabetes, including managing problems within the family or workplace.

of glucose levels. Teach the patient to have a full set of diabetes care supplies in the carry-on luggage when traveling by plane, train, or bus. This includes blood glucose monitoring equipment, insulin, noninsulin injectable agents, OAs, and syringes or insulin pens and pen needles.

Best practices for traveling with diabetes supplies and equipment change frequently. Encourage patients to check TSA guidelines before traveling at *www.diabetes.org/living-with-diabetes/know-your-rights/discrimination/public-accommodations/air-travel-and-diabetes/*. Notify screeners if an insulin pump is used so that they can inspect it while it is on the body, rather than removing it.

For patients who use insulin or OAs that can cause hypoglycemia, keep snack items and a quick-acting carbohydrate source for treating hypoglycemia in the carry-on luggage. Keep extra insulin available in case a bottle breaks or is lost. For longer trips, carry a full day's supply of food in case of canceled flights, delayed meals, or closed restaurants. If the patient is planning a trip out of the country, it is wise to have a letter from the HCP explaining that the patient has diabetes and requires all the materials, especially syringes, for ongoing health care.

When travel involves time changes, such as traveling coast to coast or across the International Date Line, the patient can contact the HCP to plan an appropriate insulin schedule. During travel, most patients find it helpful to keep watches set to the time of the city of origin until they reach their destination. The key to travel when taking insulin is to know the type of insulin being taken, its onset of action, the anticipated peak time, and mealtimes.

Patient and Caregiver Teaching. The goals of diabetes self-management education are to match the level of self-management to the patient's individual ability so that they can become the most active participant possible. Patients who actively manage their diabetes care have better outcomes than those who do not. For this reason, an educational approach that facilitates informed decision making by the patient is advocated. We call this the *empowerment approach* to education.

The empowerment approach includes eliminating messages that are judgmental and negative and replacing them with empowering, person-centered, and strengths-based language. An example includes referring to a patient as a person with diabetes versus calling them a diabetic. This places the emphasis on the person versus the disease. Other examples of words that may be perceived as negative or judgmental include compliant, uncontrolled, and poorly controlled."[18] Research has shown that people with diabetes feel the impact of negative language and would trust their HCPs more if they used empowering language and made them feel like a partner in their care.

Unfortunately, patients can encounter a variety of physical, psychologic, and emotional barriers when it comes to effectively managing their diabetes. These barriers may include feelings of inadequacy about one's own abilities, unwillingness to make behavioral changes, ineffective coping strategies, and cognitive deficits. If the patient is not able to manage the disease, a family member may be able to assume part of this role. If the patient or caregiver cannot make decisions related to diabetes management, consider a referral to a CDE, social worker, or other resources within the community. These resources can help the patient and family in outlining a feasible treatment program that meets their capabilities.

An assessment of the patient's knowledge of diabetes and lifestyle preferences is useful in planning a teaching program. Tables 48.14 and 48.15 present guidelines to use for patient and caregiver teaching. Assess the patient's knowledge base frequently so that gaps in knowledge or incorrect or inaccurate ideas can be corrected.

The ADA offers resources for patients in the form of pamphlets, booklets, books, and a monthly magazine called *Diabetes Forecast*. Affiliates of the ADA are found in all states. Most can be reached by dialing 1-800-DIABETES (800-342-2383). The ADA publishes materials and sponsors conferences for health care professionals concerned with diabetes education, research, and management of patients. The ADA website *(www.diabetes.org)* has extensive information for the public and health care professionals. The ADA also recognizes education programs that meet the national standards of diabetes education and can provide a list of these programs. Most drug companies manufacturing diabetes-related products have free educational materials for patients and HCPs. It is critical that you stay current in your diabetes knowledge so that you can effectively teach and support patients with diabetes.

◆ Evaluation
The expected outcomes are that the patient with diabetes will
- State key elements of the treatment plan
- Describe self-care measures that may prevent or slow progression of chronic complications
- Maintain a balance of nutrition, activity, and insulin availability that results in stable, safe, and healthy blood glucose levels
- Have no injury from decreased sensation in the feet
- Implement measures to increase peripheral circulation

ACUTE COMPLICATIONS OF DIABETES

The acute complications of diabetes arise from events associated with hyperglycemia and hypoglycemia. Hyperglycemia (high blood glucose) occurs when there is not enough insulin working. Hypoglycemia (low blood glucose) occurs when there is too much insulin working. Many signs and symptoms of

TABLE 48.14 Patient & Caregiver Teaching
Management of Diabetes

Include the following instructions when teaching the patient and caregiver how to manage diabetes:

Component	What to Teach
Disease process	• Introduce the pancreas and the islets of Langerhans. • Describe how insulin is made and what affects its production. • Discuss the relationship of insulin and glucose. • Explain the difference between type 1 and type 2 diabetes.
Physical activity	• Discuss the effect of regular exercise on managing blood glucose and improving cardiovascular function and general health.
Menu planning	• Stress the importance of a well-balanced diet as part of a diabetes management plan. • Explain the impact of carbohydrates on blood glucose levels.
Medication	• Ensure that the patient understands the proper use of prescribed medication (e.g., insulin [Table 48.5], OAs, noninsulin injectables). • Account for a patient's physical or other limitations or inabilities for self-medication. If necessary, involve the family or caregiver in proper use of medication. • Discuss all side effects and safety issues about medication.
Monitoring blood glucose	• Teach correct blood glucose monitoring. • Include when to check blood glucose levels, how to record them, and how to adjust insulin levels, if necessary.
Risk reduction	• Ensure that the patient understands and appropriately responds to the signs and symptoms of hypoglycemia and hyperglycemia (Table 48.16). • Stress the importance of proper foot care (Table 48.21), regular eye examinations, and consistent glucose monitoring. • Teach the patient about the effect that stress can have on blood glucose.
Psychosocial	• Help the patient identify resources that are available to help with the adjustment and answer questions about living with a chronic condition such as diabetes.

TABLE 48.15 Patient & Caregiver Teaching
Instructions for Patients With Diabetes

Include the following essential instructions for diabetes management for the patient and caregiver:

Blood Glucose
• Monitor your blood glucose at home and record results in a log.
• Take your insulin, OA, and/or noninsulin injectable agent as prescribed.
• Take insulin consistently, especially when you are sick.
• Keep an adequate supply of insulin on hand at all times.
• Obtain A1C blood test every 3–6 mo as an indicator of your long-term blood glucose levels.
• Be aware of symptoms of hypoglycemia and hyperglycemia.
• Always carry a form of rapid-acting glucose so that you can treat hypoglycemia quickly.
• Teach family members how and when to use glucagon if patient becomes unresponsive because of hypoglycemia.

Exercise
• Learn how exercise and food affect your blood glucose levels.
• Remember that exercise will usually lower your blood glucose level.
• Begin an exercise program after approval from HCP.

Food
• Work with a dietitian to create a patient specific meal plan.
• Make healthy food choices and eat regular meals at regular times.
• Choose foods low in saturated and *trans* fat. Know your cholesterol level.
• Limit the amount of alcohol you drink.
• Be aware that excess amounts of alcohol may lead to unpredictable low blood glucose events.
• Avoid fad diets.
• Limit regular soda and fruit juice.

Other Guidelines
• Obtain an annual eye examination by an ophthalmologist.
• Obtain annual urine monitoring for protein.
• Examine your feet at home.
• Wear comfortable, well-fitting shoes to help prevent foot injury. Break in new shoes gradually.
• Always carry identification that says you have diabetes.
• Have other medical problems treated, especially high BP and high cholesterol.
• Have a yearly influenza vaccination.
• Quit or never start smoking cigarettes or using nicotine products.
• Avoid applying heat or cold directly to your feet.
• Avoid going barefoot.
• Keep skin moisturized by applying cream to surfaces of feet, but not between toes.

hyperglycemia and hypoglycemia overlap. It is important for the HCP to distinguish between them because hypoglycemia worsens rapidly and is a serious threat if action is not immediately taken. Table 48.16 compares the manifestations, causes, management, and prevention of hyperglycemia and hypoglycemia.

DIABETIC KETOACIDOSIS

Etiology and Pathophysiology

Diabetes-related ketoacidosis (DKA) is caused by a profound deficiency of insulin. It is characterized by hyperglycemia, ketosis, acidosis, and dehydration. It is most likely to occur in people with type 1 diabetes. DKA may be seen in people with type 2 diabetes in conditions of severe illness or stress in which the pancreas cannot meet the extra demand for insulin. Precipitating factors include illness; infection; inadequate insulin dosage; undiagnosed type 1 diabetes; lack of education, understanding, or resources; and neglect.

When the circulating supply of insulin is insufficient, glucose cannot be properly used for energy. The body compensates by breaking down fat stores as a secondary source of fuel (Fig. 48.12). Ketones are acidic by-products of fat metabolism that can cause serious problems when they become excessive in the blood. Ketosis alters the pH balance, causing metabolic acidosis to develop. Ketonuria is a process that occurs when ketone bodies are excreted in the urine. During this process, electrolytes that are cations are also excreted with the anionic ketones to try to maintain electrical neutrality.

Insulin deficiency impairs protein synthesis and causes excessive protein degradation. This results in nitrogen losses from the tissues. Insulin deficiency stimulates the production of glucose from amino acids (from proteins) in the liver and leads to further hyperglycemia. Because of the insulin deficiency, the

TABLE 48.16 Comparison of Hyperglycemia and Hypoglycemia

Hyperglycemia	Hypoglycemia
Manifestations	
• Elevated blood glucose	• Blood glucose <70 mg/dL (3.9 mmol/L)
• Increase in urination	• Cold, clammy skin
• Increase in appetite followed by lack of appetite	• Numbness of fingers, toes, mouth
• Weakness, fatigue	• Tachycardia
• Blurred vision	• Emotional changes
• Headache	• Headache
• Glycosuria	• Nervousness, tremors
• Nausea and vomiting	• Faintness, dizziness
• Abdominal cramps	• Unsteady gait, slurred speech
• Progression to DKA or HHS	• Hunger
• Mood swings	• Changes in vision
	• Seizures, coma
Causes	
• Illness, infection	• Alcohol intake without food
• Corticosteroids	• Too little food—delayed, omitted, inadequate intake
• Too much food	• Too much diabetes medication
• Too little or no diabetes medication	• Too much exercise without adequate food intake
• Inactivity	• Diabetes medication or food taken at wrong time
• Emotional, physical stress	• Loss of weight without change in medication
• Poor absorption of insulin	• Use of β-adrenergic blockers interfering with recognition of symptoms
Clinical Course	
• More gradual onset	• More rapid onset
• Definition of elevated glucose varies by person, based on personal glucose targets	• Pattern of manifestations changes over time
Treatment	
• Get medical care	• Follow the Rule of 15 (see pp. 1134–1135).
• Continue diabetes medication as prescribed	• See Table 48.19 for emergency treatment of hypoglycemia.
• Check blood glucose frequently and check urine for ketones; record results	
• Drink fluids at least on an hourly basis	
• Contact HCP about ketonuria	
Preventive Measures	
• Take prescribed dose of medication at proper time	• Take prescribed dose of medication at proper time
• Accurately give insulin, noninsulin injectables, OA	• Accurately give insulin, noninsulin injectables, OA
• Make healthy food choices	• Coordinate eating with medications
• Follow sick-day rules when ill	• Eat adequate food intake needed for calories for exercise
• Check blood glucose routinely	• Be able to recognize symptoms and treat them immediately
• Wear or carry diabetes identification	• Carry simple carbohydrates
	• Teach family and caregiver about symptoms and treatment
	• Check blood glucose routinely
	• Wear or carry diabetes identification

PATHOPHYSIOLOGY MAP

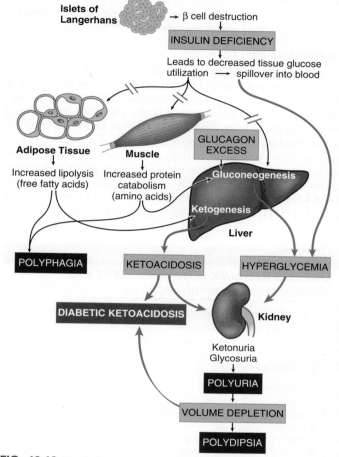

FIG. 48.12 Metabolic events leading to diabetic ketoacidosis. (Modified from Kumar V, Abbas AK, Aster JC, et al: *Robbins and Cotran pathologic basis of disease,* ed 8, Philadelphia, 2010, Saunders.)

additional glucose cannot be used and the blood glucose level rises further, adding to the osmotic diuresis.

If not treated, the patient will develop severe depletion of sodium, potassium, chloride, magnesium, and phosphate. Vomiting caused by the acidosis results in more fluid and electrolyte losses. Eventually, hypovolemia, followed by shock, will ensue. Renal failure, which may eventually occur from hypovolemic shock, causes the retention of ketones and glucose, and the acidosis progresses. Untreated, the patient becomes comatose from dehydration, electrolyte imbalance, and acidosis. If the condition is not treated, death is inevitable.

Clinical Manifestations

Dehydration occurs in DKA with manifestations of dry mucous membranes, tachycardia, and orthostatic hypotension. Early symptoms may include lethargy and weakness. As the patient becomes severely dehydrated, the skin becomes dry and loose, and the eyes become soft and sunken. Abdominal pain may be present and accompanied by anorexia, nausea, and vomiting. Acetone is noted on the breath as a sweet, fruity odor.

Kussmaul respirations (rapid, deep breathing associated with dyspnea) are the body's attempt to reverse metabolic acidosis through the exhalation of excess CO_2. (See Chapter 16 for a discussion of respiratory compensation of metabolic acidosis.) Laboratory findings include a blood glucose level of 250 mg/dL (13.9 mmol/L) or greater, arterial blood pH less than 7.30, and serum bicarbonate level less than 16 mEq/L (16 mmol/L). Moderate to large ketones are present in the urine or serum.

Interprofessional Care

Before we had SMBG, patients with DKA needed hospitalization for treatment. Today, hospitalization may not be needed. If fluid and electrolyte imbalances are not severe and blood glucose levels can be safely monitored at home, DKA can be managed on an outpatient basis (Table 48.17). Other factors to consider when deciding where the patient is managed include the presence of fever, nausea, vomiting, and diarrhea; altered mental status; the cause of the ketoacidosis; and availability of frequent communication with the HCP (every few hours). Patients with DKA who have an illness such as pneumonia or a urinary tract infection (UTI) usually need admitted to the hospital.

TABLE 48.17 Interprofessional Care

Diabetes-Related Ketoacidosis (DKA) and Hyperosmolar Hyperglycemia Syndrome (HHS)

Diagnostic Assessment
- History and physical examination
- Blood studies, including blood glucose, CBC, pH, ketones, electrolytes, BUN, arterial or venous blood gases
- Urinalysis, including specific gravity, glucose, acetone

Management
- Administration of IV fluids
- IV administration of short-acting insulin
- Electrolyte replacement
- Assessment of mental status
- Recording of intake and output
- Central venous pressure monitoring (if indicated)
- Assessment of blood glucose levels
- Assessment of blood and urine for ketones
- ECG monitoring
- Assessment of cardiovascular and respiratory status

DKA is a serious condition that proceeds rapidly and must be treated promptly. Refer to Table 48.18 for the emergency management of a patient with DKA. Because fluid imbalance is potentially life threatening, the first goal of therapy is to establish IV access and begin fluid and electrolyte replacement. Typically, the initial fluid therapy involves an IV infusion of 0.45% or 0.9% NaCl at a rate to raise BP and restore urine output to 30 to 60 mL/hr. When blood glucose levels approach 250 mg/dL (13.9 mmol/L), 5% to 10% dextrose is added to prevent hypoglycemia and a sudden drop in glucose that can be associated with cerebral edema. Overzealous rehydration, especially with hypotonic IV solutions, can cause cerebral edema.

The aim of fluid and electrolyte therapy is to replace extracellular and intracellular water and to correct deficits of sodium, chloride, bicarbonate, potassium, phosphate, and magnesium. Monitor patients with renal or cardiac compromise for fluid overload. Obtain a serum potassium level before starting insulin. If the patient is hypokalemic, giving insulin will further decrease potassium levels, making early potassium replacement essential. Although initial serum potassium may be normal or high, levels can rapidly decrease once therapy starts as insulin drives potassium into the cells, leading to life-threatening hypokalemia.

IV insulin therapy is given to correct hyperglycemia and hyperketonemia. It is important to prevent rapid drops in serum glucose to avoid cerebral edema. A blood glucose reduction of 36 to 54 mg/dL/hr (2 to 3 mmol/L/hr) will avoid complications. Insulin allows water and potassium to enter the cell along with glucose and can lead to a depletion of vascular volume and hypokalemia, so monitor the patient's fluid balance and potassium levels.

CHECK YOUR PRACTICE

A 22-yr-old female patient admitted with DKA has a blood glucose level of 554 mg/dL. You are trying to regulate her IV rate. You know that giving IV fluids too rapidly and quickly lowering of serum glucose can lead to cerebral edema. You also know that incorrect fluid replacement, especially with hypotonic fluids, can cause a sudden fall in serum sodium that can cause cerebral edema.
- What are the best clinical indicators of successful treatment of DKA?
- What is your role as a nurse in caring for this patient?

TABLE 48.18 Emergency Management

Diabetes-Related Ketoacidosis

Etiology	Assessment Findings	Interventions
- Undiagnosed diabetes - Inadequate treatment of existing diabetes - Insulin not taken as prescribed - Illness, infection - Change in eating, insulin, or exercise plan - Malfunction of insulin pump/nondelivery of insulin	- Abdominal pain - Breath odor of ketones (fruity) - Dry mouth - Eyes appearing sunken - Fever - Flushed, dry skin - Glucosuria and ketonuria - Increasing restlessness, confusion, lethargy - Labored breathing (Kussmaul respirations) - Nausea and vomiting - Rapid, weak pulse - Serum glucose >250 mg/dL (13.9 mmol/L) - Thirst - Urinary frequency	**Initial** - Ensure patent airway. - Give O$_2$ via nasal cannula or nonrebreather mask. - Establish IV access with large-bore catheter. - Begin fluid resuscitation with 0.9% NaCl solution 1 L/hr until BP stabilized and urine output 30-60 mL/hr. - Begin continuous regular insulin drip 0.1 U/kg/hr. - Identify history of diabetes, time of last food, and time and amount of last insulin injection. **Ongoing Monitoring** - Monitor vital signs, level of consciousness, ECG, O$_2$ saturation, and urine output. - Assess breath sounds for fluid overload. - Monitor serum glucose and serum potassium. - Give potassium to correct hypokalemia. - Give sodium bicarbonate if severe acidosis (pH <7.0). - Add dextrose to IV fluid for blood glucose <250 mg/dL.

HYPEROSMOLAR HYPERGLYCEMIA SYNDROME

Hyperosmolar hyperglycemia syndrome (HHS) is a life-threatening syndrome that can occur in the patient with diabetes who is able to make enough insulin to prevent DKA, but not enough to prevent severe hyperglycemia, osmotic diuresis, and extracellular fluid depletion (Fig. 48.13). HHS is less common than DKA (Table 48.17). It often occurs in patients over 60 years of age with type 2 diabetes.

Common causes of HHS are UTIs, pneumonia, sepsis, any acute illness, and newly diagnosed type 2 diabetes. HHS is often related to impaired thirst sensation and/or a functional inability to replace fluids. There is usually a history of inadequate fluid intake, increasing mental depression or cognitive impairment, and polyuria.

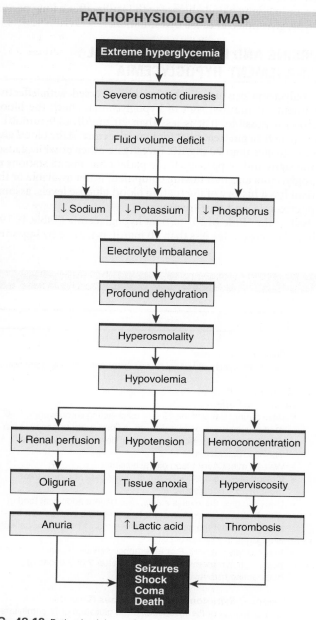

FIG. 48.13 Pathophysiology of hyperosmolar hyperglycemic syndrome. (Modified from Urden LD, Stacy KM, Lough ME: *Critical care nursing: Diagnosis and management*, ed 6, St Louis, 2010, Mosby.)

The main difference between HHS and DKA is that the patient with HHS usually has enough circulating insulin so that ketoacidosis does not occur. Because HHS has fewer symptoms in the earlier stages, blood glucose levels can climb quite high before the problem is recognized. The higher blood glucose levels increase serum osmolality and cause more severe neurologic manifestations, such as somnolence, coma, seizures, hemiparesis, and aphasia. Since these manifestations resemble a stroke, immediate determination of the glucose level is critical for correct diagnosis and treatment.

Laboratory values in HHS include a blood glucose level greater than 600 mg/dL (33.33 mmol/L) and a marked increase in serum osmolality. Ketone bodies are absent or minimal in both blood and urine.

Interprofessional Care

HHS is a medical emergency. It has a high mortality rate. The management of HHS is similar to DKA. It includes immediate IV administration of insulin and either 0.9% or 0.45% NaCl. HHS usually requires large volumes of fluid replacement. This should be done slowly and carefully. Patients with HHS are often older and may have cardiac or renal compromise, requiring hemodynamic monitoring to avoid fluid overload during fluid replacement. When blood glucose levels fall to about 250 mg/dL (13.9 mmol/L), IV fluids containing dextrose are given to prevent hypoglycemia.

Electrolytes are monitored and replaced as needed. Hypokalemia is not as significant in HHS as it is in DKA, although fluid losses may result in milder potassium deficits that require replacement. Assess vital signs, intake and output, laboratory values, and cardiac monitoring to check the efficacy of fluid and electrolyte replacement. This includes monitoring serum osmolality and frequently assessing cardiac, renal, and mental status. Once the patient is stabilized, begin attempts to detect and correct the underlying cause.

❖ NURSING MANAGEMENT: DIABETES-RELATED KETOACIDOSIS AND HYPEROSMOLAR HYPERGLYCEMIA SYNDROME

Closely monitor the hospitalized patient with appropriate blood and urine tests. You are responsible for monitoring blood glucose and urine for output and ketones and using laboratory data to determine appropriate patient care.

Monitor the administration of (1) IV fluids to correct dehydration, (2) insulin therapy to reduce blood glucose and serum ketone levels, and (3) electrolytes given to correct electrolyte imbalance. Assess renal status and cardiopulmonary status related to hydration and electrolyte levels. Monitor the level of consciousness.

Assess for signs of potassium imbalance resulting from low levels of insulin and osmotic diuresis (see Chapter 16). When insulin treatment is started, serum potassium levels may decrease rapidly as potassium moves into the cells once insulin is available. This movement of potassium into and out of extracellular fluid influences cardiac functioning. Cardiac monitoring is useful in detecting characteristic changes of potassium excess or deficit that are observable on ECG tracings (see Fig. 16.14). Assess vital signs often to identify fever, hypovolemic shock, tachycardia, and Kussmaul respirations.

HYPOGLYCEMIA

Hypoglycemia, or low blood glucose, occurs when there is too much insulin in proportion to available glucose in the blood.

This causes the blood glucose level to drop to less than 70 mg/dL (3.9 mmol/L). When glucose drops below 70 mg/dL, counterregulatory hormones are released and the autonomic nervous system is activated. Suppression of insulin secretion and production of glucagon and epinephrine provide a defense against hypoglycemia. Epinephrine release causes manifestations that include shakiness, palpitations, nervousness, diaphoresis, anxiety, hunger, and pallor. Because the brain needs a constant supply of glucose in sufficient quantities to function properly, hypoglycemia can affect mental functioning. These "neuroglycopenia" manifestations are difficulty speaking, visual changes, stupor, confusion, and coma. Manifestations of hypoglycemia can mimic alcohol intoxication. Untreated hypoglycemia can progress to loss of consciousness, seizures, coma, and death.

Hypoglycemia unawareness is a condition in which a person does not have the warning signs and symptoms of hypoglycemia until the glucose level reaches a critical point. Then the person may become incoherent and combative or lose consciousness. This is often a result of diabetes-related autonomic neuropathy that interferes with the secretion of counterregulatory hormones that cause these symptoms. Patients at risk for hypoglycemia unawareness include those who have had repeated episodes of hypoglycemia, older adults, and patients who use β-adrenergic blockers. Using intensive treatment to lower blood glucose levels in patients who have or are at risk for hypoglycemia unawareness may not be an appropriate goal. These patients usually keep blood glucose levels somewhat higher than those who can detect and manage the onset of hypoglycemia.

Causes of hypoglycemia are often related to a mismatch in the timing of food intake and the peak action of insulin or OAs that increase endogenous insulin secretion. The balance between blood glucose and insulin can be disrupted by giving too much insulin or medication, ingesting too little food, delaying the time of eating, and performing unusual or unexpected exercise. Hypoglycemia can occur at any time, but most often occurs when the OA or insulin is at its peak of action or when the patient's daily routine is disrupted without adequate adjustments in diet, drugs, and activity. Although hypoglycemia is most common with insulin therapy, it can occur with noninsulin injectable agents and OAs and may persist for an extended time because of the longer duration of action of these drugs.

Symptoms of hypoglycemia may occur when a very high blood glucose level falls too rapidly (e.g., a blood glucose level of 300 mg/dL [16.7 mmol/L] falling quickly to 150 mg/dL [10 mmol/L]). Although the blood glucose level is above normal by definition and measurement, the sudden metabolic shift can cause hypoglycemia symptoms. Aggressively managing blood glucose levels, lowering high blood glucose levels for the first time, or lowering blood glucose with insulin after a long period of hyperglycemia can cause this situation.

❖ NURSING AND INTERPROFESSIONAL MANAGEMENT: HYPOGLYCEMIA

Hypoglycemia can usually be quickly reversed with effective treatment. At the first sign of hypoglycemia, check the blood glucose, if possible. If it is less than 70 mg/dL (3.9 mmol/L), immediately begin treatment for hypoglycemia. If the blood glucose is greater than 70 mg/dL, investigate other possible causes of the signs and symptoms. If the patient has manifestations of hypoglycemia and monitoring equipment is not available or the patient has a history of fluctuating blood glucose levels, assume hypoglycemia, and start treatment.

Follow the "Rule of 15" to treat hypoglycemia (Table 48.19). A blood glucose value less than 70 mg/dL is treated by ingesting

---

✚ TABLE 48.19 Emergency Management

Hypoglycemia

Etiology	Assessment Findings	Interventions
• Too little food—delayed, omitted, inadequate intake • Too much diabetes medication • Too much exercise without adequate food intake • Diabetes medication or food taken at wrong time • Alcohol use without food intake	• Blood glucose <70 mg/dL (3.9 mmol/L) • Cold, clammy skin • Numbness of fingers, toes, mouth • Tachycardia • Emotional changes • Headache • Nervousness, tremors • Faintness, dizziness • Unsteady gait, slurred speech • Hunger • Changes in vision • Seizures, coma	**Initial** • Check blood glucose. • Determine cause of hypoglycemia (after correction of condition). **Management** ***Conscious Patient*** • Have patient eat or drink 15 g of quick-acting carbohydrate (4–6 oz of regular soda, 5–8 LifeSavers, 1 Tbsp syrup or honey, 4 tsp jelly, 4–6 oz orange juice, commercial dextrose products [per label instructions]). • Wait 15 min. Check blood glucose again. • If blood glucose is still <70 mg/dL, have patient repeat treatment of 15 g of carbohydrate. • Once the glucose level is stable, give patient additional food of carbohydrate plus protein or fat (e.g., crackers with peanut butter or cheese) if the next meal is more than 1 hr away or patient is engaged in physical activity. • Immediately notify HCP or emergency service (if patient outside hospital) if symptoms do not subside after 2 or 3 doses of quick-acting carbohydrate. ***Worsening Symptoms or Unconscious Patient*** • Subcutaneous or IM injection of 1 mg glucagon or IV administration of 20–50 mL of 50% glucose. • Turn the patient on the side to prevent aspiration.

15 g of a simple (fast-acting) carbohydrate, such as 4 to 6 oz of fruit juice or a regular soft drink. Commercial products, such as gels or tablets containing specific amounts of glucose, are convenient for carrying in a purse or pocket to be used in such situations. Recheck the blood glucose 15 minutes later. If the value is still less than 70 mg/dL, ingest 15 g more of carbohydrate and recheck the blood glucose in 15 minutes. If no significant improvement occurs after 2 or 3 doses of 15 g of simple carbohydrate, contact the HCP. After an acute episode of hypoglycemia, the patient may need a snack with carbohydrate and protein if the next meal is more than an hour away or if they are being active.

Avoid treatment with carbohydrates that contain fat, such as candy bars, cookies, whole milk, and ice cream. The fat in those foods will slow the absorption of the glucose and delay the response to treatment. Do not overtreat with large quantities of quick-acting carbohydrates because a rapid fluctuation to hyperglycemia can occur.

In an acute care setting, patients with hypoglycemia may be given 20 to 50 mL of 50% dextrose IV. If the patient is not alert enough to swallow and no IV access is available, another option is to give 1 mg of glucagon by IM or subcutaneous injection. An IM injection in a site such as the deltoid muscle will result in a quicker response. Glucagon stimulates a strong hepatic response to convert glycogen to glucose and makes glucose rapidly available. Nausea is a common reaction after glucagon injection. To prevent aspiration if vomiting occurs, turn the patient on the side until they are alert. Patients with minimal glycogen stores will not respond to glucagon. This includes patients with alcohol-related hepatic disease, starvation, and adrenal insufficiency.

Teach family members and others likely to be present if severe hypoglycemia occurs when and how to inject glucagon.

Once the acute hypoglycemia is reversed, explore with the patient the reasons why the situation developed. This assessment may indicate the need for further patient teaching to avoid future episodes of hypoglycemia.

CHRONIC COMPLICATIONS ASSOCIATED WITH DIABETES

ANGIOPATHY

Chronic complications associated with diabetes are primarily those of end-organ disease from damage to blood vessels (*angiopathy*) from chronic hyperglycemia (Fig. 48.14). Angiopathy is a leading cause of diabetes-related deaths, with about 68% of deaths caused by CVD and 16% caused by strokes for those ages 65 or older.[19] These chronic blood vessel dysfunctions are divided into 2 categories: macrovascular complications and microvascular complications.

Several theories exist as to how and why chronic hyperglycemia damages cells and tissues. Possible causes include (1) the accumulation of damaging by-products of glucose metabolism, such as sorbitol, which is associated with damage to nerve cells; (2) the formation of abnormal glucose molecules in the basement membrane of small blood vessels, such as those that circulate to the eyes and kidneys; and (3) a derangement in RBC function that leads to a decrease in oxygenation to the tissues.

The Diabetes Control and Complications Trial (DCCT), a landmark study in diabetes management, showed the risk for

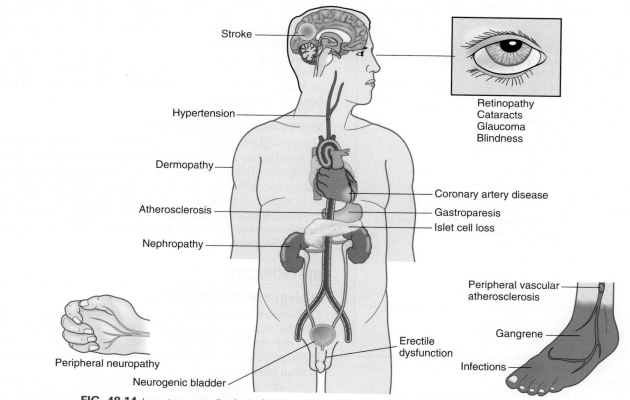

FIG. 48.14 Long-term complications of diabetes. (From Kumar V, Abbas AK, Aster JC, et al: *Robbins and Cotran pathologic basis of disease*, ed 8, Philadelphia, 2010, Saunders.)

microvascular complications could be significantly reduced in patients with type 1 diabetes by keeping blood glucose levels as near to normal as possible for as much of the time as possible *(tight or intensive therapy).*[20] Those who maintained tight glucose levels reduced their risk for developing retinopathy and nephropathy, common microvascular complications. Based on these findings, the ADA issued recommendations for diabetes management that included treatment goals to maintain blood glucose levels as near to normal as possible. Specific targets for individual patients must consider the risk for severe or undetected hypoglycemia as a side effect of intensive management.

The United Kingdom Prospective Diabetes Study (UKPDS) showed that intensive treatment of type 2 diabetes significantly lowered the risk for developing diabetes-related eye, kidney, and neurologic problems. The findings included a 25% reduction of microvascular disease and a 16% reduction in the risk for MI in those who maintained long-term blood glucose levels.[21]

Because of the devastating effects of long-term complications, patients with diabetes need scheduled and ongoing monitoring for the detection and prevention of chronic complications. The ADA recommendations for ongoing evaluation are shown in Table 48.20. It is essential that patients understand the importance of regular follow-up visits.

Macrovascular Complications

Macrovascular complications are diseases of the large and medium-size blood vessels that occur with greater frequency and with an earlier onset in people with diabetes. Macrovascular

TABLE 48.20 Monitoring for Long-Term Complications Related to Diabetes

Complication	Type of Examination	Frequency
Retinopathy	• Funduscopic: dilated eye examination • Fundus photography	• Annually
Nephropathy	• Urine for albuminuria • Serum creatinine	• Annually
Neuropathy (foot and lower extremities)	• Visual examination of foot • Comprehensive foot: • Visual examination • Sensory examination with monofilament and tuning fork • Palpation (pulses, temperature, callus formation)	• Daily by patient • Every visit to HCP • Annually*
Cardiovascular disease	• Risk factor assessment: hypertension, dyslipidemia, smoking, family history of premature coronary artery disease, and presence of albuminuria or	• Every visit • At least annually
	• Exercise stress testing (may include stress ECG, stress echocardiogram, stress nuclear imaging)	• As needed, based on risk factors

Source: American Diabetes Association: Standards of medical care in diabetes, *Diabetes Care* 41:S86, 2018.
*If patients have a history of foot ulcers, loss of sensation in their feet, or other foot abnormalities, the recommendation is to have a foot examination at every visit.

diseases include cerebrovascular, cardiovascular, and peripheral vascular disease. Women with diabetes have a 4 to 6 times increased risk for CVD. Men with diabetes have a 2 to 3 times increased risk for CVD compared with those without diabetes.[2]

Patients with diabetes can decrease several risk factors associated with macrovascular complications, such as obesity, smoking, hypertension, high fat intake, and sedentary lifestyle. The ADA recognizes that diabetes alone is a CVD risk factor. The ADA recommends yearly screening for CVD risk factors in people with diabetes.[22]

Insulin resistance is important in the development of CVD and implicated in the pathogenesis of essential hypertension and dyslipidemia. We do not completely understand the role of insulin resistance in the pathogenesis of CVD. It seems to combine with dyslipidemia in contributing to greater risk for CVD in patients with diabetes.

Optimizing BP control in patients with diabetes is significant in preventing CVD and renal disease. Treating hypertension in those with diabetes results in a decrease in macrovascular and microvascular complications. Hypertension in people with diabetes causes an increase in mortality greater than for those with hypertension without diabetes. The ADA recommends BP screening at every visit for people with diabetes. They recommend lifestyle counseling for BP greater than 130/80 mm Hg and treatment to achieve a target BP of less than 140/90 mm Hg for most patients with diabetes.[22] Hypertension is discussed in Chapter 32, and coronary artery disease is discussed in Chapter 33.)

Patients with diabetes have an increase in lipid abnormalities that contribute to their increased risk for CVD. The ADA recommends screening all adults for dyslipidemia at the time diabetes is diagnosed and starting statin therapy as needed. Dosing is based on the presence of age and other CVD risk factors. The ADA advocates treating hyperlipidemia with lifestyle interventions, including nutrition therapy, exercise, weight loss, and smoking cessation.

Smoking, which is detrimental to health in general, is especially dangerous for people with diabetes. It significantly increases their risk for blood vessel and CVD, stroke, and lower extremity amputation.

Microvascular Complications

Microvascular complications result from thickening of the vessel membranes in the capillaries and arterioles (small vessels) in response to conditions of chronic hyperglycemia. Although microangiopathy can be found throughout the body, the areas most noticeably affected are the eyes (retinopathy), kidneys (nephropathy), and nerves (neuropathy). Microvascular changes are present in some patients with type 2 diabetes at the time of diagnosis.

RETINOPATHY

Etiology and Pathophysiology

Diabetes-related retinopathy refers to the process of microvascular damage to the retina because of chronic hyperglycemia, nephropathy, and hypertension in patients with diabetes. Diabetes-related retinopathy is the leading cause of new cases of adult blindness.[2]

We classify retinopathy as nonproliferative or proliferative. In *nonproliferative retinopathy,* the most common form, partial occlusion of the small blood vessels in the retina causes microaneurysms to develop in the capillary walls. The walls of these microaneurysms are so weak that capillary fluid leaks out, causing retinal edema and eventually hard exudates or intra-retinal hemorrhages. This may cause mild to severe vision loss, depending on which parts of the retina are affected. If the center of the retina (macula) is affected, vision loss can be severe.

Proliferative retinopathy, the most severe form, involves the retina and vitreous. When retinal capillaries become occluded, the body compensates by forming new blood vessels to supply the retina with blood, a pathologic process known as *neovas-cularization.* These new vessels are extremely fragile and hemorrhage easily, producing vitreous contraction. Eventually light is prevented from reaching the retina as the vessels break and bleed into the vitreous cavity. The patient sees black or red spots or lines. If these new blood vessels pull the retina while the vitreous contracts, causing a tear, partial or complete retinal detachment will occur. If the macula is involved, vision is lost. Without treatment, more than half of patients with proliferative diabetic retinopathy will be blind.

Persons with diabetes are prone to other visual problems. Glaucoma occurs because of the occlusion of the outflow channels from neovascularization. This type of glaucoma is hard to treat and often results in blindness. Cataracts develop at an earlier age and progress more rapidly in people with diabetes.

Interprofessional Care

The earliest and most treatable stages of diabetes-related retinopathy often cause no changes in the vision. Therefore teach patients with type 2 diabetes to have a dilated eye examination by an ophthalmologist or a specially trained optometrist at the time of diagnosis and annually thereafter for early detection and treatment. Those with type 1 diabetes need to have a dilated eye examination within 5 years after the onset of diabetes and then annually.

The best approach to managing diabetes-related eye disease is to prevent it by maintaining healthy blood glucose levels and managing hypertension. Laser photocoagulation therapy can reduce the risk for vision loss in patients with proliferative retinopathy or macular edema and, sometimes, nonproliferative retinopathy. Laser photocoagulation destroys the ischemic areas of the retina that make growth factors that encourage neovascularization. A patient who develops vitreous hemorrhage and retinal detachment of the macula may need to undergo vitrectomy. *Vitrectomy* is the aspiration of blood, membrane, and fibers from the inside of the eye through a small incision just behind the cornea. (Photocoagulation and vitrectomy are discussed in Chapter 20.)

A fluocinolone acetonide intravitreal implant (Iluvien) is used to treat retinopathy. It is an injectable microinsert that provides sustained treatment through continuous delivery of corticosteroid fluocinolone acetonide for 36 months. Iluvien is injected in the back of the patient's eye with an applicator that uses a 25-gauge needle, which allows for a self-sealing wound.

Vascular endothelial growth factor (VEGF) plays a key role in the development of diabetes-related retinopathy. We are currently studying drugs injected into the eye that block the action of VEGF and reduce inflammation for their effectiveness in treating retinopathy.[23]

NEPHROPATHY

Diabetes-related nephropathy is a microvascular complication associated with damage to the small blood vessels that supply the glomeruli of the kidney. It is the leading cause of ESRD in the United States and seen in 20% to 40% of people with diabetes. Risk factors include hypertension, genetic predisposition, smoking, and chronic hyperglycemia. Keeping blood glucose levels in a healthy range is critical in the prevention and delay of diabetes-related nephropathy.[21]

Patients are screened for nephropathy annually with a random spot urine collection to assess for albuminuria and measure the albumin-to-creatinine ratio. Serum creatinine is measured to give an estimate of the glomerular filtration rate and the degree of kidney function.

Patients with diabetes who have albuminuria receive either ACE inhibitor drugs (e.g., lisinopril [Prinivil, Zestril]) or angiotensin II receptor blockers (e.g., losartan [Cozaar]). Both classifications of these drugs are used to treat hypertension and delay the progression of nephropathy in patients with diabetes. Hypertension significantly accelerates the progression of nephropathy. Therefore aggressive BP management is indicated for all patients with diabetes. See Chapter 32 for a discussion of hypertension and Chapter 46 for a discussion of renal failure.

NEUROPATHY

Diabetes-related neuropathy is nerve damage that occurs because of the metabolic imbalances associated with diabetes. About 60% to 70% of patients with diabetes have some degree of neuropathy.[2] The most common type affecting persons with diabetes is sensory neuropathy. This can lead to the loss of protective sensation in the lower extremities. Coupled with other factors, it significantly increases the risk for complications that result in a lower limb amputation. More than 60% of nontraumatic amputations in the United States occur in people with diabetes.[2] Screening for neuropathy begins at the time of diagnosis in patients with type 2 diabetes and 5 years after diagnosis in patients with type 1 diabetes.[3]

Etiology and Pathophysiology

We do not completely understand the pathophysiologic processes of diabetes-related neuropathy. Theories include metabolic, vascular, and autoimmune factors. The prevailing theory is that persistent hyperglycemia leads to an accumulation of sorbitol and fructose in the nerves that causes damage. How they cause damage is unknown. The result is reduced nerve conduction and demyelination. Ischemic damage by chronic hyperglycemia in blood vessels that supply the peripheral nerves is implicated in the development of diabetes-related neuropathy. Neuropathy can precede, accompany, or follow the diagnosis of diabetes.

Classification

The 2 major categories of diabetes-related neuropathy are *sensory neuropathy,* which affects the peripheral nervous system, and *autonomic neuropathy.* Each type has several forms.

Sensory Neuropathy. The most common form of sensory neuropathy is distal symmetric polyneuropathy, which affects the hands and/or feet bilaterally. This is sometimes called *stocking-glove neuropathy.* Characteristics include loss of sensation, abnormal sensations, pain, and paresthesias. The pain, which patients describe as burning, cramping, crushing, or tearing, is usually worse at night and may occur only at that time. The paresthesias may be associated with tingling, burning, and itching sensations. The patient may report a feeling of walking on pillows or numb feet. The skin can become so sensitive (hyperesthesia) that the patient cannot tolerate even light pressure from bed sheets. Complete or partial loss of sensitivity to touch and temperature is common. Foot injury and ulcerations can occur without the patient ever having pain (Fig. 48.15). Neuropathy can cause atrophy of the small muscles of the hands and feet, causing deformity and limiting fine movement.

Managing blood glucose is the only treatment for diabetes-related neuropathy. It is effective in many, but not all, cases. Drug therapy may be used to treat neuropathic symptoms, especially pain. At the start of therapy, symptoms usually increase, followed by relief of pain in 2 to 3 weeks.

Drugs commonly used include topical creams (e.g., capsaicin [Zostrix]), tricyclic antidepressants (e.g., amitriptyline), selective serotonin and norepinephrine reuptake inhibitors (e.g., duloxetine [Cymbalta]), and antiseizure drugs (e.g., gabapentin [Neurontin], pregabalin [Lyrica]). Capsaicin is a moderately effective topical cream made from chili peppers. It depletes the accumulation of pain-mediating chemicals in the peripheral sensory neurons. The cream is applied 3 or 4 times a day.

Tricyclic antidepressants are moderately effective in treating diabetes-related neuropathy. They work by inhibiting the reuptake of norepinephrine and serotonin, which are neurotransmitters thought to play a role in the transmission of pain through the spinal cord. We think duloxetine relieves pain by increasing the levels of serotonin and norepinephrine, which improves the body's ability to regulate pain. Antiseizure drugs decrease the release of neurotransmitters that transmit pain.[24]

Autonomic Neuropathy. Autonomic neuropathy can affect nearly all body systems and lead to hypoglycemia unawareness, bowel incontinence and diarrhea, and urinary retention. *Gastroparesis* (delayed gastric emptying) is a complication of autonomic neuropathy that can cause anorexia, nausea, vomiting, gastroesophageal reflux, and persistent feelings of fullness. Gastroparesis can trigger hypoglycemia by delaying food absorption. Cardiovascular abnormalities associated with autonomic neuropathy are postural hypotension, resting tachycardia, and painless MI. Assess patients with diabetes for postural hypotension to determine if they are at risk for falls. Teach the patient with postural hypotension to change from a lying or sitting position slowly.

Diabetes can affect sexual function in men and women. Erectile dysfunction (ED) in men with diabetes is well recognized and common, often being the first manifestation of autonomic neuropathy. ED is associated with other factors, including vascular disease, elevated blood glucose levels, endocrine disorders, psychogenic factors, and medications. Decreased libido is a problem for some women with diabetes. Candida and nonspecific vaginitis are common. ED or sexual dysfunction requires sensitive therapeutic counseling for both the patient and the patient's partner. See Chapter 55 for more about ED.

A neurogenic bladder may develop as the sensation in the inner bladder wall decreases, causing urinary retention. A patient with retention has infrequent voiding, difficulty voiding, and a weak stream of urine. Emptying the bladder every 3 hours in a sitting position helps prevent stasis and infection. Tightening the abdominal muscles during voiding and using the Credé maneuver (mild massage downward over the lower abdomen and bladder) may help with complete bladder emptying. Cholinergic agonist drugs, such as bethanechol (Urecholine), may be used. The patient may need to learn self-catheterization (see Chapter 45).

COMPLICATIONS OF FEET AND LOWER EXTREMITIES

People with diabetes are at high risk for foot ulcerations and lower extremity amputations. The development of diabetes-related foot complications can be the result of a combination of microvascular and macrovascular diseases that place the patient at risk for injury and serious infection (Fig. 48.16). Sensory neuropathy and peripheral artery disease (PAD) are risk factors for foot complications. In addition, clotting abnormalities, impaired immune function, and autonomic neuropathy have a role. Smoking has a negative effect on the health of lower extremity blood vessels and increases the risk for amputation.

Sensory neuropathy is a major risk factor for lower extremity amputation in the person with diabetes. *Loss of protective sensation* (LOPS) often prevents the patient from being aware that a foot injury has occurred. Improper footwear and injury from stepping on foreign objects while barefoot are common causes of undetected foot injury in the person with LOPS. Because the primary risk factor for lower extremity amputation is LOPS, annual screening using a *monofilament* is important.[25] This is done by applying a thin, flexible filament to several spots on the plantar surface of the foot and asking the patient to report if it

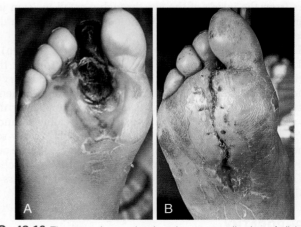

FIG. 48.16 The necrotic toe developed as a complication of diabetes. A, Before amputation. B, After amputation. (From Chew SL, Leslie D: *Clinical endocrinology and diabetes: An illustrated colour text,* Edinburgh, 2006, Churchill Livingstone.)

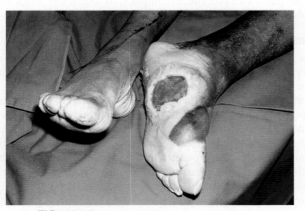

FIG. 48.15 Neuropathy: Neurotrophic ulceration.

is felt. Insensitivity to a monofilament greatly increases the risk for foot ulcers that can lead to amputation.

PAD increases the risk for amputation by causing a reduction in blood flow to the lower extremities. With decreased blood flow, oxygen, white blood cells (WBCs), and vital nutrients are not available to the tissues. Wounds take longer to heal, and the risk for infection increases. Signs of PAD include intermittent claudication, pain at rest, cold feet, loss of hair, delayed capillary filling, and dependent rubor (redness of the skin that occurs when the extremity is in a dependent position). PAD is diagnosed by history, ankle-brachial index (ABI), and angiography. Management includes reduction of risk factors, especially smoking, cholesterol intake, and hypertension. Bypass or graft surgery is indicated in some patients. PAD is discussed in Chapter 37.

If the patient has LOPS or PAD, aggressive measures must be taken to teach the patient how to prevent foot ulcers. These measures include choosing proper footwear, including protective shoes. Teach the patient to carefully avoid injury to the foot, practice diligent skin and nail care, inspect the foot thoroughly each day, and treat small problems promptly. Guidelines for patient teaching are listed in Table 48.21.

Proper care of a foot ulcer is critical for wound healing. Several forms of treatment can be used. Casting can redistribute the weight on the plantar surface of the foot. Wound care for the ulcer can include debridement, dressings, advanced wound healing products (becaplermin [Regranex]), vacuum-assisted closure, ultrasound, hyperbaric O$_2$, and skin grafting.

TABLE 48.21 Patient & Caregiver Teaching*
Foot Care

Include the following instructions when teaching the patient and caregiver about foot care:
1. Wash feet daily with a mild soap and warm water. First test water temperature with elbow.
2. Pat feet dry gently, especially between toes.
3. Examine feet daily for cuts, blisters, swelling, and red, tender areas. Do not depend on feeling sores. If eyesight is poor, have others inspect feet.
4. Use lanolin on feet to prevent skin from drying and cracking. Do not apply between toes.
5. Use mild foot powder on sweaty feet.
6. Do not use commercial remedies to remove calluses or corns.
7. Cleanse cuts with warm water and mild soap, covering with clean dressing. Do not use iodine, rubbing alcohol, or strong adhesives.
8. Report skin infections or nonhealing sores to HCP at once.
9. Cut toenails evenly with rounded contour of toes. Do not cut down corners. The best time to trim nails is after a shower or bath.
10. Separate overlapping toes with cotton or lamb's wool.
11. Avoid open-toe, open-heel, and high-heel shoes. Leather shoes are preferred to plastic ones. Wear slippers with soles. Do not go barefoot. Inspect feet, socks and shoes for foreign objects before putting on.
12. Wear clean, absorbent (cotton or wool) socks or stockings that have not been mended. Colored socks must be colorfast.
13. Do not wear clothing that leaves impressions, hindering circulation.
14. Do not use hot water bottles or heating pads to warm feet. Wear socks for warmth.
15. Guard against frostbite.
16. Exercise feet daily either by walking or by flexing and extending feet in suspended position. Avoid prolonged sitting, standing, and crossing of legs.

*This teaching guide is also appropriate for patients with peripheral vascular problems.

Neuropathic arthropathy, or *Charcot's foot,* results in ankle and foot changes that lead to joint dysfunction and footdrop. These changes occur gradually and promote an abnormal distribution of weight over the foot. This increases the chances of developing a foot ulcer as new pressure points appear. Foot deformity should be recognized early, and proper footwear fitted before ulceration occurs.

SKIN COMPLICATIONS

Up to two thirds of persons with diabetes develop skin problems. Diabetes-related dermopathy, the most common skin lesion, is characterized by reddish brown, round or oval patches. They initially are scaly, then they flatten out and become indented. The lesions appear most often on the shins but can occur on the front of the thighs, forearm, side of the foot, scalp, and trunk.

Acanthosis nigricans is a manifestation of insulin resistance. It can appear as a velvety light brown to black skin thickening, mainly on flexures, axillae, and the neck. *Necrobiosis lipoidica diabeticorum* usually appears as red-yellow lesions, with atrophic skin that becomes shiny and transparent, revealing tiny blood vessels under the surface (Fig. 48.17). This condition is uncommon. It occurs more often in young women. It may appear before other signs and symptoms of diabetes. Because the thin skin is prone to injury, special care must be taken to protect affected areas from injury and ulceration.

INFECTION

A person with diabetes is more susceptible to infections because of a defect in the mobilization of WBCs and an impaired phagocytosis by neutrophils and monocytes. Recurring or persistent infections, such as *Candida albicans*, boils, and furuncles in the undiagnosed patient often lead the HCP to suspect diabetes. Loss of sensation (neuropathy) may delay the detection of an infection.

Persistent glycosuria may predispose patients to bladder infections, especially patients with a neurogenic bladder. Decreased circulation resulting from angiopathy can prevent or delay the immune response. Antibiotic therapy has prevented

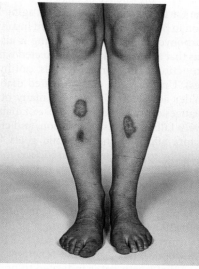
FIG. 48.17 Necrobiosis lipoidica diabeticorum. (From Chew SL, Leslie D: *Clinical endocrinology and diabetes: An illustrated colour text,* Edinburgh, 2006, Churchill Livingstone.)

infection from being a major cause of death in patients with diabetes. The treatment of infections must be prompt and vigorous. Teach patients to prevent infection by practicing good hand hygiene, avoiding exposure to persons who have a communicable illness, and getting an annual influenza vaccine and pneumococcal vaccine. (Guidelines for pneumococcal vaccine are shown in Table 27.5.)

PSYCHOLOGIC CONSIDERATIONS

Patients with diabetes have high rates of depression, anxiety, and eating disorders. Depression contributes to diminished diabetes self-care, feelings of helplessness related to chronic illness, and poor outcomes.[9] Diabetes distress is different from depression and encompasses the stress, fear, and burden of living with and managing a demanding chronic disease. Assess patients for manifestations of depression and/or diabetes distress.

Disordered eating behaviors (DEBs) can occur in people with both type 1 and type 2 diabetes. DEBs include anorexia, bulimia, binge eating, excessive restriction of calories, and intense exercise. The greatest incidence of eating disorders is seen in females. Adolescent girls with diabetes are more than twice as likely to develop DEB than those who do not have diabetes.[26] Patients may intentionally decrease their dose of insulin or omit the dose. This is called "diabulimia." It leads to weight loss, hyperglycemia, and glycosuria because the food ingested cannot be used for energy without adequate insulin. Insulin omission and DEBs can have serious consequences, including retinopathy, neuropathy, lipid abnormalities, DKA, and death.[26]

Open communication is critical to identify these behaviors early. Refer patients with eating disorders to a mental health professional with expertise in eating disorders and an understanding of diabetes management.

Gerontologic Considerations: Diabetes

Diabetes is present in more than 25% of persons over 65 years of age. This age-group is the fastest-growing segment of the population developing diabetes.[2] Older people with diabetes have higher rates of premature death, functional disability, and coexisting illnesses, such as hypertension and stroke, than those without diabetes. The prevalence of diabetes increases with age. A major reason for this is that the process of aging is associated with a reduction in β-cell function, decreased insulin sensitivity, and altered carbohydrate metabolism. Aging is also associated with conditions that are more likely to be treated with drugs that impair insulin action (e.g., corticosteroids, antihypertensives, phenothiazines). Undiagnosed and untreated diabetes is more common in older adults, partly because many of the normal physiologic changes of aging resemble those of diabetes, such as low energy levels, falls, dizziness, confusion, and chronic UTIs.

Several factors affect setting glycemic goals for an older adult. One is that hypoglycemia unawareness is more common in older adults, making them more likely to have adverse consequences from blood glucose–lowering therapy. They may have delayed psychomotor function that could interfere with the ability to treat hypoglycemia. Other factors include the patient's desire for treatment and coexisting medical problems, such as cognitive impairment. Compounding the challenge, diabetes increases the rate of decline of cognitive function. Although it is generally agreed that treatment is indicated to prevent complications, intensive diabetes management may be hard and dangerous to achieve, especially in older adults.

ETHICAL/LEGAL DILEMMAS
Durable Power of Attorney for Health Care

Situation

G.V., a 64-yr-old woman, is admitted to the intensive care unit with HF. She has many complications from a long-term history of type 1 diabetes and hypertension, including a right leg above-the-knee amputation and blindness related to retinopathy. She severed ties with her family 30 years ago. She has a life partner of 35 years whom she chose as her proxy in her signed Durable Power of Attorney. She has said many times that she would rather die than have renal dialysis. She has been sedated and intubated for 3 days. The HCP plans to extubate her and resuscitate her so that she can start dialysis. Her brother shows up at the hospital and supports the HCP's decision. Her partner disagrees with the decision. The HCP refuses to recognize her partner as proxy because she is not a blood relative.

Ethical/Legal Points for Consideration

The Patient Self-Determination Act (1990) requires all health care facilities receiving Medicare and Medicaid funding to make available advance directives allowing persons to state their preferences or refusals of health care in the event that they are incapable of consenting for themselves.

Durable Power of Attorney for health care is one type of advance directive in which people, when they are competent, identify someone else to make decisions for them, should they lose their decision-making ability in the future (see Table 9.6).

The Living Will, another type of advance directive, permits people to state their own preferences and refusals.

Many HCPs mistakenly think that proxies must be family members or blood relatives. Lesbian, gay, bisexual, and transgender (LGBT) persons often have difficulty having their partnership recognized as valid, especially if the patient's family disputes their rights.

Some families are deeply divided on decisions for their loved ones. Sometimes difficulties occur when money and property are also disputed. The passage of time may be an issue where the original documents were executed and then changes occurred (e.g., divorce, death or disability of the proxy, inability to contact the proxy, inability to find a valid original of the advance directive).

Within your scope of nursing practice, you need to know the decision-making laws and regulations in your own state and make advance directive documents available to patients. In addition, you need to (1) teach patients and their families about advance directives, (2) make sure that HCPs are aware of and follow advance directives, (3) assist the patient and family in communicating with the HCPs when a "No Code" order is requested, and (4) assist a conflicted family in obtaining appropriate counseling whenever needed.

Counsel LGBT patients on the importance of having a health care proxy and a will to legally protect their end-of-life choices.

Discussion Questions

1. How would you handle a situation in which the family and surrogate decision maker disagree?
2. How can you assess the patient and family's understanding of durable power of attorney and assist them in understanding their role in decision making?
3. What should you do when an HCP orders dialysis to be started when you know that this goes against the patient's advance directive?

Meal planning and exercise are recommended therapy for older adults with diabetes. Consider functional limitations that may interfere with physical activity and the ability to prepare meals. Because of the physiologic changes that occur with aging, the therapeutic outcome for the older adult who receives OAs may be altered. Assess renal function and creatinine clearance in those over 80 years of age taking metformin. Monitor those taking sulfonylurea drugs (e.g., glipizide) for hypoglycemia and renal and liver dysfunction. Insulin therapy may be started if OAs are not effective. However, older adults are more likely to have limitations in the manual dexterity and visual acuity necessary for accurate insulin administration. Insulin pens may be a safer alternative.

Patient education issues include those related to altered vision, mobility, cognitive status, and functional ability. Plan patient teaching based on individual needs, using a slower pace with simple printed or audio materials in patients with cognitive and functional limitations. Include the family or caregivers in the teaching. Consider the patient's financial and social situation and the effect of multiple drugs, eating habits, and quality-of-life issues.

CASE STUDY

Diabetes-Related Ketoacidosis

(© katrinaelena/ iStock/ Thinkstock.)

Patient Profile

N.B., a 48-yr-old farmer, was admitted to the emergency department after he was found unconscious by his wife in their barn. They live 40 miles from the nearest health care facility. He has a medical history of type 1 diabetes, hypertension, and diabetic neuropathy.

Subjective Data (Provided by Wife)

- Diagnosed with type 1 diabetes 15 years ago
- Takes 40 U/day of insulin via insulin pump: 5 U of lispro insulin bolus with breakfast, 5 U bolus with lunch, and 10 U bolus with dinner plus 20 U of basal insulin
- Has history of gastroenteritis for 1 wk with vomiting and anorexia
- Stopped taking meal time boluses 2 days ago when he was unable to eat
- Has not changed his infusion set in 5 days

Objective Data
Physical Examination

- Respirations deep with rate 36 breaths/min
- Fruity acetone smell on breath
- Skin flushed and dry
- Heart rate 118 beats/min; BP 98/60 mm Hg

Diagnostic Studies

- Blood glucose level 730 mg/dL (40.5 mmol/L)
- Blood pH 7.26

Discussion Questions

1. Briefly explain the pathophysiology behind N.B.'s diabetes-related ketoacidosis (DKA).
2. What factors precipitated his developing DKA?
3. What clinical manifestations of DKA does this patient exhibit?
4. What distinguishes this case history from one of hyperosmolar hyperglycemia syndrome (HHS) or hypoglycemia?
5. ***Priority Decision:*** Based on the assessment data presented, what are the priority nursing diagnoses? Are there any collaborative problems?
6. ***Priority Decision:*** What is the priority nursing intervention for N.B.?
7. ***Priority Decision:*** What is the priority teaching for this patient and his family?
8. ***Evidence-Based Practice:*** N.B.'s wife asks you if she should have given her husband insulin when he got sick. How would you respond?
9. ***Collaboration:*** How can the interprofessional team be most effective in caring for N.B?
10. ***Quality Improvement:*** What outcomes would indicate that the interprofessional team was effective in caring for N.B.?
11. Develop a conceptual care map for N.B.

Answers and a corresponding concept map are available at *http://evolve.elsevier.com/Lewis/medsurg.*

▌ B R I D G E   T O   N C L E X   E X A M I N A T I O N

The number of the question corresponds to the same-numbered outcome at the beginning of the chapter.

1. Polydipsia and polyuria related to diabetes are primarily due to
   a. the release of ketones from cells during fat metabolism.
   b. fluid shifts resulting from the osmotic effect of hyperglycemia.
   c. damage to the kidneys from exposure to high levels of glucose.
   d. changes in RBCs resulting from attachment of excess glucose to hemoglobin.

2. Which statement would be correct for a patient with type 2 diabetes who was admitted to the hospital with pneumonia?
   a. The patient must receive insulin therapy to prevent ketoacidosis.
   b. The patient has islet cell antibodies that have destroyed the pancreas's ability to make insulin.
   c. The patient has minimal or absent endogenous insulin secretion and requires daily insulin injections.
   d. The patient may have enough endogenous insulin to prevent ketosis but is at risk for hyperosmolar hyperglycemia syndrome.

3. Analyze the following diagnostic findings for your patient with type 2 diabetes. Which result will need further assessment?
   a. A1C 9%
   b. BP 126/80 mm Hg
   c. FBG 130 mg/dL (7.2 mmol/L)
   d. LDL cholesterol 100 mg/dL (2.6 mmol/L)

4. Which statement by the patient with type 2 diabetes is accurate?
   a. "I will limit my alcohol intake to 1 drink each day."
   b. "I am not allowed to eat any sweets because of my diabetes."
   c. "I cannot exercise because I take a blood glucose-lowering medication."
   d. "The amount of fat in my diet is not important. Only carbohydrates raise my blood sugar."

5. You are caring for a patient with newly diagnosed type 1 diabetes. What information is *essential* to include in your patient teaching before discharge from the hospital? *(select all that apply)*
   a. Insulin administration
   b. Elimination of sugar from diet
   c. Need to reduce physical activity
   d. Use of a portable blood glucose monitor
   e. Hypoglycemia prevention, symptoms, and treatment

6. What is the *priority* action for the nurse to take if the patient with type 2 diabetes reports blurred vision and irritability?
   a. Call the provider.
   b. Give insulin as ordered.
   c. Assess for other neurologic symptoms.
   d. Check the patient's blood glucose level.

7. A patient with diabetes has a serum glucose level of 824 mg/dL (45.7 mmol/L) and is unresponsive. After assessing the patient, the nurse suspects diabetes-related ketoacidosis rather than hyperosmolar hyperglycemia syndrome based on the finding of
   a. polyuria.
   b. severe dehydration.
   c. rapid, deep respirations.
   d. decreased serum potassium.

8. Which are appropriate therapies for patients with diabetes? *(select all that apply)*
   a. Use of statins to reduce CVD risk
   b. Use of diuretics to treat nephropathy
   c. Use of ACE inhibitors to treat nephropathy
   d. Use of serotonin agonists to decrease appetite
   e. Use of laser photocoagulation to treat retinopathy

1. b, 2. d, 3. a, 4. a, 5. a, 6. d, 7. c, 8. a, c, e

For rationales to these answers and even more NCLEX review questions, visit *http://evolve.elsevier.com/Lewis/medsurg.*

EVOLVE WEBSITE/RESOURCES LIST

http://evolve.elsevier.com/Lewis/medsurg
Review Questions (Online Only)
Key Points
Answer Keys for Questions
- Rationales for Bridge to NCLEX Examination Questions
- Answer Guidelines for Case Study on p. 1141
Student Case Studies
- Patient With Type 1 Diabetes Mellitus and Diabetes-Related Ketoacidosis
- Patient With Type 2 Diabetes Mellitus and Hyperosmolar Hyperglycemia Syndrome
Nursing Care Plans
- eNursing Care Plan 48.1: Patient With Diabetes Mellitus
Conceptual Care Map Creator
- Conceptual Care Map for Case Study on p. 1141
Audio Glossary
Supporting Media
- Animation
- Insulin Function
Content Updates

REFERENCES

1. American Diabetes Association: Statistics about diabetes. Retrieved from *www.diabetes.org/diabetes-basics/statistics.*
2. Centers for Disease Control and Prevention: 2017 National diabetes statistics report. Retrieved from *www.cdc.gov/diabetes/pdfs/data/statistics/national-diabetes-statistics-report.pdf.*
*3. American Diabetes Association: Diagnosis and classification of diabetes mellitus, *Diab Care* 41:S13, 2018.
4. Bouzid T, Hamel FG, Lim JY: Role of adipokines in controlling insulin signaling pathways in type-2 diabetes and obesity, *Int J Diabetes Res* 5:75, 2016.
5. Ben-Shmuel S, Rostoker R, Scheinman EJ, et al: Metabolic syndrome, type 2 diabetes, and cancer: Epidemiology and potential mechanisms, *Handb Exp Pharmacol* 233:355, 2016.
6. Kawada T: Risk factors for developing prediabetes, *J Diabetes Res Clin Metab* 135:232, 2018.
7. Centers for Disease Control and Prevention: Gestational diabetes. Retrieved from *www.cdc.gov/diabetes/basics/gestational.html.*
*8. Chamberlain JJ, Herman WH, Leal S, et al. Pharmacologic therapy for type 2 diabetes: Synopsis of the 2017 ADA standards of medical care in diabetes, *Ann Intern Med* 166:572, 2017.

9. American Association of Diabetes Educators: *The art and science of self-management education desk reference,* ed 4, Chicago, 2017, The Association.
10. BD Diabetes: Syringe and needle sizes. Retrieved from *www.bd.com/en-us/offerings/capabilities/diabetes-care/insulin-syringes.*
11. Joslin Diabetes Center: The advantages and disadvantages of an insulin pump. Retrieved from *www.joslin.org/info/the_advantages_and_disadvantages_of_an_insulin_pump.html.*
*12. American Diabetes Association: Lifestyle management: Standards of medical care in diabetes, *Diabetes Care* 41:S38, 2018.
13. American Diabetes Association: Food and fitness: Create your plate. Retrieved from *www.diabetes.org/food-and-fitness/food.*
*14. US Department of Health and Human Services: Physical Activity Guidelines Advisory Committee report. Retrieved from *www.cdc.gov/nccdphp/sgr/contents.htm.*
*15. American Diabetes Association: Fitness. Retrieved from *www.diabetes.org/food-and-fitness/fitness.*
16. Wood A, O'Neal D, Furler J, et al: Continuous glucose monitoring: A review of the evidence, opportunities for future use and ongoing challenges, *Internal Med J* 48:499, 2018.
17. American Diabetes Association: Prevention or delay of type 2 diabetes, *Diab Care* 40:S44, 2017.
*18. Dickinson JK, Guzman SJ, Maryniuk MD, et al: The use of language in diabetes care and education, *Diab Care* 40:1790, 2017.
19. Boucher J, Hurrell D: Cardiovascular disease and diabetes, *Diab Spect* 21:154, 2008. (Classic)
*20. Diabetes Control and Complications Trial Research Group: The effect of intensive treatment of diabetes on the development and progression of long-term complications in insulin-dependent diabetes mellitus, *N Engl J Med* 329:977, 1993. (Classic)
*21. UK Prospective Diabetes Study (UKPDS) Group: Intensive blood-glucose control with sulphonylureas or insulin compared with conventional treatment and risk of complications in patients with type 2 diabetes, *Lancet* 352:837, 1998. (Classic)
22. American Diabetes Association: Cardiovascular disease and risk management: Standards of medical care in diabetes, *Diab Care* 41:S86, 2018.
23. Bahrami B, Hong T, Gilles MC, et al: Anti-VEGF therapy for diabetic eye diseases, *Asia Pac J Ophthalmol* 6:535, 2017.
*24. Waldfogel JM, Nesbit SA, Dy SM, et al: Pharmacotherapy for diabetic peripheral neuropathy: A systematic review, *Neurology* 88:1958, 2017.
*25. American Diabetes Association: Microvascular complications and foot care: Standards of medical care in diabetes, *Diab Care* 41:S105, 2018.
26. Doyle EA, Quinn SM, Ambrosino JM, et al: Disordered eating behaviors in emerging adults with type 1 diabetes: A common problem for both men and women, *J Pediatr Health Care* 31:327, 2017.

*Evidence-based information for clinical practice.

49

Endocrine Problems

Ann Crawford

The best way to cheer yourself up is to try to cheer somebody else up.

Mark Twain

ⓔ http://evolve.elsevier.com/Lewis/medsurg

CONCEPTUAL FOCUS

Coping

Fluids and Electrolytes

Hormonal Regulation

Nutrition

Perfusion

Reproduction

Thermoregulation

Tissue Integrity

LEARNING OUTCOMES

1. Explain the pathophysiology, clinical manifestations, and interprofessional and nursing management of the patient with an imbalance of hormones made by the anterior pituitary gland.
2. Describe the pathophysiology, clinical manifestations, and interprofessional and nursing management of the patient with an imbalance of hormones made by the posterior pituitary gland.
3. Explain the pathophysiology, clinical manifestations, and interprofessional and nursing management of the patient with thyroid dysfunction.
4. Describe the pathophysiology, clinical manifestations, and interprofessional and nursing management of the patient with parathyroid dysfunction.

5. Identify the pathophysiology, clinical manifestations, and interprofessional and nursing management of the patient with an imbalance of hormones made by the adrenal cortex.
6. Describe the pathophysiology, clinical manifestations, and interprofessional and nursing management of the patient with an excess of hormones made by the adrenal medulla.
7. List the side effects of corticosteroid therapy.

KEY TERMS

acromegaly, p. 1144

Addison's disease, p. 1165

Cushing syndrome, p. 1161

diabetes insipidus (DI), p. 1148

exophthalmos, p. 1150

goiter, p. 1149

Graves' disease, p. 1150

hyperaldosteronism, p. 1167

hyperparathyroidism, p. 1159

hyperthyroidism, p. 1150

hypoparathyroidism, p. 1161

hypopituitarism, p. 1145

hypothyroidism, p. 1156

myxedema, p. 1156

pheochromocytoma, p. 1168

syndrome of inappropriate antidiuretic hormone (SIADH), p. 1147

thyroid cancer, p. 1158

thyroiditis, p. 1149

thyrotoxicosis, p. 1150

The endocrine system is made up of several organs and glands that are involved in the synthesis and secretion of hormones that affect every body system. Because hormones have a wide range of action, problems with their regulation are associated with homeostatic changes that can affect many aspects of a person's life. The severity varies widely. There may be adverse effects on perfusion, metabolism, and nutrition. Regulating fluid and electrolyte balance, skin integrity, and temperature may be difficult. The patient may have problems with growth and fertility and reproductive processes since these are hormone dependent. There may be a wide range of psychologic responses, including anxiety and depression.

DISORDERS OF ANTERIOR PITUITARY GLAND

The pituitary gland is considered the master gland of the endocrine system. The anterior pituitary gland secretes growth hormone (GH), prolactin, and tropic hormones, adrenocorticotropic hormone (ACTH), thyroid-stimulating hormone (TSH), follicle-stimulating hormone (FSH), and luteinizing hormone (LH). These hormones affect growth, sexual maturation, reproduction, metabolism, stress response, and fluid balance. As a result, pituitary gland disorders manifest in a variety of ways.

Tumors of the pituitary gland account for 5% to 20% of primary intracranial tumors.[1] The most common, a pituitary adenoma, is a slow-growing, benign tumor. It often occurs in adults between 40 and 60 years of age. Hypersecretory pituitary adenomas secrete an excess of a specific hormone causing manifestations related to the action of that hormone. The most common are prolactinomas and GH- and ACTH-secreting adenomas.[1]

ACROMEGALY

Acromegaly is a rare condition characterized by an overproduction of GH. Around 4 of every 1 million adults in the United States are diagnosed annually.[2] It affects both genders equally. The mean age at the time of diagnosis is 40 to 45 years old.

Etiology and Pathophysiology

Acromegaly most often occurs because of a benign GH-secreting pituitary adenoma. The excess GH results in an overgrowth of soft tissues and bones in the hands, feet, and face. Because the problem develops after epiphyseal closure, the bones of the arms and legs do not grow longer.

Clinical Manifestations

The changes resulting from excess GH in adults can occur slowly, over many years, and may go unnoticed by the person, family, and friends. Thickening and enlargement of the bony and soft tissues on the face, feet, and head occur (Fig. 49.1). Patients may have proximal muscle weakness and joint pain that can range from mild to crippling. Carpal tunnel syndrome and peripheral neuropathy may be present.

Tongue enlargement results in dental and speech problems. The voice deepens because of hypertrophy of the vocal cords. Sleep apnea may occur because of upper airway narrowing and obstruction from increased amounts of pharyngeal soft tissues. The skin becomes thick, leathery, and oily with acne outbreaks.

Vision changes may occur from pressure on the optic nerve from a pituitary adenoma. Headaches are common. Since GH antagonizes the action of insulin, glucose intolerance and manifestations of diabetes may occur, including *polydipsia* (increased thirst) and *polyuria* (increased urination).

The life expectancy of those with acromegaly is reduced by 5 to 10 years. They are prone to cardiovascular disease (CVD), diabetes, and colorectal cancer.[3] Even if patients are cured or the disease is well controlled, manifestations such as joint pain and deformities often remain.

Diagnostic Studies

In addition to the history and physical examination, a diagnosis requires evaluating plasma insulin-like growth factor-1 (IGF-1) levels and GH response to an oral glucose tolerance test (OGTT). IGF-1 mediates the peripheral actions of GH. As GH levels rise, so do IGF-1 levels. Since GH is released in a pulsatile fashion, several samples are needed to obtain an accurate assessment. Serum IGF-1 levels are more constant, giving a more reliable diagnostic measure of acromegaly. During an OGTT, GH concentration normally falls because glucose inhibits GH secretion. In acromegaly, GH levels do not fall and in some cases GH levels rise.

MRI or high-resolution CT scan with contrast media can detect pituitary adenomas. A complete eye examination, including visual fields, is done because a tumor may cause pressure on the optic chiasm or optic nerves.

❖ Interprofessional and Nursing Care

The patient's prognosis depends on the age at onset, age when treatment started, and tumor size. The overall goal is to return the patient's GH levels to normal. Treatment consists of surgery, radiation therapy, drug therapy, or a combination of these therapies. Treatment can stop bone growth and reverse tissue hypertrophy. However, sleep apnea, diabetes, and cardiac problems may persist.

Surgery (hypophysectomy) is the treatment of choice. It offers the best chance for a cure and optimal symptom management, especially for smaller pituitary tumors.[4] Surgery results in an immediate reduction in GH levels. IGF-1 levels fall within a few weeks. Patients with larger tumors or those with GH levels greater than 45 ng/mL may need adjuvant radiation or drug therapy. Surgery and radiation therapy for pituitary tumors are discussed later in this chapter on p. 1145.

Drug therapy is an option for patients whose surgery did not result in a cure and/or in combination with radiation therapy. The main drug used is octreotide (Sandostatin), a somatostatin analog. It reduces GH levels to normal in many patients. Octreotide is given by subcutaneous injection 3 times a week. Long-acting somatostatin analogs, octreotide (Sandostatin LAR), pasireotide (Signifor), and lanreotide SR (Somatuline Depot), are available as IM injections given every 4 weeks. GH levels are measured every 2 weeks to guide drug dosing and then every 6 months until the desired response is achieved.

Dopamine agonists (e.g., bromocriptine, cabergoline) may be given alone or with somatostatin analogs if complete remission has not been achieved after surgery. These drugs reduce the secretion of GH from the tumor.

GH antagonists (e.g., pegvisomant [Somavert]) reduce the effect of GH in the body by blocking liver production of IGF-1. Most patients taking this drug achieve normal IGF-1 levels with symptom improvement.[3]

Serial photographs showing improvement in appearance may be helpful to the patient's recovery. Psychosocial effects of acromegaly include body image problems, sexual problems, and depression. Fatigue and sleep problems may persist after surgery. Patients will need strategies for dealing with these symptoms. Referral to a support group may be helpful.

EXCESSES OF OTHER TROPIC HORMONES

Excess secretion of prolactin or the tropic hormones (e.g., ACTH, TSH) by the anterior pituitary gland will cause other endocrine glands to overproduce certain hormones. An excess

FIG. 49.1 Progressive development of facial changes associated with acromegaly. (Courtesy Linda Haas, Seattle, WA.)

of these hormones (discussed later in the chapter) can cause significant problems in metabolism and general health.

A prolactin-secreting adenoma is known as a *prolactinoma*. They account for about 40% of pituitary tumors.[5] Women with prolactinomas may have galactorrhea, anovulation, infertility, infrequent or absent menses, decreased libido, and hirsutism. In men, impotence, decreased sperm density, and libido may result. Compression of the optic chiasm can cause vision changes and signs of increased intracranial pressure, including headache, nausea, and vomiting.

Because prolactinomas do not typically progress in size, drug therapy is usually the first-line treatment. The dopamine agonists cabergoline and bromocriptine are given to block the release of prolactin. Surgery may be an option, depending on the extent and size of the tumor. Radiation therapy can reduce the risk for tumor recurrence for patients with large tumors.

HYPOFUNCTION OF PITUITARY GLAND

Hypopituitarism is a rare disorder that involves a decrease in 1 or more of the pituitary hormones. A deficiency of only 1 pituitary hormone is called *selective hypopituitarism*. Total failure of the pituitary gland results in deficiency of all pituitary hormones—a condition referred to as *panhypopituitarism*. The most common hormone deficiencies associated with hypopituitarism involve GH and gonadotropins (e.g., LH, FSH).

Etiology and Pathophysiology

The usual cause of pituitary hypofunction is a pituitary tumor. Autoimmune disorders, infections, pituitary infarction (Sheehan syndrome), or destruction of the pituitary gland (from trauma, radiation, or surgical procedures) can also cause hypopituitarism. Blacks have a higher incidence of pituitary tumors than other ethnic groups.[6]

Anterior pituitary hormone deficiencies can lead to end-organ failure. TSH and ACTH deficiencies are life threatening. ACTH deficiency can lead to acute adrenal insufficiency and hypovolemic shock from sodium and water depletion. Acute adrenal insufficiency is discussed later in this chapter on pp. 1165–1166.

Clinical Manifestations and Diagnostic Studies

The manifestations vary with the type and degree of dysfunction. Early manifestations associated with a space-occupying lesion include headaches, vision changes (decreased visual acuity or decreased peripheral vision), loss of smell, nausea and vomiting, and seizures. Manifestations associated with hyposecretion of the target glands vary widely (Table 49.1).

In addition to a history and physical examination, diagnostic studies such as MRI and CT can identify a pituitary tumor. Laboratory tests generally involve the direct measurement of pituitary hormones (e.g., TSH) or an indirect determination of the target organ hormones (e.g., triiodothyronine [T_3], thyroxine [T_4]). (See Chapter 47 for more information about diagnostic studies.)

❖ Interprofessional and Nursing Care

The treatment for hypopituitarism often consists of surgery or radiation therapy followed by lifelong hormone therapy. Surgery and radiation therapy for pituitary tumors are discussed in the

TABLE 49.1 Manifestations of Hypopituitarism

Hormone Deficiency	Manifestations
Adrenocorticotropic hormone (ACTH)	Involves cortisol deficiency: weakness, fatigue, headache, dry and pale skin, ↓ axillary and pubic hair, ↓ resistance to infection, fasting hypoglycemia
Follicle-stimulating hormone (FSH) and luteinizing hormone (LH)	*Women:* Menstrual irregularities, loss of libido, changes in secondary sex characteristics (e.g., ↓ breast size) *Men:* Testicular atrophy, ↓ spermatogenesis, loss of libido, impotence, ↓ facial hair and muscle mass
Growth hormone (GH)	Subtle, nonspecific findings: truncal obesity, osteoporosis, ↓ muscle mass and strength, weakness, fatigue, depression, or flat affect
Thyroid-stimulating hormone (TSH)	Mild form of primary hypothyroidism: fatigue, cold intolerance, constipation, lethargy, weight gain

next section. Appropriate hormone therapy is used (e.g., GH, corticosteroids, thyroid hormone). Hormone therapies for thyroid hormone and corticosteroids are discussed later in this chapter on p. 1156 and p. 1167.

Somatropin (Genotropin, Humatrope, Omnitrope), recombinant human GH, is used for long-term hormone therapy in adults with GH deficiency. These patients respond well to GH replacement. They have increased energy, increased lean body mass, a feeling of well-being, and improved body image. Mild to moderate side effects of GH include fluid retention with swelling in the feet and hands, myalgia, joint pain, and headache. GH is given daily as a subcutaneous injection (preferably in the evening). The dosing is variable and adjusted based on symptoms, IGF-1 levels, and the presence of adverse effects.

Although gonadal deficiency is not life threatening, hormone therapy will improve sexual function and general well-being. It is contraindicated in those with certain medical conditions, such as phlebitis, pulmonary embolism, breast cancer in women, and prostate cancer in men. Estrogen and progesterone replacement therapy may be given to hypogonadal women to treat hot flashes, vaginal dryness, and decreased libido. (Hormone therapy for women is discussed in Chapter 53.) Testosterone is used to treat men with gonadotropin deficiency. The benefits achieved with testosterone therapy include a return of male secondary sex characteristics; improved libido; and increased muscle mass, bone mass, and bone density. (Hormone therapy for men is discussed in Chapter 54.)

PITUITARY SURGERY

A *hypophysectomy* is the surgical removal of the pituitary gland. It is the treatment of choice for tumors in the pituitary area, especially smaller pituitary adenomas. Most surgeries are done by an endoscopic *transsphenoidal* approach (Fig. 49.2). When the entire pituitary gland is removed, there is permanent loss of all pituitary hormones. The patient will need lifelong replacement therapy of thyroid hormone, sex hormones, and glucocorticoids.

Radiation therapy can reduce the size of a tumor before surgery. It is also used when surgery does not produce a cure or

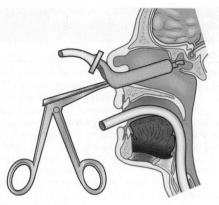

FIG. 49.2 Surgery on the pituitary gland is most often done by a transsphenoidal approach. An incision is made in the inner aspect of the upper lip and gingiva. The sella turcica is entered through the floor of the nose and sphenoid sinuses.

when patients are poor candidates for surgery. Its full effects may not be noted for months to years. Radiation therapy may lead to hypopituitarism, which then requires lifelong hormone replacement therapy. Stereotactic radiosurgery (gamma knife surgery, proton beam, linear accelerator) is an option for small, surgically inaccessible pituitary tumors or in place of conventional radiation.

❖ NURSING MANAGEMENT: PITUITARY SURGERY

After surgery, assess the patient for the formation of a hematoma compressing the optic nerve or optic chiasma. Monitor peripheral vision, visual acuity, extraocular movements, and pupillary response. Report changes at once because prompt intervention may prevent visual deterioration from becoming permanent (Table 49.2).

Cerebrospinal fluid (CSF) leaks and epistaxis are other common complications after surgery.[7] The HCP may place a petroleum jelly–coated ribbon of gauze or a balloon-tipped catheter (like an indwelling urinary catheter) in the sphenoid sinus. It is usually removed after 24 hours. It can be left in for 2 to 3 days if there is concern for bleeding or CSF leak. It is important that the patient does not blow the nose for at least 48 hours after surgery and avoids vigorous coughing, sneezing, and straining at stool.

Monitor the "moustache" dressing regularly for any drainage. Check any clear drainage with a urine dipstick for glucose and protein. If present, notify the HCP of a possible CSF leak. A sample can be sent to the laboratory. A glucose level greater than 30 mg/dL (1.67 mmol/L) indicates CSF leakage from an open connection with the brain. If this happens, the patient is at increased risk for meningitis.

A persistent and severe generalized or supraorbital headache may indicate CSF leakage into the sinuses. A CSF leak usually resolves within 72 hours when treated with head elevation and bed rest. If the leak persists, daily spinal taps may be done to reduce pressure to below-normal levels.

Other measures include elevating the head of the patient's bed at all times to a 30-degree angle. This avoids pressure on the sella turcica and decreases headaches. Monitor the pupillary response, speech patterns, and extremity strength to detect neurologic complications. Gentle mouth care every 4 hours is essential to keep the surgical area clean and free of debris. Have the patient avoid tooth brushing for at least 10 days to protect the suture line.

TABLE 49.2 Nursing Management
Care of the Patient After Pituitary Surgery

- Monitor vital signs. Assess peripheral pulses and watch for orthostatic hypotension.
- Monitor neurologic/cognitive status (e.g., level of consciousness, orientation, speech) hourly for the first 24 hr and then every 4 hr.
- Assess extremity strength and reflexes.
- Monitor field of vision, visual acuity, extraocular movements, and pupillary response. Notify HCP of any changes.
- Assess dressing for type and amount of drainage. Notify HCP for excessive bleeding or CSF drainage.
- Maintain strict intake and output and monitor fluid balance. Assess for DI or SIADH.
- Keep head of bed elevated at least 30 degrees at all times.
- Encourage deep breathing exercises and incentive spirometer use.
- Monitor for pain and give analgesic medications as prescribed.
- Encourage high-fiber diet to decrease potential for constipation.
- Perform oral care every 4 hr.
- Teach the patient to:
  - Avoid vigorous coughing, sneezing, and blowing the nose
  - Avoid bending over at the waist or straining at stool (Valsalva maneuver) due to potential increased intracranial pressure
  - Avoid use of toothbrushes until incision heals
  - Follow replacement hormone therapy plan

Fluid and electrolyte problems can occur from the development of diabetes insipidus (DI).[8] Transient DI may occur because of the loss of antidiuretic hormone (ADH), which is stored in the posterior lobe of the pituitary gland, or cerebral edema related to manipulation of the pituitary during surgery. DI may be permanent after surgery. To assess for DI, closely monitor urine output and measure specific gravity. Report a urine output of more than 200 mL/hr for more than 3 consecutive hours or a specific gravity level of <1.005. Patients with DI will have a high serum sodium and extreme thirst. DI is treated by giving desmopressin acetate (DDAVP). Fluid replacement may be needed to avoid hypovolemia related to high urine output. Syndrome of inappropriate antidiuretic hormone secretion (SIADH) can occur after any intracranial surgery. SIADH typically occurs later than DI, usually around the fourth postoperative day. It may occur due to manipulation of the pituitary and other structures causing release of ADH. The fluid retention caused by circulating ADH leads to dilutional hyponatremia. Sodium levels of less than 125 mEq/L will manifest as headache, vomiting, and decreased level of consciousness. The manifestations and treatment of DI and SIADH are discussed in the next section.

ADH, cortisol, and thyroid hormone replacement are needed after a hypophysectomy. Teach the patient about the need for lifelong therapy. Surgery may result in permanent loss or deficiencies in FSH and LH. This can lead to decreased fertility. Assist the patient in working through the grieving process associated with these losses.

DISORDERS OF POSTERIOR PITUITARY GLAND

The hormones secreted by the posterior pituitary are ADH and oxytocin. ADH, also referred to as *arginine vasopressin* (AVP) or vasopressin, has a key role in the regulation of water balance and serum osmolarity (see Chapter 47). The primary problems associated with ADH secretion are a result of either overproduction or underproduction of ADH.

SYNDROME OF INAPPROPRIATE ANTIDIURETIC HORMONE

Etiology and Pathophysiology

Syndrome of inappropriate antidiuretic hormone (SIADH) results from an overproduction of ADH or the release of ADH despite normal or low plasma osmolarity (Fig. 49.3). ADH increases the permeability of the renal distal tubule and collecting duct, which leads to the reabsorption of water into the circulation. Extracellular fluid volume expands, plasma osmolality declines, glomerular filtration rate increases, and sodium levels decline (dilutional hyponatremia).[8] Thus features of the disorder are fluid retention, serum hypoosmolality, dilutional hyponatremia, hypochloremia, and concentrated urine in the presence of normal or increased intravascular volume.

SIADH occurs more often in older adults. The most common cause is cancer, especially small cell lung cancer (Table 49.3).

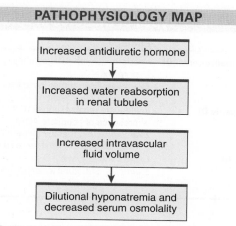

PATHOPHYSIOLOGY MAP

Increased antidiuretic hormone

↓

Increased water reabsorption in renal tubules

↓

Increased intravascular fluid volume

↓

Dilutional hyponatremia and decreased serum osmolality

FIG. 49.3 Pathophysiology of SIADH. (Modified from Urden LD, Stacy KM, Lough ME: *Critical care nursing: Diagnosis and management,* ed 6, St Louis, 2010, Mosby.)

TABLE 49.3 Causes of SIADH

Cancer
- Colorectal cancer
- Lymphoid cancers (Hodgkin's lymphoma, non-Hodgkin's lymphoma, lymphocytic leukemia)
- Pancreatic cancer
- Prostate cancer
- Small cell lung cancer
- Thymus cancer

CNS Disorders
- Brain tumors
- Cerebral atrophy
- Guillain-Barré syndrome
- Head injury (skull fracture, subdural hematoma, subarachnoid hemorrhage)
- Infection (encephalitis, meningitis)
- Stroke
- Systemic lupus erythematosus

Drug Therapy
- carbamazepine (Tegretol)
- Chemotherapy agents (vincristine, vinblastine, cyclophosphamide)
- chlorpropamide
- General anesthesia agents
- Opioids
- oxytocin
- Thiazide diuretics
- Selective serotonin reuptake inhibitor (SSRI) antidepressants
- Tricyclic antidepressants

Miscellaneous Conditions
- Adrenal insufficiency
- Chronic obstructive pulmonary disease
- HIV
- Hypothyroidism
- Lung infection (pneumonia, tuberculosis, lung abscess)
- Positive pressure mechanical ventilation

SIADH tends to be self-limiting when caused by head trauma or drugs. It can be chronic when associated with tumors or metabolic diseases.

Clinical Manifestations and Diagnostic Studies

The patient with SIADH has low urine output and increased body weight. At first, the patient has thirst, dyspnea on exertion, and fatigue. Mild hyponatremia causes muscle cramping, irritability, and headache. As the serum sodium level falls (usually below 120 mEq/L [120 mmol/L]), manifestations become more severe and include vomiting, abdominal cramps, and muscle twitching. As plasma osmolality and serum sodium levels continue to decline, cerebral edema may occur, leading to lethargy, confusion, seizures, and coma.

The diagnosis is made by simultaneous measurements of urine and serum osmolality. Dilutional hyponatremia is indicated by a serum sodium less than 135 mEq/L, serum osmolality less than 280 mOsm/kg (280 mmol/kg), and urine specific gravity greater than 1.030. A serum osmolality much lower than the urine osmolality shows the body is inappropriately excreting concentrated urine in the presence of dilute serum.

❖ Interprofessional and Nursing Care

When assessing patients at risk and those who have confirmed SIADH, be alert for low urine output with a high specific gravity, a sudden weight gain without edema, or a decreased serum sodium level. Monitor intake and output, vital signs, and heart and lung sounds. Obtain daily weights. Observe for signs of hyponatremia, including seizures, headache, vomiting, and decreased neurologic function.

Once SIADH is diagnosed, treatment is directed at the underlying cause. Medications that stimulate ADH release should be avoided or discontinued (Table 49.3). If symptoms are mild and serum sodium is greater than 125 mEq/L (125 mmol/L), the only treatment may be a fluid restriction of 800 to 1000 mL/day. This restriction should result in weight reduction and a gradual rise in serum sodium concentration and osmolality. An improvement in symptoms should accompany normalization of serum sodium and osmolality. Provide the patient with frequent oral care and distractions to decrease discomfort related to thirst from the fluid restriction.

A loop diuretic, such as furosemide (Lasix), may be used to promote diuresis. The serum sodium must be at least 125 mEq/L (125 mmol/L) because it may promote further sodium loss. Because furosemide increases potassium, calcium, and magnesium losses, supplements may be needed. Demeclocycline also may be given. This drug blocks the effect of ADH on the renal tubules, resulting in more dilute urine.

Initiate seizure and fall precautions if the patient has an altered sensorium or is having seizures. Position the head of the bed flat or elevated no more than 10 degrees. This enhances venous return to the heart and increases left atrial filling pressure, thus reducing the release of ADH. Frequent turning, positioning, and range-of-motion exercises are important to maintain skin integrity and joint mobility.

In cases of severe hyponatremia (less than 120 mEq/L), especially in the presence of neurologic manifestations, such as seizures, small amounts of IV hypertonic saline solution (3% sodium chloride) may be slowly given. It is important to correct hyponatremia slowly. The level should not increase by more than 8 to 12 mEq/L in the first 24 hours. Quickly increasing levels can cause osmotic demyelination syndrome with permanent damage to nerve cells in the brain.[8] A fluid restriction of 500 mL/day may be needed for those with severe hyponatremia.

Vasopressor receptor antagonists (drugs that block the activity of ADH) are used to treat euvolemic hyponatremia in hospitalized patients. Two drugs are FDA-approved: conivaptan (Vaprisol) and tolvaptan (Samsca). Conivaptan is given IV; tolvaptan is given orally. Neither should be given to patients with liver disease because they worsen liver function.

Help the patient with chronic SIADH in self-managing the treatment plan. In chronic SIADH, a fluid restriction of 800 to 1000 mL/day is recommended. Ice chips or sugarless chewing gum help decrease thirst. Have the patient obtain a daily weight to monitor changes in fluid balance. Have the patient supplement the diet with sodium and potassium, especially if taking loop diuretics. Teach the patient the symptoms of fluid and electrolyte imbalances, particularly those involving sodium and potassium (see Chapter 16).

DIABETES INSIPIDUS

Etiology and Pathophysiology

Diabetes insipidus (DI) is caused by a deficiency of production or secretion of ADH or a decreased renal response to ADH. The decrease in ADH results in fluid and electrolyte imbalances caused by increased urine output and increased plasma osmolality (Fig. 49.4). Depending on the cause, DI may be transient or a chronic, lifelong condition. There are several types of DI (Table 49.4). Central DI is the most common form.

Clinical Manifestations

Key features of DI are polydipsia and polyuria. The patient excretes large quantities of urine (2 to 20 L/day) with a very low specific gravity (less than 1.005) and urine osmolality of less than 100 mOsm/kg (100 mmol/kg). Serum osmolality is increased (usually greater than 295 mOsm/kg [295 mmol/kg]) because of hypernatremia (serum sodium greater than 145 mg/dL) caused by pure water loss in the kidneys. Most patients compensate for fluid loss by drinking large amounts of water so that serum osmolality stays normal or is moderately increased. The patient may be tired from nocturia and have generalized weakness. Uncorrected hypernatremia can cause brain shrinkage and intracranial bleeding.[8]

The onset of central DI is usually acute and accompanied by excess fluid loss. After intracranial surgery, central DI has a triphasic pattern: (1) an acute phase with an abrupt onset of polyuria, (2) an interphase in which urine volume normalizes, and (3) a third phase in which central DI may become permanent. The third phase occurs 10 to 14 days after surgery. Central DI from head trauma is often self-limiting and improves with treatment of the underlying problem. Although the manifestations of nephrogenic DI are like those of central DI, the onset and amount of fluid loss are less dramatic.

Severe dehydration can result if oral fluid intake cannot keep up with urinary losses. The patient will have hypotension, tachycardia, and hypovolemic shock. Increasing serum osmolality and hypernatremia can cause central nervous system (CNS) manifestations, ranging from irritability and mental dullness to coma.

Diagnostic Studies

Patients with DI excrete dilute urine at a rate greater than 200 mL/hr with a specific gravity of less than 1.005. Central DI is

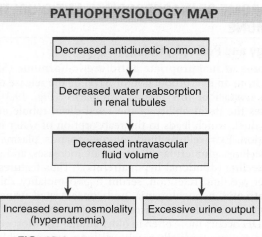

PATHOPHYSIOLOGY MAP

FIG. 49.4 Pathophysiology of diabetes insipidus.

TABLE 49.4 Types of Diabetes Insipidus

Type	Etiology
Central (neurogenic) DI	Interference with ADH synthesis, transport, or release *Examples:* Brain tumor, head injury, brain surgery, CNS infections
Nephrogenic DI	Inadequate renal response to ADH despite presence of adequate ADH *Examples:* Drug therapy (especially lithium), renal damage, hereditary renal disease
Primary DI	Excess water intake *Examples:* Structural lesion in thirst center, psychologic disorder

diagnosed by a water deprivation test. Before the test, body weight, and urine osmolality, volume, and specific gravity are measured. The patient is deprived of water for 8 to 12 hours and then given desmopressin acetate (DDAVP) subcutaneously or nasally. Patients with central DI have a dramatic increase in urine osmolality (from 100 to 600 mOsm/kg) and a significant decrease in urine volume. The patient with nephrogenic DI will not be able to increase urine osmolality to greater than 300 mOsm/kg.

Another test to distinguish central DI from nephrogenic DI is to measure the level of ADH after an analog of ADH (e.g., desmopressin) is given. If the cause is central DI, the kidneys will respond to the hormone by concentrating urine. If the kidneys do not respond in this way, the cause is nephrogenic.

❖ Interprofessional and Nursing Care

Management of the patient with DI includes early detection, maintaining adequate hydration, and patient teaching for long-term management. A therapeutic goal is maintaining fluid and electrolyte balance.

For central DI, fluid and hormone therapy are the cornerstone of treatment. Fluids are replaced orally or IV, depending on the patient's condition and ability to drink copious amounts of fluids. In acute DI, IV hypotonic saline or dextrose 5% in water (D_5W) is given and titrated to replace urine output. If IV glucose solutions are used, monitor serum glucose levels because hyperglycemia and glycosuria can lead to osmotic diuresis, which increases the fluid volume deficit. Monitoring BP, heart rate, urine output, level of consciousness, and specific gravity is essential and may be done hourly in the acutely ill patient. Assess for signs of acute dehydration. Maintain an accurate record of intake and output and daily weights to determine fluid volume status. Adjustments in fluid replacement should be made accordingly.

DDAVP, an analog of ADH, is the hormone replacement of choice for central DI. Another ADH replacement drug is aqueous vasopressin. DDAVP can be given orally, IV, subcutaneously, or as a nasal spray. Assess the response to DDAVP by monitoring pulse, BP, level of consciousness, intake and output, and specific gravity. Chlorpropamide and carbamazepine (Tegretol) can help decrease thirst associated with central DI.

Because the kidney is unable to respond to ADH in nephrogenic DI, hormone therapy has little effect. Instead, the treatment includes a low-sodium diet and thiazide diuretics (e.g., hydrochlorothiazide, chlorothiazide [Diuril]), which may reduce flow to the ADH-sensitive distal nephrons. Limiting sodium intake to no more than 3 g/day often helps decrease urine output. If a low-sodium diet and thiazide drugs are not effective, indomethacin (Indocin) may be prescribed. Indomethacin, a nonsteroidal antiinflammatory drug (NSAID), helps increase renal responsiveness to ADH.

DISORDERS OF THYROID GLAND

Problems with thyroid function are among the most common endocrine disorders. The thyroid hormones, thyroxine (T_4) and triiodothyronine (T_3), regulate energy metabolism and growth and development. Disorders of the thyroid gland include goiter, benign and malignant nodules, inflammatory conditions leading to hyperthyroidism, and hypothyroidism (Fig. 49.5).

GOITER

A **goiter** is an enlarged thyroid gland. In a person with a goiter, the thyroid cells are stimulated to grow. This may result in an overactive thyroid (hyperthyroidism) or an underactive thyroid (hypothyroidism). The most common cause of goiter worldwide is a lack of iodine in the diet.[9] In the United States, where most people use iodized salt, goiter is more often due to the overproduction or underproduction of thyroid hormones or to nodules that develop in the gland itself. *Goitrogens* (foods or drugs that contain thyroid-inhibiting substances) can cause a goiter (Table 49.5).

A nontoxic goiter is a diffuse enlargement of the thyroid gland that does not result from cancer or an inflammatory process. Normal levels of thyroid hormone are associated with this type of goiter. *Nodular goiters* are thyroid hormone–secreting nodules that function independent of TSH stimulation. There may be multiple nodules (multinodular goiter) or a single nodule (solitary autonomous nodule). The nodules are usually benign follicular adenomas. If these nodules are associated with hyperthyroidism, they are called *toxic nodular goiters*. This type of goiter is often found in patients with Graves' disease (Fig. 49.6). Toxic nodular goiters occur equally in men and women. Although they can appear at any age, they most often occur in people over 40 years of age.

TSH and T_4 levels are measured to determine whether a goiter is associated with normal thyroid function, hyperthyroidism, or hypothyroidism. Thyroid antibodies (e.g., thyroid peroxidase [TPO] antibody) show the presence of *thyroiditis* (inflammation of the thyroid). Treatment with thyroid hormone may prevent further thyroid enlargement. Surgery can remove large goiters. Goiter as a manifestation of thyroid disorders is discussed in the next sections.

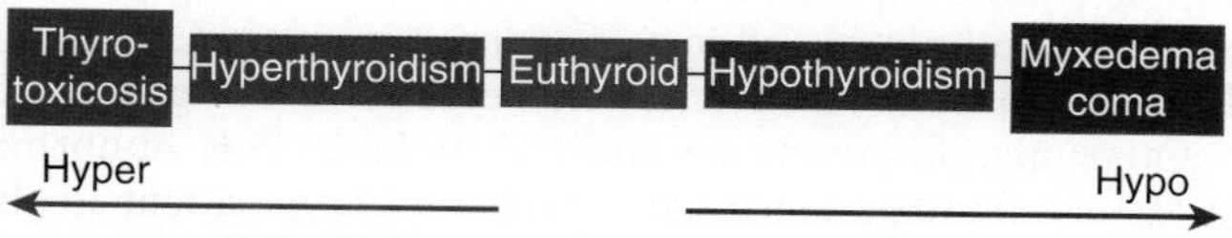

THYROIDITIS

Thyroiditis, an inflammation of the thyroid gland, encompasses several clinical disorders.[10] It is a frequent cause of goiter. *Subacute granulomatous thyroiditis* is thought to be caused by a viral infection. *Acute thyroiditis* is due to bacterial or fungal infection. Subacute and acute forms of thyroiditis have an abrupt onset. The patient reports pain localized in the thyroid or radiating to the throat, ears, or jaw. Systemic manifestations include fever, chills, sweats, and fatigue.

TABLE 49.5 Goitrogens

Thyroid Inhibitors	Select Foods
• iodine in large doses	• Broccoli
• methimazole (Tapazole)	• Brussels sprouts
• propylthiouracil (PTU)	• Cabbage
	• Cauliflower
Other Drugs	• Kale
• amiodarone	• Mustard
• lithium	• Peanuts
• *p*-aminosalicylic acid	• Strawberries
• Salicylates	• Turnips
• Sulfonamides	

FIG. 49.6 Exophthalmos and goiter of Graves' disease. (From Forbes CD, Jackson WF: *Colour atlas and text of clinical medicine,* ed 3, London, 2003, Mosby.)

Thyro-toxicosis	Hyperthyroidism	Euthyroid	Hypothyroidism	Myxedema coma

Hyper ← → Hypo

FIG. 49.5 Continuum of thyroid dysfunction.

Hashimoto's thyroiditis (chronic autoimmune thyroiditis) is caused by the destruction of thyroid tissue by antibodies.[11] It is the most common cause of hypothyroid goiters in the United States. Risk factors include female gender, a positive family history, older age, and white ethnicity. The goiter, which is the hallmark of Hashimoto's thyroiditis, may develop gradually or rapidly. If it enlarges rapidly, it may compress structures in the neck (e.g., trachea, laryngeal nerves), changing the voice and affecting breathing. As thyroid tissue is destroyed by antibodies, there may be a transient phase of hyperthyroidism due to leaking thyroid hormone from the damaged tissues.

Silent, painless thyroiditis, which may be early Hashimoto's thyroiditis, can occur in postpartum women. This condition is usually seen in the first 6 months after delivery. It may be due to an autoimmune reaction to fetal cells in the mother's thyroid gland.

T_4 and T_3 levels are initially increased in subacute, acute, and silent thyroiditis but become decreased with time. Suppressed radioactive iodine uptake (RAIU) is seen in subacute and silent thyroiditis. In Hashimoto's thyroiditis, T_4 and T_3 levels are usually low and the TSH level is high. Antithyroid antibodies are present in Hashimoto's thyroiditis.

Recovery from acute or subacute thyroiditis may be complete in weeks or months without any treatment. If the thyroiditis is bacterial in origin, treatment may include specific antibiotics or surgical drainage. In the subacute and acute forms, NSAIDs (aspirin, naproxen [Aleve]) are used to relieve symptoms. With more severe pain, corticosteroids (e.g., prednisone up to 40 mg/day) can relieve discomfort. Propranolol (Inderal) or atenolol (Tenormin) may relieve cardiovascular symptoms related to a hyperthyroid condition. The patient who is hypothyroid needs thyroid hormone therapy.

Nursing care of the patient with thyroiditis includes patient teaching about the disease process and course of treatment. Teach the patient not to stop medications abruptly. Tell the patient to remain under close health care supervision so that progress can be monitored. Teach the patient to report to the HCP any change in symptoms, such as difficulty breathing or swallowing, swelling to face and extremities, or rapid weight gain or loss. Teach those receiving thyroid hormone about the expected side effects of these drugs and ways to manage them (see p. 1158).

The patient with Hashimoto's thyroiditis is at risk for other autoimmune diseases, such as Addison's disease, pernicious anemia, or Graves' disease. Teach the patient the signs and symptoms of these disorders, particularly Addison's disease.

HYPERTHYROIDISM

Hyperthyroidism is hyperactivity of the thyroid gland with sustained increase in synthesis and release of thyroid hormones. It occurs in women more than men, with the highest frequency in persons 20 to 40 years old. The most common form is Graves' disease. Other causes include toxic nodular goiter, thyroiditis, excess iodine intake, pituitary tumors, and thyroid cancer. Since hyperthyroidism may be caused by iodinated contrast media used in CT scans and other radiologic studies, monitor those who are at risk closely after iodinated contrast media exposure.[11]

The term **thyrotoxicosis** refers to the physiologic effects or clinical syndrome of hypermetabolism resulting from excess circulating levels of T_4, T_3, or both.[12] Hyperthyroidism and thyrotoxicosis usually occur together. Subclinical hyperthyroidism

occurs when the patient has a serum TSH level below 0.4 mU/L but normal T_4 and T_3 levels. Overt hyperthyroidism is defined by low or undetectable TSH and increased T_4 and T_3 levels. The patient may or may not have symptoms of hyperthyroidism.

Etiology and Pathophysiology
Graves' Disease. Graves' disease is an autoimmune disease of unknown cause characterized by diffuse thyroid enlargement and excess thyroid hormone secretion. It accounts for 75% of the cases of hyperthyroidism. Causative factors, such as a lack of iodine, smoking, infection, and stressful life events, may interact with genetic factors to cause Graves' disease.

In Graves' disease, the patient develops antibodies to the TSH receptor. These antibodies attach to the receptors and stimulate the thyroid gland to release T_3, T_4, or both. The excess release of thyroid hormones leads to the manifestations associated with thyrotoxicosis. The disease is characterized by remissions and exacerbations, with or without treatment. It may progress to destruction of the thyroid tissue, causing hypothyroidism. Graves' disease is associated with the presence of other autoimmune disorders, including rheumatoid arthritis, pernicious anemia, systemic lupus erythematosus, Addison's disease, celiac disease, and vitiligo.

Clinical Manifestations
The manifestations are related to the effect of excess circulating thyroid hormone. It directly increases metabolism and tissue sensitivity to sympathetic nervous system stimulation.

Palpation of the thyroid gland may reveal a goiter. When the thyroid gland is excessively large, a goiter may be seen on inspection. Auscultating the thyroid gland may reveal bruits, a reflection of increased blood supply. Another common finding is *ophthalmopathy,* a term used to describe abnormal eye appearance or function. A classic finding in Graves' disease is **exophthalmos**, a protrusion of the eyeballs from the orbits that is usually bilateral (Fig. 49.6). Exophthalmos results from increased fat deposits and fluid (edema) in the orbital tissues and ocular muscles. The increased pressure forces the eyeballs outward. The upper lids are usually retracted and elevated, with the sclera visible above the iris. When the eyelids do not close completely, the exposed corneal surfaces become dry and irritated. Corneal ulcers and loss of vision can occur. Changes in the ocular muscles result in muscle weakness, causing diplopia.

Other manifestations are outlined in Table 49.6. Abnormal laboratory findings are listed in Table 49.7. A patient in the early stages of hyperthyroidism may only have weight loss and

TABLE 49.6 Manifestations of Thyroid Dysfunction

Hyperfunction	Hypofunction
Cardiovascular System	
• Systolic hypertension	• ↑ Capillary fragility
• ↑ Rate and force of cardiac contractions	• ↓ Rate and force of contractions
• Bounding, rapid pulse	• Varied changes in BP
• ↑ Cardiac output	• Cardiac hypertrophy
• Systolic murmurs	• Distant heart sounds
• Dysrhythmias	• Anemia
• Palpitations	• Heart failure
• Angina	• Angina
Gastrointestinal System	
• ↑ Appetite, thirst	• ↓ Appetite
• Weight loss	• Weight gain
• ↑ Peristalsis	• Nausea and vomiting
• Diarrhea, frequent defecation	• Constipation
• ↑ Bowel sounds	• Distended abdomen
• Splenomegaly	• Enlarged, scaly tongue
• Hepatomegaly	• Celiac disease
Musculoskeletal System	
• Fatigue	• Fatigue
• Weakness	• Weakness
• Proximal muscle wasting	• Muscular aches and pains
• Dependent edema	• Slow movements
• Osteoporosis	• Arthralgia
Nervous System	
• Hyperactive deep-tendon reflexes	• Prolonged relaxation of deep tendon reflexes
• Depression	• Anxiety, depression
• Lack of ability to concentrate	• Slowed mental processes
• Rapid speech	• Slow, slurred speech
• Insomnia	• Sleepiness
• Difficulty focusing eyes	• Apathy
• Nervousness	• Lethargy
• Fine tremor of fingers and tongue	• Forgetfulness
• Lability of mood, delirium	• Hoarseness
• Restlessness	• Stupor, coma
• Personality changes of irritability, agitation	• Paresthesias
• Stupor, coma	

Hyperfunction	Hypofunction
Reproductive System	
• Menstrual irregularities	• Prolonged menstrual periods or amenorrhea
• Amenorrhea	
• ↓ Libido	• ↓ Libido
• ↓ Fertility	• Infertility
• Impotence and gynecomastia in men	
Respiratory	
• Dyspnea on mild exertion	• Dyspnea
• ↑ Respiratory rate	• ↓ Breathing capacity
Skin	
• Warm, smooth, moist skin	• Dry, thick, inelastic, cold skin
• Thin, brittle nails detached from nail bed (onycholysis)	• Thick, brittle nails
• Hair loss (may be patchy)	• Dry, sparse, coarse hair
• Clubbing of fingers (thyroid acropachy) (Fig. 49.7)	• Poor turgor of mucosa
• Palmar erythema	• Generalized interstitial edema
• Fine, silky hair	• Puffy face
• Premature graying (in men)	• ↓ Sweating
• Diaphoresis	• Pallor
• Vitiligo	
• Pretibial myxedema (infiltrative dermopathy)	
Other	
• Goiter (Fig. 49.6)	• Goiter
• Intolerance to heat	• Intolerance to cold
• Elevated basal temperature	• ↑ Risk for infection
• Lid lag, stare	• ↑ Sensitivity to opioids, barbiturates, anesthesia
• Eyelid retraction	• ↓ Hearing
• Exophthalmos	

TABLE 49.7 Laboratory Results for Hyperthyroid and Hypothyroid Patients

Test	Hyperthyroid	HYPOTHYROID Primary	HYPOTHYROID Secondary
Thyroid-stimulating hormone (TSH)	↓	↑	↓
T$_4$ (thyroxine)	↑	↓	↓
Total cholesterol	N	↑	↑
Low-density lipoproteins (LDLs)	↓	↑	↑
Triglycerides	N	↑	↑
Creatine kinase (CK)	N	↑	↑
Basal metabolic rate (BMR)	↑	↓	↓
Thyroid peroxidase (TPO) antibody	N	+ (in autoimmune hypothyroidism)	N

N, Normal; +, positive.

increased nervousness. *Acropachy* (clubbing of the digits) may occur with advanced disease (Fig. 49.7). Manifestations (e.g., palpitations, tremors, weight loss) in older adults do not differ significantly from those of younger adults (Table 49.8). In older patients who are confused and agitated, dementia may be suspected and delay the diagnosis.

Complications

Acute thyrotoxicosis (also called *thyrotoxic crisis* or *thyroid storm*) is an acute, severe, and rare condition that occurs when excess amounts of thyroid hormones are released into the circulation. Although considered a life-threatening emergency, death is rare when treatment is started early. Acute thyroiditis is thought to result from stressors (e.g., infection, trauma, surgery) in a patient with preexisting hyperthyroidism. Patients having a thyroidectomy are at risk because manipulation of the hyperactive thyroid gland results in an increase in hormones released.

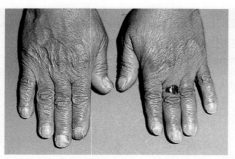

FIG. 49.7 Thyroid acropachy. Digital clubbing and swelling of fingers. (From Chew SL, Leslie D: *Clinical endocrinology and diabetes: An illustrated colour text,* Edinburgh, 2006, Churchill Livingstone.)

TABLE 49.8 Comparison of Hyperthyroidism in Younger and Older Adults

	Younger Adult	Older Adult
Common causes	Graves' disease in >90% of cases	Graves' disease or toxic nodular goiter
Common symptoms	Nervousness, irritability, weight loss, heat intolerance, warm moist skin	Anorexia, weight loss, apathy, lassitude, depression, confusion
Goiter	Present in >90% of cases	Present in about 50% of cases
Ophthalmopathy	Exophthalmos (Fig. 49.6) present in 20%–40% of cases	Exophthalmos less common
Cardiac features	Tachycardia and palpitations common, but without heart failure	Angina, dysrhythmia (especially atrial fibrillation with rapid ventricular response), heart failure may occur

In acute thyrotoxicosis, all the symptoms of hyperthyroidism are prominent and severe. Manifestations include severe tachycardia, heart failure, shock, hyperthermia (up to 106°F [41.1°C]), agitation, delirium, seizures, abdominal pain, vomiting, diarrhea, and coma.

Diagnostic Studies

The primary laboratory findings used to confirm the diagnosis of hyperthyroidism are low or undetectable TSH levels (<0.4 mU/L) and increased free thyroxine (free T_4) levels. Total T_3 and T_4 levels also may be assessed, but they are not as definitive. Total T_3 and T_4 determine both free and bound (to protein) hormone levels. The free hormone is the only biologically active form of these hormones.

The RAIU test can distinguish Graves' disease from other forms of thyroiditis. The patient with Graves' disease shows a diffuse, homogeneous uptake of 35% to 95%, while the patient with thyroiditis shows an uptake of less than 2%. The person with a nodular goiter has an uptake in the high normal range.

Interprofessional Care

The goal of management is to block the adverse effects of excess thyroid hormone, suppress oversecretion of thyroid hormone, and prevent complications. There are several treatment options, including antithyroid medications, radioactive iodine therapy,

TABLE 49.9 Interprofessional Care

Hyperthyroidism

Diagnostic Assessment
- History and physical examination
- Ophthalmologic examination
- ECG
- Laboratory tests
  - TSH levels, serum free T_4
  - Thyroid antibodies (e.g., thyroid peroxidase [TPO] antibody)
  - Total serum T_3 and T_4
- Radioactive iodine uptake (RAIU)

Management
Drug Therapy
- Antithyroid drugs
  - methimazole (Tapazole)
  - propylthiouracil
- iodine (SSKI)

Radiation Therapy
- Radioactive iodine

Surgical Therapy
- Subtotal thyroidectomy

Nutritional Therapy
- High-calorie, high-protein diet
- Frequent meals

and surgical intervention (Table 49.9). Supportive therapy is directed at managing respiratory distress, reducing fever, replacing fluid, and eliminating or managing the initiating stressor(s).

The choice of treatment is influenced by the patient's age and preferences, coexistence of other diseases, and pregnancy status. **Drug Therapy.** Drugs used to treat hyperthyroidism include antithyroid drugs, iodine, and β-adrenergic blockers. These drugs are useful in treating thyrotoxic states but are not curative. Radiation therapy or surgery may be needed.

Antithyroid Drugs. The first-line antithyroid drugs are propylthiouracil and methimazole (Tapazole).[12] These drugs inhibit thyroid hormone synthesis. Reasons for use include Graves' disease in the young patient, hyperthyroidism during pregnancy, and the need to achieve a euthyroid state before surgery or radiation therapy. Propylthiouracil is generally used for patients who are in the first trimester of pregnancy, had an adverse reaction to methimazole, or need a rapid reduction in symptoms. It is the first-line therapy in thyrotoxicosis since it blocks the peripheral conversion of T_4 to T_3. An advantage of propylthiouracil is that it achieves the therapeutic goal of being euthyroid more quickly. However, it must be taken 3 times per day. Methimazole is given in a single daily dose.

Improvement usually begins 1 to 2 weeks after the start of drug therapy. Results are usually seen within 4 to 8 weeks. Therapy is usually continued for 6 to 15 months to allow for spontaneous remission, which occurs in 20% to 40% of patients. Emphasize to the patient the importance of adhering to the drug plan. Abruptly stopping drug therapy can result in a return of hyperthyroidism.

Iodine. Iodine is available as saturated solution of potassium iodide (SSKI) and Lugol's solution. Iodine is used with other antithyroid drugs to prepare the patient for thyroidectomy or for treatment of thyrotoxicosis. Rapidly giving large doses of iodine inhibits synthesis of T_3 and T_4 and blocks the release of these hormones into circulation. It also decreases the vascularity of the thyroid gland, making surgery safer and easier. The maximal effect is usually seen within 1 to 2 weeks. Because of a reduction in the therapeutic effect, long-term iodine therapy is not effective in controlling hyperthyroidism.

Iodine is mixed with water or juice and given after meals. Sipping it through a straw decreases the chance of it staining the teeth. Assess the patient for signs of iodine toxicity, such as swelling of the buccal mucosa and other mucous membranes, excess salivation, nausea and vomiting, and skin reactions. If toxicity occurs, stop administering iodine and notify the HCP.

β-Adrenergic Blockers. β-Adrenergic blockers are used for symptomatic relief of thyrotoxicosis. These drugs block the effects of sympathetic nervous stimulation, thereby decreasing tachycardia, nervousness, irritability, and tremors. Propranolol is usually given with antithyroid agents. Atenolol is the preferred β-adrenergic blocker for use in the hyperthyroid patient with asthma or heart disease.

Radioactive Iodine Therapy. Radioactive iodine (RAI) therapy is the treatment of choice for most nonpregnant adults. RAI damages or destroys thyroid tissue, thus limiting thyroid hormone secretion. RAI has a delayed response. The maximum effect may not be seen for up to 3 months. For this reason, the patient is usually treated with antithyroid drugs and propranolol before and for 3 months after starting RAI until the effects of radiation become apparent. Although RAI is usually effective, 80% of patients have posttreatment hypothyroidism, resulting in the need for lifelong thyroid hormone therapy. Teach the patient the symptoms of hypothyroidism and to seek medical help if these symptoms occur.

RAI therapy is usually given on an outpatient basis. A pregnancy test is done before starting therapy for all women who have menstrual cycles. Tell the patient that radiation thyroiditis and parotitis are possible and may cause dryness and irritation of the mouth and throat. Relief may be obtained with frequent sips of water, ice chips, or a salt and soda gargle 3 or 4 times per day. This gargle is made by dissolving 1 tsp of salt and 1 tsp of baking soda in 2 cups of warm water. The discomfort should subside in 3 to 4 days. A mixture of antacid (Mylanta or Maalox), diphenhydramine, and viscous lidocaine can be used to swish and spit, increasing patient comfort when eating.

To limit radiation exposure to others, teach the patient receiving RAI home precautions, including (1) using private toilet facilities, if possible, and flushing 2 or 3 times after each use; (2) separately laundering towels, bed linens, and clothes daily at home; (3) not preparing food for others that requires prolonged handling with bare hands; and (4) avoiding being close to pregnant women and children for 7 days after therapy.

Surgical Therapy. A thyroidectomy is done for those who have (1) a large goiter causing tracheal compression, (2) a lack of response to antithyroid therapy, or (3) thyroid cancer (Fig. 49.8). Surgery may be done when a person is not a candidate for RAI. One advantage that thyroidectomy has over RAI is a more rapid reduction in T$_3$ and T$_4$ levels. A *subtotal thyroidectomy* is the preferred surgical procedure. It involves removing a significant portion (90%) of the thyroid gland.

Some patients may undergo minimally invasive endoscopic or robotic thyroidectomy. Endoscopic thyroidectomy is appropriate for patients with small nodules (less than 3 cm) and no evidence of cancer. Robotic surgery is best for those who are not overweight and have small nodules on only one side of the gland. Advantages of endoscopic and robotic procedures over open thyroidectomy include less scarring, less pain, and a faster return to normal activity.

Nutritional Therapy. With the increased metabolic rate in hyperthyroid patients, there is a high potential for the patient to have nutrition problems. A high-calorie diet (4000 to 5000 cal/day) may be needed to satisfy hunger, prevent tissue breakdown, and decrease weight loss. This can be achieved with 6 full meals a day and snacks high in protein, carbohydrates, minerals, and vitamins. The protein content should be 1 to 2 g/kg of ideal body weight. Increase carbohydrate intake to compensate for increased metabolism. Carbohydrates provide energy and decrease the use of body-stored protein. Teach the patient to avoid highly seasoned and high-fiber foods because they can further stimulate the already hyperactive GI tract. Have the patient avoid caffeine-containing liquids, such as coffee, tea, and cola, to decrease the restlessness and sleep problems. Refer the patient to a dietitian for help in meeting individual nutritional needs.

❖ NURSING MANAGEMENT: HYPERTHYROIDISM

◆ Nursing Assessment

Subjective and objective data you should obtain from a person with hyperthyroidism are outlined in Table 49.10.

◆ Nursing Diagnoses

Nursing diagnoses for the patient with hyperthyroidism include:
- Activity intolerance
- Impaired nutritional status

Additional information on nursing diagnoses and interventions is presented in eNursing Care Plan 49.1 for the patient with hyperthyroidism (available on the website for this chapter).

◆ Planning

The overall goals are that the patient with hyperthyroidism will (1) have relief of symptoms, (2) have no serious complications related to the disease or treatment, (3) maintain nutritional balance, and (4) cooperate with the therapeutic plan.

◆ Nursing Implementation

◆ Acute Care. Patients with hyperthyroidism are usually treated in an outpatient setting. However, those who develop acute thyrotoxicosis or undergo thyroidectomy need hospitalization and acute care.

Acute Thyrotoxicosis. Acute thyrotoxicosis requires aggressive treatment, often in an intensive care unit (ICU). Give medications (previously discussed) that block thyroid hormone production and the sympathetic nervous system. Provide supportive therapy, including monitoring for dysrhythmias and decompensation, ensuring adequate oxygenation, and giving IV fluids to replace fluid and electrolyte losses. This is especially important in the patient who has fluid losses from vomiting and diarrhea (Table 49.11).

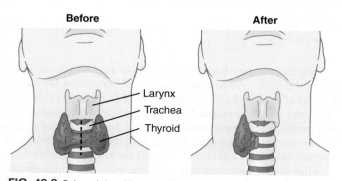

FIG. 49.8 Subtotal thyroidectomy. Part of the thyroid gland is removed.

Before   After

Larynx
Trachea
Thyroid

TABLE 49.10 Nursing Assessment

Hyperthyroidism

Subjective Data

Important Health Information

Past health history: Preexisting goiter. Recent infection or trauma, immigration from iodine-deficient area, autoimmune disease

Medications: Thyroid hormones, herbal therapies that may contain thyroid hormone

Functional Health Patterns

Health perception–health management: Positive family history of thyroid or autoimmune disorders

Nutritional-metabolic: Iodine intake, weight loss, ↑ appetite, thirst, nausea, vomiting

Elimination: Diarrhea, polyuria, sweating

Activity-exercise: Dyspnea on exertion, palpitations, muscle weakness, fatigue

Sleep-rest: Insomnia

Cognitive-perceptual: Chest pain, nervousness, heat intolerance, pruritus

Sexuality-reproductive: ↓ Libido, impotence, gynecomastia (in men), amenorrhea (in women)

Coping–stress tolerance: Emotional lability, irritability, restlessness, personality changes, delirium

Objective Data

General Observation

Agitation, rapid speech and body movements, anxiety, restlessness, hyperthermia, enlarged or nodular thyroid gland

Eyes

Exophthalmos, eyelid retraction, infrequent blinking

Skin

Warm, diaphoretic, velvety skin. Thin, loose nails. Fine, silky hair and hair loss. Palmar erythema, clubbing, white pigmentation of skin (vitiligo), diffuse edema of legs and feet

Respiratory

Tachypnea, dyspnea on exertion

Cardiovascular

Tachycardia, bounding pulse, systolic murmurs, dysrhythmias, hypertension, bruit over the thyroid gland

Gastrointestinal

↑ Bowel sounds. Increased appetite, diarrhea, weight loss, liver and/or spleen enlargement

Neurologic

Hyperreflexia; diplopia. Fine tremors of hands, tongue, eyelids

Musculoskeletal

Muscle wasting

Reproductive

Menstrual irregularities, infertility, impotence, gynecomastia in men

Possible Diagnostic Findings

↑ T_3, ↑ T_4, ↑ T_3 resin uptake, ↓ or undetectable TSH. Chest x-ray showing enlarged heart. ECG findings of tachycardia, atrial fibrillation

---

Ensuring adequate rest may be a challenge because of the patient's irritability and restlessness. Provide a calm, quiet room because increased metabolism and sensitivity of the sympathetic nervous system causes sleep problems. Other interventions may include (1) placing the patient in a cool room away from very ill patients and noisy, high-traffic areas; (2) using light bed coverings and changing the linen often if the patient is diaphoretic; and (3) encouraging and assisting with exercise involving large muscle groups (tremors can interfere with small-muscle coordination) to allow the release of nervous tension and restlessness. It is important to establish a supportive, trusting relationship to promote coping by a patient who is irritable, restless, and anxious.

If exophthalmos is present, there is a potential for corneal injury related to irritation and dryness. The patient may have orbital pain. To relieve eye discomfort and prevent corneal ulceration, apply artificial tears to soothe and moisten conjunctival membranes. Restricting salt may help reduce periorbital edema. Elevate the patient's head to promote fluid drainage from the periorbital area. The patient should sit upright as much as possible.

Dark glasses reduce glare and prevent irritation from smoke, air currents, dust, and dirt. If the eyelids cannot be closed, lightly tape them shut for sleep. To maintain flexibility, teach the patient to exercise the intraocular muscles several times a day by turning the eyes in the complete range of motion. Good grooming can help reduce the loss of self-esteem from an altered body image. If the exophthalmos is severe, treatment options include corticosteroids, radiation of retroorbital tissues, orbital decompression, or corrective lid or muscle surgery.

Thyroid Surgery. When a subtotal thyroidectomy is the treatment of choice, the patient must be adequately prepared to avoid complications. Before surgery, antithyroid drugs, iodine, and β-adrenergic blockers may be given to achieve a euthyroid state. Iodine also decreases the vascularization of the thyroid gland, reducing the risk for hemorrhage.

Before surgery, teach the patient about routine postoperative care and comfort and safety measures. Show the patient how to support the head manually while turning in bed, since this minimizes stress on the suture line after surgery. The patient should practice neck range-of-motion exercises. Tell the patient that talking is likely to be difficult for a short time after surgery. Review the importance of performing leg exercises.

Postoperative Care. Postoperative complications include hypothyroidism, damage to or inadvertent removal of parathyroid glands, causing hypoparathyroidism and hypocalcemia, hemorrhage, injury to the recurrent or superior laryngeal nerve, thyrotoxicosis, and infection.[13] Recurrent laryngeal nerve damage leads to vocal cord paralysis. If both cords are paralyzed, spastic airway obstruction will occur, requiring an immediate tracheostomy.

> **! SAFETY ALERT Airway Obstruction**
> - Although not common, airway obstruction after thyroid surgery is an emergency.
> - Keep O_2, suction equipment, and a tracheostomy tray available in the patient's room.

Respiration may become difficult because of excess swelling of the neck tissues, hemorrhage, and hematoma formation. *Laryngeal stridor* (harsh, vibratory sound) may occur because of edema of the laryngeal nerve. It also may be related to tetany from hypocalcemia, which occurs if the parathyroid glands were removed or damaged during surgery. To treat tetany, IV calcium salts (e.g., calcium gluconate) should be available.

After a thyroidectomy, assess the patient frequently for signs of hemorrhage or tracheal compression (Table 49.12).

✚ TABLE 49.11 Emergency Management

Acute Thyrotoxicosis

Etiology	Assessment Findings	Interventions

• Infection, surgery, trauma in a patient with hyperthyroidism
• Thyroidectomy
	• Abdominal pain
	• Agitation
	• Delirium
	• Diarrhea
	• Heart failure
	• Hyperthermia (up to 106° F [41.1° C])
	• Seizures
	• Severe tachycardia
	• Shock
	• Vomiting
		• Begin fluid replacement with isotonic saline infusions containing dextrose.
		• Monitor airway, breathing, and circulation.
		• Monitor vital signs at least every 30 min.
		• Apply continuous O_2 saturation and ECG monitoring.
		• Monitor serial serum electrolytes, serum glucose, ABGs, and serum calcium levels.
		• Monitor urine output hourly.
		• Apply ice packs and cooling blankets to reduce fever. Acetaminophen as needed.
		• Provide pulmonary hygiene.
		• Assess for manifestations of heart failure or pulmonary edema (e.g., extra heart sounds, adventitious lung sounds).
		• Decrease O_2 demands by decreasing anxiety and pain.
		• Restrict visitors, if needed.
		• Give prescribed drugs and monitor effects:
		  • β-Adrenergic blockers
		  • Antithyroid agents
		  • Iodine compounds
		  • Glucocorticoids

▦ TABLE 49.12 Nursing Management

Care of the Patient After Thyroid Surgery

- Assess vital signs every 15 min until stable and then every 30 min for the first 24 hr after surgery.
- Monitor airway and respiratory status (patency, rate, rhythm, depth, and effort).
- Assess the patient every 2 hr for 24 hr for signs of hemorrhage or tracheal compression (e.g., irregular breathing, neck swelling, frequent swallowing, choking, blood on the dressings, and sensations of fullness at the incision site).
- Assist the patient with coughing and deep breathing.
- Apply supplemental O_2 with humidification as ordered.
- Have suction equipment and a tracheostomy kit available for immediate use.
- Assess the ability to speak aloud, noting voice quality, tone, and any problems speaking. Notify the HCP of any permanent hoarseness or loss of vocal volume.
- Monitor calcium levels and assess for signs of tetany and hypocalcemia (e.g., tingling in toes, fingers, around the mouth; muscular twitching; apprehension) and any difficulty in speaking and hoarseness. Check Trousseau's sign and Chvostek's sign (see Fig. 16.15).
- Keep calcium salts (calcium gluconate, calcium chloride) available for immediate IV use.
- Assess condition of operative site and dressing. Monitor the area under the patient's neck and shoulders for drainage.
- Place the patient in a semi-Fowler's position. Support the head and neck with pillows. Avoid neck flexion to prevent tension on the suture line.
- Provide comfort measures and give analgesic medications as prescribed.

The patient should expect some hoarseness for 3 or 4 days after surgery because of edema. Keep the patient in a semi-Fowler's position and support the patient's head with pillows. Avoid any tension on the suture lines. Monitor vital signs and assess for any signs of hypocalcemia from hypoparathyroidism. If recovery is uneventful, the patient ambulates within hours after surgery. Fluids are allowed as soon as tolerated. A soft diet starts the day after surgery.

The appearance of the incision may be distressing to the patient. Reassure the patient that the scar will fade in color and eventually look like a normal neck wrinkle. A scarf, jewelry, a high collar, or other covering can effectively camouflage the scar.

◆ **Ambulatory Care.** Teach the patient and caregiver that thyroid hormone balance will be monitored periodically. Most patients have a period of relative hypothyroidism soon after surgery because of the substantial reduction in the size of the thyroid. However, the remaining tissue usually hypertrophies over time and recovers the ability to make hormones. Giving thyroid hormone is avoided because the exogenous hormone inhibits pituitary production of TSH and delays or prevents the restoration of normal gland function and tissue regeneration.

To prevent weight gain, caloric intake must be greatly reduced below the amount that was required before surgery. Adequate iodine is needed to promote thyroid function, but excesses can inhibit the thyroid gland. Seafood once or twice a week or normal use of iodized salt should provide enough iodine intake. Encourage regular exercise to stimulate the thyroid gland. Teach the patient to avoid high environmental temperatures because they inhibit thyroid regeneration.

Regular follow-up care is needed. The patient should see the HCP biweekly for a month and then at least semiannually to assess thyroid function. Tell the patient who had a complete thyroidectomy about the need for lifelong thyroid hormone replacement. Teach the patient the signs and symptoms of thyroid failure and to seek medical care promptly if these develop.

◆ Evaluation

The expected outcomes are that the patient with hyperthyroidism will

- Have relief of symptoms
- Have no serious complications related to the disease or treatment
- Cooperate with the therapeutic plan
- Maintain nutritional balance

HYPOTHYROIDISM

Hypothyroidism is a deficiency of thyroid hormone that causes a general slowing of the metabolic rate. About 4% of the U.S. population has mild hypothyroidism, with about 0.3% having more severe disease. Hypothyroidism is more common in women than men. Subclinical hypothyroidism occurs when the TSH is greater than 4.5 mU/L, but the T_4 levels are normal. Up to 10% of women older than 60 years have subclinical hypothyroidism.[14] Patients with overt hypothyroidism have increased TSH and decreased T_4 levels. Critically ill patients may present with nonthyroidal illness syndrome (NTIS).[15] Those with NTIS have low T_3, T_4, and TSH levels.

Etiology and Pathophysiology

We classify hypothyroidism as primary or secondary. *Primary hypothyroidism* is caused by destruction of thyroid tissue or defective hormone synthesis. *Secondary hypothyroidism* is caused by pituitary disease with decreased TSH secretion or hypothalamic dysfunction with decreased thyrotropin-releasing hormone (TRH) secretion. Hypothyroidism can be brief and related to thyroiditis or stopping thyroid hormone therapy.

Iodine deficiency is the most common cause of hypothyroidism worldwide. In the United States, the most common cause of primary hypothyroidism is atrophy of the thyroid gland. This atrophy is the result of Hashimoto's thyroiditis or Graves' disease. These autoimmune diseases destroy the thyroid gland. Hypothyroidism can develop after treatment for hyperthyroidism, specifically thyroidectomy or RAI therapy. Drugs, such as amiodarone, which contains iodine, and lithium, which blocks hormone production, can cause hypothyroidism.

Hypothyroidism that develops in infancy *(cretinism)* results from thyroid hormone deficiencies during fetal or early neonatal life. All infants in the United States are screened for decreased thyroid function at birth.

Clinical Manifestations

The systemic effects of hypothyroidism are characterized by a slowing of body processes (Table 49.6). Manifestations vary depending on the severity and the duration of thyroid deficiency and the patient's age at the onset of the deficiency. Symptoms may develop over months to years, unless hypothyroidism occurs after a thyroidectomy, after thyroid ablation, or during treatment with antithyroid drugs.

The patient is often tired and lethargic. There may be personality and mental changes, including impaired memory, slowed speech, decreased initiative, and somnolence. Many appear depressed. Weight gain is a result of a decreased metabolic rate.

Hypothyroidism may cause significant cardiovascular problems, especially in a person with a history of CVD. It is associated with decreased cardiac contractility and decreased cardiac output. The patient may have low exercise tolerance and shortness of breath on exertion. High serum cholesterol and triglyceride levels and the accumulation of mucopolysaccharides in the intima of small blood vessels can result in coronary atherosclerosis. Anemia is common.

Patients with severe, long-standing hypothyroidism may have **myxedema**. Myxedema results from the accumulation of hydrophilic mucopolysaccharides in the dermis and other tissues (Fig. 49.9). It alters the physical appearance of the skin and subcutaneous tissues with puffiness, facial and periorbital

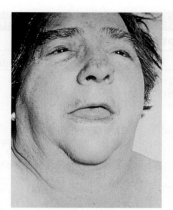

FIG. 49.9 Common features of myxedema. Dull, puffy skin; coarse, sparse hair; periorbital edema; and prominent tongue. (Courtesy Paul W. Ladenson, MD, The Johns Hopkins University and Hospital, Baltimore, MD. From Seidel HM, Ball JW, Dains JE, et al, editors: *Mosby's guide to physical examination*, ed 6, St Louis, 2006, Mosby.)

edema, and a masklike affect. Patients may have an altered self-image related to their disabilities and altered appearance.

In the older adult, we may attribute the typical manifestations of hypothyroidism (fatigue, cold and dry skin, hoarseness, hair loss, constipation, cold intolerance) to normal aging. For this reason, the patient's symptoms may not raise suspicion of an underlying condition. Older adults who have confusion, lethargy, and depression should be evaluated for thyroid disease.

Complications

The mental sluggishness, drowsiness, and lethargy of hypothyroidism may progress gradually or suddenly to a notable impairment of consciousness or coma. This situation, termed *myxedema coma*, is a medical emergency. Myxedema coma can be precipitated by infection, drugs (especially opioids, tranquilizers, and barbiturates), exposure to cold, and trauma. It is characterized by subnormal temperature, hypotension, and hypoventilation. Cardiovascular collapse can result from hypoventilation, hyponatremia, hypoglycemia, and lactic acidosis. For the patient to survive myxedema coma, vital functions must be supported and IV thyroid hormone replacement given.

Diagnostic Studies

The most reliable laboratory tests for thyroid function are TSH and free T_4. These values, correlated with symptoms obtained from the history and physical examination, confirm the diagnosis of hypothyroidism. Serum TSH levels help determine the cause of hypothyroidism. Serum TSH is high when the defect is in the thyroid and low when it is in the pituitary or the hypothalamus. The presence of thyroid antibodies suggests an autoimmune origin. Other abnormal laboratory findings are high cholesterol and triglycerides, anemia, and increased creatine kinase (Table 49.7).

Interprofessional Care

The treatment goal for a patient with hypothyroidism is to restore a euthyroid state as safely and rapidly as possible with hormone therapy (Table 49.13). A low-calorie diet can promote weight loss or prevent weight gain.

Levothyroxine (Synthroid) is the drug of choice to treat hypothyroidism. In the young and otherwise healthy patient, the maintenance replacement dosage is adjusted according to

TABLE 49.13 Interprofessional Care

Hypothyroidism

Diagnostic Assessment	Management
• History and physical examination • Serum TSH and free T_4 • Total serum T_3 and T_4 • Thyroid peroxidase (TPO) antibodies	• Thyroid hormone replacement (e.g., levothyroxine) • Monitor thyroid hormone levels and adjust dosage (if needed) • Nutritional therapy to promote weight loss • Patient and caregiver teaching (Table 49.14)

the patient's response and laboratory findings. When beginning thyroid hormone therapy, the first dosages are low to avoid increases in resting heart rate and BP. In the patient with compromised cardiac status, careful monitoring is needed when starting and adjusting the dosage because the usual dose may increase myocardial O_2 demand. This may cause angina and dysrhythmias.

DRUG ALERT Levothyroxine (Synthroid)
• Carefully monitor patients with CVD who take this drug.
• Monitor heart rate and report pulse greater than 100 beats/min or an irregular heartbeat.
• Promptly report chest pain, weight loss, nervousness, tremors, and/or insomnia.

In a patient without side effects, the dose is increased at 4- to 6-week intervals as needed based on the TSH levels. It may take up to 8 weeks before the full effect of hormone therapy is seen. Levothyroxine has a peak of action of 1 to 3 weeks. It is important that the patient regularly take replacement medication. Lifelong thyroid therapy is usually required.

Liotrix is a synthetic mix of levothyroxine (T_4) and liothyronine (T_3) in a 4:1 combination. Liotrix has a faster onset of action with a peak of 2 to 3 days. It can be used in acutely ill patients with hypothyroidism.

❖ NURSING MANAGEMENT: HYPOTHYROIDISM

◆ Nursing Assessment

Careful assessment may reveal early and subtle changes in a patient suspected of having hypothyroidism. Note any history of hyperthyroidism and treatment with antithyroid medications, RAI, or surgery. Ask the patient about using iodine-containing medications (Table 49.5). Note any changes in appetite, weight, activity level, speech, memory, and skin (e.g., increased dryness or thickening). Assess for cold intolerance, constipation, and signs of depression. Further assessment should focus on heart rate, tenderness over the thyroid gland, and edema in the extremities and face.

◆ Nursing Diagnoses

Nursing diagnoses for the patient with hypothyroidism may include:
• Activity intolerance
• Constipation
• Impaired nutritional status

Additional information on nursing diagnoses and interventions is presented in the eNursing Care Plan 49.2 for the patient with hypothyroidism (available on the website for this chapter).

◆ Planning

The overall goals are that the patient with hypothyroidism will (1) have relief of symptoms, (2) maintain a euthyroid state, (3) maintain a positive self-image, and (4) adhere with lifelong thyroid therapy.

◆ Nursing Implementation

◆ Health Promotion.
Routine screening of thyroid function is not recommended in nonpregnant, asymptomatic adults. Risk factors include being female, white ethnicity, advancing age or having type 1 diabetes, Down syndrome, family history of thyroid disease, goiter, previous hyperthyroidism, and external beam radiation in the head and neck area.[16] High-risk populations should be screened for subclinical thyroid disease.

◆ Acute Care.
Most people with hypothyroidism are treated on an outpatient basis. The person who develops myxedema coma needs acute nursing care, often in the ICU. Mechanical respiratory support and cardiac monitoring are often needed.

Give thyroid hormone therapy and all other medications IV because severe gastric hypomotility may prevent the absorption of oral agents. Monitor the core temperature for hypothermia that often occurs in myxedema and myxedema coma. Use gentle soap and moisturize often to prevent skin breakdown. Frequent position changes and a low-pressure mattress help maintain skin integrity.

Monitor the patient's progress by assessing vital signs, body weight, fluid intake and output, and edema. Cardiac assessment is especially important because the cardiovascular response to hormone therapy determines the medication regimen. Note energy level and mental alertness, which should improve within 2 to 14 days and continue a steady progression to normal levels. Neurologic status and TSH levels are used to determine continuing treatment.

◆ Ambulatory Care.
Patient teaching about medication management and identification of complications is essential (Table 49.14). At first the hypothyroid patient may have a hard time processing complex instructions. It is important to give written instructions, repeat the information often, and assess the patient's comprehension level.

Stress the need for lifelong drug therapy and avoiding abruptly stopping drugs. Caution patients against doubling up on doses for any reason. Some patients notice weight loss and are tempted to increase dosing to achieve a desired weight. Teach the patient the expected and unexpected side effects, including the signs and symptoms of hypothyroidism and hyperthyroidism (Table 49.6). The manifestations of overdose are the same as hyperthyroidism. Tell the patient to contact the HCP at once if symptoms, such as orthopnea, dyspnea, rapid pulse, palpitations, chest pain, nervousness, or insomnia, are present.

The patient with diabetes should test blood glucose levels at least daily because the return to the euthyroid state often increases insulin requirements. Thyroid drugs increase the effects of anticoagulants and decrease the effect of digitalis compounds. Teach the patient the toxic signs and symptoms of these medications and the need to remain under close medical observation until stable. Medication interactions are an important reason for patients to consult the HCP before switching brands of thyroid replacement medication. Switching brands may change bioavailability of the drug and physiologic response.

TABLE 49.14 Patient & Caregiver Teaching
Hypothyroidism

Include the following instructions when teaching the patient and caregiver about management of hypothyroidism:

1. Discuss the importance of thyroid hormone therapy:
   - Need for lifelong therapy
   - Taking thyroid hormone in the morning before food
   - Need for regular follow-up care and monitoring of thyroid hormone levels
2. Caution the patient not to switch brands of the hormone since the bioavailability of thyroid hormones may differ.
3. Emphasize the need for a comfortable, warm environment because of cold intolerance.
4. Teach ways to prevent skin breakdown. Use soap sparingly and apply lotion to skin.
5. Caution the patient, especially if an older adult, to avoid sedatives. If they must be used, suggest that the lowest dose be used. Caregiver should closely monitor mental status, level of consciousness, and respirations.
6. Discuss ways to minimize constipation, including:
   - Gradual increase in activity and exercise
   - Increased fiber in diet
   - Use of stool softeners
   - Regular bowel elimination time
   - Tell patient to avoid using enemas. They cause vagal stimulation, which can be hazardous if heart disease is present.

With treatment, striking transformations occur in both appearance and mental function. Most adults return to a normal state. Cardiovascular conditions and psychosis may persist despite corrections of the hormonal imbalance. Relapses occur if treatment is interrupted.

◆ Evaluation

The expected outcomes are that the patient with hypothyroidism will

- Have relief from symptoms
- Maintain a euthyroid state with normal thyroid hormone and TSH levels
- Avoid complications of therapy
- Adhere to lifelong therapy

THYROID NODULES AND CANCER

A *thyroid nodule* (growth in the thyroid gland) may be benign or malignant (thyroid cancer). More than 95% of all thyroid gland nodules are benign. Prevalence of thyroid nodule development increases with age. Benign nodules are usually not dangerous, but they can cause tracheal compression if they become too large.

Thyroid cancer is the most common type of cancer of the endocrine system. An estimated 62,450 new cases of thyroid cancer are diagnosed annually. The incidence of thyroid cancer has increased significantly in the past 25 years. It is the most rapidly increasing cancer in the United States. Thyroid cancer affects more women, and the incidence is higher in whites and Asian Americans.[17] Adults at risk include those who had head and neck radiation therapy during childhood, were exposed to radioactive fallout, or have a personal or family history of goiter.

Types of Thyroid Cancer

The 4 main types of thyroid cancer are papillary, follicular, medullary, and anaplastic. *Papillary* thyroid cancer is the most common type, accounting for about 70% to 80% of all thyroid cancers. Papillary cancer tends to grow slowly. It initially spreads to lymph nodes in the neck.

Follicular thyroid cancer makes up about 15% of all thyroid cancers. It tends to occur in older patients. Follicular cancer first metastasizes into the cervical lymph nodes and then spreads to the neck, lungs, and bones.

Medullary thyroid cancer, accounts for up to 10% of all thyroid cancers. It is more likely to occur in families and be associated with other endocrine problems. It is diagnosed by genetic testing for a proto-oncogene called *RET*. Medullary thyroid cancer is a type of multiple endocrine neoplasia. It is often poorly differentiated and associated with early metastasis.

Anaplastic thyroid cancer occurs in less than 2% of patients with thyroid cancer. It is the most advanced and aggressive thyroid cancer. The patient is least likely to respond to treatment and has a poor prognosis.

Clinical Manifestations and Diagnostic Studies

The primary manifestation of thyroid cancer is a painless, palpable nodule or nodules in an enlarged thyroid gland. Most nodules are found during routine palpation of the neck. The presence of firm, palpable, cervical masses suggests lymph node metastasis. Some patients may have difficulty swallowing or breathing because of tumor growth invading the trachea or esophagus. Hemoptysis and airway obstruction may occur if the trachea is involved. Patients with thyroid cancer generally are euthyroid.

Nodular enlargement of the thyroid gland or palpation of a mass requires further evaluation. Ultrasound is often the first test used. Follow-up testing may involve CT, MRI, positron emission tomography (PET), and ultrasound-guided fine-needle aspiration (FNA). An FNA is done when a tissue sample for pathologic examination is needed. A thyroid scan may be done. The scan shows whether nodules on the thyroid are "hot" or "cold." "Hot" tumors take up radioactive iodine. They are almost always benign. If the nodule does not take up the radioactive iodine, it appears as "cold" and has a higher risk for being cancer.

Increases in serum calcitonin are associated with medullary thyroid cancer. In papillary and follicular cancers, serum thyroglobulin is high. In families with a history of medullary thyroid cancer, family members are encouraged to have genetic testing and thyroid screening on a regular basis.

❖ Interprofessional and Nursing Care

Surgical removal of the tumor is the main treatment for thyroid cancer. Surgical procedures range from unilateral total lobectomy to near-total thyroidectomy with bilateral lobectomy. Lymph nodes in the neck may be removed to determine if the cancer has spread. RAI may be given to some patients to destroy any remaining cancer cells after surgery. RAI therapy improves survival rates in patients with papillary and follicular thyroid cancer. External beam radiation may be given as palliative treatment for patients with metastatic thyroid cancer.

Many thyroid cancers are TSH dependent. Thyroid hormone therapy in high doses is often prescribed to inhibit pituitary secretion of TSH. Chemotherapy, including doxorubicin, may be used for advanced disease. Vandetanib (Caprelsa), lenvatinib (Lenvima), sorafenib tosylate (Nexavar), and cabozantinib (Cometriq) are targeted therapies used for metastatic thyroid cancer. These drugs inhibit tyrosine kinases, enzymes that are involved in the growth of cancer cells.

Nursing care for the patient with thyroid cancer is similar to that of a patient undergoing thyroidectomy (see p. 1154). Because of the surgical site location and the potential for hypocalcemia, the patient needs frequent postoperative assessment. Assess the patient for airway obstruction, bleeding, and tetany since the parathyroid gland may have been disturbed or removed during surgery.

MULTIPLE ENDOCRINE NEOPLASIA

Multiple endocrine neoplasia (MEN) is an inherited condition characterized by hormone-secreting tumors.[18] It is caused by the mutation of 1 of 2 genes, *MEN1* or *RET,* that normally control cell growth. Tumors may develop in childhood or later in life.

The 2 major types of MEN are type 1 and type 2. Both types are often inherited as autosomal dominant disorders. Persons with type 1 often have parathyroid gland hyperactivity (hyperparathyroidism). Other signs may include hyperactivity of the pituitary gland (prolactinoma) and pancreas (gastrinoma). In most cases, the tumors are initially benign. Some tumors later become malignant. Persons with type 2 neoplasia often have medullary thyroid carcinoma. They may develop pheochromocytoma (tumor of the adrenal glands). Pheochromocytoma is discussed later in this chapter on p. 1168.

Treatment includes conservative management (watchful waiting), drugs to block the effects of excess hormone, and surgical removal of the gland and/or tumor. It is important for patients to have regular screening visits with the HCP so that new tumors may be detected early and existing tumors carefully monitored.

DISORDERS OF PARATHYROID GLANDS

HYPERPARATHYROIDISM

Etiology and Pathophysiology

Hyperparathyroidism is a condition involving an increased secretion of parathyroid hormone (PTH). PTH helps regulate serum calcium and phosphate levels by stimulating bone resorption of calcium, renal tubular reabsorption of calcium, and activation of vitamin D. Thus oversecretion of PTH is associated with increased serum calcium levels.

Hyperparathyroidism is classified as primary, secondary, or tertiary. *Primary hyperparathyroidism* is due to an increased secretion of PTH leading to disorders of calcium, phosphate, and bone metabolism. The most common cause is a benign tumor (adenoma) in the parathyroid gland. Patients who have previously undergone head and neck radiation have an increased risk for developing a parathyroid adenoma. Long-term lithium therapy is also associated with primary hyperparathyroidism. Primary hyperparathyroidism affects 25 of 100,000 persons per year.[19] The peak incidence is in the 40s and 50s. It affects twice as many women as men.[19]

Secondary hyperparathyroidism is a compensatory response to conditions that induce or cause hypocalcemia, the main stimulus of PTH secretion. These include vitamin D deficiencies, malabsorption, chronic kidney disease, and hyperphosphatemia.

Tertiary hyperparathyroidism occurs when there is hyperplasia of the parathyroid glands and a loss of negative feedback (see Chapter 47) from circulating calcium levels. Thus there is

autonomous secretion of PTH even with normal calcium levels. This condition is seen in patients who have had a kidney transplant after a long period of dialysis treatment for chronic kidney disease (see Chapter 46).

Excess levels of PTH usually lead to hypercalcemia and hypophosphatemia. Multiple body systems are affected (Table 49.15). Decreased bone density can occur because of the effect of PTH on osteoclastic (bone resorption) and osteoblastic (bone formation) activity. The kidneys cannot reabsorb the excess calcium. This leads to increased urinary calcium levels (hypercalciuria). This urinary calcium, along with a large amount of urinary phosphate, can lead to stone formation.

Clinical Manifestations and Complications

Manifestations range from an asymptomatic person (diagnosed through testing for unrelated problems) to a patient with overt symptoms.[19] The manifestations are associated with hypercalcemia (Table 49.15). Loss of appetite, constipation, fatigue, emotional disorders, shortened attention span, and muscle weakness, particularly in the proximal muscles of the lower extremities, often occur. Complications include osteoporosis, renal failure, kidney stones, pancreatitis, cardiac changes, and long bone, rib, and vertebral fractures.

Diagnostic Studies

PTH levels are increased in patients with hyperparathyroidism. Serum calcium levels usually exceed 10 mg/dL (2.50 mmol/L). Because of its inverse relation with calcium, the serum phosphorus level is usually less than 3 mg/dL (0.1 mmol/L). Hypercalcemia in asymptomatic cases is often identified through a routine chemistry panel.

Increases in other laboratory tests include urine calcium, serum chloride, uric acid, creatinine, amylase (if pancreatitis is present), and alkaline phosphatase (in the presence of bone disease). Bone density measurements may be used to detect bone loss. Conversely, those with bone loss on a screening dual-energy x-ray absorptiometry (DEXA) scan should be tested for hypercalcemia. MRI, CT, and/or ultrasound can detect an adenoma.

Interprofessional Care

The goal of treatment is to relieve symptoms and prevent complications caused by excess PTH. The choice of therapy depends on the urgency of the situation, degree of hypercalcemia, and underlying cause of the disorder.

Surgical Therapy. The most effective treatment of primary and secondary hyperparathyroidism is surgical intervention. Surgery involves partial or complete removal of the parathyroid glands. The most common procedure involves endoscopy and is done on an outpatient basis. Criteria for surgery include increased serum calcium levels (more than 1 mg/dL above the upper limit of normal), hypercalciuria (greater than 400 mg/day), markedly reduced bone mineral density, overt symptoms (e.g., neuromuscular effects, kidney stones), or age under 50 years. Parathyroidectomy leads to a rapid reduction of high calcium levels.

Patients who have multiple parathyroid glands removed may undergo autotransplantation of normal parathyroid tissue in the forearm or near the sternocleidomastoid muscle. This allows PTH secretion to continue with normalization of calcium levels. If autotransplantation is not possible or if it fails, the patient will need to take calcium supplements for life.

TABLE 49.15 Manifestations of Parathyroid Dysfunction

Hyperfunction	Hypofunction	Hyperfunction	Hypofunction
Cardiovascular System		**Neurologic System**	
• Hypertension	• Hypotension	• Lethargy, weakness, fatigue	• Weakness, fatigue
• Angina	• Edema	• Psychosis, depression	• Depression
• Dysrhythmias	• Dysrhythmias	• Depressed reflexes	• Hyperreflexia, muscle cramps
• Shortened ST segment	• Elongation of ST segment	• Personality changes	• Personality changes
• Shortened QT interval	• Prolonged QT interval	• Irritability	• Irritability
• ↑ Digitalis effect	• ↓ Cardiac output	• Memory impairment	• Memory impairment
		• Delirium, confusion, coma	• Disorientation, confusion (in older adult)
Gastrointestinal System		• Headache	
• Vague abdominal pain	• Abdominal cramps	• Poor coordination	• Headache, ↑ intracranial pressure
• Anorexia	• Fecal incontinence (in older adult)	• Gait abnormalities	• Tetany, seizures
• Nausea and vomiting	• Malabsorption	• Psychomotor retardation	• Positive Chvostek's and Trousseau's sign
• Constipation		• Paresthesias	• Tremor
• Pancreatitis			• Paresthesias of lips, hands, feet
• Peptic ulcer disease			
• Cholelithiasis		**Renal/Urinary System**	
• Weight loss		• Hypercalciuria	• Urinary frequency
		• Kidney stones	• Urinary incontinence
Laboratory Findings		• Urinary tract infections	
• ↑ Calcium	• ↓ Calcium	• Polyuria	
• ↓ Phosphorus	• ↑ Phosphorus		
		Skin	
Musculoskeletal System		• Skin necrosis	• Dry, scaly skin
• Weakness, fatigue	• Weakness, fatigue	• Moist skin	• Hair loss on scalp and body
• Skeletal pain	• Painful muscle cramps		• Brittle nails, transverse ridging
• Backache	• Skeletal x-ray changes, osteosclerosis		• Lack of tooth enamel
• Pain on weight bearing	• Soft tissue calcification		
• Osteoporosis	• Difficulty walking	**Visual System**	
• Pathologic fractures of long bones		• Impaired vision	• Eye changes, including lenticular opacities, cataracts, papilledema
• Compression fractures of spine; kyphosis		• Corneal calcification	
• ↓ muscle tone, muscle atrophy			

Nonsurgical Therapy. A conservative approach is often used in patients who are asymptomatic or have mild symptoms of hyperparathyroidism. Ongoing care includes regular examination with measurements of serum PTH, calcium, phosphorus, alkaline phosphatase, creatinine and blood urea nitrogen (BUN) (to assess renal function), and urinary calcium excretion. Annual x-rays and DEXA scans assess for metabolic bone loss. Continued ambulation and avoiding immobility are important. Dietary measures include high fluid and moderate calcium intake.

Severe hypercalcemia is managed with IV sodium chloride solution and loop diuretics, such as furosemide, to increase the urinary excretion of calcium. Several drugs help to lower calcium levels, but they do not treat the underlying problem. Bisphosphonates (e.g., alendronate [Fosamax]) inhibit osteoclastic bone resorption, normalizing serum calcium levels and improving bone mineral density. IV bisphosphonates (e.g., pamidronate [Aredia]) can rapidly lower serum calcium in patients with dangerously high levels. Phosphates are given if the patient has normal renal function and low serum phosphate levels.

Calcimimetic agents (e.g., cinacalcet [Sensipar]) increase the sensitivity of the calcium receptor on the parathyroid gland, resulting in decreased PTH secretion and calcium blood levels. They are useful in treating secondary hyperparathyroidism in those with chronic kidney disease on dialysis or in patients with parathyroid cancer.

❖ NURSING MANAGEMENT: HYPERPARATHYROIDISM

Nursing care for the patient after a parathyroidectomy is similar to that for a patient after thyroidectomy. The major complications are associated with hemorrhage and fluid and electrolyte problems. *Tetany,* a condition of neuromuscular hyperexcitability associated with sudden decrease in calcium levels, is another concern. It is usually apparent early in the postoperative period but may develop over several days. Mild tetany, characterized by unpleasant tingling of the hands and around the mouth, may be present but should decrease over time. If tetany becomes more severe (e.g., muscular spasms, laryngospasms), IV calcium may be given. IV calcium gluconate should be readily available for patients after parathyroidectomy in case acute tetany occurs.

Monitor intake and output to evaluate the patient's fluid status. Assess calcium, potassium, phosphate, and magnesium levels frequently, as well as Chvostek's and Trousseau's signs (see Fig. 16.15). Encourage mobility to promote bone calcification.

If surgery is not done, treatment to relieve symptoms and prevent complications is started. Help the patient to adapt the meal plan to their lifestyle. A referral to a dietitian may be useful. Because immobility can worsen bone loss, emphasize the importance of an exercise program. Encourage the patient to keep the regular follow-up appointments. Teach the patient the symptoms of hypocalcemia and hypercalcemia and to report them if they occur. Hypocalcemia and hypercalcemia are discussed in Chapter 16.

HYPOPARATHYROIDISM

Hypoparathyroidism is an uncommon condition associated with inadequate circulating PTH. It is characterized by hypocalcemia due to a lack of PTH to maintain serum calcium levels. PTH resistance at the cellular level may also occur (*pseudohypoparathyroidism*). This is caused by a genetic defect resulting in hypocalcemia despite normal or high PTH levels. It is often associated with hypothyroidism and hypogonadism.

The most common cause is iatrogenic. This may include accidental removal of the parathyroid glands or damage to the vascular supply of the glands during neck surgery (e.g., thyroidectomy). Idiopathic hypoparathyroidism resulting from the absence, fatty replacement, or atrophy of the glands is a rare disease. It usually occurs early in life and may be associated with other endocrine disorders. Affected patients may have antiparathyroid antibodies. Severe hypomagnesemia (e.g., malnutrition, chronic alcoholism, renal failure) can suppress PTH secretion. Other causes of parathyroid deficiency include tumors and heavy metal poisoning.

The features of acute hypoparathyroidism are due to hypocalcemia (Table 49.15). Sudden decreases in calcium concentration cause tetany, characterized by tingling of the lips and stiffness in the extremities. Painful tonic spasms of smooth and skeletal muscles can cause dysphagia and laryngospasms, which compromise breathing. Lethargy, anxiety, and personality changes may occur. Abnormal laboratory findings include decreased serum calcium and PTH levels and increased serum phosphate levels.

❖ Interprofessional and Nursing Care

Treatment goals are to treat acute complications, such as tetany, maintain normal serum calcium levels, and prevent long-term complications. Emergency treatment of tetany after surgery requires IV calcium administration.

Give IV calcium slowly. Use ECG monitoring when giving calcium because high serum calcium levels can cause hypotension, serious dysrhythmias, or cardiac arrest. The patient who takes digoxin is particularly vulnerable. It is important to assess IV patency before administration. Calcium chloride can cause venous irritation and inflammation. Extravasation may cause cellulitis, necrosis, and tissue sloughing.

Rebreathing may partially relieve acute neuromuscular symptoms associated with hypocalcemia, including muscle cramps and mild tetany. Have the patient breathe in and out of a paper bag or breathing mask. This reduces CO_2 excretion from the lungs, increases carbonic acid levels in the blood, and lowers the pH. A lower pH (acidic environment) enhances calcium ionization, which causes more total body calcium to be available in the active form.

Teach the patient how to manage long-term drug and nutritional therapy. PTH replacement is not recommended because of the expense and need for parenteral administration. Most patients receive oral calcium supplements, magnesium supplements, and vitamin D.

Vitamin D is used to enhance intestinal calcium absorption. Vitamin D (e.g., 1,25-dihydroxycholecalciferol, calcitriol [Rocaltrol]) increases calcium levels rapidly and is quickly metabolized. Rapid metabolism is desired because vitamin D is a fat-soluble vitamin and toxicity can cause irreversible renal impairment.

A high-calcium meal plan includes foods, such as dark green vegetables, soybeans, and tofu. Tell the patient to avoid foods containing oxalic acid (e.g., spinach, rhubarb) because they inhibit calcium absorption. Teach the patient about the need for follow-up care, including monitoring of calcium levels 3 or 4 times a year.

▌DISORDERS OF ADRENAL CORTEX

Adrenal cortex steroid hormones have 3 main classifications: glucocorticoids, mineralocorticoids, and androgens. Glucocorticoids regulate metabolism, increase blood glucose levels, and are critical in the physiologic stress response. The primary glucocorticoid is cortisol. Mineralocorticoids regulate sodium and potassium balance. The primary mineralocorticoid is aldosterone. Androgens contribute to growth and development in both genders and to sexual development in men. The term *corticosteroid* refers to any of these 3 types of hormones made by the adrenal cortex.

CUSHING SYNDROME

Etiology and Pathophysiology

Cushing syndrome is a clinical condition that results from chronic exposure to excess corticosteroids, particularly glucocorticoids.[20] Several conditions can cause Cushing syndrome. The most common cause is iatrogenic administration of exogenous corticosteroids (e.g., prednisone). About 85% of the cases of endogenous Cushing syndrome are due to an ACTH-secreting pituitary adenoma (Cushing disease). Less common causes include adrenal tumors and ectopic ACTH production by tumors (usually of the lung or pancreas) outside of the hypothalamic-pituitary-adrenal axis. Cushing disease and primary adrenal tumors are more common in women in the 20- to 40-year-old age-group. Ectopic ACTH production is more common in men.

Clinical Manifestations

Manifestations occur in most body systems and are related to excess levels of corticosteroids (Table 49.16). Although signs of glucocorticoid excess usually predominate, symptoms of mineralocorticoid and androgen excess can occur.

Corticosteroid excess causes pronounced changes in physical appearance (Fig. 49.10). Weight gain is the most common feature. It results from the accumulation of adipose tissue in the trunk (centripetal obesity), face ("moon face"), and cervical areas ("buffalo hump") (Fig. 49.11). Hyperglycemia occurs because of glucose intolerance associated with cortisol-induced insulin resistance and increased gluconeogenesis by the liver. Muscle wasting causes weakness, especially in the extremities. A loss of bone matrix leads to osteoporosis and back pain. The

---

? CHECK YOUR PRACTICE

You are caring for a 56-yr-old man admitted 18 hours ago to your clinical unit. He had a total thyroidectomy for papillary thyroid cancer. As you are preparing to give oral pain medication, he tells you he hopes he "doesn't have any trouble" taking it because his lips feel "a little numb."

• What complication do you suspect could be occurring?
• What assessments do you need to make?
• Describe the actions needed if this complication is occurring.

TABLE 49.16 Manifestations of Adrenocortical Dysfunction

System	Cushing Syndrome	Addison's Disease
Glucocorticoids		
General appearance	Truncal obesity, thin extremities, rounding of face (moon face), fat deposits on back of neck and shoulders (buffalo hump) (Fig. 49.11)	Weight loss, emaciation
Cardiovascular	Hypervolemia, hypertension, edema of lower extremities	Hypotension, tendency to develop refractory shock, vasodilation
Gastrointestinal	↑ Secretion of pepsin and HCl acid, risk for peptic ulcer disease, anorexia	Anorexia, nausea and vomiting, cramping abdominal pain, diarrhea
Immune	Inhibition of immune response, suppression of allergic response	Tendency for coexisting autoimmune diseases
Metabolic	Hyperglycemia, negative nitrogen balance, dyslipidemia	Hyponatremia, insulin sensitivity, fever
Musculoskeletal	Muscle wasting in extremities, fatigue, osteoporosis, awkward gait, back pain, weakness, compression fractures	Fatigue
Psychologic	Euphoria, irritability, depression, insomnia, anxiety	Depression, exhaustion or irritability, confusion, delusions
Renal/urinary	Glycosuria, hypercalciuria, risk for kidney stones	
Skin	Thin, fragile skin, purplish red striae (Fig. 49.12). Petechial hemorrhages, bruises. Florid cheeks (plethora), acne, poor wound healing	Bronzed or smoky hyperpigmentation of face, neck, hands (especially creases) (Fig. 49.13), buccal membranes, nipples, genitalia, and scars (if pituitary function normal). Vitiligo, alopecia
Mineralocorticoids		
Cardiovascular	Hypertension, hypervolemia	Hypovolemia, tendency toward shock, decreased cardiac output
Fluid and electrolytes	Marked sodium and water retention, edema, marked hypokalemia, alkalosis	Sodium loss, ↓ volume of extracellular fluid, hyperkalemia, salt craving
Androgens		
Musculoskeletal	Muscle wasting and weakness	↓ Muscle size and tone
Reproductive	*Women:* Menstrual irregularities and enlargement of clitoris *Men:* Gynecomastia and testicular atrophy	*Women:* ↓ Libido in women *Men:* No effect in men
Skin	Hirsutism, acne, hyperpigmentation	↓ Axillary and pubic hair (in women)

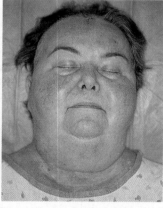

FIG. 49.10 Cushing syndrome. Facies include a rounded face ("moon face") with thin, reddened skin. Hirsutism may be present. (From Seidel HM, Ball JW, Dains JE, et al: *Mosby's guide to physical examination,* ed 6, St Louis, 2006, Mosby.)

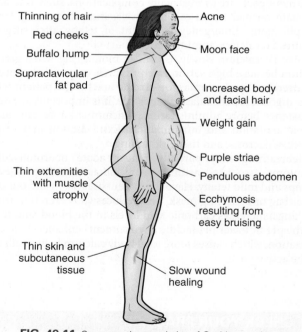

Thinning of hair — Acne
Red cheeks
Buffalo hump — Moon face
Supraclavicular fat pad
— Increased body and facial hair
— Weight gain
Thin extremities with muscle atrophy
— Purple striae
— Pendulous abdomen
— Ecchymosis resulting from easy bruising
Thin skin and subcutaneous tissue
— Slow wound healing

FIG. 49.11 Common characteristics of Cushing syndrome.

loss of collagen makes the skin weaker, thinner, and more easily bruised. Purplish red striae (usually depressed below the skin surface) appear on the abdomen, breast, or buttocks (Fig. 49.12). Catabolic processes lead to a delay in wound healing.

Mineralocorticoid excess may cause hypokalemia from potassium excretion and hypertension from fluid retention. Adrenal androgen excess may cause severe acne, the development of male characteristics in women, and feminization in men. Menstrual disorders and hirsutism in women and gynecomastia and impotence in men are seen more often in adrenal cancers.

Diagnostic Studies

Diagnosing Cushing syndrome begins with confirming increased plasma cortisol levels. We use 3 tests: (1) midnight or late-night salivary cortisol, (2) low-dose dexamethasone suppression test, and (3) 24-hour urine cortisol.[21] Urine cortisol

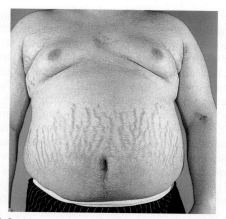

FIG. 49.12 Cushing syndrome. Truncal obesity; broad, purple striae; and easy bruising (left antecubital fossa). (From Chew SL, Leslie D: *Clinical endocrinology and diabetes: An illustrated colour text*, Edinburgh, 2006, Churchill Livingstone.)

levels higher than 100 mcg/24 hr indicate Cushing syndrome. Urine levels of 17-ketosteroids may be high. A CT scan or MRI of the pituitary and adrenal glands can detect a tumor.

Plasma ACTH levels may be low, normal, or high, depending on the underlying cause of Cushing syndrome. High or normal ACTH levels indicate Cushing disease, while low or undetectable levels indicate an adrenal or medication cause. Other findings associated with, but not diagnostic of, Cushing syndrome include leukocytosis, lymphopenia, eosinopenia, hyperglycemia, glycosuria, hypercalciuria, and osteoporosis. Hypokalemia and alkalosis are seen in ectopic ACTH syndrome and adrenal cancer.

Interprofessional Care

The primary goal of treatment is to normalize hormone secretion. The specific treatment depends on the underlying cause (Table 49.17). If the underlying cause is a pituitary adenoma, the standard treatment is surgical removal of the pituitary tumor using the transsphenoidal approach.[21] (This was discussed earlier in this chapter on p. 1145.) Radiation therapy is an option for patients who are not good surgical candidates.

An adrenalectomy is done if Cushing syndrome is caused by adrenal tumors or hyperplasia. Sometimes, bilateral adrenalectomy is needed. A laparoscopic approach is used unless a malignant adrenal tumor is suspected. An open surgical adrenalectomy is usually done for adrenal cancer.

Patients with ectopic ACTH-secreting tumors are best managed by removing the tumor (usually lung or pancreas). This is usually possible when the tumor is benign. If a cancerous tumor has already metastasized, surgical removal may not be possible or successful.

When the patient is a poor candidate for surgery or prior surgery has failed, drug therapy may be tried. The goal of drug therapy is to suppress the synthesis and secretion of cortisol from the adrenal gland (*medical adrenalectomy*). Drugs used include ketoconazole and mitotane. These are used cautiously because they are often toxic at the dosages needed to reduce cortisol secretion. Hydrocortisone or prednisone may be needed to avoid adrenal insufficiency. Mifepristone (Korlym) may be used to control hyperglycemia in patients with endogenous Cushing syndrome who have type 2 diabetes.

TABLE 49.17 Interprofessional Care
Cushing Syndrome

Diagnostic Assessment
- History and physical examination
- Dexamethasone suppression test
- 24-Hr urine for free cortisol and 17-ketosteroids
- Plasma and salivary cortisol levels
- Plasma ACTH levels
- Complete blood count (CBC) with WBC differential
- Blood chemistries for sodium, potassium, glucose
- CT scan, MRI

Management
Pituitary Adenoma
- Transsphenoidal resection
- Radiation therapy
Adrenocortical Adenoma, Cancer, or Hyperplasia
- Adrenalectomy (open or laparoscopic)
- Drug therapy (e.g., ketoconazole, mitotane, mifepristone [Korlym])
Ectopic ACTH-Secreting Tumor
- Treatment of the tumor (surgical removal or radiation)
Exogenous Corticosteroid Therapy
- Discontinue or change the dose of exogenous corticosteroids

If Cushing syndrome developed because of prolonged use of corticosteroids (e.g., prednisone), the following alternatives may be tried: (1) gradually discontinuing corticosteroid therapy, (2) reducing the corticosteroid dose, and (3) converting to alternate-day dosing. Gradual tapering of the corticosteroids is necessary to avoid potentially life-threatening adrenal insufficiency. In alternate-day dosing, twice the daily dosage of a shorter-acting corticosteroid is given every other morning to minimize hypothalamic-pituitary-adrenal suppression, growth suppression, and altered appearance. This plan is not used when the corticosteroids are given as hormone therapy.

❖ NURSING MANAGEMENT: CUSHING SYNDROME

◆ Nursing Assessment

Subjective and objective data that should be obtained from a patient with Cushing syndrome are outlined in Table 49.18.

◆ Nursing Diagnoses

Nursing diagnoses for the patient with Cushing syndrome may include:
- Risk for infection
- Impaired nutritional status
- Disturbed body image
- Impaired tissue integrity

Additional information on nursing diagnoses and interventions is presented in eNursing Care Plan 49.3 for the patient with Cushing syndrome (available on the website for this chapter).

◆ Planning

The overall goals are that the patient with Cushing syndrome will (1) have relief of symptoms, (2) avoid serious complications, (3) maintain a positive self-image, and (4) actively take part in the therapeutic plan.

TABLE 49.18 Nursing Assessment
Cushing Syndrome

Subjective Data
Important Health Information
Past health history: Pituitary tumor (Cushing disease). Adrenal, pancreatic, or pulmonary cancer. GI bleeding, frequent infections
Medications: Corticosteroids

Functional Health Patterns
Health perception–health management: Malaise
Nutritional-metabolic: Weight gain, anorexia. Prolonged wound healing, easy bruising
Elimination: Polyuria
Activity-exercise: Weakness, fatigue
Sleep: Insomnia, poor sleep quality
Cognitive-perceptual: Headache. Back, joint, bone, and rib pain. Poor concentration and memory
Self-perception–self-concept: Negative feelings about changes in personal appearance
Sexuality-reproductive: Amenorrhea, impotence, ↓ libido
Coping–stress tolerance: Anxiety, mood changes, emotional lability, psychosis

Objective Data
General
Truncal obesity, supraclavicular fat pads, buffalo hump, moon face

Skin
Hirsutism of body and face, thinning of head hair. Thin, friable skin. Acne, petechiae, purpura, hyperpigmentation. Purplish red striae on breasts, buttocks, and abdomen. Edema of lower extremities

Cardiovascular
Hypertension

Musculoskeletal
Muscle wasting, thin extremities, awkward gait

Reproductive
Gynecomastia, testicular atrophy (in men), enlarged clitoris (in women)

Possible Diagnostic Findings
Hypokalemia, hyperglycemia, dyslipidemia, polycythemia, lymphocytopenia, eosinopenia. ↑ Plasma cortisol, ↑ salivary cortisol. High, low, or normal ACTH levels. Abnormal dexamethasone suppression test. ↑ Urine free cortisol, 17-ketosteroids. Glycosuria, hypercalciuria. Osteoporosis on x-ray

◆ **Nursing Implementation**

◆ **Health Promotion.** Health promotion focuses on identifying patients at risk for Cushing syndrome. Patients receiving long-term, exogenous corticosteroids are at risk. Teaching related to using medications and monitoring side effects is an important preventive measure.

◆ **Acute Care.** The patient with Cushing syndrome is seriously ill. Because the therapy has many side effects, assessment focuses on signs and symptoms of hormone and drug toxicity and complicating conditions (e.g., CVD, diabetes, infection). Monitor vital signs, daily weight, and glucose. Assess for infection. Because signs and symptoms of inflammation (e.g., fever, redness) may be minimal or absent, assess for pain, loss of function, and purulent drainage. Monitor for signs and symptoms of thromboembolic events, such as pulmonary emboli (e.g., sudden chest pain, dyspnea, tachypnea).

Another important focus of nursing care is emotional support. Changes in appearance, such as truncal obesity, multiple bruises, hirsutism in women, and gynecomastia in men, can be distressing. The patient may feel unattractive, repulsive, or unwanted. You can help by being sensitive to the patient's feelings and offering respect and unconditional acceptance. Reassure the patient that the physical changes and much of the emotional lability will resolve when hormone levels return to normal.

If treatment involves surgical removal of a pituitary adenoma, an adrenal tumor, or one or both adrenal glands, nursing care will include preoperative and postoperative care.

Preoperative Care. Before surgery, the patient should be brought to optimal physical condition. Hypertension and hyperglycemia must be controlled. Hypokalemia must be corrected with diet and potassium supplements. A high-protein diet helps correct the protein depletion. Preoperative teaching depends on the type of surgical approach planned (hypophysectomy or adrenalectomy). Include information about the expected care after surgery.

Postoperative Care. Surgery on the adrenal glands poses great risks. Because the adrenal glands are vascular, the risk for hemorrhage is increased. After both laparoscopic and open adrenalectomy, the patient may have a nasogastric tube, a urinary catheter, IV therapy, and central venous pressure monitoring. Initiate VTE prophylaxis.

Manipulating glandular tissue during surgery may release large amounts of hormones into the circulation. This can produce marked fluctuations in the metabolic processes affected by these hormones. After surgery, BP, fluid balance, and electrolyte levels may be unstable due to these hormone fluctuations.

High doses of corticosteroids (e.g., hydrocortisone [Solu-Cortef]) are given IV during surgery and for several days afterward to ensure adequate responses to the stress of the procedure. If large amounts of endogenous hormone were released into the systemic circulation during surgery, the patient is likely to develop hypertension, increasing the risk for hemorrhage. High corticosteroid levels cause problems with glycemic control, increase risk for infection, and delay wound healing.

The critical period for circulatory instability is 24 to 48 hours after surgery. During this time, you must constantly be alert for signs of corticosteroid imbalance. Report any rapid or significant changes in BP, respirations, or heart rate. Monitor fluid intake and output carefully and assess for potential imbalances. IV corticosteroids are given, and the dosage and flow rate are adjusted to the patient's manifestations and fluid and electrolyte balance. Oral doses are given as tolerated. After IV corticosteroids are withdrawn, keep the IV line open for quick administration of corticosteroids or vasopressors. Obtain morning urine samples at the same time each morning for cortisol measurement to evaluate the surgery's effectiveness.

If corticosteroid dosage is tapered too rapidly after surgery, acute adrenal insufficiency may develop. Vomiting, increased weakness, dehydration, and hypotension are signs of hypocortisolism. The patient may have painful joints, pruritus, or peeling skin and may have severe emotional problems. Report these signs and symptoms so that drug doses can be adjusted as needed.

The patient is usually kept on bed rest until the BP stabilizes. Be alert for subtle signs of infection because the usual inflammatory responses are suppressed. To prevent infection, provide meticulous care when changing the dressing and during any other procedures that involve access to body cavities, circulation, or areas under the skin.

◆ **Ambulatory Care.** Discharge instructions are based on the patient's lack of endogenous corticosteroids and resulting inability to react physiologically to stressors. Consider a home health nurse referral, especially for older adults, because of the need for ongoing evaluation and teaching. Teach the patient to always wear a Medic Alert bracelet and carry medical identification and instructions in a wallet or purse. Teach the patient to avoid exposure to extreme temperatures, infections, and emotional situations. Stress may cause acute adrenal insufficiency because the remaining adrenal tissue cannot meet an increased hormonal demand. Teach patients to adjust their corticosteroid replacement therapy by their stress levels. Consult with the patient's HCP to determine the parameters for dosage changes if this plan is feasible. If the patient cannot adjust their own medication, or if weakness, fainting, fever, or nausea and vomiting occur, the patient should contact the HCP for a possible adjustment in corticosteroid dosage. Many patients require lifetime replacement therapy. However, patients should be prepared for it to take several months to adjust the hormone dose satisfactorily.

◆ **Evaluation**

The expected outcomes are that the patient with Cushing syndrome will

- Have no signs or symptoms of infection
- Maintain weight appropriate for height
- State acceptance of appearance and treatment plan
- Show healing of skin and maintaining intact skin

ADRENOCORTICAL INSUFFICIENCY

Etiology and Pathophysiology

Adrenocortical insufficiency (hypofunction of the adrenal cortex) may be from a primary cause (Addison's disease) or a secondary cause (lack of pituitary ACTH secretion). In Addison's disease, all 3 classes of adrenal corticosteroids (glucocorticoids, mineralocorticoids, and androgens) are reduced. In secondary adrenocortical insufficiency, corticosteroids and androgens are deficient but mineralocorticoids rarely are. ACTH deficiency may be caused by pituitary disease or suppression of the hypothalamic-pituitary axis because of the use of exogenous corticosteroids.

Up to 80% of Addison's disease cases in the United States are caused by an autoimmune response.[22] Autoimmune adrenalitis causes the adrenal cortex to be destroyed by antibodies. This results in loss of glucocorticoid, mineralocorticoid, and adrenal androgen hormones. Addison's disease can be present along with other endocrine conditions. This is known as *autoimmune polyglandular syndrome*. It is most common in white females. Those with autoimmune adrenalitis often have other autoimmune disorders, such as type 1 diabetes, autoimmune thyroid disease, pernicious anemia, and celiac disease.[23]

Although tuberculosis causes Addison's disease worldwide, it is now an uncommon cause in the United States. Other causes include amyloidosis, fungal infections (e.g., histoplasmosis), acquired immunodeficiency syndrome (AIDS), and metastatic cancer. Iatrogenic Addison's disease may be due to adrenal hemorrhage, often related to anticoagulant therapy, chemotherapy, ketoconazole therapy for AIDS, or bilateral adrenalectomy. Adrenal insufficiency most often occurs in adults younger than 60 years of age and affects both genders equally.

Clinical Manifestations

Because manifestations do not tend to become evident until 90% of the adrenal cortex is destroyed, the disease is often advanced before it is diagnosed. The manifestations have a slow (insidious) onset and include anorexia, nausea, progressive weakness, fatigue, and weight loss. Increased ACTH causes the striking feature of a bronze-colored skin hyperpigmentation. It is seen mainly in sun-exposed areas of the body; at pressure points; over joints; and in the creases, especially palmar creases (Fig. 49.13). The changes in the skin are likely due to increased secretion of β-lipotropin (which contains melanocyte-stimulating hormone [MSH]). MSH is increased because of decreased negative feedback and subsequent low corticosteroid levels. Other manifestations include abdominal pain, diarrhea, headache, orthostatic hypotension, salt craving, and joint pain. Irritability and depression may occur in primary adrenal hypofunction.

Patients with secondary adrenocortical hypofunction may have many signs and symptoms similar to those of patients with Addison's disease. However, they usually do not have hyperpigmented skin because ACTH levels are low.

Complications

Patients with adrenocortical insufficiency are at risk for acute adrenal insufficiency (*Addisonian crisis*). It is a life-threatening emergency caused by insufficient adrenocortical hormones or a sudden sharp decrease in these hormones. Addisonian crisis is triggered by (1) stress (e.g., from infection, surgery, psychologic distress), (2) the sudden withdrawal of corticosteroid hormone therapy, (3) adrenal surgery, or (4) sudden pituitary gland destruction.

During acute adrenal insufficiency, the patient has severe manifestations of glucocorticoid and mineralocorticoid deficiencies. These include hypotension, tachycardia, dehydration, hyponatremia, hyperkalemia, hypoglycemia, fever, weakness, and confusion. Hypotension may lead to shock. Circulatory collapse associated with adrenal insufficiency is often unresponsive to the usual treatment (vasopressors and fluid replacement). GI manifestations include severe vomiting, diarrhea, and pain in the abdomen. Pain may occur in the lower back and legs.

Diagnostic Studies

The ACTH stimulation test is a common test to diagnose adrenal insufficiency. Baseline cortisol and ACTH levels are measured, and the patient is given an IV injection of synthetic ACTH (cosyntropin). Cortisol and ACTH levels are rechecked after 30 and 60 minutes. The normal response is a rise in blood cortisol levels. People with Addison's disease have little or no

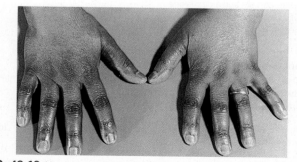

FIG. 49.13 Hyperpigmentation typically seen in Addison's disease. (From Chew SL, Leslie D: *Clinical endocrinology and diabetes: An illustrated colour text*, Edinburgh, 2006, Churchill Livingstone.)

increase in cortisol levels. Those with primary adrenal insufficiency have a high ACTH level.[22]

When the response to the ACTH test is abnormal, a corticotropin-releasing hormone (CRH) stimulation test may be done. The patient is given an IV injection of synthetic CRH, and blood is taken after 30 and 60 minutes. Those with Addison's disease have high ACTH levels but no cortisol. People with secondary adrenal insufficiency from pituitary or hypothalamus problems do not make ACTH or have a delayed response.[23]

Other abnormal laboratory findings may include hyperkalemia, hypochloremia, hyponatremia, hypoglycemia, anemia, and increased BUN levels.[23] An ECG may show low voltage and peaked T waves caused by hyperkalemia. CT scans and MRI can identify other causes, including tumors, fungal infections, tuberculosis, or adrenal calcification.

❖ Interprofessional and Nursing Care

Treatment focuses on managing the underlying cause when possible. The mainstay is often lifelong hormone therapy with glucocorticoids and mineralocorticoids (Table 49.19). Overall, patients who take their medications consistently can expect a normal life expectancy. Hydrocortisone, the most common form of hormone therapy, has both glucocorticoid and mineralocorticoid properties. Mineralocorticoids are replaced with fludrocortisone. Women need androgen replacement with dehydroepiandrosterone (DHEA) as their only source of androgen production is the adrenal glands.[23] Increased salt is added to the diet.

As a nurse, you have a key role in the long-term management of Addison's disease. The serious nature of the disease and the need for lifelong hormone therapy necessitate a comprehensive teaching plan. Table 49.20 outlines the major areas to include in a teaching plan.

Glucocorticoids are usually given in divided doses, two thirds in the morning and one third in the afternoon. Mineralocorticoids are given once daily, preferably in the morning. This schedule reflects normal circadian rhythm in endogenous hormone secretion and decreases the side effects associated with corticosteroid therapy. Teach patients using mineralocorticoid therapy (fludrocortisone) how to take their BP, increase salt intake, and report any significant changes to the HCP.

The patient with Addison's disease needs an increased dosage of corticosteroids in stressful situations to prevent Addisonian crisis. Examples of situations requiring corticosteroid adjustment are fever, influenza, tooth extraction, and rigorous physical activity, such as playing sports on a hot day or distance running. Provide written and verbal instructions on when to change the dose. Review stress management techniques. If vomiting or diarrhea occurs, as may happen with gastroenteritis, the patient should notify the HCP at once. Electrolyte replacement and parenteral administration of cortisol may be needed.

Teach patients the signs and symptoms of corticosteroid deficiency and excess (Cushing syndrome) and to report these signs to the HCP so that the drug dose can be adjusted. It is critical that the patient wear an identification bracelet (Medic Alert) and carry a wallet card saying the patient has Addison's disease so that appropriate therapy can be started in case of an emergency. The patient should always carry an emergency kit with 100 mg of IM hydrocortisone and syringes. Teach the patient and caregiver how to give an IM injection.

When the patient with Addison's disease is hospitalized, nursing management focuses on monitoring the patient while correcting fluid and electrolyte balance. Assess vital signs and neurologic status. Monitor for signs of fluid volume deficit and electrolyte imbalance. Obtain a daily weight and keep an accurate intake and output record. Take a complete medication history to determine drugs that can potentially interact with corticosteroids. These drugs include oral hypoglycemics, cardiac glycosides, oral contraceptives, anticoagulants, and NSAIDs.

Note changes in BP, weight gain, weakness, or other manifestations of Cushing syndrome. Guard the patient against exposure to infection and help with daily hygiene. Protect the patient from noise, light, and environmental temperature extremes. The patient cannot cope with these stresses because of the inability to make corticosteroids.

TABLE 49.19 Interprofessional Care
Addison's Disease

Diagnostic Assessment
- History and physical examination
- ACTH stimulation test
- Serum cortisol and ACTH
- Urine cortisol and aldosterone
- CRH suppression test
- Serum electrolytes
- CT scan, MRI

Management
- Daily glucocorticoid (e.g., prednisone, hydrocortisone) replacement (two thirds on awakening in morning, one third in late afternoon)
- Daily mineralocorticoid (fludrocortisone) in morning
- ↑ Salt in the diet
- Androgen replacement with dehydroepiandrosterone (DHEA) for women
- Salt additives for excess heat or humidity
- ↑ Doses of glucocorticoid for stress situations (e.g., surgery, hospitalization)

TABLE 49.20 Patient & Caregiver Teaching
Addison's Disease

Include the following information in the teaching plan for the patient with Addison's disease and the caregiver:
1. Names, dosages, and actions of drugs
2. Symptoms of overdosage and underdosage
3. Conditions requiring increased dosage (e.g., trauma, infection, surgery, emotional crisis)
4. Course of action to take related to changes in medication
   - Increased dose of corticosteroid
   - Self-administration of large dose of corticosteroid IM
   - Consultation with HCP
5. Preventing infection and need for prompt and vigorous treatment of existing infections
6. Need for lifelong replacement therapy
7. Need for lifelong medical supervision
8. Need to carry medical identification
9. Fall prevention
10. Adverse effects of corticosteroid therapy and prevention techniques
11. Special instruction for patients with diabetes and management of blood glucose when taking corticosteroids

Addisonian crisis is a life-threatening emergency requiring aggressive management. Treatment is directed toward shock management and high-dose hydrocortisone replacement. Large volumes of 0.9% saline solution and 5% dextrose are given to reverse hypotension and electrolyte imbalances until BP returns to normal.

CORTICOSTEROID THERAPY

Corticosteroids are effective in treating many diseases and disorders (Table 49.21). However, the long-term administration of corticosteroids at therapeutic doses often leads to serious complications and side effects (Table 49.22). For this reason, corticosteroid therapy is not recommended for minor chronic

TABLE 49.21 Drug Therapy
Diseases/Disorders Treated With Corticosteroids

Hormone Therapy
- Adrenal insufficiency
- Congenital adrenal hyperplasia

Therapeutic Effect
Allergic Reactions
- Anaphylaxis
- Bee stings
- Contact dermatitis
- Drug reactions
- Serum sickness
- Urticaria

Connective Tissue Diseases
- Mixed connective tissue disorders
- Polymyositis
- Polyarteritis nodosa
- Rheumatoid arthritis
- Systemic lupus erythematosus

Endocrine Diseases
- Hypercalcemia
- Hashimoto's thyroiditis
- Thyrotoxicosis

Gastrointestinal Diseases
- Inflammatory bowel disease
- Celiac disease

Liver Diseases
- Alcoholic hepatitis
- Autoimmune hepatitis

Neurologic Diseases
- Cerebral edema and increased intracranial pressure
- Head trauma

Pulmonary Diseases
- Aspiration pneumonia
- Asthma
- Chronic obstructive pulmonary disease

Other Diseases or Disorders
- Skin diseases
- Cancer, leukemia, lymphoma
- Immunosuppression
- Inflammation
- Nephrotic syndrome

TABLE 49.22 Drug Therapy
Effects and Side Effects of Corticosteroids

- Delayed wound healing with ↑ risk for wound dehiscence
- Fat from extremities redistributed to trunk and face
- Glucose intolerance
- Hypertension with ↑ risk for heart failure
- Hypocalcemia related to anti–vitamin D effect
- Hypokalemia
- ↑ Risk for infection
- Infection develops more rapidly and spreads more widely
- Mood and behavior changes
- Pathologic fractures, especially compression fractures of the vertebrae (osteoporosis)
- Peptic ulcer disease
- Pituitary ACTH synthesis suppressed
- Skeletal muscle atrophy and weakness
- Suppressed inflammatory response

conditions. Therapy should be reserved for diseases that have a risk for death or permanent loss of function and for conditions in which short-term therapy is likely to produce remission or recovery. The potential benefits of treatment must always be weighed against the risks.

❓ CHECK YOUR PRACTICE

You are working in the outpatient clinic. Your 39-yr-old female patient has Cushing syndrome from high doses of prednisone use for her severe systemic lupus erythematosus. At her office visit today, she tells you, "I looked in the mirror this morning and did not recognize the fat, ugly woman looking back at me."
- How would you respond to her?

A beneficial effect of corticosteroids in one situation may be a harmful one in another. For example, decreasing inflammation in arthritis is an important therapeutic effect, but increasing the risk for infection is a harmful effect. Suppressing inflammation and the immune response may help save lives in persons with anaphylaxis and in those receiving an organ transplant, but it can reactivate latent tuberculosis and increase the risk for infection and cancer. The vasopressive effect of corticosteroids is critical in allowing a person to function in stressful situations but can cause hypertension when used for drug therapy.

💊 DRUG ALERT Corticosteroids
- Teach the patient not to abruptly stop these drugs.
- Monitor the patient for signs of infection.
- Have patients with diabetes closely monitor blood glucose.

Patients receive corticosteroid therapy for many reasons. Detailed instruction is needed to ensure patient adherence. When corticosteroids are used as nonreplacement therapy, they are taken once daily or once every other day. They should be taken early in the morning with food to decrease gastric irritation. Because exogenous corticosteroid use may suppress endogenous ACTH and therefore endogenous cortisol (suppression is time and dose dependent), emphasize the danger of abruptly stopping corticosteroid therapy to patients and caregivers. Corticosteroids taken for longer than 1 week will suppress adrenal production, and oral corticosteroids must be tapered. Ensure that increased doses of corticosteroids are prescribed in acute care or home care settings in situations of physical or emotional stress.

Corticosteroid-induced osteoporosis is an important concern for patients who receive corticosteroid treatment for prolonged periods (longer than 3 months).[24] Therapies to reduce bone resorption include increased calcium intake, vitamin D supplementation, bisphosphonates (e.g., alendronate), and a low-impact exercise program. Further instruction and interventions to minimize the side effects and complications of corticosteroid therapy are outlined in Table 49.23.

HYPERALDOSTERONISM

Hyperaldosteronism (Conn's syndrome) is characterized by excess aldosterone secretion. The main effects of aldosterone are (1) sodium retention and (2) potassium and hydrogen ion excretion. Thus the hallmark of this disease is hypertension with hypokalemic alkalosis. *Primary hyperaldosteronism* (PA) is most often caused by a small solitary adrenocortical adenoma. Sometimes, multiple lesions are involved and are associated with bilateral adrenal hyperplasia.

TABLE 49.23 Patient & Caregiver Teaching

Corticosteroid Therapy

Include the following instructions when teaching the patient and caregiver to manage corticosteroid therapy:

1. Follow a diet high in protein, calcium (at least 1500 mg/day), and potassium and low in fat and concentrated simple carbohydrates, such as sugar, syrups, and candy.
2. Ensure adequate rest and sleep, such as daily naps and avoiding caffeine late in the day.
3. Take part in an exercise program to help maintain bone integrity.
4. Recognize edema and ways to restrict sodium intake to <2000 mg/day if edema occurs.
5. Monitor glucose levels and recognize symptoms of hyperglycemia (e.g., polydipsia, polyuria, blurred vision). Report hyperglycemic symptoms or capillary glucose levels >120 mg/dL (10 mmol/L).
6. Notify HCP if heartburn after meals or epigastric pain that is not relieved by antacids occurs.
7. See an eye specialist yearly to assess for cataracts.
8. Use safety measures, such as getting up slowly from bed or a chair and good lighting, to avoid accidental injury.
9. Maintain appropriate hygiene practices.
10. Avoid contact with persons with colds or other contagious illnesses to prevent infection.
11. Inform all HCPs about long-term corticosteroid use.
12. Recognize need for ↑ doses of corticosteroids in times of physical and emotional stress.
13. Never abruptly stop the corticosteroids because this could lead to Addisonian crisis and death.

PA affects women more than men and usually occurs between 30 and 50 years of age. A genetic link has been found in some patients.[25] PA causes up to 2% of all cases of hypertension. *Secondary hyperaldosteronism* occurs in response to a nonadrenal cause of increased aldosterone levels, such as renal artery stenosis, renin-secreting tumors, and chronic kidney disease.

Increased aldosterone levels are associated with sodium retention and potassium excretion. Sodium retention leads to hypernatremia, hypertension, and headache. Edema does not usually occur because the rate of sodium excretion increases, preventing more severe sodium retention. Potassium wasting leads to hypokalemia, which causes generalized muscle weakness, fatigue, dysrhythmias, glucose intolerance, and metabolic alkalosis that may lead to tetany.

Hyperaldosteronism should be suspected in hypertensive patients with hypokalemia who are not being treated with diuretics. PA is associated with increased plasma aldosterone levels, increased sodium levels, decreased serum potassium levels, and decreased plasma renin activity. A CT scan or MRI can detect an adenoma.[25] If a tumor is not found, plasma 18-hydroxycorticosterone is measured after overnight bed rest. A level greater than 50 ng/dL indicates an adenoma.

❖ Interprofessional and Nursing Care

The preferred treatment for PA is surgical removal of the adenoma (adrenalectomy). A laparoscopic approach is most often used. Before surgery, patients should be treated with potassium-sparing diuretics (e.g., spironolactone, eplerenone [Inspra]) and antihypertensive agents to normalize serum potassium levels and BP. Spironolactone and eplerenone block the binding of aldosterone to the mineralocorticoid receptor in the terminal distal tubules and collecting ducts of the kidney, thus increasing

sodium and water excretion and potassium retention. Oral potassium supplements and sodium restrictions may be needed. However, potassium supplementation and a potassium-sparing diuretic should not be started simultaneously because of the risk for hyperkalemia. Teach patients taking eplerenone to avoid grapefruit juice as it may increase potential for hyperkalemia.

Patients with bilateral adrenal hyperplasia are treated with a potassium-sparing diuretic. Calcium channel blockers may be used to control BP. Dexamethasone may be used to decrease adrenal hyperplasia.

Nursing care includes careful assessment of fluid and electrolyte balance (especially potassium) and cardiovascular status. Monitor BP frequently before and after surgery because unilateral adrenalectomy is successful in controlling hypertension in only 80% of patients with an adenoma. Tell patients receiving spironolactone about the possible side effects of gynecomastia, impotence, and menstrual disorders, as well as the signs and symptoms of hypokalemia and hyperkalemia. Teach patients how to monitor their own BP and the need for frequent monitoring. Stress the need for continued health supervision.

DISORDERS OF ADRENAL MEDULLA

PHEOCHROMOCYTOMA

Pheochromocytoma is a rare condition caused by a tumor in the adrenal medulla. It affects the chromaffin cells, resulting in an excess production of catecholamines (epinephrine, norepinephrine). The most dangerous immediate effect of the disease is severe hypertension. If left untreated, it may lead to encephalopathy, diabetes, cardiomyopathy, multiple organ failure, and death. It most often occurs in young to middle-aged adults. Pheochromocytoma may be inherited in persons with MEN.[26]

The most striking findings are severe, episodic hypertension accompanied by severe, pounding headache; tachycardia with palpitations; profuse sweating; and unexplained abdominal or chest pain. Attacks can be induced by direct trauma, mechanical pressure to the tumor, stress (e.g., surgery, exercise, defecation, sexual intercourse, alcohol consumption, smoking), or many drugs, including antihypertensives, opioids, radiologic contrast media, and tricyclic antidepressants. Attacks can last from a few minutes to several hours.

The simplest and most reliable diagnostic test is measurement of urinary fractionated metanephrines (catecholamine metabolites) and fractionated catecholamines and creatinine, usually done as a 24-hour urine collection. Values are increased in at least 95% of persons with pheochromocytoma. Serum catecholamines may be increased during an "attack." CT scans and MRI can detect tumors. Do not palpate the abdomen of a patient with suspected pheochromocytoma. It may cause the sudden release of catecholamines and severe hypertension.

❖ Interprofessional and Nursing Care

The main treatment is surgical removal of the tumor. Treatment with α- and β-adrenergic receptor blockers is required before surgery to control BP and prevent an intraoperative hypertensive crisis. Therapy begins with an α-adrenergic receptor blocker (e.g., doxazosin, prazosin, phenoxybenzamine) 10 to 14 days before surgery to reduce BP.[26] After adequate α-adrenergic blockade, β-adrenergic receptor blockers (e.g., propranolol) are used to decrease tachycardia and dysrhythmias. If β-blockers are started too early, unopposed α-adrenergic stimulation can precipitate a hypertensive crisis. Therapy can cause orthostatic hypotension. Teach the patient to make postural changes cautiously.

Surgery is usually done using a laparoscopic approach. Removing the adrenal tumor often cures the hypertension, but hypertension persists in about 10% to 30% of patients. If surgery is not an option, metyrosine (Demser) can decrease catecholamine production by the tumor.

Case finding is an important nursing role. Although pheochromocytoma is associated with several symptoms, the diagnosis is often missed. Any patient with hypertension accompanied by symptoms of sympathoadrenal stimulation should be referred to an HCP for definitive diagnosis. Assess the patient for the classic triad of symptoms of pheochromocytoma: severe pounding headache, tachycardia, and profuse sweating. Monitor the BP often if the patient is having an "attack."

Make the patient as comfortable as possible. Monitor blood glucose levels to assess for diabetes. Patients need rest, nourishing food, and emotional support during this period. Surgical care is similar to that for any patient undergoing adrenalectomy. Note that BP fluctuations from catecholamine excesses tend to be severe and must be carefully monitored. Emphasize the importance of follow-up and routine BP monitoring because hypertension may persist even when the tumor is removed.

CASE STUDY
Graves' Disease

(© Hemera Technologies/ AbleStock.com/ Thinkstock.)

Patient Profile

R.D., a 52-yr-old white woman, was admitted to the hospital with a high fever. Unable to find a source of infection, the HCP does an endocrine workup. R.D. is diagnosed with Graves' disease.

Subjective Data

- Reports recent job loss because she is no longer able to tolerate work-related stress
- Reports symptoms including fatigue, unintentional weight loss, insomnia, palpitations, vision problems, and heat intolerance

Objective Data

Physical Examination

- Fever of 104° F (40° C)
- BP of 150/80 mm Hg, pulse of 116 beats/min, and respiratory rate of 26 breaths/min
- Hot, moist skin
- Fine tremors of the hands
- 4+ deep tendon reflexes and muscle strength of 1 to 2 out of 5

Interprofessional Care

- Subtotal thyroidectomy planned for 2 months later
- Started on methimazole (Tapazole) and propranolol (Inderal LA)

Discussion Questions

1. Explain the cause of R.D.'s symptoms.
2. What diagnostic studies were probably ordered? What would the results have been to establish the diagnosis of Graves' disease?
3. Why was surgery delayed?
4. *Collaboration:* What is the interprofessional team's top priority at this time for R.D.?
5. *Quality Care:* What is the expected outcome associated with drug therapy?
6. *Priority Decision:* What are her priority teaching needs at this time?
7. *Patient-Centered Care:* What teaching will you provide after surgery so that R.D. can successfully self-manage her care?
8. *Priority Decision:* Based on the assessment data presented, what are the priority nursing diagnoses pertinent to this patient while hospitalized? Are there any collaborative problems?
9. *Evidence-Based Practice:* Why is R.D. counseled to give up her long-standing cigarette smoking habit?

Answers available at *http://evolve.elsevier.com/Lewis/medsurg.*

▮ BRIDGE TO NCLEX EXAMINATION

The number of the question corresponds to the same-numbered outcome at the beginning of the chapter.

1. After a hypophysectomy for acromegaly, immediate postoperative nursing care should focus on
   a. frequent monitoring of serum and urine osmolarity.
   b. parenteral administration of a GH-receptor antagonist.
   c. keeping the patient in a recumbent position at all times.
   d. patient teaching about the need for lifelong hormone therapy.

2. A patient with a head injury develops SIADH. Manifestations the nurse would expect to find include
   a. hypernatremia and edema.
   b. muscle spasticity and hypertension.
   c. low urine output and hyponatremia.
   d. weight gain and decreased glomerular filtration rate.

3. The health care provider prescribes levothyroxine for a patient with hypothyroidism. After teaching about this drug, the nurse determines that further instruction is needed when the patient says
   a. "I can expect the medication dose may need to be adjusted."
   b. "I only need to take this drug until my symptoms are improved."
   c. "I can expect to return to normal function with the use of this drug."
   d. "I will report any chest pain or difficulty breathing to the doctor right away."

4. After thyroid surgery, the nurse suspects damage or removal of the parathyroid glands when the patient develops
   a. muscle weakness and weight loss.
   b. hyperthermia and severe tachycardia.
   c. hypertension and difficulty swallowing.
   d. laryngospasms and tingling in the hands and feet.

5. Important nursing intervention(s) when caring for a patient with Cushing syndrome include *(select all that apply)*
   a. restricting protein intake.
   b. monitoring blood glucose levels.
   c. observing for signs of hypotension.
   d. administering medication in equal doses.
   e. protecting patient from exposure to infection.

6. An important preoperative nursing intervention before an adrenalectomy for hyperaldosteronism is to
   a. monitor blood glucose levels.
   b. restrict fluid and sodium intake.
   c. administer potassium-sparing diuretics.
   d. advise the patient to make postural changes slowly.

7. To control the side effects of corticosteroid therapy, the nurse teaches the patient who is taking corticosteroids to
   a. increase calcium intake to 1500 mg/day.
   b. perform glucose monitoring for hypoglycemia.
   c. obtain immunizations due to high risk for infections.
   d. avoid abrupt position changes because of orthostatic hypotension.

1. a, 2. c, 3. b, 4. d, 5. b, e, 6. c, 7. a

For rationales to these answers and even more NCLEX review questions, visit *http://evolve.elsevier.com/Lewis/medsurg.*

(e) EVOLVE WEBSITE/RESOURCES LIST

REFERENCES

1. American Cancer Society: About pituitary tumors. Retrieved from *www.cancer.org/cancer/pituitary-tumors/about/what-is-pituitary-tumor.html.*
2. National Institute of Diabetes and Digestive, and Kidney Diseases: Acromegaly. Retrieved from *www.niddk.nih.gov/health-information/health-topics/endocrine/acromegaly/Pages/fact-sheet.aspx.*
3. Pituitary Network Association: About acromegaly. Retrieved from *http://acromegaly.org/en/about/about-acromegaly.*
*4. Buchfelder M, Schlaffer SM: The surgical treatment of acromegaly, *Pituitary* 20:1, 2017.
*5. Auriemma RS, Grasso LS, Pivonello R, et al: The safety of treatments for prolactinomas, *Opin Drug Saf* 15:4, 2016.
*6. Molitch ME: Diagnosis and treatment of pituitary adenomas: A review, *JAMA* 317:5, 2017.
*7. Prete A, Corsello SM, Salvatori R. Current best practice in the management of patients after pituitary surgery, *Ther Adv Endocrinol Metab* 8:3, 2017.
8. Braun MM, Mahowald M, Electrolytes: Sodium disorders, *FP Essent* 459:11, 2017.
9. Vanderpump MP: Epidemiology of iodine deficiency, *Minerva Med* 108:2, 2017.
10. Dunn D, Turner C: Hypothyroidism in women, *Nurs Womens Health* 20:1, 2016.
*11. Salman F, Oktaei H, Solomon S, et al: Recurrent Graves' hyperthyroidism after prolonged radioiodine-induced hypothyroidism, *Ther Adv Endocrinol Metab* 8:7, 2017.
12. Ross DS, Burch HB, Cooper DS, et al: 2016 American Thyroid Association guidelines for diagnosis and management of hyperthyroidism and other causes of thyrotoxicosis, *Thyroid* 26:10, 2016.
*13. Caulley L, Johnson-Obaseki S, Luo L, et al: Risk factors for postoperative complications in total thyroidectomy: A retrospective, risk-adjusted analysis from the National Surgical Quality Improvement Program, *Medicine* 96:5, 2017.
14. Chaker L, Bianco AC, Jonklaas J, et al: Hypothyroidism, *Lancet* 390:10101, 2017.
*15. Kumar E, McCurdy MT, Koch CA, et al: Impairment of thyroid function in critically ill patients in the intensive care units, *Am J Med Sci* 355:3, 2018.
*16. Hennessey JV, Garber JR, Woeber KA, et al: American Association of Clinical Endocrinologists and American College of Endocrinology position statement on thyroid dysfunction, *Endocr Pract* 22:84, 2016.
17. Bibbins-Domingo K, Grossman DC, Curry SJ, et al: Screening for thyroid cancer: US Preventive Services Task Force recommendation statement, *JAMA* 317:18, 2017.
18. National Institutes of Health: Multiple endocrine neoplasia. Retrieved from *https://ghr.nlm.nih.gov/condition/multiple-endocrine-neoplasia.*
19. Markowitz ME, Underland L, Gensure R: Parathyroid disorders, *Pediatr Rev* 37:12, 2016.
*20. Sharma ST: An individualized approach to the evaluation of Cushing syndrome, *Endocr Pract* 23:6, 2017.
*21. Lonser RR, Nieman L, Oldfield EH: Cushing's disease: Pathobiology, diagnosis, and management, *J Neurosurg* 126:404, 2017.
22. Munir S, Waseem M: Addison disease, *StatPearls*, 2018. Retrieved from *www.statpearls.com/as/endocrine%20and%20metabolic/17183/.*
23. National Institute of Diabetes and Digestive and Kidney Diseases: Addison's disease. Retrieved from *www.niddk.nih.gov/health-information/health-topics/endocrine/adrenal-insufficiency-addisons-disease/Pages/fact-sheet.aspx.*
24. Arthritis Foundation: Treating corticosteroid-induced bone loss. Retrieved from *www.arthritis.org/living-with-arthritis/treatments/medication/drug-types/corticosteroids/osteoporosis-bone-loss.php.*
25. Gyamlani G, Headley CM, Naseer A, et al: Primary aldosteronism: Diagnosis and management, *Am J Med Sci* 352:4, 2016.
26. Azadeh N, Ramakrishna H, Bhatia NL, et al: Therapeutic goals in patients with pheochromocytoma: A guide to perioperative management, *Ir J Med Sci* 185:1, 2016.

*Evidence-based information for clinical practice.

50

Assessment: Reproductive System

Kim K. Choma

Be a rainbow in someone else's cloud.

Maya Angelou

🄴 http://evolve.elsevier.com/Lewis/medsurg

CONCEPTUAL FOCUS

Hormonal Regulation
Reproduction

Sexuality

LEARNING OUTCOMES

1. Describe the structures and functions of the male and female reproductive systems.
2. Outline the functions of the major hormones essential for the functioning of the male and female reproductive systems.
3. Explain the physiologic changes during the stages of sexual response for both a man and a woman.
4. Link the age-related changes of the male and female reproductive systems to the differences in assessment findings.

5. Obtain significant subjective and objective data related to the male and female reproductive systems and information about sexual function from a patient.
6. Perform a physical assessment of the male and female reproductive systems using the appropriate techniques.
7. Distinguish normal from common abnormal findings of a physical assessment of the male and female reproductive systems.
8. Describe the purpose, significance of results, and nursing responsibilities related to diagnostic studies of the male and female reproductive systems.

KEY TERMS

amenorrhea, p. 1177
ductus deferens, p. 1172
dyspareunia, p. 1181
epididymis, p. 1172
estrogen, p. 1175

gonads, p. 1171
menarche, p. 1176
menopause, p. 1177
menstrual cycle, p. 1176
progesterone, p. 1175

spermatogenesis, p. 1171
testosterone, p. 1176
uterus, p. 1173
vulva, p. 1174

STRUCTURES AND FUNCTIONS OF MALE AND FEMALE REPRODUCTIVE SYSTEMS

The reproductive systems of males and females consist of primary (or essential) organs and secondary (or accessory) organs. The primary reproductive organs are referred to as gonads. The female gonads are the ovaries. The male gonads are the testes. The main purpose of the gonads is secretion of hormones and production of gametes (ova and sperm, sex cells that unite during fertilization to form a new cell called a *zygote*). Secondary (or accessory) organs begin their maturity at puberty under the influence of sex hormones. They are responsible for (1) transporting and nourishing the ova (eggs) and sperm and (2) preserving and protecting the fertilized ova.

Male Reproductive System

The 3 main roles of the male reproductive system are (1) sperm production and transportation, (2) deposition of sperm in the female reproductive tract, and (3) hormone secretion. The primary male reproductive organs are the testes. Secondary reproductive organs include ducts (epididymis, ductus deferens, ejaculatory duct, urethra), sex glands (prostate gland, Cowper's glands, seminal vesicles), and the external genitalia (scrotum, penis) (Fig. 50.1).

Testes. The paired testes are ovoid, smooth, firm organs. They measure 1.4 to 2.2 in (3.5 to 5.6 cm) long and 0.8 to 1.2 in (2 to 3 cm) wide. They lie within the scrotum. It is a loose protective sac composed of a thin outer layer of skin over a tough connective tissue layer. Within the testes, coiled structures called the seminiferous tubules form *spermatozoa* (immature sperm). The process of sperm production is called spermatogenesis. Interstitial cells lie between the seminiferous tubules. These cells make the male sex hormone testosterone.

Ducts. Sperm formed in the seminiferous tubules move through a series of ducts. These ducts transport sperm from the testes to the outside of the body. As sperm exit the testes, they enter and pass through the epididymis, ductus deferens, ejaculatory duct, and urethra.

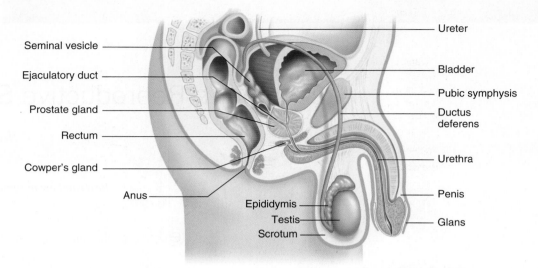

FIG 50.1 Male reproductive tract. (Modified from Patton KT, Thibodeau GA: *Anatomy and physiology*, ed 8, St Louis, 2013, Mosby.)

The **epididymis** is a comma-shaped structure found on the posterosuperior aspect of each testis within the scrotum (Figs. 50.1 and 50.2). It is a long, tightly coiled structure that measures, uncoiled, about 20 ft in length.[1] The epididymis transports sperm as they mature. Sperm exit the epididymis through a long, thick tube called the **ductus deferens**.

The ductus deferens (also called the *vas deferens*) is continuous with the epididymis within the scrotal sac. It travels upward through the scrotum and continues through the inguinal ring into the abdominal cavity. The spermatic cord is composed of a connective tissue sheath that encloses the ductus deferens, arteries, veins, nerves, and lymph vessels as it ascends through the inguinal canal (Fig. 50.2). In the abdominal cavity, the ductus deferens travels up, over, and behind the bladder. Behind the bladder the ductus deferens joins the seminal vesicle to form the ejaculatory duct (Fig. 50.1).

The ejaculatory duct passes downward through the prostate gland, connecting with the urethra. The urethra extends from the bladder, through the prostate, and ends in a slit-like opening (the meatus) on the ventral side of the *glans*, the tip of the penis. During the process of ejaculation, sperm travel through the urethra and out of the penis.

Glands. The seminal vesicles, prostate gland, and Cowper's (bulbourethral) glands are the accessory glands. These glands make and secrete seminal fluid *(semen)*, which surrounds the sperm and forms the *ejaculate*. The ejaculate fluid serves as a medium for the transport of sperm and creates an alkaline, nutritious environment that promotes sperm motility and survival.

The seminal vesicles lie behind the bladder, between the bladder and rectum. The ducts of the seminal vesicles fuse with the ductus deferens to form the ejaculatory ducts that enter the prostate gland. The prostate gland lies beneath the bladder. Its posterior surface is in contact with the rectal wall. The prostate normally measures 0.8 in (2 cm) wide and 1.2 in (3 cm) long. It is divided into right and left lateral lobes and an anteroposterior median lobe. Cowper's glands lie on each side of the urethra and slightly posterior to it, just below the prostate. The ducts of these glands enter directly into the urethra.

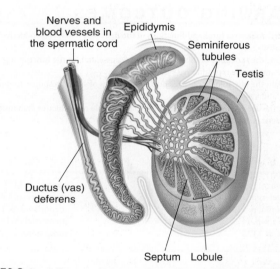

FIG 50.2 Seminiferous tubules, testis, epididymis, and ductus (vas) deferens in the male. (Modified from Patton KT, Thibodeau GA: *Anatomy and physiology*, ed 8, St Louis, 2013, Mosby.)

External Genitalia. The male external genitalia consist of the penis and scrotum. The penis consists of a shaft and tip, which is called the *glans*. The glans is covered by a fold of skin, the prepuce (or foreskin), that forms at the junction of the glans and shaft of the penis. In circumcised males the prepuce has been removed. The shaft consists of erectile tissue composed of the corpus cavernosum, corpus spongiosum (fibrous sheath that encases the erectile tissue), and urethra. The skin covering the penis is thin, loose, and hairless.

Female Reproductive System

The 3 main roles of the female reproductive system are (1) ova production, (2) hormone secretion, and (3) protect and facilitate the development of the fetus in a pregnant female. Like the male, the female has primary and secondary reproductive organs. The primary reproductive organs in the female are the

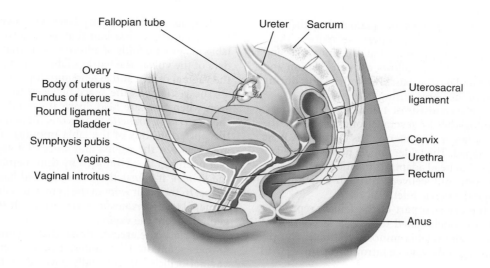

FIG 50.3 Female reproductive tract. (Modified from McKenry L, Tessier E, Hogan M: *Mosby's pharmacology in nursing,* St Louis, 2006, Mosby.)

paired ovaries. Secondary reproductive organs include the ducts (fallopian tubes), uterus, vagina, sex glands (Bartholin's glands, breasts), and external genitalia (vulva).

Pelvic Organs

Ovaries. The ovaries are found on either side of the uterus, just behind and below the fallopian tubes (Fig. 50.3). The almond-shaped ovaries are firm and solid, around 0.6 in (1.5 cm) wide and 1.2 in (3 cm) long. Their functions include ovulation and secretion of the 2 major reproductive hormones: estrogen and progesterone.

The outer zone of the ovary has follicles with germ cells, or *oocytes*. Each follicle contains a primordial (immature) oocyte surrounded by granulosa and theca cells. These 2 layers protect and nourish the oocyte until the follicle reaches maturity and ovulation occurs. However, not all follicles reach maturity. In a process termed *atresia,* most of the immature follicles become smaller and are reabsorbed by the body. Thus the number of follicles declines from 1 million at birth to about 400,000 at *menarche* (first menstruation). This is the female's lifetime supply of sex cells. In contrast, males make spermatocytes throughout their reproductive life cycle. As a woman ages, both the number and quality of the oocytes decline. Fewer than 500 oocytes are actually released by ovulation during the reproductive years of the normal healthy woman.[2]

Fallopian Tubes. The fallopian tubes transport the ovum toward the uterus, facilitating fertilization or implantation. The tubes are uterine appendages that end by curling around the ovary. The distal ends of the fallopian tubes consist of fingerlike projections called *fimbriae*. They sweep the ovum from the ruptured ovarian follicle (ovulation) into the fallopian tube. The tubes, which average 4.8 in (12 cm) in length, extend from the fimbriae to the superior lateral borders of the uterus.

Normally, each month during a woman's reproductive years, 1 ovarian follicle reaches maturity. That ovum is ovulated, or expelled, from the ovary through the stimulus of the gonadotropic hormones: follicle-stimulating hormone (FSH) and luteinizing hormone (LH). The ovum then travels through a fallopian tube, where fertilization by sperm may occur (if sperm are present). Fertilization usually takes place within the outer one third of the fallopian tubes. An ovum can be fertilized up to 72 hours after its release.

Uterus. The **uterus** is a pear-shaped, hollow, muscular organ found between the bladder and rectum (Fig. 50.3). In the mature *nulliparous* (never pregnant) woman, the uterus is about 2.4 to 3.2 in (6 to 8 cm) long and 1.6 in (4 cm) wide. The uterine walls consist of an outer serosal layer, the *perimetrium;* a middle muscular layer, the *myometrium;* and an inner mucosal layer, the *endometrium.*

The uterus consists of the fundus, body (or corpus), and cervix (Fig. 50.3). The body makes up about 80% of the uterus. It connects with the cervix at the isthmus, or neck. The cervix is the lower part of the uterus. It projects into the anterior wall of the vaginal canal. It makes up about 15% to 20% of the uterus in the nulliparous female. The cervix consists of the *ectocervix,* the outer part that protrudes into the vagina, and the *endocervix,* the canal in the opening of the cervix. The opening of the cervix is the *cervical os* (Fig. 50.4).

The ectocervix is covered with squamous epithelial cells. This gives it a smooth, pinkish appearance. The endocervix is lined with columnar epithelial cells, which give it a rough, reddened appearance. The junction at which the 2 types of epithelial cells (squamous and columnar) meet is the *squamocolumnar junction* (Fig. 50.4). Cells sampled from the squamocolumnar junction are examined as part of a Papanicolaou (Pap) test, which is a critical part of cervical cancer screening.

The cervical canal is 0.8 to 1.6 in (2 to 4 cm) long. It is relatively tightly closed. However, menses can be expelled and sperm can enter the uterus through the cervical os. The entrance of sperm into the uterus is facilitated by mucus made by the cervix under the influence of estrogen. Under normal conditions, the cervical mucus becomes watery, stretchy, and more abundant at ovulation. The postovulatory cervical mucus, under the influence of progesterone, is thick and inhibits sperm passage. The cervix can stretch to allow passage of a fetus during the birth process. The columnar epithelium, under hormonal influence, provides elasticity during labor.

Vagina. The vagina is a tubular structure 3 to 4 in (7.6 to 10 cm) long. The anterior vaginal wall lies along the urethra and bladder. The posterior vaginal wall is next to the rectum. It is lined with squamous epithelium. In reproductive-age women, the vagina has multiple transverse folds called *rugae*. Vaginal secretions consist of cervical mucus, desquamated epithelium, and, during sexual stimulation, a watery secretion. These fluids help protect against vaginal infection. The muscular and erectile tissue of the vaginal walls allows enough dilation and contraction to accommodate the passage of the fetus during labor and penetration of the penis during intercourse.

Pelvis. The female pelvis consists of 4 bones (2 pelvic bones, sacrum, coccyx) held together by several strong ligaments. The pelvis in females has a larger diameter and is circular. A male pelvis is more heart shaped. The wider female pelvis plays a key role in childbirth. The fetal head adapts its position to the pelvic dimensions during labor and delivery through rotation and flexion to pass through the pelvic inlet.[1]

External Genitalia. The external part of the female reproductive system (Fig. 50.5) is often called the vulva. It consists of the mons pubis, labia majora, labia minora, vestibule, clitoris, urethral meatus, Skene's glands, vaginal introitus (opening), and Bartholin's glands.

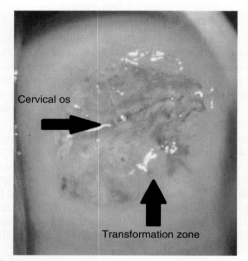

FIG 50.4 Cervical os and squamocolumnar junction (transformation zone). (Courtesy Candy Tedschi, NP, Great Neck, NY.)

The *mons pubis* is a fatty layer lying over the pubic bone. It is covered with coarse hair that lies in a triangular pattern. The labia majora are folds of adipose tissue that form the outer borders of the vulva. The hairless labia minora form the borders of the vaginal orifice and extend anteriorly to enclose the clitoris.

The *vestibule* is the space between the labia minora that is seen when they are held apart. It extends from the clitoris to the *posterior fourchette* (a mucous membrane band that forms the posterior ends of the labia minora). The perineum is the area between the vagina and anus. The vaginal introitus (vaginal opening) is surrounded by thin membranous tissue called the *hymen*. It is usually perforated and has many variations in shape. In the adult woman the hymen usually appears as folds or hymenal tags (*carunculae myrtiformes*). It separates the external genitalia from the vagina.

The *clitoris* is erectile tissue that becomes engorged during sexual excitation. It lies anterior to the urethral meatus and the vaginal orifice and is usually covered by the prepuce. Clitoral stimulation is an important part of sexual activity for many women.

Ducts of the Skene's glands lie alongside the urinary meatus and correspond to the prostate gland in males. We think they help lubricate the urinary meatus. The Bartholin's glands are found at the posterior and lateral aspects of the vaginal orifice. They secrete a thin, mucoid material we think contributes slightly to lubrication during sexual intercourse. These glands are not usually palpable unless sebaceous-like cysts form or they are swollen from an infection, such as a sexually transmitted infection (STI). Bartholin's glands correspond to Cowper's glands in males.

Breasts. The breasts are a secondary sex characteristic that develops during puberty in response to estrogen and progesterone. Cyclic hormonal changes lead to regular changes in breast tissue to prepare it for lactation when fertilization and pregnancy occur.

The breasts extend from the second to the sixth ribs. The extension of breast tissue into the upper-outer quadrant into the axilla is an area referred to as the *tail of Spence* (Fig. 50.6). The fully mature breast is dome shaped and has a pigmented center called the *areola*. The areolar region contains Montgomery's

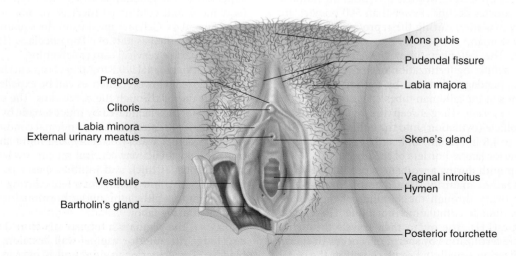

FIG 50.5 External female genitalia. (Modified from Patton KT, Thibodeau GA: *Anatomy and physiology*, ed 8, St Louis, 2013, Mosby.)

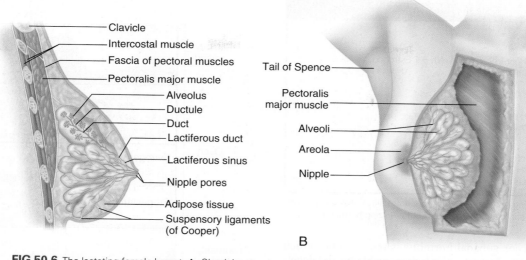

FIG 50.6 The lactating female breast. **A,** Glandular structures are anchored to the overlying skin and the pectoralis muscle by suspensory ligaments of Cooper. Each lobule of glandular tissue is drained by a lactiferous duct that eventually opens through the nipple. **B,** Anterior view of a lactating breast. In nonlactating breasts, glandular tissue is less evident, with adipose tissue making up most of the breast. (Modified from Patton KT, Thibodeau GA: *Anatomy and physiology,* ed 8, St Louis, 2013, Mosby.)

tubercles, which are similar to sebaceous glands. They help lubricate the nipple. During lactation, the alveoli secrete milk. The milk then flows into a ductal system and is transported to the lactiferous sinuses. The nipple has 15 to 20 tiny openings through which the milk flows during breastfeeding. The fibrous and fatty tissue that supports and separates the channels of the mammary duct system is primarily responsible for the varying sizes and shapes of the breasts.

Neuroendocrine Regulation of Reproductive System

The hypothalamus, pituitary gland, and gonads secrete several hormones (Fig. 50.7). (Endocrine hormones are discussed in Chapter 47.) These hormones regulate the processes of ovulation, sperm formation, and fertilization and the formation and function of the secondary sex characteristics. The hypothalamus secretes gonadotropin-releasing hormone (GnRH), which stimulates the anterior pituitary gland to secrete its hormones, including FSH and LH. LH in males is sometimes called *interstitial cell–stimulating hormone (ICSH)*. The gonadal hormones are estrogen, progesterone, and testosterone.

In women, FSH production stimulates the growth and maturity of the ovarian follicles necessary for ovulation. The mature follicle makes estrogen, which in turn suppresses the release of FSH. Another hormone, inhibin, is also secreted by the ovarian follicle. It inhibits both GnRH and FSH secretion. In men, FSH stimulates the seminiferous tubules to make sperm.

LH contributes to the ovulatory process. It causes follicles to complete maturation and undergo ovulation. It affects the development of a ruptured follicle (area where ovum exited during ovulation), which turns into a corpus luteum, which secretes progesterone. **Progesterone** plays a major role in the menstrual cycle, specifically in the secretory phase. It maintains the rich vascular state of the uterus (secretory phase) in preparation for fertilization and implantation. Adequate progesterone is necessary to maintain an implanted ovum. Like estrogen, progesterone is involved in the bodily changes associated with pregnancy. In men, LH triggers testosterone production by the

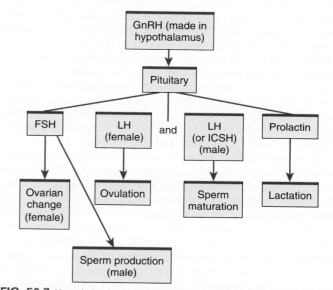

FIG 50.7 Hypothalamic-pituitary-gonadal axis. Only the major pituitary hormone actions are depicted. *FSH,* Follicle-stimulating hormone; *GnRH,* gonadotropin-releasing hormone; *ICSH,* interstitial cell–stimulating hormone; *LH,* luteinizing hormone.

interstitial cells of the testes and thus is essential for the full maturation of sperm.

In women, prolactin stimulates the development and growth of the mammary glands. During lactation, it initiates and maintains milk production. In men, prolactin has no known function.

In women the gonadal hormones, estrogen and progesterone, are made by the ovaries. Small amounts of an estrogen precursor are also made in the adrenal cortices. **Estrogen** is essential to the development and maintenance of the secondary sex characteristics, proliferative phase of the menstrual cycle immediately after menstruation, and uterine changes essential to pregnancy. In men, most estrogen is made in the adrenal cortices. We do not understand the role and importance of estrogen in men.

TABLE 50.1 Gonadal Feedback Mechanisms

Negative Feedback

Female

↓ Estrogen → ↑ GnRH → ↑ FSH (pituitary) → ↑ Estrogen
      (hypothalamus)   (ovaries)

Male

↓ Testosterone → ↑ GnRH → ↑ FSH and LH → ↑ Testosterone
         (hypothalamus) (or ICSH)   (testes)
                 (pituitary)

Positive Feedback

↑ Estrogen → ↑ GnRH → ↑ LH (pituitary)
      (hypothalamus)

FSH, Follicle-stimulating hormone; *GnRH,* gonadotropin-releasing hormone; *ICSH,* interstitial cell–stimulating hormone; *LH,* luteinizing hormone.

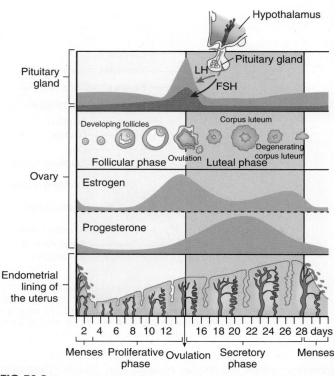

FIG 50.8 Events of the menstrual cycle. The *lines* depict the changes in blood hormone levels, the development of the follicles, and the changes in the endometrium during the cycle. (Modified from Patton KT, Thibodeau GA: *Anatomy and physiology,* ed 8, St Louis, 2013, Mosby.)

In men, the major gonadal hormone is testosterone, which is made by the testes. **Testosterone** is responsible for the development and maintenance of secondary sex characteristics and adequate spermatogenesis. In women, the adrenal glands and ovaries make small amounts of androgens.

The circulating levels of gonadal hormones are controlled primarily by a *negative feedback process.* Receptors within the hypothalamus and pituitary are sensitive to the circulating blood levels of the hormones (Table 50.1). Increased hormone levels stimulate a hypothalamic response to decrease the high circulating levels. Likewise, low circulating levels provoke a hypothalamic response that increases the low circulating levels. For example, low circulating testosterone levels stimulate the hypothalamus to secrete GnRH. This triggers the anterior pituitary to secrete greater amounts of FSH and LH, which in turn cause an increase in the testosterone production. The high level of testosterone signals a decrease in GnRH production, and thus FSH and LH.

In women, however, there is a slight variation in the control of gonadal hormones. The circulating levels are controlled through a combination of both a negative and positive feedback system. A *negative feedback control* mechanism exists similar to that described for men. Low circulating estrogen levels stimulate the hypothalamus to increase its production of GnRH. GnRH stimulates the pituitary to secrete greater amounts of FSH and LH, resulting in increased estrogen production by the ovaries. Higher levels of circulating estrogen result in a decreasing secretion of GnRH and thus a decrease in the secretion of FSH by the pituitary.

Women also have a *positive feedback control* mechanism. Here, with increased levels of circulating estrogen, more GnRH is made, resulting in an increased level of LH from the pituitary. Likewise, low estrogen levels result in a lower level of LH.

Menarche

Menarche is the first episode of menstrual bleeding, indicating that a girl has reached puberty. Menarche usually occurs at around 12 to 13 years of age but can occur as early as 10 years of age in some girls. Menstrual cycles are often irregular for the first 1 to 2 years after menarche because of *anovulatory cycles* (cycles without ovulation).

Menstrual Cycle

The major functions of the ovaries are ovulation and the secretion of hormones. These functions are accomplished during the normal **menstrual cycle,** a monthly process mediated by the hormonal activity of the hypothalamus, pituitary gland, and ovaries. Menstruation occurs during each month in which an ovum is not fertilized (Fig. 50.8). The length of the menstrual cycle ranges from 21 to 35 days, with an average of 28 days. Most women have regular cycles. Irregular cycles may occur and can be due to a variety of factors, including hormonal fluctuations, medications, or conditions, such as uterine fibroids. Table 50.2 describes characteristics of the menstrual cycle and related teaching.

The menstrual cycle is divided into 3 phases. They are labeled in relation to uterine and ovarian changes: (1) the *proliferative,* or *follicular, phase;* (2) the *secretory,* or *luteal, phase;* and (3) the *menstrual,* or *ischemic, phase.* The menstrual cycle begins on the first day of menstruation, which usually lasts 4 to 6 days. The first day of the menstrual cycle is charted as the last menstrual period (LMP). During menstruation, estrogen and progesterone levels are low, but FSH levels begin to increase. During the follicular phase, a single follicle matures fully under FSH stimulation. The mechanism that ensures that usually only 1 follicle reaches maturity is not known. The mature follicle stimulates estrogen production, causing a negative feedback with resulting decreased FSH secretion.

Although the first stage of follicular maturation is stimulated by FSH, complete maturation and ovulation occur only in the presence of LH. When estrogen levels peak on about the 12th day of the cycle, there is a surge of LH, which triggers ovulation 1 or 2 days later. After ovulation, LH promotes the development of the corpus luteum, a temporary functional cyst that forms with the ruptured follicle.

The fully developed corpus luteum continues to secrete estrogen and initiates progesterone secretion. If fertilization occurs,

TABLE 50.2 Patient Teaching

Characteristics of Menstruation

Include the following information when teaching the patient about menstruation:

Characteristic	Teaching
Menarche • Occurs between ages 10 and 16 yr • Average age at onset is 12–13 yr	• See HCP about possible endocrine or developmental abnormality when delayed.
Interval • Usually is 21–35 days • Regular cycles as short as 17 days or as long as 45 days are considered normal if pattern is consistent for the person	• Keep track of periods via an app or calendar to identify menstrual cycle pattern • Expect some irregularity in perimenopausal period • Be aware that drugs (e.g., opioids, contraceptives) and stressful life events can result in missed periods
Duration • Menstrual flow generally lasts 2–8 days	• Realize that pattern is fairly constant but that wide variations do exist
Amount • Menstrual flow varies from 20–80 mL per menses. Average is 30 mL • Amount varies among women and in same woman at different times • It is usually heaviest first 2 days	• Count pads or tampons used per day • The average tampon or pad (when completely saturated) absorbs 20–30 mL • Very heavy flow is indicated by complete soaking of 2 pads in 1–2 hr • Flow increases and then gradually decreases in perimenopausal period • IUD or drugs, such as anticoagulants and thiazides, can cause heavy menses • Women with uterine fibroids may have increased or heavy menses
Composition • Menstrual discharge is mixture of endometrium, blood, mucus, and vaginal cells • Dark red, less viscous than blood, and usually does not clot	• Clots indicate heavy flow or vaginal pooling

estrogen and progesterone continue to be secreted because of the continued activity of the corpus luteum from stimulation by human chorionic gonadotropin (hCG). If fertilization does not take place, menstruation occurs because of a decrease in estrogen production and progesterone withdrawal.

During the *follicular phase,* the endometrial lining of the uterus undergoes change. As more estrogen is made, the endometrial lining goes through proliferative changes, including an increase in the length of blood vessels and glandular tissue.

With ovulation and the resulting increased levels of progesterone, the *luteal* (or *secretory*) *phase* begins. If the corpus luteum regresses (when fertilization does not occur) and estrogen and progesterone levels fall, the endometrial lining can no longer be supported. As a result, the blood vessels contract, and tissue begins to slough (fall away). This sloughing results in the menses and the start of the menstrual phase.

Menopause

Menopause is the physiologic cessation of menses associated with declining ovarian function. It is usually considered complete after 1 year of amenorrhea (absence of menstruation). Menopause is discussed in Chapter 53.

Phases of Sexual Response

The sexual response is a complex interplay of psychologic and physiologic phenomena. It is influenced by several variables (e.g., stress, illness). The changes that occur during sexual excitement are similar for men and women. Masters and Johnson described the sexual response in terms of the excitement, plateau, orgasmic, and resolution phases.[3]

Male Sexual Response. The penis and urethra are essential to the transport of sperm into the vagina and cervix during intercourse. This transport is facilitated by penile erection in response to sexual stimulation during the *excitement phase.* Erection results from the filling of the large venous sinuses within the erectile tissue of the penis. In the flaccid state the sinuses hold only a small amount of blood. During an erection, they are congested with blood. Because the penis is richly endowed with sympathetic, parasympathetic, and pudendal nerve endings, it is readily stimulated to erection. The loose skin of the penis becomes taut from venous congestion. This tautness allows for easy insertion into the vagina.

As the man reaches the *plateau phase,* the erection is maintained. The penis increases in diameter from a slight increase in vasocongestion. Testicle size also increases. Sometimes the glans penis becomes reddish purple.

The contractions of the penile and urethral musculature during the *orgasmic phase* propel the sperm outward through the meatus. In this process, termed *ejaculation,* sperm are released into the ductus deferens. Sperm advance through the urethra, where fluids from the prostate and seminal vesicles are added to the ejaculate. The sperm continue their path through the urethra, receiving a small amount of fluid from the Cowper's glands. They are finally ejaculated through the urinary meatus. *Orgasm* is characterized by the rapid release of vasocongestion and muscular tension through rhythmic contractions. This occurs primarily in the penis, prostate gland, and seminal vesicles. After ejaculation, a man enters the *resolution phase.* The penis undergoes involution, gradually returning to its unstimulated, flaccid state.

Female Sexual Response. The changes that occur in a woman during sexual excitation are similar to those in a man. In response to stimulation, the clitoris becomes congested and vaginal lubrication increases from secretions from the cervix, Bartholin's glands, and vaginal walls. This initial response is the excitation phase.

As excitation is maintained in the plateau phase, the vagina expands, and the uterus is elevated. In the orgasmic phase, contractions occur in the uterus from the fundus to the lower uterine segment. There is a slight relaxation of the cervical os, which helps the entrance of the sperm, and rhythmic contractions of the vagina. Muscular tension is rapidly released through rhythmic contractions in the clitoris, vagina, and uterus. A resolution

TABLE 50.3 Gerontologic Assessment Differences

Reproductive Systems

Structure	Changes	Assessment Findings Abnormalities
Male		
Breasts	Enlargement	Gynecomastia (abnormal enlargement)
Penis	↓ Subcutaneous fat	Easily retractable foreskin (if uncircumcised)
		↓ Size
		Fewer sustained erections
Prostate	Benign hyperplasia	Enlargement, urinary obstruction, incontinence
Testes	↓ Testosterone production	↓ Size, firmness
Female		
Breasts	↓ Subcutaneous fat, increased fibrous tissue, ↓ skin turgor	Less resilient, looser, more pendulous tissue
		↓ Size
		Duct around nipple may feel like stringy strand
Ovaries	↓ Ovarian function	Nonpalpable ovaries are normal postmenopause
Urethra	↓ Muscle tone, mucosal thinning	Possible urinary tract infections, painful urination (dysuria), urgency, frequency, incontinence
Uterus	↓ Thickness of myometrium	Uterine prolapse
Vagina	Tissue atrophy, ↓ muscle tone, alkaline pH	Mucosa becomes pale, dry, smooth and thins
		Vagina narrows and shortens
Vulva	↓ Skin turgor	Atrophy
		↓ Amount of pubic hair
		↓ Size of clitoris and labia

phase follows, in which these organs return to their preexcitation state. However, women do not have to go through the resolution (refractory) recovery state before they can be orgasmic again. They can be multiorgasmic without resolution between orgasms.

Gerontologic Considerations: Effects of Aging on Reproductive Systems

With advancing age, changes occur in the male and female reproductive systems (Table 50.3). In women, many of these changes are related to decreased estrogen production associated with menopause.[4] Decreased estrogen and other sex steroids in postmenopausal women is associated with breast and genital atrophy, reduced bone mass, and increased rate of atherosclerosis. Vaginal dryness may occur, which can lead to urogenital atrophy and changes in the composition of the vaginal *microbiome* (the aggregate of microorganisms and their genetic material in a particular environment).[5]

Testosterone levels decline in men as they age. Manifestations of this decline are more gradual in men and can be physical, psychologic, or sexual. Changes include an increase in prostate size and a decrease in testosterone level, sperm production, muscle tone of the scrotum, and size and firmness of the testicles. Erectile dysfunction (ED) and sexual dysfunction occur in some men because of these changes.

GENDER DIFFERENCES
Effects of Aging on Sexual Function

Men	Women
• ↑ Stimulation necessary for erection	• ↓ Vaginal lubrication
• ↓ Force of ejaculation	• ↓ Sensitivity with labia shrinking and more clitoris exposed
• ↓ Ability to attain or sustain erection	• Difficulty in maintaining arousal
• ↓ Size and rigidity of the penis at full erection	• Difficulty in achieving orgasm after stimulation
• ↓ Libido and interest in sex	• ↓ Libido and interest in sex

Many factors affect sexuality in later life. Gradual changes occur in the sexual responses of men and women. The cumulative effects of these changes, as well as the negative social attitude toward sexuality in older adults, can affect the sexual practices of older adults. Illness, disability, medicines, and surgeries can affect a person's ability to take part in sexual activities.

Nurses play a vital role in providing accurate and unbiased information about sexuality and age. Emphasize the normalcy of sexual activity in older adults and refer them to resources that address such issues.

ASSESSMENT OF MALE AND FEMALE REPRODUCTIVE SYSTEMS

Subjective Data

Important Health Information. In addition to general health information, elicit information specifically related to the reproductive system. Reproduction and sexual issues are often considered extremely personal and private. The extent and depth of the interview about a patient's sexuality and reproductive health depend primarily on your expertise and on the patient's needs and willingness to discuss the topic. Assess your comfort with your own sexuality because any discomfort in questioning becomes obvious to the patient.

A professional demeanor is important when taking a reproductive or sexual history. Develop trust with the patient to elicit such information. Conduct interviews in an environment that provides reassurance, confidentiality, and a nonjudgmental attitude. Be sensitive, use gender-neutral terms when asking about

CASE STUDY
Patient Introduction

A.K. is a 21-yr-old black woman who is being evaluated for pelvic pain and irregular menstrual bleeding for the past several months. She takes oral contraceptive pills orally once daily and naproxen (Aleve) as needed for pain.

(© Benjamin A. Peterson/Mother Image/mother image/Fuse/Thinkstock.)

Discussion Questions

1. What are the possible causes for A.K.'s irregular menstrual bleeding?
2. What assessment questions would you ask A.K.?
3. How would you individualize the assessment based on her age, ethnic/cultural background, and condition?

You will learn more about A.K. and her condition as you read through this assessment chapter.
(See p. 1182 for more information on A.K.)

partners, and maintain an awareness of a patient's culture and beliefs. Begin with the least sensitive information (e.g., menstrual history) before asking questions about more sensitive issues, such as sexual practices or STIs.

Past Health History. The health history should include information about major illnesses, hospitalizations, immunizations, and surgeries. Ask about any infections involving the reproductive system, including STIs. Take a complete obstetric and gynecologic history from the female patient.

Mumps and rubella affect reproductive function. The occurrence of mumps in young men is associated with an increased risk for sterility. Bilateral testicular atrophy may occur from mumps-related orchitis. Ask male patients if they have had mumps, have been immunized with the mumps vaccine, or have any signs of sterility.

Rubella is of primary concern to women of childbearing age. Having rubella during the first 3 months of pregnancy increases the risk for congenital anomalies. So, encourage immunization for all women of childbearing age who have not been immunized for rubella or have not already had the disease. Antibody titers can determine rubella immunity. Women should not be immunized if they are already pregnant.[6] Advise women to avoid becoming pregnant for 1 month after vaccination, or ideally, when their immunity has been confirmed by antibody titers.

Ask the patient about current health status and any acute or chronic health problems. Chronic illnesses, such as cardiovascular disease, respiratory problems, anemia, cancer, and kidney and urinary tract problems, may affect the reproductive system and sexual functioning.

Ask questions relating to possible endocrine disorders, particularly diabetes, hypothyroidism, and hyperthyroidism. These disorders directly interfere with women's menstrual cycles and with sexual performance. Men with diabetes may have ED and retrograde ejaculation. In women with uncontrolled diabetes, pregnancy may pose significant health risks to both the woman and unborn fetus.

Determine if the patient has a history of a stroke. In men, strokes may cause physiologic or psychologic ED. Men who have had a myocardial infarction (MI) may have ED because of fear that sexual activity could precipitate another MI. Post MI medication, such as β-blockers, may affect a man's ability to achieve an erection.[7] Although most patients have concerns about sexual activity after an MI, many are not comfortable expressing these fears to the nurse. Be sensitive to this concern.

Document the patient's allergies, especially if the patient is allergic to latex or drugs, including sulfonamides, macrolides, cephalosporins, tetracyclines, or penicillin. These drugs are often used to treat reproductive and genitourinary (GU) problems, such as STIs and urinary tract infections (UTIs). Silicone and latex are often used in diaphragms and condoms. An allergy to these substances precludes their use as contraceptive methods.

Medications. Document all prescription and over-the-counter drugs that the patient is taking, including the reason for use, dosage, and length of time that the drug has been taken. Ask the patient about the use of herbal products and dietary and nutritional supplements.

Particularly relevant is the use of diuretics (sometimes prescribed for premenstrual edema) and psychotropic agents (which may interfere with sexual performance). Antihypertensives, such as amlodipine (Norvasc), lisinopril (Prinivil), propranolol

(Inderal), and clonidine (Catapres), may cause ED. Use of drugs such as alcohol, marijuana, barbiturates, amphetamines, or cocaine can affect the reproductive system.

In women, document the use of hormonal contraceptives and hormone therapy (HT). The long-term use of combined HT (specifically a combination of oral conjugated equine estrogen and a progestin, *medroxyprogesterone acetate*) is associated with an increased risk for stroke, breast cancer, deep vein thrombosis, and gallbladder disease. These risks are higher in women who also use tobacco products.[8] For postmenopausal women who may have symptoms, such as hot flashes, newer data that suggest that HT does not increase the risk for mortality. Women will need counseling based on their degree of symptoms and associated morbidities to help balance their quality of life with menopausal symptoms.[9]

A history of cholecystitis and hepatitis is important because these conditions may be contraindications for the use of oral contraceptives. Oral contraceptives often aggravate cholecystitis. Chronic liver inflammation generally precludes the use of estrogen products because they are metabolized by the liver. Chronic obstructive pulmonary disease may be a contraindication to oral contraceptive use because progesterone thickens respiratory secretions.

Surgery or Other Treatments. Note any surgical procedures. Common surgical procedures involving the female reproductive system are listed in Table 53.14. Record any therapeutic or spontaneous abortions and type of intervention (e.g., medical versus surgical abortion).

Functional Health Patterns. The key questions to ask a patient with a reproductive problem are outlined in Table 50.4.

Health Perception–Health Management Pattern. The primary focus of this pattern is the patient's perception of his or her own health and measures that the patient takes to maintain health. Ask about self-examination practices and screenings. Mammography and periodic cervical Pap tests are integral to a woman's health. Men are at risk for testicular and prostate cancer. However, controversy exists about the benefits of routine screening for these cancers.[10] All patients should discuss the benefits and risks of screening with their HCP.

> ## ⚕ GENETIC RISK ALERT
>
> - Breast, ovarian, uterine, and prostate cancer have known genetic risk factors.
> - Having a first-degree relative with any of these cancers significantly increases the risk for cancer for the patient.
> - The risk increases if several family members have had these cancers over succeeding generations.
> - Persons with a known hereditary predisposition to breast or ovarian cancer can use this information to make informed decisions about how to minimize their risks.

An accurate family history is avital. Ask about a history of cancer, especially cancer of the reproductive organs. Determine if the patient has a familial tendency for diabetes, hypothyroidism, hyperthyroidism, hypertension, stroke, angina, MI, endocrine disorders, or anemia.

Assessment of the reproductive system is incomplete without knowledge of the patient's lifestyle choices. Determine whether a patient has smoked or is currently smoking, the amount (if any) of alcohol consumption, or if the patient uses illicit drugs. Risks associated with smoking include ectopic pregnancy, miscarriage, an increased risk for perinatal mortality and morbidity,

TABLE 50.4 Health History

Reproductive System

Health Perception–Health Management
- How would you describe your overall health?
- Describe the health of your family members. Any history of breast, uterine, ovarian, or prostate cancer?*

Women
- Do you perform breast self-examination? Any concerns?
- What was the date of your last Pap test and the results?*
- Any prior abnormalities with your Pap tests?
- What was the date of your last mammogram and the results?*
- Any prior abnormalities with your mammograms?

Men
- Do you perform testicular self-examination? Any concerns?

Nutritional-Metabolic
- Describe what you usually eat and drink.
- Have you had any changes in weight?*
- How do you feel about your current weight?
- Do you take any nutritional supplements, such as calcium or vitamins?*
- Do you have any dietary restrictions?*

Elimination
- Do you have problems with urination (e.g., pain, burning, dribbling, incontinence, frequency)?*
- Have you had bladder infections? If so, when? How often?
- Do you have problems with bowel movements?*
- Do you have any constipation, loose stools, or blood with stools?*
- Do you use laxatives?*

Activity-Exercise
- What activities do you typically do each day?
- Do you have enough energy for your desired activities?

Sleep-Rest
- How many hours do you typically sleep each night?
- Do you feel rested after sleep?
- Do you have any problems associated with sleeping?*

Cognitive-Perceptual
- Do you have pain? If yes, where?
- Do you have pain during sexual activity or intercourse?*

Self-Perception–Self-Concept
- How would you describe yourself?
- Have there been any recent changes that have made you feel differently about yourself?*
- Are you having any problems that are affecting your sexuality?*

Role-Relationship
- Describe your living arrangements. With whom do you live?
- Do you have a significant other? If yes, is this relationship satisfying?
- Are you having any role-related problems in your family?* At work?*
- What are the relationships among your family members?

Sexuality-Reproductive
- Are you sexually active? If so, how many partners do you have?
- What kind of sex do you engage in (e.g., oral, vaginal, anal)?
- How do you protect yourself against sexually transmitted infections and unwanted pregnancy?
- Are you satisfied with your present means of sexual expression? If not, explain.
- Have you had any recent changes in your sexual practices?*

Women
- How old were you when you had your first menstrual period? (Menarche)
- What was the first day of your last menstrual period?
- Describe your period. How many days does it last? How often does it come (e.g., every 28 days)?
- Do you have pain with your period? Do you pass clots?
- Do you feel your flow is heavy or excessive?
- How old were you when you went through menopause?
- Have you had any postmenopausal bleeding or spotting?*
- Pregnancy history: How many times have you been pregnant? How many living children do you have? Have you ever had any miscarriages or abortions? Did they need medical intervention?

Men
- Do you have any problem obtaining or sustaining an erection?
- Do you have any problems with ejaculation?

Coping–Stress Tolerance
- Have there been any major changes in your life within the past couple of years?*
- What is stressful in your life right now?
- How do you handle health problems when they occur?
- Do you feel safe in your home? Work? Has anyone ever tried to hurt or harm you?

Value-Belief
- What beliefs do you have about your health and illnesses?
- Do you use home remedies?*
- Is religion an important part of your life?*
- Do you think that any of your personal beliefs or values may be compromised because of your treatment?*

*If yes, describe.

placental abnormalities, preterm delivery, and congenital facial defects of the fetus.[11] Smoking increases the risk for morbidity and mortality in women who use oral contraceptives. Smoking in women is also associated with early menopause.[5] Decreased sperm counts and ED are seen in male smokers. Smoking is a known cofactor for persistence of *human papillomavirus* (HPV) infection for oral and anogenital cancers among men and women.[12]

Nutritional-Metabolic Pattern. Anemia is a common problem in women in their reproductive years, particularly during pregnancy and the postpartum period. Evaluate the adequacy of the diet with this condition in mind. Iron-deficiency anemia is the most common cause of anemia in menstruating females.

Take a thorough nutritional and psychologic history to assess for the presence of an eating disorder. Anorexia nervosa can cause amenorrhea and other problems, such as osteoporosis, that are related to menopause. Obesity can be related to polycystic ovarian syndrome and may be a precursor to type 2 diabetes.

From early adolescence, teach women about adequate calcium and vitamin D intake to prevent osteoporosis. Estimate the patient's daily calcium intake to determine whether supplementation is needed. Evaluate folic acid intake for women in their reproductive years because a deficiency can result in spina bifida and other fetal neural tube defects.[13]

Elimination Pattern. Many gynecologic problems can result in GU problems. Urinary incontinence is common in older women. Factors associated with female incontinence include relaxation of the pelvic musculature caused by multiple births, advancing age, fibroid tumors, diabetes, obesity, and weight gain. Condom, diaphragm, and spermicide use is associated with an increased risk for UTIs. Vaginal infections, such as bacterial vaginosis (BV), facilitate the growth of *Escherichia coli,* which causes most UTIs.[14] Men may have urethritis, an inflammation of the urethra, which may be caused by an STI. Urethritis can cause painful urination. Benign prostatic hyperplasia (BPH) is common in older men. It can cause urinary retention or difficulty in starting the urinary stream.

Activity-Exercise Pattern. Record the amount, type, and intensity of activity and exercise. Lack of weight-bearing exercise is an important factor in the development of osteoporosis, especially in postmenopausal women. Adolescent females who engage in excessive leanness sports may have *female athlete triad.* It is characterized by secondary amenorrhea, low energy availability, and osteoporosis.[15] Anemia can result in fatigue and activity intolerance and interfere with satisfactory performance of activities of daily living.

Sleep-Rest Pattern. Sleep patterns for women may be affected during the postpartum period and while raising young children. Hot flashes and sweating during perimenopause can cause serious sleep interruption when the woman awakens in a drenching sweat. The need to change her nightgown and bedding further disrupts her sleep. Insomnia is common among perimenopausal women. Daytime fatigue can result from sleep problems. In men, frequent urination at night associated with prostate enlargement or hormone therapy for prostate cancer can disturb sleep.

Cognitive-Perceptual Pattern. Pelvic pain is associated with various gynecologic disorders, such as pelvic inflammatory disease, ovarian cysts, and *endometriosis.* Dyspareunia (painful intercourse) can be problematic for women in the postmenopausal period. The pain associated with intercourse can create a reluctance to take part in sexual activity and strain relationships with sexual partners. Refer women with dyspareunia to their HCP.

Self-Perception–Self-Concept Pattern. Changes that occur with aging, such as pendulous breasts and vaginal dryness in women and decreased penis size in men, may lead to emotional distress. The subtle changes associated with sexuality and advancing age may affect self-concept.

Role-Relationship Pattern. Obtain information about the family structure and occupation. Ask about recent changes in work-related relationships or family conflict. Assess the patient's role in the family as a starting point to determine family dynamics. Roles and relationships are affected by changes within the family. The addition of a new baby may change family dynamics.

Sexuality-Reproductive Pattern. For women, obtain a menstrual and a chronologic obstetric history. The menstrual history includes the first day of the LMP, description of menstrual flow, age of menarche, and, if applicable, age at menopause. Menstrual history data are used in the detection of pregnancy, infertility, and many gynecologic problems. Have the patient describe any changes in her usual menstrual pattern

TABLE 50.5 Sexual History Format

The Five Ps of Taking a Sexual History*

The 5 Ps	Questions
1. Partners	Are you currently sexually active? (yes or no) • Do you have sex with men, women, or both? • In the past 2 months, with how many partners have you had sex? • In the past 12 months, with how many partners have you had sex?
2. Practices	To understand your risk for STIs, I need to understand the kind of sex you have had recently. • Genital (penis in the vagina) • Anal (penis in the anus) • Oral (mouth on penis, vagina, or anus)
3. Protection from STIs	Do you and your partner(s) use any protection against STIs? • What kind? • How often?
4. Past history of STIs	Have you ever been diagnosed with an STI? • What type? • When? • How were you treated?
5. Prevention of pregnancy	Are you or your partner trying to get pregnant? • If not, what are you doing to prevent pregnancy?

Adapted from *www.cdc.gov/std/treatment/sexualhistory.pdf.*
*Modify this guide as needed to be culturally appropriate based on culture or gender dynamics.

to determine whether the change is transient and unimportant or connected with a more serious gynecologic problem. Terminology that describes abnormal uterine bleeding patterns is discussed in Chapter 53.

Identify changes in menstrual patterns associated with the use of oral contraceptives, intrauterine devices (IUDs), birth control patches, vaginal rings, progestin-only implants, or medroxyprogesterone injections. Oral contraceptives usually decrease the amount and duration of flow. Some IUDs can increase menstrual flow. Some IUDs are used for both contraception and as a nonsurgical treatment for heavy menstrual bleeding.

The obstetric history includes the number of pregnancies, full-term births, preterm births, stillbirths, living children, and abortions (including spontaneous [miscarriage], ectopic, or induced). Document the course of each pregnancy, including the duration of each pregnancy, date of delivery, problems that may have occurred with each pregnancy, and any medical or surgical interventions that were needed.

Table 50.5 outlines *The 5 Ps of Sexual Health* approach for taking a sexual history. Never make an assumption about a patient's sexual orientation. Ask both men and women about their general satisfaction with their sexuality. Ask the patient about sexual beliefs and practices and whether they achieve orgasm. Explore any unexplained change in sexual practices or performance. Reproductive problems can cause physiologic or psychologic problems that can lead to painful intercourse, ED, sexual dysfunction, or infertility.

Coping-Stress Tolerance Pattern. The stress related to situations such as pregnancy or menopause increases dependence on support systems. Determine whom the support people are in the patient's life. The diagnosis of an STI can cause stress for the patient and partner. Explore ways to manage this stress with patients by encouraging them to share their fears and concerns.

Value-Belief Pattern. Sexual and reproductive functioning is closely related to cultural, religious, moral, and ethical values. Be aware of your own beliefs in these areas. Recognize and sensitively react to the patient's personal beliefs associated with reproductive and sexuality issues.

CASE STUDY—cont'd
Subjective Data

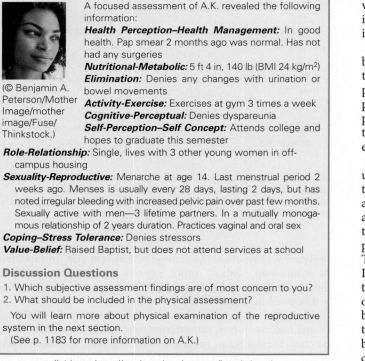

(© Benjamin A. Peterson/Mother Image/mother image/Fuse/Thinkstock.)

A focused assessment of A.K. revealed the following information:

Health Perception–Health Management: In good health. Pap smear 2 months ago was normal. Has not had any surgeries

Nutritional-Metabolic: 5 ft 4 in, 140 lb (BMI 24 kg/m²)

Elimination: Denies any changes with urination or bowel movements

Activity-Exercise: Exercises at gym 3 times a week

Cognitive-Perceptual: Denies dyspareunia

Self-Perception–Self Concept: Attends college and hopes to graduate this semester

Role-Relationship: Single, lives with 3 other young women in off-campus housing

Sexuality-Reproductive: Menarche at age 14. Last menstrual period 2 weeks ago. Menses is usually every 28 days, lasting 2 days, but has noted irregular bleeding with increased pelvic pain over past few months. Sexually active with men—3 lifetime partners. In a mutually monogamous relationship of 2 years duration. Practices vaginal and oral sex

Coping–Stress Tolerance: Denies stressors

Value-Belief: Raised Baptist, but does not attend services at school

Discussion Questions

1. Which subjective assessment findings are of most concern to you?
2. What should be included in the physical assessment?

You will learn more about physical examination of the reproductive system in the next section.

(See p. 1183 for more information on A.K.)

Objective Data

Physical Examination: Male. The examination of the male external genitalia by the nurse includes inspection and palpation of the pubis, penis, and scrotum. The patient may be lying or standing. The standing position is preferred. Sit in front of the standing patient. Use gloves during examination of the male genitalia.

If breast cancer is suspected or there is a strong family history of breast cancer in a male patient, a clinical breast examination is conducted in the same pattern for a male patient as a female breast examination (see Fig. 51.1).

Pubis. Assess for hair distribution and presence of body lice. Normally, the hair is in a diamond-shaped pattern and coarser than scalp hair. The absence of hair is not a normal finding unless the man is shaving or waxing the pubic hair. Carefully assess the skin for irritation and inflammation.

Penis and Scrotum. Inspect the penis for any lesions, bleeding, or swelling. Note the location of the urethral meatus and the presence of a foreskin. If present, retract the foreskin and note any redness, discharge, irritation, lesions, or swelling from the meatus. Replace the foreskin over the glans after observation.

Inspect the scrotum by lifting each testis to inspect all sides of the scrotal sac. Palpate the testes for tenderness or masses. The left testis usually hangs lower than the right. An undescended testis *(cryptorchidism)* is a major risk factor for testicular cancer and a potential cause of male infertility.

Anus. Note if the buttocks have any lesions, swelling, or inflammation. Spread the buttocks apart with both hands to expose the anus. Inspect the anal sphincter and perineal regions for fissures, lesions, masses, and hemorrhoids. The anus should be free from inflammation or skin changes.

Physical Examination: Female. With a chaperone present, physical examination of women often begins with inspection and palpation of the breasts and axillae then proceeds to the abdomen and genitalia. Examining the abdomen provides an opportunity to detect pain or any masses that may involve the GU system. Abdominal examination is discussed in Chapter 38.

Breasts. To perform a breast examination, first examine the breasts by visual inspection. With the patient seated, inspect the breasts for symmetry, size, shape, skin color, vascular patterns, dimpling, and unusual lesions. Ask the patient to put the arms at the sides, arms overhead, lean forward, and press hands on hips. Observe for any abnormalities during these maneuvers. Palpate the axillae and clavicular areas for enlarged lymph nodes.

After the patient assumes the supine position, place a pillow under the back on the side to be examined. Ask the patient to put the arm above and behind the head. This flattens breast tissue and make palpation easier. Then palpate the breast in a systematic fashion, preferably using a vertical line (see Fig. 51.1). Use the distal finger pads of the index, middle, and ring fingers for palpation. Include the axillary tail of Spence in the examination. This area of the breast lies adjacent to the upper outer quadrant. It is where most breast cancer develops. Palpate the area around the areolae for masses. Document the color, consistency, and odor of any discharge. For patients at average risk who have no breast symptoms, the benefit of routine clinical breast examinations to detect early breast cancer is unclear. Teach patients to be familiar with how their breasts feel and report any significant changes or concerns to an HCP.[16]

External Genitalia. The examination of a woman's genitalia by the nurse includes inspection and palpation of the mons pubis, vulva, and anus. Use gloves for the examination. Assess for hair distribution, presence of body lice, lesions, redness, edema, or discharge. Many women remove hair from the genital region via shaving, waxing, or laser hair removal and may develop folliculitis (infection of the hair follicle). Separate the labia to fully inspect the clitoris, urethral meatus, and vaginal orifice. Spread the buttocks apart to inspect the anus for fissures, lesions, and hemorrhoids.

Internal Pelvic Examination. HCPs with advanced or specialized training usually do this part of the examination. During the speculum examination, the HCP inspects the walls of the vagina and cervix for inflammation, discharge, polyps, and suspicious growths. A Pap test and specimens for nucleic acid amplification tests (NAATs) for STI sampling and microscopic examination may be obtained. After the speculum examination, a bimanual examination may be done to assess the size, shape, and consistency of the uterus and ovaries. The ovaries and tubes are not normally palpable.

Table 50.6 gives an example of a recording format for the physical assessment findings for the male and female

TABLE 50.6 Normal Physical Assessment of Reproductive System

Male	Female
Breasts	
Nipples soft. No lumps, nodules, swelling, or enlarged tissue noted.	Symmetric without dimpling. Nipples soft. No drainage, retraction, or lesions noted. No masses or tenderness. No lymphadenopathy.
External Genitalia	
Diamond-shaped hair distribution. No penile lesions or discharge noted. Scrotum symmetric, no masses, descended testes. No inguinal hernia.	Triangular hair distribution. Genitalia dark pink, no lesions, redness, swelling, or inflammation in perineal region. No vaginal discharge noted. No tenderness with palpation of Skene's ducts and Bartholin's glands.
Anus	
No hemorrhoids, fissures, or lesions noted.	No hemorrhoids, fissures, or lesions noted.

CASE STUDY—cont'd

Objective Data: Physical Examination

(© Benjamin A. Peterson/Mother Image/mother image/Fuse/Thinkstock.)

Focused assessment of A.K. reveals the following: BP is 118/76 mm Hg; her pulse is 70 beats/min and regular. Skin warm and dry without lesions. No cyanosis of lips, mucous membranes, or nail beds. Thyroid is not enlarged. Heart examination is normal. Abdomen soft and nontender. External genitalia examination is normal. Bimanual examination by the HCP is negative for cervical motion tenderness, uterine anomalies. She has pain on left side with palpation of a soft mass consistent with an ovarian cyst.

Discussion Questions

1. Based on the subjective and objective assessment findings, what diagnostic tests would you anticipate being ordered for A.K.?

You will learn more about diagnostic studies related to the reproductive system in the next section.

(See p. 1183 for more information on A.K.)

Answers available at *http://evolve.elsevier.com/Lewis/medsurg.*

reproductive systems. Tables 50.7 through 50.9 summarize assessment abnormalities of the breasts, female reproductive system, and male reproductive system, respectively.

A *focused assessment* is used to evaluate the status of previously identified reproductive problems and to monitor for signs of new problems. A focused assessment of the reproductive system is presented in the box on this page.

DIAGNOSTIC STUDIES OF REPRODUCTIVE SYSTEMS

The most common diagnostic studies used to assess the reproductive systems are described in Tables 50.10 through 50.14. Diagnostic studies of the endocrine system may also be done in a person with a reproductive system problem (see Tables 47.6 and 47.7).

FOCUSED ASSESSMENT

Reproductive System

Use this checklist to ensure the key assessment steps have been done.

Subjective

Ask the patient about any of the following and note responses.

Vaginal or vulvar: discharge, lesions, itching, unusual bleeding, odor	Y	N
Penile pain, lesions, discharge	Y	N
Medications: oral contraceptives, antihypertensives, psychotropics, hormones	Y	N
Clinical examinations of reproductive systems (breast, pelvis, testicular, prostate) and results	Y	N
Pain: abdomen, pelvis, or genitalia	Y	N

Objective: Diagnostic

Check the following for results and critical values.

Serum/urine hCG	✓
Serum PSA	✓
CBC	✓
Hormone studies (testosterone, progesterone, estrogen, FSH, LH, TSH)	✓
NAAT STI results (e.g., *Chlamydia*, gonorrhea, *Trichomonas*)	✓
In office testing (e.g., wet mounts, pH assessment)	✓
Mammography and/or ultrasound of breasts	✓
Ultrasound: abdominal, pelvic, transvaginal, prostate	✓

Objective: Physical Examination

Inspect

External genitalia for redness, swelling, discharge, lesions	✓
Breasts for swelling, dimpling, retraction, drainage, redness, skin changes, masses,	✓

Palpate

Breast tissue for masses or tenderness	✓
External genitalia: tenderness, pain	✓

hCG, Human chorionic gonadotropin; *PSA,* prostate-specific antigen.

CASE STUDY—cont'd

Objective Data: Diagnostic Studies

(© Benjamin A. Peterson/Mother Image/mother image/Fuse/Thinkstock.)

The following laboratory and diagnostic tests are ordered for A.K.:

Urine pregnancy test, urinalysis, pelvic and transvaginal ultrasound, complete blood count (CBC), thyroid stimulating hormone (TSH), gonorrhea and chlamydia NAAT testing. Her results are:

Urine pregnancy test: Negative

Urinalysis: Normal

CBC: hemoglobin, 13.2 g/dL, hematocrit, 36%

TSH: 2.3 IU/L

Gonorrhea and chlamydia tests: Negative

The pelvic and transvaginal ultrasound revealed a 4-cm ovarian cyst.

Discussion Questions

1. Which diagnostic and laboratory test results are of concern to you?
2. What patient teaching can you provide A.K. based on her diagnostic test results?

Answers available at *http://evolve.elsevier.com/Lewis/medsurg.*

TABLE 50.7 Assessment Abnormalities

Breast

Finding	Description	Possible Etiology and Significance
Dimpling	Unilateral, recent onset, no pain	Cancer
Nipple inversion or retraction	Recent onset, redness, pain, unilateral	Abscess, inflammation, cancer
	Recent onset (usually within past year), unilateral presentation, lack of tenderness	Cancer
Nipple scaling or irritation	Unilateral or bilateral presentation, crusting, possible ulceration	Paget's disease, eczema, infection
Nipple secretions		
• Galactorrhea (female)	Milky, no relationship to lactation, unilateral or bilateral, intermittent or consistent presentation	Drug therapy, especially phenothiazines, tricyclic antidepressants, methyldopa. Hypofunction or hyperfunction of thyroid or adrenal glands. Hypothalamus or pituitary tumor. Excess estrogen. Prolonged suckling or breast foreplay
• Galactorrhea (male)	Milky, bilateral presentation	Chorioepithelioma of testes, pituitary tumor
• Multicolored or dark green discharge	Thick, sticky, and often bilateral	Ductal ectasia (dilation of mammary ducts)
• Purulent	Gray-green or yellow color. Frequent unilateral presentation. Association with pain, redness, induration, nipple inversion	Puerperal (after birth) mastitis (inflammatory condition of breast) or abscess
	Same as above but usually without nipple inversion	Infected sebaceous cyst
• Serosanguineous or bloody drainage	Unilateral presentation	Papillomatosis (widespread development of nipple-like growths), intraductal papilloma, cancer (male and female)
• Serous discharge	Clear appearance, unilateral or bilateral, intermittent or consistent presentation	Intraductal papilloma
Nodules, lumps, or masses	Multiple, bilateral, well-delineated, soft or firm, mobile cysts. Pain. Premenstrual occurrence	Fibrocystic changes
	Rubbery consistency, fluid-filled interior, pain	Ductal ectasia
	Soft, mobile, well-delineated cyst, absence of pain	Lipoma, fibroadenoma
	Redness, tenderness, induration	Infected sebaceous cysts, abscesses
	Usually singular, hard, irregularly shaped, poorly delineated, nonmobile	Cancer

TABLE 50.8 Assessment Abnormalities

Female Reproductive System

Finding and Description	Possible Etiology and Significance
Vulvar Discharge	
Thin gray or white, copious flow, malodorous or fishy, vulvar irritation	Bacterial vaginosis infection
White, thick, curdy, frequent itching and inflammation, lack of odor or yeast-like smell	Candidiasis (*Candida* or yeast infection), vaginitis
Mucopurulent discharge; bloody discharge	*Chlamydia trachomatis* or *Neisseria gonorrhoeae* infection, menstruation, trauma, cancer
Frothy green or yellow color; malodorous	*Trichomonas vaginalis*
Vulvar Redness	
Bright or beefy red color, itching	*Candida albicans*, allergy, chemical vaginitis
Reddened base, painful vesicles or ulcerations	Genital herpes
Macules or papules, itching	Chancroid, contact dermatitis, scabies, pediculosis
Vulvar Growths	
Soft, fleshy growth, nontender	Condyloma acuminatum (genital warts)
Flat and warty appearance, nontender	Condyloma latum
Same as either of above, possible pain	Cancer
Reddened base, vesicles, and small erosions; pain	Lymphogranuloma venereum, genital herpes, chancroid
Indurated, firm ulcers, no pain	Chancre (syphilis), granuloma inguinale
Abdominal Pain, Tenderness, or Pelvic Masses	
Intermittent or consistent tenderness in right or left lower quadrant	Salpingitis (infection of fallopian tube), ectopic pregnancy, ruptured ovarian cyst, PID, tubal or ovarian abscess
Periumbilical location, consistent occurrence	Cystitis, endometritis (inflammation of endometrium), ectopic pregnancy
Abdominal or pelvic pain, especially with menses, which radiates to back, rectum or vagina.	Endometriosis (a disorder in which the endometrial lining grows on pelvic organs or outside the pelvis in rare cases)
Pelvic masses	Fibroids, ovarian cysts (typically benign); Cancer or metastases (requires additional testing and treatment)

PID, Pelvic inflammatory disease.

TABLE 50.9 Assessment Abnormalities

Male Reproductive System

Finding and Description	Possible Etiology and Significance
Penile Growths or Masses	
Indurated, smooth, disk-like appearance. Absence of pain. Singular presentation	Chancre (syphilis)
Papular to irregularly shaped ulceration with pus, lack of induration	Chancroid
Ulceration with induration and nodularity	Cancer
Flat, wartlike nodule	Condyloma latum
Raised, fleshy, moist, elongated projections with single or multiple projections	Condyloma acuminatum (genital warts)
Localized swelling with retracted, tight foreskin	Paraphimosis (inability to replace foreskin to its normal position after retraction), trauma
Vesicles, Erosions, or Ulcers	
Painful, reddened base. Vesicular or small erosions	Genital herpes, balanitis (inflammation of glans penis), chancroid
Painless, singular, small erosion with eventual lymphadenopathy	Lymphogranuloma venereum, cancer
Scrotal Masses	
Localized swelling with tenderness, unilateral or bilateral presentation	Epididymitis (inflammation of epididymis), testicular torsion, orchitis (mumps)
Swelling, tenderness	Incarcerated hernia
Swelling without pain. Unilateral or bilateral presentation. Translucent, cordlike or wormlike appearance	Hydrocele (accumulation of fluid in outer covering of testes), spermatocele (firm, sperm-containing cyst of epididymis), varicocele (dilation of veins that drain testes), hematocele (accumulation of blood within scrotum)
Firm, nodular testes or epididymis. Frequent unilateral presentation	Tuberculosis, cancer
Penile Discharge	
Clear to purulent color, minimal to copious flow	Urethritis or gonorrhea, *Chlamydia trachomatis* infection, trauma
Penile or Scrotal Redness	
Macules and papules	Scabies, pediculosis
Inguinal Masses	
Bulging unilateral presentation during straining	Inguinal hernia
1- to 3-cm nodules	Lymphadenopathy

TABLE 50.10 Serology Studies

Male and Female Reproductive Systems

Study	Reference Interval	Description and Purpose
Anti-müllerian hormone (AMH)	*Female:* 13–45 yr: 0.9–9.5 ng/mL >45 yr: <1.0 ng/mL	Measures ovarian function. Level reflects size of the remaining egg supply ("ovarian reserve"). May be done when a woman has manifestations of polycystic ovarian syndrome (PCOS). Used to monitor AMH-producing ovarian tumor. Females with high AMH levels have a better response to ovarian stimulation during fertility treatments.
Estradiol	*Female:* Follicular phase: 20–350 pg/mL (73–1285 pmol/L) Luteal phase: 30–450 pg/mL (110–1652 pmol/L) Postmenopause: ≤20 pg/mL (≤73 pmol/L) *Male:* 10–50 pg/mL (37–184 pmol/L)	Measures ovarian function. Useful in assessing estrogen-secreting tumors and states of precocious female puberty. May be used to confirm perimenopausal status. Increased levels in men may indicate testicular tumor.
Follicle-stimulating hormone (FSH)	In 24-hr urine samples: *Female:* Follicular phase: 2–15 U/24 hr Midcycle: 8–60 U/24 hr Luteal phase: 2–10 U/24 hr Postmenopause: 35–100 U/24 hr *Male:* 3–11 U/24 hr In blood: *Female:* Follicular phase: 1.37–9.9 mU/mL Ovulatory phase: 6.17–17.2 mU/mL Luteal phase: 1.09–9.2 mU/mL Postmenopause: 19.3–100.6 mU/mL *Male:* 1.42–15.4 mU/mL	Assesses gonadal function. Abnormal levels may indicate pituitary tumors or dysfunction. Increased in menopause. May be used to confirm menopausal status.

Continued

TABLE 50.10 Serology Studies

Male and Female Reproductive Systems—cont'd

Study	Reference Interval	Description and Purpose
Human chorionic gonadotropin (hCG)	Qualitative: Negative Quantitative: <5 mIU/mL (<5 IU/L) (males and non-pregnant females)	Detects pregnancy. Detects hydatidiform mole and chorioepithelioma (in men and women). Done with urine or blood.
Luteinizing hormone (LH)	*Female:* Premenopause: 5–25 IU/L, with higher peaks at ovulation Postmenopause: 14–52.3 IU/L *Male:* 1.8–8.6 IU/L	Associated with ovulation in women and testosterone production in men. Used in women in the workup of infertility and menstrual irregularities.
Progesterone	*Female:* Follicular phase: 15–70 ng/dL (0.5–2.2 nmol/L) Luteal phase: 200–2500 ng/dL (6.4–79.5 nmol/L) Postmenopause: <40 ng/dL (1.28 nmol/L) *Male:* 13–97 ng/dL (0.4–3.1 nmol/L)	Used to assess infertility, monitors success of drugs for infertility or the effect of progesterone treatment, determines whether ovulation is occurring. Diagnoses problems with adrenal glands and some types of cancer.
Prolactin	*Female:* 3.8–23.2 ng/mL (3.8–23.2 mg/L) *Male:* 3.0–14.7 ng/mL (3.0–14.7 mg/L)	Detects pituitary dysfunction that can cause amenorrhea, decreased libido, and impotence.
Prostate-specific antigen (PSA)	*Male:* <4 ng/mL (<4 mcg/L)	Detects prostate cancer. Used to monitor response to therapy.
Testosterone	In 24-hr urine samples: *Female:* 2–12 mcg/24 hr (6.9–41.6 nmol/24 hr) *Male:* 40–135 mcg/24 hr (139–469 nmol/24 hr) In blood: *Female:* 15–70 ng/dL (0.52–2.43 nmol/L) *Male:* 280–1100 ng/dL (10.4–38.17 nmol/L)	Detects tumors and developmental anomalies of the testicles. Used to assess male infertility.

TABLE 50.11 Radiologic Studies

Male and Female Reproductive System

Study	Description and Purpose
CT scan of pelvis	Detects tumors in the pelvis.
Mammography	X-ray image used to assess breast tissue. Detects benign and malignant masses. Mammography screening guidelines are discussed in Chapter 51.
MRI	Radio waves and magnetic field are used to assess soft tissue. Useful after an abnormal mammogram or in women with dense breast tissue. Breast MRI may be with mammography to detect breast cancer in women at high risk for breast cancer. Used to diagnose abnormalities in female and male reproductive systems.
Ultrasound (US) (breast, pelvic, testicular, transvaginal [TV], rectal [TRUS])	Measures and records high-frequency sound waves as they pass through tissues of variable density. Breast US: Used to detect fluid-filled masses and for follow-up screening after mammography in women with dense breast tissue. Pelvic and TV US: In women, used to detect pelvic masses, such as ectopic pregnancy, ovarian cysts, fibroids, and cancer. Testicular US: Detects testicular masses and testicular torsion. TRUS: Used to diagnose prostate tumors.

TABLE 50.12 Interventional Studies

Study	Description and Purpose	Nursing Responsibility
Colposcopy	Direct visualization of cervix with binocular microscope. Allows magnification of cervix and study of cellular abnormalities. Used as follow-up for abnormal Pap test and for examination of women exposed to DES in utero. Cervical biopsy(ies) may be taken. Assesses for vaginal or vulvar dysplasia.	*Before:* Teach patient about the procedure. Tell patient this test is similar to a speculum examination. *After:* If a biopsy was done, tell patient she may have some vaginal bleeding and to avoid sexual intercourse until healed.
Conization	Cone-shaped sample of squamocolumnar tissue of cervix is removed for direct study.	*Before:* Teach patient about the procedure. Requires use of surgical facilities and anesthesia. *After:* Tell patient to avoid sexual intercourse and tampons for 3–4 wk. May have some discharge or spotting for 1 wk. 3-wk follow-up necessary.
Dilation and curettage (D&C)	Operative procedure that dilates cervix and allows curetting of endometrial lining. Used in assessment of abnormal bleeding and cytologic evaluation of lining.	*Before:* Teach patient about procedure and sedation. *After:* Assess degree of bleeding with frequent pad check during first 24 hr.

TABLE 50.12 Interventional Studies—cont'd

Study	Description and Purpose	Nursing Responsibility
Hysterosalpingo-gram (HSG)	Involves instillation of contrast media through cervix into uterine cavity and through fallopian tubes. X-ray images taken to detect abnormalities of uterus and its adnexa (ovaries and tubes) as contrast progresses through them. Most useful in diagnostic assessment of fertility (e.g., to detect adhesions near ovary, abnormal uterine shape, blockage of tubal pathways).	*Before:* Teach patient about procedure and that it may be uncomfortable. Contrast medium is used. *After:* Tell patient she may have slight vaginal bleeding and cramping. Monitor for foul-smelling vaginal discharge, severe pain, fever, or chills.
Hysteroscopy	Allows visualization of uterine lining through insertion of scope through cervix. Used to diagnose and treat abnormal bleeding, such as polyps and fibroids. Biopsy may be done during procedure. May be part of infertility assessment.	*Before:* Should be NPO for at least 6 hr prior. May be done in the HCP's office or an outpatient setting. *After:* Tell patient that mild cramping and slight bloody discharge is normal.
Laparoscopy	Allows visualization of pelvic structures via fiberoptic scopes inserted through small abdominal incisions. Instillation of CO_2 into the abdominal cavity improves visualization. Used in diagnostic assessment of uterus, tubes, and ovaries (Fig. 50.9). Often used for tubal sterilization or part of infertility assessment.	*Before:* Prepare patient for vaginal operation with preoperative teaching and sedation. *After:* Tell patient referred shoulder pain is likely from residual gas in the abdomen. A heating pad may help. A slight discharge or spotting for 2–5 days is normal.
Loop electrosur-gical excision procedure (LEEP)	Excision of cervical tissue via an electrosurgical instrument. Diagnoses and treats cervical dysplasia. Minimal amount of tissue removed and preserves childbearing ability.	*Before:* Teach about procedure. May be done in the HCP's office. Patient may feel slight tingling or abdominal cramping during procedure. *After:* Tell patient that discharge, bleeding, and cramping may occur for 1–3 days.
Ultrasound-guided biopsy	Use of ultrasound guidance while performing a biopsy. Ultrasound used to direct the biopsy needle into the region of interest and obtain a sample of tissue. Can diagnose infection, inflammation, or mass.	*Before:* Teach about procedure. Usually done as an outpatient. *After:* Tell patient to monitor for signs and symptoms of infection at biopsy site.

DES, Diethylstilbestrol.

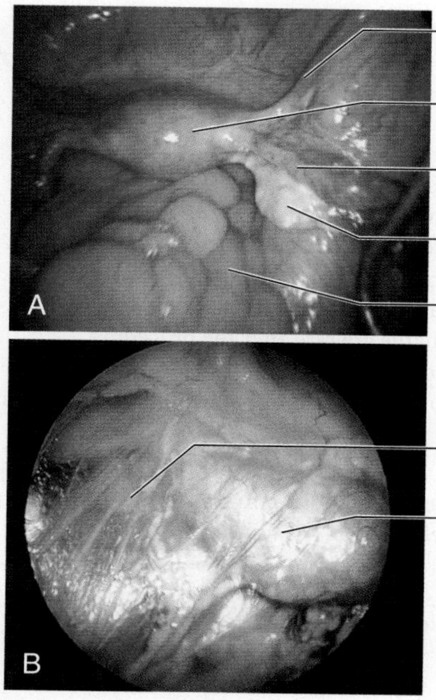

FIG 50.9 Laparoscopic views of the female pelvis. A, Normal image. B, Pelvic inflammatory disease. (Note reddish inflammatory membrane covering and fixing the ovary and uterus to the surrounding structures.) (*A,* From Abrahams P, Marks S, Hutching R: *McMinn's color atlas of human anatomy,* ed 5, Philadelphia, 2003, Saunders. *B,* From Symonds EM, MacPherson MB: *Color atlas of obstetrics and gynecology,* London, 1994, Mosby Wolfe.)

Labels for A: Round ligament; Uterus (fundus); Uterine tube; Ovary; Sigmoid colon

Labels for B: Uterus (fundus); Uterine tube (swollen)

TABLE 50.13 Cytology and Microbiologic Studies

Study	Description and Purpose
Cultures	Specimens from urine to assess for gonorrhea, chlamydia or UTIs. Rectal and throat cultures may be taken depending on data from sexual history.
Gram stain	Used for rapid detection of gonorrhea. Presence of gram-negative intracellular diplococci generally needs treatment. Not highly accurate for women. A valid alternative for chlamydia testing.
Nucleic acid amplifica-tion test (NAAT)	Nonculture test used to identify small amounts of DNA or RNA in test samples. Sensitivity similar to culture tests. Uses ligase or polymerase chain reaction that amplifies the signal of the nucleic acids in the test sample so that they are easier to identify. CDC preferred method to test for gonorrhea, chlamydia, and trichomoniasis. Can be done on a wide variety of samples, including vaginal, endocervical, urethral, urine, rectal, and pharyngeal.
Papanicolaou (Pap) test	Microscopic study of exfoliated cervical cells to detect abnormal cells. *Conventional cytology* entails fixing cells directly to a slide at the time of collection and sending the slide to the laboratory for interpretation. In *liquid-based cytology* the specimen is sent to the laboratory in a liquid solution that preserves it and is processed for microscopic evaluation at the laboratory. Testing for HPV may be done on specimen obtained for liquid-based Pap test (see Chapter 53).
Wet mounts	Direct microscopic examination of vaginal discharge specimen is done immediately after collection. Determines presence or absence and number of *Trichomonas* organisms, bacteria, white and red blood cells, and candidal buds or hyphae.

TABLE 50.14 Fertility Studies

Study	Description and Purpose
Basal body temperature assessment	Indirectly indicates whether ovulation has occurred. Temperature rises at ovulation and stays high during secretory phase of normal menstrual cycle.
Semen analysis	Assesses semen for volume (2–5 mL), viscosity, sperm count (>20 million/mL), sperm motility (60% motile), and percent of abnormal sperm (60% with normal structure).
Serum anti-müllerian hormone, estradiol, FSH, progesterone	Same as serology studies. See Table 50.10.
Urinary LH	Over-the-counter "ovulation predictor kits." Identifies midcycle LH surge that precedes ovulation by 1 to 2 days.

BRIDGE TO NCLEX EXAMINATION

The number of the question corresponds to the same-numbered outcome at the beginning of the chapter.

1. A normal male reproductive function that may be altered in a patient who undergoes an orchiectomy (removal of testes) is the production of
   a. PSA.
   b. GnRH.
   c. testosterone.
   d. seminal fluid.

2. Luteinizing hormone (LH) secretion by the anterior pituitary (*select all that apply*)
   a. results in ovulation.
   b. causes follicles to complete maturation.
   c. affects development of ruptured follicles.
   d. directly inhibits both GnRH and FSH secretion.
   e. stimulates testosterone production by interstitial cells of testes.

3. Female orgasm is characterized by
   a. resolution.
   b. increased breast size.
   c. relaxation of cervical os.
   d. vasoconstriction and dystonia.

4. An age-related finding during the assessment of the older woman's reproductive system is
   a. vaginal atrophy.
   b. increased libido.
   c. nipple enlargement.
   d. increased vulvar skin turgor.

5. Significant information about a person's health history related to the reproductive system should include (*select all that apply*)
   a. tobacco use.
   b. intellectual status.
   c. number of sexual partners.
   d. previous history of shingles.
   e. previous sexually transmitted infections.

6. Nucleic acid amplification tests (NAATs) used in the diagnosis of STIs can be obtained from (*select all that apply*)
   a. urine.
   b. vagina.
   c. urethra.
   d. rectum.
   e. endocervix.

7. An abnormal finding noted during physical assessment of the male reproductive system is
   a. descended testes.
   b. symmetric scrotum.
   c. slight clear urethral discharge.
   d. the glans covered with prepuce.

8. The nurse is caring for a patient scheduled for hysteroscopy. The nurse explains to the woman that
   a. the procedure treats cervical dysplasia.
   b. bleeding and discharge are rare after the procedure.
   c. the procedure involves curettage of the endometrial lining.
   d. the procedure allows visualization of the lining of the uterus.

1. c, 2. a, b, c, e, 3. c, 4. a, 5. a, c, e, 6. a, b, c, d, e, 7. c, 8. d

For rationales to these answers and even more NCLEX review questions, visit *http://evolve.elsevier.com/Lewis/medsurg*.

REFERENCES

1. Patton KT, Thibodeau GA: *Structure and function of the body*, ed 15, St Louis, 2016, Elsevier.
2. Strauss J. Barbieri R: *Yen and Jaffe's reproductive endocrinology: Physiology, pathophysiology, and clinical management*, ed 8, Philadelphia, 2018, Elsevier.
3. Masters WH, Johnson E: *Human sexual response*, Boston, 1966, Little Brown. (Classic)
4. Knudtson J, McLaughlin JE: Effects of aging on the female reproductive system. Retrieved from *www.merckmanuals.com/home/women-s-health-issues/biology-of-the-female-reproductive-system/effects-of-aging-on-the-female-reproductive-system*.

*5. Cobin RH, Goodman NF: American Association of Clinical Endocrinologists and American College of Endocrinology position statement on menopause—2017 update, *Endoc Pract* 23:869, 2017.

*6. Centers for Disease Control and Prevention: Pregnancy and rubella. Retrieved from *www.cdc.gov/rubella/pregnancy.html*.

7. Male reproductive endocrinology: Effects of aging. Retrieved from *https://medlineplus.gov/ency/article/004017.htm*.

8. The American College of Obstetricians and Gynecologists: The menopause years. Retrieved from *www.acog.org/Patients/FAQs/The-Menopause-Years*.

*9. Manson JE, Aragaki AK, Rossouw JE, et al: Menopausal hormone therapy and long-term all-cause and cause-specific mortality: The Women's Health Initiative randomized trials, *JAMA* 318:927, 2017.

*10. American Cancer Society: Can prostate cancer be found early? Retrieved from *www.cancer.org/cancer/prostatecancer/detailedguide/prostate-cancer-detection*.

*11. Centers for Disease Control and Prevention: Health effects of cigarette smoking. Retrieved from *www.cdc.gov/tobacco/data_statistics/fact_sheets/health_effects/effects_cig_smoking/*.

12. deSanjose S, Brotons, M, Pavon MA: The natural history of human papillomavirus infection, *Best Pract Res Clin Obstet Gynaecol* 47:2, 2018.

*13. Centers for Disease Control and Prevention: Folic acid recommendations. Retrieved from *www.cdc.gov/ncbddd/folicacid/recommendations.html*.

14. Tonolini M: *Imaging and intervention in urinary tract infections and urosepsis*, New York, 2018, Springer.

15. American College of Obstetrics and Gynecology: Opinion on the female athletic triad. Retrieved from *https://www.acog.org/Resources-And-Publications/Committee-Opinions/Committee-on-Adolescent-Health-Care/Female-Athlete-Triad*.

16. American Cancer Society: American Cancer Society recommendations for the early detection of breast cancer. Retrieved from *www.cancer.org/cancer/breast-cancer/screening-tests-and-early-detection/american-cancer-society-recommendations-for-the-early-detection-of-breast-cancer.html*.

*Evidence-based information for clinical practice.

51

Breast Disorders

Deena Dell

Caring for others is an expression of what it means to be fully human.

Hillary Clinton

http://evolve.elsevier.com/Lewis/medsurg

LEARNING OUTCOMES

1. State screening guidelines for the early detection of breast cancer.
2. Explain the types, causes, clinical manifestations, and interprofessional and nursing management of common benign breast disorders.
3. State the risk factors for breast cancer.
4. Describe the pathophysiology and clinical manifestations of breast cancer.
5. Describe the interprofessional and nursing management of breast cancer.
6. Specify the physical and psychologic aspects of nursing management for the patient undergoing breast cancer surgery.
7. Explain the indications for, types and complications of, and nursing management after reconstructive breast surgery.

KEY TERMS

ductal ectasia, p. 1194
fibroadenoma, p. 1193
fibrocystic changes, p. 1192
galactorrhea, p. 1193

gynecomastia, p. 1194
intraductal papilloma, p. 1193
lumpectomy, p. 1199
lymphedema, p. 1199

mammoplasty, p. 1207
mastalgia, p. 1191
mastitis, p. 1192
Paget's disease, p. 1196

Breast disorders are a significant health concern for women. Whether the actual diagnosis is a benign condition or a cancer, the initial discovery of a lump or change in the breast often triggers intense feelings of anxiety and fear. The potential loss of a breast, or part of a breast, may be devastating for many women because of the significant psychologic, social, sexual, and body image implications associated with it.

The most common breast disorders in women are fibrocystic changes, fibroadenoma, intraductal papilloma, ductal ectasia, and breast cancer. In a woman's lifetime, there is a 1 in 8 (12%) chance that she will be diagnosed with breast cancer.[1] Although rare, breast cancer does occur in men. Being aware of personal risk, including genetic factors, and taking part in recommended screening are important health promotion activities.

ASSESSMENT OF BREAST DISORDERS

Breast Cancer Screening Guidelines

Screening guidelines for the early detection of breast cancer vary depending on a woman's age and risk. For women at average risk for breast cancer, these are the American Cancer Society (ACS) recommended guidelines[2]:

- Women should undergo regular screening mammography starting at age 45 years.
- Women should be offered the chance to begin screening between the ages of 40 and 44.
- Women aged 45 to 54 years should be screened annually.
- Women 55 years and older should transition to biennial screening or be able to continue screening annually.
- Women should continue screening if their overall health is good, and they have a life expectancy of 10 years or longer.
- The ACS does not recommend depending on clinical breast examination (CBE) for breast cancer screening among average-risk women at any age.

Women at increased risk for breast cancer (family history, genetic link, prior breast cancer, history of thoracic radiation therapy, or certain atypical findings on a prior breast biopsy) should talk with their HCP about the benefits and limitations of starting screening earlier with 3D mammography and breast magnetic resonance imaging (MRI) and having more frequent clinical breast encounters. A clinical encounter includes an assessment of risk factors, instruction in ways to reduce the risk factors, and a CBE.[3]

Consistent breast self-examination (BSE) may be a useful way to increase self-awareness of how one's breast normally look and feel. However, research has shown that BSE has no effect on reducing deaths from breast cancer. However, you still need to teach women the importance of knowing how their breasts look and feel and to report breast changes (e.g., nipple discharge, a lump) to their HCP.[3]

If a woman wants to learn about BSE, include information related to potential benefits, limitations, and harm (chance of a false-positive test result). Allow time for questions about the procedure and a return demonstration. For women who choose to perform BSE, teach the method described at *www.breastcancer.org/symptoms/testing/types/self_exam/bse_steps*.

Diagnostic Studies

Radiologic Studies. We use several techniques to screen for breast disorders or to help diagnose a suspicious physical finding. *Mammography* is a method used to visualize the breast's internal structure using x-rays (Fig. 51.1). This generally well-tolerated procedure can detect suspicious lumps that cannot be felt. Mammography has significantly improved the early and accurate detection of breast cancer. Improved imaging technology has reduced the radiation dose from mammography.

A comparison of current and prior mammograms may show early tissue changes. Because some tumors metastasize late, early detection by mammography allows for earlier treatment and the prevention of metastasis. In younger women, mammography is less sensitive because of the greater density of breast tissue, resulting in more false-negative results.

With digital mammography x-ray images are digitally coded and stored in a computer (Fig. 51.1). Digital mammograms are more accurate than traditional film mammography in younger women with dense breasts. The availability and associated costs of digital mammography are issues related to this technology.

3D mammography, or tomosynthesis mammography, produces a 3D image of the breast. It gives a clearer view of

overlapping breast tissue structures. It can increase the numbers of cancers detected and decrease the number of false-positive results (a result stating a cancer is present when it is not).[3]

Calcifications are the most easily recognized mammogram abnormality (Fig. 51.1). These deposits of calcium crystals form in the breast for many reasons, such as inflammation, trauma, and/or aging. Although most calcifications are benign, they may be associated with breast cancer.

About 10% to 15% of all breast cancers cannot be seen on mammography. They may be detected by palpation or other breast imaging studies, such as ultrasound and MRI. If the clinical findings are suspicious and the mammogram is normal, an ultrasound or MRI may be done. Based on these findings, a biopsy may be done.

Ultrasound is used in conjunction with mammography to discern a solid mass from a cystic mass, to evaluate a mass in a pregnant or lactating woman, and to locate and biopsy a suspicious lesion. MRI is recommended as a screening tool in addition to mammography for women who are at high risk for breast cancer (e.g., first-degree relative with a *BRCA* mutation).[3]

Biopsies. A definitive diagnosis of a suspicious area is made by analyzing biopsied tissue. Biopsy techniques include *fine-needle aspiration* (FNA), core (core needle), vacuum-assisted, and excisional biopsies.

FNA biopsy is done by inserting a needle into a lesion to sample fluid from a breast cyst, remove cells from intercellular spaces, or sample cells from a solid mass. Before the procedure, the breast area is first locally anesthetized. Then the needle is placed into the breast, and fluid and cells are aspirated into a syringe. Usually 3 or 4 passes are made. If the results are negative with a suspicious lesion, another biopsy may be necessary.

A *core (core needle) biopsy* involves removing small samples of breast tissue using a hollow "core" needle. For palpable lesions, this is done by fixing the lesion with one hand and performing a needle biopsy with the other. In the case of nonpalpable lesions, *stereotactic mammography*, ultrasound, or MRI image guidance is used. Stereotactic mammography uses computers to pinpoint the exact location of a breast mass based on mammograms. With ultrasound, the HCP watches the needle on the ultrasound monitor to help guide it to the area of concern. Because a core biopsy removes more tissue than an FNA, it is more accurate.

Vacuum-assisted biopsy is a version of core biopsy that uses a vacuum technique to help collect the tissue sample. In core biopsy, several separate needle insertions are used to obtain multiple samples. During vacuum-assisted biopsy, the needle is inserted only once into the breast, and the needle can be rotated, which allows for multiple samples through a single needle insertion.

Minimally invasive breast biopsies have become the standard of care for diagnosing abnormalities found either on imaging studies or through CBE. However, in some cases an *excisional biopsy* is recommended. An excisional biopsy is done in an operating room.

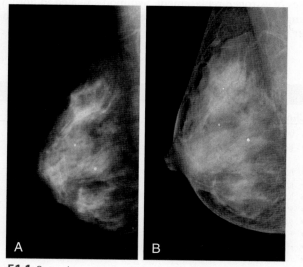

FIG. 51.1 Screening mammogram showing dense breast tissue and benign, scattered microcalcifications of a 57-year-old. **A,** Using conventional x-rays. **B,** Using digital x-rays. (From Adam A, Dixon AK, Grainger RG, et al: *Grainger and Allison's diagnostic radiology*, ed 5, St Louis, 2008, Churchill Livingstone.)

BENIGN BREAST DISORDERS

MASTALGIA

Mastalgia, or breast pain, is the most common breast-related symptom reported in women. The most common form is *cyclic mastalgia*, which coincides with the menstrual cycle.[4] Women describe it as diffuse bilateral breast tenderness or heaviness. Breast pain may last 2 or 3 days or most of the month and is related to hormonal sensitivity. The symptoms often decrease with menopause.

Noncyclic mastalgia has no relationship to the menstrual cycle and can continue into menopause. It may be constant or intermittent throughout the month and last for several years. Symptoms include a burning, aching, or soreness in the breast. It usually affects only 1 breast. The pain may be from trauma, fat necrosis, ductal ectasia, costochondritis, or arthritic pain in the chest or neck radiating to the breast.

For patients with breast pain, mammography and targeted ultrasound are often done to exclude cancer and provide information on the cause of the pain. Evidence supporting treatments for benign breast pain have yielded conflicting results. Some relief for cyclic pain may occur by reducing intake of caffeine and dietary fat; taking vitamin E or gamma-linolenic acid (evening primrose oil); and continually wearing a supportive bra. Compresses, ice, analgesics, and antiinflammatory drugs may help. Tamoxifen may provide relief with few side effects. Danazol is an FDA approved treatment. The androgenic side effects (acne, edema, hirsutism) make this therapy unacceptable for many women. Finally, you need to reassure women that mastalgia is not a usual sign of breast cancer.[4]

BREAST INFECTIONS

Mastitis

Mastitis is an inflammatory condition of the breast that occurs most often in lactating women (Table 51.1). *Lactational mastitis* presents as a localized area that is erythematous, painful, and tender to palpation. Fever is often present. The infection develops when organisms (usually staphylococci) gain access to the breast through a cracked nipple. In its early stages, mastitis can be cured with antibiotics. Breastfeeding should continue unless an abscess is forming, or there is purulent drainage. The mother may wish to use a nipple shield or to hand-express milk from the involved breast until the pain subsides. The woman should see her HCP promptly to begin a course of antibiotic therapy. Any breast that stays red, tender, and not responsive to antibiotics requires follow-up care and evaluation for inflammatory breast cancer.[4,5]

Mastitis sometimes develops in women who are not lactating. This is called *periductal mastitis*. It is seen most often in regular smokers aged late 20s to early 30s. Treatment is the same as for lactating mastitis.

Lactational Breast Abscess

If lactational mastitis persists after several days of antibiotic therapy, a lactational breast abscess may be present. In this condition, the skin may become red and edematous over the involved breast, often with a corresponding palpable mass, and the patient may have a fever. Antibiotics alone are insufficient treatment for a breast abscess. Ultrasound-guided drainage of the abscess or surgical incision and drainage are needed. The drainage is cultured, sensitivities are obtained, and therapy with the appropriate antibiotic is begun. Breastfeeding can continue in most cases with ongoing treatment of the abscess.

FIBROCYSTIC CHANGES

Fibrocystic changes in the breast are benign conditions characterized by changes in breast tissue (Fig. 51.2).[6,7] Fibrocystic changes are the most common breast disorder, occurring in more than 50% of women in North America. They occur most often in women between 30 and 50 years of age but may begin under 21 years of age in as many as 10% of women. Fibrocystic changes most often occur in women with premenstrual abnormalities, nulliparous women, women with a history of spontaneous abortion, nonusers of oral contraceptives, and women with early menarche and late menopause.

The use of the term *fibrocystic disease* is incorrect because the cluster of problems represent benign disorders. Fibrocystic changes include the development of excess fibrous tissue, hyperplasia of the epithelial lining of the mammary ducts, proliferation of mammary ducts, and cyst formation. We think these changes are due to a heightened responsiveness of breast tissue to circulating estrogen and progesterone. They may cause pain from chronic inflammation, edema, nerve irritation, and fibrosis. Pain and nodularity often increase over time. They tend to subside after menopause unless the woman is taking high doses of estrogen replacement. Symptoms related to fibrocystic changes often worsen in the premenstrual phase and subside after menstruation.

TABLE 51.1 Common Benign Breast Disorders

Disorder	Risk Factors	Clinical Manifestations
Lactational mastitis	Occurs in up to 10% of postpartum lactating mothers (both primipara and multipara), usually within first 3 mo after birth	• Warm to touch, indurated, painful, often unilateral • Most often caused by *Staphylococcus aureus*
Fibrocystic changes	Most common between ages 30 and 50	• Not usually discrete masses—nodularity instead • Usually accompanied by cyclic pain and tenderness • Mass(es) often cyclic in occurrence (movable, soft)
Cysts	Most common over age 35. Incidence decreases after menopause. Develop in over half of women in North America	• Palpable fluid-filled mass (movable, soft) • Multiple cysts can occur and recur • Rarely associated with breast cancer
Fibroadenoma	Often occurs in teens and those in their 20s	• Palpable mass (firm, movable), usually 1–3 cm in size • Rarely associated with breast cancer
Fat necrosis	Many women report a history of trauma to breast	• Usually a hard, tender, mobile, indurated mass with irregular borders
Ductal ectasia	Most common in women over 60 yr old. Considered a normal part of aging. May be due to duct obstruction or mastitis	• Nipple fixation, usually accompanied by nipple discharge of thick gray material • Often associated with breast pain

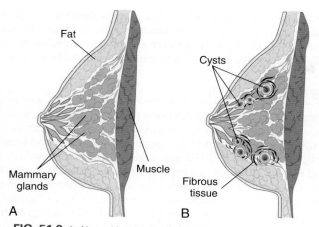

FIG. 51.2 A, Normal breast tissue. B, Fibrocystic breast tissue.

Manifestations of fibrocystic breast changes include 1 or more palpable lumps that are often round, well delineated, and freely movable within the breast (Table 51.1). Discomfort ranging from tenderness to pain may occur. The lump usually increases in size and sometimes tenderness before menstruation. Cysts may enlarge or shrink rapidly. Nipple discharge associated with fibrocystic breasts is often green or dark brown, not bloody.

Alone, fibrocystic changes are not associated with increased breast cancer risk. Masses or nodules can appear in both breasts. They often occur in the upper, outer quadrants and usually occur bilaterally.

Mammography may be helpful in distinguishing fibrocystic changes from breast cancer. However, in some women, the breast tissue is so dense that it is hard to obtain a mammogram. In these situations, ultrasound may be more useful in differentiating a fluid-filled cyst from a solid mass.

❖ Interprofessional and Nursing Care

With the discovery of a discrete mass in the breast by a woman or her HCP, aspiration or biopsy may be indicated. If the nodularity is recurrent, a wait of 7 to 10 days may be planned in order to note any changes that may be related to the menstrual cycle. With large or frequent cysts, an excisional biopsy may be preferred over repeated aspiration. An excisional biopsy may be done if (1) no fluid is found on aspiration, (2) the fluid is hemorrhagic, or (3) a residual mass remains after fluid aspiration. The biopsy is usually done in an outpatient surgery unit.

Severe fibrocystic changes may make palpation of the breast more difficult. Teach the woman with cystic changes to maintain regular follow-up care with her HCP and encourage breast self-awareness and to report any changes found so they can be evaluated.

Treatment for a fibrocystic condition is similar to that described earlier for mastalgia. Teach the woman with fibrocystic breasts that she may expect a recurrence of the cysts in 1 or both breasts until menopause, and that the cysts may enlarge or become painful just before menstruation. Reassure her that the cysts do not "turn into" cancer. Tell her that any new lump that does not respond in a cyclic manner over 1 to 2 weeks should be examined by her HCP.

FIBROADENOMA

Fibroadenoma is the most common cause of discrete benign breast lumps in young women. It generally occurs in women in their teens and twenties and is found more often in blacks than whites.

The possible cause of fibroadenoma may be increased estrogen sensitivity in a localized area of the breast. Fibroadenomas are usually small (but can be large [2 to 3 cm]), painless, round, well delineated, and very mobile. They are usually solid, firm, and rubbery in consistency. There is no accompanying retraction or nipple discharge. The fibroadenoma may appear as a single unilateral mass, although multiple bilateral fibroadenomas may occur. Growth is slow and often ceases when the size reaches 2 to 3 cm. Menstruation does not affect size. However, pregnancy can stimulate dramatic growth.

Fibroadenomas are easily detected by physical examination and may be visible on mammography and ultrasound. However, definitive diagnosis requires FNA, core, or excisional biopsy and tissue examination to exclude a cancer. Treatment can include observation with regular monitoring if cancer is not present, there are no symptoms, and the mass stays less than 3 cm. A fibroadenoma that increases in size and/or is symptomatic should be removed by surgical resection or, in some cases, cryotherapy. All new lesions should be evaluated by breast ultrasound and possible biopsy.[3]

NIPPLE DISCHARGE

Nipple discharge may occur spontaneously or because of nipple manipulation. A milky secretion is due to inappropriate lactation, or **galactorrhea**. It may be a result of certain medicines or endocrine or neurologic disorders. Nipple discharge may be idiopathic (no known cause).

Secretions can be serous, bloody, or brown to green. A cytology slide may be made of the secretion to determine the specific cause and recommended treatment. Disorders associated with nipple discharge include benign breast conditions, such as fibrocystic changes, intraductal papilloma, or ductal ectasia. In most cases, nipple discharge is not related to cancer.

ATYPICAL HYPERPLASIA

Atypical hyperplasia is usually found after a biopsy is done to evaluate a suspicious area found on a mammogram or during a CBE. It can be in either the ducts (atypical ductal hyperplasia) or in the lobules (atypical lobular hyperplasia). Both are associated with an increased risk for developing breast cancer. To follow up on a diagnosis of atypical hyperplasia, an excisional biopsy or lumpectomy may be done to remove all the affected tissue.[6]

INTRADUCTAL PAPILLOMA

An **intraductal papilloma** is a benign, soft or hard growth found in the mammary ducts. It is usually unilateral. Typically, the nipple has a bloody discharge that can be intermittent or spontaneous. Most intraductal papillomas are beneath the areola and may be difficult to palpate. They usually occur in women 30 to 50 years of age. A single duct or several ducts may be involved. Papillomas are associated with a slightly increased risk for developing breast cancer. So, a core biopsy should be done. If any abnormal cells are found, surgical excision of the papilloma and the involved duct or duct system is done.[8]

DUCTAL ECTASIA

Ductal ectasia (duct dilation) is a benign breast disease of perimenopausal and postmenopausal women involving the ducts in the subareolar area. It usually involves several bilateral ducts. Nipple discharge is the primary symptom. Ductal ectasia is initially painless but may progress to burning, itching, pain around the nipple, and swelling in the areolar area. Inflammatory signs are often present, and the nipple may retract. The discharge may become bloody in more advanced disease. It is not associated with cancer. If an abscess develops, warm compresses and antibiotics are usually effective treatments. Therapy consists of close follow-up examinations or surgical excision of the involved ducts.

MALE GYNECOMASTIA

Gynecomastia is a transient, noninflammatory enlargement of 1 or both breasts. It is the most common breast problem in men. The condition is usually temporary and benign. Gynecomastia itself is not a risk factor for breast cancer. The most common cause of gynecomastia is a change in the normal ratio of active androgen to estrogen in plasma or within the breast itself.[6]

Gynecomastia can occur in puberty. During puberty, there is often a transient relative imbalance between estrogen and testosterone, leading to gynecomastia. This condition usually resolves by age 20 years when adult androgen-to-estrogen ratios are reached. The treatment of pubertal gynecomastia is reassurance of the parent and teenager about the benign nature of the condition.

Gynecomastia can be a manifestation of other problems. It may accompany diseases such as testicular tumors, adrenal cancer, pituitary adenomas, hyperthyroidism, and liver disease. It can be a side effect of drug therapy, particularly with estrogen and androgen, digitalis, isoniazid, ranitidine, and spironolactone. Marijuana use can also cause gynecomastia.

Senescent Gynecomastia

Senescent gynecomastia occurs in many older men. The likely cause is high plasma estrogen levels with the increased conversion of androgens to estrogens in peripheral circulation. Although initially unilateral, the tender, firm, centrally located enlargement may become bilateral. A discrete, circumscribed mass with gynecomastia must be biopsied to determine if it is the rare breast cancer in males. Senescent hyperplasia needs no treatment. It usually regresses within 6 to 12 months.

Gerontologic Considerations: Age-Related Breast Changes

The loss of subcutaneous fat and structural support and the atrophy of mammary glands often result in pendulous breasts in the postmenopausal woman. Encourage older women to wear a well-fitting bra. Adequate support can improve physical appearance and reduce pain in the back, shoulders, and neck. It can also prevent *intertrigo*, dermatitis caused by friction between opposing surfaces of skin. Sagging breasts can be surgically lifted (mastopexy).

The decrease in glandular tissue makes a breast mass easier to palpate. This decreased density likely results from age-related decreases in estrogen. Rib margins may be palpable in a thin woman and can be confused with a mass. That is why it is so important that women become familiar with their own breasts and what is normal for them. Because the incidence of breast cancer increases with age, encourage breast awareness in older women. Encourage them to have an annual mammogram and CBE and have any breast-related concern evaluated by their HCP.

BREAST CANCER

Breast cancer is the most common cancer in American women except for skin cancer. It is second only to lung cancer as the leading cause of death from cancer in women. In the United States, more than 255,180 new cases of invasive breast cancer and more than 60,000 cases of in situ breast cancer are diagnosed annually. Another 2470 cases of breast cancer happen in men. About 41,070 deaths occur each year related to breast cancer.[1]

The incidence of breast cancer is slowly decreasing, with a slight drop in the number of deaths related to breast cancer. This decline may be the result of the decreased use of hormone therapy after menopause as well as earlier detection and advances in treatment. Breast cancer survivors are the largest group of any cancer survivors.[1]

Etiology and Risk Factors

Although we do not completely understand the cause, several risk factors are related to breast cancer (Table 51.2). Risk factors

TABLE 51.2 Risk Factors for Breast Cancer

Risk Factor	Comments
Age ≥50 yr	Majority found in postmenopausal women
	After age 60, ↑ in incidence
Alcohol use	Drinking ≥1 alcoholic beverage per day may have an ↑ risk
Benign breast disease with atypical epithelial hyperplasia, lobular carcinoma in situ	Atypical changes in breast biopsy ↑ risk
Early menarche (before age 12), late menopause (after age 55)	A long menstrual history ↑ risk
Exposure to ionizing radiation	Radiation damages DNA (e.g., prior treatment for Hodgkin's lymphoma)
Family history	Breast cancer in a first-degree relative, particularly when premenopausal or bilateral
Female	Women account for 99% of breast cancer cases
First full-term pregnancy after age 30, nulliparity, no breast-feeding	Prolonged exposure to unopposed estrogen ↑ risk
Genetic factors (*BRCA1, BRCA2, P53, PTEN, PALB2, ATM, CHEK2, NBM*)	Gene mutations play a role in up to 10% of breast cancer cases
Hormone use	Use of estrogen and/or progesterone as hormone therapy, especially in postmenopausal women
Long-term heavy smoking	May ↑ risk, especially in women who begin smoking before first pregnancy
Personal history of breast, colon, endometrial, or ovarian cancer	Personal history significantly ↑ risk for breast cancer, risk for cancer in other breast, and recurrence
Physical inactivity	Risk ↑s most after menopause
Weight gain and obesity after menopause	Fat cells store estrogen, which ↑ the risk for developing breast cancer

appear to be cumulative and interacting. So, the presence of multiple risk factors may greatly increase the overall risk, especially for people with a positive family history.

Risk Factors for Women. The risk factors most associated with breast cancer include female gender and advancing age. Women are at far greater risk than men, with 99% of breast cancers occurring in women. Increasing age also increases the risk for developing breast cancer. The incidence of breast cancer in women under 25 years of age is very low. Risk increases gradually until age 60. After age 60, the incidence increases dramatically.

Hormonal regulation of the breast is related to breast cancer development, but the mechanisms are poorly understood. The hormones estrogen and progesterone may act as tumor promoters to stimulate breast cancer growth if cancer changes in the cells have already occurred. The Women's Health Initiative study showed that combined hormone therapy (estrogen plus progesterone) (1) increases the risk for breast cancer after as little as 2 years use and (2) increased the risk for having a larger, more advanced breast cancer at diagnosis. Using estrogen therapy alone for longer than 15 years (for women with a prior hysterectomy) increases a woman's long-term risk for breast cancer in some studies.[9] A link also exists between oral contraceptive use and increased risk for breast cancer. This risk decreases when use stops and is gone after 10 years.

Modifiable risk factors include excess weight gain during adulthood, sedentary lifestyle, smoking, dietary fat intake, obesity, and alcohol use. Environmental factors, such as radiation exposure, may play a role.

Genetic Link

Family history of breast cancer is an important risk factor, especially if the involved family member also had ovarian cancer, was premenopausal, had bilateral breast cancer, or is a first-degree relative (i.e., mother, father, sister, brother, daughter). Having any first-degree relative with breast cancer doubles a woman's risk for breast cancer, especially if the relative was diagnosed at a young age.[10,11] A breast cancer risk assessment tool for HCPs is available *(www.cancer.gov/bcrisktool)*. Genetic counseling must be considered for a person at high risk for breast cancer.

Up to 10% of all breast cancers are hereditary. This means that specific genetic abnormalities that contribute to breast cancer development have been inherited. Most inherited cases of breast cancer are associated with mutations in 2 genes: *BRCA1* and *BRCA2*. *BRCA* stands for *BReast CAncer*. Everyone has *BRCA* genes. The *BRCA1* gene, found on chromosome 17, is a tumor suppressor gene that inhibits tumor development when functioning normally. Women who have *BRCA1* mutations have a 41% to 90% lifetime chance of developing breast cancer along with an increased risk for developing cancer in the other breast. The *BRCA2* gene, found on chromosome 11, is another tumor suppressor gene. Women with a mutation of this gene have a similar risk for breast cancer.[10,11]

In addition to *BRCA* gene mutations, we have identified many other abnormal genes that increase a person's risk for developing breast cancer. These include the tumor suppressor genes *p53* and *PTEN* (which inhibit tumor development when functioning normally), *ATM and NBM* (which help to repair damaged deoxyribonucleic acid [DNA]), *CHEK2* (which stops tumor growth), *PALB2* (which partners with *BRCA* to suppress tumor growth), and *CDH1* (which makes a protein to bind cells together).[12]

Most people who develop breast cancer do not have an abnormal breast cancer gene or a family history of breast cancer.

GENETICS IN CLINICAL PRACTICE
Breast Cancer

Genetic Basis

- Mutations occur in *BRCA1* and/or *BRCA2* genes.
- Normally, these genes are tumor suppressor genes involved in DNA repair.
- Transmission is autosomal dominant.
- Other genes (e.g., *ATM, CHEK-2, p53, PTEN, PALB2, NBM, NF1, STR11, CHD1*) may increase the risk for breast cancer.

Incidence

- Up to 10% of breast cancers are related to *BRCA1* and *BRCA2* gene mutations.
- As many as 1 in 300 to 800 women in the United States have *BRCA1* and *BRCA2* gene mutations.[11]
- Women with *BRCA1* and *BRCA2* gene mutations have a 41% to 90% lifetime risk for developing breast cancer.
- Mutations in *BRCA* genes may cause as many as 90% of all inherited breast cancers.
- *BRCA1* and *BRCA2* gene mutations are associated with early-onset breast cancer that is more likely to involve both breasts.
- Men with mutations in *BRCA1* and *BRCA2* have an increased risk for breast cancer and prostate cancer.
- Family history of both breast and ovarian cancer increases the risk for having a *BRCA* mutation.

Genetic Testing

- DNA testing is available for *BRCA1* and *BRCA2* gene mutations.
- Genetic tests can analyze an entire panel of genes in specific breast cancer patient populations.

Clinical Implications

- Most breast cancers (about 90%) are not inherited. They are associated with genetic changes that occur after a person is born (somatic mutations). There is no risk for passing on the mutated gene to children.
- Bilateral oophorectomy and/or bilateral mastectomy reduces the risk for breast cancer and ovarian cancer in women with *BRCA1* and *BRCA2* mutations.
- Women with *BRCA* mutations have a higher risk for developing ovarian, colon, pancreatic, and uterine cancers.[11]
- Genetic counseling and testing for *BRCA* mutations should be offered to patients whose personal or family history puts them at high risk for a genetic predisposition to breast cancer.

Ongoing research continues to look at the role of genes in the development of breast cancer.

Risk Factors for Men. Predisposing risk factors for breast cancer in men include hyperestrogenism, a family history of breast cancer, and radiation exposure. A thorough examination of the male breast should be a routine part of a physical examination. Men in *BRCA*-positive families should consider genetic testing. Teach men who test positive for a *BRCA* gene mutation to be aware of how their breasts look and feel and to report any changes to their HCP. They should have a CBE every year starting at age of 35. Screening mammography is not recommended as there is no evidence showing this to be of benefit. These men should begin prostate screening at age 35 as they have an increased risk for developing prostate cancer.[11]

Prophylactic Oophorectomy and Mastectomy. In women with *BRCA1* or *BRCA2* mutations, prophylactic bilateral oophorectomy can decrease the risk for breast and ovarian cancers. Removing the ovaries lowers the risk for breast cancer because the ovaries are the main source of estrogen in a premenopausal woman. Removing the ovaries does not reduce the risk for

? CHECK YOUR PRACTICE

Your best female friend calls you on the phone, and you can tell she has been crying. Her mother has just been diagnosed with stage 3A breast cancer. Between sobs, she tells you that her grandmother died of breast cancer and her aunt (her mother's sister) is receiving chemotherapy for breast cancer. She asks you, "Don't you think that I should just get mine whacked off? Then I would not have to worry anymore."
• How would you respond to her?

breast cancer in postmenopausal women because the ovaries are not the main producers of estrogen in these women. Women with *BRCA* mutations also have a higher risk for developing breast cancer in the unaffected (contralateral) breast. So, they may, as might any woman who has a high risk for developing breast cancer choose, in consultation with her HCP and genetic counselor, to undergo prophylactic bilateral mastectomy.

Pathophysiology

The main components of the breast are lobules (milk-producing glands) and ducts (milk passages that connect the lobules and the nipple). In general, breast cancer arises from the epithelial lining of the ducts *(ductal carcinoma)* or from the epithelium of the lobules *(lobular carcinoma)*. Breast cancers may be in situ (within the duct) or invasive (invading through the wall of the duct).

Metastatic breast cancer is breast cancer that has spread to other organs. The most common sites are the bone, liver, lung, and brain. Cancer growth rates can range from slow to rapid. Factors that affect cancer prognosis are tumor size, axillary node involvement (the more nodes involved, the worse the prognosis), tumor differentiation, estrogen and progesterone receptor status, and *human epidermal growth factor receptor 2* (HER-2) status. HER-2 is a protein that helps regulate cell growth.[13]

Types of Breast Cancer

Breast cancer is not just one disease, but a group of diseases characterized by different pathologic findings and clinical behaviors. Breast cancer can be classified as (1) ductal or lobular or other or (2) noninvasive or invasive (Table 51.3). We can also classify it based on hormonal status and genetic subtypes.

Noninvasive Breast Cancer. An estimated 20% of breast cancers are noninvasive. These intraductal cancers include *ductal carcinoma in situ* (DCIS) and pure Paget's disease.[13]

DCIS tends to be unilateral and may progress to invasive breast cancer if left untreated. Treatment options include breast-conserving treatment (lumpectomy) with or without radiation therapy, total mastectomy with or without sentinel lymph node biopsy, and/or hormone therapy (e.g., tamoxifen) to prevent recurrences.[14]

In the past, *lobular carcinoma in situ* (LCIS) was considered a noninvasive breast cancer. However, it has now been reclassified as a benign condition that is a risk factor for developing breast cancer.[13] No surgical or radiation treatment is indicated for LCIS. Hormone therapy may be used as a preventive measure to reduce breast cancer risk for some patients.

Invasive Ductal Carcinoma. *Invasive (infiltrating) ductal carcinoma* is the most common type of breast cancer. It accounts for about 80% of all invasive breast cancers. It starts in the milk ducts, then breaks through the walls of the duct, invading the surrounding tissue. From there it may metastasize to other parts of the body. Subtypes of invasive ductal carcinoma include

TABLE 51.3 Classification of Breast Cancer

Based on Tissue Type
• Ductal carcinoma (affects milk ducts)
  • Medullary
  • Tubular
  • Colloid (mucinous)
• Lobular carcinoma (affects milk-producing glands)
• Other
  • Inflammatory
  • Paget's disease
  • Phyllodes tumor

Based on Invasiveness
Noninvasive (In situ)
• Ductal carcinoma in situ (DCIS)
• Pure Paget's disease

Invasive (Spreading to Other Locations)
• Invasive ductal carcinoma
• Invasive lobular carcinoma

Based on Hormone Receptor and Genetic Status
Estrogen and Progesterone Receptor Status
• Estrogen receptor positive
• Estrogen receptor negative
• Progesterone receptor positive
• Progesterone receptor negative

HER-2 Genetic Status
• HER-2 positive
• HER-2 negative

medullary carcinoma, tubular carcinoma, colloid (mucinous) carcinoma, papillary carcinoma, and metaplastic carcinoma.

Invasive Lobular Carcinoma. *Invasive (infiltrating) lobular carcinoma* begins in the lobules (milk-producing glands) of the breast. It accounts for about 10% to 15% of invasive breast cancers. The cancer cells can break out of the lobule and metastasize to other areas of the body. Invasive lobular carcinoma usually presents as a subtle thickening in the upper outer quadrant of the breast. It is often not detected by mammography.

Other Types of Breast Cancer

Inflammatory Breast Cancer. *Inflammatory breast cancer* is an aggressive and fast-growing breast cancer with a high risk for metastasis. It accounts for about 1% to 3% of all breast cancers. In the early stages, it is often mistaken for mastitis. However, the inflammatory changes do not improve with antibiotics, because cancer cells block the lymph channels in the skin of the breast. Because of skin involvement, the breast looks red, feels warm, and has a thickened appearance that is often described as looking like an orange peel *(peau d'orange)*. Sometimes, the breast develops ridges and small bumps that look like hives. A breast mass may not be present. Changes may not show up on mammograms, making diagnosis difficult. Inflammatory breast cancer is associated with a worse prognosis as compared to invasive ductal and lobular breast cancers.[14]

Paget's Disease. Paget's disease is a rare breast cancer that starts in the breast ducts and spreads to the nipple and areola. It causes about 1% of all breast cancers. It is different from Paget's disease of the bone, which is discussed in Chapter 63. Most women with Paget's disease have underlying ductal carcinoma. Only in rare cases is the cancer confined to the nipple and not associated with some invasive cancer (in situ).

Itching, burning, bloody nipple discharge with superficial skin erosion and ulceration may be present. A pathologic examination of the lesion confirms the diagnosis. Nipple changes are often diagnosed as an infection or dermatitis, which can lead to treatment delays.

The treatment of Paget's disease is surgical removal of the involved tissue by either central lumpectomy or mastectomy with or without sentinel node biopsy. Radiation therapy may be used after surgery. The prognosis is good when the cancer is confined to the nipple.[14]

Phyllodes Tumor. A phyllodes tumor is a very rare tumor that develops in the connective tissue (stroma) of the breast. The tumors tend to grow quickly, within a period of weeks or months, to a size of 2 to 3 cm or sometimes larger. Although most are benign, some are cancerous. Treatment is usually excision with a wide margin. Axillary surgery is not necessary.[14]

Triple-Negative Breast Cancer. A patient whose breast cancer tests negative for all 3 receptors (estrogen, progesterone, HER-2) has *triple-negative breast cancer.* Receptor testing is discussed on p. 1198. The incidence of triple-negative breast cancer is higher in blacks, Hispanics, premenopausal women, and those with a *BRCA1* mutation. These patients tend to have more aggressive tumors with a poorer prognosis. These cancers do not respond to hormone therapy or therapy for HER-2. Chemotherapy appears to be the more successful for treating triple-negative breast cancer.

Clinical Manifestations

Breast cancer is usually detected as a lump or thickening in the breast or mammography abnormality. It occurs most often in the upper, outer quadrant of the breast, which is the location of most of the glandular tissue (Fig. 51.3). Breast cancers vary in their growth rate. If palpable, breast cancer is characteristically hard and may be irregularly shaped, poorly delineated, nonmobile, and nontender.

A small number of breast cancers cause nipple discharge. The discharge is usually unilateral and may be clear or bloody. Nipple retraction may occur. Peau d'orange may occur due to plugging of the dermal lymphatics. In large cancers, infiltration, induration, and dimpling pulling in) of the overlying skin may occur.

Complications

The main complication of breast cancer is recurrence (Table 51.4). Recurrence may be *local* or *regional* (skin or soft tissue

near the mastectomy site, axillary or internal mammary lymph nodes) or distant. Widely disseminated or metastatic disease involves the growth of cancerous breast cells in parts of the body distant from the breast (most often involving the bone, lung, brain, liver). Metastases primarily occur through the lymphatics, usually those of the axilla (Fig. 51.4). However, metastatic disease can occur anywhere.

Diagnostic Studies

In addition to radiologic and biopsy studies used to diagnose breast cancer (see earlier discussion in this chapter on p. 1191), other tests are used to predict the risk for local or systemic recurrence. These tests include axillary lymph node analysis, tumor size, estrogen and progesterone receptor status, cell-proliferative indices (number of cells that are dividing), and genomic assays.

Axillary Lymph Node Analysis. Axillary lymph node involvement is an important prognostic factor in breast cancer. *Axillary lymph nodes* are often examined to see if cancer has spread to the axilla on the same side of the breast as the cancer (Fig. 51.4). The more nodes involved, the greater the risk for recurrence.

A *sentinel lymph node biopsy* (SLNB) helps to identify the lymph node(s) that drain first from the tumor site. Those nodes are called *sentinel node(s)* (SLN). In SLNB, a radioisotope and/or blue dye, which will travel the same route as the cancer, is injected into the affected breast. Then, in surgery, the

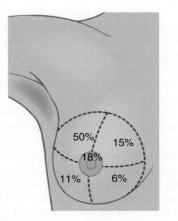

FIG. 51.3 Distribution of where breast cancer occurs.

TABLE 51.4 Sites of Breast Cancer Recurrence and Metastasis	
Site	**Manifestations**
Local Recurrence	
Skin, chest wall	Firm, discrete nodules. Sometimes pruritic, usually painless, often in or near a scar
Regional Recurrence	
Lymph nodes	Enlarged nodes in axilla or supraclavicular area, usually nontender
Distant Metastasis	
Bone marrow	Anemia, infection, ↑ bleeding, bruising, petechiae. Weakness, fatigue, mild confusion, light-headedness, dyspnea
Brain	Headache described as "different," unilateral sensory loss, focal muscular weakness, hemiparesis, incoordination (ataxia), nausea and vomiting unrelated to medication, cognitive changes
Liver	Abdominal distention. Right lower quadrant abdominal pain sometimes radiating to scapular area. Nausea and vomiting, anorexia, weight loss. Weakness and fatigue. Hepatomegaly, ascites, jaundice. Peripheral edema. High liver enzymes
Lung (including lung nodules and pleural effusions)	Shortness of breath, tachypnea, nonproductive cough
Skeletal	Localized pain of gradually increasing intensity, percussion tenderness at involved sites, pathologic fracture caused by involvement of bone cortex
Spinal cord	Progressive back pain, localized and radiating. Change in bladder or bowel function. Loss of sensation in lower extremities

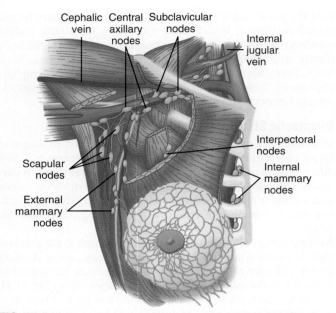

FIG. 51.4 Lymph nodes and drainage in the axilla. The sentinel lymph node is usually found in the external mammary nodes. A complete axillary dissection would remove all nodes. (From Donegan WL, Spratt JS: *Cancer of the breast,* ed 3, Philadelphia, 1988, Saunders.)

HCP determines if the radioisotope (using radioactive detector) or dye (visually see blue nodes) is found in any SLNs. A local incision is made in the axilla, and the HCP dissects the blue-stained and/or radioactive SLNs. Generally, with SLNB, 1 to 4 axillary lymph nodes are removed. The nodes are sent for pathologic analysis. If the SLNs are negative, no further axillary surgery is needed.

If the SLNs are positive, a complete *axillary lymph node dissection* (ALND) may be done. In an ALND, the HCP will typically remove 12 to 20 lymph nodes. SLNB is less invasive than ALND and is associated with lower morbidity rates compared with ALND.

Tumor Size. *Tumor size* is a prognostic variable. In general, the larger the tumor, the poorer the prognosis. The wide variety of biologic types of breast cancer explains the variability of disease behavior. In general, the more well differentiated (like the original cell type) the tumor, the less aggressive it is. The cells of poorly differentiated (unlike the original cell type) tumors appear morphologically disorganized, and they are more aggressive.

Estrogen and Progesterone Receptor Status. *Estrogen receptor (ER) and progesterone receptor (PR) status* is another diagnostic test useful for decisions about both treatment and prognosis. Receptor-positive tumors (1) often show histologic evidence of being well differentiated, (2) have a lower chance for recurrence, (3) often have a *diploid* (more normal) DNA content and low proliferative indices, and (4) are often hormone dependent and responsive to hormone therapy. Receptor-negative tumors (1) are often poorly differentiated histologically, (2) often recur, (3) have a high incidence of *aneuploidy* (abnormally high or low DNA content) and higher proliferative indices, and (4) are usually unresponsive to hormone therapy. Ploidy status (number of chromosomes in a cell) correlates with tumor aggressiveness. Diploid tumors have a much lower risk for recurrence than aneuploid tumors.

Cell-Proliferative Indices. *Cell-proliferative indices* indirectly measure the rate of tumor cell proliferation. The number of tumor cells in the synthesis (S) phase of the cell cycle (see Chapter 15, Fig. 15.1) is another important prognostic indicator. Although cell-proliferative indices are not routinely done as part of the breast cancer pathology evaluation, patients with cells that have high S-phase fractions have a higher risk for recurrence and earlier cancer death.

Genomic Assay. An important *genomic assay* is to determine HER-2, which is a prognostic indicator. Overexpression of HER-2 is associated with unusually aggressive tumor growth, a greater risk for recurrence, and a poorer prognosis. HER-2 is overexpressed in 10% to 20% of patients with breast cancer. The presence of HER-2 helps in the selection and sequence of drug therapy and predicts the patient's response to treatment.

A *genomic* test uses a sample of the breast cancer tissue to analyze the activity of a group of genes that can affect how a cancer is likely to behave and respond to treatment. Knowing whether certain genes are present or absent, or overly active or not active enough, can provide information about the risk for recurrence and the expected benefit of chemotherapy or hormone therapy. The 21-gene recurrence (OncotypeDX) test is the most often used genomic test.[15] Other genomic tests are MammaPrint, PAM50 (Prosigna), EndoPredict, and the Breast Cancer Index.

Interprofessional Care

A wide range of treatment options is available to the patient and HCPs making critical decisions about how to treat breast cancer (Table 51.5). The treatment plan is often determined by prognostic factors, the clinical stage, and biology of the cancer.

Staging of Breast Cancer. The most widely accepted staging method for breast cancer is the TNM system. This system uses traditional anatomic factors of tumor size (T), nodal involvement (N), and presence of metastasis (M) to determine the stage of disease (Table 51.6). The stages range from 0 to IV, with stage 0 being in situ cancer with no lymph node involvement and no metastasis. Stage IV indicates metastatic spread, regardless of tumor size or lymph node involvement. This system is used worldwide to communicate the size of a breast cancer and the extent to which it has spread. It provides an accurate prediction of the outcome of a group of patients.

The latest cancer staging guidelines add biologic factors in making the final determination of stage. These enable more accurate determination of prognosis and appropriate systemic therapy. These factors include tumor grade, hormone receptor expression, HER-2 overexpression and/or amplification, and genomic panels.[13]

For example, some larger tumors will now be considered stage I instead of stage II based on their biology. For patients with hormone receptor–positive, HER2-negative, lymph node–negative tumors, and a low-risk gene recurrence score, regardless of T size, place into the same prognostic category as T1a-T1b N0 M0. Patients with triple-negative tumors have survival equal to that of patients with disease 1 TNM stage higher who have ER, PR, or HER2-positive expressing tumors.

Surgical Therapy. Surgery is the primary treatment for breast cancer. Table 51.7 describes the most common surgical procedures used to treat breast cancer. The most common surgical options for operable breast cancer are (1) breast conservation surgery (lumpectomy [segmental mastectomy]) and (2) mastectomy with or without reconstruction. Most women diagnosed with early-stage breast cancer (tumors smaller than 5 cm) are candidates for either treatment choice. The overall survival rate with lumpectomy and radiation is the same as that with mastectomy.[14]

TABLE 51.5 Interprofessional Care

Breast Cancer

Diagnostic Assessment

Prediagnosis
- Health history, including risk factors
- Physical examination, including breast and lymph nodes
- Mammography
- Ultrasound (if indicated)
- Breast MRI (if indicated)
- Biopsy

Postdiagnosis
- Lymph node analysis
- Estrogen and progesterone receptor status
- Cell-proliferative indices
- HER-2 marker
- Genetic assays (e.g., MammaPrint, Oncotype DX)

Staging
- Complete blood count
- Liver function tests
- Chest x-ray (if indicated)
- CT scan of chest, abdomen, pelvis (if indicated)
- PET/CT, MRI, bone scans (if indicated)

Management

Surgical Therapy
- Breast-conserving surgery (lumpectomy) with SLNB and/or axillary lymph node dissection
- Simple (total) mastectomy with SLNB and/or axillary lymph node dissection
- Modified radical mastectomy
- Reconstructive surgery

Radiation Therapy
- External radiation
- Brachytherapy
- Palliative radiation therapy

Drug Therapy (Table 51.8)
- Chemotherapy
- Hormone therapy
- Immunotherapy
- Targeted therapy

TABLE 51.6 Staging of Breast Cancer

Stage	Tumor Size	Lymph Node Involvement	Metastasis
0	TIS (tumor in situ)	No	No
I			
A	<2 cm	No	No
B	<2 cm	<2 mm	No
II			
A	No evidence of tumor ranging to 5 cm	No, or 1–3 axillary nodes and/or internal mammary nodes	No
B	Ranging from ≤2 to >5 cm	No, or 1–3 axillary nodes and/or internal mammary nodes	No
III			
A	Ranging ≤2 to >5 cm	Yes, 1–9 axillary nodes and/or internal mammary nodes	No
B	Any size with extension to chest wall or skin	No, or 1–9 axillary nodes and/or internal mammary nodes	No
C	Any size	Yes, ≥10 axillary nodes, internal mammary nodes, or infraclavicular nodes	No
IV	Any size	Any type of nodal involvement	Yes

Adapted from Guiliano AE, Connolly JL, Edge SB, et al: Breast cancer: Major changes in the American Joint Committee on Cancer 8th edition cancer staging manual, *Cancer J Clin* 67:290, 2017.

It is important to note that breast reconstruction is an option for any woman undergoing surgical treatment for breast cancer. For women undergoing mastectomy, breast reconstruction can be done at the time of the mastectomy or delayed for months or even years. Women may opt to not have reconstruction and choose to use a breast prosthesis instead.

Breast-Conserving Surgery. Breast-conserving surgery, also called **lumpectomy**, involves removing the entire tumor along with a margin of normal surrounding tissue (Fig. 51.5, *A*). In some cases, it may take 2 or 3 more surgeries to remove all the cancer from the margins. After surgery, radiation therapy is usually delivered to the entire breast, ending with a boost to the tumor bed. If the risk for recurrence is high, chemotherapy may be given before radiation therapy.

Not everyone is a candidate for breast conservation surgery. Contraindications include breast size too small in relation to the tumor size to yield an acceptable cosmetic result, multifocal masses and calcifications, multicentric masses (in more than 1 quadrant), diffuse calcifications in more than 1 quadrant, or prior radiation therapy. Because of the time commitment (i.e., 3 to 7 weeks of daily radiation therapy treatments) and travel distances to access radiation therapy treatment centers, some patients may choose mastectomy over breast conservation surgery.

Axillary Lymph Node Analysis. SLNB is the preferred standard for axillary lymph node analysis and staging. It was described on p. 1197. However, if the SLN cannot be identified, or if the node is positive for cancer, ALND may have to be done.

Lymphedema. Lymphedema, an accumulation of lymph in soft tissue, can occur because of the lymph node sampling procedure or radiation therapy (Fig. 51.6). When the axillary nodes cannot return lymph fluid to the central circulation, the fluid accumulates in the arm, hand, or breast, causing obstructive pressure on the veins and venous return. The patient may have heaviness, impaired motor function in the arm, and numbness and paresthesia of the fingers. Cellulitis and progressive fibrosis of the skin can result from untreated lymphedema. (See further discussion on lymphedema later in this chapter on p. 1206.)

Mastectomy. A *total* or *simple mastectomy* removes the entire breast. A *modified radical mastectomy* includes removal of the breast and axillary lymph nodes. It preserves the pectoralis major muscle (Fig. 51.5, *B*). For women desiring breast reconstruction, a skin-sparing mastectomy provides the best cosmetic result and does not increase the chance of the cancer recurring. In a *nipple-sparing mastectomy*, the nipple and/or areola are left in place and the breast tissue under them is removed. Women who have a small, low-grade cancer near the outer part of the

TABLE 51.7 Surgical Procedures for Breast Cancer

Procedure	Side Effects	Complications	Patient Issues
Breast-Conserving Surgery (Lumpectomy) With Radiation Therapy			
Excision of tumor with no tumor at margins, sentinel lymph node biopsy (SLNB) and/or axillary lymph node dissection (ALND) Radiation therapy	• Breast soreness • Breast edema • Skin reactions • Arm swelling • Sensory changes in breast and arm	*Short-term:* moist desquamation,* hematoma, seroma, infection *Long-term:* fibrosis,* lymph-edema,[†] myositis, pneumoni-tis,* rib fractures*	• Prolonged treatment* • Impaired arm mobility[†] • Change in texture and sensitivity of breast
Mastectomy			
Simple Mastectomy	• Chest wall tightness, scar	*Short-term:* skin flap necrosis, seroma, hematoma, infection	• Loss of breast
Removal of breast, preservation of pectoralis muscle, SLNB may be done at same time	• Phantom breast sensations • Lymphedema • Sensory changes • Impaired range of motion	*Long-term:* sensory loss, muscle weakness, lymphedema	• Incision • Body image • Need for prosthesis • Impaired arm mobility
Modified Radical Mastectomy			
Removal of breast with ALND, pectoralis muscle is spared			
Breast Implants and Tissue Expansion			
Expander used to slowly stretch tissue. Saline gradually injected into reservoir over weeks to months Insertion of implant under muscu-lofascial layer of chest wall	• Discomfort • Chest wall tightness	*Short-term:* skin flap necrosis, wound separation, seroma, hematoma, infection *Long-term:* capsular contractions, displacement of implant	• Body image • Prolonged HCP visits to expand implants • Potential added surgeries for nipple construction, symmetry
Breast Reconstruction Tissue Flap Procedures[‡]			
Transverse Rectus Abdominis Musculocutaneous (TRAM) Flap			
Musculocutaneous flap (muscle, skin, fat, blood supply) is trans-posed from abdomen to the mastectomy site May be done concurrently with mastectomy	• Pain related to 2 surgical sites and extensive surgery	*Short-term:* delayed wound healing, infection, skin flap necrosis, abdominal hernia, hematoma	• Longer postoperative recovery
Deep Inferior Epigastric Artery Perforator (DIEP) Flap			
Free flap that transfers skin and fat from the abdomen to the chest. Differs from TRAM flap because no muscle is moved	• Requires more time in surgery than pedicle TRAM flap • Pain related to 2 surgical sites	Needs to be closely monitored first 24–48 hours after surgery. If flap fails, patient needs surgery	• Patients may have less pain and restriction of movement than with a pedicle TRAM flap.

*Specific to radiation therapy.
[†]If ALND (less likely with SLNB).
[‡]This list is not inclusive as other breast reconstruction options are available to patients.

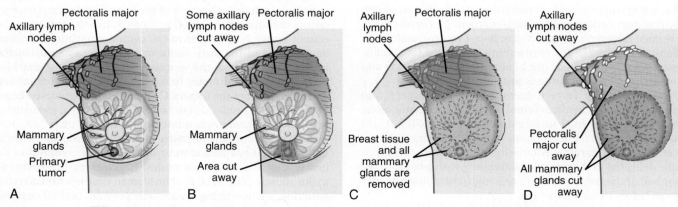

FIG. 51.5 Breast cancer surgery. **A,** Preoperative. **B,** Lumpectomy. **C,** Simple mastectomy. **D,** Modified radical mastectomy.

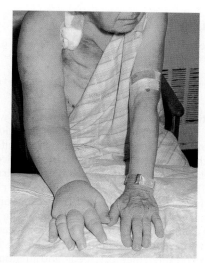

FIG. 51.6 Lymphedema. Accumulation of fluid in the tissue after excision of lymph nodes. (From Swartz MH: *Textbook of physical diagnosis: History and examination,* ed 6, Philadelphia, 2010, Saunders.)

breast, with no signs of cancer in the skin or near the nipple, may be able to have nipple-sparing surgery.[14]

For women who have a mastectomy, breast reconstruction can be done with the mastectomy or it can be delayed. Some women choose not to have reconstruction. There are 2 main types of breast reconstruction procedures: implant reconstruction or tissue flap procedures (Table 51.7). Breast reconstructive surgery is discussed on pp. 1207–1209.

Post–Breast Therapy Pain Syndrome. Post–breast therapy pain syndrome (PBTPS) occurs in some people who have had procedures for breast cancer. Most often it is caused by injury to nerves during surgery. However, it also can be due to chemotherapy and radiation therapy. The most common theory is that PBTPS results from injury to intercostobrachial nerves. These are sensory nerves that exit the chest wall muscles and provide sensation to the shoulder and upper arm.

Because of its multiple causes, PBTPS symptoms can range from mild to debilitating.[16] Common symptoms include chest and upper arm pain, tingling down the arm, continuous aching and burning, numbness, shooting or pricking pain, and unbearable itching that persists beyond the normal 3-month healing time. Edema may be present.

Treatment includes nonsteroidal antiinflammatory drugs (NSAIDs), low-dose antidepressants, topical anesthetics (e.g., EMLA [lidocaine and prilocaine]), and antiseizure drugs (e.g., gabapentin). Other treatments include biofeedback, physical therapy to prevent "frozen shoulder" syndrome from inadequate movement, guided imagery, and psychologic counseling with a therapist trained in the management of chronic pain syndromes.

Phantom Breast Pain. Phantom breast pain is feeling pain in the breast after the breast was removed via mastectomy. It occurs

for the same reasons phantom limb sensation occurs after limb amputations. The brain continues to send signals to nerves in the breast area that were cut during surgery, even though the breast is no longer physically there.

Radiation Therapy. Radiation therapy is one *adjuvant (additional)* therapy that can be used after surgery. It is used for breast cancer to (1) prevent local breast cancer recurrences after breast-conserving surgery; (2) prevent local and lymph node recurrences after mastectomy; or (3) relieve pain caused by local, regional, or distant spread of cancer.

External Radiation Therapy. When radiation therapy is a primary treatment, it is usually done after surgery for the breast cancer. The decision to use radiation therapy after mastectomy is based on the chance that local, residual cancer cells are present. Radiation of the axilla and/or supraclavicular nodes may be done when lymph nodes are involved to decrease the risk for axillary recurrence. Radiating a localized area does not prevent distant metastasis.

In traditional whole breast, and in some cases regional lymph node, radiation treatment, the area is radiated 5 days per week over the course of about 5 to 7 weeks. An external beam of radiation delivers daily fractions to a total dose of 46 to 50 Gy (4500 to 5000 cGy). Patients who have had breast-conserving surgery may receive a "boost" dose of radiation to the area where the original tumor was located. It is given by external beam and adds 4 to 8 more treatments to the total number given.[14]

Newer and preferred regimens use a type of accelerated external beam radiation called hypofractionation. This type of radiation has a shortened schedule, daily for 3 to 4 weeks, with a total dose of 40 to 42.5 Gy.[14]

Fatigue, skin changes, and breast edema may be temporary side effects of external radiation therapy. Nursing management of the patient receiving radiation therapy is discussed in Chapter 15.

Brachytherapy. Brachytherapy (internal radiation) is used for partial-breast radiation. It is an alternative to traditional external radiation treatment for some patients with early-stage breast cancer.[14] This method has the same chance for local recurrence as whole breast radiation. However, some studies show the cosmetic results are not as good.

Brachytherapy is minimally invasive. The radiation is delivered directly into the cavity left after a tumor is surgically removed by a lumpectomy. Because the radiation is concentrated and focused on the area with the highest risk for tumor recurrence, it only requires 5 treatments. Therapy is delivered using a multicatheter method or balloon-catheter system.

In the *multicatheter method* (e.g., SAVI) many very small catheters are placed in the breast at the site of the tumor. The SAVI is inserted through a small incision, and the catheter bundle expands uniformly. The ends of the catheters stick out through little holes in the skin. Small radioactive seeds are placed in the catheters. The seeds are left in place just long enough to deliver the radiation dose (e.g., 5 to 10 minutes) then removed. The radiation does not remain in the body between treatments or after the last treatment is over.

In the *balloon-catheter system,* a balloon is placed where the tumor was located. The balloon is filled with fluid, to keep it in place, then radioactive seeds are inserted (Fig. 51.7). Radiation is emitted by a tiny radioactive seed attached by a wire to an afterloader, a computer-controlled machine. The seed travels through the MammoSite applicator into the inflated balloon. As with the multicatheter system, the radiation does not remain in

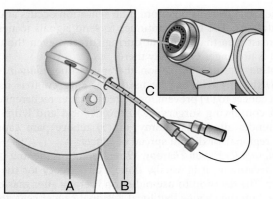

FIG. 51.7 High-dose brachytherapy for breast cancer. The MammoSite system involves the insertion of a single small balloon catheter *(B)* at the time of the lumpectomy or shortly thereafter into the tumor resection cavity (the space that is left after the HCP removes the tumor). A tiny radioactive seed *(A)* is inserted into the balloon, connected to a machine called an *afterloader (C)*, and delivers the radiation therapy.

the body between treatments or after the last treatment is over. Once the last session is done, the balloon is deflated, and the system is removed.

Palliative Radiation Therapy. In addition to reducing the primary tumor mass with a resultant decrease in pain, radiation therapy can be used to treat symptomatic metastatic lesions in such sites as bone, soft tissue organs, brain, and chest. Radiation therapy often relieves pain and is successful in controlling recurrent or metastatic disease.

Drug Therapy. Drug therapy includes chemotherapy, hormone therapy, immunotherapy, and targeted therapy. When drug therapy is given before surgery, we call it *neoadjuvant therapy.* Neoadjuvant therapy is often used to shrink the size of the tumor enough to make surgical removal possible or to allow for breast-conserving surgery in women who would have been recommended to have a mastectomy. It also allows time for genetic testing to occur (if appropriate) so a patient can make a more informed decision about what type of surgery to have. Drug therapy after surgery is called *adjuvant therapy.* Drug therapy can decrease the rate of recurrence and increase the length of survival. Because of the risk for recurrent disease, nearly all patients with evidence of node involvement, particularly those who are hormone receptor negative, will have some type of drug therapy. Some patients, particularly those with a more aggressive tumor, are known to be at higher risk for recurrent or metastatic disease. Drug therapy may be used for these patients even when there is no evidence of node involvement. Weighing the risks and benefits of drug therapy is a complex process.[14]

Chemotherapy. Chemotherapy is the use of cytotoxic drugs to destroy cancer cells. A combination of drugs is usually superior to the use of a single drug. Combination treatment is best because the drugs have different mechanisms of action and work at different parts of the cell cycle. When used in the neoadjuvant and adjuvant setting, chemotherapy is usually given for 3 to 6 months. However, when a patient has metastasis, chemotherapy may be given for the rest of the patient's life.

Common combination-therapy protocols in the adjuvant and neoadjuvant setting are (1) CMF: cyclophosphamide, methotrexate, and fluorouracil; (2) AC: doxorubicin and cyclophosphamide, with or without the addition of a taxane, such as paclitaxel (Taxol) or docetaxel (Taxotere); or (3) CEF or CAF: cyclophosphamide, epirubicin (Ellence) or doxorubicin, and fluorouracil.

💊 DRUG ALERT Doxorubicin

- Monitor for signs of cardiotoxicity and heart failure (e.g., shortness of breath, pedal edema, decreased activity tolerance, dysrhythmias, ECG changes).
- Tell the patient not to have immunizations without the HCP's approval.

Teach patients to avoid contact with those who recently received live virus vaccine and those with infections. Because chemotherapy affects healthy cells, many side effects accompany chemotherapy. The incidence and severity of common side effects are related to specific drug combination, drug schedule, and dosage. The most common side effects involve rapidly dividing cells in the gastrointestinal tract (nausea, anorexia, weight loss), bone marrow (anemia), and hair follicles (hair loss).

Cognitive changes during and after treatment can occur. This phenomenon is called *"chemobrain."* These changes include difficulties in concentration, memory, focus, and attention. Cognitive changes in cancer are discussed in Chapter 15 on p. 251.

EVIDENCE-BASED PRACTICE
Treatment for Breast Cancer

C.P. is a 56-yr-old woman who was diagnosed with stage IIIA breast cancer. Her treatment plan is to receive neoadjuvant chemotherapy and then have surgery and radiation. C.P. tells you that she is anxious and will have surgery and radiation but does not want chemotherapy because she is afraid of the side effects.

Making Clinical Decisions

Best Available Evidence. The use of chemotherapy before surgery reduces the size and extent of the tumor, thus making the surgery more likely to succeed. It reduces the chance a more extensive treatment will be needed.

Clinician Expertise. Neoadjuvant chemotherapy is usually recommended for stage IIIA breast cancer. The common side effects (e.g., nausea, vomiting, fatigue) can be managed with appropriate treatment.

Patient Preferences and Values. C.P. does not want chemotherapy and prefers to take her chances. If the cancer comes back, she will have chemotherapy.

Implications for Nursing Practice

1. Why is it important to discuss with C.P. the reason chemotherapy is recommended?
2. What information would you share with her about treatment side effects and how they can be managed?
3. You note her spouse appears attentive and supportive. How will you involve him in C.P.'s care?

Reference for Evidence

National Comprehensive Cancer Network: NCCN guidelines for patients: Invasive breast cancer, 2018. Retrieved from *www.nccn. org/patients/guidelines/breast-invasive/index.html.*

Hormone Therapy. Estrogen can promote the growth of breast cancer cells if the cells are ER positive. Hormone therapy can block the effect and source of estrogen, promoting tumor regression.

ER and PR status assays can identify women whose breast cancers are likely to respond to hormone therapy. These assays predict whether hormone therapy is a treatment option. Chances of tumor regression are significantly greater in women whose tumors have estrogen and progesterone receptors. The 21-gene recurrence score (OncotypeDX) is an excellent prognostic assay to identify which women with hormone-positive breast cancer can be treated with hormone therapy alone and do not need chemotherapy.

TABLE 51.8 Drug Therapy

Breast Cancer

Drug Class	Mechanism of Action	Indications
Hormone Therapy		
Aromatase Inhibitors		
anastrozole (Arimidex) exemestane (Aromasin) letrozole (Femara)	Prevents production of estrogen by inhibiting aromatase	ER-positive breast cancer in postmenopausal women only
Estrogen Receptor Blockers		
fulvestrant (Faslodex)	Blocks estrogen receptors (ERs)	ER-positive breast cancer in postmenopausal women only
tamoxifen	Blocks ERs	ER-positive breast cancer in premenopausal and postmenopausal women Used as a preventive measure in high-risk premenopausal and postmenopausal women
toremifene (Fareston)	Blocks ERs	ER-positive breast cancer in postmenopausal women only
Estrogen Receptor Modulator		
raloxifene (Evista)	In breast, blocks the effect of estrogen. In bone, promotes effect of estrogen and prevents bone loss	Postmenopausal women
Immunotherapy and Targeted Therapy		
ado-trastuzumab emtansine (Kadcyla)	Trastuzumab connected to a chemotherapy drug called DM1	HER-2-positive breast cancer
everolimus (Afinitor)	Binds to mechanistic target of rapamycin (mTOR), thereby suppressing T cell activation and proliferation	ER-positive, HER-2-negative breast cancer in postmenopausal women
lapatinib (Tykerb)	Inhibits HER-2 tyrosine kinase and EGFR tyrosine kinase	HER-2-positive breast cancer
abemaciclib (Verzenio) palbociclib (Ibrance) ribociclib (Kisqali)	Kinase inhibitors	ER-positive, HER-2-negative breast cancer in postmenopausal women
neratinib (Nerlynx) pertuzumab (Perjeta) trastuzumab (Herceptin) trastuzumab-pkrb (Herzuma) trastuzumab-qyyp (Trazimera)	Blocks HER-2 receptor	HER-2-positive breast cancer

Hormone therapy can (1) block ERs or (2) suppress estrogen synthesis by inhibiting aromatase, an enzyme needed for estrogen synthesis (Table 51.8). Premenopausal women with ER-positive breast cancers may benefit from the removal or suppression of their ovaries. Ovarian ablation can be done surgically or by using luteinizing hormone–releasing hormone (LHRH) analogs, such as goserelin (Zoladex) or leuprolide (Lupron).

Estrogen Receptor Blockers. ER blockers include tamoxifen, toremifene (Fareston), and fulvestrant (Faslodex). Tamoxifen has been the hormone therapy of choice in ER-positive women with all stages of breast cancer over the past 30 years. It also may be used in high-risk women to prevent breast cancer. Common side effects include hot flashes, mood swings, vaginal discharge and dryness, and other effects associated with decreased estrogen. It also increases the risk for blood clots, cataracts, stroke, and endometrial cancer in postmenopausal women.

💊 DRUG ALERT Tamoxifen

- Irregular vaginal bleeding or spotting may occur.
- Decreased visual acuity, corneal opacity, and retinopathy can occur in women receiving high doses (240–320 mg/day for >17 mo). These problems may be irreversible.
- Teach the patient to immediately report decreased visual acuity.
- Monitor for signs of deep vein thrombosis, pulmonary embolism, and stroke, including shortness of breath, leg cramps, and weakness.

Aromatase inhibitors. Aromatase inhibitor drugs interfere with the anastrozole enzyme aromatase, which is needed for the synthesis of estrogen. These drugs include anastrozole, letrozole (Femara), and exemestane (Aromasin). They are used in the treatment of breast cancer in postmenopausal women. Aromatase inhibitors do not block the production of estrogen by the ovaries. Thus they are of little benefit and may be harmful in premenopausal women.

Aromatase inhibitors have different side effects than tamoxifen. They rarely cause blood clots and do not cause endometrial cancer. Because they block the production of estrogen in postmenopausal women, osteoporosis and bone fractures may occur. These drugs have been associated with night sweats, nausea, arthralgias, and myalgias.

Estrogen receptor modulator and others. Raloxifene (Evista) is a selective ER modulator that has both estrogen-agonistic effects on bone and estrogen-antagonistic effects on breast tissue. (Raloxifene is discussed in the section on osteoporosis in Chapter 63.) Less common drugs that may be used to suppress hormone-dependent breast tumors include megestrol acetate, diethylstilbestrol, and fluoxymesterone.

Immunotherapy and Targeted Therapy. As more is known about the genetic changes in breast cancer, we have developed drugs that specifically target cells that have altered gene expression. One of these genetic changes is the overexpression of HER-2.

Tumors that overexpress the HER-2 protein tend to be more aggressive and are more likely to recur.

Trastuzumab (Herceptin) is a monoclonal antibody to HER-2. After the antibody attaches to the antigen, blocks signals that tell the cancer cells to proliferate. It can be used alone or in combination with chemotherapy agents. The most common side effects are flu-like symptoms (fever, chills, myalgia), nausea and vomiting, diarrhea, and infusion reactions. Another possible, but more serious side effect, is heart damage. Trastuzumab-qyyp (Trazimera) and trastuzumab-pkrb (Herzuma) are newly approved biosimiliars of trastuzamab.

💊 DRUG ALERT Trastuzumab (Herceptin)

- Use with caution in women with preexisting heart disease.
- Monitor for signs of ventricular dysfunction and heart failure.

Other drugs that target HER-2 include pertuzumab (Perjeta) and ado-trastuzumab emtansine (Kadcyla). Kadcyla is trastuzumab connected to a chemotherapy drug called DM1. Lapatinib (Tykerb) works inside the cell by blocking the function of the HER-2 protein. Nerotinib (Nerlynx) is an option for extended adjuvant therapy for some high-risk women. Using 2 of these agents together for neoadjuvant therapy can increase the number of tumors that become undetectable and can improve survival when used for adjuvant therapy. Other drugs that target HER-2 include pertuzumab (Perjeta), trastuzumab-qyyp (Trazimera), trastuzumab-pkrb (Herzuma), and ado-trastuzumab emtansine (Kadcyla). Kadcyla is trastuzumab connected to a chemotherapy drug called DM1. Lapatinib (Tykerb) works inside the cell by blocking the function of the HER-2 protein. Using 2 of these agents together for neoadjuvant therapy can increase the number of tumors that become undetectable.

Drugs in other classes that are used to treat breast cancer include everolimus (Afinitor) and the CDK 4 and 6 inhibitors palbociclib (Ibrance), ribociclib (Kisquali), and abemaciclib (Verzenio). Everolimus works by blocking mTOR, a protein that normally promotes cell growth and division. CDK 4 and 6 inhibitors prevent cells from dividing, thus slowing cancer growth. (The use of immunotherapy and targeted therapy is discussed in Chapter 15.)

🌐 Culturally Competent Care: Breast Cancer

Differences exist in the incidence, mortality rates, and care issues among diverse racial and ethnic groups related to breast cancer (see Promoting Health Equity box on this page). In addition,

🌐 PROMOTING HEALTH EQUITY
Breast Cancer

- White and black women have the highest incidence of breast cancer.
- Black women have lower survival rates from breast cancer than white women, even when diagnosed at an early stage.
- Hispanic and black women are more likely to be diagnosed at a later stage of breast cancer than white women.
- Triple-negative breast cancer has a higher incidence in black and Hispanic women.
- Mortality rates are lower among Hispanic and Asian/Pacific Islander women than among white and black women.
- Breast cancer is the most common diagnosed cancer among Hispanic women.
- Indian/Alaskan native women have the lowest rate of breast cancer screening of any ethnic group.

cultural differences may involve gender roles, health beliefs, religion, family structure, socioeconomic factors (e.g., poverty) and lack of health insurance. Lack of education may influence disparities related to access to health care and having recommended surveillance examinations.[17,18]

Cultural values strongly influence how a person responds to and copes with breast cancer and treatment. Diverse cultural norms influence health beliefs and behaviors. Breast cancer screening, diagnosis, and treatment are affected by the cultural values and meanings (body image, sexuality, modesty, motherhood) associated with the breasts. Women may delay screening or treatment for varying reasons, including an acceptance of disease as inevitable fate or "God's will," a mistrust of Western medicine, lack of health care benefits, fear, or the stigma of a cancer diagnosis.

❖ NURSING MANAGEMENT: BREAST CANCER

◆ Nursing Assessment

You must consider many factors when assessing a patient with a breast problem. The history of the breast disorder helps establish a diagnosis. Investigate the presence of nipple discharge, pain, rate of growth of the lump, breast asymmetry, and correlation with the menstrual cycle.

Carefully record the size and location of the lump or lumps. Assess the physical characteristics of the lesion, including consistency, mobility, and shape. If nipple discharge is present, note the color and consistency and whether it occurs from 1 or both breasts.

Subjective and objective data to obtain from a person suspected of having or diagnosed with breast cancer are outlined in Table 51.9.

◆ Nursing Diagnoses

Nursing diagnoses related to the care of a patient diagnosed with breast cancer vary. After diagnosis and before a treatment plan has been selected, the following nursing diagnoses would apply:
- Difficulty coping
- Lack of knowledge
- Disturbed body image

If surgery is planned, the nursing diagnoses and interventions may include those in eNursing Care Plan 51.1 (available on the website for this chapter).

◆ Planning

The overall goals are that the patient with breast cancer will (1) actively take part in the decision-making process related to treatment, (2) adhere to the therapeutic plan, (3) communicate about and manage the side effects of adjuvant therapy, (4) access and benefit from the support provided by significant others and HCPs, and (5) adhere to recommended follow-up and surveillance after treatment.

◆ Nursing Implementation

◆ **Health Promotion.** Review the risk factors in Table 51.2. People can reduce their risk factors by maintaining a healthy weight, exercising regularly, limiting alcohol, eating nutritious food, and never smoking (or quitting if currently smoking).

Encourage people to adhere to the breast cancer screening guidelines shown on pp. 1190–1191. A person at high risk needs to develop a personalized plan with the HCP. Early detection

TABLE 51.9 Nursing Assessment
Breast Cancer

Subjective Data

Important Health Information

Past health history: Benign breast disease with atypical changes. Previous unilateral breast cancer. Menstrual history (early menarche with late menopause), pregnancy history (nulliparity or first full-term pregnancy after age 30). Endometrial, ovarian, or colon cancer. Hyperestrogenism and testicular atrophy (in men)

Medicines: Hormones, especially as postmenopausal hormone therapy and in oral contraceptives. Infertility treatments

Surgery or other treatments: Exposure to therapeutic radiation (e.g., Hodgkin's lymphoma or thyroid radiation)

Functional Health Patterns

Health perception–health management: Family history of breast cancer (young age at diagnosis). History of abnormal mammogram or atypical prior biopsy. Palpable change found on BSE. Known *BRCA* mutation carrier, first-degree relative of *BRCA* carrier (but untested)

Nutritional-metabolic: Obesity; unexplained severe weight loss (may indicate metastasis)

Activity-exercise: Level of usual activity

Cognitive-perceptual: Changes in cognition, headache, bone pain (may indicate metastasis)

Sexuality-reproductive: Unilateral nipple discharge (clear, milky, bloody). Change in breast contour, size, or symmetry

Coping–stress tolerance: Psychologic stress

Self-perception–self-concept: Anxiety about threat to self-esteem

Objective Data

General

Axillary and supraclavicular lymphadenopathy

Integumentary

Hard, irregular, nonmobile breast lump most often in upper, outer sector, possibly fixated to fascia or chest wall. Thickening of breast. Nipple inversion or retraction, erosion. Edema ("peau d'orange"), erythema, induration, infiltration, or dimpling (in later stages). Firm, discrete nodules at mastectomy site (may indicate local recurrence). Peripheral edema (may indicate metastasis)

Respiratory

Pleural effusions (may indicate metastasis)

Gastrointestinal

Hepatomegaly, jaundice, ascites (may indicate liver metastasis)

Possible Diagnostic Findings

Finding of mass or change in tissue on breast examination. Abnormal mammogram, ultrasound, or breast MRI. Positive results of FNA or surgical biopsy; similar results with a needle biopsy

---

can decrease the morbidity and mortality associated with breast cancer.

Along with these lifestyle choices, there are other risk-reduction options for people at high risk. Genetic testing for *BRCA* and other gene mutations is available. People with a strong family history of breast cancer should talk with their HCP about the possibility of genetic testing. There is no reason for routine screening for genetic abnormalities in women without evidence of a strong family history of breast cancer.

In women with an abnormal *BRCA1* or *BRCA2* gene, prophylactic oophorectomy may reduce their risk for developing breast cancer and ovarian cancer. In deciding whether and when to undergo this surgical procedure, women should receive counseling about the risks and benefits of prophylactic oophorectomy, including fertility issues.

Prophylactic surgery decisions require a great deal of thought, patience, and discussion with the HCP, genetic counselor, and family. Patients need to consider these options and make decisions with which they feel comfortable. Removing both breasts and ovaries at a young age does not eliminate the risk for breast cancer. A small risk exists that cancer can develop in the areas where the breasts used to be. Close follow-up is necessary even after prophylactic surgery.

◆ **Acute Care.** The times of waiting for the initial biopsy results and waiting for the HCP to make treatment recommendations are difficult for patients and their families. Even after the HCP has discussed treatment options, the patient often relies on you to clarify and expand on these options. During this stressful time, the patient may not be coping effectively. Appropriate nursing interventions are to explore the patient's usual decision-making processes, help to evaluate the advantages and disadvantages of the options, provide information relevant to the decision, clarify unresolved issues with the HCP, and support the patient and family once the decision is made.

Provide the patient with enough information to ensure informed consent. Some patients seek extensive, detailed information to maintain a sense of control. Others avoid information to decrease anxiety and fear. Be sensitive to the person's need for and preferred type of information. These include (1) instructions on pain control and what to expect after surgery (e.g., dressing and drain care, turning, coughing, deep breathing), (2) a review of mobility restrictions and postoperative exercises, and (3) an explanation of the recovery period.

The woman who has breast-conserving surgery usually has an uncomplicated postoperative course with variable pain intensity. Pain depends primarily on the extent of the lymph node sampling procedure. If an ALND has been done or if the patient had a mastectomy, drains are generally left in place and patients are discharged home with them. Teach the patient and family, with a return demonstration, how to manage the drains at home.

Most patients are discharged from the hospital 24 to 48 hours after a mastectomy, depending on if reconstructive surgery was done. Restoring arm function on the affected side after breast cancer surgery is a key nursing goal. Arm and shoulder exercises, which are started gradually, may begin prior to discharge (Fig. 51.8). These exercises are designed to prevent contractures and muscle shortening, maintain muscle tone, and improve lymph and blood circulation. The difficulty and pain encountered in performing what used to be simple tasks may cause frustration and depression. The goal of all exercise is a gradual return to full range of motion.

Discomfort can be minimized by giving analgesics regularly when the patient is in pain and about 30 minutes before starting exercises. When the patient can shower, the warm water on the involved shoulder often relaxes the muscle and reduces joint stiffness.

Explain the specific follow-up plan to the patient and emphasize the importance of ongoing monitoring and self-care. After surgery, teach the patient to report symptoms, such as fever, inflammation at the surgical site, erythema, and unusual swelling. Other changes to report are new back pain, weakness, shortness of breath, and change in mental status, including confusion.

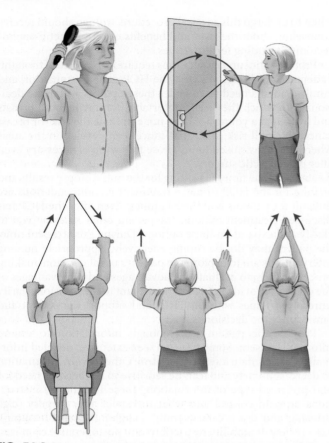

FIG. 51.8 Postoperative exercises for the patient with a mastectomy or lumpectomy with axillary lymph node sampling and/or dissection.

For women who have had a mastectomy without breast reconstruction, a variety of products are available. Your role is to present the choices and resources. Options include garments such as camisoles with soft breast prosthetic inserts or a fitted prosthesis with bra. Should the woman choose a breast prosthesis, a certified fitter can help her choose a comfortable, more permanent weighted prosthesis and bra. This is generally done 4 to 8 weeks after surgery.

Lymphedema. Upper extremity lymphedema can occur at any point after treatment for breast cancer. Teach the patient ways to prevent and reduce lymphedema. These include no BP readings, venipunctures, or injections on the affected arm, if possible. The affected arm should not be dependent for long periods. Caution should be used to prevent infection, burns, or compromised circulation on the affected side. Encourage exercise and maintaining a normal weight.

If trauma to the arm occurs, the area should be washed thoroughly with soap and water and observed. A topical antibiotic ointment and a bandage or other sterile dressing may be applied.

When lymphedema is acute (Fig. 51.6), complete decongestive therapy will be recommended. This therapy is performed by specially trained professionals. It consists of a massage-like technique to mobilize the subcutaneous accumulation of fluid. This may be followed by use of compression bandaging and an intermittent pneumatic compression sleeve. The sleeve applies mechanical massage to the arm and helps move lymph drainage up toward the heart. Elevating the arm so that it is level with the heart and performing isometric exercises reduce the fluid in the

arm. To maintain maximum volume reduction, the patient may need to wear a fitted compression sleeve during waking hours and preventively during air travel.

Psychosocial Support. Throughout history, the female breast has been a symbol of beauty, femininity, sexuality, and motherhood. The potential loss of a breast, or part of a breast, may be devastating for many women because of the significant psychologic, social, sexual, and body image implications associated with it. For men diagnosed with breast cancer, isolation and embarrassment related to the diagnosis can occur. You must be aware of resources for men (*www.malebreastcancer.org*).

As hard as it is to predict which patients will develop physical effects of treatment, it can be even more difficult to foresee the psychosocial effects of treatment. In some cases, psychosocial concerns may increase the physical effects of cancer, such as pain, fatigue, sleep problems, fear of recurrence, and cognitive changes.

Screening all cancer patients for psychosocial distress is a Commission on Cancer accreditation requirement.[19] From the time of diagnosis through treatment, survivorship, or metastatic disease, the patient may have signs of distress or tension (e.g., tachycardia, increased muscle tension, sleep problems, restlessness, changes in appetite or mood). Assess the patient's body language and affect during periods of high stress and indecision so that you can begin appropriate interventions, including referral to a mental health provider.

Remain sensitive to the complex psychologic impact that a diagnosis of cancer and breast surgery can have on patients and their families. With an accepting attitude and the offer of resources, you can help the patient cope with feelings of fear, anger, anxiety, and depression. You can help to:

- Provide a safe environment for the expression of feelings.
- Identify sources of support and strength, such as the partner, family, and spiritual or religious practices.
- Encourage the patient to identify and learn personal coping strengths.
- Promote communication among the patient, family, and friends.
- Answer questions about the disease, treatment options, and reproductive, fertility, or lactation issues (if appropriate).
- Make resources available for mental health counseling.
- Offer information about local and national community resources.

Referring patients to support resources, such as *www.Breastcancer.org*, the Cancer Support Community, or local breast cancer organizations, is valuable. The ACS and National Cancer Institute can provide excellent materials to help you in meeting the special needs of patients with breast cancer. In addition to in-person and online support programs, multiple free smart phone applications are available through national cancer organizations that provide reliable and current information for the patient and his or her family.

How the loss of part or all of the breast and cancer affect the patient's sexual identity, body image, and relationships can vary. Many HCPs do not adequately address sexual concerns. If you are comfortable, begin a discussion of sexuality by inviting questions about relationships or intimacy concerns. Often the patient's partner and/or family members need help dealing with their emotional reactions to the diagnosis and surgery before they can provide effective support for the patient. There are no physical reasons why a mastectomy would prevent sexual satisfaction. A woman taking hormone therapy may have a decreased sexual

COMPLEMENTARY & ALTERNATIVE THERAPIES

Supportive Care

Many women use complementary and integrative therapies as supportive care during cancer treatment to improve quality of life and manage treatment-related side effects.

Scientific Evidence

- There is strong evidence that practicing meditation and relaxation decreases anxiety and depression and improves quality of life.
- Stress management, yoga, massage, music therapy, and meditation decrease stress, fatigue, anxiety, and depression and improve quality of life.

Nursing Implications

- Women use a variety of integrative therapies during breast cancer treatment.
- Meditation, yoga, relaxation, stress management, massage, music therapy, and energy conservation may be especially helpful in managing symptoms and improving quality of life during treatment.

Reference for Evidence

Greenlee H, DuPont-Reyes MJ, Balneaves L, et al.: Clinical practice guidelines on the evidence-based use of integrative therapies during and after breast cancer treatment, *CA Cancer J Clin* 67:1954, 2017.

drive or vaginal dryness. She may need to use lubrication to prevent discomfort during intercourse. If difficulty in adjustment or other problems develop, single or couples counseling may be useful to deal with the emotional side of a diagnosis of cancer.

Depression and anxiety may occur with the continued stress and uncertainty of a cancer diagnosis. A patient's self-esteem and identity may be threatened. The support of family and friends and taking part in a cancer support group and/or counseling are important aspects of care that may improve the patient's quality of life.

Survivorship. Almost 3 million breast cancer survivors are alive in the United States, making this population the largest group of cancer survivors. We expect this number to grow due to an aging population and improved methods for early detection and treatment. After treatment for breast cancer, the patient will have ongoing survivorship care.[19,20]

A history and physical examination is recommended 1 to 4 times per year as clinically appropriate for 5 years, then annually thereafter. In addition, teach breast cancer survivors to perform monthly BSE and chest wall self-examination and report any changes to their HCP. Local recurrence of breast cancer is usually at the surgical site. Breast cancer survivors should have an annual mammogram. Other breast imaging studies, such as a breast ultrasound or breast MRI, should be done only as an adjunct to mammography and not for annual routine surveillance. Cancer survivorship is discussed in Chapter 15 on p. 264.

◆ Evaluation

Expected outcomes are that the patient after breast cancer surgery will

- Identify activities that can reduce postoperative edema and improve mobility
- Show effective use of coping strategies
- Discuss feelings about and the meaning of changes in physical appearance
- Identify community and online resources, personal counseling resources, and support groups

Gerontologic Considerations: Breast Cancer

A major risk for breast cancer is increasing age. More than half of all breast cancers occur in women who are age 65 or older.[1] Older women are less likely to have mammograms. Screening and treatment decisions for breast cancer should be based on a woman's general health status rather than biologic age, since health status has a greater influence on tolerance to treatment and long-term prognosis. In addition to medical co-morbidities and life expectancy, treatment decisions for the older woman with breast cancer should be based on an assessment of nutritional and functional status; vision, gait, and balance; and the presence of delirium, dementia, or depression.

Breast cancer treatment is similar for older and younger patients, including the use of surgery, radiation therapy, and drug therapy. For healthy older women, breast cancer survival rates are similar to those of younger women when matched by cancer stage.

MAMMOPLASTY

Mammoplasty is the surgical change in the size or shape of the breast. It may be done electively for cosmetic purposes to either enlarge or reduce the size of the breasts. It also may be done to reconstruct the breast after a mastectomy.

A professional, nonjudgmental attitude and clear information about surgical breast options are most useful for women engaged in decision making about mammoplasty. The desire to change the appearance of the breasts has special significance for each woman as she attempts to change or recreate her body image. Be aware of the cultural value that the woman places on the breast. Help the patient set realistic expectations about what mammoplasty can achieve and possible complications (e.g., hematoma formation, hemorrhage, infection). If an implant is involved, capsular contracture and loss of the implant are possible.

Breast Reconstruction

Breast reconstructive surgery is a type of surgery for women who have had all or part of a breast removed. It is done to achieve symmetry and to restore or preserve body image. It may be done simultaneously with a mastectomy or some time afterward. The timing of reconstructive surgery is personalized based on the patient's physical and psychologic needs.[21]

Indications. The main indication for breast reconstruction is to improve a woman's self-image, regain a sense of normalcy, and assist in coping with the loss of the breast. It restores the contour of the breast without the use of an external prosthesis. Reconstruction techniques cannot restore lactation, nipple sensation, or erectility. Although the breast will not fully resemble its premastectomy appearance, the reconstructed appearance usually is an improvement over the mastectomy scar (Fig. 51.9).

Types of Reconstruction

Breast Implants and Tissue Expansion. Implants have a silicone shell filled with either silicone gel or saline.[22] Some newer types use a cohesive gel, which is a thicker silicone gel. Implant surgery can be done in 1 or 2 stages.

In the 1-stage procedure, the implant is placed at the same time as the mastectomy. The implant is usually placed under the pectoralis muscle.

In the 2-stage procedure, a tissue expander is inserted after the mastectomy. The expander stretches the skin and muscle at the mastectomy site before inserting permanent implants (Fig. 51.10). It is placed in a pocket under the pectoralis muscle,

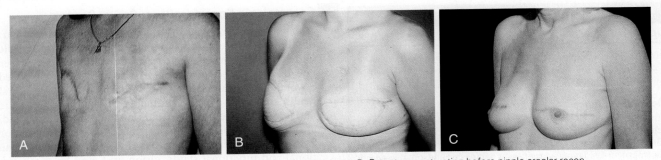

FIG. 51.9 A, Appearance of chest after bilateral mastectomy. B, Breast reconstruction before nipple-areolar reconstruction. C, Breast reconstruction after nipple-areolar reconstruction. (Courtesy Brian Davies, MD. From Fortunato N, McCullough S, eds: *Plastic and reconstructive surgery,* St Louis, 1998, Mosby.)

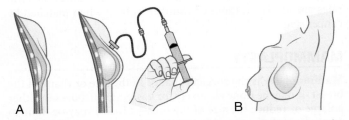

FIG. 51.10 A, Tissue expander with gradual expansion. B, Tissue expander in place after mastectomy.

which protects the implant and provides soft tissue coverage. The expander is minimally inflated, then gradually filled by weekly injections of sterile saline solution. This procedure stretches the skin and muscle and can be painful. A small magnet embedded in most expanders helps locate the port where the fluid is injected. A woman should not have an MRI with a magnet in place.

The expander can be (1) surgically removed and a permanent implant is inserted or (2) remain in place to become the implant, thus eliminating the need for a second surgical procedure. Tissue expansion does not work well in those with extensive scar tissue from surgery or radiation therapy.

The body's natural response to the presence of a foreign substance is the formation of a fibrous capsule around the implant. If excessive capsular formation occurs because of infection, hematoma, trauma, or reaction to a foreign body, a contracture can develop, resulting in deformity. Although HCPs differ in their approaches to the prevention of contracture formation, gentle manual massage around the implant is routine. Other adverse outcomes include wrinkling, scarring, asymmetry, pain, and infection at the incision site. There is a small chance of anaplastic large cell lymphoma occurring. This has mostly been associated with textured implants.[19]

Tissue Flap Procedures. Another type of breast reconstruction uses autologous (person's own) tissue to recreate a breast mound. In autologous reconstruction, tissue from the abdomen, back, thighs, or buttocks is used to create a reconstructed breast. The most common types of tissue flap procedures are *transverse rectus abdominis musculocutaneous (TRAM) flap, deep inferior epigastric artery perforator (DIEP) flap,* and *latissimus dorsi flap.*

The TRAM flap is a common flap surgery. The rectus abdominis muscles are paired flat muscles running from the rib cage down to the pubic bone. Arteries running inside the muscles provide branches at many levels, and these branches supply the fat and skin across a large expanse of the abdomen.

There are 2 different types of TRAM flaps: pedicle and free. In a pedicle flap, the tissue stays attached to the rectus muscle and is tunneled under the skin to the patient's chest (Fig. 51.11). In a free flap, the tissue is completely separated from the muscle and its blood supply and moved to the new place on the patient's chest. The tissue is molded and fashioned to form a breast. The abdominal incision is closed, giving the patient a result that is similar to having an abdominoplasty ("tummy tuck"). The procedure can last 6 to 8 hours with recovery taking 6 to 8 weeks. Some patients have report pain and fatigue for up to 3 months. Complications include bleeding, seroma, hernia, infection, and low back pain.

Perforator flaps are a type of free flap (a perforator artery connects a superficial artery with a deep one) that do not use muscle tissue. A *DIEP flap* is the type done most often. With the DIEP flap, only the skin and fat are taken from the same lower abdominal area as the TRAM flap. Patients may have less pain and restriction of movement with this procedure. The *superficial inferior epigastric artery perforator (SIEAP)* is another option using the abdominal area.

The *latissimus dorsi flap* is a pedicle flap. In this type of flap, a block of skin and muscle from the patient's back replaces tissue removed during mastectomy. A small implant may be needed under the flap to gain reasonable breast shape and size. A disadvantage of this technique is a scar on the back.

Less often, flaps are taken from the buttocks, hips, or thighs. The transverse upper gracilis flap, or inner thigh flap, is one type of free flap. Tissue, including the gracilis muscle, is taken from the bottom fold of the buttock extending into the inner thigh. The inferior or superior gluteal artery perforators are used for flaps taken from the buttocks.

Nipple-Areolar Reconstruction. Many patients undergoing breast reconstruction also have nipple-areolar reconstruction. Nipple reconstruction gives the reconstructed breast a much more natural appearance (Fig. 51.9, *C*). Nipple-areolar reconstruction is usually done a few months after breast reconstruction. Tissue to construct a nipple may be taken from the opposite breast or from a small flap of tissue on the reconstructed breast mound. Most often, the areola is tattooed with a permanent pigmented dye. Improved techniques now allow skilled tattoo artists to create a complete 3D nipple-areola complex. Polyurethane removable nipples are also available.

Breast Augmentation

In *augmentation mammoplasty* (procedure to enlarge the breasts), an implant is placed in a surgically created pocket between the capsule of the breast and pectoral fascia, or

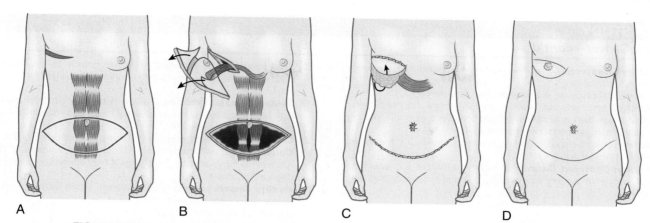

FIG. 51.11 Transverse rectus abdominis musculocutaneous (TRAM) flap. **A,** TRAM flap is planned. **B,** The abdominal tissue, while attached to the rectus muscle, nerve, and blood supply, is tunneled through the abdomen to the chest. **C,** The flap is trimmed to shape the breast. The lower abdominal incision is closed. **D,** Nipple and areola are reconstructed after the breast is healed.

ideally under the pectoralis muscle. (Implants are discussed on p. 1207.)

Breast Reduction

For some women, large breasts can be a source of physical and psychologic discomfort. They can interfere with normal daily activities, such as walking, using a computer, and driving a car. The weight of large breasts can lead to back, shoulder, and neck problems, including degenerative nerve changes. Overly large breasts can interfere with self-esteem, self-image, and comfort in wearing some clothing. Reducing breast size can have positive effects on the patient's psychologic and physical health.

Reduction mammoplasty is done by resecting wedges of tissue from the upper and lower quadrants of the breast. The excess skin is removed, and the areola and nipple are relocated on the breast. Lactation usually can be accomplished if massive amounts of tissue are not removed and the nipples are left connected during surgery.

❖ NURSING MANAGEMENT: BREAST AUGMENTATION AND REDUCTION

Breast augmentation and breast reduction may be done in the outpatient surgical area or involve overnight hospitalization. General anesthesia is used. Drains are generally placed in the surgical site to prevent hematoma formation and then removed when drainage is under 20 to 30 mL/day. Examine drainage for color and odor to detect infection or hemorrhage. Monitor the temperature. Change dressings as needed using sterile technique.

After surgery, assure the woman that the breast's appearance will improve when healing is complete. Depending on HCP preference, the patient may be told to wear a bra that provides good support continuously for 2 or 3 days after breast reduction or augmentation. Depending on the extent of the surgery, most women resume normal activities within 2 to 3 weeks. Strenuous exercise must often be avoided for several weeks.

CASE STUDY
Breast Cancer

(© XiXinXing/ iStock/ Thinkstock.)

Patient Profile

A.K., a 68-yr-old married Asian American woman, has been diagnosed with a 1.3-cm estrogen- and progesterone-positive, HER-2–negative breast cancer. She is scheduled in the morning for a lumpectomy and sentinel lymph node biopsy (SLNB) with possible axillary node dissection.

Interprofessional Care
Preoperative

- When she is seen in the clinic 1 week before surgery, she is crying uncontrollably and says, "My husband does not want to look at me anymore. He is afraid of what I am going to look like with a flat chest."
- She says, "I cannot sleep, and I just pace the floor at night."
- "My mother died of breast cancer when she was 60, and my sister got it when she was 40."
- Expresses concern that her 2 daughters (34 and 32) and their daughters are going to get "this horrible disease."

Operative Procedure

- Lumpectomy and SLNB are done
- Tumor was removed with clear margins
- No cancer cells in her sentinel lymph nodes
- 4 lymph nodes are removed
- Tissue specimen sent for a 21-gene recurrence score genomic test

Postoperative

- Does not want to leave hospital and refuses to get out of bed
- Swelling and restricted range of motion in right arm
- Pain not controlled well with pain medication

Follow-Up Findings and Treatment

- 21-Gene recurrence score is 11, low risk
- Scheduled for external radiation and a consult with medical oncologist to discuss hormone therapy

Discussion Questions

1. What in A.K.'s breast cancer experience with her family members may influence her coping response?

Continued

CASE STUDY

Breast Cancer—cont'd

2. ***Patient-Centered Care:*** How will you include cultural preferences in A.K.'s plan of care?
3. What complication did she develop after her surgery?
4. Which common exercises will A.K. need to practice after her surgery?
5. What information is important for you to provide to A.K. about her radiation treatment and hormonal therapy?
6. ***Safety:*** Describe specific nursing interventions aimed at minimizing risk for harm for A.K.
7. ***Patient-Centered Care:*** What information would you provide to A.K. about her surgery and why the 21-gene recurrence test was done?
8. What information is important for you to provide to A.K. and her daughters? What early detection measures are important for them to know?
9. ***Evidence-Based Practice:*** A.K. wants to know what the psychologic benefit may be for her daughters if they decide on a breast cancer genetic risk assessment.
10. ***Collaboration:*** What types of referrals may be indicated for A.K.?
11. ***Collaboration:*** What community resources are available to help A.K. and her family adjust to the change in her body and cope with the diagnosis of cancer?
12. ***Quality Improvement:*** What outcomes would indicate nursing interventions were successful for A.K.?
13. Develop a conceptual care map for A.K.

Answers and a corresponding conceptual care map available at *http://evolve.elsevier.com/Lewis/medsurg.*

▌ BRIDGE TO NCLEX EXAMINATION

The number of the question corresponds to the same-numbered outcome at the beginning of the chapter.

1. You are a community health nurse planning a program on breast cancer screening guidelines for women in the neighborhood. Which recommendations you would include? *(select all that apply)*
   a. Women over age 55 may have biennial screening.
   b. Screening should end when the women reaches age 65.
   c. Women aged 45 to 54 years should be screened annually.
   d. Regular screening mammography should start at age 45 years.
   e. Clinical breast examinations can be used if the woman has average risk.

2. You are caring for a young woman who has painful fibrocystic breast changes. Management of this patient would include
   a. scheduling a biopsy to rule out the presence of breast cancer.
   b. teaching that symptoms will subside if she stops using oral contraceptives.
   c. preparing her for surgical removal of the lumps, since they will become larger and more painful.
   d. explaining that restricting coffee and chocolate and supplementing with vitamin E may relieve some discomfort.

3. When discussing risk factors for breast cancer with a group of women, you emphasize that the greatest known risk factor for breast cancer is
   a. being a woman over age 60.
   b. experiencing menstruation for 30 years or more.
   c. using hormone therapy for 5 years for menopausal symptoms.
   d. having a paternal grandmother with postmenopausal breast cancer.

4. A patient with breast cancer has a lumpectomy with sentinel lymph node biopsy that is positive for cancer. You explain that, of the other tests done to determine the risk for cancer recurrence or spread, the results that support the more favorable prognosis are *(select all that apply)*
   a. well-differentiated tumor.
   b. estrogen receptor–positive tumor.
   c. overexpression of HER-2 cell marker.
   d. involvement of two to four axillary nodes.
   e. aneuploidy status from cell proliferation studies.

5. You are caring for a patient with breast cancer following a simple mastectomy. Postoperatively, to restore arm function on the affected side, you would
   a. apply heating pads or blankets to increase circulation.
   b. place daily ice packs to minimize the risk for lymphedema.
   c. teach passive exercises with the affected arm in a dependent position.
   d. emphasize regular exercises for the affected shoulder to increase range of motion.

6. Preoperatively, to meet the psychologic needs of a woman scheduled for a simple mastectomy, you would
   a. discuss the limitations of breast reconstruction.
   b. include her significant other in all conversations.
   c. promote an environment for expression of feelings.
   d. explain the importance of regular follow-up screening.

7. To prevent capsular formation after breast reconstruction with implants, teach the patient to
   a. gently massage the area around the implant.
   b. bind the breasts tightly with elastic bandages.
   c. avoid strenuous exercise until the implant has healed.
   d. exercise the arm on the affected side to promote drainage.

1. a, c, d; 2. d; 3. a, b; 4. a, b; 5. d; 6. c; 7. a

For the rationale for these answers and even more NCLEX review questions, visit *http://evolve.elsevier.com/Lewis/medsurg.*

ⓔ EVOLVE WEBSITE/RESOURCES LIST

http://evolve.elsevier.com/Lewis/medsurg
Review Questions (Online Only)
Key Points
Answer Keys for Questions
- Rationales for Bridge to NCLEX Examination Questions
- Answer Guidelines for Case Study on p. 1209

Student Case Study
- Patient With Breast Cancer

Nursing Care Plan
- eNursing Care Plan 51.1: Patient After Breast Surgery

Conceptual Care Map Creator
- Conceptual Care Map for Case Study on p. 1209

Audio Glossary
Content Updates

REFERENCES

1. American Cancer Society: Cancer facts and figures 2017. Retrieved from www.cancer.org/content/dam/cancer-org/research/cancer-facts-and-statistics/annual-cancer-facts-and-figures/2017/cancer-facts-and-figures-2017.pdf.

*2. American Cancer Society: ACS recommendations for early detection of breast cancer. Retrieved from www.cancer.org/cancer/breast-cancer/screening-tests-and-early-detection/american-cancer-society-recommendations-for-the-early-detection-of-breast-cancer.html.

*3. National Comprehensive Cancer Network: NCCN guidelines, version1, 017: Breast cancer screening and diagnosis. Retrieved from www.nccn.org/professionals/physician_gls/pdf/breast-screening.pdf.

4. Liu J, Jacobs L: The management of benign breast disease. In: Cameron J, Cameron A: Current surgical therapy, ed 12, Atlanta, 2017, Elsevier.

5. Nordqviist C. Mastitis: Treatment, causes, and symptoms. Retrieved from www.medicalnewstoday.com/articles/163876.php.

6. Bland KI, Copeland EM, Klimberg VS, et al: The breast comprehensive management of benign and malignant diseases, ed 5, Philadelphia, 2018, Elsevier.

7. Smith R: Fibrocystic breast changes. In: Netter's obstetrics and gynecology, ed 3, Philadelphia, 2018, Elsevier.

*8. American College of Obstetricians and Gynecologists: Practice bulletin: Diagnosis and management of benign breast disorders, Obstet & Gynecol 127:e141, 2016.

9. American Cancer Society: Breast cancer: Risk factors and prevention. Retrieved from www.cancer.org/cancer/breast-cancer/risk-and-prevention.html.

10. National Cancer Institute: Genetics and breast and gynecologic cancers PDQ®—Health professional version. Retrieved from www.cancer.gov/types/breast/hp/breast-ovarian-genetics-pdq.

11. National Comprehensive Cancer Network: NCCN guidelines, version 2, 2017: Genetic/familial high-risk assessment: Breast and ovarian. Retrieved from www.nccn.org/professionals/physician_gls/pdf/genetics_screening.pdf.

12. Breastcancer.org: Gene testing. Retrieved from www.breastcancer.org/symptoms/testing/genetic.

13. Guiliano AE, Connelly JL, Edge SB, et al: Breast cancer—Major changes in the American Joint Committee on Cancer 8th edition cancer staging manual, Cancer J Clin 67:290, 2017.

*14. National Comprehensive Cancer Network: NCCN guidelines, version 2, 2017: Breast cancer. Retrieved from www.nccn.org/professionals/physician_gls/pdf/breast.pdf.

15. About OncotypeDX breast DCIS score. Retrieved from www.oncotypeiq.com/en-US/breast-cancer/patients-and-caregivers/stage-0-dcis/about-the-test.

16. Post-breast therapy pain syndrome. Retrieved from www.cancersupportivecare.com/neuropathicpain.php.

17. Who gets triple negative breast cancer? Retrieved from www.breastcancer.org/symptoms/diagnosis/trip_neg/who_gets.

*18. Koç H, O'Donnell O, Van Ourti T: What explains education disparities in screening mammography in the United States? A comparison with the Netherlands, Int J Environ Res Public Health 15:1961, 2018.

19. American College of Surgeons Commission on Cancer: Cancer program standards 2016 edition: Ensuring survivor-centered care. Retrieved from www.facs.org/~/media/files/quality%20programs/cancer/coc/2016%20coc%20standards%20manual_interactive%20pdf.ashx.

20. Runowicz CD, Leach CR, Henry LH. et al: ACS/American Society of Clinical Oncology breast cancer survivorship care guideline, J Clin Oncol 34:611, 2016.

21. American Cancer Society: Breast reconstructive surgery. Retrieved from www.cancer.org/cancer/breast-cancer/reconstruction-surgery.html.

22. Food and Drug Administration: Breast implants. Retrieved from www.fda.gov/MedicalDevices/ProductsandMedicalProcedures/ImplantsandProsthetics/BreastImplants/default.htm.

*Evidence-based information for clinical practice.

52

Sexually Transmitted Infections

Daniel P. Worrall

The meaning of life is to find your gift. The purpose of life is to give it away.

Pablo Picasso

http://evolve.elsevier.com/Lewis/medsurg

CONCEPTUAL FOCUS

Infection	Reproduction
Pain	Sexuality

LEARNING OUTCOMES

1. Identify factors contributing to sexually transmitted infections (STIs) in the United States.
2. Describe the etiology, clinical manifestations, complications, and diagnostic studies for chlamydia, gonorrhea, trichomoniasis, genital herpes, genital warts, and syphilis.
3. Compare and contrast primary genital herpes with recurrent genital herpes.
4. Explain the interprofessional care and treatment of chlamydia, gonorrhea, trichomoniasis, genital herpes, genital warts, and syphilis.
5. Discuss the nursing assessment for patients who have an STI.
6. Describe the nursing management of patients with STIs.
7. Summarize the nursing role in the prevention and control of STIs.

KEY TERMS

chlamydial infections, p. 1213	gonorrhea, p. 1215	syphilis, p. 1220
genital herpes, p. 1217	sexually transmitted infections (STIs), p. 1212	trichomoniasis, p. 1216
genital warts, p. 1218		

Sexually transmitted infections (STIs) are infectious diseases that are spread through sexual contact with the penis, vagina, anus, mouth, or sexual fluids of an infected person. Many do not view STIs as a serious health threat because they are easily treated. However, the complications are serious and can include infertility and cancer. Having an STI can affect persons' well-being, their relationships, and their sexual lives. Patient education, counseling, and referral are essential nursing roles for promoting health and optimal sexual well-being.

Mucosal tissues in the genitals (urethra in men, vagina in women), rectum, and mouth are especially susceptible to the bacteria and viruses that cause STIs. A list of common STIs is shown in Table 52.1. Some STIs, such as genital human papillomavirus (HPV), can spread from direct skin-to-skin contact with an infected person. Other STIs, such as human immunodeficiency virus (HIV), may be contracted via blood or blood products or be transmitted from mother to baby during pregnancy or labor and delivery. Some STIs can spread through *autoinoculation* (spread of infection by touching or scratching an infected area and transferring it to another part of the body). STIs cannot typically be transmitted from casual contact or inanimate objects.

FACTORS AFFECTING INCIDENCE OF STIs

STIs are quite common. There are nearly 20 million new STIs diagnosed in the United States each year, resulting in an estimated 16 billion in health care costs.[1] More than 110 million Americans are infected with an STI at any given time. Having 1 STI increases the risk for getting another. A person can have more than 1 STI at the same time.

All STIs have an *incubation period*. It is the time from initial infection to the time when symptoms first appear or screening tests for the infection are positive. This can lead to the transmission of disease from an asymptomatic (but infected) person to another person, even before any symptoms or signs begin.

In the United States, all cases of gonorrhea, chlamydia, and syphilis must be reported to public health authorities for surveillance purposes for federally funded control programs and partner notification. Surveillance and partner notification are a major part of the effort to prevent and control the spread of STIs. Nurses and other HCPs play a vital role, as they are mandated to report these STIs to public health authorities. Despite this requirement, only a small number of infections are reported. This is especially important when considering that the

TABLE 52.1 Causes of Sexually Transmitted Infections (STIs)

STI	Cause
Bacterial Infections	
Chlamydial	*Chlamydia trachomatis*
Gonorrhea	*Neisseria gonorrhoeae*
Syphilis	*Treponema pallidum*
Viral Infections	
Genital herpes	Herpes simplex virus (HSV 1 or 2)
Genital warts (*condylomata acuminata*)	Human papillomavirus (HPV)
Human immunodeficiency virus infection (HIV)	Human immunodeficiency virus (HIV) (see Chapter 14)
Hepatitis B and C	Hepatitis B and C viruses (see Chapter 43)
Molluscum	Molluscum contagiosum
Parasitic/Protozoan Infection	
Trichomoniasis	*Trichomonas vaginalis*

TABLE 52.2 Risk Factors for STIs

High-Risk Behaviors
- Alcohol or drug use (inhibits judgment)
- Having new or multiple sexual partners
- Having more than 1 sexual partner
- Having sexual partners who have/have had multiple partners
- Inconsistent or incorrect use of condoms or other barrier methods
- Sharing needles used to inject drugs

High-Risk Medical History
- Having 1 STI is a risk factor for getting another
- Not being vaccinated for STIs or other infections that may be transmitted through some forms sexual activity (HPV, hepatitis A and B)
- Receiving multiple courses of nonoccupational postexposure prophylaxis for HIV infection

High-Risk Populations
- Adolescents and young adults (age <25)
- Ethnicity (e.g., black, American Indian/Alaskan Native, Native Hawaiian/Other Pacific Islander, Hispanic)[1]
- Men who have sex with men
- Persons in correctional facilities
- Transgender persons
- Victims of sexual assault
- Women

Sexually Transmitted Infections

Incidence of STIs
- In the United States, depending on their age-group and gender, blacks have[3]:
  - The highest number of chlamydial infections, occurring at a rate 3.7–8.8 times that of whites.
  - More than 50% of gonorrhea, infected at a rate 7.4–10.3 times that of whites.
  - More than 33% of cases of syphilis, infected at a rate 4.6–7.0 times that of whites.
- Non-Hispanic and black persons have a higher seroprevalence of herpes simplex type 2.[3]

Factors Influencing Disparities
- Social and economic disadvantages can make it hard for people to care for their overall health, including their sexual health.
- People who cannot afford basic necessities may have trouble accessing and affording quality sexual health services.
- Fear and distrust of HCPs and institutions can negatively affect racial and ethnic minorities from seeking health care.
- In communities in which there is a higher prevalence of STIs, it may be hard to reduce the risk for infection because with any sexual encounter a person faces a higher chance of having an infected partner than in those communities with a lower prevalence.

more than 2 million cases of gonorrhea, chlamydia, and syphilis reported in the United States annually do not represent the actual number of infections.

Many factors contribute to the high rate of STIs.[2,3] Earlier reproductive maturity and increased longevity make for a longer sexual life span. Other factors include (1) greater sexual freedom, (2) inconsistent or incorrect use of barrier methods (e.g., condoms) during sexual activity, and (3) the media's increasing emphasis on sexuality without mentioning safer sex. Substance use can further contribute to unsafe sexual practices by impairing judgment. Risk factors for STIs are outlined in Table 52.2.

STIs affect certain groups of people disproportionately. This includes youth under age 25 and those who are socially and economically disadvantaged.

Trends in methods of contraceptive use also affect the rate of STIs. The male condom is the best form of protection (other than abstinence) against STIs. Although condom use has increased in the United States, condoms are not often used in the general population. Most women use hormonal (e.g., oral contraceptive pills, patch, injectables) or long-acting reversible contraceptives (e.g., intrauterine devices, implantable devices).[4] These do not provide barrier protection against STIs.[5]

This chapter covers the most common forms of STIs. HIV infection is covered in Chapter 14. Anyone who contracts an STI may also be at risk for HIV infection. HIV preexposure prophylaxis (PrEP) or nonoccupational postexposure prophylaxis (nPEP) may be appropriate for these persons.[6] See Chapter 14 for more about PrEP and nPEP.

STIs CHARACTERIZED BY DISCHARGE, CERVICITIS, OR URETHRITIS

CHLAMYDIAL INFECTIONS

Chlamydia is the most common reportable STI in the United States. Nearly 1.6 million cases are reported annually, and incidence is on the rise. As many infections are asymptomatic, the actual number of infections is significantly higher.[1]

Etiology and Pathophysiology

Chlamydial infections are caused by *Chlamydia trachomatis*, a gram-negative bacterium and intracellular pathogen. *Chlamydia* is transmitted through exposure to sexual fluids during vaginal, anal, or oral sex. Ejaculation does not have to occur for it to be transmitted. The incubation period for chlamydia is 1 to 3 weeks. Infection with *Chlamydia* does not provide protection from reinfection. This means that people who were treated for chlamydial infection can always be reinfected.

The most common site for infection in men is the urethra. Infections in the male urethra are called *urethritis*. The most

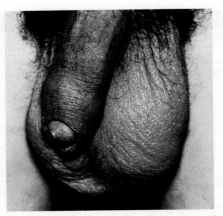

FIG. 52.1 Chlamydial epididymitis. Red, swollen scrotum. (From Morse S, Moreland A, Holmes K: *Atlas of sexually transmitted diseases and AIDS,* London, 1996, Mosby-Wolfe.)

TABLE 52.3 Interprofessional Care
Chlamydial Infections

Diagnostic Assessment
- History and physical examination
- Nucleic acid amplification test (NAAT)
- Testing for other STIs (gonorrhea, HIV, syphilis)

Management
- Azithromycin (Zithromax) or doxycycline (Vibramycin)
- Alternative regimen: erythromycin, ofloxacin, or levofloxacin (Levaquin)
- Teach to abstain from sexual contact for 7 days after completing treatment
- Treat all sexual partners, who must also wait 7 days before resuming sexual contact

common site for infection for women is the cervix. Infections in the female cervix are called *cervicitis*. Both men and women can get chlamydia of the rectum from receptive anal sex or the oropharynx from giving oral sex. Because the vagina acts as a natural reservoir for infectious secretions, STI transmission is often more efficient from men to women than it is from women to men.

There are many serotypes of the *C. trachomatis* bacteria. A subset of these strains can cause another STI, lymphogranuloma venereum (LGV). More common serotypes are often the cause of nongonococcal urethritis (NGU).

Clinical Manifestations

Patients with chlamydia often have no symptoms. However, if symptoms develop in men, they may have pain with urination or a urethral discharge. Rarely, men can have pain or swelling of the testicles caused by infection of the epididymis (Fig. 52.1). Symptoms of cervicitis include mucopurulent discharge (mucus with pus), bleeding, dysuria, and pain with intercourse. Symptoms of rectal chlamydia include anorectal pain, discharge, bleeding, pruritus, tenesmus, mucus-coated stools, or painful bowel movements.

Complications

Complications often develop from poorly managed, inaccurately diagnosed, or undiagnosed chlamydia. Chlamydia is often not diagnosed until complications occur. While men rarely have long-term complications from infection, epididymitis can result in male infertility. More often, chlamydia can affect a woman's reproductive tract, resulting in *pelvic inflammatory disease* (PID).[7] PID can damage fallopian tubes and increases a woman's risk for an ectopic pregnancy (pregnancy outside of uterus), infertility, and chronic pelvic pain. The risk for developing PID increases with repeated infection The more episodes of PID, the more likely a woman will experience infertility. Both men and women can develop a rare reactive arthritis, an autoimmune response to infection with *C. trachomatis*.

Diagnostic Studies

Diagnosis of any STI requires an accurate sexual history, a physical examination, and laboratory tests specific to each infection. The preferred method for diagnosing chlamydia is through a nucleic acid amplification test (NAAT) (Table 52.3). NAAT is used to identify small amounts of DNA or RNA in test samples. NAAT can be done on endocervical or vaginal swabs from women, urethral swabs from men, and urine from both men and women. NAATs are the recommended test for rectal and oropharyngeal screening and diagnosis.[8]

Interprofessional Care

Because of the high prevalence of asymptomatic infections, regular screening for chlamydia in high-risk populations is recommended (Table 52.2). Anyone diagnosed and treated for chlamydia needs to return for testing 3 months after treatment to be sure that they have not been reinfected or to detect treatment failure.

Drug Therapy. The preferred treatment is a single dose of azithromycin (Zithromax) or doxycycline (Vibramycin) twice a day for 7 days (Table 52.3). All sexual contacts within 60 days should be evaluated and treated to prevent reinfection and further transmission. Teach patients to abstain from sexual contact for 7 days after treatment or until all partners have been treated and have also abstained from sexual contact for 7 days. Review the ways to reduce risk for acquiring a repeat or new STI in the future. Tell patients to return if symptoms persist or recur.

DRUG ALERT Doxycycline (Vibramycin)

- Patients should avoid prolonged or excessive exposure to sunlight.
- Take doses on an empty stomach either 1 hour before eating or 2 hours after eating.
- Avoid taking with antacids, iron products, or dairy products.
- Pregnant women should not take doxycycline.

Unfortunately, there is a high rate of recurrence for chlamydia. This often occurs when the sexual partners of infected people are not treated. This "ping-pong" effect (treatment, reexposure, then reinfection) can end only when both partners are treated appropriately. Because of this issue, the CDC recommends *expedited partner therapy* (EPT).[8,9] EPT means HCPs can give drugs or prescriptions to patients with STIs to give to partners without their examining the partner. The legality of EPT varies from state to state, but few states prohibit EPT. EPT is not routinely recommended for men who have sex with men (MSM) because of a higher risk for coexisting infections in partners of MSM, especially undiagnosed syphilis or HIV. It is not recommended for female partners who are symptomatic because of the risk for PID.

GONOCOCCAL INFECTIONS

Gonorrhea is the second most common reportable STI in the United States. The incidence is on the rise. There are an estimated 820,000 cases each year, though only 468,000 cases are reported.[1]

Etiology and Pathophysiology

Gonorrhea is caused by *Neisseria gonorrhoeae,* a gram-negative, diplococcus bacterium. Gonorrhea can be transmitted by exposure to sexual fluids during vaginal, anal, or oral sex. Ejaculation does not have to occur for it to be transmitted. The incubation period ranges from 1 to 14 days. As in chlamydia, prior infection does not provide protection from reinfection. The most common site for infection for men is the urethra and for women, the cervix. Both men and women can get gonorrhea of the rectum from anal sex or of the oropharynx from oral sex.

Clinical Manifestations

The initial site of infection in men is usually the urethra. Most men will be symptomatic within a few days. The most common symptoms of gonococcal urethritis are dysuria, purulent urethral discharge (Fig. 52.2), or epididymitis. Most women who contract gonorrhea are asymptomatic or have minor symptoms that they often overlook. For women, common symptoms are increased vaginal discharge, dysuria, frequency of urination, or bleeding after sex. Often, redness and swelling can occur at the cervix or urethra along with a purulent exudate (Fig. 52.3).

Both men and women can contract rectal gonorrhea during anal intercourse or oropharyngeal gonorrhea during oral sex. Symptoms of rectal infection include mucopurulent rectal discharge or bleeding, anorectal pain, pruritus, tenesmus, mucus-coated stools, or painful bowel movements. Most patients with gonorrhea in the throat have few symptoms. Some may have a sore throat within days of performing oral sex.

Complications

Because men are often symptomatic and seek treatment early in the course of gonorrhea, they are less likely to develop serious complications than women. The complication in men is epididymitis, which can result in infertility.

Because many women are asymptomatic and seldom seek treatment, serious complications are more common and usually the reason for seeking medical care. Untreated gonorrhea can cause an infection in the Bartholin's glands or Skene's glands or result in PID. PID increases risk for ectopic pregnancy, infertility, and chronic pelvic pain.

Although rare, both men and women can develop disseminated gonococcal infection (DGI). DGI is associated with skin lesions, fever, arthralgia, arthritis, and/or endocarditis (Fig. 52.4).

Neonates can develop gonococcal conjunctivitis (*ophthalmia neonatorum*) from exposure to an infected mother during

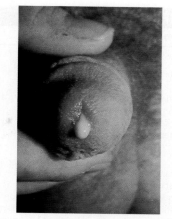

FIG. 52.2 Profuse, purulent drainage in a patient with gonorrhea. (From Marx J, Walls R, Hockberger R: *Rosen's emergency medicine: Concepts and clinical practice,* ed 7, St Louis, 2010, Mosby.)

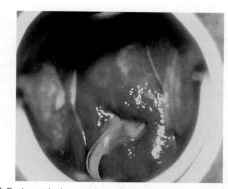

FIG. 52.3 Endocervical gonorrhea. Cervical redness and edema with discharge. (From Morse S, Moreland A, Holmes K: *Atlas of sexually transmitted diseases and AIDS,* London, 1996, Mosby-Wolfe.)

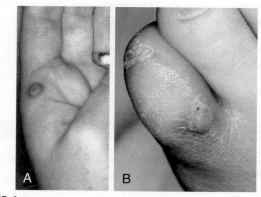

FIG. 52.4 Skin lesions with disseminated gonococcal infection. **A,** On the hand. **B,** On the fifth toe. (*A,* From Cohen J, Powderly WG: *Infectious diseases,* ed 2, St Louis, 2004, Mosby. *B,* From Mandell GL, Bennett JE, Dolin R: *Mandell, Douglas, and Bennett's principles and practice of infectious diseases,* ed 7, Philadelphia, 2010, Churchill Livingstone.)

delivery that can result in permanent blindness. Almost all states have laws or health department regulations requiring the use of prophylactic eye treatment of all newborns to prevent such infections. Because of both improved prenatal screening for gonorrhea and prophylactic treatment regimens, *ophthalmia neonatorum* caused by gonorrhea is rare.

Diagnostic Studies

For men, a presumptive diagnosis of gonorrhea is made if there is a history of sexual contact with a new or infected partner followed within a few days by urethral discharge. For women, making a diagnosis based on symptoms is difficult. Most women are asymptomatic or have symptoms that may be confused with other conditions, such as chlamydial or urinary tract infection.

A culture may be used to diagnose infection. Gram stains of urethral secretions can be used, but the sensitivity is not as good as other methods.

Interprofessional Care

Drug Therapy. Because of a short incubation period and high rates of infectivity, treatment is often given without waiting for positive test results. The first-line treatment is dual therapy with IM ceftriaxone with oral azithromycin (Zithromax) as a single dose (Table 52.4). Over the years, *N. gonorrhoeae* has developed resistance to many classes of antibiotics, including fluoroquinolones (e.g., ciprofloxacin [Cipro], levofloxacin) and tetracyclines (e.g., doxycycline [Vibramycin]).[10] Given the increasing rate of drug resistance, all patients with gonorrhea must receive treatment with at least 2 antibiotics. Patients treated with a preferred regimen but who have a positive test 7 days after treatment need antibiotic sensitivity testing.

TABLE 52.4 Interprofessional Care
Gonococcal Infections

Diagnostic Assessment
- History and physical examination
- Gram-stained smears of urethral or endocervical exudate
- Culture for *Neisseria gonorrhoeae*
- Nucleic acid amplification test (NAAT) to detect *N. gonorrhoeae*
- Testing for other STIs (syphilis, HIV, chlamydial infection)

Management
- Uncomplicated gonorrhea: ceftriaxone IM with azithromycin (Zithromax)
- Treatment of sexual contacts
- Teach to abstain from sexual contact for 7 days after treatment
- Treat all sexual partners, who must also wait 7 days before resuming sexual contact
- Reexamination if symptoms persist or recur after treatment

As with chlamydia, all sexual contacts within 60 days should be evaluated and treated to prevent reinfection and further transmission. Teach patients to abstain from sexual contact for 7 days after treatment, or until all partners have been treated and have also abstained from sexual contact for 7 days. Review the ways to reduce risk for acquiring a repeat or new STI in the future.

TRICHOMONIASIS

Trichomoniasis ("trich") is an STI caused by the protozoan parasite *Trichomonas vaginalis*. It is another common STI in the United States, affecting an estimated 3.7 million people.[1] This infection is often overlooked compared to other STIs. However, better testing methods have improved detection. It is much more common among women than men, especially among women with HIV.

Etiology and Pathophysiology

Trichomonas can be transmitted by exposure to sexual fluids during vaginal, anal, or oral sex, even if ejaculation does not occur. The incubation period is usually 1 week to 1 month but can be much longer. Prior infection does not provide protection from reinfection.

The most common site for infection in men is the urethra and in women is the cervix. It is uncommon for *Trichomonas* to infect the rectum. It is not known to infect the oropharynx. Routine screening should be considered for women in high-risk populations, including HIV-positive women and women seeking care for vaginal discharge.[8]

Clinical Manifestations

Most people do not have symptoms. Men may report burning with urination, ejaculation, or urethral discharge. Women may report painful urination, vaginal itching, painful intercourse, bleeding after sex, or a yellow-green discharge with a foul odor. The cervix can have a "strawberry" appearance.

Complications

The main complications of untreated infection are related to the inflammation and irritation that it causes in the genital tract. This inflammation makes an infected person more likely to contract or transmit another STI, particularly HIV. While gonorrhea and chlamydia are responsible for most PID, trichomoniasis is associated with PID in women with HIV.

Diagnostic Studies

The preferred method of diagnosing trichomoniasis is by NAAT testing of vaginal or endocervical secretions or urine. Other methods include culture, point-of-care testing, or direct visualization of trichomonads under the microscope. Identification of motile trichomonads in the vaginal secretions confirms infection. Tests can be done on liquid-based cervical Pap samples. In men, NAAT testing is recommended.[8]

Interprofessional Care

Drug Therapy. Patients and their partners should be treated with either metronidazole (Flagyl) or tinidazole (Tindamax). Teach patients to abstain from sexual contact for 7 days after treatment or until all sexual partners have completed a full course of treatment and abstained from sexual contact for 7 days. Tell patients to return if symptoms persist or recur. Any sexual partner within the preceding 60 days should be treated. Teach patients to use condoms or other barrier methods with every sexual contact. Because of a high rate of recurrence, repeat testing 3 months after treatment is recommended.

STIs CHARACTERIZED BY GENITAL LESIONS OR ULCERS

GENITAL HERPES INFECTIONS

Genital herpes is a common, lifelong, incurable infection. There are 2 strains of herpes: herpes simplex virus type 1 (HSV-1) and herpes simplex virus type 2 (HSV-2). Although both forms of HSV may cause anogenital infection, HSV-1 is usually associated with oral lesions. HSV-2 is more common in the genitals or anus.[8] However, an increasing proportion of anogenital herpes infections are caused by HSV-1. It is possible, but rare, to have HSV-2 infection of the mouth. Having 1 type does not protect against getting the other.

Around 50 million people in the United States have HSV-2. Most new infections are transmitted by someone who is unaware they are infected. The prevalence of new genital HSV-2 infections is twice as high among women compared to men. Hispanic and black persons are more likely to be infected.[1]

Etiology and Pathophysiology

The virus enters through the mucous membranes or breaks in the skin during contact with an infected person. The virus reproduces inside the cell and spreads to the surrounding cells. Then the virus enters the peripheral or autonomic nerve endings and ascends to the sensory or autonomic nerve ganglion near the infection site, where it often becomes dormant. Viral reactivation (recurrence or "outbreak") occurs when the virus descends to that initial site of infection, either the mucous membranes or skin.

When a person is infected with HSV-1 or HSV-2, the virus persists within the person for life. Transmission of either strain of HSV to others occurs easiest through direct contact with skin or mucous membranes when an infected person is symptomatic. However, both can be transmitted without any apparent symptoms, called *asymptomatic viral shedding*. It is impossible to predict when asymptomatic shedding will occur or for how long. HSV-2 is more likely to shed than HSV-1.

HSV-1 was primarily associated with orolabial disease, known as "cold sores" or "fever blisters" (Fig. 52.5) and HSV-2 with anogenital disease. However, there has been a shift in understanding that either HSV-1 or HSV-2 can cause genital, anal, or orolabial infections. In most cases, HSV-1 infections are more common "above the waist," involving the gingivae, dermis, upper respiratory tract, and, rarely the central nervous system (CNS). HSV-2 almost always infects sites "below the waist," the genital tract, perineum, or anus. It is important to understand that there is no absolute, single site for either virus.

Clinical Manifestations

Primary Episode. A *primary (initial) episode* of genital herpes has an incubation of 2 to 12 days. Most people do not have any recognizable symptoms of primary HSV genital infection. If symptoms do occur, they follow a series of stages. During the *prodromal stage*, the period before lesions appear, the patient may have burning, itching, or tingling at the site of inoculation. In the *vesicular stage*, few to multiple small, often painful

vesicles (blisters) may appear on the buttock, inner thigh, penis, scrotum, vulva, perineum, perianal region, vagina, or cervix. The vesicles have large quantities of infectious viral particles. Next, in the *ulcerative stage*, the lesions rupture and form shallow, moist ulcerations. In the *final stage*, spontaneous crusting and epithelialization of the erosions occur (Fig. 52.6).

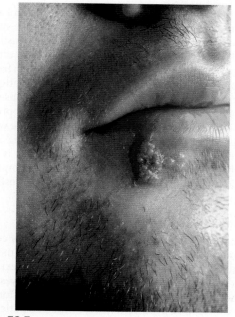

FIG. 52.5 Herpes simplex virus (HSV). (© iStock.com/zeleno.)

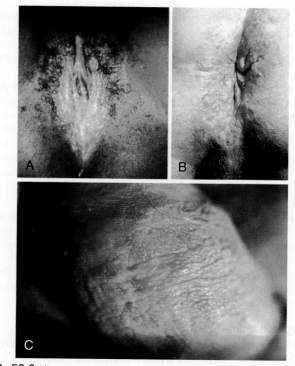

FIG. 52.6 Unruptured vesicles of herpes simplex virus type 2 (HSV-2). A, Vulvar area. B, Perianal area. C, Penile herpes simplex, ulcerative stage. (A and C, From Centers for Disease Control and Prevention. Courtesy Susan Lindsley. B, From Morse S, Moreland A, Holmes K: *Atlas of sexually transmitted diseases and AIDS*, London, 1996, Mosby-Wolfe.)

Regional (inguinal node) lymphadenopathy and systemic flu-like symptoms, including fever, headache, malaise, and myalgia may occur with the primary episode. Urination may be painful from the urine touching active lesions. The whole process from prodrome to healing varies and can take up to 3 weeks. Autoinoculation can occur if active lesions are touched or scratched, causing additional and potentially recurrent infection at extragenital sites.

Recurrent Episodes. *Recurrent genital herpes* occurs in many people during the year after the primary episode. The symptoms of recurrent episodes are less severe, and the lesions usually heal more quickly. HSV-1 genital infections recur less often than HSV-2 genital infections. Over time, both decrease in frequency.

Common triggers of recurrence include stress, fatigue, sunburn, general illness, immunosuppression, and menses. Many patients can predict a recurrence by noticing the prodromal symptoms of tingling, burning, and itching at the site where the lesions will recur. The greatest risk for transmitting infection exists when active lesions are present. However, it is possible to transmit the virus when no visible lesions or symptoms are present. Most HSV transmission occurs during these asymptomatic periods.

Complications

Both HSV-1 and HSV-2 can cause rare but serious complications, including blindness, encephalitis, and aseptic meningitis. Autoinoculation can result in the development of extragenital lesions in the buttocks, groin, thighs, fingers, and eyes. Genital ulcers increase the risk for contracting HIV. HSV lesions can be more severe and more persistent in HIV-infected patients.

Pregnant women with HSV can transmit the virus to the baby, especially if the virus is shed while the infant passes though the birth canal. Women with a primary episode of HSV near the time of delivery have the highest risk for transmitting genital herpes to the neonate. The virus can infect the neonate's skin, eyes, mouth, or the CNS or become widespread and cause significant morbidity and mortality. An active genital lesion at the time of delivery is an indication for cesarean delivery.[8]

One of the most profound consequences for people with genital herpes is the overall impact it can have on their psychologic well-being, their relationships, and their sexual lives. You can help teach patients to understand how to talk to sexual partners about HSV. Refer patients who need counseling. Teach patients with herpes that it is a common, manageable, non–life-threatening condition and help them to understand their treatment options.

Diagnostic Studies

Diagnosis is often based on the patient's reported symptoms, then confirmed by visual examination. Culture from open skin eruptions can be used to diagnose HSV and distinguish between HSV-1 and HSV-2. Highly accurate blood tests for antibodies are available for HSV-1 and HSV-2, but do not show the location of the infection. These antibodies usually appear by 12 weeks after exposure.

Interprofessional Care

Drug Therapy. Although not a cure, antiviral drugs can shorten the duration of HSV viral shedding, shorten the healing time of eruptions, and reduce the frequency of outbreaks by up to 80%.[8] Treatment of HSV should start before diagnostic results are available because early treatment reduces the duration of the ulcers and risk for transmission (Table 52.5).

TABLE 52.5 Interprofessional Care
Genital Herpes

Diagnostic Assessment
- History and physical examination
- Antibody assay for HSV type
- Viral isolation by tissue culture

Management
- Identify triggering factors
- Abstain from sexual contact while lesions are present and until fully healed
- Symptomatic care
- Confidential counseling and testing for HIV

Primary (Initial) Infection
- Acyclovir (Zovirax), valacyclovir (Valtrex) or famciclovir (Famvir)

Recurrent Episodic Infection
- Acyclovir, valacyclovir, or famciclovir for shorter duration

Suppressive Therapy
- Acyclovir, valacyclovir, or famciclovir daily at a lower dose

Severe Infection
- IV acyclovir until clinical improvement, followed by oral antiviral therapy

Three antiviral agents are available for the treatment of HSV: acyclovir (Zovirax), famciclovir (Famvir), and valaciclovir (Valtrex). These drugs inhibit herpetic viral replication. They are prescribed for both primary and recurrent infections. Taken daily at a lower dose, they can be used as suppressive therapy to decrease frequent anogenital recurrences. Teach patients with active outbreaks to maintain good hygiene, wear loose-fitting cotton undergarments, and avoid sexual contact until the outbreak has completely healed to reduce transmission to others.

The main goal is to keep eruptions clean and dry. Techniques to reduce pain with urination include pouring water onto the perineal area while voiding to dilute the urine or voiding in the shower. Pain may need a local anesthetic, such as lidocaine gel, or analgesics, such as ibuprofen, acetaminophen, acetaminophen with codeine, or aspirin. Ice packs to the affected area can give some relief.

IV acyclovir is reserved for severe or life-threatening infections in which hospitalization is needed for the treatment of ocular or widespread infections, CNS infections (e.g., meningitis), or pneumonitis.

GENITAL WARTS

Genital warts (*condylomata acuminata*) are caused by the HPV. There are around 100 types of papillomavirus, of which at least 40 strains are sexually transmitted.[8] "Low-risk" strains of the virus can cause warts on the skin. "High-risk" strains can lead to cancers of the genital tract, anus, or oropharynx in some patients. HPV types 6 and 11 cause about 90% of genital and anal wart cases. About 355,000 people are diagnosed each year. Most sexually active men and women will be infected with some type of HPV at some point in their lives. In most states, HPV is not a reportable infection. (Cervical HPV infection is discussed in Chapter 53.)

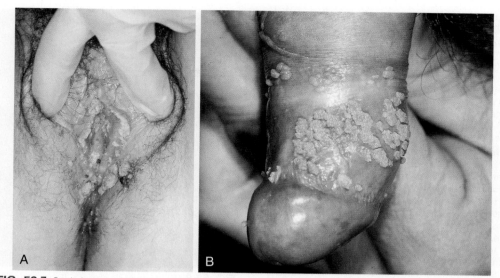

FIG. 52.7 Genital warts. **A**, Vulvar warts. **B**, Multiple warts on the penis. (From Habif TP: *Clinical dermatology*, ed 6, St Louis, 2015, Mosby.)

Etiology and Pathophysiology

HPV is transmitted by skin-to-skin contact, most often during vaginal, anal, or oral sex. It can be transmitted during nonpenetrating sexual activity. The basal epithelial cells infected with HPV undergo transformation and proliferation to form a warty growth (Fig. 52.7). The incubation period can range from weeks to months to years. Infection with 1 type of HPV does not prevent infection with another type.

In most people, HPV is considered transient (virus is "cleared" or resolves spontaneously after 1 to 2 years). However, it can persist even when the warts themselves are not visible after treatment. It is unclear whether removing visible warts helps a person to clear the virus, cures the virus, or reduces a person's ability to transmit the virus.[8]

Clinical Manifestations

Most people with HPV do not know that they are infected because they are asymptomatic. Genital or anal warts are discrete single or multiple papillary growths that are white to gray, are pink-flesh colored, or can be hyperpigmented depending on the skin type. They may grow and coalesce to form large, cauliflower-like masses. Most patients have 1 to 10 genital warts.

In men, warts occur on the penis and scrotum, inside or around the anus, or in the urethra. In women, warts occur on the inner thighs, vulva, vagina, or cervix, in the perianal area, including in the internal anal canal (Fig. 52.7). There are usually no other signs or symptoms. Itching may occur with anogenital warts. Bleeding on defecation may occur with anal warts.

Diagnostic Studies

Most early lesions caused by HPV are undetectable by visual examination. A diagnosis of genital warts can be made based on the characteristic appearance of the lesions (Fig. 52.7). Warts may be confused with *condylomata lata* of secondary syphilis, cancer, or benign growths. Testing should be done to rule out other conditions. At present, the only definitive diagnostic procedure is biopsy of any questionable growth. Testing for cervical HPV is discussed in Chapter 53.

Complications

Although genital and anal warts can grow, spread, or be transmitted to others, they have few long-term complications and are not associated with the development of cancer. Infection with "high-risk" strains of HPV (types 16 and 18) can lead to cancers of the cervix, vagina, vulva, penis, anus, and oropharynx. For some people, HPV lesions can cause psychosocial burden due to the cosmetic appearance of lesions or the need for long courses of HPV-related treatment. During pregnancy, warts tend to grow rapidly and increase in size.

Interprofessional Care

HPV Vaccines. It may be possible to eradicate some cancerous HPV types over the next few decades, especially if both girls and boys are vaccinated. Currently 3 vaccines are available to protect against HPV. A quadrivalent vaccine (Gardasil) protects against types 6, 11, 16, and 18. The bivalent vaccine Cervarix offers protection against HPV types 16 and 18. A 9-valent vaccine (Gardasil 9) protects against HPV types 6, 11, 16, 18 and 5 other HPV types. These vaccines are given in 2 or 3 IM doses over a 6-month period and have few side effects. The CDC recommends that all children, male and female, be vaccinated at age 11 to 12, but vaccination can be started as early as age 9.[11] The bivalent and quadrivalent vaccines are approved for persons up to age 26. The 9-valent vaccine is approved for girls 9 to 26 and boys 9 to 15.

These vaccines do not treat active HPV infection. Ideally, persons should receive the vaccine before the start of sexual activity. Those who are infected with HPV can still get protection against HPV types not already contracted. HPV vaccines offer protection against strains causing 90% of genital warts and 70% (Gardasil) to 90% (Gardasil-9) of cervical cancers. They may offer protection from anal and certain types of throat cancer.

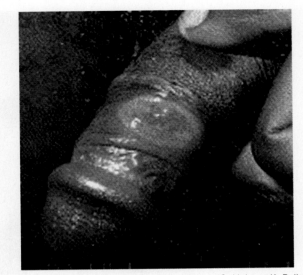

FIG. 52.8 Primary syphilis chancre. (From Morse S, Holmes K, Ballard R: *Atlas of sexually transmitted diseases and AIDS,* ed 4, London, 2010, Saunders.)

Therapy should be modified if a patient has not improved or cannot tolerate the side effects of certain treatments.

If the warts do not resolve with topical therapies, treatments such as cryotherapy with liquid nitrogen, electrocautery, laser therapy, local α-interferon injections, or surgical excision may be needed. Teach patients that because treatment does not destroy the virus (merely the infected tissue), recurrence and reinfection are possible. Long-term follow-up is advised.

SYPHILIS

Syphilis is a sexually transmitted bacterial infection that can cause serious long-term complications if not identified and treated appropriately. Over 88,000 cases of syphilis are reported annually in the United States, with a sharp increase seen in recent years. The population most affected by syphilis is MSM, with the highest rates among black MSM between 25 and 29 years old.[1]

Etiology and Pathophysiology

Syphilis is caused by *Treponema pallidum,* a bacterial spirochete. It is transmitted by direct contact with a syphilitic ulcer called a *chancre.* A chancre can occur externally on the genitals, anus, or lips or internally in the vagina, rectum, or mouth or tongue (Fig. 52.8) or through the mucosal membranes of an infected person. Transmission can occur during vaginal, anal, or oral sex. The incubation period can range from 10 to 90 days (average 21 days). Having the infection does not provide protection from reinfection, even after successful treatment. An infected pregnant woman can transmit syphilis to her fetus during her pregnancy. There is a high risk for stillbirth or having babies who develop complications after birth, including seizures and death.

Clinical Manifestations

Syphilis is called "*The Great Imitator*" because it can present with a variety of signs and symptoms that mimic other diseases.

Drug Therapy. Treatment of genital or anal warts is hampered by the high proportion of asymptomatic and undiagnosed infections and lack of curative treatment. The primary goal of treatment is the removal of symptomatic warts.

In-office treatment consists of chemical or ablative (removal with laser or electrocautery) methods. A common treatment is the use of trichloroacetic acid (TCA) or bichloroacetic acid (BCA) applied directly to the wart surface. Petroleum jelly applied with a cotton swab to the surrounding normal skin can minimize irritation. A sharp, stinging pain is often felt with initial acid contact, but this quickly subsides.

Patient-applied treatments are also available. Podofilox liquid and gel are available by prescription (Condylox, Condylox Gel). The patient applies the solution or gel for 3 successive days. Treatment can be repeated for up to 4 weeks or until resolution of the lesions. Imiquimod cream (Aldara, Zyclara) is an immune response modifier that is applied at bedtime, either 3 times per week (Aldara) or nightly for up to 16 weeks (Zyclara). Sinecatechin ointment (Veregen) is made from the extract of green tea leaves and has antioxidant properties. It is applied 3 times daily for up to 16 weeks.

Treatment of warts may or may not decrease infectivity as the HPV causing these may still be present. Anogenital warts are hard to treat and often need more than 1 treatment or modality.

TABLE 52.6 Stages of Syphilis

Primary
- *Infectivity:* Highly infectious
- Duration of stage: 3–6 wk
- Single or multiple chancres (painless indurated lesions) of penis, vulva, lips, mouth, vagina, and rectum) (Fig. 52.8). Occurs 10–90 days after inoculation
- Regional lymphadenopathy (microorganisms drain into the lymph nodes)
- Exudate and blood from chancre are highly infectious

Secondary
- *Infectivity:* Highly infectious
- *Duration of stage:* Occurs a few weeks after primary chancre heals, lasts 1–2 yr
- Flu-like symptoms: malaise, fever, sore throat, headaches, fatigue, arthralgia, generalized adenopathy
- Mucous patches in mouth (Fig. 52.9), tongue, or cervix
- Symmetric, nonpruritic rash bilaterally that appears on trunk, palms, and/or soles (Fig. 52.10)
- *Condylomata lata* (moist, weeping papules) in the anogenital area
- Weight loss, alopecia

Latent
- *Infectivity:* Early (<1 yr)—infectious; late (≥1 yr)—noninfectious
- *Duration of stage:* Throughout life or progression to late stage
- Absence of signs or symptoms
- Diagnosis based on positive specific treponemal antibody test together with normal CSF and absence of clinical manifestations

Late
- *Infectivity:* Noninfectious
- *Duration of stage:* Chronic (without treatment), occurs 1–20 years after initial infection
- Gummas (chronic, destructive lesions affecting any organ of body, especially skin, bone, liver, mucous membranes) (Fig. 52.11)
- *Cardiovascular:* Aneurysms, heart valve insufficiency, heart failure, aortitis
- *Neurosyphilis:* Can occur at any stage of syphilis
- *General paresis:* Personality changes from minor to psychotic, tremors, physical and mental deterioration
- *Tabes dorsalis* (ataxia, areflexia, paresthesias, lightning pains, damaged joints)

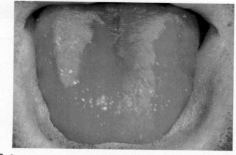

FIG. 52.9 Secondary syphilis. Mucous patch in the mouth. (From Mandell GL, Bennett JE, Dolin R: *Mandell, Douglas, and Bennett's principles and practice of infectious diseases,* ed 7, Philadelphia, 2010, Churchill Livingstone.)

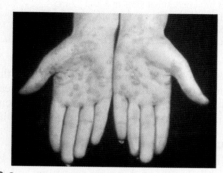

FIG. 52.10 Secondary syphilis. Palmar rash. (From Centers for Disease Control and Prevention Public Health Image Library. Courtesy Robert Sumpter.)

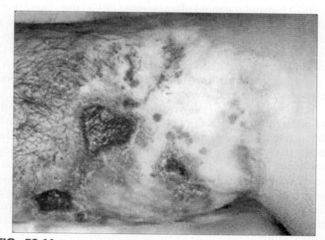

FIG. 52.11 Destructive skin gummas associated with tertiary syphilis. (From Gawkrodger D, Ardern-Jones M: *Dermatology,* ed 6, St Louis, 2016, Mosby.)

Compared with other STIs, syphilis is harder to recognize, which can delay treatment. If it is not diagnosed and treated, specific clinical stages occur with the progression of the disease (Table 52.6).

The primary stage is the development of a chancre at the site of transmission. This can appear days to months following infection. In most patients, it occurs by 3 weeks. Chancres can be found on the genitals but often go unnoticed when inside the mouth, vagina, or anus. As the chancre begins to heal or shortly after, patients will progress to the secondary stage of infection if untreated. This stage is usually characterized by a maculopapular rash. It may be coupled with other systemic symptoms. The classic rash appears on the palms of the hands or soles of the feet, but often involves the trunk or extremities. Without treatment, the rash will resolve, but the patient still has syphilis and will remain infectious for some time.

Tertiary, or late syphilis, is the final stage. Patients will not have obvious symptoms. During this stage, the organism is silently causing organ damage over many years. The formation of gummas can lead to serious complications.

Complications

Gummas may cause irreparable damage to skin, bone, or liver. In cardiovascular syphilis, the resulting aneurysm may press on structures such as the intercostal nerves, causing pain. The risk for rupture exists as the aneurysm increases in size. Scarring of the aortic valve can cause aortic valve insufficiency and heart failure.

Neurosyphilis occurs when *T. pallidum* invades the CNS. It can occur at any stage of syphilis. Visual impairment, *tabes dorsalis* (progressive locomotor ataxia), and dementia are rare, extreme manifestations.

TABLE 52.7 Interprofessional Care

Syphilis

Diagnostic Assessment
- History and physical examination
- Dark-field microscopy
- Nontreponemal and/or treponemal serologic testing
- Testing for other STIs (HIV, gonorrhea, chlamydial infection)

Management
- Antibiotic therapy:
  - Penicillin G benzathine (Bicillin LA)
  - Doxycycline or tetracycline (if penicillin contraindicated)
- Confidential counseling and testing for HIV infection
- Surveillance
- Repeat of nontreponemal tests at 6 and 12 mo
- Examination of cerebrospinal fluid at 1 yr if treatment involves alternative antibiotics or treatment failure has occurred.

Chancres on or inside the genitalia or anus enhance HIV transmission. Patients with HIV and syphilis appear to be at greatest risk for clinically significant CNS involvement and may need more intensive treatment than other patients with syphilis.

Diagnostic Studies

Syphilis is most often diagnosed by a blood test. We classify tests for syphilis as those done for screening and those done to confirm a positive screening test. Nontreponemal tests used for screening detect antibodies that are not specific for syphilis. These tests include the Venereal Disease Research Laboratory (VDRL) test and the rapid plasma reagin (RPR) test. These tests usually become positive 10 to 14 days after the appearance of a chancre. We call the fluorescent treponemal antibody absorption (FTA-Abs) test, *T. pallidum* particle agglutination (TP-PA) test, and syphilis qualitative enzyme-linked immunoassay (EIA) *treponemal tests* because they specifically detect treponemal antibodies. These tests are used to confirm a diagnosis.[8]

False-negative and false-positive test results can occur with the nontreponemal tests (VDRL, RPR). A false-negative result may occur with primary syphilis if the test is done before the person has had time to make antibodies. A false-positive finding may occur if patients have various other diseases or inflammatory conditions. Positive nontreponemal test results are always confirmed by treponemal tests. In the cerebrospinal fluid (CSF), changes such as an increased WBC count, increased total protein, and a positive treponemal antibody test are diagnostic of neurosyphilis.

If treatment with antibiotics is started early in the course of the disease based on the history and the symptoms, the serologic testing may not show syphilis. If the patient tests positive with screening serology (RPR), it will take time for this to normalize after treatment. This test is often used to ensure cure in patients. Once a person tests positive for syphilis via syphilis-specific testing (TP-PA, EIA), these findings may stay positive for an indefinite period despite successful treatment.

Interprofessional Care

Because of the serious complications associated with untreated syphilis, screening programs for high-risk groups are important for reducing morbidity and mortality. The evaluation of all patients with syphilis should include HIV testing. The CDC recommends annual syphilis testing for HIV patients (Table 52.7).[8]

Drug Therapy. Management is aimed at starting treatment early. Penicillin G benzathine (Bicillin L-A) is the recommended treatment for all stages (Table 52.7). When penicillin is contraindicated, doxycycline or tetracycline may be used. Aqueous procaine penicillin G is the treatment of choice for neurosyphilis. Treatment cannot reverse damage that is already present in the later stages of the disease. All sexual contacts from the preceding 90 days should be treated. Reexamination and follow-up testing are recommended every 6 months for up to 2 years to ensure cure. Repeat HIV testing should be done on all HIV-negative patients diagnosed with primary or secondary syphilis given the higher risk for HIV transmission during these stages.

❖ NURSING MANAGEMENT: STIs

◆ Nursing Assessment

Subjective and objective data that should be obtained from a person with an STI are outlined in Table 52.8. You must be aware of patients' gender identity and current anatomy. Screen patients based on risk history and sexual behaviors. Assess the patient's risk for contracting an STI. Questions to ask include number of partners (in the last month, year?), types of partners ("Do you have sex with men, women, or both?"), type of birth control used (if applicable), use of condoms or other barrier methods, history of an STI, use of drugs and alcohol, exchange of sex for drugs or money, and risk for violence and personal safety.[12] Plan teaching based on the responses to these questions.

Interpersonal skills necessary for this interview include respect, compassion, and a nonjudgmental attitude. Tailor your counseling to the patient. Start by asking patients how they define themselves, including their gender identity and sexual preferences. Do not assume someone is heterosexual, MSM, or women who have sex with women (WSW) based on appearance. Do not assume MSM engage in the same sexual practices. Finally, do not assume that older people are not at risk. Sex and sexuality are dynamic across the life cycle, and sexually active older adults can be at risk for STIs.[13]

? CHECK YOUR PRACTICE

You are working on the medicine unit caring for a 68-yr-old man admitted for IV penicillin for neurosyphilis. The nurse that you are working with says, "I can't believe a man that old could get syphilis."
- How would you respond?
- What should you discuss with your colleague?

◆ Nursing Diagnoses

Nursing diagnoses for the patient with an STI include:
- Impaired sexual functioning
- Risk for infection
- Lack of knowledge

◆ Planning

The overall goals are that the patient with an STI will (1) understand the mode of transmission of STIs and the risks associated with STIs, (2) complete treatment and return for appropriate follow-up, (3) notify or assist in notifying sexual contacts about their need for testing and treatment, (4) abstain from sexual contact until infection is resolved, and (5) demonstrate knowledge of safer sex practices.

TABLE 52.8 Nursing Assessment

STIs

Subjective Data

Important Health Information

Sexual health history: Sexual activity, history of STIs, multiple sexual partners, unsafe sexual practices
Medications: Allergy to antibiotics

Functional Health Patterns

Health perception–health management: Unsafe sexual practices, drug and/or alcohol use
Nutritional-metabolic: Nausea, vomiting, anorexia. Pharyngitis, oral lesions, chills. Alopecia
Elimination: Dysuria, urinary frequency, urethral discharge, pain with bowel movements
Cognitive-perceptual: Arthralgia, headache, painful, burning lesions, itching or irritation at infected site
Sexuality-reproductive: Dyspareunia, vaginal or penile discharge, bleeding with sex, genital or perianal lesions

Objective Data

General

Fever, lymphadenopathy (generalized or inguinal)

Integumentary

Syphilis: Primary: Painless, indurated genital, oral, or perianal lesions
Secondary: Bilateral, symmetric rash on palms, soles, or entire body. Mucous patches on mouth or tongue; alopecia
Genital herpes: Painful genital or anal vesicular lesions
Genital warts: Single or multiple gray or white genital or anal warts

Gastrointestinal

Rectal discharge, rectal lesions

Urinary

Urethral discharge, erythema

Reproductive

Cervical mucopurulent discharge, cervical erythema, cervical bleeding; penile purulent discharge, epididymitis, proctitis, genital lesions

Possible Diagnostic Findings

Chlamydia: Positive culture or NAAT cervical, urethral, anal, oropharyngeal, or urine samples
Gonorrhea: Positive cultures or NAAT from cervical, urethral, anal, oropharyngeal, or urine samples
Genital herpes: Positive HSV-1 or HSV-2 serum antibody test. Positive culture from active lesion indicating HSV-1 or HSV-2
Syphilis: Positive findings on VDRL and RPR, spirochetes on dark-field microscopy
Trichomoniasis: Positive increased pH and positive motile protozoa on wet preparation of discharge. Positive FDA–approved rapid test or liquid-based Pap positive for trichomoniasis

TABLE 52.9 Understanding Risk for STIs in Special Populations

When dealing with the following populations at risk for STIs, it is important to consider cultural, behavioral, and other risk factors that may place them at increased risk for STIs or not receiving appropriate screening.

Women Who Have Sex With Women (WSW)

- WSW should not be presumed to be at low or no risk for STIs based on sexual orientation.
- WSW are at risk for acquiring bacterial, viral, and protozoal infections from current and prior partners, both male and female.
- Practices involving digital-vaginal or digital-anal contact, particularly with shared penetrative sex items, present a means for transmission of infected cervicovaginal secretions.
- Female-to-female transmission of chlamydia, trichomoniasis, HIV, HPV, HSV, and syphilis have been reported.
- Report of same-sex behavior in women should not deter HCPs from screening for all STIs.

Men Who Have Sex With Men (MSM)

- MSM are at higher risk for HIV, syphilis, hepatitis C, and other viral and bacterial STIs compared to the general population.
- HIV-uninfected MSM who are diagnosed with an STI should be counseled about the options for HIV prevention, including preexposure prophylaxis (PrEP) and nonoccupational postexposure prophylaxis (nPEP).
- Rates of syphilis, gonorrhea, and chlamydia are increasing in MSM, particularly in HIV-infected MSM.
- Assess risk for STIs among MSM patients and be comfortable asking questions about sexual identity and practices, including insertive and receptive anal sex.

Transgender Persons

- *Transgender man* is a term used to describe a person born anatomically female but who identifies as male. *Transgender woman* is a term used to describe a person born anatomically male but who identifies as female.
- Rates of certain STIs, including HIV, are higher among transgender women, compared to the general population.
- Not all transgender persons have had genital reassignment surgery and may still have the genitals they were assigned at birth. Therefore screen these persons for STIs based on both risk history and current anatomy. For example, a transgender man may still have a vagina and cervix.

Source: Centers for Disease Control: Sexually transmitted disease treatment guidelines. Retrieved from *www.cdc.gov/std/tg2015/specialpops.htm*.

in which both partners have been tested for STIs can reduce the risk. Addressing issues related to drug and alcohol use is important for promoting healthy sexual behavior.

Be prepared to teach special populations, including MSM, WSW, and transgender persons, about their risks (Table 52.9). Encourage routine testing in people who are at higher risk, so STIs can be identified early. This will help decrease the potential for complications and reduce transmission to others. A teaching guide for the patient with an STI is shown in Table 52.10.

Measures to Prevent Infection. Encourage patients to take notice of a sexual partner's genitalia before sex, paying attention to any discharge, sores, blisters, lesions, or rashes. Help patients to be aware of specific signs and symptoms of infection. This can help them to make good decisions about whether to continue sexual activity with safer-sex modifications or to choose not to have sexual contact at all. Remind patients that most STIs may have no symptoms but can still be transmitted. Emphasize with patients that when they have sex, they are exposed to the infections of everyone with whom their partner has ever had sex.

◆ **Nursing Implementation**

◆ **Health Promotion.** Many approaches to stopping the spread of STIs have had varying degrees of success. Be prepared to discuss "safer" sex practices and harm reduction with all patients, not only those who are perceived to be at risk. These practices include abstinence, monogamy, avoiding high-risk sexual behaviors, and correctly using condoms and other barriers with every sexual act. Sexual abstinence is the only certain method of avoiding all STIs, but few people consider this option. Limiting sexual contacts to an established, monogamous relationship

TABLE 52.10 Patient Teaching

STIs

When teaching the patient with STIs:

1. Explain precautions to take, such as
   - Using condoms and other barrier methods with every sexual encounter
   - Being monogamous, defining what monogamy means with your partner
   - Asking potential partners about their sexual history
   - Asking potential partners if they have been tested for STIs
   - Avoiding sex with partners who have visible oral, inguinal, genital, perineal, or anal lesions or those who use IV drugs
   - Voiding and washing genitalia and surrounding area after sex to flush out/wash away organisms to reduce potential for transmitting infection
2. Explain the importance of taking all antibiotics or antiviral agents as prescribed. Symptoms will improve after 1–2 days of treatment, but organisms may still be present.
3. Teach patients diagnosed with gonorrhea, chlamydia, syphilis, or trichomoniasis that all sexual partners need to be treated to prevent transmission and reinfection.
4. Teach patients to abstain from sexual contact during and for 7 days after treatment and to use condoms or other barrier methods when sexual activity is resumed to prevent spread of infection and reinfection.
5. Explain the importance of follow-up examination and retesting at least once after treatment (if appropriate) to confirm complete cure and prevent relapse.
6. Allow patients and partners to voice their concerns and clarify areas that need explanation.
7. Teach patients about the signs and symptoms of complications and need to report problems to their HCP to ensure proper follow-up and early treatment of reinfection.
8. Tell patients of the infectious nature of these infections to avoid a false sense of security, which may result in careless sexual practices or poor personal hygiene.
9. Tell patients about health department requirements for anonymously reporting certain STIs.

Proper use of a condom is a highly effective mechanical barrier to several infections that may be transmitted by or to a penis. Partners should openly discuss any objections to condom use, such as interference with spontaneity and the presence of a barrier. Information about the mechanics of sexual arousal and incorporating a condom into sex can help in overcoming the resistance to its use. Refusing sexual activity with any partner who will not use a condom is a safe and legitimate option.

The *female condom*, a lubricated polyurethane sheath designed for vaginal use, is another option for some women. Teach patients to avoid the spermicide nonoxynol 9 (N-9), which can be used alone to prevent pregnancy or as a condom

PROMOTING POPULATION HEALTH

Preventing Sexually Transmitted Infections

- Follow "safer" sex practices every time you have sexual contact and be responsible for your own protection.
- Have sexual activity only in an established, monogamous relationship.
- Obtain vaccinations to help prevent some types of HPV.
- Know your sex partners. Be comfortable saying "no" to sexual activity.
- Limit alcohol use to moderate levels.
- If you are at risk, obtain testing regularly and encourage partners to do the same.

lubricant. Nonoxynol 9 is one of the least effective methods of birth control when used alone. It can be irritating to the vagina and rectum, increasing the risk for acquiring an STI.

Screening Programs. Screening programs are an effective means of identifying, treating, preventing, and controlling the spread of STIs. At present, there are CDC-recommended screening programs for certain populations, including young people, MSM, pregnant women, and anyone at increased risk for exposure to an STI (e.g., new partners, nonmonogamous relationships, not using condoms).[8]

Case Finding. Interviewing and case finding are other methods used to control the spread of STIs. These activities are directed toward finding and examining all sexual contacts of patients with reportable STIs so that effective treatment can be started. Public health professionals, often nurses, are aware of the social implications of STIs and the need for discretion in finding partners. Sexual contacts are not told about the origin of the information naming them as a contact or the timing of exposure to ensure patient privacy mandates.

Partner notification and treatment impose a heavy burden on public health departments. As a result, the notification often becomes the responsibility of the infected partner. The infected partner may choose not to tell sexual partners, and the partners may choose not to seek treatment. Unfortunately, this perpetuates the disease.

Educational and Research Programs. Actively encourage your community to provide better education about STIs for its citizens. High-risk populations (e.g., young people under age 25, MSM) should be a prime target for such educational programs. STI rates are rising in older adults.[13] Older adults are less likely to use condoms and often have a hard time starting discussions of sexual health issues.

Knowledge and understanding can decrease the incidence of STIs. Encourage the HPV vaccine that protects against genital warts and cervical cancer for boys and girls before the start of sexual activity. Accurate and current information may help reduce parental fears related to the vaccine. Consider stressing the prevention of cancer as a reason for the vaccine, which may be more productive and less controversial, thus making the parent and adolescent more receptive.

Acute Care

Psychologic Support. The diagnosis of an STI may be met with a variety of emotions, such as embarrassment, shame, guilt, anger, or even a desire for vengeance. Encourage the patient to voice feelings. Couples in marital or committed relationships have an added problem when an STI is diagnosed if they must face the implication of sexual activity outside the relationship. The STI raises other concerns about their relationship and may serve as an incentive for further problem solving. A referral for professional counseling to explore the impact of the STI on their relationship may be indicated.

A patient who has genital herpes is faced with the fact that future outbreaks will occur and that no cure is available. This can be frustrating and disruptive to the patient's physical, emotional, social, and sexual life. Help the patient identify and avoid any factors that may precipitate outbreaks, such as stress, local trauma, or sun exposure. Tell the patient that the frequency and severity of recurrences will decrease over time. It is important to stress that herpes is manageable and does not pose a risk to their overall health.

Genital or anal warts involve a prolonged course of treatment. Clearing the virus takes time and is not always possible. Patients can become frustrated and distressed due to frequent office visits, associated costs, potential for unpleasant side effects because of treatment, and effects of the infection on future health and sexual relationships. Support and a willingness to listen to the patient's concerns are needed. Local or online support groups are available for almost all STIs. Help patients to connect with support groups.

Follow-up. If you work in public health facilities, clinics, or other outpatient settings, you are more likely to care for a patient with an STI than if you work in a hospital setting. Whatever the setting, as a nurse, you are in a position to explain and interpret treatment measures, such as the purpose and possible side effects of prescribed drugs and the need for follow-up care (Table 52.10).

Single-dose treatment for gonorrhea, chlamydia, and syphilis helps prevent the problems associated with nonadherence with drug therapy. Give special instructions to the patient receiving multiple-dose therapy to complete the prescribed treatment. Teach the patient about problems resulting from nonadherence. All patients should return to the treatment center for a repeat culture from the infected sites or for serologic testing at designated times to determine the effectiveness of the treatment.

ETHICAL/LEGAL DILEMMAS
Confidentiality and HIPAA

Situation

P.H. is a 22-yr-old woman who recently tested positive for chlamydia. You tell her to tell her sexual partners of the infection. She refuses to tell her boyfriend because he will know that she has had sex with another partner. You later learn that the nursing student who was in the clinic for the day is a friend of her boyfriend and told him that he should have STI testing.

Ethical/Legal Points for Consideration

* Each state has requirements for reporting communicable diseases and other health-related data. Inform the patient of the reporting requirements for communicable diseases.
* Nurses and other HCPs have both a legal and an ethical obligation to maintain confidentiality of patient information. The Health Insurance Portability and Accountability Act (HIPAA) ensures the privacy of personal health information.
* The duty to maintain confidentiality is not absolute and may be limited, as needed, to protect the patient or other parties, or by law or regulation, such as mandated reporting for safety or public health reasons.
* Your main obligation is to the patient seeking care. Patient teaching is one way to establish a partnership with this woman. Share information about the effects of the disease, the consequences of reinfection, and the effect of the disease on others who may not know that they are infected. Then encourage the patient to tell her partners of the diagnosis and discuss the option of expedited partner therapy (EPT) where applicable.

Discussion Questions

* What are your state's requirements for reportable conditions?
* In your opinion, what is the best way to balance the needs of an individual patient with those of the public?
* What are the risks to agencies for the breach of confidentiality and HIPAA?

Reference

Code of Ethics for Nurses. Retrieved from *www.nursingworld.org/practice-policy/nursing-excellence/ethics/code-of-ethics-for-nurses/*.

Explaining to the patient that cures are not always obtained on the first treatment can reinforce the need for a follow-up visit. Advise the patient to inform sexual partners of the need for testing and treatment as a contact, regardless of whether they are free of symptoms or experiencing symptoms.

Hygiene Measures. Emphasize to the patient with an STI the importance of certain hygiene measures, such as frequent hand washing. Tell the patient not to scratch infection sites to avoid autoinoculation of STIs that can be spread to other parts of the body. Washing with soap and water and voiding after sex may have some benefit in decreasing the exposure to STIs but does not give adequate protection against transmission. Teach patients not to douche after sex. It can push bacteria higher into the reproductive tract or undermine local immune responses.

Sexual Activity. Sexual abstinence is needed during the communicable phase of any STI. Long-term precautions must be taken with those STIs that are chronic or recurrent. Emphasize that even single-dose treatments can take up to 1 week to clear the infection. Thus the patient is infectious during this period and should avoid all sexual contact. Emphasize the importance of using condoms or other barrier methods to help prevent the spread of infection and reinfection after treatment. Remind patients that complications can follow if sexual activity occurs before treatment completion. Patients need to discuss re-treatment or continued treatment with an HCP. During treatment, the patient can choose to relate to a partner in an intimate way that avoids penetrative, oral-genital contact, or skin-to-skin contact.

◆ **Ambulatory Care.** Because many STIs are cured with a single dose or short course of antibiotic therapy, many patients are casual about the outcome of these infections. The consequences of this attitude can include delays in treatment, nonadherence with instructions, and the development of complications, treatment failure, or reinfection. Complications are serious and costly and can include future infertility.

Surgery and prolonged therapy are needed for many patients with infection-related complications. Major surgical procedures, such as resection of an aneurysm or aortic valve replacement, may be needed to treat cardiovascular problems caused by syphilis. Pelvic surgery and procedures to correct fertility problems from an STI may be needed. If not successful, patients may need assisted reproductive technologies to achieve future pregnancy. Because young people ages 15 to 24 represent about 50% of new STIs annually, it is important to know that almost every state and the District of Columbia have laws that allow minors to consent to STI services without parental involvement (the minimum age varies by state).[8]

◆ **Evaluation**

Expected outcomes for the patient with an STI are that the patient will
* Understand the course, modes of transmission, and treatment options for the STI
* Relate the potential long-term complications of untreated infection
* Adhere with drug regimens and the follow-up protocol
* Understand the importance of partner notification and treatment
* Have no reinfection and understand STI risk-reducing behaviors and practices going forward

CASE STUDY

Gonococcal and Chlamydial Infection

(© Eyecandy Images/ Thinkstock.)

Patient Profile

C.R. is a 24-yr-old Hispanic woman seen in the outpatient clinic reporting increased yellow vaginal discharge and bleeding after sex for the past 2 weeks. She is sexually active with a new partner. She was treated in the past for chlamydial infection at age 20.

Subjective Data

- She and her partner use condoms "sometimes"
- Last menstrual period was 3 weeks ago
- Noticed her partner had some unusual discharge before they had sex
- Appears anxious and teary

Objective Data

- Cervix: erythematous
- Mucopurulent cervical discharge
- Urine pregnancy test is negative
- NAAT of the cervix is positive for *N. gonorrhoeae* and *C. trachomatis*

Interprofessional Care

- ceftriaxone 250 mg IM × 1 dose
- azithromycin 1 g PO × 1 dose

Discussion Questions

1. What were C.R.'s risk factors for acquiring gonorrhea and chlamydial infection?
2. What complications could occur if C.R.'s infections are not treated?
3. **Priority Decision:** What is the priority of care for C.R.?
4. **Priority Decision:** Based on the assessment data presented, what are the priority nursing diagnoses?
5. **Patient-Centered Care:** What instructions should C.R. receive to ensure successful treatment? To prevent reinfection? To prevent further transmission of the infection?
6. **Patient-Centered Care:** What impact is her diagnosis likely to have on C.R.'s self-image? On her relationship with her sexual partner?
7. **Safety:** C.R. tells you she is worried about how her partner will react when she discloses this information. What safety precautions should be considered?
8. **Evidence-Based Practice:** C.R. mentions she is using the spermicide nonoxynol-9 (N-9) to protect herself against STIs. Would you advise her to continue to use it?

Answers available at *http://evolve.elsevier.com/Lewis/medsurg.*

BRIDGE TO NCLEX EXAMINATION

The number of the question corresponds to the same-numbered outcome at the beginning of the chapter.

1. Which populations have a higher risk for acquiring sexually transmitted infections (STIs)? *(select all that apply)*
   a. Transgender persons
   b. Young adults (age < 25)
   c. Men who have sex with men
   d. Men in long-term care facilities
   e. Women in correctional facilities

2. The nurse is obtaining a subjective data assessment from a woman reported as a sexual contact of a man with chlamydial infection. The nurse understands that symptoms of chlamydial infection in women
   a. are often absent.
   b. are similar to those of genital herpes.
   c. include a macular palmar rash in the later stages.
   d. may involve chancres inside the vagina that are not visible.

3. A primary HSV infection differs from recurrent HSV episodes in that *(select all that apply)*
   a. only primary infections are sexually transmitted.
   b. symptoms are less severe during recurrent episodes.
   c. transmission of the virus to a fetus is less likely during primary infection.
   d. systemic manifestations, such as fever and myalgia, are more common in primary infection.
   e. lesions from recurrent HSV are more likely to transmit the virus than lesions from primary HSV.

4. Explain to the patient with gonorrhea that treatment will include both ceftriaxone and azithromycin because
   a. azithromycin helps prevent recurrent infections.
   b. some patients do not respond to oral drugs alone.
   c. coverage with more than one antibiotic will prevent reinfection.
   d. the increasing rates of drug resistance requires using at least 2 drugs.

5. In assessing patients for STIs, the nurse needs to know that many STIs can be asymptomatic. Which STIs can be asymptomatic? *(select all that apply)*
   a. Syphilis
   b. Gonorrhea
   c. Genital warts
   d. Genital herpes
   e. Chlamydial infection

6. To prevent the infection and transmission of STIs, the nurse's teaching plan would include an explanation of
   a. the appropriate use of oral contraceptives.
   b. the need for annual Pap tests for women with HPV.
   c. sexual positions that can be used to avoid infection.
   d. sexual practices that are considered high-risk behaviors.

7. Provide emotional support to a patient with an STI by
   a. offering information on how safer sexual practices can prevent STIs.
   b. showing concern when listening to the patient who expresses negative feelings.
   c. reassuring the patient that the disease is highly curable with appropriate treatment.
   d. helping the patient who received an STI from their sexual partner in forgiving the partner.

1. a, b, c, e, 2. a, 3. b, d, 4. d, 5. a, b, c, d, e, 6. d, 7. b

For rationales to these answers and even more NCLEX review questions, visit *http://evolve.elsevier.com/Lewis/medsurg.*

ⓔ EVOLVE WEBSITE/RESOURCES LIST

http://evolve.elsevier.com/Lewis/medsurg
Review Questions (Online Only)
Key Points
Answer Keys for Questions
- Rationales for Bridge to NCLEX Examination Questions
- Answer Guidelines for Case Study on p. 1226

Conceptual Care Map Creator
Audio Glossary
Content Updates

REFERENCES

1. Centers for Disease Control and Prevention: Sexually transmitted disease surveillance. Retrieved from *www.cdc.gov/std/stats/*.
2. Shannon CL, Klausner JD: The growing epidemic of sexually transmitted infections in adolescents: A neglected population, *Curr Opin Pediatr* 30:137, 2018.
3. Poteat TC, Malik M, Beyrer C: Epidemiology of HIV, sexually transmitted infections, viral hepatitis, and tuberculosis among incarcerated transgender people: A case of limited data, *Epidemiol Rev* 40:27, 2018.
4. Copen CE: Condom use during sexual intercourse among women and men aged 15-44 in the United States: 2011-2015 national survey of family growth, *Natl Health Stat Rep* 105:1, 2017.

*5. Centers for Disease Control and Prevention: US Public Health Service: Preexposure prophylaxis for the prevention of HIV infection in the United States—2017 Update. Retrieved from *www.cdc.gov/hiv/pdf/risk/prep/cdc-hiv-prep-guidelines-2017.pdf*.
*6. Centers for Disease Control and Prevention: *Updated guidelines for antiretroviral postexposure prophylaxis after sexual, injection drug use, or other nonoccupational exposure to HIV—United States*. Retrieved from *https://stacks.cdc.gov/view/cdc/38856*.
7. Centers for Disease Control and Prevention: *Pelvic inflammatory disease (PID)—CDC fact sheet*. Retrieved from *www.cdc.gov/std/pid/stdfact-pid-detailed.htm*.
*8. Centers for Disease Control and Prevention: *Sexually transmitted diseases treatment guidelines*. Retrieved from *www.cdc.gov/std/tg2015/default.htm*.
9. Centers for Disease Control and Prevention: *Expedited partner therapy*. Retrieved from *www.cdc.gov/std/ept/*.
10. Weston EJ, Wi T, Papp J: Strengthening global surveillance for antimicrobial drug-resistant *Neisseria gonorrhoeae* through the enhanced gonococcal antimicrobial surveillance program, *Emerg Infect Dis* 23:S47, 2017.
*11. Meites E, Kempe A, Markowitz LE: Use of a 2-dose schedule for human papillomavirus vaccination—Updated recommendations of the Advisory Committee on Immunization Practices, *MMWR* 65:1405, 2016.
12. Centers for Disease Control and Prevention: A guide to taking a sexual history. Retrieved from *www.cdc.gov/std/treatment/sexualhistory.pdf*.
13. Syme ML, Cohn TJ, Barnack-Tavlaris J: A comparison of actual and perceived sexual risk among older adults, *J Sex Res* 54:149, 2017.

*Evidence-based information for clinical practice.

53

Female Reproductive Problems

Kim K. Choma

Never believe that a few caring people can't change the world.

Margaret Mead

🅔 http://evolve.elsevier.com/Lewis/medsurg

LEARNING OUTCOMES

1. Summarize the etiologies of infertility and the strategies for diagnosis and treatment of the infertile woman.
2. Describe the etiology, clinical manifestations, and interprofessional and nursing management of menstrual problems and abnormal uterine bleeding.
3. Identify the risk factors, clinical manifestations, and nursing and interprofessional management of ectopic pregnancy.
4. Describe the changes related to menopause and interprofessional and nursing management of the patient with menopausal symptoms.
5. Describe the assessment and interprofessional and nursing management of women with pelvic inflammatory disease and endometriosis.
6. Explain the clinical manifestations, diagnostic studies, interprofessional care, including surgical therapy for cervical, endometrial, ovarian, and vulvar cancers.
7. Discuss the nursing management of the patient requiring surgery of the female reproductive system.
8. Distinguish among the common problems that occur with cystoceles, rectoceles, and fistulas and the related interprofessional and nursing management.
9. Summarize the clinical manifestations of sexual assault and the nursing and interprofessional management of the patient who has been sexually assaulted.

KEY TERMS

This chapter discusses several disorders, many of which are related to hormonal regulation, infection, inflammation, and cancer. Problems of the female reproductive and genital system can profoundly affect sexuality and reproduction. The consequences of these problems vary widely. Besides the obvious manifestations, a diagnosis of ovarian cancer often triggers intense feelings of anxiety and fear. An infertile couple can struggle with grief and the stress of infertility treatments. Pain and sexual dysfunction from prolapse or endometriosis can cause psychologic, social, and body image problems. We close with discussing sexual assault and the multiple physical and psychologic effects of intimate violence.

INFERTILITY

Infertility is the inability of a couple to conceive after at least 1 year of regular unprotected intercourse. Around 12% to 18% of women are not pregnant after 12 months of trying to conceive.[1] *Fecundability,* the probability of achieving a pregnancy in 1 menstrual cycle, is a more accurate label because it recognizes varying degrees of infertility. Impaired fecundity refers to women who have difficulty getting pregnant or carrying a pregnancy to term.

Etiology and Pathophysiology

Infertility may be caused by male, female, or combined factors. Of couples with infertility, 25% have male factors that affect their chances of conceiving. Conditions that cause male infertility are discussed in Chapter 54. Sometimes the cause of infertility may not be found.

Female infertility may be due to problems with ovulation, the fallopian tubes, or conditions that affect the uterus or cervix. In women the risk for infertility begins around age 30. By the time a woman reaches the age of 40, the chances of

TABLE 53.1 Interprofessional Care
Infertility

Diagnostic Assessment
- History and physical examination of both partners, including psychosocial functioning
- Review of menstrual and gynecologic history
- Assessment of possible sexually transmitted infections
- Hormone levels
  - Serum hormone levels (e.g., FSH, LH, prolactin)
  - Urinary LH
- Pap test with HPV test as indicated by age
- Ovulatory study
- Tubal patency study
  - Hysterosalpingogram
- Semen analysis
- Pelvic ultrasound
- Genetic screening

Management
- Hormone therapy
- Drug therapy (Table 53.2)
- Intrauterine insemination
- Assisted reproductive technologies (ARTs)

TABLE 53.2 Drug Therapy
Infertility

Drug	Mechanism of Action
Follicle-Stimulating Hormone Agonists	
follitropin (Gonal-f) urofollitropin (Bravelle)	Stimulates follicle growth and maturation by mimicking the body's natural FSH.
GnRH Agonists	
leuprolide (Lupron) nafarelin (Synarel)	Suppresses release of LH and FSH with continuous use. May be used in the treatment of endometriosis.
GnRH Antagonists	
cetrorelix (Cetrotide) ganirelix	Prevents premature LH surges and premature ovulation in women undergoing ovarian stimulation.
Human Chorionic Gonadotropin (hCG)	
Novarel Pregnyl Profasi	Induces ovulation by stimulating release of eggs from follicles.
Menotropins (Human Menopausal Gonadotropin)	
Humegon Pergonal Repronex	Product made of FSH and LH to promote the development and maturation of follicles in ovaries.
Selective Estrogen Receptor Modulator	
clomiphene (Clomid)	Stimulates hypothalamus to ↑ production of GnRH, which ↑ release of LH and FSH. End result is stimulation of ovulation.

TABLE 53.3 Types of Spontaneous Abortion

Type	Description
Complete abortion	All products of conception (POC) are expelled
Incomplete abortion	Parts of POC are retained
Inevitable abortion	Cervix is open and pregnancy loss cannot be prevented
Infected (septic) abortion	Endometrium (uterine lining) and POC become infected
Missed abortion	Fetus has died but has not been expelled
Threatened abortion	Unexplained bleeding with or without pain. Suggests pregnancy loss may occur

conceiving are 10% or less. For both genders, chronic diseases, genital infections, and exposure to environmental toxins can affect fertility.[2]

Diagnostic Studies

Formal evaluation of the infertile couple is usually done after 1 year of regular unprotected intercourse. Earlier evaluation may occur in women over age 35 or based on medical or physical findings. Couples who are being evaluated usually have a detailed history and physical examination. Based on the findings, diagnostic testing may be ordered (Table 53.1).

A comprehensive evaluation of the female reproductive system includes cervical, uterine, endometrial, tubal, peritoneal, and ovarian factors that could be the source of infertility. A semen sample is done to determine if the cause is related to the male partner.

❖ Interprofessional and Nursing Care

Infertility management depends on the cause. If the cause is due to ovarian function, supplemental hormone therapy may be used. Table 53.2 reviews drugs commonly used for women with infertility. Couples should be involved in fertility treatment decisions. The choices involve 4 major aspects: effectiveness (e.g., live birth rate), burdens of treatments (office visits, frequent injections), safety, (e.g., risk for multiple gestation), and costs.[3]

Assisted reproductive technology (ART) can be used to help women who are having difficulty becoming pregnant. ART includes fertility drugs for ovulation induction, artificial insemination, and surrogacy. Types of ART include (1) in vitro fertilization (IVF), (2) gamete intrafallopian transfer (GIFT), (3) zygote intrafallopian transfer (ZIFT), (4) donor gametes, (5) freezing of ova, and (6) intracytoplasmic sperm injection (ICSI), a type of IVF that is often used for couples with male factor infertility. Some types of ART, such as IVF, are expensive and can be emotionally stressful. Assisting couples with infertility is critical. You can provide teaching about the physiology of reproduction and an overview of infertility evaluation and treatments.

EARLY PREGNANCY LOSS

Early pregnancy loss is a term used to describe the loss of a pregnancy before 20 weeks of gestation.[4] **Abortion** is another term we use to describe the loss of pregnancy. Abortions are classified as *spontaneous* (those occurring naturally [e.g., miscarriage]) or *induced* (those occurring from medical intervention). *Miscarriage* is the common term for the unintended loss of a pregnancy.

Spontaneous Abortion

Spontaneous abortion is the natural loss of pregnancy before 20 weeks of gestation (Table 53.3). Nearly 20% of pregnancies result in miscarriage. The loss can be devastating for both the

TABLE 53.4 Methods for Inducing Abortions

Method	Length of Pregnancy	Description
Dilation and evacuation (D&E)	10–16 wk	Cervix is dilated, and contents of uterus are removed by vacuum cannula and use of other instruments as needed.
Medical vacuum aspiration	Usually up to 2 wk after first missed period	Catheter is inserted through cervix into uterus, and suction is applied. Contents of uterus are aspirated.
Mifepristone (Mifeprex) with misoprostol (Cytotec)	Up to 49–63 days*	Mifepristone is given orally, followed by misoprostol orally 48 hr later.
Suction aspiration (curettage)	Up to 12 wk	Cervix is dilated, uterine aspirator is introduced, and suction is applied, removing contents of uterus.

*FDA recommends 49 days. The American Congress of Obstetricians and Gynecologists guidelines state it is safe to use up to 63 days.

mother and her partner. Fetal chromosomal abnormalities cause many miscarriages before 8 weeks of gestation. Testing for chromosomal anomalies is now available for products of conception (POC) from a miscarriage. Other causes of miscarriage include endocrine abnormalities, maternal infection, uterine abnormalities (e.g., uterine fibroids, endometriosis), immunologic factors, and environmental factors.

Treatment to prevent miscarriage is limited. Although bed rest and avoiding vaginal intercourse are often recommended, there is no evidence that these measures improve the outcome. Women are told to report any bleeding to the HCP.

If the pregnancy is not viable, 2 options are considered: expectant management or medical management. *Expectant management* refers to monitoring the patient to see if the POC are expelled naturally without complications. *Medical management* may be needed if the POC do not pass completely or bleeding becomes excessive. This may involve a *dilation and curettage (D&C)* or the use of medications (e.g., misoprostol [Cytotec]) to expel the remaining contents from the uterus. The D&C involves surgically dilating the cervix and scraping the endometrium of the uterus to empty the contents of the uterus.

Women who have moderate-to-heavy bleeding and the passage of clots during pregnancy may need emergency care at a hospital. Vital signs and blood loss are monitored along with an assessment of psychologic well-being. Any heavy bleeding, severe pain, or fever that occurs after medical management should be reported to the HCP. Ovulation can occur as soon as 2 weeks after early pregnancy loss. Normal menses should return within 4 to 6 weeks.

Provide grief support as the couple deals with the psychologic distress of their loss. Encourage them to share their feelings. Referral to a pregnancy loss support group may be helpful.

Induced Abortion

Induced abortion is an elective termination of a pregnancy.[5] There are several ways to induce an abortion (Table 53.4). Deciding which method to use depends on the length of the pregnancy and the woman's condition.

Once the woman makes the decision to have an abortion, she and her partner need support and acceptance. Prepare the patient for what to expect both emotionally and physically. Grief and sadness are normal emotions after an abortion. Nursing care for a woman who terminates her pregnancy includes assessment of a woman's need for counseling and support, providing for privacy, maintaining her physical comfort, and monitoring her vital signs.

After the abortion, teach the patient the signs and symptoms of complications. These includes abnormal vaginal bleeding, severe abdominal cramping, fever, and foul-smelling drainage. Stress to the patient that as soon as 1 week after having an abortion she can become pregnant again. Normal menstruation returns in 4 to 6 weeks.

Teach patients to refrain from intercourse and putting anything into the vagina for 1 week after the abortion. The exception is for women who use NuvaRing birth control. Oral contraception can be started the day of the abortion or 1 to 2 weeks after the procedure, depending on the patient's needs and desires.

PROBLEMS RELATED TO MENSTRUATION

The normal menstrual cycle is discussed in Chapter 50. The menstrual cycle may be irregular the first few years after menarche and in the years preceding menopause. Although most women have a predictable menstrual cycle, considerable normal variation exists among women in cycle length and in duration, amount, and character of the menstrual flow (see Table 50.2). During the perimenopausal period (the years prior to menopause) as ovarian function begins to decrease, women may note a change in their menstrual patterns.

PREMENSTRUAL SYNDROME

Premenstrual syndrome (PMS) refers to a group of symptoms that occur during a woman's menstrual cycle. Many women have symptoms of PMS. They may be severe enough to affect interpersonal relationships, work responsibilities, academic performance, and social activities.

PMS includes a variety of physical, psychologic, and somatic symptoms. As many as 150 symptoms are associated with PMS. (PMDD) is the term used to describe PMS associated with a severe mood disorder.

Etiology and Pathophysiology

We do not completely understand the cause of PMS. PMS is likely due to a combination of biologic and psychosocial factors. Genetics, hormone and neurotransmitter (e.g., serotonin) imbalances, and nutrition problems are all thought to be causes of PMS.

Clinical Manifestations

PMS is extremely variable in its manifestations, frequency, and severity. Symptoms may also vary from one cycle to another. Common symptoms include breast discomfort, peripheral edema, abdominal bloating, sensation of weight gain, episodes of binge eating, headaches, anxiety, depression, irritability and moodiness, back pain, insomnia, menstrual cramps, fatigue, and generalized muscle pain.

Diagnostic Studies and Interprofessional Care

A focused health history and physical examination are done to identify any underlying conditions which may account for symptoms. These include thyroid problems, uterine fibroids, anemia, nutritional and vitamin deficiencies, autoimmune disorders, endometriosis, and depression.

To accurately diagnose PMS or PMDD, 4 factors are critical: (1) consistency of the syndrome complex, (2) occurrence of the symptoms in the luteal phase and resolution after the beginning of menses, (3) documented ovulatory cycles, and (4) symptoms that disrupt the woman's life.

A holistic approach to managing PMS symptoms for women includes stress management, dietary changes, exercise, teaching, and cognitive behavioral therapy. Mindfulness activities can help women deal with the discomforts of PMS.[6]

Drug Therapy. Selective serotonin reuptake inhibitors (SSRIs) (e.g., sertraline [Zoloft], fluoxetine [Prozac]) have provided relief to women who have anxiety, irritability, and mood changes associated with PMS. Many women choose to take oral contraceptives (OCPs) and/or nonsteroidal antiinflammatory drugs (NSAIDs) to reduce cramping, blood flow, and back pain. Vitamin B_6, calcium, and magnesium have been recommended for mood changes associated with PMS.

? CHECK YOUR PRACTICE

You are working in the gynecology outpatient clinic. Your patient is a 28-yr-old woman who reporting symptoms of PMS. She tells you, "My PMS has gotten so bad lately that I spend the entire day in bed due to pain. I am very anxious and overwhelmed. I can't function like this anymore."

- How would you respond?
- What are things she can do to relieve symptoms?

❖ NURSING MANAGEMENT: PREMENSTRUAL SYNDROME

Nursing care for the patient with PMS includes teaching her about the symptoms associated with PMS and how to manage them (Table 53.5). Acknowledging that she has PMS can be therapeutic and empowering. Teaching the woman's partner about the nature of PMS helps the partner better understand PMS and its effects. Provide the patient with support and reassure her that PMS is not an emotional disorder, but one that has a physiologic basis and can be managed.

TABLE 53.5 Interprofessional Care
Premenstrual Syndrome (PMS)

Diagnostic Assessment
- History and physical examination
- Symptom diary

Management
- Stress management
- Nutritional therapy
- Aerobic exercise

Drug Therapy
- Diuretics
- Combined OCPs
- Prostaglandin inhibitors (e.g., ibuprofen)
- SSRIs (e.g., sertraline [Zoloft])

DYSMENORRHEA

Dysmenorrhea is painful menses with abdominal cramping. The 2 types of dysmenorrhea are *primary* (no pathologic condition exists) and *secondary* (pelvic disease is the underlying cause). Dysmenorrhea is one of the most common gynecologic problems.

Etiology and Pathophysiology

Primary dysmenorrhea begins in the first few years after menarche, typically with the onset of regular menstrual cycles. It is usually related to increased levels of prostaglandin, a hormone that is found in the endometrium. Endometrial stimulation by estrogen and progesterone results in a dramatic increase in prostaglandin production. Prostaglandin stimulates the uterus to contract. Uterine contractions and constriction of small endometrial blood vessels result in tissue ischemia and increased sensitization of the pain receptors. This results in painful menstrual cramps. As menstruation continues, prostaglandin levels decrease each day and menstrual cramping lessens.

Secondary dysmenorrhea usually occurs after adolescence, most commonly at 30 to 40 years of age and worsens as a woman ages. Common pelvic conditions that cause secondary dysmenorrhea include endometriosis, chronic pelvic inflammatory disease (PID), and uterine fibroids. Because secondary dysmenorrhea can be caused by many conditions, the manifestations and severity vary. However, painful menses is the main manifestation.

Clinical Manifestations

Manifestations include menstrual pain that is most severe during the first few days of menses. Painful menstruation rarely lasts more than 2 days. Typical symptoms include lower, colicky abdominal pain that often radiates to the lower back and upper thighs. Nausea, diarrhea, fatigue, and headache may occur.

Secondary dysmenorrhea usually occurs after the woman has little to no pain during the menstrual cycle. The pain, which may be unilateral, is often more constant and continues longer than in primary dysmenorrhea. Depending on the cause, symptoms such as *dyspareunia* (painful intercourse), painful defecation, or irregular bleeding may occur at times other than menstruation.

Diagnostic Studies

Evaluation begins with a complete health history and pelvic examination. A probable diagnosis of primary dysmenorrhea is given if the history reveals an onset shortly after menarche with symptoms that are associated only with menses. The pelvic examination is otherwise normal. If the HCP finds an underlying cause of dysmenorrhea, the diagnosis is secondary dysmenorrhea.

❖ Interprofessional and Nursing Care

Treatment for primary dysmenorrhea includes pharmacologic and nonpharmacologic therapy. NSAIDs (e.g., naproxen [Naprosyn]) inhibit prostaglandins. OCPs may be used to decrease estrogen and progesterone. This results in lower prostaglandin levels, decreased monthly endometrial lining proliferation, and decreased menstrual flow.

Nonpharmacologic interventions include applying heat to the lower abdomen or back and physical exercise. Regular exercise helps to reduce prostaglandin production. Acupuncture and transcutaneous nerve stimulation may be used for women who have inadequate relief from drugs or who prefer not to take drugs.

Treatment of secondary dysmenorrhea depends on the etiology. Some patients are helped by the approaches used for primary dysmenorrhea. However, if a gynecologic problem is the main cause of secondary dysmenorrhea, then treating that underlying problem is the priority. For example, women with endometriosis who have secondary dysmenorrhea may benefit from OCPs.

Nursing interventions include teaching women with dysmenorrhea about the cause, symptoms, and treatment. This will provide women with a basis for coping with the problem and increase feelings of self-control. Teach women that during acute pain, relief may be obtained by applying heat to the abdomen or back and taking NSAIDs. Suggest noninvasive pain-relieving practices, such as relaxation breathing and guided imagery, yoga, and meditation. Other measures to reduce discomfort include regular exercise and good nutrition.

ABNORMAL UTERINE BLEEDING

Abnormal uterine bleeding (AUB) is any change in a woman's menstrual flow, including volume, duration, or cycle pattern. AUB can be classified based on the cause of bleeding (Fig. 53.1). *Heavy menstrual bleeding* (HMB) (instead of the term *menorrhagia*) describes excessive bleeding. *Intermenstrual bleeding* (instead of the term *metrorrhagia*) refers to bleeding between regular menstrual cycles.

Chronic AUB is classified as uterine bleeding that is abnormal in volume, timing, or regularity and has been present for most of the past 6 months. *Acute AUB* is an episode of heavy bleeding that requires immediate treatment.

In reproductive-age women, causes of AUB include uterine fibroids, polyps, ovulatory dysfunction, endometrial problems, or cancer. Other causes include bleeding disorders (e.g., thrombocytopenia), leukemia, medications, eating disorders, or liver failure.[7] For postmenopausal women, endometrial cancer must be considered whenever bleeding or spotting occurs after menstrual bleeding has ceased for 1 year or longer.

Anovulation is the most common reason for missing menses. Ovulation is often erratic for several years after menarche and before menopause. Bleeding in between periods (spotting) is common for women who start taking OCPs. If spotting continues beyond the first few months on OCPs, a different pill formulation may be prescribed. Spotting with long-acting progestin therapies (e.g., intrauterine devices [IUDs], Nexplanon implant, progestin-only pills [levonorgestrel, norethindrone], progesterone injections [medroxyprogesterone acetate]) is common and not usually associated with any serious complications.

Amenorrhea is the absence or abnormal interruption of menstruation (Table 53.6). *Primary amenorrhea* refers to the failure of menstrual cycles to begin by 16 years of age. *Secondary amenorrhea* occurs when menstrual cycles stop for 3 to 6 months in menstruating women. Primary amenorrhea is often associated with chromosomal or congenital abnormalities and the female athletic triad. Causes of secondary amenorrhea include primary ovarian insufficiency, polycystic ovary syndrome (PCOS), hypothalamic disorders, and hyperprolactinemia.

Diagnostic Studies and Interprofessional Care

Once it is determined that a patient has AUB, the HCP will determine if the AUB is related to a structural cause or nonstructural cause. A comprehensive history and physical examination are done to find the cause of AUB (Table 53.7). Laboratory evaluation and diagnostic procedures are based on findings from the history and physical examination. Treatment depends on the cause of the problem, degree of threat to the patient's health, her quality of life, and whether children are desired in the future.

Combined OCPs may be prescribed for a woman with amenorrhea to ensure regular shedding of the endometrium. Tranexamic acid (Lysteda) may be used during the menstrual cycle to treat heavy menstrual bleeding. This drug stabilizes a protein that helps blood to clot. The use of tranexamic acid is contraindicated in women who use combined OCPs.

Estradiol valerate/dienogest (Natazia) is the only combined OCP approved for treatment of heavy menstrual bleeding. It may be given to women who want an OCP to prevent pregnancy. Other options for treatment of heavy menstrual bleeding include NSAIDs and the Mirena IUD (progestin IUD).

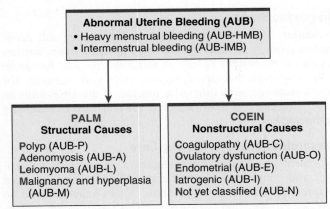

FIG. 53.1 PALM-COEIN classification system for abnormal uterine bleeding. (Used with permission. Munro MG, Critchley HO, Broder MS, et al: FIGO classification system [PALM–OEIN] for causes of AUB in nongravid women of reproductive age, *Int J Gynecol Obstet* 11:3, 2011.)

TABLE 53.6 Causes of Amenorrhea

Genetic
- Congenital absence or doubling of reproductive organ(s)
- Turner's syndrome

Hormonal Imbalance
- Polycystic ovary syndrome (PCOS)
- Pituitary tumors
- Thyroid dysfunction

Lifestyle
- Acute and chronic illness
- Excess exercise
- Low body weight
- Stress

Medications
- Antidepressants
- Antihypertensives
- Antipsychotics
- Chemotherapy
- Hormone therapy (oral or injectable contraceptives, intrauterine devices)

Natural Amenorrhea
- Breastfeeding
- Menopause
- Pregnancy

Structural Problems
- Damage or scarring to reproductive organs from infection, trauma, radiation

TABLE 53.7 Interprofessional Care
Abnormal Uterine Bleeding

Diagnostic Assessment
- History, including surgical history and medication history
- Age of menarche/menopause
- Bleeding patterns and perceived severity of bleeding (clots, soaking through clothing)
- Evaluation for obesity/hirsutism (suggestive of polycystic ovary syndrome)
- Pelvic examination
- Pregnancy test
- Complete blood count (CBC)
- Thyroid-stimulating hormone (TSH)
- STI screening
- Screening for bleeding disorders (if indicated)
- Imaging studies and tissue sampling
  - Transvaginal/pelvic ultrasound
  - Saline infusion sonohysterography
  - Endometrial biopsy
  - Hysteroscopy

Management
Based on the cause, may include:
- OCPs
- Hormonal therapy
- NSAIDS
- Mirena IUD

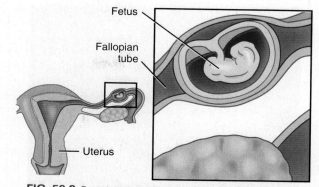

FIG. 53.2 Ectopic pregnancy occurring in the fallopian tube.

❖ NURSING MANAGEMENT: ABNORMAL UTERINE BLEEDING

Teach women about the characteristics of the menstrual cycle to help them identify variations (see Table 50.2). This knowledge can decrease apprehension and dispel misconceptions about the menstrual cycle. Encourage the patient to report excessive bleeding, passing of clots, and unusually long duration of menstrual cycles.

Teach women to avoid the prolonged use of superabsorbent tampons that can increase the risk for toxic shock syndrome (TSS). TSS is an acute life-threatening condition caused by a toxin from *Staphylococcus aureus*. TSS causes high fever, vomiting, diarrhea, weakness, myalgia, and a sunburn-like rash.

ECTOPIC PREGNANCY

An **ectopic pregnancy** is the implantation of the fertilized ovum anywhere outside the uterus. Almost all ectopic pregnancies occur within the fallopian tube. Around 3% of all pregnancies are ectopic (Fig. 53.2). Ectopic pregnancy is a life-threatening condition. Early detection can lead to successful management and reduce morbidity and mortality.

Etiology and Pathophysiology

Ectopic pregnancy can be caused by blockage of the fallopian tube(s) or reduction of tubal peristalsis that impedes or delays the fertilized ovum from passing to the uterus. After the fertilized egg implants itself in the fallopian tube, the growth of the gestational sac expands the tubal wall. Eventually the fallopian tube ruptures, leading to acute peritonitis. This occurs 6 to 8 weeks after the last normal menstrual period. Often the woman presents due to bleeding and/or pelvic pain or pressure.

Risk factors or causes for ectopic pregnancy include a history of PID, prior ectopic pregnancy, current progestin-releasing IUD, and prior pelvic or tubal surgery. Procedures used in infertility treatment (e.g., IVF, embryo transfer, ovulation induction) increase the risk.

Clinical Manifestations

The classic manifestations are abdominal or pelvic pain, missed menses, and/or irregular vaginal bleeding. Others include morning sickness, breast tenderness, gastrointestinal (GI) symptoms, malaise, and syncope. Often, the symptoms of pregnancy (e.g., nausea) decrease as the hormones level off, offering a clue early on that something is not right.

Pelvic and/or abdominal pain is almost always present. It is caused by distention of the fallopian tube. The character of the pain varies among women. It can be colicky or vague, unilateral or bilateral.

Symptom severity does not necessarily correlate with the extent of vaginal bleeding. Vaginal bleeding that may accompany ectopic pregnancy is usually described as spotting. However, bleeding may be heavier and can be confused with menses. If tubal rupture occurs, there is risk for hemorrhage and hypovolemic shock. This situation is an emergency.

Diagnostic Studies

Diagnosing an ectopic pregnancy can be challenging because of the manifestations. If the HCP suspects an ectopic pregnancy, a pelvic examination, vaginal ultrasound, and serum pregnancy test (quantitative human chorionic gonadotropin [β-hCG]) are done. Serum β-hCG levels can be measured every few days until ultrasound testing can confirm or rule out ectopic pregnancy. This is usually about 5 to 6 weeks after conception.

❓ CHECK YOUR PRACTICE

You are working in the ED. Your patient is a 29-yr-old woman who presented with acute abdominal pain. She has had in vitro fertilization. Her pain is 7 (on 0 to 10 pain scale). The HCP suspects an ectopic pregnancy. She is crying, "I am going to lose this baby, and we have been trying so hard to have one."
- As her nurse, what are your priorities?
- How would you respond to her?

❖ Interprofessional and Nursing Care

There are 2 ways to treat ectopic pregnancies: drug therapy or surgery.[8] Drug therapy is used (1) when an ectopic pregnancy is confirmed on ultrasound, (2) the woman is hemodynamically

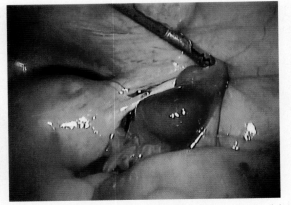

FIG. 53.3 Laparoscopic treatment of ectopic pregnancy in the right fallopian tube. (From Katz V: *Comprehensive gynecology,* ed 5, St Louis, 2007, Mosby.)

stable, (3) the woman is compliant with follow-up, and (4) the pregnancy is small and the fallopian tube has not ruptured.

Methotrexate therapy is the drug therapy of choice. Methotrexate stops the growth of rapidly dividing cells, such as embryonic, fetal, and early placenta cells, by inhibiting DNA synthesis and disrupting cell multiplication. Methotrexate can be given as a single shot or as several injections. The most common side effect is cramping abdominal pain. It usually occurs during the first 2 to 3 days of treatment. Other side effects may include vaginal bleeding, nausea, vomiting, indigestion, or dizziness.

Serum β-hCG levels are measured on posttreatment days 4 and 7. A 15% reduction in β-hCG is expected. Weekly β-hCG tests are done until negative. If at any time serum β-hCG levels plateau or increase, methotrexate may be repeated. If an ectopic pregnancy continues after 2 or 3 doses of methotrexate, surgical treatment is needed to remove the ectopic pregnancy.

If surgery is needed, a conservative approach that limits damage to the reproductive system is the goal. If the pregnancy is small, the pregnancy is removed laparoscopically (Fig. 53.3). If the tube ruptures, emergent surgery is done to stabilize the patient.

Nursing care includes closely monitoring vital signs and observing for signs of shock. Provide patient teaching to prepare her for the diagnostic procedures and drug therapy. Explain the side effects of methotrexate and tell her to avoid NSAIDs. Follow-up with weekly β-hCG tests is required. If the patient needs laparoscopic surgery, provide patient teaching and emotional support.

PERIMENOPAUSE AND POSTMENOPAUSE

Perimenopause is a normal life transition for women that begins with the first signs of change in menstrual cycles and ends after cessation of menses. Menstrual changes can include shorter or longer cycles, less frequent cycles, lighter cycles, or heavier cycles.

Menopause is a normal physiologic cessation of menses associated with declining ovarian function that ends in cessation of the menstrual cycle and ovulation. *Natural menopause* is diagnosed retrospectively after 12 months of no periods. The average age for a woman is 52 years. The age can vary from 40 to 58 years.

Induced menopause occurs after surgical intervention to remove the ovaries or from side effects of chemotherapy,

TABLE 53.8 **Manifestations of Perimenopause and Postmenopause**	
Perimenopause	**Postmenopause**
• Irregular menstrual cycles • Mood changes • Occasional vasomotor symptoms (e.g., hot flashes) • Sleep problems • Vaginal dryness	• Atrophy of genitourinary tissue (e.g., vulvar, vaginal epithelium) with decreased support • Breast tenderness • Cessation of menses • Osteopenia, osteoporosis • Vasomotor instability (e.g., hot flashes, night sweats) • Stress and urge incontinence

TABLE 53.9 **Manifestations of Estrogen Deficiency**	
Cardiovascular • ↓ High-density lipoproteins (HDLs) • ↑ Increased low-density lipoproteins (LDLs) **Genitourinary** • Atrophic vaginitis • Dyspareunia from poor lubrication • Incontinence **Musculoskeletal** • ↑ Fracture rate, especially vertebral bodies but also humerus, distal radius, and upper femur	**Psychologic** • Emotional lability • Change in sleep pattern • ↓ REM sleep **Vasomotor** • Hot flashes • Night sweats **Other** • ↓ Collagen content of skin • Breast tissue changes

radiation therapy, or other drugs. *Postmenopause* is a term that refers to the time in a woman's life after menopause.

Clinical Manifestations

Manifestations of perimenopause and menopause are outlined in Table 53.8. Perimenopause is a time of erratic hormonal fluctuation and irregular menstrual cycles. With the decrease in function of the ovaries, estrogen levels drop, and hot flashes and other symptoms begin. The signs and symptoms of decreased estrogen are listed in Table 53.9.

The loss of estrogen plays a significant role in age-related changes. Changes most critical to a woman's well-being are the increased risks for coronary artery disease (CAD) and osteoporosis (from bone density loss). Other changes include a redistribution of fat, a tendency to gain weight more easily, muscle and joint pain, loss of skin elasticity, changes in hair amount and distribution, and atrophy of external genitalia and breast tissue.

Vasomotor instability (hot flashes) and irregular menses are the main manifestations associated with menopause. A hot flash is a sudden sensation of intense heat along with perspiration and flushing. Atrophy of the vulva and vagina may occur due to decreased estrogen levels. Decreased estrogen also causes thinning of the vaginal mucosa and the disappearance of rugae. This results in a decrease in vaginal secretions and causes the secretions to become more alkaline. Because of these changes, the vagina is easily traumatized. The woman can have dyspareunia and be more susceptible to infection.

Vaginal atrophy can lead to unnecessary and premature cessation of sexual activity. This can be corrected with water-soluble lubricants or, if needed, hormonal creams (vaginal estrogen) or oral hormone replacement therapy. About half of midlife women have vaginal atrophy, but few seek care.

The woman can have atrophic changes in the lower urinary tract and the vulva, which can result in a regression of the labia minora and majora. Bladder capacity decreases. The bladder and urethral tissue lose tone. These changes can cause symptoms that mimic a bladder infection (e.g., dysuria, urgency, frequency) when no infection is present. Decreasing blood serum estrogen levels can cause an array of physical and cognitive changes during menopause that include depression, irritability, insomnia, and memory loss.

Interprofessional Care

The diagnosis of menopause should be made only after careful consideration of other possible causes for a woman's symptoms. Testing of follicle-stimulating hormone (FSH) levels in the perimenopause period is not recommended because hormone levels change throughout the menstrual cycle. However, once a woman has no periods for at least a year, FSH testing can confirm a diagnosis of menopause. FSH levels are increased in menopause. When a woman's FSH blood level is consistently elevated to 30 mIU/mL or higher, and she has not had a menstrual period for a year, it is generally accepted that she has reached menopause.

Drug Therapy. Hormone replacement therapy (HRT) using estrogen, with or without progesterone, is prescribed for some women. Women may choose to use HRT for short-term symptom management and treatment for several years (4 to 5 years) of menopausal symptoms. The risks (e.g., increased risk for breast and endometrial cancer, risk for blood clots) and benefits (e.g., minimizes bone loss, hot flashes, vaginal atrophic changes) must be carefully considered.[9]

Nonhormonal Therapy. Because of the risks associated with HRT, some women choose to use nonhormonal and nonpharmacologic interventions to manage their symptoms. For significant menopausal symptoms, nonhormonal pharmacologic agents may be used. For example, the SSRI antidepressants paroxetine (Paxil), fluoxetine, and venlafaxine (Effexor XR) are effective alternatives to HRT to reduce hot flashes.

Clonidine (Catapres), an antihypertensive drug, and gabapentin (Neurontin), an antiseizure drug, also have been shown to manage vasomotor symptoms during menopause. Selective estrogen receptor modulators (SERMs), such as raloxifene (Evista), are also used to manage menopausal symptoms. SERMs have positive benefits of estrogen, including preventing bone loss, without the negative effects (e.g., endometrial hyperplasia).

Some women seek herbal therapies to ease the symptoms they experience during menopause. While you will see a number of supplements marketed for menopause, there is no research showing that the use of any herb as a treatment for menopause symptoms is effective.

Nutritional Therapy. Good nutrition can decrease the risk for cardiovascular disease (CVD) and osteoporosis and help with vasomotor symptoms. A decrease in metabolic rate and careless eating habits can cause the weight gain and fatigue often attributed to menopause. An adequate intake of calcium and vitamin D helps maintain healthy bones and counteracts loss of bone density.

COMPLEMENTARY & ALTERNATIVE THERAPIES
Herbs and Supplements for Menopause

Herb	Scientific Evidence	Nursing Implications
Black cohosh	Mixed evidence for use in the treatment of menopausal symptoms	• Generally well tolerated in recommended doses for up to 6 mo. • Should not be used by women with a liver disorder.
Soy	Mixed evidence for treatment of menopausal symptoms	• Women with a history of breast, ovarian, or uterine cancer or endometriosis should consult with their HCP before using soy or soy products. • Soy may interact with warfarin. Patients taking warfarin should consult with their HCP before using soy or soy products.

Source: *www.nlm.nih.gov/medlineplus/herbalmedicine.html#summary.*

Postmenopausal women not taking supplemental HRT should have a daily calcium intake of at least 1500 mg. Women taking estrogen replacement need at least 1000 mg/day. Calcium supplements are best absorbed when taken with meals, but not taken as a single dose. The woman should divide the calcium she needs into 2 doses per day so that it is absorbed properly. Either dietary calcium or calcium supplements may be used (see Table 63.14).

❖ NURSING MANAGEMENT: PERIMENOPAUSE AND POSTMENOPAUSE

Menopause is a time of great transition for a woman both physically and psychologically. Many women have symptoms for years during the perimenopausal period while others transition without any difficulty. Menopause may be occurring simultaneously with role changes in the woman's personal and professional life. The combination of menopause and these changes can cause great emotional distress or a renewed sense of self and well-being.

Women in their perimenopausal and menopausal years need a lot of emotional support. Provide reassurance that symptoms can be treated and managed with either hormonal or nonhormonal therapies. It is important to teach them about strategies to prevent or reduce the risk for CVD and osteoporosis.

INFECTIONS OF LOWER GENITAL TRACT
Etiology and Pathophysiology

The female genital tract is susceptible to different types of infections, especially when the pH of the genital tract is altered. In most women, the vaginal pH is typically below 4.5, which helps prevent certain bacterial infections from occurring. The pH level of the vagina is maintained through a combination of sufficient levels of estrogen and *Lactobacillus*, a naturally occurring bacteria that colonizes the vagina.

Infection and inflammation of the vagina, cervix, and vulva often occur when estrogen levels decrease or medication use (e.g., contraceptives, antibiotics, corticosteroids) affects the microbiome of the vagina, leading to changes in the pH balance of the genital tract. For example, *Candida albicans* may be present in small numbers in the vagina. Women who take an

TABLE 53.10 Infections of the Lower Genital Tract

Infection and Etiology	Manifestations	Treatment Considerations
Bacterial Vaginosis *Corynebacterium vaginale* *Gardnerella vaginalis*	Watery discharge with fish-like odor. May or may not have other symptoms	Drug therapy based on cause: • clindamycin (Clindesse)—vaginal • metronidazole (Flagyl)—oral or intravaginal • tinidazole (Tindamax)—oral • *Lactobacillus acidophilus* taken orally by diet (e.g., yogurt, fermented soy products) or supplements can ↓ unwanted vaginal bacteria
Cervicitis *Chlamydia trachomatis* *Neisseria gonorrhoeae* (most often)	Sexually transmitted. Mucopurulent discharge with postcoital spotting from cervical inflammation	Drug therapy based on cause, common agents include azithromycin (Zithromax) and ceftriaxone. Treat patient and partner. May be reportable according to state laws.
Severe Recurrent Vaginitis (more than 4 episodes per year) *Candida albicans* (most often) or non-*albicans* strains	Depend on cause	Drug therapy based on cause. All women who are unresponsive to first-line treatment should be offered HIV testing. Common in women with uncontrolled diabetes or HIV infection.
Trichomonas Vaginitis *Trichomonas vaginalis* (protozoa)	Sexually transmitted. Itching, frothy greenish or gray discharge. Hemorrhagic spots on cervix or vaginal walls	Antifungal agents • metronidazole (Flagyl) • tinidazole (Tindamax) Treat patient and partner
Vulvovaginal Candidiasis *Candida albicans* (fungus)	Itching, thick white curd-like discharge	Antifungal agents • clotrimazole (Gyne-Lotrimin, Mycelex) • fluconazole (Diflucan) • miconazole (Monistat) • terconazole (Terazol)

antibiotic for another type of infection may have an overgrowth of *C. albicans*. This leads to a condition called *vulvovaginal candidiasis* (often called a "yeast infection").

Organisms gain entrance to the lower genital tract through contaminated hands, clothing, douching, and intercourse. Women should not douche. Douching changes the natural acidity and microbiome of the vagina, causing an overgrowth of bacteria. Most lower genital tract infections are related to sexual intercourse. Intercourse can transmit organisms, injure tissue, and change the acid-base balance of the vagina.

Table 53.10 presents the causes, manifestations, and interprofessional care of common infections of the female lower genital tract.

Clinical Manifestations

The manifestations of lower genital tract infections depend on the type of infection. Abnormal vaginal discharge and a reddened vulva are common. Women with vulvovaginal candidiasis have a curd-like discharge with intense itching and pain with urination. Women with bacterial vaginosis often have vaginal discharge that has a fishy odor. With cervicitis, there may be spotting (bleeding) after intercourse.

Common vulvar lesions include herpes infection and genital warts. Initial or primary herpes infections may be extremely painful. Herpes infections begin as a small vesicle followed by a superficial red, painful, ulcer. Genital warts, caused by the

human papillomavirus (HPV), vary in appearance. Irregularly shaped "cauliflower" lesions are common. Genital warts are painless unless traumatized. (Herpes infection and genital warts are discussed in Chapter 52.)

Postmenopausal women may develop vulvar changes, such as *lichen sclerosis*. This chronic inflammatory skin condition is associated with intense itching in the genital skin area (e.g., labia minora, clitoris). Although the vulvar changes are white with a "tissue paper" appearance initially, scratching causes changes in the appearance. The cause is unknown.

Interprofessional Care

Evaluation of genital problems includes a history, physical examination, and appropriate laboratory and diagnostic studies. Because many problems relate to sexual activity, a sexual history is essential. The nature of the problem determines the extent of the evaluation. When ulcerative lesions are present, the HCP will usually obtain a culture for herpes and a blood test for syphilis. Genital warts are usually identified by their clinical appearance. Vulvar skin conditions may be examined by colposcopy and biopsy of the skin lesion.

Problems involving vaginal discharge are evaluated by examining the discharge under a microscope or by obtaining specimens for testing. To assess for cervicitis, specimens are obtained for chlamydial, gonorrhea, and trichomonal infections. (Sexually transmitted infections [STIs] are discussed in Chapter 52.)

Drug therapy is based on the diagnosis (Table 53.10). Antibiotics taken as directed will cure bacterial infections. Teach patients how to properly take their medications and get follow-up care. Partners should be treated so that reinfection does not occur.

Women with vaginal conditions or cervical infection should abstain from intercourse for at least 1 week. Sexual partners must be evaluated and treated if the patient is diagnosed with trichomoniasis, chlamydial infection, gonorrhea, syphilis, or HIV.

Treatment of vulvar skin conditions is symptomatic because no cures are available. Treatment involves controlling the "itch-scratch cycle." High-potency topical corticosteroid ointments (e.g., clobetasol), help relieve itching. Stopping the itch-scratch cycle prevents further damage to the skin.

❖ NURSING MANAGEMENT: INFECTIONS OF LOWER GENITAL TRACT

Teach women about common infections of the genital tract and how to reduce their risks for infection. Recognize symptoms that indicate a problem, and help women seek care promptly. Discussing problems that concern the patient's genitalia or sexual intercourse is often hard. Use a nonjudgmental attitude to make women feel more comfortable while empowering them to ask questions.

When a woman is diagnosed with a genital infection, ensure that she fully understands the treatment. If a woman is using a vaginal medication for the first time, show her the applicator and how to fill it. Teach where and how the applicator should be inserted using visual aids or models. Vaginal creams should be inserted before going to bed so the medication will remain in the vagina for a long period.

PELVIC INFLAMMATORY DISEASE (PID)

Pelvic inflammatory disease (PID) is an infectious condition of the pelvic cavity. It may involve the fallopian tubes (salpingitis), ovaries (oophoritis), and pelvic peritoneum (peritonitis). A tubo-ovarian abscess may form (Fig. 53.4).

Etiology and Pathophysiology

PID is often the result of an untreated cervical infection. The organism infecting the cervix can spread into the uterus, fallopian tubes, ovaries, and peritoneal cavity. *C. trachomatis* and *N. gonorrhoeae* are the most common causative organisms of PID.[10] Other organisms include anaerobes, mycoplasma, streptococci, and enteric gram-negative rods. It is important to remember that not all cases of PID are the result of an STI. Organisms can gain entrance during sexual intercourse or after pregnancy termination, pelvic surgery, or childbirth.

Women at increased risk for chlamydia infection (e.g., younger than 24 years of age, have multiple sex partners, have a new sex partner) should be routinely tested. The infection can be asymptomatic and unknowingly transmitted during intercourse.

Clinical Manifestations

Lower abdominal pain is a common. The pain typically starts gradually and then becomes constant. The intensity may vary from mild to severe. Movement, such as walking, can increase the pain. The pain is often associated with intercourse. Spotting after intercourse and purulent cervical or vaginal discharge may occur. Fever and chills may be present.

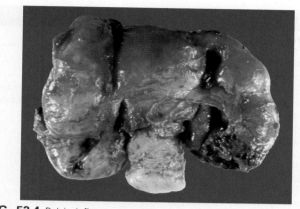

FIG. 53.4 Pelvic inflammatory disease. Acute infection of the fallopian tubes and the ovaries. The tubes and the ovaries have become an inflamed mass attached to the uterus. A tubo-ovarian abscess is present. (From Kumar V, Abbas AK, Aster JC, Fausto N: *Robbins and Cotran pathologic basis of disease,* ed 8, Philadelphia, 2010, Saunders.)

Women with less acute symptoms often notice increased cramping pain with menses, irregular bleeding, and some pain with intercourse. Women who have mild symptoms may go untreated either because they did not seek care or the HCP misdiagnoses their symptoms.

Complications

Complications of PID include septic shock, perihepatitis, tubo-ovarian abscess, peritonitis, and embolism. PID can cause adhesions and strictures in the fallopian tubes, which may lead to ectopic pregnancy. After 1 episode of PID, the risk for having an ectopic pregnancy increases nearly 10 times. Further damage can obstruct the fallopian tubes and cause infertility.

Interprofessional Care

A pelvic examination aids in the diagnosis of PID. Women with PID have lower abdominal tenderness, adnexal tenderness, and positive cervical motion tenderness.

Diagnostic testing includes examination for *N. gonorrhoeae* and *C. trachomatis* and a pregnancy test to rule out an ectopic pregnancy. When the patient's pain or obesity compromises the pelvic examination, a vaginal ultrasound may be done.

PID is usually treated on an outpatient basis. The patient is given a combination of antibiotics to provide broad coverage against the causative organisms. With effective antibiotic therapy, the pain should subside. The patient should abstain from intercourse for 3 weeks. Her partner(s) must be examined and treated. An important part of care is physical rest and oral fluids. Reevaluation in 48 to 72 hours, even if symptoms are improving, is an essential part of outpatient care.

If outpatient treatment is unsuccessful, a tubo-ovarian abscess is present, or the patient is acutely ill or in severe pain, admission to a hospital is needed. IV antibiotics are given in the hospital. Corticosteroids may be added to the antibiotic regimen to reduce inflammation, allowing for faster recovery and optimizing the chances for fertility. Application of heat to the lower abdomen or sitz baths may improve circulation and decrease pain. Bed rest in the semi-Fowler's position promotes drainage of the pelvic cavity by gravity and may prevent the development of abscesses high in the abdomen. Analgesics to relieve pain and IV fluids to prevent dehydration are used.

TABLE 53.11 Nursing Assessment

Pelvic Inflammatory Disease (PID)

Subjective Data

Important Health Information

Past health history: Use of IUD. Previous PID, gonorrhea, or chlamydial infection. Multiple sexual partners. Exposure to partner with urethritis. Infertility

Medications: Use of and allergy to any antibiotics

Surgery or other treatments: Recent abortion or pelvic surgery

Functional Health Patterns

Health perception–health management: Malaise

Nutritional-metabolic: Nausea, vomiting; chills, fever

Elimination: Urinary frequency, urgency

Cognitive-perceptual: Lower abdominal and pelvic pain, low back pain, onset of pain just after a menstrual cycle. Dysmenorrhea, dyspareunia, dysuria, vulvar pruritus

Sexuality-reproductive: Abnormal vaginal bleeding and menstrual irregularity. Vaginal discharge

Objective Data

Reproductive

Mucopurulent cervicitis, vulvar maceration, vaginal discharge (heavy and purulent to thin and mucoid), tenderness on motion of cervix and uterus. Presence of inflammatory masses on palpation

Possible Diagnostic Findings

Leukocytosis, ↑ erythrocyte sedimentation rate, positive culture of secretions or endocervical fluid, pelvic inflammation and positive endometrial biopsy on laparoscopic examination, abscess or inflammation on ultrasonography

Surgery is needed for abscesses that do not resolve with IV antibiotics. The abscess may be drained by laparoscopy or laparotomy. In extreme cases of infection or severe chronic pelvic pain, a hysterectomy may be done. When surgery is done, the capacity for childbearing is preserved whenever possible.

❖ NURSING MANAGEMENT: PELVIC INFLAMMATORY DISEASE

Subjective and objective data that should be obtained from the woman with PID are outlined in Table 53.11. Prevention, early recognition, and prompt treatment of vaginal and cervical infections can help prevent PID and its serious complications. Give accurate information about factors that place a woman at increased risk for PID. Urge women to seek medical attention for any unusual vaginal discharge or possible infection of their reproductive organs. Tell patients that not all vaginal discharge indicates infection, but early diagnosis and treatment of an infection, if present, can prevent serious complications. Teach patients methods to decrease the risk for getting STIs and to recognize the signs of infection in their partner(s).

The patient may feel guilty about having PID, especially if it is associated with an STI. She may be concerned about the complications associated with PID, such as infertility, and the increased incidence of ectopic pregnancy. Discuss with the patient her feelings and concerns to help her cope with them more effectively.

For hospitalized patients, you have a key role in implementing drug therapy, monitoring the patient's health status, and providing symptom relief and patient teaching. Record vital signs and the character, amount, color, and odor of the vaginal discharge. Assess the degree of abdominal pain to determine the effectiveness of drug therapy.

CHRONIC PELVIC PAIN

Chronic pelvic pain refers to pain in the pelvic region (below the umbilicus and between the hips) that lasts 6 months or longer. The cause of chronic pelvic pain is often hard to find. Many different conditions can cause pelvic pain. Gynecologic etiologies include PID, endometriosis, ovarian cysts, uterine fibroids, pelvic adhesions, and ectopic pregnancies. Abdominal causes include irritable bowel syndrome, interstitial cystitis, and colitis. Psychologic factors (e.g., depression, chronic stress, history of sexual or physical abuse) may increase the risk for developing chronic pelvic pain. Emotional distress makes pain worse. Living with chronic pain contributes to emotional distress.

Chronic pelvic pain has many different manifestations. These include severe and steady pain, intermittent pain, dull and achy pain, pelvic pressure or heaviness, and sharp pain or cramping. Pain may occur during intercourse or while having a bowel movement.

Determining the cause of chronic pelvic pain often involves a process of elimination. In addition to a detailed history and physical examination (including a pelvic examination), the patient may be asked to keep a journal of the onset of symptoms and any precipitating factors.

Diagnostic tests may include specimens from the cervix or vagina (used to detect STIs), ultrasound, CT scan, or MRI to detect abnormal structures or growths. Laparoscopy may be used to see the pelvic organs. This procedure is especially useful in detecting endometriosis and chronic PID.

If the cause of chronic pelvic pain is found, treatment focuses on that cause. If no cause can be found, treatment involves managing the pain. Over-the-counter pain drugs (e.g., aspirin, ibuprofen, acetaminophen) may give some relief. Sometimes stronger pain drugs may be needed. OCPs or other hormonal drugs may help relieve cyclic pelvic pain related to menstrual cycles. If an infection is the source of the problem, antibiotics are used.

Tricyclic antidepressants (e.g., amitriptyline, nortriptyline [Pamelor]) have pain-relieving and antidepressant effects. These drugs may help improve chronic pelvic pain even in women who do not have depression. Counseling can help the woman live with chronic pain.

Laparoscopic surgery may be used to remove pelvic adhesions or endometrial tissue. As a last resort, a hysterectomy may be done.

ENDOMETRIOSIS

Endometriosis is a condition in which endometrial tissue accumulates outside the endometrium of the uterus. Endometriosis is a common gynecologic problem.

The most frequent sites for endometrial tissue growth are in or near the ovaries, uterosacral ligaments, and uterovesical peritoneum (Fig. 53.5). The tissue responds to the hormones of the ovarian cycle and undergoes a "mini-menstrual cycle" similar to the uterine endometrium. Although it is not a life-threatening condition, endometriosis can cause considerable pain. It can significantly affect a woman's quality of life and ability to conceive. It also increases the risk for ovarian cancer.

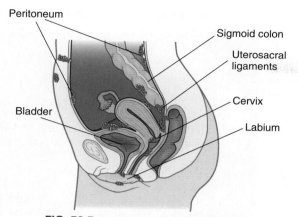

Peritoneum
Sigmoid colon
Uterosacral ligaments
Bladder
Cervix
Labium

FIG. 53.5 Common sites of endometriosis.

Etiology and Pathophysiology

We have several theories as to the cause of endometriosis. One theory is that the disorder is due to retrograde (backward) flow of endometrial tissue. Instead of flowing out the cervix, the endometrial tissue flows through the fallopian tubes, depositing endometrial tissue into the pelvis.

Other theories suggest that endometrial tissue spreads to the pelvic area through the lymph system or bloodstream. Or, there is an increased sensitivity and production of prostaglandins, which are released prior to onset of menses. Other proposed causes include a genetic predisposition and altered immune function.

Clinical Manifestations

Patients with endometriosis have a wide range of manifestations. The severity of symptoms does not always correlate with the degree of disease found. The most common ones are secondary dysmenorrhea, infertility, pelvic pain, dyspareunia, and AUB. Less common ones include backache, painful bowel movements, and dysuria. With menopause, the ovaries no longer make estrogen and the symptoms may disappear.

❖ Interprofessional and Nursing Care

Endometriosis may be suspected based on a woman's history of the characteristic symptoms and the HCP's palpation of firm nodular lumps in the adnexa on bimanual examination. Laparoscopy with a biopsy is needed for a definitive diagnosis. MRI is now being used more often prior to surgery to determine if gynecologic symptoms the woman is having are from endometriosis.

Treatment is influenced by the patient's age, desire for pregnancy, symptom severity, and extent and location of the disease. When endometriosis is the probable cause of infertility, therapy proceeds more rapidly. When symptoms are not disruptive, a "watch and wait" approach is used (Table 53.12). Teach the patient about comfort measures that may be helpful. Reassure the woman that endometriosis is not life threatening and treatment options exist. Women who have severe disabling pain, sexual difficulties from dyspareunia, and infertility may need psychologic support.

Drug Therapy. Drug therapy does not cure endometriosis but can reduce symptoms. The most common drugs used to control symptoms and cause regression of endometrial tissue are

TABLE 53.12 Interprofessional Care
Endometriosis

Diagnostic Assessment
- History and physical examination
- Pelvic examination
- Laparoscopy
- Pelvic ultrasound
- MRI

Management
Conservative Therapy
- Watch and wait

Drug Therapy
- Danazol (use is limited by the occurrence of androgenic side effects)
- GnRH agonists (e.g., leuprolide [Lupron])
- NSAIDs
- OCPs

Surgical Therapy
- Laparotomy to remove implanted tissue and adhesions
- TAH-BSO after childbearing

combined OCPs. Their continuous use causes regression of endometrial tissue. NSAIDs, such as ibuprofen, naproxen (Naprosyn), and diclofenac (Voltaren) can relieve pain.

Another class of drugs used is gonadotropin-releasing hormone (GnRH) agonists (e.g., leuprolide [Lupron], nafarelin [Synarel]). These drugs result in amenorrhea. Side effects are usually the same as those of menopause (hot flashes, vaginal dryness, emotional lability). Loss of bone density can occur in women who stay on the therapy longer than 6 months. "Add-back" therapy with norethindrone acetate (Aygestin) can ease side effects.

🌐 DRUG ALERT Leuprolide (Lupron)

- Assess patient for pregnancy before starting therapy.
- Monitor patient for dysrhythmias, palpitations.
- Teach patient to use nonhormonal contraceptive measures during therapy.

Surgical Therapy. The only cure for endometriosis is surgical removal of all endometrial tissue.[11] It involves removal or destruction of endometrial tissue and excision of adhesions by laparoscopic laser surgery or laparotomy. Definitive surgery involves removal of the uterus, fallopian tubes, ovaries, and as many endometrial implants as possible. GnRH agonist therapy can be given for 4 to 6 months to reduce the size of the lesions before surgery.

For women wishing to get pregnant, conservative surgical therapy can remove implants blocking the fallopian tube. Adhesions are removed from the tubes, ovaries, and pelvic structures. Efforts are made to conserve all tissues necessary to maintain fertility.

Patients should be actively involved in making the decision about preserving part or all their ovaries, if surgically possible. Explore the patient's feelings about maintaining her ovarian function. The HCP should assess the woman's risk for ovarian cancer and provide this information for her consideration.

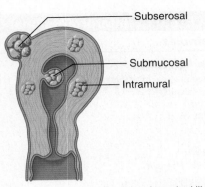

FIG. 53.6 Leiomyomas. Uterine section showing whorl-like appearance and locations of leiomyomas. (From McCance KL, Huether SE: *Pathophysiology: The biologic basis for disease in adults and children*, ed 6, St Louis, 2010, Mosby.)

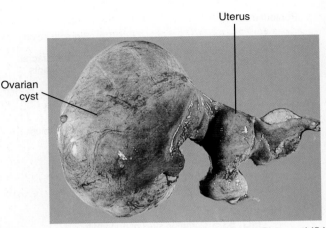

FIG. 53.7 Large ovarian cyst. (From Symonds EM, McPherson MBA: *Colour atlas of obstetrics and gynecology*, London, 1994, Mosby.)

BENIGN TUMORS OF THE FEMALE REPRODUCTIVE SYSTEM

LEIOMYOMAS

Etiology and Pathophysiology

Leiomyomas (usually called uterine fibroids) are benign smooth-muscle tumors (noncancerous) that occur during the childbearing years. Fibroids do not increase a woman's risk for endometrial cancer. They may be present inside the uterus within the endometrium, within the muscle of the uterus (myometrium), or outside on the surface of the uterus (subserosal). The size, shape, location, and number of fibroids vary among women. Some fibroids grow in spurts, while others slowly grow during the reproductive years (Fig. 53.6). They can occur at any age but often occur in women ages 30 to 40 years.

The cause of fibroids is unknown. Their growth appears to depend on estrogen and progesterone because they grow during the reproductive years and undergo atrophy after menopause. Fibroids have more estrogen and progesterone receptors than normal uterine tissue. So, they are more sensitive and grow in response to the release of these hormones.

Genetics may play a role. Identical twins and women with mothers and sisters with leiomyomas have an increased risk. Black women have increased incidence. They present with larger uterine fibroids and ones at an early age compared to other women. Other risk factors include early age of menarche, alcohol use, and a diet high in red meat and low in green vegetables.

Clinical Manifestations

Most women who have fibroids do not report any symptoms. Those who do may have abdominal and pelvic pain (i.e., dull, heaving, and/or achy pain and with pelvic pressure), painful sexual intercourse, pressure or dysuria, or frequent urination. If the fibroids are large, women may report constipation and difficulty passing stool. AUB can present as increased duration, more frequent, or increased menstrual bleeding. The pain associated with a fibroid seems to be caused from uterine blood vessel compression as the fibroid grows or from the fibroid pressing on surrounding organs.

❖ Interprofessional and Nursing Care

Diagnosis is based on the characteristic pelvic examination findings of an enlarged uterus distorted by nodular masses. Ultrasound can confirm the diagnosis. In some cases, small fibroids are found during a hysteroscopy, laparoscopy, or hysterosalpingogram when a woman is having a comprehensive workup for other gynecologic conditions, especially infertility.

The treatment depends on the manifestations, patient's age, her desire to conceive, and the location and size of the fibroid. If the symptoms are minimal, the HCP may choose to follow the patient closely for a period of time. Treatment may be needed if a woman is seeking conception, is having AUB, has pelvic pain and pressure, has anemia, or has difficulty with urination and defecation.

The most common and least invasive treatment for fibroids is the use of OCPs to maintain and slow growth and manage AUB. If surgical intervention is needed, options include a myomectomy (surgical removal of the uterine fibroid only) or a hysterectomy (surgical removal of the uterus with or without the ovaries and fallopian tubes). Myomectomies are typically done when the fibroids are small and few in number and the woman would like to preserve her uterus. Hysterectomies are done when there are multiple fibroids s, if they are large, or if their location is affecting bowel and/or bladder function.

Uterine artery embolization (UAE) is increasingly being used as an alternative treatment to treat fibroids. UAE is the process by which embolic material (small plastic or gelatin beads) is injected into the uterine artery. This process blocks blood flow to the uterus and shrinks the fibroid. Because UAE's effects on future fertility are unknown, the procedure is offered to women who no longer want children.

OVARIAN CYSTS

Ovarian cysts are usually soft and surrounded by a thin capsule. Follicular and corpus luteum cysts are common ovarian cysts (Fig. 53.7). Multiple small ovarian follicles may occur with PCOS. They are not cancerous.

Ovarian cysts are often asymptomatic until they are large enough to cause pressure in the pelvis. Depending on the tumor's size and location, constipation, menstrual irregularities, urinary frequency, a full feeling in the abdomen, anorexia, an increase in abdominal girth, and peripheral edema may occur.

Pelvic pain may be present if the tumor is growing rapidly. Severe pain results when the cyst twists on its pedicle (ovarian torsion). In some cases, an ovarian cyst can rupture. A ruptured ovarian cyst is not only extremely painful, but it can lead to serious complications, such as hemorrhage and infection, especially if large.

Pelvic examination may reveal a mass or an enlarged ovary. A pelvic ultrasound can help determine a diagnosis. In premenopausal women, ovarian cysts often resolve on their own. If the mass is cystic (does not appear cancerous) and smaller than 5 cm, the patient is asked to return for reexamination in 4 to 6 weeks. This is called "watchful waiting."

In postmenopausal women, watchful waiting may be an option depending on the results of the ultrasound. If the mass is cystic and greater than 5 cm or is solid, laparoscopic surgery or laparotomy is done. Immediate surgery is needed if ovarian torsion occurs, causing the ovary to rotate and cutting off circulation. Surgical techniques are used to save as much of the ovary as possible (if indicated).

Polycystic Ovary Syndrome

Polycystic ovary syndrome (PCOS) is a disorder that includes ovulatory dysfunction, polycystic ovaries, and hyperandrogenism.[12] It most often occurs in women under 30 years old and is a cause of infertility.

The cause of PCOS is unknown. We think it is due to the ovaries producing estrogen and excess testosterone but not progesterone. Because of this hormonal imbalance, ovulation fails, and multiple fluid-filled cysts develop from mature ovarian follicles (Fig. 53.8).

Classic manifestations of PCOS include irregular menstrual periods, amenorrhea, hirsutism, and obesity (80% of women). Of these, obesity is associated with severe symptoms, such as excess androgens, amenorrhea, and infertility. Many women start with normal menstrual periods, which become irregular after 1 to 2 years, and then the periods become infrequent. Untreated PCOS can lead to CVD and abnormal insulin resistance with type 2 diabetes.

Successful management includes early diagnosis and treatment to improve quality of life and decrease the risk for complications. Pelvic ultrasound reveals enlarged ovaries with multiple small cysts. Treatment is based on symptoms. OCPs are useful in regulating menstrual cycles. Hirsutism may be treated with spironolactone. Hyperandrogenism can be treated with flutamide and a GnRH agonist, such as leuprolide. Metformin reduces

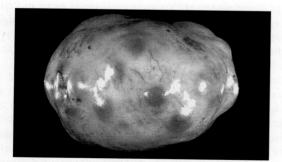

FIG. 53.8 Polycystic ovary syndrome. Multiple fluid-filled cysts in the ovary. (From Kumar V, Abbas A, Fausto N: *Robbins and Cotran pathologic basis of disease*, ed 7, Philadelphia, 2005, Saunders.)

hyperinsulinemia, improves hyperandrogenism, and can restore ovulation. For women wishing to become pregnant, fertility drugs (e.g., clomiphene [Clomid]) may induce ovulation.

Nursing management includes teaching about the importance of weight management and exercise to decrease insulin resistance. Obesity worsens problems related to PCOS. Monitor lipid profile and fasting glucose levels. Hirsutism is cosmetically distressing for many women. Support the patient as she explores measures to remove unwanted hair (e.g., depilating agents, electrolysis). Stress the importance of regular follow-up care to monitor the effectiveness of therapy and to detect any complications.

CERVICAL POLYPS

Cervical polyps are benign pedunculated (stalked) lesions that generally arise from the endocervical mucosa. Polyps are a characteristic bright cherry red and are soft and fragile. They are usually small, measuring less than 3 cm in length. They may be single or multiple. Their cause is unknown. Symptoms are usually not present, but intermenstrual bleeding after straining for a bowel movement and coitus can occur. Polyps are prone to infection.

Polyps may be seen protruding through the cervical os during a speculum examination. When the polyp is small, it can be excised in an outpatient procedure. If the point of attachment cannot be found and is not accessible to cautery, a polypectomy is done in an operating room. All tissue removed is biopsied as polyps, on rare occasion, are malignant.

CANCERS OF THE FEMALE REPRODUCTIVE SYSTEM

CERVICAL CANCER

Around 13,240 women in the United States are diagnosed with cervical cancer each year and 4100 women will die. While Hispanic women are the most likely to be diagnosed with cervical cancer, black women have the highest mortality rate from cervical cancer.[13]

Cervical cancer was once a common cause of cancer death. However, with early detection (Pap test, HPV testing), the mortality rate from cervical cancer has significantly declined.

🌐 PROMOTING HEALTH EQUITY
Cancers of the Female Reproductive System

Ovarian Cancer
- The mortality rate for black women is higher than any other ethnic group.

Endometrial Cancer
- The mortality rate for black women is higher than any other ethnic group.

Cervical Cancer
- The incidence rate is highest among Hispanic women
- Mortality rates are twice as high among black women.

Etiology and Pathophysiology

Risk factors for cervical cancer include (1) infection with high-risk strains of HPV 16 and 18, (2) immunosuppression, (3) using OCPs for a long period of time, (4) being exposed to the drug diethylstilbestrol (DES), (5) giving birth to many children, and (6) smoking.

The cervix is the lower third of the uterus that projects into the vagina. It is made up of glandular cells that line the uterine cavity and endocervical canal. Squamous epithelium lines the vagina and outer part of the cervix. These 2 cell types meet and undergo a normal physiologic process known as *squamous metaplasia*. This is the transformation of columnar epithelium into squamous epithelium, which results in an area called the *transformation zone*. This process begins at puberty and continues throughout a women's reproductive life cycle. The transformation zone moves in and out the endocervical canal, depending upon hormonal status and other factors. While the entire anogenital tract can be infected by HPV, the transformation zone is an area that is particularly susceptible to HPV-associated carcinogenesis.

Clinical Manifestations

Early cervical cancer often has no symptoms. An unusual discharge, AUB, or postcoital bleeding eventually occurs. The discharge is usually thin and watery but becomes dark and foul smelling as the disease advances. Vaginal bleeding first presents as spotting. As the tumor enlarges, bleeding becomes heavier and more frequent (Fig. 53.9). Pain is a late symptom. It is followed by weight loss, anemia, and cachexia.

Diagnostic Studies

The 2 tests used for cervical cancer screening are the Papanicolaou (Pap) test and the HPV test. The Pap test helps find changes in cervical cells that may indicate precancerous changes. Cells are obtained from the cervix during a speculum examination. HPV testing can identify high-risk HPV types 16 and 18, of which 80% are associated with cervical cancer, more than any other high-risk HPV types. The use of the HPV test is age-dependent and Pap result–dependent. To do an HPV test, cervical scrapings are tested for viral DNA or RNA.

All women should begin cervical cancer screening at age 21. Women ages 21 to 29 years should get a Pap test every 3 years. Women between the ages of 30 and 65 should have a Pap test and HPV test every 5 years. This is the preferred approach, but the woman may choose to get a Pap test without an HPV test every 3 years.[14] If both tests are negative, the risk for cervical cancer is very low, and women can wait 5 years before another screening. HPV tests may be used to provide more information when a Pap test has unclear results. Women found to have an abnormal Pap test typically need a *colposcopy* (an examination of the cervical tissue under magnification). Typically, a cervical biopsy(s) is taken and sent for further analysis by a pathologist. Other tests for gonorrhea, chlamydia, and trichomonas can be run off the Pap test.

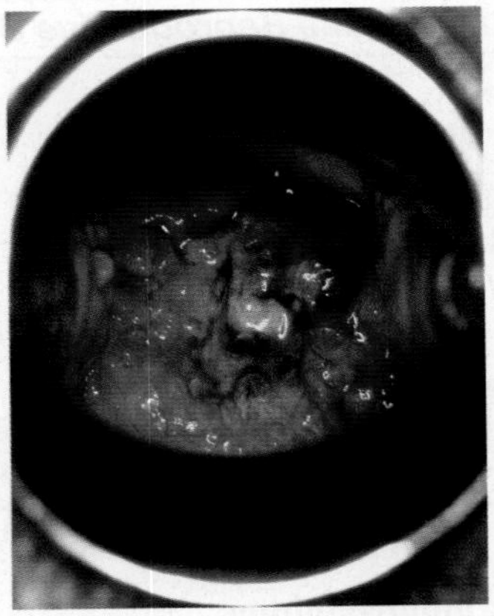

EVIDENCE-BASED PRACTICE

Pap Test and Cervical Cancer

E.V. is a 36-yr-old black woman who had a tubal ligation in the outpatient surgery unit. As you prepare her for discharge, you remind her that she needs to have regular Pap tests to screen for cervical cancer. She expresses concern over the expense of this procedure. She tells you she does not know if her health care insurance pays for screening tests. She does not remember when she last had a Pap test done.

Making Clinical Decisions

Best Available Evidence. For women 21 to 30 years a Pap test alone every 3 years is recommended. For women between the ages of 30 and 65, the screening preference for cervical cancer is a Pap test and HPV test every 5 years. A Pap test alone every 3 years is also within the recommended guidelines.

Clinician Expertise. You know the incidence and death rate of cervical cancer is twice as high for black women compared to all other ethnicities.

Patient Preferences and Values. E.V. is concerned about the costs related to her current procedure and future Pap tests. She adds that no one in her family has ever had cervical cancer.

Implications for Nursing Practice

1. How would you explain to her the current recommendations and her increased risk for cervical cancer?
2. Why is it important to encourage E.V. to learn more about her health care coverage?

Reference for Evidence

American Cancer Society: American Cancer Society guidelines for the early detection of cancer. Retrieved from *www.cancer.org/healthy/find-cancer-early/cancer-screening-guidelines/american-cancer-society-guidelines-for-the-early-detection-of-cancer.html.*

FIG. 53.9 Cervical cancer. View through a speculum inserted into the vagina. (From Drake RL, Vogl W, Mitchell AWM: *Gray's anatomy for students,* ed 2, Edinburgh, 2010, Churchill Livingstone.)

Interprofessional Care

Vaccination against HPV provides for primary prevention of cervical cancer. Teach both parents and patients about the need to complete the HPV vaccination series prior to first sexual contact. The CDC recommends that all children, males and females, be vaccinated at age 11 to 12, when the immune system has a better uptake of the vaccine. Vaccines can be given as early as age 9.

Currently 3 vaccines are available to protect against HPV. Gardasil, protects against types 6, 11, 16, and 18. Gardasil 9 protects against HPV types 6, 11, 16, 18, and 5 other HPV types. Cervarix offers protection against HPV types 16 and 18. These vaccines are given in 2 or 3 IM doses (depending upon the patient's age) over a 6-month period. They have few side effects. More specific information about HPV vaccines is discussed in Chapter 52 on p. 1219.

Women diagnosed with cervical cancer are typically referred to a gynecologic oncologist for treatment recommendations.[15] Treatment options can include surgery or a combination of chemotherapy and radiation. For patients with advanced disease, bevacizumab (Avastin), a targeted therapy drug, may be used in addition to cisplatin-based chemotherapy. Bevacizumab is an angiogenesis inhibitor. It works by interfering with the blood vessels that supply nutrients to cancer cells. (Chemotherapy, radiation therapy, and targeted therapy are discussed in Chapter 15.)

ENDOMETRIAL CANCER

Endometrial cancer is the most common gynecologic cancer. About 63,000 women are diagnosed each year with endometrial cancer, and 11,300 will die.[16] If endometrial cancer is diagnosed in the early stage, it has a low mortality rate, with survival rates over 88%. The average age of a woman diagnosed with endometrial cancer is 60. It is rare in women under the age of 45.

Etiology and Pathophysiology

The major risk factor for endometrial cancer is exposure to estrogen, especially unopposed estrogen. Obesity is a risk factor because adipose cells store estrogen, thus increasing the amount of circulating estrogen. Other risk factors include increasing age, never being pregnant, early menarche, late menopause, smoking, diabetes, and a personal or family history of hereditary nonpolyposis colorectal cancer (HNPCC) (see the Genetics in Clinical Practice box for HNPCC in Chapter 42 on p. 949). Pregnancy, use of OCPs and IUDs, and physical exercise are associated with reduced risk.

Endometrial cancer arises from the lining of the endometrium within the uterus. Most tumors are adenocarcinomas. If endometrial cancer is not diagnosed in early stages, it can invade the myometrium (muscle of the uterus) and the regional lymph nodes. If metastasis occurs, common sites include the lung, liver, bone, and brain. Prognosis depends on tumor size, cell type, degree of invasion into the myometrium, and any metastasis.[17]

Clinical Manifestations

Early manifestations include AUB, especially in postmenopausal women. Later symptoms can include dysuria, dyspareunia, unintentional weight loss, and pelvic pain.

Interprofessional Care

No routine screening test is available for endometrial cancer. Most cases are diagnosed at an early stage because of postmenopausal bleeding. An endometrial biopsy is the main diagnostic test for identifying endometrial cancer. This procedure is typically done in the office.

The National Comprehensive Cancer Network (NCCN) recommends surveillance and risk reduction for women with Lynch syndrome, a hereditary cancer associated with endometrial cancer. Hysterectomy and bilateral salpingo-oophorectomy should be offered to women who have completed childbearing and carry *MLH1, MLH2, or MLH6* mutations. For carriers of *MLH1 or MLH2*, annual endometrial biopsy is advised.

Treatment of endometrial cancer in the early stage is a total hysterectomy and bilateral salpingo-oophorectomy with lymph

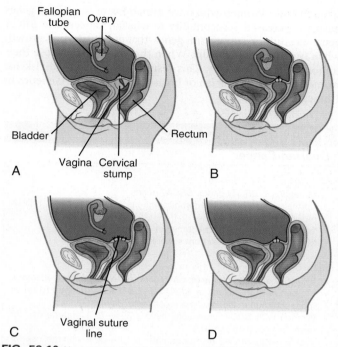

FIG. 53.10 Hysterectomies. **A,** Cross section of subtotal hysterectomy. The cervical stump, fallopian tubes, and ovaries remain. **B,** Cross section of total hysterectomy. The fallopian tubes and ovaries remain. **C,** Cross section of vaginal hysterectomy. The fallopian tubes and ovaries remain. **D,** Total hysterectomy, salpingectomy, and oophorectomy. The uterus, fallopian tubes, and ovaries are completely removed.

node biopsies. These may be done by less invasive types of surgery, including robotics and laparoscopy. (Various types of hysterectomies are shown in Fig. 53.10.) External radiation either to the pelvis or abdomen or internal radiation (brachytherapy) intravaginally follows surgery if there is local or distant metastasis.

The woman with advanced or recurrent disease may receive chemotherapy and hormonal therapy. The 5-year survival rate for stage 1 cancer is 90%, with reductions seen as the grade of the cancer increases.

OVARIAN CANCER

Ovarian cancer is the deadliest gynecologic cancer in the United States. Around 22,240 women will receive an ovarian cancer diagnosis in 2018, and about 14,070 women die. It is the fifth leading cause of cancer deaths in women in the United States. Half of women diagnosed are age 63 and older. Overall the 5- and 10-year survival rates are 45% and 35%, respectively. Most women with ovarian cancer are diagnosed when the disease is advanced, for which the 5-year survival rate is 27%.

Etiology and Pathophysiology

The cause of ovarian cancer is not known. The major risk factor is family history (1 or more first-degree relatives). A family history of breast or colon cancer is also a risk factor. Other risk factors include a personal history of breast or colon cancer and HNPCC (see the Genetics in Clinical Practice box on HNPCC in Chapter 42 on p. 949).

Genetic Link. Women who have mutations of the *BRCA* genes have an increased susceptibility to ovarian cancer. The *BRCA* genes are tumor suppressor genes that inhibit tumor growth when functioning normally. When they mutate, they lose their tumor suppressor ability. This results in an increased risk for women to develop ovarian or breast cancer (see the Genetics in Clinical Practice box).

GENETICS IN CLINICAL PRACTICE

Ovarian Cancer

Genetic Basis
- Mutations in *BRCA1* and/or *BRCA2* genes
- Normally these genes are tumor suppressor genes involved in DNA repair
- Transmission is autosomal dominant
- Mutations passed down from either mother or father

Incidence
- 5%–10% of cases of ovarian cancer are related to hereditary factors.
- Women with mutations in *BRCA1* and *BRCA2* are about 10 times more common in those who are Ashkenazi Jewish.
- Women with *BRCA1* mutations have a 35%–70% lifetime risk for developing ovarian cancer.
- Women with *BRCA2* mutations have a 10%–30% lifetime risk for developing ovarian cancer.
- Family history of both breast and ovarian cancer increases the risk for having a BRCA mutation.
- *BRCA* mutations occur in 10%–20% of patients with ovarian cancer who have no family history of breast or ovarian cancer.[18]

Genetic Testing
- DNA testing is available for *BRCA1* and *BRCA2* genetic mutations.

Clinical Implications
- Bilateral salpingectomy-oophorectomy reduces the risk for ovarian cancer in women with *BRCA1* and *BRCA2* mutations.
- Genetic counseling and testing for *BRCA* mutations should be offered to women whose personal or family history puts them at high risk for ovarian cancer.
- Women with *BRCA* mutations have a higher risk for developing breast, colon, pancreatic, and uterine cancers.

Women who have never been pregnant (nulliparity) are at higher risk. Other risk factors include increasing age, high-fat diet, increased number of ovulatory cycles (usually associated with early menarche and late menopause), HRT, and possibly the use of infertility drugs.

Breastfeeding, multiple pregnancies, OCP use (more than 5 years), and early age at first birth reduce the risk for ovarian cancer. These factors may have a protective effect because they reduce the number of ovulatory cycles and thus reduce the exposure to estrogen.

There are 3 major types of ovarian cancer. About 90% of ovarian cancers are epithelial cancers that arise from malignant transformation of the surface epithelial cells. Germ cell tumors account for another 3%, and sex cord stromal, 2%. Histologic grading is important to determine the prognosis of the disease. Tumor cells are graded according to the level of differentiation, ranging from well differentiated (grade I) to poorly differentiated (grade III) to undifferentiated (grade IV). Grade IV cells have a poorer prognosis than the other grades.

Intraperitoneal dissemination is a common characteristic of ovarian cancer. It metastasizes to the uterus, bladder, bowel, and

---

TABLE 53.13 Interprofessional Care

Ovarian Cancer

Diagnostic Assessment
- History and physical examination
- Pelvic examination
- Abdominal and transvaginal ultrasound
- CA-125 level
- Laparotomy for diagnostic staging

Management
- Surgery
  - TAH-BSO with pelvic lymph node biopsies
  - Debulking for advanced disease
- Chemotherapy
  - Adjuvant and palliative
- Radiation therapy
  - Adjuvant and palliative

---

omentum. In advanced disease, it can spread to the stomach, colon, liver, and other parts of the body.

Clinical Manifestations

Early ovarian cancer usually has no obvious symptoms. Most manifestations are vague and nonspecific. These include pelvic or abdominal pain, bloating, urinary urgency or frequency, and difficulty eating or feeling full quickly. Late-stage disease typically presents with abdominal enlargement with ascites (fluid in the abdominal cavity), unexplained weight loss or gain, and menstrual changes.

Diagnostic Studies

No accurate screening test exists for early detection of ovarian cancer. For women at high risk for ovarian cancer, screening using a combination of the tumor marker CA-125, ultrasound, and yearly pelvic examination is recommended. However, this approach is not proven to be effective in reducing ovarian cancer mortality.[18] The CA-125 test is positive in 80% of women with epithelial ovarian cancer. CA-125 is also used to monitor the course of the disease and response to treatment. The problem is that CA-125 levels can be high with other cancers (e.g., pancreatic cancer) or with benign gynecologic conditions, including fibroids and endometriosis.

Since postmenopausal women should not have palpable ovaries, a mass of any size found during a bimanual pelvic examination is considered suspicious. An abdominal or a transvaginal ultrasound can be done to detect ovarian masses (Table 53.13). An exploratory laparotomy may be used to establish the diagnosis and stage the disease.

Interprofessional Care

Options for women at high risk based on family and health history include prophylactic removal of the ovaries and fallopian tubes and the use of OCPs. While salpingo-oophorectomy significantly reduces the risk for ovarian cancer, it does not completely eliminate the risk for cancer in the peritoneum.

The initial treatment for all stages of ovarian cancer is a total abdominal hysterectomy and bilateral salpingo-oophorectomy (TAH-BSO) with removal of the omentum and as much of the tumor as possible (i.e., tumor debulking). Depending on the grade and stage of cancer, treatment options include intraperitoneal and systemic chemotherapy, intraperitoneal instillation of radioisotopes, and external abdominal and pelvic radiation therapy. Combination chemotherapy and radiation therapy should be considered before a single-modality treatment.

The chemotherapy agents most commonly used are taxanes (paclitaxel or docetaxel) and platinum agents (carboplatin or cisplatin). (See Table 15.7 for more about these drugs.)

Targeted therapy used to treat advanced ovarian cancer includes bevacizumab (Avastin) (discussed on p. 1243), rucaparib (Rubraca), and olaparib (Lynparza). Rucaparib and olaparib are poly ADP-ribose polymerase (PARP) inhibitors. They block enzymes involved in repairing damaged DNA. They are used for women with ovarian cancer that is associated with defective *BRCA* genes.

VAGINAL CANCER

Vaginal cancers are rare, with about 5170 new cases reported annually. They usually occur in women between ages 50 and 70. Vaginal tumors can be secondary sites or metastases of other gynecologic cancers, such as cervical or endometrial cancer. About 70% of vaginal cancers are squamous cell carcinomas, which begin in the squamous epithelium. Intrauterine exposure to diethylstilbestrol (DES) places a woman at risk for clear cell adenocarcinoma of the vagina.

Treatment depends on the type of cells involved, stage of the disease, and the size and location of the tumor.[19] Squamous cell carcinomas can be treated with both surgery and radiation. The process of transitioning from precancer to cancer can take many years. The term for the precancerous condition of squamous cells is *vaginal intraepithelial neoplasia* (VAIN.) There are 3 types of VAIN: VAIN 1, VAIN 2, and VAIN 3. VAIN 3 progresses closest to a true cancer.

VULVAR CANCER

Vulvar cancer is rare. There are about 6020 new cases reported each year, with an estimated 1150 deaths for 2017. Preinvasive lesions are referred to as *vulvar intraepithelial neoplasia (VIN)*, which precedes invasive vulvar cancer. The 3 types of VIN are VIN 1, VIN 2, and VIN 3. The invasive form occurs mainly in women over 60 years of age, with the highest incidence being in women in their 70s.

Patients with vulvar cancer may have symptoms of vulvar itching or burning, pain, bleeding, or discharge. Women who are immunosuppressed and/or have diabetes, hypertension, or chronic vulvar dystrophies have the highest risk for developing vulvar cancer. HPV DNA have been identified in some, but not all, vulvar cancers.

Diagnosis is based on physical examination, colposcopy, and biopsy results of the suspicious lesion. VIN can be treated topically with imiquimod cream (Aldara) or laser surgery. Surgery is the most common treatment for vulvar cancer. The goal is to remove all the cancer without any loss of the woman's sexual function.

If a woman has extensive lesions, a vulvectomy is recommended. Various types of vulvectomies are described in Table 53.14. As adjuvant measures, the patient may have chemotherapy or radiation therapy after surgery.

❖ NURSING AND INTERPROFESSIONAL MANAGEMENT: CANCERS OF FEMALE REPRODUCTIVE SYSTEM

◆ Nursing Assessment

Women with cancer of the reproductive system may have a variety of manifestations. These include leukorrhea, AUB,

---

TABLE 53.14 Surgical Procedures Involving the Female Reproductive System

Type of Surgery	Description
daVinci	Minimally invasive surgery using robotics for major gynecologic procedures.
Dilation and Curettage (D&C)	Dilation of cervix and scraping of endometrium.
Endometrial Ablation	An outpatient procedure using hot or cold energy to destroy the endometrial lining of the uterus in cases of AUB.
Hysterectomy	
Abdominal supracervical hysterectomy	Removal of uterus only with cervix remaining intact.
Radical hysterectomy	Panhysterectomy, partial vaginectomy, and dissection of lymph nodes in pelvis.
Total abdominal hysterectomy (TAH)	Uterus and cervix removed using a pfannenstiel incision (bikini cut).
Total abdominal hysterectomy and bilateral salpingo-oophorectomy (TAH-BSO)	Uterus, cervix, fallopian tubes, and ovaries removed using a pfannenstiel or a vertical incision.
Vaginal hysterectomy	Uterus and cervix removed through a cut in the top of vagina.
Laparoscopic hysterectomy	Laparoscope (video camera and small surgical instruments).
• Laparoscopic-assisted vaginal hysterectomy (LAVH)	Incision made at top of vagina. Uterus and cervix removed through the vagina. Laparoscope inserted into abdomen to assist in the procedure.
• Laparoscopic supracervical hysterectomy	Uterus removed using only laparoscopic instruments. Cervix is left intact.
Hysteroscopy	Video done with D&C to check for abnormal uterine lining, AUB, polyps.
Myomectomy	Removal of fibroid from the uterus, leaving the uterus in place.
Pelvic Exenteration	Radical hysterectomy, total vaginectomy, removal of bladder with diversion of urinary system and resection of colon and rectum with colostomy.
Vaginectomy	Removal of vagina.
Vulvectomy	Removal of part or all the vulva.
• Skinning vulvectomy	Removal of top layer of vulvar skin where the cancer is found. Skin grafts from other parts of the body may be needed to cover the area.
• Simple vulvectomy	Entire vulva is removed.
• Radical vulvectomy	Entire vulva, including clitoris, labia majora and minora, and nearby tissue, is removed. Nearby lymph nodes may be removed.

vaginal discharge, abdominal pain and pressure, bowel and bladder dysfunction, and vulvar itching and burning. Assessment for these signs and symptoms is an important nursing responsibility.

◆ Nursing Diagnoses

Nursing diagnoses for the female patient with cancer of the reproductive system include:

- Anxiety
- Acute pain
- Disturbed body image
- Impaired sexual functioning

◆ Planning

The overall goals are that the patient with cancer of the female reproductive system will (1) actively take part in treatment decisions, (2) achieve satisfactory pain and symptom management, (3) recognize and report problems promptly, (4) maintain preferred lifestyle as long as possible, and (5) continue to practice cancer detection strategies.

◆ Nursing Implementation

◆ **Health Promotion.** Through your contact with women in a variety of settings, teach women the importance of routine screening for cancers of the reproductive system. Cancer can be prevented when screening reveals precancerous conditions. Routine screening increases the chance that a cancer will be found in an early stage.

Teach women about risk factors for cancers of the reproductive system. Limiting sexual activity during adolescence, using condoms, having fewer sexual partners, and not smoking reduce the risk for cervical cancer. When high-risk behaviors are identified, help women in changing their lifestyles to decrease risk.

◆ **Acute Intervention Related to Surgery.** Types of surgery of the female reproductive tract are described in Table 53.14 and Fig. 53.10. All patients have a degree of anxiety when expecting surgery. The prospect of major gynecologic surgery increases these concerns. Some women may focus on the effect the surgery will have on their appearance and sexual functions. Discuss the woman's feelings and concerns about her surgery. Assess each patient individually. Be willing to listen since this can provide considerable psychologic support.

Preoperatively, prepare the patient physically for surgery with the standard perineal or abdominal preparation. A vaginal douche and enema may be given (based on the HCP's preference). The bladder should be emptied before the patient goes to the operating room. An indwelling catheter is often inserted.

Hysterectomy. After a hysterectomy, abdominal distention may develop from the sudden release of pressure on the intestines when a large tumor is removed or from paralytic ileus due to anesthesia and pressure on the bowel. Food and fluids may be restricted if the patient is nauseated. Ambulation will help relieve flatus.

Initiate venous thromboembolism (VTE) prophylaxis. Apply intermittent pneumatic compression devices and administer anticoagulant therapy. Frequent position changes, avoiding high-Fowler's position, and avoiding pressure under the knees minimize stasis and pooling of blood. Pay special attention to patients with varicosities. Encourage leg exercises to promote circulation.

Discharge teaching includes what to expect after surgery (e.g., she will not menstruate). Review specific activity restrictions. Intercourse should be avoided until the wound is healed (about 4 to 6 weeks). However, intercourse is not contraindicated once healing is complete. If a vaginal hysterectomy was done, tell the patient that she may have a temporary loss of vaginal sensation. Reassure her that the sensation will return in several months.

Physical restrictions are needed for a short time. Heavy lifting should be avoided for 2 months. Teach her to avoid activities that may increase pelvic congestion, such as dancing and walking swiftly, for several months. However, activities such as swimming may be both physically and mentally helpful. Assure her that once healing is complete, all previous activity can be resumed.

Salpingectomy and Oophorectomy. Care of the woman who had removal of a fallopian tube (salpingectomy) or an ovary (oophorectomy) is like that for any patient having abdominal surgery. However, if a large ovarian cyst is removed, she may have abdominal distention caused by the sudden release of pressure in the intestines. An abdominal binder may provide relief until the distention subsides.

When both ovaries are removed (bilateral oophorectomy), surgical menopause results. The symptoms are similar to those of regular menopause but may be more severe because of the sudden withdrawal of hormones.

Vulvectomy. It is important to know the extent of the vulvectomy and the significant effect it is likely to have on the patient's life. Because the surgery causes mutilation of the perineal area and the healing process is slow, the patient is likely to become discouraged. Provide opportunities for the patient to express her feelings and concerns about the operation.

Pay special attention to bowel and bladder care. A low-residue diet and stool softeners prevent straining and wound contamination. An indwelling catheter is used to provide urinary drainage. Be careful not to dislodge the catheter because extensive edema makes its reinsertion difficult. Heavy, taut sutures are often used to close the wounds, resulting in severe discomfort. In other instances, the wound may heal by granulation. Give analgesics to control pain. Carefully position the patient using strategically placed pillows to provide comfort. Initiate VTE prophylaxis.

Discharge teaching includes specific instructions in self-care. Teach her to report any unusual odor, fresh bleeding, breakdown of incision, or perineal pain. Home care nursing can help the patient during her adjustment period.

Sexual function is often retained. Whether clitoral sensation is retained may be critical to some women, particularly if it was the source of orgasmic satisfaction. Discussing alternative methods of achieving sexual satisfaction may be needed.

Pelvic Exenteration. When other forms of therapy do not control the spread of cancer and no metastases have been found outside of the pelvis, pelvic exenteration may be done. This radical surgery usually involves removal of the uterus, ovaries, fallopian tubes, vagina, bladder, urethra, and pelvic lymph nodes (Fig. 53.11). In some situations, the descending colon, rectum, and anal canal also are removed. Women who have this procedure are selected based on their likelihood of surviving the surgery and their ability to adjust to and accept the resulting limitations.

Postoperative care is similar to that of a patient who has had a radical hysterectomy, an abdominal perineal resection, and an ileostomy or a colostomy. The physical, emotional, and social adjustments to life by the woman and her family are great. There are urinary or fecal diversions in the abdominal wall, a reconstructed vagina, possible lymphedema, and the onset of menopausal symptoms.

Assess the patient's physical and emotional adjustment to the changes in body image from the surgery and her ability to carry out any treatment measures. The patient's rehabilitative process should keep pace with her acceptance of the situation. You need to provide understanding and support during a long recovery period. Gently encourage the patient to regain her independence. She needs to share her feelings about her altered body structure. Include her caregiver and family in the plan of care. Careful follow-up monitoring is needed so that early recurrence of the cancer can be identified and treated.

◆ **Acute Intervention With Radiation Therapy.** Teach the patient who is to receive external radiation to urinate immediately before the treatment to minimize radiation exposure to the bladder. Review the side effects of radiation, including enteritis and cystitis. Discuss measures that can be used to reduce their impact.

Nursing management of the patient receiving internal radiation therapy requires special considerations. Do not stay in the immediate area any longer than is necessary to give proper care and attention. (Radiation therapy is discussed in Chapter 15.)

◆ **Evaluation**

The expected outcomes are that the patient with cancer of the female reproductive system will
- Actively take part in treatment decisions
- Achieve satisfactory pain and symptom management
- Recognize and report problems promptly
- Maintain preferred lifestyle as long as possible
- Continue to practice cancer detection strategies

PELVIC ORGAN PROLAPSE

Pelvic organ prolapse (POP) involves the descent of 1 or more aspects of the uterus and vagina, allowing nearby organs, such as the bladder and rectum, to herniate into the vaginal space.[20] Although vaginal birth increases the risk for POP, it can occur in women who never went through childbirth. Obesity, chronic coughing, and straining during bowel movements can increase the risk for POP. The decreased estrogen that normally accompanies perimenopause decreases connective tissue support and increases the risk.

UTERINE PROLAPSE

Uterine prolapse is the downward displacement of the uterus into the vaginal canal (Fig. 53.12). Prolapse is rated by degrees. In first-degree prolapse, the cervix rests in the lower part of the vagina. Second-degree prolapse means the cervix is at the

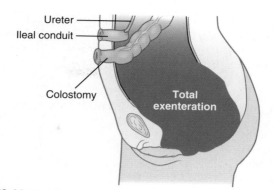

FIG. 53.11 Total exenteration is removal of all pelvic organs with creation of an ileal conduit and a colostomy.

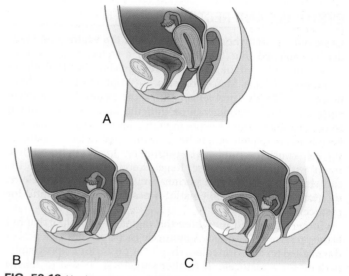

FIG. 53.12 Uterine prolapse. A, First-degree prolapse. B, Second-degree prolapse. C, Third-degree prolapse.

vaginal opening. Third-degree prolapse means the uterus protrudes through the introitus.

Symptoms vary with the degree of prolapse. The patient may describe a feeling of "something coming down." She may have dyspareunia, a dragging or heavy feeling in the pelvis, and a backache. Stress incontinence is a common and troubling problem. When third-degree uterine prolapse occurs, the protruding cervix and vaginal walls are subjected to constant irritation, and tissue changes may occur.

Therapy depends on the degree of prolapse and how much the woman's daily activities have been affected.[20] Pelvic muscle strengthening exercises (Kegel exercises) may be effective for some women (see Table 45.18). If not, a pessary may be used. A *pessary* is a device that is placed in the vagina to help support the uterus. A wide variety of shapes exist, including rings, arches, and balls. Most are made of plastic or wire coated with plastic. When a woman first receives a pessary, she needs instructions on how to clean it. Pessaries that are left in place for long periods are associated with erosion, fistulas, and vaginal cancer.

If more conservative measures are not successful, surgery is indicated. Surgery generally involves a vaginal hysterectomy with anterior and posterior repair of the vagina and the underlying fascia.

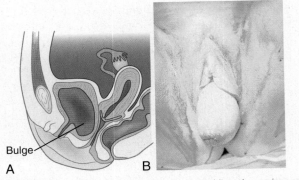

FIG. 53.13 A, Cystocele. B, Bladder has prolapsed into the vagina, causing a uterine prolapse.

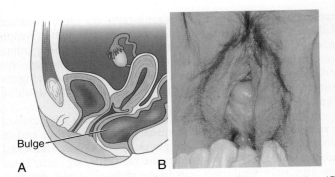

FIG. 53.14 A, Rectocele. B, Rectum has prolapsed into the vagina. (*B*, From Townsend CM: *Sabiston textbook of surgery*, ed 18, St Louis, 2009, Mosby.)

CYSTOCELE AND RECTOCELE

Cystocele occurs when support between the vagina and bladder is weakened (Fig. 53.13). Similarly, a *rectocele* results from weakening between the vagina and rectum (Fig. 53.14). Both are common problems. Many women are asymptomatic. Some have bowel and bladder problems. With large cystoceles, complete emptying of the bladder can be difficult, predisposing women to bladder infections. A woman with a large rectocele may not be able to completely empty her rectum when defecating unless she helps push the stool out by putting her fingers in her vagina.

As with uterine prolapse, Kegel exercises (see Table 45.18) can strengthen weakened perineal muscles if the cystocele or rectocele is not too problematic. A pessary may be helpful for cystoceles.

Surgery designed to tighten the vaginal wall (colporrhaphy) is the preferred treatment. A cystocele is corrected with a procedure called an anterior colporrhaphy. A posterior colporrhaphy is done for a rectocele. If further surgery is needed to relieve stress incontinence, procedures to support the urethra and restore the proper angle between the urethra and the posterior bladder wall are done.

❖ NURSING AND INTERPROFESSIONAL MANAGEMENT: PELVIC ORGAN PROLAPSE

Help women avoid or decrease problems with pelvic support by teaching them how to do Kegel exercises.[21] Women of all ages may benefit from these exercises. Teach the patient to pull in or contract her muscles as if she were trying to stop the flow of urine, control the passing of gas, or pinch off a stool (see Table 45.18).

With vaginal surgery, the preoperative preparation usually includes a cleansing douche the morning of surgery. A cleansing enema is usually given before a rectocele repair. A perineal shave may be done.

After surgery, the goals of care are to prevent wound infection and pressure on the vaginal suture line. Perineal care must be done at least twice a day and after each urination or defecation. Apply an ice pack locally to help relieve perineal discomfort and swelling. A disposable glove filled with ice and covered with a cloth works well to create an ice pack. Later, sitz baths may be used.

After an anterior colporrhaphy, an indwelling catheter is usually left in the bladder for 4 days to allow the local edema to subside. The catheter keeps the bladder empty, preventing strain on the sutures. Twice-daily catheter care with an

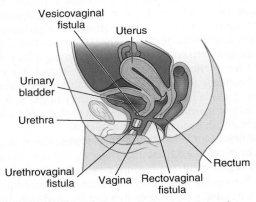

FIG. 53.15 Common fistulas involving the vagina.

antiseptic is generally done. To prevent constipation after a posterior colporrhaphy, a high-fiber diet and stool softener may be used.

Review discharge instructions before the patient leaves the hospital. These include the (1) use of mild laxative as needed; (2) restrictions on heavy lifting and prolonged standing, walking, or sitting; and (3) avoiding intercourse until the HCP gives permission. There may be a temporary loss of vaginal sensation, which can last for several months.

FISTULA

A *fistula* is an abnormal opening between internal organs or between an organ and the exterior of the body (Fig. 53.15). Gynecologic procedures cause most urinary tract fistulas. Other causes include injury during childbirth and disease processes such as cancer. Fistulas may develop between the vagina and bladder, urethra, ureter, or rectum. When *vesicovaginal* fistulas (between the bladder and vagina) develop, some urine leaks into the vagina. With *rectovaginal* fistulas (between the rectum and vagina), flatus and feces escape into the vagina. In both instances, excoriation and irritation of the vaginal and vulvar tissues occur and may lead to severe infections. In addition to wetness, offensive odors may develop, causing embarrassment and severely limiting socialization.

❖ Interprofessional and Nursing Care

Because small fistulas may heal spontaneously within a matter of months, treatment may not be needed. If the fistula does not heal, surgical repair is needed. Inflammation and tissue edema must be eliminated before surgery, which may involve a wait of many months. The fistulectomy may result in the patient having an ileal conduit or temporary colostomy. (See Chapter 45 for care of a patient with an ileal conduit and Chapter 42 for care of a patient with a colostomy.)

Perineal hygiene is of great importance before and after surgery. Cleanse the perineum every 4 hours. Warm sitz baths should be taken 3 times daily if possible. After surgery, emphasize ways to avoid stress on the repaired areas and prevent infection. Make sure the indwelling catheter, usually in place for 7 to 10 days, is draining at all times. Encourage the patient to maintain an adequate fluid intake to provide for internal catheter irrigation. Use minimal pressure and strict asepsis if catheter irrigation is needed. Change perineal pads often. The first stool after bowel surgery may be purposely delayed to prevent wound contamination. Later, give stool softeners or mild laxatives (as ordered).

Surgical repair of fistulas is not always effective, even in the best conditions. Therefore supportive nursing care for the patient and her significant others is especially important. Encouragement and reassurance are needed to help the patient cope with her problems.

SEXUAL ASSAULT

Sexual assault is the forcible perpetration of a sexual act on a person without their consent. It is a crime of violence and aggression. It can include any of the following actions: sodomy (anal or oral copulation with a person of the same or opposite sex); forced vaginal intercourse; assault with a foreign object; unwanted kissing, touching, or fondling; and serial battery and rape. The Federal Bureau of Investigation's (FBI's) definition of *rape* includes female or male victims who have experienced sexual assault that includes oral or anal penetration.

Sexual assault may be committed by a stranger or by an intimate partner. *Intimate partner violence (IPV)* is a major health problem in the United States.[22] Sexual assault that is perpetrated by a family member is termed *incest*. *Statutory rape* is consensual sexual intercourse with someone younger than a specific age. This age usually varies state to state. Most states use the criteria of a person younger than 16 years of age. Most states consider that an adolescent who is 16 years of age or older can consent to consensual sexual intercourse.

The involvement of children 14 years of age or younger in sexual activity, either consensual or forced, is termed *child sexual abuse*. Child sexual abuse is defined as the employment, persuasion, inducement, enticement, or even coercion of a person younger than 14 years of age in any sexually explicit conduct or simulation of sexual conduct. It includes behaviors that are forced onto the child for the purpose of producing video material, as well as rape, molestation, prostitution, or other forms of exploitation involving any sexual behavior.

Every 98 seconds, an American is sexually assaulted. Annually, 1.3 million rape or rape-related assaults occur to women. 18% of women report that they had been victims of an attempted or completed rape during their lifetime. Most (80%) reported that they were assaulted before the age of 25. Survivors have an array of physical and psychologic health consequences, such as suicidal thoughts and depression, after sexual violence.[23]

Clinical Manifestations

Physical. Some female victims of assault have more injuries than others. Factors that influence the severity of injury include the woman's age, if the perpetrator used a weapon, and if the victim knew the perpetrator. Physical injuries may include fractures, subdural hematomas, cerebral concussions, and intraabdominal injuries. Sexual injuries may include bruising and lacerations of the perineum, hymen, vulva, vagina, cervix, and anus. Sexual assault places women at risk for STIs and pregnancy.

Psychologic. Immediately after the assault, women may show signs of shock, numbness, denial, or withdrawal. Some women may seem unnaturally calm, while others may cry or express anger. Feelings of humiliation, degradation, embarrassment, anger, self-blame, and fear of another assault are often expressed.

These symptoms usually decrease after 2 weeks, and victims may appear to have adjusted. Yet any time from 2 to 3 weeks to months or years after the assault, symptoms may return and become more severe.

Rape trauma syndrome is a classification of posttraumatic stress disorder. Flashbacks, intrusive recall, sleep problems, GI symptoms, and numbing of feelings are common initial symptoms. Women feel embarrassment, self-blame, and powerlessness. Later symptoms include mood swings, irritability, and anger. Feelings of despair, shame, and hopelessness may be internalized and lead to depression, and the risk for suicide may increase.

Interprofessional Care

The highest priority for the victim of assault is her emotional and physical safety. Table 53.15 outlines the emergency management of the patient who has been sexually assaulted. Most emergency departments (EDs) have identified personnel who have received special training to work with women who have been assaulted. The sexual assault nurse examiner (SANE) is a registered nurse who is certified to provide care to victims of sexual assault, while ensuring evidence is safeguarded. Special procedures are followed in taking the history and conducting the examination to preserve all evidence in case of future prosecution. When the victim of an assault is in the ED or clinic, a specific chain of events occurs to collect legal evidence if the woman chooses to pursue legal action (Tables 53.15 and 53.16).

The SANE takes a comprehensive gynecologic and sexual history and an account of the assault (who, what, when, and where) and does a general physical and pelvic examination. Laboratory tests are done to identify sperm in the vagina and to screen for STIs or pregnancy. The patient receives preventive treatment for pregnancy and STIs and treatment for injuries sustained in the assault.

Follow-up physical and psychologic care is recommended. Women should return weekly for the first month after the assault. This includes the time period when a woman's psychologic reactions may be the most severe.

❖ NURSING MANAGEMENT: SEXUAL ASSAULT

Nursing care for a sexual assault victim is complex. Provide emotional and nonjudgmental support. Obtain referrals as needed for follow-up care. Part of the role of the SANE is to discuss the risk for pregnancy and STIs and offer the patient an emergency contraception pill and antibiotics (Table 53.17). A social worker or nurse case manager referral should be made by the primary nurse in the ED. They can assist the patient in securing financial compensation to help them pay for emergency services as a result of the assault, counseling services, and any missed work.

TABLE 53.15 Emergency Management

Sexual Assault

Etiology	Assessment Findings	Interventions
• Assault involving genitalia (male or female) without consent • Sexual molestation • Sodomy	• Anger • Crying • ↓ Level of consciousness • Emotional or physical manifestations of shock • Extragenital injuries • Hyperventilation • Hysteria • Pain in genital or extragenital area • Silence • Vaginal, oral, and rectal injuries	**Initial** • Treat shock and other urgent medical problems (e.g., head injury, hemorrhage, wounds, fractures). • Assess emotional state. • Contact support person (i.e., social worker, rape advocate, sexual assault nurse examiner). • Do *not* clean the patient until all evidence is collected. Make sure the patient does not wash, douche, urinate, brush teeth, or gargle. • Place sheet on floor. Then have patient stand on sheet to remove clothing. Place sheet with clothing in paper bag. • Obtain forensic evidence per local protocol (e.g., body hair, nail scrapings, tissue, dried semen, vaginal washing, blood samples). • Maintain chain of evidence for all legal specimens. Clearly label evidence and keep in locked cabinet until given to law enforcement agency. • Obtain baseline HIV, syphilis, and other STI screening. • Determine method of contraception, date of last menstrual period, and date of last tetanus immunization. • Consider tetanus prophylaxis if lacerations contain soil or dirt. • Vaccinate against hepatitis B if not already done. **Ongoing Monitoring** • Monitor vital signs and emotional status. • Provide clothing as needed. • Counsel patient about confidential HIV and STI testing.

TABLE 53.16 Evaluation of Alleged Sexual Assault

1. Medicolegal
- Valid written consent for examination, photographs, laboratory tests, release of information, and laboratory samples
- Appropriate "chain of evidence" documentation

2. History
- History of assault (who, what, when, where)
- Penetration, ejaculation, extragenital acts
- Activities since assault (e.g., changed clothes, bathed, douched)
- Inquire about safety
- Menstrual and contraceptive history
- Medical history
- Emotional status
- Current symptoms

3. General Physical Examination
- Vital signs and general appearance
- Extragenital trauma: mouth, breasts, neck
- Cuts, bruises, scratches (photographs taken)

4. Pelvic Examination
- Vulvar trauma, redness. Hymen, anal, and rectal status
- Matted hairs or free hairs
- Vaginal examination with unlubricated speculum for discharge, blood, lacerations
- Uterine size
- Adnexa, especially hematomas

5. Laboratory Samples
- Vaginal vault content sampling
- Vaginal smears: microscope evaluation for trichomonads and semen
- Oral or rectal swabs and smears (if indicated)
- Blood samples: pregnancy test; serologic testing for syphilis, HIV, and hepatitis B infection
- Freeze serum sample for later testing
- Cultures: cervix and other areas (if indicated) for gonorrhea and chlamydia infection
- Fingernail scrapings
- Pubic hair scrapings
- Clipping of matted pubic hairs

6. Treatment
- Care of injuries and emotional trauma
- Prophylaxis for STIs, tetanus, and hepatitis B (see appropriate chapters)
- If appropriate, consider levonorgestrel (Plan-B One-Step) emergency contraceptive pill up to 72 hr after assault; follow-up for pregnancy test in 2–3 wk
- Testing for HIV, syphilis, and hepatitis B may be done at 6–8 wk
- Protection of legal rights
- Recommendation of continued follow-up and services of rape crisis center

TABLE 53.17 Patient Teaching

Sexual Assault Prevention

Include the following instructions when teaching measures to prevent sexual assault:

1. Be proactive and take a self-defense class.
2. Be aware of date-rape drugs (e.g., GHB, Rohypnol, ketamine). Never leave your beverage unattended when socializing.
3. Place and maintain lights at all entrances to your home.
4. Keep your doors locked and do not open them to a stranger. Ask for identification if a service person comes to the door.
5. Do not advertise that you live alone. List only your initials with your last name in the telephone directory or on the mailbox. Never reveal to a caller that you are home alone.
6. Avoid walking alone in deserted areas. Walk to the parking lot with a friend. Be sure you see each other leave.
7. Have your keys ready as you approach your car or home.
8. Keep all doors locked and the windows up when driving.
9. Never get on an elevator with a suspicious person. Pretend you have forgotten something and get off.
10. Say what you mean in social situations. Be sure your voice and body language reflect your response.
11. Be cautious with online correspondence.
12. Carry a loud whistle and use it when you think you are in danger.
13. Yell "Fire!" if you are attacked and run toward a lighted area

CASE STUDY

Uterine Fibroids and Endometrial Cancer

(© Juanmonino/ iStock.com.)

Patient Profile

B.C. is a 49-yr-old Latina woman who has lower pelvic discomfort and anemia. She has hypertension and hypothyroidism. B.C. is the mother of 2 teenage children. She has had abnormal uterine bleeding for 5 months. Large multiple uterine fibroids were diagnosed on ultrasound. She comes to the hospital for an abdominal hysterectomy.

Subjective Data

- Was initially reluctant about surgery
- Concerned about her dyspareunia and her husband's reaction to the surgery
- States she has pelvic discomfort and vaginal spotting

Objective Data (Preoperative)

- BP 140/92 mm Hg, pulse 82 beats/min, respirations 14 breaths/min
- Height 5ft, 6 in; weight 145 lb.

Operative

- During surgery, abnormal-looking endometrial tissue was sent for pathologic analysis. The results were positive for endometrial cancer.
- Had total hysterectomy and bilateral salpingo-oophorectomy with lymph node biopsies. 5 large fibroids were found in the uterus.

Postoperative Status

- Returned to room with indwelling urinary catheter in place
- Abdominal incision
- Intermittent pneumatic compression devices on lower extremities
- Patient-controlled analgesia (PCA) pump for pain management

Discussion Questions

1. Can the manifestations of uterine fibroids be distinguished from endometrial cancer?
2. **Patient-Centered Care:** Preoperatively, B.C. asks you about the effect of the surgery on her sexuality. How would you respond, and what type of patient teaching would you do?
3. **Patient-Centered Care:** When she is told about the diagnosis of endometrial cancer, she is shocked. She cannot believe that it was not discovered before surgery. How would you respond to her?
4. **Priority Decision:** What are priorities of care for B.C.?
5. **Safety:** When assessing B.C. after you got her out of bed, you note that her abdominal dressing is saturated with blood and she says she feels weak and dizzy. What would you do?
6. What other complications (including reasons for their development) can occur after an abdominal hysterectomy?
7. **Priority Decision:** Based on the assessment data presented, what are the priority nursing diagnoses? Are there any collaborative problems?
8. Her 17-yr-old daughter asks you if she is at risk for endometrial cancer. How would you respond?

Answers available at *http://evolve.elsevier.com/Lewis/medsurg.*

BRIDGE TO NCLEX EXAMINATION

The number of the question corresponds to the same-numbered outcome at the beginning of the chapter.

1. In telling a patient with infertility what she and her partner can expect, the nurse explains that
   a. ovulatory studies can help determine tube patency.
   b. a hysterosalpingogram is a common diagnostic study.
   c. for most couples, the cause of infertility is usually not found.
   d. semen analysis is performed only if testosterone levels are low.

2. An appropriate question to ask the patient with painful menstruation to distinguish primary from secondary dysmenorrhea is
   a. "Does your pain become worse with activity or overexertion?"
   b. "Have you had a recent personal crisis or change in your lifestyle?"
   c. "Is your pain relieved by nonsteroidal antiinflammatory medications?"
   d. "When in your menstrual history did the pain with your period begin?"

3. The nurse should advise the woman recovering from surgical treatment of an ectopic pregnancy that
   a. she has an increased risk for salpingitis.
   b. maintaining bed rest for 12 hours will assist in healing.
   c. having an ectopic pregnancy increases her risk for another.
   d. intrauterine devices and infertility treatments must be avoided.

4. To prevent or decrease age-related changes that occur after menopause in a patient who chooses not to take hormone therapy, the *most* important self-care measure to teach is
   a. maintaining usual sexual activity.
   b. increasing the intake of dairy products.
   c. performing regular aerobic, weight-bearing exercise.
   d. taking vitamin E and B-complex vitamin supplements.

5. In caring for a patient with endometriosis, the nurse teaches the patient that interventions used to treat or cure this condition may include (*select all that apply*)
   a. radiation.
   b. antibiotic therapy.
   c. oral contraceptive pills.
   d. surgical removal of tissue.
   e. total abdominal hysterectomy and salpingo-oophorectomy.

6. Nursing care for the patient with endometrial cancer who had a total abdominal hysterectomy and salpingectomy and oophorectomy includes
   a. maintaining absolute bed rest.
   b. keeping the patient in high-Fowler's position.
   c. need for supplemental estrogen after removal of ovaries.
   d. encouraging movement and walking as much as tolerated.

7. Postoperative care for the patient who had an abdominal hysterectomy includes (*select all that apply*)
   a. monitoring urine output.
   b. changing position frequently.
   c. restricting all food for 24 hours.
   d. observing perineal pad for bleeding.
   e. encouraging leg exercises to promote circulation.

8. Postoperative nursing care for the woman with a gynecologic fistula includes (*select all that apply*)
   a. bed rest.
   b. bladder training.
   c. warm sitz baths.
   d. perineal hygiene.
   e. use of daily enemas.

9. The *first* nursing intervention for the patient who has been sexually assaulted is to
   a. treat urgent medical problems.
   b. contact support person for the patient.
   c. provide supplies for the patient to cleanse self.
   d. document bruises and lacerations of the perineum and the cervix.

1. b, 2. d, 3. c, 4. c, 5. c, d, e, 6. d, 7. a, b, e, 8. b, c, d, 9. a

For rationales to these answers and even more NCLEX review questions, visit *http://evolve.elsevier.com/Lewis/medsurg.*

EVOLVE WEBSITE/RESOURCES LIST

http://evolve.elsevier.com/Lewis/medsurg
Review Questions (Online Only)
Key Points
Answer Keys for Questions
- Rationales for Bridge to NCLEX Examination Questions
- Answer Guidelines for Case Study on p. 1251
Student Case Study
- Patient With Endometrial Cancer
Nursing Care Plan(s)
- eNursing Care Plan 53.1: Patient Having Abdominal Hysterectomy
Conceptual Care Map Creator
Audio Glossary
Content Updates

REFERENCES

1. National Institutes of Health: How common is infertility? Retrieved from *www.nichd.nih.gov/health/topics/infertility/conditioninfo/common.*
2. Centers for Disease Control and Prevention: What is infertility? Retrieved from *www.cdc.gov/reproductivehealth/infertility/index.htm.*
3. Barbieri RL: Female infertility. In: Strauss JF, Barbieri RL, eds: *Yen and Jaffe's reproductive endocrinology, physiology, pathophysiology, and clinical management,* ed 8, Philadelphia, 2019, Elsevier.
4. American Congress of Obstetricians and Gynecologists: Early pregnancy loss. Retrieved from *www.acog.org/~/media/For%20Patients/faq090.pdf.*
5. American Congress of Obstetricians and Gynecologists: Induced abortion. Retrieved from *www.acog.org/-/media/For-Patients/faq043.pdf?dmc=1&ts=20150208T1033249676.*

*6. Lustyk M, Gerrish W, Douglas H, et al: Relationships among premenstrual symptom reports, menstrual attitudes, and mindfulness. Retrieved from *www.uptodate.com/contents/treatments-for-female-infertility?-search=treatrnents-for-female-infertility&source=search_result&selected Title=3~132&usage_type=default&display_rank=3.*

7. American Congress of Obstetricians and Gynecologists: Abnormal uterine bleeding. Retrieved from *www.acog.org/Patients/FAQs/Abnormal-Uterine-Bleeding#abnormal.*

8. Tulundi T: Ectopic pregnancy: Choosing a treatment and methotrexate therapy. Retrieved from *www.uptodate.com/contents/ectopic-pregnancy-choosing-a-treatment-and-methotrexate-therapy?source=search_result&search=ectopic+pregnancy&selectedTitle=2~150.*

*9. Shifren JL, Gass LS: The North American Menopause Society recommendations for clinical care of midlife women. Retrieved from *www.menopause.org/publications/clinical-care-recommendations.*

10. Centers for Disease Control and Prevention: *Pelvic inflammatory disease.* Retrieved from *www.cdc.gov/std/pid/stdfact-pid-detailed.htm.*

11. Rosin M, Abrao MS: Endometriosis: From diagnosis to surgical management. In: Gomes-da-Silveira G, da Silveira G, Pessini S, eds: *Minimally invasive gynecology,* New York, 2018, Springer.

*12. Polycystic ovary syndrome guidelines. Retrieved from *https://emedicine.medscape.com/article/256806-guidelines.*

13. American Cancer Society: Cancer facts and figures 2018. Retrieved from *www.cancer.org/research/cancer-facts-statistics/all-cancer-facts-figures/cancer-facts-figures-2018.html.*

*14. American Cancer Society: The American Cancer Society guidelines for the prevention and early detection of cervical cancer. Retrieved from *www.cancer.org/cancer/cervical-cancer/prevention-and-early-detection/cervical-cancer-screening-guidelines.html.*

15. National Cancer Institute: Cervical cancer treatment. Retrieved from *www.cancer.gov/types/cervical/patient/cervical-treatment-pdq#link/_117.*

16. American Cancer Society: Key statistics for endometrial cancer. Retrieved from *www.cancer.org/cancer/endometrial-cancer/about/key-statistics.html.*

17. National Cancer Institute: Endometrial cancer treatment (PDQ)—Health professional version. Retrieved from *www.cancer.gov/types/uterine/hp/endometrial-treatment-pdq.*

18. American Cancer Society: Special section: Ovarian cancer. Retrieved from *www.cancer.org/content/dam/cancer-org/research/cancer-facts-and-statistics/annual-cancer-facts-and-figures/2018/cancer-facts-and-figures-special-section-ovarian-cancer-2018.pdf.*

19. National Cancer Institute: *Vaginal cancer treatment (PDQ)—Health professional version.* Retrieved from *www.cancer.gov/types/vaginal/hp/vaginal-treatment-pdq.*

20. American College of Obstetrics and Gynecology: Practice bulletin #176: Pelvic organ prolapse. Retrieved from *www.acog.org/Clinical%20Guidance%20and%20Publications/Practice%20Bulletins/Committee%20on%20Practice%20Bulletins%20Gynecology/Pelvic%20Organ%20Prolapse.aspx.*

21. American College of Obstetrics and Gynecology: Pelvic support problems. Retrieved from *www.acog.org/Patients/FAQs/Pelvic-Support-Problems.*

22. Centers for Disease Control and Prevention: Intimate partner violence. Retrieved from *www.cdc.gov/violenceprevention/intimatepartnerviolence.*

23. Rape, Abuse, and Incest National Network: Victims of sexual violence: Statistics. Retrieved from *www.rainn.org/statistics/victims-sexual-violence.*

*Evidence-based information for clinical practice

54

Male Reproductive Problems

Anthony Lutz

I would like my life to be a statement of love and compassion—and where it isn't, that's where my work lies.

Ram Dass

🅔 http://evolve.elsevier.com/Lewis/medsurg

CONCEPTUAL FOCUS

Cellular Regulation	Pain	Sexuality
Infection	Reproduction	

LEARNING OUTCOMES

1. Describe the pathophysiology, clinical manifestations, and interprofessional and nursing management of benign prostatic hyperplasia.
2. Describe the pathophysiology, clinical manifestations, and interprofessional care of prostate cancer.
3. Explain the nursing management of prostate cancer.
4. Specify the pathophysiology, clinical manifestations, and interprofessional and nursing management of prostatitis and problems of the penis and scrotum.

5. Explain the clinical manifestations and interprofessional care of testicular cancer.
6. Describe the pathophysiology, clinical manifestations, and interprofessional and nursing management of problems related to male sexual function.
7. Discuss the psychologic and emotional implications related to male reproductive problems.

KEY TERMS

benign prostatic hyperplasia (BPH), p. 1254
epididymitis, p. 1271
erectile dysfunction (ED), p. 1273
orchitis, p. 1271
paraphimosis, p. 1270

phimosis, p. 1270
prostate cancer, p. 1262
prostatitis, p. 1269
radical prostatectomy, p. 1265
testicular cancer, p. 1272

testicular torsion, p. 1272
transurethral resection of the prostate (TURP), p. 1260
vasectomy, p. 1273

This chapter discusses problems of the male reproductive system. These involve a variety of structures, including the prostate, penis, urethra, ejaculatory duct, scrotum, testes, epididymis, ductus (vas) deferens, and rectum (Fig. 54.1). Many of these problems can profoundly affect sexuality and reproduction. Sexual dysfunction from prostate problems or erectile dysfunction (ED) can cause psychologic and body image problems. The patient may have anxiety because of a perceived loss of his sex role, self-esteem, or quality of sexual interaction with his partner. Patient education and counseling are essential nursing roles for promoting health and optimal sexual well-being.

PROBLEMS OF THE PROSTATE GLAND

BENIGN PROSTATIC HYPERPLASIA

Benign prostatic hyperplasia (BPH) is a condition in which the prostate gland increases in size, disrupting the outflow of urine from the bladder through the urethra. Half of men will have some signs of BPH by the age of 50. That number increases to more than 70% for men 60 to 69 years old.[1] Symptoms of BPH can include bothersome lower urinary tract symptoms (LUTS), such as difficulty starting a urine stream, a decreased/weaker flow of urine, or urinary frequency. BPH with LUTS does not cause or lead to an increased risk for prostate cancer.[2]

Etiology and Pathophysiology

There are several potential factors that may play a role in the development and progression of BPH. We think that hormonal changes associated with aging are a contributing factor. Dihydroxytestosterone (DHT), one of several sex hormones, stimulates prostate cell growth. Excess amounts of DHT can cause overgrowth of prostate tissue. As men age, they have a decrease in testosterone but continue to make and accumulate high levels of DHT, resulting in prostate enlargement.

Another possible cause of BPH is an increased proportion of estrogen (as compared to testosterone). Throughout their lives, men make both testosterone and small amounts of estrogen. As men age, the amount of active testosterone in the blood decreases, leaving a higher proportion of estrogen. A higher

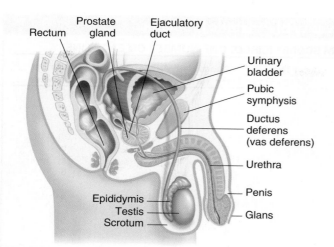

FIG. 54.1 Areas of the male reproductive system in which problems are likely to develop.

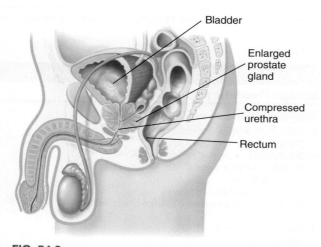

FIG. 54.2 BPH. The enlarged prostate compresses the urethra.

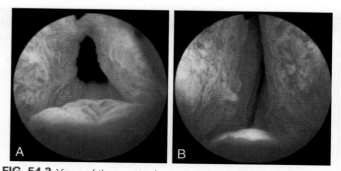

FIG. 54.3 Views of the prostate by cystoscopy. A, Normal appearance. B, Moderate BPH with urethral obstruction. (From Townsend CM, Beauchamp RD, Evers BM, et al: *Sabiston textbook of surgery*, ed 19, Philadelphia, 2012, Saunders.)

amount of estrogen within the prostate gland increases the activity of substances (including DHT) that promote prostate cell growth.

BPH usually develops in the inner part of the prostate, called the transition zone. (Prostate cancer is most likely to develop in the outer part, called the peripheral zone). As the transition zone of the prostate enlarges, it gradually compresses the urethra, leading to partial or complete obstruction (Fig. 54.2). This compression of the urethra leads to the development of clinical manifestations. There is no direct relationship between overall prostate size and the severity of manifestations or degree of obstruction.[3] The location of the enlargement is most significant in the development of obstructive symptoms (Fig. 54.3). For example, it is possible for mild prostate enlargement to cause severe obstructive symptoms or for extreme prostate enlargement to cause few obstructive symptoms.

Risk factors for BPH include aging, obesity (especially increased waist circumference), lack of physical activity, a high amount of dietary animal protein, alcohol use, ED, smoking, and diabetes. A family history of BPH in a first-degree relative also may be a risk factor.

Clinical Manifestations

Manifestations occur gradually and may not be noticed until prostate enlargement has been present for some time. Early symptoms may not cause many problems because the bladder can compensate for a small amount of resistance to urine flow. As the severity of urethral obstruction increases, symptoms gradually worsen.

Symptoms can be divided into 2 groups: irritative and obstructive. *Irritative symptoms* include nocturia, urinary frequency, urgency, dysuria, bladder pain, and incontinence. These symptoms are related to inflammation or infection. Nocturia is often the first symptom that the patient notices. *Obstructive symptoms,* caused by prostate enlargement, include a decrease in the caliber and force of the urinary stream, difficulty in starting a stream, intermittency (stopping and starting stream several times while voiding), and dribbling at the end of urination. These symptoms are due to the increased effort of the bladder as it tries to empty through the decreased diameter of the urethra. As a group, both irritative and obstructive symptoms are considered LUTS.

The American Urological Association (AUA) symptom index for BPH (Table 54.1) is a widely used tool to assess voiding symptoms from obstruction.[4] Although this tool is not diagnostic, it helps determine the extent of symptoms and guide treatment. Higher scores on this tool mean greater symptom severity.

Complications

Complications of BPH are relatively rare. Some men may have acute urinary retention. This complication is manifested by the sudden and painful inability to urinate. Treatment involves the insertion of a catheter to drain the bladder. Surgery may be indicated in severe situations.

Urinary tract infection (UTI) can be a complication of BPH. Since the bladder is unable to empty completely, bacteria can grow in the residual urine that remains in the bladder and cause infection. In more severe cases, infection can progress into the kidney and cause pyelonephritis. In severe cases, infection can spread into the bloodstream and sepsis can develop. Bladder calculi (stones) may develop because of the alkalinization of the residual urine. So, the finding of bladder stones often indicates obstruction related to BPH. The risk for kidney stones is not significantly increased in this population.

Other complications include renal failure caused by *hydronephrosis* (distention of the renal pelvis and calyces by urine that cannot flow through the ureter to the bladder) and bladder damage if treatment for acute urinary retention is delayed.

TABLE 54.1 AUA Symptom Index to Determine Severity of Prostatic Problems

	AUA SYMPTOM SCORE* (CIRCLE ONE NUMBER ON EACH LINE)					
Questions	Not At All	Less Than 1 Time in 5	Less Than Half the Time	About Half the Time	More Than Half the Time	Almost Always
Over the Past Month						
1. How often do you have the sensation that your bladder is not completely empty after you finish urinating?	0	1	2	3	4	5
2. How often do you have to urinate again, less than 2 hr after you finish urinating?	0	1	2	3	4	5
3. How often do you stop and start again several times when you urinate?	0	1	2	3	4	5
4. How often do you find it difficult to postpone urination?	0	1	2	3	4	5
5. How often do you have a weak urinary stream?	0	1	2	3	4	5
6. How often do you have to push or strain to begin urination?	0	1	2	3	4	5
7. How many times do you usually get up to urinate from the time you go to bed at night until the time you get up in the morning?	0 (None)	1 (1 time)	2 (2 times)	3 (3 times)	4 (4 times)	5 (5 times or more)
Sum of circled numbers (AUA Symptom Score): _____*						

Source: Barry MJ, Fowler FJ, O'Leary MP, et al: The AUA symptom index for benign prostatic hyperplasia, *J Urol* 148:1549, 1992. Used with permission.
*Score is interpreted as follows: 0–7, mild; 8–19, moderate; 20–35, severe.
AUA, American Urological Association.

Diagnostic Studies

A detailed history and physical examination are both important in the diagnosis. Diagnostic studies are outlined in Table 54.2. A digital rectal examination (DRE) is done to estimate the prostate size, symmetry, and consistency. In BPH, the prostate is symmetrically enlarged, firm, and smooth.

Other diagnostic testing may include a urinalysis and urine culture and sensitivities to look for bacteria, nitrites, leukocyte esterase, white blood cells (WBCs), or microscopic hematuria (RBCs), which could indicate infection or inflammation.

A prostate-specific antigen (PSA) blood test may be done to screen for prostate cancer. PSA levels may be slightly increased in patients with BPH, as PSA is released into the bloodstream by both benign and malignant prostate cells. Serum creatinine levels can assess for renal insufficiency. If creatinine levels are high, a renal ultrasound may be done to evaluate for hydronephrosis. Because symptoms of BPH are similar to those of a neurogenic bladder, a neurologic examination may be done.

In patients with an abnormal DRE and high PSA, a transrectal ultrasound (TRUS) is typically ordered. This examination allows for accurate assessment of prostate size and can help to distinguish BPH from prostate cancer. Biopsies can be taken during the ultrasound procedure. A pelvic MRI with attention to the prostate is an alternative imaging test that can be done in the setting of abnormal DRE and high PSA. If abnormal areas are seen on MRI, these areas can be specially targeted on a TRUS prostate biopsy using new software and equipment (called an MRI-fusion targeted biopsy). Currently insurance coverage of pelvic MRI can sometimes be an issue. However, recent studies have shown risk assessment with MRI prior to biopsy and MRI-targeted biopsy is superior to standard TRUS biopsy in men at risk for prostate cancer.[5]

Uroflowmetry, a study that measures the volume of urine expelled from the bladder, is helpful to determine the extent of urethral blockage and the type of treatment needed. Postvoid

TABLE 54.2 Interprofessional Care

Benign Prostatic Hyperplasia

Diagnostic Assessment
- History and physical examination
- Digital rectal examination (DRE)
- Urinalysis and urine culture and sensitivities
- Prostate-specific antigen (PSA)
- Serum creatinine
- Postvoid residual (by ultrasound)
- Renal ultrasound (if increased serum creatinine/to evaluate for hydronephrosis)
- Transrectal ultrasound (TRUS)
- Uroflowmetry
- Cystoscopy
- Urodynamic/pressure flow studies

Management

Active Surveillance
- Annual PSA and DRE
- Repeat IPSS score and postvoid residual if any symptoms change

Drug Therapy
- 5α-Reductase inhibitors (e.g., dutasteride [Avodart], finasteride [Proscar])
- α-Adrenergic receptor blockers (e.g., alfuzosin, doxazosin, tamsulosin [Flomax])
- Combination 5α-reductase inhibitor and α-adrenergic receptor blocker (e.g., dutasteride plus tamsulosin [Jalyn])
- Erectogenic drugs (e.g., tadalafil [Cialis])

Minimally Invasive Therapy
- Laser enucleation of the prostate (HoLEP or ThuLEP)
- Photoselective vaporization of the prostate (PVP)
- Prostatic urethral lift (PUL)
- Transurethral microwave thermotherapy (TUMT)
- Transurethral needle ablation (TUNA)
- Water vapor thermal therapy

Invasive (Surgery) Therapy
- Transurethral incision of the prostate (TUIP)
- Transurethral resection of the prostate (TURP)
- Simple prostatectomy (open, laparoscopic, or robotic-assisted)

residual urine volume is can determine the degree of urine flow obstruction. Cystoscopy, a procedure allowing internal visualization of the urethra and bladder, is done if the diagnosis is unclear or to see the degree of prostatic enlargement. If the diagnostic picture is unclear, urodynamic/pressure flow studies can be done to help evaluate bladder function and assess for obstruction.

Interprofessional Care

The goals of interprofessional care are to (1) restore bladder drainage, (2) relieve the patient's symptoms, and (3) prevent or treat the complications of BPH. Treatment is generally based on the degree to which the symptoms bother the patient or the presence of complications, rather than the size of the prostate. Alternatives to surgical intervention for some patients include surveillance, drug therapy, and minimally invasive procedures.

The most conservative treatment that is recommended for some patients with BPH is referred to as *active surveillance,* or watchful waiting. When the patient has mild symptoms (AUA symptom scores of 0 to 7), a wait-and-see approach is taken. Teaching patients to make lifestyle changes can help relieve early or mild symptoms. Making dietary changes (decreasing intake of bladder irritants, like caffeine, alcohol, carbonated drinks, artificial sweeteners, and spicy or acidic foods), avoiding certain drugs (e.g., decongestants, anticholinergics), and restricting evening fluid intake may improve symptoms.

In addition, a timed voiding schedule (also referred to as "bladder re-training") may reduce symptoms, eliminating the need for further intervention. If the patient begins to have signs or symptoms that indicate an increase in obstruction, further treatment is needed.

Drug Therapy. The 2 main classes of drugs that are used to treat BPH include 5α-reductase inhibitors and α-adrenergic receptor blockers. Combination therapy using both types of drugs may be more effective in reducing symptoms than using 1 drug alone. A medication in the erectogenic class of drugs also can be used to help treat BPH.

5α-Reductase Inhibitors. 5α-Reductase inhibitors work by reducing the size of the prostate gland. They block the 5α-reductase type 1 and 2 isoenzymes, which are necessary for the conversion of testosterone to DHT (main intraprostatic androgen). Prostate size is directly related to the amount of DHT. By blocking DHT, overly enlarged prostates can decrease in size. This class of medication is more effective for men with larger prostates who have bothersome symptoms.

Finasteride (Proscar) inhibits only the type 2 isoenzyme. It is an appropriate treatment option for men who have a moderate to severe symptom score on the AUA symptom index (Table 54.1). Although most men who are treated with the drug have symptom improvement, it can take up to 6 months to be effective. It must be taken on a regular basis to have an effect. Because it blocks the enzyme needed for conversion of testosterone to DHT, a common side effect is decreased libido.

Serum PSA levels may appear decreased by almost 50% when taking finasteride. Therefore, to "correct" for the apparent decrease caused by the finasteride, the HCP should double the PSA value for a patient who has been on a 5α-reductase inhibitor for at least 6 months. This allows for an accurate comparison to premedication levels, in order to track trends more accurately in the PSA.

Dutasteride (Avodart) has the same effect on prostatic tissue as finasteride. It is a dual inhibitor of 5α-reductase types 1 and 2 isoenzymes. The combination of a 5α-reductase inhibitor (dutasteride) and an α-adrenergic receptor blocker (tamsulosin) is available in a single oral medication (Jalyn).

These drugs may lower the risk for some prostate cancers. However, using them to prevent prostate cancer is not been recommended and research is currently ongoing. Patients who develop a high PSA level while taking these drugs should be referred to their HCP. Encourage the patient to discuss the need for prostate cancer screening with the HCP.

DRUG ALERT Finasteride (Proscar)
- Women who may be or are pregnant should not handle tablets due to potential risk to male fetus (anomaly).

α-Adrenergic Receptor Blockers. α-Adrenergic receptor blockers are another drug treatment option for BPH. These drugs selectively block α1-adrenergic receptors, which are abundant in the prostate, and are increased in hyperplastic prostate tissue. They offer symptom relief by relaxing the smooth muscle of the prostate that surrounds the urethra, thus facilitating urinary flow through the urethra. These medications do not decrease the overall size of the prostate.

α-adrenergic blockers used include alfuzosin (Uroxatral), doxazosin (Cardura), prazosin (Minipress), tamsulosin (Flomax), and silodosin (Rapaflo). Symptom improvement can often be seen within days to weeks of starting α-adrenergic blockers. Because they relax the smooth muscle of the prostatic urethra, one of the most common side effects is retrograde ejaculation.

Erectogenic Drugs. Tadalafil (Cialis) can be used in men who have symptoms of BPH alone or in combination with ED. It is effective in reducing symptoms for both conditions.

Herbal Therapy. Some patients take plant extracts, such as saw palmetto (*Serenoa repens*). However, research shows that saw palmetto has no benefit over a placebo.[6] Advise patients to discuss herbal therapies with their HCP.

Minimally Invasive Therapy. Minimally invasive therapies are becoming more common as an alternative to watchful waiting and invasive treatment (Table 54.3). They generally do not involve hospitalization or catheterization. They are associated with few adverse events. Many minimally invasive therapies have outcomes comparable to invasive techniques.

Photoselective Vaporization of the Prostate. Photoselective vaporization of the prostate (PVP) uses a high-power green laser light to vaporize prostate tissue. The use of laser therapy through visual or ultrasound guidance is an effective alternative to transurethral resection of the prostate (TURP) in treating BPH.[7] The laser beam is delivered transurethrally through a fiber instrument inserted into the meatus and through the urethra. It can cut, coagulate, and vaporize prostatic tissue. Improvements in urine flow and symptoms are almost immediate after the procedure. PVP works well for larger prostate glands, but irritative voiding symptoms may persist for several weeks.

Laser Enucleation of the Prostate. Laser enucleation involves delivering a laser beam transurethrally through a fiber instrument. It is used for rapid coagulation and vaporization of prostatic tissue, with better coagulative properties in the tissue compared with TURP. There are 2 types of lasers in this class: holmium laser enucleation of the prostate (HoLEP) and thulium

TABLE 54.3 Treatment for Benign Prostatic Hyperplasia

Description	Advantages	Disadvantages
Minimally Invasive		
Laser Enucleation of the Prostate Laser beams used to rapidly vaporize and coagulate prostate tissue. Laser does not penetrate deep tissue. 2 types of lasers in this class: holmium laser enucleation of the prostate (HoLEP), thulium laser enucleation of the prostate (ThuLEP).	• Outpatient procedure • Better coagulative properties in tissue compared with TURP • Comparable results to TURP and PVP • Minimal bleeding • Fast recovery time	• Catheter needed after for 24–48 hr • Irritative voiding symptoms, urinary incontinence • Hematuria • Retrograde ejaculation • May be more difficult to perform compared with PVP
Photoselective Vaporization of the Prostate (PVP) Procedure uses a laser beam to cut or destroy part of the prostate. May be more effective for small to moderate-sized prostates.	• Short procedure • Comparable results to TURP • Minimal bleeding • Fast recovery time • Rapid symptom improvement • Very effective	• Catheter needed up to 7 days after due to edema and urinary retention • Delayed sloughing of tissue • Takes several weeks to reach optimal effect • Retrograde ejaculation
Prostatic Urethral Lift (PUL) Permanent transprostatic implants/tension sutures placed transurethrally via cystoscope. Mechanically open the prostatic urethra by compressing the prostate tissue/parenchyma.	• Outpatient procedure • Erectile dysfunction, urinary incontinence, and retrograde ejaculation are minimal • No change in PSA since no prostate tissue ablated	• Lack of long-term durability/results • Treatment response rates slightly lower when compared with TURP • If unsuccessful, may need repeat PUL or TURP in the future
Transurethral Microwave Thermotherapy (TUMT) Use of microwave radiating heat to produce coagulative necrosis of the prostate.	• Outpatient procedure • Erectile dysfunction, urinary incontinence, and retrograde ejaculation are rare • Mild effects: bladder spasm, hematuria, dysuria	• Potential for damage to surrounding tissue • Urinary catheter needed after for 2–7 days • Not appropriate for men with rectal problems
Transurethral Needle Ablation (TUNA) Low-wave radiofrequency used to heat the prostate, causing necrosis.	• Outpatient procedure • Erectile dysfunction, urinary incontinence, and retrograde ejaculation are rare • Precise delivery of heat to desired area • Very little pain • Early return to activities	• Urinary retention common • Irritative voiding symptoms • Hematuria for up to a week • May need a catheter for a short time after
Transurethral Vaporization of Prostate (TUVP) Electrosurgical modification of the standard TURP. Vaporization and desiccation are used together to destroy prostatic tissue. Can use a variety of energy delivery mediums (e.g., button, rollerball, or vaportrode).	• Minimal risks • Minimal bleeding and sloughing	• Retrograde ejaculation • Intermittent hematuria
Water Vapor Thermal Therapy Heated water vapor/steam used to destroy obstructive prostate tissue. Delivered transurethrally via handheld device with a retractable needle that releases the water vapor in 9-second doses.	• Outpatient procedure • Can be done in an outpatient office setting • Erectile dysfunction, urinary incontinence, and retrograde ejaculation are rare • Precise delivery of steam to desired area • Very little pain	• Relatively new, so lack of long-term durability/results • Irritative voiding symptoms and UTI • Hematuria
Invasive (Surgery)		
Transurethral Incision of Prostate (TUIP) Involves transurethral incisions into prostatic tissue to relieve obstruction. Effective for men with small to moderate prostates.	• Outpatient procedure • Minimal complications • Low occurrence of erectile dysfunction or retrograde ejaculation • Outcomes similar to TURP	• Urinary catheter needed after procedure

TABLE 54.3 Treatment for Benign Prostatic Hyperplasia—cont'd

Description	Advantages	Disadvantages
Transurethral Resection of Prostate (TURP) Use of excision and cauterization to remove prostate tissue via cystoscope. Standard for treatment of BPH.	• Erectile dysfunction unlikely	• Bleeding, clot retention • Retrograde ejaculation • Catheter needed after
Simple Prostatectomy (open, laparoscopic, or robotic-assisted) Surgery of choice for men with large prostates (often >100 g), bladder damage, or other complicating factors. If open, involves an external incision with 2 possible approaches (either retropubic or perineal; see Fig. 54.6). If laparoscopic and/or robotic-assisted, involves several small abdominal incisions and 1 slightly larger incision near the umbilicus.	• Complete visualization of the prostate and surrounding tissue	• Erectile dysfunction • Bleeding • Pain • Risk for infection

laser enucleation of the prostate (ThuLEP). Neither penetrate deep tissue, which decreases side effects.

Prostatic Urethral Lift. Prostatic urethral lift (PUL) involves permanent transprostatic implants or tension sutures delivered transurethrally via cystoscope. They mechanically open the prostatic urethra by compressing the prostate tissue. This alters prostate anatomy without ablation of any tissue. This is a relatively new minimally invasive treatment for BPH. So far, it has been studied only in prostates less than 80 g in size and in prostates without an obstructive median lobe. This means there is a current lack of long-term data on the durability of this treatment over time and the rates of needing either repeat treatment or progression to TURP in the future.

Transurethral Microwave Thermotherapy. Transurethral microwave thermotherapy (TUMT) is an outpatient procedure that involves the delivery of microwaves directly to the prostate through a transurethral probe. The microwaves increase the temperature of the prostate tissue to about 113° F (45° C). The heat causes death of tissue, relieving the obstruction. A rectal temperature probe is used during the procedure to ensure that the temperature in the rectum is kept below 110° F (43.5° C) to prevent rectal tissue damage. The procedure takes about 90 minutes.

Urinary retention is a common complication. Patients who have a TUMT are generally sent home with an indwelling catheter for 2 to 7 days to maintain urinary flow and facilitate the passing of small clots or necrotic tissue. Antibiotics, pain medication, and bladder antispasmodic medications are used to treat and prevent postprocedure problems. Anticoagulant therapy should be stopped 10 days before treatment.

Transurethral Needle Ablation. Transurethral needle ablation (TUNA) is another procedure that increases the temperature of prostate tissue, thus causing localized necrosis. TUNA differs from TUMT in that low-wave radiofrequency is used to heat the prostate. Only prostate tissue in direct contact with the needle is affected, which allows for more precise removal of the target tissue. Most patients undergoing TUNA have an improvement in symptoms. It is done in an outpatient unit or HCP's office using local anesthesia and IV or oral sedation. The TUNA procedure lasts about 30 minutes.

Transurethral Vaporization of the Prostate. Transurethral vaporization of the prostate (TUVP) is an electrosurgical

CHECK YOUR PRACTICE

You are caring for a patient who is scheduled for a transurethral needle ablation for BPH. He appears anxious. He tells you, "I'm afraid of the pain after the procedure. They told me I might have to have a tube in my bladder. I don't know how I'll manage at home."
• What type of information and teaching would you provide him?

modification of the standard TURP, where vaporization and desiccation are used together to destroy obstructive prostatic tissue. There are a variety of energy delivery mediums that can be used to deliver the energy (e.g., button, rollerball, vaportrode). This is why it is referred to as a "button TURP." The results, side effects, and long-term outcomes are equivalent to TURP. Because TUVP uses a bipolar energy delivery surface, an energy current is not passed through the patient's body to a grounding pad. This allows for saline to be used during the procedure for irrigation, which dramatically decreases the risk for TUR syndrome (discussed on p. 1260.).

Water Vapor Thermal Therapy. Water vapor thermal therapy is another relatively new minimally invasive treatment for BPH. It uses heated water vapor/steam to destroy obstructive prostate tissue. The steam is delivered transurethrally directly into the prostate by a hand-held device with a retractable needle. It releases the heated water vapor in 9-second doses. It is potentially a good option for a patient who is looking to minimize the risk for postprocedure ED. This treatment has been studied only on prostates less than 80 g in size thus far. It lacks long-term durability data.

Invasive (Surgery) Therapy. Invasive treatment of symptomatic BPH involves surgery. The choice of the treatment approach depends on the size and location of the prostatic enlargement and patient factors, such as age and surgical risk. Invasive treatments are described in Table 54.3.

Invasive therapy is indicated when a decrease in urine flow causes discomfort, persistent residual urine, acute urinary retention because of obstruction with no reversible precipitating cause, or hydronephrosis. Intermittent catheterization or insertion of an indwelling catheter can temporarily reduce symptoms and bypass the obstruction. However, avoid long-term catheter use because of the increased risk for infection.

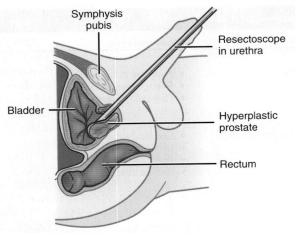

FIG. 54.4 Transurethral resection of the prostate.

Transurethral Incision of the Prostate. Transurethral incision of the prostate (TUIP) is a surgical procedure done under local anesthesia for men with moderate to severe symptoms. Several small incisions are made into the prostate gland to expand the urethra, which relieves pressure on the urethra and improves urine flow. TUIP is an option for patients with a small or moderately enlarged prostate gland.

Transurethral Resection of the Prostate. Transurethral resection of the prostate (TURP) is a surgical procedure involving the removal of prostate tissue using a resectoscope inserted through the urethra. TURP has long been considered the gold standard for surgical treatment of obstructing BPH. Most patients have marked improvements in symptoms and urinary flow rates. While in the past many TURP procedures required a longer hospital stay, many TURP procedures now are done on an outpatient basis.

In TURP no external surgical incision is made. A resectoscope is inserted through the urethra to excise and cauterize obstructing prostatic tissue (Fig. 54.4). A large 3-way indwelling catheter with a 30-mL balloon is inserted into the bladder after the procedure to provide hemostasis and to facilitate urinary drainage. If there is a large amount of hematuria with clots after surgery, then the bladder can be irrigated, either continuously or intermittently, for the first 24 hours to prevent obstruction from blood clots.

TURP was classically done with a monopolar resectoscope/loop. It sends a current through the patient during the resection to a grounding pad, so iso-osmolar fluid is used for irrigation. TURP has a relatively low risk, but caregivers must be vigilant for signs or symptoms of transurethral resection syndrome (TUR or TURP syndrome). This condition is manifested by nausea, vomiting, confusion, bradycardia, and hypertension. TUR syndrome is the result of hyponatremia due to longer operative times and prolonged intraoperative bladder irrigation with the iso-osmolar fluid. However, it is now common practice for a TURP to be done with a bipolar resectoscope/loop. This allows for saline to be used for irrigation and dramatically decreases the risk for TUR syndrome.

Other complications include bleeding and clot retention. Because bleeding is a common complication, patients taking aspirin, warfarin (Coumadin), or other anticoagulants must

TABLE 54.4 Nursing Assessment

Benign Prostatic Hyperplasia

Subjective Data
Important Health Information

Medications: Testosterone supplementation
Surgery or other treatments: Previous treatment for BPH

Functional Health Patterns

Health perception–health management: Knowledge of the condition
Nutritional-metabolic: Voluntary fluid restriction
Elimination: Urinary urgency, diminution in caliber and force of urinary stream. Hesitancy in starting voiding. Postvoid dribbling, urinary retention, urinary incontinence
Sleep-rest: Nocturia
Cognitive-perceptual: Dysuria, sensation of incomplete voiding, bladder discomfort
Sexuality-reproductive: Anxiety about sexual dysfunction

Objective Data
General
Older adult male

Urinary
Distended bladder on palpation. Smooth, firm, elastic enlargement of prostate on rectal examination

Possible Diagnostic Findings
Enlarged prostate on ultrasonography, bladder neck obstruction on cystoscopy, residual urine with postvoiding ultrasound or catheterization. WBCs, bacteria, or microscopic hematuria with bladder infection. ↑ Serum creatinine levels with renal involvement

stop taking medications several days before surgery. BPH medications are stopped after the procedure.

❖ NURSING MANAGEMENT: BENIGN PROSTATIC HYPERPLASIA

Because you will be most directly involved in care of patients with BPH having invasive therapies, the focus of nursing management in this section is on preoperative and postoperative care.

◆ Nursing Assessment

Subjective and objective data that should be obtained from a patient with BPH are outlined in Table 54.4.

Nursing Diagnoses

Nursing diagnoses for the patient with BPH before surgery may include:

- Acute pain
- Risk for infection
- Impaired urinary system function

Nursing diagnoses and interventions for the patient with BPH who has invasive therapy (surgery) are presented in eNursing Care Plan 54.1 (available on the website for this chapter).

◆ Planning

The overall preoperative goals for the patient having invasive procedures are to have (1) restoration of urinary drainage; (2)

resolution of any UTI; and (3) understanding of the upcoming procedure, implications for sexual function, and urinary control. The overall postoperative goals are to have (1) no complications, (2) restoration of urinary control, (3) complete bladder emptying, and (4) satisfying sexual expression.

◆ Nursing Implementation

◆ **Health Promotion.** The cause of BPH is largely attributed to the aging process. Health promotion focuses on early detection and treatment. The AUA currently recommends that men age 55 to 69 have the greatest potential benefit from PSA screening. The recommended screening interval is every 2 years.[8] When symptoms of BPH are present, further diagnostic screening may be needed (Table 54.2).

Some men find that consuming alcohol, caffeine, or other bladder irritants tends to increase prostatic voiding symptoms because the diuretic effect increases bladder distention and overactivity. Compounds found in common cough and cold remedies, such as pseudoephedrine (e.g., Sudafed) and phenylephrine (e.g., Allerest PE, Coricidin D), often worsen the symptoms of BPH. These drugs are α-adrenergic agonists that cause smooth muscle contraction. If this occurs, the patient should avoid these drugs.

Teach patients with obstructive symptoms to urinate every 2 to 3 hours and when they first feel the urge. This will minimize urinary stasis and acute urinary retention. Teach patients to maintain a normal level of fluid so that they do not become dehydrated. The patient may think that if he restricts his fluid intake, symptoms will be less severe, but this only increases the chances of an infection while concentrating his urine.

◆ **Acute Care.** The following discussion focuses on preoperative and postoperative care for the patient undergoing a TURP.

◆ *Preoperative Care.* Antibiotics are usually given before any invasive genitourinary (GU) procedure. Any infection of the urinary tract must be treated before surgery. Restoring urinary drainage and encouraging a high fluid intake (2 to 3 L/day unless contraindicated) are helpful in managing the infection. Prostatic obstruction may result in acute retention or inability to void. Urinary drainage must be restored before surgery.

A urethral catheter, such as a coudé (curved-tip) catheter, may be needed to restore bladder drainage. In many health care settings, 2% lidocaine gel is inserted into the urethra before catheter placement. The lidocaine gel acts as a lubricant, provides local anesthesia, and helps open the urethral lumen. If a sizable obstruction of the urethra exists, the HCP may insert a filiform catheter with enough rigidity to pass the obstruction. Aseptic technique is important to avoid introducing bacteria into the bladder. (Urinary catheters are discussed in Chapter 45.)

Patients may be concerned about the impact of the impending surgery on sexual function. Provide an opportunity for the patient and his partner to express their concerns. Tell the patient that his ejaculate volume may be decreased or absent after the procedure. Most types of prostatic surgery result in some degree of *retrograde ejaculation*. This is a condition in which some semen travels back into the bladder during orgasm instead of traveling out of the penis. This may decrease orgasmic sensations felt during ejaculation. Retrograde ejaculation is not harmful. The semen is voided during the next urination.

Postoperative Care. The main complications after surgery are hemorrhage, bladder spasms, urinary incontinence, and infection. Adjust the plan of care to the type of surgery, reasons for surgery, and patient's response to surgery.

After surgery, the patient will have a standard catheter or a triple-lumen catheter. Bladder irrigation is typically done to remove clotted blood from the bladder and ensure drainage of urine. The bladder is irrigated either manually on an intermittent basis or more often, as continuous bladder irrigation (CBI) with sterile normal saline solution or another prescribed solution. If the bladder is manually irrigated, instill 50 mL of irrigating solution and then withdraw with a syringe to remove clots that may be in the bladder and catheter. Painful bladder spasms often occur with manual irrigation.

With CBI, irrigating solution is continuously infused and drained from the bladder. The rate of infusion is based on the color of drainage. Ideally the urine drainage should be light pink without clots. Continuously monitor the inflow and outflow of the irrigant. If outflow is less than inflow, assess the catheter patency for kinks or clots. If the outflow is blocked and patency cannot be reestablished by manual irrigation, stop the CBI, and notify the HCP.

NURSING MANAGEMENT
Patient Receiving Bladder Irrigation

- Assess for bleeding and clots.
- Assess catheter patency by measuring intake and output and presence of bladder spasms.
- Manually irrigate catheter if bladder spasms or decreased outflow occurs.
- Give antispasmodics and analgesics as needed.
- Monitor catheter drainage for increased blood or clots.
- Discontinue CBI and notify HCP if obstruction occurs.
- Teach patient Kegel exercises after catheter removal.
- Provide care instructions for patient discharged with indwelling catheter.

Use careful aseptic technique when irrigating the bladder because bacteria can be easily introduced into the urinary tract. Secure the catheter to the leg with tape or a catheter strap to prevent urethral irritation and minimize the risk for bladder infection. The catheter should be connected to a closed-drainage system. Do not disconnect unless it is being removed, changed, or irrigated.

Blood clots are expected after prostate surgery for the first 24 to 36 hours. However, large amounts of bright red blood in the urine can indicate hemorrhage. Hemorrhage may occur from displacement of the catheter, dislodgment of a large clot, or increases in abdominal pressure.

Release or displacement of the catheter dislodges the balloon that provides counterpressure on the operative site. Traction on the catheter may be applied to provide counterpressure (tamponade) on the bleeding site in the prostate, thereby decreasing bleeding. Such traction can result in local necrosis if pressure is applied for too long. Pressure should be relieved on a scheduled basis by qualified personnel.

Activities that increase abdominal pressure should be avoided in the recovery period. These include sitting or walking for prolonged periods and straining to have a bowel movement (Valsalva maneuver).

Bladder spasms are a distressing complication for the patient after transurethral procedures. They occur because of irritation of the bladder mucosa from the insertion of the resectoscope, presence of a catheter, or clots leading to obstruction of the catheter. If bladder spasms develop, check the catheter for clots. If present, remove the clots by irrigation so that urine can flow freely. Tell the patient not to urinate around the catheter because this increases the chance of spasm. Belladonna and opium suppositories or other antispasmodics (e.g., oxybutynin [Ditropan XL]), along with relaxation techniques, are used to relieve the pain and decrease spasm.

The catheter is often removed 2 to 4 days after surgery. The patient should have a voiding trial after catheter removal. If he cannot urinate, he will have a catheter reinserted for a day or so or be taught to perform clean intermittent self-catheterization (see Chapter 45).

Sphincter tone may be poor right after catheter removal, resulting in urinary incontinence or dribbling. This is a common but distressing situation for the patient. Sphincter tone can be strengthened by having the patient practice Kegel exercises (pelvic floor muscle technique) 10 to 20 times per hour while awake. (Kegel exercises are discussed in Table 45.18.) Encourage the patient to practice starting and stopping the stream several times during urination. This helps the patient to target the correct pelvic floor muscles when doing Kegel exercises.

It can take several weeks to achieve urinary continence. In some instances, control of urine may never be fully regained. Continence can improve for up to 12 months. If continence has not been achieved by that time, the patient may be referred to a continence clinic. A variety of methods, including biofeedback, have been used to achieve positive results.

Teach the patient how to use a penile clamp, a condom catheter, or incontinence pads or briefs to avoid embarrassment from dribbling. In severe cases, an occlusive cuff that serves as an artificial sphincter can be surgically implanted to restore continence. Help the patient find ways to manage the problem that allow him to continue socializing and interacting with others. (Urinary incontinence is discussed in Chapter 45.)

Observe the patient for signs of infection. If an external wound is present (e.g., from an open, laparoscopic, or robotic-assisted prostatectomy), assess the area for redness, heat, swelling, and purulent drainage. Special care must be taken if a perineal incision is present because of the proximity of the anus. Avoid rectal procedures, such as rectal temperatures and enemas. The insertion of well-lubricated belladonna and opium suppositories is acceptable.

Dietary intervention and stool softeners are important to prevent the patient from straining while having bowel movements. Straining increases the intraabdominal pressure, which can lead to bleeding at the operative site. A diet high in fiber promotes the passage of stool.

◆ **Ambulatory Care.** Discharge planning and home care issues are important aspects of care after prostate surgery. Patient teaching includes (1) caring for an indwelling catheter (if one is in place), (2) managing urinary incontinence, (3) maintaining adequate oral fluid intake, (4) observing for signs and symptoms of urinary tract and wound infection, (5) preventing constipation, (6) avoiding heavy lifting (more than 10 lb [4.5 kg]), and (7) refraining from driving or intercourse after surgery as directed by the HCP.

The patient may have a change in sexual function after surgery. Recovery depends on the type of surgery done and the interval of time between when symptoms first appeared and the date of surgery. For example, it may take up to 1 to 2 years for complete sexual function to return after nerve-sparing prostatectomy. Many men have retrograde ejaculation because of trauma to the internal urethral sphincter. ED may occur if the nerves are cut or damaged during surgery. The patient may have anxiety over the change because of a perceived loss of his sex role, self-esteem, or quality of sexual interaction with his partner. Discuss these changes with the patient and his partner and allow them to ask questions and express their concerns. Sexual counseling and treatment options may be needed if ED becomes a chronic issue. (ED is discussed later in this chapter).

The bladder may take up to 2 months to return to its normal capacity. Teach the patient to drink at least 2 to 3 L of fluid per day and urinate every 2 to 3 hours to flush the urinary tract. Teach the patient to avoid or limit the amounts of bladder irritants, such as caffeine products, citrus juices, and alcohol. Because the patient may have incontinence or dribbling, he may incorrectly believe that decreasing fluid intake will relieve this problem.

Urethral strictures may result from instrumentation or catheterization. Treatment may include teaching the patient intermittent clean self-catheterization or having a urethral dilation.

Tell the patient to discuss the need for a yearly DRE with his HCP if he has had any procedure other than complete removal of the prostate. Hyperplasia or cancer can occur in the remaining prostatic tissue.

◆ **Evaluation**

The expected outcomes are that the patient with BPH who has surgery will

- Report acceptable pain control
- Report improved urinary function with no pain or incontinence

PROSTATE CANCER

Prostate cancer is a tumor of the prostate gland. Prostate cancer is the most common cancer among men, excluding skin cancer. It is the second leading cause of cancer death in men, exceeded only by lung cancer. The American Cancer Society estimates that in 2018 there will be 164,690 men diagnosed with prostate cancer, and 29,430 men will die from prostate cancer. A man has a 1 in 9 risk for developing prostate cancer in his lifetime. More than 2.9 million men in the United States are survivors of prostate cancer.[9]

Etiology and Pathophysiology

Prostate cancer is a slow-growing, androgen-dependent cancer. It can spread by 3 routes: by direct extension, through the lymph system, or through the bloodstream. Spread by direct extension involves the seminal vesicles, urethral mucosa, bladder wall, and external sphincter. The cancer later spreads through the lymphatic system to the regional lymph nodes. The bloodstream is the mode of spread to the axial skeleton (e.g., pelvic bones, head of the femur, lower lumbar spine), liver, and lungs.

Age, ethnicity, and family history are known risk factors for prostate cancer. The incidence of prostate cancer rises markedly after age 50. The median age at diagnosis is 66 years old. However, many cases occur in younger men, who sometimes have a more aggressive type of cancer.

Dietary factors and obesity may be related to prostate cancer. A diet high in red and processed meat and high-fat dairy products along with a low intake of vegetables and fruits may increase the risk for prostate cancer. Environment may play a role. There is an increased prevalence of prostate cancer in farmers and commercial pesticide applicators, possibly due to chemicals found in pesticides. It is not clear if smoking is a risk factor for prostate cancer.

PROMOTING HEALTH EQUITY

Cancers of the Male Reproductive System

Prostate Cancer
* Black men have the highest rate of prostate cancer.
* Black men are diagnosed with prostate cancer at an earlier age, have more advanced disease at the time of diagnosis, and have a higher mortality rate than do white men.
* Although the mortality rate for prostate cancer among black men is high, the mortality rate is declining.
* Asian American men have a lower incidence and lower mortality rates from prostate cancer than white men.

Testicular Cancer
* Testicular cancer occurs most often among whites than in other ethnic groups.

Genetic Link

Currently no known single gene causes prostate cancer. Some genes or gene mutations are more common in men with prostate cancer. From a genetics viewpoint, prostate cancer can be classified into 3 categories.

Most prostate cancers (about 75%) are considered *sporadic*, which means that damage to the genes occurs by chance after a person is born. Prostate cancer that runs in a family, called *familial prostate cancer*, is less common (about 20%). It occurs because of a combination of genes and environment or lifestyle factors. Familial prostate cancer is when 2 or more first-degree relatives (father, brother, son) are diagnosed with prostate cancer.

Hereditary (inherited) prostate cancer is rare (5% to 10%) and occurs when gene mutations are passed down in a family from 1 generation to the next. In hereditary prostate cancer, a family has any of the following characteristics: (1) 3 or more first-degree relatives with prostate cancer, (2) prostate cancer in 3 generations on the same side of the family, and (3) 2 or more close relatives (father, brother, son, grandfather, uncle, nephew) on the same side of the family diagnosed with prostate cancer before age 55.

Having a family history does not mean that a man will develop prostate cancer. It means that he has an increased risk. Men with a family history of prostate cancer should talk with their HCP about their concerns. It is important for the HCP to obtain a detailed family history. Depending on the findings, a referral to a genetic counselor may be appropriate.

Hereditary breast and ovarian cancer (HBOC) syndrome is associated with mutations in the *BRCA1* and/or *BRCA2* genes (BRCA stands for *BR*east *CA*ncer). Women with HBOC have an increased risk for breast and ovarian cancer. Men with HBOC have an increased risk for breast cancer and prostate cancer. Mutations in *BRCA1* and *BRCA2* cause only a small number of familial prostate cancers. Genetic testing may be appropriate for families with prostate cancer that have HBOC.

Clinical Manifestations and Complications

Prostate cancer typically has no symptoms in the early stages. Eventually, the patient may have LUTS similar to those of BPH. Pain in the lumbosacral area that radiates down to the hips or the legs, when combined with urinary symptoms, may indicate metastasis.

The tumor can spread to pelvic lymph nodes, bones, bladder, lungs, and liver. Once the tumor has spread to distant sites, the major problem becomes pain management. As the cancer

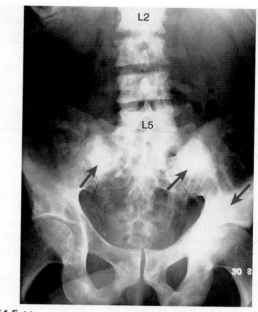

FIG. 54.5 Metastasis of prostate cancer to the pelvis and lumbar spine, indicated by *arrows*. (From Mettler F: *Essentials of radiology*, ed 2, Philadelphia, 2004, Saunders.)

spreads to the bones (common site of metastasis), pain can become severe, especially in the back and legs because of spinal cord compression and bone destruction (Fig. 54.5).

Diagnostic Studies

Most men in the United States with prostate cancer are diagnosed by PSA screening. As prostate cancer screening has become more widespread, smaller cancers are being found in older men. In most cases, slow-growing cancers probably do not need to be treated. Many men live and die *with* prostate cancer, but most will not die *from* it.

Men have a chance to make an informed decision with their HCP about whether to be screened for prostate cancer. Men should be told about the potential risks (e.g., subsequent evaluation and treatment that may not be needed) and benefits (early detection of prostate cancer) of PSA screening before being tested. After this discussion, men who want to be screened may have an annual PSA test and DRE. On DRE, an abnormal prostate may feel hard, nodular, and asymmetric.

The AUA thinks that men age 55 to 69 have the greatest potential benefit from PSA screening and recommend screening every 2 years.[8] Men at higher risk (black men, men with a first-degree relative with prostate cancer) will have an individualized screening schedule.

The American Cancer Society recommends that men should have a discussion with their HCP about screening for prostate cancer. Men should not be screened unless they have received this information. The discussion about screening should take place at:
* Age 50 for men who are at average risk for prostate cancer and are expected to live at least 10 more years.
* Age 45 for men at high risk for developing prostate cancer. This includes blacks and men who have a first-degree relative (father, brother, or son) diagnosed with prostate cancer at an early age (younger than age 65).
* Age 40 for men at even higher risk (those with more than 1 first-degree relative who had prostate cancer at an early age).

TABLE 54.5 Staging of Prostate Cancer

Stage	Tumor Size	Lymph Node Involvement	Metastasis	PSA Level	Gleason Score
I	Not felt on DRE. Not seen by visual imaging.	No	No	<10	≤6
II	Felt on DRE. Seen by imaging. Tumor confined to prostate.	No	No	10–20	6–7
III	Cancer outside prostate. Possible spread to seminal vesicles.	No	No	Any level	Any score
IV	Any size.	Any nodal involvement.	Yes	Any level	Any score

Adapted from American Cancer Society: How is prostate cancer staged? Retrieved from *www.cancer.org/Cancer/ProstateCancer/DetailedGuide/prostate-cancer-staging*.

High PSA levels do not always indicate prostate cancer. Mild elevations in PSA may occur with aging, BPH, recent ejaculation, constipation, acute or chronic prostatitis, or after long bike rides. Cystoscopy, indwelling urethral catheters, and prostate biopsies may cause transient increases in PSA levels.

Neither PSA nor DRE is a definitive diagnostic test for prostate cancer. If PSA levels are continually high or if the DRE is abnormal, a biopsy of the prostate tissue is usually done. Biopsy of prostate tissue is necessary to confirm the diagnosis of prostate cancer. The biopsy is typically done using a transrectal approach. In a transrectal ultrasound (TRUS) procedure, an ultrasound probe allows the HCP to see abnormalities in the prostate. When a suspicious area is found, biopsy needles are inserted through the wall of the rectum into the prostate to obtain tissue samples. A pathologic examination of the specimen is done to assess for malignant changes. For patients at a high risk for infection with a transrectal biopsy, or with a history of prior postbiopsy sepsis, a transperineal approach is another option if it is available at the agency. There can be a lower risk for infection with the transperineal approach as the biopsy needles do not pierce the rectal wall. It is typically done in the operating room.

Another approach for biopsies is to use an MRI/ultrasound fusion biopsy. In this approach, pelvic MRI 3-dimensional images are fused with real-time, transrectal ultrasound images. This new technique is more accurate than the traditional approach. Typically, men who are candidates for this procedure have a history of a previous negative ultrasound-guided biopsy and increasing PSA. This approach may also be used for men who are on active surveillance. However, as discussed earlier in this chapter, recent studies show risk assessment with MRI prior to biopsy and MRI-targeted biopsy to be superior to standard TRUS biopsy in men at risk for prostate cancer who have never had a prostate biopsy before.[5]

PSA is used to monitor the success of treatment. When treatment has been successful, with either prostatectomy or hormone therapy, PSA levels should fall to undetectable levels. With successful radiation therapy, the PSA level should decrease to a very low number (the nadir) and remain stable near that number. The regular measurement of PSA levels after treatment is important to evaluate the effectiveness of treatment and possible recurrence of prostate cancer.[10]

With advanced prostate cancer, serum alkaline phosphatase can be increased because of bone metastases. Other tests used to determine the location and extent of the spread of the cancer may include a nuclear medicine whole body bone scan, a CT scan of the abdomen and pelvis, and an MRI of the pelvis with special attention to the prostate.

Interprofessional Care

Chemoprevention of prostate cancer is an active area of research. As discussed earlier in this chapter, finasteride and dutasteride, used to treat BPH, may reduce the chance for getting prostate cancer. Men who are concerned about prostate cancer should discuss with their HCP the potential risks and benefits of taking finasteride or dutasteride.

Early recognition and treatment are important to control tumor growth, prevent metastasis, and preserve quality of life. Most patients (93%) with prostate cancer are diagnosed when the cancer is at a local or regional stage.[9,11] The 5-year survival rate with a diagnosis at this stage is almost 100%.

The most common classification system for determining the extent of prostate cancer is the tumor, node, and metastasis (TNM) system (Table 54.5). The tumor is graded based on tumor histology using 2 different grading systems: the Gleason scale and the Grade Group.[12] The Gleason scale grades the tumor from 1 to 5 based on the degree of glandular differentiation. Grade 1 represents the most well-differentiated or lowest grade (most like the original cells), and grade 5 represents the most poorly differentiated (unlike the original cells) or highest grade. The 2 most commonly occurring patterns of cells are graded, and the 2 scores are added together to create a Gleason score. Gleason score ranges from 6 to 10. Currently the lowest risk Gleason score is Gleason 6 (3+3).

The Grade Group system grades the cells based on their differentiation. The Grade Group assigns the tumor a number on a scale from 1 to 5. Grade Group 1 is the lowest risk and Grade Group 5 the highest risk. Currently, the Gleason score and the Grade Group system are used together. A low-risk, well-differentiated prostate cancer specimen may be graded a Grade Group 1, Gleason 6 (3+3) prostate cancer. The trend is moving toward Grade Group scoring only.

The PSA level at diagnosis and the patient's Gleason score and Grade Group are used with the TNM system to determine the stage of the tumor, which is vital to determine treatment options.

The interprofessional care of the patient with prostate cancer depends on the stage of the cancer and the patient's overall health (Table 54.6). None of these diagnostic options can predict the progression of prostate cancer. At all stages, there is more than one treatment option depending on the stage, Gleason score, and PSA. The decision of which treatment course to pursue should be made jointly by patients, their partners, and the interprofessional care team.[10,11]

Active Surveillance. Low-grade prostate cancer is relatively slow growing. Therefore a conservative approach to management of prostate cancer is active surveillance, or "watchful waiting." This strategy is appropriate when the patient has (1)

TABLE 54.6 Interprofessional Care

Prostate Cancer

Diagnostic Assessment
- History and physical examination
- Digital rectal examination (DRE)
- Prostate-specific antigen (PSA)
- Transrectal ultrasound (TRUS) or pelvic MRI
- Prostate biopsy
- CT abdomen and pelvis with contrast (to assess for metastatic disease)

Management

Active Surveillance
- Closely monitor PSA and DRE (annually, at minimum)
- Repeat/surveillance prostate biopsies
- Repeat imaging
- Consider genomic testing on biopsy tissue, if appropriate

Surgery
- Radical prostatectomy
- Cryotherapy
- Orchiectomy (for metastatic disease)

Radiation Therapy
- External beam for primary, adjuvant, and recurrent disease
- Brachytherapy

Drug Therapy
- Androgen deprivation therapy (Table 54.7)
- Chemotherapy for metastatic disease

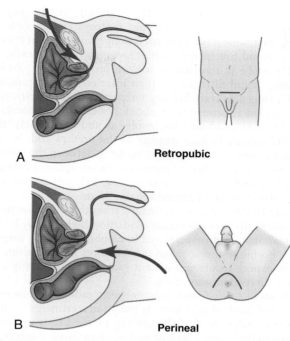

FIG. 54.6 Common approaches used to perform a prostatectomy. A, Retropubic approach involves a midline abdominal incision. B, Perineal approach involves an incision between the scrotum and the anus.

a life expectancy of less than 10 years (low risk for dying of the disease); (2) a low-grade, low-stage tumor; and (3) serious coexisting medical conditions. With active surveillance, patients are typically followed with frequent PSA measurements and DRE to monitor the progress of the disease. Significant changes in the PSA level, the DRE, or the development of symptoms, warrant a reevaluation of treatment options.

Surgical Therapy

Radical Prostatectomy. With radical prostatectomy, the entire prostate gland, seminal vesicles, and part of the bladder neck (ampulla) are removed. The entire prostate is removed because the cancer tends to be in many different places within the gland. A pelvic lymph node dissection is typically done at the same time as prostatectomy to pathologically assess for nodal metastases in the local pelvic area. Typically, a higher number of lymph nodes are removed and dissected if the prostate cancer is higher grade/higher risk on biopsy. Surgery is usually not an option for advanced-stage disease except to relieve symptoms associated with obstruction.

Traditional surgical approaches for an open radical prostatectomy include retropubic and perineal approaches (Fig. 54.6). With the *retropubic* approach, a low midline abdominal incision is made to access the prostate gland and the pelvic lymph nodes can be dissected. With the *perineal* resection, an incision is made between the scrotum and anus.

A *robotic-assisted* (e.g., da Vinci system) prostatectomy is a type of surgery in which the HCP sits at a computer console while controlling high-resolution cameras and microsurgical instruments. Robotics is being used more often since it allows for increased precision, visualization, and dexterity by the HCP when removing the prostate gland. It results in less bleeding, less pain, and a faster recovery compared with other approaches.[13]

After surgery, the patient has a large indwelling catheter with a 20-mL or 30-mL balloon placed in the bladder via the urethra. A drain is left in the surgical site to aid in removing drainage from the area. This drain is typically removed after a few days. Because the perineal approach has a higher risk for infection (because of the location of the incision related to the anus), careful dressing changes and perineal care after each bowel movement are important for comfort and to prevent infection. Depending on the type of surgery, the length of hospital stay ranges from 1 to 3 days.

Two major adverse outcomes after a radical prostatectomy are ED and urinary incontinence. The incidence of ED depends on the patient's age, preoperative sexual function, whether nerve-sparing surgery was done, and the HCP's expertise. Sexual function after surgery tends to return gradually over at least 24 months or more. Phosphodiesterase type 5 (PDE5) inhibitor medications may help improve sexual function.

Problems with urinary control may occur for the first few months after surgery because the bladder must be reattached to the urethra after the prostate is removed. Over time, the bladder adjusts, and most men regain urinary continence. Kegel exercises strengthen the pelvic floor muscles and the urinary sphincter and may help improve continence. (Kegel exercises are discussed in Table 45.18.) Other complications associated with surgery include hemorrhage, seroma, lymphocele, urinary retention, infection, wound dehiscence, and VTE.[14]

Nerve-Sparing Procedure. Near the prostate gland are neurovascular bundles that maintain erectile functioning. The preservation of these bundles during a prostatectomy is possible while still removing all the cancer. Nerve-sparing prostatectomy is not indicated for patients with cancer outside of the prostate gland. Although the risk for ED is reduced with this procedure, there is no guarantee that potency will be maintained.

Cryotherapy. *Cryotherapy* (cryoablation) is a surgical technique for prostate cancer that destroys cancer cells by freezing the tissue. It has been used both as an initial treatment and as a second-line treatment after radiation therapy has failed. A TRUS probe is inserted to see the prostate gland. Probes containing liquid nitrogen are then inserted into the prostate. Liquid nitrogen delivers freezing temperatures, thus destroying the tissue. The treatment takes about 2 hours under general or spinal anesthesia and does not involve an abdominal incision.

Complications include damage to the urethra and, in rare cases, an urethrorectal fistula (an opening between the urethra and rectum) or a urethrocutaneous fistula (an opening between the urethra and skin). Tissue sloughing, ED, urinary incontinence, prostatitis, and hemorrhage can occur.

Radiation Therapy. Radiation therapy is another common treatment option for prostate cancer. Radiation therapy may be the only treatment, or it may be used in combination with surgery or with hormone therapy. Salvage radiation therapy given for prostate cancer recurrence after a radical prostatectomy may improve survival in some men.

External Beam Radiation. External beam radiation is the most widely used method of delivering radiation treatments for men with prostate cancer. This therapy can be used to treat cancer confined to the prostate and/or surrounding tissue. Patients are usually treated on an outpatient basis 5 days a week for 4 to 8 weeks. Each treatment lasts less than 1 hour.

Side effects from radiation can be acute (occurring during treatment or within 90 days that follow) or delayed (occurring months or years after treatment). The most common side effects involve changes to the skin (dryness, redness, irritation, pain), gastrointestinal tract (diarrhea, abdominal cramping, bleeding, radiation proctitis), urinary tract (dysuria, hematuria, frequency, hesitancy, urgency, nocturia, radiation cystitis), and sexual function.[15] Fatigue may occur. There is a rare risk for secondary cancers after radiation to the pelvic area (e.g., bladder cancer, rectal cancer). In patients with localized prostate cancer, cure rates with external beam radiation are comparable to those with radical prostatectomy.

Brachytherapy. *Brachytherapy* involves placing radioactive seed implants into the prostate gland. This delivers high doses of radiation directly to the tissue while sparing the surrounding tissue (rectum and bladder). The radioactive seeds are placed in the prostate gland with a needle through a grid template guided by TRUS (Fig. 54.7) to ensure accurate placement of the seeds.

Because brachytherapy is a one-time outpatient procedure, many patients find this more convenient than external beam radiation treatment. Brachytherapy is best suited for patients with early-stage disease. The most common side effect is the development of urinary irritative or obstructive problems. Some men may have ED. The AUA Symptom Index (Table 54.1) can be used to measure urinary function for patients undergoing brachytherapy and can be incorporated into nursing management. For those with more advanced tumors, brachytherapy may be offered in combination with external beam radiation treatment.[16] (Brachytherapy is discussed in Chapter 15.)

Drug Therapy. The forms of drug therapy available for the treatment of advanced or metastatic prostate cancer are androgen deprivation (hormone) therapy, chemotherapy, or a combination of both.

Androgen Deprivation Therapy. Prostate cancer growth is largely dependent on the presence of androgens. *Androgen deprivation therapy* (ADT) reduces the levels of circulating androgens to reduce the tumor growth.[17] Androgen deprivation

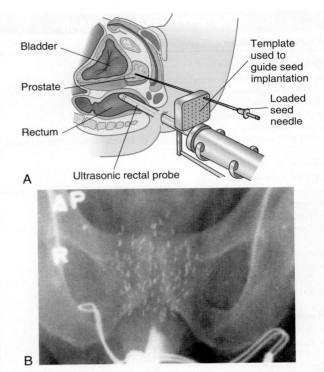

FIG. 54.7 A, Prostate brachytherapy. Implantation of radioactive seeds with a needle guided by ultrasound and a template grid. **B,** Radioactive seeds. (*B,* From Abeloff MD, Armitage JO, Niederhuber JE, et al, eds: *Abeloff's clinical oncology,* ed 4, 2008, Churchill Livingstone.)

can be produced by inhibiting androgen production or blocking androgen receptors (Table 54.7).

One of the biggest challenges with ADT is that almost all tumors treated become resistant to this therapy (*hormone refractory*) within a few years. A high PSA level is often the first sign that this therapy is no longer effective. Patients taking ADT have an increased risk for cardiovascular side effects, including high serum cholesterol and triglyceride levels and coronary artery disease.

Osteoporosis and fractures may occur in those receiving ADT. Drugs recommended to reduce bone mineral loss include zoledronic acid (Reclast) and raloxifene (Evista). Zoledronic acid is a bisphosphonate therapy given IV. A rare complication of therapy is osteonecrosis of the jaw. Denosumab (Prolia, Xgeva), a drug that slows the breakdown of bone, may be used to increase bone mass in men with nonmetastatic prostate cancer.

Androgen synthesis inhibitors. The hypothalamus produces luteinizing hormone–releasing hormone (LHRH), which stimulates the anterior pituitary to produce luteinizing hormone (LH) and follicle-stimulating hormone (FSH). LH stimulates the testicular Leydig cells to make testosterone. *LHRH agonists* super stimulate the pituitary, downregulating the LHRH receptors and leading to a refractory condition in which the anterior pituitary is unresponsive to LHRH. These drugs cause an initial, transient increase in LH and FSH; testosterone abruptly rises resulting in a *flare*. Symptoms may worsen during this time. However, with continued administration, LH and testosterone levels decrease.

LHRH agonists include goserelin (Zoladex), leuprolide (Lupron Depot, Eligard), and triptorelin (Trelstar) (Table 54.7). These drugs essentially produce a chemical castration similar to the effects of an orchiectomy. They are given by subcutaneous or IM injections on a regular basis. Viadur is an implant that is placed subcutaneously and delivers leuprolide continuously for 1 year.

TABLE 54.7 Drug Therapy
Androgen Deprivation Therapy for Prostate Cancer

Therapy	Mechanism of Action	Side Effects
Androgen Receptor Blockers bicalutamide (Casodex) enzalutamide (Xtandi) flutamide nilutamide (Nilandron)	• Block action of testosterone by competing with receptor sites	• Loss of libido, erectile dysfunction, and hot flashes • Breast pain and gynecomastia
Androgen Synthesis Inhibitors **CYP17 Enzyme Inhibitor** abiraterone (Zytiga)	• Inhibits CYP17, an enzyme needed to produce testosterone • Inhibits testosterone synthesis from testes, adrenal glands, and prostate cancer cells	• Joint swelling, fluid retention • Muscle discomfort • Hot flashes • Diarrhea
LHRH Agonists goserelin (Zoladex) leuprolide (Eligard , Lupron Depot) triptorelin (Trelstar)	• ↓ Secretion of LH and FSH • ↓ Testosterone production	• Hot flashes, gynecomastia, ↓ libido, erectile dysfunction • Depression and mood changes
LHRH Antagonist degarelix (Firmagon)	• Blocks LH receptors • Immediate testosterone suppression	• Pain, redness, and swelling at injection site • High liver enzymes

Degarelix (Firmagon) is an *LHRH antagonist* that lowers testosterone levels to castration levels. Unlike the LHRH agonists, degarelix does not cause a testosterone flare because it acts directly to block LH and FSH receptors. It is given as a subcutaneous injection. Results are seen in 3 days.

Abiraterone (Zytiga) works by inhibiting an enzyme, CYP17, which is needed to produce testosterone. This drug is given orally to men with castration-resistant prostate cancer, usually in combination with prednisone. It improves overall survival by 4 to 5 months.

Androgen receptor blockers. Androgen receptor blockers are another classification of antiandrogen drugs that compete with circulating androgens at the receptor sites. Flutamide, nilutamide (Nilandron), bicalutamide, and enzalutamide (Xtandi) are androgen receptor blockers. They are taken daily as an oral medication and can be used in combination with an LHRH agonist (e.g., goserelin, leuprolide). Combining an androgen receptor blocker with an LHRH agonist results in combined androgen blockade.

Chemotherapy. The use of chemotherapy is limited to treatment for those with hormone-refractory prostate cancer (HRPC) in late-stage disease. In HRPC the cancer is progressing despite treatment. This occurs in patients who have taken an antiandrogen for a certain period. The goal of chemotherapy is mainly palliative.

Some commonly used chemotherapy drugs for prostate cancer include cabazitaxel (Jevtana), cyclophosphamide, docetaxel (Taxotere), estramustine (Emcyt), mitoxantrone, paclitaxel (Abraxane), and vinblastine.

Men with advanced prostate cancer who have HRPC may receive a vaccine (sipuleucel-T [Provenge]). We do not know exactly how, but the vaccine stimulates the patient's system against the cancer. Use prolongs survival by about 4 months but does not reduce tumor burden. It is individually prepared for each man by a process that combines his own WBCs with granulocyte-macrophage colony-stimulating factor (GM-CSF), which then attacks the prostate tumor cells.

Radiotherapy. Radium-223 dichloride (Xofigo) can be used in the treatment of patients with castration-resistant prostate cancer, symptomatic bone metastases, and no known visceral metastatic disease. It is an alpha particle–emitting radiotherapy drug that mimics calcium and forms complexes with hydroxyapatite at areas of increased bone turnover, such as bone metastases.

Orchiectomy. A bilateral orchiectomy is the surgical removal of the testes. It may be done alone or after prostatectomy. It is the gold standard for androgen deprivation. There are no side effects to be managed. It is very low cost when compared with other options. For advanced stages of prostate cancer, an orchiectomy is an option for cancer control, with rapid relief of bone pain associated with advanced tumors.

Orchiectomy may shrink the prostate, thus relieving urinary obstruction in the later stages of disease when surgery is not an option. After an orchiectomy, weight gain and loss of muscle mass can change a man's physical appearance. These physical changes can affect self-esteem, leading to grief and depression. Because this procedure is permanent, many men prefer drug therapy over an orchiectomy.

Culturally Competent Care: Prostate Cancer

Nurses need to be aware of ethnic and cultural considerations when providing information about the risk for prostate cancer and screening recommendations. Consider not only the ethnic differences in the incidence of prostate cancer but also differences in health promotion practices.

Black men have the highest mortality rates from prostate cancer, in part because their prostate cancer often is more advanced at the time of diagnosis. Despite the availability of screening measures (PSA and DRE), black men and those in lower socioeconomic groups may not access these services. This is only partially related to knowledge levels about prostate cancer. In comparison to white men, black men with prostate cancer report more problems with financial access to transportation and health care costs. They describe using more religious coping strategies. White men are perceived as receiving more favorable treatment from their HCPs than black men.[18]

Although exposure to electronic and print media is successful in informing some men about prostate cancer, the effectiveness differs significantly based on demographic variables, such as ethnicity, age, education level, and socioeconomic level. Ideally, all men should be aware of the risks associated with prostate cancer and the screening methods available. Consider the best method to communicate this information to men of all cultures and ethnicities to promote understanding and participation in prostate cancer screening for men in at-risk groups.

❖ NURSING MANAGEMENT: PROSTATE CANCER

◆ Nursing Assessment

Subjective and objective data that should be obtained from a patient with prostate cancer are outlined in Table 54.8.

◆ Nursing Diagnoses

Nursing diagnoses for the patient with prostate cancer depend on the stage of the cancer. General ones may include:
- Lack of knowledge
- Acute pain
- Urinary retention and impaired urinary system function
- Impaired sexual functioning
- Anxiety

◆ Planning

The overall goals are that the patient with prostate cancer will (1) be an active participant in the treatment plan, (2) have acceptable pain control, (3) follow the therapeutic plan, (4) understand the effect of the therapeutic plan on sexual function, and (5) find an acceptable way to manage the impact on bladder and bowel function.

◆ Nursing Implementation

◆ Health Promotion. One of the most important roles in relation to prostate cancer is to encourage patients, in consultation with their HCPs, to have annual prostate screening (PSA and DRE). The age at which to begin screening was discussed earlier on p. 1263. Because of their increased risk for prostate cancer, black men and other men at high risk, such as those with a family history of prostate cancer, should discuss the need for annual PSA and DRE beginning at age 45.[9]

◆ Acute Care. Care of the patient having a radical prostatectomy is similar to surgical procedures for BPH. Nursing interventions for the patient who has radiation therapy and chemotherapy are discussed in Chapter 15. Another consideration is the patient's psychologic response to a diagnosis of cancer. Provide sensitive, caring support for the patient and his family to help them cope with the diagnosis. Prostate cancer support groups are available for men and their families to encourage them to be active, informed participants in their own care.

◆ Ambulatory Care. Teach catheter care if the patient is discharged with an indwelling catheter in place. Teach the patient to clean the urethral meatus with soap and water once a day; maintain a high fluid intake; keep the collecting bag lower than the bladder at all times; and keep the catheter securely anchored to the inner thigh or abdomen. Tell them to report any signs of bladder infection, such as bladder spasms, fever, or hematuria.

If urinary incontinence is a problem, encourage the patient to practice pelvic floor muscle exercises (Kegel exercises) at every urination and throughout the day. Continuous practice during the 4- to 6-week healing process improves the success

---

TABLE 54.8 Nursing Assessment
Prostate Cancer

Subjective Data
Important Health Information
Medications: Testosterone supplements. Use of any medications affecting urinary tract such as morphine, anticholinergics, monoamine oxidase inhibitors, and tricyclic antidepressants

Functional Health Patterns
Health perception–health management: Positive family history. ↑ Fatigue and malaise
Nutritional-metabolic: High-fat diet. Anorexia, weight loss (may indicate metastasis)
Elimination: Hesitancy or straining to start stream, urinary urgency, frequency, retention with dribbling, weak stream, hematuria
Sleep-rest: Nocturia
Cognitive-perceptual: Dysuria. Low back pain radiating to legs or pelvis, bone pain (may indicate metastasis). Pain level
Self-perception–self-concept: Anxiety about self-concept

Objective Data
General
Older adult male. Pelvic lymphadenopathy (late sign)

Urinary
Distended bladder on palpation. Unilaterally hard, enlarged, fixed prostate on rectal examination

Musculoskeletal
Pathologic fractures (metastasis)

Possible Diagnostic Findings
Serum PSA. Serum alkaline phosphatase. Nodular and irregular prostate on ultrasonography, positive biopsy results. Anemia

---

rate. Products used for incontinence specifically designed for men are available through home care product catalogs and retail stores. (Urinary incontinence is discussed in Chapter 45).

Palliative and end-of-life care are often appropriate and beneficial to the patient with advanced disease and his family (see Chapter 9). Common problems with advanced prostate cancer include fatigue, bladder outlet obstruction and ureteral obstruction (caused by compression of the urethra and/or ureters from tumor mass or lymph node metastasis), severe bone pain and fractures (from bone metastasis), spinal cord compression (from spinal metastasis), and leg edema (from lymphedema, VTE). Nursing interventions must focus on all these problems.

Pain management is one of the most important aspects of your care for these patients. Pain control involves ongoing pain assessment, giving prescribed medications (both opioid and nonopioid agents), and nonpharmacologic methods of pain relief (e.g., relaxation breathing). (Pain management is further discussed in Chapter 8).

◆ Evaluation

The outcomes are that the patient with prostate cancer will
- Be an active participant in the treatment plan
- Have acceptable pain control
- Follow the therapeutic plan
- Understand the effect of the treatment on sexual function
- Find an acceptable way to manage the impact on bladder or bowel function

PROSTATITIS

Etiology and Pathophysiology

Prostatitis is a broad term that describes a group of inflammatory and noninflammatory conditions affecting the prostate gland. Prostatitis is one of the most common urologic disorders. It is thought that 10% to 15% of all men in the United States will have prostatitis in their lifetime.[19] Almost 2 million men are treated for prostatitis every year.

The 4 categories of prostatitis syndromes are (1) acute bacterial prostatitis, (2) chronic bacterial prostatitis, (3) chronic prostatitis/chronic pelvic pain syndrome, and (4) asymptomatic inflammatory prostatitis. The most common type is nonbacterial.

Both acute and chronic bacterial prostatitis generally result from organisms reaching the prostate gland by ascending from the urethra, descending from the bladder, or invading via the bloodstream or the lymphatic channels. Common causative organisms are *Escherichia coli* (most common), *Klebsiella, Pseudomonas, Enterobacter, Proteus, Chlamydia trachomatis, Neisseria gonorrhoeae,* and group D streptococci.

Chronic bacterial prostatitis differs from acute prostatitis in that it involves recurrent episodes of infection. It is the most common reason for recurrent UTIs in adult men.

Chronic prostatitis/chronic pelvic pain syndrome describes a syndrome of prostate and urinary pain in the absence of an obvious infectious process. The cause of this syndrome is not known. It may occur after a viral illness, or it may be associated with sexually transmitted infections (STIs), especially in younger adults. A culture reveals no causative organisms, but leukocytes may be found in prostatic secretions.

Asymptomatic inflammatory prostatitis is usually diagnosed in those who have no symptoms but are found to have an inflammatory process in the prostate. These patients are usually diagnosed during the evaluation of other GU tract problems. Leukocytes are present in the seminal fluid from the prostate. The cause of this process is unclear.

Clinical Manifestations and Complications

Common manifestations of acute prostatitis include fever, chills, back pain, and perineal pain. In addition, acute urinary symptoms such as dysuria, urinary frequency, urgency, and cloudy urine may occur. The patient may progress to acute urinary retention caused by prostatic swelling if he remains untreated. With DRE, the prostate is extremely swollen, extremely tender, and boggy.

Complications of prostatitis are epididymitis and cystitis. Sexual function may be affected as manifested by postejaculation pain, libido problems, and ED. Prostatic abscess is a potential, but rare, complication.

In chronic bacterial prostatitis and chronic prostatitis/chronic pelvic pain syndrome, manifestations are similar but generally milder than those of acute bacterial prostatitis. These include irritative voiding symptoms (frequency, urgency, dysuria), backache, perineal and pelvic pain, and ejaculatory pain. Obstructive symptoms are rare unless there is coexisting BPH. With DRE, the prostate feels enlarged and soft or boggy and can be slightly tender with palpation. Chronic prostatitis can predispose the patient to recurrent UTIs.

The clinical features of prostatitis can mimic those of a UTI. However, it is important to remember that acute cystitis is not common in men.

Diagnostic Studies

Because patients with prostatitis have urinary symptoms, a urinalysis (UA) and urine culture and sensitivities are needed. Often WBCs and bacteria are present. The patient with a fever needs blood cultures and a complete blood count (CBC) to check the WBC count. The PSA test may be done to rule out prostate cancer. However, PSA levels are often increased with prostatic inflammation or infection. Thus, when inflammation or infection is present, the PSA may not be considered diagnostic.

Microscopic evaluation and culture of expressed prostate secretion can potentially be useful in the diagnosis of prostatitis. Expressed prostate secretion is obtained using a premassage and postmassage test. The patient is asked to void into a specimen cup just before and just after a vigorous prostate massage. Prostatic massage (for expressed prostate secretion) is becoming less common in clinical practice unless all other diagnostic options are exhausted. It should not be done if acute bacterial prostatitis is suspected, since compression is extremely painful and can increase the risk for bacterial spread. TRUS is not useful in the diagnosis of prostatitis. However, TRUS or MRI may be done to rule out an abscess in the prostate.

❖ Interprofessional and Nursing Care

Antibiotics commonly used for acute and chronic bacterial prostatitis include fluoroquinolones (e.g., ciprofloxacin [Cipro], levofloxacin, ofloxacin), clindamycin, cephalexin (Keflex), trimethoprim/sulfamethoxazole (Bactrim), doxycycline (Vibramycin), or tetracycline. Antibiotics are usually given orally for up to 4 weeks for acute bacterial prostatitis. However, if the patient has high fever or other signs of impending sepsis, he will be hospitalized and given IV antibiotics.

Men with chronic bacterial prostatitis may be given oral antibiotic therapy for 8 to 12 weeks. Antibiotics may be given for a lifetime if the patient is immunocompromised. A short course of oral antibiotics is usually prescribed for those with chronic prostatitis/chronic pelvic pain syndrome in case of bacterial infection. However, antibiotic therapy is often ineffective for patients whose prostatitis is not due to bacteria.

Patients with acute and chronic bacterial prostatitis tend to have a great amount of discomfort. The pain resolves as the infection is treated. However, they may have residual discomfort for several weeks after a course of antibiotics, as it takes time for the prostate to return to normal. Pain management for patients with chronic prostatitis/chronic pelvic pain syndrome is more difficult because the pain persists for weeks to months. No single approach provides relief for everyone. Antiinflammatory agents (e.g., ibuprofen, naproxen) may be used for pain control in prostatitis, but these drugs provide only moderate pain relief.

Warm sitz baths may help to relieve pain. Relaxation of muscle tissue in the prostate using α-adrenergic blockers (e.g., tamsulosin, alfuzosin) are effective in reducing discomfort for some men.

Acute urinary retention can develop in acute prostatitis, requiring insertion of a urinary catheter. However, passage of a catheter through an inflamed urethra is contraindicated in acute prostatitis. The placement of a suprapubic catheter may then be indicated. Repetitive prostatic massage may be recommended as adjunct therapy for prostatitis for men. This potentially relieves congestion within the prostate by squeezing out excess prostatic secretions, providing pain relief. Like massage, measures to stimulate ejaculation (masturbation and intercourse) may help to drain the prostate and provide some relief.

Because the prostate can serve as a source of bacteria, fluid intake should be kept at a high level. Encourage the patient to drink plenty of fluids. Men with acute bacterial prostatitis have increased fluid needs from fever and infection. Management of fever is an important nursing intervention.

PROBLEMS OF THE PENIS

Health problems of the penis are rare if STIs are excluded (see Chapter 52). Problems of the penis may be classified as congenital, problems of the prepuce, problems with the erectile mechanism, and cancer.

CONGENITAL PROBLEMS

Hypospadias is a urologic problem in which the urethral meatus is on the ventral surface of the penis. This can be anywhere from the corona to the perineum. Causes include hormonal influences in utero, environmental factors, and genetic factors. Surgical repair of hypospadias, especially those that are close to the scrotum or perineum, is usually done while the boy is young. Surgery may be done if it is associated with *chordee* (a painful downward curvature of the penis during erection) or if it prevents intercourse or normal urination. Surgery may be considered for cosmetic reasons or emotional well-being in older boys and adult men.

PROBLEMS OF PREPUCE

Problems of the prepuce (foreskin) are not as common in the United States as in most other countries because circumcision (surgical removal of the foreskin of the penis) is a routine procedure for many male infants. However, these conditions do occur and can be very painful and potentially an emergency. It is important to be familiar with these problems so appropriate treatment and pain relief can be promptly provided.

Phimosis is a tightness or constriction of the foreskin around the head of the penis, making retraction difficult (Fig. 54.8, *A*). It is caused by chronic inflammation of the foreskin. It is usually associated with poor hygiene techniques that allow bacterial and yeast organisms to become trapped under the foreskin. Topical corticosteroid cream, with or without an antifungal, applied 2 or 3 times daily to the exterior and interior of the tip of the foreskin may be effective in the initial treatment of inflammation. Definitive treatment is either circumcision or a dorsal slit surgical procedure.

Paraphimosis is tightness of the foreskin resulting in the inability to pull it forward from a retracted position, thus preventing normal return over the glans. It is a urologic emergency. A tightly retracted phimotic ring can compromise arterial flow to the glans. An ulcer can develop if the foreskin stays contracted (Fig. 54.8, *B*). Paraphimosis can occur when the foreskin is pulled back during bathing, use of urinary catheters, or intercourse and is not placed back in the forward position. Replacement of the foreskin after careful cleaning helps prevent this condition. The goal of treatment is to return the foreskin to its natural position over the glans penis through manual reduction. One strategy involves pushing the glans back through the prepuce by applying constant thumb pressure while the index fingers pull the prepuce over the glans. Ice and/or hand

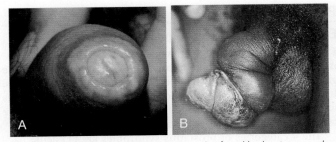

FIG. 54.8 **A,** Phimosis: inability to retract the foreskin due to secondary lesions on the prepuce (foreskin). **B,** Paraphimosis: ulcer with edema from foreskin remaining contracted over the prepuce (foreskin).

compression on the foreskin, glans, and penis may be applied before to reduce edema. Treatment may include antibiotics or warm soaks. Definitive treatment is either circumcision or a dorsal slit.

PROBLEMS OF ERECTILE MECHANISM

Priapism is a painful erection lasting longer than 4 hours. It is caused by complex vascular and neurologic factors that result in an obstruction of venous outflow in the penis. Conditions that may be associated with priapism include sickle cell disease, diabetes, trauma to the spinal cord, degenerative lesions of the spine, and drugs (e.g., cocaine, trazodone). Vasoactive drugs (e.g., alprostadil) injected into the corpora cavernosa for ED can cause priapism. Complications include penile tissue necrosis caused by lack of blood flow or hydronephrosis from bladder distention. Without immediate medical treatment, the risk for permanent ED is high.

Treatment varies depending on the cause. Patients with sickle cell disease may need a blood exchange transfusion. Other patients may be treated with sedatives, an injection of a smooth muscle relaxant directly into the penis, or aspiration and irrigation of the corpora cavernosa with a large-bore needle.

Peyronie's disease is caused by plaque formation in the corpora cavernosa of the penis that results in inelasticity during erection. The palpable, nontender, hard plaque formation may occur spontaneously or result from trauma to the penile shaft. The plaque prevents adequate blood flow into the spongy tissue, which results in a curvature during erection. The condition is not dangerous but can result in painful erections, ED, or embarrassment. Patients may improve slightly over time, stabilize, or need surgery. Collagenase clostridium histolyticum (Xiaflex) and intralesional verapamil (ILV) are medication options. Each is given as a series of injections into the plaque. The goal of therapy is to reduce the curvature and allow men to avoid surgery.

CANCER OF PENIS

Cancer of the penis is rare in the United States. More than 95% are squamous cell carcinoma. It occurs more often in men who have human papillomavirus (HPV) infection and phimosis or uncircumcised men.[20] The tumor may appear as a superficial ulceration or a pimple-like nodule. Pain is rare. This contributes to a delay in seeking treatment. The nontender warty lesion may be mistaken for a genital wart. Treatment in the early stages is laser removal of the growth. A radical resection of the penis may be done if the cancer has spread. Surgery, radiation, or chemotherapy are options, depending on the extent of the disease, lymph node involvement, or metastasis.

PROBLEMS OF SCROTUM AND TESTES

It is important for the patient to see his HCP if he feels any scrotal lumps or painful areas in his scrotum or testes. He would not be able to tell normal variations from cancer when performing self-examination. An incidental finding of a "scrotal lump" results in high anxiety for the patient.

INFLAMMATORY AND INFECTIOUS PROBLEMS

Skin Problems

The skin of the scrotum is susceptible to several common skin diseases. The most common are fungal infections, dermatitis (neurodermatitis, contact dermatitis, seborrheic dermatitis), and parasitic infections (scabies, lice). These conditions involve discomfort for the patient but are associated with few severe complications (see Chapter 23).

Epididymitis

Epididymitis is an acute, painful inflammatory process of the epididymis (Fig. 54.9). It is often due to an infectious process, trauma, or urinary reflux down the ductus (vas) deferens. It is usually unilateral. Swelling may progress to the point that the epididymis and testis are indistinguishable. In men younger than 35 years of age, the most common cause is gonorrhea or chlamydial infection. In men over 35, the most common cause is *E. coli* infection. BPH and prostatitis are common contributors in older men.

The use of antibiotics is important for both partners if the transmission is through sexual contact. Encourage patients to refrain from sexual intercourse until treatment is complete. They should use a condom if they do engage in intercourse. Conservative treatment consists of elevating the scrotum, ice packs, and analgesics. Ambulation places the scrotum in a dependent position and increases pain. Acute tenderness subsides within 1 week, although some discomfort and swelling may last for weeks or months.

Orchitis

Orchitis refers to an acute inflammation of the testis. In orchitis, the testis is painful, tender, and swollen. It generally occurs after an episode of bacterial or viral infection, such as mumps, pneumonia, tuberculosis, or syphilis. It can be a side effect of epididymitis, trauma, infectious mononucleosis, influenza, catheterization, or complicated UTI. Mumps orchitis is a condition contributing to infertility that can be avoided by childhood vaccination against mumps. Treatment is similar to that for epididymitis.

CONGENITAL PROBLEMS

Cryptorchidism (undescended testes) is failure of the testes to descend into the scrotal sac before birth. It is the most common congenital testicular condition and is more common on the right. It may occur bilaterally or unilaterally and may be a contributing factor to male infertility if corrective surgery is not done by 2 years of age. The incidence of testicular cancer is higher if the condition is not corrected before puberty. Surgery is done to locate and suture the testis or testes to the scrotum.

ACQUIRED PROBLEMS

Hydrocele

A *hydrocele* is a nontender, fluid-filled mass that results from interference with lymphatic drainage of the scrotum and swelling

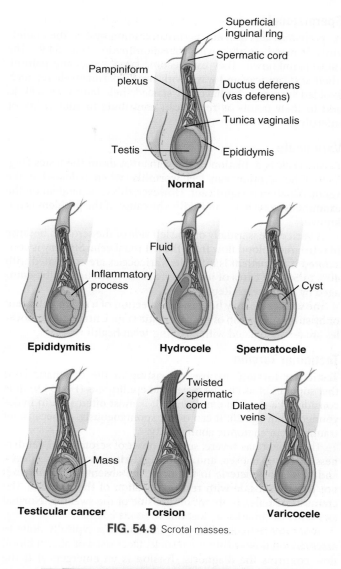

FIG. 54.9 Scrotal masses.

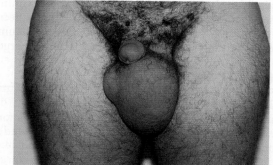

FIG. 54.10 Hydrocele. (From Swartz MH: *Textbook of physical diagnosis,* ed 6, Philadelphia, 2010, Saunders.)

of the tunica vaginalis that surrounds the testis (Fig. 54.10; also Fig. 54.9). Diagnosis is aided by shining a flashlight through the scrotum (transillumination). No treatment is needed unless the swelling becomes large and uncomfortable, then surgical repair of the hydrocele is needed. Hydrocele repair is avoided in men who have not started their family or seek to add to their family as repair can contribute to subfertility or infertility.

Spermatocele

A *spermatocele* is a firm, sperm-containing cyst of the epididymis. It may be visible with transillumination (Fig. 54.9). The cause is unknown. They can become large, tense, and painful. Their size can wax and wane with time. Spermatocele repair is avoided in men who have not started their family or seek to add to their family as repair can contribute to subfertility or infertility.

Varicocele

A *varicocele* is a dilation of the veins that drain the testes (Fig. 54.9). The scrotum can feel wormlike when palpated if the venous dilation is significant. However, this is dependent on the examiner's experience and skill. The cause of the problem is not known.

A varicocele is usually on the left side of the scrotum because of retrograde blood flow from the left renal vein. Surgery is considered if the patient is infertile. Varicoceles are associated with 40% to 50% of cases of infertility. Sperm is thought to be damaged by varicoceles. Repair of

the varicocele may be through injection of a sclerosing agent or by surgical ligation of the spermatic vein. Untreated varicoceles are not associated with any long-term health risk.

Testicular Torsion

Testicular torsion involves a twisting of the spermatic cord that supplies blood to the testes and epididymis (Fig. 54.9). It is considered a surgical emergency. It is most often seen in males younger than age 20. It can occur spontaneously, or because of trauma or an anatomic abnormality.

The patient has severe, sudden onset of scrotal pain, tenderness, swelling, nausea, and vomiting. Urinary symptoms, fever, and WBCs or bacteria in the urine are absent. The pain does not usually subside with rest or elevation of the scrotum. The cremasteric reflex is absent on the side of the swelling. Normal anatomic landmarks are lost due to tissue edema.

A scrotal/testicular Doppler ultrasound is typically done to assess blood flow within the testicle. Decreased or absent blood flow confirms the diagnosis. Torsion is an emergency! If the blood supply to the affected testicle is not restored within 4 to 6 hours, ischemia to the testis will occur, leading to necrosis. Unless the torsion resolves spontaneously, surgery to untwist the cord and restore the blood supply must be done emergently.

TESTICULAR CANCER

Etiology and Pathophysiology

Testicular cancer is overall relatively rare. It accounts for less than 1% of all cancers found in males. However, it is the most common type of cancer in young men between 15 and 44 years of age. In the United States, about 8430 new cases occur annually. The median age at diagnosis is 33 years old.[21]

Testicular tumors are more common in males who have had undescended testes (cryptorchidism) or a family history of testicular cancer or anomalies. Other predisposing factors include orchitis, human immunodeficiency virus (HIV) infection, maternal exposure to exogenous estrogen, and testicular cancer in the other testis.

Most testicular cancers develop from 2 types of embryonic germ cells: seminomas and nonseminomas. Seminoma germ cell cancers are the most common but are the least aggressive. Nonseminoma testicular germ cell tumors are rare but very aggressive. Non–germ cell tumors arise from other testicular

tissue. These include Leydig cell and Sertoli cell tumors. They account for less than 10% of testicular cancers.

Clinical Manifestations

Testicular cancer may have a slow or rapid onset depending on the type of tumor (Fig. 54.9). The patient may notice a painless lump in his scrotum, scrotal swelling, and a feeling of heaviness. The scrotal mass usually is nontender and firm. Some patients report a dull ache or heavy sensation in the lower abdomen, perianal area, or scrotum. Acute pain is the first symptom in about 10% of patients. Manifestations associated with advanced disease are varied and include lower back or chest pain, cough, and dyspnea.

Diagnostic Studies

Palpation of the scrotal contents is the first step in diagnosing testicular cancer. A cancerous mass is firm and does not transilluminate. Ultrasound of the testes is done if testicular cancer is suspected (e.g., palpable mass) or when persistent or painful testicular swelling is present. If testicular cancer is suspected, serum tumor markers should be checked to determine the serum levels of α-fetoprotein (AFP), lactate dehydrogenase (LDH), and human chorionic gonadotropin (hCG). (The tumor markers AFP and hCG are discussed in Chapter 15.)

If ultrasound is suspicious for testicular cancer, a radical inguinal orchiectomy should be done. A chest x-ray, CBC, basic metabolic panel, and liver function tests may be done before. Anemia may be present. Liver function levels may be increased in metastatic disease. If cancer is confirmed by pathology, then a CT scan of the abdomen and pelvis (and possibly the chest) can be done to further stage and assess for metastases.

❖ Interprofessional and Nursing Care

Testicular cancer is one of the most curable types of cancer. Interprofessional care generally involves a radical inguinal orchiectomy (surgical removal of the affected testis, spermatic cord, and regional lymph nodes). Some patients with early-stage disease do not need further treatment after an orchiectomy. Retroperitoneal lymph node dissection and removal also may be done in early-stage disease. These nodes are the primary route for metastasis.

Postorchiectomy treatment may involve radiation therapy, or chemotherapy, depending on the stage of the cancer. Radiation therapy is mainly used for patients with a seminoma, which is very sensitive to radiation. Radiation does not work well for nonseminomas.

Testicular germ cell tumors are more sensitive to systemic chemotherapy than any other adult solid tumor. Chemotherapy protocols use a combination of agents, including bleomycin, cisplatin, etoposide, and ifosfamide (Ifex). Retroperitoneal lymph node dissection may be done after chemotherapy as adjunct therapy in patients with advanced testicular cancer.

❓ CHECK YOUR PRACTICE

You are working on the urologic oncology unit caring for a 24-yr-old man who recently had an orchiectomy for testicular cancer. He appears quiet and nonengaged when you assess him. He says, "I'm never going to have a normal sex life."

- How would you respond? What kind of support or information would you provide?

The prognosis for patients with testicular cancer in recent years has greatly improved. 95% obtain complete remission if the disease is detected in the early stages. Because of treatment successes, many men with testicular cancer are long-term survivors.

However, some drugs used to treat testicular cancer can cause serious long-term side effects. These include pulmonary toxicity, kidney damage, nerve damage (which can cause numbness and tingling), and hearing loss (from nerve damage). Secondary cancers can occur due to chemotherapy (see Chapter 15).

All patients with testicular cancer require surveillance and regular physical examinations, chest x-rays, CT scans, and assessment of serum tumor markers (hCG, AFP, LDH). The goal is to detect relapse when the tumor burden is minimal.

Pretreatment subfertility or impaired fertility is identified at diagnosis. In treatment of testicular cancer, chemotherapy with cisplatin and/or pelvic radiation often damages the testicular germ cells. However, spermatogenesis can return in some patients. Because of the high risk for infertility, the cryopreservation of sperm in a sperm bank before treatment begins should be sensitively discussed and recommended for the man with testicular cancer.[22] Ejaculatory dysfunction may result from retroperitoneal lymph node dissection. These issues may be hard to discuss with the newly diagnosed patient. Men may think that the disease is a threat to their masculinity and self-worth.

SEXUAL FUNCTION

VASECTOMY

Vasectomy is the bilateral surgical ligation or resection of the ductus deferens performed for the purpose of sterilization (Fig. 54.11). The procedure takes only 15 to 30 minutes. It is usually done with the patient under local anesthesia on an outpatient basis. Although vasectomy is considered a permanent form of sterilization, successful vasectomy reversals (*vasovasotomy, vasoepididymostomy*) are common.

After vasectomy, the patient should not notice any difference in the look or feel of the ejaculate because its major components are seminal and prostatic fluid. The patient must use a different form of contraception until semen examination reveals no sperm. Sperm cells continue to be made by the testes but are stored in the epididymis and reabsorbed by the body rather than being passed through the ductus deferens. Vasectomy does not affect the hormone production, ability to ejaculate, or physiologic mechanisms related to erection or orgasm. Psychologic adjustment may be a problem after surgery. It may be hard for the patient to separate vasectomy from castration at a subconscious level. Some men may develop psychogenic ED or may feel the need to become more sexually active than they were in the past to prove their masculinity.

ERECTILE DYSFUNCTION

Erectile dysfunction (ED) is the inability to attain or maintain an erection that allows satisfactory sexual activity. Although sexual function is a topic that many persons are uncomfortable discussing, health care professionals must be able and willing to address ED.

ED is a condition that is significant because of its prevalence. More than 10 million men in the United States are thought to have ED. It can occur at any age, although the incidence

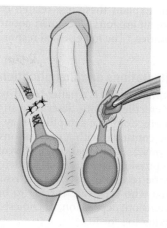

FIG. 54.11 Vasectomy procedure. The ductus deferens is ligated or resected for the purpose of sterilization.

TABLE 54.9 **Common Risk Factors for Erectile Dysfunction**	
Drug Induced • Alcohol • Antiandrogens • Antihypertensives • Antilipidemic agents • Major tranquilizers (diazepam [Valium], alprazolam [Xanax]) • Marijuana, cocaine • Nicotine • Tricyclic antidepressants (e.g., amitriptyline [Elavil])	**Neurologic** • Cerebrovascular disease • Parkinson's disease • Trauma to the spinal cord • Tumors or transection of spinal cord
Endocrine • Diabetes • Hypogonadism • Obesity	**Psychologic** • Anxiety • Depression • Stress
Genitourinary • Radical prostatectomy • Renal failure	**Vascular** • Atherosclerosis • Hypertension • Peripheral vascular disease **Other** • Aging

increases with age. In fact, it is estimated that about 50% of all men between ages 40 and 70 have at least some degree of ED. ED is increasing in all sexually active males. In younger men, the increase is attributed to substance use (e.g., recreational drugs, alcohol), stress, and anxiety. Middle-aged men are more likely to have ED due to chronic medical conditions (e.g., diabetes, hypertension) or treatment for these conditions (e.g., antihypertensive drugs) that may cause ED.

Etiology and Pathophysiology

ED can be due to many factors (Table 54.9). Common causes include diabetes, vascular disease, side effects from medications, result of surgery (e.g., prostatectomy), trauma, chronic illness, stress, difficulty in a relationship, or depression. Since ED results from reduced blood flow to the penis, there is a potential association with cardiovascular disease because the risk factors for both disorders are the same.

Normal physiologic age-related changes are associated with changes in erectile function and may be an underlying cause of ED for some men. Table 50.3 lists age-related changes in sexual function. Explain these age-related changes (if necessary) to reassure an anxious older man about normal changes in his sexual abilities. (The male sexual response is discussed in Chapter 50.)

Clinical Manifestations and Complications

The typical symptom of ED is a patient's self-report of problems associated with erectile activity, describing an inability to attain or maintain an erection. The symptoms may occur only occasionally, may be continual with a gradual onset, or may occur with a sudden onset. A gradual onset of symptoms is usually associated with physiologic factors. A sudden or rapid onset of symptoms may be related to psychologic issues. It is common for younger men who seek care for ED to be diagnosed with diabetes, hypertension, depression, or cholesterol abnormalities during their evaluation for ED.[23]

A man's inability to perform sexually can cause great distress in his interpersonal relationships and may interfere with his concept of himself as a man. It can affect the relationship between the man and his partner. Problems with ED can lead to personal issues, including anger, anxiety, and depression.

Diagnostic Studies

The first step in the diagnosis and management of ED begins with a thorough sexual, health, and psychosocial history.[24] Self-administered assessment and treatment-related questionnaires may be useful as primary screening tools. For example, the International Index of Erectile Function (IIEF) identifies a man's response to 5 key areas of male sexual function: erectile function, orgasmic function, sexual desire, intercourse satisfaction, and overall satisfaction.

Second, a physical examination should focus on secondary sexual characteristics. Note if secondary sexual characteristics reflect the person's chronologic age (Tanner stage). A DRE should be done to assess prostate size, consistency, and presence of nodules. Assessment of BP with palpation and auscultation of the femoral arteries and peripheral pulses should be included.

Further examination or diagnostic testing is typically based on findings from the history and physical examination. A serum glucose, hemoglobin A1C (Hb A1C), and lipid profile are recommended to rule out diabetes. Hormonal levels for testosterone, prolactin, LH, and thyroid hormones may help identify endocrine-related problems. PSA level and a CBC may help to identify other diseases.

Other diagnostic tests may be done to diagnose ED. Nocturnal penile tumescence and rigidity testing is a noninvasive method that involves the continuous measurement of penile circumference and axial rigidity during sleep. These are used to distinguish between physiologic or psychogenic causes of ED. Vascular studies, including penile arteriography, penile blood flow study, and duplex Doppler ultrasound studies, are used to assess penile blood inflow and outflow. These tests help to identify vascular problems interfering with erection.

❖ Interprofessional and Nursing Care

The goal of ED therapy is for the patient and his partner to achieve a satisfactory sexual relationship. The treatment for ED can be based on the underlying cause. Generally, men are moved directly into treatment without a costly workup. A variety of treatment options are available (Table 54.10). Advise

TABLE 54.10 Interprofessional Care
Erectile Dysfunction

Diagnostic Assessment	Drug Therapy
• History and physical examination	• avanafil (Stendra)
• Sexual history	• sildenafil (Viagra)
• Serum glucose and lipid profile	• tadalafil (Cialis)
• Testosterone, prolactin, and thyroid hormone levels	• vardenafil (Levitra, Staxyn)
• Nocturnal penile tumescence and rigidity testing	**Devices and Implants**
• Vascular studies	• Intraurethral medication pellet
	• Intracavernosal self-injection
Management	• Penile implants
• Modify reversible causes	• Vacuum erection device (VED)
• Sexual counseling	

patients that no option will restore ejaculation or tactile sensations if they were absent before treatment.

It is important to determine if ED is reversible before treatment is started. For example, if ED appears to be a side effect of prescribed drugs, other treatments can be explored. With an established diagnosis of testicular failure (hypogonadism), androgen replacement therapy may be part of the prescribed treatment.

For men who have ED that is psychologic in nature, counseling for the patient (with or without his partner) is recommended. This counseling should be carried out by a qualified sex therapist.

The man with ED needs a great deal of emotional support for both himself and his partner. Men often do not feel comfortable discussing their problems because of their perceptions of society's expectations of a man's sexual abilities. Reassure the patient that confidentiality will be maintained. Many men delay seeking medical care and may expect immediate solutions to their problems. The interprofessional care team should provide a support system and accurate information.

Erectogenic Drugs. Avanafil (Stendra), sildenafil (Viagra), tadalafil (Cialis), and vardenafil (Levitra, Staxyn) are erectogenic drugs. These drugs are PDE5 inhibitors. They cause smooth muscle relaxation and increased blood flow into the corpus cavernosum, promoting penile erection. They are taken orally before sexual activity. These drugs have been found to be generally safe and effective for the treatment of most types of ED but are ineffective in the absence of arousal.

Side effects include headaches, leg/back pain, dyspepsia, flushing, and nasal congestion. Rare side effects are blurred or blue-green visual problems, sudden hearing loss, and an erection lasting more than 4 hours (priapism). Teach the patient to seek immediate medical attention if any of these reactions occur. Because these drugs may potentiate the hypotensive effect of nitrates, they are contraindicated for those taking nitrates (e.g., nitroglycerin).

Be aware that increasing numbers of men are seeking other ways to obtain ED medications. This include compounding pharmacies and online pharmacies. This may be due to both the cost of ED medications and the lack of insurance coverage for them.

DRUG ALERT Phosphodiesterase Type 5 (PDE5) Inhibitors

• Should not be used with nitrates (nitroglycerin) in any form.
• Can potentiate hypotensive effects of nitrates.

Vacuum Erection Devices. Vacuum erection devices (VEDs) are suction devices that are applied to a flaccid penis then produce an erection by pulling blood up into the corporeal bodies. A penile ring or constrictive band is placed around the base of the penis to retain venous blood, preventing the erection from subsiding.

Intraurethral Devices and Intracavernosal Injections. Intraurethral devices include the use of vasoactive drugs applied as a topical gel or a medication pellet inserted into the urethra using a medicated urethral system for erection (MUSE) device. Intracavernosal self-injections may be performed, with medication injected directly into the corpus cavernosum.

Alprostadil (Caverject, Edex) is a vasoactive drug that enhances blood flow into the penile arteries. It can be given either by injection or as a transurethral pellet (suppository). When given as a suppository, the drug is placed into the opening at the tip of the penis. When injected, a needle and syringe is used to inject the drug directly into the corpus cavernosum. Trimix (a combination product) includes alprostadil, papaverine, and phentolamine.

Penile Implants. Implantation requires surgery but can sometimes be done in an outpatient setting. The devices are implanted into the corporeal bodies to provide an erection firm enough for penetration. The inflatable implant consists of cylinders in the penis, a small pump in the scrotum, and a reservoir in the lower abdomen. The main complications associated with penile prostheses are infection, erosions, and, rarely, mechanical failure.

Sexual Counseling. Sexual counseling can be recommended at any point during treatment for ED. It may be most valuable in cases with a component of psychogenic ED. Counseling should address psychologic or interpersonal factors that may enhance sexual expression, as well as other factors that are of concern. Counseling can be effective for the patient. It can include his partner, especially if he is involved in a long-term relationship.

HYPOGONADISM

Hypogonadism is a gradual decline in androgen secretion that occurs in most men as they age. The primary male androgen that is reduced is testosterone (Fig. 54.12). This has also been called *late onset-hypogonadism* or *hypogonadism of old age*. It can begin as early as age 40. It is unclear what causes a decline in testosterone. Obesity is a contributing factor.

Manifestations associated with low testosterone include decreased libido, fatigue, ED, depression and mood swings, and sleep problems. Since many of these manifestations can be associated with aging, some patients may not mention this to their HCP, or the HCP may not recognize these manifestations as signs of low testosterone. Long-term effects of low testosterone include loss of muscle mass and strength, which may contribute to an increased risk for falls and fractures.

Hypogonadism is diagnosed with a blood test and a physical examination. Normal serum testosterone levels can range from 300 to 1100 ng/dL, but often the normal ranges vary between laboratories. Replacement testosterone therapy is considered once total serum testosterone levels drop below 300 ng/dL on 2 separate early morning measurements/occasions, and the patient has manifestations of low testosterone.[25] Therapy may be started earlier depending on severity of symptoms. Testosterone replacement therapy (TRT) should not be started until the patient, in consultation with his HCP, considers the risks and benefits of therapy. Potential risks of TRT include lowered levels of high-density lipoprotein (HDL) cholesterol, increased hematocrit, and worsening sleep apnea, although these are rare. Since TRT may

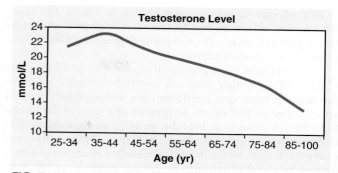

FIG. 54.12 Changes in testosterone plasma level in men as they age.

cause increased growth of prostate tissue, TRT is contraindicated in patients with unmanaged BPH or prostate cancer. Before treatment is started, a DRE and PSA test should be done. Once TRT begins, the HCP should closely monitor the patient.

Replacement therapy is available in different forms, including injection, transdermal, topical, buccal, or intranasal preparations. Oral TRT is not approved for use in the United States. IM injections, such as testosterone cypionate (Depo-Testosterone) and testosterone enanthate (Delatestryl), are available in varying doses. These drugs create a cyclic rise and fall in serum testosterone levels. The highest levels occur 2 to 3 days after the injection. Testosterone levels slowly decrease until the next injection. One side effect of this form of TRT is that men may report mood swings with the hormone fluctuations.

Transdermal preparations, including patches and gels (e.g., Androderm, Testim), are often prescribed. They are applied to the skin at product-specific sites, including the back, arm, and abdomen. Skin irritation is a common side effect. Testosterone may also be given as a buccal tablet (Striant) or intranasally (Natesto).

Emphasize to the patient the importance of hand washing with soap and water after applying testosterone preparations to the skin. Covering the area with clothing until the preparation has dried is recommended.

Women of childbearing age and children should avoid direct contact with testosterone products. Testosterone may cause early signs of puberty in young children and changes (virilization) in the external genitalia of a female fetus.

INFERTILITY

Infertility in a couple is defined as the inability to conceive after 1 year of frequent unprotected intercourse. Infertility is a disorder of a couple, not of one person. For this reason, both partners must be involved in determining the cause of infertility. Infertility is caused by factors involving the man in a significant number of cases. Some estimate 25% of cases are male-related.[26]

Problems of the hypothalamic-pituitary system, testicular disorders, and problems of the ejaculatory system can cause male infertility. The physical causes of infertility can be divided into 3 categories: pretesticular, testicular, and posttesticular. The *pretesticular* or endocrine causes occur in only about 3% of the cases. They can generally be treated with medication or surgery.

Testicular problems make up 50% of the cases. The most common cause of male infertility is a varicocele. Other factors that influence the testes include infection (e.g., mumps virus, STIs, bacterial infections), congenital anomalies, drugs, radiation, substance use (alcohol, nicotine, drugs), and environmental hazards.

Posttesticular causes account for 5% to 7% of the cases. Obstruction, infection, and the result of a surgical procedure are the primary causes. The remaining 40% are classified as *idiopathic,* or of unknown causes.

A careful health history and examination may reveal the cause of a patient's infertility. Thus the history is a starting point for determining cause and treatment. The history should include age; occupation; past injury, surgery, or infections of the genital tract; lifestyle issues (e.g., hot tubs, weight training, wearing tight undergarments); sexual practices; frequency of intercourse; and emotional factors, such as stress levels and the desire for children. Record the use of drugs, such as chemotherapeutic agents, anabolic steroids or testosterone, sulfasalazine (Azulfidine), cimetidine (Tagamet HB), and recreational drugs, since these drugs can reduce the sperm count. A physical examination may identify a varicocele, Peyronie's disease, or other physical findings.

The first test in the male infertility evaluation is a semen analysis to determine sperm concentration, motility, and morphology. Hormone studies are helpful in determining the cause, including plasma testosterone and serum LH and FSH measurements. Be tactful in dealing with the male patient undergoing infertility studies. Many cultures equate fertility and masculinity. Both male and female partners should undergo evaluation simultaneously to avoid potential treatment delays for the couple.

Treatment options for the man include drugs, conservative lifestyle changes (e.g., avoiding scrotal heat, substance use, high stress), in vitro fertilization techniques, and corrective surgery. Infertility can seriously strain a relationship. The couple may need counseling and discussion of alternatives if conception is not achieved. (Female infertility is discussed in Chapter 53.)

CASE STUDY

Benign Prostatic Hyperplasia With Acute Urinary Retention

Patient Profile

(© IPGGutenber-gUKLtd/iStock/Thinkstock.)

B.G., a 60-yr-old married black man with hypertension, COPD, and coronary artery disease, comes to the ED because of an inability to void for the past 13 hours and pain in the lower abdomen.

Subjective Data

- Reports the urge to void
- Is restless, anxious, and agitated

Objective Data

- Has prostate enlargement on digital rectal examination
- Has hematuria, bacteria, and WBCs in urine
- Has a tender and palpable bladder above the umbilicus
- PSA test: 8 ng/mL

Interprofessional Care

- Indwelling catheter inserted by a urology resident
- Admitted to the hospital for observation

Discussion Questions

1. What risk factors for prostate problems are present in B.G.?
2. Explain the cause of the manifestations that B.G. exhibited.
3. What are possible reasons for B.G.'s high PSA level?
4. Discuss the drug and surgical options available to B.G.
5. **Patient-Centered Care:** B.G. asks you about the effect of the various surgical options on his ability to have sex. How would you respond and what type of teaching would you provide?
6. **Priority Decision:** Based on the assessment data, what are the priority nursing diagnoses?
7. **Priority Decision:** What is the priority nursing intervention for B.G.?
8. **Patient-Centered Care:** On further assessment, you note that B.G. is concerned he may have incontinence if he has surgery on his prostate. How would you help him resolve this concern related to treatment options, and how would you teach him about these options?
9. **Evidence-Based Practice:** What information would you offer to B.G. when he asks if he should start taking saw palmetto to prevent future UTIs?

Answers available at *http://evolve.elsevier.com/Lewis/medsurg.*

▌ BRIDGE TO NCLEX EXAMINATION

The number of the question corresponds to the same-numbered outcome at the beginning of the chapter.

1. Postoperatively, a patient who has had a laser prostatectomy has continuous bladder irrigation with a 3-way urinary catheter with a 30-mL balloon. When he reports bladder spasms with the catheter in place, the nurse should
   a. deflate the balloon to 10 mL to decrease bulk in the bladder.
   b. deflate the balloon and then reinflate to ensure that the catheter is patent.
   c. explain that this feeling is normal and that he should not try to urinate around the catheter.
   d. stop the irrigation, assess the patient's vital signs, and notify the HCP of possible obstruction.

2. Which factors would place a patient at a higher risk for prostate cancer *(select all that apply)*?
   a. Older than 65 years
   b. Asian or Native American
   c. Long-term use of an indwelling urethral catheter
   d. Father diagnosed and treated for early-stage prostate cancer
   e. Previous history of undescended testicle and testicular cancer

3. A patient scheduled for a radical prostatectomy for prostate cancer expresses the fear that he will have erectile dysfunction. In responding to this patient, the nurse should keep in mind that
   a. PD5 inhibitors are not recommended in prostatectomy patients.
   b. erectile dysfunction can occur even with a nerve-sparing procedure.
   c. the most common complication of this surgery is bowel incontinence.
   d. the provider will place a penile implant during surgery to treat any dysfunction.

4. The nurse explains to the patient with chronic bacterial prostatitis who is undergoing antibiotic therapy that *(select all that apply)*
   a. all patients require hospitalization.
   b. pain will lessen once treatment has ended.
   c. the course of treatment is generally 1 to 2 weeks.
   d. long-term therapy may be needed in immunocompromised patient.
   e. if the condition is not treated appropriately, he is at risk for prostate cancer.

5. In assessing a patient for testicular cancer, the nurse understands that the manifestations of this disease often include
   a. urinary frequency.
   b. painless mass in the scrotal area.
   c. erectile dysfunction with retrograde ejaculation.
   d. rapid onset of dysuria with scrotal swelling and fever.
6. The nurse should explain to the patient who has erectile dysfunction (ED) that *(select all that apply)*
   a. the most common cause is benign prostatic hypertrophy.
   b. ED may be due to medications or conditions such as diabetes.
   c. only men who are 65 years or older benefit from PDE5 inhibitors.
   d. there are medications and devices that can be used to help with erections.
   e. this condition is primarily due to anxiety and best treated with psychotherapy.

7. To decrease the patient's discomfort related to discussing his reproductive organs, the nurse should
   a. relate his sexual concerns to his sexual partner.
   b. arrange to have male nurses care for the patient.
   c. give him written material and ask if he has questions.
   d. maintain a nonjudgmental attitude toward his sexual practices.

1. c, 2. a, 3. b, 4. d, 5. b, 6. b, d, 7. d

For rationales to these answers and even more NCLEX review questions, visit *http://evolve.elsevier.com/Lewis/medsurg*.

EVOLVE WEBSITE/RESOURCES LIST

http://evolve.elsevier.com/Lewis/medsurg
Review Questions (Online Only)
Key Points
Answer Keys for Questions
- Rationales for Bridge to NCLEX Examination Questions
- Answer Guidelines for Case Study on p. 1276
- Answer Guidelines for Managing Care of Multiple Patients Case Study (Section 11) on p. 1278
Student Case Study
- Patient With Benign Prostatic Hyperplasia
Nursing Care Plan
- eNursing Care Plan 54.1: Patient Having Prostate Surgery
Conceptual Care Map Creator
Audio Glossary
Supporting Media
- Animations
  - Prostatectomy
  - Vasectomy
Content Updates

REFERENCES

1. Briolat G: Benign prostatic hyperplasia. In: Lajiness M, Quallich S, eds. *The Nurse Practitioner in Urology*, Basel, Switzerland, 2016, Springer International Publishing.
*2. Al-Khalil S, Boothe D, Durdin T, et al: Interactions between benign prostatic hyperplasia (BPH) and prostate cancer in large prostates. A retrospective data review, *Int Urol Nephrol* 48:91, 2016.
*3. American Urological Association: AUA guideline: Surgical management of lower urinary tract symptoms attributed to benign prostatic hyperplasia. Retrieved from *www.auanet.org/guidelines/surgical-management-of-lower-urinary-tract-symptoms-attributed-to-benign-prostatic-hyperplasia-(2018)*.
4. Barry M, Fowler F, O'Leary M, et al: The AUA symptom index for benign prostatic hyperplasia, *J Urol* 148:1549, 1992. (Classic)
*5. Kasivisvanathan V, Rannikko A, Borghi M, et al: MRI-targeted or standard biopsy for prostate-cancer diagnosis, *N Engl J Med* 378:1767, 2018.
*6. Nabavizadeh R, Zangi M, Kim M, et al: Herbal supplements for prostate enlargement. Current state of the evidence, *Urology* 112:145, 2018.
*7. Calves J, Thoulouzan M, Perroui-Verbe MA, et al: Long-term patient reported clinical outcomes and reoperation rate after photovaporization with the CPS-180W greenlight laser, *Eur Urol Focus* 17:S2405, 2017.
*8. American Urological Association: AUA guideline: Early detection of prostate cancer. Retrieved from *www.auanet.org/guidelines/prostate-cancer-early-detection-guideline*.

9. American Cancer Society: What are the key statistics about prostate cancer? Retrieved from *www.cancer.org/cancer/prostatecancer/detailedguide/prostate-cancer-key-statistics*.
*10. Loblaw A, Souter LH, Canil C, et al: Follow-up care for survivors of prostate cancer—Clinical management: A program in evidence-based care systematic review and clinical practice guidelines, *Clin Oncol (R Coll Radiol)* 29:711, 2017.
11. National Cancer Institute: Treatment choices for men with early-stage prostate cancer. Retrieved from *www.cancer.gov/types/prostate/patient/prostate-treatment-pdq*.
*12. Montironi R, Cimadamore A, Cheng L, et al: Prostate cancer grading in 2018: Limitations, implementations, cribriform morphology, and biological markers, *Int J Biol Markers* 33:331, 2018.
*13. Coughlin GD, Yaxley JW, Chambers SK, et al: Robot-assisted laparoscopic prostatectomy versus open radical prostatectomy: 24-Month outcomes from a randomized controlled study, *Lancet Oncol* 19:1051, 2018.
*14. Barocas DA, Alvarez J, Resnick MJ, et al: Association between radiation therapy, surgery, or observation for localized prostate cancer and patient-reported outcomes after 3 years, *JAMA* 317:1126, 2017.
15. Oncolink: Possible side effects of radiation treatment for prostate cancer. Retrieved from *www.oncolink.org/cancers/prostate/treatments/possible-side-effects-of-radiation-treatment-for-prostate-cancer*.
*16. Strouthos I, Chatzikonstantinou G, Zamboglou N, et al: Combined high dose rate brachytherapy and external beam radiotherapy for clinically localized prostate cancer, *Radiother Oncol* 128:301, 2018.
17. Gamat M, McNeel DG: Androgen deprivation and immunotherapy for the treatment of prostate cancer, *Endocr Relat Cancer* 12:T297, 2017.
*18. Pollack C, Armstrong K, Mitra N, et al: A multidimensional view of racial differences in access to prostate cancer care, *Cancer* 123:4449, 2017.
19. National Institute of Diabetes and Digestive and Kidney Disorders Information Clearinghouse: Prostatitis. Retrieved from *www.niddk.nih.gov/health-information/urologic-diseases/prostate-problems/prostatitis-inflammation-prostate*.
*20. Araujo LA, De Paula AA, de Paula HD, et al: Human papillomavirus genotype distribution in penile carcinoma: Association with clinic pathological factors, *PloSOne* 6:e0199557, 2018.
21. Woldu SL, Bargrodia A: Update on epidemiologic considerations and treatment trends in testicular cancer, *Curr Opin Urol* 28:440, 2018.
22. McBride A, Lipshultz LI: Male fertility preservation, *Curr Urol Rep* 19:40, 2018.
*23. Nguyen HMT, Gabrielson AT, Hellstrom WJG: Erectile dysfunction in young men—A review of the prevalence and risk factors, *Sex Med Rev* 5:508, 2017.
*24. Burnett AL, Nehra A, Breau RH, et al: Erectile dysfunction: AUA guideline, *J Urol* 200:633, 2018.
*25. American Urological Association: AUA guideline: Evaluation and management of testosterone deficiency. Retrieved from *www.auanet.org/guidelines/evaluation-and-management-of-testosterone-deficiency*.
26. Lotti F, Maggi M: Sexual dysfunction and male infertility, *Nat Rev Urol* 15:287, 2018.

*Evidence-based information for clinical practice

CASE STUDY

Managing Care of Multiple Patients

You are working on the medical-surgical unit and have been assigned to care for the following 6 patients. You have 1 LPN and 1 UAP on your team to help you.

Patients

L.M. is a 35-yr-old Hispanic woman who went to the clinic 3 days ago saying she was just "not feeling well." She was admitted to the hospital for treatment of hypertension caused by newly diagnosed Cushing syndrome. She has been depressed and crying because of her physical appearance. Her last BP was 164/94 mm Hg.

(© iStockphoto/ Thinkstock.)

N.B. is a 48-yr-old man admitted to the ICU 2 days ago in diabetic ketoacidosis. He was transferred to the clinical unit yesterday evening. His fasting blood glucose level this morning is 296 mg/dL.

(© iStockphoto/ Thinkstock.)

A.K. is a 68-yr-old Asian American woman recently diagnosed with adenocarcinoma of her right breast. She had a lumpectomy and axillary node dissection yesterday. She has a Jackson-Pratt drain in her right chest. Her last pain medication was given 1 hour ago, at which time she rated her pain as a 7 on a scale of 0–10.

(© XiXinXing/ iStock/ Thinkstock.)

B.G. is a 60-yr-old black man who was admitted to the hospital because of an inability to void for 13 hours and pain in the lower abdomen. He has a urinary tract infection and prostatic enlargement. The urology resident inserted an indwelling catheter. B.G. is scheduled to undergo a TURP this morning.

(© IPGGutenber-gUKLtd/iStock/ Thinkstock.)

R.D. is a 52-yr-old white woman who was diagnosed with Graves' disease 2 mo ago. She was treated with antithyroid medication for 2 mo and underwent a subtotal thyroidectomy yesterday. In report it was noted that her voice has become slightly "hoarse" in the last hour.

(© Jupiterimages/ Photos.com/ Thinkstock.)

B.C. is a 49-yr-old Latina woman who had a total abdominal hysterectomy and bilateral salpingo-oophorectomy 1 day ago. She has a urinary catheter in place. Her vital signs are stable. She is not reporting any pain.

(© Juanmonino/ iStock.com.)

Discussion Questions

1. **Priority Decision:** After receiving report, which patient should you see first? Second? Provide a rationale.
2. **Collaboration:** Which tasks could you delegate to UAP? *(select all that apply)*
   a. Assist B.C. to ambulate in the hallway.
   b. Teach B.G. what to expect postoperatively.
   c. Take R.D.'s vital signs and report the results to you.
   d. Assess A.K.'s mastectomy incision for manifestations of infection.
   e. Listen to L.M. talk about her feelings while helping her with AM care.
3. **Priority Decision and Collaboration:** While you are assessing R.D., the LPN informs you that A.K.'s chest dressing is totally saturated with bloody drainage. Which *initial* action would be most appropriate?
   a. Ask the LPN to call the laboratory for a stat Hgb and Hct on A.K.
   b. Tell the LPN to reinforce the dressing with sterile 4× 4–gauze pads.
   c. Have the LPN stay with R.D. while you assess the patency of A.K.'s Jackson-Pratt drain.
   d. Ask the LPN to stay with A.K. and have the UAP monitor R.D. while you call A.K.'s HCP.

Case Study Progression

A.K.'s Jackson-Pratt drain was not functioning properly. You get it working and change the chest dressing. The incision is well approximated without signs of infection. When you leave the room, the Jackson-Pratt has a small amount of serosanguineous drainage in it. As you enter R.D.'s room, you notice she is having a carpal spasm on the same arm on which the LPN is taking her BP. You recognize this as a manifestation of hypocalcemia and notify the health care provider.

4. Which assessment findings would be *most* important to include in a discussion with the health care provider about R.D.? *(select all that apply)*
   a. Patient is anxious
   b. Hoarseness of voice
   c. Most recent Hgb and Hct
   d. Carpal spasm upon inflation of BP cuff
   e. Blood pressure of 138/76 and heart rate of 78
5. **Priority Decision:** Which intervention would be of *highest* priority in caring for L.M.?
   a. Assess her for fall risk.
   b. Assess her for signs and symptoms of hypoglycemia.
   c. Teach her the need for a high-carbohydrate, low-protein diet.
   d. Reassure her that her physical appearance will improve with treatment.
6. B.G. asks you what to expect when he returns from surgery. You explain that he will have a(n)
   a. dressing in his groin as well as a urinary catheter.
   b. 3-way urinary catheter connected to an irrigation system.
   c. patient-controlled analgesia (PCA) pump for pain control.
   d. abdominal and a perineal drain that will be recharged q4hr.
7. **Priority Decision and Management Decision:** The LPN is assigned to give medications to N.B., including his sliding scale Novolog insulin with breakfast. The UAP, who is also a senior nursing student, tells you that the LPN gave N.B.'s insulin at least 30 minutes after the patient ate his breakfast. What is your *best* initial action?
   a. Report the incident to the charge nurse for follow-up.
   b. Talk to the LPN about the importance of timely medication administration.
   c. Ask the LPN what time the insulin was given and when the patient ate breakfast.
   d. Ask the UAP to first discuss the concern with the LPN to follow proper channels of communication.

Assessment: Nervous System

Tara Shaw

Act as if what you do makes a difference. It does.

William James

ⓔ http://evolve.elsevier.com/Lewis/medsurg

CONCEPTUAL FOCUS

Cognition

Functional Ability

Intracranial Regulation

Sensory Perception

LEARNING OUTCOMES

1. Distinguish between the functions of neurons and glial cells.
2. Explain the anatomic location and functions of the cerebrum, brainstem, cerebellum, spinal cord, peripheral nerves, and cerebrospinal fluid.
3. Identify the major arteries supplying the brain.
4. Describe the functions of the 12 cranial nerves.
5. Compare the functions of the 2 divisions of the autonomic nervous system.
6. Link the age-related changes in the neurologic system to the differences in assessment findings.
7. Obtain significant subjective and objective data related to the nervous system from a patient.
8. Perform a physical assessment of the nervous system using the appropriate techniques.
9. Distinguish normal from abnormal findings of a physical assessment of the nervous system.
10. Describe the purpose, significance of results, and nursing responsibilities related to diagnostic studies of the nervous system.

KEY TERMS

autonomic nervous system (ANS), p. 1284
blood-brain barrier, p. 1285
central nervous system (CNS), p. 1279
cerebrospinal fluid (CSF), p. 1283
cranial nerves (CNs), p. 1284

dermatome, p. 1284
glial cells, p. 1280
lower motor neurons (LMNs), p. 1281
meninges, p. 1286
neurons, p. 1279

neurotransmitters, p. 1280
peripheral nervous system (PNS), p. 1279
reflex, p. 1281
synapse, p. 1280
upper motor neurons (UMNs), p. 1281

The nervous system is one of the most complex systems. It controls all the body's activities. Having a general understanding of the nervous system is critical to your being able to analyze and interpret clinical findings. This chapter reviews the structures and functions, assessment, and diagnostic studies of the nervous system.

STRUCTURES AND FUNCTIONS OF NERVOUS SYSTEM

The nervous system is responsible for the control and integration of the body's many activities. It is divided into the central nervous system and peripheral nervous system. The central nervous system (CNS) consists of the brain, spinal cord, and cranial nerves I and II. The peripheral nervous system (PNS) consists of cranial nerves III to XII, spinal nerves, and peripheral components of the autonomic nervous system (ANS).

Cells of Nervous System

The nervous system is made up of 2 types of cells: neurons and supportive glial cells.

Neurons. Neurons are the primary functional unit of the nervous system. Although neurons come in many shapes and sizes, they share 3 characteristics: (1) *excitability,* or the ability to generate a nerve impulse; (2) *conductivity,* or the ability to transmit an impulse; and (3) *influence,* or the ability to influence other neurons, muscle cells, or glandular cells.

A typical neuron consists of a cell body, multiple dendrites, and an axon (Fig. 55.1). The *cell body* contains the nucleus and cytoplasm. It is the metabolic center of the neuron. *Dendrites*

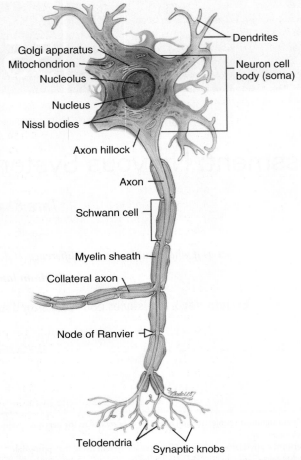

Golgi apparatus
Mitochondrion
Nucleolus
Nucleus
Nissl bodies
Axon hillock
Axon
Schwann cell
Myelin sheath
Collateral axon
Node of Ranvier
Telodendria
Synaptic knobs
Dendrites
Neuron cell body (soma)

FIG. 55.1 Structural features of neurons: dendrites, cell body, and axons. (Modified from Thibodeau GA, Patton KT: *Anatomy and physiology*, ed 8, St Louis, 2013, Mosby.)

are short processes extending from the cell body. They receive impulses or signals from other neurons and conduct them toward the cell body. The *axon* projects varying distances from the cell body. The axon carries nerve impulses to other neurons or to end organs, such as smooth and striated muscles and glands.

Many axons in the CNS and PNS are covered by a *myelin sheath*, a white, lipid protein substance that acts as an insulator for the conduction of impulses. Axons may be myelinated or unmyelinated, as in the case of smaller fibers.

Glial Cells. Glial cells (glia or neuroglia) provide support, nourishment, and protection to neurons. Glial cells make up about half of the brain and spinal cord mass. Glial cells are divided into microglia and macroglia. *Microglia,* specialized macrophages capable of phagocytosis, protect the neurons. These cells are mobile within the brain and multiply when the brain is damaged.

Macroglial cells include astrocytes, oligodendrocytes, and ependymal cells. *Astrocytes* are found mainly in gray matter. They provide structural support to neurons. Their delicate processes form the *blood-brain barrier* with the endothelium of the blood vessels. They also play a role in *synaptic transmission* (conduction of impulses between neurons). When the brain is injured, astrocytes act as phagocytes for cleaning up neuronal debris. They help restore the neurochemical milieu and provide support for repair. Proliferation of astrocytes contributes to the formation of scar tissue (*gliosis*) in the CNS.

Oligodendrocytes are specialized cells that produce the myelin sheath of nerve fibers in the CNS. They are found mainly in the white matter of the CNS. *Ependymal cells* line the brain ventricles and aid in the secretion of cerebrospinal fluid (CSF).

Neuroglia are mitotic and can replicate. In general, when neurons are destroyed, the tissue is replaced by the proliferation of neuroglial cells. Most primary CNS tumors involve glial cells. Primary cancers involving neurons are rare.

Nerve Regeneration

If the axon of the nerve cell is damaged, the cell tries to repair itself. Damaged nerve cells try to grow back to their original destinations by sprouting many branches from the damaged ends of their axons. Axons in the CNS are generally less successful than peripheral axons in regeneration.[1]

Schwann cells myelinate the nerve fibers in the PNS. Injured nerve fibers in the PNS can regenerate by growing within the protective myelin sheath of the Schwann cells if the cell body is intact and the environment is optimal.[2] The final result of nerve regeneration depends on the number of axon sprouts that join with the appropriate Schwann cell columns and reinnervate appropriate end organs.

Neurons have long been thought to be nonmitotic. That is, after being damaged, neurons could not be replaced. Recent research shows a subset of glial cells (astrocytes) proliferate after certain injuries in the CNS, and neurogenesis may occur from stem cells.[3] These findings support the expectation that the patient will have a certain amount of recovery after injury involving the neurons.

Nerve Impulse

The purpose of a neuron is to initiate, receive, and process messages about events both within and outside the body. The initiation of a neuronal message (*nerve impulse*) involves the generation of an action potential. A series of action potentials travel along the axon. When the impulse reaches the end of the nerve fiber, a chemical interaction involving neurotransmitters transmits the impulse across the junction (*synapse*) between nerve cells by. This chemical interaction generates another set of action potentials in the next neuron. These events are repeated until the nerve impulse reaches its destination.

Because of its insulating capacity, myelination of nerve axons speeds the conduction of an action potential. Many peripheral nerve axons have *nodes of Ranvier* (gaps in the myelin sheath) that allow an action potential to travel much faster by jumping from node to node. We call this *saltatory* (hopping) *conduction*. In an unmyelinated fiber, conduction is slower. The wave of depolarization travels the entire length of the axon, with each part of the membrane becoming depolarized in turn.

Synapse. A synapse is the structural and functional junction between 2 neurons. It is where the nerve impulse is transmitted from 1 neuron to another. The nerve impulse also can be transmitted from neurons to glands or muscles. The essential structures of synaptic transmission are a presynaptic terminal, synaptic cleft, and receptor site on the postsynaptic cell (Fig. 55.2).

Neurotransmitters. Neurotransmitters are chemicals that affect the transmission of impulses across the synaptic cleft. *Excitatory neurotransmitters* (e.g., epinephrine, norepinephrine, glutamate) activate postsynaptic receptors that increase the chance that an action potential will be generated. *Inhibitory neurotransmitters* (e.g., serotonin, γ-aminobutyric acid [GABA],

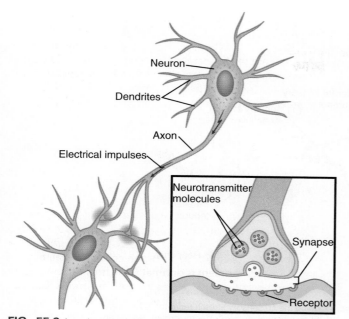

FIG. 55.2 Impulse generation between neurons. Synapse shown with neurotransmitters and receptors.

dopamine) activate postsynaptic receptors to decrease the chance that an action potential will be generated. For example, endorphins block pain transmission while substance P makes nerves more sensitive to pain.

In general, the net effect (excitatory or inhibitory) depends on the number of presynaptic neurons releasing neurotransmitters on the postsynaptic cell. A presynaptic cell that releases an excitatory neurotransmitter does not always cause the postsynaptic cell to depolarize enough to generate an action potential.

When many presynaptic cells release excitatory neurotransmitters on a single neuron, the sum of their input is enough to generate an action potential. Neurotransmitters continue to combine with the receptor sites at the postsynaptic membrane until they are inactivated by enzymes, are taken up by the presynaptic endings, or diffuse away from the synaptic region. Drugs and toxins can affect neurotransmitters by changing their function or blocking their attachment to receptor sites on the postsynaptic membrane. We can use cerebral microdialysis to measure neurotransmitter levels in the cerebral cortex (see Chapter 56).

Central Nervous System

The components of the CNS include the cerebrum (cerebral hemispheres), brainstem, cerebellum, and spinal cord.

Spinal Cord. The *spinal cord* is continuous with the brainstem and exits from the cranial cavity through the foramen magnum. A cross section of the spinal cord reveals gray matter that is centrally located in an H shape and surrounded by white matter. The gray matter contains the cell bodies of voluntary motor neurons, preganglionic autonomic motor neurons, and association neurons (interneurons). The white matter contains the axons of the ascending sensory and descending motor fibers. The myelin surrounding these fibers gives them their white appearance. The spinal pathways or tracts are named for the point of origin and the point of destination (e.g., spinocerebellar tract [ascending], corticospinal tract [descending]).

Ascending Tracts. In general, the ascending tracts carry specific sensory information to higher levels of the CNS. This information comes from special sensory receptors in the skin, muscles and joints, viscera, and blood vessels and enters the spinal cord by way of the dorsal roots of the spinal nerves. The ascending tracts are organized by sensory modality and anatomy. The fasciculus gracilis and the fasciculus cuneatus (often called the *dorsal* or *posterior columns*) carry information about touch, deep pressure, vibration, position sense, and kinesthesia (appreciation of movement, weight, and body parts). The *spinocerebellar tracts* carry information about muscle tension and body position to the cerebellum for coordination of movement. The *spinothalamic tracts* carry pain and temperature sensations.

Other ascending tracts may also carry sensory modalities. The signs and symptoms of various neurologic diseases suggest there are additional pathways for touch, position sense, and vibration.

Descending Tracts. Descending tracts carry impulses that are responsible for muscle movement. Among the most important descending tracts are the corticobulbar and corticospinal tracts, collectively termed the *pyramidal tract*. These tracts carry voluntary impulses from the cerebral cortex to the cranial and peripheral nerves. Another group of descending motor tracts carries impulses from the extrapyramidal system (all motor systems except the pyramidal) concerned with voluntary movement. It includes pathways originating in the brainstem, basal ganglia, and cerebellum. The motor output exits the spinal cord by way of the ventral roots of the spinal nerves.

Reflex Arc. A reflex is an involuntary response to stimuli. In the spinal cord, reflex arcs play an important role in maintaining muscle tone, which is essential for body posture. The components of a monosynaptic reflex arc (Fig. 55.3) are a receptor organ, afferent neuron, effector neuron, and effector organ (e.g., skeletal muscle). The afferent neuron synapses with the efferent neurons in the gray matter of the spinal cord. More complex reflex arcs have other neurons (interneurons) in addition to the afferent neuron influencing the effector neuron.

Lower and Upper Motor Neurons. Upper motor neurons (UMNs) originate in the cerebral cortex and project downward. The corticobulbar tract ends in the brainstem, and the corticospinal tract descends into the spinal cord. These neurons influence skeletal muscle movement. UMN lesions generally cause weakness or paralysis, disuse atrophy, hyperreflexia, and increased muscle tone (spasticity).

Lower motor neurons (LMNs) are the final common pathway through which descending motor tracts influence skeletal muscle. The cell bodies of LMNs, which send axons to innervate the skeletal muscles of the arms, trunk, and legs, are found in the anterior horn of the corresponding segments of the spinal cord (e.g., cervical segments contain LMNs for the arms). LMNs for skeletal muscles of the eyes, face, mouth, and throat are found in the corresponding segments of the brainstem. These cell bodies and their axons make up the somatic motor components of the cranial nerves. LMN lesions generally cause weakness or paralysis, denervation atrophy, hyporeflexia or areflexia, and decreased muscle tone (flaccidity).

Brain. The *brain* has 3 major intracranial components: cerebrum, brainstem, and cerebellum.

Cerebrum. The *cerebrum* is composed of the right and left cerebral hemispheres. It is divided into 4 lobes: frontal, temporal, parietal, and occipital (Fig. 55.4). The functions of the cerebrum are multiple and complex (Table 55.1). The *frontal lobe* controls higher cognitive function, memory retention,

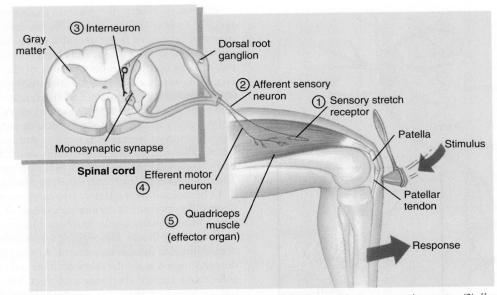

FIG. 55.3 Basic diagram of the patellar "knee jerk" reflex arc, including the *(1)* sensory stretch receptor, *(2)* afferent sensory neuron, *(3)* interneuron, *(4)* efferent motor neuron, and *(5)* quadriceps muscle (effector organ). (Modified from Thibodeau GA, Patton KT: *Anatomy and physiology,* ed 6, St Louis, 2007, Mosby.)

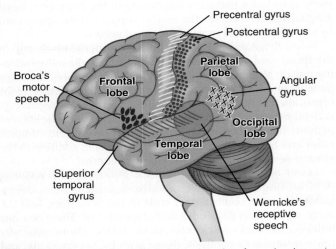

FIG. 55.4 Left hemisphere of cerebrum, lateral surface, showing major lobes and areas of the brain.

voluntary eye movements, voluntary motor movement, and motor functions involved in speech production *(Broca's area)*. The *temporal lobe* integrates somatic, visual, and auditory data and contains *Wernicke's receptive speech area*. (Language and potential functional deficits are described with strokes in Chapter 57 [see Table 57.4]).

The *parietal lobe* interprets spatial information and contains the sensory cortex. Processing of sight takes place in the *occipital lobe*.

The division of the cerebrum into lobes is useful to delineate portions of the neocortex (gray matter), which makes up the outer layer of the cerebral hemispheres. Neurons in specific parts of the neocortex are essential for various highly complex and sophisticated functions, such as language, memory, and appreciation of visual-spatial relationships.

The basal ganglia, thalamus, hypothalamus, and limbic system are also in the cerebrum. The *basal ganglia* are a group of

structures found centrally in the cerebrum and midbrain. Most of them are on both sides of the thalamus. The function of the basal ganglia includes the initiation, execution, and completion of voluntary movements, learning, emotional response, and automatic movements associated with skeletal muscle activity (e.g., swallowing saliva, blinking, swinging the arms while walking).

The *thalamus* lies directly above the brainstem (Fig. 55.5). It is the major relay center for sensory input from the body, face, retina, and cochlear and taste receptors. Motor relay nuclei in the thalamus connect the cerebellum and basal ganglia to the frontal cortex.

The *hypothalamus* is just below the thalamus and slightly in front of the midbrain. It exerts a direct influence on release of hormones from the anterior pituitary gland. It has a rich capillary connection to the pituitary gland to aid in the transport of hormones. These hormones include thyroid-stimulating hormone, growth hormone, luteinizing hormone, and prolactin-releasing hormone, which play a role in regulating reproductive function. In contrast, the supraoptic and paraventricular neurons travel directly through the pituitary stalk to the posterior pituitary, where they release vasopressin and oxytocin. The hypothalamus contains the satiety center that regulates appetite. With input from the limbic system, it also regulates body temperature, water balance (through influence on vasopressin secretion), circadian rhythm, and expression of emotion. The *limbic system* is found near the inner surfaces of the cerebral hemispheres. It is concerned with emotion, aggression, feeding behavior, and sexual response.

Brainstem. The *brainstem* includes the midbrain, pons, and medulla (Fig. 55.5). Ascending and descending fibers to and from the cerebrum and cerebellum pass through the brainstem. The nuclei of cranial nerves III through XII are in the brainstem. The vital centers concerned with respiratory, vasomotor, and heart function are in the medulla.

Also in the brainstem is the *reticular formation,* a diffusely arranged group of neurons and their axons that extends from the

TABLE 55.1 Function of Cerebrum

Part	Location	Function
Cortical Areas		
Motor		
Primary	Precentral gyrus	Motor control and movement on opposite side of body
Supplemental	Anterior to precentral gyrus	Facilitates proximal muscle activity, including activity for stance and gait, and spontaneous movement and coordination
Sensory		
Association areas	Parietal lobe	Integrates somatic and sensory input
	Posterior temporal lobe	Integrates visual and auditory input for language comprehension
	Anterior temporal lobe	Integrates past experiences
	Anterior frontal lobe	Controls higher order processes (e.g., judgment, reasoning)
Auditory	Superior temporal gyrus	Registers auditory input
Somatic	Postcentral gyrus	Sensory response from opposite side of body
Visual	Occipital lobe	Registers visual images
Language		
Comprehension	Wernicke's area in dominant posterior temporal lobe	Integrates auditory language (understanding of spoken words)
Expression	Broca's area in dominant frontal lobe	Regulates motor speech
Basal Ganglia	Near lateral ventricles of both cerebral hemispheres	Controls and refines learned and automatic movements
Thalamus	Below and slightly posterior to basal ganglia	Relays sensory and motor input to and from cerebrum
Hypothalamus	Below and anterior to thalamus	Regulates endocrine and autonomic functions
Limbic System	Lateral to hypothalamus	Influences emotional behavior and basic drives, such as feeding and sexual behavior

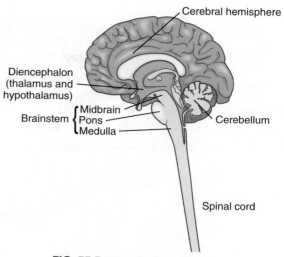

FIG. 55.5 Major divisions of the CNS.

Ventricles and Cerebrospinal Fluid. The ventricles are 4 interconnected fluid-filled cavities. The lower part of the fourth ventricle becomes the central canal in the lower part of the brainstem. The spinal canal extends centrally through the full length of the spinal cord.

Cerebrospinal fluid (CSF) is made largely in the choroid plexuses of the brain within the ventricles. It circulates within the subarachnoid space that surrounds the brain, brainstem, and spinal cord, cushioning the brain and spinal cord. CSF flows from the cranial cavity to the spinal cavity, carrying nutrients through both passive diffusion and active transport. We make CSF at an average rate of about 500 mL/day. The ventricles and central canal are filled with an average of 150 mL at any given time. Changes in the rate of CSF production or absorption can occur, leading to a change in the volume within the ventricles and central canal. Excessive buildup of CSF results in a condition known as *hydrocephalus*.

CSF circulates throughout the ventricles and seeps into the subarachnoid space surrounding the brain and spinal cord. It is absorbed primarily through the *arachnoid villi* (tiny projections into the subarachnoid space) into the intradural venous sinuses and eventually into the venous system.

The analysis of CSF composition provides useful diagnostic information related to certain nervous system diseases. We often measure CSF pressure in patients with actual or suspected intracranial injury. Increased intracranial pressure, indicated by increased CSF pressure, can force downward (central) herniation of the brain and brainstem. The signs marking this event are part of the herniation syndrome (see Chapter 56).

Peripheral Nervous System

The PNS includes all the neuronal structures that lie outside the CNS. It consists of the spinal and cranial nerves, their associated ganglia (groupings of cell bodies), and portions of the ANS.
Spinal Nerves. The spinal cord can be seen as a series of spinal segments, each on top of another with no visible boundaries. In addition to the cell bodies, each segment has a pair of dorsal (afferent) sensory nerve fibers or roots and ventral (efferent) motor fibers or roots. They innervate a specific region of the body. This combined motor-sensory nerve is called a *spinal nerve* (Fig. 55.6). The cell bodies of the voluntary motor system

medulla to the thalamus and hypothalamus. The functions of the reticular formation include relaying sensory information, influencing excitatory and inhibitory control of spinal motor neurons, and controlling vasomotor and respiratory activity. The *reticular activating system* (RAS) is a complex system that requires communication among the brainstem, reticular formation, and cerebral cortex. The RAS regulates arousal and sleep-wake transitions. The brainstem also contains the centers for sneezing, coughing, hiccupping, vomiting, sucking, and swallowing.

Cerebellum. The *cerebellum* is in the posterior cranial fossa below the occipital lobe. It coordinates voluntary movement and maintains trunk stability and equilibrium. The cerebellum receives information from the cerebral cortex, muscles, joints, and inner ear. It influences motor activity through axonal connections to the thalamus, motor cortex, and brainstem nuclei and their descending pathways.

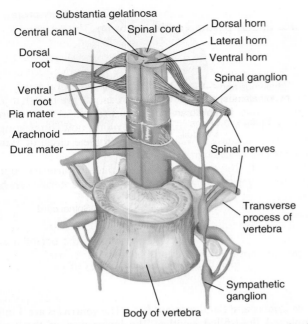

FIG. 55.6 Cross section of spinal cord showing attachments of spinal nerves and coverings of the spinal cord.

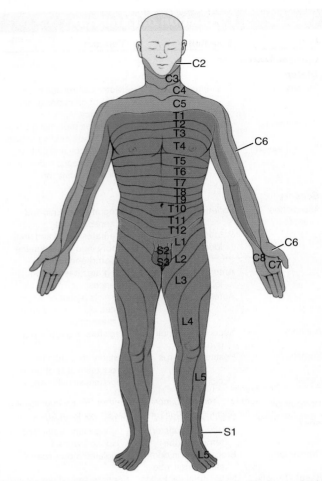

FIG. 55.7 Dermatomes of the body. (From Herlihy B: *The human body in health and illness*, ed 4, St Louis, 2011, Saunders.)

are in the anterior horn of the spinal cord gray matter. The cell bodies of the autonomic (involuntary) motor system are in the anterolateral part of the spinal cord gray matter. The cell bodies of sensory fibers are in the dorsal root ganglia just outside the spinal cord. On exiting the spinal column, each spinal nerve divides into ventral and dorsal rami, a collection of motor and sensory fibers that eventually goes to peripheral structures (e.g., skin, muscles, viscera).

A dermatome is the area of skin innervated by the sensory fibers of a single dorsal root of a spinal nerve (Fig. 55.7). The dermatomes give a general picture of somatic sensory innervation by spinal segments. A *myotome* is a muscle group innervated by the primary motor neurons of a single ventral root. The dermatomes and myotomes of a given spinal segment overlap with those of adjacent segments because of the development of ascending and descending collateral branches of nerve fibers.

Cranial Nerves. The cranial nerves (CNs) are the 12 paired nerves composed of cell bodies with fibers that exit from the cranial cavity. Unlike the spinal nerves, which always have both afferent sensory and efferent motor fibers, some CNs are only sensory, some only motor, and some both.

Table 55.4 (later in this chapter) outlines the motor and sensory components of the CNs. Fig. 55.8 shows the position of the CNs in relation to the brain and spinal cord. Just as the cell bodies of the spinal nerves are found in specific segments of the spinal cord, cell bodies (nuclei) of the CNs found in specific segments of the brainstem. Exceptions are the nuclei of the olfactory and optic nerves. The primary cell bodies of the olfactory nerve are in the nasal epithelium. The cell bodies of the optic nerve are in the retina.

Autonomic Nervous System. The autonomic nervous system (ANS) is divided into the sympathetic and parasympathetic systems. The ANS governs involuntary functions of heart muscle, smooth muscle, and glands through both efferent and afferent pathways. The 2 systems function together to maintain a relatively balanced internal environment. The preganglionic cell

bodies of the *sympathetic nervous system* (SNS) are found in spinal segments T1 through L2. The major neurotransmitter released by the postganglionic fibers of the SNS is norepinephrine. The neurotransmitter released by the preganglionic fibers is acetylcholine.

The preganglionic cell bodies of the *parasympathetic nervous system* (PSNS) are found in the brainstem and sacral spinal segments (S2 through S4). Acetylcholine is the neurotransmitter released at both preganglionic and postganglionic nerve endings.

SNS stimulation activates the mechanisms required for the "fight-or-flight" response that occurs throughout the body (Fig. 55.9). In contrast, the PSNS is geared to act in localized and discrete regions. It conserves and restores the body's energy stores. The ANS provides dual and often reciprocal innervation to many structures. For example, the SNS increases the rate and force of heart contraction and the PSNS decreases the rate and force.

Cerebral Circulation

Knowing the distribution of the brain's major arteries is essential for understanding and evaluating the signs and symptoms of cerebrovascular disease and trauma. The brain's blood supply arises from the internal carotid arteries (anterior circulation) and the vertebral arteries (posterior circulation). They are shown in Fig. 55.10.

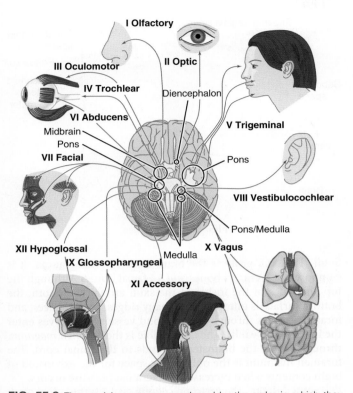

FIG. 55.8 The cranial nerves are numbered by the order in which they leave the brain. (Redrawn from McCance KL, Huether SE: *Pathophysiology: The biologic basis for disease in adults and children,* ed 6, St Louis, 2010, Mosby.)

The internal carotid arteries provide blood flow to the anterior and middle portions of the cerebrum. The vertebral arteries join to form the basilar artery, which branches to supply the middle and lower parts of the temporal lobes, occipital lobes, cerebellum, brainstem, and part of the diencephalon. The main branch of the basilar artery is the posterior cerebral artery. The *circle of Willis* is formed by communicating arteries that join the basilar and internal carotid arteries (Fig. 55.11). The circle of Willis plays a key role in cerebral blood flow. Interestingly, only 40% of us have a well-formed, complete circle of Willis. Everyone else has a degree of variation.[4]

Superior to the circle of Willis, 3 pairs of arteries supply blood to the left and right hemispheres. The anterior cerebral artery feeds the medial and anterior portions of the frontal lobes. The middle cerebral artery feeds the outer portions of the frontal, parietal, and superior temporal lobes. The posterior cerebral artery feeds the medial portions of the occipital and inferior temporal lobes. Venous blood drains from the brain through the dural sinuses, which form channels that drain into the 2 jugular veins.

Blood-Brain Barrier. The blood-brain barrier is a physiologic barrier between blood capillaries and brain tissue. This barrier protects the brain from harmful agents, while allowing nutrients and gases to enter. The structure of brain capillaries differs from that of other capillaries, so substances that normally pass into most tissues are prevented from entering brain tissue. Lipid-soluble compounds enter the brain easily. Water-soluble and ionized drugs enter the brain and the spinal cord slowly. Thus the blood-brain barrier affects the penetration of drugs. Only certain drugs can enter the CNS from the bloodstream.

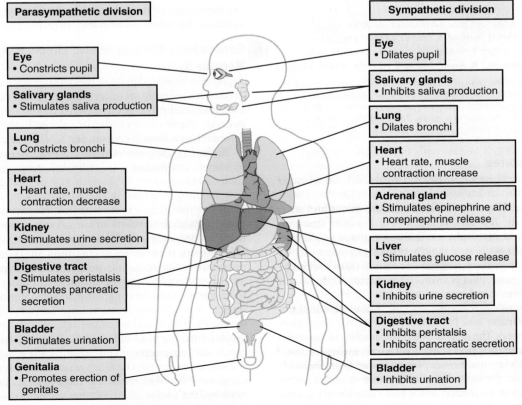

FIG. 55.9 Effects of the sympathetic and parasympathetic systems.

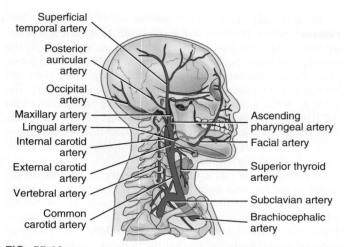

FIG. 55.10 Arteries of the head and neck. Brachiocephalic artery, right common carotid artery, right subclavian artery, and their branches. The major arteries to the head are the common carotid and vertebral arteries. (Modified from Thibodeau GA, Patton KT: *Anatomy and physiology*, ed 8, St Louis, 2013, Mosby.)

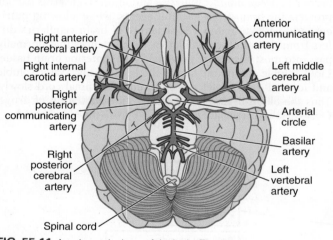

FIG. 55.11 Arteries at the base of the brain. The arteries that compose the circle of Willis are the 2 anterior cerebral arteries joined to each other by the anterior communicating cerebral artery and to the posterior cerebral arteries by the posterior communicating arteries. (Modified from Thibodeau GA, Patton KT: *Anatomy and physiology*, ed 8, St Louis, 2013, Mosby.)

Protective Structures

Meninges. The meninges consist of 3 protective membranes that surround the brain and spinal cord: the dura mater, arachnoid, and pia mater (Fig. 55.12). The thick *dura mater* forms the outermost layer. The *falx cerebri* is a fold of the dura that separates the 2 cerebral hemispheres. It slows expansion of brain tissue in conditions such as a rapidly growing tumor or acute hemorrhage. The *tentorium cerebelli* is a fold of dura that separates the cerebral hemispheres from the posterior fossa (which contains the brainstem and cerebellum).

The *arachnoid* layer is a fragile, web-like membrane that lies between the dura mater and *pia mater* (the vascular innermost layer of the meninges). The area between the arachnoid layer and pia mater (*subarachnoid space*) is filled with CSF. Structures such as arteries, veins, and cranial nerves passing to and from the brain and skull must pass through the subarachnoid space. A larger subarachnoid space in the region of the third and fourth lumbar vertebrae is the area used to obtain CSF during a lumbar puncture.

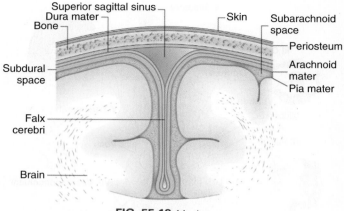

FIG. 55.12 Meninges.

Skull. The *skull* protects the brain from external trauma. It is composed of 8 cranial bones and 14 facial bones. Although the top and sides of the inside of the skull are fairly smooth, the bottom surface is uneven. It has many ridges, prominences, and foramina (holes through which blood vessels and nerves enter the intracranial vault). The largest hole is the *foramen magnum*, through which the brainstem extends to the spinal cord. The foramen magnum is the only major space for the expansion of brain contents when increased intracranial pressure occurs.

Vertebral Column. The *vertebral column* protects the spinal cord, supports the head, and provides flexibility. The vertebral column is made up of 33 individual vertebrae: 7 cervical, 12 thoracic, 5 lumbar, 5 sacral (fused into 1), and 4 coccygeal (fused into 1). Each vertebra has a central opening through which the spinal cord passes. A series of ligaments holds the vertebrae together. Intervertebral discs occupy the spaces between vertebrae, allowing movement of the column. Fig. 55.13 shows the natural curvature of the spinal column and its relation to the trunk.

Gerontologic Considerations: Effects of Aging on Nervous System

Aging affects several parts of the nervous system. In the CNS, the gradual loss of neurons in certain areas of the brainstem, cerebellum, and cerebral cortex begins in early adulthood. With loss of neurons, the ventricles widen or enlarge, brain weight decreases, cerebral blood flow decreases, and CSF production declines.

In the PNS, degenerative changes in myelin cause a decrease in nerve conduction. Coordinated neuromuscular activity, such as maintaining BP in response to changing from a lying to a standing position, is altered with aging. As a result, older adults are more likely to have orthostatic hypotension. Similarly, coordination of neuromuscular activity to maintain body temperature becomes less efficient with aging. Older adults are less able to adapt to extremes in environmental temperature and are more vulnerable to both hypothermia and hyperthermia.

Other relevant changes associated with aging include decreases in memory, vision, hearing, taste, smell, vibration, position sense, muscle strength, and reaction time. Sensory changes, including decreases in taste and smell perception, may result in decreased dietary intake in the older adult. Reduced hearing and vision can result in perceptual confusion.[5] Problems with balance and coordination can put the older adult at risk for falls.[6] Changes in assessment findings result from age-related changes in the nervous system (Table 55.2). Changes should not be attributed to aging without considering other underlying causes.

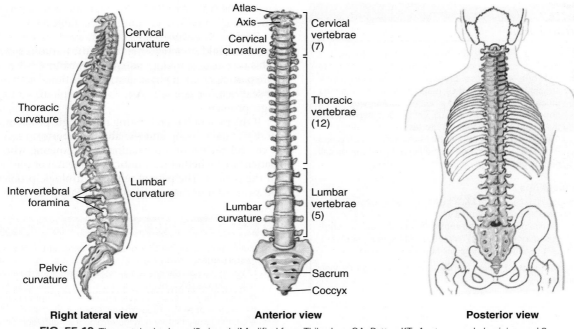

FIG. 55.13 The vertebral column (3 views). (Modified from Thibodeau GA, Patton KT: *Anatomy and physiology,* ed 8, St Louis, 2013, Mosby.)

TABLE 55.2 Gerontologic Assessment Differences

Nervous System

Component	Changes	Differences in Assessment Findings
Central Nervous System		
Brain	↓ Cerebral blood flow and metabolism Cerebral tissue atrophy and ↑ size of ventricles ↓ Efficiency of temperature-regulating mechanism ↓ Neurotransmitters, loss of neurons ↓ O₂ supply	• Altered balance, vertigo, syncope, ↑ postural hypotension • Changes in gait and ambulation • Changes in mental functioning • ↓ Kinesthetic sense • Impaired ability to adapt to environmental temperature • ↓ Proprioception, ↓ sensory input • Slowed conduction of nerve impulses, with slowed response time
Peripheral Nervous System		
Cranial and spinal nerves	Cell degeneration, death of neurons Loss of myelin and ↓ conduction time	• ↓ Reaction time in specific nerves • ↓ Speed and intensity of neuronal reflexes
Functional Divisions		
Motor *Sensory**	↓ Muscle bulk Atrophy of taste buds Degeneration and loss of fibers in olfactory bulb Degenerative changes in nerve cells in inner ear, cerebellum, and proprioceptive pathways ↓ Electrical activity ↓ Sensory receptors	• ↓ Strength and agility • ↓ Sense of touch, pain, and temperature • Slowing of or change in sensory reception • Signs of malnutrition, weight loss • ↓ Sense of smell • Poor ability to maintain balance, widened gait
Reflexes	↓ Deep tendon reflexes ↓ Sensory conduction velocity	• Below-average reflex score • Sluggish reflexes, slowed reaction time
Reticular Formation		
Reticular activating system	Modification of hypothalamic function ↓ Stage IV sleep	• Changes in sleep patterns
Autonomic Nervous System		
Sympathetic nervous system and parasympathetic nervous system	Morphologic features of ganglia Slowed autonomic nervous system responses	• Orthostatic hypotension, systolic hypertension

*Specific changes related to the eye are listed in Table 20.1. Specific changes related to the ear are listed in Table 21.1.

ASSESSMENT OF NERVOUS SYSTEM

Subjective Data

Important Health Information

Past Health History. When performing a neurologic examination, first determine if an emergency exists. For example, does the patient have decreasing level of consciousness? The neurologic assessment is done when an abnormality is identified during screening or can be expected based on patient history. Is the patient a reliable historian and able to give detailed information? If not, interview someone with first-hand knowledge of the patient's history and current problem. Avoid suggesting symptoms or asking leading questions.

Second, the mode of onset and course of the illness are especially important aspects of the history. Often these facts alone can reveal the nature of a neurologic disease process. Obtain all pertinent data in the history of the present illness, especially data related to the characteristics and progression of the symptoms. In some cases, the history may include birth injury (e.g., cerebral palsy from hypoxia) and/or other neurologic insults, such as a traumatic brain injury, stroke, or degenerative disease.

Growth and developmental history can be important in determining if nervous system dysfunction was present at an early age. Specifically, ask about major developmental tasks, such as walking and talking.

Medications. Obtain a careful medication history, especially the use of sedatives, opioids, tranquilizers, and mood-elevating drugs. Many other drugs can cause neurologic side effects. Ask the patient to describe the medication regimen to determine adherence to prescribed therapies.

Surgery or Other Treatments. Ask about any surgery involving any part of the nervous system, such as head, spine, or sensory organs. If a patient had surgery, determine the date, cause, procedure, recovery, and current status. Note any history of eye surgery to determine the relevance of abnormal pupil assessment.

Functional Health Patterns. Key questions to ask a patient with a neurologic problem are outlined in Table 55.3.

Health Perception–Health Management Pattern. Ask about the patient's health practices that affect the nervous system, such as substance use, smoking, adequate nutrition, BP management, safe participation in physical and recreational activities, and use of seat belts or helmets. Ask about hospitalizations for neurologic problems.

If the patient has an existing neurologic problem, assess how it affects daily living and the ability to perform self-care. After a careful review of information, ask someone who knows the patient well whether they notice any mental or physical changes in the patient. The patient with a neurologic problem may not be aware of it or may be a poor historian.

🧬 GENETIC RISK ALERT

- Huntington's disease is a genetically transmitted, autosomal dominant disorder.
- Major neurologic disorders that may have a genetic basis include multiple sclerosis (MS), headaches, Parkinson's disease, and Alzheimer's disease. The presence of these problems in a family history increases the chance of similar problems occurring in the patient.
- A careful family history may determine if a neurologic problem has a genetic basis.

Nutritional-Metabolic Pattern. Neurologic problems can result in poor nutrition. Problems related to chewing, swallowing, facial nerve paralysis, and muscle coordination could make it difficult for the patient to ingest adequate nutrients. Certain vitamins, such as thiamine (B_1), niacin, and pyridoxine (B_6), are essential for the health of the CNS. Deficiencies in any of these can result in nonspecific problems, such as depression, apathy, neuritis, weakness, mental confusion, and irritability. Cobalamin (vitamin B_{12}) deficiency can occur in older adults, who may have problems with vitamin absorption from supplements as well as natural food sources, such as meat, fish, and poultry. Untreated, cobalamin deficiency can cause mental function decline. In the patient with brain injury, early nutritional support can markedly improve outcomes.[7]

Elimination Pattern. Bowel and bladder problems often are associated with neurologic problems, such as stroke, head injury, spinal cord injury, MS, and dementia. To plan appropriate interventions, determine if the bowel or bladder problem was present before or after the current neurologic event. Urinary retention and incontinence of urine and feces are the most common elimination problems associated with a neurologic problem or its treatment. For example, nerve root compression (as occurs in cauda equina conditions) leads to a sudden onset of incontinence. Record key details, such as number of episodes, accompanying sensations or lack of sensations, and measures to control the problem.

Activity-Exercise Pattern. Many neurologic disorders can cause problems in the patient's mobility, strength, and coordination. These problems can affect the patient's usual activity and exercise patterns and can increase the risk for falls.[6] Assess the person's activities of daily living because neurologic diseases can affect the ability to perform motor tasks, which increases the risk for injury.

Sleep-Rest Pattern. Sleep pattern changes can be both a cause and a response to neurologic problems. Pain and reduced ability to change position because of muscle weakness and paralysis

TABLE 55.3 Health History

Nervous System

Health Perception–Health Management
- What are your usual daily activities?
- Do you use alcohol, tobacco, or recreational drugs?*
- What safety practices do you follow in a car? On a motorcycle? On a bicycle?
- Do you have hypertension? If so, how is it managed?
- Have you ever been hospitalized for a neurologic problem?*
- Do you take any medication to manage neurologic problems? If so, what?

Nutritional-Metabolic
- Are you able to feed yourself?
- Do you have any problems getting adequate nutrition because of chewing or swallowing difficulties, facial nerve paralysis, or poor muscle coordination?*
- Give a 24-hr dietary recall.

Elimination
- Do you have incontinence of your bowels or bladder?*
- Do you ever have problems with urinary hesitancy, urgency, retention?*
- Do you postpone your bowel movements?*

Activity-Exercise
- Describe any problems you have with usual activities and exercise because of a neurologic problem.
- Do you have weakness or lack of coordination?*
- Are you able to perform your personal hygiene needs alone?*

Sleep-Rest
- Describe your sleep pattern.
- When you have trouble sleeping, what do you do?

Cognitive-Perceptual
- Have you noticed any changes in your memory?*
- Do you have dizziness, heat or cold sensitivity, numbness, or tingling?*
- Do you have chronic pain?*
- Do you have any problem with verbal or written communication?*
- Have you noticed any changes in vision or hearing?*

Self-Perception–Self-Concept
- How do you feel about yourself, about who you are?
- Describe your general emotional pattern.

Role-Relationship
- Have you had changes in roles such as spouse, parent, or breadwinner?*

Sexuality-Reproductive
- Are you dissatisfied with your sexual function?*
- Are problems related to your sexual function causing tension in an important relationship?*
- Do you feel the need for professional counseling related to your sexual function?*

Coping–Stress Tolerance
- Describe your usual coping pattern.
- Do you think your present coping pattern is adequate to meet the stressors of your life?*
- What needs are unmet by your current support system?

Value-Belief
- Describe any culturally specific beliefs and attitudes that may influence your care.

*If yes, describe.

could interfere with sleep quality. Hallucinations resulting from dementia or drugs can interrupt sleep. Carefully assess and record the patient's sleep pattern and bedtime routines.

Cognitive-Perceptual Pattern. Because the nervous system controls cognition and sensory integration, many neurologic problems affect these functions. Consider culture, age, and education when assessing communication because they play a role in our interaction with others. Assess memory, language, calculation ability, problem-solving ability, insight, and judgment. Ask the patient hypothetical questions such as, "What is a reasonable price for a cup of coffee?" or "What would you do if you saw a car crash outside your house?" Consider if the patient's plans and goals match the physical and mental capabilities. Note the presence of factors affecting intellectual capacity, such as cognitive impairment, hallucinations, delusions, and dementia.

Assess a person's ability to use and understand language. Appropriateness of responses is a useful indicator of cognitive and perceptual ability. Determine the patient's understanding and ability to carry out needed treatments. Neurologic-related cognitive changes can interfere with the patient's understanding of the disease and adherence to related treatment.

Pain is common with many neurologic problems and is often the reason a patient seeks care. Carefully assess the patient's pain. (Pain and pain assessment are discussed in Chapter 8.)

Self-Perception–Self-Concept Pattern. Neurologic diseases can drastically change a patient's control over life and create dependency on others for meeting daily needs. The patient's physical appearance and emotional control can be affected. Sensitively ask about the patient's evaluation of self-worth, perception of abilities, body image, and general emotional pattern.

Role-Relationship Pattern. Physical impairments, such as weakness and paralysis, can alter or limit participation in usual roles and activities. Cognitive changes can permanently alter a person's ability to maintain previous roles. These changes can dramatically affect the patient and caregiver. Ask the patient if a role change has occurred (e.g., spouse or breadwinner) because of neurologic problems and determine how long it has lasted. Caregivers should take part in decision making when neurologic deficits prevent the patient from decisions that will affect the role.

Sexuality-Reproductive Pattern. Assess the person's ability to take part in sexual activity. Many neurologic disorders can affect sexual response. Cerebral lesions may inhibit the desire phase or the reflex responses of the excitement phase. The hypothalamus stimulates the pituitary gland to release hormones that influence sexual desire. Brainstem and spinal cord lesions may partially or completely interrupt the desire or ability to have intercourse. Neuropathies and spinal cord lesions may prevent reflex activities of the sexual response or affect sensation and decrease desire. Despite neurologically related changes in sexual function, many persons can achieve satisfying expression of intimacy and affection.

Coping–Stress Tolerance Pattern. The physical sequelae of a neurologic problem can strain a patient's coping ability. Often the problem is chronic, and the patient must learn new coping skills. Assess if the patient's coping skills are adequate to deal with the stress of this problem. Also assess the patient's support system.

Value-Belief Pattern. Many neurologic problems have serious, long-term, life-changing effects. Determine what these effects are because they can strain the patient's belief system. Assess if any religious or cultural beliefs could affect the treatment plan.

CASE STUDY—cont'd
Subjective Data

(© TatyanaGl/ iStock/ Thinkstock.)

After her admission to the hospital, a subjective assessment of J.K. revealed the following information:
Past Medical History: No history of seizures, migraine, or other headache prior to the current headaches and seizure.
Medications: lisinopril 10 mg PO daily.
Health Perception–Health Management: Never smoked. Occasional social alcohol use. Reports good health other than mild hypertension.

Nutritional-Metabolic: J.K. is 5 ft, 5 in tall; weight 145 lb.
Activity-Exercise: Moderate activity. No formal exercise or participation in sports.
Cognitive-Perceptual: Says her headaches led her to get her eyes tested. Has had only minor decrease in visual acuity.
Coping–Stress Tolerance: Is depressed and fearful. She is worried that something serious is wrong. Denies dizziness, change in hearing, or memory deficits.

Discussion Questions
1. Which subjective assessment findings are of most concern to you?
2. Based on these subjective assessment findings, what should be included in the physical assessment?

You will learn more about the physical examination of the neurologic system in the next section.
(See p. 1293 for more information on J.K.)

Objective Data
Physical Examination. The standard neurologic examination helps determine the presence, location, and nature of nervous system disease (Fig. 55.14). The examination assesses 6 categories of function: mental status, cranial nerve function, motor function, sensory function, cerebellar function, and reflexes.[8] Develop a consistent pattern of completing the neurologic examination to remember to include each element for every patient examination.

Mental Status. Assessment of mental status (cerebral function) gives a general impression of how the patient is functioning. It involves determining complex and high-level cerebral functions governed by many areas of the cerebral cortex. Complete most of the mental status examination during your interaction with the patient. For example, assess language and memory when asking the patient for details of the illness and significant past events. Consider the patient's age, cultural background, and level of education when evaluating mental status.

The components of the mental status examination include:
- *General appearance and behavior:* This includes level of consciousness (awake, asleep, comatose), motor activity, body posture, dress and hygiene, facial expression, and speech pattern. This assessment begins when you first see the patient. A patient who has deficits in self-care as shown by poor grooming is more likely to have other cognitive deficits.

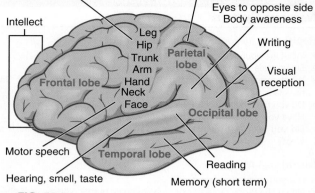

FIG. 55.14 Each area of the brain controls a particular activity.

- *Cognition:* Note orientation to time, place, person, and situation, as well as memory, general knowledge, insight, judgment, problem solving, and calculation. Common questions are "Who were the last 3 presidents?" "What do people use to cut paper?" "Can you count backward from 100 by 7s?"[8] Often a structured mental status questionnaire is used to evaluate these functions and provide baseline data for evaluating changes over time. Common tools include the Mini-Mental State Examination (MMSE) (see Table 59.10) and Montreal Cognitive Assessment (MoCA).[9] Delirium is an acute and transient disorder of cognition that can be seen at any time during a patient's illness. As discussed in Chapter 59, delirium is often an early indicator of various illnesses (see Table 59.16). The Confusion Assessment Method tool is used to assess for delirium (see Table 59.18).
- *Mood and affect:* Note any agitation, anger, depression, or euphoria, and the appropriateness of these states. Use suitable questions to reveal the patient's feelings.

Cranial Nerves. Testing each CN is an essential part of the neurologic examination (Table 55.4).

Olfactory nerve. Chronic rhinitis, sinusitis, and heavy smoking may decrease the sense of smell. Problems with the ability to smell may be associated with a tumor involving the olfactory bulb or the result of a basilar skull fracture that has damaged the olfactory fibers as they pass through the delicate cribriform plate of the skull. *Anosmia* (loss of sense of smell) is an early sign in Parkinson's disease and Alzheimer's disease.[10]

Optic nerve. Visual field defects may arise from lesions of the optic nerve, optic chiasm, or tracts that extend through the temporal, parietal, or occipital lobes. Visual field changes resulting from brain lesions include *hemianopsia* (half of the visual field is affected), *quadrantanopia* (one fourth of the visual field is affected), *bitemporal hemianopsia* (bilateral peripheral vision is affected), or monocular vision. It may be hard to test acuity if the patient does not read English or is aphasic.

Oculomotor, trochlear, and abducens nerves. Because the oculomotor (CN III), trochlear (CN IV), and abducens (CN VI) nerves help move the eye, they are tested together (Table 55.4). With weakness or paralysis of an eye muscle, the eyes do not move together, and the patient has a *disconjugate gaze*. Note the presence and direction of *nystagmus* (fine, rapid jerking movements of the eyes), even though this condition most often indicates vestibulocerebellar problems.

TABLE 55.4 Cranial Nerves

Function and Assessment

Nerve	Function	Assessment
I Olfactory	*Sensory:* from olfactory (smell)	Ask patient to close 1 nostril at a time and identify easily recognized odors (e.g., coffee). Any asymmetry in sense of smell is important.
II Optic	*Sensory:* from retina of eyes (vision)	Examine each eye independently. *Visual fields:* Position yourself opposite the patient. Ask him or her to look directly at the bridge of your nose and indicate when an object (finger, pencil tip) presented from the periphery of each of the visual fields is seen (Fig. 55.15). *Visual acuity:* Ask patient to read a Snellen chart. Record the number on the lowest line the patient can read with 50% accuracy. The patient who wears glasses should wear them during testing unless they are used only for close reading. If a Snellen chart is not available, ask the patient to read newsprint for gross assessment of acuity. Record the distance from patient to newsprint needed for accurate reading.
III Oculomotor	*Motor:* to 4 eye movement muscles and levator palpebrae muscle *Parasympathetic:* smooth muscle in eyeball	Ask the person to hold the head steady and to follow the movement of your finger, pen, or penlight only with the eyes. Hold the target back about 12 inches so that the person can focus on it comfortably. Move the target to each of the 6 positions (right and up, right, right and down, left and up, left, left and down), hold it momentarily, and then move back to center. Progress clockwise. A normal response is parallel tracking of the object with both eyes. Check for pupillary constriction and *accommodation* (pupils constricting with near vision). To test pupillary constriction, shine a light into the pupil of 1 eye; look for ipsilateral constriction of the same pupil and contralateral (consensual) constriction of the opposite eye. Note the size and shape of the pupils. The optic nerve must be intact for this reflex to occur.
IV Trochlear	*Motor:* to 1 eye movement muscle, the superior oblique muscle	See testing for CN III. Because the oculomotor (CN III), trochlear (CN IV), and abducens (CN VI) nerves help move the eye, they are tested together.
V Trigeminal • Ophthalmic branch • Maxillary branch • Mandibular branch	*Sensory:* from forehead, eye, superior nasal cavity *Sensory:* from inferior nasal cavity, face, upper teeth, mucosa of superior mouth *Sensory:* from surfaces of jaw, lower teeth, mucosa of lower mouth, and anterior tongue *Motor:* to muscles of mastication	*Sensory:* Have patient close eyes and identify light touch (cotton wisp) and pinprick in each of the 3 divisions (ophthalmic, maxillary, and mandibular) of nerve on both sides of face. *Motor:* Ask patient to clench teeth and then palpate masseter muscles just above the mandibular angle. Muscles should feel equally strong on both sides. *Corneal (blink) reflex:* Evaluates CN V and CN VII simultaneously. Sensory component (corneal sensation) is innervated by the ophthalmic division of CN V. The motor component (eye blink) is innervated by the facial nerve (CN VII). Have patient look up and away. Then from the other side, lightly touch the cornea with cotton wisp. Look for normal blink reaction of both eyes. Repeat on other side.
VI Abducens	*Motor:* to the lateral rectus muscle of the eye (1 eye movement)	See testing for CN III. Because CN III, CN IV, and CN VI nerves help move the eye, they are tested together.
VII Facial	*Motor:* to facial muscles of expression and cheek muscle *Sensory:* taste from anterior two thirds of tongue	Ask patient to raise eyebrows, close eyes tightly, purse lips, draw back the corners of mouth in an exaggerated smile, and frown. Note any asymmetry in the facial movements because this can indicate damage to nerve.
VIII Vestibulocochlear • Vestibular branch • Cochlear branch	*Sensory:* from equilibrium sensory organ (vestibular apparatus) *Sensory:* from auditory sensory organ (cochlea), hearing	Not routinely tested unless the patient has dizziness, vertigo, unsteadiness, or auditory dysfunction. Have patient close eyes and indicate when they hear the rustling of your fingertips. For more precise assessment of hearing, perform the Weber and Rinne tests or use an audiometer (see Table 21.6).
IX Glossopharyngeal	*Sensory:* from pharynx and posterior tongue, including taste *Motor:* to superior pharyngeal muscles	The glossopharyngeal and vagus nerves (CN IX and CN X) are tested together because both innervate the pharynx. To test the gag reflex, touch the sides of the posterior pharynx or soft palate with a tongue blade. If the reflex is weak or absent, the patient is in danger of aspirating food or secretions. Another test for the awake, cooperative patient is to ask the patient to say "ah," and note the bilateral symmetry of elevation of the soft palate. If a patient has an endotracheal tube, the cough reflex (elicited when the suction catheter contacts the *carina* of the respiratory tree) is a method of assessing the vagus nerve.
X Vagus	*Sensory:* from much of viscera of thorax and abdomen *Motor:* to larynx and middle and inferior pharyngeal muscles *Parasympathetic:* to heart, lungs, most of digestive system	See testing for CN IX. The glossopharyngeal and vagus nerves (CN IX and CN X) are tested together because both innervate the pharynx.
XI Accessory	*Motor:* to sternocleidomastoid and trapezius muscles	Ask patient to shrug the shoulders and to turn head to either side against resistance. Sternocleidomastoid and trapezius muscles should contract smoothly. Note symmetry, atrophy, or fasciculation of muscle.
XII Hypoglossal	*Motor:* to muscles of tongue	Ask to protrude tongue, which should protrude in midline. Next ask the patient to move the tongue up and down and side to side. Finally, the patient should be able to push the tongue to either side against the resistance of a tongue blade. Note any asymmetry, atrophy, or fasciculation.

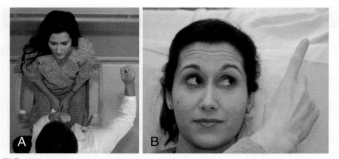

FIG. 55.15 A, Nurse checking visual fields. B, Nurse checking extraocular movement (EOM). (Courtesy DaiWai Olson, RN, PhD, CCRN, Dallas, TX.)

Because the oculomotor nerve exits at the top of the brainstem at the tentorial notch, it can be compressed easily by expanding mass lesions. When this occurs, sympathetic input to the pupil is unopposed; the pupil changes shape and becomes dilated. The lack of pupillary constriction is an early sign of central herniation (see Chapter 56).

Two abbreviations we often used to record the reaction of the pupils are *PERRL* (*Pupils are Equal* [in size], *Round*, and *Reactive to Light*) and *PERRLA* (*Pupils are Equal*, *Round*, and *Reactive to Light and Accommodation*). The *PERRL* abbreviation is appropriate when accommodation cannot be assessed, as in an unconscious patient. Convergence and accommodation are tested by having the patient focus on the examiner's finger as it moves toward the patient's nose.

Another function of the oculomotor nerve is to keep the eyelid open. Damage to the nerve can cause *ptosis* (drooping eyelid), pupillary abnormalities, and eye muscle weakness.

Motor System. The motor system examination includes assessment of strength, tone, coordination, and symmetry of the major muscle groups. Test muscle strength by asking the patient to push and pull against the resistance of your arm as it opposes flexion and extension of the patient's muscle. Ask the patient to offer resistance at the shoulders, elbows, wrists, hips, knees, and ankles. Mild weakness of the arm is demonstrated by downward drifting of the arm or pronation of the palm (*pronator drift*). The pronator drift test is especially sensitive when the patient has a potential for vasospasm or increasing edema in 1 hemisphere of the cerebrum. Ask the patient to close the eyes and hold the arms out with palms facing up (like they are holding a large pizza). The patient should hold this position for 30 seconds. Downward drift with palm pronation indicates a problem in the opposite motor cortex. Note any weakness or asymmetry of strength between the same muscle groups of the right and left sides.

Test muscle tone by passively moving the limbs through their range of motion. You should identify a slight resistance to these movements. Abnormal tone is described as *hypotonia* (flaccidity) or *hypertonia* (spasticity). Note any involuntary movements, such as tics, tremor, *myoclonus* (spasm of muscles), *athetosis* (slow, writhing, involuntary movements of extremities), *chorea* (involuntary, purposeless, rapid motions), and *dystonia* (impairment of muscle tone).

Test cerebellar function by assessing balance and coordination. A good screening test for both balance and muscle strength is to observe the patient's stature (posture while standing) and gait. Note the pace and rhythm of the gait. Observe for normal symmetric and oppositional arm swing. The patient's ability to ambulate helps to determine the level of nursing care needed and the risk for falling.

The finger-to-nose test (having the patient alternately touch the nose, then touch the examiner's finger) and the heel-to-shin test (having the patient stroke the heel of 1 foot up and down the shin of the opposite leg) assess coordination and cerebellar function. Reposition your finger while the patient is touching the nose so that the patient must adjust to a new distance each time your finger is touched. These movements should be performed smoothly and accurately. Other tests include asking the patient to pronate and supinate both hands rapidly and to do a shallow knee bend, first on 1 leg and then on the other. Note dysarthria or slurred speech because it is a sign of incoordination of the speech muscles.

Sensory System. In the somatic sensory examination, several modalities are tested. Each modality is carried by a specific ascending pathway in the spinal cord before it reaches the sensory cortex. As a rule, perform the examination with the patient's eyes closed and avoid providing the patient with clues. Ask "How does this feel?" rather than "Is this sharp?" In the routine neurologic examination, sensory testing of the anterior torso, posterior torso, and all extremities is sufficient. However, if a problem is identified in sensory function, the boundaries of that dysfunction should be carefully delineated along the dermatome.

Touch, pain, and temperature. Light touch is usually tested first using a cotton wisp or light pinprick. Gently touch each extremity and ask the patient to indicate when they feel the stimulus. Test pain by alternately touching the skin with the sharp and dull end of a pin. Tell the patient to respond "sharp" or "dull." Evaluate each limb separately.

Extinction is assessed by simultaneously touching both sides of the body symmetrically. Normally, the simultaneous stimuli are both perceived (sensed). An abnormal response occurs when the patient perceives the stimulus on only 1 side. The other stimulus is *extinguished*.

Test the sensation of temperature by applying tubes of warm and cold water to the skin and asking the patient to identify the stimuli with the eyes closed. If pain sensation is intact, you do not have to assess temperature sensation because the same ascending pathways carry both sensations.

Vibration sense. Assess vibration sense by applying a vibrating tuning fork to the fingernails and bony prominences of the hands, legs, and feet. Ask the patient if the vibration or "buzz" is felt. Then ask the patient to indicate when the vibration ceases.

Position sense. Assess position sense (*proprioception*) by placing your thumb and forefinger on either side of the patient's forefinger or great toe and gently moving his or her digit up or down. Ask the patient to close the eyes and state the direction in which the digit is moved.

Another test of proprioception is the Romberg test. Ask the patient to stand with feet together and then close his or her eyes. If the patient can maintain balance with the eyes open but sways or falls with the eyes closed (i.e., a positive Romberg test), vestibulocochlear dysfunction or disease in the posterior columns of the spinal cord may be present. Be aware of patient safety during this test.

Cortical sensory functions. Several tests evaluate cortical integration of sensory perceptions (which occurs in the parietal lobes). Explain these tests to the patient before performing

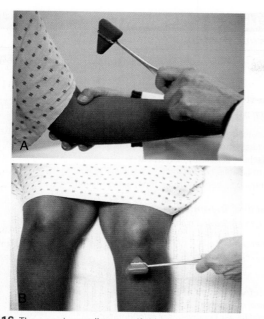

FIG. 55.16 The examiner strikes a swift blow over a stretched tendon to elicit a stretch reflex. **A**, Biceps reflex. **B**, Patellar reflex.

them, while his or her eyes are still open. Assess *two-point discrimination* by placing the 2 points of a calibrated compass on the tips of the fingers and toes. The minimum recognizable separation is 4 to 5 mm in the fingertips and a greater degree of separation elsewhere. This test is important in diagnosing diseases of the sensory cortex and PNS.

Test *graphesthesia* (ability to feel writing on skin) by having the patient identify numbers traced on the palm of the hands. Test *stereognosis* (ability to perceive the form and nature of objects) by having the patient close the eyes and identify the size and shape of easily recognized objects (e.g., coins, keys, safety pin) placed in the hands.

Reflexes. Tendons have receptors that are sensitive to stretch. A reflex contraction of the skeletal muscle occurs when the tendon is stretched. In general, we test the biceps, triceps, brachioradialis, patellar, and Achilles tendon reflexes. Initiate a simple muscle stretch reflex by briskly tapping the tendon of a stretched muscle, usually with a reflex hammer (Fig. 55.16). Measure the response (muscle contraction of the corresponding muscle) on a 0 to 5 scale as follows: 0 = absent reflex; 1 = weak response, seen only with reinforcement; 2 = normal response; 3 = brisk response; 4 = hyperreflexia with nonsustained clonus; and 5 = hyperreflexia with sustained clonus. *Clonus,* an abnormal response, is a continued rhythmic contraction of the muscle with continuous application of the stimulus.

Elicit the *biceps reflex,* with the patient's arm partially flexed and palm up, by placing your thumb over the biceps tendon in the antecubital space and striking the thumb with a hammer. The normal response is flexion of the arm at the elbow or contraction of the biceps muscle that you can feel with your thumb.

Elicit the *triceps reflex* by striking the triceps tendon above the elbow while the patient's arm is flexed. The normal response is extension of the arm or visible contraction of the triceps.

Elicit the *brachioradialis reflex* by striking the radius 3 to 5 cm above the wrist while the patient's arm is relaxed. The normal response is flexion and supination at the elbow or visible contraction of the brachioradialis muscle.

Elicit the *patellar reflex* by striking the patellar tendon just below the patella. The patient can be sitting or lying as long as the leg being tested hangs freely. The normal response is extension of the leg with contraction of the quadriceps.

Gently dorsiflex the patient's foot at the ankle. Elicit the *Achilles tendon reflex* by striking the Achilles tendon while the patient's leg is flexed at the knee. The normal response is plantar flexion at the ankle.

A *focused assessment* is used to evaluate the status of previously identified neurologic problems and to monitor for signs of new problems. A focused assessment of the neurologic system is shown in the box on p. 1294.

Table 55.5 is an example of a normal neurologic physical assessment. Abnormal assessment findings of the neurologic system are shown in Table 55.6.

DIAGNOSTIC STUDIES OF NERVOUS SYSTEM

Many diagnostic studies are available to assess the nervous system (Tables 55.7, 55.8, 55.9, and 55.10). CSF analysis provides information about a variety of CNS diseases. Normal CSF is clear, colorless, odorless, and free of red blood cells. It contains little protein. Normal CSF values are listed in Table 55.7. CSF may be obtained through lumbar puncture (LP) or, on occasion, ventriculostomy.

During LP, the HCP aspirates CSF through a needle inserted into the L3-4 or L4-5 interspace. A manometer attached to the needle is used to obtain CSF pressure. CSF is withdrawn in a series of tubes and sent for analysis. LP is contraindicated in the presence of increased intracranial pressure because of the risk for downward herniation from CSF removal or if there is infection at the intended puncture site. Nursing care of the patient undergoing LP is outlined in Table 55.8.

Biopsies of nerve, muscle, brain, and arterial tissues are useful in diagnosing several disorders (e.g., tumors, infectious disease, degenerative diseases, temporal artery for arteritis). A brain biopsy is usually done using a stereotactic procedure.

TABLE 55.5 Normal Physical Assessment of Nervous System*

Parameter	Findings
Mental status	• Alert and oriented, orderly thought processes. • Appropriate mood and affect.
Cranial nerves†	• Smell intact to soap or coffee. • Visual fields full to confrontation. • Intact extraocular movements. • No nystagmus. Pupils equal, round, reactive to light and accommodation. • Intact facial sensation to light touch and pinprick. • Facial movements full. • Hearing intact bilaterally. • Intact gag and swallow reflexes. Symmetric smile. Midline protrusion of tongue. • Full strength with head turning and shoulder shrugging.
Motor system	• Normal gait and station. Normal tandem walk. Negative Romberg test. • Normal and symmetric muscle bulk, tone, and strength. • Smooth performance of finger-nose, heel-shin movements.
Sensory system	• Intact sensation to light touch, position sense, pinprick, heat, and cold.
Reflexes‡	• Biceps, triceps, brachioradialis, patellar, and Achilles tendon reflexes 2/5 bilaterally. • Toes pointed down with plantar stimulation.

*If some part of the neurologic examination was not done, this should be indicated (e.g., "Smell not tested").
†May be recorded as "CN I to XII intact."
‡May also be recorded as drawing of stick figure showing reflex strength at appropriate sites.

FOCUSED ASSESSMENT
Nervous System

Use this checklist to make sure the key assessment steps have been done.

Subjective
Ask the patient about any of the following and note responses.

Blackouts/loss of memory	Y	N
Weakness, numbness, tingling in arms or legs	Y	N
Headaches, especially new onset	Y	N
Loss of balance/coordination	Y	N
Orientation to person, place, time, and situation	Y	N

Objective: Diagnostic
Check the following diagnostic results for critical values.

Lumbar puncture	✓
CT or MRI of brain	✓
EEG	✓

Objective: Physical Examination
Inspect/Observe

General level of consciousness/orientation	✓
Oropharynx for gag reflex and soft palate movement	✓
Peripheral sensation of light touch and pinprick (face, hands, feet)	✓
Smell with coffee or soap	✓
Eyes for extraocular movements, PERRLA, peripheral vision, nystagmus	✓
Gait for smoothness and coordination	✓

Palpate

Strength of neck, shoulders, arms, and legs for fullness and symmetry	✓

Percuss

Reflexes	✓

TABLE 55.6 Assessment Abnormalities
Nervous System

Finding	Description	Possible Etiology and Significance
Cranial Nerves		
Dysphagia	Difficulty in swallowing	Lesions involving motor pathways of CN IX and CN X (including lower brainstem)
Ophthalmoplegia	Paralysis of eye muscles	Lesions in brainstem
Eyes		
Anisocoria	Inequality of pupil size	Oculomotor nerve injury Sympathetic pathway injury
Diplopia	Double vision	Lesions affecting nerves of extraocular muscles, cerebellar damage
Homonymous hemianopsia	Loss of vision in one side of visual field	Lesions in the contralateral occipital lobe
Papilledema	"Choked disc," swelling of optic nerve head	Increased intracranial pressure
Mental Status		
Altered consciousness	Stuporous, mute, ↓ response to verbal cues or pain	Intracranial lesions, metabolic disorder, psychiatric disorders
Anosognosia	Inability to recognize bodily defect or disease	Lesions in right parietal cortex
Motor System		
Apraxia	Inability to perform learned movements despite having desire and physical ability to perform them	Cerebral cortex lesion
Ataxia	Lack of coordination of movement	Lesions of sensory or motor pathways, cerebellum Antiseizure drugs, sedatives, hypnotic drug toxicity (including alcohol)

TABLE 55.6 Assessment Abnormalities

Nervous System—cont'd

Finding	Description	Possible Etiology and Significance
Dyskinesia	Impairment of voluntary movement, resulting in fragmentary or incomplete movements	Disorders of basal ganglia, idiosyncratic reaction to psychotropic drugs
Hemiplegia	Paralysis on 1 side	Stroke and other lesions involving contralateral motor cortex
Nystagmus	Jerking or bobbing of eyes as they track moving object	Lesions in cerebellum, brainstem, vestibular system
		Antiseizure drugs, sedatives, hypnotic toxicity (including alcohol)
Reflexes		
Deep tendon reflexes	↓ or absent motor response	Lower motor neuron lesions
Extensor plantar response	Toes pointing up with plantar stimulation	Suprasegmental or upper motor neuron lesion
Sensory System		
Analgesia	Loss of pain sensation	Lesion in spinothalamic tract or thalamus. Analgesic drugs
Anesthesia	Absence of sensation	Lesions in spinal cord, thalamus, sensory cortex, or peripheral sensory nerve. Anesthesia drugs
Astereognosis	Inability to recognize form of object by touch	Lesions in parietal cortex
Paresthesia	Abnormal sensation, such as numbness or tingling	Lesions in the posterior column or sensory cortex
Speech		
Aphasia, dysphasia	Loss of or impaired language faculty (comprehension, expression, or both)	Left cerebral cortex lesion
Dysarthria	Lack of coordination in articulating speech	Cerebellar or cranial nerve lesion
		Antiseizure drugs, sedatives, hypnotic drug toxicity (including alcohol)
Spinal Cord		
Bladder dysfunction		
• Atonic (autonomous)	Absence of muscle tone and contractility, enlargement of capacity, no sensation of discomfort, overflow with large residual, inability to voluntarily empty	Early stage of spinal cord injury
• Hypertonic	↑ Muscle tone, ↓ capacity, reflex emptying, dribbling, incontinence	Lesions in pyramidal tracts (efferent pathways)
• Hypotonic	More ability than atonic bladder but less than normal	Interruption of afferent pathways from bladder
Paraplegia	Paralysis of lower extremities	Spinal cord transection or mass lesion (thoracolumbar region)
Tetraplegia (quadriplegia)	Paralysis of all extremities	Spinal cord transection or mass lesion (cervical region)

TABLE 55.7 Cerebrospinal Fluid Analysis

Parameter	Normal Value
Specific gravity	1.007
pH	7.35
Appearance	Clear, colorless
Red blood cells (RBCs)	None
White blood cells (WBCs)	0–5 cells/μL (0–5 × 10^6 cells/L)
Protein	
• Lumbar	15–45 mg/dL (0.15–0.45 g/L)
• Cisternal	15–25 mg/dL (0.15–0.25 g/L)
• Ventricular	5–15 mg/dL (0.05–0.15 g/L)
Glucose	40–70 mg/dL (2.2–3.9 mmol/L)
Microorganisms	None
Pressure	60–150 mm H$_2$O

TABLE 55.8 Nursing Management

Care of the Patient Undergoing Lumbar Puncture

Preprocedure

- Obtain vital signs and a baseline neurologic assessment. Notify HCP of signs of increased intracranial pressure.
- Assess coagulation studies to reduce the risk for epidural hematoma.
- Teach patient and caregiver about procedure. Tell the patient they may feel temporary, sharp pain or tingling radiating down the leg as a sterile needle is passed between 2 lumbar vertebrae.
- Give sedative and analgesia, as ordered.
- Have patient void.
- Place patient in a side-lying position.

Postprocedure

- Monitor neurologic signs and vital signs. Monitor for headache intensity and drainage from the puncture site.
- Apply pressure and a pressure dressing to the puncture site.
- Keep the patient in a reclining position for 1 hour or up to several hours to decrease the risk for spinal headache. The patient may to turn from side to side as long as the head is not raised.
- Ensure proper labeling of CSF specimens and send to laboratory.
- Teach the patient to report numbness, tingling, and movement of the extremities; pain at the injection site; and the inability to void.
- Encourage fluids with a straw to replace the CSF that was removed.
- Give ordered analgesia, as needed.

TABLE 55.9 Radiologic Studies

Nervous System

Study	Description and Purpose	Nursing Responsibility
Cerebral angiography	Serial x-ray visualization of intracranial and extracranial blood vessels done to detect vascular lesions (aneurysms, hematomas, arteriovenous malformations) and brain tumors (Fig. 55.17). Catheter is inserted into the femoral (sometimes brachial) artery and passed through the aortic arch into the base of a carotid or a vertebral artery for injection of contrast medium. Timed-sequence radiographic images are obtained as contrast flows through arteries, smaller vessels, and veins.	*Before:* Assess patient for stroke risk because thrombi may be dislodged during procedure. May need to be NPO. *During:* Warn patient that contrast injection may cause a feeling of being warm and flushed. Patient must lie completely still during scan. *After:* Monitor neurologic signs and VS every 15–30 min for first 2 hr, every hour for next 6 hr, then every 2 hr for 24 hr. Maintain bed rest for 6 hr (1 hr if a closure device is used). Assess for bleeding. Report any neurologic status changes.
CT scan	Provides a rapid means of obtaining radiographic images of the brain (Fig. 55.18, *A*). Computer-assisted x-ray of multiple cross sections of body parts to detect problems such as hemorrhage, tumor, cyst, edema, infarction, brain atrophy, and other abnormalities. Contrast medium may be used to enhance visualization of brain structures.	*Before:* Evaluate renal function before contrast medium used. Assess if patient is allergic to shellfish since the contrast is iodine based. Patient may need to be NPO 4 hr prior. If the patient is taking metformin, hold it the day of the test to prevent hypoglycemia or acidosis. *During:* Warn patient that contrast injection may cause a feeling of being warm and flushed. Patient must lie completely still during scan. *After:* Encourage patient to drink fluids to avoid renal problems with any contrast.
• CT angiography (CTA)	Noninvasive imaging of vascular system (e.g., aneurysms). Evaluates blood volume, flow, and mean transit time as a measure of perfusion. Has fewer complications than cerebral angiography and is less expensive.	Similar to CT (see above).
MRI	Imaging of brain, spinal cord, and spinal canal by means of magnetic energy (Fig. 55.18, *B*). Used to detect strokes, MS, tumors, trauma, herniation, and seizures. Provides greater detail than CT and improved resolution (detail) of intracranial structures. Takes a longer time to complete and may not be appropriate in life-threatening emergencies. Contrast medium may be used to enhance visualization. The contrast agent *gadolinium* has a lower incidence of allergy than iodine used in CT.	*Before:* Oral and/or IV contrast injection may be used. Check for pregnancy, allergies, and renal function. Have patient remove all metal objects. Ask about any history of surgical insertion of staples, plates, dental bridges, or other metal appliances. Remove metallic foil patches. Patient may need to be fasting. Assess for claustrophobia and the need for antianxiety medication. *During:* Patient must lie completely still.
• Magnetic resonance angiography (MRA)	Uses differential signal characteristics of flowing blood to evaluate extracranial and intracranial blood vessels. Provides both anatomic and hemodynamic information. Can be used in conjunction with contrast medium.	Similar to MRI (see above).
• Functional MRI (fMRI)	MRI technique that provides time-related (temporal) images that can evaluate how the brain responds to various stimuli. Makes it possible to detect the brain areas that are involved in a task, process, or an emotion.	Similar to MRI (see above).

TABLE 55.9 Radiologic Studies

Nervous System—cont'd

Study	Description and Purpose	Nursing Responsibility
• MR spectroscopy (MRS)	Noninvasive test for measuring biochemical changes in the brain, especially the presence of tumors. Compares the chemical composition of normal brain tissue with abnormal tumor tissue. Can detect tissue changes in stroke and epilepsy.	Similar to MRI (see above).
Myelogram	X-ray of spinal cord and vertebral column after injection of contrast medium into subarachnoid space. Used to detect spinal lesions (e.g., herniated or ruptured disc, spinal tumor).	*Before:* Give sedative as ordered. Have patient empty bladder. Tell patient that test is done with patient on tilting table that is moved during test. *After:* Patient should lie flat for 1–2 hours to prevent spinal headache. Encourage fluids. Monitor neurologic signs and VS. Headache, nausea, and vomiting may occur.
Positron emission tomography (PET)	Measures metabolic activity of brain to assess cell death or damage. Uses radioactive material that shows up as a bright spot on the image (see Fig. 15.7). Used for patients with stroke, Alzheimer's disease, seizure disorders, Parkinson's disease, and tumors.	*Before:* Explain procedure to patient. Tell patient not to take sedatives or tranquilizers. Have patient empty bladder. Insert 2 IV lines. *During:* Patient may be asked to perform different activities during test.
Single-photon emission computed tomography (SPECT)	Method of scanning similar to PET but uses more stable substances and different detectors. Radiolabeled compounds are injected, and their photon emissions can be detected. Resulting images are accumulation of labeled compound. Assesses blood flow and O$_2$ and glucose metabolism in the brain. Used to diagnose strokes, brain tumors, and seizure disorders.	Similar to PET (see above).
Skull and spine x-rays	Simple x-ray of skull and spinal column. Done to detect fractures, bone erosion, calcifications, abnormal vascularity.	*Before:* Remove any radiopaque objects that can interfere with results. Explain procedure to patient. *During:* Avoid excessive exposure of patient and self.
Ultrasound		
Carotid artery duplex scan	Noninvasive study that evaluates the degree of stenosis of carotid and vertebral arteries. Combines ultrasound and Doppler technology. Probe is placed over the carotid artery and slowly moved along the course of common carotid artery. Frequency of reflected ultrasound signal corresponds to blood velocity. Increased blood flow velocity can indicate stenosis of a vessel.	*Before:* Explain procedure to patient.
Transcranial Doppler	Same technology as carotid duplex but evaluates blood flow velocities of intracranial blood vessels. Probe is placed on skin at various "windows" in the skull (areas in the skull that have only a thin bony covering) to record velocities of the blood vessels.	*Before:* Explain procedure to patient.

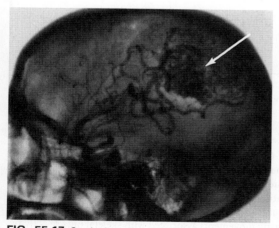

FIG. 55.17 Cerebral angiogram illustrating an arteriovenous malformation *(arrow)*. (From Chipps E, Clanin N, Campbell V: *Neurologic disorders,* St Louis, 1992, Mosby.)

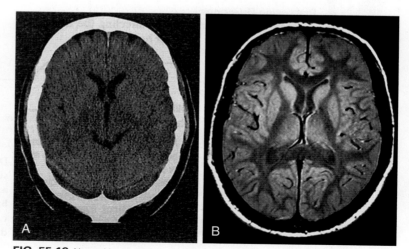

FIG. 55.18 Normal images of the brain. **A,** CT scan. **B,** MRI. (From Fuller G, Manford M: *Neurology: An illustrated colour text,* ed 3, New York, 2010, Churchill Livingstone.)

TABLE 55.10 Electrographic Studies

Nervous System

Electroencephalography (EEG)	Electrical activity of brain is recorded using scalp electrodes. Evaluates seizure disorders, cerebral disease, CNS effects of systemic diseases, brain injury, brain death. Specific tests may be done to evaluate brain's electrical response to lights and loud noises.	*Before:* Tell patient procedure is noninvasive and without danger of electric shock. Determine if any medications (e.g., tranquilizers, antiseizure drugs) should be withheld. *After:* Resume medications and have patient wash electrode paste out of hair.
Electromyography (EMG)	Recording of electrical activity associated with innervation of skeletal muscle. Needle electrodes are inserted into the muscle to record specific motor units. Normal muscle at rest shows no electrical activity. Electrical activity occurs only when the muscle contracts. Activity may be altered in diseases of muscle (e.g., myopathic conditions) or in disorders of muscle innervation (e.g., segmental or LMN lesions, peripheral neuropathic conditions).	*Before:* Explain procedure. Tell patient that pain and discomfort are associated with insertion of needles. HCPs may restrict stimulants (e.g., caffeine) 2–3 hr prior. *After:* Assess needle sites for hematoma or inflammation. Give as-needed analgesics.
Electroneurography (nerve conduction studies)	Measures nerve conduction velocity of peripheral nerves. Involves applying a brief electrical stimulus to a distal portion of a sensory nerve and recording the resulting wave of depolarization at a point proximal to the stimulation. The time between the stimulus onset and the first wave of depolarization at the recording electrode is measured. Damaged nerves have slower conduction velocities.	*Before:* Explain procedure to patient. For example, a stimulus can be applied to the forefinger and a recording electrode placed over the median nerve at the wrist will detect the speed of the conduction.
Evoked potentials	Electrical activity associated with nerve conduction along sensory pathways is recorded by electrodes placed on skin and scalp. A stimulus generates the impulse. Increases in the normal time from stimulus onset to a given peak (latency) indicate slowed nerve conduction or nerve damage. Used to diagnose disease (e.g., MS), locate nerve damage, and monitor function during surgery. Can diagnose disorders of the visual or auditory systems because it shows if a sensory impulse is reaching the right part of brain.	*Before:* Explain procedure to patient. Have patient shampoo hair before test.
Magnetoencephalography (MEG)	Uses a biomagnetometer to detect magnetic fields generated by neural activity. Can accurately pinpoint the part of the brain involved in a stroke, seizure, or other disorder or injury. Measures extracranial magnetic fields and scalp electric field (EEG).	*Before:* Explain procedure to patient. MEG, a passive sensor, does not make physical contact with patient.

CNS, Central nervous system; *LMN,* lower motor neuron.

CASE STUDY—cont'd

Objective Data: Diagnostic Studies

MRI/MRA results show a temporal-parietal glioblastoma that has extended into margins of the occipital lobes.

Discussion Questions

1. Are these the diagnostic studies that you expected to be ordered?
2. Why are these diagnostic study results of concern to you?

(© TatyanaGl/ iStock/ Thinkstock.)

This case study is continued in Chapter 57 on p. 1350.

Answers available at *http://evolve.elsevier.com/Lewis/medsurg.*

BRIDGE TO NCLEX EXAMINATION

The number of the question corresponds to the same-numbered outcome at the beginning of the chapter.

1. In a patient with a disease that affects the myelin sheath of nerves, such as multiple sclerosis, the glial cells affected are the
   a. microglia.
   b. astrocytes.
   c. ependymal cells.
   d. oligodendrocytes.

2. Drugs or diseases that impair the function of the extrapyramidal system may cause loss of
   a. sensations of pain and temperature.
   b. regulation of the autonomic nervous system.
   c. integration of somatic and special sensory inputs.
   d. automatic movements associated with skeletal muscle activity.

3. During the admitting neurologic examination, the nurse determines the patient has speech difficulties with weakness of the right arm and lower face. The nurse would expect a CT scan to show pathology in the distribution of the
   a. basilar artery.
   b. left middle cerebral artery.
   c. right anterior cerebral artery.
   d. left posterior communicating artery.

4. A patient is seen in the emergency department after diving into the pool and hitting the bottom with a blow to the face that hyperextended the neck and scraped the skin off the nose. The patient describes "having double vision" when looking down. During the neurologic examination, the nurse finds the patient is unable to abduct either eye. The nurse recognizes this finding is related to
   a. a basal skull fracture.
   b. an injury to CN VI on both sides.
   c. a stiff neck from the hyperextension injury.
   d. facial swelling from the scrape on the bottom of the pool.

5. Stimulation of the parasympathetic nervous system results in (select all that apply)
   a. constriction of the bronchi.
   b. dilation of skin blood vessels.
   c. increased secretion of insulin.
   d. increased blood glucose levels.
   e. relaxation of the urinary sphincters.

6. The nurse is assessing the muscle strength of an older adult. The nurse knows the findings cannot be compared with those of a younger adult because
   a. nutritional status is better in young adults.
   b. muscle tone and strength decrease in older adults.
   c. muscle strength should be the same for all adults.
   d. most young adults exercise more than older adults.

7. A patient is admitted with a headache, fever, and general malaise. The HCP has asked that the patient be prepared for a lumbar puncture. What is a *priority* nursing action to avoid complications?
   a. Evaluate laboratory results for changes in the white cell count.
   b. Give acetaminophen for the headache and fever before the procedure.
   c. Notify the provider if signs of increased intracranial pressure are present.
   d. Administer antibiotics before the procedure to treat the potential meningitis.

8. During neurologic testing, the patient can perceive pain elicited by pinprick. Based on this finding, the nurse may omit testing for
   a. position sense.
   b. patellar reflexes.
   c. temperature perception.
   d. heel-to-shin movements.

9. A patient's eyes jerk while the patient looks to the left. The nurse will record this finding as
   a. nystagmus.
   b. CN VI palsy.
   c. ophthalmic dyskinesia.
   d. oculocephalic response.

10. The nurse is caring for a patient with peripheral neuropathy who is scheduled for EMG studies tomorrow morning. The nurse should
    a. ensure the patient has an empty bladder.
    b. instruct the patient about the risk for electric shock.
    c. ensure the patient has no metallic jewelry or metal fragments.
    d. teach the patient that pain may be experienced during the study.

1. d, 2. d, 3. b, 4. b, 5. a, b, c, e, 6. b, 7. c, 8. c, 9. a, 10. d

For rationales to these answers and even more NCLEX review questions, visit *http://evolve.elsevier.com/Lewis/medsurg.*

EVOLVE WEBSITE/RESOURCES LIST

http://evolve.elsevier.com/Lewis/medsurg
Review Questions (Online Only)
Key Points
Answer Keys for Questions
- Rationales for Bridge to NCLEX Examination Questions
- Answer Guidelines for Case Study on pp. 1288, 1290, 1293, and 1298
Conceptual Care Map Creator
Audio Glossary
Supporting Media
- Animations
- Cervical Nerves
- Overview of Nervous System
- Parts of the Brain
- Synaptic Transmission
- The Synapse
- Vertebral Column and Spinal Nerves
- Content Updates

REFERENCES

*1. Curcio M, Bradke F: Axon regeneration in the central nervous system: Facing the challenges from the inside, *Annu Rev Cell Dev B* 8:46, 2018.

*2. Boerboom A, Dion V, Chariot A, et al: Molecular mechanisms involved in Schwann cell plasticity, *Front Mol Neurosci* 10:38, 2017.

3. Falk S, Götz M: Glial control of neurogenesis, *Curr Opin Neurobiol* 47:188, 2017.

*4. Mukherjee D, Jani ND, Narvid J, et al: The role of circle of Willis anatomy variations in cardio-embolic stroke: A patient-specific simulation-based study, *Ann Biomed Eng* 46:1128, 2018.

5. NIH MedlinePlus: Aging changes in the senses. Retrieved from *www.nlm.nih.gov/medlineplus/ency/article/004013.htm.*

6. Cuevas-Trisan R: Balance problems and fall risks in the elderly, *Phys Med Rehab Clin N Amer* 28:727, 2017.

*7. Blaser AR, Starkopf J, Alhazzani W, et al: Early enteral nutrition in critically ill patients: ESICM clinical practice guidelines, *Intens Care Med* 43:380, 2017.

8. Daroff RB, Jankovic J, Mazziotta JC, et al: *Bradley's neurology in clinical practice,* ed 7, St Louis, 2016, Elsevier.

9. Finney GR, Minagar A, Heilman KM: Assessment of mental status, *Neurol Clin* 34:1, 2016.

*10. Marin C, Vilas D, Langdon C, et al: Olfactory dysfunction in neurodegenerative diseases, *Curr Allergy Asthm R* 18:42, 2018.

*Evidence-based information for clinical practice.

56

Acute Intracranial Problems

Kristen Keller

If you want others to be happy, practice compassion.
If you want to be happy, practice compassion.

Dalai Lama XIV

e http://evolve.elsevier.com/Lewis/medsurg

CONCEPTUAL FOCUS

Cognition	Intracranial Regulation	Safety
Functional Ability	Mobility	Sensory Perception

LEARNING OUTCOMES

1. Explain the physiologic mechanisms that maintain normal intracranial pressure.
2. Describe the common etiologies, clinical manifestations, and interprofessional care of the patient with increased intracranial pressure.
3. Describe the nursing management of the patient with increased intracranial pressure.
4. Distinguish types of head injury by mechanism of injury and clinical manifestations.
5. Describe the interprofessional and nursing management of the patient with a head injury.
6. Compare the types, clinical manifestations, and interprofessional care of patients with brain tumors.
7. Discuss the nursing management of the patient with a brain tumor.
8. Describe the nursing management of the patient undergoing cranial surgery.
9. Distinguish among the primary causes and interprofessional and nursing management of brain abscess, meningitis, and encephalitis.

KEY TERMS

brain abscess, p. 1326
cerebral edema, p. 1302
coma, p. 1303
concussion, p. 1312
contusion, p. 1313
diffuse axonal injury (DAI), p. 1313

encephalitis, p. 1327
epidural hematoma, p. 1313
Glasgow Coma Scale (GCS), p. 1308
head injury, p. 1311
intracerebral hematoma, p. 1314
intracranial pressure (ICP), p. 1300

meningitis, p. 1324
nuchal rigidity, p. 1324
subdural hematoma, p. 1313
unconsciousness, p. 1303

The body has various mechanisms by which it regulates the intracranial space to promote optimal brain function. Acute intracranial problems can disrupt these processes, leading to increased intracranial pressure (ICP), reduced blood flow to the brain, and brain tissue damage. This chapter discusses the mechanisms that maintain normal ICP and problems that lead to increased ICP. Head injury, brain tumors, and cerebral infections and inflammatory disorders are common problems that disrupt intracranial regulation.

INTRACRANIAL REGULATION

Understanding the dynamics associated with ICP is important in caring for patients with different neurologic problems. The skull is an enclosed space with 3 essential volume components: brain tissue, blood, and cerebrospinal fluid (CSF) (Fig. 56.1). The intracellular and extracellular fluids of brain tissue make up about 78% of this volume. Blood in the arterial, venous, and capillary network makes up 12% of the volume. The remaining 10% is the volume of the CSF.

Primary versus secondary injury is an important concept in understanding ICP. *Primary injury* occurs at the initial time of an injury (e.g., impact of car accident, blunt-force trauma). It results in displacement, bruising, or damage to any of the components (brain tissue, blood, CSF).

Secondary injury is the resulting hypoxia, ischemia, hypotension, edema, or increased ICP that follows the primary injury. Secondary injury, which can occur several hours to days after the initial injury, is a concern when managing brain injury. Nursing management of the patient with an acute intracranial problem must include management of secondary injury and increased ICP.

Normal Intracranial Pressure

Intracranial pressure (ICP) is the hydrostatic force measured in the brain CSF compartment. Under normal conditions in which intracranial volume stays relatively constant, the balance

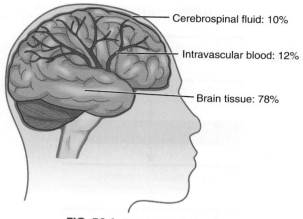

FIG. 56.1 Components of the brain.

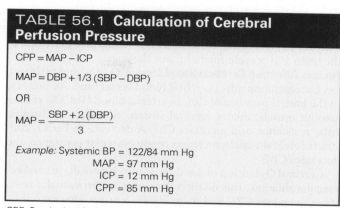

TABLE 56.1 **Calculation of Cerebral Perfusion Pressure**
CPP = MAP − ICP
MAP = DBP + 1/3 (SBP − DBP)
OR
$MAP = \dfrac{SBP + 2\,(DBP)}{3}$
Example: Systemic BP = 122/84 mm Hg
MAP = 97 mm Hg
ICP = 12 mm Hg
CPP = 85 mm Hg

CPP, Cerebral perfusion pressure; *DBP,* diastolic blood pressure; *MAP,* mean arterial pressure; *SBP,* systolic blood pressure.

among the 3 components (brain tissue, blood, CSF) maintains ICP. Factors that influence ICP under normal circumstances are changes in (1) arterial pressure; (2) venous pressure; (3) intraabdominal and intrathoracic pressure; (4) posture; (5) temperature; and (6) blood gases, particularly CO_2 levels. The degree to which these factors increase or decrease the ICP depends on the brain's ability to adapt to changes.

The Monro-Kellie doctrine states that the 3 components must stay at a relatively constant volume within the closed skull structure. If the volume of any 1 of the 3 components increases within the cranial vault and the volume from another component is displaced, the total intracranial volume will not change.[1] This hypothesis is applicable only in situations in which the skull is closed. The hypothesis is not valid in persons with displaced skull fractures or craniectomy (removal of part of the skull).

We can measure ICP in the ventricles, subarachnoid space, subdural space, epidural space, or brain tissue using a pressure transducer.[2] Normal ICP ranges from 5 to 15 mm Hg. A sustained pressure greater than 20 mm Hg is considered abnormal and must be treated.

Normal Compensatory Adaptations

In applying the Monro-Kellie doctrine, the body can adapt to volume changes within the skull in 3 different ways to maintain a normal ICP. The first compensatory mechanisms can include changes in the CSF volume. CSF volume can be changed by altering CSF absorption or production and by displacing CSF into the spinal subarachnoid space. Second, changes in intracranial blood volume can occur through the collapse of cerebral veins and dural sinuses, regional cerebral vasoconstriction or dilation, and changes in venous outflow. Third, brain tissue volume compensates through distention of the dura or compression of brain tissue.

Initially an increase in volume produces no increase in ICP because of these compensatory mechanisms. However, there is limited ability to compensate for changes in volume. As the volume increase continues, ICP rises and decompensation occurs, resulting in compression and ischemia.

Cerebral Blood Flow

Cerebral blood flow (CBF) is the amount of blood in milliliters passing through 100 g of brain tissue in 1 minute. The global CBF is about 50 mL/min/100 g of brain tissue. Maintaining blood flow to the brain is critical because the brain requires a constant supply of O_2 and glucose. The brain uses 20% of the body's O_2 and 25% of its glucose.[3]

Autoregulation of Cerebral Blood Flow. The brain regulates its own blood flow in response to its metabolic needs despite wide fluctuations in systemic arterial pressure. *Cerebral autoregulation* is the automatic adjustment in the diameter of the cerebral blood vessels by the brain to maintain a constant blood flow during changes in arterial BP. The purpose of autoregulation is to ensure a consistent CBF to provide for the metabolic needs of brain tissue and maintain cerebral perfusion pressure within normal limits.

The lower limit of systemic arterial pressure at which autoregulation is effective in a normotensive person is a mean arterial pressure (MAP) of 70 mm Hg. Below this, CBF decreases, and symptoms of cerebral ischemia, such as syncope and blurred vision, occur. The upper limit of systemic arterial pressure at which autoregulation is effective is a MAP of 150 mm Hg. When this pressure is exceeded, the vessels are maximally constricted, and further vasoconstrictor response is lost.

The *cerebral perfusion pressure* (CPP) is the pressure needed to ensure blood flow to the brain. CPP is equal to the MAP minus the ICP (CPP = MAP − ICP) (see the example in Table 56.1). Normal CPP is 60 to 100 mm Hg. As the CPP decreases, autoregulation fails and CBF decreases. A CPP of less than 50 mm Hg is associated with ischemia and neuronal death. A CPP of less than 30 mm Hg results in ischemia and is incompatible with life.

Though CPP is clinically useful, it does not consider the effect of cerebrovascular resistance. Cerebrovascular resistance, generated by the arterioles within the cranium, links CPP and blood flow as follows:

$$CPP = Flow \times Resistance$$

When cerebrovascular resistance is high, blood flow to brain tissue is impaired. Transcranial Doppler is a noninvasive technique used in intensive care units (ICUs) to monitor changes in cerebrovascular resistance.

Normally, autoregulation maintains an adequate CBF and CPP by adjusting the diameter of cerebral blood vessels and metabolic factors that affect ICP. It is critical to maintain MAP when ICP is increased.

Remember that CPP may not reflect perfusion pressure in all parts of the brain. There may be local areas of swelling and compression limiting regional perfusion pressure. Thus a higher

CPP may be needed for these patients to prevent localized tissue damage. For example, a patient with an acute stroke may need a higher BP, increasing MAP and CPP, to increase perfusion to the brain and prevent further tissue damage.

Factors Affecting Cerebral Blood Flow. CO_2, O_2, and hydrogen ion concentration affect cerebral blood vessel tone. An increase in the partial pressure of CO_2 in arterial blood ($PaCO_2$) relaxes smooth muscle, dilates cerebral vessels, decreases cerebrovascular resistance, and increases CBF. A decrease in $PaCO_2$ constricts cerebral vessels, increases cerebrovascular resistance, and decreases CBF.

Cerebral O_2 tension of less than 50 mm Hg results in cerebrovascular dilation. This dilation decreases cerebrovascular resistance, increases CBF, and increases O_2 tension. However, if O_2 tension is not increased, anaerobic metabolism begins, resulting in an accumulation of lactic acid. As lactic acid increases and hydrogen ions accumulate, the environment becomes more acidic. Within this acidic environment, further vasodilation occurs in a continued attempt to increase blood flow. The combination of a severely low partial pressure of O_2 in arterial blood (PaO_2) and increased hydrogen ion concentration (acidosis), which are both potent cerebral vasodilators, may produce a state in which autoregulation is lost and compensatory mechanisms do not meet tissue metabolic demands.

CBF can be affected by cardiac or respiratory arrest, systemic hemorrhage, and other pathophysiologic states (e.g., diabetic coma, encephalopathies, infections, toxicities). Regional CBF can be affected by trauma, tumors, cerebral hemorrhage, or stroke. When regional or global autoregulation is lost, CBF is no longer maintained at a constant level but is directly influenced by changes in systemic BP, hypoxia, or catecholamines.

INCREASED INTRACRANIAL PRESSURE

Any patient who becomes unconscious acutely, regardless of the cause, should be suspected of having increased ICP.

Mechanisms of Increased Intracranial Pressure

Increased ICP is a potentially life-threatening situation that results from an increase in any or all the 3 components (brain tissue, blood, CSF) within the skull. Increased ICP is clinically significant because it decreases CPP, increases risks for brain ischemia and infarction, and is associated with a poor prognosis.[4] Common causes of increased ICP include a mass (e.g., hematoma, contusion, abscess, tumor) and cerebral edema (from brain tumors, hydrocephalus, head injury, brain inflammation).

These cerebral insults, which may result in hypercapnia, cerebral acidosis, impaired autoregulation, and systemic hypertension, increase the formation and spread of cerebral edema. This edema distorts brain tissue, further increasing the ICP, and leads to even more tissue hypoxia and acidosis. Fig. 56.2 shows the progression of increased ICP.

It is critical to maintain CBF to preserve tissue and thus minimize secondary injury. Sustained increases in ICP result in brainstem compression and herniation of the brain. *Herniation* occurs as the brain tissue is forcibly shifted from the compartment of greater pressure to a compartment of lesser pressure.

Displacement and herniation of brain tissue can cause a potentially reversible process to become irreversible. Ischemia and edema are further increased, compounding the preexisting problem. Compression of the brainstem and cranial nerves may

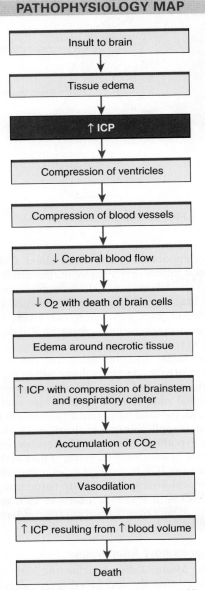

PATHOPHYSIOLOGY MAP

FIG. 56.2 Progression of increased ICP.

be fatal. Fig. 56.3 shows types of herniation. Herniation forces the cerebellum and brainstem downward through the foramen magnum. If compression of the brainstem is unrelieved, respiratory arrest will occur due to compression of the respiratory control center in the medulla. In this situation, intense pressure is placed on the brainstem. If herniation continues, brainstem death is imminent.

Cerebral Edema

There are a variety of causes of **cerebral edema** (increased accumulation of fluid in the extravascular spaces of brain tissue) (Table 56.2). Regardless of the cause, cerebral edema results in an increase in tissue volume that can increase ICP. The extent and severity of the original insult are factors that determine the degree of cerebral edema.

There are 3 types of cerebral edema: vasogenic, cytotoxic, and interstitial. The same patient may have more than 1 type.

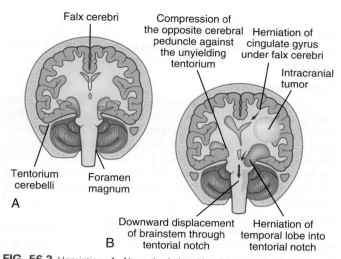

FIG. 56.3 Herniation. **A,** Normal relationship of intracranial structures. **B,** Shift of intracranial structures. (Modified from McCance KL, Huether SE: *Pathophysiology: The biologic basis for disease in adults and children,* ed 6, St Louis, 2010, Mosby.)

TABLE 56.2 Causes of Cerebral Edema

Cerebral Infections
- Encephalitis
- Meningitis

Head Injuries and Brain Surgery
- Contusion
- Hemorrhage
- Posttraumatic brain swelling

Mass Lesions
- Brain abscess
- Brain tumor (primary, metastatic)
- Hematoma (intracerebral, subdural, epidural)
- Hemorrhage (intracerebral, cerebellar, brainstem)

Toxic or Metabolic Encephalopathic Conditions
- Hepatic encephalopathy
- Lead or arsenic intoxication
- Uremia

Vascular Insult
- Anoxic and ischemic episodes
- Cerebral infarction (thrombotic or embolic)
- Venous sinus thrombosis

Vasogenic Cerebral Edema. *Vasogenic cerebral edema,* the most common type of cerebral edema, occurs mainly in the white matter. It is characterized by leakage of large molecules from the capillaries into the surrounding extracellular space. This results in an osmotic gradient that favors the flow of fluid from the intravascular to extravascular space. A variety of problems, such as brain tumors, abscesses, and ingested toxins, may increase in the permeability of the blood-brain barrier and produce an increase in the extracellular fluid volume. The speed and extent of the spread of the edema are influenced by the systemic BP, site of the brain injury, and extent of the blood-brain barrier defect.

This edema may produce a continuum of symptoms, ranging from headache to a decrease in consciousness, including coma (profound state of unconsciousness) and focal neurologic deficits.

It is important to recognize that although a headache may seem to be a benign symptom, in cases of cerebral edema it can quickly progress to coma and death. So, you must be vigilant in your assessment.

Cytotoxic Cerebral Edema. *Cytotoxic cerebral edema* results from disruption of the integrity of the cell membranes. It develops from destructive lesions or trauma to brain tissue, resulting in cerebral hypoxia or anoxia and syndrome of inappropriate antidiuretic hormone (SIADH) secretion. In this type of edema, the blood-brain barrier stays intact. Cerebral edema occurs from fluid and protein shifts from the extracellular space directly into the cells, with subsequent swelling and loss of cellular function.

Interstitial Cerebral Edema. *Interstitial cerebral edema* is usually a result of hydrocephalus. *Hydrocephalus* is a buildup of fluid in the brain. It is manifested by ventricular enlargement. It can be due to excess CSF production, obstruction of flow, or an inability to reabsorb the CSF. Hydrocephalus treatment usually consists of a ventriculostomy or ventriculoperitoneal shunt. Management of hydrocephalus is discussed later in this chapter on p. 1319.

Clinical Manifestations

The manifestations of increased ICP can take many forms, depending on the cause, location, and rate of increases in ICP.

Change in Level of Consciousness. The *level of consciousness* (LOC) is the most sensitive and reliable indicator of the patient's neurologic status. Changes in LOC are a result of impaired CBF, which causes O_2 deprivation to the cells of the cerebral cortex and reticular activating system (RAS). The RAS is found in the brainstem, with neural connections to many parts of the nervous system. An intact RAS can maintain a state of wakefulness even in the absence of a functioning cerebral cortex. Interruptions of impulses from the RAS or changes in functioning of the cerebral hemispheres can cause unconsciousness, an abnormal state of complete or partial unawareness of self or environment.

The patient's state of consciousness is defined by the patient's clinical responses and pattern of brain activity (recorded by an electroencephalogram [EEG]). A change in consciousness may be dramatic (as in coma) or subtle (e.g., flattening of affect, change in orientation, decrease in level of attention). In the deepest state of unconsciousness (e.g., coma), the patient does not respond to painful stimuli. Corneal and pupillary reflexes are absent. The patient cannot swallow or cough and is incontinent of urine and feces. The EEG pattern shows suppressed or absent neuronal activity.

Changes in Vital Signs. Increasing pressure on the thalamus, hypothalamus, pons, and medulla causes changes in vital signs.

Manifestations such as *Cushing's triad* (systolic hypertension with a widening pulse pressure, bradycardia with a full and bounding pulse, irregular respirations) may be present but often do not appear until ICP has been increased for some time or is suddenly and markedly increased (e.g., head trauma). Always recognize Cushing's triad as a medical emergency as it is a sign of brainstem compression and impending death. A change in body temperature may occur because increased ICP affects the hypothalamus.

❓ CHECK YOUR PRACTICE

You are monitoring the vital signs of an 82-yr-old woman who was admitted for a head injury after she fell while walking on the sidewalk. She hit her head on a fire hydrant. She was confused on admission, but vital signs were stable at BP 150/86, pulse 84, respirations 14/min. 2 hours after admission, her vital signs are now BP 166/74, pulse 54, respirations 10 to 16/min.

- What is your interpretation of her vital signs?

Ocular Signs. Compression of cranial nerve (CN) III, the oculomotor nerve, results in dilation of the pupil on the same side (*ipsilateral*) as the mass lesion, sluggish or no response to light, inability to move the eye upward and adduct, and ptosis of the eyelid. These signs can be the result of the brain shifting from midline, compressing the trunk of CN III, and paralyzing the muscles controlling pupillary size and shape. In this situation, a fixed, unilateral, dilated pupil is considered a neurologic emergency that indicates brain herniation.

Other cranial nerves may be affected, including the optic (CN II), trochlear (CN IV), and abducens (CN VI) nerves. Signs of problems with these cranial nerves include blurred vision, diplopia, and changes in extraocular eye movements. *Central herniation* may initially manifest as sluggish but equal pupil response. *Uncal herniation* may cause a dilated unilateral pupil. *Papilledema* (an edematous optic disc seen on retinal examination) is a nonspecific sign associated with persistent increases in ICP.

Decrease in Motor Function. As the ICP continues to rise, the patient has changes in motor ability. A *contralateral* (opposite side of the mass lesion) hemiparesis or hemiplegia may develop, depending on the location of the source of the increased ICP. If painful stimuli are used to elicit a motor response, the patient may localize to the stimuli or withdraw from it.

Noxious stimuli may elicit *decorticate* (flexor) or *decerebrate* (extensor) posturing (Fig. 56.4). Decorticate posture consists of internal rotation and adduction of the arms with flexion of the elbows, wrists, and fingers. It is a result of interruption of voluntary motor tracts in the cerebral cortex. Extension of the legs may be seen. A decerebrate posture may indicate more serious damage. It results from disruption of motor fibers in the midbrain and brainstem. In this position, the arms are stiffly extended, adducted, and hyperpronated. There is hyperextension of the legs with plantar flexion of the feet.

Headache. Although the brain itself is insensitive to pain, compression of other intracranial structures, such as arteries, veins, and cranial nerves, can cause a headache. A nocturnal headache and/or a headache in the morning is cause for concern and may indicate a tumor or other space-occupying lesion that is causing increased ICP. Straining, agitation, or movement may worsen the pain.

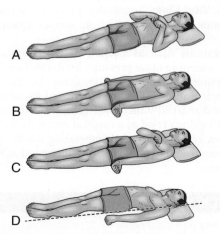

FIG. 56.4 Decorticate and decerebrate posturing. **A,** Decorticate response. Flexion of arms, wrists, and fingers with adduction in upper extremities. Extension, internal rotation, and plantar flexion in lower extremities. **B,** Decerebrate response. All 4 extremities in rigid extension, with hyperpronation of forearms and plantar flexion of feet. **C,** Decorticate response on right side of body and decerebrate response on left side of body. **D,** Opisthotonic posturing.

Vomiting. Vomiting, usually not preceded by nausea, is often a nonspecific sign of increased ICP. This is called *unexpected vomiting* and is related to pressure changes in the cranium. Projectile vomiting may occur and is related to increased ICP.

Complications

The major complications of uncontrolled increased ICP are inadequate cerebral perfusion and cerebral herniation (Fig. 56.3). To better understand cerebral herniation, 2 important structures in the brain must be described. The *falx cerebri* is a thin wall of dura that folds down between the cortex, separating the 2 cerebral hemispheres. The *tentorium cerebelli* is a rigid fold of dura that separates the cerebral hemispheres from the cerebellum (Fig. 56.3). It is called the *tentorium* (meaning tent) because it forms a tentlike cover over the cerebellum.

Tentorial herniation (central herniation) occurs when a mass lesion in the cerebrum forces the brain to herniate downward through the opening created by the brainstem. *Uncal herniation* occurs when there is lateral and downward herniation. *Cingulate herniation* occurs when there is lateral displacement of brain tissue beneath the falx cerebri.

Diagnostic Studies

Diagnostic studies can be used to identify the cause of increased ICP (Table 56.3). CT and MRI are used to discern the many conditions that can cause increased ICP and assess the effect of treatment.

TABLE 56.3 Interprofessional Care
Increased Intracranial Pressure

Diagnostic Assessment
- History and physical examination
- Vital signs, neurologic assessments, ICP measurements
- Skull, chest, and spinal x-ray studies
- CT scan, MRI, cerebral angiography, EEG, PET
- Transcranial Doppler studies
- Infrascanner
- ECG
- Evoked potential studies
- Lumbar puncture (should not be done if there is a risk for herniation)
- Laboratory studies, including CBC, coagulation profile, electrolytes, serum creatinine, ABGs, ammonia level, drug and toxicology screen, CSF analysis (for protein, WBC, and glucose)

Management
- Elevation of head of bed to 30 degrees with head in a neutral position
- Intubation and mechanical ventilation
- ICP monitoring
- Cerebral oxygenation monitoring (PbtO$_2$, SjvO$_2$)
- Maintain PaO$_2$ ≥100 mm Hg
- Maintain fluid balance and assess osmolality
- Maintain systolic arterial pressure between 100 and 160 mm Hg
- Maintain CPP >60 mm Hg
- Reduction of cerebral metabolism (e.g., high-dose barbiturates)

Drug Therapy
- Osmotic diuretic (mannitol)
- Hypertonic saline
- Antiseizure drugs (e.g., phenytoin [Dilantin])
- Corticosteroids (dexamethasone) for brain tumors, bacterial meningitis
- Histamine (H$_2$)-receptor antagonist (e.g., cimetidine) or proton pump inhibitor (e.g., pantoprazole to prevent GI ulcers and bleeding

Other tests include EEG, cerebral angiography, ICP measurement, brain tissue oxygenation measurement via the LICOX catheter (described later), positron emission tomography (PET), transcranial Doppler studies, and evoked potential studies. In general, a lumbar puncture (LP) is not done when increased ICP is suspected. The reason for this is that cerebral herniation could occur from the sudden release of the pressure in the skull from the area above the LP.

In some agencies, a hand-held near-infrared scanner (Infrascanner) is used to detect life-threatening intracranial bleeding. The scanner directs a wavelength of light that can penetrate tissue and bone. Blood from intracranial hematomas absorbs the light differently from other areas of the brain.

Monitoring ICP and Cerebral Oxygenation

Indications for Intracranial Pressure Monitoring. ICP monitoring is used to guide clinical care when the patient is at risk for or has elevations in ICP.[4] It may be used in patients with a variety of neurologic problems, including hemorrhage, stroke, tumor, infection, or traumatic brain injury (TBI). ICP should be monitored in patients admitted with a *Glasgow Coma Scale* (GCS) score of 8 or less and an abnormal CT scan or MRI. These results indicate that the patient may have bleeding, contusion, edema, or other problems. The GCS is discussed later on p. 1308.

Methods of Measuring ICP. Patients with conditions known to elevate ICP, except those with irreversible problems or advanced neurologic disease, usually undergo ICP monitoring in an ICU. Multiple methods and devices are available to monitor ICP in various sites (Fig. 56.5).

The gold standard for monitoring ICP is the *ventriculostomy,* in which a specialized catheter is inserted into the lateral ventricle and coupled to an external transducer (Figs. 56.6 and 56.7). This technique directly measures the pressure within the ventricles, facilitates removal and/or sampling of CSF, and allows for intraventricular drug administration. In this system the transducer is external. It is important to ensure that the transducer is level with the foramen of Monro (interventricular foramen). The system must also be at the ideal height (Fig. 56.8, *A*). A reference point for this foramen is the tragus of the ear. Every time the patient is repositioned, assess the system to ensure it is level.

The *fiberoptic catheter,* an alternative technology, uses a sensor transducer found within the catheter tip. The sensor tip is placed within the ventricle or the brain tissue and gives a direct measurement of brain pressure.

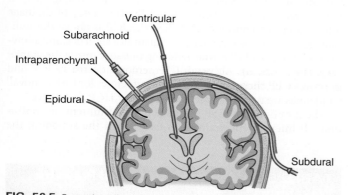

FIG. 56.5 Coronal section of brain showing potential sites for placement of ICP monitoring devices.

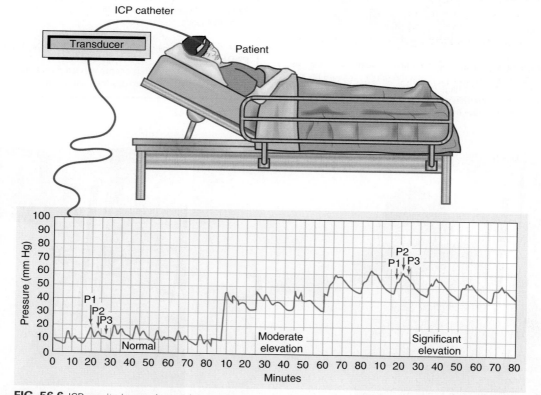

FIG. 56.6 ICP monitoring can be used to continuously measure ICP. The ICP tracing shows normal, elevated, and plateau waves. At high ICP, the P2 peak is higher than the P1 peak, and the peaks become less distinct and plateau. (Modified from Copstead-Kirkhorn LC, Banasik JL: *Pathophysiology,* ed 5, St Louis, 2013, Mosby.)

The *air pouch/pneumatic technology,* another system for monitoring ICP, has an air-filled pouch at the tip of the catheter that maintains a constant volume. The pressure changes within the cranium are transmitted through the changes exerted on this pouch to the monitor.

ICP is represented on the monitor as a mean pressure in millimeters of mercury (mm Hg). If a CSF drainage device is in place, the drain must be closed for at least 6 minutes to ensure an accurate reading. Record the waveform strip along with other pressure monitoring waveforms. The normal ICP waveform has 3 phases (Fig. 56.6 and Table 56.4). It is important to monitor the ICP waveform and the mean CPP. When ICP is normal, P1, P2, and P3 resemble a staircase. As ICP increases, P2 rises above P1. This indicates poor ventricular compliance (Fig. 56.6). Consider the rate at which changes occur and the patient's clinical condition. Neurologic deterioration may not occur until ICP elevation is pronounced and sustained. Immediately report to the HCP any ICP elevation, either as a mean increase in pressure or as an abnormal waveform configuration.

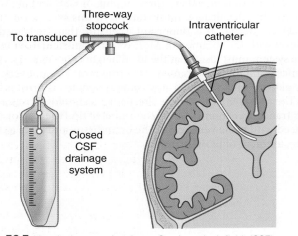

FIG. 56.7 Ventriculostomy in place. Cerebrospinal fluid (CSF) can be drained via a ventriculostomy when ICP exceeds the upper pressure parameter set by the HCP. Intermittent drainage involves opening the 3-way stopcock to allow CSF to flow into the drainage bag for brief periods (30 to 120 seconds) until the pressure is below the upper pressure parameters.

Inaccurate ICP readings can be caused by CSF leaks around the monitoring device, obstruction of the intraventricular catheter (from tissue or blood clot), a difference between the height of the catheter and the transducer, kinks in the tubing, and incorrect height of the drainage system relative to the patient's reference point. Bubbles or air in the tubing can dampen the waveform.

Infection is a serious complication with ICP monitoring. Factors that contribute to infection include ICP monitoring more than 5 days, use of a ventriculostomy, a CSF leak, and a concurrent systemic infection. Routinely assess the insertion site, use aseptic technique, and monitor the CSF for a change in drainage color or clarity.

Cerebrospinal Fluid Drainage. With the ventricular catheter, it is possible to control ICP by removing CSF (Fig. 56.7). The HCP typically orders a specific level at which to start drainage (e.g., if ICP is greater than 20 mm Hg) and the frequency of drainage (intermittent or continuous). When the ICP is above the indicated level, the system is opened by turning a stopcock and allowing the drainage of CSF, thus relieving pressure inside the cranial vault (Fig. 56.8, *B*). Although CSF removal decreases ICP and improves CPP, there are no universal guidelines for CSF removal. Guidelines are typically based on agency or HCP preference.[5]

The 2 options for CSF drainage are intermittent or continuous. If intermittent drainage is used, open the system at the

TABLE 56.4 **Normal Intracranial Pressure Waveforms***	
Waveform	**Meaning**
P1 Percussion wave	Represents arterial pulsations. Normally the highest of the 3 waveforms.
P2 Rebound wave or tidal wave	Reflects intracranial compliance or relative brain volume. When P2 is higher than P1, intracranial compliance is compromised.
P3 Dicrotic wave	Follows dicrotic notch. Represents venous pulsations. Normally the lowest waveform.

*See Fig. 56.6.

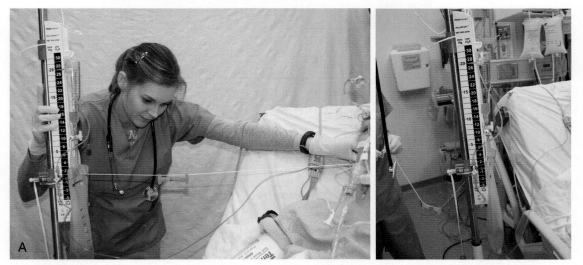

FIG. 56.8 **A,** Leveling a ventriculostomy. **B,** Cerebrospinal fluid is drained into a drainage system. (Courtesy Meg Zomorodi, RN, PhD, CNL, Raleigh, NC.)

indicated ICP and allow CSF to drain for 2 to 3 minutes. Then close the stopcock to return the ventriculostomy to a closed system. If continuous ICP drainage is ordered, carefully monitor the volume of CSF drained. Keep in mind that normal CSF production is about 20 to 30 mL/hr. There is a total CSF volume of about 150 mL within the ventricles and subarachnoid space. Post a sign above the patient's bed to notify anyone before turning, moving, or suctioning the patient to prevent the removal of too much CSF, which can result in other complications.

Complications include ventricular collapse, infection, and herniation or subdural hematoma formation from rapid decompression. Strict aseptic technique during dressing changes or sampling of CSF is crucial to prevent infection. The system must stay intact to ensure that the ICP readings are accurate because treatment is based on the pressures.

Cerebral Oxygenation Monitoring. Technology is available to measure cerebral oxygenation and assess perfusion. Three intracranial devices used in ICU settings are the LICOX catheter, Neurovent catheter, and jugular venous bulb catheter.

The LICOX and Neurovent catheters are placed in healthy white matter of the brain (Fig. 56.9). These catheters measure brain oxygenation and temperature. These systems provide continuous monitoring of the pressure of O_2 in brain tissue ($PbtO_2$). The normal range for $PbtO_2$ is 20 to 40 mm Hg. A low $PbtO_2$ level indicates ischemia.[2] These catheters can also measure brain temperature. A cooler brain temperature (96.8° F [36° C]) may produce better outcomes.

Jugular venous bulb oximetry, which measures global O_2 extraction, is used in some agencies. The jugular venous bulb catheter is placed in the internal jugular vein and positioned so that the catheter tip is in the jugular bulb. An x-ray verifies placement. This catheter provides a measurement of jugular venous O_2 saturation ($SjvO_2$), which indicates total venous brain tissue extraction of O_2. This is a measure of cerebral O_2 supply and demand. The normal $SjvO_2$ range is 60% to 75%. Values less than 50% indicate impaired cerebral oxygenation.[2]

In addition to measuring ICP and brain oxygenation, many HCPs are now looking at multimodality monitoring in TBI and intracranial hypertension. This technology includes brain microdialysis (measurement of small molecules), continuous EEG, and blood flow monitoring.

Interprofessional Care

The goals of interprofessional care (Table 56.3) are to (1) identify and treat the underlying cause of increased ICP and (2) support brain function. The earlier the condition is recognized and treated, the better the patient outcome. A careful history is important in the search for the underlying cause. The underlying cause of increased ICP is usually an increase in blood (hemorrhage), brain tissue (tumor or edema), or CSF (hydrocephalus) in the brain.

For any patient with increased ICP, it is important to maintain adequate oxygenation to support brain function and prevent secondary injury. An endotracheal tube or tracheostomy may be needed to maintain adequate ventilation. Arterial blood gas (ABG) analysis guides the O_2 therapy. The goal is to maintain the PaO_2 at 100 mm Hg or greater and to keep $PaCO_2$ in normal range at 35 to 45 mm Hg. The patient may need to be on a mechanical ventilator to ensure adequate oxygenation.

If increased ICP is caused by a mass lesion (e.g., tumor, hematoma), surgical removal of the mass is the best treatment. See the sections on brain tumors and cranial surgery later in this chapter. In aggressive situations, a craniectomy (removal of part of skull) may be done to reduce ICP and prevent herniation.

Drug Therapy. Drug therapy plays an important part in the management of increased ICP. Mannitol (Osmitrol) (25%) is an osmotic diuretic given IV. Mannitol decreases ICP in 2 ways: plasma expansion and osmotic effect. The immediate plasma-expanding effect reduces the hematocrit and blood viscosity. This increases CBF and cerebral O_2 delivery. A vascular osmotic gradient is created by mannitol. Thus fluid moves from the tissues into the blood vessels, reducing the ICP because of the decrease in the total brain fluid content. Monitor fluid and electrolyte status when osmotic diuretics are used. Mannitol may be contraindicated if renal disease is present and serum osmolality increased.

Hypertonic saline solution is another option. It produces massive movement of water out of edematous swollen brain cells and into blood vessels. This movement can reduce swelling and improve cerebral blood flow. Care during an infusion includes frequent monitoring of BP and serum sodium levels because intravascular fluid volume excess can occur. Hypertonic saline infusion is just as effective as mannitol when treating increased

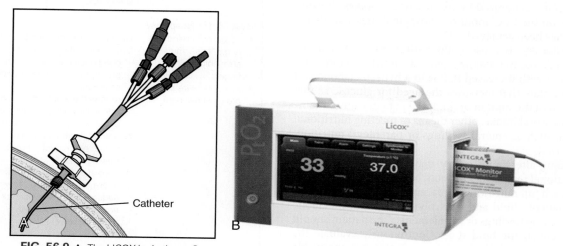

FIG. 56.9 A, The LICOX brain tissue O_2 system involves insertion of a catheter. **B,** The system measures O_2 in the brain ($PbtO_2$), brain tissue temperature, and ICP. (*B,* Courtesy of Integra LifeSciences Corporation, Plainsboro, NJ.)

ICP. They are often used concurrently when caring for a patient with a severe brain injury.[6]

Corticosteroids (e.g., dexamethasone) are used to treat vasogenic edema around tumors and abscesses. These drugs are not recommended for TBI. Corticosteroids stabilize the cell membrane and inhibit the synthesis of prostaglandins (see Fig. 11.2), preventing the formation of proinflammatory mediators. Corticosteroids also improve neuronal function by improving CBF and restoring autoregulation.

Complications associated with the use of corticosteroids include hyperglycemia, increased incidence of infections, and gastrointestinal (GI) bleeding. Regularly monitor fluid intake and sodium levels. Perform blood glucose monitoring at least every 6 hours. Patients receiving corticosteroids should receive antacid, histamine (H_2)-receptor blockers (e.g., cimetidine, ranitidine), or proton pump inhibitors (e.g., pantoprazole) to prevent GI ulcers and bleeding.

IV 0.9% sodium chloride is the preferred solution for giving secondary medications. If 5% dextrose in water or 0.45% sodium chloride is used, serum osmolarity decreases and an increase in cerebral edema may occur.

Metabolic demands, such as fever (greater than 100.4° F [38° C]), agitation or shivering, pain, and seizures, can increase ICP. Implement measures to reduce these metabolic demands to lower the ICP in the at-risk patient. Monitor patients for seizure activity. They may need prophylactic antiseizure medication. Maintain the temperature at 96.8° to 98.6° F (36° to 37° C) by using antipyretics (e.g., acetaminophen), cool baths, cooling blankets, ice packs, or intravascular cooling devices as needed. Avoid letting the patient shiver or shake, since this increases the metabolic workload on the brain. If this occurs, the patient may need sedatives or a different cooling method.

Drug therapy for reducing cerebral metabolism may be an effective way to control ICP. Reducing the metabolic rate decreases the CBF and therefore the ICP. High doses of barbiturates (e.g., pentobarbital, thiopental) are used in patients with increased ICP refractory to other treatments. Barbiturates decrease cerebral metabolism, causing a decrease in ICP and a reduction in cerebral edema. With this treatment, monitor the patient's ICP, blood flow, and EEG. Barbiturate dosing is typically based on analysis of the bedside EEG tracing and the ICP. The HCP orders the barbiturate infusion at a rate that achieves a desired level of brain wave suppression to control ICP. *Total burst suppression*, recognized by the absence of spikes showing brain activity on the EEG monitor, shows that maximal therapeutic effect has been achieved.

Nutritional Therapy. Because malnutrition promotes continued cerebral edema, maintaining optimal nutrition is important. The patient with increased ICP is in a hypermetabolic and hypercatabolic state that increases the need for glucose as fuel for metabolism of the injured brain. If the patient cannot maintain an adequate oral intake, other means of meeting nutritional requirements, such as enteral feedings or parenteral nutrition, should be started.

Early feeding after brain injury may improve patient outcome.[5] Nutritional replacement should begin within 3 days after injury and reach full nutritional replacement within 7 days after injury. The patient's fluid and electrolyte status and metabolic needs should guide feedings or supplements. The patient should be kept in a euvolemic fluid state. Continuously evaluate the patient based on clinical factors such as urine output, insensible fluid loss, serum and urine osmolality, and serum electrolytes.

❖ NURSING MANAGEMENT: INCREASED INTRACRANIAL PRESSURE

◆ Nursing Assessment

Subjective data about the patient with increased ICP can be obtained from the patient, caregiver, or family member who is familiar with the patient. Describe the LOC by noting the specific behaviors seen. Assess the LOC using the GCS. Assess body functions, especially circulation and respiration.

◆ **Glasgow Coma Scale.** The Glasgow Coma Scale (GCS) is a quick, practical, and standard system for assessing the LOC. The 3 areas assessed in the GCS are the patient's ability to (1) open the eyes when a verbal or painful stimulus is applied, (2) speak, and (3) obey commands. Specific assessments evaluate the patient's response to varying degrees of stimulus. Three indicators of response are evaluated: (1) opening of the eyes, (2) best verbal response, and (3) best motor response (Table 56.5).

TABLE 56.5 Glasgow Coma Scale

Appropriate Stimulus	Response	Score
Eyes Open		
• Approach to bedside	Spontaneous response.	4
• Verbal command	Opening of eyes to name or command.	3
• Pain	Lack of opening of eyes to previous stimuli but opening to pain.	2
	Lack of opening of eyes to any stimulus.	1
	Untestable.*	U
Best Verbal Response		
• Verbal questioning with maximum arousal	Appropriate orientation, conversant. Correct identification of self, place, year, and month.	5
	Confusion. Conversant, but disorientation in 1 or more spheres.	4
	Inappropriate or disorganized use of words (e.g., cursing), lack of sustained conversation.	3
	Incomprehensible words, sounds (e.g., moaning).	2
	Lack of sound, even with painful stimuli.	1
	Untestable.*	U
Best Motor Response		
• Verbal command (e.g., "raise your arm, hold up 2 fingers")	Obedience of command.	6
	Localization of pain, lack of obedience but presence of attempts to remove offending stimulus.	5
• Pain (pressure on proximal nail bed)	Flexion withdrawal,* flexion of arm in response to pain without abnormal flexion posture.	4
	Abnormal flexion, flexing of arm at elbow and pronation, making a fist.	3
	Abnormal extension, extension of arm at elbow usually with adduction and internal rotation of arm at shoulder.	2
	Lack of response.	1
	Untestable.*	U

*Added to the original scale by some centers.

Specific behaviors observed as responses to the testing stimulus are given a numeric value. Your responsibility is to elicit the best response on each of the scales: the higher the scores, the higher the level of brain functioning. The subscale scores are particularly important if a patient is untestable in an area. For example, severe periorbital edema may make eye opening impossible.

The total GCS score is the sum of the numeric values assigned to each of the 3 areas. The highest GCS score is 15 for a fully alert person, and the lowest possible score is 3. A GCS score of 8 or less generally indicates coma, and mechanical ventilation should be considered. Plot the results of the GCS scores on a graph, which can be used to determine whether the patient is stable, improving, or deteriorating.

The GCS offers several advantages in the assessment of the unconscious patient. It allows different health care professionals to arrive at the same conclusion about the patient's status. It can be used to determine between different or changing states.

Although the GCS is the gold standard assessment tool for LOC, other scales, such as the *Full Outline of Unresponsiveness (FOUR) scale,* are also used.[7] In cases of stroke or hemorrhage associated with increased ICP, use the NIH Stroke Scale (see Table 57.10). Other key neurologic assessments include cranial nerve assessment and motor and sensory testing. Cranial nerve assessment is outlined in Table 55.4.

◆ **Neurologic Assessment.** Compare the pupils with one another for size, shape, movement, and reactivity (Fig. 56.10). If the oculomotor nerve (CN III) is compressed, the pupil on the affected side *(ipsilateral)* becomes larger until it fully dilates. If ICP continues to increase, both pupils dilate.

Test pupillary reaction with a penlight. The normal reaction is brisk constriction when the light is shone directly into the eye. Note a consensual response (slight constriction in the opposite pupil) at the same time. A sluggish reaction can indicate early pressure on CN III. A fixed pupil unresponsive to light stimulus usually indicates increased ICP. However, note that there are other causes of a fixed pupil, including direct injury to CN III, previous eye surgery, atropine administration, and use of mydriatic eye drops.

In some agencies, HCPs are using a hand-held device *(pupillometer)* to measure the pupil reactivity and size. The device removes any subjectivity from the pupil evaluation.

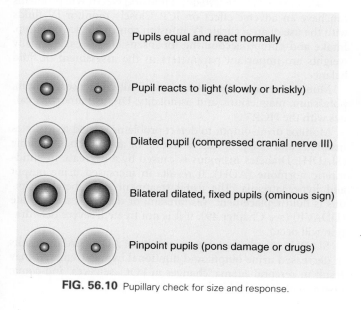

Pupils equal and react normally

Pupil reacts to light (slowly or briskly)

Dilated pupil (compressed cranial nerve III)

Bilateral dilated, fixed pupils (ominous sign)

Pinpoint pupils (pons damage or drugs)

FIG. 56.10 Pupillary check for size and response.

Assess eye movements controlled by CN III, CN IV, and CN VI in the patient who is awake and able to follow commands. They can be used to assess brainstem function. Testing the corneal reflex gives information about the functioning of CN V and CN VII. If this reflex is absent, start routine eye care to prevent corneal abrasion (see Chapter 20).

Eye movements of the uncooperative or unconscious patient can be elicited by reflex with the use of head movements (oculocephalic) and caloric stimulation (oculovestibular). To test the oculocephalic reflex (doll's eye reflex), turn the patient's head briskly to the left or right while holding the eyelids open. A normal response is movement of the eyes across the midline in the direction opposite that of the turning. Next, quickly flex and then extend the neck. Eye movement should be opposite to the direction of head movement—up when the neck is flexed and down when it is extended. Abnormal responses can help locate an intracranial lesion. This test should not be done if a cervical spine problem is suspected.

To test the oculovestibular reflex (cold caloric), the patient is positioned with the head of bed elevated. A syringe of ice-cold water is instilled into the external auditory ear canal. The patient's eyes are assessed for a total of 1 minute. The absence of eye movement or response indicates severe neurologic demise. This test requires patent external auditory ear canals and tympanic membranes.

Test motor strength by asking the awake and cooperative patient to squeeze your hands to compare strength in the hands. The pronator drift test is an excellent measure of strength in the upper extremities. The patient raises the arms in front of the body with the palms facing upward and eyes closed. If there is any weakness in the upper extremity, the palmar surface turns downward and the arm drifts down. This would indicate a problem in the opposite motor cortex. Asking the patient to raise the foot from the bed or to bend the knees up in bed is a good assessment of lower extremity strength. Test all 4 extremities for strength and for any asymmetry in strength or movement.

Assess the motor response of the unconscious or uncooperative patient by observation of spontaneous movement. If no spontaneous movement is possible, apply a pain stimulus to the patient and note the response. Resistance to movement during passive range-of-motion exercises is another measure of strength. Do not include hand squeezing as part of the assessment of motor movement in the unconscious or uncooperative patient, since this is a reflex action and can misrepresent the patient's status.

Record vital signs, including BP, pulse, respiratory rate, and temperature. Be aware of Cushing's triad, which indicates severely increased ICP. Besides recording respiratory rate, note the respiratory pattern. Specific respiratory patterns are associated with severely increased ICP (Fig. 56.11).

◆ **Nursing Diagnoses**

Nursing diagnoses for the patient with increased ICP include:
- Decreased intracranial adaptive capacity
- Ineffective tissue perfusion
- Risk for injury

Additional information on nursing diagnoses and interventions for patients with increased ICP is presented in eNursing Care Plan 56.1 (available on the website for this chapter).

◆ **Planning**

The overall goals for the patient with increased ICP are to (1) maintain a patent airway; (2) have ICP within normal limits; (3) have normal fluid, electrolyte, and nutritional balance; and (4) prevent complications from immobility and decreased LOC.

Pattern	Location of Lesion	Description
1. Cheyne-Stokes 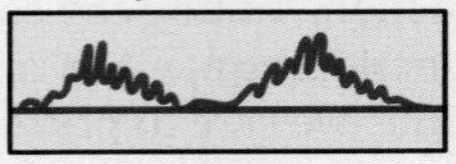	Bilateral hemispheric disease or metabolic brain dysfunction	Cycles of hyperventilation and apnea
2. Central neurogenic hyperventilation 	Brainstem between lower midbrain and upper pons	Sustained, regular rapid and deep breathing
3. Apneustic breathing 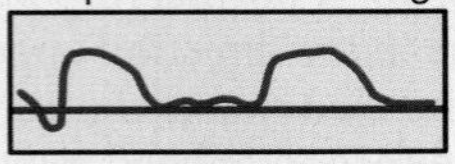	Mid or lower pons	Prolonged inspiratory phase or pauses alternating with expiratory pauses
4. Cluster breathing 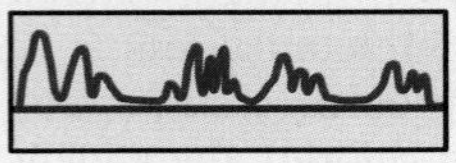	Medulla or lower pons	Clusters of breaths follow each other with irregular pauses between
5. Ataxic breathing 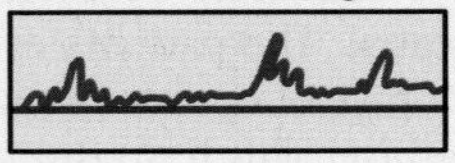	Reticular formation of the medulla	Completely irregular with some breaths deep and some shallow. Random, irregular pauses, slow rate

FIG. 56.11 Common abnormal respiratory patterns associated with coma.

◆ Nursing Implementation

◆ Acute Care

Respiratory Function. Maintaining a patent airway is critical in the patient with increased ICP and is a major nursing responsibility. As the LOC decreases, the patient is at an increased risk for airway obstruction from the tongue dropping back and occluding the airway or from accumulation of secretions.

> **! SAFETY ALERT Altered Breathing**
> • Be alert to altered breathing patterns in a patient with increased ICP.
> • Snoring sounds indicate obstruction and require immediate intervention.

Remove accumulated secretions by suctioning as needed. An oral airway facilitates breathing and provides an easier suctioning route in the comatose patient. In general, any patient with a GCS of 8 or less or an altered LOC who is unable to maintain a patent airway or effective ventilation needs intubation and mechanical ventilation.

Frequently monitor and evaluate the ABG values. Take measures to maintain the levels within prescribed or acceptable parameters. The appropriate ventilatory support can be ordered based on the PaO_2 and $PaCO_2$ values.

Prevent hypoxia and hypercapnia to minimize secondary injury. Suctioning and coughing cause transient decreases in the PaO_2 and increases in the ICP. Keep suctioning to a minimum and less than 10 seconds in duration. Give 100% O_2 before and after to prevent decreases in the PaO_2. To avoid cumulative increases in the ICP with suctioning, limit suctioning to 2 passes per suction procedure, if possible. Patients with increased ICP are at risk for lower CPP during suctioning.

Try to prevent abdominal distention, since it can interfere with respiratory function. Inserting a nasogastric (NG) tube to aspirate the stomach contents can prevent distention, vomiting, and aspiration. However, in patients with facial and skull fractures, an NG tube is contraindicated due to risk for inadvertent intracranial placement. Oral insertion of a gastric tube is preferred.

Sedation. Pain, anxiety, and fear related to the primary injury, therapeutic procedures, or noxious stimuli can increase ICP and BP, thus complicating the patient's management and recovery. The appropriate choice or combination of sedatives, paralytics, and analgesics for symptom management is a challenge. Giving these agents may alter the neurologic state, thus masking true neurologic changes. It may be necessary to temporarily stop drug therapy to appropriately assess neurologic status. The choice, dose, and combination of agents may vary depending on the patient's history, neurologic state, and overall clinical presentation.

Opioids, such as morphine sulfate and fentanyl, are rapid-onset analgesics with minimal effect on CBF or O_2 metabolism. The IV sedative propofol (Diprivan) is used to manage anxiety and agitation in the ICU because of its rapid onset and short half-life. An accurate neurologic assessment can be done soon after stopping an infusion of propofol.

Dexmedetomidine (Precedex), an α_2-adrenergic agonist, is used for continuous IV sedation of intubated and mechanically ventilated patients in the ICU setting for up to 24 hours. When using continuous IV sedatives, be aware of the side effects of these drugs, especially hypotension, since this can lower CPP.

Nondepolarizing neuromuscular blocking agents (e.g., vecuronium, cisatracurium besylate [Nimbex]) are useful for achieving complete ventilatory control in the treatment of refractory intracranial hypertension. Because these agents paralyze muscles without blocking pain or noxious stimuli, they are used in combination with sedatives, analgesics, or benzodiazepines.

Benzodiazepines, although useful for sedation, are usually avoided in the managing the patient with increased ICP because of the hypotensive effect and long half-life. They are usually given as an adjunct to neuromuscular blocking agents.

The patient should be in a quiet, calm environment with minimal noise and interruptions. Observe the patient for signs of agitation, irritation, or frustration. Teach the caregiver and family about decreasing stimulation. Coordinate with team members to minimize procedures that may cause agitation.

Fluid and Electrolyte Balance. Fluid and electrolyte problems can have an adverse effect on ICP. Closely monitor IV fluids with the use of an accurate IV infusion control device or pump. Intake and output, accounting for insensible losses, and daily weights are important parameters in the assessment of fluid balance.

Monitor serum electrolytes, especially glucose, sodium, potassium, magnesium, and osmolality. Discuss abnormal values with the HCP.

Monitor urine output to detect problems related to diabetes insipidus and inappropriate secretion of antidiuretic hormone (SIADH). Diabetes insipidus is caused by a decrease in antidiuretic hormone (ADH). It results in increased urine output and hypernatremia. The usual treatment of diabetes insipidus is fluid replacement, vasopressin, or desmopressin acetate (DDAVP) (see Chapter 49). If it is not treated, severe dehydration will occur.

SIADH is caused by excess secretion of ADH. SIADH results in decreased urine output and dilutional hyponatremia. It may result in cerebral edema, changes in LOC, seizures, and coma. (Treatment of SIADH is described in Chapter 49.)

Monitoring ICP. ICP monitoring is used in combination with other physiologic parameters to guide the care of the patient and assess the patient's response to treatment. Suctioning, hypoxemia, and arousal from sleep are factors that can increase ICP. Be alert to these factors and try to minimize them. Increased intrathoracic pressure can increase ICP by impeding the venous return. So, coughing, straining, sneezing, and the Valsalva maneuver should be avoided.

Body Position. Proper head positioning is important. Maintain the patient with increased ICP in the head-up position. Keep the head in a midline position, avoiding extreme neck flexion. Flexion can cause venous obstruction and contribute to increased ICP. Adjust the body position to decrease the ICP and improve the CPP. Elevating the head of the bed promotes drainage from the head and decreases the vascular congestion that can produce cerebral edema. However, raising the head of the bed above 30 degrees may decrease the CPP by lowering systemic BP. Carefully evaluate the effects of elevating the head of the bed on both ICP and CPP. Position the bed so that it lowers the ICP while optimizing the CPP and other indices of cerebral oxygenation.

Take care to turn the patient with slow, gentle movements. Rapid changes in position may increase ICP. Prevent discomfort when turning and positioning the patient because pain or agitation increases pressure. Avoid extreme hip flexion to decrease the risk for raising the intraabdominal pressure, which increases ICP. Decorticate or decerebrate posturing is a reflex response in some patients with increased ICP. Turning, skin care, and even passive range of motion can elicit these posturing reflexes.

Provide the physical care to minimize complications of immobility, such as atelectasis and contractures. Turn the patient at least every 2 hours.

Protection From Injury. The patient with increased ICP and decreased LOC needs protection from self-injury. Confusion, agitation, and the possibility of seizures increase the risk for injury. Use restraints judiciously in the agitated patient. If restraints are necessary to keep the patient from removing tubes or falling out of bed, they should be secure enough to be effective. Observe the skin area under the restraints regularly for irritation. Agitation may increase with the use of restraints, which indicates the need for other measures to protect the patient from injury. Light sedation with sedative agents may be needed. Having a family member stay with the patient may have a calming effect.

For the patient with seizures or the patient at risk for such activity, institute seizure precautions. These include padded side rails, an Ambu bag at the bedside, readily available suction, accurate and timely administration of antiseizure drugs, and close observation. Antiseizure prophylaxis against early seizures (within the first 7 to 10 days) is recommended in severe brain injury. This practice is controversial for mild to moderate brain injury.[8]

The patient can benefit from a quiet, nonstimulating environment. Always use a calm, reassuring approach. Touch and talk to the patient, even one who is in a coma.

Psychologic Considerations. In addition to carefully planned physical care, be aware of the psychologic well-being of patients and their families. Anxiety over the diagnosis and the prognosis can be distressing to the patient, caregiver and family, and nursing staff. Your competent and assured manner in performing care is reassuring to everyone involved. Short, simple explanations are appropriate and allow the patient and caregiver to acquire the amount of information they desire. There is a need for support, information, and teaching of both patients and families. Assess the family members' desires to help with providing care for the patient and allow for their participation as appropriate. Encourage interprofessional management (e.g., social work, chaplain) involving the patient and family in decision-making as much as possible.

◆ **Evaluation**

The expected outcomes are that the patient with increased ICP will

• Maintain ICP and cerebral perfusion within normal parameters
• Have no serious increases in ICP during or after care activities
• Have no complications of immobility

HEAD INJURY

Head injury includes any injury or trauma to the scalp, skull, or brain. A serious form of head injury is *traumatic brain injury* (TBI). Statistics about the occurrence of head injury are incomplete because many victims die at the injury scene or the condition is considered minor and health care services are not sought. An estimated 2.8 million persons are treated each year in U. S. emergency departments (EDs) for TBI. Of those, 57,000 die and 282,000 are hospitalized. Of those hospitalized, 20% will die.[9] At least 5.3 million Americans (2% of the U.S. population) currently live with disabilities resulting from TBI.

The most common causes of head injury are falls and motor vehicle accidents. Other causes of head injury include firearms, assaults, sports-related trauma, recreational injuries, and war-related injuries.[9] Men are twice as likely to sustain a TBI as women.

Head trauma has a high potential for a poor outcome. Deaths from head trauma occur at 3 points after injury: immediately after the injury, within 2 hours after injury, and about 3 weeks after injury.[10] Most deaths occur immediately after the injury, either from the direct head trauma or from massive hemorrhage and shock. Deaths occurring within a few hours of the trauma are caused by progressive worsening of the brain injury or internal bleeding.[11]

Deaths occurring 3 weeks or more after the injury result from multisystem failure. Expert nursing care in the weeks after the injury is crucial in decreasing the mortality risk and in optimizing patient outcomes.[12]

Types of Head Injuries

Scalp Lacerations. *Scalp lacerations* are an easily recognized type of external head trauma. Because the scalp contains many blood vessels with poor constrictive abilities, most scalp lacerations are associated with profuse bleeding. Even relatively small wounds can bleed significantly. The major complications associated with scalp laceration are blood loss and infection.

Skull Fractures. *Skull fractures* often occur with head trauma. Skull fractures are described in several ways: (1) linear or depressed; (2) simple, comminuted, or compound; and (3) closed or open (Table 56.6). Fractures may be closed or open, depending on the presence of a scalp laceration or extension of the fracture into the air sinuses or dura. The type and severity of a skull fracture depend on the velocity, momentum, direction, and shape (blunt or sharp) of the injuring agent and site of impact.

TABLE 56.6 Types of Skull Fractures

Type	Description	Cause
Comminuted	Multiple linear fractures with fragmentation of bone into many pieces	Direct, high-momentum impact
Compound	Depressed skull fracture and scalp laceration with communicating pathway to intracranial cavity	Severe head injury
Depressed	Inward indentation of skull	Powerful blow
Linear	Break in continuity of bone without change of relationship of parts	Low-velocity injuries
Simple	Linear or depressed skull fracture without fragmentation or communicating lacerations	Low to moderate impact

TABLE 56.7 Manifestations of Skull Fractures

Fracture Location	Manifestations
Basilar	CSF or brain otorrhea, bulging of tympanic membrane caused by blood or CSF, Battle's sign, tinnitus or hearing difficulty, rhinorrhea, facial paralysis, conjugate deviation of gaze, vertigo
Frontal	Exposure of brain to contaminants through frontal air sinus, possible association with air in forehead tissue, CSF rhinorrhea, pneumocranium (air between cranium and dura mater)
Orbital	Periorbital bruising (raccoon eyes), optic nerve injury
Parietal	Deafness, CSF or brain otorrhea, bulging of tympanic membrane caused by blood or CSF, facial paralysis, loss of taste, Battle's sign
Posterior fossa	Occipital bruising resulting in cortical blindness, visual field defects, rare appearance of ataxia or other cerebellar signs
Temporal	Boggy temporal muscle because of extravasation of blood, oval-shaped bruise behind ear in mastoid region (Battle's sign), CSF otorrhea, middle meningeal artery disruption, epidural hematoma

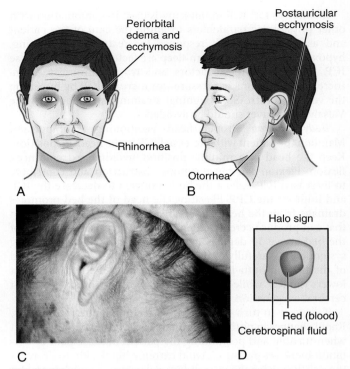

FIG. 56.12 A, Raccoon eyes and rhinorrhea. B, Battle's sign (postauricular bruising) with otorrhea. C, Battle's sign. D, Halo or ring sign (see text). (*C,* From Bingham BJG, Hawke M, Kwok P: *Clinical atlas of otolaryngology,* St Louis, 1992, Mosby.)

The location of the fracture determines the manifestations (Table 56.7). For example, a basilar skull fracture is a specialized type of linear fracture involving the base of the skull. Manifestations can evolve over the course of several hours and vary with the location and severity of fracture. These may include cranial nerve deficits, Battle's sign (postauricular bruising), and periorbital bruising (raccoon eyes) (Fig. 56.12). This fracture is often associated with a tear in the dura and subsequent leakage of CSF.

Rhinorrhea (CSF leakage from the nose) or *otorrhea* (CSF leakage from the ear) generally confirms that a fracture has traversed the dura (Fig. 56.12). Rhinorrhea may also manifest as postnasal sinus drainage. Rhinorrhea may be overlooked unless the patient is specifically assessed for this finding. The risk for meningitis is high with a CSF leak. Antibiotics should be given as a preventive measure.

Two methods of testing can be used to determine whether the fluid leaking from the nose or ear is CSF. The first method is to test the leaking fluid with a Dextrostix or Tes-Tape strip to determine whether glucose is present. CSF gives a positive reading for glucose. If blood is present in the fluid, testing for glucose is unreliable because blood also contains glucose. In this event, look for the *halo* or *ring* sign (Fig. 56.12, *D*). Allow the leaking fluid to drip onto a white gauze pad (4 × 4) or towel, and then observe the drainage. Within a few minutes, the blood coalesces into the center, and a yellowish ring encircles the blood if CSF is present. Note the color, appearance, and amount of leaking fluid because both tests can give false-positive results.

The major complications of skull fractures are intracranial infections, hematoma, and meningeal and brain tissue damage. When a basilar skull fracture is suspected, an orogastric tube should be inserted rather than a NG tube.

Head Trauma. Brain injuries are categorized as diffuse (generalized) or focal (localized). In a *diffuse* injury (e.g., concussion, diffuse axonal injury), damage to the brain is not localized to one area. In a *focal injury* (e.g., contusion, hematoma), damage is localized to a specific area of the brain. Brain injury can be classified as *minor* (GCS 13 to 15), *moderate* (GCS 9 to 12), or *severe* (GCS 3 to 8).

Diffuse Injury. Concussion, a sudden transient mechanical head injury with disruption of neural activity and a change in the LOC, is considered a minor diffuse head injury. The patient may or may not lose total consciousness with this injury.

Typical signs include a brief disruption in LOC, amnesia about the event (retrograde amnesia), and headache. The manifestations are generally of short duration. If the patient has not lost consciousness, or if the loss of consciousness lasts less than

5 minutes, the patient is usually discharged with instructions to notify the HCP if symptoms persist or if behavioral changes are noted.

Postconcussion syndrome may develop in some patients, usually from 2 weeks to 2 months after the injury. Manifestations include persistent headache, lethargy, personality and behavioral changes, shortened attention span, decreased short-term memory, and changes in intellectual ability. This syndrome can significantly affect the patient's abilities to perform activities of daily living.

Concussion is generally considered benign and usually resolves spontaneously. For some, the signs and symptoms may be the beginning of a more serious, progressive problem, especially in a patient with a history of prior concussion or head injury. At the time of discharge, it is important to give the patient and caregiver instructions for observation and accurate reporting of symptoms or changes in neurologic status.

Diffuse axonal injury. Diffuse axonal injury (DAI) is widespread axonal damage occurring after a mild, moderate, or severe TBI. The damage occurs primarily around axons in the subcortical white matter of the cerebral hemispheres, basal ganglia, thalamus, and brainstem.[13] Initially, we thought DAI occurred because the tensile forces of trauma sheared axons, resulting in axonal disconnection. There is increasing evidence that axonal damage is not preceded by an immediate tearing of the axon from the traumatic impact. Instead, the trauma changes the function of the axon, resulting in axon swelling and disconnection. This process takes 12 to 24 hours to develop and may persist longer.

The clinical signs of DAI vary. They may include a decreased LOC, increased ICP, decortication or decerebration, and global cerebral edema. About 90% of patients with DAI stay in a persistent vegetative state.[13] Patients with DAI who survive the initial event are rapidly triaged to an ICU. There, they will be vigilantly watched for signs of increased ICP and treated accordingly.

Focal Injury. Focal injury can be minor to severe and localized to an area of injury. Focal injury consists of lacerations, contusions, hematomas, and cranial nerve injuries.

Lacerations involve actual tearing of the brain tissue. They often occur in association with depressed and open fractures and penetrating injuries. Tissue damage is severe, and surgical repair of the laceration is impossible because of the nature of brain tissue. Medical management consists of antibiotics (until meningitis is ruled out) and preventing secondary injury related to increased ICP. If bleeding is deep into the brain tissue, focal and generalized signs develop.

With major head trauma, many delayed responses can occur. These include hemorrhage, hematoma formation, seizures, and cerebral edema. Intracerebral hemorrhage is generally associated with cerebral laceration. This hemorrhage manifests as a space-occupying lesion accompanied by unconsciousness, hemiplegia on the contralateral side, and a dilated pupil on the ipsilateral side. As the hematoma expands, signs of increased ICP become more severe. Subarachnoid hemorrhage and intraventricular hemorrhage can occur from head trauma.

A contusion is bruising of the brain tissue within a focal area. It is usually associated with a closed head injury and often occurs at a fracture site. A contusion may have areas of hemorrhage, infarction, necrosis, and edema.

With contusion, the phenomenon of *coup-contrecoup injury* is often noted (Fig. 56.13). Injuries can range from minor to severe. Damage from coup-contrecoup injury occurs when the

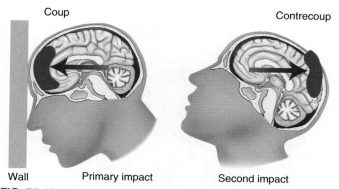

FIG. 56.13 Coup-contrecoup injury. After the head strikes the wall, a coup injury occurs as the brain strikes the skull (primary impact). The contrecoup injury (the second impact) occurs when the brain strikes the skull surface opposite the site of the original impact.

brain moves inside the skull due to high-energy or high-impact injury mechanisms. Contusions or lacerations occur both at the site of the direct impact of the brain on the skull *(coup)* and at a second area of damage on the opposite side away from injury *(contrecoup)*, leading to multiple contused areas. *Contrecoup* injuries tend to be more severe. The overall prognosis depends on the amount of bleeding around the contusion site.

Contusions may continue to bleed or rebleed and appear to "blossom" on subsequent CT scans of the brain. Bleeding worsens the neurologic outcome. Neurologic assessment may show focal and generalized manifestation, depending on the contusion's size and location. Seizures can occur because of a brain contusion, particularly when the injury involves the frontal or temporal lobes. Anticoagulant use and coagulopathy are associated with increased hemorrhage, more severe head injury, and an increased mortality rate.[14] This is especially important with older adults who are taking anticoagulants. If they fall, their contusion is likely to be more severe due to anticoagulant use. Assess for risk for falls in all patients taking anticoagulants.

Complications

Epidural Hematoma. An epidural hematoma results from bleeding between the dura and inner surface of the skull (Figs. 56.14 and 56.15). An epidural hematoma is a neurologic emergency. It is usually associated with a linear fracture crossing a major artery in the dura, causing a tear. It can have a venous or an arterial origin. Venous epidural hematomas are associated with a tear of the dural venous sinus and develop slowly. With arterial hematomas, the middle meningeal artery lying under the temporal bone is often torn. Hemorrhage occurs into the epidural space, which lies between the dura and inner surface of the skull (Fig. 56.14). Because this is an arterial hemorrhage, the hematoma develops rapidly.

Classic signs of an epidural hematoma include an initial period of unconsciousness at the scene, with a brief lucid interval followed by a decrease in LOC. Other manifestations may be a headache, nausea and vomiting, or focal findings. Rapid surgical intervention to evacuate the hematoma and prevent cerebral herniation, along with medical management for increasing ICP, dramatically improves outcomes.

Subdural Hematoma. A subdural hematoma occurs from bleeding between the dura mater and arachnoid layer of the meninges (Fig. 56.14). A subdural hematoma usually results from injury to the brain tissue and its blood vessels. The veins

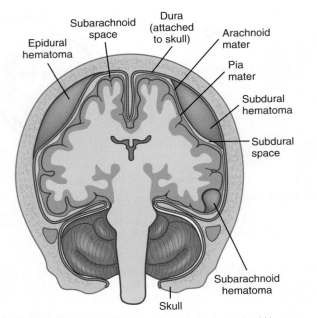

FIG. 56.14 Locations of epidural, subdural, and subarachnoid hematomas. (From Copstead-Kirkhorn LC, Banasik JL: *Pathophysiology*, ed 4, St Louis, 2010, Mosby.)

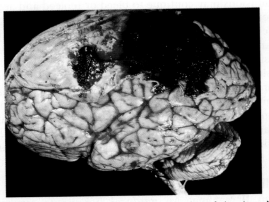

FIG. 56.15 Epidural hematoma covering a portion of the dura. Multiple small contusions are seen in the temporal lobe. (From Kumar V, Abbas AK, Aster JC, et al: *Robbins and Cotran pathologic basis of disease*, ed 8, Philadelphia, 2010, Saunders.)

that drain from the surface of the brain into the sagittal sinus are the source of most subdural hematomas. Because it is usually venous in origin, a subdural hematoma may be slower to develop. However, an arterial hemorrhage can cause a subdural hematoma, in which case it develops more rapidly.

Subdural hematomas may be acute, subacute, or chronic (Table 56.8). An *acute subdural hematoma* manifests within 24 to 48 hours of the injury.[15] The signs and symptoms are similar to those associated with brain tissue compression in increased ICP. They include decreasing LOC and headache. The size of the hematoma determines the patient's presentation and prognosis. The patient's appearance may range from drowsy and confused to unconscious. The ipsilateral pupil dilates and becomes fixed if ICP is significantly increased. Blunt-force injuries that produce acute subdural hematomas may cause significant underlying brain injury, resulting in cerebral edema. The resulting increase in ICP from the cerebral edema can increased morbidity and mortality despite surgery to evacuate the hematoma.

TABLE 56.8 Types of Subdural Hematomas

Occurrence After Injury	Progression of Symptoms	Treatment
Acute 24–48 hr after severe trauma	Immediate deterioration	Craniotomy, evacuation, and decompression
Subacute 48 hr–2 wk after severe trauma	Decline in mental status as hematoma develops. Progression dependent on size and location of hematoma	Evacuation and decompression
Chronic Weeks or months, usually >20 days after injury. Often injury seemed trivial or was forgotten by patient	Nonspecific, nonlocalizing progression. Progressive change in level of consciousness	Evacuation and decompression, membranectomy

A *subacute subdural hematoma* usually occurs within 2 to 14 days of the injury. After the initial bleeding, this hematoma may appear to enlarge over time as the breakdown products of the blood draw fluid into the subdural space.

A *chronic subdural hematoma* develops over weeks or months after a seemingly minor head injury.[15] They are more common in older adults because of a potentially larger subdural space from brain atrophy. With atrophy, the brain stays attached to the supportive structures and tension is increased. This makes it subject to tearing. Because the subdural space is larger, the presenting problem is focal symptoms (specific to a certain area of the brain) rather than signs of increased ICP.[15] Patients with a history of alcohol use are prone to subdural hematomas because of an increased incidence of falls.

Diagnosis of a subdural hematoma in the older adult may be delayed because symptoms mimic other health problems in this age-group, such as somnolence, confusion, lethargy, and memory loss. The manifestations of a subdural hematoma are often attributed to vascular disease (stroke, transient ischemic attack [TIA]) or dementia.

? CHECK YOUR PRACTICE

You are doing BP screenings in the senior center when you meet a 76-yr-old man and his wife. As you perform their BP screening, the wife tells you that her husband has been getting severe headaches, is dizzy, and sometimes has difficulty talking. Based on your advice, they go to an urgent care center, where a CT scan is done. The results show he has a chronic subdural hematoma. When you find out the diagnosis, you are puzzled because you thought he was having a stroke and cannot understand how he got a subdural hematoma.

- If you had been the nurse, what would you have done differently when screening this man?

Intracerebral Hematoma. Intracerebral hematoma occurs from bleeding within the brain tissue. It occurs in about 16% of head injuries. It usually happens in the frontal and temporal lobes, possibly from rupture of intracerebral vessels at the

✚ TABLE 56.9 Emergency Management
Head Injury

Etiology	Assessment Findings	Interventions
Blunt • Assault • Fall • Motor vehicle collision • Sports injury **Penetrating** • Arrow • Gunshot • Knife	**Surface Findings** • Bruises or contusions on face, Battle's sign (bruising behind ears) • Fracture or depressions in skull • Raccoon eyes (dependent bruising around eyes) • Scalp lacerations **Central Nervous System** • Asymmetric facial movements • Combativeness • Confusion • CSF leaking from ears or nose • Decerebrate or decorticate posturing • Decreased level of consciousness • Depressed or hyperactive reflexes • Dilated or unequal pupils, photophobia • Flaccidity • Garbled speech, abusive speech • GCS score <12 • Incontinence • Involuntary movements • Seizures **Respiratory** • Central neurogenic hyperventilation • Cheyne-Stokes respirations • Decreased O_2 saturation • Pulmonary edema	**Initial** • If unresponsive, assess circulation, airway, and breathing. • If responsive, monitor airway, breathing, and circulation. • Assume neck injury with head injury. • Stabilize cervical spine. • Apply O_2 via nonrebreather mask. • Establish IV access with 2 large-bore catheters to infuse normal saline or lactated Ringer's solution. • Intubate if GCS score <8. • Control external bleeding with sterile pressure dressing. • Remove patient's clothing. **Ongoing Monitoring** • Maintain normothermia using blankets, warm IV fluids, as needed. • Monitor vital signs, level of consciousness, O_2 saturation, cardiac rhythm, GCS score, pupil size and reactivity. • Expect intubation if gag reflex is impaired or absent. • Assess for rhinorrhea, otorrhea, scalp wounds. • Give fluids cautiously to prevent fluid overload and increasing ICP.

time of injury. The size and location of the hematoma are key in determining the patient's outcome.

Diagnostic Studies and Interprofessional Care. In general, the diagnostic studies are similar to those used for a patient with increased ICP (Table 56.3). CT scan is the best diagnostic test to evaluate for head trauma. It allows for rapid diagnosis and intervention in the acute care setting. MRI, PET, and evoked potential studies may be used to diagnose head injuries. An MRI scan is more sensitive than the CT scan in detecting small lesions. Transcranial Doppler studies allow for the measurement of cerebral blood flow (CBF) velocity. A cervical spine x-ray series, CT scan, or MRI of the spine may be done since cervical spine trauma often occurs at the same time as a head injury.

Emergency management of the patient with a head injury is outlined in Table 56.9. The principal treatment of head injuries is prompt diagnosis and surgery (if needed), In addition, we institute measures to prevent secondary injury by treating cerebral edema and managing increased ICP. For the patient with concussion and contusion, observation and management of increased ICP are the main management strategies.

The treatment of skull fractures is usually conservative. For depressed fractures and fractures with loose fragments, a craniotomy is done to elevate the depressed bone and remove the free fragments. If large amounts of bone are destroyed, the bone may be removed (craniectomy) and a cranioplasty will be needed later (see pp. 1321–1322).

In cases of large acute subdural and epidural hematomas or those associated with significant neurologic impairment, the blood must be removed through surgical evacuation. A craniotomy is generally done to see and allow control of the bleeding vessels. Burr-hole openings may be used in an extreme emergency

for a more rapid decompression, followed by a craniotomy. A drain may be placed after surgery for several days to prevent blood from reaccumulating. In cases in which extreme swelling is expected (e.g., DAI, hemorrhage), a craniectomy may be done. This involves removing a piece of skull to reduce the pressure inside the cranial vault. It reduces the risk for herniation.

❖ NURSING MANAGEMENT: HEAD INJURY

◆ **Nursing Assessment.** A patient with a head injury always has the potential to develop increased ICP, which is associated with higher mortality rates and poorer functional outcomes. Objective data are obtained by applying the GCS (Table 56.5), assessing and monitoring the neurologic status, and determining whether a CSF leak has occurred. Nursing assessment related to increased ICP is discussed on pp. 1308–1309. Nursing assessment of the patient with a head injury is outlined in Table 56.10.

◆ **Nursing Diagnoses**

Nursing diagnoses for the patient who has sustained a head injury may include:
- Decreased intracranial adaptive capacity
- Ineffective tissue perfusion
- Hyperthermia
- Risk for injury
- Anxiety

◆ **Planning**

The overall goals are that the patient with an acute head injury will (1) maintain adequate cerebral oxygenation and perfusion;

TABLE 56.10 Nursing Assessment
Head Injury

Subjective Data
Important Health Information
Past health history: Mechanism of injury: motor vehicle collision, sports injury, industrial incident, assault, falls
Medications: Anticoagulant drugs

Functional Health Patterns
Health perception–health management: Alcohol or recreational drugs. Risk-taking behaviors
Cognitive-perceptual: Headache, mood or behavioral change, mentation changes, aphasia, dysphasia, impaired judgment
Coping–stress tolerance: Fear, denial, anger, aggression, depression

Objective Data
General
Altered mental status

Integumentary
Lacerations, contusions, abrasions, hematoma, Battle's sign, periorbital edema and bruising, otorrhea, exposed brain matter

Respiratory
Rhinorrhea, impaired gag reflex, inability to maintain a patent airway. Impending herniation: altered/irregular respiratory rate and pattern

Cardiovascular
Impending herniation: Cushing's triad (systolic hypertension with widening pulse pressure, bradycardia with full and bounding pulse, irregular respirations)

Gastrointestinal
Vomiting, projectile vomiting, bowel incontinence

Urinary
Bladder incontinence

Reproductive
Uninhibited sexual expression

Neurologic
Altered level of consciousness, seizure activity, pupil dysfunction, cranial nerve deficit(s)

Musculoskeletal
Motor deficit/impairment, weakness, palmar drift, paralysis, spasticity, decorticate or decerebrate posturing, muscular rigidity or increased tone, flaccidity, ataxia

Possible Diagnostic Findings
Location and type of hematoma, edema, skull fracture, and/or foreign body on CT scan and/or MRI; abnormal EEG; positive toxicology screen or alcohol level; ↓ or ↑ blood glucose level; ↑ ICP

ETHICAL/LEGAL DILEMMAS
Brain Death

Situation
The emergency nurse receives a call from emergency response system (ERS) personnel, who are in route with R.G., a young man involved in a motorcycle crash. He was not wearing a helmet and has a large open skull fracture. Transport from the accident scene was delayed by 45 min because of a severe thunderstorm and traffic congestion. R.G. has fixed, dilated pupils and is in cardiac arrest. Estimated arrival at the hospital is still another 45 min because of the severe weather. EMS personnel request permission to stop resuscitation efforts.

Ethical/Legal Points for Consideration
- Criteria for brain death include coma or unresponsiveness, absence of brainstem reflexes, and apnea (see Chapter 9).
- The definition of death has changed with the advent of new technology, monitoring devices, and interventions.
- In a situation in which the professional responsible for determining a state of death is in remote contact with the patient, but the monitoring devices available provide virtual contact with the patient, a remote diagnosis of death may be legally acceptable.
- Brain death criteria do not address patients in a permanent vegetative state since the brainstem activity in these patients is adequate to maintain heart and lung function.
- CPR is not appropriate when survival is not expected or the patient is expected to survive without the ability to communicate. Quantitative futility implies that survival is not expected after CPR under given circumstances. In the absence of mitigating factors, prolonged resuscitative efforts are unlikely to be successful and can be stopped if there is no return of spontaneous circulation at any time during 30 minutes of cumulative advanced life support.
- It is ethical for ED personnel to stop treatment started by ERS personnel in the prehospital setting if there is valid, after-the-fact evidence that these interventions are now inappropriate.

Discussion Questions
- What are your feelings about cessation of brain function vs. cessation of heart and lung function as the criteria for death of a patient?
- What are your state's laws or practices about stopping CPR efforts by ERS personnel in the field?

♥ PROMOTING POPULATION HEALTH
Reducing the Risk for Head Injuries

- Always wear car seat belts in motor vehicles.
- Do not drive after using drugs or alcohol.
- Do not text and drive or drive distracted.
- Wear helmets while bicycling, skating, skateboarding, skiing, and playing contact sports.
- Athletes should follow safe playing techniques and the rules of the game.
- Assess home safety and implement any corrective measures needed.
- Older adults should continue to exercise regularly to improve strength and balance.
- Follow workplace safety precautions, including wearing helmets and protective gear.

(2) stay afebrile; (3) be free of discomfort; (4) be free from infection; (5) have adequate nutrition; and (6) attain maximal cognitive, motor, and sensory function.

❖ Nursing Implementation
◆ **Health Promotion.** One of the best ways to prevent head injuries is to prevent car and motorcycle accidents. Be active in campaigns that promote driving safety. Speak to driver education classes about the dangers of distracted driving and driving after drinking alcohol or using drugs. Helmets for motorcycle riders is the most effective measure for increasing survival after crashes.

◆ **Acute Care.** Management at the injury scene can have a significant impact on the outcome of a head injury. Emergency management of head injury is outlined in Table 56.9. The general goal of nursing management of the patient with head injury is to

TABLE 56.11 Patient & Caregiver Teaching

Head Injury

Include the following instructions when teaching the patient and caregiver about care during the first 2 or 3 days after a head injury:

1. Notify your HCP immediately if you have signs and symptoms that may indicate complications. These include:
   - Increased drowsiness (e.g., difficulty arousing, confusion)
   - Nausea or vomiting
   - Worsening headache or stiff neck
   - Seizures
   - Vision difficulties (e.g., blurring) or sensitivity to light (photophobia)
   - Behavioral changes (e.g., irritability, anger)
   - Motor problems (e.g., clumsiness, difficulty walking, slurred speech, weakness in arms or legs)
   - Sensory problems (e.g., numbness)
   - A heart rate <60 beats/min
2. Have someone stay with you.
3. Abstain from alcohol.
4. Check with your HCP before taking drugs that may increase drowsiness, including muscle relaxants, tranquilizers, and opioid analgesia.
5. Avoid driving, using heavy machinery, playing contact sports, and taking hot baths.

maintain cerebral oxygenation and perfusion and prevent secondary cerebral ischemia.

Surveillance or monitoring for changes in neurologic status is critically important because the patient's condition may deteriorate rapidly, requiring emergency surgery. Appropriate nursing interventions are started if surgery is anticipated. Because of the close association between hemodynamic status and cerebral perfusion, be aware of any coexisting injuries or conditions.

Explain the need for frequent neurologic assessments to both the patient and caregiver. Behavioral manifestations associated with head injury can result in a frightened, disoriented patient who is combative and resists help. Your approach should be calm and gentle. A family member may be available to stay with the patient and thus decrease anxiety and fear. An important need of the caregiver and family members in the acute injury phase is information about the patient's diagnosis, treatment plan, and reason for the interventions. Other teaching points are described in Table 56.11.

Perform neurologic assessments at intervals based on the patient's condition. The GCS is useful in assessing the LOC (Table 56.5). Report any signs of a deteriorating neurologic state, no matter how subtle, such as a decreasing LOC or decreasing motor strength, to the HCP. Monitor the patient's condition closely.

The major focus of nursing care for the patient with a brain injury relates to increased ICP (see eNursing Care Plan 56.1). However, some problems need specific nursing intervention.

Eye problems may include loss of the corneal reflex, periorbital bruising and edema, and diplopia. Loss of the corneal reflex may require lubricating eye drops or taping the eyes shut to prevent abrasion. Periorbital bruising and edema decrease with time. Cold and, later, warm compresses provide comfort and hasten the process. Wearing an eye patch can relieve diplopia. Consider a consult with an ophthalmologist.

Fever may occur from injury to or inflammation of the hypothalamus. Fever can cause increased CBF, cerebral blood volume, and ICP. Increased metabolism from fever increases metabolic waste, which in turn causes further cerebral vasodilation. Avoid fever with a goal of a temperature of 96.8° to 98.6° F (36° to 37° C) as the standard of care. Use interventions to

reduce temperature as previously discussed (see p. 1308) in conjunction with sedation to prevent shivering.

If CSF rhinorrhea or otorrhea occurs, inform the HCP at once. The head of the bed may be raised to decrease the CSF pressure so that a tear can seal. A loose collection pad may be placed under the nose or over the ear. Do not place a dressing in the nasal or ear cavities. Document the amount of drainage each shift. Teach the patient not to sneeze or blow the nose. Do not use NG tubes. Do not perform nasotracheal suctioning on these patients because of the high risk for meningitis.

Nursing measures specific to the care of the immobilized patient, such as those related to bladder and bowel function, skin care, and infection, are needed. Nausea and vomiting may be a problem and can be alleviated by antiemetic drugs. Headache can usually be controlled with acetaminophen or small doses of codeine.

If the patient's condition deteriorates, intracranial surgery may be needed (see the section on cranial surgery on pp. 1321–1323). A burr-hole opening or craniotomy may be done, depending on the underlying injury that is causing the problems. The emergency nature of the surgery may hasten the usual preoperative preparation. Consult with the HCP to determine specific preoperative nursing measures.

The patient is often unconscious before surgery, making it necessary for a family member to sign the consent form for surgery. This is a difficult and frightening time for the patient's caregiver and family and requires sensitive nursing management. The suddenness of the situation makes it especially hard for the family to cope. Use a team approach, including social workers, to help the patient and family throughout the hospitalization and recovery time.

◆ **Ambulatory Care.** Once the condition has stabilized, the patient is usually transferred for acute rehabilitation management. There may be chronic problems related to motor and sensory deficits, communication, memory, and intellectual functioning. Conditions that may need nursing and interprofessional management include nutrition problems, bowel and bladder problems, spasticity, dysphagia, and hydrocephalus. Many of the principles for managing the patient with a stroke are appropriate for these patients (see Chapter 57).

Seizure disorders may occur in patients with nonpenetrating head injury. Seizures may develop during the first week after the head injury or not until years later. Antiseizure drugs may be used prophylactically to manage posttraumatic seizure activity, but this practice is controversial.

The mental and emotional sequelae are often the most incapacitating problems. One of the consequences of TBI is that the person may not realize that a brain injury has occurred. Many patients with head injuries who were comatose for more than 6 hours undergo some personality change. They may have loss of concentration and memory and defective memory processing. Personal drive may decrease. Apathy may increase. Euphoria and mood swings, along with a seeming lack of awareness of the seriousness of the injury, may occur. The patient's behavior may indicate a loss of social restraint, judgment, tact, and emotional control.

Progressive recovery may continue for years. Specific nursing management in the posttraumatic phase depends on specific residual deficits. Being able to return to work and maintaining employment is one of the challenges during the recovery period.[16] The patient's outward physical appearance does not necessarily reflect what has happened in the brain. It is not a

TABLE 56.12 Types of Brain Tumors

Type	Tissue of Origin	Characteristics
Acoustic neuroma (schwannoma)	Cells that form myelin sheath around nerves. Often affects cranial nerve VIII	Many grow on both sides of the brain. Usually benign or low-grade.
Gliomas		
• Astrocytoma	Supportive tissue, glial cells, and astrocytes	Can range from low-grade to moderate-grade.
• Ependymoma	Ependymal epithelium	Range from benign to highly malignant. Most are benign and encapsulated.
• Glioblastoma	Primitive stem cell (glioblast)	Highly malignant and invasive. Among the most devastating of primary brain tumors.
• Medulloblastoma	Primitive neuroectodermal cell	Highly malignant and invasive. Metastatic to spinal cord and remote areas of brain.
• Oligodendroglioma	Oligodendrocytes	Benign (encapsulation and calcification).
Hemangioblastoma	Blood vessels of brain	Rare and benign. Surgery is curative.
Meningioma	Meninges	Can be benign or malignant. Most are benign.
Metastatic tumors	Lungs and breast (most common)	Malignant.
Pituitary adenoma	Pituitary gland	Usually benign.
Primary central nervous system lymphoma	Lymphocytes	Increased incidence in transplant recipients and acquired immunodeficiency syndrome (AIDS) patients.

good indicator of how well the patient will ultimately function in the home or work environment.

Give the family special consideration. They need to understand what is happening. Provide guidance and referrals for financial aid, child care, and other personal needs. Help the family in involving the patient in family activities whenever possible. Help the patient and family remain hopeful. The family often has unrealistic expectations of the patient as the coma begins to recede. The family expects full return to pretrauma status. In reality, the patient usually has a reduced awareness and ability to interpret environmental stimuli. Prepare the family for the patient's emergence from coma and explain that the process of awakening often takes several weeks. In addition, arrange for social work and chaplain consultations for the family.

When it is the time for discharge planning, the patient, caregiver, and family may benefit from specific instructions to avoid family-patient friction. Special "no" policies that may be suggested by the HCP, neuropsychologist, and nurse include no drinking of alcoholic beverages, no driving, no use of firearms, no working with hazardous implements and machinery, and no unsupervised smoking. Family members, particularly spouses, go through role transition as the role changes from that of spouse to that of caregiver.

◆ Evaluation

The expected outcomes are that the patient with a head injury will

- Maintain normal CPP
- Achieve maximal cognitive, motor, and sensory function
- Have no infection or fever

BRAIN TUMORS

There are an estimated 23,400 people diagnosed each year with brain tumors in the United States. The brain is also a frequent site for metastasis from other sites.[17] Males have a slightly higher incidence of brain tumors than females. Brain tumors most often occur in middle-aged persons, but they may be seen at any age.

🌐 PROMOTING HEALTH EQUITY

Brain Tumors

- Whites have a higher incidence of malignant brain tumors than blacks.
- White males have the highest incidence of malignant brain tumors.
- Blacks have the highest incidence of benign brain tumors (e.g., meningiomas).

Types

Brain tumors can occur in any part of the brain or spinal cord. Tumors of the brain may be *primary,* arising from tissues within the brain, or *secondary,* resulting from a metastasis of cancer from elsewhere in the body.[18]

Metastatic brain tumors are the most common brain tumor. The cancers that most often metastasize to the brain are lung and breast.

Primary brain tumors are generally classified according to the tissue from which they arise (Table 56.12). Meningiomas are the most common primary brain tumor. Other common brain tumors are gliomas (e.g., astrocytoma, glioblastoma [most common form of glioma]).

More than half of brain tumors are malignant. They infiltrate the brain tissue and are not amenable to complete surgical removal. Other tumors may be histologically benign but are located such that complete removal is not possible.

Brain tumors rarely metastasize outside the central nervous system (CNS) because they are contained by structural (meninges) and physiologic (blood-brain) barriers. Table 56.12 compares the most common brain tumors. A glioblastoma and meningioma are shown in Fig. 56.16.

Clinical Manifestations and Complications

The manifestations of brain tumors depend mainly on their location and size (Table 56.13). A wide range of manifestations are possible. Headache is common. Tumor-related headaches tend to be worse at night and may awaken the patient. The headaches are usually dull and constant but sometimes throbbing. Seizures are common in gliomas and brain metastases. Brain tumors can cause nausea and vomiting from increased ICP.

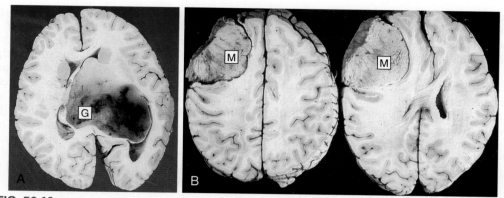

FIG. 56.16 A, A large glioblastoma *(G)* arises from one cerebral hemisphere and has grown to fill the ventricular system. B, Meningioma. These 2 different sections from different levels in the same brain show a meningioma *(M)* compressing the frontal lobe and distorting underlying brain. (From Stevens A, Lowe J: *Pathology: Illustrated review in colour,* ed 2, London, 2000, Mosby.)

TABLE 56.13 Manifestations of Brain Tumors

Tumor Location	Manifestations
Brainstem tumors	Headache on awakening, drowsiness, vomiting, ataxic gait, facial muscle weakness, hearing loss, dysphagia, dysarthria, "crossed eyes" or other visual changes, hemiparesis
Cerebellopontine tumors	Tinnitus and vertigo, deafness
Cerebral hemisphere	
• Frontal lobe (unilateral)	Unilateral hemiplegia, seizures, memory deficit, personality and judgment changes, visual changes
• Frontal lobe (bilateral)	Symptoms associated with unilateral frontal lobe tumors. Ataxic gait
• Parietal lobe	Speech problems (if tumor is in the dominant hemisphere), inability to write, spatial disorders, unilateral neglect
• Occipital lobe	Vision changes and seizures
• Temporal lobe	Few symptoms. Seizures, dysphagia, hallucinations, auras
Fourth ventricle and cerebellar tumors	Headache, nausea, and papilledema (occur from ↑ ICP). Ataxic gait and changes in coordination
Meningeal tumors	Symptoms associated with compression of the brain and depend on tumor location
Metastatic tumors	Headache, nausea, or vomiting (occur from ↑ ICP). Other symptoms depend on tumor location
Subcortical	Hemiplegia; other symptoms may depend on area of infiltration
Thalamus and sellar tumors	Headache, nausea, vision changes, papilledema, and nystagmus (occur from ↑ ICP). Diabetes insipidus may occur

Cognitive dysfunction, including memory problems and mood or personality changes, is common, especially in patients with brain metastases. Muscle weakness, sensory losses, aphasia, and visual-spatial dysfunction may occur.

If the tumor mass obstructs the ventricles or occludes the outlet, ventricular enlargement (hydrocephalus) can occur. As the brain tumor expands, it may produce manifestations of increased ICP, cerebral edema, or obstruction of the CSF pathways. Unless treated, all brain tumors eventually cause death from increasing tumor volume leading to increased ICP.

Diagnostic Studies

An extensive history and a comprehensive neurologic examination is done in the workup of a patient with a suspected brain tumor. The history and physical examination may provide data with respect to location. New onset of seizures or adult-onset migraines may indicate a brain tumor and should be investigated. Diagnostic studies are similar to those used for a patient with increased ICP (Table 56.3).

The sensitivity of techniques such as MRI and PET scans allows for detection of small tumors and may provide more reliable diagnostic information than a CT scan. CT with contrast and MRI are used to identify the lesion's location. Other tests include magnetic resonance spectroscopy, functional MRI (fMRI), and single-photon emission computed tomography (SPECT). An EEG can rule out seizures but is of less importance. An LP is seldom diagnostic and carries with it the risk for cerebral herniation. Cerebral angiography can determine blood flow to the tumor and further localize the tumor. Other studies are done to rule out a primary lesion elsewhere in the body. Endocrine studies are helpful when a pituitary adenoma is suspected (see Chapter 49).

The correct diagnosis of a brain tumor can be made by obtaining tissue for histologic study. In most patients, tissue is obtained at the time of surgery. Computer-guided stereotactic biopsy is also an option. A smear or frozen section can be done in the operating room for a preliminary interpretation of the histologic type. With this information, the HCP can make a better decision about the extent of surgery.

Interprofessional Care

Treatment goals are aimed at (1) identifying the tumor type and location, (2) removing or decreasing tumor mass, and (3) preventing or managing increased ICP.

Surgical Therapy. Surgical removal is the preferred treatment for brain tumors. Stereotactic surgical techniques are used with greater frequency to perform a biopsy and remove small brain tumors. The outcome of surgery depends on the tumor's type, size, and location. Meningiomas and oligodendrogliomas can usually be completely removed. The more invasive gliomas and medulloblastomas may only be partially removed. Computer-guided stereotactic biopsy, ultrasound, fMRI, and cortical mapping can localize brain tumors during surgery.

Complete surgical removal of brain tumors is not always possible because the tumor is not always accessible or may involve vital parts of the brain. Surgery can reduce tumor mass, which decreases ICP, provides relief of symptoms, and extends survival time.

Ventricular Shunts. Hydrocephalus due to a tumor obstructing the CSF flow can be treated with the placement of a ventricular shunt. A catheter with 1-way valves is placed in the lateral ventricle and then tunneled under the skin to drain CSF into the peritoneal cavity. Rapid decompression of ICP can cause total body collapse and weakness. Headache may be prevented by gradually introducing the patient to the upright position.

Manifestations of shunt malfunction, which are related to increased ICP, include decreasing LOC, restlessness, headache, blurred vision, or vomiting. This may require shunt revision or replacement. Infection may occur, as exhibited by high fever, persistent headache, and stiff neck. Antibiotics are used to treat the infection. In some situations, the shunt must be replaced. CSF drainage is managed with an extraventricular drainage system while the infection is treated.

Radiation Therapy and Stereotactic Radiosurgery. Radiation therapy may be used as a follow-up measure after surgery. Radiation seeds can be implanted into the brain. Cerebral edema and rapidly increasing ICP may be a complication of radiation therapy. These problems can usually be managed with high doses of corticosteroids (e.g., dexamethasone, methylprednisolone). Radiation therapy is discussed in Chapter 15.

Stereotactic radiosurgery is a method of delivering a highly concentrated dose of radiation to a precise location within the brain. Stereotactic radiosurgery may be used when conventional surgery has failed or is not an option because of the tumor location. (Radiosurgery is discussed on p. 1322.)

Chemotherapy and Targeted Therapy. The effectiveness of chemotherapy has been limited by the difficulty with getting drugs across the blood-brain barrier, tumor cell heterogeneity, and tumor cell drug resistance. Chemotherapy drugs called *nitrosoureas* (e.g., carmustine, lomustine) are used to treat brain tumors. Normally the blood-brain barrier prohibits the entry of most drugs into the brain. Cancer tumors can cause a breakdown of the blood-brain barrier in the area of the tumor, thus allowing chemotherapy agents to be used to treat the cancer. Chemotherapy-laden biodegradable wafers (e.g., Gliadel wafer [polifeprosan with carmustine implant]) implanted at the time of surgery can deliver chemotherapy directly to the tumor site. Other drugs being used include methotrexate and procarbazine (Matulane). One way used to deliver chemotherapy drugs directly to the CNS is intrathecal administration via an Ommaya reservoir.

Temozolomide (Temodar) is an oral chemotherapy agent that can cross the blood-brain barrier. In contrast with many chemotherapy drugs, which require metabolic activation to exert their effects, temozolomide can convert spontaneously to a reactive agent that directly interferes with tumor growth. It does not interact with other common drugs taken by patients with brain tumors, such as antiseizure drugs, corticosteroids, and antiemetics.

DRUG ALERT Temozolomide (Temodar)

- Causes myelosuppression. Before using, the absolute neutrophil count should be ≥1500/μL and platelet count should be ≥100,000/μL.
- To reduce nausea and vomiting, take on empty stomach or at bedtime.

Bevacizumab (Avastin) is used to treat patients with glioblastoma that continues to progress after standard therapy. Bevacizumab is a targeted therapy that inhibits the action of vascular endothelial growth factor, which helps form new blood vessels. These vessels can feed a tumor, helping it to grow, and provide a pathway for cancer cells to circulate in the body. Targeted therapy is discussed in Chapter 15 and Table 15.13.

Other Therapies. A medical device system, the Optune System, is used to treat glioblastoma that recurs or progresses after receiving chemotherapy and radiation therapy. With this system, electrodes are placed on the surface of the patient's scalp to deliver low-intensity, changing electrical fields called *tumor treatment fields* (TTFs) to the tumor site.

❖ NURSING MANAGEMENT: BRAIN TUMORS

◆ Nursing Assessment

Interview data are as important as the actual physical assessment. Ask about the medical history, intellectual abilities and educational level, and history of nervous system infections and trauma. Structure the initial assessment to provide baseline data of the patient's neurologic status. Use this information to design a realistic, patient specific care plan.

Assess the patient's LOC, motor abilities, sensory perception, integrated function (including bowel and bladder function), and balance and proprioception. Determine the presence of seizures, syncope, nausea and vomiting, and headaches or other pain. Assess the coping abilities of the patient, caregiver, and family. Watching a patient perform activities of daily living and listening to the patient's conversation can be part of the neurologic assessment. Having the patient or caregiver explain the problem can be helpful to determine the patient's limitations and obtain information about the patient's insight into the problems. Record all initial data to provide a baseline for comparison to determine whether the patient's condition is improving or deteriorating.

◆ Nursing Diagnoses

Nursing diagnoses for the patient with a brain tumor may include:

- Ineffective tissue perfusion
- Acute pain
- Anxiety
- Risk for injury

◆ Planning

The overall goals are that the patient with a brain tumor will (1) maintain normal ICP, (2) maximize neurologic functioning, (3) achieve control of pain and discomfort, and (4) be aware of the long-term implications with respect to prognosis and cognitive and physical functioning.

◆ Nursing Implementation

A tumor of the frontal lobe can cause behavioral and personality changes. Loss of emotional control, confusion, disorientation, memory loss, impulsivity, and depression may be signs of a frontal lobe lesion. The patient often does not perceive these changes. They can be disturbing and frightening to the caregiver and family. These changes can also cause a distancing to occur between the family and patient. Help the caregiver and family understand what is happening to the patient and support the family.

The confused patient with behavioral instability can be a challenge. Protecting the patient from self-harm is an important part of nursing care. Essential interventions include close supervision of activity, use of side rails, judicious use of restraints, appropriate sedatives, padding of the rails and the area around the bed, and a calm, reassuring approach.

Perceptual problems associated with frontal and parietal lobe tumors contribute to a patient's disorientation and confusion. Minimize environmental stimuli, create a routine, and use reality orientation for the confused patient. Tumors in the temporal lobe can cause hallucinations, which may be confused with dementia or delirium.

Seizures, which often occur with brain tumors, are managed with antiseizure drugs. Use seizure precautions for the patient's protection. Some behavioral changes seen in the patient are a result of seizure disorders and can improve with adequate seizure control. Patients at risk for seizures may be unable to drive, so be aware of the extra resources needed and collaborate with the social worker and family. Seizure disorders are discussed in Chapter 58.

Motor and sensory dysfunctions interfere with activities of daily living. Encourage the patient to provide as much self-care as physically possible. Self-image often depends on the patient's ability to take part in care within the limitations of the physical deficits.

Language deficits may be present. Motor (expressive) or sensory (receptive) dysphasia may occur. The problem with communication can be frustrating for the patient and may interfere with your ability to meet the patient's needs. Try to establish a communication system that both the patient and staff can use.

Nutritional intake may be decreased because of the patient's inability to eat, loss of appetite, or loss of desire to eat. Assess nutritional status and ensure adequate nutritional intake. Encourage the patient to eat. Some patients may need enteral or parenteral nutrition (see Chapter 39).

Provide help and support during the adjustment phase and in long-range planning. Social work and home health nurses may be needed to aid the caregiver with discharge planning and to help the family adjust to role changes and psychosocial and socioeconomic factors. Issues related to palliative and end-of-life care must be discussed with both the patient and family (see Chapter 9).

◆ Evaluation

The expected outcomes are that the patient with a brain tumor will

- Achieve control of pain, vomiting, and other discomforts
- Maintain ICP within normal limits
- Have maximal neurologic function given the location and extent of the tumor
- Maintain optimal nutritional status
- Accept the long-term consequences of the tumor and its treatment

CRANIAL SURGERY

Indications for cranial surgery are related to brain tumors, CNS infection (e.g., abscess), vascular abnormalities, craniocerebral trauma, seizure disorder, or intractable pain (Table 56.14).

Types

Various types of cranial surgical procedures are outlined in Table 56.15.

TABLE 56.14 Indications for Cranial Surgery

Indication	Cause	Surgical Procedure
Aneurysm repair	Dilation of weak area in arterial wall (usually near anterior portion of circle of Willis)	Dissection and clipping or coiling of aneurysm
Arteriovenous (AV) malformation	Congenital tangle of arteries and veins (often in middle cerebral artery)	Excision of malformation
Brain abscess	Bacteria that caused intracranial infection	Excision or drainage of abscess
Brain tumors	Benign or malignant cell growth	Excision or partial resection of tumor
Hydrocephalus	Overproduction of cerebrospinal fluid, obstruction to flow, defective reabsorption	Placement of ventriculoperitoneal or (rarely) ventriculoatrial shunt
Intracranial bleeding	Rupture of cerebral vessels because of trauma or stroke	Surgical evacuation through burr holes or craniotomy
Skull fractures	Trauma to skull	Debridement of fragments and necrotic tissue, elevation and realignment of bone fragments

---

TABLE 56.15 Types of Cranial Surgery

Type	Description
Burr hole	Opening into the cranium with a drill. Used to remove localized fluid and blood beneath the dura.
Craniectomy	Excision into the cranium to cut away bone flap.
Cranioplasty	Repair of cranial defect resulting from trauma, malformation, or previous surgical procedure. Artificial material used to replace damaged or lost bone.
Craniotomy	Opening into cranium with removal of bone flap and opening the dura to remove a lesion, repair a damaged area, drain blood, or relieve ↑ ICP.
Shunt procedures	Alternative pathway to redirect cerebrospinal fluid from one area to another using a tube or implanted device. Examples include ventricular shunt and Ommaya reservoir.
Stereotactic procedure	Precise localization of a specific area of the brain using a frame or frameless system based on 3-dimensional coordinates. Used for biopsy, radiosurgery, or dissection.

Craniotomy. Depending on the location of the pathologic condition, a *craniotomy* may be frontal, parietal, occipital, temporal, suboccipital, or a combination of any of these. The HCP drills a set of burr holes and uses a saw to connect the holes to remove the bone flap (Fig. 56.17). Sometimes operating microscopes are used to magnify the site. After surgery, the bone flap is secured with small plates or wired shut. Sometimes drains are placed to remove fluid and blood. Patients are usually cared for in an ICU until stable.

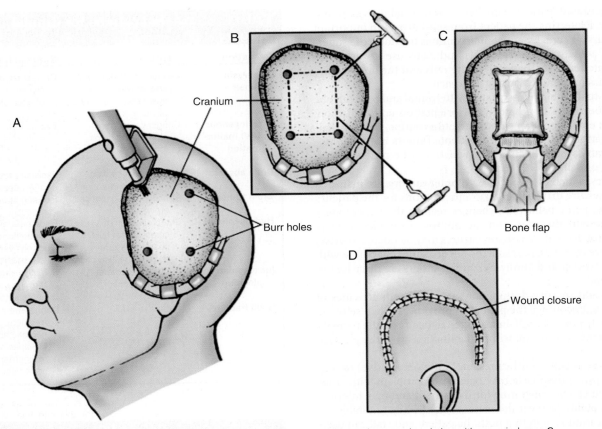

FIG. 56.17 Craniotomy. **A,** Burr holes are drill into skull. **B,** Skull is cut between burr holes with a surgical saw. **C,** Bone flap is turned back to expose cranial contents. **D,** Bone flap is replaced and wound closed. (From Monahan F, Sands J, Neighbors M, et al: *Phipps' medical-surgical nursing: Health and illness perspectives,* ed 9, St Louis, 2007, Mosby.)

Stereotactic Radiosurgery. Stereotactic procedures use a precision apparatus (often computer guided) to help the HCP precisely target an area of the brain. Stereotactic biopsy can be done to obtain tissue samples for histologic examination. CT scanning and MRI are used to image the targeted tissue. With the patient under general or local anesthesia, the HCP drills a burr hole or creates a bone flap for an entry site and then introduces a probe and biopsy needle. Stereotactic procedures are used for removal of small brain tumors and abscesses, drainage of hematomas, ablative procedures for extrapyramidal diseases (e.g., Parkinson's disease), and repair of arteriovenous malformations. A major advantage of the stereotactic approach is a reduction in damage to surrounding tissue.

Stereotactic radiosurgery is not a form of surgery in the traditional sense. Instead, radiosurgery uses precisely focused radiation to destroy tumor cells and other abnormal growths in the brain. Computers create 3-dimensional images of the brain. These images are used to guide the focused radiation while the patient's head is held still in a stereotactic frame (Fig. 56.18). Radiosurgical techniques can use ionizing radiation generated by a linear accelerator, gamma knife, or CyberKnife. In these procedures, a high dose of cobalt radiation is delivered to precisely targeted tumor tissue. The dose of radiation is delivered in a single treatment lasting a few hours or in multiple sessions. Side effects include fatigue, headache, and nausea.

In combination with stereotactic procedures to identify and localize tumor sites, surgical lasers can be used to destroy tumors. Lasers work by creating thermal energy, which destroys

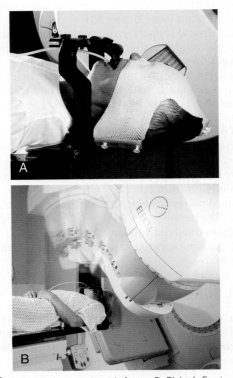

FIG. 56.18 **A,** Patient in a stereotactic frame. **B,** Elekta's Fraxion head frame helps ensure accuracy and precision in stereotactic radiation therapy (SRT) of cancer targets in the brain and cranium. (Courtesy Elekta, Stockholm, Sweden.)

the tissue on which it is focused. Laser therapy provides the benefit of reducing damage to surrounding tissue.

❖ NURSING MANAGEMENT: CRANIAL SURGERY

◆ Nursing Implementation

◆ **Acute Care.** The general preoperative and postoperative nursing care for the patient undergoing cranial surgery is similar regardless of the cause. It is similar to that for the patient with increased ICP. The patient (if conscious and coherent), caregiver, and family will be concerned about the potential physical and emotional problems that can result from surgery. The uncertainty about the prognosis and outcome requires compassionate nursing care in the preoperative period.

Preoperative teaching is important in allaying the fears of the patient, caregiver, and family and in preparing them for the postoperative period. Provide general information about the type of operation that will be done and what can be expected right after the operation. Explain that some hair may be shaved to allow for better exposure and to prevent contamination. The hair is usually removed in the operating room after induction of anesthesia. Tell them that the patient will be in an ICU or special care unit after surgery.

The main goal of care after cranial surgery is preventing increased ICP. Nursing management of the patient with increased ICP was outlined on pp. 1308–1311. Frequent assessment of the patient's neurologic status is essential during the first 48 hours. Closely monitor fluid and electrolyte levels and serum osmolality to detect changes in sodium regulation, the onset of diabetes insipidus, or severe hypovolemia.

Monitor the patient for pain and nausea. Nausea and vomiting are common after surgery and are usually treated with antiemetics. The use of promethazine is discouraged because it can increase somnolence and alter the accuracy of a neurologic assessment.

Although the brain itself does not have pain receptors, patients often report headache caused by edema or pain at the incision site. Control pain with short-acting opioids and monitor neurologic status.

The surgical dressing is usually in place for a few days. With an incision over the skull in the anterior or middle fossa, the patient will return from the operating room with the head elevated at an angle of 30 to 45 degrees. The head of the bed should stay elevated at least 30 degrees unless the surgical approach is in the posterior fossa or a burr hole has been made. In these cases, the patient is generally kept flat or at a slight elevation (10 to 15 degrees) during the postoperative phase.

Turning and positioning the patient will depend on the site of the operation. If a bone flap has been removed (craniectomy), do not position the patient on the operative side. Place a sign at the head of the bed, alerting everyone of the craniectomy site and position of the surgical site. Observe the dressing for color, odor, and amount of drainage. Notify the HCP immediately of any excess bleeding or clear drainage. Checking drains for placement and assessing the area around the dressing are important. Scalp care should include meticulous care of the incision to prevent wound infection. Cleanse the area and treat it following agency protocol or the HCP's orders. Once the dressing is removed, use an antiseptic soap for washing the scalp. The psychologic impact of hair removal can be lessened by using a wig, turban, scarves, or cap. For the patient who is receiving radiation, teach the patient to use a sunblock and head covering if any sun exposure is expected.

◆ **Ambulatory Care.** The rehabilitative potential for a patient after cranial surgery depends on the reason for the surgery, postoperative course, and patient's general state of health. Base your nursing interventions on a realistic appraisal of these factors. Specific rehabilitation potential cannot be determined until cerebral edema and increased ICP subside postoperatively. An overall goal is to foster independence for as long as possible and to the highest degree possible.

Take care to maintain as much function as possible through measures such as careful positioning, meticulous skin and mouth care, regular range-of-motion exercises, bowel and bladder care, and adequate nutrition. Address the needs and problems of each patient individually because many variables affect the plan.

Collaborate with other specialists. The physical therapist may provide an exercise plan to regain functional deficits. A speech therapist will help the patient regain communication skills. The patient's mental and physical deterioration, including seizures, personality disorganization, apathy, and wasting, is difficult for both family and health care professionals. Cognitive and emotional residual deficits are often harder to accept than are motor and sensory losses. Social workers can help the patient and family adapt to changes in their home life, work, and financial circumstances.

ETHICAL/LEGAL DILEMMAS
Withholding Treatment

Situation

C.J., a 26-yr-old patient in a permanent vegetative state, is diagnosed with her 15th bladder infection. As her home care nurse, you must determine whether to seek antibiotics for this infection. The family members have expressed a concern that no heroic measures be used to extend the life of their daughter and sister. However, they have been unwilling to stop providing enteral nutrition through a gastrostomy tube. Should antibiotics be withheld?

Ethical/Legal Points for Consideration

- Patients in a persistent vegetative state do not recover.
- The main legal issue here is who has the legal right to refuse or consent to treatment for this incapacitated patient. You need to know if a guardian has been appointed by the court or if her parents retain a form of guardianship to make health care decisions for her.
- You need to know when the vegetative state began; that is, did the patient ever have the right to consent having reached the age of majority as a competent adult or did the vegetative state begin while she was a minor? If the patient did become a competent adult before the vegetative state, did she ever express any preference for quality-of-life and end-of-life decision making?
- The courts have widespread legal precedents for accepting the decision of the patient's guardian or parents or the patient's clearly expressed preferences for quality-of-life decision making.
- Life-sustaining treatment is any treatment that serves to prolong life without reversing the underlying medical condition. Life-sustaining treatment may include, but is not limited to, mechanical ventilation, renal dialysis, chemotherapy, antibiotics, and artificial nutrition and hydration.
- There is no ethical distinction between withdrawing and withholding life-sustaining treatment. If there is not adequate evidence of the incompetent patient's preferences and values, the decision should be based on the best interests of the patient (i.e., what outcome will most likely promote the patient's well-being).

Discussion Questions

1. How would you approach C.J.'s family?
2. What are your feelings about providing nutrition, hydration, and treatments that will prolong life in a patient for whom there is no hope of recovery?
3. What options are available to the family for the care of their daughter once a decision is made about withholding antibiotics?

INFLAMMATORY CONDITIONS OF THE BRAIN

Brain abscesses, meningitis, and encephalitis are the most common inflammatory conditions of the brain and spinal cord (Table 56.16). Inflammation can be caused by bacteria, viruses, fungi, and chemicals (e.g., contrast media used in diagnostic tests, blood in the subarachnoid space). CNS infections may occur via the bloodstream, by extension from a primary site, or along cranial and spinal nerves.

The mortality rate for inflammatory conditions of the brain is about 10% to 15% in the general population, with higher rates in older and immunosuppressed patients. Some who recover have long-term neurologic deficits, including hearing loss.[19]

BACTERIAL MENINGITIS

Meningitis is an acute inflammation of the meningeal tissues surrounding the brain and spinal cord. Meningitis usually occurs in fall, winter, or early spring. It is often related to a viral respiratory disease. Older adults and persons who are debilitated are affected more often than the general population. College students living in dormitories and people living in institutions (e.g., prisoners) have a high risk for contracting meningitis. Untreated bacterial meningitis has a mortality rate of 50% to 100%.[20]

Etiology and Pathophysiology

Streptococcus pneumoniae and *Neisseria meningitidis* are the leading causes of bacterial meningitis. *N. meningitides* has at least 13 different subtypes (serogroups) with 5 of them (A, B, C, Y, W) causing most cases. *Haemophilus influenzae* was once the most common cause of bacterial meningitis. However, the use of *H. influenzae* vaccine has resulted in a significant decrease in meningitis from this organism.

The organisms usually gain entry to the CNS through the upper respiratory tract or bloodstream. However, they may enter by direct extension from penetrating wounds of the skull or through fractured sinuses in basilar skull fractures.

The inflammatory response to the infection tends to increase CSF production with a moderate increase in ICP. In bacterial meningitis the purulent secretions quickly spread to other areas of the brain through the CSF and cover the cranial nerves and other intracranial structures. If this process extends into the brain parenchyma or if concurrent encephalitis is present, cerebral edema and increased ICP become more of a problem. Closely observe all patients for manifestations of increased ICP. ICP can increase from swelling around the dura and increased CSF volume.

Clinical Manifestations

Fever, severe headache, nausea, vomiting, and **nuchal rigidity** (neck stiffness) are key signs of meningitis. Photophobia, a decreased LOC, and signs of increased ICP may be present. Coma is associated with a poor prognosis. It occurs in 5% to 10% of patients with bacterial meningitis. Seizures occur in one third of all cases. The headache becomes progressively worse and may be accompanied by vomiting and irritability.

If the infecting organism is a meningococcus, a skin rash is common. Petechiae may be seen on the trunk, lower extremities, and mucous membranes. A *tumbler test* can be done by pressing the base of a drinking glass against the rash. The rash does not blanch or fade under pressure.

Complications

The most common acute complication of bacterial meningitis is increased ICP. Most patients have increased ICP. It is the major cause of an altered mental status.

Another complication is residual neurologic dysfunction. It often involves many cranial nerves. Cranial nerve irritation can have serious sequelae. The optic nerve (CN II) is compressed by increased ICP. Papilledema is often present, and blindness may occur. When CN III, CN IV, and CN VI are irritated, ocular movements are affected. Ptosis, unequal pupils, and diplopia are common. Irritation of CN V results in sensory losses and loss of the corneal reflex. Irritation of CN VII results in facial paresis.

TABLE 56.16 Comparison of Cerebral Inflammatory Conditions

	Meningitis	Encephalitis	Brain Abscess
Cause	Bacteria (*Streptococcus pneumoniae, Neisseria meningitidis*, group B streptococci, viruses, fungi)	Bacteria, fungi, parasites, herpes simplex virus (HSV), other viruses (e.g., West Nile virus)	Streptococci, staphylococci through bloodstream
Cerebrospinal Fluid (Reference Interval)			
• Pressure (<20 mm H₂O)	Increased *Bacterial:* 200–500 *Viral:* ≤250	Normal to slight increase	Increased
• WBC count (0–5 cells/μL)	*Bacterial:* >1000/μL (mainly neutrophils) *Viral:* 25–500/μL (mainly lymphocytes)	500/μL, neutrophils (early), lymphocytes (later)	25–300/μL (neutrophils)
• Protein (15–45 mg/dL [0.15–0.45 g/L])	*Bacterial:* >500 mg/dL *Viral:* 50–500 mg/dL	Slight increase	Normal
• Glucose (50–77 mg/dL [2.2–3.9 mmol/L])	*Bacterial:* Decreased 5–40 *Viral:* Normal or low >40	Normal	Low or absent
• Appearance	*Bacterial:* Turbid, cloudy *Viral:* Clear or cloudy	Clear	Clear
Diagnostic Studies	CT scan, Gram stain, smear, culture, PCR	CT scan, EEG, MRI, PET, PCR, IgM antibodies to virus in serum or CSF	CT scan
Treatment	Antibiotics, dexamethasone, supportive care, prevention of ↑ ICP	Supportive care, prevention of ↑ ICP, acyclovir (Zovirax) for HSV	Antibiotics, incision and drainage Supportive care

*PCR is used to detect viral RNA or DNA.

IgM, immunoglobulin M; *PCR*, polymerase chain reaction.

Irritation of CN VIII causes tinnitus, vertigo, and deafness. The dysfunction usually disappears within a few weeks. However, hearing loss may be permanent.

Hemiparesis, dysphasia, and hemianopsia may occur. These signs usually resolve over time. If they do not, suspect a cerebral abscess, subdural empyema, subdural effusion, or persistent meningitis. Acute cerebral edema may cause seizures, CN III palsy, bradycardia, hypertensive coma, and death.

Headaches may occur for months after the diagnosis of meningitis until the irritation and inflammation have completely resolved. It is important to implement pain management for chronic headaches.

A noncommunicating hydrocephalus may occur if the exudate causes adhesions that prevent the normal flow of CSF from the ventricles. CSF reabsorption by the arachnoid villi may be obstructed by the exudate. In this situation, surgical implantation of a shunt is the only treatment.

Waterhouse-Friderichsen syndrome is a complication of meningococcal meningitis. The syndrome is manifested by petechiae, disseminated intravascular coagulation (DIC), adrenal hemorrhage, and circulatory collapse. DIC and shock, which are some of the most serious complications of meningitis, are associated with meningococcemia. DIC is discussed in detail in Chapter 30.

Diagnostic Studies

When a patient has manifestations suggestive of bacterial meningitis, a blood culture and CT scan should be done. Diagnosis is usually verified by doing an LP with analysis of the CSF (Table 56.16). An LP should be done only after the CT scan has ruled out an obstruction in the foramen magnum to prevent a fluid shift resulting in herniation.

Specimens of the CSF, sputum, and nasopharyngeal secretions are taken for culture before the start of antibiotic therapy to identify the causative organism. A Gram stain is done to detect bacteria. The predominant white blood cell type in the CSF with bacterial meningitis is neutrophils.

X-rays of the skull may show infected sinuses. CT scans and MRI may be normal in uncomplicated meningitis. In other cases, CT scans may reveal evidence of increased ICP or hydrocephalus.

Interprofessional Care

Bacterial meningitis is a medical emergency. Rapid diagnosis based on history and physical examination is crucial because the patient is usually in a critical state when health care is sought. When meningitis is suspected, antibiotic therapy is begun after the collection of specimens for cultures, even before the diagnosis is confirmed (Table 56.17).

Ampicillin, penicillin, vancomycin, cefuroxime (Ceftin), cefotaxime, ceftriaxone, ceftizoxime, and ceftazidime are the main drugs given to treat bacterial meningitis. Dexamethasone may be given before or with the first dose of antibiotics. Collaborate with the HCP to manage the headache, fever, and nuchal rigidity often associated with meningitis.

❖ NURSING MANAGEMENT: BACTERIAL MENINGITIS

◆ Nursing Assessment

Initial assessment should include vital signs, neurologic assessment, fluid intake and output, and evaluation of the lungs and skin.

◆ Nursing Diagnoses

Nursing diagnoses for the patient with bacterial meningitis may include:

- Decreased intracranial adaptive capacity
- Ineffective tissue perfusion
- Hyperthermia
- Acute pain

Additional information on nursing diagnoses and interventions for the patient with bacterial meningitis is presented in eNursing Care Plan 56.2 (available on the website for this chapter).

◆ Planning

The overall goals for the patient with bacterial meningitis are to (1) return to maximal neurologic functioning, (2) resolve the infection, and (3) control pain and discomfort.

◆ Nursing Implementation

◆ **Health Promotion.** Prevention of respiratory tract infections through vaccination programs for pneumococcal pneumonia and influenza is important. Meningococcal vaccines are available that protect against the serogroups of meningococcal disease that are most often seen in the United States. They will not prevent all cases. Two types of meningococcal vaccines are available in the United States:

- Meningococcal conjugate vaccines (MCV4) (Menactra, Menveo)
- Serogroup B meningococcal vaccines (Bexsero, Trumenba)

Early and vigorous treatment of respiratory tract and ear infections is important. Persons who have close contact with anyone who has bacterial meningitis should receive prophylactic antibiotics.

◆ **Acute Care.** The patient with bacterial meningitis is usually acutely ill. The fever is high, and head pain is severe. Irritation of the cerebral cortex may result in seizures. The changes in mental

---

TABLE 56.17 Interprofessional Care

Bacterial Meningitis

Diagnostic Assessment

- History and physical examination
- Analysis of CSF (for protein, WBC, and glucose), Gram stain, and culture
- CBC, coagulation profile, electrolyte levels, glucose, platelet count
- Blood culture
- CT scan, MRI, PET scan
- Skull x-ray studies

Management

- Rest
- IV fluid
- Hypothermia

Drug Therapy

- IV antibiotics
  - ampicillin, penicillin
  - cephalosporin (e.g., cefotaxime, ceftriaxone)
- codeine for headache
- dexamethasone
- acetaminophen or aspirin for temperature >100.4° F (38° C)
- phenytoin IV
- mannitol (Osmitrol) IV for diuresis

status and LOC depend on the degree of increased ICP. Assess and record vital signs, neurologic status, fluid intake and output, skin, and lung fields at regular intervals based on the patient's condition.

Head and neck pain with movement requires attention. Codeine provides some pain relief without undue sedation for most patients. Assist the patient to a position of comfort, often curled up with the head slightly extended. The head of the bed should be slightly elevated. A darkened room and a cool cloth over the eyes relieve the discomfort of photophobia.

For the patient with delirium, low lighting may decrease hallucinations. All patients have some degree of mental distortion and hypersensitivity. They may be frightened and misinterpret the environment. Make every attempt to minimize environmental stimuli and prevent injury. A familiar person at the bedside may have a calming effect. Be efficient with care while conveying an attitude of caring and unhurried gentleness. The use of touch and a soothing voice to give simple explanations of activities is helpful. If seizures occur, make appropriate observations and take protective measures. Give antiseizure drugs, such as phenytoin (Dilantin) or levetiracetam (Keppra), as ordered. Manage problems associated with increased ICP (see the section on increased ICP on pp. 1308–1311).

Fever is vigorously treated because it increases cerebral edema and the risk for seizures. In addition, neurologic damage may result from an extremely fever over a prolonged time. Acetaminophen or aspirin may be used to reduce fever. If the fever is resistant to aspirin or acetaminophen, more vigorous means are needed (e.g., cooling blanket). Take care not to reduce the temperature too rapidly because shivering may result, causing a rebound effect and increasing the temperature and ICP. Wrap the extremities in soft towels or a blanket covered with a sheet to reduce shivering. If a cooling blanket is not available or desirable, tepid sponge baths with water may be effective in lowering the temperature. Protect the skin from excessive drying and injury and prevent breaks in the skin.

Because high fever increases the metabolic rate and thus insensible fluid loss, assess the patient for dehydration and adequacy of fluid intake. Diaphoresis further increases fluid losses and should be noted on the output record. Calculate replacement fluids as 800 mL/day for respiratory losses and 100 mL for each degree of temperature above 100.4° F (38° C). Supplemental feeding (e.g., enteral nutrition) to maintain adequate nutritional intake may be needed. Follow the designated antibiotic schedule to maintain therapeutic blood levels.

Meningitis generally requires respiratory isolation until the cultures are negative. Meningococcal meningitis is highly contagious, while other causes of meningitis may pose minimal to no infection risk with patient contact. However, standard precautions are essential to protect the patient and nurse.

◆ **Ambulatory Care.** After the acute period has passed, the patient needs several weeks of recovery before resuming normal activities. In this period, stress the importance of adequate nutrition, with an emphasis on a high-protein, high-calorie diet in small, frequent feedings.

Muscle rigidity may persist in the neck and backs of the legs. Progressive range-of-motion exercises and warm baths are useful. Have the patient gradually increase activity as tolerated but encourage adequate rest and sleep.

Residual effects can result in sequelae such as dementia, seizures, deafness, hemiplegia, and hydrocephalus. Assess vision, hearing, cognitive skills, and motor and sensory abilities after

recovery, with appropriate referrals as indicated. Throughout the acute and recovery periods, be aware of the anxiety and stress felt by the caregiver and other family members.

◆ **Evaluation**

The expected outcomes are that the patient with bacterial meningitis will
- Have appropriate cognitive function
- Be oriented to person, place, and time
- Maintain body temperature within normal range
- Report satisfaction with pain control

VIRAL MENINGITIS

The most common causes of viral meningitis are enteroviruses, arboviruses, human immunodeficiency virus, and herpes simplex virus (HSV). Enteroviruses most often spread through direct contact with respiratory secretions. Viral meningitis usually presents as a headache, fever, photophobia, and stiff neck.[19] The fever may be moderate or high.

The Xpert EV test can rapidly diagnose viral meningitis. A sample of CSF is used to determine if enterovirus is present, and results are available within hours of symptom onset.[20]

The CSF can be clear or cloudy, and the typical finding is lymphocytosis. Organisms are not seen on Gram stain or acid-fast smears. Polymerase chain reaction (PCR) used to detect viral-specific deoxyribonucleic acid (DNA) or ribonucleic acid (RNA) is a sensitive method for diagnosing CNS viral infections.

Antibiotics should be given after the LP while awaiting the results of the CSF analysis. Antibiotics are the best defense for bacterial meningitis. We can easily discontinue them if the meningitis is found to be viral.

Viral meningitis is managed symptomatically because the disease is self-limiting. Full recovery is expected. Rare sequelae include persistent headaches, mild mental impairment, and incoordination.

BRAIN ABSCESS

Brain abscess is an accumulation of pus within the brain tissue from a local or systemic infection. Direct extension from an ear, tooth, mastoid, or sinus infection is the main cause. Other causes for brain abscess formation include spread from a distant site (e.g., pulmonary infection, bacterial endocarditis), skull fracture, and prior brain trauma or surgery. Streptococci and *Staphylococcus aureus* are the most common infective organisms.

Manifestations are similar to those of meningitis and encephalitis and include headache, fever, and nausea and vomiting. Signs of increased ICP may include drowsiness, confusion, and seizures. Focal symptoms may reflect the local area of the abscess. For example, visual field defects or psychomotor seizures are common with a temporal lobe abscess. Visual impairment and hallucinations may accompany an occipital abscess. CT and MRI are used to diagnose a brain abscess.

Antimicrobial therapy is the primary treatment for brain abscess. Other manifestations are treated symptomatically. If drug therapy is not effective, the abscess may have to be drained or removed if it is encapsulated.

Nursing measures are similar to those for management of meningitis or increased ICP. If surgical drainage or removal is the treatment of choice, nursing care is similar to that of a patient having cranial surgery.

ENCEPHALITIS

Encephalitis, an acute inflammation of the brain, is a serious and sometimes fatal disease. Several thousand cases occur in the United States each year. It is usually caused by a virus. Many different viruses can cause encephalitis. Some are associated with certain seasons of the year or endemic to certain geographic areas.

Ticks and mosquitoes transmit epidemic encephalitis. Examples of encephalitis include eastern equine, La Crosse, St. Louis, West Nile, and western equine.[21] Nonepidemic encephalitis may occur as a complication of measles, chickenpox, or mumps. HSV encephalitis is the most common cause of acute nonepidemic viral encephalitis. Cytomegalovirus encephalitis occurs in patients with acquired immunodeficiency syndrome (AIDS).

Clinical Manifestations and Diagnostic Studies

Encephalitis can be acute or subacute. The onset is typically nonspecific, with fever, headache, nausea, and vomiting. Signs of encephalitis appear on day 2 or 3 and may vary from minimal changes in mental status to coma. Virtually any CNS abnormality can occur, including hemiparesis, tremors, seizures, cranial nerve palsies, personality changes, memory impairment, amnesia, and dysphasia.

Early diagnosis and treatment of viral encephalitis are essential for favorable outcomes. Diagnostic findings are shown in Table 56.16. Brain imaging techniques include CT, MRI, and PET. PCR tests allow for early detection of HSV and West Nile encephalitis. West Nile virus should be strongly considered in adults over 50 years old who develop encephalitis or meningitis in summer or early fall. The best diagnostic test for West Nile virus is a blood test that detects viral RNA. This test is also used to screen donated blood, organs, cells, and tissues.

❖ Interprofessional and Nursing Care

Prevention of encephalitis focuses on mosquito control. Measures include cleaning rain gutters, removing old tires, draining bird baths, and removing water where mosquitoes can breed. Insect repellent should be used during mosquito season.

Interprofessional and nursing management of encephalitis, including West Nile virus infection, is symptomatic and supportive. In the initial stages of encephalitis, many patients need intensive care.

Acyclovir (Zovirax) is used to treat encephalitis caused by HSV infection. Its use reduces mortality rates, although neurologic complications may still occur. For maximal benefit, treatment should start before the onset of coma. Treat seizure disorders with antiseizure drugs. Prophylactic treatment with antiseizure drugs may be used in severe cases of encephalitis. Treatment of cytomegalovirus encephalitis in AIDS patients is discussed in Chapter 14.

CASE STUDY

Traumatic Brain Injury

(© Comstock/ Thinkstock.)

Patient Profile

C.G. is a 24-yr-old black man who has just returned from a 15-month army deployment to Afghanistan. He comes to the outpatient clinic with a report of chronic headaches (pain rating of 8 [0- to 10-point scale]) and trouble sleeping. His wife has noticed some personality changes since his return from deployment and is concerned that he has posttraumatic stress disorder (PTSD).

Subjective Data

- Reports that he has been depressed lately but attributes it to headache and difficulty returning home
- Headache is worse in the morning or when he lies down
- Uses tobacco and drinks coffee throughout the day
- Has trouble sleeping
- Reports "incidents" of heavy combat and blasts with a loss of consciousness. Cannot remember how many times
- Unable to obtain a more through history as he becomes quite agitated

Objective Data

- During your assessment, you note that C.G. is looking around the room and jumps when the phone rings next door
- Loss of short-term memory (remembers 1 of 3 items)
- Heart rate ranges from 100 to 130 beats/min
- ECG strip is shown below:

- Systolic BP ranges from 120 to 160 mm Hg
- Right pupil, 3 mm sluggishly reactive; left pupil, 3 mm briskly reactive

Diagnostic Studies

- CT of the head: negative for skull fracture, hematoma, or hemorrhage. Cerebral edema present, with cingulate herniation on the right side
- MRI of the head: Mild diffuse axonal injury

Discussion Questions

1. What could be the cause of C.G.'s hypertension, tachycardia, and ECG rhythm?
2. In addition to PTSD, what do his manifestations suggest?
3. ***Priority Decision:*** Based on the assessment data presented, what are the priority nursing diagnoses? Are there any collaborative problems?
4. ***Priority Decision:*** What are the priority nursing interventions that should be implemented?
5. ***Collaboration:*** How can the interprofessional team work together to meet his needs?
6. ***Safety:*** Are there any safety concerns for this patient or his wife?
7. ***Evidence-Based Practice:*** What interventions and support can help his wife?

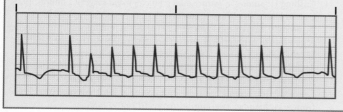

BRIDGE TO NCLEX EXAMINATION

The number of the question corresponds to the same-numbered outcome at the beginning of the chapter.

1. Vasogenic cerebral edema increases intracranial pressure by
   a. shifting fluid in the gray matter.
   b. altering the endothelial lining of cerebral capillaries.
   c. leaking molecules from the intracellular fluid to the capillaries.
   d. altering the osmotic gradient flow into the intravascular component.

2. A patient with intracranial pressure monitoring has a pressure of 12 mm Hg. The nurse understands that this pressure reflects
   a. a severe decrease in cerebral perfusion pressure.
   b. an alteration in the production of cerebrospinal fluid.
   c. the loss of autoregulatory control of intracranial pressure.
   d. a normal balance among brain tissue, blood, and cerebrospinal fluid.

3. A nurse plans care for the patient with increased intracranial pressure with the knowledge that the *best* way to position the patient is to
   a. keep the head of the bed flat.
   b. elevate the head of the bed to 30 degrees.
   c. maintain patient on the left side with the head supported on a pillow.
   d. use a continuous-rotation bed to continuously change patient position.

4. The nurse is alerted to a possible acute subdural hematoma in the patient who
   a. has a linear skull fracture crossing a major artery.
   b. has focal symptoms of brain damage with no recollection of a head injury.
   c. develops decreased level of consciousness and a headache within 48 hours of a head injury.
   d. has an immediate loss of consciousness with a brief lucid interval followed by decreasing level of consciousness.

5. During admission of a patient with a severe head injury to the emergency department, the nurse places the *highest* priority on assessment for
   a. patency of airway.
   b. presence of a neck injury.
   c. neurologic status with the Glasgow Coma Scale.
   d. cerebrospinal fluid leakage from the ears or nose.

6. A patient is suspected of having a brain tumor. The signs and symptoms include memory deficits, visual changes, weakness of right upper and lower extremities, and personality changes. The nurse determines that the tumor is *most* likely located in the
   a. frontal lobe.
   b. parietal lobe.
   c. occipital lobe.
   d. temporal lobe.

7. Nursing management of a patient with a brain tumor includes *(select all that apply)*
   a. discussing with the patient methods to control inappropriate behavior.
   b. using diversion techniques to keep the patient stimulated and motivated.
   c. assisting and supporting the family in understanding any changes in behavior.
   d. limiting self-care activities until the patient has regained maximum physical functioning.
   e. planning for seizure precautions and teaching the patient and the caregiver about antiseizure drugs.

8. The nurse on the clinical unit is assigned to four patients. Which patient should she assess *first*?
   a. Patient with a skull fracture whose nose is bleeding
   b. An older patient with a stroke who is confused and whose daughter is present
   c. Patient with meningitis who is suddenly agitated and reporting a headache of 10 on a 0- to 10 scale
   d. Patient 2 days postoperative after a craniotomy for a brain tumor who has had continued vomiting

9. A nursing measure that can reduce the potential for seizures and increased intracranial pressure in the patient with bacterial meningitis is
   a. administering codeine for relief of head and neck pain.
   b. controlling fever with prescribed drugs and cooling techniques.
   c. maintaining strict bed rest with the head of the bed slightly elevated.
   d. keeping the room dark and quiet to minimize environmental stimulation.

1. b, 2. d, 3. b, 4. c, 5. a, 6. a, 7. c, e, 8. c, 9. b

For rationales to these answers and even more NCLEX review questions, visit *http://evolve.elsevier.com/Lewis/medsurg.*

ⓔ EVOLVE WEBSITE/RESOURCES LIST

http://evolve.elsevier.com/Lewis/medsurg
Review Questions (Online Only)
Key Points
Answer Keys for Questions
- Rationales for Bridge to NCLEX Examination Questions
- Answer Guidelines for Case Study on p. 1327
Student Case Studies
- Patient With Head Injury
- Patient With Meningitis
Nursing Care Plans
- eNursing Care Plan 56.1: Patient With Increased Intracranial Pressure
- eNursing Care Plan 56.2: Patient With Meningitis
Conceptual Care Map Creator

Audio Glossary
Supporting Media
- Animation
  - Parts of the Brain Controlling Body Function
Content Updates

REFERENCES

1. Cushing H: *Studies in intracranial physiology and surgery,* London, 1925, Oxford University Press. (Classic)
*2. Tasneem N, Samaniego E, Pieper C, et al: Brain multimodality monitoring: A new tool in neurocritical care of comatose patients, *Crit Care Res Pract* 17, 2017. Retrieved from *www.hindawi.com/journals/ccrp/2017/6097265/.*
3. Seidman R: Cerebrovascular disease. Retrieved from *https://medicine.stonybrookmedicine.edu/pathology/neuropathology/chapter2.*
*4. LeRoux P: Intracranial pressure monitoring and management. Retrieved from *www.hindawi.com/journals/ccrp/2017/6097265/.*

*5. Brain Trauma Foundation: Guidelines for the management of severe traumatic brain injury. Retrieved from *https://braintrauma.org/uploads/03/12/Guidelines_for_Management_of_Severe_TBI_4th_Edition.pdf.*

*6. Peters NA, Farrell LB, Smith JP: Hyperosmolar therapy for the treatment of cerebral edema, *US Pharm* 43:HS8, 2018.

*7. Nair SS, Surendran A, Prabhakar RB, et al: Comparison between FOUR score and GCS in assessing patients with traumatic head injury: A tertiary centre study, *Int Surg J* 4:656, 2017.

*8. Surgical Critical Care: Seizure prophylaxis in patients with traumatic brain injury. Retrieved from *www.surgicalcriticalcare.net/Guidelines/Seizure%20prophylaxis%20in%20TBI%202017.pdf.*

9. Taylor CA, Bell JM, Breiding MJ, et al: Traumatic brain injury–related emergency department visits, hospitalizations, and deaths—United States, 2007 and 2013, *MMWR* 66:1, 2017.

*10. Sobrino J, Shafi S: Timing and causes of death after injuries, *Proc Bayl Univ Med Cent* 26:2, 2013. (Classic)

11. American Association of Neurological Surgeons: Traumatic brain injury. Retrieved from *www.aans.org/Patients/Neurosurgical-Conditions-and-Treatments/Traumatic-Brain-Injury.*

*12. Varghese R, Chakrabarty J, Menon G: Nursing management of adults with severe traumatic brain injury: A narrative review, *Indian J Crit Care Med* 21:10, 2017.

13. Wasserman J, Koenigsberg RA: Diffuse axonal injury. Retrieved from *https://emedicine.medscape.com/article/339912-overview.*

*14. Narun S, Brors O, Stokland O, et al: Mortality among head trauma patients taking preinjury antithrombotic agents: A retrospective cohort analysis from a level 1 trauma centre, *BMC Emerg Med* 16:29, 2016.

15. Subdural hematoma. Retrieved from *https://emedicine.medscape.com/article/1137207-overview.*

*16. Rumrill P, Hendriks DJ, Elias E, et al: Cognition and return to work after mild/moderate traumatic brain injury: A systematic review, *Work* 58:1, 2017.

17. National Cancer Institute. Brain tumor. Retrieved from *www.cancer.gov/cancertopics/types/brain.*

18. National Brain Tumor Society: Understanding brain tumors. Retrieved from *http://braintumor.org/brain-tumor-information/understanding-brain-tumors/.*

19. National Institute of Neurological Disorders and Stroke: Meningitis and encephalitis fact sheet. Retrieved from *www.ninds.nih.gov/Disorders/Patient-Caregiver-Education/Fact-Sheets/Meningitis-and-Encephalitis-Fact-Sheet.*

20. World Health Organization: Meningococcal meningitis. Retrieved from *www.who.int/mediacentre/factsheets/fs141/en/.*

21. National Institute of Neurologic Disorders and Stroke: Meningitis and encephalitis. Retrieved from *www.ninds.nih.gov/Disorders/Patient-Caregiver-Education/Fact-Sheets/Meningitis-and-Encephalitis-Fact-Sheet.*

*Evidence-based information for clinical practice.

57

Stroke

Michelle Bussard

One person caring about another represents life's greatest value.

John Rohn

http://evolve.elsevier.com/Lewis/medsurg

CONCEPTUAL FOCUS

Family Dynamics	Intracranial Regulation	Safety
Functional Ability	Mobility	Sensory Perception

LEARNING OUTCOMES

1. Describe the incidence of and risk factors for stroke.
2. Explain mechanisms that affect cerebral blood flow.
3. Compare and contrast the etiology and pathophysiology of ischemic and hemorrhagic strokes.
4. Correlate the clinical manifestations of stroke with the underlying pathophysiology.

5. Identify diagnostic studies done for patients with strokes.
6. Distinguish among the interprofessional care, drug therapy, and surgical therapy for patients with ischemic strokes and hemorrhagic strokes.
7. Describe the acute nursing management of a patient with a stroke.
8. Describe the rehabilitative nursing management of a patient with a stroke.
9. Explain the psychosocial impact of a stroke on the patient, caregiver, and family.

KEY TERMS

aneurysm, p. 1335
aphasia, p. 1336
cerebrovascular accident (CVA), p. 1330
dysarthria, p. 1336
dysphasia, p. 1336

embolic stroke, p. 1333
hemorrhagic strokes, p. 1334
intracerebral hemorrhage, p. 1334
ischemic stroke, p. 1333
stroke, p. 1330

subarachnoid hemorrhage (SAH), p. 1335
thrombotic stroke, p. 1333
transient ischemic attack (TIA), p. 1332

Stroke occurs when there is (1) *ischemia* (inadequate blood flow) to a part of the brain or (2) *hemorrhage* (bleeding) into the brain that results in death of brain cells. In a stroke, functions such as movement, sensation, thinking, talking, or emotions that were controlled by the affected area of the brain are lost or impaired. The severity of the loss of function varies according to the location and extent of the brain damage.

The terms *brain attack* and **cerebrovascular accident (CVA)** are also used to describe stroke. The term *brain attack* communicates the urgency of recognizing the warning signs of a stroke and treating it as a medical emergency, as we would do with a heart attack (Table 57.1). After the onset of a stroke, immediate medical attention is crucial to decrease disability and the risk for death.

Stroke is a major public health concern. An estimated 7 million people over the age of 20 in the United States have had a stroke.[1] With an aging population, we can expect a further increase in the incidence of strokes. However, stroke can occur at any age. About 34% of strokes occur in people younger than 65 years old.[2]

Stroke is currently the fifth most common cause of death in the United States. More than 137,000 deaths occur each year

from stroke.[3] While deaths due to stroke have declined, stroke is the leading cause of serious long-term disability. About 800,000 people have a stroke each year, and 15% to 30% have a permanent disability.[4]

Common long-term disabilities include *hemiparesis* (partial paralysis on one side), inability to walk, complete or partial dependence for activities of daily living (ADLs), *aphasia* (dysfunction in communication), and depression. In addition to the physical, cognitive, and emotional impact of the stroke on the survivor, the stroke affects the lives of the stroke victim's caregiver and family. A stroke is a lifelong change for both the stroke survivor and family. Be mindful of this impact when caring for patients who survive stroke.

PATHOPHYSIOLOGY OF STROKE

Anatomy of Cerebral Circulation

Blood is supplied to the brain by 2 major pairs of arteries: internal carotid arteries (anterior circulation) and vertebral arteries (posterior circulation). The carotid arteries branch to supply most of the (1) frontal, parietal, and temporal lobes; (2) basal

TABLE 57.1 Patient & Caregiver Teaching

FAST for Warning Signs of Stroke

FAST is an easy way to remember the signs of stroke. Include the following information in the teaching plan for a patient at risk for stroke and the patient's caregiver:

F	Face drooping	Does one side of the face droop or is it numb? Ask the person to smile. Is the smile uneven?
A	Arm weakness	Is one arm weak or numb? Ask the person to raise both arms. Does one arm drift downward?
S	Speech difficulties	Is speech slurred? Is the person unable to speak or hard to understand? Ask the person to repeat a simple sentence like "The sky is blue." Is the sentence repeated correctly?
T	Time	Time is CRITICAL! If someone shows any of these signs (even if they go away), call 911 and get the person to the hospital. Note the time when the signs first appeared.

In addition, report the sudden onset of the following:
- Confusion
- Numbness or weakness, especially in 1 side of the body
- Severe headache with no known cause
- Trouble seeing in one or both eyes
- Trouble walking, dizziness, loss of balance or coordination

Source: American Stroke Association: FAST. Retrieved from www.strokeassociation.org/STROKEORG/WarningSigns/Stroke-Warning-Signs-and-Symptoms_UCM_308528_SubHomePage.jsp.

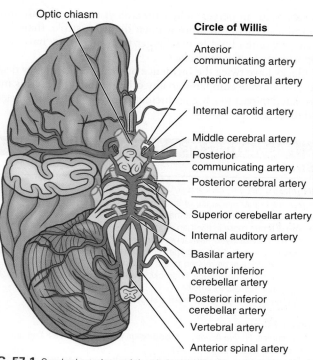

FIG. 57.1 Cerebral arteries and the circle of Willis. The top of the temporal lobe has been removed to show the course of the middle cerebral artery.

Optic chiasm

Circle of Willis
- Anterior communicating artery
- Anterior cerebral artery
- Internal carotid artery
- Middle cerebral artery
- Posterior communicating artery
- Posterior cerebral artery

- Superior cerebellar artery
- Internal auditory artery
- Basilar artery
- Anterior inferior cerebellar artery
- Posterior inferior cerebellar artery
- Vertebral artery
- Anterior spinal artery

ganglia; and (3) part of the diencephalon (thalamus and hypothalamus). The major branches of the carotid arteries are the middle cerebral and anterior cerebral arteries. The vertebral arteries join to form the basilar artery, which branches to supply the middle and lower parts of the temporal lobes, occipital lobes, cerebellum, brainstem, and part of the diencephalon. The main branch of the basilar artery is the posterior cerebral artery. The anterior and posterior cerebral circulation is connected at the *circle of Willis* by the anterior and posterior communicating arteries (Fig. 57.1). Fig. 55.11 shows the arteries at the base of the brain. Genetic variations in this area are common, and all connecting vessels may not be present.

Regulation of Cerebral Blood Flow

The brain needs a continuous supply of blood to provide the O_2 and glucose that neurons need to function. Blood flow must be maintained at 750 to 1000 mL/min (55 mL/100 g of brain tissue), or 20% of the cardiac output, for optimal brain functioning. If blood flow to the brain is totally interrupted (e.g., cardiac arrest), neurologic metabolism is altered in 30 seconds, metabolism stops in 2 minutes, and cell death occurs in 5 minutes.

The brain is normally protected from changes in mean systemic arterial BP over a range from 50 to 150 mm Hg by a mechanism known as *cerebral autoregulation*. This involves changes in the diameter of cerebral blood vessels in response to changes in pressure so that the blood flow to the brain stays constant. When cerebral ischemia occurs, autoregulation may be impaired, making the brain dependent on systemic BP. CO_2 is a potent cerebral vasodilator. Changes in arterial CO_2 levels have a dramatic effect on cerebral blood flow (CBF). Increased CO_2 levels increase CBF. Decreased CO_2 levels decrease CBF. Very low arterial oxygen (O_2) levels (partial pressure of arterial

O_2 less than 50 mm Hg) or increases in hydrogen ion concentration also increase CBF.

Factors that affect blood flow to the brain include systemic BP, cardiac output, and blood viscosity. During normal activity, O_2 requirements vary considerably. Changes in cardiac output, vasomotor tone, and distribution of blood flow normally maintain adequate blood flow to the brain. Cardiac output must be reduced by one third before CBF is reduced. Changes in blood viscosity affect CBF, with decreased viscosity increasing blood flow.

Collateral circulation may develop over time to compensate for a decrease in CBF. An area of the brain can potentially receive blood supply from another blood vessel even if blood supply from the original vessel has been cut off (e.g., because of thrombosis). In other words, the vessels in the brain make an "alternative route" for blood flow to reach damaged areas, thus preventing a stroke.

Intracranial pressure (ICP) influences CBF. Increased ICP causes brain compression and reduced CBF. One of your major goals when caring for a stroke patient is to reduce secondary injury related to increased ICP (see Chapter 56).

RISK FACTORS FOR STROKE

The most effective way to decrease the burden of stroke is prevention and teaching, especially about risk factors. We divide risk factors into nonmodifiable and modifiable. Stroke risk increases with multiple risk factors. Thus, the primary prevention of stroke focuses on reducing modifiable risk factors, which can dramatically reduce the morbidity and mortality of stroke.[5]

Nonmodifiable Risk Factors

Nonmodifiable risk factors include age, gender, ethnicity or race, and family history or heredity. Stroke risk increases with age, doubling each decade after 55 years of age. Two thirds of all strokes occur in persons older than 65 years. Strokes are more common in men, but more women die from stroke than men. Because women tend to live longer than men, they have more opportunity to have a stroke.[2]

Blacks have twice the incidence of stroke and a higher death rate from stroke compared to any other ethnic group. This may be related in part to a higher incidence of hypertension, obesity, and diabetes.[2]

🌐 PROMOTING HEALTH EQUITY

Stroke

Blacks
- Have a higher incidence of strokes than whites
- Have a rate of first strokes that is twice that of any other ethnic group
- Are 3 times more likely than whites to have an ischemic stroke and 4 times more likely to have a hemorrhagic stroke
- Have increased rates of hypertension, diabetes, and sickle cell anemia, which may be related to the high incidence of strokes
- Have a higher incidence of smoking and obesity than whites, which are 2 risk factors for stroke
- Are twice as likely to die from a stroke as whites

Other Ethnicities
- Hispanics, Native Americans, and Asian Americans have a higher incidence of strokes than whites.
- Hispanics have a high incidence of diabetes, an important risk factor for strokes.
- Native Americans are more likely than whites to have at least 2 risk factors for stroke.

Genetic risk factors are important in the development of all vascular diseases, including stroke. A person with a family history of stroke has an increased risk for having a stroke. We think that genes encoding products involved in lipid metabolism, thrombosis, and inflammation are genetic factors for stroke. People who have at least 2 first-degree relatives with a history of subarachnoid hemorrhage (SAH) or aneurysm should be screened to rule out anomalies in their cerebral vasculature.[6]

Modifiable Risk Factors

Modifiable risk factors are those that can potentially be altered through lifestyle changes and medical treatment, thus reducing the risk for stroke. They include hypertension, heart disease, diabetes, smoking, obesity, sleep apnea, metabolic syndrome, lack of physical exercise, poor diet, and drug and alcohol use. We think modifiable risk factors cause 90% of strokes.[6]

Hypertension is the single most important modifiable risk factor. It is often undetected and inadequately treated. Increases in systolic BP (SBP) and diastolic BP (DBP) independently increase stroke risk. The proper treatment of hypertension reduces stroke risk up to 50%. New recommendations by the American Heart Association (AHA) include home BP monitoring with a goal of SBP less than 140 mm Hg.[4]

Heart disease, including atrial fibrillation, myocardial infarction (MI), cardiomyopathy, cardiac valve abnormalities, and congenital heart defects, such as patent foramen ovale, is a risk factor for stroke. Atrial fibrillation is responsible for about 25% of all strokes.[7] People with atrial fibrillation are 5 times more likely to have a stroke than people with a regular heart rhythm.[8] The incidence of atrial fibrillation increases with age. Oral anticoagulants (e.g., warfarin, dabigatran) and adherence to their therapy play a vital role in stroke prevention.[4,9]

Diabetes is a significant risk factor for stroke. Stroke risk in people with diabetes is 5 times higher than in the general population.[7]

Smoking nearly doubles the risk for ischemic stroke. Smokers are 4 times as likely to have a hemorrhagic stroke than nonsmokers.[5] The risk associated with smoking decreases substantially over time after the smoker quits. After 5 to 10 years of no tobacco use, former smokers have the same risk for stroke as nonsmokers.

The effect of alcohol on stroke risk appears to depend on the amount consumed. Women who drink more than 1 alcoholic drink per day and men who drink more than 2 alcoholic drinks per day are at higher risk for hypertension, which increases their chance of stroke. Illicit drug use, especially cocaine use, increases stroke risk.[6]

A waist circumference to hip circumference ratio equal to or above the mid-value for the population increases the risk for ischemic stroke 3-fold. In addition, obesity is associated with hypertension, high blood glucose, and increased blood lipid levels, all of which increase stroke risk.[6] An association of physical inactivity and increased stroke risk is present in both men and women. Benefits of physical activity can occur with even light to moderate regular activity. The American Stroke Association recommends 40 minutes of exercise 3 to 4 days per week to reduce risk for stroke.[9] Nutrition teaching is important, since a diet high in fat and low in fruits and vegetables may increase stroke risk.

The early forms of birth control pills that had high levels of progestin and estrogen increased a woman's chance of having a stroke, especially if the woman smoked heavily. Newer, low-dose oral contraceptives have lower risks for stroke except in those who have hypertension and smoke. The AHA recommends smoking cessation and alternatives to estrogen oral contraceptives for those women to reduce the incidence of stroke.[4]

Women who have migraines with aura have an increased risk for stroke. Other conditions that may increase the stroke risk include inflammatory conditions (e.g., rheumatoid arthritis), sickle cell disease, and blood clotting disorders, such as factor V Leiden mutation.[5]

Transient Ischemic Attack

Another risk factor associated with stroke is a history of a transient ischemic attack (TIA). A TIA is a transient episode of neurologic dysfunction caused by focal brain, spinal cord, or retinal ischemia, but without acute infarction of the brain. Symptoms typically last less than 1 hour.

It is important to teach the patient to seek treatment for any stroke symptoms, since there is no way to predict if a TIA will resolve or if it will progress to a stroke. In general, one third of those who had a TIA do not have another, one third have more TIAs, and one third progress to stroke.[10]

TIAs may be due to microemboli that temporarily block the blood flow. TIAs are a warning sign of progressive cerebrovascular disease. The signs and symptoms of a TIA depend on the blood vessel that is involved and the area of the brain that is ischemic. If the carotid system is involved, patients may have a temporary loss of vision in 1 eye (*amaurosis fugax*), transient hemiparesis, numbness or loss of sensation, or a sudden inability to speak. Signs of a TIA involving the vertebrobasilar system may include tinnitus, vertigo, darkened or blurred vision, diplopia, ptosis, dysarthria, dysphagia, ataxia, and unilateral or bilateral numbness or weakness.

CHECK YOUR PRACTICE

You are talking with your uncle at your family reunion. He knows that you are a nurse and seems very eager to talk with you. He tells you that earlier this morning he was having problems talking, got dizzy, and then "blanked" out for a while. He found himself just lying on the floor in his room.
- He says, "I think it is just all the excitement of the reunion, but what do you think?"

A TIA is treated as a medical emergency since it can lead to an ischemic stroke. Teach people at risk for TIAs to seek medical attention at once with any stroke-like symptom and to identify the time of onset of symptoms. The ABCD[2] score is a tool used to predict stroke risk for a person after a TIA (Table 57.2).[11]

TYPES OF STROKE

Unlike a TIA, in which ischemia occurs without infarction, a stroke results in infarction (cell death). Strokes are classified as ischemic or hemorrhagic based on the cause and underlying pathophysiologic findings (Fig. 57.2 and Table 57.3).

Ischemic Stroke

An ischemic stroke results from inadequate blood flow to the brain from partial or complete occlusion of an artery.[12] Ischemic strokes are classified as thrombotic or embolic strokes.

Thrombotic Stroke. A thrombotic stroke occurs from injury to a blood vessel wall and formation of a blood clot (Fig. 57.2, A). The lumen of the blood vessel becomes narrowed, and, if it becomes occluded, infarction occurs. Thrombosis develops readily where atherosclerotic plaques have already narrowed blood vessels. Thrombotic stroke is the most common cause of stroke. It accounts for about 60% of strokes.[2] They are more common in older adults, especially those with high cholesterol, atherosclerosis, or diabetes. Most thrombotic strokes are associated with hypertension or diabetes, both of which accelerate atherosclerosis. Many times, a TIA precedes thrombotic strokes.[7]

The extent of the stroke depends on rapidity of onset, size of the damaged area, and presence of collateral circulation. Most patients with ischemic stroke do not have a decreased level of consciousness (LOC) in the first 24 hours, unless it is due to a brainstem stroke or other condition, such as seizure, increased ICP, or hemorrhage. Manifestations of ischemic stroke may progress in the first 72 hours as infarction and cerebral edema increase.

Embolic Stroke. Embolic stroke occurs when an embolus lodges in and occludes a cerebral artery, resulting in infarction and edema of the area supplied by the involved vessel (Fig. 57.2, B). Embolism is the second most common cause of stroke.[2] Most emboli originate in the endocardial (inside) layer of the heart, when a plaque breaks off from the endocardium and enters the circulation. The embolus travels upward to the cerebral circulation and lodges where a vessel narrows or bifurcates (splits). Heart conditions, including atrial fibrillation, MI, infective endocarditis, rheumatic heart disease, valvular heart prostheses, patent foramen ovale, and atrial septal defects, account for most embolic ischemic strokes.[2] Less common causes of emboli include air and fat from long bone (e.g., femur) fractures.

TABLE 57.2 ABCD² Score

The ABCD² score is a risk assessment tool. It is designed to predict the risk for stroke 2 days after a transient ischemic attack (TIA). Calculate the score by adding up points for 5 factors.

Risk Factor	Points
Age ≥60 yr	1
Systolic BP ≥140 mm Hg *OR* diastolic BP ≥90 mm Hg	1
Clinical features of TIA (choose 1)	
Unilateral weakness with or without speech impairment *OR*	2
Speech impairment without unilateral weakness	1
Duration	
TIA duration ≥60 min *OR*	2
TIA duration 10–59 min	1
Diabetes	1
Total ABCD² Score	0–7

ABCD² score	2-Day Stroke Risk (%)	Care Needed
0–3	1.0	Hospitalization not needed unless there is another indication (e.g., new atrial fibrillation)
4–5	4.1	Hospitalization in most situations
6–7	8.1	Hospitalization

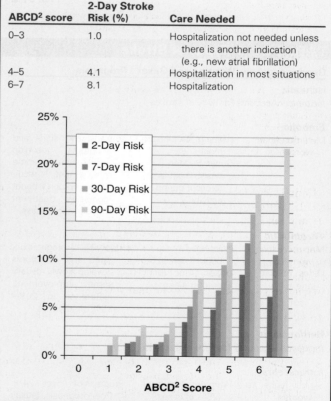

Permission obtained from National Stroke Association. Retrieved from *www.stroke.org*.

The patient with an embolic stroke often has severe manifestations that occur suddenly. Embolic strokes can affect any age-group. Rheumatic heart disease is a cause of embolic stroke in young to middle-aged adults. An embolus arising from an atherosclerotic plaque is more common in older adults.

Warning signs are less common with embolic than with thrombotic stroke. The embolic stroke often occurs rapidly, giving little time to accommodate to an obstructed blood vessel with the development of collateral circulation. The patient is usually conscious, although they may have a headache. The effects of the emboli are initially characterized by severe neurologic deficits, which can be temporary if the clot breaks up and allows blood to flow. Smaller emboli then continue to obstruct

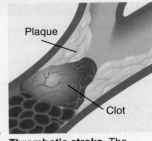

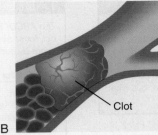

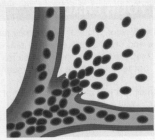

Thrombotic stroke. The process of clot formation (thrombosis) results in a narrowing of the lumen, which blocks the passage of the blood through the artery.

Embolic stroke. An embolus is a blood clot or other debris circulating in the blood. When it reaches an artery in the brain that is too narrow to pass through, it lodges there and blocks the flow of blood.

Hemorrhagic stroke. A burst blood vessel may allow blood to seep into and damage brain tissues until clotting shuts off the leak.

FIG. 57.2 Major types of stroke.

TABLE 57.3 Types of Stroke

Gender and Age	Warning and Onset	Prognosis
Ischemic _Incidence:_ Accounts for 87% of strokes		
Embolic Men more than women	_Warning:_ TIA (uncommon) _Onset:_ Sudden onset, most likely to occur during activity	Single event, signs and symptoms develop quickly, usually some improvement, recurrence common without aggressive treatment of underlying disease.
Thrombotic Men more than women Oldest median age	_Warning:_ TIA (30%–50% of cases) _Onset:_ Often during or after sleep	Stepwise progression, signs and symptoms develop slowly, usually some improvement, recurrence in 20%–25% of survivors.
Hemorrhagic _Incidence:_ Accounts for 13% of strokes		
Intracerebral Slightly higher in women	_Warning:_ Headache (25% of cases) _Onset:_ Activity (often)	Progression over 24 hr. Poor prognosis, fatality more likely with presence of coma.
Subarachnoid Slightly higher in women Youngest median age	_Warning:_ Headache (common) _Onset:_ Activity (often), sudden onset, most often related to head trauma	Usually single sudden event, fatality more likely with presence of coma.

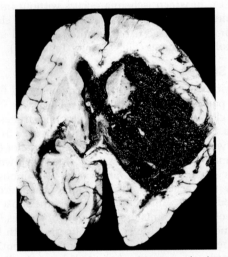

FIG. 57.3 Massive hypertensive hemorrhage rupturing into a lateral ventricle of the brain. (From Kumar V, Abbas AK, Aster JC, et al: _Robbins and Cotran pathologic basis of disease,_ ed 8, Philadelphia, 2010, Saunders.)

Hemorrhagic Stroke

Hemorrhagic strokes result from bleeding into the brain tissue itself (intracerebral or intraparenchymal hemorrhage) or into the subarachnoid space or ventricles (SAH or intraventricular hemorrhage).

Intracerebral Hemorrhage. Intracerebral hemorrhage is bleeding within the brain caused by a rupture of a vessel (usually in the basal ganglia) (Fig. 57.2, C). The prognosis of patients with intracerebral hemorrhage is poor. The 30-day mortality rate is 40% to 80%. Half of the deaths occur within the first 48 hours.[2]

Hypertension is the most common cause of intracerebral hemorrhage (Fig. 57.3). Other causes include vascular malformations, coagulation disorders, anticoagulant and thrombolytic drugs, trauma, brain tumors, and ruptured aneurysms. Hemorrhage often occurs during periods of activity. Most often there is a sudden onset of symptoms, with progression over minutes to hours because of ongoing bleeding.

Manifestations include neurologic deficits, headache, nausea, vomiting, decreased LOC, and hypertension. The extent of the symptoms varies depending on the amount, location, and

smaller vessels, which in turn involve smaller portions of the brain with fewer deficits noted.

The prognosis is related to the amount of brain tissue deprived of its blood supply. Recurrence of embolic stroke is common unless the underlying cause is aggressively treated.

duration of the bleeding. A blood clot within the closed skull can result in a mass that causes pressure on brain tissue, displaces brain tissue, and decreases CBF, leading to ischemia and infarction.

Most intracerebral hemorrhages occur in the cerebral lobes, cerebellum, pons, thalamus, subcortical white matter, internal capsule, or a part of the basal ganglia called the putamen. At first, patients have a severe headache with nausea and vomiting. Manifestations of putaminal and internal capsule bleeding include weakness of one side (including the face, arm, and leg), slurred speech, and deviation of the eyes. Progression of symptoms related to a severe hemorrhage includes hemiplegia, fixed and dilated pupils, abnormal body posturing, and coma. Thalamic hemorrhage results in hemiplegia with more sensory than motor loss. Bleeding into the subthalamic areas of the brain leads to problems with vision and eye movement. Cerebellar hemorrhages are characterized by severe headache, vomiting, loss of ability to walk, dysphagia, dysarthria, and eye movement changes.

Hemorrhage in the pons is the most serious because basic life functions (e.g., respiration) are rapidly affected. Hemorrhage in the pons can be characterized by hemiplegia leading to complete paralysis, coma, abnormal body posturing, fixed pupils, hyperthermia, and death.

Subarachnoid Hemorrhage. Subarachnoid hemorrhage (SAH) occurs when there is intracranial bleeding into the cerebrospinal fluid (CSF)–filled space between the arachnoid and pia mater membranes on the surface of the brain. SAH is often caused by rupture of a cerebral aneurysm (congenital or acquired weakness and ballooning of vessels). Aneurysms may be saccular or berry aneurysms, ranging from a few millimeters to 20 to 30 mm in size, or fusiform atherosclerotic aneurysms. Most aneurysms are in the circle of Willis. Other causes of SAH include trauma and illicit drug (cocaine) use. The incidence of SAH increases with age and is higher in women than men.

The patient may have warning signs and symptoms if the ballooning artery applies pressure to brain tissue. Minor warning symptoms may result from leaking of an aneurysm before major rupture. In general, cerebral aneurysms are viewed as a "silent killer," since people do not have warning signs or symptoms of an aneurysm until rupture has occurred.

? CHECK YOUR PRACTICE

You are watching your husband's "for fun" soccer game. He leaves the game and is kneeling on the ground. When you try to assess what is going on he says, "I've got a terrible headache. It just started." Knowing that he sometimes gets headaches when he is stressed, you ask him if he is feeling stressed. He almost screams back at you, "NO! This is the worst headache of my life!"

- What should you do?

Loss of consciousness may or may not occur. The patient's LOC may range from alert to comatose, depending on the severity of the bleed. Other manifestations include focal neurologic deficits (including cranial nerve deficits), nausea, vomiting, seizures, and stiff neck.

Complications of aneurysmal SAH include rebleeding before surgery or other therapy is started and cerebral vasospasm (narrowing of the blood vessels), which can result in cerebral infarction. Cerebral vasospasm is likely due to an interaction between the metabolites of blood and the vascular smooth muscle. This occurs when the subarachnoid blood clots break

---

TABLE 57.4 Stroke Manifestations Related to Artery Involvement

Artery	Manifestations
Anterior cerebral	Motor and/or sensory deficit (contralateral), sucking or rooting reflex, rigidity, gait problems, loss of proprioception and fine touch
Middle cerebral	*Dominant side:* Aphasia, motor and sensory deficit, hemianopsia *Nondominant side:* Neglect, motor and sensory deficit, hemianopsia
Posterior cerebral	Hemianopsia, visual hallucination, spontaneous pain, motor deficit
Vertebral	Cranial nerve deficits, diplopia, dizziness, nausea, vomiting, dysarthria, dysphagia, and/or coma

---

down or dissolve, releasing metabolites that can cause endothelial damage and vasoconstriction. The release of endothelin (a potent vasoconstrictor) may play a key role in the induction of cerebral vasospasm after SAH. Patients with SAH who are at risk for vasospasm are often kept in the intensive care unit (up to 14 days) until the threat of vasospasm is reduced. Peak time for vasospasm is 6 to 10 days after the initial bleed.

Despite improvements in surgical techniques and management, many patients with SAH die. Some die almost immediately when a rupture occurs. Others die from subsequent bleeding. Survivors may be left with significant morbidity, including cognitive problems.

CLINICAL MANIFESTATIONS OF STROKE

Neurologic manifestations do not significantly differ between ischemic and hemorrhagic stroke. The reason for this is that destruction of neural tissue is the basis for neurologic dysfunction caused by both types of stroke. The manifestations are related to the location of the stroke. Specific manifestations related to the type of stroke were discussed in the previous section. The general manifestations of ischemic and hemorrhagic stroke are discussed together here.

A stroke can affect many body functions, including motor activity, bladder and bowel elimination, intellectual function, spatial-perceptual changes, personality, affect, sensation, swallowing, and communication. The functions affected are directly related to the artery involved and area of the brain that it supplies (Table 57.4). Manifestations related to right- and left-brain damage differ somewhat. These are shown in Fig. 57.4.

Motor Function

Motor deficits are the most obvious effect of stroke. Motor deficits include impairment of (1) mobility, (2) respiratory function, (3) swallowing and speech, (4) gag reflex, and (5) self-care abilities. Symptoms are caused by the destruction of motor neurons in the pyramidal pathway (nerve fibers from the brain that pass through the spinal cord to the motor cells). The characteristic motor deficits include loss of skilled voluntary movement (*akinesia*), impaired integration of movements, changes in muscle tone, and altered reflexes. The initial *hyporeflexia* (depressed reflexes) progresses to *hyperreflexia* (hyperactive reflexes) for most patients.

Motor deficits after a stroke follow certain specific patterns. Because the pyramidal pathway crosses at the level of the

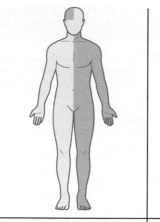

Right-brain damage
(stroke on right side of the brain)
- Paralyzed left side: hemiplegia
- Left-sided neglect
- Spatial-perceptual deficits
- Tends to deny or minimize problems
- Rapid performance, short attention span
- Impulsive, safety problems
- Impaired judgment
- Impaired time concepts

Left-brain damage
(stroke on left side of the brain)
- Paralyzed right side: hemiplegia
- Impaired speech/language aphasias
- Impaired right/left discrimination
- Slow performance, cautious
- Aware of deficits: depression, anxiety
- Impaired comprehension related to language, math

FIG. 57.4 Manifestations of right-brain and left-brain stroke.

TABLE 57.5 Types of Aphasia

Type	Characteristics
Broca's	• Type of nonfluent aphasia • Damage to frontal lobe of brain • Often speak in short phrases that make sense but take great effort • Often omit small words (e.g., is, and, the) • May say, "Walk dog," meaning, "I will take the dog for a walk," or "Book 2 table," for "There are 2 books on the table" • Typically understands others' speech • Often aware of their difficulties and can become easily frustrated
Global	• Type of nonfluent aphasia • Results from damage to extensive portions of language areas of brain • Have severe communication difficulties • May be extremely limited in ability to speak or understand language
Wernicke's	• Type of fluent aphasia • Damage occurs in left temporal lobe, although it can result from damage to right lobe • May speak in long sentences that have no meaning, add unnecessary words, and even create made-up words • May say, "You know that smoodle pinkered and that I want to get him round and take care of him like you want before" • Usually have great difficulty understanding speech • Often unaware of their mistakes • Often difficult to follow what person is trying to say
Other	• Results from damage to different language areas in brain • Some may have difficulty repeating words and sentences, even though they can speak and understand the meaning of the word or sentence • May have difficulty naming objects, even though they know what the object is and what its use is

medulla, a lesion on one side of the brain affects motor function on the opposite side of the body (contralateral). The arms and legs of the affected side may be weakened or paralyzed to different degrees depending on which part of and to what extent the cerebral circulation was compromised. A stroke affecting the middle cerebral artery leads to a greater weakness in the upper extremity than the lower extremity. The affected shoulder tends to rotate internally, and the hip rotates externally. The affected foot is plantar flexed and inverted. An initial period of flaccidity may last from days to several weeks and is related to nerve damage. Spasticity of the muscles, which follows the flaccid stage, is related to interruption of upper motor neuron influence.

Communication

The left hemisphere is dominant for language skills in right-handed persons and in most left-handed persons.[12] Language disorders involve expression and comprehension of written and spoken words. The patient may have aphasia. Types of aphasia include *receptive aphasia* (loss of comprehension), *expressive aphasia* (inability to produce language), or *global aphasia* (total inability to communicate). Aphasia occurs when a stroke damages the dominant hemisphere of the brain.

Dysphasia refers to impaired ability to communicate. However, in most settings the terms *aphasia* and *dysphasia* are used interchangeably. Aphasia is the more common term used. Patterns of aphasia may differ since the stroke affects different portions of the brain. Aphasia may be classified as *nonfluent* (minimal speech activity with slow speech that requires obvious effort) or *fluent* (speech is present but has little meaningful communication) (Table 57.5). Most types of aphasia are mixed, with impairment in both expression and understanding. A massive stroke may result in global aphasia.

Many stroke patients have dysarthria, a problem with the muscular control of speech. Impairment may involve pronunciation, articulation, and phonation. Dysarthria does not affect the meaning of communication or the comprehension of language, but it does affect the mechanics of speech. Some patients have a combination of aphasia and dysarthria.

Affect

Patients who had a stroke may have a hard time controlling their emotions. Emotional responses may be exaggerated or unpredictable. Depression and feelings associated with changes in body image and loss of function can make this worse.[13] Mobility and communication problems increase frustration.

❓ CHECK YOUR PRACTICE

You are working in the outpatient stroke clinic, counseling the family of one of your favorite patients. He is a well-respected 65-yr-old businessman who has returned home after a stroke. His family tells you that during meals he becomes frustrated and begins to cry because of the difficulty getting food into his mouth and chewing. His family cannot understand why a previously very competent man is so emotional.

- How should you counsel the family? What teaching is needed?

Intellectual Function

A stroke may impair both memory and judgment. These impairments can occur with strokes affecting either side of the brain. A left-brain stroke is more likely to result in memory problems related to language. Patients with a left-brain stroke often are cautious in making judgments.

The patient with a right-brain stroke tends to be impulsive and to move quickly. An example is that they try to rise quickly from a wheelchair without locking the wheels or raising the footrests. On the other hand, people with a left-brain stroke would move slowly and cautiously from the wheelchair. Patients with either type of stroke may find it hard to make generalizations, interfering with their ability to learn.

Spatial-Perceptual Problems

Those who had a stroke on the right side of the brain are more likely to have problems with spatial-perceptual orientation. However, this can also occur in people with left-brain stroke.

Spatial-perceptual problems may be divided into 4 categories.

- The first results from damage of the parietal lobe. It causes the patient to have an incorrect perception of self and illness. In this situation, patients may deny their illnesses or not recognize their own body parts.
- The second category occurs when the patient neglects all input from the affected side (erroneous perception of self in space). This may be worsened by *homonymous hemianopsia,* in which blindness occurs in the same half of the visual fields of both eyes. The patient also has difficulty with spatial orientation, such as judging distances.
- The third spatial-perceptual deficit is *agnosia,* the inability to recognize an object by sight, touch, or hearing.
- The fourth deficit is *apraxia,* the inability to carry out learned sequential movements on command. Patients may or may not be aware of their spatial-perceptual problems. You need to assess for this potential problem as it will affect rehabilitation and recovery.

Elimination

Most problems with urinary and bowel elimination are temporary. When a stroke affects one hemisphere of the brain, the prognosis for normal bladder function is excellent. At least partial sensation for bladder filling remains, and voluntary urination is present. At first the patient may have frequency, urgency, and incontinence. Although motor control of the bowel is usually not a problem, patients are often constipated. Constipation is associated with immobility, weak abdominal muscles, dehydration, and decreased response to the defecation reflex. Elimination problems may also be related to inability to state the need to eliminate and difficulty managing clothing (resulting in incontinence). Scheduled toileting and clothes that are easily removed encourage independence.

DIAGNOSTIC STUDIES FOR STROKE

When manifestations of a stroke occur, diagnostic studies (Table 57.6 and 57.7) are done to (1) confirm that it is a stroke and not another type of brain lesion and (2) identify the likely cause of the stroke. Diagnostic study results also guide decisions about therapy. A key assessment is to determine the time of the onset of symptoms. This is important for all types of stroke, especially ischemic strokes since the time can affect treatment decisions.

TABLE 57.6 Diagnostic Studies

Stroke

Diagnosis of Stroke (Including Extent of Involvement)
- CT scan
- CT angiography (CTA)
- CT/MRI perfusion and diffusion imaging
- MRI
- Magnetic resonance angiography (MRA)

Cerebral Blood Flow
- Carotid angiography
- Carotid duplex scanning
- Cerebral angiography
- Digital subtraction angiography
- Transcranial Doppler ultrasonography

Cardiac Assessment
- Cardiac markers (troponin, creatine kinase-MB)
- Chest x-ray
- Echocardiography (transthoracic, transesophageal)
- ECG

Additional Studies
- Coagulation studies: prothrombin time, activated partial thromboplastin time
- CBC (including platelets)
- Electrolyte panel with blood glucose
- Lipid profile
- Renal and hepatic studies

Once the person suspected of TIA or stroke arrives in the emergency department, it is important for the patient to rapidly undergo either a noncontrast head CT or MRI. These important diagnostic tests can rapidly distinguish between ischemic and hemorrhagic stroke. They help determine the size and location of the stroke and treatment options. MRI is more effective in identifying ischemic stroke than CT scans. However, a CT scan is a rapid diagnostic tool to rule out hemorrhage. Serial scans may be used to assess the effectiveness of treatment and to evaluate recovery.

CT angiography (CTA) provides visualization of cerebral blood vessels. It can be done after or at the same time as the noncontrast CT scan. CTA can give an estimate of perfusion and detect filling defects in the cerebral arteries. Magnetic resonance angiography (MRA) can detect vascular lesions and blockages, similar to CTA. CT/MRI perfusion and diffusion imaging may be done.

If the suspected cause of the stroke includes emboli from the heart, diagnostic cardiac tests should be done. Cardiac imaging is recommended because many strokes are caused by blood clots from the heart. Blood tests can help identify conditions contributing to stroke and to guide treatment (Table 57.6).

Angiography can identify cervical and cerebrovascular occlusion, atherosclerotic plaques, and malformation of vessels. Cerebral angiography can definitively identify the source of SAH. Risks of angiography include dislodging an embolus, causing vasospasm, inducing further hemorrhage, and provoking an allergic reaction to contrast media.

Intraarterial digital subtraction angiography (DSA) involves the injection of a contrast agent to visualize blood vessels in the neck and the large vessels of the circle of Willis. It reduces the dose of contrast material, uses smaller catheters, and shortens

TABLE 57.7 Interprofessional Care

Acute Stroke

Diagnostic Assessment
- History and physical examination
- Diagnostic studies (Table 57.6)

Management
Drug Therapy
- Platelet inhibitors (e.g., aspirin)
- Anticoagulation therapy for patients with atrial fibrillation

Surgical Therapy
- Carotid endarterectomy
- Stenting of carotid artery
- Transluminal angioplasty
- Surgical interventions for aneurysms at risk for bleeding

Acute Care
- Maintenance of airway
- Fluid therapy
- Treatment of cerebral edema
- Prevention of secondary injury

Ischemic Stroke
- Tissue plasminogen activator (tPA) IV or intraarterial
- Endovascular therapy

Hemorrhagic Stroke
- Surgical decompression if indicated
- Clipping or coiling of aneurysm

Role of Interprofessional Team Members
Speech Therapy
- Assess swallowing reflex
- Evaluate patient for communication defects (e.g., aphasia)

Occupational Therapy
- Evaluate ability to perform self-care
- Teach to perform activities of daily living and adapting tasks

Physical Therapy
- Recommend functional position
- Assess function and together with patient, plan a rehabilitation program

the length of the procedure compared with conventional angiography. It is considered safer than cerebral angiography because there is less vascular manipulation.

Transcranial doppler (TCD) ultrasonography is a noninvasive study that measures the velocity of blood flow in the major cerebral arteries. TCD is effective in detecting microemboli and vasospasm. It is ideal for the patient suspected of having an SAH. Carotid duplex scanning is used to detect the cause of the stroke and stratify patients for either medical management or carotid intervention if they have carotid stenosis.

An LP can determine if red blood cells are present in the CSF if we suspect a SAH but the CT does not show hemorrhage. An LP is avoided if the patient is suspected of having an obstruction in the foramen magnum or other signs of increased ICP because of the danger of herniation of the brain downward. This could lead to pressure on cardiac and respiratory centers in the brainstem and potentially death.

The LICOX system may be used as a diagnostic tool to evaluate the progression of stroke. LICOX measures brain

oxygenation and temperature (see discussion in Chapter 56 on p. 1307 and Fig. 56.9). Secondary brain injury adds significantly to mortality risk and poor functional outcome after a stroke.

INTERPROFESSIONAL CARE FOR STROKE

Preventive Therapy

Primary prevention is a priority for decreasing morbidity and mortality risk from stroke. The goals of stroke prevention include health promotion for a healthy lifestyle and management of modifiable risk factors to prevent a stroke. Health promotion focuses on (1) healthy diet, (2) weight control, (3) regular exercise, (4) no smoking, (5) limiting alcohol consumption, (6) BP management, and (7) routine health assessments. Patients with known risk factors (e.g., diabetes, hypertension, obesity, high serum lipids, cardiac dysfunction) need close management.

♥ PROMOTING POPULATION HEALTH

Stroke Prevention

- Reduce salt and sodium intake.
- Maintain a normal body weight.
- Follow a diet low in saturated fat and high in fruits and vegetables.
- Limit alcohol use to moderate levels.
- Maintain an SBP less than 140 mm Hg.
- Exercise 40 minutes 3 to 4 days per week.
- Avoid cigarette smoking and tobacco products.
- Maintain a normal blood glucose level and control diabetes.
- Follow the prescribed treatment plan for diagnosed cardiac problems.

Preventive Drug Therapy. Measures to prevent the development of a thrombus or an embolus are used in patients with TIAs, since they are at high risk for stroke. Antiplatelet drugs are usually the chosen treatment to prevent stroke in patients who had a TIA. Aspirin, at a dose of 81 mg/day, is the most often used antiplatelet agent. Other agents include ticlopidine, clopidogrel (Plavix), dipyridamole (Persantine), and combined dipyridamole and aspirin (Aggrenox).

 DRUG ALERT Ticlopidine and Clopidogrel (Plavix)
- Inform all HCPs and dentists that the medication is being taken before scheduling surgery or major dental procedures.
- They may have to be discontinued 10 to 14 days before surgery if antiplatelet effect is not desired.

For patients with atrial fibrillation, oral anticoagulation can include warfarin (Coumadin) and the direct factor Xa inhibitors: rivaroxaban (Xarelto), dabigatran (Pradaxa), and apixaban (Eliquis). The primary advantage of direct factor Xa inhibitors compared to warfarin is that they do not need close monitoring or dosage adjustments. Statins (e.g., simvastatin, lovastatin) are effective in stroke prevention for those with high cholesterol levels who had a TIA.[10]

Left Atrial Appendage Occlusion. The left atrial appendage (LAA) is a pouch that extends off the left atrium. We think the LAA is the source of many stroke-causing emboli in patients with atrial fibrillation. Removing or occluding the LAA decreases the incidence of strokes. LAA occlusion is a treatment strategy to prevent blood clot formation in patients with atrial fibrillation. It is an alternative for patients who cannot use oral anticoagulants, such as warfarin. After LAA occlusion, patients may be able to stop taking anticoagulants.[9]

A special stapler can be used to remove the LAA. Or, the HCP can place sutures that manually occlude the LAA. There are also special LAA occlusion devices (e.g., AtriClip, Watchman).[9] These devices are positioned around the LAA and then closed, like a clamp that is used to shut off the blood supply. This prevents blood from flowing into and out of the LAA.

Patent Foramen Ovale. Patients with a patent foramen ovale are at increased risk for an ischemic stroke. In this condition, there is a hole between the left and right atriums. Blood clots can pass through this opening and go to the brain, leading to ischemia. An occlusion device implanted in this opening can prevent clot dislodgment (e.g. Amplatzer PFO).[14]

Surgical/Endovascular Therapy for TIA and Stroke Prevention. Surgical interventions for the patient with TIAs due to carotid disease include carotid endarterectomy, transluminal angioplasty, and stenting. In a *carotid endarterectomy* (CEA), the atheromatous lesion is removed from the carotid artery to improve blood flow.

Transluminal angioplasty is the insertion of a balloon to open a stenosed artery in the brain and improve blood flow. The balloon is threaded up to the carotid artery through a catheter inserted in the femoral artery.

Stenting involves intravascular placement of a stent to try to maintain patency of the artery (Fig. 57.5). The stent can be inserted during an angioplasty. Once in place, the system can be used with a tiny filter that opens like an umbrella. The filter catches and removes the debris that is stirred up during the stenting procedure before it floats to the brain, where it can trigger a stroke. Stenting is a less invasive strategy for revascularization in patients unable to withstand the CEA because of coexisting medical conditions.

Postoperative nursing care includes neurovascular assessment and BP management. Assess for complications, including stent occlusion and retroperitoneal hemorrhage. Minimize the risk for bleeding at the insertion site by keeping the patient's leg straight for the prescribed time.

Acute Care for Ischemic Stroke

During initial evaluation, the single most important point in the patient's history is the time of onset of symptoms. Interprofessional goals during the acute phase are preserving life, preventing further brain damage, and reducing disability (Table 57.7).

Table 57.8 outlines the emergency management of the patient with a stroke. In the unresponsive person, acute care begins with assessing circulation, airway, and breathing. Patients may have difficulty keeping an open and clear airway because of a decreased level of consciousness or decreased or absent gag and swallowing reflexes. Maintaining adequate oxygenation is important. O_2 administration, artificial airway insertion, intubation, and mechanical ventilation may be needed. Baseline neurologic assessment is carried out, and patients are monitored closely for signs of increasing neurologic deficit. Many patients may worsen in the first 24 to 48 hours.

For emergency care, patients should be transported to the closest certified stroke center. If one is not available, they should be sent to the closest facility offering emergency stroke care.[15] The AHA recommends that acute care facilities have stroke teams in place. The stroke team generally consists of a registered nurse, neurologist, radiologist, and radiologic technician.

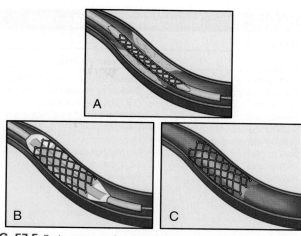

FIG. 57.5 Brain stent used to treat blockages in cerebral blood flow. **A**, A balloon catheter is used to implant the stent into an artery of the brain. **B**, The balloon catheter is moved to the blocked area of the artery and then inflated. The stent expands due to inflation of the balloon. **C**, The balloon is deflated and withdrawn, leaving the stent permanently in place holding the artery open and improving the flow of blood.

Elevated BP is common immediately after a stroke. It may be a protective response to maintain cerebral perfusion. However, it can be detrimental. In patients with an ischemic stroke who do not receive fibrinolytic therapy (discussed later), the use of drugs to lower BP is recommended only if BP is markedly increased (SBP greater than 220 mm Hg or DBP greater than 120 mm Hg). In a patient who is going to have fibrinolytic therapy, the BP must be less than 185/110 mm Hg and then maintained at or below 180/105 mm Hg for at least 24 hours after fibrinolytic therapy. In an acute stroke, IV antihypertensives, such as labetalol and nicardipine (Cardene), are preferred. Although low BP right after a stroke is uncommon, we correct hypotension and hypovolemia if present.

Fluid and electrolyte balance must be controlled carefully. The goal is to keep the patient adequately hydrated to promote perfusion and decrease further brain injury. Overhydration may compromise perfusion by increasing ICP and cerebral edema. Adequate fluid intake during acute care via oral, IV, or tube feedings is a priority. Monitor urine output to make sure the patient does not become dehydrated.

If secretion of antidiuretic hormone (ADH) increases in response to the stroke, urine output decreases and fluid is retained. Low serum sodium (hyponatremia) may occur. IV solutions with glucose and water are avoided because they are hypotonic and may further increase cerebral edema and ICP. Glycemic control should be maintained to avoid extreme hypoglycemia or hyperglycemia. In general, decisions about fluid and electrolyte replacement therapy are based on the extent of intracranial edema, manifestations of increased ICP, central venous pressure levels, electrolyte levels, and intake and output.

Increased ICP is more likely to occur with hemorrhagic strokes but can occur with ischemic strokes. Increased ICP from cerebral edema usually peaks in 72 hours and may cause brain herniation. Management of increased ICP includes practices that improve venous drainage. These include elevating the head of the bed, keeping head and neck in alignment, and avoiding hip flexion. Other measures for reducing ICP include managing fever (goal temperature of 96.8° to 98.6° F [36° to 37° C]), drug therapy to prevent seizures, pain management, and preventing

✚ TABLE 57.8 Emergency Management

Stroke

Etiology	Assessment Findings	Interventions
• Aneurysm • Arteriovenous malformation • Embolism • Hemorrhage • Sudden vascular compromise causing disruption of blood flow to brain • Thrombosis • Trauma	• Altered level of consciousness • Bladder or bowel incontinence • Difficulty swallowing • Facial drooping on affected side • Heart rate ↑ or ↓ • Hypertension • Numbness, weakness, or paralysis of part of body • Respiratory distress • Seizures • Severe headache • Speech or visual changes • Unequal pupils • Vertigo	**Initial** • If unresponsive, assess circulation, airway, and breathing. • If responsive, monitor airway, breathing, and circulation. • Call stroke code or stroke team. • Remove dentures. • Perform pulse oximetry. • Maintain adequate oxygenation (SaO_2 >95%) with supplemental O_2, if needed. • Establish IV access with normal saline. • Maintain BP according to guidelines. • Remove clothing. • Obtain CT scan or MRI. • Perform baseline laboratory tests (including blood glucose) immediately and treat if hypoglycemic. • Position head in midline. • Elevate head of bed 30 degrees if no symptoms of shock or injury. • Institute seizure precautions. • Anticipate thrombolytic therapy for ischemic stroke. • Keep patient NPO until swallow reflex evaluated. **Ongoing Monitoring** • Monitor vital signs and neurologic status, including level of consciousness (NIH Stroke Scale), motor and sensory function, pupil size and reactivity, SaO_2, and cardiac rhythm. • Reassure patient and family.

NIH, National Institutes of Health; *SaO_2,* arterial O_2 saturation.

constipation. CSF drainage may be used in some patients to reduce ICP. The specific management of increased ICP is discussed in Chapter 56.

Drug Therapy for Ischemic Stroke. Fibrinolytic therapy should not be delayed. Recombinant tissue plasminogen activator (tPA) is used to produce localized fibrinolysis by binding to the fibrin in the thrombi. The fibrinolytic action of tPA occurs as the plasminogen is converted to plasmin, whose enzymatic action then digests fibrin and fibrinogen, thus breaking down the clot. Other fibrinolytic agents cannot be substituted for tPA. (Fibrinolytic [thrombolytic] therapy is discussed in Chapter 33.)

tPA is given IV to reestablish blood flow through a blocked artery to prevent cell death in patients with the acute onset of ischemic stroke. tPA must be given within 3 to 4½ hours of the onset of signs of ischemic stroke.[16] Patients are screened carefully before tPA can be given. Screening includes a noncontrast CT scan or MRI to rule out hemorrhagic stroke; blood tests for coagulation disorders; screening for recent history of gastrointestinal (GI) bleeding, stroke, or head trauma within the past 3 months; major surgery within 14 days; or recent active internal bleeding within 22 days.[16]

During tPA infusion, closely monitor the patient's vital signs and neurologic status to assess for improvement or for potential deterioration related to intracerebral hemorrhage. Control of BP (SBP less than 185 mm Hg) is critical during treatment and for 24 hours following.

Intraarterial infusion of tPA may be used for patients with an ischemic stroke when mechanical thrombectomy is not an option. To be effective, intraarterial tPA must be given within 6 hours of the onset of stroke symptoms. In the intraarterial tPA procedure, the neurovascular specialist inserts a thin, flexible catheter into an artery (usually the femoral artery) and guides the catheter (using angiogram) to the area of the clot. The tPA is given through the catheter and immediately targets the clot. Less tPA is needed when it is delivered directly to the clot, which can reduce the chance for intracranial hemorrhage.

The use of anticoagulants (e.g., heparin) in the emergency phase after an ischemic stroke is not recommended because of the risk for intracranial hemorrhage. Aspirin at a dose of 325 mg may be started within 24 to 48 hours after the onset of an ischemic stroke. Complications of higher dose aspirin include GI bleeding. Aspirin should be given cautiously if the patient has a history of peptic ulcer disease.

After the patient has stabilized and to prevent further clot formation, patients with strokes caused by thrombi and emboli may be treated with anticoagulants and platelet inhibitors (see discussion on stroke prevention on p. 1338.). For patients with atrial fibrillation, oral anticoagulants include warfarin and the direct factor Xa inhibitors: rivaroxaban (Xarelto), dabigatran (Pradaxa), and apixaban (Eliquis). Platelet inhibitors include aspirin, ticlopidine, clopidogrel, and dipyridamole. The use of statins is effective for the patient after an ischemic stroke.[9]

Endovascular Therapy for Ischemic Stroke. Stent retrievers are a way of opening blocked arteries in the brain by using a removable stent system.[17] During the procedure, a catheter is used to guide the small stent from the femoral artery in the groin area to the affected artery in the brain. The stent is guided (using neuroimaging) into the part of the artery where a blood clot has formed. The stent expands the interior walls of the artery and allows blood to get to the patient's brain immediately to prevent as much brain damage as possible. The clot seeps into the mesh of the stent. Then, after a few minutes the stent and clot are removed together. Stent retrievers are becoming the most effective way of managing ischemic stroke.[17]

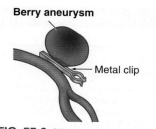

FIG. 57.6 Clipping of aneurysms.

The ENROUTE device accesses the carotid arteries through the neck, rather than the groin. It allows the surgeon to maintain blood flow to the brain while performing carotid angioplasty and stenting.[18]

Acute Care for Hemorrhagic Stroke

Drug Therapy for Hemorrhagic Stroke. Anticoagulants and platelet inhibitors are contraindicated in patients with hemorrhagic strokes. The main drug therapy for patients with hemorrhagic stroke is the management of hypertension. Oral and IV agents may be used to maintain BP within a normal to high-normal range (SBP less than 160 mm Hg). Seizure prophylaxis in the acute period after intracerebral and subarachnoid hemorrhages is situation specific and decided among the interprofessional care team.[19]

Surgical Therapy for Hemorrhagic Stroke. Surgical interventions for hemorrhagic stroke include immediate evacuation of aneurysm-induced hematomas or cerebellar hematomas larger than 3 cm. Those who have an arteriovenous malformation (AVM) may have a hemorrhagic stroke if the AVM ruptures. The treatment of AVM is surgical resection and/or radiosurgery (i.e., gamma knife). Interventional neuroradiology to embolize the blood vessels that supply the AVM may be done prior.

With SAH, bleeding from a damaged vessel causes blood to accumulate between the brain and skull. The leaked blood can irritate, damage, or destroy the surrounding brain cells. When blood enters the subarachnoid space, it mixes with the CSF. This can block CSF circulation, thus causing increased pressure on the brain. The open spaces in the brain (ventricles) may enlarge, resulting in hydrocephalus. This further increases ICP (due to the large accumulation of blood) and can result in further brain injury. Inserting a ventriculostomy for CSF drainage can dramatically improve these situations by reducing the ICP.[20] Goals for managing ICP are the same for patients with SAH as they are for patients dealing with acute stroke. The management of ICP is discussed in Chapter 56.

SAH is usually caused by a ruptured aneurysm. Patients may have multiple aneurysms. Treatment of an aneurysm involves clipping or coiling the aneurysm to prevent rebleeding (Figs. 57.6 and 57.7). In *clipping* the aneurysm, the neurosurgeon places a metallic clip on the neck of the aneurysm to block blood flow and prevent rupture. The clip stays in place for life.

In the procedure known as *coiling*, a hydrogel-coated platinum coil is inserted into the lumen of the aneurysm via interventional neuroradiology (Fig. 57.7). Guglielmi detachable coils (GDCs) give immediate protection against hemorrhage by reducing the blood pulsations within the aneurysm. Eventually, a thrombus forms within the aneurysm. Then the aneurysm becomes sealed off from the parent vessel by the formation of an endothelialized layer of connective tissue.

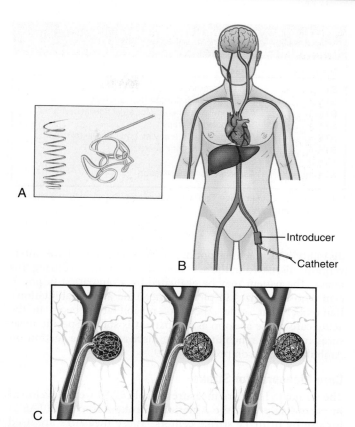

FIG. 57.7 Guglielmi detachable coil (GDC). **A,** A coil is used to occlude an aneurysm. Coils are made of soft, springlike platinum. The softness of the platinum allows the coil to assume the shape of irregularly shaped aneurysms while posing little threat of rupture of the aneurysm. **B,** A catheter is inserted through an introducer (small tube) in an artery in the leg. The catheter is threaded up to the cerebral blood vessels. **C,** Platinum coils attached to a thin wire are inserted into the catheter and then placed in the aneurysm until the aneurysm is filled with coils. Packing the aneurysm with coils prevents the blood from circulating through the aneurysm, reducing the risk for rupture.

After aneurysmal occlusion via clipping or coiling, hyperdynamic therapy (hemodilution-induced hypertension using vasoconstricting agents, such as phenylephrine or dopamine, and hypervolemia) may be started to increase the mean arterial pressure and cerebral perfusion. Volume expansion is achieved with crystalloid or colloid solutions.

Patients with SAH may receive the calcium channel blocker nimodipine to treat cerebral vasospasms and minimize cerebral damage. It may be given either before or after aneurysm clipping or coiling. Nimodipine restricts the influx of calcium ions into cells by reducing the number of open calcium channels. Although nimodipine is a calcium channel blocker, we do not know its exact mechanism of action in reducing vasospasm.

💊 DRUG ALERT Nimodipine

- Assess BP and apical pulses before administration.
- If pulse is ≤60 beats/min or SBP is <90 mm Hg, hold the medication and contact the provider.

Rehabilitation Care

After the stroke patient has stabilized for 12 to 24 hours, interprofessional care shifts from preserving life to lessening

TABLE 57.9 Stroke (STK) Core Measure Set

Measure	Topic
STK-1	Venous thromboembolism (VTE) prophylaxis
STK-2	Discharged on antithrombotic therapy
STK-3	Anticoagulation therapy for atrial fibrillation/flutter
STK-4	Thrombolytic therapy
STK-5	Antithrombotic therapy by end of hospital day 2
STK-6	Discharged on statin medication
STK-8	Stroke education
STK-10	Assessed for rehabilitation

Source: The Joint Commission. Stroke core measures. Retrieved from *www.joint-commission.org/stroke*.

disability and reaching optimal function. Many of the interventions discussed in the acute phase are continued during this phase. The patient may be evaluated by a physiatrist (a physician who specializes in physical medicine and rehabilitation). Remember that some aspects of rehabilitation begin in the acute care phase as soon as the patient is stable. Specific measures related to rehabilitation are discussed in the section on Ambulatory Care on pp. 1347–1349.

Core Measures for Stroke

The stroke (STK) core measures (Table 57.9) were developed in partnership with the American Stroke Association (ASA) for use by primary stroke centers. These measures are used by hospitals for accreditation and certification. The measures align with guidelines supported by the AHA Get With The Guidelines (GWTG) stroke patient management tool and the CDC's Paul Coverdell National Acute Stroke Registry (PCNASR).

❖ NURSING MANAGEMENT: STROKE

◆ Nursing Assessment

Subjective and objective data that you should obtain from a person who has had a stroke are detailed in Table 57.10. Primary assessment focuses on cardiac and respiratory status and neurologic assessment. If the patient is stable, the nursing history is obtained as follows: (1) description of the current illness with attention to initial symptoms, especially symptom onset and duration, nature (intermittent or continuous), and changes; (2) history of having had similar symptoms previously; (3) current medications; (4) history of risk factors and other illnesses, such as hypertension; and (5) family history of stroke, aneurysm, or cardiovascular diseases. Obtain this information through interviewing the patient and caregivers.

Secondary assessment includes a comprehensive neurologic examination. The primary assessment tool to evaluate and document neurologic status in acute stroke patients is the NIHSS, which measures stroke severity (Table 57.11).[21] The NIHSS is a predictor of both short- and long-term outcomes of stroke patients. It also serves as a data collection tool for planning patient care and exchanging information among HCPs. Other assessment data includes (1) LOC; (2) cognition; (3) motor abilities; (4) cranial nerve function; (5) sensation; (6) proprioception; (7) cerebellar function; and (8) deep tendon reflexes. Clear documentation of initial and ongoing neurologic examinations is essential to note changes in the patient's status.

TABLE 57.10 Nursing Assessment

Stroke

Subjective Data

Important Health Information

Past health history: Hypertension, previous stroke, TIA, aneurysm, cardiac disease (including recent MI, dysrhythmias, heart failure, valvular heart disease, infective endocarditis. Hyperlipidemia, polycythemia, blood clotting disorders, diabetes, gout

Family history: Neurologic disorders, aneurysms, stroke, TIA, diabetes, hypertension, coronary artery disease

Medications: Oral contraceptives; use of and adherence with antihypertensive and anticoagulant therapy; illicit substance use

Functional Health Patterns

Health perception–health management: Alcohol use, smoking, drug use

Nutritional-metabolic: Anorexia, nausea, vomiting. Dysphagia, altered sense of taste and smell

Elimination: Change in bowel and bladder patterns

Activity-exercise: Loss of movement and sensation. Syncope, weakness on one side, generalized weakness, easy fatigability

Cognitive-perceptual: Numbness, tingling of one side of the body, loss of memory. Change in speech, language, problem-solving ability. Pain, headache (possibly sudden and severe) (hemorrhage). Visual changes. Denial of illness

Objective Data

General

Emotional lability, lethargy, apathy or combativeness, fever

Respiratory

Loss of cough reflex, labored or irregular respirations, tachypnea, wheezes (aspiration), airway occlusion (tongue), apnea, coughing when eating or delayed coughing

Cardiovascular

Hypertension, tachycardia, carotid bruit

Gastrointestinal

Loss of gag reflex, bowel incontinence, decreased or absent bowel sounds, constipation

Urinary

Frequency, urgency, incontinence

Neurologic

Contralateral motor and sensory deficits, including weakness, paresis, paralysis, anesthesia. Unequal pupils, hand grasps. Akinesia, aphasia (expressive, receptive, global), dysarthria (slurred speech), agnosia, apraxia, visual deficits, perceptual or spatial problems, altered level of consciousness (drowsiness to deep coma) and Babinski's sign, ↓ followed by ↑ deep tendon reflexes, flaccidity followed by spasticity, amnesia, ataxia, personality change, nuchal rigidity, seizures

Possible Diagnostic Findings

Positive CT, CTA, MRI, MRA, or other neuroimaging scans showing size, location, and type of lesion. Positive Doppler ultrasonography and angiography showing stenosis

◆ Nursing Diagnoses

Nursing diagnoses for the person with a stroke may include:
- Decreased intracranial adaptive capacity
- Impaired communication
- Difficulty coping
- Risk for aspiration
- Impaired physical mobility
- Risk for injury

TABLE 57.11 National Institutes of Health Stroke Scale (NIHSS)

Description
The NIH Stroke Scale (NIHSS) is a 15-item neurologic examination used to evaluate the effect of an acute stroke. Total scores on the NIHSS range from 0 to 42, with higher values reflecting more severity.

Procedure for Use
A trained observer rates the patient's ability to answer questions and perform activities. Ratings for each item are scored, and there is an allowance for untestable (UN) items. If an item is left untested, a detailed explanation must be clearly written on the form. Training can be completed free at www.nihstrokescale.org.

Item	Scale Definition
Level of consciousness	0 = Alert 1 = Not alert, but arousable by minor stimulation 2 = Not alert, requires repeated stimulation to get attention 3 = Responds only with reflex motor or autonomic effects or totally unresponsive, flaccid, areflexic
Level of consciousness questions	0 = Answers both questions correctly 1 = Answers 1 question correctly 2 = Answers neither question correctly
Level of consciousness commands	0 = Performs both tasks correctly 1 = Performs 1 task correctly 2 = Performs neither task correctly
Best gaze	0 = Normal 1 = Partial gaze palsy 2 = Forced deviation, or total gaze paresis
Visual	0 = No visual loss 1 = Partial hemianopsia 2 = Complete hemianopsia 3 = Bilateral hemianopsia or blind
Facial palsy	0 = Normal symmetric movement 1 = Minor paralysis 2 = Partial paralysis 3 = Complete paralysis of 1 or both sides
Motor and drift (for each extremity)	0 = No drift 1 = Drift 2 = Some effort against gravity 3 = No effort against gravity, limb falls 4 = No movement UN = Amputation
Limb ataxia	0 = Absent 1 = Present in 1 limb 2 = Present in 2 limbs
Sensory	0 = Normal 1 = Mild to moderate sensory loss 2 = Severe to total sensory loss
Best language	0 = No aphasia, normal 1 = Mild to moderate aphasia 2 = Severe aphasia 3 = Mute, no usable speech or auditory comprehension
Dysarthria	0 = Normal 1 = Mild to moderate 2 = Severe UN = Intubated or other physical barrier
Extinction or inattention	0 = No abnormality 1 = Inattention or extinction to bilateral stimulation 2 = Does not recognize own hand
Distal motor function	0 = Normal (no flexion after 5 sec) 1 = At least some extension but not fully extended 2 = No voluntary extension after 5 sec

Source: National Institutes of Health: NIH stroke scale. Retrieved from www.stroke.nih.gov/resources/scale.htm.

Additional information on nursing diagnoses and interventions are presented in eNursing Care Plan 57.1 (available on the website for this chapter).

◆ Planning
Establish the goals of nursing care together with the patient, caregiver, and family. Typical goals are that the patient will (1) maintain a stable or improved level of consciousness, (2) attain maximum physical functioning, (3) attain maximum self-care abilities and skills, (4) maintain stable body functions (e.g., bladder control), (5) maximize communication abilities, (6) maintain adequate nutrition, (7) avoid complications of stroke, and (8) maintain effective personal and family coping.

◆ Nursing Implementation
◆ Health Promotion. You have a key role in promoting a healthy lifestyle. Teaching should focus on stroke prevention, especially for persons with known risk factors. Most strokes are caused by modifiable risk factors. Nursing measures to reduce risk factors for stroke are similar to those for coronary artery disease (see Chapter 33) and were discussed earlier in this chapter on p. 1338.

Uncontrolled or undiagnosed hypertension is the primary cause of stroke. Therefore you need to be involved in BP screening and ensuring that patients adhere to using their antihypertensive drugs and home BP monitoring. If a person has diabetes, it is important that it is well controlled. If a person has atrial fibrillation, an anticoagulant (see p. 1338) or aspirin may reduce the risk for stroke. Because smoking is a major risk factor for stroke, you need to be actively involved in helping patients to stop smoking (see Chapter 10, Tables 10.4 to 10.6).

Another important aspect of health promotion is teaching patients and families about early symptoms associated with stroke or TIA. Table 57.1 presents information on when to seek health care for these symptoms.

◆ Acute Care
Respiratory System. During the acute phase after a stroke, management of the respiratory system is a nursing priority. Stroke patients are vulnerable to respiratory problems. Advancing age and immobility increase the risk for atelectasis and pneumonia.

Nursing interventions to support adequate respiratory function are tailored to meet the patient's specific needs (Table 57.12). Some stroke patients, especially those with brainstem or hemorrhagic stroke, may need endotracheal intubation and mechanical ventilation. An oropharyngeal airway in a comatose patient may prevent the tongue from falling back and obstructing the airway and provide access for suctioning. Alternatively, a nasopharyngeal airway may be used to provide airway protection and access. When an artificial airway is needed for a prolonged time, a tracheostomy may be done.

Nursing interventions include frequently assessing airway patency and function, providing oxygenation, suctioning, promoting patient mobility, positioning the patient to prevent aspiration, and encouraging deep breathing. In patients who are on mechanical ventilation, oral care at least every 2 hours reduces the occurrence of ventilator-assisted pneumonia.

Risk for aspiration pneumonia is high because of impaired consciousness or dysphagia. Dysphagia after stroke is common. Airway obstruction can occur because of problems with chewing and swallowing, food pocketing (food remaining in the buccal cavity of the mouth), and the tongue falling back. Enteral nutrition (EN) places the patient at risk for aspiration

---

TABLE 57.12 Nursing Management

Caring for the Patient With an Acute Stroke

- Assess manifestations of stroke and determine when the they started.
- Screen patient for contraindications for tissue plasminogen activator (tPA) therapy.
- Infuse tPA for patients with ischemic stroke who meet the criteria for tPA administration.
- Assess respiratory status and start needed actions, such as O_2, oropharyngeal or nasopharyngeal airways, suctioning.
- Position patient to prevent aspiration and atelectasis.
- Assess neurologic status, including intracranial pressure (ICP), if needed.
- Monitor cardiovascular status, including hemodynamic monitoring, if needed.
- Calculate intake and output, noting imbalances.
- Regulate IV infusions and adjust fluid intake to patient needs.
- Assess patient's ability to swallow in conjunction with the speech therapist.
- Give scheduled anticoagulant and antiplatelet drugs.
- Implement measures to prevent VTE and skin breakdown.
- Delegate to UAP:
  - Obtain vital signs and report these to RN.
  - Measure and record urine output.
  - Help with proper positioning and turning patient at least every 2 hr.
  - Perform passive and active ROM exercises.

---

pneumonia. Screen all patients for their ability to swallow. Keep them NPO until dysphagia is ruled out.

Patients who have an unclipped or uncoiled aneurysm may have rebleeding and further increased ICP with coughing or suctioning, so nursing management is aimed at reducing these interventions while maintaining a proper airway.

Neurologic System. Perform ongoing neurologic assessments, including the NIHSS, mental status, pupillary response, and extremity movement and strength. Closely monitor vital signs. A decreasing level of consciousness may indicate increasing ICP. Monitor ICP and cerebral perfusion pressure if the patient is in a critical care environment. Record your nursing assessment promptly to communicate the patient's neurologic status to the stroke team.

Cardiovascular System. Nursing goals for the cardiovascular system are aimed at maintaining homeostasis. Many patients with stroke have decreased cardiac reserves from cardiac disease. Fluid retention, overhydration, dehydration, or BP changes may further compromise cardiac efficiency. Central venous pressure, pulmonary artery pressure, or hemodynamic monitoring may be used to monitor fluid balance and cardiac function in the critical care unit.

Nursing interventions include (1) monitoring vital signs frequently; (2) monitoring cardiac rhythms; (3) calculating intake and output, noting imbalances; (4) regulating IV infusions; (5) adjusting fluid intake to individual patient needs; (6) monitoring lung sounds for crackles and wheezes, indicating pulmonary congestion; and (7) monitoring heart sounds for murmurs. Bedside monitors or telemetry may record cardiac rhythms.

Hypertension sometimes occurs after a stroke as the body tries to increase CBF. It is important to monitor for orthostatic hypotension before ambulating the patient for the first time. Neurologic changes can occur with a sudden decrease in BP.

The patient is at risk for venous thromboembolism (VTE), especially in the weak or paralyzed lower extremity. VTE is related to immobility, loss of venous tone, and decreased muscle

pumping activity in the leg. The most effective prevention is to keep the patient moving. Teach the patient active range-of-motion (ROM) exercises if the patient has voluntary movement in the affected extremity. For the patient with hemiplegia, perform passive ROM exercises several times a day. Other measures to prevent VTE include positioning to minimize the effects of dependent edema and using intermittent pneumatic compression devices. VTE prophylaxis may include low-molecular-weight heparin (e.g., enoxaparin [Lovenox]).[22] The nursing assessment includes measuring the calf and thigh daily, observing for swelling of the lower extremities, noting unusual warmth of the leg, and asking the patient about pain in the calf.

Musculoskeletal System. The nursing goal for the musculoskeletal system is to maintain optimal function by preventing joint contractures and muscular atrophy. In the acute phase, ROM exercises and positioning are important nursing interventions. Passive ROM exercise is begun on the first day of hospitalization. Muscle atrophy from lack of innervation and activity can develop after stroke, so exercise is an important intervention for rehabilitation and recovery.

The paralyzed or weak side needs special attention when the patient is positioned. Position each joint higher than the joint proximal to it to prevent dependent edema. Specific deformities on the weak or paralyzed side that may be present in patients with stroke include internal rotation of the shoulder; flexion contractures of the hand, wrist, and elbow; external rotation of the hip; and plantar flexion of the foot. Subluxation of the shoulder on the affected side is common. Careful positioning and moving of the affected arm may prevent development of a painful shoulder condition. Immobilization of the affected upper extremity may precipitate a painful shoulder-hand syndrome.

Nursing interventions to optimize musculoskeletal function include (1) trochanter roll at the hip to prevent external rotation; (2) hand cones (not rolled washcloths) to prevent hand contractures; (3) arm supports with slings and lap boards to prevent shoulder displacement; (4) avoidance of pulling the patient by the arm to avoid shoulder displacement; (5) posterior leg splints, footboards, or high-top tennis shoes to prevent footdrop; and (6) hand splints to reduce spasticity.

Using a footboard for the patient with spasticity is controversial. Rather than preventing plantar flexion (footdrop), the sensory stimulation of a footboard against the bottom of the foot increases plantar flexion. Likewise, experts disagree on whether hand splints decrease spasticity. The decision about using footboards or hand splints is made on an individual patient basis.

Integumentary System. The skin of the patient with stroke is susceptible to breakdown related to loss of sensation, decreased circulation, and immobility. Advanced age, poor nutrition, dehydration, edema, and incontinence compound the risk.

Measures to prevent skin breakdown includes (1) pressure relief by position changes, special mattresses, or wheelchair cushions; (2) good skin hygiene; (3) emollients applied to dry skin; and (4) early mobility. An example of a position change schedule is side-back-side, with a maximum duration of 2 hours for any position. Position the patient on the weak or paralyzed side for only 30 minutes. Controlling pressure is the main factor in both preventing and treating skin breakdown. Use pillows under lower extremities to reduce pressure on the heels. See more information on preventing pressure injuries in Chapter 11.

Gastrointestinal System. The most common bowel problem for the stroke patient is constipation. Fluid and fiber intake goals are determined with the stroke team based on the patient's nutritional and fluid status. Patients may be prophylactically placed on stool softeners and/or fiber (psyllium [Metamucil]). Laxatives, suppositories, or additional stool softeners may be ordered if the patient does not respond to increased fluid and fiber. Enemas are used only if suppositories and digital stimulation are ineffective because they cause vagal stimulation and increase ICP. Physical activity promotes bowel function. If a patient has liquid stools, check for stool impaction.

Bowel retraining may be needed and continued into the rehabilitation phase. A bowel management program consists of placing the patient on the bedpan or bedside commode or taking the patient to the bathroom at a regular time daily to reestablish bowel regularity. A good time for a bowel movement is 30 minutes after breakfast because eating stimulates the gastrocolic reflex and peristalsis. The timing may have to be adjusted as individual bowel habits may vary.

Urinary System. In the acute stage of stroke, the primary urinary problem is poor bladder control, resulting in incontinence. Take steps to promote normal bladder function and avoid the use of indwelling catheters. If an indwelling catheter is used initially, remove it as soon as the patient is medically and neurologically stable. Long-term use of an indwelling catheter is associated with urinary tract infections and delayed bladder retraining.

Avoid bladder overdistention. An intermittent catheterization program may be used for patients with urinary retention to lower the incidence of urinary infections. An alternative to intermittent catheterizations for a male patient is an external catheter. External catheters do not address problems with urine retention.

Often the patient has functional incontinence, which is associated with communication, mobility, and dressing problems. A bladder retraining program consists of (1) adequate fluid intake, with most of it given between 7:00 AM and 7:00 PM; (2) scheduled toileting every 2 hours using bedpan, commode, or bathroom while encouraging the usual position for urinating (standing for men and sitting for women); (3) observing for signs of restlessness, which may indicate the need for urination; and (4) assessing for bladder distention by palpation. Encourage patients to wear pants without drawstrings, buttons, or zippers. These can be hard to manage if motor or sensory deficits exist.

Assessing postvoid residual volume is often done using bladder ultrasound. The ultrasound measures how much urine is in the bladder after voiding. If urine stays in the bladder, incomplete emptying is a problem and may cause urinary tract infections. A coordinated program by the entire nursing staff is needed to achieve urinary continence.

Nutrition. The patient's nutritional needs require quick assessment and treatment. The patient may initially receive IV infusions to maintain fluid and electrolyte balance and to give drugs. Patients with severe impairment may need EN or parenteral nutrition. Patients should have their nutritional needs addressed in the first 24 hours of admission to the hospital because nutrition is important for recovery and healing.[23]

Many patients have dysphagia after a stroke. Keep patients NPO until a speech therapist performs a swallowing evaluation. This should be done in the first 24 hours after the stroke.[23] You or another member of the interprofessional team may perform the screen if a speech therapist cannot perform the formal evaluation.

! SAFETY ALERT Oral Feeding After Stroke
- Dysphagia is common after stroke.
- Keep the patient on NPO status until a speech therapist does a swallowing evaluation.

Before starting feeding, assess the gag reflex by gently stimulating the back of the throat with a tongue blade. If the gag reflex is present, the patient will gag spontaneously. If it is absent, defer the feeding and begin exercises to stimulate swallowing. The speech therapist or occupational therapist is usually responsible for designing this program. However, you may be involved in helping to develop the program in some clinical settings.

To assess swallowing ability, elevate the head of the bed to an upright position (unless contraindicated). Give the patient a small amount of crushed ice or ice water to swallow. If the gag reflex is present and the patient can swallow safely, you may proceed with feeding.

The speech therapist may recommend various dietary items. Foods should be easy to swallow and provide enough texture, temperature (warm or cold), and flavor to stimulate a swallow reflex. Crushed ice can be used as a stimulant. Pureed foods are not usually the best choice because they are often bland or too smooth. Thin liquids are often hard to swallow and may promote coughing. We can thicken thin liquids with a commercially available thickening agent (e.g., Thick-It). Avoid milk products because they tend to increase the viscosity of mucus and increase salivation.

Mouth care before feeding helps stimulate sensory awareness and salivation and can help swallowing. Keep the patient in the high-Fowler's position, preferably in a chair, for the feeding and 30 minutes afterward. While feeding, keep the head flexed forward. Place food in the unaffected side of the mouth. Teach the patient to swallow and then swallow again. Follow feedings with good oral hygiene because food may collect in the affected side of the mouth.

During the acute and rehabilitation phase of the stroke, a dietitian can help determine the appropriate daily caloric intake based on the patient's size, weight, and activity level. If the patient is unable to take in an adequate oral diet and dysphagia persists, a percutaneous endoscopic gastrostomy (PEG) tube may be used for nutritional support. EN is described in Chapter 39.

The inability to feed one's self can be frustrating and may result in malnutrition and dehydration. Interventions to promote self-feeding include using the unaffected upper extremity to eat; employing assistive devices, such as rocker knives, plate guards, and nonslip pads for dishes (Fig. 57.8); and removing unnecessary items from the tray or table, which can reduce spills. Provide a calm environment (e.g., turn off the television) to decrease sensory overload and distraction. The effectiveness of the dietary program is evaluated in terms of maintenance of weight, adequate hydration, and patient satisfaction. Introduce these interventions in the acute care setting so that maximum rehabilitation can occur once the patient is discharged.

Communication. During the acute stage of stroke, your role in meeting the patient's psychologic needs is primarily supportive. Speech, comprehension, and language deficits are the most difficult problems for the patient and caregiver. Assess the patient for both the ability to speak and the ability to understand. The patient's response to simple questions can guide you in structuring explanations and instructions. If the patient cannot understand words, use gestures to support verbal cues. Collaborate with the speech therapist to assess and formulate a plan of care to enhance communication.

Nursing interventions that support communication include (1) communicating often and meaningfully; (2) allowing time for the patient to comprehend and answer; (3) using simple,

FIG. 57.8 Assistive devices for eating. **A,** The rounded plate helps keep food on the plate. Special grips and weighted handles are helpful for some persons. The cup shape allows drinking without having to tilt the head. **B,** Knives with rounded blades are rocked back and forth to cut food. The person does not need a fork in one hand and a knife in the other. **C,** Plate guards help keep food on the plate. **D,** Cup with special handles promotes independence. (Products *A, B,* and *C* courtesy of Performance Health, Warrenville, IL. *D,* Courtesy of Granny Jo Products, Lakeland, FL.)

short sentences; (4) using visual cues; (5) structuring conversation so that it permits simple answers by the patient; and (6) praising the patient honestly for improvements with speech.

An alert patient is usually anxious because of lack of understanding about what has happened and because of problems with communication or the inability to communicate. Verbal stimuli can easily overwhelm the patient with aphasia. Give the patient extra time to understand and respond to communication. Guidelines for communicating with a patient who has aphasia are outlined in Table 57.13. A picture board may be helpful for communicating with the stroke patient. The speech therapist often does further evaluation and treatment of language and communication deficits once the patient has stabilized. It is important to teach the caregiver and family these communication strategies.

Sensory-Perceptual Problems. Patients who had a stroke often have perceptual deficits. Patients with a stroke on the right side of the brain usually have difficulty judging position, distance, and rate of movement. These patients are often impulsive and impatient and tend to deny problems related to strokes. They may fail to correlate spatial-perceptual problems with the inability to perform activities, such as guiding a wheelchair through the doorway. They best understand directions given verbally. Break

down the task into simple steps for ease of understanding. The patient with a right-brain stroke and left hemiplegia is at higher risk for injury because of mobility problems. Environmental control (e.g., removing clutter, using good lighting) aids in concentration and safer mobility. Provide nonslip socks at all times. One-sided neglect is common for people with right-brain stroke. You may need to help or remind the patient to dress the weak or paralyzed side or shave the forgotten side of the face.

Patients with a left-brain stroke (right hemiplegia) often are slower in organizing and performing tasks. They tend to have impaired spatial discrimination. These patients usually admit to deficits and have a fearful, anxious response to a stroke. Their behaviors are slow and cautious. Nonverbal cues and instructions are helpful for patients who had a left-brain stroke.

Homonymous hemianopsia (blindness in the same half of each visual field) is common after a stroke. Persistent disregard of objects in part of the visual field should alert you to this possibility. At first, help the patient to compensate by arranging the environment within the patient's perceptual field, such as arranging the food tray so that all foods are on the right side or the left side to accommodate for field of vision (Fig. 57.9). Later, the patient learns to compensate for the visual defect by consciously attending to or by scanning the neglected side. Weak

TABLE 57.13 Communicating With a Patient With Aphasia

The following are guidelines for communicating with a patient with aphasia:

1. Decrease environmental stimuli that may be distracting and disrupting to communication efforts.
2. Treat the patient as an adult.
3. Speak with normal volume and tone.
4. Present a single thought or idea at a time.
5. Keep questions simple or ask questions that can be answered with "yes" or "no."
6. Let the person speak. Do not interrupt. Allow time for the person to complete thoughts.
7. Make use of gestures as an alternative form of communication. Encourage this by saying, "Show me . . . ." or "Point to what you want."
8. Do not pretend to understand the person if you do not. Calmly say you do not understand. Encourage the use of nonverbal communication or ask the person to write out what they want.
9. Give the patient time to process information and generate a response before repeating a question or statement.
10. Allow body contact (e.g., clasp of a hand, touching) as much as possible. Realize that touching may be the only way the patient can express feelings.
11. Organize the patient's day by preparing and following a schedule (the more familiar the routine, the easier it will be).
12. Do not push communication if the person is tired or upset. Aphasia worsens with fatigue and anxiety.
13. Teach communication techniques to caregiver and family members.

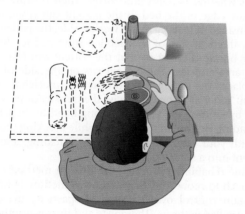

FIG. 57.9 Spatial and perceptual deficits in stroke. Perception of a patient with homonymous hemianopsia shows that food on the left side is not seen and thus is ignored. (Modified from Hoeman SP: *Rehabilitation nursing*, ed 2, St Louis, 1995, Mosby.)

or paralyzed extremities are carefully checked for adequacy of dressing, hygiene, and trauma.

In the clinical situation, it is often hard to distinguish between a visual field cut and a neglect syndrome. Both problems may occur with strokes affecting either the right or the left side of the brain. A person may be unfortunate enough to have both homonymous hemianopsia and a neglect syndrome, which increases the inattention to the weak or paralyzed side. A neglect syndrome results in decreased safety awareness and places the patient at high risk for injury. Immediately after the stroke, anticipate safety hazards and provide protection from injury. Safety measures include closely observing the patient, elevating side rails, lowering the height of the bed, and using video monitors. Avoid using restraints and soft vests because this may agitate the patient.

Other visual problems may include *diplopia* (double vision), loss of the corneal reflex, and *ptosis* (drooping eyelid), especially if the stroke is in the vertebrobasilar distribution. Diplopia is often treated with an eye patch. If the corneal reflex is absent, the patient is at risk for corneal abrasion and should be observed closely and protected against eye injuries. Prevent corneal abrasions with artificial tears or gel to keep the eyes moist and an eye shield (especially at night). We usually do not treat ptosis unless it inhibits vision.

Coping. A stroke is usually a sudden, extremely stressful event for the patient, caregiver, family, and significant others. Stroke is often a family disease, affecting the family emotionally, socially, and financially and changing roles and responsibilities within the family. The stroke patient and family may perceive the stroke as a threat to life and their accustomed lifestyle. Reactions to this threat vary considerably but may involve fear, apprehension, denial of the severity of stroke, depression, anger, and sorrow. During the acute phase of caring for the stroke patient and caregiver, nursing interventions designed to promote coping involve providing information and emotional support.

Explanations to the patient about what has happened and diagnostic and therapeutic procedures should be clear and understandable. Reinforce as needed. Decision making and upholding the patient's wishes during this challenging time are of upmost importance. Advance directives should be honored. Update the family daily and hold family meetings about feeding tube placement or tracheostomy.

Give the caregiver and family a careful, detailed explanation of what has happened to the patient. However, if the family is extremely anxious and upset during the acute phase, explanations may have to be repeated later. Because family members usually have not had time to prepare for the illness, they may need help in arranging care for family members or pets and for transportation and finances. A social services referral is often helpful.

It is challenging to keep the patient with aphasia adequately informed. Use demeanor and touch to convey support. When communicating with a patient who has a communication deficit, speak in a normal volume and tone, keep questions simple, and present one thought or idea at a time. To decrease frustration, always let the patient speak without interruption and make use of gestures. Use writing and communication boards.

◆ Ambulatory Care

Care Transitions. The patient is usually discharged from the acute care setting to home, an intermediate- or long-term care facility, or a rehabilitation facility. Ideally, discharge planning with the patient and caregiver starts early in the hospitalization and promotes a smooth transition between care settings. The stroke team provides guidance for the appropriate care needed after discharge. Factors that are considered include the patient's medical needs and independence in performing ADLs, caregiver's capacity to provide care, and community setting.[24] If the patient needs a short- or long-term health care facility, the team can make appropriate referrals that allow time to select and arrange for care.

If the patient is returning home, the team can make referrals for needed equipment and services in preparation for discharge. You can prepare the patient and caregiver for discharge through teaching and evaluating the transition plan for any barriers. Follow-up care is carefully planned to allow continuing nursing care; physical, occupational, and speech therapy; and medical care. Identify community resources to provide recreational activities, group support, spiritual assistance, respite care, adult day care, and home assistance based on the patient's needs.

Rehabilitation. *Rehabilitation* is the process of maximizing the patient's capabilities and resources to promote optimal functioning related to physical, mental, and social well-being. The goals of rehabilitation are to prevent deformity and maintain and improve function. Ongoing rehabilitation is essential to maximize the patient's abilities. Most patients recover in the first 6 months after a stroke, with maximum benefit 1 year after a stroke.[1]

Rehabilitation requires a team approach so that the patient and caregiver can benefit from the combined, expert care of an interprofessional team. The team must communicate and coordinate care to achieve the patient's goals. As a nurse, you can facilitate this process and are often the key to successful rehabilitation efforts. The rehabilitation team is composed of many members. These include nurses, physicians, psychiatrist, physical therapist, occupational therapist, speech therapist, registered dietitian, respiratory therapist, vocational therapist, recreational therapist, social worker, psychologist, pharmacist, and chaplain.

Physical therapy focuses on mobility, progressive ambulation, transfer techniques, and equipment needed for mobility. Occupational therapy emphasizes retraining for skills of daily living, including eating, dressing, hygiene, and cooking. Occupational therapists are skilled in cognitive and perceptual evaluation and training. Speech therapy focuses on speech, communication, cognition, and eating abilities.

INFORMATICS IN PRACTICE

Video Games for Stroke Recovery

- Patients dealing with the effects of a stroke often find it hard to perform activities of daily living.
- Playing active video games, such as Nintendo Wii or Xbox Kinect, brings some fun into stroke recovery and may get patients to spend more time in therapy.
- Gaming helps patients regain lost strength, improve motor skills, and improve problem solving and short- and long-term memory.
- Patients can play with their families, including children, making gaming a way to involve others in rehabilitation.

The rehabilitation nurse assesses the patient, caregiver, and family with attention to the (1) patient's rehabilitation potential, (2) physical status of all body systems, (3) complications caused by the stroke or other chronic conditions, (4) patient's cognitive status, (5) family resources and support, and (6) expectations of the patient and caregiver related to the rehabilitation program. Many interventions started in the acute phase of care continue throughout rehabilitation.

Musculoskeletal Function. The initial assessment consists of determining the stage of recovery of muscle function. If the muscles are still flaccid several weeks after the stroke, the prognosis for regaining function is poor, and care focuses on preventing further loss.

Most patients begin to show signs of spasticity with exaggerated reflexes within 48 hours after the stroke. Spasticity at this phase denotes progress toward recovery. As improvement continues, small voluntary movements of the hip or shoulder may be accompanied by involuntary movements in the rest of the extremity (*synergy*). The last stage of recovery occurs when the patient has voluntary control of isolated muscle groups.

FIG. 57.10 A patient who had a stroke works with a physical therapist to improve arm strength. (© Thinkstock 78783452.)

Interventions for the musculoskeletal system advance in a manner of progressive activity. Balance training is the first step. It begins with the patient sitting up in bed or dangling the legs over the edge of the bed. Assess tolerance by noting dizziness or syncope caused by vasomotor instability. Loss of postural stability is common after stroke. When the nondominant hemisphere is involved, walking apraxia and loss of postural control are usually apparent. The patient may be unable to sit upright and tends to fall sideways. Provide proper support with pillows or cushions.

Assess whether patients autocorrect their posture when sitting on the edge of the bed. If the patient can straighten their posture instead of leaning to the weaker side, the patient may be ready for the next step of transferring from bed to chair. Place the chair beside the bed so that the patient can lead with the stronger arm and leg. The patient sits on the side of the bed, stands, places the strong hand on the far wheelchair arm, and sits down. You may either supervise the transfer or provide minimal aid by guiding the patient's strong hand to the wheelchair arm, standing in front of the patient while blocking the patient's knees with your knees to prevent knee buckling, and guiding the patient into a sitting position.

In some rehabilitation units, the Bobath method is used as an approach to mobility. The goal of this method is to help the patient gain control over patterns of spasticity by inhibiting abnormal reflex patterns. Therapists and nurses use the Bobath approach to encourage normal muscle tone, normal movement, and bilateral function of the body. An example is to have the patient transfer into the wheelchair using the weak or paralyzed side and the stronger side to facilitate more bilateral functioning.

Another approach to stroke rehabilitation is *constraint-induced movement therapy* (CIMT). CIMT encourages the patient to use the weakened extremity by restricting movement of the normal extremity. This approach can be challenging for patients. It is used only under the supervision of physical or occupational therapy. Movement training, skill acquisition, stretching, and exercise are other therapies offered for rehabilitation of the stroke patient.[25]

Supportive or assistive equipment, such as canes, walkers, and leg braces, may be needed on a short- or long-term basis for mobility. The physical therapist usually selects the proper supportive device(s) to meet individual needs and instructs the patient about use. Incorporate physical therapy activities into the patient's daily routine for added practice and repetition of rehabilitation efforts (Fig. 57.10).

EVIDENCE-BASED PRACTICE
Virtual Reality Training and Stroke

You are a nurse working in an outpatient rehabilitation setting with C.W., a 62-yr-old woman who had a stroke 2 months ago. She has left-sided weakness especially in her lower extremity that affects her balance and mobility. She tells you she misses not being able to fully engage with friends with whom she regularly walked with each morning until her stroke.

Making Clinical Decisions

Best Available Evidence. Impaired gait is highly linked with balance disorders in patients with stroke. Reduced balance is a major obstacle to achieving independence in activities of daily living after stroke. A loss of balance often results in falls and even serious injuries. Virtual reality (VR) training on gait and balance ability showed significant benefits on gait speed, Berg Balance Scale scores, and Timed "Up & Go" scores when compared to traditional physical therapy. VR training can improve mobility and daily functioning in patients undergoing rehabilitation for stroke.

Clinician Expertise. You know that a walking program can be an important part of stroke rehabilitation. Improvements in mobility reach their maximum potential in the first year after a stroke. You note the benefit of VR training for practicing daily activities that may currently be unsafe, such as walking, showering, and dressing.

Patient Preferences and Values. C.W. states that she is willing to "try something new" as part of her treatment.

Implications for Nursing Practice

1. What parameters will you use to assess C.W.'s progress with the VR training?
2. Why is it important for you to determine with C.W. if VR training translates into the actual performance of her previous activities?
3. As you coordinate her rehabilitation care, how will you promote communication among interprofessional team members?

References for Evidence

de Rooij IJM, van de Port IGL, Meijer J-WG: Effect of virtual reality training on balance and gait ability in patients with stroke: Systematic review and meta-analysis, *Phys Ther* 96:1905, 2016.

Li Z, Han XG, Sheng J, et al: Virtual reality for improving balance in patients after stroke: A systematic review and meta-analysis, *Clin Rehabil* 30:432, 2016.

Stroke Survivorship and Coping. Patients who had a stroke often have emotional responses that are not appropriate or typical for the situation. They may appear apathetic, depressed, fearful, anxious, weepy, frustrated, and angry. Some patients, especially those with a stroke on the left side of the brain (right hemiplegia), have exaggerated mood swings. The patient may be unable to control emotions and may suddenly burst into tears or laughter. This behavior is out of context and often is unrelated to the patient's underlying emotional state. Nursing interventions for atypical emotional response are to (1) distract the patient who suddenly becomes emotional, (2) explain to the patient and family that emotional outbursts may occur after a stroke, (3) maintain a calm environment, and (4) avoid shaming or scolding the patient during emotional outbursts.

The patient with a stroke may have many losses, including sensory, intellectual, communicative, functional, role behavior, emotional, social, and vocational losses. The patient, caregiver, and family often go through the process of grief and mourning associated with the losses. Some patients develop long-term

depression with symptoms, including anxiety, weight loss, fatigue, poor appetite, and sleep problems. The time and energy needed to perform previously simple tasks can result in anger and frustration.

The patient, caregiver, and family need help coping with the losses associated with stroke. Provide assistance by (1) supporting communication between the patient and family; (2) discussing lifestyle changes resulting from stroke deficits; (3) discussing changing roles and responsibilities within the family; (4) being an active listener to allow the expression of fear, frustration, and anxiety; (5) including the family and patient in short- and long-term goal planning and patient care; (6) supporting family conferences, and (7) identifying support groups and referrals as needed.

Maladjusted dependence with inadequate coping occurs when the patient does not maintain optimal functioning for self-care, family responsibilities, decision making, or socialization. This situation can cause resentment from both the patient and family with a negative cycle of interpersonal dependency and control. Caregivers and family members must cope with 3 aspects of the patient's behavior: (1) recognition of behavioral changes resulting from neurologic deficits that are not changeable, (2) responses to multiple losses by both the patient and family, and (3) behaviors that may have been reinforced during the early stages of stroke as continued dependency.

The patient, caregiver, and family may express guilt over not living healthy lifestyles or not seeking professional help sooner. Family therapy is a helpful adjunct to rehabilitation. Open communication, information about the total effects of stroke, teaching about stroke treatment, and therapy are helpful. Stroke support groups in rehabilitation facilities and the community are helpful in terms of mutual sharing, education, coping skills, and understanding.

Sexual Function. A patient who had a stroke may be concerned about the loss of sexual function. Many patients are comfortable talking about their anxieties and fears about sexual function if you are comfortable and open to the topic. You can start a discussion about the topic with the patient and spouse or significant other. Common concerns include impotence and the chance of another stroke occurring during sex. Nursing interventions include teaching about (1) optional positioning of partners, (2) timing for peak energy periods, and (3) patient and partner counseling.

Community Integration. Traditionally, successful community integration after stroke is hard for the patient because of persistent problems with cognition, coping, physical deficits, and emotional changes that interfere with functioning. Older adults who had a stroke often have more severe deficits and multiple health problems. Failure to continue the rehabilitation regimen at home may result in deterioration and further complications.

Community resources can be an asset to patients and their families. The National Stroke Association provides information, resources, referral services, and quarterly newsletters on stroke. The American Stroke Association, a division of the AHA, has information about stroke, hypertension, diet, exercise, and assistive devices. This association sponsors self-help groups in many areas. Easter Seals supplies wheelchairs and other assistive devices for stroke patients. Local groups can offer more daily help with meals and transportation.

Gerontologic Considerations: Stroke

Stroke is a significant cause of death and disability. The majority (66%) of strokes that require hospitalization occur in adults over age 65.[4] Stroke can result in a profound disruption in the life of an older adult. The magnitude of disability and changes in total function can leave patients wondering if they can ever return to their "old self." Loss of independence may be a major concern. The ability to perform ADLs may require many adaptive changes because of physical, emotional, perceptual, and cognitive deficits. Home management may be challenging if the patient's caregiver is also older or has health problems. There may be limited family members, including adult children, living nearby to provide help.

The rehabilitative phase and helping the older patient deal with the residual deficits of stroke, as well as aging, can be a challenging nursing experience. Patients may become fearful and depressed because they think they may have another stroke or die. The fear can become immobilizing and interfere with effective rehabilitation.

Changes may occur in the patient-spouse relationship. The dependency resulting from a stroke may threaten the relationship. The spouse may have chronic medical problems that can affect their ability to care for the stroke survivor. The patient may not want anyone other than the spouse to provide care, thus putting a significant burden on the spouse.

You can help the patient and caregiver in the transition through acute hospitalization, rehabilitation, long-term care, and home care. The needs of the patient, caregiver, and family require ongoing nursing assessment and adaptation of interventions in response to changing needs to optimize quality of life for them all.

CASE STUDY

Stroke

(© iStockphoto/ Thinkstock.)

Patient Profile

J.K. is a 57-yr-old white woman who was referred to the neurosurgery service for management of a temporal-parietal glioblastoma (see the Case Study in Chapter 55 on p. 1298). She was diagnosed after presenting with persistent headaches, a seizure in her HCP's office, and left-side upper visual field loss and neglect. Her MRI/MRA showed a temporal-parietal glioblastoma that extends into the occipital lobes. She was scheduled for surgery to debulk the tumor. J.K. lives alone and holds a management position. She was concerned about her ability to return to work after her surgery.

J.K. returned from surgery to the neurosurgery unit drowsy but following commands. Her pupils were equal and responded to light. During the night J.K. developed left-sided weakness of both arm and leg. She is now having difficulty with answering questions.

Subjective Data

- Left arm and leg are weak and feel numb
- She is trying to answer questions but looks confused and cannot follow commands

Objective Data

- BP 150/90 mm Hg
- Right gaze preference
- Left homonymous hemianopsia
- Left arm weakness (3/5) greater than leg weakness (4/5)

- Decreased sensation on both left arm and leg
- Has speech but not clear. Difficulty with word finding and following commands
- CT scan shows a hemorrhagic stroke into the site of the tumor bed, and temporal-parietal and anterior occipital areas extending into the thalamus

Discussion Questions

1. How did J.K.'s diagnosis (glioblastoma) put her at risk for a stroke?
2. **Priority Decision:** What potential complications is J.K. at highest risk for developing?
3. **Priority Decision:** Based on the assessment data provided, what are the priority nursing diagnoses? Are there any collaborative problems?
4. **Priority Decision:** What are the priority nursing interventions for J.K.?
5. **Collaboration:** What nursing interventions for J.K. can the RN delegate to UAP?
6. What strategies can you implement to improve communication for J.K.?
7. **Collaboration:** How would you involve other interprofessional team members in J.K.'s care?
8. **Safety:** How can you ensure safety for J.K. in light of her homonymous hemianopsia and left-sided neglect?
9. **Patient-Centered Care:** How can you address J.K.'s concerns about her finances and self-care?
10. Develop a conceptual care map for J. K.

Answers available at *http://evolve.elsevier.com/Lewis/medsurg.*

BRIDGE TO NCLEX EXAMINATION

The number of the question corresponds to the same-numbered outcome at the beginning of the chapter.

1. Which patient has the highest risk for a having a stroke?
   a. An obese 45-yr-old Native American.
   b. A 65-yr-old black man with hypertension
   c. A 35-yr-old Asian American woman who smokes.
   d. A 32-yr-old white woman taking oral contraceptives.

2. The factor related to cerebral blood flow that *most* often determines the extent of cerebral damage from a stroke is the
   a. O_2 content of the blood.
   b. amount of cardiac output.
   c. level of CO_2 in the blood.
   d. degree of collateral circulation.

3. Information provided by the patient that would help distinguish a hemorrhagic stroke from a thrombotic stroke includes
   a. sensory changes.
   b. a history of hypertension.
   c. presence of motor weakness.
   d. sudden onset of severe headache.

4. A patient is having word finding difficulty and weakness in his right arm. What area of the brain is *most* likely involved?
   a. brainstem.
   b. vertebral artery.
   c. left middle cerebral artery.
   d. right middle cerebral artery.

5. The nurse explains to the patient with a stroke who is scheduled for angiography that this test is used to determine the
   a. presence of increased ICP.
   b. site and size of the infarction.
   c. patency of the cerebral blood vessels.
   d. presence of blood in the cerebrospinal fluid.

6. A patient having TIAs is scheduled for a carotid endarterectomy. The nurse explains that this procedure is done to
   a. decrease cerebral edema.
   b. reduce the brain damage that occurs during a stroke in evolution.
   c. prevent a stroke by removing atherosclerotic plaques blocking cerebral blood flow.
   d. provide a circulatory bypass around thrombotic plaques obstructing cranial circulation.

7. For a patient who is suspected of having a stroke, the *most* important piece of information that the nurse can obtain is
   a. time of the patient's last meal.
   b. time at which stroke symptoms first appeared.
   c. patient's hypertension history and management.
   d. family history of stroke and other cardiovascular diseases.

8. Bladder training in a male patient who has urinary incontinence after a stroke includes
   a. limiting fluid intake.
   b. helping the patient to stand to void.
   c. keeping a urinal in place at all times.
   d. catheterizing the patient every 4 hours.

9. Common psychosocial problems a patient may have post stroke include *(select all that apply)*
   a. depression.
   b. disassociation.
   c. sleep problems.
   d. intellectualization
   e. denial of severity of stroke.

1. b, 2. d, 3. d, 4. c, 5. c, 6. c, 7. b, 8. b, 9. a, c, e

For rationales to these answers and even more NCLEX review questions, visit *http://evolve.elsevier.com/Lewis/medsurg.*

EVOLVE WEBSITE/RESOURCES LIST

http://evolve.elsevier.com/Lewis/medsurg
Review Questions (Online Only)
Key Points
Answer Keys for Questions
- Rationales for Bridge to NCLEX Examination Questions
- Answer Guidelines for Case Study on p. 1350
Student Case Studies
- Patient With Hypertension and Stroke
- Patient With Stroke
eNursing Care Plans
- eNursing Care Plan 57.1: Patient With Stroke
Conceptual Care Map Creator
- Conceptual Care Map for Case Study on p. 1350
Audio Glossary
Content Updates

REFERENCES

1. National Stroke Association: *Stroke survivors.* Retrieved from *www.stroke.org/we-can-help/survivors.*
2. Center for Disease Control and Prevention: *Stroke facts.* Retrieved from *www.cdc.gov/stroke/facts.htm.*
3. American Heart Association: Stroke falls to no. 5 killer in US. Retrieved from *www.heart.org/en/news/2018/05/01/stroke-falls-to-no-5-killer-in-us.*
4. Vega C: Updated guidelines available for primary prevention of stroke. Retrieved from *www.medscape.org/viewarticle/834329.*
*5. Boehme AK, Esenwa C, Elkind MS: Stroke risk factors, genetics, and prevention, *Cir Res* 120:472, 2017.
*6. O'Donnell MJ, Chin SL, Rangarajan, et al: Global and regional effects of potentially modifiable risk factors associated with acute stroke in 32 countries: A case-control study, *Lancet* 388:761, 2016.
*7. Meschia J, Bushnel C, Boden-Albala B, et al: Guidelines for the primary prevention of stroke: A statement for healthcare professionals from the AHA/American Stroke Association, *Stroke* 45:12, 2014. (Classic).
8. National Institute of Neurological Disorders and Stroke: Brain basics: Preventing stroke. Retrieved from *www.ninds.nih.gov/Disorders/Patient-Caregiver-Education/Preventing-Stroke.*
9. Watchman: Left atrial appendage closure implant. Retrieved from *www.watchman.com/atrial-fibrillation-stroke/atrial-fibrillation-afib.html.*

10. American Heart Association/American Stroke Association: Transient ischemic attacks. Retrieved from *www.strokeassociation.org/STROKEORG/AboutStroke/TypesofStroke/TIA/TIA-Transient-Ischemic-Attack_UCM_310942_Article.jsp.*
11. National Stroke Association: ABCD² score. Retrieved from *www.stroke.org/tia-abcd2-tool/.*
12. American Heart Association/American Stroke Association: Ischemic strokes. Retrieved from *www.strokeassociation.org/STROKEORG/AboutStroke/TypesofStroke/IschemicClots/Ischemic-Strokes-Clots_UCM_310939_Article.jsp.*
*13. Eriksen S, Gay C, Lerdal A: Acute phase factors associated with the course of depression during the first 18 months after first ever stroke, *Disabil Rehabil* 38:30, 2016.
14. Amplatzer PFO Occluder. Retrieved from *www.pfoamplatzer.com.*
*15. Gross H, Grose N. Emergency neurological life support: Acute ischemic stroke, *Neurocrit Care* 27:102, 2017.
16. Anderson JA: Acute ischemic stroke: The golden hour, *Nursing2017 CritCare* 11:36, 2016.
*17. Hentschel KA, Daou B, Chalouhi N, et al: Comparison of non–stent retriever and stent retriever mechanical thrombectomy devices for the endovascular treatment of acute ischemic stroke, *JNS* 126:1123, 2017.
18. Malas MB, Leal J, Kashyap V, et al: Technical aspects of transcarotid artery revascularization using the ENROUTE transcarotid neuroprotection and stent system, *J Vasc Surg* 31:916, 2017.
*19. Al-Mufti F, Dancour E, Amuluru K, et al: Neurocritical care of emergent large-vessel occlusion: The era of a new standard of care, *J Intensive Care Med* 19:373, 2016.
20. Watson J: Subarachnoid hemorrhage surgery. Retrieved from *https://emedicine.medscape.com/article/247090-overview.*
21. American Stroke Association: NIH Stroke Scale International. Retrieved from *www.nihstrokescale.org.*
*22. Goshgarian C, Gorelick PB: DVT prevention in stroke, *Curr Neurol Neurosci* 17:81, 2017.
*23. Fedder WN: Review of evidenced-based nursing protocols for dysphagia assessment, *Stroke* 48:e99, 2017.
*24. Camicia M, Lutz BJ: Nursing's role in successful transitions across settings, *Stroke* 47:e246, 2016.
*25. Han P, Zhang W, Kang L, et al: Clinical evidence of exercise benefits for stroke. In: Xiao J, ed: *Exercise for cardiovascular disease prevention and treatment,* Singapore, 2017, Springer.

*Evidence-based information for clinical practice.

58

Chronic Neurologic Problems

Madona D. Plueger and Dottie Roberts

Compassion is a verb.

Thich Nhat Hanh

ⓔ http://evolve.elsevier.com/Lewis/medsurg

CONCEPTUAL FOCUS

Cognition

Coping

Functional Ability

Inflammation

Intracranial Regulation

Mobility

Safety

LEARNING OUTCOMES

1. Compare and contrast the etiology, clinical manifestations, and interprofessional and nursing management of tension-type, migraine, and cluster headaches.
2. Distinguish the etiology, clinical manifestations, diagnostic studies, and interprofessional and nursing management of seizure disorder, multiple sclerosis, Parkinson's disease, and myasthenia gravis.

3. Describe the clinical manifestations and nursing and interprofessional management of restless legs syndrome, amyotrophic lateral sclerosis, and Huntington's disease.
4. Explain the potential impact of chronic neurologic disease on physical and psychologic well-being.
5. Outline the major goals of treatment for the patient with a chronic, progressive neurologic disease.

KEY TERMS

absence seizure, p. 1359
amyotrophic lateral sclerosis (ALS), p. 1379
aura, p. 1353
cluster headache, p. 1355
focal-onset seizures, p. 1359
generalized-onset seizures, p. 1359
headache, p. 1352

Huntington's disease (HD), p. 1379
migraine headache, p. 1353
multiple sclerosis (MS), p. 1366
myasthenia gravis (MG), p. 1377
myasthenic crisis, p. 1377
Parkinson's disease (PD), p. 1371
restless legs syndrome (RLS), p. 1365

seizure, p. 1358
seizure disorder, p. 1358
status epilepticus, p. 1360
tension-type headache, p. 1353
tonic-clonic seizure, p. 1359

This chapter discusses headaches, chronic neurologic disorders, and degenerative neurologic disorders. Chronic neurologic disorders include seizure disorder and restless legs syndrome (RLS). *Degenerative nerve diseases* lead to nerve damage that worsens as the diseases progress. Most of these neurologic problems have no cure. Treatment aims to reduce symptoms and help the patient maintain optimal function. Many have a genetic basis.

Degenerative nerve diseases include multiple sclerosis, Parkinson's disease, myasthenia gravis, amyotrophic lateral sclerosis, and Huntington's disease. They affect many activities, including balance, movement, speech, and respiratory and heart function. Patients with these diseases have similar concerns and problems. They must deal not only with their disease but also with the impact of the disease on their quality of life. Many patients have concerns about safety, mobility, self-care, and coping. Patients and their caregivers often need psychosocial support, especially as the disease progresses and disability gets worse.

HEADACHES

Headache is the most common type of pain that people have. Most people have functional headaches, such as migraine or tension-type headaches. Others have organic headaches caused by intracranial or extracranial disease. Headaches tend to occur more often in women than in men.

Pain-sensitive structures in the head include venous sinuses, dura, and cranial blood vessels. In addition, there are 3 divisions of the trigeminal nerve (cranial nerve [CN] V), facial nerve (CN VII), glossopharyngeal nerve (CN IX), vagus nerve (CN X), and the first 3 cervical nerves. Because these nerves have both motor and sensory functions, increased pain intensity and symptoms can occur when a person moves.

Headaches are classified as primary or secondary headache. *Primary headache* includes tension-type, migraine, and cluster headaches. Primary headaches are not caused by a disease or another medical condition. The type of primary headache is determined using the International Headache Society

(IHS) guidelines based on characteristics of the headache (Table 58.1).[1] *Secondary headaches* are caused by another condition or disorder, such as sinus infection, neck injury, and brain tumor.

A patient may have more than 1 type of headache. The history and neurologic examination are diagnostic keys to determine the type of headache. The examination of a person with a headache is often normal. Unexplained abnormal findings require further diagnostic studies to identify the underlying cause.

TENSION-TYPE HEADACHE

Tension-type headache (TTH), also called *stress headache,* is the most common type of headache. This type of headache is characterized by its bilateral location and pressing or tightening quality. TTH is usually of mild or moderate intensity. It can last from minutes to days. TTHs are divided by frequency into episodic or chronic.[1] Chronic TTH can become a serious problem that leads to decreased quality of life and severe disability.

Etiology and Pathophysiology

We do not know the cause TTH. It may have a neurobiologic basis similar to migraine headaches. For some, episodic headaches evolve into chronic headaches. Increased frequency, though, does not necessarily increase headache intensity. Headaches may occur intermittently for weeks, months, or even years.

Clinical Manifestations

Patients often have a bilateral frontal-occipital headache described as a constant, dull pressure or a bandlike headache associated with neck pain. There may be increased tone in the cervical and neck muscles. The headache may involve sensitivity to light *(photophobia)* or sound *(phonophobia)* but not nausea or vomiting. There are no *premonitory symptoms* (warning symptoms of impending headache). Physical activity does not worsen symptoms.

Many patients have a combination of migraine headache and TTH, with features of both occurring together. Patients with migraine headaches may have TTH between migraine attacks. Fig. 58.1 shows the location of pain for common headache syndromes.

Diagnostic Studies

Careful history taking may be the most useful tool for diagnosing TTH (Table 58.2). If TTH is present during physical examination, increased resistance to passive movement of the head and tenderness of the head and neck may be seen. Electromyography (EMG) may show sustained contraction of neck, scalp, or facial muscles. However, the patient may not have increased muscle tension with an EMG, even when it is done during a headache. Imaging is ordered when symptoms raise concern about a possible pathologic cause.

MIGRAINE HEADACHE

Migraine headache is a recurring headache characterized by unilateral throbbing pain. Migraines are most common between the ages of 25 and 55. 12% of the population has migraines.[2] Many people who have migraines have a family history of migraines. Other risk factors include age, female gender, obesity, low level of education, depression, and stressful life events. Overuse of medications for acute migraine or ineffective acute treatment can contribute to chronic migraine headache.[3]

The IHS subdivides migraines into categories. *Migraine without aura* (formerly called *common migraine*) is the most common type. *Migraine with aura* (formerly called *classic migraine*) occurs in 25% to 30% of migraine headache episodes.[4]

GENDER DIFFERENCES
Headaches

Men
- Cluster headaches are 3 times more common than in women.
- Have more exercise-induced headaches than women.

Women
- Migraine headaches are 3 times more common than in men.
- Have more tension headaches than men.

Etiology and Pathophysiology

Although there are many theories about the cause of migraine headaches, we do not know the exact cause. Current theory suggests a complex series of neurovascular events starts the headache. People who have migraines have a state of neuron hyperexcitability in the cerebral cortex, especially in the occipital cortex. Genetics appear to play a role. Risk for migraine headache increases 50% to 75% if even 1 parent has a history of migraine.[5]

Migraine is associated with seizure disorder, ischemic stroke, asthma, depression, anxiety, myocardial infarction, Raynaud's syndrome, and irritable bowel syndrome. In many cases, migraine headaches have no known precipitating events. For some patients, specific factors may trigger a headache. *Triggers* for migraine headaches include bright lights, sound, hormone fluctuations, certain smells, poor sleep, or high stress.[6] Common food triggers include chocolate, cheese, oranges, tomatoes, onions, monosodium glutamate, aspartame, and alcohol (especially red wine).

Clinical Manifestations

Premonitory symptoms and an aura may precede the headache phase by several hours or days. Premonitory symptoms occur before the onset of aura or headache. They may include sensory experiences (e.g., photophobia, phonophobia); mood, sleep, or cognitive changes (e.g., poor concentration, irritability, fatigue); and homeostatic changes (e.g., thirst and cravings, change in bowel habits).[7] An aura is a complex of neurologic symptoms that occur before a headache for some patients. Visual symptoms, such as bright lights, scotomas (patchy blindness), visual distortions, or zigzag lines, are the most common type of aura.[1] They occur in over 90% of patients in at least some attacks. Sensory (voices or sounds that do not exist, strange smells) and/or motor phenomena (e.g., weakness, paralysis, feeling that limbs are moving) may be part of an aura.

A migraine headache may last 4 to 72 hours. Patients often describe the headache as a steady, throbbing pain that is synchronous with the pulse. Although the headache is usually unilateral, it may switch to the opposite side in another episode. During the headache, patients may try to avoid noise, light, odors, people, and problems.

TABLE 58.1   Interprofessional Care

Headaches

Tension-Type Headaches	Migraine Headache	Cluster Headache
Location Bilateral, bandlike pressure at base of skull	Unilateral in 60%, may switch sides; often anterior location	Unilateral, radiating up or down from 1 eye
Quality Constant, squeezing tightness	Throbbing, synchronous with pulse	Severe, bone crushing
Frequency Cycles for many years	Periodic, cycles of several months and years	May have months or years between attacks Attacks occur in clusters over a period of 2–12 wk
Duration 30 min–7 days	4–72 hr	5 min–3 hr
Time and Mode of Onset Not related to time	May be preceded by premonitory symptoms or aura Onset after awakening Improves with sleep	Nocturnal, often awakens person from sleep
Associated Symptoms Palpable neck and shoulder muscle tension Stiff neck Tenderness	Irritability, sweating Nausea, vomiting Photophobia Phonophobia Premonitory symptoms: sensory, motor, or psychic phenomena	Facial flushing or pallor Unilateral lacrimation, ptosis, rhinitis
Treatment: Abortive and Symptomatic Drugs Nonopioid analgesics: aspirin, acetaminophen, NSAIDS Analgesic combinations • butalbital/acetaminophen/caffeine • butalbital/aspirin/caffeine (Fiorinal) • dichloralphenazone/acetaminophen/ isometheptene Muscle relaxants	Nonopioid analgesics: aspirin, NSAIDs Serotonin receptor agonists • almotriptan (Axert) • eletriptan (Relpax) • frovatriptan (Frova) • naratriptan (Amerge) • rizatriptan (Maxalt) • sumatriptan (Imitrex) • zolmitriptan (Zomig) Combination • sumatriptan/naproxen (Treximet) α-Adrenergic blockers • ergotamine tartrate (Ergomar) • dihydroergotamine nasal spray (Migranal) Analgesic combinations • acetaminophen/caffeine/aspirin Corticosteroids • dexamethasone	α-Adrenergic blockers • ergotamine tartrate Serotonin receptor agonists • almotriptan • eletriptan • frovatriptan • naratriptan • rizatriptan • sumatriptan • zolmitriptan O_2 100% inhalation via mask
Treatment: Preventive Tricyclic antidepressants • amitriptyline • nortriptyline (Pamelor) • doxepin Selective serotonin reuptake inhibitors • fluoxetine (Prozac) • paroxetine (Paxil) β-Adrenergic blocker: • propranolol (Inderal) Antiseizure drugs • topiramate (Topamax) • divalproex (Depakote) Other drugs • mirtazapine (Remeron) Biofeedback Psychotherapy Muscle relaxation training	β-Adrenergic blocker • propranolol (Inderal) Antidepressants • amitriptyline (Elavil) • imipramine (Tofranil) Antiseizure drugs • divalproex • gabapentin • topiramate • valproic acid (Depakene) Botulinum toxin A Calcium channel blocker • nifedipine (Procardia) • verapamil Biofeedback Relaxation therapy Cognitive-behavioral therapy	α-Adrenergic blockers • ergotamine tartrate Corticosteroid • prednisone Calcium channel blocker • verapamil Lithium Biofeedback

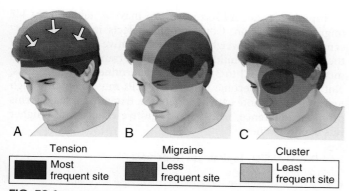

FIG. 58.1 Location of pain for common headache syndromes. **A,** Tension headache is often described as feeling of a weight in or on the head or a band squeezing the head. **B,** Migraine headache is usually unilateral, in the temple on 1 side of the head. The pain can be bilateral. **C,** Cluster headache pain is focused in and around 1 eye.

TABLE 58.2 Diagnostic Studies

Headaches

History and Physical Examination
- Neurologic examination (often negative)
- Inspection for local infection
- Palpation of head for tenderness, bony swellings
- Auscultation for bruits over major arteries, especially neck

Routine Laboratory Studies
- CBC (may show anemia, infection)
- Electrolytes (may show dehydration, other illnesses)
- Urinalysis (may show infection, other medical diagnoses [e.g., diabetes])
- Other diagnostic studies to assess evidence of disease, deformity, or infection: angiography, EMG, EEG, MRA, MRI, LP

Diagnostic Studies

The diagnosis of migraine headache is usually based on the patient history. Neurologic and other diagnostic examinations are often normal (Table 58.2).

No specific laboratory or radiologic test can diagnose migraine headache. Neuroimaging techniques (e.g., head CT scan with or without contrast, MRI) are not part of the routine evaluation of headache unless the neurologic examination is abnormal. If atypical features are present, further testing is done to rule out a secondary headache.

CLUSTER HEADACHE

Cluster headache is the most severe form of primary headache. It is classified as a trigeminal autonomic cephalalgia (TAC). This reflects its effect on the trigeminal nerve (CN V) and associated autonomic symptoms (e.g., runny or stuffy nose).[8] Repeated headaches occur in clusters, generally at the same time of day or night. Age at onset is typically 20 to 50 years, but they can start at any age. They affect men more than women. They occur more often in persons who smoke.[9] Less than 1% of people in the United States have cluster headache.

Etiology and Pathophysiology

Neither the cause nor how cluster headache occurs is fully known. The patterns of cluster headache suggest dysfunction of the hypothalamus. Many attacks occur at night, waking the person 1 to 2 hours after falling asleep. This may mean there is a circadian rhythm problem. Alcohol is a dietary trigger. Pain often starts within an hour of a drink. Strong odors (e.g., gasoline, paint fumes) can trigger cluster headache.[10]

Clinical Manifestations

Patients with cluster headache have severe, intense pain lasting from a few minutes to 3 hours. In contrast to the pulsing pain of migraine headache, the pain of cluster headache is sharp and stabbing. The pain is usually around the eye, radiating to the temple, forehead, cheek, nose, or gums. Other manifestations may include swelling around the eye, lacrimation (tearing), facial flushing or pallor, nasal congestion, and miosis (pupil constriction). Most patients have at least 3 of these symptoms. During the headache, the patient may be agitated and restless, unable to sit still or relax.

Cluster headaches can occur every other day and as often as 8 times a day. A cluster typically lasts 2 weeks to 3 months, and then the patient goes into remission for months to years. Typically, 2 cluster periods a year may be separated by months without symptoms. Because cluster periods often occur seasonally, headaches may be mistaken for symptoms of allergies. A small number of patients (10% to 15%) have chronic headaches without remission.[1]

Diagnostic Studies

The diagnosis of cluster headache is based on the patient history according to IHS criteria.[1] Asking patients to keep a headache diary can be useful. CT scan, MRI, or magnetic resonance angiography (MRA) may rule out an aneurysm, tumor, or infection. A lumbar puncture (LP) may rule out other disorders that may cause similar symptoms.

OTHER TYPES OF HEADACHES

Other types of headaches can occur. A headache may be the first symptom of a more serious illness. Headache can accompany subarachnoid hemorrhage; brain tumors; intracranial masses; vascular abnormalities; trigeminal neuralgia (tic douloureux); diseases of the eyes, nose, and teeth; and systemic illness (e.g., infection, carbon monoxide poisoning, altitude sickness, polycythemia vera). Because of the varied causes of headache, thorough clinical evaluation is important. It should include assessment of personality, life adjustment, environment, and living situation, as well as a comprehensive evaluation of neurologic and physical condition.

INFORMATICS IN PRACTICE

Social Media Use for Patients With Migraine Headaches

- Many people with migraine headaches think others do not understand their pain and its impact on their quality of life.
- Encourage patients to take part in a social media outlet where people who have migraines share their experiences.
- Patients can describe their physical and emotional pain on social media. It can help them cope better and improve their quality of life.

INTERPROFESSIONAL CARE FOR HEADACHES

If no systemic disease is the cause, the type of headache guides therapy. Table 58.2 outlines the general assessment of a patient with headaches to rule out any intracranial or extracranial disease. Table 58.1 shows therapies for preventing and managing different types of headaches.

Cognitive-behavioral therapy and relaxation therapy used alone or in conjunction with drug therapy may help some patients (see Chapter 6). Biofeedback involves the use of physiologic monitoring equipment that gives the patient information about muscle tension and peripheral blood flow (e.g., skin temperature of the fingers). The patient is trained to relax the muscles and raise the finger temperature. Reinforcement occurs when the patient makes these changes. Acupuncture, acupressure, and hypnosis are options for some patients.

Drug Therapy

Tension-Type Headache. Drug therapy for TTH usually involves aspirin, acetaminophen (Tylenol), or nonsteroidal antiinflammatory drugs (NSAIDs) used alone or in combination with caffeine, a sedative, or a muscle relaxant. Treatment is often disappointing. These analgesics may be only partly effective, even with use of the maximum dose. Stronger analgesics provide no additional benefit. For some, analgesics can make the headache worse.[11]

Many of these drugs have serious side effects. Caution the patient about the long-term use of aspirin or aspirin-containing drugs because they can cause gastrointestinal (GI) bleeding and coagulation abnormalities in some patients. Drugs containing acetaminophen can cause kidney damage with chronic use and liver damage when taken in large doses or when combined with alcohol. To decrease the recurrence of TTH, many patients take an antidepressant. Common drugs include tricyclic agents (e.g., amitriptyline, nortriptyline); mirtazapine (Remeron), a nonadrenergic serotonergic antidepressant; and venlafaxine (Effexor XR). Antiseizure drugs, such as topiramate (Topamax) or divalproex (Depakote), also may be used.

Migraine Headache. The aim of drug treatment of an acute migraine is stopping or decreasing the symptoms. Many people with mild or moderate migraine headache can get relief with NSAIDs, aspirin, or caffeine-containing analgesics. For moderate to severe headaches, triptans are the first line of therapy.

Triptans (e.g., sumatriptan [Imitrex]) affect selected serotonin receptors. They reduce neurogenic inflammation of cerebral blood vessels and cause vasoconstriction (Table 58.1). Some patients respond better to a certain triptan than to others. Triptans are most effective when taken at the start of a migraine headache or during the aura. Sumatriptan is available in several dosage forms and delivery systems (oral, subcutaneous, nasal spray, transdermal). It is also the only ultrafast-acting triptan. A combination of oral sumatriptan and naproxen sodium (Treximet) is more effective for symptom relief than either medication alone. Because triptans cause vasoconstriction, they may not be appropriate for people with heart disease (e.g., hypertension, high cholesterol) or history of stroke. When triptans are contraindicated or ineffective, other drugs can be used (Table 58.1).

DRUG ALERT Sumatriptan (Imitrex)
- Should not be given to patients with a history of:
  - Ischemic cardiac, cerebrovascular, or peripheral vascular problems.
  - Uncontrolled hypertension (may increase BP).
- Excess dosage may cause tremor and decrease respirations.

Preventive treatment is important in managing migraine headache. The decision to start preventive treatment is made based on frequency, severity, and disability related to headaches. Several different classes of medications are used.

Topiramate, an antiseizure drug, may be taken daily for migraine prevention. Common side effects include hypoglycemia, paresthesia, weight loss, and cognitive changes. Usually these side effects are mild to moderate and transient. Topiramate must be taken for 2 to 3 months to determine its effectiveness. Not all patients become pain free. HCPs must offer thorough teaching to promote patient adherence. Extended-release forms promote adherence, with fewer cognitive effects and a higher rate of effectiveness.[12]

DRUG ALERT Topiramate (Topamax)
Teach patient to:
- Not abruptly stop therapy because this may cause seizures.
- Avoid tasks that require alertness (e.g., driving, operating heavy machinery) until response to the drug is known.
- Take adequate fluids to decrease risk for developing renal stones.
- Tell the HCP if you are pregnant or want to become pregnant.

β-Blockers have been effective in migraine prevention. Commonly prescribed agents include metoprolol (Lopressor) and propranolol (Inderal). Propranolol is similar to amitriptyline in its efficacy. Atenolol (Tenormin) and nadolol (Corgard) are other options for migraine prevention.

Botulinum toxin A (Botox) may be an effective prophylactic treatment for adults who have chronic migraines at least 15 days each month or migraines that do not respond to other medications. Botox is given by multiple injections around the head and neck into the pain fibers involved in headaches. Maximum benefit may not be seen for up to 6 months. During this time, the patient should continue their regular medications. Injections are usually given every 3 months. The most common reactions are neck pain and headache. A slight risk exists for the toxin to migrate from the injection site to other areas of the face and neck, causing swallowing and breathing difficulties. Teach the patient to seek immediate medical attention if this occurs.

Cluster Headache. Triptans are the standard of treatment for occasional cluster headache. Nasal administration or subcutaneous injection is appropriate. However, as discussed earlier, they are contraindicated for patients with vascular risk factors due to their vasoconstrictive effects.

High-flow 100% O_2 by non-rebreather mask is well-tolerated, safe, and effective as an alternative treatment. O_2 delivered at a rate of 6 to 8 L/min for 10 minutes may relieve headache by causing vasoconstriction and increasing synthesis of serotonin in the central nervous system (CNS). Treatment can be repeated after a 5-minute rest. A drawback to this treatment is that the patient must have continuous access to the O_2 supply.

Those with chronic cluster headache often need preventive treatment. High-dose verapamil is the first-choice drug. It is typically given at double or more the dose used for other disorders.[8] Because of its effects on cardiac conduction, verapamil should be started only after careful consideration of the risks. Careful monitoring is needed during treatment. An electrocardiogram (ECG) should be done with every dose increase and every 6 months during treatment for patient safety. Other drug options may include lithium, ergotamine, antiseizure drugs (e.g., topiramate), and melatonin. Options for patients with refractory cluster headaches include invasive nerve blocks, deep brain stimulation, and ablative neurosurgical procedures (e.g., percutaneous radiofrequency).

Other Headaches. Patients with frequent headaches may overuse analgesics or other medications used for headache treatment. *Medication overuse headache* (MOH) is the term used to describe a new type of headache or marked worsening of a preexisting headache condition. Drugs known to cause this problem are acetaminophen, aspirin, NSAIDs (e.g., ibuprofen), triptans, ergotamine, and opioids.[1] Headache often occurs daily and is present on wakening. Patients may have nausea, restlessness, weakness, lack of energy, decreased memory, difficulty concentrating, depression, and irritability. Treatment involves abrupt withdrawal of the offending drug (except for opioids, which must be tapered) and using alternative drugs, such as amitriptyline.

Some people have chronic headaches that are difficult to treat. IV medication administration with novel therapies, such as ketamine and lidocaine, and neurostimulation are emerging as options.

❖ NURSING MANAGEMENT: HEADACHES

◆ Nursing Assessment

Table 58.3 outlines subjective and objective data to obtain from a patient with headaches. The history is key and focused on specific details of the headaches. These include location and type of pain, onset, frequency, duration, relation to events (emotional, psychologic, physical), and time of day of the occurrence. Ask about illnesses, surgery, trauma, allergies, family history, and response to medication. A thorough history may suggest headache is due to other drug therapies or a condition other than headache. For example, estrogen withdrawal headache is possible during the drug-free interval of an oral contraceptive.

Ask the patient to keep a diary of headaches with specific details. This record can help identify the type of headache and precipitating events. If there is a history of migraine, TTH, or cluster headache, ask the patient if the character, intensity, or location of the headache has changed. The answer may be an important clue about the cause of the headache.

◆ Nursing Diagnoses

Nursing diagnoses for the patient with headaches may include:
- Acute pain
- Lack of knowledge

Additional information on nursing diagnoses and interventions is presented in eNursing Care Plan 58.1 for the patient with headaches (available on the website for this chapter).

◆ Planning

The overall goals are that the patient with headaches will (1) have reduced or no pain, (2) understand triggering events and treatments, (3) use positive coping strategies to deal with pain, and (4) have increased quality of life and decreased disability.

◆ Nursing Implementation

An inability to cope with daily stresses can cause headaches. Thus effective treatment may involve helping the patient examine the daily routine, recognize stressful situations, and develop effective coping strategies. Help the patient identify precipitating factors and develop ways to avoid or minimize them. Encourage daily exercise, relaxation periods, and socialization as ways to decrease headaches. Suggest relaxation, medication, yoga, and other ways to address headache pain.

TABLE 58.3 Nursing Assessment
Headaches

Subjective Data
Important Health Information

Past health history: Seizures, cancer, recent fall or other trauma, cranial infection, stroke. Asthma or allergies. Relationship of headache to overwork, stress, menstruation, exercise, food, sexual activity, travel, bright lights, or noxious environmental stimuli
Medications: Hydralazine, bromides, nitroglycerin, ergotamine (withdrawal), NSAIDs (in high daily doses), estrogen preparations, oral contraceptives, OTC medications
Surgical interventions or other treatments: Craniotomy, sinus surgery, facial surgery

Functional Health Pattern

Health perception–health management: Positive family history. Malaise
Nutritional-metabolic: Ingestion of alcohol, caffeine, cheese, chocolate, monosodium glutamate, aspartame, lunch meats (nitrites in cured meats), sausage, hot dogs, onions, avocados. History of anorexia, nausea, vomiting (migraine premonitory symptom); unilateral lacrimation (cluster)
Activity-exercise: Vertigo, fatigue, weakness, paralysis, fainting
Sleep-rest: Insomnia
Cognitive-perceptual
- *Tension type:* Bilateral, bandlike, dull and persistent, base-of-skull headache, neck tenderness
- *Migraine:* Aura. Unilateral, severe, throbbing headache (possible switching of side). Visual changes, photophobia, phonophobia, dizziness, tingling or burning sensations
- *Cluster:* Unilateral and severe, nocturnal headache. Nasal stuffiness
Self-perception–self-concept: Depression
Coping–stress tolerance: Stress, anxiety, irritability, withdrawal

Objective Data
General

Anxiety, apprehension

Integumentary

Migraine: Generalized edema (premonitory symptom) pallor, diaphoresis
Cluster: Forehead diaphoresis, pallor, unilateral facial flushing with cheek edema, conjunctivitis

Neurologic

Horner's syndrome, restlessness (cluster), hemiparesis (migraine)

Musculoskeletal

Resistance of head and neck movement, nuchal rigidity (meningeal, tension type), palpable neck and shoulder muscle tension (tension type)

Possible Diagnostic Findings

Evidence of disease, deformity, or infection on brain imaging (CT, MRI, MRA), cerebral angiogram, LP, EEG, EMG

Teach the patient about drugs prescribed for preventive and symptomatic treatment of headache. The patient should be able to describe the purpose, action, dosage, and side effects of the drugs. To prevent accidental overdose, urge the patient to make a written note of each dose of drug or headache remedy. In addition to using analgesics and analgesic combinations to relieve headache, encourage the patient with migraines to seek a quiet, dimly lit environment. Massage and moist hot packs to the neck and head can help a patient with TTH.

Provide dietary counseling for the patient with headaches triggered by food. Encourage the patient to eliminate foods that

---

TABLE 58.4 Patient & Caregiver Teaching

Headaches

Include the following instructions when teaching the patient with a headache and the patient's caregiver:

1. Keep a diary or calendar of headaches and possible precipitating events.
2. Avoid possible triggers for a headache:
   - Foods containing amines (cheese, chocolate), nitrites (meats, such as hot dogs), vinegar, onions, monosodium glutamate
   - Fermented or marinated foods
   - Caffeine
   - Oranges
   - Tomatoes
   - Aspartame
   - Nicotine
   - Ice cream
   - Alcohol (especially red wine)
   - Emotional stress
   - Fatigue
   - Drugs, such as ergot-containing preparations (ergotamine tartrate) and monoamine oxidase inhibitors (e.g., rasagiline [Azilect])
3. Learn the purpose, action, dosage, and side effects of drugs taken.
4. Self-administer sumatriptan subcutaneously, if prescribed.
5. Use stress management techniques (see Chapter 6).
6. Take part in regular exercise.
7. Contact HCP if any of the following occur:
   - Symptoms become more severe, last longer than usual, or are resistant to medication
   - Nausea and vomiting (if severe or not typical), change in vision, or fever occurs with the headache
   - Problems occur with any drugs

---

may provoke headaches. Active challenge and provocative testing (designed specifically to provoke symptoms) with suspect foods may help determine specific causative agents. However, teach the patient that food triggers may change over time.

Teach patients to avoid smoking and exposure to triggers, such as strong perfumes and gasoline fumes. Cluster headaches may occur at high altitudes with low O_2 levels during air travel. Ergotamine, taken before the plane takes off, may decrease this risk. See Table 58.4 for a teaching guide for the patient with a headache.

◆ Evaluation

Expected outcomes are that the patient with headaches will
- Report satisfaction with pain management
- Use drug and nondrug measures appropriately to manage pain

CHRONIC NEUROLOGIC DISORDERS

SEIZURE DISORDER

Seizure disorder, also known as *epilepsy*, is a group of neurologic diseases marked by recurring seizures. It is the fourth most common neurologic disorder. Only migraine, stroke, and Alzheimer's disease occur more often. About 3.4 million Americans have seizure disorder. 1 in 26 people will develop seizure disorder during their lifetime.[13]

Seizure is a transient, uncontrolled electrical discharge of neurons in the brain that interrupts normal function. Seizures may accompany a variety of disorders, or they may occur without any apparent cause. Seizures from systemic and metabolic problems are not considered seizure disorder if they stop when the underlying problem is corrected. Metabolic problems that may cause seizures include acidosis, electrolyte imbalances, hypoglycemia, hypoxia, alcohol and barbiturate withdrawal, dehydration, and water intoxication. Extracranial disorders that may cause seizures include systemic lupus erythematosus; diabetes; hypertension; sepsis; and heart, lung, liver, or kidney diseases.

Etiology and Pathophysiology

Seizure disorder has many possible causes. The most common ones vary by age. Common causes during the first 6 months of life are severe birth injury, congenital defects involving the CNS, infection, and inborn errors of metabolism. In those 2 to 20 years of age, the main causes are birth injury, infection, head trauma, and genetic factors. In young adults 20 to 30 years of age, seizure disorder usually occurs from structural lesions, such as trauma, brain tumors, or vascular disease. After 50 years of age, the main causes are stroke and metastatic brain tumors. However, one third of all cases are idiopathic. This means they cannot be attributed to a specific cause. These cases are known as *idiopathic generalized epilepsy (IGE)*.

Seizure disorder is characterized by a group of abnormal neurons that seem to fire without a clear cause. Any stimulus that causes the neuron's cell membrane to depolarize can cause this firing. It spreads by physiologic pathways to involve near or distant areas of the brain. Localization of the *seizure focus* (the place where the seizure originates) is critical to the success of any possible surgical treatment.

Besides neuron alterations, changes in the function of astrocytes may play several key roles in recurring seizures. Activation of astrocytes by hyperactive neurons is one of the crucial factors that causes nearby neurons to generate an epileptic discharge. We continue to learn about abnormal neural antibodies that can cause seizures. *N*-methyl-D-aspartate (NMDA) receptor antibodies are present in the cerebrospinal fluid (CSF) in 80% of patients. The emerging concept of autoimmune seizure disorder may lead to better outcomes for those resistant to drug therapy.[14]

Genetic Link

Genetic abnormalities may be an important factor contributing to IGE. The role of genetics in seizure disorder is complex because it is hard to separate genetic from environmental or acquired influences. In some types, families carry a predisposition to seizure disorder through a naturally low threshold to stimuli, such as trauma, disease, and high fever. Other types of IGE are related to changes in specific genes that control the flow of ions in and out of cells, regulate neuron signaling, or are involved with protein and carbohydrate metabolism.

Sometimes seizure disorder is related to a specific genetic disorder that affects various parts of the body and causes seizures. Many cause brain abnormalities or metabolic disorders (e.g., phenylketonuria [PKU]) and have seizures as a major feature. Other seizures are known to have a genetic basis, but we have not found the gene that causes them.[15]

Clinical Manifestations

Specific manifestations of seizure are determined by the site of the electrical disturbance. The preferred way of classifying seizures is based on the clinical and electroencephalographic (EEG) manifestations. This system divides seizures into 3 major

TABLE 58.5 Classification of Seizures

Generalized Onset Seizure (Involves both hemispheres of brain)	Focal-Onset Seizure (Limited to 1 hemisphere of brain)

• Motor seizure
  • Tonic
  • Clonic
  • Tonic-clonic
  • Myoclonic
  • Myoclonic-tonic-clonic
  • Myoclonic-atonic
  • Atonic
  • Epileptic spasms
• Nonmotor (Absence) seizure
  • Typical
  • Atypical
  • Myoclonic
  • Eyelid myoclonia
	• Aware (no impairment of awareness/consciousness)
	• Impaired awareness (impairment of awareness/consciousness)
	• Motor onset
	  • Automatisms
	  • Atonic
	  • Clonic
	  • Epileptic spasms
	  • Hyperkinetic
	  • Myoclonic
	  • Tonic
	• Nonmotor onset
	  • Autonomic
	  • Behavior arrest
	  • Cognitive
	  • Emotional
	  • Sensory
	
	Unknown Onset Seizure
	(Due to inadequate information or inability to assign to other categories above)

Adapted from Fisher RS, Cross JH, D'Souza C, et al: Instruction manual for the ILAE 2017 operational classification of seizure types, *Epilepsia* 58:4, 2017.

classes: *generalized onset, focal onset,* and *unknown onset* (Table 58.5).[16] They are further described under each classification as *motor* or *nonmotor*. Descriptors address what occurs during the seizure.

Depending on the type, a seizure may occur in four phases: (1) *prodromal phase,* with sensations or behavior changes that precede a seizure by hours or days; (2) *aural phase,* with a sensory warning that is similar each time a seizure occurs and is considered part of the seizure; (3) *ictal phase,* from first symptoms to the end of seizure activity; and (4) *postictal phase,* the recovery period after the seizure.

Generalized-Onset Seizures. Generalized-onset seizures start over wide areas of both sides of the brain. They are characterized by bilateral, synchronous epileptic discharges from the onset of the seizure. In most cases, the patient has impaired awareness for a few seconds to several minutes.

Tonic-Clonic Seizure. Tonic-clonic seizure (formerly called grand mal) is the most common generalized-onset motor seizure. During a tonic-clonic seizure, the patient loses consciousness and falls to the ground, if upright. The body stiffens (tonic phase) for 10 to 20 seconds and the extremities jerk (clonic phase) for another 30 to 40 seconds. Cyanosis, excessive salivation, tongue or cheek biting, and incontinence may occur during the seizure.

In the postictal phase, the patient usually has muscle soreness, feels tired, and may sleep for several hours. Some patients may not feel normal for several hours or days after a seizure. The patient has no memory of the seizure.

Other Generalized-Onset Motor Seizures. Other types of generalized-onset motor seizures include tonic and clonic. A tonic seizure involves a sudden onset of increased tone in the extensor muscles, contributing to sudden stiff movements.

Tonic seizures most often occur in sleep and affect both sides of the body. Patients will fall if they are standing when the seizure occurs. Tonic seizures usually last less than 20 seconds. The patient usually stays aware. Clonic seizures begin with loss of awareness and sudden loss of muscle tone, followed by rhythmic limb jerking that may or may not be symmetric. Clonic seizures are rare.

A generalized *atonic seizure* (or *drop attack*) involves either a tonic episode or a paroxysmal loss of muscle tone. It begins suddenly with the person falling to the ground. Seizures typically last less than 15 seconds. The person usually stays conscious and can resume normal activity immediately. Patients with atonic seizure are at great risk for head injury. They often have to wear protective helmets.

Generalized-Onset Nonmotor (Absence) Seizures. Absence seizure usually occurs only in children and rarely beyond adolescence. This type of seizure may stop altogether as the child matures, or it may evolve into another type of seizure. A *typical absence seizure* is marked by a brief staring spell that resembles daydreaming. It often goes unnoticed because it lasts less than 10 seconds. Usually the patient is unresponsive when spoken to during the seizure.[16] The EEG has a classic spike-wave pattern with 3 per second.

In *atypical absence seizure,* the staring spell is accompanied by other signs and symptoms, such as eye blinking or jerking movements of the lips. This type of seizure often lasts more than 10 seconds (as much as 30 seconds), with a gradual beginning and end. If the patient has existing cognitive impairment, it may be hard to tell seizure activity from usual behavior. Atypical absence seizures usually continue into adulthood. An EEG shows atypical spike-and-wave patterns, with fewer than 3 per second.

Other generalized-onset nonmotor seizures include myoclonic and eyelid myoclonia. The *myoclonic absence seizure* is characterized by rhythmic arm abduction (3 movements per second) leading to progressive arm elevation. It usually lasts 10 to 60 seconds. *Eyelid myoclonia* refers to jerking of the eyelids (at least 3 per second), often with upward eye deviation. It usually lasts less than 10 seconds.[16]

Focal-Onset Seizures. Focal-onset seizures (formerly called *partial* or *partial focal seizures*) are the other major class of seizures (Table 58.5). Focal seizures begin in 1 hemisphere of the brain in a specific region of the cortex, as shown by the EEG. They cause sensory, motor, cognitive, or emotional manifestations based on the function of the involved area of the brain. For example, if the discharging focus is in the medial aspect of the postcentral gyrus, the patient may have paresthesia in the leg on the side opposite the focus. This can help distinguish the type of seizure event.

Focal-onset seizures may be described by level of awareness (*aware* or *impaired awareness*). However, this is optional and applied only when awareness is known. *Focal awareness seizures* were called simple partial seizures. Patients are conscious and alert but have unusual feelings or sensations that can take many forms. They may have sudden and unexplainable feelings of joy, anger, sadness, or nausea. They may hear, smell, taste, see, or feel things that are not real.

In a *focal impaired awareness seizure* (previously called complex partial seizures), patients have a loss of consciousness or a change in their awareness, producing a dreamlike state. Their eyes are open. They make movements that may seem purposeful, but they cannot interact with observers. During a seizure, some people may do things that can be dangerous or embarrassing, such as walking into traffic or removing their clothes. They may continue an activity started before the seizure, such as counting coins or choosing items from a grocery shelf. After the seizure they do not remember the activity performed during the seizure. Seizures usually last 1 to 2 minutes. Patients may be tired or confused after the seizure and may not return to normal activity for hours.

The degree of awareness can be unspecified, and a seizure classified as *motor* or *nonmotor*. Motor activities include atonic (loss of tone), tonic (sustained stiffening), clonic (rhythmic jerking), myoclonic (irregular, brief jerking), or epileptic spasms (flexion or extension of arms with flexion of trunk). Some people show strange behavior, such as lip smacking or other repetitive, purposeless actions *(automatisms)*. With a focal nonmotor seizure, the patient can have emotional manifestations, such as fear or joy, strange feelings, or symptoms such as a racing heart, goose bumps, or waves of heat or cold.

Psychogenic Nonepileptic Seizures (PNES). Because of the close resemblance, psychogenic seizures may be misdiagnosed as seizure disorder. Proper diagnosis usually requires video-EEG monitoring to identify associated events. If the diagnosis of seizure disorder is excluded, history of emotional or physical abuse or a specific traumatic event often emerges. Some patients may have both psychogenic seizures and seizure disorder. Care provided by a specialist is essential. Once the diagnosis is made, the treatment of choice is psychological intervention.[17]

Complications

Physical. Status epilepticus (SE) is a state of continuous seizure activity or a condition in which seizures recur in rapid succession without return to consciousness between seizures. SE is defined as any seizure lasting longer than 5 minutes. The longer a seizure lasts, the less likely it is to stop without drug therapy.

SE is a neurologic emergency that can occur with any type of seizure. The highest incidence occurs in children and older adults. During repeated seizures, the brain uses more energy than can be supplied. As neurons become exhausted and cease to function, permanent brain damage may result. *Convulsive status epilepticus* (CSE) is the most common form. It occurs with prolonged or repeated tonic-clonic seizures. The goal of therapy is to rapidly end clinical and electrical seizure activity. Without effective, timely treatment, CSE can lead to fatal respiratory insufficiency, hypoxemia, dysrhythmias, hyperthermia, and systemic acidosis. The prognosis for CSE is related to its duration and the patient's age.[18]

The term *nonconvulsive status epilepticus* is used to described long or repeated focal impaired awareness seizures. Symptoms may be subtle, making it hard to tell recovery from seizure symptoms. No consistent time frame dictates when this state is considered an emergency. It depends on the length and frequency of seizure activity.

Refractory status epilepticus (RSE) is continuous seizure activity despite administration of first- and second-line therapy. RSE carries a high risk for mortality and neurologic damage. This highlights the need for careful, rapid escalation of treatment for CSE to avoid progression. *Super refractory SE* is a refractory condition that continues or recurs 24 hours or more after starting anesthetic treatment. It also includes cases in which seizure activity returns after withdrawal of anesthetic drugs or persists after 7 days of continuous general anesthesia. About 15% of patients who enter the hospital with SE become super-refractory.[19]

Subclinical seizures are a form of SE in which a sedated patient seizes but there are no external signs because of sedative use. For example, a patient under sedation for ventilatory support in the intensive care unit (ICU) could have a seizure without physical movements and we miss the seizure occurrence.

People with seizure disorder have a higher mortality rate than the general population. Severe injury, and even death, can result from trauma suffered during a seizure. Patients who lose consciousness during a seizure are at greatest risk. Other deaths are due to accidents during seizures, suicide, treatment-related death, death from an underlying disease, or sudden unexpected death in epilepsy (SUDEP).

SUDEP affects about 1 in 150 persons with uncontrolled seizures each year.[20] It is almost always associated with tonic-clonic seizures. Occurrence is higher in males, in persons taking multiple antiseizure drugs, and patients with poorly managed seizure activity. The exact cause is not known. It could be related to respiratory dysfunction, dysrhythmias, or cerebral depression. Specific teaching about medication adherence and disease awareness is critical for at-risk people.

Psychosocial. Perhaps the most common complication of seizure disorder is the effect on a patient's lifestyle. Patients may have ineffective coping methods because of psychosocial problems related to having seizure disorder. An increased incidence of depression occurs in people who have seizures that are difficult to control. Many antiseizure drugs have side effects that overlap with depressive symptoms.

Although attitudes have improved in recent years, a diagnosis of seizure disorder still carries a social stigma. Patients may be victims of discrimination in employment and educational opportunities. Transportation may be difficult if state law does not allow the person to drive. Screen patients often for depression. Encourage them to pursue available treatment options.

Diagnostic Studies

A diagnosis of seizure disorder may have many socioeconomic, physical, and psychologic consequences for the patient. Accurate diagnosis is crucial. The most useful diagnostic tool is an accurate, comprehensive description of seizures and the patient's health history (Table 58.6). Information from caregivers can be helpful.

The EEG is useful, but only if it shows abnormalities. Abnormal findings help determine the type of seizure and

---

TABLE 58.6 Interprofessional Care

Seizure Disorder

Diagnostic Assessment	Diagnostic Studies
History and Physical Examination	• CBC, urinalysis, electrolytes, creatinine, fasting blood glucose
• Birth and developmental history	• LP for CSF analysis
• Significant illnesses and injuries	• CT, MRI, MRA, MRS, PET scan
• Family history	• EEG
• Febrile seizures	
• Comprehensive neurologic assessment	**Management**
	• Antiseizure drugs (Table 58.8)
Seizure History	• Surgery
• Precipitating factors	• Vagal nerve stimulation
• Antecedent events	• Psychosocial counseling
• Seizure description (including onset, duration, frequency, postictal state)	• Physical therapy

pinpoint the seizure focus. Ideally, an EEG should be done within 24 hours of a suspected seizure. However, only a small number of patients with seizure disorder have abnormal EEG findings the first time the test is done. Repeated EEGs or continuous EEG monitoring may be needed to detect abnormalities. An EEG is not a definitive test because some patients without seizure disorder have abnormal patterns on their EEGs. Many patients with seizure disorder have normal EEG results between seizures. If abnormal discharges do not occur during the 30 to 40 minutes of sampling during EEG, the test may not show an abnormality. Magnetoencephalography (MEG) may be done with the EEG. This test has greater sensitivity in detecting small magnetic fields of neuron activity.

A complete blood count (CBC), serum chemistries, studies of liver and kidney function, and urinalysis should be done to rule out metabolic disorders. A CT scan or MRI should be done in any new-onset seizure to rule out a structural lesion. Cerebral angiography, single-photon emission computed tomography (SPECT), magnetic resonance spectroscopy (MRS), MRA, and positron emission tomography (PET) may be done in certain situations. If an MRI shows a spot or lesion but EEG results differ, MEG can determine if the brain waves are coming from the lesion. MEG can be helpful in a patient with prior brain surgery as EEG results may be affected by changes in the scalp and brain.

The International League Against Epilepsy has developed specific diagnostic criteria for each type of seizure, including conditions that resolve over time *(www.ilae.org)*. If a patient is diagnosed with seizure disorder, the seizure type must be correctly identified to determine the appropriate treatment.

Interprofessional Care

Most seizures do not require emergency medical care because they are self-limiting and rarely cause bodily injury. However, if SE or significant bodily harm occurs, or if the event is a first-time seizure, medical care should be sought immediately. Table 58.6 outlines the diagnostic studies and interprofessional care of seizure disorder. Table 58.7 summarizes emergency care of the patient with a tonic-clonic seizure, the seizure most likely to need emergency medical care.

Drug Therapy. The main treatment for seizure disorder is antiseizure drugs (Table 58.8). Because a cure is not possible, the goal of therapy is to prevent seizures with minimal drug side effects. Drugs generally stabilize nerve cell membranes and prevent spread of the epileptic discharge. Therapy should begin with a single drug based on the patient's age and weight and type, frequency, and cause of seizure. Dosage should be increased until seizures are under control or toxic side effects occur. Antiseizure drugs successfully control seizures for about 70% of patients.

✚ TABLE 58.7 Emergency Management

Tonic-Clonic Seizures

Etiology	Assessment Findings	Interventions
Drug-Related Processes • Ingestion, inhalation • Overdose • Withdrawal of alcohol, opioids, antiseizure drugs **Head Trauma** • Cerebral contusion • Epidural hematoma • Intracranial hematoma • Subdural hematoma • Traumatic birth injury • Idiopathic **Infectious Processes** • Encephalitis • Meningitis • Sepsis **Intracranial Events** • Brain tumor • Hypertensive crisis • Increased ICP due to clogged shunt • Stroke • Subarachnoid hemorrhage **Medical Disorders** • Heart, liver, lung, or kidney disease • Systemic lupus erythematosus **Metabolic Imbalances** • Fluid and electrolyte imbalance • Hypoglycemia **Other** • Cardiac arrest • High fever • Psychiatric disorders	**Aural Phase** • Bowel and bladder incontinence • Diaphoresis • Loss of consciousness • Pallor, flushing, or cyanosis • Peculiar sensations that precede seizure • Tachycardia • Warm skin **Tonic Phase** • Continuous muscle contractions **Hypertonic Phase** • Extreme muscular rigidity lasting 5–15 sec **Clonic Phase** • Rigidity and relaxation alternating in rapid succession **Postictal Phase** • Altered level of consciousness, lethargy • Confusion and headache • Repeated tonic-clonic seizures for several min	**Initial** • Ensure patent airway. • Protect patient from injury during seizure. *Do not restrain.* Pad side rails. • Remove or loosen tight clothing. • Establish IV access. • Stay with patient until seizure has passed. • Anticipate giving phenobarbital, phenytoin (Dilantin), benzodiazepines (e.g., diazepam [Valium], midazolam [Versed], lorazepam [Ativan]) to try to stop seizures. • Suction as needed. • Assist ventilations if patient does not breathe spontaneously after seizure. • Anticipate need for intubation if gag reflex absent. **Ongoing Monitoring** • Monitor vital signs, level of consciousness, O_2 saturation, Glasgow Coma Scale results, pupil size and reactivity. • Reassure and orient patient after seizure. • Never force an airway between patient's clenched teeth. • Give IV dextrose for hypoglycemia.

If seizure control is not achieved with a single drug, dosage or timing of administration may be changed or a second drug may be added. About one third of patients need a combination regimen for enough control. Patients should discuss new treatments with their HCPs to provide the best control with the least amount of medication.

The therapeutic range for each drug is the serum level above which most patients have toxic side effects and below which most continue to have seizures. Therapeutic drug ranges are only guides for therapy. If the patient's seizures are well controlled with a subtherapeutic level, the drug dosage does not have to be increased. Likewise, if a drug level is above the therapeutic range and the patient has good seizure control without toxic side effects, the drug dosage does not have to be decreased. Serum drug levels are monitored if seizures continue to occur, frequency increases, or drug adherence is questioned. Because they have a large therapeutic range, many newer drugs do not require drug-level monitoring.

The main drugs to treat tonic-clonic and focal-onset seizures are phenytoin (Dilantin), carbamazepine (Tegretol), phenobarbital, and divalproex. The drugs used most often to treat generalized-onset nonmotor and myoclonic seizures include ethosuximide (Zarontin), divalproex, and clonazepam (Klonopin). Table 58.8 lists other drugs used for seizure treatment. Some drugs are effective for multiple seizure types. Pregabalin (Lyrica) is used as an additional treatment for focal aware or impaired awareness seizures not successfully controlled with 1 medication.

💊 **DRUG ALERT** Carbamazepine (Tegretol)
• Do not take with grapefruit juice.
• Teach patient to report visual changes (e.g., blurry or double vision).
• Abrupt withdrawal after long-term use may cause seizures.

Treatment of SE requires a rapid-acting IV antiseizure drug. The drugs most often used are lorazepam (Ativan) and diazepam (Valium). Because these are short-acting drugs, their administration is followed with long-acting drugs, such as phenytoin or phenobarbital.

Because many antiseizure drugs (e.g., phenytoin, phenobarbital, ethosuximide, lamotrigine, topiramate) have a long half-life, they can be given once or twice a day. This simplifies the drug plan and increases the patient's adherence because the drug does not have to be taken at work or school. Unnecessary combination therapy is avoided whenever possible. Medications

should be reviewed routinely and the least effective medication discontinued by tapering.

💊 **DRUG ALERT** Antiseizure Drugs
• Abrupt withdrawal after long-term use may cause seizures.
• If weaning is to occur, the patient must be seizure free for a prolonged period (e.g., 2 to 5 yr) and have a normal neurologic examination and EEG.

Side effects of antiseizure drugs involve the CNS. They include diplopia, drowsiness, ataxia, and mental slowness. Neurologic assessment for dose-related toxicity involves testing the eyes for nystagmus and evaluating hand and gait coordination, cognitive functioning, and general alertness.

As a nurse, you need to be knowledgeable about drug side effects, so you can teach patients and start proper treatment. For example, common side effects of phenytoin are gingival hyperplasia (excess growth of gingival tissue) and hirsutism, especially in young adults. Good dental hygiene, including regular tooth brushing and flossing, can decrease gingival hyperplasia. If gingival hyperplasia is extensive, the hyperplastic tissue may be surgically removed (gingivectomy) and phenytoin replaced with another antiseizure drug.

Medication nonadherence can be a problem in people with seizure disorder, often due to undesirable side effects. Take measures to increase adherence to the prescribed drug plan. If HCPs are aware of nonadherence, they can work with the patient to find an acceptable drug plan. For example, using pregabalin as an adjunct medication in some cases may allow a decreased dose of the primary antiseizure drug and thus decrease side effects.

👥 **Gerontologic Considerations: Drug Therapy for Seizure Disorder**

Many older adults have a first single seizure, then do not have another seizure. To be considered for antiseizure drug therapy, older adults should have recurrent seizures, an obvious structural predisposition for seizures, or onset of seizure disorder presenting as SE. Older adults are more responsive to antiseizure drugs than younger adults, but they also are more likely to have side effects at lower serum drug concentrations.

Age-related changes in liver enzymes decrease the liver's ability to metabolize drugs. Because the liver metabolizes phenytoin, it should not be used in older patients with liver problems. The potential effects on cognitive function make phenobarbital, carbamazepine, and primidone less desirable for older adults. Carbamazepine, phenytoin, phenobarbital, or primidone can increase the risk for osteomalacia, osteopenia, and osteoporosis. Several newer antiseizure drugs offer greater treatment benefit to older adults. Compared with older drugs, gabapentin, lamotrigine, oxcarbazepine (Trileptal), and levetiracetam may be safer, have fewer effects on cognitive function, and have fewer interactions with other drugs.

Surgical Therapy. Despite availability of newer drugs with fewer side effects, no solution has been found for *medically refractory epilepsy* (not responsive to drug therapy). About 30% of patients do not respond to antiseizure drugs. For people with a defined site of seizure origin (epileptogenic zone), research shows the benefit of surgical resection of that focal area over continued use of different antiseizure drugs. About 80% are seizure free 5 years after surgery, with 72% still seizure free at 10 years.

Not all patients benefit from surgery. An extensive preoperative evaluation is important, including continuous EEG monitoring and other tests to ensure precise localization of the focal

---

TABLE 58.8 Drug Therapy

Seizure Disorder

• brivaracetam (Briviact)	• levetiracetam (Keppra)
• carbamazepine (Tegretol)	• lorazepam (Ativan)
• clonazepam (Klonopin)	• oxcarbazepine (Trileptal)
• daclizumab (Zinbryta)	• perampanel (Fycompa)
• diazepam (Diastat)	• phenytoin (Dilantin)
• divalproex (Depakote)	• pregabalin (Lyrica)
• eslicarbazepine (Aptiom)	• primidone (Mysoline)
• ethosuximide (Zarontin)	• tiagabine (Gabitril)
• ezogabine (Potiga)	• topiramate (Topamax)
• felbamate (Felbatol)	• valproic acid (Depakene)
• gabapentin (Neurontin)	• vigabatrin (Sabril)
• lacosamide (Vimpat)	• zonisamide (Zonegran)
• lamotrigine (Lamictal)	

point. Surgical candidates must meet 3 requirements: (1) a confirmed diagnosis of seizure disorder, (2) an adequate trial with drug therapy without satisfactory results, and (3) a defined electroclinical syndrome (type of seizure disorder).

Other Therapies. *Vagal nerve stimulation* (VNS), a form of neuromodulation, is used as an adjunct to drugs when an accessible focal point cannot be identified for surgical removal. The exact mechanism of action is unknown. It may increase blood flow to specific brain areas. It could raise levels of neurotransmitters important to seizure control and change EEG patterns during a seizure. In VNS, a surgically implanted electrode in the neck is programmed to deliver electrical impulses to the vagus nerve, usually on the left side. The patient activates the electrode with a magnet when they sense a seizure is imminent. Newer devices respond to an increasing heart rate, which is often associated with seizures. Adverse effects include coughing, hoarseness, dyspnea, and tingling in the neck. Battery life is 5 to 10 years, and surgical replacement is needed. Benefits of VNS can be seen within 24 months after implantation. Contraindications include a history of dysrhythmias or sleep apnea.

Responsive neurostimulation (Neuropace RNS System) is similar to a cardiac pacemaker. It continually monitors the EEG to detect abnormalities, then responds to seizure activity by delivering electrical stimulation to a precise location. The device is placed under the skin, outside the skull, with connections to electrodes over the area of seizure focus. The HCP uses a programmable wand to download information about seizure activity. This is used to assess treatment efficacy and guide care. This modality is an option for persons who are not surgical candidates or have multiple areas of seizure focus.

A *ketogenic diet* is a special high-fat, low-carbohydrate diet that helps control seizures in some people. A person on this diet produces ketones that pass into the brain, where they replace glucose as an energy source. Meals are carefully planned to restrict the amount of protein and carbohydrate in the diet. Patients on this diet who use anticoagulants need close monitoring for bleeding. Although HCPs are more likely to recommend the diet for children than adults, the diet can work equally well in both age-groups. Most people must continue their use of antiseizure medication but may take smaller doses or fewer medications. Seizures may worsen if the diet is stopped abruptly. Long-term effects of the diet are not clear.

Biofeedback to control seizures is aimed at teaching the patient to maintain a certain brain wave frequency that is refractory to seizure activity. Further trials are needed to assess the effectiveness of biofeedback for seizure control.

❖ NURSING MANAGEMENT: SEIZURE DISORDER

◆ Nursing Assessment

Subjective and objective data to obtain from a patient with seizure disorder are outlined in Table 58.9. Obtain data related to a specific seizure episode from a witness.

TABLE 58.9 Nursing Assessment
Seizure Disorder

Subjective Data

Important Health Information

Past health history: Seizures, birth defects or injuries, anoxic episodes. CNS trauma, tumors, or infections. Stroke, metabolic disorders, alcohol use, exposure to metals and carbon monoxide, hepatic or renal failure, fever, pregnancy, systemic lupus erythematosus

Medications: Adherence to antiseizure medication plan. Barbiturate or alcohol withdrawal. Use and overdose of cocaine, amphetamines, lidocaine, theophylline, penicillin, lithium, phenothiazines, tricyclic antidepressants, benzodiazepines

Functional Health Patterns

Health perception–health management: Positive family history
Cognitive-perceptual: Headaches, aura, mood or behavioral changes before seizure. Mentation changes. Abdominal pain, muscle pain (postictal)
Self-perception–self-concept: Anxiety, depression. Loss of self-esteem, social isolation
Sexuality-reproductive: Decreased sexual drive, erectile dysfunction. Increased sexual drive (postictal)

Objective Data

General

Precipitating factors, including severe metabolic acidosis or alkalosis, hyperkalemia, hypoglycemia, dehydration, or water intoxication

Integumentary

Bitten tongue, soft tissue damage, cyanosis, diaphoresis (postictal)

Respiratory

Abnormal respiratory rate, rhythm, or depth. Apnea (ictal). Absent or abnormal breath sounds, possible airway occlusion

Cardiovascular

Hypertension, tachycardia or bradycardia (ictal)

Gastrointestinal

Bowel incontinence, excessive salivation

Urinary

Incontinence

Neurologic

Generalized Onset

Tonic-clonic: Loss of consciousness, muscle tightening, then jerking. Dilated pupils. Hyperventilation, then apnea. Postictal somnolence
Absence: Altered consciousness (5–30 sec), minor facial motor activity

Focal Onset

Aware: Aura. Focal sensory, motor, cognitive, or emotional phenomena (focal motor)
Impaired awareness: Altered consciousness with inappropriate behaviors, automatisms, amnesia of event

Musculoskeletal

Weakness, paralysis, ataxia (postictal)

Possible Diagnostic Findings

Positive toxicology screen or blood alcohol level. Altered serum electrolytes, acidosis or alkalosis, very low blood glucose, ↑ blood urea nitrogen or serum creatinine, abnormal liver function tests, ammonia; abnormal CT scan or MRI of head, abnormal findings from LP. Abnormal discharges on EEG

◆ Nursing Diagnoses

Nursing diagnoses for the patient with seizure disorder may include:

- Impaired breathing
- Difficulty coping
- Risk for fall-related injury

Additional information on nursing diagnoses and interventions for the patient with seizure disorder is presented in eNursing Care Plan 58.2 (available on the website for this chapter).

◆ Planning

The overall goals are that the patient with seizure disorder will (1) be free from injury during a seizure, (2) have optimal mental and physical functioning while taking antiseizure drugs, and (3) have satisfactory psychosocial functioning.

◆ Nursing Implementation

◆ **Health Promotion.** Following general safety measures (e.g., wearing helmets in situations involving risk for head injury) can prevent some seizure disorders. Improved perinatal care has reduced fetal trauma and hypoxia and thus brain damage leading to seizure disorder.

The patient with seizure disorder should practice good general health habits (e.g., maintain proper diet, get adequate rest, exercise). Help the patient identify events or situations that cause seizures and provide suggestions for avoiding them or handling them better. Teach the patient to avoid excess alcohol use, fatigue, and loss of sleep. Help the patient handle stress constructively.

◆ **Acute Care.** Nursing care for a hospitalized patient with seizure disorder or a patient who has had seizures due to other factors involves observation and treatment of the seizure, patient and caregiver teaching, and psychosocial intervention.

? CHECK YOUR PRACTICE

You are making your morning rounds and go to check your 22-yr-old female patient, who was admitted the night before with increased seizure activity. When you go to her room, her roommate is yelling, "Help, help!" You find the patient is on the floor jerking and stiffening and not responding to you.

- What should you do?

When a seizure occurs, carefully observe and record details of the event because the diagnosis and subsequent treatment often rest on the seizure description. What events preceded the seizure? When did the seizure occur? How long did each phase (aural [if any], ictal, postictal) last? What occurred during each phase?

All subjective data (usually the only type of data in the aural phase) and objective data are important. Note the exact onset of the seizure (which body part was affected first and how); the course and nature of the seizure activity (loss of consciousness, tongue biting, automatisms, stiffening, jerking, total lack of muscle tone); body parts involved and their sequence of involvement; and autonomic signs, such as dilated pupils, excessive salivation, altered breathing, cyanosis, flushing, diaphoresis, or incontinence. Assessment of the postictal period should include a detailed description of the level of consciousness, vital signs, pupil size and position of the eyes, memory loss, muscle soreness, speech disorders (aphasia, dysarthria), weakness or paralysis, sleep period, and the duration of each sign or symptom.

⚠ SAFETY ALERT Seizure

During a seizure, you should:

- Maintain a patent airway for the patient.
- Protect the patient's head, turn the patient to the side, loosen constrictive clothing, ease patient to the floor (if seated).
- Do not restrain the patient.
- Do not place any objects in the patient's mouth

After the seizure, the patient may need repositioning (to open and maintain the airway), suctioning, and O_2. A seizure can be frightening for the patient and others who witnessed it. Assess their level of understanding and provide information about how and why the event occurred. This is an excellent chance for you to dismiss many common misconceptions about seizures.

▦ NURSING MANAGEMENT
Caring for the Patient With Seizure Disorder

Role of the RN

- Teach patient about factors that increase risk for seizures.
- Teach patient about prescribed antiseizure medications, including drug plan, side effects, and monitoring of drug levels.
- Assess and record details of seizure events, including events preceding the seizure; length of each phase of the seizure; course and nature of seizure activity; and level of consciousness, vital signs, and activity during the postictal period.
- Assess airway patency, and position patient to maintain airway during and after seizures.
- Give IV antiseizure medications to the patient with SE.
- Give oral antiseizure medications as scheduled.
- Make appropriate referrals to community agencies to help the patient with the financial impact of seizure disorder, work training, employment, and living arrangements.
- Teach caregivers about management of seizures and SE.
- In the ambulatory and home care setting, evaluate patient self-management of medications and lifestyle.
- Oversee UAP:
  - Place suction equipment, bag-valve-mask, and O_2 at the patient's bedside.
  - Remove potentially harmful objects from the bedside and pad side rails.
  - Immediately report any seizure activity to the RN.
  - Obtain vital signs during the postictal period.

Collaborate With Other Team Members
Respiratory Therapist

- Assess airway patency and suction as needed.
- Assist ventilations if patient does not breathe spontaneously after seizure.
- Assist with intubation if gag reflex absent.

Occupational Therapist

- Help patient with increasing self-care measures, including eating and dressing.

Social Worker

- Help patient identify and obtain needed resources.
- Offer counseling to develop positive coping skills.

◆ **Ambulatory Care.** Prevention of recurring seizures is the major goal of treatment. Help the patient understand that for treatment to be effective, drugs must be taken regularly and consistently. Review details of the drug plan and what to do if a dose is missed. Usually the dose is made up if the omission is remembered within 24 hours. Caution the patient not to adjust drug dosages without HCP guidance because this can increase seizure frequency and cause SE. Encourage the patient to report any medication side effects and keep regular appointments with the HCP.

TABLE 58.10 Patient & Caregiver Teaching

Seizure Disorder

Include the following information in the teaching plan for the patient with seizure disorder:

1. Take antiseizure medications as prescribed. Report all drug side effects to the HCP.
2. When needed, blood is drawn to ensure therapeutic drug levels. Schedule regular visits with the HCP to discuss treatment options.
3. Use nondrug techniques, such as relaxation therapy, to try to reduce the number of seizures.
4. Be aware of community and online resources for education and help with tracking and explaining seizure activity.
5. Wear a medical alert bracelet or necklace and carry an identification card.
6. Avoid excess alcohol use, fatigue, and loss of sleep.
7. Eat regular meals and snacks in between if feeling shaky, faint, or hungry.
8. Be knowledgeable as a woman of childbearing age about antiseizure medications and contraceptive use.

Caregivers should receive the following information:

Focal-Onset Seizures

1. Stay calm. Guide patient to safety to prevent injury but do not restrain.
2. Observe for asymmetry of activity and focus on specific actions, such as lip smacking and abnormal movements.
3. Assess patient's level of consciousness and ability to converse and respond appropriately.
4. Note the time the seizure started and stopped. Take note of the time of return to baseline.
5. Provide respect and explanation of occurrence.

Generalized-Onset Tonic-Clonic Seizures

1. When seizure occurs outside the hospital setting, activate ERS if (1) the duration is greater than 5 minutes; (2) events recur without the patient recovering to baseline; (3) the patient is unable to establish a normal breathing pattern, is injured or pregnant; or (4) you do not know if this is a first-time seizure event.
2. Maintain patient safety. Lower the patient to the floor or bed, remove glasses if worn, and loosen restrictive clothing.
3. Do not place anything in the patient's mouth. Patient's teeth/dentures may be damaged, and caregiver may be bitten.
4. Position patient on side (if possible) to improve the patient's ability to release oral secretions.
5. Note the time the seizure started and stopped. Take note of the time of return to baseline.
6. Assess for any injury and lingering motor weakness.

You have a vital role in teaching the patient and caregiver. Review the guidelines for teaching shown in Table 58.10. Teach caregivers the emergency management of tonic-clonic seizures (Table 58.7). Remind them it is not necessary to call an ambulance or send a person to the hospital after a single seizure unless the seizure is prolonged, another seizure immediately follows, extensive injury has occurred, or it is unknown if this was a first-time seizure.

Patients with seizure disorder may have concerns or fears related to recurrent seizures, incontinence, or loss of self-control. Support patients through teaching and by helping them use effective coping mechanisms.

Perhaps the greatest challenge for a patient with seizure disorder is adjusting to the limitations imposed by the illness. Discrimination in employment is a serious problem facing the person with seizure disorder. For issues relating to job discrimination, refer patients to the state department of vocational rehabilitation or the U.S. Equal Employment Opportunity Commission (EEOC).

Help the patient find appropriate resources. If you think associating with others who have seizure disorder would be beneficial, refer the patient to the local chapter of the Epilepsy Foundation (EF). This volunteer agency offers varied services to patients with a seizure disorder (www.epilepsy.com). Refer the patient who is an eligible veteran to a Department of Veterans Affairs medical center that provides comprehensive care. If intensive psychologic counseling is needed, refer the patient to a community mental health center.

Social workers and welfare agencies can help with financial implications and living arrangements. State agencies specializing in vocational rehabilitation services can provide vocational assessment, counseling, and funding for training. They can help with job placement for patients whose seizures are not well controlled. They offer financial assistance for transportation and medical costs related to vocational rehabilitation or job maintenance.

Driving laws for patients who have had a seizure vary from state to state. For example, some states require a 3-month seizure-free period before issuing or reissuing a driver's license. Others require up to 1 year. The EF provides current information on driving laws for each state.

Tell the patient that medical alert bracelets, necklaces, and identification cards are available through the EF, local pharmacies, or companies specializing in identification devices (e.g., Medic Alert). Using medical identification is optional. Some patients have found them beneficial, but others do not want to be identified as having seizure disorder.

Encourage the patient to learn more about seizures through self-education. The EF provides informational pamphlets, has an extensive website, and may offer support groups. Many agencies that offer services to patients with seizure disorder offer teaching aids and support.

◆ Evaluation

Expected outcomes are that the patient with seizure disorder will

- Have a breathing pattern adequate to meet O_2 needs
- Have no seizure-related injury
- Express acceptance of seizure disorder by adhering to treatment plan

RESTLESS LEGS SYNDROME

Etiology and Pathophysiology

Restless legs syndrome (RLS) *(Willis-Ekbom disease)* is a relatively common sleep and movement disorder with unpleasant sensory (paresthesia) and motor abnormalities of 1 or both legs. About 8% of the U.S. population has RLS.[21] A small number have severe symptoms that affect their quality of life and require medication for treatment. RLS is more common in older adults and in women.

There are 2 distinct types of RLS: primary (idiopathic) and secondary. Most people have primary RLS. Secondary RLS can occur with metabolic problems associated with iron deficiency, renal disease and hemodialysis, and neuropathy. Sleep deprivation, sleep apnea, pregnancy (especially third trimester), and use of certain medications (e.g., antiemetics, antidepressants that increase serotonin), can cause or worsen symptoms.

We do not know the exact pathophysiology of primary RLS. We think it is related to a dysfunction in the brain's basal ganglia circuits that use the neurotransmitter dopamine (DA), which controls movements. In RLS, this dysfunction causes the urge to move the legs. RLS has a genetic link. Those with primary RLS often report a positive family history, with symptoms that start before age 40.[21]

Clinical Manifestations

The severity of RLS sensory symptoms ranges from infrequent minor discomfort (numbness, tingling, "pins and needles" sensation) to severe pain. Sensory symptoms often appear first. Some patients compare the sensations to bugs creeping or crawling on the legs. The leg pain is localized within the calf muscles. Patients can have pain in the upper extremities and trunk. The discomfort occurs when the patient is inactive. It is most common in the evening or at night.

Pain at night can disrupt sleep. Physical activity, such as walking, stretching, rocking, or kicking, often relieves the pain. In the most severe cases, patients sleep only a few hours at night. This causes daytime fatigue and disrupts the daily routine. Motor problems associated with RLS include voluntary restlessness and stereotyped, periodic, involuntary movements. The involuntary movements usually occur during sleep. Fatigue further worsens symptoms. RLS worsens over time. Symptoms become more frequent and last longer.

Diagnostic Studies

RLS is diagnosed largely based on the patient's history or the report of the bed partner about nighttime activities. Diagnosis of RLS can be made when the patient meets all 5 specific criteria: (1) overwhelming urge to move the legs, often accompanied by uncomfortable or unpleasant sensations in the legs; (2) urge to move the legs worsens during rest or inactivity; (3) urge to move the legs is partially or totally relieved by movement, as long as the activity continues; (4) urge to move the legs becomes worse in the evening or night; and (5) these features are not due to another medical or behavioral condition.[21]

The patient may have polysomnography studies during sleep to distinguish RLS from other clinical conditions that can disturb sleep (e.g., sleep apnea). While periodic leg movements in sleep can support the diagnosis of RLS, they are not exclusive to RLS. Blood tests, such as a CBC, serum ferritin, and renal function tests (e.g., serum creatinine), may help exclude secondary causes of RLS. A patient with diabetes may have paresthesia caused by peripheral neuropathy related to diabetes or RLS.

❖ Interprofessional and Nursing Care

The goal of interprofessional management is to reduce patient discomfort and distress and improve sleep quality. When RLS is due to renal failure or iron deficiency, treating these conditions may decrease symptoms. Lifestyle changes may help persons with mild to moderate RLS. For example, decreasing the use of alcohol or tobacco, maintaining regular sleep habits, exercising, and massaging and stretching the legs may be helpful. The patient should avoid antihistamine-containing medications (e.g., diphenhydramine).

If nondrug measures fail, drug therapy is an option. No single medication effectively manages RLS for all patients. The main drugs used to treat RLS aim to increase the amount of DA in the brain. They include DA precursors (e.g., carbidopa/levodopa) and DA agonists (e.g., ropinirole [Requip], pramipexole [Mirapex], rotigotine [Neupro]). The antiseizure drug gabapentin enacarbil (Horizant) may decrease the sensory sensations and nerve pain. The patient with iron-deficiency anemia may need to start iron supplementation.

Other drugs may relieve some symptoms of RLS. Very low doses of opioids (e.g., oxycodone) may help patients with severe symptoms who do not respond to other drug therapies. The main side effect of opioids is constipation, so patients may need to take a stool softener or laxative. Clonidine (Catapres) and propranolol (Inderal) are effective in some patients. Benzodiazepines (e.g., lorazepam [Ativan]) may help patients obtain more restful sleep. However, they are last-line treatments due to their side effects.[21]

Using a Relaxis device may help some patients. It produces vibration, providing counter stimulation that competes with and decreases RLS sensations. The patient places the legs on the Relaxis pad. It provides 30 minutes of uninterrupted vibration after being activated, then it slowly winds down over another 5 minutes to complete a 35-minute therapy cycle. If needed, it may be restarted one more time. The patient chooses the vibration intensity based on symptoms.

DEGENERATIVE NEUROLOGIC DISORDERS

MULTIPLE SCLEROSIS

Multiple sclerosis (MS) is a chronic, progressive, degenerative disorder of the CNS characterized by disseminated demyelination of nerve fibers of the brain and spinal cord. MS can affect people of any age. The onset of MS is usually between 20 and 50 years of age, with symptoms first appearing at an average of 30 to 35 years of age. People diagnosed at 50 years of age or older generally have more progressive disease. MS affects women 2 to 3 times more often than men. Around 400,000 people in the United States have MS, with 10,000 new cases diagnosed annually.[22]

MS is more prevalent in temperate climates (between 45 and 65 degrees of latitude), such as those found in the northern United States, Canada, and Europe. People who are born in a high-risk area and move to a low-risk area before age 15 assume the risk of their new home. We suspect exposure to some environmental agent before puberty may cause a person to develop MS later in life. MS is less common in Hispanics, Asians, and people of African descent. It rarely occurs in some ethnic groups, including Alaskan Natives and Aborigines.

Etiology and Pathophysiology

While we do not know the cause of MS, it is unlikely due to a single cause. We think MS develops in a genetically susceptible person after an environmental exposure, such as an infection. The inherited susceptibility to MS likely involves multiple genes. Having a first-degree relative with MS increases a person's risk for developing the disease. We have found common genetic factors in families with more than 1 affected member.[23]

Possible precipitating factors include infection, smoking, physical injury, emotional stress, excessive fatigue, pregnancy, and a poor state of health. The role of factors such as exposure to pathogens is controversial. We have investigated more than a dozen viruses and bacteria but have not proven any cause MS.

MS is marked by 3 processes: chronic inflammation, demyelination, and gliosis in the CNS. The primary condition is an autoimmune process driven by activated T cells. An unknown trigger in a genetically susceptible person may start this process.

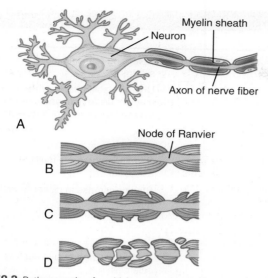

FIG. 58.2 Pathogenesis of multiple sclerosis. **A,** Normal nerve cell with myelin sheath. **B,** Normal axon. **C,** Myelin breakdown. **D,** Myelin totally disrupted; axon not functioning.

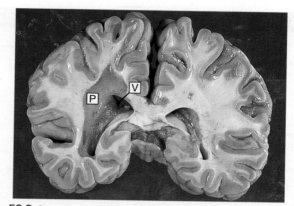

FIG. 58.3 Chronic multiple sclerosis. Demyelination plaque *(P)* at gray-white junction and adjacent partially remyelinated shadow plaque *(V)*. (From Stevens A, Lowe J: *Pathology: Illustrated review in colour,* ed 2, London, 2000, Mosby.)

The activated T cells in the systemic circulation go to the CNS and disrupt the blood-brain barrier. This may be the first event in the development of MS. Subsequent antigen-antibody reaction within the CNS activates the inflammatory response and leads to axon demyelination.

Attacks on the myelin sheaths of the neurons in the brain and spinal cord first cause damage to the myelin sheath (Fig. 58.2, *A* to *C*). The nerve fiber is not affected. Transmission of nerve impulses still occurs, but it is slowed. The patient may have a noticeable impairment of function (e.g., weakness). However, myelin can still regenerate. When it does, symptoms disappear. At that point, the patient has a remission.

As inflammation continues, nearby oligodendrocytes are affected. Myelin loses the ability to regenerate. Eventually damage occurs to the underlying axon. Nerve impulse transmission is disrupted, and nerve function is lost permanently (Fig. 58.2, *D*). As inflammation subsides, glial scar tissue replaces damaged tissue. This leads to the formation of hard, rigid plaques (Fig. 58.3). These plaques are found throughout the white matter of the CNS.

The average life expectancy after the onset of symptoms is more than 25 years. Death usually occurs due to infectious complications of immobility (e.g., pneumonia) or because of an unrelated disease.

Clinical Manifestations

The onset of MS is often slow and gradual. Vague symptoms occur periodically over months or years. Because they do not prompt the patient to seek medical attention, MS may not be diagnosed until long after the first symptom. For some patients, MS is marked by rapid, progressive deterioration. Others have remissions and exacerbations. With repeated exacerbations, the overall trend is progressive deterioration in neurologic function.

Because changes from MS have a spotty distribution in the CNS, symptoms vary with each patient based on the areas of the CNS involved. Some patients have severe, long-lasting symptoms early in the course of the disease. Others have only occasional, mild symptoms for several years after onset. A classification scheme of MS, with 4 primary patterns, has been developed based on the clinical course (Table 58.11).

The first symptom of MS may be blurred or double vision, red-green color distortion, or even blindness in 1 eye (Fig. 58.4). Many patients describe extremity muscle weakness and problems with coordination and balance. Those symptoms may affect walking or standing. MS can cause partial or complete paralysis in the worst cases. Most have numbness and tingling. *Lhermitte's sign* is a temporary sensory symptom described as an electric shock going down the spine or into the limbs with neck flexion. Some patients report pain, especially in the low thoracic and abdominal regions. Other frequent problems include speech impairments, hearing loss, tremors, and dizziness. Possible cerebellar signs include nystagmus, ataxia, dysarthria, and dysphagia. Many patients have severe, even disabling fatigue. This is worsened by heat, humidity, deconditioning, and medication side effects.

A rigid plaque is in areas of the CNS that control elimination can bowel and bladder function. Bowel problems usually involve constipation. Urinary problems vary. A common problem in patients with MS is a *spastic* (uninhibited) bladder. The bladder has a small capacity for urine, and its contractions are unchecked. The result is urinary urgency and frequency, often with dribbling or incontinence.

A *flaccid* (hypotonic) bladder occurs with a lesion in the reflex arc controlling bladder function. The patient generally has urinary retention because there is no sensation or desire to void, no pressure, and no pain. Urgency and frequency may be present. A combination of spastic and flaccid bladder can occur. Urinary problems can be diagnosed with urodynamic studies.

Sexual problems occur in many people with MS. Physiologic erectile dysfunction may result from spinal cord involvement in men. Women may have decreased desire for sexual activity (libido), difficulty with orgasm, painful intercourse, and decreased vaginal lubrication. Decreased sensation can prevent a normal sexual response in men and women. The emotional effects of chronic illness and the loss of self-esteem contribute to loss of sexual response. Some women with MS have remission or an improvement in their symptoms during pregnancy. Hormonal changes associated with pregnancy appear to affect the immune system.

About half of people with MS have problems with cognitive function. Most involve problems with short-term memory, attention, information processing, planning, visual perception, and word finding. General intellect stays unchanged and

TABLE 58.11 Patterns of Multiple Sclerosis

Category	Characteristics
Relapsing-remitting	• Clearly defined attacks of worsening neurologic function *(relapses)* with partial or complete recovery *(remission)*. • 85% of people first diagnosed with this type of MS.
Primary-Progressive	• Steadily worsening neurologic function from the beginning with minor improvements but no distinct relapses or remissions. • 10% of people first diagnosed with this type of MS.
Secondary-progressive	• A relapsing-remitting initial course, followed by progression with or without occasional relapses, minor remissions, and plateaus. • New treatments may slow progression. • Most people initially diagnosed with relapsing-remitting MS eventually transition to this type.
Progressive-relapsing	• Progressive disease from onset, with clear acute relapses, with or without full recovery. Periods between relapses are characterized by continuing progression. • 5% of people with MS.

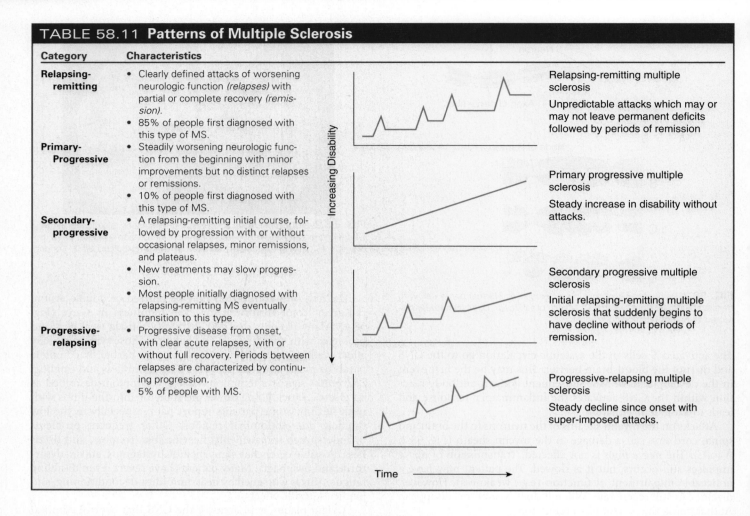

Relapsing-remitting multiple sclerosis

Unpredictable attacks which may or may not leave permanent deficits followed by periods of remission

Primary progressive multiple sclerosis

Steady increase in disability without attacks.

Secondary progressive multiple sclerosis

Initial relapsing-remitting multiple sclerosis that suddenly begins to have decline without periods of remission.

Progressive-relapsing multiple sclerosis

Steady decline since onset with super-imposed attacks.

Increasing Disability → *Time* →

---

intact. This includes long-term memory, conversational skills, and reading comprehension. Symptoms can be mild and thus easily overlooked. However, about 5% to 10% of patients with MS have such severe cognitive changes that they significantly impair the person's ability to perform activities of daily living (ADLs). Most of the time, cognitive difficulties occur later in the course of the disease. However, they can occur early and sometimes are present at the onset of MS.

People with MS may have emotional changes, such as anger, depression, or euphoria. Physical and emotional trauma, fatigue, and infection may worsen or trigger signs and symptoms.

Diagnostic Studies

Because there is no definitive diagnostic test for MS, the history, manifestations, and results of certain diagnostic tests are important (Table 58.12). Imaging in MS is vital. An MRI of the brain and spinal cord may show plaques, inflammation, atrophy, and tissue breakdown and destruction. CSF analysis may show an increase in immunoglobulin G and the presence of oligoclonal banding.[24] Evoked potential responses are often delayed because of decreased nerve conduction from the eye and ear to the brain.

To be diagnosed with MS, the patient must have (1) evidence of at least 2 inflammatory demyelinating lesions in at least 2 different locations within the CNS, (2) damage or an attack occurring at different times (usually 1 month or more apart), and (3) all other possible diagnoses ruled out. If evidence exists for only 1 lesion, or only 1 clinical attack has occurred, the HCP will monitor the patient for another attack or for an attack at a different site in the CNS.

Interprofessional Care

Drug Therapy. Because no cure currently exists for MS, interprofessional care is aimed at treating the disease process and providing symptomatic relief (Table 58.12). No cases of MS are alike, so we tailor therapy to the disease pattern and symptoms of each patient (Table 58.13). Disease-modifying therapy has been found to be more effective when started early in the course of MS. Delays in treatment are linked to poor outcomes.

Treatment of MS begins with use of immunomodulator drugs to modify disease progression and prevent relapses. These drugs include (1) interferon β-1a (Rebif, Plegridy, Avonex), (2) interferon β-1b (Betaseron, Extavia), and (3) glatiramer acetate (Copaxone, Glatopa).

> 💊 **DRUG ALERT** β-Interferon
>
> • Rotate injection sites with each dose.
> • Assess for depression and suicidal ideation.
> • Teach patient to wear sunscreen and protective clothing when exposed to sun.
> • Tell the patient that flu-like symptoms are common after starting therapy.

Teriflunomide (Aubagio) is an immunomodulatory agent with antiinflammatory properties. The exact mechanism of

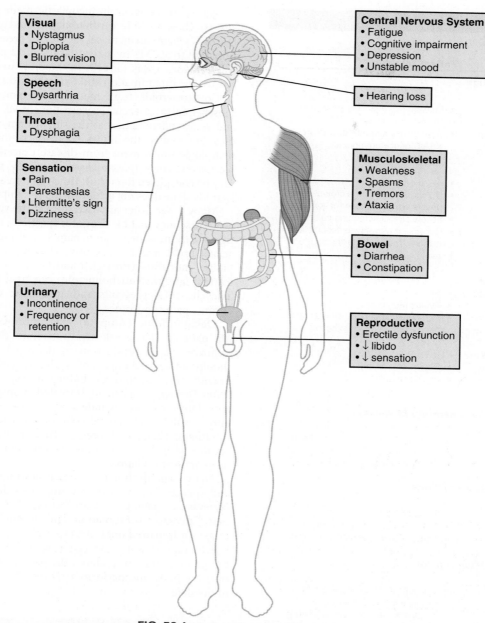

Visual
- Nystagmus
- Diplopia
- Blurred vision

Speech
- Dysarthria

Throat
- Dysphagia

Sensation
- Pain
- Paresthesias
- Lhermitte's sign
- Dizziness

Urinary
- Incontinence
- Frequency or retention

Central Nervous System
- Fatigue
- Cognitive impairment
- Depression
- Unstable mood

- Hearing loss

Musculoskeletal
- Weakness
- Spasms
- Tremors
- Ataxia

Bowel
- Diarrhea
- Constipation

Reproductive
- Erectile dysfunction
- ↓ libido
- ↓ sensation

FIG. 58.4 Manifestations of multiple sclerosis.

TABLE 58.12 Interprofessional Care

Multiple Sclerosis

Diagnostic Assessment	Management
• History and physical examination	• Drug therapy (Table 58.13)
• CSF analysis	• Surgical therapy
• CT scan	• Thalamotomy (unmanageable tremor)
• MRI, MRS (magnetic resonance spectroscopy)	• Neurectomy, rhizotomy, cordotomy (unmanageable spasticity)
• Evoked potential testing	• Physical therapy
• Somatosensory evoked potential (SSEP)	• Occupational therapy
• Auditory evoked potential (AEP)	
• Visual evoked potential (VEP)	

action is unknown. It may reduce the number of activated lymphocytes in the CNS. Fingolimod (Gilenya) and siponimod (Mayzent)reduce MS disease activity by preventing lymphocytes from reaching the CNS and causing damage. These drugs are used to treat relapsing forms of MS.

For more active and aggressive forms of MS, natalizumab (Tysabri), alemtuzumab (Lemtrada), mitoxantrone, ocrelizumab (Ocrevus), and dimethyl fumarate (Tecfidera) may be used. Natalizumab is given when patients have had an inadequate response to other drugs. An adverse effect of natalizumab is the increased risk for a potentially fatal viral infection of the brain (progressive multifocal leukoencephalopathy). Because of its safety profile, alemtuzumab is reserved for patients who have an inadequate response to 2 or more drugs used for the treatment of MS.

TABLE 58.13 Drug Therapy

Multiple Sclerosis

Drug	Patient Teaching
Disease-Modifying Drugs	
Immunomodulators	
β-1a interferon (Rebif, Plegridy, Avonex) β-1b interferon (Betaseron, Extavia) glatiramer acetate (Copaxone)	• Perform self-injection techniques. • Report side effects. • Treat flu-like symptoms with an NSAID or acetaminophen.
mavenclad (Cladribine) teriflunomide (Aubagio)	• Avoid pregnancy. • No contact with large crowds and people who have an infection. • Follow cancer screening guidelines. • Because it may cause serious liver disease, monitor liver tests. • Avoid pregnancy.
Immunosuppressants	
dimethyl fumarate (Tecfidera) mitoxantrone	• Report side effects. • Avoid pregnancy. • No contact with large crowds and people who have an infection.
Monoclonal Antibody	
alemtuzumab (Lemtrada) daclizumab (Zinbryta) natalizumab (Tysabri)	• Report side effects. • Avoid pregnancy.
Sphingosine 1-Phosphate Receptor Modulators	
fingolimod (Gilenya) siponimod (Mayzent)	• Report side effects. • Monitor blood pressure and heart rate regularly. • Avoid pregnancy.
Drugs for Managing Exacerbations	
Corticosteroids	
ACTH methylprednisolone prednisone	• Restrict salt intake. • Do not abruptly stop therapy. • Know drug interactions.
Drugs for Symptom Management	
Anticholinergics	
oxybutynin (Ditropan XL) propantheline	• Consult HCP before using other drugs, especially sleeping aids, antihistamines (possibly leading to potentiated effect).
Cholinergics	
bethanechol (Urecholine) neostigmine	• Consult with HCP before using other drugs, including OTC drugs.
Muscle Relaxants	
baclofen (Lioresal) dantrolene (Dantrium) diazepam (Valium) tizanidine (Zanaflex)	• Avoid driving and similar activities because of sedative effects. • Do not abruptly stop therapy. • Do not use with tranquilizers and alcohol.
Nerve Conduction Enhancer	
dalfampridine (Ampyra)	• Be aware that it may cause seizures, especially at higher doses. • Take the tablet whole. Do not take more than 2 in 24 hr.

Mitoxantrone is an antineoplastic medication with serious effects. These include cardiotoxicity, leukemia, and infertility. Use of ocrelizumab increases the risk for breast cancer. Dimethyl fumarate treats MS by activating the Nrf2 pathway. This pathway provides a way for cells in the body to defend themselves against the inflammation and oxidative stress caused by MS.

Corticosteroids (e.g., methylprednisolone, prednisone) are most helpful to treat acute exacerbations of MS. They reduce edema and acute inflammation at the site of demyelination. However, they do not affect the ultimate outcome or the degree of residual neurologic impairment from disease exacerbation. Therapeutic plasma exchange (*plasmapheresis*) and IV immunoglobulin G may be considered for a short time when treatment with corticosteroids alone does not achieve symptom improvement.

Many other drugs are used to treat the various symptoms of MS. These may include drugs for spasticity, fatigue, tremor, vertigo or dizziness, depression, pain, bowel and bladder problems, sexual problems, and cognitive changes. For example, amantadine, modafinil (Provigil), and fluoxetine (Prozac) are used to treat fatigue. Anticholinergics can treat bladder symptoms. Tricyclic antidepressants and antiseizure drugs are used for chronic pain syndromes.

Dalfampridine (Ampyra) may improve walking speed in MS patients. It is a selective potassium channel blocker that improves nerve conduction in damaged nerve segments. It should not be used in patients with a history of seizure disorder or with moderate to severe kidney disease.

Other Therapies. Spasticity is treated mainly with muscle relaxants. Other options include surgery (e.g., neurectomy, rhizotomy, cordotomy), dorsal-column electrical stimulation, or intrathecal baclofen (Lioresal). Tremors that become unmanageable with drugs are sometimes treated by thalamotomy or deep brain stimulation.

Neurologic dysfunction sometimes improves with physical and speech therapy. Exercise improves daily functioning for patients not having an exacerbation. Exercise decreases spasticity, increases coordination, and retrains unaffected muscles to act for impaired ones. An especially beneficial type of physical therapy is water exercise (Fig. 58.5). Water, which gives buoyancy to the body, allows the patient to have more control over the body and perform activities that would otherwise be impossible.

FIG. 58.5 Water therapy provides exercise and recreation for the patient with a chronic neurologic disease. (© Photos.com/AbleStock.com/Thinkstock.)

❖ NURSING MANAGEMENT: MULTIPLE SCLEROSIS

◆ Nursing Assessment

Subjective and objective data that should be obtained from a patient with MS are outlined in Table 58.14.

◆ Nursing Diagnoses

Nursing diagnoses for the patient with MS may include:
- Impaired physical mobility
- Difficulty coping
- Urinary retention

Additional information on nursing diagnoses and interventions for the patient with MS is presented in the eNursing Care Plan 58.3 (available on the website for this chapter).

◆ Planning

The overall goals are that the patient with MS will (1) maximize neuromuscular function, (2) maintain independence in ADLs for as long as possible, (3) manage fatigue, (4) optimize psychosocial well-being, (5) adjust to the illness, and (6) reduce factors that precipitate exacerbations.

TABLE 58.14 Nursing Assessment

Multiple Sclerosis

Subjective Data

Important Health Information

Past health history: Recent or past viral infections or vaccinations, other recent infections, residence in cold or temperate climates, recent physical or emotional stress, pregnancy, exposure to extremes of heat and cold

Medications: Adherence to regimen of corticosteroids, immunomodulators, immunosuppressants, cholinergics, anticholinergics, antispasmodics

Functional Health Patterns

Health perception–health management: Positive family history; malaise
Nutritional-metabolic: Weight loss; difficulty in chewing, dysphagia
Elimination: Urinary frequency, urgency, dribbling or incontinence, retention; constipation
Activity-exercise: Generalized muscle weakness, muscle fatigue; tingling and numbness; ataxia (clumsiness)
Cognitive-perceptual: Eye, back, leg, joint pain; painful muscle spasms; vertigo; blurred or lost vision; diplopia; tinnitus
Sexuality-reproductive: Impotence, decreased libido
Coping–stress tolerance: Anger, depression, euphoria, social isolation

Objective Data

General

Apathy, inattentiveness

Integumentary

Pressure ulcers

Neurologic

Nystagmus, ataxia, tremor, spasticity, hyperreflexia, decreased hearing

Musculoskeletal

Muscle weakness, paresis, paralysis, spasms, foot dragging, dysarthria

Possible Diagnostic Findings

↓ T suppressor cells, demyelinating lesions on MRI or MRS scans, ↑ IgG or oligoclonal banding in CSF, delayed evoked potential responses

IgG, Immunoglobulin G; *MRS,* magnetic resonance spectroscopy.

◆ Nursing Implementation

The patient with MS should be aware of triggers that may cause worsening of the disease. These include infection (especially upper respiratory and urinary tract infections [UTIs]), trauma, immunization, childbirth, stress, and change in climate. Each person responds differently to triggers. Help the patient identify triggers and develop ways to avoid them or decrease their effects.

During the diagnostic phase, reassure the patient that certain diagnostic studies must be done to rule out other neurologic disorders, even if a tentative diagnosis of MS has been made. Help the patient to deal with anxiety caused by a diagnosis of a disabling illness. The patient with recently diagnosed MS may need help with the grieving process.

During an acute exacerbation, the patient may be immobile and confined to bed. The focus of nursing interventions at this phase is to prevent complications of immobility. These include respiratory and UTIs and pressure injuries.

Focus patient teaching on general resistance to illness. This includes avoiding fatigue, extremes of heat and cold, and exposure to infection. Encourage early treatment of infection when it occurs. Teach the patient to seek a good balance of exercise and rest; minimize caffeine intake; and eat nutritious, well-balanced meals. The patient should know the treatment plan, drug side effects, how to identify and manage side effects, and drug interactions with over-the-counter (OTC) drugs. The patient should consult the HCP before taking any OTC drugs.

Bladder control is a major problem for many patients with MS. Anticholinergics may help some patients to decrease spasticity. You may need to teach others self-catheterization. Constipation is common. A diet high in fiber may help relieve constipation.

The patient with MS and caregivers need to make many emotional adjustments because of disease unpredictability, the need for lifestyle changes, and the challenge of avoiding or decreasing precipitating factors. The uncertainty of disease progression, along with fatigue and decreased mobility, can cause anxiety and depression. The National Multiple Sclerosis Society and its local chapters offer a variety of services to meet the needs of patients with MS.

◆ Evaluation

The expected outcomes are that the patient with MS will
- Maintain or improve muscle strength and mobility
- Use assistive devices appropriately for ambulation and mobility
- Maintain urinary continence
- Make decisions about health and lifestyle modifications to manage MS

PARKINSON'S DISEASE

Parkinson's disease (PD) is a chronic, progressive neurodegenerative disorder characterized by slowness in the initiation and execution of movement (*bradykinesia*), increased muscle tone (*rigidity*), tremor at rest, and gait changes. It is the most common form of *parkinsonism* (a syndrome characterized by similar symptoms).

Up to 1 million Americans will be living with PD by 2020. 60,000 persons are diagnosed each year. Incidence of PD increases with age, though 4% of people with PD are diagnosed before age 50 years. Men are 1.5 times more likely to have PD than women.[25]

Etiology and Pathophysiology

The exact cause of PD is unknown. Although we do not consider PD a hereditary condition, genetic risk factors should be evaluated for their interplay with environmental factors. Exposure to well water, pesticides, herbicides, industrial chemicals, and wood pulp mills may increase risk for PD. Rural residence is considered a risk factor.[25]

Many forms of secondary *(atypical)* parkinsonism exist other than PD. Symptoms of parkinsonism have occurred after exposure to a variety of chemicals, including carbon monoxide and manganese (among copper miners). Drug-induced parkinsonism can follow therapy with metoclopramide (Reglan), reserpine, methyldopa, lithium, haloperidol (Haldol), and chlorpromazine. It can be seen after the use of illicit drugs, including amphetamine and methamphetamine. After stopping these drugs, symptoms of parkinsonism generally disappear. One notable exception is irreversible parkinsonism that follows exposure to the product of meperidine analog synthesis (MTPT). Other causes include hydrocephalus, other neurodegenerative disorders, hypoparathyroidism, infections, stroke, tumor, and trauma.

Many changes found in the brains of people with PD may play a part in development of the disease, including a lack of DA. The pathologic process of PD involves degeneration of the DA-producing neurons in the substantia nigra of the midbrain (Figs. 58.6 to 58.8). This in turn disrupts the normal balance between DA and acetylcholine (ACh) in the basal ganglia. The neurotransmitter DA is essential for normal functioning of the extrapyramidal motor system, including control of posture, support, and voluntary motion. Manifestations of PD do not occur until 80% of neurons in the substantia nigra are lost.

Unusual clumps of protein called *Lewy bodies* are found in the brains of patients with PD. It is not known what causes Lewy bodies to form. Their presence indicates abnormal brain functioning. Lewy body dementia is discussed in Chapter 59.

Genetic Link

We do not fully understand how genetic changes cause PD or influence the risk for developing PD. Around 15% of patients with PD have a family history of PD. Many autosomal dominant and recessive genes are linked to familial PD. Autosomal dominant PD is rare, affecting only 1% to 2% of people with PD. Examples include the *SNCA* and *LRRK2* genes.[25] Mutations in the *LRRK2* gene also appear to have a role in noninherited (sporadic) cases of PD. Recessive genes include parkin (*PARK2, PARK7*), and *PINK1*. Mutations in these genes are often associated with a younger age of disease onset. They also have more manifestations compared to those typically seen with age-related PD. *PINK1* mutations are related to a rare, early-onset form of PD.

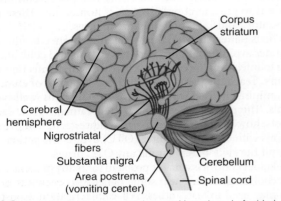

FIG. 58.6 Nigrostriatal disorders produce parkinsonism. Left-sided view of the human brain showing the substantia nigra and the corpus striatum *(shaded area)* lying deep within the cerebral hemisphere. Nerve fibers extend upward from the substantia nigra, divide into many branches, and carry dopamine to all regions of the corpus striatum.

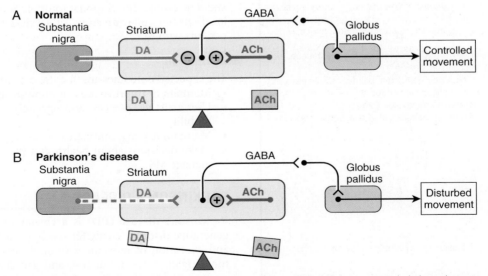

FIG. 58.7 A deficit in dopamine *(DA)* exists in Parkinson's disease. This deficit creates an imbalance between DA and the excitatory neurotransmitter acetylcholine. **A,** In a healthy person, DA released from neurons in the substantia nigra inhibits the firing of neurons in the striatum that release γ-aminobutyric acid *(GABA).* Conversely, neurons in the striatum, which release acetylcholine *(ACh),* excite the GABAergic neurons. Under normal conditions, inhibitory actions of DA are balanced by excitatory actions of ACh, and controlled movement results. **B,** In Parkinson's disease, neurons in the substantia nigra that supply DA to the striatum degenerate. When a deficit of DA occurs, excitatory effects of ACh go unopposed and disturbed movements (tremor, rigidity) result. (From Lehne RA: *Pharmacology for nursing care,* ed 8, St Louis, 2013, Saunders.)

Clinical Manifestations

The onset of PD is gradual, with an ongoing progression. Only 1 side of the body may be involved at first. Classic manifestations can be remembered by the mnemonic *TRAP* (**t**remor, **r**igidity, **a**kinesia, **p**ostural instability). Early in the disease, only a mild tremor, a slight limp, or a decreased arm swing may be seen. Later, the patient may have a shuffling gait and appear unable to stop. The patient's arms are flexed, and postural reflexes seem to be lost. The patient may have speech problems *(hypokinetic dysarthria)* that can affect communication and quality of life.

Tremor. *Tremor* is often the first sign. It may be minimal at first, so the patient is the only one who notices it. This tremor can affect handwriting, causing it to trail off, especially toward the ends of words. Parkinsonian tremor is more prominent at rest. It is worsened by emotional stress or increased concentration. The hand tremor is described as "pill rolling" because the thumb and forefinger appear to move in a rotary fashion as if rolling a pill, coin, or other small object. Tremor can involve the diaphragm, tongue, lips, and jaw. It rarely causes shaking of the head.

Unfortunately, in many people a benign *essential tremor* is mistakenly diagnosed as PD. Essential tremor occurs during voluntary movement, has a more rapid frequency than parkinsonian tremor, and is often familial.

Rigidity. *Rigidity* is the increased resistance to passive motion when the limbs are moved through their range of motion (ROM). Parkinsonian rigidity is typified by a jerky quality *(cogwheel rigidity)*, as if there were occasional catches in the passive movement of a joint. Sustained muscle contraction causes the rigidity and results in muscle soreness; feeling tired and achy; or pain in the head, upper body, spine, or legs. Slow movement is another result of rigidity because the alternating contraction and relaxation in opposing muscle groups (e.g., biceps and triceps) is inhibited.

Akinesia. *Akinesia* is the absence or loss of control of voluntary muscle movements. In PD, *bradykinesia* (slowness of movement) is especially evident in the loss of automatic movements. This occurs because of the physical and chemical change of the basal ganglia and other structures in the extrapyramidal portion of the CNS. In the unaffected patient, automatic movements are involuntary and occur subconsciously. They include blinking of the eyelids, swinging of the arms while walking, swallowing saliva, using facial and hand movements for self-expression, and making minor movements to adjust posture.

The patient with PD does not perform these movements and lacks natural activity. This accounts for the stooped posture, masked face (deadpan expression), drooling of saliva, and shuffling gait *(festination)* that are typical of a person with PD. The posture is that of a slowed "old man" image, with the head and trunk bent forward and the legs constantly flexed (Fig. 58.9).

Postural Instability. *Postural instability* is common. Patients may describe being unable to stop themselves from going forward *(propulsion)* or backward *(retropulsion)*. Assessment of postural instability includes the "pull test." The examiner stands behind the patient and gives a tug backward on the shoulder, causing the patient to lose their balance and fall backward.

Many nonmotor symptoms are common. They include depression, anxiety, apathy, fatigue, pain, urinary retention, constipation, erectile dysfunction, and memory changes. Sleep problems are common. They include difficulty staying asleep at night, restless sleep, nightmares, and drowsiness or sudden sleep onset during the day. Rapid eye movement (REM) sleep behavior disorder is a preparkinsonian state that occurs in about one third of patients with PD. It is characterized by violent dreams and potentially dangerous motor activity during REM sleep. It may cause harm to the patient or bed partner.[26]

Complications

As PD progresses, complications increase. These include motor symptoms (e.g., dyskinesias [spontaneous, involuntary movements], weakness, neurologic problems (e.g., dementia), and neuropsychiatric problems (e.g., depression, hallucinations, psychosis). As PD progresses, dementia often results and is associated with increased mortality.

As swallowing becomes more difficult (dysphagia), malnutrition or aspiration may result. Increasing weakness may lead to pneumonia, UTIs, and skin breakdown. Orthostatic hypotension is common. Along with loss of postural reflexes, it can cause falls or other injury. The patient's increased fall risk means caregivers must be aware of environmental conditions that may contribute to falls.

Diagnostic Studies

Because no specific diagnostic test exists for PD, diagnosis is based on the patient's history and clinical features. Clinical diagnosis requires the presence of TRAP and asymmetric onset. Confirmation of PD is a positive response to antiparkinsonian drugs (levodopa or DA agonist). MRI and CT have a limited role in diagnosis of PD because they do not show a specific pathologic finding. However, they can rule out a stroke or brain tumor.

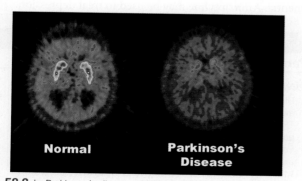

FIG. 58.8 In Parkinson's disease, PET scan showing reduced fluorodopa uptake in the basal ganglia *(right)* compared with a normal control *(left)*. (From Aminoff MJ, Daroff RB: *Encyclopedia of the neurological sciences*, Waltham, MA, 2003, Academic Press.)

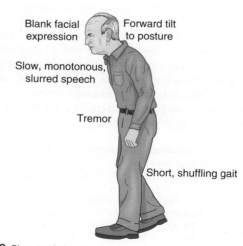

Blank facial expression

Forward tilt to posture

Slow, monotonous, slurred speech

Tremor

Short, shuffling gait

FIG. 58.9 Characteristic appearance of a patient with Parkinson's disease.

Exercise and Parkinson's Disease

You are a nurse working with T.K., a 77-yr-old man who has had Parkinson's disease (PD) for 5 years. You note he has a moderate tremor, shuffling gait, and decreased arm flexion. He asks you what types of physical activity he can do to improve his mobility and balance.

Making Clinical Decisions

Best Available Evidence. Patients with mild to moderately severe PD have improvements in gait performance and health-related quality of life after taking part in exercise programs. Facility-based programs produce greater effects on improving balance and mobility over the short and long term. Exercise training to improve balance and gait ability may prevent falls in people with PD.

Clinician Expertise. You know it is important to promote and encourage patients with PD to take part in physical exercise to help improve or maintain functional mobility and prevent falls. You are aware that we should design exercise programs around physical activities the person enjoys.

Patient Preferences and Values. T.K. says that in years past, he enjoyed dancing with his wife and currently likes to walk in his neighborhood.

Implications for Nursing Practice

1. What information will you provide to T.K. about muscle atrophy and joint contractures and the importance of physical activity?
2. How will you help T.K. and his wife in exploring community resources and programs related to physical activities that support his interests?

References for Evidence

Lee JH, Choi M, Yoo Y: A meta-analysis of nonpharmacological interventions for people with Parkinson's disease, *Clin Nurs Res* 26:608, 2017.

Shen X, Wong-Yu IS, Mak MK: Effects of exercise on falls, balance, and gait ability in Parkinson's disease: A meta-analysis, *Neurorehabil Neural Repair* 30:512, 2016.

Interprofessional Care

Because PD has no cure, interprofessional care focuses on symptom management (Table 58.15).

Drug Therapy. Drug therapy for PD is aimed at correcting the imbalance of neurotransmitters within the CNS. Antiparkinsonian drugs either enhance the release or supply of DA (dopaminergic) or block the effects of the overactive cholinergic neurons in the striatum (anticholinergic) (Fig. 58.7). Levodopa with carbidopa (Sinemet) is the primary treatment for symptomatic patients. Levodopa is a chemical precursor of DA and can cross the blood-brain barrier. It is converted to DA in the basal ganglia. Sinemet is the preferred drug because it also contains carbidopa, an agent that inhibits the enzyme dopa-decarboxylase in the peripheral tissues. Dopa-decarboxylase breaks down levodopa before it reaches the brain. The net result of using this combination is that more levodopa reaches the brain. Thus less drug is needed. Levodopa has many side effects and drug interactions. Prolonged use often results in dyskinesias and "off/on" periods when the medication will unpredictably stop or start working.

DRUG ALERT Carbidopa/Levodopa (Sinemet)
- Monitor for signs of dyskinesia.
- Monitor for short-term adverse effects of nausea, vomiting, and light-headedness.
- Stress that effects may be delayed for several weeks to months.
- Teach patient or caregiver to report any uncontrolled movement of face, eyelids, mouth, tongue, arms, hands, or legs; mental changes; palpitations; and difficulty urinating.
- Do not give levodopa with food because protein reduces absorption.

Many patients receive Sinemet early in the disease course for the management of motor symptoms. However, some HCPs think that, after a few years of therapy, the effectiveness of Sinemet wears off. Therefore they prefer to start therapy with a DA receptor agonist, a drug that directly stimulates DA receptors. Ropinirole (Requip) and pramipexole (Mirapex) may be used alone or in combination with Sinemet. Many of these medications are available in extended-release forms that improve patients' ability to adhere to treatment plans. Rotigotine (Neupro), another DA receptor agonist, is available as a transdermal patch applied once daily. It is an adjunctive therapy for patients taking Sinemet.

DRUG ALERT Pramipexole (Mirapex)
- Take the drug with food to decrease nausea.
- Notify the HCP immediately if uncontrollable urges, confusion, muscle rigidity, excess urination, shortness of breath, or vision changes occur.

The antiviral agent amantadine is a weak antagonist of NMDA-type glutamate receptors. It increases DA release and blocks DA reuptake. It may be useful as a single therapy for early PD. It can be used later with levodopa. As a single treatment, amantadine often becomes less effective after a few months.[27] Withdrawal of amantadine even after extended therapy can worsen dyskinesia.

Anticholinergic drugs, such as trihexyphenidyl and benztropine (Cogentin), decrease the activity of ACh, providing balance between cholinergic and dopaminergic actions.[27] Antihistamines (e.g., diphenhydramine) with anticholinergic properties may be used to manage tremors.

Selegiline (Eldepryl), rasagiline (Azilect), and safinamide (Xadago) are monoamine oxidase type B (MAO-B) inhibitors that may be used in combination with Sinemet.[27] By inhibiting MAO-B, the enzyme that degrades DA, these agents increase the levels of DA and prolong the half-life of levodopa. Rasagiline can be used alone as therapy in early PD. However, MAO-B inhibitors are less effective at treating motor symptoms than DA receptor agonists.

Entacapone (Comtan) and tolcapone (Tasmar) block the enzyme catechol O-methyltransferase (COMT), which breaks down levodopa in the peripheral circulation. Thus, they prolong the effect of Sinemet and are used only as adjuncts. They are often used when the patient's response to levodopa is wearing off at the end of the dosing interval. Tolcapone is rarely prescribed because it is associated with fatal hepatotoxicity.[27]

Rivastigmine (Exelon) or donepezil (Aricept) is used to treat dementia. Amitriptyline may be used to treat depression.

TABLE 58.15 Interprofessional Care
Parkinson's Disease

Diagnostic Assessment	Management
- History and physical examination - TRAP (tremor, rigidity, akinesia, postural instability) - Positive response to antiparkinsonian drugs - MRI - Rule out side effects of phenothiazines, reserpine, benzodiazepines, haloperidol	- Antiparkinsonian drugs (Table 58.16) - Surgical therapy - Deep brain stimulation - Ablation surgery - Physical therapy - Occupational therapy - Dietitian consult for nutritional therapy

Table 58.16 outlines the drugs commonly used in PD. The use of only 1 drug is preferred because fewer side effects occur and the drug dosage is easier to adjust than when several drugs are used. However, as PD progresses, combination therapy is often needed. Excessive amounts of dopaminergic drugs can worsen rather than relieve symptoms (*paradoxical intoxication*).

Within 3 to 5 years of standard PD treatments, many patients have episodes of hypomobility (e.g., inability to rise from chair, speak, or walk; also called *off episodes*). Off episodes can occur toward the end of a dosing interval with standard medications (so-called *end-of-dose wearing off*) or at unpredictable times (spontaneous "on/off"). A combination of carbidopa, levodopa, and entacapone (Stalevo) is available for patients with end-of-dose wearing off. It can be prescribed to make dosing easier, with 1 pill substituting for 3. Stalevo is typically prescribed for patients with advanced PD with intense motor fluctuations. The injectable DA receptor agonist apomorphine (Apokyn) can improve movement in hypomobility episodes. Apomorphine must be taken with an antiemetic drug because it causes severe nausea and vomiting when taken alone. It cannot be taken with antiemetics in the serotonin (5-HT3) receptor antagonist class (e.g., ondansetron [Zofran]). This combination can lead to very low BP and loss of consciousness.

Surgical Therapy. Surgical procedures to relieve symptoms of PD are usually used in patients who are not responsive to drug therapy or who have developed severe motor complications. Surgical procedures fall into 3 categories: deep brain stimulation (DBS), ablation (destruction), and transplantation. The most common surgical treatment is DBS. This involves placing an electrode in the thalamus, globus pallidus, or subthalamic nucleus and connecting it to a generator placed in the upper chest (similar to a pacemaker) (Fig. 58.10). The device is programmed to deliver a specific current to the targeted brain location. DBS is preferred to ablation procedures because it is reversible and programmable. It can be safely done bilaterally. DBS reduces the increased neuronal activity produced by DA depletion. It can improve motor function and reduce dyskinesia and medication use. DBS is most effective when patients are carefully selected and screened.[27]

Ablation surgery involves finding, targeting, and destroying an area of the brain affected by PD. The goal is to destroy tissue that produces abnormal chemical or electrical impulses leading to tremors or other symptoms. Typical targets of ablation are the thalamus (*thalamotomy*) and globus pallidus (*pallidotomy*).[27] Newer treatments, such as the gamma knife and focused ultrasound, are noninvasive options.

Transplantation of fetal neural tissue into the basal ganglia was designed to provide DA-producing cells in the brains of patients with PD. Research of this therapy was largely abandoned after mixed results over several decades. In the last few years, better transplant techniques have renewed interest in this as a potential option.

Nutritional Therapy. Diet is of major importance to patients with PD because malnutrition and constipation can result from poor nutrition. Patients who have dysphagia and bradykinesia need appetizing foods that are easy to chew and swallow. The diet should contain adequate fiber and fruit to reduce constipation.

Eating 6 small meals a day may be less tiring than eating 3 large meals a day. Plan ample time for eating to avoid frustration. Cut food into bite-sized pieces. Protein ingestion and vitamin B_6 can impair the absorption of levodopa. Limiting protein intake to the evening meal can decrease this problem. They may need to consult with the HCP about including vitamin B_6 in a multivitamin and fortified cereals.

Drug	Mechanism of Action
TABLE 58.16 Drug Therapy	
Parkinson's Disease	
Dopaminergics	
Dopamine Precursors	
levodopa (L-dopa) levodopa/carbidopa (Sinemet)	Converted to dopamine in basal ganglia
Dopamine Receptor Agonists	
pramipexole (Mirapex) ropinirole (Requip, Requip XL) rotigotine (Neupro [transdermal patch])	Stimulate dopamine receptors
Dopamine Agonists	
amantadine	Blocks NMDA-type glutamate receptors, increases dopamine release, and blocks dopamine reuptake
apomorphine (Apokyn)	Stimulates postsynaptic dopamine receptors
Anticholinergics	
benztropine (Cogentin) trihexyphenidyl	Block cholinergic receptors, thus helping to balance cholinergic and dopaminergic activity
Antihistamine	
diphenhydramine	Has anticholinergic effect
Monoamine Oxidase Inhibitors	
rasagiline (Azilect) safinamide (Xadago) selegiline (Eldepryl)	Block breakdown of dopamine
Catechol O-Methyltransferase (COMT) Inhibitors	
entacapone (Comtan) tolcapone (Tasmar)	Block COMT and slow the breakdown of levodopa, thus prolonging the action of levodopa

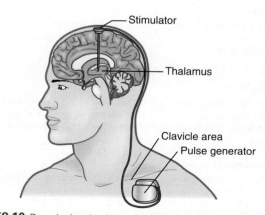

FIG. 58.10 Deep brain stimulation (DBS) can be used to treat tremors and uncontrolled movements of Parkinson's disease. Electrodes are surgically placed in the brain and connected to a neurostimulator (pacemaker device) in the chest.

❖ NURSING MANAGEMENT: PARKINSON'S DISEASE

◆ Nursing Assessment

Subjective and objective data that should be obtained from a patient with PD are outlined in Table 58.17.

◆ Nursing Diagnoses

Nursing diagnoses for the patient with PD may include:

- Impaired physical mobility
- Impaired nutritional status
- Risk for fall-related injury
- Impaired sleep pattern

Additional information on nursing diagnoses and interventions for the patient with PD is presented in eNursing Care Plan 58.4 (available on the website for this chapter).

TABLE 58.17 Nursing Assessment

Parkinson's Disease

Subjective Data

Important Health Information

Past health history: CNS trauma, cerebrovascular disorders, exposure to metals and carbon monoxide, encephalitis or other infections
Medications: Major tranquilizers, especially haloperidol (Haldol), and phenothiazines, reserpine, methyldopa, amphetamines

Functional Health Patterns

Health perception–health management: Fatigue
Nutritional-metabolic: Excessive salivation, dysphagia, weight loss
Elimination: Constipation, incontinence, excessive sweating
Activity-exercise: Difficulty in initiating movements, frequent falls, loss of dexterity, micrographia (handwriting deterioration)
Sleep-rest: Insomnia, nightmares, daytime sleepiness
Cognitive-perceptual: Diffuse pain in head, shoulders, neck, back, legs, and hips. Muscle soreness and cramping
Self-perception–self-concept: Depression, mood swings, hallucinations

Objective Data

General

Blank (masked) facial expression, slow and monotonous speech, infrequent blinking

Integumentary

Seborrhea, dandruff; ankle edema

Cardiovascular

Postural hypotension

Gastrointestinal

Drooling

Neurologic

Tremor at rest, first in hands (pill rolling), later in legs, arms, face, and tongue. Aggravation of tremor with anxiety, absence in sleep. Poor coordination, cognitive impairment and dementia, impaired postural reflexes

Musculoskeletal

Cogwheel rigidity, dysarthria, bradykinesia, contractures, stooped posture, shuffling gait

Possible Diagnostic Findings

No specific tests. Diagnosis based on history and physical findings and ruling out of other diseases

◆ Planning

The overall goals are that the patient with PD will (1) maximize neurologic function, (2) maintain independence in ADLs for as long as possible, and (3) optimize psychosocial well-being.

◆ Nursing Implementation

Because PD is a chronic degenerative disorder with no acute exacerbations, teaching and nursing care are directed toward maintaining good health, encouraging independence, and avoiding complications, such as contractures and falls. Problems due to bradykinesia can be addressed by relatively simple measures.

❓ CHECK YOUR PRACTICE

You are working in a rehabilitation facility with a new patient, a 78-yr-old man with Parkinson's disease. He was at your facility briefly 6 months ago with a fractured hip after falling in his yard. The family has asked to talk with you about their fear of taking him for a walk in the hallways because he is so unstable.

- What advice would you give to the family?

Promoting physical exercise and a well-balanced diet are major nursing concerns. Exercise can limit the effects of decreased mobility, such as muscle atrophy, contractures, and constipation. The American Parkinson Disease Association (www.apdaparkinson.org) publishes booklets and fact sheets with helpful exercises that can be used by caregivers and health care professionals.

A physical therapist can design a personal exercise program to strengthen and stretch specific muscles. Overall muscle tone and specific exercises to strengthen the muscles involved with speaking and swallowing should be included. Although exercise will not stop disease progress, it will enhance the patient's functional ability. An occupational therapist can help the patient with ways to increase self-care measures, including eating and dressing.

⚠ SAFETY ALERT Preventing Falls

For patients who are at risk for falling and tend to "freeze" while walking, have them do the following:

- Consciously think about stepping over an imaginary object on the floor.
- Rock from side to side before stepping forward.
- Walk to a beat, such as with music.
- Try to swing both arms from front to back.
- Take 1 step backward and 2 steps forward.

Work closely with the patient's caregivers to find creative ways to promote independence and self-care. The patient can get out of a chair better by using an upright chair with arms and placing the back legs of the chair on small (2-inch) blocks. Encourage environmental changes to improve safety. These include removing rugs and excess furniture to avoid stumbling, using an elevated toilet seat to help the patient get on and off the toilet, and elevating the legs of an ottoman to decrease dependent ankle edema. Clothing can be simplified by using slip-on shoes and Velcro hook-and-loop fasteners or zippers on clothing, instead of buttons.

Effective management of sleep problems can greatly improve the quality of life for patients with PD. Some patients find the use of satin nightwear or satin sheets helpful. Information on teaching about sleep hygiene practices is discussed in Chapter 7.

In the early stages of PD, many patients have depression and anxiety. Patients need to adjust their lifestyle, including work and home responsibilities. As PD progresses, the impact on the patient's psychologic well-being increases. Assist the patient by listening, providing teaching, gently correcting distorted thoughts, and encouraging social interactions. Psychologic therapy and counseling can be helpful. Ensure that patients with PD receive prescribed medications on time to avoid on-off effects.

In the early stage of PD, the patient may have subtle changes in cognitive function that can progress to dementia. This causes increased caregiver burden and may lead to long-term care placement. Information on care of the patient with dementia is provided in Chapter 59.

Family members (e.g., spouse, children) care for most patients with PD. Their burden increases as the disease progresses. This often occurs while the caregiver's physical and mental health also decline. Help them find appropriate resources.

◆ Evaluation

The expected outcomes are that the patient with PD will
- Maintain optimal muscle function
- Use assistive devices appropriately for ambulation and mobility
- Maintain nutritional intake adequate for metabolic needs
- Have unimpaired swallowing of fluids and/or solids
- Use methods of communication that allow interaction with others

MYASTHENIA GRAVIS

Myasthenia gravis (MG) is an autoimmune disease of the neuromuscular junction marked by fluctuating weakness of certain skeletal muscle groups. This weakness increases with muscle use. MG can occur in anyone. An estimated 60,000 people have MG in the United States. In women, the MG starts before age 40 years. Men usually develop MG after age 60.[28]

Etiology and Pathophysiology

MG is caused by an autoimmune process in which antibodies attack ACh receptors. This results in fewer ACh receptor (AChR) sites at the neuromuscular junction. This prevents ACh molecules from attaching to receptors and stimulating muscle contraction. Anti-AChR antibodies are found in the serum of 90% of patients with generalized MG. In the 10% of patients who lack autoantibodies to AChR, muscular weakness may be related to autoantibodies to muscle-specific tyrosine kinase or to other unknown antigens.[29] Thymic hyperplasia and tumors are common in patients with MG, suggesting autoantibody production occurs in the thymus.[28]

Clinical Manifestations and Complications

The key feature is fluctuating weakness of skeletal muscles. MG usually affects multiple muscle groups. This includes muscles used to move the eyes and eyelids, chew, swallow, speak, and breathe. Muscles are generally strongest in the morning and become exhausted with continued activity. Muscle weakness is prominent by the end of the day. A period of rest usually restores strength.

In more than half of patients, the first muscles involved are the ocular muscles, causing ptosis (drooping of the eyelids) in 1 or both eyes and double vision (Fig. 58.11).[29] MG does not progress beyond the ocular muscles in about 20% of patients. When facial muscles are affected, facial mobility and expression can be impaired. Patients may have difficulty chewing and swallowing food. Speech is affected, and the voice often fades after a long conversation. The muscles of the trunk and limbs are sometimes affected. Of these, the proximal muscles of the neck, shoulder, and hip are more often affected than the distal muscles. No other neural problems accompany MG. No sensory loss occurs, reflexes are normal, and muscle atrophy is rare.

The course of MG is highly variable. Some patients may have short-term remissions, and others may stabilize. Others may have severe, progressive involvement. Fatigue, pregnancy, illness, trauma, temperature extremes, stress, and hypokalemia can exacerbate MG. Certain drugs, including β-adrenergic blockers, quinidine, phenytoin (Dilantin), certain anesthetics, and aminoglycoside antibiotics, can worsen MG.[29]

Myasthenic crisis is an acute worsening of muscle weakness triggered by respiratory infection, surgery, emotional distress, pregnancy, exposure to certain drugs, or beginning treatment with corticosteroids. The major complications of MG result from muscle weakness in areas that affect swallowing and breathing. This results in aspiration, respiratory insufficiency, and respiratory tract infection.

Diagnostic Studies

The diagnosis of MG can be made based on history and physical examination. Other tests may be used for confirmation. EMG may show a decreased response to repeated stimulation of the hand muscles that shows muscle fatigue. Single-fiber EMG is sensitive in confirming MG. Use of drugs and serologic testing for specific antibodies is useful.

The response to a Tensilon test can indicate MG. A patient with MG has rapid improvement in muscle strength after IV injection of edrophonium chloride (Tensilon). Edrophonium is an anticholinesterase agent. It blocks the enzyme acetylcholinesterase, the enzyme that breaks down ACh. This test also helps diagnose a cholinergic crisis (from an overdose of anticholinesterase drug), which occurs due to excessive cholinesterase inhibition. In a cholinergic crisis, edrophonium may increase muscle weakness. Atropine, a cholinergic antagonist, should be readily available to counteract the effects of edrophonium when it is used diagnostically. In patients with a confirmed diagnosis of MG, a chest CT scan may be done to evaluate the thymus.

Interprofessional Care

Drug Therapy. Drug therapy for MG includes anticholinesterase drugs, alternate-day corticosteroids, and immunosuppressants

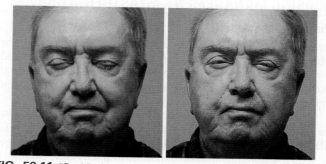

FIG. 58.11 "Peek" sign in myasthenia gravis. During sustained forced eyelid closure, he is unable to bury his eyelashes *(left)* and, after 30 sec, he is unable to keep the lids fully closed *(right)*. (From Sanders DB, Massey JM: Clinical features of myasthenia gravis. In AG Engel, ed: *Neuromuscular junction disorders: Handbook of clinical neurology*, New York, 2008, Elsevier.)

TABLE 58.18 Interprofessional Care

Myasthenia Gravis

Diagnostic Assessment	Management

• History and physical examination
• Fatigability with prolonged upward gaze (2–3 min)
• Muscle weakness
• EMG
• Tensilon test
• Acetylcholine receptor antibodies
• Chest x-ray
	• Drug therapy
	  • Anticholinesterase agents
	  • Corticosteroids
	  • Immunosuppressive agents
	• Surgery (thymectomy)
	• Plasmapheresis
	• IV immunoglobulin G

TABLE 58.19 Comparison of Myasthenic and Cholinergic Crises

Myasthenic Crisis	Cholinergic Crisis
Causes	
Exacerbation of myasthenia after precipitating factors, failure to take drug as prescribed, or drug dose too low	Overdose of anticholinesterase drugs resulting in ↑ acetylcholine at the receptor sites, remission (spontaneous or after thymectomy)
Differential Diagnosis	
Improved strength after IV administration of anticholinesterase drugs	Weakness within 1 hr after ingestion of anticholinesterase drugs
↑ Weakness of skeletal muscles manifesting as ptosis, bulbar signs (e.g., difficulty swallowing, difficulty articulating words), or dyspnea	↑ Weakness of skeletal muscles manifesting as ptosis, bulbar signs, dyspnea
	Effects on smooth muscle include pupillary miosis, salivation, diarrhea, nausea or vomiting, abdominal cramps, ↑ bronchial secretions, sweating, or lacrimation

(Table 58.18). Anticholinesterase drugs enhance transmission at the neuromuscular junction. Inhibiting acetylcholinesterase with an anticholinesterase inhibitor prolongs the action of ACh and improves impulse transmission at the neuromuscular junction. Pyridostigmine (Mestinon) is the most successful drug of this group in the long-term treatment of MG.

Tailoring the dose to avoid a myasthenic or cholinergic crisis often presents a clinical challenge. Corticosteroids (specifically prednisone) are used to suppress the immune response. Other drugs used for immunosuppression include azathioprine (Imuran), mycophenolate (CellCept), and cyclosporine (Sandimmune). Up to 80% of patients who receive corticosteroids have complete cessation of symptoms or marked improvement. Some patients become weaker for a brief time before regaining strength. These benefits must be weighed with concerns about chronic use of these medications.

Surgical Therapy. Because the thymus gland in the patient with MG appears to enhance the production of AChR antibodies, removing the thymus gland causes improvement in most patients. Thymectomy is indicated for almost all patients with thymoma, patients with generalized MG between puberty and about age 65 years, and patients with purely ocular MG.

Other Therapies. Plasmapheresis and IV immunoglobulin G can yield short-term improvement in symptoms. They are indicated for patients in myasthenic crisis or in preparation for surgery when corticosteroids must be avoided. Plasmapheresis directly removes circulating AChR antibodies, leading to a decrease in symptoms. (Plasmapheresis is discussed in Chapter 13.) It is not certain how IV immunoglobulin works. It is probably related to a decrease in antibody production.

❖ NURSING MANAGEMENT: MYASTHENIA GRAVIS

◆ Nursing Assessment

Assess the severity of MG by asking the patient about fatigue, what body parts are affected, and how severely they are affected. Some patients become so fatigued they are no longer able to work or even walk. Assess the patient's coping abilities and understanding of MG.

Obtain a thorough medication history. Many drugs are contraindicated or must be used with caution in patients with MG. Classes of drugs that should be carefully evaluated before use include β-adrenergic blockers, quinidine, phenytoin (Dilantin), certain anesthetics, and aminoglycoside antibiotics.[29]

Objective data should include respiratory rate and depth, O_2 saturation, arterial blood gas analyses, and pulmonary function tests. Assess for any evidence of respiratory distress in patients with acute myasthenic crisis. Assess muscle strength of all face and limb muscles, swallowing, speech (volume and clarity), and cough and gag reflexes.

◆ Nursing Diagnoses

Nursing diagnoses for the patient with MG may include:
- Impaired airway clearance
- Activity intolerance
- Risk for aspiration
- Disturbed body image

◆ Planning

The overall goals are that the patient with MG will (1) have a return of normal muscle strength, (2) manage fatigue, (3) avoid complications, and (4) maintain a quality of life appropriate to the disease course.

◆ Nursing Implementation

The patient with MG who is admitted to the hospital usually has a respiratory tract infection or is in acute myasthenic crisis. Nursing care is aimed at maintaining adequate ventilation, continuing drug therapy, and watching for side effects of therapy. Be able to distinguish cholinergic from myasthenic crisis (Table 58.19) because the causes and treatment of these conditions differ greatly. Features of a cholinergic crisis include involuntary muscle contraction, sweating, excessive salivation, and constricted pupils.

As with other chronic illnesses, focus care on the neurologic deficits and their impact on daily living. Teach the patient about a balanced diet that can easily be chewed and swallowed. Semisolid foods may be easier to eat than solids or liquids. Scheduling doses of drugs to reach peak action at mealtime may make eating easier. Arrange diversional activities that need little physical effort and match the patient's interests. Help the patient plan ADLs to avoid fatigue. Focus teaching on adherence to the treatment plan, complications, potential adverse reactions to specific drugs, complications of therapy (crisis conditions), and what to do about them. Explore community resources, such as the Myasthenia Gravis Foundation of America and MG support groups.

◆ **Evaluation**

The expected outcomes are that the patient with MG will

- Maintain optimal muscle function
- Be free from side effects of drugs
- Have no complications (myasthenic or cholinergic crises) from MG
- Maintain a quality of life appropriate to the disease course

AMYOTROPHIC LATERAL SCLEROSIS

Amyotrophic lateral sclerosis (ALS) is a rare progressive neuromuscular disorder marked by loss of motor neurons. ALS usually leads to death 2 to 5 years after diagnosis, but a few patients may survive for more than 10 years. This disease became known as *Lou Gehrig's disease* after the famous baseball player was stricken with it in 1939. Perhaps the best-known patient with ALS is British theoretical physicist Stephen Hawking. He was diagnosed at age 21 years and lived with ALS for over 50 years, dying at age 76. The typical onset is between age 55 and 75 years. ALS is most common in whites, men, and veterans of the Gulf War. About 20,000 Americans have ALS.[30]

In ALS, motor neurons in the brainstem and spinal cord gradually degenerate for unknown reasons. Dead motor neurons cannot produce or transport signals to muscles. Consequently, electrical and chemical messages originating in the brain do not reach the muscles to activate them.

Genetic Link

About 5% to 10% of ALS cases are genetic. Mutations in more than a dozen genes have been found to cause familial ALS (FALS). One gene is "chromosome 9 open reading frame 72," or *C9ORF72*. People with FALS from a *C9ORF72* mutation often develop ALS earlier. This same gene also causes frontotemporal dementia (FTD). A few people have both ALS and dementia (ALS-FTD). Other times FALS results from mutations in the gene that gives instructions to make the enzyme copper-zinc superoxide dismutase 1 (*SOD1*).[31]

Progressive muscle weakness and atrophy are the classic sign of ALS. Early symptoms of weakness vary. For some, symptoms initially affect the arms or legs ("limb-onset" ALS). The person may have trouble with tasks requiring fine motor skills (e.g., writing, typing) or notice they are tripping, dropping things, or stumbling more often. Those who first have problems with slurred speech or swallowing have "bulbar onset" ALS.

Muscle wasting and involuntary contractions result from the denervation of the muscles and lack of stimulation and use. Other symptoms include pain, sleep disorders, spasticity and hyperreflexia, drooling, emotional lability, constipation, and esophageal reflux. ALS does not affect a patient's intelligence but affected people may have depression and problems with decision making and memory. Death often results from compromised respiratory function due to muscle weakness and paralysis.

INFORMATICS IN PRACTICE

Voice Banking Applications for ALS

- For patients with ALS, the loss of voice and the ability to communicate can be isolating.
- Patients can take part in voice banking programs and record key words and phrases in their own voices.
- Voice banking is meant to be an alternative communication tool when patients may not be able to speak.

No cure exists for ALS. Treatment options are limited. Riluzole (Rilutek) slows the progression of ALS. This drug reduces damage to motor neurons by decreasing the release of glutamate (an excitatory neurotransmitter) in the brain. Edaravone (Radicava), approved by FDA in May 2017, is the first new drug treatment for ALS in 20 years. This drug is given IV daily for 14 days, followed by a 14-day drug-free period. Subsequent dosing is over 10 to 14 days, again followed by a 14-day drug-free period. Edaravone is a free radical scavenger that we think relieves effects of oxidative stress, a likely factor in progression of ALS.[32]

The illness trajectory for ALS is devastating because the patient is cognitively intact while wasting away. Guide the patient in the use of moderate-intensity, endurance-type exercises for the trunk and limbs because this may help to reduce ALS spasticity. Nursing interventions include (1) facilitating communication, (2) reducing aspiration risk, (3) early identification of respiratory insufficiency, (4) decreasing pain from muscle weakness, (5) decreasing risk for fall-related injury, and (6) providing diversional activities, such as reading and companionship.

Support the patient and caregivers emotionally. This includes grieving related to the loss of motor function and impending death. Discuss advance directives and artificial methods of ventilation with the patient and caregiver.

HUNTINGTON'S DISEASE

Huntington's disease (HD) is a progressive, degenerative brain disorder. It is a genetically transmitted, autosomal dominant disorder. The offspring of a person with HD have a 50% risk for inheriting it. The onset of HD is usually between ages 30 and 50 years. Diagnosis is often made after the affected person has had children. About 25,000 to 30,000 Americans are symptomatic and 150,000 or more are at risk for HD.[33] It affects men and women equally across races.

The diagnostic process begins with a review of the family history and clinical symptoms. Genetic testing confirms the disease in a person with symptoms. People who are asymptomatic but who have a positive family history of HD must decide if they want genetic testing. If the test is positive, the person will develop HD. However, when the disease will develop cannot be determined.

Like PD, the pathologic process of HD involves the basal ganglia and extrapyramidal motor system. However, instead of a deficiency of DA, HD involves a deficiency of the neurotransmitters ACh and γ-aminobutyric acid (GABA). The net effect is an excess of DA, which leads to symptoms that are the opposite of those of parkinsonism.

Manifestations include movement disorder and cognitive and psychiatric problems. The movement disorder is marked by abnormal and excessive involuntary movements (*chorea*). These are writhing, twisting movements of the face, limbs, and body. The movements get worse as the disease progresses. Because facial movements involving speech, chewing, and swallowing are affected, aspiration and malnutrition are likely. The gait deteriorates, and ambulation eventually becomes impossible. Eventually all psychomotor processes, including the ability to eat and talk, are impaired.

Psychiatric symptoms are often present in the early stage of HD, even before the onset of motor symptoms. Depression is common. Other psychiatric symptoms include anxiety,

GENETICS IN CLINICAL PRACTICE

Huntington's Disease (HD)

Genetic Basis
- Autosomal dominant disorder.
- Caused by mutation in *HTT* gene found on chromosome 4.
- A single copy of altered gene (heterozygous) is enough to cause HD.
- Offspring of a person with HD have a 50% chance of inheriting the disease-causing allele.

Incidence
- Occurs in 3 to 7 in 100,000 people of European ancestry.
- Less common in other populations, including people of Japanese, Chinese, and African descent.

Genetic Testing
- DNA testing is available.
- DNA testing can be done on fetal cells obtained by amniocentesis or chorionic villus sampling.
- Preimplantation genetic diagnosis can be done on embryos before implantation and pregnancy.
- No test is available to predict when symptoms will develop.

Clinical Implications
- Consider genetic counseling if there is a family history of HD.
- Because HD is an autosomal dominant disorder, those at risk have a strong motivation to seek genetic testing.
- A positive result is not considered a diagnosis because it may be obtained decades before symptoms begin.
- A negative test means the person does not carry the mutated gene and will not develop HD.

agitation, impulsivity, apathy, social withdrawal, and obsessiveness. Cognitive deterioration is more variable. It involves perception, memory, attention, and learning.

Death usually occurs 10 to 30 years after the onset of symptoms.[33] The most common cause of death is pneumonia, followed by suicide. Other causes of death include injuries related to falls and other complications.

Because HD has no cure, treatment is palliative. Drugs are available to control movements and behavioral problems. Tetrabenazine (Xenazine) is used to treat chorea. It decreases the amount of DA available at synapses in the brain and thus reducing the involuntary movements of chorea. If chorea is accompanied by other symptoms, tetrabenazine may not be the treatment of choice. For example, tetrabenazine can worsen depression. Deutetrabenazine (Austedo) is related to tetrabenazine. It is also approved for the treatment of chorea. Research suggests this drug is better tolerated than tetrabenazine.[34] Other medications for the movement disorder include neuroleptics (e.g., haloperidol, risperidone), benzodiazepines, and DA-depleting agents, such as reserpine.

Cognitive disorders are treated as needed with nondrug therapies (e.g., counseling, memory books). Psychiatric disorders can be treated with selective serotonin reuptake inhibitors, such as sertraline (Zoloft) and paroxetine (Paxil). Antipsychotic medication, such as haloperidol or risperidone, may be needed.

HD presents a great challenge to health care professionals. The goal of nursing management is to provide the most comfortable environment possible for the patient and caregiver by maintaining physical safety, treating physical symptoms, and providing emotional and psychologic support.

Because of the chorea, caloric requirements are high. The patient may need as many as 4000 to 5000 cal/day to maintain body weight. As HD progresses, meeting caloric needs becomes a greater challenge when the patient has difficulty swallowing and holding the head still. Depression and mental deterioration can compromise nutritional intake. Enteral or parenteral nutrition may be needed as the disease progresses.

End-of-life issues need to be discussed with the patient and caregiver. These include care in the home or long-term care facility, artificial methods of feeding, advance directives and cardiopulmonary resuscitation (CPR), use of antibiotics to treat infections, and guardianship. Address these topics throughout the course of the disease as the patient and caregiver adapt to increasing disability.

CASE STUDY

Seizure Disorder With Headache

(© Purestock/Thinkstock.)

Patient Profile

C.S. is a 24-yr-old woman who was diagnosed with seizure disorder at age 15. At that time, she had a generalized-onset tonic-clonic seizure and was given a prescription for valproate (Depakote). She had a second witnessed seizure 4 months later but has since been seizure free. C.S. now reports headaches and says she is afraid her seizures are going to return. She is single, lives alone, and describes her job as stressful.

Subjective Data
- Describes headache pain on the left side of her forehead as throbbing
- Has vomited with headache
- Describes changes in vision, including flashing lights
- Headache occurs nearly every month on a regular cycle

Objective Data
- Alert and oriented to person
- Neurologic examination negative
- Serum valproate levels within normal limits
- EEG normal
- CT of head normal

Discussion Questions

1. What is seizure disorder?
2. What is the pathophysiology of seizure disorder?
3. What is the significance of the laboratory and diagnostic findings?
4. Is the headache related to seizure activity?
5. **Safety:** To ensure C.S.'s safety, what nursing interventions are needed?
6. **Patient-Centered Care:** What teaching will you include in the plan of care for C.S. about the course of the disease?
7. **Priority Decision:** Based on the assessment data, what are the priority nursing diagnoses?
8. **Evidence-Based Practice:** Based on current treatment guidelines, what medication may be effective in managing both C.S.'s seizure disorder and her migraine headaches?
9. Develop a conceptual care map for C.S.

▪ BRIDGE TO NCLEX EXAMINATION

The number of the question corresponds to the same-numbered outcome at the beginning of the chapter.

1. A 50-yr-old man reports recurring headaches. He describes them as sharp, stabbing, and around his left eye. He says his left eye seems to swell and get teary when these headaches occur. Based on this history, you suspect he has
   a. cluster headaches.
   b. tension headaches.
   c. migraine headaches.
   d. medication overuse headaches.

2. A 65-yr-old woman was just diagnosed with Parkinson's disease. The priority nursing intervention is
   a. searching the Internet for educational videos.
   b. helping the caregiver explore respite care options.
   c. promoting physical exercise and a well-balanced diet.
   d. teaching about the benefits and risks of ablation surgery.

3. The nurse finds an 87-yr-old patient is continually rubbing, flexing, and kicking her legs throughout the day. The night shift reports this same behavior escalates at night, preventing her from obtaining sleep. The next step the nurse should take is to
   a. ask the provider for a daytime sedative for the patient.
   b. request soft restraints to prevent her from falling out of her bed.
   c. ask the provider for a nighttime sleep medication for the patient.
   d. perform an assessment, suspecting a disorder such as restless legs syndrome.

4. Possible social effects of a chronic neurologic disease include (select all that apply)
   a. divorce.
   b. job loss.
   c. depression.
   d. role changes.
   e. loss of self-esteem.

5. The nurse is reinforcing teaching with a patient newly diagnosed with amyotrophic lateral sclerosis (ALS). Which statement would be appropriate to include in the teaching?
   a. "Even though the symptoms you have are severe, most people recover with treatment."
   b. "ALS results from excess chemicals in the brain, so symptoms can be controlled with medication."
   c. "You need to consider advance directives now, because you will lose cognitive function as the disease progresses."
   d. "This is a progressing disease that eventually results in permanent paralysis, though you will not lose any cognitive function."

1. a, 2. c, 3. d, 4. a, b, c, d, 5. d

For rationales to these answers and even more NCLEX review questions, visit *http://evolve.elsevier.com/Lewis/medsurg*.

ⓔ EVOLVE WEBSITE/RESOURCES LIST

http://evolve.elsevier.com/Lewis/medsurg
Review Questions (Online Only)
Key Points
Answer Keys for Questions
- Rationales for Bridge to NCLEX Examination Questions
- Answer Guidelines for Case Study on p. 1380
Student Case Studies
- Patient With Parkinson's Disease and Hip Fracture
- Patient With Seizures
Nursing Care Plans
- eNursing Care Plan 58.1: Patient With Headaches
- eNursing Care Plan 58.2: Patient With Seizure Disorder
- eNursing Care Plan 58.3: Patient With Multiple Sclerosis
- eNursing Care Plan 58.4: Patient With Parkinson's Disease
Conceptual Care Map Creator
- Conceptual Care Map for Case Study on p. 1380
Audio Glossary
Content Updates

REFERENCES

1. Headache Classification Committee of the International Headache Society: *The international classification of headache disorders*. Retrieved from *www.ichd-3.org/*.
2. Migraine Research Foundation: Migraines. Retrieved from *http://migraineresearchfoundation.org/about-migraine/migraine-facts/*.
3. May A, Schulte LH: Chronic migraine: Risk factors, mechanisms, and treatment, *Nat Rev Neurol* 12:8, 2016.
4. American Migraine Foundation: Understanding migraine with aura. Retrieved from *https://americanmigrainefoundation.org/understanding-migraine/understanding-migraine-aura/*.
5. American Migraine Foundation: The genetics of migraine. Retrieved from *https://americanmigrainefoundation.org/understanding-migraine/the-genetics-of-migraine/*.
6. American Migraine Foundation: Living with migraine. Retrieved from *https://americanmigrainefoundation.org/living-with-migraine/*.
7. Karsan N, Prabhakar P, Goadsby PJ: Premonitory symptoms of migraine in children and adolescents, *Curr Pain Headache Rep* 21:7, 2017.
8. American Migraine Foundation: Cluster headache. Retrieved from *https://americanmigrainefoundation.org/understanding-migraine/cluster-headache/*.
9. National Institute of Neurological Disorders and Stroke: Headache: Hope through research. Retrieved from *www.ninds.nih.gov/Disorders/Patient-Caregiver-Education/Hope-Through-Research/Headache-Hope-Through-Research*.
10. The Migraine Trust: Cluster headache. Retrieved from *www.migrainetrust.org/about-migraine/types-of-migraine/other-headache-disorders/cluster-headache/*.
11. Warren E: Neurological symptoms in primary care: Part 3: Headache, *Pract Nurs* 47:3, 2017.
12. Silberstein SD: Topiramate in migraine prevention: A 2016 perspective, *Headache* 57:1, 2017.
13. Centers for Disease Control and Prevention: Epilepsy fast facts. Retrieved from *www.cdc.gov/epilepsy/about/fast-facts.htm*.
14. Gaspard N: Autoimmune epilepsy, *CONTINUUM* 22:1, 2016.
15. Epilepsy Foundation: Genetic testing. Retrieved from *www.epilepsy.com/learn/diagnosis/genetic-testing*.
16. Fisher RS, Cross JH, D'Souza C, et al: Instruction manual for the ILAE 2017 operational classification of seizure types, *Epilepsia* 58:4, 2017.
*17. Hingray C, El-Hage W, Duncan R, et al: Access to diagnostic and therapeutic facilities for psychogenic nonepileptic seizures: An international survey by the ILAE PNES Task Force, *Epilepsia* 59:1, 2018.
18. Epilepsy Foundation: Status epilepticus. Retrieved from *www.epilepsy.com/information/professionals/about-epilepsy-seizures/classifying-seizures/status-epilepticus*.

*19. Glauser T, Shinnar S, Gloss D, et al: Evidence-based guideline: Treatment of convulsive status epilepticus in children and adults: Report of the Guideline Committee of the American Epilepsy Society, *Epilepsy Curr* 16:1, 2016.

*20. Harden C, Tomson T, Gloss D, et al: Practice guideline summary: Sudden unexpected death in epilepsy incidence rates and risk factors, *Neurol* 88:17, 2017.

21. National Institute of Neurological Disorders and Stroke: Restless legs syndrome fact sheet. Retrieved from *www.ninds.nih.gov/Disorders/Patient-Caregiver-Education/Fact-Sheets/Restless-Legs-Syndrome-Fact-Sheet.*

22. Multiplesclerosis.net: MS statistics. Retrieved from *http://multiplesclerosis.net/what-is-ms/statistics.*

23. National Multiple Sclerosis Society: What causes MS? Retrieved from *www.nationalmssociety.org/What-is-MS/What-Causes-MS.*

*24. Thompson AJ, Banwell BL, Barkhof F, et al: Diagnosis of multiple sclerosis: 2017 Revisions of the McDonald criteria, *Lancet* 391:1622, 2018.

25. Parkinson's Foundation: Statistics. Retrieved from *http://parkinson.org/Understanding-Parkinsons/Causes-and-Statistics/Statistics.*

*26. Jennum P, Christensen JA, Zoetmulder M: Neurophysiological basis of rapid eye movement sleep behavior disorder: Informing future drug development, *Nat Sci Sleep* 15:107, 2018.

27. Gonzalez-Usigli HA: Parkinson disease. Retrieved from *www.merckmanuals.com/professional/neurologic-disorders/movement-and-cerebellar-disorders/parkinson-disease#section_15.*

28. National Institute of Neurological Disorders and Stroke: Myasthenia gravis fact sheet. Retrieved from *www.ninds.nih.gov/Disorders/Patient-Caregiver-Education/Fact-Sheets/Myasthenia-Gravis-Fact-Sheet#4.*

29. Mayo Clinic: Myasthenia gravis. Retrieved from *www.mayoclinic.org/diseases-conditions/myasthenia-gravis/symptoms-causes/syc-20352036.*

30. ALS Association: ALS. Retrieved from *www.alsa.org/.*

31. National Institute of Neurological Disorders and Stroke: Amyotrophic lateral sclerosis fact sheet. Retrieved from *www.ninds.nih.gov/disorders/amyotrophiclateralsclerosis/detail_ALS.htm.*

32. Almeida MJ: Edaravone (Radicava) for amyotrophic lateral sclerosis. Retrieved from *https://alsnewstoday.com/edaravone-radicava-for-als/.*

33. Mayo Clinic: Huntington's disease. Retrieved from *www.mayoclinic.org/diseases-conditions/huntingtons-disease/symptoms-causes/syc-20356117.*

34. Heo YA, Scott LJ. Deutetrabenazine: A review in chorea associated with Huntington's disease, *Drugs* 77:1857, 2017.

*Evidence-based information for clinical practice.

59

Dementia and Delirium

Janice Smolowitz

*You treat a disease you win, you lose. You treat a person,
I guarantee you'll win, no matter what the outcome.*

Patch Adams

ⓔ http://evolve.elsevier.com/Lewis/medsurg

CONCEPTUAL FOCUS

Cognition
Family Dynamics

Functional Ability
Safety

Stress

LEARNING OUTCOMES

1. Define *dementia* and *delirium*.
2. Classify the different etiologies of dementia.
3. Explain the pathophysiology for different types of dementia.
4. Discuss the clinical manifestations of mild cognitive impairment.
5. Describe the clinical manifestations, diagnostic studies, and nursing and interprofessional care for a patient with dementia.

6. Discuss the clinical manifestations, diagnostic studies, and nursing and interprofessional care for a patient with Alzheimer's disease.
7. Explain the etiology, pathophysiology, clinical manifestations, diagnostic studies, and nursing and interprofessional care for a patient with delirium.

KEY TERMS

Alzheimer's disease (AD), p. 1386
delirium, p. 1398
dementia, p. 1383
dementia with Lewy bodies (DLB), Table 59.3, p. 1385

frontotemporal lobar degeneration (FTLD), Table 59.3, p. 1385
mild cognitive impairment (MCI), p. 1389
mixed dementia, p. 1384
neurofibrillary tangles, p. 1387

retrogenesis, p. 1388
sundowning, p. 1395

This chapter discusses the cognitive disorders of dementia and delirium, with a focus on the nursing management of patients with Alzheimer's disease (AD). Cognitive impairment refers to any deficit in intellectual functioning, including problems with memory, orientation, attention, and concentration. The consequences of cognitive impairment can be devastating for the person and caregivers. Ultimately, dementia adversely affects functional ability and the person's ability to work, fulfill responsibilities, and perform activities of daily living (ADLs). There is a high risk for many problems, including injury, impaired nutrition, and social isolation.

Persons with dementia and delirium may have symptoms of depression. Depression and dementia are often mistaken for each another, especially among older adults. Manifestations of depression, especially among older adults, may include sadness, difficulty concentrating, fatigue, apathy, feelings of despair, and inactivity. When depression is severe, poor concentration and attention may result, causing memory and functional impairment. When dementia and depression occur together there can be marked intellectual deterioration. Table 59.1 compares key

features of dementia, delirium, and depression. Your ability to interview the patient and family members about presenting symptoms and signs can aide in early diagnosis and treatment.

DEMENTIA

Dementia is a disorder characterized by a decline from previous level of function in 1 or more cognitive domains: complex attention, executive function, language, learning and memory, perceptual-motor, and social cognition.[1] The cognitive decline interferes with ability to function and perform daily activities. This decline does not occur with onset of an acute state of confusion, such as delirium, or the onset of another major mental disorder, such as depression.

As the average life span increases, the number of patients diagnosed with dementia is increasing. AD is the most common form of dementia. It accounts for 60% to 80% of all cases of dementia (Fig. 59.1). In 2018, 5.7 million Americans over age 65 were living with AD. We expect this number to reach 14 million by 2050.[2]

TABLE 59.1 Comparison of Dementia, Delirium, and Depression

Feature	Dementia	Delirium	Depression
Onset	Usually insidious	Abrupt, although initially can be subtle	Often coincides with life changes. Often abrupt
Progression	Slow	Abrupt. Can fluctuate from day to day	Variable, rapid to slow but may be uneven
Duration	Years (average of 8 yr but can be much longer)	Hours to days to weeks. Can be prolonged in some	Can be several months to years, especially if not treated
Thinking	Difficulty with abstract thinking, impaired judgment, words difficult to find	Disorganized, distorted. Slow or accelerated incoherent speech	Intact but with apathy, fatigue. May be indecisive. Feels sense of hopelessness. May not want to live
Perception	Misperceptions often present. Delusions and hallucinations	Distorted. Delusions and hallucinations	May deny or be unaware of depression. May have feelings of guilt
Psychomotor behavior	May pace or be hyperactive. As disease progresses, may not be able to perform tasks or movements when asked	Variable. Can be hyperactive or hypoactive, or mixed	Often withdrawn and hypoactive
Sleep-wake cycle	Sleeps during day. Frequent awakenings at night. Fragmented sleep	Disturbed sleep. Reversed sleep-wake cycle	Disturbed, often with early morning awakening

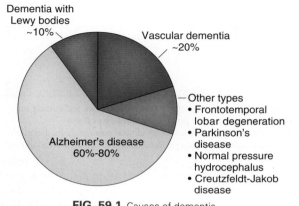

FIG. 59.1 Causes of dementia.

Dementia with Lewy bodies ~10%
Vascular dementia ~20%
Alzheimer's disease 60%-80%
Other types
• Frontotemporal lobar degeneration
• Parkinson's disease
• Normal pressure hydrocephalus
• Creutzfeldt-Jakob disease

Etiology and Pathophysiology

Dementia is caused by treatable and untreatable conditions. Table 59.2 describes the types of dementia and their underlying causes. Treatable causes may initially be reversible. However, with prolonged exposure or disease, irreversible changes may occur.

The most common causes of dementia are neurodegenerative conditions that cannot be reversed (Table 59.3). Most of these are due to AD. Other causes include dementia with Lewy bodies (DLB), frontotemporal dementia (FTD), and Parkinson's disease with dementia (PDD). Vascular, or multiinfarct dementia (VaD), is a loss of cognitive function caused by cardiovascular disease (CVD). The prevalence of VaD is higher among blacks and those with hypertension and diabetes. VaD may be caused by a single infarct (stroke) or multiple strokes.

Mixed dementia occurs when 2 or more types of dementia are present at the same time. It is characterized by the hallmark abnormalities of AD and another type of dementia. Usually the other type of dementia is VaD, but it can be other types.

Normal pressure hydrocephalus is a rare disorder characterized by an obstruction in the flow of cerebrospinal fluid (CSF). This causes a buildup of CSF in the brain. Manifestations include dementia, urinary incontinence, and difficulty walking. Meningitis, encephalitis, or head injury may cause the condition. If diagnosed early, it is treatable by surgery in which a shunt is inserted to divert the fluid away from the brain.

TABLE 59.2 Causes of Dementia

Type of Dementia	Cause
Neurodegenerative disorders	• AD • Amyotrophic lateral sclerosis (ALS) • Dementia with Lewy bodies (DLB) • Down syndrome • Frontotemporal lobar degeneration (FTLD) • Huntington's disease • Parkinson's disease
Vascular diseases	• Chronic subdural hematoma* • Subarachnoid hemorrhage* • Vascular (multiinfarct) dementia
Immunologic diseases or infections	• Multiple sclerosis • Systemic exertion intolerance disease • Infections (e.g., Creutzfeldt-Jakob disease) • Acquired immunodeficiency syndrome (AIDS) • Meningitis* • Encephalitis* • Neurosyphilis* • Systemic lupus erythematosus*
Medications†	• Anticholinergics • Antiparkinsonian drugs • Cardiac drugs: digoxin, methyldopa • Cocaine • Heroin • Hypnotics • Opioids • phenytoin (Dilantin) • Tranquilizers
Metabolic or nutritional diseases	• Alcohol use disorder • Cobalamin (vitamin B_{12}) deficiency* • Folate deficiency* • Hyperthyroidism* • Hypothyroidism* • Thiamine (vitamin B_1) deficiency*
Systemic diseases	• Dialysis dementia* • Hepatic encephalopathy* • Uremic encephalopathy* • Wilson's disease
Trauma	• Head injury*
Tumors	• Brain tumors (primary)* • Metastatic tumors*
Ventricular disorders	• Hydrocephalus*

*Potentially reversible.
†These are examples of drugs that may cause cognitive impairment that is potentially reversible.

TABLE 59.3 Neurodegenerative Causes of Dementia

Neurodegenerative Disorder	Characteristics	Management
Dementia With Lewy Bodies (DLB) • Characterized by presence of Lewy bodies (abnormal deposits of protein α-synuclein) in brainstem and cortex • Has features of both AD and Parkinson's disease. • Imperative that a correct diagnosis is made	• Diagnosis is based on manifestations • Typically have manifestations of parkinsonism (extrapyramidal signs [bradykinesia, rigidity, postural instability, but not always a tremor]), hallucinations, short-term memory loss, unpredictable cognitive shifts, and sleep problems • Pneumonia is a common complication	• Drugs may include levodopa/carbidopa and acetylcholinesterase inhibitors • Manage dementia and problems related to dysphagia and immobility • Swallowing problems can lead to impaired nutrition • At risk for falls from impaired mobility and balance
Down Syndrome • Genetic disorder caused by presence of all or part of a third copy of chromosome 21	• Typically associated with physical growth delays, characteristic facial features, and mild to moderate intellectual disability	• Much higher risk for developing dementia • Estimated 80% will develop dementia
Frontotemporal Lobar Degeneration (FTLD) • Associated with atrophy of frontal and temporal lobes of brain • In Pick's disease, a type of FTLD, brain may have abnormal microscopic deposits called *Pick bodies* • Often misdiagnosed as a psychiatric problem because of strange behaviors	• Changes in behavior, sleep, and eventually memory • Progresses relentlessly and may lead to language impairment, erratic behavior, and dementia • Tends to occur at a younger age than does AD, typically about age 60	• No specific treatment • Antidepressants and antipsychotics to treat behavioral manifestations
Parkinson's Disease, Huntington's Disease, and Amyotrophic Lateral Sclerosis • Chronic, progressive, and incurable diseases	• Associated with development of dementia in the later stages of disease	• See Chapter 58

Clinical Manifestations

The onset of manifestations varies depending on the cause. Manifestations associated with neurologic degeneration usually occur gradually and progress over time. Symptoms of VaD may appear abruptly or progress in a stepwise pattern. While the cause of dementia cannot be determined based only on the history of symptom progression, patterns can guide your thinking about the different causes. An acute change that occurs over days to weeks or subacute change that occurs over weeks to months may indicate an infectious or metabolic cause of dementia, such as encephalitis, meningitis, hypothyroidism, or drug-related dementia. Other manifestations of dementia are discussed in the section on clinical manifestations of AD on p. 1387.

Diagnostic Studies

The diagnosis of dementia is focused on determining the cause (e.g., reversible versus irreversible factors). An important first step is a thorough medical, neurologic, and psychologic history. During the history, special attention is given to reviewing the cognitive and behavioral changes that have occurred. Family members and significant others can give important information. Elicit information about (1) problems with judgment; (2) reduced interest in hobbies/activities; (3) repeating questions, stories, or statements; (4) trouble learning how to use a tool or appliance; (5) forgetting the correct month or year; (6) problems handling financial affairs; (7) difficulty remembering appointments; and (8) consistent problems with thinking and/or memory.

Obtain a complete medication history, including the use of prescribed and over-the-counter medications, herbal supplements, and recreational substances. Ask about drugs that can impair cognition, such as analgesics, anticholinergics, psychotropics, and sedative-hypnotics.

A thorough physical assessment is done to rule out other potential medical conditions. For example, slow movement, rigidity, asymmetric tremor of an extremity, and shuffling gait are suggestive of Parkinsonism. Dementia, urinary incontinence, and ataxic gait suggest normal pressure hydrocephalus. The neurologic assessment includes a mental status examination or screening test. Agreement among findings from the assessment, screening tests, and history can help confirm the presence of dementia.

Based on history and physical assessment findings, diagnostic studies are ordered to confirm the most likely cause and exclude other possible conditions. The American Academy of Neurology (AAN) recommends routine screening tests, including an electrolyte panel, liver function tests, serum vitamin B_{12} level, complete blood count, and thyroid function tests.[3] Specialized laboratory tests, such as red blood cell folate in a patient with alcoholism or ionized serum calcium in a patient with multiple myeloma, are ordered based on history. Neuroimaging with a head CT or MRI scan is important for patients with acute onset of cognitive impairment, rapid neurologic deterioration, or findings that suggest a subdural hematoma, thrombotic stroke, or cerebral hemorrhage.

❖ Interprofessional and Nursing Care

Management of patients with dementia is similar to the management of patients with AD, which is described later in this chapter. Preventive measures for VaD include treatment of risk factors, such as hypertension, diabetes, smoking, hypercholesterolemia, and dysrhythmias. Stroke is discussed in Chapter 57. Drugs that are used for patients with AD are also useful for patients with VaD. Drug therapy is discussed on p. 1392 later in this chapter.

ALZHEIMER'S DISEASE

Alzheimer's disease (AD) is a chronic, progressive, neurodegenerative brain disease. It is thought that 11% of people age 65 and older, and nearly one third of those over age 85, have AD. Only a small number of people younger than 60 years of age develop AD. When AD develops in someone younger than 60 years, it is referred to as *early-onset AD*. AD that occurs in people over 60 years old is called *late-onset AD*.

Ultimately the disease is fatal. Death typically occurs 4 to 8 years after diagnosis, although some patients have lived for 20 years. AD is the sixth leading cause of death in the United States.[2] It is the only cause of death among the top 10 in the United States that cannot be prevented or cured, nor its progression slowed.

The burden of caring for a patient with AD is well documented. 25% of AD caregivers are caring for both someone with the disease and a child or grandchild. 60% of family caregivers describe high or very high emotional stress.[2] More than 1 in 6 family caregivers report they had to stop working due to caregiving responsibilities. 74% of caregivers described becoming "somewhat concerned" to "very concerned" about maintaining their own health since becoming caregivers.

GENDER DIFFERENCES

Alzheimer's Disease and Dementia

Men
- Men have a higher incidence of VaD than women.

Women
- Nearly two thirds of people with AD are women.
- Women are more likely to develop AD than men, mainly because they live longer.
- About twice as many women as men die each year from AD.

⊕ PROMOTING HEALTH EQUITY

Alzheimer's Disease

- Older blacks are about twice as likely to have AD as older whites.
- Older Hispanics are about 1½ times as likely to have AD as older whites.
- Variations in health, lifestyle, and socioeconomic risk factors across ethnic groups account for most of the differences in risk.
- Increased rates of CVD and diabetes may be related to the increased prevalence of AD in blacks and Hispanics.
- Lower levels of education and other socioeconomic characteristics may increase risk.[2]

Source: Alzheimer's Association: 2018 Alzheimer's disease facts and figures, *Alzheimers Dement* 14:367, 2018.

Etiology

The exact cause of AD is unknown. It is likely a combination of multiple factors.

Aging. The greatest risk factor for AD is age. Most people with AD are diagnosed at age 65 or older. While age is the greatest risk factor, AD is not a normal part of aging and age alone does not cause the disease.[2]

Family History. Family history of AD is an important risk factor.[1] Persons with a first-degree relative (parent or sibling) with dementia are more likely to develop the disease. Those who have more than 1 first-degree relative with dementia are at even higher risk for developing AD.

⚕ Genetic Link

Persons with a clear pattern of inheritance within a family have familial AD (FAD). FAD is associated with onset before age 60 and a more rapid disease course. Cases are referred to as sporadic when there is no familial connection. The pathogenesis of FAD and sporadic AD is similar.

The first gene associated with late-onset and sporadic forms of AD was the epsilon (E)-4 allele of the apolipoprotein E *(ApoE)* gene on chromosome 19. *ApoE* contains the instructions to make a protein that helps to carry cholesterol and other types of fat in the bloodstream. *ApoE* may have a role in clearing amyloid plaques. Mutations in this gene result in more amyloid deposits.

ApoE comes in several different alleles or forms. Three alleles occur most often. People inherit 1 allele (e.g., *ApoE-2, ApoE-3, ApoE-4*), from each parent. The presence of *ApoE-4*, which is a risk-factor gene, increases the risk for developing late-onset AD. *ApoE* testing is controversial. Not all people with *ApoE-4* develop AD. Among patients with dementia who meet the clinical criteria for AD, finding *ApoE-4* increases the reliability of diagnosis.

In patients with early-onset AD, 3 genes have been identified as important: presenilin-1 *(PSEN1),* presenilin-2 *(PSEN2),* and amyloid precursor protein *(APP)* (see the Genetics in Clinical Practice box). When these genes mutate, they cause brain cells to overproduce β-amyloid.[2] *PSEN1* mutations cause AD before age 60 and often before age 50. *PSEN2* causes early-onset FAD.

Cardiovascular Factors. Brain health is closely linked to the health of the heart and blood vessels. Brain functioning depends on a good blood supply and nutrients delivered to it by that blood supply.

Many factors increase the risk for CVD. These include diabetes, hypertension, obesity, hypercholesterolemia, and smoking. Diabetes dramatically increases the risk for developing AD and other types of dementia. Diabetes can contribute to dementia in several ways. Chronic high levels of insulin and glucose may be directly toxic to brain cells. Insulin resistance, which causes high blood glucose and can lead to type 2 diabetes, may interfere with the body's ability to break down amyloid, a protein that forms brain plaques in AD. High blood glucose and high cholesterol have a role in atherosclerosis, which contributes to VaD.[4]

Diabetes may contribute to poor memory and decreased mental function in other ways. The disease causes microangiopathy, which damages small blood vessels throughout the body. Ongoing damage to blood vessels in the brain may be one reason why people with diabetes are at a higher risk for cognitive problems as they age.[5] People with diabetes may lose brain volume, especially gray matter, as the disease progresses.

Head Trauma. Head trauma is a risk factor for dementia. Professional football players and military veterans who had traumatic brain injury or posttraumatic stress disorder have an increased risk for AD and other types of dementia.[6]

Pathophysiology

Characteristic findings of AD related to changes in the brain's structure and function include (1) amyloid plaques, (2) neurofibrillary tangles, (3) loss of connections between neurons, and (4) neuron death.[7] Fig. 59.2 shows the pathologic changes in AD.

As part of aging, people develop some plaques in their brain tissue. In AD, more plaques appear in certain parts of

GENETICS IN CLINICAL PRACTICE
Alzheimer's Disease

Genetic Basis

Early Onset (Familial) (<60 Yr Old at Onset)
- Autosomal dominant disorder
- Various mutations in the following genes:
  - Amyloid precursor protein *(APP)* gene on chromosome 21
  - Presenilin-1 *(PSEN1)* gene on chromosome 14
  - Presenilin-2 *(PSEN2)* gene on chromosome 1

Late Onset (Sporadic) (>60 Yr Old at Onset)
- Genetically more complex than early-onset AD.
- Apolipoprotein E-4 *(ApoE-4)* allele on chromosome 19 increases the chance for developing AD.
- Presence of *ApoE-2* allele is associated with a lower risk for AD.

Incidence

Early Onset
- Rare form of AD, accounting for <5% of cases.
- 50% risk for disease for children of affected parents.
- May occur in people as young as 30 yr.

Late Onset
- *ApoE-4* is present in 40% to 65% of people with late-onset AD.
- Many *ApoE-4*–positive people do not develop AD, and many *ApoE-4*–negative people do.

Genetic Testing

Early Onset
- Genetic screening is available for mutations on chromosomes 1, 14, and 21.

Late Onset
- Blood test can identify which *ApoE* allele a patient has but cannot predict who will develop disease.
- In a patient who meets the clinical criteria for AD, finding *ApoE-4* increases the reliability of the diagnosis.

Clinical Implications
- Genetic testing for family members of patients with early-onset AD may be appropriate.
- Testing should be done only with formal genetic counseling, especially when asymptomatic family members are involved.
- If a patient tests positive for *ApoE-4*, it does not mean that the patient will develop AD.

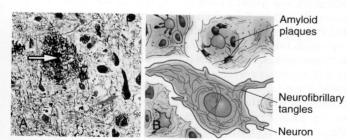

FIG. 59.2 Pathologic changes in AD. **A,** Plaque with central amyloid core *(white arrow)* next to a neurofibrillary tangle *(red arrow)* on the histologic specimen from a brain autopsy. **B,** Schematic representation of amyloid plaque and neurofibrillary tangle.

the brain. These plaques consist of clusters of insoluble deposits of a protein called β-amyloid, other proteins, remnants of neurons, non-nerve cells such as microglia (cells that surround and digest damaged cells or foreign substances), and other cells, such as astrocytes.

β-Amyloid is cleaved from amyloid precursor protein (APP), which is associated with the cell membrane (Fig. 59.3). The normal function of APP is unknown. Genetic factors may play a critical role in how the brain processes the β-amyloid protein. Overproduction of β-amyloid is an important risk factor for AD. Abnormally high levels of β-amyloid cause cell damage either directly or by eliciting an inflammatory response and ultimately neuron death.

In AD, plaques develop first in areas of the brain used for memory and cognitive function, including the hippocampus (a structure that is important in forming and storing short-term memories). Eventually AD attacks the cerebral cortex, especially the areas responsible for language and reasoning.

Neurofibrillary tangles are abnormal collections of twisted protein threads inside nerve cells. The main component of these structures is a protein called tau. Tau proteins in the central nervous system (CNS) are involved in providing support for intracellular structure through their support of microtubules. Tau proteins hold the microtubules together like railroad ties. In AD tau protein is altered. As a result, the microtubules twist together in a helical fashion (Fig. 59.3). This ultimately forms the neurofibrillary tangles found in the neurons of people with AD.

Plaques and neurofibrillary tangles are not unique to patients with AD or dementia. They are also found in the brains of people without cognitive impairment. However, they are more abundant in the brains of those with AD.

The other feature of AD is the loss of connections between neurons and neuron death. These processes result in structural damage. Affected parts of the brain begin to shrink in a process called brain atrophy. By the final stage of AD, brain tissue has shrunk significantly (Fig. 59.4).

Clinical Manifestations

Research suggests AD causes pathologic changes in the brain at least 15 years before the manifestations of AD appear.[8] The Alzheimer's Association has developed a list of 10 warning signs that are common manifestations of AD (Table 59.4).

Symptoms do not always directly relate to abnormal changes in the brain caused by AD. The stages of AD can be categorized as mild, moderate, and severe (Table 59.5). The rate of progression from mild to severe is highly variable and ranges from 3 to 20 years.

The initial manifestations are usually related to changes in cognitive functioning. The person may have memory loss, mild disorientation, or trouble with words and numbers. Often a family member reports the patient's declining memory to the HCP.

Normal age-related memory decline is characterized by mild changes that do not interfere with ADLs (Table 59.6). In AD the memory loss initially relates to recent events, with remote memories still intact. With time and progression of AD, memory loss includes both recent and remote memory and affects the ability to perform self-care.

As AD progresses, personal hygiene deteriorates, as does the ability to concentrate and maintain attention. Ongoing loss of neurons in AD can cause the person to act in unpredictable ways. Behavioral manifestations, such as agitation or aggression, result from changes that take place within the brain. These behaviors are neither intentional nor controllable by the person with the disease. Some people develop delusions and hallucinations.

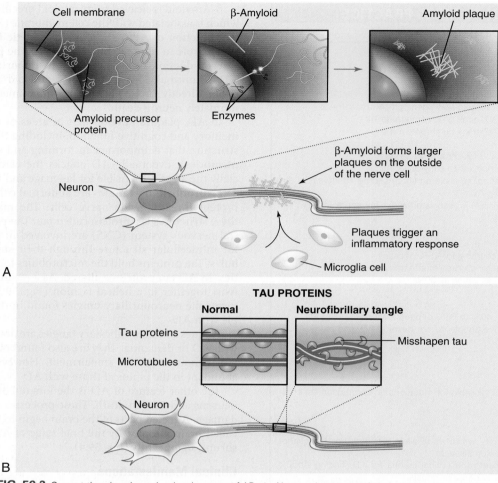

FIG. 59.3 Current theories about the development of AD. **A,** Abnormal amounts of β-amyloid are cleaved from the amyloid precursor protein *(APP)* and released into the circulation. The β-amyloid fragments come together in clumps to form plaques that attach to the neuron. Microglia react to the plaque, and an inflammatory response results. **B,** Tau proteins provide structural support for the neuron microtubules. Chemical changes in the neuron cause structural changes in tau proteins. This results in twisting and tangling (neurofibrillary tangles).

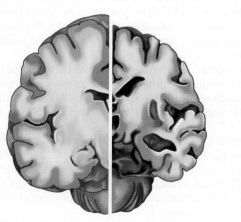

FIG. 59.4 Effects of AD on the brain. This figure compares a normal brain *(left)* with a brain affected by AD *(right).*

With progression of AD, more cognitive impairments occur. These include dysphasia (difficulty comprehending language and oral communication), apraxia (inability to manipulate objects or perform purposeful acts), visual agnosia (inability to recognize objects by sight), and dysgraphia (difficulty communicating by writing). Eventually long-term memories cannot be recalled, and the person may not recognize family members and friends. Later in the disease, the ability to communicate and perform ADLs is lost. Some tend to wander. In the late stages of AD, the person is unresponsive, incontinent, and needs total care.

Retrogenesis. Retrogenesis is the process in which the decline in AD mirrors, in reverse order, brain development that occurs from birth.[9] Thus it compares the developmental stages of childhood with the deterioration of patients with AD. As seen in Fig. 59.5, a relationship exists between the developmental stage and deterioration of function. For example, it is appropriate for a patient with AD in the moderate stage to feel good about putting together puzzles that belong to his 3-yr-old grandson. In fact, they may play well together on the same task or project.

Diagnostic Criteria for Alzheimer's Disease

The National Institute on Aging and the Alzheimer's Association have criteria and guidelines for diagnosing AD.[10] Guidelines address the use of imaging and biomarkers that may help determine whether changes are due to AD.

TABLE 59.4 Patient & Caregiver Teaching

Early Warning Signs of Alzheimer's Disease

Include the following information in the teaching plan for the patient with Alzheimer's disease:

1. Memory loss that affects job skills
   - Frequent forgetfulness or unexplainable confusion at home or in the workplace may signal that something is wrong.
   - This type of memory loss goes beyond forgetting an assignment, colleague's name, deadline, or phone number.
2. Problems with abstract thinking
   - For the patient with AD, this goes beyond challenges, such as balancing a checkbook.
   - The patient with AD may not be able to recognize numbers or do basic calculations.
3. Difficulty doing familiar tasks
   - It is normal for most people to become distracted and to forget something (e.g., leave something on the stove too long).
   - People with AD may cook a meal, then forget not only to serve it but also that they made it.
4. Poor or decreased judgment
   - Many people from time to time may choose not to dress appropriately for the weather (e.g., not bringing a coat or sweater on a cold evening).
   - The patient with AD may dress inappropriately in more noticeable ways, such as wearing a bathrobe to the store or a sweater on a hot day.
5. Problems with language
   - Most people have trouble finding the "right" word from time to time.
   - People with AD may forget simple words or substitute inappropriate words, making their speech difficult to understand.
6. Misplacing things
   - For many people, temporarily misplacing keys, purses, or wallets is a normal, albeit frustrating, event.
   - The patient with AD may put items in inappropriate places (e.g., eating utensils in clothing drawers) but have no memory of how they got there.
7. Changes in mood
   - Most people have mood changes.
   - The patient with AD tends to have more rapid mood swings for no apparent reason.
8. Changes in personality
   - As most people age, they may have some change in personality (e.g., become less tolerant).
   - The patient with AD can change dramatically, either suddenly or over time. For example, someone who is easygoing may become angry, suspicious, or fearful.
9. Loss of initiative
   - The patient with AD may become and remain uninterested and uninvolved in many or all of his or her usual pursuits.

Adapted from Alzheimer's Association: *Early warning signs*, Chicago, The Association. Retrieved from *www.alz.org/alzheimers_disease_know_the_10_signs.asp.*

AD is considered on a spectrum (Table 59.7). The stages are preclinical AD, mild cognitive impairment, and dementia due to AD.[10] Dementia marks the terminal stage of the disease.

Preclinical Stage. A long lag exists between pathologic changes in the brain and manifestations of AD. The future goal would be to modify the disease process of AD before it becomes symptomatic. Once plaques and tangles have formed in sufficient quantity, it may be too late to intervene to prevent the disease or its progression. Although current attempts at modifying the disease process have not been successful, research is ongoing.

Mild Cognitive Impairment. Mild cognitive impairment (MCI) is the second stage in the AD spectrum. It is a state of cognitive function in which persons have problems with memory, language, or other essential cognitive functions. The problems are severe enough to be noticed by the person having them and by others and can be found on screening tests. Family members may see changes in the person's abilities (Table 59.6). To the casual observer, the person with MCI may seem normal. Because the problems do not interfere with daily activities, the patient does not meet the criteria for being diagnosed with dementia.

We classify MCI based on the cognitive skills affected. MCI that primarily affects memory is called amnestic MCI. With amnestic MCI, a person may forget important information that they would have recalled easily, such as appointments. The person is often aware of the change in memory.

MCI that affects other cognitive skills is nonamnestic MCI. Skills that may be affected include the ability to make sound decisions or complete a complex task.[11]

Between 15% and 20% of people 65 years and older have MCI. They are at high risk for developing AD. Some people with MCI show no progression and do not go on to develop AD. An estimated 15% of people with MCI will eventually develop AD.[2]

No drugs have been approved for the treatment of MCI. There is little evidence that drugs used in AD, such as cholinesterase inhibitors, affect progression to dementia or improve cognitive test scores in people with MCI.[11]

The primary treatment of MCI consists of ongoing monitoring. Monitoring the patient with MCI for changes in memory and thinking skills that indicate a worsening of symptoms or a progression to AD or other dementia is critical (Table 59.4).

Diagnostic Studies

No definitive diagnostic test exists for AD. The diagnosis is primarily a diagnosis of exclusion. In patients with cognitive impairment, there is increased emphasis on early and careful evaluation. As discussed earlier, many conditions can cause

---

TABLE 59.5 Stages of Alzheimer's Disease

Mild	Moderate	Severe
- Forgetfulness beyond what is seen in a normal patient	- Memory loss and confusion become more obvious	- Severe impairment of all cognitive functions
- Short-term memory impairment, especially for new learning	- Has more trouble organizing, planning, and following directions	- Little memory, unable to process new information
- Loss of initiative and interests	- May need help getting dressed	- Unable to perform self-care activities
- May forget recent events or the names of people or things	- May start having episodes of incontinence	- Often needs help with daily needs
- Impatient	- Trouble recognizing family members and friends	- May not be able to talk
- May no longer be able to solve simple math problems	- Agitation, restlessness	- Cannot understand words
- Slowly loses the ability to plan and organize	- May lack judgment and begin to wander, gets lost	- May have problems eating, swallowing
	- May have trouble sleeping	- May not be able to walk or sit up without help
	- Delusions, hallucinations, paranoia	- Immobility
	- Behavioral problems	- Incontinence

TABLE 59.6 Comparison of Normal Forgetfulness and Memory Loss

Normal Forgetfulness	Memory Loss in Mild Cognitive Impairment	Memory Loss in Alzheimer's Disease
• Sometimes misplaces keys, eyeglasses, or other items	• Often misplaces items	• Forgets what an item is used for or puts it in an inappropriate place
• Momentarily forgets an acquaintance's name	• Often forgets people's names and is slow to recall them	• May not remember knowing a person
• Sometimes has to search for a word	• Has increasing difficulty finding desired words	• Begins to lose language skills and may withdraw from social interaction
• Sometimes forgets to run an errand	• Begins to forget important events and appointments	• Loses sense of time, does not know what day it is
• May forget an event from the distant past	• May forget recent events or newly learned information	• Seriously impaired recent memory and problems learning and remembering new information
• When driving, may momentarily forget where to turn, but quickly orients self	• Becomes temporarily lost more often, may have trouble understanding and following a map	• Becomes easily disoriented or lost in familiar places, sometimes for hours
• Jokes about memory loss	• Worries about memory loss, family and friends notice lapses	• May have little or no awareness of cognitive problems

Adapted from Rabins P: Memory. In *The Johns Hopkins white papers,* Baltimore, 2007, Johns Hopkins University.

Stage	Alzheimer's Disease	Reisberg Stage*	Developmental Age	Diversion/Distraction Activities
Mild	No difficulty at all	1		
	Some memory trouble begins to affect job/home. Forgets familiar names.	2		
	Much difficulty maintaining job performance. Withdrawal from difficult situations.	3	12+ yr	Can function with understanding. Enjoy things previously enjoyed—watch TV, play and listen to music, play games.
	Can no longer hold a job, plan and prepare meals, handle personal finances, etc. Driving becomes difficult, although can drive to familiar places.	4	8–12 yr	Can still enjoy simple games, watch TV and videos. Enjoys family photos and memories.
Moderate	Can no longer select proper clothing for occasion or season. Needs help to remain safe in home. Forgets to bathe.	5	5–7 yr	Needs age-appropriate toys and games.
	Requires assistance with dressing.	6a	4–5 yr	Enjoy many of the same activities as preschoolers.
	Requires assistance with bathing.	6b	4–5 yr	
	Can no longer use toilet without assistance.	6c	4 yr	
	Urinary incontinence	6d	3–4.5 yr	
	Fecal incontinence	6e	2–3 yr	
Severe	Speech now limited to about words per day.	7a	15 mo	Enjoys infant toys, mobiles, dangling ribbons.
	Speech now limited to 1 word per day.	7b	1 yr	
	Can no longer walk without assistance.	7c	1 yr	
	Can no longer sit up without assistance.	7d	6–10 mo	
	Can no longer smile.	7e	2–4 mo	
	Can no longer hold up head.	7f	1–3 mo	

FIG. 59.5 Retrogenesis (back to birth) in AD. (*Based on Functional Assessment Staging. From Reisberg B: Functional assessment staging [FAST], *Psychopharmacol Bull* 24:653, 1988.)

TABLE 59.7 Diagnostic Criteria for Alzheimer's Disease

	Stage and Description	Recommendations for Biomarkers
Preclinical Alzheimer's disease (AD)	• Brain changes, including amyloid buildup and other early neuron changes, may already be in process • At this point, significant symptoms are not yet evident • In some people, amyloid buildup can be detected with PET scans and cerebrospinal fluid (CSF) analysis	• Use of imaging and biomarker tests at this stage are recommended only for research • Biomarkers are still being developed and standardized, and are not used by clinicians in general practice
Mild cognitive impairment (MCI) due to AD	• MCI stage is marked by symptoms of memory problems, enough to be noticed and measured, but not compromising a patient's independence • May or may not progress to AD	• Used primarily by researchers • May be used in specialized clinical settings to supplement standard tests to help determine possible causes of MCI • May help confirm that the patient's impairment is related to AD
Dementia due to Alzheimer's disease	• Characterized by memory, thinking, and behavioral symptoms that impair a patient's ability to function in daily life • Dementia marks the terminal stage of AD • Encompasses all stages shown in Table 59.5	• Can increase the level of certainty about a diagnosis of AD • May be used to distinguish AD from other dementias

Source: National Institute on Aging: Diagnostic criteria for Alzheimer's disease. Retrieved from *www.nia.nih.gov/health/alzheimers-disease-diagnostic-guidelines.*

manifestations of dementia, some of which are treatable or reversible (Table 59.2).

When all other possible conditions that can cause cognitive impairment have been excluded, a clinical diagnosis of AD can be made. A comprehensive evaluation includes a complete health history, physical examination, neurologic and mental status assessments, and laboratory tests (Table 59.8). A definitive diagnosis of AD requires an examination of brain tissue at autopsy and findings of neurofibrillary tangles and plaques.

Neuroimaging techniques allow for detection of changes early in the disease and monitoring of treatment response. In AD, multiple brain structures atrophy and the volume of the brain correlates with neurodegeneration. Brain imaging tests, such as CT or MRI, may show brain atrophy in the later stages of the disease. This finding occurs in other diseases and can be seen in people without cognitive impairment. PET scanning can help distinguish AD from other forms of dementia (Fig. 59.6). PET determines brain metabolism using glucose tracers. PET can also detect amyloid.

Guidelines identify 2 biomarker categories: (1) biomarkers showing the level of β-amyloid accumulation in the brain and (2) biomarkers showing that nerve cells in the brain are injured or actually degenerating. Biomarkers include (1) CSF neurochemical markers: β-amyloid and tau proteins, and (2) imaging biomarkers: volumetric MRI and PET. The level of tau in the CSF is an indication of neurodegeneration. Plasma levels of tau or β-amyloid are not of any value in diagnosing AD.

Some imaging biomarkers are used in specialized clinical settings. CSF biomarkers are mainly used for research. Biomarkers may be used in some cases to increase the level of certainty about a diagnosis of AD and to distinguish AD from other dementias. However, we need to do more research with biomarkers before they can be routinely used in practice.

Neuropsychologic testing is important for diagnostic purposes and to establish a baseline for evaluating changes over time. They are repeated at regular intervals during the course of care to assess changes in the patient's cognitive status. Common tools include the Mini-Cog (Table 59.9), Mini-Mental State Examination (MMSE) (Table 59.10), and Montreal Cognitive Assessment (MoCA). Brief screenings, such as the Mini-Cog, are useful for ongoing screening, especially when time is limited. The clock drawing test can be used as part of the Mini-Cog or by itself to assess cognitive

TABLE 59.8 Interprofessional Care
Alzheimer's Disease

Diagnostic Assessment
• History and physical assessment, including psychologic evaluation
• Neuropsychologic testing, including Mini-Cog (Table 59.9), Mini-Mental State Examination (Table 59.10)
• Brain imaging tests: CT, MRI, MRS, PET
• CBC
• ECG
• Serum glucose, creatinine, blood urea nitrogen
• Serum levels of vitamins B_1, B_6, B_{12}
• Thyroid function tests
• Liver function tests
• Screening for depression

Management
• Drug therapy for cognitive problems (Table 59.11)
• Behavioral modification
• Moderate exercise
• Assistance with functional independence
• Assistance and support for caregiver

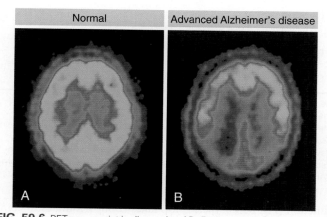

Normal	Advanced Alzheimer's disease

FIG. 59.6 PET scan assist in diagnosing AD. Radioactive fluorine is applied to glucose (fluorodeoxyglucose), and the yellow areas show metabolically active cells. **A,** A normal brain. **B,** Advanced AD is recognized by hypometabolism in many areas of the brain. (From Roberts GS: *Neuropsychiatric disorders,* London, 1993, Mosby-Wolfe.)

TABLE 59.9 The Mini-Cog

The Mini-Cog is used as a brief assessment tool for cognitive impairment. It can be quickly administered and can guide the need for further evaluation.

Administration

- Tell the patient to listen carefully to and remember 3 unrelated words and then to repeat the words. *Example:* apple, table, penny. (This initial step is not scored.) The same 3 words may be repeated to the patient up to 3 tries to register all 3 words.
- Tell the patient to draw the face of a clock, either on a blank sheet of paper or on a sheet with the clock circle already drawn on the page. After the patient puts the numbers on the clock face, ask them to draw the hands of the clock to read a specific time (11:10). The test is considered normal if all numbers are present in the correct sequence and position and the hands readably display the requested time.
- Ask the patient to repeat the 3 previously stated words.

Scoring (out of total of 5 points)

Give 1 point for each recalled word after the clock drawing test.

- Patients recalling none of the 3 words are classified as cognitively impaired (score = 0).
- Patients recalling all 3 words are classified as not cognitively impaired (score = 3).
- Patients with intermediate word recall of 1 or 2 words are classified on the clock drawing test:
  The clock drawing test is scored 2 if normal and 0 if abnormal.

Interpretation of results

0–2: Positive screen for dementia
3–5: Negative screen for dementia

Source: Borson S, Scanlan J, Brush M, et al: The Mini-Cog: A cognitive "vital signs" measure for dementia screening in multi-lingual elderly, *Intern J Geriatr Psychiatry* 15:1021, 2000.

TABLE 59.10 Mini-Mental State Examination (MMSE)

Sample Items

Orientation to Time
"What is the date?"

Registration
"Listen carefully, I am going to say 3 words. You say them back after I stop. Ready? Here they are . . . HOUSE (pause), CAR (pause), LAKE (pause). Now repeat those words back to me." (Repeat up to 5 times but score only the first trial.)

Naming
"What is this?" (Point to a pencil or pen.)

Reading
"Please read this and do what it says." (Show examinee the words CLOSE YOUR EYES on the stimulus form.)

Reproduced by special permission of the Publisher, Psychological Assessment Resource, Inc., 16204 North Florida Avenue, Lutz, FL. 33549, from the Mini-Mental State Examination, by Marshal Folstein and Susan Folstein, Copyright 1975, 1998, 2001 by Mini-Mental, LLC, Inc. Published 2001 by Psychological Assessment Resources, Inc. Further reproduction is prohibited without permission from PAR, Inc. The MMSE can be purchased from PAR, Inc., by calling 813-968-3003.

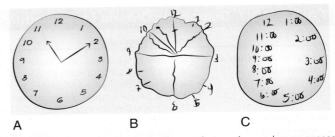

A   B   C

FIG. 59.7 Clock drawing is a simple test that can be used as an assessment technique in dementia. The patient is asked to draw a clock, put in all the numbers, and set the hands at 11:10. **A,** A clock drawn by a patient with no dementia. **B** and **C** Clocks drawn by people with AD. (Modified from Stern TA: *Massachusetts General Hospital comprehensive clinical psychiatry,* Philadelphia, 2008, Mosby.)

TABLE 59.11 Drug Therapy

Alzheimer's Disease

Problem	Drugs
Decreased memory and cognition	Cholinesterase inhibitors • donepezil (Aricept) • galantamine (Razadyne) • rivastigmine (Exelon) *N*-methyl-D-aspartate (NMDA) receptor antagonist • memantine (Namenda)
Depression	Selective serotonin reuptake inhibitors (SSRIs) • citalopram (Celexa) • fluoxetine (Prozac) • sertraline (Zoloft) • fluvoxamine (Luvox) Atypical antidepressants • mirtazapine (Remeron) • trazodone
Behavioral problems (e.g., agitation, physical aggression, disinhibition)	Antipsychotics* • aripiprazole (Abilify) • haloperidol (Haldol) • olanzapine (Zyprexa) • quetiapine (Seroquel) • risperidone (Risperdal) Benzodiazepines • clonazepam (Klonopin) • lorazepam (Ativan)
Sleep problems	• zolpidem (Ambien)

*The use of these drugs in older patients with dementia is associated with an increased risk for death.

Interprofessional Care

At this time there is no cure for AD. Treatment does not stop the deterioration of brain cells. Interprofessional care of patients with AD is aimed at controlling undesirable behavioral manifestations and providing support for family caregivers.

Drug Therapy. Although medication for AD is available (Table 59.11), these drugs do not cure or reverse the progression of the disease. They help many people for a period of time by leading to a modest decrease in the rate of decline of cognitive function. There is no effect on overall disease progression.[2]

Cholinesterase inhibitors block cholinesterase, the enzyme responsible for the breakdown of acetylcholine in the synaptic cleft (Fig. 59.8). Cholinesterase inhibitors include donepezil (Aricept), rivastigmine (Exelon), and galantamine (Razadyne). Rivastigmine is available as a patch.

function (Fig. 59.7). The MMSE takes about 7 minutes to complete. It gives information about orientation, recall, attention, calculation, language manipulation, and constructional praxis. The MoCA takes about 10 minutes to do. It assesses memory, language, attention, visuospatial, and executive functions.

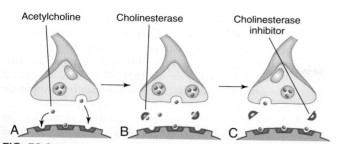

FIG. 59.8 Mechanism of action of cholinesterase inhibitors. **A,** Acetylcholine is released from the nerve synapses and carries a message across the synapse. **B,** Cholinesterase breaks down acetylcholine. **C,** Cholinesterase inhibitors block cholinesterase, thus giving acetylcholine more time to transmit the message.

Memantine (Namenda) protects the brain's nerve cells against excess amounts of glutamate, which is released in large amounts by cells damaged by AD. The attachment of glutamate to *N*-methyl-D-aspartate (NMDA) receptors permits calcium to flow freely into the cell, which in turn may lead to cell degeneration. Memantine may prevent this destructive sequence by blocking the action of glutamate.

Treating the depression that is often associated with AD may improve cognitive ability. Depression is often treated with selective serotonin reuptake inhibitors, including fluoxetine (Prozac), sertraline (Zoloft), fluvoxamine (Luvox), and citalopram (Celexa). The antidepressant trazodone may help with problems related to sleep.

Antipsychotic drugs approved for treating psychotic conditions have been used for the management of agitation and aggressive behavior, which occurs in some patients with AD. These drugs have been shown to increase the risk for death and cognitive decline in patients with AD. They should be used only in patients with AD when agitation and psychosis symptoms are severe, are dangerous, and/or cause significant distress to the patient.[12]

❖ NURSING MANAGEMENT: ALZHEIMER'S DISEASE

◆ Nursing Assessment

Subjective and objective data that should be obtained from a patient with AD are outlined in Table 59.12. Useful questions for the patient and caregiver are, "When did you first notice the memory loss?" and "How has the memory loss progressed since then?"

◆ Nursing Diagnoses

Nursing diagnoses for AD may include:
- Confusion
- Risk for injury
- Altered perception

Additional information on nursing diagnoses and interventions for the patient with AD is presented in eNursing Care Plan 59.1 (available on the website for this chapter).

◆ Planning

The overall goals are for the patient with AD to (1) maintain functional ability for as long as possible, (2) be in a safe environment with a minimum of injuries, (3) have personal care needs met, and (4) have dignity maintained. The overall goals for the caregiver of a patient with AD are to (1) reduce caregiver stress, (2) maintain personal, emotional, and physical health, and (3) cope with the long-term effects of caregiving.

TABLE 59.12 Nursing Assessment
Alzheimer's Disease

Subjective Data

Important Health Information

Past health history: Repeated head trauma, stroke, CNS infection, family history of dementia

Medications: Use of any drug to decrease symptoms (e.g., tranquilizers, hypnotics, antidepressants, antipsychotics)

Functional Health Patterns

Health perception–health management: Positive family history. Emotional lability

Nutritional-metabolic: Anorexia, malnutrition, weight loss

Elimination: Incontinence

Activity-exercise: Poor personal hygiene, gait instability, weakness, inability to perform activities of daily living

Sleep-rest: Frequent nighttime awakening, daytime napping

Cognitive-perceptual: Forgetfulness, inability to cope with complex situations, difficulty with problem solving (early signs), depression, withdrawal, suicidal ideation (early)

Objective Data

General

Disheveled appearance, agitation

Neurologic

Mild: Loss of recent memory, disorientation to date and time, flat affect, lack of spontaneity. Impaired abstraction, cognition, and judgment

Moderate: Agitation, impaired ability to recognize close family and friends, loss of remote memory, confusion, apraxia, agnosia, alexia (inability to understand written language); aphasia, inability to do simple tasks

Severe: Inability to do self-care, incontinence, immobility, limb rigidity, flexor posturing

Possible Diagnostic Findings

Diagnosis by exclusion, cerebral cortical atrophy on CT scan, poor scores on mental status tests, hippocampal atrophy on MRI scan, abnormal changes on PET

◆ Nursing Implementation

◆ Health Promotion.
Can AD be prevented? Although there is no known definitive way to prevent AD, there are several things that we can do to keep our brain healthy and modify the risk for developing dementia (Table 59.13).

Early recognition and treatment of AD are important. You have a responsibility to inform patients and their families about the early signs of AD (Table 59.4). In the early stages of AD, patients are often aware that their memory is faulty and do things to mask the problem.

◆ Acute Care.
The diagnosis of AD is traumatic for both the patient and family. It is not unusual for the patient to have depression, denial, worry, fear, and feelings of loss and dread.[13] You are in an important position to assess for depression. Antidepressant drugs and counseling may be needed. Family caregivers may be in denial and may not seek medical attention early in the disease. You can assess family caregiver's ability to accept and cope with the diagnosis.

Although there is no treatment that reverses AD, ongoing monitoring of both the patient and caregiver is important. Patients with AD move through the stages at variable rates. HCPs collaborate with caregivers and patients to manage manifestations, which change over time.

TABLE 59.13 Patient & Caregiver Teaching

Decreasing Risk for Cognitive Decline

The following are tips to reduce the risk for cognitive decline and dementia:

1. Avoid harmful substances
   Excessive drinking and drug use can damage brain cells. Stop smoking because it increases the risk for cognitive decline.
2. Challenge your mind
   Read often, do crossword puzzles. Keep mentally active. Learn new skills. Go back to school. This strengthens the brain connections and promotes new ones.
3. Exercise regularly
   Even low to moderate level activity, such as walking or gardening 3 to 5 times per week, can make you feel better. Daily physical activity, even in older adults, can decrease the risk for cognitive decline.
4. Stay socially active
   Pursue social activities that have meaning to you. Family, friends, church, and a sense of community may all contribute to better brain health.
5. Avoid trauma to the brain
   Because traumatic brain injury may be a risk factor for developing AD, promote safety in physical activities and driving. Use the car seat belt. Wear a helmet when playing contact sports or riding a bike. Fall proof your home.
6. Take care of mental health
   Recognize and treat depression early. Depression may cause or worsen memory loss and other cognitive impairment.
7. Treat diabetes.
   Better blood glucose control can help to prevent the cognitive decline associated with diabetes.
8. Take care of your heart
   Risk factors for cardiovascular disease and stroke (hypertension, obesity) negatively affect your cognitive health. Heart health is linked to brain health.
9. Get enough sleep
   Not getting enough sleep may result in problems with memory and thinking.
10. Get the right fuel
   A healthy and balanced diet low in fats and high in vegetables and fruits helps to reduce the risk for cognitive decline.

Adapted from Alzheimer's Association: 10 Ways to love your brain. Retrieved from *www.alz.org/help-support/brain_health/10_ways_to_love_your_brain;* and Baumgart M, Snyder HM, Carrillo MC, et al: Summary of evidence on modifiable risk factors for cognitive decline and dementia: A population-based perspective, *Alzheimers Dement* 11:718, 2015.

The nursing care needed by the patient with AD changes as the disease progresses, which emphasizes the need for regular assessment and support. The severity of the problems and amount of nursing care needed increase over time. The specific manifestations of the disease depend on the area of the brain involved. Nursing care focuses on decreasing manifestations, preventing harm, and supporting the patient and caregiver throughout the disease process.

Patients with AD may have other acute and chronic illnesses that require hospitalization or surgical interventions. Hospitalization can be traumatic for the patient with AD and the caregiver. Hospitalization can precipitate a worsening of dementia or development of delirium among patients with AD. Caregivers and health care professionals need to help patients who have difficulty explaining their symptoms or recalling their health and medical histories. In the acute care setting, patients with AD need to be observed more closely because of concerns for their safety. They should be frequently reassured and oriented to place and time. Anxiety or disruptive behavior may be reduced with using consistent nursing staff.

◆ **Ambulatory Care.** Currently, family members and friends care for many people with AD in their homes. Other patients with AD live in various types of facilities, including long-term care and assisted living facilities. A facility that is good for one patient may not be suitable for another. What is helpful for a patient at one point in the disease process may be completely different from what is best when the disease progresses.

After the initial diagnosis, patients need to be aware that the progression of the disease is variable. Effective management of the disease may slow symptom progression and decrease the burden on the patient, caregiver, and family. Decisions related to care should be made with the patient, family members, and interprofessional care team early in the disease. You have a role in advising the patient and caregiver to initiate health care decisions, including advance directives, while the patient has the capacity to do so. This can ease the burden for the caregiver as the disease progresses.

In the early stages of AD, memory aids, such as calendars, may be beneficial. Patients often become depressed during this phase. Depression may be related to the diagnosis of an incurable disorder and the impact of the disease on ADLs, including driving, socializing, and taking part in recreational activities. Nurses teach caregivers to perform tasks needed to maximize quality of life and safety of the patient with AD.

Adult day care is one of the options available to the patient with AD. Although programs vary in size, structure, physical environment, and staff experience, the common goals of all day care programs are to provide respite for the family and a protective environment. During the early and moderate stages of AD, the patient can still benefit from stimulating activities that encourage independence and decision making in a protective environment. The patient returns home tired, content, less frustrated, and ready to be with the family. The respite from the demands of care allows the caregiver to be more responsive to the patient's needs.

As the disease progresses, the demands on the caregiver eventually exceed the resources, and the patient with AD may need to be placed in a long-term care facility. Special dementia units are becoming increasingly common. The dementia unit is designed with an emphasis on safety. Many facilities have designated areas that allow the patient to walk freely within the unit, while the unit is secured so that the patient cannot wander outside.

As the disease progresses to the late stage, the patient is severely impaired, having difficulty with basic functions, including walking and talking. Total care is needed for this patient. Specific problems relate to the care of the patient with AD in all phases of the disease. These problems are described next.

Behavioral Problems. Behavioral problems occur in about 90% of patients with AD. These problems include repetitiveness or asking the same question repeatedly, delusions, hallucinations, agitation, aggression, altered sleeping patterns, wandering, hoarding, and resisting care. Many times, these behaviors are unpredictable and may challenge caregivers. Caregivers must be aware that these behaviors are not intentional and are often difficult to control. Behavioral problems are often the reason that patients are placed in institutional care settings.[14]

These behaviors are often the patient's way of responding to pain, frustration, temperature extremes, or anxiety. When these behaviors become problematic, you must plan interventions carefully. Assess the patient's physical status. Check for changes in vital signs, urinary and bowel patterns, and pain that could account for behavioral problems. Assess the environment to identify factors that may trigger behavior disruptions. Extremes in temperature or excessive noise may lead to behavior changes. When environmental conditions are agitating the patient, either move the patient or remove the stimulus.

When a patient resists or pulls tubes or dressings, cover these items with stretch tube gauze or remove them from the visual field. Reassure the patient that you are present to keep him or her safe. Do not ask challenging "why" questions. The patient with AD cannot think logically. If the patient cannot state distress, validate their mood. Rephrase the patient's statement to validate its meaning. Closely observe the patient's emotional state.

Nursing strategies that address difficult behavior include redirection, distraction, and reassurance. When a patient is restless or agitated, redirecting involves changing the patient's focus by having them perform activities, such as sweeping, raking, or dusting. Providing snacks, taking a car ride, sitting on a porch swing or rocker, listening to favorite music, watching videotapes, looking at family photographs, or walking may distract an agitated patient. Reassure patients by telling them that they will be protected from danger, harm, or embarrassment. Repetitive activities, including songs, poems, music, massage, aromas, or a favorite object can be soothing.

Do not threaten to restrain an agitated patient. Ask a calming family member to stay with the patient. Monitor the patient frequently and record all interventions. As verbal skills decline, you and the caregiver must rely more on the patient's body language to communicate care needs. The use of positive nursing actions can reduce the use of chemical (drug therapy) restraints.

Disruptive behaviors have been treated with antipsychotic drugs (Table 59.11). However, as discussed on p. 1393, these have adverse side effects. All other measures of treating behavioral issues should be exhausted before drug treatment is started.

? CHECK YOUR PRACTICE

You are working in a secure Alzheimer's unit. While making rounds at 4 PM you see Dan, one of the UAPs, screaming at an 84-yr-old male resident. When you approach Dan and the resident, you ask what is going on. Dan responds, "Every day about this time he gets so agitated and starts yelling at me, so I yell back."
- How would you handle the situation? What teaching does Dan need?

A specific type of agitation, termed *sundowning*, is when the patient becomes more confused and agitated in the late afternoon or evening. Behaviors related to sundowning include agitation, aggressiveness, wandering, resistance to redirection, and increased verbal activity, such as yelling. The cause of sundowning is unclear. It may be due to a disruption of circadian rhythms. Other causes include pain, hunger, unfamiliar environment and noise, medications, reduced lighting, and fragmented sleep.[15]

Managing sundowning can be challenging for you, the patient, and the family. When a patient has sundowning, remain calm and avoid confrontation. Assess the situation for possible causes of the agitation. Nursing interventions that may be helpful include (1) creating a quiet, calm environment; (2) maximizing exposure to daylight by opening blinds and turning on lights during the day; (3) evaluating medications to determine if any could cause sleep problems; (4) limiting naps and caffeine; and (5) consulting with the HCP about drug therapy.

👥 NURSING MANAGEMENT
Caring for the Patient With Alzheimer's Disease

The RN is responsible for ongoing assessment of the patient's level of function and for developing the plan of care. Since most patients with AD are cared for at home or in long-term care settings, many routine nursing activities are performed by licensed practical/vocational nurses (LPN/VNs), unlicensed assistive personnel (UAP), or family caregivers.

- Assess patients' memory and level of function.
- Teach patients and caregivers about using memory enhancement aids, such as calendars or notes.
- Monitor for physiologic problems, such as pain, swallowing difficulties, urinary tract infection, pneumonia, skin breakdown, and constipation.
- Assess nutritional and fluid intake and develop a plan to ensure adequate intake.
- Evaluate safety risk factors.
- Determine possible precipitating factors for behavioral changes and develop strategies to address difficult behavior.
- Assess family caregivers' stress level and coping strategies.
- Make referrals for community services, such as adult day care and respite care.
- Delegate to LPN/VN:
  - Monitor for behavioral changes that may indicate physiologic problems.
  - Check the environment for potential safety hazards.
  - Give enteral feedings to patients who are unable to swallow, if ordered.
  - Give ordered medications.
- Oversee UAP:
  - Help patients to use the toilet, commode, or bedpan at frequent intervals.
  - Provide personal hygiene, skin care, and oral care.
  - Help patients with eating.
  - Aid patients with daily activities.
  - Use bed alarms and surveillance to decrease risk for falls.

Collaborate With Other Team Members
Dietitian
- Assess nutrition status and provide prescribed nutritional support.
- Offer practical suggestions to enhance dietary intake.

Occupational Therapist
- Suggest ways to help patients retain self-care ability as long as possible.

Social Worker
- Help caregivers identify and obtain needed resources.
- Provide support and counseling to caregivers.

Safety. The patient with AD is at risk for problems related to personal safety. Potential hazards include falling, ingesting dangerous substances, wandering, injuring others and self with sharp objects, being burned, and being unable to respond to crisis situations. These concerns require careful attention in the home environment to minimize risk. Supervision is needed. As the patient's cognitive function declines over time, they may have problems navigating physical spaces and interpreting environmental cues. Help the caregiver assess the home environment for safety risks.

⚠ SAFETY ALERT Preventing Falls
Teach the caregiver to take the following steps:
- Have stairwells well lit.
- Make sure the patient can grasp the handrails.
- Tack down carpet edges.
- Remove throw rugs and extension cords.
- Use nonskid mats in tub or shower.
- Install handrails in the bath and by the commode.

Wandering is a major concern for caregivers. Wandering may be related to loss of memory or to side effects of medications. It may be an expression of a physical or emotional need, restlessness, curiosity, or stimuli that trigger memories of earlier routines. As with other behaviors, observe for factors or events that may precipitate wandering. For example, the patient may be sensitive to stress and tension in the environment. In such cases, wandering may reflect an attempt to leave.

When someone with AD is discovered missing, every second counts. To assist caregivers with finding them, the Alzheimer's Association and the MedicAlert Foundation have created an alliance called MedicAlert + Alzheimer's Association Safe Return.[16] This program includes identification products (e.g., bracelet, necklace, wallet cards), a national photo and information database, a 24-hour toll-free emergency crisis line, local chapter support, and wandering behavior education and training for caregivers and families.

Tracking devices (e.g., global positioning system [GPS]) can be used to find people who wander. These devices can be placed in shoes, sewn into pockets, worn as a bracelet or pendant, or clipped to a belt.

Pain Management. Because of difficulties with oral and written language, patients with AD may have a hard time expressing physical problems, including pain. You need to rely on other clues, such as the patient's behavior. Pain can result in changes in behavior, including increased vocalization, agitation, withdrawal, and changes in function. Pain should be recognized and treated promptly and the patient's response monitored.

Eating and Swallowing Difficulties. Undernutrition is a problem in the moderate and severe stages of AD. Loss of interest in food and decreased ability to self-feed (*feeding apraxia),* as well as co-morbid conditions, can result in significant nutritional problems. In long-term care facilities, inadequate aid with feeding may add to the problem.

Use pureed foods, thickened liquids, and nutritional supplements when chewing and swallowing become problematic for the patient. The patient may need reminders to chew their food and to swallow. A quiet and unhurried environment without distractions (e.g., television) at mealtimes can be helpful. Low lighting, music, and simulated nature sounds may improve eating behaviors. Easy-grip eating utensils and finger foods may allow the patient to self-feed. Liquids should be offered frequently.

When oral feeding is not possible, explore alternative routes. Nasogastric (NG) feeding may be used for short periods. However, for the long term, the NG tube is uncomfortable and may add to the patient's agitation. A percutaneous endoscopic gastrostomy (PEG) tube is another option (see Fig. 39.7). PEG tubes can be problematic since patients with AD are vulnerable to aspiration of feeding formula and tube dislodgment. The potential positive outcomes to be gained from nutritional therapies are considered in light of overall outcome goals and potential adverse effects of the specific therapy. Nutritional support therapies are described in Chapter 39.

Oral Care. In the late stages of AD, the patient is unable to perform oral self-care. With decreased tooth brushing and flossing, dental problems are likely to occur. Because of swallowing difficulties, patients may retain food in the mouth, adding to the potential for tooth decay. Dental caries and tooth abscess can cause discomfort or pain and increase agitation. Inspect the mouth regularly and provide mouth care to those patients unable to perform self-care.

Infection Prevention. Urinary tract infection and pneumonia are the most common infections in patients with AD. Such infections are the cause of death in many patients with AD. Because of feeding and swallowing problems, the patient is at risk for aspiration pneumonia. Immobility can predispose the patient to pneumonia.

Reduced fluid intake, prostate enlargement in men, poor hygiene, and urinary drainage devices can predispose patients to bladder infection. Any manifestations of infection, such as a change in behavior, fever, cough, or pain on urination, require prompt evaluation and treatment.

Skin Care. It is important to monitor the patient's skin over time. Note and treat rashes, areas of redness, and skin breakdown. In the late stages, incontinence along with immobility and undernutrition can place the patient at risk for skin breakdown. Keep the skin clean and dry. Change the patient's position regularly to avoid areas of pressure over bony prominences.

Elimination Problems. During the moderate and severe stages of AD, urinary and fecal incontinence lead to increased need for nursing care. When possible, behavioral retraining of bladder and bowel function by scheduled toileting may help decrease episodes of incontinence.

Another common elimination problem is constipation. Causes may relate to immobility, reduced fiber intake, and decreased fluid intake. Increased dietary fiber, fiber supplements, and stool softeners are the first lines of management. The combination of aging, other health problems, and swallowing difficulties may increase the risk for complications associated with the use of mineral oil, stimulants, osmotic agents, and enemas. Management of constipation is discussed in Chapter 42.

Caregiver Support. More than 16 million Americans provide unpaid care for people with AD or other dementias.[2] Most of these are family members providing care in the home (Fig. 59.9). AD disrupts all aspects of patient and family life. Caregivers for people with AD describe it as very stressful. They often have adverse consequences relating to their own emotional and physical health.

The chronic and often severe stress associated with dementia caregiving increases the risk for the development of dementia in spouse caregivers.[17] One mechanism proposed is that the detrimental effects of the chronic stress of caregiving can affect the hippocampus, a region of the brain responsible for memory.

FIG. 59.9 Caregivers of patients with dementia face an incredible challenge that often causes deterioration in their own physical and emotional health. (© iStock/Thinkstock.)

As the disease progresses, the relationship between the caregiver and patient with AD changes. Family roles may be altered or reversed. A child may care for a parent. Decisions must be made, including when to tell the patient about the diagnosis, have the patient stop driving or doing activities that may have become dangerous, ask for assistance, and place the patient in adult day care or a long-term care facility. With early-onset AD, the patient is affected during their most productive years in terms of career and family. The consequences can be devastating to the patient and family.

Sexual relations for couples are seriously affected by AD. As the disease progresses, sexual interest may decline for both the patient and partner. Several reasons account for this, including fatigue, memory impairment, and episodes of incontinence. Some patients become sexually driven and uninhibited as the disease progresses.

Work with the caregiver to assess stressors and identify coping strategies to reduce the burden of caregiving. For example, ask which behaviors are most disruptive to family life at a given time. This is likely to change as the disease progresses. Determining what is most disruptive or distressful to the caregiver can help establish priorities.

Patient safety is a high priority. It is important to assess what the caregiver's expectations are about the patient's behavior.

Are the expectations reasonable given the progression of the disease? A family and caregiver teaching guide based on the disease stages is provided in Table 59.14. Other tips for caregivers are listed in Table 59.15. A nursing care plan for the family caregiver (eNursing Care Plan 59.2) is available on the website for this chapter.

Support groups for caregivers and family members (Fig. 59.10) can provide an atmosphere of understanding and give current information about the disease itself and related topics, such as safety, legal, ethical, and financial issues. The Alzheimer's Association has many educational and support systems available to help family caregivers (*www.alz.org*).

TABLE 59.14 Patient & Caregiver Teaching

Alzheimer's Disease

Include the following instructions when teaching families and caregivers the management of the patient with Alzheimer's disease:

Mild Stage

- Many treatable (and potentially reversible) conditions can mimic dementia (Table 59.2). Try to establish a diagnosis.
- Get the patient to stop driving. Confusion and poor judgment can impair driving skills and potentially put others at risk.
- Encourage activities such as visiting with friends and family, listening to music, enjoying hobbies, and exercising.
- Provide cues in the home, establish a routine, and determine a specific location where essential items (e.g., glasses) must be kept.
- Do not correct misstatements or faulty memory.
- Register with MedicAlert + Alzheimer's Association Safe Return, a program established by the MedicAlert Foundation and the Alzheimer's Association to locate those who wander from their homes.
- Make plans in terms of advance directives, care options, financial concerns, and personal preference for care.

Moderate Stage

- Install door locks for patient safety.
- Provide protective wear for urinary and fecal incontinence.
- Ensure that the home has good lighting, install handrails in stairways and bathroom, and remove area rugs.
- Label drawers and faucets (hot and cold) to ensure safety.
- Develop ways, such as distraction and diversion, to cope with behavioral problems. Identify and reduce potential triggers (e.g., reduce stress, extremes in temperature) for disruptive behavior.
- Provide memory triggers, such as pictures of family and friends.

Severe Stage

- Follow a regular schedule for toileting to reduce incontinence.
- Provide care to meet needs, including oral care and skin care.
- Monitor diet and fluid intake to ensure their adequacy.
- Continue communication through talking and touching.
- Consider placement in a long-term care facility when providing total care becomes too difficult.

TABLE 59.15 Nursing Management

Assisting Patients With Dementia

Do

- Treat the adult with respect and dignity, even when behavior is childlike.
- Use gentle touch and direct eye contact.
- Remain patient, flexible, calm, and understanding.
- Expect challenging behaviors, since the patient's ability to think logically is affected.
- Give directions using gestures or pictures.
- Simplify tasks. Focus on one thing at a time.
- Avoid questions or topics that require extensive thought, memory, or words.
- Be flexible. If one approach does not work, try another.
- Use distraction, changing the subject, redirecting to another activity.
- Provide reassurance. Praise sincerely for success.

Do Not

- Criticize, correct, or argue.
- Rush or hurry the patient.
- Force participation in activities or events.
- Talk about the patient as if they are not there.
- Blame the patient with AD. Instead, blame the disease.
- Take challenging behaviors patiently. These behaviors are due to the disease.
- Use condescending terms, such as "honey" or "sweetie."
- Use threatening gestures.
- Overreact to the patient with AD.
- Try to explain "why" or rationalize.

FIG. 59.10 Support groups are an effective way to help caregivers cope. (© iStockphoto/Thinkstock.)

◆ Evaluation

Expected outcomes are that the patient with AD will:

- Function at the highest level of cognitive ability
- Perform basic personal care ADLs, by self or with assistance, as needed
- Have no injury
- Stay in a restricted area during ambulation and activity

DELIRIUM

Delirium is a state of confusion that develops over days to hours.[1] The patient has decreased ability to direct, focus, sustain, and shift attention and awareness. Deficits in memory, orientation, language, visuospatial ability, or perception may be present. The patient may be hypoactive or hyperactive. Emotional problems include fear, depression, euphoria, or perplexity. Sleep may be disturbed.

These symptoms represent a change from the patient's baseline and tend to fluctuate throughout the day. They do not occur in the context of a severely reduced level of arousal, such as coma, and cannot be explained by another preexisting, evolving, or established neurocognitive disorder.

Etiology and Pathophysiology

We do not know the exact cause of delirium. A main contributing factor is impairment of cerebral oxidative metabolism, in which the brain gets less oxygen and has problems using it. Multiple neurotransmitter abnormalities may be involved. Cholinergic deficiency, excess release of dopamine, and both increased and decreased serotonin activity may contribute to delirium. Proinflammatory cytokines, including interleukin-1 (IL-1), IL-2, IL-6, tumor necrosis factor-α (TNF-α), cytokines, and interferon, appear to play a role.

Delirium is rarely caused by a single factor. It most often occurs among hospitalized older adults. Up to 60% of older adults hospitalized for medical conditions have delirium at some time during their hospitalization.[18] Stress, surgery, and sleep deprivation have been linked to delirium. Delirium is the most common surgical complication among older adults. The incidence is 15% to 25% after major elective surgery and 50% after high-risk procedures, such as hip fracture repair and heart surgery.[19] Pain and depression contribute to delirium, especially among older adults.[19]

Delirium is often the result of the interaction of the patient's underlying condition with a precipitating event. Delirium can occur after a relatively minor insult in a vulnerable patient. For example, a patient with underlying health problems, such as heart failure (HF), cancer, cognitive impairment, or sensory limitations, may develop delirium in response to a minor change, such as use of a sleeping medication. In other less vulnerable patients, it may take a combination of factors, such as anesthesia, major surgery, mechanical ventilation, infection, and prolonged sleep deprivation, to precipitate delirium. Delirium can be a symptom of a serious medical illness, such as bacterial meningitis.

Dementia is the leading risk factor for delirium. Furthermore, delirium is a risk factor for developing dementia. Delirium may cause permanent neuronal damage and lead to dementia.[20]

Understanding factors that can lead to delirium can help determine effective interventions. Common factors that can precipitate delirium are listed in Tables 59.16 and 59.17. Many of these factors are more common among older adults. Older adults have limited compensatory mechanisms to deal with physiologic insults, such as hypoxia, hypoglycemia, and dehydration. They

TABLE 59.16 Factors That Precipitate Delirium

Demographic Characteristics	**Functional Status**
• Age 65 year or older	• Functional dependence
• Male gender	• History of falls
	• Immobility
Cognitive Status	**Medical Conditions**
• Cognitive impairment	• Acute infection, sepsis, fever
• Dementia	• Chronic kidney or liver disease
• Depression	• Electrolyte imbalances
• History of delirium	• Fracture or trauma
	• History of stroke
Decreased Oral Intake	• Neurologic disease
• Dehydration	• Severe acute illness
• Malnutrition	• Terminal illness
Drugs	**Sensory**
• Alcohol or drug use or withdrawal	• Sensory deprivation
• Aminoglycosides	• Sensory overload
• Anticholinergics	• Visual or hearing impairment
• Opioids	
• Sedative-hypnotics	**Surgery**
• Treatment with multiple drugs	• Cardiac surgery
	• Noncardiac surgery
Environmental	• Orthopedic surgery
• Admission to ICU	• Prolonged cardiopulmonary bypass
• Emotional stress	
• Pain (especially untreated)	
• Sleep deprivation	
• Use of physical restraints	

TABLE 59.17 Mnemonic for Causes of Delirium

Dementia, dehydration
Electrolyte imbalances, emotional stress
Lung, liver, heart, kidney, brain
Infection, intensive care unit
Rx drugs
Injury, immobility
Untreated pain, unfamiliar environment
Metabolic disorders

are more susceptible to drug-induced delirium, in part because of their increased use of multiple drugs. Many drugs, including sedative-hypnotics, opioids (especially meperidine [Demerol]), benzodiazepines, and anticholinergics, can cause or contribute to delirium, especially in older or vulnerable patients.[21]

Clinical Manifestations

Patients with delirium can have a variety of manifestations, ranging from hypoactivity and lethargy to hyperactivity, agitation, and hallucinations. Patients can have mixed delirium, with both hypoactive and hyperactive symptoms. Delirium can develop over the course of hours to days. It usually develops over a 2- to 3-day period. The early manifestations often include inability to concentrate, disorganized thinking, irritability, insomnia, loss of appetite, restlessness, and confusion. Later manifestations may include agitation, misperception, misinterpretation, and hallucinations.

Delirium can last from 1 to 7 days. However, delirium may persist for months or years. Some patients do not completely recover.

TABLE 59.18 Confusion Assessment Method (CAM)

Delirium is diagnosed with the presence of features 1 and 2, and either 3 or 4.

Feature 1
Acute Onset and Fluctuating Course
Data usually obtained from a family member or nurse.
Shown by positive responses to the following questions:
- Is there evidence of an acute change in mental status from the patient's baseline?
- Did the (abnormal) behavior fluctuate during the day (i.e., tend to come and go, or increase and decrease in severity)?

Feature 2
Inattention
Shown by positive response to the following question:
- Did the patient have problem focusing attention (e.g., being easily distractible, or having problem keeping track of what was being said)?

Feature 3
Disorganized Thinking
Shown by a positive response to the following question:
- Was the patient's thinking disorganized or incoherent, such as rambling or irrelevant conversation, unclear or illogical flow of ideas, or unpredictable switching from subject to subject?

Feature 4
Altered Level of Consciousness
Shown by any answer other than "alert" to the following question:
- Overall, how would you rate this patient's level of consciousness (alert [normal], vigilant [hyper alert], lethargic [drowsy, easily aroused], stupor [difficult to arouse], or coma [unarousable])?

Adapted from Inouye S, van Dyck C, Alessi C, et al: Clarifying confusion: The Confusion Assessment Method, *Ann Intern Med* 113:941, 1990.

Manifestations of delirium are sometimes confused with those of dementia. A key distinction between them is that the patient who has sudden cognitive impairment, disorientation, or clouded sensorium is more likely to have delirium rather than dementia. A comparison of delirium and dementia is shown in Table 59.1.

Diagnostic Studies

Diagnosing delirium is complicated because many critically ill patients cannot communicate their needs. A careful medical and psychologic history and physical assessment are the first steps in diagnosing delirium and its underlying cause. This includes careful attention to medications, both prescription and OTC. The Confusion Assessment Method (CAM) is a reliable tool for assessing delirium (Table 59.18). The version of the CAM may vary depending on the clinical setting. It is important to distinguish whether the delirium is part of underlying dementia.

Once delirium has been diagnosed, explore potential causes. Carefully review the patient's health history and medication record. Laboratory tests include complete blood count, serum electrolytes, blood urea nitrogen, and creatinine levels; ECG; urinalysis; liver and thyroid function tests; and oxygen saturation level. Drug and alcohol levels may be obtained. If unexplained fever or nuchal rigidity is present and meningitis or encephalitis is suspected, a lumbar puncture may be done. CSF is examined for glucose, protein, and bacteria. If the patient's history includes head injury, appropriate x-rays or scans may be ordered. In general, brain imaging studies, such as CT and MRI, are used only when head injury is known or suspected.

ETHICAL/LEGAL DILEMMAS
Board of Nursing Disciplinary Action

Situation
The state board of nursing has received multiple complaints about J.R., an RN who works in a long-term care facility. J.R. has signed off on 3 controlled substances count sheets that have been determined to be inaccurate. During an investigation it was discovered that several members of the nursing staff knew about J.R.'s reported behavior, but they did not report their observations to the unit administrator because the administrator is J.R.'s aunt. After the investigation, the board of nursing subpoenas J.R. to a meeting to discuss charges in preparation for a disciplinary hearing.

Ethical/Legal Points for Consideration
Regulation of professional nursing practice is the right of each of the 50 states. Most have regulatory agencies charged with writing regulations and rules to implement the state nurse practice act. The regulations approved by these agencies carry the weight of law. Failure to behave accordingly places a nurse at risk for disciplinary action.

The RN who is charged with unprofessional behavior has been charged with an offense and is entitled to the same legal rights as any other person, including a fair and timely hearing, opportunity to confront the accusers, right to be represented by an attorney, and right to prepare a defense.

Possible disciplinary actions include temporary suspension of the nursing license, revocation of the nursing license, mandatory rehabilitation for substance use, and mandated supervision and evaluation of practice. Sometimes the disciplinary action includes fines and requires reeducation. The state board of nursing may report the action to the state attorney general if evidence suggests that a crime has been committed. The RN who is found guilty of unprofessional practice must report this action on all future applications for nursing positions.

All RNs should be familiar with their state's nurse practice act and regulations, and the composition and actions of the state board of nursing. Nurses should pay attention to the regulation that lists examples of actionable behavior and disciplinary actions sanctioned by the state.

RNs have a legal and ethical obligation to report suspected illegal behavior to their administrators and to continue reporting until the situation is resolved. By failing to report, the RN may be charged as an accessory to the act or aiding and abetting the behavior. This RN may be charged with unprofessional behavior and risks losing his or her nursing license. Shifting the obligation to someone else to report or failure to continue reporting each incident does not satisfy this duty.

Discussion Questions
1. How would you handle a situation in which retaliation for reporting unprofessional behavior may occur?
2. What would you do if the nurse suspected of illegal behavior is related to someone in the administrative hierarchy?

❖ NURSING AND INTERPROFESSIONAL MANAGEMENT: DELIRIUM

Treatment is important as many cases of delirium are potentially reversible. In caring for the patient with delirium, you are responsible for prevention, early recognition, and treatment. Prevention of delirium involves recognition of patients at high risk, including those with neurologic disorders, such as dementia, stroke, CNS infection, and Parkinson's disease.[22] Other risk factors include sensory impairment, older age, surgery, hospitalization in an intensive care unit (ICU), and untreated pain. Risk factors are listed in Table 59.16.

Care of the patient with delirium focuses on eliminating precipitating factors. If it is drug induced, medications are discontinued. Keep in mind that delirium can accompany drug and alcohol withdrawal. Depending on the history, drug screening may be done. Fluid and electrolyte imbalances and nutritional deficiencies (e.g., thiamine) are corrected if appropriate. If the problem is related to an overstimulating or understimulating environment, then changes should be made. If delirium is from infection, appropriate antibiotic therapy is started. Similarly, if delirium is due to chronic illness, such as chronic kidney disease or HF, treatment focuses on these conditions.

CHECK YOUR PRACTICE

You are working in the medical ICU. Your patient is an 82-yr-old man who had a hip replacement 3 days ago. He was doing well after surgery and then developed bilateral pneumonia. He was transferred to the ICU yesterday. When you walk into his room, you notice his daughter is staring out the window and does not respond to your greeting. When you approach her, you notice she is very upset. When you ask her what is wrong, she bursts out crying, "How can this be? My dad was always such a vibrant and brilliant man. Now look at him. He talks to himself. He screams at me. He thinks I am his wife. Mom died 5 years ago. What happened to him?"

- How would you assess the situation?
- What can you do to help the daughter?

Care of the patient with delirium includes protecting the patient from harm. Give priority to creating a calm and safe environment. This may include encouraging family members to stay at the bedside, providing familiar objects and family photos, transferring the patient to a private room or one closer to the nurses' station, and planning for consistent nursing staff if possible. Use reorientation and behavioral interventions in patients with delirium. Provide the patient with reassurance and reorienting information as to place, time, and procedures. Clocks, calendars, and lists of scheduled activities are helpful. Reduce environmental stimuli, including noise and light levels.

Personal contact through touch and verbal communication can be an important reorienting strategy. If the patient uses eyeglasses or a hearing aid, they should be readily available because sensory deprivation can precipitate delirium. Avoid the use of restraints. Other interventions, including relaxation techniques, music therapy, and massage, may be appropriate for some patients with delirium.

Comprehensive interventions to prevent delirium should be implemented by the health care team.[23] The team may address issues related to polypharmacy, pain, nutritional status, and potential for incontinence. The patient with delirium is at risk for the adverse consequences of immobility, including skin breakdown. Give attention to increasing physical activity or providing range-of-motion exercises, when appropriate, and maintaining skin integrity.

Focus on supporting the family and caregivers during episodes of delirium. Family members need to understand factors that may have precipitated the delirium, as well as the potential outcomes. Patient education materials are available at *www. ICUdelirium.org.*

◆ Drug Therapy

Drug therapy is reserved for patients with severe agitation, especially when it interferes with needed medical treatments. Agitation can put the patient at risk for falls and injury. Medication therapy is used cautiously because many of the drugs used to manage agitation have psychoactive properties.

Drugs should be used only when nonpharmacologic interventions have failed.

Dexmedetomidine (Precedex), an α-adrenergic receptor agonist, has been used in ICU settings for sedation. The use of low-dose antipsychotics (e.g., haloperidol, risperidone [Risperdal], olanzapine [Zyprexa], quetiapine [Seroquel]), though common practice, is controversial.[24] Research suggests their use does not change the duration of delirium or the length of hospitalization.[24]

Haloperidol can be given IV, IM, or orally and will produce sedation. Other side effects include hypotension; extrapyramidal side effects, including *tardive* dyskinesia (involuntary muscle movements of face, trunk, and arms) and *athetosis* (involuntary writhing movements of the limbs); muscle tone changes; and anticholinergic effects. Carefully monitor older patients receiving antipsychotic agents.

Short-acting benzodiazepines (e.g., lorazepam [Ativan]) can be used to treat delirium associated with sedative and alcohol withdrawal or in conjunction with antipsychotics to reduce extrapyramidal side effects. However, these drugs may worsen delirium caused by other factors and must be used cautiously.

CASE STUDY

Alzheimer's Disease

(© iStock/ Thinkstock.)

Patient Profile

M.Y., a 78-yr-old Asian American man, was diagnosed with Alzheimer's disease (AD) 3 years ago shortly after his wife died. Today his 45-yr-old son brings him to the emergency department because he wandered from his son's home, fell, and injured his left hip.

Subjective Data

- Can say his name, confused as to place and time
- Denies memory of wandering or falling
- Agitated, trying to get up
- Denies pain

Objective Data

Physical Examination

- Left leg shorter than right leg
- Tense and anxious

Diagnostic Studies

- X-ray of left hip indicates a fracture
- Mini-Cog testing indicates cognitive impairment

Discussion Questions

1. What is the pathogenesis of AD?
2. What precipitating factors may have resulted in M.Y.'s fall?
3. **Safety:** What safety precautions need to be taken regarding the inpatient care of M.Y.?
4. **Patient-Centered Care:** What is the priority nursing intervention for M.Y.?
5. **Patient-Centered Care:** What teaching plan should you develop for M.Y. and his son?
6. Surgery is planned to repair his fractured hip. Why is he at risk for delirium?
7. **Priority Decision:** Based on the assessment data, what are the priority nursing diagnoses? Are there any collaborative problems?
8. **Collaboration:** What nursing activities can the RN delegate to unlicensed assistive personnel (UAP)?
9. **Evidence-Based Practice:** M.Y.'s son asks you if he should give his father ginkgo to help his memory. How would you respond?

Answers available at *http://evolve.elsevier.com/Lewis/medsurg.*

BRIDGE TO NCLEX EXAMINATION

The number of the question corresponds to the same-numbered outcome at the beginning of the chapter.

1. Dementia is defined as a
   a. syndrome that results only in memory loss.
   b. disease associated with abrupt changes in behavior.
   c. disease that is always due to reduced blood flow to the brain.
   d. syndrome characterized by cognitive dysfunction and loss of memory.

2. Vascular dementia is associated with
   a. transient ischemic attacks.
   b. bacterial or viral infection of neuronal tissue.
   c. cognitive changes secondary to cerebral ischemia.
   d. abrupt changes in cognitive function that are irreversible.

3. Dementia with Lewy bodies (DLB) is characterized by
   a. remissions and exacerbations over many years.
   b. memory impairment, muscle jerks, and blindness.
   c. parkinsonian symptoms, including muscle rigidity.
   d. increased intracranial pressure from decreased CSF drainage.

4. Which statement(s) accurately describe(s) mild cognitive impairment? *(select all that apply)*
   a. Cannot be detected by screening tests
   b. The person may appear normal to the casual observer
   c. Family members may see changes in the patient's abilities
   d. Problems that the person is experiencing interfere with daily activities
   e. The person is usually aware that there is a problem with his or her memory

5. The clinical diagnosis of dementia is based on
   a. CT or MRS.
   b. brain biopsy.
   c. electroencephalogram.
   d. patient history and cognitive assessment.

6. A *priority* goal of treatment for the patient with Alzheimer's disease is to
   a. maintain patient safety.
   b. maintain or increase body weight.
   c. return to a higher level of self-care.
   d. enhance functional ability over time.

7. Which patient is *most* at risk for developing delirium?
   a. A 50-yr-old woman with cholecystitis
   b. A 19-yr-old man with a fractured femur
   c. A 42-yr-old woman having an elective total hysterectomy
   d. A 78-yr-old man admitted to the medical unit with complications of heart failure

1. d, 2. c, 3. c, 4. b, c, e, 5. d, 6. a, 7. d

For rationales to these answers and even more NCLEX review questions, visit *http://evolve.elsevier.com/Lewis/medsurg.*

ⓔ EVOLVE WEBSITE/RESOURCES LIST

http://evolve.elsevier.com/Lewis/medsurg
Review Questions (Online Only)
Key Points
Answer Keys for Questions
- Rationales for Bridge to NCLEX Examination Questions
- Answer Guidelines for Case Study on p. 1400
Student Case Study
- Patient With Alzheimer's Disease
eNursing Care Plans
- eNursing Care Plan 59.1: Patient With Alzheimer's Disease
- eNursing Care Plan 59.2: Family Caregivers
Conceptual Care Map Creator
Audio Glossary
Content Updates

REFERENCES

1. American Psychiatric Association: *Diagnostic and statistical manual of mental disorders,* ed 5, Arlington, VA, 2013, American Psychiatric Association. (Classic)
2. Alzheimer's Association: 2018 *Alzheimer's Association facts and figures report.* Retrieved from *www.alz.org/alzheimers-dementia/facts-figures.*
3. American Academy of Neurology: Detection, diagnosis, and management of dementia. Retrieved from *http://tools.aan.com/professionals/practice/pdfs/dementia_guideline.pdf.*
*4. Yang T, Sun Y, Lu Z, et al: The impact of cerebrovascular aging on vascular cognitive impairment and dementia, *Ageing Res Rev* 34:15, 2017.
5. Munshi MN: Cognitive dysfunction in older adults with diabetes: What a clinician needs to know, *Diabetes Care* 40:461, 2017.

*6. Mendez MF: What is the relationship of traumatic brain injury to dementia? *J Alzheimers Dis* 57:667, 2017.
7. Heuther S, McCance KL: *Understanding pathophysiology,* ed 6, St Louis, 2017, Elsevier.
8. Aisen PS, Cummings J, Jack CR, et al: On the path to 2025: Understanding the Alzheimer's disease continuum, *Alzheimers Res Ther* 1:60, 2017.
*9. Ahmed S, Kaur A, Venigalla H, et al: The retrogenesis model in Alzheimer's disease: Evidence and practical applications, *Curr Psych Rev* 13:35, 2017.
*10. McKhann GM, Knopman DS, Chertkow H, et al: The diagnosis of dementia due to Alzheimer's disease: Recommendations from the National Institute on Aging and the Alzheimer's Association workgroup, *Alzheimers Dement* 7:263, 2011. (Classic)
11. Alzheimer's Association: Mild cognitive impairment. Retrieved from *www.alz.org/alzheimers-dementia/what-is-dementia/related_conditions/mild-cognitive-impairment.*
*12. Reus VI, Fochtmann LJ, Eyler AE, et al: The American Psychiatric Association practice guideline on the use of antipsychotics to treat agitation or psychosis in patients with dementia, *Amer J Psych* 173:543, 2016.
*13. Kristiansen PJ, Normann HK, Norberg A, et al: How do people in the early stage of Alzheimer's disease see their future? *Dementia* 16:145, 2017.
*14. Connors MH, Ames D, Woodward M, et al: Psychosis and clinical outcomes in Alzheimer disease: A longitudinal study, *Amer J Geriat Psychiat* 26:304, 2018.
*15. Canevelli M, Valletta M, Trebbastoni A, et al: Sundowning in dementia: Clinical relevance, pathophysiological determinants, and therapeutic approaches, *Front Med (Lausanne)* 27:73, 2016.
16. Alzheimer's Association: MedicAlert + Alzheimer's Association Safe Return. Retrieved from *https://alz.org/help-support/caregiving/safety/medicalert-safe-return.*
*17. Dassel KB, Carr DC, Vitaliano P: Does caring for a spouse with dementia accelerate cognitive decline? Findings from the Health and Retirement Study, *Gerontologist* 57:319, 2017.

18. Oh ES, Fong TG, Hshieh TT, et al: Delirium in older persons: Advances in diagnosis and treatment, *JAMA* 318:1161, 2017.

19. Marcantonio ER: Delirium in hospitalized older adults, *NEJM* 377:1456, 2017.

*20. Oldham MA, Flanagan NM, Khan A, et al: Responding to ten common delirium misconceptions with best evidence: An educational review for clinicians, *J Neuropsychiatry Clin Neurosci* 30:51, 2017.

*21. American Geriatrics Society Expert Panel on Postoperative Delirium in Older Adults: Postoperative delirium in older adults: Best practice statement from the American Geriatrics Society, *J Am Coll Surg* 220:136, 2015. (Classic)

22. Delirium prevention and safety: Starting with the ABCDEF's. Retrieved from *www.icudelirium.org/medicalprofessionals.html.*

23. Flaherty JH, Yue J, Rudolph JL: Dissecting delirium: Phenotypes, consequences, screening, diagnosis, prevention, treatment, and program implementation, *Clin Ger Med* 33:393, 2017.

*24. Neufeld KJ, Yue J, Robinson TN et al: Antipsychotic medication for prevention and treatment of delirium in hospitalized adults: A systematic review and meta-analysis, *J Am Geriatric Soc* 64:705, 2016.

*Evidence-based information for clinical practice.

60

Spinal Cord and Peripheral Nerve Problems

Cindy Sullivan

It only takes a split second to smile and forget, yet to someone that needed it, it can last a lifetime.

Steve Maraboli

http://evolve.elsevier.com/Lewis/medsurg

CONCEPTUAL FOCUS

Family Dynamics
Functional Ability

Mobility
Pain

Sensory Perception

LEARNING OUTCOMES

1. Outline the classification of spinal cord injuries and associated clinical manifestations.
2. Describe the clinical manifestations and interprofessional and nursing management of neurogenic and spinal shock.
3. Relate the clinical manifestations of spinal cord injury to the level of disruption and rehabilitation potential.
4. Describe the nursing management of the patient with a spinal cord injury.
5. Explain the types, clinical manifestations, and interprofessional and nursing management of spinal cord tumors.

6. Explain the etiology, clinical manifestations, and interprofessional and nursing management of trigeminal neuralgia and Bell's palsy.
7. Describe the etiology, clinical manifestations, and interprofessional and nursing management of Guillain-Barré syndrome/acute inflammatory demyelinating polyneuropathy.
8. Explain the etiology, clinical manifestations, and interprofessional and nursing management of chronic inflammatory demyelinating polyneuropathy.

KEY TERMS

acute inflammatory demyelinating polyneuropathy (AIDP), p. 1424
autonomic dysreflexia, p. 1414
Bell's palsy, p. 1423
botulism, p. 1426
chronic inflammatory demyelinating polyneuropathy (CIDP), p. 1425

Guillain-Barré syndrome (GBS), p. 1424
neurogenic bladder, p. 1407
neurogenic bowel, p. 1407
neurogenic (vasogenic) shock, p. 1404
paraplegia, p. 1405
spinal cord injury (SCI), p. 1403
spinal shock, p. 1404

tetanus, p. 1425
tetraplegia, p. 1405
trigeminal neuralgia (TN), p. 1421

This chapter discusses spinal cord and peripheral nerve problems, including spinal cord injuries, spinal cord tumors, cranial nerve disorders, and polyneuropathies. A focus of this chapter is the nursing management of the problems encountered by the patient with spinal cord injury (SCI). The potential for disruption of individual growth and development, altered family dynamics, economic loss from unemployment, and the high cost of rehabilitation and long-term health care make SCI a major problem. While many people with SCI can care for themselves independently, those with the highest level of injury need around-the-clock care at home or in a long-term care facility. The nurse's role in providing holistic care can have a significant impact on the patient's general health and well-being.

SPINAL CORD PROBLEMS

SPINAL CORD INJURY

Spinal cord injury (SCI) is caused by trauma or damage to the spinal cord. It can result in temporary or permanent alteration in the function of the spinal cord. About 17,000 Americans have SCIs each year. Some 282,000 persons in the United States are living with SCI. The average life expectancy for persons with SCI is less than those without SCI and has not improved since the 1980s. Mortality rates are high in the first year after injury with a 30% rehospitalization rate.[1]

Etiology and Pathophysiology

SCI is usually a result of trauma. The 4 most common causes are motor vehicle collisions (38%), falls (30.5%), violence (13.5%), and sports injuries (9%).[1]

Types of Injury. Neurologic damage caused by SCI occurs in 2 phases: *primary injury* (initial physical disruption of the spinal cord) and *secondary injury* (from processes, such as ischemia, hypoxia, hemorrhage, edema).

Primary Injury. Primary injury results from direct physical trauma to the spinal cord due to blunt or penetrating trauma. Trauma can cause spinal cord compression by bone displacement, interruption of blood supply, or distraction from pulling. Penetrating trauma, such as gunshot and stab wounds, can cause tearing and transection.

Secondary Injury. Secondary injury refers to the ongoing, progressive damage that occurs after the primary injury. Secondary injury causes further permanent damage. It begins a few minutes after injury and lasts for months. Fig. 60.1 shows the cascade of events causing secondary injury. These events result in edema, ischemia, and inflammation. They result in cell death, disruption of the blood-brain barrier, and demyelination. This can extend the level of deficit and worsen long-term outcome.

Seconds after the insult, mechanical disruption leads to small hemorrhages in the white and gray matter, damage to the axons, and cell membrane destruction.[2,3] Over the next minutes to hours, neuron destruction occurs. Blood-spinal barrier disruption allows for an influx of inflammatory cytokines. This further increases spinal cord edema and promotes ongoing inflammation.[4] Edema due to the inflammatory response is especially harmful because of limited space for tissue expansion. Thus compression of the spinal cord occurs. Edema extends above and below the injury, increasing ischemic damage. Within 24 hours, permanent damage may occur from edema.

The resulting hypoxia reduces O_2 levels below the metabolic needs of the spinal cord. Lactate metabolites and an increase in vasoactive substances, including norepinephrine, serotonin, and dopamine, occur. High levels of these substances cause vasospasms and hypoxia with subsequent necrosis. Unfortunately, the spinal cord has minimal ability to adapt to vasospasm.

Apoptosis (programmed cell death) continues for weeks. It contributes to postinjury demyelination. The inflammatory response at the site of the initial injury focuses on clearing up the initial cellular debris without damaging normal tissue. This results in a central non-neural core of connective tissue that we refer to as a glial scar (Fig. 60.2). The glial scar creates a physical barrier. It restricts the cells in the spinal cord from migration and regeneration. This leads to irreversible nerve damage and permanent neurologic deficit.

Spinal and Neurogenic Shock. Spinal shock may occur shortly after acute SCI. It is characterized by loss of deep tendon and sphincter reflexes, loss of sensation, and flaccid paralysis below the level of injury. This syndrome lasts days to weeks. It often masks postinjury neurologic function.[3]

In contrast to spinal shock, neurogenic (vasogenic) shock can occur in cervical or high thoracic injury (T6 or higher). It occurs from unopposed parasympathetic response due to loss of sympathetic nervous system (SNS) innervation. It causes peripheral vasodilation, venous pooling, and decreased cardiac output. Manifestations include significant hypotension (< 90 mmHg), bradycardia, and temperature dysregulation. Neurogenic shock can continue for 1 to 3 weeks.[5] Hypotension can result in poor perfusion and oxygenation to the spinal cord and worsen spinal cord ischemia.[6]

Classification of Spinal Cord Injury. SCI is classified by the (1) mechanism of injury, (2) level of injury, and (3) degree of injury.

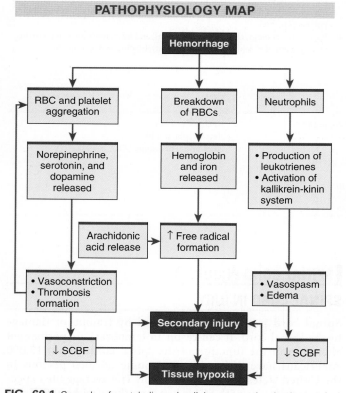

PATHOPHYSIOLOGY MAP

FIG. 60.1 Cascade of metabolic and cellular events that leads to spinal cord ischemia and hypoxia of secondary injury. *RBCs,* Red blood cells; *SCBF,* spinal cord blood flow. (Modified from Marciano FF, Greene KA, Apostolides PJ, et al: Pharmacologic management of spinal cord injury: Review of the literature, *BNI Q* 11:11, 1995. In KL McCance, SE Huether, editors: *Pathophysiology: The biologic basis for disease in adults and children,* ed 5, St Louis, 2006, Mosby.)

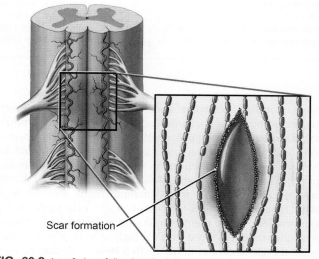

Scar formation

FIG. 60.2 1 to 2 days following the injury, astrocytes proliferate and surround the edges of the fibrotic scar to confine inflammation to the area of injury. This process may take 7 to 10 days. It protects neighboring neural tissue from further damage. (Used with permission from Barrow Neurological Institute, Phoenix, AZ.)

Mechanisms of Injury. The major mechanisms of injury include flexion, flexion-rotation, hyperextension, vertical compression, extension-rotation, and lateral flexion (Fig. 60.3). Flexion-rotation injury is the most unstable because ligaments that stabilize the spine are torn. This injury most often contributes to severe neurologic deficits.

Level of Injury. *Skeletal level* of injury is the vertebral level with the most damage to vertebra and related ligaments. *Neurologic level* is the lowest segment of the spinal cord with normal sensory and motor function on both sides of the body. The level of injury may be cervical, thoracic, lumbar, or sacral. Cervical and lumbar injuries are most common because those areas of the spine are associated with the greatest flexibility and movement.

Injury from C1 to T1 can cause paralysis of all 4 extremities, resulting in tetraplegia (formerly called *quadriplegia*). The degree of impairment in the arms after cervical injury depends on the level of injury. The lower the level, the more function is retained in the arms.

Paraplegia (paralysis and loss of sensation in the legs) can occur in SCI below the level of T2.[2] Fig. 60.4 shows affected structures and functions at different levels of cord injury.

Degree of Injury. The degree of spinal cord involvement may be complete or incomplete (partial). *Complete cord involvement* results in total loss of sensory and motor function below the level of injury. *Incomplete cord involvement* results in a mixed loss of voluntary motor activity and sensation and leaves some tracts intact. The degree of sensory and motor loss depends on the level of injury and reflects specific damaged nerve tracts.

Five major syndromes are associated with incomplete injuries: central cord syndrome, anterior cord syndrome, Brown-Séquard syndrome, cauda equina syndrome, and conus medullaris syndrome (Table 60.1).

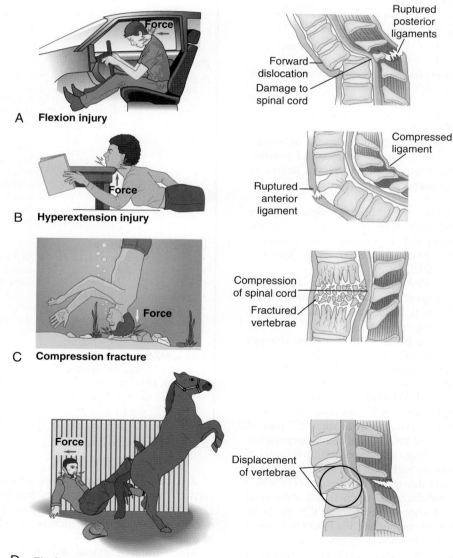

FIG. 60.3 Examples of mechanisms of spinal cord injury. **A,** Flexion injury of the cervical spine ruptures the posterior ligaments. **B,** Hyperextension injury of the cervical spine ruptures the anterior ligaments. **C,** Compression fractures crush the vertebrae and force bony fragments into the spinal canal. **D,** Flexion-rotation injury of the cervical spine often results in tearing of ligamentous structures that normally stabilize the spine. (*A, B,* and *C,* From Copstead-Kirkhorn LC, Banasik JL: *Pathophysiology,* ed 5, St Louis, 2014, Mosby.)

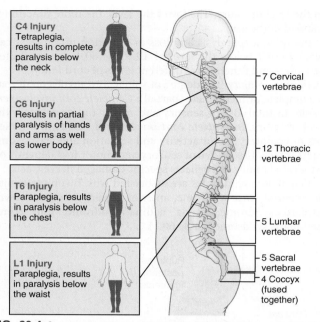

C4 Injury
Tetraplegia, results in complete paralysis below the neck

C6 Injury
Results in partial paralysis of hands and arms as well as lower body

T6 Injury
Paraplegia, results in paralysis below the chest

L1 Injury
Paraplegia, results in paralysis below the waist

7 Cervical vertebrae

12 Thoracic vertebrae

5 Lumbar vertebrae

5 Sacral vertebrae
4 Coccyx (fused together)

FIG. 60.4 Symptoms, degree of paralysis, and potential for rehabilitation depend on level of spinal injury.

Clinical Manifestations

Manifestations of SCI are generally the direct result of trauma that causes cord compression, ischemia, edema, and possible cord transection. They are related to the level and degree of injury. The patient with an incomplete injury may have a mix of manifestations.

Motor and Sensory Effects. The American Spinal Injury Association (ASIA) Impairment Scale is used to classify the severity of impairment from SCI. It combines assessments of motor and sensory function to determine neurologic level and completeness of injury (Fig. 60.5).[7]

The sensory regions are called *dermatomes*. Each segment of the spinal cord innervates a specific area of skin. A dermatome map is shown in Fig. 55.7 on p. 1284. Each dermatome has a recommended point for testing.

The ASIA Impairment Scale is useful for recording changes in neurologic status. It also helps us identify rehabilitation goals. Movement and rehabilitation potential related to specific locations of SCI are described in Table 60.2. In general, sensory function closely matches motor function at all levels.

Respiratory System. Respiratory complications closely correspond to the level of injury. Cervical injuries above C3 present special problems because of the total loss of respiratory muscle function. These patients have respiratory arrest within minutes of injury if not intubated. Patients with high cervical injury (C3-5) have respiratory insufficiency due to loss of phrenic nerve innervation to the diaphragm and decreases in chest and abdominal wall strength.[8] Patients with complete SCI above C5 should be intubated at once. Patients with incomplete SCI injury will have a high degree of variability in their respiratory function.

Cervical and thoracic injuries cause paralysis of abdominal muscles and often the intercostal muscles. The patient cannot cough effectively enough to remove secretions, increasing the risk for aspiration, atelectasis, and pneumonia. Hypoventilation and impairment of the intercostal muscles lead to a decrease in vital capacity and tidal volume.

TABLE 60.1	**Incomplete Spinal Cord Injury Syndromes**
Description	**Manifestations**
Anterior Cord Syndrome	
• Damage to anterior spinal artery • Results in compromised blood flow to anterior spinal cord • Typically results from acute compression of anterior part of the spinal cord • Common with flexion injury	• Motor paralysis and loss of pain and temperature sensation below level of injury • Since posterior cord tracts are not injured, sensations of touch, position, vibration, and motion remain intact
Brown-Séquard Syndrome	
• Damage to half of the spinal cord • Typically results from penetrating injury to spinal cord	• *Contralateral* (opposite side of injury): Loss of pain and temperature sensation below level of injury • *Ipsilateral* (same side as injury): Loss of motor function, light touch, pressure, position, and vibratory sense
Cauda Equina Syndrome	
• Damage to cauda equina (lumbar and sacral nerve roots)	• Asymmetric distal weakness, patchy sensation in lower extremities • May cause flaccid paralysis of lower extremities • Complete loss of sensation between legs and over buttocks, inner thighs, and backs of legs (*saddle area*) • Areflexic (flaccid) bladder and bowel • Severe, radicular, asymmetric pain
Central Cord Syndrome	
• Damage to central spinal cord • Occurs most often in cervical cord region • More common in older adults • Caused by hyperextension injury in people with degenerative disease	• Motor weakness and altered sensation present in upper extremities • Lower extremities not usually affected • Burning pain in upper extremities
Conus Medullaris Syndrome	
• Damage to conus medullaris (lowest part of spinal cord)	• Motor function in legs may be preserved, weak, or flaccid • Decrease in or loss of sensation in perianal area • Areflexic bowel and bladder • Impotence

Associated traumatic injuries, such as lung contusions, can further compromise pulmonary function. Fluid overload can cause pulmonary edema. Neurogenic pulmonary edema may occur due to a dramatic increase in SNS activity at the time of injury.

Maintaining an arterial saturation above 92% reduces hypoxemia, which can lead to bradycardia and worsen secondary injury. Patients are assessed for manifestations of respiratory distress, including dyspnea, decreased vital capacity, and pCO_2 > 20mm Hg above baseline, which would indicate the need for intubation.

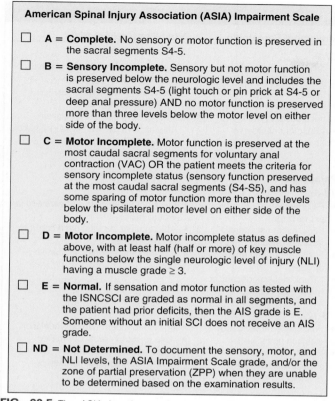

American Spinal Injury Association (ASIA) Impairment Scale

☐ **A = Complete.** No sensory or motor function is preserved in the sacral segments S4-5.

☐ **B = Sensory Incomplete.** Sensory but not motor function is preserved below the neurologic level and includes the sacral segments S4-5 (light touch or pin prick at S4-5 or deep anal pressure) AND no motor function is preserved more than three levels below the motor level on either side of the body.

☐ **C = Motor Incomplete.** Motor function is preserved at the most caudal sacral segments for voluntary anal contraction (VAC) OR the patient meets the criteria for sensory incomplete status (sensory function preserved at the most caudal sacral segments (S4-S5), and has some sparing of motor function more than three levels below the ipsilateral motor level on either side of the body.

☐ **D = Motor Incomplete.** Motor incomplete status as defined above, with at least half (half or more) of key muscle functions below the single neurologic level of injury (NLI) having a muscle grade ≥ 3.

☐ **E = Normal.** If sensation and motor function as tested with the ISNCSCI are graded as normal in all segments, and the patient had prior deficits, then the AIS grade is E. Someone without an initial SCI does not receive an AIS grade.

☐ **ND = Not Determined.** To document the sensory, motor, and NLI levels, the ASIA Impairment Scale grade, and/or the zone of partial preservation (ZPP) when they are unable to be determined based on the examination results.

FIG. 60.5 The ASIA Impairment Scale. (From American Spinal Injury Association.)

Cardiovascular System. Any cord injury above T6 leads to dysfunction of the SNS. The result may be bradycardia, peripheral vasodilation, and hypotension (neurogenic shock). Peripheral vasodilation causes relative hypovolemia because of the increase in the capacity of the dilated veins. It reduces venous return of blood to the heart. Cardiac output then decreases, leading to hypotension. Other injuries can cause hemorrhagic shock and further reduce BP. It is important to identify all causes of hypotension in the person with SCI. Those on β-blockers, young healthy patients, and older adults may not be tachycardic with hemorrhage.[8]

Urinary System. Urinary dysfunction occurs in most patients after SCI. Neurogenic bladder describes any type of bladder dysfunction related to abnormal or absent bladder innervation. After SCI, the ability for the bladder muscles and the micturition center in the brain to transmit information is impaired. Both the detrusor muscle (bladder wall) and sphincter muscle (a valve around the top of the urethra) may be overactive due to the lack of brain control. This may cause high bladder pressures and urinary retention. Incontinence results from reflex emptying and failure to store urine.

Depending on the injury, a neurogenic bladder may (1) have no reflex detrusor contractions (*flaccid, hypotonic),* which can result in bladder stretching from overdistention; (2) have hyperactive reflex detrusor contractions (*spastic),* seen in SCI above T12, leading to incontinence; or (3) lack coordination between detrusor contraction and urethral relaxation (*dyssynergia),* resulting in reflux of urine into the kidneys. Reflux into the kidneys can lead to stone formation, hydronephrosis, pyelonephritis, and renal failure.[9]

Gastrointestinal System. Decreased gastrointestinal (GI) motor activity contributes to gastric distention and the development of paralytic ileus. Gastric emptying may be delayed, especially in patients with higher level SCI. Excessive release of hydrochloric acid (HCl) in the stomach may cause stress ulcers. Dysphagia may be present in patients who need mechanical ventilation, tracheostomy, and anterior spine surgery.

Intraabdominal bleeding may be hard to diagnose because the person with SCI may not have pain or tenderness. Continued hypotension and decreases in hemoglobin and hematocrit may be the only signs of bleeding. Expanding abdominal girth may be seen.

Loss of voluntary control of the bowel after SCI results in neurogenic bowel. SCI above the level of the conus medullaris results in a *hyperreflexic* bowel with increased rectal and sigmoid compliance. Combined with increased anal sphincter tone and the inability to sense a full rectum, this causes stool retention and constipation.[10] SCI at or below the conus medullaris causes the bowel to be *areflexic.* Peristalsis is impaired and stool movement is slow. The defecation reflex may be damaged and anal sphincter tone relaxed. This leads to constipation, increased risk for incontinence, and possible impaction, ileus, or megacolon. Hemorrhoids can occur over time.

Integumentary System. The risk for skin breakdown over bony prominences in areas of decreased or absent sensation is a major consequence of immobility related to SCI. Pressure injuries can occur quickly and lead to infection and sepsis.

Thermoregulation. *Poikilothermia* is the inability to maintain a constant core temperature, with the patient assuming the temperature of the environment. It occurs in SCI because interruption of the SNS prevents peripheral temperature sensations from reaching the hypothalamus. There is a decreased ability to sweat or shiver below the level of injury, which affects the ability to regulate body temperature. The degree of poikilothermia depends on the level of injury. Cervical injuries are associated with a greater loss of ability to regulate temperature than are thoracic or lumbar injuries.

Metabolic Needs. The person with SCI has increased nutritional needs due to increased metabolism and more protein breakdown. Lean body mass decreases and muscles atrophy, leading to weight loss. In the acute injury phase, stress on the body from hemodynamic instability and medical interventions, such as surgery, can worsen stress. Nutritional support should start early. Enteral nutrition (EN) or parenteral nutrition (PN) can supply the person's caloric, protein, and micronutrient requirements needs.[11] Adequate nutrition helps prevent skin breakdown, reduce infection, and decrease the rate of muscle atrophy.

Peripheral Vascular Problems. Venous thromboembolism (VTE) is a common problem after SCI due to hypercoagulability, venous stasis, and venous endothelial injury.[12] Immobilization promotes venous stasis and thrombi of the lower extremities. Detecting a deep venous thrombosis (DVT) may be hard in a person with SCI because usual signs and symptoms, such as pain and tenderness, are not present.

Pain. Pain after SCI differs in type and severity. The patient's physical functioning and emotions influence pain. The pain can be nociceptive or neuropathic.

Nociceptive pain in SCI can result from musculoskeletal, visceral, and/or other types of injury (e.g., skin ulceration, headache). Patients often describe musculoskeletal pain as dull or aching. It starts or worsens with movement. Visceral pain is in

TABLE 60.2 Level of Spinal Cord Injury and Rehabilitation Potential

Movement Remaining	Rehabilitation Potential	Movement Remaining	Rehabilitation Potential
Tetraplegia **C1-3** • Often fatal • Movement in neck and above, loss of innervation to diaphragm, absence of independent respiratory function	• Able to drive electric wheelchair equipped with portable ventilator by using chin control or mouth stick, headrest to stabilize head • Computer use with mouth stick, head wand, or noise control • Attendant care 24 hr/day, able to instruct others	**C7-8** • All triceps to elbow extension, finger extensors and flexors • Good grasp with some decreased strength • ↓ Respiratory reserve	• Able to transfer self to wheelchair • Roll over and sit up in bed • Push self on most surfaces • Perform most self-care • Independent use of wheelchair • Able to drive car with powered hand controls (in some patients) • Attendant care 0–6 hr/day
C4 • Sensation and movement in neck and above • May be able to breathe without ventilator	• Same as C1-3	**Paraplegia** **T1-6** • Full innervation of upper extremities • Back, essential intrinsic muscles of hand • Full strength and dexterity of grasp • ↓ Trunk stability, decreased respiratory reserve	• Full independence in self-care and in wheelchair • Able to drive car with hand controls (in most patients) • Independent standing in standing frame
C5 • Full neck, partial shoulder, back, biceps • Gross elbow, inability to roll over or use hands • ↓ Respiratory reserve	• Able to drive electric wheelchair with mobile hand supports • Indoor mobility in manual wheelchair • Able to feed self with setup and adaptive equipment • Attendant care 10 hr/day	**T6-12** • Full, stable thoracic muscles and upper back • Functional intercostal muscles, resulting in ↑ respiratory reserve	• Full independent use of wheelchair • Able to stand erect with full leg brace, ambulate on crutches with swing (although gait difficult) • Unable to climb stairs
C6 • Shoulder and upper back abduction and rotation at shoulder • Full biceps to elbow flexion, wrist extension, weak grasp of thumb • ↓ Respiratory reserve	• Able to help with transfer and perform some self-care • Feed self with hand devices • Push wheelchair on smooth, flat surface • Drive adapted van from wheelchair • Independent computer use with adaptive equipment • Attendant care 6 hr/day	**L1-2** • Varying control of legs and pelvis • Instability of lower back	• Good sitting balance • Full use of wheelchair • Ambulation with long leg braces
		L3-4 • Quadriceps and hip flexors • Absence of hamstring function, flail ankles	• Completely independent ambulation with short leg braces and canes • Unable to stand for long periods

the thorax, abdomen, and/or pelvis. It may be dull, tender, or cramping.

Neuropathic pain in SCI occurs from damage to the spinal cord or nerve roots. The pain can be at or below the level of injury. Patients often describe the pain as hot, burning, tingling, pins and needles, cold, and/or shooting. They may be extremely sensitive to stimuli. Even light touch can cause significant pain. (Pain is discussed in Chapter 8.)

Diagnostic Studies

CT scan is the preferred imaging study to diagnose the location and degree of injury and the degree of spinal canal compromise. Cervical x-rays are done when CT scan is not readily available. However, it is hard to see C7 and T1 on a cervical x-ray, decreasing the ability to fully evaluate a cervical spine injury.

MRI is used to assess soft tissue injury, neurologic changes, unexplained neurologic deficits, or worsening neurologic condition. MRI results guide clinical decisions about surgery.[2] Perform a comprehensive neurologic examination with assessment of the head, chest, and abdomen for other injuries or trauma. Patients with cervical injuries who have altered mental status may need a CT angiogram to rule out vertebral artery damage. Table 37.9 presents the diagnostic studies used to determine the site or location and extent of a VTE.

Interprofessional Care

Prehospital. Goals immediately after injury include maintaining a patent *airway*, adequate ventilation/*breathing*, and adequate *circulating* blood volume (ABCs) and preventing extension of spinal cord damage (secondary injury). Table 60.3 outlines emergency management of the patient with SCI. Spinal motion should be restricted with a combination of a rigid cervical collar and a supportive backboard with straps. Patients should be kept supine and may be logrolled for transfers. Uncooperative patients may need chemical sedation or physical restraints to protect them from further injury.[13] Reverse Trendelenburg position may be used if necessary. Spinal immobilization in patients with penetrating trauma should be tried as long as it does not affect resuscitation efforts.[13]

Intubation to secure the airway is done as soon as possible for patients with respiratory distress. Using end-tidal CO_2 monitoring can help determine the need for rapid sequence intubation (RSI). Patients with stable airways in the field may need intubation at the medical facility. Systemic and neurogenic shock are treated with IV fluids and vasopressors to maintain systolic BP (SBP) greater than 90 mm Hg. After cervical injury, all body systems must be maintained until the full extent of the damage can be evaluated. After stabilization at the injury scene, the person should be transferred to the nearest medical facility.

✚ TABLE 60.3 Emergency Management
Spinal Cord Injury

Etiology	Assessment Findings	Interventions
Blunt Trauma • Compression, flexion, extension, or rotation injuries to spinal column • Diving • Falls • Motor vehicle crash • Pedestrian accidents • Sports injuries **Penetrating Trauma** • Gunshot wounds • Stab wounds • Stretched, torn, crushed, or lacerated spinal cord	• Respiratory distress/difficulty breathing • Neurogenic shock: hypotension, bradycardia, cool or warm dry skin • Spinal shock • Muscle weakness, paralysis, or flaccidity • Changes in sensation: temperature, light touch, deep pressure, proprioception • Numbness, paresthesia • Pain, tenderness, deformities, or muscle spasms adjacent to vertebral column • Cuts; bruises; open wounds on head, face, neck, or back • Bowel and bladder incontinence • Urinary retention • Priapism • Decreased rectal sphincter tone	**Initial** • Ensure patent airway and adequate breathing. • Maintain SaO_2 >90%: • Apply O_2 via nasal cannula, nonrebreather mask, or endotracheal tube. • Maintain SBP >90 mm Hg. • Establish IV access with 2 large-bore catheters to infuse normal saline or lactated Ringer's solution. • Immobilize and stabilize cervical spine. • Assess for other injuries. • Control external bleeding. • Obtain appropriate imaging. **Ongoing Monitoring** • Monitor vital signs, level of consciousness, motor and sensory function, O_2 saturation, cardiac rhythm, urine output. • Anticipate need for intubation if in respiratory distress or gag reflex absent. • Maintain normal temperature.

The preferred facility is one that specializes in acute SCI care. A thorough assessment determines the degree of deficit and the level and degree of injury.

Acute Care. Interprofessional care during the acute phase for a patient with a cervical injury is described in Table 60.4. Compared to cervical injury, patients with SCI of the thoracic and lumbar vertebrae need less intense support. At this level of injury, respiratory compromise is not as severe, and bradycardia is usually not a problem. Other problems are treated symptomatically.

Obtain a history, with emphasis on how the incident occurred. Assess the extent of injury perceived by the patient or by the emergency response system (ERS) personnel right after the event. Initial assessment occurs in the emergency department (ED). It includes managing the person's ABCs and vital signs to ensure a secure airway and maintain oxygenation saturation (SaO_2) greater than 92% and mean arterial pressure (MAP) greater than 85 mm Hg. Avoid SBP less than 90 mm Hg. Appropriate medical interventions and diagnostics are implemented to ensure the patient is hemodynamically stable.

Perform a complete neurologic assessment using the ASIA tool (Fig. 60.5). Muscle groups are tested with and against gravity, alone and against resistance, on both sides of the body. Record strength, symmetry, and spontaneous movement. Complete a sensory examination, including touch and pain, as tested by pinprick. Start at the toes and work upward toward the head. Assess rectal tone and note the presence of *priapism*. Voluntary anal contractions indicate incomplete SCI. If time and conditions permit, assess position sense and vibration.

Mechanisms of injury that cause spinal cord trauma, especially involving the cervical cord, may result in brain injury and/or vertebral artery injury. Assess for a history of unconsciousness, signs of concussion, and increased intracranial pressure (see Chapter 56). Carefully assess for musculoskeletal injuries and trauma to internal organs. Because the patient may have altered or no muscle, bone, or visceral sensations below the level of injury, the only clue to internal trauma with hemorrhage may be a rapidly decreasing BP and increasing pulse. Check urine for hematuria, which indicates internal injuries.

Move the patient in alignment as a unit *(logroll)* during transfers and when repositioning to prevent further injury. Monitor respiratory, cardiac, urinary, and GI functions. The patient may go directly to surgery after the initial evaluation or to the intensive care unit (ICU) for monitoring and management.

Nonoperative Stabilization. Nonoperative treatments involve stabilization of the injured spinal segment and decompression, either through traction or realignment. Stabilization eliminates damaging motion at the injury site. It is meant to prevent secondary spinal cord damage caused by narrowing of the spinal canal, or continued contusion or compression of the spinal cord at the level of the injury. Early realignment of an unstable fracture-dislocation injury by closed reduction through craniocervical traction is effective and safe.

Surgical Therapy. Surgical treatment after acute SCI is used to manage instability and decompress the spinal cord. It may reduce secondary injury and improve the patient's outcome. Early surgery (within 24 hours after the injury) is recommended for persons with central cord syndrome and for adults with an acute SCI at any level.[2] The type of surgery depends on the severity and level of the injury, mechanism of injury, and location and degree of compression.

Surgery to stabilize the spine can be done from the back of the spine *(posterior approach)* or from the front of the spine *(anterior approach)*. In some cases, both approaches may be needed. Fixation involves attaching metal screws, plates, or other devices to the bones of the spine to help keep them aligned. This procedure is usually done when 2 or more vertebrae are injured. Small pieces of bone may be attached to the injured bones to help them fuse into 1 solid piece. The bone used is obtained from the patient's spinal bone harvested during surgery, from another bone in the patient's body, or from donor bone. (Specific surgical and nursing interventions for these techniques are discussed in Chapter 63 on pp. 1488–1489.)

Drug Therapy. Current evidence for the use of methylprednisolone is mixed. Guidelines for managing spinal cord injuries issued by both the American Association of Neurological Surgeons and Congress of Neurological Surgeons do not recommend its use for treating acute SCI.[14] The FDS no longer approves its use either. However, recommendations in the AOSPine 2017 Guidelines suggest a 24-hour infusion of high-dose methyl-prednisolone within 8 hours of acute SCI.[2] So, some HCPs may consider this option.

VTE prophylaxis with low-molecular-weight heparin (LMWH) (e.g., enoxaparin [Lovenox]) or fixed, low-dose heparin should start within 72 hours after injury, unless contraindicated. Contraindications include internal or external bleeding and recent surgery. For those with abnormal kidney function, heparin is best as LMWH is mainly excreted via the kidneys.

Vasopressor agents (e.g., phenylephrine, norepinephrine) are used in the acute phase of injury as adjuvants to treatment. They maintain the MAP to improve perfusion to the spinal cord. Use of vasopressors has significant risk for complications. These include ventricular tachycardia, troponin elevation, metabolic acidosis, and atrial fibrillation. Dopamine has more complications than phenylephrine in SCI. Considerations for vasopressor selection include level of injury, patient age, and comorbidities (e.g., heart problems).

TABLE 60.4 Interprofessional Care
Cervical Cord Injury

Diagnostic Assessment
- History and physical examination, including complete neurologic examination
- ABGs
- Electrolytes, serum glucose, coagulation profile, hemoglobin and hematocrit
- Urinalysis
- CT scan, MRI, EMG (measure evoked potentials)
- Anteroposterior, lateral, and odontoid spinal x-rays
- Serial bedside pulmonary function tests (PFTs)

Management
Acute Care
- Immobilization and stabilization of vertebral column
- ABCs (airway, breathing, circulation)
- O_2 by high-humidity mask (PaO_2 >60 mm Hg)
- Intubation (if indicated by ABGs and PFTs)
- Maintain heart rate (e.g., atropine) and BP (e.g., dopamine) (SBP >90 mm Hg, MAP >85)
- Administer IV fluids
- Insert NG tube and attach to suction.
- Assessment and management of nutrition
- Maintain normal body temperature
- Indwelling urinary catheter
- Pain management
- VTE prophylaxis
- Pressure injury prevention
- Stress ulcer prophylaxis
- Bowel and bladder care and training
- Mobilization once spine stabilized
- Physical, occupational, speech therapy and physiatrist consults

Rehabilitation and Home Care
- Physical therapy (ROM, mobility, strength, equipment)
- Occupational therapy (splints, ADLs training)
- Speech therapy (swallow and cognition)
- Pain management
- Spasticity management
- Bowel and bladder training
- Autonomic dysreflexia prevention
- Pressure injury prevention
- Recreational therapy
- Patient and caregiver teaching

❖ NURSING MANAGEMENT: SPINAL CORD INJURY

◆ Nursing Assessment

Subjective and objective data you should obtain from a patient with recent SCI are outlined in Table 60.5.

TABLE 60.5 Nursing Assessment
Spinal Cord Injury

Subjective Data
Important Health Information
Past health history: Motor vehicle crash, sports injury, industrial incident, gunshot or stabbing injury, falls

Functional Health Patterns
Health perception–health management: Use of alcohol or recreational drugs. Risk-taking behaviors
Activity-exercise: Loss of strength, movement, and sensation below level of injury. Dyspnea, inability to breathe adequately ("air hunger")
Cognitive-perceptual: Tenderness, pain at or above level of injury. Numbness, tingling, burning, twitching of extremities
Coping–stress tolerance: Fear, denial, anger, depression

Objective Data
General
Poikilothermia (unable to regulate body heat)

Integumentary
Warm, dry skin below level of injury (neurogenic shock)

Respiratory
Injury at C1-3: Apnea, inability to cough
Injury at C4: Poor cough, diaphragmatic breathing, hypoventilation
Injury at C5-T6: ↓ Respiratory reserve

Cardiovascular
Injury above T6: Bradycardia, hypotension, postural hypotension, absence of vasomotor tone

Gastrointestinal
↓ Or absent bowel sounds (paralytic ileus in injuries above T5), abdominal distention, constipation, fecal incontinence, fecal impaction

Urinary
Retention (for injuries at T1-L2), flaccid bladder (acute stages), spasticity with reflex bladder emptying (later stages)

Reproductive
Priapism, altered sexual function

Neurologic
Complete: Areflexic, flaccid paralysis and anesthesia below level of injury resulting in tetraplegia (injuries above C8) or paraplegia (injuries below C8), hyperactive deep tendon reflexes and bilaterally positive Babinski test (after resolution of spinal shock)
Incomplete: Mixed loss of voluntary motor activity and sensation

Musculoskeletal
Muscle atony (in flaccid state), contractures (in spastic state)

Pain
Neuropathic, musculoskeletal, and/or visceral

Possible Diagnostic Findings
Location of level and type of bony involvement on spinal x-ray. Injury, edema, compression on CT scan and MRI; positive finding on myelogram

◆ Nursing Diagnoses

Nursing diagnoses for the patient with SCI depend on the severity of the injury and level of dysfunction. Nursing diagnoses for a patient with SCI may include:

- Impaired breathing
- Impaired nutritional status
- Ineffective tissue perfusion
- Impaired tissue integrity
- Impaired urinary system function
- Constipation
- Difficulty coping

Additional information on nursing diagnoses and interventions for the patient with complete cervical SCI is presented in eNursing Care Plan 60.1 (available on the website for this chapter).

◆ Planning

Overall goals are that the patient with an SCI will (1) maintain an optimal level of neurologic functioning; (2) have minimal or no complications of immobility; (3) learn new skills, gain new knowledge, and acquire new behaviors to be able to care for self or direct others to do so; and (4) return home at an optimal level of functioning.

◆ Nursing Implementation

◆ **Health Promotion.** Nursing interventions for the prevention of SCI include identifying high-risk persons and providing teaching. Support measures to combat distracted and impaired driving. Teach people to use child safety seats and helmets for motorcyclists and bicyclists. Promote programs for older adults (e.g., STEADI) aimed at preventing accidental death and injury.[15]

Emphasize the importance of health promotion and screening behaviors after SCI. Health-promoting behaviors after SCI can have significant impact on the general health and well-being of the person with SCI. Nursing interventions include (1) teaching and counseling; (2) referring to programs such as smoking cessation classes, recreation programs, and alcohol treatment programs; and (3) performing routine physical examinations for non-neurologic problems. Promotion and screening programs must be accessible to and accommodate people with SCI. Nurses should advocate for wheelchair-accessible examination rooms, adjustable-height examination tables, and appointment scheduling that allows extra time if needed.

◆ **Acute Care.** High cervical cord injury caused by flexion-rotation is the most complex SCI. It is the focus of this section. Interventions for this type of injury can be modified for patients with less severe injuries.

Immobilization. To restrict spinal motion, maintain the neck in a neutral position. For cervical injuries, closed reduction with skeletal traction is used for early realignment *(reduction)* of the injury. Crutchfield (Fig. 60.6) or Gardner-Wells tongs or halo (halo ring) can provide this type of traction. A rope extends from the center of the device over a pulley to weights attached at the end. Traction must be maintained at all times. Possible displacement of the skull pins is a disadvantage of tongs. If pin displacement occurs, hold the patient's head in a neutral position and get help. Immobilize the head while the HCP reinserts the tongs.

> ⚠️ **SAFETY ALERT Cervical Spine Injuries**
> - Always keep the patient's body in correct alignment.
> - Turn the patient as a unit (e.g., logrolling) to prevent movement of the spine.

No specific guidelines address the maximum weight for traction. The HCP may start with 10 lb and add 5 lb for each level to the injury. The goal is spinal reduction. Awake patients are monitored with x-ray and neurologic and pain assessment. Comatose patients need serial x-rays to evaluate the effects of traction. The need for surgery is determined after the spine is reduced. After cervical fusion or other stabilization surgery, the patient may have a hard cervical collar or sternal-occipital-mandibular immobilizer brace (Fig. 60.7).

Some patients with spinal fractures with or without acute SCI may not be able to have surgery but still need immobilization for their cervical fracture. In these patients, the halo frame can be attached to a special vest (Halo vest) (Fig. 60.8). This allows the patient to move and ambulate while cervical bones fuse. Surgery is used instead of the halo if the patient has ligament instability from the injury; has severe cervical deformity; or is morbidly obese, older, cachectic, or noncompliant.

Infection at the tong or pin insertion sites is a potential problem. Preventive care is based on agency protocol. A common protocol involves cleansing sites twice a day with chlorhexidine. Antibiotic ointment is then applied to act as a mechanical barrier to the entrance of bacteria. Patient and caregiver teaching for a patient with a halo vest is outlined in Table 60.6.

Patients with stable thoracic or lumbar spine injuries may be immobilized with a custom thoracolumbar sacral orthosis (TLSO or body jacket) to limit spinal flexion, extension, and rotation. A Jewett brace may be used instead to restrict forward flexion. Unstable injuries may require surgical decompression and fusion in addition to the TLSO or lumbosacral orthotic (LSO).

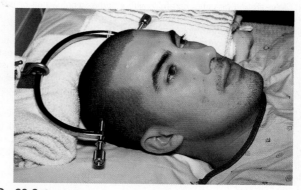

FIG. 60.6 Cervical traction is attached to tongs inserted in the skull. (Courtesy Michael S. Clement, MD, Mesa, AZ.)

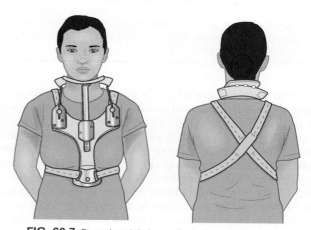

FIG. 60.7 Sternal-occipital-mandibular immobilizer brace.

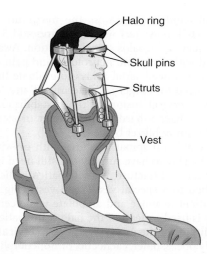

FIG. 60.8 Halo vest. The halo traction brace immobilizes the cervical spine, which allows the patient to ambulate and take part in self-care. (Modified from Urden LD, Stacy KM, Lough ME: *Priorities in critical care nursing,* ed 6, St Louis, 2012, Mosby.)

TABLE 60.6 Patient & Caregiver Teaching

Halo Vest Care

Include the following instructions when teaching the patient and caregiver management of a halo vest:

1. Inspect the pins on the halo traction ring. Report to HCP if pins are loose or signs of infection are present, including redness, tenderness, swelling, or drainage at insertion sites.
2. Clean around pin sites carefully with chlorhexidine, water, or half-strength peroxide on a cotton swab as directed.
3. Apply antibiotic ointment as prescribed.
4. For skin care, have patient lie down with the head resting on a pillow to reduce pressure on the brace. Loosen 1 side of the vest. Gently wash the skin under the vest with soap and water, rinse area, and then dry it thoroughly. At the same time, check the skin for pressure points, redness, swelling, bruising, or chafing. Close the open side and repeat the procedure on the other side.
5. If the vest becomes wet or damp, carefully dry it with a blow dryer.
6. Encourage patient to use assistive device (e.g., cane, walker) to improve balance; encourage use of flat shoes.
7. Teach patient to turn the entire body, not just the head and neck, when trying to look sideways.
8. In case of an emergency, always keep a set of wrenches close to the halo vest.
9. Mark the vest strap to maintain consistent buckling and fit.
10. Avoid grabbing bars or vest to help the patient.
11. Keep sheepskin pad under vest. Change and wash pad at least weekly.
12. If perspiration or itching is a problem, encourage patient to wear a cotton T-shirt under the sheepskin. The T-shirt can be modified with a Velcro seam closure on one side.

The effects of immobility can be great. Thorough skin care is important because decreased sensation and circulation increase the risk for skin breakdown. Remove the patient's backboard as soon as possible. Replace it with other forms of immobilization to prevent skin breakdown in the coccygeal and occipital areas. Fit cervical collars properly. Carefully assess areas under any device used for immobilization. We often place patients on special beds (Fig. 60.9). Kinetic therapy involves continuous side-to-side rotation of a patient to 40 degrees or more to help prevent lung complications. This lateral rotation also redistributes pressure, helping prevent pressure injuries.

FIG. 60.9 The RotoRest Therapy System helps prevent and treat lung complications for immobile patients, including those with unstable cervical, thoracic, and lumbar fractures. Kinetic therapy, the continual side-to-side bilateral rotation of the patient, redistributes pulmonary blood flow and mobilizes secretions to improve ventilation and perfusion matching. The therapy system helps to prevent pressure injuries. (Courtesy Arjo Huntleigh, Addison, IL.)

Respiratory Dysfunction. Respiratory complications are the leading acute and chronic causes of morbidity and mortality in SCI.[16] Respiratory dysfunction is present in up to 65% of patients with cervical SCI. During the first 48 hours after injury, spinal cord edema may increase the level of dysfunction, and respiratory distress may occur. Injury at or above C4 affects the phrenic nerve, which leads to the diaphragm, and breathing can stop.

Monitor the patient carefully for respiratory compromise and be prepared for quick action if arrest occurs. Regularly assess (1) breath sounds, (2) arterial blood gases (ABGs), (3) tidal volume, (4) vital capacity, (5) skin color, (6) breathing patterns (especially use of accessory muscles), (7) subjective comments about the ability to breathe, and (8) amount and color of sputum. A PaO_2 greater than 60 mm Hg and a $PaCO_2$ less than 45 mm Hg are acceptable values in a patient with uncomplicated tetraplegia. A patient who is unable to count to 20 aloud without taking a breath needs immediate attention.

In addition to ongoing assessment, intervene to maintain ventilation. Apply O_2 and provide appropriate ventilatory support until ABGs stabilize. If the patient is exhausted from labored breathing or ABGs show inadequate oxygenation or ventilation, endotracheal intubation or tracheostomy and mechanical ventilation is needed. Patients who have chest trauma or difficulty weaning from the ventilator may need a tracheostomy for airway management.

Clearing secretions is vital in reducing the risk for lung complications and possible respiratory failure.[16] Perform tracheal suctioning if crackles or coarse breath sounds are present. Chest physiotherapy and assisted (augmented) coughing can help. Perform assisted coughing either manually, by placing the heels of both hands just below the xiphoid process and exert firm upward pressure to the area timed with the patient's efforts to cough (see Fig. 67.6), or mechanically with an insufflation-exsufflation device. Encourage the use of incentive spirometry.

The older adult has more difficulty responding to hypoxia and hypercapnia. Thus aggressive chest physiotherapy, adequate oxygenation, and proper pain management are essential to maximize respiratory function and gas exchange.

Cardiovascular Instability. Heart rate is slowed, often to less than 60 beats/min, because of unopposed vagal response. Any increase in vagal stimulation, as occurs with turning or suctioning, can cause cardiac arrest. Loss of SNS tone in peripheral vessels results in chronic low BP with potential orthostatic hypotension. The lack of muscle tone to aid venous return can cause sluggish blood flow and predispose the patient to VTE. Dysrhythmias may occur.

Frequently assess vital signs. If bradycardia is symptomatic, give an anticholinergic drug, such as atropine. A temporary or permanent pacemaker may be inserted in some patients. Maintain SBP greater than 90 mm Hg and keep MAP between 85 and 90 mm Hg for the first 7 days after SCI. Manage hypotension with fluid replacement and a vasopressor agent, such as phenylephrine or norepinephrine.

Maintain a normal blood volume. If blood loss has occurred from other injuries, monitor hemoglobin and hematocrit and give blood according to protocol. Assess the patient for signs of hypovolemic shock from hemorrhage.

Orthostatic hypotension is likely to occur in the patient with injury at T6 and above. The patient may have light headedness, dizziness, and nausea. Assess orthostatic BP when mobilizing the patient. Some lose consciousness when moved from the bed to a chair. For symptomatic patients, use an abdominal binder and graduated compression stockings to promote venous return. Drugs used to increase intravascular volume include salt tablets and fludrocortisone. Midodrine may be given to promote blood vessel contraction and increase venous return.

Consider the effects of aging on the cardiovascular system of the older adult. The older patient is less able to manage the stress of traumatic injury because heart contractions weaken, and cardiac output is reduced. Maximum heart rate is reduced. The older adult may also have cardiovascular disease.

Use LMWH or low-dose heparin in combination with intermittent pneumatic compression devices or graduated compression stockings to promote venous return and reduce the risk for VTE. Remove stockings every 8 hours for skin care. Assess thighs and calves every shift for signs of VTE. Regularly perform range-of-motion (ROM) exercises and stretching. Continue VTE prophylaxis for 3 months after injury.

Fluid and Nutritional Management. During the first 48 to 72 hours after the injury, the GI tract may stop functioning (*paralytic ileus*). A nasogastric (NG) tube must be inserted if ileus occurs. Because the patient cannot have oral intake, monitor fluid and electrolyte status.

Nutrition should be started within the first 72 hours after injury. Specific solutions and additives are determined by individual requirements. Due to severe catabolism, a high-protein, high-calorie diet is needed for energy and tissue repair. If the patient cannot be fed through the GI system, either orally or through EN, PN should be started to reduce nitrogen losses that occur during the hypermetabolic state.

Once bowel sounds are present or flatus is passed, and the patient is not receiving mechanical ventilation, a formal swallow evaluation is done. If no risk for aspiration is identified, gradually introduce oral food and fluids. If the patient fails the swallow evaluation or is unable to eat due to an endotracheal tube or tracheostomy, a more secure feeding tube may be placed in the stomach or jejunum (see Chapter 39).

? CHECK YOUR PRACTICE

You are working in the spinal cord unit. Your 28-yr-old male patient with SCI at T6 weighs 168 lb. When he was admitted 3 weeks ago he weighed 186 lb. He asks you, "Well, what is my weight? Are you gonna make me eat now? You know you can't do that."
- What assessment data are important for you to obtain?
- What interventions would help him avoid further weight loss and regain lean body mass?

Patients may have anorexia due to depression, boredom with agency food, or discomfort at being fed (often by a hurried person). Some patients have a normally small appetite. Sometimes refusal to eat is a way of asserting control. If the patient is not eating adequately, assess the cause.

Based on assessment findings, make a contract with the patient with mutual goal setting for the diet. This contract gives the patient increased control and often results in improved nutritional intake. General measures also may be effective. For example, provide a pleasant eating environment, allow adequate time to eat (including any self-feeding the patient can achieve), encourage the family to bring in special foods, and plan social rewards for eating.

Consult a dietitian to ensure evaluation of the appropriate laboratory markers and develop the treatment plan. Keep a calorie count and record the patient's daily weight to evaluate progress. If possible, the patient should take part in recording calorie intake. Dietary supplements may be needed to meet nutritional goals. Include increased dietary fiber to promote bowel function.

Bladder and Bowel Management. Immediately after the injury, urine retention occurs because of the loss of autonomic and reflex control of the bladder and sphincter (*neurogenic bladder*). Because there is no sensation of fullness, overdistention of the bladder can result in reflux into the kidney and cause renal failure. Bladder overdistention may even result in rupture of the bladder. Thus an indwelling catheter may be inserted soon after injury. Ensure patency of the catheter by frequent inspection and irrigation, if needed. In some agencies, an HCP's order is required for this procedure. Strict aseptic technique for catheter care is essential to prevent infection. During the period of indwelling catheterization, encourage a large fluid intake. Check the catheter to prevent kinking and ensure free flow of urine.

Catheter-acquired urinary tract infection (CAUTI) is a common problem. The best way to prevent CAUTI is regular and complete bladder drainage. Once the patient is stabilized, assess the best means of managing long-term urinary function. Clean intermittent catheterization (CIC) is the preferred method for emptying the bladder. CAUTI and CIC are discussed in Chapter 45.

CIC should be done 4 to 6 times daily to prevent bacterial overgrowth from urinary stasis. Keep urine residuals under 500 mL to prevent bladder distention. If the urine is cloudy or has a strong odor or if the patient develops symptoms of a urinary tract infection (UTI) (e.g., chills, fever, malaise), send a specimen for culture.

Consider age-related changes in renal function. The older adult is more likely to develop renal stones. Older men may have benign prostatic hyperplasia, which may interfere with urinary flow and complicate management of urinary problems. It can affect the ability to complete CIC.

Start a bowel program to combat constipation from neurogenic bowel. This involves inserting a rectal stimulant (suppository or small-volume enema) daily at a regular time, followed by gentle digital stimulation or manual evacuation until evacuation is complete. At first, the program may be done in bed with the patient in the side-lying position. However, as soon as the patient has resumed sitting, the patient should be in the upright position on a padded bedside commode chair. These programs typically take 30 to 60 minutes to complete. Measures to reduce constipation include adequate fluid intake, a diet high in fiber and vegetables, and increased activity and exercise.

Temperature Control. Monitor the environment closely to maintain an appropriate temperature. Regularly assess the patient's body temperature. Do not use excess covers or unduly expose the patient (e.g., during bathing). If an infection with high fever develops, more aggressive methods for temperature control may be needed (e.g., a cooling blanket).

Stress Ulcers. Stress ulcers can occur in the patient with SCI because of the physiologic response to severe trauma and psychologic stress. Peak incidence of stress ulcers is 6 to 14 days after injury. Test stool and gastric contents daily for blood. Monitor the hematocrit for a slow drop. Histamine (H$_2$)-receptor blockers (e.g., ranitidine) or proton pump inhibitors (e.g., pantoprazole, omeprazole) given prophylactically decreases the secretion of HCl acid and prevents ulcers.

Sensory Deprivation. To prevent sensory deprivation, compensate for the patient's absent sensations by stimulating the patient above the level of injury. Conversation, music, and interesting foods can be a part of the nursing care plan. If the head of the bed must stay flat, provide prism glasses to help the patient read and watch television.

Help the patient avoid withdrawing from the environment. Promote adequate rest and sleep. Assess for changes in mood. Depression is common (discussed later in chapter on p. 1418).

Pain Management. Musculoskeletal nociceptive pain can develop from injuries to bones, muscles, and ligaments. The pain is worse with movement or palpation. Antiinflammatory drugs, such as ibuprofen (Motrin), may help with pain. Opioids may be used to manage nociceptive pain.

Visceral nociceptive pain is a dull, tender, or cramping pain in the thorax, abdomen, or pelvis. It may originate in the bladder or bowel. Assess the patient's bowel and bladder function to avoid bladder distention or constipation. Other causes of nociceptive pain include UTI and renal stones. Notify the HCP if the patient has persistent pain despite treatment. Diagnostic imaging may be needed to determine the cause.

Neuropathic pain in the initial phase is usually at the level of SCI. It may occur on 1 or both sides of the body within the affected dermatome and up to 3 levels below. The patient will describe hot, burning, tingling, shooting, electric pain. Pregabalin (Lyrica) is used to reduce symptoms.

Neuropathic pain can occur months or years after SCI, become chronic, and negatively affect sleep. The patient's mood, sudden noise, constipation, and infection can affect the pain. Teach the patient and caregiver about possible pain triggers and offer relaxation therapy. Other modes of treatment may include tricyclic antidepressants, intrathecal drugs, antiseizure drugs, epidural stimulation, and destructive surgical intervention.

Skin Care. The most common long-term complication in SCI is pressure injury (PI) formation. Healthy skin requires adequate blood circulation. Constant pressure in 1 position can compress blood vessels and limit blood supply, causing cell death and PI. Little evidence addresses interventions for prevention and treatment of PI in SCI.[17] Factors associated with increased risk for PI formation include heart and renal disease, smoking, alcohol or drug use, diabetes, hypoxia, hypotension, and pneumonia, UTI, and other infections.[18]

Prevention of PI requires diligent nursing care. Perform a risk assessment for PI formation with a daily comprehensive visual and tactile examination of the skin. Areas most vulnerable to breakdown include the sacrum, ischia, trochanters, and heels. Assess surgical incisions for healing and skin integrity under collars and braces. Regularly assess nutritional status. Both weight loss and gain can contribute to skin breakdown. Teach the patient and caregiver about the causes and risk factors for PI development.[19]

A consult with the wound, ostomy, continence nurse (WOCN) can assist with prevention and management strategies (e.g., surface overlays).[19] Monitor incontinence and implement appropriate neurogenic bowel and bladder management interventions. Apply skin barrier creams.

Carefully position and reposition the patient at least every 2 hours. Gradually increase the times between turns if no redness over bony prominences is seen when turning. While the patient is supine in bed, float the heels to reduce pressure. Consider prophylactic dressings to prevent sacral and heel wounds. Move the patient carefully during turns and transfers to avoid stretching and folding of soft tissues (*shear*) or abrasion.

Many patients are placed on specialty mattresses.[17] When the patient is moved to a chair or wheelchair, use pressure-relieving cushions. Pressure relief should be scheduled every 15 to 20 minutes when the patient is in a chair and should last 30 to 60 seconds each time.

Reflexes. Once spinal cord shock is resolved, return of reflexes may complicate rehabilitation. Lacking control from the higher brain centers, reflexes are often hyperactive and have exaggerated responses. Penile erection can occur from a variety of stimuli, causing embarrassment and discomfort. Spasms ranging from mild twitches to convulsive movements below the level of injury may occur. The patient or caregiver may interpret this reflex activity as a return of function. Tactfully explain the reason for the activity. Tell the patient of the positive use of these reflexes in sexual, bowel, and bladder retraining. Antispasmodic drugs, such as baclofen (Lioresal), dantrolene (Dantrium), and tizanidine (Zanaflex), may help control spasms. Botulism toxin injections may be given to treat severe spasticity.

Autonomic Dysreflexia. The return of reflexes after the resolution of spinal shock means patients with injury at T6 or higher may develop autonomic dysreflexia. Autonomic dysreflexia (AD) is a massive, uncompensated cardiovascular reaction mediated by the SNS. It involves stimulation of sensory receptors below the level of the SCI. The intact SNS below the level of injury responds to the stimulation with a reflex arteriolar vasoconstriction that increases BP. The parasympathetic nervous system is unable to directly counteract these responses via the injured spinal cord. Baroreceptors in the carotid sinus and aorta sense the hypertension and stimulate the parasympathetic system. This causes a decrease in heart rate. Visceral and peripheral vessels do not dilate because efferent impulses cannot pass through the injured spinal cord. It most often presents in the chronic phase after SCI.[20]

The most common precipitating cause of AD is a distended bladder or rectum. However, any sensory stimulation, including contraction of the bladder or rectum, stimulation of the skin, or stimulation of pain receptors can cause AD. AD is a life-threatening condition that requires immediate resolution. Proper identification and elimination of the inciting stimulus for AD can resolve the event. If uncorrected, it can lead to status epilepticus, stroke, myocardial infarction, and even death.

Manifestations include hypertension, throbbing headache, marked diaphoresis above the level of injury, bradycardia (30 to 40 beats/min), piloerection from pilomotor spasm, flushing of the skin above the level of injury, blurred vision or spots in the visual fields, nasal congestion, anxiety, and nausea. Measure BP when a patient with SCI reports a headache. Suspect AD in adults with SBP elevation of 20 to 40 mm Hg above baseline.[20]

Immediate nursing interventions include elevating the head of the bed 45 degrees or sitting the patient upright (to lower the BP) and determining the cause (bowel impaction, urinary retention, UTI, PI, tight clothing). Notify the HCP. The most common cause is bladder irritation. Immediate catheterization to relieve bladder distention may be needed. Instill lidocaine jelly in the urethra before catheterization. If a catheter is already in place, check it for kinks or folds. If it is plugged, perform small-volume irrigation slowly and gently to open the catheter or insert a new catheter.

Stool impaction can cause AD. Apply an anesthetic ointment to avoid increasing symptoms, then perform a digital rectal examination (if trained). Remove all skin stimuli, such as constrictive clothing and tight shoes. Monitor BP often during the episode. If symptoms persist after the source has been relieved, give a rapid-onset and short-duration agent, such as nitroglycerin, nitroprusside, or hydralazine. Continue careful monitoring until vital signs stabilize.

Teach the patient and caregiver to recognize causes and symptoms of AD (Table 60.7). They must understand the life-threatening nature of AD, know how to relieve the cause, and activate the ERS, if needed.

Rehabilitation and Home Care. Rehabilitation of the person with SCI is complex. With physical and psychologic care and intensive and specialized rehabilitation, the patient with SCI can learn to function at the highest level of wellness. All patients with a new SCI should receive comprehensive inpatient rehabilitation in a rehabilitation unit or center that specializes in SCI rehabilitation.[2] Rehabilitation is an interprofessional team effort. Team members include rehabilitation nurses, HCPs, physical therapists, occupational therapists, speech therapists, vocational counselors, psychologists, therapeutic recreation specialists, prosthetists, orthotists, case managers, social workers, and dietitians.

Many of the problems that begin in the acute period become chronic and continue throughout life. Rehabilitation focuses on retraining physiologic processes as well as extensive patient and caregiver teaching about how to manage the physiologic and life changes resulting from the injury (Fig. 60.10).

Rehabilitation care is organized around the patient's goals and needs. The patient is expected to be involved in therapies and learn self-care for several hours each day. Such intensive work at a time when the patient is dealing with the sudden change in health and function can be stressful. Progress may be slow. The rehabilitation nurse has a key role in providing encouragement, specialized nursing care, and patient and caregiver teaching and in helping to coordinate efforts of the rehabilitation team.

Respiratory Rehabilitation. The patient with mechanical ventilation will need around-the-clock caregivers who are knowledgeable about respiratory hygiene and tracheostomy care. The rehabilitation nurse and respiratory therapist should teach patients and caregivers about home ventilator and tracheostomy care. The patient may need chest percussion or postural drainage to manage secretions to lower the risk for atelectasis and pneumonia. Refer to appropriate community agencies as needed.

Some patients with high cervical SCI have improved respiratory function with phrenic nerve stimulators or electronic diaphragmatic pacemakers.[21] These devices are not appropriate for all ventilator-dependent patients but are safe and effective for those with an intact phrenic nerve. Some ventilators are portable, allowing ventilator-dependent patients with tetraplegia to be mobile and less dependent.

If the patient was weaned from the ventilator during hospitalization, downsizing (gradual decrease in size) and removal of the tracheostomy will be done during rehabilitation. Teach assisted coughing, regular use of incentive spirometry, and

---

TABLE 60.7 Patient & Caregiver Teaching

Autonomic Dysreflexia

For a patient at risk for autonomic dysreflexia, include the following information in the teaching plan for the patient and caregiver:

1. Signs and symptoms
   - Sudden onset of acute headache.
   - Elevation in BP and/or reduction in pulse rate.
   - Flushed face and upper chest (above level of injury) and pale extremities (below level of injury).
   - Sweating above level of injury.
   - Nasal congestion.
   - Feeling of apprehension.
   - Immediate interventions.
   - Raise the person to a sitting position.
   - Remove the noxious stimulus (fecal impaction, kinked urinary catheter, tight clothing).
   - Call the HCP if above actions do not relieve the signs and symptoms.
2. Measures to decrease the incidence of autonomic dysreflexia
   - Maintain regular bowel function.
   - If manual rectal stimulation is used to promote bowel function, use a local anesthetic to prevent autonomic dysreflexia.
   - Monitor urine output.
   - Teach the patient to wear a Medic Alert bracelet indicating a history of risk for autonomic dysreflexia.

FIG. 60.10 A spinal cord injury has a major effect on a person's physical, emotional, and psychologic health.

TABLE 60.8 Types of Neurogenic Bladder

Type	Characteristics	Causes	Manifestations
Uninhibited bladder (spastic, overactive)	• No inhibitions influence time and place of voiding • Bladder empties in response to stretching of bladder wall	• Results from lesions above the pons • Observed in stroke, brain tumor, brain trauma	• Incontinence, frequency, urgency • Voiding is unpredictable and incomplete

Upper motor neuron bladder (flaccid, spastic/overactive)	• *Mixed A type* (most common):
	  • Bladder is flaccid and external sphincter is spastic, leading to urinary retention.
	• *Mixed B type:*
	  • Bladder is spastic with flaccid external sphincter leading to urinary incontinence.
		• Results from lesions between pons and sacral spinal cord
		• Seen in SCI or multiple sclerosis involving the cervicothoracic spinal cord
			• Detrusor-sphincter dyssynergia
			• Can lead to high bladder pressures and kidney damage from urinary reflux
			• Sensory function impaired

Lower motor neuron bladder (flaccid, underactive, areflexic)	• Bladder acts as if all motor functions were paralyzed • Bladder fills without emptying	• Results from lower motor neuron injury caused by trauma involving S2-4 or below • Lesions of cauda equina, pelvic nerves	• If sensory function intact, patient feels bladder distention and hesitancy • No control of micturition, resulting in urinary retention, over distention of bladder, overflow incontinence, and UTI

breathing exercises to the patient who is not ventilator dependent. They should limit exposure to persons with fever, cold, and cough. Adhering to swallowing precautions (e.g., proper positioning of head and neck) and diet recommendations can prevent aspiration.

Neurogenic Bladder. Types of neurogenic bladder are described in Table 60.8. The type of bladder dysfunction determines management options. After the patient's overall condition is stable and assessment shows return of neurologic reflexes, urodynamic testing (see Table 44.11) and a urine culture may be done. Diagnostic and interprofessional care of neurogenic bladder is described in Table 60.9.

The patient with SCI and a neurogenic bladder needs a comprehensive program to manage bladder function. The goal is to improve quality of life and safety through preserving renal function, minimizing UTI and bladder stones, and developing a plan for urinary continence. Many factors are considered when selecting a bladder management strategy. These include patient preference, upper extremity function, and caregiver availability. For the selected strategy, teach the patient and caregiver successful self-management. Teach them about the various management techniques, how to obtain supplies, care of supplies and equipment, and when to seek health care.

Various drugs can be used to treat patients with a neurogenic bladder. Anticholinergic drugs (e.g., oxybutynin, tolterodine [Detrol]) may be used to suppress bladder contraction. α-Adrenergic blockers (e.g., terazosin, doxazosin [Cardura]) can relax the urethral sphincter. Antispasmodic drugs (e.g., baclofen) may decrease spasticity of pelvic floor muscles. *Botulinum toxin* is an effective alternative in patients with neurogenic detrusor overactivity who cannot tolerate or had an inadequate response to anticholinergic drugs.[22]

Numerous drainage methods are possible. These include bladder reflex retraining (if partial voiding control remains), indwelling catheter, CIC, and external catheter (condom catheter). Evaluate long-term use of an indwelling catheter because of the associated high incidence of CAUTI, fistula formation, and diverticula. However, this is the best option for some patients. Patients with indwelling catheters need to have adequate fluid intake (at least 3 to 4 L/day). Regularly check the patency of the indwelling catheter. Frequency of routine catheter changes

TABLE 60.9 Interprofessional Care

Neurogenic Bladder

Diagnostic Assessment
- History and physical examination, including neurologic and pelvic examinations
- Laboratory: Urinalysis, urine culture and sensitivity, blood urea nitrogen, serum creatinine, creatinine clearance
- Urodynamic testing (postvoid residual, cystometric testing, EMG, urethral pressure profile)

Management
- Patient teaching
- Voiding diary
- Bladder retraining: time voiding, manual expression, intermittent catheterization
- Fluid schedule: intake of 1800–2000 mL/day
- Indwelling urinary catheter

Drug Therapy
- Tricyclic antidepressants
- Anticholinergic drugs
- α-Adrenergic blockers
- Antispasmodics
- Botulinum toxin injection into bladder wall

Bladder and/or Urethral Surgical Therapy
- Bladder augmentation
- Sphincter resection or removal (*sphincterotomy*)
- Electrode placement for electrical stimulation
- Urinary diversion
- Urethral stents and balloon dilation
- Artificial urinary sphincter

ranges widely depending on the type of catheter used and agency policy.

CIC is recommended as the first-line option for bladder management (see Chapter 45). Nursing assessment is important in selecting the time interval between catheterizations. At first, catheterization is done every 4 hours. Measure bladder volume before catheterization using a bladder ultrasound machine. If less than 200 mL of urine is present, the time interval until

TABLE 60.10 Patient & Caregiver Teaching

Bowel Management After Spinal Cord Injury

For the patient with a spinal cord injury, include the following information about bowel management in the teaching plan for the patient and caregiver:

1. Optimal nutritional intake includes the following:
   - 3 well-balanced meals each day
   - 2 servings from the milk group
   - 2 or more servings from the meat group, including beef, pork, poultry, eggs, fish
   - 4 or more servings from the vegetable and fruit groups
   - 4 or more servings from the bread and cereal group
2. Fiber intake should be about 20–30 g/day. Increase the amount of fiber eaten gradually over 1–2 wk.
3. Consume at least 2–3 L of fluid per day unless contraindicated. Drink water or fruit juices (fluid softens hard stools). Limit caffeinated beverages, such as coffee, tea, and cola (caffeine stimulates fluid loss through urination).
4. Avoid foods that produce gas (e.g., beans) or upper GI upset (e.g., spicy foods).
5. *Timing:* Follow a regular schedule for bowel elimination. A good time is 30 min after the first meal of the day.
6. *Position:* If possible, an upright position with feet flat on the floor or on a step stool enhances bowel evacuation. Staying on the toilet, commode, or bedpan for longer than 20–30 min may cause skin breakdown. Based on stability, someone may need to stay with the patient.
7. *Activity:* Exercise is important for bowel function. In addition to improving muscle tone, it increases appetite and GI transit time. Exercise muscles, including stretching, ROM, position changing, and functional movement.
8. *Drug treatment:* Suppositories may be needed to stimulate a bowel movement. Manual stimulation of the rectum may be helpful in starting defecation. Use stool softeners as needed to regulate stool consistency. Use oral laxatives only if necessary.

catheterization may be extended. If more than 500 mL of urine is present, the time interval is shortened. CIC is usually done 4 to 6 times daily.

Suprapubic catheters are a safe option in select patients. Because of personal preference or the inability to catheterize due to neurologic dysfunction, 30% of patients with SCI use indwelling urethral or suprapubic catheters. The incidence of bacteriuria after catheter introduction is 5% to 10% per day.

Traditional bladder management options include *urinary diversion surgery* for the recurrent UTI patient with renal involvement or repeated stones. Surgical treatment of neurogenic bladder includes bladder neck revision (sphincterotomy), bladder augmentation (augmentation cystoplasty), perineal ureterostomy, cystotomy, vesicostomy, and anterior urethral transplantation. Placement of a sacral cord stimulator, penile prosthesis, or artificial sphincter is possible. Urinary diversion procedures are discussed in Chapter 45.

Neurogenic Bowel. Careful management of bowel evacuation is necessary in the patient with SCI because voluntary control may be lost. Usual measures for preventing constipation include high-fiber diet and adequate fluid intake (see Table 42.10). Patient and caregiver teaching is needed to promote successful independent bowel management. Guidelines related to bowel management are outlined in Table 60.10.

These measures may not be adequate to stimulate evacuation. Suppositories (e.g., bisacodyl [Dulcolax], glycerin) or small-volume enemas and digital stimulation (done 20 to 30 minutes

after suppository insertion) by the nurse or patient may be needed. In the patient with an upper motor neuron injury, digital stimulation can relax the external sphincter to promote defecation. A stool softener, such as docusate sodium (Colace), can help regulate stool consistency. Oral stimulant laxatives should be used only if absolutely necessary and not on a regular basis.

Valsalva maneuver and manual stimulation are useful in patients with lower motor neuron injuries. Because the Valsalva maneuver requires intact abdominal muscles, it is used in patients with injuries below T12. In general, a bowel movement every other day is considered adequate. However, consider preinjury patterns. Fecal incontinence can result from too much stool softener or a fecal impaction.

Timing of defecation is important. Planning bowel evacuation for 30 to 60 minutes after the first meal of the day may enhance success by taking advantage of the gastrocolic reflex induced by eating. This reflex may also be stimulated by drinking a warm beverage right after the meal. Discuss timing of the bowel program among the interprofessional team so there are no interruptions when the patient is doing therapy (e.g., swimming pool therapy).

Record all bowel movements, including amount, time, and consistency. Consider using the International Spinal Cord Injury Bowel Function Data Set. This is a 16-item, comprehensive, standardized format for assessing bowel function in the patient with SCI.[23]

Spasticity. Spasticity can be both beneficial and undesirable. It aids with mobility, especially for the patient with incomplete SCI. Spasticity improves circulation by promoting venous return, decreasing orthostatic hypotension and the risk for VTE. Unfortunately, the patient with marked spasticity and tone may have difficulty with positioning and mobility from spasms. Spasms can cause significant pain and make activities of daily living (ADLs) difficult for the patient.

The Ashworth and Modified Ashworth Scales are used to evaluate spasticity. Treatment includes ROM exercises to prevent muscle and joint tightness and reduce the risk for contracture. Antispasmodic drugs, such as baclofen or tizanidine, may be given. Botulinum toxin injection is useful for specific muscle involvement.

Skin Care. Prevention of PI is part of the lifelong treatment plan after SCI. Nurses in rehabilitation are responsible for teaching the patient and caregiver about daily skin care. PI may not be noticed until severe damage has occurred. Include information on the importance of adequate nutrition to skin condition. Anticipatory guidance about potential risks is essential. Patient and caregiver teaching related to skin care is outlined in Table 60.11.

Pain Management. The acute pain of the initial injury may persist during the first few weeks of rehabilitation. Chronic pain can result from overuse of muscles in the shoulders and arms for movement and repositioning. Pain often disrupts sleep. Assess, evaluate, and treat pain routinely. Use analgesics and interventions, such as massage and repositioning, to help the patient during therapy. Patients may benefit from referral to a pain management specialist.

Sexuality. Sexuality is an important issue regardless of the patient's age or sex. Open discussion with the patient about sexual rehabilitation is essential. A nurse or other rehabilitation professional trained in sexual counseling should provide support for the patient and the partner. Alternative methods of obtaining sexual satisfaction, such as oral-genital sex, may be

TABLE 60.11 Patient & Caregiver Teaching

Skin Care After Spinal Cord Injury

To prevent skin breakdown in a patient with spinal cord injury, include the following instructions when teaching the patient and caregiver:

Change Position Frequently
- If in a wheelchair, lift self and shift weight every 15–30 min.
- If in bed, change position with a regular turning schedule (at least every 2 hr) that includes sides, back, and abdomen.
- Use pressure-reducing mattresses and wheelchair cushions (not egg-crate).
- Use pillows to protect bony prominences when in bed.

Monitor Skin Condition
- Inspect skin often for areas of redness, swelling, and breakdown.
- If a wound develops, follow standard wound care procedures.

Protect Skin
- Do not sit too close to fires, space heaters, or other sources of heat.
- Use sunscreen liberally when outdoors.
- Keep fingernails trimmed to avoid scratches and abrasions.
- Do not wear clothes that are too tight or too loose.
- Dress warmly in cold weather to prevent frostbite.
- Do not put hot foot in your lap without protection.

suggested. Explicit films may help, such as a film showing sexual activities of a patient with paraplegia and a nondisabled partner. Use graphics cautiously because they may focus too much on the mechanics of sex rather than on the relationship.

Knowledge of the level and completeness of injury is needed to understand the male patient's potential for orgasm, erection, and fertility, and the patient's capacity for sexual satisfaction. Men normally have 2 types of erections: psychogenic and reflex. The process of *psychogenic erection* begins in the brain with sexual thoughts. Signals from the brain are sent through the nerves of the spinal cord to the T10-L2 levels. The signals are then relayed to the penis and trigger an erection. Men with low-level incomplete injuries are more likely to have psychogenic erection than men with higher level incomplete injuries. Men with complete injuries are less likely to have psychogenic erection.[24]

A *reflex erection* occurs with direct physical contact to the penis or other erotic areas. This short lived, uncontrolled, erection is involuntary and does not require sexually stimulating thoughts. Most men with SCI can have a reflex erection with physical stimulation if the S2-S4 nerve pathways are not damaged.

Treatment for erectile dysfunction includes drugs, vacuum devices, and surgical procedures. Phosphodiesterase inhibitors (e.g., sildenafil [Viagra]) have become the first-line treatment in men with SCI between T6 and L5. Sexual stimulation is needed to get an erection after taking the medication. Penile injection of vasoactive substances (papaverine, alprostadil, or a combination) is another medical treatment. Risks include scarring, bruising, and infection. Use may lead to priapism. Vacuum suction devices use negative pressure to encourage blood flow into the penis. Erection is maintained by a constriction band placed at the base of the penis. The main surgical option is implantation of a penile prosthesis.[24] (Erectile dysfunction is discussed in Chapter 54.)

SCI affects male fertility, causing poor sperm motility and ejaculatory dysfunction. Recent advances in methods of sperm retrieval include penile vibratory stimulation and rectal probe electroejaculation. Surgical removal of sperm is a last resort for sperm retrieval. Once retrieved, sperm can be directly injected into an egg via intracytoplasmic sperm injection (ICSI). These techniques have changed the prognosis for men with SCI to father children from unlikely to a reasonable chance of successful outcomes.[24]

The effect of SCI on female sexual response is less clear. A woman of childbearing age with SCI usually stays fertile. The injury does not affect the ability to become pregnant or deliver normally through the birth canal. Menses may cease for as long as 6 months after injury. If sexual activity is resumed, protection against unplanned pregnancy is needed. Pregnancy is associated with increased risk for diabetes and UTI and higher rates of AD, PI, increased spasticity, and catheter-related issues. Labor and delivery have high rates of complications.[25]

Care should be taken not to dislodge an indwelling catheter during sexual activity. A patient with an external catheter should refrain from fluids and remove the catheter before sexual activity. Teach patients about the risk for AD. The bowel program should include evacuation the morning of sexual activity. Encourage the patient to tell the partner that incontinence is always possible. The woman may need a water-soluble lubricant to supplement decreased vaginal secretions and ease vaginal penetration. Women with some residual pelvic innervation can achieve normal orgasm. Use of the Eros device may help with orgasmic dysfunction.[25]

Grief and Depression. Depression after SCI is common and disabling. Patients with SCI may feel an overwhelming sense of loss. They may temporarily lose control over everyday activities as they depend on others for ADLs and for life-sustaining measures. Patients may feel they are useless and burdens to their families. At a life stage when independence is of great importance, they may be totally dependent on others.

Working through grief is a hard, lifelong process for which the patient needs support and encouragement. Table 60.12 outlines the grief response to SCI and appropriate nursing interventions. Your role in grief work is to support the patient and family and to allow mourning as part of the rehabilitation process. Maintaining hope is important during the grieving process and should not be interpreted as denial. With recent advances in rehabilitation, the patient is often independent physically and discharged from the rehabilitation center before completing the grief process.

The goal of recovery is related more to adjustment than to acceptance. *Adjustment* implies the ability to go on with living with certain limitations. Problem-based strategies are effective in supporting positive adjustment. When the patient accepts the current new normal, levels of coping and adjustment are improved. Nonacceptance is more predictive of psychologic distress, disengagement, denial, fantasy, and dependence on drugs and alcohol.

When the patient is depressed, be patient. Sympathy is not helpful. Treat the patient as an adult and encourage participation in care planning.[26] A primary nurse relationship is helpful. To adjust, the patient needs continual support throughout the rehabilitation process in the form of acceptance, affection, and caring. Be attentive when the patient needs to talk and sensitive to needs at various stages of the grief process.

Although depression during the grief process usually lasts days to weeks, some patients become clinically depressed and need treatment for depression. Evaluation by a psychiatric nurse or psychiatrist is recommended. Treatment may include drugs and therapy. Treatment is maximized when the patient's personal preferences are identified, and care is tailored to patient needs.

ETHICAL/LEGAL DILEMMAS
Right to Refuse Treatment

Situation
R.D., a 25-yr-old man, had a SCI to C7-8 after a motorcycle accident. He was diagnosed with anterior cord syndrome and has motor paralysis, which may prevent him from riding motorcycles again. He has become extremely depressed and no longer wishes to live. Because of his emotional state, R.D. is now refusing to eat. Can he be forced to receive EN?

Ethical/Legal Points for Consideration
- Withholding treatment in a newly injured but otherwise healthy young adult may present an ethical dilemma for some nurses. They may consider it assisted suicide and believe that it violates the ethical principles of beneficence and nonmaleficence.
- A competent adult has the right to consent to or refuse medical treatment under the right to privacy, the Fourteenth Amendment of the Constitution, and case law.*
- Case law has supported the concept that forced treatment is battery (unlawful use of force on somebody). A mentally competent, physically incapacitated adult can refuse EN. The health agency must follow the patient's wishes.†
- To be competent to take part in informed consent or refusal, an adult must be able to understand the information provided about the procedure or treatment, consider choices among available alternatives, and make a choice based on his values and preferences. Depression may not be a factor in determining competency to make informed treatment choices.
- If, after adequate evaluation and treatment for pain, depression, or other medical conditions, the patient persists in his refusal, his wishes must be respected.
- Refusal to eat or drink has never been upheld as illegal, and the alternative—forced eating and drinking—is clearly a violation of patient rights and the criminal act of battery.

Discussion Questions
1. What are your feelings about requests to withhold treatment in a young person with a newly acquired disability?
2. What resources are available to help R.D., his family, and nursing staff deal with this emotionally charged and ethically complex situation?

*Cruzan v. Director, Missouri Department of Health, 497 U.S. 261, 1990. Retrieved from www.supreme.justia.com/cases/federal/us/497/261.
†Bouvia v. Superior Court, 1986. Retrieved from http://law.justia.com/cases/california/calapp3d/179/1127.html.

TABLE 60.12 Grief Response in Spinal Cord Injury

Patient Behavior	Nursing Intervention
Shock and Denial Struggle for survival, complete dependence, excessive sleep, withdrawal, fantasies, unrealistic expectations	• Provide honest information. • Use simple diagrams to explain injury. • Encourage patient to begin road to recovery. • Establish agreement to use and improve all current abilities while not denying the possibility of future improvement.
Anger Refusal to discuss paralysis, ↓ self-esteem, manipulation, hostile and abusive language	• Coordinate care with patient and encourage self-care. • Support family members. • Use humor appropriately. • Allow patient outbursts of emotions. • Do not allow fixation on injury.
Depression Sadness, pessimism, anorexia, nightmares, insomnia, agitation, "blues," suicidal preoccupation, refusal to take part in any self-care activities	• Encourage family involvement and use of community resources. • Plan graded steps in rehabilitation to give success with minimal opportunity for frustration. • Give cheerful and willing assistance with ADLs. • Avoid sympathy. • Use firm kindness.
Adjustment and Acceptance Planning for future, actively taking part in therapy, finding personal meaning in experience and continuation of growth, returning to premorbid personality	• Remember patients have unique personalities. • Balance support systems to encourage independence. • Set goals with patient input. • Emphasize potential.

Caregivers need counseling to avoid promoting dependency in the patient through guilt or misplaced sympathy. They have intense grieving. A support group of family members and friends of patients with SCI can help them increase their participation and knowledge of the grieving process, physical problems, rehabilitation plan, and meaning of the disability.

◆ Evaluation
Expected outcomes are that the patient with SCI will
- Maintain adequate ventilation and have no signs of respiratory distress
- Maintain adequate circulation and BP
- Maintain intact skin over bony prominences
- Maintain adequate nutrition
- Establish a bowel management program based on neurologic function and personal preference
- Establish a bladder management program based on neurologic function, caregiver status, and lifestyle choices
- Have no episodes of AD

Gerontologic Considerations: Spinal Cord Injury
Because of increased work and recreational activities among older adults, more of them have SCI (Fig. 60.11). Falls are the leading cause of SCI for people age 65 and older. Older adults with traumatic injuries have more complications than younger patients, are hospitalized longer, and have higher mortality rates.

Chronic illnesses associated with aging can have a serious impact on older adults living with SCI. As patients with SCI age, both individual aging changes and length of time since injury can affect functional ability. For example, bowel and bladder dysfunction can increase with the duration and severity of SCI.

Health promotion and screening are important for the older patient with SCI. Daily skin inspections and UTI prevention measures are critical. Regular breast examinations for women and prostate cancer screening for men are recommended. Heart disease is the most common cause of morbidity and mortality among older adults with SCI. The lack of sensation, including chest pain, in persons with high-level injuries may mask acute myocardial ischemia. Altered autonomic nervous system function and decreases in physical activity can place patients at risk for heart problems, including hypertension.

Rehabilitation for the older adult with SCI may take longer because of preexisting conditions and poorer health status at the time of initial injury. An interprofessional approach to rehabilitation is essential in preventing secondary complications.

FIG. 60.11 An increasing number of older adults are living with a chronic spinal cord injury. (© WavebreakmediaLtd/WavebreakMedia/Thinkstock.)

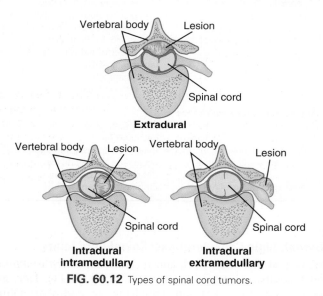

FIG. 60.12 Types of spinal cord tumors.

SPINAL CORD TUMORS

Spinal cord tumors can have a devastating impact due to spinal compression and neurologic dysfunction. Tumors are classified as *primary* (arising from some part of spinal cord, dura, nerves, or vessels) or *secondary* (from primary growths in other places in the body that have metastasized to the spinal cord).

Etiology and Pathophysiology

Spinal cord tumors are either *extradural* (outside the dura), *intradural-extramedullary* (between the spinal cord and dura), and *intramedullary* (within the substance of spinal cord itself) (Fig. 60.12 and Table 60.13).

Extradural tumors include metastatic cancer and benign schwannomas. Many patients with cancer will have metastasis to the spine. Metastatic lesions can invade intradurally and compress the spinal cord. Tumors that often metastasize to the spinal epidural space are those that spread to bone, such as prostate, breast, lung, and kidney cancer. Intradural-extramedullary lesions include meningiomas that develop in the arachnoid membrane, schwannomas and neurofibromas that extend from the nerve root, and ependymomas found at the end of the spinal cord. Intramedullary tumors arise from glial or ependymal cells found throughout the entire spinal cord. The most common lesions are astrocytes and ependymomas.[27]

Many spinal cord tumors are slow growing. Their symptoms are due to the mechanical effects of slow compression and irritation of nerve roots, displacement of the spinal cord, or gradual obstruction of the blood supply. The slowness of growth does not cause secondary injury as in traumatic SCI. Thus complete functional restoration may be possible when the tumor is removed.

Clinical Manifestations

Both sensory and motor problems may result, with the location and extent of the tumor determining the severity and extent of the problem. The most common early symptom of a spinal cord tumor is back pain or pain radiating along the compressed nerve route.[28] Location of the pain depends on the level of compression. Pain may worsen with activity, coughing, straining, and/or lying down. There may be slowly increasing clumsiness, weakness, and spasticity. Paralysis can develop. Sensory disruption occurs as coldness, numbness, and tingling

TABLE 60.13 **Classification of Spinal Cord Tumors**			
Type	**Incidence**	**Treatment**	**Prognosis**
Extradural Outside spinal cord in extradural space	Metastatic lesions and benign schwannomas	Relief of cord pressure by surgical laminectomy, radiation, chemotherapy, or combination approach	*Benign:* Excellent with resection *Metastatic:* Poor, treatment usually palliative
Intradural Extramedullary Within dura mater but outside spinal cord	Mostly benign. Meningiomas, neurofibromas, schwannomas	Complete surgical removal of tumor (if possible) Partial removal followed by radiation	Usually very good if no damage to cord from compression
Intramedullary Within spinal cord	Mostly benign. Astrocytomas, ependymomas	Complete surgical removal of tumor (if possible) Partial removal followed by radiation	Usually very good if no damage to cord from compression Complete surgical resection of astrocytomas difficult

in 1 or more extremities. Neurogenic bowel and bladder are marked by incontinence, constipation, and urgency with difficulty in starting the flow, progressing to retention with overflow incontinence.

❖ Interprofessional and Nursing Care

Extradural tumors can be seen on routine spinal x-rays. Intradural extramedullary and intramedullary tumors require MRI, CT scan, or CT myelogram for detection. CSF analysis may reveal tumor cells. Patients with tumors suspicious for metastatic disease need an oncology referral and further diagnostic testing to identify the primary cancer.[27]

Spinal cord compression is an emergency. Relief of ischemia related to the compression is the goal of therapy. Corticosteroids (e.g., dexamethasone) are generally given immediately to relieve tumor-related edema.[29]

Indications for surgery depend on the type of tumor and neurologic deficit. Emergency surgery may be needed to decompress the spinal cord, obtain tissue for biopsy, and help to determine appropriate treatment.[27] Primary spinal tumors may be removed with the goal of cure. In patients with metastatic tumors, treatment is mainly palliative. The goal is to restore or preserve neurologic function, stabilize the spine, and alleviate pain. Radiation and/or chemotherapy may be used to treat the tumor.

Relieving pain and maximizing neurologic function are the ultimate goals of treatment. Assess the patient's neurologic status before and after treatment. Giving analgesia as needed is an important nursing responsibility. Depending on the amount of neurologic dysfunction, care of the patient may be similar to that of a patient recovering from SCI.

CRANIAL NERVE DISORDERS

Cranial nerve disorders are often classified as peripheral neuropathies. The 12 pairs of cranial nerves are considered the peripheral nerves of the brain. The disorders usually involve the motor and/or sensory branches of a single nerve (*mononeuropathies*). Causes of cranial nerve problems include tumors, trauma, infection, inflammatory processes, and idiopathic (unknown) causes. The 2 cranial nerve disorders discussed here are trigeminal neuralgia and Bell's palsy.

TRIGEMINAL NEURALGIA

Trigeminal neuralgia (TN) (*tic douloureux*) is characterized by sudden, usually unilateral, severe, brief, stabbing, recurrent episodes of pain in the distribution of the trigeminal nerve. It occurs in about 12 per 100,000 Americans each year. TN affects more women than men. It occurs most often in people over age 50.

We classify TN as *classic* (TN 1) or *atypical* (TN 2). Patients may have both types. The pain intensity and lifestyle disruption that accompany TN can cause marked physical and psychologic dysfunction.

Etiology and Pathophysiology

The trigeminal nerve, the fifth cranial nerve (CN V), has both motor and sensory branches. TN most often affects the sensory (afferent) branches of the second and third division (maxillary and mandibular branches) of CN V (Fig. 60.13).

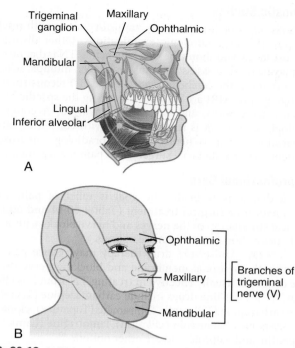

FIG. 60.13 A, Trigeminal (fifth cranial) nerve and its 3 main divisions: ophthalmic, maxillary, and mandibular nerves. B, Cutaneous innervation of the head. (Modified from Patton KT, Thibodeau GA: *Anatomy and physiology*, ed 8, St Louis, 2013, Mosby.)

Most cases result from vascular compression of the trigeminal nerve root by an abnormal loop of the superior cerebellar artery. This artery compresses the nerve as it exits the brainstem. Constant compression appears to lead to chronic injury, causing flattening and atrophy of the nerve and damage to the myelin sheath.[30] In some cases, TN may be related to underlying pathology, such as multiple sclerosis, shingles, or masses in the cerebellum or brainstem.

Clinical Manifestations

The first episode of TN is sudden with a memorable onset. In TN 1, the patient has an abrupt onset of waves of excruciating pain. It is described as a burning, knifelike, or lightning-like shock in the lips, upper or lower gums, cheek, forehead, or side of the nose.[31] Facial twitching, grimacing, and frequent blinking and tearing of the eye can occur during the acute attack (giving rise to the term *tic douloureux*). Some patients may have facial sensory loss. Attacks are usually brief, lasting only seconds to 2 or 3 minutes. Frequency ranges from 1 to over 50 times a day.[31]

Pain episodes are usually started by a triggering mechanism of light touch at a specific point (*trigger zone*) along the distribution of the nerve branches. Precipitating stimuli include chewing, brushing the teeth, feeling a hot or cold blast of air on the face, washing the face, yawning, or even talking. As a result, the patient may eat improperly, neglect hygienic practices, wear a cloth over the face, and withdraw from interaction with others. The patient may sleep excessively as a means of coping with pain.

TN 2 manifests as constant aching, burning, crushing, or stabbing pain. The pain has a lower intensity and does not subside completely.[32] The distinct attacks associated with TN 1 do not occur in TN 2.

Diagnostic Studies

Diagnosis is based almost entirely on history, along with results from physical and neurologic examinations. Other disorders that cause facial pain should be ruled out before TN is diagnosed. MRI may be used to assess for sinusitis, cancer, multiple sclerosis, or masses in the cerebellopontine angle. 3D reconstruction and angiography MRI are helpful with seeing the specific brain anatomy, nerve roots, and vasculature involved. A complete neurologic assessment is required along with consulting other subspecialties, such as neurology, neuroradiology, neurosurgery, dentistry, maxillofacial surgery, and pain management.

Interprofessional Care

Once a diagnosis is made, the goal is relief of pain with either medical or surgical treatment (Tables 60.14 and 60.15). Electrical stimulation of the nerves and nerve blocks with local anesthetics or botulinum toxin are options.

Drug Therapy. Antiseizure drug therapy may reduce pain by stabilizing the neuronal membrane and blocking nerve firing. These drugs are usually effective in treating TN 1 but less effective in TN 2. First-line drugs include carbamazepine (Tegretol) and oxcarbazepine (Trileptal). Topiramate (Topamax), clonazepam (Klonopin), phenytoin (Dilantin), lamotrigine (Lamictal), gabapentin, and valproic acid are other options.[30]

Tricyclic antidepressants, such as amitriptyline or nortriptyline, can help treat the constant burning or aching pain. Analgesics or opioids are usually not effective in controlling pain in TN 1 but may help with pain in TN 2.[30]

Surgical Therapy. If a conservative approach is ineffective or the patient is unable to tolerate adverse effects of medications, surgical therapy is available (Table 60.15). In percutaneous procedures, affected nerve fibers are damaged to eliminate pain. Although most patients are pain-free after any of the procedures, pain relief lasts longest with microvascular decompression. About half of treated patients develop recurrent pain within 12 to 15 years.[30]

◆ NURSING MANAGEMENT: TRIGEMINAL NEURALGIA

Patients usually receive outpatient treatment. Assess the attacks in detail, including triggering factors, characteristics, frequency, and pain management techniques. This information helps you to plan patient care. Evaluate the degree of pain and its effects on the patient's lifestyle, drug use, emotional state, and suicidal tendencies. Note behavior (including withdrawal).

Monitor the patient's response to drug therapy and note any side effects. Discuss complementary pain management measures, such as acupuncture, biofeedback, and yoga. Environmental assessment is essential during an acute period to decrease triggering stimuli. The room should be kept at an even, moderate temperature and free of drafts. The patient may prefer to complete all self-care activities, fearing someone else will inadvertently cause injury.

Assess the patient's nutritional status and hygiene (especially oral). Teach the patient about the importance of nutrition, hygiene, and oral care. Convey understanding if oral neglect is apparent. A small, soft-bristled toothbrush or a warm mouthwash helps promote oral care. Hygiene activities are best done when analgesia is at its peak.

TABLE 60.14 Interprofessional Care
Trigeminal Neuralgia

Diagnostic Assessment
- History and physical examination (including neurologic examination)
- MRI

Management
- Drug therapy
  - Antiseizure drugs (e.g., carbamazepine, oxcarbazepine [Trileptal], gabapentin [Neurontin])
  - Tricyclic antidepressants (e.g., amitriptyline)
- Local nerve block
- Surgical therapy (Table 60.15)

TABLE 60.15 Surgical Therapy for Trigeminal Neuralgia

Procedure	Description
Percutaneous Procedures	
Balloon compression	• Cannula is inserted through cheek and guided to a natural opening in the base of skull. • Soft catheter with a balloon tip is threaded through cannula. • Balloon is inflated and mechanical compression damages trigeminal nerve.
Glycerol rhizotomy (injection into 1 or more branches of trigeminal nerve) (Fig. 60.14)	• Thin needle inserted through puncture in cheek and guided through natural opening in base of skull. • Glycerol is injected into trigeminal ganglion. • Procedure can be repeated multiple times.
Radiofrequency thermal lesioning	• Needle is passed through cheek thorough a natural opening in base of skull. • Patient is awakened, then a small electric current is passed through the needle, causing tingling. • When the needle is positioned so the tingling occurs in the same area of pain, patient is sedated again, then radiofrequency current is used to destroy part of the nerve. • Can result in facial numbness (although some degree of sensation may be retained), corneal anesthesia, and trigeminal motor weakness
Surgical Procedures	
Microvascular decompression, with or without neurectomy	• Small craniotomy done behind the ear (suboccipital craniotomy). • Blood vessels that appear to be compressing the nerve at the root entry zone where it exits the pons are then displaced and repositioned. • If there is no compression, cutting of the nerve (neurectomy) may be done.
Stereotactic radiosurgery (gamma knife, cyber knife)	• Uses stereotactic localization to focus high doses of radiation to area where trigeminal nerve exits the brainstem. • Radiation causes slow formation of a lesion on nerve and disrupts transmission of pain signals to brain. • Pain relief from this procedure may take several months. (Radiosurgery is discussed in Chapter 56.)

Encourage food that is high in protein and calories and easy to chew. Food should be served lukewarm and offered frequently. If oral intake is sharply reduced and the patient's nutritional status is compromised, an NG tube can be inserted on the unaffected side for EN.

Appropriate teaching related to surgical procedures depends on the type of procedure planned (e.g., percutaneous). The patient needs to know they will be awake during local procedures in order to cooperate when corneal and ciliary reflexes and facial sensations are checked. After the procedure, compare the patient's pain with the preoperative intensity. Evaluate the corneal reflex, extraocular muscles, hearing, sensation, and facial nerve function often (see Chapter 55). If the corneal reflex is impaired, take special care to protect the eyes. This includes using artificial tears or eye shields.

After a percutaneous radiofrequency procedure, apply an ice pack to the jaw on the operative side for 3 to 5 hours. To avoid injuring the mouth, the patient should not chew on the operative side until sensation has returned. If intracranial surgery was done, general postoperative nursing care after a craniotomy is appropriate. (Nursing care related to craniotomy is discussed in Chapter 56.)

Plan for regular follow-up care. Teach the patient about any medications. Although pain may be relieved, encourage the patient to keep environmental stimuli to a moderate level and to use stress management techniques. Long-term management after surgical intervention depends on residual effects of the procedure. If anesthesia is present or the corneal reflex is altered, teach the patient to (1) chew on the unaffected side; (2) avoid hot foods or beverages, which can burn the mucous membranes; (3) check the oral cavity after meals to remove food particles; (4) practice meticulous oral hygiene and continue with semiannual dental visits; (5) protect the face against extremes of temperature; (6) use an electric razor; (7) wear a protective eye shield and avoid rubbing eyes; and (8) examine eye regularly for symptoms of infection or irritation.

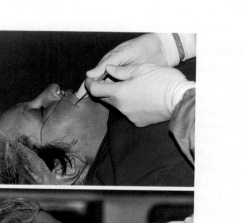

FIG. 60.14 Glycerol rhizotomy for the treatment of trigeminal neuralgia. **A,** Patient with trigeminal neuralgia having needle placed. **B,** HCP injecting glycerol. (Courtesy Joe Rothrock, Media, PA.)

BELL'S PALSY

Bell's palsy is an acute, usually temporary, facial paresis (or palsy) resulting from damage or trauma of the facial nerve (CN VII). It usually affects only 1 side of the face, but both sides can be affected.

Bell's palsy is the most common facial nerve disorder.[33] Each year about 40,000 Americans are diagnosed with Bell's palsy. It occurs equally between men and women and can affect any age-group. The peak incidence is between ages 15 and 60 years. There is a high incidence during pregnancy and in persons with upper respiratory tract conditions (e.g., flu, colds), obesity, diabetes, and hypertension.[33]

Etiology and Pathophysiology

We do not know the exact cause. Several theories exist. Some think it is a reactivation of herpes simplex virus isoform (HSV-1) and/or herpes zoster virus (HZV). The viral infection causes inflammation, leading to nerve compression and the subsequent clinical features (Fig. 60.15). Another cause may be acute demyelination similar to what happens in Guillain-Barré syndrome.

The prognosis for persons with Bell's palsy is generally very good. The extent of nerve damage determines the extent of recovery. Most begin to get better within 2 weeks after the onset and recover some or all facial function within 6 months. In some cases, there may be residual effects, including facial asymmetry or abnormal facial movements.

Clinical Manifestations

CN VII is a mixed cranial nerve with motor, sensory, and autonomic function, which accounts for the manifestations. The key feature of Bell's palsy is the acute onset of unilateral lower motor facial weakness. 50% to 60% have pain around and behind the ear and neck. Other manifestations include drooping of the eyelid and corner of the mouth, drooling, facial twitching, dryness of the eye or mouth, facial numbness, altered taste, hearing loss, and excessive tearing in 1 eye.[33] Most often these symptoms begin suddenly and reach their peak within 48 to 72 hours.

Quality of life is often decreased due to problems with eating, swallowing, speech, and taste. Patients may have psychologic withdrawal because of changes in appearance, malnutrition, dehydration, mucous membrane trauma, corneal abrasions, muscle stretching, and facial spasms and contractures.

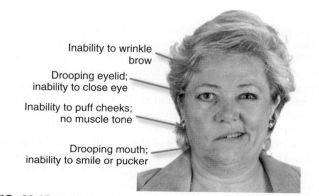

Inability to wrinkle brow

Drooping eyelid; inability to close eye

Inability to puff cheeks; no muscle tone

Drooping mouth; inability to smile or pucker

FIG. 60.15 Facial characteristics of a person with Bell's palsy. (© Jo Ann Snover/123RF Stock Photo/123rf.com.)

Diagnostic Studies

Bell's palsy is a clinical diagnosis. No definitive diagnostic test exists. The diagnosis and prognosis are indicated by clinical examination and observing the typical pattern of onset. Current guidelines do not support routine laboratory, imaging, or neurophysiologic testing at first presentation of Bell's palsy. If indicated, MRI and CT can eliminate other causes for facial paralysis. Blood tests can diagnose infections or other diseases. Electromyography (EMG) can confirm the presence of nerve damage. Patients should be referred to a neurologist or otolaryngologist as soon as possible to exclude other neurologic conditions.

Interprofessional Care

The patient with Bell's palsy is treated as an outpatient. Care focuses on relieving symptoms, preventing complications, and protecting the eye on the affected side.

Treatment is often started to try to improve the chance of a complete recovery. Oral corticosteroid therapy to reduce inflammation and swelling should be started within 72 hours of onset.[34] Some patients should receive an antiviral agent, such as acyclovir (Zovirax), in addition to the steroid therapy. Surgical decompression of the facial nerve is controversial but is considered in refractory cases.

❖ NURSING MANAGEMENT: BELL'S PALSY

Mild analgesics can relieve pain. Moist heat can reduce discomfort and aid circulation. Electrical stimulation of the nerve, facial massage, and physical therapy help maintain muscle tone and ease pain. A facial sling may be helpful to support affected muscles, improve lip alignment, and facilitate eating. The facial sling is usually made and fitted by a physical or occupational therapist. When function begins to return, active facial muscle exercises are done several times a day. Tell the patient to protect the face from cold and drafts because trigeminal *hyperesthesia* (extreme sensitivity to pain or touch) may occur.

? CHECK YOUR PRACTICE

You are working in the outpatient neurology clinic. Your patient is a 68-yr-old woman with Bell's palsy. Her main problem today is dry eyes. When you are doing an assessment, she tells you, "I hate the way I look. I cannot go anywhere, and I am afraid to leave the house. I am ugly and scary looking."

- How can you help her cope with her disorder?
- What can you suggest to increase moisture in the affected eye?

Eye protection is important. The patient may wear dark glasses for protective and cosmetic reasons. Artificial tears (methylcellulose) should be instilled often during the day to prevent drying of the cornea. Ointment and an impermeable eye shield can be used at night to retain moisture. In some patients, taping the lids closed at night may be needed. Teach the patient to report ocular pain, drainage, or discharge.

Maintaining good nutrition is important. Teach the patient to chew on the unaffected side of the mouth to avoid trapping food and to enjoy the taste of food. Thorough oral hygiene must be done after each meal to prevent parotitis, caries, and periodontal disease from accumulated residual food.

The change in physical appearance from Bell's palsy can be devastating. Reassure the patient that a stroke did not occur and that chances for a full recovery are good. Enlisting support from family and friends is important. Tell the patient most people recover within 3 to 6 months after onset of symptoms.

▮ POLYNEUROPATHIES

GUILLAIN-BARRÉ SYNDROME

Guillain-Barré syndrome (GBS) is an autoimmune process that occurs a few days or weeks after a viral or bacterial infection. GBS is rare, affecting about 1 person in every 100,000.[35] It can occur at any age, but those over age 50 are at greatest risk.[36] The most common type of GBS is acute inflammatory demyelinating polyneuropathy (AIDP). Other types include acute motor axonal neuropathy (AMAN) and acute motor sensory axonal neuropathy (AMSAN). AMAN is more common in children.

Etiology and Pathophysiology

The cause of GBS is unknown. Both cellular and humoral immune responses likely play a role in AIDP. Humoral responses appear to cause AMAN.[36] Following an infection, immune responses cause injury to either the myelin sheath (AIDP) or the nerve axon itself (AMAN). There is edema and inflammation of affected nerves. The result is segmental loss of the myelin sheath with exposed nerve membranes in nerve terminals and the nodes of Ranvier. Transmission of nerve impulses is stopped or slowed. This leads to flaccid paralysis with muscle denervation and atrophy. In the recovery phase, remyelination occurs slowly. Neurologic function returns in a proximal-to-distal pattern.

Most cases of GBS follow a viral or bacterial infection of the GI or upper respiratory tract. Cytomegalovirus is the most common viral cause. *Campylobacter jejuni* gastroenteritis is the most common bacterial cause, especially for AMAN. Other related infections include Epstein-Barr virus, *Mycoplasma pneumoniae*, *Haemophilus influenza*, hepatitis (A, B, E), and Zika virus.[35] Surgery and trauma may trigger GBS.

Clinical Manifestations and Complications

The main features of GBS include acute, ascending, rapidly progressive, symmetric weakness of the limbs. The first symptoms are weakness, *paresthesia* (numbness and tingling), and *hypotonia* (reduced muscle tone) of the limbs. Reflexes in the affected limbs are weak or absent. Maximal weakness is reached in 4 weeks.

Autonomic nervous system dysfunction occurs with AIDP and AMSAN, causing orthostatic hypotension, hypertension, and abnormal vagal responses (bradycardia, heart block, asystole). Other autonomic dysfunction effects include bowel and bladder dysfunction, facial flushing, and diaphoresis. Cranial nerve involvement manifests as facial weakness and paresthesia, extraocular eye movement problems, and dysphagia.

Pain is common. It can include paresthesia, muscular aches and cramps, and hyperesthesia. It is often worse at night. Pain may contribute to decreased appetite and interfere with sleep.

The most serious complication of GBS is respiratory failure. It occurs if the paralysis progresses to nerves that innervate the thoracic area. Frequently assess the respiratory system by checking respiratory rate and depth to determine the need for immediate intervention, including intubation and mechanical ventilation. Respiratory infection or UTI may occur. Immobility from paralysis can cause paralytic ileus, muscle atrophy, VTE, PIs, orthostatic hypotension, and nutritional deficiencies.[37]

Diagnostic Studies

Diagnosis is based mainly on the patient's history and clinical signs. Clinical features required for diagnosis include progressive weakness of more than 1 limb and decreased or absent reflexes. Electrolyte levels, liver function tests, creatinine phosphokinase, and erythrocyte sedimentation rates are evaluated. Cerebrospinal fluid (CSF) analysis helps exclude other causes. In GBS the CSF has more protein than normal.[37] Results of EMG and nerve conduction studies (NCS) are used after 2 weeks to confirm the diagnosis. NCS allow the HCP to diagnose the subtype. NCS in AIDP show demyelination. This information helps with prognosis, as patients with demyelination often need mechanical ventilation and have a poorer outcome.[38]

❖ Interprofessional and Nursing Care

The management of GBS is supportive. Ventilatory support is critical during the acute phase. Patients may be in ICU for hemodynamic monitoring. Immunomodulating treatments, such as plasma exchange (PE) *(plasmapheresis)* or high-dose IV immunoglobulin (IVIG), are most effective if used within the first 2 weeks of symptom onset. They are equally effective. PE removes antibodies and other immune factors. It is used 5 times either daily or every other day in the first 2 weeks. (PE is discussed in Chapter 13.) IVIG interferes with antigen presentation. It is given over 5 days. It is readily available and is the preferred treatment in many centers.[39] After 4 weeks past disease onset, PE and IVIG therapies have little value. Corticosteroids have little effect on the prognosis or duration of the disease.

Assessment is the most important aspect of nursing care during the acute phase. During the neurologic assessment, evaluate motor and sensory function. Report changes in motor function (e.g., ascending paralysis), reflexes, cranial nerve function (gag, cornea, swallow), and level of consciousness.

Carefully assess respiratory and cardiac function. Monitor ABGs and vital capacity. Closely monitor BP and cardiac rate and rhythm during the acute phase because dysrhythmias, orthostatic hypotension, and increased or decreased BP and heart rate may occur. Vasopressor agents and volume expanders may be needed to treat the low BP. If fever develops, obtain sputum and blood cultures to identify the pathogen. Appropriate antibiotic therapy is then started.

Nutritional needs must be met despite possible problems associated with delayed gastric emptying, paralytic ileus, and potential for aspiration if the gag reflex is lost. In addition to testing for the gag reflex, note drooling and other problems with secretions that may indicate an inadequate gag reflex. EN or PN may be used to ensure adequate caloric intake.

Throughout the course of the illness, provide support and encouragement to the patient and caregivers. Early referrals should be made for physical, occupational, and speech therapy. Counseling may help the patient adjust to the sudden disabling syndrome and dependence on others.

Most patients with GBS will start to recover spontaneously at about 28 days. 80% of patients walk independently at 6 months with 60% making a full recovery in 1 year. GBS patients who have a GI infection, are older in age, have a rapid clinical onset, have a hospital length of stay longer than 11 days, have poor upper extremity motor strength, or need mechanical ventilation have a poorer prognosis.[39]

CHRONIC INFLAMMATORY DEMYELINATING POLYNEUROPATHY

Chronic inflammatory demyelinating polyneuropathy (CIDP) is a motor and sensory neuropathy. CIDP is a rare autoimmune disorder, affecting 1 to 2 persons per 100,000.[40] CIDP is more common in those in their 50s and 60s and in men more than women.[41]

Like GBS, there are different types of CIDP. CIDP differs from GBS in that symptoms gradually occur over 8 weeks and there is not an acute onset. CIDP is not self-limiting (with an end to the acute phase). Early recognition and treatment can help the patient avoid significant disability.

Etiology and Pathophysiology

We do not know the exact cause of CIDP. There is evidence to support the theory that like GBS, it has an autoimmune basis.[40] CIDP seems to be associated with infection, HIV, hepatitis C, Sjögren's syndrome, inflammatory bowel disease, melanoma, lymphoma, and diabetes.

Clinical Manifestations and Diagnostic Studies

It is important to recognize the differences between CIPD and GBS to prevent incorrect or delayed treatment. The classic presentation of patients with CIPD includes progressive symptoms lasting over 2 months, more weakness than sensory deficits, symmetric weakness in the arms and legs, impaired sensation (from distal to proximal), paresthesia and dysesthesia, and absent or decreased reflexes in all extremities. Tremors, facial weakness, and papilledema may be present. Sensory ataxia and impaired vibration and pinprick sensation occur more often in CIDP.

CIDP diagnostic tests are similar to those for GBS. CSF shows high protein levels. MRI may show changes. Key identifying features of CIDP include nerve conduction block and slowed conduction velocity, possibly due to demyelination. Nerve biopsy is done when other studies do not confirm a diagnosis.[41]

❖ Interprofessional and Nursing Care

Early recognition and diagnosis of CIDP are key to reducing permanent disability. The goal of treatment is to halt the immune response and stop nerve inflammation and demyelination. Use of IVIG, high-dose corticosteroids, or plasma exchange are all effective treatments.[41]

Patients continue therapy until maximum clinical improvement is achieved or until they reach a clinical plateau. Patients will need maintenance therapy to prevent relapse or progression. Appropriate referrals to rehabilitation should be made early in the patient's care to promote maximum recovery. Therapy may improve muscle strength, function, and mobility while minimizing muscle atrophy and joint distortion.[40]

TETANUS

Tetanus (lockjaw) is a severe infection of the nervous system affecting spinal and cranial nerves. In the United States, because of widespread immunization and careful wound care, there are only about 30 cases per year.[42] The annual worldwide incidence is between 500,000 and 1 million cases.[43]

Tetanus results from the effects of a potent neurotoxin (tetanospasmin) released by the anaerobic bacillus *Clostridium tetani*. The spores of the bacillus are present in soil, garden mold, and manure. Tetanospasmin binds to motor nerves and enters the axons. From there it can travel to the brain and spinal cord and stop the release of inhibitory neurotransmitters. The result is sustained muscle contraction. If the toxin reaches the blood or lymph system, many different muscles can be affected.[42]

C. tetani enters the body through a wound that provides an appropriate low-O$_2$ environment for the organisms to mature and make toxin. Examples of such wounds include IV drug use injection sites, human and animal bites, puncture wounds from stepping on a nail, gardening injuries, burns, frostbite, open fractures, and gunshot wounds. The incubation period is typically 4 to 14 days. The shorter the period, the more severe the symptoms.

The hallmark feature of generalized tetanus is muscle rigidity and spasms. Patients may have muscle soreness, cramping, or difficulty swallowing. Facial muscles are affected first with stiffness in the jaw *(trismus)*. Patients may have a sardonic smile *(risus sardonicus)* due to facial muscle contractions. As the disease progresses, the neck muscles, back, abdomen, and extremities become increasingly rigid. In severe forms, continuous tonic seizures may occur with *opisthotonos* (extreme arching of the back and retraction of the head).[42] Laryngeal and respiratory spasms cause apnea and anoxia. The slightest noise, jarring motion, or bright light can set off a painful seizure.

Tetanus prevention and immunizations, which are the most important factors influencing incidence, are outlined in Table 68.6. Adults should receive a tetanus and diphtheria toxoid booster every 10 years.[43] Teach the patient that immediate, thorough cleansing of all wounds with soap and water is important to prevent tetanus. If an open wound occurs and the patient has not been immunized within 5 years, contact the HCP so that a tetanus booster can be given.

Tetanus is a medical emergency that requires hospitalization. Patients are given immediate treatment with tetanus immune globulin (TIG). It provides temporary immunity by directly providing antitoxin.[43] Drugs to control spasms are essential.

Diazepam (Valium) or barbiturates are given to promote sedation and skeletal muscle relaxation. In severe cases, neuromuscular blocking agents (e.g., vecuronium) are given to paralyze skeletal muscles. Opioid analgesics, such as morphine or fentanyl, are used for pain management. A 10- to 14-day course of penicillin, metronidazole (drug of choice), tetracycline, or doxycycline is recommended to inhibit further growth of *C. tetani*.

Because of laryngospasm and the potential need for neuromuscular blocking drugs, the patient is placed on mechanical ventilation. Sedative agents and opioid analgesics are given to all patients who are pharmacologically paralyzed. IV fluids are needed for proper hydration due to sustained muscle contraction. Any wound should be debrided or abscess drained. Antibiotics may be given to prevent secondary infections.

BOTULISM

Botulism is a rare, but the most serious type, of food poisoning. It is caused by GI absorption of a neurotoxin made by *Clostridium botulinum*. This organism is found in the soil, and the spores are hard to destroy. It can grow in any food contaminated with the spores. Improper home canning of foods is often the cause.

We think the neurotoxin destroys or inhibits the neurotransmission of acetylcholine at the myoneural junction, resulting in disturbed muscle innervation. Neurologic manifestations can develop rapidly or evolve over several days. They include a descending paralysis with muscle incoordination and weakness, difficulty swallowing, and seizures. Respiratory muscle weakness can quickly lead to respiratory and/or cardiac arrest.

The manifestations, prevention, and treatment are described in Table 41.24. Patient and caregiving teaching related to food poisoning are outlined in Table 41.25. Nursing care during the acute illness is like that for GBS. Supportive nursing interventions include rest, activities to maintain respiratory function, adequate nutrition, and preventing loss of muscle mass.

CASE STUDY

Spinal Cord Injury

(© Comstock-Images/Stockbyte/Thinkstock.)

Patient Profile

Acute Phase

S.W., an 18-yr-old white woman, is admitted to the ED with the diagnosis of a cervical spinal cord injury (SCI). S.W. was swimming at a neighbor's backyard pool. She dove into the shallow end, striking her head on the bottom of the pool. Her friends noticed she did not resurface. They rescued her and brought her to the side of the pool. They maintained neck immobilization until the rescue crews arrived.

Subjective Data

- Awake and alert
- Reporting neck pain
- Anxious and asking why she cannot move her legs
- Asking to see her family

Objective Data

Physical Examination

- Weak elbow flexion (biceps) movement bilaterally
- No triceps movement bilaterally
- Gross shoulder movement present bilaterally

- No movement in bilateral lower extremities
- Decreased sensation from the shoulders down
- No bladder or bowel control
- BP 85/50 mm Hg; pulse 56 beats/min; respirations 32 breaths/min and labored

Diagnostic Studies

- CT C-spine shows C5 subluxation and compression fracture
- MRI C-spine shows severe spinal cord compression at C5-6

Interprofessional Care

- Intubated in the ED
- Started on mechanical ventilation
- Placed in tongs and traction on arrival to the ICU

Discussion Questions (Acute Phase)

1. **Priority Decision:** What nursing activities would be a priority on S.W.'s arrival in the ICU?
2. What physiologic problems are causing S.W. to have hypotension and bradycardia?
3. What would be the initial treatment for S.W.'s hypotension and bradycardia?

CASE STUDY—cont'd

Spinal Cord Injury

4. **Safety:** What signs and symptoms would indicate respiratory distress? What physiologic problem would cause respiratory distress in S.W.'s injury state?
5. **Collaboration:** What can the interprofessional team do to decrease S.W.'s anxiety?
6. **Priority Decision:** Based on the assessment data provided, what are the priority nursing diagnoses? What are the collaborative problems?
7. **Collaboration:** Identify activities that can be delegated to unlicensed assistive personnel (UAP).

Patient Profile

Rehabilitation Phase

S.W. is now 1-month postinjury and has been admitted to a local inpatient SCI rehabilitation agency. She has been extubated and uses a wheelchair to mobilize. She eats 3 meals a day with help and is on a strict bowel and bladder program.

Subjective Data

- Awake and alert but anxious
- Reporting a severe headache, blurred vision, and nausea

Objective Data

Physical Examination

- Flushed and diaphoretic above the level of injury
- No bowel movement for 2 days
- BP 235/106 mm Hg, pulse 32 beats/min, respirations 30 breaths/min and labored

Discussion Questions (Rehabilitation Phase)

1. **Priority Decision:** What initial priority nursing interventions would be appropriate?
2. What physiologic problem is causing S.W.'s hypertension and bradycardia?
3. Once the HCP has been notified, what other interventions would be appropriate?
4. **Quality Improvement:** What outcomes would indicate that nursing interventions were successful?
5. **Patient-Centered Care:** Patient and caregiver involvement in the rehabilitation process is vital. What teaching will you provide about bowel management?
6. **Evidence-Based Practice:** S.W. and her family are concerned about the risk for autonomic dysreflexia. What effective strategies to prevent autonomic dysreflexia would you discuss with them?

Answers available at *http://evolve.elsevier.com/Lewis/medsurg.*

BRIDGE TO NCLEX EXAMINATION

The number of the question corresponds to the same-numbered outcome at the beginning of the chapter.

1. During rehabilitation, a patient with spinal cord injury begins to ambulate with long leg braces. Which level of injury does the nurse associate with this degree of recovery?
   a. L1-2
   b. T6-7
   c. T1-2
   d. C7-8

2. A patient with a T4 spinal cord injury has neurogenic shock due to sympathetic nervous system dysfunction. What would the nurse recognize as characteristic of this condition?
   a. Tachycardia
   b. Hypotension
   c. Increased cardiac output
   d. Peripheral vasoconstriction

3. A patient with spinal cord injury has severe neurologic deficits. What is the *most* likely mechanism of injury for this patient?
   a. Compression
   b. Hyperextension
   c. Flexion-rotation
   d. Extension-rotation

4. A patient undergoing rehabilitation for a C7 spinal cord injury tells the nurse he must have the flu because he has a bad headache and nausea. The nurse's *first priority* is to
   a. call the health care provider.
   b. check the patient's temperature.
   c. measure the patient's blood pressure.
   d. elevate the head of the bed to 90 degrees.

5. The most common early symptom of a spinal cord tumor is
   a. urinary incontinence.
   b. back pain that worsens with activity.
   c. paralysis below the level of involvement.
   d. impaired sensation of pain, temperature, and light touch.

6. During assessment of the patient with trigeminal neuralgia, the nurse should *(select all that apply)*
   a. inspect all aspects of the mouth and teeth.
   b. assess the gag reflex and respiratory rate and depth.
   c. lightly palpate the affected side of the face for edema.
   d. test for temperature and sensation perception on the face.
   e. ask the patient to describe factors that initiate an episode.

7. During routine assessment of a patient with Guillain-Barré syndrome, the nurse finds the patient is short of breath. The patient's respiratory distress is caused by
   a. elevated protein levels in the CSF.
   b. immobility resulting from ascending paralysis.
   c. degeneration of motor neurons in the brainstem and spinal cord.
   d. paralysis ascending to the nerves that stimulate the thoracic area.

8. A nurse is caring for a patient newly diagnosed with chronic inflammatory demyelinating polyneuropathy (CIDP). Which statement can the nurse accurately use to teach the patient about CIDP?
   a. "Corticosteroids have little effect on this disease."
   b. "Maintenance therapy will be needed to prevent relapse."
   c. "You will go into remission in approximately eight weeks."
   d. "You should be able to walk without help within three months."

1. a, 2. b, 3. c, 4. c, 5. b, 6. a, d, e, 7. d, 8. b.

For rationales to these answers and even more NCLEX review questions, visit *http://evolve.elsevier.com/Lewis/medsurg.*

℮ EVOLVE WEBSITE/RESOURCES LIST

http://evolve.elsevier.com/Lewis/medsurg

Review Questions (Online Only)

Key Points

Answer Keys for Questions
- Rationales for Bridge to NCLEX Examination Questions
- Answer Guidelines for Case Study on p. 1426

Student Case Study
- Patient With Spinal Cord Injury

Nursing Care Plan
- eNursing Care Plan 60.1: Patient With a Spinal Cord Injury

Conceptual Care Map Creator

Audio Glossary

Content Updates

REFERENCES

1. The National SCI Statistical Center: Spinal cord injury (SCI) facts and figures at a glance. Retrieved from *www.nscisc.uab.edu/Public/Facts%20 2016.pdf*.
*2. Fehlings MG, Tetreault LA, Wilson JR, et al: A clinical practice guideline for the management of acute spinal cord injury: Introduction, rationale, and scope, *AOspine* 7:845, 2017.
3. Hachem LD, Ahuja CS, Fehling MG: Assessment and management of acute spinal cord injury: From point of injury to rehabilitation, *J Spinal Cord Med* 40:665, 2017.
4. Ulndreaj A, Chio JC, Ahuja CS, et al : Modulating the immune response in spinal cord injury, *Expert Re Neurother* 16:1127, 2016.
5. Ruiz IA, Squair JW, Phillips AA, et al: Incidence and natural progression of neurogenic shock after traumatic spinal cord injury, *J Neurotrauma* 35:461, 2018.
6. Dave S, Cho JJ: Shock: Neurogenic shock, Treasure Island, FL, 2018, StatPearls Publishing. Retrieved from *www.ncbi.nlm.nih.gov/books/ NBK459361/*.
7. Roberts TT, Leonard GR, Cepela DJ : Classifications in brief: ASIA Impairment Scale, *Clin Orthop Relat Res* 475:1499, 2017.
8. Stein DM, Knight WA: Emergency neurological life support: Traumatic spine injury, *Neurocrit Care* 27:S170, 2017.
*9. Neseyo U, Santiago-Lastra Y: Long-term complications of the neurogenic bladder, *Ur Clin N Am* 44:355, 2017.
10. Martinez L, Neshatican L, Khavari R: Neurogenic bowel dysfunction in patients with neurogenic bladder, *Curr Bladder Dysfunct Rep* 11:334, 2017.
*11. Felleiter P, Krebs J: Post-traumatic changes in energy expenditure and body composition in patients with acute spinal cord injury, *J Rehabil Med* 49:579, 2017.
*12. Fehlings MG, Tetreault LA, Jefferson RW, et al: A clinical practice guideline for management of patients with acute spinal cord injury: Recommendations on the type and timing of anticoagulant thromboprophylaxis, *AOSpine* 7:2125, 2017.
13. Yue JK, Winkler EA, Rick JW, et al: Update on critical care for acute spinal cord injury in the setting of polytrauma, *Neurosurg Focus* 43:E19, 2017.
*14. Evanie N, Belley-Cote EP, Falla N, et al: Methylprednisolone for the treatment of patients with acute spinal cord injuries: A systematic review and meta-analysis, *J Neurotraum* 33:468, 2016.
15. STEADI: Stopping elderly accidents, deaths and injuries. Retrieved from *www.cdc.gov/steadi/index.html*.
*16. Kumar N, Pieri-Davies N, Chowdury JR, et al: Evidence-based respiratory management strategies required to preen complications and improve outcome in acute spinal cord injury patients, *Trauma* 19:23, 2017.
*17. Atkinson RA, Cullum NA: Interventions for pressure ulcers: A summary of evidence for prevention and treatment, *Spin Cord* 56:186, 2017.
*18. Brienza D, Krishnan S, Karg P, et al: Predictors of pressure ulcer incidence following traumatic spinal cord injury: A secondary analysis of a prospective longitudinal study, *Spin Cord* 56:28, 2018.
*19. Wound, Ostomy and Continence Nurses Society: Guidelines for prevention and management of pressure ulcers, *J Wound Ostomy Continence Nurs* 44:241, 2017.
*20. Eldahan KC, Rabchevsky AG: Autonomic dysreflexia after spinal cord injury: Systemic pathophysiology and methods of management, *Auton Neurosci* 209:59, 2018.
*21. Garara B, Wood A, Marcus HJ, et al: Intramuscular diaphragmatic stimulation for patient with traumatic high cervical injuries and ventilator dependent respiratory failure: A systematic review of safety and effectiveness, *Injury* 47:539, 2016.
*22. Cho YS, Kim KH: Botulinum toxin in spinal cord injury patients with neurogenic detrusor overactivity, *J Exerc Rehabil* 12:624, 2018.
23. Krogh K, Emmanuel A, Perrouin-Verbe B, et al: International Spinal Cord Bowel Function Basic Data Set (Version 2.0), *Spin Cord* 55:692, 2017.
24. Christopher & Dana Reeve Foundation Paralysis Resource Center: Sexual health for men. Retrieved from *www.christopherreeve.org/living-with-paralysis/health/sexual-health/sexual-health-for-men*.
25. Christopher & Dana Reeve Foundation Paralysis Resource Center: Sexual health for women. Retrieved from *www.christopherreeve.org/ living-with-paralysis/health/sexual-health/sexual-health-for-women*.
*26. Kornhabe R, Mclean L, Betivas V, et al: Resilience and the rehabilitation of adult spinal cord injury survivors: A qualitative systematic review, *J Adv Nurs* 74:23, 2018.
27. Kretzer RM: Intradural spinal cord tumors, *Spine* 42:22, 2017.
28. American Association of Neurological Surgeons: Spinal tumors. Retrieved from *www.aans.org/Patients/Neurosurgical-Conditions-and-Treatments/Spinal-Tumors*.
29. Kumar A, Weber MH, Gokaslan Z, et al: Metastatic spinal cord compression and steroid treatment, *Clin Spine Surg* 30:156, 2017.
30. National Institute of Health: Trigeminal neuralgia fact sheet. Retrieved from *www.ninds.nih.gov/Disorders/Patient-Caregiver-Education/Fact-Sheets/Trigeminal-Neuralgia-Fact-Sheet*.
*31. Crucca G, Finnerup NB, Jensen TS, et al: Trigeminal neuralgia: New classification of diagnostic grading for practice and research, *Am Acad Neurol* 87:220, 2016.
*32. Spina A, Mortini P, Alemanno F, et al: Trigeminal neuralgia: Toward a multimodal approach, *World Neurosurg* 103:220, 2017.
33. National Institute of Neurologic Disorders and Stroke: Bell's palsy information page. Retrieved from *www.ninds.nih.gov/Disorders/All-Disorders/Bells-Palsy-Information-Page*.
*34. Thielker J, Geibler K, Granitzka T, et al: Acute management of Bells palsy, *Curr Otorhinolaryngol Rep* 6:161, 2018.
35. National Institute of Neurologic Disorders and Stroke: Guillain-Barré fact sheet. Retrieved from *www.ninds.nih.gov/Disorders/Patient-Caregiver-Education/Fact-Sheets/Guillain-Barr%C3%A9-Syndrome-Fact-Sheet*.
36. Centers for Disease Control and Prevention (CDC): Guillain-Barré syndrome. Retrieved from *www.cdc.gov/campylobacter/guillain-barre.html*.
37. Andary MT, Klein MJ: Guillain-Barré syndrome updated. Retrieved from *https://emedicine.medscape.com/article/315632-overview*.
38. Wilson HJ, Jacobs BC, van Doorn PA: Guillain-Barre syndrome, *Lancet* 388:717, 2016.
39. Verboon C, van Doorn PA, Jacobs BC. Treatment dilemma in Guillain-Barr syndrome, *J Neurol Neurosurg Psychiatry* 88:346, 2017.
40. National Institute of Neurologic Disorders and Stroke: Chronic inflammatory demyelinating polyneuropathy. Retrieved from *www.ninds. nih.gov/Disorders/All-Disorders/Chronic-Inflammatory-Demyelinating-Polyneuropathy-CIDP-Information-Page*.
41. Daroff RB, Jankovic J, Mazziotta JC, et al: Bradley's neurology in clinical practice, ed 7, St Louis, 2016, Elsevier.
42. Davis DP, Stoppler MC: Tetanus. Retrieved from *www.emedicinehealth. com/tetanus/article_em.htm#facts_on_tetanus*.
43. Centers for Disease Control and Prevention (CDC): Tetanus. Retrieved from *www.cdc.gov/tetanus/clinicians.html*.

*Evidence-based information for clinical practice.

61

Assessment: Musculoskeletal System

Colleen Walsh

It takes strength to be gentle and kind.

Steven Morrissey

http://evolve.elsevier.com/Lewis/medsurg

CONCEPTUAL FOCUS

Functional Ability
Mobility

Safety

LEARNING OUTCOMES

1. Describe the gross and microscopic anatomy of bone.
2. Explain the classification system for joints and movements at synovial joints.
3. Describe the functions of cartilage, muscles, ligaments, tendons, fascia, and bursae.
4. Link age-related changes in the musculoskeletal system to the differences in assessment findings.
5. Obtain significant subjective and objective assessment data related to the musculoskeletal system from a patient.

6. Perform a physical assessment of the musculoskeletal system using appropriate techniques.
7. Distinguish normal from abnormal findings of a physical assessment of the musculoskeletal system.
8. Describe the purpose, significance of results, and nursing responsibilities related to diagnostic studies of the musculoskeletal system.

KEY TERMS

ankylosis, Table 61.6, p. 1439
arthrocentesis, Table 61.9, p. 1442
arthroscopy, Table 61.9, p. 1442
atrophy, Table 61.6, p. 1439
bone remodeling, p. 1430

contracture, Table 61.6, p. 1439
crepitation, Table 61.6, p. 1439
isometric contractions, p. 1432
isotonic contractions, p. 1432
kyphosis, Table 61.6, p. 1439

lordosis, Table 61.6, p. 1439
range of motion (ROM), p. 1437
scoliosis, p. 1438
x-ray, p. 1440

The musculoskeletal system is composed of voluntary muscle and 6 types of connective tissue: bone, cartilage, ligaments, tendons, fascia, and bursae. The purpose of the musculoskeletal system is to protect body organs, provide support and stability for the body, store minerals, and allow coordinated movement. This chapter reviews the structure and function of the musculoskeletal system to facilitate nursing assessment and evaluation of the assessment findings.

STRUCTURES AND FUNCTIONS OF MUSCULOSKELETAL SYSTEM

Bone

Function. The main functions of bone are support, protection of internal organs, voluntary movement, blood cell production, and mineral storage. Bones provide the supporting framework that keeps the body from collapsing. It allows the body to bear weight. Bones protect underlying vital organs and tissues. For example, the skull encloses the brain and vertebrae surround the spinal cord. The rib cage protects the lungs and heart.

Bones serve as a point of attachment for muscles and ligaments. Muscles are connected to bones by tendons. Bones act as a lever for muscles. Movement occurs because of muscle contractions applied to these levers. Ligaments provide stability to joints. Bone marrow contains hematopoietic tissue responsible for making red and white blood cells. Bones serve as a storage site for inorganic minerals, including calcium and phosphorus.

Bone is a dynamic tissue that continuously changes form and composition. It contains both organic material (collagen) and inorganic material (calcium, phosphate). The internal and external growth and remodeling of bone are ongoing processes. **Microscopic Structure.** Bone is classified according to structure as *cortical* (compact and dense) or *cancellous* (spongy). In *cortical bone,* cylindrical structural units called *osteons (Haversian systems)* fit closely together to create a dense bone structure (Fig. 61.1, *A*). Within the systems, the Haversian canals run parallel to the bone's long axis. They contain the blood vessels that travel to the bone's interior from the periosteum. Surrounding each osteon are concentric rings known as *lamellae,* which

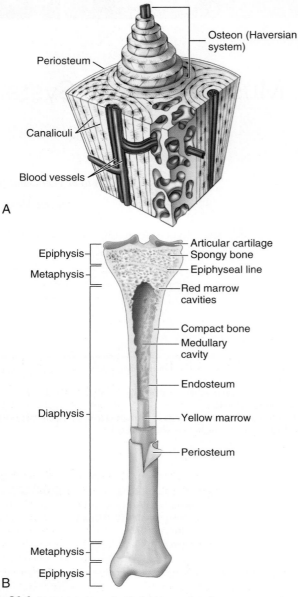

FIG. 61.1 Bone structure. A, Cortical bone showing numerous structural units called osteons. B, Anatomy of a long bone (tibia) showing cancellous and compact bone. (*A,* From Herlihy B, Maebius N: *The human body in health and illness,* ed 4, Philadelphia, 2011, Saunders. *B,* From Patton KT, Thibodeau GA: *Anatomy and physiology,* ed 8, St Louis, 2013, Mosby.)

indicate mature bone. Smaller canals *(canaliculi)* extend from the Haversian canals to the *lacunae,* where mature bone cells are embedded.

Cancellous bone has a different structure than cortical bone. The lamellae are not arranged in concentric rings. Instead, they occur along the lines of maximum stress placed on the bone. Cancellous bone is filled with red or yellow marrow. Blood reaches the bone cells by passing through spaces in the marrow.

The 3 types of bone cells are osteoblasts, osteocytes, and osteoclasts.[1] *Osteoblasts* synthesize organic bone matrix (collagen) and are the basic bone-forming cells. *Osteocytes* are mature bone cells. *Osteoclasts* take part in bone remodeling by helping in the breakdown of bone tissue. Bone remodeling is the removal of old bone by osteoclasts *(resorption)* and the deposit

of new bone by osteoblasts *(ossification).* The inner layer of bone is made mostly of osteoblasts with a few osteoclasts.

Gross Structure. The anatomic structure of bone is best represented by a typical long bone, such as the tibia (Fig. 61.1, *B*). Each long bone consists of the epiphysis, diaphysis, and metaphysis. The *epiphysis,* the widened area at each end of a long bone, is made mostly of cancellous bone. The wide epiphysis allows greater weight distribution and provides stability for the joint. The epiphysis is a primary location of muscle attachment. Articular cartilage covers the ends of the epiphysis. It provides a smooth, low-friction surface for joint movement.

The *diaphysis* is the main shaft of the long bone. It provides structural support and is composed of cortical bone. The tubular structure of the diaphysis allows it to withstand bending and twisting forces more easily.

The *metaphysis* is the flared area between the epiphysis and diaphysis. Like the epiphysis, it is composed of cancellous bone.

The *epiphyseal plate* (physis or growth plate) is the cartilaginous area between the epiphysis and metaphysis. In skeletally immature children who still have open growth plates, the epiphyseal plate actively makes chondrocytes that become mature bone. Division of the chondrocytes causes longitudinal bone growth in children. Injury to the epiphyseal plate in a growing child can cause the formation of new bone to stop at the growth plate. This leads to a shorter extremity and may contribute to significant functional problems. In the adult, the metaphysis and epiphysis become joined when chondrocyte formation at the growth plate stops and bone formation is complete.

The *periosteum* is composed of fibrous connective tissue that covers the bone. Tiny blood vessels penetrate the periosteum to bring nutrition to underlying bone. Musculotendinous fibers attach to the outer layer of the periosteum. Collagen bundles attach the inner layer of the periosteum to the bone. There is no periosteum on the articular surfaces of long bones. These bone ends are covered by articular cartilage.

The medullary *(marrow)* cavity in the center of the diaphysis contains either red or yellow bone marrow.[2] In adults, red marrow is found mainly in the *flat bones,* such as the pelvis, skull, sternum, cranium, ribs, vertebrae, and scapulae, and *cancellous* ("spongy") bone at the epiphyseal ends of long bones, such as the femur and humerus. Red bone marrow is involved in blood cell production (hematopoiesis). In the adult, the medullary cavity of long bones contains yellow bone marrow (mainly adipose tissue). Yellow marrow is involved in hematopoiesis in times of great blood cell need.

Types. The skeleton consists of 206 bones. They are classified according to shape as long, short, flat, or irregular.

Long bones have a central shaft *(diaphysis)* and 2 widened ends *(epiphyses)* (Fig. 61.1, *B*). Examples include the femur, humerus, and tibia. *Short bones* are composed of cancellous bone covered by a thin layer of compact bone. Examples include the carpals in the hand and tarsals in the foot.

Flat bones have 2 layers of compact bone separated by a layer of cancellous bone. Examples include the ribs, skull, scapula, and sternum. The spaces in the cancellous bone contain bone marrow. *Irregular bones* appear in a variety of shapes and sizes. Examples include the sacrum, mandible, and ear ossicles.

Joints

A *joint* (articulation) is a place where the ends of 2 bones are close and move in relation to each other. Joints are classified by the degree of movement that they allow (Fig. 61.2).

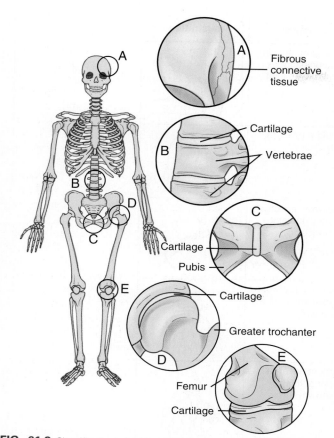

FIG. 61.2 Classification of joints. **A** to **C,** Synarthrotic (immovable) and amphiarthrotic (slightly movable) joints. **D** and **E,** Diarthrodial (*freely* movable) joints.

The most common joint is the freely movable *diarthrodial* (synovial) type. Each joint is enclosed in a capsule of fibrous connective tissue, which joins the 2 bones together to form a cavity (Fig. 61.3). The capsule is lined by a synovial membrane, which secretes thick synovial fluid. This fluid lubricates the joint, reduces friction, and allows opposing surfaces to slide smoothly over each other. The end of each bone is covered with articular (hyaline) cartilage. Supporting structures (e.g., ligaments, tendons) reinforce the joint capsule. They provide limits and stability to joint movement. Types of diarthrodial joints are shown in Fig. 61.4.

Cartilage

The 3 types of *cartilage* are hyaline, elastic, and fibrous. *Hyaline cartilage* is the most common. It has a moderate amount of collagen fibers. It is found in the trachea, bronchi, nose, epiphyseal plate, and articular surfaces of bones.

Elastic cartilage, which has both collagen and elastic fibers, is more flexible than hyaline cartilage. It is found in the ear, epiglottis, and larynx.

Fibrous cartilage (fibrocartilage) consists mostly of collagen fibers. It is a tough tissue that often functions as a shock absorber. Fibrous cartilage is found between the vertebral discs. It also forms a protective cushion between the bones of the pelvic girdle, knee, and shoulder.

Cartilage in synovial joints serves as a support for soft tissue and provides the articular surface for joint movement. It protects underlying tissues. Because articular cartilage is avascular,

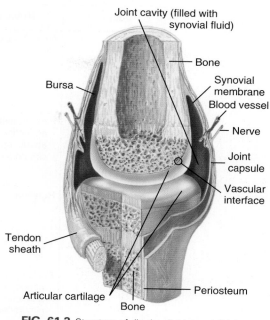

FIG. 61.3 Structure of diarthrodial (synovial) joint.

it must receive nourishment by the diffusion of material from the synovial fluid. The lack of a direct blood supply contributes to the slow metabolism of cartilage cells and explains why healing and repair of cartilage tissue occur slowly. The cartilage in the epiphyseal plate is also involved in the growth of long bones before physical maturity is reached.

Muscle

Types. The 3 types of muscle tissue are cardiac (striated, involuntary), smooth (nonstriated, involuntary), and skeletal (striated, voluntary) muscle. *Cardiac muscle* is found only in the heart. Its spontaneous contractions pump blood through the circulatory system. *Smooth muscle* is found in the walls of hollow structures, such as airways, arteries, gastrointestinal (GI) tract, urinary bladder, and uterus. Smooth muscle contraction is controlled by neuronal and hormonal influences. *Skeletal muscle,* which requires neuronal stimulation for contraction, accounts for about half of a human's body weight. It is the focus of the following discussion.

Structure. The skeletal muscle is enclosed by the *epimysium,* a continuous layer of deep fascia. The epimysium helps muscles slide over nearby structures. Connective tissue surrounding and extending into the muscle can be subdivided into fiber bundles (*fasciculi*). These bundles are covered by *perimysium* and an innermost connective tissue layer called the *endomysium* that surrounds each fiber (Fig. 61.5).

The structural unit of skeletal muscle is the muscle cell or muscle fiber. It is highly specialized for contraction. Skeletal muscle fibers are long, multinucleated cylinders that contain many mitochondria to support their high metabolic activity. Muscle fibers are composed of myofibrils, which in turn are made up of protein contractile filaments. The *sarcomere* is the contractile unit of the myofibrils. Each sarcomere consists of *myosin* (thick) filaments and *actin* (thin) filaments. The arrangement of the thin and thick filaments causes the characteristic banding of muscle seen under a microscope. Muscle contraction occurs as thick and thin filaments slide past each other, causing the sarcomeres to shorten.

Joint	Movement	Examples	Illustration
Hinge joint	Flexion, extension	Elbow joint (shown), interphalangeal joints, knee joint	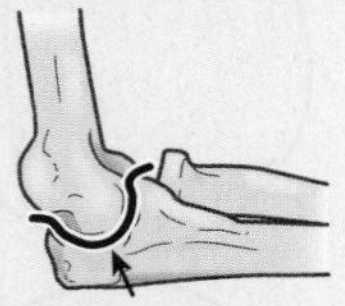
Ball and socket (spheroidal)	Flexion, extension; adduction, abduction; circumduction	Shoulder (shown), hip	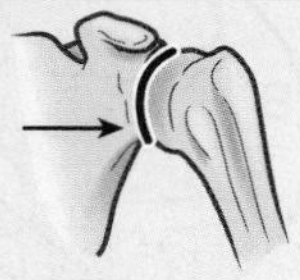
Pivot (rotary)	Rotation	Atlas-axis, proximal radioulnar joint (shown)	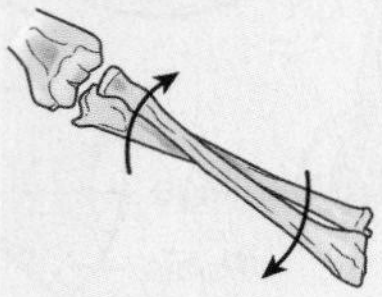
Condyloid	Flexion, extension; abduction, adduction; circumduction	Wrist joint (between radial and carpals) (shown)	
Saddle	Flexion, extension; abduction, adduction; circumduction, thumb-finger opposition	Carpometacarpal joint of thumb (shown)	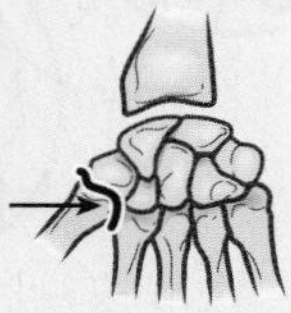
Gliding	One surface moves over another surface	Between tarsal bones, sacroiliac joint, between articular processes of vertebrae, between carpal bones (shown)	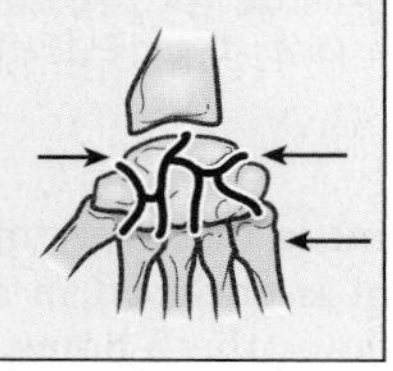

FIG. 61.4 Types of diarthrodial (synovial) joints.

Contractions. Skeletal muscle contractions allow posture maintenance, body movement, and facial expressions. Isometric contractions increase the tension within a muscle but do not produce movement. Isotonic contractions shorten a muscle to produce movement. Most contractions are a combination of tension generation *(isometric)* and shortening *(isotonic)*. Repeated isometric and/or isotonic contractions provide stress to stimulate muscle growth. Muscular *atrophy* (decrease in size) occurs with the absence of contractions that results from immobility or decreased neuronal stimulation. Increased muscular activity leads to *hypertrophy* (increase in size).

Skeletal muscle fibers are divided into 2 groups based on the type of activity they show. *Slow-twitch muscle fibers* support prolonged muscle activity, such as marathon running. Because they also support the body against gravity, they help in posture maintenance. *Fast-twitch muscle fibers* are used for rapid muscle contraction needed for activities, such as blinking the eye, jumping, or sprinting. Fast-twitch fibers tend to tire more quickly than slow-twitch fibers.

Neuromuscular Junction. Skeletal muscle fibers require a nerve impulse to contract. A nerve fiber and the skeletal muscle fibers it stimulates are called a *motor endplate.* The junction between the axon of the nerve cell and the adjacent muscle cell is called the *myoneural* or *neuromuscular junction* (Fig. 61.6).

Presynaptic neurons release acetylcholine. It diffuses across the neuromuscular junction to bind with receptors on the motor endplate of the muscle. In response to this stimulation, the sarcoplasmic reticulum releases calcium ions into the cytoplasm. The presence of calcium triggers the contraction in the myofibrils. When calcium is low, *tetany* (involuntary contractions of skeletal muscle) can occur.

Energy Source. The direct energy source for muscle fiber contractions is adenosine triphosphate (ATP). ATP is synthesized by cellular oxidative metabolism in the numerous mitochondria found close to the myofibrils. It is rapidly depleted through conversion to adenosine diphosphate (ADP) and must be rephosphorylated. Phosphocreatine provides a rapid source for the resynthesis of ATP, but it is, in turn, converted to creatine. Glycolysis can serve as a source of ATP when the O_2 supply is inadequate for metabolic needs of the muscle tissue. In this process, 1 glucose molecule is broken down to 2 ATP molecules.

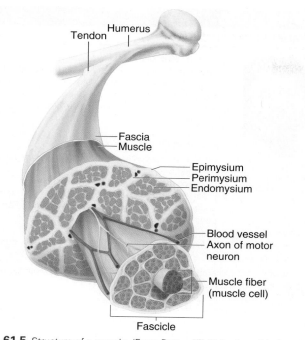

FIG. 61.5 Structure of a muscle. (From Patton KT, Thibodeau GA, Douglas M: *Essentials of anatomy and physiology*, St Louis, 2012, Mosby.)

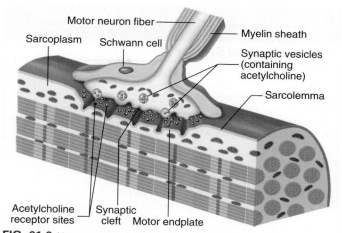

FIG. 61.6 Neuromuscular junction. (From Patton KT, Thibodeau GA: *Anatomy and physiology*, ed 8, St Louis, 2013, Mosby.)

Ligaments and Tendons

Ligaments and tendons are composed of dense, fibrous connective tissue with bundles of closely packed collagen fibers arranged in the same plane for additional strength. *Tendons* attach muscles to bones as an extension of the muscle sheath that adheres to the periosteum. *Ligaments* connect bones to bones (e.g., tibia to femur at knee joint). They have a higher elastic content than tendons.[3] Ligaments provide stability while allowing controlled movement at joints.

Ligaments and tendons have a relatively poor blood supply. This can make tissue repair a slow process after injury. For example, the stretching or tearing of ligaments that occurs with a sprain may require a long time to mend.

Fascia

Fascia refers to layers of connective tissue with intermeshed fibers that can withstand limited stretching. Superficial fascia lies right under the skin. Deep fascia is a dense, fibrous tissue that surrounds muscle bundles, nerves, and blood vessels. It also encloses individual muscles, allowing them to act independently and to glide over each other during contraction. In addition, fascia provides strength to muscle tissues.

Bursae

Bursae are small sacs of connective tissue lined with synovial membrane and containing viscous synovial fluid. They are found at bony prominences or joints to relieve pressure and decrease friction between moving parts.[4] For example, bursae are found between the (1) patella and skin (prepatellar bursae), (2) olecranon process of the elbow and skin (olecranon bursae), (3) head of the humerus and acromion process of the scapula (subacromial bursae), and (4) greater trochanter of the proximal femur and skin (trochanteric bursae). *Bursitis* is an inflammation of a bursa sac. The inflammation may be acute or chronic.

Gerontologic Considerations: Effects of Aging on Musculoskeletal System

Many functional problems experienced by the older adult are related to changes in the musculoskeletal system. Although some changes begin in early adulthood, obvious signs of musculoskeletal impairment may not appear until later adult years. Changes may affect the older adult's ability to complete self-care tasks and pursue other usual activities. Effects of musculoskeletal changes may range from mild discomfort and decreased ability to perform ADLs to severe, chronic pain and immobility.

The bone remodeling process changes in the aging adult. Increased bone resorption and decreased bone formation cause a loss of bone density. This contributes to the development of osteopenia and osteoporosis (see Chapter 63). Muscle mass and strength decrease. Almost 30% of muscle mass is lost by age 70. A loss of motor neurons can cause problems with skeletal muscle movement. Tendons and ligaments become less flexible, making movement more rigid.

Perform a musculoskeletal assessment with an emphasis on exercise practices. Obtain information on the type of exercise performed, including frequency and warm-up activities. Determine the impact of age-related changes of the musculoskeletal system on functional status. Specifically ask about changes in self-care habits and ability to be independent in the home environment. Functional limitations that are accepted by the older adult as a normal part of aging can often be addressed with appropriate preventive strategies (see Table 62.1).

The risk for falls increases in the older adult due in part to loss of strength. Aging can also bring changes in the patient's balance, making the person unsteady. *Proprioception* (awareness of self in relation to the environment) may be altered. Identify any musculoskeletal changes that increase the patient's risk for falls. Discuss fall prevention strategies.

Osteoarthritis is more likely to affect joints in the aging adult (see Chapter 64).[5] Metabolic bone diseases involve the deterioration of bone tissue (osteoporosis) and destruction of cartilage (osteoarthritis). Carefully distinguish between expected changes and the effects of disease in the aging adult. Symptoms of disease can be treated in many cases, helping the older adult to return to a higher functional level. Age-related changes in the musculoskeletal system and differences in assessment findings are outlined in Table 61.1.

TABLE 61.1 Gerontologic Assessment Differences

Musculoskeletal System

Changes	Differences in Assessment Findings
Bone	
• ↓ Bone density and strength • Slowed remodeling process	• Loss of height and deformity, such as dowager's hump (kyphosis), from vertebral compression and degeneration • Back pain, stiffness • Bony prominences more pronounced • ↑ Risk for osteopenia and osteoporosis
Joints	
• ↑ Risk for cartilage erosion that leads to direct contact between bone ends and overgrowth of bone around joint margins • Loss of water from discs between vertebrae, ↓ height of intervertebral spaces	• Joint stiffness, ↓ mobility, limited ROM, possible crepitation on movement • Pain with motion and/or weight bearing • Loss of height and shortening of trunk from disc compression. Posture change
Muscles	
• ↓ Number and diameter of muscle cells. Replacement of muscle cells by fibrous connective tissue • Loss of elasticity and deterioration of cartilage • ↓ Ability to store glycogen. ↓ Ability to release glycogen as quick energy during stress • ↓ Basal metabolic rate	• ↓ Muscle strength and mass • Abdominal protrusion • ↑ Rigidity in neck, shoulders, back, hips, and knees • ↓ Fine motor dexterity, ↓ agility • Slowed reaction times and reflexes from slowed conduction of nerve impulses along motor units • Earlier fatigue with activity

ASSESSMENT OF MUSCULOSKELETAL SYSTEM

Subjective Data

Important Health Information.

Past Health History. The most common manifestations of musculoskeletal impairment include pain, weakness, deformity, limitation of movement, stiffness, and joint crepitation (crackling sound). Ask the patient about changes in sensation or in the size of a muscle.

Questions should focus on symptoms of arthritic and connective tissue diseases (e.g., gout, psoriatic arthritis, systemic lupus erythematosus [SLE]), osteomalacia, osteomyelitis, and fungal infection of bones or joints. Ask the patient about sources of a secondary bacterial infection, such as ears, tonsils, teeth, sinuses, lungs, or genitourinary tract. These infections can enter the bones, resulting in osteomyelitis or joint destruction. Get a detailed account of the course and treatment of any of these problems.

Certain illnesses are known to affect the musculoskeletal system directly or indirectly. Ask the patient about medical problems, such as tuberculosis, poliomyelitis, diabetes, parathyroid problems, hemophilia, rickets, soft tissue infection, and neuromuscular disability.

Trauma to the musculoskeletal system is a common reason for seeking medical care. The patient who is a good historian

CASE STUDY

Patient Introduction

(© pixelhead-photo/iStock/Thinkstock.)

G.A. is a 58-yr-old black woman whose husband brought her to the emergency department (ED) this morning after she awoke with a sudden onset of excruciating pain in her left great toe. She denies any injury to her foot. She says she has never had this type of pain before.

Discussion Questions

1. What are the possible causes for G.A.'s acute pain in her great toe?
2. Is this condition stable or an emergency?
3. What type of assessment would be most appropriate for G.A.: comprehensive, focused, or emergency? What is the basis for your decision?
4. What assessment questions will you ask G.A.?
5. How will you individualize the assessment based on her age, ethnic/cultural background, and condition?

You will learn more about how to assess G.A.'s condition as you read through this chapter.

See p. 1436 for more information on G.A.

Answers available at *http://evolve.elsevier.com/Lewis/medsurg.*

can recount minor and major injuries of the musculoskeletal system. Record information chronologically and include:

- Mechanism and circumstances of the injury (e.g., twist, crush, stretch)
- Methods and duration of treatment
- Current status related to the injury
- Need for assistive devices
- Interference with ADLs

Medications. Ask the patient about prescription and over-the-counter drugs, herbal products, and nutritional supplements. Get detailed information about each treatment, including its name, dose and frequency, length of time it was taken, reason for use, and any possible side effects. Ask about the use of skeletal muscle relaxants, opioids, nonsteroidal antiinflammatory drugs, corticosteroids, and calcium and vitamin D supplements.

Review the use of drugs that can have detrimental effects on the musculoskeletal system. Some of these and their potential side effects include antiseizure drugs (osteomalacia), phenothiazines (gait changes), corticosteroids (avascular necrosis, decreased bone and muscle mass), and potassium-depleting diuretics (muscle cramps and weakness). Ask postmenopausal women about the use of hormone therapy.

Surgery or Other Treatments. Ask about any hospitalizations related to a musculoskeletal problem. Document the reason for hospitalization; the date and duration; and the treatment, including ongoing rehabilitation. Record details of emergency treatment for musculoskeletal injuries. Get specific information about any surgical procedure, postoperative course, and complications. Ask the patient about past total knee or total hip replacement. If the patient had a period of prolonged immobilization, consider the possible development of disuse osteoporosis and muscle atrophy.

Functional Health Patterns. Past or developing musculoskeletal problems can affect the patient's overall health. The use of functional health patterns helps organize assessment data. Table 61.2 outlines specific questions to ask in relation to functional health patterns.

TABLE 61.2   Health History

Musculoskeletal System

Health Perception–Health Management Pattern
- Describe your usual daily activities.
- Do you have any problems performing these activities?* Describe what you do if you have trouble dressing, preparing meals and feeding yourself, performing basic hygiene, writing or using the phone, or maintaining your home.
- Do you have to lift heavy objects? Do your work or exercise habits require repetitive motion or joint stress? Describe any special equipment you use or wear when you work or exercise that helps protect you from injury.
- Do you take any drugs or herbal products to manage your musculoskeletal problem? If so, what are their names and what are the expected effects?

Nutritional-Metabolic Pattern
- What is your usual daily intake of food and snacks?
- Do you have problems preparing your food?
- What dietary supplements do you take? Do you take calcium or vitamin D supplements?
- What is your weight? Describe any recent weight loss or gain.

Elimination Pattern
- Does your musculoskeletal problem make it hard for you to reach the toilet in time?*
- Do you need any assistive devices or equipment to manage toileting?*
- Do you have constipation related to decreased mobility or drugs taken for your musculoskeletal problem?*

Activity-Exercise Pattern
- Do you need help in completing your usual daily activities because of a musculoskeletal problem?*
- Describe your usual exercise pattern. Do you have musculoskeletal symptoms before, during, or after exercising?*
- Are you able to move all your joints comfortably through full range of motion?
- Do you use any prosthetic or orthotic devices?*

Sleep-Rest Pattern
- Do you have any problems sleeping because of a musculoskeletal problem?*
- Do you need frequent position changes at night?*
- Do you wake up at night because of musculoskeletal pain?*
- Do you use complementary and alternative therapies to help you sleep at night?*

Cognitive-Perceptual Pattern
- Describe any musculoskeletal pain you have. How do you manage your pain? Ask about adjunctive therapies, such as heat and cold, or complementary and alternative therapies, such as acupuncture.

Self-Perception–Self-Concept Pattern
- Have changes in your musculoskeletal system (posture, walking, muscle strength) and decreased ability to do certain things affected how you feel about yourself?*
- Have these changes affected your lifestyle?*

Role-Relationship Pattern
- Do you live alone?
- Describe how family, friends, or others help you with your musculoskeletal problem.
- Describe the effect of your musculoskeletal problem on your work and your social relationships.

Sexuality-Reproductive Pattern
- Describe any sexual concerns related to your musculoskeletal problem.

Coping–Stress Tolerance Pattern
- Describe how you deal with problems such as pain, weakness, or immobility that have resulted from your musculoskeletal problem.

Value-Belief Pattern
- Describe any cultural practices or religious beliefs that may influence the treatment of your musculoskeletal problem.

*If yes, describe.

Health Perception–Health Management Pattern. Ask about the patient's health practices related to the musculoskeletal system. This includes maintaining normal body weight, avoiding excessive stress on muscles and joints, and using proper body mechanics when lifting objects. Ask the patient about tetanus, pertussis, and polio immunizations.

Safety practices can affect the patient's predisposition for certain injuries and illnesses. Ask the patient about safety practices related to the work environment, home life, recreation, and exercise. For example, if the patient is a computer programmer, ask about ergonomic adaptations in the office that decrease the risk for carpal tunnel syndrome or low back pain. Identifying problems in this area will direct your plan for patient teaching.

Get a family history of rheumatoid arthritis, SLE, ankylosing spondylitis, osteoarthritis, gout, osteoporosis, and scoliosis. A patient may have a genetic predisposition to these or other musculoskeletal disorders.

Nutritional-Metabolic Pattern. The patient's description of a typical day's diet gives clues to areas of nutritional concern that can affect the musculoskeletal system. Adequate intake of vitamins C and D, calcium, and protein is essential for a healthy musculoskeletal system. Abnormal nutritional patterns can contribute to problems such as osteomalacia and osteoporosis. Maintaining normal weight is an important nutritional goal.

GENETIC RISK ALERT

Autoimmune Diseases

- Many autoimmune diseases of the musculoskeletal system have a genetic basis involving human leukocyte antigens (HLAs).
- These diseases include ankylosing spondylitis, rheumatoid arthritis, and SLE.

Osteoporosis
- Genetic factors contribute to osteoporosis by influencing bone mineral density, and bone size, quality, and turnover.

Osteoarthritis, Gout, and Scoliosis
- A genetic predisposition is a contributing risk factor in all these diseases.

Muscular Dystrophy
- The most common types of muscular dystrophy are X-linked recessive disorders.

Obesity places added stress on weight-bearing joints, such as the knees, hips, and spine. This increases the risk for cartilage deterioration and ligament instability.

Elimination Pattern. Questions about the patient's mobility may reveal problems with ambulating to the toilet. Ask the patient if an assistive device, such as an elevated toilet seat or a grab bar, is needed to manage toileting. Decreased mobility from a musculoskeletal problem can lead to constipation. Musculoskeletal problems can contribute to bowel or bladder incontinence when ambulation is a problem.

Activity-Exercise Pattern. Many musculoskeletal problems can affect the patient's activity-exercise pattern. Get a detailed account of the type, duration, and frequency of exercise and recreational activities. Compare daily, weekend, and seasonal patterns because occasional exercise can be more of a problem than regular exercise. Ask the patient about clumsiness or limitations in movement, pain, weakness, crepitus, or any change in bones or joints that interferes with daily activities.

Extremes of activity related to occupation can affect the musculoskeletal system. For example, a desk job can negatively affect muscle flexibility and strength. Jobs that require heavy lifting or pushing can lead to damage of joints and supporting structures. Specifically ask the patient about work-related musculoskeletal injuries, including treatment and time lost from work.

Sleep-Rest Pattern. The discomfort caused by musculoskeletal problems can interfere with the patient's normal sleep pattern and lead to fatigue.[6] Ask the patient about any changes in sleep patterns. If the patient describes poor sleep related to a musculoskeletal problem, ask about the type of bedding and pillows used, bedtime routine, sleeping partner, and sleeping positions.

Cognitive-Perceptual Pattern. Fully discuss any pain reported by the patient due to a musculoskeletal problem. To give a baseline for later reassessment, ask the patient to describe the intensity of the pain on a numeric scale from 0 to 10 (0 = no pain, 10 = most severe pain imaginable). Reassessments over time help to determine the effectiveness of any treatment plan. Ask the patient about measures used to manage pain. Also ask about related problems, such as joint swelling or muscle weakness, and any adjustments that help with the problem. (Pain is discussed in Chapter 8.)

Self-Perception–Self-Concept Pattern. Many chronic musculoskeletal problems lead to deformities and a reduction in activities. This can have a serious negative impact on the patient's body image and sense of personal worth.[6] Assess the patient's feelings about these changes and any effect on interactions with family and friends.

Role-Relationship Pattern. Impaired mobility and chronic pain from musculoskeletal problems can negatively affect the patient's ability to perform in roles of spouse, parent, and/or employee. The ability to pursue and maintain meaningful social and personal relationships also can be affected by musculoskeletal problems. Carefully ask the patient about role performance and relationships.

If the patient lives alone, any musculoskeletal problem and rehabilitation may make it hard or impossible to continue to do so. Assess how much help is available from family, friends, and other caregivers. Find out if other resources are needed, such as physical therapy and home health care.

Sexuality-Reproductive Pattern. Ask women about their menstrual history. Episodes of premenopausal amenorrhea can contribute to the development of osteoporosis.[7] The pain of musculoskeletal problems can affect the patient's ability to obtain sexual satisfaction. Explore this area in a sensitive and nonjudgmental way. Help the patient feel comfortable discussing any sexual problems related to pain, movement, and positioning. More information on obtaining patient data in this area is discussed in Chapter 50.

Coping–Stress Tolerance Pattern. Mobility limitations and pain are serious potential stressors that challenge the patient's coping resources. Recognize the potential for difficulty coping in the patient and family or significant other. Additional questions will help to determine if a musculoskeletal problem is causing difficulties in coping and adjusting.

Value-Belief Pattern. Ask the patient about cultural or religious beliefs that may influence acceptance of treatment for the musculoskeletal problem. These may include recommendations for diet, exercise, medication, and lifestyle modifications.

CASE STUDY—cont'd

Subjective Data

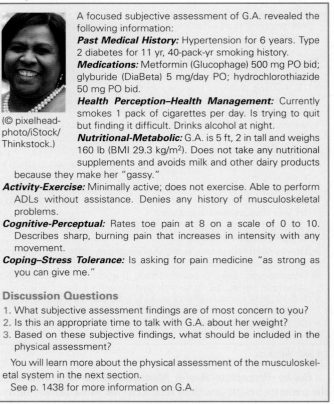

(© pixelhead-photo/iStock/Thinkstock.)

A focused subjective assessment of G.A. revealed the following information:

Past Medical History: Hypertension for 6 years. Type 2 diabetes for 11 yr, 40-pack-yr smoking history.

Medications: Metformin (Glucophage) 500 mg PO bid; glyburide (DiaBeta) 5 mg/day PO; hydrochlorothiazide 50 mg PO bid.

Health Perception–Health Management: Currently smokes 1 pack of cigarettes per day. Is trying to quit but finding it difficult. Drinks alcohol at night.

Nutritional-Metabolic: G.A. is 5 ft, 2 in tall and weighs 160 lb (BMI 29.3 kg/m^2). Does not take any nutritional supplements and avoids milk and other dairy products because they make her "gassy."

Activity-Exercise: Minimally active; does not exercise. Able to perform ADLs without assistance. Denies any history of musculoskeletal problems.

Cognitive-Perceptual: Rates toe pain at 8 on a scale of 0 to 10. Describes sharp, burning pain that increases in intensity with any movement.

Coping–Stress Tolerance: Is asking for pain medicine "as strong as you can give me."

Discussion Questions

1. What subjective assessment findings are of most concern to you?
2. Is this an appropriate time to talk with G.A. about her weight?
3. Based on these subjective findings, what should be included in the physical assessment?

You will learn more about the physical assessment of the musculoskeletal system in the next section.

See p. 1438 for more information on G.A.

Answers available at *http://evolve.elsevier.com/Lewis/medsurg.*

Objective Data

Physical Examination. The basic musculoskeletal physical examination involves inspection, palpation, neurovascular assessment, and range of motion, strength, and reflex testing. Other special tests can be used to assess for specific conditions. Conduct a general overview. While obtaining a careful health history, choose areas to concentrate on during the local examination. Take specific measurements as indicated by the local examination.

Inspection. A systematic inspection is done, starting at the head and neck then moving to the upper extremities, lower extremities, and trunk. The regular use of a systematic approach is important to avoid missing important aspects of the examination. Inspect the skin for general color, scars, or other overt signs of previous injury or surgery. Certain skin lesions require further investigation because they can indicate underlying disorders. For example, butterfly rash over the cheeks and nose is characteristic of SLE.

Note the patient's general posture and body build, muscle size and symmetry, and symmetry and contour of joints. Observe for any swelling, deformity, nodules or masses, and discrepancies in limb length or muscle size. Use the patient's opposite body part for comparison when you suspect an abnormality.

If the patient can move independently, assess posture and gait by watching the patient walk, stand, and sit. Musculoskeletal and neurologic problems can result in abnormal gait patterns.

Palpation. As with inspection, palpation usually proceeds head to toe. Examine the neck, shoulders, elbows, wrists, hands, back, hips, knees, ankles, and feet. Warm your hands to prevent muscle spasm, which can interfere with identifying essential landmarks or soft tissue structures. Carefully palpate any specific areas of concern because of a subjective report or abnormal appearance on inspection.

Both superficial and deep palpation are usually done consecutively. Consider the underlying anatomy structures and landmarks you are palpating. Purposefully palpate both muscles and joints to evaluate skin temperature, local tenderness, swelling, and crepitation. Establish the relationship of adjacent structures. Evaluate the general contour, abnormal prominences, and local landmarks. Note the specific anatomic location of any abnormal findings.

Motion. When assessing the patient's joint mobility, carefully evaluate active and passive **range of motion** (ROM). ROM is the full movement potential of a joint. Measurements should be similar for active and passive maneuvers. *Active ROM* means the patient takes their own joints through all movements without assistance. *Passive ROM* occurs when someone else moves the patient's joints without their assistance through the full ROM. Be careful in performing passive ROM because of the risk for injury to underlying structures. If pain or resistance occurs, stop at once.

If you note deficits in active or passive ROM, assess functional ROM to determine if joint changes are affecting the ability to perform ADLs. Ask the patient if activities, such as eating, grooming, dressing, and bathing, require help or cannot be done at all.

We use a goniometer to accurately assess ROM. It measures the angle of the joint (Fig. 61.7). We do not usually measure specific degrees of ROM of all joints. If a specific musculoskeletal problem has been identified, measure ROM of the affected joint. A less exact but valuable assessment method is simply to compare the ROM of 1 extremity with that on the opposite side. Common movements that occur at the synovial joints, including *abduction, adduction, flexion,* and *extension,* are described in Table 61.3.

Muscle-Strength Testing. Grade the strength of individual muscles or groups of muscles during contraction on a 5-point scale (Table 61.4). Grade normal muscle strength with full resistance to opposition as a 5/5 bilaterally. To test resistance to opposition, have the patient apply resistance as you exert a force. For example, have the patient try to extend the elbow while you try to flex it. Compare muscle strength with the strength of the opposite extremity. Note any subtle variations in muscle strength when comparing the patient's dominant and nondominant sides. Variations in strength also exist when comparing people.

Measurement. When limb length discrepancies or subjective problems are noted, measure limb length and circumferential muscle mass. For example, when gait disorders are observed, measure leg length between the anterosuperior iliac crest and the bottom of the medial malleolus. Then compare it with the similar measurement of the opposite extremity. Measure muscle

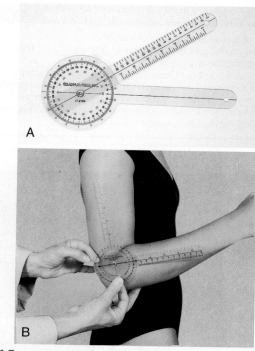

FIG. 61.7 A, Goniometer. B, Measurement of joint ROM using a goniometer. (*A,* From Wilson SF, Giddens JF: *Health assessment for nursing practice,* ed 5, St Louis, 2013, Mosby. *B,* From Barkauskas V, Baumann L, Stoltenberg-Allen K, et al: *Health and physical assessment,* ed 2, St Louis, 1998, Mosby.)

TABLE 61.3 Synovial Joint Movements	
Movement	**Description**
Abduction	Movement of part away from midline of body
Adduction	Movement of part toward midline of body
Circumduction	Circular motion of a body part from a combination of flexion, abduction, extension, and adduction
Dorsiflexion	Flexion of the ankle and toes toward the shin
Eversion	Turning of sole outward away from midline of body
Extension	Straightening of joint that ↑ angle between 2 bones
External rotation	Movement along longitudinal axis away from midline of body
Flexion	Bending of joint from muscle contraction that causes ↓ angle between 2 bones
Hyperextension	Extension in which angle exceeds 180 degrees
Internal rotation	Movement along longitudinal axis toward midline of body
Inversion	Turning of sole inward toward midline of body
Opposition	Moving the first and fifth metacarpals anteriorly from a flattened palm ("cupping position"); makes it possible to hold objects between the thumb and fingers
Plantar flexion	Flexion of the ankle and toes toward the plantar surface of the foot ("toes pointed")
Pronation	Turning of palm downward
Supination	Turning of palm upward

mass circumferentially at the largest area of the muscle. When recording measurements, record the exact location at which the measurements were obtained (e.g., the left quadriceps muscle was measured 15 cm above the patella). This tells the next examiner of the exact area to measure and ensures consistency during reassessment.

TABLE 61.4 Muscle Strength Scale

0/5	No detection of muscular contraction
1/5	Barely detectable flicker or trace of contraction with observation or palpation
2/5	Active movement of body part with elimination of gravity
3/5	Active movement against gravity only and not against resistance
4/5	Active movement against gravity and some resistance
5/5	Active movement against full resistance without evident fatigue (normal muscle strength)

TABLE 61.5 Normal Physical Assessment of the Musculoskeletal System

- Ordinary spinal curvatures
- No muscle atrophy or asymmetry
- No joint swelling, deformity, or crepitation
- No tenderness on palpation of spine, joints, or muscles
- Full ROM of all joints without pain or laxity
- Muscle strength of 5/5

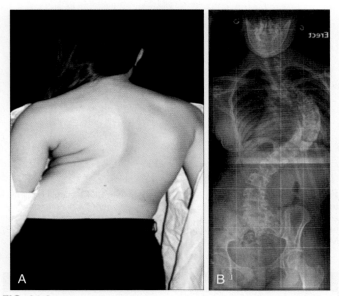

FIG. 61.8 **A,** Thoracic scoliosis. **B,** X-ray of same patient showing scoliosis greater than 90 degrees. (From Hawary R, Chukwunyerenwa C: *Update on evaluation and treatment of scoliosis, Pediatr Clin North Am* 61:1223, 2014.)

A *focused assessment* is used to evaluate previously identified musculoskeletal problems and to monitor for signs of new problems. See the Focused Assessment of the Musculoskeletal System box.

CASE STUDY—cont'd

Objective Data: Physical Examination

A focused assessment of G.A. reveals the following: BP 128/94, heart rate 88, respiratory rate 26, temp 96.8° F, O₂ saturation 98%. Alert and oriented × 3. Lungs are clear bilaterally. Left great toe is red and swollen. No open wounds. Tremendous pain on palpation and with any movement of the left great toe. +1 Pedal pulses bilaterally.

(© pixelhead-photo/iStock/Thinkstock.)

Discussion Questions

1. What physical assessment findings concern you most?
2. Based on results of the subjective and physical assessment, what diagnostic studies might you expect to be ordered for G.A.?

You will learn more about diagnostic studies related to the musculoskeletal system in the next section.

See p. 1442 for more information on G.A.

Other. Note the patient's use of an assistive device, such as a walker or cane. Assess the patient for proper fit while reviewing the safe and correct technique for using these devices. Regularly review with the patient the use of the assistive device to be sure it is still appropriate and safe. Ask the patient if the assistive device is used regularly. If not, determine possible reasons for inconsistent use.[8]

Scoliosis is a lateral S-shaped curvature of the thoracic and lumbar spine. Unequal shoulder and scapula height is usually noted when the patient is observed from the back (Fig. 61.8). Ask the patient to place the hands together above the head as if diving into a swimming pool and slowly bend forward at the waist, allowing assessment of thoracic rib prominence or paravertebral muscle prominence in the lumbar spine. Advanced scoliosis can impair lung and heart function.

The *straight-leg-raising test* is done on the supine patient with sciatica or leg pain. Passively raise the patient's leg 60 degrees or less. The test is positive if the patient reports pain along the distribution of the sciatic nerve. A positive test shows nerve root irritation from intervertebral disc prolapse and herniation, especially at level L4-5 or L5-S1.

Assessment of reflexes is discussed in Chapter 55. Table 61.5 shows an example of how to record a normal physical assessment of the musculoskeletal system. Abnormal assessment findings of the musculoskeletal system are described in Table 61.6.

FOCUSED ASSESSMENT

Musculoskeletal System

Use this checklist to be sure key assessment steps have been done.

Subjective

Ask the patient about any of the following and note responses.

Joint pain or stiffness	Y	N
Muscle weakness	Y	N
Bone pain	Y	N

Objective: Diagnostic

Check the results of the following diagnostic studies.

X-ray	✓
MRI or CT scan	✓
Bone scan	✓

Objective: Physical Examination
Inspect and Palpate

Spine and extremities (compare sides) for alignment, contour, symmetry, size, gross deformities	✓
Joints for ROM, tenderness or pain, heat, crepitus, swelling	✓
Muscles (compare sides) for size, symmetry, tone, tenderness, or pain	✓
Bones for tenderness or pain	✓

TABLE 61.6 Assessment Abnormalities

Musculoskeletal System

Finding	Description	Possible Etiology and Significance
Achilles tendonitis	Pain in ankle and posterior calf, initially when running or walking. Can progress to pain at rest.	Stress on Achilles tendon over time causing inflammation.
Ankylosis	Stiffness and fixation of a joint.	Chronic joint inflammation and destruction (e.g., rheumatoid arthritis).
Antalgic gait	Shortened stride with minimal weight bearing on the affected side, resulting in a limp.	Pain or discomfort in the lower extremity on weight bearing. Can be due to trauma or other disorders.
Ataxic gait	Staggering, uncoordinated gait often with sway.	Neurogenic disorders (e.g., spinal cord lesion).
Atrophy	↓ Size and strength of muscle leading to ↓ function and tone.	Muscle denervation, contracture, prolonged disuse from immobilization.
Boutonnière deformity	Finger abnormality, flexion of proximal interphalangeal (PIP) joint and hyperextension of the distal interphalangeal (DIP) joint of the fingers (see Fig. 64.4, B).	Typical deformity of rheumatoid and psoriatic arthritis caused by disruption of extensor tendons over the fingers.
Contracture	Resistance of movement of muscle or joint due to fibrosis of supporting soft tissues.	Shortening of muscle or ligaments, tightness of soft tissue, incorrect positioning of immobilized extremity.
Crepitation (crepitus)	Frequent, audible crackling sound with palpable grating that accompanies movement.	Fracture, dislocation, temporomandibular joint dysfunction, osteoarthritis.
Dislocation	Separation of 2 bones from their normal position within a joint.	Trauma, disorders of surrounding soft tissues.
Festinating gait	While walking, neck, trunk, and knees flex and the body is rigid. Delayed start with short, quick, shuffling steps. Speed may ↑ as if patient is unable to stop (festination).	Neurogenic disorders (e.g., Parkinson's disease).
Ganglion cyst	Small fluid-filled mass over a tendon sheath or joint, usually on dorsal surface of wrist or foot.	Inflammation of tissues around a joint, which can increase in size or disappear.
Kyphosis (dowager's hump)	Exaggerated thoracic curvature.	Poor posture, tuberculosis, arthritis, osteoporosis, growth disturbance of vertebral epiphyses, vertebral fractures.
Lateral epicondylitis (tennis elbow)	Dull ache along outer aspect of elbow, worsens with twisting and grasping motions.	Injury, inflammation, and/or partial tearing of tendon at its insertion on epicondyle.
Limited range of motion (ROM)	Joint does not achieve expected degrees of motion.	Injury, inflammation, contracture.
Lordosis (swayback)	Exaggerated lumbar curvature.	Other spinal deformities, muscular dystrophy, obesity, flexion contracture of hip, congenital dislocation of hip.
Muscle spasticity	↑ Muscle tone (rigidity) with sustained muscle contractions (spasms); stiffness or tightness may interfere with gait, movement, speech.	Neuromuscular disorders, such as multiple sclerosis (MS) or cerebral palsy.
Myalgia	General muscle tenderness and pain.	Chronic pain syndromes (e.g., fibromyalgia). Overuse, injury, or strain. May result from statin therapy.
Paresthesia	Numbness and tingling, often described as a "pins and needles" sensation.	Compromised sensory nerves, often due to edema in a closed space (e.g., cast, bulky dressing). Spinal stenosis.
Pes planus (flatfoot)	Abnormal flatness of the sole and arch of the foot.	Hereditary, muscle paralysis, mild cerebral palsy, early muscular dystrophy, injury to posterior tibial tendon.
Plantar fasciitis	Burning, sharp pain on heel and sole of foot. Worse in the morning with first step out of bed.	Chronic degenerative/reparative cycle resulting in inflammation.
Scoliosis	Asymmetric elevation of shoulders, scapulae, and iliac crests with lateral spine curvature (Fig. 61.8).	Idiopathic or congenital condition, neuromuscular, fracture or dislocation, osteomalacia.
Short-leg gait	A limp, unless corrective footwear used.	Leg length discrepancy ≥1 in, generally of structural origin (arthritis, fracture).
Spastic gait	Short steps with dragging of foot. Jerky, uncoordinated, cross-knee (scissor) movement.	Neurogenic (e.g., cerebral palsy, hemiplegia).
Steppage gait	↑ Hip and knee flexion to clear the foot from the floor. Foot drop is evident, foot slaps down and along walking surface.	Neurogenic disorders (e.g., peroneal nerve injury, paralyzed dorsiflexor muscles).
Subluxation	Partial dislocation of joint.	Instability of joint capsule and supporting ligaments (e.g., trauma, arthritis).
Swan neck deformity	Hyperextension of the PIP joint with flexion of the metacarpophalangeal (MCP) and DIP joints of the fingers (see Fig. 64.4, D).	Typical deformity of rheumatoid and psoriatic arthritis caused by contracture of muscles and tendons.
Swelling	Enlargement, often of a joint due to fluid collection. Usually leads to pain, stiffness.	Trauma or inflammation.
Tenosynovitis	Superficial swelling, pain, and tenderness along a tendon sheath.	Inflammation that often occurs with infection, injury, or overuse.
Torticollis (wryneck)	Neck is rotated and laterally bent in unusual position to one side.	Prolonged contraction of neck muscles (congenital or acquired).
Ulnar deviation (ulnar drift)	Fingers drift to ulnar side of forearm (see Fig. 64.4, A).	Typical deformity of rheumatoid arthritis due to tendon contracture.
Valgum deformity (knock-knees)	When knees are together and there is <1 in (2.5 cm) between the medial malleoli.	Poliomyelitis, congenital deformity, arthritis.
Varum deformity (bowlegs)	When knees are apart and the medial malleoli are together, a space of >1 in (2.5 cm) exists.	Arthritis, congenital deformity.

DIAGNOSTIC STUDIES OF MUSCULOSKELETAL SYSTEM

Many diagnostic studies are used to assess the musculoskeletal system. Tables 61.7, 61.8, and 61.9 present the most common studies. Select studies are described in more detail next.

The use of studies such as x-rays, MRI, and bone scans has greatly improved orthopedic care. The x-ray is the most common diagnostic study used to assess musculoskeletal problems and to monitor treatment effectiveness. Because bones are denser than other tissues and contain calcium, most x-rays are absorbed by the bone tissue and do not penetrate it. Dense areas show as white on the standard x-ray. X-rays provide information about bone deformity, joint congruity, bone density, and calcification in soft tissue. X-rays are useful for diagnosing fractures. They also help evaluate genetic, developmental, infectious, inflammatory, malignant, metabolic, and degenerative disorders.

Aspirated synovial fluid is assessed for volume, color, clarity, viscosity, and mucin clot formation. Normal synovial fluid is transparent and colorless or straw colored. It should be scant in amount and of low viscosity. Fluid from an infected joint may be purulent and thick or gray and thin. In gout, the fluid may be whitish yellow. Blood may be aspirated if there is hemarthrosis due to injury or a bleeding disorder.

The mucin clot test indicates the character of the protein portion of the synovial fluid. Normally a white, ropelike mucin clot is formed. In the presence of inflammation, the clot fragments easily. The fluid is examined grossly for floating fat globules, which indicate bone injury. In septic arthritis, protein content is increased, and glucose is considerably decreased. Presence of uric acid crystals suggests a diagnosis of gout. A Gram stain and culture also may be done to assess for the presence and type of infection.

TABLE 61.7 Serology Studies

Musculoskeletal System

Test	Reference Intervals	Description and Purpose
Aldolase	22–59 mU/L	Useful in monitoring muscular dystrophy, dermatomyositis.
Alkaline phosphatase	30–120 U/L (0.5–2.0 µkat/L)	Enzyme made by osteoblasts, needed for mineralization of organic bone matrix. ↑ Levels found with healing fractures, bone cancers, osteoporosis, osteomalacia, Paget's disease.
Anticyclic citrullinated peptide (anti-CCP)	Negative or <20.0 U	Assesses presence of CCP antibodies. More specific for rheumatoid arthritis than rheumatoid factor. Positive result indicates high likelihood of RA.
Anti-DNA antibody	<5 IU/mL	Detects serum antibodies that react with DNA. Most specific test for SLE.
Antinuclear antibody (ANA)	Negative at 1:40 dilution	Assesses presence of antibodies capable of destroying nucleus of tissue cells. Positive in 95% of patients with SLE. May be positive in those with scleroderma, rheumatoid arthritis, small number of normal persons.
Calcium	9.0–10.5 mg/dL (2.25–2.62 mmol/L)	Bone is primary organ for calcium storage. Calcium provides bone with rigid structure. ↓ Level found in osteomalacia, kidney disease, hypoparathyroidism. ↑ Level found in hyperparathyroidism, some bone tumors.
C-reactive protein (CRP)	<1.0 mg/dL	Used to diagnose inflammatory diseases, infections, active widespread cancer. Synthesized by liver. Present in large amounts in serum 18–24 hr after onset of tissue damage.
Creatine kinase (CK)	*Male:* 55–170 U/L *Female:* 30–135 U/L	Highest concentration found in skeletal muscle. ↑ Level in progressive muscular dystrophy, polymyositis, traumatic injuries.
Human leukocyte antigen (HLA)–B27	Negative	Antigen often present in autoimmune disorders, such as ankylosing spondylitis and rheumatoid arthritis.
Potassium	3.5–5.0 mEq/L (3.5–5.0 mmol/L)	Released into serum with cell destruction. ↑ Level with muscle trauma.
Phosphorus	3.0–4.5 mg/dL (0.97–1.45 mmol/L)	Amount present is indirectly related to calcium metabolism. ↓ Level found in osteomalacia. ↑ Level found in chronic kidney disease, healing fractures, osteolytic metastatic tumor.
Rheumatoid factor (RF)	Negative or titer <1:17	Presence of autoantibody (rheumatoid factor) in serum. Not specific for rheumatoid arthritis. Seen in other connective tissue diseases and in a small number of normal persons.

TABLE 61.8 Diagnostic Studies

Musculoskeletal System

Study	Description and Purpose	Nursing Responsibilities
Basic x-ray	Evaluates structural or functional changes of bones and joints. Can give a general impression of bone density. In anteroposterior view, x-ray beam passes from front to back, allowing 1-dimensional view. Lateral position provides 2-dimensional view.	*Before:* Remove any radiopaque objects that can interfere with results. Explain procedure to patient. *During:* Avoid excessive exposure of patient and self.
Bone scan	Involves injection of radioisotope (usually technetium [Tc]-99m) that is taken up by bone. Uniform uptake of isotope is normal. ↑ Uptake seen in osteomyelitis, primary and metastatic cancer of bone, certain fractures. ↓ Uptake seen in areas of avascular necrosis.	*Before:* Explain that radioisotope is given 2 hr before procedure. Have patient void before scan. Tell patient that no harm will result from isotopes. *During:* Patient must lie completely still during scan. *After:* Increase fluids after scan.

TABLE 61.8 Diagnostic Studies—cont'd

Musculoskeletal System

Study	Description and Purpose	Nursing Responsibilities
Computed tomography (CT) scan	X-ray beam used with a computer to provide a 3D picture. Used to identify soft tissue abnormalities, bony abnormalities, and various types of musculoskeletal trauma.	*Before:* Evaluate renal function before contrast medium used. Assess if patient is allergic to shellfish since the contrast is iodine based. Patient may need to be NPO 4 hr prior to study. If the patient is taking metformin, hold it the day of the test to prevent hypoglycemia or lactic acidosis. *During:* Warn patient that contrast injection may cause a feeling of being warm and flushed. Patient must lie completely still during scan. *After:* Encourage patient to drink fluids to avoid renal problems with any contrast.
Discogram	X-ray of cervical or lumbar intervertebral disc is done after injection of contrast media into nucleus pulposus. Permits visualization of intervertebral disc abnormalities.	*Before:* Assess patient for allergy to contrast medium. Explain procedure. *After:* May have mild back pain for 1–2 days. Use as-needed analgesics.
Dual energy x-ray absorptiometry (DEXA)	Measures bone mineral density of spine, femur, forearm, total body. Allows assessment of bone density with minimal radiation exposure. Used to diagnose metabolic bone disease (e.g., osteoporosis), monitor changes in bone density with treatment.	*Before:* Remove any radiopaque objects that can interfere with results. Explain procedure to patient.
Electromyogram (EMG)	Evaluates electrical potential associated with skeletal muscle contraction. Small-gauge needles are inserted into certain muscles. Needle probes are attached to leads that send information to EMG machine. Recordings of electrical activity of muscle are traced on audio transmitter and on oscilloscope and recording paper. Provides information related to lower motor neuron dysfunction and primary muscle disease.	*Before:* Explain procedure. Tell patient that pain and discomfort are associated with insertion of needles. Some HCPs may restrict stimulants (e.g., caffeine) 2–3 hr prior. *After:* Assess needle sites for hematoma or inflammation. Use as-needed analgesics.
MRI	Radio waves and magnetic field used to view soft tissue. Used to diagnose avascular necrosis, disc disease, tumors, osteomyelitis, ligament tears, cartilage tears. Patient placed inside scanning chamber. Gadolinium may be injected IV to enhance visualization of structures.	*Before:* Oral and/or IV contrast injection may be used. Check for pregnancy, allergies, and renal function before test. Have patient remove all metal objects. Ask about any history of surgical insertion of staples, plates, dental bridges, or other metal appliances. Remove metallic foil patches. Patient may need to be fasting. Assess for claustrophobia and the need for antianxiety medication. *During:* Patient must lie completely still during test.
Myelogram with or without CT	Involves injecting a radiographic contrast medium into sac around nerve roots. CT scan may follow to show how bone is affecting the nerve roots. Sensitive test for nerve impingement, can detect subtle lesions and injuries.	*Before:* Give sedative as ordered. Have patient empty bladder. Tell patient that test is done with patient on tilting table that is moved during test. *After:* Keep patient flat for 1–2 hr after procedure to prevent spinal headache. Encourage fluids. Monitor neurologic signs and VS. Headache, nausea, and vomiting may occur after procedure.
Somatosensory evoked potential (SSEP)	Evaluates evoked potential of muscle contractions. Electrodes are placed on skin and provide recordings of electrical activity of muscle. Used to identify subtle dysfunction of lower motor neuron and primary muscle disease. Measures nerve conduction along pathways not accessible by EMG. Transcutaneous or percutaneous electrodes applied to the skin help identify neuropathy and myopathy. Used during spinal surgery for scoliosis to detect neurologic compromise when patient is under anesthesia.	*Before:* Tell patient that procedure is like an EMG but does not involve needles. Electrodes are applied to the skin.
Thermography	Uses infrared detector to measure degree of heat radiating from skin surface. Used to evaluate cause of inflamed joint and determine patient response to antiinflammatory drug therapy.	*Before:* Tell patient that procedure is painless and noninvasive.
Quantitative ultrasound (QUS)	Evaluates bone mineral density, elasticity, and strength of bone using ultrasound rather than radiation. Used to assess heel.	*Before:* Tell patient that procedure is painless and noninvasive.

TABLE 61.9 Interventional Studies

Musculoskeletal System

Study	Description and Purpose	Nursing Responsibilities
Arthrocentesis	Incision or puncture of joint capsule to obtain samples of synovial fluid or to remove excess fluid. Local anesthesia and aseptic preparation are used before needle is inserted into joint and fluid aspirated. Used to diagnose joint inflammation, infection, meniscal tears, and subtle fractures.	*Before:* Explain procedure to patient. HCP may have patient be NPO prior. Usually done at bedside or in examination room. *After:* Send samples of synovial fluid to laboratory for examination (if indicated). Apply compression dressing and ice to decrease pain and swelling. Observe for leakage of blood or fluid on dressing. Assess the joint for any pain, fever, or swelling. Review activity restrictions.
Arthroscopy	Involves insertion of arthroscope into joint to see interior of joint cavity. Can be used for surgery (removal of loose bodies, biopsy); repair of joint structures; and diagnosis of abnormalities of meniscus, articular cartilage, ligaments, or joint capsule. Structures that can be seen through an arthroscope include knee, shoulder, elbow, wrist, jaw, hip, and ankle (Fig. 61.9).	*Before:* Explain the procedure to the patient. Can be done in outpatient setting. Local or general anesthesia may be used. HCP may have patient be NPO prior. *After:* Cover wound with sterile dressing. Apply ice to decrease pain and swelling. Observe for bleeding. Assess the joint for any pain, weakness, or swelling. Review activity restrictions.

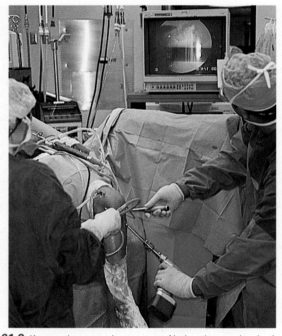

FIG. 61.9 Knee arthroscopy in progress. Notice the monitor in the background. (From Miller MD, Howard RF, Plancher KD: *Surgical atlas of sports medicine*, Philadelphia, 2003, Saunders.)

CASE STUDY—cont'd

Objective Data: Diagnostic Studies

(© pixelheadphoto/iStock/Thinkstock.)

The HCP in the ED immediately orders the following diagnostic studies:
- X-ray of left foot
- CBC, electrolytes
- Aspiration of the great toe

The x-ray of the foot shows minor soft tissue swelling but no evidence of fracture. Very mild arthritis is noted at the interphalangeal joint of the great toe. CBC and electrolytes are within normal limits.

Aspiration of the interphalangeal joint shows clear synovial fluid. Protein and glucose are within normal limits. Microscopic analysis of the synovial fluid shows urate crystals.

Discussion Questions

1. Which diagnostic results are abnormal?
2. What diagnostic study results are of most concern to you?

Answers available at *http://evolve.elsevier.com/Lewis/medsurg*.

▌ BRIDGE TO NCLEX EXAMINATION

The number of the question corresponds to the same-numbered outcome at the beginning of the chapter.

1. The bone cells that function in the formation of new bone tissue are called
   a. osteoids.
   b. osteocytes.
   c. osteoclasts.
   d. osteoblasts.
2. While performing passive range of motion for a patient, the nurse puts the elbow joint through the movements of *(select all that apply)*
   a. flexion and extension.
   b. inversion and eversion.
   c. pronation and supination.
   d. flexion, extension, abduction, and adduction.
   e. pronation, supination, rotation, and circumduction.

3. A patient with a torn ligament in the knee asks what the ligament does. The nurse's response is based on the knowledge that ligaments
   a. connect bone to bone.
   b. provide strength to muscle.
   c. lubricate joints with synovial fluid.
   d. relieve friction between moving parts.
4. The increased risk for falls in the older adult is likely due to *(select all that apply)*
   a. changes in balance.
   b. decrease in bone mass.
   c. loss of ligament elasticity.
   d. erosion of articular cartilage.
   e. decrease in muscle mass and strength.

5. The nurse is obtaining a health history of a patient with a fracture. Which condition poses the most concern related to the musculoskeletal system?
   a. Diabetes
   b. Hypertension
   c. Chronic bronchitis
   d. Nephrotic syndrome

6. When grading muscle strength, the nurse records a score of 3/5, which indicates
   a. no detection of muscular contraction.
   b. a barely detectable flicker of contraction.
   c. active movement against full resistance without fatigue.
   d. active movement against gravity but not against resistance.

7. An abnormal assessment finding of the musculoskeletal system is
   a. equal leg length bilaterally.
   b. ulnar deviation and subluxation.
   c. full range of motion in all joints.
   d. muscle strength of 5/5 in all muscles.

8. A patient is scheduled for a bone scan. The nurse explains that this diagnostic test involves
   a. incision or puncture of the joint capsule.
   b. insertion of small needles into certain muscles.
   c. administration of a radioisotope before the procedure.
   d. placement of skin electrodes to record muscle activity.

1. d, 2. c, 3. a, 4. a, b, c, 5. a, 6. d, 7. b, 8. c

For rationales to these answers and even more NCLEX review questions, visit *http://evolve.elsevier.com/Lewis/medsurg*.

ⓔ EVOLVE WEBSITE/RESOURCES LIST

http://evolve.elsevier.com/Lewis/medsurg
Review Questions (Online Only)
Key Points
Answer Keys for Questions
- Rationales for Bridge to NCLEX Examination Questions
- Answer Guidelines for Case Study on pp. 1434, 1436, 1438, and 1442
Conceptual Care Map Creator
Audio Glossary
Supporting Media
- Animation
- Overview of the Musculoskeletal System
Content Updates

REFERENCES

1. Crowther-Radulewicz CL: The musculoskeletal system. In McCance KL, Heuther SE, eds: *Pathophysiology: The biologic basis for disease in adults and children*, ed 8, St Louis, 2019, Mosby.
2. Chan BY, Gill, KG, Rebsamen SL, et al: MR imaging of pediatric bone marrow, *RadioGraphics* 36:1911, 2016.
3. Rachna C: Difference between tendons and ligaments. Retrieved from *https://biodifferences.com/difference-between-tendons-and-ligaments.html*.
4. Khodaee M: Common superficial bursitis, *Am Fam Physician* 95:224, 2017.
*5. Roberts S, Colombier P, Sowman A, et al: Ageing in the musculoskeletal system: Cellular function and dysfunction throughout life, *Acta Orthopaedica* 363:15, 2016.
*6. Hawker GA: The assessment of musculoskeletal pain, *Clinic Exp Rheumatol* 35:8, 2017.
*7. Langdahl BL: Osteoporosis in premenopausal women, *Cur Opin in Rheum* 29:410, 2017.
*8. Luz C, Bush T, Shen X: Do canes or walkers make any difference? Non-use and fall injuries, *The Gerontologist* 57:2, 2017.

*Evidence-based information for clinical practice.

62

Musculoskeletal Trauma and Orthopedic Surgery

Matthew C. Price

Never look down on anybody unless you're helping him up.

Jesse Jackson

http://evolve.elsevier.com/Lewis/medsurg

CONCEPTUAL FOCUS

Functional Ability	**Mobility**	**Perfusion**
Infection	**Pain**	**Safety**

LEARNING OUTCOMES

1. Distinguish the etiology, pathophysiology, manifestations, and interprofessional and nursing management of soft tissue injuries.
2. Relate the sequence of events involved in fracture healing.
3. Compare closed reduction, cast immobilization, open reduction, and traction in terms of purpose, complications, and nursing management.
4. Assess the neurovascular condition of an injured extremity.
5. Explain common complications associated with a fracture and fracture healing.
6. Describe the interprofessional and nursing management of patients with various kinds of fractures.
7. Describe indications for and interprofessional and nursing management of the patient with an amputation.
8. Describe types of joint replacement surgery.
9. Prioritize management of the patient having joint replacement surgery.

KEY TERMS

amputation, p. 1469
arthrodesis, p. 1474
arthroplasty, p. 1472
bursitis, p. 1450
carpal tunnel syndrome (CTS), p. 1448
compartment syndrome, p. 1460

debridement, p. 1472
dislocation, p. 1447
fat embolism syndrome (FES), p. 1461
fracture, p. 1450
osteotomy, p. 1472
phantom limb sensation, p. 1470

repetitive strain injury (RSI), p. 1447
sprain, p. 1445
strain, p. 1445
subluxation, p. 1447
synovectomy, p. 1472
traction, p. 1452

The most common cause of musculoskeletal injury is a traumatic event resulting in fracture, dislocation, subluxation, and/or soft tissue injury. Most of these injuries are not fatal. However, the cost in terms of pain, disability, medical expense, and lost wages is enormous. Accidents are 1 of the top 3 causes of death for persons ages 1 to 64 years.[1] Nurses play a key role in teaching the public about basic principles of safety and accident prevention.

This chapter discusses musculoskeletal problems resulting from trauma and common orthopedic surgical procedures. Following trauma or surgery, the injured area is often immobilized while healing occurs. The nurse's role in preventing complications (e.g., pressure injuries, constipation, infection, venous thromboembolism [VTE]) and promoting functional ability in patients with fractures and orthopedic surgery is emphasized.

HEALTH PROMOTION

Teach people in the community to take proper safety precautions to prevent injuries while at home or work, driving, or taking part in sports. The morbidity associated with accidents can be significantly reduced if people are aware of environmental hazards, use proper safety equipment, and apply safety and traffic rules. In the work setting, teach employees and employers about use of proper safety equipment and avoiding hazardous working situations.

♥ PROMOTING POPULATION HEALTH
Reducing the Risk for Musculoskeletal Injuries

- Regularly wear seatbelts.
- Drive within posted speed limits.
- Avoid distracted driving (e.g., no texting, eating, talking on a cell phone).
- Do not drive under the influence of alcohol or drugs (prescribed or illicit).
- Warm up muscles before exercise.
- Use protective athletic equipment (helmets and knee, wrist, and elbow pads).
- Use proper safety equipment at work.

Encourage people, especially older adults, to take part in moderate exercise to help maintain muscle strength and balance. Ways to prevent common musculoskeletal problems in the older adult are listed in Table 62.1. To reduce risk for falls, urge them to wear nonskid, hard-soled footwear and assess their living environment for safety risks (e.g., remove throw rugs, ensure adequate lighting, maintain clear paths to the bathroom for nighttime use). Stress the importance of adequate calcium and vitamin D intake for bone health.

⚠️ SAFETY ALERT Falls
- Falls cause many musculoskeletal injuries in the home.
- Provide preventive teaching to high-risk persons (e.g., people with gait instability, visual or cognitive impairment).
- Stress the importance of wearing shoes with functional, stable soles and heels.
- Remind patients to avoid wet or slippery surfaces.
- Encourage removal of throw rugs in the home.

TABLE 62.1 Patient & Caregiver Teaching
Prevention of Musculoskeletal Problems in Older Adults

To prevent musculoskeletal problems, include the following instructions when teaching older adults and their caregivers:
1. Use ramps in buildings and at street corners instead of steps to prevent falls.
2. Remove throw rugs from the home.
3. Treat pain and discomfort from osteoarthritis.
   - Rest in positions that decrease discomfort.
   - Use medication as prescribed for pain.
4. Use a walker or cane to help prevent falls.
5. Eat the amount and kind of foods needed to prevent weight gain. Obesity adds stress to joints, which may predispose to osteoarthritis.
6. Get regular and frequent exercise.
   - ADLs provide range-of-motion exercises. Tai Chi may be helpful.
   - Hobbies (e.g., jigsaw puzzles, needlework, model building) exercise finger joints and prevent stiffness.
   - Do daily weight-bearing exercise (e.g., walking) to improve bone health.
7. Use shoes with good support for safety and comfort.
8. Avoid sudden change in position. Rise slowly to a standing position to prevent dizziness, falls, and fractures.
9. Do not walk on uneven surfaces and wet floors.

SOFT TISSUE INJURIES

Soft tissue injuries include sprains, strains, dislocations, and subluxations. They usually result from trauma. As more people have become involved in fitness programs or sports, the incidence of soft tissue injuries has increased. Common sports-related injuries are described in Table 62.2. Sports injuries that often result in a visit to the emergency department (ED) for younger patients include sprains and strains, growth plate injuries, and repetitive motion injuries.[2]

SPRAINS AND STRAINS

Sprains and strains often result from abnormal stretching or twisting forces during vigorous activities. These injuries tend to occur around joints and in the spinal musculature.

A **sprain** is an injury to the ligaments surrounding a joint. Sprains are usually caused by a wrenching or twisting motion. Most occur in the ankle, wrist, and knee joints.[3] A sprain is classified according to the degree of ligament damage. A *first-degree (mild) sprain* involves tears in only a few fibers, with mild tenderness and minimal swelling. A *second-degree (moderate) sprain* results in partial disruption of the involved tissue with more swelling and tenderness. A *third-degree (severe) sprain* is a complete tear of the ligament with moderate to severe swelling.

A **strain** is an excessive stretching of a muscle and its fascial sheath, often involving the tendon. Most strains occur in the large muscle groups, including the lower back, calf, and hamstrings. Strains are classified as first degree (mild or slightly pulled muscle), second degree (moderate or moderately torn muscle), and third degree (severely torn or ruptured muscle). A defect in the muscle may be apparent or palpated through the skin if the muscle is torn. Because areas around joints are rich in nerve endings, the injury can be very painful.

Manifestations of sprains and strains are similar. They include pain, edema, decreased function, and bruising. Continued use of the joint, tendon, or ligament makes pain worse. Edema develops in the injured area because of the local inflammatory response.

Mild sprains and strains are usually self-limiting. Full function generally returns within 3 to 6 weeks. X-rays of the affected part may be taken to rule out a fracture. A severe sprain can

TABLE 62.2 Soft Tissue Injuries

Injury	Description	Treatment
Anterior cruciate ligament tear	Tearing of ligament by deceleration forces with pivoting or odd positions of the knee or leg.	PT with rehabilitation, knee brace. If knee instability or further injury, reconstructive surgery may be done.
Impingement syndrome	Entrapment of soft tissues and nerves under coracoacromial arch of shoulder.	NSAIDs. Rest until symptoms ↓, then begin gradual ROM and strengthening exercises.
Ligament injury	Tearing or stretching of ligament. Usually occurs from inversion, eversion, shearing, or torque applied to a joint. Characterized by sudden pain, swelling, and instability.	Rest, ice, elevation of extremity if possible, NSAIDs. Protect affected extremity by use of brace. If symptoms persist, surgical repair may be needed.
Meniscus injury	Injury to fibrocartilage discs in knee. Characterized by popping, clicking, tearing sensation, effusion, and/or swelling.	Rest, ice, elevation of extremity if possible, NSAIDs. Gradual return to regular activities. If symptoms persist, MRI to assess meniscus injury. Possible arthroscopic surgery.
Rotator cuff tear	Tear within muscle, tendons, or ligaments around shoulder.	*If minor tear:* rest, NSAIDs, and gradual mobilization with ROM and strengthening exercises. *If major tear:* surgical repair.
Shin splints	Inflammation of periosteal bone (*periostitis*) along anterior calf. Caused by improper shoes, overuse, or running on hard pavement.	Rest, ice, NSAIDs, proper shoes. Gradual ↑ in activity. If pain persists, x-ray to rule out tibial stress fracture.
Tendonitis	Inflammation of tendon due to overuse or incorrect use.	Rest, ice, NSAIDs. Gradual return to sport activity. Protective brace (*orthosis*) may be needed if symptoms recur.

cause an *avulsion fracture,* in which the ligament pulls loose a fragment of bone. The joint structure may become unstable, causing subluxation or dislocation. At the time of injury, *hemarthrosis* (bleeding into a joint space or cavity) or disruption of the synovial lining may occur. Severe strains may need surgical repair of the muscle, tendon, or surrounding fascia.

❖ NURSING MANAGEMENT: SPRAINS AND STRAINS

◆ Nursing Implementation

◆ **Health Promotion.** Warming up muscles before exercising and vigorous activity, followed by stretching, may significantly reduce the risk for sprains and strains. Strength, balance, and endurance exercises are important. Strengthening exercises that involve working against resistance build muscle strength and bone density. Balance exercises, which may overlap with some strengthening exercises, help prevent falls. Endurance exercises should start at a low level of effort and progress gradually to a moderate level.

💙 PROMOTING POPULATION HEALTH

Health Impact of Regular Physical Activity

- Helps with weight management.
- Increases lean muscle and decreases body fat.
- Helps maintain and improve bone mass.
- Increases muscle strength, flexibility, and endurance.
- Helps prevent high BP.
- Reduces the risk for heart disease, diabetes, and colon cancer.
- Enhances sense of well-being and reduces risk for depression.

◆ **Acute Care.** If an injury occurs, immediate care focuses on (1) stopping the activity and limiting movement to the injured part, (2) applying ice packs to the injured area, (3) compressing the involved area, (4) elevating the extremity, and (5) providing analgesia as needed (Table 62.3). Most sprains and strains are treated in the outpatient setting.

RICE (*R*est, *I*ce, *C*ompression, *E*levation) may decrease local inflammation and pain for most musculoskeletal injuries. Movement should be restricted, and the extremity rested as soon as pain is felt. Unless the injury is severe, prolonged rest is usually not needed.

There are several forms of cold therapy (*cryotherapy*) we can use. Cold causes vasoconstriction in the soft tissue and reduces the transmission and perception of nerve pain impulses. These changes also reduce muscle spasms, inflammation, and edema. Cold is most useful when applied immediately after an injury has occurred and used for 24 to 28 hours. Apply ice no more than 20 to 30 minutes at a time. Do not apply ice directly to the skin.

Compression helps decrease edema and pain. We often use an elastic compression bandage. It can be wrapped around the injured part. To prevent edema and encourage fluid return, wrap the bandage starting distally (at the point farthest from the trunk of the body) and progress proximally (toward the trunk of the body). The bandage is too tight if there is numbness or tingling below the area of compression or pain or more swelling occurs beyond the edge of the bandage. Leave the bandage in place for 30 minutes, then remove it for 15 minutes. Use of an elastic wrap may provide extra support during training, athletic, and work activities.

Elevate the injured part above heart level, even during sleep, for 24 to 48 hours to help mobilize excess fluid from the area and prevent further edema. Mild analgesics and nonsteroidal antiinflammatory drugs (NSAIDs) may be used to manage patient discomfort.

After the acute phase (usually 24 to 48 hours), apply warm, moist heat to the affected part to reduce swelling and provide comfort. Heat applications should not exceed 20 to 30 minutes, allowing a "cool-down" time between applications. Encourage the patient to use the limb if the joint is protected by a cast, brace, splint, or taping. Joint movement maintains nutrition to the cartilage. Muscle contraction improves circulation and helps

➕ TABLE 62.3 Emergency Management

Acute Soft Tissue Injury

Etiology	Assessment Findings	Interventions
• Crush injury • Direct blows • Falls • Motor vehicle crashes • Sports injuries	• Bruising • ↓ Movement with limited function or inability to bear weight (lower extremity) • ↓ Pulse, coolness, capillary refill >2 sec • ↓ Sensation • Edema • Muscle spasms • Pain, tenderness • Pallor • Shortening or rotation of extremity	**Initial** • Ensure airway, breathing, and circulation. • Perform neurovascular assessment of involved limb. • Elevate involved limb. • Apply compression bandage unless dislocation present. • Apply ice packs to affected area. • Immobilize affected extremity in the position found. Do *not* try to realign or reinsert protruding bones. • Anticipate x-rays of injured extremity. • Give analgesia as needed. • Give tetanus prophylaxis if there is an open fracture. • Give antibiotic prophylaxis for open fracture, large tissue defects, or mangled extremity injury. **Ongoing Monitoring** • Monitor for changes in neurovascular condition. • Implement weight-bearing restrictions as ordered for lower extremity involvement. • Anticipate compartment pressure monitoring if neurovascular assessment changes and compartment syndrome suspected.

resolve bruising and swelling. Movement also helps to prevent *contracture* (stiffening) of tendons and ligaments.

Emphasize the importance of strengthening and conditioning exercises to prevent reinjury.[4] The physical therapist may help with pain relief by using ultrasound or other interventions. The therapist may also teach the patient exercises to improve flexibility and strength.

DISLOCATION AND SUBLUXATION

Dislocation is the complete displacement or separation of the articular surfaces of the joint. Subluxation is a partial or incomplete displacement of the joint surface. Symptoms of subluxation are similar to those of a dislocation but are less severe. Multiple structures contribute to the stability of a joint. Injury to, or excessive laxity of, ligaments is a major factor in dislocations or subluxations. Weak or atrophied muscles can cause chronic joint instability. Fibrocartilage structures, such as the labrum around hip and shoulder sockets and the meniscus at the knee, play an important role in joint stability. Even small tears to these structures can result in recurrent, chronic dislocations or subluxations.

Dislocations typically result from forces on the joint that disrupt the surrounding soft tissue support structures. The joints most often dislocated in the upper extremity include the thumb, elbow, and shoulder. The shoulder most often dislocates anteriorly. Posterior shoulder dislocations are rare. They typically only happen after electrocution or seizure. In the lower extremity, the hip is vulnerable to dislocation from severe trauma, often associated with motor vehicle crashes (Fig. 62.1). The knee-cap *(patella)* may dislocate because of a sharp, direct blow or after a sudden twisting inward motion while the planted foot is pointed outward.[5]

The most obvious sign of a dislocation is deformity. For example, if the hip dislocates in a posterior (or backward) direction, the affected limb may be shorter and internally rotated. Other manifestations include local pain, tenderness, loss of function of the injured part, and swelling of soft tissues near the joint. Major complications of a dislocated joint are open joint injuries, *intraarticular* fractures (within the joint), *avascular necrosis* (bone cell death from blood supply), and damage to adjacent nerves and blood vessels.

X-rays can determine the extent of displacement. The joint may be aspirated to assess for hemarthrosis or fat cells. Fat cells in the aspirate indicate a probable intraarticular fracture.

❖ Interprofessional and Nursing Care

A dislocation requires prompt attention. It is often considered an orthopedic emergency because it may be associated with significant vascular injury. The longer the joint is dislocated, the greater the risk for avascular necrosis. The femoral head of the hip joint is especially susceptible to avascular necrosis. Compartment syndrome (discussed on p. 1460) may occur after dislocation due to vascular injury and resulting ischemia. Neurovascular assessment is critical (see pp. 1455–1456).

The first goal of management of a dislocation is to realign the dislocated part of the joint to its original anatomic position. Closed reduction (no incision) may be done under local or general anesthesia or IV moderate to deep sedation. Anesthesia is often needed to relax the muscle so that the bones can be manipulated. Sometimes, open reduction (joint visualized through surgical incision) may be needed. After

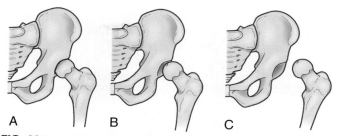

FIG. 62.1 Soft tissue injury of the hip. A, Normal. B, Subluxation (partial dislocation). C, Dislocation.

reduction, the extremity is immobilized by a brace, splint, or sling or by taping to allow torn ligaments and surrounding tissue to heal.

Nursing management is directed toward pain management and support and protection of the injured joint. After the joint has been reduced and immobilized, motion is usually restricted. A carefully monitored rehabilitation program can prevent further instability and joint dysfunction. Gentle range-of-motion (ROM) exercises may be done if the joint is stable and well supported. An exercise program slowly restores the joint to its original ROM without causing another dislocation. The patient should gradually return to normal activities.

A patient who has dislocated a joint may be at greater risk for repeated dislocations because of damage or laxity to the previously mentioned structures. Activity restrictions may be imposed on the affected joint to decrease the risk for repeated dislocations.

REPETITIVE STRAIN INJURY

Repetitive strain injury (RSI) and *cumulative trauma disorder* are terms used to describe injuries resulting from prolonged force or repetitive movements and awkward postures. RSI is also called *repetitive trauma disorder, nontraumatic musculoskeletal injury, overuse syndrome* (sports medicine), *regional musculoskeletal disorder,* and *work-related musculoskeletal disorder.* Repeated movements strain the tendons, ligaments, and muscles, causing tiny tears that become inflamed. The exact cause of these disorders is unknown. No specific diagnostic tests exist, and diagnosis is often difficult.

Persons at risk for RSI include musicians, dancers, butchers, grocery clerks, vibratory tool workers, and those who frequently use a computer mouse and keyboard. Competitive athletes and poorly trained athletes may develop RSI. Swimming, overhead throwing (e.g., baseball), weight lifting, gymnastics, tennis, skiing, and kicking sports (e.g., soccer) require repetitive motion. Overtraining compounds the effects of RSI.

Other factors related to RSI include poor posture and positioning, poor workspace ergonomics, badly designed workplace equipment (e.g., computer keyboard), and repetitive lifting of heavy objects without sufficient muscle rest. Inflammation, swelling, and pain in the muscles, tendons, and nerves of the neck, spine, shoulder, forearm, and hand may result. Symptoms of RSI include pain, weakness, numbness, or impaired motor function.

RSI can be prevented through education and *ergonomics* (the science that promotes efficiency and safety in the interaction of humans and their work environment). For example, ergonomic considerations for those who work at a desk and use a computer

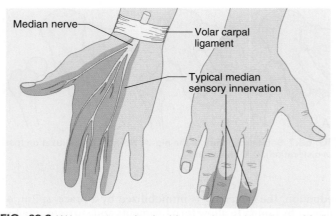

FIG. 62.2 Wrist structures involved in carpal tunnel syndrome. Median nerve distribution. *Shaded areas* show the locations of pain in carpal tunnel syndrome. (From Buttaravoli P: *Minor emergencies,* ed 3, Philadelphia, 2012, Saunders.)

include keeping the hips and knees flexed to 90 degrees with the feet flat, keeping the wrist straight to type, having the top of the computer monitor even with the forehead, and taking at least hourly stretch breaks.

Once RSI is diagnosed, treatment consists of (1) identifying the precipitating activity; (2) modifying equipment and/or activity; (3) pain management, including heat or cold therapy and NSAIDs; (4) rest; (5) physical therapy (PT) for strengthening and conditioning exercises; and (6) lifestyle changes.

CARPAL TUNNEL SYNDROME

Carpal tunnel syndrome (CTS) is caused by compression of the median nerve, which enters the hand at the wrist through the narrow carpal tunnel (Fig. 62.2). The carpal tunnel is formed by ligaments and bones. CTS is the most common compression neuropathy in the upper extremity. It is associated with hobbies or work that require continuous wrist movement (e.g., musicians, carpenters, computer operators).

CTS is often caused by pressure from trauma or edema (due to inflammation of a tendon *[tenosynovitis]*), cancer, rheumatoid arthritis (RA), or soft tissue masses, such as ganglia. Hormones may be involved because CTS often occurs during the premenstrual period, pregnancy, and menopause. Persons with diabetes, peripheral vascular disease (PVD), and RA have a higher incidence of CTS because of swelling that changes blood flow to the nerve and narrows the carpal tunnel.[6] Women are more likely than men to develop CTS, possibly because of a smaller carpal tunnel.

Manifestations of CTS are impaired sensation, pain, numbness, or weakness in the distribution of the median nerve (Fig. 62.2). Numbness and tingling may awaken the patient at night. Shaking the hands often relieves these symptoms. Clumsiness in performing fine hand movements is common.

The patient may have a positive Tinel's sign and Phalen's sign. *Tinel's sign* can be elicited by tapping over the median nerve as it passes through the carpal tunnel in the wrist. A positive response is a sensation of tingling in the distribution of the median nerve over the hand. *Phalen's sign* can be elicited by allowing the wrists to fall freely into maximum flexion and maintain the position for longer than 60 seconds. A positive response is a sensation of

tingling in the distribution of the median nerve over the hand. In late stages, atrophy of the muscles around the base of the thumb results in recurrent pain and eventual dysfunction of the hand.

❖ Interprofessional and Nursing Care

To prevent CTS, teach employees and employers to identify risk factors. Adaptive devices, such as wrist splints, may be worn to hold the wrist in a slight extension and relieve pressure on the median nerve. Special keyboard pads and computer mice that help prevent repetitive pressure on the median nerve are available for computer users. Other ergonomic changes include workstation modifications, change in body positions, and frequent breaks from work-related activities.

Care of the patient with CTS is directed toward relieving the underlying cause of the nerve compression. Early symptoms of CTS can usually be relieved by stopping the aggravating movement and by resting the hand and wrist by immobilization in a hand splint. Splints worn at night help keep the wrist in a neutral position and may reduce night pain and numbness. PT with hand and wrist exercises may lessen symptom severity. A corticosteroid injection directly into the carpal tunnel may give short-term relief. The patient may need to consider a change in occupation because of discomfort and sensory changes.

Carpal tunnel release is generally done if symptoms last more than 6 months or if there is significant impairment to conduction on electromyography (EMG). Surgery involves severing the band of tissue around the wrist to reduce pressure on the median nerve (Fig. 62.2). Surgery is done in the outpatient setting using local anesthesia. The types of carpal tunnel release surgery include open release and endoscopic surgery. In *open release surgery*, an incision is made in the wrist and then the carpal ligament is cut to enlarge the carpal tunnel. *Endoscopic carpal tunnel release* is performed through 1 or more small puncture incisions in the wrist and palm. A camera is attached to a tube, and the carpal ligament is cut. The endoscopic approach may allow a faster recovery and cause less discomfort than traditional open release surgery.

Although symptoms may be relieved right after surgery, full recovery may take months. After surgery, assess the hand's neurovascular status. Teach the patient about wound care and assessments to perform at home.

ROTATOR CUFF INJURY

The rotator cuff is made up of 4 muscles in the shoulder: the supraspinatus, infraspinatus, teres minor, and subscapularis muscles. These muscles stabilize the humeral head in the glenoid fossa while assisting with ROM of the shoulder joint and rotation of the humerus.

A tear in the rotator cuff may occur as a gradual, degenerative process due to aging, repetitive stress (especially overhead arm motions), or injury to the shoulder. In sports, repetitive overhead motions, such as in swimming, weight lifting, and swinging a racquet (tennis, racquetball), often cause injury. The rotator cuff can tear because of sudden adduction forces applied to the cuff while the arm is held in abduction. Other causes include (1) falling onto an outstretched arm and hand, (2) a blow to the upper arm, (3) heavy lifting, or (4) repetitive work motions.

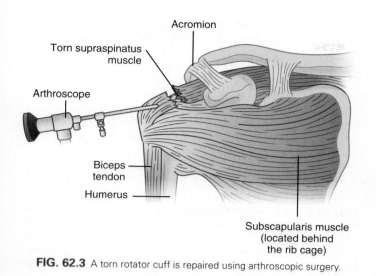

FIG. 62.3 A torn rotator cuff is repaired using arthroscopic surgery.

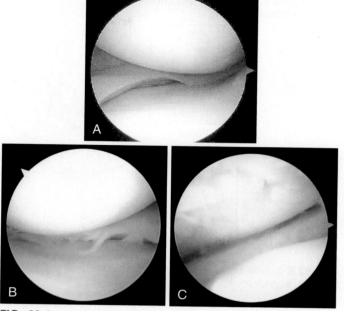

FIG. 62.4 Arthroscopic views of the meniscus. A, Normal meniscus. B, Torn meniscus. C, Surgically repaired meniscus. (A, From David Lintner, MD, Houston, TX, *www.drlintner.com. B* and *C,* Courtesy Peter Bonner, Placitas, NM.)

Manifestations include shoulder weakness, pain, and decreased ROM. The patient usually has severe pain when the arm is abducted between 60 and 120 degrees (the painful arc). A positive *drop arm test* is a sign of rotator cuff injury. In this test, the arm is abducted 90 degrees, and the patient is asked to slowly lower the arm to the side. If the arm falls suddenly, rotator cuff injury is suspected. An x-ray alone is not helpful in the diagnosis. A tear can usually be confirmed by MRI.

The patient with a partial tear or cuff inflammation may be treated conservatively with rest, ice and heat, NSAIDs, corticosteroid injections into the subacromial space, ultrasound, and PT. If the patient does not respond to conservative treatment or if a complete tear is present, surgical repair may be needed. Most surgical repairs are done as outpatient procedures through an arthroscope (Fig. 62.3). If the tear is extensive, part of the acromion may be surgically removed *(acromioplasty)* to relieve compression of the rotator cuff during movement. A shoulder immobilizer with an abduction pillow is typically used for 6 weeks after surgery to limit shoulder movement. However, the shoulder should not be immobilized for too long because "frozen" shoulder *(arthrofibrosis)* may occur. Pendulum exercises and other passive exercises typically begin the first postoperative day. Active PT starts after 6 weeks of immobilization. Weight restrictions for lifting are usually given. Full recovery may take 6 to 12 months.

MENISCUS INJURY

The menisci are crescent-shaped pieces of fibrocartilage in the knee. Menisci are also found in other joints, including the acromioclavicular (AC), sternoclavicular, and temporomandibular joints. Meniscus injuries are associated with ligament sprains common among athletes in sports such as basketball, football, soccer, and hockey.[7] These activities produce rotational stress when the knee is in varying degrees of flexion and the foot is planted or fixed. A blow to the knee can cause shearing of the meniscus between the femoral condyles and tibial plateau, causing a torn meniscus. Older adults and people who have jobs that require squatting or kneeling are at risk for degenerative tears.[7]

Meniscus injuries alone do not usually cause significant edema because most cartilage is avascular. However, an acutely torn meniscus may present with localized tenderness, pain, and effusion (Fig. 62.4). Pain occurs with flexion, internal rotation, and then extension of the knee *(McMurray's test).* The patient may feel that the knee is unstable and often reports that the knee "clicks," "pops," "locks," or "gives way." Quadriceps atrophy is usually present if the injury has been present for some time. Traumatic arthritis may occur from repeated meniscus injury and chronic inflammation.

MRI can confirm the diagnosis before arthroscopy. The patient's age, occupation, sport activities, degree of knee pain, and dysfunction may affect the decision whether to have surgery.

❖ Interprofessional and Nursing Care

Most meniscus injuries are treated in an outpatient setting. The acutely injured knee should be examined within 24 hours of injury. Initial care involves ice application, immobilization, and use of crutches with weight bearing as tolerated. Using a knee brace or immobilizer during the first few days after the injury protects the knee and offers some pain relief.

After acute pain has decreased, PT can help the patient regain knee flexion and muscle strength to aid in returning to full function. Teach athletes to do warm-up exercises to reduce the risk for sports-related injuries. In older adults with degenerative meniscus tears, progressive exercise therapy may improve neuromuscular function and muscle strength.[8]

Surgical repair or excision of part of the meniscus *(meniscectomy)* may be needed (Fig. 62.4). Meniscal surgery is done by arthroscopy. Pain relief may include NSAIDs or other analgesics. Rehabilitation starts soon after surgery, including quadriceps and hamstring strengthening exercises and ROM. When the patient's strength is back to its preinjury level, normal activities may be resumed.

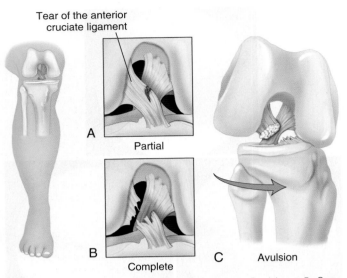

FIG. 62.5 Anterior cruciate ligament (ACL) injury. A, Partial tear. B, Complete tear. C, Avulsion.

ANTERIOR CRUCIATE LIGAMENT INJURY

Knee injuries account for more than 50% of all sports injuries. The most commonly injured knee ligament is the anterior cruciate ligament (ACL). ACL injuries are usually noncontact injuries that occur when the athlete pivots, lands from a jump, or stops abruptly when running. Patients often report coming down on the knee, twisting, and hearing a pop, followed by acute knee pain and swelling. The knee may feel unstable. Athletes usually cannot continue playing. Injury to the ACL can result in a partial tear, a complete tear, or an *avulsion* (tearing away) from the bones that form the knee (Fig. 62.5).

A positive *Lachman's test* suggests an ACL tear. This test is done by flexing the knee 15 to 30 degrees and pulling the tibia forward while the femur is stabilized. The test is considered positive for an ACL tear if forward motion of the tibia occurs with the feeling of a soft or indistinct endpoint. MRI is often used to diagnose an ACL tear and coexisting conditions, including a fracture, meniscus tearing, and collateral ligament injuries.

❖ Interprofessional and Nursing Care

Prevention programs can significantly reduce ACL injuries in athletes. Conservative treatment for an intact ACL injury includes rest, ice, NSAIDs, elevation, and ambulation as tolerated with crutches. If present, a tight, painful effusion may be aspirated. A knee immobilizer or hinged knee brace may provide support. PT often helps the patient maintain knee joint motion and muscle tone.

Reconstructive surgery is usually recommended for physically active patients who have sustained severe injury to the ACL and meniscus. In reconstruction, the torn ACL tissue is removed and replaced with graft tissue. ROM is encouraged soon after surgery. The knee is placed in a brace or immobilizer. Rehabilitation with PT is critical, with progressive weight bearing determined by the degree of surgical repair. A safe return to the patient's prior level of physical functioning may take 6 to 8 months.

BURSITIS

Bursae are closed sacs that are lined with synovial membrane and contain a small amount of synovial fluid. They are found at sites of friction, such as between tendons and bones and near the joints. Bursitis (inflammation of the bursa) results from repeated or excessive trauma or friction, gout, RA, or infection.

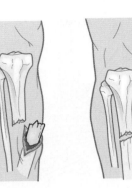

Open fracture   Closed fracture

FIG. 62.6 Fracture classification according to communication with the external environment.

Symptoms of bursitis include warmth, pain, swelling, and limited ROM in the affected part. Common sites are the hands, elbows, shoulders, knees, and greater trochanters of the hip. Improper body mechanics, repetitive kneeling (carpet layers, coal miners, and gardeners), jogging in worn-out shoes, and prolonged sitting with crossed legs are common precipitating activities.

Try to determine and correct the cause of the bursitis. Rest is often the only treatment needed. The affected part may be immobilized in a compression dressing or splint. Ice and NSAIDs can reduce pain and inflammation.[9] Aspiration of the bursal fluid and intraarticular corticosteroid injection may be needed. If the bursal wall has become thickened and continues to interfere with normal joint function, surgical excision (*bursectomy*) may be done. Septic bursae may be treated with oral antibiotics, but usually need surgical incision and drainage.

FRACTURES

Classification

A fracture is a disruption or break in the continuity of bone. Although traumatic injuries cause most fractures, some fractures are due to a disease process, such as cancer or osteoporosis (*pathologic fracture*).

We classify fractures in several ways. Fractures are described as *open* or *closed* based on communication with the external environment (Fig. 62.6). In an *open fracture*, the skin is broken and bone exposed, causing soft tissue injury. In a *closed fracture*, the skin is intact over the site.

We also describe fractures as complete or incomplete. A fracture is *complete* if the break goes completely through the bone. An *incomplete* fracture occurs partly across a bone shaft, but the bone is still intact. An incomplete fracture is often the result of bending or crushing forces applied to a bone.

Fractures are identified according to the direction of the fracture line. Types include linear, oblique, transverse, longitudinal, and spiral fractures (Fig. 62.7).

Finally, fractures can be classified as displaced or nondisplaced. In a *displaced* fracture, the 2 ends of the broken bone are separated from each other and out of their normal positions. Displaced fractures are often *comminuted* (more than 2

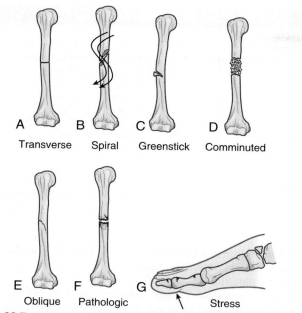

FIG. 62.7 Types of fractures. **A**, Transverse fracture: the line of the fracture extends across the bone shaft at a right angle to the longitudinal axis. **B**, Spiral fracture: the line of the fracture extends in a spiral direction along the bone shaft. **C**, Greenstick fracture: an incomplete fracture with 1 side splintered and the other side bent. **D**, Comminuted fracture: a fracture with more than 2 fragments. The smaller fragments appear to be floating. **E**, Oblique fracture: the line of the fracture extends across and down the bone. **F**, Pathologic fracture: a spontaneous fracture at the site of a diseased bone. **G**, Stress fracture: occurs in normal or abnormal bone that is subject to repeated stress, such as from jogging or running.

fragments) or *oblique* (Fig. 62.7). In a *nondisplaced* fracture, the bone fragments stay in alignment. Nondisplaced fractures are usually transverse, spiral, or greenstick (Fig. 62.7).

Manifestations

Manifestations include immediate localized pain, decreased function, and inability to bear weight or use the affected part (Table 62.4). The patient guards and protects the extremity against movement. Obvious bone deformity may be present.

Fracture Healing

Knowledge of the stages of fracture healing (Fig. 62.8) is needed to provide appropriate interventions. Bone goes through a complex multistage healing process *(union)* that occurs in 6 stages:

1. *Fracture hematoma:* When a fracture occurs, bleeding creates a hematoma that surrounds the ends of the bone fragments. The hematoma is composed of extravasated blood that changes from a liquid to a semisolid clot in the first 72 hours after injury.[10]
2. *Granulation tissue:* During this stage, active phagocytosis absorbs the products of local necrosis. The hematoma converts to granulation tissue. Granulation tissue (consisting of new blood vessels, fibroblasts, and osteoblasts) forms the basis for new bone substance *(osteoid)* during days 3 to 14 after injury.
3. *Callus formation:* As minerals (calcium, phosphorus, and magnesium) and new bone matrix are deposited in the osteoid, an unorganized network of bone is formed and woven about the fracture parts. *Callus* is primarily composed of

TABLE 62.4 Manifestations of Fracture

Manifestation	Significance
Bruising Discoloration of skin from extravasation of blood in subcutaneous tissues.	May appear immediately after injury and distal to injury. Reassure patient that process is normal, and discoloration will resolve.
Crepitation Grating or crunching of bony fragments, producing palpable or audible crunching or popping sensation.	May ↑ chance for nonunion if bone ends are allowed to move excessively. Micromovement of fragments (postfracture) helps in osteogenesis (new bone growth).
Deformity Abnormal position of extremity or part from original forces of injury and action of muscles pulling fragment into abnormal position. Seen as a loss of normal bony contours.	Classic sign of fracture. If uncorrected, it may cause problems with bony union and restoration of function of injured part.
Edema and Swelling Disruption or penetration of skin or soft tissues by bone fragments, or bleeding into surrounding tissues.	Unchecked bleeding and swelling in closed space can occlude blood vessels and damage nerves (e.g., ↑ risk for compartment syndrome).
Loss of Function Disruption of bone or joint, preventing functional use of limb or part.	Fracture must be managed properly to ensure restoration of function to limb or part.
Muscle Spasm Irritation of tissues and protective response to injury and fracture.	May displace nondisplaced fracture or prevent it from reducing spontaneously.
Pain and Tenderness Muscle spasm due to involuntary reflex action of muscle, direct tissue trauma, ↑ pressure on nerves, movement of fracture fragments.	Prompt the patient to splint muscle around fracture and reduce motion of injured area.

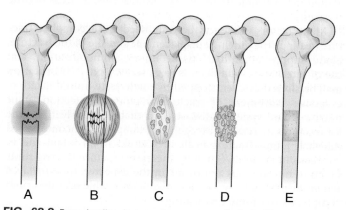

FIG. 62.8 Bone healing (schematic representation). **A**, Bleeding at fractured ends of the bone with hematoma formation. **B**, Organization of hematoma into fibrous network. **C**, Invasion of osteoblasts, lengthening of collagen strands, and deposition of calcium. **D**, Callus formation: new bone is built up as osteoclasts destroy dead bone. **E**, Remodeling is accomplished as excess callus is resorbed and trabecular bone is laid down.

TABLE 62.5 Complications of Fracture Healing

Complication	Description
Angulation	Fracture heals in abnormal position in relation to midline of structure (type of malunion).
Delayed union	Fracture healing progresses more slowly than expected. Healing eventually occurs.
Malunion	Fracture heals in expected time but in unsatisfactory position. May cause deformity or dysfunction.
Myositis ossificans	Deposition of calcium in muscle tissue at site of significant blunt muscle trauma or repeated muscle injury.
Nonunion	Fracture does not heal despite treatment. No x-ray evidence of callus formation.
Pseudoarthrosis	Type of nonunion occurring at fracture site in which a false joint is formed with abnormal movement at site.
Refracture	New fracture occurs at original fracture site.

TABLE 62.6 Interprofessional Care

Fractures

Diagnostic Assessment
- History and physical examination
- X-ray
- CT scan, MRI

Management
Fracture Reduction
- Manual traction
- Closed reduction
- Skeletal traction
- Open reduction

Fracture Immobilization
- Casting or splinting
- Skeletal traction
- External fixation
- Internal fixation

Open Fractures
- Surgical debridement and irrigation
- Tetanus and diphtheria immunization
- Prophylactic antibiotic therapy

cartilage, osteoblasts, calcium, and phosphorus. It usually appears by the end of the second week after injury. An x-ray can show evidence of callus formation.

4. *Ossification:* Ossification of the callus occurs from 3 weeks to 6 months after the fracture and continues until the fracture has healed. Callus ossification is sufficient to prevent movement at the fracture site when the bones are gently stressed. However, the fracture is still evident on x-ray. During this stage of *clinical union,* the patient may be allowed limited mobility, or the cast may be removed.

5. *Consolidation:* As callus continues to develop, the distance between bone fragments decreases and eventually closes. Ossification continues and can be equated with *radiologic union,* which occurs when an x-ray shows complete bony union. This phase can occur up to 1 year after injury.

6. *Remodeling:* Excess bone tissue is resorbed in the last stage of bone healing, and union is complete. Gradual return of the injured bone to its preinjury structural strength and shape occurs. Bone remodels in response to physical loading stress (Wolff's law). Initially, stress is provided through exercise. Weight bearing is gradually introduced. New bone is deposited in sites subjected to stress and resorbed at areas of little stress.

Many factors influence the time needed for complete fracture healing. They include displacement and site of the fracture, blood supply, other local tissue injury, immobilization, and use of internal fixation devices (e.g., screws, pins). Ossification may be slowed or even stopped by inadequate immobilization, excessive movement of fracture fragments, infection, poor nutrition, and systemic disease (e.g., diabetes).[11] Healing time for fractures increases with age. For example, an uncomplicated midshaft femur fracture heals in 3 weeks in an infant and in 20 weeks in an adult. Smoking increases fracture healing time. Fracture healing may not occur in the expected time *(delayed union)* or may not occur at all *(nonunion).* Table 62.5 describes complications of fracture healing.

Interprofessional Care

The overall goals of fracture treatment are (1) anatomic realignment of bone fragments through reduction, (2) immobilization to maintain realignment, and (3) restoration of normal or near-normal function of the injured part. Table 62.6 outlines the interprofessional care of fractures.

Fracture Reduction

Closed Reduction. Closed reduction is the nonsurgical, manual realignment of bone fragments to their anatomic position. Traction and countertraction are manually applied to the bone fragments to restore position, length, and alignment. Closed reduction is usually done while the patient is under local or general anesthesia. Traction, casting, splints, or orthoses (braces) may be used after reduction to maintain alignment and immobilize the injured part until healing occurs.

Open Reduction. Open reduction is the correction of bone alignment through a surgical incision. It usually includes internal fixation of the fracture with wires, screws, pins, plates, intramedullary rods, or nails. The type and location of the fracture, patient age, and concurrent disease influence the decision to use open reduction. The main risks of open reduction are infection, complications associated with anesthesia, and effects of preexisting medical conditions (e.g., diabetes). However, open reduction internal fixation (ORIF) facilitates early ambulation, thus decreasing the risk for complications related to prolonged immobility.

Traction. Traction is the application of a pulling force to an injured or diseased body part or extremity. Traction is used to (1) prevent or reduce pain and muscle spasm (e.g., whiplash, unrepaired hip fracture), (2) immobilize a joint or part of the body, (3) reduce a fracture or dislocation, and (4) treat a pathologic joint condition (e.g., tumor, infection). Traction is also used to (1) provide immobilization to prevent soft tissue damage, (2) promote active and passive exercise, (3) expand a joint space during arthroscopic procedures, and (4) expand a joint space before major joint reconstruction.

Traction devices apply a pulling force on a fractured extremity to attain realignment while *countertraction* pulls in the opposite direction. The most common types of traction are skin traction and skeletal traction. *Skin traction* is generally used for short-term treatment (48 to 72 hours) until skeletal traction or surgery is possible. Tape, boots, or splints are applied directly to the skin, mainly to help decrease muscle spasms in the injured extremity. Traction weights are usually 5 to 10 lb (2.3 to 4.5 kg). *Buck's traction* is a type of skin traction sometimes used for the patient with a hip, knee, or femur fracture (Fig. 62.9).[12] Pelvic or cervical skin traction may require heavier weights applied intermittently. In skin traction, regular assessment of the skin is a priority because pressure points

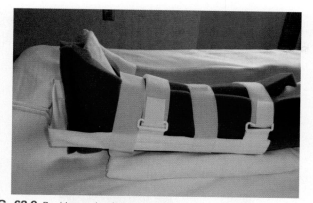

FIG. 62.9 Buck's traction is most often used for fractures of the hip and femur. (Courtesy Mary Wollan, RN, BAN, ONC, Spring Park, MN.)

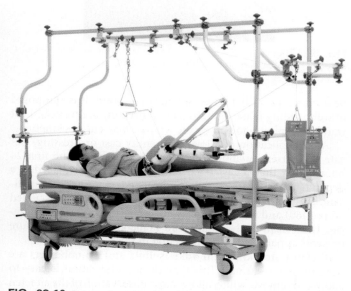

FIG. 62.10 Balanced suspension skeletal traction. Most often used for fractures of the femur, hip, and lower leg. (Courtesy Zimmer, Inc.)

and skin breakdown may develop quickly. Assess key pressure points every 2 to 4 hours.

Skeletal traction is used to align injured bones and joints or to treat joint contractures and congenital hip dysplasia. It provides a long-term pull that keeps the injured bones and joints aligned. To apply skeletal traction, the HCP inserts a pin or wire into the bone, and weights are attached to align and immobilize the injured body part. Weight for skeletal traction ranges from 5 to 45 lb (2.3 to 20.4 kg). The use of too much weight can result in delayed union or nonunion. The major complications of skeletal traction are infection at the pin insertion site and the effects of prolonged immobility.

A common type of skeletal traction is balanced suspension traction (Fig. 62.10). Fracture alignment depends on the correct positioning and alignment of the patient while the traction forces stay constant. For extremity traction to be effective, forces also must be pulling in the opposite direction (*countertraction*). Countertraction is supplied by the patient's body weight or by weights pulling in the opposite direction. Elevating the end of the bed can help. Traction must be maintained continuously. Keep the weights off the floor and moving freely through the pulleys.

Fracture Immobilization. Fracture immobilization is achieved with casts, braces, splints, immobilizers, and external and internal fixation devices.

Casts. A *cast* is a temporary immobilization device often applied after closed reduction. It allows the patient to perform many normal ADLs while providing enough immobilization to ensure stability. A cast generally immobilizes the joints above and below a fracture. This restricts tendon and ligament movement, thus assisting with joint stabilization while the fracture heals. The 2 most common cast materials are natural (plaster of Paris) and fiberglass. We use fiberglass casts most often because they are lighter, relatively waterproof, and longer wearing than plaster of Paris.[13] They also allow early weight bearing. Plaster of Paris is now used primarily for contact casting in the treatment of diabetic foot ulcers.[14]

To apply a cast on an extremity, first cover the affected part with stockinette that is cut longer than the extremity. Then place cotton padding over the stockinette, with extra padding for bony prominences. If using plaster of Paris, immerse it in warm water and then wrap and mold it around the affected part. The number of layers of plaster bandage and the technique of application determine the strength of the cast. The plaster sets within 15 minutes, so the patient may move around without difficulty. However, it is not strong enough for weight bearing until about 36 to 72 hours after application.[13] The decision about the patient's weight bearing is made by the HCP. Casts made of fiberglass or other synthetic materials (thermolabile plastic, thermoplastic resins, polyurethane) are activated by submersion in cool or tepid water. Then they are molded to fit the torso or extremity.

Leave a fresh plaster cast uncovered to allow air circulation. Covering the cast allows heat to build up in the cast. This may cause a burn and delay drying. Avoid direct pressure on the cast during the drying period. Handle the cast gently with an open palm to avoid denting the cast. Once the cast is thoroughly dry, the rough edges may be *petaled* to minimize skin irritation. Petaling also prevents plaster of Paris debris from falling into the cast and causing irritation or pressure necrosis. Place several strips (petals) of tape over the rough areas to ensure a smooth cast edge.

Upper extremity injuries. An acute fracture or soft tissue injury of the upper extremity can be immobilized by using a (1) sugar-tong splint, (2) posterior splint, (3) short arm cast, or (4) long arm cast (Fig. 62.11). The *sugar-tong splint* is applied for acute wrist injuries or injuries that may result in significant swelling. Splints are placed over a well-padded forearm, beginning at the phalangeal joints of the hand, extending up the dorsal aspect of the forearm around the distal humerus, and then down the volar aspect of the forearm to the distal palmar crease. The splinting material is wrapped with either elastic bandage or bias stockinette. The sugar-tong posterior splint accommodates early swelling in the fractured extremity.

The *short arm cast* is often used for the treatment of stable wrist or metacarpal fractures. An aluminum finger splint can be built into the short arm cast for treatment of phalangeal injuries. The short arm cast is a circular cast extending from the distal palmar crease to the proximal forearm. This cast immobilizes the wrist and allows unrestricted elbow motion.

The *long arm cast* is often used for stable forearm or elbow fractures and unstable wrist fractures. It is similar to the short arm cast but extends to the proximal humerus, restricting motion at the wrist and elbow. Support the extremity and

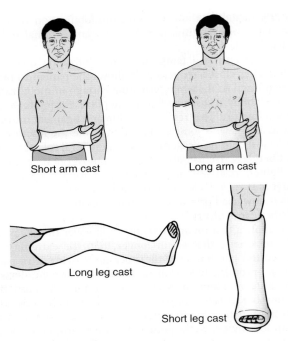

Short arm cast

Long arm cast

Long leg cast

Short leg cast

FIG. 62.11 Common types of casts.

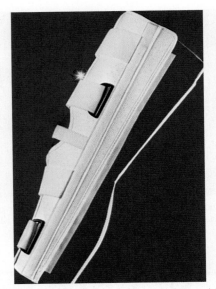

FIG. 62.12 Knee immobilizer. (From Maher AB, Salmond SW, Pellino T, editors: *Orthopedic nursing,* ed 3, Philadelphia, 2002, Saunders.)

reduce edema by elevating the extremity with a sling. However, when a hanging arm cast is used for a proximal humerus fracture, avoid elevation or use of a supportive sling. The hanging provides traction and maintains fracture alignment.

When a sling is used, ensure the axillary area is well padded to prevent skin breakdown from direct skin-to-skin contact. Apply the sling carefully to avoid putting undue pressure on the neck. Encourage movement of the fingers (unless contraindicated) to decrease edema by enhancing the pumping action of blood vessels. Teach the patient to actively move joints of the upper extremity if not immobilized to prevent stiffness and contractures.

Vertebral injuries. The *body jacket brace* is used for immobilization and support for stable spine injuries of the thoracic or lumbar spine. The brace goes around the chest and abdomen, extending from above the nipple line to the pubis. After application of the brace, assess the patient for the development of superior mesenteric artery syndrome (*cast syndrome*). This condition occurs if the brace is too tight, compressing the superior mesenteric artery against the duodenum. The patient generally has abdominal pain, abdominal pressure, nausea, and vomiting. Assess the abdomen for decreased bowel sounds (there may be a window in the brace over the umbilicus). Treatment of cast syndrome includes gastric decompression with a nasogastric (NG) tube and suction. Assess respiratory status, bowel and bladder function, and areas of pressure over the bony prominences, especially the iliac crest. The brace may have to be adjusted or removed if any complications occur.

Lower extremity injuries. Injuries to the lower extremity can be immobilized with a long leg cast, short leg cast, cylinder cast, or prefabricated splint or immobilizer. The usual indications for a long leg cast are an unstable ankle fracture, soft tissue injuries, a fractured tibia, and knee injuries. The cast usually extends from the base of the toes to the groin and gluteal crease. The short leg cast is used for stable ankle and foot injuries. A cylinder cast is used for knee injuries or fractures. It extends from the groin to the malleoli of the ankle. A Robert Jones dressing may

be used temporarily to limit mobility of a joint. It is composed of soft padding materials (absorption dressing and cotton sheet wadding), splints, and an elastic wrap or bias-cut stockinette.

After application of a lower extremity cast or dressing, elevate the extremity above the heart on pillows for the first 24 hours. After that, a casted extremity should not be placed in a dependent position as this may increase edema. After cast application, observe for signs of compartment syndrome (discussed on p. 1460) and increased pressure, especially in the heel, anterior tibia, head of the fibula, and malleoli. Increased pressure presents as pain or a burning feeling in these areas.

Prefabricated knee and ankle splints and immobilizers are used in many settings. This type of immobilization is easy to apply and remove, which allows close observation of the affected joint for swelling and skin breakdown (Fig. 62.12). Depending on the injury, removal of the splint or immobilizer promotes ROM of the affected joint and faster return to function.

The *hip spica cast* is mainly used for femur fractures in children to immobilize the affected extremity and trunk. It extends from above the nipple line to the base of the foot (single spica) and may include the opposite extremity up to an area above the knee (spica and a half) or both extremities (double spica). Assess the patient with a hip spica cast for the same problems associated with the body jacket brace.

External Fixation. An *external fixator* is composed of metal pins and wires that are inserted into the bone and attached to external rods to stabilize the fracture while it heals (Fig. 62.13). It can be used to apply traction or to compress fracture fragments and immobilize reduced fragments when the use of a cast or traction is not appropriate. The external device holds fracture fragments in place similar to a surgically implanted internal device. External fixation is used mainly for complex fractures with extensive soft tissue damage, correction of congenital bony defects, nonunion or malunion, and limb lengthening.

External fixation is often used to try to salvage extremities that otherwise may require amputation. Because the use of an external device is a long-term process, ongoing assessment for pin loosening and infection is critical. Infection may require removal of the device. Teach the patient and caregiver about

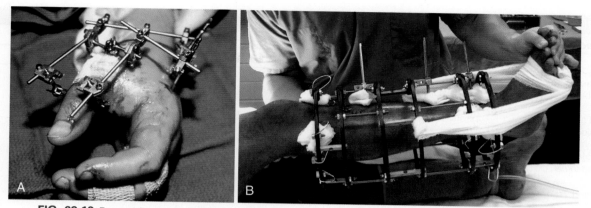

FIG. 62.13 External fixators. **A,** Stabilization of hand injury. **B,** Stabilization of a tibial fracture. (*A,* Courtesy Howmedica, Inc, Allendale, PA. *B,* From Canale ST, Beaty JH: *Campbell's operative orthopedics,* ed 12, Philadelphia, 2013, Mosby.)

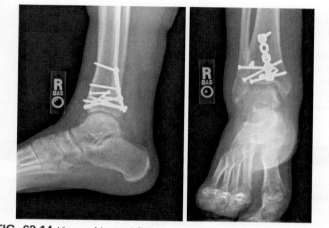

FIG. 62.14 Views of internal fixation devices to stabilize a fractured tibia and fibula. (From Jeremy Lewis, MD, Albuquerque, NM.)

meticulous pin care. Although each HCP has a protocol for pin care cleaning, chlorhexidine is often used.[15]

Internal Fixation. Internal fixation devices (pins, plates, intramedullary rods, metal and bioabsorbable screws) are surgically inserted to realign and maintain position of bony fragments (Fig. 62.14). These metal devices are biologically inert and made from stainless steel, vitallium, or titanium. Proper alignment and bone healing are evaluated regularly by x-rays.

Electrical Bone Growth Stimulation. Electrical bone growth stimulation can promote healing, especially with fracture nonunion or delayed union. The mechanism of action may include (1) increasing calcium uptake and the production of bone growth factors, (2) increasing collagen synthesis, and (3) promoting the growth of new blood vessels.[16]

There are noninvasive, semi-invasive, and invasive methods of electrical bone growth stimulation. Noninvasive stimulators use direct current or pulsed electromagnetic fields (PEMFs) to generate a weak electrical current. Electrodes are typically in a band applied over the patient's skin or cast and worn 10 to 12 hours each day, usually while the patient is sleeping. Semi-invasive or percutaneous bone growth stimulators use an external power supply and electrodes that are inserted through the skin and into the bone. Invasive stimulators require surgical implantation of a current generator in an IM or subcutaneous space. An electrode is implanted in the bone fragments.

Drug Therapy. Patients with fractures have varying degrees of pain associated with muscle spasms. Central and peripheral muscle relaxants, such as carisoprodol (Soma), cyclobenzaprine, or methocarbamol (Robaxin), may be given to manage pain associated with muscle spasms.

Give tetanus and diphtheria toxoid or tetanus immunoglobulin to the patient with an open fracture who has not been previously immunized or whose immunization is expired (see Table 68.6). Bone-penetrating antibiotics, such as a cephalosporin (e.g., cefazolin), are used prophylactically before surgery.

Nutritional Therapy. Proper nutrition is essential to ensure optimal soft tissue and bone healing. An adequate energy source is needed to promote muscle strength and tone, build endurance, and provide energy for ambulation and gait-training skills. The patient's dietary requirements must include adequate protein (e.g., 1 g/kg of body weight), vitamins (especially B, C, and D), calcium, phosphorus, and magnesium. Low serum protein and vitamin C deficiencies interfere with tissue healing. Immobility and bone healing increase calcium needs.

A fluid intake of 2000 to 3000 mL/day promotes optimal bladder and bowel function. Adequate fluid and a high-fiber diet with fruits and vegetables prevent constipation. If immobilized in bed with skeletal traction or in a body jacket brace, the patient should eat 6 small meals. This helps avoid overeating that can cause abdominal pressure and cramping.

❖ NURSING MANAGEMENT: FRACTURES

◆ Nursing Assessment

A brief history of the traumatic episode, mechanism of injury, and position in which the patient was found can be obtained from the patient or witnesses. As soon as possible, the patient should be transported to an ED, where thorough assessment can be done and treatment started (Table 62.7). Subjective and objective data that should be obtained from a person with a fracture are outlined in Table 62.8.

If a fracture is suspected, the extremity is immobilized in the position in which it is found. Unnecessary movement increases risk for damage to adjacent nerves and blood vessels. It may also convert a closed fracture to an open fracture.

◆ Neurovascular Assessment. A thorough neurovascular assessment of the affected extremity, distal to the fracture site, is a primary concern. Musculoskeletal injuries may cause changes in the neurovascular status of an injured extremity. Poor

✚ **TABLE 62.7 Emergency Management**

Fractured Extremity

Etiology	Assessment Findings	Interventions
Blunt Trauma • Direct blow • Fall • Forced flexion or hyper-extension • Motor vehicle crash • Pedestrian event • Twisting force **Penetrating Trauma** • Blast • Gunshot **Other** • Pathologic condition • Violent muscle contraction (seizures) • Crush injury	• Bruising • ↓ Distal pulses • Deformity or unnatural position of affected limb • Edema • Grating (crepitus) • Loss of function • Muscle spasm • Numbness, tingling • Tenderness, pain • Warmth at site • Wound over injured site, exposure of bone	**Initial** • Treat life-threatening injuries first. • If unresponsive, assess circulation, airway, and breathing. • If responsive, monitor airway, breathing, and circulation. • Control external bleeding with direct pressure or sterile pressure dressing and elevation of the extremity. • Assess neurovascular condition distal to injury before and after splinting. • Elevate injured limb if possible. • Do not try to straighten fractured or dislocated joints. • Do not manipulate protruding bone ends. • Apply ice packs to affected area. • Obtain x-rays of affected limb. • Give tetanus prophylaxis if there is a break in skin integrity. • Mark location of pulses to aid repeat assessment. • Splint fracture site, including joints above and below fracture site. **Ongoing Monitoring** • Assess vital signs, level of consciousness, O_2 saturation, neurovascular condition, pain. • Assess for compartment syndrome (excessive pain, pain with passive stretch of the affected extremity muscles, pallor, paresthesia, with late signs of paralysis and pulselessness). • Assess for FES (dyspnea, chest pain, temperature elevation).

TABLE 62.8 Nursing Assessment

Fracture

Subjective Data

Important Health Information

Past health history: Traumatic injury, long-term repetitive forces (stress fracture), bone or systemic diseases, prolonged immobility, osteopenia, osteoporosis

Medications: Corticosteroids (osteoporotic fractures); analgesics

Surgery or other treatments: First aid treatment of fracture, musculoskeletal surgeries

Functional Health Patterns

Health perception–health management: Calcium and vitamin D supplementation

Activity-exercise: Loss of motion or weakness of affected part, muscle spasms

Cognitive-perceptual: Sudden and severe pain in affected area; numbness, tingling, loss of sensation distal to injury; ongoing pain that increases with activity (stress fracture)

Objective Data

General

Apprehension, guarding of injured site

Integumentary

Skin lacerations, pallor and cool skin or bluish and warm skin distal to injury; bruising, edema at fracture site

Cardiovascular

Reduced or absent pulse distal to injury, ↓ skin temperature, delayed capillary refill

Neurovascular

Paresthesia, absent or ↓ sensation, hypersensation

Musculoskeletal

Restricted or lost function of affected part; local bony deformities, abnormal angulation; shortening, rotation, or crepitation of affected part; muscle weakness

Possible Diagnostic Findings

Identification and extent of fracture on x-ray, bone scan, CT scan, or MRI

positioning, physiologic responses to the traumatic injury, and application of a cast or constrictive dressing can cause nerve or vascular damage, usually distal to the injury. Record clinical findings before fracture treatment. This way if a problem occurs later, it will help determine if it was missed during the original examination or a result of treatment.

The neurovascular assessment consists of *peripheral vascular assessment* (color, temperature, capillary refill, peripheral pulses, edema) and *peripheral neurologic assessment* (sensation, motor function, pain). Throughout the neurovascular assessment, compare both extremities to obtain an accurate assessment.

Assess an extremity's color (pink, pale, cyanotic) and temperature (hot, warm, cool, cold) around the injury. Pallor or a cool-to-cold extremity below the injury could indicate arterial insufficiency. A warm, cyanotic extremity could indicate poor venous return. Next, assess capillary refill. A delay in returning to its original color (greater than 3 seconds) can occur with arterial insufficiency.[17]

Compare pulses on the unaffected and injured extremities to identify differences in rate or quality. This contralateral evaluation is critical. A decreased or absent pulse distal to the injury can indicate vascular dysfunction and insufficiency. Assess peripheral edema. Pitting edema may be present with severe injury.

Assess ulnar, median, and radial nerve function to evaluate sensation and motor innervation in the upper extremity. Assess motor function by asking the patient to (1) abduct the fingers (ulnar nerve), (2) oppose the thumb and small finger (median nerve), and (3) flex and extend the wrist (or the fingers, if in a cast) (radial nerve). In the lower extremity, assess the patient's ability to perform dorsiflexion (peroneal nerve) and plantar flexion (tibial nerve). Evaluate sensory function of the peroneal nerve by touching the web space between the great and second toes. Stroke the plantar surface (sole) of the foot to assess sensory function of the tibial nerve.

The patient may report *paresthesia* (abnormal sensation [e.g., numbness, tingling]) and hypersensation or hyperesthesia. Partial or full loss of sensation (paresis or paralysis) may be a late sign of neurovascular damage. Teach the patient to immediately report any changes in sensation or the ability to move the digits in the affected extremity.

◆ Nursing Diagnoses

Nursing diagnoses for the patient with a fracture may include:
- Impaired physical mobility
- Risk for infection
- Acute pain

Additional information on nursing diagnoses and interventions for the patient with a fracture is presented in eNursing Care Plan 62.1 (on the website for this chapter).

◆ Planning

The overall goals are that the patient with a fracture will (1) have healing with no associated complications, (2) have acceptable pain relief, and (3) achieve maximal rehabilitation potential.

◆ Nursing Implementation

Acute Care. Patients with fractures may be treated in an ED or an HCP's office and released to home care. They also may need hospitalization for varying amounts of time. Specific nursing measures depend on the setting and type of treatment.

Preoperative Care. If surgical intervention is needed to treat a fracture, patients must be prepared. In addition to the usual preoperative nursing care (see Chapter 17), teach the patient about the type of immobilization and assistive devices that will be used. Discuss expected activity limitations after surgery. Assure them that nursing staff will help meet their personal needs until they can resume self-care. Review pain management strategies.

Postoperative Care. In general, nursing care after surgery involves monitoring vital signs and applying general principles of postoperative nursing care (see Chapter 19). Frequent neurovascular assessment of the affected extremity is needed to detect early and subtle changes. Carefully follow any limitations related to turning, positioning, and extremity support. Minimize pain and discomfort through proper alignment and positioning. Frequently observe dressings or casts for any signs of bleeding or drainage. Report a significant increase in size of the drainage area to the HCP. If a wound drainage system is in place, regularly measure the volume of drainage and assess its character (e.g., bloody, purulent). Report increased or purulent drainage at once to the HCP. Maintain the patency of any drainage systems, using aseptic technique to avoid contamination.

Other nursing responsibilities depend on the type of immobilization used. A blood salvage and reinfusion system may be used to allow recovery and reinfusion of the patient's own blood. The blood is retrieved from a joint space or cavity; then the patient receives this blood in the form of an autotransfusion. (Autotransfusion is discussed in Chapter 30.)

Other Measures. Patients often have reduced mobility because of a fracture. Plan care to decrease risk for the many possible complications of immobility. Prevent constipation by increasing patient activity. Maintain high fluid intake (more than 2500 mL/day unless contraindicated by the patient's health status) and a diet high in bulk and roughage (fresh fruits and vegetables). If these measures are not effective in continuing the patient's normal bowel elimination pattern, give stool softeners, laxatives, or suppositories. Maintain a regular time for elimination to promote bowel regularity.

Renal stones can develop from bone demineralization due to reduced mobility. Hypercalcemia from demineralization causes a rise in urine pH and stone formation from calcium precipitation. Unless contraindicated, maintain a fluid intake of 2500 mL/day to decrease the risk for stone formation. (Renal stones are discussed in Chapter 45.)

Rapid deconditioning of the cardiopulmonary system can occur from prolonged bed rest, resulting in orthostatic hypotension and decreased lung capacity. Unless contraindicated, decrease these effects by having the patient sit on the side of the

---

NURSING MANAGEMENT
Caring for the Patient With a Cast or Traction

- Perform neurovascular assessment on the affected extremity.
- Monitor pain intensity and give prescribed analgesics.
- Determine correct body alignment to enhance traction.
- Monitor skin integrity around cast and at traction pin sites.
- Monitor cast during drying for denting or flattening.
- Teach patient and caregiver about cast care or traction and measures to prevent complications (e.g., ROM exercises).
- Assess for complications associated with immobility (e.g., constipation, VTE, kidney stones, atelectasis) and develop a plan to minimize those complications.
- Oversee unlicensed assistive personnel (UAP):
  - Position casted extremity above heart level as directed by RN.
  - Apply ice to cast as directed by RN.
  - Maintain body position and integrity of traction (if trained in this procedure).
  - Help patient with passive and active ROM exercises.
  - Notify RN about patient reports of pain, tingling, or decreased sensation in the affected extremity.

Collaborate With Physical Therapist
- Assess patient's current mobility and need for assistance.
- Teach safe ambulation with assistive device based on patient's weight-bearing restrictions.
- Establish exercise plan and teach patient to perform exercises safely.
- Coordinate PT with RN so that patient can receive timely analgesia.
- Discuss home environment with patient and identify modifications to promote safety (e.g., stair training).

Collaborate With Occupational Therapist
- Assess impact of patient's condition on ability to perform ADLs.
- Teach patient use of assistive devices (e.g., long-handled reacher, shoe donner) to promote self-care while maintaining activity restrictions.

bed, allowing the patient's lower limbs to dangle over the bedside, and having the patient perform standing transfers. When the patient is allowed to increase activity, assess for orthostatic hypotension. Assess patients for signs of VTE. VTE is discussed in Chapter 37.

Traction. When slings are used with traction, regularly inspect exposed skin areas. Pressure over a bony prominence created by wrinkled sheets or blankets may cause pressure necrosis. Persistent skin pressure may impair blood flow and cause injury to peripheral nerves and blood vessels. Assess skeletal traction or external fixation pin sites for signs of infection. Pin site care may vary. It often includes regularly cleansing with chlorhexidine, rinsing with sterile saline, and drying the area with sterile gauze.

External rotation of the affected extremity is a classic assessment finding for a patient with unrepaired hip fracture. If skin traction is ordered before surgery, apply traction without trying to reposition or realign the extremity. Movement of fracture fragments can occur during repositioning, causing increased pain and possible nerve impingement. Keep the patient in the center of the bed in a supine position to provide adequate countertraction.

Discuss specific patient activity with the HCP. If exercise is allowed, encourage patient participation in a simple exercise program based on activity restrictions. Have the patient perform frequent position changes, ROM exercises of unaffected joints, deep-breathing exercises, and isometric exercises. These activities should be done several times each day. Teach the patient to use the trapeze bar (if permitted) to raise the body off the bed for linen changes and placement of the bedpan. Encourage and help the hospitalized patient to stay connected with friends and family by telephone or through social media resources.

◆ **Ambulatory Care**

Cast Care. Most uncomplicated fractures are treated in an outpatient setting. Whatever the type of cast material, a cast can interfere with circulation and nerve function if it is applied too tightly or excess edema occurs after application. Frequent neurovascular assessment of the immobilized extremity is critical. Teach the patient to recognize and promptly report tightness of the cast and areas of pressure or discomfort. Explain the importance of elevating the extremity above heart level to promote venous return and applying ice to control or prevent edema during the initial phase. However, if compartment syndrome is suspected, do not elevate the extremity above the heart.

Patient and caregiver teaching is important to prevent complications. Table 62.9 describes patient and caregiver instructions for cast care. Teach the patient to exercise joints above and below the cast. Tell the patient not to scratch or place anything inside the cast because this may cause skin injury and infection. For itching, direct a hair dryer on a cool setting under the cast. Confirm the patient's and caregiver's understanding of these instructions before discharge. A follow-up phone call is appropriate. Home care nursing visits may be needed, especially for the patient with a body jacket brace.

The cast is typically removed in the outpatient setting. Patients often fear being cut by the oscillating blade of the cast saw. Reassure the patient that damage to the skin is unlikely. Teach the patient about possible changes in the appearance of the extremity beneath the cast (e.g., dry, wrinkled skin; atrophied muscle; foul odor). The patient may be scared to use the injured extremity after cast removal.

Ambulation. Know the overall goals of PT in relation to the patient's abilities, needs, and tolerance. The physical therapist

---

TABLE 62.9   Patient & Caregiver Teaching

Cast Care

After a cast is applied, include the following instructions when teaching the patient and the caregiver:

Do

1. Apply ice directly over fracture site for first 24 hr (avoid getting cast wet by keeping ice in plastic bag and protecting cast with cloth).
2. Check with HCP before getting fiberglass cast wet.
3. Dry cast thoroughly if inadvertently exposed to water.
   - Blot dry with towel.
   - Use hair dryer on low setting until cast is thoroughly dry.
4. Elevate extremity above heart level for first 48 hr.
5. Regularly move joints above and below cast.
6. Use hair dryer on cool setting for itching inside the cast.
7. Report signs of possible problems to HCP:
   - Increasing pain despite elevation, ice, analgesia.
   - Swelling associated with pain and discoloration of toes or fingers.
   - Pain during movement.
   - Burning or tingling under cast.
   - Sores or foul odor under cast.
8. Keep appointment to have fracture and cast checked.

Do Not

1. Get cast wet.
2. Remove any padding.
3. Insert any objects inside cast.
4. Bear weight on new cast for 48 hr (not all casts are made for weight bearing; check with HCP when unsure).
5. Cover cast with plastic for prolonged periods.

---

is responsible for mobility training and teaching about the use of assistive aids (cane, crutches, walker). Reinforce these instructions to the patient. The patient with lower extremity fractures usually starts mobility training when able to sit in bed and dangle the feet over the side. Work with the physical therapist to give analgesia before a PT session.

When the patient begins to ambulate, know the patient's weight-bearing status and the correct technique if the patient is using an assistive device. Ambulation occurs in different degrees of weight-bearing: (1) non–weight bearing (no weight on the involved extremity), (2) touch-down/toe-touch weight bearing (contact with floor for balance but no weight borne), (3) partial–weight-bearing ambulation (25% to 50% of patient's weight borne), (4) weight bearing as tolerated (based on patient's pain and tolerance), and (5) full–weight-bearing ambulation (no limitations).

Assistive Devices. Devices for ambulation range from a cane (can relieve up to 40% of the weight normally borne by a lower limb) to a walker or crutches (may allow for complete non–weight-bearing ambulation). The HCP decides which device is best, balancing the need for maximum stability and safety with the need for maneuverability in small spaces, such as bathrooms. Discuss with the patient lifestyle requirements and help select a device that allows the patient to feel most secure and independent. The technique for using assistive ambulation devices varies. The involved limb is usually advanced at the same time or immediately after advance of the device. The uninvolved limb is advanced last. Canes are held in the hand opposite the involved extremity.

Place a transfer belt (gait belt) around the patient's waist to provide stability while teaching the patient how to use an assistive device. Discourage the patient from reaching for furniture or relying on another person for support. A patient with inadequate upper limb strength or poorly fitted crutches bears weight at the axilla rather than at the hands. This can damage the neurovascular bundle that passes across the axilla. If verbal coaching does not correct the problem, teach the patient another form of ambulation (e.g., walker) until strength is adequate.

Patients who must ambulate without weight bearing need enough upper limb strength to lift their own weight at each step. Because the muscles of the shoulder girdle and upper arm may not be accustomed to this work, patients require focused training for this task. Push-ups, pull-ups using the overhead trapeze bar, and weight lifting develop the triceps and biceps muscles. Straight-leg raises and quadriceps-setting exercises strengthen the quadriceps muscles.

Psychosocial Concerns. Short-term rehabilitative goals address the transition from dependence to independence in performing simple ADLs. They are directed at preserving or increasing strength and endurance. Long-term rehabilitative goals are aimed at preventing problems associated with musculoskeletal injury (Table 62.10). During the rehabilitative phase, help the patient adjust to any problems caused by the injury (e.g., separation from family, financial impact of medical care, loss of income from inability to work, potential for disability). Assess patients for posttraumatic stress disorder. This is especially important if significant injury to others or fatalities were associated with the patient's injuries.

The caregiver may have a key role in providing long-term care. Teach the caregiver how to help with strength and endurance exercises, mobility, and promoting activities that enhance the quality of daily living. Offer support and encouragement while actively listening to the patient's and caregiver's concerns.

◆ Evaluation

The expected outcomes are that the patient with a fracture will
- Report satisfactory pain management
- Show proper care of cast or immobilizer
- Have uncomplicated bone healing

COMPLICATIONS OF FRACTURES

Most fractures heal without complications. Complications of fractures may be direct or indirect. *Direct complications* include problems with bone infection, bone union, and avascular necrosis. *Indirect complications* include compartment syndrome, VTE, fat embolism syndrome (FES), breakdown of skeletal muscle *(rhabdomyolysis),* and hypovolemic shock. Most musculoskeletal injuries are not life threatening. Death after a fracture is usually due to damage to underlying organs and vascular structures or complications of the fracture or immobility. Open fractures, fractures with severe blood loss, and fractures that damage vital organs (e.g., lung, heart) are medical emergencies requiring immediate attention.

Infection

Open fractures and soft tissue injuries have a high rate of infection. An open fracture usually results from severe external forces. Communication of the fracture site with the outside environment can contaminate the fracture site with microorganisms or foreign bodies. Damage to the surrounding soft tissue and blood vessels impairs the ability of defense mechanisms to respond to microorganisms.[18] Dying or contaminated tissue is an ideal medium for many common pathogens, including anaerobic bacilli, such as *Clostridium tetani.* Measures to prevent infection and osteomyelitis are important.

TABLE 62.10 Problems Associated With Musculoskeletal Injuries

Problem	Description	Nursing Considerations
Atrophy	• ↓ Muscle mass occurs from disuse after prolonged immobilization. • Loss of nerve function can cause muscle atrophy.	• Isometric muscle-strengthening exercises as able with immobilization device helps reduce amount of atrophy. • Muscle atrophy interferes with and prolongs rehabilitation process.
Contracture	• Abnormal condition of joint characterized by flexion and fixation. • Caused by atrophy and shortening of muscle fibers and ligaments or by loss of normal elasticity of skin over joint.	• Can be prevented by frequent position change, correct body alignment, active-passive ROM exercises several times a day. • Intervention requires gradual progressive stretching of muscles or ligaments in region of joint.
Footdrop	• Plantar-flexed position of the foot occurs when Achilles tendon in ankle shortens because it has been allowed to assume an unsupported position. • Peroneal nerve palsy (a compression neuropathy) can cause footdrop and spinal nerve compression.	• For patient with long-term injuries, support foot in neutral position to ↓ risk for footdrop. • Once footdrop has developed, can significantly hinder ambulation and gait training. • May need splint to keep feet in neutral position. • High-top athletic shoes may help. Apply at scheduled times to keep feet in neutral position.
Muscle spasms	• Caused by involuntary muscle contraction after fracture, muscle strain, or nerve injury. • May last several weeks. • Pain associated with muscle spasms is often intense and can last from several seconds to several minutes.	• Measures to ↓ intensity of muscle spasms are similar to actions for pain management. • Do not massage muscle spasms. Massage may stimulate muscle tissue contraction that ↑ spasm and pain. • Thermotherapy, especially heat, may reduce muscle spasm.
Pain	• Common with fractures, edema, muscle spasm. • May be mild to severe and described as aching, dull, burning, throbbing, sharp, or deep.	• Causes include incorrect positioning and alignment of extremity, incorrect support of extremity, sudden movement of extremity, immobilization device that is applied too tightly or incorrectly, constrictive dressings, motion at fracture site. • Determine causes of pain so that corrective action can be taken.

Open fractures require aggressive surgical debridement. The wound is initially cleaned by saline lavage in the operating room. Gross contaminants are irrigated and mechanically removed. Contused, contaminated, and devitalized tissue (muscle, subcutaneous fat, skin, and bone fragments) is surgically excised (*debridement*). The amount of soft tissue damage determines if the wound is closed at the time of surgery or if it needs repeat debridement, closed suction drainage, and/or skin grafting. During surgery, the open wound may be irrigated with antibiotic solution. Antibiotic-impregnated beads also may be placed in the surgical site. Patients usually receive IV antibiotics for at least 3 days.[18] In conjunction with aggressive surgical management, antibiotics have greatly reduced the occurrence of infection.

Compartment Syndrome

Compartment syndrome is a condition in which swelling causes increased pressure within a limited space (muscle compartment). Because the fascia surrounding the muscle has limited ability to stretch, continued swelling can cause pressure that compromises the function of blood vessels and nerves in the compartment. Capillary perfusion is reduced below a level needed for tissue life. Compartment syndrome often involves the leg but can occur in any muscle group.

There are 38 compartments in the upper and lower extremities. Two basic causes of compartment syndrome are (1) decreased compartment size resulting from restrictive dressings, splints, casts, excessive traction, or premature closure of fascia; and (2) increased compartment contents due to bleeding, inflammation, edema, or IV infiltration.

Edema can create enough pressure to obstruct circulation and cause venous occlusion, which further increases edema. Arterial flow is eventually compromised, causing ischemia in the extremity. As ischemia continues, muscle and nerve cells are destroyed. Fibrotic tissue eventually replaces healthy tissue. Contracture, disability, and loss of function can occur. Delays in diagnosis and treatment may lead to irreversible muscle and nerve ischemia. The extremity may become functionally useless or severely impaired.

Compartment syndrome is usually associated with fractures (especially of long bones), extensive soft tissue damage, and crush injury.[19] Fractures of the distal humerus and proximal tibia are the most common fractures associated with compartment syndrome. Compartment injury can also occur after knee or leg surgery. Prolonged pressure on a muscle compartment may result when someone is trapped under a heavy object or a person's limb is trapped beneath the body because of response to drugs or alcohol.

Clinical Manifestations. Compartment syndrome may occur initially from the body's physiologic response to the injury, or it may be delayed for several days after the original insult or injury. Ischemia can occur within 4 to 8 hours after the onset of compartment syndrome.

One or more of the "6 Ps" are specific to compartment syndrome: (1) *pain* out of proportion to the injury that is not managed by opioid analgesics, and *pain* on passive stretch of muscle in the compartment; (2) increasing *pressure* in the compartment; (3) *paresthesia* (numbness and tingling); (4) *pallor*, coolness, and loss of normal color of the extremity; (5) *paralysis* or loss of function; and (6) *pulselessness* (decreased or absent peripheral pulses).

Interprofessional Care. Prompt diagnosis of compartment syndrome is critical.[19] Perform and document regular neurovascular assessment on all patients with fractures, especially those with injury of the extremities or soft tissue in these areas. Early recognition and effective treatment of compartment syndrome are essential to avoid permanent damage to muscles and nerves.

Carefully assess the location, quality, and intensity pain (see Chapter 8). Evaluate the patient's pain intensity on a scale of 0 to 10. Pain unrelieved by drugs and out of proportion to the level of injury is one of the *first* signs of compartment syndrome. Paresthesia is also an early sign. Notify the HCP immediately of these changes in the patient's condition. Relieving the source of pressure (e.g., cast is cut [bivalved] or dressing loosened by order of the HCP) typically decreases pain and paresthesia and can avoid compartment syndrome. Reducing traction weight may also decrease external pressures on the extremity. Pulselessness and paralysis are later signs of compartment syndrome. Do not wait until these late signs occur to contact the HCP. Amputation may be needed due to prolonged ischemia.

With suspected compartment syndrome, do not elevate the extremity above the heart. Similarly, do not apply cold compresses. They may cause vasoconstriction and worsen compartment syndrome.

Surgical decompression (e.g., fasciotomy) of the involved compartment may be needed (Fig. 62.15).[19] The fasciotomy site is left open for several days to allow adequate soft tissue decompression. Infection resulting from delayed wound closure is a potential problem after fasciotomy. In severe cases of compartment syndrome, amputation is done.

Venous Thromboembolism

Veins of the lower extremities and pelvis are at great risk for clot (thrombus) formation after a fracture, especially a hip fracture. VTE may also occur after total hip or total knee replacement surgery. In patients with limited mobility, inactivity of muscles that normally help pump venous blood from the extremities to the heart worsens venous stasis.

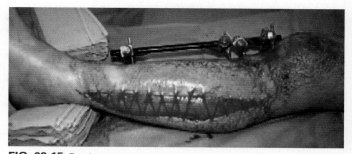

FIG. 62.15 Fasciotomy associated with compartment syndrome. Stabilization of fracture with external fixator. (From Browner BD, Jupiter JB, Levine AM, Trafton P: *Skeletal trauma: Fractures, dislocations, ligamentous injuries,* ed 4, Philadelphia, 2009, Saunders.)

Because of the high risk for VTE in the orthopedic surgical patient, prophylactic anticoagulant drugs should be given for at least 10 to 14 days.[20] The most common agents used include (1) warfarin (Coumadin), (2) low-molecular-weight heparin (LMWH) (e.g., enoxaparin [Lovenox], fondaparinux), (3) aspirin, or (4) a factor Xa inhibitor (e.g., rivaroxaban [Xarelto], apixaban).[20] Besides wearing compression gradient stockings (antiembolism hose) or using intermittent pneumatic compression devices, the patient should dorsiflex and plantar flex the ankle of an affected lower extremity against resistance and perform ROM exercises on the unaffected leg. For upper extremity injuries, have the patient flex and extend the wrist if not immobilized by a cast or splint and perform ROM exercises on the unaffected arm. VTE is discussed in Chapter 37.

> **⚠ SAFETY ALERT Anticoagulant Therapy**
> - Monitor for signs of external bleeding (e.g., nosebleeds) or internal bleeding (e.g., tea-colored urine).
> - Teach patient signs of bleeding and what to do if bleeding occurs.
> - Teach patient safe self-injection if taking an injectable anticoagulant after discharge.
> - Encourage patient to keep appointments for laboratory testing to monitor effects of warfarin (if prescribed).

Fat Embolism Syndrome

Fat embolism syndrome (FES) is characterized by fat globules entering the circulatory system from fractures. They collect in areas with abundant blood vessels, especially the lungs and brain.[21] FES contributes to mortality associated with fractures. The fractures most often associated with FES are those of the long bones, ribs, tibia, and pelvis. FES can also occur after total joint replacement, spinal fusion, liposuction, crush injuries, and bone marrow transplantation.

Two theories about FES exist. According to the mechanical theory, fat emboli originate from fat released from the marrow of injured bone. The fat enters systemic circulation, where it travels to other organs. As fat droplets become stuck in small blood vessels, local ischemia and inflammation occur. The biochemical theory suggests hormonal changes caused by trauma or sepsis stimulate systemic release of free fatty acids (e.g., chylomicrons) that form the fat emboli.

Clinical Manifestations. Early recognition of FES is crucial to prevent patient death. Most patients have symptoms within 24 to 48 hours after injury. Severe forms have occurred within hours of injury. Fat emboli in the lungs cause hemorrhagic interstitial pneumonitis with signs and symptoms of acute respiratory distress syndrome (ARDS). These include chest pain, tachypnea, cyanosis, dyspnea, apprehension, tachycardia, and hypoxemia.[21] These symptoms are caused by poor O_2 exchange. Changes in mental status due to hypoxemia are common. Petechiae on the neck, anterior chest wall, axilla, buccal membrane, and conjunctiva of the eye may help distinguish FES from other problems. They may appear due to intravascular thromboses caused by decreased oxygenation. However, petechiae occur in only 20% to 60% of cases of FES. They may fade before they are noticed.[21]

The clinical course of FES may be rapid and acute. In a short time, skin color can change from pallor to cyanosis. The patient may become comatose. No specific laboratory tests aid in the diagnosis. However, certain abnormalities may be present.

These include fat cells in blood, urine, or sputum; a decrease of PaO_2 to less than 60 mm Hg; ST segment and T-wave changes on ECG; decreased platelet count and hematocrit; and high erythrocyte sedimentation rate (ESR). A chest x-ray may show bilateral pulmonary infiltrates.

Interprofessional Care. Management of FES is supportive and related to managing symptoms. Treatment includes fluid administration to prevent hypovolemic shock, correction of acidosis, and blood transfusions. Dobutamine and nitrous oxide may be given for hemodynamic support.[21] Use of corticosteroids to prevent or treat FES is controversial.

The patient needs appropriate respiratory support. Administer O_2 to treat hypoxia. Intubation or intermittent positive pressure ventilation may be an option if satisfactory PaO_2 cannot be obtained with supplemental O_2 alone. Some patients develop pulmonary edema and/or ARDS, leading to increased mortality. Most persons survive FES with few complications.

Preventing the development of FES is important. Careful immobilization and handling of a long bone fracture are the most important factors in preventing FES. Reposition the patient as little as possible before fracture immobilization or stabilization to decrease the risk of dislodging fat droplets into the general circulation.

> **❓ CHECK YOUR PRACTICE**
>
> You are caring for a 24-yr-old male patient who had a femur fracture in a motorcycle accident last night. He is scheduled for ORIF later today. While doing your assessment, you notice that he seems very restless. You note some axillary petechiae.
> - What complication would you suspect is occurring?
> - Why is this patient particularly at risk for this complication?
> - What is the most important intervention for a patient with this complication?

Rhabdomyolysis

Rhabdomyolysis is a syndrome caused by the breakdown of damaged skeletal muscle cells. This breakdown causes the release of myoglobin into the bloodstream. Myoglobin precipitates and causes obstruction in renal tubules. This results in acute tubular necrosis and acute kidney injury (AKI). Because of possible muscle damage, assess urine output. Common signs are dark reddish-brown urine and symptoms of AKI (see Chapter 46).

TYPES OF FRACTURES

COLLES' FRACTURE

A *Colles' fracture* is a fracture of the distal radius. The styloid process of the ulna may be involved as well. The injury usually occurs when the patient falls on an outstretched arm and hand. It is one of the most common types of fractures in adults. It most often occurs in patients over 50 years old whose bones are osteoporotic (*fragility fracture*) (Fig. 62.16). A younger person with a Colles' fracture caused by a low-energy force should be referred for an osteoporosis evaluation.

Symptoms include pain in the immediate area of injury, pronounced swelling, and dorsal displacement of the distal fragment (silver-fork deformity). This displacement appears as an

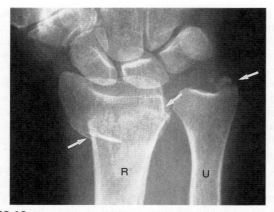

FIG. 62.16 Colles' fracture. Fracture of the distal radius *(R)* and ulnar *(U)* styloid from patient falling on the outstretched hand. (From Mettler FA: *Essentials of radiology*, ed 2, Philadelphia, 2005, Saunders.)

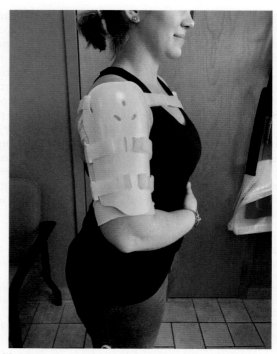

FIG. 62.17 Humeral cuff brace. (Courtesy Matthew C. Price, MS, RN, CNP, ONP-C, RNFA, Columbus, OH.)

obvious deformity of the wrist. The major complication is vascular insufficiency from edema. CTS can be a later complication.

A Colles' fracture is usually managed with closed reduction of the fracture and application of a splint or cast. If displaced, the fracture is typically managed with open reduction and internal or external fixation. Nursing management includes frequent neurovascular assessment and measures to reduce edema. Provide support and protect the extremity. Encourage active movement of the thumb and fingers to reduce edema and increase venous return. Teach the patient to perform active movements of the shoulder to prevent stiffness or contracture.

HUMERAL SHAFT FRACTURE

Fractures involving the shaft of the humerus are common among young and middle-aged adults. The most common symptoms are obvious displacement of the humeral shaft, shortened extremity, abnormal mobility, and pain. Complications associated include radial nerve injury and injury to the brachial artery due to laceration, transection, or muscle spasm.

Treatment depends on the specific fracture location and displacement. Nonoperative treatment may include a hanging arm cast, shoulder immobilizer, sling and swathe (a type of immobilizer that prevents shoulder movement), or humeral cuff brace (Fig. 62.17).

The humeral cuff brace is typically used to stabilize midshaft humerus fractures. Two pieces of molded plastic are fitted together in a clam-shell configuration and held together with Velcro straps. The humeral cuff brace is a good option for nonoperative fracture management if the patient is at increased risk for intraoperative complications.

When these devices are used, elevate the head of the bed to assist gravity in reducing the fracture. Allow the arm to hang freely when the patient is sitting or standing. Provide measures to protect the axilla and prevent skin breakdown. Carefully place absorbable composite dressing pads (e.g., ABD pads) in the axilla. Change them twice daily or as needed. Skin or skeletal traction may be used for reduction and immobilization.

During the rehabilitative phase, an exercise program to improve strength and motion of the injured extremity is extremely important. Exercises should include assisted motion of the hand and fingers. The shoulder can be exercised if the fracture is stable. This helps prevent stiffness from frozen shoulder or fibrosis of the shoulder capsule.

PELVIC FRACTURE

Pelvic fractures range from relatively minor to life threatening, depending on the mechanism of injury and associated vascular damage. Although only a small number of fractures are pelvic fractures, this type of injury is associated with a high mortality rate. Attention to more obvious injuries at the time of a traumatic event may result in oversight of pelvic injuries.

Pelvic fractures may cause serious intraabdominal injury, including laceration and hemorrhage of the urethra, bladder, or colon. They can cause acute pelvic compartment syndrome. Paralytic ileus may occur after pelvic fracture. Patients may survive the pelvic injury, only to die from sepsis, FES, or VTE.

Abdominal assessment may show local swelling, tenderness, deformity, unusual pelvic movement, and bruising. Assess the neurovascular condition of the lower extremities and determine associated injuries. Pelvic fractures are diagnosed by x-ray and CT scan.

Treatment depends on the severity of the injury. Stable, nondisplaced fractures require little intervention. Ambulation with weight bearing as tolerated is typically encouraged.[22] Complex or displaced fractures (e.g., open book fracture) need external fixation alone or combined with ORIF (e.g., screws), often done emergently. Use extreme care in handling or moving the patient, to prevent further injury. Turn the patient only when ordered by the HCP. Because a pelvic fracture can damage other organs, assess bowel and urinary elimination. Regularly perform distal neurovascular assessment. Provide back care with adequate help or while the patient is raised from the bed by independent use of a trapeze.

ETHICAL/LEGAL DILEMMAS
Entitlement to Treatment

Situation

D.C., a 35-yr-old English tourist, was in a hang-gliding accident while touring the United States. She was taken to the regional trauma center for treatment of internal injuries, blood loss, and severe pelvic fractures. She has become septic, is now in renal failure, and has ARDS. She has no health insurance. Despite a poor chance of survival, her husband and parents want all possible measures to be taken.

Ethical/Legal Points for Consideration

- Federal law requires hospitals receiving federal funds through Medicare and Medicaid to provide emergency evaluation and treatment to stabilize patients (Emergency Medical Treatment and Active Labor Act [EMTALA]). Once the patient is stabilized, they are under no obligation to continue treatment and may transfer the patient to another facility.
- Discussions with the family must occur to clarify treatment goals (e.g., recovery, survival, continued biologic existence, nonabandonment of the patient) and what they mean by wanting "everything done." There is no legal or ethical obligation to continue medical treatment when treatment goals cannot be met.
- Contact with the English consulate may result in collaboration to stabilize the patient and transport her to England.
- Neither HCPs nor hospitals are required to provide medically futile care (care that provides no benefit to the patient).
- Although her home country (England) offers universal health care, D.C. assumed the risk when engaging in a potentially dangerous activity and did not obtain international health insurance coverage for her visit to a foreign country.

Discussion Questions

1. How can the nurse facilitate discussions with the family about treatment goals for D.C.?
2. Are family members able to state D.C.'s wishes for her own care in such a situation?

HIP FRACTURE

Hip fractures are common in older adults. 95% of hip fractures result from a fall.[23] More than 320,000 patients are admitted to hospitals each year because of a hip fracture. Up to 37% of those patients die within 1 year of injury. Many older adults develop disabilities that require long-term care. By age 90, about 33% of all women and 17% of all men will have had a hip fracture. In adults over 65 years old, hip fracture occurs more often in women than in men because of osteoporosis.

Hip fracture refers to a fracture of the proximal (upper) third of the femur, which extends 5 cm below the lesser trochanter (Fig. 62.18). Fractures within the hip joint capsule are *intracapsular fractures*. Intracapsular fractures are further identified by their specific locations: (1) *capital* (fracture of the head of the femur), (2) *subcapital* (fracture just below the head of the femur), and (3) *transcervical* (fracture of the femoral neck). These fractures, which are often associated with osteoporosis and minor trauma, are called *fragility fractures*.

Extracapsular fractures occur outside the joint capsule. They are either (1) *intertrochanteric* (in a region between the greater and lesser trochanter) or (2) *subtrochanteric* (below the lesser trochanter). Most are caused by severe direct trauma or a fall.

Clinical Manifestations

Manifestations include external rotation, muscle spasm, shortening of the affected extremity, and severe pain and tenderness

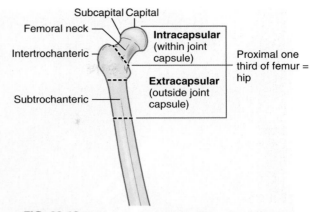

FIG. 62.18 Femur with location of various types of fracture.

around the fracture site. Displaced femoral neck fractures may disrupt blood supply to the femoral head, resulting in avascular necrosis of the femoral head.

Interprofessional Care

Immediate surgery is the standard of care. Initially the affected extremity may be immobilized with Buck's traction (Fig. 62.9) if the patient's physical condition needs stabilized before surgery can be done. Buck's traction can be used for 24 to 48 hours to relieve painful muscle spasms.

Surgical treatment allows early mobilization and decreases the risk for major complications. The type of surgery depends on the location and severity of the fracture and the person's age. Surgical options include (1) closed reduction with percutaneous pinning (CRPP) (minimally invasive surgery to stabilize the femoral neck and head with screws), (2) repair with internal fixation devices (e.g., hip compression screw, intramedullary devices), (3) replacement of the femoral head with a prosthesis (partial hip replacement or *hemiarthroplasty*, often used for fracture of the femoral neck) (Fig. 62.19), and (4) total hip replacement (involves both the femur and acetabulum) (Fig. 62.20).

❖ NURSING MANAGEMENT: HIP FRACTURE

◆ Nursing Implementation

◆ **Preoperative Care.** In addition to the usual preoperative nursing care (see Chapter 17), teaching may be done in the ED. Most patients are medically stable and thus do not have an overnight preoperative period in which to receive instructions. Most people who have hip fractures are older adults. When planning treatment of the hip fracture, consider the patient's chronic health problems (e.g., diabetes, heart and pulmonary disease). Surgery may be delayed briefly until the patient's general health is stabilized. Begin to consider discharge plans because the length of stay after surgery will be no more than a few days.

Before surgery, severe muscle spasms can increase pain. Analgesics or muscle relaxants, comfortable positioning (unless contraindicated), and properly applied traction (if used) can help to manage the spasms.

◆ **Postoperative Care.** Similar principles of patient care apply to any of the surgical procedures for hip fractures. In the initial postoperative period, assess vital signs, intake, and output. Monitor respiratory function and encourage deep breathing and coughing. Assess pain and give pain medication. Observe

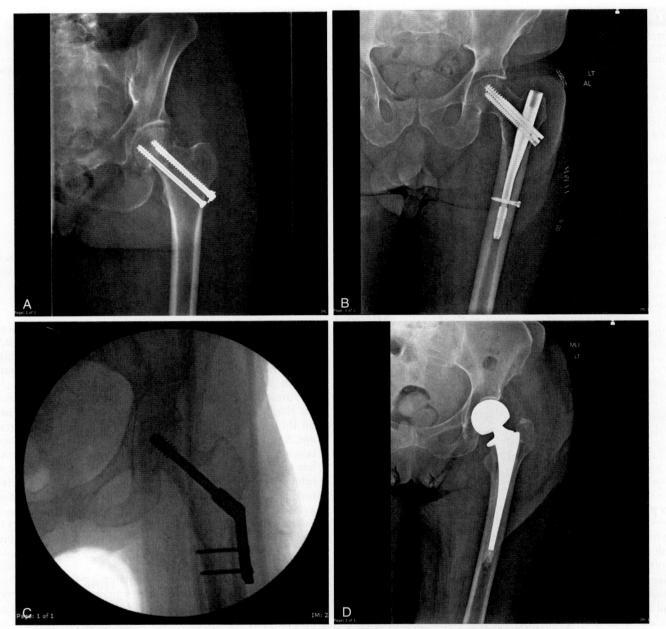

FIG. 62.19 Types of surgical repair for a hip fracture: **A**, Closed reduction with percutaneous pinning. **B**, Intramedullary nail. **C**, Sliding hip screw. **D**, Hemiarthroplasty. (Courtesy Matthew C. Price, MS, RN, CNP, ONP-C, RNFA, Columbus, OH.)

the dressing and incision for signs of bleeding. See eNursing Care Plan 62.2 for the orthopedic surgical patient (available on the website for this chapter).

Neurovascular impairment is possible. Assess the patient's extremity for (1) color, (2) temperature, (3) capillary refill, (4) distal pulses, (5) edema, (6) sensation, (7) motor function, and (8) pain. Decrease edema by elevating the leg when the patient is in bed or in a chair. Pain in the affected extremity can be reduced by maintaining limb alignment with pillows between the patient's knees when turning the patient to the nonoperative side.

Encourage the patient to use the overhead trapeze bar and the opposite side rail to help in position changes. Avoid turning the patient to the affected side unless approved by the HCP. A

physical therapist can teach the patient how to transfer out of the bed to a chair. Have the patient exercise the unaffected leg and both arms

If hemiarthroplasty or total joint replacement was done by a *posterior approach* (incision posterior to the midline of the greater trochanter down the femoral shaft), measures to prevent dislocation must be used (Table 62.11). Tell the patient and caregiver about positions and activities that increase the patient's risk for dislocation (more than 90 degrees of flexion, adduction across the midline [crossing of legs and ankles], internal rotation of hip). Many daily activities may reproduce these positions: (1) putting on shoes and socks, (2) crossing the legs or feet while seated, (3) assuming the side-lying position incorrectly, (4) standing up or sitting down while the hip is flexed more than

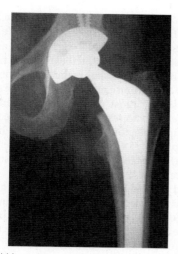

FIG. 62.20 Total hip replacement (arthroplasty) with cementless femoral prosthesis of metal alloy with plastic acetabular socket.

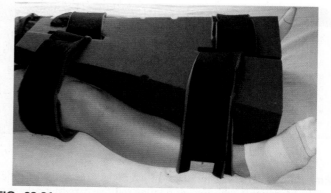

FIG. 62.21 Maintaining abduction after total hip replacement. (Courtesy Mary Wollan, RN, BAN, ONC, Spring Park, MN.)

TABLE 62.11 Patient & Caregiver Teaching

Posterior Hip Replacement

After a hip replacement by posterior surgical approach, include the following instructions when teaching a patient and caregiver:

Do

- Use an elevated toilet seat.
- Place chair inside shower or tub and remain seated while washing.
- Use pillow between legs for first 6 wk after surgery when lying on nonoperative side or when supine.
- Keep hip in neutral, straight position when sitting, walking, or lying.
- Notify HCP at once if severe pain, deformity, or loss of function occurs.
- Discuss personal risk factors for prosthetic joint infection with HCP and dentist before dental work.

Do Not

- Flex hip greater than 90 degrees (e.g., sitting in low chairs or toilet seats).
- Adduct hip (e.g., bring legs together at knees).
- Internally rotate hip (e.g., turn toward planted foot on affected side).
- Cross legs at knees or ankles.
- Put on own shoes or stockings without adaptive device (e.g., long-handled shoehorn or stocking-helper) for 4–6 wk after surgery.
- Sit on chairs without arms. The arms of chairs will help the patient rise to a standing position.

90 degrees relative to the chair, and (5) sitting on low seats, especially low toilet seats. Teach the patient to avoid these activities until the soft tissue capsule around the hip has healed enough to stabilize the prosthesis (usually at least 6 weeks).

Elevated toilet seats and chair alterations (e.g., raising the seat with a folded blanket, keeping a straight back) are needed. Avoid placing a soft pillow in the patient's seat because sitting on it can cause internal rotation. If a foam abduction wedge is ordered to prevent joint dislocation, place it between the patient's legs (Fig. 62.21). Apply the top straps above the knee to avoid putting pressure on the peroneal nerve at the lateral tibial tubercle. Some HCPs want the patient to keep the abductor wedge in place except when bathing or walking.

If hemiarthroplasty or total joint replacement was done by an *anterior approach* (incision is made in the front of the hip with patient lying on the back), the hip muscles are left intact. This approach generally provides a more stable hip in the postoperative period with a lower rate of complications. Precautions related to motion and weight bearing are few. They typically include instructions to avoid hyperextension.

Weight bearing on the involved extremity varies. Limited weight bearing is typically the only restriction for the patient who had ORIF of the hip fracture. Weight bearing after ORIF is generally restricted until x-ray examination shows adequate healing, usually 6 to 12 weeks. Tell the patient and caregiver about the weight-bearing status after surgery.

Taking a tub bath and driving a car are not allowed for 4 to 6 weeks. An occupational therapist (OT) may teach the patient to use assistive devices, such as long-handled shoehorns, sock assists, and reachers or grabbers, to avoid bending over to pick up something on the floor. The knees must be kept apart. Teach the patient to never cross the legs or twist to reach behind.

The physical therapist usually supervises exercises for the affected extremity and ambulation when the HCP allows it. The patient is usually out of bed the first postoperative day. In collaboration with the physical therapist, monitor the patient's ambulation for proper use of crutches or a walker. To be discharged home, the patient must show proper use of crutches or a walker over a functional distance (about 150 ft). The patient must be able to transfer to and from a chair and bed and to go up and down stairs.

Complications associated with femoral neck fracture include nonunion, avascular necrosis, dislocation, and osteoarthritis (OA). The affected leg may be shorter if the patient had an intertrochanteric fracture. A cane or shoe lift may be needed for safe ambulation.

Sudden severe pain, a lump in the buttock, limb shortening, and external rotation indicate prosthesis dislocation. This requires closed reduction with moderate to deep sedation or open reduction under general anesthesia to realign the femoral head in the acetabulum. If any of these signs occur (regardless of the setting), keep the patient NPO in anticipation of surgical intervention.

Help the patient and caregiver to adjust to restrictions and dependence because of the hip fracture. Anxiety and depression can easily occur, but creative nursing care and awareness of potential problems can help to prevent them. Tell the patient and caregiver about community services that can help with rehabilitation after hospital discharge.

◆ **Ambulatory Care.** Hospitalization averages 3 or 4 days. Older adults or patients who live alone may require care in a subacute rehabilitation unit, at a skilled nursing facility, or in an acute rehabilitation facility for a few weeks before returning home. If the patient has skilled nursing needs or is homebound for PT after discharge from postacute care, the HCP may order follow-up home health care.

Home care considerations include ongoing assessment of pain management, monitoring for infection, and prevention of VTE. If incision is closed with metal staples, they will be removed at the HCP's office. Teach the patient who is receiving an anticoagulant to report signs of bleeding to the HCP (see Chapter 37). Review how to administer an injectable anticoagulant (if needed). Teach the patient receiving warfarin about required laboratory testing.

Exercises to restore strength and tone in the quadriceps and muscles around the hip are essential to improve function and ROM. These include quadriceps setting (e.g., pressing the kneecap down), gluteal muscle setting (e.g., tightening the buttocks), leg raises in supine and prone positions, and abduction exercises from the supine and standing positions (e.g., swinging the leg out but never crossing midline). The patient continues these exercises for many months after discharge. Teach the exercise program to the caregiver who will be encouraging the patient at home.

A physical therapist assesses ROM, ambulation, and adherence to the exercise program. The patient gradually increases the number of exercise repetitions and may add ankle weights. Swimming and stationary cycling may tone quadriceps and improve cardiovascular fitness. Teach the patient to avoid high-impact exercises and sports, such as jogging and tennis, because they may loosen the implant. A physical therapist may perform a home assessment to identify hazards that may cause the patient to fall again.

◆ **Evaluation**

The expected outcomes are that the patient with a hip fracture will
- Report satisfactory pain management
- Have uncomplicated bone healing
- Take part in exercise therapy

Gerontologic Considerations: Hip Fracture

Factors that increase the risk for a hip fracture in older adults include (1) increased risk for falling due to an altered center of gravity and inability to correct a postural imbalance, (2) decreased fat and muscle to act as local tissue shock absorbers, and (3) reduced skeletal strength. Other factors that increase the older adult's risk for falling include (1) gait and balance problems, (2) altered vision and hearing, (3) slowed reflexes, (4)

orthostatic hypotension, and (5) medication use. Homes can be made safer by (1) eliminating tripping hazards (e.g., throw rugs, uneven surfaces), (2) adding grab bars inside and outside the tub or shower, and beside the toilet, (3) adding railings on both sides of the stairs, and (4) installing better lighting.[23]

Many falls occur when getting in or out of a chair or bed. Falls to the side, the most common type seen in frail older adults, are more likely to result in a hip fracture than a forward fall. External hip protectors may help prevent hip fractures in the frail older patient.[24] Older adults may have low bone density (*osteopenia*) or osteoporosis, which increases their risk for fragility fractures.

Calcium and vitamin D supplementation are given to patients with osteopenia or osteoporosis. A bisphosphonate drug (e.g., alendronate [Fosamax]) may be prescribed to decrease bone loss or increase bone density. This reduces the chance of fracture. (Osteoporosis is discussed in Chapter 63.)

FEMORAL SHAFT FRACTURE

Because the femur can bend slightly to absorb stress, femoral shaft fracture occurs from a severe direct force. The force exerted to cause the fracture (e.g., from a motor vehicle crash or gunshot wound) often also damages the adjacent soft tissue. These injuries may be more serious than the bone injury. Young adults have a high incidence of this type of fracture.

Displacement of fracture fragments often causes increased soft tissue damage. Considerable blood loss (1 to 1.5 L) can occur. The most common types of femoral shaft fracture include transverse, spiral, comminuted, oblique, and open (Figs. 62.6 and 62.7).

A femoral shaft fracture is marked by pain, notable deformity and angulation, shortening of the extremity, and inability to move the hip or knee. Complications include FES; nerve and vascular injury; and problems associated with bone union, open fracture, and soft tissue damage.

Initial management involves patient stabilization and fracture immobilization. Traction may be used as a temporary measure before surgery or in the patient unable to have surgery. Placement of an *intramedullary rod* is the most common surgical treatment for femoral shaft fracture. The metal rod is placed into the marrow canal of the femur. The rod passes across the fracture to keep fragments in position. Plates and screws also may be used. Internal fixation is preferred because it reduces the hospital stay and complications associated with prolonged bed rest. External fixation may be used for an open fracture.

After surgery, gluteal and quadriceps isometric exercises will promote and maintain strength in the affected extremity. Encourage the patient to perform ROM and strengthening exercises for all uninvolved extremities to prepare for ambulation. The patient may be allowed to begin non–weight-bearing activities with an assistive device (e.g., walker, crutches). Full weight bearing is usually restricted until x-rays show union of fracture fragments. Teach the patient to carefully follow the HCP's instructions for weight bearing.

TIBIAL FRACTURE

Although the tibia is vulnerable to injury because it lacks a covering of anterior muscle, strong force is needed to cause a fracture. As a result, soft tissue damage, devascularization, and open fracture are common. The tibia is also a common site for stress fracture. Complications of tibial fractures include compartment syndrome, FES, delayed union or nonunion, and possible infection with an open fracture.

Recommended management for closed tibial fractures is closed reduction followed by immobilization in a long leg cast. ORIF with intramedullary rods, plate fixation, or external fixation is needed for complex fractures and those with extensive soft tissue damage. An emphasis of care is maintaining quadriceps strength.

Assess the neurovascular condition of the affected extremity at least every 2 hours during the first 48 hours. Have the patient perform active ROM exercises with the uninvolved leg and the upper extremities to build the strength needed for crutch walking. When the HCP has determined the patient is ready for gait training, review principles of crutch walking introduced by the physical therapist. The patient may be non–weight bearing for 6 to 12 weeks, depending on healing. Home nursing visits may be needed to monitor the patient's progress if the patient is homebound.

STABLE VERTEBRAL FRACTURE

In a stable fracture, the fracture fragments are unlikely to move or cause spinal cord damage. This type of injury is often confined to the vertebral body (anterior part of the spinal column) in the lumbar region. Sometimes it involves the cervical and thoracic regions. Vertebral bodies are usually protected from displacement by intact spinal ligaments. Stable fractures of the vertebral column are usually caused by motor vehicle crashes, falls, diving, or sports injuries. Patients with osteoporosis have more than 700,000 vertebral compression fractures annually, many of which are stable.

Most patients with stable fractures have only brief periods of disability. However, if spinal ligaments are significantly disrupted, dislocation of the vertebrae may occur. Instability and injury to the spinal cord may result (unstable fracture). These injuries generally require surgery. The most serious complication of vertebral fractures is fracture displacement, which can cause damage to the spinal cord (see Chapter 60). Although stable vertebral fractures are not associated with abnormal spinal cord pathology, all spinal injuries should be considered unstable and potentially serious until diagnostic tests determine the fracture to be stable.

The patient usually has pain and tenderness in the affected region of the spine. There may be a kyphotic deformity (flexion angulation of thoracic vertebrae) known as a *dowager's hump*. This deformity is readily identified during the physical examination (see Fig. 63.9). *Lordosis* (extreme inward curve of lumbar spine) and cervical spine involvement are possible. Sudden loss of function below the fracture indicates spinal cord impingement and paraplegia. Bowel and bladder dysfunction may occur if there is interruption of the autonomic nervous system nerves or injury to the spinal cord.

The overall goal in managing stable vertebral fractures is to keep the spine in good alignment until union is achieved. Many nursing interventions are aimed at assessing for spinal cord trauma (see Chapter 60). Regularly evaluate vital signs and bowel and bladder function. Monitor the motor and sensory function of peripheral nerves distal to the injured region. Promptly report any deterioration in the patient's neurovascular condition.

Treatment includes pain medication followed by early mobilization and bracing. The patient's mattress should be firm to support the spinal column, relax muscles, decrease edema, and prevent potential compression on nerve roots. Teach the patient to keep the spine straight when turning by moving the shoulders and pelvis together. The patient will need nursing help to learn the technique of logrolling. Several days after the initial injury, the HCP may apply a specially constructed orthotic device (e.g., thoracolumbar sacral orthosis [TLSO]), a jacket cast, or a removable corset if there is no evidence of neurologic deficit. The device gives extra support during healing and is used for a short period of time.

Lightweight bracing (e.g., Jewett or Bähler-Vogt brace) may be used for patients with stable vertebral compression fractures due to osteoporosis. Patients with osteoporosis also may be treated with 2 outpatient procedures: vertebroplasty or balloon kyphoplasty. *Vertebroplasty* uses radioimaging to guide the injection of bone cement into a fractured vertebral body. When hardened, the cement stabilizes the vertebra and prevents further compression. *Balloon kyphoplasty* involves first inserting a balloon into the vertebral body and then inflating it. This creates a cavity that is filled with bone cement under low pressure to restore the height of the vertebral body. Kyphoplasty is now the surgical treatment of choice for compression fractures. This is due to the decreased incidence of bone cement leakage into nearby structures (e.g., colon, lung) compared to vertebroplasty. Patients have decreased pain almost at once with these procedures. However, later compression fractures of adjacent vertebrae are a risk.

If the fracture is in the cervical spine, the patient may wear a hard cervical collar. Some cervical fractures are immobilized by use of a halo vest (see Fig. 60.8). This consists of a plastic jacket or cast fitted about the chest and attached to a halo held in place by skeletal pins inserted into the cranium. These devices immobilize the spine in the fracture area while allowing the patient to ambulate.

The patient with a stable vertebral fracture is discharged after (1) showing safe ambulation, (2) learning care of the cast or orthotic device, and (3) stating ways to address safety and security concerns related to the injury and treatment. Unstable vertebral fractures and spinal cord injuries are the subject of Chapter 60.

FACIAL FRACTURE

Any bone of the face can be fractured from trauma, such as a motor vehicle crash, an assault, or a fall. After facial injury it is critically important to establish and maintain a patent airway and provide adequate ventilation. Suctioning may be needed to remove foreign material and blood. A surgically created airway (*tracheostomy*) may be needed if a patent airway cannot be maintained.

Facial fractures and cervical spine injuries often occur together. All patients with facial injuries should be treated as if they have a cervical injury until proven otherwise by examination and CT scan or x-ray. Table 62.12 describes clinical manifestations of common facial fractures.

Related soft tissue injury often makes assessment of facial injury difficult. Perform oral and facial examinations after any life-threatening situations have been treated. Carefully assess ocular muscles and cranial nerves III, IV, and VI. X-rays help determine the extent of the injury. CT scanning helps distinguish between bone and soft tissue injury.

Suspect injury to the eye when facial injury occurs, especially if the injury is near the orbit. If an eye-globe rupture is suspected, stop and place a protective shield over the eye. Signs

TABLE 62.12 Manifestations of Facial Fractures

Fracture	Manifestation
Frontal bone	Rapid edema that may mask underlying fractures
Mandible	Tooth fractures, bleeding, limited motion of mandible
Maxilla	Segmental motion (instability) of maxilla and tooth fracture at socket
Nasal bone	Displacement of nasal bones, nosebleed (*epistaxis*)
Periorbital bone	Possible frontal sinus involvement, entrapment of ocular muscles
Zygomatic arch	Depression of cheek bone (*zygomatic arch*) and entrapment of ocular muscles

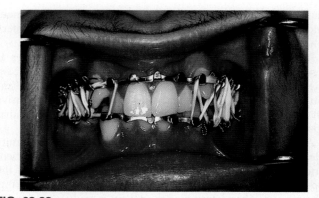

FIG. 62.22 Intermaxillary fixation. (Courtesy R.A. Weinstein, Denver, CO.)

of rupture include vitreous humor forced out of the eye. Brown tissue (iris or ciliary body) may be seen on the surface of the globe or penetrating through a laceration, with an off-center or teardrop-shaped pupil.

Specific treatment depends on the site and extent of the facial fracture and associated soft tissue injury. Immobilization or surgical stabilization may be needed. Maintain a patent airway and adequate nutrition throughout the recovery period.

Be sensitive about changes in appearance that may occur after facial fracture. Changes in appearance may be drastic. Edema and discoloration subside with time, but soft tissue injuries can cause permanent scarring.

MANDIBULAR FRACTURE

Mandibular fracture may result from trauma to the face or jaw. Maxillary fractures may also occur, but they are less common than mandibular fractures. The mandibular fracture may be simple, with no bone displacement, or may involve loss of tissue and bone. The fracture may need immediate treatment to ensure the patient's survival. Long-term treatment is sometimes needed to restore satisfactory appearance and function.

Mandibular fractures may be done therapeutically to correct an underlying alignment problem (*malocclusion*) that cannot be adjusted by orthodontics alone. The mandible is resected during surgery and manipulated forward or backward to correct the occlusion problem.

Surgery for a mandibular fracture includes immobilization, usually by wiring the jaws (*intermaxillary fixation*). Internal fixation may be done with screws and plates. In a simple fracture with no loss of teeth, the lower jaw is wired to the upper jaw. Wires are placed around the teeth, and then cross-wires or rubber bands are used to hold the lower jaw tight against the upper jaw (Fig. 62.22). Arch bars may be placed on the maxillary and mandibular arches of the teeth. Vertical wires placed between the arch bars hold the jaws together. If teeth are missing or bone is displaced, other forms of fixation may be needed (e.g., metal arch bars in the mouth or insertion of a pin in the bone). Bone grafting may be needed. Immobilization is usually needed for only 4 to 6 weeks because the fractures often heal rapidly.

❖ NURSING MANAGEMENT: MANDIBULAR FRACTURE

Teach the patient before surgery about what is involved in the surgical procedure, how the face will look afterward, and

changes caused by the surgery. Reassure the patient about the ability to breathe normally, speak, and swallow liquids. Hospitalization for respiratory monitoring is brief unless there are other injuries or problems.

Postoperative care focuses on a patent airway, oral hygiene, communication, pain management, and adequate nutrition. Two potential problems in the immediate postoperative period are airway obstruction and aspiration of vomitus. Because the patient cannot open the jaws, an airway must be maintained. Observe for signs of respiratory distress (e.g., dyspnea; changes in rate, quality, and depth of respirations). After surgery place the patient on the side with the head slightly elevated.

Tape a wire cutter or scissors (for rubber bands) to the head of the bed. Send it with the patient to all appointments and examinations away from the bedside. The wire cutter or scissors may be used to cut the wires or elastic bands in case of an emergency requiring access to the pharynx or lungs (e.g., cardiac arrest or respiratory distress). In the care plan include a picture with the appropriate wires to cut in an emergency. In some cases, cutting the wires may cause the entire facial and upper jaw structure to shift or collapse and worsen the problem. A tracheostomy or endotracheal tray should always be available.

If the patient begins to vomit or choke, try to clear the mouth and airway. Suction via the nasopharyngeal or oral route, depending on the extent of injury and type of repair. An NG tube can remove fluids and gas from the stomach to help prevent vomiting and aspiration. The NG tube can later be used as a feeding tube. Antiemetics may be given. Teach the patient to clear secretions and vomitus.

Oral hygiene is very important. Teach the patient to remove food debris by rinsing the mouth often, especially after meals and snacks. Warm normal saline solution, water, or alkaline mouthwashes may be used. A syringe and soft irrigation catheter or a Water Pik may be effective for thorough oral cleansing. Inspect the mouth several times a day to see that it is clean. Use a tongue depressor to retract the cheeks. Keep the lips, corners of the mouth, and buccal mucosa moist. Cover any sharp edges of the wires with dental wax to prevent irritation of the buccal mucosa.

Communication may be a problem, especially in the early postoperative period. Establish an effective way of communicating before surgery (e.g., use of dry erase board, pad and pencil). Usually the patient can speak well enough to be understood, especially a few days after surgery.

Intake of adequate nutrients may be a challenge because the diet must be liquid. The patient easily tires of sucking through a straw or laboriously using a spoon. Work with the dietitian and patient to plan a diet with adequate calories, protein, and fluids. Liquid protein supplements may improve the patient's nutrition. The low-bulk, high-carbohydrate diet and intake of air through the straw contribute to constipation and gas. Ambulation, prune juice, and bulk-forming laxatives may help relieve these problems.

The patient is usually discharged with the wires in place. Encourage the patient to share feelings about the changes in appearance. Discharge teaching should include oral care, diet, how to handle secretions, how and when to use wire cutters or scissors, and when to notify the HCP about concerns and problems.

AMPUTATION

An amputation is the removal of a body extremity by trauma or surgery. About 2 million Americans are living with limb loss.[25] About 185,000 amputations occur each year in the United States. Most amputations are done due to PVD, especially in older patients with diabetes. These patients often have peripheral neuropathy that progresses to deep ulcers and gangrene. Amputation in young people is usually due to trauma (e.g., motor vehicle crashes, farm-related injury). Battle injuries have affected over 1700 veterans since 2003, with several losing more than 1 limb.[26] Other common reasons for amputation include thermal injuries, tumors, osteomyelitis, and congenital limb disorders.

Diagnostic Studies

Diagnostic studies depend on the underlying reason for the amputation (Table 62.13). An increased white blood cell (WBC) count with abnormal differential may show infection. Vascular tests such as arteriography, Doppler studies, and venography give information about circulation in the extremity.

Interprofessional Care

If amputation is planned or elective, as for the patient with PVD, carefully assess the patient's general health. Chronic illnesses and infection must be managed before an amputation is done. Help the patient and caregiver understand the need for the amputation. Assure them that rehabilitation can help with quality of life. If the amputation is done emergently after trauma, patient management is physically and emotionally more complicated.

The goal of surgery is to preserve the greatest extremity length and function while removing all infected, pathologic, or ischemic tissue. Levels of amputation of upper and lower extremities are shown in Fig. 62.23. The type of amputation depends on the reason for the surgery. A closed amputation creates a weight-bearing *residual limb* (or stump). An anterior skin flap with dissected soft tissue padding covers the bony part of the residual limb. The skin flap is sutured posteriorly so that the suture line will not be in a weight-bearing area. Take special care to prevent accumulation of drainage, which can cause pressure and harbor bacteria that may cause infection.

Disarticulation is an amputation done through a joint. A *Syme's amputation* is a form of disarticulation at the ankle. After an open amputation (*guillotine amputation*), the surface of the residual limb is left uncovered with skin. This type of surgery is generally done to control actual or potential infection. The wound is usually closed later by a second surgical procedure or closed by skin traction surrounding the residual limb.

TABLE 62.13 **Interprofessional Care**
Amputation

Diagnostic Assessment	**Management**
• History and physical examination	***Medical***
• Physical appearance of soft tissues	• Appropriate management of underlying disease
• Skin temperature	• Stabilization of trauma victim
• Sensory function	
• Quality of peripheral pulses	***Surgical***
• Arteriography	• Residual limb management
• Venography	• Immediate or delayed prosthesis fitting
• Plethysmography (measures blood flow in the arms or legs)	
• Transcutaneous ultrasonic Doppler recordings	***Rehabilitation***
	• Coordination of prosthesis-fitting and gait-training activities
	• Coordination of muscle-strengthening and PT programs

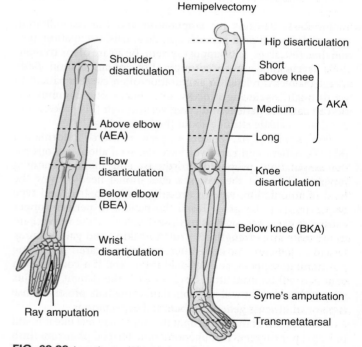

FIG. 62.23 Location and description of amputation sites of the upper and lower extremities. *AKA,* Above-the-knee amputation.

Labels: Hemipelvectomy; Hip disarticulation; Shoulder disarticulation; Short above knee; Medium; Long; AKA; Above elbow (AEA); Elbow disarticulation; Knee disarticulation; Below elbow (BEA); Below knee (BKA); Wrist disarticulation; Syme's amputation; Ray amputation; Transmetatarsal

❖ NURSING MANAGEMENT: AMPUTATION

◆ Nursing Assessment

Assess for any preexisting illnesses. Because most amputations are done for vascular problems, assessment of vascular and neurologic condition is especially important (see Chapters 31 and 55).

◆ Nursing Diagnoses

Nursing diagnoses for the patient with an amputation may include:
• Disturbed body image
• Impaired tissue integrity
• Chronic pain
• Impaired physical mobility

◆ Planning

The overall goals are that the patient with an amputation will (1) have adequate relief from the underlying health problem, (2) have satisfactory pain management, (3) reach maximum rehabilitation potential (with the use of a prosthesis, if indicated), (4) cope with the body image changes, and (5) make satisfying lifestyle adjustments.

◆ Nursing Implementation

◆ **Health Promotion.** Control of illnesses, such as PVD, diabetes, chronic osteomyelitis, and pressure injuries, can eliminate or delay the need for amputation. Teach patients with these problems to carefully examine their lower extremities daily for signs of infection or skin breakdown. If the patient cannot do this, the caregiver should help. Teach the patient and caregiver to report changes in the feet or toes to the HCP. These include decreased or absent sensation, tingling, burning pain, cuts, or abrasions, and changes in skin color or temperature.

Review safety precautions for people taking part in recreational activities and potentially hazardous work. This responsibility is especially important for the occupational health nurse.

◆ **Acute Care.** Reasons for amputation and the rehabilitation potential depend on a person's age, diagnosis, occupation, personality, resources, and support system. Be aware of the tremendous psychologic and social implications of amputation. Body image problems related to amputation often cause a patient to go through a grieving process. Use therapeutic communication to help the patient and caregiver through this process and develop a realistic attitude about the future.

Preoperative Care. Before surgery, reinforce information that the patient and caregiver have received about reasons for the amputation, proposed prosthesis, and mobility-training program. To meet the patient's educational needs, know the level of amputation, type of dressings to be applied, and type of prosthesis to be used. Teach the patient to perform upper extremity exercises, such as push-ups in bed or the wheelchair, to promote arm strength for crutch walking and gait training. Discuss general postoperative nursing care, including positioning, support, and residual limb care. If a compression bandage will be used after surgery, teach the patient about its purpose and how it will be applied. If immediate prosthesis use is planned, discuss general ambulation expectations.

Tell the patient that the amputated limb may feel like it is still present after surgery. This phenomenon, termed phantom limb sensation, occurs in many amputees. (Nursing management of phantom limb sensation is discussed in the next section.)

Postoperative Care. General care for the patient who had an amputation depends largely on the patient's age and general state of health and the reason for the amputation. Monitor patients who had an amputation due to a traumatic injury for posttraumatic stress disorder because they may have had no time to prepare or even take part in the decision to have a limb amputated.

Prevention and detection of complications are important after surgery. Carefully monitor the patient's vital signs. Assess dressings for hemorrhage. Use sterile technique during dressing changes to reduce the risk for wound infection.

If an *immediate* postoperative prosthesis has been applied, carefully observe the surgical site. If excess bleeding occurs, notify the HCP at once. Keep a surgical tourniquet available for emergency use.

FIG. 62.24 A double amputee fitted with prostheses. (Photo courtesy US Army.)

The *delayed* prosthetic fitting may be the best choice for older adults, patients with infection, or patients who have had amputations above the knee or below the elbow (Fig. 62.24). Appropriate timing for the use of a prosthesis depends on satisfactory healing of the residual limb and the patient's general condition. A temporary prosthesis may be used for partial weight bearing after sutures are removed. If there are no problems, the patient can bear full weight on a permanent prosthesis about 3 months after amputation.

Not all patients are candidates for prostheses. The seriously ill or debilitated patient may not have the upper body strength and energy needed to use a lower extremity prosthesis. Mobility with a wheelchair may be the most realistic goal for this patient.

Patients are often extremely worried about phantom limb sensation because they still perceive pain in the missing part of the limb. As recovery and ambulation progress, phantom limb sensation and pain usually subside. However, the pain may become chronic. The patient may have shooting, burning, or crushing pain as well as feelings of coldness, heaviness, and cramping,

Unfortunately, there is no one therapy for phantom limb sensation. Mirror therapy reduces symptoms in some patients (Fig. 62.25).[27] We do not know why looking in the mirror at the remaining limb would improve symptoms. The mirror is thought to give visual information to the brain, replacing sensory feedback expected from the missing limb. Mirror therapy may also improve patient function after a stroke.

Success of the rehabilitation program depends on the patient's physical and emotional health. Chronic illness and deconditioning can complicate rehabilitation. Physical and occupational therapy must be a central part of the patient's overall plan of care.

Flexion contractures may delay rehabilitation. The most common and debilitating contracture is hip flexion. Hip adduction contracture is rare. To prevent flexion contractures, have patients avoid sitting in a chair for more than 1 hour with hips

FIG. 62.25 Mirror therapy, a type of treatment that may reduce phantom limb sensation and pain. (US Navy photo courtesy Mass Communication Specialist Seaman Joseph A. Boomhower.)

TABLE 62.14 Patient & Caregiver Teaching

Lower Extremity Amputation

After lower extremity amputation, include the following instructions when teaching the patient and caregiver:

1. Inspect the residual limb daily for signs of skin irritation, especially redness, abrasion, and odor. Especially evaluate areas prone to pressure.
2. Stop using the prosthesis if irritation develops. Have the area checked before resuming use of the prosthesis.
3. Wash the residual limb thoroughly each night with warm water and bacteriostatic soap. Rinse thoroughly and dry gently. Expose the residual limb to air for 20 min.
4. Do not use lotions, alcohol, powders, or oil on residual limb unless prescribed by the HCP.
5. Wear only a residual limb sock in good condition and supplied by the prosthetist.
6. Change residual limb sock daily. Launder in mild soap, squeeze, lay flat to dry.
7. Use prescribed pain management techniques.
8. Perform ROM to all joints daily. Perform general strengthening exercises (including for upper extremities) daily.
9. Do not elevate residual limb on a pillow.
10. Lay prone with hip in extension for 30 min 3 or 4 times daily.

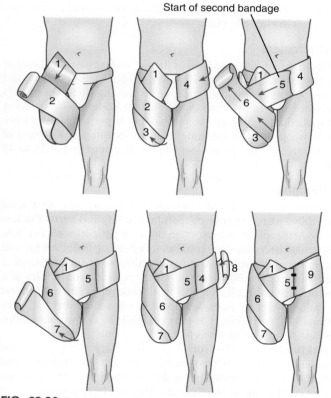

Start of second bandage

FIG. 62.26 Bandaging for the above-the-knee amputation residual limb. Figure-8 style covers progressive areas of the residual limb; 2 elastic wraps used.

flexed or having pillows under the surgical extremity. Unless contraindicated, patients should lie on their abdomen for 30 minutes 3 or 4 times each day and position the hip in extension while prone.

Proper bandaging ensures the residual limb is shaped and molded for eventual prosthesis fitting (Fig. 62.26). The HCP usually orders a compression bandage to be applied right after surgery to support soft tissues, reduce edema, hasten healing, and minimize pain. Compression also promotes residual limb shrinkage and maturation. This bandage may be an elastic roll applied to the residual limb or a residual limb shrinker, which is an elastic stocking that fits tightly over the residual limb.

At first, the patient always wears the compression bandage except during PT and bathing. Remove and reapply the bandage several times daily. Take care to apply it snugly but not so tight as to interfere with circulation. Wash and change shrinker bandages daily. After the residual limb is healed, bandage it only when the patient is not wearing the prosthesis. Teach the patient to avoid dangling the residual limb over the bedside to decrease edema.

As the patient's overall condition improves, the HCP and physical therapist start and supervise an exercise program. Active ROM exercises for all joints should be started as soon as possible after surgery. To prepare for mobility, the patient should increase triceps and shoulder strength for lower limb support. The patient will need to learn to balance the altered body. The lost weight of an amputated limb requires adaptation of the patient's proprioception and coordination to prevent falls and injury.

Crutch walking starts as soon as the patient is physically able. Follow orders for weight bearing carefully to avoid injury to the skin flap and delay of tissue healing. Before discharge, teach the patient and caregiver about residual limb care, ambulation, contracture prevention, recognition of complications, exercise, and follow-up care (Table 62.14).

◆ **Ambulatory Care.** When healing has occurred satisfactorily, and the residual limb is well molded, the patient is ready for prosthesis fitting. A prosthetist makes a mold of the residual limb and measures landmarks for creation of the prosthesis. The molded limb socket allows the residual limb to fit snugly into the prosthesis. The residual limb is covered with a stocking to ensure good fit and prevent skin breakdown. If the limb continues to shrink, causing a loose fit, a new socket has to be made. The patient may need to have the prosthesis adjusted to prevent rubbing and friction between the residual limb and socket. Excessive movement of a loose prosthesis can cause severe skin irritation, breakdown, and gait problems.

Artificial limbs become an integral part of the patient's changed body image. Teach the patient to clean the prosthesis socket daily with mild soap and rinse thoroughly to remove irritants. Leather and metal parts of the prosthesis should not get wet. Encourage the patient to have regular maintenance on the prosthesis. Consider the condition of the patient's shoe. A badly worn shoe alters the gait and can damage the prosthesis.

◆ **Special Considerations in Upper Limb Amputation.** Emotional implications of an upper limb amputation are often more devastating than for lower limb amputation. Despite technologic advances, we cannot replicate the movements and functional capacity of our hands with upper extremity prostheses.[28] The enforced dependency due to being 1-handed may be depressing and frustrating to the patient. Because most upper extremity amputations result from trauma, the patient likely had little time to adjust psychologically or be a part of the decision-making process.

Both immediate and delayed prosthetic fittings are possible for the below-the-elbow amputee. Prosthetic fitting is delayed for the above-the-elbow amputee. The usual functional prosthesis is the arm and hook. A cosmetic hand is available but has limited functional value. As with the lower limb prosthesis, patient motivation and perseverance are major factors contributing to a satisfactory outcome.

◆ **Evaluation**

The expected outcomes are that the patient with an amputation will

- Accept changed body image and integrate changes into lifestyle
- Have no evidence of skin breakdown
- Have reduction or absence of pain
- Become mobile within limitations imposed by amputation

Gerontologic Considerations: Amputation

If a lower limb amputation has been done on an older adult, the patient's previous ability to ambulate may affect the extent of recovery. Using a prosthesis requires significant strength and energy for ambulation. For example, walking with a below-the-knee prosthesis requires 40% more energy than walking on 2 legs. An above-the-knee prosthesis requires 60% more. Older adults whose general health is weakened by disorders such as heart or lung disease may not be able to use a prosthesis. The patient's ability to ambulate may be limited. If possible, discuss these issues with the patient and caregiver before surgery so that realistic expectations can be set.

COMMON JOINT SURGICAL PROCEDURES

Surgery plays a vital role in the treatment and rehabilitation of patients with various joint problems. The goals of surgery are to relieve chronic pain, improve joint motion, correct deformity and misalignment, and remove diseased cartilage. If the joint problem is not corrected, contraction with permanent limitation of motion may occur. Limited joint motion can be noted on physical examination. Joint-space narrowing can be seen on x-rays.

TYPES OF JOINT SURGERIES

Synovectomy

Synovectomy (removal of synovial membrane) is done to remove inflamed tissue that is causing unacceptable pain or limiting ROM in RA. A synovectomy is best done early in the disease process when there is minimal bone or cartilage destruction. Removing the thickened synovium does not cure RA but may relieve symptoms temporarily. Common sites for this surgery include the elbow, wrist, and fingers. Synovectomy in the knee is done less often because knee joint replacement is usually done.

Osteotomy

An osteotomy involves removing a wedge or slice of bone to restore alignment (joint and vertebral) and to shift weight bearing, thus relieving pain. Cervical osteotomy may be used to correct a kyphotic deformity in patients with ankylosing spondylitis. Halo vests and body jacket braces are worn until fusion occurs (3 to 4 months). Osteotomy is not effective in patients with inflammatory joint disease. However, femoral osteotomy may provide some pain relief and improve motion in select patients with hip osteoarthritis (OA). Tibial osteotomy also provides pain relief in some patients with knee instability or OA.[29]

Care of a patient who had an osteotomy is similar to that of a patient with ORIF of a fracture at a comparable site. Internal wires, screws and plates, bone grafts, or an external fixator usually fixes the bone in place.

Debridement

Debridement is the removal of debris, such as pieces of bone or cartilage (loose bodies) or osteophytes, from a joint using a fiberoptic arthroscope. This procedure is usually done on an outpatient basis on the knee or shoulder. A compression dressing is applied after surgery. Weight bearing is permitted after knee arthroscopy. Patient teaching includes monitoring for signs of infection, managing pain, and restricting activity for 24 to 48 hours.

Arthroplasty

Arthroplasty is the reconstruction or replacement of a joint to relieve pain, improve or maintain ROM, and correct deformity. Arthroplasty is most often done on patients with OA, RA, avascular necrosis, congenital deformities or dislocations, and other systemic problems. Types of arthroplasty include surgical reshaping of the bones of the joints, replacement of part of a joint (hemiarthroplasty), and total joint replacement. Around 1 million Americans have knee and hip replacement surgery annually.[30] Arthroplasty is also available for elbows, shoulders, fingers, wrists, ankles, and feet.

Total Hip Arthroplasty. Total hip arthroplasty (THA), or a total hip replacement, provides significant relief of pain and improved function for patients with joint deterioration from OA, RA, and other conditions. THA is also used to treat hip fractures.

In THA, the prosthesis (implant) replaces the ball-and-socket joint formed by the upper shaft of the femur and pelvis (Fig. 62.27). Both the ball-and-socket components can be cemented in place with polymethyl methacrylate, which bonds to the bone. They may also be inserted without cement (cementless). Cementless THA may provide longer stability by enabling ingrowth of new bone tissue into the porous surface coating of the prosthesis. Cementless devices are recommended for younger, more active patients and patients with good bone quality so that bone ingrowth into the components can be readily achieved.

The nursing care for a patient who had a THA is discussed in the section on nursing management of a patient with a hip fracture on pp. 1463–1466.

Partial hip replacement   Total hip replacement

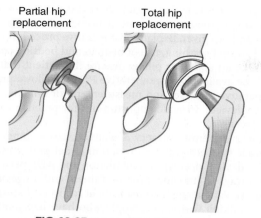

FIG 62.27 Types of hip replacements.

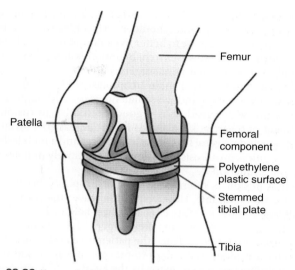

FIG. 62.28 Knee arthroplasty components. Up to 3 bone surfaces can be replaced in a total knee replacement. (Modified from Odom-Forren J: *Drain's perianesthesia nursing,* ed 7, St Louis, 2018, Elsevier.)

INFORMATICS IN PRACTICE

Web-Based Knee and Hip Replacement Community

- Most hospitals offer preoperative classes for patients undergoing joint replacement surgery, but fewer resources are available after discharge.
- Online knee and hip replacement communities offer the patient a place to share experiences and receive social support. The patient is likely to feel relieved knowing that others have similar experiences.
- Encourage patients to confirm any advice with the HCP before taking action.

Hip Resurfacing Arthroplasty. An alternative to hip replacement is hip resurfacing arthroplasty. It preserves and reshapes the femoral head (ball) rather than replacing it as in THA. The resurfaced femoral head is then capped by a metal prosthesis. Hip resurfacing may be an option for patients younger than age 60 with larger frames. A small number of patients will have a femoral neck fracture after hip resurfacing. This is not possible with THA. In addition, metal ions may be released into the bloodstream from the prosthesis. Patients may develop sensitivity or allergy to these ions.[31] Patients receiving a smaller femoral head (including many women) have a higher failure rate with a resurfaced implant when compared with patients receiving THA.

Knee Arthroplasty. Unrelieved pain and instability due to severe deterioration of the knee joint are the main reasons for total knee arthroplasty (TKA), or a total knee replacement (Fig. 62.28). Partial arthroplasty can be done on a patient with osteoarthritis limited to 1 part (compartment) of the knee.

Immediately after surgery a compression dressing may be used to immobilize the knee in extension. This dressing is removed before discharge. If the patient is unable to perform a straight-leg raise, a knee immobilizer or posterior plastic shell to maintain extension may be used during ambulation and at rest for about 4 weeks.

After surgery, emphasis is on pain management and PT. Managing pain is a primary nursing goal. Doing so decreases the patient's risk for complications and hastens the return to function.[32] Adequate analgesia should be ordered at discharge to allow the patient to continue with the exercise program. Effective pain management is key to achieving positive rehabilitation outcomes.

PT begins early with isometric quadriceps setting. Therapy progresses to straight-leg raises and gentle ROM to increase muscle strength and obtain 90-degree knee flexion. Active flexion exercises or passive flexion exercises with a continuous passive motion (CPM) machine may promote joint mobility. Ambulation starts early and typically progresses to full weight bearing before discharge. An active home exercise program involves progressive ROM with muscle strengthening and flexibility exercises. After TKA, many older patients with advanced OA show significant improvement in mobility, motor function tests, and ability to complete daily tasks.

Finger Joint Arthroplasty. A silicone rubber arthroplastic device is used to restore function in the fingers of the patient with RA. Ulnar deviation often causes severe functional limitations of the hand. The goal of hand surgery is primarily to restore function related to grasp, pinch, stability, and strength rather than to correct cosmetic deformity. Before surgery, the patient is taught hand exercises, including flexion, extension, abduction, and adduction of the fingers.

After surgery, a bulk dressing is placed and the hand is kept elevated. Perform regular neurovascular assessment and monitor for signs of infection. Success of the surgery depends largely on the postoperative treatment plan, which is usually implemented by an OT. After the dressing is removed, a guided splinting program is started. The patient is discharged with splints to use while sleeping and hand exercises to do at least 3 or 4 times a day for 10 to 12 weeks. Teach the patient to avoid lifting heavy objects.

Elbow and Shoulder Arthroplasty. Total replacement of elbow and shoulder joints is not as common as other forms of arthroplasty. Shoulder replacements are done in patients with severe pain because of RA, OA, avascular necrosis, or trauma. A specialized type of shoulder replacement, called a reverse total shoulder arthroplasty, may be done for pain and dysfunction caused by massive, irreparable, rotator cuff tears. Shoulder replacement is usually considered if the patient has adequate surrounding muscle strength and bone density. If joint replacement is needed for both elbow and shoulder, the elbow is usually done first because a severely painful elbow interferes with the shoulder rehabilitation program.

Most patients have no pain at rest or minimal pain with activity after elbow and shoulder arthroplasty. Functional improvements contribute to better hygiene and increased ability to perform ADLs. However, rehabilitation is longer and more difficult than with other joint surgeries.

Ankle Arthroplasty. Total ankle arthroplasty (TAA) is indicated for RA, OA, trauma, and avascular necrosis. Although use of TAA is not widespread, it is a good alternative to fusion for treatment of severe ankle arthritis in certain patients. Available devices include several fixed-bearing devices and a mobile-bearing cementless prosthesis. This device more closely imitates natural ankle function.

Ankle fusion is often done over arthroplasty because the result is more durable. However, fusion leaves the patient with a stiff foot and the inability to change heel height. TAA achieves a more normal gait pattern. After surgery, the patient may not bear weight for 6 weeks. Teach the patient to elevate the extremity to reduce edema, take steps to prevent infection, and maintain immobilization as directed by the HCP.

Arthrodesis

Arthrodesis is the surgical fusion of a joint. This procedure is done only if articular surfaces are too severely damaged or infected to allow joint replacement or if reconstructive surgery fails. Arthrodesis relieves pain and provides a stable but immobile joint. The fusion is usually done by removing the articular hyaline cartilage and adding bone grafts across the joint surface. The affected joint must be immobilized until bone healing has occurred. Common areas fused are wrist, ankle, cervical spine, lumbar spine, and metatarsophalangeal (MTP) joint of the great toe.

Complications of Joint Surgery

Infection is a serious complication of joint surgery, especially joint replacement surgery. The most common causative organisms are gram-positive aerobic streptococci and staphylococci. Infection may lead to pain and loosening of the prosthesis, generally requiring further surgery. Efforts to reduce infection include the use of specially designed self-contained operating suites, operating rooms with laminar airflow, and prophylactic antibiotic administration.

VTE is another potentially serious complication after joint surgeries, especially those involving the lower extremities. Provide prophylactic measures, such as anticoagulant drugs, use of intermittent pneumatic compression devices, and early ambulation. Assess patients for signs of VTE. VTE is discussed in Chapter 37.

NURSING AND INTERPROFESSIONAL MANAGEMENT: JOINT SURGERY

Preoperative Management

The primary goal of preoperative assessment is to identify risk factors for postoperative complications so we can implement measures to promote optimal outcomes. A careful history includes (1) medical diagnoses and complications, such as diabetes and VTE; (2) pain tolerance and management preferences; (3) current functional level and expectations after surgery; (4) current social support; and (5) home care needs after discharge. The patient should be free from infection and acute joint inflammation.

Preoperative teaching about the expected hospital course and postoperative management at home is important for the patient and caregiver. Explain postoperative procedures, such as turning, deep breathing, use of bedpan and bedside commode, and use of an abductor pillow. Assure the patient that analgesia will be available. A preoperative PT visit allows practice of postoperative exercises and measurement for crutches or other assistive devices. Provide opportunities for practice with assistive devices.

If lower extremity surgery is planned, assess upper extremity muscle strength and joint function to determine the type of assistive devices needed for ambulation and ADL performance. Discuss ways to maximize the usefulness and longevity of the prosthesis. Patients need to realize that recovery does not occur rapidly. Talking with other people who have had joint arthroplasty may help the patient better understand the reality of rehabilitation.

Discharge planning begins immediately. Discuss the duration of the hospital stay and the expected postoperative events so that the patient and caregiver can prepare. Discuss the safety and accessibility of the home environment (e.g., throw rugs, cords). Are the bathroom and bedroom on the first floor? Are door frames wide enough to accommodate a walker? Assess the patient's social support. Is a friend or family member available to help the patient at home? Will the patient need homemaker or meal services? The older patient may need to be discharged to a subacute or extended care facility for a few weeks to regain independent living skills.

Postoperative Management

Regularly perform neurovascular assessment postoperatively. Give ordered anticoagulant medication, analgesia, and parenteral antibiotics. Pain management strategies may include epidural or intrathecal analgesia, femoral nerve block, patient-controlled IV analgesia, and oral opioids or NSAIDs. Assess patient comfort often during the postoperative period. Monitor for postoperative complications. Nursing interventions for the patient having orthopedic surgery are presented in eNursing Care Plan 62.2 (available on the website for this chapter).

Assess ROM at regular intervals to facilitate the goal of improved functional performance. In general, the affected joint is exercised and ambulation is encouraged as early as possible to prevent complications of immobility. Specific protocols vary according to the patient, type of prosthesis, and HCP preference. Depending on the surgical approach, an abduction pillow may be used after THA.

The hospital stay after arthroplasty is about 3 days depending on the patient's course and need for PT. Some patients are discharged in 1 to 2 days. Some knee replacement surgeries are done at ambulatory surgical centers. Teach the patient to report complications, including infection (e.g., fever, increased pain, drainage) and dislocation of the prosthesis (e.g., pain, loss of function, shortening or malalignment of an extremity).

PT and ambulation enhance mobility, build muscle strength, and reduce the risk for VTE. Prophylactic anticoagulant drugs should be given for at least 10 to 14 days.[20] Some patients need therapy for up to 35 days. If the patient is taking warfarin, therapy starts on the day of surgery and the INR and prothrombin times are measured daily. Therapy with LMWH (e.g., enoxaparin), apixaban, or rivaroxaban usually starts the morning after surgery.[33]

CASE STUDY
Periprosthetic Hip Fracture and Revision Arthroplasty

(© aronaze/
iStock.com.)

Patient Profile

M.C. is a 64-yr-old white man who has had both hips replaced (left 6 years ago, right 2 years ago). He has a history of hypothyroidism. He was admitted to the ED after tripping over a short retaining wall in his backyard while gardening. He landed on his right side.

Subjective Data

- Acute, severe pain in right hip, unable to bear weight on right leg
- Takes cholecalciferol (vitamin D₃) 1000 IU every day without calcium supplement. States calcium upsets his stomach
- Reports loss of about 30 lb in the last year through diet and exercise. Exercises 3 times a week
- Lives in multilevel house with his wife. Bedrooms are on the second level
- Has smoked ½ pack of cigarettes a day for the past 30 years
- Describes himself as "a very light social drinker"

Objective Data

- 5 ft, 9 in tall, 175 lb

Diagnostic Studies

- X-rays show periprosthetic right proximal femur fracture at the greater trochanter with loss of fixation in the femoral part of the THA
- Normal CBC, chest x-ray
- Serum calcium 8.1 mg/dL

Interprofessional Care

- Revision of femoral part of his right total hip replacement with open reduction of the femoral fracture and fixation with 3 wires
- IV hydromorphone (Dilaudid) 1 mg IV every 3 hr as needed
- Cefazolin 1 gram IV every 8 hr for 24 hr
- Enoxaparin (Lovenox) 40 mg subcutaneous daily for 4 wk
- Calcium citrate 600 mg plus 800 IU vitamin D orally daily
- Levothyroxine (Synthroid) 125 mcg orally daily
- PT for transfers, gait, and stair training
- Occupational therapy for ADLs training
- Discharge planning based on mobility limitations and need for continued PT and OT

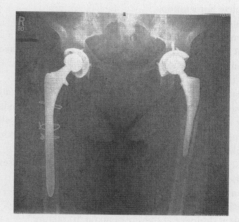

Discussion Questions

1. ***Patient-Centered Care:*** How do M.C.'s previous total joint surgeries affect his recovery after this surgery?
2. ***Priority Decision:*** As you plan care for M.C., what are the perioperative priority nursing interventions?
3. What are the most likely postoperative complications M.C. could develop?
4. In considering M.C.'s patient profile, what issues can you identify that may affect his bone healing?
5. ***Priority Decision:*** What are the priority assessments that should be done prior to discharge?
6. ***Collaboration:*** What is the interprofessional team's top priority at this time for M.C.?
7. ***Quality Improvement:*** What outcomes would indicate interprofessional care was effective?
8. ***Safety:*** What safety precautions should be considered for M.C.?
9. ***Evidence-Based Practice:*** Why is satisfactory pain management an important postoperative nursing goal for M.C.?

Answers available at *http://evolve.elsevier.com/Lewis/medsurg.*

BRIDGE TO NCLEX EXAMINATION

The number of the question corresponds to the same-numbered outcome at the beginning of the chapter.

1. The nurse suspects an ankle sprain when a patient at the urgent care center describes
   a. being hit by another soccer player during a game.
   b. having ankle pain after sprinting around the track.
   c. dropping a 10-lb weight on his lower leg at the health club.
   d. twisting his ankle while running bases during a baseball game.

2. A patient with a humeral fracture is returning for a 4-week checkup. The nurse explains that initial evidence of healing on x-ray is indicated by
   a. formation of callus.
   b. complete bony union.
   c. hematoma at the fracture site.
   d. presence of granulation tissue.

3. A patient with a comminuted fracture of the tibia is to have an open reduction with internal fixation (ORIF) of the fracture. The nurse explains that ORIF is indicated when
   a. the patient is unable to tolerate prolonged immobilization.
   b. the patient cannot tolerate the surgery for a closed reduction.
   c. other nonsurgical methods cannot achieve adequate alignment.
   d. a temporary cast would be too unstable to provide normal mobility.

4. The nurse suspects a neurovascular problem based on assessment of
   a. exaggerated strength with movement.
   b. increased redness and heat below the injury.
   c. decreased sensation distal to the fracture site.
   d. purulent drainage at the site of an open fracture.

5. A patient with a stable, closed humeral fracture has a temporary splint with bulky padding applied with an elastic bandage. The nurse notifies the provider of possible early compartment syndrome when the patient has
   a. increasing edema of the limb.
   b. muscle spasms of the lower arm.
   c. bounding pulse at the fracture site.
   d. pain when passively extending the fingers.

6. A patient with a pelvic fracture should be monitored for
   a. changes in urine output.
   b. petechiae on the abdomen.
   c. a palpable lump in the buttock.
   d. sudden increase in blood pressure.

7. The nurse teaches the patient with an above-the-knee amputation that the residual limb should not be routinely elevated because this position promotes
   a. hip flexion contracture.
   b. clot formation at the incision.
   c. skin irritation and breakdown.
   d. increased risk for wound dehiscence.

8. A patient with osteoarthritis is scheduled for total hip arthroplasty. The nurse explains the purpose of this procedure is to (select all that apply)
   a. fuse the joint.
   b. replace the joint.
   c. prevent further damage.
   d. improve or maintain ROM.
   e. decrease the amount of destruction in the joint.

9. A patient is scheduled for total ankle replacement. The nurse should tell the patient that after surgery he should avoid
   a. lifting heavy objects.
   b. sleeping on the back.
   c. abduction exercises of the affected ankle.
   d. bearing weight on the affected leg for 6 weeks.

1. d, 2, a, 3, c, 4, c, 5, d, 6, a, 7, a, 8, b, d, 9. d

For rationales to these answers and even more NCLEX review questions, visit *http://evolve.elsevier.com/Lewis/medsurg*.

EVOLVE WEBSITE/RESOURCES LIST

http://evolve.elsevier.com/Lewis/medsurg
Review Questions (Online Only)
Key Points
Answer Keys for Questions
- Rationales for Bridge to NCLEX Examination Questions
- Answer Guidelines for Case Study on p. 1475
Student Case Studies
- Patient With Musculoskeletal Trauma
- Patient With Parkinson's Disease and Hip Fracture
Nursing Care Plans
- eNursing Care Plan 62.1: Patient With a Fracture
- eNursing Care Plan 62.2: Patient Having Orthopedic Surgery
Concept Map Creator
Audio Glossary
Supporting Media
- Animations
  - ORIF Ankle
  - Total Knee Replacement
Content Updates

REFERENCES

1. Centers for Disease Control and Prevention (CDC): Leading causes of death, 2016. Retrieved from *www.cdc.gov/injury/wisqars/facts.html*.
2. National Institute of Arthritis and Musculoskeletal and Skin Diseases: Preventing sports injuries in youth: A guide for parents. Retrieved from *www.niams.nih.gov/Health_Info/Sports_Injuries/child_sports_injuries.asp*.
3. American Academy of Orthopaedic Surgeons (AAOS): Sprains, strains, and other soft-tissue injuries. Retrieved from *www.orthoinfo.org/topic.cfm?topic=A00111*.
*4. Silva PV, Kamper SJ, Costa LD: Exercise-based intervention for prevention of sports injuries (PEDro synthesis), *Br J Sports Med* 52:408, 2018.
5. American Academy of Orthopaedic Surgeons (AAOS): Common knee injuries. Retrieved from *http://orthoinfo.aaos.org/topic.cfm?topic=A00325*.
6. Mayo Clinic: Carpal tunnel syndrome. Retrieved from *www.mayoclinic.org/diseases-conditions/carpal-tunnel-syndrome/basics/definition/con-20030332*.
7. Mayo Clinic: Rotator cuff injury: Diagnosis and treatment. Retrieved from *www.mayoclinic.org/diseases-conditions/rotator-cuff-injury/symptoms-causes/syc-20350225*.
8. Mayo Clinic: Torn meniscus: Diagnosis and treatment. Retrieved from *www.mayoclinic.org/diseases-conditions/torn-meniscus/symptoms-causes/syc-20354818*.

9. Mayo Clinic: Bursitis. Retrieved from *www.mayoclinic.org/diseases-conditions/bursitis/basics/definition/con-20015102.*

10. Schell H, Duda GN, Peters A, et al: The hematoma and its role in bone healing, *J Exp Orthop* 4:5, 2017.

11. Pountos I, Giannoudis PV: Fracture healing: Back to basics and latest advances. In *Fracture reduction and fixation techniques,* New York, 2018, Springer.

*12. Matullo KS, Gangavalli A, Nwachuku C: Review of lower extremity traction in current orthopedic trauma, *JAAOS* 24:600, 2016.

13. Szostakowski B, Smitham P, Khan WS: Plaster of Paris: Short history of casting and injured limb immobilization, *Open Orthop J* 11:291, 2017.

14. American Orthopedic Foot and Ankle Society: Foot ulcers and the total contact cast. Retrieved from *www.aofas.org/footcaremd/conditions/diabetic-foot/Pages/Foot-Ulcers-and-the-Total-Contact-Cast.aspx.*

*15. Kazmers NH, Fragomen AT, Rozbruch SR: Prevention of pin site infection in external fixation: A review of the literature, *Strategies Trauma Limb Reconstr* 11:75, 2016.

*16. Gichuru M, Philips M, Yardley D, et al: A network meta-analysis evaluating different bone stimulation technologies on fracture healing outcomes, *Ann Orthop Trauma Rehab* 1:117, 2017.

17. Curtis K, Ramsden C: *Emergency and trauma care for nurses and nurse practitioners,* ed 2, St Louis, 2016, Elsevier.

*18. Zalavras CG: Prevention of infection in open fractures, *Infect Dis Clin* 31:339, 2017.

19. American Academy of Orthopaedic Surgeons (AAOS): Compartment syndrome. Retrieved from *https://orthoinfo.aaos.org/en/diseases--conditions/compartment-syndrome/.*

*20. Lieberman JR, Heckmann N: VTE in total hip arthroplasty and total knee arthroplasty patients: From guidelines to practice, *JAAOS* 25:789, 2017.

21. Fukumoto LE, Fukumoto KD: Fat embolism syndrome, *Nurs Clin* 53:335, 2018.

22. Baumgartner RE, Billow DG, Olson SA: Pelvic ring injury. In *Orthopedic traumatology,* New York, 2018, Springer.

23. Centers for Disease Control and Prevention (CDC): Hip fractures among older adults. Retrieved from *www.cdc.gov/HomeandRecreationalSafety/Falls/adulthipfx.html.*

*24. Santesso N, Carrasco-Labra A, Brignardello-Petersen R: Hip protectors for preventing hip fracture in older people. Retrieved from *www.cochrane.org/CD001255/MUSKINJ_hip-protectors-for-preventing-hip-fractures-in-older-people.*

25. Amputee Coalition: Limb loss statistics. Retrieved from *www.amputee-coalition.org/limb-loss-resource-center/resources-by-topic/limb-loss-statistics/limb-loss-statistics.*

26. Armstrong AJ, Hawley CE, Darter B, et al: Operation Enduring Freedom and Operation Iraqi Freedom veterans with amputation: An exploration of resilience, employment, and individual characteristics, *JVR* 48:167, 2018.

*27. Ambron E, Miller A, Kuchenbecker KJ, et al: Immersive low-cost virtual reality treatment for phantom limb pain: Evidence from two cases, *Front Neurol* 9:67, 2018.

28. Pierrie SN, Gaston RG, Loeffler BJ: Current concepts in upper-extremity amputation, *J Hand Surg* 43:657, 2018.

*29. Saltzman BM, Rao A, Erickson BJ, et al: A systematic review of 21 tibial tubercle osteotomy studies and more than 1000 knees: Indications, clinical outcomes, complications, and reoperations, *Pathology* 6:10, 2017.

30. American Joint Replacement Registry: Fourth AJRR annual report on hip and knee arthroplasty data. Retrieved from: *www.ajrr.net/images/annual_reports/AJRR-2017-Annual-Report---Final.pdf.*

31. American Academy of Orthopaedic Surgeons (AAOS): Hip resurfacing. Retrieved from *http://orthoinfo.aaos.org/topic.cfm?topic=A00586.*

*32. McDonald LT, Corbiere NC, DeLisle JA, et al: Pain management after total joint arthroplasty, *AORN J* 103:605, 2016.

33. Lieberman JR: Deep vein thrombosis prophylaxis: State of the art, *J Arthroplasty* 33:3107, 2018.

*Evidence-based information for clinical practice.

63

Musculoskeletal Problems

Diane Ryzner

*Courage is very important. Like a muscle, it is
strengthened by use.*

Ruth Gordon

http://evolve.elsevier.com/Lewis/medsurg

LEARNING OUTCOMES

1. Describe the pathophysiology, clinical manifestations, and interprofessional and nursing management of osteomyelitis.
2. Distinguish among the types, pathophysiology, clinical manifestations, and interprofessional management of bone cancer.
3. Distinguish between the causes and characteristics of acute and chronic low back pain.
4. Explain the conservative and surgical treatment of intervertebral disc damage.
5. Describe the postoperative nursing management of a patient who has undergone vertebral disc surgery.
6. Discuss the etiology and nursing management of common foot disorders.
7. Describe the etiology, pathophysiology, clinical manifestations, and nursing and interprofessional management of osteomalacia, osteoporosis, and Paget's disease.

KEY TERMS

degenerative disc disease (DDD), p. 1486
hallux valgus, p. 1490
herniated disc, p. 1486
low back pain, p. 1484
muscular dystrophy (MD), p. 1483

osteochondroma, p. 1482
osteomalacia, p. 1491
osteomyelitis, p. 1478
osteopenia, p. 1493
osteoporosis, p. 1492

osteosarcoma, p. 1482
Paget's disease, p. 1495
sarcoma, p. 1482

We were made to move! This chapter reviews a variety of acute and chronic musculoskeletal problems unrelated to trauma that affect the musculoskeletal system. These include osteomyelitis, bone cancer, foot disorders, back pain, and metabolic bone diseases. These problems can lead to changes in mobility that affect almost every system in the body. They are a common source of pain and physical limitations that restrict the ability to fully take part in activities of daily living (ADLs), leading to disability. The nurse plays a key role in assessing pain and functional ability and initiating interventions to prevent injury and maintain mobility.

OSTEOMYELITIS

Etiology and Pathophysiology

Osteomyelitis is a severe infection of the bone, bone marrow, and surrounding soft tissue. Although *Staphylococcus aureus* is the most common cause of infection, a variety of pathogens can cause osteomyelitis (Table 63.1).[1]

Infecting microorganisms can invade by indirect or direct entry. *Indirect entry* (hematogenous) is usually associated with infection with 1 microorganism. Indirect injury accounts for only 20% of all cases. It most often affects children younger than 17 years. Risk factors in adults are older age, debilitation, hemodialysis, sickle cell disease, and IV drug use. The vertebrae are the most common site of infection in adults.[2]

Direct entry osteomyelitis most often affects adults. It can occur when an open wound (e.g., penetrating wounds, fractures, surgery) allows microorganisms to enter the body. Osteomyelitis also may be related to a foreign body, such as an implant or an orthopedic prosthetic device (e.g., plate, total joint prosthesis). It may occur in the feet of patients with diabetes or vascular disease–related ulcers or in the hips or sacrum near a pressure injury. More than 1 microorganism is usually involved.[1]

After entering the blood, microorganisms grow and pressure increases because of the nonexpanding nature of most bone. This increasing pressure eventually leads to ischemia and vascular compromise of the periosteum. The infection spreads

TABLE 63.1 Organisms Causing Osteomyelitis

Organism	Predisposing Problem
Staphylococcus aureus	Pressure injury, penetrating wound, open fracture, orthopedic surgery, disorders with vascular insufficiency (e.g., diabetes, atherosclerosis)
Staphylococcus epidermidis	Indwelling prosthetic devices (e.g., joint replacements, fracture fixation devices)
Streptococcus viridans	Abscessed tooth, gingival disease
Escherichia coli	Urinary tract infection
Mycobacterium tuberculosis	Tuberculosis
Neisseria gonorrhoeae	Gonorrhea
Pseudomonas	Puncture wounds, IV drug use
Salmonella	Sickle cell disease
Fungi, mycobacteria	Immunocompromised host

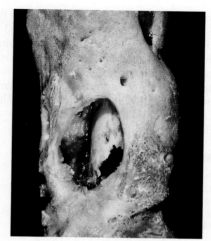

FIG. 63.2 Resection of femur due to osteomyelitis. (From Thibodeau GA, Patton KT: *The human body in health and disease,* ed 5, St Louis, 2010, Mosby.)

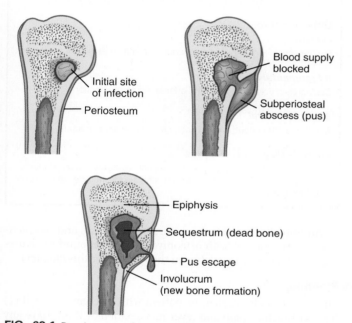

FIG. 63.1 Development of osteomyelitis infection with involucrum and sequestrum.

through the bone cortex and marrow cavity, obstructing blood flow and causing and necrosis.

Bone death occurs due to ischemia. The area of dead bone eventually separates from the surrounding living bone, forming *sequestra.* The part of the periosteum that continues to have a blood supply forms new bone called *involucrum* (Fig. 63.1). Antibiotics or white blood cells (WBCs) have difficulty reaching the sequestrum through the blood. Thus sequestrum may become a reservoir for microorganisms that spread to other sites, including the lungs and brain. If the sequestrum does not resolve or is not debrided surgically, a sinus tract may develop. Chronic, purulent cutaneous drainage from the tract results.

Clinical Manifestations and Complications

Acute osteomyelitis refers to the initial infection or an infection of less than 1 month in duration. Local manifestations of acute osteomyelitis include constant bone pain that worsens with activity and is unrelieved by rest; swelling, tenderness,

and warmth at the infection site; and restricted movement of the affected part. Systemic manifestations include fever, night sweats, chills, restlessness, nausea, and malaise. Later signs include drainage from cutaneous sinus tracts or the fracture site.

Chronic osteomyelitis refers to a bone infection that lasts longer than 1 month or an infection that did not respond to initial antibiotic treatment. Chronic osteomyelitis may be a continuous, persistent problem (a result of inadequate acute treatment) or a process of exacerbations and remissions (Fig. 63.2). Systemic manifestations are lessened. Local signs of infection become more common, including constant bone pain and swelling and warmth at the infection site. Over time, granulation tissue turns to scar tissue. The avascular scar tissue is an ideal site for continued microorganism growth because it cannot be penetrated by antibiotics.

Long-term, and mostly rare, complications of osteomyelitis include septicemia, septic arthritis, pathologic fractures, and amyloidosis.

Diagnostic Studies

Bone or soft tissue biopsy is the definitive way to identify the causative agent. The patient's blood and wound cultures are often positive. Increased WBC count and erythrocyte sedimentation rate (ESR) may occur. High C-reactive protein (CRP) may occur with acute infection. Signs of osteomyelitis usually do not appear on x-rays until 2 to 4 weeks after the initial clinical symptoms. By this time, the disease will have progressed. Compared to x-rays, CT scan may be more helpful in assessing the extent of infection. In the acute phase, MRI may be more sensitive than CT in detecting bone marrow edema, which is an early sign of osteomyelitis. Radionuclide bone scans (technetium-99m) also show abnormalities earlier than x-rays. A WBC scan (indium-111–labeled cells) may help pinpoint the area of infection.[2]

Interprofessional Care

Aggressive, prolonged IV antibiotic therapy is the treatment of choice for acute osteomyelitis if bone ischemia has not yet occurred. Cultures or a bone biopsy should be done, if possible, before starting drug therapy. Any related soft tissue abscess or ulceration often needs surgical debridement or drainage.

IV antibiotic therapy starts in the hospital and then continues at home for 4 to 6 weeks. A few persons need therapy for 3 to 6 months. Patients may be discharged to home care or a skilled nursing facility so the antibiotics can be given through a central venous access device (CVAD). (CVADs are discussed in Chapter 16.) A variety of antibiotics are used, depending on the culture results and likelihood of resistance. These include oxacillin, nafcillin, clindamycin, vancomycin, ceftriaxone, cefazolin, ceftazidime, gentamicin, and linezolid.

🔲 DRUG ALERT   Gentamicin

- Assess patient for dehydration before starting therapy.
- Ensure renal function testing is done before starting therapy, especially in older patients.
- Monitor peak and trough blood levels to achieve therapeutic effect and minimize renal and inner ear toxicity.
- Teach patient to notify HCP if any vision, hearing, or urinary problems develop.

Treatment of chronic osteomyelitis includes (1) surgical removal of the poorly perfused tissue and dead bone and (2) extended use of antibiotics. In adults with chronic osteomyelitis, oral therapy with a fluoroquinolone (e.g., ciprofloxacin [Cipro]) for 6 to 8 weeks may be prescribed instead of IV antibiotics. Oral antibiotics also may be given for 4 to 8 weeks after acute IV therapy is done to ensure the infection is resolved. The patient's response to drug therapy is monitored through bone scans and ESR testing.

Acrylic bead chains containing antibiotics may be implanted to help combat the infection. After debridement of the dead, infected tissue, a suction irrigation system may be inserted, and the wound closed. Intermittent or constant irrigation of the area with antibiotics may be used. Another option for wound management is negative-pressure wound therapy (discussed in Chapter 11). Casts or braces may be applied to protect the limb or the surgical site.

Hyperbaric O_2 may be given as an adjunct therapy in refractory cases of chronic osteomyelitis. It stimulates new blood growth and healing in the infected tissue (see p. 167 in Chapter 11).

If an orthopedic prosthetic device is the source of chronic infection, it must be removed. Muscle flaps or skin grafts provide wound coverage over the dead space (cavity) in the bone. Bone grafts may help to restore blood flow. However, flaps or grafts should never be placed in the presence of active or suspected infection.

Amputation of the extremity may be needed if bone destruction is extensive. Amputation should improve quality of life and may save the patient's life if systemic complications are developing.

❖ NURSING MANAGEMENT: OSTEOMYELITIS

◆ Nursing Assessment

Subjective and objective data that should be obtained from a person with osteomyelitis are outlined in Table 63.2.

◆ Nursing Diagnoses

Nursing diagnoses for the patient with osteomyelitis may include:

- Acute pain
- Impaired physical mobility
- Lack of knowledge

TABLE 63.2   Nursing Assessment

Osteomyelitis

Subjective Data

Important Health Information

Past health history: Bone trauma, open fracture, open or puncture wounds, other infections (e.g., streptococcal sore throat, bacterial pneumonia, sinusitis, skin or tooth infection, chronic urinary tract infection)

Medications: Analgesics or antibiotics

Surgery or other treatments: Bone surgery

Functional Health Patterns

Health perception–health management: IV drug and alcohol use. Malaise

Nutritional-metabolic: Anorexia, weight loss. Chills

Activity-exercise: Weakness, paralysis, muscle spasms around affected area

Cognitive-perceptual: Local tenderness over affected area, increased pain with movement of affected area

Coping–stress tolerance: Irritability, withdrawal, dependency, anger

Objective Data

General

Restlessness. High, spiking temperature. Night sweats

Integumentary

Diaphoresis. Erythema, warmth, edema at site of infection

Musculoskeletal

Restricted movement; wound drainage. Spontaneous fracture

Possible Diagnostic Findings

Leukocytosis, positive blood and/or wound cultures, ↑ ESR. Presence of sequestrum and involucrum on x-rays, radionuclide bone scans, CT, and MRI

Additional information on nursing diagnoses and interventions for the patient with osteomyelitis can be found in eNursing Care Plan 63.1 (available on the website for this chapter).

◆ Planning

The overall goals are that the patient with osteomyelitis will (1) have satisfactory pain and fever management, (2) not have any complications associated with osteomyelitis, (3) adhere to the treatment plan, and (4) maintain a positive outlook on the outcome of the disease.

◆ Nursing Implementation

◆ Health Promotion.
Control of other current infections (e.g., urinary or respiratory tract, pressure injuries) is important in preventing osteomyelitis. Persons at risk for osteomyelitis are those who are immunocompromised or have diabetes, orthopedic prosthetic implants, or vascular insufficiency. Teach the at-risk patient about the local and systemic signs of osteomyelitis. Encourage the patient to contact the HCP about bone pain, fever, swelling, and restricted limb movement so that treatment can be started. Teach caregivers about their role in monitoring the patient's health.

◆ Acute Care.
Some immobilization of the affected limb (e.g., splint, traction) is usually needed to decrease pain and reduce risk for further injury. Carefully handle the limb and avoid undue manipulation. This may increase pain and cause a pathologic fracture. Assess the patient's pain. Muscle spasms may cause minor to severe pain. Nonsteroidal antiinflammatory

NURSING MANAGEMENT
Caring for the Patient With Osteomyelitis

- Give IV antibiotics as ordered.
- Assess wound for signs of worsening infection.
- Teach patient and caregiver about antibiotic side effects and length of treatment, signs and symptoms of worsening infection, and use of hyperbaric O_2 if ordered.
- Assess for muscle spasms and give muscle relaxant as ordered. Assess patient response.
- Assess pain intensity and give analgesics as ordered. Assess patient response.
- Handle affected limb carefully to decrease pain and additional injury.
- Assess neurovascular condition of affected limb and immediately inform HCP of significant changes.
- Oversee UAP:
  - Handle affected limb carefully based on RN instruction.
  - Help patient with passive ROM of adjacent joints and active ROM exercises of unaffected limb.
  - Notify RN about patient reports of pain, tingling, or decreased sensation in the affected extremity.

Collaborate With Physical Therapist

- Assess patient's current mobility and need for aid.
- Teach safe ambulation with assistive device based on patient's weight-bearing restrictions.
- Establish exercise plan and teach patient to perform exercises safely.
- Coordinate PT so that patient can receive timely analgesia.
- Discuss home environment with patient and identify modifications to promote recovery (e.g., stair training, bed placement on first level).

Collaborate With Occupational Therapist

- Assess impact of patient's condition on ability to perform ADLs.
- Teach patient use of assistive devices (e.g., long-handled reacher, shoe donner) to promote self-care while maintaining activity restrictions.

drugs (NSAIDs), opioid analgesics, and muscle relaxants may be given. Encourage nondrug approaches to pain management (e.g., guided imagery, relaxation breathing) (see Chapter 6).

Dressings are used to absorb drainage from wounds and debride dead tissue from the wound bed. These include dry, sterile dressings; dressings saturated in saline or antibiotic solution; wet-to-dry dressings; and dressings applied with negative-pressure wound therapy. Sterile technique is essential when changing the dressing. Handle soiled dressings carefully to prevent transfer of bacteria to other areas of the wound. Discard dressings appropriately to prevent spread of infection to other patients.

The patient is often placed on bed rest in the early stages of acute infection. Good body alignment and frequent position changes promote comfort and prevent complications related to immobility. Flexion contracture of the affected lower extremity is common as the patient often positions the leg in a flexed position to promote comfort. Footdrop can develop quickly due to Achilles tendon contracture if the foot is not supported in a neutral position by a splint or boot. A tight splint or dressing may compress and injure the peroneal nerve.

Teach the patient the possible adverse and toxic reactions associated with prolonged high-dose antibiotic therapy. These reactions include hearing deficit, impaired renal function, and neurotoxicity (e.g., limb weakness or numbness, cognitive changes, vision changes, headache, behavioral problems). Reactions associated with cephalosporins (e.g., cefazolin) include hives, severe or watery diarrhea, blood in stools, and throat or mouth sores.

Tendonitis or tendon rupture (especially the Achilles tendon) can occur with use of fluoroquinolones (e.g., ciprofloxacin). Monitor peak and trough blood levels of most antibiotics to avoid adverse effects. Lengthy antibiotic therapy can cause an overgrowth of *Candida albicans* and *Clostridium difficile* in the genitourinary (GU) and gastrointestinal (GI) tracts, especially in immunosuppressed and older adult patients. Teach the patient to report any changes in the oral cavity (e.g., whitish yellow, curdlike lesions) or the GU tract (e.g., perianal itching, discharge).

? CHECK YOUR PRACTICE

Your patient on the orthopedic unit is a 22-yr-old man who was in a serious all-terrain vehicle accident in a remote area 4 days ago. He is now slowly recovering from his head injury and surgical repair of an open fracture of the femur. Yesterday, he was diagnosed with acute osteomyelitis. He is very angry and at times disoriented. When you try to assess his leg, he yells at you, "It hurts. Leave it alone!"
- What are your priorities of care?
- What signs and symptoms would suggest the patient's condition is worsening?

The patient and caregivers may be anxious and discouraged because of the serious nature of osteomyelitis, the uncertainty of the outcome, and the long, costly treatment. Continued psychologic and emotional support is an integral part of nursing management.

◆ **Ambulatory Care.** IV antibiotics can be given to the patient in a skilled nursing facility or home setting. If at home, teach the patient and caregiver how to manage the CVAD. Review how to administer the antibiotic and reinforce the need for follow-up laboratory testing. Stress the importance of continuing to take the full course of antibiotics prescribed, even after symptoms have improved.

Dressing changes are often needed if the patient has an open wound. The patient and caregiver may need supplies and instruction for completing the dressing change. If the osteomyelitis becomes chronic, the patient needs continued physical and psychologic support.

◆ **Evaluation**

The expected outcomes are that the patient with osteomyelitis will
- Have satisfactory pain management
- Adhere to the recommended treatment plan
- Show a consistent increase in mobility and range of motion

BONE TUMORS

Primary bone tumors, both benign and malignant, are rare in adults. They account for only about 3% of all tumors. Metastatic bone cancer, in which cancer has spread from another site, is a more common problem.

BENIGN BONE TUMORS

Benign bone tumors are more common than primary malignant tumors. The main types of benign bone tumors are osteochondroma, osteoclastoma, and enchondroma (Table 63.3). They are often removed surgically.

Osteochondroma

Osteochondroma is the most common primary benign bone tumor. It is characterized by an overgrowth of cartilage and bone near the end of the bone at the growth plate. They most often occur in the pelvis, scapula, or long bones of the leg.

Manifestations include a painless, hard, immobile mass; shorter-than-normal height for age; soreness of muscles close to the tumor; one leg or arm longer than the other; and pressure or irritation with exercise. Some may be asymptomatic. Diagnosis is confirmed using x-ray, CT scan, and MRI.

No treatment is needed for asymptomatic osteochondroma. Patients should have regular screening examinations to detect progression to cancer as soon as possible. If the tumor is causing pain or neurologic manifestations because of compression, surgical removal is usually done.

MALIGNANT BONE TUMORS

A sarcoma is a malignant tumor that develops in bone, muscle, fat, nerve, or cartilage. The most common types of sarcomas are osteosarcoma, chondrosarcoma, and Ewing's sarcoma (Table 63.3). In 2018, 3450 new cases of bone and joint cancer are expected in the United States, with an estimated 1590 deaths.[3] Primary malignant tumors occur most often during childhood and young adulthood. They cause bone destruction and have rapid metastasis.

Osteosarcoma

Osteosarcoma is an extremely aggressive primary bone cancer that rapidly spreads to distant sites. It usually occurs in the pelvis or metaphyseal region of the long bones of extremities, especially in the distal femur, proximal tibia, and proximal humerus (Fig. 63.3, A). Osteosarcoma is the most common bone cancer affecting children and young adults. It can occur in older adults, but not as often. It is most often associated with Paget's disease (discussed on p. 1495) and prior radiation.

The gradual onset of pain and swelling in the affected bone are the most common manifestations. The pain may be worse at night and increase with activity. A minor injury does not cause the cancer but may bring it to medical attention. Metastasis is present in 10% to 20% of people at the time of diagnosis.

Diagnosis is confirmed from tissue biopsy, increased serum alkaline phosphatase and calcium, x-ray, CT or PET scans, and MRI.

Preoperative chemotherapy may be used to decrease tumor size before surgery. Limb salvage procedures are usually considered if a clear (no cancer present) 6- to 7-cm margin surrounds the lesion. Limb salvage is usually not possible if the patient has major nerve or blood vessel involvement, pathologic fracture, infection, or extensive muscle involvement.

The use of adjunct chemotherapy after amputation or limb salvage has increased the 5-year survival rate to 70% in people without metastasis. Chemotherapy includes combinations of methotrexate, doxorubicin, cisplatin, ifosfamide, cyclophosphamide, and etoposide.[4]

Metastatic Bone Cancer

The most common type of malignant bone tumor occurs because of spread (metastasis) from a primary tumor at another site. Common primary sites include breast, colon, prostate, lungs, kidney, and thyroid.[5] Metastatic cancer cells travel from the primary tumor to the bone via the lymph and blood supply.

TABLE 63.3	Types of Primary Bone Tumors
Types	**Description**
Benign	
Enchondroma	• Intramedullary cartilage tumor usually found in cavity of a single hand or foot bone • Rarely transforms to cancer • If tumor becomes painful, surgical resection is done • Peak incidence in people ages 10–20 yr
Osteochondroma	• Most common benign bone tumor • Often found in pelvis, scapula, or metaphyseal part of long bones • Occurs most often in people ages 10–25 yr • May transform to cancer (chondrosarcoma)
Osteoclastoma (giant cell tumor)	• Arises in cancellous ends of arm and leg bones • About 10% are locally aggressive and may spread to lungs • High rate of local recurrence after surgery and chemotherapy
Malignant	
Chondrosarcoma	• Most often occurs in cartilage in arm, leg, and pelvic bones of adults ages 50–70 yr • Can arise from benign bone tumors (osteochondromas) • Wide surgical resection is typically done as tumor rarely responds to radiation and chemotherapy • Survival rate depends on stage, size, and grade of tumor (Fig. 63.3, B)
Ewing's sarcoma	• Develops in medullary cavity of pelvis and long bones, especially femur, humerus, and tibia • Usually occurs in children and teenagers • Use of wide surgical resection, radiation, and chemotherapy has improved 5-yr survival rate to 60%
Osteosarcoma	• Most common primary bone cancer • Occurs mostly in males ages 10–25 • Most often in pelvis or bones of arms, legs (Fig. 63.3, A)

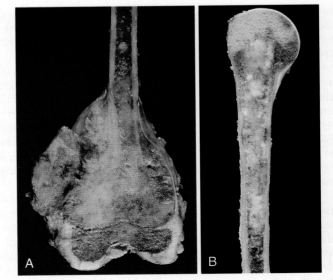

FIG. 63.3 A, Osteosarcoma. B, Chondrosarcoma. (From Damjanov I, Linder J: *Anderson's pathology*, ed 10, St Louis, 1996, Mosby.)

Metastatic bone lesions often occur in the spine, ribs, or pelvis.[5] Pathologic fractures at the site of metastasis are common because the bone is weakened. High serum calcium occurs as damaged bones release calcium.

Once a primary lesion has been found, radionuclide bone scans are often done to detect metastatic lesions before they are visible on x-ray. Metastatic bone lesions may occur at any time (even years later) after diagnosis and treatment of the primary tumor. Bone metastasis should be suspected in any patient who has local bone pain and a history of cancer. Surgical stabilization of the bone may be indicated for fracture or to prevent fracture in a high-risk patient. Prognosis depends on the primary type of cancer and any other sites of metastasis. Possible palliative treatment consists of radiation and pain management (see Chapter 15).

❖ NURSING MANAGEMENT: BONE CANCER

Nursing care of the patient with bone cancer does not differ significantly from the care provided to the patient with cancer of any other body system (see Chapter 15). Monitor the tumor site for swelling, changes in circulation, and decreased movement, sensation, or joint function.

Use special care to prevent pathologic fractures and reduce the complications associated with them. Prevent fractures by careful handling and support of the affected extremity and log-rolling the patient on bed rest. Note weakness caused by anemia and decreased mobility.

Treatment for hypercalcemia may be started if bone decalcification occurs. The patient may be unwilling to exercise or take part in activities because of weakness from the disease and treatment, fear of falling and fracturing a bone, and fear of pain. Provide regular rest periods between activities.

Assess the patient for the location and severity of pain. The pain associated with bone cancer can be severe. It is often caused by the tumor pressing against nerves and other organs near the bone. New onset or changes in pain severity may indicate pathologic fracture. Ensure adequate pain medication is provided. Sometimes radiation therapy is used as a palliative therapy to shrink the tumor and decrease pain.

Assist the patient and caregiver in accepting the prognosis associated with bone cancer. Give special attention to problems of pain and disability, side effects of chemotherapy, and postoperative care (e.g., after spinal cord decompression or amputation). As with all types of cancer, stress the importance of follow-up examinations.

MUSCULAR DYSTROPHY

Muscular dystrophy (MD) is a group of genetic diseases characterized by progressive symmetric wasting of skeletal muscles without evidence of neurologic involvement. A gradual loss of strength with increasing disability and deformity occurs with all forms of MD. The types of MD differ in the groups of muscles affected, age of onset, rate of progression, and mode of genetic inheritance (Table 63.4). Duchenne MD is the most common type.

Genetic Link

Duchenne and Becker MD are X-linked recessive disorders usually seen only in males. (X-linked recessive disorders are discussed in Chapter 12.) These disorders are caused by a mutation of the dystrophin (DMD) gene. Dystrophin is a protein that

TABLE 63.4   Select Types of Muscular Dystrophy

Type	Genetic Basis	Manifestations
Becker	• X-linked • Mutation of dystrophin gene	• Very similar but less severe than Duchenne MD • Onset ages 5–15 • Slower course of pelvic and shoulder muscle wasting than Duchenne • Cardiomyopathy • Respiratory failure • May survive into 50s
Duchenne	• X-linked • Mutation of dystrophin gene	• Most common form of MD • Primarily affects boys • Onset before age 5 • Progressive weakness of pelvic and shoulder muscles • Unable to walk by age 12 • Cardiomyopathy • Respiratory failure in 20s • Mental impairment
Facioscapulohumeral	• Autosomal dominant • Deletion of chromosome 4q35	• Onset before age 20 • Slowly progressive weakness of face, shoulder muscles, and upper arms and lower legs • Can affect vision and hearing
Limb-girdle	• Autosomal recessive or autosomal dominant • Mutation in any of at least 15 genes affecting proteins needed for muscle function	• Group of disorders affecting voluntary muscles, especially those of hips and shoulders • Onset ranges from early childhood to early adulthood or later • Slow progressive weakness of hip and shoulder muscles

helps keep skeletal muscle fibers intact. Abnormal dystrophin can cause defects in the muscle fiber and muscle fiber degeneration. Genetic testing can detect a mutation in the *DMD* gene and confirm a diagnosis.[6]

Other diagnostic studies for MD include muscle serum enzymes (especially creatine kinase), electromyogram (EMG) testing, and muscle fiber biopsy. Classic findings on muscle biopsy include fat and connective tissue deposits, muscle fiber degeneration and necrosis, and a deficiency of dystrophin. An ECG may show abnormalities that suggest cardiomyopathy.

No definitive therapy is available to stop progressive muscle wasting of MD. Corticosteroid therapy is part of the standard of care. It may slow disease progression for up to 2 years.[7] In 2017 the FDA approved 2 new medications to treat MD. Deflazacort (Emflaza) is the first corticosteroid approved to treat Duchene MD. Eteplirsen (Exondys 51) is the first disease-modifying drug to treat Duchene MD patients who have a certain dystrophin gene mutation.[8] Other clinical trials underway involve gene therapy and stem cell transplantation.

The main treatment goals are to preserve mobility and independence through exercise, physical therapy, and use of assistive devices. Progressive muscle weakening around the trunk can cause spinal collapse. The patient may be fitted early with an orthotic jacket to give stability and prevent further deformity or injury.[9]

Life expectancy is increasing due to advances in cardiac and respiratory care. Cardiomyopathy often occurs and causes heart failure. Dysrhythmias are a frequent cause of death.[6] Gradual decreases in respiratory function often lead to the use of continuous positive airway pressure (CPAP). Eventually tracheostomy and mechanical ventilation are needed to support respiratory function.

Encourage communication between the patient and family to cope with the emotional and physical demands of MD. Teach the patient and caregiver range-of-motion (ROM) exercises, principles of good nutrition, and signs of disease progression. Genetic testing and counseling may be recommended for persons with a family history of MD.

GENETICS IN CLINICAL PRACTICE
Duchenne and Becker Muscular Dystrophy (MD)

Genetic Basis
- Caused by various mutations in the dystrophin (DMD) gene
- Gene provides instructions for making dystrophin, a protein that helps keep muscle fibers intact
- Dystrophin is found mainly in skeletal and cardiac muscle
- Inherited in an X-linked recessive pattern
- Females in affected families have a 50% chance of inheriting and passing the defective gene to their children

Incidence
- Between 400 and 600 boys are born with MD each year in the United States.
- Together these disorders affect 1 in 3500 to 5000 newborn males worldwide.

Genetic Testing
- DNA testing for mutations in dystrophin gene is available.
- Genetic testing and counseling should be considered for those with a family history of MD.

Clinical Implications
- Because there are many types of MD with different genetic bases, knowing the type of MD is important to determine treatment and possible genetic counseling recommendations.

Focus care on keeping the patient active as long as possible. Prolonged bed rest should be avoided because immobility can cause more muscle wasting. As the disease progresses, teach the patient to limit sedentary periods to prevent skin breakdown and respiratory complications. Ongoing medical and nursing care is needed throughout the patient's life.

The Muscular Dystrophy Association (www.mda.org) is an important resource with information about support services for the patient and caregivers. The website gives updates about the latest clinical trials and treatment advances.

⚠ SAFETY ALERT Muscular Dystrophy
- Support respiratory function as needed.
- Fit patient with an orthotic jacket or brace to prevent deformity or injury.

LOW BACK PAIN

Low back pain is most often due to a musculoskeletal problem. It may be localized or diffuse. In *localized pain,* patients feel soreness or discomfort when a specific area of the lower back is palpated or pressed. *Diffuse pain* occurs over a larger area and comes from deep tissue.

Low back pain may be radicular or referred. *Radicular pain* is caused by irritation of a nerve root. Radicular pain is not isolated to a single location. Instead, it radiates or moves along a nerve distribution. Sciatica is an example of radicular pain. *Referred pain* is felt in the lower back, but the source of the pain is another location (e.g., kidneys, lower abdomen).

Low back pain affects about 80% of adults in the United States at least once during their lives. Backache is second only to headache as the most common pain problem. It is the leading cause of job-related disability and a major contributor to missed work days.[10]

Low back pain is common because the lumbar region (1) bears most of the weight of the body, (2) is the most flexible region of the spinal column, (3) has nerve roots that are at risk for injury or disease, and (4) has a naturally poor biomechanical structure. Risk factors include lack of muscle tone, excess body weight, stress, poor posture, smoking, pregnancy, prior compression fracture of the spine, spinal problems since birth, and a family history of back pain. Jobs that require repetitive heavy lifting, vibration (such as a jackhammer operator), and extended periods of sitting are associated with low back pain.

The causes of low back pain of musculoskeletal origin include (1) acute lumbosacral strain, (2) instability of the lumbosacral bony mechanism, (3) osteoarthritis of the lumbosacral vertebrae, (4) degenerative disc disease, and (5) herniation of an intervertebral disc.

Health care personnel who perform direct patient care activities are at high risk for developing low back pain.[11] Lifting and moving patients, excessive bending or leaning forward, and frequent twisting can result in low back pain that causes lost time and productivity and disability. Nurses should follow the agency's safe patient handling standards to avoid injury.[12]

ACUTE LOW BACK PAIN

Acute low back pain lasts 4 weeks or less. Most acute low back pain is caused by trauma or an activity that produces undue stress (often hyperflexion) on the lower back. Examples of trauma or activities that cause acute back pain are heavy lifting; overuse of back muscles during yard work; a sports injury; or a sudden jolt, as in a motor vehicle crash.

Often symptoms do not appear at the time of injury. They develop later (usually within 24 hours) because of a gradual increase in pressure on the nerve from an intervertebral disc and/or associated edema. Symptoms may range from muscle ache to shooting or stabbing pain, limited flexibility or ROM, or an inability to stand upright.

Few definitive diagnostic abnormalities are present with nerve irritation and muscle strain. One test is the straight-leg-raising test (see Chapter 61, p. 1438). MRI and CT scans are not done unless trauma or systemic disease (e.g., cancer, spinal infection) is suspected. MRI findings may be limited in the acute phase of an injury due to increased edema near the injury.

NURSING AND INTERPROFESSIONAL
❖ MANAGEMENT: ACUTE LOW BACK PAIN

◆ Nursing Assessment
Subjective and objective data that should be obtained from the patient with low back pain are outlined in Table 63.5.

TABLE 63.5 Nursing Assessment

Low Back Pain

Subjective Data

Important Health Information

Past health history: Acute or chronic lumbosacral strain/trauma, osteoarthritis, degenerative disc disease, obesity
Medications: Opioid analgesics and NSAIDs, muscle relaxants, corticosteroids, over-the-counter remedies (e.g., topical ointments, patches)
Surgery or other treatments: Back surgery, epidural corticosteroid injections

Functional Health Patterns

Health perception–health management: Smoking, lack of exercise
Nutritional-metabolic: Obesity
Activity-exercise: Poor posture, muscle spasms, activity intolerance
Elimination: Constipation
Sleep-rest: Interrupted sleep
Cognitive-perceptual: Pain in back, buttocks, or leg associated with walking, turning, straining, coughing, leg raising. Numbness or tingling of legs, feet, toes
Role-relationship: Occupations requiring heavy lifting, vibrations, or extended driving. Change in role within family structure due to inability to work and provide income

Objective Data

General

Guarded movement

Neurologic

Depressed or absent Achilles tendon reflex or patellar tendon reflex. Positive straight-leg-raising test, positive crossover straight-leg-raising test, positive Trendelenburg test

Musculoskeletal

Tense, tight paravertebral muscles on palpation, ↓ range of motion in spine

Possible Diagnostic Findings

Localization of site of lesion or disorder on myelogram, CT scan, or MRI. Determination of nerve root impingement on EMG

TABLE 63.6 Patient & Caregiver Teaching

Low Back Problems

Include the following instructions when teaching the patient and caregiver how to manage low back problems:

Do

- Maintain healthy body weight.
- Maintain a neutral pelvic position if standing. Place 1 foot on a low stool if standing for long periods.
- Choose a seat with good lower back support, armrests, and a swivel base. Place a pillow at the lumbar spine to maintain normal curvature. Keep knees and hips level.
- Sleep in a side-lying position with knees and hips bent, and a pillow between the knees for support.
- Sleep on back with a lift under knees and legs or on back with 10-in–high pillow under knees to flex hips and knees.
- Use proper body mechanics when lifting heavy objects. Bend at the knees, not at the waist, and stand up slowly while holding object close to your body.
- Take part in regular strength and flexibility training and low-impact aerobic exercise.
- Use local heat and cold application to relieve muscle tension.

Do Not

- Lean forward without bending knees.
- Lift anything above level of elbows.
- Stand unmoving for prolonged time.
- Sleep on abdomen or on back or side with legs out straight.
- Exercise without consulting HCP if having severe pain.
- Exceed prescribed amount and type of exercises without consulting HCP.
- Smoke or use tobacco products.

a supine or side-lying position with knees and hips flexed prevents pressure on support muscles, ligaments, and lumbosacral joints. Recommend use of a firm mattress.

Teach patients the importance of smoking cessation. Tobacco use impairs circulation to the intervertebral discs and contributes to low back pain.

◆ **Acute Care.** If acute muscle spasms and accompanying pain are not severe and unbearable, the patient is treated as an outpatient with NSAIDs and muscle relaxants (e.g., cyclobenzaprine). Massage and back manipulation, acupuncture, and the application of cold and hot compresses may help some patients. Severe pain may require a brief course of corticosteroids or opioid analgesics.

Some people may need a brief period (1 to 2 days) of rest at home but should avoid prolonged bed rest. Most patients do better if they continue their regular activities. Patients should refrain from activities that increase the pain, including lifting, bending, twisting, and prolonged sitting. Symptoms of acute low back pain usually improve within 2 weeks and often resolve without treatment.

Teach the patient about the cause of the pain and ways to prevent further episodes. Muscle stretching and strengthening exercises may be part of the management plan. Although the physical therapist often teaches the exercises, reinforce the type and frequency of prescribed exercise and the reason for the program.

Other nursing interventions for the patient with low back pain are detailed in eNursing Care Plan 63.2 (available on the website for this chapter).

Ambulatory Care. The goal of management is to make an episode of acute low back pain an isolated incident. If the lumbosacral

◆ **Nursing Implementation**

◆ **Health Promotion.** Serve as a role model by always using proper body mechanics. This includes increasing the patient's bed height, bending at the knees, asking for help in lifting and moving patients, and using lifting devices.

Assess the patient's use of body mechanics and offer advice when the person does activities that could produce back strain. Some HCPs refer patients with back pain to a program called "Back School." This formal program is usually taught by an HCP, nurse, or physical therapist. It is designed to teach the patient how to minimize back pain and avoid repeat episodes of pain. Tips for prevention of back injury are listed in Table 63.6. Referral to a physical therapist or personal trainer to address posture and core and abdomen strength may be appropriate. Recommend flat shoes or shoes with low heels and shock-absorbing shoe inserts for women.

Advise patients to maintain a healthy body weight. Excess body weight places more stress on the lower back. It weakens abdominal muscles that support the lower back. Sleeping position is important in preventing low back pain. Teach patients to avoid sleeping in a prone position because it causes excessive lumbar lordosis, placing stress on the lower back. Sleeping in

area is unstable, repeated episodes are likely. Obesity, poor posture, poor muscle support, older age, or trauma may weaken the lumbosacral spine, so it is unable to meet the demands placed on it without strain. Exercise is aimed at strengthening the supporting muscles.

Persistent use of poor body mechanics may result in repeated episodes of low back pain. If the strain is work related, occupational counseling may be needed. Low back pain can cause frustration, pain, and disability. Provide emotional support and understanding care of the patient.

CHRONIC LOW BACK PAIN

Chronic low back pain lasts more than 3 months or involves a repeated incapacitating episode. It is often progressive, and the cause can be hard to determine. Causes include (1) degenerative conditions, such as arthritis or disc disease; (2) osteoporosis or other metabolic bone diseases; (3) weakness from the scar tissue of prior injury; (4) chronic strain on lower back muscles from obesity, pregnancy, or stressful postures on the job; and (5) congenital spine problems.

Spinal Stenosis

Spinal stenosis is a narrowing of the spinal canal, which holds the spinal cord. Stenosis in the lumbar spine is a common cause of chronic low back pain. Spinal stenosis can be acquired or inherited. A common acquired cause is osteoarthritis. Arthritic changes (bone spurs, calcification of spinal ligaments, disc degeneration) narrow the space around the spinal canal and nerve roots, eventually leading to compression. Inflammation caused by the compression results in pain, weakness, and numbness.

Other acquired conditions that may cause spinal stenosis include rheumatoid arthritis, spinal tumors, Paget's disease, and traumatic damage to the vertebral column. Inherited conditions that lead to spinal stenosis include congenital spinal stenosis and scoliosis.

The pain associated with lumbar spinal stenosis often starts in the lower back and then radiates to the buttock and leg. It is worse with walking or prolonged standing. Numbness, tingling, weakness, and heaviness in the legs and buttocks may be present. History of decreased pain when the patient bends forward or sits is often a sign of spinal stenosis. In most cases, stenosis slowly progresses.

❖ Interprofessional and Nursing Care

The management and treatment of chronic low back pain are similar to those for acute low back pain. Manage the patient's pain and stiffness with mild analgesics, such as NSAIDs, for daily comfort. Antidepressants (e.g., duloxetine [Cymbalta]) may help with pain management and sleep problems. The antiseizure drug gabapentin (Neurontin) may improve walking and relieve leg symptoms.

Weight reduction, rest periods, local heat or cold application, physical therapy, and exercise and activity throughout the day help keep the muscles and joints mobilized. Cold, damp weather worsens the back pain. Pain can be decreased with rest and local heat application. Complementary and alternative therapies, such as biofeedback, acupuncture, and yoga, may help reduce the pain. "Back School" (discussed on p. 1485) can significantly reduce pain and improve body posture.

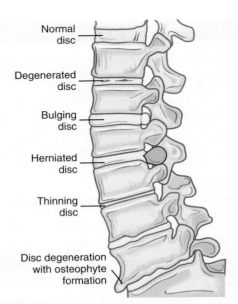

FIG. 63.4 Common causes of degenerative disc damage.

Minimally invasive treatments, such as epidural corticosteroid injections and implanted devices that deliver pain medication, are options for those with chronic low back pain that does not respond to the usual therapeutic options. Surgical intervention may be indicated in patients with severe chronic low back pain who receive no benefit from conservative care and/or have continued neurologic deficits. (Surgery for low back pain is discussed on p. 1488.)

INTERVERTEBRAL DISC DISEASE

Intervertebral discs separate the vertebrae and help absorb shock for the spine. *Intervertebral disc disease* involves the deterioration, herniation, or other dysfunction of the intervertebral discs. Disc disorders can affect the cervical, thoracic, and lumbar spine.

Etiology and Pathophysiology

Degenerative disc disease (DDD) results from loss of fluid in the intervertebral discs with aging. The discs lose their elasticity, flexibility, and shock-absorbing abilities. Unless it is accompanied by pain, DDD is a normal process.[13] The discs become thinner as the *nucleus pulposus* (gelatinous center of the disc) starts to dry out and shrink. This change limits the disc's ability to distribute pressure between vertebrae. The pressure is then transferred to the *annulus fibrosus* (strong outside part of the disc), causing progressive destruction. When the disc is damaged, the nucleus pulposus may seep through a torn or stretched annulus. This is called a **herniated disc** *(slipped disc)*, a condition in which a spinal disc bulges outward between the vertebrae (Fig. 63.4).

A herniated disc can result from degeneration with age or repeated stress and trauma to the spine. The most common sites of herniation are the lumbosacral discs, specifically L4-5 and L5-S1. Disc herniation may also occur at C5-6 and C6-7. It may be the result of spinal stenosis, in which narrowing of the spinal canal forces the intervertebral disc to bulge.

The spinal nerves emerge from the spinal column through an opening *(intervertebral foramen)* between adjacent vertebrae.

TABLE 63.7 Manifestations of Lumbar Disc Herniation*

Intervertebral Level	Pain	Affected Reflex	Motor Function	Sensation
L3-4	Back to buttocks to posterior thigh to inner calf	Patellar	Quadriceps, anterior tibialis	Inner aspect of lower leg, anterior part of thigh
L4-5	Back to buttocks to dorsum of foot and big toe	None	Anterior tibialis, extensor hallucis longus, gluteus medius	Dorsum of foot and big toe
L5-S1	Back to buttocks to sole of foot and heel	Achilles	Gastrocnemius, hamstring, gluteus maximus	Heel and lateral foot

*A disc herniation can involve pressure on more than 1 nerve root.

Herniated discs can press against these nerves ("pinched nerve") causing *radiculopathy* (radiating pain, numbness, tingling, decreased strength and/or range of motion).

Osteoarthritis (OA) of the spine is associated with DDD and the stresses placed on the vertebrae. As the poorly lubricated joints rub against each other, the protective cartilage is damaged and painful bone spurs occur as one of the changes found in OA.

Clinical Manifestations

In *lumbar disc disease,* the most common manifestation is low back pain. Radicular pain that radiates down the buttock and below the knee, along the distribution of the sciatic nerve, generally indicates disc herniation. Specific manifestations of lumbar disc herniation are outlined in Table 63.7. A positive straight-leg-raising test may indicate nerve root irritation (see Chapter 61, p. 1438). Back or leg pain may be reproduced by raising the leg.

Low back pain from other causes may not be accompanied by leg pain. Reflexes may be depressed or absent, depending on the spinal nerve root involved. Numbness and tingling *(paresthesia)* or muscle weakness in the legs, feet, or toes may occur.

Multiple lumbar nerve root compressions *(cauda equina syndrome)* from a herniated disc, tumor, or an epidural abscess may be marked by (1) severe low back pain, (2) progressive weakness, (3) increased pain, and (4) bowel and bladder incontinence or retention. Saddle anesthesia (loss of or altered sensation of the perineum, buttocks, inner thighs and back of the legs [saddle area]) may be present. Symptoms of cauda equina syndrome may develop suddenly or evolve slowly over time. They may vary in intensity. Cauda equina is a medical emergency that requires surgical decompression to reduce pressure on the nerves and prevent permanent paralysis.[14]

In *cervical disc disease,* pain radiates into the arms and hands, following the pattern of the involved nerve. Like lumbar disc disease, reflexes may or may not be present. The handgrip is often weak. Because manifestations of cervical disc disease may include shoulder pain and dysfunction, the HCP must rule out shoulder disorders as part of the diagnosis.

Diagnostic Studies

X-rays are done to detect any structural defects. A myelogram, MRI, or CT scan is helpful in localizing the damaged site. An epidural venogram or diskogram may be needed if other diagnostic studies are inconclusive. An EMG of the extremities can be done to determine the severity of nerve irritation or to rule out other conditions, such as peripheral neuropathy.

TABLE 63.8 Interprofessional Care

Intervertebral Disc Disease

Diagnostic Assessment
- History and physical examination
- X-ray
- CT scan
- MRI
- Myelogram
- Diskogram
- EMG

Management
Conservative Therapy
- Restricted activity for several days, limited total bed rest
- Local ice or heat
- Physical therapy
- Analgesics (e.g., tramadol [Ultram])
- NSAIDs
- Muscle relaxants (e.g., cyclobenzaprine)
- Antiseizure drugs (e.g., gabapentin)
- Antidepressants (e.g., pregabalin)
- Epidural corticosteroid injections

Surgical Therapy
- Intradiscal electrothermoplasty (IDET)
- Radiofrequency discal nucleoplasty
- Interspinous process decompression system (X-Stop)
- Laminectomy with or without spinal fusion
- Discectomy
- Percutaneous laser discectomy
- Artificial disc replacement (e.g., Charité disc)
- Spinal fusion with instrumentation (e.g., plates, screws) or without instrumentation

Interprofessional Care

The patient with suspected disc damage is usually managed with conservative therapy (Table 63.8). This includes limitation of extremes of spinal movement (e.g., brace, corset, belt), local heat or ice, ultrasound and massage, traction, and transcutaneous electrical nerve stimulation (TENS). Drug therapy to manage pain includes NSAIDs, short-term oral corticosteroids, opioid analgesics, muscle relaxants, antiseizure drugs, and antidepressants.[15] Epidural corticosteroid injections may reduce inflammation and relieve acute pain. However, pain tends to recur if the underlying cause remains.

When symptoms subside, the patient should begin back-strengthening exercises twice a day and continue for life. Teach the patient the principles of good body mechanics. Discourage extremes of flexion and torsion. With a conservative treatment plan, most patients heal after 6 months.

Surgical Therapy. If conservative treatment is unsuccessful, radiculopathy becomes worse, or loss of bowel or bladder control occurs, surgery may be considered. Surgery for a damaged disc is generally done if the patient is in constant pain and/or has a persistent neurologic deficit.

Intradiscal electrothermoplasty (IDET) is a minimally invasive outpatient procedure for treatment of back and sciatic pain. A needle is inserted into the affected disc with x-ray guidance. A wire is then threaded through the needle and into the disc. As the wire is heated, small nerve fibers that have invaded the degenerating disc are destroyed. The heat also partially melts the annulus fibrosus. This causes the body to generate new reinforcing proteins in the fibers of the annulus.

Another outpatient technique is *radiofrequency discal nucleoplasty* (coablation nucleoplasty). A needle is inserted into the disc similar to IDET. Instead of a heated wire, a special radiofrequency probe is used. The probe generates energy that breaks the molecular bonds of the gel in the nucleus pulposus. Up to 20% of the nucleus is removed. This decompresses the disc and reduces pressure on the disc and surrounding nerve roots. Subsequent pain relief varies.

A third procedure involves use of an *interspinous process decompression system* (X-Stop). This titanium device fits onto a mount that is placed on vertebrae in the lower back. The X-Stop is used in patients with pain due to lumbar spinal stenosis. The device works by lifting vertebrae off the pinched nerve.

Laminectomy is a common, traditional surgical procedure for lumbar disc disease. It involves surgical excision of part of the vertebra (referred to as the *lamina*) to access and remove the protruding disc.[13] Laminectomy is often done as an outpatient procedure. However, a hospital stay of 1 to 3 days is not uncommon.

Discectomy also can be done to decompress the nerve root. Microsurgical discectomy is a version of the standard procedure. The HCP uses a microscope to better see the disc and disc space, which helps in removal of the damaged portion. This helps maintain bony stability of the spine.

Percutaneous discectomy is a safe and effective outpatient surgical procedure. A tube is passed through the retroperitoneal soft tissues to the disc with the aid of fluoroscopy. A laser is then used on the damaged part of the disc. Minimal blood loss occurs because of access through small stab wounds. The procedure decreases rehabilitation time.

The goals of artificial disc replacement surgery are to restore movement and eliminate pain. The *Charité disc* is used in patients with lumbar disc damage associated with DDD. This artificial disc has a high-density core sandwiched between 2 cobalt-chromium endplates (Fig. 63.5). After removing the damaged disc, the device is surgically placed in the spine (usually through a small incision below the umbilicus). The disc restores movement at the level of the implant. The *ProDisc-L* is another type of artificial lumbar disc used to treat DDD.[16]

Options for treatment of DDD of the cervical spine include the Prestige cervical disc, Mobi-C disc, and Secure-C artificial cervical disc.

A *spinal fusion* may be needed if the spine is unstable. The spine is stabilized by creating *ankylosis* (fusion) of adjacent vertebrae with a bone graft from the patient's fibula or iliac crest (*autograft*) or from donated cadaver bone (*allograft*). Metal fixation with rods, plates, or screws may be placed to give more stability and decrease vertebral motion. A posterior lumbar fusion may be done to give extra support for bone grafting or a prosthetic device.

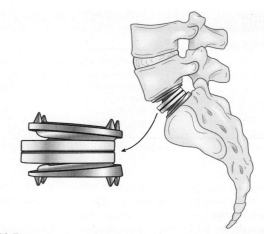

FIG. 63.5 The Charité artificial disc, used to replace a damaged intervertebral disc in degenerative disc disease of the lumbar spine. A movable high-density plastic core is placed between 2 cobalt-chromium alloy endplates. The disc's design helps realign the spine and preserve movement.

Bone morphogenetic protein (BMP), a genetically engineered protein, may be used to stimulate bone growth of the graft in spinal fusions.[17] A dissolvable sponge soaked with BMP is implanted into the spine. BMP on the sponge stimulates the body's cells to become active and produce bone, promoting fusion. The body absorbs the sponge, leaving living bone behind.

❖ NURSING MANAGEMENT: VERTEBRAL DISC SURGERY

After vertebral disc surgery, a key focus of nursing interventions is maintaining proper alignment of the spine until it has healed. Depending on the type and extent of surgery and the HCP's preference, the patient may be able to dangle the legs at the side of the bed, stand, or even ambulate the day of surgery.

After lumbar fusion, place pillows under the patient's thighs when supine and between the legs when in the side-lying position to provide comfort and ensure alignment. The patient often fears turning or any movement that may increase pain by stressing the surgical area. Have the patient logroll when changing position in bed. Reassure the patient that proper technique is being used to maintain body alignment. Remove the bed trapeze, if present, since use is contraindicated for spinal surgery patients. Enough staff should be available to move the patient without undue pain or strain for the patient or staff.

After surgery, most patients need opioids, such as morphine IV, for 24 to 48 hours. Patient-controlled analgesia (PCA) allows maintenance of optimal analgesic levels and is the preferred method of continuous pain management. Once the patient receives oral fluids, oral drugs, such as acetaminophen with codeine, hydrocodone, or oxycodone (Percocet), may be used. Diazepam (Valium) may be prescribed for muscle relaxation. Assess and document pain intensity and pain management effectiveness.

Because the spinal canal may be entered during surgery, cerebrospinal fluid (CSF) leakage is possible. Immediately report leakage of CSF on the dressing or if the patient reports a severe headache. CSF appears as clear or slightly yellow drainage on the dressing. It has a high glucose concentration and is positive for glucose when tested with a dipstick. Note the amount, color, and characteristics of drainage.

Frequently assess the patient's peripheral neurologic condition. Movement of the arms and legs and assessment of sensation should at least equal the preoperative status. Repeat these assessments every 2 to 4 hours during the first 48 hours after surgery and compare with the preoperative assessment. Paresthesia may not be relieved right after surgery. Report any new muscle weakness or paresthesia at once to the HCP and record this finding in the patient's medical record. Assess extremity circulation using skin temperature, capillary refill, and pulses.

Paralytic ileus and interference with bowel function may occur for several days. Opioids can slow bowel elimination. Assess if the patient is passing gas, has bowel sounds in all quadrants, and has a flat, soft abdomen. Stool softeners (e.g., docusate [Colace]) and laxatives may prevent and relieve constipation.

Emptying the bladder may be hard due to activity restrictions, opioids, or anesthesia. Encourage men to dangle the legs over the side of the bed or stand to urinate if allowed by the HCP. Urge patients to use a bedside commode or ambulate to the bathroom when allowed to promote bladder emptying. Intermittent catheterization or an indwelling urinary catheter may be needed by patients who have problems urinating.

Loss of sphincter tone or bladder tone may indicate nerve damage. Monitor for incontinence or problems with bowel or bladder elimination. Immediately report problems to the HCP.

In addition to nursing care appropriate for a patient who had a laminectomy, other nursing activities are needed if the patient has also had a spinal fusion. Because a bone graft is usually involved, the healing time is prolonged compared with a laminectomy. Activity limitations may be needed for an extended time. A rigid orthosis (thoracolumbar sacral orthosis [TLSO] or chairback brace) is often used during this period. Some HCPs want patients to learn to apply and remove the brace by logrolling in bed. Others allow their patients to apply the brace in a sitting or standing position. Verify the preferred method before starting this activity.

With cervical spine surgery, be alert for signs of spinal cord edema, such as respiratory distress and a worsening neurologic condition of the upper extremities. After surgery, the patient's neck may be immobilized in a soft or hard cervical collar.

In addition to the primary surgical site, regularly assess the bone graft donor site. The posterior iliac crest is the most often used donor site, although the fibula may be used. The donor site usually causes greater pain than the spinal fusion area. The donor site is bandaged with a pressure dressing to prevent excessive bleeding. If the donor site is the fibula, frequent neurovascular assessment of the extremity is a key nursing intervention.

After spinal fusion, the patient may have some immobility of the spine at the fusion site. Teach the patient to use proper body mechanics and avoid sitting or standing for prolonged periods. Encourage activities that include walking, lying down, and shifting weight from one foot to the other when standing. Teach the patient about any lifting restrictions. Encourage the patient to think through an activity before starting any potentially injurious task, such as bending or stooping. Any twisting movement of the spine is contraindicated. Teach the patient to use the thighs and knees, rather than the back, to absorb the shock of activity and movement. A firm mattress or bed board is essential.

NECK PAIN

Neck pain occurs almost as often as low back pain, affecting 10% to 20% of adults at any point in time.[18] Neck pain may result from many different conditions, including benign (e.g., poor posture) and serious (e.g., herniated cervical disc) (Table 63.9).

TABLE 63.9 Causes of Neck Pain

- Degenerative disc disease, including herniation
- Meningitis
- Osteomyelitis
- Osteoporosis
- Poor posture
- Rheumatoid arthritis
- Spondylosis
- Strain or sprain
- Trauma (e.g., fractures, subluxation)
- Tumor

TABLE 63.10 Patient & Caregiver Teaching

Neck Exercises

When teaching the patient exercises for neck pain, include the following instructions for the patient and caregiver:
- Bend your head backward until you are looking up at the ceiling. Repeat slowly 5 times. Stop if dizziness occurs.
- Bring your head forward so that your chin touches your chest and your face is looking down at the floor. Repeat slowly 5 times.
- With your head facing forward, bend your ear down toward one shoulder. Alternate this movement with your other ear. Repeat slowly 5 times on each side.
- Turn your head slowly around to one side as far as it will go. Repeat toward the other side. Repeat exercise 5 times on each side.

Cervical neck sprains and strains occur from hyperflexion and hyperextension injuries. Patients have stiffness and neck pain with possible radicular pain into the arm and hand. Pain may radiate to the head, anterior chest, thoracic spine region, and shoulders. Weakness or paresthesia of the arm and hand suggests cervical nerve root compression from stenosis, DDD, or herniation.

The cause of neck pain is diagnosed by history, physical examination, x-ray, MRI, CT scan, and myelogram. An EMG of the upper extremities may diagnose cervical radiculopathy.

Conservative treatment for neck pain in patients without an underlying disorder includes head support using a soft cervical collar, gentle traction, heat and ice applications, massage, rest until symptoms subside, ultrasound, and NSAIDs. Therapeutic neck exercises and acupuncture also may be used for pain relief.[19] Most neck pain resolves without surgical intervention.

Preventing neck pain that occurs with everyday activities, such as prolonged sitting at a computer or television, sleeping in nonaligned spinal positions, or making jarring movements during exercise, is important. Encourage patients to practice good posture and maintain neck flexibility (Table 63.10).

FOOT DISORDERS

The foot is the platform that supports the weight of the body and absorbs shock when the person ambulates. It is a complicated structure composed of bony structures, muscles, tendons, and ligaments. The foot can be affected by (1) congenital conditions; (2) structural weakness; (3) traumatic and stress injuries; and (4) systemic conditions, such as diabetes and rheumatoid arthritis. Table 63.11 outlines common foot disorders.

Footwear is used to (1) provide support, foot stability, protection, shock absorption, and a foundation for orthotics; (2) increase friction with the walking surface; and (3) treat foot abnormalities. Poorly fitting shoes cause or worsen a great deal of the pain, deformity, and disability from foot disorders.[20] Shoes may cause crowding and angulation of the toes and inhibit normal movement of foot muscles.

TABLE 63.11 Common Foot Disorders

Disorder	Description	Treatment
Forefoot **Hallux rigidus**	Painful stiffness of first MTP joint caused by osteoarthritis or local trauma.	• Conservative treatment includes intraarticular corticosteroids and passive manual stretching of first MTP joint. • Shoe with a stiff sole decreases pain in the joint during walking. • Surgical treatment is joint fusion or arthroplasty with silicone rubber implant.
Hallux valgus (bunion)	Painful deformity of great toe with lateral angulation of great toe toward second toe, bony enlargement of medial side of first metatarsal head, swelling of bursa and formation of callus over bony enlargement (Fig. 63.6).	• Conservative treatment includes wearing shoes with wide forefoot or "bunion pocket" and use of bunion pads to relieve pressure on bursal sac. • Surgical treatment involves removal of bursal sac and bony enlargement and correction of lateral angulation of great toe. • May include temporary or permanent internal fixation.
Hammer and claw toes	Hammer toe is a deformity of PIP joint on 2nd to 5th toes causing toe to be permanently bent, resembling a hammer. Mallet toe is a similar condition affecting the DIP joint. Claw toe is a similar deformity with dorsiflexion of the proximal phalanx on the MTP joint combined with flexion of both PIP and DIP joints. Symptoms include burning on bottom of foot and pain and difficulty walking when wearing shoes.	• Conservative treatment includes passive manual stretching of PIP joint and use of metatarsal arch support. • Surgical correction consists of resection of base of middle phalanx and head of proximal phalanx, bringing raw bone ends together. • Kirschner wire maintains straight position.
Morton's neuroma (Morton's toe or plantar neuroma)	Neuroma in web space between third and fourth metatarsal heads, causing sharp, sudden attacks of pain and burning sensations.	• Surgical excision is the usual treatment.
Midfoot **Pes cavus** **Pes planus** (flatfoot)	Elevation of longitudinal arch of foot resulting from contracture of plantar fascia or bony deformity of arch. Loss of metatarsal arch causing pain in foot or leg.	• Surgical correction is needed if condition interferes with ambulation. • Symptoms are relieved by use of resilient longitudinal arch supports. • Surgical treatment consists of triple arthrodesis or fusion of subtalar joint.
Hindfoot **Calcaneus stress fracture** **Heel pain**	Heel pain after moderate walking. Common causes are overtraining, running on hard surfaces, or osteoporosis. Heel pain with weight bearing. Common causes are plantar bursitis, plantar fasciitis, or bone spur.	• Rest, ice, shoe heel pad, and NSAIDs. • See HCP to assess for osteoporosis. • Corticosteroids are injected locally into inflamed bursa, and sponge-rubber heel cup is used. • Surgical excision of bursa or spur is done. • Stretching exercises, ice, shoe heel cup, shock-wave therapy, NSAIDs, and corticosteroids are used for plantar fasciitis.
Other Problems **Callus**	Localized thickening of skin. Covers wide area and usually found on weight-bearing part of foot.	• Softened with warm water or preparations containing salicylic acid and trimmed with razor blade or scalpel. • Pressure on bony prominences caused by shoes is relieved.
Corn	Localized thickening of skin caused by continual pressure over bony prominences, especially metatarsal head, often causing localized pain.	• Same as with callus.
Plantar wart	Painful papillomatous growth caused by virus that may occur on any part of skin on sole of foot. Warts tend to cluster on pressure points.	• Remedies containing salicylic acid (e.g., Compound W), excision with electrocoagulation, or surgical removal. • Laser treatments. • May disappear without treatment.
Soft corn	Painful lesion caused by bony prominence of a toe pressing against adjacent toe. Usual location is web space between toes. Softness caused by secretions keeping web space relatively moist.	• Pain is relieved by placing cotton or spacers between toes to separate them. • Surgical treatment is excision of projecting bone spur (if present).

DIP, Distal interphalangeal; *MTP*, metatarsophalangeal; *PIP*, proximal interphalangeal.

❖ NURSING MANAGEMENT: FOOT DISORDERS

◆ Nursing Implementation

◆ **Health Promotion.** Well-made and properly fitted shoes are essential for healthy, pain-free feet. Women's footwear is often influenced by current styles instead of comfort and support. Stress the importance of having a shoe that conforms to the foot rather than to fashion trends. The shoe must be long enough and wide enough to avoid crowding the toes and forcing the great toe into a position of hallux valgus (Fig. 63.6). At the metatarsal head, the shoe should be wide enough to allow foot muscles to move freely and toes to bend. The shank (narrow part of sole under the instep) of the shoe should be rigid enough to give good support. The height of the heel should be realistic in relation to the shoe's purpose. Ideally, the heel of the shoe should not rise more than 1 inch higher than the forefoot

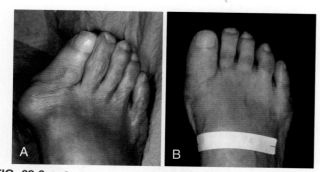

FIG. 63.6 A, Severe hallux valgus with bursa formation. B, Postoperative correction. (From Canale ST, Beaty JH: *Campbell's operative orthopaedics*, ed 12, Philadelphia, 2013, Mosby.)

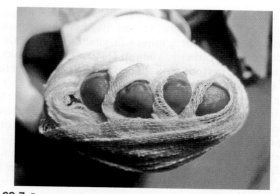

FIG. 63.7 Postoperative supportive dressing for treatment of moderate forefoot deformity. Dressing must be conforming and binding enough to hold toe in exact position. (From Canale ST, Beaty JH: *Campbell's operative orthopaedics*, ed 12, Philadelphia, 2013, Mosby.)

support. Wearing higher heeled shoes with a narrow toe box will cause hammertoes and corns over time.

Prolonged use of improper footwear can also cause a *Morton's neuroma*. They cause compression of an intermetatarsal plantar nerve, resulting in paresthesia and burning. At first, patients with Morton's neuroma may describe feeling as if a sock is rolled up under their toes. Neuromas usually occur between the third and fourth toes.

◆ **Acute Care.** Many foot problems require referral to a podiatrist. Depending on the problem, conservative therapies are tried first (Table 63.11). These include NSAIDs, ice, physical therapy, footwear changes, stretching, warm soaks, orthotics, ultrasound, and corticosteroid injections. If these methods do not help, surgery may be needed.

❓ CHECK YOUR PRACTICE

A 53-yr-old woman is scheduled for surgical correction of a bunion after a diagnosis of hallux valgus. You are doing her preoperative assessment. She asks you, "Do you think I caused this problem? I love shoes and have a whole closet full of fancy ones. Now I have to wear this ugly bunion shoe. I am not sure I can handle taking care of myself after surgery."

• How will you respond to the patient?
• What teaching will you provide about her postoperative care?

Depending on the type of surgery, pins or wires may extend through the toes, or a protective splint may be placed over the end of the foot. After surgery, the foot is usually immobilized by a bulky dressing (Fig. 63.7), short leg cast, slipper (plaster) cast, or a platform shoe that fits over the dressing and has a rigid sole (also known as a *bunion shoe*).

Elevate the foot with the heel off the bed to reduce discomfort and prevent edema. Assess neurovascular condition frequently during the immediate postoperative period. Inserted devices may interfere with assessment for movement. Be aware that evaluating sensation may be hard because the patient may be unable to distinguish surgical pain from pain caused by nerve pressure or circulatory impairment.

The type and extent of surgery determine the orders for ambulation. Crutches, a walker, or a cane may be needed. The patient may have pain or a throbbing sensation when lowering the affected leg. Reinforce instructions from the physical therapist. Teach the patient the importance of walking with an erect posture with proper weight distribution. Report gait problems or continued pain to the HCP. Encourage frequent rest periods with the foot elevated.

◆ **Ambulatory Care.** Teach the patient to perform daily hygienic foot care and wear clean stockings. Stockings should be long enough to avoid wrinkling and causing pressure areas. Trimming toenails straight across helps prevent ingrown toenails and reduces the risk for infection. Provide detailed instruction to patients with impaired circulation or diabetes to prevent serious complications from blisters, pressure areas, and infection. (See Table 48.21 for guidelines on foot care.)

🧍 Gerontologic Considerations: Foot Problems

The older adult is prone to foot problems because of poor circulation, atherosclerosis, and decreased sensation in the lower extremities. This is especially true for those with diabetes. A patient may develop an open wound but not feel it because of altered sensation from peripheral vascular disease or diabetic neuropathy. Teach older adults to inspect their feet daily and report any open wounds or breaks in the skin to their HCP.[21]

Untreated wounds may become infected, lead to osteomyelitis, and need surgical debridement. If the infection becomes widespread, lower limb amputation may be needed. Teach the caregiver of the older adult who needs help with hygiene practices the importance of carefully assessing the feet at regular intervals.

METABOLIC BONE DISEASES

Normal bone metabolism is affected by hormones, nutrition, and genetics. When dysfunction occurs in any of these factors, generalized reduction in bone mass and strength may result. Metabolic bone diseases include osteomalacia, osteoporosis, and Paget's disease.

OSTEOMALACIA

Osteomalacia is caused by a vitamin D deficiency that causes bone to lose calcium and become soft. The disease is uncommon in the United States. It is the same disorder as rickets in children, except the epiphyseal growth plates are closed in adults. Vitamin D is required for the absorption of calcium from the intestine. Insufficient vitamin D intake can interfere with normal bone mineralization. With little or no calcification, bones become soft.

Causes include limited sun exposure (ultraviolet rays needed for vitamin D synthesis), GI malabsorption (post weight loss surgery, celiac disease), chronic diarrhea, and pregnancy. Residents of long-term care settings may have inadequate sun exposure and thus poor synthesis of vitamin D. Persons with dark skin do not synthesize vitamin D as easily as persons with fair skin. Obese persons are at higher risk because of decreased physical activity. Chronic liver, kidneys, and small intestine disease may contribute to vitamin D deficiency. Long-term use of antiseizure drugs (e.g., phenytoin) and phosphate-binding antacids (e.g., Maalox) may decrease calcium and vitamin D absorption.[22]

Common manifestations are bone pain and muscle weakness. The pain is often worse at night and affects the lower back, pelvis, hips, legs, and ribs.[23] Muscle weakness and progressive deformity of weight-bearing bones (e.g., spine, extremities) can lead to problems walking and a waddling gait. Fractures are common and indicate delayed bone healing.

Laboratory findings include decreased serum calcium or phosphorus, decreased serum 25-hydroxyvitamin D, and increased serum alkaline phosphatase. X-rays may show effects of generalized bone demineralization, especially loss of calcium in the bones of the pelvis and associated bone deformity. *Looser's transformation zones* (ribbons of decalcification in bone found on x-ray) are diagnostic of osteomalacia. However, significant osteomalacia may exist without x-ray changes.

Interprofessional care is directed toward correcting the vitamin D deficiency. The patient often has a dramatic response when vitamin D_3 (cholecalciferol) and vitamin D_2 (ergocalciferol) supplements are used. Calcium or phosphorus supplements may be prescribed. Encourage dietary intake of eggs, meat, and oily fish (e.g., salmon, tuna). Milk and breakfast cereals fortified with calcium and vitamin D should be part of the diet. Exposure to sunlight and weight-bearing exercise are valuable as well. Assess patients who had weight loss surgery to treat obesity for osteomalacia. Any vitamin D deficiencies should be corrected.[24]

OSTEOPOROSIS

Osteoporosis is a chronic, progressive metabolic bone disease marked by low bone mass and deterioration of bone tissue, leading to increased bone fragility (Fig. 63.8). More than 54 million persons in the United States have decreased bone density or osteoporosis.[25] Osteoporosis is known as the "silent thief" because it slowly robs the skeleton of its banked resources. Bones eventually become so fragile that they cannot withstand normal mechanical stress.

Osteoporosis is more common in women. This is for several reasons: (1) women tend to have lower calcium intake than men throughout their lives (men between 15 and 50 years of age consume twice as much calcium as women); (2) women have less bone mass because of their generally smaller frames; (3) bone resorption begins at an earlier age in women and becomes more rapid at menopause; (4) pregnancy and breastfeeding deplete a woman's skeletal reserve unless calcium intake is adequate; and (5) longevity increases the risk for osteoporosis.

Current guidelines recommend an initial bone density test in all women over age 65 years. If results are normal and the person is at low risk for osteoporosis, another test is not needed for 15 years. Women who are younger than 65 and at high risk (e.g., low body weight, smoker, prior fractures) should have a bone density test earlier. Testing should also start earlier and be done more often if a person is at high risk for fractures. Currently there is not enough evidence that shows any benefit for screening men.[26]

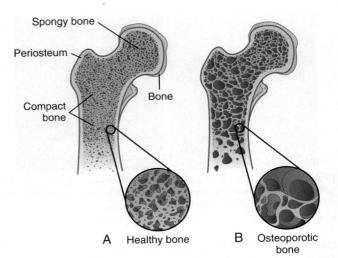

FIG. 63.8 A, Normal bone. B, Osteoporotic bone.

TABLE 63.12 Risk Factors for Osteoporosis

- Advancing age (>65 yr)
- Female gender
- Low body weight
- White or Asian ethnicity
- Cigarette smoking
- Sedentary lifestyle
- Estrogen deficiency in women (surgical or age-related menopause)
- Family history of osteoporosis
- Diet low in calcium or vitamin D deficiency
- Excess use of alcohol (>2 drinks/day)
- Low testosterone in men
- Long-term use of corticosteroids, thyroid replacement, heparin, long-acting sedatives, or antiseizure drugs

PROMOTING HEALTH EQUITY
Osteoporosis

- White and Asian American women have the highest incidence of osteoporosis.
- Black women begin menopause with more bone mass and have the lowest rate of bone loss after menopause.
- Risk for fracture is highest in white women.

Etiology and Pathophysiology

Risk factors for osteoporosis are listed in Table 63.12. Decreased risk is associated with regular weight-bearing exercise and adequate intake of fluoride, calcium, and vitamin D. Low testosterone is a major risk factor in men.

Peak bone mass (maximum bone tissue) is typically achieved before age 20. It is largely determined by 4 factors: heredity, nutrition, exercise, and hormone function. Heredity may be responsible for up to 70% of a person's peak bone mass. Genetic factors also influence bone size, quality, and turnover. Bone loss from midlife (ages 35 to 40 years) onward is inevitable, but the rate of loss varies. At menopause, women have rapid bone loss when the decline in estrogen production is the greatest. The rate of loss then slows and eventually matches the rate of bone lost by men ages 65 to 70 years.

Bone is continuously being deposited by osteoblasts and resorbed by osteoclasts, a process called *remodeling*. Rates of bone deposition and resorption are normally equal, so total bone mass stays constant.[27] In osteoporosis, bone resorption exceeds bone deposition.

Diseases associated with osteoporosis include inflammatory bowel disease, intestinal malabsorption, kidney disease, rheumatoid arthritis, hyperthyroidism, alcohol use disorder, cirrhosis, hypogonadism, and diabetes. Many drugs can interfere with bone metabolism, including corticosteroids, antiseizure drugs (e.g., divalproex sodium [Depakote], phenytoin), aluminum-containing antacids, heparin, some chemotherapy drugs, and excess thyroid hormones. When one of these drugs is prescribed, teach the patient about this possible side effect. Long-term corticosteroid use is a major contributor to osteoporosis.

GENDER DIFFERENCES
Osteoporosis

Men	Women
• Men are underdiagnosed and undertreated for osteoporosis compared with women. • 1 in 4 men over age 50 will have an osteoporosis-related fracture in his lifetime.	• Osteoporosis is 8 times more common in women than in men. • 1 in 2 women over age 50 years will have an osteoporosis-related fracture in her lifetime.

Clinical Manifestations

Osteoporosis occurs most often in bones of the spine, hips, and wrists. Typical early manifestations are back pain and spontaneous fractures. The loss of bone mass causes the bone to become mechanically weaker and prone to spontaneous fractures or fractures from minimal trauma. A person who has a vertebral fracture due to osteoporosis has an increased risk for having a second vertebral fracture within 1 year. Over time, vertebral fractures and wedging cause gradual loss of height and a humped thoracic spine (*kyphosis,* or "dowager's hump") (Fig. 63.9).

Diagnostic Studies

Osteoporosis often goes unnoticed because it cannot be detected by conventional x-ray until 25% to 40% of calcium in the bone is lost. Serum calcium, phosphorus, and alkaline phosphatase levels usually are normal. Alkaline phosphatase may be increased after a fracture.

Bone mineral density (BMD) measurements are typically expressed as grams of mineral per unit volume. BMD is determined by peak bone mass and amount of bone loss. (Procedures for BMD measurement are described in Table 61.8.) BMD may be measured by quantitative ultrasound (QUS) and dual-energy x-ray absorptiometry (DEXA). QUS uses sound waves to measure bone density in the heel, kneecap, or shin. DEXA (considered the gold standard of BMD studies by the World Health Organization) measures bone density in the spine, hips, and forearm.[28] These represent the most common sites of fragility fractures from osteoporosis. DEXA studies are useful to evaluate changes in bone density over time and assess effectiveness of osteoporosis treatment.

The BMD test results are compared to the ideal or peak bone mineral density of a healthy 30-yr-old adult and reported as T-scores. A T-score of 0 means the BMD is equal to the norm for a healthy young adult. Differences between the BMD and that of the healthy young adult norm are measured in units called *standard deviations (SDs)*. The more standard deviations below 0 (indicated as negative numbers), the lower the BMD and the higher the risk for fracture.

A T-score between +1 and −1 is normal. A T-score between −1 and −2.5 indicates osteopenia (bone loss that is more than normal, but not yet at the level for a diagnosis of osteoporosis). A T-score of −2.5 or lower indicates osteoporosis. The greater the negative number, the more severe the osteoporosis.[28]

Sometimes the HCP uses a Z-score instead of a T-score. In this case a person is compared with someone their own age, gender, and/or ethnic group instead of a healthy 30-yr-old person. Among older adults, Z-scores can be misleading because decreased bone density is common. If the Z-score is −2 or lower, it may suggest that something other than aging is causing abnormal bone loss.

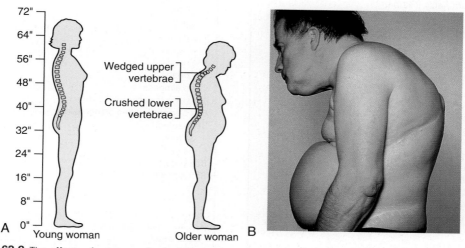

FIG. 63.9 The effects of osteoporosis. **A,** Comparison of young woman with an older woman. **B,** Severe fixed kyphosis producing a question-mark appearance. (*A,* From Phillips N: *Berry & Kohn's operating room technique,* ed 12, St Louis, 2013, Mosby. *B,* Courtesy Mir MA. In Kanski JJ: *Clinical diagnosis in ophthalmology,* St Louis, 2006, Mosby.)

❖ NURSING AND INTERPROFESSIONAL MANAGEMENT: OSTEOPOROSIS

Interprofessional care focuses on proper nutrition, calcium and vitamin D supplementation, exercise, prevention of falls and fractures, and drugs (Table 63.13). The National Osteoporosis Foundation recommends treatment for osteoporosis for post-menopausal women with (1) a T-score of less than −2.5, (2) a T-score between −1 and −2.5 with additional risk factors (Table 63.12), or (3) prior history of a hip or vertebral fracture.

A patient's risk for fracture from osteoporosis also can be calculated with the Fracture Risk Assessment (FRAX) tool. The FRAX considers BMD and other clinical factors when assessing fracture risk.[29]

The recommended calcium intake is 1000 mg/day for women ages 19 to 50 years and men ages 19 to 70 years and 1200 mg/day in women age 51 years or older and men 71 years or older. Foods high in calcium include milk, yogurt, turnip greens, cottage cheese, ice cream, sardines, and spinach (Table 63.14). If dietary intake of calcium is inadequate, supplemental calcium may be given.

It is difficult for us to absorb calcium in single doses greater than 500 mg. Teach the patient the importance of taking calcium supplements as divided doses to increase absorption. The amount of elemental calcium varies in calcium preparations. Calcium carbonate has 40% elemental calcium. It should be taken with meals because stomach acid is needed to dissolve and absorb this supplement. Calcium citrate has about 20% elemental calcium but is less dependent on stomach acid for absorption. It is better absorbed by patients taking a proton pump inhibitor (e.g., esomeprazole [Nexium]) or histamine receptor blocker (e.g., cimetidine) for acid reflux. Calcium lactate and calcium gluconate are not recommended because they have small amounts of elemental calcium.

Vitamin D is important in calcium absorption and function and may have a role in bone formation. Most people get enough vitamin D from their diet or naturally through synthesis in the skin from exposure to sunlight. Being in the sun for 20 minutes a day is generally enough. However, supplemental vitamin D (800 IU) is recommended for postmenopausal women, older men, persons who are homebound or in long-term care settings, and those in northern climates due to decreased sun exposure.

Regular physical activity is important to build and maintain bone mass. Exercise increases muscle strength, coordination, and balance. The best exercises are weight-bearing exercises that force a person to work against gravity. These include walking, hiking, weight training, stair climbing, tennis, and dancing. Walking is preferred to high-impact aerobics or running. Both may put too much stress on the bones and cause stress fractures. Encourage patients to walk 30 minutes 3 times a week. Teach patients to quit smoking and decrease alcohol use to minimize negative effects on bone mass.

Encourage patients with osteoporosis to remain ambulatory to prevent further loss of bone density due to immobility. Treatment may also involve the use of a gait aid to walk safely and protect areas of potential pathologic fractures. For example, a TLSO may be used to maintain the spine in proper alignment after fracture or treatment of a vertebral fracture. (Fractures are discussed in Chapter 62.)

Vertebroplasty and *kyphoplasty* are minimally invasive procedures used to treat osteoporotic vertebral fractures (see Chapter 62).[30] In vertebroplasty, bone cement is injected into

---

TABLE 63.13 Interprofessional Care

Osteoporosis

Diagnostic Assessment
- History and physical examination
- Serum calcium, phosphorus, alkaline phosphatase, vitamin D
- Bone mineral densitometry
- Dual-energy x-ray absorptiometry (DEXA)

Management
- Adequate dietary calcium (Table 63.14)
- Calcium supplements
- Sun exposure or vitamin D supplements
- Exercise program

Drug Therapy
- Bisphosphonates (recommended)
  - alendronate (Fosamax, Binosto)
  - risedronate (Actonel)
  - zoledronic acid (Reclast)
- Monoclonal antibodies
  - denosumab (Prolia)
  - romosozumab (Evenity)
- Bisphosphonates (other available agents)
  - etidronate (Didronel)
  - ibandronate (Boniva)
  - pamidronate (Aredia)
- Recombinant parathyroid hormone (e.g., teriparatide [Forteo], abaloparatide [Tymlos])

Minimally Invasive Procedures
- Vertebroplasty
- Kyphoplasty

TABLE 63.14 Nutritional Therapy

Sources of Calcium

Food	Calcium (mg)
Good Sources	
1 cup milk	
• Whole	279
• Skim	299
1 oz cheese	
• Mozzarella	222
• Cheddar	214
• Cottage	138
1 cup almonds	304
1 cup ice cream	168
6 oz calcium-fortified orange juice	261
3 oz seafood	
• Salmon	181
• Sardines	325
8 oz yogurt	313–384
Soft serve frozen yogurt	206
Poor Sources	
Egg	28
3 oz beef, pork, poultry	10
Apple, banana	10
1 med carrot	14
1 med potato	14
¼ head lettuce	27

the collapsed vertebra to stabilize the spine and improve the patient's pain. This procedure does not restore vertebral height or correct deformity. In kyphoplasty, a small balloon is inserted into the collapsed vertebra and inflated to restore vertebral body height before injection of bone cement. Kyphoplasty is the preferred surgical treatment for vertebral compression fractures.

◆ Drug Therapy

The recommended drug therapies for the prevention and treatment of osteoporosis are the bisphosphonates alendronate, risedronate, and zoledronic acid, or denosumab. Bisphosphonates inhibit osteoclast-mediated bone resorption and slow the cycle of bone remodeling. Although a modest increase in BMD is typical, bone remodeling may be suppressed to the extent that normal bone formation is impaired and fracture risk increases. Treatment should continue for 5 years (Table 63.13).[31]

Common side effects are anorexia, weight loss, and gastritis. Teach the patient to take the medication correctly to improve its absorption (see Drug Alert). These precautions also decrease GI side effects (especially esophageal irritation). A rare, but serious, side effect of bisphosphonates is *osteonecrosis* (bone death) of the jaw. Its cause is unknown. Those with dental disease, cancer, Paget's disease, or renal disease are most at risk for this complication. Patients should see a dentist before beginning treatment and then annually to ensure good oral health.

🔲 DRUG ALERT Bisphosphonates

Teach patient to:
- Take with full glass of water.
- Take 30 min before food or other medications.
- Remain upright for at least 30 min after taking.

Alendronate (Fosamax) is available as a daily or weekly oral tablet. The immediate-release form of risedronate (Actonel) is given daily, weekly, or monthly, based on the dose. Zoledronic acid (Reclast) is given as a once-yearly or every-other-year IV infusion. Renal function tests and serum calcium must be assessed before administration. Other bisphosphonates are shown in Table 63.13.

Denosumab (Prolia) may be given to postmenopausal women with osteoporosis who are at high risk for fractures. It is a monoclonal antibody that binds to a protein (RANKL) involved in the formation and function of osteoclasts. Denosumab is given as a subcutaneous injection every 6 months.

Other agents used include the new monoclonal antibody romosozumab (Evenity). It inhibits the action of sclerostin, a regulatory factor in bone metabolism. This increases bone formation and, to a lesser extent, decreases bone resorption. It is given by subcutaneous injection every month for a total of 12 doses.

Raloxifene (Evista)is a selective estrogen receptor modulator (SERM). This drug mimics the effect of estrogen on bone by reducing bone resorption without stimulating the tissues of the breast or uterus. Raloxifene reduces the risk for vertebral, but not hip, fractures. Side effects, including leg cramps, hot flashes, and increased risk for blood clots, limit use.[31]

Teriparatide (Forteo) is a recombinant form of human parathyroid hormone (PTH) that increases the action of osteoblasts. This drug is used to treat osteoporosis in men and postmenopausal women at high risk for fractures, including risk related to long-term corticosteroid use.[31] Side effects include leg cramps and dizziness. Teriparatide is the first drug approved to stimulate new bone formation in osteoporosis. Most drugs only prevent further bone loss. It is self-administered daily by subcutaneous injection from a preloaded pen.

Women no longer routinely use estrogen replacement therapy or estrogen with progesterone after menopause to prevent osteoporosis because of the increased risk for heart disease and breast and uterine cancer. A woman who takes short-term estrogen therapy to treat menopausal symptoms, such as hot flashes, may receive some protection against bone loss and hip and vertebrae fractures.[32] We think estrogen inhibits osteoclast activity, leading to decreased bone resorption.

Medical management of patients receiving corticosteroids includes prescribing the lowest effective dose for the shortest possible time. Ensure an adequate intake of calcium and vitamin D, including supplements, when osteoporosis drugs are prescribed. If osteopenia is present on bone densitometry in people who are taking corticosteroids, treatment with bisphosphonates may be considered.

PAGET'S DISEASE

Paget's disease (*osteitis deformans*) is a chronic skeletal bone disorder in which excessive bone resorption is followed by replacement of normal marrow by vascular, fibrous connective tissue. The new bone is larger, disorganized, and weaker. Areas commonly affected include the pelvis, long bones, spine, ribs, sternum, and skull. Up to 5% of adults in the United States are affected by Paget's disease.[33] Men are affected twice as often as women. Paget's disease is uncommon in people under age 40.

We do not know exactly what causes Paget's disease. The cause may be viral or genetic. Up to 40% of all patients with the disease have at least 1 relative with the disorder.

In milder forms of Paget's disease, patients do not have any symptoms. The disease may be found incidentally through x-ray or serum chemistry findings of high alkaline phosphatase.[34] Bone pain may develop gradually and progress to severe intractable pain. Other early manifestations include fatigue and progressive development of a waddling gait. Patients report becoming shorter or their heads are becoming larger. Headaches, dementia, vision deficits, and loss of hearing can result from an enlarged, thickened skull. Increased bone volume in the spine can cause spinal cord or nerve root compression.

Pathologic fracture is the most common complication and may be the first sign of Paget's disease. Other complications include osteosarcoma, fibrosarcoma, and osteoclastoma (giant cell) tumors.

Serum alkaline phosphatase is markedly increased in advanced disease, showing high bone turnover.[34] X-rays may show curvature of an affected bone. The bone cortex becomes thicker and irregular, especially in weight-bearing bones and the cranium. Bone scans using a radiolabeled bisphosphonate show increased uptake in the affected skeletal areas.

Interprofessional care is usually limited to symptomatic and supportive care, with correction of secondary deformities by surgical intervention or braces. Bisphosphonate drugs (Table 63.13) are used to slow bone resorption. Zoledronic acid may be given specifically to build bone. Calcium and vitamin D can decrease hypocalcemia, a common side effect of drug therapy. Monitor drug effectiveness by regular assessment of serum alkaline phosphatase.

Calcitonin is an option for patients who cannot tolerate bisphosphonates. Human calcitonin inhibits osteoclastic activity, prevents bone resorption, relieves acute symptoms, and lowers serum alkaline phosphatase. This drug is available as a subcutaneous injection. Salmon calcitonin is 1 form. It has a longer half-life and greater milligram potency than human calcitonin. Response to calcitonin therapy is not permanent and often ends when therapy stops.

Pain is usually managed with NSAIDs. Orthopedic surgery for fractures, hip and knee replacement, and knee realignment may be needed.

A firm mattress can provide back support and relieve pain. The patient may need to wear a corset or light brace to relieve back pain and give support when upright. Teach the patient to correctly apply the device and regularly examine the skin for friction damage. Discourage lifting and twisting. Good body mechanics are essential. Physical therapy may increase muscle strength. A well-balanced diet is important in management of metabolic bone disorders. Vitamin D, calcium, and protein are especially important to ensure available components for bone formation. To decrease risk for falls and related fractures, teach the patient to use an assistive device and make environmental changes (e.g., do not use throw rugs).

! SAFETY ALERT   Paget's Disease

To reduce the risk for patient harm from falls:
- Assess environmental fall risk factors (poor lighting, clutter, pets in the home).
- Identify personal risk factors for falls, including drugs and uncorrected vision.
- Take action to address any identified risks.

Gerontologic Considerations: Metabolic Bone Diseases

Osteoporosis and Paget's disease are common in older adults. Teach patients proper nutrition to decrease risk for further bone loss. Keep the patient as active as possible to slow demineralization of bone from disuse or extended immobilization.

Because metabolic bone disorders increase the risk for pathologic fractures, use extreme caution when turning or moving the patient. Hip fractures, in particular, may decrease quality of life and lead to admission to a long-term care facility. A supervised exercise program is essential to osteoporosis treatment. Encourage ambulation if the patient's condition permits.

CASE STUDY

Metastatic Bone Tumor/Pathologic Fracture

(© Christopher-Robbins/Photodisc/Thinkstock.)

Patient Profile

L.R. is a 60-yr-old white woman with a history of hypertension, hypothyroidism, and osteoporosis. Four years ago, she was diagnosed with stage 3a breast cancer and treated with surgery, radiation therapy, and chemotherapy. Today she was admitted to the emergency department after falling down 2 stairs.

Subjective Data

- Denies hitting her head or loss of consciousness
- States she was able to bear weight on her lower extremities but has significant left thigh pain after the fall
- Describes recent insidious onset of generalized weakness and fatigue
- Denies alcohol or tobacco use
- Takes levothyroxine (Synthroid) and atenolol (Tenormin) every morning. Takes risedronate (Actonel) once a month

Objective Data

- Left lower extremity slightly shorter and externally rotated compared to right lower extremity
- Moderate edema with associated ecchymosis on left thigh
- Thigh soft, compressible to palpation
- Reports pain with internal/external rotation of left lower extremity
- 2+ dorsalis pedis and posterior tibialis pulses bilaterally
- Gross motor/sensation intact in affected extremity

Diagnostic Studies

- X-ray shows oblique mid-shaft left femur fracture with lytic lesion in the femoral neck
- Normal CBC and blood chemistry results, slightly increased liver function tests
- CT scans of the chest, abdomen, and pelvis show multiple bony metastases throughout the pelvis, as well as lesions of the liver and spleen, widespread abdominal cancer, compression fractures with lesions of T11 vertebral body, and bilateral rib fractures with associated lesions.

- Whole body bone scan consistent with findings from x-ray and CT
- CT-guided biopsy of femur fracture site showed poorly differentiated cells consistent with breast cancer

Interprofessional Care

- Diagnosed with stage IV breast cancer
- Intramedullary nail for femur fracture
- Pain management
- Postoperative chemotherapy and hormone therapy
- High-protein, high-calcium, nutrient-rich diet
- Depression assessment and management
- Ambulation evaluation with gait aids as needed

Discussion Questions

1. Why did a relatively low-energy injury cause L.R.'s fracture?
2. *Patient-Centered Care:* What factors could result in inadequate caloric intake after surgery? How could you help L.R. increase her intake of protein and calcium?
3. What factors increase L.R.'s risk for delayed union or nonunion of the fracture?
4. *Priority Decision:* What are the priority teaching needs for L.R.?
5. *Collaboration:* Which persons on the interprofessional team should be responsible for L.R.'s home care instructions? Who should be responsible for ambulation and home safety teaching and assessments? Who should help L.R. with transfers and ambulation during her hospital stay?
6. *Priority Decision:* Based on the assessment data, what are the priority nursing diagnoses?
7. *Quality Improvement:* What outcomes would indicate that interprofessional care was effective?
8. *Safety:* What safety precautions should be considered for this patient?
9. *Evidence-Based Practice:* L.R asks why it is important for her to have daily injections of enoxaparin after surgery. How do you respond?

Answers available at *http://evolve.elsevier.com/Lewis/medsurg.*

BRIDGE TO NCLEX EXAMINATION

The number of the question corresponds to the same-numbered outcome at the beginning of the chapter.

1. A patient with osteomyelitis undergoes surgical debridement with implantation of antibiotic beads. When the patient asks why the beads are used, the nurse answers (select all that apply)
   a. "Oral or IV antibiotics are not effective in most cases of bone infection."
   b. "The beads are an adjunct to debridement and antibiotics for deep infections."
   c. "The beads are used to deliver antibiotics directly to the site of the infection."
   d. "This is the safest method to deliver long-term antibiotic therapy for bone infection."
   e. "Ischemia and bone death related to osteomyelitis are impenetrable to IV antibiotics."

2. A patient with osteosarcoma of the humerus shows understanding of his treatment options when he states
   a. "I accept that I have to lose my arm with surgery."
   b. "The chemotherapy before surgery will shrink the tumor."
   c. "This tumor is related to the melanoma I had 3 years ago."
   d. "I'm glad they can take out the cancer with such a small scar."

3. Which persons are at high risk for chronic low back pain? (select all that apply)
   a. A 63-yr-old man who is a long-distance truck driver
   b. A 30-yr-old nurse who works on an orthopedic unit and smokes
   c. A 55-yr-old construction worker who is 6 ft, 2 in and weighs 250 lb
   d. A 44-yr-old female chef with prior compression fracture of the spine
   e. A 28-yr-old female yoga instructor who is 5 ft, 6 in and weighs 130 lb

4. A patient with suspected disc herniation has acute pain and muscle spasms. The nurse's responsibility is to
   a. encourage total bed rest for several days.
   b. teach principles of back strengthening exercises.
   c. stress the importance of straight-leg raises to decrease pain.
   d. promote use of cold and hot compresses and pain medication.

5. In caring for a patient after a spinal fusion, the nurse would report which finding to the health care provider?
   a. The patient has a single episode of emesis.
   b. The patient is unable to move the lower extremities.
   c. The patient is nauseated and has not voided in 4 hours.
   d. The patient reports of pain at the bone graft donor site.

6. A patient who has had surgical correction of bilateral hallux valgus is being discharged from the same-day surgery unit. The nurse will teach the patient to
   a. rest frequently with the feet elevated.
   b. wear shoes continually except when bathing.
   c. soak the feet in warm water several times a day.
   d. expect the feet to be numb for the next few days.

7. What is most important to include in the teaching plan for a patient with osteopenia?
   a. Lose weight.
   b. Stop smoking.
   c. Eat a high-protein diet.
   d. Start swimming for exercise.

1. b, c, 2. b, 3. a, b, c, d, 4. d, 5. b, 6. a, 7. b

For rationales to these answers and even more NCLEX review questions, visit *http://evolve.elsevier.com/Lewis/medsurg.*

ⓔ EVOLVE WEBSITE/RESOURCES LIST

http://evolve.elsevier.com/Lewis/medsurg
Review Questions (Online Only)
Key Points
Answer Keys for Questions
- Rationales for Bridge to NCLEX Examination Questions
- Answer Guidelines for Case Study on p. 1496
Student Case Study
- Patient With Osteoporosis
Nursing Care Plans
- eNursing Care Plan 63.1: Patient With Osteomyelitis
- eNursing Care Plan 63.2: Patient With Low Back Pain
Conceptual Care Map Creator
Audio Glossary
Supporting Media
- Animations
  - Diskectomy
  - Kyphoplasty
Content Updates

REFERENCES

1. Kavanagh N, Ryan EJ, Widaa A, et al: Staphylococcal osteomyelitis. Disease progression, treatment challenges, and future directions, *Clinical Microbiology Reviews* 31:e84, 2018.
2. Schmitt S: Osteomyelitis. Retrieved from *www.merckmanuals.com/ professional/musculoskeletal-and-connective-tissue-disorders/infections-of-joints-and-bones/osteomyelitis#.*
*3. Siegel RL, Miller KD, Jemal, A: Cancer statistics, *CA Cancer J Clin* 68:1, 2018.
4. American Cancer Society: Osteosarcoma. Retrieved from *www.cancer. org/cancer/osteosarcoma.html.*
5. Itano JK: *Core curriculum for oncology nursing,* ed 5, St Louis, 2016, Elsevier.
6. Muscular Dystrophy Association: Duchenne muscular dystrophy. Retrieved from *www.mda.org/disease/duchenne-muscular-dystrophy.*
*7. Matthews E, Brassington R, Kuntzer T, et al: Corticosteroids for the treatment of Duchenne muscular dystrophy, *The Cochrane Library* May 5(5):CD003725, 2016.
8. Sarepta Therapeutics: Exondys 51. Retrieved from *www.exondys51hcp.com/.*
9. Centers for Disease Control and Prevention: Duchene muscular dystrophy care considerations. Retrieved from *www.cdc.gov/features/muscular-dystrophy-care.*
10. National Institute of Neurological Disorders and Stroke: Low back pain fact sheet. Retrieved from *www.ninds.nih.gov/disorders/backpain/detail_ backpain.htm.*
*11. Nourollahi M, Afshari D, Dianat I: Awkward trunk postures and their relationship with low back pain in hospital nurses, *Work* 59:317, 2018.
*12. Andrews VD, Southard EP: Safe patient handling: Keeping health care workers safe, *Med-Surg Matters* 26:4, 2017.
13. Cleveland Clinic: Degenerative back conditions. Retrieved from *https:// my.clevelandclinic.org/health/diseases/16912-degenerative-back-conditions.*
14. American Academy of Orthopedic Surgeons: Cauda equina syndrome. Retrieved from *https://orthoinfo.aaos.org/en/diseases--conditions/cauda-equina-syndrome/.*
15. Mayo Clinic: Herniated disc. Retrieved from *www.mayoclinic.org/ diseases-condtions/herniated-disc/diagnosis/treatment/drc-20354101.*
16. An HS, Juarez KK: Artificial disc replacement. Retrieved from *www. spineuniverse.com/treatments/surgery/artificial-disc-replacement.*

*17. Lee DD, Kim YM: A comparison of radiographic and clinical outcomes of anterior lumbar interbody fusion performed with either a cellular bone allograft containing multipotent adult progenitor cells or recombinant human bone morphogenetic protein-2, *J Orthop Surg Res* 12:126, 2017.

*18. Blanpied PR, Gross AR, Elliott JM, et al: Neck pain: Clinical practice guidelines linked to the international classification of functioning, disability and health from the orthopedic section of the American Physical Therapy Association, *J Orthop Sports Phys Ther* 47:A1, 2017.

*19. Gross AR, Paquin JP, Dupont G, et al: Exercises for mechanical neck disorders: A Cochrane review update, *Man Ther* 24:25, 2016.

*20. Buldt AK, Menz HB: Incorrectly fitted footwear, foot pain and foot disorders: A systematic search and narrative review of the literature, *JFAR* 11:43, 2018.

*21. Guidelines abstracted from the American Geriatrics Society Guidelines for improving the care of older adults with diabetes mellitus: 2013 Update, *JAGS* 61:2020, 2013. (Classic)

22. Bartl R, Bartl C: Drug-induced osteomalacia. In *Bone disorders,* New York, 2017, Springer.

23. Mayo Clinic: Osteomalacia. Retrieved from *www.mayoclinic.org/diseases-conditions/osteomalacia/symptoms-causes/syc-20355514?p=1.*

*24. Liu C, Wu D, Zhang JF, et al: Changes in bone metabolism in morbidly obese patients after bariatric surgery: A meta-analysis, *Obes Surg* 26:91, 2016.

25. National Osteoporosis Foundation: What is osteoporosis and what causes it? Retrieved from *www.nof.org/patients/what-is-osteoporosis/.*

*26. US Preventive Services Task Force: Osteoporosis to prevent fractures: Screening. Retrieved from *www.uspreventiveservicestaskforce.org/Page/Document/UpdateSummaryFinal/osteoporosis-screening1.*

27. Cleveland Clinic: Osteoporosis. Retrieved from *https://my.clevelandclinic.org/health/diseases/4443-osteoporosis.*

28. World Health Organization: WHO criteria for diagnosis of osteoporosis. Retrieved from *www.4bonehealth.org/education/world-health-organization-criteria-diagnosis-osteoporosis/.*

29. McCloskey EV, Harvey NC, Johansson H, et al: FRAX updates 2016, *Curr Opin Rheumatol* 28:433, 2016.

30. McCarthy J, Davis A: Diagnosis and management of vertebral compression fractures, *Am Fam Physician* 94:44, 2016.

*31. Qaseem A, Forciea MA, McLean RM, et al: Treatment of low bone density or osteoporosis to prevent fractures in men and women: A clinical practice guideline update from the American College of Physicians, *Ann Intern Med* 166:818, 2017.

*32. Schmidt P: The 2017 hormone therapy position statement of the North American Menopause Society, *Menopause* 24:728, 2017.

33. NIH Osteoporosis and Related Bone Diseases National Resource Center: What is Paget's disease of bone? Retrieved from *www.bones.nih.gov/health-info/bone/pagets/pagets-disease-ff#who.*

*34. Appelman-Dijkstra NM, Papapoulos SE: Paget's disease of bone. *Best Pract Res Clin Endocrinol Metab* 32:657, 2018.

*Evidence-based information for clinical practice.

64

Arthritis and Connective Tissue Diseases

Dottie Roberts

No one is useless in the world who lightens the burdens of another.

Charles Dickens

http://evolve.elsevier.com/Lewis/medsurg

CONCEPTUAL FOCUS

Fatigue	Mobility	Stress
Functional Ability	Pain	
Inflammation	Self-Management	

LEARNING OUTCOMES

1. Outline the sequence of events leading to joint destruction in osteoarthritis and rheumatoid arthritis.
2. Detail the clinical manifestations and interprofessional and nursing management of osteoarthritis and rheumatoid arthritis.
3. Describe the pathophysiology, clinical manifestations, and interprofessional care of gout, Lyme disease, and septic arthritis.
4. Discuss the pathophysiology, clinical manifestations, and interprofessional and nursing management of ankylosing spondylitis, psoriatic arthritis, and reactive arthritis.

5. Describe the pathophysiology, clinical manifestations, and interprofessional and nursing management of systemic lupus erythematosus, scleroderma, polymyositis, dermatomyositis, and Sjögren's syndrome.
6. Explain the drug therapy and related nursing management associated with arthritis and connective tissue diseases.
7. Relate possible etiologies, clinical manifestations, and interprofessional and nursing management of fibromyalgia and systemic exertion tolerance disease.

KEY TERMS

ankylosing spondylitis (AS), p. 1517
arthritis, p. 1499
CREST syndrome, p. 1523
dermatomyositis (DM), p. 1525
fibromyalgia, p. 1527
gout, p. 1513
Lyme disease, p. 1515

myofascial pain syndrome, p. 1527
osteoarthritis (OA), p. 1499
polymyositis (PM), p. 1525
psoriatic arthritis (PsA), p. 1518
Raynaud's phenomenon, p. 1523
rheumatoid arthritis (RA), p. 1505
septic arthritis, p. 1516

scleroderma, p. 1523
Sjögren's syndrome, p. 1526
spondyloarthropathies, p. 1517
systemic exertion intolerance disease (SEID), p. 1528
systemic lupus erythematosus (SLE), p. 1519

This chapter discusses *rheumatic diseases,* which primarily affect body joints, tendons, ligaments, muscles, and bones. These diseases are often marked by inflammation, pain, and loss of function in 1 or more of the body's connecting or supporting structures. The patient may be challenged by problems of limited function and fatigue, loss of self-esteem, altered body image, and fear of disability. More than 100 kinds of rheumatic diseases have been identified.[1] Over 54 million people in the United States have rheumatic conditions.[2]

ARTHRITIS

Arthritis involves inflammation of a joint or joints. Most forms of arthritis affect women more often than men in every age-group.[2] Osteoarthritis is the most common chronic condition of the joints.[3] Other forms include rheumatoid arthritis (RA), fibromyalgia, systemic lupus erythematosus (SLE), and gout.

OSTEOARTHRITIS

Osteoarthritis (OA) is a slowly progressive noninflammatory disorder of the diarthrodial *(synovial)* joints. Currently OA affects 30 million Americans. This number is expected to greatly increase as the population ages.[2]

Etiology and Pathophysiology

OA involves the gradual loss of articular cartilage with formation of bony outgrowths (spurs or osteophytes) at the joint margins.[3] OA is not a normal part of the aging process, but aging is one risk factor for disease development. Cartilage destruction

TABLE 64.1 Causes of Osteoarthritis

Cause	Effects on Joint Cartilage
Drugs	Drugs, such as indomethacin, colchicine, and corticosteroids, can stimulate collagen-digesting enzymes in joint synovium.
Hematologic or endocrine disorders	Chronic hemarthrosis (e.g., from hemophilia) contributes to cartilage deterioration.
Inflammation	Release of enzymes in response to local inflammation can affect cartilage health.
Joint instability	Damage to supporting structures causes instability, placing uneven stress on joint cartilage.
Mechanical stress	Repetitive physical activities (e.g., sports) cause cartilage deterioration.
Neurologic disorders	Pain and loss of reflexes from neurologic disorders, such as diabetic neuropathy and Charcot joint, cause abnormal movements that contribute to cartilage deterioration.
Skeletal deformities	Congenital or acquired conditions (e.g., dislocated hip) contribute to cartilage deterioration.
Trauma	Dislocations or fractures may lead to avascular necrosis or uneven stress on cartilage.

likely begins between ages 20 and 30. Most adults are affected by age 40. Few patients have symptoms until after age 50 or 60. More than half of those over age 65 have x-ray evidence of OA in at least 1 joint.[2]

OA may be caused by a known event or condition that directly damages cartilage or causes joint instability (Table 64.1). However, we cannot identify a single cause for many persons with OA. In these situations, various genetic traits may contribute to the development of cartilage defects. People with hand OA are more likely to develop knee OA.[2]

Decreased estrogen at menopause may contribute to the increased incidence of OA in aging women. Obesity is a modifiable risk factor that contributes to hip and knee OA. It increases mechanical stress on the joints. Regular moderate exercise, which helps with weight management, decreases the risk for disease development and progression. Anterior cruciate ligament injury from quick stops and pivoting, as in football and soccer, are linked to an increased risk for knee OA.[3] Work that requires frequent kneeling and stooping also increase the risk for knee OA.

GENDER DIFFERENCES
Osteoarthritis (OA)

Men
- Except for traumatic arthritis, men do not have OA as often as women until age 70 or 80 years.
- Hip OA is more common in men.

Women
- OA affects women more often.
- Hand OA (interphalangeal joints and thumb base) is more common in women.
- Knee OA is more common in women, especially after menopause. It is likely to be more severe.

The development of OA is complex. Genetic, metabolic, and local factors interact to cause cartilage deterioration from damage at the level of the chondrocytes (Fig. 64.1). The normally smooth, white, translucent articular cartilage becomes dull, yellow, and granular as the disease progresses. Affected cartilage steadily becomes softer and less elastic. It is less able to resist wear with heavy use.

The body's attempts at cartilage repair cannot keep up with the destruction of OA. As the collagen structure in the cartilage changes, articular surfaces become cracked and worn. While central cartilage becomes thinner, cartilage at the joint edges becomes thicker and osteophytes form. Joint surfaces become uneven, affecting the distribution of stress across the joint and causing reduced motion.

Although inflammation is not typical of OA, secondary synovitis may occur when phagocytes try to rid the joint of small pieces of cartilage torn from the joint surface. These changes cause the early pain and stiffness of OA. Pain in later disease occurs when articular cartilage is lost, and bony joint surfaces rub each other.

Clinical Manifestations

Joints. Manifestations range from mild discomfort to significant disability. Joint pain is the main symptom and the typical reason the patient seeks medical attention. Pain generally gets worse with joint use. In early stages of OA, joint pain is relieved by rest. However, the patient with advanced disease may have pain at rest or have trouble sleeping due to increased joint pain. Pain may worsen as the barometric pressure falls before the onset of severe weather.

As OA progresses, increasing pain can contribute greatly to disability and loss of function. The pain of OA may be referred to the groin, buttock, or outside of the thigh or knee. Sitting down becomes hard, as does rising from a chair when the hips are lower than the knees. As OA develops in the intervertebral (*apophyseal*) joints of the spine, local pain and stiffness are common.

Unlike pain, which typically worsens with activity, joint stiffness occurs after periods of rest or an unchanged position. Early morning stiffness is common. It generally resolves within 30 minutes. This distinguishes OA from inflammatory joint disorders, such as RA. Overactivity can cause a mild joint swelling that temporarily increases stiffness. *Crepitation,* a grating sensation caused by loose cartilage particles in the joint cavity, can cause stiffness. Crepitation is common in patients with knee OA.

OA usually affects joints on 1 side of the body (*asymmetrically*) rather than in pairs. For example, the left knee may be affected and the right knee unchanged. The distal interphalangeal (DIP) and proximal interphalangeal (PIP) joints of the fingers, and the metacarpophalangeal (MCP) joint of the thumb are often affected. Weight-bearing joints (hips, knees), the metatarsophalangeal (MTP) joint of the foot, and the cervical and lower lumbar vertebrae are often involved (Fig. 64.2).

Deformity. Deformity or instability associated with OA is specific to the involved joint. For example, *Heberden's nodes* occur on the DIP joints due to osteophyte formation and loss of joint space (Fig. 64.1, *D*). They can appear as early as age 40 and tend to be seen in family members. *Bouchard's nodes* on the PIP joints indicate similar disease involvement. Heberden's and Bouchard's nodes are often red, swollen, and tender. Although they usually do not cause significant loss of function, the visible deformity may bother the patient.

Knee OA often leads to obvious joint deformity due to cartilage loss in 1 joint compartment. For example, the patient

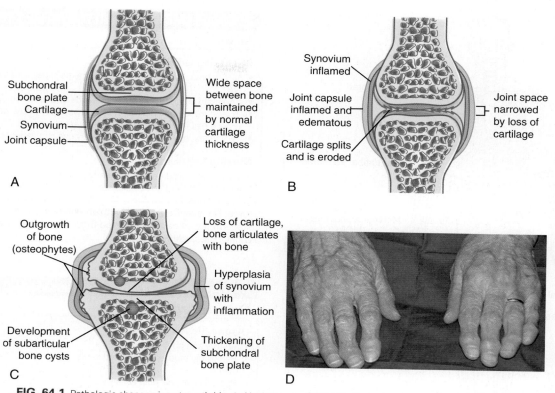

FIG. 64.1 Pathologic changes in osteoarthritis. **A,** Normal synovial joint. **B,** Early change in osteoarthritis is destruction of articular cartilage and narrowing of the joint space. There is inflammation and thickening of the joint capsule and synovium. **C,** With time, thickening of subarticular bone occurs, caused by constant friction of the 2 bone surfaces. Osteophytes form around the periphery of the joint by irregular overgrowths of bone. **D,** In osteoarthritis of the hands, osteophytes on the distal interphalangeal joints of the fingers, termed *Heberden's nodes,* appear as small nodules. (*D,* From Forbes CD, Jackson WF: *Color atlas and text of clinical medicine,* ed 3, London, 2003, Mosby.)

becomes bowlegged *(varus deformity)* in response to medial joint arthritis. Lateral joint arthritis causes a knock-kneed appearance *(valgus deformity).* In advanced hip OA, 1 leg may become shorter as the joint space narrows.

Systemic. Fatigue, fever, and organ involvement are not present in OA. This is an important distinction between OA and inflammatory joint disorders, such as rheumatoid arthritis.

Diagnostic Studies

A bone scan, CT scan, or MRI may be used to diagnose OA. These tests can detect early joint changes. X-rays help confirm disease and stage joint damage. As OA progresses, x-rays often show joint space narrowing and increasingly dense bone. Osteophytes may be visible. However, these changes do not always reflect the degree of pain the patient has. Despite strong x-ray evidence of disease, the patient may be relatively free of symptoms. Another patient may have severe pain with only slight x-ray changes.

No laboratory tests or biomarkers can be used to diagnose OA. The erythrocyte sedimentation rate (ESR) is normal except for slight increases during acute inflammation. Other routine blood tests (e.g., CBC, renal and liver function tests) are useful only in screening for related conditions or for establishing baseline values before starting treatment. Synovial fluid analysis helps distinguish OA from other types of inflammatory arthritis. In OA, the fluid is clear yellow with little or no sign of inflammation.

Interprofessional Care

OA has no cure. Interprofessional care focuses on managing pain and inflammation, preventing disability, and maintaining and improving joint function (Table 64.2). Nondrug interventions are the basis of OA management. They should be maintained throughout the patient's treatment. Drug therapy supplements nondrug treatments.

Rest and Joint Protection. Teach the patient with OA to balance rest and activity. Encourage rest of the affected joint during periods of acute inflammation. Keep joints in a functional position with splints or braces if needed. Avoid immobilization for more than 1 week because of the risk for joint stiffness with inactivity. Review how to modify usual activities to decrease stress on affected joints. Teach the patient with knee OA to avoid standing, kneeling, or squatting for long periods. Using an assistive device, such as a cane, walker, or crutches, can decrease joint stress.

Heat and Cold Applications. Apply heat and cold to help reduce pain and stiffness. Ice is not used as often as heat in OA treatment. Ice can be helpful if the patient has acute inflammation. Heat therapy is especially useful for stiffness. Treatments include hot packs, whirlpool baths, ultrasound, and paraffin wax baths.

Nutritional Therapy and Exercise. If the patient is overweight, a weight-reduction program is a critical part of the treatment plan. Help the patient evaluate the current diet to make needed changes. (Chapter 40 discusses ways to help the patient attain and maintain a healthy body weight.) Since mobilizing the joint

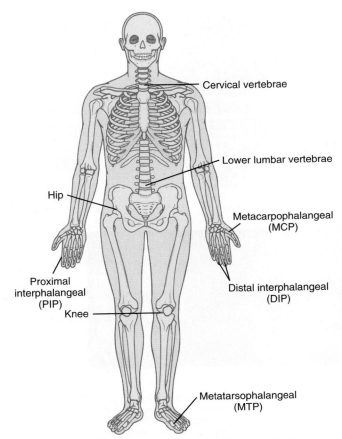

FIG. 64.2 Joints most often involved in osteoarthritis.

preserves articular cartilage health, exercise is an important part of OA management. Aerobic conditioning, range-of-motion (ROM) exercises, and programs to strengthen muscles around the affected joint help many patients.

Complementary and Alternative Therapies. Complementary and alternative therapies for OA symptom management are popular with patients who have not found relief through traditional medical care. Teach the patient to carefully research any alternative therapies and avoid replacing conventional OA treatments with unproven complementary approaches. Acupuncture, massage, and Tai Chi may reduce arthritis pain and improve joint mobility.

Some nutritional supplements may have antiinflammatory effects (e.g., fish oil, ginger, SAM-e). However, results of studies on glucosamine and chondroitin are mixed. The American College of Rheumatology (ACR) and American Academy of Orthopaedic Surgeons (AAOS) does not recommend their use.[4] Teach patients to discuss any supplement use with their HCP to identify possible interactions with prescribed medications.

Drug Therapy. Drug therapy is based on the severity of the patient's symptoms (Table 64.3). The patient with mild to moderate joint pain may get relief from acetaminophen (Tylenol).

A topical agent, such as capsaicin cream, may be helpful, alone or with acetaminophen. It blocks pain by locally interfering with substance P. It is responsible for the transmission of pain impulses. A concentrated product is available by prescription. Creams of 0.025% to 0.075% capsaicin are available over the counter (OTC). OTC products that contain camphor, eucalyptus oil, and menthol (e.g., Bengay, Arthricare) may provide

COMPLEMENTARY & ALTERNATIVE THERAPIES

Tai Chi

Scientific Evidence
- Tai Chi brought short-term improvements in pain and stiffness in knee OA.
- Some studies found improved balance or decreased depression.
- In a study comparing Tai Chi to physical therapy, patients in both groups had improved pain for a full year.
- Temporary increase of knee pain may occur in patients with knee OA.

Nursing Implications
- Generally considered to be safe practices.
- Avoid overuse of affected joints.

Source: National Center for Complementary and Alternative Medicine: Osteoarthritis: in depth. Retrieved from *www.nccih.nih.gov/health/arthritis/osteoarthritis#hed3.*

TABLE 64.2 Interprofessional Care

Osteoarthritis

Diagnostic Assessment
- History and physical examination
- Radiologic studies of involved joints (e.g., x-ray, CT scan, MRI, bone scan)
- Possible synovial fluid analysis

Management
- Nutritional and weight management counseling
- Rest and joint protection, use of assistive devices
- Therapeutic exercise
- Heat and cold applications
- Complementary and alternative therapies
  - Herbs and nutritional supplements (e.g., fish oil, ginger, SAM-e)
  - Movement therapies (e.g., yoga, Tai Chi)
  - Acupuncture
  - Massage
- Transcutaneous electrical nerve stimulation (TENS)
- Reconstructive joint surgery

Drug Therapy (Table 64.3)
- acetaminophen
- NSAIDs
- Intraarticular corticosteroids

temporary pain relief. Topical salicylates (e.g., Aspercreme) may be an option for patients who cannot take aspirin-containing medication. Several applications may be needed daily because topical agents have short-acting effects.

If a patient does not get adequate pain management with acetaminophen, has moderate to severe OA pain, or has signs of joint inflammation, a nonsteroidal antiinflammatory drug (NSAID) may be more effective. NSAID therapy typically is started in low-dose OTC strengths (e.g., ibuprofen 200 mg up to 4 times daily). The dose may be increased if needed. If the patient is at risk for or develops gastrointestinal (GI) side effects with an NSAID, adding a protective agent, such as misoprostol (Cytotec), may be needed. Arthrotec, a combination of misoprostol and the NSAID diclofenac, is available. Diclofenac gel may be applied to the affected joint. Teach the patient who is taking an oral NSAID to avoid use of a topical NSAID because of increased risk for adverse effects.

TABLE 64.3 Drug Therapy

Osteoarthritis

Drug	Mechanism of Action	Nursing Considerations
Corticosteroids		
Intraarticular Injections		
methylprednisolone acetate (Depo-Medrol) triamcinolone (Aristospan)	Antiinflammatory Analgesic Act by inhibiting synthesis and/or release of inflammatory mediators	Use strict aseptic technique for corticosteroid injection. Tell patient that joint may temporarily feel worse right after injection. Teach patient to avoid overusing affected joint right after injection. Tell patient improvement lasts weeks to months after injection.
Systemic		
dexamethasone hydrocortisone (Solu-Cortef) methylprednisolone (Solu-Medrol) prednisone triamcinolone	Antiinflammatory Analgesic Act by inhibiting synthesis and/or release of inflammatory mediators	Use only in life-threatening exacerbation or when symptoms persist after treatment with less potent antiinflammatory drugs. Give for limited time only, tapering dose slowly. Be aware that worsening of symptoms occurs with abrupt withdrawal of drug. Monitor BP, weight, CBC, and serum potassium. Limit sodium intake. Report signs of infection.
Nonsteroidal Antiinflammatory Drugs (NSAIDs)		
celecoxib (Celebrex) diclofenac ibuprofen (Advil) indomethacin ketoprofen meclofenamate meloxicam (Mobic) nabumetone naproxen (Aleve) oxaprozin (Daypro) piroxicam (Feldene) sulindac tolmetin	Antiinflammatory Analgesic Fever reducer (antipyretic) Act by inhibiting prostaglandin synthesis	Give drug with food, milk, or antacids (as prescribed). Report signs of bleeding (e.g., tarry stools, bruising, petechiae, nosebleeds), edema, skin rashes, persistent headaches, visual problems. Monitor BP for elevations related to fluid retention. Must be used regularly for maximal effect.
Salicylate		
aspirin, salicylate (salsalate)	Antiinflammatory Analgesic Fever reducer (antipyretic) Act by inhibiting prostaglandin synthesis	Give with food, milk, antacids (as prescribed), or full glass of water. May use enteric-coated aspirin. Report signs of bleeding (e.g., tarry stools, bruising, petechiae, nosebleeds).
Topical Analgesics		
capsaicin cream	Depletes substance P from nerve endings, interrupting pain signals to the brain	Must be used at regular intervals for maximal effect. Aloe vera cream may decrease burning sensation. Teach patient not to use cream with external heat source (heating pad) because of risk for burns. Available in OTC and prescriptive strengths.
diclofenac sodium (Voltaren gel)	Antiinflammatory Analgesic	Teach patient to avoid sun and ultraviolet (UV) light exposure. Should not be used in combination with oral NSAIDs or aspirin due to risk for increased side effects.

All NSAIDs inhibit the production of cyclooxygenase-1 (COX-1) and cyclooxygenase-2 (COX-2). These enzymes convert arachidonic acid into prostaglandins (see Fig. 8.5). Inhibiting COX-1 causes many of the untoward effects of NSAIDs, including the risk for bleeding and GI irritation.[5] Patients taking an anticoagulant (e.g., warfarin [Coumadin]) and an NSAID are at high risk for bleeding. Long-term NSAID treatment may affect cartilage metabolism, especially in older patients who may have poor cartilage integrity. As an alternative to traditional NSAIDs, the COX-2 inhibitor celecoxib (Celebrex) may be considered in selected patients.

When given in equivalent doses, all NSAIDs are comparably effective but vary widely in cost. Individual responses to NSAIDs also vary. Some patients still prefer aspirin, but it is no longer a common treatment. It should be used cautiously with NSAIDs because both inhibit platelet function and prolong bleeding time. Intraarticular injections of corticosteroids may be needed for those with local inflammation and swelling. Four or more injections without relief suggest the need for more intervention. Systemic corticosteroids are not used as they may actually hasten the disease process.

Injection of hyaluronic acid (viscosupplementation) has been a common treatment for knee OA. However, its effectiveness is not clear. Neither the ACR nor the AAOS recommends against using hyaluronates.[6] Research on the long-term effects continues.

Drugs thought to slow the progression of OA or support joint healing are known as disease-modifying osteoarthritis drugs (DMOADs). To date, no drugs have been approved to modify OA progression despite many clinical trials. Strontium ranelate, an approved treatment for osteoporosis, is being researched for effects on OA. Because it reduces levels of a cartilage turnover marker, it may be helpful in OA treatment.[5]

Surgical Therapy. Symptoms of disease are often managed conservatively for many years. However, the patient's loss of joint function, unmanaged pain, and decreased independence in self-care may lead to consideration of surgery. Patients with knee OA used to undergo arthroscopy to remove loose bodies from the joint. However, it does not have any benefit over physical therapy and medical treatment.[7] Reconstructive surgical procedures (e.g., hip and knee replacements) are discussed in Chapter 62.

❖ NURSING MANAGEMENT: OSTEOARTHRITIS

◆ Nursing Assessment

Carefully assess and document the type, location, severity, frequency, and duration of the patient's joint pain and stiffness. Determine what makes the pain better or worse. Ask the patient how these symptoms affect the ability to perform activities of daily living (ADLs). Review the patient's pain management practices. Ask about success of each treatment. Assess tenderness, swelling, limitation of movement, and crepitation of affected joints. Compare an involved joint with the opposite joint if it is not affected.

◆ Nursing Diagnoses

Nursing diagnoses for the patient with OA may include:
- Acute and chronic pain
- Impaired physical mobility
- Difficulty coping

◆ Planning

Overall goals are that the patient with OA will (1) maintain or improve joint function through a balance of rest and activity, (2) use joint protection measures (Table 64.4) to improve activity tolerance, (3) achieve independence in self-care and maintain optimal role function, and (4) use drug and nondrug strategies to manage pain satisfactorily.

◆ Nursing Implementation

◆ **Health Promotion.** Prevention of OA is possible in some cases. Focus community education on altering modifiable risk factors. For example, encourage the patient to lose weight and reduce occupational or recreational hazards. For athletic instruction and physical fitness programs, include safety measures that protect and reduce trauma to the joints. Prompt treatment of traumatic joint injuries decreases the risk for OA.

> ### ♥ PROMOTING POPULATION HEALTH
> #### Preventing Osteoarthritis
>
> - Avoid cigarette smoking.
> - Promptly treat any joint injury.
> - Maintain healthy weight and eat a balanced diet.
> - Use safety measures to protect and decrease risk for joint injury.
> - Exercise regularly, including strength and endurance training.

Acute Care. The patient with OA usually is treated as an outpatient. The interprofessional team involved may include an internal medicine physician or family HCP, a rheumatologist, a nurse, an occupational therapist, and a physical therapist. Health assessment questionnaires can pinpoint areas of decreased function. They are completed at regular intervals to

> ### TABLE 64.4 Patient & Caregiver Teaching
> #### Joint Protection and Energy Conservation
>
> Include the following instructions when teaching patients with arthritis to protect joints and conserve energy:
> - Maintain healthy weight.
> - Use assistive devices, if needed.
> - Avoid forceful repetitive joint movements.
> - Avoid awkward positions that stress joints.
> - Use good posture and body mechanics.
> - Seek help with needed tasks that may cause pain.
> - Organize routine tasks and pace yourself to decrease fatigue and joint pain.
> - Modify home and work environment to perform tasks in less stressful ways.

document disease and treatment progression. Treatment goals can be based on data from the questionnaires and physical examination, with specific interventions for identified problems. The patient is usually hospitalized only if having joint surgery (see Chapter 62).

Drugs are given for the treatment of pain and inflammation. Nondrug strategies to decrease pain and disability may include massage, use of heat (thermal packs) or cold (ice packs), meditation, and yoga.[8] Splints may be prescribed to rest and stabilize painful or inflamed joints.

Once an acute flare has subsided, a physical therapist can give valuable assistance in planning an exercise program. The therapist may recommend Tai Chi as a low-impact form of exercise. Tai Chi can be done by patients of all ages and may be done in a wheelchair. Stress the importance of warming up before any exercise to decrease risk for injury.

Patient and caregiver teaching related to OA is an important nursing responsibility. Provide information about the nature and treatment of the disease, pain management, body mechanics, correct use of assistive devices (e.g., cane, walker), principles of joint protection and energy conservation (Table 64.4), nutritional choices, weight and stress management, and an exercise program.

Assure the patient that OA is a localized disease and severe deforming arthritis is not the usual course. The patient may gain support and understanding of the disease process through community resources, such as the Arthritis Foundation's self-help course (*www.arthritis.org*).

> ### ❓ CHECK YOUR PRACTICE
>
> A 54-yr-old woman has OA of the left knee. She received an intraarticular corticosteroid injection in the left knee and a prescription for diclofenac 50 mg twice daily. She receives a prescription for physical therapy.
> - What information will you provide about diclofenac to ensure the patient's safe, effective use?
> - What type of exercises will be appropriate for this patient?
> - The patient asks about complementary therapies for osteoarthritis. What will you tell her?

Ambulatory Care. Adjust home management goals to meet the patient's needs. Include the caregiver, family members, and significant others in goal setting and teaching. Discuss home and work environment modification for patient safety, accessibility, and self-care. Measures include removing throw rugs, placing rails at the stairs and bathtub, using night-lights, and wearing well-fitting supportive shoes. Assistive devices, such as canes, walkers, elevated toilet seats, and grab bars, reduce the load on an affected joint and promote safety. Urge the patient to continue all prescribed therapies at home and be open to new approaches to symptom management.

Sexual counseling may help the patient and significant other to enjoy physical closeness by introducing the idea of alternative positions and timing for sexual activity. Discussion also increases awareness of each partner's needs. Encourage the patient to take analgesics or a warm bath to decrease joint stiffness before sexual activity.

◆ Evaluation

The expected outcomes are that the patient with OA will
- Have adequate rest and activity
- Achieve acceptable pain management
- Maintain joint flexibility and muscle strength through joint protection and therapeutic exercise

RHEUMATOID ARTHRITIS

Rheumatoid arthritis (RA) is a chronic, systemic autoimmune disease characterized by inflammation of connective tissue in the diarthrodial (synovial) joints. RA is typically marked by periods of remission and exacerbation. RA often has extraarticular manifestations. RA has long been considered one of the most disabling forms of arthritis. Symptoms and outcomes can vary greatly. Without adequate treatment, patients may need mobility aids or joint reconstruction. They may have loss of independence and self-care ability.

RA occurs globally, affecting all ethnic groups. It can occur at any time of life. However, incidence increases with age, peaking between ages 30 and 50 years. RA affects around 1.5 million adult Americans. Almost 3 times as many women have the disease as men.[9]

Etiology and Pathophysiology

We do not know the exact cause of RA. It likely results from a combination of genetics and environmental triggers. An autoimmune cause is currently the most widely accepted theory. This theory suggests changes of RA begin when a genetically susceptible person has an initial immune response to an antigen. Although a bacterium or virus could be the possible antigen, no infection or organism has been found to date.

⊕ PROMOTING HEALTH EQUITY

Arthritis and Connective Tissue Disorders

- Arthritis is most common in whites and blacks.
- Hispanics and blacks have the highest incidence of arthritis-related activity limitations.
- Some Native Americans (e.g., Pima, Chippewa, Yakima) have a higher incidence of RA than other ethnic groups in North America.
- Ankylosing spondylitis is most common in whites and certain Native American groups.
- SLE is more common and more severe among black, Hispanic, Asian American, and Native American women than white women.
- Black and Hispanic women are at greater risk than white women for developing scleroderma.

The antigen, which is probably not the same in all patients, triggers formation of an abnormal immunoglobulin G (IgG). RA is marked by autoantibodies to this abnormal IgG. The

autoantibodies are known as *rheumatoid factor (RF)*. They combine with IgG to form immune complexes that initially deposit on synovial membranes or superficial articular cartilage in the joints. Immune complex formation leads to the activation of complement and an inflammatory response. (Complement activation is discussed in Chapter 11. Immune complex formation is discussed in Chapter 13.)

Neutrophils are attracted to the site of inflammation, where they release proteolytic enzymes that damage articular cartilage and cause the synovial lining to thicken (Fig. 64.3). Other inflammatory cells include T helper (CD4) cells, which stimulate cell-mediated immune responses. Activated CD4 cells cause monocytes, macrophages, and synovial fibroblasts to secrete the proinflammatory cytokines interleukin-1 (IL-1), IL-6, and tumor necrosis factor (TNF). These cytokines drive the inflammatory response in RA.

Some patients report a precipitating stressful event, such as infection, work stress, physical exertion, childbirth, surgery, or emotional upset. However, research has been unable to directly correlate such events with RA onset.

Genetic Link

Genetic predisposition is important in the development of RA. The strongest evidence for a genetic influence is the role of human leukocyte antigens (HLA), especially the HLA-DR4 and HLA-DR1 antigens. (HLA is discussed in Chapter 13.) Smoking increases the risk for RA for persons who are genetically predisposed to the disease. It may interfere with treatment for diagnosed persons.[10]

Clinical Manifestations

Joints. The onset of RA is typically subtle. Nonspecific manifestations, such as fatigue, anorexia, weight loss, and generalized stiffness, may precede the onset of joint symptoms. Stiffness becomes more localized in the following weeks to months.

Specific joint involvement is marked by pain, stiffness, limited motion, and signs of inflammation (e.g., heat, swelling, tenderness). Joint symptoms occur symmetrically and often affect the small joints of the hands (PIP and MCP) and feet (MTP). Larger peripheral joints such as wrists, elbows, shoulders, knees, hips, ankles, and jaw may be involved. The cervical spine may be affected, but the axial skeleton (spine and bones connected to it) is generally spared. Table 64.5 compares RA and OA.

The patient typically has joint stiffness after periods of inactivity. Morning stiffness may last from 60 minutes to several hours or more, depending on disease activity. MCP and PIP joints are typically swollen. In early disease, the fingers may become spindle shaped from synovial hypertrophy and thickening of the joint capsule. Joints are tender, painful, and warm to the touch. Joint pain increases with motion. It varies in intensity. It may not be related to the degree of inflammation. Tenosynovitis often affects the extensor and flexor tendons around the wrists. This causes symptoms of carpal tunnel syndrome and makes it hard for the patient to grasp objects.

As the disease progresses, inflammation and fibrosis of the joint capsule and supporting structures may cause deformity and disability. Muscle atrophy and tendon destruction cause 1 joint surface to slip past the other (*subluxation*). Metatarsal head dislocation and subluxation in the feet may cause pain and walking disability (Fig. 64.3, *D*). Ulnar drift ("zig-zag deformity"), swan neck, and boutonnière deformities are common in the hands (Fig. 64.4).

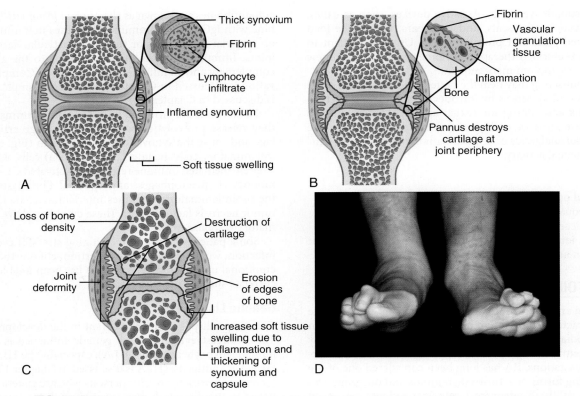

FIG. 64.3 RA. **A,** Early pathologic change is rheumatoid synovitis. Synovium becomes inflamed. Lymphocytes and plasma cells increase greatly. **B,** Over time, articular cartilage destruction occurs, and vascular granulation tissue grows across the cartilage surface (pannus) from the edges of the joint. Joint surface shows loss of cartilage beneath the extending pannus, most marked at joint margins. **C,** Inflammatory pannus causes focal destruction of bone. Osteolytic destruction of bone occurs at joint edges, causing erosions seen on x-rays. This phase is associated with joint deformity. **D,** Multiple deformities of the foot from rheumatoid arthritis. (*D,* From Canale ST, Beaty JH: *Campbell's operative orthopaedics,* ed 12, Philadelphia, 2013, Mosby.)

TABLE 64.5 Comparison of Rheumatoid Arthritis and Osteoarthritis

Parameter	Rheumatoid Arthritis	Osteoarthritis
Age at onset	Young to middle age.	Usually older than 40 years.
Gender	Female-to-male ratio is 2:1 or 3:1. Less marked sex difference after age 60.	Females 2:1 after age 60; except for traumatic arthritis, men less affected until age 70 or 80.
Weight	Lost or maintained weight.	Often overweight or obese.
Disease	Systemic disease with exacerbations and remissions.	Localized disease with variable, progressive course.
Affected joints	Small joints typically affected first (PIPs, MCPs, MTPs), wrists, elbows, shoulders, knees. Usually bilateral, symmetric joint involvement.	Weight-bearing joints of knees and hips, small joints (MCPs, DIPs, PIPs), cervical and lumbar spine. Often asymmetric.
Pain characteristics	Stiffness lasts 1 hr to all day and may ↓ with use. Pain is variable, may disrupt sleep.	Stiffness occurs on arising but usually subsides after 30 min. Pain gradually worsens with joint use and disease progression, relieved with joint rest but may disrupt sleep.
Effusions	Common.	Uncommon.
Nodules	Present, especially on extensor surfaces.	Heberden's (DIPs) and Bouchard's (PIPs) nodes.
Synovial fluid	WBC count 5000–60,000/μL with mostly neutrophils; ↓ viscosity.	WBC count <2000/μL (mild leukocytosis); normal viscosity.
X-rays	Joint space narrowing and erosion with bony overgrowths, subluxation with advanced disease. Osteoporosis related to decreased activity, corticosteroid use.	Joint space narrowing, osteophytes, subchondral cysts, sclerosis.
Laboratory findings	Rheumatoid factor positive in 70%–90% of patients; negative titers in early disease for about 25% of patients. ↑ In ANA titer likely. Positive anti-CCP in 60%–80% of patients ↑ ESR, CRP indicative of active inflammation.	Rheumatoid factor negative. ANA negative. Anti-CCP negative. Transient elevation in ESR related to synovitis.

ANA, Antinuclear antibodies; *anti-CCP,* anti-citrullinated peptide; *DIPs,* distal interphalangeal; *MCPs,* metacarpophalangeals; *MTPs,* metatarsophalangeals; *PIPs,* proximal interphalangeals.

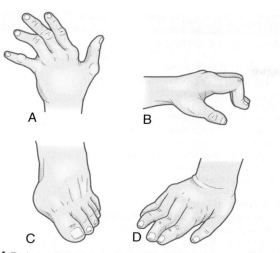

FIG. 64.4 Typical deformities of RA. **A,** Ulnar drift. **B,** Boutonnière deformity. **C,** Hallux valgus. **D,** Swan neck deformity.

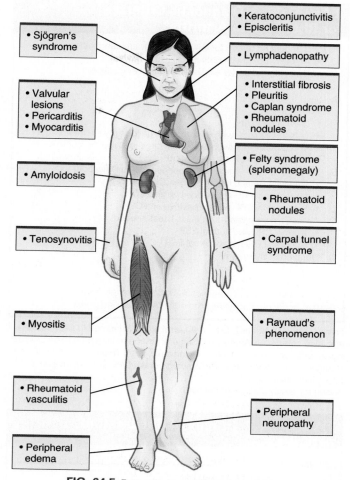

- Keratoconjunctivitis
- Episcleritis
- Sjögren's syndrome
- Lymphadenopathy
- Valvular lesions
- Pericarditis
- Myocarditis
- Interstitial fibrosis
- Pleuritis
- Caplan syndrome
- Rheumatoid nodules
- Amyloidosis
- Felty syndrome (splenomegaly)
- Rheumatoid nodules
- Tenosynovitis
- Carpal tunnel syndrome
- Myositis
- Raynaud's phenomenon
- Rheumatoid vasculitis
- Peripheral neuropathy
- Peripheral edema

FIG. 64.5 Extraarticular manifestations of RA.

Extraarticular Manifestations. RA can affect nearly every body system (Fig. 64.5). Extraarticular manifestations are more likely to occur in the person with high levels of biomarkers, such as RF.

Rheumatoid nodules develop in about half the patients with RA.[11] Rheumatoid nodules appear under the skin as firm, non-tender masses. They are often found on bony areas exposed to pressure, such as the fingers and elbows. Nodules at the base of the spine and back of the head are common in older adults. Treatment is usually not needed. However, these nodules can break down, like pressure injuries. Cataracts and vision loss can result from scleral nodules. Nodular myositis and muscle fiber degeneration can cause pain like that of vascular insufficiency. In later disease, nodules in the heart and lungs can cause pleurisy, pleural effusion, pericarditis, pericardial effusion, and cardiomyopathy.

Sjögren's syndrome can occur by itself or with other arthritic disorders, such as RA and SLE. The inflammation of RA can damage the tear-producing (lacrimal) glands, making the eyes feel dry and gritty.[11] Affected patients may have photosensitivity. (Sjögren's syndrome is discussed later in this chapter on p. 1526.)

Felty syndrome is rare but can occur in those with long-standing RA. It is characterized by an enlarged spleen and low white blood cell (WBC) count. Patients with Felty syndrome are at increased risk for infection and lymphoma.

Flexion contractures and hand deformities cause decreased grasp strength and affect the patient's ability to perform self-care tasks. Depression may occur. However, it is unclear if the patient becomes depressed from struggling with chronic pain and disability or if depression is part of the autoimmune disease process. Levels of C-reactive protein (CRP), a marker of inflammation, are higher in patients with depression compared to those with no symptoms of depression.[12]

Diagnostic Studies

Accurate diagnosis is critical to prompt initiation of treatment to decrease the risk for disability. A diagnosis is often made based on history and physical findings. Criteria for diagnosis of RA in a newly presenting patient are described in Table 64.6. Laboratory tests are used to confirm diagnosis and monitor disease progression (Tables 64.7 and 64.8).

Positive RF occurs in 80% of adults with RA. Titers rise during active disease. ESR and CRP are increased as general indicators of active inflammation. Testing for the antibodies to citrullinated peptide (anti-CCP) is more specific than RF for RA. Anti-CCP is present in 60% to 80% of patients with RA. It can be found in patients' blood 5 to 10 years before they have symptoms of RA. If the patient's symptoms are consistent with RA, the presence of anti-CCP and RF makes a strong case for early, accurate diagnosis. An increase in antinuclear antibody (ANA) titers is an indicator of autoimmune reaction.

Synovial fluid analysis in early disease often shows slightly cloudy, straw-colored fluid with many fibrin flecks. The enzyme MMP-3 is increased in the synovial fluid. It may be a marker of progressive joint damage. The WBC count of synovial fluid is increased. Tissue biopsy can confirm inflammatory changes in the synovial membrane.

X-rays alone are not diagnostic of RA. They may show only soft tissue swelling and possible bone demineralization in early disease. A narrowed joint space, articular cartilage destruction, erosion, subluxation, and deformity are seen in later disease. Poor alignment and fusion may be seen in advanced disease. Baseline x-rays may be used to monitor disease progression and treatment effectiveness. Bone scans are more useful in detecting early joint changes and confirming diagnosis so that RA treatment can be started.

TABLE 64.6 Diagnostic Criteria for Rheumatoid Arthritis*

Patients should be tested for RA who initially are seen with:
- At least 1 joint with definite clinical synovitis
- Synovitis not better explained by another disease

	Score
A. Joint Involvement	
• 1 large joint	0
• 2–10 large joints	1
• 1–3 small joints (with or without large joint involvement)	2
• 4–10 small joints (with or without large joint involvement)	3
• >10 joints (at least 1 small joint)	5
B. Serology (at least 1 test result needed for classification)	
• Negative RF *and* negative anti-CCP	0
• Low-positive RF *or* low-positive anti-CCP	2
• High-positive RF *or* high-positive anti-CCP	3
C. Acute Phase Reactants (at least 1 test needed)	
• Normal CRP *and* normal ESR	0
• Abnormal CRP *or* abnormal ESR	1
D. Duration of Symptoms	
• <6 wk	0
• ≥6 wk	1

Scoring: Add score of categories A–D. Scores range from 0–10. A score of ≥6 indicates the definitive presence of RA.

From Aletaha D, Neogi T, Silman AJ, et al: 2010 Rheumatoid arthritis classification criteria: An American College of Rheumatology/European League Against Rheumatism Collaborative Initiative, *Arthr Rheum* 62:2569, 2010. Retrieved from *www.rheumatology.org/Portals/0/Files/2010_revised_criteria_classification_ra.pdf.*
*Used for newly diagnosed patients.

TABLE 64.7 Stages of Rheumatoid Arthritis

Stage	Characteristics

I	• Synovitis marked by:
	  • Synovial membrane swelling with excess blood
	  • Membrane containing small areas of lymphocyte infiltration
	  • High WBC counts in synovial fluid (5000–60,000/μL)
	  • X-ray results: soft tissue swelling, possible osteoporosis; no evidence of joint destruction

II	• ↑ Joint inflammation, spreading across cartilage into joint cavity • Signs of gradual destruction in joint cartilage • Narrowing joint space from loss of cartilage
III	• Formation of synovial pannus • Joint cartilage becomes eroded, bone exposed • X-ray results: extensive cartilage loss, erosion at joint margins, possible deformity
IV	• End-stage: inflammatory process subsides • Loss of joint function • Formation of subcutaneous nodules

Source: Rheumatoid Arthritis.net: A health union community: Understanding RA stages and progressions. Retrieved from *http://rheumatoidarthritis.net/what-is-ra/stages-and-progression.*

Interprofessional Care

An individualized treatment plan considers disease activity, joint function, age, sex, family and social roles, and response to previous treatment (Table 64.8). Treatment advances have improved the prognosis for patients with newly diagnosed RA. The progression of joint damage can be slowed or stopped with aggressive, early treatment.[13] A caring, long-term relationship with an interprofessional health care team can promote the patient's self-esteem and positive coping.

TABLE 64.8 Interprofessional Care

Rheumatoid Arthritis

Diagnostic Assessment
- History and physical examination
- Complete blood count (CBC)
- ESR
- C-reactive protein (CRP)
- Rheumatoid factor (RF)
- Antibodies to citrullinated peptide (anti-CCP)
- Antinuclear antibody (ANA)
- X-rays of involved joints
- Possible synovial fluid analysis

Management
- Nutritional and weight management counseling
- Therapeutic exercise
- Psychologic support
- Rest and joint protection, use of assistive devices
- Heat and cold applications
- Complementary and alternative therapies
  - Herbal products and nutritional supplements
  - Acupuncture
- Reconstructive surgery

Drug Therapy
- Disease-modifying antirheumatic drugs (DMARDs) (Table 64.9)
- Biologic response modifiers (BRMs) (Table 64.9)
- NSAIDs (Table 64.3)
- Intraarticular or systemic corticosteroids (Table 64.3)

Drug Therapy

Disease-Modifying Antirheumatic Drugs. Drugs are the cornerstone of RA treatment (Table 64.9). Because irreversible joint changes can occur as early as the first year of RA, HCPs aggressively prescribe disease-modifying antirheumatic drugs (DMARDs). These drugs may slow disease progression and decrease risk for joint erosion and deformity. The choice of drug is based on disease activity, the patient's functional level, and lifestyle considerations, such as the wish to become pregnant.

Methotrexate is preferred for early treatment of patients diagnosed with RA.[13] It has a lower risk for toxicity than other drugs. Rare but serious side effects include bone marrow suppression and hepatotoxicity. Methotrexate therapy requires frequent laboratory monitoring, including CBC and blood chemistry. The patient begins to see therapeutic effects within 4 to 6 weeks. However, not everyone gets adequate relief from methotrexate alone. It can be given with other DMARDs or biologic response modifiers.

Sulfasalazine (Azulfidine) and the antimalarial drug hydroxychloroquine (Plaquenil) may be effective DMARDs for mild to moderate disease. They are rapidly absorbed, relatively safe, and well-tolerated. Teach the patient taking sulfasalazine to drink adequate fluids to avoid crystal formation in the urine. Urge the patient to wear sunscreen with sun exposure. For those taking hydroxychloroquine, a baseline eye examination with follow-up every 6 to 12 months is needed because of the risk for vision loss.

The synthetic DMARD leflunomide (Arava) blocks immune cell overproduction. Its efficacy and side effects are similar to those of methotrexate and sulfasalazine. Because the drug is teratogenic, pregnancy in women of childbearing age must be excluded before therapy is started. Using 2 kinds of birth control is recommended during treatment.

Tofacitinib (Xeljanz), a JAK (Janus kinase) inhibitor, is used to treat moderate to severe active RA. The drug interferes with JAK enzymes that contribute to joint inflammation in RA. Live vaccinations should not be given to the patient receiving tofacitinib.

Biologic Response Modifiers. Biologic response modifiers *(BRMs)* (also called *biologics* or *immunotherapy*) are used to slow disease progression in RA. BRMs are classified based on their mechanism of action (Table 64.9). They can be used to treat patients with moderate to severe RA who have not responded to DMARDs. They can be used alone or in combination therapy with a DMARD, such as methotrexate.[13]

TNF inhibitors include etanercept (Enbrel), infliximab (Remicade), adalimumab (Humira), certolizumab (Cimzia), and golimumab (Simponi). Etanercept is a biologically engineered copy of the TNF cell receptor. It binds to TNF in circulation before TNF can bind to the cell surface receptor. Thus it inhibits the inflammatory response. This drug is given as a subcutaneous injection.

Infliximab and adalimumab are monoclonal antibodies that bind to TNF, preventing it from binding to TNF receptors on cells. Infliximab is given IV in combination with methotrexate. Adalimumab is given subcutaneously.

Certolizumab and golimumab are TNF inhibitors that improve symptoms in patients with moderate to severe RA. Both drugs are given in combination with methotrexate.

⚕ DRUG ALERT Tumor Necrosis Factor Inhibitors

- Perform tuberculin test and chest x-ray before starting therapy.
- Monitor for signs of infection. Stop the drug temporarily and notify HCP if acute infection develops.
- Teach patients to avoid live vaccination while taking drug.
- Report bruising, bleeding, or persistent fever and other signs of infection.

Anakinra (Kineret) is an IL-1 receptor antagonist (IL-1Ra) created from new combinations of genetic material. It blocks the biologic activity of IL-1 by competitively inhibiting its ability to bind to the IL-1 receptor. Anakinra is given as a subcutaneous injection. It is used to reduce pain and swelling of moderate to severe RA. It can be used in combination with DMARDs but not with other TNF inhibitors. Using these agents together can lead to serious infection and neutropenia.

Tocilizumab (Actemra) and sarilumab (Kevzara) block the action of IL-6, a cytokine that contributes to inflammation. They are used to treat patients with moderate to severe RA who have not responded to or cannot tolerate other drugs for the disease.

Abatacept (Orencia) blocks T-cell activation. It is recommended for patients who have inadequate response to DMARDs or TNF inhibitors. It is given IV. Like anakinra, it should not be used with TNF inhibitors.

Rituximab (Rituxan) is a monoclonal antibody that targets B cells. It may be used in combination with methotrexate for patients with moderate to severe RA not responding to TNF inhibitors. It is given IV.

Other Drug Therapy. Other DMARDS include immunosuppressants (azathioprine), penicillamine (Cuprimine), and gold preparations. These medications are used less often because they are weak treatments compared to other DMARDs and biologics.

Corticosteroid therapy can be used to manage symptoms during disease flares. Intraarticular injections may temporarily reduce acute pain and inflammation. Low-dose oral corticosteroids may be used for a limited time to decrease disease activity

until the effects of DMARDs or biologics are seen. However, they are inadequate as a sole therapy because they do not affect disease progression. Their long-term use should not be a mainstay of RA treatment. Complications include osteoporosis and avascular necrosis.

Various NSAIDs and salicylates are used to treat arthritis pain and inflammation. Aspirin may be used in dosages of 3 to 4 g/day in 3 to 4 doses. Blood salicylate levels should be monitored in a patient taking more than 3600 mg daily. NSAIDs have antiinflammatory and analgesic effects. Some relief may be seen within days of starting treatment with NSAIDs. Full effect may take 2 to 3 weeks. NSAIDs may be used when the patient cannot tolerate aspirin. The patient may be able to better follow the treatment plan if using an antiinflammatory drug that can be taken only once or twice a day (Table 64.3). Celecoxib (Celebrex), the only available COX-2 inhibitor, is effective in RA as well as OA. All nonaspirin NSAIDs can increase the risk for blood clots, heart attack, and stroke.

Nutritional Therapy. Although no special diet is needed for RA, balanced nutrition is important. Fatigue, pain, and depression may cause a loss of appetite. Limited endurance and mobility may make it hard to shop for and prepare food. Weight loss may result. The occupational therapist can help the patient modify the home environment and use assistive devices for easier food preparation.

Corticosteroid therapy and decreased mobility due to pain may cause unwanted weight gain. Corticosteroids increase the appetite, leading to higher caloric intake. A sensible weight loss program with balanced nutrition and exercise reduces stress on affected joints. The patient taking corticosteroids may become distressed as signs and symptoms of Cushing syndrome (e.g., moon face, redistribution of fatty tissue to the trunk) change the physical appearance. Encourage the patient not to change the dose or stop therapy abruptly. Weight will return to normal several months after treatment ends. Remind the patient to continue to eat a balanced diet.

Surgical Therapy. Surgery may be needed to relieve severe pain and improve the function of severely deformed joints. Removal of the joint lining *(synovectomy)* is one type of surgery. Total joint replacement *(arthroplasty)* can be done for many different joints in the body. Joint surgery is discussed in Chapter 62.

❖ NURSING MANAGEMENT: RHEUMATOID ARTHRITIS

◆ Nursing Assessment

Subjective and objective data to obtain from the patient with RA are outlined in Table 64.10. Begin with a careful physical assessment (e.g., joint pain, swelling, ROM, general health status). Assess psychosocial needs (e.g., family support, sexual satisfaction, emotional stress, financial constraints, vocational and career limitations). Assess for environmental concerns (e.g., transportation, home or work modifications). After identifying the patient's problems, carefully plan a program for rehabilitation and education with the interprofessional care team.

◆ Nursing Diagnoses

Nursing diagnoses for the patient with RA may include:
- Impaired physical mobility
- Chronic pain
- Disturbed body image

Additional information on nursing diagnoses and interventions for the patient with RA is provided in eNursing Care Plan 64.1 (available on the website for this chapter).

TABLE 64.9 Drug Therapy

Rheumatoid Arthritis

Drug	Mechanism of Action	Nursing Considerations
Disease-Modifying Antirheumatic Drugs (DMARDs)		
Antimalarial		
hydroxychloroquine (Plaquenil)	Exact mechanism unknown but may suppress formation of antigens	Monitor CBC and liver function. Tell patient therapeutic response may not occur for up to 6 mo. Teach patient to report visual changes, muscular weakness, and ↓ hearing or tinnitus.
Gold Compounds		
Oral: auranofin (Ridaura) *Parenteral:* gold sodium thiomalate, myochrysine, aurothioglucose	Alter immune responses, suppressing synovitis of active RA	Rule out pregnancy before beginning treatment. Monitor CBC, urinalysis, and liver and renal function. Tell patient therapeutic response may not occur for 3–6 mo. Teach patient to report pruritus, rash, sore mouth, indigestion, or metallic taste.
Immunosuppressants		
azathioprine (Imuran) cyclophosphamide	Inhibit DNA, RNA, protein synthesis	Assess for ↓ pain, swelling, stiffness, and ↑ joint mobility. Teach patient to report unusual bleeding or bruising. Tell patient therapeutic response may take up to 12 wk. Teach women of childbearing age to avoid pregnancy. Encourage ↑ fluid intake to ↓ risk for hemorrhagic cystitis.
mycophenolate mofetil (CellCept)	Inhibits DNA synthesis	Monitor blood count and liver function tests every 2–4 wk for first 3 mo of treatment, thereafter every 1–3 mo. Teach patient about ↑ infection risk. Tell patients not to take antacids at same time because they may interfere with drug absorption.
JAK (Janus Kinase) Inhibitor		
tofacitinib (Xeljanz)	Inhibits action of JAK enzymes, signaling pathways inside the cell with a key role in inflammation of RA	Tell patient of ↑ infection risk, including opportunistic infections. Monitor patient for any sign or symptom of infection for early treatment.
Miscellaneous		
leflunomide (Arava)	Antiinflammatory Immunomodulatory agent that inhibits proliferation of lymphocytes	Monitor liver function. Assess for ↓ pain, swelling, stiffness, and ↑ joint mobility. Teach women of childbearing age to avoid pregnancy.
methotrexate (Trexall)	Antimetabolite Inhibits DNA, RNA, protein synthesis	Monitor CBC and liver and renal function. Teach patient to report signs of anemia (fatigue, weakness). Keep patient well hydrated. Due to teratogenic effects, have female patient use effective contraception during and 3 mo after treatment.
penicillamine (Cuprimine, Depen)	Antiinflammatory Exact mechanism unknown but may suppress cell-mediated immune response	Monitor WBC count, platelets, urinalysis. Tell patient to take medication 1 hr before or 2 hr after meals, and at least 1 hr away from any other drug, food, or milk.
sulfasalazine (Azulfidine)	Sulfonamide Antiinflammatory Blocks prostaglandin synthesis	Tell patient drug may cause orange-yellow discoloration of urine or skin. Space doses evenly around the clock, taking drug after food with 8 oz water. Treatment may be continued even after symptoms are relieved. Monitor CBC.
Biologic Response Modifiers (Biologics, Immunotherapy)		
B-Cell Depleting Agent		
rituximab (Rituxan)	Monoclonal antibody that binds to CD20, an antigen on B cells, destroying B cells and suppressing immune response	Monitor for infection and bleeding. Tell patient to not receive live virus vaccines with treatment. Monitor for low BP if taking BP medication. Teach patient fatigue is common.
Interleukin-1 Receptor Antagonist		
anakinra (Kineret)	Blocks the action of interleukin-1, ↓ inflammatory response	Assess for ↓ pain, swelling, stiffness, and ↑ joint mobility. Injection site reaction generally occurs in first month of treatment and decreases with continued therapy. Assess renal function. Monitor for infection. Tell patient to not take drug with TNF inhibitors.
Interleukin-6 Receptor Antagonist		
sarilumab (Kevzara) tocilizumab (Actemra)	Blocks action of interleukin-6, thus ↓ inflammatory response	Given to patients with RA for whom other therapies have failed. Monitor BP and for infection. Tell patient of GI effects (e.g., perforation). Monitor liver enzyme and serum low-density lipoprotein (LDL).
T-Cell Activation Inhibitor		
abatacept (Orencia)	Inhibits T-cell activation, thus suppressing immune response	Not recommended for concomitant use with TNF inhibitors. Assess for ↓ pain, swelling, stiffness, and ↑ joint mobility.

TABLE 64.9 Drug Therapy—cont'd
Rheumatoid Arthritis

Drug	Mechanism of Action	Nursing Considerations
Tumor Necrosis Factor (TNF) Inhibitors		
adalimumab (Humira) certolizumab (Cimzia) etanercept (Enbrel) golimumab (Simponi) infliximab (Remicade)	Bind to TNF, blocking its interaction with cell surface receptors. Decrease inflammatory and immune responses	Assess for ↓ pain, swelling, stiffness, and ↑ joint mobility. Tell patient of ↑ risk for tuberculosis. Teach patient to have yearly PPD. Monitor for infection, bleeding, and emergence of cancers. Injection site reaction generally occurs in first month of treatment and ↓ with continued therapy. Teach patient to not receive live virus vaccines during treatment.
Other Agents **Antibiotics**		
doxycycline (Vibramycin)	↓ Action of enzymes on cartilage degradation	Possible treatment alternative for mild disease.
minocycline (Minocin)	Antirheumatic effect possibly related to immunomodulatory/antiinflammatory properties	

TABLE 64.10 Nursing Assessment
Rheumatoid Arthritis

Subjective Data

Important Health Information

Past health history: Recent infections. Precipitating factors, such as emotional upset, infections, overwork, childbirth, surgery. Pattern of remissions and exacerbations
Medications: Aspirin, NSAIDs, corticosteroids, DMARDs, BRMs
Surgery or other treatments: Any joint surgery

Functional Health Patterns

Health perception–health management: Positive family history for RA or other autoimmune disorders. Malaise, ability to take part in treatment plan. Impact of disease on functional ability
Nutritional-metabolic: Anorexia, weight loss, dry mucous membranes of mouth and pharynx
Activity-exercise: Stiffness and joint swelling, muscle weakness, difficulty walking, fatigue
Cognitive-perceptual: Paresthesia of hands and feet, loss of sensation; symmetric joint pain and aching that ↑ with motion or stress on joint, may interfere with rest

Objective Data

General

Lymphadenopathy, fever

Integumentary

Scleritis, uveitis, Sjögren's syndrome. Subcutaneous rheumatoid nodules on forearms, elbows. Skin ulcers. Shiny, taut skin over involved joints. Peripheral edema

Cardiovascular

Symmetric pallor and cyanosis of fingers (Raynaud's phenomenon). Distant heart sounds, murmurs, dysrhythmias

Respiratory

Bronchiectasis, pleural effusion, tuberculosis, interstitial lung disease

Gastrointestinal

Splenomegaly (Felty syndrome)

Musculoskeletal

Symmetric joint involvement with swelling, erythema, heat, tenderness. Deformities (with later disease). Enlargement of PIP and MCP joints. Limitation of joint movement, muscle contractures, muscle atrophy

Possible Diagnostic Findings

Positive RF, ANA, Anti-CCP. ↑ ESR; anemia. ↑ WBCs in synovial fluid. On x-ray evidence of joint space narrowing, bony erosion, deformity, possible osteoporosis

ANA, Antinuclear antibody; *anti-CCP*, antibodies to citrullinated peptide; *BRMs*, biologic response modifiers; *DMARDs*, disease-modifying antirheumatic drugs; *MCP*, metacarpophalangeal; *PIP*, proximal interphalangeal; *RF*, rheumatoid factor.

◆ **Planning**

The overall goals are that the patient with RA will (1) have acceptable pain management, (2) have minimal loss of function of affected joints, (3) take part in planning and implementing the treatment plan, (4) maintain a positive self-image, and (5) perform self-care to the maximum amount possible.

◆ **Nursing Implementation**

◆ **Health Promotion.** Prevention of RA is not possible. Early treatment can help prevent further joint damage. Community education programs should focus on symptom recognition to promote early diagnosis and treatment. The Arthritis Foundation offers many publications, classes, and support activities to help persons with RA.

◆ **Acute Care.** The patient newly diagnosed with RA is usually treated on an outpatient basis. Hospitalization may be needed for the patient who has systemic complications or needs surgery for decreased functional ability. Work closely with the HCP, physical and occupational therapists, and social worker to help the patient regain function and adjust to chronic illness.

NURSING MANAGEMENT
Caring for the Patient With Rheumatoid Arthritis

- Give drug therapy as ordered.
- Teach patient and caregiver about drug therapy, including increased risk for infection with disease-modifying agents.
- Assess disease impact on quality of life and joint function.
- Assess pain intensity and give analgesics as ordered. Assess patient response.
- Develop program for rehabilitation and education with the interprofessional team.
- Teach patient about need for balance of rest and activity, with use of joint protective strategies.
- Oversee UAP
  - Aid patient with passive ROM of affected joints.
  - Help patient with self-care needs.

Collaborate With Interprofessional Team Members
Physical Therapist
- Assess patient's current mobility and need for assistance (e.g., walker).
- Develop exercise plan and teach patient to perform exercises safely.
- Coordinate PT with RN so that patient can receive timely analgesia.
- Recommend and apply thermal therapies.

Occupational Therapist
- Assess impact of patient's condition on ability to perform ADLs.
- Teach patient in use of assistive devices (e.g., long-handled reacher, long-handled shoe horn) to improve self-care ability without increasing stress on joints.
- Identify modifications to improve role performance (e.g., kitchen modifications for meal preparation).

Social Worker
- Assist with obtaining durable medical equipment (e.g., walker).
- Assess psychosocial and financial impact of disease. Arrange vocational retraining if needed.

Ambulatory Care. Care of the patient with RA includes a broad program of drug therapy, balance of rest and activity with joint protection, use of heat and cold applications, exercise, and patient and caregiver teaching. Nondrug management may include the use of therapeutic heat and cold, rest, relaxation techniques, joint protection (Tables 64.4 and 64.11), biofeedback, transcutaneous electrical nerve stimulation (see Chapter 8), and hypnosis. Allow the patient and caregiver to choose therapies that promote optimal comfort and fit their lifestyle.

Rest. Alternating scheduled rest periods with activity throughout the day helps relieve fatigue and pain. The amount of rest needed varies based on disease severity and the patient's limitations. The patient should rest before becoming exhausted. Total bed rest is rarely necessary. It should be avoided to prevent stiffness and other effects of immobility. A patient with mild disease may need daytime rest plus 8 to 10 hours of sleep at night.

Help the patient find ways to change daily activities to avoid overexertion and fatigue, which can worsen disease activity. For example, the patient may be able to prepare meals more easily while sitting on a high stool in front of the sink.

Teach the patient to maintain good body alignment during rest through use of a firm mattress or bed board. Encourage positions of extension. Teach the patient to avoid positions of flexion. To decrease the risk for joint contracture, never place pillows under the knees. Use a small, flat pillow under the head and shoulders if needed.

TABLE 64.11 Patient & Caregiver Teaching
Protection of Small Joints

Include the following instructions when teaching the patient with arthritis how to protect small joints:
1. Maintain joint in neutral position to minimize deformity.
   - Press water from a sponge instead of wringing.
2. Use strongest joint available for any task.
   - When rising from chair, push with palms rather than fingers.
   - Carry laundry basket in both arms rather than with fingers.
3. Distribute weight over many joints instead of stressing a few.
   - Slide objects instead of lifting them.
   - Hold packages close to body for support.
4. Change positions often.
   - Do not hold book or grip steering wheel for long periods without resting.
   - Avoid grasping pencil or cutting vegetables with knife for extended periods.
5. Avoid repetitious movements.
   - Do not knit or sew for long periods.
   - Rest between rooms when vacuuming.
   - Use faucets and doorknobs that are pushed rather than turned.
6. Modify chores to avoid stress on joints.
   - Avoid heavy lifting.
   - Sit on stool instead of standing during meal preparation.

Joint Protection. Protecting joints from stress is important. Help the patient find ways to alter routine tasks to put less stress on joints (Table 64.11). Energy conservation requires careful planning. The emphasis is on work simplification. Work for short periods with scheduled rest breaks to avoid fatigue (pacing). Organize activities to avoid going up and down stairs repeatedly. Use carts to carry supplies. Store frequently used materials in a convenient, easy-to-reach area. Use joint-protective devices (e.g., electric can opener) whenever possible. Teach patients to delegate tasks to other family members.

An occupational therapist helps the patient maintain upper extremity function and encourages use of splints or other assistive devices for joint protection. Lightweight splints may be prescribed to rest an inflamed joint and prevent deformity from muscle spasms and contractures. Remove the splints regularly to assess skin and perform ROM exercises. After assessment and supportive care, reapply splints as prescribed.

Occupational therapy may increase patient independence with assistive devices that simplify tasks (e.g., built-up utensils, buttonhooks, modified drawer handles, lightweight plastic dishes, raised toilet seats). Encourage the patient to make dressing easier by wearing shoes with Velcro fasteners and clothing with buttons or a zipper in the front instead of the back. Use a cane or a walker for support and decreased pain when walking.

Cold and Heat Therapy and Exercise. Cold and heat applications can help relieve stiffness, pain, and muscle spasm. Heat and cold can be used several times a day as needed. Ice is especially helpful during periods of increased disease activity. Cold application should not exceed 10 to 15 minutes at a time. Plastic bags of small frozen vegetables (peas or kernel corn) can easily mold around the shoulder, wrists, or knees to be an effective home treatment. The patient can use ice cubes or small paper cups of frozen water to massage areas on either side of a painful joint. Moist heat offers better relief for chronic stiffness. However, heat application should not exceed 20 minutes at a time.

Heating pads, moist hot packs, paraffin baths, and warm baths or showers can relieve stiffness to allow the patient to take part in therapeutic exercise. Alert the patient to the risk for a burn and the need to avoid using a heat-producing cream (e.g., capsaicin) with an external heat device. Sitting or standing in a warm shower, sitting in a tub with warm towels around the shoulders, or simply soaking the hands in a basin of warm water may relieve joint stiffness and allow the patient to perform ADLs more comfortably.

Individualized exercise is an important part of the treatment plan. A physical therapist may develop a therapeutic exercise program to improve flexibility and strength of affected joints and increase the patient's endurance. Encourage program participation and reinforce correct performance of the exercises. Progressive joint immobility and muscle weakness can occur if the patient does not move the joints. Overaggressive exercise can cause increased pain, inflammation, and joint damage. Emphasize that taking part in a recreational exercise program (e.g., walking, swimming) or doing usual daily activities does not take the place of therapeutic exercise to maintain adequate joint motion.

Gentle ROM exercises are usually done daily to keep joints functional. The patient should practice exercises with supervision. Exercising in warm water (78° to 86° F [25° to 30° C]) allows easier joint movement because of the buoyancy and warmth of the water. Although movement seems easier, water provides 2-way resistance that makes muscles work harder than they would on land. During acute inflammation, limit exercise to 1 or 2 repetitions.

Patient and Caregiver Teaching. Care of the patient with RA begins with a thorough program of education and drug therapy. Teach the patient and caregiver about the disease process and home management strategies. Inflammation may be managed through administration of NSAIDs, DMARDs, and BRMs. Careful timing of drug administration is critical to maintain a therapeutic drug level and reduce early morning stiffness. Discuss the action and side effects of each prescribed drug and any needed laboratory monitoring. Many patients with RA take several different drugs, so make the drug regimen as understandable as possible. Encourage patients to develop a way to remember to take their medications (e.g., pill containers).

Psychologic Support. For effective self-management and adherence to an individualized home treatment program, help the patient understand the nature and course of RA and the goals of therapy. Consider the patient's value system and perception of the disease.

Discuss changes in sexuality. Chronic pain or loss of function may make the patient vulnerable to claims of false advertising about unproven or even dangerous remedies. Help the patient recognize fears and concerns faced by all people who live with chronic illness.

Evaluate the family support system. Financial planning may be needed. Consider community resources, such as a home care nurse, homemaker services, and vocational rehabilitation. Self-help groups are helpful for some patients.

Living with chronic pain may lead to depression. To decrease depressive symptoms, suggest activities such as listening to music, reading, exercising, and counseling. Hypnosis and biofeedback may be useful.

Gerontologic Considerations: Arthritis

The prevalence of arthritis in older adults is high. The disease is accompanied by problems unique to this age-group. Areas of concern for older adults include:

- The high incidence of OA in older adults may keep the HCP from considering other types of arthritis.
- Age alone causes changes that make interpretation of laboratory values, such as RF and ESR, more difficult. Drugs taken for co-morbid conditions can affect laboratory values.
- Musculoskeletal pain syndromes and weakness may have no physical cause. Instead, they may be related to depression and physical inactivity.
- Diseases such as SLE, which often occur in younger adults, can develop in a milder form in older adults.

Physical and metabolic changes of aging may increase the older patient's sensitivity to both therapeutic and toxic effects of some drugs. The older adult who takes NSAIDs has an increased risk for side effects, especially GI bleeding and renal toxicity. Using NSAIDs with a shorter half-life may need more frequent dosing and have fewer side effects in the older patient with altered drug metabolism.

Polypharmacy in the older adult is a concern. Use of drugs in RA treatment may increase the chance of unexpected drug interactions. The drug regimen should be as simple as possible to increase adherence (e.g., limited number of drugs with decreased frequency of administration). This is especially important for those who lack regular assistance.

Osteopenia from corticosteroid use can worsen the problem of decreased bone density from aging and inactivity. The risk for pathologic fractures is increased, especially vertebral compression fractures. Myopathy related to corticosteroid use can be minimized by an age-appropriate exercise program. An adequate support system for the older adult is critical to the ability to follow a treatment plan.

GOUT

Gout is a type of arthritis characterized by elevation of uric acid (*hyperuricemia*) and the deposit of uric acid crystals in 1 or more joints. Sodium urate crystals may be found in articular, periarticular, and subcutaneous tissues. Unlike other forms of arthritis, gout is marked by painful flares lasting days to weeks followed by long periods without symptoms. More than 8 million Americans have gout. Blacks have a higher incidence compared to whites.[14]

GENDER DIFFERENCES
Gout

Men
- Occurs 3 times more often in men than in women until age 60.
- Usually develops in men ages 30 to 50.

Women
- Rarely develop gout before menopause.

Etiology and Pathophysiology

Uric acid is the major end product of purine catabolism. It is primarily excreted by the kidneys. Gout occurs when either the kidneys cannot excrete enough uric acid or there is too much being made for the kidneys to handle effectively.

We classify hyperuricemia as primary or secondary. *Primary hyperuricemia* is genetic. A hereditary error of purine metabolism leads to the overproduction or retention of uric acid. *Secondary hyperuricemia* may be caused by conditions that

TABLE 64.12 Causes of Hyperuricemia

- Acidosis or ketosis
- Alcohol use, especially beer and red wine
- Cancer
- Chemotherapy drugs
- Diabetes
- Drug-induced renal impairment
- Hyperlipidemia
- Hypertension
- Lead exposure
- Metabolic syndrome
- Myeloproliferative disorders
- Obesity
- Renal insufficiency
- Sickle cell anemia
- Starvation
- Use of certain common drugs (aspirin, ACE inhibitors, β-blockers, loop or thiazide diuretics, niacin)

FIG. 64.6 Tophi associated with chronic gout. Painless nodules are filled with uric acid crystals. (Courtesy John Cook, MD. From Goldstein BG, Goldstein AE: *Practical dermatology*, ed 2, St Louis, 1997, Mosby.)

increase uric acid production or decrease uric acid excretion or drugs that inhibit uric acid excretion (e.g., loop diuretics, β-blockers). Organ transplant recipients receiving immunosuppressive agents are at risk for hyperuricemia (Table 64.12).

Gout is likely caused by the interaction of several factors. The most important is metabolic syndrome (obesity, insulin resistance, hypertension, hyperlipidemia). Increased intake of foods containing purines (e.g., red and organ meat, shellfish, fructose drinks) can trigger gout. High uric acid may result from prolonged fasting or excessive alcohol use because they increase the production of keto acids, which inhibit uric acid excretion.

Not everyone with high uric acid levels develops gout. Two processes are essential for a person to develop gout: crystallization and inflammation. As urate levels increase and saturate the synovial fluid or soft tissues, the excess urate coalesces into crystals. These trigger inflammation. Monocytes and macrophages try to remove the crystals through phagocytosis. This causes the release of inflammatory mediators into the surrounding area, causing more inflammation and tissue damage.[15]

Clinical Manifestations and Complications

Gout may occur acutely in 1 or more joints (usually less than 4). Inflammation of the great toe (*podagra*) is the most common initial problem. Other affected joints may include wrists, knees, ankles, and the midfoot. Olecranon bursae may be involved. Affected joints may appear dusky or cyanotic and are extremely tender. Acute gout arthritis is usually triggered by events such as trauma, surgery, alcohol use, or systemic infection. Symptom onset typically occurs at night with sudden swelling and severe pain peaking within several hours. The painful area is highly sensitive to light touch. Low-grade fever is common.

An attack usually ends in 2 to 10 days with or without treatment. The affected joint returns to normal, and patients have no symptoms between attacks.

Chronic gout is characterized by multiple joint involvement and visible deposits of sodium urate crystals called tophi. Tophi are hard white nodules. They are typically seen in subcutaneous tissue, synovial membranes, tendons, and soft tissues (Fig. 64.6). Tophi generally occur many years after the onset of disease.

The severity of gout arthritis varies. The clinical course may involve infrequent mild attacks or multiple severe episodes (up to 12 per year) marked by slowly progressive disability. In general, tophi appear earlier, and the patient has more frequent,

severe episodes of gout if serum uric acid is high. Chronic inflammation may cause joint deformity, and cartilage destruction may lead to secondary OA. Large urate crystal deposits may pierce overlying skin, producing draining sinuses that often become infected.

Excessive uric acid excretion may lead to stone formation in the kidneys or urinary tract. Pyelonephritis related to sodium urate deposits and obstruction contributes to kidney disease.

Diagnostic Studies

In gout, serum uric acid is usually increased above 6 mg/dL. However, hyperuricemia is not specifically diagnostic of gout because serum values may be normal during an acute gout attack.[15] Increased uric acid may be related to various drugs or an asymptomatic abnormality in the general population A 24-hour urine uric acid can determine if the disease is caused by decreased renal excretion or overproduction of uric acid.

The gold standard for diagnosis of gout is synovial fluid aspiration. Affected fluid contains needle-like monosodium urate crystals. This procedure is done in only a small number of patients because diagnosis can typically be made on clinical symptoms alone. However, it is the only reliable way to tell gout from septic arthritis or *pseudogout* (calcium phosphate crystal formation). Aspiration may decrease pain by relieving pressure in a swollen joint capsule.

X-rays appear normal in the early stages of gout. In chronic disease, tophi may appear as eroded areas in the bone.

❖ INTERPROFESSIONAL AND NURSING MANAGEMENT: GOUT

Goals for the care of the patient with gout (Table 64.13) include ending an acute attack with an antiinflammatory agent, such as colchicine. Hyperuricemia and gout are chronic problems that can be controlled with effective patient education and careful adherence to a treatment program. Drug therapy is the primary way to treat acute and chronic gout.

◆ Drug Therapy

Acute gout is treated with oral colchicine (Colcrys, Mitigare) and NSAIDs. Because colchicine has antiinflammatory effects but is not an analgesic, an NSAID is added for pain management. Colchicine generally produces dramatic pain relief when given within 12 hours of an attack. This helps in diagnosis because good response to this drug is further evidence of gout.

TABLE 64.13 Interprofessional Care
Gout

Diagnostic Assessment
- History and physical examination
- Family history of gout
- Sodium urate crystals in synovial fluid
- Increased serum uric acid
- Increased uric acid in 24-hr urine
- X-ray of affected joints

Management
- Joint immobilization
- Local application of heat and cold
- Joint aspiration and intraarticular corticosteroids
- Avoid food and fluids with high purine content (e.g., anchovies, liver, wine, beer)

Drug Therapy
- colchicine
- NSAIDs (e.g., naproxen [Naprosyn])
- Xanthine oxidase inhibitors: allopurinol (Zyloprim), febuxostat (Uloric)
- Uricosurics: probenecid, lesinurad (Zurampic)
- pegloticase (Krystexxa)
- Corticosteroids (e.g., prednisone)
- Intraarticular corticosteroids (methylprednisolone)
- Adrenocorticotropic hormone (ACTH)

Corticosteroids (orally or by intraarticular injection) can be helpful in treating an acute attack. Systemic corticosteroids may be used only if routine therapies are contraindicated or ineffective. Adrenocorticotropic hormone (ACTH) may be used for acute treatment of patients for whom NSAIDs, colchicine, or steroids may be problematic.

Future attacks of gout are prevented in part by a maintenance dose of a xanthine oxidase inhibitor. These drugs decrease the production of uric acid. Allopurinol is the most commonly used drug and the first choice for therapy. It is used for patients with uric acid kidney stones or renal impairment. Serious adverse effects limit the use of febuxostat (Uloric).

DRUG ALERT Febuxostat
- May cause heart-related death and liver failure.
- Encourage patient with cardiovascular disease to take low-dose aspirin therapy.
- Monitor liver function tests before starting therapy and during treatment.
- Teach patient to notify HCP if symptoms of liver or heart problems occur.

The ACR recommends therapy with probenecid if allopurinol or febuxostat are contraindicated or the patient has intolerance to either.[15] Probenecid is a uricosuric, increasing uric acid excretion in the urine. Aspirin inactivates its effect, resulting in urate retention, and must be avoided during treatment. Acetaminophen can be used safely if analgesia is needed. Lesinurad (Zurampic), a new uricosuric agent, can be taken with a xanthine oxidase inhibitor for those with persistent, increased uric acid levels. Duzallo, a fixed-dose combination of lesinurad and allopurinol, is taken once daily.

Uricosurics can cause renal impairment. They are ineffective when creatinine clearance is reduced, as can occur in patients over age 60 years or with renal impairment. They should be taken in the morning with food and water. Teach patients to stay well hydrated and to drink about 2 L of liquid a day when taking the drug.

Patients who cannot take or do not respond to drugs that lower serum uric acid may be given pegloticase (Krystexxa). This drug is an enzyme that metabolizes uric acid into a harmless chemical excreted in the urine. It is given IV, usually for at least 6 months. Life-threatening anaphylactic and infusion reactions can occur.

The angiotensin II receptor antagonist losartan (Cozaar) may be effective for treating older patients with gout and hypertension. Losartan promotes urate excretion and may normalize serum urate. Combination therapy with losartan and allopurinol may be used.

Serum uric acid must be checked regularly to monitor treatment effectiveness. Explain the importance of drug therapy and the need for regular assessment of serum uric acid. Dietary restrictions that limit alcohol and foods high in purine help minimize uric acid production (see Table 45.12). Adequate urine volume with normal renal function (2 to 3 L/day) must be maintained to prevent precipitation of uric acid in the renal tubules. Teach obese patients in a carefully planned weight-reduction program (see Chapter 40). Teach the patient about other factors that may cause an attack, including fasting, drug use (e.g., diuretics), and major medical events (e.g., surgery, heart attack).

Nursing interventions for the patient with acute gout include supportive care of the inflamed joints. Avoid causing pain by careless handling of an inflamed joint. Bed rest may be appropriate to immobilize affected joints as needed. Use a cradle or footboard to protect a painful lower extremity from the weight of bed linens. Assess motion limitations and degree of pain.

CHECK YOUR PRACTICE

A patient is admitted to the medical unit with acute gout. The right great toe is swollen, red, and painful. He is prescribed colchicine.
- What nursing interventions will you use to protect the foot and decrease pain?
- What will you discuss with the patient about possible dietary changes to decrease risk for future attacks?

LYME DISEASE

Lyme disease is an infection caused by the spirochete *Borrelia burgdorferi*. It is transmitted by the bite of an infected deer tick. It was first identified in 1975 in Lyme, Connecticut, after an unusual occurrence of arthritis in children. It is the most common vector-borne disease in the United States, with 7.9 cases per 100,000 persons.[16] The tick typically feeds on mice, dogs, cats, cows, horses, deer, and humans. Person-to-person transmission does not occur.

The summer months are the peak season for human infection. Most U.S. cases occur in 3 areas: along the northeastern states from Maryland to northern Massachusetts, in the midwestern states of Wisconsin and Minnesota, and along the northwestern coast of California and Oregon.[16] Reinfection is common.

Symptoms mimic those of other diseases, such as multiple sclerosis, mononucleosis, and meningitis. The most characteristic clinical symptom of early localized disease is *erythema migrans* (EM). This "bull's-eye rash" occurs in about 80% of infected persons. It appears at the site of the tick bite within 1 month after exposure (Fig. 64.7). It may occur anywhere else on the body as the disease progresses. The EM lesion begins as

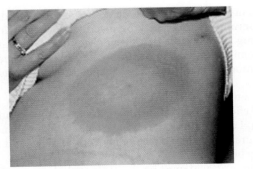

FIG. 64.7 Erythema migrans. Typical skin lesion of Lyme disease occurs at the site of tick bite. (From Marx J, Hockberger R, Walls R: *Rosen's emergency medicine*, ed 7, Philadelphia, 2009, Mosby.)

a central red macule or papule that slowly expands to include a red outer ring of up to 12 in, resembling a bull's eye. It may be warm to the touch but is not itchy or painful. The rash often occurs with acute flu-like symptoms: (1) low-grade fever, (2) headache, (3) neck stiffness, (4) fatigue, (5) loss of appetite, and (6) migratory joint and muscle pain. Flu-like symptoms generally resolve over weeks or months, even if untreated.

If not treated, the spirochete can spread within several weeks or months to the heart, joints, heart, and central nervous system (CNS). Arthritis is the second most common manifestation of Lyme disease. About 60% of persons with untreated infection develop chronic arthritic pain and swelling in the large joints, mainly the knee. Cardiac symptoms, such as heart block and pericarditis, may require hospitalization.[16] Bell's palsy is the most common neurologic effect. Other problems include short-term memory loss, cognitive impairment, shooting pains, and numbness and tingling in the feet.

Diagnosis is often based on the manifestations, especially EM, and a history of exposure in an at-risk area. The CDC recommends a 2-step laboratory testing process to confirm the diagnosis.[17] The first step is the enzyme immunoassay (EIA). It will be positive for most people with Lyme disease. If the EIA is positive or inconclusive, then a Western blot test is done. Results are diagnostic of Lyme disease only if both tests are positive. The CDC does not recommend the Western blot test alone. False-positive results lead to incorrect diagnosis and treatment. In those with neurologic involvement, cerebrospinal fluid should be examined.

Active lesions are treated with oral antibiotics. Doxycycline (Vibramycin), cefuroxime, and amoxicillin are often effective in treating early-stage infection and preventing later stages of the disease. Short-term therapy of 10 to 21 days of doxycycline is preferred. It treats both Lyme disease and human granulocytic anaplasmosis, which can be transmitted as a co-infection with a single tick bite. While other antibiotics can be used for those who cannot tolerate any of these drugs, they all are less effective. Patients with certain neurologic or cardiac complications may need IV therapy with ceftriaxone or penicillin.

A small number of persons treated with antibiotics may have lingering fatigue or joint and muscle pain. Antibiotic treatment should be extended as needed because the risks of untreated Lyme disease outweigh those of long-term antibiotic therapy.[18]

Reducing exposure to ticks is the best way to prevent Lyme disease. Patient and caregiver teaching for people living in endemic areas is outlined in Table 64.14. No vaccine is available for Lyme disease.

TABLE 64.14 Patient & Caregiver Teaching

Prevention and Early Treatment of Lyme Disease

Include the following instructions when teaching patients how to prevent Lyme disease:
- Do not walk through tall grasses and low brush or sit on logs.
- Mow grass. Remove brush around paths, buildings, and campsites to create tick-safe zones.
- Move woodpiles and bird feeders away from your house. Discourage deer (main source of food for adult ticks) from being in the area.
- Wear long pants or nylon tights of tightly woven, light-colored fabric so that you can easily see ticks.
- Tuck pants into boots or long socks, wear long-sleeved shirts tucked into pants, and wear closed toed shoes when hiking.
- Check often for ticks crawling from pant legs to open skin.
- Thoroughly inspect and wash clothes. Placing clothing in dryer on high heat kills ticks.
- Spray insect repellent containing DEET sparingly on skin or clothing. Apply permethrin to clothing and camping gear; protects for several hours.
- Have pets wear tick collars and inspect them often. Do not allow pets on furniture or beds.

Include the following instructions when teaching patients and caregivers living in endemic areas:
- Remove attached ticks with fine-tipped tweezers (not fingers). Grasp tick's mouth parts as close to skin as possible and pull straight out with steady, even pressure. Do not twist or jerk. Avoid folk solutions, such as painting the tick with nail polish or petroleum jelly (see Fig. 68.5).
- Save the tick in a bottle of alcohol (if you need it later for identification). Never crush a tick with your fingers.
- Wash bitten area with soap and water, iodine scrub, or rubbing alcohol. Apply antiseptic. Wash hands.
- See an HCP if flu-like symptoms or a bull's-eye rash appears within 2–30 days after removal of tick.

Adapted from Centers for Disease Control and Prevention: Prevent Lyme disease. Retrieved from *www.cdc.gov/features/lymedisease;* and Centers for Disease Control and Prevention: Tick removal and testing. Retrieved from *www.cdc.gov/lyme/removal/index.html.*
DEET, N,N-diethyl-m-toluamide.

SEPTIC ARTHRITIS

Septic arthritis (infectious or bacterial arthritis) is caused by microorganisms invading the joint cavity. Bacteria can travel through the bloodstream from another site of active infection, resulting in seeding of the joint. Organisms also can be introduced directly through trauma or surgical incision.

Any infectious agent can cause septic arthritis (bacteria, viruses, mycobacteria, fungi), especially in the immunocompromised patient. *Staphylococcus aureus* is the most common causative organism. Factors that increase the risk for infection include (1) diseases with decreased host resistance (e.g., RA, SLE), (2) treatment with corticosteroids or immunosuppressive drugs, and (3) debilitating chronic illness (e.g., diabetes).

Large joints, such as the knee and hip, are most often affected. Inflammation of the joint cavity causes severe pain, redness, and swelling. Septic arthritis of the hip can cause avascular necrosis. Because infection has often spread from a primary site elsewhere in the body, fever or shaking chills often accompany joint problems. Diagnosis may be made by joint aspiration (*arthrocentesis*) and synovial fluid culture. WBC count may be low early in the infectious process, especially in those who are immunosuppressed, so diagnosis is not possible solely based on WBC count. Blood cultures for aerobic and anaerobic organisms should be obtained.

Emergent aspiration or surgical drainage is a cornerstone of successful treatment. Irreversible joint damage can occur without rapid, appropriate treatment of septic arthritis. In some cases, damage can occur despite treatment. Broad-spectrum antibiotics are typically started before culture results have been received. Once the organism is identified, more specific treatment can be determined. IV antibiotics are typically transitioned to oral antibiotics, with total treatment of 4 to 6 weeks.

Assess and monitor joint inflammation, pain, and fever. To manage pain, use resting splints or traction to immobilize affected joints. Local hot compresses can decrease pain. Start gentle ROM exercises as soon as tolerated to prevent muscle atrophy and joint contractures. Explain the need for antibiotics and the importance of their continued use until the infection is resolved. Support the patient who needs joint drainage. Use strict aseptic technique when assisting with joint aspiration.

SPONDYLOARTHROPATHIES

The **spondyloarthropathies** are a group of multisystem inflammatory disorders that affect the spine, peripheral joints, and periarticular structures. These disorders include ankylosing spondylitis, psoriatic arthritis, and reactive arthritis. They are all negative for RF so we call them *seronegative arthropathies*.

Inheritance of human leukocyte antigen (HLA) B27 is strongly associated with these diseases. Both genetic and environmental factors play a role in their development. (HLAs and their relationship to autoimmune diseases are discussed in Chapter 13.)

The spondyloarthropathies share clinical and laboratory characteristics that may make it hard to distinguish among them in early disease. These include absence of antibodies in the serum, peripheral joint involvement (mainly of the lower extremities), low back pain *(sacroiliitis)*, pain and redness of the eyes *(uveitis)*, intestinal inflammation, and psoriasis.[19]

ANKYLOSING SPONDYLITIS

Ankylosing spondylitis (AS) is a chronic inflammatory disease that primarily affects the axial skeleton, including the sacroiliac joints, intervertebral disc spaces, and costovertebral articulations. Onset of AS is usually in the third decade of life, but onset in adolescence is fairly common. Men are 3 times more likely to develop AS. The disease may go undetected in women because of a milder course.

Etiology and Pathophysiology

We do not know the exact cause of AS. HLA-B27 antigen is found in about 90% of whites with AS, but only 8% of whites without the disease.[20] This suggests genes play a key role in AS. Along with whites, Asians and Hispanics are more likely to have AS than other ethnic groups. Inflammation in the joints and adjacent tissue causes the formation of granulation tissue *(pannus)* and dense fibrous scars that can cause joint fusion. Inflammation can affect the eyes, lungs, heart, kidneys, and peripheral nervous system.

Clinical Manifestations and Complications

AS is characterized by symmetric sacroiliitis and progressive inflammatory arthritis of the axial skeleton. Symptoms of inflammatory spine pain are the first clues to AS. The patient often has low back pain, stiffness, and limitation of motion that

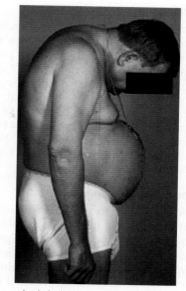

FIG. 64.8 Advanced ankylosing spondylitis. Kyphotic posture causes many patients to have a bulging abdomen due to pulmonary restriction. (From Kim DH, Henn J, Vaccaro AR, Dickman C: *Surgical anatomy and techniques to the spine,* Philadelphia, 2006, Saunders.)

GENETICS IN CLINICAL PRACTICE
Ankylosing Spondylitis

Genetic Basis
- Inheritance of HLA-B27 increases susceptibility to developing AS.
- We do not know how HLA-B27 increases the risk for AS.

Incidence
- HLA-B27 antigen is found in about 90% of whites with AS.
- Inheriting HLA-B27 does not mean a person will develop AS.
- 80% of those who inherit HLA-B27 from a parent do not develop the disease.

Genetic Testing
- Testing for HLA-B27 antigen is available.

Clinical Implications
- Diagnosis of AS usually occurs in the third decade of life.
- Multiple genetic and environmental factors play a role in pathogenesis of disease.

is worse during the night and in the morning but improves with mild activity. In women, early symptoms may include pain and stiffness in the neck rather than the lower back. Uveitis is the most common nonskeletal symptom. It can appear as an initial presentation of the disease years before arthritic symptoms develop. Patients with AS may have distressing chest pain and sternal/costal cartilage tenderness.

Severe postural abnormalities and deformity can cause significant disability (Fig. 64.8). Impaired spinal ROM and fusion, along with vision problems, raise concerns about safe ambulation. Aortic insufficiency and pulmonary fibrosis are common complications. Cauda equina syndrome (compression of the nerves at the end of the spinal cord) can occur. This contributes to lower extremity weakness and bladder dysfunction. The patient is at risk for spinal fracture from associated osteoporosis.

Diagnostic Studies

X-rays are the most important radiographic technique for the diagnosis and follow up of AS. However, x-rays are limited in detecting early sacroiliitis or subtle changes in posterior vertebrae. MRI is useful in assessing early cartilage abnormalities. CT scan is appropriate in specific situations (e.g., cases with subtle x-ray changes). Changes on later spinal films include the appearance of "bamboo spine," the result of calcifications (*syndesmophytes*) that bridge from one vertebra to another. An increased ESR and mild anemia may be seen. When the suspicion for AS is high, the presence of the HLA-B27 antigen improves the likelihood of the diagnosis.

❖ Interprofessional and Nursing Care

Prevention of AS is not possible. Families with other diagnosed HLA-B27–positive rheumatic diseases (e.g., psoriatic arthritis, juvenile spondyloarthritis) should be alert to signs of low back pain for early identification and treatment of AS.

Care of the patient with AS is aimed at maintaining maximal skeletal mobility while decreasing pain and inflammation. Heat applications can help relieve local symptoms. NSAIDs and salicylates are often prescribed. DMARDs, such as sulfasalazine or methotrexate, have little effect on spinal disease but help with peripheral joint disease. Local corticosteroid injections may be helpful in relieving symptoms.

TNF, which promotes inflammation, is increased in the blood and certain tissues of patients with AS. Etanercept, a BRM, binds TNF and inhibits its action. Etanercept reduces active inflammation and improves spinal mobility. Other anti-TNF inhibitors (infliximab, adalimumab, golimumab) may be effective.

Once pain and stiffness are managed, exercise is essential. Good posture is important to minimize spinal deformity. The exercise plan should include back, neck, and chest stretches. Hydrotherapy (e.g., sauna, steam bath) can decrease pain and facilitate spinal extension. Surgery may be needed for severe deformity and mobility impairment. Spinal osteotomy and total joint replacement are the most common procedures (see Chapter 62).

A key nursing responsibility is to teach the patient with AS about the disease and principles of therapy. The home management program should include regular exercise and attention to posture, local moist heat applications, and informed use of drugs.

Assess chest expansion (using breathing exercises) as part of baseline ROM assessment. Encourage smoking cessation to decrease the risk for lung complications in persons with reduced chest expansion. Ongoing PT includes gentle, graded stretching and strengthening exercises. These preserve ROM and improve thoracolumbar flexion and extension.

Discourage excessive physical exertion during periods of increased disease activity. Proper positioning at rest is essential. Encourage the patient to use a firm mattress. They should sleep on the back with a flat pillow, avoiding positions that encourage flexion deformity. Emphasize the need to avoid spinal flexion (e.g., leaning over a desk); heavy lifting; and prolonged walking, standing, or sitting. Encourage sports that involve natural stretching, such as swimming and racquet games. Family counseling and vocational rehabilitation are important.

PSORIATIC ARTHRITIS

Psoriatic arthritis (PsA) is a progressive inflammatory disease that affects about 30% of people with psoriasis.[21] *Psoriasis* is a common, benign, inflammatory skin disorder characterized by red, irritated, and scaly patches. Both PsA and psoriasis appear to have a genetic link with HLA antigens in many patients. Although the exact cause of PsA is unknown, we suspect a combination of immune, genetic, and environmental factors.

PsA can occur in different forms. *Distal arthritis* mainly involves the ends of the fingers and toes, with pitting and color changes in the fingernails and toenails. *Asymmetric arthritis* involves different joints on each side of the body. *Symmetric psoriatic arthritis* resembles RA. It affects joints on both sides of the body at the same time. It accounts for about 50% of cases. *Psoriatic spondylitis* is marked by pain and stiffness in the spine and neck. *Arthritis mutilans* affects only 5% of people with PsA. It is the most severe form of the disease, causing complete destruction of small joints.[21]

On x-ray, the cartilage loss and erosion are similar to RA. Advanced cases often show widened joint spaces. A "pencil in cup" deformity is common in the DIP joints due to thinning, weakened bone. In this deformity, the narrowed ends of the metacarpals or phalanges insert into the expanded end of the other bone sharing the joint. Increased ESR, mild anemia, and increased serum uric acid can be seen in some patients. Thus the diagnosis of gout must be excluded.

Treatment includes splinting, joint protection, and PT. NSAIDs given early in the course of the disease may help with inflammation. Drug therapy includes the DMARDs, such as methotrexate, which is effective for both articular and cutaneous manifestations. Sulfasalazine, cyclosporine, and BRMs (e.g., etanercept, golimumab, adalimumab, infliximab) may be used. Apremilast (Otezla), an inhibitor of the enzyme phosphodiesterase-4, can treat adults with active PsA.

REACTIVE ARTHRITIS

Reactive arthritis (Reiter's syndrome) occurs more often in young men. It is associated with a symptom complex that includes urethritis, conjunctivitis, and mucocutaneous lesions. Although we do not know the exact cause, it appears to be a reaction triggered in the body after exposure to specific genitourinary or GI tract infections. *Chlamydia trachomatis* spreads by sexual contact. Reactive arthritis is associated with GI infections from *Shigella, Salmonella, Campylobacter,* or *Yersinia* species and other pathogens.[22]

Those who are positive for HLA-B27 are at increased risk for developing reactive arthritis after sexual contact or exposure to certain GI pathogens. This finding supports the suggestion of genetic predisposition.

Urethritis develops within 1 to 2 weeks after sexual contact or GI infection. In women, symptoms include cervicitis. Low-grade fever, conjunctivitis, and arthritis may occur over the next several weeks. This type of arthritis tends to be asymmetric. It often involves the toes and the large joints of the lower extremities. Lower back pain may occur with severe disease. Lesions involving the skin and mucous membranes often occur as small, painless, superficial ulcerations on the tongue, oral mucosa, and glans penis. Soft tissue manifestations include Achilles tendinitis or plantar fasciitis. Few laboratory abnormalities occur, although the ESR may be increased.

Most patients recover within a few months of initial symptoms. Because reactive arthritis is often associated with *C. trachomatis* infection, treatment with doxycycline is widely recommended for patients and their sexual partners. Antibiotics have no effect on arthritis or other symptoms. Topical ophthalmic corticosteroids may be prescribed for treatment of uveitis. Conjunctivitis and lesions generally do not need treatment. NSAIDs and DMARDs may be used if joint symptoms do not resolve. PT may be helpful during recovery.

Most patients have complete remission with return of full joint function. Some patients may develop chronic arthritis, but the condition is often mild. X-ray changes in chronic reactive arthritis closely resemble those of AS. Treatment is based on symptoms.

SYSTEMIC LUPUS ERYTHEMATOSUS

Systemic lupus erythematosus (SLE) is a multisystem inflammatory autoimmune disease. It is a complex disorder of multifactorial origin resulting from interactions among genetic, hormonal, environmental, and immunologic factors. SLE typically affects the skin, joints, and serous membranes (pleura, pericardium). Renal, hematologic, and neurologic systems are also affected. SLE is marked by a chronic unpredictable course with alternating periods of remission and exacerbation.

About 1.5 million people in the United States have SLE. Blacks, Asian Americans, Hispanics, and Native Americans are more likely than whites to develop the disease. While SLE can affect anyone, 90% of those with SLE are women ages 15 to 45 years.[23]

Etiology and Pathophysiology

The cause of the abnormal immune response in SLE is unknown. Based on the high prevalence of SLE among family members, we suspect a genetic influence. Multiple genes from the HLA complex, including *HLA-DR2* and *HLA-DR3*, are associated with SLE.

Hormones are known to play a role in SLE. Onset or worsening of disease symptoms may occur after the start of menses, with the use of oral contraceptives, and during and after pregnancy. The disease tends to become worse in the immediate postpartum period.

Environmental factors are thought to contribute to SLE. These include sun or ultraviolet light exposure, stress, and exposure to some chemicals and toxins. Infectious agents, such as viruses, may stimulate immune hyperactivity. More than 45 drugs currently in use may trigger SLE. Most cases have been related to procainamide, hydralazine, and quinidine. Drug-induced SLE should not be confused with medication side effects, which typically occur within a few hours or days of short-term drug use. SLE generally occurs months to years after continuous therapy with a causative drug.[24]

In SLE, varied autoantibodies are made against nucleic acids (e.g., single- and double-stranded DNA), erythrocytes, coagulation proteins, lymphocytes, platelets, and many other self-proteins. Autoimmune reactions (antinuclear antibodies [ANA]) are typically directed against elements of the cell nucleus, especially DNA.

Circulating immune complexes with antibodies against DNA are deposited in the basement membranes of capillaries in the kidneys, heart, skin, brain, and joints. These complexes trigger inflammation that causes tissue destruction. Overaggressive autoimmune responses are related to activation of B and T cells. Specific disease effects depend on the involved cell types or organs. SLE is a type III hypersensitivity response (see Chapter 13).

Clinical Manifestations and Complications

Severity of SLE is extremely variable. It ranges from a relatively mild disorder to a rapidly progressive disease affecting many body systems (Fig. 64.9). No characteristic pattern occurs in the progression of SLE. The circulating immune complexes can affect any organ. The most commonly involved tissues are the skin and muscle, lining of the lungs, heart, nervous tissue, and kidneys. General complaints, such as fever, weight loss, joint pain, and excessive fatigue, may precede worsened disease activity.

Dermatologic Problems. Vascular skin lesions can appear anywhere. They are most likely to develop on sun-exposed areas. Severe skin reactions can occur in people who are sensitive to sunlight (*photosensitivity*). The classic butterfly rash over the cheeks and bridge of the nose occurs in about half of patients at some time during the disease (Fig. 64.10). SLE-specific skin disease can occur in people who do not have full-blown SLE, but the presence of skin disease increases the risk for developing SLE later in life. Some patients have *chronic cutaneous lupus* (CCLE) with discoid (round, coin-shaped) lesions. About 10% of patients have *subacute cutaneous lupus* (SCLE). Lesions in SCLE usually do not scar or itch and are not thick and scaly.[25]

Oral or nasopharyngeal ulcers occur in one third of patients with SLE. Alopecia is common, with or without related scalp lesions. The hair may grow back during remission, but hair loss may be permanent over lesions. The scalp becomes dry, scaly, and atrophied.

Musculoskeletal Problems. Arthritis occurs in many patients with SLE. Pain in multiple joints (*polyarthralgia*) with morning stiffness is often the first complaint. It may precede the onset of multisystem disease by many years. Diffuse swelling occurs with joint and muscle pain and some stiffness. SLE-related arthritis is generally nonerosive but may cause deformities (e.g., swan neck deformity of the fingers [Fig. 64.4, *D*], ulnar deviation, subluxation with joint laxity). Patients have increased risk for bone loss and fracture.

Cardiopulmonary Problems. Tachypnea and cough suggest the presence of lung disease. Pleurisy is possible. Cardiac involvement may include dysrhythmias due to fibrosis of the sinoatrial and atrioventricular nodes. This shows advanced disease and is the leading cause of death among patients with SLE. Inflammation can lead to pericarditis, myocarditis, and endocarditis. Hypertension and hypercholesterolemia from steroid use need aggressive treatment and careful monitoring. People with SLE are at risk for secondary *antiphospholipid syndrome*. This coagulation disorder causes clots in the arteries and veins. It increases the risk for stroke, gangrene, and heart attack.

Renal Problems. About 40% of persons with SLE develop kidney problems that need medical evaluation and treatment. Renal involvement is usually present within the first 5 years after diagnosis.[26] Manifestations vary from mild proteinuria to rapidly progressive glomerulonephritis. Scarring and permanent damage can lead to end-stage renal disease (ESRD).

The main goal is to slow the progression of nephropathy and preserve renal function by managing the underlying disease. The need for a renal biopsy is controversial, but findings can help guide treatment. Effective treatments include corticosteroids,

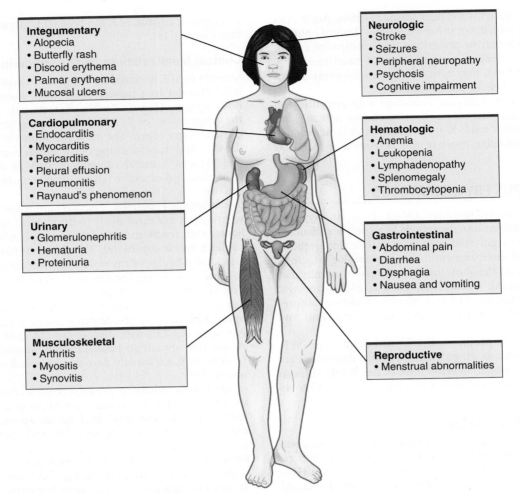

Integumentary
- Alopecia
- Butterfly rash
- Discoid erythema
- Palmar erythema
- Mucosal ulcers

Cardiopulmonary
- Endocarditis
- Myocarditis
- Pericarditis
- Pleural effusion
- Pneumonitis
- Raynaud's phenomenon

Urinary
- Glomerulonephritis
- Hematuria
- Proteinuria

Musculoskeletal
- Arthritis
- Myositis
- Synovitis

Neurologic
- Stroke
- Seizures
- Peripheral neuropathy
- Psychosis
- Cognitive impairment

Hematologic
- Anemia
- Leukopenia
- Lymphadenopathy
- Splenomegaly
- Thrombocytopenia

Gastrointestinal
- Abdominal pain
- Diarrhea
- Dysphagia
- Nausea and vomiting

Reproductive
- Menstrual abnormalities

FIG. 64.9 Multisystem involvement in SLE.

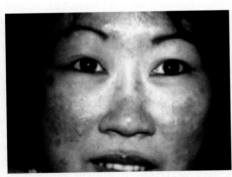

FIG. 64.10 Butterfly rash of SLE. (From Firestein GS, Budd RC, Gabriel SE, McInnes IB: *Kelley's textbook of rheumatology*, ed 9, Philadelphia, 2012, Saunders.)

cytotoxic agents (cyclophosphamide), and immunosuppressive agents (azathioprine, cyclosporine, mycophenolate mofetil [CellCept]). Oral prednisone or pulsed IV methylprednisolone may be used, especially in the initial treatment period when cytotoxic agents have not yet taken effect.

Nervous System Problems. Neuropsychiatric manifestations are common in SLE. About 15% of patients with SLE have generalized-onset or focal-onset seizures. Seizures are generally controlled by corticosteroids or antiseizure drugs. Peripheral neuropathy can occur, leading to sensory and motor deficits.

Cognitive problems may result from the deposit of immune complexes within the brain. There may be disordered thinking, disorientation, and memory deficits. Various psychiatric problems may occur, including depression, mood disorders, anxiety, and psychosis. However, they may be related to the stress of having a major illness or to associated drug therapies. Sometimes SLE may cause a stroke or aseptic meningitis. Headaches are common and can become severe during a disease flare.

Hematologic Problems. Blood problems are common due to formation of antibodies against blood cells. Anemia, leukopenia, thrombocytopenia, and coagulation disorders (excess bleeding or clotting) are often present.[27] Many patients benefit from high-intensity treatment with warfarin.

Infection. Patients with SLE appear to have increased susceptibility to infection. Risk may be due to impaired ability to eliminate invading bacteria, deficient antibody production, and immunosuppressive effects of many antiinflammatory drugs. Pneumonia is the most common infection. Fever may indicate an underlying infection rather than SLE activity alone. Vaccinations are generally safe for patients with SLE. Patients receiving corticosteroids or cytotoxic drugs must avoid live virus vaccines.

Diagnostic Studies

Diagnosis of SLE is based on distinct criteria (Table 64.15). No specific test is diagnostic for SLE, but a variety of abnormalities

TABLE 64.15 Diagnostic Criteria for Systemic Lupus Erythematosus

A person is classified as having SLE if 4 or more of the criteria are pres-ent, serially or simultaneously, during any interval of observation:

- Antinuclear antibody: abnormal titer
- Discoid rash: raised patches with scaling follicular plugging; scarring in older lesions
- Hematologic disorder: hemolytic anemia, leukopenia, lymphopenia, or thrombocytopenia
- Immunologic disorder: anti-DNA antibody or antibody to Sm (Smith) nuclear antigen or positive antiphospholipid antibodies
- Malar rash: fixed erythema, flat or raised (butterfly rash)
- Oral ulcers: usually painless
- Nonerosive arthritis: 2 or more peripheral joints with tenderness, swelling, effusion
- Pleuritis or pericarditis
- Neurologic disorder: seizures or psychosis (in the absence of caus-ative drugs or known metabolic disorders)
- Photosensitivity: skin rash as unusual reaction to light
- Renal disorder: persistent proteinuria or cellular casts in urine

Source: American College of Rheumatology: 1997 Update of the 1982 American College of Rheumatology revised criteria for classification of systemic lupus erythematosus. Retrieved from *www.rheumatology.org/ Portals/0/Files/1997%20Update%20of%201982%20Revised.pdf.*

TABLE 64.16 Interprofessional Care
Systemic Lupus Erythematosus

Diagnostic Assessment

- History and physical examination
- Antibodies (e.g., ANA, anti-DNA, anti-Sm, antiphospholipid)
- CBC count
- Serum complement
- Urinalysis
- X-ray of affected joints
- Chest x-ray
- ECG to determine cardiac involvement

Management
Drug Therapy

- NSAIDs for mild disease
- Steroid-sparing drugs (e.g., methotrexate)
- Antimalarials (e.g., hydroxychloroquine [Plaquenil])
- Corticosteroids for flares and severe disease
- Immunosuppressive drugs (e.g., cyclophosphamide, mycophenolate mofetil [CellCept])

may be present in the blood. SLE is marked by the presence of ANA in 97% of persons with the disease.[28]

Anti-DNA antibodies are found in half the persons with SLE. Anti-Smith (Sm) antibodies are found in 30% to 40% of persons with SLE and are almost always considered diagnostic. Nearly 30% of people with SLE will have antiphospholipid antibod-ies. Antibodies to histone are most often seen in people with drug-induced SLE. Increased ESR and CRP indicate inflamma-tion but are not diagnostic of SLE. They may be used to monitor disease activity and treatment effectiveness.[28]

Interprofessional Care

A major challenge in the treatment of SLE is managing active disease while preventing complications of treatment. Age, race, sex, socioeconomic status, co-morbid conditions, and disease severity influence survival. Prognosis can be improved with early diagnosis, ongoing assessment and prompt recognition of serious organ involvement, and effective treatment plans.

Drug Therapy. NSAIDs continue to be an important interven-tion, especially for patients with mild joint pain. Monitor the patient on long-term NSAID therapy for GI and renal effects.

Antimalarial agents, such as hydroxychloroquine and chloro-quine, are often used to treat fatigue and skin and joint problems. They repress the immune system but do not cause immunosup-pression. These drugs may reduce occurrence of flares. Patients taking hydroxychloroquine should have eye examinations by an ophthalmologist every 6 to 12 months. Retinopathy can develop with high doses of these drugs. It generally reverses when they are stopped. If the patient cannot tolerate an antimalarial agent, an antileprosy drug, such as dapsone, may be used.

Use of corticosteroids should be limited to the lowest dose for the shortest possible time. For example, steroids can be used for a few weeks until a slower acting medication becomes effec-tive. Taper the patient's dose of steroid slowly rather than stop-ping the medication abruptly. High doses of corticosteroids may be especially appropriate for the patient with severe cutaneous SLE.

Immunosuppressive drugs, such as azathioprine and cyclo-phosphamide, may be used to suppress the immune system and reduce end-organ damage. Monitor closely to decrease the risk for drug toxicity and side effects. Because blood clots can be a life-threatening complication of SLE, anticoagulants, such as warfarin, may be prescribed. Belimumab (Benlysta) is a B-lymphocyte stimulator that inhibits the inflammation of SLE.

Topical immunomodulators can be used instead of cortico-steroids to treat serious skin conditions. Tacrolimus (Protopic, Prograf) and pimecrolimus (Elidel) suppress immune activity in the skin, affecting the butterfly rash and discoid lesions.

Disease management is appropriately monitored by serial anti-DNA titers and serum complement (Table 64.16). Simpler, less costly tests, such as ESR or CRP, may be helpful.

❖ NURSING MANAGEMENT: SYSTEMIC LUPUS ERYTHEMATOSUS

◆ Nursing Assessment

Subjective and objective data to obtain from the patient with SLE are outlined in Table 64.17. In particular, assess the effect of pain and fatigue on ability to perform ADLs.

◆ Nursing Diagnoses

Nursing diagnoses for the patient with SLE may include:

- Fatigue
- Impaired tissue integrity
- Difficulty coping

Additional information on nursing diagnoses and interven-tions for the patient with SLE is presented in eNursing Care Plan 64.2 (available on the website for this chapter).

◆ Planning

Overall goals are that the patient with SLE will (1) have accept-able pain management, (2) show awareness of and avoid activi-ties that worsen the disease, and (3) maintain optimal role function and positive self-image.

◆ Nursing Implementation

The unpredictable nature of SLE presents many challenges for the patient and caregiver. Physical, psychologic, and sociocultural

TABLE 64.17 Nursing Assessment

Systemic Lupus Erythematosus

Subjective Data

Important Health Information

Past health history: Exposure to ultraviolet light, drugs, chemicals, viral infections. Physical or psychologic stress. States of ↑ estrogen activity, including early onset of menses, pregnancy, and postpartum period. Pattern of remissions and flares

Medications: Oral contraceptives, procainamide, hydralazine, isoniazid, antiseizure drugs, antibiotics, corticosteroids, NSAIDs

Functional Health Patterns

Health perception–health management: Family history of autoimmune disorders, frequent infections, malaise, impact of disease on functional ability

Nutritional-metabolic: Weight loss, oral and nasal ulcers, nausea and vomiting, dry mouth *(xerostomia)*, dysphagia, photosensitivity with rash, frequent infections

Elimination: ↓ Urine output, diarrhea or constipation

Activity-exercise: Morning stiffness, joint swelling and deformity, shortness of breath *(dyspnea)*, excessive fatigue

Sleep-rest: Insomnia

Cognitive-perceptual: Vision problems, vertigo, headache, arthralgia, chest pain (pericardial, pleuritic), abdominal pain. Painful, throbbing, cold fingers with numbness and tingling

Sexuality-reproductive: Amenorrhea, irregular menstrual periods

Coping–stress tolerance: Depression, withdrawal

Objective Data

General

Fever, lymphadenopathy, periorbital edema

Integumentary

Alopecia. Dry, scaly scalp. Keratoconjunctivitis, butterfly rash, palmar or discoid erythema, hives (urticaria), erythema at fingernails or toenails, purpura, or petechiae. Leg ulcers

Respiratory

Pleural friction rub, ↓ breath sounds

Cardiovascular

Vasculitis, pericardial friction rub, hypertension, edema, dysrhythmias, murmurs. Bilateral, symmetric pallor and cyanosis of fingers (Raynaud's phenomenon)

Gastrointestinal

Oral and pharyngeal ulcers; splenomegaly

Neurologic

Facial weakness, peripheral neuropathies, papilledema, dysarthria, confusion, hallucination, disorientation, psychosis, seizures, aphasia, hemiparesis

Musculoskeletal

Myopathy, myositis, arthritis

Urinary

Proteinuria

Possible Diagnostic Findings

Presence of anti-DNA, anti-Sm, and antinuclear antibodies. Anemia, leukopenia, thrombocytopenia. ↑ ESR, ↑ serum creatinine. Microscopic hematuria, cellular casts in urine. Pericarditis or pleural effusion on chest x-ray

---

problems linked to long-term management require varied approaches and skills from the interprofessional team.

During a disease flare, the patient may quickly become very ill. Assess fever pattern, joint inflammation, limitation of motion, location and degree of discomfort, and fatigue. Monitor the patient's weight and fluid intake and output. This is especially important if corticosteroids are prescribed because of related fluid retention and possible renal failure. Collect 24-hour urine samples for protein and creatinine clearance as ordered. Observe for signs of bleeding due to drug therapy (e.g., pallor, skin bruising, petechiae, tarry stools).

Carefully assess neurologic function. Observe for vision problems, headaches, personality changes, seizures, and memory loss. Psychosis may result from CNS disease or be an effect of corticosteroid therapy. Nerve irritation of the extremities *(peripheral neuropathy)* may cause numbness, tingling, and weakness of the hands and feet.

Explain the nature of the disease, treatments, and all diagnostic procedures. When teaching patients about their prescribed drugs, include indications for use, proper administration, and side effects. Help patients understand that abruptly stopping a medication may worsen disease activity. Provide emotional support for the patient and caregiver, especially during a disease flare.

Emphasize the importance of patient involvement for successful home management. Help the patient understand that even strong adherence to the treatment plan is no guarantee against flares in this unpredictable disease. Several factors may increase disease activity, such as fatigue, sun exposure,

TABLE 64.18 Patient & Caregiver Teaching

Systemic Lupus Erythematosus

Include the following information in the teaching plan for a patient with SLE and the caregiver:

- Disease process
- Names of drugs, actions, side effects, dosage, administration
- Pain management strategies
- Energy conservation and pacing techniques
- Therapeutic exercise, heat therapy for arthralgia
- Relaxation therapy
- Avoid physical and emotional stress
- Avoid exposure to those with infection
- Avoid drying soaps, powders, household chemicals
- Use sunscreen protection (at least SPF 15) and protective clothing, with minimal sun exposure from 11:00 AM to 3:00 PM
- Regular medical and laboratory follow-up
- Marital and pregnancy counseling as needed
- Community resources and health care agencies

SPF, Sun protection factor.

emotional stress, infection, drugs, and surgery. Help the patient and caregiver eliminate or reduce exposure to such factors (Table 64.18).

SLE and Pregnancy. Because SLE is most common in women of childbearing age, treatment during pregnancy must be considered. The HCP and obstetrician should discuss with the woman her desire to become pregnant. Infertility may have resulted from renal involvement and use of high-dose corticosteroids and immunosuppressive drugs. The patient should understand spontaneous abortion, stillbirth, and intrauterine growth restriction are common problems. They occur because immune complexes are deposited in the placenta and inflammation occurs in placental blood vessels.

Renal, cardiovascular, lung, and central nervous systems may be affected during pregnancy. Women who already show serious effects in these systems should be counseled against pregnancy. For the best outcome, pregnancy should be planned when disease activity is minimal. Flares are common during the postpartum period. Therapeutic abortion offers the same risk for postdelivery exacerbation as carrying the fetus to term.

Psychosocial Issues. The patient with SLE may face many psychosocial issues. Disease onset and symptoms may be vague, and SLE may be undiagnosed for a long time. Supportive therapies may be as important as medical treatment in helping the patient cope with the disease. Tell the patient and caregiver that SLE has a good prognosis for most people.

Stress the importance of planning both recreational and work activities. The young adult may find sun restrictions and physical limitations hard to follow. Help the patient develop and achieve reasonable goals for improving or maintaining mobility, energy, and self-esteem.

Families worry about hereditary aspects and want to know if their children will have SLE. Many couples need pregnancy and sexual counseling. Those making decisions about marriage and careers worry how SLE will interfere with their plans. Teach employers, teachers, and co-workers as needed about the impact of SLE.

◆ Evaluation

The expected outcomes are that the patient with SLE will
- Use energy-conservation techniques
- Adapt lifestyle to current energy
- Maintain skin integrity with use of topical treatments
- Prevent disease flare with use of sunscreens and limited sun exposure

SCLERODERMA

Scleroderma (systemic sclerosis) is a disorder of connective tissue characterized by fibrotic, degenerative, and, sometimes, inflammatory changes in the skin, blood vessels, synovium, skeletal muscle, and internal organs.

Scleroderma occurs in all ethnic groups. It is more common in blacks, Native Americans, and persons of Japanese descent. Although symptoms may begin at any age, the usual age at onset is between 30 and 50 years. Scleroderma is relatively rare. Only about 300,000 Americans have the disease. Incidence in women is 4 times more common than in men.[3]

Two types of disease exist: localized scleroderma, which is the more common form, and systemic scleroderma. Skin changes of localized disease are usually limited to a few places on the skin or muscle without involvement of the trunk or internal organs. The prognosis of patients with limited disease is better than for those with systemic disease. Skin and connective tissue changes progress rapidly during the first months of systemic scleroderma, which is associated with internal organ involvement.[29]

Etiology and Pathophysiology

The exact cause of scleroderma is unknown. We think immunologic and vascular abnormalities play a role in the development of systemic disease. Risk factors include environmental or occupational exposure to coal, plastics, and silica dust.

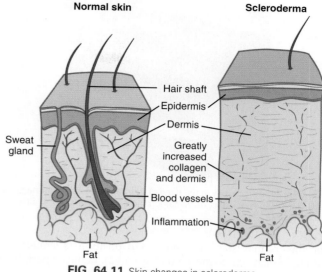

FIG. 64.11 Skin changes in scleroderma.

In scleroderma, the body makes too much collagen (protein that gives normal skin its strength and elasticity) (Fig. 64.11). This leads to progressive tissue fibrosis and occlusion of blood vessels. Collagen overproduction also disrupts normal function of internal organs, such as the lungs, kidney, heart, and GI tract.

Vascular problems, which mainly involve the small arteries and arterioles, are almost always present. These changes are some of the earliest changes in scleroderma.

Clinical Manifestations

Manifestations of scleroderma range from benign limited skin disease to diffuse skin thickening with rapidly progressive and widespread organ involvement. Localized disease is often marked by the CREST syndrome:

Calcinosis: painful deposits of calcium in skin of fingers, forearms, pressure points

Raynaud's phenomenon: intermittent vasospasm of fingertips in response to cold or stress

Esophageal dysfunction: difficulty swallowing due to internal scarring

Sclerodactyly: tightening of skin on fingers and toes

Telangiectasia: red spots on hands, forearms, palms, face, and lips from capillary dilation

Raynaud's Phenomenon. Raynaud's phenomenon (sudden vasospasm of the digits) is the most common first complaint in localized scleroderma. Patients have decreased blood flow to the fingers and toes when exposed to cold (blanching or white phase). This is followed by cyanosis as hemoglobin releases O_2 to the tissues (blue phase), then erythema during rewarming (red phase). Numbness and tingling often occur. Raynaud's phenomenon may precede the onset of systemic disease by months, years, or even decades. Raynaud's phenomenon is described in detail in Chapter 37.

Skin and Joint Changes. Symmetric painless swelling or thickening of the skin of the fingers and hands may progress to diffuse scleroderma of the trunk. In localized disease, skin thickening generally does not extend above the elbow or knee, although the face may be affected. In diffuse disease, the skin loses elasticity and becomes taut and shiny. This causes the typical expressionless face with tightly pursed lips. Skin changes in the face may contribute to reduced ROM in the temporomandibular joint.

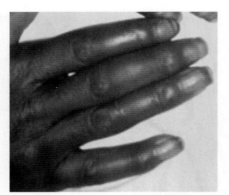

FIG. 64.12 Sclerodactyly in the hand of a patient with scleroderma. (From Zitelli BJ, Davis HW: *Atlas of pediatric physical diagnosis,* ed 4, St Louis, 2002, Mosby.)

The fingers may stay in a semiflexed position *(sclerodactyly),* with tightened skin to the wrist (Fig. 64.12). Reduced peripheral joint function may be an early symptom of arthritis.

Internal Organ Involvement. About 20% of people with systemic scleroderma and a few with localized disease develop secondary Sjögren's syndrome, a condition associated with dry eyes and dry mouth. Dysphagia, gum disease, and dental decay can result. Frequent reflux of gastric acid can occur due to esophageal fibrosis. If swallowing becomes difficult, the patient is likely to decrease food intake and lose weight. GI effects include constipation from colonic hypomotility and diarrhea due to malabsorption from bacterial overgrowth.

Lung problems include pleural thickening, pulmonary fibrosis, and abnormal pulmonary function. The patient develops a cough and dyspnea. Pulmonary arterial hypertension and interstitial lung disease may occur. Lung disease is the main cause of death in scleroderma.

Heart disease includes pericarditis, pericardial effusion, and dysrhythmias. Heart failure from myocardial fibrosis occurs most often in patients with systemic disease.

Renal disease was a major cause of death in systemic scleroderma. Because malignant hypertension associated with rapidly progressive, irreversible renal insufficiency can occur, early recognition of renal involvement and initiation of therapy are critical. Recent improvements in dialysis, bilateral nephrectomy in patients with uncontrollable hypertension, and kidney transplant have offered hope to patients with renal failure. Use of angiotensin-converting enzyme (ACE) inhibitors (e.g., lisinopril [Prinivil]) has had a marked effect on the ability to treat renal disease.

Diagnostic Studies

Laboratory results in scleroderma are relatively normal. Blood studies may show mild hemolytic anemia from RBC damage in diseased small vessels. Anticentromere antibodies related to CREST syndrome are found in about 45% to 50% of people with localized scleroderma. They are rare in people with systemic disease. Antibodies to topoisomerase-1 are present in about 30% of people with diffuse disease.[30] Presence of either antibody is highly specific for diagnosis. If renal involvement is present, urinalysis may show proteinuria, microscopic hematuria, and casts. Serum creatinine may be increased. X-ray evidence of subcutaneous calcification, distal esophageal hypomotility, or bibasilar pulmonary fibrosis is diagnostic of scleroderma. Pulmonary function studies show decreased vital capacity and lung compliance.

TABLE 64.19 Interprofessional Care

Scleroderma

Diagnostic Assessment
- History and physical examination
- Antibodies to topoisomerase-1
- Anticentromere antibody
- Nail bed capillary microscopy
- Chest x-ray
- Skin or organ biopsy
- Urinalysis (proteinuria, hematuria, casts)
- Pulmonary function tests
- ECG

Management
- Physical therapy
- Occupational therapy

Drug Therapy
- Vasoactive agents: reserpine, bosentan, epoprostenol
- Calcium channel blockers: diltiazem, nifedipine
- ACE inhibitors: lisinopril (Prinivil)
- Immunosuppressive drugs: cyclophosphamide, mycophenolate mofetil (CellCept)

Interprofessional Care

There is no specific treatment (Table 64.19). Supportive care is directed toward preventing or treating secondary complications of involved organs. PT helps to maintain joint mobility and preserve muscle strength. Occupational therapy assists the patient in maintaining functional abilities.

Drug Therapy. Vasoactive agents are often prescribed in early disease. Calcium channel blockers (nifedipine [Procardia], diltiazem [Cardizem]) and the angiotensin II blocker losartan are common treatments for Raynaud's phenomenon. Reserpine, an α-adrenergic blocking agent, increases blood flow to the fingers. Bosentan (Tracleer), an endothelin-receptor antagonist, and the vasodilator epoprostenol (Flolan) may improve blood flow to the lung.[31]

NSAIDs and topical agents may give some relief from joint pain. Capsaicin cream may be useful, not only as a local analgesic but also as a vasodilator. Other therapies prescribed to treat specific systemic problems include (1) tetracycline for diarrhea caused by bacterial overgrowth, (2) histamine (H_2) receptor blockers (e.g., cimetidine) and proton pump inhibitors (e.g., omeprazole) for esophageal symptoms, and (3) antihypertensive agent (e.g., captopril, propranolol, methyldopa) for hypertension with renal involvement. Immunosuppressive drugs (e.g., cyclophosphamide, mycophenolate mofetil) are used in severe cases.

❖ NURSING MANAGEMENT: SCLERODERMA

Nursing interventions often begin during hospitalization for diagnosis. Assess vital signs, weight, intake and output, respiratory and bowel function, and joint ROM regularly to plan appropriate care. Emotional stress and cold ambient temperatures may aggravate Raynaud's phenomenon. Teach patients with scleroderma to avoid finger-stick blood testing because of compromised circulation and poor healing.

Teaching is an important nursing intervention throughout the disease. Obvious changes in the face and hands often lead to poor self-image and loss of mobility and function. Teach the patient to regularly take part in therapeutic exercises at home to prevent skin retraction and promote vascularization. Mouth excursion (yawning with an open mouth) is a good exercise to help with temporomandibular joint function. Isometric exercises are best if the patient has arthropathy because no joint movement occurs. Encourage the use of moist heat applications or paraffin baths to promote skin flexibility in the hands and feet. Teach the patient to use assistive devices as needed and organize activities to preserve strength and reduce disability.

Teach the patient to protect the hands and feet from cold exposure. Protect against burns or cuts that may heal slowly. Encourage the patient to avoid smoking because of its vasoconstricting effect. Report signs of infection promptly. Use alcohol-free lotions to improve skin dryness and cracking. They must be rubbed in for a long time to be absorbed through the thick skin.

Remind the patient to reduce dysphagia by eating small, frequent meals, chewing carefully and slowly, and drinking fluids. A consultation with a dietitian is helpful. Decrease risk for heartburn by using antacids 45 to 60 minutes after each meal and sitting upright for at least 2 hours after eating. Using extra pillows or raising the head of the bed on blocks may reduce gastroesophageal reflux during the night.

Job alterations are often needed due to problems with climbing stairs, using a computer, writing, and being exposed to cold. The patient may be socially withdrawn as skin tightening changes the appearance of the face and hands. Dining out may become socially embarrassing because of the patient's small mouth, swallowing difficulty, and reflux. Some persons with scleroderma wear gloves to protect fingertip ulcers and provide extra warmth. Emphasize daily oral hygiene to avoid increased tooth and gum problems. The patient needs a dentist who is familiar with scleroderma and able to adapt care to a small mouth.

Psychologic support, biofeedback training, and relaxation can reduce stress and improve sleeping habits. Sexual problems from body changes, pain, muscular weakness, limited mobility, decreased self-esteem, erectile dysfunction, and decreased vaginal secretions may require sensitive counseling.

? CHECK YOUR PRACTICE

A 34-yr-old woman hospitalized for aspiration pneumonia has a 5-year history of scleroderma.
- How could scleroderma have contributed to the aspiration pneumonia?
- What strategies will you suggest to decrease the risk for pneumonia recurrence?
- What other self-care strategies will you reinforce with this patient?

POLYMYOSITIS AND DERMATOMYOSITIS

Polymyositis (PM) is diffuse, idiopathic, inflammatory myopathy of striated muscle. It causes bilateral weakness, usually most severe in the proximal or limb girdle muscles. When muscle changes associated with PM are accompanied by distinctive skin changes, the disorder is called dermatomyositis (DM).

These relatively rare disorders can be similar in signs, symptoms, and treatment, but they are 2 distinct diseases. They typically affect adults age 20 years and older. They rarely occur in

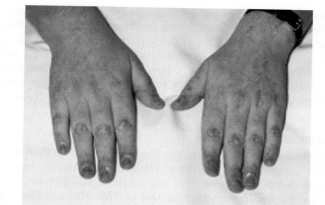

FIG. 64.13 Dermatomyositis skin changes indicating Gottron's papules. (From Firestein GS, Budd RC, Gabriel SE, McInnes IB: *Kelley's textbook of rheumatology*, ed 9, Philadelphia, 2012, Saunders.)

people under age 18 years. PM and DM occur twice as often in women as in men. Patients with PM generally have more severe disease than those with DM.

Etiology and Pathophysiology

The exact cause of PM and DM is unknown. Evidence suggests an autoimmune origin with T cell–mediated destruction of unidentified muscle antigens. Environmental factors are likely, including viral and bacterial infection, certain drugs, supplements, vaccines, medical implants, and occupational exposure.

Clinical Manifestations and Complications

Muscular. The patient with PM and DM has weight loss and increasing fatigue, with gradually developing muscle weakness that causes difficulty in performing ADLs. The most commonly affected muscles are in the shoulders, legs, arms, and pelvic girdle. The patient may have difficulty rising from a chair or bathtub, climbing stairs, combing hair, or reaching into a high cupboard. Repetitive movements are more likely to cause trouble than a single strength exercise. The patient may be unable to raise the head from a pillow as neck muscles weaken. Muscle discomfort or tenderness is uncommon. Muscle examination shows an inability to move against resistance or even gravity. Weak pharyngeal muscles may cause dysphagia and dysphonia (nasal or hoarse voice).

Dermal. Rashes are typical with DM. They usually prompt earlier recognition of DM than PM, which has no rashes. Skin changes of DM include a classic red or purple symmetric rash (*heliotrope*) with edema around the eyelids. The typical skin rash is not often found with other disorders. A scaly, smooth, or raised rash may be seen on the knuckles and sides of the hands (*Gottron's papules*) (Fig. 64.13). Reddened, smooth, or scaly patches appear with the same symmetric distribution but sparing the interphalangeal spaces (*Gottron's sign*). The rash can be confused with psoriasis or seborrheic dermatitis. A red, scaling rash (*poikiloderma*) may develop as a late finding on the back, buttocks, and a V-shaped area of the anterior neck and chest.

Hyperemia and telangiectasia are often present at the nail beds. Calcium nodules (*calcinosis cutis*) can develop throughout the skin and are especially common in long-standing DM.

Other Manifestations. Joint redness, pain, and inflammation often occur. They contribute to limited joint ROM in PM and DM. Contractures and muscle atrophy may occur with advanced disease. Weakened pharyngeal muscles can lead to poor cough effort, difficulty swallowing, and increased risk for aspiration pneumonia. Interstitial lung disease is a common complication. All patients should be evaluated routinely with a chest x-ray and pulmonary function tests. People with DM have increased risk for cancer and should receive age- and gender-appropriate screenings. PM and DM may be associated with other connective tissue disorders (e.g., scleroderma).

Diagnostic Studies

Biopsy is the gold standard for diagnosis of PM or DM after other neuromuscular diseases are excluded. Muscle biopsy shows necrosis, degeneration, regeneration, and fibrosis with pathologic findings distinct for DM or PM. MRI can identify areas of inflammation and guide the biopsy site selection.[32] Laboratory tests are helpful, but not diagnostic of either disease. Increased muscle enzymes (e.g., creatine kinase, myoglobin) reflect muscle damage but will decrease to normal or near normal with treatment. An EMG suggestive of PM shows bizarre high-frequency discharges and spontaneous fibrillation, with positive spikes at rest. Increased ESR or CRP occurs with active disease.

❖ Interprofessional and Nursing Care

PM and DM are treated initially with high-dose oral corticosteroids, with the dose tapered based on patient response. Most patients respond well to treatment. Long-term corticosteroid therapy may be needed because relapses are common when the drug is withdrawn.

Immunosuppressive drugs (methotrexate, azathioprine, tacrolimus, cyclophosphamide) may be used in combination with steroids or as a second-line therapy if the patient does not respond to steroids. IV immunoglobulin (IVIG) may be given with corticosteroids or immunosuppressants, but it is not a first-line treatment.

> **💊 DRUG ALERT IV Immunoglobulin (IVIG)**
> * Give by slow infusion to decrease risk for thromboembolic complications.
> * Hydrate patient well during infusion to decrease risk for renal failure.
> * Treat transient adverse effects, such as headache.

Injection of synthetic ACTH (repository corticotropin injection [Acthar]) helps with muscle spasms. The exact mechanism of action is unknown. Limited data are available on its effectiveness.[32]

PT can be helpful and is tailored to disease activity. Use massage and passive movement during active disease. Delay more aggressive exercises until disease activity is minimal based on low serum muscle enzymes.

Teach the patient about the disease, prescribed therapies, diagnostic tests, and the need for regular medical care. Help the patient understand that the benefits of therapy are often delayed. For example, weakness may increase during the first few weeks of corticosteroid therapy. Encourage the use of assistive devices to decrease risk for falls. To prevent aspiration, encourage the patient to rest before meals, maintain an upright position when eating, and choose easily swallowed foods.

Help the patient to organize activities and use pacing techniques to conserve energy. Encourage daily ROM exercises to prevent contractures. When inflammation is decreased, start muscle-strengthening (repetitive) exercises. Home care and bed rest may be needed during acute PM, when the patient may not be able to complete ADLs because of profound muscle weakness.

MIXED CONNECTIVE TISSUE DISEASE

Patients having a combination of clinical features of several rheumatic diseases are described as having *mixed connective tissue disease*. The term describes a disorder with features primarily of SLE, scleroderma, and PM. This disease occurs most often in women in their 20s and 30s.

About 25% of persons with a connective tissue disease develop another related disease over the course of several years, which is known as *overlap syndrome*.[33]

SJÖGREN'S SYNDROME

Sjögren's syndrome is a relatively common autoimmune disease that targets the moisture-producing exocrine glands. This leads to *xerostomia* (dry mouth) and *keratoconjunctivitis sicca* (dry eyes).[34] The nose, throat, airways, and skin can become dry. The disease may affect other glands, including those in the stomach, pancreas, and intestines (extraglandular involvement). The disease is usually diagnosed in people over age 40 but can be found in all age-groups. Women are 10 times more likely than men to have Sjögren's syndrome.

In primary Sjögren's syndrome, problems occur with lacrimal and salivary glands. However, up to 40% of patients have extended disease affecting the lungs, liver, kidneys, and skin. This occurrence increases the risk for non-Hodgkin's lymphoma.[34]

Sjögren's syndrome appears to be caused by genetic and environmental factors. A particular gene predisposes whites to the disease. Other genes are linked to the disease in people of Japanese, Chinese, and African-American ethnicity. The trigger may be a viral or bacterial infection that adversely stimulates the immune system. In Sjögren's syndrome, lymphocytes attack and damage the lacrimal and salivary glands.

Decreased tearing causes dry eyes, which leads to a gritty sensation in the eyes, burning, blurred vision, and photosensitivity. Dry mouth causes buccal membrane fissures, changes in taste, dysphagia, and increased mouth infection or dental decay. Dry skin and rashes, joint and muscle pain, and thyroid problems may be present. Other exocrine glands can be affected. For example, vaginal dryness may lead to painful intercourse (*dyspareunia*).

Autoimmune thyroid disorders, including Graves' disease and Hashimoto's thyroiditis, are common with Sjögren's syndrome. Histologic study shows lymphocyte infiltration of salivary and lacrimal glands. The disease may become more generalized and involve the lymph nodes, bone marrow, and visceral organs (pseudolymphoma).

Ophthalmologic examination (Schirmer's test for tear production), measures of salivary gland function, and lower lip biopsy of minor salivary glands aid in diagnosis. Treatment is symptomatic, including (1) instillation of preservative-free artificial tears or ophthalmic antiinflammatory drops (e.g., cyclosporine [Restasis]) as needed for adequate hydration and lubrication, (2) surgical punctal occlusion, and (3) increased fluids with meals. Dental hygiene is important.

Pilocarpine (Salagen) and cevimeline (Evoxac) can ease the dry mouth. Increased humidity at home may reduce respiratory tract infections. Vaginal lubrication with a water-soluble product, such as K-Y Jelly, may increase comfort during intercourse.

> **⚠ SAFETY ALERT** Sjögren's Syndrome
> To help with chewing and swallowing:
> • Moisten food with mayonnaise, sauces, gravy, or yogurt.
> • Thin foods with skim milk or broth.
> • Use a food processor or blender to finely chop or liquefy foods.
> • Try soft, creamy foods (e.g., mashed potatoes, macaroni and cheese).
> • Drink high-calorie cold liquids (e.g., breakfast drinks).
> • Avoid salty, acidic, or spicy foods.

MYOFASCIAL PAIN SYNDROME

Myofascial pain syndrome is a chronic form of muscle pain and tenderness, typically in the chest, neck, shoulders, hips, and lower back. Referred pain from these muscle groups can travel to the buttocks, hands, and head, causing severe headaches. Temporomandibular joint pain may originate in myofascial pain. Regions of pain are often within the connective tissue (fascia) that covers skeletal muscles. Trigger or tender points are thought to activate a characteristic pattern of pain that worsens with activity or stress.

Myofascial pain syndrome occurs more often in middle-aged adults and in women. Patients report deep, aching pain with a sensation of burning, stinging, and stiffness.

A typical PT treatment is the "spray and stretch" method. The painful area is iced or sprayed with a coolant, such as ethyl chloride and then stretched. Positive results have been seen with topical patches and injection of the trigger points with a local anesthetic (e.g., 1% lidocaine). Massage, dry needling, and ultrasound therapy have helped some patients.[35]

FIBROMYALGIA

Fibromyalgia is a chronic central pain syndrome marked by widespread, nonarticular musculoskeletal pain and fatigue with multiple tender points. Fibromyalgia is a common musculoskeletal disorder and a major cause of disability. It affects more than 3.7 million Americans. Most are women ages 40 to 75 years.[36] Fibromyalgia and systemic exertion intolerance disease (SEID) (formerly called chronic fatigue syndrome) share many common features (Table 64.20).

Etiology and Pathophysiology

Fibromyalgia involves abnormal central processing of nociceptive pain input. The increased pain is due to abnormal sensory processing in the CNS. Multiple physiologic abnormalities have been found. They include (1) increased levels of substance P in the spinal fluid, (2) low blood flow to the thalamus, (3) dysfunction of the hypothalamic-pituitary-adrenal (HPA) axis, (4) low serotonin and tryptophan, and (5) abnormal cytokine function. Serotonin and substance P play a role in mood regulation, sleep, and pain perception. Changes in the HPA axis can negatively affect a person's physical and mental health. An increased incidence of depression and decreased response to stress occur. Genetic factors contribute to the development of fibromyalgia, as a familial tendency exists. Recent illness or trauma may be a trigger in susceptible people.

TABLE 64.20 Common Features of Fibromyalgia and Systemic Exertion Intolerance Disease (SEID)
Occurrence Previously healthy, young and middle-aged women
Etiology (Theories) Infectious trigger, dysfunction in HPA axis, CNS problem
Clinical Manifestations Generalized musculoskeletal pain, malaise and fatigue, cognitive problems, headaches, sleep problems, depression, anxiety, fever
Disease Course Variable intensity of symptoms, fluctuates over time
Diagnosis No definitive laboratory tests or joint and muscle examinations Mainly a diagnosis of exclusion
Management Symptomatic treatment may include antidepressant drugs, such as amitriptyline and fluoxetine (Prozac). Nondrug measures include heat, massage, regular stretching, biofeedback, stress management, and relaxation training

HPA, Hypothalamic-pituitary-adrenal.

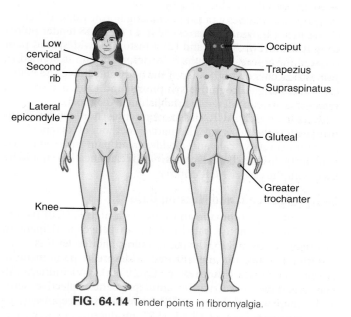

FIG. 64.14 Tender points in fibromyalgia.

Clinical Manifestations and Complications

The patient reports widespread burning pain that fluctuates through the course of a day. The patient often cannot determine if pain occurs in the muscles, joints, or soft tissues. Head or facial pain often results from stiff or painful neck and shoulder muscles. The pain can accompany temporomandibular joint dysfunction, which affects about one third of patients with fibromyalgia.

Physical examination typically shows point tenderness at 11 or more of 18 identified sites (Fig. 64.14). Patients with fibromyalgia are sensitive to painful stimuli throughout the body, not just at the identified tender sites. They may have pain in response to a stimulus that does not typically cause pain (allodynia). Point tenderness can vary from day to day. Sometimes, the patient may respond to fewer than 11 tender points. At other times, palpation of all sites may cause pain.

Cognitive effects range from difficulty concentrating to memory lapses and a feeling of being overwhelmed when dealing with multiple tasks. Many report migraine headaches. Depression and anxiety often occur and may require drug therapy. Stiffness, nonrefreshing sleep, fatigue, and numbness or tingling in the hands or feet often accompany fibromyalgia. Restless legs syndrome is typical. Some describe an irresistible urge to move the legs when at rest or lying down.

Irritable bowel syndrome with constipation and/or diarrhea, abdominal pain, and bloating is common. Patients may have difficulty swallowing, perhaps because of problems in esophageal smooth muscle function. Increased frequency of urination and urinary urgency, in the absence of a bladder infection, may occur. Women with fibromyalgia may have more difficult menstruation, with disease symptoms worse during this time.

Diagnostic Studies

A definitive diagnosis of fibromyalgia is often hard to establish. Lack of knowledge about the disease and its manifestations among HCPs may cause delays in diagnosis and treatment.

Laboratory results in most cases help rule out other suspected disorders. Muscle biopsy may show a nonspecific moth-eaten appearance or fiber atrophy.

The ACR classifies a person as having fibromyalgia if 2 criteria are met: (1) pain is experienced in 11 of the 18 tender points on palpation (Fig. 64.14) and (2) a history of widespread pain is noted for at least 3 months.[37] Widespread pain is defined as pain that occurs on both sides of the body and above and below the waist. Fatigue, cognitive symptoms, and extensive somatic symptoms are considered in establishing a diagnosis.

A more recent ACR classification uses non–tender point diagnostic criteria as an alternative method of diagnosis. A symptom severity scale and a widespread pain index are used to identify disease characteristics.[38] This classification should be used with the earlier ACR criteria.

❖ Interprofessional and Nursing Care

Treatment is symptomatic and requires a high level of patient motivation. Teach the patient to be an active participant in treatment. Rest can help the pain, aching, and tenderness.

Drug therapy for the chronic widespread pain includes pregabalin (Lyrica), duloxetine (Cymbalta), and milnacipran (Savella). Low-dose tricyclic antidepressants, selective serotonin reuptake inhibitors (SSRIs), or benzodiazepines (e.g., diazepam) may be prescribed. SSRI antidepressants (e.g., sertraline [Zoloft], paroxetine [Paxil]) tend to be reserved for patients who also have depression. SSRIs may have to be prescribed at higher doses than when used to treat depression. Antidepressants and muscle relaxants (e.g., baclofen) have sedative effects that can improve nighttime rest for the patient with fibromyalgia.

Long-acting opioids are not recommended unless other therapies are not successful. In some patients, pain may be managed with OTC analgesics, such as acetaminophen, ibuprofen, or naproxen (Aleve). Nonopioids, such as tramadol (Ultram), may be used. Zolpidem (Ambien) or trazodone is sometimes given for short-term intervention in patients with severe sleep problems.

Because of the chronic nature of fibromyalgia, the patient needs consistent support from interprofessional team members. Massage is often combined with ultrasound or use of alternating heat and cold packs to soothe tense, sore muscles and increase blood circulation. Gentle stretching to relieve muscle tension and spasm can be done by a physical therapist or practiced by the patient at home. Yoga and Tai Chi are often helpful. Low-impact aerobic exercise, such as walking, can help prevent muscle atrophy.

Patients may consider limiting intake of sugar, caffeine, and alcohol because they may be muscle irritants. Vitamin and mineral supplements may help combat stress, correct deficiencies, and support the immune system. However, unproven miracle diets or supplements should be carefully investigated by the patient and discussed with the HCP before using them. Teach the patient that some foods and supplements can cause serious or even dangerous side effects when mixed with certain drugs.

Pain and the related symptoms of fibromyalgia can cause significant stress. Patients with fibromyalgia may not cope well with stress. Effective relaxation strategies include biofeedback, imagery, meditation, and cognitive-behavioral therapy. Patients need initial training for these interventions, but they can continue to practice in their own homes. (Stress management is discussed in Chapter 6.) Psychologic counseling (individual or group) and a support group may be helpful.

SYSTEMIC EXERTION INTOLERANCE DISEASE (SEID)

Systemic exertion intolerance disease (SEID), formerly called *chronic fatigue syndrome,* is a serious, complex, multisystem disease in which exertion of any sort (physical, emotional, cognitive) is impaired and accompanied by profound fatigue.[39] SEID is a poorly understood condition that can have a devastating impact on the lives of patients and their families.

SEID affects at least 1 million people in the United States. The condition is 3 to 4 times more common in women than men. SEID occurs in all ethnic and socioeconomic groups, but the illness is more common in minorities and socioeconomically disadvantaged groups. The true prevalence of SEID is unknown because many people with the disease have not been diagnosed.[39]

Etiology and Pathophysiology

Despite efforts to determine the cause and pathology of SEID, we do not know the cause. Many theories exist about the cause of SEID. Neuroendocrine abnormalities have been implicated involving a hypofunction of the HPA axis and hypothalamic-pituitary-gonadal (HPG) axis, which together regulate the stress response and reproductive hormone levels. Several microorganisms have been investigated as causative agents, including herpes viruses (e.g., Epstein-Barr virus [EBV], cytomegalovirus [CMV]), retroviruses, enteroviruses, *Candida albicans,* and mycoplasma. Because many patients have cognitive deficits (e.g., decreased memory, attention, concentration), changes in the CNS have been suggested as the cause of SEID.

Clinical Manifestations

Diagnosis of SEID requires that the patient have the following 3 symptoms

1. Impaired function with profound fatigue lasting at least 6 months

2. Malaise after exertion: total exhaustion after even minor physical or mental exertion that the patient sometimes describes as a "crash"

3. Unrefreshing sleep

At least 1 of the following manifestations is also required:

1. Cognitive impairment ("brain fog," confusion)
2. *Orthostatic intolerance* (lightheadedness, dizziness, imbalance, fainting)

Severe fatigue is the most common symptom and the problem that causes the patient to seek health care.

SEID is often hard to distinguish from fibromyalgia because many clinical features are similar (Table 64.20). In about half the cases, SEID develops slowly, or the patient may have periodic episodes that gradually become chronic. SEID can arise suddenly in a previously active, healthy person. An unremarkable flu-like illness or other acute stress is often identified as a trigger. Associated symptoms may vary in intensity over time.

The patient may become angry and frustrated with HCPs who cannot diagnose a problem. The disorder may have a major impact on work and family responsibilities. Some people may need help with ADLs.

Diagnostic Studies

Physical examination and diagnostic studies can be used to rule out other possible causes of the patient's symptoms. No laboratory test can diagnose SEID or measure its severity. SEID is a diagnosis of exclusion.

❖ Interprofessional and Nursing Care

Because no definitive treatment exists for SEID, supportive management is essential. Tell the patient what we know about the disease.

NSAIDs can be used to treat headaches, muscle and joint aches, and fever. Because many patients with SEID have allergies and sinusitis, antihistamines and decongestants can be used to treat allergic symptoms. Tricyclic antidepressants (e.g., doxepin, amitriptyline) and SSRIs (e.g., fluoxetine, paroxetine) can improve mood and sleep. Clonazepam (Klonopin) can be used to treat sleep problems and panic disorders. Use of low-dose hydrocortisone to decrease fatigue and disability is being studied.

Teach the patient to avoid total rest because it can create a self-image of the patient as an invalid. On the other hand, strenuous exertion can worsen the exhaustion. Urge the patient to plan a carefully graduated exercise program. Encourage a well-balanced diet, including fiber and fresh dark-colored fruits and vegetables for antioxidant action. Behavioral therapy may be used to promote a positive outlook and improve overall disability and fatigue.

One major problem facing many patients is loss of livelihood and economic security. When the illness strikes, they cannot work or must decrease the amount of work. Loss of a job often leads to loss of medical insurance. Obtaining disability benefits can be frustrating because of the difficulty of establishing a definitive diagnosis of SEID. Patients with SEID may have severe psychosocial losses, including social pressure and isolation from being labelled as lazy or crazy.

SEID does not appear to progress. Although most patients recover or at least gradually improve, some do not show substantial improvement. Recovery is more common in persons with a sudden onset of SEID.

CASE STUDY

Rheumatoid Arthritis

(© iStockphoto/ Thinkstock.)

Patient Profile

K.R., a 42-yr-old married white woman, comes to the rheumatology clinic with tenderness and pain in the small joints of her hands.

Subjective Data
- Reports tenderness, joint pain, and stiffness in her hands for the last 3 mo
- Having fatigue, anorexia, and morning stiffness
- Mother diagnosed with ankylosing spondylitis 8 yr ago
- Expresses doubt about her ability to manage the disease

Objective Data
Physical Examination
- Swelling, warmth, and tenderness of third and fourth metacarpophalangeal joints of both hands
- Mild pain with neck motion
- Tenosynovitis

Diagnostic Studies
- Positive ESR, RF, and anti-CCP
- Mild bone demineralization present bilaterally in hand x-rays

Interprofessional Care
- Diagnosed with RA
- Started on methotrexate 7.5 mg PO once per week, etanercept (Enbrel) 50 mg subcutaneously once per week, prednisone 10 mg/day

Discussion Questions
1. How will you explain the pathophysiology of RA to K.R.?
2. K.R. asks you if genetic factors are related to a diagnosis of RA. How will you respond?
3. **Safety:** What are some home and work modifications you can suggest to K.R. to reduce her symptoms?
4. **Patient-Centered Care:** What suggestions can you make to K.R. about coping with fatigue?
5. **Collaboration:** What referrals may be needed for K.R.?
6. **Priority Decision:** Based on the assessment data presented, what are the priority nursing diagnoses?
7. **Quality Improvement**: What outcomes would indicate interprofessional care was effective?
8. **Evidence-Based Practice:** Why is an exercise program important in the treatment plan for K.R.?
9. Develop a conceptual care map for K.R.

Answers and a corresponding conceptual care map are available at *http://evolve.elsevier.com/Lewis/medsurg.*

BRIDGE TO NCLEX EXAMINATION

The number of the question corresponds to the same-numbered outcome at the beginning of the chapter.

1. In assessing the joints of a patient with osteoarthritis, the nurse understands that Bouchard's nodes
   a. are often red, swollen, and tender.
   b. indicate osteophyte formation at the PIP joints.
   c. are the result of pannus formation at the DIP joints.
   d. occur from deterioration of cartilage by proteolytic enzymes.

2. A patient with rheumatoid arthritis has articular involvement. The nurse recognizes these characteristic changes include (select all that apply)
   a. bamboo-shaped fingers.
   b. metatarsal head dislocation in feet.
   c. noninflammatory pain in large joints.
   d. asymmetric involvement of small joints.
   e. morning stiffness lasting 60 minutes or more.

3. When administering medications to the patient with chronic gout, the nurse recognizes which drug is used as a treatment for this disease?
   a. Colchicine
   b. Allopurinol
   c. Sulfasalazine
   d. Cyclosporine

4. The nurse should teach the patient with ankylosing spondylitis the importance of
   a. avoiding extremes in environmental temperatures
   b. regularly exercising and maintaining proper posture.
   c. maintaining patient's usual physical activity during flares.
   d. applying hot and cool compresses for relief of local symptoms.

5. In teaching a patient with systemic lupus erythematosus about the disorder, the nurse knows the pathophysiology includes
   a. circulating immune complexes formed from IgG autoantibodies reacting with IgG.
   b. an autoimmune T-cell reaction that results in destruction of the deep dermal skin layer.
   c. immunologic dysfunction leading to chronic inflammation in the cartilage and muscles.
   d. the production of a variety of autoantibodies directed against components of the cell nucleus.

6. In teaching a patient with Sjögren's syndrome about drug therapy for this disorder, the nurse includes instruction about the use of which drug?
   a. Pregabalin (Lyrica)
   b. Etanercept (Enbrel)
   c. Cyclosporine (Restasis)
   d. Cyclobenzaprine (Flexeril)

7. Teach the patient with fibromyalgia the importance of limiting intake of which foods? (select all that apply)
   a. Sugar
   b. Alcohol
   c. Caffeine
   d. Red meat
   e. Root vegetables

1. b, 2. b, e, 3. b, 4. b, 5. d, 6. c, 7. a, b, c

For rationales to these answers and even more NCLEX review questions, visit *http://evolve.elsevier.com/Lewis/medsurg.*

ⓔ EVOLVE WEBSITE/RESOURCES LIST

http://evolve.elsevier.com/Lewis/medsurg
Review Questions (Online Only)
Key Points
Answer Keys for Questions
- Rationales for Bridge to NCLEX Examination Questions
- Answer Guidelines for Case Study on p. 1529
- Answer Guidelines for Managing Care of Multiple Patients Case Study (Section 12) on p. 1532
Students Case Studies
- Patient With Obesity and Osteoarthritis
- Patient With Rheumatoid Arthritis
- Patient With Systemic Lupus Erythematosus
Nursing Care Plans
- eNursing Care Plan 64.1: Patient With Rheumatoid Arthritis
- eNursing Care Plan 64.2: Patient With Systemic Lupus Erythematosus
Conceptual Care Map Creator
- Conceptual Care Map for Case Study on p. 1529
Audio Glossary
Content Updates

REFERENCES

1. Arthritis Foundation: Understanding arthritis. Retrieved from *www.arthritis.org/about-arthritis/understanding-arthritis/.*
2. Centers for Disease Control and Prevention: Arthritis. Retrieved from *www.cdc.gov/arthritis/.*
3. Arthritis Foundation: Osteoarthritis. Retrieved from *www.arthritis.org/about-arthritis/types/osteoarthritis/.*
4. National Center for Complementary and Integrative Health: Osteoarthritis: In depth. Retrieved from *https://nccih.nih.gov/health/arthritis/osteoarthritis#hed3.*
*5. Karsdal MA, Michaelis M, Ladel C, et al: Disease-modifying treatments for osteoarthritis (DMOADs) of the knee and hip: Lessons learned from failures and opportunities for the future, *Osteoarthritis Cartilage* 24:2013, 2016.
*6. American Academy of Orthopaedic Surgeons: Treatment of osteoarthritis of the knee: Evidence-based guidelines, ed 2. Retrieved from *www.aaos.org/research/guidelines/TreatmentofOsteoarthritisoftheKneeGuideline.pdf.*
7. Goodman B: Arthroscopic knee surgery little help for arthritis. Retrieved from *www.arthritis.org/living-with-arthritis/treatments/joint-surgery/types/knee/arthroscopic-knee-surgery.php.*
8. Arthritis Foundation: Other natural therapies for osteoarthritis. Retrieved from *www.arthritis.org/living-with-arthritis/treatments/natural/other-therapies/.*
9. Arthritis Foundation: What is rheumatoid arthritis? Retrieved from *www.arthritis.org/about-arthritis/types/rheumatoid-arthritis/what-is-rheumatoid-arthritis.php.*
10. Harrison P: Rheumatoid arthritis: Smoking exacerbates disease activity. Retrieved from *www.medscape.com/viewarticle/821446.*
11. Arthritis Foundation: More than just joints: How rheumatoid arthritis affects the rest of your body. Retrieved from *www.arthritis.org/about-arthritis/types/rheumatoid-arthritis/articles/rhemuatoid-arthritis-affects-body.php.*
12. Arthritis Foundation: The arthritis-depression connection. Retrieved from *www.arthritis.org/living-with-arthritis/comorbidities/depression-and-arthritis/depression-rheumatoid-arthritis.php.*
*13. Agency for Healthcare Research and Quality: Drug therapy for early rheumatoid arthritis: A systematic review update. Retrieved from *https://effectivehealthcare.ahrq.gov/topics/rheumatoid-arthritis-medicine-update/final-report-update-2018.*

*14. Kumar B, Lenert P: Gout and African Americans: Reducing disparities, *Cleve Clin J Med* 83:665, 2016.

15. Harding M: An update on gout for primary care providers, *Nurse Pract* 17:14, 2016.

*16. Armstrong AD, Hubbard MC: *Essentials of musculoskeletal care*, ed 5, Chicago, 2016, American Academy of Orthopaedic Surgeons.

17. Centers for Disease Control and Prevention: Two-step laboratory testing process. Retrieved from *www.cdc.gov/lyme/diagnosistesting/labtest/twostep/index.html.*

18. International Lyme and Associated Diseases Society: Lyme disease basics for providers. Retrieved from *www.ilads.org/research-literature/lyme-disease-basics-for-providers/.*

19. Arthritis Foundation: Spondyloarthritis: What is spondyloarthritis? Retrieved from *www.arthritis.org/about-arthritis/types/spondyloarthritis.*

20. Arthritis Foundation: What is ankylosing spondylitis? Retrieved from *www.arthritis.org/about-arthritis/types/ankylosing-spondylitis/what-is-ankylosing-spondylitis.php.*

21. Arthritis Foundation: What is psoriatic arthritis? Retrieved from *www.arthritis.org/about-arthritis/types/psoriatic-arthritis/what-is-psoriatic-arthritis.php.*

22. Arthritis Foundation: What is reactive arthritis? Retrieved from *www.arthritis.org/about-arthritis/types/reactive-arthritis/what-is-reactive-arthritis.php.*

23. Arthritis Foundation: What is lupus? Retrieved from *www.arthritis.org/about-arthritis/types/lupus/what-is-lupus.php.*

24. Lupus Foundation of America: Medications that can cause drug-induced lupus. Retrieved from *https://resources.lupus.org/entry/causes-of-drug-induced-lupus.*

25. The Johns Hopkins Lupus Center: Lupus-specific skin disease and skin problems. Retrieved from *www.hopkinslupus.org/lupus-info/lupus-affects-body/skin-lupus/.*

26. Lupus Foundation of America: Lupus kidney disease: Did you know? Retrieved from *https://resources.lupus.org/entry/lupus-kidney-disease.*

27. Feltz M, Wickam MB: Systemic lupus erythematosus, *Clin Rev* 26:38, 2016.

28. Lupus Foundation of America: Lab tests for lupus? Retrieved from *https://resources.lupus.org/entry/lab-tests.*

29. Scleroderma Foundation: *What is scleroderma?* Retrieved from *www.scleroderma.org/site/PageNavigator/patients_whatis.html#.W4nYpLgnZPY.*

30. Jimenez SA: Scleroderma. Retrieved from *https://emedicine.medscape.com/article/331864.overview.*

31. The Johns Hopkins Scleroderma Center: Scleroderma treatment options. Retrieved from *www.hopkinsscleroderma.org/patients/scleroderma-treatment-options/.*

32. National Organization for Rare Disorders: Polymyositis. Retrieved from *https://rarediseases.org/rare-diseases/polymyositis/.*

33. Cleveland Clinic: Mixed connective tissue disease. Retrieved from *https://my.clevelandclinic.org/health/diseases/15039-mixed-connective-tissue-disease.*

*34. Papageorgiou A, Ziogas DZ, Mavragani CP, et al: Predicting the outcome of Sjögren's syndrome-associated non-Hodgkin's lymphoma patients, *PLosONE* 10:e0116189, 2015.

35. Mayo Clinic: Myofascial pain syndrome. Retrieved from *www.mayoclinic.org/diseases-conditions/myofascial-pain-syndrome/diagnosis-treatment/drc-20375450.*

36. Arthritis Foundation: What is fibromyalgia? Retrieved from *www.arthritis.org/about-arthritis/types/fibromyalgia/what-is-fibromyalgia.php.*

37. Wolfe F, Smythe HA, Yunus MB, et al: The American College of Rheumatology 1990 criteria for the classification of fibromyalgia, *Arthr Rheum* 33:160, 1990. (Classic)

38. Wolfe F, Clauw DJ, Fitzcharles MA, et al: 2016 Revisions to the 2010/2011 fibromyalgia diagnostic criteria, *Semin Arthritis Rheum* 46:319, 2016.

39. Institute of Medicine of the National Academies: Beyond myalgic encephalomyelitis/chronic fatigue syndrome: Redefining an illness. Retrieved from *www.nationalacademies.org/hmd/~/media/Files/Report%20Files/2015/MECFS/MECFScliniciansguide.pdf.*

*Evidence-based information for clinical practice.

CASE STUDY

Managing Care of Multiple Patients

You are working on the medical-surgical unit and have been assigned to care for the following 5 patients. You have 1 LPN/VN and 1 UAP on your team to help you.

Patients

J.K. is a 57-yr-old white woman who had debulking surgery for a temporal-parietal glioblastoma. Her MRI/MRA showed a temporal-parietal glioblastoma that extended into the occipital lobes. 4 days ago, she had a hemorrhagic stroke into the site of the tumor bed extending into the thalamus. She now has left homonymous hemianopsia and left-sided weakness.

© iStockphoto/Thinkstock.

J.P. is a 24-yr-old woman who fell and hit her head during a tonic-clonic seizure. Her boyfriend found her lying unconscious on the floor of her apartment. She had an emergency evacuation of a subdural hematoma and was initially in the ICU. She was transferred to the medical-surgical unit yesterday and is scheduled for a rehabilitation evaluation. She is oriented to person only and is somewhat restless. A safety sitter is at the bedside at all times.

© Purestock/Thinkstock.

M.Y., an 78-yr-old Asian American man, had an ORIF 2 days ago for a fractured left hip. He has a 3-yr history of Alzheimer's disease and is confused to place and time. He has been pleasant and cooperative. He has a personal alarm and bed alarm on for safety. His hip dressing is dry and intact and the drainage in the Hemovac drain is minimal.

© iStockphoto/Thinkstock.

S.W., an 18-yr-old woman, sustained a C5 cervical spinal cord injury when she dove into the shallow end of a pool and struck her head on the bottom. She was initially placed in cervical traction, intubated, and mechanically ventilated. She has since undergone surgical stabilization and the traction was removed. After spending 1 week in an inpatient SCI rehabilitation facility, she was transferred to the medical-surgical unit this morning with severe headache, blurred vision, and nausea.

© iStockphoto/Thinkstock.

M.C. is a 64-yr-old white man who had a right femoral fracture of the greater trochanter after falling while gardening. He previously had both hips replaced. He had surgery 4 days ago to repair the femoral component of his right total hip replacement. Discharge home is planned today.

© aronaze/iStock.com.

Discussion Questions

1. **Priority Decision:** After receiving report, which patient should you see first? Provide a rationale.
2. **Collaboration:** Which tasks could you delegate to UAP? *(select all that apply)*
   a. Explain discharge instructions to M.C.
   b. Change the dressing on M.Y.'s left hip.
   c. Obtain vital signs on M.C. before discharge.
   d. Sit with J.P. while the safety sitter takes a break.
   e. Assess J.K.'s ability to swallow before feeding her breakfast.

3. **Priority and Collaboration:** When you enter the room to assess S.W., you find her diaphoretic with a flushed face and pale extremities. Her BP is 200/102 mm Hg. Which 2 initial actions would be *most* appropriate?
   a. Ask the UAP to obtain a stat bladder scan.
   b. Have the LPN administer her oral antihypertensive meds stat.
   c. Elevate the head of the bed while assessing for any noxious stimuli.
   d. Ask the LPN to stay with S.W. while you stat page S.W.'s provider.
   e. Insert rectal suppository after applying lidocaine to the area around the rectum.

Case Study Progression

S.W.'s bladder scan showed 700 mL of urine. After you have the LPN catheterize her using a local anesthetic gel, her symptoms subside. You take this time to further teach S.W. about the manifestations of autonomic dysreflexia and the need to report any symptom as soon as it appears. You discuss bladder training strategies and how to avoid bladder distention. S.W. is grateful for the information and your caring attitude. Just as you are finishing, the UAP tells you that M.Y. has pulled out his Hemovac drain.

4. What should be your *initial* intervention for M.Y.?
   a. Reinsert the Hemovac drain.
   b. Assess the incision site for a hematoma.
   c. Notify M.Y.'s provider that the drain was removed.
   d. Apply pressure to the incisional site where the drain had been placed.
5. Which intervention would be *most* appropriate in caring for J.K.?
   a. Place her left arm in a sling for support.
   b. Arrange the food tray so that all foods are on the right side.
   c. Position her left leg so that the ankle is lower than the knee.
   d. Call the provider to get an order of warfarin to prevent VTE.
6. When teaching J.P.'s boyfriend about what to expect during recovery from a head injury, which statement is *most* accurate?
   a. "You can tell by how great she looks physically that she will ultimately function well at the home."
   b. "One good thing that will come out of this injury is that her seizures should occur less frequently."
   c. "Most patients are transferred out of the hospital for acute rehabilitation management to prepare them for going home."
   d. "She can expect a full recovery without any chronic problems, but it may take a few months to achieve that goal."
7. **Priority Decision:** You receive the morning laboratory data. Which finding should you report to the provider immediately?
   a. J.K. has a platelet level of 170,000 μ/L.
   b. M.C.'s INR after his first dose of warfarin is 1.4.
   c. M.Y.'s WBC has increased from 7000 yesterday to 10,800.
   d. S.W. who is receiving enteral nutrition, has a glucose level of 142 mg/dL.
8. **Management Decision:** As you enter M.C.'s room to discuss his discharge plans, you find him all packed up and ready to go. He tells you the UAP already told him what he needed to do. What is your *best* initial action?
   a. Ask M.C. if he has any further questions.
   b. Call the UAP to M.C.'s room to find out what she told him.
   c. Review discharge instructions with M.C. to ascertain correct understanding.
   d. Give M.C. a telephone number to call in case he has any concerns when he gets home.

Answers and rationales available at *http://evolve.elsevier.com/Lewis/medsurg*.

65

Critical Care

Megan Ann Brissie

Those who are happiest are those who do the most for others.

Booker T. Washington

http://evolve.elsevier.com/Lewis/medsurg

CONCEPTUAL FOCUS

Cognition	Perfusion	Sleep
Gas Exchange	Sensory Perception	Technology and Informatics
Nutrition		

LEARNING OUTCOMES

1. Discuss the various certification opportunities for critical care registered nurses.
2. Select appropriate nursing interventions to manage common problems and needs of critically ill patients.
3. Develop strategies to manage issues related to caregivers of critically ill patients.
4. Apply the principles of hemodynamic monitoring to the nursing and interprofessional management of patients receiving monitoring.
5. Discern the purpose of, indications for, and function of circulatory assist devices and related nursing and interprofessional management.
6. Distinguish the indications for and modes of mechanical ventilation.
7. Select appropriate nursing interventions related to the care of an intubated patient.
8. Relate the principles of mechanical ventilation to the nursing and interprofessional management of patients receiving this intervention.

KEY TERMS

arterial pressure–based cardiac output (APCO), p. 1541
assist-control ventilation (ACV), p. 1554
circulatory assist devices (CADs), p. 1545
continuous positive airway pressure (CPAP), p. 1547
endotracheal (ET) intubation, p. 1548

hemodynamic monitoring, p. 1537
high-frequency oscillatory ventilation (HFOV), p. 1557
intraaortic balloon pump (IABP), p. 1545
mechanical ventilation, p. 1553
negative pressure ventilation, p. 1553
positive end-expiratory pressure (PEEP), p. 1556

positive pressure ventilation (PPV), p. 1553
pressure support ventilation (PSV), p. 1556
synchronized intermittent mandatory ventilation (SIMV), p. 1556
ventricular assist device (VAD), p. 1547
volume ventilation, p. 1553
weaning, p. 1561

This chapter focuses on the role of the critical care registered nurse (RN) in the management of critically ill patients in an intensive care setting. The chapter reviews concepts related to cardiovascular and respiratory dynamics that support perfusion and gas exchange. We emphasize the interprofessional care and nursing management of ill patients requiring advanced care modalities. These include hemodynamic monitoring, circulatory assist devices (CADs), artificial airways, and mechanical ventilation.

CRITICAL CARE NURSING

The American Association of Critical-Care Nurses (AACN) defines *critical care nursing* as a specialty that manages human responses to life-threatening problems.[1] Critical care RNs care for patients with acute and unstable physiologic problems and their caregivers. This involves assessing life-threatening conditions, starting appropriate interventions, evaluating the outcomes of interventions, and providing teaching and emotional support to caregivers.

Critical Care Units

Critical care units (CCUs) or *intensive care units* (ICUs) are designed to meet the special needs of acutely and critically ill patients. In many hospitals, the concept of ICU care has expanded from delivering care in a standard unit to bringing care to patients wherever they may be. For example, the *electronic* or *teleICU* helps the bedside ICU team by monitoring the patient from a remote location (Fig. 65.1).

FIG. 65.1 eICU team members monitor patients from a remote site. (From Amelung PJ, Doerfler, ME: VISICU and the e ICU Program. In Le Roux PD, Levine J, Kofke WA: *Monitoring in neurocritical care,* St Louis, 2013, Elsevier.)

Similarly, *rapid response teams* (RRTs) deliver advanced care by an interprofessional team. The team is usually composed of a critical care RN, critical care physician or an advanced practice registered nurse (APRN), and a respiratory therapist (RT). RRTs bring rapid and immediate care to unstable patients in noncritical care settings. Patients often show early and subtle signs of deterioration (e.g., mild confusion, tachypnea, vital sign changes) 6 to 8 hours before cardiac or respiratory arrest. RRT intervention has made significant advances in reducing mortality rates in these patients.[2]

The technology available in the ICU is extensive and always evolving. It is possible to continuously monitor a patient's electrocardiogram (ECG), BP, O_2 saturation, cardiac output (CO), intracranial pressure (ICP), and temperature. Advanced monitoring devices can measure cardiac index (CI), stroke volume (SV), stroke volume variation (SVV), ejection fraction (EF), end-tidal carbon dioxide ($EtCO_2$), and O_2 consumption. Patients may receive ongoing support from mechanical ventilators, intraaortic balloon pumps (IABPs), CADs, or dialysis machines.

Progressive care units (PCUs), also called *intermediate care* or *step-down units,* are a transition between the ICU and the general unit. Generally, PCU patients are at risk for serious complications, but their risk is lower than that of ICU patients. Examples of patients in PCUs include those scheduled for interventional heart procedures (e.g., stent placement), awaiting heart transplant, receiving stable doses of vasoactive IV drugs (e.g., diltiazem [Cardizem]), being weaned from prolonged mechanical ventilation, or who recently had tracheostomy placement. Monitoring capabilities in PCUs may include continuous ECG, arterial BP, O_2 saturation, and $EtCO_2$.

Critical Care Registered Nurse

A critical care RN has in-depth knowledge of anatomy, physiology, pathophysiology, and pharmacology; advanced assessment skills; and the ability to use advanced technology. As a critical care RN, you perform frequent assessments to monitor trends in the patient's physiologic parameters (e.g., BP, ECG, O_2 saturation). This allows you to rapidly recognize and manage complications while aiding healing and recovery. You provide psychologic support to the patient and/or caregiver. To be effective, you must be able to communicate and collaborate with all interprofessional team members.

As a critical care RN, you will face ethical dilemmas related to the care of your patients. Moral distress over perceived issues

of delivering futile or nonbeneficial care can lead to emotional exhaustion or burnout. Consequently, it is important that all members of the interprofessional care team coexist in a healthy work environment.

Specialization in critical care nursing requires a preceptored clinical orientation, often over several months. The AACN Certification Corporation offers (1) critical care certification (CCRN) in direct care adult, pediatric, and neonatal critical care nursing; (2) progressive care certification (PCCN); (3) critical care certification knowledge (CCRN-K) or progressive care certification knowledge (PCCN-K) for those who do not provide direct care but influence care delivery in their role; and (4) teleICU certification (CCRN-E). Other certifications are available in cardiac medicine (CMC) and cardiac surgery (CSC). Certification requires RN licensure, practice experience in the related area, and successful completion of a written test. It validates basic knowledge of critical or progressive care nursing.

APRNs in critical care function in a variety of roles: patient and staff educators, consultants, administrators, researchers, or expert practitioners.[3] The APRN who is a clinical nurse specialist (CNS) typically provides advanced nursing care to meet the needs of adult-gerontology, pediatric, or neonatal patient populations. Certification for the CNS in acute and critical care is available through the AACN.

Another APRN role is the adult-gerontology acute care nurse practitioner (AG-ACNP). This APRN provides comprehensive care to select critically ill patients and their caregivers. The AG-ACNP conducts comprehensive assessments, orders and interprets diagnostic tests, manages health problems, prescribes treatments, and coordinates care among interprofessional care teams and during transitions in care settings. Certification as an AG-ACNP is available through the AACN. Prescriptive authority and licensure regulations for APRNs vary by state.

Critical Care Patient

A critically ill patient is one whose need for care is acute in nature, requiring intense and vigilant nursing care. A patient is generally admitted to the ICU for 1 of 3 reasons. First, the patient may be physiologically unstable, requiring advanced clinical judgments by you or another HCP. Second, the patient may be at risk for serious complications and need frequent assessments and often invasive interventions. Third, the patient may need intensive and complicated nursing support related to the use of IV medications (e.g., sedation, drugs requiring titration [e.g., vasopressors], or thrombolytics) and advanced technology (e.g., hemodynamic monitoring, mechanical ventilation, continuous renal replacement therapy [CRRT], ICP monitoring). The incidence of death is higher in ICU patients than in non-ICU patients. In general, nonsurvivors are older, have co-morbidities (e.g., liver disease, obesity), and have longer ICU stays.

ICU patients may be clustered by disease condition (e.g., cardiology, burns, neurology) or age-group (e.g., neonatal, pediatrics, adult). Those with medical emergencies (e.g., sepsis, diabetic ketoacidosis, drug overdoses) are treated in a medical ICU. Sometimes we cluster patients by acuity (e.g., critical and unstable versus chronic but technology dependent and stable). Patients commonly treated in the ICU include those with respiratory failure, myocardial infarction (MI), or acute neurologic impairment or those requiring care after major surgery (e.g., heart or brain surgery, organ transplantation). Fig. 65.2 shows a typical ICU bed with monitors.

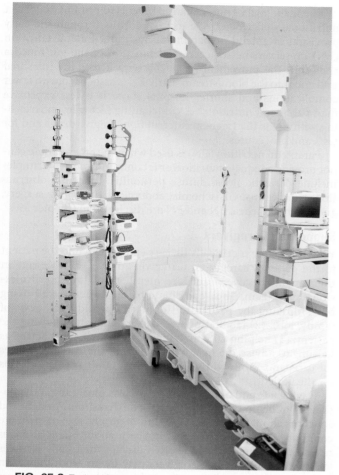

FIG. 65.2 Typical ICU bed with monitors. (© danutela/iStock.com.)

The patient who we do not expect to recover from an illness is usually not admitted to an ICU. For example, the ICU is not typically used to care for the patient in a persistent, vegetative state or to prolong the natural process of death. ICUs will manage patients who have brain death or who meet criteria for donation after cardiac death to optimize the opportunity for organ donation. Sometimes patients may be managed in the ICU to allow for end-of-life decisions or transitions of care to occur in a private, dignified setting. So, it is important that critical care RNs are skilled in palliative and end-of-life care (see Chapter 9).

Common Problems of Critical Care Patients. The patient in the ICU is at risk for many complications and special problems. Critically ill patients are often intubated and mechanically ventilated, immobile, and at high risk for skin problems (see Chapter 23) and venous thromboembolism (VTE) (see Chapter 37). The use of multiple, invasive devices predisposes the patient to health care–associated infections (HAIs). Sepsis and multiple organ dysfunction syndrome (MODS) may follow (see Chapter 66). Other special problems relate to anxiety, pain, impaired communication, sensory-perceptual problems, sleep, and nutrition.

Anxiety. Anxiety is a common problem for ICU patients. The main sources of anxiety include the perceived or expected threat to health or life, loss of control of body functions, and a foreign environment. Many patients and caregivers feel uncomfortable in the ICU with its complex equipment, high noise and light levels, and intense pace of activity. Pain, impaired communication, sleeplessness, immobilization, and loss of control all enhance anxiety.

To help reduce anxiety, have patients and caregivers express concerns, ask questions, and state their needs. Include them in all conversations and explain the purpose of equipment and procedures. Structure the patient's environment in a way that decreases anxiety. For example, encourage caregivers to bring in photographs and personal items. Antianxiety drugs (e.g., lorazepam [Ativan]) and relaxation techniques (e.g., music therapy) may reduce the stress response that anxiety can trigger.

Pain. The control of pain in the ICU patient is very important. Unrelieved pain is common among ICU patients and can lead to poor outcomes.[4] Inadequate pain control is linked with agitation, fear, and anxiety and adds to the stress response. ICU patients at high risk for pain include those who (1) have medical conditions that include ischemic, infectious, or inflammatory processes; (2) are immobilized; (3) have invasive monitoring devices, including endotracheal tubes (ETs); and (4) undergo procedures.

For many critically ill patients (e.g., those intubated), continuous IV sedation (e.g., propofol [Diprivan]) and an analgesic agent (e.g., fentanyl) are used for sedation and pain control. However, patients getting deep sedation are often unresponsive. This prevents you and other HCPs from fully assessing the patient's neurologic status. To address this issue, all patients who can safely tolerate an interruption in sedation usually receive a daily, scheduled interruption of sedation, or "sedation holiday." These allow you to awaken the patient to conduct a neurologic examination.[5] Pain management is discussed in Chapter 8.

Impaired Communication. Inability to communicate is distressing for patients who cannot speak because of sedative and paralyzing drugs, an ET, or the inability to communicate from a neurologic impairment. As part of every procedure, explain what will happen or is happening to the patient. When the patient cannot speak, explore other methods of communication, such as picture boards, notepads, magic slates, or computers. When speaking with the patient, look directly at the patient and use hand gestures when appropriate. For those who do not speak English, you must use an approved interpreter or interpreter phone service when providing care or instructions (see Chapter 2).

Nonverbal communication is important. High levels of procedure-related touch and lower levels of comfort-related touch often characterize the ICU environment. Patients have different levels of tolerance for being touched, usually related to culture and personal history. If appropriate, use comforting touch with ongoing evaluation of the patient's response. Encourage the caregiver to talk to the patient, even if the patient is intubated, is sedated, or appears comatose. Hearing is often the last sense to decrease. Even if the patient cannot respond, they may still be able to hear.

Sleep. Nearly all ICU patients have sleep problems. Patients may have difficulty falling asleep or have disrupted sleep because of noise, anxiety, pain, frequent monitoring, treatments, or care needs. Sleep problems can cause delirium and delayed recovery.

Arrange the environment to promote the patient's sleep-wake cycle. Measures include scheduling rest periods, bundling care, limiting noise and visitors, getting physiologic measurements without disturbing the patient, opening curtains during the daytime and dimming lights at nighttime, providing eye masks/ear plugs to encourage sleep, and providing comfort measures (e.g., massage).[6] If needed, use benzodiazepines (e.g., temazepam), benzodiazepine-like drugs (e.g., zolpidem [Ambien]), or natural hormones (e.g., melatonin), especially for an older adult, to aid and maintain sleep. Promoting sleep is discussed in Chapter 7.

Sensory-Perceptual Problems. Acute and reversible sensory-perceptual changes are common in ICU patients. We used to call the combination of changes in mentation (e.g., delusions, short attention span, loss of recent memory), psychomotor behavior (e.g., restlessness, lethargy), and sleep-wake cycle (e.g., daytime sleepiness, nighttime agitation) *ICU psychosis.* The patient with these changes is not psychotic but has *delirium.* Delirium is an acute change in mental status. The prevalence of delirium in ICU patients is as high as 87%.[7] It is associated with longer hospital stays and higher mortality rates.

Major risk factors for delirium include increased age, pre-existing dementia, hypertension, alcohol use, and severe illness on admission. Environmental factors that can contribute to delirium include sleep deprivation, anxiety, sensory overload, and immobilization. Physical conditions such as hemodynamic instability, hypoxemia, electrolyte imbalances, and severe infections can lead to delirium. Last, certain drugs (e.g., sedatives [benzodiazepines], analgesics [opioids], vasopressors) are linked with delirium. Chapter 59 discusses delirium.

Monitor all ICU patients for delirium using a valid tool and initiate prevention strategies. Assessment tools for adult ICU patients include the Confusion Assessment Method for the ICU (CAM-ICU) (see Table 59.18) and the Intensive Care Delirium Screening Checklist (ICDSC). It is critical to address physiologic factors (e.g., correction of oxygenation, perfusion, electrolyte problems). Clocks and calendars can help orient the patient. Reorient patients who are confused during assessments to provide comfort and direction. The presence of a caregiver may help. Removing lines no longer needed and early mobility are effective.[8] If the patient has hyperactivity, insomnia, or delusions, treatment with sedative drugs with anxiolytic effects (e.g., dexmedetomidine [Precedex]) can be used.

Sensory overload can result in patient distress and anxiety. Environmental noise levels are high in the ICU. Help the patient understand we cannot prevent noise. Conversation is an especially stressful noise, especially when the discussion concerns the patient and is held in the presence of, but without participation from, the patient. Reduce this source of stress by finding suitable places for patient-related discussions. Whenever possible, include the patient and caregiver in the discussion.

You can limit noise levels by muting phones, setting alarms based on the patient's condition, and reducing unnecessary alarms. For example, silence the BP alarm when handling invasive lines and then reset the alarm when done. Similarly, silence ventilator alarms when suctioning. Last, limit overhead paging and all unnecessary noise in patient care areas.

Nutrition. Patients often arrive at ICUs with conditions that result in either hypermetabolic states (e.g., burns, sepsis) or catabolic states (e.g., acute kidney injury). Other times, patients are in severely malnourished states (e.g., chronic heart, lung, or liver disease). In general, inadequate nutrition increases mortality and morbidity rates. Determining whom to feed, what to feed, when to feed, and how to feed (e.g., route of administration) is crucial when caring for critically ill patients.[9] Collaborate with the HCP and dietitian to decide how best to meet the nutritional needs of the ICU patient.

The main goal of nutritional support is to prevent or correct nutritional deficiencies. We usually do this through the early provision of enteral or parenteral nutrition. Enteral nutrition (EN) preserves the structure and function of the gut mucosa and stops the movement of gut bacteria across the intestinal wall and into the bloodstream. Early EN is associated with fewer complications and shorter hospital stays. It is less expensive than parenteral nutrition.[9] A contributing factor to underfeeding with EN is the frequent interruptions to give drugs and for tests and procedures.

Parenteral nutrition (PN) is used when the enteral route cannot provide adequate nutrition or is contraindicated.[9] Examples include paralytic ileus, diffuse peritonitis, intestinal obstruction, pancreatitis, GI ischemia, abdominal trauma or surgery, and severe diarrhea. EN and PN are discussed in Chapter 39.

Supporting Caregivers

When someone is critically ill, care extends beyond the patient to the patient's caregivers. Caregivers play a valuable role in the patient's recovery and are members of the interprofessional care team. They contribute to the patient's well-being by (1) linking the patient to the outside world (e.g., news of family, job); (2) facilitating decision making and advising the patient; (3) helping with activities of daily living; (4) acting as liaisons to advise the health care team of the patient's wishes for care; and (5) providing safe, caring, familiar relationships for the patient.

Having a friend or relative in the ICU is physically and emotionally difficult, often to the point of exhaustion. Anxiety and concerns about the patient's condition, prognosis, and pain are common. Caregivers may have concern about financial issues related to hospital stay. They often disrupt their daily routines to support the patient. Caregivers may be far from their own home, friends, and relatives. Consulting with the case manager or social worker is helpful in these instances.

Caregivers of the critically ill are in crisis, and family-centered care is essential. Caregivers need your guidance and support. You must be skilled in crisis intervention to provide effective family-centered care. Conduct a family assessment and intervene as needed. Strategies include active listening, reduction of anxiety, and support for those who become upset or angry. Recognize the caregivers' feelings, listen to them openly and without being judgmental, and acknowledge their decisions. Consult other team members (e.g., chaplains, psychologists, patient representatives) as needed to help caregivers cope.

The major needs of caregivers of critically ill patients include information, communication, and access.[10] Lack of information is a major source of anxiety. Assess their understanding of the patient's status, treatment plan, and prognosis and provide information as appropriate. Identify a spokesperson to help coordinate information exchange between the interprofessional care team and caregivers.

Holding routine interprofessional conferences with caregivers improves satisfaction with communication and trust in clinicians and reduces conflict between clinicians and family members.[10] Have them meet the interprofessional care team. Include them in rounds and patient care conferences. It helps caregivers accept and cope with problems when they see that the team is caring and competent, decisions are deliberate, and their input is valued. If the patient has an advance directive, the caregiver needs to see that the patient's wishes are followed. If the patient has a durable power of attorney for health care, this person must be involved in the patient's plan of care.

Caregivers need access to the patient. The AACN strongly recommends less restrictive and more individualized visiting policies. Achieve this goal by assessing the patient's and caregiver's needs and preferences and incorporating these into the patient's plan of care.

ETHICAL/LEGAL DILEMMAS
Visitation and Caregiver Presence in the Adult ICU

Situation
B.W., a new RN, is undergoing orientation in the surgical ICU. He asks his preceptor why the patients' families are allowed on the unit throughout the day and even the night. B.W. states that, in his last position, visiting hours in the ICU were 10 AM to 12 PM and 4 PM to 6 PM. He adds that families make him nervous when they watch what he is doing and ask him many questions. B.W. says that he plans to tell the visitors to leave the patient's room when he is giving care.

Ethical/Legal Points for Consideration
- We used to think that visitation caused the patient stress, interfered with care, was mentally exhausting to patients and caregivers, and contributed to increased infection rates. Evidence does not support any of these beliefs.[1,2]
- Evidence suggests several positive benefits of flexible visitation for the patient: decreased anxiety, confusion, and agitation; fewer cardiovascular complications; shorter ICU length of stay; and reports that patients feel more secure and satisfied with care.[1]
- Similar evidence exists for the benefits of flexible visitation for caregivers: increased satisfaction, decreased anxiety, better communication, and increased opportunities for patient and caregiver teaching as caregivers are more involved in care.[1]
- Some conditions may require restricting visitation: a documented legal reason; visitor behavior presents a risk to the patient, staff, or others; visitor behavior disrupts the functioning of the unit; visitor has a contagious illness or has been exposed to a contagious disease that could endanger the patient's health; or the patient requests fewer or no visitors.

Discussion Questions
1. How should the preceptor respond to B.W.'s statement of his intentions?
2. Does B.W. have an ethical or legal obligation to allow visitation regardless of his personal concerns? Defend your position.

References
1. Davidson JE, Aslakson RA, Long AC, et al.: Guidelines for family-centered care in the neonatal, pediatric, and adult ICU, *CCM* 45:103, 2017.
2. Clark AP, Guzzetta CE: A paradigm shift for patient/family-centered care in intensive care units: Bring in the family, *Crit Care Nurse* 37(96), 2017.

The first time that caregivers visit, it is important for you to prepare them for the experience. Briefly describe the patient's appearance and physical environment (e.g., equipment, noise). Join caregivers as they enter the room. Observe the responses of the patient and caregivers. Invite the caregivers to take part in the patient's care if they want. Be prepared that people may respond differently to seeing their loved one in the ICU for the first time.

In some ICUs, visitation includes animal-assisted therapy or pet visitation, most often therapy dogs. The positive benefits (e.g., decreases in BP and anxiety) far outweigh the risks (e.g.,

transmission of infection from animal to patient). Pet therapy should be a part of the ICUs visitation policy.

Caregivers should also have the option to be present at the bedside when patients are undergoing invasive procedures (e.g., central line insertion) or cardiopulmonary resuscitation (CPR). Even when the outcomes are not favorable, being present helps caregivers to (1) overcome doubts about the patient's condition, (2) reduce their anxiety and fear, (3) meet their need to be together with and to support their loved one, and (4) begin the grief process if death occurs. Be a part of initiatives to develop policies and procedures that offer the option of caregiver presence during invasive procedures and CPR.[11]

Culturally Competent Care: Critical Care Patients

Providing culturally competent care to critically ill patients and caregivers can be challenging. Often, meeting the patient's physiologic needs is a priority and overshadows the influence of the patient's culture on the illness experience. It is important to consider the cultural aspects of the meaning of sickness and health, pain, dying and death, and grief when caring for critically ill patients and their caregivers (see Chapter 2).

Cultural perspectives on dying and death are complex. Some view a discussion about advance directives as a legal way to withhold, withdraw, or deny care. Customs surrounding dying and death vary. Caregiver requests may range from asking you to leave a window open so that the spirit of the deceased can leave to giving the final bath for the deceased. Ask caregivers about their cultural traditions when caring for the dying patient.

Several variables influence the expressions of grief that follow the loss of a loved one. These include the relationship between the grieving person and the deceased, whether the loss is sudden or expected, the support systems available to the grieving person, past experiences with loss, and the person's religious and cultural beliefs. Proceed cautiously when approaching patients facing death and their caregivers. Asking patients, "What do you want to know?" and "Who do you want with you when discussing options?" are good starting points. Chapter 9 provides detailed information about end-of-life care.

HEMODYNAMIC MONITORING

Hemodynamic monitoring is the measurement of pressure, flow, and oxygenation within the cardiovascular system. The purpose of hemodynamic monitoring is to assess heart function, fluid balance, and the effects of fluids and drugs on CO. Both invasive (internally placed devices) and noninvasive (externally placed devices) obtain hemodynamic parameters (values). These include systemic and pulmonary arterial pressures, central venous pressure (CVP), pulmonary artery wedge pressure (PAWP) (also known as pulmonary artery occlusive pressure [PAOP]), CO/CI, SV/SV index (SVI), SVV, O_2 saturation of the hemoglobin of arterial blood (SaO_2), and mixed venous O_2 saturation (SvO_2).

From these measurements, you can calculate several values. These include the resistance of the systemic and pulmonary arterial vasculature and O_2 content, delivery, and consumption. When you combine these data, you get a picture of the patient's hemodynamic status and the effect of therapy over time (trends). Take all measurements with attention to accuracy. Inaccurate data can result in unnecessary or inappropriate treatment.

Hemodynamic Terminology

Cardiac Output and Cardiac Index. *Cardiac output* (CO) is the volume of blood in liters pumped by the heart in 1 minute. *Cardiac index* (CI) is the measurement of CO adjusted for body surface area (BSA). It is a more precise measurement of the efficiency of the heart's pumping action. Although minor beat-to-beat variations may occur, the left and right ventricles pump the same volume. The volume ejected with each heartbeat is the SV. Like CI, *stroke volume index* (SVI) is the measurement of SV adjusted for BSA.

CO and the forces opposing blood flow determine BP. *Systemic vascular resistance* (SVR) (opposition encountered by the left ventricle) or *pulmonary vascular resistance* (PVR) (opposition encountered by the right ventricle) is the resistance to blood flow by the vessels. Preload, afterload, and contractility determine SV, and thus CO (see Chapter 31). It is essential that you understand these concepts and the physiologic effects of manipulating each of these variables. Table 65.1 presents the formulas and values for common hemodynamic parameters.

Preload. *Preload* is the volume within the ventricle at the end of diastole. Unfortunately, chamber volume measurements are hard to obtain. Instead, we use various pressures to estimate the volume. Left ventricular preload is called *left ventricular end-diastolic pressure.* PAWP, a measurement of pulmonary capillary pressure, reflects left ventricular end-diastolic pressure under normal conditions (i.e., when there is no mitral valve dysfunction, intracardiac defect, or dysrhythmia). CVP is measured in the right atrium or in the vena cava close to the heart. It is the right ventricular preload or right ventricular end-diastolic pressure when there is no tricuspid valve dysfunction, intracardiac defect, or dysrhythmia.

Frank-Starling's law explains the effects of preload. It says that the more a myocardial fiber is stretched during filling, the more it shortens during systole and the greater the force of the contraction. As preload increases, force generated in the subsequent contraction increases and SV and CO increase. The greater the preload, the greater the myocardial stretch and the greater the myocardial O_2 requirement. Thus increases in CO from increased preload require increased delivery of O_2 to the myocardium. The clinical measurement made is not a direct measurement of the muscle length. The measurement is of the pressure at the time of the peak stretch (end diastole) (Table 65.1). This pressure indirectly indicates the amount of stretch and the volume. It is also important because it indicates pressure

in the blood vessels of the lungs or in the blood returning to the heart. Diuresis and vasodilation decrease preload. Fluid administration increases preload.

Afterload. *Afterload* refers to the forces opposing ventricular ejection. These forces include systemic arterial pressure, the resistance offered by the aortic valve, and the mass and density of the blood. SVR and arterial pressure are indices of left ventricular afterload, though clinically they do not include all the components of afterload. Similarly, PVR and pulmonary arterial pressure are indices of right ventricular afterload. Increased afterload often results in a decreased CO and increased O_2 demand. CO can be improved and myocardial O_2 needs reduced by decreasing afterload (i.e., decreasing forces opposing contraction). For example, vasodilator drug therapy (e.g., milrinone) can reduce afterload.

Vascular Resistance. SVR is the resistance of the systemic vascular bed. PVR is the resistance of the pulmonary vascular bed. Both these measures reflect afterload as described earlier and can be adjusted for body size (Table 65.1).

Contractility. *Contractility* describes the strength of contraction. Contractility increases when preload is unchanged and the heart contracts more forcefully. Epinephrine, norepinephrine, isoproterenol (Isuprel), dopamine, dobutamine, digitalis-like drugs, calcium, and milrinone increase or improve contractility. We call these drugs *positive inotropes.* Increased contractility results in increased SV and increased myocardial O_2 requirements. *Negative inotropes* reduce contractility. These include certain drugs (e.g., calcium channel blockers, β-adrenergic blockers) and clinical conditions (e.g., acidosis).

There are no direct clinical measures of cardiac contractility. Measuring the patient's preload (PAWP) and CO and graphing the results indirectly indicate contractility. If preload, heart rate (HR), and afterload remain constant and CO changes, contractility is changed. Contractility is reduced in the failing heart.

Principles of Invasive Pressure Monitoring

Invasive lines are used in the ICU to measure systemic and pulmonary BPs. Fig. 65.3 shows the parts of a typical invasive arterial BP monitoring system. The catheter, pressure tubing, flush system, and transducer are disposable.

Pressure monitoring equipment is referenced and zero balanced to the environment, and dynamic response characteristics are optimized for accuracy.[12] *Referencing* means placing the transducer so that the zero-reference point is at the level of the atria of the heart. The stopcock nearest the transducer is used for the zero reference. To place this level with the atria, use an external landmark, the phlebostatic axis. To find the *phlebostatic axis,* draw 2 imaginary lines with the patient supine (Fig. 65.4, *A*). Draw a horizontal line down from the axilla, midway between the anterior and posterior chest walls. Draw a vertical line laterally through the fourth intercostal space along the chest wall. The phlebostatic axis is the intersection of the 2 imaginary lines. Mark this location on the patient's chest with a permanent marker. Position the port of the stopcock nearest the transducer level at the phlebostatic axis. Tape the transducer to the patient's chest at the phlebostatic axis or ideally mount it on a bedside pole (Fig. 65.4, *B*).

Zeroing confirms that when pressure within the system is zero, the monitor reads 0. To do this, open the reference stopcock to room air (off to the patient) and observe the monitor for a reading of 0. This allows the monitor to use

TABLE 65.1 Resting Hemodynamic Parameters

Indicators	Normal Range
Preload	
Pulmonary artery diastolic pressure (PADP)	4–12 mm Hg
Pulmonary artery wedge pressure (PAWP) or left atrial pressure (LAP)	6–12 mm Hg
Right atrial pressure (RAP) or central venous pressure (CVP)	2–8 mm Hg
Right ventricular end-diastolic volume $(RVEDV) = \dfrac{\text{Stroke volume (SV)}}{\text{Right ventricular ejection fraction (RVEF)}}$	100–160 mL
Afterload	
$MAP = \dfrac{\text{Systolic blood pressure} + 2\,(\text{Diastolic blood pressure})}{3}^{*}$	70–105 mm Hg
$PAMP = \dfrac{\text{Pulmonary artery styolic pressure (PASP)} + 2PADP}{3}^{*}$	10–20 mm Hg
Pulmonary vascular resistance $(PVR) = \dfrac{(\text{Pulmonary artery pressure [PAMP]} - PAWP) \times 80}{\text{Cardiac output (CO)}}$	<250 dynes/sec/cm^{-5}
Pulmonary vascular resistance index $(PVRI) = \dfrac{[PAMP - PAWP] \times 80}{\text{Cardiac index (CI)}}$	160–380 dynes/sec/cm^{-5}/m^2
Systemic vascular resistance $(SVR) = \dfrac{(\text{Mean arterial pressure [MAP]} - CVP) \times 80}{CO}$	800–1200 dynes/sec/cm^{-5}
Systemic vascular resistance index $(SVRI) = \dfrac{(MAP - CVP) \times 80}{CI}$	1970–2390 dynes/sec/cm^{-5}/m^2
Other	
$CI = \dfrac{CO}{\text{Body surface area (BSA)}}$	2.2–4 L/min/m^2
$CO = SV \times HR$	4–8 L/min
Heart rate	60–100 beats/min
$RVEF = \dfrac{SV}{RVEDV \times 100}$	40%–60%
Stroke volume $= \dfrac{CO}{\text{Heart rate}}$	60–150 mL/beat
Stroke volume index $(SVI) = \dfrac{CI}{\text{Heart rate}}$	30–65 mL/beat/m^2
Stroke volume variation $(SVV) = \dfrac{SV_{max} - SV_{min}}{SV_{mean}}$	<13%
Oxygenation	
Arterial hemoglobin O$_2$ saturation	95%–100%
Mixed venous hemoglobin O$_2$ saturation	60%–80%
Venous hemoglobin O$_2$ saturation	70%

*This formula is an approximation because it does not take into consideration the heart rate. The monitor looks at the area under the pressure curve, as well as the heart rate, to calculate MAP and PAMP.

the atmospheric pressure as a reference for 0. Zero the transducer during the initial setup, immediately after insertion of the arterial line, when the transducer has been disconnected from the pressure cable or the pressure cable has been disconnected from the monitor and when the accuracy of the measurements is questioned. Always follow the manufacturer's guidelines.

Optimizing dynamic response characteristics involves checking that the equipment reproduces, without distortion, a signal that changes rapidly. Perform a *dynamic response test (square wave test)* every 8 to 12 hours, when the system is opened to air, or when you question the accuracy of the measurements. It involves activating the fast flush and checking that the equipment reproduces a distortion-free signal (Fig. 65.5).

! SAFETY ALERT Positioning the Zero Reference Stopcock
- Mark the location of the phlebostatic axis on the patient's chest with a permanent marker.
- Recheck the leveling of the zero-reference stopcock to the phlebostatic axis with any change in the patient's position.
- Transducers placed higher than the phlebostatic axis will produce falsely low BP readings.
- Transducers placed lower than the phlebostatic axis will produce falsely high BP readings.

Types of Invasive Pressure Monitoring

Arterial BP. Continuous arterial BP monitoring is indicated for patients in many situations, including acute hypotension and hypertension, respiratory failure, shock, neurologic injury,

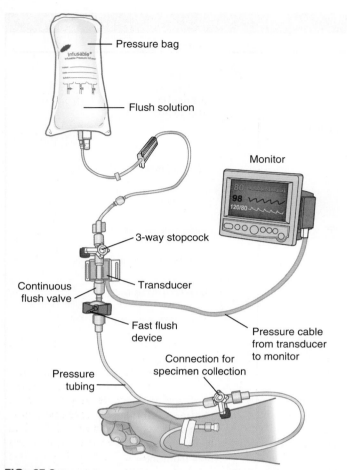

FIG. 65.3 Parts of a pressure monitoring system. The cannula, shown entering the radial artery, is connected via pressure (nondistensible) tubing to the transducer. The transducer converts the pressure wave into an electronic signal. The transducer is wired to the electronic monitoring system, which amplifies, conditions, displays, and records the signal. Stopcocks are inserted into the line for specimen withdrawal and for referencing and zero-balancing procedures. A flush system, consisting of a pressurized bag of IV fluid, tubing, and a flush device, is connected to the system. The flush system provides continuous slow (about 3 mL/hr) flushing and a mechanism for fast flushing of lines.

coronary interventional procedures, continuous infusion of vasoactive drugs (e.g., norepinephrine), and frequent arterial blood gas (ABG) sampling.[12] A nontapered Teflon catheter is typically used to cannulate an artery (e.g., radial, femoral) using a percutaneous approach. After insertion, the HCP usually sutures the catheter in place. You should immobilize the insertion site to prevent dislodging or kinking the catheter line.

Measurements. Use the arterial line to obtain systolic, diastolic, and mean arterial pressure (MAP) (Fig. 65.6). Table 65.2 outlines the steps in obtaining BP measurements with an invasive line. Obtain measurements from both digital and printed analog outputs. Readings from a printed pressure tracing at the end of expiration (to limit the effect of the respiratory cycle on arterial BP) are most accurate. When possible, position the patient supine for initial readings. Values with the head of the bed elevated up to 45 degrees are generally equal to measurements with the patient supine unless the patient's BP is extremely sensitive to orthostatic changes. It is important to keep the zero-reference stopcock level with the phlebostatic axis to ensure accurate continuous measurements.

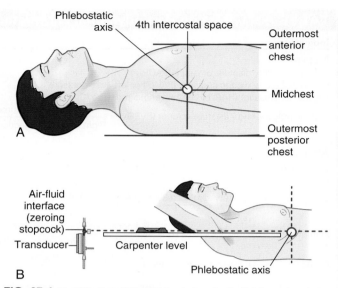

FIG. 65.4 Identification of the phlebostatic axis. A, Phlebostatic axis is an external landmark used to identify the level of the atria in the supine patient. It is defined as the intersection of 2 imaginary lines: 1 drawn horizontally from the axilla, midway between the anterior and posterior chest walls, and the other drawn vertically through the 4th intercostal space along the lateral chest wall. B, Air-fluid interface (zeroing the stopcock) is level with the phlebostatic axis using a carpenter's or laser level.

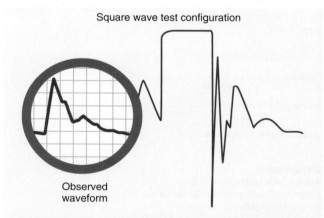

When the fast flush of the continuous flush system is activated and quickly released, a sharp upstroke terminates in a flat line at the maximal indicator on the monitor and hard copy. This is then followed by an immediate rapid downstroke extending below baseline with just 1 or 2 oscillations within 0.12 second (minimal ringing) and a quick return to a baseline. The patient's pressure waveform is also clearly defined with all components of the waveform, such as the dicrotic notch on an arterial waveform, clearly visible.

FIG. 65.5 Optimally damped system. Dynamic response test (square wave test) using the fast flush system: normal response. No adjustment in the monitoring system is needed. (From Darovic GO, Vanriper S, Vanriper J: Fluid-filled monitoring systems. In Darovic GO: *Hemodynamic monitoring,* ed 2, Philadelphia, 1995, Saunders.)

The high- and low-pressure alarms are set based on the patient's status. Various patient conditions will change the pressure tracings. In heart failure (HF), the systolic upstroke may be slower. In volume depletion, systolic pressure varies with mechanical ventilation, decreasing during inspiration. Observe simultaneous ECG and pressure tracings with dysrhythmias.

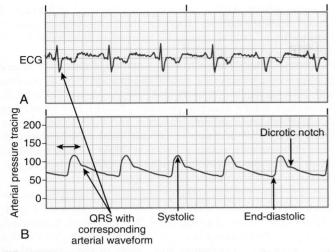

FIG. 65.6 A, Simultaneously recorded ECG tracing. B, Systemic arterial pressure tracing. Systolic pressure is the peak pressure. The *dicrotic notch* indicates aortic valve closure. Diastolic pressure is the lowest value before contraction. Mean pressure is the average pressure over time calculated by the monitoring equipment. (Modified from Urden LD, Stacy KM, Lough ME: *Critical care nursing: Diagnosis and management*, ed 6, St Louis, 2010, Mosby.)

TABLE 65.2 Invasive Arterial Blood Pressure Measurement

1. Explain the procedure to the patient.
2. Position the patient supine and flat or (if appropriate) with the head of the bed less than 45 degrees or prone.
3. Confirm that the zero reference (port of the stopcock nearest the transducer) is at the level of the phlebostatic axis (Fig. 65.4). If the reference stopcock is not taped to the patient's chest, use a leveling device to position the stopcock on a bedside pole at the point level with the phlebostatic axis.
4. Observe the monitor tracing and assess the quality of the tracing. Perform a dynamic response test (Fig. 65.5).
5. Obtain an analog printout (if available) and measure the systolic and diastolic pressures at end expiration (Fig. 65.6). If no printout is available, freeze the tracing on the oscilloscope screen and use the cursor to measure the pressures at end expiration.
6. Record the pressure measurements promptly, including (if available) the printout marked to identify the points read.

Dysrhythmias that significantly decrease arterial BP are more urgent than those that cause only a slight decrease in systolic amplitude.

Complications. Arterial lines carry the risk for hemorrhage, infection, thrombus formation, neurovascular impairment, and loss of limb. Hemorrhage is most likely to occur if the catheter dislodges or the line disconnects. To avoid this complication, use Luer-Lok connections, always check the arterial waveform, and activate alarms. If the pressure in the line falls (e.g., when the line is disconnected), the low-pressure alarm sounds immediately, allowing you to promptly correct the problem.

To limit the risk for catheter-related infection, inspect the insertion site for local signs of inflammation. Monitor the patient for signs of systemic infection. Change the pressure tubing, flush bag, and transducer every 96 hours or according to agency policy. If you suspect infection, notify the HCP, remove the catheter, and replace the equipment.

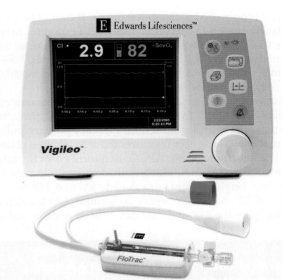

FIG. 65.7 FloTrac sensor and Vigileo monitor. (Courtesy Edwards Lifesciences, Irvine, CA.)

Circulatory impairment can result from formation of a thrombus around the catheter, release of an embolus, spasm, or occlusion of the circulation by the catheter. Before inserting a line into the radial artery, perform an *Allen test* to confirm that ulnar circulation to the hand is adequate. Apply pressure to the radial and ulnar arteries simultaneously. If the patient is able, ask the patient to open and close the hand repeatedly. The hand should blanch. Release the pressure on the ulnar artery while maintaining pressure on the radial artery. If pinkness does not return within 6 seconds, the ulnar artery is not adequate. You should not use the radial artery on that limb for line insertion.

Once the catheter is inserted, assess the neurovascular status distal to the arterial insertion site hourly. The limb with compromised arterial flow will be cool and pale, with capillary refill time longer than 3 seconds. The patient may have symptoms of neurovascular impairment (e.g., paresthesia, pain, paralysis). If present, it can result in the loss of a limb. This, this is an emergency and must be reported to the HCP at once.

To maintain line patency and limit thrombus formation, assess the flush system every 1 to 4 hours to determine that the (1) pressure bag is inflated to 300 mm Hg, (2) flush bag contains fluid, and (3) system is delivering a continuous slow (1 to 3 mL/hr) flush. Follow agency policy for adding heparin to the flush solution.[13]

Arterial Pressure–Based Cardiac Output. Arterial pressure–based cardiac output (APCO) measurement is a minimally invasive technique to determine *continuous CO (CCO)/continuous CI (CCI)*. This technology uses a specialized sensor that attaches to a standard arterial pressure line and a monitor (Fig. 65.7).

APCO can assess a patient's ability to respond to fluids by increasing SV (*preload responsiveness*) (Table 65.1). This is determined by using SVV or by measuring the percent increase in SV after a fluid bolus.[14] SVV is the variation of the arterial pulsation caused by the heart-lung interaction. It is a sensitive indicator of preload responsiveness in certain patients. SVV helps predict whether a patient would benefit from an IV fluid challenge that may help optimize hemodynamic status.

APCO is only used with adult patients. It cannot be used in patients who are on IABP therapy. The APCO monitor may not be able to filter certain dysrhythmias, specifically atrial fibrillation, thus limiting the use of SVV in these patients.[14] SVV is used only with patients on controlled mechanical ventilation with a fixed respiratory rate and a tidal volume (V_T).

Measurements. Arterial pressure is the force generated by the ejection of blood from the left ventricle into the arterial circulation. The heart's contractions (systole) produce pulsatile pressure waves. The sensor measures the arterial pulse pressure, which is proportional to SV. APCO monitoring uses the arterial waveform characteristics, along with demographic data (e.g., gender, age, height, weight) to calculate SV, and HR to calculate CCO/CCI and SV/SVI every 20 seconds. CO is calculated by multiplying the HR and calculated SV. It is displayed on a

continuous basis. APCO monitoring is often used with a central venous oximetry catheter. Together, these allow for continuous monitoring of central venous O_2 saturation ($ScvO_2$) and SVR that is derived from the CVP.

Pulmonary Artery Flow-Directed Catheter. Pulmonary artery (PA) pressure monitoring guides the management of patients with select complicated heart and lung problems (Table 65.3). Pulmonary artery diastolic pressure (PADP) and PAWP are sensitive indicators of heart function and fluid volume status. PADP and PAWP increase in HF and fluid volume overload. They decrease with volume depletion. Fluid therapy based on PA pressures can restore fluid balance while limiting overcorrection or undercorrection of the problem.

A PA flow-directed catheter (e.g., Swan-Ganz) is used to measure PA pressures, including PAWP. The standard PA catheter has multiple lumens (Fig. 65.8). When properly positioned, the distal lumen port (catheter tip) is within the PA. We use this port to monitor PA pressures and sample mixed venous blood (e.g., to monitor O_2 saturation).

A balloon connected to an external valve surrounds the distal lumen port. Balloon inflation has 2 purposes: (1) to allow blood to "float" the catheter forward and (2) to allow PAWP measurement. There are 1 or 2 proximal lumens, with exit ports in the right atrium or right atrium and right ventricle (if 2). The right atrium port is used for CVP measurement, injecting fluid for CO measurement, and withdrawing blood specimens. The second proximal port (if available) is for infusing fluids and drugs or for blood sampling. A temperature sensor is near the distal tip. It monitors core temperature and is used for the thermodilution method of measuring CO.[13]

An advanced technology PA catheter can continuously monitor the patient's SvO_2. CCO and right ventricular ejection fraction (RVEF) can be measured using advanced thermodilution technology. RVEF gives information about RV function and helps to assess right heart contractility. RV end-diastolic volume is assessed by dividing SV by RVEF (Table 65.1). This is a key indicator of preload.

TABLE 65.3 Common Indications and Contraindications for Pulmonary Artery Catheterization

Indications
- Assessment of response to therapy in patients with pulmonary hypertension and mixed types of shock
- Cardiogenic shock
- Differential diagnosis of pulmonary hypertension
- MI with complications (e.g., HF, cardiogenic shock)
- Potentially reversible systolic HF (e.g., fulminant myocarditis)
- Severe chronic HF requiring inotropic, vasopressor, and vasodilator therapy
- Transplantation workup

Contraindications
- Coagulopathy (may be overlooked in emergency situations)
- Endocardial pacemaker
- Endocarditis
- Mechanical tricuspid or pulmonic valve
- Right heart mass (e.g., thrombus, tumor)

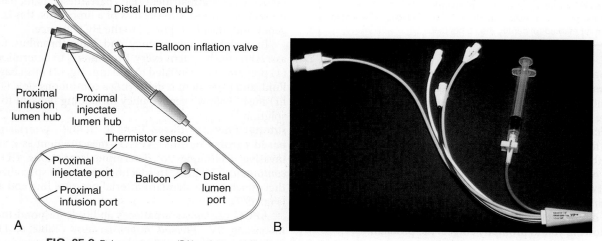

FIG. 65.8 Pulmonary artery (PA) catheter. **A,** Illustrated catheter has 5 lumens. When properly positioned, the distal lumen exit port is in the PA and the proximal lumen ports are in the right atrium and right ventricle. The distal and 1 of the proximal ports are used to measure PA and CVP, respectively. A balloon surrounds the catheter near the distal end. The balloon inflation valve is used to inflate the balloon with air to allow reading of the PAWP. A thermistor near the distal tip senses PA temperature and measures thermodilution cardiac output when solution cooler than body temperature is injected into a proximal port. **B,** Photo of an actual catheter. (*B,* Courtesy Edwards Critical Care Division, Baxter Healthcare Corporation, Santa Ana, CA.)

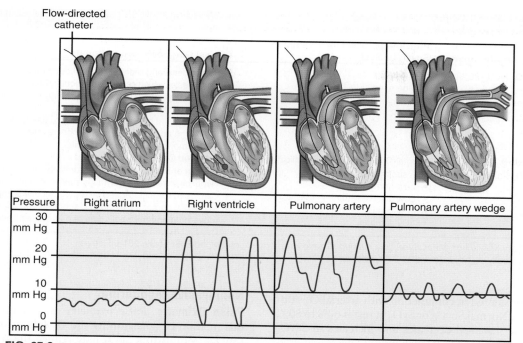

Flow-directed
catheter

Pressure	Right atrium	Right ventricle	Pulmonary artery	Pulmonary artery wedge
30 mm Hg				
20 mm Hg				
10 mm Hg				
0 mm Hg				

FIG. 65.9 Position of the pulmonary artery flow-directed catheter during progressive stages of insertion with corresponding pressure waveforms. (Modified from Urden LD, Stacy KM, Lough ME: *Critical care nursing: Diagnosis and management*, ed 6, St Louis, 2010, Mosby.)

The use of PA pressure monitoring has decreased dramatically. This is due, in part, to risks associated with this invasive technology (e.g., dysrhythmias, infection) and the development of less invasive techniques (e.g., APCO monitoring, bedside echocardiography).

The HCP often inserts a PA catheter at the bedside. Preparation includes arranging the monitor, cables, and infusion and pressurized flush solutions. The system is leveled and zero-referenced to the phlebostatic axis. Note the patient's electrolyte, acid-base, oxygenation, and coagulation status. Imbalances such as hypokalemia, hypomagnesemia, hypoxemia, or acidosis can make the heart more irritable. This can increase the risk for ventricular dysrhythmia during catheter insertion. Coagulopathy increases the risk for hemorrhage.

During insertion, a key nursing role is to observe the characteristic waveforms on the monitor as the HCP moves the catheter through the heart to the PA (Fig. 65.9). Monitor the ECG continuously because of the risk for dysrhythmias, especially when the catheter reaches the right ventricle. After insertion and before using the PA catheter, obtain a chest x-ray to confirm catheter placement. Note and record the measurement at the exit point. Apply an occlusive sterile dressing and change it according to agency policy.

Central Venous or Right Atrial Pressure Measurement. CVP is a measurement of right ventricular preload and reflects fluid volume status. We most often measure it with a central venous catheter placed in the internal jugular or subclavian vein. It can be measured with a PA catheter using the proximal lumen in the right atrium. CVP waveforms (Fig. 65.10) are similar to PAWP waveforms. CVP is measured as a mean pressure at the end of expiration.[13] A high CVP indicates right ventricular failure or volume overload. A low CVP indicates hypovolemia.

Venous Oxygen Saturation Monitoring. In critically ill patients, measuring the O_2 saturation of hemoglobin in venous blood

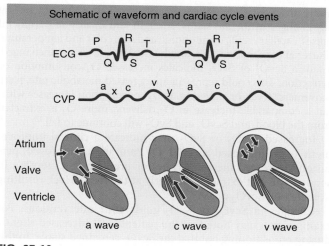

Schematic of waveform and cardiac cycle events

FIG. 65.10 Cardiac events that produce the CVP waveform with *a, c,* and *v* waves. The *a* wave represents atrial contraction. The *x* descent represents atrial relaxation. The *c* wave represents the bulging of the closed tricuspid valve into the right atrium during ventricular systole. The *v* wave represents atrial filling. The *y* descent represents opening of the tricuspid valve and filling of the ventricle. (Modified from Urden LD, Stacy KM, Lough ME: *Critical care nursing: Diagnosis and management*, ed 6, St Louis, 2010, Mosby.)

helps to determine the adequacy of tissue oxygenation. The O_2 saturation of venous blood from the CVP catheter is called *central venous O_2 saturation* ($ScvO_2$). Similarly, the O_2 saturation of blood from the PA catheter is the *mixed venous O_2 saturation* (SvO_2). $ScvO_2$ and SvO_2 reflect the balance among oxygenation of the arterial blood, tissue perfusion, and tissue O_2 consumption.[13] This gives a global indicator of the balance between O_2 delivery and O_2 consumption. $ScvO_2$ and SvO_2 are useful in assessing hemodynamic status and response to treatments or

TABLE 65.4 Interpreting ScvO₂ and SvO₂* Measurements

ScvO₂ and SvO₂ Measurement	Physiologic Basis for Change in ScvO₂ or SvO₂	Clinical Diagnosis and Rationale
High ScvO₂ or SvO₂ (80%–95%)	↑ O_2 supply ↓ O_2 demand	• Patient receiving more O_2 than needed by clinical condition • Anesthesia, which causes sedation and ↓ muscle movement • Hypothermia, which ↓ metabolic demand (e.g., with cardiopulmonary bypass) • Sepsis caused by ↓ ability of tissues to use O_2 at the cellular level • False high positive because pulmonary artery catheter is wedged in a pulmonary capillary (SvO₂ only)
Normal ScvO₂ or SvO₂ (60%–80%)	Normal O_2 supply and metabolic demand	• Balanced O_2 supply and demand
Low ScvO₂ or SvO₂ (<60%)	↓ O_2 supply caused by • Low hemoglobin • Low arterial saturation (SaO₂) • Low cardiac output • ↑ O_2 demand	• Anemia or bleeding with compromised cardiopulmonary system • Hypoxemia resulting from ↓ O_2 supply or lung disease • Cardiogenic shock caused by left ventricular pump failure • Metabolic demand exceeds O_2 supply in conditions that ↑ muscle movement and metabolic rate (e.g., seizures, fever)

Source: Urden LD, Stacy KM, Lough ME: *Critical care nursing: Diagnosis and management,* ed 8, St Louis, 2018, Elsevier.
*ScvO₂ values are generally slightly higher than SvO₂ values.

activities when considered in conjunction with arterial O_2 saturation (Table 65.4). Normal ScvO₂ or SvO₂ at rest is 60% to 80%.

Carefully review sustained decreases and increases in ScvO₂ or SvO₂. Decreased ScvO₂ or SvO₂ may indicate decreased arterial oxygenation, low CO, low hemoglobin level, or increased O_2 consumption or extraction. If the ScvO₂ or SvO₂ falls below 60%, determine which of these factors has changed. Observe for changes in arterial oxygenation (e.g., monitor pulse oximetry, ABGs) and indirectly assess CO and tissue perfusion. This is done by noting any changes in mental status, strength and quality of peripheral pulses, capillary refill, urine output, and skin color and temperature. If arterial oxygenation, CO, and hemoglobin level are unchanged, a fall in ScvO₂ or SvO₂ indicates increased O_2 consumption or extraction. This could represent an increased metabolic rate, pain, movement, fever, or shivering. If O_2 consumption increases without a comparable increase in O_2 delivery, more O_2 is extracted from the blood, and ScvO₂ and SvO₂ will continue to fall.[13]

Increased ScvO₂ or SvO₂ may indicate a clinical improvement (e.g., increased arterial O_2 saturation, improved perfusion, decreased metabolic rate) or problem (e.g., sepsis). In sepsis, O_2 is not extracted properly at the tissue level, resulting in increased ScvO₂ or SvO₂.

Changes in ScvO₂ or SvO₂ guide your interventions. For example, you may note that the patient's HR increased slightly during repositioning but that the ScvO₂ remained stable. In this case, you would conclude that the patient tolerated the position change. If the ScvO₂ dropped, this would be a sign to stop the activity until the ScvO₂ returned to baseline.

In many cases, as activity or metabolism increases, HR and CO increase, and ScvO₂ or SvO₂ stays constant or varies slightly. However, critically ill patients often have conditions (e.g., HF, shock) that prevent substantial increases in CO. In these cases, ScvO₂ or SvO₂ can be a useful indicator of the balance between O_2 delivery and consumption.

? CHECK YOUR PRACTICE

You are caring for a 38-yr-old woman admitted with sepsis due to a ruptured ectopic pregnancy. She has CVP and ScvO₂ monitoring in place. Trends in ScvO₂ have shown a slow, steady decline, with the most recent reading being 55%.
• What assessment data would you obtain to explain this change?

Noninvasive Monitoring

Pulse Oximetry. *Pulse oximetry* is a noninvasive, continuous method of determining the O_2 saturation of hemoglobin (SpO₂). Monitoring SpO₂ may reduce the frequency of ABG sampling (see Chapter 25). SpO₂ is normally 95% to 100%. Accurate SpO₂ measurements may be hard to obtain on patients who are hypothermic, are receiving IV vasopressor therapy (e.g., norepinephrine), or have hypoperfusion or vasoconstriction (e.g., shock).

A common use for pulse oximetry is to assess the effectiveness of O_2 therapy. Decreased SpO₂ indicates inadequate oxygenation of the blood in the pulmonary capillaries. You can correct this by increasing the fraction of inspired O_2 (FIO₂) and evaluating the patient's response. Similarly, use SpO₂ to monitor how the patient tolerates decreases in FIO₂ and responds to interventions. For example, if SpO₂ falls when you place the patient in a left lateral recumbent position, plan position changes that pose less risk for the patient.

Impedance Cardiography. *Impedance cardiography (ICG)* is a continuous or intermittent, noninvasive method of obtaining CO and assessing thoracic fluid status. Based on the concepts of *impedance* (the resistance to the flow of electric current [Ω]), ICG uses 4 sets of external electrodes to deliver a high-frequency, low-amplitude current that is like that used in apnea monitors. Blood is an excellent conductor of electricity (lower impedance), and pulsatile blood flow generates electrical impedance changes. ICG measures the change in impedance (dΩ) in the ascending aorta and left ventricle over time (dt). It is represented as dΩ/dt. Ωo is the measurement of the average impedance of the fluid in the thorax. We can calculate impedance-based hemodynamic parameters (CO, SV, SVR) from Ωo, dΩ/dt, MAP, CVP, and ECG.

Major uses of ICG include (1) detecting early signs and symptoms of pulmonary or cardiac problems, (2) determining cardiac or pulmonary cause of shortness of breath, (3) evaluating the cause and managing hypotension, (4) monitoring after removing a PA catheter or justifying insertion of a PA catheter, (5) evaluating drug therapy, and (6) diagnosing rejection after heart transplantation. ICG is not accurate in patients who have generalized edema or third spacing because the excess volume interferes with the signals.

❖ NURSING MANAGEMENT: HEMODYNAMIC MONITORING

Assessment of hemodynamic status requires integrating data from many sources and trending data over time. Comprehensive nursing observations give important clues about the patient's hemodynamic status.

Begin by obtaining baseline data about the patient's general appearance, level of consciousness, skin color and temperature, vital signs, peripheral pulses, capillary refill, and urine output. Does the patient appear tired, weak, exhausted? There may be too little cardiac reserve to sustain even minimum activity. Pallor, cool skin, and decreased pulses may indicate decreased CO. Changes in mental status may reflect problems with cerebral perfusion or oxygenation. Monitor urine output to determine the adequacy of perfusion to the kidneys. The patient with decreased perfusion to the GI tract may develop hypoactive or absent bowel sounds. If the patient is bleeding and developing shock, the BP may be stable at first. The patient may become increasingly pale and cool from peripheral vasoconstriction. Conversely, the patient with septic shock may be warm and pink yet have tachycardia and BP instability. Increased HRs are common in stressed, compromised, critically ill patients. However, sustained tachycardia increases myocardial O_2 demand and can result in decreased CO.

Always correlate observational data with data obtained from technology (e.g., ECG, arterial and PA pressures, $ScvO_2$, SvO_2). Single hemodynamic values are rarely helpful. You must monitor trends in these values over time and evaluate the whole clinical picture with the goals of recognizing early clues and intervening before problems escalate.

CIRCULATORY ASSIST DEVICES

Mechanical **circulatory assist devices (CADs)** are used to decrease cardiac work and improve organ perfusion in patients with HF when conventional drug therapy is no longer adequate. CADs include **intraaortic balloon pumps (IABPs)** and left or right ventricular assist devices (VADs).

The type of device used depends on the extent and nature of the heart problem. CADs provide support in 3 situations: (1) the left, right, or both ventricles require support while recovering from acute injury (e.g., postcardiotomy); (2) the patient must be stabilized before surgical repair of the heart (e.g., a ruptured septum); and (3) the heart has failed, and the patient is awaiting heart transplantation. All CADs decrease cardiac workload, increase myocardial perfusion, and augment circulation.

Intraaortic Balloon Pump

The IABP provides temporary circulatory assistance by reducing afterload (through reducing systolic pressure) and augmenting the aortic diastolic pressure. This improves coronary blood flow. Table 65.5 lists common indications for an IABP.

The IABP consists of a sausage-shaped balloon, a pump that inflates and deflates the balloon, a control panel for synchronizing the balloon inflation to the cardiac cycle, and fail-safe features. The balloon is inserted percutaneously or surgically into the femoral artery. It is moved toward the heart and placed in the descending thoracic aorta just below the left subclavian artery and above the renal arteries (Fig. 65.11). After placement, an x-ray confirms the position.

A pneumatic device fills the balloon with helium at the start of diastole (immediately after aortic valve closure) and deflates

---

TABLE 65.5 Common Indications and Contraindications for IABP Therapy

Indications
- Acute MI with any of the following*:
  - Ventricular aneurysm accompanied by ventricular dysrhythmias
  - Acute ventricular septal defect
  - Acute mitral valve dysfunction
  - Cardiogenic shock
  - Refractory chest pain with or without ventricular dysrhythmias
- High-risk interventional cardiology procedures
- Preoperative, intraoperative, and postoperative cardiac surgery (e.g., prophylaxis before surgery, failure to wean from cardiopulmonary bypass, left ventricular failure after cardiopulmonary bypass)
- Unstable angina unresponsive to drug therapy
- Short-term bridge to heart transplantation

Contraindications
- Abdominal aortic and thoracic aneurysms
- Generalized peripheral vascular disease (e.g., aortoiliac disease)†
- Irreversible brain damage
- Major coagulopathy (e.g., disseminated intravascular coagulation [DIC])
- Moderate to severe aortic insufficiency
- Terminal or untreatable diseases of any major organ system

*Allows time for emergent angiography and corrective heart surgery to be done.
†May inhibit placement of balloon and is considered a relative contraindication; sheathless insertion may be used.

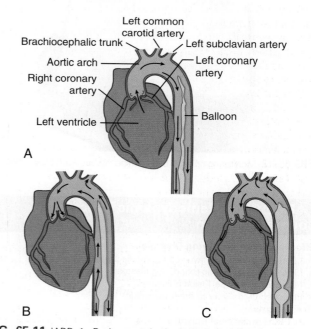

FIG. 65.11 IABP. **A,** During systole the balloon is deflated, which helps with ejection of blood into the periphery. **B,** In early diastole, the balloon begins to inflate. **C,** In late diastole, the balloon is totally inflated, which augments aortic pressure and increases the coronary perfusion pressure. This increases coronary and cerebral blood flow.

---

it just before the next systole. The ECG is the trigger used to start the deflation on the upstroke of the R wave (of the QRS) and inflation on the T wave. The dicrotic notch of the arterial pressure tracing is used to refine timing (Fig. 65.12).

IABP therapy is known as *counterpulsation* because the timing of balloon inflation is opposite the ventricular contraction. The IABP assist ratio is 1:1 in the acute phase of treatment, meaning that 1 IABP cycle of inflation and deflation occurs for every heartbeat.

Effects of Counterpulsation. In late diastole when the balloon is totally inflated, blood is forcibly displaced distal to the extremities and proximal to the coronary arteries and main branches of the aortic arch. Diastolic arterial pressure rises (diastolic augmentation). This increases coronary artery perfusion pressure and perfusion of vital organs. The rise in coronary artery perfusion pressure increases blood flow to the myocardium. The balloon is rapidly deflated just before systole. This creates a vacuum that causes aortic pressure to drop. When aortic resistance to left ventricular ejection is reduced (reduced afterload), the left ventricle empties more easily and completely. SV increases while myocardial O_2 consumption decreases. Table 65.6 describes the hemodynamic effects of IABP therapy.

Complications With IABP Therapy. Vascular injuries, such as aortic dissection and compromised distal circulation, are common with IABP therapy. Thrombus and embolus formation add to the risk for circulatory compromise to the extremity. The action of the IABP can destroy platelets and cause thrombocytopenia. Movement of the balloon can block the left subclavian, renal, or mesenteric arteries. This can result in a weak or absent radial pulse, decreased urine output, and reduced or absent bowel sounds. Patients receiving IABP therapy are prone to infection. Local or systemic signs of infection require catheter removal. To reduce these complications, perform cardiovascular, neurovascular, and hemodynamic assessments every 15 to 60 minutes, depending on the patient's status (Table 65.7).[13]

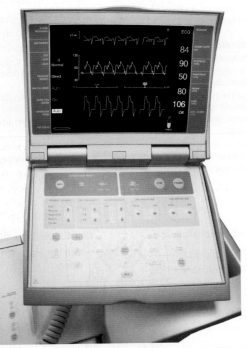

FIG 65.12 Monitoring on an IABP machine. (© beerkoff/iStock.com.)

TABLE 65.6 Hemodynamic Effects of Counterpulsation

Effects of Inflation During Diastole
- ↑ Diastolic pressure (may exceed systolic pressure)
- ↑ Pressure in the aortic root during diastole
- ↑ Coronary artery perfusion pressure
- Improved O_2 delivery to the myocardium
  - ↓ Angina
  - ↓ ECG evidence of ischemia
  - ↓ Ventricular ectopy

Effects of Deflation During Systole
- ↓ Afterload
- ↓ Peak systolic pressure
- ↓ Myocardial O_2 consumption
- ↑ Stroke volume, possibly associated with:
  - Improved mentation
  - Warm skin
  - ↑ Urine output
  - ↓ HR
- ↑ Forward flow of blood, ↓ preload
  - ↓ Pulmonary artery pressures, including PAWP
  - ↓ Crackles

TABLE 65.7 Managing Complications of IABP Therapy

Potential Complications	Nursing Interventions
Balloon leak or rupture	• Prepare for emergent removal and possible reinsertion.
Arterial trauma caused by insertion or displacement of balloon	• Assess and mark peripheral pulses before inserting balloon to use as baseline for assessing pulses after insertion. • Assess perfusion to both upper and lower extremities at least every hour. • Measure urine output at least every hour (occlusion of renal arteries causes severe ↓ in urine output). • Observe arterial waveforms for sudden changes. • Keep head of bed no higher than 45 degrees. • Do not flex cannulated leg at the hip. • Immobilize cannulated leg to prevent flexion using a draw sheet tucked under the mattress, soft ankle restraint, or knee immobilizer.
Hematologic problems due to platelet aggregation along the balloon (e.g., thrombocytopenia)	• Monitor coagulation profiles, hematocrit, and platelet count.
Hemorrhage from insertion site	• Check site for bleeding at least every hour. • Monitor vital signs for signs of hypovolemia with each check.
Infection at site	• Use strict aseptic technique for insertion and dressing changes for all lines. • Cover all insertion sites with occlusive dressings. • Give prescribed prophylactic antibiotic for entire course of therapy.
Issues related to immobilization (e.g., pressure injuries)	• Reposition patient at least q2hr, being careful to maintain proper positioning. • Use appropriate pressure-relieving devices.
VTE caused by trauma, balloon obstruction of blood flow distal to catheter	• Give prophylactic heparin therapy (if ordered). • Assess pulses, urine output, and level of consciousness at least every hour. • Check circulation, sensation, and movement in both legs at least every hour.

Mechanical complications from IABP are rare but can occur. Improper timing of balloon inflation may cause increased afterload, decreased CO, myocardial ischemia, and increased myocardial O_2 demand. If the balloon develops a leak, the pump will automatically stop. The catheter needs to be promptly removed to avoid an embolus. Signs of a leak include less effective augmentation, repeated alarms for gas loss, and blood backing up into the catheter. A malfunction of the balloon or console triggers fail-safe alarms and automatically shuts down the unit. You must be able to recognize complications immediately and report them to the HCP.

The patient with an IABP is relatively immobile, limited to side-lying or supine positions with the head of bed (HOB) elevated less than 45 degrees. The patient may be receiving mechanical ventilation and will likely have multiple invasive lines. All of this increases the risk for pressure injury and makes it hard to find comfortable positioning. The patient may have sleep problems and anxiety. Adequate sedation, pain relief, skin care, and comfort measures are essential.

As the patient improves, circulatory support provided by the IABP is gradually reduced. Weaning involves reducing the IABP assist ratio from 1:1 to 1:2 and assessing the patient's response. If the patient remains stable, the ratio is changed from 1:2 to 1:3 until the IABP catheter is removed. Pumping must continue until the line is removed even if the patient is stable. This reduces the risk for clot formation around the catheter.

Ventricular Assist Devices

A **ventricular assist device (VAD)** provides short- and long-term support for the failing heart and allows more mobility than the IABP. VADs are inserted into the path of flowing blood to augment or replace the action of the ventricle. Some VADs are implanted internally (e.g., peritoneum). Others are positioned externally. A typical VAD shunts blood from the left atrium or ventricle to the device and then to the aorta. Some VADs provide right or biventricular support (Fig. 65.13).

Failure to wean from cardiopulmonary bypass (CPB) after surgery is a key indicator for VAD support. VADs can support patients with HF caused by MI and patients awaiting heart transplantation. A VAD is a temporary device that can partially or totally support circulation until the heart recovers or a donor heart is found.

Appropriate patient selection for VAD therapy is critical. Indications include (1) failure to wean from CPB or postcardiotomy cardiogenic shock, (2) a bridge to recovery or heart transplantation, and (3) patients with New York Heart Association Class IV heart disease (see Table 34.3) who have failed medical therapy. Relative contraindications for VAD therapy include (1) BSA less than manufacturer's limit (e.g., 1.2 m^2), (2) irreversible end-stage organ damage, and (3) co-morbidities that would limit life expectancy to less than 3 years.[13]

Implantable Artificial Heart

Every year, about 2200 patients receive heart transplants, yet the demand for donor hearts far exceeds the supply. Research on mechanical CADs has led to the development of a fully implantable artificial heart that can sustain the body's circulatory system. This device can provide a bridge to transplantation or replace the hearts of patients who are not eligible for a transplant and have no other treatment options. A major advantage of the artificial heart is that patients do not need immunosuppression therapy and thus avoid its inevitable, long-term effects. Risks include infection, thrombus, and stroke. Patients need lifelong anticoagulation and ongoing care from the interprofessional team.[15]

❖ NURSING AND INTERPROFESSIONAL MANAGEMENT: CIRCULATORY ASSIST DEVICES

The patient with an IABP needs highly skilled care. Perform frequent and thorough cardiovascular assessments. These include measuring hemodynamic parameters (e.g., arterial BP, CO/CI, SVR), auscultating the heart and lungs, and evaluating the ECG (e.g., rate, rhythm). Assess for adequate tissue perfusion (e.g., skin color and temperature, mental status, capillary refill, peripheral pulses, urine output, bowel sounds) at regular intervals. IABP therapy should improve these findings.

Nursing care of the patient with a VAD is like that of the patient with an IABP. Observe the patient for bleeding, cardiac tamponade, ventricular failure, infection, dysrhythmias, renal failure, hemolysis, and VTE. The patient with VAD may be mobile and need an activity plan. In some cases, patients with VADs may go home. Preparation for discharge is complex and needs in-depth teaching about the device and support equipment (e.g., battery chargers). A competent caregiver must always be present.

Ideally, patients with CADs will recover, receive an artificial heart, or undergo heart transplantation. However, many patients die, or the decision is made to no longer seek treatment and death follows. Both the patient and caregiver need emotional support. Consult other team members, such as social workers or clergy, as needed.

NONINVASIVE VENTILATION

At times, patients may need ventilator support, without the placement of an ET tube. Noninvasive ventilation (NIV) uses a mask, instead of an ET tube, to oxygenate and ventilate a patient. These masks can be full face or a nasal piece. There are 2 common modes used for NIV.

Continuous Positive Airway Pressure

Continuous positive airway pressure (CPAP) restores functional residual capacity (FRC) and is similar to positive end-expiratory pressure (PEEP). However, the pressure in CPAP is delivered continuously during spontaneous breathing, preventing the patient's airway pressure from falling to 0. For example, if CPAP is 5 cm H_2O, airway pressure during expiration is 5 cm H_2O. During inspiration, we generate 1 to 2 cm H_2O of negative pressure. This reduces airway pressure to 3 or 4 cm H_2O.

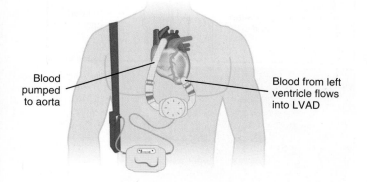

FIG. 65.13 Schematic diagram of a biventricular assist device (BVAD). (From Urden LD, Stacy KM, Lough ME: *Critical care nursing: Diagnosis and management,* ed 8, St Louis, 2018, Mosby.)

Blood pumped to aorta

Blood from left ventricle flows into LVAD

CPAP is often used to treat obstructive sleep apnea. It is a non-invasive modality, delivered through a tight-fitting face mask, nasal mask, or nasal pillows. CPAP increases *work of breathing* (WOB) because the patient must forcibly exhale against the CPAP. Therefore it must be used with caution in patients with myocardial compromise. The patient must be able to remove a mask independently due to the risk for vomiting. Those with increased secretions or the inability to control their airway are not good candidates for CPAP due to the risk for aspiration.[13]

Bilevel Positive Airway Pressure

In addition to O$_2$, *bilevel positive airway pressure (BiPAP)* provides 2 levels of positive pressure support: higher inspiratory positive airway pressure and lower expiratory positive airway pressure.[13] Like CPAP, the patient must be able to spontaneously breathe and cooperate with this treatment (Fig. 65.14).

BiPAP is used for COPD patients with HF and acute respiratory failure and for patients with sleep apnea. Its use after extubation can help prevent reintubation. Patients with shock, altered mental status, or increased airway secretions cannot use BiPAP because of the risk for aspiration and the inability to remove the mask.

ARTIFICIAL AIRWAYS

Patients in the ICU often need mechanical assistance to maintain airway patency. Inserting a tube into the trachea, bypassing upper airway and laryngeal structures, creates an artificial airway. The tube is placed into the trachea via the mouth or nose past the larynx (**endotracheal [ET] intubation**) or through a stoma in the neck (*tracheostomy*). Fig. 65.15 shows the parts of an ET tube.

ET intubation is common in ICU patients requiring mechanical ventilation for short periods of time (e.g., less than 2 weeks). Other indications for intubation include (1) upper airway obstruction (e.g., burns, tumor, bleeding), (2) apnea, (3) high risk for aspiration, (4) ineffective clearance of secretions, and (5) respiratory distress. ET intubation is done quickly and safely at the bedside by an HCP or RT.

A *tracheotomy* is a surgical procedure that is done when the need for an artificial airway is expected to be prolonged. Early tracheotomy (done within 10 days) appears to have advantages over delayed tracheotomy. These include fewer ventilator dependent days, reduced length of stays, decreased pain, and improved communication.[16] Chapter 26 discusses tracheostomy tubes and related nursing management.

Endotracheal Tubes

In *oral intubation,* the ET tube is passed through the mouth and vocal cords and into the trachea with the aid of a laryngoscope or a bronchoscope. Oral ET intubation is preferred for most emergencies because the airway can be secured rapidly. A larger diameter tube is used. A larger tube reduces the WOB because of less airway resistance. It is easier to remove secretions and perform bronchoscopy, if needed. In *nasal ET intubation,* the ET is placed blindly (i.e., without seeing the larynx) through the nose, nasopharynx, and vocal cords. We rarely use nasal ET intubation. It may be done when oral intubation is not possible (e.g., unstable cervical spine injury, dental abscess, epiglottitis).

There are risks associated with oral ET intubation. It is hard to place the tube with limited head and neck mobility

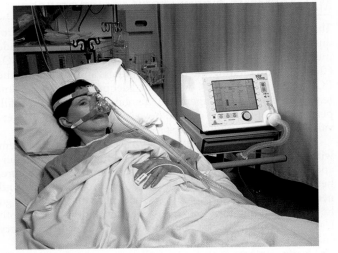

FIG. 65.14 BiPAP delivered through a face mask. (Courtesy Respironics Inc., Murrysville, PA.)

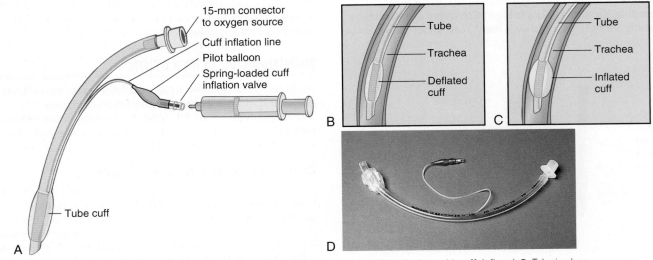

15-mm connector to oxygen source

Cuff inflation line

Pilot balloon

Spring-loaded cuff inflation valve

Tube cuff

Tube
Trachea
Deflated cuff

Tube
Trachea
Inflated cuff

FIG. 65.15 Endotracheal tube. **A,** Parts of an endotracheal tube. **B,** Tube in place with cuff deflated. **C,** Tube in place with the cuff inflated. **D,** Photo of tube before placement. (*A,* From Beare PG, Myers JL: *Adult health nursing,* ed 3, St Louis, 1998, Mosby.)

(e.g., spinal cord injury). Teeth can be chipped or accidentally removed during the procedure. Salivation increases, and swallowing is difficult. Patients can obstruct the ET tube by biting down on the tube. Sedation, along with a bite block or oropharyngeal airway, may be used to prevent obstruction. Mouth care is a challenge because of limited space in the oral cavity.

Endotracheal Intubation Procedure

Unless ET intubation is emergent, consent for the procedure is obtained. Tell the patient and caregiver the reason for ET intubation and steps in the procedure. Explain that, while intubated, the patient will not be able to speak, but that you will provide other means of communication. Tell them that the patient's hands may have removable mitts placed or wrists may have soft restraints placed to remind them not to touch the airway.

Have a self-inflating *bag-valve-mask* (BVM) (e.g., *Ambu bag*) attached to O_2, suctioning equipment ready at the bedside, and IV access. The BVM has a reservoir that is filled with O_2 so that it delivers concentrations of 90% to 95%. The slower the bag is deflated and inflated, the higher the O_2 concentration that is delivered. Assemble and check the equipment, remove the patient's dentures or partial plates (for oral intubation), and give medications as ordered. Premedication varies depending on the patient's level of consciousness (e.g., awake, obtunded), urgency (e.g., emergent, nonemergent), and the HCP's preferences.

For oral intubation, place the patient supine with the head extended and the neck flexed ("sniffing position"). This position allows the HCP to better see the vocal cords. For nasal intubation, the nasal passages may be sprayed with a local anesthetic and vasoconstrictor (e.g., lidocaine with epinephrine) to reduce trauma and bleeding. Before intubation is started, preoxygenate the patient using the BVM and 100% O_2 for 3 to 5 minutes. Each intubation attempt is limited to less than 30 seconds. Ventilate the patient between successive attempts using the BVM and 100% O_2.

Rapid-sequence intubation (RSI) is the rapid, concurrent administration of both a sedative and a paralytic drug during emergency airway management to induce unconsciousness for intubation. It decreases the risks for aspiration and injury to the patient. RSI is not indicated in patients who are in cardiac arrest or have a known difficult airway. A sedative-hypnotic-amnesic (e.g., propofol, etomidate [Amidate]) is given to induce unconsciousness, along with a rapid-onset opioid (e.g., fentanyl) to blunt the pain of the procedure. This is followed with a drug (e.g., rocuronium) to produce skeletal muscle paralysis.[17] Monitor the patient's O_2 status during the procedure with pulse oximetry. Adhere to the agency policy about RSI medication administration.

After intubation, inflate the cuff. Confirm the placement of the ET tube while continuing to manually ventilate the patient using the BVM with 100% O_2. Use an EtCO2 detector to confirm proper placement by noting the presence of exhaled CO_2 from the lungs (Fig. 65.16). Place the detector between the BVM and ET tube and look for a color change (indicating the presence of CO_2) or a number. At least 5 or 6 exhalations with a consistent CO_2 level must be present to confirm tube placement in the trachea.[13] Auscultate the lungs for bilateral breath sounds and the epigastrium for the absence of air sounds. Observe the chest for symmetric chest wall movement. SpO2 should be stable or improved.

If the findings support proper ET tube placement, connect the ET tube to a mechanical ventilator and secure the tube per

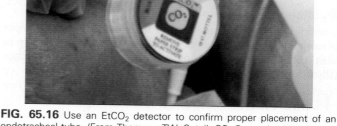

FIG. 65.16 Use an EtCO2 detector to confirm proper placement of an endotracheal tube. (From Thomsen TW, Setnik GS: Orotracheal intubation, *Procedures Consult*, 2017.)

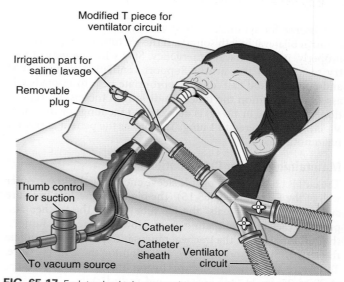

FIG. 65.17 Endotracheal tube secured to a closed tracheal suction system.

agency policy (Fig. 65.17). Suction the ET tube and pharynx. Insert a bite block, if needed, and secure it separately from the ET tube to the face. Obtain a chest x-ray to confirm tube location (2 to 6 cm above the carina in the adult). This position allows the patient to move the neck without moving the tube or causing it to enter the right mainstem bronchus. Once proper positioning is confirmed with x-ray, record and mark the position of the tube at the lip or teeth or nose.

Obtain ABGs 15 to 30 minutes after intubation to determine baseline oxygenation and ventilation status. ABG values are used to guide oxygenation and ventilation changes. Continuous pulse oximetry gives data about arterial oxygenation. EtCO2 monitoring provides data related to ventilation.

❖ NURSING AND INTERPROFESSIONAL MANAGEMENT: ARTIFICIAL AIRWAY

Managing a patient with an artificial airway is often a shared responsibility between you and the RT. Agency policy dictates specific management tasks. Nursing responsibilities for the patient with an artificial airway may include: (1) maintaining correct tube placement, (2) maintaining proper cuff inflation, (3) monitoring oxygenation and ventilation, (4) maintaining tube patency, (5) providing oral care and maintaining skin integrity, (6) fostering comfort and communication, and (7) assessing for complications. See eNursing Care Plan 65.1 for the patient on a mechanical ventilator (available on the website for this chapter).

◆ Maintaining Correct Tube Placement

Continuously monitor the patient with an ET tube for proper placement. If the tube moves or is dislodged, it could end up in the pharynx or enter the esophagus or right mainstem bronchus (thus ventilating only the right lung).

> **⚠ SAFETY ALERT** **Endotracheal Tube Placement**
> - Maintain proper ET tube position by recording and marking the position of the tube at the lip or teeth (usually 21 cm for women, 23 cm for men).
> - Confirm that the mark stays constant while at rest and during patient care, repositioning, and transport.

Observe for symmetric chest wall movement. Auscultate to confirm bilateral breath sounds. If the ET tube is not positioned properly, it is an airway emergency. Stay with the patient and try to maintain the airway. Support ventilation with a BVM and 100% O_2 and call for the appropriate help to immediately assess or reposition the tube. If a dislodged tube is not repositioned, minimal or no O_2 is delivered to the lungs or the entire V_T is being delivered to 1 lung. This places the patient at risk for pneumothorax.

◆ Maintaining Proper Cuff Inflation

The cuff is an inflatable, pliable sleeve encircling the lower, outer wall of the ET tube (Fig. 65.15). The high-volume, low-pressure cuff stabilizes and "seals" the ET tube within the trachea and prevents escape of ventilating gases. However, excess volume in the cuff can damage the tracheal mucosa. To prevent this, inflate the cuff with air and measure and monitor the cuff pressure. To ensure adequate tracheal perfusion, maintain cuff pressure at 20 to 25 cm H_2O.[13] Measure and record cuff pressure after intubation and on a routine basis (e.g., every 8 hours) using the *minimal occluding volume* (MOV) *technique* or *the minimal leak technique* (MLT).

To perform the MOV technique, first, in the mechanically ventilated patient, place a stethoscope over the trachea and inflate the cuff to MOV by adding air until you hear no air at peak inspiratory pressure (end of ventilator inspiration). For the spontaneously breathing intubated patient, you inflate until you hear no sound after a deep breath or after inhalation with a BVM. Second, use a manometer to verify that cuff pressure is between 20 and 25 cm H_2O and record cuff pressure in the chart. If adequate cuff pressure cannot be maintained or larger volumes of air are needed to keep the cuff inflated, there could be a leak in the cuff or tracheal dilation at the cuff site. In these situations, notify the HCP. The procedure for MLT is similar with 1 exception. You remove a small amount of air from the cuff until you hear a slight air leak at peak inflation.

◆ Monitoring Oxygenation and Ventilation

Closely monitor the patient with an ET tube for adequate oxygenation by assessing clinical findings, ABGs, SpO_2, and, if available, $ScvO_2$ or SvO_2. Assess for signs of hypoxemia, such as a change in mental status (e.g., confusion), dusky skin,

and dysrhythmias. Periodic ABGs and continuous SpO_2 provide objective data about oxygenation. Lower PaO_2 values are expected in patients with some disease states, such as chronic obstructive pulmonary disease (COPD). CVP or PA catheters with $ScvO_2$ or SvO_2 capability provide an indirect measure of the patient's tissue oxygenation status (Table 65.4).

Indicators of ventilation include clinical findings, $PaCO_2$, and continuous partial pressure of $EtCO_2$ ($PETCO_2$). Assess the patient's respirations for rate, rhythm, and use of accessory muscles. The patient who is hyperventilating will be breathing rapidly and deeply and may have circumoral and peripheral numbness and tingling. The patient who is hypoventilating will be breathing shallowly or slowly and may appear dusky. $PaCO_2$ is the best indicator of alveolar hyperventilation (e.g., decreased $PaCO_2$, increased pH indicates respiratory alkalosis) or hypoventilation (e.g., increased $PaCO_2$, decreased pH indicates respiratory acidosis).

$PETCO_2$ monitoring *(capnography)* is done by analyzing exhaled gas directly at the patient-ventilator circuit *(mainstream sampling)* or by transporting a sample of gas via a small-bore tubing to a bedside monitor *(sidestream sampling)*. Continuous $PETCO_2$ monitoring can assess the patency of the airway and presence of breathing. Gradual changes in $PETCO_2$ values may accompany an increase in CO_2 production (e.g., sepsis, hypoventilation, neuromuscular blockade) or a decrease in CO_2 production (e.g., hypothermia, decreased CO, metabolic acidosis). In patients with normal ventilation-to-perfusion ratios (see Chapter 67), we can use $PETCO_2$ to estimate $PaCO_2$. $PETCO_2$ is generally 2 to 5 mm Hg lower than $PaCO_2$.[13] However, in patients with unusually large dead air space or serious mismatch between ventilation and perfusion (e.g., COPD, pulmonary embolism), $PETCO_2$ is not a reliable estimate of $PaCO_2$.

◆ Maintaining Tube Patency

Do not routinely suction a patient.[13] Regularly assess the patient to determine if suctioning is needed. Indications for suctioning include (1) visible secretions in the ET tube, (2) sudden onset of respiratory distress, (3) suspected aspiration of secretions, (4) increase in respiratory rate or frequent coughing, and (5) sudden decrease in SpO_2. Other signs that indicate the patient needs suctioning include an increase in peak airway pressure and auscultating adventitious breath sounds over the trachea or bronchi.[13]

Table 65.8 describes 2 recommended suctioning methods, the *closed-suction technique* (CST) and the *open-suction technique* (OST). The CST uses a suction catheter that is enclosed in a plastic sleeve connected directly to the patient-ventilator circuit (Fig. 65.17). With the CST, oxygenation and ventilation are maintained during suctioning, and exposure to the patient's secretions and infection is reduced for the patient's and HCP's safety. The CST should be used for patients who (1) require PEEP, (2) have high levels of FIO_2, (3) have bloody or infected pulmonary secretions, (4) require frequent suctioning, and (5) have clinical instability with the OST.[13]

Potential complications associated with suctioning include hypoxemia, bronchospasm, increased ICP, dysrhythmias, hypertension, hypotension, mucosal damage, pulmonary bleeding, pain, and infection. Closely assess the patient before, during, and after suctioning. If the patient does not tolerate suctioning (e.g., decreased SpO_2, increased or decreased BP, sustained coughing, development of dysrhythmias), stop at once. Continue to reassess the patient until hemodynamic stability is achieved,

TABLE 65.8 Suctioning Procedures for Patient on Mechanical Ventilator

General Measures for Open- and Closed-Suction Techniques

1. Gather all equipment.
2. Wash hands and don personal protective equipment and gloves.
3. Explain procedure and patient's role in assisting with secretion removal by coughing.
4. Monitor patient's cardiopulmonary status (e.g., vital signs, SpO₂, SvO₂ or ScvO₂, ECG, level of consciousness) before, during, and after suctioning.
5. Turn on suction and set vacuum to 100–120 mm Hg.
6. Pause ventilator alarms.

Open-Suction Technique

7. Open sterile catheter package using the inside of the package as a sterile field. NOTE: Suction catheter should be no wider than half the diameter of the ET tube (e.g., for a 7-mm ET tube, select a 10F suction catheter).
8. Fill the sterile solution container with sterile normal saline or water.
9. Don sterile gloves.
10. Pick up sterile suction catheter with dominant hand. Using nondominant hand, secure the connecting tube (to suction) to the suction catheter.
11. Check equipment for proper functioning by suctioning a small volume of sterile saline solution from the container. **(Go to step 13.)**

Closed-Suction Technique

12. Connect the suction tubing to the closed suction port.
13. Hyperoxygenate the patient for 30 seconds using 1 of the following methods:
    - Activate the suction hyperoxygenation setting on the ventilator using nondominant hand. This is the safest method to hyperoxygenate the patient and should be used when available.
    - Increase FIO₂ to 100%. NOTE: Remember to return FIO₂ to baseline level when done suctioning, if not done automatically after preset time by ventilator.
    - Disconnect the ventilator tubing from the ET tube and provide manual ventilation to the patient with 100% O₂ using a BVM device. Attach a PEEP valve to the BVM for patients on >5 cm H₂O PEEP. Give 5 or 6 breaths over 30 seconds. Having a second person deliver the manual breaths significantly increases the V_T delivered.
14. With suction off, gently and quickly insert the catheter using the dominant hand. When you meet resistance, pull back ½ in.
15. Apply continuous or intermittent suction using the nondominant thumb. Withdraw the catheter over 10 seconds or less.
16. Hyperoxygenate once more for another 30 seconds as described in step 13.
17. If secretions remain and the patient has tolerated suctioning, perform 2 or 3 suction passes as described in steps 14 and 15. NOTE: Rinse the suction catheter with sterile saline solution between suctioning passes as needed. Maintaining a closed circuit at all times is best to reduce the risk for infection.
18. Reconnect patient to ventilator (open-suction technique).
19. Rinse the catheter and connecting tubing with the sterile saline solution.
20. Suction oral pharynx. NOTE: Use a separate catheter for this step when using the closed-suction technique.
21. Discard the suction catheter and rinse the connecting tubing with the sterile saline solution (open-suction technique).
22. Reset FIO₂ (if needed) and ventilator alarms.
23. Reassess patient for signs of effective suctioning.

Adapted from Wiegand DL: *AACN procedure manual for high acuity, progressive, and critical care*, ed 7, St Louis, 2017, Elsevier.

the patient recovers, and/or the situation resolves before trying to suction again. Prevent hypoxemia by hyperoxygenating the patient before and after each suctioning pass and limiting each pass to 10 seconds or less (Table 65.8). Assess both the ECG and SpO₂ before, during, and after suctioning.

Causes of dysrhythmias during suctioning include (1) hypoxemia resulting in myocardial ischemia; (2) vagal stimulation caused by tracheal irritation; and (3) sympathetic nervous system stimulation caused by anxiety, discomfort, or pain. Dysrhythmias include tachydysrhythmias and bradydysrhythmias, premature beats, and asystole. Stop suctioning if any new dysrhythmias develop. Avoid excessive suctioning in patients with severe hypoxemia or bradycardia.

Tracheal mucosal damage may occur due to excessive suction pressures (greater than 120 mm Hg), overly vigorous catheter insertion, and the suction catheter itself. Blood streaks or tissue shreds in aspirated secretions may indicate mucosal damage. This increases the risk for infection and bleeding, especially if the patient is receiving anticoagulants. We can prevent trauma to the mucosa by following the steps described in Table 65.8.

Secretions may be thick and hard to suction because of inadequate hydration or humidification, infection, or inaccessibility of the lower airways. Maintain adequate hydration when clinically indicated (e.g., IV fluids) and provide supplemental humidification of inspired gases through the mechanical ventilator to help thin secretions. Mobilize and turn the patient (e.g., every 2 hours) to help move secretions into larger airways. If infection is the cause of thick secretions, give the patient appropriate antibiotics.

◆ Providing Oral Care and Maintaining Skin Integrity

When an oral ET tube is in place, the patient's mouth is always open. Moisten the lips, tongue, and gums with saline or water swabs to prevent mucosal drying. Proper oral care provides comfort and prevents injury to the gums and plaque formation (Table 65.9). If space is limited in the oral cavity, use smaller or pediatric-sized oral products for providing oral care.

Frequent assessment and meticulous care are needed to prevent skin breakdown on the face, lips, tongue, and nares because

TABLE 65.9 Oral Care for Patient on Mechanical Ventilator

General Measures

1. Gather all equipment.
2. Wash hands and don personal protective equipment and gloves.
3. Explain procedure to the patient and caregiver (if present).
4. Perform oral care every 2–4 hours using a suction toothbrush and toothpaste or gel for 1–2 minutes, suctioning often. Assess for plaque buildup and any potential infection.
5. Use 0.12% chlorhexidine oral rinse twice daily.
6. Apply a mouth moisturizer to oral mucosa and lips with each cleaning.
7. Suction oral cavity and pharynx when needed. Fig. 65.18 shows an endotracheal tube that can provide continuous or intermittent subglottic suctioning.

NOTE:
- Change all oral suction equipment and suction tubing every 24 hr.
- Rinse nondisposable oral suction apparatus with sterile normal saline after each use and place on a dry paper towel.

Adapted from Wiegand DL *AACN procedure manual for high acuity, progressive, and critical care*, ed 7, St Louis, 2017, Elsevier.

of pressure from the ET tube or the method used to secure the ET tube to the patient's face. Ongoing assessment is shared between the RN and RT. Reposition and re-tape the ET tube (per agency policy) and as needed to prevent skin breakdown. Repositioning the ET tube may be limited to the RT. Two staff members should always perform repositioning to prevent accidental ET tube dislodgment. Monitor the patient for any signs of respiratory distress throughout the procedure.

For the nasally intubated patient, remove the old tape and clean the skin around the ET tube with saline-soaked gauze. For the orally intubated patient, remove the bite block (if present) and the old tape. Provide oral hygiene, then reposition the ET tube to the opposite side of the mouth. Replace the bite block (if appropriate) and reconfirm proper cuff inflation and tube placement. Secure the ET tube again (per agency policy).

We often use commercial ET holders. These may increase the risk for skin breakdown compared to tape.[18] If one is used, follow the manufacturer's directions for maintaining tube position, providing skin care, and preventing skin breakdown.

◆ Fostering Comfort and Communication

Intubation is a major stressor for the patient.[19] Intubated patients have stress from not being able to talk and communicate their needs. This can be frustrating for the patient, caregiver, and interprofessional care team. To communicate more effectively, use a variety of methods. (See Common Problems of Critical Care Patients earlier in this chapter on p. 1535.)

The physical discomfort associated with ET intubation and mechanical ventilation often requires sedating the patient and giving an analgesic until the ET tube is removed. Assess the drugs' effectiveness in achieving an acceptable level of patient comfort by using a valid pain scale, sedation scale (e.g., Richmond Agitation and Sedation Scale [RASS], Sedation Agitation Scale [SAS]), and/or delirium scale.[20] Consider using relaxation techniques (e.g., music therapy) to complement drug therapy.

◆ Complications of Endotracheal Intubation

Two major complications of ET intubation are unplanned extubation and aspiration. Unplanned *extubation* (i.e., removal of the ET tube from the trachea) may complicate the patient's recovery. Unplanned extubation can be due to patient removal of the ET tube or accidental removal during movement or a procedure. Usually, the unplanned extubation is obvious (i.e., the patient is holding the ET tube). Other times, the tip of the ET tube is in the hypopharynx or esophagus and the extubation is not obvious. You are responsible for preventing unplanned extubation by ensuring that the ET tube is secured and observing and supporting the ET tube during repositioning, procedures, and patient transfers. Giving adequate sedation and analgesia and using standardized weaning protocols decrease the incidence of self-extubation.[21]

The use of restraints to immobilize the patient's hands is a deterrent to self-extubation.[21] Be sure to explain to the patient and caregiver when you use short-term restraints for patient safety and discuss the use of alternatives. Reassess for the continued need of restraints (per agency policy) and limit restraint use when possible.

Should an unplanned extubation occur, stay with the patient and call for help. Interventions are aimed at maintaining the patient's airway, supporting ventilation (e.g., manually ventilating the patient with a BVM and 100% O_2), securing the

appropriate help to reintubate the patient (if needed), and providing psychologic support to the patient.

> **! SAFETY ALERT Unplanned Extubation**
> Observe for signs of unplanned extubation:
> - Activation of the low-pressure ventilator alarm
> - Decreased or absent breath sounds
> - Respiratory distress
> - Auditory cuff leak
>
> What to do during an unplanned extubation:
> - Stay with the patient
> - Support the patient's oxygenation as needed by applying an adjunct therapy, such as a nasal cannula or manually ventilating the patient with a BVM and 100% O_2
> - Notify the HCP and RT
> - Assess for respiratory distress and listen for stridor
> - Assess the patient's ability to cough and/or vocalize
> - Assess the patient's ability to maintain secretions
> - Assess the patient's need for reintubation
> - If the patient is unable to protect their airway or is in respiratory distress, prepare for reintubation

Aspiration is another potential hazard for the patient with an ET tube. The ET tube passes through the epiglottis, splinting it in an open position. Thus the intubated patient cannot protect the airway from aspiration. The high-volume, low-pressure ET cuff cannot totally prevent the trickle of oral or gastric secretions into the trachea.[22] Further, secretions collect above the cuff. When the cuff is deflated, those secretions can move into the lungs. Some ET tubes provide continuous suctioning of secretions above the cuff (Fig. 65.18).

Oral intubation increases salivation, yet swallowing is difficult, so suction the patient's mouth often. Use a Yankauer (tonsil-tip) suction catheter or a sterile single-use catheter. Other factors contributing to aspiration include improper cuff inflation, patient positioning, and decreased gastric mobility and bowel function if receiving EN. The patient with an ET tube is at risk for aspiration of gastric contents. Even when the cuff is properly inflated, take precautions to prevent vomiting, which can lead to aspiration.

Often, a nasogastric (NG) or an orogastric (OG) tube is inserted and connected to low, intermittent suction when a patient is first intubated. An OG tube is preferred over an NG tube to reduce the risk for sinusitis. All intubated patients who

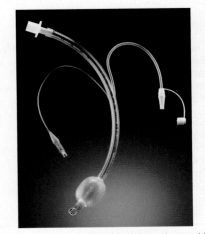

FIG. 65.18 Continuous subglottal suctioning can be provided by the Hi Lo Evac Tube. A dorsal lumen above the cuff allows for suctioning of secretions from the subglottic area. (Reprinted by permission of Nellcor Puritan Bennett Inc, Pleasanton, CA.)

are receiving EN should have the HOB elevated a minimum of 30 to 45 degrees, unless medically contraindicated.

MECHANICAL VENTILATION

Mechanical ventilation is the process by which the FIO_2 (21% [room air] or more) is moved in and out of the lungs by a mechanical ventilator. Mechanical ventilation is not curative. It is a means of supporting patients until they recover the ability to breathe independently. It can also serve as a bridge to long-term mechanical ventilation or until a decision is made to stop ventilatory support.

Indications for mechanical ventilation include (1) apnea, (2) inability to breathe or protect the airway, (3) acute respiratory failure (see Chapter 67), (4) severe hypoxia, and (5) respiratory muscle fatigue. Patients with chronic lung disease and their caregivers should be given the opportunity to discuss mechanical ventilation before end-stage respiratory failure develops. Encourage all patients, especially those with chronic illnesses, to discuss the subject of life-sustaining measures, including mechanical ventilation, with their families and HCPs. The patient's wishes about end-of-life treatment should be recorded in an advance directive.

The decision to use, withhold, or stop mechanical ventilation must be made carefully, respecting the wishes of the patient. When the interprofessional care team, patient, and/or caregiver disagree over the treatment plan that the patient desires, conferences are essential to keep the lines of communication open and discuss options. You may need to consult the agency's ethics committee for assistance.

Types of Mechanical Ventilation

The 2 major types of mechanical ventilation are negative pressure and positive pressure ventilation.

Negative Pressure Ventilation. Negative pressure ventilation involves the use of chambers that encase the chest or body and surround it with intermittent subatmospheric (or negative) pressure. The "iron lung" was the first form of negative pressure ventilation. It was developed during the polio epidemic. Intermittent negative pressure around the chest wall pulls the chest outward, reducing intrathoracic pressure. Air rushes in via the upper airway, which is outside the sealed chamber. Expiration is passive. The machine cycles off, allowing chest retraction. This type of ventilation is like normal ventilation in that decreased intrathoracic pressures produce inspiration, and expiration is passive. Negative pressure ventilation is noninvasive and does not need an artificial airway.

Several portable negative pressure ventilators are available for home use. They are mainly for patients with neuromuscular diseases, central nervous system disorders, diseases and injuries of the spinal cord, and severe COPD. They are not routinely used for acutely ill patients.

🖊 DRUG ALERT Oxygen

- O_2 is considered a drug, and overexposure can lead to O_2 toxicity.
- Mechanically ventilated patients receiving high levels of FIO_2 for prolonged periods of time (e.g., 60% FIO_2 for >24 hours) are at risk for O_2 toxicity.
- Target FIO_2 levels are to maintain SpO_2 >92% and PaO_2 between 60 and 80 mm Hg.
- Assess ABGs for evidence of excess O_2.
- Monitor patient for signs of O_2 toxicity: uncontrolled coughing, chest pain, and dyspnea.

Positive Pressure Ventilation. Positive pressure ventilation (PPV) is the main method used with acutely ill patients (Fig. 65.19). During inspiration the ventilator pushes air into the lungs under positive pressure. Unlike spontaneous ventilation, intrathoracic pressure is raised during lung inflation rather than lowered. Expiration occurs passively as in normal expiration. There are 2 categories of PPV: volume and pressure ventilation.[13]

Volume Ventilation. With volume ventilation, a predetermined V_T is delivered with each inspiration. The amount of pressure needed to deliver the breath varies based on compliance and resistance factors of the patient-ventilator system. So, the V_T is consistent from breath to breath, but airway pressures vary.

Pressure Ventilation. With *pressure ventilation,* the peak inspiratory pressure is predetermined. The V_T delivered to the patient varies based on the selected pressure and compliance and resistance factors of the patient-ventilator system. Careful attention must be given to the V_T to prevent unplanned hyperventilation or hypoventilation. For example, when the patient breathes out of synchrony with the ventilator, the pressure limit may be reached quickly, and the volume of gas delivered may be small.

Settings of Mechanical Ventilators

Mechanical ventilator settings regulate rate, V_T, O_2 concentration, and other characteristics of ventilation (Table 65.10, Fig. 65.20). Settings are based on the patient's status (e.g., ABGs, ideal body weight, current physiologic state, level of consciousness, respiratory muscle strength). Settings are evaluated and adjusted until oxygenation and ventilation targets have been reached.

It is important that you check that all ventilator alarms are always on. Alarms alert the staff to potentially dangerous situations, such as mechanical malfunction, apnea, unplanned extubation, or patient asynchrony with the ventilator (Table 65.11). On many ventilators, the alarms can be temporarily suspended or silenced for up to 2 minutes for suctioning or testing while a staff member is in the room. After that time, the alarm system automatically turns back on.

❗ SAFETY ALERT Alarm Fatigue

- Alarm fatigue can develop in those who hear an excess number of alarms, resulting in sensory overload.
- This can cause a delayed response to alarms or dismissing them altogether and can lead to serious adverse events (e.g., patient death).
- One way to reduce alarm fatigue includes customizing alarm parameters based on patient specific needs.[23]

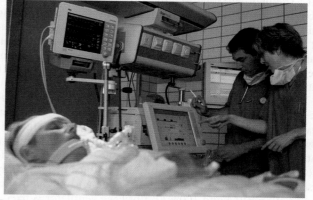

FIG. 65.19 Patient receiving mechanical ventilation. (Courtesy Draeger Medical, Houston, TX.)

TABLE 65.10 Settings of Mechanical Ventilation

Parameter	Description
Respiratory rate (f)	Number of breaths the ventilator delivers per minute. *Usual setting:* 12–20 breaths/min
Tidal volume (V_T)	Volume of gas delivered to patient during each ventilator breath. *Usual volume:* 6–8 mL/kg, 4–8 mL/kg in ARDS
O_2 concentration (FIO_2)	Fraction of inspired O_2 (FIO_2) delivered to patient. May be set between 21% (essentially room air) and 100%. *Usually adjusted* to maintain PaO_2 level >60–80 mm Hg or SpO_2 level >92%
Positive end-expiratory pressure (PEEP)	Positive pressure applied at the end of expiration of ventilator breaths. *Usual setting:* 5 cm H_2O
Pressure support	Positive pressure used to augment patient's inspiratory pressure. *Usual setting:* 5–10 cm H_2O
I/E ratio	Duration of inspiration (I) to duration of expiration (E). *Usual setting:* 1:2 to 1:1.5 unless inverse ratio ventilation is desired
Inspiratory flow rate and time	Speed with which the V_T is delivered. *Usual setting:* 40–80 L/min and time is 0.8–1.2 sec
Sensitivity	Determines the amount of effort the patient must generate to initiate a ventilator breath. It may be set for pressure triggering or flow triggering. *Usual setting:* A pressure trigger is set 0.5–1.5 cm H_2O below baseline pressure and a flow trigger is set 1–3 L/min below baseline flow
High-pressure limit	Regulates the maximal pressure the ventilator can generate to deliver the V_T. When the pressure limit is reached, the ventilator ends the breath and spills the undelivered volume into the atmosphere. *Usual setting:* 10–20 cm H_2O above peak inspiratory pressure

Adapted from Urden LD, Stacy, KM, Lough ME: *Critical care nursing: Diagnosis and management,* ed 8, St Louis, 2018, Elsevier.

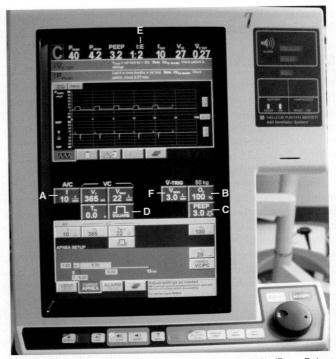

FIG. 65.20 Ventilator control panel (Puritan Bennett 840). (From Roberts JR: *Roberts and Hedges' clinical procedures in emergency medicine and acute care,* ed 7 ed, St Louis, 2019, Elsevier.)

Ventilator Alarms. Mechanical ventilators may become disconnected or malfunction. Most deaths from accidental ventilator disconnection occur while the alarm is off. Most accidental disconnections are discovered by low-pressure alarms. The most frequent site for disconnection is between the tracheal tube and the adapter. Push connections together and then twist to secure more tightly. Be certain that alarms are always set and activated. Chart that this is the case. You can pause alarms (not inactivate) during suctioning or removal from the ventilator, but you must reactivate them before leaving the patient's bedside.

Ventilator malfunction may occur. Although most agencies have emergency generators in case of a power failure and newer ventilators may have battery backup, power failure is always a possibility. Have a plan for manually ventilating all patients who depend on a ventilator. If, at any time, you decide the ventilator is malfunctioning (e.g., failure of O_2 supply), disconnect the patient from the machine and manually ventilate with a BVM and 100% O_2 until the ventilator is fixed or replaced.

Modes of Volume Ventilation

The ways by which the patient and ventilator interact to deliver effective ventilation are called *ventilator modes.* The selected ventilator mode is based on how much WOB the patient should or can perform. WOB is the inspiratory effort needed to overcome the elasticity and viscosity of the lungs along with the airway resistance. The mode is determined by the patient's ventilatory status, respiratory drive, and ABGs. Generally, ventilator modes are controlled or assisted.

With controlled ventilatory support, the ventilator does all the WOB for the patient. With assisted ventilatory support, the ventilator and patient share the WOB. Historically, volume modes, such as controlled mandatory ventilation (CMV), assist-control ventilation (ACV), and synchronized intermittent mandatory ventilation (SIMV), have been used to treat critically ill patients. Pressure modes, such as pressure support ventilation (PSV), pressure-control ventilation (PCV), and inverse ratio ventilation (PC-IRV) are becoming more common.[24] Table 65.12 describes ventilator modes.

Assist-Control Ventilation. With **assist-control ventilation (ACV)**, the ventilator delivers a preset V_T at a preset frequency. When the patient initiates a spontaneous breath, the ventilator senses a decrease in intrathoracic pressure and then delivers the preset V_T. The patient can breathe faster than the preset rate but not slower. ACV has the advantage of allowing the patient some control over ventilation while providing some assistance. It is used in patients with a variety of conditions, including neuromuscular disorders (e.g., Guillain-Barré syndrome), pulmonary edema, and acute respiratory failure.

With ACV, the patient has the potential for hyperventilation. The spontaneously breathing patient can easily be overventilated, resulting in hyperventilation. If the volume or minimum rate is set too low and the patient is apneic or weak, the patient

TABLE 65.11 Managing Mechanical Ventilation Alarms

Alarm	Possible Causes	Interventions
High-pressure limit	• Secretions, coughing, or gagging • Patient fighting ventilator (ventilator asynchrony) • Condensate (water) in tubing • Kinked or compressed tubing (e.g., patient biting on ET tube) • ↑ Resistance (e.g., bronchospasm) • ↓ Compliance (e.g., pulmonary edema, ARDS, tension pneumo-thorax, atelectasis, pneumonia) • Improper alarm setting • ET tube inserted too far (e.g., right mainstem bronchus or carina)	• Clear secretions and ↑ sedation • Reassure patient • Remove water from ventilator tubing • Unkink tubing, insert bite block, or reposition patient • Give bronchodilator • Assess breath sounds, obtain chest x-ray • Adjust ET tube
Low-pressure limit	• Total or partial ventilator disconnect • Loss of airway (e.g., total or partial extubation) • ET tube or tracheotomy cuff leak (e.g., patient speaking, grunting)	• Check connections • Confirm adequate tidal volume and ET tube position with chest x-ray • Reinflate cuff
Apnea	• Respiratory arrest • Oversedation • Change in patient condition • Loss of airway (e.g., total or partial extubation)	• ↓ Sedation • ↓ Analgesia • Reverse sedation or analgesia • Confirm ET tube placement or reintubate
High V_T, minute venti-lation, or respira-tory rate	• Pain, anxiety • Change in patient condition (e.g., ↑ metabolic demand, fever, hypoxia, hypercapnia) • Excess condensate or secretions in tubing (i.e., false reading)	• Treat pain • Assess patient for change in condition • Obtain an ABG • Remove water or secretions from tubing
Low V_T or minute ventilation	• Change in patient's breathing efforts (e.g., rate and volume) • Patient disconnection, loose connection, or leak in circuit • ET tube or tracheotomy cuff leak (e.g., air leak) • Insufficient gas flow	• Assess patients respiratory and neurologic status. Reduce sedation. • Assess ventilator circuit for leaks • Reassess cuff to ensure cuff is adequately inflated • Check ventilator settings
Ventilator inoperative or low battery	• Machine malfunction • Unplugged, power failure, or internal battery not charged	• Ensure mechanical ventilator is plugged into right power source • Disconnect patient from mechanical ventilator and use bag- valve-mask to ventilate until machine is properly functioning

Adapted from Urden LD, Stacy KM, Lough ME: *Critical care nursing: Diagnosis and management,* ed 8, St Louis, 2018, Elsevier.

TABLE 65.12 Modes of Mechanical Ventilation

Mode of Ventilation	Ventilator Settings	Nursing Implications
Volume Modes		
Assist-control (AC) or assisted mandatory ventilation (AMV)	• Requires rate, V_T, inspiratory time, and PEEP set for the patient • The ventilator sensitivity is set, so when the patient initiates a sponta-neous breath, a full-volume breath is delivered	• Hyperventilation can occur • To limit spontaneous breaths, sedation may be needed • Muscle fatigue may occur due to ↑ work of breathing
Intermittent mandatory ventilation (IMV) and synchronized inter-mittent mandatory ventilation (SIMV)	• Requires rate, V_T, inspiratory time, sensitivity, and PEEP set for the patient • Between "mandatory breaths," patients spontaneously breathe at their own rates and V_T • With SIMV, the ventilator synchronizes the mandatory breaths with the patient's own inspirations	
Pressure Modes		
Pressure support ventilation (PSV)	• Provides an augmented inspiration to a spontaneously breathing patient • HCP selects inspiratory pressure level, PEEP, and sensitivity • When the patient initiates a breath, a high flow of gas is delivered to the preselected pressure level, and pressure is maintained throughout inspira-tion • Patient determines V_T, rate, and inspiratory time	• Reduces patients work of breathing and ↑ ventilator synchrony • Monitor patient for hypercapnia
Pressure-control inverse ratio ventilation (PC-IRV)	• Combines pressure-limited ventilation with an inverse ratio of inspiration to expiration • HCP selects the pressure level, rate, inspiratory time (1:, 2:1, 3:1, 4:1), and PEEP level • With the prolonged inspiratory times, auto-PEEP may result • Auto-PEEP may be a desirable outcome of the inverse ratios	• Requires sedation and/or pharmacologic paralysis to oxygenate and ventilate patient due to discomfort • Air trapping can occur due to ↑ intra-thoracic pressure, leading to a ↓ cardiac output • Monitor for hypercapnia
Airway pressure release ventilation (APRV)	• Provides 2 levels of continuous positive airway pressure (CPAP) with timed releases • Permits spontaneous breathing throughout the respiratory cycle • HCP selects both pressure (high, low) and time (high, low). V_T is not a set variable and depends on the CPAP level, the patient's compliance and resistance, and spontaneous breathing effort	

Modified from Wiegand DL: *AACN procedure manual for high acuity, progressive, and critical care,* ed 7, St Louis, 2017, Elsevier; and Urden LD, Stacy, KM, Lough ME: *Critical care nursing: Diagnosis and management,* ed 8, St Louis, 2018, Elsevier.

can be hypoventilated. Thus these patients need vigilant assessment and monitoring of ventilatory status, including respiratory rate, ABGs, SpO_2, and $ScvO_2$ or SvO_2. It is important that the sensitivity, or amount of negative pressure needed to start a breath, is appropriate to the patient's condition. For example, if it is too hard for the patient to begin a breath, the WOB is increased and the patient may tire (i.e., the patient "rides" the ventilator) or develop ventilator dyssynchrony (i.e., the patient "fights" the ventilator).

Synchronized Intermittent Mandatory Ventilation. With **synchronized intermittent mandatory ventilation (SIMV)**, the ventilator delivers a preset V_T at a preset frequency in synchrony with the patient's spontaneous breathing. Between ventilator-delivered breaths, the patient can breathe spontaneously through the ventilator circuit. Thus the patient receives the preset FIO_2 during the spontaneous breaths but self-regulates the rate and V_T of those breaths. SIMV is used during continuous ventilation and during weaning from the ventilator. It may be combined with PSV (described later). Potential benefits of SIMV include improved patient-ventilator synchrony, lower mean airway pressure, and prevention of muscle atrophy as the patient takes on more of the WOB.

SIMV has disadvantages. If spontaneous breathing decreases when the preset rate is low, ventilation may not be adequately supported. Only patients with regular, spontaneous breathing should use low-rate SIMV. Weaning with SIMV demands close monitoring and may take longer because the rate of breathing is gradually reduced. Patients being weaned with SIMV may have increased muscle fatigue associated with spontaneous breathing efforts.

Modes of Pressure Ventilation

Pressure Support Ventilation. With **pressure support ventilation (PSV)**, positive pressure is applied to the airway only during inspiration and is used with the patient's spontaneous respirations. The patient must be able to initiate a breath in this modality. The level of positive airway pressure is preset so that the gas flow rate is greater than the patient's inspiratory flow rate. As the patient starts a breath, the machine senses the spontaneous effort and supplies a rapid flow of gas at the initiation of the breath and variable flow throughout the breath. With PSV, the patient determines inspiratory length, V_T, and respiratory rate. V_T depends on the pressure level and airway compliance.

PSV is used with continuous ventilation and during weaning. It also may be used with SIMV during weaning. PSV is not often used as ventilatory support during acute respiratory failure because of the risk for hypoventilation and apnea. Advantages include increased patient comfort, decreased WOB (because inspiratory efforts are augmented), decreased O_2 consumption (because inspiratory work is reduced), and increased endurance conditioning (because the patient is exercising respiratory muscles).

Pressure-Control and Pressure-Control Inverse Ratio Ventilation. *Pressure-control ventilation (PCV)* provides a pressure-limited breath delivered at a set rate. It may permit spontaneous breathing. The V_T is not set. It is determined by the pressure limit set. *Pressure-control inverse ratio ventilation (PC-IRV)* combines pressure-limited ventilation with an inverse ratio of inspiration (I) to expiration (E). Some HCPs use PC without IRV.

The *I/E ratio* is the ratio of duration of inspiration to the duration of expiration. This ratio is normally 1:2 or 1:3. With IRV, the I/E ratio begins at 1:1 and may progress to 4:1. Prolonged positive pressure is applied, increasing inspiratory time. IRV gradually expands collapsed alveoli. The short expiratory time

has a PEEP-like effect, preventing alveolar collapse. Because IRV imposes a nonphysiologic breathing pattern, the patient needs sedation and often paralysis.

PC-IRV is used for patients with acute respiratory distress syndrome (ARDS) who continue to have hypoxemia despite high levels of PEEP. Not all patients with poor oxygenation respond to PC-IRV.

Airway Pressure Release Ventilation. *Airway pressure release ventilation (APRV)* permits spontaneous breathing at any point during the respiratory cycle with a preset CPAP with short timed pressure releases. The CPAP level (pressure high, pressure low) is adjusted to keep oxygenation goals while the timed releases (time high, time low) are increased or decreased to meet ventilation goals.[25] V_T is not set. It varies depending on the CPAP level, the patient's compliance and resistance, and spontaneous breathing effort. This mode is best for patients who need high pressure levels for alveolar recruitment (open collapsed alveoli). An advantage is that it allows for spontaneous respirations. This may reduce the need for deep sedation or paralytics.

Positive End-Expiratory Pressure. **Positive end-expiratory pressure (PEEP)** is a ventilatory maneuver, or mechanical ventilator setting, in which positive pressure is applied to the airway during exhalation. Normally during exhalation, airway pressure drops to near 0, and exhalation occurs passively. With PEEP, exhalation is passive but pressure falls to a preset level, often 3 to 20 cm H_2O. Lung volume during expiration and between breaths is greater than normal with PEEP. This increases FRC and often improves oxygenation by restoring the lung volume that normally remains at the end of passive exhalation. The mechanisms by which PEEP increases FRC and oxygenation include increased aeration of patent alveoli, aeration of previously collapsed alveoli, and prevention of alveolar collapse throughout the respiratory cycle.

PEEP is titrated to the point that oxygenation improves without compromising hemodynamics. We call this *optimal PEEP*. Often 5 cm H_2O PEEP (referred to as *physiologic PEEP*) is used prophylactically to replace the glottic mechanism, help maintain a normal FRC, and prevent alveolar collapse. PEEP of 5 cm H_2O is used for patients with a history of alveolar collapse during weaning. PEEP improves gas exchange, vital capacity, and inspiratory force when used during weaning.

In contrast, *auto-PEEP* is not purposely set on the ventilator but is a result of inadequate exhalation time. Auto-PEEP is more PEEP over what is set by the HCP. This added PEEP may result in increased WOB, barotrauma, and hemodynamic instability. Interventions to limit auto-PEEP include sedation and analgesia, large-diameter ET tube, bronchodilators, short inspiratory times, and decreased respiratory rates. Reducing water accumulation in the ventilator circuit by frequent emptying or use of heated circuits also limits auto-PEEP. In patients with short exhalation times and early airway closure (e.g., asthma), setting PEEP above auto-PEEP can offset auto-PEEP effects by splinting the airway open during exhalation and preventing "air trapping."

FIO_2 often can be reduced when PEEP is used. PEEP is generally indicated in all patients who are mechanically ventilated. The classic indication for PEEP therapy is ARDS (see Chapter 67). PEEP is used with caution in patients with increased ICP, low CO, and hypovolemia. In these cases, the adverse effects of high PEEP may outweigh the benefits.

Other Modes. Advances in ventilator technology have led to the development of other pressure modes. However, the names and features of these other options are manufacturer specific. The superiority of these modes has not been proven. Some examples include *volume-assured pressure ventilation* and *adaptive support ventilation*.

Other Methods to Improve Oxygenation and Ventilation

Automatic Tube Compensation. *Automatic tube compensation (ATC)* is an adjunct designed to overcome WOB through an artificial airway. It is currently available on many ventilators. ATC is increased during inspiration and decreased during expiration. It is set by entering the internal diameter of the patient's airway and the desired number for compensation. ATC may be less effective in patients with excess secretions or who need longer term ventilation.

High-Frequency Oscillatory Ventilation. **High-frequency oscillatory ventilation (HFOV)** involves delivery of a small V_T (usually 1 to 5 mL/kg of body weight) at rapid respiratory rates (100 to 300 breaths/min). The goals are to recruit (e.g., alveolar expansion) and maintain lung volume and reduce intrapulmonary shunting. While HFOV may be a useful mode for patients with life-threatening hypoxia, it has not improved survival of patients with ARDS.[26] Patients receiving HFOV must be sedated and may need to be paralyzed to suppress spontaneous respiration.

Nitric Oxide. *Nitric oxide* (NO) is a gaseous molecule that is made intravascularly and takes part in the regulation of pulmonary vascular tone. Inhibiting NO production results in pulmonary vasoconstriction. Administering continuous inhaled NO results in pulmonary vasodilation. NO may be given through an ET tube, a tracheostomy, or a face mask. Currently, NO is used as a diagnostic screening tool for pulmonary hypertension and to improve oxygenation during mechanical ventilation in this patient population. The use of NO does not reduce mortality in patients with ARDS and may cause kidney injury.[27]

Prone Positioning. *Prone positioning* is the repositioning of a patient from a supine or lateral position to a prone (on the stomach, face down) position. This repositioning improves lung recruitment through various mechanisms. Gravity reverses the effects of fluid in the dependent parts of the lungs as the patient is moved from supine to prone. The heart rests on the sternum, away from the lungs, contributing to an overall uniformity of pleural pressures. The prone position requires increased sedation and is nurse-intensive. It is an effective supportive therapy used in critically ill patients with severe ARDS to improve oxygenation.[28]

Extracorporeal Membrane Oxygenation. *Extracorporeal membrane oxygenation* (ECMO) is an alternative form of pulmonary support for the patient with severe respiratory failure (Fig. 65.21).[13] It is used most often in the pediatric and neonatal populations but is increasingly being used in adults. ECMO is a modification of cardiac bypass. It involves partially removing

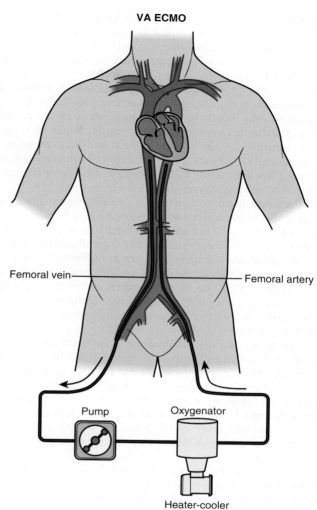

FIG. 65.21 ECMO circuit. The circuit consists of a pump, oxygenator, and heating-cooling element. Circulatory access is typically obtained through the femoral vein and artery. (From Mann DL, Zipes DP, Libby P, et al: *Braunwald's heart disease: A textbook of cardiovascular medicine*, ed 11, St Louis, 2019, Saunders.)

blood from a patient with large-bore catheters, infusing O_2, removing CO_2, and returning the blood to the patient. This intensive therapy requires systemic anticoagulation and is a time-limited intervention. A skilled team of specialists, including a perfusionist, must be continuously at the bedside.

Complications of Positive Pressure Ventilation

Although PPV may be essential to maintain ventilation and oxygenation, it can cause adverse effects. It may be hard to distinguish complications of mechanical ventilation from the underlying disease.

Cardiovascular System. PPV can affect circulation because of the transmission of increased mean airway pressure to various structures in the thorax. Increased intrathoracic pressure compresses the thoracic vessels. This compression causes decreased venous return to the heart, left ventricular end-diastolic volume (preload), and CO, resulting in hypotension. Mean airway pressure is further increased if PEEP is being titrated (greater than 5 cm H_2O) to improve oxygenation.

If the lungs are noncompliant (e.g., ARDS), airway pressures are not as easily transmitted to the heart and blood vessels. Thus effects of PPV on CO are reduced. Conversely, with compliant lungs (e.g., COPD), there is increased danger of transmission of high airway pressures and negative effects on hemodynamics.

Hypovolemia (e.g., hemorrhage) and decreased venous tone (e.g., sepsis, spinal shock) can further compromise venous return. Restoring and maintaining the circulating blood volume are important in minimizing cardiovascular complications.

Pulmonary System

Barotrauma. As lung inflation pressures increase, risk for *barotrauma* increases. Barotrauma results when the increased airway pressure distends the lungs and possibly ruptures fragile alveoli or emphysematous blebs. Patients with noncompliant lungs (e.g., COPD) are at greatest risk for barotrauma. Patients with stiff lungs (e.g., ARDS) who are given high inspiratory pressures and high levels of PEEP (greater than 5 cm H_2O) or have a lung abscess from necrotizing organisms (e.g., staphylococci) are also at risk.

Air can escape into the pleural space from alveoli or the interstitium and become trapped. Pleural pressure increases and collapses the lung, causing a pneumothorax (see Chapter 27 for more about pneumothorax.) The lungs receive air during inspiration but cannot expel it during expiration. Respiratory bronchioles are larger on inspiration than expiration. They may close on expiration, and air becomes trapped. With PPV, a simple pneumothorax can become a life-threatening tension pneumothorax. The mediastinum and contralateral lung are compressed, reducing CO. Immediate treatment of the pneumothorax is required.

Pneumomediastinum usually begins with rupture of alveoli into the lung interstitium. Progressive air movement occurs into the mediastinum and subcutaneous neck tissue, and a pneumothorax often follows. New, unexplained subcutaneous emphysema is an indication for immediate chest x-ray. Pneumomediastinum and subcutaneous emphysema may be too small to detect on x-ray or clinically before the development of a pneumothorax.

Volutrauma. The concept of *volutrauma* in PPV relates to the lung injury that occurs when a large V_T is used to ventilate noncompliant lungs. Volutrauma results in alveolar rupture and movement of fluids and proteins into the alveolar spaces. Low-volume ventilation should be used in patients with ARDS to protect the lungs.

Alveolar Hypoventilation. Alveolar hypoventilation can be caused by inappropriate ventilator settings, leakage of air from the ventilator tubing or around the ET tube or tracheostomy cuff, lung secretions or obstruction, and low ventilation/perfusion ratio. A low V_T or respiratory rate decreases minute ventilation. This results in hypoventilation, atelectasis, and respiratory

acidosis. A leaking cuff or tubing that is not secured may cause air leakage and lower V_T. Mobilizing the patient, turning the patient at least every 2 hours, encouraging deep breathing and coughing, and suctioning (as needed) may limit lung secretions. Increasing the V_T, adding small increments of PEEP, and adding a preset number of *sighs* to the ventilator settings (i.e., a deeper than normal breath incorporated into the respiratory cycle) can help reduce the risk for atelectasis.

Alveolar Hyperventilation. Respiratory alkalosis can occur if the respiratory rate or V_T is set too high (*mechanical overventilation*) or if the patient receiving assisted ventilation is *hyperventilating*. It is easy to overventilate a patient on PPV. Especially at risk are patients with chronic alveolar hypoventilation and CO_2 retention. For example, the patient with COPD may have a chronic $PaCO_2$ elevation (acidosis) and compensatory bicarbonate retention by the kidneys. When the patient is ventilated, the patient's "normal baseline" rather than the standard normal values is the therapeutic goal. If the COPD patient is returned to a standard normal $PaCO_2$, the patient will develop alkalosis because of the retained bicarbonate. Such a patient could move from compensated respiratory acidosis to serious metabolic alkalosis.

The presence of alkalosis makes weaning from the ventilator difficult. Alkalosis, especially if the onset is abrupt, can have serious consequences, including hypokalemia, hypocalcemia, and dysrhythmias. Usually the patient with COPD who is supported on the ventilator does better with a short inspiratory and longer expiratory time.

If hyperventilation is spontaneous, it is important to determine the cause and treat it. Common causes include hypoxemia, pain, fear, anxiety, or compensation for metabolic acidosis. Patients who fight the ventilator or breathe out of synchrony may be anxious or in pain. If the patient is anxious and fearful, sitting with the patient and verbally coaching the patient to breathe with the ventilator or weaning the ventilator to a more appropriate setting may help. If these measures fail, manually ventilating the patient slowly with a BVM and 100% O_2 may slow breathing enough to bring it in synchrony with the ventilator.

Ventilator-Associated Pneumonia. The risk for HAI pneumonia is highest in patients requiring mechanical ventilation because the ET or tracheostomy tube bypasses normal upper airway defenses. Poor nutrition, immobility, and the underlying disease process (e.g., immunosuppression, organ failure) make the patient more prone to infection. *Ventilator-associated pneumonia* (VAP) is pneumonia that occurs 48 hours or more after ET intubation.[29] It occurs in as many as 27% of all intubated patients. Patients who develop VAP have significantly longer hospital stays and higher mortality rates than those who do not. Half of the patients develop early VAP (VAP that occurs within 96 hours of mechanical ventilation).

In those with early VAP, sputum cultures often grow gram-negative bacteria (e.g., *E coli, Klebsiella, Streptococcus pneumoniae, H influenzae*). Organisms associated with late VAP include antibiotic-resistant organisms, such as *Pseudomonas aeruginosa* and oxacillin-resistant *Staphylococcus aureus*. These organisms are abundant in the hospital environment and the patient's GI tract. They can spread in a number of ways, including contaminated respiratory equipment, inadequate hand washing, adverse environmental factors (e.g., poor room ventilation, high traffic flow), and decreased patient ability to cough and clear secretions. Colonization of the oropharynx tract by gram-negative organisms predisposes the patient to gram-negative pneumonia.

Clinical signs that suggest VAP include fever, high white blood cell count, purulent or odorous sputum, crackles or wheezes on auscultation, and pulmonary infiltrates noted on chest x-ray. The patient is given antibiotics after appropriate cultures are taken by tracheal suctioning or bronchoscopy and when infection is evident.

Guidelines for VAP prevention include (1) minimizing sedation, including daily spontaneous awakening trials (SATs) and daily spontaneous breathing trials (SBTs), (2) early exercise and mobilization, (3) use of ET tubes with subglottic secretion drainage ports for patients likely to be intubated greater than 48 to 72 hours, (4) HOB elevation at a minimum of 30 to 45 degrees unless medically contraindicated, (5) oral care with chlorhexidine, and (6) no routine changes of the patient's ventilator circuit tubing.[30]

Other preventive measures include strict hand washing before and after suctioning, whenever ventilator equipment is touched, and after contact with any respiratory secretions (see Nursing Management: Artificial Airway earlier in this chapter). Always wear gloves when in contact with the patient and change gloves between activities (e.g., emptying urinary catheter drainage, hanging an IV drug). Last, always drain the water that collects in the ventilator tubing away from the patient as it collects.

! SAFETY ALERT *VAP Prevention Strategies*
- Practice good hand hygiene techniques before and after suctioning.
- Wear gloves when providing oral hygiene.
- Suction patients as needed for comfort.
- Keep the HOB elevated >30 to 45 degrees.
- Turn patient according to agency policy (e.g., side to side every 2 hours).
- Initiate early mobilization.
- Follow agency policy for limiting sedation with SAT.
- Perform daily SBT unless contraindicated.[31]

Psychosocial Needs. The patient receiving mechanical ventilation often has physical and emotional stress. In addition to the problems related to critical care patients discussed at the beginning of this chapter, the patient supported by a mechanical ventilator is unable to speak, eat, move, or breathe normally. Tubes and machines cause pain, fear, and anxiety. Usual activities, such as eating, elimination, and coughing, are extremely complicated.

The ABCDEF Bundle is an evidence-based practice of providing care that strives to attain an environment in which all patients receiving mechanical ventilation are calm, delirium free, and able to express their needs for pain control, positioning, and reassurance. The ABCDEF Bundle ensures (1) **A**ssessment, (2) **B**oth SATs and SBTs are done, (3) correct **C**hoice of analgesia and sedation, (4) **D**elirium prevention and management, (5) **E**arly mobility, and (6) **F**amily engagement.[32]

Feeling safe is an overpowering need of patients on mechanical ventilation. Work to strengthen the various factors that affect feeling safe. Encourage hope, as appropriate, and build trusting relationships with both the patient and caregiver. Involve them in decision making as much as possible.[19]

Sedation and Analgesia. Patients receiving PPV may need sedation (e.g., propofol) and/or analgesia (e.g., fentanyl) to help with optimal ventilation. Before starting sedation or analgesia in the mechanically ventilated patient who is agitated or anxious, identify the cause of distress. Common problems that can result in patient agitation or anxiety include PPV, nutritional

deficits, pain, hypoxemia, hypercapnia, drugs, and environmental stressors (e.g., sleep deprivation).

At times, the decision is made to paralyze the patient with a neuromuscular blocking agent (e.g., cisatracurium [Nimbex]) to provide more effective synchrony with the ventilator and improve oxygenation. Remember that the paralyzed patient can hear, see, and feel. It is essential to give IV sedation and analgesia concurrently when the patient is paralyzed. Sedated or paralyzed patients may be aware of their surroundings. You should always address them as if they were awake and alert.

Monitoring patients receiving these drugs is challenging. Assess the patient using train-of-four (TOF) peripheral nerve stimulation, physiologic signs of pain or anxiety (e.g., changes in HR and BP), and ventilator synchrony. The TOF assessment involves using a peripheral nerve stimulator to deliver 4 successive stimulating currents to elicit muscle twitches (Fig. 65.22).[33] The number of twitches varies with the amount of neuromuscular blockade. The usual goal is 1 or 2 twitches out of 4 currents.

Noninvasive electroencephalogram technology (e.g., bispectral index monitoring [BIS]) can be used to guide sedative and analgesic therapy.[34] Excess administration of neuromuscular blocking agents may predispose the patient to prolonged paralysis and muscle weakness even after these agents are stopped.

Neurologic System. In patients with head injury, PPV, especially with PEEP, can impair cerebral blood flow. The increased intrathoracic positive pressure impedes venous drainage from the brain. This results in jugular venous distention. The patient may have increases in ICP due to the impaired venous return and subsequent increase in cerebral volume. Elevating the HOB and keeping the patient's head in alignment may reduce the harmful effects of PPV on ICP.

Sodium and Water Imbalance. Progressive fluid retention often occurs after 48 to 72 hours of PPV, especially PPV with PEEP. Fluid retention is associated with decreased urine output and increased sodium retention. Fluid balance changes may be due to decreased CO, which causes decreased renal perfusion. This stimulates the release of renin with the subsequent production of angiotensin and aldosterone (see Chapter 44, Fig. 44.4). This results in sodium and water retention. It is possible that pressure changes within the thorax are associated with decreased release of atrial natriuretic peptide, which also causes sodium retention. Less insensible water loss occurs via the airway because ventilated

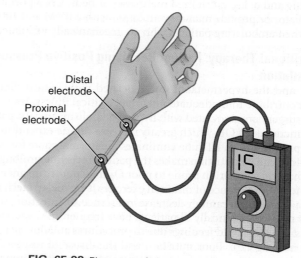

Distal electrode
Proximal electrode

FIG. 65.22 Placement of electrodes along ulnar nerve.

delivered gases are humidified with body-temperature water. As a part of the stress response, release of antidiuretic hormone (ADH) and cortisol contributes to sodium and water retention.

Gastrointestinal System. Patients receiving PPV are stressed because of the serious illness, immobility, or discomforts associated with the ventilator. This places the patient at risk for developing stress ulcers and GI bleeding. Patients with a preexisting ulcer or those receiving corticosteroids have a higher risk. Any circulatory compromise, including reduced CO caused by PPV, may contribute to ischemia of the gastric and intestinal mucosa and increase the risk for translocation of GI bacteria.

Stress ulcer prophylaxis includes giving histamine (H_2)-receptor blockers (e.g., ranitidine), proton pump inhibitors (PPIs) (e.g., esomeprazole), or EN to decrease gastric acidity and reduce the risk for stress ulcer and hemorrhage. PPIs may increase the risk for *Clostridium difficile infection*.[35] (This is discussed in Chapter 41 on p. 898.)

Gastric and bowel dilation may occur because of gas accumulation in the GI tract from swallowed air. The irritation of an artificial airway may cause excessive air swallowing and gastric dilation. Gastric or bowel dilation may put pressure on the vena cava, decrease CO, and prohibit adequate diaphragmatic excursion during spontaneous breathing. Elevation of the diaphragm from a paralytic ileus or bowel dilation leads to compression of the lower lobes of the lungs. This may cause atelectasis and compromise respiratory function. Decompression of the stomach is done by inserting an OG or NG tube.

Immobility, sedation, circulatory impairment, decreased oral intake, use of opioid pain medicines, and stress contribute to decreased peristalsis. The patient's inability to exhale against a closed glottis may make defecation difficult. As a result, the ventilated patient is at risk for constipation. A bowel regimen should be started to help with motility.

Musculoskeletal System. Maintaining muscle strength and preventing complications associated with immobility are important. Adequate analgesia and nutrition can enhance exercise tolerance. Plan for early and progressive mobility of appropriate patients receiving PPV.[8] In collaboration with physical and occupational therapy, perform passive and active exercises to maintain muscle tone in the upper and lower extremities. Simple maneuvers, such as leg lifts, knee bends, or arm circles, are appropriate. Prevent contractures, pressure injuries, footdrop, and external rotation of the hip and legs by proper positioning and using specialized mattresses or beds. Use a portable ventilator or provide manual ventilation with a BVM and 100% O_2 when ambulating patients who are mechanically ventilated.

Nutritional Therapy: Patient Receiving Positive Pressure Ventilation

PPV and the hypermetabolism associated with critical illness can contribute to inadequate nutrition. Critical illness, trauma, and surgery are associated with hypermetabolism, anxiety, pain, and increased WOB, which greatly increase caloric expenditure. The presence of an ET tube eliminates the normal route for eating. Inadequate nutrition makes the patient receiving prolonged mechanical ventilation prone to poor O_2 transport from anemia and to poor tolerance of minimal exercise. It can delay mechanical ventilation weaning, decrease resistance to infection, and slow recovery. Critically ill patients have frequent EN interruptions. We often hold feedings due to procedures and during routine nursing care. Poor nutrition and the disuse of respiratory muscles contribute to decreased respiratory muscle strength.

Serum protein levels (e.g., albumin, prealbumin, transferrin, total protein) are usually decreased.

Patients unlikely to be able to eat independently for 3 to 5 days should have a nutritional assessment and EN started within 24 to 48 hours of admission.[9] EN is the preferred method to meet caloric needs of mechanically ventilated patients (see Chapter 39 for discussion of EN). Consult the dietitian to determine the caloric and nutrient needs of these patients.

❖❖ NURSING MANAGEMENT
Caring for the Patient Requiring Mechanical Ventilation

In the critically ill patient who requires mechanical ventilation, the RN and RT provide most of the care. Some patients who need chronic mechanical ventilation may be in long-term care settings or at home. In these settings, the RN and RT assess the patient and plan and evaluate care, but implementation of some activities may be delegated.

- Develop plan for communication with the patient who has an ET tube or tracheostomy.
- Give sedatives, analgesics, and paralytic drugs as needed.
- Teach patient and caregiver about mechanical ventilation and weaning procedures.
- Auscultate breath sounds and respiratory effort, assessing for decreased ventilation or adventitious sounds.
- Monitor ventilator settings and alarms.
- Determine need for ET tube suctioning and suction patients as needed.
- Reposition and secure ET tube (based on agency policy).
- Monitor oxygenation level and signs of respiratory fatigue during weaning procedure.
- Provide enteral nutrition.
- Oversee UAP:
  - Obtain vital signs and report to the RN.
  - Provide personal hygiene, skin care, and oral care, as directed by RN.
  - Assist with frequent position changes, including ambulation, as directed by the RN.
  - Help to perform passive or active range-of-motion (ROM) exercises.

Collaborate With Respiratory Therapist (RT)
- Auscultate breath sounds and respiratory effort, assessing for decreased ventilation or adventitious sounds.
- Monitor ventilator settings and alarms.
- Change ventilator settings as needed or ordered by HCP.
- Maintain appropriate cuff inflation on ET tube.
- Determine need for ET tube suctioning and suction patients as needed.
- Reposition and secure ET tube (based on agency policy).
- Monitor oxygenation level and signs of respiratory fatigue during weaning procedure.

Collaborate With Physical and Occupational Therapist
- Perform ROM exercises.
- Assist with early and progressive ambulation as directed by the RN.

Collaborate With Dietitian
- Assess and monitor patient's nutritional status.
- Recommend formulations for enteral and/or parenteral nutrition as needed.

Collaborate With Speech Therapist
- Perform swallowing studies.
- Assess patient's cognitive function and assist with communication.
- Provide teaching for patient with a long-term tracheostomy.

Collaborate With Social Worker
- Work with the patient and caregiver to identify care needs.
- Help the patient with transitions through the health care system.
- Teach the patient the various levels of care and seek to optimize outcomes in a cost-effective manner.

When eating with a tracheostomy tube in place, the patient should tilt the head slightly forward to assist with swallowing and to prevent aspiration. The diet may be restricted to soft foods (e.g., puddings, ice cream) and thickened liquids. Patients with a long-term tracheostomy will likely have a tube placed in the stomach (gastrostomy) or small bowel (jejunostomy) for nutritional support (see Chapter 39). Patients may be able to eat normally once the tracheostomy site heals and they meet criteria that will allow them to take oral intake. Swallowing studies and a speech therapy consultation are done to assess the patient's readiness for oral intake.

Weaning From Positive Pressure Ventilation and Extubation

Weaning is the process of reducing ventilator support and resuming spontaneous breathing. The weaning process differs for patients on short-term ventilation (up to 3 days) versus long-term ventilation (longer than 3 days). Those with short-term ventilation (e.g., after heart surgery) have a linear weaning process. Patients with prolonged PPV (e.g., patients with COPD who develop respiratory failure) often have a weaning process that consists of alternating gains and losses. Preparation for weaning begins when PPV is started and involves a team approach (e.g., HCP, RT, RN, patient).

Weaning consists of 3 phases: the *preweaning phase*, the *weaning process*, and the *outcome phase*. The preweaning, or assessment phase, looks at the patient's ability to breathe spontaneously. Assessment depends on a combination of respiratory and nonrespiratory factors (Table 65.13). Note the resolution of the primary problem that prompted patient admission. The patient's lungs should be reasonably clear on auscultation and chest x-ray. Weaning assessment parameters should include criteria to assess muscle strength (negative inspiratory force) and endurance (spontaneous V_T, vital capacity, minute ventilation, rapid shallow breathing index). There should be minimal secretions, the ability to cough and gag, and a cuff leak when the ET tube cuff is deflated.

Nonrespiratory factors include the patient's neurologic status; hemodynamics; fluid, electrolytes, and acid-base balance; nutrition; and hemoglobin. It is important to have an alert, well-rested, and well-informed patient relatively free from pain and anxiety who can cooperate with the weaning plan. This does not mean complete withdrawal from sedatives or analgesics. Instead, drugs should be titrated to achieve comfort without causing excessive drowsiness.

TABLE 65.13 Indicators for Weaning

Weaning Readiness

Patients receiving mechanical ventilation for respiratory failure should undergo a formal assessment of weaning potential if the following are satisfied*:

1. Reversal of the underlying cause of respiratory failure
2. Adequate oxygenation
   - PaO_2/FIO_2 >150–200
   - SpO_2 ≥90%
   - PEEP ≤5–7 cm H_2O
   - FIO_2 ≤40%–50%
   - pH ≥7.25

3. Hemodynamically stabile
   - Absence of myocardial ischemia
   - Absence of clinically significant hypotension (low dose or no vasopressor therapy)
4. Patient ability to initiate respirations
5. Optional criteria
   - Hemoglobin ≥7–10 g/dL
   - Core temperature ≤100.4° F (38° C) to 101.3° F (38.5° C)
   - Mental status awake and alert or easily arousable

WEANING ASSESSMENT

Measurement	Significance	Normal Values	Indices for Weaning
Spontaneous respiratory rate (RR)	Respiratory rate/frequency over 1 min.	12–20 breaths/min	<35 breaths/min
Spontaneous tidal volume (V_T)	Amount of air exchanged during normal breathing at rest. Measure of muscle endurance.	>5–7 mL/kg	≥5 mL/kg
Minute ventilation (V_E)	V_T multiplied by respiratory rate over 1 min. *For example:* 0.350 (V_T) × 28 (f) = 9.8 L/min.	>10 L/min	>10 L/min
Negative inspiratory force or pressure (NIF, NIP)	Amount of negative pressure that a patient can generate to initiate spontaneous respirations. *Measured by clinician:* After complete occlusion of inspiratory valve, a pressure manometer is attached to airway or mouth for 10–20 sec while negative inspiratory efforts are noted.	<−50 cm H_2O	<−20 cm H_2O The more negative the number, the better indication for weaning.
Positive expiratory pressure (PEP)	Measure of expiratory muscle strength and ability to cough. *Measured by clinician:* After complete occlusion of expiratory valve, a pressure manometer is attached to the airway or mouth for 10–20 sec while positive expiratory efforts are noted.	60–85 cm H_2O	≥30 cm H_2O
Rapid shallow breathing index RSBI (f/V_T)	Spontaneous respiratory rate over 1 min divided by V_T (in liters). *For example:* 30 (f)/0.400 (V_T) = 75/L	<40/L	<105/L
Spontaneous breathing trial (SBT)	If patient passes daily weaning screen, assess patient during SBT with little or no ventilator assistance. Trial should be at least 30 min to a maximum of 120 min.		Successful completion of trial is based on an integrated patient assessment.
Vital capacity (VC)	Maximum inspiration and then measurement of air during maximal forced expiration. Measure of respiratory muscle endurance or reserve or both. Requires patient cooperation.	65–75 mL/kg	≥10–15 mL/kg

Adapted from Urden LD, Stacy, KM, Lough ME: *Critical care nursing: Diagnosis and management*, ed 8, St Louis, 2018, Elsevier.
*The decision to use these criteria are personalized to the patient.

A SAT and an SBT are recommended in patients who meet a daily safety screen. A SAT should be done by stopping all sedatives and, in patients without active pain, all opioids. Sedation should be restarted at 50% of the previous dose in patients who "fail" the SAT and remain off in patients who "pass."

EVIDENCE-BASED PRACTICE
Early Mobilization and Critically Ill Patients

W.R. is a 68-yr-old man who has been in the ICU for 2 days. He is receiving mechanical ventilation, and weaning trials are planned. You have started passive exercises and dangling with W.R. You prepare to discuss early mobilization with him and his partner.

Making Clinical Decisions

Best Available Evidence. Implementing an early exercise and mobilization protocol for stable, mechanically ventilated patients is safe and well tolerated. Early mobilization improves patient outcomes (e.g., prevention of ICU-acquired weakness, maintenance of long-term function, preservation of quality of life) and reduces the length of hospital stays. Involving patients and families in decision-making around care (e.g., early mobilization) is an identified priority among this group.

Clinician Expertise. Your unit has successfully implemented AACN's **ABCDEF** bundle related to delirium, immobility, sedation/analgesia, and ventilator management in the ICU. You know that patients and their families often worry about ambulating with complex equipment attached to them.

Patient Preferences and Values. W.R. writes on the computer that he does not want to get out of bed until his "breathing tube is out." His partner tells you he is "afraid of falling."

Implications for Nursing Practice

1. What will you tell W.R. and his partner about the benefits of and protocol for early mobilization?
2. How will you involve them in the decision to take part in the program?

Reference for Evidence

McKenzie E, Potestio ML, Boyd JM, et al.: Reconciling patient and provider priorities for improving the care of critically ill patients: a consensus method and qualitative analysis of decision making, *Health Expect* 20:1367, 2017.

An SBT should last at least 30 minutes but no more than 120 minutes.[13] It may be done with low levels of PEEP, low levels of PSV, or FIO_2. Tolerance of the trial may lead to extubation. Failure to tolerate an SBT should prompt a search for reversible or complicating factors and a return to a nonfatiguing ventilator modality. The SBT should be tried daily, unless contraindicated.

All health care team members should be familiar with the weaning plan. The use of a weaning protocol decreases ventilator days.[13] The ventilator settings are not as important as the use of a daily protocol to prevent delays in weaning. The patient receiving SIMV can have the ventilator breaths gradually reduced as ventilatory status permits. PEEP or PSV can be added to SIMV. PSV is thought to provide gentle, slow respiratory muscle conditioning. It may be especially beneficial for patients who are deconditioned or have heart problems.

Weaning may be tried at any time of day. It is usually done after a period of time when the patient has been ventilated in a rest mode. The rest mode should be a stable, nonfatiguing, and comfortable form of support for the patient. It is important to allow the patient's respiratory muscles to rest between weaning trials. Once the respiratory muscles become fatigued, they may need 12 to 24 hours to recover.

The patient and caregiver need ongoing emotional support. Explain the weaning process to them to keep them informed of progress. Place the patient in a comfortable sitting or semirecumbent position. Obtain baseline vital signs and respiratory parameters. During the weaning trial, closely monitor the patient for signs and symptoms that may signal a need to end the trial (e.g., tachypnea, dyspnea, tachycardia, dysrhythmias, sustained desaturation [SpO_2 less than 90%], hypertension or hypotension, agitation, diaphoresis, anxiety, sustained V_T less than 5 mL/kg, changes in mental status). Record the patient's tolerance throughout the weaning process. Include statements about the patient's and the caregiver's feelings.

The weaning outcome phase is the period when the patient is ready for extubation or weaning is stopped because progress is not being made. The patient who is ready for extubation should receive hyperoxygenation and suctioning (e.g., oropharynx, ET tube) prior to extubation. Loosen the ET tapes or commercial holder. Have the patient take a deep breath, and at the peak of inspiration, deflate the ET tube cuff and remove the tube in one motion. After removal, encourage the patient to deep breath and cough. Suction the oropharynx as needed. Have the patient say their name to assess vocalization. Give supplemental O_2 and provide naso-oral care. Carefully monitor vital signs, respiratory status, and oxygenation immediately after extubation, within 1 hour, and per agency policy. If the patient does not tolerate extubation (e.g., decreased SpO_2 levels, tachypnea or bradypnea, tachycardia, decreased level of consciousness, decrease in PaO_2, increase in $PaCO_2$), immediate reintubation or a trial of noninvasive ventilation may be needed.

Chronic Mechanical Ventilation

Mechanical ventilators are now a part of long-term and home care. In some instances, terminally ill, ventilated patients may be discharged to hospice. The emphasis on controlling hospital costs has increased the number of patients discharged early from the acute care setting and the need to provide highly technical care, such as mechanical ventilation, in home settings. The success of home mechanical ventilation depends, in part, on careful predischarge assessment and planning for the patient and caregivers. Patients must first meet criteria to be discharged on mechanical ventilation (e.g., tracheostomy, stabile mechanical ventilator settings).

Both negative pressure and positive pressure ventilators can be used in the home. Negative pressure ventilators do not require an artificial airway and are less complicated to use. Several types of small, portable (battery-powered) positive pressure ventilators are available. They can be attached to a wheelchair or placed on a bedside table. Settings and alarms on these ventilators are simpler to use than on the standard ICU ventilators.

Home mechanical ventilation has advantages and disadvantages. Having the patient in the home eliminates the strain that the hospital setting imposes on family dynamics. Caregivers may feel helpless when they first hear about the need for long-term mechanical ventilation. However, these feelings are often balanced by the opportunity to take part in the patient's care in the home setting. At home, the patient may be able to take part in more activities of daily living around a personalized schedule. Because of the smaller size of the home ventilator, the patient may be more mobile. Another advantage is a lower risk for HAIs.

Disadvantages include problems related to equipment, reimbursement, caregiver stress and fatigue, and the patient's complex needs. Ventilated patients are usually dependent, requiring extensive nursing care, at least initially. Disposable products may not be reimbursable. Carefully assess financial resources when arranging home ventilation. Schedule a meeting with the interprofessional care team (e.g., social worker, home health care RN, RT) before starting a discharge teaching plan. Caregivers may seem enthusiastic about caring for their loved one in the home but may not understand the sacrifices they may have to make financially and in personal time and commitment. Encourage caregivers to consider respite care to periodically relieve their stress and fatigue.

OTHER CRITICAL CARE CONTENT

Table 65.14 lists critical care content discussed in other chapters of this book.

TABLE 65.14 Cross-References to Critical Care Content

Topic	Discussed in Chapter	Topic	Discussed in Chapter
Acute coronary syndrome (ACS)	33	Enteral nutrition (EN)	39
Acute heart failure	34	Head injury and ICP monitoring	56
Acute respiratory distress syndrome (ARDS)	67	Multiple organ dysfunction syndrome (MODS)	66
Acute respiratory failure	67	Myocardial infarction (MI)	33
Basic life support and CPR	Appendix A	Oxygen delivery	28
Burns	24	Pain management	8
Cardiac pacemakers	35	Parenteral nutrition (PN)	39
Cardiac surgery	33	Pulmonary edema	34
Central venous access device (CVAD)	16	Renal dialysis	46
Continuous renal replacement therapy (CRRT)	46	Shock	66
Delirium	59	Stroke	57
Dysrhythmias	35	Systemic inflammatory response syndrome (SIRS)	66
Emergencies	68	Tracheostomy	26
End-of-life (EOL) care	9	Trauma	68

CASE STUDY

Critical Care and Mechanical Ventilation

Patient Profile

R.K. is a 72-yr-old white man who collapsed in his home. He was found by his daughter, and she activated the emergency response system. He was unresponsive on admission to the emergency department and is still unresponsive on arrival to the ICU. He has an oral ET tube in place and is receiving mechanical ventilation. A large-bore, peripheral IV has been placed and fluids are infusing.

(© Thinkstock.)

Subjective Data

None. Patient has no eye opening. He is intubated and is unresponsive to painful stimuli.

Objective Data

Physical Examination

- Noninvasive BP 100/75 mm Hg; apical-radial HR 128; temperature 102° F (38.8° C); SpO$_2$ is 98%
- ECG: atrial fibrillation with a rapid ventricular response
- Purulent secretions suctioned from ET tube
- Breath sounds: coarse crackles bilaterally, decreased breath sounds on the right
- Weight: 168 lb. (76 kg)

Diagnostic Studies

- Chest x-ray shows right lower lung consolidation
- ABGs: pH 7.48; PaO$_2$ 94 mm Hg; PaCO$_2$ 30 mm Hg; HCO$_3$ 34 mEq/L
- CT scan is positive for a hemorrhagic stroke

Interprofessional Care

- Positive pressure ventilation settings: assist-control mode
- Settings: FIO$_2$ 70%, V$_T$ 700 mL, respiratory rate 16 breaths/min, PEEP 5 cm H$_2$O

- Orogastric tube. EN at 25 mL/hr, increase by 20 mL/hr every 2 hr with a goal of 80 mL/hr to start on day 2
- External condom catheter for urinary drainage and measurement
- HOB elevated at 40 degrees
- Reposition at least every 2 hr
- Azithromycin (Zithromax) 500 mg IV q24hr
- Cefotaxime 2 gram IV q6hr
- NS at 75 mL/hr

Discussion Questions

1. Identify 2 reasons for intubating and providing mechanical ventilation for R.K.
2. What does R.K.'s ABG indicate, and which ventilator setting(s) should be changed to prevent barotrauma?
3. R.K.'s BP drops to 80 mm Hg. Despite increasing doses of vasopressors and fluid challenges, his BP is still low. A central venous catheter and an arterial line are inserted. Arterial pressure–based cardiac output (APCO) monitoring is started. What would be the purpose of hemodynamic monitoring in this patient?
4. ***Priority Decision:*** What are 2 priority nursing considerations for a patient with invasive monitoring?
5. R.K.'s pulmonary condition deteriorates. PaO$_2$ drops to 60 mm Hg, and SpO$_2$ is 89%. PEEP is increased to 7.5 cm H$_2$O. What implications does this have for R.K. given his hemodynamic status? What other intervention could be done to improve oxygenation?
6. ***Collaboration:*** What patient care activities can you delegate to unlicensed assistive personnel?
7. ***Evidence-Based Practice:*** R.K.'s caregivers want to know why he is to receive tube feedings. What would you tell them? What is the evidence to support the use of EN?
8. ***Patient-Centered Care:*** After 4 days, R.K. is still unresponsive and has developed renal failure. The HCP thinks the patient will not recover from his neurologic injury and wishes to discuss goals of care with the patient's caregivers. What would be your role in this meeting?

Answers available at *http://evolve.elsevier.com/Lewis/medsurg.*

BRIDGE TO NCLEX EXAMINATION

The number of the question corresponds to the same-numbered outcome at the beginning of the chapter.

1. Certification in critical care nursing (CCRN) by the American Association of Critical-Care Nurses indicates that the nurse
   a. is an advanced practice nurse who cares for acutely and critically ill patients.
   b. may practice independently to provide symptom management for the critically ill.
   c. has earned a master's degree in the field of advanced acute and critical care nursing.
   d. has practiced in critical care and successfully completed a test of critical care knowledge.

2. What are appropriate nursing interventions for the patient with delirium in the ICU? *(select all that apply)*
   a. Use clocks and calendars to maintain orientation.
   b. Encourage round-the-clock presence of caregivers at the bedside.
   c. Silence all alarms, reduce overhead paging, and avoid conversations around the patient.
   d. Sedate the patient with appropriate drugs to protect the patient from harmful behaviors.
   e. Identify physiologic factors that may be contributing to the patient's confusion and irritability.

3. The critical care nurse recognizes that an ideal plan for caregiver involvement includes
   a. having a caregiver at the bedside at all times.
   b. allowing caregivers at the bedside at preset, brief intervals.
   c. a personally devised plan to involve caregivers with care and patient needs.
   d. restriction of visiting in the ICU because the environment is overwhelming to caregivers.

4. To establish hemodynamic monitoring for a patient, the nurse zeros the
   a. cardiac output monitoring system to the level of the left ventricle.
   b. pressure monitoring system to the level of the catheter tip in the patient.
   c. pressure monitoring system to the level of the atrium, or the phlebostatic axis.
   d. pressure monitoring system to the level of the atrium, or the midclavicular line.

5. The hemodynamic changes the nurse expects to find after successful initiation of intraaortic balloon pump therapy in a patient with cardiogenic shock include *(select all that apply)*
   a. decreased SV.
   b. decreased SVR.
   c. decreased PAWP.
   d. increased diastolic BP.
   e. decreased myocardial O_2 consumption.

6. The purpose of adding PEEP to positive pressure ventilation is to
   a. increase functional residual capacity and improve oxygenation.
   b. increase FIO_2 to try to help wean the patient and avoid O_2 toxicity.
   c. determine if the patient can be weaned and avoid pneumomediastinum.
   d. determine if the patient is in synchrony with the ventilator or needs to be paralyzed.

7. The nursing management of a patient with an artificial airway includes
   a. maintaining ET tube cuff pressure at 35 cm H_2O.
   b. routine suctioning of the tube at least every 2 hours.
   c. observing for cardiac dysrhythmias during suctioning.
   d. preventing tube dislodgment by limiting mouth care to lubrication of the lips.

8. The nurse monitors the patient with positive pressure mechanical ventilation for
   a. paralytic ileus because pressure on the abdominal contents affects bowel motility.
   b. diuresis and sodium depletion because of increased release of atrial natriuretic peptide.
   c. signs of cardiovascular insufficiency because pressure in the chest impedes venous return.
   d. respiratory acidosis in a patient with COPD because of alveolar hyperventilation and increased PaO_2 levels.

1. d, 2. a, d, e, 3. c, 4. c, 5. b, c, d, e, 6. a, 7. c, 8. c

For rationales to these answers and even more NCLEX review questions, visit *http://evolve.elsevier.com/Lewis/medsurg*.

ⓔ EVOLVE WEBSITE/RESOURCES LIST

http://evolve.elsevier.com/Lewis/medsurg
Review Questions (Online Only)
Key Points
Answer Keys to Questions
- Rationales for Bridge to NCLEX Examination Questions
- Answer Guidelines for Case Study on p. 1563
Student Case Study
- Patient With Pulmonary Embolism and Respiratory Failure
Nursing Care Plan
- eNursing Care Plan 65.1: Patient on Mechanical Ventilation
Conceptual Care Map Creator
Audio Glossary
Supporting Media
- Animation
- Endotracheal Intubation
Content Updates

REFERENCES

1. American Association of Critical-Care Nurses: AACN scope and standards for acute and critical care nursing. Retrieved from *www.aacn.org/nursing-excellence/standards/aacn-scope-and-standards-for-acute-and-critical-care-nursing-practice*.
*2. Tirkkonen J, Tamminen T, Skrifvars MB: Outcome of adult patients attended by rapid response teams: A systematic review of the literature, *Resuscitation* 112:43, 2017.
3. American Association of Critical-Care Nurses: Frequently asked questions about APRN Consensus Model—For nurse practitioners. Retrieved from *www.aacn.org/wd/certifications/content/aprn-nurses-np-faqs.pcms?menu=certification*.
4. Papathanassoglou ED, Hadjibalassi M, Miltiadous P, et al: Effects of an integrative nursing intervention on pain in critically ill patients, *Amer J Crit Care* 27:172, 2018.
5. Hariharan U, Garg R: Sedation and analgesia in critical care, *J Anesth Crit Care Open Access* 7:262, 2017.
*6. Boyko Y, Jennum P, Toft P: Sleep quality and circadian rhythm disruption in the intensive care unit: A review, *Nat Sci Sleep* 9:277, 2017.

*7. Kanova M, Sklienka P, Kula R, et al: Incidence and risk factors for delirium development in ICU patients. A prospective observational study, *Biomedical Paper* 161:187, 2017.

*8. Blair GJ, Mehmood T, Rudnick M, et al: Nonpharmacologic and medication minimization strategies for the prevention and treatment of ICU delirium: A narrative review, *J Intensive Care Med* 34:183, 2019.

*9. McClave SA, Taylor BE, Martindale RG, et al: Guidelines for the provision and assessment of nutrition support therapy in the adult critically ill patient, *J Parenter Enteral Nutr* 40:159, 2016.

*10. Davidson JE, Aslakson RA, Long AC, et al: Guidelines for family-centered care in the neonatal, pediatric, and adult ICU, *CCM* 45:103, 2017.

11. Clark AP, Guzzetta CE: A paradigm shift for patient/family-centered care in intensive care units: Bring in the family, *Crit Care Nurse* 37:96, 2017.

12. Edwards Lifesciences: Hemodynamic monitoring. Retrieved from *www.edwards.com/devices/hemodynamic-monitoring*.

*13. Wiegand DL: *AACN procedure manual for high acuity, progressive, and critical care*, ed 7, St Louis, 2017, Elsevier.

14. Baird MB: *Manual of critical care nursing*, ed 7, St Louis, 2016, Elsevier.

*15. Cook JL, Colvin M, Francis GS, et al: Recommendations for the use of mechanical circulatory support. Ambulatory and community patient care. A scientific statement from the AHA, *Circulation* 135:e1, 2017.

16. Herritt B, Chaudhuri D, Thavorn K, et al: Early vs. late tracheostomy in intensive care settings: Impact on ICU and hospital costs, *J Crit Care* 44:285, 2018.

17. Dean C, Chapman E: Induction of anaesthesia, *Anaesth Intensive Care,* 19:383, 2018.

*18. Hampson J, Green C, Stewart J, et al: Impact of the introduction of an endotracheal tube attachment device on the incidence and severity of oral pressure injuries in the intensive care unit: A retrospective observational study, *BMC Nursing* 17:4, 2018.

*19. Holm A, Dreyer P: Intensive care unit patients' experience of being conscious during endotracheal intubation and mechanical ventilation, *Nurs Crit Care* 22:81, 2017.

20. Au G, Johnson JR, Chlan LL: Time for a paradigm shift: Assessing for anxiety in patients receiving mechanical ventilation, *Heart & Lung* 46:135, 2017.

21. Mohammed HM, Ali AA: Nursing issues of unplanned extubation in ICU, *IJNSS* 8:17, 2018.

*22. Sousa AS, Ferrito C, Paiva JA: Intubation-associated pneumonia: An integrative review, *Intensive Crit Care Nurs* 44:45, 2018.

*23. Allan SH, Doyle PA, Sapirstein A, et al: Data-driven implementation of alarm reduction interventions in a cardiovascular surgical ICU, *Jt Comm J Qual Patient Saf* 43:62, 2017.

24. Pham T, Brochard LJ, Slutsky AS: Mechanical ventilation: State of the art, *Mayo Clin Proc* 92:1382, 2017.

25. Bein T, Wrigge H: Airway pressure release ventilation (APRV): Do good things come to those who can wait? *J Thorac Dis* 10:667, 2018.

26. Ng J, Ferguson ND: High-frequency oscillatory ventilation: Still a role? *Curr Opin Crit Care* 23:175, 2017.

*27. Karam O, Gebistorf F, Wetterslev J, et al: The effect of inhaled nitric oxide in acute respiratory distress syndrome in children and adults: A Cochrane systematic review with trial sequential analysis, *Anaesthesia* 72:106, 2017.

*28. Fan E, Del Sorbo L, Goligher E, et al: An official American Thoracic Society/European Society of Intensive Care Medicine/Society of Critical Care Medicine Clinical Practice guideline: Mechanical ventilation in adult patients with acute respiratory distress syndrome, *Amer J Resp Crit Care Med* 195:1253, 2017.

29. Centers for Disease Control and Prevention (CDC): Pneumonia (ventilator-associated [VAP] and non-ventilator-associated pneumonia [PNEU]) event. Retrieved from *www.cdc.gov/nhsn/pdfs/pscmanual/6pscvapcurrent.pdf*.

*30. American Association of Critical Care Nurses: Ventilator assisted pneumonia. Retrieved from *www.aacn.org/clinical-resources/practice-alerts/ventilator-associated-pneumonia-vap*.

31. Larrow V, Klich-Heartt EI: Prevention of ventilator-associated pneumonia in the intensive care unit: Beyond the basics, *J Neuroscience Nurs* 48:160, 2016.

*32. Marra A, Ely EW, Pandharipande PP, Patel MB: The ABCDEF bundle in critical care, *Crit Care Clin* 33:225, 2017.

33. Naguib M, Brull SJ, Johnson KB: Conceptual and technical insights into the basis of neuromuscular monitoring, *Anaesthesia* 72:16, 2017.

34. Faritous Z, Barzanji A, Azarfarin R, et al: Comparison of bispectral index monitoring with the critical-care pain observation tool in the pain assessment of intubated adult patients after cardiac surgery, *Anesthesiol Pain Med* 6:e38334, 2016.

*35. Watson T, Hickok J, Fraker S, et al: Evaluating the risk factors for hospital-onset *Clostridium difficile* infections in a large healthcare system. *Clin Infect Dis* 66:1957, 2018.

*Evidence-based information for clinical practice.

66

Shock, Sepsis, and Multiple Organ Dysfunction Syndrome

Helen Miley

You have not lived until you have done something for someone who can never repay you.

John Bunyen

e http://evolve.elsevier.com/Lewis/medsurg

CONCEPTUAL FOCUS

Anxiety	Gas Exchange	Perfusion
Fluids and Electrolytes	Immunity	

LEARNING OUTCOMES

1. Relate the pathophysiology to the clinical manifestations of the different types of shock: cardiogenic, hypovolemic, distributive, and obstructive.
2. Compare the effects of shock, sepsis, systemic inflammatory response syndrome, and multiple organ dysfunction syndrome on the major body systems.
3. Compare the interprofessional care, drug therapy, and nursing management of patients with different types of shock.
4. Describe the interprofessional care and nursing management of a patient experiencing multiple organ dysfunction syndrome.

KEY TERMS

anaphylactic shock, p. 1569
cardiogenic shock, p. 1566
hypovolemic shock, p. 1568
multiple organ dysfunction syndrome
 (MODS), p. 1584

neurogenic shock, p. 1568
obstructive shock, p. 1571
sepsis, p. 1569
septic shock, p. 1569
shock, p. 1566

systemic inflammatory response syndrome
 (SIRS), p. 1583

Shock, systemic inflammatory response syndrome (SIRS), sepsis, and multiple organ dysfunction syndrome (MODS) are serious and interrelated problems (Fig. 66.1). **Shock** is a syndrome characterized by decreased tissue perfusion and impaired cellular metabolism. This results in an imbalance between the supply of and demand for O_2 and nutrients. The exchange of O_2 and nutrients at the cellular level is essential to life. When cells are hypoperfused, the demand for O_2 and nutrients exceeds the supply at the microcirculatory level. Ischemia can occur, leading to cell injury and death. Thus shock of any cause is life-threatening. This chapter gives an overview of the different types of shock, SIRS, sepsis, and MODS and the related management of each.

SHOCK

Classification of Shock

The 4 main categories of shock are cardiogenic, hypovolemic, distributive, and obstructive (Table 66.1). Although the cause, initial presentation, and management vary for each type, the physiologic responses of the cells to hypoperfusion are similar.

Cardiogenic Shock. Cardiogenic shock occurs when either systolic or diastolic dysfunction of the heart's pumping action results in reduced cardiac output (CO), stroke volume (SV), and BP. These changes compromise myocardial perfusion, further depress myocardial function, and decrease CO and perfusion. Causes of cardiogenic shock are shown in Table 66.1. Mortality rates for patients with cardiogenic shock are around 50%.[1] It is the leading cause of death from acute myocardial infarction (MI).[1]

The heart's inability to pump the blood forward is called *systolic dysfunction*. This inability results in a low CO (less than 4 L/min) and *cardiac index* (less than 2.5 L/min/m²). Systolic dysfunction primarily affects the left ventricle since systolic pressure is greater on the left side of the heart. The most common cause of systolic dysfunction is acute MI. When systolic dysfunction affects the right side of the heart, blood flow through the pulmonary circulation is reduced. Decreased filling of the heart results in decreased SV. Causes of diastolic dysfunction are shown in Table 66.1.

Fig. 66.2 describes the pathophysiology of cardiogenic shock. Whether the first event is myocardial ischemia, a structural

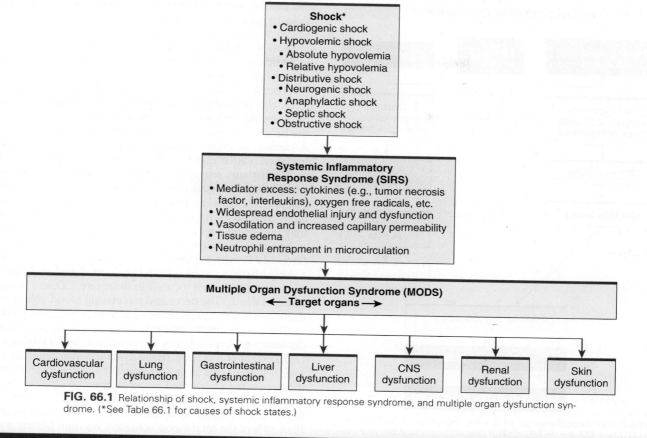

FIG. 66.1 Relationship of shock, systemic inflammatory response syndrome, and multiple organ dysfunction syndrome. (*See Table 66.1 for causes of shock states.)

TABLE 66.1 Classification of Shock States

Types and Causes	Associated Conditions	Types and Causes	Associated Conditions
Cardiogenic Shock		**Distributive Shock**	
		Anaphylactic Shock	
• Diastolic dysfunction: inability of the heart to fill	Cardiac tamponade, ventricular hypertrophy, cardiomyopathy	• Hypersensitivity (allergic) reaction to a sensitizing substance	Contrast media, blood or blood products, drugs, insect bites, anesthetic agents, food or food additives, vaccines, environmental agents, latex
• Dysrhythmias	Bradydysrhythmias, tachydysrhythmias		
• Structural factors	Valvular stenosis or regurgitation, ventricular septal rupture, tension pneumothorax		
• Systolic dysfunction: inability of the heart to pump blood forward	MI, cardiomyopathy, blunt cardiac injury, severe systemic or pulmonary hypertension, myocardial depression from metabolic problems	**Neurogenic Shock**	
		• Hemodynamic consequence of spinal cord injury and/or disease at or above T5	Severe pain, drugs, hypoglycemia, injury
Hypovolemic Shock		• Spinal anesthesia	
Absolute Hypovolemia		• Vasomotor center depression	
• External loss of whole blood	Hemorrhage from trauma, surgery, GI bleeding		
• Loss of other body fluids	Vomiting, diarrhea, excessive diuresis, diabetes insipidus, diabetes	**Septic Shock**	
		• Infection	Pneumonia, peritonitis, urinary tract, invasive procedures, indwelling lines and catheters
Relative Hypovolemia		• At-risk patients	Older adults, patients with chronic diseases (e.g., diabetes, chronic kidney disease, HF), patients receiving immunosuppressive therapy or who are malnourished or debilitated
• Fluid shifts	Burn injuries, ascites		
• Internal bleeding	Fracture of long bones, ruptured spleen, hemothorax, severe pancreatitis		
• Massive vasodilation	Sepsis		
• Pooling of blood or fluids	Bowel obstruction		
		Obstructive Shock	
		• Physical obstruction impeding the filling or outflow of blood resulting in reduced CO	Cardiac tamponade, tension pneumothorax, superior vena cava syndrome, abdominal compartment syndrome, pulmonary embolism

PATHOPHYSIOLOGY MAP

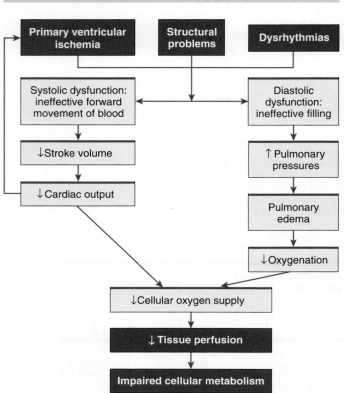

FIG. 66.2 The pathophysiology of cardiogenic shock. (Modified from Urden LD, Stacy KM, Lough ME: *Critical care nursing: Diagnosis and management,* ed 6, St Louis, 2010, Mosby.)

problem (e.g., valvular disorder, ventricular septal rupture), or dysrhythmias, the physiologic responses are similar. The patient has impaired tissue perfusion and cellular metabolism.

The early presentation of a patient with cardiogenic shock is similar to that of a patient with acute decompensated heart failure (HF) (see Chapter 34). The patient may have tachycardia and hypotension. Pulse pressure may be narrowed due to the heart's inability to pump blood forward during systole and increased volume during diastole. An increase in systemic vascular resistance (SVR) increases the workload of the heart. This increases myocardial O_2 consumption.

On assessment, the patient is tachypneic and has crackles on auscultation of breath sounds because of pulmonary congestion. The hemodynamic profile shows an increase in the pulmonary artery wedge pressure (PAWP), stroke volume variation (SVV), and pulmonary vascular resistance.

Signs of peripheral hypoperfusion (e.g., cyanosis, pallor, diaphoresis, weak peripheral pulses, cool and clammy skin, delayed capillary refill) occur. Decreased renal blood flow results in sodium and water retention and decreased urine output. Anxiety, confusion, and agitation may develop with impaired cerebral perfusion. Tables 66.2 and 66.3 describe the laboratory findings and clinical presentation of a patient with cardiogenic shock.

Hypovolemic Shock. Hypovolemic shock occurs from inadequate fluid volume in the intravascular space to support adequate perfusion (Table 66.1).[2] The volume loss may be either an absolute or a relative volume loss. *Absolute hypovolemia* results when fluid is lost through hemorrhage, gastrointestinal (GI) loss (e.g., vomiting, diarrhea), fistula drainage, diabetes insipidus, or

diuresis. In *relative hypovolemia,* fluid volume moves out of the vascular space into the extravascular space (e.g., intracavitary space). We call this type of fluid shift *third spacing.* One example of relative volume loss is fluid leaking from the vascular space to the interstitial space from increased capillary permeability, as seen in burns (see Chapter 24).

Whether the loss of intravascular volume is absolute or relative, the physiologic consequences are similar. The reduced intravascular volume results in a decreased venous return to the heart, decreased preload, decreased SV, and decreased CO. A cascade of events results in decreased tissue perfusion and impaired cellular metabolism, the hallmarks of shock (Fig. 66.3).

The patient's response to acute volume loss depends on several factors, including extent of injury, age, and general state of health. The clinical presentation of hypovolemic shock is consistent (Table 66.3). An overall assessment of physiologic reserves may indicate the patient's ability to compensate. A patient may compensate for a loss of up to 15% of the total blood volume (around 750 mL). Further loss of volume (15% to 30%) results in a sympathetic nervous system (SNS)–mediated response.[2] This response results in an increase in heart rate, CO, and respiratory rate and depth. The decreased circulating blood volume causes decreases in SV, central venous pressure (CVP), and PAWP.[3]

The patient may appear anxious. Urine output begins to decrease. If hypovolemia is corrected by crystalloid fluid replacement at this time, tissue dysfunction is generally reversible. If volume loss is greater than 30%, compensatory mechanisms may fail and immediate replacement with blood products should be started. Loss of autoregulation in the microcirculation and irreversible tissue destruction occur with loss of more than 40% of the total blood volume. Common laboratory studies and assessments that are done include serial measurements of hemoglobin and hematocrit levels, electrolytes, lactate, blood gases, mixed central venous O_2 saturation (SvO_2), and hourly urine outputs (Table 66.2).

Distributive Shock

Neurogenic Shock. Neurogenic shock is a hemodynamic phenomenon that can occur within 30 minutes of a spinal cord injury and last up to 6 weeks. Neurogenic shock related to spinal cord injuries is generally associated with a cervical or high thoracic injury. The injury results in a massive vasodilation without compensation because of the loss of SNS vasoconstrictor tone.[4] This massive vasodilation leads to a pooling of blood in the blood vessels, tissue hypoperfusion, and impaired cellular metabolism (Fig. 66.4).

In addition to spinal cord injury, spinal anesthesia can block transmission of impulses from the SNS. Depression of the vasomotor center of the medulla from drugs (e.g., opioids, benzodiazepines) can decrease the vasoconstrictor tone of the peripheral blood vessels, resulting in neurogenic shock (Table 66.1).

The classic manifestations are hypotension (from the massive vasodilation) and bradycardia (from unopposed parasympathetic stimulation).[4] The patient may not be able to regulate body temperature. Combined with massive vasodilation, the inability to regulate temperature promotes heat loss. At first, the patient's skin is warm due to the massive vasodilation. As the heat disperses, the patient is at risk for hypothermia. Later, the patient's skin may be cool or warm depending on the ambient temperature (*poikilothermia,* taking on the temperature of the environment). In either case, the skin is usually dry. Tables 66.2 and 66.3 further describe the laboratory findings and clinical presentation of a patient with neurogenic shock.

TABLE 66.2 Diagnostic Studies

Shock

Study	Finding	Significance of Finding
Arterial blood gasses	Respiratory alkalosis	Found in early shock due to hyperventilation
	Metabolic acidosis	Occurs later in shock when lactate accumulates in blood from anaerobic metabolism
Base deficit	>−6	Acid production due to hypoxia
Blood cultures	Growth of organisms	May grow organisms in patients who are in septic shock
BUN	↑	Impaired kidney function caused by hypoperfusion from severe vasoconstriction, or occurs due to cell catabolism (e.g., trauma, infection)
Creatine kinase	↑	Trauma, MI in response to cellular damage and/or hypoxia
Creatinine	↑	Impaired kidney function caused by hypoperfusion because of severe vasoconstriction
DIC screen		Acute DIC can develop within hours to days after an initial assault on the body (e.g., shock)
• Fibrin split products (FSP)	↑	
• Fibrinogen level	↓	
• Platelet count	↓	
• PTT and PT	↑	
• INR	↑	
• Thrombin time	↑	
• D-dimer	↑	
Glucose	↑	Found in early shock because of release of liver glycogen stores in response to sympathetic nervous system stimulation and cortisol. Insulin insensitivity develops
	↓	Depleted glycogen stores with liver dysfunction possible as shock progresses
Electrolytes (serum)		
• Sodium	↑	Found in early shock because of ↑ secretion of aldosterone, causing renal retention of sodium
	↓	May be iatrogenic if excess hypotonic fluid is given after fluid loss
• Potassium	↑	Results when dead cells release potassium. Occurs in acute kidney injury and acidosis
	↓	Found in early shock because of ↑ secretion of aldosterone, causing renal excretion of potassium
Lactate level	↑	Usually ↑ once significant hypoperfusion and impaired O_2 use at the cellular level have occurred. By-product of anaerobic metabolism
Liver enzymes (ALT, AST, GGT)	↑	Liver cell destruction in progressive stage of shock
Procalcitonin (PCT)	↑	Biomarker released in response to bacterial infections
RBC count, hematocrit, hemoglobin	Normal	Remains within normal limits in shock because of relative hypovolemia and pump failure and in hemorrhagic shock before fluid resuscitation
	↓	Hemorrhagic shock after fluid resuscitation when fluids other than blood are used
	↑	Nonhemorrhagic shock caused by actual hypovolemia and hemoconcentration
Troponin	↑	MI
White blood cell count	↑, ↓	Infection, septic shock

ALT, Alanine aminotransferase; *AST,* aspartate aminotransferase; *GGT,* γ-glutamyl transferase; *INR,* international normalized ratio; *PT,* prothrombin time; *PTT,* partial thromboplastin time.

Although spinal shock and neurogenic shock often occur in the same patient, they are not the same disorder. *Spinal shock* is a transient condition that is present after an acute spinal cord injury (see Chapter 60). The patient with spinal shock has an absence of all voluntary and reflex neurologic activity below the level of the injury.

Anaphylactic Shock. Anaphylactic shock is an acute, life-threatening hypersensitivity (allergic) reaction to a sensitizing substance (e.g., drug, chemical, vaccine, food, insect venom).[5] The reaction quickly causes massive vasodilation, release of vasoactive mediators, and an increase in capillary permeability. As capillary permeability increases, fluid leaks from the vascular space into the interstitial space.

Anaphylactic shock can lead to respiratory distress due to laryngeal edema or severe bronchospasm and circulatory failure from the massive vasodilation. The patient has a sudden onset of symptoms, including dizziness, chest pain, incontinence, swelling of the lips and tongue, wheezing, and stridor. Skin changes include flushing, pruritus, urticaria, and angioedema. The patient may be anxious and confused and have a sense of impending doom.

A patient can have a severe allergic reaction, possibly leading to anaphylactic shock, after contact, inhalation, ingestion, or injection with an antigen (allergen) to which the person has previously been sensitized (Table 66.1). IV administration of the antigen (allergen) is the route most likely to cause anaphylaxis. However, oral, topical, and inhalation routes can cause anaphylactic reactions. Tables 66.2 and 66.3 describe the laboratory findings and clinical presentation of a patient in anaphylactic shock. Quick and decisive action is critical to prevent an allergic reaction from progressing to anaphylactic shock. (Anaphylaxis is discussed in Chapter 13.)

Septic Shock. Sepsis is a life-threatening syndrome in response to an infection. It is characterized by a dysregulated patient response along with new organ dysfunction related to the infection (Table 66.4).[6] In as many as 30% of patients with sepsis, the causative organism is not identified. Sepsis and septic shock have a high incidence worldwide, with a mortality rate of 25% or higher.[7]

Septic shock is a subset of sepsis. It has an increased mortality risk due to profound circulatory, cellular, and metabolic abnormalities. Septic shock is characterized by persistent hypotension, despite adequate fluid resuscitation, and inadequate tissue perfusion that results in tissue hypoxia.[6,7] The main organisms that cause sepsis are gram-negative and gram-positive bacteria.

TABLE 66.3 Clinical Presentation of Types of Shock

Cardiogenic Shock	Hypovolemic Shock	DISTRIBUTIVE SHOCK			Obstructive Shock
		Neurogenic Shock	Anaphylactic Shock	Septic Shock	
Cardiovascular System					
Tachycardia	Tachycardia	Bradycardia	Tachycardia	Tachycardia	Tachycardia
↓ BP	↓ Preload	↓ BP	↑ CO	↓/↑ Temperature	↓ BP
↓ SV, CO	↓ CO, CVP, PAWP	↓ CO, CVP, SVR	↓ CVP, PAWP	Myocardial dysfunction	↓ Preload
↑ SVR, PAWP, CVP	↑ SVR	↓/↑ Temperature	Chest pain	Biventricular dilation	↓ CO
↓ Capillary refill	↓ Capillary refill		Third spacing of fluid	↓ Ejection fraction	↑ SVR, CVP
Respiratory System					
Tachypnea	Tachypnea →	Dysfunction related	Shortness of breath	Hyperventilation	Tachypnea →
Crackles	bradypnea (late)	to level of injury	Edema of larynx and	Crackles	bradypnea (late)
Cyanosis			epiglottis	Respiratory alkalosis →	Shortness of
			Wheezing	respiratory acidosis	breath
			Stridor	Hypoxemia	
			Rhinitis	Respiratory failure	
				ARDS	
				Pulmonary hypertension	
Renal System					
↑ Na+ and H2O retention	↓ Urine output	Bladder dysfunction	Incontinence	↓ Urine output	↓ Urine output
↓ Renal blood flow					
↓ Urine output					
Skin					
Pallor	Pallor	↓ Skin perfusion	Flushing	Warm and flushed →	Pallor
Cool, clammy	Cool, clammy	Cool or warm	Pruritus	cool and mottled	Cool, clammy
		Dry	Urticaria	(late)	
			Angioedema		
Neurologic System					
↓ Cerebral perfusion:	↓ Cerebral perfusion:	Flaccid paralysis	Anxiety	Change in men-	↓ Cerebral
• Anxiety	• Anxiety	below the level	Feeling of impending	tal status (e.g.,	perfusion:
• Confusion	• Confusion	of the lesion	doom	confusion)	• Anxiety
• Agitation	• Agitation	Loss of reflex	Confusion	Agitation	• Confusion
		activity	↓ LOC	Coma (late)	• Agitation
			Metallic taste		
Gastrointestinal System					
↓ Bowel sounds	Absent bowel sounds	Bowel dysfunction	Cramping	GI bleeding	↓ To absent bowel
Nausea, vomiting			Abdominal pain	Paralytic ileus	sounds
			Nausea		
			Vomiting		
			Diarrhea		
Diagnostic Findings*					
↑ Cardiac biomarkers	↓ Hematocrit		Sudden onset	↑/↓ WBC	Specific to cause
↑ b-Type natriuretic pep-	↓ Hemoglobin		History of allergies	↓ Platelets	of obstruction
tide (BNP)	↑ Lactate		Exposure to contrast	↑ Lactate	
↑ Blood glucose	↑ Urine specific gravity		media	↑ Blood glucose	
↑ BUN	Changes in electro-			↑ Procalcitonin	
ECG (e.g., dysrhythmias)	lytes			↑ Urine specific gravity	
Echocardiogram (e.g., left				↓ Urine Na+	
ventricular dysfunction				Positive blood cultures	
Chest x-ray (e.g., pulmo-					
nary infiltrates)					

*Also see Table 66.2.

Parasites, fungi, and viruses can also cause sepsis and septic shock.[6] Fig. 66.5 presents the pathophysiology of septic shock.

When a microorganism enters the body, the normal immune or inflammatory responses are triggered. However, in sepsis and septic shock the body's response to the microorganism is exaggerated. Both proinflammatory and antiinflammatory responses are activated, coagulation increases, and fibrinolysis decreases.[6] Endotoxins from the microorganism cell wall stimulate the release of cytokines. These include tumor necrosis factor (TNF), interleukin-1 (IL-1), and other proinflammatory mediators that act through secondary mediators, such as platelet-activating factor, IL-6, and IL-8.[6] (See Chapter 11 for discussion of the inflammatory response.) The release of platelet-activating factor results in

PATHOPHYSIOLOGY MAP

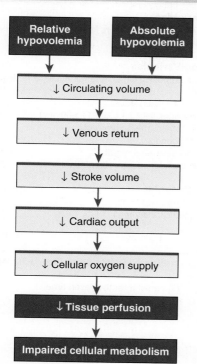

FIG. 66.3 The pathophysiology of hypovolemic shock. (Modified from Urden LD, Stacy KM, Lough ME: *Critical care nursing: Diagnosis and management,* ed 6, St Louis, 2010, Mosby.)

PATHOPHYSIOLOGY MAP

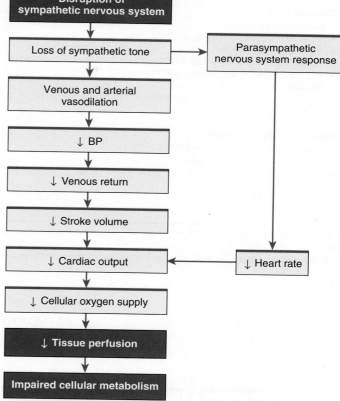

FIG. 66.4 The pathophysiology of neurogenic shock. (Modified from Urden LD, Stacy KM, Lough ME: *Critical care nursing: Diagnosis and management,* ed 6, St Louis, 2010, Mosby.)

the formation of microthrombi and obstruction of the microvasculature. The combined effects of the mediators result in damage to the endothelium, vasodilation, increased capillary permeability, and neutrophil and platelet aggregation and adhesion to the endothelium.

Septic shock has 3 major pathophysiologic effects: vasodilation, maldistribution of blood flow, and myocardial depression. Patients may be euvolemic, but because of acute vasodilation and shifting of fluids out of the intravascular space, relative hypovolemia and hypotension occur. Blood flow in the microcirculation is decreased, causing poor O_2 delivery and tissue hypoxia. We think the combination of TNF and IL-1 has a role in sepsis-induced myocardial dysfunction. The ejection fraction (EF) is decreased for the first few days after the initial insult. Because of a decreased EF, the ventricles dilate to maintain the SV. The EF typically improves, and ventricular dilation resolves over 7 to 10 days. Persistent high CO and a low SVR beyond 24 hours is an ominous finding. It is often associated with an increased development of hypotension and MODS. Coronary artery perfusion and myocardial O_2 metabolism are not primarily altered in septic shock.

Respiratory failure is common. The patient initially hyperventilates as a compensatory mechanism, causing respiratory alkalosis. Once the patient can no longer compensate, respiratory acidosis develops. Respiratory failure develops in 85% of patients with sepsis, and 40% develop acute respiratory distress syndrome (ARDS) (see Chapter 67). These patients may need to be intubated and mechanically ventilated.

Other signs of septic shock include changes in neurologic status, decreased urine output, and GI dysfunction, such as GI

bleeding and paralytic ileus. Table 66.3 gives the clinical presentation of a patient with septic shock.

Obstructive Shock. Obstructive shock develops when a physical obstruction to blood flow occurs with a decreased CO (Fig. 66.6). This can be caused by restricted diastolic filling of the right ventricle from compression (e.g., cardiac tamponade, tension pneumothorax, superior vena cava syndrome). Other causes include *abdominal compartment syndrome,* in which increased abdominal pressures compress the inferior vena cava. This decreases venous return to the heart. Pulmonary embolism and right ventricular thrombi cause an outflow obstruction as blood leaves the right ventricle through the pulmonary artery. This leads to decreased blood flow to the lungs and decreased blood return to the left atrium.

Patients have a decreased CO, increased afterload, and variable left ventricular filling pressures depending on the obstruction. Other signs include jugular venous distention and pulsus paradoxus. Rapid assessment and treatment are important to prevent further hemodynamic compromise and possible cardiac arrest (Fig. 66.6).

Stages of Shock

In addition to understanding the underlying pathogenesis of the type of shock the patient has, management is guided by knowing where the patient is on the shock "continuum." We categorize

TABLE 66.4 Diagnostic Criteria for Sepsis

Infection, documented or suspected, and some of the following:

General Variables
- Altered mental status
- Fever (temperature >100.9°F [38.3°C])
- Heart rate >90 beats/min
- Hyperglycemia (blood glucose >140 mg/dL) in the absence of diabetes
- Hypothermia (core temperature <97.0°F [36°C])
- Systolic BP ≤100 mm Hg
- Significant edema or positive fluid balance (>20 mL/kg over 24 hr)
- Tachypnea (respiratory rate ≥22/min)

Inflammatory Variables
- Leukocytosis (WBC count >12,000/μL)
- Leukopenia (WBC count <4000/μL)
- Normal WBC count with >10% immature forms (bands)
- Elevated C-reactive protein
- Elevated procalcitonin

Hemodynamic Variables
- Arterial hypotension (SBP <90 mm Hg, MAP <70 mm Hg, or a decrease in SBP >40 mm Hg)

Organ Dysfunction Variables
- Acute oliguria (urine output <0.5 mL/kg/hr for at least 2 hr despite adequate fluid resuscitation)
- Arterial hypoxemia (PaO_2/FIO_2 <300)
- Coagulation abnormalities (INR >1.5 or PTT >60 sec)
- Hyperbilirubinemia (total bilirubin >4 mg/dL)
- Ileus (absent bowel sounds)
- Serum creatinine increase >0.5 mg/dL
- Thrombocytopenia (platelet count <100,000/μL)

Tissue Perfusion Variables
- Hyperlactatemia (>1 mmol/L)
- Mottling or decreased capillary refill

Source: Singer M, Deutschman CS, Seymour CW, et al: The third international consensus definitions for sepsis and septic shock (Sepsis-3), *JAMA* 315:801, 2016.

FIO_2, Fraction of inspired O_2; *INR,* international normalized ratio; PaO_2, partial pressure of arterial O_2; *PTT,* partial thromboplastin time.

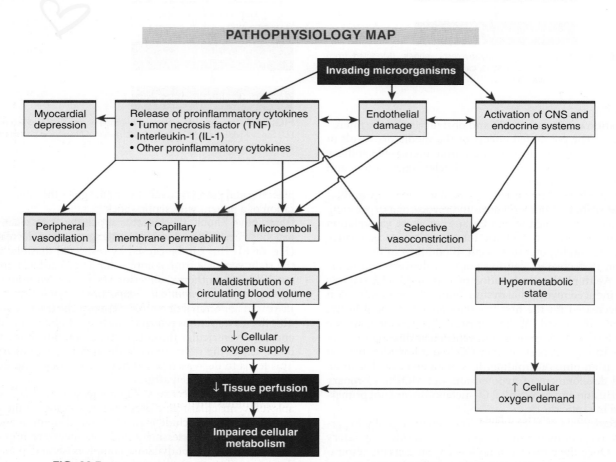

FIG. 66.5 The pathophysiology of septic shock. (Modified from Urden LD, Stacy KM, Lough ME: *Critical care nursing: Diagnosis and management,* ed 6, St Louis, 2010, Mosby.)

PATHOPHYSIOLOGY MAP

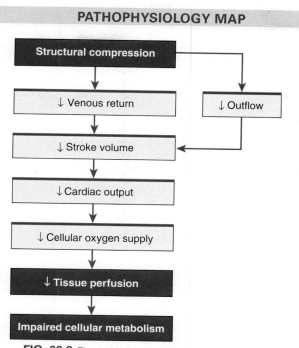

FIG. 66.6 The pathophysiology of obstructive shock.

shock into 4 overlapping stages: (1) initial stage, (2) compensatory stage, (3) progressive stage, and (4) refractory stage.[6]

Initial Stage. The continuum begins with the *initial stage* of shock that occurs at a cellular level. This stage is usually not clinically apparent. Metabolism changes at the cellular level from aerobic to anaerobic, causing lactic acid buildup. Lactic acid is a waste product that is removed by the liver. However, this process requires O_2, which is unavailable because of the decrease in tissue perfusion.

Compensatory Stage. In the *compensatory stage* the body activates neural, hormonal, and biochemical compensatory mechanisms to try to overcome the increasing consequences of anaerobic metabolism and maintain homeostasis. The patient's clinical presentation begins to reflect the body's responses to the imbalance in O_2 supply and demand (Table 66.5).

A classic sign of shock is a drop in BP. This occurs because of a decrease in CO and a narrowing of the pulse pressure. The baroreceptors in the carotid and aortic bodies immediately respond by activating the SNS. The SNS stimulates vasoconstriction and the release of the potent vasoconstrictors epinephrine and norepinephrine. Blood flow to the heart and brain is maintained. Blood flow to the nonvital organs, such as kidneys, GI tract, skin, and lungs, is diverted or shunted.

The myocardium responds to the SNS stimulation and the increase in O_2 demand by increasing the heart rate and contractility. Increased contractility increases myocardial O_2 consumption. The coronary arteries dilate to try to meet the increased O_2 demands of the myocardium.

Shunting blood away from the lungs has an important clinical effect in the patient in shock. Decreased blood flow to the lungs increases the patient's physiologic dead space. *Physiologic dead space* is the anatomic dead space (the amount of air that will not reach gas-exchanging units) and any inspired air that cannot take part in gas exchange. The clinical result of an increase in dead space ventilation is a *ventilation-perfusion mismatch*. Some

areas of the lungs that are being ventilated will not be perfused because of the decreased blood flow to the lungs. Arterial O_2 levels will decrease, and the patient will have a compensatory increase in the rate and depth of respirations (see Chapter 67).

The shunting of blood from other organ systems results in clinically important changes. The decrease in blood flow to the GI tract results in impaired motility and a slowing of peristalsis. This increases the risk for a paralytic ileus.

Decreased blood flow to the skin results in the patient feeling cool and clammy. The exception is the patient in early septic shock who may feel warm and flushed because of a hyperdynamic state. Decreased blood flow to the kidneys activates the renin-angiotensin system. Renin stimulates angiotensinogen to make angiotensin I, which is then converted to angiotensin II (see Fig. 44.4). Angiotensin II is a potent vasoconstrictor that causes both arterial and venous vasoconstriction. The net result is an increase in venous return to the heart and an increase in BP. Angiotensin II stimulates the adrenal cortex to release aldosterone. This results in sodium and water reabsorption and potassium excretion by the kidneys. The increase in sodium reabsorption raises the serum osmolality and stimulates the release of antidiuretic hormone (ADH) from the posterior pituitary gland. ADH increases water reabsorption by the kidneys, further increasing blood volume. The increase in total circulating volume results in an increase in CO and BP.

A multisystem response to decreasing tissue perfusion starts during the compensatory stage of shock. At this stage, the body can compensate for the changes in tissue perfusion. If the cause of the shock is corrected, the patient will recover with little or no residual effects. If the cause of the shock is not corrected and the body is unable to compensate, the patient enters the progressive stage of shock.

Progressive Stage. The *progressive stage* of shock begins as compensatory mechanisms fail. Changes in the patient's mental status are important findings in this stage. Patients must be moved to the intensive care unit (ICU), if not already there, for advanced monitoring and treatment.

The cardiovascular system is profoundly affected in the progressive stage of shock. CO begins to fall, resulting in a decrease in BP and coronary artery, cerebral, and peripheral perfusion. Continued decreased cellular perfusion and resulting altered capillary permeability are the distinguishing features of this stage. Altered capillary permeability allows fluid and protein to leak out of the vascular space into the surrounding interstitial space. In addition to the decrease in circulating volume, there is an increase in systemic interstitial edema. The patient may have *anasarca* (diffuse profound edema). Fluid leakage from the vascular space affects the solid organs (e.g., liver, spleen, GI tract, lungs) and peripheral tissues by further decreasing perfusion.

Sustained hypoperfusion results in weak peripheral pulses, and ischemia of the distal extremities eventually occurs. Myocardial dysfunction from decreased perfusion results in dysrhythmias, myocardial ischemia, and possibly MI. The result is a complete deterioration of the cardiovascular system.

The pulmonary system is often the first system to display signs of critical dysfunction. During the compensatory stage, blood flow to the lungs is already reduced. In response to the decreased blood flow and SNS stimulation, the pulmonary arterioles constrict, resulting in increased pulmonary artery (PA) pressure. As the pressure within the pulmonary vasculature increases, blood flow to the pulmonary capillaries decreases and ventilation-perfusion mismatch worsens.

TABLE 66.5 Manifestations of Stages of Shock*

Compensatory Stage	Progressive Stage	Refractory Stage
Neurologic System		
Oriented to person, place, time	↓ Cerebral perfusion pressure	Unresponsive
Restless, apprehensive, confused	↓ Cerebral blood flow	Areflexia (loss of reflexes)
Change in level of consciousness	↓ Responsiveness to stimuli	Pupils nonreactive and dilated
	Delirium	
Cardiovascular System		
Sympathetic nervous system response:	↑ Capillary permeability → systemic interstitial edema	Profound hypotension
• Release of epinephrine/norepinephrine (vasoconstriction)	↓ CO → ↓ BP and ↑ HR	↓ CO
• ↑ MVO$_2$	MAP <60 mm Hg (or 40 mm Hg drop in BP from baseline)	Bradycardia, irregular rhythm
• ↑ Contractility	↓ Coronary perfusion → dysrhythmias, myocardial ischemia, MI	↓ BP inadequate to perfuse vital organs
• ↑ HR	↓ Peripheral perfusion → ischemia of distal extremities, ↓ pulses, ↓ capillary refill	
Coronary artery dilation		
Narrowed pulse pressure		
↓ BP		
Respiratory System		
↓ Blood flow to the lungs:	ARDS:	Severe refractory hypoxemia
• ↑ Physiologic dead space	• ↑ Capillary permeability	Respiratory failure
• ↑ Ventilation-perfusion mismatch	• Pulmonary vasoconstriction	
• Hyperventilation	• Pulmonary interstitial edema	
• ↑ Minute ventilation (V$_E$)	• Alveolar edema	
• Tachypnea	• Diffuse infiltrates	
	• Tachypnea	
	• ↓ Compliance	
	• Moist crackles	
Gastrointestinal System		
↓ Blood supply	Vasoconstriction and ↓ perfusion → ischemic gut (e.g., stomach, small and large intestines, gallbladder, pancreas):	Ischemic gut
↓ GI motility	• Erosive ulcers	
Hypoactive bowel sounds	• GI bleeding	
↑ Risk for paralytic ileus	• Translocation of GI bacteria	
	• Impaired absorption of nutrients	
Renal System		
↓ Renal blood flow	Renal tubules become ischemic → acute tubular necrosis	Anuria
↑ Renin resulting in release of angiotensin (vasoconstrictor)	↓ Urine output	
↑ Aldosterone resulting in Na$^+$ and H$_2$O reabsorption	↑ BUN-to-creatinine ratio	
↑ Antidiuretic hormone resulting in H$_2$O reabsorption	↑ Urine sodium	
	↓ Urine osmolality and specific gravity	
	↓ Urine potassium	
	Metabolic acidosis	
Hepatic System		
	Failure to metabolize drugs and waste products	Metabolic changes from accumulation of waste products (e.g., NH$_3$, lactate, CO$_2$)
	Cell death (↑ liver enzymes)	
	Jaundice (↓ clearance of bilirubin)	
	↑ NH$_3$ (ammonia) and lactate	
Hematologic System		
	DIC:	DIC progresses
	• Thrombin clots in microcirculation	
	• Consumption of platelets and clotting factors	
Temperature		
Normal or abnormal	Hypothermia or hyperthermia	Hypothermia
Skin		
Pale and cool	Cold and clammy	Mottled, cyanotic
Warm and flushed		

*The shock continuum begins with the *initial stage* of shock. This stage occurs at the cellular level and is usually not clinically apparent. Also see Table 66.2 and Table 66.3.

MVO$_2$, myocardial O$_2$ consumption.

Another key response in the lungs is the movement of fluid from the pulmonary vasculature into the interstitial space. As capillary permeability increases, the movement of fluid to the interstitial spaces results in interstitial edema, bronchoconstriction, and a decrease in functional residual capacity. With further increases in capillary permeability, fluid moves into the alveoli, causing alveolar edema and a decrease in surfactant production. The combined effects of pulmonary vasoconstriction and bronchoconstriction are impaired gas exchange, decreased compliance, and worsening ventilation-perfusion mismatch. Clinically, the patient has tachypnea, crackles, and an overall increased work of breathing.

The GI system is affected by prolonged decreased tissue perfusion. As the blood supply to the GI tract is decreased, the normally protective mucosal barrier becomes ischemic. This ischemia predisposes the patient to ulcers and GI bleeding (see Chapter 41). It increases the risk for bacterial migration from the GI tract to the blood and lungs. The decreased perfusion to the GI tract leads to a decreased ability to absorb nutrients.

The effect of prolonged hypoperfusion on the kidneys is renal tubular ischemia. The resulting acute tubular necrosis may lead to acute kidney injury (AKI). This can be worsened by nephrotoxic drugs (e.g., certain antibiotics, anesthetics, diuretics) (see Chapter 46). The patient has decreased urine output and increased blood urea nitrogen (BUN) and serum creatinine. Metabolic acidosis occurs from the kidneys' inability to excrete acids (especially lactic acid) and reabsorb bicarbonate.

The sustained hypoperfusion in the progressive stage of shock greatly affects other organs. The loss of the functional ability of the liver leads to a failure of the liver to metabolize drugs and waste products (e.g., lactate, ammonia). Jaundice results from an accumulation of bilirubin. As the liver cells die, liver enzymes increase. The liver loses its ability to function as an immune organ. Kupffer cells no longer destroy bacteria from the GI tract. Instead, they are released into the bloodstream, increasing the possibility of bacteremia.

Dysfunction of the hematologic system adds to the complexity of the clinical picture. The patient is at risk for disseminated intravascular coagulation (DIC). The consumption of the platelets and clotting factors with secondary fibrinolysis results in clinically significant bleeding from many orifices. These include the GI tract, lungs, and puncture sites (see Chapter 30). Altered laboratory values in DIC are shown in Table 66.3.

In this stage, aggressive interventions are needed to prevent the development of MODS.

Refractory Stage. In the last stage of shock, the *refractory stage*, decreased perfusion from peripheral vasoconstriction and decreased CO worsen anaerobic metabolism. The accumulation of lactic acid contributes to increased capillary permeability and dilation. Increased capillary permeability allows fluid and plasma proteins to leave the vascular space and move to the interstitial space. Blood pools in the capillary beds due to the constricted venules and dilated arterioles. The loss of intravascular volume worsens hypotension and tachycardia and decreases coronary blood flow. Decreased coronary blood flow leads to worsening myocardial depression and a further decline in CO. Cerebral blood flow cannot be maintained and cerebral ischemia results.

The patient in this stage of shock has profound hypotension and hypoxemia. The failure of the liver, lungs, and kidneys results in an accumulation of waste products, such as lactate, urea, ammonia, and CO_2. The failure of 1 organ system affects several other organ systems. Recovery is unlikely in this stage. The organs are in failure and the body's compensatory mechanisms are overwhelmed (Table 66.5).

Diagnostic Studies

There is no single diagnostic study to determine whether a patient is in shock. The diagnosis starts with a history and physical examination. Obtaining a thorough medical and surgical history and a history of recent events (e.g., surgery, chest pain, trauma) gives valuable data.

Decreased tissue perfusion in shock leads to an increased lactate with a base deficit (the amount needed to bring the pH back to normal). These laboratory changes reflect an increase in anaerobic metabolism.[8] Table 66.2 outlines laboratory findings seen in shock.

Other diagnostic studies include a 12-lead electrocardiogram (ECG), continuous ECG monitoring, chest x-ray, continuous pulse oximetry, and invasive and noninvasive hemodynamic monitoring. Chapter 65 discusses hemodynamic monitoring)

Interprofessional Care

Critical factors in the successful management of a patient in shock relate to the early recognition and treatment of the shock state. Prompt intervention in the early stages of shock may prevent the decline to the progressive or irreversible stage. Successful management of the patient in shock includes (1) identification of patients at risk for the development of shock; (2) integration of the patient's history, physical examination, and clinical findings to establish a diagnosis; (3) interventions to control or eliminate the cause of the decreased perfusion; (4) protecting target and distal organs from dysfunction; and (5) providing multisystem supportive care.

Table 66.6 provides an overview of the initial assessment findings and interventions for the emergency care of patients in shock. General management strategies begin with ensuring that the patient is responsive and has a patent airway. Once the airway is established, either naturally or with an endotracheal tube, O_2 delivery must be optimized. Supplemental O_2 and mechanical ventilation may be needed to maintain an arterial O_2 saturation of 90% or more (PaO_2 greater than 60 mm Hg) to avoid hypoxemia (see Chapter 65). The mean arterial pressure (MAP) and circulating blood volume are optimized with fluid replacement and drug therapy.

Oxygen and Ventilation. O_2 delivery depends on CO, available hemoglobin, and arterial O_2 saturation (SaO_2). Methods to optimize O_2 delivery are directed at increasing supply and decreasing demand. Supply is increased by (1) optimizing the CO with fluid replacement and/or drug therapy, (2) increasing the hemoglobin through transfusion of whole blood or packed red blood cells (RBCs), and/or (3) increasing the arterial O_2 saturation with supplemental O_2 and mechanical ventilation.

Plan care to avoid disrupting the balance of O_2 supply and demand. Space activities that increase O_2 consumption (e.g., endotracheal suctioning, position changes) appropriately for O_2 conservation. Intermittent or continuous monitoring of $ScvO_2$ by a central venous catheter or mixed venous O_2 saturation (SvO_2) may be helpful. Both reflect the dynamic balance between O_2 supply and demand. Assess these values along with related hemodynamic measures (e.g., arterial pressure–based cardiac output [APCO], O_2 consumption, hemoglobin) to evaluate the patient's response to treatments and activities (see Chapter 65).

✚ TABLE 66.6 Emergency Management

Shock

Etiology*	Assessment Findings	Interventions
Surgical • Aortic dissection • GI bleeding • Postoperative bleeding • Ruptured ectopic pregnancy or ovarian cyst • Ruptured organ or vessel • Vaginal bleeding **Medical** • Addisonian crisis • Dehydration • Diabetes • Diabetes insipidus • MI • Pulmonary embolus • Sepsis **Trauma** • Fractures, spinal injury • Multiorgan injury • Ruptured or lacerated vessel or organ (e.g., spleen)	• Anxiety • Chills • Confusion • Cool, clammy skin (warm skin in early onset of septic and neurogenic shock) • Cyanosis • Decreased level of consciousness • Decreased O_2 saturation • Dysrhythmias • Extreme thirst • Feeling of impending doom • Hypotension • Narrowed pulse pressure • Nausea and vomiting • Obvious hemorrhage or injury • Pallor • Rapid, weak, thready pulses • Restlessness • Tachypnea, dyspnea, or shallow, irregular respirations • Temperature dysregulation • Weakness	**Initial** • If unresponsive, assess circulation, airway, and breathing (CAB). • If responsive, monitor airway, breathing, and circulation (ABC). • Stabilize cervical spine as appropriate. • Control any external bleeding with direct pressure or pressure dressing. • Give high-flow O_2 (100%) by nonrebreather mask or bag-valve-mask. • Anticipate need for intubation and mechanical ventilation. • Establish IV access with 2 large-bore catheters (14- to 16-gauge) or an intraosseous access device; aid with central line insertion. • Begin fluid resuscitation with crystalloids (e.g., 30 mL/kg repeated until hemodynamic improvement is seen). • Draw blood for laboratory studies (e.g., blood cultures, lactate, WBC). • Assess for life-threatening injuries (e.g., cardiac tamponade, liver laceration, tension pneumothorax). • Consider vasopressor therapy if hypotension persists after fluid resuscitation. • Insert an indwelling urinary catheter and nasogastric tube. • Start antibiotic therapy after blood cultures if sepsis is suspected. • Obtain 12-lead ECG and treat dysrhythmias. **Ongoing Monitoring** • ABCs • Level of consciousness • Vital signs, including pulse oximetry; peripheral pulses, capillary refill, skin color and temperature • Respiratory status • Heart rate and rhythm • Urine output

*See Table 66.1 for other causes of shock.

Fluid Resuscitation. The cornerstone of therapy for septic, hypovolemic, and anaphylactic shock is volume expansion with administration of the appropriate fluid (Table 66.7). Fluid resuscitation should start using 1 or 2 large-bore (e.g., 14- to 16-gauge) IV catheters, an intraosseous (IO) access device, or a central venous catheter.

> ⚠ **SAFETY ALERT Intraosseous (IO) Access**
> • Use an IO access device for emergency resuscitation when IV access cannot be obtained.
> • Insertion sites include the sternum, proximal and distal tibia, and proximal and distal humerus.
> • Remove IO devices within 24 hours of insertion or as soon as possible after peripheral or central IV access is obtained.
> • Monitor for complications: extravasation of drugs and fluids into the soft tissue, fractures caused during insertion, and osteomyelitis.

The choice of resuscitation fluid is based on the type and volume of fluid lost and the patient's clinical status. The ideal choice of fluid is controversial. Currently, normal saline is most often used in the initial resuscitation of shock. Large-volume resuscitation with normal saline can lead to hyperchloremic metabolic acidosis. Lactated Ringer's solution can cause serum lactate levels to increase because the failing liver cannot convert lactate to bicarbonate.[9] Transfusions of RBCs may be given to treat hypovolemic shock due to bleeding. Colloids (4% to 5%) have not been shown to improve patient outcomes.[9]

Fluid responsiveness is determined by clinical assessment. This includes vital signs, cerebral and abdominal perfusion pressures, capillary refill, skin temperature, and urine output. Hemodynamic parameters, such as SVV or CO, are also used. Monitor trends in BP with an automatic BP cuff or an arterial catheter to assess the patient's response. Use an indwelling urinary catheter to monitor urine output during resuscitation.

The goal for fluid resuscitation is to restore tissue perfusion. Although BP helps determine whether the patient's CO is adequate, an assessment of end-organ perfusion (e.g., urine output, neurologic function, peripheral pulses) provides more relevant data.

> ⚠ **SAFETY ALERT Complications of Fluid Resuscitation**
> • Warm crystalloid and colloid solutions during massive fluid resuscitation to prevent hypothermia.
> • When giving large volumes of packed RBCs, remember that they do not contain clotting factors.
> • Replace clotting factors based on the clinical situation and laboratory studies.

Drug Therapy. The goal of drug therapy for shock is to correct decreased tissue perfusion. Decisions on which drug to use should be based on the physiologic goal. Drugs used to improve perfusion in shock are given IV via an infusion pump and central venous line. Many of these drugs have vasoconstrictor properties that are harmful if the drug leaks into the tissues while being infused peripherally (Table 66.8).

TABLE 66.7 Fluid Therapy in Shock

Fluid Type	Mechanism of Action	Type of Shock	Nursing Implications
Crystalloids			
Isotonic			
• 0.9% NaCl, normal saline solution (NSS) • Lactated Ringer's (LR) solution	Fluid primarily stays in the intravascular space, ↑ intravascular volume.	Used for initial volume replacement in most types of shock.	Monitor patient closely for circulatory overload. Do not use LR in patients with liver failure. LR may be used if hyperchloremic acidosis develops from use of NSS in fluid resuscitation.
Hypertonic			
• 1.8%, 3%, 5% NaCl	Fluid stays in the intravascular space, increases serum osmolarity, shifts fluid volume from intracellular space to extracellular space to intravascular space.	May be used for initial volume expansion in hypovolemic shock.	Monitor patient closely for signs of hypernatremia (e.g., disorientation, seizures). Central line preferred for infusing saline solutions ≥3%, since these may damage veins.
Blood or Blood Products			
Packed red blood cells Fresh frozen plasma Platelets	Replaces blood loss, increases O_2-carrying capability. Replaces coagulation factors. Helps control bleeding caused by thrombocytopenia.	All types.	Same precautions as any blood administration (see Chapter 30).
Colloids			
Human serum albumin (5% or 25%)	Can increase plasma colloid osmotic pressure. Rapid volume expansion.	All types except cardiogenic and neurogenic shock.	Use 5% solution in hypovolemic patients. Use 25% solution in patients with fluid and sodium restrictions. Monitor for circulatory overload. Mild side effects of chills, fever, and urticaria may develop. More expensive than crystalloids.
dextran (dextran 40)	Hyperosmotic glucose polymer.	Limited use because of side effects, including reducing platelet adhesion, diluting clotting factors.	Increases risk for bleeding. Monitor patient for allergic reactions and AKI. Has maximum volume recommendations per manufacturer.

Sympathomimetic Drugs. Many of the drugs used in the treatment of shock influence the SNS. Drugs that mimic the action of the SNS are called *sympathomimetic.* The effects of these drugs are mediated through their binding to α- or β-adrenergic receptors. The various drugs differ in their relative α- and β-adrenergic effects.[10]

Many of these drugs cause peripheral vasoconstriction and are called *vasopressor drugs* (e.g., norepinephrine, dopamine, phenylephrine). These drugs can cause severe peripheral vasoconstriction and an increase in SVR, further risking tissue perfusion. The increased SVR increases the workload of the heart and myocardial O_2 demand. It can harm a patient in cardiogenic shock by causing further myocardial damage and increasing the risk for dysrhythmias.[1] Use of vasopressor drugs is limited to patients who do not respond to fluid resuscitation. Adequate fluid resuscitation must be achieved before starting vasopressors because the vasoconstrictor effects in patients with low blood volume will cause further reduction in tissue perfusion. Typically, if the patient has persistent hypotension after adequate fluid resuscitation, a vasopressor (e.g., norepinephrine, dopamine) and/or an inotrope (e.g., dobutamine) is given.

The goal of vasopressor therapy is to achieve and maintain a MAP of greater than 65 mm Hg.[10] Continuously monitor end-organ perfusion (e.g., urine output, level of consciousness) and serum lactate levels (e.g., every 3 hours for the first 6 hours) to ensure that tissue perfusion is adequate.

Vasodilator Drugs. Patients in cardiogenic shock have decreased myocardial contractility, and vasodilators may be needed to decrease afterload. This reduces myocardial workload and O_2 requirements. Although generalized sympathetic vasoconstriction is a useful compensatory mechanism for maintaining BP, excessive constriction can reduce tissue blood flow and increase the workload of the heart. The reason for using vasodilator therapy for a patient in shock is to break the harmful cycle of widespread vasoconstriction causing a decrease in CO and BP, resulting in further sympathetic-induced vasoconstriction.

The goal of vasodilator therapy, as in vasopressor therapy, is to maintain the MAP greater than 65 mm Hg. Monitor hemodynamic parameters (e.g., CVP, CO, $ScvO_2$/SvO_2, SV, PA pressures) and assessment findings so that fluids can be increased or vasodilator therapy decreased if a serious fall in CO or BP occurs. The vasodilator agent most often used for the patient in cardiogenic shock is nitroglycerin. Vasodilation may be enhanced with nitroprusside or nitroglycerin in noncardiogenic shock.

Nutritional Therapy. Protein-calorie malnutrition is common because of hypermetabolism. Nutrition is vital to reducing mortality. Enteral nutrition (EN) should be started within the first 24 hours. However, full calorie replacement is not recommended for previously well-nourished adults early in a critical illness.[11] Start the patient on a *trophic feeding.* This is a small amount of EN (e.g., 10 mL/hr). Early EN enhances the perfusion of the

TABLE 66.8 Drug Therapy

Shock

Drug*	Mechanism of Action	Type of Shock	Nursing Implications
angiotensin II (Giapreza)	↑ BP, ↑ MAP ↑SVR	Septic and other distributive shock	Give via central line. Monitor for thromboembolic events. VTE prophylaxis is recommended.
dobutamine	↑ Myocardial contractility ↓ Ventricular filling pressures ↓ SVR, PAWP ↑ CO, SV, CVP ↑/↓ HR	Used in cardiogenic shock with severe systolic dysfunction Used in septic shock to increase O₂ delivery and raise ScvO₂ or SvO₂ to 70% if Hgb >7 g/dL or Hct ≥30%	Give via central line (infiltration leads to tissue sloughing). Do not give in same line with NaHCO₃. Monitor HR, BP (hypotension may worsen, requiring addition of a vasopressor). Stop infusion if tachydysrhythmias develop.
Dopamine	Positive inotropic effects: ↑ Myocardial contractility ↑ Automaticity ↑ Atrioventricular conduction ↑ HR, CO ↑ BP, ↑ MAP ↑ MVO₂ Can cause progressive vasoconstriction at high doses	Cardiogenic shock	Give via central line (infiltration leads to tissue sloughing). Do not give in same line with NaHCO₃. Monitor for tachydysrhythmias. Monitor for peripheral vasoconstriction (e.g., paresthesias, coldness in extremities) at moderate to high doses.
epinephrine (Adrenalin)	*Low doses:* β-Adrenergic agonist (cardiac stimulation, bronchodilation, peripheral vasodilation) ↑ HR, contractility, CO ↓ SVR *High doses:* α-Adrenergic agonist (peripheral vasoconstriction) ↑ SV, SVR ↑ Systolic/↓ diastolic BP, widened pulse pressure ↑ CVP, PAWP	Cardiogenic shock Anaphylactic shock Septic shock, if 2nd agent needed after norepinephrine Cardiac arrest, pulseless ventricular tachycardia, ventricular fibrillation, asystole	Monitor for HR >110 beats/min. Monitor for dyspnea, pulmonary edema. Monitor for chest pain, dysrhythmias from ↑ MVO₂. Monitor for renal failure due to ischemia.
hydrocortisone (Solu-Cortef)	↓ Inflammation, reverses ↑ capillary permeability ↑ BP, HR	Septic shock requiring vasopressor therapy (despite fluid resuscitation) to maintain adequate BP Anaphylactic shock if hypotension persists after initial therapy	Monitor for hypokalemia, hyperglycemia. Consider use as continuous infusion.
nitroglycerin	Venous dilation Dilates coronary arteries ↓ Preload, MVO₂, SVR, BP	Cardiogenic shock	Continuously monitor BP and HR, since reflex tachycardia may occur. Glass bottle recommended for infusion.
norepinephrine (Levophed)	β₁-Adrenergic agonist (cardiac stimulation) α-Adrenergic agonist (peripheral vasoconstriction) Renal and splanchnic vasoconstriction ↑ BP, MAP, CVP, PAWP, SVR ↑/↓ CO	Cardiogenic shock after MI Septic shock—first drug of choice for BP unresponsive to adequate fluid resuscitation	Give via central line (infiltration leads to tissue sloughing). Monitor for dysrhythmias due to ↑ MVO₂ requirements.
phenylephrine	α-Adrenergic agonist (peripheral vasoconstriction) Renal, mesenteric, splanchnic, cutaneous, and pulmonary blood vessel constriction ↑ HR, BP, SVR ↑/↓ CO	Neurogenic shock	Monitor for reflex bradycardia, headache, restlessness. Monitor for renal failure from ↓ renal blood flow. Give via central line (infiltration leads to tissue sloughing).
sodium nitroprusside	Arterial and venous vasodilation ↓ Preload, afterload ↓ CVP, PAWP ↑/↓ CO ↓ BP	Cardiogenic shock with ↑ SVR	Continuously monitor BP. Protect solution from light. Wrap infusion bottle with opaque covering. Give with D₅W only. Monitor serum cyanide levels and for signs of cyanide toxicity (e.g., metabolic acidosis, tachycardia, altered level of consciousness, seizures, coma, almond smell on breath).
vasopressin	Antidiuretic hormone Nonadrenergic vasoconstrictor ↑ MAP ↑ Urine output	Shock states (most often septic shock) refractory to other vasopressors	Given with norepinephrine and in low doses. Infusions are not titrated. Monitor hemodynamic pressures and urine output.

*Consult agency guidelines, pharmacist, pharmacology references, and drug manufacturer's materials for more information and dosing recommendations.
CVP, Central venous pressure; *MVO₂,* myocardial O₂ consumption; *PAWP,* pulmonary artery wedge pressure; *PT,* prothrombin time; *PTT,* partial thromboplastin time; *SVR,* systemic vascular resistance.

GI tract and helps maintain the integrity of the gut mucosa. Advance feedings as tolerated and as prescribed. Parenteral nutrition (PN) is used only if EN is contraindicated. Chapter 39 discusses enteral and parenteral nutrition.

Weigh the patient daily on the same scale (usually the bed scale) at the same time of day. If the patient has a significant weight loss, rule out dehydration before adding more calories. Large weight gains are common because of third spacing of fluids. Therefore daily weights serve as a better indicator of fluid status than caloric needs. Serum protein, total albumin, prealbumin, BUN, serum glucose, and serum electrolytes are all used to assess nutritional status.

Measures Specific to Type of Shock

Cardiogenic Shock. For a patient in cardiogenic shock, the overall goal is to restore heart function and the balance between O_2 supply and demand in the myocardium. Cardiac catheterization is done as soon as possible after the initial insult.[1] Specific measures to restore blood flow include angioplasty with stenting, emergency revascularization, and valve replacement (see Chapter 33). Until these interventions are done, we must support the heart to optimize SV and CO to achieve optimal perfusion (Tables 66.8 and 66.9).

Hemodynamic management of a patient in cardiogenic shock aims to reduce the workload of the heart through drug therapy and/or mechanical interventions. Drug choice is based on the clinical goal and a thorough understanding of each drug's mechanism of action. Drugs can be used to decrease the workload of the heart by dilating coronary arteries (e.g., nitrates), reducing preload (e.g., diuretics), afterload (e.g., vasodilators), and heart rate and contractility (e.g., β-adrenergic blockers).

The patient may benefit from a circulatory assist device (e.g., intraaortic balloon pump, ventricular assist device [VAD]) (see Chapter 65). The goals of this intervention are to decrease SVR and left ventricular workload so that the heart can heal.[12] A VAD may be used as a temporary measure for the patient in cardiogenic shock who is awaiting heart transplantation. Heart transplantation is an option for a small, select group of patients with cardiogenic shock.

Hypovolemic Shock. The underlying principles of managing patients with hypovolemic shock focus on stopping the loss of fluid and restoring the circulating volume. We often calculate the initial fluid resuscitation using a 3:1 rule (3 mL of isotonic crystalloid for every 1 mL of estimated blood loss). Table 66.7 describes types of fluid used for volume resuscitation, the mechanisms of action, and specific nursing implications for each fluid type.

Septic Shock. Patients in septic shock need large amounts of fluid replacement. The overall goal of fluid resuscitation is to restore the intravascular volume and organ perfusion. Initial volume resuscitation is achieved by giving 30 mL/kg of an isotonic crystalloid solution. Albumin 4% to 5% may be added when patients need substantial volumes.

A fluid challenge technique (e.g., a minimum of 30 mL/kg of crystalloids) may be used and repeated until hemodynamic improvement (e.g., increase in MAP and/or CVP, change in SVV) is seen. Table 66.9 shows predetermined end points of fluid resuscitation along with methods to reassess volume status.

One of these methods is a *passive leg raise* (PLR) challenge along with hemodynamic measures to monitor response.[13] A PLR challenge provides a transient increase in fluid volume of 150 to 500 mL by placing the patient supine and raising the legs to 45 degrees (Fig. 66.7). Response is monitored within 1 to 2 minutes by measuring CO, CI, SV, SVV, or other parameters for improvement. If the response is positive, the patient is fluid responsive and should receive more fluids. To optimize and evaluate large-volume fluid resuscitation, hemodynamic monitoring with various noninvasive or invasive monitors is needed.

If the patient is hypotensive after initial volume resuscitation and no longer fluid responsive, vasopressors may be added. The first drug of choice is norepinephrine.[14] Vasodilation and low CO, or vasodilation alone, can cause low BP despite adequate fluid resuscitation. Vasopressin may be added for those who are refractory to initial vasopressor therapy.[14] Exogenous vasopressin can replace the stores of physiologic vasopressin that are often depleted in septic shock.

DRUG ALERT Vasopressin

- Given along with norepinephrine.
- Infuse at low doses (e.g., 0.03 units/min) using an IV pump.
- Do not titrate infusion.
- Use cautiously in patients with coronary artery disease.

Vasopressor drugs may increase BP but can decrease SV. An inotropic agent (e.g., dobutamine) may be added to offset the decrease in SV and increase tissue perfusion (Table 66.8). IV corticosteroids may be considered for patients in septic shock who cannot maintain an adequate BP despite vasopressor therapy and fluid resuscitation.

To try to meet the increasing tissue demands coupled with a low SVR, the patient initially has a normal or high CO. If the patient is unable to achieve and maintain an adequate CO and has unmet tissue O_2 demands, CO may have to be increased using drug therapy (e.g., dopamine). $ScvO_2$ or SvO_2 monitoring is used to assess the balance between O_2 delivery and consumption, and the adequacy of the CO (see Chapter 65). If balance is maintained, the tissue demands will be met.

Broad-spectrum antibiotics are an important and early part of therapy. They should be started within the first hour of sepsis or septic shock.[15] Obtain cultures (e.g., blood, wound, urine, stool, sputum) before antibiotics are started. However, this should not delay the start of antibiotics within the first hour. Specific antibiotics may be ordered once the organism has been identified.

Glucose levels should be maintained below 180 mg/dL (10.0 mmol/L) for patients in shock.[16] Monitor glucose levels in all patients in septic shock according to agency policy. Stress ulcer prophylaxis with proton pump inhibitors (e.g., pantoprazole) and VTE prophylaxis (e.g., heparin, enoxaparin [Lovenox]) are recommended.[17]

Neurogenic Shock. The specific treatment of neurogenic shock is based on the cause. If the cause is spinal cord injury, general measures to promote spinal stability (e.g., spinal precautions, cervical stabilization with a collar) are initially used. Once the spine is stabilized, treatment of the hypotension and bradycardia is essential to prevent further spinal cord damage. Treatment involves the use of vasopressors (e.g., phenylephrine) to maintain BP and organ perfusion (Table 66.8). Bradycardia may be treated with atropine. Infuse fluids cautiously as the cause of the hypotension is not related to fluid loss. The patient with a spinal cord injury is monitored for hypothermia caused by hypothalamic dysfunction (Table 66.9).

Anaphylactic Shock. The first strategy in managing patients at risk for anaphylactic shock is prevention. A thorough history

TABLE 66.9 Interprofessional Care

Shock

Oxygenation	Circulation	Drug Therapies	Supportive Therapies
Cardiogenic Shock • Provide supplemental O_2 (e.g., nasal cannula, nonrebreather mask) • Intubation and mechanical ventilation, if needed • Monitor $ScvO_2$ or SvO_2	• Restore blood flow with angioplasty with stenting, emergent coronary revascularization • Reduce workload of heart with circulatory assist devices: IABP, VAD	• Nitrates (e.g., nitroglycerin) • Inotropes (e.g., dobutamine) • Diuretics (e.g., furosemide) • β-Adrenergic blockers (contraindicated with ↓ ejection fraction)	• Treat dysrhythmias

Hypovolemic Shock
• Provide supplemental O_2
• Monitor $ScvO_2$ or $ScvO_2$
	• Rapid fluid replacement using 2 large-bore (14–16 gauge) peripheral IV lines, an intraosseous access device, or central venous catheter
	• Restore fluid volume (e.g., blood or blood products, crystalloids)
	• End points of fluid resuscitation:
	  • CVP 15 mm Hg
	  • PAWP 10–12 mm Hg
		• No specific drug therapy	• Correct the cause (e.g., stop bleeding, GI losses)
			• Use warmed IV fluids, including blood products (if appropriate)

Septic Shock
• Provide supplemental O_2
• Intubation and mechanical ventilation, if needed
• Monitor $ScvO_2$ or SvO_2
	• Aggressive fluid resuscitation (e.g., 30 mL/kg of crystalloids repeated if hemodynamic improvement is noted)
	• End points of fluid resuscitation are based on:
	  • Focused physical examination including vital signs, cardiopulmonary assessment, capillary refill, peripheral pulses, and skin or any 2 of the following:
	    • $ScvO_2$ >70 or SvO_2 >65
	    • CVP 8–12 mm Hg
	    • Cardiovascular ultrasound
	    • Assessment of fluid responsiveness with passive leg raise or fluid challenge
		• Antibiotics as ordered
		• Vasopressors (e.g., norepinephrine)
		• Inotropes (e.g., dobutamine)
		• Anticoagulants (e.g., low-molecular-weight heparin)
			• Obtain cultures (e.g., blood, wound) before beginning antibiotics
			• Monitor temperature
			• Control blood glucose
			• Stress ulcer prophylaxis

Neurogenic Shock • Maintain patent airway • Provide supplemental O_2 • Intubation and mechanical ventilation (if needed)	• Cautious administration of fluids	• Vasopressors (e.g., phenylephrine) • Atropine (for bradycardia)	• Minimize spinal cord trauma with stabilization • Monitor temperature
Anaphylactic Shock • Maintain patent airway • Optimize oxygenation with supplemental O_2 • Intubation and mechanical ventilation, if needed	• Aggressive fluid resuscitation with colloids	• Epinephrine (IM or IV) • Antihistamines (e.g., diphenhydramine) • Histamine (H_2)-receptor blockers (e.g., ranitidine [Zantac]) • Bronchodilators: nebulized (e.g., albuterol) • Corticosteroids (if hypotension persists)	• Identify and remove offending cause • Prevent via avoidance of known allergens • Premedicate with history of prior sensitivity (e.g., contrast media)
Obstructive Shock • Maintain patent airway • Provide supplemental O_2 • Intubation and mechanical ventilation, if needed	• Restore circulation by treating cause of obstruction • Fluid resuscitation may provide temporary improvement in CO and BP	• No specific drug therapy	• Treat cause of obstruction (e.g., pericardiocentesis for cardiac tamponade, needle decompression or chest tube insertion for tension pneumothorax, embolectomy for pulmonary embolism)

CVP, central venous pressure; *PAWP*, pulmonary artery wedge pressure.

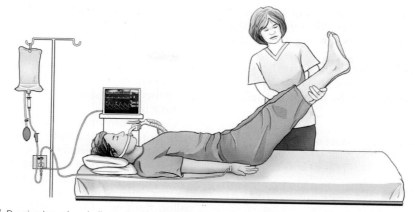

FIG. 66.7 Passive leg raise challenge in a patient with septic shock. (From Lough, M.E. *Hemodynamic monitoring: Evolving technologies and clinical practice*, Philadelphia, 2016, Elsevier.)

is key to avoiding risk factors for anaphylaxis (Table 66.1). The clinical presentation of anaphylactic shock is dramatic, and immediate intervention is required. Epinephrine is the first drug of choice to treat anaphylactic shock.[5] It causes peripheral vasoconstriction and bronchodilation and opposes the effect of histamine. Diphenhydramine and histamine receptor blockers (e.g., famotidine) are given as adjunctive therapies to block the ongoing release of histamine from the allergic reaction.

Maintaining a patent airway is important because the patient can quickly develop airway compromise from laryngeal edema or bronchoconstriction. Nebulized bronchodilators are highly effective. Aerosolized epinephrine can reduce treat laryngeal edema. Endotracheal intubation may be needed to secure and maintain a patent airway.

Hypotension results from leakage of fluid out of the intravascular space into the interstitial space because of increased vascular permeability and vasodilation. Aggressive fluid resuscitation, usually with crystalloids, is needed. IV corticosteroids may be helpful in anaphylactic shock if significant hypotension persists after 1 to 2 hours of aggressive therapy (Tables 66.8 and 66.9).

Obstructive Shock. The main strategy in treating obstructive shock is early recognition and treatment to relieve or manage the obstruction (Table 66.1). Mechanical decompression for pericardial tamponade, tension pneumothorax, and hemopneumothorax may be done by needle or tube insertion. Obstructive shock from a pulmonary embolism requires immediate anticoagulation therapy or pulmonary embolectomy. Superior vena cava syndrome, a compression or obstruction of the outflow tract of the mediastinum, may be treated by radiation, debulking, or removal of the mass or cause. A decompressive laparotomy may be done for abdominal compartment syndrome for patients with high intraabdominal pressures and hemodynamic instability.

❖ NURSING MANAGEMENT: SHOCK

◆ Nursing Assessment

Your role is vital in caring for patients who are at risk for developing shock or are in a state of shock. Focus your assessment on the ABCs: airway, breathing, and circulation. Next, assess for tissue perfusion. This includes evaluating vital signs, level of consciousness, peripheral pulses, capillary refill, skin (e.g., temperature, color, moisture), and urine output. As shock

progresses, the patient's neurologic status declines, urine output decreases, skin becomes cooler and mottled, and peripheral pulses decrease.

To understand the complexity of the patient's clinical status, integrate all the assessment data. It is essential to obtain a brief history from the patient or caregiver, including a description of the events leading to the shock state, time of onset and duration of symptoms, and health history (e.g., medications, allergies). In addition, obtain details about any care the patient received before hospitalization.

◆ Nursing Diagnoses

Nursing diagnoses for the patient in shock may include:
- Impaired cardiac output
- Ineffective tissue perfusion
- Anxiety

Additional information on nursing diagnoses and interventions for the patient with shock is presented in eNursing Care Plan 66.1 (available on the website for this chapter).

◆ Planning

The overall goals for a patient in shock include (1) evidence of adequate tissue perfusion, (2) restoration of normal or baseline BP, (3) recovery of organ function, (4) avoiding complications from prolonged states of hypoperfusion, and (5) preventing health care–associated complications of disease management and care.

◆ Nursing Implementation

◆ Health Promotion. You have a vital role in the prevention of shock, beginning with the identification of patients at risk. In general, patients who are older, are immunocompromised, or have chronic illnesses are at an increased risk. Any person who has surgery or trauma is at risk for shock resulting from hemorrhage, spinal cord injury, sepsis, and other problems (Table 66.1).

Planning is essential to help prevent shock after you identify an at-risk person. For example, a person with an acute anterior wall MI is at high risk for cardiogenic shock.[1] The main goal for this patient is to limit the infarct size. This is done by restoring coronary blood flow through percutaneous coronary intervention, thrombolytic therapy, or surgical revascularization. Rest, analgesics, and sedation can reduce the myocardial demand for O_2. Modify the ICU environment to provide care at intervals that will not increase the patient's O_2 demand. For example, if the patient becomes tired with bathing, perform this care at a time that does not interfere with tests or other activities that may also increase O_2 demand.

A person with certain severe allergies, such as to drugs, shellfish, insect bites, and latex, is at increased risk for anaphylactic shock. This risk can be decreased if the patient is carefully assessed for allergies.

> **⚠ SAFETY ALERT Preventing Allergic Reactions**
> • Always confirm the patient's allergies before giving drugs or starting diagnostic procedures (e.g., CT scan with contrast media).
> • Premedicate (e.g., diphenhydramine, methylprednisolone) patients who need a drug to which they are at high risk for an allergic reaction (e.g., contrast media).
> • Encourage patients with allergies to obtain and wear a medical alert device and report their allergies to their HCPs.
> • Tell patients about the availability of kits that contain equipment and drugs (e.g., epinephrine [EpiPen]) for the treatment of acute allergic reactions.

Careful monitoring of fluid balance can help prevent hypovolemic shock. Ongoing monitoring of intake and output and daily weights is important. Identifying trends in the patient's condition is more meaningful than any single piece of clinical information.

Carefully monitor all patients for infection. Progression from an infection to sepsis and septic shock depends on the patient's defense mechanisms. Patients who are immunocompromised are at high risk for opportunistic infections. Strategies to decrease the risk for health care–associated infections (HAIs) include decreasing the number of invasive catheters (e.g., central lines, bladder catheters), using aseptic technique during invasive procedures, and paying strict attention to hand washing. Change equipment per agency policy. Thoroughly sanitize or discard (if disposable) equipment between patient use.

Evidence-based guidelines are available to reduce the risk for HAIs (e.g., ventilator-associated pneumonia, central line infections, catheter-associated urinary tract infections). These guidelines, called *care bundles,* outline key interventions aimed at reducing infections.[18]

◆ **Acute Care.** Your role in shock involves (1) monitoring the patient's ongoing physical and emotional status, (2) identifying trends to detect changes in the patient's condition, (3) planning and implementing nursing interventions and therapy, (4) evaluating the patient's response to therapy, (5) providing emotional support to the patient and caregiver, and (6) collaborating with other members of the interprofessional team to coordinate care.

Neurologic Status. Assess the patient's neurologic status, including orientation and level of consciousness using a valid tool, at least every 1 to 2 hours. The patient's neurologic status is the best indicator of cerebral blood flow. Be aware of the clinical manifestations of neurologic involvement (e.g., changes in behavior, restlessness, blurred vision, confusion, paresthesias). Note any subtle changes in the patient's mental status (e.g., mild agitation) and report them to the HCP.

Orient the patient to person, place, time, and events on a regular basis. Orientation to the ICU environment is especially important. Reduce noise and light levels to control sensory input. Keep a day-night cycle of activity and rest as much as possible. Sensory overload and disruption of the patient's diurnal cycle may contribute to delirium (see Chapter 59).

Cardiovascular Status. Most of the therapy for shock is based on information about the patient's cardiovascular status.

If the patient is unstable, continuously assess heart rate and rhythm, BP, CVP, and PA pressures, including CO, SVR, SV, and SVV (if available). Monitoring trends in hemodynamic parameters provides more important information than single values. Integration of hemodynamic data with physical assessment data is essential in planning strategies to manage the patient with shock. Chapter 65 discusses hemodynamic monitoring.

Continuously monitor the patient's ECG to detect dysrhythmias that may result from the cardiovascular and metabolic abnormalities associated with shock. Assess heart sounds for an S_3 or S_4 sound or new murmurs. An S_3 sound usually indicates HF. Monitor the patient's skin (e.g., upper and lower extremities) for signs of adequate perfusion. Changes in temperature, pallor, flushing, cyanosis, diaphoresis, and piloerection may indicate hypoperfusion.

Give the prescribed therapy to correct cardiovascular system problems. Assess the patient's response to fluid and drug administration as often as every 5 to 10 minutes. Make appropriate adjustments (e.g., drug titration) as needed. Once tissue perfusion is restored and the patient is stabilized, you can decrease the frequency of monitoring and slowly wean the patient off drugs to support BP and tissue perfusion.

> **❓ CHECK YOUR PRACTICE**
>
> A 69-yr-old male patient has just been admitted to the ICU with a diagnosis of sepsis. Your assessment shows that he is confused, with weak peripheral pulses and a BP of 84/50.
> • What fluids would you expect to be ordered?
> • How much fluid would you expect to infuse to improve his BP?
> • Despite aggressive fluid resuscitation, the patient is still hypotensive. What drug would you expect to be given to improve tissue perfusion?

Respiratory Status. Frequently assess the respiratory status of the patient in shock to ensure adequate oxygenation, detect complications early, and provide data about the patient's acid-base status. At first, monitor the rate, depth, and rhythm of respirations as often as every 15 to 30 minutes. Increased rate and depth provide information about the patient's attempts to correct metabolic acidosis. Assess breath sounds every 1 to 2 hours and as needed for any changes that may indicate fluid overload or accumulation of secretions.

Use pulse oximetry to continuously monitor O_2 saturation. Pulse oximetry using a patient's finger may not be accurate in a shock state because of poor peripheral circulation. Instead, attach the probe to the ear, nose, or forehead (according to the manufacturer's guidelines). Arterial blood gases (ABGs) give definitive information on ventilation and oxygenation status and acid-base balance. Initial interpretation of ABGs is often your responsibility. A PaO_2 below 60 mm Hg (in the absence of chronic lung disease) indicates hypoxemia and the need for higher O_2 concentrations or for a different mode of O_2 administration. Low $PaCO_2$ with a low pH and low bicarbonate level may mean that the patient is trying to compensate for metabolic acidosis from increasing lactate levels.

A rising $PaCO_2$ with a persistently low pH and PaO_2 indicates the need for advanced pulmonary management. Many patients in shock are intubated and on mechanical ventilation. Maintaining a patent airway and monitoring for ventilator-related complications are critical. Chapter 65 discusses artificial airways and mechanical ventilation.

Renal Status. At first, measure urine output every 1 to 2 hours to assess the adequacy of renal perfusion. Inserting an indwelling urinary catheter helps measure during resuscitation. Urine output below 0.5 mL/kg/hr may indicate inadequate perfusion of the kidneys. Use trends in serum creatinine values to assess renal function. Serum creatinine is a better indicator of renal function than BUN levels, since BUN is affected by the patient's catabolic state.

Body Temperature. Monitor temperature every 4 hours if normal. In the presence of a high or subnormal temperature, obtain hourly core temperatures (e.g., urinary, esophageal, PA catheter). Use light covers and control the room temperature to keep the patient comfortably warm. If the patient's temperature rises above 101.5°F (38.6°C) and the patient becomes uncomfortable or shows cardiovascular compromise, treat the fever with antipyretic drugs (e.g., ibuprofen, acetaminophen) and remove some of the patient's covers. Consider a cooling device if fever persists despite treatment.

Gastrointestinal Status. Auscultate bowel sounds at least every 4 hours. Monitor for abdominal distention. If a nasogastric tube is present, measure drainage and check for occult blood. Check all stools for occult blood.

Skin Integrity. Hygiene is especially important for the patient in shock because impaired tissue perfusion predisposes the patient to skin breakdown and infection. Perform bathing and other nursing measures carefully because a patient in shock has problems with O_2 delivery to tissues. Use clinical judgment in determining priorities of care to limit the demands for increased O_2. Monitor trends in O_2 consumption (e.g., SpO_2, $ScvO_2/SvO_2$) during all nursing interventions to assess the patient's tolerance of activity.

The increased O_2 demand that occurs during bathing and repositioning of patients with limited O_2 reserves makes the prevention of pressure injuries challenging. Turn the patient at least every 1 to 2 hours. Maintain good body alignment. Use a pressure-relieving or pressure-reducing mattress or a specialty bed as needed. Perform passive range of motion 3 or 4 times a day to maintain joint mobility and help prevent breakdown.

Oral care is essential because mucous membranes may become dry and fragile in the volume-depleted patient. The intubated patient usually has difficulty swallowing, resulting in pooled secretions in the mouth. Apply a water-soluble lubricant to the lips to prevent drying and cracking. Brush the patient's teeth or gums with a soft toothbrush every 12 hours. Swab the lips and oral mucosa with a moisturizing solution every 2 to 4 hours.

Emotional Support and Comfort. Do not underestimate the effects of fear and anxiety when the patient and caregiver are faced with a critical, life-threatening situation (see Chapter 65). Fear, anxiety, and pain may worsen respiratory distress and increase the release of catecholamines. When implementing care, monitor the patient's mental state and level of pain using valid assessment tools. Give drugs to decrease anxiety and pain as needed. Continuous infusions of a benzodiazepine (e.g., lorazepam) and an opioid or sedative (e.g., morphine, propofol [Diprivan]) are extremely helpful in decreasing anxiety and pain.[19]

Do not overlook the patient's spiritual needs. Patients may want a visit from a chaplain, priest, rabbi, or minister. One way to provide support is to offer to call a member of the clergy rather than wait for the patient or caregiver to express a wish for spiritual counseling.

Caregivers need to be kept informed of the patient's condition. Give the patient and caregiver simple explanations of all procedures before you carry them out and information about

---

the plan of care. If they ask questions about progress and prognosis, give simple and honest answers.

If possible, the same nurses should continually care for the patient. This decreases anxiety, limits conflicting information, and increases trust. If the prognosis becomes grave, support the patient's caregiver when making tough decisions, such as withdrawing life support. The interprofessional care team must promote realistic expectations and outcomes. Remember, compassion is as essential as scientific and technical expertise in the total care of the patient and caregiver.

Ensure that the caregiver can spend time with the patient, provided the patient perceives this time as comforting.[20] Explain in simple terms the purpose of any tubes and equipment attached to or surrounding the patient. Tell them what they may and may not touch. If possible, place the patient's hands and arms outside the sheets to encourage therapeutic touch. Encourage caregivers to perform simple comfort measures if desired. Provide privacy as much as possible while assuring the patient and caregiver that help is readily available should it be needed. Always position the call light in reach of the patient or caregiver.

◆ **Ambulatory Care.** Rehabilitation of the patient who had a critical illness requires (1) correction of the precipitating cause, (2) prevention or early treatment of complications, and (3) teaching focused on disease management or prevention of recurrence based on the initial cause of shock. Continue to monitor the patient for complications throughout the recovery period. These may include decreased range of motion, muscle weakness, decreased physical endurance, AKI (see Chapter 46), and fibrotic lung disease (from ARDS) (see Chapter 67). Patients recovering from shock often need diverse services after discharge. These can include admission to transitional care units (e.g., for mechanical ventilation weaning), rehabilitation centers (inpatient or outpatient), or home health care agencies. Start planning for a safe transition from hospital to home as soon as the patient is admitted to the hospital.

◆ **Evaluation**

The expected outcomes are that the patient who has shock will have:
- Adequate tissue perfusion with restoration of normal or baseline BP
- Normal organ function with no complications from hypoperfusion
- Decreased fear and anxiety and increased psychologic comfort

SYSTEMIC INFLAMMATORY RESPONSE SYNDROME AND MULTIPLE ORGAN DYSFUNCTION SYNDROME

Etiology and Pathophysiology

Systemic inflammatory response syndrome (SIRS) is a systemic inflammatory response to a variety of insults, including infection (referred to as *sepsis*), ischemia, infarction, and injury.[21] Generalized inflammation in organs remote from the initial insult characterizes SIRS. Many different mechanisms can trigger SIRS. These include:

- Mechanical tissue trauma: burns, crush injuries, surgical procedures
- Abscess formation: intraabdominal, extremities
- Ischemic or necrotic tissue: pancreatitis, vascular disease, MI
- Microbial invasion: bacteria, viruses, fungi, parasites
- Endotoxin release: gram-negative and gram-positive bacteria
- Global perfusion deficits: postcardiac resuscitation, shock states
- Regional perfusion deficits: distal perfusion deficits

Multiple organ dysfunction syndrome (MODS) is the failure of 2 or more organ systems in an acutely ill patient such that homeostasis cannot be maintained without intervention.[22] MODS results from SIRS. These 2 syndromes represent the ends of a continuum. Transition from SIRS to MODS does not occur in a clear-cut manner (Fig. 66.1).

Organ and Metabolic Dysfunction. When the inflammatory response is activated, consequences include the release of mediators, direct damage to the endothelium, and hypermetabolism. Vascular permeability increases. This allows mediators and protein to leak out of the endothelium and into the interstitial space. White blood cells begin to digest the foreign debris, and the coagulation cascade is activated (see Chapter 29). Hypotension, decreased perfusion, microemboli, and redistributed or shunted blood flow eventually compromise organ perfusion.

The respiratory system is often the first system to show signs of dysfunction in SIRS and MODS.[22] Inflammatory mediators have a direct effect on the pulmonary vasculature. The endothelial damage from the release of inflammatory mediators causes increased capillary permeability. This causes movement of fluid from the pulmonary vasculature into the pulmonary interstitial spaces. The fluid then moves to the alveoli, causing alveolar edema. Type I pneumocytes (alveolar cells) are destroyed. Type II pneumocytes are damaged, and surfactant production is decreased. The alveoli collapse. This creates an increase in *shunt* (blood flow to the lungs that does not take part in gas exchange) and worsening ventilation-perfusion mismatch. The result is ARDS. Patients with ARDS need aggressive pulmonary management with mechanical ventilation. See Chapter 67 for a complete discussion of ARDS.

Cardiovascular changes include myocardial depression and massive vasodilation in response to increasing tissue demands. Vasodilation results in decreased SVR and BP. The baroreceptor reflex causes release of *inotropic* (increasing force of contraction) and *chronotropic* (increasing heart rate) factors that enhance CO. To compensate for hypotension, CO increases by an increase in heart rate and SV. Increases in capillary permeability cause a shift of albumin and fluid out of the vascular space. This further reduces venous return and thus preload. The patient becomes warm and tachycardic with a high CO and a low SVR. Other signs include decreased capillary refill, skin mottling, increased CVP and PAWP, and dysrhythmias. $ScvO_2$ or SvO_2 may be abnormally high because the patient is perfusing areas not consuming much O_2 (e.g., skin, nonworking muscle). Other areas may have blood shunted away from them. Eventually, either perfusion of vital organs becomes insufficient or the cells are unable to use O_2 and their function is further compromised.

Neurologic dysfunction in SIRS and MODS often presents as mental status changes. These acute changes can be an early sign of SIRS or MODS. The patient may be confused and agitated, combative, disoriented, lethargic, or comatose. These changes are due to hypoxemia, the effects of inflammatory mediators, and impaired perfusion.

AKI is common in SIRS and MODS. Hypoperfusion and the effects of the mediators can cause AKI. Decreased perfusion to the kidneys activates the SNS and the renin-angiotensin system.[22] Stimulation of the renin-angiotensin system causes systemic vasoconstriction and aldosterone-mediated sodium and water reabsorption. Another risk factor for the development of AKI is the use of nephrotoxic drugs. Many antibiotics used to treat gram-negative bacteria (e.g., aminoglycosides) can be nephrotoxic. Careful monitoring of drug levels is essential to avoid the nephrotoxic effects.

The GI tract plays a key role in the development of MODS. GI motility is often decreased in critical illness, causing abdominal distention and paralytic ileus. In the early stages of SIRS and MODS, blood is shunted away from the GI mucosa, making it highly vulnerable to ischemic injury. Decreased perfusion leads to a breakdown of this normally protective mucosal barrier. This increases the risk for ulceration, GI bleeding, and bacterial movement from the GI tract into circulation.[21]

Metabolic changes are pronounced in SIRS and MODS. Both syndromes trigger a hypermetabolic response. Glycogen stores are rapidly converted to glucose (glycogenolysis). Once glycogen is depleted, amino acids are converted to glucose (gluconeogenesis), reducing protein stores. Fatty acids are mobilized for fuel. Catecholamines and glucocorticoids are released and cause hyperglycemia and insulin resistance. The net result is a catabolic state with a loss of lean body mass (muscle).

The hypermetabolism associated with SIRS and MODS may last for several days and cause liver dysfunction. Liver dysfunction in MODS may begin long before clinical evidence of it is present. Protein synthesis is impaired. The liver cannot make albumin, one of the key proteins in maintaining plasma oncotic pressure. This changes plasma oncotic pressure, causing fluid and protein to leak from the vascular spaces to the interstitial space. At this point, giving albumin does not normalize oncotic pressure in these patients.

As the state of hypermetabolism persists, the patient cannot convert lactate to glucose and lactate accumulates (lactic acidosis). Despite increases in glycogenolysis and gluconeogenesis, eventually the liver cannot maintain an adequate glucose level and the patient becomes hypoglycemic. Hypoglycemia can also develop due to acute adrenal insufficiency.

DIC may result from dysfunction of the coagulation system. DIC causes microvascular clotting and bleeding at the same time because of the depletion of clotting factors and excessive fibrinolysis. (Chapter 30 discusses DIC.)

Electrolyte imbalances are common and result from the hormonal and metabolic changes and fluid shifts. These changes worsen mental status changes, neuromuscular dysfunction, and dysrhythmias. The release of ADH and aldosterone results in sodium and water retention. Aldosterone increases urinary potassium loss, and catecholamines cause potassium to move into the cell, resulting in hypokalemia. Hypokalemia is associated with dysrhythmias and muscle weakness. Metabolic acidosis results from impaired tissue perfusion, hypoxia, and the shift to anaerobic metabolism. This increases lactate levels. Progressive renal dysfunction also contributes to metabolic acidosis. Hypocalcemia, hypomagnesemia, and hypophosphatemia are common.

Clinical Manifestations of SIRS and MODS

The clinical manifestations of SIRS and MODS are described in Table 66.10.

❖ NURSING AND INTERPROFESSIONAL MANAGEMENT: SIRS AND MODS

The prognosis for the patient with MODS is poor, with mortality rates of 40% to 60%.[22] Mortality increases as more organ systems fail. The most common cause of death continues to be sepsis. Survival improves with early, goal-directed therapy. So, the most important goal is to prevent SIRS from progressing to MODS.

A critical part of your role is vigilant assessment and ongoing monitoring to detect early signs of deterioration or organ dysfunction. Interprofessional care for patients with SIRS and MODS focuses on (1) prevention and treatment of infection, (2) maintaining tissue oxygenation, (3) nutritional and metabolic support, and (4) appropriate support of individual failing organs. Table 66.10 outlines the management for patients with SIRS and MODS.

TABLE 66.10 Manifestations and Management of SIRS and MODS

Manifestations	Management	Manifestations	Management
Respiratory System		**Renal System**	
Development of ARDS (see Chapter 67):	Optimize O_2 delivery and minimize O_2 consumption	*Prerenal:* renal hypoperfusion	Diuretics
• Bilateral fluffy infiltrates on chest x-ray	Mechanical ventilation (see Chapter 65)	• BUN/creatinine ratio >20:1	• Loop diuretics (e.g., furosemide [Lasix])
• Decreased compliance	• Positive end-expiratory pressure	• ↓ Urine Na+ <20 mEq/L	• May need to ↑ dosage due to ↓ glomerular filtration rate
• Dyspnea (severe)	• Lung protective modes (e.g., pressure-control inverse ratio ventilation, low tidal volumes)	• ↑ Urine osmolality	Continuous renal replacement therapy (see Chapter 46)
• Increased minute ventilation		• Urine specific gravity >1.020	
• PaO_2/FIO_2 ratio <200			
• PAWP <18 mm Hg	• Permissive hypercapnia	*Intrarenal:* acute tubular necrosis	
• Pulmonary hypertension	• Positioning (e.g., continuous lateral rotation therapy, prone positioning)	• BUN/creatinine ratio <10:1–15:1	
• Refractory hypoxemia		• ↑ Urine Na+ >20 mEq/L	
• Tachypnea		• ↓ Urine osmolality	
• Ventilation-perfusion (V/Q) mismatch		• Urine specific gravity ~1.010	
		GI System	
Cardiovascular System		GI bleeding	Stress ulcer prophylaxis
Biventricular failure	Volume management to ↑ preload	Hypoperfusion → ↓ peristalsis, paralytic ileus	• Antacids (e.g., Maalox)
↓ BP, MAP, SVR	Hemodynamic monitoring	Mucosal ischemia	• Proton pump inhibitors (e.g., omeprazole [Prilosec])
↑ HR, CO, SV	Arterial pressure monitoring to maintain MAP >65 mm Hg	• ↓ Intramucosal pH	• sucralfate (Carafate)
Massive vasodilation	Vasopressors	• Potential translocation of gut bacteria	Monitor abdominal distention, intraabdominal pressures
Myocardial depression	Intermittent or continuous $ScvO_2$ or SvO_2 monitoring	• Potential abdominal compartment syndrome	Dietitian consult
Systolic, diastolic dysfunction	Balance O_2 supply and demand	Mucosal ulceration on endoscopy	Enteral nutrition
	Continuous ECG monitoring		Stimulate mucosal activity
	Circulatory assist devices		Provide essential nutrients and optimal calories
	VTE prophylaxis		
		Hepatic System	
		Bilirubin >2 mg/dL (34 µmol/L)	Maintain adequate tissue perfusion
Central Nervous System		Hepatic encephalopathy	Provide nutritional support (e.g., enteral nutrition)
Acute change in neurologic status	Evaluate for hepatic or metabolic encephalopathy	Jaundice	Careful use of drugs metabolized by liver
Confusion, disorientation, delirium	Optimize cerebral blood flow	↑ Liver enzymes (ALT, AST, GGT)	
Fever	↓ Cerebral O_2 requirements	↓ Serum albumin, prealbumin, transferrin	
Hepatic encephalopathy	Prevent secondary tissue ischemia	↑ Serum NH_3 (ammonia)	
Seizures	Calcium channel blockers (reduce cerebral vasospasm)	**Hematologic System**	
		↑ Bleeding times, ↑ PT, ↑ PTT	Observe for bleeding from obvious and/or occult sites
		↑ D-dimer	Replace factors being lost (e.g., platelets)
Endocrine System		↑ Fibrin split products	Minimize traumatic interventions (e.g., IM injections, multiple venipunctures)
Hyperglycemia → hypoglycemia	Provide continuous infusion of insulin and glucose to maintain blood glucose 140–180 mg/dL (7.77–10.0 mmol/L)	↓ Platelet count (thrombocytopenia)	

ALT, Alanine aminotransferase; *AST,* aspartate aminotransferase; *GGT,* γ-glutamyl transferase; *PA,* pulmonary artery; *PAWP,* pulmonary artery wedge pressure; *PT,* prothrombin time; *PTT,* partial thromboplastin time; *ScvO₂,* O_2 saturation in venous blood; *SvO₂,* O_2 saturation in mixed venous blood; *SVR,* systemic vascular resistance.

◆ Prevention and Treatment of Infection

Aggressive infection control strategies are essential to decrease the risk for HAIs. Early, aggressive surgery is recommended to remove necrotic tissue (e.g., early debridement of burn tissue) that can provide a culture medium for microorganisms. Aggressive pulmonary management, including early mobilization, can reduce the risk for infection. Strict asepsis can decrease infections related to intraarterial lines, endotracheal tubes, indwelling urinary catheters, IV lines, and other invasive devices or procedures. Daily assessment of the ongoing need for invasive lines and other devices is an important strategy to prevent or limit HAIs.

Despite aggressive strategies, infection may develop. Once an infection is suspected, begin interventions to treat the cause. Send appropriate cultures and start broad-spectrum antibiotic therapy, as ordered. Adjust therapy based on the culture results, if needed.

◆ Maintenance of Tissue Oxygenation

Hypoxemia often occurs because patients have greater O_2 needs and decreased O_2 supply to the tissues. Interventions that decrease O_2 demand and increase O_2 delivery are essential. Sedation, mechanical ventilation, analgesia, and rest may decrease O_2 demand and should be considered. Treating fever, chills, and pain decrease O_2 demand. O_2 delivery may be optimized by using individualized tidal volumes with positive end-expiratory pressure, increasing preload (e.g., fluids) or myocardial contractility to enhance CO, or reducing afterload to increase CO.

◆ Nutritional and Metabolic Needs

Hypermetabolism can result in profound weight loss, cachexia, and further organ failure. Protein-calorie malnutrition is a key sign of hypermetabolism. Total energy expenditure is often increased 1.5 to 2.0 times the normal metabolic rate. Because of their short half-life, monitor plasma transferrin and prealbumin levels to assess hepatic protein synthesis.

The goal of nutritional support is to preserve organ function. Providing early and optimal nutrition decreases morbidity and mortality rates. EN is preferred. If it cannot be used, PN should be considered. (Chapter 39 discusses EN and PN.) Provide glycemic control with a goal of ≤180 mg/dL with insulin infusions in these patients.[21]

◆ Support of Failing Organs

Support of any failing organ is a goal of therapy. For example, the patient with ARDS requires aggressive O_2 therapy and mechanical ventilation (see Chapter 67). DIC should be treated appropriately (e.g., blood products) (see Chapter 30). Renal failure may require dialysis. Continuous renal replacement therapy is better tolerated than hemodialysis, especially in a patient with hemodynamic instability (see Chapter 46).

A final consideration may be that further interventions are futile. It is important to maintain communication between the health care team and the patient's caregiver about realistic goals and likely outcomes for the patient with MODS. Withdrawal of life support and starting end-of-life care may be the best options for the patient.

CASE STUDY

Shock

Patient Profile

K.L., a 25-yr-old Korean American, was not wearing his seat belt when he was driving a motor vehicle involved in a crash. The windshield was broken, and K.L. was found 10 ft from his car. He was face down, conscious, and moaning. His wife and daughter were in the car with their seat belts on. They sustained minor injuries and were very frightened and upset. All passengers were taken to the ED. This information pertains to K.L.

(© Thinkstock.)

Subjective Data

*   States, "I can't breathe"
*   Cries out when abdomen is palpated

Objective Data

Physical Examination

*   *Cardiovascular:* BP 80/56 mm Hg; apical pulse 138 but no palpable radial or pedal pulses; carotid pulse 1+. ECG is below:

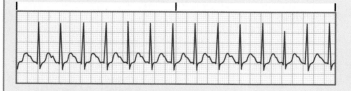

*   *Respiratory:* respiratory rate 35 breaths/min; labored breathing with shallow respirations; asymmetric chest wall movement; absence of breath sounds on left side. Trachea deviated slightly to the right
*   *Abdomen:* slightly distended and left upper quadrant painful on palpation
*   *Musculoskeletal:* open compound fracture of the lower left leg

Diagnostic Studies

*   Chest x-ray: hemothorax and 6 rib fractures on left side
*   Hematocrit: 28%

Interprofessional Care (in the ED)

*   Intraosseous access in right proximal tibia placed prehospital
*   Left chest tube placed, draining bright red blood
*   Fluid resuscitation started with crystalloids
*   High-flow O_2 via nonrebreather mask

Emergency Surgical Procedures

*   Splenectomy
*   Repair of torn intercostal artery
*   Repair of compound fracture

Discussion Questions

1. What types of shock is K.L. experiencing? What clinical manifestations did he display that support your answer?
2. What were the causes of K.L.'s shock states? What are other causes of these types of shock?
3. **Priority Decision:** What are the priority nursing responsibilities for K.L.?
4. **Priority Decision:** What ongoing nursing assessment parameters are essential for this patient?
5. What are his potential complications?
6. **Patient-Centered Care:** K.L.'s parents arrive. English is their second language. They are very anxious and asking about their son. What can you do to provide culturally competent family-centered care?
7. **Priority Decision:** Based on the assessment data presented, what are the priority nursing diagnoses?
8. **Collaboration:** Identify the tasks that could be delegated to unlicensed assistive personnel (UAP).
9. **Evidence-Based Practice:** You are orienting a new graduate RN. He asks you why crystalloids are used for fluid resuscitation. What is your response?

BRIDGE TO NCLEX EXAMINATION

The number of the question corresponds to the same-numbered outcome at the beginning of the chapter.

1. A patient has a spinal cord injury at T4. Vital signs include falling blood pressure with bradycardia. The nurse recognizes that the patient is experiencing
   a. a relative hypervolemia.
   b. an absolute hypovolemia.
   c. neurogenic shock from low blood flow.
   d. neurogenic shock from massive vasodilation.

2. A 78-yr-old man with a history of diabetes has confusion and temperature of 104° F (40° C). There is a wound on his right heel with purulent drainage. After an infusion of 3 L of normal saline solution, his assessment findings are BP 84/40 mm Hg; heart rate 110; respiratory rate 42 and shallow; CO 8 L/min; and PAWP 4 mm Hg. This patient's symptoms are *most* likely indicative of
   a. sepsis.
   b. septic shock.
   c. multiple organ dysfunction syndrome.
   d. systemic inflammatory response syndrome.

3. Treatment modalities for the management of cardiogenic shock include (*select all that apply*)
   a. dobutamine to increase myocardial contractility.
   b. vasopressors to increase systemic vascular resistance.
   c. circulatory assist devices such as an intraaortic balloon pump.
   d. corticosteroids to stabilize the cell wall in the infarcted myocardium.
   e. Trendelenburg positioning to facilitate venous return and increase preload.

4. The *most* accurate assessment parameters for the nurse to use to determine adequate tissue perfusion in the patient with MODS are
   a. blood pressure, pulse, and respirations.
   b. breath sounds, blood pressure, and body temperature.
   c. pulse pressure, level of consciousness, and pupillary response.
   d. level of consciousness, urine output, and skin color and temperature.

1. d, 2. b, 3. a, c, 4. d

For rationales to these answers and even more NCLEX review questions, visit *http://evolve.elsevier.com/Lewis/medsurg*.

(e) EVOLVE WEBSITE/RESOURCES LIST

REFERENCES

1. Tewelde SZ, Liu SS, Winters ME: Cardiogenic shock, *Cardiol Clin* 28:53, 2018.
2. Good VS, Kirkwood PL: *Advanced critical care nursing*, ed 2, St Louis, 2017, Elsevier.
3. Hamlin S, Strauss P, Chen H, et al: Microvascular fluid resuscitation in circulatory shock, *Nurs Clin North Am* 52:291, 2017.
4. Taylor MP, Wrenn P, O'Donnell AD: Presentation of neurogenic shock within the emergency department, *Emerg Med J* 34:157, 2016.
*5. Lee SE: Management of anaphylaxis, *Otolaryngol Clin North Am* 50: 1175, 2017.
6. Kleinpell R, Schorr C, Balk R: The new sepsis definitions: Implications for critical care practitioners, *Amer J Crit Care* 25:457, 2016.
*7. Singer M, Deutschman C, Seymour C, et al: The third international consensus definitions for sepsis and septic shock (Sepsis-3), *JAMA* 315:801, 2016.
8. O'Shaughnessy J, Grzelak M, Dontsova A, et al: Early sepsis identification, *MEDSURG Nursing* 26:248, 2017.

*9. Winters ME, Sherwin R, Vilke GM, et al: What is the preferred resuscitation fluid for patients with severe sepsis and septic shock? *J Emerg Med* 53:928, 2017.
*10. Stratton L, Verlin D, Arbo J: Vasopressors and inotropes in sepsis. *Emerg Med Clin North Am* 35:75, 2017.
11. McClave SA, Taylor BE, Martindale RG, et al: Guidelines for the provision and assessment of nutrition support therapy in the adult critically ill patient: Society of Critical Care Medicine (S.C.C.M.) and American Society for Parenteral and Enteral Nutrition (A.S.P.E.N.), *J Parenter Enteral Nutr* 40:159, 2016.
12. Jakovijevi D, Lip-Burn M, Scheueler S, et al: Left ventricular assist device as a bridge to recovery for patient with advanced heart failure, *J Am Coll Cardiol* 69:1924, 2017.
*13. Pickett J, Bridges E, Kritek P, et al: Passive leg-raising and prediction of fluid responsiveness: Systematic review, *Crit Care Nurse* 37:32, 2017.
14. Timmerman RA: Managing vasoactive infusions to restore hemodynamic stability, *Nursing2019 Critical Care*, 11:35, 2016.
15. Sherwin R, Winters ME, Vilke GM, et al: Does early and appropriate antibiotic administration improve mortality in patients with severe sepsis or septic shock? *J Emerg Med* 53:588, 2017.
16. Gunst J, Van den Berghe G: Blood glucose control in the ICU. How tight? *Ann Transl Med* 5:76, 2017.
*17. Rhodes A, Evans LE, Alhazzani W, et al: Surviving sepsis campaign. International guidelines for management of sepsis and septic shock, *Intens Care Med* 43:304, 2017.
18. Institute for Healthcare Improvement: Evidence-based care bundles. Retrieved from *www.ihi.org/topics/Bundles/Pages/default.aspx*.
19. Hariharan U, Garg R: Sedation and analgesia in critical care, *J Anesth Crit Care Open Access* 7:262, 2017.
20. Davidson JE, Aslakson RA, Long AC, et al: Guidelines for family-centered care in the neonatal, pediatric, and adult ICU, *Crit Care Med* 45:103, 2017.
21. Sauaia A, Moore FA, Moore EE: Postinjury inflammation and organ dysfunction, *Crit Care Clin* 33:167, 2017.
22. Gordy S: Multiple organ failure. In Moore L, Todd S, eds: *Common problems in acute care surgery*, New York, 2017, Springer.

*Evidence-based information for clinical practice.

67

Acute Respiratory Failure and Acute Respiratory Distress Syndrome

Eugene Mondor

The closest thing to being cared for is to care for someone else.

Carson McCullers

ⓔ http://evolve.elsevier.com/Lewis/medsurg

CONCEPTUAL FOCUS

Acid-Base Balance
Anxiety

Gas Exchange

LEARNING OUTCOMES

1. Discuss the etiology, pathophysiology, and clinical manifestations of hypoxemic and hypercapnic acute respiratory failure.
2. Describe the nursing and interprofessional management of hypoxemic or hypercapnic respiratory failure.
3. Discuss the pathophysiology and clinical manifestations of acute respiratory distress syndrome (ARDS).
4. Describe the nursing and interprofessional management of ARDS.
5. Select measures to prevent and manage complications of acute respiratory failure and ARDS.

KEY TERMS

acute respiratory distress syndrome (ARDS), p. 1597
acute respiratory failure (ARF), p. 1588
alveolar hypoventilation, p. 1590
chronic respiratory failure, p. 1589

hypercapnic respiratory failure, p. 1588
hypoxia, p. 1591
hypoxemia, p. 1588
hypoxemic respiratory failure, p. 1588
PaO_2/FIO_2 (P/F) ratio, p. 1599

permissive hypercapnia, p 1601
refractory hypoxemia, p. 1598
shunt, p. 1590
V/Q mismatch, p. 1589
work of breathing (WOB), p. 1591

This chapter discusses acute respiratory failure (ARF) and acute respiratory distress syndrome (ARDS). Nursing and interprofessional management of patients with ARF and ARDS focus on interventions to promote adequate oxygenation, ensure effective ventilation, identify and treat the underlying causes, and prevent complications. When respiratory function is insufficient, all body systems are affected

ACUTE RESPIRATORY FAILURE

The major function of the respiratory system is gas exchange. **Acute respiratory failure (ARF)** occurs when oxygenation, ventilation, or both are inadequate. ARF is not a disease. It is a symptom that reflects lung function. For example, not enough O_2 is transferred to the blood or inadequate CO_2 is removed from the lungs (Fig. 67.1). ARF occurs because of disorders involving the lungs or other body systems (Table 67.1).

Conditions that interfere with adequate O_2 transfer result in **hypoxemia**. This causes a decrease in arterial O_2 (PaO_2) and saturation (SaO_2) to less than the normal values. Insufficient CO_2 removal results in hypercapnia. It causes an increase in arterial CO_2 ($PaCO_2$). Arterial blood gases (ABGs) are used to assess changes in pH, PaO_2, $PaCO_2$, bicarbonate, and SaO_2. We use pulse oximetry to assess arterial O_2 saturation (SpO_2).

We classify ARF as hypoxemic or hypercapnic (Fig. 67.2). **Hypoxemic respiratory failure** is a PaO_2 less than 60 mm Hg when the patient is receiving an inspired O_2 concentration of 60% or more.[1] In hypoxemic respiratory failure (also called *oxygenation failure*), the main problem is inadequate exchange of O_2 between the alveoli and pulmonary capillaries. The PaO_2 level shows inadequate O_2 saturation. A less than optimal PaO_2 level exists despite supplemental O_2.

Hypercapnic respiratory failure (or *ventilatory failure*) is a $PaCO_2$ greater than 50 mm Hg with acidemia (arterial pH less than 7.35).[2] The main problem is insufficient CO_2 removal. This causes the $PaCO_2$ to be higher than normal. For whatever reason, the body is unable to compensate for the increase. This allows acidemia to occur.

Patients may have both types of respiratory failure at the same time. For example, a patient with chronic obstructive

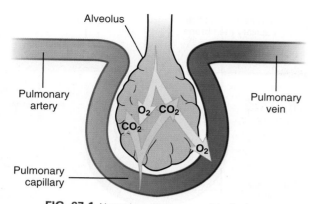

FIG. 67.1 Normal gas exchange unit in the lung.

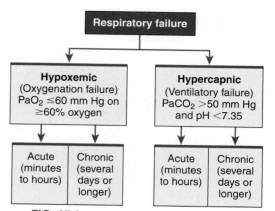

FIG. 67.2 Classification of respiratory failure.

TABLE 67.1 Common Causes of Respiratory Failure

Hypoxemic Respiratory Failure	Hypercapnic Respiratory Failure
Respiratory System	**Respiratory System**
• ARDS	• Asthma
• Hepatopulmonary syndrome (e.g., low-resistance flow state, V/Q mismatch)	• COPD
	• Cystic fibrosis
• Massive pulmonary embolism (e.g., thrombus emboli, fat emboli)	**Central Nervous System**
• Pneumonia	• Brainstem injury or infarction
• Pulmonary artery laceration and hemorrhage	• Sedative and opioid overdose
• Toxic inhalation (e.g., smoke inhalation)	• Spinal cord injury
	• Severe head injury
Cardiac System	**Chest Wall**
• Anatomic shunt (e.g., ventricular septal defect)	• Kyphoscoliosis
• Cardiogenic pulmonary edema	• Pain
	• Severe obesity
• Cardiogenic shock (decreasing blood flow through pulmonary vasculature)	• Thoracic trauma (e.g., flail chest)
	Neuromuscular System
• High cardiac output states: diffusion limitation	• Amyotrophic lateral sclerosis
	• Critical illness polyneuropathy
	• Guillain-Barré syndrome
	• Muscular dystrophy
	• Multiple sclerosis
	• Myasthenia gravis
	• Phrenic nerve injury
	• Poliomyelitis
	• Toxin exposure or ingestion (e.g., tree tobacco, acetylcholinesterase inhibitors, carbamate or organophosphate poisoning)

pulmonary disease (COPD) who has pneumonia could have "acute-on-chronic" respiratory failure. In other words, the patient has an underlying chronic respiratory problem. The new infection, in addition to the chronic problem, results in the "acute-on-chronic" clinical picture.

Significant changes in PaO_2 and $PaCO_2$ occur with ARF. These may develop over several minutes to a few hours to 1 or 2 days. The patient may have hemodynamic instability (e.g. tachycardia, hypotension), increased respiratory effort, and decreased level of consciousness. Urgent intervention is required. Chronic respiratory failure develops more slowly, over days to weeks. The patient is usually more stable as the

body had time to compensate for the small, but subtle, changes that have occurred.

Etiology and Pathophysiology

Hypoxemic Respiratory Failure. Four physiologic mechanisms may cause hypoxemia and hypoxemic respiratory failure: (1) mismatch between ventilation (V) and perfusion (Q), often referred to as V/Q mismatch; (2) shunt; (3) diffusion limitation; and (4) alveolar hypoventilation. The most common causes are V/Q mismatch and shunt.

Ventilation-Perfusion Mismatch. In normal lungs, the volume of blood perfusing the lungs and the amount of gas reaching the alveoli are almost identical. So, when you compare normal alveolar ventilation (4 to 6 L/min) to pulmonary blood flow (4 to 6 L/min), you have a V/Q ratio of 0.8 to 1.2.[3] In a perfect match, ventilation and perfusion would yield a V/Q ratio of 1:1, expressed as V/Q = 1. When the match is not 1:1, a V/Q mismatch occurs.

This example implies that ventilation and perfusion are perfectly matched in all areas of the lung. This situation does not normally exist. In reality, some regional mismatch occurs. For example, at the apex of the lung, V/Q ratios are greater than 1 (more ventilation than perfusion). At the base of the lung, V/Q ratios are less than 1 (less ventilation than perfusion). Because changes at the lung apex balance changes at the base, the net effect is a close overall match (Fig. 67.3).

Many diseases and conditions cause a V/Q mismatch (Fig. 67.4). The most common are those in which increased secretions are present in the airways (e.g., COPD) or alveoli (e.g., pneumonia) or bronchospasm is present (e.g., asthma). V/Q mismatch may result from pain, alveolar collapse (atelectasis), or pulmonary emboli.

Pain interferes with chest and abdominal wall movement and increases muscle tension. This often compromises ventilation. The patient is often unwilling to take big, deep breaths. As a result, short, shallow respirations contribute to the development of atelectasis. This worsens V/Q mismatch.

Pain activates the stress response, increasing baseline metabolic state. This increases O_2 consumption and CO_2 production (as a by-product of cellular and tissue metabolism). The increased O_2 demand, increased CO_2, and decreased O_2 supply increase ventilation demands. Since there is no effect on blood flow to the lungs, the result is V/Q mismatch.

Pulmonary emboli affect the perfusion part of the V/Q relationship. When a pulmonary embolus occurs, it limits blood

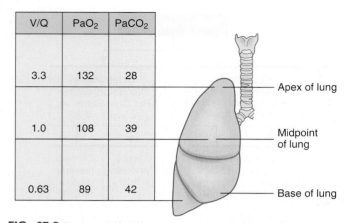

V/Q	PaO$_2$	PaCO$_2$
3.3	132	28
1.0	108	39
0.63	89	42

— Apex of lung

— Midpoint of lung

— Base of lung

FIG. 67.3 Regional V/Q differences in the normal lung. This difference causes the PaO$_2$ to be higher at the apex of the lung and lower at the base. Values for PaCO$_2$ are the opposite (i.e., lower at the apex and higher at the base). Blood that exits the lung is a mixture of these values.

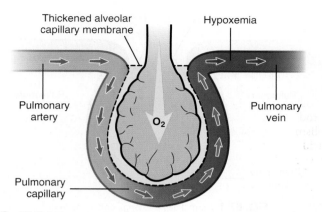

FIG. 67.5 Diffusion limitation. Exchange of CO$_2$ and O$_2$ cannot occur because of the thickened alveolar-capillary membrane.

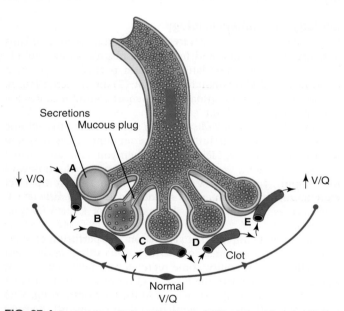

FIG. 67.4 Range of ventilation to perfusion (V/Q) relationships. A, Absolute shunt, no ventilation because of fluid filling the alveoli. B, V/Q mismatch, ventilation partially compromised by secretions in the airway. C, Normal lung unit. D, V/Q mismatch, perfusion partially compromised by emboli obstructing blood flow. E, Dead space, no perfusion because of obstruction of the pulmonary capillary.

flow distal to the occlusion. Areas of normal lung ventilation remain, but there is decreased perfusion due to the vessel occlusion. This results in a V/Q mismatch. If the embolus is large, it can cause hemodynamic instability due to blockage of a large pulmonary artery.

O$_2$ therapy is an appropriate first step to reverse hypoxemia caused by V/Q mismatch. O$_2$ therapy increases the PaO$_2$ in the blood leaving normal gas exchange units, causing a higher-than-normal PaO$_2$. This blood mixes with the poorly oxygenated blood from damaged areas, raising the overall PaO$_2$ level in the blood leaving the lungs. The best way to treat hypoxemia caused by a V/Q mismatch is to treat the cause.

Shunt. A **shunt** occurs when blood exits the heart without having taken part in gas exchange. A shunt is an extreme V/Q mismatch. There are 2 types of shunt: anatomic and

intrapulmonary. An *anatomic shunt* occurs when blood passes through an anatomic channel in the heart (e.g., a ventricular septal defect) and bypasses the lungs.[4] An *intrapulmonary shunt* occurs when blood flows through the pulmonary capillaries without taking part in gas exchange.[4] It is seen in conditions in which the alveoli fill with fluid (e.g., pneumonia) and gas exchange is severely impaired at the alveolar-capillary membrane.

O$_2$ therapy alone is not effective at increasing the PaO$_2$ if hypoxemia is due to shunt. Patients with a shunt are usually more hypoxemic than patients with V/Q mismatch. They often need mechanical ventilation with a high fraction of inspired O$_2$ (FIO$_2$) to improve gas exchange.

Diffusion Limitation. *Diffusion limitation* occurs when gas exchange across the alveolar-capillary membrane is compromised by a process that damages or destroys the alveolar membrane or affects blood flow through the pulmonary capillaries (Fig. 67.5).[5] Conditions that cause the alveolar-capillary membrane to become thicker (fibrotic) slow gas transport. These include pulmonary fibrosis, interstitial lung disease, and ARDS. The accumulation of fluid, white blood cells, or protein in the alveoli can decrease gas exchange between the alveolus and the capillary bed. A common example is pulmonary edema.

The classic sign of diffusion limitation is hypoxemia that is present during exercise but not at rest. During exercise, blood moves more quickly through the lungs. This decreases the time for diffusion of O$_2$ across the alveolar-capillary membrane. Diffusion limitation can occur in conditions in which CO is markedly increased (e.g., high-output heart failure [HF], severe traumatic brain injury [TBI]). As blood circulates rapidly through the pulmonary capillary bed, there is less time for gas exchange to occur.

Alveolar Hypoventilation. Alveolar hypoventilation is a decrease in ventilation that results in an increase in the PaCO$_2$. It may be caused by central nervous system (CNS) conditions, chest wall dysfunction, acute asthma, or restrictive lung diseases. Although alveolar hypoventilation is mainly a mechanism of hypercapnic respiratory failure, it contributes to hypoxemia.

Interrelationship of Mechanisms. Rarely is acute hypoxemic respiratory failure caused by a single factor. More often, it is a combination of 2 or more factors. For example, the patient with ARF from pneumonia may have a V/Q mismatch and shunt. Inflammation, edema, and exudate obstruct the airways (V/Q mismatch) and fill the alveoli with exudate (shunt). Other contributing factors include increases in O_2 demand with anxiety and unrelieved pain.

Consequences of Hypoxemia. Hypoxemia can lead to hypoxia if not corrected. Hypoxia occurs when the PaO_2 falls enough to cause signs and symptoms of inadequate oxygenation. If hypoxia or hypoxemia is severe, the cells shift from aerobic to anaerobic metabolism. Anaerobic metabolism uses more fuel, produces less energy, and is less efficient than aerobic metabolism. The waste product of anaerobic metabolism is lactic acid. Lactic acid is harder to remove from the body than CO_2, because it must be buffered with sodium bicarbonate. When the body does not have enough sodium bicarbonate to buffer the lactic acid, metabolic acidosis occurs. Left uncorrected, tissue and cell dysfunction, and ultimately cell death, occurs.

Hypercapnic Respiratory Failure. In acute hypercapnic respiratory failure, sometimes referred to as *ventilatory failure*, the lungs are often normal. In this situation, the respiratory system cannot keep CO_2 levels maintained within normal limits. This often occurs from an increase in CO_2 production or a decrease in alveolar ventilation. Hypercapnic respiratory failure can be acute or chronic. It often reflects significant problems with the respiratory system.

Many conditions can cause impaired ventilation. We group into 4 categories: (1) CNS problems, (2) neuromuscular conditions, (3) chest wall abnormalities, and (4) problems affecting the airways and/or alveoli. Acute hypercapnic respiratory failure can occur with CNS problems, neuromuscular conditions, and chest wall abnormalities in the presence of normal lungs.

Central Nervous System Problems. A number of CNS problems can suppress the drive to breathe. A common example is an overdose of a respiratory depressant drug (e.g., opioids). In a dose-related manner, CNS depressants decrease CO_2 reactivity in the brainstem. This allows arterial CO_2 levels to rise. A brainstem infarction or TBI may interfere with normal function of the respiratory center in the medulla. Patients are then at risk for acute hypercapnic respiratory failure because the medulla does not change the respiratory rate in response to a change in $PaCO_2$.

High-level spinal cord injuries can affect nerve supply to the respiratory muscles of the chest wall and diaphragm. Brain injury with a decreased level of consciousness can hinder the patient's ability to protect the airway, breathe, or manage secretions.

Neuromuscular Conditions. Various neuromuscular problems place patients at risk for respiratory failure. For example, patients with Guillain-Barré syndrome and multiple sclerosis have respiratory muscle weakness or paralysis. As a result, they cannot eliminate CO_2 and maintain normal $PaCO_2$ levels. Exposure to toxins (e.g., carbamate/organophosphate pesticides, chemical nerve agents) can interfere with the nerve supply to muscles and lung ventilation. Respiratory muscle weakness can occur from muscle wasting during a critical illness or peripheral nerve damage.

Chest Wall Abnormalities. Several conditions can prevent normal movement of the chest wall or diaphragm and limit lung expansion. In patients with flail chest, fractures prevent the rib cage from expanding normally. With kyphoscoliosis, the change in spinal configuration compresses the lungs and prevents normal expansion of the chest wall. In those with severe obesity, the weight of the chest and abdominal contents limit lung expansion.

Problems of the Airway and Alveoli. Patients with asthma, COPD, and cystic fibrosis have a high risk for hypercapnic respiratory failure because the underlying pathophysiology results in airflow obstruction and air trapping. Respiratory muscle fatigue and ventilatory failure occur from the added work of breathing needed to inspire air against increased airway resistance and air trapped within the alveoli.

Consequences of Hypercapnia. The body can tolerate increased CO_2 levels far better than low O_2 levels. This is because with slow changes in $PaCO_2$, the body may have time for compensation to occur. For example, consider the patient with COPD who has a slow increase in $PaCO_2$ after an upper respiratory tract infection. Because the change occurred over several days, there is time for the kidneys to compensate (e.g., by retaining bicarbonate). This will initially minimize the change in arterial pH. Unless the primary cause is identified and corrected, the patient's condition will likely get worse. (See Chapter 16 for a discussion of renal compensation for acid-base disorders.)

Clinical Manifestations

Respiratory failure may develop suddenly (acute, minutes or hours) or gradually (chronic, several days or weeks). A sudden decrease in PaO_2 and/or a rapid rise in $PaCO_2$ implies a serious respiratory condition, which can rapidly become a life-threatening emergency. An example is the patient with asthma who develops severe bronchospasm and a marked decrease in airflow, resulting in respiratory muscle fatigue, acidemia, and ARF.

Signs of respiratory failure are related to the extent of change in PaO_2 or $PaCO_2$, the speed of change (acute versus chronic), and the patient's ability to compensate for this change. When the patient's compensatory mechanisms fail, respiratory failure occurs. Because clinical signs vary, frequent patient assessment is a priority.

A lack of O_2 affects all body systems (Table 67.2). For example, a decreased level of consciousness may occur without enough blood, O_2, and glucose supplied to the brain. Permanent brain damage can result if hypoxia is severe and prolonged. Gastrointestinal (GI) system changes include tissue ischemia and increased intestinal wall permeability. Bacteria can migrate from the GI tract into systemic circulation. Renal function may be impaired. Sodium retention, peripheral edema, and acute kidney injury may occur.

One of the first signs of acute hypoxemic respiratory failure is a change in mental status. Mental status changes occur early because the brain is extremely sensitive to changes in O_2 (and to a lesser degree CO_2) levels and acid-base balance. Restlessness, confusion, and agitation suggest inadequate O_2 delivery to the brain. On the other hand, a morning headache and slow respiratory rate with decreased level of consciousness may indicate problems with CO_2 removal.

Tachycardia, tachypnea, slight diaphoresis, and mild hypertension are early signs of ARF.[6] These changes indicate attempts by the heart and lungs to compensate for decreased O_2 delivery and rising CO_2 levels. It is important to understand that cyanosis is an unreliable indicator of hypoxemia. It is a late sign in ARF. It often does not occur until hypoxemia is severe (PaO_2 45 mm Hg or less).[7]

The priority for the patient with ARF is immediate assessment of the patient's ability to breathe and providing any assistive measures needed. Depending on the severity of the respiratory failure and hemodynamic status, this may involve intubation and starting mechanical ventilation.

Observing the patient's position helps assess the effort associated with the **work of breathing (WOB)**. WOB is the effort needed by the respiratory muscles to inhale air into the lungs.

TABLE 67.2 Common Manifestations of Hypoxemia and Hypercapnia

Specific	Nonspecific
Hypoxemia	
Respiratory	*Central Nervous*
Dyspnea	Agitation
Tachypnea	Confusion
Prolonged expiration	Disorientation
Nasal flaring	Restless, combative behavior
Intercostal muscle retraction	Delirium
Use of accessory muscles in respiration	↓ Level of consciousness
	Coma (late)
↓ SpO_2 (<90%)	
Paradoxical chest or abdominal wall movement with respiratory cycle (late)	*Cardiovascular*
	Tachycardia
	Hypertension
Cyanosis (late)	Skin cool, clammy, and diaphoretic
	Dysrhythmias (late)
	Hypotension (late)
	Other
	Fatigue
	Inability to speak in complete sentences without pausing to breathe
Hypercapnia	
Respiratory	*Central Nervous*
Dyspnea	Morning headache
Use of tripod position	Disorientation, confusion
Pursed-lip breathing	Agitation
Limited chest wall movement	Progressive somnolence
↓ Respiratory rate or rapid rate with shallow respirations	↑ ICP
	Coma (late)
↓ Tidal volume	
↓ Minute ventilation	*Cardiovascular*
	Dysrhythmias
	Hypertension
	Tachycardia
	Bounding pulse
	Neuromuscular
	Muscle weakness
	↓ Deep tendon reflexes
	Tremors, seizures (late)

Patients with mild distress may be able to lie down. In moderate distress, patients may be able to lie down but prefer to sit. With severe distress they may be unable to breathe unless sitting upright. The tripod position helps decrease the WOB in patients with moderate to severe COPD and ARF. The patients sit with the arms propped on the overbed table or on the knees. Propping the arms increases the anteroposterior diameter of the chest and changes pressure in the thorax.

The patient in ARF may have a rapid, shallow breathing pattern (hypoxemia) or a slower respiratory rate (hypercapnia). Both changes predispose the patient to insufficient O_2 delivery and CO_2 removal. Increased respiratory rates require a substantial amount of work and can lead to respiratory muscle fatigue. A change from a rapid rate to a slower rate in a patient in respiratory distress, such as that seen with acute asthma, suggests severe respiratory muscle fatigue. There is an increased chance for respiratory arrest.

The patient's ability to speak is related to the severity of dyspnea. The dyspneic patient may be able to speak only a few words at a time between breaths. For example, the patient may have "2-word" or "3-word" dyspnea. This means the patient can say only 2 or 3 words before pausing to breathe.

You may see dyspneic patients using pursed-lip breathing (see Table 28.12). This technique increases SaO_2 by slowing respirations, increasing time for expiration, and preventing small bronchioles from collapsing. You may see *retraction* (inward movement) of the intercostal spaces or supraclavicular area and use of the accessory muscles (e.g., sternocleidomastoid) during inspiration or expiration. Use of the accessory muscles often signifies a moderate degree of respiratory distress.

Paradoxical breathing occurs with severe respiratory distress. Normally, the thorax and abdomen move outward on inspiration and inward on exhalation. With paradoxical breathing, the abdomen and chest move in the opposite manner—outward during exhalation and inward during inspiration. Paradoxical breathing results from maximal use of the accessory muscles of respiration. The patient may be extremely diaphoretic from the increased WOB.

Auscultate breath sounds. Note the presence and location of any abnormal breath sounds. Fine crackles may occur with pulmonary edema. Coarse crackles heard on expiration indicate fluid in the airways. This may be a sign of pneumonia or a degree of HF. Absent or decreased breath sounds occur with atelectasis, pleural effusion, or hypoventilation. Bronchial breath sounds over the lung periphery occur with lung consolidation from pneumonia. You may hear a pleural friction rub if pneumonia involves the pleura.

Diagnostic Studies

The most common diagnostic studies used to evaluate ARF are chest x-ray and ABG analysis. A chest x-ray helps identify possible causes of respiratory failure (e.g., atelectasis, pneumonia). ABGs evaluate oxygenation (PaO_2) and ventilation ($PaCO_2$) status and acid-base (pH, bicarbonate) balance. Pulse oximetry monitors oxygenation status indirectly.

Other diagnostic studies that may be done include a complete blood cell count, serum electrolytes, urinalysis, and 12-lead ECG. Blood and sputum cultures (Gram stain, culture and sensitivity) may reveal infection. A CT scan or V/Q lung scan may be done if a pulmonary embolus is suspected. For the patient in severe ARF who needs intubation, end-tidal CO_2 ($EtCO_2$) may be used during ventilator management to assess trends in lung ventilation.[8]

❖ NURSING AND INTERPROFESSIONAL MANAGEMENT: ACUTE RESPIRATORY FAILURE

Because many different problems cause ARF, initial management and specific care varies. Factors taken into consideration include patient age, severity of onset of respiratory failure, underlying co-morbidities, and suspected or most likely cause of the respiratory failure. We then tailor management strategies to what best meets the patient's unique needs. This section discusses general assessment and interventions most commonly used for patients with ARF. In acute care settings, collaboration between nursing and the interprofessional team (e.g., ICU physicians, respiratory therapists, pharmacists) is essential.

In severe ARF, the patient will be cared for in an intensive care unit (ICU). ICU care will include central venous pressure (CVP) and arterial BP monitoring. Arterial BP will be monitored at least hourly. Central or mixed venous O_2 saturation

[ScvO$_2$ or SvO$_2$] data help determine the adequacy of tissue perfusion and the patient's response to treatment. The patient may need advanced hemodynamic monitoring to evaluate parameters such as CO and pulmonary capillary wedge pressure (PCWP). Chapter 65 discusses hemodynamic monitoring.

◆ Nursing Assessment

Table 67.3 presents subjective and objective data that you should obtain from the patient with ARF. A thorough assessment may result in early detection of respiratory insufficiency. This allows us to intervene sooner and can prevent worsening respiratory failure. Monitor patients with preexisting cardiac and/or respiratory disease closely. A slight change in their overall condition can cause significant decompensation.

It is important to observe trends in ABGs, pulse oximetry, and assessment findings. You must identify the changes that are occurring from hypoxemia or hypercarbia. Your ability to detect problems, notify the HCP, implement appropriate treatment, and evaluate response to therapy is essential.

◆ Nursing Diagnoses

Nursing diagnoses for the patient with ARF may include:
- Impaired gas exchange
- Impaired respiratory system function

Additional information on nursing diagnoses and interventions for the patient with ARF is presented in eNursing Care Plan 67.1 (available on the website for this chapter).

◆ Planning

The overall goals for the patient with ARF include (1) independently maintain a patent airway, (2) absence of dyspnea or recovery to baseline breathing patterns, (3) effectively cough and able to clear secretions, (4) normal ABG values or values within the patient's baseline, and (5) breath sounds within the patient's baseline.

◆ Nursing Implementation

◆ Prevention.
For the patient at risk for ARF, prevention and early recognition of respiratory distress are important. This is especially important for patients with neuromuscular diseases, cardiac problems, or respiratory problems (e.g., COPD). Do a thorough history and physical assessment to identify risk factors, then start appropriate interventions. Early strategies may include teaching patients about deep breathing and coughing, use of incentive spirometry, and early ambulation.

Preventing atelectasis, pneumonia, and complications of immobility, and optimizing hydration and nutrition, can decrease the risk for ARF. Those patients at high risk should be assessed more often with attention given to preventive measures.

◆ Respiratory Therapy

The goals of respiratory care include maintaining adequate oxygenation and ventilation and correcting acid-base imbalance. Interventions include O$_2$ therapy, mobilization of secretions, and positive pressure ventilation (PPV) (Table 67.4).

TABLE 67.3 Nursing Assessment
Acute Respiratory Failure

Subjective Data

Important Health Information

Past health history: Age, weight, altered level of consciousness, tobacco use (pack-years), alcohol or drug use, hospitalizations related to either acute or chronic lung disease, thoracic or spinal cord trauma, occupational exposures to lung toxins

Medications: Use of home O$_2$, inhalers (bronchodilators), home nebulization, over-the-counter drugs; immunosuppressant (e.g., corticosteroid) therapy, CNS depressants, illicit substances

Surgery or other treatments: Intubation and mechanical ventilation, recent thoracic or abdominal surgery

Functional Health Patterns

Health perception–health management: Exercise, self-care activities, immunizations (flu, pneumonia, hepatitis)

Nutritional-metabolic: Eating habits, bloating, indigestion; recent weight gain or loss, change in appetite. Use of vitamins or herbal supplements

Activity-exercise: Fatigue, dizziness, dyspnea at rest or with activity, wheezing, cough (productive or nonproductive), sputum (volume, color, viscosity), palpitations, swollen feet, change in exercise tolerance

Sleep-rest: Changes in sleep pattern, use of CPAP

Cognitive-perceptual: Headache, chest pain or tightness, chronic pain

Coping–stress tolerance: Anxiety, depression, feelings of hopelessness. Risk for drug and/or alcohol use, nicotine withdrawal

Objective Data

General

Restlessness, agitation

Integumentary

Pale, cool, clammy skin or warm, flushed skin. Peripheral and central cyanosis. Peripheral dependent edema

Respiratory

Shallow, increased respiratory rate progressing to decreased rate. Use of accessory muscles with evidence of retractions, increased diaphragmatic excursion or asymmetric chest expansion, paradoxical chest and abdominal wall movement. Tactile fremitus, crepitus, or deviated trachea on palpation. Absent, decreased, or adventitious breath sounds. Pleural friction rub. Bronchial or bronchovesicular sounds heard in other than normal location, inspiratory stridor

Cardiovascular

Tachycardia progressing to bradycardia, dysrhythmias, extra heart sounds (S$_3$, S$_4$). Bounding pulse. Hypertension progressing to hypotension. Pulsus paradoxus, jugular venous distention, pedal edema

Gastrointestinal

Abdominal distention, ascites, epigastric tenderness, hepatojugular reflex

Neurologic

Somnolence, confusion, slurred speech, restlessness, delirium, agitation, tremors, seizures, coma, asterixis, ↓ deep tendon reflexes, papilledema

Possible Diagnostic Findings

↓/↑ pH, ↑/↓ PaCO$_2$, ↑/↓ bicarbonate, ↓ PaO$_2$, ↓ SaO$_2$, abnormal hemoglobin, ↑ WBC count, changes in serum electrolytes. Abnormal findings on chest x-ray. Abnormal central venous or pulmonary artery pressures. Initially cardiac output may be ↑ due to the stress response. As hypoxemia, hypercapnia, and acidosis become more severe, cardiac output will ↓.

TABLE 67.4 Interprofessional Care

Acute Respiratory Failure

Diagnostic Assessment

- Vital signs
- History and physical examination
- Arterial blood gases (ABGs)
- Pulse oximetry
- Chest x-ray
- CBC and differential
- Serum electrolytes
- 12-Lead ECG
- Blood, sputum, and/or urine cultures (if indicated)
- Hemodynamic monitoring: CVP, SVV, PAWP (if indicated)

Management

Respiratory Therapy

- O_2 therapy
- Mobilization of secretions
  - Positioning
  - Effective coughing
  - Chest physiotherapy
  - Suctioning of the airway
  - Oral and/or IV hydration
  - Humidification (of O_2)
  - Ambulation (early mobility)
  - Positioning: head of bed elevated
- Positive pressure ventilation (PPV)
  - Noninvasive positive pressure ventilation (e.g. CPAP, BiPAP)
  - Intubation with positive pressure ventilation

Drug Therapy

- Reduce airway inflammation (e.g., corticosteroids)
- Relief of bronchospasm (e.g., albuterol)
- Reduce pulmonary congestion (e.g., furosemide [Lasix], morphine)
- Treat pulmonary infections (e.g., antibiotics)
- Reduce anxiety, pain, and restlessness (e.g., lorazepam, fentanyl, morphine)

Supportive Therapy

- Management of the underlying cause of respiratory failure
- Monitor hemodynamic status
- Optimize balance between activity and rest
- Monitor for deterioration in patient condition

CVP, Central venous pressure; *SVV,* stroke volume variation; *PAWP,* pulmonary artery wedge pressure.

◆ **Oxygen Therapy.** The primary goal of O_2 therapy is to correct hypoxemia. This requires O_2 administration. Always administer O_2 at the lowest possible FIO_2 (O_2 concentration) needed to keep SpO_2 and PaO_2 within patient-specific goals. Never withhold O_2 from a patient. It is essential to observe the patient's response to O_2 therapy. Closely monitor patients for changes in mental status, respiratory rate, and ABGs, until their PaO_2 level has reached their baseline normal value.

Several methods are available to provide O_2 to patients in ARF. Chapter 28 and Table 28.19 discuss O_2 delivery devices. The device selected depends upon the patient's overall condition, degree of respiratory failure, ability to maintain a patent airway, the amount of FIO_2 that the device can deliver, and, most importantly, the patient's ability to breathe spontaneously. Ideally, the selected O_2 delivery device must maintain PaO_2 at 60 mm Hg or higher and SaO_2 at 90% or higher.

The patient is often agitated, disoriented, and restless. A face mask, though appropriate, may cause anxiety from feelings of claustrophobia. Anxiety can cause dyspnea and increase O_2 consumption and CO_2 production. The patient may try to remove the mask. In this case, you need to explore other O_2 therapy options.

Breathing high O_2 concentrations for prolonged periods is not without potential adverse effects. Exposure to higher FIO_2 (greater than 60%) for longer than 48 hours poses a risk for O_2 *toxicity.* In this situation, oxygen free radicals from the high O_2 levels cause inflammation and cell death, by disrupting the alveolar-capillary membrane. *Absorption atelectasis* is another risk. O_2 has the ability to replace nitrogen and other gases normally present in the alveoli. Without nitrogen to help maintain size and shape of the alveolus, structural support is lost and the alveolus collapses. Other effects of prolonged exposure to high levels of O_2 include increased pulmonary capillary permeability, decreased surfactant production, surfactant inactivation, and fibrotic changes in the alveoli.[9]

Another risk of O_2 therapy is specific to patients with chronic hypercapnia (e.g., patient with COPD). Chronic hypercapnia blunts the response of chemoreceptors to high CO_2 levels as a respiratory stimulant. Initial O_2 therapy may be provided to patients with chronic hypercapnia through a low-flow device, such as a nasal cannula at 1 to 2 L/min or a Venturi mask at 24% to 28%. The patient with COPD who does not respond to O_2 therapy or other interventions may need mechanical ventilation with higher FIO_2.

◆ **Mobilization of Secretions.** Retained pulmonary secretions may cause or worsen ARF. This occurs because the movement of O_2 into the alveoli and removal of CO_2 is severely limited or blocked. Secretions can be mobilized by proper positioning, effective coughing, chest physiotherapy, suctioning, humidification, hydration, and, when possible, early ambulation.

Patient Positioning. Position the patient upright, either by elevating the head of the bed at least 30 degrees or by using a reclining chair or chair bed. This helps maximize respiratory expansion, decrease dyspnea, and mobilize secretions. A sitting position improves pulmonary function by promoting downward movement of the lungs. When lungs are upright, ventilation and perfusion are best in the lung bases. If there is a chance for aspiration, position the patient side-lying.

Patients with one-sided lung disorders may be placed in a lateral or side-lying position. This position, called *good lung down,* allows for improved V/Q matching in the affected lung. Pulmonary blood flow and ventilation are better in dependent lung areas. This position allows secretions to drain out of the affected lung so they can be removed with suctioning. For example, place a patient with right-sided pneumonia on the left side. This will maximize ventilation and perfusion in the "good" lung and aid in secretion removal from the affected lung (postural drainage). Patients with ARF often have problems with both lungs. They may need repositioning at regular intervals on both sides to optimize air movement and drainage of secretions.

Effective Coughing. When secretions are present, encourage the patient to cough. Unfortunately, not all patients will have enough strength or force to produce a cough that will clear the airway of secretions. *Augmented coughing (quad coughing)* may benefit some patients. To aid with augmented coughing, place 1 or both hands at the anterolateral base of the patient's lungs (Fig. 67.6). As you observe deep inspiration end and expiration begin, move your hands forcefully upward. This increases abdominal pressure and helps the patient cough. It increases expiratory flow and promotes secretion clearance.

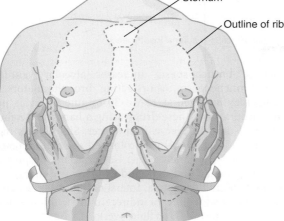

FIG. 67.6 Augmented coughing is performed by placing 1 or both hands on the anterolateral base of the lungs. After the patient takes a deep inspiration and at the beginning of expiration, move the hand(s) forcefully upward. This increases abdominal pressure and helps produce a forceful cough. (From American Association of Critical Care Nurses: *AACN advanced critical care nursing*, St Louis, 2009, Mosby.)

Huff coughing is a series of coughs performed while saying the word "huff" (see Table 28.21).[10] This technique prevents the glottis from closing during the cough. The patient takes a deep breath, holds the breath for 2 or 3 seconds, and then exhales. The huff cough is effective in clearing central airways. It may help move secretions upward. COPD patients generate higher flow rates with a huff cough than with a normal cough, and it is less tiring.

The *staged cough* also helps clear secretions. To perform a staged cough, the patient assumes a sitting position, breathes in and out 3 or 4 times through the mouth, then coughs while bending forward and pressing a pillow inward against the diaphragm.

Chest Physiotherapy. Chest physiotherapy is indicated for all patients who are producing sputum or have evidence of severe atelectasis or pulmonary infiltrates on chest x-ray. Postural drainage, percussion, and vibration to the affected lung segments help move secretions to the larger airways. Then, they can be removed by coughing or suctioning. Chest physiotherapy is discussed in Chapter 28.

Contraindications include TBI and increased intracranial pressure (ICP), unstable orthopedic injuries (e.g., spinal fractures, fractured ribs, fractured sternum), and recent hemoptysis.[11]

Suctioning. Suctioning may be needed if the patient is unable to expectorate secretions. Suctioning through an artificial airway (e.g., endotracheal tube [ET], tracheostomy) is done only as needed (see Chapters 26 and 65). Perform suctioning beyond the posterior oropharynx with caution, while monitoring the patient for complications. These include hypoxia, increased ICP, dysrhythmias, hypotension (from sudden elevation in intrathoracic pressure), hypertension and tachycardia (from noxious stimulation), and bradycardia (possible vasovagal response).

Humidification. Humidification is an adjunct in secretion management. We can thin secretions with aerosols of sterile normal saline or mucolytic drugs (e.g., acetylcysteine mixed with a bronchodilator) given by nebulizer. O_2 given by aerosol mask can thin secretions and promote their removal. Aerosol therapy may cause bronchospasm and severe coughing, causing

a decrease in PaO_2. Frequent assessment of the patient's tolerance to therapy is critical. Closely monitor the patient's respiratory status.

Hydration. Thick, viscous secretions are hard to expel. Unless contraindicated, adequate fluid intake (2 to 3 L/day) keeps secretions thin and easier to remove. The patient who is unable to take enough fluids orally needs IV hydration. Assess cardiac and renal status to determine whether the patient can tolerate the IV fluid volume and avoid HF and pulmonary edema. Regularly assess for signs of fluid overload (e.g., crackles, dyspnea, increased CVP).

❓ CHECK YOUR PRACTICE

You are caring for a 72-yr-old male patient admitted with acute hypoxemic respiratory failure. He has a history of atrial flutter and COPD. A chest x-ray shows left-sided pneumonia. Your patient is awake but mildly confused. He has a productive cough (thick, yellow-green purulent sputum).
- What respiratory interventions would you expect to be ordered?

◆ **Positive Pressure Ventilation.** If initial measures do not improve oxygenation and ventilation, enhanced ventilatory assistance may be needed. Noninvasive positive pressure ventilation (NIPPV) is one option for patients with acute or chronic respiratory failure. During NIPPV, a mask is placed tightly over the patient's nose or nose and mouth (Fig. 67.7). When the patient breathes spontaneously, a mechanical ventilator or table-top unit delivers PPV to the patient. With NIPPV, it is possible to provide O_2 and decrease WOB, avoiding the need for endotracheal intubation.

NIPPV is most useful in managing chronic respiratory failure in those with chest wall or neuromuscular problems. It may be used with patients with a chronic respiratory problem that is worse due to cardiac problems or infection. It is an option for patients who refuse intubation, but still want some degree of ventilatory support (e.g., patients with end-stage COPD). NIPPV is not appropriate for patients who have a decreased level of consciousness, high O_2 requirements, facial trauma, hemodynamic instability, or excessive secretions. NIPPV used after extubation can help avoid reintubation.

There are 2 forms of NIPPV used for patients with ARF. Continuous positive airway pressure (CPAP) delivers 1 level of pressure—a constant pressure—to the patient's airway during inspiration and expiration. Bilevel positive airway pressure (BiPAP) uses 2 different levels of positive pressure (one on inspiration, another on expiration) (Fig. 67.8). With both CPAP and BiPAP, the patient must be awake and alert, have stable vital signs, and be able to support spontaneous ventilation.

The most often used NIPPV for ARF is BiPAP.[12] BiPAP provides O_2 therapy and humidification, decreases WOB, and reduces respiratory muscle fatigue. It helps open collapsed airways and decrease shunt. If respiratory status worsens with NIPPV, PPV via mechanical ventilation and higher O_2 concentrations is needed. Chapter 65 discusses mechanical ventilation.

◆ **Drug Therapy**

Drug therapy depends on several factors. These include the cause of ARF, the patient's preexisting medical condition, and whether infection is present. Goals of drug therapy include to (1) reduce airway inflammation and bronchospasm, (2) relieve

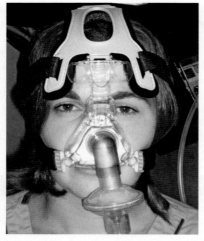

FIG. 67.7 Noninvasive bilevel positive airway pressure ventilation. A mask is placed over the nose or nose and mouth. Positive pressure from a mechanical ventilator aids the patient's breathing efforts, decreasing the work of breathing. (Courtesy Richard Arbour, RN, MSN, CCRN, CNRN, CCNS, FAAN and Anna Kirk, RN, MSN.)

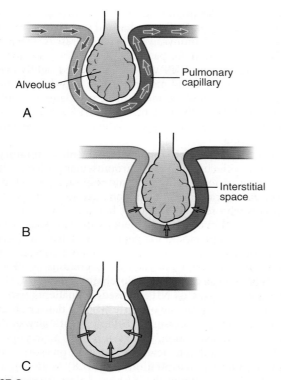

FIG. 67.8 Stages of edema formation in ARDS. **A,** Normal alveolus and pulmonary capillary. **B,** Interstitial edema occurs with increased flow of fluid into the interstitial space. **C,** Alveolar edema occurs when the fluid crosses the alveolar-capillary membrane.

pulmonary congestion; (3) treat infection; and (4) reduce anxiety, pain, and restlessness.

◆ **Reduce Airway Inflammation and Bronchospasm.** Corticosteroids (e.g., IV methylprednisolone [Solu-Medrol]) are often used in combination with other drugs, such as bronchodilators, for relief of inflammation and bronchospasm. It may take several hours to see their effects. Inhaled corticosteroids require 4 to 5 days for optimum therapeutic effects, so they will not relieve ARF.

> **DRUG ALERT** IV Corticosteroids
>
> - Monitor potassium levels. Corticosteroids worsen hypokalemia caused by diuretics.
> - Prolonged use causes adrenal insufficiency.

Relief of bronchospasm increases alveolar ventilation. In acute bronchospasm, short-acting bronchodilators (e.g., albuterol), may be given at 15- to 30-minute intervals until a response occurs. Give these drugs using a hand-held nebulizer or a metered-dose inhaler with a spacer. Side effects include tachycardia and hypertension. Prolonged use can increase the risk for dysrhythmias and cardiac ischemia. It is important to monitor the patient's vital signs and ECG for any changes.

◆ **Relieve Pulmonary Congestion.** Interstitial fluid can accumulate in the lungs because of direct or indirect injury to the alveolar capillary membrane from HF or fluid overload. Use of IV diuretics (e.g., furosemide [Lasix]), morphine, or nitroglycerin can decrease pulmonary congestion caused by HF. Use extreme caution when giving these drugs. Changes in heart rate and rhythm and significant decreases in BP are common. (Chapter 34 discusses HF.)

◆ **Treat Infection.** Lung infections (e.g., pneumonia, acute bronchitis) can result in excessive mucus production, fever, increased O_2 consumption, and inflamed, fluid-filled, and/or collapsed alveoli. Alveoli that are fluid filled or collapsed cannot take part in gas exchange. Consequently, pulmonary infections can either cause or worsen ARF. IV antibiotics are often given to treat infection. Chest x-rays can show the location and extent of an infection. Sputum cultures help identify the organisms causing the infection and their sensitivity to antimicrobial drugs.

◆ **Reduce Anxiety, Pain, and Restlessness.** Anxiety, pain, and restlessness may result from hypoxia. They increase O_2 consumption and CO_2 production (from an increased metabolic rate) and increase WOB. For the nonintubated patient, this may cause tachypnea and ineffective ventilation. For the intubated patient, this may cause ventilator dyssynchrony and increase the risk for unplanned extubation. We promote patient comfort in several ways.

Benzodiazepines (e.g., lorazepam, midazolam), and opioids (e.g., morphine, fentanyl) may decrease anxiety, restlessness, and pain. They are often given IV. For the nonintubated patient, they should be started at the lowest dose possible. Address treatable causes of restlessness (e.g., hypoxemia, pain, delirium). Often, restlessness and mental status changes are the first signs of hypoxemia or ventilator dyssynchrony. You should address the causes and not depend solely on the use of analgesics and sedatives.

> **!** **SAFETY ALERT** Managing Restlessness and Sedation
> - Pain, hypoxemia, electrolyte imbalance, TBI, and drug reactions can cause restlessness.
> - Assess and aggressively treat all reversible causes of restlessness.
> - Monitor patients closely for CNS, cardiac, and respiratory depression when giving sedative and analgesic drugs, especially in the nonintubated patient.
> - Sedative and analgesic drugs may have a prolonged effect in critically ill patients. This can delay weaning from mechanical ventilation and increase length of stay.

◆ **Medical Supportive Therapy**

Goals and interventions targeted to improving the patient's oxygenation and ventilation status are essential to improve O_2 delivery. The primary goal is to treat the underlying cause of the

ARF. Patients with V/Q mismatch, shunting, or diffusion limitation are managed differently, depending on the underlying cause. Patients are continuously monitored for their response to therapy, including changes in respiratory status, trends in ABGs, and signs of clinical improvement.

◆ Nutritional Therapy

Maintaining protein and energy stores is especially important in patients with ARF. The hypermetabolic state in critical illness increases the caloric requirements needed to maintain a stable body weight and muscle mass. Nutritional depletion causes a loss of muscle mass, including the respiratory muscles, which may delay recovery. The dietitian often determines the best method of feeding and optimal caloric and fluid requirements. Ideally, enteral or parenteral nutrition should be started within 24 to 48 hours (see Chapter 39).

◆ Evaluation

The expected outcomes are that the patient with ARF will
- Independently maintain a patent airway
- Achieve normal or baseline respiratory system function
- Maintain adequate oxygenation as shown by normal or baseline ABGs
- Have normal hemodynamic status

Gerontologic Considerations: Acute Respiratory Failure

Many factors contribute to an increased risk for respiratory failure in older adults. The reduced ventilatory capacity that accompanies aging places the older adult at risk for ARF. Physiologic changes in the lungs include alveolar dilation, larger air spaces, and loss of surface area for gas exchange. Decreased elastic recoil within the airways, decreased chest wall compliance, and decreased respiratory muscle strength occur.[13]

In older adults, the PaO_2 falls further and the $PaCO_2$ rises to a higher level before the respiratory system is stimulated to change the rate and depth of breathing. This delayed response contributes to the development of respiratory insufficiency. A history of tobacco use is a major risk factor that can accelerate age-related respiratory changes. Poor nutritional status and less physiologic reserve in the cardiopulmonary system increases the risk for further compromising respiratory function and leading to ARF.

ACUTE RESPIRATORY DISTRESS SYNDROME

Acute respiratory distress syndrome (ARDS) is a sudden and progressive form of ARF in which the alveolar-capillary membrane becomes damaged and more permeable to intravascular fluid (Fig. 67.8). Next to septic shock, ARDS is one of the most common conditions seen in the adult ICU. ARDS accounts for about 10% of all adult ICU admissions.[14] The incidence of ARDS in the United States is estimated at more than 200,000 cases each year.[14] Despite supportive therapy, the mortality rate from ARDS is around 50%.

Etiology

Table 67.5 lists conditions that predispose patients to developing ARDS. The most common cause is sepsis. ARDS may also develop because of multiple organ dysfunction syndrome (MODS). Patients with multiple risk factors are 3 or 4 times more likely to develop ARDS.

Either a direct or indirect lung injury causes ARDS. In direct lung injury, the pathogen comes into contact with the tissue of

TABLE 67.5 Predisposing Conditions to ARDS

Direct Lung Injury	Indirect Lung Injury
Common Causes	
• Aspiration of gastric contents or other substances • Bacterial or viral pneumonia • Sepsis	• Sepsis (especially gram-negative infection) • Severe massive trauma • Severe TBI • Shock states (hypovolemic, cardiogenic, septic)
Less Common Causes	
• Chest trauma (blunt or penetrating) • Embolism: fat, air, amniotic fluid, thrombus • Inhalation of toxic substances • Near-drowning • O_2 toxicity • Radiation pneumonitis	• Acute pancreatitis • Cardiopulmonary bypass • Disseminated intravascular coagulation • Opioid drug overdose (e.g., heroin) • Transfusion-related acute lung injury (e.g., multiple blood transfusions) • Urosepsis

the lung. For example, aspiration of gastric contents into the lung will immediately initiate the inflammatory response. In an indirect injury, ARDS develops due to a problem somewhere else in the body. For example, necrotizing pancreatitis or bowel obstruction with perforation cause widespread inflammation and infection. As a result, septic mediators gain entrance to the bloodstream and often move toward the lungs, which provide a favorable, dark, moist environment for their proliferation. This is the beginning of acute lung injury.

Pathophysiology

The pathophysiologic changes in ARDS are divided into 3 phases: (1) injury or exudative phase, (2) reparative or proliferative phase, and (3) fibrotic or fibroproliferative phase. The pathophysiology of ARDS is shown in Fig. 67.9.

Injury or Exudative Phase. The *injury or exudative phase* usually occurs 24 to 72 hours after the initial insult (direct or indirect).[15] It generally lasts up to 7 days. Engorgement of the peribronchial and perivascular interstitial space causes interstitial edema. Fluid in the parenchyma of the lung surrounding the alveoli crosses the alveolar membrane and enters the alveolar space. V/Q mismatch and intrapulmonary shunt develop because the alveoli fill with fluid. Blood in the capillary network cannot be oxygenated.

The exact cause for the damage to the alveolar-capillary membrane is not known. Some think it is caused by stimulation of the inflammatory and immune systems. This stimulation attracts neutrophils to the pulmonary interstitium. The neutrophils release biochemical, humoral, and cellular mediators that produce changes in the lung. These changes include increased pulmonary capillary membrane permeability, destruction of collagen, formation of pulmonary microemboli, and pulmonary artery vasoconstriction.

Hypoxemia and the stimulation of juxtacapillary receptors in the stiff lung parenchyma (*J reflex*) initially cause an increase in respiratory rate and a decrease in tidal volume (V_T). This breathing pattern increases CO_2 removal, producing respiratory alkalosis. CO increases in response to hypoxemia, a compensatory effort to increase pulmonary blood flow. However, as atelectasis, pulmonary edema, and pulmonary shunt increase, compensation fails and hypoventilation, decreased CO, and decreased tissue O_2 perfusion occur.

PATHOPHYSIOLOGY MAP

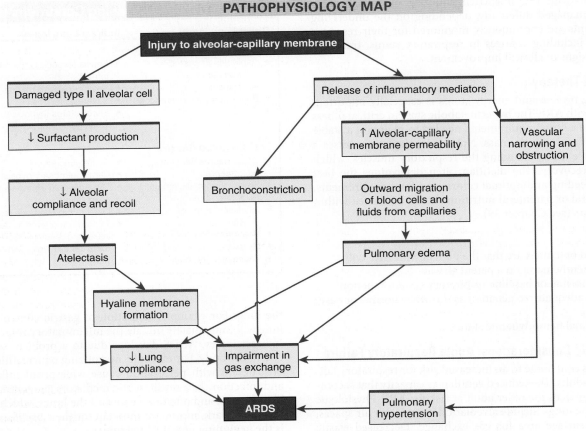

FIG. 67.9 Pathophysiology of ARDS.

The changes caused by ARDS damage both alveolar type I cells and alveolar type II cells (which make surfactant). This damage, in addition to fluid and protein accumulation, results in surfactant dysfunction. The function of *surfactant* is to maintain alveolar stability and prevent alveolar collapse. When surfactant synthesis is decreased or surfactant becomes inactivated, alveoli become unstable and collapse (*atelectasis*). Widespread atelectasis further decreases lung compliance, compromises gas exchange, and contributes to hypoxemia.

Necrotic cells, protein, and fibrin form hyaline membranes that line the inside of each alveolus. These thick hyaline membranes contribute to the development of fibrosis and atelectasis, leading to a further decrease in gas exchange capability and reduced lung compliance.

Severe V/Q mismatch and shunting of pulmonary capillary blood result in hypoxemia unresponsive to increasing concentrations of O_2. This is the classic signs of ARDS, called **refractory hypoxemia**. In other words, despite receiving higher concentrations of O_2, the patient's condition does not improve but continues to get worse. Diffusion limitation, caused by hyaline membrane formation, contributes to and worsens hypoxemia. As the lungs become less compliant because of decreased surfactant, pulmonary edema, and atelectasis, the patient must generate higher airway pressures to inflate "stiff" lungs. Reduced lung compliance increases the patient's WOB. At this point, the patient needs mechanical ventilation.

Reparative or Proliferative Phase. The *reparative* or *proliferative phase* of ARDS begins 1 to 2 weeks after the initial lung injury.[16] During this phase, there continues to be an influx of

neutrophils, monocytes, lymphocytes, and fibroblasts as part of the inflammatory response. Increased pulmonary vascular resistance and pulmonary hypertension may occur because fibroblasts and inflammatory cells destroy the pulmonary vasculature. Lung compliance continues to decrease due to interstitial fibrosis. Hypoxemia worsens because of the thickened alveolar membrane. This causes V/Q mismatch, diffusion limitation, and shunting. Airway resistance is severely increased from fluid in the lungs and secretions in the airways. The proliferative phase is complete when the diseased lung is replaced by dense, fibrous tissue. If the reparative phase persists, widespread fibrosis results. If the reparative phase stops, the lesions will often resolve.

Fibrotic or Fibroproliferative Phase. The *fibrotic phase* (*chronic or late phase*) of ARDS occurs 2 to 3 weeks after the initial lung injury. Not all patients who develop ARDS enter the fibrotic stage. For those who never fully recover from ARDS, the lung is completely remodeled by collagenous and fibrous tissues. Diffuse scarring of the lungs, interstitial fibrosis, and alveolar duct fibrosis result in decreased lung compliance.[17] This reduces the surface area for gas exchange because the interstitium is fibrotic, and hypoxemia continues. Varying degrees of pulmonary hypertension may result from pulmonary vascular destruction and fibrosis.

Clinical Progression

Progression of ARDS varies among patients. Some survive the acute phase of lung injury. Pulmonary edema resolves, and complete recovery occurs within a week or so. The chance for survival is poorer in those who enter the fibrotic stage. Patients may need several weeks of long-term mechanical ventilation. It is not known why injured lungs repair and recover in some patients and in others ARDS progresses. Several factors are important in determining the course of ARDS. These include the nature of the initial injury, extent and severity of comorbidities, and pulmonary complications (e.g., pneumothorax). Genetics may account for a person's predisposition to developing ARDS.[18]

Clinical Manifestations and Diagnostic Studies

The initial presentation of ARDS is often subtle. At the time of the initial injury, and for 24 to 72 hours, the patient may not have respiratory symptoms or may have only mild dyspnea, tachypnea, cough, and restlessness. Lung auscultation may be normal or reveal fine, scattered crackles. ABGs may show mild hypoxemia and respiratory alkalosis caused by hyperventilation. The chest x-ray may be normal or reveal diffusely scattered, but minimal, interstitial infiltrates.

As ARDS progresses, symptoms worsen because of fluid in the lung parenchyma and alveoli and increased secretion accumulation in the airways. Respiratory distress becomes evident as WOB increases. Tachypnea and intercostal and suprasternal retractions may be present. Tachycardia, diaphoresis, changes in mental status, cyanosis, and pallor may occur. Lung auscultation usually reveals scattered to diffuse crackles and coarse crackles on expiration. After 72 hours, the chest x-ray often shows diffuse and extensive bilateral interstitial and alveolar infiltrates (Fig. 67.10).

As ARDS progresses, ABGs reflect changes in oxygenation and ventilation. Refractory hypoxemia is the hallmark characteristic of ARDS. Hypercapnia often signifies that respiratory muscle fatigue and hypoventilation have severely affected gas exchange, and respiratory failure is imminent.

To help evaluate the severity of hypoxemia in ARDS, we can calculate the **PaO₂/FIO₂ (P/F) ratio**. This measure reflects the ratio of the patient's PaO_2 to the FIO_2 that the patient is receiving. Under normal circumstances (e.g., PaO_2 80 to 100 mm Hg; FIO_2 0.21 [room air]), the P/F ratio is greater than 400 (e.g., 95/0.21 = 452). With the onset and progression of lung injury and impairment in O_2 delivery through the alveolar-capillary membrane, the PaO_2 may remain lower than expected despite increased FIO_2. The P/F ratio distinguishes among mild (<300), moderate (<200), and severe (<100) ARDS (Table 67.6).

❓ CHECK YOUR PRACTICE

You are caring for a 26-yr-old woman with ARDS who experienced near-drowning 4 days ago. She is mechanically ventilated and receiving continuous IV infusions of analgesia and sedation. The ventilator settings are: full support (control mode), FIO_2 = 90%, PEEP = 15 cm H_2O, V_T = 350 mL, respiratory rate 12 breaths/min (patient taking no breaths above the set rate on the ventilator), peak pressure = 35 cm H_2O. The patient's PaO_2 is 83 mm Hg.
• Calculate and interpret the PaO_2/FIO_2 (P/F) ratio.

As ARDS progresses, it is associated with profound dyspnea, hypoxemia, increased WOB, and respiratory distress, which require endotracheal intubation and PPV. The chest x-ray is often called "whiteout" (or white lung) because consolidation and infiltrates are widespread throughout the lungs, leaving few recognizable air spaces. Pleural effusions may be present. Severe hypoxemia, hypercapnia, metabolic acidosis, and organ dysfunction often accompany ARDS and provide additional challenges.

Complications

Complications may develop because of ARDS itself or its treatment (Table 67.7). Besides the lungs, the vital organs most often involved are the kidneys, liver, and heart. The main cause of death in ARDS is MODS, often accompanied by sepsis.

Abnormal Lung Function. Most patients will recover from ARDS within 6 months. Many will have normal to near normal lung function. However, not all patients regain normal lung function. Sometimes, abnormal lung function can persist for years. The severity of scarring and changes within the lungs are key factors. Mechanical ventilation, the duration of time ventilated, and use of extracorporeal life support (ECLS) may be contributing factors.[19] Patients may report extreme tiredness, chest pain, shortness of breath after minimal activity, and persistent dyspnea post-ARDS.

Ventilator-Associated Pneumonia. Risk factors for ventilator-associated pneumonia (VAP) include impaired host defenses, invasive monitoring devices, aspiration of GI contents (especially in patients receiving enteral nutrition), and

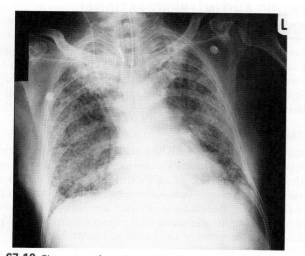

FIG. 67.10 Chest x-ray of a patient with ARDS. The x-ray shows new, bilateral, diffuse, homogeneous pulmonary infiltrates without cardiac failure, fluid overload, chest infection, or chronic lung disease. (From Cohen J, Powderly WG: *Infectious diseases*, ed 2, St Louis, 2004, Mosby.)

TABLE 67.6 Berlin Definition of ARDS

Timing
Within 1 week of a known clinical insult or new or worsening respiratory symptoms

Chest X-Ray
Bilateral opacities: not fully explained by effusions, lobar/lung collapse, or nodules

Oxygenation
Mild ARDS: PaO_2/FIO_2 ratio ≤300 with PEEP or CPAP ≥5 cm H_2O
Moderate ARDS: PaO_2/FIO_2 ratio ≤200 with PEEP or CPAP ≥5 cm H_2O
Severe ARDS: PaO_2/FIO_2 ratio <100 with PEEP or CPAP ≥5 cm H_2O

Modified from Pneumatikos L, Papaioannou VE: The new Berlin definition: What is, finally, the ARDS? *Pneumon* 25:365, 2012.

prolonged mechanical ventilation. Implement a ventilator bundle protocol (Table 67.8).

Common strategies to prevent VAP include elevating the head of bed 30 to 45 degrees, strict infection control measures (e.g., hand washing, sterile technique during endotracheal suctioning) and frequent oral care.

Barotrauma. *Barotrauma* occurs when fragile alveoli are overdistended with excess pressure during mechanical ventilation. The high peak airway pressures needed to ventilate the lungs predispose patients with ARDS to this complication. Barotrauma results in alveolar air escaping from ruptured alveoli. This can lead to pulmonary interstitial emphysema, pneumothorax, subcutaneous emphysema, pneumopericardium, and tension pneumothorax. Providing ventilation with a smaller V_T (e.g., 4 to 8 mL/kg) and varying amounts of PEEP minimizes the risk for barotrauma.

Stress Ulcers. Patients with ARF and ARDS are at high risk for stress ulcers because of blood being diverted from the GI to respiratory system to help meet the body's demand for O_2. Management strategies include correcting predisposing conditions, such as hypotension, shock, and acidosis. Prophylactic management includes antiulcer drugs, such as proton pump inhibitors (e.g., pantoprazole [Protonix]) and mucosal-protecting drugs (e.g., sucralfate [Carafate]). Early initiation of enteral nutrition helps prevent mucosal damage.

Venous Thromboembolism (VTE). ARDS patients are susceptible to the effects of immobility and venous stasis. They are at risk for deep vein thrombosis (DVT) and pulmonary emboli. Prophylactic management may include intermittent pneumatic compression stockings, anticoagulation (e.g. low-molecular-weight heparin), and, when possible, early ambulation.

Acute Kidney Injury. Acute kidney injury (AKI) can occur from decreased renal perfusion and subsequent decreased delivery of O_2 to the kidneys. This most often occurs in ARDS because of hypotension in septic shock. It may also result from hypoxemia or nephrotoxic drugs (e.g., vancomycin) used to treat ARDS-related infections. Management strategies for AKI include careful monitoring of intake and output, obtaining daily creatinine and urea levels, and, when needed, dialysis therapy.

Continuous renal replacement therapy (CRRT) is often used. Patients with ARDS are often hemodynamically unstable and need vasopressors and/or inotropes to maintain heart rate and BP. They cannot tolerate the large volumes of fluid that would be removed during traditional hemodialysis. CRRT is slow, gentle, and continuous. The patient can receive CRRT 24 hours a day. The overall mortality rate for ARDS patients is higher in those who need CRRT.[20]

Psychological Issues. Recovery is far from complete for the patient who survives ARDS. Survivors may have anxiety, issues with memory and attention, inability to focus, nightmares, depression, and in some instances, various degrees of posttraumatic stress disorder (PTSD). PTSD can occur in ARDS survivors up to 5 years later.[21]

❖ NURSING AND INTERPROFESSIONAL MANAGEMENT: ARDS

Management of a patient with ARF (Table 67.4) and the nursing care plan for ARF (eNursing Care Plan 67.1 [available on the website for this chapter]) apply to patients with ARDS. The next section discusses additional interprofessional care for the patient with ARDS (Table 67.9).

◆ Nursing Assessment

Because ARDS causes ARF, the subjective and objective data that you should obtain from someone with ARDS are the same as those for ARF (Table 67.3). Patient information may not be possible to obtain on admission due to the urgent need to protect the airway (intubation), initiate mechanical ventilation, monitor vital signs, and assist with urgent treatments and procedures (e.g., insertion of an arterial and central line).

◆ Planning

With appropriate therapy, overall goals include a PaO_2 of 60 mm Hg or higher and adequate lung ventilation to maintain normal pH. Specific goals for a patient with ARDS include (1)

TABLE 67.7 Complications Associated With ARDS

Cardiac
- ↓ Cardiac output
- Dysrhythmias

Central Nervous System and Psychologic
- Delirium
- PTSD

Gastrointestinal
- Hypermetabolic state, dramatically ↑ nutrition requirements
- Paralytic ileus
- Pneumoperitoneum
- Stress ulceration and hemorrhage

Hematologic
- Anemia
- Disseminated intravascular coagulation
- Thrombocytopenia
- VTE

Infection
- Catheter-related infection (e.g., central and peripheral IV catheters, urinary catheters)
- Sepsis

Renal
- AKI

Respiratory
- Pulmonary emboli
- Pulmonary fibrosis
- Ventilator associated: volutrauma, barotrauma
- VAP

TABLE 67.8 Components of a Ventilator Bundle

- Good hand washing before, during (as needed), and after delivery of patient care
- Elevate head of the bed 30 to 45 degrees
- Daily assessment of readiness for extubation (see Chapter 65)
- Stress ulcer prophylaxis (see Chapter 41)
- VTE prophylaxis (see Chapter 37)
- Daily oral care with chlorhexidine (0.12%) solution (see Table 65.9)

Source: Institute for Healthcare Improvement: How-to guide: Prevent VAP. Retrieved from *www.ihi.org/resources/Pages/Tools/HowtoGuidePreventVAP.aspx.*

TABLE 67.9 Interprofessional Care

Acute Respiratory Distress Syndrome

Diagnostic Assessment
See Table 67.6.

Management
General Care
- Identify and treat underlying cause
- Hemodynamic monitoring
- Proper patient positioning

Respiratory Therapy
- O_2 administration
- Mechanical ventilation (see Chapter 65)
- Low V_T ventilation
- Permissive hypercapnia
- PEEP
- Positioning strategies (e.g., prone)
- Extracorporeal membrane oxygenation (ECMO)

Supportive Care
- Nutrition therapy
- VTE prophylaxis
- VAP prophylaxis
- Inotropic and vasopressor drugs
  - norepinephrine (Levophed)
  - dopamine
  - dobutamine
- IV fluid administration
- Analgesia and sedation
- Neuromuscular blocking agents

PaO_2 within normal limits for age or at baseline on room air, (2) SaO_2 greater than 90%, (3) resolution of the precipitating factor(s), and (4) clear lungs on auscultation.

Implementation

Patients with moderate to severe ARDS receive care in an ICU. Even with appropriate therapy, the clinical course of ARDS is complex and unpredictable. Patients with ARDS often need several days of mechanical ventilation to allow time for the overwhelming inflammation and fluid accumulation in the lungs to begin resolving. Best practices for care of the patient with ARDS include (1) O_2 administration, (2) mechanical ventilation, (3) low V_T ventilation, (4) permissive hypercapnia, (5) PEEP, (6) prone positioning, and (7) extracorporeal membrane oxygenation (ECMO). Many of these practices are detailed in the *Acute Respiratory Distress Syndrome Clinical Network (ARDSNet) protocol.*[22]

Respiratory Therapy

Oxygen Administration. The primary goal of O_2 therapy is to correct hypoxemia. Initially, the use of a high-flow system that delivers higher O_2 concentrations to maximize O_2 delivery may be all that is needed. Continuously monitor SpO_2 to assess the effectiveness of O_2 therapy. However, for most patients diagnosed with ARDS, high-flow O_2 delivery, including BiPAP, is only a temporary measure. As respiratory failure worsens, high-flow O_2 will be not be able to keep the PaO_2 within acceptable ranges. Patients with moderate to severe ARDS and refractory hypoxemia need mechanical ventilation to keep the PaO_2 at or close to near-normal levels. However, even with mechanical ventilation, the patient may need an FIO_2 of 70%, 80%, or

higher to keep the PaO_2 at least 60 mm Hg. Most HCPs agree that in the injury and reparative phases, they may have to accept a lower than normal PaO_2 (e.g. PaO_2 55 to 80 mm Hg) and SpO_2 (88% to 95%).

Mechanical Ventilation. Mechanical ventilation is often delivered via a pressure-control type of ventilation. Pressure-control ventilation helps to keep the inspiratory and plateau pressures from becoming too high. This prevents alveolar overdistention and rupture. By reducing the amount of pressure going into the stiff, noncompliant lungs, we can help prevent further lung injury. However, no mode of mechanical ventilation is superior to the others.[23] Chapter 65 provides additional information on mechanical ventilation.

Low Tidal Volume (V_T) Ventilation. Patients with ARDS are ventilated with a low V_T of 4 to 8 mL/kg.[22] The delivery of a large V_T into stiff lungs is associated with volutrauma and barotrauma. Volutrauma causes *alveolar fractures* (damage or tears in the alveoli) and movement of fluids and protein into the alveolar spaces. Low V_T ventilation has reduced mortality and the risk for volutrauma.

Permissive Hypercapnia. As a result of delivering a lower than normal V_T to the patient with ARDS, the $PaCO_2$ level will slowly rise above normal limits. This is known as **permissive hypercapnia**. A $PaCO_2$ of up to 60 mm Hg is acceptable in the early phase of ARDS. The patient usually tolerates this rise in $PaCO_2$ if it is gradual, allowing the brain and systemic circulation to compensate. Permissive hypercapnia is not used for the patient with TBI or increased ICP.

Frequent ABG samples are needed, with careful monitoring of the pH, PaO_2, and $PaCO_2$ values. As per the ARDSNet protocol, the pH is kept between 7.30 and 7.45. CO_2 is a powerful stimulant to breathe. When permissive hypercapnia is used, the patient is usually given continuous IV analgesia and sedation.

Positive End-Expiratory Pressure (PEEP). During PPV, it is common to apply PEEP at 5 cm H_2O to compensate for loss of glottic function caused by the ET. PEEP increases functional residual capacity, or the volume of air left in the lungs at the end of a normal expiration. PEEP also helps open up ("recruit") collapsed alveoli.

We typically apply PEEP in increments of 3 to 5 cm H_2O until oxygenation is adequate, with an FIO_2 of 60% or less (if possible). PEEP may improve ventilation in respiratory units that collapse at low airway pressures, thus allowing the FIO_2 to be lowered. Patients with ARDS may need higher levels of PEEP (e.g., 10 to 20 cm H_2O). There is no identified optimal level of PEEP for patients with ARDS.

PEEP is not without complications. The added intrathoracic and intrapulmonic pressures generated by positive pressure remaining in the lungs and transmitted to surrounding structures (e.g., inferior vena cava, heart) at end expiration can compromise venous return. This in turn has the potential to decrease the amount of blood returning to both the right and left sides of the heart. Dramatic reductions in preload, CO, and BP can occur. High levels of PEEP or excess inspiratory pressures can cause barotrauma and volutrauma.

Prone Positioning. In the early phases of ARDS, fluid moves freely throughout the lung. Because of gravity, fluid pools in dependent regions of the lung. As a result, some alveoli are fluid filled (dependent areas) while others are air filled (nondependent areas). When the patient is supine, the heart and mediastinal contents place added pressure on the lungs. Consequently, the supine position predisposes all patients, including those with ARDS, to atelectasis.

Prone positioning is an option for patients with refractory hypoxemia who do not respond to other strategies to increase PaO_2. By turning the patient prone, perfusion may be better matched to ventilation. Air-filled alveoli in the anterior part of the lung become dependent. Alveoli in the posterior part of the lungs are "recruited" (given the opportunity to reexpand), improving oxygenation.

Some patients will have a big improvement in PaO_2 when prone with no change in FIO_2. The improvement in ventilation may be enough to allow a reduction in FIO_2 or PEEP. You may see hemodynamic instability (dysrhythmias, a decrease in BP) from fluid shifts when the patient is prone. There may be more need for airway suctioning as secretions are mobilized. Best practice suggests that patients be positioned prone early in the course of ARDS. They can stay in the prone position for up to 16 hours per day.[24] Placing a patient prone requires the presence of an ICU intensivist, respiratory therapist, and at least 3 to 4 nurses. Special attention must be given to securing the airway. Once prone, the patient should be positioned in a side-lying position.

◆ **Extracorporeal Membrane Oxygenation (ECMO).** Extracorporeal membrane oxygenation (ECMO) is used most often in specialized ICUs in major cities. Like hemodialysis, a large blood vessel is cannulated (most often the internal jugular, femoral artery, or femoral vein) and a catheter is inserted. The catheter is then connected to a device that allows the blood to exit the patient and pass across a gas-exchanging membrane outside the body. Within the ECMO unit, O_2 is delivered into the blood and CO_2 removed. Oxygenated blood is returned back to the patient. $ECCO_2R$ is like ECMO. It does not require as high of blood flow rates. It is only used to enhance oxygenation. Both ECMO and $ECCO_2R$ are expensive and require specially trained nurses and other personnel.

◆ **Medical Supportive Therapy**

The entire interprofessional team have important roles in the care of the patient with ARDS. All mechanically ventilated patients with ARDS in the ICU will have continuous heart rate, respiratory rate, BP, MAP, and SpO_2 monitoring. $EtCO_2$ monitoring is standard in the care of ARDS patients.[8]

Other positioning strategies for patients with ARDS include continuous lateral rotation therapy (CLRT) and kinetic therapy. CLRT provides continuous, slow, side-to-side turning of the patient by rotating the actual bed frame less than 40 degrees. The bed's lateral movement is maintained for 18 of every 24 hours to simulate postural drainage and help mobilize pulmonary secretions. The bed may contain a vibrator pack that provides chest physiotherapy. This feature assists with secretion mobilization and removal (Fig. 67.11). Kinetic therapy is like CLRT in that patients are rotated side-to-side 40 degrees or more. It is important to obtain baseline assessments of the patient's pulmonary status (e.g., respiratory rate and rhythm, breath sounds, ABGs, SpO_2) and continue to monitor the patient throughout the therapy.

Analgesia and Sedation. Analgesia and sedation, either by direct IV or continuous IV infusion, are important. Analgesia and sedation decrease the discomfort associated with the presence of an ET tube, help reduce WOB, and prevent ventilator dyssynchrony.

Patients who breathe asynchronously with mechanical ventilation may benefit from an adjustment of ventilator inspiratory flow rates or other settings. Patients who stay asynchronous with mechanical ventilation despite aggressive analgesia and sedation

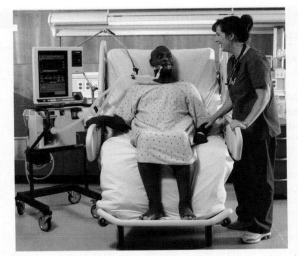

FIG. 67.11 TotalCare SpO2RT Bed System offers continuous lateral rotation therapy and percussion and vibration therapies. Patients can easily and quickly be repositioned. (© 2006 Hill-Rom Services, Inc. Reprinted with permission. All rights reserved.)

may need a neuromuscular blocking agent (NMBA). These drugs, such as vecuronium, pancuronium (Pavulon) or cisatracurium (Nimbex), relax skeletal muscles and promote synchrony with mechanical ventilation. Remember that a patient receiving neuromuscular blockade can appear to be asleep, but still be awake and in pain. For this reason, simultaneous administration of analgesia and sedation with NMBAs is essential.

> **! SAFETY ALERT** Neuromuscular Blockade
> - Always give concurrent analgesia and sedation to patients receiving a NMBA. This eliminates patient awareness, ensures patient comfort, and avoids the terrifying experience of being awake and in pain while paralyzed.
> - Use a NMBA for the shortest duration and at the lowest dose possible to avoid complications.

Monitoring levels of sedation in patients receiving NMBA is challenging. Levels of drug paralysis are monitored primarily by clinical assessment, including heart rate and BP, but more importantly, respiratory rate and whether the patient is taking breaths above the set rate on the ventilator.

◆ **Promoting Tissue Perfusion.** Patients with ARDS are at risk for hemodynamic compromise. Those on PPV and PEEP often have decreased CO. One cause is decreased venous return from the PEEP-induced increase in intrathoracic pressure. Impaired contractility and decreased preload can decrease CO. Changes in intrathoracic or intrapulmonary pressures from PPV can also decrease CO. Patients with an exacerbation of COPD or asthma and those receiving PPV are at risk for alveolar hyperinflation, increased right ventricular afterload, and excess intrathoracic pressures. These changes can limit blood flow from the right side of the heart, through the pulmonary vasculature, to the left side of the heart, and cause hemodynamic compromise (e.g., decreased CO). Blood return from the systemic circulation to the right side of the heart may be impaired, decreasing preload and CO.

Hemodynamic monitoring (e.g., CVP, CO, $ScvO_2$, SvO_2) is essential. This allows you to see trends, detect changes, and adjust therapy as needed. BP and mean arterial pressure (MAP) are important indicators of the adequacy of CO. Closely monitor BP and indicators of CO and tissue perfusion (SaO_2, mixed venous O_2 saturation) with the start of or changes in mechanical ventilation. A decrease in CO is treated by giving IV fluids, drugs, or both. (Chapter 66 discusses drugs used to treat decreased CO and shock.)

◆ **Maintaining Fluid Balance and Nutrition.** Maintaining fluid balance and nutrition is challenging. Increasing pulmonary capillary permeability results in fluid in the lungs and causes pulmonary edema. At the same time, the patient may be intravascularly volume depleted and at risk for hypotension and decreased CO from mechanical ventilation and PEEP.

Monitor hemodynamic parameters (e.g., CVP, stroke volume variation) and daily weights to assess the patient's fluid volume status. Monitor intake and output hourly. Keep the ARDS patient on the "dry" side. In other words, avoid aggressive resuscitation with IV fluids. ARDS patients typically have increased WOB because the alveoli, lungs, and spaces between the alveoli are partially or completely fluid filled. Since ARDS is an inflammatory process, diuretics play a minimal role.

Maintaining protein and energy stores is important. Nutritional depletion causes a loss of muscle mass, including the respiratory muscles, which may prolong mechanical ventilation and delay recovery. Ideally, enteral or parenteral nutrition should be started within 24 to 48 hours.

◆ **Evaluation**

The expected outcomes for the patient with ARDS are similar to those for a patient with ARF (see p. 1597). It is essential that the patient with ARDS be able to maintain and sustain adequate oxygenation and ventilation with decreasing amounts of O_2, be hemodynamically stable, and be free of complications.

CASE STUDY

Acute Respiratory Distress Syndrome

(© Thinkstock.)

Patient Profile

J.N. is a 58-yr-old white man who was admitted 36 hours ago to the surgical ICU after emergent surgery for a small-bowel obstruction, acute ischemic bowel, and perforated colon.

Past Medical History

- Mild obesity, hypertension, type 2 diabetes
- Lumbar spine surgery 5 years ago
- Chronic back pain controlled with oxycodone (Oxy-Contin) 15 mg PO 3 times daily

Operative Procedure

- Surgical procedure relieved small bowel obstruction, resected 2 feet of intestine, repaired the perforated colon, irrigated the abdominal cavity
- HR was 102 to 135, BP dropped to 70 mm Hg for 6 minutes, SpO$_2$ was greater than 90% for the duration of surgery
- Received 6 units of packed red blood cells and 4 L of 0.9% saline

Postoperative Status

J.N.'s pulmonary status worsened over the first 24 hours in the ICU. He required progressively higher FIO$_2$ via the mechanical ventilator. J.N. continued to have declining SaO$_2$ levels, increased WOB, and worsening hemodynamic status. He became more tachycardic. Despite direct IV analgesia and sedation, his respiratory rate increased and he was often "out-of-sync" with the ventilator. A chest x-ray showed bilateral pleural effusions and a right-sided pneumothorax, requiring chest tube placement. Immediately after chest tube placement, his SpO$_2$ decreased to 80% for 4 minutes. J.N. stayed dyssynchronous with the ventilator so continuous IV analgesia and sedation infusions were ordered. Neuromuscular blockade was started to decrease his WOB and achieve ventilator synchrony.

Current Status

J.N.'s oxygenation continues to worsen. He is still mechanically ventilated and is receiving 100% FIO$_2$ with PEEP 15 cm H$_2$O. Urine output has greatly decreased over the past 6 hours. He was diagnosed with AKI. His wife has brought in a copy of his advance directives. They state he does not want to be kept alive by artificial means. His wife and 2 adult children are at the bedside and voicing concerns about his status.

Objective Data
Physical Examination

- *General:* Sedated, paralyzed. Head of bed elevated 30 degrees. Skin cool, temperature 101° F (38.3° C) rectally
- *Respiratory:* ET tube in place with PPV. No accessory muscle use, retractions, or paradoxical breathing. Respiratory rate 18 breaths/min and in sync with ventilator. SpO$_2$ 88%, coarse crackles bilaterally throughout all lung fields. Ventilator settings: V$_T$ 350 mL, FIO$_2$ 100%, rate 18/min, PEEP 15 cm H$_2$O, peak inspiratory pressure 35 cm H$_2$O
- *Cardiovascular:*
- Apical-radial pulse equal, BP 96/54 mm Hg. 2+ carotid, radial, and femoral pulses; 1+ dorsalis pedis pulses. ECG is below:

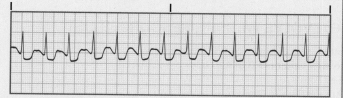

- *Gastrointestinal:* Surgical dressing dry and intact; colostomy draining a moderate amount of serosanguineous drainage
- *Urologic:* Indwelling bladder catheter draining concentrated, dark amber urine less than 30 mL/hr

Diagnostic Findings

- Current ABG: pH 7.23, PaO$_2$ 59 mm Hg, PaCO$_2$ 57 mm Hg, HCO$_3$ 16 mEq/L, O$_2$ saturation 88%.
- Hemoglobin 6.9 g/dL (69g/L), WBC 20.6/μL (20.6 × 10^9/L)
- BUN and creatinine values are increased
- Chest x-ray: Bilateral, scattered interstitial infiltrates compatible with ARDS

Discussion Questions

1. What is the cause of ARDS for J.N? Is this a direct or indirect cause?
2. How does the pathophysiology of ARDS predispose him to refractory hypoxemia?
3. What manifestations does J.N. have that support a diagnosis of ARDS?
4. Calculate the PaO$_2$/FIO$_2$ ratio. What does this value tell you about the seriousness of his condition?
5. What other complications is J.N. at risk for developing from ARDS?
6. ***Evidence-Based Practice:*** You are orienting a new nurse, who asks you why you allowed J.N.'s family to stay at the bedside during your physical assessment and morning rounds with the ICU team. How would you respond?
7. ***Priority Decision:*** What priority interventions should be implemented to improve J.N.'s respiratory status and hypoxemia?
8. ***Patient-Centered Care:*** What information would you give to J.N.'s family about his status?
9. ***Patient-Centered Care:*** Given the guidelines in the patient's advance directive, what ethical/legal issues could you encounter?

BRIDGE TO NCLEX EXAMINATION

The number of the question corresponds to the same-numbered outcome at the beginning of the chapter.

1. Which signs and symptoms distinguish hypoxemic from hypercapnic respiratory failure? *(select all that apply)*
   a. Cyanosis
   b. Tachypnea
   c. Morning headache
   d. Paradoxical breathing
   e. Use of pursed-lip breathing

2. An important consideration in selecting an O_2 delivery device for the patient with acute hypoxemic respiratory failure is to
   a. always start with noninvasive positive pressure ventilation.
   b. apply a low-flow device, such as a nasal cannula or face mask.
   c. be able to correct the PaO_2 to a normal level as quickly as possible.
   d. base the selection on the patient's condition and amount of FIO_2 needed.

3. The *most* common early clinical manifestations of ARDS that the nurse may see are
   a. dyspnea and tachypnea.
   b. cyanosis and apprehension.
   c. respiratory distress and frothy sputum.
   d. bradycardia and increased work of breathing

4. Interventions used in managing the patient with ARDS include *(select all that apply)*
   a. IV injection of surfactant.
   b. aggressive IV fluid resuscitation.
   c. giving adequate analgesia and sedation.
   d. elevating the head of bed 30 to 45 degrees when supine.
   e. monitoring hemodynamic parameters and daily weights.

5. Which intervention is *most* likely to prevent or limit volutrauma in the patient with ARDS who is mechanically ventilated?
   a. Increasing PEEP
   b. Increasing the inspiratory flow rate
   c. Use of low tidal volume ventilation
   d. Suctioning the patient via endotracheal tube hourly

1. a, b, d. 2. d. 3. a. 4. c, d, e. 5. c.

For rationales to these answers and even more NCLEX review questions, visit *http://evolve.elsevier.com/Lewis/medsurg.*

---

e EVOLVE WEBSITE/RESOURCES LIST

http://evolve.elsevier.com/Lewis/medsurg
Review Questions (Online Only)
Key Points
Answer Keys to Questions
- Rationales for Bridge to NCLEX Examination Questions
- Answer Guidelines for Case Study on p. 1603
Student Case Studies
- Patient With Acute Respiratory Failure and Ventilatory Management
- Patient With Pulmonary Embolism and Respiratory Failure
Nursing Care Plans
- eNursing Care Plan 67.1: Patient With Acute Respiratory Failure
Conceptual Care Map Creator
Audio Glossary
Content Updates

REFERENCES

1. Kaynar AM: Respiratory failure. Retrieved from *https://emedicine. medscape.com/article/167981-overview.*
2. Baird MS: *Manual of critical care nursing: Nursing interventions and collaborative management.* 7 ed, St Louis: Elsevier; 2016.
3. Levitzky MG: *Pulmonary physiology,* 9th ed, New York: McGraw-Hill; 2018.
4. Hess DR, Kacmarek RM: *Essentials of mechanical ventilation,* ed 3, New York, 2014, McGraw-Hill.
5. Sarkar M, Nirarjan N, Banyal PK: Mechanisms of hypoxemia, *Lung India* 34:47, 2017.
6. Patel BK: Acute hypoxemic respiratory failure. Retrieved from *www. merckmanuals.com/en-ca/professional/critical-care-medicine/respiratory-failure-and-mechanical-ventilation/acute-hypoxemic-respiratory-failure-ahrf,-ards.*
7. Davis TM, Olff C: Acute respiratory failure and acute lung injury. In Good VS, Kirkwood PL: *Advanced critical care nursing,* ed 2, St Louis, 2018, Elsevier.
8. Kerslake I, Kelly F: Uses of capnography in the critical care unit, *BMJ Education* 17:178, 2017.
9. DeWit S, Stromberg H, Dallred C: *Medical-surgical nursing: Concepts and practice,* ed 3, St Louis, 2017, Elsevier.
10. Cystic Fibrosis Foundation: Coughing and huffing. Retrieved from *www. cff.org/Life-With-CF/Treatments-and-Therapies/Airway-Clearance/ Coughing-and-Huffing/.*
11. Field JB: Chest physiotherapy. Retrieved from *www.merckmanuals.com/ en-ca/professional/pulmonary-disorders/pulmonary-rehabilitation/ chest-physiotherapy.*
12. Scala R, Pisani L: Non-invasive ventilation in acute respiratory failure: Which recipe for success? *Eur Resp Rev* 27:180029, 2018.
13. Knight J, Nigam Y: Anatomy and physiology of ageing 2: The respiratory system, *Nurs Times* 113:53, 2017.
14. Fan E, Brodie D, Slutsky AS: Acute respiratory distress syndrome: Advances in diagnosis and treatment, *JAMA* 319:698, 2018.
15. Stacy KM: Pulmonary disorders. In Urden LD, Stacy KM, Lough ME: *Critical care nursing: Diagnosis and management,* ed 8, St Louis, 2018, Elsevier.
16. European Respiratory Society: Acute respiratory distress syndrome. Retrieved from *www.erswhitebook.org/chapters/acute-respiratory-distress-syndrome/.*
17. Adigun M, McIntosh C, Onyilofor C: Treatment considerations for acute respiratory distress syndrome, *US Pharm* 41:HS6, 2016.
18. Reilly JP, Christie JD, Meyer NJ: Fifty years of research in ARDS: Genomic contributions and opportunities, *Am J Respir Crit Care Med* 196:1113, 2017.
19. Herridge MS, Moss M, Hough CL, et al: Recovery and outcomes after the acute respiratory distress syndrome (ARDS) in patients and their family caregivers, *Intensive Care Med* 42:725, 2016.
20. Tignanelli CJ, Wiktor AJ, Vatsaas CJ: Outcomes of acute kidney injury in patients with severe ARDS due to influenza A (H1N1) pdmo9 virus, *Am J Crit Care* 27:67, 2018.
21. Bienvenu OJ, Friedman LA, Colantuoni E: Psychiatric symptoms after acute respiratory distress syndrome: A 5-year longitudinal study, *Intensive Care Med* 44:38, 2018.
22. Fan E, Del Sorbo L, Goligher EC, et al: An official American Thoracic Society/European Society of Intensive Care Medicine/Society of Critical Care Medicine clinical practice guideline: Mechanical ventilation in adult patients with acute respiratory distress syndrome, *Am J Respir Crit Care Med* 195:1253, 2017.
23. Bein T, Grasso S, Moerer O, et al: The standard of care of patients with ARDS: Ventilatory settings and rescue therapies for refractory hypoxemia, *Intensive Care Med* 42:699, 2016.
24. Chiumello D, Coppola S, Froio S: Prone position in ARDS: A simple maneuver still underused, *Intensive Care Med* 44: 241, 2018.

68

Emergency and Disaster Nursing

Cathy Edson and Amy Meredith

The simple act of caring is heroic.

Edward Albert

ⓔ http://evolve.elsevier.com/Lewis/medsurg

CONCEPTUAL FOCUS

Gas Exchange   Perfusion
Interpersonal Violence   Thermoregulation

LEARNING OUTCOMES

1. Apply the steps in triage, the primary survey, and the secondary survey to a patient with a medical, surgical, or traumatic emergency.
2. Relate the pathophysiology to the assessment and interprofessional care of select environmental emergencies.
3. Relate the pathophysiology to the assessment and interprofessional care of select toxicologic emergencies.
4. Select appropriate nursing interventions for victims of violence.
5. Distinguish among the responsibilities of health care providers, the community, and select federal agencies in emergency and mass casualty incident preparedness.

KEY TERMS

drowning, p. 1615
emergency, p. 1620
family presence, p. 1607
frostbite, p. 1613
heat cramps, p. 1611

heat exhaustion, p. 1611
heatstroke, p. 1612
hypothermia, p. 1613
jaw-thrust maneuver, p. 1607
mass casualty incident (MCI), p. 1620

primary survey, p. 1607
secondary survey, p. 1609
submersion injury, p. 1615
terrorism, p. 1620
triage, p. 1606

Entire books are dedicated to the nursing care of emergency patients. It is a unique specialty that requires a solid understanding of basic nursing concepts and specific approaches to patient problems. Nurses unaccustomed to the emergency department (ED) often describe the flow as "chaotic" and uncertain. Certainly, it may have this appearance. The challenge of the ED is that the nurse does not know what patient will come through the doors. The trained ED nurse must be prepared to meet this challenge. This chapter presents an overview of the triage process and care of select emergency patients. Common emergency situations discussed include heat- and cold-related emergencies, submersion injuries, bites and stings, and various types of poisonings. The chapter concludes with a discussion of terrorism, mass casualty incidents, and the methods of response.

The emergency management of various medical, surgical, and traumatic emergencies is discussed throughout this book. Tables outline the emergency management of specific problems. Table 68.1 lists these emergency management tables by title, chapter number, and page.

More than 141 million people visit EDs each year.[1] Of these, 11.2 million patients are admitted to the hospital. This number is increasing for several reasons. These include (1) the inability to see a HCP, (2) an aging population, (3) shorter hospital stays resulting in frequent readmissions, (4) acute mental health crises, (5) ED and hospital closures, and (6) lack of or inadequate health insurance or a HCP. These factors result in overcrowding and long wait times.[2]

ED nurses care for patients of all ages with a variety of problems. However, some EDs specialize in certain patient populations or conditions, such as pediatric ED or trauma ED. The Emergency Nurses Association (ENA) is the specialty organization aimed at advancing emergency nursing practice. The ENA provides standards of care for nurses working in the ED. They offer a certification process that allows nurses to become certified emergency nurses (CENs).[3]

CARE OF EMERGENCY PATIENT

Recognizing life-threatening illness or injury is one of the most important goals of emergency nursing. Initiating interventions to reverse or prevent a crisis is often a priority before making a medical diagnosis. This process begins with your first contact with a patient. Prompt identification of patients who need immediate treatment and determining appropriate interventions are essential nurse competencies.

Triage

Triage, a French word meaning "to sort," refers to the process of rapidly determining patient acuity.[4] It is one of the most important assessment skills needed by ED nurses. Most often you will confront multiple patients who have a variety of problems. The triage process works on the premise that we must treat patients who have a threat to life before other patients.

A *triage system* identifies and categorizes patients so that the most critically ill are treated first. The ENA and American College of Emergency Physicians support the use of a 5-level triage system.[5] The *Emergency Severity Index* (ESI) is a 5-level triage system that incorporates concepts of illness severity and resource use (e.g., electrocardiogram [ECG], laboratory tests, radiology studies, IV fluids) to determine who should be treated first (Table 68.2). The ESI includes a triage algorithm that directs you to assign an ESI level to patients coming into the ED. The triage algorithm can be found in the ESI Implementation Handbook.[5]

First, assess the patient for any threats to life (ESI-1). Ask "Is the patient in imminent danger of dying?" Or, for ESI-2, is this a high-risk patient who should not wait to be seen? Next, evaluate patients who do not meet the criteria for ESI-1 or ESI-2 for the number of anticipated resources they may need. Assign patients to ESI-3, ESI-4, or ESI-5 based on this determination. Vital signs are important. Patients assigned to ESI-3 must have normal vital signs. Patients with abnormal vital signs may be reassigned to ESI-2.[5]

✚ TABLE 68.1 Emergency Management

Emergency Management Tables

Title	Chapter	Page
Abdominal Trauma	42	936
Acute Abdominal Pain	42	934
Acute GI Bleeding	41	919
Acute Soft Tissue Injury	62	1446
Acute Thyrotoxicosis	49	1155
Anaphylactic Shock	13	199
Chemical Burns	24	438
Chest Injuries	27	523
Chest Pain	33	723
Chest Trauma	27	523
Depressant Toxicity	10	149
Diabetic Ketoacidosis	48	1132
Dysrhythmias	35	760
Electrical Burns	24	437
Eye Injury	21	361
Fractured Extremity	62	1446
Head Injury	56	1315
Hyperthermia	68	1612
Hypoglycemia	48	1134
Hypothermia	68	1614
Inhalation Injury	24	437
Sexual Assault	53	1246
Shock	66	1576
Spinal Cord Injury	60	1409
Stimulant Toxicity	10	148
Stroke	57	1340
Submersion Injuries	68	1616
Thermal Burns	24	436
Tonic-Clonic Seizures	58	1361

❓ CHECK YOUR PRACTICE

You are working in the ED with your preceptor, who is a triage nurse. A 24-yr-old man arrives and states, "I think I have food poisoning. I've been vomiting all night and now I have diarrhea." The patient reports abdominal cramping that he rates as 6/10. He denies fever or chills. Vital signs: T = 97.8° F (36.6°C), HR = 94, RR = 16, BP = 121/74 mm Hg.
• Assign a triage acuity rating using the ESI.

After you complete the initial focused assessment to determine the presence of actual or potential threats to life, proceed with a more detailed assessment. A systematic approach to this assessment decreases the time needed to identify potential threats to life and limits the risk for overlooking a life-threatening condition. A primary and secondary survey is the approach used for all trauma patients. For nontrauma patients, the primary survey is followed by a focused assessment. Focused assessments are discussed in Chapter 3.

TABLE 68.2 Five-Level Emergency Severity Index (ESI)

Definition	ESI-1	ESI-2	ESI-3	ESI-4	ESI-5
Stability of vital functions (ABCs)	Unstable	Threatened	Stable	Stable	Stable
Life threat or organ threat	Obvious	Likely but not always obvious	Unlikely but possible	No	No
How soon should the HCP see the patient	Immediately	Within 10 min	Up to 1 hr	Could be delayed	Could be delayed
Expected resource intensity	High resource intensity Staff at bedside continuously Often mobilization of team response	High resource intensity Multiple, often complex diagnostic studies Frequent consultation Continuous monitoring	Medium to high resource intensity Multiple diagnostic studies (e.g., multiple laboratory studies, x-rays) or brief observation Complex procedure (e.g., IV fluids, drugs)	Low resource intensity 1 simple diagnostic study (e.g., x-ray) or simple procedure (e.g., sutures)	Low resource intensity Examination only
Examples	Cardiac arrest, intubated trauma patient, overdose with bradypnea, severe respiratory distress	Chest pain from ischemia, multiple trauma unless responsive	Abdominal pain or gynecologic disorders unless in severe distress, hip fracture in older patient	Closed extremity trauma, simple laceration, cystitis	Cold symptoms, minor burn, recheck (e.g., wound), prescription refill

Modified and reprinted with permission. © 1999, Richard C. Wuerz, MD, and David R. Eitel, MD.

Primary Survey

The primary survey (Table 68.3) focuses on airway, breathing, circulation (ABC), disability, exposure, facilitation of adjuncts and family, and other resuscitation aids. If uncontrolled external hemorrhage is noted, the usual ABC assessment format may be reprioritized to <C>ABC. The <C> stands for catastrophic hemorrhage. If present, it must be controlled first.[6] Apply direct pressure with a sterile dressing followed by a pressure dressing to any obvious bleeding sites.

The primary survey aims to identify life-threatening conditions so that appropriate interventions can be started (Table 68.4). You may identify life-threatening conditions related to ABCs at any point during the primary survey. When this occurs, start interventions immediately, before moving to the next step of the survey.

A = Alertness and Airway. Nearly all immediate trauma deaths occur because of airway obstruction. Saliva, bloody secretions, vomitus, laryngeal trauma, dentures, facial trauma, fractures, and the tongue can obstruct the airway. Patients at risk for airway compromise include those who drown or have seizures, anaphylaxis, foreign body obstruction, or cardiopulmonary arrest. If an airway is not maintained, obstruction of airflow, hypoxia, and death will result. Signs and symptoms in a patient with a compromised airway include dyspnea, inability to speak, gasping (agonal) breaths, foreign body in the airway, and trauma to the face or neck. The patient's alertness level is a crucial factor for choosing the right airway interventions. Determine level of consciousness (LOC) by assessing the patient's response to verbal and/or painful stimuli. A simple mnemonic to remember is *AVPU: A* = alert, *V* = responsive to voice, *P* = responsive to pain, and *U* = unresponsive.[6]

Airway maintenance should progress rapidly from the least to the most invasive method. Treatment includes opening the airway using the jaw-thrust maneuver (avoiding hyperextension of the neck) (Fig. 68.1), suctioning and/or removal of foreign body, inserting a nasopharyngeal or oropharyngeal airway (in unconscious patients only), and endotracheal intubation. If intubation is impossible because of airway obstruction, an emergency cricothyroidotomy or tracheotomy is done (see Chapter 26). Ventilate patients with 100% O_2 using a bag-valve-mask (BVM) device before intubation or cricothyroidotomy.[6]

Rapid-sequence intubation is the preferred procedure for securing an unprotected airway in the ED. It involves the use of sedatives and paralytic drugs. These drugs aid in intubation and reduce the risk for aspiration and airway trauma. (See Chapter 65 for more information on intubation.)

If the patient has a suspected spinal cord injury and is not already immobilized, the cervical spine must be stabilized at the same time as the assessment of the airway. This can be done with manual stabilization or the use of a rigid cervical collar (C collar). Keep the bed flat and continue to monitor airway patency and breathing effectiveness.

B = Breathing. Adequate airflow through the upper airway does not ensure adequate ventilation. Many problems cause breathing changes. Common ones include fractured ribs, pneumothorax, penetrating injury, allergic reactions, pulmonary emboli, and asthma attacks. Patients with these conditions may have a variety of signs and symptoms. The patient may have dyspnea, paradoxical or asymmetric chest wall movement, decreased or absent breath sounds on the affected side, visible wounds to the chest wall, cyanosis, tachycardia, and hypotension.

Every critically injured or ill patient has an increased metabolic and O_2 demand and should receive supplemental O_2. Give high-flow O_2 (100%) via a nonrebreather mask and monitor the patient's response. Life-threatening conditions (e.g., flail chest, tension pneumothorax) can severely and quickly compromise ventilation. Interventions may include BVM ventilation with 100% O_2, needle decompression, intubation, and treatment of the underlying cause.

C = Circulation. An effective circulatory system includes the heart, intact blood vessels, and adequate blood volume. Uncontrolled internal or external bleeding places a person at risk for hemorrhagic shock (see Chapter 66). Check either a femoral or carotid pulse. Peripheral pulses may be absent due to direct injury or vasoconstriction. Assess the quality and rate of the pulse if found. Assess the skin for color, temperature, and moisture. Altered mental status and delayed capillary refill (longer than 3 seconds) are common signs of shock. When evaluating capillary refill in cold environments, remember that a cold temperature delays refill.

Insert IV lines into veins in the upper extremities unless contraindicated, such as in an open fracture or an injury that affects limb circulation. Insert 2 large-bore (14- to 16-gauge) IV catheters. Start aggressive fluid resuscitation using normal saline or lactated Ringer's solution. Consider intraosseous or central venous access if unable to rapidly obtain venous access. (See Chapter 66 for more information on hypovolemic shock and fluid resuscitation.)

The HCP may order type-specific packed red blood cells if needed. In an emergency (life-threatening) situation, give blood that is not cross-matched (e.g., O negative) if immediate transfusion is needed.

D = Disability. Conduct a brief neurologic examination as part of the primary survey. The patient's LOC is a measure of the degree of disability. Use the Glasgow Coma Scale (GCS) to determine the LOC (see Table 56.5).[7] This allows for consistent communication among the interprofessional care team. Remember! The GCS is not accurate for intubated or aphasic patients. Last, assess the pupils for size, shape, equality, and reactivity.

E = Exposure and Environmental Control. Remove clothing from all trauma patients to perform a thorough physical assessment. This often requires cutting off the patient's clothing. Be careful not to cut through any area that is forensic evidence (e.g., bullet hole). Do not remove any impaled objects (e.g., knife). Removing these could result in serious bleeding and further injury. Once the patient is exposed, use warming blankets, overhead warmers, and warmed IV fluids to limit heat loss, prevent hypothermia, and maintain privacy.

Obtain a full set of vital signs, including BP, heart rate, respiratory rate, O_2 saturation, and temperature after the patient is exposed. If the patient has sustained or is suspected of having sustained chest trauma, or if the BP is abnormally high or low, obtain a BP in both arms.

F = Facilitate Adjuncts and Family. Research supports the benefits for patients, caregivers, and staff of allowing family presence during resuscitation and invasive procedures.[8] Patients report that caregivers provide comfort, serve as advocates for them, and help remind the care team of their "personhood." Caregivers who wish to be present during invasive procedures and resuscitation view themselves as active participants in the care process. They believe that they comfort the patient and that it is their right to be with the patient. Nurses report that family members serve as "patient helpers" and "staff

TABLE 68.3   Emergency Assessment

Primary Survey

Assessment	Interventions
Alertness and Airway With Cervical Spine Stabilization and/or Immobilization	
• Assess for catastrophic external bleeding. • Assess alertness (e.g., AVPU). • Assess for respiratory distress. • Determine airway patency. • Check for loose teeth or foreign bodies. • Assess for bleeding, vomitus, or edema.	• Control bleeding with direct pressure and pressure dressings. • Open airway using jaw-thrust maneuver. • Remove or suction any foreign bodies. • Insert oropharyngeal or nasopharyngeal airway, tracheostomy. • Initiate rapid sequence intubation. • Immobilize cervical spine using rigid cervical collar and cervical immobilization device.
Breathing	
• Assess ventilation. • Scan chest for signs of breathing. • Look for paradoxical movement of the chest wall during inspiration and expiration. • Note use of accessory muscles or abdominal muscles. • Observe and count respiratory rate. • Note color of nail beds, mucous membranes. • Auscultate lungs. • Assess for jugular venous distention and trachea position.	• Give supplemental O_2 via appropriate delivery system (e.g., nonrebreather mask). • Ventilate with bag-valve-mask with 100% O_2 if respirations are inadequate or absent. • Prepare to intubate if severe respiratory distress (e.g., agonal breaths) or arrest. • Have suction available. • If absent breath sounds, prepare for needle thoracostomy and chest tube insertion.
Circulation	
• Check carotid or femoral pulse. • Palpate pulse for quality and rate. • Assess skin color, temperature, moisture. • Check capillary refill.	• If absent pulse, start cardiopulmonary resuscitation and advanced life support measures. • If shock symptoms or hypotensive, start 2 large-bore (14- to 16-gauge) IVs and start infusions of normal saline or lactated Ringer's solution. • Consider intraosseous or central venous access if IV access cannot be rapidly obtained. • Give blood products if ordered.
Disability	
• Assess level of consciousness by determining response to verbal and/or painful stimuli (e.g., Glasgow Coma Scale). • Assess pupils for size, shape, equality, and reactivity.	• Periodically reassess level of consciousness, mental status, and pupil size and reactivity.
Exposure and Environmental Control	
• Assess full body for determination of additional or related injuries. • Assess environment.	• Remove clothing for adequate examination. • Stabilize any impaled objects. • Keep patient warm with blankets, warmed IV fluids, overhead lights to prevent heat loss, if appropriate. • Maintain privacy.
Facilitate Adjuncts and Family	
• Assess vital signs and pulse oximetry. • Determine caregiver's desire to be present during invasive procedures and/or cardiopulmonary resuscitation.	• Obtain bilateral blood pressures if patient has sustained or is suspected of having sustained chest trauma, or if the BP is abnormal. • Assign health team member to support caregiver(s). • Provide emotional support to patient and caregiver.
Get Resuscitation Adjuncts	
• Determine need for adjunct measures for monitoring the patient's condition.	• Obtain laboratory tests, such as type and crossmatch, CBC and metabolic panel, blood alcohol, toxicology screening, ABGs, coagulation profile, cardiac biomarkers, pregnancy. • Continuously monitor ECG. • Insert NG tube; insert orogastric tube in a patient with significant head or facial trauma. • Monitor oxygenation and ventilation (e.g., continuous pulse oximetry, capnography). • Manage pain with pharmacologic (e.g., NSAIDs, IV opioids) and non-pharmacologic (e.g., distraction, positioning, music) pain management strategies. • Provide comfort measures as appropriate (e.g., ice, position of comfort, warm blanket).

AVPU, A = alert, V = responsive to voice, P= responsive to pain, and U = unresponsive.

TABLE 68.4 Potential Life-Threatening Conditions Found During Primary Survey*

Airway
- Inhalation injury (e.g., fire victim)
- Obstruction (partial or complete) from foreign bodies, debris (e.g., vomitus), or tongue
- Penetrating wounds and/or blunt trauma to upper airway structures

Breathing
- Anaphylaxis
- Flail chest with pulmonary contusion
- Hemothorax
- Pneumothorax (e.g., open, tension)

Circulation
- Direct cardiac injury (e.g., myocardial infarction, trauma)
- Pericardial tamponade
- Shock (e.g., massive burns, hypovolemia)
- Uncontrolled external hemorrhage
- Hypothermia

Disability
- Head injury
- Stroke

* List is not all-inclusive.

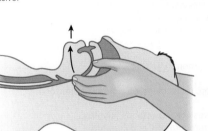

FIG. 68.1 Jaw-thrust maneuver is the recommended procedure for opening the airway of an unconscious patient with a possible neck or spinal injury. With the patient lying supine, kneel at the top of the head. Place 1 hand on each side of the patient's head, resting your elbows on the surface. Grasp the angles of the patient's lower jaw and lift the jaw forward with both hands without tilting the head.

helpers." It is essential to assign an interprofessional team member to explain the care being delivered and answer questions if a caregiver is present during resuscitation or invasive procedures.

G = Get Resuscitation Adjuncts. Start adjunct measures for monitoring the patient's condition, if not already done. Use the mnemonic "LMNOP" to remember these resuscitation aids:

L: Laboratory tests, such as type and crossmatch, complete blood count (CBC) and metabolic panel, blood alcohol, toxicology screening, arterial blood gases (ABGs), coagulation profile, cardiac biomarkers, pregnancy test, and urinalysis.

M: Monitor ECG for heart rate and rhythm.

N: Nasogastric (NG) tube to decompress and empty the stomach, reduce the risk for aspiration, and test the contents for blood. Place an orogastric tube in a patient with significant head or facial trauma since an NG tube could enter the brain.

O: Oxygenation and ventilation assessment. Continuously monitor O_2 saturation and end-tidal CO_2 ($EtCO_2$) if the patient is intubated (see Chapter 65).

P: Pain assessment and management

Most patients who come to the ED report pain.[9] Providing comfort measures is critical when caring for patients in the ED. Many EDs have pain management protocols for nurses to use to treat pain early, beginning at triage. Pain management strategies should include a combination of pharmacologic and nonpharmacologic measures. You are the advocate in ensuring comfort measures for the patient.

Secondary Survey

The secondary survey begins after addressing each step of the primary survey and starting any lifesaving interventions. The secondary survey is a brief, systematic process that aims to identify *all* injuries (Table 68.5). It is valuable for discovering unknown problems in patients with a poor or confusing history.[6]

H = History and Head-to-Toe Assessment. Obtain a history and mechanism of the injury or illness. These details provide clues to the cause and guide specific assessment and interventions. The patient may not be able to give a history. However, caregivers, friends, bystanders, and prehospital personnel can often give necessary information.

SAMPLE is a memory aid that prompts you to ask about:

S: Symptoms associated with the injury or illness

A: Allergies (e.g., drugs, food, latex, environment) and tetanus status

M: Medication history

P: Past health history (e.g., preexisting medical or psychiatric conditions, surgeries, smoking history, recent use of drugs or alcohol, last menstrual period, baseline mental status)

L: Last meal/oral intake

E: Events or environmental factors leading to the illness or injury

Details of the incident are important because the mechanism of injury and injury patterns can predict specific injuries. For example, a restrained front-seat passenger may have knee or femur fractures from hitting the dashboard and a chest injury from the airbag. Those who fell off a ladder or roof may have fractures, spinal cord injury, or head trauma.

Head, Neck, and Face. Check eyes for extraocular movements. A disconjugate gaze is a sign of neurologic damage. Battle's sign, or bruising directly behind the ears, may indicate a fracture of the base or posterior part of the skull. "Raccoon eyes," or periorbital bruising, usually occurs with a fracture of the base of the frontal part of the skull. Check the ears for blood and cerebrospinal fluid. Do not block clear drainage from the ear or nose.

Chest. Inspection and palpation of the chest will clue the nurse for heart and lung injuries. These may be life threatening and need immediate intervention.

Abdomen and Flanks. Frequent evaluation for subtle changes in the abdomen is essential. Motor vehicle crashes and assaults can cause blunt trauma. Penetrating trauma tends to injure specific organs. Stabilize, but do not remove, any impaled objects. They must be removed in a controlled environment, such as the operating room.

If the patient has blunt abdominal trauma or you suspect intraabdominal hemorrhage, perform a *focused abdominal sonography for trauma* (FAST).[6] This procedure can identify blood in the peritoneal space and assess cardiac function. It is noninvasive and done quickly at the bedside. However, a FAST cannot rule out a retroperitoneal bleed. If one is suspected, a CT scan is usually done.

Pelvis and Perineum. Inspect and gently palpate the pelvis. Do not rock the pelvis. Pain may indicate a pelvic fracture and the need for imaging. Assess for bladder distention, hematuria, dysuria, or inability to void. The HCP may perform a rectal examination to check for blood, prostate gland problems, and loss of sphincter tone (e.g., spinal cord injury).

Extremities. Assess the upper and lower extremities for point tenderness, crepitus, and deformities. If not done prehospital,

TABLE 68.5 Emergency Assessment

Secondary Survey

Assessment	Interventions
History and Head-to-Toe Assessment	
History	• Obtain details of the incident/illness, mechanism and pattern of injury, length of time since incident occurred, injuries suspected, treatment provided and patient's response, level of consciousness.
	• Use the mnemonic **SAMPLE** to determine **S**ymptoms associated with injury or illness; **A**llergies, including tetanus status; **M**edication history; **P**ast health history (e.g., preexisting medical/psychiatric conditions, last menstrual period); **L**ast meal/oral intake; and **E**vents/Environment preceding illness or injury.
Head, neck, and face	• Note general appearance, including skin color.
	• Assess face and scalp for lacerations, bone or soft tissue deformity, tenderness, bleeding, foreign bodies.
	• Inspect eyes, ears, nose, and mouth for bleeding, foreign bodies, drainage, pain, deformity, bruising, lacerations.
	• Palpate head for depressions of cranial or facial bones, contusions, hematomas, areas of softness, bony crepitus.
	• Assess neck for stiffness, pain in cervical vertebrae, tracheal deviation, distended neck veins, bleeding, edema, difficulty swallowing, bruising, subcutaneous emphysema, bony crepitus.
Chest	• Observe rate, depth, and effort of breathing, including chest wall movement and use of accessory muscles.
	• Palpate for bony crepitus and subcutaneous emphysema.
	• Auscultate breath sounds.
	• Obtain 12-lead ECG and chest x-ray.
	• Inspect for external signs of injury: petechiae, bleeding, cyanosis, bruises, abrasions, lacerations, old scars.
Abdomen and flanks	• Look for symmetry of abdominal wall and bony structures.
	• Inspect for external signs of injury: bruises, abrasions, lacerations, punctures, old scars.
	• Auscultate for bowel sounds.
	• Palpate for masses, guarding, femoral pulses.
	• Note type and location of pain, rigidity, or distention of abdomen.
Pelvis and perineum	• Gently palpate pelvis.
	• Assess genitalia for blood at the meatus, priapism, bruising, rectal bleeding, anal sphincter tone.
	• Determine ability to void.
Extremities	• Inspect for signs of external injury: deformity, bruising, abrasions, lacerations, swelling.
	• Observe skin color and palpate skin for pain, tenderness, temperature, and crepitus.
	• Evaluate movement, strength, and sensation in arms and legs.
	• Assess quality and symmetry of peripheral pulses.
Inspect posterior surfaces	• Logroll and inspect and palpate back for deformity, bleeding, lacerations, bruises. Maintain cervical spine immobilization, if appropriate.

splint injured extremities above and below the injury to decrease further soft tissue injury and pain. The HCP should realign grossly deformed, pulseless extremities before splinting. Check pulses before and after movement or splinting of an extremity. A pulseless extremity is a time-critical emergency. Immobilize and elevate injured extremities and apply ice packs. Antibiotics are given for open fractures to prevent infection.

Assess extremities for *compartment syndrome*. This occurs over several hours as pressure and swelling increase inside a muscle compartment of an extremity. This compromises the viability of the muscles, nerves, and arteries. Potential causes include crush injuries, fractures, edema, and hemorrhage.

I = Inspect Posterior Surfaces. An often overlooked part of the assessment is the back of the patient. Logroll the trauma patient while protecting the cervical spine. Up to 4 or more people with 1 person supporting the head may be needed to complete this assessment.

Acute Care and Evaluation

Once the secondary survey is complete, record all findings. Give tetanus prophylaxis based on vaccination history and the condition of any wounds (Table 68.6).[10]

Ongoing monitoring and evaluation are critical. Provide appropriate care and assess the patient's response. The evaluation of airway patency and the effectiveness of breathing is always the highest priority. Monitor respiratory rate and rhythm, O_2 saturation, and ABGs (if ordered) to evaluate the patient's respiratory status. A portable chest x-ray is done to confirm exact placement of tubes.

Closely monitor LOC; vital signs; quality of peripheral pulses; and skin temperature, color, and moisture for key information about circulation and perfusion. When indicated, insert an indwelling catheter to decompress the bladder, monitor urine output, and check for hematuria. Notify the HCP for any changes that may occur to the patient during this ongoing assessment process.

Depending on the patient's injuries or illness, the patient may be (1) transported for diagnostic tests (e.g., CT scan, angiography) or to the operating room for immediate surgery; (2) admitted; or (3) transferred to another facility. You may go with critically ill patients on transports. You are responsible for monitoring the patient during transport, notifying the HCP should the patient's condition become unstable, and starting life-support measures as needed.

Cardiac Arrest and Targeted Temperature Management

Many patients arrive at the ED in cardiac arrest. Patients with nontraumatic, out-of-hospital cardiac arrest benefit from a combination of good chest compressions and rapid defibrillation (see Appendix A), targeted temperature management (TTM), and supportive care. TTM for at least 24 hours after the return of spontaneous circulation (ROSC) decreases mortality rates and improves neurologic outcomes in many patients.[11] It is recommended for all patients who are comatose or who do not follow commands after ROSC.

TTM, also called therapeutic hypothermia, involves 3 phases: induction, maintenance, and rewarming. The induction phase begins in the ED. The goal core temperature is 89.6°

TABLE 68.6 Tetanus Vaccines and TIG for Wound Management

Vaccination History	TYPE OF WOUND	
	Clean, Minor Wounds	All Other Wound
Age 11 and Older*		
Unknown or <3 doses of tetanus toxoid-containing vaccine	Tdap and recommend catch-up vaccination	Tdap and recommend catch-up vaccination TIG
≥3 doses of tetanus toxoid-containing vaccine *and* <5yr since last dose	No indication	No indication
≥3 doses of tetanus toxoid-containing vaccine *and* 5–10yr since last dose	No indication	Tdap preferred (if not yet received) or Td
≥3 doses of tetanus toxoid–containing vaccine *and* >10yr since last dose	Tdap preferred (if not yet received) or Td	Tdap preferred (if not yet received) or Td

Source: Centers for Disease Control and Prevention: Tetanus. Retrieved from *www.cdc.gov/tetanus/clinicians.html.*

*Pregnant women: As part of standard wound management care to prevent tetanus, a tetanus toxoid–containing vaccine might be recommended for wound management in a pregnant woman if ≥5 yr have elapsed since previous Td booster. If a Td booster is indicated for a pregnant woman, Tdap should be given.

Td, Tetanus-diphtheria toxoid absorbed; *Tdap,* tetanus toxoid, reduced diphtheria toxoid, and acellular pertussis vaccine; *TIG,* tetanus immune globulin (human).

to 96.8°F (32° to 36°C). We use a variety of methods to cool patients. These include cold saline infusions and surface cooling devices (e.g., Arctic Sun).[12] Patients need intubation, mechanical ventilation, and invasive monitoring and require continuous assessment.[12] Protocols often direct the care of these patients.

Death in the Emergency Department

The loss of life in the ED is a stressful event. Many times, death is sudden and happens after an accident or unexpected illness (e.g., myocardial infarction [MI]). Sudden death is by its nature unexpected and thus shocking for family and friends.[13] It is important for you to identify and manage your feelings about sudden death so you can help them begin the grieving process (see Chapter 9).

You play a key role in providing comfort. Provide a private area for them to say goodbye, and, if appropriate, arrange for a visit from a chaplain. Assist the family by collecting the personal belongings and making mortuary arrangements. At times, you may need to contact the medical examiner or coroner. An autopsy may be done at the family's request, or if death occurred within 24 hours of ED admission, from suspected trauma or violence, or in an unusual way.

Many patients who die in the ED could potentially be candidates for *non–heart-beating donation.* We can harvest certain tissues and organs (e.g., corneas, heart valves, skin, bone, and kidneys) from patients after death. *Organ procurement organizations* aid in screening potential donors, counseling donor families, obtaining informed consent, and harvesting organs from patients who are on life support or who die in the ED.[14] Approaching caregivers about donation after an unexpected death can be distressing to both the staff and caregivers. However, for many, the act of donation may be the first positive step in the grieving process.

Gerontologic Considerations: Emergency Care

People older than 65 account for 16% of all ED visits.[15] Regardless of a patient's age, aggressive interventions are provided for all injuries or illnesses unless the patient has a preexisting terminal illness, an extremely low chance for survival, or an advance directive indicating a different course of action.

Understanding the physiologic and psychosocial aspects of aging will improve the care delivered to older adults in the ED (see Chapter 5). Many older adults dismiss their symptoms as simply "normal for their age." It is important to fully explore any complaint by an older adult.

The older population is at high risk for injury because of the many changes that occur with aging. Falls are the leading cause of injury.[16] The most common causes of falls in older adults are generalized weakness, environmental hazards, syncope, and orthostatic hypotension. When assessing a patient who has fallen, determine whether the physical findings may have caused the fall or are due to the fall itself. For example, a patient may come to the ED with acute confusion. The confusion may be due to a stroke that caused the patient to fall. Or, the patient may have a head injury because of a fall from tripping on a rug.

ENVIRONMENTAL EMERGENCIES

Increased interest in outdoor activities, such as running, cycling, skiing, and swimming, has increased the number of environmental emergencies seen in the ED. Illness or injury may be caused by the activity, exposure to weather, or attack from various animals or humans. Specific environmental emergencies discussed in this section include heat-related emergencies, cold-related emergencies, submersion injuries, bites, stings, and envenomation.

HEAT-RELATED EMERGENCIES

Brief exposure to intense heat or prolonged exposure to less intense heat leads to heat stress. This occurs when thermoregulatory mechanisms, such as sweating, vasodilation, and increased respirations, cannot compensate for exposure to increased ambient temperatures. Ambient temperature is a product of environmental temperature and humidity. Strenuous activities in hot or humid environments, clothing that interferes with perspiration, high fevers, and preexisting illnesses predispose people to heat stress (Table 68.7). Table 68.8 presents the management of heat-related emergencies.

Heat Cramps

Heat cramps are severe cramps in large muscle groups fatigued by heavy work. Cramps are brief and intense and tend to occur during rest after exercise or heavy labor. Nausea, tachycardia, pallor, weakness, and profuse diaphoresis are often present. The condition is seen most often in healthy, acclimated athletes with inadequate fluid intake. Cramps resolve rapidly with rest and oral or parenteral replacement of sodium and water. Elevation, gentle massage, and analgesia minimize pain associated with heat cramps. Tell the patient to avoid strenuous activity for at least 12 hours. Discharge teaching should emphasize salt replacement during strenuous exercise in hot, humid environments. You can recommend the use of commercially prepared electrolyte solutions.

Heat Exhaustion

Prolonged exposure to heat over hours or days leads to **heat exhaustion.** This is a clinical syndrome characterized by fatigue, nausea, vomiting, extreme thirst, and feelings of anxiety. Hypotension, tachycardia, elevated body temperature, dilated pupils, mild confusion, ashen color, and profuse diaphoresis are present. Heat exhaustion usually occurs in people engaged in strenuous activity in hot, humid weather.

Always correlate fluid replacement to clinical and laboratory findings. Place a moist sheet over the patient to decrease core temperature through evaporative heat loss. Consider hospital admission for older adults, the chronically ill, or those who do not improve within 3 to 4 hours.

Heatstroke

Heatstroke is the most serious form of heat stress and is a medical emergency. It results from failure of the hypothalamic thermoregulatory processes. Increased sweating, vasodilation, and increased respiratory rate deplete fluids and electrolytes, specifically sodium. Eventually, sweat glands stop functioning. Core temperature increases rapidly, within 10 to 15 minutes. The brain is extremely sensitive to thermal injuries. Cerebral edema and hemorrhage may occur from direct thermal injury to the brain and decreased cerebral blood flow. Death from heatstroke is directly related to the amount of time that the patient's body temperature is high.[6] Prognosis is related to age, baseline health status, and length of exposure. Older adults and those with diabetes, chronic kidney disease, heart disease, pulmonary disease, or other physiologic compromise are particularly prone.

Interprofessional Care. Treatment focuses on stabilizing the patient's ABCs, rapidly reducing the core temperature, and monitoring for dysrhythmias. Give 100% O_2 to compensate for the patient's hypermetabolic state. Ventilation with a BVM or intubation and mechanical ventilation may be needed. Place the patient on continuous ECG monitoring and pulse oximetry. Monitor laboratory findings. Correcting electrolyte imbalances and coagulation abnormalities is critical.

Place the patient in a cool environment. Promote evaporative cooling by removing clothing and spraying the patient with lukewarm water in front of a large fan.[6] Other cooling methods include conductive cooling (e.g., immersing the patient in a cool

---

TABLE 68.7 Risk Factors for Heat-Related Emergencies

Alcohol

Age
- Infants
- Older adults

Environmental Conditions
- High environmental temperatures
- High relative humidity

Preexisting Illness
- Cardiovascular disease
- Cystic fibrosis
- Dehydration
- Diabetes
- Obesity
- Skin disorders (e.g., large burn scars)
- Stroke or other CNS lesion

Prescription Drugs
- Anticholinergics
- Antihistamines
- Antiparkinsonian drugs
- Antispasmodics
- β-Adrenergic blockers
- Butyrophenones
- Diuretics
- Phenothiazines
- Tricyclic antidepressants

Street Drugs
- Amphetamines
- Jimson weed
- Lysergic acid diethylamide (LSD)
- Phencyclidine (PCP)
- 3,4-Methylenedioxymethamphetamine (MDMA, Ecstasy)

Adapted from Howard PK, Steinmann RA, eds: *Sheehy's emergency nursing*, ed 6, St Louis, 2010, Mosby.

✚ TABLE 68.8 Emergency Management

Hyperthermia

Etiology	Assessment Findings	Interventions
Environmental • Lack of acclimatization • Physical exertion, especially during hot weather • Prolonged exposure to extreme temperatures **Trauma** • Head injury • Spinal cord injury **Metabolic** • Dehydration • Diabetes • Thyrotoxicosis **Drugs** • Amphetamines • Antihistamines • β-Adrenergic blockers • Diuretics • Phenothiazines • Tricyclic antidepressants **Other** • Alcohol • Cardiovascular disease • CNS disorders	**Heat Cramps** • Severe muscle contractions in exerted muscles • Thirst **Heat Exhaustion** • Altered mental status (e.g., anxiety) • Ashen, pale skin • Extreme thirst • Fatigue, weakness • Hypotension • Profuse sweating • Tachycardia • Temperature (99.6° to 105.8°F [37.5° to 41°C]) • Weak, thready pulse **Heatstroke** • Altered mental status (ranging from confusion to coma) • Hot, dry skin • Hypotension • Tachycardia • Tachypnea • Temperature >105.8°F (41°C) • Weakness	**Initial** • Manage and maintain ABCs. • Provide high-flow O_2 via nonrebreather mask or BVM. • Establish IV access and begin fluid replacement for significant heat injury. • Place patient in a cool environment. • For patient with heatstroke, start rapid cooling measures: remove patient's clothing, place wet sheets over patient, and place in front of fan; immerse in a cool water bath; give cool IV fluids or lavage with cool fluids. • Obtain 12-lead ECG. • Obtain blood for electrolytes and CBC. • Insert urinary catheter. **Ongoing Monitoring** • Monitor ABCs, temperature and vital signs, level of consciousness. • Monitor heart rhythm, O_2 saturation, and urine output. • Replace electrolytes as needed. • Monitor urine for development of myoglobinuria. • Monitor clotting studies for development of disseminated intravascular coagulation.

water bath); applying ice packs to the groins and axillae; and, in refractory cases, peritoneal or rectal lavage with iced fluids.

Closely monitor the patient's temperature and control shivering. Shivering increases core temperature due to the heat generated by muscle activity. This complicates cooling efforts. The HCP may order drugs to control shivering.

Heat stroke places the patient at risk for kidney injury due to *rhabdomyolysis*. It is a serious syndrome caused by the breakdown of skeletal muscle. Carefully monitor the urine for color, amount, pH, and myoglobin.

Patient and caregiver teaching focuses on how to avoid future problems. Stress the importance of proper hydration during hot weather and physical exercise. Teach patients the early signs of and interventions for heat-related stress.

COLD-RELATED EMERGENCIES

Cold injuries may be localized (e.g., frostbite) or systemic (e.g., hypothermia). Contributing factors include age, duration of exposure, environmental temperature, homelessness, preexisting conditions, drugs that suppress shivering, and alcohol intoxication. Smokers have an increased risk for cold-related injury because of the vasoconstrictive effects of nicotine.

Frostbite

Frostbite is true tissue freezing that results in the formation of ice crystals in the tissues and cells. Peripheral vasoconstriction is the first response to cold stress and results in a decrease in blood flow and vascular stasis. As cell temperature decreases, and ice crystals form in intracellular spaces, the organelles are damaged, and the cell membrane destroyed. This results in edema.

Depth of frostbite depends on ambient temperature, length of exposure, type and condition (wet or dry) of clothing, and contact with metal surfaces. Other factors that affect severity include skin color (those with dark skin are more prone to frostbite), lack of acclimatization, previous episodes, exhaustion, and poor peripheral vascular status.

Superficial frostbite involves the skin and subcutaneous tissue, usually the ears, nose, fingers, and toes. The skin appearance ranges from waxy pale yellow to blue to mottled. The skin feels crunchy and frozen. The patient may report tingling, numbness, or a burning sensation. Handle the area carefully and never squeeze, massage, or scrub the injured tissue because it is easily damaged. Swelling will occur with thawing. So, remove clothing and jewelry as they may constrict the extremity and decrease circulation.

Immerse the affected area in circulating water that is temperature controlled (98.6° to 104°F) [37° to 40°C]). Use warm soaks for the face. The patient often has a warm, stinging sensation as tissue thaws. Blisters form within a few hours (Fig. 68.2). The blisters should be debrided, and a sterile dressing applied.[17] Avoid heavy blankets and clothing because friction and weight can lead to sloughing of damaged tissue. Rewarming is extremely painful. Residual pain may last weeks or even years. Give analgesia and tetanus prophylaxis as appropriate. Evaluate the patient with superficial frostbite for systemic hypothermia.

Deep frostbite involves muscle, bone, and tendon. The skin is white, hard, and insensitive to touch. The area has the appearance of deep thermal injury with mottling gradually progressing to gangrene (Fig. 68.3). Immerse the affected extremity in a temperature-controlled, circulating water bath (98.6° to 104°F [37° to 40°C]) until flushing occurs distal to the injured area.

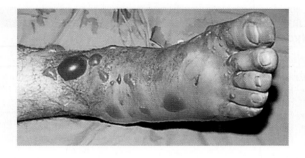

FIG. 68.2 Edema and blister formation 24 hours after frostbite injury occurring in an area covered by a tightly fitted boot. (Courtesy Cameron Bangs, MD. From Auerbach PS, Donner HJ, Weiss EA: *Field guide to wilderness medicine*, ed 2, St Louis, 2003, Mosby.)

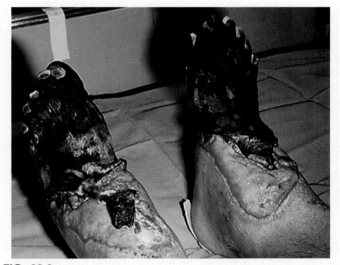

FIG. 68.3 Gangrenous necrosis 6 weeks after the frostbite injury shown in Fig. 68.2. (Courtesy Cameron Bangs, MD. From Auerbach PS, Donner HJ, Weiss EA: *Field guide to wilderness medicine*, ed 2, St Louis, 2003, Mosby.)

After rewarming, elevate the extremity to reduce edema. Significant edema may begin within 3 hours, with blistering in 6 hours to days. IV analgesia is needed in severe frostbite because of the pain associated with tissue thawing. All patients should start on nonsteroidal antiinflammatory drugs (NSAIDs) because of their dual affect as an analgesic and antiinflammatory. Give tetanus prophylaxis and evaluate the patient for systemic hypothermia.

Amputation may be needed if the injured area is untreated or treatment is unsuccessful. It may take as long as 90 days to determine the final necrotic area. The patient may be admitted to the hospital for observation with bed rest, elevation of the injured part, and prophylactic antibiotics if the wound is at risk for infection.

Hypothermia

Hypothermia is a core temperature below 95°F (35°C).[6] It occurs when heat produced by the body cannot compensate for heat lost to the environment. Most body heat is lost as radiant energy, with the greatest loss from the head, thorax, and lungs (with each breath). Wet clothing increases evaporative heat loss to 5 times greater than normal. Immersion in cold water (e.g., drowning) increases evaporative heat loss to 25 times greater than normal. Environmental exposure to freezing temperatures,

---

✚ TABLE 68.9 **Emergency Management**

Hypothermia

Etiology	Assessment Findings	Interventions

Environmental
• Inadequate clothing for environmental temperature
• Prolonged exposure to cold
• Prolonged immersion or near-drowning
 	
Metabolic
• Hypoglycemia
• Hypothyroidism
 	
Health Care Associated
• Administration of neuromuscular blocking agents
• Blood administration
• Cold IV fluids
• Inadequate warming or rewarming in the ED or operating room
 	
Other
• Alcohol
• Barbiturates
• Phenothiazines
• Shock
• Trauma
	• Core body temperature:
	  • *Mild hypothermia:* 93° to 95°F (33.9° to 35°C)
	  • *Moderate hypothermia:* 86° to 93°F (30° to 33.9°C)
	  • *Severe hypothermia:* <86°F (30°C)
	• Shivering, decreased or absent at core body temperatures ≤86°F (30°C)
	• Altered mental status (ranging from confusion to coma)
	• Areflexia (absence of reflexes)
	• Blue, white, or frozen extremities
	• Cyanotic, pale skin
	• Dysrhythmias: bradycardia, atrial fibrillation, ventricular fibrillation, asystole
	• Fixed, dilated pupils
	• Hypotension
	• Hypoventilation
		Initial
		• Remove patient from cold environment.
		• Manage and maintain ABCs.
		• Provide high-flow O₂ via nonrebreather mask or BVM.
		• Anticipate intubation for decreased or absent gag reflex.
		• Establish IV access with 2 large-bore catheters for fluid resuscitation.
		• Rewarm patient:
		  • *Passive:* Remove wet clothing, apply dry clothing and warm blankets, use radiant lights.
		  • *Active external:* Apply heating devices (e.g., air or fluid-filled warming blankets), use warm water immersion.
		  • *Active internal:* Provide warmed IV fluids; heated, humidified O₂. Peritoneal lavage with warmed fluids. Extracorporeal circulation (e.g., cardiopulmonary bypass, rapid fluid infuser, hemodialysis).
		• Obtain 12-lead ECG.
		• Anticipate need for defibrillation.
		• Warm central trunk first in patients with severe hypothermia to limit rewarming shock.
		• Assess for other injuries.
		• Keep patient's head covered with warm, dry towels or stocking cap to limit loss of heat.
		• Treat patient gently to avoid increased cardiac irritability.
		
		Ongoing Monitoring
		• Monitor ABCs, temperature, level of consciousness, vital signs
		• Monitor O₂ saturation, heart rate and rhythm.
		• Monitor electrolytes, glucose.

cold winds, and wet terrain plus physical exhaustion, inadequate clothing, and inexperience predisposes people to hypothermia. Older adults are prone to hypothermia because of decreased body fat, decreased energy reserves, decreased basal metabolic rate, decreased shivering response, chronic medical conditions, and drugs that alter body defenses. Peripheral vasoconstriction is the body's first attempt to conserve heat. As cold temperatures persist, shivering and movement are the body's only mechanisms for producing heat.

Assessment findings are variable and depend on core temperature (Table 68.9). Patients with *mild hypothermia* (93° to 95°F [33.9° to 35°C]) have shivering, lethargy, confusion, rational to irrational behavior, and minor heart rate changes. *Moderate hypothermia* (86° to 93°F [30° to 33.9°C]) causes rigidity, bradycardia, slowed respiratory rate, BP obtainable only by Doppler, metabolic and respiratory acidosis, and hypovolemia. Shivering decreases or disappears at core temperatures of 86°F (30°C).[6]

As core temperature drops, metabolic rate decreases 2 to 3 times. The cold myocardium is extremely irritable, making it vulnerable to dysrhythmias (e.g., atrial and ventricular fibrillation). Decreased renal blood flow decreases glomerular filtration rate, which impairs water reabsorption and leads to dehydration. The hematocrit increases as intravascular volume decreases. Cold blood becomes thick and acts as a thrombus, placing the patient at risk for stroke, MI, pulmonary emboli, and renal failure. Decreased blood flow leads to hypoxia, anaerobic metabolism, lactic acid accumulation, and metabolic acidosis.

Severe hypothermia (below 86°F [30°C]) makes the person appear dead and is a potentially life-threatening situation. Metabolic rate, heart rate, and respirations are so slow that they may be hard to detect. Reflexes are absent, and the pupils fixed and dilated. Profound bradycardia, ventricular fibrillation, or pulseless electrical activity may be present. Effort is made to try to warm the patient to at least 86°F (30°C) before the person is pronounced dead. The cause of death is usually refractory ventricular fibrillation.

Interprofessional Care. Treatment focuses on managing and maintaining ABCs, rewarming the patient, correcting dehydration and acidosis, and treating dysrhythmias. Mildly hypothermic patients may be rewarmed with passive and active external measures since their risk for dysrhythmia is low. Those with more severe hypothermia need active internal rewarming measures.

Carefully monitor core temperature during rewarming procedures. Rewarming places the patient at risk for *afterdrop*, a further drop in core temperature. This occurs when cold peripheral blood returns to the central circulation. Rewarming shock can produce hypotension and dysrhythmias. Thus patients with moderate to severe hypothermia should have the core warmed before the extremities. Discontinue active rewarming once the core temperature reaches 90° to 95°F (32.2° to 35°C).

Patient teaching focuses on how to avoid future cold-related problems. Essential information includes dressing in layers for cold weather, covering the head, carrying high-carbohydrate foods for extra calories, and developing a plan for survival should an injury occur when in an extreme environment.

SUBMERSION INJURIES

Submersion injury results when a person becomes hypoxic from submersion in a liquid, usually water.[6] Around 3500 deaths from drowning occur each year in the United States. Most of the victims are children younger than 5 years of age or boys and men between ages 15 and 25.[18] The main risk factors for submersion injury include inability to swim, use of alcohol or drugs, trauma, seizures, hypothermia, stroke, and child neglect. Aggressive resuscitation efforts (e.g., airway and ventilation management), especially in the prehospital phase, improve survival of drowning victims.

Drowning is the process of experiencing respiratory impairment after submersion in water or other fluid. Submersion in cold water (below 32°F [0°C]) may slow the progression of hypoxic brain injury.

Most drowning victims do not aspirate any liquid due to laryngospasm. If liquid is aspirated, it is in small amounts. Drowning victims who do aspirate water develop pulmonary edema, which can cause acute respiratory distress syndrome (see Chapter 67).

The osmotic gradient caused by aspirated fluid leads to fluid imbalances in the body (Fig. 68.4). Hypotonic fresh water is rapidly absorbed into the circulatory system through the alveoli. Fresh water is often contaminated with chlorine, mud, or algae. This causes the breakdown of lung surfactant, fluid seepage, and pulmonary edema.

Hypertonic saltwater draws fluid from the vascular space into the alveoli, impairing alveolar ventilation and causing hypoxia. The body tries to compensate for hypoxia by shunting blood to the lungs. This results in increased pulmonary pressures and deteriorating respiratory status. More and more blood is shunted through the alveoli. Since the blood is not adequately oxygenated, and hypoxemia worsens. This can result in cerebral injury, edema, and brain death.

Interprofessional Care

Treatment focuses on correcting hypoxia and fluid imbalances, supporting basic physiologic functions, and rewarming when hypothermia is present. Initial evaluation involves assessment of airway, cervical spine, breathing, and circulation (Table 68.10). Mechanical ventilation with positive end-expiratory pressure or continuous positive airway pressure can improve gas exchange across the alveolar-capillary membrane when significant pulmonary edema is present. Ventilation and oxygenation are the main techniques for treating respiratory failure (see Chapters 65 and 67).

Deterioration in neurologic status suggests cerebral edema, worsening hypoxia, or profound acidosis. Drowning victims may have head and neck injuries that cause changes in the LOC. Complications can develop in patients who are free of symptoms immediately after the drowning episode. Consequently,

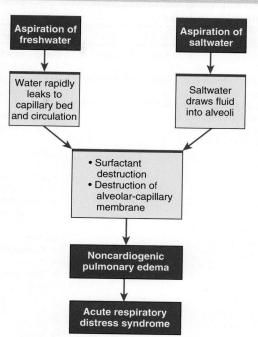

FIG. 68.4 Pathophysiology of submersion injury.

observe all victims of drowning in a hospital for a minimum of 23 hours. Additional observation is needed for patients with co-morbidities.

Patient teaching focuses on water safety and how to reduce the risks for drowning. Remind patients and caregivers to lock all swimming pool gates; use life jackets on all watercrafts, including inner tubes and rafts; and learn water survival skills. Emphasize the dangers of combining alcohol and drugs with swimming and other water sports.

STINGS AND BITES

Animals, spiders, snakes, and insects cause injury and even death by biting or stinging. Morbidity is a result of either direct tissue damage or lethal toxins. Direct tissue damage is a product of animal size, characteristics of the animal's teeth, and strength of the jaw. Tissue is lacerated, crushed, or chewed, while teeth, fangs, stingers, spines, or tentacles release toxins that have local or systemic effects. Death associated with animal bites is due to blood loss, allergic reactions, or lethal toxins. Injuries caused by select insects, ticks, animals, and humans are described here.

Hymenopteran Stings

The *Hymenoptera* family includes bees, yellow jackets, hornets, wasps, and fire ants. Stings can cause mild discomfort or life-threatening anaphylaxis (see Chapter 66). Venom may be cytotoxic, hemolytic, allergenic, or vasoactive. Symptoms may begin immediately or be delayed up to 48 hours. Reactions are more severe with multiple stings. Most hymenopterans sting repeatedly. However, the domestic honey bee stings only once, usually leaving a barbed stinger with an attached venom sac in the skin so that venom release continues.

African honey bees (killer bees) look like domestic bees. If threatened, these bees aggressively swarm and can repeatedly sting their victims. These attacks can be fatal.

✚ TABLE 68.10 Emergency Management

Submersion Injuries

Etiology	Assessment Findings	Interventions
• Entrapment or entanglement with objects in water • Inability to swim or exhaustion while swimming • Loss of ability to move secondary to trauma, stroke, hypothermia, MI • Poor judgment due to alcohol or drugs • Seizure while in water	**Respiratory** • Cough with pink-frothy sputum • Crackles, rhonchi • Cyanosis • Dyspnea • Respiratory distress • Respiratory arrest **Cardiac** • Bradycardia • Dysrhythmia • Hypotension • Tachycardia • Cardiac arrest **Other** • Exhaustion • Coma • Coexisting illness (e.g., MI) or injury (e.g., cervical spine injury) • Core temperature slightly elevated or below normal, depending on water temperature and length of submersion • Panic	**Initial** • Manage and maintain ABCs. • Assume cervical spine injury in all drowning victims and stabilize or immobilize cervical spine. • Provide 100% O_2 via nonrebreather mask or BVM. • Anticipate need for intubation and mechanical ventilation if airway is compromised (e.g., absent gag reflex). • Establish IV access with 2 large-bore catheters for fluid resuscitation and infuse warmed fluids, if appropriate. • Obtain 12-lead ECG. • Assess for other injuries. • Remove wet clothing and cover with warm blankets. • Obtain temperature and begin rewarming, if needed. • Obtain cervical spine and chest x-rays. • Insert gastric tube and urinary catheter. **Ongoing Monitoring** • Monitor ABCs, vital signs, level of consciousness. • Monitor O_2 saturation, heart rate and rhythm. • Monitor temperature and maintain normothermia. • Monitor for signs of acute respiratory failure.

BVM, Bag-valve-mask.

⚠ SAFETY ALERT Hymenopteran Stings
• Remove the stinger using a scraping motion with thin, flat object, like a fingernail, knife, or credit card.
• Do not use tweezers because they may squeeze the stinger and release more venom.
• Remove rings, watches, or any restrictive clothing around the sting site.

Manifestations of mild reactions include stinging, burning, swelling, and itching. More severe reactions may present with edema, headache, fever, syncope, malaise, nausea, vomiting, wheezing, bronchospasm, laryngeal edema, and hypotension. Treatment depends on the severity of the reaction. Treat mild reactions with elevation, cool compresses, antipruritic lotions, and oral antihistamines. More severe reactions require IM or IV antihistamines, subcutaneous epinephrine, and corticosteroids. Chapter 13 discusses allergic reactions and related patient teaching.

Snake Bites

There are more than 45,000 snakebites each year in the United States. *Envenomation* (poisoning by venom) occurs in only 8000 cases, with only 5 to 10 deaths each year.[19] The 2 families of venomous snakes found in the United States are Crotalidae or pit vipers (rattlesnakes, copperheads, cottonmouths) and Elapidae (coral snakes). Almost all the venomous bites are from pit vipers.

Snake venom may be hemolytic, neurotoxic, vascular toxic, or any combination of these. When bites occur, you will see fang or puncture marks. The patient often has severe pain at the site. There may be swelling, discoloration and blistering. If moderate envenomation has occurred, the patient will have paresthesias, lymphadenopathy, and nausea and vomiting. Treatment includes wound care and tetanus prophylaxis. Immobilize the affected extremity. Remove potentially constricting clothing. Most bites are minor and resolve without antivenom therapy. Patients with suspected envenomation are observed for at least 8 hours to ensure no life- or limb-threatening symptoms develop.

Manifestations of severe envenomation include profound edema, tachycardia, blurred vision, headache, chills, paresthesias, hypotension, and muscle twitching. The patient may report a metallic taste in the mouth. As symptoms progress, pulmonary edema, coagulopathy, thrombocytopenia, and hemorrhage may develop. Treatment of severe envenomation requires close patient monitoring. The ABCs are the most vital part of nursing management. Limb circumference and the advancing edema should be marked and monitored every 30 minutes. Anticipate fluid resuscitation, respiratory support, monitoring of laboratory results, and antivenom therapy. On rare occasions, the patient will need a fasciotomy.[6] The need to give antivenom is made in conjunction with a snake venom expert. Antivenom is given only if symptom progression occurs and platelet and coagulation studies are abnormal.

Snakebites from exotic snake species are primarily neurotoxic. They result in autonomic dysfunction, paralysis, and dysrhythmias. The bite should be discussed with your regional poison control center as there is specific antivenom therapy, often obtained from a zoo, for each species.

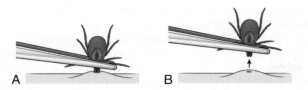

FIG. 68.5 Tick removal. **A,** Use tweezers to grasp the tick close to the skin. **B,** With a steady motion, pull the tick's body up and away from the skin. Do not be alarmed if the tick's mouthparts stay in the skin. Once the mouthparts are removed from the rest of the tick, it can no longer transmit disease.

Tick Bites

Ticks live throughout the United States. Specific types are more prevalent in certain regions. Tick-borne pathogens can be passed to humans by the bite of an infected tick. Common tick-borne illnesses include Lyme disease, Rocky Mountain spotted fever, anaplasmosis, Southern tick-associated rash illness, tick-borne relapsing fever, and tularemia.

Ticks transmit pathogens that cause disease through their feeding process. The infected tick attaches to its host and can slowly feed for up to several days. During this time, saliva from the tick can be transferred to the host. Tick saliva may harbor pathogens acquired by the tick from a prior host. The tick should be removed as soon as possible to stop the flow of saliva. Use forceps or tweezers to grasp the tick close to the point of attachment and pull upward in a steady motion (Fig. 68.5). After you remove the tick, clean the skin with soap and water. Do not use a hot match, petroleum jelly, nail polish, or other products to remove the tick. These measures may cause a tick to salivate, thus increasing the risk for infection.[20]

Lyme disease is the most common tick-borne disease in the United States. In 2016, more than 22,500 confirmed and 37,000 probable cases were reported to the CDC.[20] It is caused by the bacterium *Borrelia burgdorferi* that lives on the tick. In most cases, the tick must be attached for at least 36 hours to transmit the bacterium. Symptoms usually appear in about 7 days. The first stage begins with flu-like symptoms (e.g., headache, stiff neck, fatigue). Some patients may develop a characteristic bull's-eye rash. This is a circular area of redness 5 cm or more in diameter. Treatment at this stage includes doxycycline, cefuroxime, or amoxicillin.[20] The rash, if it develops, will disappear even if the patient is not treated.

Monoarticular arthritis, meningitis, and neuropathies occur days or weeks after the initial manifestations. Treatment at this stage involves IV ceftriaxone or penicillin. Chronic arthritis, heart disease, and peripheral nerve problems occur with the later stage of the disease. These illnesses can last several months to years after the initial skin lesion. (Chapter 64 discusses Lyme disease.)

Rocky Mountain spotted fever is caused by *Rickettsia rickettsia*. It is a bacterium that is spread to humans by the ixodid tick. The incubation period is 2 to 14 days. A pink, macular rash appears on the palms, wrists, soles, feet, and ankles within 10 days of exposure. Other symptoms include fever, chills, malaise, muscle pain, and headache. It is hard to diagnosis in the early stages. Without treatment, the disease can be fatal. Antibiotic therapy with doxycycline is the treatment of choice.

Animal and Human Bites

Every year more than 5 million animal bites are reported in the United States. Animal bites from dogs and cats are most

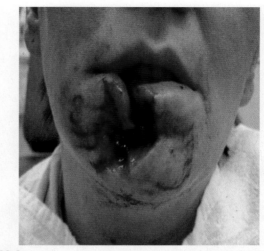

FIG. 68.6 Dog bite wound. (From Mannion C, Kanatas A, Telfer MR: One dog bite too far, *Brit J Oral Max Surg* 49:159, 2011.)

common. Wild or domestic rodents (e.g., squirrels, hamsters) follow as the third most common offenders. The few bite deaths (15 to 20) are mostly from dogs. The greatest problems associated with animal bites are infection and mechanical destruction of skin, muscle, tendons, blood vessels, and bone. The bite may cause a simple laceration or be associated with crush injury, puncture wound, or tearing of multiple layers of tissue (Fig 68.6). The severity of injury depends on animal size, victim size, and anatomic location of the bite. Children are at greatest risk.

Dog bites usually occur on the extremities. Facial bites are common in small children. Cat bites result in deep puncture wounds. They can involve tendons and joint capsules. There is a greater risk for infection than with dog bites. Septic arthritis, osteomyelitis, and tenosynovitis can occur. The most common infectious organisms from dog and cat bites are the *Pasteurella* species (e.g., *Pasteurella multocida*). Most healthy cats and dogs carry this organism in their mouths.

The human jaw has great crushing ability, causing laceration, puncture, crush injury, soft tissue tearing, and even amputation (Fig. 68.7). Hands, fingers, ears, nose, vagina, and penis are the most common sites of human bites. Often these injuries are due to violence or sexual activity. There is a high risk for infection from oral bacterial flora, most often *Staphylococcus aureus, Streptococcus* organisms, and hepatitis virus. Infection rates are as high as 50% when victims do not seek medical care within 24 hours of injury.

Interprofessional Care. Initial treatment for animal and human bites includes cleaning, copious irrigation, debridement, tetanus prophylaxis, and analgesics as needed. Prophylactic antibiotics are used for animal and human bites at risk for infection, such as wounds over joints, those older than 6 to 12 hours, puncture wounds, and bites of the hand or foot. People at greatest risk for infection are infants, older adults, immunosuppressed patients, patients with substance or alcohol use disorder, people living with diabetes, or those taking corticosteroids.

Leave puncture wounds open. Splint wounds over joints. Lacerations may be loosely sutured. Plastic surgery consultation may be needed for disfiguring facial wounds. The patient often receives prophylactic antibiotics. Report animal and human bites to the police as required.

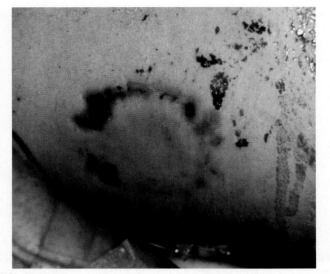

FIG. 68.7 Human bite injury. (From Stevens MR, Emam HA, Cunningham L: *Oral & maxillofacial trauma*, ed 4, St Louis, 2013, Elsevier.)

Consider *rabies postexposure prophylaxis* in the management of all animal bites. Rabies is caused by a neurotoxic virus in the saliva of an infected animal. Most rabies carriers are wild animals, like raccoons, skunks, bats, foxes, and coyotes. Rabies is usually transmitted through the saliva via a bite by the infected animal. If the saliva from the infected animal has come in contact with its claws, theoretically rabies may be transmitted through a scratch. The virus spreads through the central nervous system (CNS) via peripheral nerves. People who develop rabies may have flu-like symptoms, confusion, paresthesias, or numbness resulting in death.

Consider rabies exposure if an animal attack was not provoked, involves a wild animal, or involves a domestic animal not immunized against rabies. Always provide postexposure vaccinations when the animal is not found or a wild animal causes the bite. The series of 4 injections of rabies vaccine (human diploid cell rabies vaccine [HDCV, Imovax Rabies]) are given on days 0, 3, 7, and 14 to provide active immunity.[21] Give an initial, weight-based dose of rabies immune globulin (RIG [HyperRab S/D]) to provide passive immunity at the same time as the first dose of vaccine.

Since rabies is nearly always fatal, management efforts are directed at preventing the transmission and onset of the disease. Although death from rabies is significant worldwide, it is rare in the United States. Rabies vaccine is encouraged for persons who travel globally, since it is a serious world health concern. Notify your local health department for any suspected cases.

🗲 DRUG ALERT Rabies Postexposure Prophylaxis

- If possible, give the calculated dose of RIG via infiltration around the wound edges.
- Give any remaining volume of RIG IM at a site distant from the vaccine site (e.g., gluteal site for bite wounds on the arm).
- Give the HDCV IM in the deltoid.

POISONINGS

A poison is any chemical that harms the body. More than 5 million cases of human poisonings occur each year in the United States. Poisonings can be accidental, occupational, recreational,

or intentional. Natural or manufactured toxins can be ingested, inhaled, injected, splashed in the eye, or absorbed through the skin. Chapter 10 discusses other poisonings related to the use of drugs, such as amphetamines, opioids, and hallucinogens. Poisoning also may be due to toxic plants or contaminated foods. (Chapter 41 discusses food poisoning.)

Severity of the poisoning depends on type, concentration, and route of exposure (Table 68.11). Toxins can affect every tissue of the body, so symptoms can be seen in any body system. Specific management of toxins involves decreasing absorption, enhancing elimination, and implementing toxin-specific interventions. Consult the local poison control center (available 24 hours a day) for the most current treatment protocols for specific poisons.[22]

Decontamination takes priority over all interventions except those needed for life support. Wear *personal protective equipment (PPE)* for decontamination to prevent secondary exposure. In some cases, decontamination is done by those specially trained in hazardous material decontamination before the patient arrives at the hospital and again at the hospital, if needed.

Skin and ocular decontamination involves removing the toxins from skin and eyes using copious amounts of water or saline. Most toxins can be safely removed with water or saline. As a rule, brush dry substances from the skin and clothing before using water. Do not remove powdered lime or mustard gas with water. Lime should just be brushed off. Water mixes with mustard gas and releases chlorine gas.

Under the guidance of the Poison Control Center, binding agents, such as activated charcoal, cathartics, whole-bowel irrigation, hemodialysis, urine alkalinization, chelating agents, and antidotes, may be given to increase the elimination of poisons.[22] Focus patient teaching for toxic emergencies on how the poisoning occurred. Arrange for an evaluation and follow-up by a mental health professional for all patients who have poisoning because of a suicide attempt or substance use.

Many health care workers (e.g., nurses, housekeepers) are at risk for exposure to hazardous materials (e.g., antineoplastic drugs, cleaning agents). Always consult the Material Safety Data Sheet (required by the Occupational Health and Safety Administration [OSHA]) for specific information about hazardous agents in the workplace. OSHA should evaluate all poisoning related to a workplace hazard.

VIOLENCE

Violence is the acting out of the emotions of fear and/or anger to cause harm to someone or something. It may be the result of organic disease (e.g., temporal lobe epilepsy), psychosis (e.g., schizophrenia), or criminal behavior (e.g., assault, murder). The patient cared for in the ED may be the victim or the perpetrator of violence. Violence can take place in a variety of settings, including the home, community, and workplace.

EDs are high-risk areas for *workplace violence*.[23] Measures to protect staff include the use of on-site security personnel and police officers, metal detectors, surveillance cameras, self-defense training, and locked access doors. The ENA recommends comprehensive workplace violence prevention plans be in place in every ED.[24]

Awareness of *family and intimate partner violence* (IPV) along with the possibility of a patient being a victim or perpetrator of human trafficking is a critical part of the ED nurse's role. IPV and human trafficking are patterns of coercive behavior

TABLE 68.11 Common Poisons

Poison	Manifestations	Treatment
acetaminophen (Tylenol)	*Phase 1* (within 24 hr of ingestion): Malaise, diaphoresis, nausea and vomiting *Phase 2* (24–28 hr after ingestion): Right upper quadrant pain, ↓ urine output, ↓ nausea, increase in LFTs *Phase 3* (72–96 hr after ingestion): Nausea and vomiting, malaise, jaundice, hypoglycemia, enlarged liver, possible coagulopathies, including DIC *Phase 4* (7-8 days after ingestion): Recovery, resolution of symptoms or permanent liver damage, LFT results remain high	Activated charcoal, *N*-acetylcysteine (oral form may cause vomiting, IV form can be used)
Acids and Alkalis • *Acids:* Toilet bowl cleaners, antirust compounds • *Alkalis:* Drain cleaners, dishwashing detergents, ammonia	Excess salivation, dysphagia, epigastric pain, pneumonitis; burns of mouth, esophagus, and stomach	Immediate dilution (water, milk), corticosteroids (for alkali burns), induced vomiting is contraindicated
• Aspirin and aspirin-containing drugs	Tachypnea, tachycardia, fever, seizures, pulmonary edema, occult bleeding or hemorrhage, metabolic acidosis	Activated charcoal, gastric lavage, urine alkalinization, hemodialysis for severe acute ingestion, intubation and mechanical ventilation, supportive care
Bleaches	Irritation of lips, mouth, and eyes, superficial injury to esophagus; chemical pneumonia and pulmonary edema	Washing of exposed skin and eyes, dilution with water and milk, gastric lavage, prevention of vomiting and aspiration
Carbon monoxide	Dyspnea, headache, tachypnea, confusion, impaired judgment, cyanosis, respiratory depression	Remove from source, apply 100% O₂ via nonrebreather mask, BVM, or intubation and mechanical ventilation; consider hyperbaric O₂ therapy
Cyanide	Almond odor to breath, headache, dizziness, nausea, confusion, hypertension, bradycardia followed by hypotension and tachycardia, tachypnea followed by bradypnea and respiratory arrest	Amyl nitrate (nasally), IV sodium nitrate, IV sodium thiosulfate, supportive care
Ethylene glycol	Sweet aromatic odor to breath, nausea and vomiting, slurred speech, ataxia, lethargy, respiratory depression	Activated charcoal, gastric lavage, supportive care
Iron	Vomiting (often bloody), diarrhea (often bloody), fever, hyperglycemia, lethargy, hypotension, seizures, coma	Gastric lavage, chelation therapy (deferoxamine [Desferal])
NSAIDs	Gastroenteritis, abdominal pain, drowsiness, nystagmus, hepatic and renal damage	Activated charcoal, gastric lavage, supportive care
Tricyclic antidepressants (e.g., amitriptyline)	*In low doses:* Anticholinergic effects, agitation, hypertension, tachycardia *In high doses:* CNS depression, dysrhythmias, hypotension, respiratory depression	Multidose activated charcoal, gastric lavage, serum alkalinization with sodium bicarbonate, intubation and mechanical ventilation, supportive care; never induce vomiting
Alcohol, barbiturates, benzodiazepines, cocaine, hallucinogens, stimulants	See Chapter 10	See Chapter 10

BVM, Bag-valve-mask; *DIC,* disseminated intravascular coagulation; *LFT,* liver function test.

in relationships that involve fear, humiliation, intimidation, neglect, or intentional physical, emotional, financial, or sexual injury (see Chapter 53 for information on sexual assault). Trafficking can involve being kidnapped or even being sold by family. It may also involve coercion of runaways into a "safe" situation that results in anything but safety.

IPV is found in all cultures, socioeconomic groups, age-groups, and genders. Although men can be victims of family violence and IPV, most victims are women, children, and older adults. Each year, more than 5 million women and 3 million men are treated in EDs for *battery* (assault) by spouses, caregivers, or persons known to them. IPV is most common among women of reproductive age.[25]

In the ED, screening for family violence and IPV (e.g., Do you feel safe at home? Is anyone hurting you?) is required. Barriers to effective screening include lack of privacy, fear of offending the patient, lack of time, and discomfort with the topic. Developing and implementing policies, procedures, and staff education programs improve screening practices.

With over 100 million people worldwide affected by human trafficking, it is likely that the ED nurse will come in contact with either a victim or perpetrator of human trafficking. Interviews with former victims suggest that over 85% had come in contact with the health care system at some time during their captivity.[26] ED nurses are uniquely positioned to help identify and report a trafficking victim or perpetrator to the appropriate authorities.

Be sensitive when gathering information about suspected abuse and trafficking as it may have potential for increasing the patient's risk. Start appropriate interventions for patients who you suspect or find are victims of abuse or trafficking. This includes making referrals, notifying appropriate agencies, providing emotional support, and informing victims about their options. The ENA encourages ED nurses to become certified *sexual assault nurse examiners* (SANEs). SANEs provide expert emergency care, collect and document evidence, take part in staff and community education, and advocate for sexual assault and rape victims.[27]

AGENTS OF TERRORISM

Terrorism involves overt actions, such as the dispensing of nuclear, biologic, or chemical (NBC) agents as weapons, for the express purpose of causing harm. Prompt recognition and identification of potential health hazards are essential in the preparedness of health care professionals.

Biologic agents most often used in terrorist attacks include anthrax, smallpox, botulism, plague, tularemia, and hemorrhagic fever. Anthrax, plague, and tularemia are treated effectively with antibiotics if enough supplies are available and the organisms are not resistant.[28] Vaccines are available for most of these agents.

Chemicals used as agents of terrorism are categorized by their target organ or effect. For example, sarin is a highly toxic nerve gas that can cause death within minutes of exposure.[29] The radioactive dust and smoke can spread and cause illness if inhaled. Since radiation cannot be seen, smelled, felt, or tasted, you should start measures to limit contamination and provide for decontamination. *Ionizing radiation,* such as that from a nuclear bomb or damage to a nuclear reactor, is a serious threat to the safety of victims and the environment. Exposure to ionizing radiation may include skin contamination with radioactive material. Begin decontamination procedures immediately if external radioactive contaminants are present.

Explosive devices cause blast, crush, and/or penetrating injuries. Blast injuries result from the supersonic pressurization shock wave caused by the explosion. This shock wave primarily damages the lungs, GI tract, and middle ear. Crush injuries often result from explosions in confined spaces causing structural collapse. Some explosive devices contain materials that are projected during the explosion, leading to penetrating injuries.

PENETRATING TRAUMA

Penetrating trauma is an injury that occurs when an object pierces the skin and enters the body creating an open wound. When the object goes all the way through, creating and entry and exit wound, it is a perforating injury. The most common causes of penetrating and perforating injuries in the United States are gunshot and stab wounds. The severity of the injury largely depends on the body part involved. Patients with penetrating trauma have the best outcome when they are thoroughly evaluated and promptly treated. All victims must first have a primary assessment to maintain airway, breathing, and circulation; control bleeding; and evaluate neurologic status.

Penetrating head trauma is a traumatic brain injury (TBI) that has a high mortality rate. Most deaths from TBI are from gunshot wounds. Other causes include stab wounds, motor vehicle accidents, or occupational accidents. Those who survive penetrating head trauma often have permanent neurologic deficits.

Patients with penetrating neck trauma are at risk for injury to major blood vessels, airway, and spinal cord. Anticipate bleeding, respiratory, and neurologic problems. Chest wounds can damage the heart, lungs, esophagus, diaphragm, or trachea. Penetrating wounds to the heart are almost 80% fatal. Lung injury can cause pneumothorax or hemothorax requiring emergent decompression and chest tube insertion.

Penetrating wounds to the abdomen often result from gunshot wounds. Severity and prognosis depend on the organs injured. Mortality from abdominal wounds is about 5%. Death usually occurs later due to hemorrhage or infection.

FIG. 68.8 American Red Cross. (Photo used with the permission of the American Red Cross.)

Extremity trauma is usually not life threatening but can cause permanent disability. Blood vessels may be affected, leading to hemorrhage. Angulated fractures can cause penetrating trauma. Nerves, tendons, ligaments, and muscles can be injured. Early interventions include control of bleeding and stabilization of the injured extremity.

EMERGENCY AND MASS CASUALTY INCIDENT PREPAREDNESS

The term emergency usually refers to any extraordinary event that requires a rapid and skilled response and that the community's existing resources can manage. An emergency is different from a mass casualty incident (MCI) in that an MCI is a human-made (e.g., involving NBC agents) or natural (e.g., hurricane) event or disaster that overwhelms a community's ability to respond with existing resources. MCIs usually involve large numbers of victims, physical and emotional suffering, and permanent changes within a community. MCIs always require assistance from resources outside the affected community (Fig. 68.8).

When an emergency or an MCI occurs, first responders are sent to the scene. Triage of victims of an emergency or an MCI differs from the usual ED triage. Several systems exist. Many use colored tags to designate both the seriousness of the injury and the chance for survival. One system uses green for minor injuries and yellow for urgent but not life-threatening injuries. Red means a life-threatening injury requiring immediate intervention. Blue indicates those who are expected to die, and black identifies the dead.[30]

Triage of victims of an emergency or an MCI must be done in less than 15 seconds. Victims need to be treated and stabilized and, if there is known or suspected contamination, decontaminated at the scene. After this, they are moved to hospitals. Many other victims arrive at hospitals on their own. The total number of victims a hospital can expect is estimated by doubling the number of victims who arrive in the first hour.

ETHICAL/LEGAL DILEMMAS
Good Samaritan

Situation

You are a registered nurse, employed as a charge nurse at a subacute rehabilitation facility. It is midnight, and you are driving home from work when you see a motor vehicle crash with a person at the side of the road waving and yelling for help. You stop and call 911 to report the incident. What do you do next?

Ethical/Legal Points for Consideration

• As a licensed health care professional, you are under no legal obligation to stop and give aid.
• If you do stop, you assume an obligation not to leave the scene until sufficiently trained first responders arrive and assume control.
• Many states encourage health care professionals to stop and give aid by having "Good Samaritan" laws. These laws, which vary somewhat from state to state, offer immunity from lawsuit for bystanders who offer aid in emergencies except in the case of gross negligence.
• A Good Samaritan must not be in the place of employment or under employment conditions.
• An example of gross negligence may be refusing to help someone who obviously had a serious hemorrhage in favor of a person with a minor injury because the bleeding person looked old or disheveled.
• Immunity covers only the scene of the accident and not later care under the supervision of HCPs.
• If there is a national disaster, an act of terrorism, or a major emergent need for HCPs, you may be required to go to an assigned site to offer aid. You would not be covered by the Good Samaritan Act under these circumstances.

Discussion Questions

1. What factors do you think contribute to a health care professional's decision whether to stop to provide aid?
2. What basic aid would you feel comfortable providing if you do not have an emergency or trauma background?
3. Would your professional liability (malpractice) insurance cover you if someone claimed that you acted negligently while giving aid?

In addition to the services provided by first responders, many communities have developed *community emergency response teams* (CERTs). CERTs are recognized by the Federal Emergency Management Agency (FEMA) as important partners in emergency preparedness. The CERT training helps citizens understand their personal responsibility in preparing for a natural or human-made disaster. Participants learn what to expect after a disaster and how to safely help themselves, their family, and their neighbors. Training includes lifesaving skills with emphasis on decision making and rescuer safety. CERTs are an extension of the first responder services. They can offer immediate help to victims and organize untrained volunteers to assist until professional services arrive.[31]

All HCPs have a role in emergency and MCI preparedness. Knowledge of the hospital's *emergency response plan* is essential. This includes individual roles and responsibilities of the members of the response team plus participation in emergency/MCI preparedness drills on a regular basis. Several types of drills can assess a hospital's level of emergency preparedness. These include hospital disaster drills, computer simulations, and table-top exercises. Drills allow HCPs to become familiar with the emergency response procedures.

Response to MCIs often requires the aid of a federal agency. The National Incident Management System (NIMS), American Red Cross, FEMA, and National Disaster Medical System (NDMS) are examples of federal resources.

All disasters result in psychologic stress to those involved. This stress can persist for an extended period. It is influenced, in part, by the nature of the event, the person's age, preexisting coping mechanisms, role in the event, and medical and mental health history. Many hospitals have a *critical incident stress management unit*. This unit arranges group discussions to allow participants to share their feelings about the experience. This is important for emotional recovery.

CASE STUDY
Trauma

(© Thinkstock.)

Patient Profile

D.F., a 20-yr-old Hispanic female trauma victim, is brought to the ED in an ambulance. She was the driver in a motor vehicle crash and was not wearing a seat belt. Two unrestrained children in the car were pronounced dead at the scene. The paramedics said there was significant damage to the car on the driver's side.

Subjective Data

• Patient asks, "What happened? Where am I?"
• Reports of shortness of breath and leg pain

Objective Data
Physical Examination

• Vital signs: BP = 85/40 mm Hg, HR = 140 beats/min, RR = 36 breaths/min; O_2 saturation = 85% with 100% nonrebreather mask
• Decreased breath sounds on left side of chest
• Asymmetric chest wall movement
• Glasgow Coma Score = 14; pupils slightly unequal
• Badly deformed left lower leg with significant swelling and a pedal pulse by Doppler only
• 4-cm head laceration, bleeding controlled

Discussion Questions

1. What are D.F.'s most likely life-threatening injuries?
2. *Priority Decision:* What is the priority of care for D.F.?
3. *Priority Decision:* What interventions does this patient need immediately?
4. What other interventions should you consider?
5. *Collaboration:* What activities could you delegate to unlicensed assistive personnel (UAP)?
6. *Patient-Centered Care:* Several family members have arrived in the ED, including the mother of 1 of the children who died. The second child who died was the patient's child. How should you approach the family?
7. *Priority Decision:* Based on assessment data presented, what are the priority nursing diagnoses? Are there any collaborative problems?
8. *Evidence-Based Practice:* What are the best practice guidelines for fluid resuscitation in patients with hypovolemic shock?

Answers available at *http://evolve.elsevier.com/Lewis/medsurg.*

■ BRIDGE TO NCLEX EXAMINATION

The number of the question corresponds to the same-numbered outcome at the beginning of the chapter.

1. An older man arrives in triage disoriented and dyspneic. His skin is hot and dry. His wife states that he was fine earlier today. The nurse's next *priority* would be to
   a. assess his vital signs.
   b. obtain a brief medical history from his wife.
   c. start supplemental O_2 and have the provider see him.
   d. determine the kind of insurance he has before treating him.

2. A patient has a core temperature of 90° F (32.2° C). The *most* appropriate rewarming technique would be
   a. passive rewarming with warm blankets.
   b. active internal rewarming using warmed IV fluids.
   c. passive rewarming using air-filled warming blankets.
   d. active external rewarming by submersing in a warm bath.

3. What are effective interventions to decrease absorption or increase elimination of an ingested poison? *(select all that apply)*
   a. Hemodialysis
   b. Eye irrigation
   c. Hyperbaric O_2
   d. Gastric lavage
   e. Activated charcoal

4. An older woman arrives in the ED reporting severe pain in her right shoulder. The nurse notes her clothes are soiled with urine and feces. She tells the nurse that she lives with her son and that she "fell." She is tearful and asks you if she can be admitted. What possibility should the nurse consider?
   a. Dementia
   b. Possible cancer
   c. Family violence
   d. Orthostatic hypotension

5. A chemical explosion occurs at a nearby industrial site. First responders report that victims are being decontaminated at the scene and about 125 workers will need medical evaluation and care. The first action of the nurse receiving this report should be to
   a. issue a code blue alert.
   b. activate the hospital's emergency response plan.
   c. notify the Federal Emergency Management Agency (FEMA).
   d. arrange for the American Red Cross to provide aid to victims.

1. a, 2. b, 3. a, d, e, 4. c, 5. b

For rationales to these answers and even more NCLEX review questions, visit *http://evolve.elsevier.com/Lewis/medsurg*.

ⓔ EVOLVE WEBSITE/RESOURCES LIST

http://evolve.elsevier.com/Lewis/medsurg
Review Questions (Online Only)
Key Points
Answer Keys for Questions
  • Rationales for Bridge to NCLEX Examination Questions
  • Answer Guidelines for Case Study on p. 1621
  • Answer Guidelines for Managing Care of Multiple Patients Case Study (Section 13) on p. 1623
Student Case Study
  • Patient With Musculoskeletal Trauma
Conceptual Care Map Creator
Audio Glossary
Content Updates

REFERENCES

1. Centers for Disease Control and Prevention (CDC): Emergency department visits. Retrieved from *www.cdc.gov/nchs/fastats/emergency-department.htm*.
2. American College of Emergency Physicians: Only 5.5% of emergency visits are nonurgent and wait times continue to improve, CDC says. Retrieved from *http://newsroom.acep.org/2018-04-23-ACEP-Only-5-5-Percent-of-Emergency-Visits-Are-Nonurgent-and-Wait-Times-Continue-to-Improve-CDC-Says*.
3. Board of Certification for Emergency Nurses: Get certified—CEN. Retrieved from *www.bcencertifications.org/Get-Certified/CEN.aspx*.
4. Rund DA, Rausch TS: *Triage*, St Louis, 1981, Mosby. (Classic)
*5. Gilboy N, Tanabe P, Travers DA, et al: Emergency Severity Index (ESI): A triage tool for emergency department care. Retrieved from *www.ahrq.gov/professionals/systems/hospital/esi/esihandbk.pdf*.
6. Sweet V: Emergency nursing core curriculum, ed 7, St Louis, 2018, Elsevier.
*7. Nair SS, Surendran A, Prabhakar RB, et al: Comparison between FOUR score and GCS in assessing patients with traumatic head injury: A tertiary centre study, *Int Surg J* 4:656, 2017.

*8. Davidson JE, Aslakson RA, Long AC, et al: Guidelines for family-centered care in the neonatal, pediatric, and adult ICU, *CCM* 45:103, 2017.
*9. Motov SM, Nelson LS: Advanced concepts and controversies in emergency department pain management, *Anesthesiol Clin* 34:271, 2016.
10. Centers for Disease Control and Prevention (CDC): Tetanus: Prevention. Retrieved from *www.cdc.gov/tetanus/about/prevention.html*.
*11. Tisherman SA: Targeted temperature management after cardiac arrest: When, how deep, how long? *JTD* 9:4840, 2017.
*12. Madden LK, Hill M, May TL, et al: The implementation of targeted temperature management: An evidence-based guideline from the Neurocritical Care Society, *Neurocrit Care* 27:468, 2017.
*13. Mayer D: Improving the support of the suddenly bereaved, *Curr Opin Support Palliat Care* 11:1, 2017.
14. United Network for Organ Sharing: What every patient needs to know. Retrieved from *www.unos.org/wp-content/uploads/unos/WEPNTK.pdf*.
15. Centers for Disease Control and Prevention (CDC): National hospital ambulatory medical care survey: 2015 Emergency department summary tables. Retrieved from *www.cdc.gov/nchs/data/nhamcs/web_tables/2015_ed_web_tables.pdf*.
16. National Council on Aging: Fall prevention facts. Retrieved from *www.ncoa.org/news/resources-for-reporters/get-the-facts/falls-prevention-facts/*.
17. Handford C, Thomas O, Imray CH: Frostbite, *Emerg Med Clin North Am* 35:281, 2017.
18. Centers for Disease Control and Prevention (CDC): Unintentional drowning. Retrieved from *www.cdc.gov/homeandrecreationalsafety/water-safety/waterinjuries-factsheet.html*.
19. Centers for Disease Control and Prevention (CDC): Venomous snakes. Retrieved from *www.cdc.gov/niosh/topics/snakes/default.html*.
20. Centers for Disease Control and Prevention (CDC): Tick removal. Retrieved from *www.cdc.gov/ticks/removing_a_tick.html*.
21. Centers for Disease Control and Prevention (CDC): Rabies VIS. Retrieved from *www.cdc.gov/vaccines/hcp/vis/vis-statements/rabies.html*.
22. National Capital Poison Control Center: Act fast. Retrieved from *www.poison.org*.
*23. Nikathil S, Olaussen A, Gocentas RA, et al: Workplace violence in the emergency department: A systematic review and meta analysis, *EMA* 29:265, 2017.

*24. Emergency Nurses Association: Workplace violence. Retrieved from *www.ena.org/practice-resources/workplace-violence*.

25. Agency for Healthcare Research and Quality: Intimate partner violence screening. Retrieved from *www.ahrq.gov/professionals/prevention-chronic-care/healthier-pregnancy/preventive/partnerviolence.html*.

26. Gibbons P, Stoklosa H: Identification and treatment of human trafficking victims in the emergency department, *JEM* 50:715, 2016.

*27. Emergency Nurses Association: Joint position statement: Adult and adolescent sexual assault patients in the emergency setting. Retrieved from *www.ena.org/docs/default-source/resource-library/practice-resources/position-statements/joint-statements/adultandadolescentsexualassaultpatientser.pdf?sfvrsn=234258f1_6*.

28. Centers for Disease Control and Prevention (CDC): Anthrax. Retrieved from *www.cdc.gov/anthrax/medical-care/prevention.html*.

29. Agency for Toxic Substances and Disease Registry: Medical management guidelines for nerve agents: Tabun, sarin, soman, and VX. Retrieved from *www.atsdr.cdc.gov/mmg/mmg.asp?id=523&tid=93*.

30. Ryan JM, Doll D, Giannou C: Mass casualties and triage in military and civilian environment. In Velmahos G, Degiannis E, Doll D: *Penetrating trauma,* Berlin, 2017, Springer.

31. Department of Homeland Security: Community emergency response team. Retrieved from *www.ready.gov/community-emergency-response-team*.

*Evidence-based information for clinical practice.

CASE STUDY
Managing Care of Multiple Patients

You are working in a 12-bed ICU and have been assigned to care for the following 2 patients. There is 1 UAP available to help as needed.

Patients

(© Thinkstock.)

R.K. is a 72-yr-old white man who was admitted with a massive stroke after collapsing at his home. He is unresponsive, even to painful stimuli. He has an oral endotracheal (ET) tube in place and is receiving mechanical ventilation (assist-control mode, FIO$_2$ 70%, V$_T$ 700 mL, respiratory rate 16 breaths/min, PEEP 7.5 cm H$_2$O). His chest x-ray shows right lower lung consolidation. A subclavian central line was placed to monitor central venous pressure (CVP) and give fluids and IV antibiotics. His cardiac rhythm on admission was atrial fibrillation with a rapid ventricular response. He is receiving IV diltiazem (Cardizem), and his ventricular response has slowed to 84 bpm. His temperature is increased despite receiving acetaminophen (Tylenol) q4hr. Enteral nutrition is running at 25 mL/hr via orogastric feeding tube. R.K. has a catheter for urinary drainage.

(© Thinkstock.)

J.N. is a 58-yr-old white man who was admitted 24 hours ago after emergent surgery for an acutely ischemic bowel. The surgical procedure involved extensive abdominal surgery to repair a perforated colon, irrigate the abdominal cavity, and provide hemostasis. During surgery, his systolic BP dropped to 70 mm Hg and is still in the low 90s. He is in sinus tachycardia at a rate of 128 bpm. His pulmonary status worsened over the first 24 hr in ICU. He developed a right-sided pneumothorax and a chest tube was placed at that time. His hypoxemia has rapidly progressed and is now refractory to 100% FIO$_2$ and 15 cm H$_2$O PEEP. His laboratory tests show kidney and liver failure. He has an advance directive that states he does not want to be kept alive by artificial means, but he currently is full code status. He is sedated, paralyzed, and unable to communicate. His urinary catheter is draining concentrated urine <30 mL/hr. He has a central line in place with 0.9% saline running at 125 mL/hr. His most recent ABGs are as follows: pH 7.12, PaO$_2$ 59 mm Hg, PaCO$_2$ 62 mm Hg, HCO$_3^-$ 17 mEq/L, and O$_2$ saturation 84%, and his chest x-ray shows worsening bilateral interstitial infiltrates compatible with an ARDS pattern.

Discussion Questions

1. *Priority Decision:* After receiving report, which patient should you see first? Provide rationale.
2. *Collaboration:* Which tasks could you delegate to the UAP? *(select all that apply)*

a. Record vital signs on R.K. and J.N.
b. Drain the water from J.N.'s ventilator tubing.
c. Change suction tubing on R.K.'s ET tubes as needed.
d. Titrate the diltiazem IV drip based on R.K.'s heart rate.
e. Talk to J.N.'s family about his advance directive and current code status.

3. *Priority Decision and Collaboration:* As you are assessing J.N., the UAP informs you that R.K. just vomited all over his bed. Which *initial* action would be *most* appropriate?
a. Ask the UAP to give R.K. a bath while you finish assessing J.N.
b. Turn off R.K.'s enteral nutrition pump and auscultate his breath sounds.
c. Ask the UAP to inform the HCP about J.N.'s ABG results while you assess R.K.
d. Finish assessing R.K., then suction R.K.'s endotracheal tube to remove any emesis.

Case Study Progression

R.K.'s lungs are clear to auscultation. Evaluation of his GI status reveals minimal bowel sounds and a gastric residual of 200 mL even after his emesis. You elevate the head of his bed to 60 degrees, place the enteral nutrition on hold, and notify his HCP.

4. Which intervention would you expect the HCP to order for R.K.?
a. Morphine sulfate 2 mg IV stat
b. Metoclopramide (Reglan) 10 mg IV every 6 hr
c. Restart enteral nutrition and maintain HOB elevation at 90 degrees
d. Hold enteral nutrition for 1 hour and restart with half-strength fluid at same rate
5. J.N.'s ABG results reflect a worsening of his ARDS. You correctly identify that these results demonstrate
a. uncompensated respiratory acidosis.
b. uncompensated respiratory alkalosis.
c. partially compensated respiratory acidosis.
d. partially compensated respiratory alkalosis.
6. Calculate and interpret J.N.'s PaO$_2$/FIO$_2$ ratio.
7. What aspects of care would be the same for J.N. and R.K. since they are both receiving mechanical ventilation? *(select all that apply)*
a. Obtaining daily arterial blood gasses.
b. Monitoring pulse oximetry continuously.
c. Administering an IV proton-pump inhibitor.
d. Suctioning the endotracheal tube every 2 hours.
e. Applying intermittent pneumatic compression stockings.
8. *Management Decision:* You walk into J.N.'s room and find his wife whispering in his ear with her hand on the ventilator tubing, appearing to be ready to disconnect him from life support. What is your *best* initial action?
a. Ask J.N.'s wife to leave the room immediately.
b. Report the incident to the charge nurse and security at once.
c. Ask J.N.'s wife if you could talk to her about her husband's condition.
d. Report the incident to J.N.'s health care provider to address J.N.'s code status.

Answers and rationales available at *http://evolve.elsevier.com/Lewis.*

Basic Life Support for Health Care Providers

Mariann M. Harding

Basic life support (BLS) for health care professionals consists of a series of actions and skills performed by the rescuer(s) based on assessment findings. The first action the rescuer performs upon finding an adult victim is assessing for responsiveness. This is done by tapping or shaking the victim's shoulder and asking, "Are you all right?" If the victim does not respond, simultaneously scan the victim's chest for signs of breathing and perform a pulse check (described later).

If the rescuer is alone, the rescuer shouts for help. If someone responds, the rescuer asks him or her to activate the *emergency response system* (ERS) (e.g., through the use of a mobile phone) and get an *automatic external defibrillator* (AED) (if available). If no one responds and the rescuer does not have a mobile phone, the rescuer should leave to activate the ERS, get an AED (if available), and return to the victim before beginning *cardiopulmonary resuscitation* (CPR) and defibrillation if necessary.[1]

CARDIOPULMONARY RESUSCITATION

Cardiac arrest is characterized by the absence of a pulse and breathing in an unconscious victim. The current approach for CPR is the chest *compressions-airway-breathing* (CAB) sequence.[1]

The first step in CPR is to perform a pulse check by palpating the carotid pulse for at least 5 but no more than 10 seconds. While maintaining a head-tilt position with 1 hand on the victim's forehead, locate the victim's trachea using 2 or 3 fingers of your other hand. Slide these fingers into the groove between the trachea and neck muscles where the carotid pulse can be felt. The technique is more easily performed on the side nearest you.

If a pulse is felt, give 1 rescue breath every 5 to 6 seconds (10 to 12 breaths/min) and recheck the pulse every 2 minutes (Fig. A.1). If no pulse is felt, start CAB.[1,2]

Chest Compressions

The proper technique for providing chest compressions is shown in Fig. A.2. Chest compression technique consists of fast and deep applications of pressure on the lower half of the sternum. The victim must be in the supine position when compressions are performed. The victim must be lying on a flat, hard surface, such as a CPR board (specially designed for use in CPR), a headboard from a unit bed, or, if necessary, the floor. Position yourself close to the side of the victim's chest. More frequently, mechanical chest compression devices are being used to provide chest compressions both prehospital and in the emergency department.

Chest compressions are combined with rescue breathing for an effective resuscitation effort of the adult victim of cardiac arrest. The compression-to-ventilation ratio for 1- or 2-rescuer CPR is 30 compressions to 2 breaths (Table A.1). However, if the patient has an advanced airway (e.g., endotracheal tube, laryngeal mask airway), do not pause between compressions for breaths and deliver 1 breath every 6 seconds (10 breaths/min).[1]

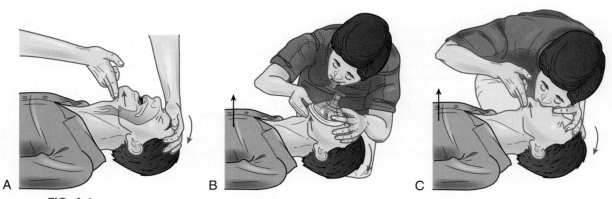

FIG. A.1 The head tilt–chin lift maneuver is used to open the victim's airway to give rescue breaths. **A,** Rescuer places 1 hand on the victim's forehead and applies firm, backward pressure with the palm to tilt the head back. The chin is lifted and brought forward with the fingers of the other hand. **B,** Mouth-to-barrier device: Rescuer places the device tightly over the victim's mouth and nose and delivers a regular breath. **C,** Mouth-to-mouth technique: Rescuer pinches the victim's nostrils, tightly seals mouth over victim's mouth, and delivers a regular breath. *Note:* Rescuer should observe for a rise in the victim's chest *(black arrows).*

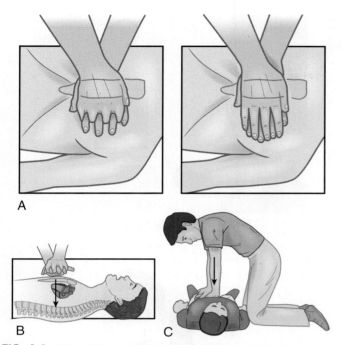

FIG. A.2 CPR. **A,** Position of the hands on the lower half of the sternum during chest compressions. **B,** When pressure is applied, the sternum is displaced posteriorly with the heel of the hand. **C,** Arms are kept straight, and the rescuer pushes deep (at least 2 in [5 cm]) and fast (a rate of 100 to 120 compressions per minute).

If a mechanical chest compression device is not used, it is preferable to have 2 persons performing CPR. One rescuer, positioned at the victim's side, performs chest compressions while the second rescuer, positioned at the victim's head, maintains an open airway and performs ventilations. To maintain the quality and rate of compressions, rescuers should change roles every 2 minutes.[2] Interruptions in CPR should be limited.

Defibrillation

When the AED or advanced cardiovascular life support (ACLS) team arrives, assess the victim's rhythm. If the victim has a shockable rhythm (e.g., ventricular tachycardia, ventricular fibrillation), deliver 1 shock and immediately resume CPR for about 2 minutes before checking the rhythm again. If the rhythm is not a shockable rhythm, immediately resume CPR and recheck the rhythm after 2 minutes. CPR should continue between rhythm checks and shocks and until the ACLS team arrives or the victim shows signs of movement.[1]

The American Heart Association includes training in the use of AEDs with BLS instruction of HCPs and laypersons. Survival from cardiac arrest is the highest when immediate CPR is provided and defibrillation occurs within 3 to 5 minutes.[2] AEDs are found in many out-of-hospital, public settings (Fig. A.3).

Airway and Breathing

If a victim has a pulse but is gasping (e.g., agonal breathing) or not breathing, establish an open airway and begin rescue breathing. Open an adult's airway by hyperextending the head (Fig. A.1). Use the *head tilt–chin lift maneuver.* This involves tilting the head back with 1 hand and lifting the chin forward with the fingers of the other hand. Use the *jaw-thrust maneuver* if you suspect a cervical spine injury (see Fig. 68.1). Try to

TABLE A.1 Adult 1- and 2-Rescuer Basic Life Support With Automatic External Defibrillator (AED)

Assess
- Determine unresponsiveness: tap or shake victim's shoulder; shout, "Are you all right?"
- Check for no breathing or abnormal breathing (e.g., gasping) while simultaneously performing a pulse check (5–10 sec).

Activate Emergency Response System (ERS)
- Activate ERS (e.g., call 911) and get the AED (if available) (outside of hospital).
- Call a code and ask for the AED or crash cart (in hospital).

Begin High-Quality CPR
- If victim has a pulse but is not breathing or not breathing adequately, begin rescue breathing at a rate of 1 breath every 3–5 sec, or about 12–20/min (Fig. A.1). Recheck the pulse every 2 min.*
- If there is no pulse, expose the victim's chest and immediately begin chest compressions (Fig. A.2).
- Deliver compressions at a rate of 100–120/min.
- Compress the chest at least 2 in (5 cm) but not greater than 2.4 in (6 cm).
- Allow for complete chest recoil after each compression.
- Deliver a compression-ventilation ratio of 30 compressions to 2 breaths.†
- Minimize interruptions in compressions by delivering the 2 breaths in <10 sec.

Deliver Effective Breaths
- Open airway adequately (Fig. A.1, *A*).
- Deliver breath to produce a visible chest rise (Fig. A.1, *B, C*).
- Avoid excessive ventilation.

Integrate Prompt Use of the AED
- Use AED as soon as possible.
- If rhythm is shockable, deliver 1 shock and then resume chest compressions immediately after delivery of shock.
- If the rhythm is not shockable, resume CPR and recheck rhythm every 5 cycles.

Continue CPR
- Continue CPR between rhythm checks and shocks, and until ACLS providers arrive or the victim shows signs of movement.

Source: American Heart Association: *BLS for healthcare providers: student manual,* Dallas, 2015, The Association.
ACLS, Advanced cardiovascular life support.
*If possible opioid overdose, give naloxone if available and per protocol.
†For patients with ongoing CPR and an advanced airway in place, a ventilation rate of 1 breath every 6 seconds (10 breaths per minute) with no interruption in compressions is recommended.

provide ventilation to the victim using a mouth-to-barrier (recommended) device (e.g., face mask or bag-valve-mask) or mouth-to-mouth resuscitation (Fig. A.1, *B, C*).[2]

For mouth-to-mouth resuscitation give ventilations with the victim's nostrils pinched. Take a regular (not deep) breath and tightly seal your lips around the victim's mouth. Give 1 breath and watch for a rise in the victim's chest. Continue rescue breaths at a rate of 10 to 12 per minute. When the victim has a tracheostomy, give ventilations through the stoma.

If the victim cannot be ventilated, proceed with CPR. When providing the next rescue breaths, look for any objects in the victim's mouth. If any objects are visible, remove them (Table A.2).

TABLE A.2 Management of the Adult Choking Victim

Conscious Adult Choking Victim

Assess Victim for Severe Airway Obstruction
Look for any of the following signs:
- Poor or no air exchange
- Clutching the neck with the hands, making the universal choking sign
- Weak, ineffective cough or no cough at all
- High-pitched noise while inhaling or no noise at all
- Increased respiratory difficulty
- Possible cyanosis

Ask the victim if he or she is choking. If the victim nods yes and cannot talk or has any of the symptoms noted above, severe airway obstruction is present and you must take immediate action.

Abdominal Thrusts (Heimlich Maneuver) With Standing or Sitting Victim (Fig. A.4)
1. Stand or kneel behind victim and wrap arms around the victim's waist.
2. Make fist with 1 hand.
3. Place thumb side of fist against victim's abdomen. Position fist midline, slightly above navel and well below breastbone.
4. Grasp fist with other hand and press fist into victim's abdomen with a quick, forceful upward thrust.
5. Give each new thrust with a separate, distinct movement to relieve the obstruction. *CAUTION:* If victim is pregnant or obese, give chest thrusts instead of abdominal thrusts. Position hands (as described) over lower portion of the breastbone and apply quick backward thrusts.
6. Repeat thrusts until object is expelled or victim becomes unresponsive.

Unconscious Adult Choking Victim
If you see a choking victim collapse and become unresponsive:
1. Activate the emergency response system.
2. Lower the victim to the ground and begin CPR, starting with compressions (do not check for a pulse).
3. Open the victim's mouth wide each time you prepare to give breaths. Look for the object. If you see the object and can easily remove it, do so with your fingers. If you do not see the object, continue with CPR using the chest compression–airway-breathing sequence (Table A.1).
4. If efforts to ventilate are unsuccessful, continue with CPR.

Source: American Heart Association: *BLS for healthcare providers: Student manual,* Dallas, 2015, The Association.

FIG. A.3 AED located in an airport.

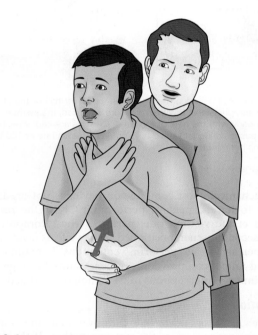

FIG. A.4 Abdominal thrusts (Heimlich maneuver) administered to a conscious (standing) choking victim.

HANDS-ONLY CPR

Hands-only CPR can be used to help adult victims who suddenly collapse from cardiac arrest outside of a health care setting. If an untrained person witnesses the event, the person should provide compression-only CPR. If you are trained and witness the event (as a bystander), you should provide conventional CPR (described previously). If you are unable to do so, provide chest compressions only (push fast and deep in the center of the chest). Both methods are effective when done in the first few minutes of an out-of-hospital cardiac arrest.[1]

REFERENCES*

1. American Heart Association: *Highlights of the 2015 American Heart Association guidelines update for CPR and ECC,* Dallas, 2015, The Association.
2. American Heart Association: *BLS for healthcare providers: Student manual,* Dallas, 2015, The Association.

*CPR guidelines are updated on an ongoing basis and are available at *https://eccguidelines.heart.org/index.php/circulation/cpr-ecc-guidelines-2.*

Nursing Diagnoses

1. Activity Intolerance: Lack of ability or energy to endure or complete daily activities.
2. Acute Confusion: Confusion occurring abruptly, over a short time interval.
3. Acute Pain: Pain occurring abruptly, over a short time interval.
4. Altered Blood Pressure: Any change in the systolic or diastolic BP.
5. Altered Perception: Change in the response to sensory stimuli, awareness of objects, or other data through the senses.
6. Anxiety: Feelings of threat, fear, apprehension, danger, or distress.
7. Chronic Pain: Pain occurring over time, long-standing.
8. Confusion: Memory impairment with disorientation in relation to person, place, or time.
9. Constipation: Decrease in the frequency of defecation accompanied by difficult or incomplete passage of stool; passage of excessively hard, dry stool.
10. Death Anxiety: Anxiety associated with the awareness of death.
11. Decreased Intracranial Adaptive Capacity: Compromised intracranial fluid volumes.
12. Diarrhea: Passage of loose, liquid, unformed stools, increased frequency of elimination accompanied by increased bowel sounds, cramping, and urgency of defecation.
13. Difficulty Coping: Inadequate personal ability to manage problems, stress, or responsibilities.
14. Disturbed Body Image: Disturbance in the mental picture of one's own body or physical appearance.
15. Electrolyte Imbalance: High or low serum electrolyte levels.
16. Fatigue: Feelings of decreased strength or endurance, weariness, mental or physical tiredness, and listlessness with lower capacity for physical or mental work.
17. Fluid Imbalance: Any change in or modification of body fluid balance.
18. Hyperglycemia: Increased serum glucose levels.
19. Hyperthermia: Increased body temperature.
20. Hypoglycemia: Decreased serum glucose levels.
21. Hypothermia: Reduced body temperature.
22. Impaired Airway Clearance: Impaired ability to keep air passage open from mouth to lung alveoli due to inability to clear secretions or obstructions from the respiratory tract.
23. Impaired Breathing: Inadequate inhalation or exhalation.
24. Impaired Cardiac Output: Any change in or modification of the pumping action of the heart.
25. Impaired Communication: Impediment or blockage to exchanging thoughts, messages, or information.
26. Impaired Gas Exchange: Impairment of the alveolar exchange of oxygen and carbon dioxide.
27. Impaired Hearing: Change in the ability to hear.
28. Impaired Nutritional Intake: Impaired ability to take in nutrients necessary for growth, normal functioning, and maintaining of life.
29. Impaired Nutritional Status: Impairment of weight and body mass in relation to intake of nutrition and specific nutrients estimated according to height, body build, and age.
30. Impaired Peripheral Neurovascular Function: Change in or modification of neurovascularization of the extremities.
31. Impaired Mobility: Diminished ability to perform independent movement.
32. Impaired Respiratory System Function: Any change in respiratory system function that influences oxygenation and breathing.
33. Impaired Sexual Functioning: Change negatively affecting a person's sexual response and the ability to participate in intercourse.
34. Impaired Sleep Pattern: Imbalance in the normal sleep/wake cycle.
35. Impaired Tissue Integrity: Damage, inflammation, or lesion to the skin or underlying structures.
36. Ineffective Tissue Perfusion: Change in the movement of blood through periphery tissues resulting in ineffective delivery of oxygen, fluids, and nutrients at the cellular level.
37. Impaired Urinary System Function: Any change in urinary system function that affects the ability to excrete waste.
38. Lack of Knowledge: Lack of information, understanding, skills, or comprehension.
39. Nausea: Sensation of feeling sick with an inclination to vomit.
40. Obesity: Condition of high body weight and body mass usually of more than 20% over ideal weight, abnormal increase in proportion of fat cells mainly in viscera and subcutaneous tissues.
41. Risk for Aspiration: Risk for inhaling gastric or external substances into the trachea or lungs.
42. Risk for Bleeding: Risk for loss of blood, externally or internally.
43. Risk for Fall-Related Injury: Risk for injury from the descent of a body from higher to lower level.
44. Risk for Infection: Risk for invasion of the body by pathogenic microorganisms that cause disease.
45. Risk for Injury: Risk for intentional or accidental physical harm or damage to tissues.

46. Sleep Deprivation: Lack of a normal sleep/wake cycle.
47. Substance Abuse: Misuse of chemically active substance for a nontherapeutic effect that may be harmful to health and cause addiction.
48. Surgical Wound: Cut of tissue made by sharp surgical instrument to create an opening into a body space or an organ.
49. Urinary Retention: Involuntary accumulation of urine in the bladder or incomplete emptying of the bladder.
50. Vomiting: Expulsion of stomach contents through the esophagus and out of mouth.

REFERENCES

International Council of Nurses: *ICNP®—English*, Geneva, 2017, The Association.

International Council of Nurses: International Classification for Nursing Practice catalogue: CCC-ICNP equivalency table for nursing diagnoses. Retrieved from *www.icn.ch/sites/default/files/inline-files/CCC-ICNP_Equivalency_Table_for_Nursing_Diagnoses.pdf*.

International Council of Nurses: Nursing diagnoses and outcome statements. Retrieved from *www.icn.ch/sites/default/files/inline-files/icnp2017-dc.pdf*.

Laboratory Reference Intervals

The tables in this appendix list some of the most common tests, their reference intervals (formally referred to as *normal values*), and possible etiologies of abnormal results. Laboratory results may vary depending on different techniques or different laboratories. Abbreviations appearing in the tables are defined as follows:

mEq = milliequivalent
mm Hg = millimeter of mercury
mm = millimeter
mOsm = milliosmole
L = liter
dL = deciliter (10^{-1} liter)
mL = milliliter (10^{-3} liter)
μL = microliter (10^{-6} liter, 10^{-3} milliliter)
fL = femtoliter (10^{-15} liter, 10^{-12} milliliter)
g = gram

mg = milligram (10^{-3} gram)
mcg = microgram (10^{-6} gram)
ng = nanogram (10^{-9} gram)
pg = picogram (10^{-12} gram)
U = unit
μU = microunit
IU = international unit
mU = milliunit
mmol = millimole (10^{-3} mole)
μmol = micromole (10^{-6} mole)
nmol = nanomole (10^{-9} mole)
pmol = picomole (10^{-12} mole)
kPa = kilopascal
μkat = microkatal

Source: Rafai N, Horvath AR ER, Wittwer CT: *Tietz textbook of clinical chemistry and molecular diagnostics*, ed 6, St Louis, 2018, Elsevier.

TABLE C.1 Serum, Plasma, and Whole Blood Chemistries

Test	REFERENCE INTERVALS		POSSIBLE ETIOLOGY	
	Conventional Units	SI Units	High	Low
Aldolase	22–59 mU/L	22–59 mU/L	Skeletal muscle disease	Muscle-wasting disease
α_1-Antitrypsin	85–213 mg/dL	0. 85–2.13 g/L	Acute and chronic inflammation, arthritis	Early-onset emphysema, malnutrition, nephrotic syndrome
α_1-Fetoprotein	<40 ng/mL	<40 mcg/L	Cancer of testes, ovaries, and liver	
Ammonia	10–80 mcg/dL	6–47 μmol/L	Severe liver disease	
Amylase	60–120 Somogyi U/dL	30–220 U/L	Acute and chronic pancreatitis, salivary gland disease, perforated ulcers	Acute alcoholism, cirrhosis of liver, extensive destruction of pancreas
Bicarbonate	21–28 mEq/L	21–28 mmol/L	Compensated respiratory acidosis, metabolic alkalosis	Compensated respiratory alkalosis, metabolic acidosis
b-Type natriuretic peptide (BNP)	<100 pg/mL	<100 pmol/L	Heart failure	
Bilirubin			Biliary obstruction, hemolytic anemia, impaired liver function, pernicious anemia	
• Total	0.3–1.0 mg/dL	5.1–17 μmol/L		
• Indirect	0.2–0.8 mg/dL	3.4–12.0 μmol/L		
• Direct	0.1–0.3 mg/dL	1.7–5.1 μmol/L		
Blood gases*				
• Arterial pH	7.35–7.45	7.35–7.45	Alkalosis	Acidosis
• Venous pH	7.31–7.41	7.31–7.41		
• $PaCO_2$	35–45 mm Hg	4.66–5.98 kPa	Compensated metabolic alkalosis	Compensated metabolic acidosis
• $PvCO_2$	40–50 mm Hg	5.06–7.32 kPa	Respiratory acidosis	Respiratory alkalosis
• PaO_2	80–100 mm Hg	10.6–13.33 kPa	Administration of high concentration of O_2	Chronic lung disease, decreased cardiac output
• PvO_2	40–50 mm Hg	5.04–5.57 kPa		
Calcium (total)	9.0–10.5 mg/dL	2.25–2.62 mmol/L	Hyperthyroidism, hyperparathyroidism, vitamin D intoxication, multiple myeloma	Pancreatitis, hypoparathyroidism, malabsorption syndrome, renal failure, vitamin D deficiency
Calcium (ionized)	4.5–5.6 mg/dL	1.05–1.3 mmol/L	Acidosis	Alkalosis
Chloride	98–106 mEq/L	98–106 mmol/L	Metabolic acidosis, respiratory alkalosis, corticosteroid therapy, uremia	Addison's disease, vomiting, metabolic alkalosis, respiratory acidosis

Continued

TABLE C.1 Serum, Plasma, and Whole Blood Chemistries—cont'd

Test	REFERENCE INTERVALS		POSSIBLE ETIOLOGY	
	Conventional Units	**SI Units**	**High**	**Low**
Cholesterol	<200 mg/dL	<5.2 mmol/L	Biliary obstruction, hypothyroidism, idiopathic hypercholesterolemia, renal disease, uncontrolled diabetes	Extensive liver disease, hyperthyroidism, malnutrition, malabsorption
• High-density lipoproteins (HDLs)	*Male:* >45 mg/dL	*Male:* >0.75 mmol/L	Excessive exercise	Metabolic syndrome, liver disease
	Female: >55 mg/dL	*Female:* >0.91 mmol/L		
• Low-density lipoproteins (LDLs)	*Recommended:* <130 mg/dL		Chronic liver disease, familial hypercholesterolemia, nephrotic syndrome	Hyperthyroidism
• Very low-density lipoproteins (VLDLs)	7–32 mg/dL		Familial hypercholesterolemia, nephrotic syndrome	Hyperthyroidism
Cortisol	8 AM: 5–23 mcg/dL 4 PM: 3–13 mcg/dL	8 AM: 138–635 nmol/L 4 PM: 83–359 nmol/L	Cushing syndrome, hyperthyroidism	Adrenal insufficiency, panhypopituitary states
Creatine kinase (CK)	*Male:* 55–170 U/L *Female:* 30–135 U/L	*Male:* 55–170 U/L *Female:* 30–135 U/L	Musculoskeletal injury or disease, myocardial infarction, severe myocarditis, exercise, numerous IM injections	
• CK-MB	<4%–6% of total CK	<0.4–0.6	Acute myocardial infarction	
Creatinine	*Male:* 0.6–1.2 mg/dL *Female:* 0.5–1.1 mg/dL	*Male:* 53–106 µmol/L *Female:* 44–97 µmol/L	Severe renal disease	Decreased muscle mass, dehabilitation
Ferritin	*Male:* 12-300 ng/mL *Female:* 10-150 ng/mL	*Male:* 12–300 mcg/L *Female:* 10–150 mcg/L	Anemia of chronic disease, sideroblastic anemia	Iron-deficiency anemia
Folic acid (folate)	5–25 ng/mL	11–57 nmol/L	Hypothyroidism, pernicious anemia	Alcoholism, hemolytic anemia, inadequate diet, malabsorption syndrome, megaloblastic anemia
γ-Glutamyl transferase (GGT)	*Male and Female >45:* 8–38 U/L *Female <45:* 5–27 U/L	*Male and Female >45:* 8–38 U/L *Female <45:* 5–27 U/L	Liver disease, infectious myocardial infarction, pancreatitis, hyperthyroidism	Hypothyroidism
Glucose (fasting)	74–106 mg/dL	4.1–5.9 mmol/L	Acute stress, Cushing disease, diabetes, hyperthyroidism, pancreatic insufficiency	Addison's disease, hepatic disease, hypothyroidism, insulin overdosage, pancreatic tumor, pituitary hypofunction
Haptoglobin	50–220 mg/dL	0.5–2.2 g/L	Infectious and inflammatory processes, cancer	Hemolytic anemia, malnutrition, chronic liver disease
Insulin (fasting)	6–26 µU/mL	43–186 pmol/L	Acromegaly, adenoma of pancreatic islet cells, Cushing syndrome	Diabetes, hypopituitarism
Iron, total	*Male:* 80–180 mcg/dL *Female:* 60-160 mcg/dL	*Male:* 14–32 µmol/L *Female:* 11–29 µmol/L	Excess RBC destruction, hepatitis, massive blood transfusion	Anemia of chronic disease, iron-deficiency anemia, cancer
(Total) iron-binding capacity	250–460 mcg/dL	45–82 µmol/L	Iron-deficient state, polycythemia	Cirrhosis, chronic infections, pernicious anemia
Lactic acid (L-Lactate), venous	5–20 mg/dL	0.6–2.2 mmol/L	Acidosis, liver disease, sepsis, shock	
Lactic dehydrogenase (LDH)	100–190 U/L	100–190 U/L	Heart failure, hemolytic disorders, hepatitis, metastatic cancer of liver, myocardial infarction, pernicious anemia, pulmonary embolus, skeletal muscle damage	
Lactic dehydrogenase isoenzymes				
• LDH₁	17%–27%	0.17–0.27	Myocardial infarction, pernicious anemia	
• LDH₂	27%–37%	0.27–0.37	Pulmonary embolus, sickle cell crisis	
• LDH₃	18%–25%	0.18–0.25	Malignant lymphoma, pulmonary embolus	
• LDH₄	3%–8%	0.03–0.08	Systemic lupus erythematosus, pulmonary infarction	

TABLE C.1 Serum, Plasma, and Whole Blood Chemistries—cont'd

Test	REFERENCE INTERVALS		POSSIBLE ETIOLOGY	
	Conventional Units	SI Units	High	Low
• LDH₅	0%–5%	0.00–0.05	Heart failure, hepatitis, pulmonary embolus and infarction, skeletal muscle damage	
Lipase	0–160 U/L	0–160 U/L	Acute pancreatitis, hepatic disorders, perforated peptic ulcer	
Magnesium	1.3–2.1 mEq/L	0.65–1.05 mmol/L	Addison's disease, hypothyroidism, renal failure	Chronic alcoholism, severe malabsorption
Osmolality	285–295 mOsm/kg	285–295 mmol/kg	Chronic renal disease, diabetes, diabetes insipidus	Addison's disease, diuretic therapy, SIADH, hypervolemia
O₂ saturation (arterial) (SaO₂)	>95%	>0.95	Polycythemia	Anemia, cardiac decompensation, respiratory disorders
Phosphatase, alkaline	30–120 U/L	0.5–2.0 μkat/L	Biliary system obstruction, bone diseases, marked hyperparathyroidism, rickets	Excess vitamin D ingestion, hypothyroidism
Phosphorus (phosphate)	3.0–4.5 mg/dL	0.97–1.45 mmol/L	Bone cancer, hypoparathyroidism, renal disease, vitamin D intoxication, hypocalcemia	Diabetes, hyperparathyroidism, vitamin D deficiency
Potassium	3.5–5.0 mEq/L	3.5–5.0 mmol/L	Addison's disease, diabetic ketosis, massive tissue destruction, renal failure, infection, dehydration	Cushing syndrome, diarrhea (severe), diuretic therapy, gastrointestinal fistula, starvation, vomiting
Progesterone (Female)				
• Follicular phase	<50 ng/dL	0.5–2.2 nmol/L	Adrenal hyperplasia, choriocarcinoma of ovary, pregnancy, cysts of ovary	Threatened abortion, hypogonadism, amenorrhea, ovarian tumor
• Luteal phase	300-2500 ng/dL	6.4–79.5 nmol/L		
• Postmenopause	<40 ng/dL	1.28 nmol/L		
Prostate-specific antigen (PSA)	<4.0 ng/mL	<4.0 mcg/L	Prostate cancer, prostatitis, benign prostatic hypertrophy	
Proteins			Burns, cirrhosis (globulin fraction), dehydration	Liver disease, malabsorption
• Total	6.4–8.3 g/dL	64–83 g/L		
• Albumin	3.5–5.0 g/dL	35–50 g/L		
• Globulin	2.3–3.4 g/dL	23–34 g/L		
• Albumin/globulin ratio	1.5:1–2.5:1	1.5:1–2.5:1	Multiple myeloma (globulin fraction), shock, vomiting	Malnutrition, nephrotic syndrome, proteinuria, renal disease, severe burns
Sodium	136–145 mEq/L	136–145 mmol/L	Dehydration, impaired renal function, primary aldosteronism, corticosteroid therapy	Addison's disease, diabetic ketoacidosis, diuretic therapy, excessive loss from GI tract, excessive perspiration, water intoxication
Testosterone (total)	Male: 280–1080 ng/dL Female: <70 ng/dL	Male: 280–1080 ng/dL Female: <70 ng/dL	Hyperthyroidism Polycystic ovary, virilizing tumors	Hypofunction of testes, hypogonadism
T₄ (thyroxine), total	Male: 4–12 mcg/dL Female: 5–12 mcg/dL	Male: 59–135 nmol/L Female: 71–142 nmol/L	Hyperthyroidism, thyroiditis, hepatitis, Graves' disease, thyroid cancer	Cretinism, hypothyroidism, myxedema, Cushing syndrome, renal failure
T₄ (thyroxine), free	0.8–2.8 ng/dL	10–36 pmol/L		
T₃ uptake	24%–34%	0.24–0.34	Hyperthyroidism	Hypothyroidism
T₃ (triiodothyronine), total	Age 20–50: 70–205 ng/dL Age >50: 40–180 ng/dL	1.2–3.4 nmol/L 0.60–2.8 nmol/L	Hyperthyroidism	Hypothyroidism
Thyroid-stimulating hormone (TSH)	2.0–10 μU/mL	2.0–10 mU/L	Myxedema, primary hypothyroidism	Secondary hypothyroidism, hyperthyroidism
Transaminases				
• Aspartate aminotransferase (AST)	0–35 U/L	0–0.58 μkat/L	Liver disease, myocardial infarction, pulmonary infarction, acute hepatitis	Acute renal disease, diabetic ketoacidosis
• Alanine aminotransferase (ALT)	4–36 U/L	4–36 U/L	Liver disease, shock	
Transferrin	Male: 215–365 mg/dL Female: 250–380 mg/dL	Male: 2.15–3.65 g/L Female: 2.5–3.8 g/L	Iron-deficiency anemia, polycythemia vera	Cirrhosis, pernicious anemia, sickle cell disease
Transferrin saturation (%)	Male: 20%–50% Female: 15%–50%	Male: 20%–50% Female: 15%–50%	Hemolytic anemia, iron overdose	Malnutrition

Continued

TABLE C.1   Serum, Plasma, and Whole Blood Chemistries—cont'd

| Test | REFERENCE INTERVALS | | POSSIBLE ETIOLOGY | |
	Conventional Units	SI Units	High	Low
Triglycerides	*Male:* 40–160 mg/dL *Female:* 35–135 mg/dL	*Male:* 0.45–1.81 g/L *Female:* 0.40–1.52 g/L	Diabetes, hyperlipidemia, hypothyroidism, liver disease	Malnutrition
Troponins (cardiac)			Myocardial infarction, myocardial injury	
• Troponin T (cTnT)	<0.1 ng/mL	<0.1 mcg/L		
• Troponin I (cTnI)	<0.03 ng/mL	<0.03 mcg/L		
Urea nitrogen (BUN)	10–20 mg/dL	3.6–7.1 mmol/L	Increase in protein catabolism (fever, sepsis, stress), renal disease, heart failure, myocardial infarction	Malnutrition, severe liver damage
Uric acid	*Male:* 4.0–8.5 mg/dL *Female:* 2.7–7.3 mg/dL	*Male:* 0.24–0.51 mmol/L *Female:* 0.16–0.43 mmol/L	Gout, gross tissue destruction, high-protein weight reduction diet, leukemia, renal failure	Administration of uricosuric drugs
Vitamin B$_{12}$ (cobalamin)	160–950 pg/mL	118–701 pmol/L	Chronic myeloid leukemia	Strict vegetarianism, malabsorption syndrome, pernicious anemia, total or partial gastrectomy
Vitamin C (ascorbic acid)	0.4–2.0 mg/dL	23–114 μmol/L	Excessive ingestion of vitamin C	Connective tissue disorders, hepatic disease, renal disease, rheumatic fever, vitamin C deficiency
Vitamin D	25–80 ng/dL	25–80 ng/dL	Excess dietary supplement	Liver disease, malabsorption syndromes, osteoporosis, renal disease

*Because arterial blood gases are influenced by altitude, the value for PaO$_2$ decreases as altitude increases. The lower value is normal for an altitude of 1 mile.
PaCO$_2$, Partial pressure of CO$_2$ in arterial blood; *PaO$_2$,* partial pressure of oxygen in arterial blood; *PvCO$_2$,* partial pressure of CO$_2$ in venous blood; *PvO$_2$,* partial pressure of oxygen in venous blood; *RBC,* red blood cell; *SaO$_2$,* arterial oxygen saturation.

TABLE C.2 Hematology

Test	REFERENCE INTERVALS		POSSIBLE ETIOLOGY	
	Conventional Units	SI Units	High	Low
Bleeding time	1–9 min	60–540 sec	Aspirin ingestion, ineffective platelet function, thrombocytopenia, vascular disease, von Willebrand disease	
Activated partial thromboplastin time (aPTT)	30–40 sec*	30–40 sec*	Deficiency of factors I, II, V, VIII, IX, X, XI, XII; hemophilia, heparin therapy, liver disease	Early DIC, extensive cancer
Prothrombin time (protime, PT)	11–12.5 sec*	11–12.5 sec*	Deficiency of factors I, II, V, VII, and X; liver disease; vitamin K deficiency; warfarin therapy	
Fibrinogen	200–400 mg/dL	2–4 g/L	Burns (after first 36 hr), inflammatory disease, stroke, myocardial infarction	Burns (during first 36 hr), DIC, severe liver disease, malnutrition
Fibrin split (degradation) products	<10 mcg/mL	<10 mg/L	Acute DIC, massive hemorrhage, primary fibrinolysis	
D-Dimer	<250 ng/mL	<250 mcg/L	DIC, myocardial infarction, VTE, unstable angina, cancer	
Erythrocyte count† (altitude dependent)	*Male:* 4.7–6.1 × 10⁶/µL *Female:* 4.2–5.4 × 10⁶/µL	*Male:* 4.7–6.1 × 10¹²/L *Female:* 4.2–5.4 × 10¹²/L	Dehydration, high altitudes, polycythemia vera, severe COPD	Anemia, leukemia, hemorrhage, cancer, chronic illness, kidney disease
Red blood indices				
• Mean corpuscular volume (MCV)	80–95 fL	80–95 fL	Alcoholism, liver disease, macrocytic anemia	Microcytic anemia, thalassemia
• Mean corpuscular hemoglobin (MCH)	27–31 pg	27–31 pg	Macrocytic anemia	Microcytic anemia
• Mean corpuscular hemoglobin concentration (MCHC)	32%–36%	32–36 g/dL	Spherocytosis	Iron deficiency anemia, thalassemia
Erythrocyte sedimentation rate (ESR)	<20 mm/hr (some gender variation)	<20 mm/hr (some gender variation)	*Moderate increase:* acute hepatitis, myocardial infarction; rheumatoid arthritis *Marked increase:* acute and severe bacterial infections, cancer, pelvic inflammatory disease	Malaria, severe liver disease, sickle cell anemia
Hematocrit† (altitude dependent)	*Male:* 42%–52% *Female:* 37%–47%	*Male:* 0.42–0.52 *Female:* 0.37–0.47	Dehydration, high altitudes, polycythemia, COPD	Anemia, hemorrhage, overhydration, cirrhosis, kidney disease
Hemoglobin† (altitude dependent)	*Male:* 14–18 g/dL *Female:* 12–16 g/dL	*Male:* 140–180 g/L *Female:* 120–160 g/L	COPD, high altitudes, polycythemia, dehydration, burns	Anemia, hemorrhage, kidney disease, cancer
Hemoglobin, glycosylated (A1C)	4.0%–5.6%	4.0%–5.6%	Diabetes, pre–diabetes	Sickle cell anemia, chronic renal failure, pregnancy
Platelets (thrombocytes)	150–400 × 10³/µL	150–400 × 10⁹/L	Acute infections, chronic granulocytic leukemia, chronic pancreatitis, cirrhosis, collagen disorders, polycythemia, postsplenectomy	Acute leukemia, DIC, thrombocytopenic purpura
Reticulocyte count	0.5%–2.0% of RBC	0.5%–2.0% of RBC	Hemolytic anemia, polycythemia vera	Hypoproliferative anemia, macrocytic anemia, microcytic anemia
White blood cell count†	5000–10000/mm³	5.0–10.0 × 10⁹/L	Inflammatory and infectious processes, leukemia	Aplastic anemia, side effects of chemotherapy and irradiation
WBC differential				
• Segmented neutrophils	55%–70%	0.55–0.70	Bacterial infections, collagen diseases, Hodgkin's lymphoma	Aplastic anemia, viral infections
• Band neutrophils	0–8%	0–0.08	Acute infections	
• Lymphocytes	20%–40%	0.20–0.40	Chronic infections, lymphocytic leukemia, mononucleosis, viral infections	Corticosteroid therapy, whole body irradiation
• Monocytes	2%–8%	0.02–0.08	Chronic inflammatory disorders, malaria, monocytic leukemia, acute infections, Hodgkin's lymphoma	
• Eosinophils	1%–4%	0.01–0.04	Allergic reactions, eosinophilic and chronic granulocytic leukemia, parasitic disorders, Hodgkin's lymphoma	Corticosteroid therapy
• Basophils	0.5%–1%	0.005–0.01	Hypothyroidism, ulcerative colitis, myeloproliferative diseases	Hyperthyroidism, stress

*Values depend on reagent and instrumentation used.
†Components of complete blood count (CBC).
COPD, Chronic obstructive pulmonary disease; *DIC,* disseminated intravascular coagulation.

TABLE C.3 Serology-Immunology

Test	REFERENCE INTERVALS		POSSIBLE ETIOLOGY	
	Conventional Units	SI Units	High/Positive	Low
Antinuclear antibody (ANA)	Negative at 1:40 dilution	Negative at 1:40 dilution	Chronic hepatitis, rheumatoid arthritis, scleroderma, systemic lupus erythematosus	
Anti-DNA antibody	<5 IU/mL	<5 IU/mL	Systemic lupus erythematosus	
Anti-Sm (Smith)	Negative	Negative	Systemic lupus erythematosus	
C-reactive protein (CRP)	<1.0 mg/dL	<10.0 mg/L	Acute infections, any inflammatory condition, widespread cancer	
Carcinoembryonic antigen (CEA)	*Nonsmoker:* <3 ng/mL *Smoker:* <5 ng/mL	*Nonsmoker:* <3 mcg/L *Smoker:* <5 mcg/L	Cancer of colon, liver, pancreas; cigarette smoking; inflammatory bowel disease	
Complement, total hemolytic (CH$_{50}$)	30–75 U/mL	30–75 U/mL	Cancer, ulcerative colitis	Bacterial endocarditis, glomerulonephritis, rheumatoid arthritis, systemic lupus erythematosus
Direct Coombs or direct antihuman globulin test (DAT)	Negative	Negative	Acquired hemolytic anemia, drug reactions, transfusion reactions	
Fluorescent treponemal antibody absorption (FTA-Abs)	Negative or nonreactive	Negative or nonreactive	Syphilis	
Hepatitis A antibody	Negative	Negative	Hepatitis A	
Hepatitis B surface antigen (HB$_s$Ag)	Negative	Negative	Hepatitis B	
Hepatitis C antibody	Negative	Negative	Hepatitis C	
Monospot or monotest	Negative	Negative	Infectious mononucleosis	
Rheumatoid factor (RF)	Negative or titer <1:17	Negative or titer <1:17	Rheumatoid arthritis, Sjögren's syndrome, systemic lupus erythematosus	
RPR	Negative or nonreactive	Negative or nonreactive	Leprosy, malaria, rheumatoid arthritis, systemic lupus erythematosus, syphilis,	
VDRL	Negative or nonreactive	Negative or nonreactive	Syphilis	

RPR, Rapid plasma reagin test; *VDRL,* Venereal Disease Research Laboratory test.

TABLE C.4 Urine Chemistry

Test	Specimen	Units	SI Units	POSSIBLE ETIOLOGY High	Low
Acetone	Random	Negative	Negative	Diabetes, high-fat and low-carbohydrate diets, starvation	
Aldosterone	24 hr	2–26 mcg/day	6–72 nmol/day	*Primary aldosteronism:* adrenocortical tumors *Secondary aldosteronism:* cirrhosis, heart failure hyperkalemia, hyponatremia	ACTH deficiency, Addison's disease, corticosteroid therapy, hypokalemia
Amylase	24 hr	<5000 Somogyi U/day	6.5–48.1 U/hr	Acute pancreatitis	
Bence Jones protein	Random	<0.68 mg/dL	<0.68 mg/dL	Multiple myeloma	
Bilirubin	Random	Negative	Negative	Liver disorders	
Catecholamines	24 hr			Heart failure, pheochromocytoma, progressive muscular dystrophy	
• Epinephrine		<20 mcg/day	<109 nmol/day		
• Norepinephrine		<100 mcg/day	<590 nmol/day		
Cortisol	24 hr	<100 mcg/day	<276 nmol/day	Adrenal cancer, Cushing syndrome, hyperthyroidism, obesity, stress	Addison's disease, hypothyroidism, liver disease
Creatinine clearance	24 hr	*Male:* 107–139 mL/min *Female:* 87–107 mL/min	*Male:* 1.78–2.32 mL/sec *Female:* 1.45–1.78 mL/sec	Exercise, pregnancy	Cirrhosis, heart failure, renal disease
Estrogens	24 hr			Gonadal or adrenal tumor	Endocrine disturbance, ovarian dysfunction, menopause
• Female					
• Nonpregnant		4–60 mcg/day	4–60 mcg/day		
• Postmenopause		<20 mcg/day	<20 mcg/day		
• Male		4–25 mcg/day	4–25 mcg/day		
Glucose	Random	Negative	Negative	Diabetes, pituitary disorders	
Hemoglobin	Random	Negative	Negative	Extensive burns, glomerulonephritis, hemolytic anemia, hemolytic transfusion reaction	
5-Hydroxyindole acetic acid (5-HIAA)	24 hr	2–8 mg/day	10–40 µmol/day	Malignant carcinoid syndrome	
Ketones	Random	Negative	Negative	Diabetes, starvation, dehydration	
Metanephrine	24 hr	<1.3 mg/day	<7 µmol/day	Pheochromocytoma	
Myoglobin	Random	Negative	Negative	Crushing injuries, electric injuries, extreme physical exertion	
Osmolality	Random	50–1200 mOsm/kg	50–1200 mmol/kg	Heart failure, liver disease, shock, SIADH	Aldosteronism, diabetes insipidus, hypokalemia, pyelonephritis
pH	Random	4.6–8.0	4.6–8.0	Urinary tract infection, urine allowed to stand at room temperature	Respiratory or metabolic acidosis
Protein	Random	0–8 mg/dL	0–8 mg/dL	Acute and chronic renal disease, heart failure	
Protein (quantitative)	24 hr	50–80 mg/day	50–80 mg/day	Heart failure, inflammatory process of urinary tract, nephritis, nephrosis, strenuous exercise	
Sodium	24 hr	40–220 mEq/day	40–220 mmol/day	Acute tubular necrosis	Hyponatremia
Specific gravity	Random	1.005–1.030	1.005–1.030	Albuminuria, dehydration, glycosuria, fever	Diabetes insipidus, hypothermia, diuresis
Uric acid	24 hr	250–750 mg/day	1.48–4.43 mmol/day	Gout, leukemia	Nephritis
Urobilinogen	Random	Negative	Negative	Hemolytic disease, hepatic parenchymal cell damage, liver disease	Complete bile duct obstruction
Vanillylmandelic acid	24 hr	<6.8 mg/day	<35 µmol/day	Pheochromocytoma	

ACTH, Adrenocorticotropic hormone.

TABLE C.5 Fecal Analysis

Test	REFERENCE INTERVALS Conventional Units	SI Units	POSSIBLE ETIOLOGY High
Fecal fat	2–6 g/24 hr	7–21 mmol/day	Common bile duct obstruction, malabsorption syndrome, pancreatic disease
Mucus	Negative	Negative	Mucous colitis, spastic constipation
Pus	Negative	Negative	Chronic bacillary dysentery, chronic ulcerative colitis, localized abscesses
Blood*	Negative	Negative	Anal fissures, gastrointestinal cancer, hemorrhoids, inflammatory bowel disease, peptic ulcer disease
Color			
• Brown			Various color depending on diet
• Clay			Biliary obstruction, presence of barium sulfate
• Tarry			More than 100 mL of blood in gastrointestinal tract
• Red			Blood in large intestine
• Black			Blood in upper gastrointestinal tract, iron medication

*Ingestion of meat may produce false-positive results. Patient may be placed on a meat-free diet for 3 days before the test.

TABLE C.6 Cerebrospinal Fluid Analysis

Test	REFERENCE INTERVALS Conventional Units	SI Units	POSSIBLE ETIOLOGY High	Low
Pressure	<20 mm H_2O	<20 mm H_2O	Hemorrhage, intracranial tumor, meningitis	Head injury, spinal tumor, subdural hematoma
Blood	Negative	Negative	Intracranial hemorrhage	
Cell count (age dependent)			CNS infection or inflammation	
• WBC	0–5 cells/μL	0–5 × 10^6 cells/L		
• RBC	Negative	Negative		
Chloride	700–750 mg/dL	118–132 mmol/L	Uremia	CNS bacterial infection
Glucose	50–75 mg/dL	2.2–3.9 mmol/L	CNS viral infection, diabetes	Bacterial infection, CNS tuberculosis
Protein				
• Lumbar	15–45 mg/dL	0.15–0.45 g/L	Guillain-Barré syndrome, poliomyelitis, trauma	
• Cisternal	15–25 mg/dL	0.15–0.25 g/L	CNS syphilis	
• Ventricular	5–15 mg/dL	0.05–0.15 g/L	Acute meningitis, brain tumor, chronic CNS infection, multiple sclerosis	

CNS, Central nervous system.

Note: Disorder names and key terms are in **boldface**. Page numbers in **boldface** indicate main discussions. Page numbers followed by *f* or *b* indicate figures or boxes/tables, respectively.

ABBREVIATIONS

ABG	arterial blood gas
ACE	angiotensin-converting enzyme
ACLS	advanced cardiac life support
ACS	acute coronary syndrome
ACTH	adrenocorticotropic hormone
ADH	antidiuretic hormone
AED	automatic external defibrillator
AIDS	acquired immunodeficiency syndrome
AKA	above-knee amputation
AKI	acute kidney injury
ALI	acute lung injury
ALL	acute lymphocytic leukemia
ALS	amyotrophic lateral sclerosis
AMI	acute myocardial infarction
ANA	antinuclear antibody
ANS	autonomic nervous system
AORN	Association of periOperative Room Nurses
APD	automated peritoneal dialysis
aPTT	activated partial thromboplastin time
ARDS	acute respiratory distress syndrome
ATN	acute tubular necrosis
BCLS	basic cardiac life support
BKA	below-knee amputation
BMI	body mass index
BMR	basal metabolic rate
BMT	bone marrow transplantation
BPH	benign prostatic hyperplasia
BSE	breast self-examination
BUN	blood urea nitrogen
CABG	coronary artery bypass graft
CAD	coronary artery disease; circulatory assist device
CAPD	continuous ambulatory peritoneal dialysis
CAVH	continuous arteriovenous hemofiltration
CBC	complete blood count
CCU	coronary care unit; critical care unit
CDC	Centers for Disease Control and Prevention
CIS	carcinoma in situ
CKD	chronic kidney disease
CLL	chronic lymphocytic leukemia
CML	chronic myelocytic leukemia
CMP	cardiomyopathy
CN	cranial nerve
CNS	central nervous system
CO	cardiac output
COPD	chronic obstructive pulmonary disease
CPAP	continuous positive airway pressure
CPR	cardiopulmonary resuscitation
CRRT	continuous renal replacement therapy
CRNA	certified registered nurse anesthetist
CSF	cerebrospinal fluid
CT	computed tomography
CVA	cerebrovascular accident; costovertebral angle
CVAD	central venous access device
CVI	chronic venous insufficiency
CVP	central venous pressure
D&C	dilation and curettage
DDD	degenerative disk disease
DI	diabetes insipidus
DIC	disseminated intravascular coagulation
DJD	degenerative joint disease
DKA	diabetic ketoacidosis

DM	diabetes mellitus; diastolic murmur
DRE	digital rectal examination
DVT	deep vein thrombosis
ECF	extracellular fluid
ECG	electrocardiogram
ED	emergency department; erectile dysfunction
EEG	electroencephalogram
EMG	electromyogram
EMS	emergency medical services
ENT	ear, nose, and throat
ERCP	endoscopic retrograde cholangiopancreatography
ERT	estrogen replacement therapy
ESKD	end-stage kidney disease
ESR	erythrocyte sedimentation rate
ET	endotracheal
FEV	forced expiratory volume
FRC	functional residual capacity
FUO	fever of unknown origin
GCS	Glasgow Coma Scale
GERD	gastroesophageal reflux disease
GFR	glomerular filtration rate
GH	growth hormone
GI	glycemic index
GTT	glucose tolerance test
GU	genitourinary
GYN, Gyn	gynecologic
HAI	health care–associated infection
HAV	hepatitis A virus
Hb, Hgb	hemoglobin
HBV	hepatitis B virus
Hct	hematocrit
HCV	hepatitis C virus
HD	hemodialysis, Huntington's disease
HDL	high-density lipoprotein
HF	heart failure
HIV	human immunodeficiency virus
H&P	history and physical examination
HPV	human papillomavirus
HSCT	hematopoietic stem cell transplantation
IABP	intraaortic balloon pump
IBS	irritable bowel syndrome
ICP	intracranial pressure
I&D	incision and drainage
IE	infective endocarditis
IFG	impaired fasting glucose
IGT	impaired glucose tolerance
INR	international normalized ratio
IOP	intraocular pressure
IPPB	intermittent positive-pressure breathing
ITP	idiopathic thrombocytopenic purpura
IUD	intrauterine device
IV	intravenous
IVP	intravenous push; intravenous pyelogram
JVD	jugular venous distention
KS	Kaposi sarcoma
KUB	kidney, ureters, and bladder (x-ray)
KVO	keep vein open
LAD	left anterior descending
LDL	low-density lipoprotein
LGV	lymphogranuloma venereum
LLQ	left lower quadrant